PEOPLE, PLACES, & THINGS ALONG THE WAY

THE STEP STONE BIBLE

COMMON
ENGLISH
BIBLE

ISBN 978-1-60926-063-7

14 15 16 17 18 19 20 21 22 23—10 9 8 7 6 5 4 3 2 1
Printed in China

CONTENTS

OLD TESTAMENT

CONTENTS

NEW TESTAMENT

ABBREVIATIONS AND TERMS

Aram Aramaic
BCE Before the Common Era; traditionally BC: before Christ
CE Common Era; traditionally Anno Domini: year since the Lord's birth
cf compare
chap chapter
DSS Dead Sea Scrolls found at Qumran
   (1QIsaª) Isaiah scroll *a* in Cave 1 of the Dead Sea Scrolls
   (1QDeutᵇ) Deuteronomy scroll *b* in Cave 1 of the Dead Sea Scrolls
   (4QDeutᵇ) Deuteronomy scroll *b* in Cave 4 of the Dead Sea Scrolls
   (4QDeutʰ) Deuteronomy scroll *h* in Cave 4 of the Dead Sea Scrolls
   (4QDeutʲ) Deuteronomy scroll *j* in Cave 4 of the Dead Sea Scrolls
   (4QDeut�q) Deuteronomy scroll *q* in Cave 4 of the Dead Sea Scrolls
   (4QPhylⁿ) Phylactery scroll *n* in Cave 4 of the Dead Sea Scrolls
   (4QSamª) Samuel scroll *a* in Cave 4 of the Dead Sea Scrolls
   (4QSamᵇ) Samuel scroll *b* in Cave 4 of the Dead Sea Scrolls
   (4QSamᶜ) Samuel scroll *c* in Cave 4 of the Dead Sea Scrolls
   (4QTest) Testimonia in Cave 4 of the Dead Sea Scrolls
   (8QMez) Mezuza scroll in Cave 8 of the Dead Sea Scrolls
   (11QPsª) Psalms scroll *a* in Cave 11 of the Dead Sea Scrolls
Eth Ethiopic translation of 2 Esdras in the Ge'ez language
Gk Greek
   Gk uncertain The meaning of the Greek text is uncertain.
Heb Hebrew
   Heb uncertain The meaning of the Hebrew text is uncertain.
Josephus *Ant*. Works of Flavius Josephus: Antiquities of the Jews
Kethib Aramaic term meaning what is written (the written consonantal text)
Lat Latin
LXX Septuagint; Greek translation of Hebrew Bible by seventy translators
   LXXᴬ In Samuel, the Greek uncial Alexandrinus
   LXXᴮ In Samuel, the Greek uncial Vaticanus
   LXXᴸ In Samuel, Lucianic Greek manuscripts
   LXXᴹ In Samuel, the Greek uncial Coislinianus
   LXXᴺ In Samuel, the Greek uncials Basilianus and Vaticanus
   LXX¹ In Tobit, the Greek uncial Sinaiticus
   LXX² In Tobit, the Greek uncials Alexandrinus and Vaticanus
   LXXª in Sirach the Greek uncials Sinaiticus, Alexandrinus, and Vaticanus
   LXXᵇ In Sirach the Origenic and Lucianic Greek manuscripts
MT Masoretic Text; the Hebrew Bible
NT New Testament
OL Old Latin; manuscripts in Latin prior to the Vulgate
OT Old Testament
pl plural
Qere Aramaic term meaning what is read aloud (the vocalized text)
Sam Samaritan Hebrew text of the Old Testament
Selah Musical direction of uncertain meaning found in Psalms
Sym Greek version of the Old Testament translated by Symmachus
Syr Syriac, a translation known as the Peshitta in a dialect of the Aramaic language
Tg Targum; Aramaic translation of Hebrew Bible
Vulg Vulgate; standardized Latin version of the Bible

MEASURES

Capacity and linear measures

ammah *length of a forearm, standardized at eighteen inches; traditionally a cubit*

bath *a liquid measure equivalent to approximately twenty quarts*

ephah *a dry measure for flour or grains, approximately twenty quarts (five gallons)*

etsbah *length of the finger or thumb; traditionally a fingerbreadth*

hin *a liquid measure for wine or water, approximately one gallon*

homer *the largest dry measure, fifty gallons, equivalent to ten ephah*

issaron *one-tenth of an unknown weight; possibly an equivalent for omer*

kab *an unknown measure in 2 Kgs 6:25*

kor *a dry measure for grain, possibly equal to a homer; approximately fifty gallons as a liquid measure in Ezekiel*

litra *a Roman pound equal to approximately twelve ounces dry*

log *a liquid measure for oil in Leviticus, approximately two-thirds of a pint*

metretes *a liquid measure of approximately ten gallons*

milion *a mile; a Roman mile was 1,000 paces or approximately 4,855 feet*

omer *one-tenth of an ephah or two quarts dry*

pechon *approximately eighteen inches; traditionally a cubit*

pim *two-thirds of a shekel*

qaneh *a measuring rod in Ezekiel equivalent to six ammah or nine feet*

seah *a dry measure of grain, possibly seven and a half quarts but may be smaller amount in Genesis*

shearim *an unknown dry measure of grain*

stadion *a Roman linear measurement of approximately 607 feet*

tefakh or tofakh *width of the hand at the base of the fingers; traditionally a handbreadth or a palm*

tsimdo *traditionally an acre, the area that a team can plow in a day*

zereth *distance between tip of thumb to little finger; traditionally a span*

Monetary measures

beqa *one-half shekel, typically one-fifth of an ounce; ten or twelve gerahs*

daric *a gold Persian coin named after Darius 1, weighing one-third of an ounce*

denarion, denaria (pl) *a coin equivalent in value to one day's work*

drachme, drachmen (pl) *a silver coin equivalent in value to a denarion; also possibly a daric*

gerah *one-twentieth or one twenty-fourth of a shekel*

kikkar *a unit of weight in the common shekel system; traditionally a talent*

kodrantes *a coin equivalent to two lepta*

lepto *a coin equivalent to one-128th of a denarion*

maneh *in the Old Testament possibly fifty or sixty sanctuary shekels; in the New Testament a monetary unit equivalent to one hundred denaria*

shekel *basic measure, typically two-fifths of an ounce, for three monetary weight systems attested in the Old Testament: the royal shekel, the sanctuary shekel, and the common shekel*

talanta *a coin equivalent to six thousand denaria; traditionally a talent. In the Greek period, one talent is approximately 57 pounds of weight.*

qesitah *an unknown monetary weight*

PREFACE

The King James Version of the Bible was published in 1611. For two centuries the KJV competed for readership with the Geneva Bible. However, by the nineteenth century in America, the KJV would be described as the "common English Bible," because it was the most widely used translation of Christian scripture. Numerous translations have appeared since that time. However, it has proved difficult to combine concern for accuracy and accessibility in one translation that the typical reader or worshipper would be able to understand. Therefore, readers in the twenty-first century, four hundred years after the creation of the KJV, need and deserve a new translation that is suitable for personal devotion, for communal worship, and for classroom study.

The Common English Bible (CEB), completed in 2011, is a fresh translation of the Bible. Some editions include the books of the Apocrypha that are used in Anglican, Orthodox, and Catholic congregations. The translation is sponsored by the Common English Bible Committee, which is an alliance of denominational publishers, including Presbyterian (USA), Episcopalian, United Methodist, Disciples of Christ, and United Church of Christ representatives.

One hundred twenty biblical scholars from twenty-two faith traditions worked as translators for the CEB. In addition, members of seventy-seven reading groups from congregations throughout North America reviewed and responded to early drafts of the translation. As a result, more than five hundred individuals were integrally involved in the preparation of the CEB. These individuals represent the sorts of diversity that permit this new translation to speak to people of various religious convictions and different social locations.

The translators, reviewers, and editors represent the following faith communities: African Methodist Episcopal Church, American Baptist, Anglican, Baptist, Baptist General Conference, Church of the Nazarene, Disciples of Christ, Episcopal Church, Evangelical Free Church, Evangelical Lutheran Church, Free Methodist, Mennonite, Moravian, National Baptist, Presbyterian (USA), Progressive National Baptist, Quaker, Reformed Church in America, Reform Judaism, Roman Catholic Church, Seventh-day Adventist, United Churches of Christ, and United Methodist. The CEB is truly a Bible created by churches and for the Church.

Accuracy and clarity. The CEB translators balance rigorous accuracy in the rendition of ancient texts with an equally passionate commitment to clarity of expression in the target language. Translators create sentences and choose vocabulary that will be readily understood when the biblical text is read aloud. Two examples illustrate this concern for accuracy and clarity.

First, *ben 'adam* (Hebrew) and *huios tou anthrōpou* (Greek) are best translated as "human being" (rather than "son of man") except in cases of direct address, where CEB renders "human one" (instead of "son of man" or "mortal"; e.g., Ezek 2:1). When *ho huios tou anthrōpou* is used as a title for Jesus, the CEB refers to Jesus as "the Human One." People who have grown accustomed to hearing Jesus refer to himself in the Gospels as "the Son of Man" may find this jarring. Why "Human One"? Jesus' primary language would have been Aramaic, so he would have used the Aramaic phrase *bar enosha*. This phrase has the sense of "a human" or "a human such as I." This phrase was taken over into Greek in a phrase that might be translated woodenly as "son of humanity." However, Greek usage often refers to "a son of x" in the sense of "one who has the character of x." For example, Luke 10:6 refers in Greek to "a son of peace," a phrase that has the sense of "one who shares in peace." In the Greek of Acts 13:10 Paul calls a sorcerer "a son of the devil." This is not a reference to the sorcerer's actual ancestry, but it serves to identify his character. He is devilish—or more simply in English "a devil." *Human* or *human one* represents accurately the Aramaic and Greek idioms and reflects common English usage. Finally, many references to Jesus as "the Human One" refer back to Daniel 7:13, where Daniel "saw one like a human being" (Greek *huios anthropou*). By using the title Human One in the Gospels and Acts, the CEB preserves this connection to Daniel's vision.

Second, the phrase "Lord of hosts" (*Yahweh sebaoth* in Hebrew; *Kyrios sabaoth* in Greek) appears hundreds of times in older Bibles and persists as an idiom in translations that preserve King James usage. This archaic translation is no longer meaningful to most English speakers. The CEB renders *Yahweh sebaoth* and *Kyrios sabaoth* as "Lord of heavenly forces," which conveys accurately the meaning of the Hebrew and Greek phrases by using contemporary English language.

English speakers, especially when telling a story, writing a letter, or engaging in conversation, make frequent use of contractions. As a result, translators have often used contractions, particularly in direct speech, in the CEB. However, formal genres of literature typically do not include contractions. As a result, translators did not include contractions in contexts such as (a) formal trials or royal interviews (socially formal situations), (b) much divine discourse (e.g., Hos 11:9; Exod 24:12), and (c) poetic and/or liturgical discourse (several types of psalms).

Texts. Translators of the Old Testament used as their base text the Masoretic Text (MT) as found in Biblia Hebraica Stuttgartensia and the published fascicles of Biblia Hebraica Quinta. For some books the Hebrew University Bible Project was consulted. Judicious departures from the Masoretic Text, based on ancient manuscript (e.g., reading with the Dead Sea Scrolls in 1 Sam 10:27*b* or Deut 32:8) and versional evidence (e.g., reading with the Septuagint in Gen 4:8), were sometimes necessary. In those situations, in which one may postulate two literary editions of a biblical book, or in which there are major or lengthy differences between the Masoretic Text and other texts or versions (e.g., 1 Sam 17), the CEB translated the edition that became canon in the Masoretic Text.

Translators of the New Testament used as their base text the eclectic Greek text known as Nestle Aland, the twenty-seventh edition, which was published in 1993.

Translators of the Apocrypha faced a more complicated set of choices. Translators generally used the base text presented in the Göttingen Septuagint. For those books not yet published in the fascicles of the Göttingen Septuagint, translators used the 2006 revised edition of Rahlfs' Septuaginta, edited by Robert Hanhart. However, in those instances in which Hebrew texts have survived and offer a better reading (e.g., in Sirach and Tobit), the translator noted alternative readings to the Greek Septuagint. Second Esdras presents a special problem, explained in a footnote about the Latin text.

Footnotes. Translators decided, in certain instances, that they should explain their translations or textual decisions. However, notes are kept to a minimum and are rendered with utmost concision. Such notes when present offer: (a) evidence from ancient texts and versions (e.g., LXX; MT *men of*); (b) brief philological comment (e.g., Heb uncertain); (c) explanations of anomalies in versification (e.g., Acts 8:37: Critical editions of the Gk New Testament do not include 8:37 *Philip said to him, "If you believe with your whole heart, you can be." The eunuch answered, "I believe that Jesus Christ is God's Son"*); (d) citations of the Old Testament in the New Testament; and rarely (e) alternative translations (e.g., Or *everyone*). In those instances in which the Old Testament is cited in the New Testament, the quoted text is set in italic font.

Measurements. When possible, the CEB converts linear and spatial dimensions to feet and inches. Thus archaic terms such as rods, cubits, spans, handbreadths, and fingerbreadths are replaced with feet and inches. For example, Genesis 6:15 gives the dimensions of Noah's ark in *'ammah* or "forearms." Most translations since the KJV use the archaic English cubit to translate *'ammah:* "the length of the ark three hundred cubits, its width fifty cubits, and its height thirty cubits." The CEB translates the dimensions of the ark as "four hundred fifty feet long, seventy-five feet wide, and forty-five feet high."

The CEB prefers to transliterate (rather than translate) measurements of capacity, both wet (e.g., bath) and dry (e.g., homer), as well as measurements of weight (e.g., kikkar). When feasible, a footnote is allowed to calculate the rough equivalent in a U.S. English measurement, such as quarts.

Monetary values are inherently relative, and prices are constantly changing. Therefore, the CEB prefers to transliterate (rather than translate) monetary weights (e.g., shekel) and coins (e.g., denarion).

Months in the biblical lunar calendar are transliterated, with a footnote to indicate the approximate month or months in the Gregorian solar calendar (e.g., Nisan is March–April).

Pronouns. In ancient Hebrew and Greek a pronoun is often bound with the verb. If the translator is too literal, the English reader loses the antecedent of the pronoun so that one cannot tell who is speaking or acting in the sentence or paragraph. This problem occurs throughout much biblical literature. The CEB addresses this issue by substituting a noun for a pronoun, but only when the antecedent is clear. Because this problem and its resolution are so common, the CEB usually does not offer footnotes to identify these substitutions. CEB translators also use gender-inclusive or neutral syntax for translating pronouns that refer to humans, unless context requires otherwise.

Consistency. Although translators often try to use the same English word for a Hebrew or Greek word, many words in any language offer a breadth of meanings that do not readily correlate with a single word in the target language. For example, the Hebrew word *torah*, which has often been translated as Law, is often better translated as Instruction. The same could be said for *Sheol* (Hebrew) and *Hades* (Greek). The CEB translates these two terms as "grave" or "death" and "underworld" or "hell," respectively depending on context. A mechanical selection of any one term for words that involve semantic breadth would preclude a translation sensitive to the originating literary context.

The women and men who participated in the creation of the CEB hope that those who read and study it will find the translation to be an accurate, clear, and inspiring version of Christian scripture.

The Editorial Board of the Common English Bible
www.CommonEnglishBible.com

OLD TESTAMENT

OLD TESTAMENT

GENESIS

The book of Genesis is a book about how the universe, the earth and its creatures, faith, and the community of faith all began. At its heart, however, Genesis is a statement of faith. The stories in this book testify that all reality begins with God and that nothing exists except by the will and power of God. These stories tell us that, if we push each question of "Why?" or "How?" about our world to its ultimate end, the answer must be: God.

The book of Genesis is also about relationships. From the beginning, relationships are established between God and creation and among the different parts of creation. No part exists in isolation. The relationship that receives the most attention in Genesis is the relationship between God and the community of faith. This community was born in the relationship established between God and Abraham, and it continues to this day.

TITLE, DATE, AND AUTHORSHIP

The Hebrew title of Genesis comes from the first word in the text, which means "in the beginning (of)," and the name *Genesis* comes from the title in the Septuagint (the oldest Greek translation of the Old Testament). Genesis is part of the Pentateuch, the first five books of the Old Testament, which is also called the Torah ("Law" or "Instruction"). These books are traditionally referred to as the "five books of Moses." The close association of Moses with the law and the specific records he did write (see, for example, Exodus 17:14) have helped to foster the idea that Moses wrote the Pentateuch. Most scholars agree, however, that Moses was not the author of the Pentateuch. Indeed, there is much evidence within the books themselves that more than one person contributed to them.

The sources and writers of the Pentateuch, and of Genesis in particular, are still the objects of much study and debate. There are, however, some generally accepted opinions about how the books came about:

(1) Before much of the material in these books was written it was preserved in oral form. This is the "oral tradition," the stories, history, laws, prayers, and poems that were passed from one generation to the next before they were written down and collected.

(2) At least four sources of this tradition are found in the Pentateuch. Each source has a characteristic style, language, and perspective that (in many cases) allow it to be identified. There is no definite agreement concerning

which parts of the scripture belong to which source, and some commentators find more than four sources within the text.

(3) The four most widely accepted sources are called J, E, P, and D. J gets its name from the characteristic use of Yahweh (Jehovah) as the name for God in this source. E uses the name Elohim (divine being) for God. P stands for "priestly" because much of the material from this source focuses on the interests of priests and on the sanctuary. D stands for Deuteronomistic and is associated with much of the material in the book of Deuteronomy. J, E, and P are found in the book of Genesis.

(4) The writers who put together each of these sources probably used both oral and written material, much of which was ancient even in their day. Exact dates for J, E, P, and D are not known, nor do we know exactly when the book of Genesis was put into the form we know today. Estimates have been made, however, about the general dates for these sources. J perhaps took shape during the reigns of King David and King Solomon (1000–922 BCE), E may have developed during the 8th century BCE, P may come from the time of the exile (587–539 BCE) or soon after, and D in its earliest form probably comes from approximately 650 BCE.

(5) Some scholars believe that one person collected these various sources (and other material—for example, from "the scroll of the LORD's wars," Numbers 21:14) and formed them into the books we have today. Others believe that the collection and formation were done over a number of years by more than one person.

(6) Genesis and the other books of the Pentateuch were put together sometime during or after the Jewish exile in Babylon (587–539 BCE). The process of writing and organizing the text may have continued for a long time, but the process was completed before 250 BCE when the Septuagint translation of the Old Testament was begun.

THE CONTENT OF GENESIS

The content of Genesis can be divided into three broad sections: the primeval history (Creation through the tower of Babel), the patriarchal history (Abraham, Isaac, and Jacob), and the story of Joseph.

Each of these sections is a collection of different kinds of materials such as stories, genealogical lists, prayers, and poems. The biggest part of Genesis is taken up with stories about particular people in specific circumstances and times. These stories, however, also have an application and a point beyond the individual lives involved. Genesis is like a "family history" for the community of faith.

Though we use the word *history* in relation to the events described in Genesis, we do not mean history in our modern sense of the word. The writers of Genesis did not produce objective, footnoted, cross-referenced documents with specific dates for the people and events they described. They had a very definite perspective from which they wrote the book, and this perspective is that all reality, and specifically the reality of the community of faith, is grounded in the will and power of God. They wrote a theological history that seeks to preserve the experiences, remembrances, and beliefs of this earliest community.

This is not to say, however, that what they wrote is not true or historical. The trend of archaeological and other historical research in recent years has been to illuminate more fully this ancient world and to confirm the scriptural account. To be sure, many questions remain unanswered, and, to our twenty-first-century minds hungry for facts on which to base our beliefs, there may never be enough answers. The writers of Genesis, however, are calling us beyond this issue to larger questions that they do indeed answer: How did this world come to be? What is our place in the world? How did the community of faith begin?

GENESIS

World's creation in seven days

1 When God began to create[a] the heavens and the earth—²the earth was without shape or form, it was dark over the deep sea, and God's wind swept over the waters—³God said, "Let there be light." And so light appeared. ⁴God saw how good the light was. God separated the light from the darkness. ⁵God named the light Day and the darkness Night.

There was evening and there was morning: the first day.

⁶God said, "Let there be a dome in the middle of the waters to separate the waters from each other." ⁷God made the dome and separated the waters under the dome from the waters above the dome. And it happened in that way. ⁸God named the dome Sky.

There was evening and there was morning: the second day.

⁹God said, "Let the waters under the sky come together into one place so that the dry land can appear." And that's what happened. ¹⁰God named the dry land Earth, and he named the gathered waters Seas. God saw how good it was. ¹¹God said, "Let the earth grow plant life: plants yielding seeds and fruit trees bearing fruit with seeds inside it, each according to its kind throughout the earth." And that's what happened. ¹²The earth produced plant life: plants yielding seeds, each according to its kind, and trees bearing fruit with seeds inside it, each according to its kind. God saw how good it was.

¹³There was evening and there was morning: the third day.

¹⁴God said, "Let there be lights in the dome of the sky to separate the day from the night. They will mark events, sacred seasons, days, and years. ¹⁵They will be lights in the dome of the sky to shine on the earth." And that's what happened. ¹⁶God made the stars and two great lights: the larger light to rule over the day and the smaller light to rule over the night. ¹⁷God put them in the dome of the sky to shine on the earth, ¹⁸to rule over the day and over the night, and to separate the light from the darkness. God saw how good it was.

¹⁹There was evening and there was morning: the fourth day.

²⁰God said, "Let the waters swarm with living things, and let birds fly above the earth up in the dome of the sky." ²¹God created the great sea animals and all the tiny living things that swarm in the waters, each according to its kind, and all the winged birds, each according to its kind. God saw how good it was. ²²Then God blessed them: "Be fertile and multiply and fill the waters in the seas, and let the birds multiply on the earth."

²³There was evening and there was morning: the fifth day.

²⁴God said, "Let the earth produce every kind of living thing: livestock, crawling things, and wildlife." And that's what happened. ²⁵God made every kind of wildlife, every kind of livestock, and every kind of creature that crawls on the ground. God saw how good it was. ²⁶Then God said, "Let us make humanity in our image to resemble us so that they may take charge of the fish of the sea, the birds in the sky, the livestock, all the earth, and all the crawling things on earth."

²⁷ God created humanity
in God's own image,
in the divine image
God created them,[b]
male and female God created them.

²⁸God blessed them and said to them, "Be fertile and multiply; fill the earth and master it. Take charge of the fish of the sea, the birds in the sky, and everything crawling on the ground." ²⁹Then God said, "I now give to you all the plants on the earth that yield seeds and all the trees whose fruit produces its seeds within it. These will be your food. ³⁰To all wildlife, to all the birds in the sky, and to everything crawling on the ground—to everything that breathes—I give all the green grasses for food." And

---

[a]Or *In the beginning, God created*   [b]Heb has singular *him,* referring to *humanity.*

that's what happened. [31]God saw everything he had made: it was supremely good.

There was evening and there was morning: the sixth day.

2 The heavens and the earth and all who live in them were completed. [2]On the sixth[c] day God completed all the work that he had done, and on the seventh day God rested from all the work that he had done. [3]God blessed the seventh day and made it holy, because on it God rested from all the work of creation.[d] [4]This is the account of the heavens and the earth when they were created.

World's creation in the garden

On the day the LORD God made earth and sky—[5]before any wild plants appeared on the earth, and before any field crops grew, because the LORD God hadn't yet sent rain on the earth and there was still no human being[e] to farm the fertile land, [6]though a stream rose from the earth and watered all of the fertile land—[7]the LORD God formed the human[f] from the topsoil of the fertile land[g] and blew life's breath into his nostrils. The human came to life. [8]The LORD God planted a garden in Eden in the east and put there the human he had formed. [9]In the fertile land, the LORD God grew every beautiful tree with edible fruit, and also he grew the tree of life in the middle of the garden and the tree of the knowledge of good and evil.

[10]A river flows from Eden to water the garden, and from there it divides into four headwaters. [11]The name of the first river is the Pishon. It flows around the entire land of Havilah, where there is gold. [12]That land's gold is pure, and the land also has sweet-smelling resins and gemstones.[h] [13]The name of the second river is the Gihon. It flows around the entire land of Cush. [14]The name of the third river is the Tigris, flowing east of Assyria; and the name of the fourth river is the Euphrates.

[15]The LORD God took the human and settled him in the garden of Eden to farm it and to take care of it. [16]The LORD God commanded the human, "Eat your fill from all of the garden's trees; [17]but don't eat from the tree of the knowledge of good and evil, because on the day you eat from it, you will die!" [18]Then the LORD God said, "It's not good that the human is alone. I will make him a helper that is perfect for him." [19]So the LORD God formed from the fertile land all the wild animals and all the birds in the sky and brought them to the human to see what he would name them. The human gave each living being its name. [20]The human named all the livestock, all the birds in the sky, and all the wild animals. But a helper perfect for him was nowhere to be found.

[21]So the LORD God put the human into a deep and heavy sleep, and took one of his ribs and closed up the flesh over it. [22]With the rib taken from the human, the LORD God fashioned a woman and brought her to the human being. [23]The human[i] said,

"This one finally is bone from my bones
and flesh from my flesh.

---

[c]LXX, Sam, Syr; MT *seventh*   [d]Or *from all his work, which God created to do*   [e]Or *man* (Heb *adam*)   [f]Heb *adam*   [g]Heb *adamah*   [h]Heb uncertain   [i]Or *man* (Heb *adam*)

ADAM

The first man. Yahweh forms Adam ("human") from the ground and places him in the garden. Adam and Eve break Yahweh's one rule against eating the forbidden fruit and are expelled from the garden and cursed with pain, work, and mortality. In the NT, Paul portrays Adam as a type for Jesus Christ, the "last Adam," who reverses the exile and death brought by the "first" Adam (1 Cor 15:22, 45; Rom 5:14).

She will be called a woman[j]
  because from a man[k] she was taken."

²⁴This is the reason that a man leaves his father and mother and embraces his wife, and they become one flesh. ²⁵The two of them were naked, the man and his wife, but they weren't embarrassed.

Knowledge, not eternal life

3 The snake was the most intelligent[l] of all the wild animals that the LORD God had made. He said to the woman, "Did God really say that you shouldn't eat from any tree in the garden?"

²The woman said to the snake, "We may eat the fruit of the garden's trees ³but not the fruit of the tree in the middle of the garden. God said, 'Don't eat from it, and don't touch it, or you will die.'"

⁴The snake said to the woman, "You won't die! ⁵God knows that on the day you eat from it, you will see clearly and you will be like God, knowing good and evil." ⁶The woman saw that the tree was beautiful with

[j]Or *wife* (Heb *ishshah*) [k]Or *husband* (Heb *ish*) [l]Heb sounds like *naked*.

EVE

The name Eve, meaning "life," appears only once in the story of Eden (3:20). At first, God creates one human without sexual differentiation. In time, the Lord God observes that the singularity of the human is not "good" and decides to make a partner (Gen 2:18-20). God's first attempt to provide the human with a companion fails. God then puts the human to sleep, takes a part from its side, and closes up the place with flesh (Gen 2:21-25). God "builds" the part removed into "woman." With her creation, the sexually undifferentiated human is no more. Instead, from the leftovers of the divine surgery, man the male emerges.

In the following scene of disobedience (Gen 3:1-7), the woman figures prominently. As spokesperson for the human couple, she replies to the devious question that the serpent asks about God's command not to eat the fruit of a particular tree. To the command she attaches the prohibition "and don't touch it." In this way she becomes a faithful interpreter of divine law. She shows intelligence and thoughtfulness as she ponders the wholesome possibilities that the fruit offers: nourishment, pleasure, and wisdom. Without consulting the man, "who was with her," she eats. Then, behaving like a faithful wife, she "gave some" of the fruit to him. (The verb suggests neither trickery nor seduction.) Unlike her, he does not think about it at all but simply eats. Throughout the scene the strong, active, and independent role of the woman contrasts with the weak, passive, and acquiescent role of the man.

The contrast continues in a trial, with God questioning the couple (Gen 3:8-19). Though asked only about his disobedience, the man betrays the woman and blames both her and God. In her answer, the woman does not implicate the man but blames the serpent for beguiling her. God proceeds to describe (not prescribe) the consequences of disobedience. God curses the serpent directly and the man indirectly through the ground (Gen 3:14, 17). But God does not curse the woman. The consequences for her consist of increased pain in childbirth (a physical sign) and rule by the man (a cultural sign). Neither consequence defines her in creation.

delicious food and that the tree would provide wisdom, so she took some of its fruit and ate it, and also gave some to her husband, who was with her, and he ate it. [7] Then they both saw clearly and knew that they were naked. So they sewed fig leaves together and made garments for themselves.

[8] During that day's cool evening breeze, they heard the sound of the LORD God walking in the garden; and the man and his wife hid themselves from the LORD God in the middle of the garden's trees. [9] The LORD God called to the man and said to him, "Where are you?"

[10] The man[m] replied, "I heard your sound in the garden; I was afraid because I was naked, and I hid myself."

[11] He said, "Who told you that you were naked? Did you eat from the tree, which I commanded you not to eat?"

[12] The man said, "The woman you gave me, she gave me some fruit[n] from the tree, and I ate."

[13] The LORD God said to the woman, "What have you done?!"

And the woman said, "The snake tricked me, and I ate."

[14] The LORD God said to the snake,

"Because you did this,
　you are the one cursed
　　out of all the farm animals,
　　out of all the wild animals.
　On your belly you will crawl,
　　and dust you will eat
　　every day of your life.
[15] I will put contempt
　between you and the woman,
　between your offspring and hers.
They will strike your head,
　but you will strike at their heels."
[16] To the woman he said,
"I will make your pregnancy very painful;
　in pain you will bear children.
You will desire your husband,
　but he will rule over you."
[17] To the man he said, "Because you listened to your wife's voice and you ate from the tree that I commanded, 'Don't eat from it,'

cursed is the fertile land because of you;
　in pain you will eat from it
　every day of your life.
[18] Weeds and thistles will grow for you,
　even as you eat the field's plants;
[19] by the sweat of your face
　you will eat bread—
　　until you return to the fertile land,
　　since from it you were taken;
　you are soil,
　　to the soil you will return."

[20] The man named his wife Eve[o] because she is the mother of everyone who lives. [21] The LORD God made the man and his wife leather clothes and dressed them. [22] The LORD God said, "The human being[p] has now become like one of us, knowing good and evil." Now, so he doesn't stretch out his hand and take also from the tree of life and eat and live forever, [23] the LORD God sent him out of the garden of Eden to farm the fertile land from which he was taken. [24] He drove out the human. To the east of the garden of Eden, he stationed winged creatures wielding flaming swords to guard the way to the tree of life.

Cain and Abel

4 The man Adam knew his wife Eve intimately. She became pregnant and gave birth to Cain, and said, "I have given life to[q] a man with the LORD's help." [2] She gave birth a second time to Cain's brother Abel. Abel cared for the flocks, and Cain farmed the fertile land.

[3] Some time later, Cain presented an offering to the LORD from the land's crops [4] while Abel presented his flock's oldest offspring with their fat. The LORD looked favorably on Abel and his sacrifice [5] but didn't look favorably on Cain and his sacrifice. Cain became very angry and looked resentful. [6] The LORD said to Cain, "Why are you angry, and why do you look so resentful? [7] If you do the right thing, won't you be accepted? But if you don't do the right thing, sin will be waiting at the door ready to strike! It will entice you, but you must rule over it."

---

[m]Or He [n]Heb lacks some fruit. [o]Heb sounds like live. [p]Or man (Heb adam) [q]Or created; Heb sounds similar to Cain.

⁸Cain said to his brother Abel, "Let's go out to the field."ʳ When they were in the field, Cain attacked his brother Abel and killed him.

⁹The LORD said to Cain, "Where is your brother Abel?"

Cain said, "I don't know. Am I my brother's guardian?"

¹⁰The LORD said, "What did you do? The voice of your brother's blood is crying to me from the ground. ¹¹You are now cursed from the ground that opened its mouth to take your brother's blood from your hand. ¹²When you farm the fertile land, it will no longer grow anything for you, and you will become a roving nomad on the earth."

¹³Cain said to the LORD, "My punishment is more than I can bear. ¹⁴Now that you've driven me away from the fertile land and I am hidden from your presence, I'm about to become a roving nomad on the earth, and anyone who finds me will kill me."

¹⁵The LORD said to him, "It won't happen;ˢ anyone who kills Cain will be paid back seven times. The LORD put a sign on Cain so that no one who found him would assault him. ¹⁶Cain left the LORD's presence, and he settled down in the land of Nod, east of Eden.

Cain's descendants

¹⁷Cain knew his wife intimately. She became pregnant and gave birth to Enoch. Cain built a city and named the city after his son Enoch.

¹⁸Irad was born to Enoch. Irad fathered Mehujael, Mehujael fathered Methushael, and Methushael fathered Lamech. ¹⁹Lamech took two wives, the first named Adah and the second Zillah. ²⁰Adah gave birth to Jabal; he was the ancestor of those who live in tents and own livestock. ²¹His brother's name was Jubal; he was the ancestor of those who play stringed and wind instruments. ²²Zillah also gave birth to Tubal-cain, the ancestor ofᵗ blacksmiths and all artisans of bronze and iron. Tubal-cain's sister was Naamah.

²³Lamech said to his wives,
"Adah and Zillah,
    listen to my voice;
    wives of Lamech,
    pay attention to my words:
I killed a man for wounding me,
    a boy for striking me;
²⁴ so Cain will be paid back seven times
    and Lamech seventy-seven times."

²⁵Adam knew his wife intimately again, and she gave birth to a son. She named him Sethᵘ "because God has given me another child in place of Abel, whom Cain killed." ²⁶Seth also fathered a son and named him Enosh. At that time, people began to worship in the LORD's name.

Adam's descendants

5 This is the record of Adam's descendants. On the day God created humanity, he made them to resemble God ²and created them male and female. He blessed them and called them humanityᵛ on the day they were created. ³When Adam was 130 years old, he became the father of a son in his image, resembling him, and named him Seth. ⁴After Seth's birth, Adam lived 800 years; he had other sons and daughters. ⁵In all, Adam lived 930 years, and he died.

⁶When Seth was 105 years old, he became the father of Enosh. ⁷After the birth of Enosh, Seth lived 807 years; and he had other sons and daughters. ⁸In all, Seth lived 912 years, and he died.

⁹When Enosh was 90 years old, he became the father of Kenan. ¹⁰After Kenan's birth, Enosh lived 815 years; and he had other sons and daughters. ¹¹In all, Enosh lived 905 years, and he died.

¹²When Kenan was 70 years old, he became the father of Mahalalel. ¹³After the birth of Mahalalel, Kenan lived 840 years; and he had other sons and daughters. ¹⁴In all, Kenan lived 910 years, and he died.

¹⁵When Mahalalel was 65 years old, he became the father of Jared. ¹⁶After

---

ʳLXX, Syr, Vulg, Sam; MT lacks *Let's go out to the field.* ˢLXX, Syr, Vulg; MT *therefore* ᵗHeb lacks *the ancestor of.* ᵘSounds like the Heb verb *gave* ᵛHeb *adam*

Jared's birth, Mahalalel lived 830 years; and he had other sons and daughters. ¹⁷In all, Mahalalel lived 895 years, and he died.

¹⁸When Jared was 162 years old, he became the father of Enoch. ¹⁹After Enoch's birth, Jared lived 800 years; and he had other sons and daughters. ²⁰In all, Jared lived 962 years, and he died.

²¹When Enoch was 65 years old, he became the father of Methuselah. ²²Enoch walked with God. After Methuselah's birth, Enoch lived 300 years; and he had other sons and daughters. ²³In all, Enoch lived 365 years. ²⁴Enoch walked with God and disappeared because God took him.

²⁵When Methuselah was 187 years old, he became the father of Lamech. ²⁶After Lamech's birth, Methuselah lived 782 years; and he had other sons and daughters. ²⁷In all, Methuselah lived 969 years, and he died.

²⁸When Lamech was 182 years old, he became the father of a son ²⁹and named him Noah, saying, "This one will give us relief^w from our hard work, from the pain in our hands, because of the fertile land that the LORD cursed." ³⁰After Noah's birth, Lamech lived 595 years; and he had other sons and daughters. ³¹In all, Lamech lived 777 years, and he died.

³²When Noah was 500 years old, Noah became the father of Shem, Ham, and Japheth.

Ancient heroes

6 When the number of people started to increase throughout the fertile land, daughters were born to them. ²The divine beings saw how beautiful these human women were, so they married the ones they chose. ³The LORD said, "My breath^x will not remain in humans forever, because they are flesh. They will live one hundred twenty years." ⁴In those days, giants^y lived on the earth and also afterward, when divine beings and human daughters had sexual relations and gave birth to children. These were the ancient heroes, famous men.

Great flood

⁵The LORD saw that humanity had become thoroughly evil on the earth and that every idea their minds thought up was always completely evil. ⁶The LORD regretted making human beings on the earth, and he was heartbroken. ⁷So the LORD said, "I will wipe off of the land the human race that I've created: from human beings to livestock to the crawling things to the birds in the skies, because I regret I ever made them." ⁸But as for Noah, the LORD approved of him.

⁹These are Noah's descendants. In his

^w Heb resembles the sound of Noah's name.   ^x Or spirit   ^y Or the Nephilim

ENOCH

1. The first son of Cain and the father of Irad. The first city was named after Enoch (Gen 4:17-18).

2. In the seventh generation from Adam through Seth, Enoch was the son of Jared and the father of Methuselah (Gen 5:18-21; 1 Chron 1:2-3; Luke 3:37). Although the text pattern in the Genesis 5 genealogy says in turn that each patriarch "died," uniquely Enoch "walked with God" (Gen 5:22-24). Later interest in Enoch's nondeath is apparent, as when he is cited as an example of faith (Heb 11:5). Much as Elijah's ascension stirred expectations of his return, the fact that Enoch did not die meant that he was available in the future for use by God (Jude 14), giving rise to an abundance of visionary and prophetic literature, including three books of Enoch.

generation, Noah was a moral and exemplary man; he[z] walked with God. [10]Noah had three sons: Shem, Ham, and Japheth. [11]In God's sight, the earth had become corrupt and was filled with violence. [12]God saw that the earth was corrupt, because all creatures behaved corruptly on the earth.

[13]God said to Noah, "The end has come for all creatures, since they have filled the earth with violence. I am now about to destroy them along with the earth, [14]so make a wooden ark.[a] Make the ark with nesting places and cover it inside and out with tar. [15]This is how you should make it: four hundred fifty feet long, seventy-five feet wide, and forty-five feet high. [16]Make a roof[b] for the ark and complete it one foot from the top.[c] Put a door in its side. In the hold below, make the second and third decks.

[17]"I am now bringing the floodwaters over the earth to destroy everything under the sky that breathes. Everything on earth is about to take its last breath. [18]But I will set up my covenant with you. You will go into the ark together with your sons, your wife, and your sons' wives. [19]From all living things—from all creatures—you are to bring a pair, male and female, into the ark with you to keep them alive. [20]From each kind of bird, from each kind of livestock, and from each kind of everything that crawls on the ground—a pair from each will go in with you to stay alive. [21]Take some from every kind of food and stow it as food for you and for the animals."

[22]Noah did everything exactly as God commanded him.

7 The LORD said to Noah, "Go into the ark with your whole household, because among this generation I've seen that you are a moral man. [2]From every clean animal, take seven pairs, a male and his mate; and from every unclean animal, take one pair, a male and his mate; [3]and from the birds in the sky as well, take seven pairs, male and female, so that their offspring will survive throughout the earth. [4]In seven days from

now I will send rain on the earth for forty days and forty nights. I will wipe off from the fertile land every living thing that I have made."

[5]Noah did everything the LORD commanded him.

[6]Noah was 600 years old when the floodwaters arrived on earth. [7]Noah, his sons, his wife, and his sons' wives with him entered the ark to escape the floodwaters. [8]From the clean and unclean animals, from the birds and everything crawling on the ground, [9]two of each, male and female, went into the ark with Noah, just as God commanded Noah. [10]After seven days, the floodwaters arrived on the earth. [11]In the six hundredth year of Noah's life, in the second month, on the seventeenth day—on that day all the springs of the deep sea erupted, and the windows in the skies opened. [12]It rained on the earth forty days and forty nights. [13]That same day Noah, with his sons Shem, Ham, and Japheth, Noah's wife, and his sons' three wives, went into the ark. [14]They and every kind of animal—every kind of livestock, every kind that crawls on the ground, every kind of bird[d]—[15]they came to Noah and entered the ark, two of every creature that breathes. [16]Male and female of every creature went in, just as God had commanded him. Then the LORD closed the door behind them.[e]

[17]The flood remained on the earth for forty days. The waters rose, lifted the ark, and it rode high above the earth. [18]The waters rose and spread out over the earth. The ark floated on the surface of the waters. [19]The waters rose even higher over the earth; they covered all of the highest mountains under the sky. [20]The waters rose twenty-three feet high, covering the mountains. [21]Every creature took its last breath: the things crawling on the ground, birds, livestock, wild animals, everything swarming on the ground, and every human being. [22]Everything on dry land with life's breath in its nostrils died. [23]God wiped away every living thing that was on the fer-

[z]Heb Noah [a]Or ark of gopher wood, an unknown species of tree [b]Or window [c]Heb uncertain [d]LXX; MT every bird, every winged thing [e]Heb lacks the door.

tile land—from human beings to livestock to crawling things to birds in the sky. They were wiped off the earth. Only Noah and those with him in the ark were left. [24] The waters rose over the earth for one hundred fifty days.

8 God remembered Noah, all those alive, and all the animals with him in the ark. God sent a wind over the earth so that the waters receded. [2] The springs of the deep sea and the skies[f] closed up. The skies held back the rain. [3] The waters receded gradually from the earth. After one hundred fifty days, the waters decreased; [4] and in the seventh month, on the seventeenth day, the ark came to rest on the Ararat mountains. [5] The waters decreased gradually until the tenth month, and on the first day of the tenth month the mountain peaks appeared.

[6] After forty days, Noah opened the window of the ark that he had made. [7] He sent out a raven, and it flew back and forth until the waters over the entire earth had dried up. [8] Then he sent out a dove to see if the waters on all of the fertile land had subsided, [9] but the dove found no place to set its foot. It returned to him in the ark since waters still covered the entire earth. Noah stretched out his hand, took it, and brought it back into the ark. [10] He waited seven more days and sent the dove out from the ark again. [11] The dove came back to him in the evening, grasping a torn olive leaf in its beak. Then Noah knew that the waters were subsiding from the earth. [12] He waited seven more days and sent out the dove, but it didn't come back to him again. [13] In Noah's six hundred first year, on the first day of the first month, the waters dried up from the earth. Noah removed the ark's hatch and saw that the surface of the fertile land had dried up. [14] In the second month, on the seventeenth day, the earth was dry.

[15] God spoke to Noah, [16] "Go out of the ark, you and your wife, your sons, and your sons' wives with you. [17] Bring out with you all the animals of every kind—birds, livestock, everything crawling on the ground—so that they may populate the earth, be fertile, and multiply on the earth." [18] So Noah went out of the ark with his sons, his wife, and his sons' wives. [19] All the animals, all the livestock,[g] all the birds, and everything crawling on the ground, came out of the ark by their families.

God's promise for the earth

[20] Noah built an altar to the LORD. He took some of the clean large animals and some of the clean birds, and placed entirely burned offerings on the altar. [21] The LORD smelled the pleasing scent, and the LORD thought to himself, I will not curse the fertile land anymore because of human beings since the ideas of the human mind are evil from their youth. I will never again destroy every living thing as I have done.

[22] As long as the earth exists,
seedtime and harvest,
cold and hot,
summer and autumn,
day and night
will not cease.

God's covenant with all life

9 God blessed Noah and his sons and said to them, "Be fertile, multiply, and fill

[f] Or *the windows of the skies* [g] LXX; MT lacks *all the livestock.*

FLOOD

The flood story of Genesis 6–9 forms a key component of the Bible's primordial history (Gen 1–11). The flood story is an ancient Israelite adaptation of time-honored Near Eastern lore and establishes the core theological theme of God's governance over a conflicted world.

the earth. [2]All of the animals on the earth will fear you and dread you—all the birds in the skies, everything crawling on the ground, and all of the sea's fish. They are in your power. [3]Everything that lives and moves will be your food. Just as I gave you the green grasses, I now give you everything. [4]However, you must not eat meat with its life, its blood, in it.

[5] I will surely demand your blood
 for a human life,
 from every living thing I will demand it.
 From humans,
 from a man for his brother,
 I will demand something
 for a human life.
[6] Whoever sheds human blood,
 by a human his blood will be shed;
 for in the divine image
 God made human beings.

[7]As for you, be fertile and multiply. Populate the earth and multiply in it." [8]God said to Noah and to his sons with him, [9]"I am now setting up my covenant with you, with your descendants, [10]and with every living being with you—with the birds, with the large animals, and with all the animals of the earth, leaving the ark with you.[h] [11]I will set up my covenant with you so that never again will all life be cut off by floodwaters. There will never again be a flood to destroy the earth."

[12]God said, "This is the symbol of the covenant that I am drawing up between me and you and every living thing with you, on behalf of every future generation. [13]I have placed my bow in the clouds; it will be the symbol of the covenant between me and the earth. [14]When I bring clouds over the earth and the bow appears in the clouds, [15]I will remember the covenant between me and you and every living being among all the creatures. Floodwaters will never again destroy all creatures. [16]The bow will be in the clouds, and upon seeing it I will remember the enduring covenant between God and every living being of all the earth's creatures." [17]God said to Noah,

"This is the symbol of the covenant that I have set up between me and all creatures on earth."

Shem's blessing and Canaan's curse

[18]Noah's sons Shem, Ham, and Japheth came out of the ark. Now Ham was Canaan's father. [19]These were Noah's three sons, and from them the whole earth was populated. [20]Noah, a farmer, made a new start and planted a vineyard. [21]He drank some of the wine, became drunk, and took off his clothes in his tent. [22]Ham, Canaan's father, saw his father naked and told his two brothers who were outside. [23]Shem and Japheth took a robe, threw it over their shoulders, walked backward, and covered their naked father without looking at him because they turned away. [24]When Noah woke up from his wine, he discovered what his youngest son had done to him. [25]He said,

"Cursed be Canaan:
 the lowest servant
 he will be for his brothers."
[26] He also said,
"Bless the LORD,
 the God of Shem;
 Canaan will be his servant.
[27] May God give space[i] to Japheth;
 he will live in Shem's tents,
 and Canaan will be his servant."

[28]After the flood, Noah lived 350 years. [29]In all, Noah lived 950 years; then he died.

Noah's descendants

10 These are the descendants of Noah's sons Shem, Ham, and Japheth, to whom children were born after the flood. [2]Japheth's sons: Gomer, Magog, Madai, Javan, Tubal, Meshech, and Tiras. [3]Gomer's sons: Ashkenaz, Riphath, and Togarmah. [4]Javan's sons: Elishah, Tarshish, Kittim, and Rodanim.[j] [5]From these the island-nations were divided into their own countries, each according to their languages and their clans within their nations.

[6]Ham's sons: Cush, Egypt, Put, and Canaan. [7]Cush's sons: Seba, Havilah,

---

[h]LXX; MT includes *for all the animals of the earth.* [i]Heb sounds like *Japheth.* [j]LXX, Sam, 1 Chron 1:7; MT *Dodanim*

Sabtah, Raamah, and Sabteca. Raamah's sons: Sheba and Dedan. ⁸Cush fathered Nimrod, the first great warrior on earth. ⁹The LORD saw him as a great hunter, and so it is said, "Like Nimrod, whom the LORD saw as a great hunter." ¹⁰The most important cities in his kingdom were Babel, Erech, Accad, and Calneh in the land of Shinar. ¹¹Asshur left that land and built Nineveh, Rehoboth City, Calah, ¹²and Resen, the great city between Nineveh and Calah. ¹³Egypt fathered Ludim, Anamim, Lehabim, Naphtuhim, ¹⁴Pathrusim, Casluhim, and Caphtorim,ᵏ from which the Philistines came.

¹⁵Canaan fathered Sidon his oldest son, and Heth, ¹⁶the Jebusites, the Amorites, the Girgashites, ¹⁷the Hivites, the Arkites, the Sinites, ¹⁸the Arvadites, the Zemarites, and the Hamathites. After this the Canaanite clans were dispersed. ¹⁹The Canaanite boundary extends from Sidon by way of Gerar to Gaza and by way of Sodom, Gomorrah, Admah, and Zeboiim to Lasha. ²⁰These are Ham's sons according to their clans, their languages, their lands, and their nations.

²¹Children were also born to Shem the father of all Eber's children and Japheth's older brother.

²²Shem's sons: Elam, Asshur, Arpachshad, Lud, and Aram. ²³Aram's sons: Uz, Hul, Gether, and Mash. ²⁴Arpachshad fathered Shelah, and Shelah fathered Eber. ²⁵To Eber were born two sons: The first was named Peleg,ˡ because during his lifetime the earth was divided. His brother's name was Joktan. ²⁶Joktan fathered Almodad, Sheleph, Hazarmaveth, Jerah, ²⁷Hadoram, Uzal, Diklah, ²⁸Obal, Abimael, Sheba, ²⁹Ophir, Havilah, and Jobab. All of these were Joktan's sons. ³⁰Their settlements extended from Mesha by way of Sephar, the eastern mountains. ³¹These are Shem's sons according to their clans, their languages, their lands, and their nations.

³²These are the clans of Noah's sons according to their generations and their nations. From them the earth's nations branched out after the flood.

Origin of languages and cultures

11 All peopleᵐ on the earth had one language and the same words. ²When they traveled east,ⁿ they found a valley in the land of Shinar and settled there. ³They said to each other, "Come, let's make bricks and bake them hard." They used bricks for stones and asphalt for mortar. ⁴They said, "Come, let's build for ourselves a city and a tower with its top in the sky, and let's make a name for ourselves so that we won't be dispersed over all the earth."

⁵Then the LORD came down to see the city and the tower that the humans built. ⁶And the LORD said, "There is now one people and they all have one language. This is what they have begun to do, and now

ᵏOr *Casluhim, from which the Philistines set out, and Caphtorim* ˡOr *separation* ᵐHeb lacks *people.* ⁿOr *from the east*

BABEL

Genesis 11:1-9 explains how Babylon got its name and why God establishes the earth with different races and languages. The inhabitants of the earth, who are all speaking one language, come together in a plain in Shinar to build a city whose showpiece is a tower reaching skyward (vv. 1-4). Their aim was to stay together in one place with a single culture and a single language. To celebrate and show preference for diversity in race and language, God ends this project (vv.5-9). God confuses the common language (vv. 7, 9) and then scatters the peoples well beyond the borders of Shinar.

all that they plan to do will be possible for them. ⁷Come, let's go down and mix up their language there so they won't understand each other's language." ⁸Then the LORD dispersed them from there over all of the earth, and they stopped building the city. ⁹Therefore, it is named Babel, because there the LORD mixed up° the language of all the earth; and from there the LORD dispersed them over all the earth.

Shem's descendants

¹⁰These are Shem's descendants.

When Shem was 100 years old, he became the father of Arpachshad, two years after the flood. ¹¹After Arpachshad

°Heb *balal*, wordplay on Babel

was born, Shem lived 500 years; he had other sons and daughters.

¹²When Arpachshad was 35 years old, he became the father of Shelah. ¹³After Shelah was born, Arpachshad lived 403 years; he had other sons and daughters.

¹⁴When Shelah was 30 years old, he became the father of Eber. ¹⁵After Eber was born, Shelah lived 403 years; he had other sons and daughters.

¹⁶When Eber was 34 years old, he became the father of Peleg. ¹⁷After Peleg was born, Eber lived 430 years; he had other sons and daughters.

¹⁸When Peleg was 30 years old, he became the father of Reu. ¹⁹After Reu was

ABRAHAM

Abraham is the first of the Genesis patriarchs and has lived up to the meaning of his name ("the ancestor of many nations," according to Gen 17:5). His earlier name, Abram (probably "exalted ancestor"), is used exclusively in Genesis 11:26–17:5, 1 Chronicles 1:27, and Nehemiah 9:7. He is given his new identity in view of a covenant relationship with God (Gen 17:1-8). The formula "The God of Abraham" (e.g., Exod 4:5; 1 Kgs 18:36; 1 Chron 29:18) repeatedly links Israel with Abraham's God. Indeed, Israel is known as "the people of Abraham's God" (Ps 47:9). God's promises to Abraham are repeated to Isaac (Gen 26:3-4, 24) and to Jacob (28:4, 13-14; 35:11-12), through Joseph to the 12 sons of Jacob (50:24), and to Moses and the people of Israel (Exod 6:3-8; 33:1). Moses understands that God's covenant with Abraham takes precedence over the covenant with Israel at Sinai (Exod 32:13), remaining in place in spite of Israel's apostasy. Other texts make similar claims (e.g., Lev 26:42; Deut 4:31; 2 Kgs 13:23; Jer 33:25-26; Mic 7:20; Gal 3:29).

Next to Moses, Abraham is the most frequently named figure from the OT in the NT. Abraham is the ancestor of the Jews (Matt 1:1-2; Luke 13:16; 16:24; 19:9; Acts 13:26; Rom 4:1; 11:1). New Testament writings acknowledge Abraham's centrality in the history of salvation: Abraham receives the covenant and the promise of God's support for his descendants (Luke 1:55, 73; Acts 3:25; 7:2, 17). God is frequently called the God of Abraham and Isaac and Jacob, particularly when God's abiding presence with his people is expressed (Matt 22:32; Mark 12:26; Luke 20:37; Acts 3:13; 7:32). Abraham is not important simply as a past example. He is the symbol of future blessing for his true descendants (Matt 8:11; Luke 13:28; 16:19-31; Heb 2:16; 6:13). This blessing is seen as fulfilled in Abraham's descendant Jesus (Matt 1:1–17; Luke 3:34; Gal 3:16).

born, Peleg lived 209 years; he had other sons and daughters.

²⁰When Reu was 32 years old, he became the father of Serug. ²¹After Serug was born, Reu lived 207 years; he had other sons and daughters.

²²When Serug was 30 years old, he became the father of Nahor. ²³After Nahor was born, Serug lived 200 years; he had other sons and daughters.

²⁴When Nahor was 29 years old, he became the father of Terah. ²⁵After Terah was born, Nahor lived 119 years; he had other sons and daughters.

²⁶When Terah was 70 years old, he became the father of Abram, Nahor, and Haran.

²⁷These are Terah's descendants. Terah became the father of Abram, Nahor, and Haran. Haran became the father of Lot. ²⁸Haran died while with his father Terah in his native land,ᵖ in Ur of the Chaldeans. ²⁹Abram and Nahor both married; Abram's wife was Sarai, and Nahor's wife was Milcah the daughter of Haran, father of both Milcah and Iscah. ³⁰Sarai was unable to have children. ³¹Terah took his son Abram, his grandson Lot (son of Haran), and his son Abram's wife, Sarai his daughter-in-law. They left Ur of the Chaldeans for the land of Canaan, and arriving at Haran, they settled there. ³²Terah lived 205 years, and he died in Haran.

Abram's family moves to Canaan

12 The LORD said to Abram, "Leave your land, your family, and your father's household for the land that I will show you. ²I will make of you a great nation and will bless you. I will make your name respected, and you will be a blessing.

³ I will bless those who bless you,
   those who curse you I will curse;
   all the families of the earth
   will be blessed because of you."�q

⁴Abram left just as the LORD told him, and Lot went with him. Now Abram was 75 years old when he left Haran. ⁵Abram took his wife Sarai, his nephew Lot, all of their possessions, and those who became members of their household in Haran; and they set out for the land of Canaan. When they arrived

ᵖOr *birthplace* �q Or *will bless themselves because of you;* or *will find a blessing because of you*

LOT

Lot is the son of Abraham's dead brother Haran. He travels and lives with his uncle, who protects him. Eventually he moves to Sodom, but his uncle's presence continues to influence his life.

Lot accompanies his uncle Abraham and Sarah when they leave Haran for Canaan in response to God's promise to Abraham in Genesis 12:1-3, 7. However, when they go to Egypt (Gen 12:10-20), Lot does not accompany them. When Abraham and Sarah return to Canaan, they rejoin Lot (Gen 13:1-13). The men have large flocks and their servants fight for use of the land. Abraham asks Lot to choose where he will settle and promises to move elsewhere. Lot chooses the best-irrigated land: the Jordan Valley. Lot will find difficulty in the land of his choice while God will renew his promise to Abraham in 13:14-18. Lot's choice includes the cities of Sodom and Gomorrah, which God destroys in Genesis 19. Lot and his daughters are the only survivors; Abraham witnesses the destruction. Thinking that all human life has been destroyed, the daughters have sex with their father when he is drunk in order to repopulate the earth. Lot's daughters bear their father two sons: Moab and Ben-Ammi, understood to be the ancestors of the Moabites and Ammonites (Gen 19:30-38).

in Canaan, [6] Abram traveled through the land as far as the sacred place at Shechem, at the oak of Moreh. The Canaanites lived in the land at that time. [7] The LORD appeared to Abram and said, "I give this land to your descendants," so Abram built an altar there to the LORD who appeared to him. [8] From there he traveled toward the mountains east of Bethel, and pitched his tent with Bethel on the west and Ai on the east. There he built an altar to the LORD and worshipped in the LORD's name. [9] Then Abram set out toward the arid southern plain, making and breaking camp as he went.

Abram and Sarai visit Egypt

[10] When a famine struck the land, Abram went down toward Egypt to live as an immigrant since the famine was so severe in the land. [11] Just before he arrived in Egypt, he said to his wife Sarai, "I know you are a good-looking woman. [12] When the Egyptians see you, they will say, 'This is his wife,' and they will kill me but let you live. [13] So tell them you are my sister so that they will treat me well for your sake, and I will survive because of you."

[14] When Abram entered Egypt, the Egyptians saw how beautiful his wife was. [15] When Pharaoh's princes saw her, they praised her to Pharaoh; and the woman was taken into Pharaoh's household. [16] Things went well for Abram because of her: he acquired flocks, cattle, male donkeys, men servants, women servants, female donkeys, and camels. [17] Then the LORD struck Pharaoh and his household with severe plagues because of Abram's wife Sarai. [18] So Pharaoh summoned Abram and said, "What's this you've done to me? Why didn't you tell me she was your wife? [19] Why did you say, 'She's my sister,' so that I made her my wife? Now, here's your wife. Take her and go!" [20] Pharaoh gave his men orders concerning Abram, and they expelled him with his wife and everything he had.

Abram and Lot separate

13 Abram went up from Egypt toward the arid southern plain with his wife, with everything he had, and with Lot. [2] Abram was very wealthy in livestock, silver, and gold. [3] Abram traveled, making and breaking camp, from the arid southern plain to Bethel and to the sacred place there, where he had first pitched his tent between Bethel and Ai, [4] that is, to the place at which he had earlier built the altar. There he worshipped in the LORD's name. [5] Now Lot, who traveled with Abram, also had

CANAAN/CANAANITES

1. Ham's son and the grandson of Noah (Gen 9:18-27; 10:6). He is the ancestor of the Canaanite people. Noah curses Canaan to be literally "a slave of slaves" among his kin (Gen 9:22, 25-27).

2. A word for "trader" or merchant (e.g., Hos 12:7; Prov 31:24; Job 41:6). The association of commerce with Canaanites continues with the mercantile power of the Phoenicians in the Iron Age.

3. In the Bible there are many references to the land of Canaan and to its inhabitants. *Canaan* and *Canaanite* were terms still used in the NT (Acts 7:11; 13:19). As a geographical term, Canaan refers to the eastern Mediterranean coastal area approximating the modern states of Lebanon and Israel (inclusive of the disputed territories) and parts of Syria, such as its southern coast and the lower reaches of the Orontes Valley. In the OT, Canaan is depicted as both the land of promise and the location of a corrupting culture.

flocks, cattle, and tents. [6]They had so many possessions between them that the land couldn't support both of them. They could no longer live together. [7]Conflicts broke out between those herding Abram's livestock and those herding Lot's livestock. At that time the Canaanites and the Perizzites lived in the land.

[8]Abram said to Lot, "Let's not have disputes between me and you and between our herders since we are relatives. [9]Isn't the whole land in front of you? Let's separate. If you go north, I will go south; and if you go south, I will go north." [10]Lot looked up and saw the entire Jordan Valley. All of it was well irrigated, like the garden of the LORD, like the land of Egypt, as far as Zoar (this was before the LORD destroyed Sodom and Gomorrah). [11]So Lot chose for himself the entire Jordan Valley. Lot set out toward the east, and they separated from each other. [12]Abram settled in the land of Canaan, and Lot settled near the cities of the valley and pitched his tent close to Sodom. [13]The citizens of Sodom were very evil and sinful against the LORD.

[14]After Lot separated from him, the LORD said to Abram, "From the place where you are standing, look up and gaze to the north,

south, east, and west, [15]because all the land that you see I give you and your descendants forever. [16]I will make your descendants like the dust of the earth. If someone could count the bits of dust on the earth, then they could also count your descendants. [17]Stand up and walk around through the length and breadth of the land because I am giving it to you." [18]So Abram packed his tent and went and settled by the oaks of Mamre in Hebron. There he built an altar to the LORD.

Abram rescues Lot

14 While Amraphel was king of Shinar, Ellasar's King Arioch, Elam's King Chedorlaomer, and Goiim's King Tidal [2]declared war on Sodom's King Bera, Gomorrah's King Birsha, Admah's King Shinab, Zeboiim's King Shemeber, and the king of Bela, that is, Zoar. [3]These latter kings formed an alliance in the Siddim Valley (that is, the Dead Sea[r]). [4]For twelve years they had served Chedorlaomer, and in the thirteenth year they revolted. [5]In the fourteenth year, Chedorlaomer and the kings of his alliance came and attacked the Rephaim in Ashteroth-karnaim, the Zuzim in Ham, the Emim in Shaveh-kiriathaim, [6]and the

[r]Or *Salt Sea*

MELCHIZEDEK

Melchizedek ("Zedek's king") is the first priest mentioned in Genesis (14:18) and for that reason has been the object of speculation over the centuries despite his relatively minor role in the story of the celebration of Abram's victory over Chedorlaomer in Genesis 14:17-20. Melchizedek was king of Salem and priest of El Elyon. As king, he brought out bread and wine to Abram. As priest, he blessed Abram by El Elyon, "creator of heaven and earth" (14:19). These events occurred in the King's Valley, a site possibly near Jerusalem (2 Sam 18:18). In Psalm 110:4 the king of Judah receives eternal priesthood "in line with Melchizedek."

Given the secondary role of Melchizedek in Genesis and Psalms, readers of the Letter to the Hebrews may be surprised to find that Melchizedek and his priesthood are given great significance there (Heb 5:6, 10; 6:20–7:17), providing Christ a priestly order and prefiguring its superiority to the Jewish priesthood.

Horites in the mountains of Seir as far as El-paran near the desert. ⁷Then they turned back, came to En-mishpat (that is, Kadesh), and attacked the territory of the Amalekites, as well as the Amorites who lived in Hazazon-tamar.

⁸Then the kings of Sodom, Gomorrah, Admah, Zeboiim, and Bera (that is, Zoar) took up battle positions in the Siddim Valley ⁹against King Chedorlaomer of Elam, King Tidal of Goiim, King Amraphel of Shinar, and King Arioch of Ellasar, four kings against five.

¹⁰Now the Siddim Valley was filled with tar pits. When the kings of Sodom and Gomorrah retreated, they fell into them; and the rest fled to the mountains. ¹¹They took everything from Sodom and Gomorrah, including its food supplies, and left. ¹²They also took Lot, Abram's nephew who lived in Sodom, and everything he owned, and took off. ¹³When a survivor arrived, he told Abram the Hebrew, who lived near the oaks of the Amorite Mamre, who was the brother of Eshcol and Aner, Abram's treaty partners.

¹⁴When Abram heard that his relative had been captured, he took all of the loyal men born in his household, three hundred eighteen, and went after them as far as Dan. ¹⁵During the night, he and his servants divided themselves up against them, attacked, and chased them to Hobah, north of Damascus. ¹⁶He brought back all of the looted property, together with his relative Lot and Lot's property, wives, and people.

Abram blessed by Melchizedek

¹⁷After Abram returned from his attack on Chedorlaomer and the kings who were with him, the king of Sodom came out to the Shaveh Valley (that is, the King's Valley) to meet him. ¹⁸Now Melchizedek the king of Salem and the priest of El Elyon⁵ had brought bread and wine, ¹⁹and he blessed him,

"Bless Abram by El Elyon,
    creator of heaven and earth;
²⁰ bless El Elyon,
    who gave you the victory
        over your enemies."

Abram gave Melchizedek one-tenth of everything. ²¹Then the king of Sodom said to Abram, "Give me the people and take the property for yourself."

²²But Abram said to the king of Sodom, "I promised the LORD, El Elyon, creator of heaven and earth, ²³that I wouldn't take even a thread or a sandal strap from anything that was yours so that you couldn't say, 'I'm the one who made Abram rich.' ²⁴The only exception is that the young men may keep whatever they have taken to eat, and the men who went with me—Aner, Eshcol, and Mamre—may keep their share."

God's covenant with Abram

15 After these events, the LORD's word came to Abram in a vision, "Don't be afraid, Abram. I am your protector.ᵗ Your reward will be very great."

²But Abram said, "LORD God, what can you possibly give me, since I still have no children? The head of my household is Eliezer, a man from Damascus."ᵘ ³He continued, "Since you haven't given me any children, the head of my household will be my heir."

⁴The LORD's word came immediately to him, "This man will not be your heir. Your heir will definitely be your very own biological child." ⁵Then he brought Abram outside and said, "Look up at the sky and count the stars if you think you can count them. He continued, "This is how many children you will have." ⁶Abram trusted the LORD, and the LORD recognized Abram's high moral character.

⁷He said to Abram, "I am the LORD, who brought you out of Ur of the Chaldeans to give you this land as your possession."

⁸But Abram said, "LORD God, how do I know that I will actually possess it?"

⁹He said, "Bring me a three-year-old female calf, a three-year-old female goat, a three-year-old ram, a dove, and a young pigeon." ¹⁰He took all of these animals, split them in half, and laid the halves facing each other, but he didn't split the birds. ¹¹When vultures swooped down on the carcasses,

---

⁵Or *God Most High* ᵗOr *shield* or *benefactor* ᵘHeb uncertain

Abram waved them off. ¹²After the sun set, Abram slept deeply. A terrifying and deep darkness settled over him.

¹³Then the LORD said to Abram, "Have no doubt that your descendants will live as immigrants in a land that isn't their own, where they will be oppressed slaves for four hundred years. ¹⁴But after I punish the nation they serve, they will leave it with great wealth. ¹⁵As for you, you will join your ancestors in peace and be buried after a good long life. ¹⁶The fourth generation will return here since the Amorites' wrongdoing won't have reached its peak until then."

¹⁷After the sun had set and darkness had deepened, a smoking vessel with a fiery flame passed between the split-open animals. ¹⁸That day the LORD cut a covenant with Abram: "To your descendants I give this land, from Egypt's river to the great Euphrates, ¹⁹together with the Kenites, the Kenizzites, the Kadmonites, ²⁰the Hittites, the Perizzites, the Rephaim, ²¹the Amorites, the Canaanites, the Girgashites, and the Jebusites."

Hagar and the Ishmaelites' origins

16 Sarai, Abram's wife, had not been able to have children. Since she had an Egyptian servant named Hagar, ²Sarai said to Abram, "The LORD has kept me from giving birth, so go to my servant. Maybe she will provide me with children." Abram did just as Sarai said. ³After Abram had lived ten years in the land of Canaan, Abram's wife Sarai took her Egyptian servant Hagar and gave her to her husband Abram as his wife. ⁴He slept with Hagar, and she became pregnant. But when she realized that she was pregnant, she no longer respected her mistress. ⁵Sarai said to Abram, "This harassment is your fault. I allowed you to embrace my servant, but when she realized she was pregnant, I lost her respect. Let the LORD decide who is right, you or me."

⁶Abram said to Sarai, "Since she's your servant, do whatever you wish to her." So Sarai treated her harshly, and she ran away from Sarai.

⁷The LORD's messenger found Hagar at a spring in the desert, the spring on the road to Shur, ⁸and said, "Hagar! Sarai's servant! Where did you come from and where are you going?"

She said, "From Sarai my mistress. I'm running away."

⁹The LORD's messenger said to her, "Go back to your mistress. Put up with her harsh treatment of you." ¹⁰The LORD's messenger also said to her,

"I will give you many children,
   so many they can't be counted!"

UR

Ur was a very ancient and important city of lower Mesopotamia, located at modern Tell el-Muqayyar, just southwest of the modern city of Nasiriyah, Iraq. Though Tell el-Muqayyar lies in the desert at some distance from the Euphrates and quite removed from the head of the Persian Gulf, this is due to changes in the course of the Euphrates and to a receding coastline. An ancient bed of the Euphrates runs along the western and northern walls of Ur, and in its heyday Ur was served by both a western and a northern harbor on the right bank of the river. Ur was a large and powerful city for about 4,000 years.

The Bible mentions Ur four times as the original home of Abraham, always in the expression "Ur of the Chaldeans" (Gen 11:28, 31; 15:7; Neh 9:7). Abraham first emigrated from Ur to Haran in upper Mesopotamia and eventually from there to Canaan.

[11]The LORD's messenger said to her,
   "You are now pregnant
      and will give birth to a son.
   You will name him Ishmael[v]
      because the LORD has heard about
         your harsh treatment.
[12] He will be a wild mule of a man;
      he will fight everyone,
         and they will fight him.
      He will live at odds
         with all his relatives."[w]

[13]Hagar named the LORD who spoke to her, "You are El Roi"[x] because she said, "Can I still see after he saw me?"[y] [14]Therefore, that well is called Beer-lahai-roi;[z] it's the well between Kadesh and Bered. [15]Hagar gave birth to a son for Abram, and Abram named him Ishmael. [16]Abram was 86 years old when Hagar gave birth to Ishmael for Abram.

God's covenant with Abraham

17When Abram was 99 years old, the LORD appeared to Abram and said to him, "I am El Shaddai.[a] Walk with me and be trustworthy. [2]I will make a covenant between us and I will give you many, many descendants." [3]Abram fell on his face, and God said to him, [4]"But me, my covenant is with you; you will be the ancestor of many nations. [5]And because I have made you the ancestor of many nations, your name will no longer be Abram[b] but Abraham.[c] [6]I will make you very fertile. I will produce nations from you, and kings will come from you. [7]I will set up my covenant with you and your descendants after you in every generation as an enduring covenant. I will be your God

and your descendants' God after you. [8]I will give you and your descendants the land in which you are immigrants, the whole land of Canaan, as an enduring possession. And I will be their God."

[9]God said to Abraham, "As for you, you must keep my covenant, you and your descendants in every generation. [10]This is my covenant that you and your descendants must keep: Circumcise every male. [11]You must circumcise the flesh of your foreskins, and it will be a symbol of the covenant between us. [12]On the eighth day after birth, every male in every generation must be circumcised, including those who are not your own children: those born in your household and those purchased with silver from foreigners. [13]Be sure you circumcise those born in your household and those purchased with your silver. Your flesh will embody my covenant as an enduring covenant. [14]Any uncircumcised male whose flesh of his foreskin remains uncircumcised will be cut off from his people. He has broken my covenant."

[15]God said to Abraham, "As for your wife Sarai, you will no longer call her Sarai. Her name will now be Sarah. [16]I will bless her and even give you a son from her. I will bless her so that she will become nations, and kings of peoples will come from her."

[17]Abraham fell on his face and laughed. He said to himself, Can a 100-year-old man become a father, or Sarah, a 90-year-old woman, have a child? [18]To God Abraham said, "If only you would accept Ishmael!"

[19]But God said, "No, your wife Sarah will give birth to a son for you, and you

---

[v]Or God hears [w]Or He will reside near all his relatives. [x]Or God who sees or God whom I've seen [y]Heb uncertain; or Have I really seen God and survived? [z]Or the Well of the Living One who sees me or whom I've seen [a]Or God Almighty or God of the Mountain [b]Or exalted ancestor [c]Or ancestor of a multitude

ISHMAEL/ISHMAELITES

Ishmael was the son of Abraham and Hagar (the servant of Abraham's wife Sarah) and the older half-brother of Isaac. The Ishmaelites were an ancient tribe who, according to the Bible, were the descendants of Ishmael.

will name him Isaac.[d] I will set up my covenant with him and with his descendants after him as an enduring covenant. [20]As for Ishmael, I've heard your request. I will bless him and make him fertile and give him many, many descendants. He will be the ancestor of twelve tribal leaders, and I will make a great nation of him. [21]But I will set up my covenant with Isaac, who will be born to Sarah at this time next year."

[22]When God finished speaking to him, God ascended, leaving Abraham alone.

[23]Abraham took his son Ishmael, all those born in his household, and all those purchased with his silver—that is, every male in Abraham's household—and he circumcised the flesh of their foreskins that same day, just as God had told him to do. [24]Abraham was 99 years old when he circumcised the flesh of his foreskin, [25]and

[d]Or he laughs

COVENANT (OT)

A covenant is a formal commitment made by one party to another party, or by two parties to each other. Its seriousness is normally shown by an oath or rite undertaken before God or before other people.

The first covenant is made by God to Noah and his descendants, and thus with all future humanity, including all other living creatures (Gen 6:18; 9:8-17). This covenant is a one-sided commitment on God's part, by which God undertakes to never again flood the earth and thus destroy life on earth.

God first makes a covenant with Abraham to give the land of Canaan to his descendants (Gen 15:18-21). In God's second covenant with Abraham (Gen 17), the focus of the covenant lies on the promise of offspring. Like the Noah covenant, this Abraham covenant issues entirely from God's initiative but leaves ambiguous the relationship between divine commitment and human obligation.

In Exodus 6:6-8, God refers to delivering Israel from slavery, establishing the mutual relationship, and taking them to the land. When they reach Sinai, in Exodus 19:1-8 God points out that the first undertaking has been fulfilled; it is therefore possible to move on to the second. This will involve Israel's keeping God's covenant. The phrase recurs from Genesis 17:9-10, and the people could understandably reckon that God is simply reasserting the demand for circumcision; this might explain the ease with which they agree, "Everything that the LORD has said we will do" (Exod 19:8). Actually, it will become clear that keeping the covenant will now have much broader implications.

In his "last words" David says that God "has made an eternal covenant with me, laid out and secure in every detail" (2 Sam 23:5). The Bible has not recorded this, though one could see God's promise in 2 Samuel 7 as covenant-like.

Beyond the calamity of exile God declares the intention of making a new covenant with both Judah and Israel (Jer 31:31-34). It will be new because the thing God intends to do is different; it is new as the Sinai covenant was new over against the Abraham covenant.

his son Ishmael was 13 years old when the flesh of his foreskin was circumcised. ²⁶That same day Abraham and his son Ishmael were circumcised. ²⁷All the men of his household, those born in his household and those purchased with silver from foreigners, were circumcised with him.

Isaac's birth announced

18 The LORD appeared to Abraham at the oaks of Mamre while he sat at the entrance of his tent in the day's heat. ²He looked up and suddenly saw three men standing near him. As soon as he saw them, he ran from his tent entrance to greet them and bowed deeply. ³He said, "Sirs, if you would be so kind, don't just pass by your servant. ⁴Let a little water be brought so you may wash your feet and refresh yourselves under the tree. ⁵Let me offer you a little bread so you will feel stronger, and after that you may leave your servant and go on your way—since you have visited your servant."

They responded, "Fine. Do just as you have said."

⁶So Abraham hurried to Sarah at his tent and said, "Hurry! Knead three seahs^e of the finest flour and make some baked goods!" ⁷Abraham ran to the cattle, took a healthy young calf, and gave it to a young servant, who prepared it quickly. ⁸Then Abraham took butter, milk, and the calf that had been prepared, put the food in front of them, and stood under the tree near them as they ate.

⁹They said to him, "Where's your wife Sarah?"

And he said, "Right here in the tent."

¹⁰Then one of the men said, "I will definitely return to you about this time next year. Then your wife Sarah will have a son!"

Sarah was listening at the tent door behind him. ¹¹Now Abraham and Sarah were both very old. Sarah was no longer menstruating. ¹²So Sarah laughed to herself, thinking, I'm no longer able to have children and my husband's old.

¹³The LORD said to Abraham, "Why did Sarah laugh and say, 'Me give birth? At my age?' ¹⁴Is anything too difficult for the LORD? When I return to you about this time next year, Sarah will have a son."

¹⁵Sarah lied and said, "I didn't laugh," because she was frightened.

But he said, "No, you laughed."

Abraham pleads for Sodom

¹⁶The men got up from there and went over to look down on Sodom. Abraham was walking along with them to send them off ¹⁷when the LORD said, "Will I keep from Abraham what I'm about to do? ¹⁸Abraham will certainly become a great populous nation, and all the earth's nations will be blessed because of him. ¹⁹I have formed a relationship with him so that he will instruct his children and his household after him. And they will keep to the LORD's path, being moral and just so that the LORD can do for Abraham everything he said he would." ²⁰Then the LORD said, "The cries of injustice from Sodom and Gomorrah are countless, and their sin is very serious! ²¹I will go down now to examine the cries of injustice that have reached me. Have they really done all this? If not, I want to know."

²²The men turned away and walked toward Sodom, but Abraham remained standing in front of the LORD.^f ²³Abraham approached and said, "Will you really sweep away the innocent^g with the guilty?^h ²⁴What if there are fifty innocent people in the city? Will you really sweep it away and not save the place for the sake of the fifty innocent people in it? ²⁵It's not like you to do this, killing the innocent with the guilty as if there were no difference. It's not like you! Will the judge of all the earth not act justly?"

²⁶The LORD said, "If I find fifty innocent people in the city of Sodom, I will save it because of them."

²⁷Abraham responded, "Since I've already decided to speak with my Lord, even though I'm just soil and ash, ²⁸what if

---

^e One seah is seven and a half quarts. ^f Some ancient manuscripts read *but the LORD remained standing in front of Abraham.* ^g Or *righteous* ^h Or *wicked* there are five fewer innocent people than fifty? Will you destroy the whole city over just five?"

The LORD said, "If I find forty-five there, I won't destroy it."

²⁹Once again Abraham spoke, "What if forty are there?"

The LORD said, "For the sake of forty, I will do nothing."

³⁰He said, "Don't be angry with me, my Lord, but let me speak. What if thirty are there?"

The LORD said, "I won't do it if I find thirty there."

³¹Abraham said, "Since I've already decided to speak with my Lord, what if twenty are there?"

The LORD said, "I won't do it, for the sake of twenty."

³²Abraham said, "Don't be angry with me, my Lord, but let me speak just once more. What if there are ten?"

And the LORD said, "I will not destroy it because of those ten." ³³When the LORD finished speaking with Abraham, he left; but Abraham stayed there in that place.

Lot leaves Sodom

19 The two messengers entered Sodom in the evening. Lot, who was sitting at the gate of Sodom, saw them, got up to greet them, and bowed low. ²He said, "Come to your servant's house, spend the night, and wash your feet. Then you can get up early and go on your way."

But they said, "No, we will spend the night in the town square." ³He pleaded earnestly with them, so they went with him and entered his house. He made a big meal for them, even baking unleavened bread, and they ate.

⁴Before they went to bed, the men of the city of Sodom—everyone from the youngest to the oldest—surrounded the house ⁵and called to Lot, "Where are the men who arrived tonight? Bring them out to us so that we may have sex with them."

⁶Lot went out toward the entrance, closed the door behind him, ⁷and said, "My brothers, don't do such an evil thing. ⁸I've got two daughters who are virgins. Let me bring them out to you, and you may do to them whatever you wish. But don't do anything to these men because they are now under the protection of my roof."

⁹They said, "Get out of the way!" And they continued, "Does this immigrant want to judge us? Now we will hurt you more than we will hurt them." They pushed Lot back and came close to breaking down the door. ¹⁰The men inside reached out and pulled Lot back into the house with them

SODOM/SODOMITES

Sodom is first mentioned in the list of nations in Genesis 10:1-32. It appears in a geographical description of Canaan (10:19) and as the land of the cursed descendants of Noah's son Ham, the Canaanites (see 9:22-27). One boundary extends to the southeast in the direction of Lasha, as far as, but not including, "Sodom, Gomorrah, Admah, and Zeboiim" (10:19; cf. Gen 13:10, 12-13; 14:2, 8). These four cities, with a fifth, Bela, later called Zoar (13:10; 14:2, 8; 19:22-23, 30), form a region known collectively as the "cities of the valley" (Gen 13:12).

These cities play an important role in Genesis, because they show a contrast with the life Abraham leaves to his descendants. They are notable for their attractiveness (to Lot and to later Israelites), their proverbial wickedness (as homes to every sin), and their deserved destruction (an ever-present threat to an "evil and sinful" people of God [Gen 13:13]).

and slammed the door. [11]Then the messengers blinded the men near the entrance of the house, from the youngest to the oldest, so that they groped around trying to find the entrance.

[12]The men said to Lot, "Who's still with you here? Take away from this place your sons-in-law, your sons, your daughters, and everyone else you have in the city [13]because we are about to destroy this place. The LORD has found the cries of injustice so serious that the LORD sent us to destroy it."

[14]Lot went to speak to his sons-in-law, married to his daughters, and said, "Get up and get out of this place because the LORD is about to destroy the city." But his sons-in-law thought he was joking.

[15]When dawn broke, the messengers urged Lot, "Get up and take your wife and your two daughters who are here so that you are not swept away because of the evil in this city." [16]He hesitated, but because the LORD intended to save him, the men grabbed him, his wife, and two daughters by the hand, took him out, and left him outside the city.

[17]After getting them out, the men said, "Save your lives! Don't look back! And don't stay in the valley. Escape to the mountains so that you are not swept away."

[18]But Lot said to them, "No, my lords, please. [19]You've done me a favor and have been so kind to save my life. But I can't escape to the mountains since the catastrophe might overtake me there and I'd die. [20]This city here is close enough to flee to, and it's small. It's small, right? Let me escape there, and my life will be saved."

[21]He said to Lot, "I'll do this for you as well; I won't overthrow the city that you have described. [22]Hurry! Escape to it! I can't do anything until you get there." That is why the name of the city is Zoar.[i]

Sodom and Gomorrah destroyed

[23]As the sun rose over the earth, Lot arrived in Zoar; [24]and the LORD rained down burning asphalt from the skies onto Sodom and Gomorrah. [25]The LORD destroyed these cities, the entire valley, everyone who lived in the cities, and all of the fertile land's vegetation. [26]When Lot's wife looked back, she turned into a pillar of salt.

[27]Abraham set out early for the place where he had stood with the LORD, [28]and looked out over Sodom and Gomorrah and over all the land of the valley. He saw the smoke from the land rise like the smoke from a kiln.

Origin of Moab and Ammon

[29]When God destroyed the cities in the valley, God remembered Abraham and sent Lot away from the disaster that overtook the cities in which Lot had lived. [30]Since Lot had become fearful of living in Zoar, he and his two daughters headed up from Zoar and settled in the mountains where he and his two daughters lived in a cave. [31]The older daughter said to the younger, "Our father is old, and there are no men in the land to sleep with us as is the custom everywhere. [32]Come on, let's give our father wine to drink, lie down with him, and we'll have children from our father." [33]That night they served their father wine, and the older daughter went in and lay down with her father, without him noticing when she lay down or got up. [34]The next day the older daughter said to the younger, "Since I lay down with our father last night, let's serve him wine tonight too, and you go in and lie down with him so that we will both have children from our father." [35]They served their father wine that night also, and the younger daughter lay down with him, without him knowing when she lay down or got up. [36]Both of Lot's daughters became pregnant by their father. [37]The older daughter gave birth to a son and named him Moab. He is the ancestor of today's Moabites. [38]The younger daughter also gave birth to a son and named him Ben-ammi.[j] He is the ancestor of today's Ammonites.

Abraham and Sarah visit Gerar

20Abraham traveled from there toward the land of the arid southern

---

[i]Or small   [j]Or son of my people

plain, and he settled as an immigrant in Gerar, between Kadesh and Shur. ²Abraham said of his wife Sarah, "She's my sister." So King Abimelech of Gerar took her into his household.

³But God appeared to Abimelech that night in a dream and said to him, "You are as good as dead because of this woman you have taken. She is a married woman."

⁴Now Abimelech hadn't gone near her, and he said, "Lord, will you really put an innocent nation to death? ⁵Didn't he say to me, 'She's my sister,' and didn't she—even she—say, 'He's my brother'? My intentions were pure, and I acted innocently when I did this."

⁶God said to him in the dream, "I know that your intentions were pure when you did this. In fact, I kept you from sinning against me. That's why I didn't allow you to touch her. ⁷Now return the man's wife. He's a prophet; he will pray for you so you may live. But if you don't return her, know that you and everyone with you will die!"

⁸Abimelech got up early in the morning and summoned all of his servants. When he told them everything that had happened, the men were terrified. ⁹Then Abimelech summoned Abraham and said to him, "What have you done to us? What sin did I commit against you that you have brought this terrible sin to me and my kingdom, by doing to me something that simply isn't done?" ¹⁰Abimelech said to Abraham, "What were you thinking when you did this thing?"

¹¹Abraham said, "I thought to myself, No one reveres God here and they will kill me to get my wife. ¹²She is, truthfully, my sister—my father's daughter but not my mother's daughter—and she's now my wife. ¹³When God led me away from my father's household, I said to her, 'This is the loyalty I expect from you: in each place we visit, tell them, "He is my brother."'"

¹⁴Abimelech took flocks, cattle, male servants, and female servants, and gave them to Abraham; and Abimelech returned his wife Sarah. ¹⁵Abimelech said, "My land

is here available to you. Live wherever you wish." ¹⁶To Sarah, he said, "I've given your brother one thousand pieces of silver. It means that neither you nor anyone with you has done anything wrong. Everything has been set right." ¹⁷Abraham prayed to God; and God restored Abimelech, his wife, and his women servants to health, and they were able to have children. ¹⁸Because of the incident with Abraham's wife Sarah, the LORD had kept all of the women in Abimelech's household from having children.

Isaac's birth

21 The LORD was attentive to Sarah just as he had said, and the LORD carried out just what he had promised her. ²She became pregnant and gave birth to a son for Abraham when he was old, at the very time God had told him. ³Abraham named his son—the one Sarah bore him—Isaac.ᵏ ⁴Abraham circumcised his son Isaac when he was eight days old just as God had commanded him. ⁵Abraham was 100 years old when his son Isaac was born. ⁶Sarah said, "God has given me laughter. Everyone who hears about it will laugh with me."ˡ ⁷She said, "Who could have told Abraham that Sarah would nurse sons? But now I've given birth to a son when he was old!"

Hagar and Ishmael evicted

⁸The boy grew and stopped nursing. On the day he stopped nursing, Abraham prepared a huge banquet. ⁹Sarah saw Hagar's son laughing, the one Hagar the Egyptian had borne to Abraham. ¹⁰So she said to Abraham, "Send this servant away with her son! This servant's son won't share the inheritance with my son Isaac."

¹¹This upset Abraham terribly because the boy was his son. ¹²God said to Abraham, "Don't be upset about the boy and your servant. Do everything Sarah tells you to do because your descendants will be traced through Isaac. ¹³But I will make of your servant's son a great nation too, because he is also your descendant." ¹⁴Abraham got up early in the morning, took some bread and a

---

ᵏOr he laughs ˡOr God has made a joke of me. Everyone who hears about it will laugh at me.

flask of water, and gave it to Hagar. He put the boy in her shoulder sling and sent her away.

She left and wandered through the desert near Beer-sheba. ¹⁵Finally the water in the flask ran out, and she put the boy down under one of the desert shrubs. ¹⁶She walked away from him about as far as a bow shot and sat down, telling herself, I can't bear to see the boy die. She sat at a distance, cried out in grief, and wept.

¹⁷God heard the boy's cries, and God's messenger called to Hagar from heaven and said to her, "Hagar! What's wrong? Don't be afraid. God has heard the boy's cries over there. ¹⁸Get up, pick up the boy, and take him by the hand because I will make of him a great nation." ¹⁹Then God opened her eyes, and she saw a well. She

went over, filled the water flask, and gave the boy a drink. ²⁰God remained with the boy; he grew up, lived in the desert, and became an expert archer. ²¹He lived in the Paran desert, and his mother found him an Egyptian wife.

Abraham's treaty with the Philistines

²²At that time Abimelech, and Phicol commander of his forces, said to Abraham, "God is with you in everything that you do. ²³So give me your word under God that you won't cheat me, my children, or my descendants. Just as I have treated you fairly, so you must treat me and the land in which you are an immigrant."

²⁴Abraham said, "I give you my word." ²⁵Then Abraham complained to Abimelech

ISAAC

Son of Abraham and Sarah. Promised in Genesis 17–18, Isaac next appears in Genesis 20–22. At first, he is only implicitly involved in the story, but the issue of his birth nonetheless features when Abraham attempts to pass Sarah off as his sister to Abimelech, king of Gerar.

The issues of Abraham's bizarre offer of his own wife to Abimelech when she was about to bear Isaac, his callous attitude toward the life of his older son (Ishmael) as well as that son's mother (Hagar), and his willingness to make covenant with a human sovereign all converge as a strong undercurrent of doubt about his character by the time Genesis 22 begins "After these events, God tested Abraham." Taking the chapter out of its context makes what happens seem unmotivated, an arbitrary test of loyalty arising from God's nature alone, rather than from Abraham's character. In Genesis 22, Abraham is not the noble figure of later tradition, but the subject of testing, because his actions and their motivations have been dubious. God prevents Abraham from sacrificing Isaac. The story emphasizes at its climax that Abraham and his descendants will go on to live out the promise made by the Lord (vv. 16-18) and that Abraham is not to do anything whatever to harm Isaac (vv. 12-14). When he returns to Beer-sheba at the close (v. 19), Abraham does so on the basis of his covenant with the Lord, not with Abimelech, and with a complete dedication to Isaac as his and Sarah's son.

Abraham accordingly secures Rebekah as a wife for Isaac, because she is not a Canaanite but a woman of Abraham's own land and kin (Gen 24). Isaac rather than Ishmael is the progeny of the covenant, not only by virtue of his residence in the land of promise, but also because of the union he came from and the marriage he entered.

about a well that Abimelech's servants had seized. [26]Abimelech said, "I don't know who has done this, and you didn't tell me. I didn't even hear about it until today." [27]Abraham took flocks and cattle, gave them to Abimelech, and the two of them drew up a treaty.[m] [28]Abraham set aside, by themselves, seven female lambs from the flock. [29]So Abimelech said to Abraham, "What are these seven lambs you've set apart?"

[30]Abraham said, "These seven lambs that you take from me will attest that I dug this well." [31]Therefore, the name of that place is Beer-sheba[n] because there they gave each other their word. [32]After they drew up a treaty[o] at Beer-sheba, Abimelech, and Phicol commander of his forces, returned to the land of the Philistines. [33]Abraham planted a tamarisk tree in Beer-sheba, and he worshipped there in the name of the LORD, El Olam.[p] [34]Abraham lived as an immigrant in the Philistines' land for a long time.

Binding of Isaac

22 After these events, God tested Abraham and said to him, "Abraham!"

Abraham answered, "I'm here."

[2]God said, "Take your son, your only son whom you love, Isaac, and go to the land of Moriah. Offer him up as an entirely burned offering there on one of the mountains that I will show you." [3]Abraham got up early in the morning, harnessed his donkey, and took two of his young men with him, together with his son Isaac. He split the wood for the entirely burned offering, set out, and went to the place God had described to him.

[4]On the third day, Abraham looked up and saw the place at a distance. [5]Abraham said to his servants, "Stay here with the donkey. The boy and I will walk up there, worship, and then come back to you."

[6]Abraham took the wood for the entirely burned offering and laid it on his son Isaac. He took the fire and the knife in his hand, and the two of them walked on together. [7]Isaac said to his father Abraham, "My father?"

Abraham said, "I'm here, my son."

Isaac said, "Here is the fire and the wood, but where is the lamb for the entirely burned offering?"

[8]Abraham said, "The lamb for the entirely burned offering? God will see to it,[q] my son." The two of them walked on together.

[9]They arrived at the place God had described to him. Abraham built an altar there and arranged the wood on it. He tied up his son Isaac and laid him on the altar on top of the wood. [10]Then Abraham stretched out his hand and took the knife to kill his son as a sacrifice. [11]But the LORD's messenger called out to Abraham from heaven, "Abraham? Abraham?"

Abraham said, "I'm here."

[12]The messenger said, "Don't stretch out your hand against the young man, and don't do anything to him. I now know that you revere God and didn't hold back your son, your only son, from me." [13]Abraham looked up and saw a single ram[r] caught by its horns in the dense underbrush. Abraham went over, took the ram, and offered it as an entirely burned offering instead of his son. [14]Abraham named that place "the LORD sees."[s] That is the reason people today say, "On this mountain the LORD is seen."[t]

[15]The LORD's messenger called out to Abraham from heaven a second time [16]and said, "I give my word as the LORD that because you did this and didn't hold back your son, your only son, [17]I will bless you richly and I will give you countless descendants, as many as the stars in the sky and as the grains of sand on the seashore. They will conquer their enemies' cities. [18]All the nations of the earth will be blessed because of your descendants, because you obeyed me." [19]After Abraham returned to the young men, they got up and went to Beer-sheba where Abraham lived.

---

[m]Or *covenant* [n]Or *Well of seven;* or *Well of giving one's word* [o]Or *covenant* [p]Or *the eternal God* [q]Or *God will see;* or *God will provide* [r]LXX, Sam, Syr, Tg; MT *a ram behind* [s]Or *the LORD is seen;* or *the LORD provides* [t]Or *the LORD sees;* or *on the LORD's mountain, it will be provided*

Abraham's nephews in Syria

²⁰ After these events, Abraham was told: "Milcah has now also given birth to sons for your brother Nahor. ²¹ They are Uz his oldest son, Buz his brother, Kemuel the father of Aram, ²² Chesed, Hazo, Pildash, Jidlaph, and Bethuel." ²³ Bethuel became the father of Rebekah. These are the eight Milcah bore for Nahor, Abraham's brother. ²⁴ His secondary wife's name was Reumah, and she gave birth to Tebah, Gaham, Tahash, and Maacah.

Sarah's death and burial site

23 Sarah lived to be 127 years old; this was how long she lived. ² She died in Kiriath-arba, that is, in Hebron, in the land of Canaan; and Abraham cried out in grief and wept for Sarah. ³ After he got up from embracing his deceased wife, he spoke with the Hittites: ⁴ "I am an immigrant and a temporary resident with you. Give me some property for a burial plot among you so that I can bury my deceased wife near me."

⁵ The Hittites responded to Abraham, ⁶ "Listen to us, sir. You are an eminent man of God among us. Bury your dead in one of our own select burial sites. None of us will keep our own burial plots from you to bury your dead."

⁷ Abraham rose, bowed to the local citizens the Hittites, ⁸ and spoke with them: "If you yourselves allow me to bury my dead near me, listen to me and ask Ephron, Zohar's son, ⁹ to give me his own cave in Machpelah at the edge of his field. Let him give it to me for the full price, to be witnessed by you, as my own burial property."

¹⁰ Now Ephron was a native Hittite. So Ephron the Hittite responded to Abraham publicly in order that the Hittites and everyone at his city's gate could hear: ¹¹ "No, sir. Listen, I will give you the field, and I will give you the cave in it. In front of my people's witnesses, I will give it to you. Bury your dead!"

¹² Abraham bowed before the local citizens ¹³ and spoke to Ephron publicly in the presence of the local citizens: "If only you would accept my offer. I will give you the price of the field. Take it from me so that I can bury my dead there."

¹⁴ Ephron responded to Abraham, ¹⁵ "Sir, what is four hundred shekels of silver between me and you for the land so that you can bury your dead?" ¹⁶ Abraham accepted Ephron's offer and weighed out for Ephron the silver he requested publicly before the Hittites: four hundred shekels of silver at the current rate of exchange.

¹⁷ So the field of Ephron in Machpelah near Mamre—the field and the cave in it, and all the trees within the field's boundaries—was officially transferred ¹⁸ to Abraham as his property in the presence of the Hittites and of everyone at his city's gate. ¹⁹ After this, Abraham buried his wife Sarah in the cave in the field of Machpelah near Mamre, that is, Hebron, in the land of Canaan. ²⁰ The field and the cave in it were officially transferred from the Hittites to Abraham as his burial property.

Isaac marries Rebekah

24 As the days went by and Abraham became older, the LORD blessed Abraham in every way. ² Abraham said to the oldest servant of his household, who was in charge of everything he owned, "Put your hand under my thigh. ³ By the LORD, God of heaven and earth, give me your word that you won't choose a wife for my son from the Canaanite women among whom I live. ⁴ Go to my land and my family and find a wife for my son Isaac there."

⁵ The servant said to him, "What if the woman doesn't agree to come back with me to this land? Shouldn't I take your son back to the land you left?"

⁶ Abraham said to him, "Be sure you don't take my son back there. ⁷ The LORD, God of heaven—who took me from my father's household and from my family's land, who spoke with me and who gave me his word, saying, 'I will give this land to your descendants'—he will send his messenger in front of you, and you will find a wife for my son there. ⁸ If the woman won't agree to come back with you, you will be free from this obligation to me. Only don't take my son back there." ⁹ So the servant put his hand under his master Abraham's thigh and gave him his word about this mission.

[10] The servant took ten of his master's camels and all of his master's best provisions, set out, and traveled to Nahor's city in Aram-naharaim. [11] He had the camels kneel down outside the city at the well in the evening, when women come out to draw water. [12] He said, "LORD, God of my master Abraham, make something good happen for me today and be loyal to my master Abraham. [13] I will stand here by the spring while the daughters of the men of the city come out to draw water. [14] When I say to a young woman, 'Hand me your water jar so I can drink,' and she says to me, 'Drink, and I will give your camels water too,' may she be the one you've selected for your servant Isaac. In this way I will know that you've been loyal to my master." [15] Even before he finished speaking, Rebekah—daughter of Bethuel the son of Milcah wife of Nahor, Abraham's brother—was coming out with a water jar on her shoulder. [16] The young woman was very beautiful, old enough to be married, and hadn't known a man intimately. She went down to the spring, filled her water jar, and came back up.

[17] The servant ran to meet her and said, "Give me a little sip of water from your jar." [18] She said, "Drink, sir." Then she quickly lowered the water jar with her hands and gave him some water to drink. [19] When she finished giving him a drink, she said, "I'll draw some water for your camels too, till they've had enough to drink." [20] She emptied her water jar quickly into the watering trough, ran to the well again to draw water, and drew water for all of the camels. [21] The man stood gazing at her, wondering silently if the LORD had made his trip successful or not.

[22] As soon as the camels had finished drinking, the man took out a gold ring, weighing a half shekel,[u] and two gold bracelets for her arms, weighing ten shekels. [23] He said, "Please tell me whose daughter you are. Is there room in your father's house for us to spend the night?"

[24] She responded, "I'm the daughter of Bethuel, who is the son of Milcah and Nahor." [25] She continued, "We have plenty of straw and feed for the camels, and a place to spend the night."

[26] The man bowed down and praised the LORD: [27] "Bless the LORD, God of my master Abraham, who hasn't given up his loyalty and his faithfulness to my master. The LORD has shown me the way to the household of my master's brother."

[28] The young woman ran and told her mother's household everything that had happened. [29] Rebekah had a brother named Laban, and Laban ran to the man outside

[u] Heb *beqa*

REBEKAH

Rebekah (or "Rebecca," Rom 9:10-12) is the second matriarch in the Hebrew family line after Sarah. She is the wife of Isaac, the mother of Jacob and Esau, and the daughter of Bethuel, son of Nahor and Milcah. Rebekah is an independent, assertive, clever character who overshadows her husband Isaac, about whom we learn much less than we do about his wife.

In the NT, Paul contends that Abraham's only true heirs are those born to him as a result of a promise (Gen 18:10). He further illustrates this concept with Sarah and Hagar, two mothers, and with Rebekah, one mother with two sons, of whom God promises that the elder will serve the younger (Rom 9:10-12).

by the spring. ³⁰When he had seen the ring and the bracelets on his sister's arms, and when he had heard his sister Rebekah say, "This is what the man said to me," he went to the man, who was still standing by the spring with his camels. ³¹Laban said, "Come in, favored one of the LORD! Why are you standing outside? I've prepared the house and a place for the camels." ³²So the man entered the house. Then Laban unbridled the camels, provided straw and feed for them and water to wash his feet and the feet of the men with him, ³³and set out a meal for him.

But the man said, "I won't eat until I've said something."

Laban replied, "Say it."

³⁴The man said, "I am Abraham's servant." ³⁵The LORD has richly blessed my master, has made him a great man, and has given him flocks, cattle, silver, gold, men servants, women servants, camels, and donkeys. ³⁶My master's wife Sarah gave birth to a son for my master in her old age, and he's given him everything he owns. ³⁷My master made me give him my word: 'Don't choose a wife for my son from the Canaanite women, in whose land I'm living. ³⁸No, instead, go to my father's household and to my relatives and choose a wife for my son.' ³⁹I said to my master, 'What if the woman won't come back with me?' ⁴⁰He said to me, 'The LORD, whom I've traveled with everywhere, will send his messenger with you and make your trip successful; and you will choose a wife for my son from my relatives and from my father's household. ⁴¹If you go to my relatives, you will be free from your obligation to me. Even if they provide no one for you, you will be free from your obligation to me.'

⁴²"Today I arrived at the spring, and I said, 'LORD, God of my master Abraham, if you wish to make the trip I'm taking successful, ⁴³when I'm standing by the spring and the young woman who comes out to draw water and to whom I say, "Please give me a little drink of water from your jar," ⁴⁴and she responds to me, "Drink, and I will draw water for your camels too," may she be the woman the LORD has selected for

my master's son.' ⁴⁵Before I finished saying this to myself, Rebekah came out with her water jar on her shoulder and went down to the spring to draw water. And I said to her, 'Please give me something to drink.' ⁴⁶She immediately lowered her water jar and said, 'Drink, and I will give your camels something to drink too.' So I drank and she also gave water to the camels. ⁴⁷Then I asked her, 'Whose daughter are you?' And she said, 'The daughter of Bethuel, Nahor's son whom Milcah bore him.' I put a ring in her nose and bracelets on her arms. ⁴⁸I bowed and worshipped the LORD and blessed the LORD, the God of my master Abraham, who led me in the right direction to choose the granddaughter of my master's brother for his son. ⁴⁹Now if you're loyal and faithful to my master, tell me. If not, tell me so I will know where I stand either way."

⁵⁰Laban and Bethuel both responded, "This is all the LORD's doing. We have nothing to say about it. ⁵¹Here is Rebekah, right in front of you. Take her and go. She will be the wife of your master's son, just as the LORD said." ⁵²When Abraham's servant heard what they said, he bowed low before the LORD. ⁵³The servant brought out gold and silver jewelry and clothing and gave them to Rebekah. To her brother and to her mother he gave the finest gifts. ⁵⁴He and the men with him ate and drank and spent the night.

When they got up in the morning, the servant said, "See me off to my master."

⁵⁵Her brother and mother said, "Let the young woman stay with us not more than ten days, and after that she may go."

⁵⁶But he said to them, "Don't delay me. The LORD has made my trip successful. See me off so that I can go to my master."

⁵⁷They said, "Summon the young woman, and let's ask her opinion." ⁵⁸They called Rebekah and said to her, "Will you go with this man?"

She said, "I will go."

⁵⁹So they sent off their sister Rebekah, her nurse, Abraham's servant, and his men. ⁶⁰And they blessed Rebekah, saying to her,

"May you, our sister, become
    thousands of ten thousand;

may your children possess
their enemies' cities."

⁶¹Rebekah and her young women got up, mounted the camels, and followed the man. So the servant took Rebekah and left.

⁶²Now Isaac had come from the region of ᵛ Beer-lahai-roi and had settled in the arid southern plain. ⁶³One evening, Isaac went out to inspect the pasture,ʷ and while staring he saw camels approaching. ⁶⁴Rebekah stared at Isaac. She got down from the camel ⁶⁵and said to the servant, "Who is this man walking through the pasture to meet us?"

The servant said, "He's my master." So she took her headscarf and covered herself. ⁶⁶The servant told Isaac everything that had happened. ⁶⁷Isaac brought Rebekah into his mother Sarah's tent. He received Rebekah as his wife and loved her. So Isaac found comfort after his mother's death.

Abraham and Keturah's children

25 Abraham married another wife, named Keturah. ²The children she bore him were Zimran, Jokshan, Medan, Midian, Ishbak, and Shuah. ³Jokshan became the father of Sheba and Dedan. Dedan's sons were Asshurim, Letushim, and Leummim. ⁴Midian's sons were Ephah, Epher, Enoch, Abida, and Eldaah. All of these were Keturah's sons. ⁵Abraham gave everything he owned to Isaac. ⁶To the sons of Abraham's secondary wives, Abraham gave gifts and, while he was still living, sent them away from his son Isaac to land in the east.

Abraham's death

⁷Abraham lived to the age of 175. ⁸Abraham took his last breath and died after a good long life, a content old man, and he was placed with his ancestors. ⁹His sons Isaac and Ishmael buried him in the cave in Machpelah, which is in the field of Zohar's son Ephron the Hittite, near Mamre. ¹⁰Thus Abraham and his wife Sarah were both buried in the field Abraham had purchased from the Hittites. ¹¹After Abraham's death, God blessed his son Isaac, and Isaac lived in Beer-lahai-roi.

Ishmael's descendants

¹²These are the descendants of Ishmael, Abraham's son, whom Hagar the Egyptian, Sarah's servant, bore for Abraham. ¹³These are the names of Ishmael's sons, by their names and according to their birth order: Nebaioth, Ishmael's oldest son; Kedar; Adbeel; Mibsam; ¹⁴Mishma; Dumah; Massa; ¹⁵Hadad; Tema; Jetur; Naphish; and Kedemah. ¹⁶These are Ishmael's sons. These are their names by their villages and their settlements: twelve tribal leaders according to their tribes. ¹⁷Ishmael lived to the age of 137. He took his last breath and died, and was placed with his ancestors. ¹⁸He established camps˟ from Havilah to Shur, which is near Egypt on the road to Assyria. He diedʸ among all of his brothers.

Jacob and Esau are born

¹⁹These are the descendants of Isaac, Abraham's son. Abraham became the father of Isaac. ²⁰Isaac was 40 years old when he

---

ᵛHeb uncertain; LXX *through the desert of* ʷHeb uncertain; possibly *to walk around in the pasture* or *to meditate in the pasture* ˟LXX; MT *they established camps* ʸOr *He fell*

JACOB

Jacob belongs to the third generation of Israelites and becomes the ancestor of the whole group. He is one of the patriarchs of Israel. His name was changed to Israel (Gen 32:28), giving his name to the subsequent people and nation. Jacob is the ancestor of Jesus (Matt 1:2-16; Luke 3:34-36). Jesus refers to Jacob as one of the three foundational patriarchs several times in his public preaching (Matt 8:11; 22:32; Mark 12:26; Luke 13:28; 20:37).

married Rebekah the daughter of Bethuel the Aramean and the sister of Laban the Aramean, from Paddan-aram. [21]Isaac prayed to the LORD for his wife, since she was unable to have children. The LORD was moved by his prayer, and his wife Rebekah became pregnant. [22]But the boys pushed against each other inside of her, and she said, "If this is what it's like, why did it happen to me?"[z]

So she went to ask the LORD. [23]And the LORD said to her,

"Two nations are in your womb;
    two different peoples will emerge
        from your body.
One people will be stronger
    than the other;
    the older will serve the younger."

[24]When she reached the end of her pregnancy, she discovered that she had twins. [25]The first came out red all over, clothed with hair, and she named him Esau. [26]Immediately afterward, his brother came out gripping Esau's heel, and she named him Jacob. Isaac was 60 years old when they were born.

Jacob acquires the oldest son's rights

[27]When the young men grew up, Esau became an outdoorsman who knew how to hunt, and Jacob became a quiet man who stayed at home. [28]Isaac loved Esau because he enjoyed eating game, but Rebekah loved Jacob. [29]Once when Jacob was boiling stew, Esau came in from the field hungry [30]and said to Jacob, "I'm starving! Let me devour some of this red stuff." That's why his name is Edom.[a]

[31]Jacob said, "Sell me your birthright[b] today."

[32]Esau said, "Since I'm going to die anyway, what good is my birthright to me?"

[33]Jacob said, "Give me your word today." And he did. He sold his birthright to Jacob. [34]So Jacob gave Esau bread and lentil stew. He ate, drank, got up, and left, showing just how little he thought of his birthright.

Isaac and Rebekah visit Gerar

26 When a famine gripped the land, a different one from the first famine that occurred in Abraham's time, Isaac set out toward Gerar and toward King Abimelech of the Philistines. [2]The LORD appeared to him and said, "Don't go down to Egypt but settle temporarily in the land that I will show you. [3]Stay in this land as an immigrant, and I will be with you and bless you because I will give all of these lands to you and your descendants. I will keep my word, which I gave to your father Abraham. [4]I will give you as many descendants as the stars in the sky, and I will give your descendants all of these lands. All of the nations of the earth will be blessed because of your descendants. [5]I will do this because Abraham obeyed me and kept my orders, my commandments, my statutes, and my instructions."

[6]So Isaac lived in Gerar. [7]When the men who lived there asked about his wife, he said, "She's my sister," because he was afraid to say, "my wife," thinking, The men who live there will kill me for Rebekah because she's very beautiful. [8]After Isaac had lived there for some time, the Philistines' King Abimelech looked out his window and saw Isaac laughing together with his wife Rebekah.

---

[z]Heb uncertain [a]Or red [b]Or oldest son's rights

ABIMELECH

The king of Gerar in association with Abraham in Genesis 20:1-18; 21:22-34; and with Isaac in Genesis 26:1-11, 26-31. In both cases, the patriarch tries to save himself from some perceived threat by claiming his wife is his sister (also Abram in Egypt [Gen 12:10-20]).

[9] So Abimelech summoned Isaac and said, "She's your wife, isn't she? How could you say, 'She's my sister'?"

Isaac responded, "Because I thought that I might be killed because of her."

[10] Abimelech said, "What are you trying to do to us? Before long, one of the people would have slept with your wife; and you would have made us guilty." [11] Abimelech gave orders to all of the people, "Anyone who touches this man or his wife will be put to death!"

Isaac's treaty with the Philistines

[12] Isaac planted grain in that land and reaped one hundred shearim[c] that year because the LORD had blessed him. [13] Isaac grew richer and richer until he was extremely wealthy. [14] He had livestock, both flocks and cattle, and many servants. As a result, the Philistines envied him. [15] The Philistines closed up and filled with dirt all of the wells that his father's servants had dug during his father Abraham's lifetime. [16] Abimelech said to Isaac, "Move away from us because you have become too powerful among us."

[17] So Isaac moved away from there, camped in the valley of Gerar, and lived there. [18] Isaac dug out again the wells that were dug during the lifetime of his father Abraham. The Philistines had closed them up after Abraham's death. Isaac gave them the same names his father had given them. [19] Isaac's servants dug wells in the valley and found a well there with fresh water. [20] Isaac's shepherds argued with Gerar's shepherds, each claiming, "This is our water." So Isaac named the well Esek[d] because they quarreled with him. [21] They dug another well and argued about it too, so he named it Sitnah.[e] [22] He left there and dug another well, but they didn't argue about it, so he named it Rehoboth[f] and said, "Now the LORD has made an open space for us and has made us fertile in the land."

[23] Then he went up from Gerar to Beer-sheba. [24] The LORD appeared to him that night and said, "I am the God of your father Abraham. Don't be afraid because I am with you. I will bless you, and I will give you many children for my servant Abraham's sake." [25] So Isaac built an altar there and worshipped in the LORD's name. Isaac pitched his tent there, and his servants dug a well.

[26] But Abimelech set out toward him from Gerar, with Ahuzzath his ally and Phicol the commander of his forces. [27] Isaac said to him, "Why have you come after me? You resented me and sent me away from you."

[28] They said, "We now see that the LORD was with you. We propose that there be a formal agreement between us and that we draw up a treaty[g] with you: [29] you must not treat us badly since we haven't harmed you and since we have treated you well at all times. Then we will send you away peacefully, for you are now blessed by the LORD." [30] Isaac prepared a banquet for them, and they ate and drank. [31] They got up early in the morning, and they gave each other their word. Isaac sent them off, and they left peacefully.

[32] That day Isaac's servants informed him about the well that they had been digging and said to him, "We found water." [33] He called it Shibah;[h] therefore, the city's name has been Beer-sheba[i] until today.

Esau's wives

[34] When Esau was 40 years old, he married Judith daughter of Beeri the Hittite, and Basemath daughter of Elon the Hittite. [35] They made life very difficult for Isaac and Rebekah.

Jacob acquires his father's blessing

27 When Isaac had grown old and his eyesight was failing, he summoned his older son Esau and said to him, "My son?"

And Esau said, "I'm here."

[2] He said, "I'm old and don't know when I will die. [3] So now, take your hunting gear, your bow and quiver of arrows, go out to the field, and hunt game for me. [4] Make me

---

[c] An unknown measure of grain [d] Or *quarrel* [e] Or *accusation* [f] Or *open spaces* [g] Or *covenant* [h] Or *giving one's word* or *seven* [i] Or *Well of giving one's word* or *Well of seven*

the delicious food that I love and bring it to me so I can eat. Then I can bless you before I die."

⁵Rebekah was listening when Isaac spoke to his son Esau. When Esau went out to the field to hunt game to bring back, ⁶Rebekah said to her son Jacob, "I just heard your father saying to your brother Esau, ⁷'Bring me some game and make me some delicious food so I can eat, and I will bless you in the LORD's presence before I die.' ⁸Now, my son, listen to me, to what I'm telling you to do. ⁹Go to the flock and get me two healthy young goats so I can prepare them as the delicious food your father loves. ¹⁰You can bring it to your father, he will eat, and then he will bless you before he dies."

¹¹Jacob said to his mother Rebekah, "My brother Esau is a hairy man, but I have smooth skin. ¹²What if my father touches me and thinks I'm making fun of him? I will be cursed instead of blessed."

¹³His mother said to him, "Your curse will be on me, my son. Just listen to me: go and get them for me." ¹⁴So he went and got them and brought them to his mother, and his mother made the delicious food that his father loved. ¹⁵Rebekah took her older son Esau's favorite clothes that were in the house with her, and she put them on her younger son Jacob. ¹⁶On his arms and smooth neck she put the hide of young goats, ¹⁷and the delicious food and the bread she had made she put into her son's hands.

¹⁸Jacob went to his father and said, "My father."

And he said, "I'm here. Who are you, my son?"

¹⁹Jacob said to his father, "I'm Esau your oldest son. I've made what you asked me to. Sit up and eat some of the game so you can bless me."

²⁰Isaac said to his son, "How could you find this so quickly, my son?"

He said, "The LORD your God led me right to it."ʲ

²¹Isaac said to Jacob, "Come here and let me touch you, my son. Are you my son Esau or not?" ²²So Jacob approached his father

Isaac, and Isaac touched him and said, "The voice is Jacob's voice, but the arms are Esau's arms." ²³Isaac didn't recognize him because his arms were hairy like Esau's arms, so he blessed him.

²⁴Isaac said, "Are you really my son Esau?"

And he said, "I am."

²⁵Isaac said, "Bring some food here and let me eat some of my son's game so I can bless you." Jacob put it before him and he ate, and he brought him wine and he drank. ²⁶His father Isaac said to him, "Come here and kiss me, my son." ²⁷So he came close and kissed him. When Isaac smelled the scent of his clothes, he blessed him,

"See, the scent of my son
    is like the scent of the field
      that the LORD has blessed.
²⁸ May God give you
    showers from the sky,
    olive oil from the earth,
    plenty of grain and new wine.
²⁹ May the nations serve you,
    may peoples bow down to you.
Be the most powerful man
    among your brothers,
      and may your mother's sons
      bow down to you.
Those who curse you will be cursed,
    and those who bless you
      will be blessed."

Esau receives a secondary blessing

³⁰After Isaac had finished blessing Jacob, and just as Jacob left his father Isaac, his brother Esau came back from his hunt. ³¹He too made some delicious food, brought it to his father, and said, "Let my father sit up and eat from his son's game so that you may bless me."

³²His father Isaac said to him, "Who are you?"

And he said, "I'm your son, your oldest son, Esau."

³³Isaac was so shocked that he trembled violently. He said, "Who was the hunter just here with game? He brought me food, and I ate all of it before you came. I blessed him, and he will stay blessed!"

ʲOr made something good happen for me

³⁴When Esau heard what his father said, he let out a loud agonizing cry and wept bitterly. He said to his father, "Bless me! Me too, my father!"

³⁵Isaac said, "Your brother has already come deceitfully and has taken your blessing."

³⁶Esau said, "Isn't this why he's called Jacob? He's taken me[k] twice now: he took my birthright, and now he's taken my blessing." He continued, "Haven't you saved a blessing for me?"

³⁷Isaac replied to Esau, "I've already made him more powerful than you, and I've made all of his brothers his servants. I've made him strong with grain and wine. What can I do for you, my son?"

³⁸Esau said to his father, "Do you really have only one blessing, Father? Bless me too, my father!" And Esau wept loudly.

³⁹His father Isaac responded and said to him,

"Now, you will make a home
   far away from the olive groves
      of the earth,
   far away from the showers
      of the sky above.
⁴⁰ You will live by your sword;
   you will serve your brother.
But when you grow restless,[l]
   you will tear away his harness
      from your neck."

Jacob sent away for protection

⁴¹Esau was furious at Jacob because his father had blessed him, and Esau said to himself, When the period of mourning for the death of my father is over, I will kill my brother. ⁴²Rebekah was told what her older son Esau was planning, so she summoned her younger son Jacob and said to him, "Esau your brother is planning revenge. He plans to kill you. ⁴³So now, my son, listen to me: Get up and escape to my brother Laban in Haran. ⁴⁴Live with him for a short while until your brother's rage subsides, ⁴⁵until your brother's anger at you goes away and he forgets what you did to him. Then I will

send for you and bring you back from there. Why should I suffer the loss of both of you on one day?"

⁴⁶Rebekah then said to Isaac, "I really loathe these Hittite women. If Jacob marries one of the Hittite women, like the women of this land, why should I go on living?"

28

So Isaac summoned Jacob, blessed him, and gave him these orders: "Don't marry a Canaanite woman. ²Get up and go to Paddan-aram, to the household of Bethuel, your mother's father, and once there, marry one of the daughters of Laban, your mother's brother. ³God Almighty[m] will bless you, make you fertile, and give you many descendants so that you will become a large group of peoples. ⁴He will give you and your descendants Abraham's blessing so that you will own the land in which you are now immigrants, the land God gave to Abraham." ⁵So Isaac sent Jacob off, and he traveled to Paddan-aram, to Laban son of Bethuel the Aramean and brother of Rebekah, Jacob and Esau's mother.

⁶Esau understood that Isaac had blessed Jacob and sent him to Paddan-aram to marry a woman from there. He recognized that, when Isaac blessed Jacob, he had ordered him, "Don't marry a Canaanite woman," ⁷and that Jacob had listened to his father and mother and gone to Paddan-aram. ⁸Esau realized that his father Isaac considered Canaanite women unacceptable. ⁹So he went to Ishmael and married Mahalath daughter of Abraham's son Ishmael and sister of Nebaioth, in addition to his other wives.

Jacob's dream at Bethel

¹⁰Jacob left Beer-sheba and set out for Haran. ¹¹He reached a certain place and spent the night there. When the sun had set, he took one of the stones at that place and put it near his head. Then he lay down there. ¹²He dreamed and saw a raised staircase, its foundation on earth and its top touching the sky, and God's messengers were ascending and descending on it.

---

[k]Heb ya'acob, a wordplay on Jacob   [l]Heb uncertain   [m]Heb El Shaddai or God of the Mountain

[13]Suddenly the LORD was standing on it[n] and saying, "I am the LORD, the God of your father Abraham and the God of Isaac. I will give you and your descendants the land on which you are lying. [14]Your descendants will become like the dust of the earth; you will spread out to the west, east, north, and south. Every family of earth will be blessed because of you and your descendants. [15]I am with you now, I will protect you everywhere you go, and I will bring you back to this land. I will not leave you until I have done everything that I have promised you."

[16]When Jacob woke from his sleep, he thought to himself, The LORD is definitely in this place, but I didn't know it. [17]He was terrified and thought, This sacred place is awesome. It's none other than God's house and the entrance to heaven. [18]After Jacob got up early in the morning, he took the stone that he had put near his head, set it up as a sacred pillar, and poured oil on the top of it. [19]He named that sacred place Bethel,[o] though Luz was the city's original name. [20]Jacob made a solemn promise: "If God is with me and protects me on this trip I'm taking, and gives me bread to eat and clothes to wear, [21]and I return safely to my father's household, then the LORD will be my God. [22]This stone that I've set up as a sacred pillar will be God's house, and of everything you give me I will give a tenth back to you."

Jacob meets Rachel

29 Jacob got to his feet and set out for the land of the easterners. [2]He saw a well in the field in front of him, near which three flocks of sheep were lying down. That well was their source for water because the flocks drank from that well. A huge stone covered the well's opening. [3]When all of the flocks were gathered there, the shepherds would roll the stone from the well's opening, water the sheep, and return the stone to its place at the well's opening. [4]Jacob said to them, "Where are you from, my brothers?"

They said, "We're from Haran."

[5]Then he said to them, "Do you know Laban, Nahor's grandson?"

They said, "We know him."

[6]He said to them, "Is he well?"

They said, "He's fine. In fact, this is his daughter Rachel now, coming with the flock."

[7]He said to them, "It's now only the middle of the day. It's not time yet to gather the animals. Water the flock, and then go, put them out to pasture."

[8]They said to him, "We can't until all the herds are gathered, and then we[p] roll the stone away from the well's opening and water the flock."

[9]While he was still talking to them, Rachel came with her father's flock since she was its shepherd. [10]When Jacob saw Rachel the daughter of Laban his uncle, and the flock of Laban, Jacob came up, rolled the stone from the well's opening, and watered the flock of his uncle Laban. [11]Jacob kissed Rachel and wept aloud. [12]Jacob told Rachel that he was related to her father and that he was Rebekah's son. She then ran to tell her father. [13]When Laban heard about Jacob his sister's son, he ran to meet him. Laban embraced him, kissed him, and invited him into his house, where Jacob recounted to Laban everything that had happened. [14]Laban said to him, "Yes, you are my flesh and blood."

Jacob marries Leah and Rachel

After Jacob had stayed with Laban for a month, [15]Laban said to Jacob, "You shouldn't have to work for free just because you are my relative. Tell me what you would like to be paid."

[16]Now Laban had two daughters: the older was named Leah and the younger Rachel. [17]Leah had delicate eyes,[q] but Rachel had a beautiful figure and was good-looking. [18]Jacob loved Rachel and said, "I will work for you for seven years for Rachel, your younger daughter."

[19]Laban said, "I'd rather give her to you than to another man. Stay with me."

[20]Jacob worked for Rachel for seven years, but it seemed like a few days because

---

[n]Or *beside it* or *beside him* [o]Or *God's house* [p]Or *they* [q]Heb uncertain; perhaps *Leah had poor eyesight*

he loved her. [21]Jacob said to Laban, "The time has come. Give me my wife so that I may sleep with her." [22]So Laban invited all the people of that place and prepared a banquet. [23]However, in the evening, he took his daughter Leah and brought her to Jacob, and he slept with her. [24]Laban had given his servant Zilpah to his daughter Leah as her servant. [25]In the morning, there she was— Leah! Jacob said to Laban, "What have you done to me? Didn't I work for you to have Rachel? Why did you betray me?"

[26]Laban said, "Where we live, we don't give the younger woman before the oldest. [27]Complete the celebratory week with this woman. Then I will give[r] you this other woman too for your work, if you work for me seven more years." [28]So that is what Jacob did. He completed the celebratory week with this woman, and then Laban gave him his daughter Rachel as his wife. [29]Laban had given his servant Bilhah to his daughter Rachel as her servant. [30]Jacob slept with Rachel, and he loved Rachel more than Leah. He worked for Laban seven more years.

Jacob's sons are born

[31]When the LORD saw that Leah was unloved, he opened her womb; but Rachel was unable to have children. [32]Leah became pregnant and gave birth to a son. She named him Reuben[s] because she said, "The LORD saw my harsh treatment, and now my husband will love me." [33]She became pregnant again and gave birth to a son. She said, "The LORD heard that I was unloved, so he gave me this son too," and she named him Simeon.[t] [34]She became pregnant again and gave birth to a son. She said, "Now, this time my husband will embrace me,[u] since I have given birth to three sons for him." So she named him Levi.[v] [35]She became pregnant again and gave birth to a son. She said,

[r]LXX, Sam, Syr, Tg, Vulg; MT *we will give* [s]Or *see, a son* [t]Sounds like the Heb verb *hear* [u]Or *be connected to me* [v]Sounds like the Heb verb *embrace*, or *connect*

LEAH

Leah, daughter of Laban and wife of Jacob, is the third matriarch. She appears only in Genesis (mostly Gen 29–30) and in a blessing in Ruth 4:11. First described as possessing "weak" or "soft" eyes (29:17, CEB "delicate"), Leah is deceitfully given to Jacob as a wife instead of his dearly loved Rachel, her younger sister. The narrator subsequently states that Leah was "unloved" but adds that God blessed her with fertility (29:31).

Competition between Leah and Rachel results in the birth of Israel's 12 tribes. Leah proves to be the fertile wife and biological mother of seven children, including Judah and Levi, as well as their only named sister, Dinah. The names Leah gives her children (including those of her woman servant Zilpah) repeatedly express longing to be loved by her husband. She resents Rachel, accusing her of stealing Jacob's love (30:15). Nevertheless, Leah assists Rachel (in exchange for a night with Jacob) by letting her have mandrakes that purportedly help fertility (Gen 30:14-17).

According to Gen 49:29-31, Jacob buries Leah in the family's cave of Machpelah and instructs his sons to bury him with her. Yet Jacob's words and actions repeatedly indicate that he prefers Rachel.

"This time I will praise the LORD." So she named him Judah.[w] Then she stopped bearing children.

30 When Rachel realized that she could bear Jacob no children, Rachel became jealous of her sister and said to Jacob, "Give me children! If you don't, I may as well be dead." ²Jacob was angry at Rachel and said, "Do you think I'm God? God alone has kept you from giving birth!" ³She said, "Here's my servant Bilhah. Sleep with her, and she will give birth for me. Because of her, I will also have children." ⁴So Rachel gave her servant Bilhah to Jacob as his wife, and he slept with her. ⁵Bilhah became pregnant and gave birth to a son for Jacob. ⁶Rachel said, "God has judged in my favor, heard my voice, and given me a son." So she named him Dan.[x] ⁷Rachel's servant Bilhah became pregnant again and gave birth to a second son for Jacob. ⁸Rachel said, "I've competed fiercely with my sister, and now I've won." So she named him Naphtali.[y]

⁹When Leah realized that she had stopped bearing children, she took her servant Zilpah and gave her to Jacob as his wife. ¹⁰Leah's servant Zilpah gave birth to a son for Jacob, ¹¹and Leah said, "What good luck!" So she named him Gad.[z] ¹²Leah's servant Zilpah gave birth to a second son for Jacob, ¹³and Leah said, "I'm happy now because women call me happy." So she named him Asher.[a]

¹⁴During the wheat harvest, Reuben found some erotic herbs[b] in the field and brought them to his mother Leah. Rachel said to Leah, "Give me your son's erotic herbs."

¹⁵Leah replied, "Isn't it enough that you've taken my husband? Now you want to take my son's erotic herbs too?"

---

[w]Sounds like the Heb verb *praise*   [x]Or *he judged*   [y]Or *my competition* or *my wrestling*   [z]Or *good fortune*
[a]Or *happy*   [b]Or *mandrakes*

RACHEL

Means "ewe." Rachel is the younger daughter of Laban and the sister of Leah. As Jacob's wife, she was the biological mother of Joseph and Benjamin and the grandmother of Ephraim and Manasseh, heads of the tribes that became the northern kingdom of Israel.

Best known, perhaps, as the object of her cousin Jacob's great love (Jacob is smitten from the moment he sees her and immediately kisses her [Gen 29:10-11]), Rachel is depicted as a complex figure. Genesis introduces her as having "a beautiful figure" and being "good-looking" (29:17) and also as a shepherd (29:9), the only woman in the Bible who explicitly holds this position. She is portrayed on the one hand as a resourceful figure (who dares, for example, to steal her father's household divine images) and also a barren woman who desperately longs for children (Gen 30:1). She eventually gets her wish, but she also tragically dies young in childbirth. Jacob, who seeks refuge in her father's house, falls in love with Rachel and offers to work seven years for her father in order to marry her (Gen 29:18). At the end of those years, however, her father switches brides, and Jacob discovers in the morning that he has married her sister Leah instead (Gen 29:23-25). Beloved Rachel becomes Jacob's bride a week later, but Jacob must work for her father an additional seven years.

Rachel said, "For your son's erotic herbs, Jacob^c may sleep with you tonight."

¹⁶When Jacob came back from the field in the evening, Leah went out to meet him and said, "You must sleep with me because I've paid for you with my son's erotic herbs." So he slept with her that night.

¹⁷God responded to Leah. She became pregnant and gave birth to a fifth son for Jacob. ¹⁸Leah said, "God gave me what I paid for, what I deserved for giving my servant to my husband." So she named him Issachar.^d ¹⁹Leah became pregnant again and gave birth to a sixth son for Jacob, ²⁰and she said, "God has given me a wonderful gift. Now my husband will honor me since I've borne him six sons." So she named him Zebulun.^e ²¹After this, she gave birth to a daughter and named her Dinah.

²²Then God remembered Rachel, responded to her, and let her conceive. ²³She became pregnant and gave birth to a son and said, "God has taken away my shame." ²⁴She named him Joseph,^f saying to herself, May the LORD give me another son.

God blesses Jacob and Laban

²⁵After Rachel gave birth to Joseph, Jacob said to Laban, "Send me off so that I can go to my own place and my own country. ²⁶Give me my wives and children whom I've worked for, and I will go. You know the work I've done for you."

²⁷Laban said to him, "Do me this favor. I've discovered by a divine sign that the LORD has blessed me because of you, ²⁸so name your price and I will pay it."

²⁹Jacob said to him, "You know how I've worked for you, and how well your livestock have done with me. ³⁰While in my care, what little you had has multiplied a great deal. The LORD blessed you wherever I took your livestock.^g Now, when will I be able to work for my own household too?"

³¹Laban said, "What will I pay you?"

Jacob said, "Don't pay me anything. If you will do this for me, I will take care of your flock again, and keep a portion.^h ³²I will go through the entire flock today, taking out all of the speckled and spotted sheep, all of the black male lambs, and all of the spotted and speckled female goats. That will be my price. ³³I will be completely honest with you: when you come to check on our agreement, every female goat with me that isn't speckled or spotted and every male lamb with me that isn't black will be considered stolen."

³⁴Laban said, "All right; let's do it." ³⁵However, on that very day Laban took out the striped and spotted male goats and all of the speckled and spotted female goats—any with some white in it—and all of the black male lambs, and gave them to his sons. ³⁶He put a three-day trip between himself and Jacob, while Jacob was watching the rest of Laban's flock.

³⁷Then Jacob took new branches from poplar, almond, and plane trees; and he peeled white stripes on them, exposing the branches' white color. ³⁸He set the branches that he had peeled near the watering troughs so that they were in front of the flock when they drank, because they often mated when they came to drink. ³⁹When the flock mated in front of the branches, they gave birth to striped, speckled, and spotted young. ⁴⁰Jacob sorted out the lambs, turning the flock to face the striped and black ones in Laban's flock but keeping his flock separate, setting them apart from Laban's flock. ⁴¹Whenever the strongest of the flock mated, Jacob put the branches in front of them near the watering troughs so that they mated near the branches. ⁴²But he didn't put branches up for the weakest of the flock. So the weakest became Laban's and the strongest Jacob's. ⁴³The man Jacob became very, very rich: he owned large flocks, female and male servants, camels, and donkeys.

Jacob's household leaves Laban

31 Jacob heard that Laban's sons were saying, "Jacob took everything our father owned and from it he produced all of this wealth." ²And Jacob saw that Laban no longer liked him as much as he used to.

^c Or he ^d Or there is payment ^e Or honor ^f Or he adds ^g Or them ^h Heb uncertain

³Then the LORD said to Jacob, "Go back to the land of your ancestors and to your relatives, and I will be with you."

⁴So Jacob sent for Rachel and Leah and summoned them into the field where his flock was. ⁵He said to them, "I am aware that your father no longer likes me as much as he used to. But my father's God has been with me. ⁶You know that I've worked for your father as hard as I could. ⁷But your father cheated me and changed my payment ten times. Yet God didn't let him harm me. ⁸If he said, 'The speckled ones will be your payment,' the whole flock gave birth to speckled young. And if he said, 'The striped ones will be your payment,' the whole flock gave birth to striped young. ⁹God took away your father's livestock and gave them to me. ¹⁰When the flocks were mating, I looked up and saw in a dream that the male goats that mounted the flock were striped, speckled, and spotted. ¹¹In the dream, God's messenger said to me, 'Jacob!' and I said, 'I'm here.' ¹²He said, 'Look up and watch all the striped, speckled, and spotted male goats mounting the flock. I've seen everything that Laban is doing to you. ¹³I am the God of Bethel, where you anointed a sacred pillar and where you made a solemn promise to me. Now, get up and leave this country and go back to the land of your relatives.'"

¹⁴Rachel and Leah answered him, "Is there any share or inheritance left for us in our father's household? ¹⁵Doesn't he think of us as foreigners since he sold us and has even used up the payment he received for us? ¹⁶All of the wealth God took from our father belongs to us and our children. Now, do everything God told you to do."

¹⁷So Jacob got up, put his sons and wives on the camels, ¹⁸and set out with all of his livestock and all of his possessions that he had acquiredⁱ in Paddan-aram in order to return to his father Isaac in the land of Canaan. ¹⁹Now, while Laban was out shearing his sheep, Rachel stole the household's divine images that belonged to her father. ²⁰Moreover, Jacob deceived Laban the Aramean by not sending word to him that he was leaving. ²¹So Jacob and his entire household left. He got up, crossed the river, and set out directly for the mountains of Gilead.

²²Three days later, Laban found out that Jacob had gone, ²³so Laban took his brothers with him, chased Jacob for seven days, and caught up with him in the mountains of Gilead. ²⁴That night, God appeared to Laban the Aramean in a dream and said, "Be careful and don't say anything hastily to Jacob one way or the other."

²⁵Laban reached Jacob after Jacob had pitched his tent in the mountains. So Laban and his brothers also pitched theirs in the mountains of Gilead. ²⁶Laban said to Jacob, "What have you done? You have deceived me and taken off with my daughters as if they were prisoners of war. ²⁷Why did you leave secretly, deceiving me, and not letting me know? I would've sent you off with a celebration, with songs and tambourines and harps. ²⁸You didn't even let me kiss my sons and my daughters good-bye. Now you've acted like a fool, ²⁹and I have the power to punish you. However, your

---

ⁱLXX; MT includes *he had acquired, the livestock in his possession.*

GILEAD

Jacob settled in the region called Gilead (Gen 31:23), a place centrally located east of the Jordan between the river Yarmuk and the Dead Sea. Moses defeated Og and Sihon, two Amorite kings controlling all Gilead and Bashan (Deut 4:47-49).

father's God told me yesterday, 'Be careful and don't say anything hastily to Jacob one way or the other.' [30]You've rushed off now because you missed your father's household so much, but why did you steal my gods?"

[31]Jacob responded to Laban, "I was afraid and convinced myself that you would take your daughters away from me. [32]Whomever you find with your divine images won't live. Identify whatever I have that is yours, in front of your brothers, and take it." Jacob didn't know that Rachel had stolen them. [33]Laban went into Jacob's tent, Leah's tent, and her two servants' tent and didn't find them.

So he left Leah's tent and went into Rachel's. [34]Now Rachel had taken the divine images and put them into the camel's saddlebag and sat on them. Laban felt around in the whole tent but couldn't find them. [35]Rachel said to her father, "Sir, don't be angry with me because I can't get up for you; I'm having my period." He searched but couldn't find the divine images.

[36]Jacob was angry and complained to Laban, "What have I done wrong and what's my crime that you've tracked me down like this? [37]You've now felt through all of my baggage, and what have you found from your household's belongings? Put it in front of our relatives, and let them decide between us. [38]For these twenty years I've been with you, your female sheep and goats haven't miscarried, and I haven't eaten your flock's rams. [39]When animals were killed, I didn't bring them to you but took the loss myself. You demanded compensation from me for any animals poached during the day or night. [40]The dry heat consumed me during the day, and the frost at night; I couldn't sleep. [41]I've now spent twenty years in your household. I worked for fourteen years for your two daughters and for six years for your flock, and you changed my pay ten times. [42]If the God of my father—the God of Abraham and the awesome one of Isaac—hadn't been with me, you'd have no

doubt sent me away without anything. God saw my harsh treatment and my hard work and reprimanded you yesterday."

Jacob and Laban's treaty

[43]Laban responded and told Jacob, "The daughters are my daughters, the children are my children, and the flocks are my flocks. Everything you see is mine. But what can I do now about my daughters and about their sons? [44]Come, let's make a treaty, you and me, and let something be our witness."[j]

[45]So Jacob took a stone, set it up as a sacred pillar, [46]and said to his relatives, "Gather stones." So they took stones, made a mound, and ate there near the mound. [47]Laban called it Jegar-sahadutha,[k] but Jacob called it Galeed.[l]

[48]Laban said, "This mound is our witness today," and, therefore, he too named it Galeed. [49]He also named it Mizpah,[m] because he said, "The LORD will observe both of us when we are separated from each other. [50]If you treat my daughters badly and if you marry other women, though we aren't there, know that God observed our witness."

[51]Laban said to Jacob, "Here is this mound and here is the sacred pillar that I've set up for us. [52]This mound and the sacred pillar are witnesses that I won't travel beyond this mound and that you won't travel beyond this mound and this pillar to do harm. [53]The God of Abraham and the God of Nahor[n] will keep order between us." So Jacob gave his word in the name of the awesome one of his father Isaac. [54]Jacob offered a sacrifice on the mountain, and invited his relatives to a meal. They ate together and spent the night on the mountain. [55][o]Laban got up early in the morning, kissed his sons and daughters, blessed them, and left to go back to his own place.

Jacob prepares to meet Esau

32 Jacob went on his way, and God's messengers approached him. [2]When Jacob saw them, he said, "This is God's

---

[j]Or convenant or testimony   [k]Or mound of witness (Aram)   [l]Or mound of witness   [m]Or observation   [n]LXX; MT includes their father's God.   [o]32:1 in Heb

camp," and he named that sacred place Mahanaim.P ³Jacob sent messengers ahead of him to his brother Esau, toward the land of Seir, the open country of Edom. ⁴He gave them these orders: "Say this to my master Esau. This is the message of your servant Jacob: 'I've lived as an immigrant with Laban, where I've stayed till now. ⁵I own cattle, donkeys, flocks, men servants, and women servants. I'm sending this message to my master now to ask that heq be kind.'"

⁶The messengers returned to Jacob and said, "We went out to your brother Esau, and he's coming to meet you with four hundred men."

⁷Jacob was terrified and felt trapped, so he divided the people with him, and the flocks, cattle, and camels, into two camps. ⁸He thought, If Esau meets the first camp and attacks it, at least one camp will be left to escape.

⁹Jacob said, "LORD, God of my father Abraham, God of my father Isaac, who said to me, 'Go back to your country and your relatives, and I'll make sure things go well for you,' ¹⁰I don't deserve how loyal and truthful you've been to your servant. I went away across the Jordan with just my staff, but now I've become two camps. ¹¹Save me from my brother Esau! I'm afraid he will come and kill me, the mothers, and their children. ¹²You were the one who told me, 'I will make sure things go well for you, and I will make your descendants like the sand of the sea, so many you won't be able to count them.'"

¹³Jacob spent that night there. From what he had acquired, he set aside a gift for his brother Esau: ¹⁴two hundred female goats and twenty male goats, two hundred ewes and twenty rams, ¹⁵thirty nursing camels with their young, forty cows and ten bulls, and twenty female donkeys and ten male donkeys. ¹⁶He separated these herds and gave them to his servants. He said to them, "Go ahead of me and put some distance between each of the herds." ¹⁷He ordered the first group, "When my brother Esau meets you and asks you, 'Who are you with? Where are you going? And whose herds are these in front of you?' ¹⁸say, 'They are your servant Jacob's, a gift sent to my master Esau. And Jacob is actually right behind us.'" ¹⁹He also ordered the second group, the third group, and everybody following the herds, "Say exactly the same thing to Esau when you find him. ²⁰Say also, 'Your servant Jacob is right behind us.'" Jacob thought, I may be able to pacify Esau with the gift I'm sending ahead. When I meet him, perhaps he will be kind to me. ²¹So Jacob sent the gift ahead of him, but he spent that night in the camp.

Jacob wrestles with God

²²Jacob got up during the night, took his two wives, his two women servants, and his eleven sons, and crossed the Jabbok River's shallow water. ²³He took them and everything that belonged to him, and he helped them cross the river. ²⁴But Jacob stayed apart by himself, and a man wrestled with him until dawn broke. ²⁵When the man saw that he couldn't defeat Jacob, he grabbed Jacob's thigh and tore a muscle in Jacob's thigh as he wrestled with him. ²⁶The man said, "Let me go because the dawn is breaking."

But Jacob said, "I won't let you go until you bless me."

POr *two camps* qOr *you*

ESAU/EDOMITES

Esau is the brother of Jacob, the son of Isaac and Rebekah, ancestor of the people of Edom. Esau and Jacob experienced significant conflict through most of their lives (Gen 25:21-34; 27; 32–33).

[27] He said to Jacob, "What's your name?" and he said, "Jacob." [28] Then he said, "Your name won't be Jacob any longer, but Israel,[r] because you struggled with God and with men and won."

[29] Jacob also asked and said, "Tell me your name."

But he said, "Why do you ask for my name?" and he blessed Jacob there. [30] Jacob named the place Peniel,[s] "because I've seen God face-to-face, and my life has been saved." [31] The sun rose as Jacob passed Penuel, limping because of his thigh. [32] Therefore, Israelites don't eat the tendon attached to the thigh muscle to this day, because he grabbed Jacob's thigh muscle at the tendon.

Esau forgives Jacob

33 Jacob looked up and saw Esau approaching with four hundred men. Jacob divided the children among Leah, Rachel, and the two women servants. [2] He put the servants and their children first, Leah and her children after them, and Rachel and Joseph last. [3] He himself went in front of them and bowed to the ground seven times as he was approaching his brother. [4] But Esau ran to meet him, threw his arms around his neck, kissed him, and they wept. [5] Esau looked up and saw the women and children and said, "Who are these with you?"

Jacob said, "The children that God generously gave your servant." [6] The women servants and their children came forward and bowed down. [7] Then Leah and her servants also came forward and bowed, and afterward Joseph and Rachel came forward and bowed.

[8] Esau said, "What's the meaning of this entire group of animals that I met?"

Jacob said, "To ask for my master's kindness."

[9] Esau said, "I already have plenty, my brother. Keep what's yours."

[10] Jacob said, "No, please, do me the kindness of accepting my gift. Seeing your face is like seeing God's face, since you've accepted me so warmly. [11] Take this present that I've brought because God has been generous to me, and I have everything I need." So Jacob persuaded him, and he took it.

[12] Esau said, "Let's break camp and set out, and I'll go with you."

[13] But Jacob said to him, "My master knows that the children aren't strong and that I am responsible for the nursing flocks and cattle. If I push them hard for even one day, all of the flocks will die. [14] My master, go on ahead of your servant, but I've got to take it easy, going only as fast as the animals in front of me and the children are able to go, until I meet you in Seir."

[15] Esau said, "Let me leave some of my people with you."

But Jacob said, "Why should you do this since my master has already been so kind to me?" [16] That day Esau returned on the road to Seir, [17] but Jacob traveled to Succoth. He built a house for himself but made temporary shelters for his animals; therefore, he named the place Succoth.[t]

Dinah and the conflict at Shechem

[18] Jacob arrived safely at the city of Shechem in the land of Canaan on his trip from Paddan-aram, and he camped in front of the city. [19] He bought the section of the field where he pitched his tent from the sons of Hamor, Shechem's father, for one hundred qesitahs.[u] [20] Then he set up an altar there and named it El Elohe Israel.[v]

34 Dinah, the daughter whom Leah had borne to Jacob, went out to meet the women of that country. [2] When Shechem the son of the Hivite Hamor and the country's prince saw her, he took her, slept with her, and humiliated her. [3] He was drawn to Dinah, Jacob's daughter. He loved the young woman and tried to win her heart. [4] Shechem said to his father Hamor, "Get this girl for me as my wife." [5] Now Jacob heard that Shechem defiled his daughter Dinah; but his sons were with the animals in the countryside, so he decided to keep quiet until they got back. ⁶Meanwhile, Hamor, Shechem's father, went out to Jacob to speak with him. ⁷Just then, Jacob's sons got back from the countryside. When they heard what had happened, they were deeply offended and very angry, because Shechem had disgraced Israel by sleeping with Jacob's daughter. Such things are simply not done.

⁸Hamor said to them, "My son Shechem's heart is set on your daughter. Please let him marry her. ⁹Arrange marriages with us: give us your daughters and take our daughters for yourselves. ¹⁰Live with us. The land is available to you: settle down, travel through it, and buy property in it."

¹¹Shechem said to Dinah's father and brothers, "If you approve of me, tell me what you want, and I will give it to you. ¹²Make the bride price and marriage gifts as large as you like, and I will pay whatever you tell me. Then let me marry the young woman."

¹³Jacob's sons responded deviously to Shechem and his father Hamor because Shechem defiled their sister Dinah. ¹⁴They said to them, "We can't do this, allowing our sisters to marry uncircumcised men, because it's disgraceful to us. ¹⁵We can only agree to do this if you circumcise every male as we do. ¹⁶Then we will give our daughters to you, and we will take your daughters for ourselves. We will live with you and be one people. ¹⁷But if you don't listen to us and become circumcised, we will take our daughter and leave."

¹⁸Their idea seemed like a good one to Hamor and Hamor's son Shechem. ¹⁹The young man didn't waste any time doing this because he liked Jacob's daughter so much. He was more respected than anyone else in his father's household. ²⁰Hamor and his son Shechem went to their city's gate and spoke to the men of their city: ²¹"These men want peace with us. Let them live in the land and travel through it; there's plenty of land for them. We will marry their daughters and give them our daughters. ²²But the men will agree to live with us and become one people only if we circumcise every

male just as they do. ²³Their livestock, their property, and all of their animals—won't they be ours? Let's agree with them and let them live with us." ²⁴Everyone at the city gate agreed with Hamor and his son Shechem, so every able-bodied male in the city was circumcised.

²⁵On the third day, when they were still in pain, two of Jacob's sons and Dinah's brothers Simeon and Levi took their swords, came into the city, which suspected nothing, and killed every male. ²⁶They killed Hamor and his son Shechem with their swords, took Dinah from Shechem's household, and left. ²⁷When Jacob's other sons discovered the dead, they looted the city that had defiled their sister. ²⁸They took their flocks, their cattle, and their donkeys, whether in the city or in the fields nearby. ²⁹They carried off their property, their children, and their wives. They looted the entire place. ³⁰Jacob said to Simeon and Levi, "You've put me in danger by making me offensive to those who live here in the land, to the Canaanites and the Perizzites. I have only a few men. They may join forces, attack me, and destroy me, me and my household."

³¹They said, "But didn't he treat our sister like a prostitute?"

Jacob establishes worship at Bethel

35 God said to Jacob, "Get up, go to Bethel, and live there. Build an altar there to the God who appeared to you when you ran away from your brother Esau."

²Jacob said to his household and to everyone who was with him, "Get rid of the foreign gods you have with you. Clean yourselves and change your clothes. ³Then let's rise and go up to Bethel so that I can build an altar there to the God who answered me when I was in trouble and who has been with me wherever I've gone." ⁴So they gave Jacob all of the foreign gods they had, as well as the rings in their ears, and Jacob buried them under the terebinth at Shechem. ⁵When they set out, God made all of the surrounding cities fearful so that they didn't pursue Jacob's sons. ⁶Jacob and all of the people with him arrived in Luz,

otherwise known as Bethel, in the land of Canaan. [7]He built an altar there and named the place El-bethel,[w] because God had revealed himself to him there when he ran away from his brother. [8]Rebekah's nurse Deborah died and was buried at Bethel under the oak, and Jacob named it Allon-bacuth.[x]

[9]God appeared to Jacob again, while he was on his way back from Paddan-aram, and blessed him. [10]God said to him, "Your name is Jacob, but your name will be Jacob no longer. No, your name will be Israel." And he named him Israel. [11]God said to him, "I am El Shaddai.[y] Be fertile and multiply. A nation, even a large group of nations, will come from you; kings will descend from your own children. [12]The land I gave to Abraham and to Isaac, I give to you; and I will give the land to your descendants after you." [13]Then God ascended, leaving him alone in the place where he spoke to him. [14]So Jacob set up a sacred pillar, a stone pillar, at the place God spoke to him. He poured an offering of wine on it and then poured oil over it. [15]Jacob named the place Bethel where God spoke to him.

Benjamin's birth and Rachel's death

[16]They left Bethel, and when they were still some distance from Ephrath, Rachel went into hard labor. [17]During her difficult labor, the midwife said to her, "Don't be afraid. You have another son." [18]As her life faded away, just before she died, she named him Ben-oni,[z] but his father named him Benjamin.[a] [19]Rachel died and was buried near the road to Ephrath, that is, Bethlehem. [20]Jacob set up a pillar on her grave. It's the pillar on Rachel's tomb that's still there today. [21]Israel continued his trip and pitched his tent farther on near the tower of Eder.

Jacob's family

[22]While Israel stayed in that place, Reuben went and slept with Bilhah his father's secondary wife, and Israel heard about it.

Jacob had twelve sons. [23]The sons of Leah were Reuben, Jacob's oldest son, and Simeon, Levi, Judah, Issachar, and Zebulun. [24]The sons of Rachel were Joseph and Benjamin. [25]The sons of Bilhah, Rachel's servant, were Dan and Naphtali. [26]The sons of Zilpah, Leah's servant, were Gad and Asher. These were Jacob's sons born to him in Paddan-aram.

Isaac's death

[27]Jacob came to his father Isaac at Mamre, that is, Kiriath-arba. This is Hebron, where Abraham and Isaac lived as immigrants. [28]At the age of 180 years, [29]Isaac took his last breath and died. He was buried with his ancestors after a long, satisfying life. His sons Esau and Jacob buried him.

Esau's descendants

36 These are the descendants of Esau, that is, Edom. [2]Esau married Canaanite women: Adah the daughter of the Hittite Elon; Oholibamah the daughter of Anah son of the Hittite Zibeon,[b] [3]and Basemath the daughter of Ishmael and sister of Nebaioth. [4]Adah gave birth to Eliphaz for Esau, Basemath gave birth to Reuel, [5]and Oholibamah gave birth to Jeush, Jalam, and Korah. These are Esau's sons born to him in the land of Canaan.

[6]Esau took his wives, his sons, his daughters, and everyone in his household, and his livestock, all of his animals, and all of the property he had acquired in the land of Canaan; and he moved away from the land of Canaan[c] and from his brother Jacob. [7]They had so many possessions that they couldn't live together. The land where they lived as immigrants couldn't support all of their livestock. [8]So Esau, that is, Edom, lived in the mountains of Seir.

[9]These are the descendants of Esau, the ancestor of Edom, which lies in the mountains of Seir. [10]These are the names of Edom's sons: Eliphaz son of Esau's wife Adah, and Reuel son of Esau's wife Basemath. [11]Eliphaz's sons were Teman, Omar,

---

[w]Or *God of Bethel*   [x]Or *oak of weeping*   [y]Or *God Almighty* or *God of the Mountain*   [z]Or *my suffering son*   [a]Or *right-hand son* or *strong son*   [b]LXX, Sam, Syr; MT *daughter*   [c]LXX, Sam; MT *to a land*

Zepho, Gatam, and Kenaz. [12]Timna was the secondary wife of Eliphaz, Esau's son, and she gave birth to Amalek for Eliphaz. These are the sons of Esau's wife Adah. [13]These are Reuel's sons: Nahath, Zerah, Shammah, and Mizzah. These are the sons of Esau's wife Basemath. [14]These are the sons of Esau's wife Oholibamah, the daughter of Anah, Zibeon's son:[d] she gave birth to Esau, Jeush, Jalam, and Korah.

[15]These are the tribal chiefs from Esau's sons. The sons of Eliphaz, Esau's oldest son: Chief Teman, Chief Omar, Chief Zepho, Chief Kenaz, [16]Chief Korah, Chief Gatam, and Chief Amalek. These are the tribal chiefs of Eliphaz in the land of Edom; they are Adah's sons. [17]These are the sons of Reuel, Esau's son: Chief Nahath, Chief Zerah, Chief Shammah, and Chief Mizzah. These are the tribal chiefs of Reuel in the land of Edom; they are the sons of Esau's wife Basemath. [18]These are the sons of Esau's wife Oholibamah: Chief Jeush, Chief Jalam, and Chief Korah. They are the tribal chiefs of Esau's wife Oholibamah the daughter of Anah. [19]These are the sons of Esau, who is Edom, and these are their tribal chiefs.

[20]These are the sons of Seir, the Horite, who live in the land: Lotan, Shobal, Zibeon, Anah, [21]Dishon, Ezer, and Dishan. These are the Horite tribal chiefs, Seir's sons, in the land of Edom. [22]Lotan's sons are Hori and Heman, and Lotan's sister was Timna. [23]These are Shobal's sons: Alvan, Manahath, Ebal, Shepho, and Onam. [24]These are Zibeon's sons: Aiah and Anah. Anah is the one who found water[e] in the desert while pasturing his father Zibeon's donkeys. [25]These are Anah's children: Dishon and Anah's daughter Oholibamah. [26]These are Dishon's[f] sons: Hemdan, Eshban, Ithran, and Cheran. [27]These are Ezer's sons: Bilhan, Zaavan, and Akan. [28]These are Dishan's sons: Uz and Aran. [29]These are the Horite tribal chiefs: Chiefs Lotan, Shobal, Zibeon, Anah, [30]Dishon, Ezer, and Dishan. These are

the Horite tribal chiefs, listed according to their chiefs in the land of Seir.

[31]These are the kings who ruled in the land of Edom before a king ruled over the Israelites. [32]Bela, Beor's son, ruled in Edom; his city's name was Dinhabah. [33]After Bela died, Jobab son of Zerah from Bozrah became king. [34]After Jobab died, Husham from the land of the Temanites became king. [35]After Husham died, Hadad, Bedad's son who defeated Midian in the countryside of Moab, became king; his city's name was Avith. [36]After Hadad died, Samlah from Masrekah became king. [37]After Samlah died, Shaul from Rehoboth on the river became king. [38]After Shaul died, Baal-hanan, Achbor's son, became king. [39]After Baal-hanan, Achbor's son, died, Hadar became king; his city's name was Pau and his wife's name was Mehetabel the daughter of Matred and granddaughter of Me-zahab.

[40]These are the names of Esau's tribal chiefs according to their families, their locations, and their names: Chief Timna, Chief Alvah, Chief Jetheth, [41]Chief Oholibamah, Chief Elah, Chief Pinon, [42]Chief Kenaz, Chief Teman, Chief Mibzar, [43]Chief Magdiel, and Chief Iram. These are Edom's tribal chiefs according to their settlements in the land they possessed. This is Esau, the ancestor of the Edomites.

Joseph dreams of power

37 Jacob lived in the land of Canaan where his father was an immigrant. [2]This is the account of Jacob's descendants. Joseph was 17 years old and tended the flock with his brothers. While he was helping the sons of Bilhah and Zilpah, his father's wives, Joseph told their father unflattering things about them. [3]Now Israel loved Joseph more than any of his other sons because he was born when Jacob was old. Jacob had made for him a long[g] robe. [4]When his brothers saw that their father loved him more than any of his broth-

[d]LXX, Sam, Syr; MT *daughter*   [e]Syr; Heb uncertain   [f]Sam, Syr; MT *Dishan's*   [g]LXX *many-colored*

ers, they hated him and couldn't even talk nicely to him.

⁵Joseph had a dream and told it to his brothers, which made them hate him even more. ⁶He said to them, "Listen to this dream I had. ⁷When we were binding stalks of grain in the field, my stalk got up and stood upright, while your stalks gathered around it and bowed down to my stalk."

⁸His brothers said to him, "Will you really be our king and rule over us?" So they hated him even more because of the dreams he told them.

⁹Then Joseph had another dream and described it to his brothers: "I've just dreamed again, and this time the sun and the moon and eleven stars were bowing down to me."

¹⁰When he described it to his father and brothers, his father scolded him and said to him, "What kind of dreams have you dreamed? Am I and your mother and your brothers supposed to come and bow down to the ground in front of you?" ¹¹His brothers were jealous of him, but his father took careful note of the matter.

Joseph's brothers take revenge

¹²Joseph's brothers went to tend their father's flocks near Shechem. ¹³Israel said to Joseph, "Aren't your brothers tending the sheep near Shechem? Come, I'll send you to them."

And he said, "I'm ready."

¹⁴Jacob said to him, "Go! Find out how your brothers are and how the flock is, and report back to me."

So Jacob sent him from the Hebron Valley. When he approached Shechem, ¹⁵a man found him wandering in the field and asked him, "What are you looking for?"

¹⁶Joseph said, "I'm looking for my brothers. Tell me, where are they tending the sheep?"

¹⁷The man said, "They left here. I heard them saying, 'Let's go to Dothan.'" So Joseph went after his brothers and found them in Dothan.

¹⁸They saw Joseph in the distance before he got close to them, and they plotted to kill him. ¹⁹The brothers said to each other, "Here comes the big dreamer. ²⁰Come on

now, let's kill him and throw him into one of the cisterns, and we'll say a wild animal devoured him. Then we will see what becomes of his dreams!"

²¹When Reuben heard what they said, he saved him from them, telling them, "Let's not take his life." ²²Reuben said to them, "Don't spill his blood! Throw him into this desert cistern, but don't lay a hand on him." He intended to save Joseph from them and take him back to his father.

²³When Joseph reached his brothers, they stripped off Joseph's long robe, ²⁴took him, and threw him into the cistern, an empty cistern with no water in it. ²⁵When they sat down to eat, they looked up and saw a caravan of Ishmaelites coming from Gilead, with camels carrying sweet resin, medicinal resin, and fragrant resin on their way down to Egypt. ²⁶Judah said to his brothers, "What do we gain if we kill our brother and hide his blood? ²⁷Come on, let's sell him to the Ishmaelites. Let's not harm him because he's our brother; he's family." His brothers agreed. ²⁸When some Midianite traders passed by, they pulled Joseph up out of the cistern. They sold him to the Ishmaelites for twenty pieces of silver, and they brought Joseph to Egypt.

²⁹When Reuben returned to the cistern and found that Joseph wasn't in it, he tore his clothes. ³⁰Then he returned to his brothers and said, "The boy's gone! And I—where can I go now?"

³¹His brothers took Joseph's robe, slaughtered a male goat, and dipped the robe in the blood. ³²They took the long robe, brought it to their father, and said, "We found this. See if it's your son's robe or not."

³³He recognized it and said, "It's my son's robe! A wild animal has devoured him. Joseph must have been torn to pieces!" ³⁴Then Jacob tore his clothes, put a simple mourning cloth around his waist, and mourned for his son for many days. ³⁵All of his sons and daughters got up to comfort him, but he refused to be comforted, telling them, "I'll go to my grave mourning for my son." And Joseph's father wept for him. ³⁶Meanwhile the Midianites had sold Joseph to the Egyptians, to Potiphar,

Pharaoh's chief officer, commander of the royal guard.

Tamar's place in Judah's family

38 At that time, Judah moved away from his brothers and settled near an Adullamite named Hirah. [2]There Judah saw the daughter of a Canaanite whose name was Shua, and he married her. After he slept with her, [3]she became pregnant and gave birth to a son, whom she[h] named Er. [4]She became pregnant again, gave birth to a son, and named him Onan. [5]Then she gave birth to one more son and named him Shelah. She was in Chezib when she gave birth to him.

[6]Judah married his oldest son Er to a woman named Tamar. [7]But the LORD considered Judah's oldest son Er immoral, and the LORD put him to death. [8]Judah said to Onan, "Go to your brother's wife, do your duty as her brother-in-law, and provide children for your brother." [9]Onan knew the children wouldn't be his so when he slept with his brother's wife, he wasted his semen on the ground, so he wouldn't give his brother children. [10]The LORD considered what he did as wrong and put him to death too. [11]Judah said to Tamar his daughter-in-law, "Stay as a widow in your father's household until my son Shelah grows up." He thought Shelah would die like his brothers had. So Tamar went and lived in her father's household.

[12]After a long time, Judah's wife the daughter of Shua died. Then, after a period of mourning, he and his neighbor Hirah the Adullamite went up to Timnah, to those who were shearing his sheep. [13]Tamar was told, "Your father-in-law is now on his way up to Timnah to shear his sheep." [14]So Tamar took off the clothing she wore as a widow, covered herself with a veil, put on makeup,[i] and sat down at the entrance to Enaim on the road to Timnah, since she realized that although Shelah had already grown up, she hadn't been given to him as a wife.

[15]Judah saw her and thought she was a prostitute because she had covered her face. [16]He turned to her beside the road and said, "Let me sleep with you," because he didn't know she was his daughter-in-law.

She said, "What will you give me for sleeping with you?"

[17]He said, "I will give you a kid goat from my flock."

She said, "Only if you give me some deposit, as security to guarantee that you will send it."

[18]He said, "What kind of deposit should I give you?"

And she said, "Your seal, its cord, and the staff in your hand." He gave these to her, slept with her, and she became pregnant by him.

[19]Then she got up, left, and took off her veil, dressing once again in the clothing she wore as a widow. [20]Judah sent the kid goat with his neighbor the Adullamite so he could take back the deposits from the woman, but he couldn't find her. [21]He asked the locals of that place, "Where's the consecrated worker[j] who was at Enaim on the road?"

But they said, "There's no consecrated worker here."

---

[h]Sam, Tg; MT *he* [i]Or *perfumed herself* or *wrapped herself up* [j]Traditionally *cultic prostitute*

TAMAR

In Genesis 38, Tamar is the wife of Judah's oldest son Er, then the wife of Judah's second son Onan, and then the mother of Judah's twin sons Perez and Zerah. The story tells of Tamar's persistence in seeking justice after the wickedness or neglect of the men in Judah's family. Her name is used as a blessing in Ruth 4:12, and she is listed as an ancestor of Jesus in Matthew 1:3.

²²So he went back to Judah and said, "I couldn't find her. The locals even said, 'There's no holy woman here.'"

²³Judah said, "Let her keep everything so we aren't laughed at. I did send this kid goat, but you couldn't find her."

²⁴About three months later, Judah was told, "Your daughter-in-law Tamar has become a prostitute and is now pregnant because of it."

And Judah said, "Bring her out so that she may be burned."

²⁵When she was brought out, she sent this message to her father-in-law, "I'm pregnant by the man who owns these things. See if you recognize whose seal, cord, and staff these are."

²⁶Judah recognized them and said, "She's more righteous than I am, because I didn't allow her to marry my son Shelah." Judah never knew her intimately again.

²⁷When she gave birth, she discovered she had twins in her womb. ²⁸At birth, one boy put out his hand, and the midwife took it and tied a red thread on his hand, saying, "This one came out first." ²⁹As soon as he pulled his hand back, his brother came out, and she said, "You've burst out on your own." So he was named Perez.ᵏ ³⁰Afterward, his brother with the red thread on his hand came out, and he was named Zerah.ˡ

Joseph's rise and betrayal

39 When Joseph had been taken down to Egypt, Potiphar, Pharaoh's chief officer, the commander of the royal guard and an Egyptian, purchased him from the Ishmaelites who had brought him down there. ²The LORD was with Joseph, and he became a successful man and served

in his Egyptian master's household. ³His master saw that the LORD was with him and that the LORD made everything he did successful. ⁴Potiphar thought highly of Joseph, and Joseph became his assistant; he appointed Joseph head of his household and put everything he had under Joseph's supervision. ⁵From the time he appointed Joseph head of his household and of everything he had, the LORD blessed the Egyptian's household because of Joseph. The LORD blessed everything he had, both in the household and in the field. ⁶So he handed over everything he had to Joseph and didn't pay attention to anything except the food he ate.

Now Joseph was well-built and handsome. ⁷Some time later, his master's wife became attracted to Joseph and said, "Sleep with me."

⁸He refused and said to his master's wife, "With me here, my master doesn't pay attention to anything in his household; he's put everything he has under my supervision. ⁹No one is greater than I am in this household, and he hasn't denied me anything except you, since you are his wife. How could I do this terrible thing and sin against God?" ¹⁰Every single day she tried to convince him, but he wouldn't agree to sleep with her or even to be with her.

¹¹One day when Joseph arrived at the house to do his work, none of the household's men were there. ¹²She grabbed his garment, saying, "Lie down with me." But he left his garment in her hands and ran outside. ¹³When she realized that he had left his garment in her hands and run outside, ¹⁴she summoned the men of her house and said to them, "Look, my husband brought us

---

ᵏOr *bursting out* ˡOr *dawn*

POTIPHAR'S WIFE

The wife of Potiphar, the Egyptian who purchased Joseph (Gen 37:36; 39:1). While she is unnamed in the biblical text, some later Jewish and Islamic sources refer to her as "Zulaikha" (with various spellings).

a Hebrew to ridicule us. He came to me to lie down with me, but I screamed. ¹⁵When he heard me raise my voice and scream, he left his garment with me and ran outside." ¹⁶She kept his garment with her until Joseph's master came home, ¹⁷and she told him the same thing: "The Hebrew slave whom you brought to us, to ridicule me, came to me; ¹⁸but when I raised my voice and screamed, he left his garment with me and ran outside."

¹⁹When Joseph's master heard the thing that his wife told him, "This is what your servant did to me," he was incensed. ²⁰Joseph's master took him and threw him in jail, the place where the king's prisoners were held. While he was in jail, ²¹the LORD was with Joseph and remained loyal to him. He caused the jail's commander to think highly of Joseph. ²²The jail's commander put all of the prisoners in the jail under Joseph's supervision, and he was the one who determined everything that happened there. ²³The jail's commander paid no attention to anything under Joseph's supervision, because the LORD was with him and made everything he did successful.

Joseph interprets dreams in prison

40Some time later, both the wine steward and the baker for Egypt's king offended their master, the king of Egypt. ²Pharaoh was angry with his two officers, the chief wine steward and the chief baker, ³and he put them under arrest with the commander of the royal guard in the same jail where Joseph was imprisoned. ⁴The commander of the royal guard assigned Joseph to assist them. After they had been under arrest for some time, ⁵both of them—the wine steward and the baker for Egypt's king who were imprisoned in the jail—had dreams one night, and each man's dream had its own meaning. ⁶When Joseph met them in the morning, he saw that they were upset. ⁷He asked the officers of Pharaoh who were under arrest with him in his master's house, "Why do you look so distressed today?"

⁸They answered, "We've both had dreams, but there's no one to interpret them."

Joseph said to them, "Don't interpretations belong to God? Describe your dreams to me."

⁹The chief wine steward described his dream to Joseph: "In my dream there was a vine right in front of me, ¹⁰and on the vine were three branches. When it budded, its blossoms appeared, and its clusters ripened into grapes. ¹¹Pharaoh's cup was in my hand, so I took the grapes, crushed them into Pharaoh's cup, and put the cup in Pharaoh's hand."

¹²Joseph said to him, "This is the dream's interpretation: The three branches are three days. ¹³After three days, Pharaoh will give you an audience and return you to your position. You will put Pharaoh's cup in his hand, just the way things were before when you were his wine steward. ¹⁴But please, remember me when you are doing well and be loyal to me. Put in a good word for me to Pharaoh, so he sets me free from this prison. ¹⁵I was stolen from the land of the Hebrews, and here too I've done nothing to be thrown into this dungeon."

¹⁶When the chief baker saw that the interpretation was favorable, he said to Joseph, "It was the same for me. In my dream, there were three baskets of white bread^m on my head. ¹⁷In the basket on top there were baked goods for Pharaoh's food, but birds were eating them out of the basket on my head."

¹⁸Joseph responded, "This is the dream's interpretation: The three baskets are three days. ¹⁹After three days, Pharaoh will give you an audience and will hang you from a tree where birds will peck your flesh from you."

²⁰The third day was Pharaoh's birthday, and he gave a party for all of his servants. Before all of his servants, he gave an audience to the chief wine steward and the chief baker. ²¹He returned the chief wine steward to his position, and he placed the cup in Pharaoh's hand. ²²But the chief baker he hanged, just as Joseph had said would hap-

---

^m Heb uncertain

pen when he interpreted their dreams for them. [23]But the chief wine steward didn't remember Joseph; he forgot all about him.

Joseph interprets Pharaoh's dreams

41 Two years later, Pharaoh dreamed that he was standing near the Nile. [2]In front of him, seven healthy-looking, fattened cows climbed up out of the Nile and grazed on the reeds. [3]Just then, seven other cows, terrible-looking and scrawny, climbed up out of the Nile after them and stood beside them on the bank of the Nile. [4]The terrible-looking, scrawny cows devoured the seven healthy-looking, fattened cows. Then Pharaoh woke up. [5]He went back to sleep and had a second dream, in which seven ears of grain, full and healthy, grew on a single stalk. [6]Just then, seven ears of grain, scrawny and scorched by the east wind, sprouted after them, [7]and the scrawny ears swallowed up the full and well-formed ears. Then Pharaoh woke up and realized it was a dream. [8]In the morning, he was disturbed and summoned all of Egypt's religious experts[n] and all of its advisors. Pharaoh described his dreams[o] to them, but they couldn't interpret them for Pharaoh.

[9]Then the chief wine steward spoke to Pharaoh: "Today I've just remembered my mistake. [10]Pharaoh was angry with his servants and put me and the chief baker under arrest with the commander of the royal guard. [11]We both dreamed one night, he and I, and each of our dreams had its own interpretation. [12]A young Hebrew man, a servant of the commander of the royal guard, was with us. We described our dreams to

him, and he interpreted our dreams for us, giving us an interpretation for each dream. [13]His interpretations came true exactly: Pharaoh restored me to my position but hanged him."

[14]So Pharaoh summoned Joseph, and they quickly brought him from the dungeon. He shaved, changed clothes, and appeared before Pharaoh. [15]Pharaoh said to Joseph, "I had a dream, but no one could interpret it. Then I heard that when you hear a dream, you can interpret it." [16]Joseph answered Pharaoh, "It's not me. God will give Pharaoh a favorable response."

[17]So Pharaoh said to Joseph, "In my dream I was standing on the bank of the Nile. [18]In front of me, seven fattened, stout cows climbed up out of the Nile and grazed on the reeds. [19]Just then, seven other cows, weak and frail and thin, climbed up after them. I've never seen such awful cows in all the land of Egypt. [20]Then the thin, frail cows devoured the first seven, fattened cows. [21]But after they swallowed them whole, no one would have known it. They looked just as bad as they had before. Then I woke up. [22]I went to sleep again[p] and saw in my dream seven full and healthy ears of grain growing on one stalk. [23]Just then, seven hard and thin ears of grain, scorched by the east wind, sprouted after them, [24]and the thin ears swallowed up the healthy ears. I told the religious experts,[q] but they couldn't explain it to me."

[25]Joseph said to Pharaoh, "Pharaoh has actually had one dream. God has announced to Pharaoh what he is about to do. [26]The seven healthy cows are seven

[n]Or magicians   [o]Sam; MT dream   [p]LXX, Syr, Vulg; MT lacks I went to sleep again.   [q]Or magicians

DREAMS

Dreams used to be considered messages from deities, demons, or the deceased. Neither Hebrew nor Greek made a sharp distinction between dreams and visions, and both considered these to be potentially revelations of God (Num 12:6).

years, and the seven healthy ears of grain are seven years. It's actually one dream. ²⁷The seven thin and frail cows, climbing up after them, are seven years. The seven thin ears of grain, scorched by the east wind, are seven years of famine. ²⁸It's just as I told Pharaoh: God has shown Pharaoh what he is about to do. ²⁹Seven years of great abundance are now coming throughout the entire land of Egypt. ³⁰After them, seven years of famine will appear, and all of the abundance in the land of Egypt will be forgotten. The famine will devastate the land. ³¹No one will remember the abundance in the land because the famine that follows will be so very severe. ³²The dream occurred to Pharaoh twice because God has determined to do it, and God will make it happen soon.

Joseph's rise to power

³³"Now Pharaoh should find an intelligent, wise man and give him authority over the land of Egypt. ³⁴Then Pharaoh should appoint administrators over the land and take one-fifth of all the produce of the land of Egypt during the seven years of abundance. ³⁵During the good years that are coming, they should collect all such food and store the grain under Pharaoh's control, protecting the food in the cities. ³⁶This food will be reserved for the seven years of famine to follow in the land of Egypt so that the land won't be ravaged by the famine."

³⁷This advice seemed wise to Pharaoh and all his servants, ³⁸and Pharaoh said to his servants, "Can we find a man with more God-given gifts[r] than this one?" ³⁹Then Pharaoh said to Joseph, "Since God has made all this known to you, no one is as intelligent and wise as you are. ⁴⁰You will be in charge of my kingdom,[s] and all my people will obey[t] your command. Only as the enthroned king will I be greater than you." ⁴¹Pharaoh said to Joseph, "Know this: I've given you authority over the entire land of Egypt." ⁴²Pharaoh took his signet ring from

his hand and put it on Joseph's hand, he dressed him in linen clothes, and he put a gold necklace around his neck. ⁴³He put Joseph on the chariot of his second-in-command, and everyone in front of him cried out, "Attention!"[u] So Pharaoh installed him over the entire land of Egypt. ⁴⁴Pharaoh said to Joseph, "I am Pharaoh; no one will do anything or go anywhere in all the land of Egypt without your permission." ⁴⁵Pharaoh renamed Joseph, Zaphenath-paneah, and married him to Asenath, the daughter of Potiphera the priest of Heliopolis.[v]

Then Joseph assumed control of the land of Egypt. ⁴⁶Joseph was 30 years old when he began to serve Pharaoh, Egypt's king, when he left Pharaoh's court and traveled through the entire land of Egypt. ⁴⁷During the seven years of abundance, the land produced plentifully. ⁴⁸He collected all of the food during the seven years of abundance[w] in the land of Egypt, and stored the food in cities. In each city, he stored the food from the fields surrounding it. ⁴⁹Joseph amassed grain like the sand of the sea. There was so much that he stopped trying to measure it because it was beyond measuring. ⁵⁰Before the years of famine arrived, Asenath the daughter of Potiphera, priest of Heliopolis,[x] gave birth to two sons for Joseph. ⁵¹Joseph named the oldest son Manasseh,[y] "because," he said, "God has helped me forget all of my troubles and everyone in my father's household." ⁵²He named the second Ephraim,[z] "because," he said, "God has given me children in the land where I've been treated harshly."

⁵³The seven years of abundance in the land of Egypt came to an end, ⁵⁴and the seven years of famine began, just as Joseph had said. The famine struck every country, but the entire land of Egypt had bread. ⁵⁵When the famine ravaged the entire land of Egypt and the people pleaded to Pharaoh for bread, Pharaoh said to all of the Egyptians, "Go to Joseph. Do whatever he tells you." ⁵⁶The famine covered every part of

---

[r]Or like this one, in whom is the spirit of God [s]Or house [t]LXX; Heb uncertain, perhaps submit themselves to your command [u]An Egyptian loanword similar to the Heb word kneel [v]Heb On [w]LXX; MT lacks of abundance. [x]Heb On [y]Or making forget [z]Sounds like has given me children

the land, and Joseph opened all of the granaries[a] and sold grain to the Egyptians. In the land of Egypt, the famine became more and more severe. [57]Every country came to Egypt to buy grain from Joseph, because in every country the famine had also become more severe.

Joseph's brothers arrive in Egypt

42 When Jacob learned that there was grain in Egypt, he said to his sons, "Why are you staring blankly at each other? [2]I've just heard that there's grain in Egypt. Go down there and buy some for us so that we can survive and not starve to death." [3]So Joseph's ten brothers went down to buy grain in Egypt. [4]However, Jacob didn't send Joseph's brother Benjamin along with his brothers because he thought something bad might happen to him. [5]Israel's sons came to buy grain with others who also came since the famine had spread to the land of Canaan.

[6]As for Joseph, he was the land's governor, and he was the one selling grain to all the land's people. When Joseph's brothers arrived, they bowed down to him, their faces to the ground. [7]When Joseph saw his brothers, he recognized them, but he acted like he didn't know them. He spoke to them with a harsh tone and said, "Where have you come from?"

And they said, "From the land of Canaan to buy food."

[8]Joseph recognized his brothers, but they didn't recognize him. [9]Joseph remembered the dreams he had dreamed about them, and said to them, "You are spies. You've come to look for the country's weaknesses."

[10]They said to him, "No, Master. Your servants have just come to buy food. [11]We are all sons of one man. We are honest men. Your servants aren't spies."

[12]He said to them, "No. You've come to look for the country's weaknesses."

[13]They said, "We, your servants, are twelve brothers, sons of one man in the land of Canaan. The youngest is now with our father, but one is gone."

[14]Joseph said to them, "It's just as I've said to you. You are spies! [15]But here is how to prove yourselves: As Pharaoh lives, you won't leave here until your youngest brother arrives. [16]Send one of you to get your brother, but the rest of you will stay in prison. We will find out if your words are true. If not, as Pharaoh lives, you are certainly spies."

Joseph's brothers return to Canaan

[17]He put them all in prison for three days. [18]On the third day, Joseph said to them, "Do this and you will live, for I'm a God-fearing man. [19]If you are honest men, let one of your brothers stay in prison, and the rest of you, go, take grain back to those in your households who are hungry. [20]But bring your youngest brother back to me so that your words will prove true and you won't die."

So they prepared to do this. [21]The brothers said to each other, "We are clearly guilty for what we did to our brother when we saw his life in danger and when he begged us for mercy, but we didn't listen. That's why we're in this danger now."

[22]Reuben responded to them, "Didn't I tell you, 'Don't do anything wrong to the boy'? But you wouldn't listen. So now this is payback for his death." [23]They didn't know that Joseph was listening to them because they were using an interpreter. [24]He stepped away from them and wept. When he returned, he spoke with them again. Then he took Simeon from them and tied him up in front of them.

[25]Then Joseph gave orders to fill their bags with grain, to put back each man's silver into his own sack, and to give them provisions for their trip, and it was done. [26]They loaded their grain onto their donkeys, and they set out. [27]When they stopped to spend the night, one of them opened his sack to feed his donkey, and he saw his silver at the top of his sack. [28]He said to his brothers, "My silver's been returned. It's right here in my sack." Their hearts stopped. Terrified, they said to each other, "What has God done to us?"

[a]LXX, Syr; MT *what was in them*

²⁹When they got back to their father Jacob in the land of Canaan, they described to him everything that had happened to them: ³⁰"The man, the country's governor, spoke to us with a harsh tone and accused us of being spies in the country. ³¹We told him, 'We're honest men, not spies. ³²We are twelve brothers, all our father's sons. One of us is gone, but the youngest is right now with our father in the land of Canaan.' ³³The man, the country's governor, told us, 'This is how I will know you are honest men: Leave one of your brothers with me, take grain for those in your households who are hungry, and go. ³⁴But bring back your youngest brother to me. Then I will know that you are not spies but honest men. I will give your brother back to you, and you may travel throughout the country.'"

³⁵When they opened their sacks, each man found a pouch of his silver in his sack. When they and their father saw their pouches of silver, they were afraid. ³⁶Their father Jacob said to them, "You've taken my children from me. Joseph's gone. Simeon's gone. And you are taking Benjamin. All this can't really be happening to me!"

³⁷Reuben said to his father, "You may put both of my sons to death if I don't bring him back to you. Make him my responsibility, and I will make sure he returns to you."

³⁸But Jacob said to him, "My son won't go down with you because his brother's dead and he's been left all alone. If anything were to happen to him on the trip you are taking, you would send me—old as I am—to my grave in grief."

Joseph's brothers return with Benjamin

43 The famine was severe in the land, ²and when they had eaten all the grain that they brought from Egypt, their father said to them, "Go back and buy us a little food."

³Judah said to him, "The man was absolutely serious when he said, 'You may not see me again without your brother with you.' ⁴If you agree to send our brother with us, then we will go down and buy you food.

⁵But if you don't agree to send him, then we can't go down because the man said to us, 'You may not see me again without your brother with you.'"

⁶Israel said, "Why have you caused me such pain by telling the man you had another brother?"

⁷They said, "The man asked us pointedly about our family: 'Is your father still alive? Do you have a brother?' So we told him just what we've said. How were we to know he'd say, 'Bring your brother down here'?"

⁸Judah said to his father Israel, "Send the young man with me. Let's get ready to leave so that we can stay alive and not die— we, you, and our children. ⁹I will guarantee his safety; you can hold me responsible. If I don't bring him back to you and place him here in front of you, it will be my fault forever. ¹⁰If we hadn't waited so long, we would've returned twice by now."

¹¹Their father Israel said to them, "If it has to be, then do this. Take in your bags some of the land's choice produce, and bring it down to the man as a gift: a little medicinal resin, a little honey, gum, resin, pistachios, and almonds. ¹²Take twice as much silver with you, and take back the silver returned in the top of your sacks. It might have been a mistake. ¹³And take your brother, get ready, and go back to the man. ¹⁴May God Almighty[b] make the man compassionate toward you so that he may send back our other brother and Benjamin with you. But me, if I'm left childless, then I'm left childless."

¹⁵So the men took this gift. They took twice as much silver with them, together with Benjamin. They left, traveled down to Egypt, and received an audience with Joseph. ¹⁶When Joseph saw Benjamin with them, he said to the manager of his household, "Bring the men to the house and slaughter an animal and prepare it because the men will have dinner with me at noon." ¹⁷The man did as Joseph told him and brought the men to Joseph's house.

¹⁸When they were brought to Joseph's house, the men were frightened and said,

[b] Heb *El Shaddai* or *God of the Mountain*

"We've been brought here because of the silver put back in our sacks on our first trip so he can overpower us, capture us, make slaves of us, and take our donkeys."

[19]They approached the man who was Joseph's household manager and spoke to him at the house's entrance: [20]"Please, Master, we came down the first time just to buy food, [21]but when we stopped to spend the night and opened our sacks, there was the exact amount of each man's silver at the top of his sack. We've brought it back with us, [22]and we've brought down with us additional silver to buy food. We don't know who put our silver in our sacks."

[23]He said, "You are fine. Don't be afraid. Your God and your father's God must have hidden a treasure in your sacks. I received your money." Then he brought Simeon out to them.

[24]The manager brought the men into Joseph's house and gave them water to wash their feet and feed for their donkeys. [25]They prepared the gift, anticipating Joseph's arrival at noon, since they had heard that they would have a meal there. [26]When Joseph came into the house, they presented him the gift they had brought with them into the house, and they bowed low in front of him. [27]He asked them how they were and said, "How is your elderly father, about whom you spoke? Is he still alive?"

[28]They said, "Your servant our father is fine. He's still alive." And they bowed down again with deep respect.

[29]Joseph looked up and saw his brother Benjamin, his own mother's son, and he said, "Is this your youngest brother whom you told me about? God be gracious to you, my son." [30]Joseph's feelings for his brother were so strong he was about to weep, so he rushed to another room and wept there. [31]He washed his face, came back, pulled himself together, and said, "Set out the dinner." [32]So they set out his food by himself, their food by themselves, and the Egyptians' who ate with him by themselves because Egyptians don't allow themselves to eat with Hebrews; the Egyp-

tians think it beneath their dignity. [33]They were seated in front of him from the oldest to the youngest in their exact birth order, and the men looked at each other with amazement. [34]Portions of food from Joseph's table were brought to them, but Benjamin's portion was five times as large as theirs. So they drank together and were at ease.

Joseph tests his brothers

44Joseph gave commands to his household manager: "Fill the men's sacks with as much food as they'll hold, and put each man's silver at the top of his sack. [2]Put my cup, the silver cup, on top of the youngest brother's sack, together with the silver for his grain." So he did just as Joseph told him to do.

[3]At dawn, the men and their donkeys were sent off. [4]They had left the city but hadn't gone far when Joseph said to his household manager, "Get ready, go after the men and catch up with them! Ask them, 'Why have you repaid hospitality with ingratitude?[c] [5]Isn't this the cup[d] my master drinks from and uses to discover God's plans?[e] What you've done is despicable.'"

[6]When he caught up to them, he repeated these words. [7]They replied, "Why does my master talk to us like this? Your servants would never do such a thing. [8]The silver that we found at the top of our sacks, we've just brought back to you from the land of Canaan. We didn't steal silver or gold from your master's house. [9]Whoever of your servants is found with it will be put to death, and we'll be my master's slaves."

[10]He said, "Fine. We'll do just as you've said. Whoever is found with it will be my slave, and the rest of you will go free." [11]Everyone quickly lowered their sacks down to the ground and each opened his sack. [12]He searched the oldest first and the youngest last, and the cup was found in Benjamin's sack. [13]At this, they tore their clothing. Then everyone loaded their donkeys, and they returned to the city.

[14]When Judah and his brothers arrived

---

[c]LXX adds *Why have you stolen my silver cup?* [d]Syr; MT lacks *cup.* [e]Or *uses for divination*

at Joseph's house, he was still there, and they fell to the ground in front of him. [15] Joseph said to them, "What's this you've done? Didn't you know someone like me can discover God's plans?"[f]

[16] Judah replied, "What can we say to my master? What words can we use? How can we prove we are innocent? God has found your servants guilty. We are now your slaves, all of us, including the one found with the cup."

[17] Joseph said, "I'd never do such a thing. Only the man found with the cup will be my slave. As for the rest of you, you are free to go back to your father."

Judah appeals for Benjamin

[18] Judah approached him and said, "Please, my master, allow your servant to say something to my master without getting angry with your servant since you are like Pharaoh himself. [19] My master asked his servants, 'Do you have a father or brother?'

[20] And we said to my master, 'Yes, we have an elderly father and a young brother, born when he was old. His brother is dead and he's his mother's only child. But his father loves him.' [21] You told your servants, 'Bring him down to me so I can see him.' [22] And we said to my master, 'The young man can't leave his father. If he leaves, his father will die.' [23] You said to your servants, 'If your youngest brother doesn't come down with you, you'll never see my face again.'

[24] "When we went back to my father your servant, we told him what you said. [25] Our father told us, 'Go back and buy for us a little food.' [26] But we said, 'We can't go down. We will go down only if our youngest brother is with us. We won't be able to gain an audience with the man without our youngest brother with us.' [27] Your servant my father said to us, 'You know that my wife gave birth to two sons for me. [28] One disappeared and I said, "He must have been torn up by a wild animal," and I haven't seen him

[f] Or *can practice divination*

JUDAH/JUDAHITES

    1. Judah, the fourth son of Jacob; born to Leah (Gen 29:35). As a character in Genesis, Judah can be seen in a sympathetic light. For instance, Judah entreats his brothers to sell Joseph rather than kill him (Gen 37:26-27), though the story reports a mercenary motive on Judah's part. Also, when Joseph threatens to imprison Benjamin in Egypt, Judah pleads for him and offers himself in Benjamin's stead (Gen 44:18-34).

    2. Judah, the territory, was located in the southern part of the Levant. Joshua 15 describes its ideal expanse: Its eastern border was the Dead Sea, and its northern boundary ran basically from the northern edge of the Dead Sea to the Mediterranean, its western border. Judah's southern border met the Mediterranean at the Wadi (or "border") of Egypt, perhaps the Wadi Besor or the Wadi el-Arish.

    The general area of Judah became known as Yehud in the Persian Period and eventually as Judea in NT times. Judah is the location of Jesus' birth according to Matthew 2:6 (cf. Mic 5:2). Hebrews mentions the tribe of Judah twice; once to affirm that Jesus is not a levitical priest (as he was a Judahite, Heb 7:14), and once in a quotation of Jeremiah 31:31 (Heb. 8:8). Revelation 5:5 symbolically refers to Jesus as "the Lion of the tribe of Judah," and Revelation 7:5 lists 12,000 "sealed" from Judah.

since. [29]And if you take this one from me too, something terrible will happen to him, and you will send me—old as I am—to my grave in despair.' [30]When I now go back to your servant my father without the young man—whose life is so bound up with his— [31]and when he sees that the young man isn't with us,[g] he will die, and your servants will have sent our father your servant—old as he is—to his grave in grief. [32]I, your servant, guaranteed the young man's safety to my father, telling him, 'If I don't bring him back to you, it will be my fault forever.' [33]Now, please let your servant stay as your slave instead of the young man so that he can go back with his brothers. [34]How can I go back to my father without the young man? I couldn't bear to see how badly my father would be hurt."

Joseph reveals his identity

45 Joseph could no longer control himself in front of all his attendants, so he declared, "Everyone, leave now!" So no one stayed with him when he revealed his identity to his brothers. [2]He wept so loudly that the Egyptians and Pharaoh's household heard him. [3]Joseph said to his brothers, "I'm Joseph! Is my father really still alive?" His brothers couldn't respond because they were terrified before him.

[4]Joseph said to his brothers, "Come closer to me," and they moved closer. He said, "I'm your brother Joseph! The one you sold to Egypt. [5]Now, don't be upset and don't be angry with yourselves that you sold me here. Actually, God sent me before you to save lives. [6]We've already had two years of famine in the land, and there are five years left without planting or harvesting. [7]God sent me before you to make sure you'd survive[h] and to rescue your lives in this amazing way. [8]You didn't send me here; it was God who made me a father to Pharaoh, master of his entire household, and ruler of the whole land of Egypt.

[9]"Hurry! Go back to your father. Tell him this is what your son Joseph says: 'God has made me master of all of Egypt.

Come down to me. Don't delay. [10]You may live in the land of Goshen, so you will be near me, your children, your grandchildren, your flocks, your herds, and everyone with you. [11]I will support you there, so you, your household, and everyone with you won't starve, since the famine will still last five years.' [12]You and my brother Benjamin have seen with your own eyes that I'm speaking to you. [13]Tell my father about my power in Egypt and about everything you've seen. Hurry and bring my father down here." [14]He threw his arms around his brother Benjamin's neck and wept, and Benjamin wept on his shoulder. [15]He kissed all of his brothers and wept, embracing them. After that, his brothers were finally able to talk to him.

Joseph's brothers return for Jacob

[16]When Pharaoh's household heard the message "Joseph's brothers have arrived," both Pharaoh and his servants were pleased. [17]Pharaoh said to Joseph, "Give your brothers these instructions: Load your pack animals and go back to the land of Canaan. [18]Get your father and your households and come back to me. Let me provide you with good things from the land of Egypt so that you may eat the land's best food. [19]Give them these instructions too: Take wagons from the land of Egypt for your children and wives, and pick up your father and come back. [20]Don't worry about your possessions because you will have good things from the entire land of Egypt."

[21]So Israel's sons did that. Joseph gave them wagons as Pharaoh instructed, and he gave them provisions for the road. [22]To all of them he gave a change of clothing, but to Benjamin he gave three hundred pieces of silver and five changes of clothing. [23]To his father he sent ten male donkeys carrying goods from Egypt, ten female donkeys carrying grain and bread, and rations for his father for the road. [24]He sent his brothers off; and as they were leaving, he told them, "Don't be worried about the trip."[i] [25]So they left Egypt and returned to

---

[g]Sam, LXX; MT lacks *with us.*   [h]Or *survive on earth*   [i]Or *Don't quarrel during the trip.*

their father Jacob in the land of Canaan. [26]They announced to him, "Joseph's still alive! He's actually ruler of all the land of Egypt!" Jacob's heart nearly failed, and he didn't believe them.

[27]When they told him everything Joseph had said to them, and when he saw the wagons Joseph had sent to carry him, Jacob recovered. [28]Then Israel said, "This is too much! My son Joseph is still alive! Let me go and see him before I die."

Jacob's household moves to Egypt

46 Israel packed up everything he owned and traveled to Beer-sheba. There he offered sacrifices to his father Isaac's God. [2]God said to Israel in a vision at night, "Jacob! Jacob!" and he said, "I'm here." [3]He said, "I am El,[j] your father's God. Don't be afraid to go down to Egypt because I will make a great nation of you there. [4]I will go down to Egypt with you, and I promise to bring you out again. Joseph will close your eyes when you die." [5]Then Jacob left Beer-sheba. Israel's sons put their father Jacob, their children, and their wives on the wagons Pharaoh had sent to carry him. [6]They took their livestock and their possessions that they had acquired in the land of Canaan, and arrived in Egypt, Jacob and all of his children with him. [7]His sons and grandsons, his daughters and his granddaughters—all of his descendants he brought with him to Egypt.

[8]These are the names of the Israelites who went to Egypt, including Jacob and his sons. Jacob's oldest son was Reuben. [9]Reuben's sons were Hanoch, Pallu, Hezron, and Carmi. [10]Simeon's sons were Jemuel, Jamin, Ohad, Jachin, Zohar, and Shaul, whose mother was a Canaanite. [11]Levi's sons were Gershon, Kohath, and Merari. [12]Judah's sons were Er, Onan, Shelah, Perez, and Zerah. Er and Onan both died in the land of Canaan. Perez's sons were Hezron and Hamul. [13]Issachar's sons were Tola, Puvah, Iob, and Shimron. [14]Zebulun's sons were Sered, Elon, and Jahleel. [15]These are the sons Leah bore to Jacob in Paddan-aram. Her daughter was Dinah. All of these persons, including his sons and daughters, totaled 33.

[16]Gad's sons were Ziphion, Haggi, Shuni, Ezbon, Eri, Arodi, and Areli. [17]Asher's sons were Imnah, Ishvah, Ishvi, Beriah, and their sister Serah. Beriah's sons were Heber and Malchiel. [18]These are the sons of Zilpah, whom Laban gave to his daughter Leah. She bore these to Jacob, a total of 16 persons.

[19]The sons of Jacob's wife Rachel were Joseph and Benjamin. [20]To Joseph, in the land of Egypt, were born Manasseh and Ephraim. Asenath daughter of Potiphera, priest of Heliopolis,[k] bore them to him. [21]Benjamin's sons were Bela, Becher, Ashbel, Gera, Naaman, Ehi, Rosh, Muppim, Huppim, and Ard. [22]These are Rachel's sons who were born to Jacob, a total of 14 persons.

[23]Dan's son[l] was Hushim. [24]Naphtali's sons were Jahzeel, Guni, Jezer, and Shillem. [25]These are the sons of Bilhah, whom Laban gave to his daughter Rachel. She bore these to Jacob, a total of 7 persons. [26]All of the persons going to Egypt with Jacob—his own children, excluding Jacob's sons' wives—totaled 66 persons. [27]Joseph's sons born to him in Egypt were 2 persons. Thus, all of the persons in Jacob's household going to Egypt totaled 70.

[28]Israel had sent Judah ahead to Joseph so that Joseph could explain the way to Goshen. Then they arrived in the land of Goshen. [29]Joseph hitched up his chariot and went to meet his father Israel in Goshen. When he arrived, he threw his arms around his neck and wept, embracing him for a long time. [30]Israel said to Joseph, "I can die now after seeing your face. You are really still alive!"

Jacob's household settles in Egypt

[31]Joseph said to his brothers and to his father's household, "Let me go up and inform Pharaoh and tell him, 'My brothers and my father's household who were in the

---

[j]Or God [k]Heb On [l]Or sons

land of Canaan have arrived. ³²The men are shepherds, because they own livestock. They've brought with them their flocks and herds and everything they own.' ³³When Pharaoh summons you and says, 'What do you do?' ³⁴say, 'Your servants have owned livestock since we were young, both we and our ancestors,' so that you will be able to settle in the land of Goshen, since Egyptians think all shepherds are beneath their dignity."

47 Joseph went to inform Pharaoh and said, "My father and brothers with their flocks, herds, and everything they own have come from the land of Canaan and are now in the land of Goshen." ²From all of his brothers, he selected five men and presented them before Pharaoh.

³Pharaoh said to Joseph's brothers, "What do you do?"

They said to Pharaoh, "Your servants are shepherds, both we and our ancestors." ⁴They continued, "We've come to the land as immigrants because the famine is so severe in the land of Canaan that there are no more pastures for your servants' flocks. Please allow your servants to settle in the land of Goshen."

⁵Pharaoh said to Joseph, "Since your father and brothers have arrived, ⁶the land of Egypt is available to you. Settle your father and brothers in the land's best location. Let them live in the land of Goshen. And if you know capable men among them, put them in charge of my own livestock."

⁷Joseph brought his father Jacob and gave him an audience with Pharaoh. Jacob blessed Pharaoh, ⁸and Pharaoh said to Jacob, "How old are you?"

⁹Jacob said to Pharaoh, "I've been a traveler for 130 years. My years have been few and difficult. They don't come close to the years my ancestors lived during their travels." ¹⁰Jacob blessed Pharaoh and left Pharaoh's presence. ¹¹Joseph settled his father and brothers and gave them property in the land of Egypt, in the best location in the land of Rameses, just as Pharaoh had ordered. ¹²Joseph provided food for his father, his brothers, and his father's entire household, in proportion to the number of children.

Joseph centralizes power in Egypt

¹³There was no food in the land because the famine was so severe. The land of Egypt and the land of Canaan dried up from the famine. ¹⁴Joseph collected all of the silver to be found in the land of Egypt and in the land of Canaan for the grain, which people came to buy, and he deposited it in Pharaoh's treasury. ¹⁵The silver from the land of Egypt and from the land of Canaan had been spent, and all of the Egyptians came to Joseph and said, "Give us food. Why should we die before your eyes, just because the silver is gone?"

¹⁶Joseph said, "Give me your livestock, and I will give you food for your livestock if the silver is gone." ¹⁷So they brought their livestock to Joseph, and Joseph gave them food for the horses, flocks, cattle, and donkeys. He got them through that year with food in exchange for all of their livestock.

¹⁸When that year was over, they came to him the next year and said to him, "We can't hide from my master that the silver is spent and that we've given the livestock to my master. All that's left for my master is our corpses and our farmland. ¹⁹Why should we die before your eyes, we and our

JOSEPH (OT)

Joseph belongs to the third generation of descendants of Abraham and Sarah; he is the older son of Jacob and Rachel (Gen 35:24) and the father of Ephraim and Manasseh. Joseph is one of the patriarchs of Israel, and in some lists his name is used for one of the 12 tribes.

farmland too? Buy us and our farms for food, and we and our farms will be under Pharaoh's control. Give us seed so that we can stay alive and not die, and so that our farmland won't become unproductive." [20] So Joseph bought all of Egypt's farmland for Pharaoh because every Egyptian sold his field when the famine worsened. So the land became Pharaoh's. [21] He moved the people to the cities[m] from one end of Egypt to the other. [22] However, he didn't buy the farmland of the priests because Pharaoh allowed the priests a subsidy, and they were able to eat from the subsidy Pharaoh gave them. Therefore, they didn't have to sell their farmland.

[23] Joseph said to the people, "Since I've now purchased you and your farmland for Pharaoh, here's seed for you. Plant the seed on the land. [24] When the crop comes in, you must give one-fifth to Pharaoh. You may keep four-fifths for yourselves, for planting fields, and for feeding yourselves, those in your households, and your children." [25] The people said, "You've saved our lives. If you wish, we will be Pharaoh's slaves." [26] So Joseph made a law that still exists today: Pharaoh receives one-fifth from Egypt's farmland. Only the priests' farmland didn't become Pharaoh's.

Jacob blesses Ephraim and Manasseh

[27] Israel lived in the land of Egypt, in the land of Goshen. They settled in it, had many children, and became numerous. [28] After Jacob had lived in the land of Egypt for seventeen years, and after he had lived a total of 147 years, [29] Israel's death approached. He summoned his son Joseph and said to him, "If you would be so kind, lay your hand under my thigh, and be loyal and true to me. Don't bury me in Egypt. [30] When I lie down with my fathers, carry me from Egypt and bury me in their grave."

Joseph said, "I will do just as you say." [31] Israel said, "Give me your word!" and Joseph gave his word. Then Israel slumped down at the head of the bed.

48 After this happened, Joseph was told,[n] "Your father is getting weaker," so he took his two sons Manasseh and Ephraim with him. [2] When Jacob was informed,[o] "Your son Joseph is here now," he[p] pulled himself together and sat up in bed. [3] Jacob said to Joseph, "God Almighty[q] appeared to me in Luz in the land of Canaan. He blessed me [4] and said to me, 'I am about to give you many children, to increase your numbers, and to make you a large group of peoples. I will give this land to your descendants following you as an enduring possession.' [5] Now, your two sons born to you in the land of Egypt before I arrived in Egypt are my own. Ephraim and Manasseh are just like Reuben and Simeon to me. [6] Your family who is born to you after them are yours, but their inheritance will be determined under their brothers' names. [7] When I came back from Paddan-aram,[r] Rachel died, to my sorrow, on the road in the land of Canaan, with some distance yet to go to Ephrathah, so I buried her there near the road to Ephrathah,[s] which is Bethlehem."

[8] When Israel saw Joseph's sons, he said, "Who are these?"

[9] Joseph told his father, "They're my sons, whom God gave me here."

Israel said, "Bring them to me and I will bless them." [10] Because Israel's eyesight had failed from old age and he wasn't able to see, Joseph brought them close to him, and he kissed and embraced them.

[11] Israel said to Joseph, "I didn't expect I'd see your face, but now God has shown me your children too." [12] Then Joseph took them from Israel's knees, and he bowed low with his face to the ground. [13] Joseph took both of them, Ephraim in his right hand at Israel's left hand, and Manasseh in his left hand at Israel's right hand, and brought them close to him. [14] But Israel put out his right hand and placed it on the head of Ephraim, the younger one, and his left hand on Manasseh's head, crossing his hands because Manasseh was the oldest son. [15] He blessed them[t] and said,

---

[m] Sam, LXX *he made the people slaves*   [n] LXX, Syr, Tg, Vulg; MT *he told*   [o] LXX; MT *he informed*   [p] Heb *Israel*
[q] Heb *El Shaddai* or *God of the Mountain*   [r] Sam, LXX, Syr; MT lacks *aram.*   [s] Sam; MT *Ephrath*   [t] LXX; MT *Joseph*

"May the God before whom my fathers
  Abraham and Isaac walked,
may the God who was my shepherd
  from the beginning until this day,
[16] may the divine messenger
  who protected me from all harm,
    bless the young men.
Through them may my name
  be kept alive
  and the names of my fathers
    Abraham and Isaac.
May they grow into a great multitude
  throughout the land."

[17] When Joseph saw that his father had placed his right hand on Ephraim's head, he was upset and grasped his father's hand to move it from Ephraim's head to Manasseh's head. [18] Joseph said to his father, "No, my father! This is the oldest son. Put your right hand on his head."

[19] But his father refused and said, "I know, my son, I know. He'll become a people too, and he'll also be great. But his younger brother will be greater than he will, and his descendants will become many nations." [20] Israel blessed them that day, saying,

"Through you, Israel will pronounce
  blessings, saying,
    'May God make you
    like Ephraim and Manasseh.'"
So Israel put Ephraim before Manasseh.

[21] Then Israel said to Joseph, "I'm about to die. God will be with you and return you to the land of your fathers. [22] I'm giving you one portion more than to your brothers,[u] a portion that I took from the Amorites with my sword and my bow."

Jacob reveals his sons' destinies

49

Jacob summoned his sons and said, "Gather around so that I can tell you what will happen to you in the coming days. [2] Assemble yourselves and listen, sons of Jacob;
  listen to Israel your father.

[3] Reuben, you are my oldest son,
  my strength and my first contender,[v]
  superior in status and superior in might.
[4] As wild as the waters, you won't endure,
  for you went up to your father's bed,
  you went up[w] and violated my couch.

[5] Simeon and Levi are brothers,
  weapons of violence their stock in trade.
[6] May I myself never enter their council.
  May my honor never be linked
    to their group;
  for when they were angry,
    they killed men,
  and whenever they wished,
    they maimed oxen.

---

[u] Heb uncertain   [v] Or *first of my power*   [w] LXX; MT *he went up*

RIGHT HAND

In Hebrew, the phrase "right hand" can simply mean to the right (as opposed to left) side literally (Num 20:17) or metaphorically as departing from the commandments to the right or left (Josh 1:7). It also represents the literal right hand (Gen 48:13; 2 Sam 20:9). The right hand was apparently the main hand for giving a blessing (Gen 48:14, 17-18).

The right or strong hand represents the power of God (Exod 15:6; cf. Job 40:14; Ps 20:6 [Heb. 20:7]).

Being at someone's right hand or right side is to occupy a place of honor (Ps 45:9 [Heb. 45:10]; 110:1). In the NT, being at the right hand often refers to Psalm 110:1 and is used especially of Jesus at God's right hand (Matt 26:64; Acts 2:33; Heb 12:2).

⁷ Cursed be their anger; it is violent,
    their rage; it is relentless.
I'll divide them up within Jacob
    and disperse them within Israel.
⁸ Judah, you are the one
    your brothers will honor;
    your hand will be
      on the neck of your enemies;
    your father's sons will bow down to you.
⁹ Judah is a lion's cub;
    from the prey, my son, you rise up.
He lies down and crouches like a lion;
    like a lioness—who dares disturb him?
¹⁰ The scepter won't depart from Judah,
    nor the ruler's staff
      from among his banners.ˣ
Gifts will be brought to him;
    people will obey him.
¹¹ He ties his male donkey to the vine,
    the colt of his female donkey
      to the vine's branches.
He washes his clothes in wine,
    his garments in the blood of grapes.
¹² His eyes are darker than wine,
    and his teeth whiter than milk.
¹³ Zebulun will live at the seashore;
    he'll live at the harbor of ships,
    his border will be at Sidon.
¹⁴ Issachar is a sturdy donkey,
    bedding down
      beside the village hearths.ʸ

¹⁵ He saw that a resting place was good
    and that the land was pleasant.
He lowered his shoulder to haul loads
    and joined the work gangs.

¹⁶ Danᶻ will settle disputes
    for his people,
    as one of Israel's tribes.
¹⁷ Dan will be a snake on the road,
    a serpent on the path,
biting a horse's heels,
    so its rider falls backward.

¹⁸ I long for your victory, LORD.

¹⁹ Gadᵃ will be attacked by attackers,
    but he'll attack their back.

²⁰ Asherᵇ grows fine foods,
    and he will supply
      the king's delicacies.

²¹ Naphtali is a wild doe
    that gives birth to beautiful fawns.ᶜ

²² Joseph is a young bull,ᵈ
    a young bull by a spring,
    who strides with oxen.ᵉ
²³ They attacked him fiercely
    and fired arrows;
    the archers attacked him furiously.
²⁴ But his bow stayed strong,
    and his forearms were nimble,ᶠ

ˣSam; MT *his feet*   ʸOr *stubbornly lying beneath its saddlebags*   ᶻOr *he judges,* or *settles disputes*   ᵃOr *he attacks* or *good fortune*   ᵇLXX, Syr, Vulg; MT *from Asher*   ᶜOr *who gives beautiful words*   ᵈHeb uncertain   ᵉHeb uncertain   ᶠHeb uncertain; or *flexible*

NAMES OF GOD

    The question of divine identity is a theologically critical one in the Bible, because the people of the OT and the NT worshipped neither an inanimate object nor an impersonal being but someone with whom they related. Since in ancient Israel the name of a person signified that person's nature and character, a survey of the various names of God will give some insights about how God was understood. While Yahweh (the LORD) is the distinctive name by which Israel's God was known, there are numerous other designations such as father, mother, brother, husband, holy one, mighty one, fear of Isaac, shield, and rock.

by the hands
  of the strong one of Jacob,
by the name of the shepherd,
  the rock of Israel,
  [25] by God, your father,
    who supports you,
  by the Almighty[g] who blesses you
    with blessings from the skies above
    and blessings
      from the deep sea below,
    blessings from breasts and womb.
[26] The blessings of your father exceed
  the blessings
    of the eternal mountains,[h]
    the wealth of the everlasting hills.
  May they all rest on Joseph's head,
  on the forehead of the one
    set apart from his brothers.

[27] Benjamin is a wolf who hunts:
  in the morning he devours the prey;
  in the evening he divides the plunder."

[28] These are the twelve tribes of Israel, and this is what their father said to them. He blessed them by giving each man his own particular blessing.

Jacob's death and burial

[29] Jacob ordered them, "I am soon to join my people. Bury me with my ancestors in the cave that's in the field of Ephron the Hittite; [30] in the cave that's in the field of Machpelah near Mamre in the land of Canaan that Abraham bought from Ephron the Hittite as a burial property. [31] That is where Abraham and his wife Sarah are buried, and where Isaac and his wife Rebekah are buried, and where I buried Leah. [32] It is the field and the cave in it that belonged to the Hittites." [33] After he finished giving orders to his sons, he put his feet up on the bed, took his last breath, and joined his people.

50

Joseph fell across his father's body, wept over him, and kissed him. [2] Joseph then ordered the physicians in his service to embalm his father, and the physicians embalmed Israel. [3] They mourned for him forty days because that is the period required for embalming. Then the Egyptians mourned him for seventy days. [4] After the period of mourning had passed, Joseph spoke to Pharaoh's household: "If you approve my request, give Pharaoh this message: [5] My father made me promise, telling me, 'I'm about to die. You must bury me in the tomb I dug for myself in the land of Canaan.' Now, let me leave and let me bury my father, and then I will return."

[6] Pharaoh replied, "Go, bury your father as you promised."

[7] So Joseph left to bury his father. All of Pharaoh's servants went with him, together with the elder statesmen in his household and all of the elder statesmen in the land of Egypt, [8] Joseph's entire household, his brothers, and his father's household. Only the children, flocks, and cattle remained in the land of Goshen. [9] Even chariots and horsemen went with him; it was a huge collection of people. [10] When they arrived at the threshing floor of Atad on the other side of the Jordan River, they observed a solemn, deeply sorrowful period of mourning. He grieved seven days for his father. [11] When the Canaanites who lived in the land saw the observance of grief on Atad's threshing floor, they said, "This is a solemn observance of grief by the Egyptians." Therefore, its name is Abel-mizraim.[i] It is on the other side of the Jordan River. [12] Israel's sons did for him just as he had ordered. [13] His sons carried him to the land of Canaan and buried him in the cave in the field of Machpelah near Mamre, which Abraham had purchased as burial property from Ephron the Hittite. [14] Then[j] Joseph returned to Egypt, he, his brothers, and everyone who left with him to bury his father.

Joseph and his brothers in Egypt

[15] When Joseph's brothers realized that their father was now dead, they said, "What

---

[g] Heb *Shaddai* or *the Mountain One*   [h] LXX; Heb uncertain   [i] Or *the Egyptians' observance of grief*   [j] LXX; MT includes *after he buried his father.*

if Joseph bears a grudge against us, and wants to pay us back seriously for all of the terrible things we did to him?" [16]So they approached[k] Joseph and said, "Your father gave orders before he died, telling us, [17]'This is what you should say to Joseph. "Please, forgive your brothers' sins and misdeeds, for they did terrible things to you. Now, please forgive the sins of the servants of your father's God."'" Joseph wept when they spoke to him.

[18]His brothers wept[l] too, fell down in front of him, and said, "We're here as your slaves."

[19]But Joseph said to them, "Don't be afraid. Am I God? [20]You planned something bad for me, but God produced something good from it, in order to save the lives of many people, just as he's doing today. [21]Now, don't be afraid. I will take care of you and your children." So he put them at ease and spoke reassuringly to them.

[22]Thus Joseph lived in Egypt, he and his father's household. Joseph lived 110 years [23]and saw Ephraim's grandchildren. The children of Machir, Manasseh's son, were also born on Joseph's knees. [24]Joseph said to his brothers, "I'm about to die. God will certainly take care of you and bring you out of this land to the land he promised to Abraham, to Isaac, and to Jacob." [25]Joseph made Israel's sons promise, "When God takes care of you, you must bring up my bones out of here." [26]Joseph died when he was 110 years old. They embalmed him and placed him in a coffin in Egypt.

---

[k]LXX, Syr; MT *they commanded* [l]Or *came*

EXODUS

HISTORICAL BACKGROUND

The book of Exodus concerns events in the history of the people of Israel that likely took place sometime between 1450 and 1200 BCE. The events follow the Genesis account of the entry of Jacob (Israel) and his descendants into Egypt.

Hundreds of years after Jacob entered Egypt, his descendants had been enslaved. Exodus is the story of how these enslaved people were delivered from the Egyptian bondage. Deliverance was not accomplished by the power of human beings. It was the result of the hand of God in the affairs of humankind. It involved confrontation between the God of the Hebrews and the ruler of Egypt, the pharaoh. The confrontation ended in a dramatic defeat for Pharaoh.

The story also involves the development of a special relationship between God and the children of Israel. This relationship is based on a mutual agreement called a covenant. As a result of the establishment of the covenant, the book closes with God coming to live among the slaves that have been freed.

THE NAME OF THE BOOK

Exodus means "the going out." The English word comes from the name for the book in Greek translation of the Old Testament called the Septuagint. The Hebrew title is *Shemot*, meaning "names." It is taken from the first phrase in the book, "These are the names of." Naming books in this way was a common ancient practice.

THE LITERARY HISTORY OF THE BOOK

Traditionally, the book was considered a single work written by Moses. A careful analysis has led many scholars to observe differing elements in Exodus which they attribute to several sources: J (Yahwist), E (Elohist), and D (Deuteronomist). It is believed that these were finally combined by P (Priestly writer) during the Babylonian Exile. A base of Mosaic material underlies these sources.

THE CONTENT OF THE BOOK

Chapters 1–5: The book of Exodus opens with the descendants of the twelve sons of Jacob enslaved in Egypt. Pharaoh orders that all Hebrew male children shall be slain at birth. Moses is born and concealed. He is set adrift on a river and is found by the daughter of Pharaoh. The princess has him brought up in the royal court.

Moses, seeing an Egyptian smiting a Hebrew, kills the Egyptian. He flees for his life to Midian in the Sinai wilderness. There he meets and marries Zipporah, the daughter of a Midianite priest named Jethro. As Moses tends Jethro's flock, God appears to him in a burning bush on Mount Horeb. God commissions Moses to deliver Israel. Moses is reluctant to accept the commission. God gives Moses confirmatory signs: God changes the rod of Moses into a serpent, then back to a rod; God makes Moses' hand leprous, then cures it.

Aaron, Moses' brother, is appointed first assistant. Moses and Aaron, in the name of God, ask Pharaoh to permit the people to go into the wilderness for three days to hold a sacrificial feast to their God. Pharaoh refuses and then increases the burdens of the Israelites.

Chapters 6–10: A series of plagues. At the height of each plague, Pharaoh promises to let the people go. As soon as the plague ends, he refuses to honor his pledge. The following are the ten plagues: water turned to blood, an invasion of frogs, an invasion of lice, an invasion of insects, death of the livestock, a plague of skin sores and blisters, hail and thunder, invasion of locusts, thick darkness, and the death of the firstborn.

Chapters 11–15: As the Lord slays the firstborn of Egypt, the Hebrew slaves make a hasty departure. At this point, the P author introduces the festival of the Passover and gives directions for its observance. Led by God, who appears to them in a column of cloud by day and in a column of lightning by night, the Israelites proceed to the Reed Sea. Pharaoh pursues and the Israelites murmur against Moses. At this point, God intervenes. The waters of the Reed Sea are parted, the Israelites cross over in safety, and the host of the Egyptians is drowned.

The journey from the sea to Mount Sinai follows. It is a series of crises. The people of Israel are unable to drink the bitter waters of Marah, and in their thirst they again murmur against Moses. Moses casts a tree into the waters, and the waters are made sweet.

Chapters 16–19: The Israelites now wander through the wilderness of Sin. The people complain of lack of food. God sends quails and manna daily to feed the people. On the sixth day of the week they gather a double portion, for on the seventh day there is to be no gathering.

From the wilderness of Sin, the Israelites proceed to Rephidim, where there is a lack of water. The people complain. Moses strikes the rock and abundant water flows.

The Israelites are attacked in Rephidim by Amalek. Moses, meanwhile, ascends a hill. As long as he holds aloft his hand, Israel prevails; and when he lets his hand down, Amalek prevails. Aaron and Hur hold Moses' hand up until Joshua completely routs Amalek.

Jethro, Moses' father-in-law, comes to visit him. He finds that all of Moses' time is consumed in acting as judge in all kinds of petty disputes. He counsels Moses to appoint a minor judiciary to settle unimportant cases, and himself to judge only the most important.

From Rephidim, the Israelites proceed to the Wilderness of Sinai where they encamp before Mount Sinai. Moses meets God on the mountain. Through Moses, God commands the people to obey. If they do so, they will prosper. They agree to do so. With Mount Sinai in a state of volcanic eruption, with the people warned not to approach the mountain, Moses ascends the mountain for secret conversation with God.

Chapter 20:1-17: The Ten Commandments. Some biblical scholars believe the commandments were first written down during the time of David. However, Egypt, the land where Moses lived, was a world acquainted with writing. The moral intensity and the spirit, if not the actual form, certainly go back to a period much before the Israelite monarchy. The germ of this morality goes back to the Mosaic period.

Chapters 20:22-23:33: The Covenant Code. This code is divisible into four parts: (1) ritual legislation, 20:22-26; 22:28-31; 23:10-19; (2) philanthropic laws, 22:21-27; 23:1-9; (3) civil and penal laws, 21:1-22:20; (4) conclusion, 23:20-33.

The nucleus of the Covenant Code is the ritual legislation, particularly the last two sections. Some of the laws in the Covenant Code are as follows: idolatry is forbidden; laws concerning kindly treatment of servants; concerning crimes of violence, arson, and immorality; treatment of the stranger; the sabbatical year; the sabbath; and three annual feasts—unleavened bread, harvest, and gathering.

Chapter 24: Sacrifices are made to God. The covenant is read to the people by Moses. They promise obedience. Moses ascends the mountain a second time, this time for forty days.

Chapters 25-31: This section is surely the work of P. It contains technical instructions regarding the building of the chest of the covenant, the table for the bread of the presence, and the lampstand, curtains of the dwelling, its boards and bars, the veil, the screen, the altar of burnt offering, and the perpetual lamp. Aaron and his sons are appointed priests. A description is given of their priestly garments. God gives Moses the two stone tablets.

Chapters 32-34: While Moses is on the mountain, the people begin to murmur. Aaron makes them a gold calf to which they offer sacrifices. God is very angry, and is placated by Moses. When Moses comes down from the mountain, he breaks the tablets, destroys the golden calf, strews it upon the water, and makes the people drink it. The sons of Levi put to death the apostates.

God tells the people to march on and behave. God withdraws from among the people, but when Moses remonstrates, God returns. Moses again ascends Mount Sinai and the two tablets are renewed.

Chapter 34:10-26: A form of the Ten Commandments provided by J. Included are five laws on religious festivals. Also there are five laws on sacrifice. The primitive law of sacrificing firstborn male children has been changed; the firstborn is now redeemed by the sacrifice of an animal.

Chapters 35-40: When Moses comes down from the mountain, he transmits to the people the instructions of God regarding the building of the chest containing the covenant. The people all contribute gifts to carry out this project. There follows now a detailed description of the building of the chest, curtains, veil and screen, boards and bars, candlestick, and so forth. This description of the building of the chest corresponds to the instructions given in chapters 25 through 31.

In chapter 40, the work is completed. A cloud covers the tent of meeting and the glory of God fills the dwelling. When the cloud is taken up, the Israelites march on; when it abides over the tent, they pause.

WHAT THE BOOK OF EXODUS TEACHES

The book of Exodus teaches that by the victory over Pharaoh, the God of the Hebrews was shown to be indeed the God of all heaven and earth, and the great lover of the chosen people Israel. Having delivered them from bondage, God providentially supplied their physical needs. And God gave them guidelines for living that would allow them to exist forever in a special relationship of covenantal love.

The core of the covenant, the Ten Commandments, was summed up by Jesus as love for God and love for one's neighbor (Matthew 22:37-40). The theme of deliverance from slavery permeates the New Testament. The deliverance, however, is from spiritual bondage.

The theme of the presence of God based on a covenant relationship is also carried into the New Testament. A new covenant is established by Christ. People are able to have fellowship with God and to experience God's abiding presence because they have been purified by the blood of Christ. They thereby become "a chosen race, a royal priesthood, a holy nation, a people who are God's own possession. You have become this people so that you may speak of the wonderful acts of the one who called you out of darkness into his amazing light" (1 Peter 2:9).

EXODUS

1 These are the names of the Israelites who came to Egypt with Jacob along with their households: ²Reuben, Simeon, Levi, and Judah, ³Issachar, Zebulun, and Benjamin, ⁴Dan and Naphtali, Gad and Asher. ⁵The total number in Jacob's family was seventy. Joseph was already in Egypt. ⁶Eventually, Joseph, his brothers, and everyone in his generation died. ⁷But the Israelites were fertile and became populous. They multiplied and grew dramatically, filling the whole land.

Israel is oppressed

⁸Now a new king came to power in Egypt who didn't know Joseph. ⁹He said to his people, "The Israelite people are now larger in number and stronger than we are. ¹⁰Come on, let's be smart and deal with them. Otherwise, they will only grow in number. And if war breaks out, they will join our enemies, fight against us, and then escape from the land." ¹¹As a result, the Egyptians put foremen of forced work gangs over the Israelites to harass them with hard work. They had to build storage cities named Pithom and Rameses for Pharaoh. ¹²But the more they were oppressed, the more they grew and spread, so much so that the Egyptians started to look at the Israelites with disgust and dread. ¹³So the Egyptians enslaved the Israelites. ¹⁴They made their lives miserable with hard labor, making mortar and bricks, doing field work, and by forcing them to do all kinds of other cruel work.

¹⁵The king of Egypt spoke to two Hebrew midwives named Shiphrah and Puah:

¹⁶"When you are helping the Hebrew women give birth and you see the baby being born, if it's a boy, kill him. But if it's a girl, you can let her live." ¹⁷Now the two midwives respected God so they didn't obey the Egyptian king's order. Instead, they let the baby boys live.

¹⁸So the king of Egypt called the two midwives and said to them, "Why are you doing this? Why are you letting the baby boys live?"

¹⁹The two midwives said to Pharaoh, "Because Hebrew women aren't like Egyptian women. They're much stronger and give birth before any midwives can get to them." ²⁰So God treated the midwives well, and the people kept on multiplying and became very strong. ²¹And because the midwives respected God, God gave them households of their own.

²²Then Pharaoh gave an order to all his people: "Throw every baby boy born to the Hebrews into the Nile River, but you can let all the girls live."

Moses' birth

2 Now a man from Levi's household married a Levite woman. ²The woman became pregnant and gave birth to a son. She saw that the baby was healthy and beautiful, so she hid him for three months. ³When she couldn't hide him any longer, she took a reed basket and sealed it up with black tar. She put the child in the basket and set the basket among the reeds at the riverbank. ⁴The baby's older sister stood watch nearby to see what would happen to him.

MIDIAN/MIDIANITES

Abraham's descendants through Keturah (Gen 25:2) included six sons, one named Midian. Genesis 25:1-6 states that Abraham sent his six sons born by Keturah away from Canaan to the east. The Midianites became a tribal and ethnic entity whose territory consisted of the desert regions of the southern Transjordan, south and east of the Dead Sea. Thus, the Midianites are understood to be part of the ancestry and precursors of the Arabic-speaking tribes of the Western Arabian Desert.

⁵Pharaoh's daughter came down to bathe in the river, while her women servants walked along beside the river. She saw the basket among the reeds, and she sent one of her servants to bring it to her. ⁶When she opened it, she saw the child. The boy was crying, and she felt sorry for him. She said, "This must be one of the Hebrews' children."

⁷Then the baby's sister said to Pharaoh's daughter, "Would you like me to go and find one of the Hebrew women to nurse the child for you?"

⁸Pharaoh's daughter agreed, "Yes, do that." So the girl went and called the child's mother. ⁹Pharaoh's daughter said to her, "Take this child and nurse it for me, and I'll pay you for your work." So the woman took the child and nursed it. ¹⁰After the child had grown up, she brought him back to Pharaoh's daughter, who adopted him as her son. She named him Moses, "because," she said, "I pulled him outᵃ of the water."

Moses runs away to Midian

¹¹One day after Moses had become an adult, he went out among his people and he saw their forced labor. He saw an Egyptian beating a Hebrew, one of his own people. ¹²He looked around to make sure no one else was there. Then he killed the Egyptian and hid him in the sand.

¹³When Moses went out the next day, he saw two Hebrew men fighting with each other. Moses said to the one who had started the fight, "Why are you abusing your fellow Hebrew?"

¹⁴He replied, "Who made you a boss or judge over us? Are you planning to kill me like you killed the Egyptian?"

Then Moses was afraid when he realized: They obviously know what I did. ¹⁵When Pharaoh heard about it, he tried to kill Moses.

But Moses ran away from Pharaoh and settled down in the land of Midian. One day Moses was sitting by a well. ¹⁶Now there was a Midianite priest who had seven daughters. The daughters came to draw water and fill the troughs so that their father's flock could drink. ¹⁷But some shepherds came along and rudely chased them away. Moses got up, rescued the women, and gave their flock water to drink.

¹⁸When they went back home to their father Reuel,ᵇ he asked, "How were you able to come back home so soon today?"

¹⁹They replied, "An Egyptian man rescued us from a bunch of shepherds. Afterward, he even helped us draw water to let the flock drink."

ᵃHeb *mashah* sounds like Moses (*moshe*).   ᵇAlso called Jethro

I AM

A name for the God of Israel taken from God's initial revelation to Moses (Exod 3:13-15), deriving from an attempt to translate the Hebrew phrase "I am who I am," or "I will be what I will be." God tells Moses to inform the Israelites that "I Am has sent me to you." In its original context, the self-description may show that God was reluctant to reveal the precise name (as in Jacob's struggle with a divine being in Gen 32:29).

The passage is important in the history of interpretation. Based on the Greek translation of the Old Testament, Jews during the Greek period before Jesus' time understood the title to say that the God of Israel is "pure being." Jesus' self-description in the Gospel of John by means of "I am" sayings (e.g., John 6:35, 41, 48, 51) is also be grounded in the phrase. (See esp. the enigmatic statement of Jesus, "Before Abraham was, I Am," in John 8:58.)

²⁰Reuel said to his daughters, "So where is he? Why did you leave this man? Invite him to eat a meal with us."

²¹Moses agreed to come and live with the man, who gave his daughter Zipporah to Moses as his wife. ²²She gave birth to a son, and Moses named him Gershom, "because," he said, "I've been an immigrant[c] living in a foreign land."

²³A long time passed, and the Egyptian king died. The Israelites were still groaning because of their hard work. They cried out, and their cry to be rescued from the hard work rose up to God. ²⁴God heard their cry of grief, and God remembered his covenant with Abraham, Isaac, and Jacob. ²⁵God looked at the Israelites, and God understood.

Moses at the burning bush

3 Moses was taking care of the flock for his father-in-law Jethro,[d] Midian's priest. He led his flock out to the edge of the desert, and he came to God's mountain called Horeb. ²The LORD's messenger appeared to him in a flame of fire in the middle of a bush. Moses saw that the bush was in flames, but it didn't burn up. ³Then Moses said to himself, Let me check out this amazing sight and find out why the bush isn't burning up.

⁴When the LORD saw that he was coming to look, God called to him out of the bush, "Moses, Moses!"

Moses said, "I'm here."

⁵Then the LORD said, "Don't come any closer! Take off your sandals, because you are standing on holy ground." ⁶He contin-ued, "I am the God of your father, Abraham's God, Isaac's God, and Jacob's God." Moses hid his face because he was afraid to look at God.

⁷Then the LORD said, "I've clearly seen my people oppressed in Egypt. I've heard their cry of injustice because of their slave masters. I know about their pain. ⁸I've come down to rescue them from the Egyptians in order to take them out of that land and bring them to a good and broad land, a land that's full of milk and honey, a place where the Canaanites, the Hittites, the Amorites, the Perizzites, the Hivites, and the Jebusites all live. ⁹Now the Israelites' cries of injustice have reached me. I've seen just how much the Egyptians have oppressed them. ¹⁰So get going. I'm sending you to Pharaoh to bring my people, the Israelites, out of Egypt."

¹¹But Moses said to God, "Who am I to go to Pharaoh and to bring the Israelites out of Egypt?"

¹²God said, "I'll be with you. And this will show you that I'm the one who sent you. After you bring the people out of Egypt, you will come back here and worship God on this mountain."

God's special name

¹³But Moses said to God, "If I now come to the Israelites and say to them, 'The God of your ancestors has sent me to you,' they are going to ask me, 'What's this God's name?' What am I supposed to say to them?"

¹⁴God said to Moses, "I Am Who I Am.[e] So say to the Israelites, 'I Am has sent me to

---

[c]Heb *ger* sounds like *Gershom*.   [d]Also called Reuel   [e]Or *I Will Be Who I will Be*.

BURNING BUSH

Moses sees a burning bush that is not destroyed by the fire (Exod 3:2-4; see also Deut 33:16). In the NT the bush is mentioned in Mark 12:26 and Luke 20:37. Stephen mentions it in his sermon where Moses appears as a deliverer rejected by his people (Acts 7:30, 35; see Exod 2:14). The bush is located in Horeb/Sinai at the site of future worship, covenant making, and revelation of Law and Instruction.

you.'" [15]God continued, "Say to the Israelites, 'The LORD, the God of your ancestors, Abraham's God, Isaac's God, and Jacob's God, has sent me to you.' This is my name forever; this is how all generations will remember me.

[16]"Go and get Israel's elders together and say to them, 'The LORD, the God of your ancestors, the God of Abraham, of Isaac, and of Jacob, has appeared to me. The LORD said, "I've been paying close attention to you and to what has been done to you in Egypt. [17]I've decided to take you away from the harassment in Egypt to the land of the Canaanites, the Hittites, the Amorites, the Perizzites, the Hivites, and the Jebusites, a land full of milk and honey."' [18]They will accept what you say to them. Then you and Israel's elders will go to Egypt's king and say to him, 'The LORD, the Hebrews' God, has met with us. So now let us go on a three-day journey into the desert so that we can offer sacrifices to the LORD our God.' [19]However, I know that Egypt's king won't let you go unless he's forced to do it. [20]So I'll use my strength and hit Egypt with dramatic displays of my power. After that, he'll let you go.

[21]"I'll make it so that when you leave Egypt, the Egyptians will be kind to you and you won't go away empty-handed. [22]Every woman will ask her neighbor along with the immigrant in her household for their silver and their gold jewelry as well as their clothing. Then you will put it on your sons and daughters, and you will rob the Egyptians."

Signs of power

4 Then Moses replied, "But what if they don't believe me or pay attention to me? They might say to me, 'The LORD didn't appear to you!'"

[2]The LORD said to him, "What's that in your hand?"

Moses replied, "A shepherd's rod."

[3]The LORD said, "Throw it down on the ground." So Moses threw it on the ground, and it turned into a snake. Moses jumped back from it. [4]Then the LORD said to Moses, "Reach out and grab the snake by the tail." So Moses reached out and grabbed it, and it turned back into a rod in his hand. [5]"Do this so that they will believe that the LORD, the God of their ancestors, Abraham's God, Isaac's God, and Jacob's God has in fact appeared to you."

[6]Again, the LORD said to Moses, "Put your hand inside your coat." So Moses put his hand inside his coat. When he took his hand out, his hand had a skin disease flaky like snow. [7]Then God said, "Put your hand back inside your coat." So Moses put his hand back inside his coat. When he took it back out again, the skin of his hand had returned to normal. [8]"If they won't believe you or pay attention to the first sign, they may believe the second sign. [9]If they won't believe even these two signs or pay attention to you, then take some water from the Nile River and pour it out on dry ground. The water that you take from the Nile will turn into blood on the dry ground."

[10]But Moses said to the LORD, "My Lord, I've never been able to speak well, not yesterday, not the day before, and certainly not now since you've been talking to your servant. I have a slow mouth and a thick tongue."

[11]Then the LORD said to him, "Who gives people the ability to speak? Who's responsible for making them unable to speak or hard of hearing, sighted or blind? Isn't it I, the LORD? [12]Now go! I'll help you speak, and I'll teach you what you should say."

[13]But Moses said, "Please, my Lord, just send someone else."

[14]Then the LORD got angry at Moses and said, "What about your brother Aaron the Levite? I know he can speak very well. He's on his way out to meet you now, and he's looking forward to seeing you. [15]Speak to him and tell him what he's supposed to say. I'll help both of you speak, and I'll teach both of you what to do. [16]Aaron will speak for you to the people. He'll be a spokesperson for you, and you will be like God for him. [17]Take this shepherd's rod with you too so that you can do the signs."

Moses goes back to Egypt

[18]Moses went back to his father-in-law Jethro and said to him, "Please let me go

back to my family in Egypt and see whether or not they are still living."

Jethro said to Moses, "Go in peace."

¹⁹The LORD said to Moses in Midian, "Go back to Egypt because everyone there who wanted to kill you has died." ²⁰So Moses took his wife and his children, put them on a donkey, and went back to the land of Egypt. Moses also carried the shepherd's rod from God in his hand.

²¹The LORD said to Moses, "When you go back to Egypt, make sure that you appear before Pharaoh and do all the amazing acts that I've given you the power to do. But I'll make him stubborn so that he won't let the people go. ²²Then say to Pharaoh, 'This is what the LORD says: Israel is my oldest son. ²³I said to you, "Let my son go so he could worship me." But you refused to let him go. As a result, now I'm going to kill your oldest son.'"

²⁴During their journey, as they camped overnight, the LORD met Moses[f] and tried to kill him. ²⁵But Zipporah took a sharp-edged flint stone and cut off her son's foreskin. Then she touched Moses' genitals[g] with it, and she said, "You are my bridegroom because of bloodshed." ²⁶So the LORD let him alone. At that time, she announced, "A bridegroom because of bloodshed by circumcision."

²⁷The LORD said to Aaron, "Go into the desert to meet Moses." So he went, and Aaron met him at God's mountain and greeted him with a kiss. ²⁸Moses told Aaron what the LORD had said about his mission and all the signs that the LORD had told him to do. ²⁹Then Moses and Aaron called together all the Israelite elders. ³⁰Aaron told them everything that the LORD had told to Moses, and he performed the signs in front of the people. ³¹The people believed. When they heard that the LORD had paid attention to the Israelites and had seen their oppression, they bowed down and worshipped.

First meeting with Pharaoh

5 Afterward, Moses and Aaron went to Pharaoh and said, "This is what the LORD, Israel's God, says: 'Let my people go so that they can hold a festival for me in the desert.'"

²But Pharaoh said, "Who is this LORD whom I'm supposed to obey by letting Israel go? I don't know this LORD, and I certainly won't let Israel go."

³Then they said, "The Hebrews' God has appeared to us. Let us go on a three-day journey into the desert so we can offer sacrifices to the LORD our God. Otherwise, the LORD will give us a deadly disease or violence."

⁴The king of Egypt said to them, "Moses and Aaron, why are you making the people slack off from their work? Do the hard work yourselves!" ⁵Pharaoh continued, "The land's people are now numerous. Yet you want them to stop their hard work?"

⁶On the very same day Pharaoh commanded the people's slave masters and

[f] Or him [g] Or his feet

AARON

The brother of Moses and Miriam. As God prepares Moses for confrontation with Pharaoh, Aaron is given as his spokesperson (Exod 4:14-16). Elsewhere Aaron functions as an assistant for Moses, so that "Moses and Aaron" work together as a team throughout the conflict with Pharaoh (Exod 5–12). He is also considered the primary ancestor of the Jerusalem priesthood (Exod 28–29; Lev 1–8; Num 6:22-27). His traditional gravesite was Mount Hor in Edom (Num 20:12, 22-29; Deut 10:6). Like Moses, he died outside the promised land as a punishment (Deut 32:50).

supervisors, [7]"Don't supply the people with the straw they need to make bricks like you did before. Let them go out and gather the straw for themselves. [8]But still make sure that they produce the same number of bricks as they made before. Don't reduce the number! They are weak and lazy, and that's why they cry, 'Let's go and offer sacrifices to our God.' [9]Make the men's work so hard that it's all they can do, and they can't focus on these empty lies."

[10]So the people's slave masters and supervisors came out and spoke to the people, "This is what Pharaoh says, 'I'm not giving you straw anymore. [11]Go and get the straw on your own, wherever you can find it. But your work won't be reduced at all.'" [12]So the people spread out all through the land of Egypt to gather stubble for straw. [13]The slave masters drove them hard and said, "Make sure you make the same daily quota as when you had the straw." [14]The Israelite supervisors, whom Pharaoh's slave masters had set over them, were also beaten and asked, "Why didn't you produce the same number of bricks yesterday and today as you did before?"

[15]Then the Israelite supervisors came and pleaded to Pharaoh, "Why do you treat your servants like this? [16]No straw is supplied to your servants, yet they say to us, 'Make bricks!' Look at how your servants are being beaten! Your own people are to blame!"

[17]Pharaoh replied, "You are lazy bums, nothing but lazy bums. That's why you say, 'Let us go and offer sacrifices to the LORD.' [18]Go and get back to work! No straw will be given to you, but you still need to make the same number of bricks."

[19]The Israelite supervisors saw how impossible their situation was when they were commanded, "Don't reduce your daily quota of bricks." [20]When they left Pharaoh, they met Moses and Aaron, who were waiting for them. [21]The supervisors said to them, "Let the LORD see and judge what you've done! You've made us stink in the opinion of Pharaoh and his servants. You've given them a reason to kill us."

[22]Then Moses turned to the LORD and said, "My Lord, why have you abused this people? Why did you send me for this? [23]Ever since I first came to Pharaoh to speak in your name, he has abused this people. And you've done absolutely nothing to rescue your people."

God reassures Moses

6 The LORD replied to Moses, "Now you will see what I'll do to Pharaoh. In fact, he'll be so eager to let them go that he'll drive them out of his land by force."

[2]God also said to Moses: "I am the LORD. [3]I appeared to Abraham, Isaac, and Jacob as God Almighty,[h] but I didn't reveal myself to them by my name 'The LORD.' [4]I also set up my covenant with them to give them the land of Canaan where they lived as immigrants. [5]I've also heard the cry of grief of the Israelites, whom the Egyptians have

[h]Heb El Shaddai or God of the Mountain

PHARAOH

A title for the king of ancient Egypt. In biblical usage, pharaoh is a synonym for "king of Egypt," following 1st-millennium BCE Egyptian convention. The Egyptian king is referred to alternately as "king of Egypt," "Pharaoh," or "Pharaoh king of Egypt." Any of these formulations can be used with the king's name: Shishak king of Egypt (1 Kgs 11:40); Pharaoh Neco (2 Kgs 23:33); Pharaoh Hophra king of Egypt (Jer 44:30). The formal similarity between "Shishak king of Egypt" and "Pharaoh king of Egypt" lends the appearance that Pharaoh is the king's name.

turned into slaves, and I've remembered my covenant. [6]Therefore, say to the Israelites, 'I am the LORD. I'll bring you out from Egyptian forced labor. I'll rescue you from your slavery to them. I'll set you free with great power and with momentous events of justice. [7]I'll take you as my people, and I'll be your God. You will know that I, the LORD, am your God, who has freed you from Egyptian forced labor. [8]I'll bring you into the land that I promised to give to Abraham, Isaac, and Jacob. I'll give it to you as your possession. I am the LORD.'" [9]Moses told this to the Israelites. But they didn't listen to Moses, because of their complete exhaustion and their hard labor.

[10]Then the LORD said to Moses, [11]"Go and tell Pharaoh, Egypt's king, to let the Israelites out of his land." [12]But Moses said to the LORD, "The Israelites haven't even listened to me. How can I expect Pharaoh to listen to me, especially since I'm not a very good speaker?" [13]Nevertheless, the LORD spoke to Moses and Aaron about the Israelites and Pharaoh, Egypt's king, giving them orders to let the Israelites go from the land of Egypt.

Family line of Moses and Aaron

[14]These were the leaders of their households.

The descendants of Reuben, Israel's oldest son: Hanoch, Pallu, Hezron, and Carmi. These were Reuben's clans. [15]The Simeonites: Jemuel, Jamin, Ohad, Jachin, Zohar, and Shaul, a Canaanite woman's son. These were Simeon's clans. [16]These were the Levites' names by their generations: Gershon, Kohath, and Merari. Levi lived 137 years. [17]The Gershonites: Libni and Shimei and their clans. [18]The Kohathites: Amram, Izhar, Hebron, and Uzziel. Kohath lived 133 years. [19]The Merarites: Mahli and Mushi. These were the Levite clans by their generations. [20]Amram married Jochebed, his father's sister. She gave birth to Aaron and Moses. Amram lived 137 years. [21]The Izharites: Korah, Nepheg, and Zichri. [22]The Uzzielites:

Mishael, Elzaphan, and Sithri. [23]Aaron married Elisheba, Amminadab's daughter and Nahshon's sister. She gave birth to Nadab, Abihu, Eleazar, and Ithamar. [24]The Korahites: Assir, Elkanah, and Abiasaph. These were the Korahite clans. [25]Aaron's son Eleazar married one of Putiel's daughters. She gave birth to Phinehas. These were the leaders of Levite households by their clans.

[26]It was this same Aaron and Moses whom the LORD commanded, "Bring the Israelites out of the land of Egypt in military formation." [27]It was also this same Moses and Aaron who spoke to Pharaoh king of Egypt to bring the Israelites out of Egypt. [28]At the time the LORD spoke to Moses in the land of Egypt, [29]the LORD said to him, "I am the LORD. Tell Pharaoh, Egypt's king, everything that I've said to you." [30]But Moses replied to the LORD, "Look, I'm not a very good speaker. How is Pharaoh ever going to listen to me?"

7 The LORD said to Moses, "See, I've made you like God to Pharaoh, and your brother Aaron will be your prophet. [2]You will say everything that I command you, and your brother Aaron will tell Pharaoh to let the Israelites out of his land. [3]But I'll make Pharaoh stubborn, and I'll perform many of my signs and amazing acts in the land of Egypt. [4]When Pharaoh refuses to listen to you, then I'll act against Egypt and I'll bring my people the Israelites out of the land of Egypt in military formation by momentous events of justice. [5]The Egyptians will come to know that I am the LORD, when I act against Egypt and bring the Israelites out from among them." [6]Moses and Aaron did just as the LORD commanded them. [7]Moses was 80 years old and Aaron was 83 when they spoke to Pharaoh.

Turning rods into snakes

[8]The LORD said to Moses and Aaron, [9]"When Pharaoh says to you, 'Do one of your amazing acts,' then say to Aaron, 'Take your shepherd's rod and throw it down in front of Pharaoh, and it will turn into a cobra.'"[i]

[i]Or serpent

¹⁰So Moses and Aaron went to Pharaoh and did just as the LORD commanded. Aaron threw down his shepherd's rod in front of Pharaoh and his officials, and it turned into a cobra. ¹¹Then Pharaoh called together his wise men and wizards, and Egypt's religious experts^j did the same thing by using their secret knowledge. ¹²Each one threw down his rod, and they turned into cobras. But then Aaron's rod swallowed up each of their rods. ¹³However, Pharaoh remained stubborn. He wouldn't listen to them, just as the LORD had said.

Water into blood

¹⁴Then the LORD said to Moses, "Pharaoh is stubborn. He still refuses to let the people go. ¹⁵Go to Pharaoh in the morning.

^jOr magicians

SERPENT

There are several terms used to denote snakes within the OT, variously translated as serpent, snake, dragon, poisonous serpent, fiery serpent, asp, adder, or viper. Snakes that appear in the stories in the Bible have magical or mythological characteristics. In Genesis 3, the snake is introduced at the beginning of the chapter as "the most intelligent" (also meaning "shrewd" or "sensible") "of all the wild animals that the LORD God had made" (v. 1). Magical snakes appear in the exodus narrative. In Exodus 4:3 (part of Moses' call narrative), God turns Moses' staff into a snake as a reassuring sign that God will be with him. This staff is alluded to again in Exodus 7:15. In other references in Exodus 7, Aaron's staff changes to a snake in competition with the magicians of Egypt. Aaron's staff/snake wins the competition by swallowing those of the Egyptians.

Numbers 21:4-9 describes an episode in the wilderness when the Israelites complain about the food, and the Lord responds by sending poisonous snakes that bite and kill the people.

Serpent language is used by the prophets to describe God's judgment. In these instances, serpents are always depicted as dangerous or malevolent (Isa 14:29; Jer 8:17; Amos 5:19). Serpent language is also used in descriptions of hope and restoration. In these cases, serpents are still viewed as dangerous animals. In Isaiah 11:8 (a description of a peaceful reign under the Davidic monarch) and Isaiah 65:25 (a vision of a new creation), snakes, among other dangerous creatures such as wolves, leopards, lions, and bears, will live in harmony and will not be harmful to humans. Micah 7:17 describes Judah's enemies as snakes that will fear God and the people of Judah.

In the NT, snakes are dangerous or evil (Matt 7:10; Luke 10:19; 11:11; 1 Cor 10:9; 2 Cor 11:3).

In Revelation, the devil is called "the old snake" (Rev 12:9; 20:2).

Jesus and John the Baptist are portrayed as condemning the Pharisees and their religious practices as hypocritical with the phrase "you children of snakes" (Matt 3:7; 12:34; 23:33; Luke 3:7).

As he is going out to the water, make sure you stand at the bank of the Nile River so you will run into him. Bring along the shepherd's rod that turned into a snake. ¹⁶Say to him, The LORD, the Hebrews' God, has sent me to you with this message: Let my people go so that they can worship me in the desert. Up to now you still haven't listened. ¹⁷This is what the LORD says: By this you will know that I am the LORD. I'm now going to hit the water of the Nile River with this rod in my hand, and it will turn into blood. ¹⁸The fish in the Nile are going to die, the Nile will stink, and the Egyptians won't be able to drink water from the Nile." ¹⁹The LORD said to Moses, "Say to Aaron, 'Take your shepherd's rod and stretch out your hand over Egypt's waters—over their rivers, their canals, their marshes, and all their bodies of water—so that they turn into blood. There will be blood all over the land of Egypt, even in wooden and stone containers.'"

²⁰Moses and Aaron did just as the LORD commanded. He raised the shepherd's rod and hit the water in the Nile in front of Pharaoh and his officials, and all the water in the Nile turned into blood. ²¹The fish in the Nile died, and the Nile began to stink so that the Egyptians couldn't drink water from the Nile. There was blood all over the land of Egypt. ²²But the Egyptian religious experts did the same thing with their secret knowledge. As a result, Pharaoh remained stubborn, and he wouldn't listen to them, just as the LORD had said. ²³Pharaoh turned and went back to his palace. He wasn't impressed even by this. ²⁴Meanwhile, all the Egyptians had to dig for drinking water along the banks of the Nile River, because they couldn't drink the water of the Nile itself. ²⁵Seven days went by after the LORD had struck the Nile River.

Invasion of frogs

8 ᵏThen the LORD said to Moses, "Go to Pharaoh and tell him: This is what the LORD says: Let my people go so that they can worship me. ²If you refuse to let them

go, then I'll send a plague of frogs over your whole country. ³The Nile will overflow with frogs. They'll get into your palace, into your bedroom and onto your bed, into your officials' houses, and among all your people, and even into your ovens and bread pans. ⁴The frogs will crawl up on you, your people, and all your officials." ⁵Andˡ the LORD said to Moses, "Tell Aaron, 'Stretch out your hand with your shepherd's rod over the rivers, the canals, and the marshes, and make the frogs crawl up all over the land of Egypt.'" ⁶So Aaron stretched out his hand over the waters of Egypt. The frogs crawled up and covered the land of Egypt. ⁷However, the Egyptian religious experts were able to do the same thing by their secret knowledge. They too made frogs crawl up onto the land of Egypt.

⁸Then Pharaoh called for Moses and Aaron, and said, "If you pray to the LORD to get rid of the frogs from me and my people, then I'll let the people go so that they can offer sacrifices to the LORD."

⁹Moses said to Pharaoh, "Have it your way. When should I pray for you and your officials and your people to remove the frogs from your houses, courtyards, and fields? They'll stay only in the Nile."

¹⁰Pharaoh said, "Tomorrow!"

Moses said, "Just as you say! That way you will know that there is no one like the LORD our God. ¹¹The frogs will leave you, your houses, your officials, and your people. They'll stay only in the Nile." ¹²After Moses and Aaron had left Pharaoh, Moses cried out to the LORD about the frogs that the LORD had brought on Pharaoh. ¹³The LORD did as Moses asked. The frogs died inside the houses, out in the yards, and in the fields. ¹⁴They gathered them together in big piles, and the land began to stink. ¹⁵But when Pharaoh saw that the disaster was over, he became stubborn again and wouldn't listen to them, just as the LORD had said.

Swarming lice

¹⁶Then the LORD said to Moses, "Tell Aaron, 'Stretch out your shepherd's rod

ᵏ7:26 in Heb ˡ8:1 in Heb

and hit the land's dirt so that lice[m] appear in the whole land of Egypt.'" [17]They did this. Aaron stretched out his hand with his shepherd's rod, hit the land's dirt, and lice appeared on both people and animals. All the land's dirt turned into lice throughout the whole land of Egypt.

[18]The religious experts[n] tried to produce lice by their secret knowledge, but they weren't able to do it. There were lice on people and animals. [19]The religious experts said to Pharaoh, "This is something only God could do!" But Pharaoh was stubborn, and he wouldn't listen to them, just as the LORD had said.

Insects fill Egypt

[20]The LORD said to Moses, "Get up early in the morning and confront Pharaoh as he goes out to the water. Say to him, This is what the LORD says: Let my people go so that they can worship me. [21]If you refuse to let my people go, I'll send swarms of insects[o] on you, your officials, your people, and your houses. All Egyptian houses will be filled with swarms of insects and also the ground that they cover. [22]But on that day I'll set apart the land of Goshen, where my people live. No swarms of insects will come there so you will know that I, the LORD, am in this land. [23]I'll put a barrier between my people and your people. This sign will happen tomorrow." [24]The LORD did this. Great swarms of insects came into the houses of Pharaoh and his officials and into the whole land of Egypt. The land was ruined by the insects.

[25]Then Pharaoh called in Moses and Aaron and said, "Go, offer sacrifices to your God within the land."

[26]Moses replied, "It wouldn't be right to do that, because the sacrifices that we offer to the LORD our God will offend Egyptians. If we openly offer sacrifices that offend Egyptians, won't they stone us to death? [27]We need to go for a three-day journey into the desert to offer sacrifices to the LORD our God as he has ordered us."

[28]So Pharaoh said, "I'll let you go to offer sacrifices to the LORD your God in the desert, provided you don't go too far away and you pray for me."

[29]Moses said, "I'll leave you now, and I'll pray to the LORD. Tomorrow the swarms of insects will leave Pharaoh, his officials, and his people. Just don't let Pharaoh lie to us again and not let the people go to offer sacrifices to the LORD."

[30]So Moses left Pharaoh and prayed to the LORD. [31]The LORD did as Moses asked and removed the swarms of insects from Pharaoh, from his officials, and from his people. Not one insect remained. [32]But Pharaoh was stubborn once again, and he wouldn't let the people go.

Animals sick and dying

9 Then the LORD said to Moses, "Go to Pharaoh and say to him, This is what the LORD, the Hebrews' God, says: Let my people go so that they can worship me. [2]If you refuse to let them go and you continue to hold them back, [3]the LORD will send a very deadly disease on your livestock in the field: on horses, donkeys, camels, cattle, and flocks. [4]But the LORD will distinguish Israel's livestock from Egypt's livestock so that not one that belongs to the Israelites will die." [5]The LORD set a time and said, "Tomorrow the LORD will do this in the land." [6]And the next day the LORD did it. All of the Egyptian livestock died, but not one animal that belonged to the Israelites died. [7]Pharaoh asked around and found out that not one of Israel's livestock had died. But Pharaoh was stubborn, and he wouldn't let the people go.

Skin sores and blisters

[8]Then the LORD said to Moses and Aaron, "Take handfuls of ashes from a furnace and have Moses throw it up in the air in front of Pharaoh. [9]The ashes will turn to soot over the whole land of Egypt. It will cause skin sores that will break out in blisters on people and animals in the whole land of Egypt." [10]So they took ashes from the furnace, and they stood in front of Pha-

---

[m]Heb uncertain [n]Or *magicians* [o]Heb uncertain

raoh. Moses threw the ash up in the air, and it caused skin sores and blisters to break out on people and animals. [11]The religious experts[p] couldn't stand up to Moses because of the skin sores, because there were skin sores on the religious experts as well as on all the Egyptians. [12]But the LORD made Pharaoh stubborn, and Pharaoh wouldn't listen to them, just as the LORD had said to Moses.

Hail and thunder

[13]Then the LORD said to Moses, "Get up early in the morning and confront Pharaoh. Say to him, This is what the LORD, the God of the Hebrews, says: Let my people go so that they can worship me. [14]This time I'm going to send all my plagues on you, your officials, and your people so that you will know that there is no one like me in the whole world. [15]By now I could have used my power to strike you and your people with a deadly disease so that you would have disappeared from the earth. [16]But I've left you standing for this reason: in order to show you my power and in order to make my name known in the whole world. [17]You are still abusing your power against my people, and you refuse to let them go. [18]Tomorrow at this time I'll cause the heaviest hail to fall on Egypt that has ever fallen from the day Egypt was founded until now. [19]So bring under shelter your livestock and all that belongs to you that is out in the open. Every person or animal that is out in the open field and isn't brought inside will die when the hail rains down on them." [20]Some of Pharaoh's officials who took the LORD's word seriously rushed to bring their servants and livestock inside for shelter. [21]Others who didn't take the LORD's word to heart left their servants and livestock out in the open field.

[22]The LORD said to Moses, "Raise your hand toward the sky so that hail will fall on the whole land of Egypt, on people and animals and all the grain in the fields in the land of Egypt." [23]Then Moses raised his shepherd's rod toward the sky, and the LORD sent thunder and hail, and lightning struck the earth. The LORD rained hail on the land of Egypt. [24]The hail and the lightning flashing in the middle of the hail were so severe that there had been nothing like it in the entire land of Egypt since it first became a nation. [25]The hail beat down everything that was in the open field throughout the entire land of Egypt, both people and animals. The hail also beat down all the grain in the fields, and it shattered every tree out in the field. [26]The only place where hail didn't fall was in the land of Goshen where the Israelites lived.

[27]Then Pharaoh sent for Moses and Aaron and said to them, "This time I've sinned. The LORD is right, and I and my people are wrong. [28]Pray to the LORD! Enough of God's thunder and hail! I'm going to let you go. You don't need to stay here any longer."

[29]Moses said to him, "As soon as I've left the city, I'll spread out my hands to the LORD. Then the thunder and the hail will stop and won't return so that you will know that the earth belongs to the LORD. [30]But I know that you and your officials still don't take the LORD God seriously." ([31]Now the flax and the barley were destroyed, because the barley had ears of grain and the flax had buds. [32]But both durum and spelt wheat weren't ruined, because they hadn't come up.) [33]Moses left Pharaoh and the city, and spread out his hands to the LORD. Then the thunder and the hail stopped, and the rain stopped pouring down on the earth. [34]But when Pharaoh saw that the rain, hail, and thunder had stopped, he sinned again. Pharaoh and his officials became stubborn. [35]Because of his stubbornness, Pharaoh refused to let the Israelites go, just as the LORD had told Moses.

Invasion of locusts

10 Then the LORD said to Moses, "Go to Pharaoh. I've made him and his officials stubborn so that I can show them my signs [2]and so that you can tell your children and grandchildren how I overpowered the

Egyptians with the signs I did among them. You will know that I am the LORD."

³So Moses and Aaron went to Pharaoh and said to him, "This is what the LORD, the Hebrews' God, says: How long will you refuse to respect me? Let my people go so that they can worship me. ⁴Otherwise, if you refuse to let my people go, I'm going to bring locusts into your country tomorrow. ⁵They will cover the landscape so that you won't be able to see the ground. They will eat the last bit of vegetation that was left after the hail. They will eat all your trees growing in the fields. ⁶The locusts will fill your houses and all your officials' houses and all the Egyptians' houses. Your parents and even your grandparents have never seen anything like it during their entire lifetimes in this fertile land." Then Moses turned and left Pharaoh.

⁷Pharaoh's officials said to him, "How long will this man trap us in a corner like this? Let the people go so that they can worship the LORD their God. Don't you get it? Egypt is being destroyed!"

⁸So Moses and Aaron were brought back to Pharaoh, and he said to them, "Go! Worship the LORD your God! But who exactly is going with you?"

⁹Moses said, "We'll go with our young and old, with our sons and daughters, and with our flocks and herds, because we all must observe the LORD's festival."

¹⁰Pharaoh said to them, "Yes, the LORD will be with you, all right, especially if I let your children go with you! Obviously, you are plotting some evil scheme. ¹¹No way! Only your men can go and worship the LORD, because that's what you asked for." Then Pharaoh had them chased out of his presence.

¹²Then the LORD said to Moses: "Stretch out your hand over the land of Egypt so that the locusts will swarm over the land of Egypt and eat all of the land's grain and everything that the hail left." ¹³So Moses stretched out his shepherd's rod over the land of Egypt, and the LORD made an east wind blow over the land all that day and all that night. When morning came, the east wind had carried in the locusts. ¹⁴The locusts swarmed over the whole land of Egypt and settled on the whole country. Such a huge swarming of locusts had never happened before and would never happen ever again. ¹⁵They covered the whole landscape so that the land turned black with them. They ate all of the land's grain and all of the orchards' fruit that the hail had left. Nothing green was left in any orchard or in any grain field in the whole land of Egypt.

¹⁶Pharaoh called urgently for Moses and Aaron and said, "I've sinned against the LORD your God and against you. ¹⁷Please forgive my sin this time. Pray to the LORD your God just to take this deathly disaster away from me."

¹⁸So Moses left Pharaoh and prayed to the LORD. ¹⁹The LORD turned the wind into a very strong west wind that lifted the

LOCUST

An insect widely known in the ancient Near East for its periodic swarming, at which times it ate most kinds of vegetation in its path. Because of the destructiveness of locusts, biblical writers sometimes saw them as punishment from God (see Exod 10:3-20), even of end-time proportions (Rev 9:1-12), while at other times they constituted a mere natural calamity on account of which Israelites were to ask for God's help (2 Chron 6:28). Writers could also use locusts as symbols of military destruction (see Joel 1:4; 2:25). The dietary regulations also defined locusts, crickets, and grasshoppers as ritually clean food, suitable for eating (Lev 11:22).

locusts and drove them into the Reed Sea.^q Not a single locust was left in the whole country of Egypt. ²⁰But the LORD made Pharaoh stubborn so that he wouldn't let the Israelites go.

Darkness covers Egypt

²¹Then the LORD said to Moses, "Raise your hand toward the sky so that darkness spreads over the land of Egypt, a darkness that you can feel." ²²So Moses raised his hand toward the sky, and an intense darkness fell on the whole land of Egypt for three days. ²³People couldn't see each other, and they couldn't go anywhere for three days. But the Israelites all had light where they lived.

²⁴Then Pharaoh called Moses and said, "Go! Worship the LORD! Only your flocks and herds need to stay behind. Even your children can go with you."

²⁵But Moses said, "You need to let us have sacrifices and entirely burned offerings to present to the LORD our God. ²⁶So our livestock must go with us. Not one animal can be left behind. We'll need some of them for worshipping the LORD our God. We won't know which to use to worship the LORD until we get there."

²⁷But the LORD made Pharaoh stubborn so that he wasn't willing to let them go. ²⁸Pharaoh said to him, "Get out of here! Make sure you never see my face again, because the next time you see my face you will die."

²⁹Moses said, "You've said it! I'll never see your face again!"

God announces the final disaster

11 The LORD said to Moses, "I'll bring one more disaster on Pharaoh and on Egypt. After that, he'll let you go from here. In fact, when he lets you go, he'll eagerly chase you out of here. ²Tell every man to ask his neighbor and every woman to ask her neighbor for all their silver and gold jewelry." ³The LORD made sure that the Egyptians were kind to the Hebrew people. In addition, Pharaoh's officials and the

Egyptian people even came to honor Moses as a great and important man in the land.

⁴Moses said, "This is what the LORD says: At midnight I'll go throughout Egypt. ⁵Every oldest child in the land of Egypt will die, from the oldest child of Pharaoh who sits on his throne to the oldest child of the servant woman by the millstones, and all the first offspring of the animals. ⁶Then a terrible cry of agony will echo through the whole land of Egypt unlike any heard before or that ever will be again. ⁷But as for the Israelites, not even a dog will growl at them, at the people, or at their animals. By this, you will know that the LORD makes a distinction between Egypt and Israel. ⁸Then all your officials will come down to me, bow to me, and say, 'Get out, you and all your followers!' After that I'll leave." Then Moses, furious, left Pharaoh.

⁹The LORD said to Moses, "Pharaoh won't listen to you so that I can perform even more amazing acts in the land of Egypt." ¹⁰Now Moses and Aaron did all these amazing acts in front of Pharaoh, but the LORD made Pharaoh stubborn so that he didn't let the Israelites go from his land.

First Passover

12 The LORD said to Moses and Aaron in the land of Egypt, ²"This month will be the first month; it will be the first month of the year for you.^r ³Tell the whole Israelite community: On the tenth day of this month they must take a lamb for each household, a lamb per house. ⁴If a household is too small for a lamb, it should share one with a neighbor nearby. You should divide the lamb in proportion to the number of people who will be eating it. ⁵Your lamb should be a flawless year-old male. You may take it from the sheep or from the goats. ⁶You should keep close watch over it until the fourteenth day of this month. At twilight on that day, the whole assembled Israelite community should slaughter their lambs. ⁷They should take some of the blood and smear it on the two doorposts and on the beam over the door of the houses in

which they are eating. [8]That same night they should eat the meat roasted over the fire. They should eat it along with unleavened bread and bitter herbs. [9]Don't eat any of it raw or boiled in water, but roasted over fire with its head, legs, and internal organs. [10]Don't let any of it remain until morning, and burn any of it left over in the morning. [11]This is how you should eat it. You should be dressed, with your sandals on your feet and your walking stick in your hand. You should eat the meal in a hurry. It is the Passover of the LORD. [12]I'll pass through the land of Egypt that night, and I'll strike down every oldest child in the land of Egypt, both humans and animals. I'll impose judgments on all the gods of Egypt. I am the LORD. [13]The blood will be your sign on the houses where you live. Whenever I see the blood, I'll pass over[s] you. No plague will destroy you when I strike the land of Egypt.

[14]"This day will be a day of remembering for you. You will observe it as a festival to the LORD. You will observe it in every generation as a regulation for all time. [15]You will eat unleavened bread for seven days. On the first day you must remove yeast from your houses because anyone who eats leavened bread anytime during those seven days will be cut off from Israel. [16]The first day and the seventh day will be a holy occasion for you. No work at all should be done on those days, except for preparing the food that everyone is going to eat. That is the only work you may do. [17]You should observe the Festival of Unleavened Bread, because on this precise day I brought you out of the land of Egypt in military formation. You should observe this day in every generation as a regulation for all time. [18]In the first month, from the evening of the fourteenth day until the evening of the twenty-first day, you should eat unleavened bread. [19]For seven days no yeast should be found in your houses because whoever eats leavened bread will be cut off from the Israelite community, whether the person is an immigrant or a native of the land. [20]You should not eat anything made with yeast in all your settlements. You should eat only unleavened bread."

[21]Then Moses called together all of Israel's elders and said to them, "Go pick out one of the flock for your families, and slaughter the Passover lamb. [22]Take a bunch of hyssop, dip it into the blood that is in the bowl, and touch the beam above the door and the two doorposts with the blood in the bowl. None of you should go out the door of your house until morning. [23]When the LORD comes by to strike down the Egyptians and sees the blood on the beam above the door and on the two doorposts, the LORD will pass over that door. He won't let the destroyer enter your houses to strike you down. [24]You should observe this ritual as a regulation for all time for you and your children. [25]When you enter the land that the LORD has promised to give you, be sure that you observe this ritual. [26]And when your children ask you, 'What does this ritual mean to you?' [27]you will say, 'It is the Passover sacrifice to the LORD, for the LORD passed over the houses of the Israelites in Egypt. When he struck down the Egyptians, he spared our houses.'" The people then bowed down and worshipped. [28]The Israelites went and did exactly what the LORD had commanded Moses and Aaron to do.

Death of Egypt's oldest children

[29]At midnight the LORD struck down all the first offspring in the land of Egypt, from the oldest child of Pharaoh sitting on his throne to the oldest child of the prisoner in jail, and all the first offspring of the animals. [30]When Pharaoh, all his officials, and all the Egyptians got up that night, a terrible cry of agony rang out across Egypt because every house had someone in it who had died. [31]Then Pharaoh called Moses and Aaron that night and said, "Get up! Get away from my people, both you and the Israelites! Go! Worship the LORD, as you said! [32]You can even take your flocks and herds, as you asked. Just go! And bring a blessing on me as well!"

---

[s]Heb verb of the noun *Passover*

Israel set free

[33] The Egyptians urged the people to hurry and leave the land because they thought, We'll all be dead. [34] So the people picked up their bread dough before the yeast made it rise, with their bread pans wrapped in their robes on their shoulders. [35] The Israelites did as Moses had told them and asked the Egyptians for their silver and gold jewelry as well as their clothing. [36] The LORD made sure that the Egyptians were kind to the people so that they let them have whatever they asked for. And so they robbed the Egyptians.

[37] The Israelites traveled from Rameses to Succoth. They numbered about six hundred thousand men on foot, besides children. [38] A diverse crowd also went up with them along with a huge number of livestock, both flocks and herds. [39] They baked unleavened cakes from the dough they had brought out of Egypt. The dough didn't rise because they were driven out of Egypt and they couldn't wait. In fact, they didn't have time to prepare any food for themselves.

[40] The length of time that the Israelites had lived in Egypt was four hundred thirty years. [41] At the end of four hundred thirty years, on that precise day, all the LORD's people in military formation left the land of Egypt. [42] For the LORD, that was a night of intent watching, to bring them out of the land of Egypt. For all Israelites in every generation, this same night is a time of intent watching to honor the LORD.

Instructions for observing Passover

[43] The LORD said to Moses and Aaron: This is the regulation for the Passover. No foreigner may eat it. [44] However, any slave who has been bought may eat it after he's been circumcised. [45] No temporary foreign

PASSOVER AND FESTIVAL OF UNLEAVENED BREAD

The Passover and Festival of Unleavened Bread are two consecutive festivals that are treated as one holiday in some biblical passages. The traditional celebration of Passover is called the Seder.

In the lists of pilgrimage festivals (Exod 23:14-17; 34:18, 22-24) only the Festival of Unleavened Bread, not Passover, is mentioned; it is said to last seven days during which only unleavened bread is to be eaten. The feast lists in Leviticus 23 and Numbers 28–29 present a different picture: in them there are two separate but contiguous holidays. The two festivals—Passover and Unleavened Bread—are distinguished in other scriptural sources but are regularly mentioned side by side. In the narratives that introduce them in Exodus 12–13, they are related to the tenth plague on Egypt, the death of all the firstborn children. The destructive event happened around midnight (Exod 11:4) in the very night when the Israelites were celebrating the first Passover. The legislation in Exodus 12 highlights these divine instructions to Moses regarding the Passover.

The Passover plays a central role in the NT, and the Festival of Unleavened Bread is mentioned a few times. The most famous instance is in the accounts of the Last Supper, which is presented as a Passover meal (Seder) in Matthew, Mark and Luke.

resident or day laborer may eat it. ⁴⁶It should be eaten in one house. You shouldn't take any of the meat outside the house, and you shouldn't break the bones. ⁴⁷The whole Israelite community should observe it. ⁴⁸If an immigrant who lives with you wants to observe the Passover to the LORD, then he and all his males should be circumcised. Then he may join in observing it. He should be regarded as a native of the land. But no uncircumcised person may eat it. ⁴⁹There will be one Instruction for the native and for the immigrant who lives with you.

⁵⁰All the Israelites did just as the LORD had commanded Moses and Aaron. ⁵¹On that precise day, the LORD brought the Israelites out of the land of Egypt in military formation.

13 The LORD said to Moses: ²Dedicate to me all your oldest children. Each first offspring from any Israelite womb belongs to me, whether human or animal.

Unleavened bread

³Moses said to the people, "Remember this day which is the day that you came out of Egypt, out of the place you were slaves, because the LORD acted with power to bring you out of there. No leavened bread may be eaten. ⁴Today, in the month of Abib,ᵗ you are going to leave. ⁵The LORD will bring you to the land of the Canaanites, the Hittites, the Amorites, the Hivites, and the Jebusites. It is the land that the LORD promised your ancestors to give to you, a land full of milk and honey. You should perform this ritual in this month. ⁶You must eat unleavened bread for seven days. The seventh day is a festival to the LORD. ⁷Only unleavened bread should be eaten for seven days. No leavened bread and no yeast should be seen among you in your whole country. ⁸You should explain to your child on that day, 'It's because of what the LORD did for me when I came out of Egypt.'

⁹"It will be a sign on your hand and a reminder on your forehead so that you will often discuss the LORD's Instruction, for the LORD brought you out of Egypt with great power. ¹⁰So you should follow this regulation at its appointed time every year.

Dedication of Israel's oldest offspring

¹¹"When the LORD brings you into the land of the Canaanites and gives it to you as promised to you and your ancestors, ¹²you should set aside for the LORD whatever comes out of the womb first. All of the first males born to your animal belong to the LORD. ¹³But every first male donkey you

ᵗMarch–April, named Nisan after the exile

LAMB

A young sheep, usually less than a year old. Most OT references to lambs are sacrificial. Lambs were a daily entirely burned offering in the temple (e.g., Num 15:1-13), and they were the animals offered at Passover (Exod 12:3-4). Lambs could be sacrificed as offerings for purification and reparation (Lev 4:32; Num 6:12; "purification" and "compensation" offerings). However, bulls and goats were the more common offerings for these purposes (Lev 4:1-31).

In the NT, *lamb* is used only metaphorically. The 70 disciples in Luke are sent out as "lambs" (Luke 10:3), indicating their vulnerability in a hostile environment. Jesus instructs Peter to "feed my lambs" (John 21:15); here the lambs are followers for whom Peter should provide care. Primarily, however, lamb in the NT is a metaphor for Christ (e.g., John 1:29; 1 Pet 1:19; Rev 5:6).

should ransom with a sheep. If you don't ransom it, you must break its neck. You should ransom every oldest male among your children. [14]When in the future your child asks you, 'What does this mean?' you should answer, 'The LORD brought us with great power out of Egypt, out of the place we were slaves. [15]When Pharaoh refused to let us go, the LORD killed all the oldest offspring in the land of Egypt, from the oldest sons to the oldest male animals. That is why I offer to the LORD as a sacrifice every male that first comes out of the womb. But I ransom my oldest sons.' [16]It will be a sign on your hand and a symbol on your forehead that the LORD brought us out of Egypt with great power."

God leads the way

[17]When Pharaoh let the people go, God didn't lead them by way of the land of the Philistines, even though that was the shorter route. God thought, If the people have to fight and face war, they will run back to Egypt. [18]So God led the people by the roundabout way of the Reed Sea[u] desert. The Israelites went up out of the land of Egypt ready for battle. [19]Moses took with him Joseph's bones just as Joseph had made Israel's sons promise when he said to them, "When God takes care of you, you must carry my bones out of here with you." [20]They set out from Succoth and camped at Etham on the edge of the desert. [21]The LORD went in front of them during the day in a column of cloud to guide them and at night in a column of lightning to give them light. This way they could travel during the day and at night. [22]The column of cloud during the day and the column of lightning at night never left its place in front of the people.

Israel crossing the sea

14 Then the LORD said to Moses: [2]Tell the Israelites to turn back and set up camp in front of Pi-hahiroth, between Migdol and the sea in front of Baal-zephon. You should set up camp in front of it by the sea. [3]Pharaoh will think to himself, The Israelites are lost and confused in the land. The desert has trapped them. [4]I'll make Pharaoh stubborn, and he'll chase them. I'll gain honor at the expense of Pharaoh and all his army, and the Egyptians will know that I am the LORD. And they did exactly that.

[5]When Egypt's king was told that the people had run away, Pharaoh and his officials changed their minds about the people. They said, "What have we done, letting Israel go free from their slavery to us?" [6]So he sent for his chariot and took his army with him. [7]He took six hundred elite chariots and all of Egypt's other chariots with captains on all of them. [8]The LORD made Pharaoh, Egypt's king, stubborn, and he chased the Israelites, who were leaving confidently. [9]The Egyptians, including all of Pharaoh's horse-drawn chariots, his cavalry, and his army, chased them and caught up with them as they were camped by the sea, by Pi-hahiroth in front of Baal-zephon.

[10]As Pharaoh drew closer, the Israelites looked back and saw the Egyptians marching toward them. The Israelites were terrified and cried out to the LORD. [11]They said to Moses, "Weren't there enough graves in Egypt that you took us away to die in the desert? What have you done to us by bringing us out of Egypt like this? [12]Didn't we tell you the same thing in Egypt? 'Leave us alone! Let us work for the Egyptians!' It would have been better for us to work for the Egyptians than to die in the desert."

[13]But Moses said to the people, "Don't be afraid. Stand your ground, and watch the LORD rescue you today. The Egyptians you see today you will never ever see again. [14]The LORD will fight for you. You just keep still."

[15]Then the LORD said to Moses, "Why do you cry out to me? Tell the Israelites to get moving. [16]As for you, lift your shepherd's rod, stretch out your hand over the sea, and split it in two so that the Israelites can go into the sea on dry ground. [17]But me, I'll make the Egyptians stubborn so that they will go in after them, and I'll gain honor at

[u]Or Red Sea

the expense of Pharaoh, all his army, his chariots, and his cavalry. [18]The Egyptians will know that I am the LORD, when I gain honor at the expense of Pharaoh, his chariots, and his cavalry."

[19]God's messenger, who had been in front of Israel's camp, moved and went behind them. The column of cloud moved from the front and took its place behind them. [20]It stood between Egypt's camp and Israel's camp. The cloud remained there, and when darkness fell it lit up the night. They didn't come near each other all night.

[21]Then Moses stretched out his hand over the sea. The LORD pushed the sea back by a strong east wind all night, turning the sea into dry land. The waters were split into two. [22]The Israelites walked into the sea on dry ground. The waters formed a wall for them on their right hand and on their left. [23]The Egyptians chased them and went into the sea after them, all of Pharaoh's horses, chariots, and cavalry. [24]As morning approached, the LORD looked down on the Egyptian camp from the column of lightning and cloud and threw the Egyptian camp into a panic. [25]The LORD jammed their chariot wheels so that they wouldn't

REED SEA

The exodus story climaxes at the *Yam Suf* (Exod 14:1–15:19), traditionally translated "Red Sea," but translated as "Reed Sea" in much modern scholarship. *Suf* is a term for weeds, reeds, or other such water plants (Exod 2:3, 5; Isa 19:6; Jonah 2:5).

The exodus route had three legs: Rameses to Yam Suf, Yam Suf to Sinai, and Sinai to Kadesh-barnea. (See Exod 12:37–19:25; parts of Num 10; 20–21; and 33:1-49; and brief statements in Deut 1–2.) The biblical record gives us a lot of place-names but few details to help locate them. Succoth appears to be a region in the area of the Wadi Tumilat. Etham and the Wilderness of Etham are near the sea (Num 33:8) and so must be near Yam Suf. The traditional site of Yam Suf is the northern end of the Gulf of Suez, but that location is far to the south of Succoth and would have given Pharaoh's army too much time to catch the Israelites.

At times Yam Suf refers to the Gulf of Aqaba (1 Kgs 9:26-28; Exod 23:31; Judg 11:16; Jer 49:21). Uncertain references (Exod 10:19; 13:18; Num 33:10-11) could refer to Aqaba. References to God's victory over the Egyptians include Exodus 15:4; Psalm 106:7, 9; Acts 7:36; Hebrews 11:29. Apparently this body of water covered the large marshy area that once existed east of Baal-zephon. Or it could be that the waters of the Gulf of Suez (itself sometimes identified as Yam Suf) extended farther north than they do today.

The Yam Suf in the exodus account represents a barrier, a hazard insurmountable by the Israelites. Whether the narrative has in mind a reedy marsh in the delta, an arm of the Red Sea, or the indeterminate cosmic ocean, the importance of the events at the Yam Suf was clearly understood by Israel: there God definitively demonstrated power over the forces of nature, the forces of chaos, and the forces of Pharaoh; there also God showed his unequivocal favor and intent to care for Israel.

turn easily. The Egyptians said, "Let's get away from the Israelites, because the LORD is fighting for them against Egypt!"

²⁶ Then the LORD said to Moses, "Stretch out your hand over the sea so that the water comes back and covers the Egyptians, their chariots, and their cavalry." ²⁷ So Moses stretched out his hand over the sea. At daybreak, the sea returned to its normal depth. The Egyptians were driving toward it, and the LORD tossed the Egyptians into the sea. ²⁸ The waters returned and covered the chariots and the cavalry, Pharaoh's entire army that had followed them into the sea. Not one of them remained. ²⁹ The Israelites, however, walked on dry ground through the sea. The waters formed a wall for them on their right hand and on their left.

³⁰ The LORD rescued Israel from the Egyptians that day. Israel saw the Egyptians dead on the seashore. ³¹ Israel saw the amazing power of the LORD against the Egyptians. The people were in awe of the LORD, and they believed in the LORD and in his servant Moses.

Moses' victory song

15 Then Moses and the Israelites sang this song to the LORD:

I will sing to the LORD,
    for an overflowing victory!
    Horse and rider he threw into the sea!
² The LORD is my strength and my power;ᵛ
    he has become my salvation.
    This is my God, whom I will praise,
    the God of my ancestors,
    whom I will acclaim.
³ The LORD is a warrior;
    the LORD is his name.

⁴ Pharaoh's chariots and his army he
    hurled into the sea;
    his elite captains were sunk
    in the Reed Sea.ʷ
⁵ The deep sea covered them;
    they sank into the deep waters
    like a stone.

⁶ Your strong hand, LORD,
    is dominant in power;
    your strong hand, LORD,
    shatters the enemy!
⁷ With your great surge
    you overthrow your opponents;
    you send out your hot anger;
    it burns them up like straw.
⁸ With the breath of your nostrils
    the waters swelled up,
    the floods surged up in a great wave;
    the deep waters foamed
    in the depths of the sea.
⁹ The enemy said, "I'll pursue, I'll overtake,
    I'll divide the spoils of war.
    I'll be overfilled with them.
    I'll draw my sword;
    my hand will destroy them."
¹⁰ You blew with your wind;
    the sea covered over them.
    They sank like lead
    in the towering waters.
¹¹ Who is like you among the gods, LORD?
    Who is like you, foremost in holiness,
    worthy of highest praise,
    doing awesome deeds?
¹² You raised your strong hand;
    earth swallowed them up.

¹³ With your great loyalty
    you led the people you rescued;
    with your power you guided them
    to your sanctuary.
¹⁴ The peoples heard, they shook in terror;
    horror grabbed hold
    of Philistia's inhabitants.
¹⁵ Then Edom's tribal chiefs were terrified;
    panic grabbed hold of Moab's rulers;
    all of Canaan's inhabitants
    melted in fear.
¹⁶ Terror and fear came over them;
    because of your great power,
    they were as still as a stone
    until your people, LORD, passed by,
    until the people you made your own
    passed by.
¹⁷ You brought them in and planted them
    on your own mountain,

ᵛ Or song ʷ Or Red Sea

the place, LORD,
   that you made your home,
   the sanctuary, LORD,
   that your hand created.
¹⁸ The LORD will rule forever and always.

¹⁹ When Pharaoh's horses, chariots, and cavalry went into the sea, the LORD brought back the waters of the sea over them. But the Israelites walked through the sea on dry ground.

Miriam's victory song
²⁰ Then the prophet Miriam, Aaron's sister, took a tambourine in her hand. All the women followed her playing tambourines and dancing. ²¹ Miriam sang the refrain back to them:

Sing to the LORD,
   for an overflowing victory!
Horse and rider he threw into the sea!

Turning bitter water sweet
²² Then Moses had Israel leave the Reed Sea^x and go out into the Shur desert. They traveled for three days in the desert and found no water. ²³ When they came to Marah, they couldn't drink Marah's water because it was bitter. That's why it was called Marah.^{y} ²⁴ The people complained against Moses, "What will we drink?" ²⁵ Moses cried out to the LORD, and the LORD pointed out a tree to him. He threw it into the water, and the water became sweet.

The LORD made a regulation and a ruling there, and there he tested them. ²⁶ The LORD said, "If you are careful to obey the LORD your God, do what God thinks is right, pay attention to his commandments, and keep all of his regulations, then I won't bring on you any of the diseases that I brought on the Egyptians. I am the LORD who heals you."

²⁷ Then they came to Elim, where there were twelve springs of water and seventy palm trees. They camped there by the water.

Wilderness food: manna and quail
16 The whole Israelite community set out from Elim and came to the Sin desert, which is located between Elim and Sinai. They set out on the fifteenth day of the second month^z after they had left the land of Egypt. ² The whole Israelite community complained against Moses and Aaron in the desert. ³ The Israelites said to them, "Oh, how we wish that the LORD had just put us to death while we were still in the land of Egypt. There we could sit by the pots cooking meat and eat our fill of bread. Instead, you've brought us out into this desert to starve this whole assembly to death."

⁴ Then the LORD said to Moses, "I'm going to make bread rain down from the sky for you. The people will go out each day and gather just enough for that day. In this way, I'll test them to see whether or not they follow my Instruction. ⁵ On the sixth day, when they measure out what they have collected, it will be twice as much as they collected on other days." ⁶ So Moses and Aaron said to all the Israelites, "This evening you will know that it was the LORD who brought you out of the land of Egypt. ⁷ And in the morning you will see the LORD's glorious presence, because your complaints against the LORD have been heard. Who are we? Why blame us?" ⁸ Moses continued, "The LORD will give you meat to eat in the evening and your fill of bread in the morning because the LORD heard the complaints you made against him. Who are we? Your complaints aren't against us but against the LORD."

⁹ Then Moses said to Aaron, "Say to the whole Israelite community, 'Come near to the LORD, because he's heard your complaints.'" ¹⁰ As Aaron spoke to the whole Israelite community, they turned to look toward the desert, and just then the glorious presence of the LORD appeared in the cloud.

¹¹ The LORD spoke to Moses, ¹²"I've heard the complaints of the Israelites. Tell them, 'At twilight you will eat meat. And in the morning you will have your fill of bread. Then you will know that I am the LORD your God.'"

¹³ In the evening a flock of quail flew

down and covered the camp. And in the morning there was a layer of dew all around the camp. [14]When the layer of dew lifted, there on the desert surface were thin flakes, as thin as frost on the ground. [15]When the Israelites saw it, they said to each other, "What[a] is it?" They didn't know what it was.

Moses said to them, "This is the bread that the LORD has given you to eat. [16]This is what the LORD has commanded: 'Collect as much of it as each of you can eat, one omer[b] per person. You may collect for the number of people in your household.'" [17]The Israelites did as Moses said, some collecting more, some less. [18]But when they measured it out by the omer, the ones who had collected more had nothing left over, and the ones who had collected less had no shortage. Everyone collected just as much as they could eat. [19]Moses said to them, "Don't keep any of it until morning." [20]But they didn't listen to Moses. Some kept part of it until morning, but it became infested with worms and stank. Moses got angry with them. [21]Every morning they gathered it, as much as each person could eat. But when the sun grew hot, it melted away.

[22]On the sixth day the people collected twice as much food as usual, two omers per person. All the chiefs of the community came and told Moses. [23]He said to them, "This is what the LORD has said, 'Tomorrow is a day of rest, a holy Sabbath to the LORD. Bake what you want to bake and boil what you want to boil. But you can set aside and keep all the leftovers until the next morning.'" [24]So they set the leftovers aside until morning, as Moses had commanded. They didn't stink or become infested with worms. [25]The next day Moses said, "Eat it today, because today is a Sabbath to the LORD. Today you won't find it out in the field. [26]Six days you will gather it. But on the seventh day, the Sabbath, there will be nothing to gather."

[27]On the seventh day some of the people went out to gather bread, but they found nothing. [28]The LORD said to Moses, "How long will you refuse to obey my commandments and instructions? [29]Look! The LORD has given you the Sabbath. Therefore, on the sixth day he gives you enough food for two days. Each of you should stay where you are and not leave your place on the seventh day." [30]So the people rested on the seventh day.

[31]The Israelite people called it manna. It was like coriander seed, white, and tasted like honey wafers. [32]Moses said, "This is what the LORD has commanded: 'Let an omer of it be kept safe for future generations so that they can see the food that I used to feed you in the desert when I brought you out of the land of Egypt.'"

[33]Moses said to Aaron, "Take a jar, and put one full omer of manna in it. Then set it in the LORD's presence, where it should be kept safe for future generations." [34]Aaron did as the LORD commanded Moses, and he put it in front of the covenant document for safekeeping. [35]The Israelites ate manna for forty years, until they came to a livable land. They ate manna until they came to the border of the land of Canaan. ([36]An omer[c] is one-tenth of an ephah.)

Water from a rock

17 The whole Israelite community broke camp and set out from the Sin desert to continue their journey, as the LORD commanded. They set up their camp at Rephidim, but there was no water for the people to drink. [2]The people argued with Moses and said, "Give us water to drink."

Moses said to them, "Why are you arguing with me? Why are you testing the LORD?"

[3]But the people were very thirsty for water there, and they complained to Moses, "Why did you bring us out of Egypt to kill us, our children, and our livestock with thirst?"

[4]So Moses cried out to the LORD, "What should I do with this people? They are getting ready to stone me."

[5]The LORD said to Moses, "Go on ahead of the people, and take some of Israel's elders with you. Take in your hand the shepherd's rod that you used to strike the Nile River, and go. [6]I'll be standing there

---

[a]Heb *man* (= *What?*); cf Exod 16:31   [b]Two quarts   [c]Two quarts

in front of you on the rock at Horeb. Hit the rock. Water will come out of it, and the people will be able to drink." Moses did so while Israel's elders watched. [7]He called the place Massah[d] and Meribah,[e] because the Israelites argued with and tested the LORD, asking, "Is the LORD really with us or not?"

Israel defeats Amalek

[8]Amalek came and fought with Israel at Rephidim. [9]Moses said to Joshua, "Choose some men for us and go fight with Amalek. Tomorrow I'll stand on top of the hill with the shepherd's rod of God in my hand." [10]So Joshua did as Moses told him. He fought with Amalek while Moses, Aaron, and Hur went up to the top of the hill. [11]Whenever Moses held up his hand, Israel would start winning the battle. Whenever Moses lowered his hand, Amalek would start winning. [12]But Moses' hands grew tired. So they took a stone and put it under Moses so he could sit down on it. Aaron and Hur held up his hands, one on each side of him so that his hands remained steady until sunset. [13]So Joshua defeated Amalek and his army with the sword.

[14]Then the LORD said to Moses, "Write this as a reminder on a scroll and read it to Joshua: I will completely wipe out the memory of Amalek under the sky."

[15]Moses built an altar there and called it, "The LORD is my banner." [16]He said, "The power of the LORD's banner![f] The LORD is at war with Amalek in every generation."

Sharing the burden of leadership

18 Jethro, Midian's priest and Moses' father-in-law, heard about everything that God had done for Moses and for God's people Israel, how the LORD had brought Israel out of Egypt. [2]Moses' father-in-law Jethro took with him Zipporah, Moses' wife whom he had sent away, [3]along with her two sons. One was named Gershom because he said, "I have been an immigrant[g] living in a foreign land." [4]The other was named Eliezer[h] because he said, "The God of my ancestors was my helper who rescued me from Pharaoh's sword." [5]Jethro, Moses' father-in-law, brought Moses' sons and wife back to him in the desert where he had set up camp at God's mountain. [6]He sent word to Moses: "I, your father-in-law Jethro, am coming to you along with your wife and her two sons." [7]Moses went out to meet his father-in-law, and he bowed down and kissed him. They asked each other how they were doing, and then they went into the tent. [8]Moses then told his father-in-law everything that the LORD had done to Pharaoh and to the Egyptians on Israel's behalf, all the difficulty they had on their journey, and how the LORD had rescued them. [9]Jethro was glad about all the good things that the LORD had done for Israel in saving them from the Egyptians' power.

[10]Jethro said, "Bless the LORD who rescued you from the Egyptians' power and from Pharaoh's power, who rescued the people from Egypt's oppressive power.

[d]Or test [e]Or argument [f]Heb uncertain [g]Heb ger sounds like Gershom. [h]Or my God is a helper.

AMALEK/AMALEKITES

Amalekites were descendants of Amalek, Esau's grandson born to Eliphaz and his secondary wife Timna (Gen 36:12, 16; 1 Chron 1:36). They are one of the peoples living in and around Canaan and are described as opponents of the Israelites as they moved from Egypt into the wilderness (Exod 17:8-16). They remained enemies after Israel's settlement in the promised land. A deep-seated hatred existed between Amalek and Israel that pervades most references to them.

[11]Now I know that the LORD is greater than all the gods, because of what happened when the Egyptians plotted against them." [12]Then Jethro, Moses' father-in-law, brought an entirely burned offering and sacrifices to God. Aaron came with all of Israel's elders to eat a meal with Moses' father-in-law in God's presence.

[13]The next day Moses sat as a judge for the people, while the people stood around Moses from morning until evening. [14]When Moses' father-in-law saw all that he was doing for the people, he said, "What's this that you are doing for the people? Why do you sit alone, while all the people are standing around you from morning until evening?"

[15]Moses said to his father-in-law, "Because the people come to me to inquire of God. [16]When a conflict arises between them, they come to me and I judge between the two of them. I also teach them God's regulations and instructions."

[17]Moses' father-in-law said to him, "What you are doing isn't good. [18]You will end up totally wearing yourself out, both you and these people who are with you. The work is too difficult for you. You can't do it alone. [19]Now listen to me and let me give you some advice. And may God be with you! Your role should be to represent the people before God. You should bring their disputes before God yourself. [20]Explain the regulations and instructions to them. Let them know the way they are supposed to go and the things they are supposed to do. [21]But you should also look among all the people for capable persons who respect God. They should be trustworthy and not corrupt. Set these persons over the people as officers of groups of thousands, hundreds, fifties, and tens. [22]Let them sit as judges for the people at all times. They should bring every major dispute to you, but they should decide all of the minor cases themselves. This will be much easier for you, and they will share your load. [23]If you do this and God directs you, then you will be able to endure. And all these people will be able to go back to their homes much happier."

[24]Moses listened to his father-in-law's suggestions and did everything that he had said. [25]Moses chose capable persons from all Israel and set them as leaders over the people, as officers over groups of thousands, hundreds, fifties, and tens. [26]They acted as judges for the people at all times. They would refer the hard cases to Moses, but all of the minor cases they decided themselves. [27]Then Moses said good-bye to his father-in-law, and Jethro went back to his own country.

Arrival at Mount Sinai

19 On exactly the third-month anniversary of the Israelites' leaving the land of Egypt, they came into the Sinai desert. [2]They traveled from Rephidim, came into the Sinai desert, and set up camp there. Israel camped there in front of the mountain [3]while Moses went up to God. The LORD called to him from the mountain, "This is what you should say to Jacob's household and declare to the Israelites: [4]You saw what I did to the Egyptians, and how I lifted you up on eagles' wings and brought you to me. [5]So now, if you faithfully obey me and stay true to my covenant, you will be my most precious possession out of all the peoples, since the whole earth belongs to me. [6]You will be a kingdom of priests for me and a holy nation. These are the words you should say to the Israelites."

[7]So Moses came down, called together the people's elders, and set before them all these words that the LORD had commanded him. [8]The people all responded with one voice: "Everything that the LORD has said we will do." Moses reported to the LORD what the people said.

Preparing for a divine encounter

[9]Then the LORD said to Moses, "I'm about to come to you in a thick cloud in order that the people will hear me talking with you so that they will always trust you."

Moses told the LORD what the people said, [10]and the LORD said to Moses: "Go to the people and take today and tomorrow to make them holy. Have them wash their clothes. [11]Be ready for the third day, because on the third day the LORD will come down on Mount Sinai for all the people to see. ¹²Set up a fence for the people all around and tell them, 'Be careful not to go up the mountain or to touch any part of it.' Anyone who even touches the mountain must be put to death. ¹³No one should touch anyone who has touched it, or they must be either stoned to death or shot with arrows. Whether an animal or a human being, they must not be allowed to live. Only when the ram's horn sounds may they go up on the mountain."

¹⁴So Moses went down the mountain to the people. He made sure the people were holy and that they washed their clothes. ¹⁵He told the men, "Prepare yourselves for three days. Don't go near a woman."

¹⁶When morning dawned on the third day, there was thunder, lightning, and a thick cloud on the mountain, and a very loud blast of a horn. All the people in the camp shook with fear. ¹⁷Moses brought the people out of the camp to meet God, and they took their place at the foot of the mountain. ¹⁸Mount Sinai was all in smoke because the LORD had come down on it with lightning. The smoke went up like the smoke of a hot furnace, while the whole mountain shook violently. ¹⁹The blasts of the horn grew louder and louder. Moses would speak, and God would answer him with thunder. ²⁰The LORD came down on Mount Sinai to the top of the mountain. The LORD called Moses to come up to the top of the mountain, and Moses went up. ²¹The LORD said to Moses, "Go down and warn the people not to break through to try to see the LORD, or many of them will fall dead. ²²Even the priests who come near to the LORD must keep themselves holy, or the LORD will break loose against them."

²³Moses said to the LORD, "The people aren't allowed to come up on Mount Sinai because you warned us and said, 'Set up a fence around the mountain to keep it holy.'"

²⁴The LORD said to him, "Go down, and

MOUNT SINAI

Mount Sinai (Horeb) is the mountain in the wilderness at which God appeared to the Israelites and gave them laws and a covenant on their way from Egypt to the land of promise of Canaan in the books of Exodus, Leviticus, and Numbers. It is the definitive place of God's revelation to Israel at the foundation of its life as a people. God's powerful but veiled presence on the mountain is marked by dazzling visual signs.

The precise location of Mount Sinai has been a matter of considerable debate from ancient times to the present. At least 12 different mountains have been nominated as the location, but two main options have been suggested. The first connects Mount Sinai with the region of Midian, a region or city in northwest Arabia. This location lies east of the Sinai Peninsula, south and east of the land of Israel. Paul seems to reflect this tradition of identifying Sinai with Arabia (Gal 4:24-25).

The second major proposal is that Mount Sinai is in the southern end of the Sinai Peninsula, which lies just east of Egypt. This part of the peninsula contains the highest mountains of the region. Already in the 4th century CE, Christian interpreters argued for this location. The early Christian monastery of Saint Catherine (built around 530 CE) was established at the foot of Jebel Musa (Arabic for "mountain of Moses"), which Christian monks and pilgrims identified as Mount Sinai.

bring Aaron back up with you. But the priests and the people must not break through and come up to the LORD. Otherwise, the LORD will break loose against them." ²⁵So Moses went down to the people and told them.

The Ten Commandments

20 Then God spoke all these words: ²I am the LORD your God who brought you out of Egypt, out of the house of slavery.

³You must have no other gods before[i] me.

⁴Do not make an idol for yourself—no form whatsoever—of anything in the sky above or on the earth below or in the waters under the earth. ⁵Do not bow down to them or worship them, because I, the LORD your God, am a passionate God. I punish children for their parents' sins even to the third and fourth generations of those who hate me. ⁶But I am loyal and gracious to the thousandth generation[j] of those who love me and keep my commandments.

⁷Do not use the LORD your God's name as if it were of no significance; the LORD won't forgive anyone who uses his name that way.

⁸Remember the Sabbath day and treat it as holy. ⁹Six days you may work and do all your tasks, ¹⁰but the seventh day is a Sabbath to the LORD your God. Do not do any work on it—not you, your sons or daughters, your male or female servants, your animals, or the immigrant who is living with you. ¹¹Because the LORD made the heavens and the earth, the sea, and everything that is in them in six days, but rested on the seventh day. That is why the LORD blessed the Sabbath day and made it holy.

¹²Honor your father and your mother so that your life will be long on the fertile land that the LORD your God is giving you.

¹³Do not kill.[k]

¹⁴Do not commit adultery.

¹⁵Do not steal.

¹⁶Do not testify falsely against your neighbor.

¹⁷Do not desire your neighbor's house. Do not desire and try to take your neighbor's wife, male or female servant, ox, donkey, or anything else that belongs to your neighbor.

¹⁸When all the people witnessed the thunder and lightning, the sound of the horn, and the mountain smoking, the people shook with fear and stood at a distance. ¹⁹They said to Moses, "You speak to us, and we'll listen. But don't let God speak to us, or we'll die."

²⁰Moses said to the people, "Don't be afraid, because God has come only to test you and to make sure you are always in awe of God so that you don't sin." ²¹The people stood at a distance while Moses approached the thick darkness in which God was present.

Instructions about worship

²²The LORD said to Moses: "Say this to the Israelites: You saw for yourselves how I spoke with you from heaven. ²³Don't make alongside me gods of silver or gold for yourselves. ²⁴Make for me an altar from fertile soil on which to sacrifice your entirely burned offerings, your well-being sacrifices, your sheep, and your oxen. I will come to you and bless you in every place where I make sure my name is remembered. ²⁵But if you do make for me an altar from stones, don't build it with chiseled stone since using your chisel on the stone will make it impure. ²⁶Don't climb onto my altar using steps: then your genitals won't be exposed by doing so."

Instructions about slaves

21 These are the case laws that you should set before them:

²When you buy a male Hebrew slave, he will serve you for six years. But in the seventh year, he will go free without any payment. ³If he came in single, he will leave single. If he came in married, then his wife will leave with him. ⁴If his master gave him

---

[i]Or besides   [j]Or to thousands   [k]Or murder

a wife and she bore him sons or daughters, the wife and her children will belong to her master. He will leave single. ⁵However, if the slave clearly states, "I love my master, my wife, and my children, and I don't want to go free," ⁶then his master will bring him before God. He will bring him to the door or the doorpost. There his master will pierce his ear with a pointed tool, and he will serve him as his slave for life.

⁷When a man sells his daughter as a slave, she shouldn't be set free in the same way as male slaves are set free. ⁸If she doesn't please her master who chose her for himself, then her master must let her be bought back by her family. He has no right to sell her to a foreign people since he has treated her unfairly. ⁹If he assigns her to his son, he must give her the rights of a daughter. ¹⁰If he takes another woman for himself, he may not reduce her food, clothing, or marital rights. ¹¹If he doesn't do these three things for her, she will go free without any payment, for no money.

Instructions about human violence

¹²Anyone who hits and kills someone should be put to death. ¹³If the killing wasn't on purpose but an accident allowed by God, then I will designate a place to which the killer can run away. ¹⁴But if someone plots and kills another person on purpose, you should remove the killer from my altar and put him to death.

¹⁵Anyone who violently hits their father or mother should be put to death.

¹⁶Anyone who kidnaps a person, whether they have been sold or are still being held, should be put to death.

¹⁷Anyone who curses their father or mother should be put to death.

¹⁸When two people are fighting and one hits the other with a stone or with his fist so that he is in bed for a while but doesn't die—¹⁹if he recovers and is able to walk around outside with a cane, then the one who hit him shouldn't be punished, except to pay for the loss of time from work and to pay for his full recovery.

²⁰When a slave owner hits a male or female slave with a rod and the slave dies immediately, the owner should be punished. ²¹But if the slave gets up after a day or two, the slave owner shouldn't be punished because the slave is the owner's property.

²²When people who are fighting injure a pregnant woman so that she has a miscarriage but no other injury occurs, then the guilty party will be fined what the woman's husband demands, as negotiated with the judges. ²³If there is further injury, then you will give a life for a life, ²⁴an eye for an eye, a tooth for a tooth, a hand for a hand, a foot for a foot, ²⁵a burn for a burn, a bruise for a bruise, a wound for a wound.

²⁶When a slave owner hits and blinds the eye of a male or female slave, he should let the slave go free on account of the eye. ²⁷If he knocks out a tooth of a male or female slave, he should let the slave go free on account of the tooth.

Instructions about animals and property

²⁸When an ox gores a man or a woman to death, the ox should be stoned to death, and the meat of the ox shouldn't be eaten. But the owner of the ox shouldn't be punished. ²⁹However, if the ox had gored people in the past and its owner had been warned but didn't watch out for it, and the ox ends up killing a man or a woman, then the ox should be stoned to death, and its owner should also be put to death. ³⁰If the owner has to pay compensation instead, he must pay the agreed amount to save his life. ³¹If the ox gores a boy or a girl, this same case law applies to the owner. ³²If the ox gores a male or female slave, the owner will pay thirty silver shekels to the slave's owner, and the ox will be stoned to death.

³³When someone leaves a pit open or digs a pit and doesn't cover it and an ox or a donkey falls into the pit, ³⁴the owner of the pit must make good on the loss. He should pay money to the ox's owner, but he may keep the dead animal.

³⁵When someone's ox hurts someone else's ox and it dies, then they should sell the live ox and divide its price. They should also divide the dead animal between them. ³⁶But if the ox was known for goring in the

past and its owner hadn't watched out for it, the owner must make good the loss, an ox for an ox, but may keep the dead animal.

22 [l]When someone steals an ox or a sheep and then slaughters or sells it, the thief must pay back five oxen for the one ox or four sheep for the one sheep.

[m]2If the thief is caught breaking in and is beaten and dies, the one who killed him won't be guilty of bloodshed. 3However, if this happens in broad daylight, then the one who killed him is guilty of bloodshed. For his part, the thief must make good on what he stole. If he has nothing, he must be sold to pay for his theft. 4If an animal (whether ox, donkey, or sheep) is found alive in the thief's possession, he must pay back double.

5When someone lets an animal loose to eat in another person's field and causes the field or vineyard to be stripped of its crop, the owner must pay them back with the best from his own field or vineyard.

6When someone starts a fire and it catches in thorns and then spreads to someone else's stacked grain, standing grain, or a whole field, the one who started the fire must fully repay the loss.

7When someone entrusts money or other items to another person to keep safe and they are stolen from the other person's house and the thief is caught, the thief must pay back double. 8If the thief isn't caught, the owner of the house should be brought before God to determine whether or not the owner stole the other's property. 9When any dispute of ownership over an ox, donkey, sheep, piece of clothing, or any other loss arises in which someone claims, "This is mine," the cases of both parties should come before God. The one whom God finds at fault must pay double to the other.

10When someone gives a donkey, ox, sheep, or any other animal to another person to keep safe, and the animal dies or is injured or taken and no one saw what happened, 11the person should swear a solemn pledge before the LORD in the presence of the owner that he didn't touch the other's property. The owner must accept that, and no payment needs to be made. 12But if the animal was stolen, the person must make full payment to its owner. 13If the animal was attacked and ripped apart and its torn body is brought as evidence, no payment needs to be made.

14When someone borrows an animal from another and it is injured or dies while the owner isn't present, full payment must be made. 15If the owner was present, no payment needs to be made. If the animal was hired, only the fee for hiring the animal is due.

Instructions about social and religious matters

16When a man seduces a young woman who isn't engaged to be married yet and he sleeps with her, he must marry her and pay the bride-price for her. 17But if her father absolutely refuses to let them marry, he must still pay the same amount as the bride-price for young women.

18Don't allow a female sorcerer to live.

19Anyone who has sexual relations with an animal should be put to death.

20Anyone who offers sacrifices to any god, other than the LORD alone, should be destroyed.

21Don't mistreat or oppress an immigrant, because you were once immigrants in the land of Egypt. 22Don't treat any widow or orphan badly. 23If you do treat them badly and they cry out to me, you can be sure that I'll hear their cry. 24I'll be furious, and I'll kill you with the sword. Then your wives will be widows, and your children will be orphans.

25If you lend money to my people who are poor among you, don't be a creditor and charge them interest. 26If you take a piece of clothing from someone as a security deposit, you should return it before the sun goes down. 27His clothing may well be his only blanket to cover himself. What else will that person have to sleep in? And if he cries out to me, I'll listen, because I'm compassionate.

[l]21:37 in Heb [m]22:1 in Heb

²⁸Don't say a curse against God, and don't curse your people's chief.

²⁹Don't delay offering the produce of your vineyards and winepresses. Give me your oldest son. ³⁰Do the same with your oxen and with your sheep. They should stay with their mother for seven days. On the eighth day, you should give them to me. ³¹You are holy people to me. Don't eat any meat killed by wild animals out in the field. Throw it to the dogs instead.

23 Don't spread false rumors. Don't plot with evil people to act as a lying witness. ²Don't take sides with important people to do wrong. When you act as a witness, don't stretch the truth to favor important people. ³But don't privilege unimportant people in their lawsuits either.

⁴When you happen to come upon your enemy's ox or donkey that has wandered off, you should bring it back to them.

⁵When you see a donkey that belongs to someone who hates you and it's lying down under its load and you are inclined not to help set it free, you must help set it free.

⁶Don't undermine the justice that your poor deserve in their lawsuits. ⁷Stay away from making a false charge. Don't put an innocent person who is in the right to death, because I will not consider innocent those who do such evil. ⁸Don't take a bribe, because a bribe blinds the clear-sighted and subverts the cause of those who are in the right.

⁹Don't oppress an immigrant. You know what it's like to be an immigrant, because you were immigrants in the land of Egypt.

Sabbaths and festivals

¹⁰For six years you should plant crops on your land and gather in its produce. ¹¹But in the seventh year you should leave it alone and undisturbed so that the poor among your people may eat. What they leave behind, the wild animals may eat. You should do the same with your vineyard and your olive trees.

¹²Do your work in six days. But on the seventh day you should rest so that your ox and donkey may rest, and even the child of your female slave and the immigrant may be refreshed.

¹³Be careful to obey everything that I have said to you. Don't call on the names of other gods. Don't even mention them.

¹⁴You should observe a festival for me three times a year. ¹⁵Observe the Festival of Unleavened Bread, as I commanded you. Eat unleavened bread for seven days at the appointed time in the month of Abib,ⁿ because it was in that month that you came out of Egypt.

No one should appear before me empty-handed. ¹⁶Observe the Harvest Festival for the early produce of your crops that you planted in the field, and the Gathering Festival at the end of the year, when you gather your crop of fruit from the field. ¹⁷All your males should appear three times a year before the Lord God.

¹⁸Don't offer the blood of my sacrifice with anything leavened. Don't let the fat of my festival offering be left over until the morning.

¹⁹Bring the best of your land's early produce to the Lord your God's temple.

Don't boil a young goat in its mother's milk.

God's promise: messenger and land

²⁰I'm about to send a messenger in front of you to guard you on your way and to bring you to the place that I've made ready. ²¹Pay attention to him and do as he says. Don't rebel against him. He won't forgive the things you do wrong because Iᵒ am with him. ²²But if you listen carefully to what he says and do all that I say, then I'll be an enemy to your enemies and fight those fighting you.

²³When my messenger goes in front of you and brings you to the Amorites, the Hittites, the Perizzites, the Canaanites, the Hivites, and the Jebusites, and I wipe them out, ²⁴don't bow down to their gods, worship them, or do what they do. Instead, you should completely destroy them and smash their sacred stone pillars to bits.

ⁿMarch–April, named Nisan after the exile ᵒOr *my name*

²⁵If you worship the LORD your God, the LORD will bless your bread and your water. I'll take sickness away from you, ²⁶and no woman will miscarry or be infertile in your land. I'll let you live a full, long life. ²⁷My terrifying reputation will precede you, and I'll throw all the people that you meet into a panic. I'll make all your enemies turn their backs to you. ²⁸I'll send insect swarms in front of you and drive out the Hivites, the Canaanites, and the Hittites before you. ²⁹I won't drive them out before you in a single year so the land won't be abandoned and the wild animals won't multiply around you. ³⁰I'll drive them out before you little by little, until your numbers grow and you eventually possess the land. ³¹I'll set your borders from the Reed Seaᴾ to the Philistine Sea and from the desert to the River. I'll hand the inhabitants of the land over to you, and you will drive them out before you. ³²Don't make any covenants with them or their gods. ³³Don't allow them to live in your land, or else they will lead you to sin against me. If you worship their gods, it will become a dangerous trap for you.

Covenant at Sinai

24 Then the LORD said to Moses, "Come up to the LORD, you and Aaron, Nadab and Abihu, and seventy of Israel's elders, and worship from a distance. ²Only Moses may come near to the LORD. The others shouldn't come near, while the people shouldn't come up with him at all."

ᴾOr Red Sea

³Moses came and told the people all the LORD's words and all the case laws. All the people answered in unison, "Everything that the LORD has said we will do." ⁴Moses then wrote down all the LORD's words. He got up early in the morning and built an altar at the foot of the mountain. He set up twelve sacred stone pillars for the twelve tribes of Israel. ⁵He appointed certain young Israelite men to offer entirely burned offerings and slaughter oxen as well-being sacrifices to the LORD. ⁶Moses took half of the blood and put it in large bowls. The other half of the blood he threw against the altar. ⁷Then he took the covenant scroll and read it out loud for the people to hear. They responded, "Everything that the LORD has said we will do, and we will obey."

⁸Moses then took the blood and threw it over the people. Moses said, "This is the blood of the covenant that the LORD now makes with you on the basis of all these words."

Covenant meal with God

⁹Then Moses and Aaron, Nadab and Abihu, and seventy elders of Israel went up, ¹⁰and they saw Israel's God. Under God's feet there was what looked like a floor of lapis-lazuli tiles, dazzlingly pure like the sky. ¹¹God didn't harm the Israelite leaders, though they looked at God, and they ate and drank.

¹²The LORD said to Moses, "Come up to me on the mountain and wait there. I'll give

COVENANT SCROLL

This title for the collection of laws in Exodus 20:22–23:33 comes from Exodus 24:7. The collection contains rules governing altars to Yahweh (Exod 20:23-26), judgments covering crimes against persons and property (Exod 21:1–22:17), religious and moral transgressions (Exod 22:18-20, 28-31) mixed with duties to care for the poor and vulnerable (22:21-27), and a table of holy times and feasts (23:10-19), followed by instructions for departure from Sinai/Horeb. Both the style and content suggest this code is the oldest in the first five books of the Bible.

you the stone tablets with the instructions and the commandments that I've written in order to teach them."

¹³So Moses and his assistant Joshua got up, and Moses went up God's mountain. ¹⁴Moses had said to the elders, "Wait for us here until we come back to you. Aaron and Hur will be here with you. Whoever has a legal dispute may go to them."

¹⁵Then Moses went up the mountain, and the cloud covered the mountain. ¹⁶The LORD's glorious presence settled on Mount Sinai, and the cloud covered it for six days. On the seventh day the LORD called to Moses from the cloud. ¹⁷To the Israelites, the LORD's glorious presence looked like a blazing fire on top of the mountain. ¹⁸Moses entered the cloud and went up the mountain. Moses stayed on the mountain for forty days and forty nights.

Gifts offered for the dwelling

25 The LORD said to Moses: ²Tell the Israelites to collect gift offerings for me. Receive my gift offerings from everyone who freely wants to give. ³These are the gift offerings that you should receive from them: gold, silver, and copper; ⁴blue, purple, and deep red yarns; fine linen; goats' hair; ⁵rams' skins dyed red; beaded leather;�q acacia wood; ⁶oil for the lamps; spices for the anointing oil and for the sweet-smelling incense; ⁷gemstones; and gems for setting in the priest's vestʳ and chest piece. ⁸They should make me a sanctuary so I can be present among them. ⁹You should follow the blueprints that I will show you for the dwelling and for all its equipment.

Instructions for building the chest containing the covenant

¹⁰Have them make an acacia-wood chest. It should be forty-five inches long, twenty-seven inches wide, and twenty-seven inches high. ¹¹Cover it with pure gold, inside and out, and make a gold molding all around it. ¹²Cast four gold rings for it and put them on its four feet, two rings on one side and two rings on the other. ¹³Make acacia-wood poles and cover them with gold. ¹⁴Then put the poles into the rings on the chest's sides and use them to carry the chest. ¹⁵The poles should stay in the chest's rings. They shouldn't be taken out of them. ¹⁶Put the covenant document that I will give you into the chest.

¹⁷Then make a cover of pure gold, forty-five inches long and twenty-seven inches wide. ¹⁸Make two winged heavenly creatures of hammered gold, one for each end of the cover. ¹⁹Put one winged heavenly creature at one end and one winged heavenly creature at the other. Place the winged heavenly creatures at the cover's two ends. ²⁰The heavenly creatures should have their wings spread out above, shielding the cover with their wings. The winged heavenly creatures should face each other toward the cover's center. ²¹Put the gold cover on top of the chest and put the covenant document that I will give you inside the chest. ²²There I will meet with you. From there above the cover, from between the two winged heavenly creatures that are on top of the chest containing the covenant, I will deliver to you all that I command you concerning the Israelites.

qOr *dolphin skins*   ʳHeb *ephod*

ACACIA

A tree or shrub common in the desert areas of Egypt, Arabia, Sinai, and the southern plain. Due to its exceptional durability, acacia wood was used for the covenant chest, the furnishings of the covenant dwelling, and the altar (Exod 25–27; 30; 35–38; cf. Deut 10:3).

Instructions for the table

²³Make an acacia-wood table, three feet long, eighteen inches wide, and twenty-seven inches high. ²⁴Cover it with pure gold and make a gold molding all around it. ²⁵Make a frame around it that is four inches wide and a gold molding around the frame. ²⁶Make four gold rings for the table. Fasten the rings to the four corners at its four legs. ²⁷The rings that house the poles used for carrying the table should be close to the frame. ²⁸Make the poles from acacia wood and cover them with gold. The table should be carried with these poles. ²⁹Make its plates, dishes, jars, and bowls for pouring drink offerings. Make them of pure gold. ³⁰Set the bread of the presence on the table so it is always in front of me.

Instructions for the lampstand

³¹Make a lampstand of pure hammered gold. The lampstand's base, branches, cups, flowers, and petals should all be attached to it. ³²It should have six branches growing out from its sides, three branches on one side of the lampstand and three branches on the other side of the lampstand. ³³One branch will have three cups shaped like almond blossoms, each with a flower and petals, and the next branch will also have three cups shaped like almond blossoms, each with a flower and petals. So it will be

for the six branches that grow out of the lampstand. ³⁴In addition, on the lampstand itself there will be four cups shaped like almond blossoms, each with its flower and petals. ³⁵There will be a flower attached under the first pair of branches, a flower attached under the next pair of branches, and a flower attached under the last pair of branches. So it will be for the six branches that grow out of the lampstand. ³⁶Their flowers and their branches will be permanently attached to it. The whole lampstand should be one piece of pure hammered gold. ³⁷Make its seven lamps and set up its lamps so that they direct their light in front of the lampstand. ³⁸You should also make its tongs and fire pans out of pure gold. ³⁹All these items should be made from pure gold weighing one kikkar. ⁴⁰See to it that you make them according to the blueprint for them that you were shown on the mountain.

Instructions for building the dwelling

26 Make the dwelling with ten curtains of fine twisted linen and blue, purple, and deep red yarns. Work figures of winged heavenly creatures into their design. ²Each curtain should be forty-two feet long and each curtain six feet wide. All the curtains should be the same size. ³Five curtains will be joined to each other as one set,

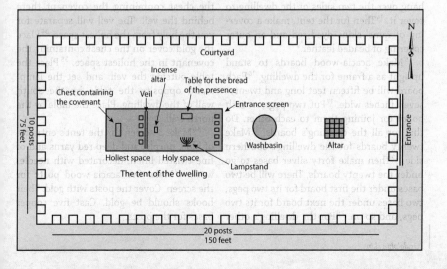

Courtyard

Incense altar

Table for the bread of the presence

Chest containing the covenant

Veil

Entrance screen

Holiest space   Holy space

The tent of the dwelling

Lampstand

Washbasin

Altar

Entrance

10 posts / 75 feet

20 posts / 150 feet

N

while the other five curtains will be joined together as a second set. ⁴Make loops of blue thread on the edge of the outer curtain in the first set. Do the same on the edge of the outer curtain in the second set. ⁵Make fifty loops on the one curtain in the first set and fifty loops on the edge of the curtain that is in the second set. The loops should be opposite each other. ⁶Then make fifty gold clasps. Join the curtains to each other with the clasps so that the dwelling becomes one whole structure.

⁷You should also make curtains of goats' hair for a tent over the dwelling. Make eleven curtains. ⁸Each curtain should be forty-five feet long and each curtain six feet wide. The eleven curtains should all be the same size. ⁹Join five of the curtains together, and join the six other curtains together. Double over the sixth curtain at the front of the tent. ¹⁰Make fifty loops on the edge of the outer curtain in one set and fifty loops on the edge of the outer curtain in the second set.

¹¹Make fifty copper clasps. Put the clasps into the loops and join the tent together so that it becomes one whole structure. ¹²The extra cloth that is left over from the tent curtains, that is, the half curtain that remains, should hang over the back of the dwelling. ¹³Eighteen inches on one side and eighteen inches on the other side of the leftover length of the tent's curtains will hang over the two sides of the dwelling to cover it. ¹⁴Then for the tent, make a covering of rams' skins dyed red and an outer covering of beaded leather.ˢ

¹⁵Make acacia-wood boards to stand upright as a frame for the dwelling. ¹⁶Each board will be fifteen feet long and twenty-seven inches wide. ¹⁷Put two pegs on each board for joining them to each other. Do this for all the dwelling's boards. ¹⁸Make twenty boards for the dwelling's southern side. ¹⁹Then make forty silver bases to go under the twenty boards. There will be two bases under the first board for its two pegs, two bases under the next board for its two pegs, and so on. ²⁰For the dwelling's other side on the north, make twenty boards ²¹and their forty silver bases, two bases under the first board, two bases under the next board, and so on. ²²For the back of the dwelling on the west, make six boards. ²³Make two additional boards for the dwelling's rear corners. ²⁴They should be spread out at the bottom but joined together at the top with one ring. In this way, these two boards will form the two corners. ²⁵And so there will be eight boards with their sixteen silver bases, two bases under the first board, two bases under the next board, and so on.

²⁶You should also make acacia-wood bars: five for the boards on one side of the dwelling, ²⁷five bars for the boards on the other side of the dwelling, and five bars for the boards on the back wall of the dwelling on the west. ²⁸The middle bar, halfway up the boards, should run from one end to the other. ²⁹Cover the boards with gold. Make gold rings to house the bars. Cover the bars with gold. ³⁰Then set up the dwelling according to the plan for it that you were shown on the mountain.

³¹Make a veil of blue, purple, and deep red yarns and of fine twisted linen. Work figures of winged heavenly creatures into its design. ³²Hang it on four acacia-wood posts covered in gold. They should have gold hooks and stand on four silver bases. ³³Hang the veil under the clasps, and put the chest containing the covenant there behind the veil. The veil will separate for you the holy from the holiest space. ³⁴Place the gold cover on the chest containing the covenant in the holiest space. ³⁵Place the table outside the veil, and set the lampstand opposite the table by the south wall of the dwelling. Place the table by the north wall.

³⁶Make a screen for the tent's entrance of blue, purple, and deep red yarns and of fine twisted linen, decorated with needlework. ³⁷Make five acacia-wood posts for the screen. Cover the posts with gold. Their hooks should be gold. Cast five copper bases for the posts.

ˢOr *dolphin skin*

Instructions for the altar

27 Make an acacia-wood altar. The altar should be square, seven and a half feet long and seven and a half feet wide. It should be four and a half feet high. ²Make horns for the altar and attach them to it, one horn on each of its four corners. Cover it with copper. ³Make pails for removing its ashes and its shovels, bowls, meat forks, and trays. Make all its equipment out of copper. ⁴Make for the altar a grate made of copper mesh. Make four copper rings for each of the four corners of the mesh. ⁵Slide the mesh underneath the bottom edge of the altar and then extend the mesh halfway up to the middle of the altar. ⁶Make acacia-wood poles for the altar and cover them with copper. ⁷Put the poles through the rings so that the poles will be on the two sides of the altar when it is carried. ⁸Make the altar with planks but hollow inside. All these should be made just as you were shown on the mountain.

Instructions for the dwelling's courtyard

⁹You should also set up the dwelling's courtyard. The courtyard's south side should have drapes of fine twisted linen stretching one hundred fifty feet on that side, ¹⁰with twenty posts, twenty copper bases, and silver hooks and bands for the posts. ¹¹Likewise along the north side the drapes should stretch one hundred fifty feet, with twenty posts, twenty copper bases, and silver hooks and bands for the posts. ¹²The courtyard's width on the west side should consist of seventy-five feet of drapes with their ten posts and their ten bases. ¹³The courtyard's width on the front, facing east should be seventy-five feet. ¹⁴There should be twenty-two and a half feet of drapes on one side with three posts and three bases for them. ¹⁵There should be twenty-two and a half feet of drapes on the other side with three posts and three bases for them. ¹⁶For the gate into the courtyard there will be a screen thirty feet long, made of blue, purple, and deep red yarns and of fine twisted linen, decorated with needlework. It will have four posts with their four bases. ¹⁷All the posts around the courtyard will have silver bands, silver hooks, and copper bases. ¹⁸The courtyard will be one hundred fifty feet long and seventy-five feet wide. Its walls' height will be seven and a half feet of fine twisted linen and its copper bases. ¹⁹All the dwelling's equipment for any use and all its tent pegs and all the courtyard's tent pegs will be made of copper.

Olive oil for the lampstand

²⁰You must require the Israelites to bring you pure oil of crushed olives for the light so that the lamp may be set up to burn continually. ²¹In the meeting tent, outside the veil that hangs in front of the covenant document, Aaron and his sons will tend the lamp from evening to morning in the LORD's presence. It will be a permanent regulation for the Israelites in every generation.

Instructions for the priests' clothing

28 Summon to you your brother Aaron and his sons from among the Israelites to serve me as priests—Aaron and Aaron's sons, Nadab and Abihu, and Eleazar and Ithamar. ²Make holy clothing that will give honor and dignity to your brother Aaron. ³Tell all who are skilled, to whom I have given special abilities, to make clothing for Aaron for his dedication to serve me as a priest. ⁴These are the articles of clothing that they should make: a chest pendant, a vest, a robe, a woven tunic, a turban, and a sash. When they make this holy clothing for your brother Aaron and his sons to serve me as priests, ⁵they should use gold, blue, purple, and deep red yarns and fine linen.

Priest's ornamental vest

⁶They should make the vest of gold, of blue, purple, and deep red yarns and of fine twisted linen with embroidered designs. ⁷The vest will have two shoulder pieces attached to its two edges so that they may be joined together. ⁸The vest's belt should be attached to it and made in the same way of gold, of blue, purple, and deep red yarns and fine twisted linen. ⁹Take two gemstones and engrave on them the names of Israel's sons, ¹⁰six names on one stone and the other six names on the other stone, in

the order of their birth. [11]Like a gem cutter who engraves official seals, you will engrave the two stones with the names of Israel's sons. Mount them in gold settings. [12]Attach the two stones to the vest's shoulder pieces as stones of reminder for the Israelites. Aaron will carry into the LORD's presence their names on his two shoulders as a reminder. [13]Then make gold settings [14]along with two chains of pure gold, twisted like cords. Attach the corded chains to the gold settings.

Priest's chest pendant used for making decisions

[15]Make an embroidered chest pendant used for making decisions. Make it in the style of the vest, using gold, blue and purple and deep red yarns, and fine twisted linen. [16]It will be square and doubled, nine inches long and nine inches wide. [17]Set in it four rows of gemstone settings. The first row will be a row of carnelian, topaz, and emerald stones. [18]The second row will be a turquoise, a sapphire, and a moonstone. [19]The third row will be a jacinth, an agate, and an amethyst. [20]The fourth row will be a beryl, an onyx, and a jasper. Their settings will be made of decorative gold. [21]There will be twelve stones with names corresponding to the names of Israel's sons. They will be engraved like official seals, each with its name for the twelve tribes.

[22]Make chains of pure gold twisted like cords for the chest pendant. [23]Make two gold rings for the chest pendant and attach the two rings to the two edges of the chest pendant. [24]Attach the two gold cords to the two rings at the edges of the chest pendant. [25]Then fasten the two ends of the cords to the two settings, which you should attach to the vest's two front shoulder pieces. [26]Make two gold rings and attach them to the two ends of the chest pendant on its inside edge facing the vest. [27]Make two gold rings and fasten them on the front of the lower part of the two shoulder pieces of the vest, at its seam just above the vest's belt. [28]The chest pendant should be held in place by a blue cord binding its rings to the vest's rings so that the chest pendant rests on the vest's belt and won't come loose from the vest. [29]In this way, Aaron will carry the names of Israel's sons on the chest pendant for making decisions over his heart when he goes into the sanctuary as a reminder before the LORD at all times. [30]Put into the chest pendant used for making decisions the Urim and the Thummim, so they will be over Aaron's heart when he goes into the LORD's presence. In this way, Aaron will carry the means to make decisions for the Israelites over his heart when in the LORD's presence at all times.

Instructions for other priestly clothing

[31]You will make the robe for the vest all of blue. [32]The opening for the head should be in the middle of it. The opening should be reinforced by a woven binding, a strong border so that it doesn't tear. [33]On its lower hem add pomegranates made of blue, purple, and deep red yarns all around the lower hem, with gold bells between the pomegranates all around it. [34]A gold bell and a pomegranate should alternate all around the lower hem of the robe. [35]Aaron will wear the robe when he ministers as a priest. Its sound will be heard when he goes into the sanctuary in the LORD's presence and when he comes out, so that he will not die.

[36]Make a flower ornament of pure gold and engrave on it like an official seal: "Holy to the LORD." [37]You should fasten it on the turban with a blue cord. It should be on the front of the turban. [38]It will be on Aaron's forehead, and Aaron will take on himself any guilt connected with the holy offerings that the Israelites give as their sacred donations. It will always be on his forehead so that the people may be remembered favorably in the LORD's presence.

[39]Weave the tunic out of fine linen. Make the turban out of fine linen. Make a sash decorated with needlework. [40]For Aaron's sons, you should also make tunics, sashes, and turbans to mark their honor and dignity. [41]Put these garments on your brother Aaron and on his sons with him. Anoint them with oil, ordain them, and make them holy to serve me as priests. [42]You should also make linen undergar-

ments for them to cover their naked skin from their hips to their thighs. ⁴³Aaron and his sons should wear this clothing when they go into the meeting tent or when they approach the altar to minister as priests in the sanctuary. Otherwise, they will bring guilt on themselves and die. This will be a permanent regulation for him and for his descendants after him.

Instructions for the priests' ordination

29 Now this is what you should do to make them holy in order to serve me as priests. Take a young bull and two flawless rams. ²Take unleavened bread, unleavened flatbread made with oil, and unleavened wafers spread with oil. Make them out of high-quality wheat flour. ³Put them all in one basket and present them in the basket along with the bull and the two rams. ⁴Present Aaron and his sons at the entrance to the meeting tent and wash them with water. ⁵Then take the priestly clothes and put them on Aaron: the tunic, the vest's robe, the vest itself, and the chest pendant. Put the vest on him with the vest's belt. ⁶Set the turban on his head and place the holy crown on the turban. ⁷Take the anointing oil and pour it on his head to anoint him. ⁸Then present his sons and put the tunics on them. ⁹Tighten the sashes on them, on both Aaron and his sons. Wrap the turbans on their heads. It will be a permanent regulation that the duties of priesthood belong to them. In this way, you will ordain Aaron and his sons.

¹⁰Present the bull at the front of the meeting tent. Aaron and his sons will lay their hands on the bull's head. ¹¹Then slaughter the bull in the LORD's presence at the meeting tent's entrance. ¹²Take some of the bull's blood and smear it on the altar's horns with your finger. Pour out the rest of the blood at the altar's base. ¹³Then take all the fat that covers the inner organs, the lobe of the liver, and the two kidneys along with the fat that is on them, and burn them up in smoke on the altar. ¹⁴Burn the rest of the meat of the bull, its hide, and the intestines with their contents with a fire outside the camp. It is a purification offering.

¹⁵Choose one of the rams, and have Aaron and his sons lay their hands on the ram's head. ¹⁶Then slaughter the ram. Take its blood and throw it against all the altar's sides. ¹⁷Cut up the ram into parts. Wash its inner organs and legs, and put them together with its parts and its head. ¹⁸Then turn the entire ram into smoke by burning it on the altar. It is an entirely burned offering for the LORD, a soothing smell, a food gift for the LORD.

¹⁹Take the second ram, and have Aaron and his sons lay their hands on the ram's head. ²⁰Slaughter the ram. Take some of its blood and smear it on the right earlobes of Aaron and his sons, on the thumbs of their right hands, and on the big toes of their right feet. Throw the rest of the blood against all the altar's sides. ²¹Then take some of the blood on the altar and some of the anointing oil and sprinkle them on Aaron and on his clothes and on his sons and on his sons' clothes. In this way, Aaron, his sons, and all their priestly garments will be holy.

²²Take the fatty parts of the ram: the fat tail, the fat around the inner organs, the lobe of the liver, the two kidneys with the fat around them, and the right thigh (because it is a ram for ordination). ²³Add one loaf of bread, one flatbread made with oil, and one wafer from the basket of unleavened bread that was presented to the LORD. ²⁴Place all of these in the hands of Aaron and his sons, and lift them as an uplifted offering in the LORD's presence. ²⁵Then take them from their hands and turn them into smoke by burning them on the altar with the entirely burned offering as a soothing smell in the LORD's presence. It is a food gift for the LORD.

²⁶Take the breast of the ram for Aaron's ordination and lift it as an uplifted offering in the LORD's presence. It will be your portion. ²⁷Make holy the breast that was lifted for the uplifted offering and the thigh that was raised for the gift offering from the ram for the ordination. They belong to Aaron and his sons. ²⁸Those parts will be given to Aaron and his sons from the Israelites as a permanent provision, because they

are a gift offering. They will be a gift offering from the Israelites, their gift offering to the LORD from their well-being sacrifices.

29 Aaron's holy clothes should be passed on to his sons after him. His sons should be anointed in them and ordained in them. 30 The son who is priest in his place should wear them seven days when he comes into the meeting tent to minister in the sanctuary. 31 Take the ram for the ordination and boil its meat in a holy place. 32 Aaron and his sons will eat the ram's meat and the bread that is in the basket at the meeting tent's entrance. 33 They alone should eat the food that was used to purify them, to ordain them, and to make them holy. No one else should eat it because it is holy. 34 If any meat for the ordination or any of the bread is left over until morning, then you should burn the leftovers with fire. It shouldn't be eaten because it's holy.

35 Treat Aaron and his sons just as I have commanded you. Ordain them for seven days. 36 Every day you should offer a bull as a purification offering for reconciliation. You should remove the sin from the altar through a ritual of reconciliation, and you should anoint the altar to make it holy. 37 Seven days you should perform the ritual of reconciliation for the altar and make it holy. In this way, the altar will become most holy, and whatever touches the altar will also become holy.

Instructions for daily entirely burned offerings

38 Now this is what you should offer on the altar: two one-year-old lambs regularly every day. 39 Offer one lamb in the morning and offer the other lamb at twilight. 40 With the first lamb, add one-tenth of a measure of the high-quality flour mixed with a quarter of a hin[t] of oil from crushed olives and a quarter of a hin of wine for a drink offering. 41 With the second lamb offered at twilight, again include a grain offering and its drink offering as in the morning as a soothing smell, a gift offering for the LORD. 42 This should be the regular entirely burned offering in every generation at the meeting tent's entrance in the LORD's presence. There I will meet with you, and there I will speak to you. 43 I will meet with the Israelites there, and it will be made holy by my glorious presence. 44 I will make the meeting tent and the altar holy. Likewise, I will make Aaron and his sons holy to serve me as priests. 45 I will be at home among the Israelites, and I will be their God. 46 They will know that I am the LORD their God, who brought them out of the land of Egypt so that I could make a home among them. I am the LORD their God.

Instructions for the incense altar

30 Make an acacia-wood altar for burning incense. 2 The altar should be square, eighteen inches long and eighteen inches wide. It should be three feet high. Its horns should be permanently attached. 3 Cover the altar with pure gold, including its top, all its sides, and its horns. You should also make a gold molding all around it. 4 Make two gold rings and attach them under the molding on two opposite sides of the altar. They will house the poles used to carry the altar. 5 Make acacia-wood poles and cover them with gold. 6 Place the incense altar in front of the veil that hangs before the chest containing the covenant, in front of the cover that is on top of the covenant document where I will meet with you. 7 Aaron will burn sweet-smelling incense on the incense altar every morning when he takes care of the lamps. 8 And again when Aaron lights the lamps at twilight, he will burn incense. It should be a regular incense offering in the LORD's presence in every generation. 9 Don't offer the wrong incense on the altar or an entirely burned offering or a grain offering. Don't pour a drink offering on it. 10 Once a year Aaron should perform a ritual of reconciliation on its horns with the blood of the purification offering for reconciliation. Once a year in every generation he should perform a ritual of reconciliation at the altar. It is most holy to the LORD.

[t] One hin is approximately one gallon.

Census and compensation

[11]The LORD spoke to Moses: [12]When you take a census of the Israelites to count them, each of them should pay compensation for their life to the LORD when they are counted. Then no plague will descend on them when they are counted. [13]Every one who is counted should pay a half shekel according to the official shekel of the sanctuary (the shekel is twenty gerahs). The half shekel is a gift offering to the LORD. [14]Every one who is counted, from 20 years old and above, should present a gift offering to the LORD. [15]When you bring this gift offering to the LORD to pay compensation for your lives, the rich shouldn't give more and the poor shouldn't give less than the half shekel. [16]Take the compensation money from the Israelites and use it to support the service of the meeting tent. It will serve for the Israelites as a reminder in the LORD's presence of the compensation paid for your lives.

Instructions for the washbasin

[17]The LORD spoke to Moses: [18]Make a copper basin for washing along with its copper stand. Put it between the meeting tent and the altar, and put water in it. [19]Aaron and his sons will use it to wash their hands and their feet. [20]When they go into the meeting tent or approach the altar to minister and to offer a food gift to the LORD, they must wash with water so that they don't die. [21]They must wash their hands and their feet so that they don't die. This will be

[u]One hin is approximately one gallon.

a permanent regulation for them, for Aaron and his descendants in every generation.

Instructions for oil and incense

[22]The LORD spoke to Moses: [23]Now take for yourself high-quality spices: five hundred weight of solid myrrh; half as much of sweet-smelling cinnamon, that is, two hundred fifty; two hundred fifty weight of sweet-smelling cane; [24]five hundred of cassia—measured by the sanctuary shekel— and a hin[u] of olive oil. [25]Prepare a holy anointing oil, blending them like a skilled perfume maker to produce the holy anointing oil. [26]Use it to anoint the meeting tent, the chest containing the covenant, [27]the table and all its equipment, the lampstand and its equipment, the incense altar, [28]the altar for entirely burned offerings and all its equipment, and the washbasin with its stand. [29]Make them holy so that they may be perfectly holy. Whatever touches them will become holy. [30]Then anoint Aaron and his sons and make them holy to serve me as priests. [31]Say to the Israelites: This will be my holy anointing oil in every generation. [32]Don't allow anyone else to use this oil. Don't make another oil like it by using the same formula. This oil is holy, and you should regard it as holy. [33]Whoever blends an oil like it or whoever uses the oil on someone else will be cut off from the people.

[34]The LORD said to Moses: Take an equal amount of each of these spices: gum resin,

INCENSE

Incense is a material made of spices, gum, aromatic wood, or other perfumed substances burned to produce a fragrant smoke. Incense refers both to the aromatic substance to be burned and to the fragrant odor that results. In Israel and its neighboring cultures, the burning of incense was a cultic practice associated with sacrifice, offering, and worship. The burning of incense was also associated with prayer (Ps 141:2; Luke 1:10; Rev 5:8; 8:3-4). Incense, like spice, was a valuable trade commodity (Rev 18:11-13).

onycha, galbanum, and pure frankincense. [35]Like a skilled perfume maker, carefully blend them together and make incense, seasoned with salt, pure and holy. [36]Beat some of it into a fine powder and put part of it in front of the covenant document in the meeting tent where I will meet with you. You should regard it as perfectly holy. [37]When you make incense according to this formula, you shouldn't make any of it for your own use. You should regard it as holy to the LORD. [38]Whoever makes incense with this same formula to enjoy its fragrance will be cut off from the people.

Construction leaders: Bezalel and Oholiab

31 The LORD spoke to Moses: [2]Look, I have chosen Bezalel, Uri's son and Hur's grandson from the tribe of Judah. [3]I have filled him with the divine spirit, with skill, ability, and knowledge for every kind of work. [4]He will be able to create designs; do metalwork in gold, silver, and copper; [5]cut stones for setting; carve wood; and do every kind of work. [6]I have also appointed with him Oholiab, Ahisamach's son from the tribe of Dan. To all who are skillful, I have given the skill to make everything that I have commanded you: [7]the meeting tent, the chest containing the covenant, the cover that is on top of it, all the tent's furnishings, [8]the table and its equipment, the pure lampstand with all its equipment, the incense altar, [9]the altar for entirely burned offerings with all its equipment, the washbasin with its stand, [10]the woven clothing, the holy clothes for Aaron the priest and for his sons for their service as priests, [11]the anointing oil, and the sweet-smelling incense for the sanctuary. They will do just as I have commanded you.

Instructions for keeping the Sabbath

[12]The LORD said to Moses: [13]Tell the Israelites: "Be sure to keep my sabbaths, because the Sabbath is a sign between me and you in every generation so you will know that I am the LORD who makes you holy.

[14]Keep the Sabbath, because it is holy for you. Everyone who violates the Sabbath will be put to death. Whoever does any work on the Sabbath, that person will be cut off from the people. [15]Do your work for six days. But the seventh day is a Sabbath of complete rest that is holy to the LORD. Whoever does any work on the Sabbath day will be put to death. [16]The Israelites should keep the Sabbath. They should observe the Sabbath in every generation as a covenant for all time. [17]It is a sign forever between me and the Israelites that in six days the LORD made the heavens and the earth, and on the seventh day the LORD rested and was refreshed."

[18]When God finished speaking with Moses on Mount Sinai, God gave him the two covenant tablets, the stone tablets written by God's finger.

Worshipping the gold bull calf

32 The people saw that Moses was taking a long time to come down from the mountain. They gathered around Aaron and said to him, "Come on! Make us gods[v] who can lead us. As for this man Moses who brought us up out of the land of Egypt, we don't have a clue what has happened to him."

[2]Aaron said to them, "All right, take out the gold rings from the ears of your wives, your sons, and your daughters, and bring them to me." [3]So all the people took out the gold rings from their ears and brought them to Aaron. [4]He collected them and tied them up in a cloth.[w] Then he made a metal image of a bull calf, and the people declared, "These are your gods, Israel, who brought you up out of the land of Egypt!"

[5]When Aaron saw this, he built an altar in front of the calf. Then Aaron announced, "Tomorrow will be a festival to the LORD!" [6]They got up early the next day and offered up entirely burned offerings and brought well-being sacrifices. The people sat down to eat and drink and then got up to celebrate.

[7]The LORD spoke to Moses: "Hurry up and go down! Your people, whom you

---

[v]Or *a god* [w]Or *formed them into a mold* or *engraved them with a stylus*

brought up out of the land of Egypt, are ruining everything! [8]They've already abandoned the path that I commanded. They have made a metal bull calf for themselves. They've bowed down to it and offered sacrifices to it and declared, 'These are your gods, Israel, who brought you up out of the land of Egypt!'" [9]The LORD said to Moses, "I've been watching these people, and I've seen how stubborn they are. [10]Now leave me alone! Let my fury burn and devour them. Then I'll make a great nation out of you."

[11]But Moses pleaded with the LORD his God, "LORD, why does your fury burn against your own people, whom you brought out of the land of Egypt with great power and amazing force? [12]Why should the Egyptians say, 'He had an evil plan to take the people out and kill them in the mountains and so wipe them off the earth'? Calm down your fierce anger. Change your mind about doing terrible things to your own people. [13]Remember Abraham, Isaac, and Israel, your servants, whom you yourself promised, 'I'll make your descendants as many as the stars in the sky. And I've promised to give your descendants this whole land to possess for all time.'" [14]Then the LORD changed his mind about the terrible things he said he would do to his people.

[15]Moses then turned around and came down the mountain. He carried the two covenant tablets in his hands. The tablets were written on both sides, front and back.

[16]The tablets were God's own work. What was written there was God's own writing inscribed on the tablets. [17]When Joshua heard the noise of the people as they shouted, he said to Moses, "It sounds like war in the camp."

[18]But Moses said,

"It isn't the sound of a victory song.

It isn't the sound of a song of defeat.

The sound of party songs is what I hear."

[19]When he got near the camp and saw the bull calf and the dancing, Moses was furious. He hurled the tablets down and shattered them in pieces at the foot of the mountain. [20]He took the calf that they had made and burned it in a fire. Then he ground it down to crushed powder, scattered it on the water, and made the Israelites drink it.

[21]Moses said to Aaron, "What did these people do to you that you led them to commit such a terrible sin?"

[22]Aaron replied, "Don't get angry with me, sir. You know yourself that these people are out of control.[x] [23]They said to me, 'Make us gods who can lead us. As for this man Moses who brought us up out of the land of Egypt, we don't have a clue what has happened to him.' [24]So I said to them, 'Whoever has gold, take it off!' So they gave it to me, I threw it into the fire, and out came this bull calf!"

[25]Moses saw that the people were out of control because Aaron had let them get out of control, making them an easy

---

[x]Sam; MT *evil*

GOLD CALF

Ancient Near Eastern bull and calf icons were used as symbols of fertility or war. Bull icons were dedicated to El, the chief god of the Canaanites. Icons were also used as pedestals, with a god astride them or with no god visible. The biblical texts associated with the story of the gold calf (Exod 32; Deut 9; 1 Kgs 11–12; Hosea) reflect diverse political and religious interests in the centuries following the division of Solomon's kingdom (ca. 920 BCE), possibly including differences between followers of Moses and those of Aaron. Traditional interpreters have long considered the episode as a sign of the Israelites' betrayal of the covenant.

target for their enemies. ²⁶So Moses stood at the camp's gate and said, "Whoever is on the LORD's side, come to me!" All the Levites gathered around him. ²⁷Moses said to them, "This is what the LORD, Israel's God, says: Each of you, strap on your sword! Go back and forth from one end of the camp to the other. Each of you, kill your brother, your friend, and your neighbor!" ²⁸The Levites did as Moses commanded. About three thousand people were killed that day. ²⁹Moses said, "Today you've been ordained to the LORD, each one of you at the cost of a son or a brother. Today you've gained a special blessing for yourselves."

³⁰The next day Moses said to the people, "You've committed a terrible sin. So now I will go up to the LORD. Maybe I can arrange reconciliation on account of your sin." ³¹So Moses went back to the LORD and said, "Oh, what a terrible sin these people have committed! They made for themselves gods[y] of gold. ³²But now, please forgive their sin! And if not, then wipe me out of your scroll that you've written."

³³But the LORD said to Moses, "The ones I'll wipe out of my scroll are those who sinned against me. ³⁴Now go and lead the people to the place I described to you. My messenger here will go in front of you. When the day of reckoning comes, I'll count their sin against them." ³⁵Then the LORD sent a plague on the people because of what they did with the bull calf that Aaron made.

The LORD: "I can't go"

33 The LORD said to Moses, "Go and leave this place, you and the people whom you brought up out of the land of Egypt. Go to the land I promised to Abraham, Isaac, and Jacob when I said, 'I'll give it to your descendants.' ²I'll send a messenger before you. I'll drive out the Canaanites, the Amorites, the Hittites, the Perizzites, the Hivites, and the Jebusites. ³Go to this land full of milk and honey. But I won't go up with you because I would end up destroying you along the way since you are a stubborn people."

⁴When the people heard the bad news, they were sorry. No one put on any jewelry, ⁵because the LORD had said to Moses, "Tell the Israelites, 'You are a stubborn people. If I were to go up with you even for a single moment, I would destroy you. So now take off your jewelry, while I figure out what to do with you.'" ⁶So after leaving Mount Horeb the Israelites rid themselves of their jewelry.

Speaking with the LORD at the meeting tent

⁷Moses took the tent and pitched it outside the camp, far away from the camp. He called it the meeting tent. Everyone who wanted advice from the LORD would go out to the meeting tent outside the camp. ⁸Whenever Moses went out to the tent, all the people would rise and stand at the entrance to their tents and watch Moses until he had gone into the tent. ⁹When Moses entered the tent, the column of cloud would come down and stand at the tent's entrance while the LORD talked with Moses. ¹⁰When all the people saw the column of cloud standing at the tent's entrance, they would all rise and then bow down at the entrances to their tents. ¹¹In this way the LORD used to speak to Moses face-to-face, like two people talking to each other. Then Moses would come back to the camp. But his young assistant Joshua, Nun's son, wouldn't leave the tent.

Moses pleads with God

¹²Moses said to the LORD, "Look, you've been telling me, 'Lead these people forward.' But you haven't told me whom you will send with me. Yet you've assured me, 'I know you by name and think highly of you.' ¹³Now if you do think highly of me, show me your ways so that I may know you and so that you may really approve of me. Remember too that this nation is your people."

¹⁴The LORD replied, "I'll go myself, and I'll help you."

¹⁵Moses replied, "If you won't go your-

---

[y] Or a god

self, don't make us leave here. ¹⁶Because how will anyone know that we have your special approval, both I and your people, unless you go with us? Only that distinguishes us, me and your people, from every other people on the earth."

¹⁷The LORD said to Moses, "I'll do exactly what you've asked because you have my special approval, and I know you by name."

¹⁸Moses said, "Please show me your glorious presence."

¹⁹The LORD said, "I'll make all my goodness pass in front of you, and I'll proclaim before you the name, 'The LORD.' I will be kind to whomever I wish to be kind, and I will have compassion to whomever I wish to be compassionate. ²⁰But," the LORD said, "you can't see my face because no one can see me and live." ²¹The LORD said, "Here is a place near me where you will stand beside the rock. ²²As my glorious presence passes by, I'll set you in a gap in the rock, and I'll cover you with my hand until I've passed by. ²³Then I'll take away my hand, and you will see my back, but my face won't be visible."

A deeper revealing of God's character

34 The LORD said to Moses, "Cut two stone tablets like the first ones. I'll write on these tablets the words that were on the first tablets, which you broke into pieces. ²Get ready in the morning and come up to Mount Sinai. Stand there on top of the mountain in front of me. ³No one else can come up with you. Don't allow anyone even to be seen anywhere on the mountain. Don't even let sheep and cattle graze in front of the mountain." ⁴So Moses cut two stone tablets like the first ones. He got up early in the morning and climbed up Mount Sinai, just as the LORD had commanded him. He carried the two stone tablets in his hands. ⁵The LORD came down in the cloud and stood there with him, and proclaimed the name, "The LORD." ⁶The LORD passed in front of him and proclaimed:

"The LORD! The LORD!
a God who is
compassionate and merciful,

very patient,
full of great loyalty and faithfulness,
⁷showing great loyalty
to a thousand generations,
forgiving every kind of sin
and rebellion,
yet by no means clearing the guilty,
punishing for their parents' sins
their children and their grandchildren,
as well as the third
and the fourth generation."

⁸At once Moses bowed to the ground and worshipped. ⁹He said, "If you approve of me, my Lord, please go along with us.ᶻ Although these are stubborn people, forgive our guilt and our sin and take us as your own possession."

Renewing the broken covenant

¹⁰The LORD said: I now make a covenant. In front of all your people, I'll perform dramatic displays of power that have never been done before anywhere on earth or in any nation. All the people who are around you will see what the LORD does, because I will do an awesome thing with you.

¹¹Be sure to obey what I command you today. I'm about to drive out before you the Amorites, the Canaanites, the Hittites, the Perizzites, the Hivites, and the Jebusites. ¹²Be careful that you don't make a covenant with the inhabitants of the land to which you are going, or it will become a dangerous trap for you. ¹³You must tear down their altars, smash their sacred stone pillars, and cut down their sacred poles. ¹⁴You must not bow down to another god, because the LORD is passionate: the LORD's name means "a passionate God." ¹⁵Don't make a covenant with those who live in the land. When they prostitute themselves with their gods and sacrifice to their gods, they may invite you and you may end up eating some of the sacrifice. ¹⁶Then you might go and choose their daughters as wives for your sons. And their daughters who prostitute themselves with their gods might lead your sons to prostitute themselves with their gods.

ᶻLXX; MT adds *my Lord.*

¹⁷Don't make metal gods for yourself.

¹⁸Observe the Festival of Unleavened Bread. You should eat unleavened bread for seven days, as I commanded you, at the set time in the month of Abib,ᵃ because it was in the month of Abib that you came out of Egypt.

¹⁹Every first offspring is mine. That includes all your male livestock, the oldest offspring of cows and sheep. ²⁰But a donkey's oldest offspring you may ransom with a sheep. Or if you don't ransom it, you must break its neck. You should ransom all of your oldest sons.

No one should appear before me empty-handed.

²¹You should do your work for six days, but on the seventh day you should rest. Even during plowing or harvesttime you should rest. ²²You should observe the Festival of Weeks, for the early produce of the wheat harvest, and the Gathering Festival at the end of the year. ²³All your males should appear three times a year before the LORD God, Israel's God. ²⁴I will drive out nations before you and extend your borders. No one will desire and try to take your land if you go up and appear before the LORD your God three times a year.

²⁵Don't slaughter the blood of my sacrifice with anything leavened. The sacrifice of the Passover Festival shouldn't be left over until the morning.

²⁶Bring the best of the early produce of your farmland to the LORD your God's temple.

Don't boil a young goat in its mother's milk.

²⁷The LORD said to Moses: "Write down these words because by these words I hereby make a covenant with you and with Israel." ²⁸Moses was there with the LORD forty days and forty nights. He didn't eat any bread or drink any water. He wrote on the tablets the words of the covenant, the ten words.

Moses' brightly shining face

²⁹Moses came down from Mount Sinai. As he came down from the mountain with the two covenant tablets in his hand, Moses didn't realize that the skin of his face shone brightly because he had been talking with God. ³⁰When Aaron and all the Israelites saw the skin of Moses' face shining brightly, they were afraid to come near him. ³¹But Moses called them closer. So Aaron and all the leaders of the community came back to him, and Moses spoke with them. ³²After that, all the Israelites came near as well, and Moses commanded them everything that the LORD had spoken with him on Mount Sinai. ³³When Moses finished speaking with them, he put a veil over his face. ³⁴Whenever Moses went into the LORD's presence to speak with him, Moses would take the veil off until he came out again. When Moses came out and told the Israelites what he had been commanded, ³⁵the Israelites would see that the skin of Moses' face was shining brightly. So Moses would put the veil on his face again until the next time he went in to speak with the LORD.

35 Moses gathered together the whole Israelite community and said to them: These are the things that the LORD has commanded you to do:

Instructions for the Sabbath

²Do your work for six days, but the seventh day should be holy to you, a Sabbath of complete rest for the LORD. Whoever does any work on the Sabbath will be put to death. ³Don't start a fire in any of your homes on the Sabbath day.

Preparing to build the dwelling

⁴Moses said to the whole Israelite community, This is what the LORD has commanded: ⁵Collect gift offerings for the LORD from all of you. Whoever freely wants to give should bring the LORD's gift offerings: gold, silver, and copper; ⁶blue, purple, and deep red yarns; fine linen; goats' hair; ⁷rams' skins dyed red; beaded leather;ᵇ acacia wood; ⁸the oil for the light; spices for the anointing oil and for the sweet-smelling incense; ⁹gemstones; and gems for set-

---

ᵃMarch–April, named Nisan after the exile　ᵇOr dolphin skins

ting in the priest's vest[c] and in the priest's chest pendant.

[10]All of you who are skilled in crafts should come forward and make everything that the LORD has commanded: [11]the dwelling, its tent and its covering, its clasps, its boards, its bars, its posts, and its bases, [12]the chest with its poles and its cover, the veil for a screen, [13]the table with its poles and all its equipment, the bread of the presence, [14]the lampstand for light with its equipment and its lamps, the oil for the light, [15]the incense altar with its poles, the anointing oil and the sweet-smelling incense, the entrance screen for the dwelling's entrance, [16]the altar for entirely burned offerings with its copper grate, its poles, and all its equipment, the washbasin with its stand, [17]the courtyard's drapes, its posts, and its bases, and the screen for the courtyard gate, [18]the dwelling's tent pegs and the courtyard's tent pegs, and their cords, [19]the woven clothing for ministering in the sanctuary, and the holy clothes for Aaron the priest and his sons for their service as priests.

Gifts for building the dwelling

[20]The whole Israelite community left Moses. [21]Everyone who was excited and eager to participate brought the LORD's gift offerings to be used for building the meeting tent and all its furnishings and for the holy clothes. [22]Both men and women came forward. Everyone who was eager to participate brought pins, earrings, rings, and necklaces, all sorts of gold objects. Ev-

eryone raised an uplifted offering of gold to the LORD. [23]And everyone who had blue or purple or deep red yarn or fine linen or goats' hair or rams' skins dyed red or beaded leather brought them. [24]Everyone who could make a gift offering of silver or copper brought it as the LORD's gift offering. Everyone who had acacia wood that could be used in any kind of building work brought it. [25]All the skilled women spun cloth with their hands, and brought what they had spun in blue and purple and deep red yarns and fine linen. [26]All the women who were eager to use their skill spun the goats' hair. [27]The chiefs brought gemstones and gems to be set in the priest's vest and the chest pendant, [28]spices and oil for light and for the anointing oil, and for the sweet-smelling incense. [29]All the Israelite men and women who were eager to contribute something for the work that the LORD had commanded Moses to do brought it as a spontaneous gift to the LORD.

Moses introduces Bezalel and Oholiab

[30]Then Moses said to the Israelites: "Look, the LORD has chosen Bezalel, Uri's son and Hur's grandson from the tribe of Judah. [31]The LORD has filled him with the divine spirit that will give him skill, ability, and knowledge for every kind of work. [32]He will be able to create designs, do metalwork in gold, silver, and copper, [33]cut stones for setting, carve wood, do every kind of creative work, [34]and have the ability to teach others. Both he and Oholiab, Ahisamach's son from the tribe of Dan, [35]have been

[c]Heb ephod

COVENANT DWELLING

The portable tent sanctuary built by the people of Israel in the wilderness of Sinai according to instructions God gave to Moses on Mount Sinai after God made a covenant with Israel (Exod 25–31; 35–40). Together with its priests and its rituals, the covenant dwelling is the original and purest model for worship in the OT. Along with the temple in Jerusalem, the covenant dwelling has shaped the worship of Judaism and Christianity.

given the skill to do every kind of work done by a gem cutter or a designer or a needleworker in blue, purple, and deep red yarns and in fine linen or a weaver or anyone else doing work or creating designs.

36 "Let Bezalel, Oholiab, and every other skilled worker whom the LORD has given skill, ability, and knowledge for the work of building the sanctuary do all that the LORD has commanded."

² Moses then called together Bezalel, Oholiab, and every skilled person whom the LORD had given skill and who was eager to come and do the work. ³ Moses gave them all the gift offerings that the Israelites had contributed to the work on the sanctuary. They kept bringing him spontaneous gifts, morning after morning.

⁴ Finally, all the skilled workers building the sanctuary left their work that they were doing one by one to come ⁵ and say to Moses, "The people are contributing way too much material for doing the work that the LORD has commanded us to do."

⁶ So Moses issued a command that was proclaimed throughout the camp: "Every man and woman should stop making gift offerings for the sanctuary project." So the people stopped bringing anything more ⁷ because what they had already brought was more than enough to do all the work.

Construction of the dwelling

⁸ All the skilled workers made the dwelling out of ten curtains of fine twisted linen and blue, purple, and deep red yarns, with figures of winged heavenly creatures worked into their design. ⁹ Each curtain was forty-two feet long and six feet wide. All the curtains were the same size.

¹⁰ They joined five of the curtains to each other and joined the other five curtains to each other. ¹¹ They made loops of blue thread on the edge of the outer curtain of the first set. They did the same on the edge of the outer curtain of the second set. ¹² They made fifty loops on the one curtain and fifty loops on the outer curtain that was in the second set. The loops were opposite each other. ¹³ They also made fifty gold clasps, and they used the clasps to join the

curtains to each other so that the dwelling was one whole structure.

¹⁴ They also made curtains of goats' hair for a tent over the dwelling. They made eleven curtains. ¹⁵ Each curtain was forty-five feet long and each curtain six feet wide. All eleven curtains were the same size. ¹⁶ They joined five curtains together and the six other curtains together. ¹⁷ They made fifty loops on the edge of the outer curtain of the one set and fifty loops on the edge of the other set of curtains. ¹⁸ They made fifty copper clasps to join the tent together so that it would be one whole structure. ¹⁹ They also made a covering for the tent of rams' skins dyed red and an outer covering of beaded leather.

²⁰ Then they made acacia-wood boards to stand upright as a frame for the dwelling. ²¹ Each board was fifteen feet long and twenty-seven inches wide. ²² Each board had two pegs for joining them to each other. They did this for all the dwelling's boards. ²³ They made twenty boards for the dwelling's southern side. ²⁴ They made forty silver bases under the twenty boards, with two bases under the first board for its two pegs, two bases under the next board for its two pegs, and so on. ²⁵ For the dwelling's other side on the north, they made twenty boards ²⁶ and forty silver bases, two bases under the first board, two bases under the next board, and so on. ²⁷ For the back of the dwelling on the west, they made six boards. ²⁸ They made two additional boards for the dwelling's rear corners. ²⁹ They were spread out at the bottom but joined together at the top with one ring. In this way, these two boards formed the two corners. ³⁰ And so there were eight boards with their sixteen silver bases, with two bases under every board.

³¹ They also made acacia-wood bars: five for the boards on one side of the dwelling, ³² five bars for the boards on the other side of the dwelling, and five bars for the boards on the back wall of the dwelling on the west. ³³ They made the middle bar, which was halfway up the boards, run from one end to the other. ³⁴ They covered the boards with gold. They made gold rings to house the bars and covered the bars with gold.

³⁵ They made the veil of blue, purple, and deep red yarns and fine twisted linen, with figures of winged heavenly creatures worked into its design. ³⁶ They made for it four acacia-wood posts covered in gold with gold hooks and cast four silver bases for them. ³⁷ They made a screen for the entrance to the tent of blue, purple, and deep red yarns and fine twisted linen, decorated with needlework. ³⁸ They made its five posts with hooks. They covered their tops and bands with gold, but made their five bases out of copper.

Building the chest containing the covenant document

37 Bezalel made the chest of acacia wood. It was forty-five inches long, twenty-seven inches wide, and twenty-seven inches high. ²He covered the chest with pure gold inside and out, and made a gold molding all around it. ³He cast four gold rings for it and put them on its four feet, two rings on one side and two rings on the other. ⁴He made acacia-wood poles and covered them with gold. ⁵He put the poles into the rings on the chest's sides to use to carry the chest. ⁶He made a cover for the chest out of pure gold, forty-five inches long and twenty-seven inches wide.

⁷He made two winged heavenly creatures of hammered gold for the two ends of the cover, ⁸one winged heavenly creature at one end and one winged heavenly creature at the other. He placed the winged heavenly creatures at the cover's two ends. ⁹The winged heavenly creatures spread out their wings above, shielding the cover with their wings. The winged heavenly creatures faced each other toward the cover's center.

Constructing the table and lampstand

¹⁰He also made the table of acacia wood, three feet long, eighteen inches wide, and twenty-seven inches high. ¹¹He covered it with pure gold and made a gold molding all around it. ¹²He made a frame around it that was four inches wide and gold molding around the frame. ¹³He made four gold rings for the table. He fastened the rings to the four corners at its four legs. ¹⁴The rings that housed the poles used for carrying the table were close to the frame. ¹⁵He made the poles used to carry the table out of acacia wood, and he covered them with gold. ¹⁶He made the containers of pure gold that were to be on the table: its plates, dishes, bowls, and jars for pouring drink offerings.

LAMPSTAND

When lamplight was needed above ground level, ceramic stands were sometimes used to hold lamps. These stands were typically hollow cylinders, approximately three to five inches in diameter and up to a foot high, with flaring bases. They are similar to stands used for holding incense dishes and other vessels without flat bases. Ceramic lampstands were probably uncommon household items since few have been found in archaeological digs. Lamps in most houses would have been elevated by placing them in niches in the stone walls.

Accordingly, the use of *lampstand* in the Bible refers most often to the single golden menorah of the covenant dwelling or the ten of the Jerusalem temple (Exod 25; 1 Kgs 7:49; cf. Heb 9:2). Building on the symbolism of the golden menorahs of the OT and perhaps suggesting a temple setting, the NT (in the visions of Rev 1 and 2) refers to seven golden lampstands representing the seven churches and also to two golden lampstands (Rev 11:4; cf. Zech 4:2-3).

[17] He also made the lampstand of pure, hammered gold. The lampstand's base, branches, cups, flowers, and petals were all attached to it. [18] It had six branches growing out from its sides, three branches on one side of the lampstand and three branches on the other side of the lampstand. [19] One branch had three cups shaped like almond blossoms, each with a flower and petals, and the next branch also had three cups shaped like almond blossoms, each with a flower and petals. A total of six branches grew out of the lampstand. [20] In addition, on the lampstand itself there were four cups shaped like almond blossoms, each with its flower and petals. [21] There was a flower attached under the first pair of branches, a flower attached under the next pair of branches, and a flower attached under the last pair of branches. [22] Their flowers and their branches were attached to it. The whole lampstand was one piece of pure hammered gold. [23] He made its seven lamps and its tongs and its fire pans out of pure gold. [24] He made the lampstand and all its equipment from pure gold weighing one kikkar.

Making the incense altar, incense, and oil

[25] He made the incense altar out of acacia wood. The altar was square, eighteen inches long by eighteen inches wide. It was three feet high, and its horns were permanently attached. [26] He covered it with pure gold, including its top, all its sides, and its horns. He also made a gold molding all around it. [27] He made two gold rings, and he attached them under the molding on two opposite sides of the altar. They housed the poles used to carry it. [28] He made the poles of acacia wood, and he covered them with gold.

[29] He also made the holy anointing oil and the pure sweet-smelling incense like a skilled perfume maker.

Making the altar for entirely burned offerings

38 He made the altar for entirely burned offerings out of acacia wood. The altar was square, seven and a half feet long and seven and a half feet wide. It was four and a half feet high. [2] He made horns for it, one horn on each of its four corners. Its horns were attached to the altar, and he covered it with copper. [3] He made all the altar's equipment: the pails, the shovels, the bowls, the meat forks, and the trays. He made all its equipment out of copper. [4] He made a grate for the altar of copper mesh underneath its bottom edge and extending halfway up to the middle of the altar. [5] He made four rings for each of the four corners of the copper grate to house the poles. [6] He made the poles out of acacia wood, and he covered them with copper. [7] He put the poles through the rings so that the poles were on the two sides of the altar when it was carried. He made the altar with planks but hollow inside.

[8] He made the copper washbasin with its copper stand from the copper mirrors among the ranks of women assigned to the meeting tent's entrance.

Constructing the dwelling's plaza

[9] He also set up the courtyard. The courtyard's south side had drapes of fine twisted linen stretching one hundred fifty feet [10] with twenty posts, twenty copper bases, and silver hooks and bands for the posts. [11] Likewise the north side stretched one hundred fifty feet, with twenty posts, twenty copper bases, and silver hooks and bands for the posts. [12] On the west side the drapes stretched seventy-five feet, with their ten posts, their ten bases, and silver hooks and bands for the posts. [13] The front side facing east was seventy-five feet. [14] There were twenty-two and a half feet of drapes on one side with three posts and three bases for them. [15] Likewise, there were twenty-two and a half feet of drapes on the other side of the plaza's gate with three posts and three bases for them. [16] All the drapes around the courtyard were made of fine twisted linen. [17] The bases for the posts were made of copper, but the hooks for the posts and their bands were made of silver. The tops of the posts were covered with silver, and all the posts surrounding the courtyard had silver bands. [18] The screen for the gate into the

courtyard was made with blue, purple, and deep red yarns and fine twisted linen, decorated with needlework. It was thirty feet long and, along the width of it, seven and a half feet high, corresponding to the courtyard's drapes. ¹⁹It had four posts, their four copper bases, their silver hooks, and their tops and bands covered with silver. ²⁰All the tent pegs for the dwelling and for the courtyard all around were made of copper.

A listing of materials used

²¹These are the accounts of the dwelling, the covenant dwelling, that were recorded at Moses' instructions. They are the work of the Levites, under the direction of Ithamar, Aaron the priest's son. ²²Bezalel, Uri's son and Hur's grandson from the tribe of Judah, made everything that the LORD had commanded Moses to make. ²³Working with Bezalel was Oholiab, Ahisamach's son from the tribe of Dan, who was a gem cutter, a designer, and a needleworker in blue, purple, and deep red yarns and in fine linen.

²⁴The total amount of the gold that was used for construction of the whole sanctuary, gold from the uplifted offerings, was twenty-nine kikkars and seven hundred thirty shekels in weight, measured by the sanctuary shekel. ²⁵The silver from the community census totaled one hundred kikkars and one thousand seven hundred seventy-five shekels in weight, measured by the sanctuary shekel. ²⁶They gave a beqa per person (that is, half a shekel, measured by the sanctuary shekel) for everyone who was counted in the census, 20 years old and above, 603,550 men. ²⁷One hundred kikkars of silver were used to cast the bases for the sanctuary and the bases for the veil, one hundred bases from one hundred kikkars of silver, one kikkar for every base. ²⁸He used one thousand seven hundred seventy-five shekels of silver[d] to make the hooks for the posts, cover their tops, and make bands for them. ²⁹The amount of copper from the uplifted offering was seventy kikkars and two thousand four hundred shekels in weight. ³⁰He used it to make the bases for the meeting tent's entrance, the copper altar, its copper grate, and all the altar's equipment, ³¹the bases all around the courtyard, and the bases for the courtyard's gate, all the dwelling's tent pegs, and all the tent pegs used around the courtyard.

Making the priests' clothing

39 They used the blue, purple, and deep red yarns to make the woven clothing for those ministering as priests in the sanctuary. They made the holy clothes for Aaron as the LORD had commanded Moses.

²They made the vest[e] of gold, of blue, purple, and deep red yarns, and of fine twisted linen. ³They beat out thin sheets of gold and cut them into threads to work into designs among the blue, purple, and deep red yarns and the fine linen. ⁴They made shoulder pieces for it attached to its two edges so that they could be joined together. ⁵The vest's belt was attached to it and made in the same way of gold, of blue, purple, and deep red yarns, and of fine twisted linen, just as the LORD had commanded Moses.

⁶They prepared the gemstones by mounting them in gold settings and engraving on them the names of Israel's sons, like an official seal is engraved. ⁷The stones were attached to the vest's shoulder pieces as reminder stones for the Israelites, just as the LORD had commanded Moses.

⁸They made the embroidered chest pendant in the style of the vest, using gold, blue, purple, and deep red yarns, and fine twisted linen. ⁹They made the chest pendant square and doubled, nine inches long and nine inches wide when doubled. ¹⁰They set in it four rows of gemstones. The first row was a row of carnelian, topaz, and emerald stones. ¹¹The second row was a turquoise, a sapphire, and a moonstone. ¹²The third row was a jacinth, an agate, and an amethyst. ¹³The fourth row was a beryl, an onyx, and a jasper. The settings around them were decorative gold. ¹⁴There were twelve stones with names corresponding to the names of Israel's sons. They were engraved like official seals, each with its name

---

[d]Heb lacks *shekels of silver*.   [e]Heb *ephod*

for the twelve tribes. ¹⁵They made chains of pure gold, twisted like cords, for the chest pendant. ¹⁶They made two gold settings and two gold rings. They attached the two rings to the two edges of the chest pendant. ¹⁷They attached the two gold cords to the two rings at the edges of the chest pendant. ¹⁸Then they fastened the two ends of the two cords to the two gold settings and attached them to the front of the vest's shoulder pieces. ¹⁹They made two gold rings, and they attached them to the two edges of the chest pendant, on its inside edge facing the vest. ²⁰They made two gold rings and fastened them on the front of the lower part of the two shoulder pieces of the vest, at its seam just above the vest's belt. ²¹The chest pendant was held in place by a blue cord binding its rings to the vest's rings so that the chest pendant rested on the vest's belt and didn't come loose from the vest, just as the LORD had commanded Moses.

²²They also made the vest's robe, woven completely in blue. ²³The opening of the robe in the middle of it was reinforced with a strong border so that it didn't tear. ²⁴On the robe's lower hem, they added pomegranates made of blue, purple, and deep red yarns and of fine twisted linen. ²⁵They also made pure gold bells and sewed the bells between the pomegranates, all around the robe's lower hem, ²⁶with a bell and a pomegranate alternating all around the lower hem of the robe that is used for ministering as a priest, just as the LORD had commanded Moses.

²⁷They also made the tunics woven out of fine linen for Aaron and his sons, ²⁸the turban of fine linen, the decorated turbans of fine linen, the linen undergarments of fine twisted linen, ²⁹the sashes of fine twisted linen, and of blue, purple, and crimson yarns, decorated with needlework, just as the LORD had commanded Moses.

³⁰They made the flower ornament for the holy crown out of pure gold. Like the engraving on an official seal, they engraved on it the saying "Holy to the LORD." ³¹They fastened to it a blue cord to tie it to the top of the turban, just as the LORD had commanded Moses.

Completion of dwelling construction

³²In this way all the work of the meeting tent dwelling was finished. The Israelites did everything just exactly as the LORD had commanded Moses. ³³Then they brought to Moses the dwelling, the tent, and all its equipment:

its clasps, its boards, its bars, its posts, and its bases,

³⁴the covering of rams' skins dyed red, the covering of beaded leather, and the veil for a screen,

³⁵the chest containing the covenant with its poles and the cover,

³⁶the table with all its equipment and the bread of the presence,

³⁷the pure lampstand with its lamps set on it and all its equipment, and the oil for the light,

³⁸the gold altar, the anointing oil, and the sweet-smelling incense,

the screen for the tent's entrance,

³⁹the copper altar and its copper grate, its poles, and all its equipment, the washbasin with its stand,

⁴⁰the courtyard's drapes, its posts, and its bases,

the screen for the plaza's gate, its cords, and its tent pegs,

and all the other equipment for the service of the dwelling, for the meeting tent,

⁴¹the woven clothes for ministering as priests in the sanctuary, the holy clothes for the priest Aaron and the clothes for his sons to serve as priests.

⁴²The Israelites did all of the work just as the LORD had commanded Moses. ⁴³When Moses saw that they in fact had done all the work exactly as the LORD had commanded, Moses blessed them.

Moses sets up the dwelling

40 The LORD spoke to Moses: ²Set up the meeting tent dwelling on the first day of the first month.^f ³Place the

^fMarch–April, Abib

chest containing the covenant inside the dwelling. Hide the chest from view with the veil. ⁴Bring in the table and arrange its items. Bring in the lampstand and set up its lamps. ⁵Place the gold altar for burning incense in front of the chest containing the covenant. Set up the screen at the dwelling's entrance. ⁶Put the altar for entirely burned offerings in front of the entrance to the meeting tent dwelling. ⁷Put the washbasin between the meeting tent and the altar and put water in it. ⁸Set up the courtyard all around. Hang up the screen at the courtyard gate. ⁹Then take the anointing oil and anoint the dwelling and everything in it. Make holy the dwelling and all its equipment, and it will be holy. ¹⁰Anoint the altar for entirely burned offerings and all its equipment. Make the altar holy, and the altar will be most holy. ¹¹Anoint the washbasin with its stand and make it holy.

¹²Then bring Aaron and his sons to the meeting tent's entrance and wash them with water. ¹³Dress Aaron in the holy clothes. Anoint him and make him holy so that he may serve me as priest. ¹⁴Then bring his sons and dress them in tunics. ¹⁵Anoint them like you anointed their father so that they may serve me as priests. Their anointing is to the priesthood for all time in every generation.

¹⁶Moses did everything exactly as the LORD had commanded him. ¹⁷In the first month in the second year, on the first day of the month, the dwelling was set up. ¹⁸Moses set up the dwelling. He laid out its bases. He set up its boards, inserted its bars, and raised up its posts. ¹⁹He spread the tent out over the dwelling, and he put the covering of the tent over it, just as the LORD had commanded Moses. ²⁰He took the covenant document and placed it inside the chest. He put the poles on the chest, and he set the cover on top of the chest. ²¹He brought the chest into the dwelling. He set up the veil as a screen to hide from view the chest containing the covenant,

just as the LORD had commanded Moses. ²²He placed the table in the meeting tent, on the north side of the dwelling, outside the veil. ²³He set the bread in its proper place on the table in the LORD's presence, just as the LORD had commanded Moses. ²⁴He put the lampstand in the meeting tent, opposite the table on the south side of the dwelling. ²⁵He set up the lamps in the LORD's presence, just as the LORD had commanded Moses. ²⁶He put the gold altar in the meeting tent in front of the veil. ²⁷He burned sweet-smelling incense on it, just as the LORD had commanded Moses. ²⁸He also set up the screen at the entrance to the dwelling. ²⁹He placed the altar for entirely burned offerings at the entrance to the meeting tent dwelling. He offered the entirely burned offering and the grain offering on it, just as the LORD had commanded Moses. ³⁰He put the washbasin between the meeting tent and the altar, and put water in it for washing. ³¹Moses, Aaron, and his sons used it to wash their hands and their feet. ³²Whenever they went into the meeting tent and whenever they approached the altar, they washed themselves, just as the LORD had commanded Moses. ³³He set up the courtyard around the dwelling and the altar, and he hung up the screen at the courtyard's gate.

God's presence fills the dwelling!

When Moses had finished all the work, ³⁴the cloud covered the meeting tent and the LORD's glorious presence filled the dwelling. ³⁵Moses couldn't enter the meeting tent because the cloud had settled on it, and the LORD's glorious presence filled the dwelling. ³⁶Whenever the cloud rose from the dwelling, the Israelites would set out on their journeys. ³⁷But if the cloud didn't rise, then they didn't set out until the day it rose. ³⁸The LORD's cloud stayed over the dwelling during the day, with lightning in it at night, clearly visible to the whole household of Israel at every stage of their journey.

The book of Leviticus is the third of the five books of Moses. The name comes from the Vulgate, an early Latin translation. But the Vulgate title is based on the earlier Greek translation, the Septuagint. The Greek title means "The [Book] of the Levites" because it contains so much instruction of value to the priestly family of Israel, the Levites. The Hebrew name for the book is *Wayyikra*, after the opening phrase, "Then [the LORD] called [to Moses]."

THE PURPOSE OF THE BOOK

The purpose of Leviticus is to help the people of Israel be the holy people of God. God is holy, and God requires a people with a high level of holiness.

HISTORICAL BACKGROUND

The book of Leviticus, like much of Exodus before it, is set at the base of Mount Sinai. It continues the instructions of the Lord to Moses for the people of Israel.

The book of Exodus closes with the completion of the tent of dwelling. The Lord's presence indicated approval, for the glory of the Lord filled the dwelling. The instructions in Leviticus relate to the use of the dwelling place. It is God's home among the people of Israel. But it is also a sanctuary for worship and atonement. The regulations in Leviticus are intended to help the people live holy lives according to the covenant relationship.

In Leviticus God speaks to Moses from the tent of meeting, the place where God's presence is manifested and where God communicates with the people.

LITERARY BACKGROUND

According to tradition, the first five books of the Bible, including Leviticus, were written by Moses. There may be a core of materials in Leviticus from Moses. The current form of the book is probably an expansion on the basic Mosaic material.

Leviticus as it now stands is likely the result of priestly editors (P). These devout men were at work before and during the Babylonian Exile (about 650–550 BCE). They collected, preserved, edited, and arranged the ancient laws and traditions. Their purpose was to make certain that God's people never again aroused the wrath of the Lord against them by ignoring the call to be holy people.

The ritual regulations of Leviticus were followed during the Second Temple period (515 BCE to 70 CE). But they were viewed as having been in effect during the period of the tabernacle. They were understood as God's revelation to Moses at Mount Sinai.

THE CONTENT OF THE BOOK OF LEVITICUS

Chapters 1–7: These chapters contain laws and directions pertaining to sacrifices. Included here are directions for entirely burned offerings, grain offerings, well-being offerings, and purification offerings. Also included is a manual of priestly directions, describing the function of the priest in the sacrifice.

Chapters 8–9: In accordance with the instructions in Exodus 29, Aaron and his sons are consecrated priests. In chapter 9, Aaron offers official sacrifice.

Chapter 10: Nadab and Abihu, sons of Aaron, offer unauthorized fire to the Lord and are immediately killed. This injected piece of narrative serves to emphasize the importance of precise ritual.

Chapters 11–16: This section deals with laws of purification and reconciliation. It begins with a list of clean and unclean animals. Then follows a set of rules for purification of women after childbirth. Chapters 13 and 14 are concerned with the tests for skin disease, purification of the infection, and the treatment of those with incurable diseases, their clothes, and their homes. Chapter 15 is concerned with activities that result in ceremonial uncleanness: sexual intercourse, menstruation, and so forth. Chapter 16 gives a detailed description of the ceremonies of the Day of Reconciliation.

Chapters 17–26: This section is known as the Holiness Code, or simply as the H Code. The theme that runs through this section is *You shall be holy unto me*. In its present form, this code was probably written in the Babylonian Exile by a priest and intended for the layperson. It likely existed as an independent collection of laws until it was incorporated into the book.

The principle of holiness is partly ceremonial and partly moral. The author intends that Israel, as the chosen people, shall be set apart for the service of God and distinguished from all other peoples by the attribute of holiness. The code begins with laws concerning the slaughter of beasts and the prohibition of eating meat with blood. Incest and kindred impurities are forbidden.

Chapter 19 contains some of the loftiest ethical precepts in the Old Testament. Provision is made for charity for the poor and the immigrant. Also, there are laws regarding kindly treatment for employees. The famous expression *You shall love your neighbor as yourself* appears here. The ethic of the Ten Commandments is here given renewed expression.

Chapter 20 forbids Molech worship (that is, sacrifice of children). There follow laws against unchastity; general rules regarding cleanness; general precepts for the priests; laws concerning religious festivals; and the law of the sabbatical year and the year of jubilee. The taking of interest is forbidden and provision is made for the redemption of servants.

The concluding chapter (chapter 26) lists the blessings that will be showered on Israel if God's words are obeyed. Then follows a list of the curses that will result from disobedience. In conclusion, mercy is promised to the repentant sinner.

The H Code is put in a homiletic setting purporting to be a sermon of Moses. The author of the H code regarded the calamity of exile in 586 BCE as resulting from the wrong kind of worship. In order to avoid future calamity, he sets about to fix the ritual.

The conception of holiness in H is derived largely from Ezekiel. The author retains many primitive rites, but at the same time he includes much that is best in the prophetic teaching.

Chapter 27: Laws concerning dedications and tithes.

THE CONCEPT OF GOD IN LEVITICUS

Leviticus teaches that everything in Israel belongs to God. God owns all land. God reserves only a small portion, that on which the temple stands. The Israelite is permitted to use all other land, but he must pay taxes to God, that is, tithes of his crops to the clergy.

The principle of the sabbatical year and the jubilee year is likewise based on this conception of God as the possessor of all land. God owns all time. God allows the people to use time freely, but reserves a fraction of time, that is, the Sabbath and the festival days. It is a sin to take this time which God has reserved and use it for one's private business.

God owns all souls. God allows the parents to redeem the firstborn with an animal offering. Each man redeems his own soul by payment of one third of a shekel per year. Beyond this, the priests, by devoting themselves exclusively to the service of God, redeem all Israel. The conception of God in Leviticus is that of a supreme ruler, and Israel is a state within a state, a theocracy.

Because God is ruler, God must be paid taxes and fines. Sacrifices are both public and private. The public sacrifices are offered at appointed times as part of the official cult. Private sacrifices are offered both as taxes and as fines.

LEVITICUS AND THE NEW TESTAMENT

The teachings of Leviticus were an integral part of the world of Jesus. Religious Jews were intent on the correct observance of the Sabbath, ceremonial washings, keeping the set feasts, paying the temple tax, tithing, and the like. The Gospels testify to the controversies that arose between Jesus and other Jewish teachers over the meaning of such things.

Leviticus focuses upon sin, guilt, and reconciling sacrifices carried out by the Levitical priesthood. The New Testament writers understood the life and death of Jesus as the full realization of the purposes of Leviticus. Jesus was the once-and-for-all-time sufficient sacrifice for sin. His blood opened a way for believers into the most holy place, God's presence in heaven itself. And Christ was the true high priest. The connections between Christ and Leviticus are most clearly spelled out in the letter to the Hebrews.

LEVITICUS

1 Then the LORD called to Moses and said to him from the meeting tent, [2] Speak to the Israelites and say to them: When any of you present a livestock offering to the LORD, you can present it from either the herd or the flock.

The entirely burned offering

[3] If the offering is an entirely burned offering from the herd, you must present a flawless male, bringing it to the meeting tent's entrance for its acceptance before the LORD. [4] You must press your hand on the head of the entirely burned offering so that it will be accepted for you, to make reconciliation for you. [5] Then you will slaughter the bull before the LORD. Aaron's sons the priests will present the blood and toss it against every side of the altar at the meeting tent's entrance. [6] Then the entirely burned offering will be skinned and cut up into pieces. [7] The sons of Aaron the priest[a] will light the altar and

[a] Some Heb sources, Sam, LXX, Syr, and some Tg sources have *Aaron's sons, the priests*, as in 1:5, 8.

SACRIFICES AND OFFERINGS

The Priestly traditions provide the most detailed instructions concerning the sacrificial offerings, esp. Exodus 25–40; Leviticus; and Numbers 5; 15. The primary sacrifices are the entirely burned offering, the grain offering, the well-being offering, the purification offering, the ordination offering, and the compensation offering. The offerer must bring sacrifices and offerings to the correct altar; a priest must put the blood on the altar (grain offerings are exceptions) and burn the specified parts.

Jesus participated in or referred to temple sacrifices (Matt 8:1-4; 17:24-27; Mark 1:40-45; Luke 5:12-16), but argued that true purity was also related to inner beliefs (Mark 7:1-23; cf. Matt 15:1-20). Jesus' visit to Jerusalem near the end of his life disrupted the normal temple activities (Mark 11:15-19; 13:1-8).

The Gospels interpret the Last Supper in sacrificial terms. This very likely expresses the efforts of the early church to make sense of Jesus' death. His death did not bring the end; it was a sacrificial death on behalf of the world.

Paul's statements concerning sacrifice are for the most part limited to theological interpretations of the death of Christ (e.g., Gal 2:15-21; Rom 3:21-26; 5:18-21; 6:1-11). In Romans Paul states, "God displayed Jesus as the place of sacrifice where mercy is found by means of his blood" (3:25).

The writer of Hebrews approaches the matter in very different terms. The writer argues that God established a new covenant through the blood and death of Christ. Following his death, Jesus entered into the heavenly sanctuary, contrasted repeatedly with the earthly tent of the wilderness, and sat at the right side of God (1:3; 6:19-20; 9:1-28). God set up the heavenly sanctuary, of which the earthly one is but a sketch and a shadow (8:2-5). Jesus is high priest (4:14–5:10; 7:1-28) and makes a sacrifice of reconciliation for the sins of the people (2:17; 9:26). His sacrifice, unlike the repeated ones of the Israelite priests, was offered once (7:26-28).

lay wood on the fire. [8]Then Aaron's sons the priests will arrange the pieces, the head, and the fat on the wood that is on the altar fire, [9]but the animal's insides and lower legs must be washed with water. The priest will then completely burn all of it on the altar as an entirely burned offering, a food gift[b] of soothing smell to the LORD.

[10]If the offering is an entirely burned offering from the flock—whether sheep or goat—you must present a flawless male. [11]You must slaughter it on the north side of the altar before the LORD. Aaron's sons the priests will toss its blood against every side of the altar. [12]Once it has been cut into pieces, including the head and the fat, the priest will arrange these out on the wood that is on the altar fire, [13]but its insides and lower legs must be washed with water. Then the priest will present all of it and completely burn it on the altar. It is an entirely burned offering, a food gift of soothing smell to the LORD.

[14]If the offering for the LORD is an entirely burned offering from the birds, you can present your offering from the doves or pigeons. [15]The priest will bring it to the altar. He will tear off its head and completely burn it on the altar. Its blood will be drained against the side of the altar. [16]Then the priest will remove its throat along with its contents[c] and throw it by the east side of the altar, into the place for the ashes. [17]He will then tear the bird open by its wings, without splitting it. The priest will completely burn it on the altar, on the wood that is on the altar fire. It is an entirely burned offering, a food gift of soothing smell to the LORD.

The grain offering

2 When anyone presents a grain offering to the LORD, the offering must be of choice flour. They must pour oil on it and put frankincense on it, [2]then bring it to Aaron's sons, the priests. A priest will take a handful of its choice flour and oil, along with all of its frankincense, and will completely burn this token portion on the altar as a food gift of soothing smell to the LORD. [3]The rest of the grain offering belongs to Aaron and his sons as a most holy portion from the LORD's food gifts.

[4]When you present a grain offering baked in an oven, it must be of choice flour: unleavened flatbread mixed with oil or unleavened wafers spread with oil. [5]If your offering is grain prepared on a griddle, it must be of choice flour mixed with oil and it must be unleavened. [6]Crumble it into pieces and pour oil on it; it is a grain offering. [7]If your offering is grain prepared in a pan, it must be made of choice flour with oil. [8]You will bring the grain offering made in one of these ways to the LORD, presenting it to the priest, who will then bring it to the altar. [9]The priest will remove from the grain offering the token portion and completely burn it on the altar as a food gift of soothing smell to the LORD. [10]The rest of the grain offering belongs to Aaron and his sons as a most holy portion from the LORD's food gifts.

[11]No grain offering that you give to the LORD can be made with yeast. You must not completely burn any yeast or honey as a food gift for the LORD. [12]You can present those as first-choice offerings to the LORD, but they must not be entirely burned up on the altar as a soothing smell.

[13]You must season all your grain offerings with salt. Do not omit the salt of your God's covenant from your grain offering. You must offer salt with all your offerings.

[14]If you present a grain offering to the LORD from the first produce, you must make such an offering from the crushed heads of newly ripe grain, roasted with fire. [15]You must put oil and frankincense on it; it is a grain offering. [16]The priest will completely burn the token portion—some of the crushed new grain and oil along with all of the frankincense—as a food gift for the LORD.

The well-being sacrifice

3 If the offering is a communal sacrifice of well-being,[d] the one who offers

---

[b]Or (here and throughout Leviticus) *offering by fire* (cf 3:11)   [c]Heb uncertain   [d]Or *peace offering*

the herd animal—whether it is male or female—must present a flawless specimen before the LORD. [2]You must press your hand on the head of the offering and slaughter it at the meeting tent's entrance. Aaron's sons the priests will toss the blood against every side of the altar. [3]Then you can offer a food gift to the LORD from the communal sacrifice of well-being: the fat that covers and surrounds the insides; [4]the two kidneys and the fat around them at the loins; and the lobe on the liver, which should be removed with the kidneys. [5]Aaron's sons will completely burn all of this on the altar—along with the entirely burned offering on the wood that is on the altar fire—as a food gift of soothing smell to the LORD.

[6]If the offering for a communal sacrifice of well-being for the LORD is from the flock—whether it is male or female—you must present a flawless specimen. [7]If you present a sheep as the offering, you must present it before the LORD. [8]You must press your hand on the head of the offering and slaughter it before the meeting tent. Aaron's sons will toss the blood against every side of the altar. [9]Then you may offer the fat from the communal sacrifice of well-being as a food gift for the LORD: the whole fat

UNLEAVENED BREAD

Unleavened bread figures in several places in the OT. Since bread of this type lacked a leavening agent and therefore did not require time for the dough to rise, it was convenient to prepare for a visitor, especially an unexpected one. Scriptural examples are Lot, who served the two angels who came to Sodom (Gen 19:3); Gideon, who presented it to his angelic guest (Judg 6:19-22); and the medium of Endor, who baked it for Saul (1 Sam 28:24).

The most familiar references to unleavened bread occur in the exodus from Egypt. Exodus 12 provides the legislation for both the Passover meal, which included unleavened bread (12:8), and the Festival of Unleavened Bread when, for the seven days after Passover, unleavened bread was to be eaten and no leaven was to be found among the Israelites (12:15, 17-20; 13:3-8; see also Exod 23:15; 34:18; Lev 23:6; Num 28:17; Deut 16:3-4, 8, 16; Ezek 45:21). Eating unleavened bread was also the rule at the second Passover (Num 9:11).

The other context in which unleavened bread plays a role is the priestly legislation about the grain offering. Leviticus 2 provides the rules covering the different forms these sacrifices could take. If the offering is prepared in an oven, there is to be "unleavened flatbread mixed with oil or unleavened wafers spread with oil" (2:4); there is also to be unleavened bread if it is heated on a griddle (vv. 5-6; see also 1 Chron 23:29). The implication is that there is something objectionable about leaven (and honey) with its fermenting properties in a sacrificial context; exactly what is objectionable about it is not explained here (cf. Matt 16:6-12, where Jesus warns the disciples against "the yeast of the Pharisees and Sadducees"). See also Leviticus 6–8.

In 1 Corinthians 5:8, the apostle Paul contrasts "the unleavened bread of honesty and truth" with "the yeast of evil and wickedness" in warning the Corinthians to "clean out the old yeast" (v. 7).

tail, which should be removed close to the tailbone; the fat that covers and surrounds the insides; [10]the two kidneys and the fat around them at the loins; and the lobe on the liver, which should be removed with the kidneys. [11]The priest will then completely burn all of this on the altar as food—as a food gift for the LORD.

[12]If the offering is a goat, you must present it before the LORD. [13]You must press your hand on its head and slaughter it before the meeting tent. Aaron's sons will toss its blood against every side of the altar. [14]Then you may present as your offering—a food gift for the LORD—the fat that covers and surrounds the insides; [15]the two kidneys and the fat around them at the loins; and the lobe on the liver, which should be removed with the kidneys. [16]The priest will then completely burn all of this on the altar as food—as a food gift for a soothing smell.

All fat belongs to the LORD. [17]This is a permanent rule for your future generations, wherever you live: you must not eat any fat or blood.

The purification offering

4 The LORD said to Moses, [2]Say to the Israelites: Do the following whenever someone sins unintentionally against any of the LORD's commands, doing something that shouldn't be done:

[3]If it is the anointed priest who has sinned, making the people guilty of sin, he must present to the LORD a flawless bull from the herd as a purification offering[e] for the sin he has committed. [4]He will bring the bull before the LORD at the entrance to the meeting tent and press his hand on the bull's head. Then he will slaughter the bull before the LORD. [5]The anointed priest will take some of the bull's blood and take it into the meeting tent. [6]The priest will dip his finger into the blood and sprinkle some of it seven times before the LORD, toward the sanctuary's inner curtain. [7]Then the priest will put some of the blood on the horns of the altar of perfumed incense, which is in the meeting tent before the LORD. But he will pour out all the rest of the bull's blood at the base of the altar of entirely burned offerings, which is at the meeting tent's entrance. [8]Then he will remove all the fat from the bull for the purification offering: the fat that covers and surrounds the insides; [9]the two kidneys and the fat around them at the loins; and the lobe on the liver, which he will remove with the kidneys, [10]just as this is removed from the ox for the communal sacrifice of well-being. Then the priest will completely burn these on the altar of entirely burned offerings. [11]But the bull's hide and all of its flesh, along with its head, lower legs, en-

[e]Or sin offering (Heb hatta't, which recurs frequently in Leviticus)

BULL

The offering of bulls as sacrifices and offerings or as gifts was a central part of Israelite worship. Bulls were considered the pride of the herd in the Israelite sacrificial system.

Without necessarily becoming idolatrous or worshipping other gods, the Israelites used bulls as poetic symbols of power. Yet danger was present, because the religion of Israel's Canaanite neighbors included bull cults dedicated to the chief god of the Canaanite pantheon, El, and his son Baal, representing virility, fertility, the weather, and war. The prophets denounced the use of bull icons in the northern kingdom as marks of apostasy (Amos 4:4; 5:5; 7:9; Hos 8:4-6; 10:5; 12:11; 13:2).

trails, and dung—[12]all that remains of the bull—will be taken to a clean location outside the camp, to the ash heap. It should be burned there at the ash heap on a wood fire.

[13]If it is the entire Israelite community that has done something wrong unintentionally and the deed escapes the assembly's notice—but they've done something that shouldn't be done in violation of the LORD's commands, becoming guilty of sin—[14]once the sin that they committed becomes known, the assembly must present a bull from the herd as a purification offering. They will bring it before the meeting tent. [15]The community elders will press their hands on the bull's head before the LORD and then slaughter it before the LORD. [16]The anointed priest will take some of the bull's blood into the meeting tent. [17]The priest will dip his finger into the blood and sprinkle it seven times before the LORD toward the inner curtain. [18]Then he will put some of the blood on the horns of the altar that is before the LORD in the meeting tent. But he will pour all the rest of the blood out at the base of the altar of entirely burned offerings that is at the meeting tent's entrance. [19]Then he will remove all the fat from it and completely burn it on the altar. [20]He will do the same with this bull as he did with the other bull for the purification offering; that is exactly what he must do. In this way, the priest will make reconciliation for them, and they will be forgiven. [21]Then the priest will take the bull outside the camp and burn it, just as the first bull was burned. It is the purification offering for the assembly.

[22]If a leader sins by unintentionally breaking any of the commands of the LORD his God, doing something that shouldn't be done, and becomes guilty of sin—[23]once the sin that he committed is made known to him—he must bring as his offering a flawless male goat. [24]He will press his hand on the goat's head. It will be slaughtered[f] at the place where an entirely burned offering would be slaughtered before the LORD. It is

a purification offering. [25]The priest will take some of the blood from the purification offering and, using his finger, will put it on the horns of the altar of entirely burned offerings. But he will pour the rest of the blood out at the base of the altar of entirely burned offerings. [26]He will completely burn all of its fat on the altar just as the fat of the communal sacrifice of well-being is burned. In this way the priest will make reconciliation for the leader to remove his sin, and he will be forgiven.

[27]If any ordinary person[g] sins unintentionally by breaking one of the LORD's commands, doing something that shouldn't be done, and becomes guilty of sin—[28]once the sin they committed is made known to them—they must bring as their offering a flawless female goat because of the sin that was committed. [29]They will press their hand on the head of the purification offering. It will be slaughtered[h] at the place for the entirely burned offerings. [30]The priest will take some of its blood and, using his finger, will put it on the horns of the altar of entirely burned offerings. But he will pour all the rest of the blood out at the base of the altar. [31]He will remove all of its fat, just as the fat from a communal sacrifice of well-being is removed. Then the priest will completely burn it on the altar as a soothing smell to the LORD. In this way, the priest will make reconciliation for them, and they will be forgiven.

[32]If you offer a sheep as a purification offering, it must be a flawless female. [33]You must press your hand on the head of the purification offering. It will be slaughtered[i] as a purification offering in the place where the entirely burned offering is slaughtered. [34]Then the priest will take some of the blood from the purification offering and, using his finger, will put it on the horns of the altar of entirely burned offerings. But he will pour all the rest of the blood out at the base of the altar. [35]He will remove all of its fat, just as the fat of a sheep would be removed from the communal sacrifice of

[f]Or He will slaughter it . . . where he would slaughter   [g]Or one of the people of the land   [h]Or They will slaughter it.
[i]Or You will slaughter it.

well-being. Then the priest will completely burn it on the altar along with the LORD's food gifts. In this way, the priest will make reconciliation for you for the sin you committed, and you will be forgiven.

Unintentional sin

5 If you sin:

by not providing information after hearing a public solemn pledge even though you are a witness, knowing something, or having seen something so that you become liable to punishment; [2] or by touching some unclean thing—the dead body of an unclean wild animal, unclean livestock, or unclean swarming creature—but the fact goes unknown so that you become unclean and guilty of sin; [3] or by touching human uncleanness—any uncleanness that makes one unclean—and the fact goes unknown, but you later learn of it and become guilty of sin; [4] or by carelessly swearing to do something, whether bad or good—whatever one might swear carelessly—and the fact goes unknown, but you later learn of it and become guilty of sin concerning one of these things— [5] at that point, when you have become guilty of sin in one of these ways, you must confess how you have sinned [6] and bring to the LORD as compensation for the sin that was committed a female from the flock, either a sheep or goat, as a purification offering. The priest will then make reconciliation for you, to remove your sin.

Alternative offerings

[7] If you can't afford an animal from the flock, you can bring to the LORD as compensation for your sin two doves or two pigeons, one as a purification offering and the other as an entirely burned offering. [8] You will bring them to the priest, who will first present the one for the purification offering. He will pinch off its head at the back of its neck without splitting it.

[9] Then he will sprinkle some of the blood of the purification offering on the side of the altar. The rest of the blood will be drained out at the base of the altar. It is a purification offering. [10] Then, with the second bird, the priest will perform an entirely burned offering according to the regulation. In this way, the priest will make reconciliation for you because of the sin you committed, and you will be forgiven.

[11] If you cannot afford two doves or two pigeons, you can bring as the offering for your sin a tenth of an ephah[j] of choice flour as a purification offering. You must not put any oil on it, nor any frankincense, because it is a purification offering. [12] You will bring it to the priest, and the priest will take a handful from it—the token portion—and will burn it completely on the altar along with the food gifts for the LORD. It is a purification offering. [13] In this way, the priest will make reconciliation for you for whichever one of the sins you committed, and you will be forgiven. The rest of the offering will belong to the priest like the grain offering.

The compensation offering

[14] The LORD said to Moses, [15] Whenever you commit wrongdoing, unintentionally sinning against any of the LORD's holy things, you must bring to the LORD as your compensation a flawless ram from the flock, its value calculated in silver shekels according to the sanctuary's shekel, as a compensation offering. [16] You will make amends for the way you have sinned against the holy thing: you will add one-fifth to its value and give it to the priest. Then the priest will make reconciliation for you with the ram for the compensation offering, and you will be forgiven.

[17] If you sin by breaking any of the LORD's commands, but without realizing it, doing something that shouldn't be done, and then become guilty and liable to punishment, [18] you must bring a flawless ram from the flock, at the standard value, as a compensation offering to the priest. The

[j] Two quarts; one ephah is approximately twenty quarts dry.

priest will make reconciliation for you for the unintentional fault that you committed, even though you didn't realize it, and you will be forgiven. [19]It is a compensation offering. You have definitely become guilty before the LORD.

6 [k]The LORD said to Moses, [2]If you sin: by acting unfaithfully against the LORD;

by deceiving a fellow citizen concerning a deposit or pledged property;

by cheating a fellow citizen through robbery;

[3]or, though you've found lost property, you lie about it;

or by swearing falsely about anything that someone might do and so sin,

[4]at that point, once you have sinned and become guilty of sin, you must return the property you took by robbery or fraud, or the deposit that was left with you for safekeeping, or the lost property that you found, [5]or whatever it was that you swore falsely about. You must make amends for the principal amount and add one-fifth to it. You must give it to the owner on the day you become guilty. [6]You must bring to the priest as your compensation to the LORD a flawless ram from the flock at the standard value as a compensation offering. [7]The priest will make reconciliation for you before the LORD, and you will be forgiven for anything you may have done that made you guilty.

Priestly instructions

[8]The LORD said to Moses: [9]Command Aaron and his sons: This is the Instruction for the entirely burned offering—the entirely burned offering that must remain on the altar hearth all night until morning, while the fire is kept burning. [10]The priest will dress in his linen robe, with linen undergarments on his body. Because the fire will have devoured the entirely burned offering on the altar, he must remove the ashes and place them beside the altar. [11]The priest will then take off his clothes, dress in a different set of clothes, and take the ashes outside the camp to a clean location. [12]The altar fire must be kept burning; it must not go out. Each morning the priest will burn wood on it, will lay out the entirely burned offering on it, and will completely burn the fat of the well-being offering on it. [13]A continuous fire must be kept burning on the altar; it must not go out.

[14]This is the Instruction for the grain offering: Aaron's sons will present it before the LORD in front of the altar. [15]The priest will remove a handful of the choice flour and oil from the grain offering, and all of the frankincense that is on it, and burn this token portion completely on the altar as a soothing smell to the LORD. [16]Aaron and his sons will eat the rest of it. It must be eaten as unleavened bread in a holy place; the priests must eat it in the meeting tent's courtyard. [17]It must not be baked with leaven. I have made it the priests' share from my food gifts. It is most holy like the purification offering and the compensation offering. [18]Only the males from Aaron's descendants can eat it as a permanent portion from the LORD's food gifts throughout your future generations. Anything that touches these food gifts will become holy.

[19]The LORD said to Moses, [20]This is the offering that Aaron and his sons must present to the LORD on the day of his anointment: one-tenth of an ephah[m] of choice flour as a regular grain offering, half in the morning and half in the evening. [21]It must be prepared on a griddle with oil. You must bring it thoroughly mixed up and must present it as a grain offering of crumbled pieces[n] as a soothing smell to the LORD. [22]The priest who is anointed from among Aaron's sons to succeed him will prepare the offering as a permanent portion for the LORD. It will be completely burned as a complete offering. [23]Every priestly grain offering must be a complete offering; it must not be eaten.

[24]The LORD said to Moses, [25]Say to Aaron and his sons: This is the Instruction for the purification offering: The purification offering must be slaughtered before

[k]5:20 in Heb   [l]6:1 in Heb   [m]Two quarts; an ephah is approximately twenty quarts dry.   [n]Heb uncertain

the LORD at the same place the entirely burned offering is slaughtered; it is most holy. ²⁶The priest who offers it as a purification offering will eat it. It must be eaten in a holy place, in the meeting tent's courtyard. ²⁷Anything that touches the purification offering's flesh will become holy. If some of its blood splashes on a garment, you must wash the bloodied part in a holy place. ²⁸A pottery container in which the purification offering is cooked must be broken, but if it is cooked in a bronze container, that must be scrubbed and rinsed with water. ²⁹Any male priest can eat it; it is most holy. ³⁰But no purification offering can be eaten if blood from it is brought into the meeting tent to make reconciliation in the holy place; it must be burned with fire.

7This is the Instruction for the compensation offering: It is most holy. ²The compensation offering must be slaughtered at the same place where the entirely burned offering is slaughtered, and its blood must be tossed against all sides of the altar. ³All of its fat will be offered: the fat tail; the fat that covers the insides; ⁴the two kidneys and the fat around them at the loins; and the lobe on the liver, which must be removed with the kidneys. ⁵The priest must burn them completely on the altar as a food gift for the LORD; it is a compensation offering. ⁶Any male priest can eat it. It must be eaten in a holy place; it is most holy.

⁷The compensation offering is like the purification offering—they share the same Instruction: It belongs to the priest who makes reconciliation with it. ⁸The hide of

CHART OF MAJOR OFFERINGS (LEVITICUS 1–9)

Offering name	Materials	Distribution	Blood ritual	Result
entirely burned	cattle, sheep, goats, pigeons (1:1-17)	entirely burned (1:9), priest gets hide (7:8)	blood on sides of altar (1:5, 11, 15)	soothing smell (1:9, 13, 17), reconciliation (1:4)
grain	flour, unleavened bread, crushed grain (2:1-16)	token burned, priest gets the rest (2:2-3, 9-10, 16; 6:15-18; 7:9-10)	none	soothing smell (2:2, 9)
well-being sacrifice	cattle, sheep, goats (3:1-17)	fat & organs burned, priest gets breast & right thigh, worshippers get the rest (7:15-34)	blood on sides of altar (3:2, 8, 13)	soothing smell (3:5, 16)
purification	cattle, sheep, goats, pigeons, grain (4:1–5:13)	fat & organs burned, priest gets the rest (6:24-26)	blood sprinkled inside meeting tent (4:5-7, 16-18) or outside on altar horns (4:25, 30, 34), the rest at altar base	reconciliation (4:20, 26, 31, 35; 5:10, 13)
compensation	ram (5:14-19)	fat & organs burned, priest gets the rest (7:3-7)	blood on sides of altar (7:1-2)	reconciliation (5:16, 18)
anointment	unleavened bread (6:20-21)	entirely burned (6:19-23)	none	
grain well-being	unleavened & leavened bread (7:12-13)	priest gets one of each kind, worshippers get the rest (7:11-14)	none	

the entirely burned offering that a priest has offered belongs to the priest who offered it. ⁹Any grain offering that is baked in an oven or that is prepared in a pan or on a griddle also belongs to the priest who offered it. ¹⁰But every other grain offering, whether mixed with oil or dry, will belong to all of Aaron's sons equally.

¹¹This is the Instruction for the communal sacrifice of well-being that someone may offer to the LORD: ¹²If you are offering it for thanksgiving, you must offer the following with the communal sacrifice of thanksgiving: unleavened flatbread mixed with oil, unleavened thin loaves spread with oil, and flatbread of choice flour thoroughly mixed with oil. ¹³You must present this offering, plus the leavened flatbread, with the communal thanksgiving sacrifice of well-being. ¹⁴From this you will present one of each kind of offering as a gift to the LORD. It will belong to the priest who tosses the blood of the well-being offering.

¹⁵The flesh of your communal thanksgiving sacrifice of well-being must be eaten on the day you offer it; you cannot save any of it until morning. ¹⁶But if your communal sacrifice of well-being is payment for a solemn promise or if it is a spontaneous gift, it may be eaten on the day you offer it as your communal sacrifice, and whatever is left over can be eaten the next day. ¹⁷But whatever is left over of the flesh of the communal sacrifice on the third day must be burned with fire. ¹⁸If any of it is eaten on the third day, it will not be accepted. It will not be credited to the one who offered it. It will be considered foul, and the person who eats of it will be liable to punishment.

¹⁹Flesh that touches any unclean thing must not be eaten; it must be burned with fire. Any clean person may eat the flesh, ²⁰but anyone who eats the flesh of a communal sacrifice of well-being that belongs to the LORD while in an unclean state will be cut off from their people. ²¹Whenever anyone touches any unclean thing—whether it is human uncleanness, an unclean animal, or any unclean and disgusting creature—and then eats the flesh of a communal sacrifice of well-being that belongs to the LORD, that person will be cut off from their people.

²²The LORD said to Moses: ²³Tell the Israelites: You must not eat the fat of an ox, sheep, or goat. ²⁴The fat of an animal that has died naturally or the fat of an animal that was killed by another animal may be put to any use, but you must definitely not eat it. ²⁵If anyone eats the fat of an animal from which a food gift could be offered to the LORD, that person will be cut off from their people. ²⁶You must not consume any blood whatsoever—whether bird or animal blood—wherever you may live. ²⁷Any person who consumes any blood whatsoever will be cut off from their people.

²⁸The LORD said to Moses: ²⁹Say to the Israelites: If you wish to offer a communal sacrifice of well-being to the LORD, you are allowed to bring your offering to the LORD as your communal sacrifice of well-being.° ³⁰Your own hands must bring the LORD's food gifts. You will bring the fat with the breast so that the breast can be lifted as an uplifted offering before the LORD. ³¹The priest will completely burn the fat on the altar, but the breast will go to Aaron and his sons. ³²You will give the right thigh of your communal sacrifice of well-being to the priest as a gift. ³³The right thigh will belong to the son of Aaron who offers the blood and fat of the well-being offering. ³⁴I have taken the breast of the uplifted offering and the thigh that is given by the Israelites from their communal sacrifices of well-being, and have given them to Aaron the priest and to his sons as a permanent portion from the Israelites.

³⁵This is what Aaron and his sons are allotted from the LORD's food gifts once they have been presented to serve the LORD as priests. ³⁶The LORD commanded that these things be given to the priests by the Israelites, following their anointment. It is their permanent portion throughout their future generations.

°Heb uncertain

Conclusion concerning offerings

[37] This concludes the Instructions for the entirely burned offering, the grain offering, the purification offering, the compensation offering, the ordination offering, and the communal sacrifice of well-being, [38] which the LORD commanded Moses at Mount Sinai on the day when he ordered the Israelites to present their offerings to the LORD, in the Sinai desert.

The priests' ordination

8 The LORD said to Moses, [2] Take Aaron and his sons with him, the priestly clothing, the anointing oil, a bull for the purification offering, two rams, and a basket of unleavened bread, [3] and assemble the whole community at the meeting tent's entrance.

[4] Moses did as the LORD commanded him, and the community assembled at the meeting tent's entrance. [5] Moses said to the community, "This is what the LORD has commanded us to do." [6] Then Moses brought Aaron and his sons forward and washed them in water. [7] Moses put the tunic on Aaron, tied the sash around him, and dressed him in the robe. Moses then put the priestly vest on Aaron, tied the woven waistband of the vest around him, and secured the vest to him with it. [8] Then Moses placed the chest piece on Aaron and set the Urim and Thummim into the chest piece. [9] Moses placed the turban on Aaron's head and put the gold flower ornament, the holy crown, on the turban's front, just as the LORD had commanded him.

[10] Moses then took the anointing oil and anointed the dwelling[p] and everything in it, making them holy by doing so. [11] He sprinkled some of the oil on the altar seven times, and anointed the altar and all its equipment, as well as the basin and its base, to make them holy. [12] He poured some of the anointing oil on Aaron's head, thereby anointing him to make him holy. [13] Then Moses brought Aaron's sons forward, dressed them in tunics, tied sashes around them, and wrapped headbands on

them, just as the LORD had commanded him.

[14] Next Moses brought forward the bull for the purification offering. Aaron and his sons pressed their hands on its head. [15] Moses slaughtered it, then took the blood and, using his finger, put it on all of the altar's horns, purifying the altar. He poured the rest of the blood out at the altar's base. Then he made the altar holy so that reconciliation could be performed on it.[q] [16] Moses removed all the fat that was around the insides, the lobe of the liver, the two kidneys and their fat, and he completely burned it on the altar. [17] But the rest of the bull, including its hide, its flesh, and its dung, he burned with fire outside the camp just as the LORD had commanded him.

[18] Then Moses presented the ram for the entirely burned offering, and Aaron and his sons pressed their hands on its head. [19] Moses slaughtered it, then tossed the blood against all sides of the altar. [20] He cut up the ram into pieces, and then completely burned the head, pieces, and fat. [21] After he washed the insides and lower legs with water, Moses completely burned the whole ram on the altar. It was an entirely burned offering for a soothing smell; it was a food gift for the LORD, as the LORD had commanded Moses.

[22] Moses then presented the second ram, the ram for ordination, and Aaron and his sons pressed their hands on its head. [23] Moses slaughtered it, then took some of its blood and put it on Aaron's right earlobe, on his right thumb, and on his right big toe. [24] Then Moses brought forward Aaron's sons and put some of the blood on their right earlobes, their right thumbs, and their right big toes. Moses tossed the rest of the blood against all of the altar's sides. [25] Then he took the fat—the fat tail, all the fat that was around the insides, the lobe of the liver, the two kidneys and their fat—as well as the right thigh. [26] From the basket of unleavened bread that was before the LORD, he took one loaf of unleavened flatbread, one loaf of flatbread made with

---

[p] Or tabernacle   [q] Or to make reconciliation for it (i.e., the altar)

oil, and one unleavened wafer, and he placed these on the fat pieces and on the right thigh. [27]Moses set all of this in Aaron's and his sons' hands, then lifted them as an uplifted offering before the LORD. [28]Next Moses took this out of their hands and completely burned it on the altar, along with the entirely burned offering. This was an ordination offering for a soothing smell; it was a food gift for the LORD. [29]Next Moses took the breast from the ram for the ordination offering and lifted it as an uplifted offering before the LORD. It belonged to Moses as his portion, just as the LORD had commanded him. [30]Moses took some of the anointing oil and some of the blood that was on the altar and sprinkled it

on Aaron and his clothes, and on his sons and their clothes as well. In this way, Moses made holy Aaron, his clothing, and Aaron's sons and their clothing.

[31]Moses said to Aaron and his sons: "Cook the meat at the meeting tent's entrance. You may eat it there along with the bread that is in the basket of the ordination offering, just as I was commanded,[r] 'Aaron and his sons can eat it.' [32]But you must burn whatever is left over of the meat and bread with fire. [33]You must not leave the meeting tent's entrance for seven days, until the period of your ordination is completed, because your ordination takes seven days. [34]What was done today was commanded by the LORD, to make

[r]LXX, Syr, Tg; cf 8:35; MT *as I commanded*

OIL

While Deuteronomy 8:7-8 lists seven products of Canaan that make it a desirable, fertile, and well-watered land (wheat, barley, grape vines, figs, pomegranates, olive oil, and honey), the most versatile and economically important is the olive from which oil is extracted. The economic triad of olive, grape, and wheat made life possible in ancient Canaan.

Olive oil was everywhere in ancient Near Eastern society, as can be seen by the many uses to which it was put. Lighting people's paths at night, their homes, and their temples were oil lamps that were carried in the hand (Matt 25:3-8), placed on a table or in a niche (2 Kgs 4:10), or placed in a lampstand before the altar (Lev 24:2). Sacred objects and persons were set apart by anointing them with oil (Jacob's pillar at Bethel in Gen 28:18; Samuel's anointing of kings in 1 Sam 10:1 and 16:13). Oil was one of the items regularly offered on God's altar (Lev 2:2-7). Wheat or barley flour was mixed with oil to produce cakes, both for sacred purposes (Exod 29:2) and for one's daily bread (1 Kgs 17:12).

Oil was used to anoint the sick (Mark 6:13), as medicine on sores (Isa 1:6), in the bindings of wrapped wounds (Luke 10:34), and possibly as a liniment for sore joints (Ps 109:18). Customarily, olive oil was used after bathing to maintain skin tone, to soothe the spirit (Ps 133:2), and to make "the face shine" (Ps 104:15). Cosmetics to color the eyes, lips, and hair and perfumes used by both genders depended upon oil as a base mixed with a variety of spices, roots, and dyes. The fragrant ointments, spices, and unguents used to honor the dead and mask the smell associated with their bodies were also oil-based (Mark 16:1).

reconciliation for you. [35]You must stay at the meeting tent's entrance for seven days, day and night, observing the LORD's requirement so you don't die, because that's what I was commanded."

[36]Aaron and his sons did everything the LORD commanded through Moses.

The priests' initiation

9 On the eighth day, Moses called for Aaron, Aaron's sons, and Israel's elders. [2]He said to Aaron, "Take a young bull from the herd as a purification offering and a ram as an entirely burned offering, both flawless animals, and bring them before the LORD. [3]Then tell the Israelites, 'Take a male goat as a purification offering; a young bull and a sheep—both one-year-old flawless animals—as an entirely burned offering; [4]an ox and a ram as a well-being sacrifice before the LORD; and a grain offering mixed with oil, because today the LORD will appear to you.'"

[5]They brought what Moses had commanded to the front of the meeting tent. Then the whole community came forward and stood before the LORD. [6]Moses said, "The LORD has ordered you to do this so that the LORD's glorious presence will appear to you." [7]Moses said to Aaron, "Come up to the altar and perform your purification offering and your entirely burned offering, making reconciliation for yourself and the people. Then perform the people's offering in order to make reconciliation for them, just as the LORD commanded."

[8]Aaron went to the altar and slaughtered the young bull for his purification offering. [9]Then Aaron's sons presented the blood to him, and he dipped his finger into the blood and put it on the altar's horns. He poured the rest of the blood out at the altar's base. [10]He completely burned on the altar the fat, kidneys, and lobe of the liver from the purification offering, just as the LORD commanded Moses. [11]But he burned the flesh and hide with fire outside the camp.

[12]Then Aaron slaughtered the entirely burned offering. Aaron's sons handed him the blood, and he tossed it against all sides of the altar. [13]They handed him the entirely burned offering in pieces, including the head, and he completely burned them on the altar. [14]Then he washed the insides and lower legs and completely burned them on the altar along with the rest of the entirely burned offering.

[15]Next, Aaron presented the people's offering. He took the male goat for the people's purification offering, slaughtered it, and offered it as a purification offering like the first purification offering. [16]He presented the entirely burned offering and did with it according to the regulation. [17]Then he presented the grain offering, took a handful from it, and completely burned it on the altar, in addition to the morning's entirely burned offering.

[18]Aaron then slaughtered the ox and the ram—the people's communal sacrifice of well-being. Aaron's sons handed him the blood, which he tossed against all sides of the altar, [19]and the fat pieces of the ox and ram—the fat tail, the covering fat, the kidneys, and the lobe of the liver. [20]They placed these fat pieces on the animals' breasts, and Aaron completely burned them on the altar. [21]But Aaron lifted up the breasts and the right thigh as an uplifted offering before the LORD, just as Moses had commanded.

[22]Aaron then raised his hands toward the people and blessed them. After performing the purification offering, the entirely burned offering, and the well-being sacrifice, he came down. [23]Moses and Aaron then entered the meeting tent. When they came out, they blessed the people, and the LORD's glorious presence appeared to all the people. [24]Fire flew out from before the LORD and devoured the entirely burned offering and the fat pieces on the altar. All the people saw it. They shouted for joy and fell facedown.

Nadab and Abihu

10 Now Nadab and Abihu, two of Aaron's sons, each took an incense pan. They put fire and incense on them and offered unauthorized fire before the LORD, which he had not commanded them. [2]Then fire flew out from before the LORD and devoured them, and they died before the LORD.

³Moses said to Aaron, "When the LORD said, 'I will show that I am holy among those near me, and before all the people I will manifest my glorious presence,' this is what he meant!" But Aaron was silent.

⁴Then Moses called Mishael and Elzaphan the sons of Uzziel, Aaron's uncle, and told them, "Go carry your relatives out from the front of the sanctuary to a place outside the camp." ⁵So they went forward and carried Nadab and Abihu out by their tunics to a place outside the camp, just as Moses had ordered. ⁶Moses then said to Aaron and his sons, Eleazar and Ithamar, "Don't dishevel your hair and don't rip your clothes into pieces, or you will die and bring anger upon the whole community. Your family—all of Israel's house—will mourn the burning the LORD has done. ⁷But you must not leave the meeting tent, or you will die because the LORD's anointing oil is on you." So they did what Moses ordered.

Priestly drinking and eating

⁸The LORD said to Aaron: ⁹Both you and your sons must not drink wine or beer when you enter the meeting tent so that you don't die—this is a permanent rule throughout your future generations—¹⁰so that you can distinguish between the holy and the common, and between the unclean and the clean, ¹¹and so that you can teach the Israelites all the rules that the LORD spoke to them through Moses.

¹²Moses then told Aaron and his remaining sons, Eleazar and Ithamar, "Take the grain offering that is left over from the LORD's food gifts and eat it unleavened next to the altar, because it is most holy. ¹³You must eat it in a holy place because it is your portion and your sons' portion from the LORD's food gifts, as I have been commanded. ¹⁴You must eat the breast for the uplifted offering and the thigh for the gift offering in a clean place—both you and your sons and daughters. These things are designated as your portion and your chil-

dren's portion from the Israelites' communal sacrifices of well-being. ¹⁵The Israelites must bring the thigh for the gift and the breast for the uplifted offering along with the food gifts of the fat pieces, to be lifted up as an uplifted offering before the LORD. These will belong to both you and your children as a permanent portion, just as the LORD has commanded."

¹⁶Then Moses asked about the male goat for the purification offering, and discovered that it had already been burned. He was angry with Eleazar and Ithamar, Aaron's remaining sons, and asked, ¹⁷"Why didn't you eat the purification offering in the holy area? It's most holy, and it was assigned to you for bearing the community's punishment by making reconciliation for them before the LORD. ¹⁸Since its blood wasn't brought into the sanctuary's interior, you were to have eaten it in the sanctuary, just as I was commanded."ˢ

¹⁹"Look," Aaron said to Moses, "today they offered their purification offerings and their entirely burned offerings before the LORD, but these things still happened to me! Would the LORD have approved if I had eaten a purification offering today?" ²⁰When Moses heard that, he approved.ᵗ

Dietary rules

11 The LORD said to Moses and Aaron: ²Say to the Israelites: These are the creatures that you are allowed to eat from the land animals: ³You can eat any animal that has divided hoofs, completely split, and that rechews food. ⁴But of animals that rechew food and have divided hoofs you must not eat the following: the camel—though it rechews food, it does not have divided hoofs, so it is unclean for you; ⁵the rock badger—though it rechews food, it does not have divided hoofs, so it is unclean for you; ⁶the hare—though it rechews food, it does not have divided hoofs, so it is unclean for you; ⁷the pig—though it has completely divided hoofs, it does not rechew food, so it is unclean for you. ⁸You must not eat the flesh of these animals or

---

ˢSyr, Tg, Vulg; MT *as I commanded*; cf 8:31   ᵗOr *he was satisfied.*

touch their dead bodies; they are unclean for you. ⁹You are allowed to eat the following from all water animals: You may eat anything in the water that has fins and scales, whether in sea or stream. ¹⁰But anything in the seas or streams that does not have fins and scales—whether it be any of the swarming creatures in the water or any of the other living creatures in the water—is detestable to you ¹¹and must remain so. You must not eat their flesh, and you must detest their dead bodies. ¹²Anything in the water that does not have fins or scales is detestable to you.

¹³Of the birds, the following are the ones you must detest—they must not be eaten; they are detestable: the eagle, the black vulture, the bearded vulture, ¹⁴the kite, any kind of falcon, ¹⁵any kind of raven, ¹⁶the eagle owl, the short-eared owl, the long-eared owl, any kind of hawk, ¹⁷the tawny owl, the fisher owl, the screech owl, ¹⁸the white owl, the scops owl, the osprey, ¹⁹the stork, any kind of heron, the hoopoe, and the bat.ᵘ

²⁰Any flying insect that walks on four feet is detestable to you, ²¹but you can eat four-footed flying insects that have jointed legs above their feet with which they hop on the ground. ²²Of these you can eat the following: any kind of migrating locust, any kind of bald locust, any kind of cricket, and any kind of grasshopper. ²³But every other flying insect that has four feet is detestable to you.

Unclean animals

²⁴You make yourself unclean by the following animals—whoever touches their dead bodies will be unclean until evening, ²⁵and anyone who carries any part of their dead bodies must wash their clothes and will be unclean until evening: ²⁶All animals that have divided hoofs, but they are not completely split, and that do not rechew food are unclean for you—whoever touches them will be unclean. ²⁷Of all the animals

that walk on four feet, the ones that walk on their paws are unclean for you—anyone who touches their dead bodies will be unclean until evening. ²⁸Anyone who carries one of their dead bodies must wash their clothes and will be unclean until evening; these animals are unclean for you.

²⁹The following are unclean for you among the small creatures that move about on the ground: the rat, the mouse, any kind of large lizard, ³⁰the gecko, the spotted lizard, the lizard, the skink, and the chameleon.ᵛ ³¹Of all small moving creatures, these are unclean for you—anyone who touches them when they are dead will be unclean until evening. ³²Moreover, anything on which one of these creatures falls when it is dead will be unclean, whether it is wood, cloth, skin, or funeral clothing—any such item that can be used to do work. It must be put into water and will be unclean until evening. Then it will be clean again. ³³If any of these creatures fall into a pottery jar, everything inside it will be unclean; you must smash the pot. ³⁴If water from such a jar gets on any edible food, it will be unclean; any drinkable beverage in such a jar will be unclean. ³⁵Anything on which a part of these animals' dead bodies might fall will be unclean. If it is an oven or stove, it must be destroyed; they are unclean for you and must remain that way. ³⁶Now, a spring or cistern that collects water is clean, but anyone who touches one of these animals' dead bodies in it will be unclean.ʷ ³⁷If any part of these animals' dead bodies falls on seed that is to be planted, the seed is still clean. ³⁸But if water is poured on some seed and part of their dead bodies falls on it, it is unclean for you.

³⁹If one of the animals that you are allowed to eat dies naturally, anyone who touches its dead body will be unclean until evening. ⁴⁰Anyone who eats from the dead body must wash their clothes and will be unclean until evening. Anyone who carries such a dead body must wash their clothes and will be unclean until evening.

ᵘMany of the species in 11:13-19 cannot be identified with certainty. ᵛMany of the species in 11:29-30 cannot be identified with certainty. ʷHeb lacks in it.

⁴¹Every creature that swarms on the earth is detestable; it must not be eaten. ⁴²Among all such creatures that swarm on the earth, you must not eat anything that moves on its belly or anything that walks on four or more feet because they are detestable. ⁴³Do not make yourselves detestable by means of any swarming creatures. Do not make yourselves unclean with them or be made unclean by them. ⁴⁴I am the LORD your God. You must keep yourselves holy and be holy, because I am holy. You must not make yourselves unclean by any swarming creature that crawls on the ground. ⁴⁵I am the LORD, who brought you up from the land of Egypt to be your God. You must be holy, because I am holy.

Conclusion concerning animals and diet

⁴⁶This concludes the Instruction concerning animals, birds, all creatures that live in water, and all the creatures that swarm on the earth, ⁴⁷in order to distinguish between the unclean and the clean and between creatures that can be eaten and those that cannot.

Purification after childbirth

12 The LORD said to Moses: ²Say to the Israelites: If a woman conceives a child and gives birth to a son, she will be unclean for seven days—just as she is during her menstrual period. ³On the eighth day, the flesh of the boy's foreskin must be circumcised. ⁴For thirty-three days the mother will be in a state of blood purification. She must not touch anything holy or enter the sacred area until her time of purification is completed. ⁵But if the woman gives birth to a daughter, she will be unclean for two weeks—just as she is during her menstrual period—and will be in a state of blood purification^x for sixty-six days.

⁶When the time of purification is complete, whether for a son or a daughter, the mother must bring a one-year-old lamb as an entirely burned offering and a pigeon or turtledove as a purification offering to the priest at the meeting tent's entrance. ⁷The priest will present it before the LORD and make reconciliation for her. She will then be cleansed from her blood flow. This is the Instruction for any woman who has a child, male or female. ⁸But if the mother cannot afford a sheep, she can bring two turtledoves or two pigeons—one for the entirely burned offering and the other for the purification offering. The priest will then make reconciliation for her, and she will be clean.

Diagnosis of skin disease

13 The LORD said to Moses and Aaron, ²When a person has a swelling, a scab, or a shiny spot on their skin, and it becomes an infection of skin disease^y on their skin, they will be brought to the priests, either to Aaron or one of his sons. ³The priest will examine the infection on the skin. If hair in the infected area has turned white and the infection appears to be deeper than the skin, then it is an infection of skin disease. Once the priest sees this, he will declare the person unclean. ⁴But if the shiny spot on the skin is white and does not appear to be deeper than the skin and the hair has not turned white, the priest will quarantine the infected person for seven days. ⁵On the seventh day the priest will again examine the infection. If he sees that it has remained the same—the infection has not spread on the skin—the priest will quarantine the person for seven more days. ⁶On the seventh day the priest will examine it again. If the infection has faded and has not spread over the skin, the priest will declare the person clean; it is just a rash. The person must wash their clothes, then they will be clean again. ⁷But if the rash continues to spread over the skin after they appeared before the priest for purification, they must again show themselves to the priest. ⁸If the priest sees that the rash has spread over the skin, the priest will declare the person unclean; it is a case of skin disease.

⁹Whenever someone has an infection

---

^x Heb uncertain ^y The precise meaning is uncertain; traditionally *leprosy*—a term used for several different skin diseases.

of skin disease, they will be brought to the priest. [10]If the priest sees that there is a white swelling on the skin, it has turned the hair white, and there is a patch of raw flesh in the swelling, [11]then it is a case of chronic skin disease on their skin. The priest will declare the person unclean. The priest will not quarantine such persons, because they are already unclean. [12]But if the skin disease continues to break out so that the disease covers all of the infected person's skin from head to toe, as far as the priest can tell—[13]then the priest will make an examination. If the skin disease has covered the person's whole body, the priest will declare the infected person clean. The person has turned entirely white; he is clean. [14]But as soon as raw flesh appears in the swelling, they will be unclean. [15]When the priest sees the raw flesh, he will declare the person unclean. Raw flesh is unclean; it is a case of skin disease. [16]But if the raw flesh turns white again, the person will go back to the priest. [17]The priest will examine it. If the infection has turned white, the priest will declare the infected person clean; at that point, the person is clean.

[18]Whenever someone has a boil on their skin, it heals, [19]and in place of the boil there is a white swelling or reddish-white shiny spot, it must be shown to the priest. [20]If the priest sees that it appears to be lower than the skin, and its hair has turned white, the priest will declare the person unclean. It is an infection of skin disease that has broken out in the boil. [21]But if the priest examines it and there is no white hair in it, it is not lower than the skin, and it is faded, the priest will quarantine the person seven days. [22]If it continues to spread over the skin, the priest will declare the person unclean; it is an infection. [23]But if the shiny spot remains where it was and does not spread, it is just a scar from the boil. The priest will declare the person clean.

[24]Whenever there is a burn on someone's skin, and the raw patch of the burn becomes a reddish-white or white shiny spot, [25]the priest will examine it. If the hair has turned white in the shiny spot, and it appears to be deeper than the skin, it is a case of skin disease that has broken out in the burn. The priest will declare the person unclean; it is an infection of skin disease. [26]But if the priest examines it, and there is no white hair in the shiny spot, it is not lower than the skin, and it is faded, the priest will quarantine the person seven days. [27]On the seventh day the priest will again examine it. If it has continued to spread over the skin, the priest will declare the person unclean; it is an infection of skin disease. [28]But if the shiny spot remains where it was, has not spread over the skin, and is faded, it is just swelling from the burn. The priest will declare the person clean, because it is just the scar from the burn.

[29]Whenever a man or woman has an infection, whether on the head or in the beard, [30]the priest will examine it. If it appears to be deeper than the skin, and there is thin yellow hair in it, the priest will declare the person unclean; it is a case of scabies—a skin disease of the head or beard. [31]When the priest examines the scabies infection, if it does not appear to be deeper than the skin, but there is no black hair in it, the priest will quarantine the person with the scabies infection for seven days. [32]On the seventh day the priest will examine the infection again. If the scabies has not spread, there is no yellow hair in it, and it does not appear to be deeper than the skin, [33]the person must shave the area, without shaving the scabies. The priest will then quarantine that person another seven days. [34]On the seventh day the priest will again examine the scabies. If it has not spread over the skin and does not appear to be deeper than the skin, the priest will declare the person clean. They must wash their clothes; then they will be clean again. [35]But if the scabies continues to spread over the skin after the person's purification, [36]the priest must examine it again. If the scabies has spread over the skin at all, the priest does not need to look for the yellow hair; the person is unclean. [37]But if the priest sees that the scabies has remained the same, and black hair has grown in it, the scabies has healed. The person is clean, and the priest will declare them to be so.

³⁸Whenever a man or woman has many white shiny spots on their skin, ³⁹if the priest sees that there are faded white shiny spots on the skin of the body, it is just a rash that has broken out on the skin; the person is clean.

⁴⁰If someone loses their hair, they are bald, but they are clean. ⁴¹If the hair is lost at the sides of the forehead, the person has a receding hairline, but they are clean. ⁴²But whenever there is a reddish-white infection in the bald spot or in the receding hairline, it is a case of skin disease breaking out there. ⁴³The priest must examine it. If the swelling of the infection is reddish white in the bald spot or receding hairline and resembles skin disease on the body, ⁴⁴the person is afflicted with skin disease; they are unclean. The priest must declare them unclean on account of the head infection.

⁴⁵Anyone with an infection of skin disease must wear torn clothes, dishevel their hair, cover their upper lip, and shout out, "Unclean! Unclean!" ⁴⁶They will be unclean as long as they are infected. They are unclean. They must live alone outside the camp.

Articles with skin disease

⁴⁷Whenever there is an infection of skin disease on clothing—on wool or linen clothing, ⁴⁸in the weaving of the linen or wool, or on a skin or skin item—⁴⁹and the infection is greenish or reddish on the clothing, the weaving, or the skin or skin item, it is an infection of skin disease. It must be shown to the priest. ⁵⁰The priest will examine the infection and quarantine the infected item seven days. ⁵¹On the seventh day he will examine the infection again. If the infection has spread in the clothing, the weaving, or the skin, whatever it is used for, the infection is a case of infectious skin disease; the item is unclean. ⁵²The priest will burn the clothing, the weaving of the wool or linen, or whatever skin item in which the infection was found, because it is an infectious skin disease; it must be burned with fire.

⁵³But if the priest sees that the infection has not spread in the clothing, the weaving, or on any skin item, ⁵⁴the priest will order that the infected piece be washed, and he will quarantine it for another seven days. ⁵⁵After it has been washed, if the priest sees that the infection has not changed its appearance, even though the infection has not spread, it is unclean. You must burn it with fire. It is a fungus,^z whether it is on the inside or outside.

⁵⁶But if, after it is washed, the priest sees that the infection has faded, he will tear the infected part out of the cloth, the weaving, or the skin. ⁵⁷If it appears again in the cloth, the weaving, or any item of skin, it is starting to break out. You must burn the infected item with fire. ⁵⁸But if the infection disappears from the cloth, the weaving, or any item of skin that you washed, it must be washed again. Then it will be clean.

⁵⁹This concludes the Instruction about the infection of skin disease in a woolen or linen cloth, weaving, or any skin item, in order to declare whether it is clean or unclean.

Persons with skin disease

14 The LORD said to Moses, ²This will be the Instruction for anyone with skin disease^a at the time of purification: When it has been reported to the priest, ³he will go outside the camp. If the priest sees that the person afflicted with skin disease has been healed of the infection, ⁴the priest will order that two birds—wild^b and clean—and cedarwood, crimson yarn, and hyssop be brought for the person who needs purification. ⁵The priest will order that one bird be slaughtered over fresh water in a pottery jar. ⁶He will then take the other wild bird, along with the cedarwood, crimson yarn, and hyssop, and will dip all of this into the blood of the bird that was slaughtered over the fresh water. ⁷He will sprinkle the person who needs purification from skin disease seven times and declare that they are clean. Then the priest will release the wild bird into the countryside. ⁸The person

---

^zHeb uncertain ^aThe precise meaning is uncertain; traditionally *leprosy*—a term used for several different skin diseases. ^bOr *live* or *healthy;* also in 14:6-7

who needs purification will then wash their clothes, shave off all of their hair, and bathe in water; at that point, they will be clean. After that, they can return to the camp, but they must live outside their tent for seven days. [9] On the seventh day, the person must shave off all their hair again: head, beard, and eyebrows—everything. They must wash their clothes and bathe in water; then they will be clean again.

[10] On the eighth day, that person must take two flawless male sheep, one flawless one-year-old ewe, a grain offering of three-tenths of an ephah[c] of choice flour mixed with oil, and one log[d] of oil. [11] The priest performing the purification will place these and the person needing purification before the LORD at the meeting tent's entrance.

[12] The priest will take one of the male sheep and present it as a compensation offering, along with the log of oil, and will lift them as an uplifted offering before the LORD. [13] The priest will slaughter the sheep at the same place where the purification offering and the entirely burned offering are slaughtered: in the holy area. The compensation offering, like the purification offering, belongs to the priest; it is most holy. [14] The priest will take some of the blood from the compensation offering and

will put it on the right earlobe, the right thumb, and the right big toe of the person needing purification. [15] Then the priest will take some of the log of oil and pour it into his left palm. [16] The priest will then dip his right finger into the oil and sprinkle some of it with his finger seven times before the LORD. [17] Then the priest will put some of the oil that is left in his hand on the right earlobe, the right thumb, and the right big toe of the person needing purification—this oil will be placed on top of the blood of the compensation offering. [18] The priest will put whatever is left of the oil in his hand on the head of the person needing purification. In this way, the priest will make reconciliation for the person before the LORD.

[19] The priest will then perform the purification offering and make reconciliation for the person needing purification from their uncleanness. After that, the entirely burned offering will be slaughtered. [20] The priest will offer up the entirely burned offering and the grain offering on the altar. In this way, the priest will make reconciliation for the person, and they will be clean again.

[21] Now if the person is poor and cannot afford these things, they can bring one male sheep as a compensation offering, to be lifted up in order to make reconciliation

---

[c] Heb lacks *ephah*; an ephah is approximately twenty quarts dry.   [d] Heb *log*; two-thirds of a pint; also in 14:12, 15, 21, 24

SHAVING

Israelite men usually wore beards, and shaving was limited to special circumstances. Levites prepared for their consecration by shaving their whole bodies (Num 8:7). At the completion of their vows, nazirites shaved their heads and burned the hair (Num 6:13-20). During a visit to Jerusalem, Paul sought to show his respect for the Instruction of Moses by making a nazirite vow, which included shaving his head (Acts 21:23-24; cf. 18:18). Shaving was employed in the diagnosis of "scabies infection" or "skin disease" (Lev 13:31-33) and in subsequent purification (e.g., Lev 14:8-9). Forcefully shaving another's beard was a means of humiliation carried out on enemies, prisoners, or slaves (e.g., 2 Sam 10:4; Isa 7:20; Jer 48:37; cf. 1 Cor 11:5-6). Occasionally the Lord commanded shaving as a sign of mourning over sinfulness (Isa 22:12; Amos 8:10).

for them; a grain offering of one-tenth of an ephah of choice flour mixed with oil; a log of oil; ²²and two turtledoves or two pigeons, whatever they can afford—one as a purification offering and the other as an entirely burned offering. ²³On the eighth day, they must bring these items for their purification to the priest at the meeting tent's entrance before the LORD.

²⁴The priest will take the male sheep for the compensation offering and the log of oil, and will lift them as an uplifted offering before the LORD. ²⁵The priest will slaughter the sheep for the compensation offering and will take some of its blood and put it on the right earlobe, the right thumb, and the right big toe of the person needing purification. ²⁶The priest will pour some of the oil into his left palm. ²⁷Next, the priest will sprinkle some of the oil seven times before the LORD using his right finger. ²⁸The priest will then put some of the oil that is in his hand on the right earlobe, the right thumb, and the right big toe of the person needing purification—on top of the same places as the blood of the compensation offering. ²⁹The priest will put whatever is left of the oil in his hand on the head of the person needing purification, to make reconciliation for them before the LORD.

³⁰The person will then offer one of the turtledoves or pigeons, whatever they can afford—³¹one as a purification offering and the other as an entirely burned offering along with the grain offering.^e In this way, the priest will make reconciliation before the LORD for the person needing purification.

³²This is the Instruction concerning those who have an infection of skin disease but who cannot afford the normal means of purification.

Houses with skin disease

³³The LORD said to Moses and Aaron: ³⁴When you enter the land of Canaan, which I am giving to you as a possession, and I put an infection of skin disease on a house in the land you possess, ³⁵the homeowner must come and tell the priest, "I

think some sort of infection is in my house." ³⁶The priest will order that the house be emptied before he comes to examine it so that nothing else in the house will become unclean. After that, the priest will come to examine the house. ³⁷If he examines the infection, and the infection in the walls of the house consists of greenish or reddish depressions, which appear to be deeper than the surface of the wall, ³⁸the priest will exit the house, go to the front door, and quarantine the house for seven days. ³⁹On the seventh day, the priest will return. If he finds that the infection has spread over the walls of the house, ⁴⁰the priest will order the stones in which the infection is found to be pulled out and discarded outside the city in an unclean area. ⁴¹The inside of the house will then be scraped on all sides, and the plaster that has been scraped off must be dumped outside the city in an unclean area. ⁴²Then different stones will be used in place of the first ones, and new coating will be used to replaster the house.

⁴³If the infection breaks out again in the house after the stones have been pulled out and the house scraped and replastered, ⁴⁴the priest will return. If he finds that the infection has spread throughout the house, it is a case of infectious skin disease in the house; the house is unclean. ⁴⁵The house must be destroyed—its stones, wood, and all the plaster in the house. All of it must be taken outside the city to an unclean area. ⁴⁶Anyone who enters the house during the entire period when it is quarantined will be unclean until evening. ⁴⁷Anyone who lies down in the house must wash their clothes. Anyone who eats in the house must also wash their clothes.

⁴⁸But if the priest arrives and finds that the infection has not spread after the house was replastered, the priest will declare the house clean because the infection has been healed. ⁴⁹To cleanse the house, the priest will take two birds, cedarwood, crimson yarn, and hyssop. ⁵⁰He will slaughter one bird over fresh water in a pottery jar. ⁵¹He will then take the cedarwood, hyssop, and

^eLXX, Syr; MT repeats *whatever they can afford* at the beginning of 14:31.

crimson yarn, along with the wild[f] bird, and will dip all of this into the fresh water and into the blood of the bird that was slaughtered. He will then sprinkle the house seven times. [52] In this way, the priest will cleanse the house with the blood of the bird, the fresh water, the wild bird, the cedarwood, the hyssop, and the crimson yarn. [53] Then he will release the wild bird outside the city into the countryside. In this way, he will make reconciliation for the house, and it will be clean.

Conclusion concerning skin disease

[54] This concludes the Instruction concerning every infection of skin disease: for scabies, [55] for skin disease on clothing or in houses, [56] and for swelling, scabs, or shiny spots, [57] in order to determine when it is unclean or clean. This concludes the Instruction concerning skin disease.

Male genital emissions

15 The LORD said to Moses and Aaron: [2] Speak to the Israelites and say to them: Whenever a man has a genital emission, that emission is unclean. [3] This is the nature of the uncleanness brought about by his emission: regardless of whether his genital organ allows his emission to flow or blocks the flow, it is unclean to him. [4] Any bed on which someone with an emission lies will be unclean, and any object on which that person sits will be unclean. [5] Anyone who touches such a bed must wash their clothes, bathe in water, and will be unclean until evening. [6] Anyone who sits on something that the one with the emission also sat on must wash their clothes, bathe in water, and will be unclean until evening. [7] Anyone who touches the body of the one with the emission must wash their clothes, bathe in water, and will be unclean until evening. [8] If the one with the emission spits on a clean person, the clean person must wash their clothes, bathe in water, and will be unclean until evening. [9] Every saddle on which the person with the emission rode will be unclean. [10] Anyone who touches anything that has been under such a person will be unclean until evening. Anyone who carries such items must wash their clothes, bathe in water, and will be unclean until evening. [11] If the one with the emission touches someone without first rinsing his hands with water, that person must wash their clothes, bathe in water, and will be unclean until evening. [12] Any pottery jar that the one with the emission touches must be broken, and any wooden tool must be rinsed with water.

[13] When the man with the emission is cleansed of his emission, he will count off seven days for his purification. He must wash his clothes and bathe his body in running water; then he will be clean again. [14] On the eighth day he will take two turtledoves or two pigeons and come before the LORD to the meeting tent's entrance and give these to the priest. [15] The priest will offer them, one as a purification offering and the other as an entirely burned offering. In this way, the priest will make reconciliation for him before the LORD because of his emission.

[16] If it is an emission of semen, the man must bathe his whole body in water and will be unclean until evening. [17] Any clothing or skin on which there is an emission of semen must be washed in water and will be unclean until evening. [18] If a man lies with a woman and has an emission of semen, both of them must bathe in water and will be unclean until evening.

Female genital emissions

[19] Whenever a woman has a discharge of blood that is her normal bodily discharge, she will be unclean due to her menstruation for seven days. Anyone who touches her will be unclean until evening. [20] Anything on which she lies or sits during her menstruation will be unclean. [21] Anyone who touches her bed must wash their clothes, bathe in water, and will be unclean until evening. [22] Anyone who touches anything on which she has sat must wash their clothes, bathe in water, and will be unclean until evening.

[f] Or live or healthy

²³Whenever anyone touches something—whether it was on the bed or where she has been sitting—they will be unclean until evening. ²⁴If a man has sexual intercourse with her and her menstruation gets on him, he will be unclean for seven days. Any bed he lies on will be unclean.

²⁵Whenever a woman has a bloody discharge for a long time, which is not during her menstrual period, or whenever she has a discharge beyond her menstrual period, the duration of her unclean discharge will be like the period of her menstruation; she will be unclean.

²⁶Any bed she lies on during the discharge should be treated like the bed she uses during her menstruation; and any object she sits on will be unclean, as during her menstruation. ²⁷Anyone who touches these things will be unclean. They must wash their clothes, bathe in water, and will be unclean until evening.

²⁸When the woman is cleansed of her discharge, she will count off seven days; after that, she will be clean again. ²⁹On the eighth day she will take two turtledoves or two pigeons and bring them to the priest at the meeting tent's entrance. ³⁰The priest will perform a purification offering with one and an entirely burned offering with the other. In this way, the priest will make reconciliation for her before the LORD because of her unclean discharge.

³¹You must separate the Israelites from their uncleanness so that they don't die on account of it, by making my dwelling^g unclean, which is in their midst.

³²This concludes the Instruction concerning those with discharges: men with

emissions of semen that make them unclean, ³³women during their menstruation, men or women with discharges, and men who have had sexual intercourse with an unclean woman.

The Day of Reconciliation

16 After the death of Aaron's two sons, which happened when they approached the LORD and died, the LORD spoke to Moses: ²Tell your brother Aaron that he cannot come whenever he wants into the holy area inside the inner curtain, to the front of the cover^h that is on the chest, or else he will die, because I am present^i in the cloud above the cover. ³No, but Aaron must enter the holy area as follows: with a bull from the herd as a purification offering and a ram as an entirely burned offering. ⁴Aaron must dress in a holy linen tunic and wear linen undergarments on his body. He must tie a linen sash around himself and wrap a linen turban around his head. These are holy clothes—Aaron will first bathe his body in water and then put them on. ⁵He will take from the Israelite community two male goats for a purification offering and one ram for an entirely burned offering.

⁶Aaron will offer the bull as a purification offering to make reconciliation for himself and his household. ⁷He will take the two male goats and place them before the LORD at the meeting tent's entrance. ⁸Aaron will cast lots over the two goats: one lot labeled "the LORD's" and the other lot labeled "Azazel's."^j ⁹Aaron will present the goat selected by the LORD's lot and perform a purification offering with it. ¹⁰But the goat

---

^gOr tabernacle   ^hOr mercy seat or perhaps reconciliation cover (Heb kapporet)   ^iOr I am seen or I appear
^jOr scapegoat

MOST HOLY PLACE

The inner sanctum behind a veil in the tent of meeting where the Israelites kept the covenant chest. The high priest alone was allowed to enter the most holy place once a year, on Reconciliation Day (see Lev 16).

selected by Azazel's lot will be left standing alive before the LORD in order to make reconciliation upon it[k] by sending it away into the wilderness to Azazel.

[11] Aaron will offer the bull for his purification offering to make reconciliation for himself and his household. He will slaughter the bull for his purification offering. [12] Then he will take an incense pan full of burning coals from the altar, from before the LORD, and two handfuls of finely ground perfumed incense and bring them inside the inner curtain. [13] He will put the incense on the fire before the LORD so that the cloud of incense conceals the cover that is on top of the covenant document, or else he will die. [14] He will take some of the bull's blood and sprinkle it with his finger on the cover from the east side. He will then sprinkle some of the blood with his finger seven times in front of the cover. [15] Then he will slaughter the goat for the people's purification offering, bring the blood inside the inner curtain, and do with it as he did with the bull's blood: he will sprinkle it on the cover and in front of the cover. [16] In this way, he will make reconciliation for the inner holy area because of the pollution of the Israelites and because of their rebellious sins, as well as for all their other sins.

Aaron must do the same for the meeting tent, which is with them among their pollution. [17] No one can be in the meeting tent from the time Aaron enters to make reconciliation in the inner holy area until the time he comes out. He will make reconciliation for himself, for his household, and for the whole assembly of Israel.

[18] Aaron will then go to the altar that is before the LORD and make reconciliation for it: He will take some of the bull's blood and some of the goat's blood and put it on each of the altar's horns. [19] He will sprinkle some of the blood on the altar with his finger seven times. In this way, he will purify it and make it holy again from the Israelites' pollution.

[20] When Aaron has finished reconciling the inner holy area, the rest of the meeting tent, and the altar, he will bring forward the live goat. [21] Aaron will press both his hands on its head and confess over it all the Israelites' offenses and all their rebellious sins, as well as all their other sins, putting all these on the goat's head. Then he will send it away into the wilderness with someone designated for the job.[l] [22] The goat will carry on itself all their offenses to a desolate region, then the goat will be released into the wild.

[23] After this, Aaron will enter the meeting tent, take off the linen clothes he was wearing when he entered the inner holy area, and will leave them there. [24] He will bathe his body in water in a holy place and dress in his priestly clothing. Then he will go out and perform the entirely burned offerings for himself and for the people. In this way, he will make reconciliation for himself and for the people. [25] He will completely burn the fat of the purification offering on the altar. [26] The one who set the goat free for Azazel must wash their clothes and bathe their body in water; after that they can return to the camp. [27] The bull and the goat for the purification offerings, whose blood was brought in to make reconciliation in the inner holy area, will be taken outside the camp. Their hides, flesh, and dung will be burned with fire. [28] The person who burns them must wash their clothes and bathe their body in water; after that, they can return to the camp.

[29] This will be a permanent rule for you: On the tenth day of the seventh month,[m] you must deny yourselves. You must not do any work—neither the citizen nor the immigrant who lives among you. [30] On that day reconciliation will be made for you in order to cleanse you. You will be clean before the LORD from all your sins. [31] It will be a Sabbath of special rest for you, and you will deny yourselves. This is a permanent rule.

Conclusion concerning the Day of Reconciliation

[32] The priest who is anointed and ordained to serve as priest after his father will perform the reconciliation, wearing the

---

[k] Or *over it* or *for it* or *with it* [l] Heb uncertain [m] September–October, Tishrei

holy linen clothes. [33]He will reconcile the holiest part of the sanctuary and will do the same for the meeting tent and the altar. He will make reconciliation for the priests and for all the people of the assembly. [34]This will be a permanent rule for you, in order to make reconciliation for the Israelites from all their sins once a year.

It was done just as the LORD commanded Moses.

Sacrifice at the sanctuary

17 The LORD said to Moses, [2]Say to Aaron, to his sons, and to all the Israelites: This is what the LORD has commanded: [3]Anyone from the house of Israel who slaughters an ox, sheep, or goat inside or outside the camp [4]but does not bring it to the meeting tent's entrance to present it as an offering to the LORD in front of the LORD's dwelling[n] will be considered guilty of bloodshed; they have spilled blood. They will be cut off from their people. [5]This will make the Israelites bring the communal sacrifices, which they are sacrificing in the countryside, to the LORD, to the priest at the meeting tent's entrance, and sacrifice them as communal sacrifices of well-being to the LORD. [6]The priest will toss the blood against the LORD's altar at the meeting tent's entrance and burn the fat completely as a soothing smell to the LORD. [7]The Israelites must no longer sacrifice their communal sacrifices to the goat demons that they follow so faithlessly.[o] This will be a permanent rule for them throughout their future generations. [8]You will also say to them: Anyone from Israel's house or from the immigrants who live with you who offers up an entirely burned offering or communal sacrifice [9]without bringing it to the meeting tent's entrance in order to offer it to the LORD will be cut off from their people.

Consuming blood forbidden

[10]I will oppose the person who consumes blood—whether they are from Israel's house or from the immigrants who live with you—and I will cut them off from their people. [11]A creature's life is in the blood. I have provided you the blood to make reconciliation for your lives on the altar, because the blood reconciles by means of the life.[p] [12]That is why I have told the Israelites: No one among you can consume blood, nor can the immigrant who lives with you consume blood.

[13]Anyone who hunts any animal or bird that can be eaten—whether the hunter is an Israelite or an immigrant who lives with you—must drain its blood out and cover it with dirt. [14]Again: for every creature's life, its blood is its life. That is why I have told the Israelites: You must not consume any creature's blood because every creature's life is its blood. Anyone who consumes it will be cut off.

Eating meat

[15]Anyone, whether citizen or immigrant, who eats an animal that has died naturally or that was killed by another animal, must wash their clothes, bathe in water, and will be unclean until evening. At that time, they will be clean again. [16]If they do not wash or bathe their body, they will be liable to punishment.

Sexual conduct

18 The LORD said to Moses, [2]Speak to the Israelites and say to them: I am the LORD your God. [3]You must not do things like they are done in the land of Egypt, where you used to live. And you must not do things like they are done in the land of Canaan, where I am bringing you. You must not follow the practices[q] of those places. [4]No, my regulations and my rules are the ones you must keep by following them: I am the LORD your God. [5]You must keep my rules and my regulations; by doing them one will live; I am the LORD.

[6]No one is allowed to approach any blood relative for sexual contact:[r] I am the LORD. [7]You must not uncover your father's nakedness, which is your mother's nakedness. She is your mother; you must not have sexual contact with her. [8]You must

---

[n]Or tabernacle [o]Or promiscuously [p]Or as life [q]Or rules or customs [r]Or to uncover nakedness

not uncover the nakedness of your father's wife; it is your father's nakedness. ⁹You must not have sexual contact with your sister—regardless of whether she is your father's daughter or your mother's daughter, whether born into the same household as you or outside it. ¹⁰You must not have sexual contact with your son's daughter or your daughter's daughter, because their nakedness is your own nakedness.ˢ ¹¹You must not have sexual contact with the daughter of your father's wife, who was born into your father's family; she is your sister. ¹²You must not have sexual contact with your father's sister; she is your father's blood relative. ¹³You must not have sexual contact with your mother's sister because she is your mother's blood relative. ¹⁴You will not uncover the nakedness of your father's brother—that is, you will not approach his wife for sex; she is your aunt. ¹⁵You must not have sexual contact with your daughter-in-law; she is your son's wife. You must not have sexual contact with her. ¹⁶You will not uncover the nakedness of your brother's wife; it is your brother's nakedness.

¹⁷You must not have sexual contact with a woman and her daughter. You will not marry her son's daughter or her daughter's daughter, thereby uncovering her nakedness. They are her blood relatives; it is shameful. ¹⁸You must not marry your wife's sister as a rival and have sexual contact with her while her sister is alive. ¹⁹You must not approach a woman for sexual contact during her menstrual uncleanness. ²⁰You must not have sexual relations with the wife of your fellow Israelite, becoming unclean by it.

²¹You must not give any of your childrenᵗ to offer them over to Molech so that you do not defile your God's name: I am the LORD. ²²You must not have sexual intercourse with a man as you would with a woman; it is a detestable practice. ²³You will not have sexual relations with any animal, becoming unclean by it. Nor will a woman present herself before an animal to mate with it; it is a perversion.

Warning against uncleanness and moral pollution

²⁴Do not make yourselves unclean in any of these ways because that is how the nations that I am throwing out before you became unclean. ²⁵That is also how the land became unclean, and I held it liable for punishment, and the land vomited out its inhabitants. ²⁶But all of you must keep my rules and my regulations. You must not do any of these detestable things, neither citizen nor immigrant who lives with you (²⁷because the people who had the land before you did all of these detestable things and the land became unclean), ²⁸so that the land does not vomit you out because you have made it unclean, just as it vomited out the nations that were before you. ²⁹Anyone who does any of these detestable things will be cut off from their people. ³⁰You must keep my requirement of not doing any of the detestable practicesᵘ that were done before you arrived so that you don't make yourselves unclean by them; I am the LORD your God.

Living as holy people

19 The LORD said to Moses, ²Say to the whole community of the Israelites: You must be holy, because I, the LORD your God, am holy. ³Each of you must respect your mother and father, and you must keep my sabbaths; I am the LORD your God. ⁴Do not turn to idols or make gods of cast metal for yourselves; I am the LORD your God. ⁵When you sacrifice a communal sacrifice of well-being to the LORD, offer it so that it will be accepted on your account. ⁶It must be eaten on the day of your sacrifice or the following day; whatever is left over on the third day must be burned with fire. ⁷If any of it is eaten on the third day, it is foul; it will not be accepted. ⁸Anyone who eats it will be liable to punishment, because they defiled what is holy to the LORD. That person will be cut off from their people. ⁹When you harvest your land's produce, you must not harvest all the way to the edge of your field; and don't gather up every remaining

---

ˢHeb uncertain ᵗOr *seed* ᵘOr *rules* or *customs*

bit of your harvest. ¹⁰Also do not pick your vineyard clean or gather up all the grapes that have fallen there. Leave these items for the poor and the immigrant; I am the LORD your God.

¹¹You must not steal nor deceive nor lie to each other. ¹²You must not swear falsely by my name, desecrating your God's name in doing so; I am the LORD. ¹³You must not oppress your neighbors or rob them. Do not withhold a hired laborer's pay overnight. ¹⁴You must not insult a deaf person or put some obstacle in front of a blind person that would cause them to trip. Instead, fear your God; I am the LORD.

¹⁵You must not act unjustly in a legal case. Do not show favoritism to the poor or deference to the great; you must judge your fellow Israelites fairly. ¹⁶Do not go around slandering your people.ᵛ Do not stand by while your neighbor's blood is shed;ʷ I am the LORD. ¹⁷You must not hate your fellow Israelite in your heart. Rebuke your fellow Israelite strongly, so you don't become responsible for his sin.ˣ ¹⁸You must not take revenge nor hold a grudge against any of your people; instead, you must love your neighbor as yourself; I am the LORD.

¹⁹You must keep my rules. Do not crossbreed your livestock, do not plant your field with two kinds of seed, and do not wear clothes made from two kinds of material. ²⁰If a man has sexual relations with a woman who is a slave engaged to another man, who hasn't yet been released or given her freedom, there must be a punishment.ʸ But they will not be put to death because she had not yet been freed. ²¹The man must bring as his compensation to the LORD at the meeting tent's entrance a ram for a compensation offering. ²²The priest will use the ram for the compensation offering to make reconciliation for him before the LORD on account of the sin he committed. Then he will be forgiven of the sin that he committed.

²³When you enter the land and plant any fruit tree, you must consider its fruit off-limits.ᶻ For three years it will be off-limits to you;ᵃ it must not be eaten. ²⁴In the fourth year, all of the tree's fruit will be holy, a celebration for the LORD. ²⁵In the fifth year you can eat the fruit. This is so as to increase its produce for you; I am the LORD your God.

²⁶You must not eat anything with its blood. You must not participate in divination or fortune-telling. ²⁷You must not cut off the hair on your forehead or clip the ends of your beard. ²⁸Do not cut your bodies for the deadᵇ or put marks onᶜ yourselves; I am the LORD. ²⁹Do not defile your daughter by making her sexually promiscuous or else the land will become promiscuousᵈ and full of shame. ³⁰You must keep my sabbaths and treat my sanctuary with respect; I am the LORD. ³¹Do not resort to dead spirits or inquire of spirits of divination—you will be made unclean by them; I am the LORD your God. ³²You must rise in the presence of an old person and respect the elderly. You must fear your God; I am the LORD.

³³When immigrants live in your land with you, you must not cheat them. ³⁴Any immigrant who lives with you must be treated as if they were one of your citizens. You must love them as yourself, because you were immigrants in the land of Egypt; I am the LORD your God. ³⁵You must not act unjustly in a legal case involving measures of length, weight, or volume. ³⁶You must have accurate scales and accurate weights, an accurate ephahᵉ and an accurate hin.ᶠ I am the LORD your God, who brought you out of the land of Egypt. ³⁷You must keep all my rules and all my regulations, and do them; I am the LORD.

Worship of Molech forbidden

20 The LORD said to Moses, ²You will also say to the Israelites: Any

---

ᵛHeb uncertain ʷHeb uncertain ˣOr *strongly, but don't become liable for punishment because of it*; Heb uncertain
ʸOr *an inquiry* ᶻOr *treat its fruit as a foreskin* ᵃOr *uncircumcised to you* ᵇOr *for the living* ᶜOr *tattoo*; Heb
uncertain ᵈOr *making her a prostitute so that the land won't become a prostitute* ᵉApproximately twenty quarts
ᶠApproximately one gallon of liquid

Israelite or any immigrant living in Israel who gives their children to Molech must be executed. The common people will stone such a person. ³Moreover, I will set my own face against such a person, cutting them off from their people, because they gave their children to Molech, making my sanctuary unclean and degrading my holy name by doing so. ⁴But if the common people choose to look the other way when someone gives their children to Molech and do not execute such a person, ⁵I will set my own face against such a person and their extended family, cutting off from their people—both the guilty party and anyone with them who faithlessly followed Molech. ⁶I will also oppose anyone who resorts to dead spirits or spirits of divination and faithlessly follows those things. I will cut such an individual off from their people.

Sexual prohibitions

⁷You must be holy and keep yourselves holy because I am the LORD your God. ⁸You will keep my rules and do them; I am the LORD, who makes you holy. ⁹If anyone curses their father or mother, they must be executed. They have cursed their own father and mother; that person's blood is on their own heads. ¹⁰If a man commits adultery with a married woman, committing adultery with a neighbor's wife, both the adulterer and the adulteress must be executed. ¹¹If a man has sexual intercourse with his father's wife, he has uncovered his father's nakedness. Both of them must be executed; their blood is on their own heads. ¹²If a man has sexual intercourse with his daughter-in-law, both of them must be executed. They have acted

perversely; their blood is on their own heads. ¹³If a man has sexual intercourse with a man as he would with a woman, the two of them have done something detestable. They must be executed; their blood is on their own heads. ¹⁴If a man marries a woman and her mother as well, it is shameful. They will be burned with fire—the man and the two women—so that no such shameful thing will be found among you. ¹⁵If a man has sexual relations with an animal, he must be executed and you must kill the animal. ¹⁶If a woman approaches any kind of animal to mate with it, you must kill the woman and the animal. They must be executed; their blood is on their own heads. ¹⁷If a man marries his sister—his father's daughter or his mother's daughter—and they have sexual contact with each other, it is a disgrace. They will be cut off in the sight of their people. Such a man has had sexual contact with his sister; he will be liable to punishment. ¹⁸If a man sleeps with a woman during her menstrual period and has sexual contact with her, he has exposed the source of her blood flow and she has uncovered the same. Both of them will be cut off from their people. ¹⁹You must not have sexual contact with your mother's sister or your father's sister, because that exposes your own close relative; both of you will be liable to punishment. ²⁰If a man has sexual intercourse with his aunt, he has uncovered his uncle's nakedness. The man and the aunt will be liable to punishment; they will die childless. ²¹If a man marries his brother's wife, it is indecent. He has uncovered his brother's nakedness; the man and the woman will be childless.

MOLECH/MOLOCH

Molech occurs several times in the OT as the name of a detested god associated with child sacrifice (Lev 18:21; 20:2-5; 2 Kgs 23:10; Jer 32:35; see also Isa 30:33; 57:9; Jer 7:31; 19:5; Molech in 1 Kgs 11:7 is a slip for "Milcom," cf. vv. 5 and 33).

Conclusion concerning conduct

²²You must keep all my rules and all my regulations, and do them so that the land I am bringing you to, where you will live, won't vomit you out. ²³You must not follow the practices[g] of the nations that I am throwing out before you, because they did all these things and I was disgusted with them. ²⁴But I have told you, "You will certainly possess their fertile land; I am giving it to you to possess. It is a land full of milk and honey." I am the LORD your God, who has separated you from all other peoples. ²⁵So you must separate between clean and unclean animals, and between clean and unclean birds. Do not become detestable through some animal, bird, or anything that moves on the fertile ground that I have separated from you as unclean. ²⁶You must be holy to me, because I the LORD am holy, and I have separated you from all other peoples to be my own. ²⁷If someone, whether male or female, is a medium with the dead or a diviner,[h] they must be executed. They will be stoned; their blood is on their own head.

Rules for priests

21 The LORD said to Moses, Say to the priests, Aaron's sons: None of you are allowed to make yourselves unclean by any dead person among your community ²except for your closest relatives: for your mother, father, son, daughter, brother; ³also for your unmarried sister, who is close to you because she isn't married—you may be polluted for her sake. ⁴You must not make yourself unclean for in-laws, defiling yourself by doing so.

⁵Priests must not shave bald patches on their heads or cut off the ends of their beards or make gashes in their bodies. ⁶They must be holy to their God so that they do not make their God's name impure. They must be holy because they offer the LORD's food gifts, their God's food. ⁷Priests must not marry a woman who is promiscuous and defiled, nor can they marry a woman divorced from her husband, because priests must be[i] holy to their God. ⁸You will treat the priests as holy, because they offer your God's food. The priests will be holy to you, because I am the holy LORD, who makes you holy. ⁹If the daughter of a priest defiles herself by being promiscuous, she defiles her father. She must be burned with fire.

¹⁰The high priest[j]—the one whose head has been anointed with the anointing oil and who is ordained to dress in the priestly clothing—must not dishevel his hair or tear his clothing. ¹¹He must not go near any dead bodies and cannot make himself unclean even for his father or mother. ¹²He must not exit the sanctuary, making his God's sanctuary impure by doing so, because his God's anointing oil, which separates,[k] is upon him; I am the LORD. ¹³The high priest must marry a woman who is a virgin. ¹⁴He cannot marry a widow, a divorced woman, or a woman defiled by promiscuity. He can only marry a virgin from his own people ¹⁵so that he doesn't make his children impure among his people, because I am the LORD, who makes him holy.

¹⁶The LORD said to Moses, ¹⁷Say to Aaron: None of your future descendants who have some kind of imperfection are allowed to offer their God's food. ¹⁸No one who has an imperfection will be allowed to make an offering: this includes anyone who is blind, crippled, disfigured, or deformed; ¹⁹anyone who has a broken foot or hand; ²⁰anyone who is a hunchback or too small; anyone who has an eye disease, a rash, scabs, or a crushed testicle.[l] ²¹No descendant of Aaron the priest who has an imperfection will be allowed to offer the LORD's food gifts; since he has an imperfection, he will not be allowed to offer his God's food. ²²He may, of course, eat of his God's most holy or holy food, ²³but since he has an imperfection, he cannot enter toward the inner curtain or officiate at the altar, making these parts of my sanctuary impure by doing so. I am the LORD, who makes them holy.

---

[g]Or *rules* or *customs*   [h]Or *has a spirit of the dead or a spirit of divination*   [i]Or *are*   [j]Or *the priest who is greater than his brothers*   [k]Or *consecrates*   [l]The meaning of several words in 21:18-20 is uncertain.

²⁴This is what Moses said to Aaron, his sons, and to all the Israelites.

Priestly uncleanness

22 The LORD said to Moses: ²Tell Aaron and his sons to be very careful how they treat the holy things that the Israelites devote to me so that they do not make my holy name impure: I am the LORD. ³Say to them: If any descendant of yours should ever come near the holy things that the Israelites have dedicated to the LORD while he is in an unclean state, he will be cut off from before me; I am the LORD. ⁴Any descendant of Aaron who is afflicted with skin disease^m or has a discharge cannot eat of the holy things until he is clean. Anyone who touches anything made unclean by a dead body, or who has an emission of semen, ⁵or who touches any swarming creature or another person who makes him unclean—whatever the uncleanness might be—⁶the person who touches these things will be unclean until evening. He must not eat of the holy things unless he has bathed his body in water. ⁷Once the sun has set and he has become clean again, he may eat of the holy things, for that is his food. ⁸He must not eat an animal that has died naturally or that was killed by another animal, becoming unclean by doing so; I am the LORD. ⁹The priests must keep my requirement so that they don't become liable to punishment and die for having made it impure.^n I am the LORD, who makes them holy.

Unauthorized eating

¹⁰No layperson is allowed to eat the holy offerings. No foreign guest or hired laborer of a priest can eat it. ¹¹But if a priest purchases a servant, that person can eat it, and servants born into the priest's household can also eat his food. ¹²If a priest's daughter marries a layman, she is not allowed to eat the holy offerings. ¹³But if a priest's daughter is a widow or divorced and has no children and so returns to her father's household as when she was young, she can eat her father's food. But, again, no layperson is allowed to eat it. ¹⁴If someone eats a holy offering unintentionally, they must provide the priest with an equal item, plus one-fifth. ¹⁵The Israelites must not make the holy offerings impure that they offer up to the LORD ¹⁶or make themselves liable to punishment requiring compensation by eating their own holy offerings. I am the LORD, who makes them holy.

Unacceptable animal offerings

¹⁷The LORD said to Moses: ¹⁸Tell Aaron, his sons, and all the Israelites: Whenever someone from Israel's house or from the immigrants in Israel presents their offering to the LORD as an entirely burned offering—whether it is payment for a solemn promise or a spontaneous gift—¹⁹for it to be acceptable on your behalf, it must be a flawless male from the herd, the sheep, or the goats. ²⁰You must not present anything that has an imperfection, because it will not be acceptable on your behalf. ²¹Whenever someone presents a communal sacrifice of well-being to the LORD from the herd or flock—whether it is payment for a solemn promise or a spontaneous gift—it must be flawless to be acceptable; it must not have any imperfection. ²²You must not present to the LORD anything that is blind or that has an injury, mutilation, warts, a rash, or scabs. You must not put any such animal on the altar as a food gift for the LORD. ²³You can, however, offer an ox or sheep that is deformed or stunted as a spontaneous gift, but it will not be acceptable as payment for a solemn promise. ²⁴You must not offer to the LORD anything with bruised, crushed, torn, or cut-off testicles. You must not do that in your land. ²⁵You are not allowed to offer such animals as your God's food even if they come from a foreigner. Because these animals have blemishes and imperfections in them, they will not be acceptable on your behalf.

---

^mThe precise meaning is uncertain; traditionally *leprosy*—a term used for several different skin diseases.   ^nVulg; MT *and die in it*

Additional rules for sacrifice

²⁶The LORD said to Moses: ²⁷When an ox or sheep or goat is born, it must remain with its mother for seven days. From the eighth day on it will be acceptable as an offering, a food gift for the LORD. ²⁸But you will not slaughter an ox or sheep and its offspring on the same day. ²⁹When you sacrifice a communal sacrifice of thanksgiving for the LORD, you must sacrifice it so that it will be acceptable on your behalf. ³⁰It must be eaten on the same day; you must not leave any of it until morning; I am the LORD. ³¹You must keep my commands and do them; I am the LORD. ³²You must not make my holy name impure so that I will be treated as holy by the Israelites. I am the LORD—the one who makes you holy ³³and who is bringing you out of the land of Egypt to be your God; I am the LORD.

Sacred times

23 The LORD said to Moses: ²Speak to the Israelites and say to them: These are my appointed times, the LORD's appointed times, which you will declare to be holy occasions: ³Work can be done for six days, but the seventh day is a Sabbath of special rest, a holy occasion. You must not do any work on it; wherever you live, it is a Sabbath to the LORD. ⁴These are the LORD's

°March–April, Nisan ᴾFour quarts dry; also in 23:17

appointed times, holy occasions, which you will celebrate at their appointed times:

⁵The LORD's Passover is on the fourteenth day of the first month° at twilight. ⁶The LORD's Festival of Unleavened Bread is on the fifteenth day of the same month. You must eat unleavened bread for seven days. ⁷On the first day you will hold a holy occasion and must not do any job-related work. ⁸You will offer food gifts to the LORD for seven days. The seventh day will be a holy occasion; you must not do any job-related work.

⁹The LORD said to Moses: ¹⁰Speak to the Israelites and say to them: When you enter the land that I am giving you and harvest its produce, you must bring the first bundle of your harvest to the priest. ¹¹The priest will lift up the bundle before the LORD so that it will be acceptable on your behalf. The priest will do this on the day after the Sabbath. ¹²On the day the bundle is lifted up for you, you must offer a flawless one-year-old lamb as an entirely burned offering to the LORD. ¹³The accompanying grain offering must be two-tenths of an ephahᴾ of choice flour mixed with oil, as a food gift for the LORD, a soothing smell. The accompanying drink offering must be a quarter of a hin of wine. ¹⁴You must not eat any bread, roasted grain, or fresh grain until the exact

FESTIVAL OF WEEKS

The Festival of Weeks is one of the three required pilgrimage festivals in the OT. Exodus 23:16, part of the Covenant Code, mentions a "Harvest Festival for the early produce of your crops that you planted in the field," while the parallel in Exodus 34:22 provides its name and identifies the crop: "the Festival of Weeks, for the early produce of the wheat harvest." Neither of these texts specifies a date for the festival; only in Deuteronomy 16:9-12 and Leviticus 23:15-16 are there instructions for determining when it was to be celebrated. According to Deuteronomy, one should count seven weeks, beginning from the time the sickle is set to the standing grain, and then celebrate the Festival of Weeks with a freewill offering and rejoicing by all the population, free or slave, native or sojourner. Leviticus 23 also mentions the seven weeks but adds other details.

day when you bring your God's offering. This is a permanent rule throughout your future generations, wherever you live. [15]You must count off seven weeks starting with the day after the Sabbath, the day you bring the bundle for the uplifted offering; these must be complete. [16]You will count off fifty days until the day after the seventh Sabbath. Then you must present a new grain offering to the LORD. [17]From wherever you live, you will bring two loaves of bread as an uplifted offering. These must be made of two-tenths of an ephah of choice flour, baked with leaven, as early produce[q] to the LORD. [18]Along with the bread you must present seven flawless one-year-old lambs, one bull from the herd, and two rams. These will be an entirely burned offering to the LORD, along with their grain offerings and drink offerings, as a food gift of soothing smell to the LORD. [19]You must also offer one male goat as a purification offering and two one-year-old lambs as a communal sacrifice of well-being. [20]The priest will lift up the two sheep, along with the bread of the early produce, as an uplifted offering before the LORD. These will be holy to the LORD and will belong to the priest. [21]On that very same day you must make a proclamation; it will be a holy occasion for you. You must not do any job-related work. This is a permanent rule wherever you live throughout your future generations. [22]When you harvest your land's produce, you must not harvest all the way to the edge of your field; and don't gather every remaining bit of your harvest. Leave these items for the poor and the immigrant; I am the LORD your God.

[23]The LORD said to Moses: [24]Say to the Israelites: On the first day of the seventh month,[r] you will have a special rest, a holy occasion marked by a trumpet signal. [25]You must not do any job-related work, and you must offer a food gift to the LORD.

[26]The LORD said to Moses: [27]Note that the tenth day of this seventh month is the Day of Reconciliation. It will be a holy occa-sion for you. You must deny yourselves and offer a food gift to the LORD. [28]You must not do any work that day because it is a Day of Reconciliation to make reconciliation for you before the LORD your God. [29]Anyone who does not deny themselves on that day will be cut off from their people. [30]Moreover, I will destroy from their people anyone who does any work on that day. [31]You must not do any work! This is a permanent rule throughout your future generations wherever you live. [32]This is a Sabbath of special rest for you, and you must deny yourselves. You will observe your Sabbath on the ninth day of the month from evening to the following evening.

[33]The LORD said to Moses: [34]Say to the Israelites: The Festival of Booths to the LORD will start on the fifteenth day of the seventh month and will last for seven days. [35]The first day is a holy occasion. You must not do any job-related work. [36]For seven days you will offer food gifts to the LORD. On the eighth day you will have a holy occasion and must offer a food gift to the LORD. It is a holiday: you must not do any job-related work.

[37]These are the LORD's appointed times that you will proclaim as holy occasions, offering food gifts to the LORD: entirely burned offerings, grain offerings, communal sacrifices, and drink offerings—each on its proper day. [38]This is in addition to the LORD's sabbaths and in addition to your presents, all the payments for solemn promises, and all the spontaneous gifts that you give to the LORD.

[39]Note that on the fifteenth day of the seventh month, when you have gathered the land's crops, you will celebrate the LORD's festival for seven days. The first day and the eighth day are days of special rest. [40]On the first day you must take fruit from majestic trees,[s] palm branches, branches of leafy trees,[t] and willows of the streams, and rejoice before the LORD your God for seven days. [41]You will celebrate this festival to the LORD for seven days each year; this

---

[q]Or firstfruits; also in 23:20   [r]September–October, Tishrei; also in 23:27, 33, 39, 41   [s]Or hadar trees
[t]Heb uncertain

is a permanent rule throughout your future generations. You will celebrate it in the seventh month. ⁴²For seven days you must live in huts. Every citizen of Israel must live in huts ⁴³so that your future generations will know that I made the Israelites live in huts when I brought them out of the land of Egypt; I am the LORD your God.

⁴⁴So Moses announced the LORD's appointed times to the Israelites.

The sanctuary's lamp and bread

24 The LORD said to Moses: ²Command the Israelites to bring pure, pressed olive oil to you for the lamp, to keep a light burning constantly. ³Aaron will tend the lamp, which will be inside the meeting tent but outside the inner curtain of the covenant document, from evening until morning before the LORD. This is a permanent rule throughout your future generations. ⁴Aaron must continually tend the lights on the pure lampstandᵘ before the LORD.

⁵You will take choice flour and bake twelve loaves of flatbread, two-tenths of an ephahᵛ for each loaf. ⁶You must place them in two stacks, six in a stack, on the pure tableʷ before the LORD. ⁷Put pure frankincense on each stack, as a token portion for the bread; it is a food gift for the LORD. ⁸Aaron will always set it out before the LORD, Sabbath after Sabbath, on behalf ofˣ the Israelites, as a permanent covenant. ⁹It will belong to Aaron and his sons. They must eat it in a holy place because it is the most holy part of their share of the LORD's food gifts, a permanent portion.

Assault and blasphemy

¹⁰The son of an Israelite mother and an Egyptian father came out among the Israelites. A fight broke out between this half-Israeliteʸ and another Israelite man in the camp, ¹¹during which the half-Israelite blasphemed the Lord's name and cursed. So he was brought to Moses. (His mother's name was Shelomith, Dibri's daughter from the tribe of Dan.) ¹²He was put under guard until they could determine the LORD's verdict.

¹³Then the LORD said to Moses: ¹⁴Take the one who cursed outside the camp. All who heard him will press their hands on his head. Then the whole community will stone him. ¹⁵Tell the Israelites: Anyone who curses God will be liable to punishment. ¹⁶And anyone who blasphemes the LORD's name must be executed. The whole community will stone that person. Immigrant and citizen alike: whenever someone blasphemes the Lord's name, that person will be executed.

ᵘPerhaps *pure gold lampstand* ᵛApproximately four quarts dry ʷPerhaps *pure gold table* ˣOr *from* or *as a gift of*; Heb uncertain ʸOr *Israelite woman's son*; also in 24:11

STONING

A type of capital punishment via pelting of stones, stoning typically involved taking a person outside the camp or the city (Lev 24:14; Deut 17:5), where the person was stoned initially by witnesses of the offense and, if death did not ensue, by onlookers (Deut 17:7). In biblical times, it was one of three types of lethal punishments, the others being burning and hanging. Stoning was the punishment for several crimes, including idolatry or seduction of others to idolatry (Lev 20:2; Deut 13:6-10); blasphemy (Lev 24:14); and breaking the Sabbath (Num 15:32-36). Both Stephen (Acts 7:58) and Paul (Acts 14:19) were stoned, the former with a fatal end. A woman also escaped a possible stoning by virtue of Jesus' challenges to her accusers (John 8:7). Stoning was also prominent among the Persians and the Greeks.

¹⁷If anyone kills another person, they must be executed. ¹⁸Someone who kills an animal may make amends for it: a life for a life. ¹⁹If someone injures a fellow citizen, they will suffer the same injury they inflicted: ²⁰broken bone for broken bone, an eye for an eye, a tooth for a tooth. The same injury the person inflicted on the other will be inflicted on them. ²¹Someone who kills an animal must make amends for it, but whoever kills a human being must be executed. ²²There is but one law on this matter for you, immigrant or citizen alike, because I am the LORD your God.

²³Moses told this to the Israelites. So they took the one who had cursed outside the camp and stoned him. The Israelites did just as the LORD commanded Moses.

The sabbatical year

25 The LORD said to Moses on Mount Sinai, ²Speak to the Israelites and say to them: Once you enter the land that I am giving you, the land must celebrate a sabbath rest to the LORD. ³You will plant your fields for six years, and prune your vineyards and gather their crops for six years. ⁴But in the seventh year the land will have a special sabbath rest, a Sabbath to the LORD: You must not plant your fields or prune your vineyards. ⁵You must not harvest the secondary growth of your produce or gather the grapes of your freely growing vines. It will be a year of special rest for the land. ⁶Whatever the land produces during its sabbath will be your food—for you, for your male and female servants, and for your hired laborers and foreign guests who live with you, ⁷as well as for your livestock and for the wild animals in your land. All of the land's produce can be eaten.

The Jubilee year

⁸Count off seven weeks of years—that is, seven times seven—so that the seven weeks of years totals forty-nine years. ⁹Then have the trumpet^z blown on the tenth day of the seventh month.^a Have the trumpet blown throughout your land on the Day of Reconciliation. ¹⁰You will make the fiftieth year holy, proclaiming freedom throughout the land to all its inhabitants. It will be a Jubilee year^b for you: each of you must return to your family property and to your extended family. ¹¹The fiftieth year will be a Jubilee year for you. Do not plant, do not harvest the secondary growth, and do not gather from the freely growing vines ¹²because it is a Jubilee: it will be holy to you. You can eat only the produce directly out of the field. ¹³Each of you must return to your family property in this year of Jubilee.

¹⁴When you sell something to or buy something from your fellow citizen, you must not cheat each other. ¹⁵You will buy from your fellow citizen according to the number of years since the Jubilee; he will sell to you according to the number of years left for harvests. ¹⁶You will raise the price if there are more years, or lower the price if there are less years because it is the number of harvests that are being sold to you. ¹⁷You must not cheat each other but fear your God because I am the LORD your God. ¹⁸You will observe my rules, and you will keep my regulations and do them so that you can live securely on the land.

Food during fallow years

¹⁹The land will give its fruit so that you can eat your fill and live securely on it. ²⁰Suppose you ask, "What will we eat in the seventh year if we don't plant or gather our crops then?" ²¹I will send my blessing on you in the sixth year so that it will make enough produce for three years. ²²You can plant again in the eighth year and eat food from the previous year's produce until the ninth year. Until its produce comes, you will eat the food from the previous year.

Buying back family property

²³The land must not be permanently sold because the land is mine. You are just immigrants and foreign guests of mine.

²⁴Throughout the whole land that you possess, you must allow for the land to be

---

^zHeb *shofar* ^aSeptember–October, Tishrei ^bHeb *yobel*

bought back. [25]When one of your fellow Israelites faces financial difficulty and must sell part of their family property, the closest relative[c] will come and buy back what their fellow Israelite has sold. [26]If the person doesn't have someone to buy it back, but then manages to afford buying it back, [27]they must calculate the years since its sale and refund the balance to the person to whom they sold it. Then it will go back to the family property.[d] [28]If they cannot afford to make a refund to the buyer, whatever was sold will remain in the possession of the buyer until the Jubilee year. It will be released in the Jubilee year, at which point it will return to the family property.

[29]When a person sells a home in a walled city, it may be bought back until a year after its sale. The period for buying it back will be one year. [30]If it is not bought back before a full year has passed, the house in the walled city will belong to the buyer permanently and their descendants forever. It will not be released at the Jubilee. [31]But houses in settlements that are unwalled will be considered as if they were country fields. They can be bought back, and they must be released at the Jubilee.

[32]Levites will always have the right to buy back homes in the levitical cities that are part of their family property. [33]Levite property that can be bought back—houses sold in a city that is their family property—must be released at the Jubilee, because homes in levitical cities are the Levites' family property among the Israelites. [34]But the pastureland around their cities cannot be sold, because that is their permanent family property.

Poor Israelites and slavery

[35]If one of your fellow Israelites faces financial difficulty and is in a shaky situation with you,[e] you must assist them as you would an immigrant or foreign guest so that they can survive among you. [36]Do not take interest from them, or any kind of profit from interest, but fear your God so that your fellow Israelite can survive among you. [37]Do not lend a poor Israelite money with interest or lend food at a profit. [38]I am the LORD your God, who brought you out from the land of Egypt to give you Canaan's land and to be your God.

[39]If one of your fellow Israelites faces financial difficulty with you and sells themselves to you, you must not make him work as a slave. [40]Instead, they will be like a hired laborer or foreign guest to you. They will work for you until the Jubilee year, [41]at which point the poor Israelite along with their children will be released from you. They can return to their extended family and to their family property. [42]You must do this because these people are my servants—I brought them out of Egypt's land. They must not be sold as slaves. [43]You will not harshly rule over them but must fear your God.

[c]Or next of kin; traditionally redeemer   [d]Or they will go back to their family property; also in 25:28.
[e]Heb uncertain

JUBILEE YEAR

The Jubilee year is the final year of a cycle of seven "sabbatical" periods of seven years each. The name derives from the ram's horn with which the Jubilee year is inaugurated on Reconciliation Day (Lev 25:9). Land is left fallow (Lev 25:11, 19-22), debts for fellow Israelites are forgiven (Lev 25:24-34), and Israelite slaves held by other Israelites are freed (Lev 25:39-46). Jubilee laws also include general rules governing fair commercial practices (e.g., Lev 25:14) and attention to the economically disadvantaged, particularly among one's own relatives (25:35-55).

⁴⁴Regarding male or female slaves that you are allowed to have: You can buy a male or a female slave from the nations that are around you. ⁴⁵You can also buy them from the foreign guests who live with you and from their extended families that are with you, who were born in your land. These can belong to you as property. ⁴⁶You can pass them on to your children as inheritance that they can own as permanent property. You can make these people work as slaves, but you must not rule harshly over your own people, the Israelites.

⁴⁷If an immigrant or foreign guest prospers financially among you, but your fellow Israelite faces financial difficulty and so sells themselves to the immigrant or foreign guest, or to a descendant of a foreigner, ⁴⁸the Israelite will have the right to be bought back after they sold themselves. One of their relatives can buy them back: ⁴⁹their uncle or cousin can buy them back; one of their blood relatives from their family can buy them back; or they may be able to afford their own purchase. ⁵⁰The Israelite will calculate with their owner the time from the year they were sold until the Jubilee year. The price of their release will be based on the number of years they were with the owner, as in the case of a hired laborer. ⁵¹If there are many years left before the Jubilee, the Israelite will pay for their purchase in proportion to their purchase price. ⁵²If only a few years are left, they will calculate that and pay for their purchase according to the years of service. ⁵³Regardless, the Israelite will be to the buyer like a yearly laborer; the buyer must not harshly rule over them in your sight. ⁵⁴If the Israelite is not bought back in one of these ways, they and their children must be released in the Jubilee year ⁵⁵because the Israelites belong to me as servants. They are my servants—I brought them out of Egypt's land; I am the LORD your God.

Covenant blessings

26 You must not make any idols, and do not set up any divine image or sacred pillar. You must not place any carved[f] stone in your land, bowing down to it, because I am the LORD your God. ²You must keep my sabbaths and respect my sanctuary; I am the LORD.

³If you live according to my rules, keep my commands, and do them, ⁴I will give you rain at the proper time, the land will produce its yield, and the trees of the field will produce their fruit. ⁵Your threshing season will last until the grape harvest, and the grape harvest will last until planting time. You will eat your fill of food and live securely in your land. ⁶I will grant peace in the land so that you can lie down without anyone frightening you. I will remove dangerous animals from the land, and no sword will pass through it. ⁷You will chase your enemies, and they will fall before you in battle. ⁸Five of you will chase away a hundred, and a hundred of you will chase away ten thousand, and your enemies will fall before you in battle. ⁹I will turn my face to you, will make you fruitful and numerous, and will keep my covenant with you. ¹⁰You will still be eating the previous year's harvest when the time will come to clear it out to make room for the new! ¹¹I will place my dwelling[g] among you, and I will not despise you. ¹²I will walk around among you; I will be your God, and you will be my people. ¹³I am the LORD your God, who brought you out of Egypt's land—who brought you out from being Egypt's slaves. I broke your bonds and made you stand up straight.

Covenant curses

¹⁴But if you do not obey me and do not carry out all these commands—¹⁵if you reject my rules and despise my regulations, not doing all my commands and breaking my covenant—¹⁶then I will do the following to you:

I will bring horrific things:[h] wasting diseases and fevers that make the eyes fail and drain life away.

You will plant seed for no reason because your enemies will eat the food.

¹⁷I will turn my face against you: you will

---

[f]Heb uncertain [g]Or *tabernacle* [h]Precise nature of the diseases uncertain

be defeated by your enemies; those who hate you will rule over you; and you will run away even when no one is chasing you.

¹⁸If, despite all that, you still do not obey me, I will punish you for your sins seven more times: ¹⁹I will destroy your prideful power. I will turn your sky to iron and your land to bronze ²⁰so that your strength will be spent for no reason: your land will not produce its yield, and the trees of the land won't produce their fruit.

²¹If you continue to oppose me and are unwilling to obey me, I will strike you for your sins seven more times: ²²I will send wild animals against you, and they will kill your children and destroy your livestock. They will make you so few in number that your roads will seem deserted.

²³If, despite these things, you still do not accept my discipline and continue to oppose me, ²⁴then I will continue to oppose you. I will strike you for your sins seven more times: ²⁵I will bring the sword against you, avenging the breaking of the covenant.ⁱ If you retreat into your cities, I will send a plague on you, and you will be handed over to the enemy. ²⁶When I destroy your food supply, ten women will bake bread in a single oven, and they will ration out bread by weight. You will eat but will never get full.

²⁷If, despite all this, you still do not obey me and continue to oppose me, ²⁸then I will continue to oppose you—with anger! I will punish you for your sins seven more times: ²⁹You will eat the flesh of your own sons and daughters. ³⁰I will eliminate your shrines, chop down your incense altars, and pile your dead bodies on the dead bodies of your idols. I will despise you. ³¹I will turn your cities into ruins, I will devastate your sanctuaries, and I will not smell the soothing smells of your offerings. ³²I will personally devastate the land so much that your enemies who resettle it will be astonished by it. ³³I will scatter you among the nations. I will unsheathe my sword against you. Your land will be devastated and your cities will be ruins.

³⁴At that time, while it is devastated and you are in enemy territory, the land will enjoy its sabbaths. At that time, the land will rest and enjoy its sabbaths. ³⁵During the whole time it is devastated, it will have the rest it didn't have during the sabbaths you lived in it.

³⁶I will bring despair into the hearts of those of you who survive in enemy territory. Just the sound of a windblown leaf will put them to running, and they will run scared as if running from a sword! They will fall even when no one is chasing them! ³⁷They will stumble over each other as they would before a sword, even though no one is chasing them! You will have no power to stand before your enemies. ³⁸You will disappear among the nations—the land of your enemies will devour you. ³⁹Any of you who do survive will rot in enemy territory on account of their guilty deeds. And they will rot too on account of their ancestors' guilty deeds.

Covenant and restoration

⁴⁰But if they confess their and their ancestors' guilt for the wrongdoing they did to me, and for their continued opposition to me—⁴¹which made me oppose them, so I took them into enemy territory—or if their uncircumcised hearts are humbled and they make up for their guilt, ⁴²then I will remember my covenant with Jacob. I will also remember my covenant with Isaac. And my covenant with Abraham. And I will remember the land. ⁴³The land will be absent of them and will be enjoying its sabbaths while it lies devastated, free of them. They will be making up for their guilty deeds for no other reason than the fact that they rejected my regulations and despised my rules. ⁴⁴But despite all that, when they are in enemy territory, I will not reject them or despise them to the point of totally destroying them, breaking my covenant with them by doing so, because I am the LORD their God. ⁴⁵But for their sake I will remember the covenant with the first generation, the ones I brought out of Egypt's land in

ⁱOr *executing covenant vengeance*

the sight of all the nations, in order to be their God; I am the LORD.

⁴⁶These are the rules, regulations, and instructions between the LORD and the Israelites that he gave through Moses on Mount Sinai.

Dedications

27 The LORD said to Moses, ²Speak to the Israelites and say to them: When a person makes a solemn promise to the LORD involving the value of a person, ³if it is the value for a male between 20 and 60 years old, his value is fifty silver shekels according to the sanctuary's shekel. ⁴If the person is a female, her value is thirty shekels. ⁵If the age of the person is between 5 and 20 years, the value for a male is twenty shekels, for a female ten shekels. ⁶If the age of the person is between one month and 5 years, the value for a male is five silver shekels, for a female three silver shekels. ⁷If the age of the person is 60 years or more, the value is fifteen shekels if the person is male, ten shekels for a female. ⁸But if financial difficulty prevents the promise maker from giving the full value, they must set the person before the priest. The priest will assign the person a value according to what the promise maker can afford.

⁹If a solemn promise involves livestock that can be offered to the LORD, any such animal given to the LORD will be considered holy. ¹⁰The promise maker cannot replace or substitute for it, either good for bad or bad for good. But if one should substitute one animal for another, both it and the substitute will be holy. ¹¹If the solemn promise involves any kind of unclean animal that cannot be offered to the LORD, the promise maker must set the animal before the priest. ¹²The priest will assign it a value, whether high or low.ʲ Its value will be what the priest says. ¹³If the promise maker wishes to buy it back, they must add one-fifth to its value.

¹⁴When someone dedicates their house to the LORD as holy, the priest will as-

sign a value to it, whether high or low. The value is fixed, whatever value the priest assigns to it. ¹⁵If the one who dedicates the house wishes to buy it back, they must add one-fifth to its valued price, and it will be theirs again.

¹⁶If a person dedicates part of the land from their family property to the LORD, the value will be set according to the seed needed to plant it: fifty silver shekels per homer of barley seed. ¹⁷If the person dedicates the piece of land during the Jubilee year, its value will stay fixed. ¹⁸But if the person dedicates the piece after the Jubilee year, the priest will calculate the price according to the years that are left until the next Jubilee year, and the value will be reduced. ¹⁹If the one who dedicates the land wishes to buy it back, they must add one-fifth to its valued price, and it will be theirs again. ²⁰But if they do not buy it back or if it was sold to someone else, it is no longer able to be bought back. ²¹When the piece of land is released in the Jubilee year, it will be holy to the LORD like a piece of devoted land; it will be the priest's property. ²²If the person dedicates land they purchased to the LORD—land that is not part of their family property—²³the priest will calculate the amount of its value until the Jubilee year. The person must pay the value on that day as a holy donation to the LORD. ²⁴In the Jubilee year the piece of land will return to the seller, to the one who is the original owner of the family property. ²⁵Every value will be according to the sanctuary's shekel. The shekel will be twenty gerahs.

²⁶But note that a person cannot dedicate any oldest offspring from livestock, which already belongs to the LORD because it is the oldest. Whether ox or sheep, it belongs to the LORD. ²⁷If it is an unclean animal, it may be bought back at its value plus twenty percent. If it is not bought back, it will be sold at its set value.

²⁸Also note that everything someone devotesᵏ to the LORD from their possessions—whether humans, animals, or pieces

---

ʲOr *good or bad*; also in 27:14   ᵏOr *places under the ban* (also in 27:29), a technique of holy war, in which all is dedicated to the deity who helps in the battle; it often involved total destruction.

of land from their family property—cannot be sold or bought back. Every devoted thing is most holy to the LORD. ²⁹No human beings that have been devoted can be bought back; they must be executed.

³⁰All tenth-part gifts[1] from the land, whether of seed from the ground or fruit from the trees, belong to the LORD; they are holy to the LORD. ³¹If someone wishes to buy back part of their tenth-part gift, they must add one-fifth to it. ³²All tenth-part gifts from a herd or flock—every tenth animal that passes under the shepherd's staff—will be holy to the LORD. ³³The one bringing the tenth-part gift must not pick out the good from the bad, and cannot substitute any animal. But if one should substitute an animal, both it and the substitute will be holy and cannot be bought back.

³⁴These are the commands that the LORD gave Moses on Mount Sinai for the Israelites.

---

[1] Or tithes

NUMBERS

The book of Numbers is the fourth book in the series often called "the five books of Moses" (Genesis–Deuteronomy). Numbers continues the historical narrative that began at Exodus 1:1.

In the original Hebrew, the name of this book is actually *In the desert* or *wilderness*. This name fits the contents of the book well, since the book of Numbers narrates events during the time of the Israelites' desert wanderings. The English title, *Numbers*, was given to this book because its earliest words have to do with the numbers of people in the census taken by Moses (chapter 1).

THE CONTENT OF THE BOOK

The book of Numbers may be divided into three parts: (1) the Israelites prepare to depart from Mount Sinai, chapters 1–10; (2) the Israelites journey to Kadesh, chapters 11–21; and (3) the Israelites approach the land of Canaan, chapters 22–36.

Numbers 1:1 continues the narrative that began in the book of Exodus. The people of Israel have left Egypt, have journeyed to Sinai, and are receiving instructions about life and worship in the promised land. These instructions begin with the Ten Commandments (Exodus 20:1–17) and continue through the tenth chapter of Numbers, when the people finally pull up stakes and continue their journey to the promised land.

THE DATE OF NUMBERS

The book of Numbers is part of the Pentateuch, or the five books of Moses. This group of narratives was written over a period of many years (900–500 BCE) and was compiled in its final form sometime during the exile.

MAJOR THEMES IN NUMBERS

Theological themes in Numbers include the people's complaining against Moses while they are wandering in the desert, God's continued presence with them during this time, the people's disobedience and lack of trust in God, and what the covenant relationship promises the people and what it requires of them.

NUMBERS

First census

1 The LORD spoke to Moses in the Sinai desert in the meeting tent on the first day of the second month,[a] in the second year after they left the land of Egypt: ² Take a census of the entire Israelite community by their clans and their households, recording the name of every male, ³ 20 years old and above, who is eligible for military service in Israel. These you and Aaron will enlist in their military units. ⁴ Take with you one man from each tribe who is the head of his household. ⁵ These are the names of the men who will assist you:

from Reuben, Elizur, Shedeur's son;
⁶ from Simeon, Shelumiel,
  Zurishaddai's son;
⁷ from Judah, Nahshon,
  Amminadab's son;
⁸ from Issachar, Nethanel, Zuar's son;
⁹ from Zebulun, Eliab, Helon's son;
¹⁰ from Joseph's sons:
  from Ephraim, Elishama,
    Ammihud's son;
  from Manasseh, Gamaliel,
    Pedahzur's son;
¹¹ from Benjamin, Abidan, Gideoni's son;
¹² from Dan, Ahiezer, Ammishaddai's son;
¹³ from Asher, Pagiel, Ochran's son;
¹⁴ from Gad, Eliasaph, Deuel's son;
¹⁵ from Naphtali, Ahira, Enan's son.

¹⁶ These are the ones appointed from the community, chiefs of their ancestral tribes and leaders of the divisions of Israel.

¹⁷ Moses and Aaron took these men who were selected by name ¹⁸ and they assembled the entire community on the first day of the second month. They registered them by their clans and their households, recording the name of each male 20 years old and above. ¹⁹ Moses enlisted them in the Sinai desert just as the LORD commanded him.

²⁰ There were the descendants of Reuben, Israel's oldest, registered by their clans and their households. Every man 20 years old and above eligible for military service was individually recorded by name. ²¹ Those enlisted from the tribe of Reuben were 46,500.

²² There were the descendants of Simeon, registered by their clans and their households. Every male 20 years old and above eligible for military service was individually recorded by name. ²³ Those enlisted from the tribe of Simeon were 59,300.

²⁴ There were the descendants of Gad, registered by their clans and their households. The men 20 years old and above eligible for military service were recorded by name. ²⁵ Those enlisted from the tribe of Gad were 45,650.

²⁶ There were the descendants of Judah, registered by their clans and their households. The men 20 years old and above eligible for military service were recorded by name. ²⁷ Those enlisted from the tribe of Judah were 74,600.

²⁸ There were the descendants of Issachar, registered by their clans and their households. The men 20 years old and above eligible for military service were recorded by name. ²⁹ Those enlisted from the tribe of Issachar were 54,400.

³⁰ There were the descendants of Zebulun, registered by their clans and their households. The men 20 years old and above eligible for military service were recorded by name. ³¹ Those enlisted from the tribe of Zebulun were 57,400.

³² From Joseph's descendants there were the descendants of Ephraim, registered by their clans and their households. The men 20 years old and above eligible for military service were recorded by name. ³³ Those enlisted from the tribe of Ephraim were 40,500.

³⁴ There were the descendants of Manasseh, registered by their clans and their households. The men 20 years old and above eligible for military service were recorded by name. ³⁵ Those enlisted from the tribe of Manasseh were 32,200.

[a] April–May, Iyar

³⁶There were the descendants of Benjamin, registered by their clans and their households. The men 20 years old and above eligible for military service were recorded by name. ³⁷Those enlisted from the tribe of Benjamin were 35,400.

³⁸There were the descendants of Dan, registered by their clans and their households. The men 20 years old and above eligible for military service were recorded by name. ³⁹Those enlisted from the tribe of Dan were 62,700.

⁴⁰There were the descendants of Asher, registered by their clans and their households. The men 20 years old and above eligible for military service were recorded by name. ⁴¹Those enlisted from the tribe of Asher were 41,500.

⁴²There were the descendants of Naphtali, registered by their clans and their households. The men 20 years old and above eligible for military service were recorded by name. ⁴³Those enlisted from the tribe of Naphtali were 53,400.

⁴⁴These are the ones who were enlisted by Moses, Aaron, and the twelve chiefs of Israel, each from his own household. ⁴⁵All the Israelites 20 years old and above eligible for military service in Israel were enlisted by their households. ⁴⁶All those enlisted were 603,550. ⁴⁷But the Levites, belonging to their own ancestral tribe, weren't enlisted along with them.

The Levites' exclusion from the census

⁴⁸The LORD spoke to Moses: ⁴⁹You must not enlist the tribe of Levi, nor should you take their census along with the Israelites. ⁵⁰Rather, assign the Levites to the covenant dwelling, to all its equipment, and to everything that belongs to it. They will carry the dwelling and all its equipment, perform its religious ceremonies, and camp around the dwelling. ⁵¹When it's time to break camp, the Levites will take down the dwelling; and when it's time to make camp, the Levites will set up the dwelling. Any other person who approaches will be put to death. ⁵²The Israelites will camp each in their own place under the banner of their own military unit. ⁵³But the Levites will camp around the covenant dwelling so that God's anger will not strike the Israelite community. The Levites will guard the covenant dwelling.

⁵⁴The Israelites did everything exactly as the LORD commanded Moses.

The wilderness camp's arrangement

2 The LORD spoke to Moses and Aaron: ²The Israelites will camp each under the banner with the symbol of their household.

CENSUS

A census in the Bible is the enrollment and numbering of a group of people, tribe, or nation for various purposes: the numbering of the 70 members of Jacob's clan who came to Egypt in the time of Joseph (Gen 46:26-27; Exod 1:1-7), taxation for religious or governmental purposes (Exod 30:13-16; 38:24-26; Luke 2:1-5), assignment of duties to clans of priestly Levites (Num 3:1-39), finding the number of Levites available as substitutes for Israel's firstborn males (Num 3:40-51), counting of troops for war (Num 1:2-3; 26:2; 2 Sam 24:1-9; 1 Chron 21:1-6), distribution of the land of Canaan according to the size of Israelite tribes and clans (Num 26:3-56), and the counting of former exiles who returned from Babylon to Judah (Ezra 2:1-67). The three most significant census-taking events in the Bible are the wilderness census lists in Numbers 1 and 26, David's census in 2 Samuel 24 and 1 Chronicles 21, and the census associated with Jesus' birth in Luke 2.

They will camp around the meeting tent some distance from it.

The camp's east side

[3]On the east side toward the sunrise will be the banner of Judah's camp with its military units. The chief of the people of Judah is Nahshon, Amminadab's son. [4]His military unit and those enlisted in it are 74,600. [5]Those camping on one side of him are the tribe of Issachar. The chief of the people of Issachar is Nethanel, Zuar's son. [6]His military unit and those enlisted in it are 54,400. [7]On the other side, the tribe of Zebulun: the chief of the people of Zebulun is Eliab, Helon's son. [8]His military unit and those enlisted in it are 57,400. [9]All those enlisted in Judah's camp with their military units are 186,400. They will march first.

The camp's south side

[10]On the south side will be the banner of Reuben's camp with its military units. The chief of the people of Reuben is Elizur, Shedeur's son. [11]His military unit and those enlisted in it are 46,500. [12]Those camping on one side of him are the tribe of Simeon. The chief of the people of Simeon is Shelumiel, Zurishaddai's son. [13]His military unit and those enlisted in it are 59,300. [14]On the other side, the tribe of Gad: the chief of the people of Gad is Eliasaph, Reuel's son. [15]His military unit and those enlisted in it are 45,650. [16]All those enlisted in Reuben's camp with their military units are 151,450. They will march second.

The camp's center

[17]The meeting tent and the Levites' camp will march in the center of the camps. They will march in the same order as they camp: each in position under his banner.

The camp's west side

[18]On the west will be the banner of Ephraim's camp with its military units. The chief of the people of Ephraim is Elishama, Ammihud's son. [19]His military unit and those enlisted in it are 40,500. [20]On one side of him is the tribe of Manasseh. The chief of the people of Manasseh is Gamaliel, Pedahzur's son. [21]His military unit and those enlisted in it are 32,200. [22]On the other side, the tribe of Benjamin: the chief of the people of Benjamin is Abidan, Gideoni's son. [23]His military unit and those enlisted in it are 35,400. [24]All those enlisted in Ephraim's camp with their military units are 108,100. They will march third.

The camp's north side

[25]On the north will be the banner of Dan's camp with its military units. The chief of the people of Dan is Ahiezer, Ammishaddai's son. [26]His military unit and those enlisted in it are 62,700. [27]Those camping on one side of him are the tribe of Asher. The chief of the people of Asher is Pagiel, Ochran's son. [28]His military unit and those enlisted in it are 41,500. [29]On the other side, the tribe of Naphtali: the chief of the people of Naphtali is Ahira, Enan's son. [30]His military unit and those enlisted in it are 53,400. [31]All those enlisted in the camp of Dan are 157,600. They will march last under their banners.

[32]These are the enlisted Israelites by their households. The total enlisted in the camps with their military units is 603,550. [33]But the Levites weren't enlisted among the Israelites, as the LORD had commanded Moses. [34]The Israelites did everything exactly as the LORD had commanded Moses: they camped under their banners and they marched by their clans and by their households.

Aaron's sons

3 These are the descendants of Aaron and Moses at the time when the LORD spoke with Moses on Mount Sinai. [2]These are the names of Aaron's sons: Nadab the oldest, and Abihu, Eleazar, and Ithamar. [3]These are the names of Aaron's sons, who are the anointed priests and ordained to the priesthood. [4]Nadab and Abihu died before the LORD when they made an unauthorized offering to the LORD in the Sinai desert. They didn't have any sons. Eleazar and Ithamar served as priests during the lifetime of their father Aaron.

The Levites' first census

⁵The LORD spoke to Moses: ⁶Bring near the tribe of Levi and place them before Aaron the priest. They will assist him. ⁷They will perform duties for him and for the entire community before the meeting tent, doing the work of the dwelling. ⁸They will be responsible for all the equipment of the meeting tent and the duties on behalf of the Israelites when they do the work of the dwelling. ⁹You will give the Levites to Aaron and his sons. They have been assigned as a gift to him from the Israelites. ¹⁰You will appoint Aaron and his sons to be responsible for the priesthood. Any other person who approaches will be put to death.

¹¹The LORD spoke to Moses: ¹²I claim the Levites from the Israelites in place of all the oldest males who open an Israelite womb. The Levites are mine ¹³because all the oldest males are mine. When I killed all the oldest males in the land of Egypt, I reserved for myself all the oldest males in Israel, both humans and animals. They are mine; I am the LORD.

¹⁴The LORD spoke to Moses in the Sinai desert: ¹⁵Enroll the Levites by their households and their clans. You will enroll all the males over one month old. ¹⁶Moses enrolled them according to the LORD's word as he was commanded. ¹⁷These were Levi's sons by name: Gershon, Kohath, and Merari. ¹⁸These were the names of Gershon's sons by their clans: Libni and Shimei. ¹⁹Kohath's sons by their clans: Amram, Izhar, Hebron, and Uzziel. ²⁰Merari's sons by their clans: Mahli and Mushi. These were the clans of Levi by their households.

²¹To Gershon belonged the clans of Libni and Shimei. These were the clans of the Gershonites. ²²Their enrollment, according to the number of males over one month old, was 7,500. ²³The clans of the Gershonites were to camp behind the dwelling on the west side. ²⁴The chief of the household of the Gershonites was Eliasaph, Lael's son. ²⁵In the dwelling, the Gershonites were responsible for the meeting tent, the tent with its covering, the screen for the entrance of the meeting tent, ²⁶the curtains of the courtyard, the screen for the entrance of the courtyard surrounding the meeting tent and the altar, and its cords—all these structures.

²⁷To Kohath belonged the clans of the Amramites, Izharites, Hebronites, and Uzzielites. These were the clans of the Kohathites. ²⁸The number of males over one month old, who would perform duties for the sanctuary, was 8,600. ²⁹The clans of the Kohathites were to camp on the south side of the dwelling. ³⁰The chief of the household representing the clans of the Kohathites was Elizaphan, Uzziel's son. ³¹They were responsible for the chest, the table, the lampstand, the altars, the equipment of the sanctuary with which they would minister, and the screen—all these furnishings. ³²The head chief over the chiefs of the Levites was Eleazar the son of Aaron the priest. He was supervisor over those performing the duties of the sanctuary.

³³To Merari belonged the clans of Mahli and Mushi. These were the clans of the Merarites. ³⁴Their enrollment, according to the number of males over one month old, was 6,200. ³⁵The chief of the household representing the clans of the Merarites was Zuriel, Abihail's son. They were to camp on the north side of the dwelling. ³⁶The Merarites were assigned responsibility for the frames of the dwelling, its bars, pillars, bases, and all its equipment—all these items—³⁷and the pillars of the courtyard all around, their bases, pegs, and cords.

³⁸Those camping in front of the dwelling eastward (that is, before the meeting tent on the east side) were Moses, Aaron, and his sons, who performed the duties of the sanctuary as service for the Israelites. Anyone else who approached would be put to death. ³⁹The total enrollment of the Levites, all the males over one month old whom Moses and Aaron enrolled by orders from the LORD, according to their clans, was 22,000.

Levites rescue
the oldest male Israelites

⁴⁰The LORD said to Moses: Enroll all the oldest males of the Israelites over one month of age and record their names.

⁴¹Take the Levites for me, in place of all the oldest sons of the Israelites, for I am the LORD, and the cattle of the Levites in place of all the oldest cattle of the Israelites. ⁴²Moses enrolled all the oldest males of the Israelites as the LORD commanded. ⁴³All the oldest males over one month old, recorded by name according to their enrollment, were 22,273.

⁴⁴Then the LORD spoke to Moses: ⁴⁵Take the Levites in place of all the oldest Israelites and the cattle of the Levites in place of their cattle. The Levites are mine; I am the LORD. ⁴⁶To rescue the 273 remaining oldest Israelites over and above the number of Levites, ⁴⁷you will receive five shekels each. You will receive them according to the sanctuary shekel of twenty gerahs to the shekel. ⁴⁸You will give the money for their rescue to Aaron and his sons.

⁴⁹So Moses took the money from those rescued over and above the ones rescued by the Levites. ⁵⁰He took the money from the oldest of the Israelites, 1,365 shekels, according to the sanctuary shekel. ⁵¹Moses gave the money for those rescued to Aaron and his sons according to the LORD's word, as the LORD commanded Moses.

Second census and the Levites' duties

The Kohathites' duties

4 The LORD spoke to Moses and Aaron: ²Take a census of the Kohathites from among the Levites by their clans and their households, ³from 30 to 50 years old, all who are eligible for service to do the work of the meeting tent. ⁴These are the responsibilities of the Kohathites in the meeting tent: the most holy things.

⁵When it's time to break camp, Aaron and his sons will enter and take down the screening curtain, and they will cover the chest containing the covenant with it. ⁶Then they will place a covering of fine leather[b] on it. They will spread a whole cloth of blue over it, and they will set its poles in place. ⁷They will spread a blue cloth on the presentation table and place on it the plates, the dishes, the bowls, and the container for the drink offering. The usual bread will be on it. ⁸They will spread on them a red cloth, cover it with fine leather, and set its poles in place. ⁹They will take a blue cloth and cover the lampstand used for light, its lamps, its extinguishers, its trays, and all the containers for oil that are used in its service. ¹⁰They will place it and its equipment in a covering of fine leather, and then place it on the carrying frame. ¹¹They will spread a blue cloth on the gold altar and cover it with fine leather. ¹²They will take all the service equipment used in the sanctuary, place it in a blue cloth, and cover it with fine leather. Then they will place it on the carrying frame. ¹³They will remove the ashes from the altar and spread a purple cloth on it. ¹⁴They will place on it all the equipment used for servicing it, the censers, the meat fork, the shovels, the bowls, all the equipment of the altar. They will spread a covering of fine leather over it and then set its poles in place.

¹⁵Aaron and his sons will finish covering the sanctuary and all the equipment of the sanctuary when it is time to break camp. After that the Kohathites will enter to carry it, but they will not touch the sanctuary, lest they die. These are the objects in the dwelling that the Kohathites are to carry. ¹⁶But Eleazar son of Aaron the priest will have oversight of the oil for lighting, the fragrant incense, the regular grain offering, and the anointing oil, as well as oversight of the entire dwelling and everything in it related to the sanctuary and its equipment.

¹⁷The LORD spoke to Moses and Aaron: ¹⁸You must not let the tribe of the Kohathite clans be eliminated from the Levites. ¹⁹This is what you must do for them so that they stay alive and don't die when they approach the most holy things. Aaron and his sons will enter and assign each of them his work and his load. ²⁰But they may not enter to look at the sanctuary even for a moment, lest they die.

---

b Or *dolphin skin*; see also 4:8, 10-12.

The Gershonites' duties

[21]The LORD spoke to Moses: [22]Take a census of the Gershonites also, by their households and their clans. [23]You will enroll those from 30 to 50 years old, all who are eligible for service to do work in the dwelling. [24]This is the duty of the Gershonite clans for work and for carrying the load: [25]They will carry the fabric of the dwelling, the meeting tent with its covering, the outer covering of fine leather, the screen for the entrance of the meeting tent, [26]the curtains of the courtyard, the screen of the entrance at the gate of the courtyard that surrounds the meeting tent and the altar, their cords, and all their equipment for their work. They will do everything that needs to be done with these objects.

[27]All the duties of the Gershonites for carrying their load and for their work will be at the command of Aaron and his sons. You will assign to them the responsibility to carry their load. [28]This is the work of the Gershonite clans in the dwelling. Their responsibility will be under Ithamar son of Aaron the priest.

The Merarites' duties

[29]You will enroll the Merarites by their clans and their households. [30]You will enroll those from 30 to 50 years old, all who are eligible for service to do work in the meeting tent. [31]This is what they are responsible to carry as their work in the meeting tent: the frames of the meeting tent, its bars, pillars, and bases; [32]the pillars of the courtyard all around, with their bases, pegs, cords, and all the equipment used with them. You will list by name the objects they are required to carry. [33]This is the duty of the Merarite clans for all their work in the meeting tent under the supervision of Ithamar son of Aaron the priest.

Summary of the census

[34]So Moses, Aaron, and the chiefs of the community enrolled the Kohathites by their clans and their households, [35]those from 30 to 50 years old who were eligible for work in the meeting tent. [36]Their enrollment by their clans was 2,750. [37]These are the enrolled of the Kohathite clans, all who worked in the meeting tent and whom Moses and Aaron enrolled according to the LORD's command through Moses.

[38]The enrollment of the Gershonites by their clans and their households, [39]those 30 to 50 years old who were eligible for work in the meeting tent: [40]their enrollment by their clans and their households

KOHATH/KOHATHITES

Kohath was the second-born son of Levi and head of one of the three levitical divisions (Gen 46:11). The Kohathites were prominent among the Levites and were given the most important duties, including carrying the sacred furniture housed in the meeting tent, notably the covenant chest (Num 3:30-31). Because these objects were sacred, however, the Kohathites could not enter the meeting tent until the Aaronic priests had covered the objects with cloth (Num 4:15). Unlike the Gershonites and Merarites, the Kohathites were not given carts for their work because the sacred objects had to be carried on their shoulders (Num 7:9). They camped on the south side of the meeting tent, forming a barrier between it and the people so that the Israelites would not violate the sacred precincts (Num 3:29). The Kohathites were divided into four clans according to the sons of Kohath: Amram, Izhar, Hebron, and Uzziel (Exod 6:18; Num 3:19). Kohathites served as musicians in Solomon's temple in Jerusalem (1 Chron 6:33-38).

was 2,630. [41]These are the enrolled of the Gershonite clans, all who worked in the meeting tent, and whom Moses and Aaron enrolled according to the LORD's command.

[42]The enrollment of the Merarite clans by their clans and their households, [43]those 30 to 50 years old who were eligible for work in the meeting tent: [44]their enrollment by their clans was 3,200. [45]These are the enrolled of the Merarite clans, whom Moses and Aaron enrolled according to the LORD's command through Moses.

[46]All the enrolled Levites whom Moses, Aaron, and the chiefs of Israel enrolled by their clans and their households, [47]those 30 to 50 years old who were eligible to do the work and to carry the load of the meeting tent: [48]their enrollment was 8,580. [49]Each was enrolled by the LORD's command through Moses to work and to carry his load. Each was assigned just as the LORD had commanded Moses.

Instructions about purity in the camp

5 The LORD spoke to Moses: [2]Command the Israelites to send out from the camp anyone with a skin disease, an oozing discharge, or who has become unclean from contact with a corpse. [3]You must send out both male and female. You must send them outside the camp so that they will not make their camp, where I live among them, unclean.

[4]The Israelites did so and sent them outside the camp. The Israelites did just what the LORD said to Moses.

[5]The LORD spoke to Moses: [6]Tell the Israelites: When a man or a woman commits any sin against anyone else, thus breaking faith with the LORD, that person becomes guilty. [7]Such persons will confess the sin they have done. Each will make payment for his guilt, add one-fifth more, and give it to the injured party. [8]If the person has no close relative to whom the payment can be made, then the compensation payment will go to the LORD for the priest. This is in addition to the ram of reconciliation by which the guilty party himself is reconciled. [9]Any

gift offering from all the sacred donations that the Israelites offer will be the property of the priest. [10]The sacred donations belong to each person alone; whatever anyone gives to the priest will be his.

A woman accused of adultery

[11]The LORD spoke to Moses: [12]Speak to the Israelites and say to them: A man may suspect that his wife has had an affair[c] and has broken faith with him, [13]that a man has had intercourse with her unknown to her husband and that she has defiled herself in secret—even though there are no witnesses and she isn't caught. [14]If jealousy overcomes him and he is jealous of his wife who has defiled herself, or if jealousy overcomes him and he is jealous of his wife who hasn't defiled herself, [15]then the man will bring his wife to the priest. He will bring the offering required for her, one-tenth of an ephah[d] of barley flour. He will not pour oil on it, nor offer frankincense with it, because it is a grain offering for jealousy, a grain offering for recognition in order to recognize guilt. [16]The priest will bring her close and make her stand before the LORD [17]The priest will take holy water in a clay jar, and taking dust from the floor of the dwelling, the priest will place it in the water. [18]The priest will make the woman stand before the LORD, let the hair of the woman hang down, and place the grain offering for recognition, that is, the grain offering for jealousy, in her hands. The water of bitterness that brings the curse will be in the hands of the priest.

[19]Then the priest will make her swear a solemn pledge, saying to the woman, "If no man has slept with you and if you haven't had an affair, becoming defiled while married to your husband, then be immune from the water of bitterness that brings these curses. [20]But if you have had an affair while married to your husband, if you have defiled yourself, and a man other than your husband has had intercourse with you"— [21]then the priest must make the woman utter the curse and say to the woman,

---

[c]Or *goes astray*; see also 5:19-20, 29.   [d]Two quarts; one ephah is approximately twenty quarts dry.

"May the LORD make you a curse and a harmful pledge among your people, when the LORD induces a miscarriage and your womb discharges. ²²And may the water that brings these curses enter your stomach and make your womb discharge and make you miscarry."

And the woman will say, "I agree, I agree."

²³The priest will write these curses in the scroll and wipe them off into the water of bitterness. ²⁴Then he will make the woman drink the water of bitterness that brings the curse. And the water that brings the curse will enter her, causing bitterness. ²⁵The priest will take the grain offering for jealousy from the woman's hands, elevate the grain offering before the LORD, and bring it to the altar. ²⁶The priest will take a handful of the grain offering as a token part of it and turn it into smoke on the altar. And afterward he will make the woman drink the water. ²⁷When he has made her drink the water, if she has defiled herself and has broken faith with her husband, then the water that brings the curse will enter her, causing bitterness, and her womb will discharge and she will miscarry. The woman will be a curse among her people. ²⁸But if the woman hasn't defiled herself and she is pure, then she will be immune and able to conceive.

²⁹These are the instructions about jealousy, when a wife has an affair while married to her husband and defiles herself, ³⁰or when jealousy overcomes a man and he is jealous of his wife. The priest will make the woman stand before the LORD and will follow all these instructions concerning her. ³¹The man will be free from guilt, but the woman will bear her guilt.

Instructions for the nazirite

6 The LORD spoke to Moses: ²Speak to the Israelites and say to them: If a man or a woman makes a binding promise to be a nazirite in order to be dedicated to the LORD, ³that person must refrain from wine and brandy. He or she may not drink wine vinegar or brandy vinegar, nor drink any grape juice or eat grapes, whether fresh or dried. ⁴While a nazirite, the person may not eat anything produced from the grapevine, not even its seeds or skin.

⁵For the term of the nazirite promise, no razor may be used on the head until the period of dedication to the LORD is fulfilled. The person is to be holy, letting his or her hair grow untrimmed. ⁶The period of dedication to the LORD also requires that the person not go near a corpse, ⁷whether father, mother, brother, or sister. Nazirites should not defile themselves because of the death of these people, because they bear the sign of their dedication to God on their heads.

⁸While a nazirite, the person is holy to the LORD. ⁹If someone suddenly dies nearby, defiling the head of the nazirite, he or she will shave the head on the day of cleansing; they will shave it on the seventh day. ¹⁰On the eighth day the person will bring two turtledoves or two young doves to the priest at the entrance of the meeting tent. ¹¹The priest will offer one for a purification offering and the other as an entirely burned offering. He will seek reconciliation for the person on account of the guilt acquired from the corpse, and he will make the head holy again on that same day. ¹²The person will be rededicated to the LORD as a nazirite and bring a one-year-old male lamb for a compensation offering. The previous period will be invalid, because the nazirite promise was defiled.

¹³This is the Instruction for the nazirite. When the term as a nazirite is completed, the person will be brought to the entrance of the meeting tent ¹⁴and offer a gift to the LORD, consisting of a flawless one-year-old male lamb as an entirely burned offering, a flawless one-year-old female lamb as a purification offering, one flawless ram as a well-being sacrifice, ¹⁵and a basket of loaves of unleavened bread made with fine flour and mixed with oil, and unleavened wafers spread with oil, along with their grain offering and their drink offering. ¹⁶The priest will come close to the LORD and offer the purification and entirely burned offerings. ¹⁷The ram he will offer as a well-being sacrifice to the LORD with the basket of unleavened bread; then the priest will offer the

grain offering and the drink offering. [18]The nazirite will shave his ordained head at the meeting tent's entrance, take the hair from his ordained head, and put it in the fire under the well-being sacrifice. [19]The priest will take the shoulder from the ram after it is boiled, one piece of unleavened bread from the basket, and one unleavened wafer, and place them in the hands of the nazirite after the ordained head is shaved. [20]Then the priest will raise them as an uplifted offering before the LORD; they are holy to the priest, with the breast of the uplifted offering and the thigh of the gift offering. After this the nazirite may drink wine.

[21]This is the instruction for the nazirite who takes the solemn promise. That person's offering to the LORD will be in accordance with the nazirite promise, in addition to whatever else the person may have offered. The person must do just as they have promised, in adherence with the nazirite promise.

Priestly blessing

[22]The LORD spoke to Moses: [23]Tell Aaron and his sons: You will bless the Israelites as follows. Say to them:
[24]The LORD bless you and protect you.
[25]The LORD make his face shine on you
   and be gracious to you.
[26]The LORD lift up his face to you and
   grant you peace.
[27]They will place my name on the Israelites, and I will bless them.

The dwelling's dedication

7On the day when Moses finished setting up the dwelling, he anointed and made it holy. All its equipment, as well as the altar

NAZIR/NAZIRITES

Nazirites appear early in the OT record and are found in both the NT period and rabbinic Judaism. Nazirites demonstrated their devotion to God through distinctive behaviors, commonly observing prohibitions against cutting their hair, drinking wine, or touching the dead. The earliest nazirites appear to have adopted the role as a life calling. In later periods, a practice developed in which one could become a nazirite for a temporary period as payment of a vow. Early nazirites were either called by God or dedicated by their parents to a lifelong state of consecration to God, outwardly identified by their unshorn hair. The oldest biblical account of a nazirite is that of Samson, in the period of the judges (11th–12th centuries BCE). Before his conception, the Lord's messenger instructed Samson's mother to rear her child as a nazirite: "Don't allow a razor to shave his head, because the boy is going to be a nazirite for God from birth" (Judg 13:5). Samson's mother was instructed to avoid wine, strong drink, and unclean foods (Judg 13:4), but the only restriction spelled out for the child was that his hair not be cut. Samson drank at his wedding feast (which typically involved fermented drinks) "as was the custom for young men" (Judg 14:10) and had no compunction about touching dead bodies (Judg 14:19). When Delilah relieved Samson of his hair, however, he lost the supernatural strength emblematic of his special relationship with God (Judg 16:19-20).

Samuel (11th century BCE) may also have been considered a nazirite. When his mother Hannah prayed for a son, she vowed to return him to the Lord: "I'll give him to the LORD for his entire life. No razor will ever touch his head" (1 Sam 1:11).

and all its equipment, he also anointed and made holy. ²The chiefs of Israel, the leaders of their households, made their presentations. They were the tribal chiefs and those who were in charge of the enlistment. ³They brought their offerings before the LORD: six covered wagons and twelve oxen—a wagon for every two chiefs, and an ox for every chief. They brought them near before the dwelling.

⁴The LORD said to Moses: ⁵Take these from them and use them for service in the meeting tent. Give them to the Levites according to their duties.

⁶So Moses took the wagons and the oxen, and he gave them to the Levites. ⁷Two wagons and four oxen he gave to the Gershonites for their duty. ⁸Four wagons and eight oxen he gave to the Merarites for their duty under the supervision of Ithamar, Aaron the priest's son. ⁹But to the Kohathites he gave nothing because their duty concerned the holy things that had to be carried on the shoulders. ¹⁰The chiefs made their presentations for the dedication of the altar on the day it was anointed. The chiefs presented their offerings before the altar.

¹¹The LORD said to Moses: One chief per day will present their offering for the dedication of the altar.

¹²The one presenting his offering on the first day was Nahshon, Amminadab's son, from the tribe of Judah. ¹³His offering was one silver dish weighing one hundred thirty shekels, one silver basin weighing seventy shekels according to the sanctuary shekel, both of them full of fine flour mixed with oil for a grain offering; ¹⁴one gold bowl weighing ten shekels full of incense; ¹⁵one bull from the herd, one ram, and one year-old male lamb for an entirely burned offering; ¹⁶one male goat for a purification offering; ¹⁷and for the well-being sacrifice two oxen, five rams, five male goats, and five male lambs a year old. This was the offering of Nahshon, Amminadab's son.

¹⁸On the second day Nethanel, Zuar's son, the chief of Issachar, presented his offering. ¹⁹He presented as his offering one silver dish weighing one hundred thirty shekels, one silver basin weighing seventy shekels according to the sanctuary shekel, both of them full of fine flour mixed with oil for a grain offering; ²⁰one gold bowl weighing ten shekels full of incense; ²¹one bull from the herd, one ram, and one year-old male lamb for an entirely burned offering; ²²one male goat for a purification offering; ²³and for the well-being sacrifice two oxen, five rams, five male goats, and five male lambs a year old. This was the offering of Nethanel, Zuar's son.

²⁴On the third day Zebulun's Chief Eliab, Helon's son: ²⁵his offering was one silver dish weighing one hundred thirty shekels, one silver basin weighing seventy shekels according to the sanctuary shekel, both of them full of fine flour mixed with oil for a grain offering; ²⁶one gold bowl weighing ten shekels full of incense; ²⁷one bull from the herd, one ram, and one year-old male lamb for an entirely burned offering; ²⁸one male goat for a purification offering; ²⁹and for the well-being sacrifice, two oxen, five rams, five male goats, and five male lambs a year old. This was the offering of Eliab, Helon's son.

³⁰On the fourth day Reuben's Chief Elizur, Shedeur's son: ³¹his offering was one silver dish weighing one hundred thirty shekels, one silver basin weighing seventy shekels according to the sanctuary shekel, both of them full of fine flour mixed with oil for a grain offering; ³²one gold bowl weighing ten shekels full of incense; ³³one bull from the herd, one ram, and one year-old male lamb for an entirely burned offering; ³⁴one male goat for a purification offering; ³⁵and for the well-being sacrifice two oxen, five rams, five male goats, and five male lambs a year old. This was the offering of Elizur, Shedeur's son.

³⁶On the fifth day Simeon's Chief Shelumiel, Zurishaddai's son: ³⁷his offering was one silver dish weighing one hundred thirty shekels, one basin weighing seventy shekels according to the sanctuary shekel, both of them full of fine flour mixed with oil for a grain offering; ³⁸one gold bowl weighing ten shekels full of incense; ³⁹one bull from the herd, one ram, and one year-old male

lamb for an entirely burned offering; ⁴⁰one male goat for a purification offering; ⁴¹and for the well-being sacrifice two oxen, five rams, five male goats, and five male lambs a year old. This was the offering of Shelumiel, Zurishaddai's son.

⁴²On the sixth day Gad's Chief Eliasaph, Deuel's son: ⁴³his offering was one silver dish weighing one hundred thirty shekels, one silver basin weighing seventy shekels according to the sanctuary shekel, both of them full of fine flour mixed with oil for a grain offering; ⁴⁴one gold bowl weighing ten shekels full of incense; ⁴⁵one bull from the herd, one ram, and one year-old male lamb for an entirely burned offering; ⁴⁶one male goat for a purification offering; ⁴⁷and for the well-being sacrifice two oxen, five rams, five male goats, and five male lambs a year old. This was the offering of Eliasaph, Deuel's son.

⁴⁸On the seventh day Ephraim's Chief Elishama, Ammihud's son: ⁴⁹his offering was one silver dish weighing one hundred thirty shekels, one silver basin weighing seventy shekels according to the sanctuary shekel, both of them full of fine flour mixed with oil for a grain offering; ⁵⁰one gold bowl weighing ten shekels full of incense; ⁵¹one bull from the herd, one ram, and one year-old male lamb for an entirely burned offering; ⁵²one male goat for a purification offering; ⁵³and for the well-being sacrifice two oxen, five rams, five male goats, and five male lambs a year old. This was the offering of Elishama, Ammihud's son.

⁵⁴On the eighth day Manasseh's Chief Gamaliel, Pedahzur's son: ⁵⁵his offering was one silver dish weighing one hundred thirty shekels, one silver basin weighing seventy shekels by the sanctuary scale, both of them full of fine flour mixed with oil for a grain offering; ⁵⁶one gold bowl weighing ten shekels full of incense; ⁵⁷one bull from the herd, one ram, and one year-old male lamb for an entirely burned offering; ⁵⁸one male goat for a purification offering; ⁵⁹and for the well-being sacrifice two oxen, five rams, five male goats, and five male lambs a year old. This was the offering of Gamaliel, Pedahzur's son.

⁶⁰On the ninth day Benjamin's Chief Abidan, Gideoni's son: ⁶¹his offering was one silver dish weighing one hundred thirty shekels, one silver basin weighing seventy shekels according to the sanctuary shekel, both of them full of fine flour mixed with oil for a grain offering; ⁶²one gold bowl weighing ten shekels full of incense; ⁶³one bull from the herd, one ram, and one year-old male lamb for an entirely burned offering; ⁶⁴one male goat for a purification offering; ⁶⁵and for the well-being sacrifice two oxen, five rams, five male goats, and five male lambs a year old. This was the offering of Abidan, Gideoni's son.

⁶⁶On the tenth day Dan's Chief Ahiezer, Ammishaddai's son: ⁶⁷his offering was one silver dish weighing one hundred thirty shekels, one silver basin weighing seventy shekels according to the sanctuary shekel, both of them full of fine flour mixed with oil for a grain offering; ⁶⁸one gold bowl weighing ten shekels full of incense; ⁶⁹one bull from the herd, one ram, and one year-old male lamb for an entirely burned offering; ⁷⁰one male goat for a purification offering; ⁷¹and for the well-being sacrifice two oxen, five rams, five male goats, and five male lambs a year old. This was the offering of Ahiezer, Ammishaddai's son.

⁷²On the eleventh day Asher's Chief Pagiel, Ochran's son: ⁷³his offering was one silver dish weighing one hundred thirty shekels, one silver basin weighing seventy shekels according to the sanctuary shekel, both of them full of fine flour mixed with oil for a grain offering; ⁷⁴one gold bowl weighing ten shekels full of incense; ⁷⁵one bull from the herd, one ram, and one year-old male lamb for an entirely burned offering; ⁷⁶one male goat for a purification offering; ⁷⁷and for the well-being sacrifice two oxen, five rams, five male goats, and five male lambs a year old. This was the offering of Pagiel, Ochran's son.

⁷⁸On the twelfth day Naphtali's Chief Ahira, Enan's son: ⁷⁹his offering was one silver dish weighing one hundred thirty shekels, one silver basin weighing seventy shekels according to the sanctuary shekel, both of them full of fine flour mixed with

oil for a grain offering; [80]one gold bowl weighing ten shekels full of incense; [81]one bull from the herd, one ram, one year-old male lamb for an entirely burned offering; [82]one male goat for a purification offering; [83]and for the well-being sacrifice two oxen, five rams, five male goats, and five male lambs a year old. This was the offering of Ahira, Enan's son.

[84]This is what the Israelite chiefs provided for the dedication of the altar on the day it was anointed: twelve silver dishes, twelve silver basins, and twelve gold bowls; [85]each silver dish weighing one hundred thirty shekels and each basin seventy shekels—all the silver equipment weighed two thousand four hundred shekels according to the sanctuary shekel; [86]the twelve gold bowls full of incense weighing ten shekels each according to the sanctuary shekel—all the gold of the bowls weighed one hundred twenty shekels; [87]all the animals for the entirely burned offering were twelve bulls, twelve rams, twelve male lambs a year old, with their grain offering; twelve male goats for the purification offering; [88]and all the animals for the well-being sacrifice were twenty-four bulls, sixty rams, sixty male goats, and sixty male lambs a year old. This was the dedication offering for the altar after it was anointed.

Moses in the dwelling

[89]When Moses entered the meeting tent to speak with the LORD,[e] he would hear the voice speaking to him from above the cover[f] that was on the chest containing the covenant, from between the two winged creatures. In this way he spoke to Moses.

The lampstand

8 The LORD spoke to Moses: [2]Speak to Aaron and say to him: When you set them up, the seven lamps will give light in front of the lampstand.

[3]Aaron did so. He set up its lamps in front of the lampstand as the LORD commanded Moses. [4]This is how the lampstand was made: it was hammered gold; from its base to its flower it was hammered. Moses made the lampstand according to the vision that the LORD had shown Moses.

Dedication of the Levites

[5]The LORD spoke to Moses: [6]Separate the Levites from the Israelites and cleanse them. [7]This is what you will do to them to cleanse them: Sprinkle water of purification on them, have them shave their bodies, wash their clothes, and cleanse themselves. [8]They will take a bull from the herd, with its grain offering of fine flour mixed with oil. You will take a second bull from the herd for a purification offering. [9]You will bring the Levites before the meeting tent and gather the entire Israelite community. [10]Then you will bring the Levites into the LORD's presence, and the Israelites will lay their hands on the Levites. [11]Aaron will present the Levites as an uplifted offering in the LORD's presence from the Israelites so that they may do the LORD's service. [12]Then the Levites will lay their hands on the heads of the bulls, and Aaron will offer one as a purification offering and the other as an entirely burned offering to the LORD in order to seek reconciliation for the Levites.

[13]You will have the Levites stand before Aaron and his sons and you will present them as an uplifted offering to the LORD. [14]You will separate the Levites from the Israelites, and the Levites will be mine. [15]The Levites will enter to serve the meeting tent, after you have cleansed them and presented them as an uplifted offering. [16]They are given over to me from the Israelites in place of all the newborn, the oldest of all the Israelites. I take them for myself. [17]Every oldest male among the Israelites is mine, whether human or animal. When I killed all the oldest males in the land of Egypt, I dedicated them to myself. [18]I have taken the Levites in place of all the oldest among the Israelites. [19]I have selected the Levites from the Israelites for Aaron and his sons to perform the service of the Israelites in the meeting tent and to seek reconciliation for the

Israelites so that there will not be a plague when the Israelites approach the sanctuary.

²⁰Moses, Aaron, and the entire Israelite community carried out for the Levites everything the LORD had commanded Moses. That is what the Israelites did for the Levites. ²¹The Levites purified themselves and washed their clothes. Aaron presented them as an uplifted offering in the LORD's presence, and he sought reconciliation for them in order to cleanse them. ²²After this the Levites went in to perform their service in the meeting tent before Aaron and his sons. They did for the Levites just as the LORD had commanded Moses concerning them.

²³The LORD spoke to Moses: ²⁴This rule applies[g] to the Levites: Everyone 25 years old and above will enter into service, performing the duties for the meeting tent. ²⁵At 50 years old each will retire from service. They will perform their duties no longer. ²⁶Each may assist his fellow Levites in the meeting tent with some responsibilities, but he may not perform service. This is how you should assign responsibilities to the Levites.

Passover

9 The LORD spoke to Moses in the Sinai desert in the first month[h] of the second year after they had left the land of Egypt: ²Let the Israelites keep the Passover at its appointed time. ³On the fourteenth day of this month at twilight you will keep it at its appointed time. Keep it according to all its regulations and its customary practices.

⁴Moses instructed the Israelites to keep the Passover. ⁵At twilight on the fourteenth day of the first month[i] they kept the Passover in the Sinai desert. The Israelites did everything just as the LORD commanded Moses.

⁶But there were persons who were unclean from contact with a human corpse, and they were unable to keep the Passover on that day. They approached Moses and Aaron that day. ⁷These persons said to him, "Although we are unclean from contact

with a human corpse, why must we be prohibited from presenting the LORD's offering at its appointed time with the rest of the Israelites?"

⁸Moses said to them, "Wait while I listen for what the LORD will command concerning you."

⁹The LORD spoke to Moses: ¹⁰Tell the Israelites: When any of you or your descendants are unclean from contact with a corpse or are on a long trip, they may still keep the Passover to the LORD. ¹¹They will keep it at twilight on the fourteenth day of the second month.[j] They will eat the Passover lamb with unleavened bread and bitter herbs. ¹²They must not leave any of it until morning, nor break any of its bones. They will keep the Passover according to all its regulations. ¹³But any persons who are clean and not on a trip, yet don't keep the Passover, those persons will be cut off from their people, because they didn't present the LORD's offering at its appointed time. Those persons will bear their sin. ¹⁴If an immigrant resides among you and wishes to keep the Passover to the LORD, that one also will keep it according to its regulations and its customary practices. There will be one set of regulations for both of you, for the immigrant and for the native of the land.

Cloud over the dwelling

¹⁵On the day the dwelling was erected, the cloud covered the dwelling, the covenant tent. At night until morning, the cloud appeared with lightning over the dwelling. ¹⁶It was always there. The cloud covered it by day,[k] appearing with lightning at night. ¹⁷Whenever the cloud ascended from the tent, the Israelites would march. And the Israelites would camp wherever the cloud settled. ¹⁸At the LORD's command, the Israelites would march, and at the LORD's command they would camp. As long as the cloud settled on the dwelling, they would camp. ¹⁹When the cloud lingered on the meeting tent for many days, the Israelites would observe the LORD's direction

---

[g]Heb lacks *rule applies.*   [h]March–April, Nisan   [i]March–April, Nisan   [j]April–May, Iyar   [k]LXX; MT lacks *by day.*

and they wouldn't march. ²⁰Sometimes the cloud would be over the dwelling for a number of days, so they would camp at the LORD's command, marching again only at the LORD's command. ²¹Sometimes the cloud would settle only overnight, and they would march when the cloud ascended in the morning. Whether it was day or night, they would march when the cloud ascended. ²²Whether it was two days, or a month, or a long time, the Israelites would camp so long as the cloud lingered on the dwelling and settled on it. They wouldn't march. But when it ascended, they would march. ²³They camped at the LORD's command and they marched at the LORD's command. They followed the LORD's direction according to the LORD's command through Moses.

Trumpets

10 The LORD spoke to Moses: ²Make two silver trumpets and make them from hammered metalwork. Use them for summoning the community and for breaking camp. ³When both are blown, the entire community will meet you at the entrance of the meeting tent. ⁴When one is blown, the chiefs, the leaders of Israel's divisions, will meet you. ⁵When you blow a series of short blasts, the camp on the east side will march. ⁶And when you blow a second series of short blasts, the camp on the south side will march. You will blow a series of short blasts to announce their march.

⁷To gather the assembly, blow a long blast, not a series of short blasts. ⁸Aaron's sons the priests will blow the trumpets. This will be a permanent regulation for you throughout time.

⁹When you go to war in your land against an enemy who is attacking you, you will blow short blasts with the trumpets so that you may be remembered by the LORD your God and be saved from your enemies. ¹⁰On your festival days, your appointed feasts, and at the beginning of your months, you will blow the trumpets over your entirely burned offerings and your well-being sacrifices. They will serve as a reminder of you to your God. I am the LORD your God.

Organization of the wilderness march

¹¹On the twentieth day of the second month in the second year, the cloud ascended from the covenant dwelling. ¹²The Israelites set out on their march from the Sinai desert, and the cloud settled in the Paran desert.

¹³They marched for the first time at the LORD's command through Moses. ¹⁴The banner of Judah's camp marched first with its military units. Nahshon, Amminadab's son, commanded its military. ¹⁵Nethanel, Zuar's son, commanded the military of the tribe of Issachar. ¹⁶Eliab, Helon's son, commanded the military of the tribe of Zebulun. ¹⁷The dwelling was taken down, and the Gershonites and the Merarites, who carried the dwelling, marched. ¹⁸The banner of Reuben's camp marched with its military units. Elizur, Shedeur's son, commanded its military. ¹⁹Shelumiel, Zurishaddai's son, commanded the military of the tribe of Simeon. ²⁰Eliasaph, Deuel's son, commanded the military of the tribe of Gad. ²¹The Kohathites, who carried the holy things, marched. The dwelling would be set up before their arrival. ²²The banner of Ephraim's camp marched with its military units. Elishama, Ammihud's son, commanded its military. ²³Gamaliel, Pedahzur's son, commanded the military of the tribe of Manasseh. ²⁴Abidan, Gideoni's son, commanded the military of the tribe of Benjamin. ²⁵The banner of Dan's camp, at the rear of the whole camp, marched with its military units. Ahiezer, Ammishaddai's son, commanded its military. ²⁶Pagiel, Ochran's son, commanded the military of the tribe of Asher. ²⁷Ahira, Enan's son, commanded the military of the tribe of Naphtali. ²⁸This was the order of departure of the Israelites with their military units when they set out.

The chest leads

²⁹Moses said to Hobab the Midianite, Reuel's son and Moses' father-in-law, "We're marching to the place about which the LORD has said, 'I'll give it to you.' Come with us and we'll treat you well, for the LORD has promised to treat Israel well."

³⁰Hobab said to him, "I won't go; I'd rather go to my land and to my folk."

³¹Moses said, "Please don't abandon us, for you know where we can camp in the desert, and you can be our eyes. ³²If you go with us, whatever good the LORD does for us, we'll do for you."

³³They marched from the LORD's mountain for three days. The LORD's chest containing the covenant marched ahead of them for three days to look for a resting place for them. ³⁴Now the LORD's cloud was over them by day when they marched from the camp. ³⁵When the chest set out, Moses would say, "Arise, LORD, let your enemies scatter, and those who hate you flee." ³⁶When it rested, he would say, "Return, LORD of the ten thousand thousands of Israel."

Complaint at Taberah

11 When the people complained intensely in the LORD's hearing, the LORD heard and became angry. Then the LORD's fire burned them and consumed the edges of the camp. ²When the people cried out to Moses, Moses prayed to the LORD, and the fire subsided. ³The name of that place was called Taberah,¹ because the LORD's fire burned against them.

Complaint over the lack of meat

⁴The riffraff among them had a strong craving. Even the Israelites cried again and said, "Who will give us meat to eat? ⁵We remember the fish we ate in Egypt for free, the cucumbers, the melons, the leeks, the onions, and the garlic. ⁶Now our lives are wasting away. There is nothing but manna in front of us."

⁷The manna was like coriander seed and its color was like resin. ⁸The people would roam around and collect it and grind it with millstones or pound it in a mortar. Then they would boil it in pots and make it into cakes. It tasted like cakes baked in olive oil. ⁹When the dew fell on the camp during the night, the manna would fall with it.

Moses' complaint about leadership

¹⁰Moses heard the people crying throughout their clans, each at his tent's entrance. The LORD was outraged, and Moses was upset. ¹¹Moses said to the LORD, "Why have you treated your servant so badly? And why haven't I found favor in your eyes, for you have placed the burden of all these people on me? ¹²Did I conceive all these people? Did I give birth to them, that you would say to me, 'Carry them at the breast, as a nurse carries an unweaned child,' to the fertile land that you promised their ancestors? ¹³Where am I to get meat for all these people? They are crying before me and saying, 'Give us meat, so we can eat.' ¹⁴I can't bear this people on my own. They're too heavy for me. ¹⁵If you're going to treat me like this, please kill me. If I've found favor in your eyes, then don't let me endure this wretched situation."

¹⁶The LORD said to Moses, "Gather before me seventy men from Israel's elders,

¹Or *the place of burning*

ELDER (OT)

Elder appears in the OT writers more than 140 times. In a few passages it merely denotes persons of advanced years (Lev 19:32; Ezek 9:6; Joel 2:16, 28), but it more typically refers to traditional but unofficial leaders of tribal communities or professional groups. Such individuals acquire knowledge and wisdom through years of experience; consequently, they gain the respect of—and typically exercise authority over—the members of their community or group.

whom you know as elders and officers of the people. Take them to the meeting tent, and let them stand there with you. [17]Then I'll descend and speak with you there. I'll take some of the spirit that is on you and place it on them. Then they will carry the burden of the people with you so that you won't bear it alone. [18]To the people you will say, 'Make yourselves holy for tomorrow; then you will eat meat, for you've cried in the LORD's hearing, "Who will give us meat to eat? It was better for us in Egypt." The LORD will give you meat, and you will eat. [19]You won't eat for just one day, or two days, or five days, or ten days, or twenty days, [20]but for a whole month until it comes out of your nostrils and nauseates you. You've rejected the LORD who's been with you and you have cried before him, saying, "Why did we leave Egypt?" '"

[21]Moses said, "The people I'm with are six hundred thousand on foot and you're saying, 'I will give them meat, and they will eat for a month.' [22]Can flocks and herds be found and slaughtered for them? Or can all the fish in the sea be found and caught for them?"

[23]The LORD said to Moses, "Is the LORD's power too weak? Now you will see whether my word will come true for you or not."

[24]So Moses went out and told the people the LORD's words. He assembled seventy men from the people's elders and placed them around the tent. [25]The LORD descended in a cloud, spoke to him, and took some of the spirit that was on him and placed it on the seventy elders. When the spirit rested on them, they prophesied, but only this once. [26]Two men had remained in the camp, one named Eldad and the second named Medad, and the spirit rested on them. They were among those registered, but they hadn't gone out to the tent, so they prophesied in the camp. [27]A young man ran and told Moses, "Eldad and Medad are prophesying in the camp."

[28]Joshua, Nun's son and Moses' assistant since his youth, responded, "My master Moses, stop them!"

[29]Moses said to him, "Are you jealous for my sake? If only all the LORD's people were prophets with the LORD placing his spirit on them!"

Quail from the sea

[30]Moses and Israel's elders were assembled in the camp. [31]A wind from the LORD blew up and brought quails from the sea. It let them fall by the camp, about a day's journey all around the camp and about three feet deep on the ground. [32]Then the people arose and gathered the quail all that day, all night, and all the next day. The least collected was ten homers,[m] and they laid them out around the camp. [33]While the meat was still between their teeth and not yet consumed, the LORD's anger blazed against the people. The LORD struck the people with a very great punishment. [34]The name of that place was called Kibroth-hattaavah,[n] because there they buried the people who had the craving.

Miriam and Aaron challenge Moses

[35]From Kibroth-hattaavah the people marched to Hazeroth.

12 When they were in Hazeroth, Miriam and Aaron criticized Moses on account of the Cushite woman whom he had married—for he had married a Cushite woman. [2]They said, "Has the LORD spoken only through Moses? Hasn't he also spoken through us?" The LORD heard it. [3]Now the man Moses was humble, more so than anyone on earth.

The LORD defends Moses

[4]Immediately, the LORD said to Moses, Aaron, and Miriam, "You three go out to the meeting tent." So the three of them went out. [5]Then the LORD descended in a column of cloud, stood at the entrance of the tent, and called to Aaron and Miriam. The two of them came forward. [6]He said, "Listen to my words: If there is a prophet of the LORD among you,[o] I make myself known to him in visions. I speak to

---

[m]Five hundred gallons; one homer is two hundred quarts. [n]Or graves of craving [o]Heb uncertain; LXX If there is a prophet of you for the Lord

him in dreams. [7]But not with my servant Moses. He has proved to be reliable with all my household. [8]I speak with him face-to-face, visibly, not in riddles. He sees the LORD's form. So why aren't you afraid to criticize my servant Moses?" [9]The LORD's anger blazed against them, and they went back.

The LORD punishes Miriam

[10]When the cloud went away from over the tent, Miriam suddenly developed a skin disease flaky like snow. Aaron turned toward Miriam and saw her skin disease. [11]Then Aaron said to Moses, "Oh, my master, please don't punish us for the sin that we foolishly committed. [12]Please don't let her be like the stillborn, whose flesh is half eaten as it comes out of the mother's womb."

[13]So Moses cried to the LORD, "God, please heal her!"

[14]The LORD said to Moses, "If her father had spit in her face, would she not be shamed for seven days? Let her be shut out of the camp for seven days, and afterward she will be brought back." [15]So they shut Miriam out of the camp seven days. And the people didn't march until Miriam was brought back. [16]Afterward the people marched from Hazeroth, and they camped in the Paran desert.

Leaders explore the land of Canaan

13 The LORD spoke to Moses: [2]Send out men to explore the land of Canaan, which I'm giving to the Israelites. Send one man from each ancestral tribe, each a chief among them. [3]So Moses sent them out from the Paran desert according to the LORD's command. All the men were leaders among the Israelites. [4]These are their names:

from the tribe of Reuben, Shammua, Zaccur's son;

[5]from the tribe of Simeon, Shaphat, Hori's son;

[6]from the tribe of Judah, Caleb, Jephunneh's son;

[7]from the tribe of Issachar, Igal, Joseph's son;

[8]from the tribe of Ephraim, Hoshea, Nun's son;

[9]from the tribe of Benjamin, Palti, Raphu's son;

[10]from the tribe of Zebulun, Gaddiel, Sodi's son;

[11]from the tribe of Joseph:

from the tribe of Manasseh, Gaddi, Susi's son;

[12]from the tribe of Dan, Ammiel, Gemalli's son;

[13]from the tribe of Asher, Sethur, Michael's son;

[14]from the tribe of Naphtali, Nahbi, Vophsi's son;

[15]from the tribe of Gad, Geuel, Machi's son.

[16]These are the names of the men whom Moses sent out to explore the land. Moses changed the name of Hoshea, Nun's son, to Joshua.

[17]When Moses sent them out to explore the land of Canaan, he said to them, "Go up there into the arid southern plain and into the mountains. [18]You must inspect the land. What is it like? Are the people who live in it strong or weak, few or many? [19]Is the land in which they live good or bad? Are the towns in which they live camps or fortresses? [20]Is the land rich or poor? Are there trees in it or not? Be courageous and bring back the land's fruit." It was the season of the first ripe grapes.

[21]They went up and explored the land from the Zin desert to Rehob, near Lebo-hamath. [22]They went up into the arid southern plain and entered Hebron, where Ahiman, Sheshai, and Talmai, the descendants of the Anakites, lived. (Hebron was built seven years before Tanis[P] in Egypt.) [23]Then they entered the Cluster[q] ravine, cut down from there a branch with one cluster of grapes, and carried it on a pole between them. They also took pomegranates and figs. [24]That place was called the Cluster ravine because of the cluster of grapes that the Israelites cut down from there.

[P]Heb Zoan   [q]Or cluster of grapes

Report about the land of Canaan

²⁵They returned from exploring the land after forty days. ²⁶They went directly to Moses, Aaron, and the entire Israelite community in the Paran desert at Kadesh. They brought back a report to them and to the entire community and showed them the land's fruit. ²⁷Then they gave their report: "We entered the land to which you sent us. It's actually full of milk and honey, and this is its fruit. ²⁸There are, however, powerful people who live in the land. The cities have huge fortifications. And we even saw the descendants of the Anakites there. ²⁹The Amalekites live in the land of the arid southern plain; the Hittites, Jebusites, and Amorites live in the mountains; and the Canaanites live by the sea and along the Jordan."

³⁰Now Caleb calmed the people before Moses and said, "We must go up and take possession of it, because we are more than able to do it."

³¹But the men who went up with him said, "We can't go up against the people because they are stronger than we." ³²They started a rumor about the land that they had explored, telling the Israelites, "The land that we crossed over to explore is a land that devours its residents. All the people we saw in it are huge men. ³³We saw there the Nephilim (the descendants of Anak come from the Nephilim). We saw ourselves as grasshoppers, and that's how we appeared to them."

The Israelites' complaint

14 The entire community raised their voice and the people wept that night. ²All the Israelites criticized Moses and Aaron. The entire community said to them, "If only we had died in the land of Egypt or if only we had died in this desert! ³Why is the LORD bringing us to this land to fall by the sword? Our wives and our children will be taken by force. Wouldn't it be better for us to return to Egypt?" ⁴So they said to each other, "Let's pick a leader and let's go back to Egypt."

⁵Then Moses and Aaron fell on their faces before the assembled Israelite community. ⁶But Joshua, Nun's son, and Caleb, Jephunneh's son, from those who had explored the land, tore their clothes ⁷and said to the entire Israelite community, "The land we crossed through to explore is an exceptionally good land. ⁸If the LORD is pleased with us, he'll bring us into this land and give it to us. It's a land that's full of milk and honey. ⁹Only don't rebel against the LORD and don't be afraid of the people of the land. They are our prey.ʳ Their defense has deserted them, but the LORD is with us. So don't be afraid of them." ¹⁰But the entire community intended to stone them.

The LORD's anger and Moses' intercession

Then the LORD's glory appeared in the meeting tent to all the Israelites. ¹¹The LORD said to Moses, "How long will these people disrespect me? And how long will they doubt me after all the signs that I performed among them? ¹²I'll strike them down with a plague and disown them. Then I'll make you into a great nation, stronger than they."

¹³Moses said to the LORD, "The Egyptians will hear, for with your power you brought these people up from among them. ¹⁴They'll tell the inhabitants of this land. They've heard that you, LORD, are with this people. You, LORD, appear to them face-to-face. Your cloud stands over them. You go before them in a column of cloud by day and in a column of lightning by night. ¹⁵If you kill these people, every last one of them, the nations who heard about you will say, ¹⁶'The LORD wasn't able to bring these people to the land that he solemnly promised to give them. So he slaughtered them in the desert.' ¹⁷Now let my master's power be as great as you declared when you said, ¹⁸'The LORD is very patient and absolutely loyal, forgiving wrongs and disloyalty. Yet he doesn't forgo all punishment, disciplining the grandchildren and great-grandchildren for their ancestors' wrongs.' ¹⁹Please for-

ʳOr our bread

give the wrongs of these people because of your absolute loyalty, just as you've forgiven these people from their time in Egypt until now."

²⁰Then the LORD said, "I will forgive as you requested. ²¹But as I live and as the LORD's glory fills the entire earth, ²²none of the men who saw my glory and the signs I did in Egypt and in the desert, but tested me these ten times and haven't listened to my voice, ²³will see the land I promised to their ancestors. All who disrespected me won't see it. ²⁴But I'll bring my servant Caleb into the land that he explored, and his descendants will possess it because he has a different spirit, and he has remained true to me. ²⁵Since the Amalekites and the Canaanites live in the valley, tomorrow turn and march into the desert by the route of the Reed Sea."ˢ

The Israelites' punishment

²⁶The LORD spoke to Moses and Aaron: ²⁷How long will this wicked community complain against me? I've heard the Israel-ites' dissent as they continue to complain against me. ²⁸Say to them, "As I live," says the LORD, "just as I've heard you say, so I'll do to you. ²⁹Your dead bodies will fall in this desert. None of you who were enlisted and were registered from 20 years old and above, who complained against me, ³⁰will enter the land in which I promisedᵗ to settle you, with the exception of Caleb, Jephunneh's son, and Joshua, Nun's son. ³¹But your children, whom you said would be taken by force, I'll bring them in and they will know the land that you rejected. ³²Your bodies, however, will fall in this desert, ³³and your children will be shepherds in the desert for forty years. They will suffer for your unfaithfulness, until the last of your bodies fall in the desert. ³⁴For as many days as you explored the land, that is, forty days, just as many years you'll bear your guilt, that is, forty years. This is how you will understand my frustration." ³⁵I the LORD have spoken. I will do this to the entire wicked community who gathered against me. They will die in this desert. There they'll meet their end.

ˢOr Red Sea ᵗOr raised my hand

DESERT

Desert denotes a range of landscapes, from open plains and rugged mountains offering seasonal pasturage to scrub to scorched, toxic land incapable of supporting vegetation. It is unsettled and uncultivated land, the natural habitation of wild animals but not of humans, a place through which shepherds and Bedouin pass following pasturage and travelers hasten to safer havens.

Desert usually designates a place, but it is also an evocative symbol with layers of meaning. The Bible never romanticizes the desert. Except when using it for travel, biblical characters seek out the desert primarily as a refuge from harassment or as a place to prepare for the advent of God's kingdom. The desert is preeminently the place of Israel's 40-year sojourn between Egypt and the land of promise, and the most frequent and significant references to the desert in the OT pertain to Israel's experiences there.

In the Gospels, the writers record that Jesus withdrew to the desert to teach ever-growing crowds (Mark 1:45), to rest alone (Matt 14:13; Luke 4:42; John 6:15) or with his disciples (Mark 6:31-32), or to pray (Mark 1:35; Luke 5:16; "up onto a mountain" [Matt 14:23; Mark 6:46; Luke 6:12]).

³⁶The men whom Moses sent out to explore the land had returned and caused the entire community to complain against him by starting a rumor about the land. ³⁷These men died by a plague in the LORD's presence on account of their false rumor. ³⁸But Joshua, Nun's son, and Caleb, Jephunneh's son, survived from those men who went to explore the land.

³⁹Moses spoke these words to all the Israelites, and the people mourned bitterly. ⁴⁰They rose early in the morning and went up to the top of the mountain range, saying, "Let's go up to the place the LORD told us to, for we have sinned."

⁴¹But Moses said, "Why do you disobey the LORD's command? It won't succeed. ⁴²Don't go up, for the LORD isn't with you. Don't be struck down before your enemies. ⁴³The Amalekites and the Canaanites will be there in front of you and you will fall by the sword because you turned away from the LORD, and the LORD is no longer with you." ⁴⁴Yet they recklessly[u] ascended toward the top of the mountains, even though Moses and the LORD's chest containing the covenant didn't depart from the camp. ⁴⁵Then the Amalekites and the Canaanites, who lived in those mountains, descended, struck them down, and beat them all the way to Hormah.

Immigrants in the land of Canaan

15 The LORD spoke to Moses: ²Speak to the Israelites and say to them: When you enter the land where you will live, which I am giving you, ³and you make a food gift[v] to the LORD as a soothing smell for the LORD from the herd or the flock—whether an entirely burned offering, or a sacrifice to fulfill a solemn promise, or a spontaneous gift, or at your sacred seasons—⁴the one presenting the offering to the LORD will bring a grain offering of one-tenth of fine flour mixed with one-fourth of a hin[w] of oil. ⁵You will also offer one-fourth of a hin of wine as a drink offering with either the entirely burned offering or the sacrifice, for each lamb. ⁶For a ram you will offer a grain offering of two-tenths of a measure of fine flour mixed with one-third of a hin of oil. ⁷You will also present one-third of a hin of wine for a drink offering as a soothing smell for the LORD. ⁸When you offer a bull for an entirely burned offering, or a sacrifice to fulfill a solemn promise, or a well-being sacrifice to the LORD, ⁹you will present[x] with the bull a grain offering of three-tenths of a measure of fine flour mixed with a half hin of oil. ¹⁰You will present a half hin of wine for a drink offering as a food gift that is a soothing smell to the LORD. ¹¹So will it be done with each ox, each ram, or for any sheep or goat. ¹²However many you offer, you will do the same for each one.

¹³Every citizen will perform these rituals in bringing a food gift that is a soothing smell to the LORD. ¹⁴If an immigrant lives with you or has settled among you for many years and would also like to offer a food gift that is a soothing smell to the LORD, that person must do just as you do. ¹⁵The assembly will have the same regulation for you and for the immigrant. The regulation will be permanent for all time. You and the immigrant will be the same in the LORD's presence. ¹⁶There will be one set of instructions and one legal norm for the immigrant and for you.

¹⁷The LORD spoke to Moses: ¹⁸Speak to the Israelites and say to them: When you enter the land to which I'm bringing you, ¹⁹whenever you eat the land's food you will present a gift offering to the LORD. ²⁰You will present a gift offering from the first bread you bake just like you present a gift offering from the threshing floor. ²¹You will give a gift offering from the first bread you bake for all time.

Offerings for accidental sin

²²If by accident you don't obey all these commands that the LORD spoke to Moses, ²³or everything that the LORD commanded you through Moses from the day of the LORD's command onward for all time, ²⁴then if it was done unintentionally without the knowledge of the community, the

---

entire community must offer one bull from the herd as an entirely burned offering, a soothing smell to the LORD, with its grain and drink offering according to the specific instruction, and one male goat for a purification offering. [25] The priest will seek reconciliation for the entire Israelite community. They will be forgiven, because it was unintentional and because they brought their food gift to the LORD, along with their purification offering in the LORD's presence for their accidental error. [26] The entire Israelite community and the immigrant residing among them will be forgiven, because all the people acted unintentionally.

[27] If an individual sins unintentionally, that person must present a one-year-old female goat for a purification offering. [28] The priest will seek reconciliation in the LORD's presence for the person who sinned unintentionally, when the sin is an accident, seeking reconciliation so that person will be forgiven. [29] There will be one set of instructions for the Israelite citizen and the immigrant residing with you for anyone who commits an unintentional sin.

Punishment for intentional sin

[30] But the person who acts deliberately,[y] whether a citizen or an immigrant, and insults the LORD, that person will be cut off from the people [31] for despising the LORD's word and breaking his commands. That person will be completely cut off and bear the guilt.

Instructions for Sabbath observance

[32] When the Israelites were in the desert, they found a man gathering wood on the Sabbath day. [33] Those who found him gathering wood brought him to Moses, Aaron, and the entire community. [34] They placed him in custody, because it wasn't clear what should be done to him. [35] Then the LORD said to Moses: The man should be put to death. The entire community should stone him outside the camp. [36] The entire community took him outside the camp and stoned him. He died as the LORD had commanded Moses.

Fringes on garments

[37] The LORD said to Moses: [38] Speak to the Israelites and say to them: Make fringes on the edges of your clothing for all time. Have them put blue cords on the fringe on the edges. [39] This will be your fringe. You will see it and remember all the LORD's commands and do them. Then you won't go exploring the lusts of your own heart or your eyes. [40] In this way you'll remember to do all my commands. Then you will be holy to your God. [41] I am the LORD your God, who brought you out of the land of Egypt to be your God. I am the LORD your God.

A challenge to the priesthood

16 Korah—Izhar's son, Kohath's grandson, and Levi's great-grandson—with Dathan and Abiram, Eliab's sons, and On, Peleth's son, descendants of Reuben, [2] rose up against Moses, along with two hundred fifty Israelite men, leaders of the community, chosen by the assembly, men of reputation. [3] They assembled against Moses and Aaron and said to them, "You've gone too far, because the entire community is holy, every last one of them, and the LORD is with them. Why then do you exalt yourselves above the LORD's assembly?"

[4] When Moses heard this, he fell on his face. [5] He spoke to Korah and all his community, "In the morning the LORD will make known who is his, who is holy, and who is able to approach him. The one he chooses for himself is the one who will be able to approach him. [6] This is what must be done. Korah and your entire community: Take censers for yourselves. [7] Tomorrow put fire in them and place incense on them in the LORD's presence. The man whom the LORD chooses, that one is holy. You Levites have gone too far!" [8] Moses said to Korah, "Listen, you Levites, [9] isn't it enough for you that Israel's God has separated you from the Israelite community to allow you to approach him, to perform the service of the LORD's dwelling, and to serve before the community by ministering for them? [10] He has allowed you and all your fellow Levites

---

[y] Or *with a high hand*

with you to approach him. Yet you also seek the priesthood? [11]Thus you and your entire community have assembled against the LORD. But Aaron, what is he that you complain about him?"

Test of priesthood

[12]Moses sent for Dathan and Abiram, Eliab's sons. But they said, "We won't come up! [13]Isn't it enough that you've brought us up from a land full of milk and honey to kill us in the desert so that you'd also dominate us? [14]Moreover, you haven't brought us to a land full of milk and honey, nor given us the inheritance of field and vineyard. Would you also gouge out the eyes of these men? We won't come up!"

[15]Moses became very angry and he said to the LORD, "Pay no attention to their offering. I haven't taken a single donkey from them, nor have I wronged any one of them."

[16]Moses said to Korah, "You and your entire community should appear before the LORD tomorrow, you, they, and Aaron. [17]Every person should take his censer, place incense on it, and present it before the LORD. Each person will carry his censer, two hundred fifty censers in all, including you and Aaron." [18]Then every person took his censer, placed fire on it, put incense on it, and stood at the entrance of the meeting tent with Moses and Aaron. [19]Korah gathered the entire community with them to the entrance of the meeting tent.

Then the LORD's glory appeared to the entire community. [20]The LORD spoke to Moses and Aaron, [21]"Separate yourselves from this community so that I may consume them in a moment."

[22]They fell on their faces and said, "God, the God of all living things. If one person sins, should you become angry with the entire community?"

[23]The LORD said to Moses, [24]"Speak to the community and say, 'Withdraw from around the dwellings of Korah, Dathan, and Abiram.'"

[25]Moses rose and went to Dathan and Abiram. Israel's elders followed him. [26]He spoke to the community: "Move away from the tents of these wicked men and don't touch anything of theirs, lest you too be wiped out for all their sins." [27]They withdrew from around the dwellings of Korah, Dathan, and Abiram. Then Dathan and Abiram came out and stood at the entrance of their tents with their wives, children, and little ones. [28]Moses said, "By this you will know that the LORD sent me to do these deeds and that it wasn't my own desire. [29]If all these people die a natural death, or if their fate be that of all humans, then the LORD hasn't sent me. [30]But if the LORD performs an act of creation, and the ground opens its mouth and swallows them and everything that belongs to them, so that they descend alive to their graves, then you'll know that these men disrespected the LORD."

The rebels' punishment

[31]As soon as he finished speaking these words, the ground under them split open. [32]The earth opened its mouth and swallowed them and their households, including every human that belonged to Korah and all their possessions. [33]They along with all their possessions descended alive to their graves, and the earth closed over them. They perished in the middle of the assembly. [34]All the Israelites who were around them fled at their cry, for they said, "The earth may swallow us." [35]Then fire went out from the LORD and consumed the two hundred fifty men offering incense.

The reminder of the censers

[36z]The LORD spoke to Moses: [37]Tell Eleazar, Aaron the priest's son, to raise the censers from the fire and scatter the ashes about, because they are holy. [38]Hammer the censers of those who sinned and lost their lives into thin plates for the altar. Since they presented them in the LORD's presence, they had become holy. They will be a sign for the Israelites.

[39]Eleazar the priest took the bronze

censers presented by those who had been consumed by fire and hammered them into a covering for the altar, [40]just as the LORD instructed him through Moses. This was a reminder for the Israelites that no outsider who isn't one of Aaron's descendants should approach to burn incense in the LORD's presence, so as not to be like Korah and his community.

[41]On the next day the entire Israelite community complained to Moses and Aaron, "You killed the LORD's people." [42]When the community assembled against Moses and Aaron, they turned toward the meeting tent. At that moment the cloud covered it, and the LORD's glory appeared. [43]Moses and Aaron came to the front of the meeting tent, [44]and the LORD spoke to Moses: [45]Get away from this community, so that I may consume them in an instant.

They fell on their faces, [46]and Moses said to Aaron, "Take the censer, put fire from the altar on it, place incense on it, go quickly to the community, and seek reconciliation for them. Indeed, the LORD's anger has gone out. The plague has begun." [47]Aaron took it as Moses said and ran into the middle of the assembly, for the plague had already begun among the people. He burned incense and sought reconciliation for the people. [48]He stood between the dead and the living, and the plague stopped. [49]Those who died from the plague were fourteen thousand seven hundred, in addition to those who died because of Korah. [50]Aaron returned to Moses at the entrance of the meeting tent once the plague stopped.

[a]17:16 in Heb

Aaron's budding staff

17[a]The LORD spoke to Moses: [2]Speak to the Israelites and take from them a staff from each household, from each of the chiefs of their households, twelve staffs. Write each person's name on his staff. [3]Write Aaron's name on Levi's staff, for there will be one staff for the leader of each household. [4]Then you will place them in the meeting tent in front of the chest containing the covenant, where I meet you. [5]The staff of the person I choose will sprout. Then I will rid myself of the Israelites' complaints that they make against you.

[6]Moses spoke to the Israelites, and each of their chiefs gave him a staff, one staff for each chief and his household, twelve staffs, and the staff of Aaron was with their staffs. [7]Moses placed the staffs before the LORD in the meeting tent. [8]The next day Moses entered the covenant tent, and Aaron's staff of Levi's household had sprouted. It grew shoots, produced blossoms, and bore almonds. [9]Moses brought out all the staffs from the LORD's presence to the Israelites. They saw what happened, and each person took back his staff.

[10]Then the LORD said to Moses, "Return Aaron's staff in front of the chest containing the covenant to serve as a sign to the rebels so that their complaints against me end and they don't die." [11]Moses did exactly as the LORD commanded him.

[12]The Israelites said to Moses, "We are perishing. We are being destroyed. All of us are being destroyed. [13]Anyone who approaches the LORD's dwelling will die. Are we doomed to perish?"

AARON'S STAFF

Aaron's staff is an instrument of power in the confrontation with Pharaoh and the plagues (Exod 7:8-12, 19; 8:5-6, 16-17). In Numbers 17, a staff representing Levi is inscribed with Aaron's name. It blossoms, proving that the Aaronites are the only legitimate priests. It is preserved in the sanctuary as a warning to rival factions.

The priests' and Levites' duties

18 The LORD said to Aaron: You, your sons, and your household will bear the guilt of offenses connected with the sanctuary. You and your sons will bear the guilt of offenses connected with your priesthood. ²Bring with you your brothers from the tribe of Levi, your father's tribe, so that they can assist you and serve you and your sons before the covenant tent. ³They will perform their duties for you and the service for the entire tent. But they will not approach the holy equipment of the sanctuary or the altar, lest both they and you die. ⁴They will assist you and they will perform the duties of the meeting tent with regard to all the work of the tent. But no outsider may accompany you. ⁵You will perform the duties of the sanctuary and the altar. Then there will no longer be any anger against the Israelites. ⁶I have taken your brothers, the Levites, from the Israelites. They are a gift to you, dedicated to the LORD to perform the service of the meeting tent. ⁷You and your sons must perform the duties of your priesthood for all the matters of the altar and the area behind the curtain. I give you your priestly service as a gift. But an outsider who approaches will die.

The priests' compensation

⁸The LORD spoke to Aaron: I now place you in charge of my gifts, including all the Israelites' sacred offerings. I have given them to you and your sons as an allowance. This is a permanent regulation. ⁹This is what belongs to you from the most holy offerings, from the offerings by fire: all their offerings, including their grain offerings, their purification offerings, and their compensation offerings. The most holy offerings that they bring to me will be yours and your sons'. ¹⁰You will eat it as a most holy thing. Every male may eat it. It will be holy to you. ¹¹This will also belong to you, your sons, and your daughters: I'm giving you the gift offerings and all the Israelites' uplifted offerings. This is a permanent regulation. Anyone who is clean in your household may eat it. ¹²All the choice oil, new wine, and the grain's first harvest that they give to the LORD, I'm giving to you. ¹³The early produce of everything in their land, which they bring to the LORD, will be yours. Anyone who is clean in your household may eat it. ¹⁴Everything that is devoted to the LORD in Israel will be yours. ¹⁵Any oldest male from the womb of any living thing that is presented to the LORD, whether human or animal, will be yours. However, you will redeem the oldest males of humans and of unclean animals. ¹⁶Their redemption price from one month of age you will calculate at five shekels of silver according to the sanctuary shekel, which is twenty gerahs. ¹⁷But the oldest offspring of a cow, sheep, or goat you may not redeem. They are holy. You must dash their blood on the altar and turn their fat into smoke for a soothing smell to the LORD. ¹⁸But their meat is yours. It will be yours just as the breast of the uplifted offering and the right thigh are yours. ¹⁹All the holy gift offerings that the Israelites raise to the LORD I have given to you, your sons, and your daughters. This is a permanent regulation. It is a covenant of salt forever in the LORD's presence, for you and your descendants.

²⁰The LORD said to Aaron: You will have no inheritance in their land, nor will you have a share among them. I am your share and your inheritance among the Israelites.

The Levites' compensation

²¹I have given all the one-tenth portions in Israel to the Levites as an inheritance. They are a reward for performing their service in the meeting tent. ²²The Israelites will no longer be able to approach the meeting tent, or they will be responsible for their sin and die. ²³The Levites will perform the service of the meeting tent, and they will be responsible for their own sins. This is a permanent regulation for all time. But they will not inherit land among the Israelites ²⁴because I've given the Israelites' one-tenth portion, which they have raised to the LORD as a gift offering, as an inheritance to the Levites. Therefore, I've said to them, "They won't inherit land among the Israelites."

²⁵The LORD spoke to Moses: ²⁶Speak to

the Levites and say to them: When you receive from the Israelites the one-tenth portion that I have given you from them as your inheritance, you also must present a gift offering to the LORD from it, a tenth from the one-tenth portion. [27] It will be considered your gift offering, like the grain of the threshing floor and what fills the winepress. [28] In this way you will also present a gift offering to the LORD from all the one-tenth portions that you take from the Israelites. You will provide from it a gift offering to the LORD for Aaron the priest. [29] You will present each gift offering to the LORD from all your gifts, from its best portions and its holiest parts.

[30] You will say to them: When you have presented the best portion, it will be considered for the Levites equivalent to the produce of the grain and the produce of the winepress. [31] You and your household may eat it anywhere, because it is payment for your service in the meeting tent. [32] You will not bear guilt after you have presented the best portion. But you must not make the sacred gifts of the Israelites impure, on penalty of death.

Instructions about the red cow and the water of purification

19 The LORD spoke to Moses and Aaron: [2] This is the regulation in the Instruction that the LORD commanded. Tell the Israelites that they must bring you a red cow without defect, which is flawless and on which no yoke has been laid. [3] You will give it to Eleazar the priest, and he will take

it outside the camp and slaughter it in front of him. [4] Eleazar the priest will take some of its blood with his finger and sprinkle it seven times in front of the meeting tent. [5] Then he will burn the cow in front of him, its skin, flesh, and blood, with its dung. [6] The priest will take cedarwood, hyssop, and crimson cloth and throw them into the fire where the cow is burning. [7] Then the priest will wash his clothes and bathe his body in water. Afterward the priest will enter the camp, but he will be unclean until evening. [8] The one who burned the cow will wash his clothes in water and bathe his body in water, but he will be unclean until evening. [9] A person who is clean will gather the ashes of the cow and place them outside the camp in a clean place. They will be kept for the water of purification for the Israelite community as a purification offering. [10] The one who gathers the ashes of the cow will wash his clothes but will be unclean until evening. This will be a permanent regulation for the Israelites and for the immigrant who lives among them.

Contact with a dead body

[11] The person who touches the dead body of any human will be unclean for seven days. [12] That person must be cleansed with water on the third and seventh days to be clean. If he fails to be cleansed with water on the third and seventh days, he will not be clean. [13] Anyone who touches the body of a human who has died and doesn't cleanse himself defiles the LORD's dwelling. Such persons must be cut off from Israel because

RED COW

According to the book of Numbers, the ashes of a special red cow were used to purify those defiled by death, the strongest contaminant in the Israelite system of impurities. A corpse was irrevocably impure, and those who had been in contact with it were required to purify themselves under penalty of death by divine agency. If one was not properly purified, corpse impurity became a danger to the sanctuary, even if no direct contact with it was made (Num 19:2-10, 13, 20).

the water of purification wasn't sprinkled on them. They remain unclean.

[14]This is the instruction: When anyone dies in a tent, all who go into the tent and all who are in the tent are unclean for seven days. [15]Any open jar without a sealed cover on it is unclean. [16]Anyone in the open field who touches a person slain by the sword, or who died naturally, or a human bone or a grave, will be unclean for seven days. [17]For the unclean person, they will take some of the ashes of the purification offering and place fresh water with it in a jar. [18]Then a clean person will take hyssop, dip it into the water, and sprinkle it on the tent, on all the jars, on the people who were there, and on anyone who touched bone, the slain, the dead, or the grave. [19]On the third day and the seventh day the clean person will sprinkle it on the unclean, so that he will have purified him on the seventh day. He will then wash his clothes, bathe in water, and be clean at evening. [20]Any person who is unclean and didn't cleanse himself will be cut off from the assembly, because he has defiled the LORD's sanctuary. He didn't have the water of purification sprinkled on him. He is unclean. [21]This will be a permanent regulation for them. The one who sprinkles the water of purification will wash his own clothes. Anyone who touches the water of purification will be unclean until evening. [22]Whoever the unclean person touches will be unclean, and the one who touches the unclean will be unclean until evening.

Lawsuit over water and Moses' disobedience

20 In the first month,[b] the entire Israelite community entered the Zin desert and the people stayed at Kadesh. Miriam died and was buried there. [2]Now there was no water for the community, and they assembled against Moses and Aaron. [3]Then the people confronted Moses and said to him, "If only we too had died when our brothers perished in the LORD's presence! [4]Why have you brought the LORD's assembly into this desert to kill us and

our animals here? [5]Why have you led us up from Egypt to bring us to this evil place without grain, figs, vines, or pomegranates? And there's no water to drink!"

[6]Moses and Aaron went away from the assembly to the entrance of the meeting tent and they fell on their faces. Then the LORD's glory appeared to them. [7]The LORD spoke to Moses: [8]"You and Aaron your brother, take the staff and assemble the community. In their presence, tell the rock to provide water. You will produce water from the rock for them and allow the community and their animals to drink."

[9]Moses took the staff from the LORD's presence, as the LORD had commanded him. [10]Moses and Aaron gathered the assembly before the rock. He said to them, "Listen, you rebels! Should we produce water from the rock for you?" [11]Then Moses raised his hand and struck the rock with his staff twice. Out flooded water so that the community and their animals could drink.

[12]The LORD said to Moses and Aaron, "Because you didn't trust me to show my holiness before the Israelites, you will not bring this assembly into the land that I am giving them." [13]These were the waters of Meribah,[c] where the Israelites confronted the LORD with controversy and he showed his holiness to them.

The Israelites confront Edom

[14]Moses sent messengers from Kadesh to the king of Edom: "This is what your brother Israel says: 'You know all the adversity that has happened to us. [15]How our ancestors went down to Egypt and lived in Egypt for a long time. The Egyptians oppressed us as they had our ancestors, [16]and we cried out to the LORD. He heard our voice, sent a messenger, and brought us out of Egypt. Now here we are in Kadesh, a city on the edge of your border. [17]Please let us cross through your land. We won't pass through any field or vineyard, or drink water from any well. We will walk on the King's Highway and not turn to the right or to the left until we have crossed your border.'"

---

[b]March–April, Nisan   [c]Or confrontation

¹⁸Edom said to him, "You won't cross through, or I will come out against you with a sword."

¹⁹The Israelites said to him, "We'll go up by the road. If we drink from your water, either we or our livestock, we'll pay for it. It's a small matter. We would only ask to cross on foot."

²⁰But he said, "You won't cross." Then Edom came out against them with a powerful army and a strong hand. ²¹Edom refused to allow Israel to cross his border. And Israel turned away from him. ²²They marched from Kadesh.

Aaron's death at Mount Hor

The entire Israelite community came to Mount Hor. ²³The LORD said to Moses and Aaron at Mount Hor on the border of the land of Edom: ²⁴Aaron will join his ancestors, for he may not enter the land that I've given to the Israelites, because you rebelled against my command at the waters of Meribah. ²⁵Take Aaron and his son Eleazar, and bring them up Mount Hor. ²⁶Strip Aaron of his clothes and put them on Eleazar his son. Then Aaron will die there.

²⁷Moses did as the LORD commanded. They went up Mount Hor in the sight of the entire community. ²⁸Moses stripped Aaron of his clothes and put them on Eleazar his son. Aaron died there at the top of the mountain. Then Moses and Eleazar descended from the mountain. ²⁹When the entire community saw that Aaron had died, the entire household of Israel wept thirty days for Aaron.

Defeat of the Canaanite king of Arad

21 When the Canaanite king of Arad, who ruled in the arid southern plain, heard that the Israelites were coming on the Atharim road, he fought against Israel and took some of them captive. ²Then Israel made a solemn promise to the LORD and said, "If you give this people into our hands, we will completely destroy their city." ³The LORD heard the voice of Israel and handed the Canaanites over. They completely destroyed them and their cities, so the name of the place is called Hormah.^d

The bronze snake's healing power

⁴They marched from Mount Hor on the Reed Sea^e road around the land of Edom. The people became impatient on the road. ⁵The people spoke against God and Moses: "Why did you bring us up from Egypt to kill us in the desert, where there is no food or water. And we detest this miserable bread!" ⁶So the LORD sent poisonous^f snakes among the people and they bit the people. Many of the Israelites died.

⁷The people went to Moses and said, "We've sinned, for we spoke against the LORD and you. Pray to the LORD so that he will send the snakes away from us." So Moses prayed for the people.

⁸The LORD said to Moses, "Make a poisonous snake and place it on a pole. Whoever is bitten can look at it and live." ⁹Moses made a bronze snake and placed it on a pole. If a snake bit someone, that person could look at the bronze snake and live.

March around Moab

¹⁰Then the Israelites marched and they camped at Oboth. ¹¹They marched from Oboth and camped at Iye-abarim in the desert on the border of Moab toward the east. ¹²From there they marched and camped in the Zered ravine. ¹³From there they marched and camped across the Arnon in the desert that extends from the border of the Amorites, for the Arnon was the border of Moab, between Moab and the Amorites. ¹⁴For this reason the scroll of the LORD's wars says:

Waheb in Suphah and the ravines.
The Arnon ¹⁵and the ravines
that extend to the settlement of Ar
and lie along the border of Moab.

¹⁶From there they marched to Beer, the well where the LORD said to Moses, "Gather the people, and I'll give them water." ¹⁷Then the Israelites sang this song:

"Well, flow up!
Sing about it!

^dOr destruction   ^eOr Red Sea   ^fHeb uncertain

18 The well that the officials dug,
 that the officials of the people
  hollowed out
 with the ruler's scepter and their staffs."
They marched from the desert to Mattanah; 19from Mattanah to Nahaliel; from Nahaliel to Bamoth; 20from Bamoth to the valley in the Moabite countryside, to the top of Pisgah overlooking Jeshimon.g

Wars against Sihon and Og

21Then the Israelites sent messengers to Sihon the Amorite king: 22"Let us pass through your land. We won't turn aside into a field or vineyard. We won't drink water from a well. We will walk on the King's Highway until we cross your border." 23But Sihon wouldn't allow the Israelites to cross his border. Sihon gathered all his people and went out to meet the Israelites in the desert. When he came to Jahaz, he attacked the Israelites. 24The Israelites struck him down with their swords and took possession of his land from the Arnon to the Jabbok, as far as the Ammonites, for the border of the Ammonites was fortified. 25The Israelites took all these cities. Then the Israelites settled in all the cities of the Amorites, in Heshbon and all its villages.

26Now Heshbon was the city of Sihon the Amorite king who had fought against the former king of Moab. He had taken all his land from him as far as the Arnon. 27Therefore, the poets say:

"Come to Heshbon, let it be built.
 Let the city of Sihon be established.

28 Fire went out from Heshbon,
 flame from Sihon's city.
 It consumed Ar of Moab
 and swallowed up
  the shrines of the Arnon.
29 You are doomed, Moab!
 You are destroyed, people of Chemosh!
 He gave his sons as fugitives,
 and his daughters as captives
  to the Amorite king Sihon.
30 Yet we have thrown them down,
 destroying themh
 from Heshbon to Dibon.
 We brought ruin until Nophah,
 which is by Medeba."

31Israel settled in the land of the Amorites. 32Moses sent spies to Jazer. They captured its villages and took possession of the Amorites who were there. 33Then they turned and ascended the road of Bashan. Og, Bashan's king, came out at Edrei to meet them in battle, he and all his people. 34The LORD said to Moses: Don't be afraid of him, for I have handed over all his people and his land. Do to him as you did to Sihon the Amorite king who ruled in Heshbon. 35They slaughtered Og, his sons, and all his people until there were no survivors. Then they took possession of his land.

Balak summons Balaam to curse the Israelites

22 The Israelites marched and camped in the plains of Moab across the Jordan from Jericho. 2Balak, Zippor's son, saw everything that the Israelites did to the Amorites. 3The Moabites greatly feared

gOr wasteland   hHeb uncertain; LXX their posterity has perished

BEER

The Hebrew word for "well" (Gen 26:15-33). During the Israelites' desert wandering, after they left Moab and traveled along the Arnon River they came to a place called "Beer" (Num 21:16), and they celebrated it as God's gift to Israel (21:17-18). Its precise location remains unknown. Jotham fled to Beer from his brother Abimelech's rampage against all of Jerubaal's sons (Judg 9:21).

the people, for they were so numerous. The Moabites were terrified of the Israelites. [4]The Moabites said to the elders of Midian, "Now this assembly will devour everything around us, as an ox eats up the grass in the field."

Balak, Zippor's son, was king of Moab at that time. [5]He sent messengers to Balaam, Beor's son, at Pethor, which is by the river in the land of his people,[i] to summon him: "A people has come out of Egypt, and they have now covered the land. They have settled next to me. [6]Now please come and curse this people for me because they are stronger than I am. Perhaps I'll be able to destroy them and drive them from the land, for I know that whomever you bless is blessed and whomever you curse is cursed."

[7]So the elders of Moab and Midian went with the payment for divination in their hands. They came to Balaam and told him Balak's words. [8]He said to them, "Spend the night here and I'll bring back to you a word exactly as the LORD speaks to me." So the officials of Moab stayed with Balaam.

[9]God came to Balaam and said, "Who are these men with you?"

[10]Balaam said to God, "Moab's King Balak, Zippor's son, sent them to me with the message, [11]'A people has come out of Egypt and covered the land. Now come and curse them for me. Perhaps I'll be able to fight against them and drive them out.'"

[12]God said to Balaam, "Don't go with them. Don't curse the people, because they are blessed."

[13]Then Balaam arose in the morning and said to Balak's officials, "Go to your land, for the LORD has refused to allow me to go with you."

[14]The officials of Moab arose, they went to Balak, and they said, "Balaam refused to come with us."

[15]Balak continued to send other officials more numerous and important than these. [16]They came to Balaam and said to him, "This is what Balak, Zippor's son, says: 'Please let nothing hold you back from com-

ing to me, [17]for I'll greatly honor you and I'll do anything you ask of me. Please come and curse this people for me.'"

[18]Balaam answered and said to Balak's servants, "If Balak were to give me his house full of silver and gold, I wouldn't be able to do anything, small or great, to break the command of the LORD my God. [19]Now you also must remain the night here so that I may know what else the LORD may say to me."

[20]God came to Balaam in the night and said to him, "If the men have come to summon you, arise and go with them. But you must do only what I tell you to do." [21]So Balaam arose in the morning, saddled his donkey, and went with the officials of Moab.

Balaam and the LORD's messenger

[22]Then God became angry because he went. So while he was riding on his donkey accompanied by his two servants, the LORD's messenger stood in the road as his adversary. [23]The donkey saw the LORD's messenger standing in the road with his sword drawn in his hand, so the donkey turned from the road and went into the field. Balaam struck the donkey in order to turn him back onto the road. [24]Then the LORD's messenger stood in the narrow path between vineyards with a stone wall on each side. [25]When the donkey saw the LORD's messenger, it leaned against the wall and squeezed Balaam's foot against the wall, so he continued to beat it. [26]The LORD's messenger persisted and crossed over and stood in a narrow place, where it wasn't possible to turn either right or left. [27]The donkey saw the LORD's messenger and lay down underneath Balaam. Balaam became angry and beat the donkey with the rod. [28]Then the LORD opened the donkey's mouth and it said to Balaam, "What have I done to you that you've beaten me these three times?"

[29]Balaam said to the donkey, "Because you've tormented me. If I had a sword in my hand, I'd kill you now."

[30]The donkey said to Balaam, "Am I not your donkey, on whom you've often ridden

to this day? Have I been in the habit of doing this to you?"

Balaam said, "No."

31 Then the LORD uncovered Balaam's eyes, and Balaam saw the LORD's messenger standing in the road with his sword drawn in his hand. Then he bowed low and worshipped. 32 The LORD's messenger said to him, "Why have you beaten your donkey these three times? I've come out here as an adversary, because you took the road recklessly in front of me. 33 The donkey saw me and turned away from me these three times. If it hadn't turned away from me, I would just now have killed you and let it live."

34 Balaam said to the LORD's messenger, "I've sinned, because I didn't know that you were standing against me in the road. Now, if you think it's wrong, I'll go back."

35 The LORD's messenger said to Balaam, "Go with the men. But don't say anything. Say only that which I tell you." So Balaam went with Balak's officials.

Balaam and Balak meet

36 When Balak heard that Balaam was coming, he went out to meet him at Ir-moab, which is on the border of the Arnon at the farthest point of the border. 37 Balak said to Balaam, "Didn't I send urgently and summon you? Why didn't you come to me? Am I really not able to honor you?"

38 Balaam said to Balak, "I've now come to you. But I'm only able to speak whatever word God gives me to say. That is what I will speak."

Balaam's first blessing of the Israelites

39 Then Balaam went with Balak and they came to Kiriath-huzoth. 40 Balak sacrificed oxen and sheep and sent them to Balaam and the officials who were with him. 41 In the morning Balak took Balaam and brought him up to Bamoth-baal, where he could see part of the people.

23 Balaam said to Balak, "Build me seven altars here and prepare for me seven bulls and seven rams." 2 Balak did as Balaam had said. Then Balak and Balaam offered a bull and a ram on each altar. 3 Balaam said to Balak, "Stay by your entirely burned offering. I will go and perhaps the LORD will grant me an appearance and speak. Whatever he shows me, I will tell you." Then he went off to a high outlook.

4 God granted Balaam an appearance. Balaam said to him, "I have arranged seven altars and I have sacrificed a bull and a ram on each altar."

5 The LORD gave Balaam something to say, and said to him, "Return to Balak and say this."

6 Balaam returned to him, while he and all the officials of Moab were standing next to his entirely burned offering. 7 Then he raised his voice and made his address:

"From Aram Balak led me,
  the king of Moab,
    from the eastern mountains.
  Come, curse Jacob for me;
    come, denounce Israel.
8 How can I curse
    whom God hasn't cursed?
  How can I denounce
    whom God hasn't denounced?
9 From the top of the rocks I see him;
    from the hills I gaze on him.
  Here is a people living alone;
    it doesn't consider itself
      among the nations.

BALAK

King of Moab, son of Zippor. Fearing the Israelites, Balak sends for Balaam, the seer, to curse the Israelites. Balaam curses the Moabites instead (Num 22–24). References to Balak also appear in Joshua 24:9; Judges 11:25; Micah 6:5; and Revelation 2:14.

¹⁰ Who can count the dust of Jacob,
  or number a fourth of Israel?
Let me die the death
  of those who do right,
  and let my end be like his."

¹¹Then Balak said to Balaam, "What have you done to me? I took you to curse my enemy. But now you've blessed him."

¹²He answered and said, "Don't I have to take care to speak whatever the Lord gives me to say?"

Balaam's second blessing of the Israelites

¹³Then Balak said to Balaam, "Come with me, please, to another place where you'll see them. You'll see only part of them. You won't see all of them. Then curse them for me from there." ¹⁴He took him to the field of Zophim, to the top of Pisgah. He built seven altars and offered a bull and a ram on each altar.

¹⁵Then Balaam said to Balak, "Stand here by your entirely burned offering, while I seek an appearance over there."

¹⁶The Lord granted Balaam an appearance and gave him a message. He said, "Return to Balak and say this."

¹⁷Balaam approached Balak, who was standing by his entirely burned offering with the officials of Moab. Balak said to him, "What did the Lord say?"

¹⁸Then Balaam raised his voice and made his address:

"Arise, Balak, and listen;
  hear me out, Zippor's son.
¹⁹ God isn't a man that he would lie,
  or a human being that he would
    change his mind.
Has he ever spoken and not done it,
  or promised and not fulfilled it?
²⁰ I received a blessing, and he blessed.
  I can't take it back.
²¹ He hasn't envisioned misfortune
    for Jacob,
  nor has he seen trouble for Israel.
The Lord his God is with him,
  proclaimed as his king.
²² God, who brought them out of Egypt,

is like a magnificent wild bull for him.
²³ There is no omen against Jacob,
  no divination against Israel.
Instantly it is told to Jacob,
  and to Israel, what God performs.
²⁴ A people now rises like a lioness,
  like a lion it stands up.
It doesn't lie down until it eats the prey
  and drinks the blood of the slain."

²⁵Then Balak said to Balaam, "Don't curse them or bless them."

²⁶But Balaam answered and said to Balak, "Didn't I say to you, 'I'll do whatever the Lord tells me to'?"

Balaam's third blessing of the Israelites

²⁷Balak said to Balaam, "Please come and I'll take you to another place. Perhaps God will prefer it, so that you could curse him for me from there."

²⁸So Balak took Balaam to the top of Peor, which overlooks Jeshimon.^j ²⁹Balaam said to Balak, "Build me seven altars here and prepare for me seven bulls and seven rams." ³⁰Balak did just as Balaam said. He offered a bull and a ram on each altar.

24 Balaam saw that it pleased the Lord to bless the Israelites, so he didn't go as the other times to seek omens. Instead, he turned toward the desert. ²Balaam looked up and saw Israel camping by tribes. Then God's spirit came on him. ³He raised his voice and made his address:

"The oracle of Balaam, Beor's son;
  the oracle of a man whose eye is open.^k
⁴ The oracle of one who hears God's speech,
  who perceives the Almighty's^l visions,
  who falls down with eyes uncovered.
⁵ How beautiful are your tents, Jacob,
  your camps, Israel!
⁶ Like palm groves that stretch out,
  like gardens next to a river,
  like eaglewood trees
    that the Lord has planted,
  like cedar trees next to water.
⁷ Water will drip from his branches;
  his seed will have plenty of water;
  his king will be higher than Agag,
  and his kingdom will be lifted up.

---

^jOr wasteland ^kHeb uncertain ^lHeb Shaddai or Mountain One

8 God, who brought him from Egypt,
   is like a magnificent wild bull
   for him.
He will devour enemy nations
   and break their bones;
   he will strike with his arrows.
9 He crouched and lay down like a lion;
   like a lioness, who can make her rise?
The one blessing you will be blessed,
   and the one cursing you will be cursed."

10 Balak was angry with Balaam. He pounded his fists. Balak said to Balaam, "I summoned you to curse my enemies, but now you've given a blessing these three times. 11 Now get out of here and go home. I told you I'd greatly honor you, but the LORD has denied you any honor."

Balaam predicts Moab's destruction

12 Balaam said to Balak, "Didn't I tell your messengers, whom you sent to me, 13 'If Balak would give me his house full of silver and gold, I wouldn't be able to break the LORD's command for good or ill by my own will. I'll say whatever the LORD says'? 14 So now I'm going to my people. Let me advise you what this people will do to your people in the days to come." 15 He raised his voice and made his address:

m Heb *Elyon*   n Heb *Shaddai* or *Mountain One*

"The oracle of Balaam, Beor's son,
   the oracle of a man whose eye is open.
16 The oracle of one who hears
      God's speech,
   and understands
      the Most High's[m] knowledge,
   who perceives the Almighty's[n] visions,
   who falls down with eyes uncovered.
17 I see him, but not now;
   I look at him, but not nearby.
A star comes from Jacob;
   a scepter arises from Israel,
      smashing Moab's forehead,
      the head of all the Sethites.
18 Edom will become a possession,
   Seir a possession of its enemies.
   But Israel acts powerfully.
19 Someone from Jacob will rule
   and destroy the survivors from Ir."

20 He looked at Amalek
   and raised his voice
   and gave his address:
"Amalek is foremost among the nations,
   but its end is to perish forever."
21 He looked at the Kenites
   and raised his voice
   and gave his address:

ORACLE

A direct message from God delivered through a prophet. Although the word *oracle* often carries with it the idea of a divine answer given in response to an inquiry (e.g., the Oracle of Delphi), the terms translated as "oracle" in the Bible do not necessarily carry this connotation. Some biblical oracles are given in response to a question or petition presented to the deity (1 Kgs 22:15; 2 Chron 20:5-19), a practice that is also known from Mesopotamia, and in such cases the prophetic activity often takes place within a cultic setting (1 Chron 25:1). But the means by which the majority of oracles in the OT were received is unknown, as most are presented in their canonical form without reference to the process of intermediation that produced them.

This term as used in the NT does not necessarily refer to prophetic activity. It is used in later Christian literature to refer to the sayings of Christ and the teachings of the early church.

"Your dwelling is secure;
  your nest is set in the rock.
²² Yet Kain will burn
  when Asshur takes you away captive."

²³ He raised his voice
  and made his address:
"How terrible!
  Who will live when God does this?
²⁴ Ships from Kittim will attack Asshur;
  they will attack Eber,
  and even he will perish forever."

²⁵Then Balaam arose, set out, and returned home. Balak also went on his way.

Israelites and Moabites intermarry

25 When the Israelites lived at Shittim, the people made themselves impure by having illicit sex with Moabite women. ²The Moabite women invited the people to the sacrifices for their god. So the people ate a meal, and they worshipped their god. ³Israel became attached to the Baal of Peor, and the LORD was angry at the Israelites. ⁴The LORD said to Moses: Take all the leaders of the people and kill them on behalf of the LORD in broad daylight, so that the LORD's anger turns away from Israel.

⁵Then Moses said to Israel's officials, "Each of you: kill your men who are attached to the Baal of Peor."

Israelites and Midianites intermarry

⁶An Israelite man brought a Midianite woman to his brothers in the sight of Moses and the entire Israelite community, who were weeping at the entrance of the meeting tent. ⁷When Phinehas (Eleazar's son and Aaron the priest's grandson) saw

this, he arose in the middle of the community, took a spear in his hand, ⁸went after the Israelite man into the chamber, and stabbed the two of them, the Israelite man and the woman, through the stomach. Then the plague stopped spreading among the Israelites. ⁹Yet those who died by the plague numbered twenty-four thousand.

¹⁰The LORD spoke to Moses: ¹¹Phinehas (Eleazar's son and Aaron the priest's grandson) has turned back my rage toward the Israelites. Because he was jealous for me among you, I didn't consume the Israelites due to my jealousy. ¹²Therefore, say: I'm now giving him my covenant of well-being. ¹³It will be for him and his descendants a covenant of permanent priesthood, because he was jealous for his God and sought reconciliation for the Israelites.

¹⁴The name of the slain Israelite man who was killed with the Midianite woman was Zimri the son of Salu, chief of Simeon's household. ¹⁵The name of the slain Midianite woman was Cozbi the daughter of Zur, a tribal leader of a Midianite household. ¹⁶The LORD spoke to Moses: ¹⁷Go after the Midianites and destroy them ¹⁸because they went after you by the deception they devised for you at Peor with Cozbi, the Midianite chief's daughter and their sister, who was killed on the same day as the plague during the events at Peor.

Second census of the Israelite tribes

26 °After the plague ᵖthe LORD said to Moses and Eleazar, Aaron the priest's son: ²Take a census of the entire Israelite community, from 20 years old and above by their households, to determine

°25:19 in Heb ᵖ26:1 in Heb

SHITTIM

Means "acacia trees." Located approximately 8 miles northeast of the Jordan River's mouth and 8 miles west-northwest of Heshbon. Numbers 25:1 has Israel staying at Shittim at the end of their 40 years of wandering and prior to their entrance into the land of Canaan.

everyone in Israel who is eligible for military service.

[3] Moses and Eleazar the priest spoke to the people on the plains of Moab by the Jordan opposite Jericho: [4] "Take a census of those 20 years old and above as the LORD commanded Moses." The Israelites who left the land of Egypt were:

[5] Reuben, Israel's oldest son.

Reuben's descendants: from Hanoch, the Hanochite clan; from Pallu, the Palluite clan; [6] from Hezron, the Hezronite clan; from Carmi, the Carmite clan. [7] These are the Reubenite clans. Their enrollment was 43,730.

[8] Pallu's descendants: Eliab.

[9] Eliab's descendants: Nemuel, Dathan, and Abiram. These are the Dathan and Abiram chosen by the community who fought against Moses and Aaron with the community of Korah, when they fought against the LORD. [10] The earth opened its mouth and swallowed them, along with Korah, when the community died and fire devoured 250 persons. They became a warning sign. [11] But Korah's descendants didn't die.

[12] Simeon's descendants according to their clans: from Nemuel, the Nemuelite clan; from Jamin, the Jaminite clan; from Jachin, the Jachinite clan; [13] from Zerah, the Zerahite clan; from Shaul, the Shaulite clan. [14] These are the Simeonite clans, 22,200.

[15] Gad's descendants according to their clans: from Zephon, the Zephonite clan; from Haggi, the Haggite clan; from Shuni, the Shunite clan; [16] from Ozni, the Oznite clan; from Eri, the Erite clan; [17] from Arod, the Arodite clan; from Areli, the Arelite clan. [18] These are the Gadite clans. Their enrollment was 40,500.

[19] Judah's descendants: Er and Onan. Er and Onan died in the land of Canaan. [20] Judah's descendants according to their clans: from Shelah, the Shelanite clan; from Perez, the Perezite clan; from Zerah, the Zerahite clan.

[21] Perez's descendants: from Hezron, the Hezronite clan; from Hamul, the Hamulite clan. [22] These are the Judahite clans. Their enrollment was 76,500.

[23] Issachar's descendants according to their clans: from Tola, the Tolaite clan; from Puvah, the Punite clan; [24] from Jashub, the Jashubite clan; from Shimron, the Shimronite clan. [25] These are the Issacharite clans. Their enrollment was 64,300.

[26] Zebulun's descendants according to their clans: from Sered, the Seredite clan; from Elon, the Elonite clan; from Jahleel, the Jahleelite clan. [27] These are the Zebulunite clans. Their enrollment was 60,500.

[28] Joseph's descendants according to their clans: Manasseh and Ephraim.

[29] Manasseh's descendants: from Machir, the Machirite clan. Machir fathered Gilead. From Gilead, the Gileadite clan. [30] These are Gilead's descendants: from Iezer, the Iezerite clan; from Helek, the Helekite clan; [31] from Asriel, the Asrielite clan; from Shechem, the Shechemite clan; [32] from Shemida, the Shemidaite clan; and from Hepher, the Hepherite clan. [33] But Zelophehad, Hepher's son, had no sons, only daughters. The names of Zelophehad's daughters were Mahlah, Noah, Hoglah, Milcah, and Tirzah. [34] These are the Manassehite clans. Their enrollment was 52,700.

[35] These are Ephraim's descendants according to their clans: from Shuthelah, the Shuthelahite clan; from Becher, the Becherite clan; from Tahan, the Tahanite clan. [36] These are Shuthelah's descendants: from Eran, the Eranite clan. [37] These are Ephraim's descendants. Their enrollment was 32,500. These are Joseph's descendants according to their clans.

[38] Benjamin's descendants according to their clans: from Bela, the Belaite clan; from Ashbel, the Ashbelite clan; from Ahiram, the Ahiramite clan; [39] from Shupham,[q] the Shuphamite clan; from Hupham, the Huphamite clan. [40] Bela's

descendants were Ard and Naaman: from Ard, the Ardite clan; from Naaman, the Naamite clan. ⁴¹These are Benjamin's descendants according to their clans. Their enrollment was 45,600.

⁴²These are Dan's descendants according to their clans: from Shuham, the Shuhamite clan. These are the Danite clans according to their clans. ⁴³All the Shuhamite clans according to their enrollment were 64,400.

⁴⁴Asher's descendants according to their clans: from Imnah, the Imnite clan; from Ishvi, the Ishvite clan; from Beriah, the Beriite clan. ⁴⁵From Beriah's descendants: from Heber, the Heberite clan; from Malchiel, the Malchielite clan. ⁴⁶The name of Asher's daughter was Serah. ⁴⁷These are the clans of Asher's descendants. Their enrollment was 53,400.

⁴⁸Naphtali's descendants according to their clans: from Jahzeel, the Jahzeelite clan; from Guni, the Gunite clan; ⁴⁹from Jezer, the Jezerite clan; from Shillem, the Shillemite clan. ⁵⁰These are Naphtali's clans according to their clans. Their enrollment was 45,400.

⁵¹These are the ones enrolled as Israelites: 601,730.

⁵²The LORD spoke to Moses: ⁵³The land will be apportioned to these as an inheritance according to the number of names. ⁵⁴To a large clan you will give a large inheritance, and to a small clan you will give a small inheritance. Each will be given its inheritance according to the number of its enrollment. ⁵⁵The land, however, will be apportioned by lot. They will inherit according to the names of their ancestral tribes. ⁵⁶Whether they are large or small, each tribe will inherit by means of the lot.

Second census of the Levites

⁵⁷These are the ones enrolled as Levites according to their clans: from Gershon, the Gershonite clan; from Kohath, the Kohathite clan; from Merari, the Merarite clan. ⁵⁸These are the Levite clans: the Libnite clan, the Hebronite clan, the Mahlite clan, the Mushite clan, and the Korahite clan. Now Kohath fathered Amram. ⁵⁹The name of Amram's wife was Jochebed, Levi's daughter, who was born to Levi in Egypt. She gave birth for Amram to Aaron, Moses, and Miriam their sister. ⁶⁰To Aaron were born Nadab, Abihu, Eleazar, and Ithamar. ⁶¹Nadab and Abihu died when they made an unauthorized offering to the LORD. ⁶²Their enrollment was 23,000, consisting of every male one month old and above. They weren't enrolled with the Israelites because no inheritance of land was given to them among the Israelites.

Summary

⁶³These are the ones whom Moses and Eleazar the priest enrolled. They enrolled the Israelites on the plains of Moab by the Jordan opposite Jericho. ⁶⁴There wasn't one person among these from those enrolled by Moses and Aaron the priest when they enrolled the Israelites in the Sinai desert. ⁶⁵The LORD had said to them, "They will die in the desert." Not one of them remained, except Caleb, Jephunneh's son, and Joshua, Nun's son.

Zelophehad's daughters' inheritance

27 The daughters of Zelophehad, Hepher's son, Gilead's grandson, Machir's great-grandson, and Manasseh's great-great-grandson, belonging to the clan of Manasseh and son of Joseph, came forward. His daughters' names were Mahlah, Noah, Hoglah, Milcah, and Tirzah. ²They stood before Moses, Eleazar the priest, the chiefs, and the entire community at the entrance of the meeting tent and said, ³"Our father died in the desert. He wasn't part of the community who gathered against the LORD with Korah's community. He died for his own sin, but he had no sons. ⁴Why should our father's name be taken away from his clan because he didn't have a son? Give us property among our father's brothers."

⁵Moses brought their case before the LORD. ⁶The LORD said to Moses: ⁷Zelophehad's daughters are right in what they are saying. By all means, give them property as

an inheritance among their father's brothers. Hand over their father's inheritance to them. ⁸Speak to the Israelites and say: If a man dies and doesn't have a son, you must hand his inheritance over to his daughters. ⁹If he doesn't have a daughter, you will give his inheritance to his brothers. ¹⁰If he doesn't have any brothers, you should give his inheritance to his father's brothers. ¹¹If his father had no brothers, you should give his inheritance to his nearest relative from his clan. He will take possession of it. This will be a regulation and a case law for the Israelites, as the LORD commanded Moses.

Announcement of Moses' death

¹²The LORD said to Moses, "Go up this mountain, Abarim, and look at the land that I've given to the Israelites. ¹³You will see it and then join your ancestors just as Aaron your brother has, ¹⁴because in the Zin desert, when the community confronted you, you rebelled against my command to show them my holiness by means of the water." (These are the waters of Meribah[r] of Kadesh in the Zin desert.)

¹⁵Moses spoke to the LORD: ¹⁶"Let the LORD, the God of all living things, appoint someone over the community ¹⁷who will go out before them and return before them, someone who will lead them out and bring them back, so that the LORD's community won't be like sheep without their shepherd."

¹⁸The LORD said to Moses, "Take Joshua, Nun's son, a man who has the spirit, and lay your hand on him. ¹⁹Place him before Eleazar the priest and the entire community and commission him before them. ²⁰You will give him some of your power so that the entire Israelite community may obey. ²¹He will stand before Eleazar the priest, who will determine for him the decision by lot before the LORD. At his command, he and all the Israelites with him, the entire community, will go out, and at his command they will return."

²²Moses did as the LORD commanded him. He took Joshua and placed him before Eleazar the priest and the entire community. ²³He laid his hands on him and commissioned him as the LORD had spoken through Moses.

Daily offering

28 The LORD spoke to Moses: ²Command the Israelites and say to them: Make sure to offer to me my offering, my food, my food gift as a soothing smell to me at its appointed time.

³You will say to them: This is the food gift that you must present to the LORD: two flawless one-year-old lambs as the regular entirely burned offering every day. ⁴One lamb you will offer in the morning and the second at twilight, ⁵with a tenth of an ephah[s] of fine flour for a grain offering mixed with a fourth of a hin[t] of beaten oil. ⁶It is the regular entirely burned offering begun at Mount Sinai, a food gift that is a soothing smell to the LORD. ⁷Their drink offering will be a fourth of a hin for each lamb. In the sanctuary a drink offering of brandy will be poured out for the LORD. ⁸The second lamb you will offer at twilight like the grain offering and the drink offering in the morning. You will offer a food gift that is a soothing smell to the LORD.

⁹On the Sabbath day: two flawless one-year-old male lambs and two-tenths of fine flour for a grain offering, mixed with oil, and its drink offering. ¹⁰This is the entirely burned offering for every Sabbath, in addition to the regular entirely burned offering and its drink offering.

Monthly offering

¹¹At the beginning of every month you will present an entirely burned offering to the LORD: two bulls from the herd, one ram, and seven one-year-old male lambs, all flawless. ¹²Use three-tenths of fine flour for a grain offering mixed with oil for each bull, two-tenths of fine flour for a grain offering mixed with oil for each ram, ¹³and one-tenth of fine flour for a grain offering mixed with oil for each lamb. It is an entirely burned offering with a soothing

---

[r]Or *confrontation* [s]One ephah is approximately twenty quarts. [t]One hin is approximately one gallon.

smell, a food gift to the LORD. [14]Their drink offerings will be half a hin of wine for a bull, a third a hin of wine for a ram, and a fourth a hin of wine for a lamb. This is the monthly entirely burned offering for every month through the months of the year. [15]There will be one male goat for a purification offering to the LORD in addition to the regular entirely burned offering and its drink offering.

Yearly offerings

Passover and unleavened bread

[16]On the fourteenth day of the first month[u] there will be a Passover offering to the LORD. [17]On the fifteenth day of this month there will be a festival. For seven days unleavened bread will be eaten. [18]The first day will be a holy occasion. You will not do any job-related work. [19]You will bring a food gift, an entirely burned offering to the LORD: two bulls from the herd, one ram, and seven male lambs one year old. They will be flawless. [20]Their grain offering will be fine flour mixed with oil. You will offer three-tenths for the bull, two-tenths for the ram, [21]and one-tenth for each of the seven lambs, [22]along with one male goat for a purification offering to seek reconciliation for yourselves. [23]You will offer these in addition to the entirely burned offering of the morning, which is the regular entirely burned offering. [24]Like these, you will also offer each day for seven days a food gift as a soothing smell to the LORD. It will be offered in addition to the regular entirely burned offering and its drink offering. [25]The seventh day will be a holy occasion for you. You will not do any job-related work.

Festival of Weeks

[26]The day of the early produce, when you present your new grain offering to the LORD at your Festival of Weeks, will be a holy occasion for you. You will not do any job-related work. [27]You will present an entirely burned offering as a soothing smell to the LORD: two bulls from the herd, one ram, and seven male lambs one year old. [28]Their grain offering will be fine flour mixed with oil: three-tenths for each bull, two-tenths for the one ram, [29]and one-tenth for each of the seven lambs. [30]Offer one male goat to seek reconciliation for yourselves. [31]You will offer these in addition to the regular entirely burned offering, its grain offering and drink offerings. They will be flawless.

Blowing of the trumpet

29 The first day of the seventh month[v] will be a holy occasion for you. You will not do any job-related work. It will be for you a day of the trumpet's sound. [2]You will offer an entirely burned offering as a soothing smell to the LORD: one bull from the herd, one ram, and seven male lambs one year old, all flawless. [3]Their grain offering will be fine flour mixed with oil, three-tenths for the bull, two-tenths for the ram, [4]and one-tenth for each of the seven lambs. [5]There will be one male goat for a purification offering to seek reconciliation for yourselves. [6]This is in addition to the monthly entirely burned offering with its grain offering, and the regular entirely burned offering with its grain offering and drink offerings as prescribed. It will be a soothing smell, a food gift to the LORD.

Day of Reconciliation

[7]The tenth day of this seventh month will be a holy occasion for you. You will deny yourselves and not do any work. [8]You will present an entirely burned offering to the LORD as a soothing smell: one bull from the herd, one ram, and seven male lambs one year old. They will be flawless. [9]Their grain offering will be fine flour mixed with oil, three-tenths for the bull, two-tenths for the one ram, [10]and one-tenth for each of the seven lambs. [11]There will be one male goat for a purification offering in addition to the purification offering of reconciliation, and the regular entirely burned offering with its grain offering and drink offerings.

[u]March–April, Nisan   [v]September–October, Tishrei

Festival of Booths

¹²The fifteenth day of the seventh month[w] will be a holy occasion for you. You will not do any job-related work. You will celebrate a festival to the LORD for seven days. ¹³You will present an entirely burned offering, a food gift as a soothing smell to the LORD: thirteen bulls from the herd, two rams, and fourteen male lambs one year old. They will be flawless. ¹⁴Their grain offering will be fine flour mixed with oil: three-tenths for each of the thirteen bulls, two-tenths for each of the two rams, ¹⁵and one-tenth for each of the fourteen lambs. ¹⁶There will be one male goat for a purification offering in addition to the regular entirely burned offering with its grain offering and its drink offering.

¹⁷On the second day: twelve bulls from the herd, two rams, and fourteen male lambs one year old, all flawless. ¹⁸The grain offering and drink offerings for the bulls, rams, and lambs will be as prescribed for their number. ¹⁹There will be one male goat for a purification offering in addition to the regular entirely burned offering with its grain offering and drink offerings.

²⁰On the third day: eleven bulls, two rams, and fourteen male lambs one year old, all flawless. ²¹The grain offering and drink offerings for the bulls, rams, and lambs will be as prescribed for their number. ²²There will be one male goat for a purification offering in addition to the regular entirely burned offering with its grain offering and drink offering.

[w]September–October, Tishrei

²³On the fourth day: ten bulls, two rams, and fourteen male lambs one year old, all flawless. ²⁴The grain offering and drink offerings for the bulls, rams, and lambs will be as prescribed for their number. ²⁵There will be one male goat for a purification offering in addition to the regular entirely burned offering with its grain offering and drink offering.

²⁶On the fifth day: nine bulls, two rams, and fourteen male lambs one year old, all flawless. ²⁷The grain offering and their drink offerings for the bulls, rams, and lambs will be as prescribed for their number. ²⁸There will be one male goat for a purification offering in addition to the regular entirely burned offering with its grain offering and drink offering.

²⁹On the sixth day: eight bulls, two rams, and fourteen male lambs one year old, all flawless. ³⁰The grain offering and their drink offerings for the bulls, rams, and lambs will be as prescribed for their number. ³¹There will be one male goat for a purification offering in addition to the regular entirely burned offering with its grain offering and its drink offerings.

³²On the seventh day: seven bulls, two rams, and fourteen male lambs one year old, all flawless. ³³The grain offering and their drink offering for the bulls, rams, and lambs will be as prescribed for their number. ³⁴There will be one male goat for a purification offering in addition to the regular entirely burned offering with its grain offering and its drink offering.

FESTIVALS

Each major festival in the OT represents a week of harvest: one in the spring, one in the summer, and one in the autumn. Spring brings early grain, especially barley, and is also time to move the flocks on from one pasture to another. Summer sees the larger grain-harvest of wheat. Autumn is the last time of gathering for the cycle, and the grapes and olives and nuts of that season make it the most joyous time of all.

[35] On the eighth day you will have a holiday. You will not do any job-related work. [36] You will present an entirely burned offering, a food gift as a soothing smell to the LORD: one bull, one ram, and seven male lambs one year old, all without blemish. [37] The grain offering and their drink offerings for the bull, ram, and lambs will be as prescribed for their number. [38] There will be one male goat for a purification offering in addition to the regular entirely burned offering with its grain offering and its drink offering.

[39] These you will offer to the LORD at your appointed times in addition to your payments for solemn promises, your spontaneous gifts, your entirely burned offerings, your grain offerings, your drink offerings, and your well-being sacrifices.

[40x] Moses told the Israelites everything that the LORD commanded Moses.

Solemn promises by men

30 Moses spoke to the leaders of the tribes of the Israelites: This is what the LORD has commanded: [2] When a man makes a solemn promise to the LORD or swears a solemn pledge of binding obligation for himself, he cannot break his word. He must do everything he said.

Solemn promises by women

[3] When a woman makes a solemn promise to the LORD or a binding obligation while she is young and in her father's household, [4] and her father hears her solemn promise or her binding obligation for herself and keeps silent[y]—then all her solemn promises and any of her binding obligations for herself will stand. [5] But if her father expresses disapproval to her on the day that he hears her, none of her solemn promises nor any of her binding obligations for herself will stand. The LORD will forgive her, because her father expressed disapproval to her.

[6] If she marries while her solemn promise is in effect or makes a statement by which she binds herself, [7] and her husband hears it and on the day he hears it keeps silent—her solemn promises will stand as well as her binding obligations for herself. [8] But if on the day that her husband hears it he expresses disapproval to her, he can break her solemn promise and the statement by which she bound herself. Then the LORD will forgive her.

[9] Every solemn promise of a widow or a divorced woman who makes a binding obligation for herself will stand.

[10] If a woman makes a solemn promise in her husband's household or makes a binding obligation for herself with a solemn pledge, [11] and her husband hears, keeps silent, and doesn't express disapproval to her—then all her solemn promises will stand and all her binding obligations for herself will stand. [12] If her husband breaks them on the day he hears them, then whatever she said with regard to her solemn promises or the binding obligations for herself will not stand. Her husband has broken them. The LORD will forgive her.

[13] Her husband may allow any solemn promise or any binding pledge of self-denial to stand or be broken. [14] But if her husband keeps silent from one day to the next, he has upheld all her solemn promises, or all her binding obligations. He has upheld them because he remained silent on the day he heard them. [15] If he breaks them after he has heard them, he will assume her guilt.

[16] These are the regulations that the LORD commanded Moses concerning a husband and his wife and between a father and his daughter while she is young and in her father's household.

War against the Midianites

31 The LORD spoke to Moses: [2] Take just reparations for the Israelites from the Midianites. Afterward you will join your ancestors.

[3] Moses spoke to the people: "Equip some of your men for battle so that they may go against Midian and execute the LORD's just punishment against Midian. [4] You will send out for battle one thousand from each of the tribes of Israel."

---

[x] 30:1 in Heb   [y] Or *her father is deaf to her.*

⁵From the thousands of Israel, one thousand from each tribe were selected. Twelve thousand were equipped for battle. ⁶Moses sent them to battle, one thousand from each tribe, along with Phinehas, Eleazar the priest's son, who carried the sanctuary equipment and the trumpets for sounding the alarm in his hand. ⁷They battled against Midian as the LORD had commanded Moses, and they killed every male. ⁸They killed the kings of Midian: Evi, Rekem, Zur, Hur, and Reba, the five kings of Midian, along with others slain. They also killed Balaam, Beor's son, with the sword. ⁹The Israelites took captive the Midianite women, their little ones, all their cattle, their herds, and their possessions. ¹⁰They burned all the cities where they lived and their encampments. ¹¹They took all the spoils of war and the valuable property, both human and animal, ¹²and they brought the captives, the valuable property, and the spoils of war to Moses, Eleazar the priest, and the Israelite community, at the camp on the plains of Moab by the Jordan across from Jericho.

Purification from war

¹³Moses, Eleazar the priest, and the chiefs of the community went to meet them outside the camp. ¹⁴Moses became angry with the commanders of the army, the officers of thousands and the officers of hundreds, who came back from the battle. ¹⁵Moses said to them, "Have you let all the women live? ¹⁶These very women, on Balaam's advice, made the Israelites break faith with the LORD in the affair at Peor, so there was a plague among the LORD's community. ¹⁷Now kill every male child and every female who has known a man intimately by sleeping with him. ¹⁸But all the young girls who have not known a man intimately by sleeping with him, spare for yourselves. ¹⁹You will remain outside the camp for seven days. Everyone among you or your captives who has killed a person or touched a corpse must purify themselves on the third and seventh days. ²⁰You must also purify every garment, and everything made of leather, goats' hair, or wood."

Instructions about the spoils of war

²¹Eleazar the priest said to the men of battle who had gone out to war, "This is the regulation in the Instruction that the LORD commanded Moses: ²²Gold, silver, copper, iron, tin, and lead—²³anything that can withstand fire—you will put through the fire and it will be clean. It will also be purified with the water of purification. Anything that isn't able to withstand fire, you will immerse in water. ²⁴You must wash your clothes on the seventh day and you will be clean. Afterward you may enter the camp."

²⁵The LORD said to Moses: ²⁶You, Eleazar the priest, and the leaders of the community's households must take an inventory of the valuable property and the captives, both human and animals, ²⁷and divide the valuable property between the warriors who went into battle and the entire community. ²⁸You will offer as tribute to the LORD from each warrior who went into battle one living being in five hundred, whether human, oxen, donkeys, or flocks. ²⁹Take it from the warriors' half and give it to Eleazar the priest as a gift offering to the LORD. ³⁰But from the Israelites' half you will take one out of every fifty, whether from human, oxen, donkeys, or flock—all the animals. You will give them to the Levites who carry out the duties of the LORD's dwelling.

³¹Moses and Eleazar the priest did as the LORD commanded Moses. ³²The valuable property remaining from the spoils of war that the people of the army had taken was 675,000 sheep, ³³72,000 oxen, ³⁴61,000 donkeys, ³⁵and 32,000 women who hadn't known a man intimately by sleeping with him. ³⁶The half-share of those who had gone out to battle numbered 337,500 sheep, ³⁷of which the LORD's tribute was 675. ³⁸The oxen were 36,000, of which LORD's tribute was 72. ³⁹The donkeys were 30,500, of which the LORD's tribute was 61. ⁴⁰Humans were 16,000, of which the LORD's tribute was 32 persons. ⁴¹Moses gave the tribute, a gift offering for the LORD, to Eleazar the priest as the LORD had commanded Moses.

⁴²As for the half-share of the Israelites that Moses divided from those who had

gone out to battle: [43]the community's half-share was 337,500 sheep, [44]36,000 oxen, [45]30,500 donkeys, [46]and 16,000 humans. [47]Moses took from the Israelites' half one out of every fifty, from humans and animals. He gave them to the Levites who carry out the duties of the LORD's dwelling, just as the LORD had commanded Moses.

[48]The commanders over the thousands of the army, officers over thousands and officers over hundreds, approached Moses [49]and said to Moses, "Your servants have counted the warriors in our charge and not one of us is missing. [50]We have brought the LORD's offering that each found, gold articles—anklets, bracelets, signet rings, earrings, and necklaces—to seek reconciliation for ourselves before the LORD." [51]Moses and Eleazar the priest took all the gold articles from them. [52]All the gold for the gift offering that was presented to the LORD from the officers of thousands and the officers of hundreds was sixteen thousand seven hundred fifty shekels. [53]Each of the men of battle took spoils of war for himself. [54]Yet Moses and Eleazar the priest also received the gold from the officers of thousands and of hundreds, and they brought it to the meeting tent as a memorial for the Israelites before the LORD.

Reuben and Gad request land

32 The livestock owned by the Reubenites and the Gadites were unusually vast and numerous. They saw that the land of Jazer and the land of Gilead were exactly the place for livestock. [2]So the Gadites and the Reubenites came and said to Moses, Eleazar the priest, and the chiefs of the community: [3]"Ataroth, Dibon, Jazer, Nimrah, Heshbon, Elealeh, Sebam, Nebo, and Beon is [4]the land that the LORD struck down before the Israelite community. It is a land for livestock, and your servants have livestock." [5]They said, "If you approve our request, give this land to your servants as property. Don't make us cross the Jordan."

[6]Moses said to the Gadites and the Reubenites, "Should your brothers go to war, while you stay here? [7]Why would you destroy the Israelites' resolve to cross into the land that the LORD gave them? [8]Your ancestors did this, when I sent them from Kadesh-barnea to inspect the land. [9]They went up to the Cluster ravine, saw the land, and destroyed the Israelites' resolve to enter the land that the LORD had given them. [10]The LORD became angry on that day and promised, [11]'None of the persons that went up from Egypt, those 20 years old and above, will see the fertile ground that I promised to Abraham, Isaac, and Jacob, because they didn't remain true to me, [12]except Caleb, Jephunneh the Kenizzite's son, and Joshua, Nun's son, because they remained true to the LORD.' [13]The LORD became angry with the Israelites and made them wander in the desert for forty years until the entire generation had died, which had done evil in the LORD's eyes. [14]Now you've taken the place of your ancestors, a group of sinful men, to intensify the LORD's anger against Israel. [15]If you turn away from him, he will turn away again to abandon Israel in the desert. Then you will destroy this entire people."

Conditions for possession of the land

[16]So they approached him and said, "We will build walled enclosures here for our livestock and towns for our children. [17]Then we will eagerly fight in front of the Israelites until we have brought them into their place. Our children will live in the fortified cities because of the land's inhabitants. [18]And we won't return to our homes until each one of the Israelites takes possession of his property. [19]We won't inherit land with them there across the Jordan, because we've received our property on the east side of the Jordan."

[20]Moses said to them, "Do this and fight before the LORD in war. [21]All of you who are equipped for war, cross the Jordan before the LORD until he has driven his enemies out before him [22]and the land is subdued in the LORD's presence. Then you may return innocently before the LORD and Israel, and this land will be your property before the LORD. [23]But if you don't do this, you've sinned against the LORD. Know that your sin will find you. [24]So build

towns for your children and walled enclosures for your flocks, but do what you have promised."

25 The Gadites and the Reubenites said to Moses, "Your servants will do as my master has commanded. 26 Our children, wives, livestock, and all of our animals will remain in the cities of Gilead. 27 But your servants, everyone equipped for war before the LORD, will go over to do battle as my master said."

28 Moses made demands for them to Eleazar the priest, to Joshua, Nun's son, and to the leaders of the households of the Israelite tribes. 29 Moses said to them, "If the Gadites and the Reubenites cross the Jordan with you, each equipped for battle before the LORD, and the land is subdued before you, then you will give them the land of Gilead as a possession. 30 If, however, they don't cross with you, equipped for war, they will take possession of property with you in the land of Canaan."

31 The Gadites and the Reubenites answered, "We'll do just as the LORD has spoken to your servants. 32 We'll cross into the land of Canaan before the LORD, equipped for war. But the property we inherit will be across the Jordan."

Territory of Gad, Reuben, and half the tribe of Manasseh

33 So Moses gave to them—to the Gadites, the Reubenites, and half the tribe of Manasseh, Joseph's son—the kingdom of Sihon the king of the Amorites, and the kingdom of Og the king of Bashan, including the land, its cities, and the territory surrounding the land's cities. 34 The Gadites built Dibon, Ataroth, Aroer, 35 Atroth-shophan, Jazer, Jogbehah, 36 Beth-nimrah, and Beth-haran, fortified cities and walled enclosures for flocks. 37 The Reubenites built Heshbon, Elealeh, Kiriathaim, 38 Nebo, and Baal-meon (whose names were changed), and Sibmah. They named the cities that they built. 39 The descendants of Machir, Manasseh's son, went to Gilead, captured it, and drove

out the Amorites who were there. 40 So Moses gave Gilead to Machir, Manasseh's son, and he lived there. 41 Manasseh's son Jair went and captured their villages and named them Havvoth-jair.ᶻ 42 Nobah went and captured Kenath and its surrounding villages. He renamed it Nobah after himself.

March out of Egypt and through the sea

33 These were the stages by which the Israelites marched when they left the land of Egypt, according to their military units under the leadership of Moses and Aaron. 2 Moses recorded the points of departure for each stage of the march at the LORD's command. These are the stages of their march according to their points of departure.

3 They marched from Rameses on the fifteenth day of the first month.ᵃ On the day after the Passover the Israelites went out defiantlyᵇ in the sight of all the Egyptians, 4 while the Egyptians were burying their oldest males, whom the LORD had killed. The LORD also executed judgments against their gods. 5 The Israelites marched from Rameses and they camped at Succoth. 6 They marched from Succoth and camped at Etham on the edge of the desert. 7 They marched from Etham and turned back to Pi-hahiroth, which faces Baal-zephon, and they camped before Migdol. 8 They marched from Pi-hahiroth and they crossed through the sea toward the desert.

March through the southern desert

Then they traveled three days in the Etham desert and they camped at Marah. 9 They marched from Marah and arrived at Elim. At Elim there were twelve springs of water and seventy palm trees and they camped there. 10 They marched from Elim and camped by the Reed Sea.ᶜ 11 They marched from the Reed Sea and camped in the Sin desert. 12 They marched from the Sin desert and camped at Dophkah.

ᶻ Or the villages of Jair   ᵃ March–April, Nisan   ᵇ Or with a high hand   ᶜ Or Red Sea

¹³They marched from Dophkah and camped at Alush.

¹⁴They marched from Alush and camped at Rephidim, where there was no water for the people to drink.

¹⁵They marched from Rephidim and camped in the Sinai desert.

¹⁶They marched from the Sinai desert and camped at Kibroth-hattaavah.

¹⁷They marched from Kibroth-hattaavah and camped at Hazeroth.

¹⁸They marched from Hazeroth and camped at Rithmah.

¹⁹They marched from Rithmah and camped at Rimmon-perez.

²⁰They marched from Rimmon-perez and camped at Libnah.

²¹They marched from Libnah and camped at Rissah.

²²They marched from Rissah and camped at Kehelathah.

²³They marched from Kehelathah and camped at Mount Shepher.

²⁴They marched from Mount Shepher and camped at Haradah.

²⁵They marched from Haradah and camped at Makheloth.

²⁶They marched from Makheloth and camped at Tahath.

²⁷They marched from Tahath and camped at Terah.

²⁸They marched from Terah and camped at Mithkah.

²⁹They marched from Mithkah and camped at Hashmonah.

³⁰They marched from Hashmonah and camped at Moseroth.

³¹They marched from Moseroth and camped at Bene-jaakan.

³²They marched from Bene-jaakan and camped at Hor-haggidgad.

³³They marched from Hor-haggidgad and camped at Jotbathah.

³⁴They marched from Jotbathah and camped at Abronah.

³⁵They marched from Abronah and camped at Ezion-geber.

³⁶They marched from Ezion-geber and camped in the Zin desert (that is, Kadesh).

March through the Transjordan region

³⁷They marched from Kadesh and camped at Mount Hor, on the edge of the land of Edom. ³⁸Aaron the priest ascended Mount Hor at the LORD's command, and he died there in the fortieth year on the first day of the fifth month^d after the Israelites left the land of Egypt. ³⁹Aaron was 123 years old when he died on Mount Hor. ⁴⁰The Canaanite king of Arad, who ruled in the arid southern plain in the land of Canaan, heard of the Israelites' coming.

⁴¹They marched from Mount Hor and camped at Zalmonah.

⁴²They marched from Zalmonah and camped at Punon.

⁴³They marched from Punon and camped at Oboth.

⁴⁴They marched from Oboth and camped at Iye-abarim in the territory of Moab.

⁴⁵They marched from Iyim and camped at Dibon-gad.

⁴⁶They marched from Dibon-gad and camped at Almon-diblathaim.

⁴⁷They marched from Almon-diblathaim and camped in the Abarim mountains in front of Nebo.

⁴⁸They marched from the Abarim mountains and camped in the plains of Moab by the Jordan across from Jericho. ⁴⁹They camped by the Jordan from Beth-jeshimoth to Abel-shittim in the plains of Moab.

Divine instruction about the land

⁵⁰The LORD spoke to Moses on the plains of Moab by the Jordan across from Jericho: ⁵¹Speak to the Israelites and say to them: When you cross the Jordan into the land of Canaan, ⁵²you will drive out all the inhabitants of the land before you. You will destroy all their carved figures. You will also destroy all their cast images. You will eliminate all their shrines. ⁵³You will take possession of the land and live in it, because I've given the land to you to possess. ⁵⁴You will divide up the land by lot according to

^dJuly–August, probably Av

your clans. To the large you will make its inheritance large, and to the small you will make its inheritance small. To whomever the lot falls, that place will be his. You will inherit land according to your ancestral tribes. ⁵⁵But if you don't drive out the inhabitants of the land before you, then those you allow to remain will prick your eyes and be thorns in your side. They will harass you in the land in which you are living. ⁵⁶Then what I intended to do to them, I'll do to you.

Boundaries of the land of Canaan

34 The LORD said to Moses: ²Command the Israelites and say to them: When you enter the land of Canaan, this is the land that will fall to you as an inheritance. The land of Canaan according to its boundaries:

³Your southern boundary extends from the Zin desert alongside Edom. Your southern border extends from the edge of the Dead Sea on the east. ⁴Your border will turn south of the ascent of Akrabbim and cross toward Zin. Its limit will be south of Kadesh-barnea. It will go out to Hazar-addar and cross toward Azmon. ⁵The border will then turn from Azmon to the Egypt ravine. Its limit will be at the Mediterranean Sea.

⁶Your western border will be the Mediterranean Sea. This will be your western border.

⁷This will be your northern border: From the Mediterranean Sea you will mark out your boundary to Mount Hor. ⁸From Mount Hor you will mark out your boundary to Lebo-hamath. The limit of the border will be Zedad. ⁹The border will go out to Ziphron. Its limit will be Hazar-enan. This will be your northern border.

¹⁰You will mark out your eastern border from Hazar-enan to Shepham. ¹¹The border will descend from Shepham to Riblah on the east side of Ain. The border will go down and meet the eastern slope of the Galilee Sea. ¹²The border will descend to the Jordan. Its limit will be the Dead Sea.

This will be your land with its borders all around.

¹³Moses commanded the Israelites: This is the land that you will inherit by lot, which the LORD has commanded to give to the nine and a half tribes, ¹⁴because the tribe of Reuben by their households and the tribe of Gad by their households, and half the tribe of Manasseh have taken their inheritance. ¹⁵The two and a half tribes have taken their inheritance across the Jordan at Jericho toward the east.

Appointment of leaders to assign the inheritance

¹⁶The LORD spoke to Moses: ¹⁷These are the names of the men who will assign the inheritance of the land: Eleazar the priest and Joshua, Nun's son. ¹⁸You will also take one chief from each tribe to apportion the land. ¹⁹These are the names of the men: from the tribe of Judah, Caleb, Jephunneh's son; ²⁰from the tribe of the Simeonites, Shemuel, Ammihud's son; ²¹from the tribe of Benjamin, Elidad, Chislon's son; ²²from the tribe of the Danites, a chief, Bukki, Jogli's son; ²³from Joseph's descendants: of the tribe of the Manassites, a chief, Hanniel, Ephod's son; ²⁴and from the tribe of the Ephraimites, a chief, Kemuel, Shiphtan's son; ²⁵from the tribe of the Zebulunites, a chief, Elizaphan, Parnach's son; ²⁶from the tribe of the Issacharites, a chief, Paltiel, Azzan's son; ²⁷from the tribe of the Asherites, a chief, Ahihud, Shelomi's son; ²⁸from the tribe of the Naphtalites, a chief, Pedahel, Ammihud's son.

²⁹These are the ones whom the LORD commanded to assign the inheritance of the Israelites in the land of Canaan.

Cities and pastures of the Levites

35 The LORD spoke to Moses in the Moab plains by the Jordan across from Jericho: ²Command the Israelites that they give cities from their inherited property to the Levites in which to live. You will also give the Levites pastures around their cities. ³The cities will be theirs in which to live. Their pastures will be for their cattle, their possessions, and all their animals.

⁴The pastures of the cities that you must give to the Levites will extend from the wall of the city outward for one thousand five hundred feet in all directions. ⁵You will measure outside the city on the east side three thousand feet, on the south side three thousand feet, on the west side three thousand feet, and on the north side three thousand feet, with the city in the middle. These will be their cities' pastures.

⁶Six of the cities that you give to the Levites will be refuge cities. You will allow the person who kills someone to flee there. In addition to these you will give them forty-two cities. ⁷All the cities that you give to the Levites will total forty-eight, along with their pastures. ⁸As for the cities that you give from the property of the Israelites, you will take more from the larger tribes and less from the smaller. Each in proportion to its inheritance will give cities to the Levites.

Refuge cities

⁹The LORD spoke to Moses: ¹⁰Speak to the Israelites and say to them: When you cross the Jordan into the land of Canaan, ¹¹identify for yourselves cities to be refuge cities, where a person who kills someone by accident may flee. ¹²The cities will be for you a place of refuge from the close relative of the dead. The person who killed someone may not be put to death until he stands before the community for judgment. ¹³You will establish six refuge cities for yourselves. ¹⁴You will establish three cities across the Jordan and three cities in the land of Canaan. They will be the refuge cities. ¹⁵These six cities will be refuge for Israelites, immigrants, and temporary residents, as a place to flee for anyone who kills a person by accident.

¹⁶But if someone strikes a person with an iron object and he dies, he is a murderer. The murderer must definitely be put to death. ¹⁷If someone strikes another with a stone in hand that could cause death and he dies, he is a murderer. The murderer must definitely be put to death. ¹⁸Or if someone strikes with a wood object in hand that could cause death, he is a murderer. The murderer must definitely be put to death. ¹⁹The close relative responsible for the blood^e of the dead is the one who will put the murderer to death. When he meets him, he will execute him. ²⁰If in hatred someone hits another or throws something at him with premeditation, he will be put to death. ²¹Or if in hostility someone strikes another with his hand and he dies, the one who struck is a murderer and he will be put to death. The close relative will put the murderer to death when he meets him.

²²But if suddenly and without hostility someone hits another or throws any object at him without premeditation, ²³or accidentally drops any stone on him that could cause death and he dies—even though they weren't enemies and no evil was intended—²⁴then the community must come to a verdict between the killer and the close relative in accordance with these case laws. ²⁵The community will protect

---

^eOr (here and throughout Num 36) *the close relative of the blood*

LEVITICAL CITIES/TOWNS

Moses denied the Levites an allotment of land among the rest of the tribes (Num 18:20), yet decreed that they were to be given 48 cities, with attached grazing lands, when Israel took possession of Canaan (Num 35:1-8). Joshua 21:1-42 reports on the fulfillment of Moses' decree and designates each of the cities within a scheme that places the levitical clans among particular tribal groups. The Chronicler uses a corresponding and derivative list to conclude a section on the organization of the Levites (1 Chron 6:54-81).

the killer from the hand of the close relative and return him to the refuge city where he fled. He will live there until the death of the high priest who was anointed with holy oil. ²⁶ But if the killer ever goes outside the boundaries of the refuge city where he fled ²⁷ and the close relative finds him outside the boundary of his refuge city and kills him, he will not be responsible for his blood. ²⁸ The killer must live in his refuge city until the high priest's death. After the high priest's death the killer may return to the land he owns.

²⁹ These will be the regulations and case laws for all time in all your settlements.

³⁰ Anyone who kills another will be executed on the evidence of witnesses. But one witness alone cannot testify against a person for a death sentence. ³¹ You may not accept a ransom for the life of a killer, who is guilty of a capital crime, for he must definitely be put to death. ³² You may not accept a ransom for someone who has fled to his refuge city so that he can return and live in the land before the priest's death. ³³ You may not pollute the land in which you live, for the blood pollutes the land. There can be no recovery[^f] for the land from the blood

[^f]: Or *reconciliation*

that is shed in it, except by the blood of the one who shed it. ³⁴ You will not make the land in which you live unclean, the land in the middle of which I reside, for I the LORD reside among the Israelites.

Inheritance of Zelophehad's daughters

36 The leaders of the households of the clans of Gilead, Machir's son and Manasseh's grandson, of Joseph's clans, approached and spoke before Moses and the chiefs, who were the leaders of the Israelite households. ² They said, "The LORD commanded my master to give the land as an inheritance by lot to the Israelites. But my master was also commanded by the LORD to give the inheritance of Zelophehad our brother to his daughters. ³ If they are married to someone from another Israelite tribe, their inheritance will be taken away from our household and given to another tribe into which they marry. Then it will be taken away from the lot of our inheritance. ⁴ At the Israelite Jubilee, their inheritance will be added to the inheritance of the tribe into which they married. Then their inheritance will be taken away from the inheritance of our ancestral tribe."

TRIBE

The social system of ancient Israel was divided into about a dozen large groupings called "tribes." The tribes were made up of "clans," which were in turn made up of families. The institution of the tribe happened before state formation in Israel but continued to function alongside the monarchy. As a way of organizing affiliations and resources, tribes share functions with states but have few if any institutions and minimal hierarchy. Israel's tribes seem to have been used to organize resources and defend territory. They covered larger areas and more diverse means of food production than individual clans or families, so they could distribute resources efficiently and provide a cushion in times of scarcity.

The effective unit of organization above the family level was not the tribe but the clan. Both legal and narrative texts show that clans functioned as independent, active entities. Clans were territorial, economic, and biological associations of families claiming descent from a common ancestor. Marriage was to be outside one's family and inside one's clan.

⁵Then Moses commanded the Israelites according to the LORD's word: "The tribe of Joseph's descendants are correct in what they're saying. ⁶This is the word that the LORD commands to Zelophehad's daughters: They may marry whomever seems best to them, but they may only marry into one of the clans of their ancestral tribe, ⁷so that the inheritance of the Israelites doesn't transfer from one tribe to another. The Israelites will each retain the tribal inheritance of his ancestral tribe. ⁸Every daughter who inherits land from an Israelite tribe must marry into one of the clans of her father's tribe. In this way each Israelite will own the land of his ancestors. ⁹An inheritance of land may not be transferred from one tribe to another, for the Israelite tribes will each retain its own inheritance."

¹⁰Zelophehad's daughters did as the LORD commanded Moses. ¹¹Mahlah, Tirzah, Hoglah, Milcah, and Noah, Zelophehad's daughters, married their cousins. ¹²They married into the clan of Manasseh, Joseph's son. Their inheritance remained in the tribe of their father's clan.

Conclusion

¹³These are the commandments and the case laws that the LORD commanded the Israelites through Moses in the plains of Moab by the Jordan across from Jericho.

DEUTERONOMY

TITLE AND IMPORTANCE

Our name "Deuteronomy" came from the Greek translation of the Old Testament (the Septuagint) by way of the Latin Vulgate. The Septuagint mistranslated the Hebrew phrase "a copy of this law" in Deuteronomy 17:18 as "second [or repeated] law" (*deuteronomion*).

This word apparently became the name of the book because it indicates a prominent aspect of the material: a repetition by Moses of the deeds of God and the content of God's Instruction for the benefit of the generation about to enter the promised land.

Deuteronomy is one of the four Old Testament books most quoted in the New Testament (the others are Isaiah, Psalms, and Genesis). Jesus used its words when resisting the tempter in the wilderness (Matthew 4:4, 7, 10). Like the Jewish teachers of his time, he summarized God's primary demand by quoting Deuteronomy 6:5: "Love the LORD your God with all your heart, all your being, and all your strength" (Matthew 22:37; Mark 12:30; Luke 10:27-28).

Deuteronomy was early regarded as canonical, that is, as containing an authoritative standard for the life of the covenant people.

CONTENTS

Deuteronomy is not a book of law in a narrow sense. It is a book of sermons about the gracious deeds of God for Israel and *how* Israel should respond to God's gracious deeds and *why*.

The theme of the preaching is: In view of God's love for the chosen people, God's gracious deliverance of them from the bondage of Egypt, and the gift of the covenant at Horeb (Sinai), they should respond by loving God, remaining staunchly loyal to God, and wholeheartedly obeying God's will as expressed in the terms of the covenant. If they obey God's laws, God will bless them with rich life in the new land; if they do not, they will be blighted with a horrible curse and perish in the land.

CIRCUMSTANCES OF WRITING

Most scholars believe that Deuteronomy, in whole or in part, was the book found in the temple by Hilkiah the priest in the time of King Josiah.

This book became the basis of a sweeping religious reformation (2 Kings 22–23). The reforms instituted by Josiah—the rooting out of polytheism, the reestablishment of exclusive worship of the ancestral God of Israel, and the centralization of worship in one sanctuary in Jerusalem—are in line with the teaching of Deuteronomy. The threats and promises of the book (chapters 27 and 28) seem to have had a profound effect on Josiah (2 Kings 22:11-13; 23:1-3).

We do not know how long the book had been in existence before its discovery in the temple. Many scholars believe that Deuteronomy is part of a great theological interpretation of Israel's history that reaches from the book of Deuteronomy to the end of 2 Kings. This interpretation happened in stages but was complete around the time of the Babylonian Exile (about 550 BCE). But there is a growing consensus that much of the material in Deuteronomy is older than the time of Hezekiah or Josiah (about 622 BCE). According to one hypothesis, reminiscences of the words of Moses may have been carried in oral or written form, preserved by Levitical preachers of the covenant in northern Israel, and enshrined in Deuteronomy (or part of it) in the time of Hezekiah or Josiah. Thus the book may be both early and late in origin.

THEOLOGICAL EMPHASES

(1) Yahweh is the Lord of the nations and of history. Yahweh has assigned all people their lands and their forms of worship (2:5, 9; 4:19; 32:8).

(2) Out of Yahweh's love, Israel was chosen as God's special possession (7:6-8). God gave Israel a godly land, a law to govern its life, a form of worship, and the promise of a magnificent future (28:1-14).

(3) Israel must give exclusive loyalty to Yahweh (4:1-40). It must eliminate idolatrous peoples and the worship of other gods from its land (7:1-5), centralize the worship at the one sanctuary in Jerusalem (12:2-28), and faithfully perform the ceremonies prescribed by God (14:22–16:17).

(4) God's love should be reciprocated with love, and this love should bring about obedience to God's righteous will in all areas of personal and national life.

Members of the covenant community must be loving and faithful both to God and to one another. Lost property is to be restored to its owner (22:1-4). Money should be lent to a neighbor without interest (23:19-20). The coat that a poor man pawns must be returned before nightfall (24:12-13). A widow's coat must not be taken as security (24:17). Fellow Israelites are not to be forced into slavery or sold (24:7). Withholding wages from servants is strictly forbidden (24:14-15). Honest weights and measures have to be used in all transactions (25:13-15). God's love and mercy requires love and mercy of those who live in fellowship with God.

IMPORTANCE

On the historical side, Deuteronomy is to the teaching of Moses what the Gospel of John is to the teaching of Jesus. Authentic notes of each teacher are undoubtedly preserved in each writing, but both bodies of teaching have been transposed into a different key and made to apply to new situations. Moses stands behind Deuteronomy, even as Jesus stands behind the Fourth Gospel.

Deuteronomy stands at the center of Jewish and Christian theology. The heart of the gospel in both Testaments is that we should love and serve God because God first loved and redeemed us. Deuteronomy presents God's deeds as the basis of God's requirements, a point made strongly by both Jesus and Paul. And that true ethical behavior springs from a loving, dedicated heart is a profound and important insight.

DEUTERONOMY

The first heading: Introducing Deuteronomy

1 These are the words that Moses spoke to all Israel across the Jordan River, in the desert, on the plain across from Suph, between Paran and Tophel, Laban, Hazeroth, and Di-zahab. ([2]It is eleven days from Horeb to Kadesh-barnea along the Mount Seir route.) [3]It was in the fortieth year, on the first day of the eleventh month, that Moses spoke to the Israelites precisely what the LORD had commanded him for them. ([4]This was after the defeat of Sihon, the Amorite king who ruled in Heshbon, and Og, Bashan's king, who ruled in Ashtaroth and[a] Edrei.) [5]Beyond the Jordan, in the land of Moab, Moses began to explain this Instruction. He said the following:

Leaving Mount Horeb

[6]At Horeb, the LORD our God told us: You've been at this mountain long enough. [7]Get going! Enter the hills of the Amorites and the surrounding areas in the desert, the highlands, the lowlands, the arid southern region, and the seacoast—the land of the Canaanites—and the Lebanon range, all the way to the great Euphrates River. [8]Look, I have laid the land before you. Go and possess the land that I[b] promised to give to your ancestors Abraham, Isaac, and Jacob, as well as to their descendants after them. [9]At that same time, I told you: I can't handle all of you by myself. [10]The LORD your God has multiplied your number—you are now as countless as the stars in the sky. [11]May the LORD, your ancestors' God, continue to multiply you—a thousand times more! And may God bless you, just as he promised. [12]But how can I handle all your troubles, burdens, and disputes by myself? [13]Now, for each of your tribes, choose wise, discerning, and well-regarded individuals. I will appoint them as your leaders.

[14]You answered me: "What you have proposed is a good idea."

[15]So I took leading individuals from your tribes, people who were wise and well-regarded, and I set them up as your leaders. There were commanders over thousands, hundreds, fifties, and tens, as well as officials for each of your tribes. [16]At that same time, I commanded your judges: Listen to your fellow tribe members and judge fairly, whether the dispute is between one fellow tribe member or between a tribe member and an immigrant. [17]Don't show favoritism in a decision. Hear both sides out, whether the person is important or not. Don't be afraid of anyone because the ruling belongs to God. Any dispute that is too difficult for you to decide, bring to me and I will take care of it. [18]So at that time, I commanded you concerning everything you were to do.

The spy disaster

[19]We left Horeb and journeyed through that vast and terrifying desert you saw, on the way to the hills of the Amorites, exactly as the LORD our God commanded us. Then we arrived at Kadesh-barnea. [20]I said to you: You have come to the hills of the Amorites, which the LORD our God is giving to us. [21]Look! The LORD your God has laid out the land before you. Go up and take it, just as the LORD, your ancestors' God, has promised you. Don't be afraid! Don't be frightened!

[22]Then all of you approached me, saying, "Let's send spies ahead of us—they can check out the land for us. Then they can return with word about the route we should use and bring a report about the cities that we'll be entering."

[23]This idea seemed good to me, so I selected twelve men, one from each tribe. [24]These set out and went up into the hills, going as far as the Cluster[c] ravine. They walked all around that area. [25]They took some of the land's fruit and then came back down to us. They reported to us: "The

---

[a]LXX, Syr, Vulg; MT lacks *and.* [b]Sam, LXX; MT *the Lord* [c]Heb *Eshcol* means *bunch, a cluster* (of grapes); cf Num 13:23-24; 32:9.

land that the LORD our God is giving to us is wonderful!" ²⁶But you weren't willing to go up. You rejected the LORD your God's instruction. ²⁷You complained in your tents, saying things like, "The LORD hates us! That's why he brought us out of Egypt—to hand us over to the Amorites, to destroy us! ²⁸What are we doing? Our brothers have made our hearts sick by saying, 'People far stronger and much taller than we live there, and the cities are huge, with walls sky-high! Worse still, we saw the descendants of the Anakites there!'"

²⁹But I said to you: Don't be terrified! Don't be afraid of them! ³⁰The LORD your God is going before you. He will fight for you just as he fought for you in Egypt while you watched, ³¹and as you saw him do in the desert. Throughout your entire journey, until you reached this very place, the LORD your God has carried you just as a parent carries a child.

³²But you had no faith in the LORD your God about this matter, ³³even though he went ahead of you, scouting places where you should camp, in fire by night, so you could see the road you were taking, and in cloud during the daytime.

³⁴The LORD heard what you said. He was angry and he swore: ³⁵Not even one of these people—this wicked generation!—will see the wonderful land that I promised to give to your ancestors. ³⁶The only exception is Caleb, Jephunneh's son. He will see it. I will give the land he walked on to him and his children for this reason: he was completely devoted to the LORD.

(³⁷The LORD was even angry with me because of what you did. "You won't enter the land either," God said. ³⁸"But Nun's son Joshua, your assistant, will enter it. Strengthen him because he's the one who will help Israel inherit the land.")

³⁹Now as for your toddlers, those you said would be taken in war, and your young children who don't yet know right and wrong—they will enter the land. I will give it to them. They will possess it! ⁴⁰But you all must now turn around. Head back toward the wilderness along the route of the Reed Sea.ᵈ

⁴¹You replied to me: "We've sinned against the LORD! We will go up! We will fight, just as the LORD our God commanded." Each one of you grabbed your weapons. You thought it would be easyᵉ to go up into the hills. ⁴²But the LORD told me: Tell them: Don't go up! Don't fight because I will not be with you. You will be defeated by your enemies.

⁴³I reported this to you but you wouldn't listen. You disobeyed the LORD's instruction. Hotheadedly, you went up into the hills. ⁴⁴And the Amorites who lived in those hills came out to meet you in battle. They chased you like bees give chase! They gave you a beating from Seir all the way to Hormah. ⁴⁵When you came back, you cried before the LORD, but he wouldn't respond to your tears or give you a hearing.

⁴⁶And so you stayed in Kadesh-barnea for quite some time.

Journeys in Transjordan

2 Next, we turned around and headed back toward the wilderness along the Reed Seaᶠ road, exactly as the LORD instructed me. We traveled all around Mount Seir for a long time.

²Eventually the LORD said: ³You've been traveling around this mountain long enough. Head north. ⁴Command the people as follows: You are about to enter into the territory of your relatives who live in Seir: Esau's descendants. They will be afraid of you, so watch yourselves most carefully. ⁵Don't fight with them because I will not give the tiniest parcel of their land to you. I have given Mount Seir to Esau's family as their property. ⁶Of course you may buy food from them with money so you can eat, and also water with money so you can drink.

⁷No doubt about it: the LORD your God has blessed you in all that you have done. He watched over your journey through that vast desert. Throughout these forty years the LORD your God has been with you. You haven't needed a thing.

ᵈOr *Red Sea* ᵉHeb uncertain ᶠOr *Red Sea*

[8]So we passed through the territory of our relatives who live in Seir, Esau's descendants, leaving the desert road from Elath and from Ezion-geber. Next we turned and went along the Moab wilderness route. [9]The LORD said to me: Don't aggravate Moab. Don't fight them in battle because I won't give any part of their land to you as your own. I have given Ar to Lot's descendants as their property.

([10]Now the Emim[g] had lived there before. They were big and numerous and tall—just like the Anakim. [11]Most people thought the Emim were Rephaim, like the Anakim were. But the Moabites called them "Emim." [12]Additionally, the Horim[h] had lived in Seir previously, but Esau's descendants took possession of their area, eliminating them altogether and settling in their place. That is exactly what Israel did in the land it took possession of, which the LORD gave to them.)

[13]"So then, get going. Cross the Zered ravine."

So we crossed the Zered ravine.

[14]It took us a total of thirty-eight years to go from Kadesh-barnea until we crossed the Zered ravine. It was at that point that the last of the previous generation, every one of fighting age in the camp, had died, just as the LORD had sworn about them. [15]In fact, the LORD's power was against them, to rid the camp of them, until they were all gone.

[16]Now as soon as all those of fighting age had died, [17]the LORD said to me: [18]Today you are crossing through the territory of Moab and Ar [19]and you will come close to the Ammonites. Don't aggravate them. Don't fight with them because I won't give any part of the Ammonites' land to you as your own. I've given it to Lot's descendants as their property.

[20]Now people thought that land was Rephaim territory as well. The Rephaim had lived there previously. But the Ammonites called them "Zamzummim."[i] [21]They were large, numerous, and tall, just like the Anakim. But the LORD completely destroyed the Zamzummim before the Ammonites, and they took possession of that area, settling in their place. [22]That is exactly what God did for Esau's descendants, who live in Seir, when he completely destroyed the Horites in their presence, and they took possession of the Horites' area, settling in their place to this very day. [23]The Avvim,[j] who had lived in settlements around Gaza, were completely destroyed by the Caphtorim, who had come from Caphtor. They replaced the Avvim there.

Victories in Transjordan

[24]"So get going. Cross the Arnon ravine. I have handed Sihon the Amorite king of Heshbon and his land over to you. It's time to possess the area! It's time to fight him in battle! [25]Starting right now, I am making everyone everywhere afraid of you and scared of you. Once they hear news of you, they will be shaking and worrying because of you."

[g]Or *Frighteners*   [h]Or *Cave-dwellers* or *Hurrians*   [i]Or *Mumblers*   [j]Or *Ruiners*

REPHAIM

Rephaim is an ethnic term designating a people who once occupied portions of the Levant, especially the Transjordan. The translation of *Rephaim* as "giants" is probably derived from two differing traditions. One was their association with the Anakim, a people described as exceedingly tall (Deut 1:28; 2:11; 9:2). The second was the identification of Og, king of Bashan, as one of the Rephaim (Josh 12:4; 13:12), whose bed was reported to have been 13.5 ft. by 6 ft. (Deut 3:11) and whose land was called "Rephaim Country" (Deut 3:13).

[26] I then sent messengers from the Kedemoth desert to Sihon, Heshbon's king, with words of peace: [27] "Please let us[k] pass through your land. We promise to stay on the road. We won't step off it, right or left. [28] Please sell us food for money so we can eat; sell us water for money so we can drink. Let us pass through on foot—[29] just as Esau's descendants who live in Seir and the Moabites who live in Ar did for me—until we cross the Jordan River into the land that the LORD our God is giving to us."

[30] But Sihon, Heshbon's king, wasn't willing to let us pass through his land because the LORD your God had made his spirit hard and his heart inflexible so that God could hand him over to you, which is exactly how it happened. [31] The LORD said to me: Look! Right now I'm laying Sihon and his land before you. It's time to take possession of his land!

[32] Sihon and all his forces came out to meet us in battle at Jahaz. [33] But the LORD our God gave him to us. We struck him down, along with his sons, and all his forces. [34] At that time, we captured all of Sihon's cities, and we placed every town—men, women, and children—under the ban.[l] We left no survivors. [35] The only things we kept for ourselves were the animals and the plunder from the towns we had taken. [36] From Aroer, which is on the edge of the Arnon Ravine, to the town that is in the valley there,[m] even as far as Gilead, there wasn't a city that could resist us. The LORD our God laid everything out before us. [37] But you didn't go near the Ammonite lands or hillside cities alongside the Jabbok River, in compliance with all[n] that the LORD our God had commanded.

3 Next we turned and went up along the road to Bashan. Og, Bashan's king, came out with all his forces to meet us in battle at Edrei. [2] The LORD said to me: Don't be afraid of him! I have handed him, all his forces, and his land over to you. Do the same thing to him that you did to Sihon, the Amorite king who ruled in Heshbon.

[3] And so the LORD our God also handed Og, Bashan's king, along with his forces, over to us. We struck them down until no survivor was left. [4] We also captured all of Og's towns at that time. There wasn't a single city that we didn't take from them—a total of sixty towns, the entire region of Argob, the whole kingdom of Og in Bashan. [5] Each of these towns was fortified with high walls, double gates, and crossbars. Outside the towns there were also a great number of villages.[o] [6] We placed them under the ban, just as we did with Sihon, Heshn's king. Every town—men, women, and children—was under the ban.[p] [7] The only

[k] Heb here and through 2:29a is singular me, I. [l] A technique of holy war that often involves total destruction, in which everything that is destroyed is dedicated to the deity who helps in the battle [m] Heb uncertain [n] LXX, Tg Jonathan; MT and all [o] Heb uncertain [p] See note at 2:34.

BASHAN

Bashan (Batanae in the Roman world, today roughly corresponding with the Golan Heights) is a region that rests generally north of the Yarmuk River, south of Mount Hermon, and east of the Galilee Sea until reaching the desert and the basalt lava beds of the northwest Arabian Desert. An important agricultural center, Bashan runs about 20 mi. (30 km) east to west, and about 40 mi. (65 km) north to south. After rising about 2,600 ft. out of the Galilee basin, Bashan is a flat region of rich, fertile soil, whose 20–24 in. of annual rainfall supports forests and grasslands, making it famous in the ancient world for its livestock and trees.

things we kept for ourselves were the animals and the plunder from the towns.

[8] So at that time, we took the land that had belonged to the two Amorite kings beyond the Jordan, all the way from the Arnon Ravine to Mount Hermon ([9] Sidonians call Hermon "Sirion," but the Amorites call it "Senir"), [10] including all the towns on the plateau, in the regions of Gilead and Bashan, and all the way to Salecah and Edrei—all the towns that belonged to Og's kingdom in Bashan.

([11] By the way, Bashan's King Og was the last of the Rephaim. His bed was made of iron. Isn't it still in the Ammonite town of Rabbah? By standard measurements, it was thirteen and a half feet long and six feet wide.)

[12] So this is the land we possessed at that time. I gave some of it, from Aroer, which is beside the Arnon River, up through half of the Gilead highlands, along with its cities, to the Reubenites and the Gadites. [13] The rest of the Gilead region and all of Bashan, Og's kingdom, I gave to half the tribe of Manasseh.

(Now the whole Argob area, including all of Bashan, was often called Rephaim Country. [14] Jair, from the tribe of Manasseh, took possession of the entire Argob region, as far as the border with the Geshurites and the Maacathites. He named the Bashan area after himself, Jair's Settlement. That's what it's still called today.)

[15] I also gave Gilead to Machir. [16] To the Reubenites and the Gadites, I gave land from the Gilead, as far as the Arnon River—the middle of the river being the boundary line—to the Jabbok River, which is the boundary line with the Ammonites. [17] Also the desert plain, with the Jordan River as the boundary, from the Galilee Sea[q] down to the desert sea (the Dead Sea[r]) below the slopes of Mount Pisgah on the east.

[18] Then I commanded you: Although the LORD your God has given you this land to possess, you must now cross over before the rest of your Israelite relatives as a fighting force ready for battle! [19] However, your wives, children, and herds—I know

you have lots of herds!—may remain in the towns that I have given to you. [20] Once the LORD settles your relatives, as you have been settled, and they also possess the land that the LORD your God is giving them across the Jordan River, each of you can return to the property that I have given to you.

[21] It was at that same time that I commanded Joshua: You saw everything that the LORD your God did to these two kings. That is exactly what the LORD will do to all the kingdoms where you're going! [22] Don't be afraid of them because the LORD your God is the one who will be fighting for you.

Moses' prayer

[23] It was also at that same time that I begged the LORD: [24] Please, LORD God! You have only begun to show your servant your greatness and your mighty hand. What god in heaven or on earth can act as you do or can perform your deeds and powerful acts? [25] Please let me cross over the Jordan River so I can see the wonderful land that lies beyond it: those beautiful highlands, even the Lebanon region.

[26] But the LORD was angry with me because of you! He wouldn't listen to me. He said to me: That's enough from you! Don't ever ask me about this again! [27] Go up to the top of Mount Pisgah. Look west, north, south, and east. Have a good look, but you will not cross the Jordan River. [28] Instead, command Joshua, strengthen him, and encourage him because he's the one who will cross the river before this people. He's the one who will make sure they inherit the land you will see.

[29] After that, we stayed in the valley across from Beth-peor.

The events at Mount Horeb

4 Now, Israel, in light of all that, listen to the regulations and the case laws that I am teaching you to follow, so that you may live, enter, and possess the land that the LORD, your ancestors' God, is giving to you. [2] Don't add anything to the word that I am commanding you, and don't take anything

---

[q] Heb *Chinnereth*   [r] Or *the Salt Sea*

away from it. Instead, keep the commands of the LORD your God that I am commanding all of you.

³You saw with your own eyes what the LORD did concerning the Baal of Peor. The LORD your God destroyed everyone who followed the Baal of Peor, ⁴but all of you who stayed true to the LORD your God are alive today. ⁵So pay attention! I am teaching all of you the regulations and the case laws exactly as the LORD my God commanded me. You must do these in the land you are entering to possess. ⁶Keep them faithfully because that will show your wisdom and insight to the nations who will hear about all these regulations. They will say, "Surely this great nation is a wise and insightful people!" ⁷After all, is there any great nation that has godsˢ as close to it as the LORD our God is close to us whenever we call to him? ⁸Or does any great nation have regulations and case laws as righteous as all this Instruction that I am setting before you today?

⁹But be on guard and watch yourselves closely so that you don't forget the things your eyes saw and so they never leave your mind as long as you live. Teach them to your children and your grandchildren. ¹⁰Remember thatᵗ day when you stood before the LORD your God at Horeb, when the LORD said to me: "Gather the people to me. I will declare my words to them so that they will learn to fear me every day of their lives on the fertile land, and teach their children to do the same." ¹¹Then you all came close and stood at the foot of the mountain. The mountain was blazing with fire up to the sky, with darkness, cloud, and thick smoke! ¹²The LORD spoke to you out of the very fire itself. You heard the sound of words, but you didn't see any form. There was only a voice. ¹³The LORD declared his covenant to you, which he commanded you to do—the Ten Commandmentsᵘ—and wrote them on two stone tablets. ¹⁴At that time, the LORD commanded me to teach you all the regulations and the case laws that you must keep in the land that you are entering to possess.

¹⁵So watch your conduct closely, because you didn't see any form on the day the LORD spoke to you at Horeb out of the very fire itself. ¹⁶Don't ruin everything and make an idol for yourself: a form of any image, any likeness—male or female—¹⁷or any likeness whatsoever, whether of a land animal, a bird that flies in the sky, ¹⁸an insect that crawls on the earth, or a fish that lives in the sea. ¹⁹Don't look to the skies, to the sun or the moon or the stars, all the heavenly bodies, and be led astray, worshipping and serving them. The LORD your God has granted these things to all the nations who live under heaven. ²⁰But the LORD took you and brought you out of that iron furnace, out of Egypt, so that you might be his own treasured people, which is what you are right now.

²¹The LORD was angry with me because of your deeds and swore that I couldn't cross the Jordan River or enter the wonderful land that the LORD your God is giving you as an inheritance. ²²I will die here in this land. I won't cross the Jordan River.

ˢMT; LXX, Syr, Tg *a god so close*   ᵗHeb lacks *remember that.*   ᵘOr *the ten words*

BAAL

In the OT the word occurs both as a noun meaning "lord, master, husband" and as the proper name of a deity. Used in the second sense, Baal is the pagan god most frequently mentioned in the Bible and the archetypical rival of Yahweh; the classic indictment of the Israelites says that, instead of serving Yahweh, they "worshipped," "followed," or "have gone after" Baal or the Baals (e.g., Deut 4:3; Judg 8:33; 1 Kgs 18:18; Jer 2:23; 9:14).

But you will, and you will take possession of that wonderful land. ²³So all of you, watch yourselves! Don't forget the covenant that the LORD your God made with you by making an idol or an image of any kind or anything the LORD your God forbids, ²⁴because the LORD your God is an all-consuming fire. He is a passionate God.

Warnings and teachings about future disobedience

²⁵Once you have had children and grandchildren and have grown old on the land, if you ruin things by making an idol, in any form whatsoever, and do what is evil in the eyes of the LORD your God and anger him, ²⁶I call heaven and earth as my witnesses against you today: You will definitely disappear—and quickly—from the land that you are crossing over the Jordan River to possess. You won't extend your time there but will instead be totally destroyed. ²⁷The LORD will scatter you among the nations. Only a very few of you will survive in the countries where the LORD will drag you. ²⁸There you will worship other^v gods, made of wood and stone by human hands—gods that cannot see, listen, eat, or smell. ²⁹You will seek the LORD your God from there, and you will find him^w if you seek him with all your heart and with all your being. ³⁰In your distress, when all these things happen to you in the future, you will return to the LORD your God and you will obey his voice, ³¹because the LORD your God is a compassionate God. He won't let you go, he won't destroy you, and he won't forget the covenant that he swore to your ancestors.

³²Now look into it: into days long past, before your time—all the way back to the day God first created human beings on earth, from one end of heaven to the other. Has anything this amazing ever happened? Has anything like it ever been heard of before? ³³Has any people ever listened to a god's voice speaking out of fire, as each of you have, and survived? ³⁴Or has any god ever tried to take one nation out of another nation using tests, miracles, wonders, war, a strong hand and outstretched arm, or awesome power like all that the LORD your God did for you in Egypt while you watched? ³⁵You were shown these things so that you would know this: The LORD is the only God. There's no other god except him. ³⁶From heaven he made you hear his voice in order to discipline you. On earth he showed you his great fire. You heard his words from that very fire. ³⁷And because he loved your ancestors and chose their descendants after them, God brought you out of Egypt with his own presence, by his own great power, ³⁸in order to remove larger and stronger nations from before you and bring you into their land, giving it to you as an inheritance. That's where things stand right now. ³⁹Know then today and keep in mind that the LORD is the only God in heaven above or on earth below. There is no other. ⁴⁰Keep the Lord's regulations and his commandments. I'm commanding them to you today for your well-being and for the well-being of your children after you, so that you may extend your time on the fertile land that the LORD your God is giving you forever.

Cities of refuge

⁴¹Then Moses set aside three cities on the eastern side of the Jordan River ⁴²so that anyone who killed someone accidentally and without prior hatred could flee to one of these cities and be safe: ⁴³Bezer in the wilderness on the plateau for the Reubenites, Ramoth in Gilead for the Gadites, and Golan in Bashan for the Manassites.

The second heading: Recounting the Horeb covenant

⁴⁴Now this is the Instruction that Moses set before the Israelites. ⁴⁵These are the laws and the regulations and the case laws that Moses spoke to the Israelites when they came out of Egypt. ⁴⁶This took place across the Jordan River, in the valley opposite Beth-peor, in the land of Sihon the Amorite king who ruled in Heshbon, whom Moses and the Israelites defeated when they came

---

^vLXX; MT lacks *other*.   ^wHeb lacks *him*.

out of Egypt. [47]They took possession of his land and the land of Og, Bashan's king—the two Amorite kings across the Jordan River to the east—[48]from Aroer, which is on the banks of the Arnon River, all the way to Mount Sion,[x] also known as Hermon, [49]and all the desert regions across the Jordan River, on the east, down to the Dead Sea, beneath the slopes of Mount Pisgah.

Ten Commandments

5 Moses called out to all Israel, saying to them: "Israel! Listen to the regulations and the case laws that I'm recounting in your hearing right now. Learn them and carefully do them. [2]The LORD our God made a covenant with us at Mount Horeb. [3]The LORD didn't make this covenant with our ancestors but with us—all of us who are here and alive right now. [4]The LORD spoke with you face-to-face on the mountain from the very fire itself. [5]At that time, I was standing between the LORD and you, declaring to you the LORD's word, because you were terrified of the fire and didn't go up on the mountain."

The LORD said:

[6]I am the LORD your God, who brought you out of Egypt, out of the house of slavery.

[7]You must have no other gods before[y] me. [8]Do not make an idol for yourself—no form whatsoever—of anything in the sky above or on the earth below or in the waters under the earth. [9]Do not bow down to them or worship them because I, the LORD your God, am a passionate God. I punish children for their parents' sins—even to the third and fourth generations of those who hate me. [10]But I am loyal and gracious to the thousandth generation[z] of those who love me and keep my commandments.

[11]Do not use the LORD your God's name as if it were of no significance; the LORD won't forgive anyone who uses his name that way.

[12]Keep the Sabbath day and treat it as holy, exactly as the LORD your God commanded: [13]Six days you may work and do all your tasks, [14]but the seventh day is a Sabbath to the LORD your God. Don't do any work on it—not you, your sons or daughters, your male or female servants, your oxen or donkeys or any of your animals, or the immigrant who is living among you—so that your male and female servants can rest just like you. [15]Remember that you were a slave in Egypt, but the LORD your God

[x]Syr *Sirion;* see 3:9. [y]Or *besides* [z]Or *to thousands*

TEN COMMANDMENTS

Literally "the ten words" (Exod 34:28; Deut 4:13; 10:4), which is the source of the alternative designation "Decalogue." A body of divine instruction in the form of eight prohibitions and two positive commandments preceded by a brief self-presentation formula on the part of the deity: "I am the LORD your God who brought you out of Egypt, out of the house of slavery" (Exod 20:2; Deut 5:6).

The Ten Commandments appear in two versions: Exodus 20:1-17, where they are the Lord's direct address to all the people of Israel at Mount Sinai after they have escaped from Egypt; and Deuteronomy 5:6-21, where the commandments are repeated, though not precisely in the same form as in Exodus 20, this time by Moses on the plains of Moab prior to Israel's entering the land of Canaan.

brought you out of there with a strong hand and an outstretched arm. That's why the LORD your God commands you to keep the Sabbath day.

¹⁶Honor your father and your mother, exactly as the LORD your God requires, so that your life will be long and so that things will go well for you on the fertile land that the LORD your God is giving you.

¹⁷Do not kill.^a

¹⁸Do not commit adultery.

¹⁹Do not steal.

²⁰Do not testify falsely against your neighbor.

²¹Do not desire and try to take your neighbor's wife.

Do not crave your neighbor's house, field, male or female servant, ox, donkey, or anything else that belongs to your neighbor.

²²Those are the words the LORD spoke to your entire assembly with a loud voice while on the mountain, from the midst of the fire, the cloud, and the thick smoke. He added no more. God wrote them on two stone tablets, then gave them to me.

Moses' intercessory role

²³Now once you heard the voice from the darkness while the mountain was blazing with fire, you came to me—more specifically, all the chiefs of your tribes and your elders came—²⁴and you said: "Look here! The LORD our God has shown us his glory and greatness. We've heard his voice come out of the very fire itself. We've seen firsthand that God can speak to a human being and they can survive! ²⁵But why should we die? Surely this massive fire will consume us! If we hear any more of the LORD our God's voice, we will die. ²⁶Is there anyone who has heard the living God's voice speaking out of the very fire itself, like we have, and survived? ²⁷You go and listen to all that the LORD our God says. Then tell us all that the LORD our God speaks to you. We'll listen and we'll do it."

²⁸The LORD heard what you said, when you said this to me. The LORD then told me: I heard what the people said when they spoke with you. Everything they suggest is good. ²⁹If only their minds were like this: always fearing me and keeping all my commandments so that things would go well for them and their children forever! ³⁰Go and tell them: You may go back to your tents. ³¹But you, Moses, must stay here with me. I will tell you all the commandments,^b the regulations, and the case laws that you must teach the Israelites to do in the land that I am giving them to possess.

³²So you must carefully do exactly what the LORD your God commands you. Don't deviate even a bit! ³³You must walk the precise path that the LORD your God indicates for you so that you will live, and so that things will go well for you, and so you will extend your time on the land that you will possess.

The great commandment

6 Now these are the commandments, the regulations, and the case laws that the LORD your God commanded me to teach you to follow in the land you are entering to possess, ²so that you will fear the LORD your God by keeping all his regulations and his commandments that I am commanding you—both you and your sons and daughters—all the days of your life and so that you will lengthen your life. ³Listen to them, Israel! Follow them carefully so that things will go well for you and so that you will continue to multiply exactly as the LORD, your ancestors' God, promised you, in a land full of milk and honey.

⁴Israel, listen! Our God is the LORD! Only the LORD!^c

⁵Love the LORD your God with all your heart, all your being, and all your strength. ⁶These words that I am commanding you today must always be on your minds. ⁷Recite them to your children. Talk about them when you are sitting around your house and when you are out and about, when you

---

^aOr *murder*   ^bHeb is singular, *commandment* (see 6:1).   ^cOr *The LORD is our God, the LORD only;* or *The LORD is our God, the LORD alone;* or *The LORD our God is one LORD;* or *The LORD our God, the LORD is one;* or *The LORD is our God, the LORD is one.*

are lying down and when you are getting up. [8]Tie them on your hand as a sign. They should be on your forehead as a symbol.[d] [9]Write them on your house's doorframes and on your city's gates.

[10]Now once the LORD your God has brought you into the land that he swore to your ancestors, to Abraham, Isaac, and Jacob, to give to you—a land that will be full of large and wonderful towns that you didn't build, [11]houses stocked with all kinds of goods that you didn't stock, cisterns that you didn't make, vineyards and olive trees that you didn't plant—and you eat and get stuffed, [12]watch yourself! Don't forget the LORD, who brought you out of Egypt, out of the house of slavery. [13]Revere the LORD your God, serve him, and take your solemn pledges in his name! [14]Don't follow other gods, those gods of the people around you—[15]because the LORD your God, who is with you and among you, is a passionate God. The LORD your God's anger will burn against you, and he will wipe you off the fertile land. [16]Don't test the LORD your God the way you frustrated him at Massah. [17]You must carefully follow the LORD your God's commands along with the laws and regulations he has given you. [18]Do what is right and good in the LORD's sight so that things will go well for you and so you will enter and take possession of the wonderful land that the LORD swore to your ancestors, [19]and so the LORD will drive out all your enemies from before you, just as he promised.

The next generation

[20]In the future, your children will ask you, "What is the meaning of the laws,[e] the regulations, and the case laws that the LORD our God commanded you?" [21]tell them: We were Pharaoh's slaves in Egypt. But the LORD brought us out of Egypt with a mighty hand. [22]Before our own eyes, the LORD performed great and awesome deeds of power[f] against Egypt, Pharaoh, and his entire dynasty. [23]But the Lord brought us

out from there so that he could bring us in, giving us the land that he swore to our ancestors. [24]Then the LORD commanded us to perform all these regulations, revering the LORD our God, so that things go well for us always and so we continue to live, as we're doing right now. [25]What's more, we will be considered righteous if we are careful to do all this commandment before the LORD our God, just as he commanded us.

Dealing with foreign worship

7Now once the LORD your God brings you into the land you are entering to take possession of, and he drives out numerous nations before you—the Hittites, the Girgashites, the Amorites, the Canaanites, the Perizzites, the Hivites, and the Jebusites: seven nations that are larger and stronger than you—[2]once the LORD your God lays them before you, you must strike them down, placing them under the ban.[g] Don't make any covenants with them, and don't be merciful to them. [3]Don't intermarry with them. Don't give your daughter to one of their sons to marry, and don't take one of their daughters to marry your son, [4]because they will turn your child away from following me so that they end up serving other gods. That will make the LORD's anger burn against you, and he will quickly annihilate you.

[5]Instead, this is what you must do with these nations: rip down their altars, smash their sacred stones, cut down their sacred poles,[h] and burn their idols [6]because you are a people holy to the LORD your God. The LORD your God chose you to be his own treasured people beyond all others on the fertile land. [7]It was not because you were greater than all other people that the LORD loved you and chose you. In fact, you were the smallest of peoples! [8]No, it is because the LORD loved you and because he kept the solemn pledge he swore to your ancestors that the LORD brought you out with a strong hand and saved you from the house of slavery, from the power of

---

[d]Heb uncertain; cf Exod 13:16; Syr *sign* or *mark*; Tg *phylacteries*   [e]Or *What are the laws . . . ?*   [f]Or *signs and wonders*   [g]See note at 2:34.   [h]Heb *asherim*, perhaps objects devoted to the goddess Asherah

Pharaoh, Egypt's king. ⁹Know now then that the LORD your God is the only true God! He is the faithful God, who keeps the covenant and proves loyal to everyone who loves him and keeps his commands—even to the thousandth generation! ¹⁰He is the God who personally repays anyone who hates him, ultimately destroying that kind of person. The LORD does not waste time with anyone who hates him; he repays them personally. ¹¹So make sure you carefully keep the commandment, the regulations, and the case laws that I am commanding you right now.

¹²If you listen to these case laws and follow them carefully, the LORD your God will keep the covenant and display the loyalty that he promised your ancestors. ¹³He will love you, bless you, and multiply you. He will bless the fruit of your wombs and the fruit of your fertile land—all your grain, your wine, your oil, and the offspring of your cattle and flocks—upon the very fertile land that he swore to your ancestors to give to you. ¹⁴You will be more blessed than any other group of people. No one will be sterile or infertile—not among you or your animals. ¹⁵The LORD will remove all sickness from you. As for all those dreadful Egyptian diseases you experienced, the Lord won't put them on you but will inflict them on all who hate you. ¹⁶You will destroy all the peoples that the LORD your God is handing over to you. Show them no pity. And don't serve their gods because that would be a trap for you.

Against power and lack of trust

¹⁷If you happen to think to yourself, These nations are greater than we are; how can we possibly possess their land? ¹⁸don't be afraid of them! Remember, instead, what the LORD your God did to Pharaoh and all Egypt: ¹⁹the great trials that you saw with your own eyes, the signs and wonders, and the strong hand and outstretched arm the LORD your God used to rescue you. That's what the LORD your God will do to any people you fear. ²⁰The LORD your God will send terrorⁱ on them until even the survivors and those hiding from you are destroyed. ²¹Don't dread these nations because the LORD your God, the great and awesome God, is with you and among you. (²²The LORD your God will drive out these nations before you bit by bit. You won't be able to finish them off quickly; otherwise, the wild animals would become too much for you to handle.) ²³The LORD your God will lay these nations before you, throwing them into a huge panic until they are destroyed. ²⁴He will hand their kings over to you, and you will wipe their names out from under the skies. No one will be able to stand before you; you will crush them.

²⁵Burn the images of their gods. Don't desire the silver or the gold that is on them and take it for yourself, or you will be trapped by it. That is detestable to the LORD your God. ²⁶Don't bring any detestable thing into your house, or you will be placed under the ban too, just like it is! You must utterly detest these kinds of things,

---

ⁱHeb uncertain; perhaps *wasp*, *plague*, or *pestilence*

BAN

The "ban" ("devoted thing," "devoted to destruction") is a category or status for things or people consecrated irrevocably into God's ownership and unavailable for secular use. Leviticus 27:21, 28-29 applies this status to fields, animals, and enslaved people as a result of voluntary dedication. Things that were banned became priestly property according to Numbers 18:14 and Ezekiel 44:29. People who were banned were put to death (Lev 27:29).

despising them completely, because they are under the ban.

8 You must carefully perform all of the commandment that I am commanding you right now so you can live and multiply and enter and take possession of the land that the LORD swore to your ancestors. ²Remember the long road on which the LORD your God led you during these forty years in the desert so he could humble you, testing you to find out what was in your heart: whether you would keep his commandments or not. ³He humbled you by making you hungry and then feeding you the manna that neither you nor your ancestors had ever experienced, so he could teach you that people don't live on bread alone. No, they live based on whatever the LORD says.ʲ ⁴During these forty years, your clothes didn't wear out and your feet didn't swell up. ⁵Know then in your heart that the LORD your God has been disciplining you just as a father disciplines his children. ⁶Keep the commandments of the LORD your God by walking in his ways and by fearing him, ⁷because the LORD your God is bringing you to a wonderful land, a land with streams of water, springs, and wells that gush up in the valleys and on the hills; ⁸a land of wheat and barley, vines, fig trees, and pomegranates; a land of olive oil and honey; ⁹a land where you will eat food without any shortage—you won't lack a thing there—a land where stone is hard as iron and where you will mine copper from the hills. ¹⁰You will eat, you will be satisfied, and you will bless the LORD your God in the wonderful land that he's given you.

Against wealth and overconfidence

¹¹But watch yourself! Don't forget the LORD your God by not keeping his commands or his case laws or his regulations that I am commanding you right now. ¹²When you eat, get full, build nice houses, and settle down, ¹³and when your herds and your flocks are growing large, your silver and gold are multiplying, and every-

ʲOr whatever comes out of the LORD's mouth

MANNA

Manna is the bread that God made "rain down from the sky" (Exod 16:4) for Israel during their journey through the desert on the way to the land of promise. The name manna (Exod 16:31) sounds like the Hebrew for Israel's question: "What is it?" (Exod 16:15). According to Exodus, the manna could be baked or boiled to form bread that "tasted like honey wafers" (Exod 16:23, 31). Compare the alternative view in Numbers 11:8 that the manna tasted like "cakes baked in olive oil." Moses, acting as interpreter, explained to the people that this white, fine substance that looked like coriander seed (Exod 16:14, 31) and that came every morning with the dew was the gracious gift of food that God had provided (v. 15).

Several stories in the NT build on the tradition of God's provision of manna to Israel in the wilderness. Scholars have shown connections between Exodus 16 and the Gospel accounts of Jesus providing food to the crowds of followers (Matt 14:15-21; Mark 6:35-44; Luke 9:10-17). Particularly, in John 6:22-59 we find an in-depth exposition of the manna story when Jesus makes a connection between himself and the bread from heaven. Not only does Jesus provide the life-giving bread that comes from God, Jesus identifies himself as "the bread of life" (v. 35).

thing you have is thriving, ¹⁴don't become arrogant, forgetting the LORD your God:

the one who rescued you from Egypt, from the house of slavery;

¹⁵the one who led you through this vast and terrifying desert of poisonous snakes and scorpions, of cracked ground with no water;

the one who made water flow for you out of a hard rock;

¹⁶the one who fed you manna in the wilderness, which your ancestors had never experienced, in order to humble and test you, but in order to do good to you in the end.

¹⁷Don't think to yourself, My own strength and abilities have produced all this prosperity for me. ¹⁸Remember the LORD your God! He's the one who gives you the strength to be prosperous in order to establish the covenant he made with your ancestors—and that's how things stand right now. ¹⁹But if you do, in fact, forget the LORD your God and follow other gods, serving and bowing down to them, I swear to you right now that you will be completely destroyed. ²⁰Just like the nations that the LORD is destroying before you, that's exactly how you will be destroyed—all because you didn't obey the LORD your God's voice.

Against false piety and immodesty

9 Listen, Israel! Today you will cross the Jordan River to enter and take possession of nations larger and more powerful than you, along with huge cities with fortifications that reach to the sky. ²These people are large and tall—they are the Anakim. You know and have heard what people say: "Who can stand up to the Anakim?" ³Know right now that the LORD your God, who is crossing over before you, is an all-consuming fire! He will wipe them out! He will subdue them before you! Then you will take possession of their land, eliminating them quickly, exactly as the LORD told you. ⁴Once the LORD your God has driven them out before you, don't think to yourself, It's because I'm righteous that the LORD brought me in to possess this land. It is instead because of these nations' wick-

edness that the LORD is removing them before you. ⁵You aren't entering and taking possession of their land because you are righteous or because your heart is especially virtuous; rather, it is because these nations are wicked—that's why the LORD your God is removing them before you, and because he wishes to establish the promise he made to your ancestors: to Abraham, Isaac, and Jacob.

Gold calf

⁶Know then that the LORD your God isn't giving you this excellent land for you to possess on account of your righteousness—because you are a stubborn people! ⁷Remember—don't ever forget!—how you made the LORD your God furious in the wilderness. From the very first day you stepped out of Egypt until you arrived at this place, you have been rebels against the LORD. ⁸Even at Horeb you angered the LORD! He was so enraged by you that he threatened to wipe you out. ⁹When I went up on the mountain to get the stone tablets, the covenant tablets that the LORD made with you, I was up there forty days and forty nights. I ate no bread, drank no water. ¹⁰The LORD gave me the two stone tablets, written by God's finger, and on them were all the words that the LORD had said to you on the mountain, out of the very fire itself, on the day we assembled. ¹¹At the end of those forty days and nights, the LORD gave me the two stone tablets—the covenant tablets. ¹²Then the LORD said to me, "Get going! Get down from here quickly because your people, whom you brought out of Egypt, have ruined everything! They couldn't wait to turn from the path I commanded them! They've made themselves an idol out of cast metal."

¹³The LORD said more to me: "I have seen this people. Look! What a stubborn people they are! ¹⁴Now stand back. I am going to wipe them out. I will erase their name from under heaven, then I will make a nation out of you—one stronger and larger than they were."

¹⁵So I went down the mountain while it was blazing with fire. The two covenant

tablets were in my two hands. [16]It was then that I saw how you sinned against the LORD your God: you made yourselves a calf, an idol made of cast metal! You couldn't wait to turn from the path the LORD commanded you! [17]I grabbed the two tablets and threw them down with my own hands, shattering them while you watched. [18]Then I fell before the LORD as I had done the previous forty days and forty nights. I ate no bread and drank no water, all because of the sin that you had committed by doing such evil in the LORD's sight, infuriating him. [19]I was afraid of the massive anger and rage the LORD had for you—he was going to wipe you out! However, the LORD listened to me again in that moment.

[20]But the LORD was furious with Aaron—he was going to wipe him out! So I also prayed hard for Aaron at that time. [21]And as for that sinful thing you made, that calf, I took it and I burned it with fire. Then I smashed it, grinding it thoroughly until it was as fine as dust. Then I dumped the dust into the stream that ran down the mountain.

[22]Also at Taberah, again at Massah, and then again at Kibroth-hattaavah, you have been the kind of people who make the LORD angry. [23]And then, when the LORD sent you from Kadesh-barnea, telling you: "Go up and take possession of the land that I'm giving you," you disobeyed the LORD your God's command. You didn't trust him. You didn't obey God's voice. [24]You've been rebellious toward the LORD from the day I[k] met you.

Moses' intercessory prayer

[25]But I fell on my knees in the LORD's presence forty days and forty nights, lying flat out, because the LORD planned on wiping you out. [26]But I prayed to the LORD! I said: LORD, my Lord! Don't destroy your people, your own possession, whom you saved by your own power, whom you brought out of Egypt with a strong hand! [27]Remember your servants: Abraham, Isaac, and Jacob! Don't focus on this people's stubbornness, wickedness, and

sin. [28]Otherwise, that land out of which you brought us will say: The LORD wasn't strong enough to bring them into the land he'd promised them. Because he didn't care for them in the least, he brought them out to die in the desert. [29]But these are your people! Your own possession! The people you brought out by your great power and by your outstretched arm!

New tablets

10 At that time the LORD told me: Carve two stone tablets, just like the first ones, and hike up the mountain to me. Construct a wooden chest as well. [2]I will write on the tablets the words that were on the first tablets—the ones you smashed—then you will place them in the chest.

[3]So I built a chest out of acacia wood and carved two stone tablets just like the first ones. Then I hiked up the mountain holding the two tablets in my hands. [4]God wrote on the new tablets what had been written on the first set: the Ten Commandments that the LORD spoke to you on the mountain, from the very fire itself, on the day we assembled there. Then the LORD gave them to me.

[5]So I came back down the mountain. I put the tablets in the chest that I'd made, and that's where they are now, exactly as the LORD commanded me.

([6]Now, the Israelites had set out from Beeroth-bene-jaakan[l] to Moserah. It was there that Aaron died and was buried. His son Eleazar succeeded him in the priestly role. [7]From there the Israelites traveled to Gudgodah, then from Gudgodah to Jotbathah, which is a land with flowing streams. [8]At that time, the LORD selected the tribe of Levi to carry the chest containing the LORD's covenant, to minister before the LORD, to serve him, and to offer blessings in his name. That's the way things are right now. [9]That's why the Levites don't have a stake or inheritance with the rest of their relatives. The LORD is the Levites' inheritance, just as the LORD your God promised them.)

[k]LXX, Sam *he (God) met you* [l]Or *from the wells of the Jaakanites*

¹⁰Just as the first time, I remained on the mountain forty days and nights. And the LORD listened to me again in this instance. The LORD wasn't willing to destroy you. ¹¹Then the LORD told me: Get going. Lead the people so they can enter and take possession of the land that I promised I'd give to their ancestors.

What the LORD requires

¹²Now in light of all that, Israel, what does the LORD your God ask of you? Only this: to revere the LORD your God by walking in all his ways, by loving him, by serving the LORD your God with all your heart and being, ¹³and by keeping the LORD's commandments and his regulations that I'm commanding you right now. It's for your own good! ¹⁴Clearly, the LORD owns the sky, the highest heavens, the earth, and everything in it. ¹⁵But the LORD adored your ancestors, loving them and choosing the descendants that followed them—you!—from all other people. That's how things still stand now. ¹⁶So circumcise your hearts[m] and stop being so stubborn, ¹⁷because the LORD your God is the God of all gods and Lord of all lords, the great, mighty, and awesome God who doesn't play favorites and doesn't take bribes. ¹⁸He enacts justice for orphans and widows, and he loves immigrants, giving them food and clothing. ¹⁹That means you must also love immigrants because you were immigrants in Egypt. ²⁰Revere the LORD your God, serve him, cling to him, swear by his name alone! ²¹He is your praise, and he is your God—the one who performed these great and awesome acts that you witnessed with your very own eyes. ²²Your ancestors went down to Egypt with a total of seventy people, but now look! The LORD your God has made you as numerous as the stars in the nighttime sky!

11 So love the LORD your God and follow his instruction, his regulations, his case laws, and his commandments always. ²And know right now what your children haven't known or yet witnessed:[n]

The LORD your God's discipline, his power, his mighty hand and outstretched arm;

³the signs and the acts that he performed in the heart of Egyptian territory, against Egypt's King Pharaoh and all his land;

⁴what God did to the Egyptian army, to its horses and chariots—how he made the water of the Reed Sea[o] flow over their heads when they chased after you, but the LORD destroyed them, and that's how things stand right now;

⁵what the Lord did for you in the desert, until you arrived at this place;

⁶and what he did to Dathan and Abiram, the descendants of Eliab the Reubenite, when the ground opened up its mouth and swallowed them, their families, their tents, and every living thing they possessed in the presence of all Israel.

⁷Your own eyes witnessed each of these powerful acts the LORD performed. ⁸So keep every part of the commandment that I am giving you today so that you stay strong to enter and take possession of the land that you are crossing over to possess, ⁹and so that you might prolong your life on the fertile land that the LORD swore to your ancestors to give to them and their descendants—a land full of milk and honey.

¹⁰The land you are about to enter and possess is definitely not like the land of Egypt, where you came from, where you sowed your seed and irrigated it by hand[p] like a vegetable garden. ¹¹No, the land you are entering to possess is a land of hills and valleys, where your drinking water will be rain from heaven. ¹²It's a land that the LORD cares for: the LORD's eyes are on it constantly from the first of the year until the very end of the year.

¹³Now, if you completely obey God's[q] commandments that I am giving you right now, by loving the LORD your God and by serving him with all your heart and all your being, ¹⁴then he[r] will provide rain for your

---

[m]Or the foreskin of your hearts; cf 30:6 [n]Heb uncertain [o]Or Red Sea [p]Or foot [q]LXX his; MT my [r]Sam, LXX, DSS (8QMez); Heb, Vulg, Syr, Tg, and several DSS I, in which case the text shifts to direct divine discourse.

land at the right time—early rain and late rain—so you can stock up your grain, wine, and oil. [15] He[s] will also make your fields lush for your livestock, and you will eat and be satisfied. [16] But watch yourselves! Otherwise, your heart might be led astray so you stray away, serving other gods and worshipping them. [17] Then the LORD's anger would burn against you. He will close the sky up tight. There won't be any rain, and the ground won't yield any of its crops. You will quickly disappear off the wonderful land the LORD is giving to you.

[18] Place these words I'm speaking on your heart and in your very being. Tie them on your hand as a sign. They should be on your forehead as a symbol.[t] [19] Teach them to your children, by talking about them when you are sitting around your house and when you are out and about, when you are lying down and when you are getting up. [20] Write them on your house's doorframes and on your city's gates. [21] Do all that so your days and your children's days on the fertile land the LORD swore to give to your ancestors are many—indeed, as many as the number of days that the sky's been over the earth!

[22] It's true: if you carefully keep all this commandment that I'm giving you, by doing it, by loving the LORD your God, by walking in all his ways, and by clinging to him, [23] then the LORD will clear out all these nations before you. You will inherit what belonged to nations that are larger and stronger than you are. [24] Every place you set foot on will be yours: your territory will run from the wilderness all the way to the Lebanon range, and from the Euphrates River all the way to the Mediterranean Sea. [25] No one will be able to stand up to you. Just as he promised, the LORD your God will make the entire land deathly afraid of you wherever you advance in it.

Ceremony on Mount Gerizim and Mount Ebal

[26] Pay attention! I am setting blessing and curse before you right now: [27] the blessing if you obey the LORD your God's commandments that I am giving you right now, [28] but the curse if you don't obey the LORD your God's commandments and stray from the path that I am giving you today by following other gods that you have not known. [29] Now when the LORD your God brings you into the land that you are entering to take possession of, put the blessing on Mount Gerizim and the curse on Mount Ebal. ([30] Aren't both of these mountains across the Jordan River, down along the western road in the region of the Canaanites who live in the desert plain, across from Gilgal, next to the Moreh Oak Grove?) [31] So then, once you cross the Jordan River to enter and possess the land that the LORD your God is giving you, and you take possession of it, settling down in it, [32] you must carefully follow the regulations and the case laws that I am laying out before you right now.

Regulations and the case laws:

Worship at the location the LORD selects

12 These are the regulations and the case laws that you must carefully keep in the fertile land the LORD, your ancestors' God, has given to you to possess for as long as you live on that land: [2] You must completely destroy every place where the nations that you are displacing worshipped their gods—whether on high mountains or hills or under leafy green trees. [3] Rip down their altars and shatter their sacred stones. Burn their sacred poles[u] with fire. Hack their gods' idols into pieces. Wipe out their names from that place. [4] Don't act like they did toward the LORD your God! [5] Instead, you must search for the location the LORD your God will select from all your tribes to put his name there, as his residence, and you must go there. [6] You must bring your entirely burned offerings, your sacrifices, your tenth-part gifts, your contributions,[v] your payments for solemn

---

[s] Sam, LXX, two DSS; Heb, four DSS, Syr, Tg *I*, in which case the text shifts to direct divine discourse. [t] Heb uncertain; cf Exod 13:16; Syr *sign* or *mark*; Tg *phylacteries* [u] Heb *asherim*, perhaps objects devoted to the goddess Asherah [v] Or *the contribution of your hands*; also in 12:11, 17

promises, your spontaneous gifts, and the oldest offspring of your herds and flocks to that place. ⁷You will have a feast there, each of you and your families, in the LORD your God's presence, and you will celebrate all you have done because the LORD your God has blessed you. ⁸Don't act like we've been acting here lately—everyone doing what seems right to them—⁹because up to this point you haven't yet reached the place of rest or the inheritance the LORD your God is giving you. ¹⁰But you are about to cross the Jordan River and will settle in the land the LORD your God is giving you as your inheritance. Then he will give you rest from all your enemies on every side so that you live safely and securely. ¹¹At that point, you must bring all that I am commanding you, your entirely burned offerings, your sacrifices, your tenth-part gifts, your contributions, and all your best payments that you solemnly promised to the LORD, to the location the LORD your God selects for his name to reside. ¹²Then you will rejoice in the LORD your God's presence: each of you, your sons and daughters, your male and female servants, and the Levites who dwell in your cities because they have no designated inheritance.

¹³But watch yourself! Make sure you don't offer up your entirely burned offerings in just any place you see. ¹⁴No, only at the location the LORD selects from one of your tribal areas—that's where you must offer up your entirely burned offerings and that's where you must perform everything I'm telling you. ¹⁵However, whenever you wish, you may slaughter and eat meat, as the LORD your God sees fit to bless you with such in your cities. People who are polluted and people who are purified can join in the feast, as they would if they were eating gazelle or deer. ¹⁶But you must not consume any of the animals' blood. Pour it out on the ground, just like water.

¹⁷Within your cities you are not allowed to eat any of the following: your tenth-part gifts of grain, wine, and oil; the oldest offspring of your herds and flocks; any of the payments you have solemnly promised; your spontaneous gifts or your contributions. ¹⁸Only in the presence of the LORD your God, at the location the LORD your God selects, can you eat these things—that holds true for you, your son and daughter, your male and female servant, and the Levite who lives in your city. Then celebrate all you have done in the LORD your God's presence. ¹⁹But watch yourself: as long as you are on the land, don't forget about the Levites.

²⁰Once the LORD your God has enlarged your territory, as he promised you, and you think to yourself, I'd like to eat some meat (because you have the desire to do so), feel free to do so whenever you want. ²¹But if the location that the LORD your God will choose to put his name is far away from where you live, then slaughter an animal from your herd or flock that the LORD has given you, just as I have commanded you, and eat it in your cities whenever you wish. ²²But be sure to eat it as if it were gazelle or deer. People who are polluted and people who are purified can feast on it together.

²³Furthermore, make sure that you don't consume any of the blood, because blood is life. You must not consume the life along with the meat. ²⁴You must not consume any of it. Pour it out on the ground, just like water. ²⁵You must not consume any of it so that things go well for you and for your children later because you did what was right in the LORD's eyes.

²⁶Note that you must bring your sacred offerings and your payments for solemn promises to the location the LORD selects, ²⁷offering up your entirely burned sacrifices—both meat and blood—on the LORD your God's altar. The blood from your sacrifices must be poured out on the LORD your God's altar, but you are allowed to eat the meat. ²⁸Observe and obey all these words that I am commanding you so that things always go well for you and your children later because you did what was good and right in the LORD your God's eyes.

²⁹Once the LORD your God has removed from before you all the nations that you are entering and taking possession of, and you have displaced them and are living in their land, ³⁰then watch yourself! Don't be

trapped by following their practices after they've been wiped out before you. Don't go investigating their gods, thinking, How did these nations worship their gods? I want to do the very same thing!

³¹Don't act like they did toward the LORD your God because they did things for their gods that are detestable to the LORD, which he hates. They even burned their own sons and daughters with fire for their gods!

³²ʷEverything I'm commanding you, you must do it with utmost care! Don't add anything to it or take anything away from it.

False prophets and false gods

13 ˣNow if a prophet or a dream interpreter appears among you and performs a sign or wonder for you, ²and the sign or wonder that was spoken actually occurs; if he says: "Come on! We should follow other gods"—ones you haven't experienced—"and we should worship them," ³you must not listen to that prophet's or dream interpreter's words, because the LORD your God is testing you to see if you love the LORD your God with all your mind and all your being. ⁴You must follow the LORD your God alone! Revere him! Follow his commandments! Obey his voice! Worship him! Cling to him—no other! ⁵That prophet or dream interpreter must be executed because he encouraged you to turn away from the LORD your God who brought you out of Egypt, who redeemed you from the house of slavery; they tried to lead you away from the path the LORD your God commanded you to take. Removeʸ such evil from your community!

⁶Similarly, if one of your relatives—even one of your own siblings—or your own son or daughter or your dear spouse or best friend entices you secretly, if someone like that says: "Come on! We should follow and worship other gods"—ones that neither you nor your ancestors have experienced, ⁷gods from all the neighboring peoples, whether nearby or far away, from one end of the earth to the other—⁸don't give in to them! Don't obey them! Don't have any mercy on them! Don't have compassion on them and don't protect them! ⁹Instead, you must execute them. Your own hand must be against them from the beginning of the execution; the hand of all the people will be involved at the end. ¹⁰Stone them until they are dead because they desired to lead you away from the LORD your God, the one who brought you out of Egypt, out of the house of slavery. ¹¹All Israel will hear about this and be afraid. They won't do that sort of evil thing among you again.

¹²Or if you hear about one of your towns the LORD your God is giving you to inhabit, that ¹³certain wicked people have gone out from your community and they've led the citizens of their town astray by saying: "Come on! We should follow and worship other gods"—ones you haven't experienced before; ¹⁴at that point you must look into this situation very carefully to see if it's true. And if it's definitely true that this detestable thing was done in your community, ¹⁵you must completely strike down the inhabitants of that city with the sword. Place it and all that is in it under the ban.ᶻ Put its animals to the sword. ¹⁶Gather all the plunder into the middle of the town's square. Then burn the city and all of its plunder as an entirely burned offering to the LORD your God. It must remain a heap of rubble forever. It must not be rebuilt. ¹⁷Don't hold on to any of the banned items—this will ensure that the LORD turns from his great anger and is compassionate to you, showing you mercy and multiplying you just like he swore to your ancestors. ¹⁸You must definitely obey the LORD your God's voice, keeping all his commandments that I am giving you right now, by doing what is right in the LORD your God's eyes!

Complete devotion to the LORD

14 You are the LORD's children. Don't cut yourselves and don't shave your foreheads for the dead, ²because you are a people holy to the LORD your God. You

ʷ13:1 in Heb ˣ13:2 in Heb ʸOr burn ᶻSee note at 2:34.

are the ones whom the LORD selected to be his own, to be a treasured people out of all other people on earth.

Dietary laws

[3]Don't eat any detestable thing. [4]Here's a list of animals you are allowed to eat: ox, sheep, goat, [5]deer, gazelle, roebuck, wild goat, ibex, antelope, and mountain sheep. [6]You are also allowed to eat any animal with a divided hoof—the hoof being divided into two parts—and that rechews food among the various kinds of animals. [7]However, here's a list of animals that either rechew food or have hooves divided in two parts that you are not allowed to eat:

the camel, the hare, and the rock badger—because these rechew food but don't have divided hoofs, they are off-limits for you;

[8]and the pig—because it has a divided hoof but doesn't rechew food, it's off-limits for you.

You may not eat these animals' meat, and you must not touch their carcasses.

[9]Here's a list of the water animals you are allowed to eat: you can eat anything that has fins and scales. [10]But you aren't allowed to eat anything that lacks scales or fins. These are off-limits for you.

[11]You are allowed to eat any clean bird. [12]Here's a list of those you are not allowed to eat: the eagle, the vulture, the osprey, [13]the red kite, the black kite, and any kind of bird of prey, [14]any kind of raven, [15]the ostrich, the nighthawk, the seagull, any kind of hawk, [16]the small owl and the large owl, the water hen, [17]the desert owl, the carrion vulture, the cormorant, [18]the stork, any kind of heron, the hoopoe, and the bat.[a]

[19]Also, all winged insects are off-limits for you. They are not to be eaten. [20]Any clean winged creature can be eaten, however.

[21]You must not eat any decayed animal flesh because you are a people holy to the LORD your God. You can give decayed animal flesh to the immigrants who live in your cities, and they can eat it; or you can sell it to foreigners.

Don't cook a lamb in its own mother's milk.

Tenth part

[22]You must reserve a tenth part of whatever your fields produce each year. [23]Eat the tenth part of your grain, wine, oil, oldest offspring of your herds and flocks in the presence of the LORD your God in the location he selects for his name to reside so that you learn to fear the LORD your God at all times. [24]But if the trip is too long, because the location the LORD your God has selected to put his name is far away from where you live so that you can't transport the tenth part—because the LORD your God will certainly bless you—[25]then you can convert it to money. Take the money with you and go to the location the LORD your God selects. [26]Then you can use the money for anything you want: cattle, sheep, wine, beer, or whatever else you might like. Then you should feast there and celebrate in the presence of the LORD your God, along with your entire household. [27]Only make sure not to neglect the Levites who are living in your cities because they don't have a designated inheritance like you do.

[28]Every third year you must bring the tenth part of your produce from that year and leave it at your city gates. [29]Then the Levites, who have no designated inheritance like you do, along with the immigrants, orphans, and widows who live in your cities, will come and feast until they are full. Do this so that the LORD your God might bless you in everything you do.

Year of canceled debts

15 Every seventh year you must cancel all debts. [2]This is how the cancellation is to be handled: Creditors will forgive the loans of their fellow Israelites. They won't demand repayment from their neighbors or their relatives because the LORD's year of debt cancellation has been announced. [3]You are allowed to demand payment from foreigners, but whatever is owed you from your fellow Israelites you must forgive.

---

[a]The species of many of the birds in 14:12-18 is uncertain.

⁴Of course there won't be any poor persons among you because the LORD will bless you in the land that the LORD your God is giving you to possess as an inheritance, ⁵but only if you carefully obey the LORD your God's voice, by carefully doing every bit of this commandment that I'm giving you right now. ⁶Once the LORD your God has blessed you, exactly as he said he would, you will end up lending to many different peoples but won't need to borrow a thing. You will dominate many different peoples, but they won't dominate you.

⁷Now if there are some poor persons among you, say one of your fellow Israelites in one of your cities in the land that the LORD your God is giving you, don't be hardhearted or tightfisted toward your poor fellow Israelites. ⁸To the contrary! Open your hand wide to them. You must generously lend them whatever they need. ⁹But watch yourself! Make sure no wicked thought crosses your mind, such as, The seventh year is coming—the year of debt cancellation—so that you resent your poor fellow Israelites and don't give them anything. If you do that, they will cry out to the LORD against you, and you will be guilty of sin. ¹⁰No, give generously to needy persons. Don't resent giving to them because it is this very thing that will lead to the LORD your God's blessing you in all you do and work at. ¹¹Poor persons will never disappear from the earth. That's why I'm giving you this command: you must open your hand generously to your fellow Israelites, to the needy among you, and to the poor who live with you in your land.

¹²If any of your fellow Hebrews, male or female, sell themselves into your service, they can work for you for six years, but in the seventh year you must set them free from your service. ¹³Furthermore, when you set them free from your service, you must not let them go empty-handed. ¹⁴Instead, provide for them fully from your flock, food, and wine. You must give to them from that with which the LORD your God has blessed you. ¹⁵Remember how each of you were slaves in Egypt and how the LORD your God saved you. That's why I am commanding you to do this right now. (¹⁶Now if your male servant says to you: "I don't want to leave your service" because he loves you and your family and because life is good for him in your service, ¹⁷then you may take a needle and pierce his ear with it into the doorframe. From that point on, he will be your permanent servant. Do the same thing for female servants.) ¹⁸Don't consider it a hardship to set these servants free from your service, because they worked for you for six years—at a value double that of a paid worker. The LORD

SABBATICAL YEAR

Observance of the sabbatical year is a practice to regulate slavery and agricultural land management practices to help the poor and encourage piety. While Deuteronomy 15 understands the seventh year primarily as a time of freeing slaves, Leviticus 25 develops ancient practices of fallowing land in rotation (see also Exod 23:10-11) by connecting them to the Jubilee, a scheme for ensuring just distribution of wealth in Israel.

Whether the sabbatical year was ever implemented in the Iron Age is unknown, though statewide manumission of slaves, the central feature of the year in Deuteronomy, was a common practice in antiquity, known also in ancient Israel (see Jer 34:8-16). It is difficult to see how the land-fallowing practices described by Leviticus could have been achievable, especially if the Jubilee Year succeeded a sabbatical year.

your God will bless you in everything that you do.

[19]You must devote every oldest male animal from your herds or flocks to the LORD your God. Don't plow with your oldest male ox and don't shear your oldest male sheep. [20]Year after year, you and your family are allowed to eat these animals in the presence of the LORD your God, in the location the LORD selects. [21]But if there is any defect in it, lameness, blindness, any flaw whatsoever, you must not sacrifice it to the LORD your God. [22]You are allowed to eat those in your own cities, whether you are polluted or purified, just as you would eat gazelle or deer. [23]Even so, don't consume any blood. Pour it out on the ground, like water.

Passover celebration

16Wait for the month of Abib,[b] at which time you must perform the Passover for the LORD your God, because the LORD your God brought you out of Egypt at nighttime during the month of Abib. [2]Offer a Passover sacrifice from the flock or herd to the LORD your God at the location the LORD selects for his name to reside. [3]You must not eat anything containing yeast along with it.[c] Instead, for seven days you must eat unleavened bread, bread symbolizing misery, along with it because you fled Egypt in a great hurry. Do this so you remember the day you fled Egypt for as long as you live. [4]No dough with yeast should appear in any of your territory for seven days. Furthermore, none of the meat that you sacrificed on the first night should remain until morning. [5]You are not permitted to offer the Passover sacrifice in any of the cities that the LORD your God is giving you. [6]Instead, you must offer the Passover sacrifice at the location the LORD your God selects for his name to reside, at evening time, when the sun sets, which was the time you fled Egypt. [7]Cook it and eat it in the location that the LORD your God selects. The next morning you can return to your tents. [8]For six days you will eat unleavened bread. The seventh day will be a cele-

bration for the LORD your God. Don't do any work.

Festival of Weeks

[9]Count out seven weeks, starting the count from the beginning of the grain harvest. [10]At that point, perform the Festival of Weeks for the LORD your God. Offer a spontaneous gift in precise measure with the blessing the LORD your God gives you. [11]Then celebrate in the presence of the LORD your God—you, your sons, your daughters, your male and female servants, the Levites who live in your cities, the immigrants, the orphans, and the widows who are among you—in the location the LORD your God selects for his name to reside. [12]Remember how each of you was a slave in Egypt, so follow these regulations most carefully.

Festival of Booths

[13]Once you have collected the food and drink you need, perform the Festival of Booths for seven days. [14]Celebrate your festival: you, your sons, your daughters, your male and female servants, the Levites, the immigrants, the orphans, and the widows who live in your cities. [15]Seven days you must perform the festival for the LORD your God in the location the LORD selects because the LORD your God will bless you in all you do and in all your work. You will be overjoyed.

[16]Three times a year every male among you must appear before the presence of the LORD your God in the location he will select: at the Festival of Unleavened Bread, the Festival of Weeks, and the Festival of Booths. They must not appear before the LORD's presence empty-handed. [17]Each one should have his gift in hand, in precise measure with the blessing the LORD your God gives you.

Judges and officials

[18]Appoint judges and officials for each of your tribes in every city that the LORD your God gives you. They must judge the people fairly. [19]Don't delay justice; don't show

[b]March–April; called Nisan in post-exilic period [c]It, the Passover sacrifice

favoritism. Don't take bribes because bribery blinds the vision of the wise and twists the words of the righteous. [20]Righteousness! Pursue righteousness so that you live long and take possession of the land that the LORD your God is giving you.

Rules for worship

[21]Don't plant any tree to serve as a sacred pole[d] next to the altar you make for the LORD your God. [22]Don't set up any sacred stone either, because the LORD your God hates such things. **17** [1]Don't sacrifice to the LORD your God any oxen or sheep that have defects of any kind, because that is detestable to the LORD your God.

Capital punishment

[2]If someone, whether male or female, is found in your community—in one of the cities the LORD your God is giving you—who does evil in the LORD your God's eyes, by breaking God's covenant, [3]by following and serving other gods, and by bowing down to them, to the sun or the moon or any of the heavenly bodies that I haven't permitted—[4]and you hear news about it, then you must look into this situation very carefully. And if it's definitely true that this detestable thing was done in Israel, [5]then you must bring out the man or woman who has done this evil thing to the gates of the city. Stone that person until he or she is dead.

[6]Capital punishment must be decided by two or three witnesses. No one may be executed on the basis of only one testimony. [7]In the execution, the hands of the witnesses must be against the guilty person from the start; the hand of all the people will be involved at the end. Remove[e] such evil from your community!

Legal disputes

[8]If some legal dispute in your cities is too difficult for you to decide—say, between different kinds of bloodshed, different kinds of legal ruling, or different kinds of injury—then take it to the location the LORD your God selects. [9]Go to the levitical priests and to the head judge in office at that time and look into things there. They will announce to you the correct ruling. [10]You must then act according to the ruling they announced to you from that location, the one the LORD selects. You must follow very carefully everything they instruct you to do. [11]Act precisely according to the instruction they give you and the ruling they announce to you. Don't deviate even a bit from the word they announce. [12]And whoever acts rashly by not listening to the priest who is in office serving the LORD your God or to the head judge will die. Remove[f] such evil from Israel! [13]All the people will hear about this and be afraid. They won't act arrogantly anymore.

Law of the king

[14]Once you have entered the land the LORD your God is giving you and you have taken possession of it and settled down in it, you might say: "Let's appoint a king over us, as all our neighboring nations have done." [15]You can indeed appoint over you a king that the LORD your God selects. You can appoint over you a king who is one of your fellow Israelites. You are not allowed to appoint over you a foreigner who is not one of your fellow Israelites. [16]That granted, the king must not acquire too many horses, and he must not return the people to Egypt in order to acquire more horses, because the LORD told you: "You will never go back by that road again." [17]The king must not take numerous wives so that his heart doesn't go astray. Nor can the king acquire too much silver and gold. [18]Instead, when he sits on his royal throne, he himself must write a copy of this Instruction on a scroll in the presence of the levitical priests. [19]That Instruction must remain with him, and he must read in it every day of his life so that he learns to revere the LORD his God by keeping all the words of this Instruction and these regulations, by doing them, [20]by not being overbearing toward his fellow Israelites, and by not deviating even a bit

[d]Heb *asherah*, perhaps an object devoted to the goddess Asherah [e]Or *burn* [f]Or *burn*

from the commandment. If the king does all that, he will ensure lasting rule in Israel for himself and for his successors.

Priests and Levites

18 Neither the levitical priests nor any Levite tribe member will have a designated inheritance in Israel. They can eat the sacrifices offered to the LORD, which are the LORD's portion,[g] [2]but they won't share an inheritance with their fellow Israelites. The LORD alone is the Levites' inheritance—just as God promised them.

[3]Now this is what the priests may keep from the people's sacrifices of oxen or sheep: They must give the priest the shoulder, the jaws, and the stomach. [4]You must also give the priest the first portions of your grain, wine, and oil, and the first of your sheep's shearing [5]because the LORD your God selected Levi from all of your tribes to stand and minister in the LORD's name—both him and his descendants for all time.

[6]Now if a Levite leaves one of your cities or departs from any location in Israel where he's been living and, because he wants to, comes to the location the LORD selects [7]and ministers in the LORD his God's name, just like his relatives—the other Levites serving there in the LORD's presence—[8]he is allowed to eat equal portions, despite the finances he has from his family.[h]

Communicating with God

[9]Once you enter the land that the LORD your God is giving you, don't try to imitate the detestable things those nations do. [10]There must not be anyone among you who passes his son or daughter through fire; who practices divination, is a sign reader, fortune-teller, sorcerer, [11]or spell caster; who converses with ghosts or spirits or communicates with the dead. [12]All who do these things are detestable to the LORD! It is on account of these detestable practices that the LORD your God is driving these nations[i] out before you.

[13]Instead, you must be perfect before the LORD your God. [14]These nations you are displacing listened to sign readers and diviners, but the LORD your God doesn't permit you to do the same! [15]The LORD your God will raise up a prophet like me from your community, from your fellow Israelites. He's the one you must listen to. [16]That's exactly what you requested from the LORD your God at Horeb, on the day of the assembly, when you said, "I can't listen to the LORD my God's voice anymore or look at this great fire any longer. I don't want to die!"

[17]The LORD said to me: What they've said is right. [18]I'll raise up a prophet for them from among their fellow Israelites—one just like you. I'll put my words in his mouth, and he will tell them everything I command him. [19]I myself will hold accountable anyone who doesn't listen to my words, which that prophet will speak in my name. [20]However, any prophet who arrogantly speaks a word in my name that I haven't commanded him to speak, or who speaks in the name of other gods—that prophet must die.

[g]Heb uncertain [h]Heb uncertain [i]Or them

LEVI/LEVITES

In the OT, Levi is the third son of Jacob by Leah (Gen 29:34) and the ancestor of the tribe of Levi and all priests. The descendants of Levi were called Levites. The evidence of the Levites' nature, function, and destiny vis-à-vis the priesthood appears chiefly in Deuteronomy through Judges, Ezekiel, and Chronicles.

[21]Now, you might be wondering, How will we know which word God hasn't spoken? [22]Here's the answer: The prophet who speaks in the LORD's name and the thing doesn't happen or come about—that's the word the LORD hasn't spoken. That prophet spoke arrogantly. Don't be afraid of him.[j]

Cities of refuge

19 Once the LORD your God has eliminated those nations—whose land the LORD your God is giving you—and you displace them, settling into their cities and their houses, [2]you must designate three cities for your use in the land the LORD your God is giving you to possess. [3]Mark out the roads to them[k] and divide the regions of the land the LORD your God is apportioning to you into three parts. These cities are the places to which a person who has killed can escape. [4]Here is the rule concerning a person who killed someone and is permitted to escape to one of these cities and live:

If it is someone who killed his neighbor accidentally, without having hated that person previously; [5]or if someone goes into the forest with a neighbor to chop some wood, and while swinging an ax to cut down the tree, the axhead flies off its handle and hits the neighbor, who subsequently dies—these kinds of killers may escape to one of these cities and live. [6]Otherwise, the blood avenger will chase after the killer out of rage and—especially if the distance to one of these cities[l] is too far—might catch and kill him, even though a death sentence was not in order because the killer didn't have prior malice toward the other. [7]This is why I am commanding you as follows: Designate three cities for your use.

[8]Now if the LORD your God enlarges your territory, as he swore to your ancestors—and he will give you all the land he swore to give to them [9]as long as you keep all this commandment that I am giving you right now by doing it, by loving the LORD your God, and by always walking in his ways—

you can add three more cities for your use along with the first three. [10]Innocent blood must not be spilled in the land the LORD your God is giving to you as an inheritance, or it will be bloodshed that will be required of you.

[11]But if someone does hate a neighbor and ambushes him, rising up against him and attacking him so he dies, and then escapes to one of these cities, [12]elders from the killer's hometown will send word, and the killer will be sent back from there. They will then hand him over to the blood avenger, and he will be executed. [13]Show no mercy to such killers. Remove[m] innocent bloodshed from Israel so that things go well for you.

Property laws

[14]Now in the land the LORD your God is giving you, in your allotted property that you will receive there, you must not tamper with your neighbor's property line, which has been previously established.

Rules for testimony

[15]A solitary witness against someone in any crime, wrongdoing, or in any sort of misdeed that might be done is not sufficient. The decision must stand by two or three witnesses. [16]Now if a spiteful witness comes forward against someone, so as to testify against them falsely, [17]the two persons who have a legal suit must stand before the LORD, before the priests, and before the judges that are in office at that time. [18]The judges will look into the situation very carefully. If it turns out that the witness is a liar—that the witness has given false testimony against his fellow Israelite—[19]then you must do to him what he had planned to do to his fellow Israelite. Remove[n] such evil from your community! [20]The rest of the people will hear about this and be afraid. They won't do that sort of evil thing among you again. [21]Show no mercy on this point: life for life, eye for eye, tooth for tooth, hand for hand, foot for foot.

---

[j]Or *bothered by it* (the prophecy)   [k]Heb uncertain and lacks *to them.*   [l]Heb lacks *to one of these cities.*   [m]Or *burn*
[n]Or *burn*

Rules for warfare

20 When you march out to battle your enemies and you see horses, chariots, and a fighting force larger than yours, don't be afraid of them, because the LORD your God, the one who brought you up from Egypt, is with you. [2] As you advance toward the war, the priest will come forward and will address the troops. [3] He will say to them: "Listen, Israel: Right now you are advancing to wage war against your enemies. Don't be discouraged! Don't be afraid! Don't panic! Don't shake in fear on account of them, [4] because the LORD your God is going with you to fight your enemies for you and to save you."

[5] The officials will also say to the troops: "Is there anyone here who has just built a new house but hasn't yet dedicated it? He can leave and go back to his house; otherwise, he might die in the war and someone else would dedicate the house. [6] Or is there anyone here who has planted a vineyard but hasn't yet put it to good use? He can leave and go back to his house; otherwise, he might die in the battle and someone else would use the vineyard. [7] Or is there anyone here who is engaged but not yet married? He may leave and go back to his house; otherwise, he might die in the battle and someone else would marry his fiancée."

[8] The officials will continue to address the troops, stating: "Is there anyone here who is afraid and discouraged? He can leave and go back to his house; otherwise, his comrades might lose courage just as he has." [9] Once the officials have completed their speech to the troops, the army commanders will assume leadership of the forces.

[10] When you approach a city to fight against it, you should first extend peaceful terms to it. [11] If the city responds with peaceful terms and surrenders to you, then all the people in the city will serve you as forced laborers. [12] However, if the city does not negotiate peacefully with you but makes war against you, you may attack it. [13] The LORD your God will hand it over to you; you must kill all the city's males with the sword.

[14] However, you can take for yourselves the women, the children, the animals, and all that is in the city—all its plunder. You can then enjoy your enemies' plunder, which the LORD your God has given you.

[15] That's what you must do to all the cities that are located far away from you—specifically, those cities that don't belong to these nations here. [16] But in the case of any of the cities of these peoples—the ones the LORD your God is giving you as an inheritance—you must not spare any living thing. [17] Instead, you must place these under the ban:[o] Hittites, Amorites, Canaanites, Perizzites, Hivites, and Jebusites—just as the LORD your God commanded you. [18] Then they can't teach you to do all the detestable things they did for their gods, with the result that you end up sinning against the LORD your God.

[19] Now if you have been attacking a city for some time, fighting against it and trying to conquer it, don't destroy its trees by cutting them down with axes. You can eat from those trees; don't cut them down! Do you think a tree of the field is some sort of warrior to be attacked by you in battle? [20] That said, if you know that a tree is not a food-producing tree, you are allowed to destroy it, cutting it down and using it in the siege against the city that is fighting against you until it falls.

Unsolved homicides

21 If a corpse is found on the ground the LORD your God is giving you to possess, lying in a field, and the identity of the killer is unknown, [2] your elders and judges must come out and measure the distances to the cities nearest the body. [3] Once it is determined which city is closest to the dead body, its elders must take a young cow that hasn't been used or yet pulled a plow, [4] and those elders will take the cow down to a ravine with a flowing stream—one that has not been plowed or planted—and they will break the cow's neck right there in the river valley. [5] Then the priests, the descendants of Levi, will step forward because the LORD your God selected them to minister for

[o]See note at Deut 2:34.

him and to bless in the LORD's name, and because every legal dispute and case of assault is decided by them. [6]All the elders of the city closest to the corpse will wash their hands over the cow whose neck was broken in the river valley. [7]They will then solemnly state: "Our hands did not shed this blood. Our eyes did not see it happen. [8]LORD, please forgive your people Israel, whom you saved. Don't put the guilt of innocent bloodshed on your people Israel."

Then the bloodguilt will be forgiven them.

[9]But you must remove[p] innocent bloodshed from your community; do only what is right in the LORD's eyes.

Foreign wives

[10]When you wage war against your enemies and the LORD hands them over to you and you take prisoners, [11]if you see among the captives a beautiful woman, and you fall in love with her and take her as your wife, [12]bringing her into your home, she must shave her head, cut her nails, [13]remove her prisoner's clothing, and live in your house, mourning her father and her mother for one month. After that, you may consummate the marriage. You will be her husband, and she will be your wife. [14]But if you aren't pleased with her, you must send her away as she wishes. You are not allowed to sell her for money or treat her as a slave because you have humiliated her.

Right of the oldest son

[15]Now suppose a man has two wives—one of them loved and the other unloved. Both wives bear children, but the oldest male is the unloved wife's child. [16]On the day when the man decides what will go to each of his children as an inheritance, he isn't allowed to treat his loved wife's son as the oldest male rather than his unloved wife's son, who is the real oldest male. [17]Instead, he must acknowledge the unloved wife's son as the oldest male, giving to him two-thirds of everything that he owns, because that son is the earliest produce of his physical power. The oldest male's rights belong to that son.

Rebellious children

[18]Now if someone has a consistently stubborn and rebellious child, who refuses to listen to their father and mother—even when the parents discipline him, he won't listen to them—[19]the father and mother will take the son before the elders of that city at its gates. [20]Then they will inform the city's elders: "This son of ours is consistently stubborn and rebellious, refusing to listen to us. What's more, he's wild and a drunkard."

[21]Then all the people of that town will stone him until he dies.

Remove[q] such evil from your community! All Israel will hear about this and be afraid.

Hanging

[22]Now if someone is guilty of a capital crime, and they are executed, and you then hang them on a tree, [23]you must not leave the body hanging on the tree but must bury it the same day because God's curse is on those who are hanged.[r] Furthermore, you

---

[p]Or burn [q]Or burn [r]LXX, Vulg, Tg Neofiti *God's curse is on those who are hanged;* Syr, Tg Onqelos *those who curse God are to be hanged;* Heb uncertain

---

BIRTHRIGHT

The special privilege assigned to the oldest male offspring of any father. This meant, in the first place, that he inherited two portions, that is, double the portions for the other males. (Females inherited only when there were no males.) See Deuteronomy 21:15-17; on females, Numbers 27:1-11.

must not pollute the ground that the LORD your God is giving to you as an inheritance.

Rules for property and mixtures

22 Don't just watch your fellow Israelite's ox or sheep wandering around and do nothing about it. You must return the animal to its owner. ²If the owner doesn't live nearby, or you don't know who owns the animal, then you must take care of it. It should stay with you until your fellow Israelite comes looking for it, at which point you must return it to him. ³Do the same thing in the case of a donkey. Do the same thing in the case of a piece of clothing. Do the same thing in the case of anything that your fellow Israelite loses and you end up finding. You are not allowed to sit back and do nothing about it.

⁴Don't just watch your fellow Israelite's donkey or ox fall down in the road and do nothing about it. You must help your fellow Israelite get the animal up again.

⁵Women must not wear men's clothes, and men must not wear women's clothes. Everyone who does such things is detestable to the LORD your God.

⁶If you come across a bird's nest along your way, whether in a tree or on the ground, with baby birds or eggs, and the mother is sitting on the baby birds or eggs, do not remove the mother from her young. ⁷You must let the mother go, though you may take the young for yourself so that things go well for you and so you can prolong your life.

⁸Whenever you build a new house, you must build a railing for the roof so that you don't end up with innocent blood on your hands because someone fell off of it.

⁹Don't plant your vineyards with two types of seed; otherwise, the entire crop that you have planted and the produce of the vineyard will be unusable.ˢ

¹⁰Don't plow with an ox and a donkey together.

¹¹Don't wear clothes that mix wool and linen together.

¹²Make tassels for the four corners of the coat you wear.

Virgin bride

¹³Suppose a man gets married and consummates the marriage but subsequently despises his wife. ¹⁴He then spreads false claims about her to the point that she has a bad reputation, because he said such things as, "I married this woman, but when I went to have sex with her, I couldn't find any proof that she was a virgin."

ˢOr *sanctified*

DIVORCE

Leviticus 21:7, 14 and Ezekiel 44:22 prohibit priests from marrying a divorced woman. Deuteronomy 21:14 deals with provisions for a man to marry a woman taken captive in war. If the man is not satisfied with her, he can divorce her and set her free; he cannot sell her for money or treat her as a slave. Deuteronomy 22:19 and 22:29 deal with cases in which a man may never divorce his wife. In each case, the aggrieved party is the father of the "young woman" (Deut 22:19, 28-29), to whom the man must pay a fine. These laws may also protect the woman, who would otherwise be ineligible to marry another man (see also Deut 24:1-4). Divorce is used as a prophetic metaphor in Isaiah 50:1; 54:5-8; Jeremiah 3–4; and Malachi 2:16. Paul argues against three specific cases of divorce in 1 Corinthians 7:10-16. Jesus' teachings on divorce are found in Matthew 5:31-32; 19:1-12; Mark 10:2-12; Luke 16:18.

¹⁵At that point, the young woman's father and mother will bring proof of her virginity to the city's elders at the city gate. ¹⁶The young woman's father will say to the elders: "I gave my daughter to this man to be his wife, but he doesn't like her anymore. ¹⁷That's why he has spread false claims about her, saying, 'I couldn't find any proof that your daughter was a virgin.' But look! Here's proof of my daughter's virginity." At that point they will spread out the blanket in front of the city's elders. ¹⁸The city's elders must then take that husband and punish him. ¹⁹They will fine him one hundred silver shekels, giving that to the young woman's father, because that husband gave one of Israel's virgin daughters a bad reputation. Moreover, she must remain his wife; he is never allowed to divorce her.

²⁰However, if the claim is true and proof of the young woman's virginity can't be produced, ²¹then the city's elders will bring the young woman to the door of her father's house. The citizens of that city must stone her until she dies because she acted so sinfully in Israel by having extramarital sex while still in her father's house.

Remove[t] such evil from your community!

Inappropriate sexual behavior

²²If a man is found having sex with a woman who is married to someone else, both of them must die—the man who was having sex with the woman and the woman herself.

Remove such evil from Israel!

²³If a young woman who is a virgin is engaged to one man and another man meets up with her in a town and has sex with her, ²⁴you must bring both of them to the city gates there and stone them until they die—the young woman because she didn't call for help in the city, and the man because of the fact that he humiliated his neighbor's wife.

Remove such evil from your community!

²⁵But if the man met up with the engaged woman in a field, grabbing her and having sex with her there, only the man will die. ²⁶Don't do anything whatsoever to the young woman. She hasn't committed any capital crime—rather, this situation is exactly like the one where someone attacks his neighbor and kills him.[u] ²⁷Since the man met up with her in a field, the engaged woman may well have called out for help, but there was no one to rescue her.

²⁸If a man meets up with a young woman who is a virgin and not engaged, grabs her and has sex with her, and they are caught in the act, ²⁹the man who had sex with her must give fifty silver shekels to the young woman's father. She will also become his wife because he has humiliated her. He is never allowed to divorce her.

³⁰[v]A man cannot marry his father's former wife so that his father's private matters are not exposed.[w]

The Lord's assembly

23[x]No man whose testicles are crushed or whose penis is cut off can belong to the Lord's assembly. ²No one born of an illegitimate marriage[y] can belong to the Lord's assembly either. Not even the tenth generation of such children can belong to the Lord's assembly. ³Ammonites and Moabites can't belong to the Lord's assembly. Not even the tenth generation of such people can belong to the Lord's assembly, as a rule, ⁴because they didn't help you with food or water on your journey out of Egypt, and because they hired Balaam, Beor's son, from Pethor of Mesopotamia to curse you. ⁵But the Lord your God wasn't interested in listening to Balaam. The Lord your God turned that curse into a blessing because the Lord your God loves you. ⁶So don't be concerned with their health and well-being as long as you live.

⁷Don't detest Edomites, because they are your relatives. Don't detest Egyptians because you were immigrants in their land. ⁸Children born to them are permitted to belong to the Lord's assembly starting with the third generation.

---

[t]Or *burn*; so also 22:22, 24 [u]See 19:11. [v]23:1 in Heb [w]Or *so that he doesn't uncover his father's skirt* [x]23:2 in Heb [y]Heb uncertain

Rules for the war camp

⁹When you are camped in battle against your enemies, guard yourself from every possible evil. ¹⁰If an individual in the camp becomes polluted due to a nighttime emission, he must exit the camp area and not reenter. ¹¹When the next evening arrives, he must wash with water; and when the sun sets, he can come back to the camp.

¹²The latrinesᶻ must be outside the camp. You will use them there, outside the camp. ¹³Carry a shovel with the rest of your gear; once you have relieved yourself, use it to dig a hole, then refill it, covering your excrement.

¹⁴Do these things because the LORD your God travels with you, right in the middle of your camp, ready to save you and to hand your enemies over to you. For this reason your camp must be holy. The LORD must not see anything indecent among you, or he will turn away from you.

Escaped slaves

¹⁵Don't return slaves to owners if they've escaped and come to you. ¹⁶They can stay with you: in your own community or in any place they select from one of your cities, whatever seems good to them. Don't oppress them.

Consecrated workers

¹⁷No Israelite daughter is allowed to be a consecrated worker.ᵃ Neither is any Israelite son allowed to be a consecrated worker.ᵇ ¹⁸Don't bring a female prostitute's fee or a male prostitute'sᶜ payment to the LORD your God's temple to pay a solemn promise because both of these things are detestable to the LORD your God.

Charging interest

¹⁹Don't charge your fellow Israelites interest—whether on money, provisions, or anything one might loan. ²⁰You can charge foreigners interest, but not your fellow Israelite. Do this so that the LORD your God blesses you in all your work on the land you are entering to possess.

Solemn promise

²¹When you make a promise to the LORD your God, don't put off making good on it, because the LORD your God will certainly be expecting it from you; delaying would make you guilty. ²²Now if you simply don't make any promises, you won't be guilty of anything. ²³But whatever you say, you should be sure to make good on, exactly according to the promise you freely made to the LORD your God because you promised it with your own mouth.

Neighbor's goods

²⁴If you go into your neighbor's vineyard, you can eat as many grapes as you like, until full, but don't carry any away in a basket. ²⁵If you go into your neighbor's grain field, you can pluck ears by hand, but you aren't allowed to cut off any of your neighbor's grain with a sickle.

Marriage and divorce

24 Let's say a man marries a woman, but she isn't pleasing to him because he's discovered something inappropriate about her. So he writes up divorce papers, hands them to her, and sends her out of his house. ²She leaves his house and ends up marrying someone else. ³But this new husband also dislikes her, writes up divorce papers, hands them to her, and sends her out of his house (or suppose the second husband dies). ⁴In this case, the first husband who originally divorced this woman is not allowed to take her back and marry her again after she has been polluted in this way because the LORD detests that. Don't pollute the land the LORD your God is giving to you as an inheritance.

⁵A newly married man doesn't have to march in battle. Neither should any related duties be placed on him. He is to live free of such responsibilities for one year, so he can bring joy to his new wife.

ᶻLXX, Syr, Vulg *place of the hand* (a euphemism); MT has only *hand*. ᵃTraditionally *cultic prostitute* ᵇTraditionally *cultic prostitute* ᶜOr *a dog*

Pawning

[6] Millstones or even just the upper millstone must not be pawned, because that would be pawning someone's livelihood.

Kidnapping

[7] If someone is caught kidnapping their fellow Israelites, intending to enslave the Israelite or sell them, that kidnapper must die. Remove[d] such evil from your community!

Skin disease

[8] Be on guard against outbreaks of skin disease[e] by being very careful about what you do. You must carefully do everything the levitical priests teach you, just as I have commanded them. [9] Remember, after all, what the LORD your God did to Miriam on your departure from Egypt!

Loans

[10] When you make any type of loan to your neighbor, don't enter their house to receive the collateral. [11] You must wait outside. The person to whom you are lending will bring the collateral to you out there. [12] Moreover, if the person is poor, you are not allowed to sleep in their pawned coat. [13] Instead, be certain to give the pawned coat back by sunset so they can sleep in their own coat. They will bless you, and you will be considered righteous before the LORD your God.

Payment for workers

[14] Don't take advantage of poor or needy workers, whether they are fellow Israelites or immigrants who live in your land or your cities. [15] Pay them their salary the same day, before the sun sets, because they are poor, and their very life depends on that pay, and so they don't cry out against you to the LORD. That would make you guilty.

Generational punishment

[16] Parents shouldn't be executed because of what their children have done; neither should children be executed be-cause of what their parents have done. Each person should be executed for their own guilty acts.

Rights of widows, orphans, and immigrants

[17] Don't obstruct the legal rights of an immigrant or orphan. Don't take a widow's coat as pledge for a loan. [18] Remember how you were a slave in Egypt but how the LORD your God saved you from that. That's why I'm commanding you to do this thing.

[19] Whenever you are reaping the harvest of your field and you leave some grain in the field, don't go back and get it. Let it go to the immigrants, the orphans, and the widows so that the LORD your God blesses you in all that you do. [20] Similarly, when you beat the olives off your olive trees, don't go back over them twice. Let the leftovers go to the immigrants, the orphans, and the widows. [21] Again, when you pick the grapes of your vineyard, don't pick them over twice. Let the leftovers go to the immigrants, the orphans, and the widows. [22] Remember how you were a slave in Egypt. That's why I am commanding you to do this thing.

Corporal punishment

25 Now two people have a disagreement and they enter into litigation and their case is decided, with the judges declaring one person legally right and the other legally liable. [2] If the guilty party is to be beaten, the presiding judge will have that person lie down and be punished in his presence—the number of blows in measure with the guilt determined. [3] Give no more than forty blows. If more than that is given, your fellow Israelite would be completely disgraced in your eyes.

Working oxen

[4] Don't muzzle an ox while it is threshing grain.

The brother-in-law's duty

[5] If brothers live together and one of them dies without having a son, the dead

---

[d] Or *burn* [e] Heb uncertain; traditionally *leprosy*—a term used for several different skin diseases

man's wife must not go outside the family and marry a stranger. Instead, her brother-in-law should go to her and take her as his wife. He will then consummate the marriage according to the brother-in-law's duty. [6]The brother-in-law will name the oldest male son that she bears after his dead brother so that his brother's legacy will not be forgotten in Israel. [7]If the brother does not want to marry his sister-in-law, she can go to the elders at the city gate, informing them: "My brother-in-law refuses to continue his brother's legacy in Israel. He's not willing to perform the brother-in-law's duty with me." [8]The city's elders will summon him and talk to him about this. If he doesn't budge, insisting, "I don't want to marry her," [9]then the sister-in-law will approach him while the elders watch. She will pull the sandal off his foot and spit in his face. Then she will exclaim: "That's what's done to any man who won't build up his own brother's family!" [10]Subsequently, that man's family will be known throughout Israel as "the house of the removed sandal."

Improper touching

[11]If two men are fighting with each other—a man and his fellow Israelite—and the wife of one of them gets into the fight, trying to save her husband from his attacker and does so by reaching out and grabbing his genitals, [12]you must cut off her hand. Show no mercy.

Honest business practices

[13]Don't have two different types of money weights in your bag, a heavy one and a light one. [14]Don't have two different types of ephahs in your house, a large one and a small one. [15]Instead, you must have only one weight, complete and correct, and only one ephah, also complete and correct, so that your life might be long in the fertile land the LORD your God is giving you. [16]What's more, all who do such things, all who do business dishonestly, are detestable to the LORD your God. [17]Remember, after all, what Amalek did to you on your departure from Egypt: [18]how he met up with you on the way, striking from behind those who were lagging back because you were weak and tired, and because he didn't fear God. [19]So once the LORD your God gives you relief from all the enemies that surround you in the land the LORD your God is giving you as an inheritance to possess, you must wipe out Amalek's memory from under the heavens. Don't forget this!

The ceremony upon entering the land

26 Once you have entered the land the LORD your God is giving you as an inheritance, and you take possession of it and are settled there, [2]take some of the early produce of the fertile ground that you have harvested from the land the LORD your God is giving you, and put it in a basket. Then go to the location the LORD your God selects for his name to reside. [3]Go to

SANDALS AND SHOES

Basic footwear consisted of a sturdy leather sole tied to the foot or ankle (Mark 1:7). More serviceable sandals with leggings were used during construction work or heavy labor, although slaves generally were forced to go barefoot. The well-dressed individual was one who had quality sandals (Song 7:1 [Heb. 7:2]; Ezek 16:10). However, since sandals protected the feet and walked through the debris associated with the secular world, they were to be removed when one wished to enter sacred space (Exod 3:5; Josh 5:15; Acts 7:33).

the priest who is in office at that time and say to him: "I am declaring right now before the LORD my[f] God that I have indeed arrived in the land the LORD swore to our ancestors to give us."

[4] The priest will then take the basket from you and place it before the LORD your God's altar. [5] Then you should solemnly state before the LORD your God:

"My father was a starving Aramean. He went down to Egypt, living as an immigrant there with few family members, but that is where he became a great nation, mighty and numerous. [6] The Egyptians treated us terribly, oppressing us and forcing hard labor on us. [7] So we cried out for help to the LORD, our ancestors' God. The LORD heard our call. God saw our misery, our trouble, and our oppression. [8] The LORD brought us out of Egypt with a strong hand and an outstretched arm, with awesome power, and with signs and wonders. [9] He brought us to this place and gave us this land—a land full of milk and honey. [10] So now I am bringing the early produce of the fertile ground that you, LORD, have given me."

Set the produce before the LORD your God, bowing down before the LORD your God. [11] Then celebrate all the good things the LORD your God has done for you and your family—each one of you along with the Levites and the immigrants who are among you.

[12] When you have finished paying the entire tenth part of your produce on the third year—that is the year for paying the tenth-part—you will give it to the Levites, the immigrants, the orphans, and the widows so they can eat in your cities until they are full. [13] Then announce before the LORD your God: "I have removed the holy portion from my[g] house, and I have given it to the Levites, the immigrants, the orphans, and the widows—in full compliance with your entire commandment that you commanded me. I haven't broken your commandments. I haven't forgotten one! [14] I haven't eaten from the holy portion

while mourning, nor did I remove it while I was polluted, nor have I dedicated any of it to the dead. I've obeyed the LORD my God's voice. I've done everything just as you commanded me. [15] Please look down from your holy home, from heaven itself, and bless your people Israel and the fertile land that you have given us—a land full of milk and honey—just like you promised our ancestors."

Conclusion to the regulations and case laws

[16] This very moment the LORD your God is commanding you to keep these regulations and case laws. So keep them and do them with all your mind and with your entire being! [17] Today you have affirmed that the LORD will be your God and that you will walk in his ways and follow his regulations, his commandments, and his case laws, and that you will obey his voice. [18] Today the LORD has gotten your agreement[h] that you will be his treasured people, just like he promised—by keeping his commandments—[19] in order to set you high above all the other nations that he made in praise, fame, and honor; and so that you are a people holy to the LORD your God, just as he said you would be.

Stones of the Instruction

27 Then Moses and Israel's elders commanded the people:

Keep all of the commandment that I am giving you right now. [2] The same day you cross the Jordan River to enter the land the LORD your God is giving you, set up large stones and cover them with plaster. [3] Once you have crossed over, write on the stones all the words of this Instruction because you will have entered[i] the land the LORD your God is giving to you—a land full of milk and honey—exactly as the LORD, your ancestors' God, promised you. [4] Once you have crossed over the Jordan River, set up these stones that I'm telling you about right now on Mount Ebal. Cover

---

[f] LXX; MT and most versions read *your*.   [g] LXX, Vulg; MT lacks *my*.   [h] Heb uncertain   [i] Or *in order that you might enter*; Heb uncertain

them with plaster ⁵and build an altar there for the LORD your God—an altar of stones that haven't been cut with iron tools. ⁶(You must build the LORD your God's altar with uncut stones.) Then offer up on that altar entirely burned sacrifices to the LORD your God. ⁷Offer up well-being sacrifices and eat them there, celebrating in the LORD your God's presence. ⁸Make sure to write all the words of this Instruction on the stones plainly and clearly.

⁹Then Moses and the levitical priests said to all Israel: Quiet down and listen, Israel! This very moment you have become the people of the LORD your God. ¹⁰So obey the LORD your God's voice. Do his commandments and his regulations that I'm giving you right now.

Ceremony on Mount Gerizim and Mount Ebal

¹¹That same day Moses commanded the people: ¹²Once you have crossed over the Jordan River, the following tribes will stand on Mount Gerizim to bless the people: Simeon, Levi, Judah, Issachar, Joseph, and Benjamin. ¹³And these are the tribes that will stand on Mount Ebal for the cursing: Reuben, Gad, Asher, Zebulun, Dan, and Naphtali. ¹⁴The Levites will address every individual Israelite with a loud voice:

¹⁵"Cursed is anyone who makes an idol or an image—things detestable to the LORD, made by artisans—and sets it up secretly."

All the people will reply: "We agree!"ʲ

¹⁶"Cursed is anyone who belittles their father or mother."

All the people will reply: "We agree!"

¹⁷"Cursed is anyone who tampers with their neighbor's property lines."

All the people will reply: "We agree!"

¹⁸"Cursed is anyone who misleads a blind person on a road."

All the people will reply: "We agree!"

¹⁹"Cursed is anyone who obstructs the legal rights of immigrants, orphans, or widows."

All the people will reply: "We agree!"

²⁰"Cursed is anyone who has sex with his father's wife, because that exposes his father's private matters."ᵏ

All the people will reply: "We agree!"

²¹"Cursed is anyone who has sex with any kind of animal."

All the people will reply: "We agree!"

²²"Cursed is anyone who has sex with his sister, whether his father's daughter or his mother's daughter."

All the people will reply: "We agree!"

²³"Cursed is anyone who has sex with his mother-in-law."

All the people will reply: "We agree!"

²⁴"Cursed is anyone who kills his neighbor in secret."

All the people will reply: "We agree!"

²⁵"Cursed is anyone who accepts money to kill an innocent person."

All the people will reply: "We agree!"

²⁶"Cursed is anyone who doesn't support the words of this Instruction by carrying them out."

All the people will reply: "We agree!"

Future blessing

28 Now if you really obey the LORD your God's voice, by carefully keeping all his commandments that I am giving you right now, then the LORD your God will set you high above all nations on earth. ²All these blessings will come upon you and find you if you obey the LORD your God's voice: ³You will be blessed in the city and blessed in the field. ⁴Your own fertility, your soil's produce, and your livestock's offspring—the young of both cattle and flocks—will be blessed. ⁵Your basket and your kneading bowl will be blessed. ⁶You will be blessed when you are out and about and blessed when you come back. ⁷The LORD will defeat any enemies who attack you. They will come against you from one direction but will run for their lives away from you in seven different directions. ⁸The LORD will command the blessing to be with you—in your barns and on all the work you do—and he will bless you on the land the LORD your God is giving you. ⁹The LORD will establish you as his own, a holy nation, just as he swore to

---

ʲHeb *Amen*; also in the following verses   ᵏOr *because that uncovers his father's skirt* you, if you keep the LORD your God's commandments and walk in his ways. [10]All the earth's peoples will see that you are called by the LORD's name, and they will be in awe of you. [11]The LORD will make good things abound for you—whether the fertility of your womb, your livestock's offspring, or your fertile soil's produce—on the very land that the LORD swore to your ancestors to give to you. [12]The LORD will open up for you his own well-stocked storehouse, the heavens, providing your land with rain at just the right time and blessing all your work. You will lend to many nations, but you won't have any need to borrow. [13]The LORD will make you the head of things, not the tail; you will be at the top of things, not the bottom, as long as you obey the LORD your God's commandments that I'm commanding you right now, by carefully doing them. [14]Don't deviate even a bit from any of these words that I'm commanding you right now by following other gods and serving them.

Future curses

[15]But if you don't obey the LORD your God's voice by carefully doing all his commandments and his regulations that I am commanding you right now, all these curses will come upon you and find you. [16]You will be cursed in the city and cursed in the field. [17]Your basket and kneading bowl will be cursed. [18]Your own fertility, your soil's produce, your cattle's young, and your flock's offspring will be cursed. [19]You will be cursed when you are out and about and cursed when you come back. [20]The LORD will send calamity, confusion, and frustration on you no matter what work you are doing until you are wiped out and until you disappear—it'll be quick!—because of the evil acts by which you have abandoned him.[l] [21]The LORD will make a plague stick to you until he has totally wiped you off the fertile land you are entering to possess. [22]The LORD will strike you with consumption, fever, and inflammation; with scorching heat and

drought;[m] with destruction and disease for your crops.[n] These things will chase you until you are dead and gone. [23]The sky over your head will be as hard as bronze; the earth under your feet will be like iron. [24]The LORD will turn the rain on your land into dust. Only dirt will fall down on you from the sky until you are completely wiped out. [25]The LORD will hand you over defeated to your enemies. You will go out against them by one direction, but you will run for your life away from them in seven different directions. All the earth's kingdoms will be horrified by you. [26]Your corpses will be food for every bird in the sky and animal on earth; no one will frighten them off. [27]The LORD will afflict you with Egyptian inflammation, hemorrhoids,[o] rash, and itch. You will be untreatable. [28]The LORD will make you go crazy, make you blind, make your mind confused. [29]You will fumble around at high noon as blind people fumble around in darkness. Your plans won't prosper. Instead, you will be constantly oppressed and taken advantage of without any savior. [30]You might get engaged to a woman, but another man will have sex with her. You might build a house, but you won't get to live in it. You might plant a vineyard, but you won't enjoy it. [31]Your ox will be slaughtered while you watch, but you won't get to eat any of it. Your donkey will be stolen right out from under you, and it won't come back. Your flocks will be given to your enemies. No one will save you. [32]Your sons and daughters will be given to another nation while you watch; you will long for them constantly, but you won't have the power to do anything about it. [33]The produce of your land and all your hard work will be consumed by people you don't know. You will be nothing but oppressed and mistreated constantly. [34]The sights your eyes see will drive you insane. [35]The LORD will strike you with horrible inflammation in your knees and legs, from the sole of your foot to the top of your head. You will be untreatable. [36]The LORD will send you and the king

---

[l]Or me, in which case the text shifts to direct divine discourse.   [m]Heb uncertain   [n]Or blight and mildew
[o]Qere; Kethib tumors

that you appoint over you far away to a nation that neither you nor your ancestors have known. There you will worship other gods made of wood and stone. [37]You will become a horror, fit only for use in proverbs and in insults by all the nations where the LORD drives you. [38]You might scatter a lot of seed on the field, but you will gather almost nothing because the locusts will eat it all. [39]You might plant lots of vineyards and work hard in them, but you won't drink any wine or harvest the grapes because worms will devour them. [40]You might have many olive trees throughout your territories, but you won't cover yourself with their oil because your olive trees will fail. [41]You might have sons and daughters, but they won't be yours for long because they will be taken away as prisoners. [42]Crickets will take over all your trees and your soil's produce. [43]The immigrants who live among you will be promoted over you, higher and higher! But you will be demoted, lower and lower! [44]They will lend to you, but you will have nothing to lend to them. They will be the head of things; you will be the tail.

[45]That's how all these curses will come over you, pursuing you, reaching you until you are completely wiped out, because you didn't obey the LORD your God's voice by keeping his commandments and his regulations that he gave you. [46]These things will be a sign and a wonder on you and your descendants forever. [47]Because you didn't serve the LORD your God joyfully and gladly above all else,[P] [48]you will serve your enemies—the ones the LORD will send against you—during famine, drought, nakedness, and total depravation. God will put an iron yoke on your neck until he has wiped you out. [49]The LORD will bring a distant nation—one from the far ends of the earth—against you as fast as the eagle flies: a nation that speaks a language you can't understand, [50]a stern nation that doesn't go easy on the very old or show pity to the very young. [51]That nation will devour your livestock's offspring and your soil's produce until you yourselves are destroyed because

you will have no grain, wine, or oil left—nor any young from your cattle or offspring from your flocks—that is, until that nation annihilates you. [52]That nation will attack you in all your cities until your high, reinforced walls that you thought were so safe fall down across your entire countryside. That nation will attack you in all your cities throughout the land the LORD your God has given you. [53]You will eat the offspring of your own womb—the flesh of your own sons and daughters, whom the LORD your God gave you—because of the desperate and dire circumstances that your enemy has brought on you.

[54]Even the most gentle and refined man among you will scowl at his brother or his own dear wife, or the last of his surviving children. [55]He won't want to give them any of his children's flesh that he will be eating because he has no other food due to the desperate and dire circumstances that your enemy has brought on you in all your cities. [56]Even the most gentle and refined woman among you, who is so refined and gentle she wouldn't stomp her foot on the ground, will scowl at her own dear husband, her son, or her daughter—[57]not wanting to give them any of the afterbirth she pushed out or the babies she bore, because she will be eating them secretly while starving due to the desperate and dire circumstances that your enemy will bring on you in your cities.

[58]If you don't carefully keep all the words of this Instruction that are written in this scroll, by fearing the awesome and glorious name of the LORD your God—[59]the LORD will overwhelm you and your descendants with severe and chronic afflictions, and with terrible and untreatable sicknesses. [60]He'll put on you all the Egyptian diseases about which you were so afraid; they will stick to you! [61]What's more, the LORD will bring on you all the other diseases and plagues that aren't written in this Instruction scroll until you are completely wiped out. [62]Once as countless as the stars in the night sky, only a few of you will be left alive—all because you didn't

PHeb uncertain

obey the LORD your God's voice. ⁶³And just as before, the LORD enjoyed doing good things for you and increasing your numbers, now the LORD will enjoy annihilating and destroying you. You will be torn off the very fertile land you are entering to possess. ⁶⁴The LORD will scatter you among every nation, from one end of the earth to the other. There you will serve other gods that neither you nor your ancestors have known—gods of wood and stone. ⁶⁵Among those nations you will have no rest and no place to call your own.�q There the LORD will give you an agitated mind, failing eyes, and a depressed spirit. ⁶⁶Your life will seem to dangle before your very eyes. You will be afraid night and day. You won't be able to count on surviving for long. ⁶⁷In the morning you will say: "I wish it was nighttime," but at nighttime you will say, "I wish it was morning"—on account of your tortured mind, which will be terrified, and because of the horrible sights that your eyes will see. ⁶⁸Finally, the LORD will take you back to Egypt in ships, by the route I promised you would never see again. There you will try to sell yourselves as slaves—both male and female—but no one will want to buy you.

The third heading:
The new covenant at Moab

29 ¹These are the words of the covenant the LORD commanded Moses to make with the Israelites in the land of Moab in addition to the covenant he had made with them at Horeb. ²ˢMoses summoned all Israel, saying to them:

You've seen with your own eyes everything the LORD did in Egypt, to Pharaoh, his servants, and all his land—³the great trials your eyes witnessed, those awesome signs and wonders! ⁴But until this very moment, the LORD hasn't given you insight to understand, eyes to see, or ears to hear. ⁵I've led you in the wilderness forty years now; neither the clothes on your back nor the sandals on your feet have worn out.

⁶Neither have you eaten bread nor drunk wine or beer during this time—so that you would know that I am the LORD your God.ᵗ ⁷When you arrived here, Sihon, Heshbon's king, and Og, Bashan's king, marched out to fight against us, but we defeated them. ⁸We took possession of their land and gave it as an inheritance to the Reubenites, Gadites, and half of Manasseh's tribe. ⁹So then keep the words of this covenant and do them so you can succeed in all you do.

¹⁰Right now, all of you are in the presence of the LORD your God—the leaders of your tribes,ᵘ your elders, and your officials, all the Israelite males, ¹¹your children, your wives, and the immigrants who live with you in your camp, the ones who chop your wood and those who draw your water— ¹²ready to enter into the LORD your God's covenant and into the agreement that the LORD your God is making with you right now. ¹³That means the Lord will make you his own people right now—he will be your God just as he promised you and just as he swore to our ancestors: to Abraham, Isaac, and Jacob. ¹⁴But I'm not making this covenant and this agreement with you alone ¹⁵but also with those standing here with us right now before the LORD our God, and also with those who aren't here with us right now.

¹⁶You know firsthand how we used to live in Egypt and how we passed right through the nations that you passed through. ¹⁷You saw the horrific things, the filthy idols of wood and stone, silver and gold, that they had with them. ¹⁸Make sure there isn't any one among you right now—male or female, clan or tribe—whose mind is turning from being with the LORD our God in favor of going to serve these nations' gods. Make sure there isn't any root among you that is sprouting poison and bitterness. ¹⁹When that kind of person hears the words of this agreement, they congratulate themselves, thinking: I'll be fine even though I insist on being stubborn. This would cause something wet to dry up and become like

�q Or resting place for the sole of your foot　ʳ 28:69 in Heb　ˢ 29:1 in Heb　ᵗ Or that I, the LORD, am your God.
ᵘ LXX, Syr; MT your leaders, your tribes

something parched.[v] [20]The LORD won't be willing to forgive that kind of person; instead, the LORD's anger and passion will smolder against that person. Every curse written in this scroll will stretch out over them, and the LORD will wipe out their name from under the heavens. [21]Out of all Israel's tribes, the LORD will single them out for disaster in compliance with all the covenant curses that are written in this Instruction scroll.

[22]Future generations, your children after you, or foreigners from distant lands will say: Look[w] at all that land's plagues and the sicknesses that the LORD laid on it! [23]Look at all its land burned by sulfur and salt, unsuitable for planting, unable to grow or produce any vegetation, as devastated as Sodom and Gomorrah, Admah and Zeboiim, which the LORD devastated in anger and wrath! [24]Indeed, all nations will ask: Why did the LORD do this to this land? What led to this terrible display of anger? [25]They will deduce: It was because those people abandoned the covenant of the LORD, their ancestors' God, which he made with them when he brought them out of Egypt. [26]They followed other gods, serving them and worshipping them—other gods that they hadn't experienced before and that the Lord hadn't designated for them. [27]Then the LORD's anger burned against that land, and he brought against it every curse written in this scroll. [28]The LORD ripped them off their land in anger, wrath, and great fury. He threw them into other lands, and that's how things still stand today.

[29]The secret things belong to the LORD our God. The revealed things belong to us and to our children forever: to keep all the words of this covenant.

30 Now, once all these things happen to you, the blessing and the curse that I'm setting before you, you must call them to mind as you sit among the various nations where the LORD your God has driven you; [2]and you must return to the LORD your God, obeying his voice, in line with all that I'm commanding you right now—you and your children—with all your mind and with all your being. [3]Then the LORD your God will restore you as you were before and will have compassion on you, gathering you up from all the peoples where the LORD your God scattered you. [4]Even if he has driven you to the far end of heaven, the LORD your God will gather you up from there; he will take you back from there. [5]The LORD your God will bring you home to the land that your ancestors possessed; you will possess it again. And he will do good things for you and multiply you— making you more numerous even than your ancestors!

[6]Then the LORD your God will circumcise your hearts and the hearts of your descendants so that you love the LORD your God with all your mind and with all your being in order that you may live. [7]The LORD your God will put all these curses on your enemies and on those who hate you and chase you. [8]But you will change and obey the LORD's voice and do all his commandments that I'm commanding you right now. [9]The LORD your God will help you succeed in everything you do—in your own fertility, your livestock's offspring, and your land's produce—everything will be great! Because the LORD will once again enjoy doing good things for you just as he enjoyed doing them for your ancestors, [10]and because you will be obeying the LORD your God's voice, keeping his commandments and his regulations that are written in this Instruction scroll, and because you will have returned to the LORD your God with all your heart and all your being.

[11]This commandment that I'm giving you right now is definitely not too difficult for you. It isn't unreachable. [12]It isn't up in heaven somewhere so that you have to ask, "Who will go up for us to heaven and get it for us that we can hear it and do it?" [13]Nor is it across the ocean somewhere so that you have to ask, "Who will cross the

---

[v]Heb uncertain; perhaps the agricultural imagery of 29:18 is continued here or the terms are metaphors for human states. [w]Or *after they see*

ocean for us and get it for us that we can hear it and do it?" [14]Not at all! The word is very close to you. It's in your mouth and in your heart, waiting for you to do it.

Life and death

[15]Look here! Today I've set before you life and what's good versus death and what's wrong. [16]If you obey the LORD your God's commandments that[x] I'm commanding you right now by loving the LORD your God, by walking in his ways, and by keeping his commandments, his regulations, and his case laws, then you will live and thrive, and the LORD your God will bless you in the land you are entering to possess. [17]But if your heart turns away and you refuse to listen, and so are misled, worshipping other gods and serving them, [18]I'm telling you right now that you will definitely die. You will not prolong your life on the fertile land that you are crossing the Jordan River to enter and possess. [19]I call heaven and earth as my witnesses against you right now: I have set life and death, blessing and curse before you. Now choose life—so that you and your descendants will live—[20]by loving the LORD your God, by obeying his voice, and by clinging to him. That's how you will survive and live long on the fertile land the LORD swore to give to your ancestors: to Abraham, Isaac, and Jacob.

Moses announces his death

31 Then Moses said[y] these words to all Israel, [2]telling them:

I'm 120 years old today. I can't move around well anymore. Plus, the LORD told me "You won't cross the Jordan River." [3]But the LORD your God, he's the one who will cross over before you! He's the one who will destroy these nations before you so you can displace them. Joshua too will cross over before you just like the LORD indicated. [4]The LORD will do to these enemies the same thing he did to the Amorite kings Sihon and Og, and to their land, when he destroyed them. [5]The LORD will lay them out before you, and you will do to them exactly what the command I've given you dictates. [6]Be strong! Be fearless! Don't be afraid and don't be scared by your enemies, because the LORD your God is the one who marches with you. He won't let you down, and he won't abandon you.

[7]Then Moses called Joshua and, with all Israel watching, said to him: "Be strong and fearless because you are the one who will lead[z] this people to the land the LORD swore to their ancestors to give to them; you are the one who will divide up the land for them. [8]But the LORD is the one who is marching before you! He is the one who will be with you! He won't let you down. He won't abandon you. So don't be afraid or scared!"

Regular reading of the Instruction

[9]Then Moses wrote this Instruction down and gave it to the priests—the Levites who carry the chest containing the LORD's covenant—and to all of the Israelite elders. [10]Moses then commanded them:

At the end of seven years, at the appointed time in the year of debt cancellation, during the Festival of Booths, [11]when all Israel comes to appear before the LORD your God at the location he selects, you must read this Instruction aloud, in the hearing of all the people. [12]Gather everyone—men, women, children, and the immigrants who live in your cities—in order that they hear it, learn it, and revere the LORD your God, carefully doing all the words of this Instruction, [13]and so that their children, who don't yet know the Instruction, may hear it and learn to revere the LORD your God for as long as you live on the ground you are crossing the Jordan River to possess.

Joshua commissioned

[14]Then the LORD said to Moses: "It's almost time for you to die. Summon Joshua. The two of you must present yourselves at the meeting tent so I can command him."

---

[x]LXX; MT lacks *if you obey the LORD your God's commandments.* [y]LXX, DSS (1QDeut[b]) *When Moses had finished speaking* [z]Sam, Vulg, Syr; MT, Tg *accompany*

So Moses and Joshua went and presented themselves at the meeting tent. [15]The LORD appeared in the tent in a pillar of cloud; the cloud pillar stood at the tent's entrance. [16]The LORD then said to Moses:

"Soon you will rest with your ancestors, and the people will rise up and act unfaithfully, going after strange gods of the land they are entering. They will abandon me, breaking my covenant that I made with them. [17]At that point my anger will burn against them, and I'll be the one who abandons them! I'll hide my face from them. They will become nothing but food for their enemies,[a] and all sorts of bad things and misfortunes will happen to them. Then they will say: 'Haven't these terrible things happened to us because our God is no longer with us?' [18]But I will hide my face at that time because of the many wrong things they have done, because they have turned to other gods! [19]So in light of all that, you must write down this poem and teach it to the Israelites. Put it in their mouths so that the poem becomes a witness for me against them. [20]When I bring the Israelites to the land I swore to their ancestors, which is full of milk and honey, and they eat, get full, then fat, and then turn toward other gods, serving them and disrespecting me and breaking my covenant, [21]then, when all kinds of bad things and misfortunes happen to them, this poem will witness against them, giving its testimony, because it won't be lost from the mouths of their descendants. Yes, I know right now what they are inclined to do, even before I've brought them into the land I swore."

[22]So Moses wrote this poem down that very day, and he taught it to the Israelites.

[23]Then the Lord commissioned Joshua, Nun's son: "Be strong and fearless because you are the one who will bring the Israelites to the land I swore to them. I myself will be with you."

Life after Moses

[24]Once Moses had finished writing in their entirety all the words of this Instruction scroll, [25]he commanded the Levites who carry the chest containing the LORD's covenant as follows:

[26]"Take this Instruction scroll and put it next to the chest containing the LORD your God's covenant. It must remain there as a witness against you [27]because I know how rebellious and hardheaded you are. If you are this rebellious toward the LORD while I'm still alive, it's bound to get worse once I'm dead! [28]Assemble all of your tribes' elders and your officials in front of me, so I can speak these words in their hearing, and

---

[a]Heb lacks *for their enemies.*

JOSHUA

The political successor to Moses and the commander who leads the Israelite invasion of Canaan. Joshua, described as the assistant of Moses and one of his "assembled seventy men" (Num 11:24, 28), is put in command of the Israelite defensive action against the Amalekites at Rephidim (Exod 17:9). As they approach the land of Canaan, Moses includes Joshua among the spies sent to scout the land and to gauge the possibility of capturing the region from its inhabitants (Num 13:16-20). As the desert wanderings come to a close, God tells Moses to pass "some of" his power to Joshua "so that the entire Israelite community may obey" (Num 27:20). Moses commissions Joshua in this position of authority by placing his hands on him in front of the entire congregation. This is a sign of transferring identity and authority, as in the hand-laying ceremony in the purification offering (e.g., Lev 4:15).

so I can call heaven and earth as my witnesses against them, ²⁹because I know that after I'm dead, you will ruin everything, departing from the path I've commanded you. Terrible things will happen to you in the future because you will do evil in the LORD's eyes, aggravating him with the things your hands have made."

The poem of Instruction

³⁰Then Moses recited in their entirety the words of this poem in the hearing of the entire assembly of Israel:

32 Heaven! Pay attention
and I will speak;
Earth! Listen to the words of my mouth.
² My teaching will fall like raindrops;
my speech will settle like dew—
like gentle rains on grass,
like spring showers on all that is green—
³ because I proclaim the LORD's name:
Give praise to our God!

⁴ The rock: his acts are perfection!
No doubt about it: all his ways are right!
He's the faithful God, never deceiving;
altogether righteous and true is he.
⁵ But children who weren't his own[b]
sinned against him with their defects;[c]
they are a twisted
and perverse generation.
⁶ Is this how you thank the LORD,
you stupid, senseless people?
Isn't he your father, your creator?
Didn't he make you and establish you?

⁷ Remember the days long past;
consider the years long gone.
Ask your father,
he will tell you about it;
ask your elders,
they will give you the details:
⁸ When God Most High
divided up the nations—
when he divided up humankind—
he decided the people's boundaries
based on the number of the gods.[d]

⁹ Surely the LORD's property
was his people;
Jacob was his part of the inheritance.
¹⁰ God found[e] Israel in a wild land—
in a howling desert wasteland—
he protected him, cared for him,
watched over him with his very own eye.
¹¹ Like an eagle protecting its nest,
hovering over its young,
God spread out his wings,
took hold of Israel,
carried him on his back.
¹² The LORD alone led Israel;
no foreign god assisted.
¹³ God[f] made Israel[g] glide over the highlands;
he fed him[h] with food from the field,
nursed him with honey from a boulder,
with oil from a hard rock:
¹⁴ curds from the herd,
milk from the flock,
along with the best of lambs,
rams from Bashan, he-goats too,
along with the finest wheat—
and for drink,
wine from the juiciest grapes!

¹⁵ Jacob ate until he was stuffed;[i]
Jeshurun[j] got fat, then rebellious.[k]
It was you who got fat, thick, stubborn![l]

Jeshurun[m] gave up
on the God who made him,
thought the rock of his salvation
was worthless.
¹⁶ They made God[n] jealous
with strange gods,
aggravated him
with detestable things.
¹⁷ They sacrificed to demons, not to God,
to deities of which
they had no knowledge—
new gods only recently on the scene,
ones about which your ancestors
had never heard.[o]
¹⁸ You deserted[p] the rock that sired you;

[b]Heb uncertain [c]LXX, Vulg; Heb uncertain [d]DSS (4QDeut¹), LXX; MT *the Israelites* [e]Vulg, Syr, and others; Sam, LXX, Tg Onkelos *sustained him* [f]Or *he* [g]Or *him* [h]Sam, Syr, LXX, Tg; MT *he ate* [i]DSS (4QPhyl ⁿ), Sam, LXX; MT lacks *Jacob ate until he was stuffed.* [j]A poetic name for Israel; see also 33:5, 26. [k]Or *kicked* [l]Heb uncertain [m]Or *he* [n]Or *him* [o]Heb uncertain [p]LXX, Vulg; Heb uncertain

you forgot the God
who gave birth to you!

19 The LORD saw this and rejected
out of aggravation
his sons and his daughters.[q]

20 He said: I will hide my face from them—
I will see what becomes of them—
because they are a confused generation;
they are children lacking loyalty.

21 They provoked me with "no-gods,"
aggravated me with their pieces of junk.
So I am going to provoke them
with "No-People,"
aggravate them with a nation of fools.

22 A fire burns in me—
it will blaze to the depths of the grave;[r]
it will destroy the land and its crops;
it will blacken the base of the mountains.

23 I'll throw[s] on them
disaster after disaster;
I'll destroy them with my arrows:

24 devastating hunger, consuming plague,
bitter sickness.
I'll send animal fangs after them,
venom from dust crawlers too.

25 Outside, in the streets,
the sword will bereave!
Inside, in the safest room,
there will be terror
for young men and women,
nursing baby and senior citizen.

26 I thought about it:
I could have struck them down,[t]
erased them from human memory,

27 but their enemies' rage concerned me;
their opponents might misunderstand.
They might say, "Our strong hands,
not the LORD's, did all this,"

28 because they are not
a thoughtful nation;
they lack any insight.

29 If they had any wisdom,
they would understand this;
they would discern
what will become of them.

30 How could one person
chase off a thousand in battle?

How could two people make ten
thousand flee for their lives?
Only because their rock sold them off,
only because the LORD
handed them over!

31 But, no, their rocks
can't compare to our rock!
Our enemies are completely stupid.[u]

32 Their roots run straight from Sodom—
from the fields of Gomorrah!
Their grapes are pure poison;
their grape clusters, nothing but bitter;

33 their wine is snake poison,
venom from a cruel cobra.

34 Don't I have this stored up,
sealed in my vaults?

35 Revenge is my domain,
so is punishment-in-kind,
at the exact moment their step slips up,
because the day of their destruction
is just around the corner;
their final destiny is speeding on its way!

36 But the LORD will acquit his people,
will have compassion
on those who serve him,
once he sees that their strength
is all gone,
that both prisoners and free people
are wiped out.[v]

37 The Lord will ask, "Where are their gods—
the rocks they trusted in—

38 who ate up the fat of their sacrifices,
who drank their sacred wine?
They should stand up and help you!
They should protect you now!

39 Now, look here: I myself, I'm the one;
there are no other gods with me.
I'm the one who deals death
and gives life;
I'm the one who wounded,
but now I will heal.
There's no escaping my hand.

40 But now I'm lifting my hand to heaven—
I swear by my own eternity:

41 when I sharpen my blazing sword
and my hand grabs hold of justice,
I'll pay my enemies back;

---

[q]Or, following LXX, DSS (4QPhyl[n]), and correcting the LORD saw this and was jealous; he spurned his sons and daughters. [r]Heb Sheol [s]LXX [t]Heb uncertain; LXX scattered them [u]LXX; Heb uncertain [v]Heb uncertain

I'll punish in kind
    everyone who hates me.
⁴² I'll make my arrows drink much blood,
    while my sword devours flesh,
    the blood of the dead and captured,
    flowing from the heads
        of enemy generals."ʷ

⁴³ Heavens:ˣ Rejoice with God!ʸ
    All you gods: bow down to the Lord!ᶻ
    Because he will avenge
        his children'sᵃ blood;
    he will pay back his enemies;
    he will punish in kind
        those who hate him;ᵇ
    he will cleanse his people's land.ᶜ

⁴⁴ So Moses came and recited all the words of this poem in everyone's hearing; Joshua,ᵈ Nun's son, joined him. ⁴⁵When Moses finished speaking all these words to all Israel, ⁴⁶he told them: Set your mind on all these words I'm testifying against you right now, because you must command your children to perform carefully all the words of this Instruction. ⁴⁷This is no trivial matter for you—this is your very life! It is by this meansᵉ alone that you will prolong your life on the fertile land you are crossing the Jordan River to possess.

Moses' death imminent

⁴⁸The Lord spoke to Moses that very same day: ⁴⁹"Hike up the Abarim mountains, to Mount Nebo, which is in the land of Moab opposite Jericho. Take a good look at the land of Canaan, which I'm giving to the Israelites as their property. ⁵⁰You will die on the mountain you have hiked up, and you will be gathered to your people just like your brother Aaron, who died on Mount Hor and was gathered to his people, ⁵¹because the two of you were unfaithful toward me in front of the Israelites at the waters of Meribath-kadesh, in the Zin wilderness, because you didn't treat me with proper respect before the Israelites. ⁵²You can look at the land from the other side of the river,ᶠ but you won't enter there."ᵍ

The fourth heading: Moses' blessing

33 This is the blessing that Moses the man of God gave the Israelites before he died. ²He said:

The Lord came from Sinai:
    from Seir he shone
        like the dawn on us,ʰ
    from Paran Mountain
    he beamed down.
    Thousands of holy ones were with him;ⁱ
        his warriors were next to him, ready.ʲ
³ Yes, those who loveᵏ the nations—
    all his holy ones—
        were at your command;
    they followed your footsteps;
    they got moving when you said so.

⁴ Moses gave the Instruction to us—
    it's the prized possession
        of Jacob's assembly.
⁵ A king came to rule in Jeshurun,
    when the people's leaders
        gathered together,
    when Israel's tribes were one.

⁶ "I pray that Reuben lives, doesn't die,
    though his numbers are so few."

⁷ Moses said this to Judah:
    "Lord, listen to Judah's voice!
    Bring him back to his own people,
        strengthen his hands;ˡ
        be his help against every enemy."

⁸ Then he told Levi:
    "Give your Thummim to Levi,ᵐ
    your Urim to your faithful one—

ʷHeb uncertain ˣDSS (4QDeut�q), LXX; MT *nations* ʸDSS (4QDeut�q), LXX; MT *his people* ᶻThis line is missing in Heb; it is found in DSS (4QDeut�q); LXX *him for the Lord.* ᵃDSS (4QDeut�q), LXX; MT *his servants* ᵇDSS (4QDeut�q), LXX; MT lacks this line. ᶜSam, DSS (4QDeut�q), LXX, Vulg; MT *his land his people* or *his land for his people;* or, correcting, *he will wipe away his people's tears.* ᵈSam, Syr, Tg Neofiti; MT *Hoshea* ᵉOr *word* ᶠHeb lacks *of the river.* ᵍLXX; MT, Sam, Vulg, Syr, Tg add *to the land that I am giving to the Israelites* ʰCorrecting with LXX, Vulg, Syr, Tg Onkelos (see 33:4); MT and Sam *on them* ⁱCorrection; cf LXX, Sam, Syr, Vulg; MT *he came from Riboboth-kadesh* ʲLXX *angels;* Heb uncertain ᵏCorrection; MT *lover of* ˡOr *with his hands he contended* ᵐDSS (4QDeutʰ, 4QTest) and LXX; MT lacks *Give to Levi.*

the one you tested at Massah,
   the one you challenged
      by Meribah's waters;
9 the one who said
   of his own mother and father:
      'I don't consider them as such';
   of their siblings:
      'I don't recognize them';
   of their own children,
      'I don't know them'—
   but who obeyed your words
   and who guarded your covenant!
10 They teach your case laws to Jacob,
   your Instruction to Israel.
   They hold sweet incense to your nose;
   put the entirely burned offering
      on your altar.
11 I pray that the LORD
   blesses Levi's strength,
   favors his hard work,
   and crushes the insides
      of his enemies
   so that those who hate him
      can't fight anymore."
12 He said to Benjamin:
   "The LORD's dearest one
   rests safely on him.
   The Lord always shields him;
   he rests on God's chest."
13 Then he told Joseph:
   "I pray that his land is blessed by God:
   with heaven's gifts from above,ⁿ
   with the deep waters
      stretching out underneath;
14 with the gifts produced by the sun,
   with the gifts generated by the moon;ᵒ
15 with the best fruit
      from ancient mountains,
   with the gifts of eternal hills;
16 with the gifts of the earth
      and all that fills it,
   and the favor of the one
      who lives on Sinai.ᵖ

I pray that all these rest on Joseph's head,
   on the crown of that prince
      among brothers.
17 A firstborn bull�q—
   that's how majestic he is!
   A wild ox's horns—
      those are his horns!
   With them he gores all peoples
      completely, to the far ends of the earth!
   His hornsʳ are Ephraim's
      tens of thousands.
   His horns are Manasseh's thousands."
18 Then he told Zebulun:
   "Zebulun: celebrate
      when you are out and about;
   Issachar: celebrate when you are
      at home in your tents!
19 They call all sorts of people
      to the mountain,
   where they offer right sacrifices.
   It's true: They're nourished
      on the sea's abundance;
   they are nourished
      on buried treasures in the sand."
20 Then he told Gad:
   "May Gad's broad landsˢ be blessed!
   He lives like a lion:
   he rips an arm, even a head!
21 He chose the best part for himself
      because there, where the commander's
         portion was,
      the leaders of the people
         gathered together.ᵗ
   Gad executed the LORD's justice
   and the Lord's judgments for Israel."ᵘ
22 Then he told Dan:
   "Dan is a lion cub.
   He jumps up from Bashan."
23 Then he told Naphtali:
   "Naphtali—you are full of favor,
   overflowing with the LORD's blessing—
   go possess the west and the south!"

ⁿOr from the dew ᵒOr moons or months ᵖOr lives in a bush qSam, LXX, Vulg; DSS (4QDeutʰ) and Heb the oldest offspring of his bull ʳOr they; also in the next line ˢOr the one who makes Gad large ᵗCf LXX; MT there the commander's portion was reserved; he came at the front of the people or there was the portion of the respected commander; the people's leaders came. ᵘHeb uncertain

²⁴ Finally, he told Asher:
  "Asher is the most blessed of sons.
    I pray that he's his brothers' favorite—
    one who dips his foot in fine oil.
²⁵ I pray that your dead bolts
    are iron and copper,
    and that your strength
    lasts all your days."ᵛ

²⁶ Jeshurun! No one compares to God!
    He rides through heaven to help you,
      rides majestically through the clouds.
²⁷ The most ancient God
    is a place of safety;ʷ
    the eternal arms are a support.ˣ
  He drove out the enemy before you.
  He commanded: "Destroy them!"
²⁸ So Israel now lives in safety—
    Jacob's residenceʸ is secure—
    in a land full of grain and wine,
      where the heavens drip dew.

²⁹ Happy are you, Israel! Who is like you?
    You are a people saved by the LORD!
  He's the shield that helps you,
    your majestic sword!

Your enemies will come crawling
  on their knees to you,
    but you will stomp on their backs!ᶻ

Moses' death

34 Then Moses hiked up from the Moabite plains to Mount Nebo, the peak of the Pisgah slope, which faces Jericho. The LORD showed him the whole land: the Gilead region as far as Dan's territory; ²all the parts belonging to Naphtali along with the land of Ephraim and Manasseh, as well as the entirety of Judah as far as the Mediterranean Sea; ³also the arid southern plain, and the plain—including the Jericho Valley, Palm City—as far as Zoar.

⁴Then the LORD said to Moses: "This is the land that I swore to Abraham, Isaac, and Jacob when I promised: 'I will give it to your descendants.' I have shown it to you with your own eyes; however, you will not cross over into it."

⁵Then Moses, the LORD's servant, died—right there in the land of Moab, according to the LORD's command. ⁶The Lord buried him in a valley in Moabite country

---

ᵛHeb uncertain ʷOr *He humiliates the oldest gods.* ˣOr *He shatters the most ancient forces.* ʸOr *fountain*
ᶻOr *their shrines*

MOSES

Moses is the leader of the people of Israel as portrayed in the OT books of Exodus, Leviticus, Numbers, and Deuteronomy. He combines characteristics of the founding ruler, judge, lawgiver, scribe, teacher, prophet, intercessor, healer, and savior for Israel. He led Israel out of slavery in Egypt in the exodus (Exod 14–15). He had a uniquely close relationship with Israel's God, speaking directly with God "face-to-face" (Exod 33:11; Num 12:8; Deut 34:10). He transmitted the Ten Commandments and other laws from God on Mount Sinai to the Israelites (Exod 19–20). He led the runaway Israelite slaves from Egypt through 40 years of wandering until they reached the eastern boundary of the promised land of Canaan, a land he would see from a distance but not enter (Deut 34:4-5). He taught a new generation of young Israelites the essentials of their faith, leaving behind a written "Instruction" to be read and studied by each new generation (Deut 31:9-13). Moses has retained his prominence and importance in both Jewish and Christian imaginations throughout their history, extending as well to Islam and the wider culture up to modern times.

across from Beth-peor. Even now, no one knows where Moses' grave is.

⁷Moses was 120 years old when he died. His eyesight wasn't impaired, and his vigor hadn't diminished a bit.

⁸Back down in the Moabite plains, the Israelites mourned Moses' death for thirty days. At that point, the time for weeping and for mourning Moses was over.

⁹Joshua, Nun's son, was filled with wisdom because Moses had placed his hands

on him. So the Israelites listened to Joshua, and they did exactly what the LORD commanded Moses.

¹⁰No prophet like Moses has yet emerged in Israel; Moses knew the LORD face-to-face! ¹¹That's not even to mention all those signs and wonders that the LORD sent Moses to do in Egypt—to Pharaoh, to all his servants, and to his entire land—¹²as well as all the extraordinary power that Moses displayed before Israel's own eyes!

JOSHUA

The sixth book of our Bible is named for Joshua, the central figure in its story. That story is the story of Israel's conquest of Canaan. Joshua is a great leader in these events, yet he is not a hero in the usual sense. Joshua does not accomplish great deeds by his own ability. Instead, Joshua appears as God's instrument. It is God who is the real hero here.

Jews have traditionally classed Joshua as the first of the books called the Former Prophets (Joshua–2 Kings). These are not prophetic books as we know them, but they received the name for two reasons: (1) After a time, people began to call all great religious leaders prophets, and (2) these books reflect a prophetic view of history.

Christians, on the other hand, usually classify Joshua as a historical book, because Joshua tells the history of Israel's conquest and settlement of the promised land. More than that, though, this book tells of God's action in and through specific historical events. Joshua gives us both history and a religious interpretation of that history.

RELATIONSHIP TO OTHER BIBLICAL BOOKS

The book of Joshua stands as an essential part of the whole historical sequence sweeping from Genesis to Nehemiah. As one portion of the ongoing story of God's action in Israel's history, Joshua has strong ties to many biblical books. In Joshua we see God's fulfillment of the Genesis promises to Abraham. Joshua carries forth the themes of law and covenant so basic to the book of Exodus. Sometimes the man Joshua even appears as a parallel to the Exodus leader, Moses. The Psalms often mention the conquest story in poetic praise of God for mighty acts. As mentioned before, Joshua shares a religious viewpoint with many of the prophets. The book has its closest ties, however, with a literary unit that runs from Deuteronomy through 2 Kings. Style and theology show that this whole epic was probably written by one school of writers who maintained a standard outlook and formula for expression. So Joshua does not stand alone; it is part of a much larger biblical picture.

AUTHORSHIP

Literary and theological evidence show that someone (probably just one person) from the Deuteronomy–2 Kings school composed the final version of Joshua. We do not know this author's name. Instead, for convenience, we usually call any writer from this school "D" and say Joshua was written by D. It's not quite that simple, however. The book is now a well-organized whole, but there are signs that the author used many older sources for his work. He has blended together many stories, some of them ancient tribal traditions whose originators are unknown. This blending has left a few contradictions. For instance, in 4:8, twelve stones are carried out of the Jordan. But in 4:9, twelve stones are set up in the river. Either way, the writer still makes his point. His concern to glorify God comes through.

THEOLOGY

The book of Joshua shows us a God of unlimited power, justice, and grace. God acts in historical events of this world. Israel is God's chosen instrument in the world. Obedience to God's command gives Israel success; disobedience brings failure. God's promises are true and worthy of trust. The covenant is both God's gracious gift and Israel's moral responsibility.

For special reasons, God wants Israel to possess the land of Canaan. God has promised it and works with the faithful people to bring this about. The conquest is thus a gift, not Joshua's or Israel's achievement. God's will for the people is freedom and self-determination, and God follows through to give Israel a homeland.

Most of us probably find little quarrel with such a theology. Yet underneath there are some problems. One has been the over-simplification of the "obedience equals success" theory. Some have taken this belief to mean that (1) we can win God's favor by good works, or (2) that every misfortune is proof of sin. Seeing these problems, many have supposed that the writer was a shallow thinker who had perhaps not even considered the problem of innocent suffering. So they have written him off. But perhaps the writer was speaking only of the nation's long-term well-being, not of individual short-term events.

Another problem that often bothers readers of Joshua is the picture they see of God as a God of violence and bloodshed, a God who seems to advocate pure mayhem if it suits the divine purposes. Since this is not the God we know through Jesus, many simply dismiss Joshua as primitive religious fanaticism. Others suggest that Israel's religious understanding had just not developed far enough to see God as a God of consistent love toward everyone. But we must remember that peace was always offered before a town was destroyed. The writer may actually be expressing a much deeper thought: that this God is one who works through the people and institutions of this world as they are, good or evil. God uses war, even though it is evil, because God works with what is here, not what we might wish were here.

DATES

In Joshua there are two dates to consider: the date of the events and the date when the writer wrote them down.

The date of the events themselves is fairly clear. After the Exodus from Egypt and the wilderness wanderings, Israel finally established a home in Canaan. This probably happened in the late thirteenth century BCE.

The date of writing is more complex. We cannot tell how old the ancient sources may be. Scholars are fairly sure, however, that the final writing took place in the sixth or seventh century BCE. Most place it during the Babylonian Exile (587–538 BCE). Some commentators place the writing just before the fall of Jerusalem in 587 BCE. In either case we find that someone living 600 to 700 years after the event had determined to tie this story together, to preserve his nation's history, and to interpret that history in the light of faith.

JOSHUA

Orders from the LORD

1 After Moses the LORD's servant died, the LORD spoke to Joshua, Nun's son. He had been Moses' helper. ² "My servant Moses is dead. Now get ready to cross over the Jordan with this entire people to the land that I am going to give to the Israelites. ³ I am giving you every place where you set foot, exactly as I promised Moses. ⁴ Your territory will stretch from the desert and the Lebanon as far as the great Euphrates River, including all Hittite land, up to the Mediterranean Sea on the west. ⁵ No one will be able to stand up against you during your lifetime. I will be with you in the same way I was with Moses. I won't desert you or leave you. ⁶ Be brave and strong, because you are the one who will help this people take possession of the land, which I pledged to give to their ancestors.

⁷ "Be very brave and strong as you carefully obey all of the Instruction that Moses my servant commanded you. Don't deviate even a bit from it, either to the right or left. Then you will have success wherever you go. ⁸ Never stop speaking about this Instruction scroll. Recite it day and night so you can carefully obey everything written in it. Then you will accomplish your objectives and you will succeed. ⁹ I've commanded you to be brave and strong, haven't I? Don't be alarmed or terrified, because the LORD your God is with you wherever you go."

Joshua gives orders

¹⁰ Then Joshua gave orders to the people's officers: ¹¹ "Go through the camp and give orders to the people. Say, 'Get supplies ready for yourselves because in three days you will be crossing over the Jordan to enter the land and take it over. The LORD your God is going to give it to you as your possession.'"

¹² Then Joshua addressed the Reubenites, the Gadites, and half the tribe of Manasseh: ¹³ "Remember the command that Moses the LORD's servant gave you: 'The LORD your God will give you rest and give you this land.' ¹⁴ Your wives, children, and cattle may re-main in the land that Moses has given you on the east side of the Jordan. But all you brave fighters, organized for war, must cross over in front of your fellow Israelites. You must help them ¹⁵ until the LORD gives a rest like yours to your fellow Israelites and they too take possession of the land that the LORD your God is giving them. Then you may return and take over the land that belongs to you, which Moses the LORD's servant has given you on the east side of the Jordan."

¹⁶ They answered Joshua, "We will obey everything you have commanded us and go anywhere you send us. ¹⁷ We will obey you in the same way that we obeyed Moses. Just let the LORD your God be with you as he was with Moses! ¹⁸ Anybody who stubbornly opposes what you declare and doesn't obey any of your commands will be put to death. Be brave and strong!"

Joshua sends spies

2 Joshua, Nun's son, secretly sent two men as spies from Shittim. He said, "Go. Look over the land, especially Jericho." They set out and entered the house of a prostitute named Rahab. They bedded down there.

² Someone told the king of Jericho, "Men from the Israelites have come here tonight to spy on the land."

³ So the king of Jericho sent word to Rahab: "Send out the men who came to you, the ones who came to your house, because they have come to spy on the entire land."

Rahab takes action

⁴ But the woman had taken the two men and hidden them. Then she said, "Of course the men came to me. But I didn't know where they were from. ⁵ The men left when it was time to close the gate at dark, but I don't know where the men went. Hurry! Chase after them! You might catch up with them." ⁶ But she had taken them up to the roof and hidden them under the flax stalks that she had laid out on the roof. ⁷ The men from Jericho[a] chased after them in the

---

[a] Heb lacks *from Jericho*.

direction of the Jordan up to the fords. As soon as those chasing them went out, the gate was shut behind them.

Rahab sets terms

[8] Before the spies bedded down, Rahab went up to them on the roof. [9] She said to the men, "I know that the LORD has given you the land. Terror over you has overwhelmed us. The entire population of the land has melted down in fear because of you. [10] We have heard how the LORD dried up the water of the Reed Sea[b] in front of you when you left Egypt. We have also heard what you did to Sihon and Og, the two kings of the Amorites on the other side of the Jordan. You utterly wiped them out. [11] We heard this and our hearts turned to water. Because of you, people can no longer work up their courage. This is because the LORD your God is God in heaven above and on earth below. [12] Now, I have been loyal to you. So pledge to me by the LORD that you in turn will deal loyally with my family. Give me a sign of good faith. [13] Spare the lives of my father, mother, brothers, and sisters, along with everything they own. Rescue us from death."

[14] The men said to her, "We swear by our own lives to secure yours. If you don't reveal our mission, we will deal loyally and faithfully with you when the LORD gives us the land."

The spies escape

[15] So she lowered the spies on a rope through the window. Her house was on the outer side of the city wall, and she lived inside the wall. [16] Then she said to them, "Go toward the highlands so that those chasing you don't run into you. Hide there for three days until those chasing you return. Then you may go on your way."

[17] The men said to her, "We won't be responsible for this pledge you made us swear [18] unless, when we come into the land, you tie this red woven cord in the window through which you lowered us. Gather your father, your mother, your brothers, and your whole family into the house with you. [19] Those who go outside the doors of your house into the street will have only themselves to blame for their own deaths. We won't be responsible. If anyone lays a hand on those who are with you in the house, we will take the blame for their death. [20] But if you reveal our mission, we won't be responsible for this pledge you made us swear."

[b] Or Red Sea

RAHAB

1. The woman who helps Joshua's spies in Jericho (Josh 2). Although most English translations describe Rahab as a "prostitute," the exact meaning of the Hebrew description is debated. Rahab, it seems, is a woman who sells access to her body in exchange for money or goods. She owns her own house, perhaps a kind of bordello, which may have led Greek interpreters to call her an "innkeeper."

There are three verses that mention Rahab in the NT. First, Matthew puts her in the genealogy that links Jesus to Abraham (Matt 1:5). According to Matthew, she is the mother of Boaz (the husband of Ruth). The author of Hebrews praises Rahab for her faith (Heb 11:31), while the author of James lauds her for her works (Jas 2:25).

2. A dragon or chaos monster, known in ancient Near Eastern traditions as well as the OT (Job 26:12; Ps 89:7-13 [Heb. 89:8-14]).

[21]She said, "These things will happen just like you said." She sent them away and they went off. Then she tied the red cord in the window.

Mission accomplished

[22]The spies went out and entered the highlands. They stayed there for three days until those chasing them came back. Those chasing them had searched all along the road but never found them. [23]Then the two men came back down from the highlands. They crossed the Jordan and came to Joshua, Nun's son. They told him everything that had happened to them. [24]They said to Joshua, "The LORD has definitely given the entire land into our power. In addition, all of the land's population has melted down in fear because of us."

Directions for crossing the Jordan

3 Joshua took down the camp early in the morning. He and all the Israelites marched out of Shittim and came to the Jordan, where they stayed overnight before crossing. [2]At the end of three days the officers went through the middle of the camp. [3]They commanded the people, "As soon as you see the LORD your God's chest containing the covenant and the levitical priests carrying it, you are to march out from your places and follow it. [4]But let there be some distance between you and it, about three thousand feet. Don't come near it! You will know the way you should go, even though you've never traveled this way before."

[5]Joshua said to the people, "Make yourselves holy! Tomorrow the LORD will do wonderful things among you." [6]Then Joshua said to the priests, "Lift up the covenant chest. Go along in front of the people."

So they lifted up the covenant chest and went in front of the people.

[7]The LORD said to Joshua, "Today I will begin to make you great in the opinion of all Israel. Then they will know that I will be with you in the same way that I was with Moses. [8]You are to command the priests who carry the covenant chest, 'As soon as you come to the bank of the Jordan, stand still in the Jordan.'"

[9]Joshua said to the Israelites, "Come close. Listen to the words of the LORD your God." [10]Then Joshua said, "This is how you will know that the living God is among you and will completely remove the Canaanites, Hittites, Hivites, Perizzites, Girgashites, Amorites, and Jebusites before you. [11]Look! The covenant chest of the ruler of the entire earth is going to cross over in front of you in the Jordan. [12]Now pick twelve men from the tribes of Israel, one per tribe. [13]The soles of the priests' feet, who are carrying the chest of the LORD, ruler of the whole earth, will come to rest in the water of the Jordan. At that moment, the water of the Jordan will be cut off. The water flowing downstream will stand still in a single heap."

Marching across the Jordan

[14]The people marched out from their tents to cross over the Jordan. The priests carrying the covenant chest were in front of the people. [15]When the priests who were carrying the chest came to the Jordan, their feet touched the edge of the water. The Jordan had overflowed its banks completely, the way it does during the entire harvest season. [16]But at that moment the water of the Jordan coming downstream stood still. It rose up as a single heap very far off, just below Adam, which is the city next to

ADONAI/ADONAY

"Lord" or "the ruler of the entire earth" was an epithet of God (Josh 3:11). The term began as a title; however, Adonai became an alternate name for God, often used in parallel with *Yahweh* or as a substitute for this name when *Yahweh* was deemed too sacred to be pronounced.

Zarethan. The water going down to the desert sea (that is, the Dead Sea) was cut off completely. The people crossed opposite Jericho. [17] So the priests carrying the LORD's covenant chest stood firmly on dry land in the middle of the Jordan. Meanwhile, all Israel crossed over on dry land, until the entire nation finished crossing over the Jordan.

Twelve stones at Gilgal

4 When the entire nation had finished crossing over the Jordan, the LORD said to Joshua, [2] "Pick twelve men from the people, one man per tribe. [3] Command them, 'Pick up twelve stones from right here in the middle of the Jordan, where the feet of the priests had been firmly planted. Bring them across with you and put them down in the camp where you are staying tonight.'"

[4] Joshua called for the twelve men he had appointed from the Israelites, one man per tribe. [5] Joshua said to them, "Cross over into the middle of the Jordan, up to the LORD your God's chest. Each of you, lift up a stone on his shoulder to match the number of the tribes of the Israelites. [6] This will be a symbol among you. In the future your children may ask, 'What do these stones mean to you?' [7] Then you will tell them that the water of the Jordan was cut off before the LORD's covenant chest. When it crossed over the Jordan, the water of the Jordan was cut off. These stones will be an enduring memorial for the Israelites."

[8] The Israelites did exactly what Joshua ordered. They lifted twelve stones from the middle of the Jordan, matching the number of the tribes of the Israelites, exactly as the LORD had said to Joshua. They brought them over to the camp and put them down there. [9] Joshua also set up twelve stones in the middle of the Jordan where the feet of the priests had stood while carrying the covenant chest. They are still there today.

Crossing completed

[10] Meanwhile, the priests carrying the chest were standing in the middle of the Jordan. They stood there until every command that the LORD had ordered Joshua to tell the people had been carried out. This was exactly what Moses had commanded Joshua. The people crossed over quickly. [11] As soon as all the people had finished crossing, the LORD's chest crossed over. The priests then moved to the front of the people. [12] The people of Reuben, the people of Gad, and half the tribe of Manasseh crossed over, organized for war ahead of the Israelites, exactly as Moses had told them. [13] Approximately forty thousand armed for war crossed over in the LORD's presence to

GILGAL

A shrine from the time of Joshua up through them time of Saul. The clues in the Bible about the location of Gilgal are somewhat contradictory. Most of the references are consistent with a location on the eastern border of Jericho, but some (Deut 11:30; Josh 12:23; 15:7; 2 Kgs 2:1) are not. For this reason, many scholars think that there were at least three different sites named Gilgal. But the site near Jericho, which accounts for all the references to Gilgal except those noted above, was the national shrine and sanctuary for the Israelites. It was here that Joshua set up the first national monument in the promised land (Josh 4:19-20), likely a stone circle that gave the place its name ("Gilgal" comes from the Hebrew root for "round"). This was also the site of the communal circumcision and Passover celebration (Josh 5). Gilgal served as the Israelites' base camp during their conquest of Canaan (Josh 10). Later, Saul was confirmed as king at Gilgal (1 Sam 11).

the plains of Jericho, ready for battle. ¹⁴The LORD made Joshua great in the opinion of all Israel on that day. So they revered him in the same way that they had revered Moses during all of his life.

¹⁵The LORD said to Joshua, ¹⁶"Command the priests carrying the chest containing the testimony to come up out of the Jordan."

¹⁷So Joshua commanded the priests, "Come up from the Jordan." ¹⁸The priests carrying the LORD's covenant chest came up from the middle of the Jordan, and the soles of their feet touched dry ground. At that moment, the water of the Jordan started flowing again. It ran as before, completely over its banks. ¹⁹The people came up out of the Jordan on the tenth day of the first month.ᶜ They camped at Gilgal on the east border of Jericho.

Stones at Gilgal

²⁰Joshua set up at Gilgal those twelve stones they had taken from the Jordan. ²¹He said to the Israelites, "In the future your children will ask their parents, 'What about these stones?' ²²Then you will let your children know: 'Israel crossed over the Jordan here on dry ground.' ²³This was because the LORD your God dried up the water of the Jordan before you until you crossed over. This was exactly what the LORD your God did to the Reed Sea.ᵈ He dried it up before us until we crossed over. ²⁴This happened so that all the earth's peoples might know that the LORD's power is great and that you may always revere the LORD your God."

Enemy kings react

5 All the Amorite kings on the west side of the Jordan and all the Canaanite kings near the sea heard that the LORD had dried up the water of the Jordan before the Israelites until they had crossed over. Then their hearts melted. They lost all courage because of the Israelites.

Circumcision

²At that time the LORD said to Joshua, "Make yourself flint knives. Circumcise the Israelites for a second time." ³So Joshua made flint knives for himself. He circumcised the Israelites at Foreskins Hill. ⁴This is the reason Joshua did so: All the people who went out of Egypt, that is, all the men who were soldiers, had died in the desert on the way after they left Egypt. ⁵All the people who went out were circumcised. But none of the people born in the desert on the way after they had left Egypt had been circumcised. ⁶This was because the Israelites journeyed forty years in the desert until the whole nation died off. These were the men old enough to fight who went out from Egypt and who hadn't obeyed the LORD. The LORD had pledged to them never to show them the land that the LORD had pledged to their ancestors to give us. It is a land full of milk and honey. ⁷Joshua circumcised their children, the ones the LORD had set in their place. They were uncircumcised because they hadn't been circumcised on the way. ⁸After the whole nation had undergone circumcision, they remained in the camp until they got well again. ⁹Then the LORD said to Joshua, "Today I have rolled away from you the disgrace of Egypt." So the place was called Gilgal,ᵉ as it is today.

Passover

¹⁰The Israelites camped in Gilgal. They celebrated Passover on the evening of the fourteenth day of the monthᶠ on the plains of Jericho. ¹¹On the very next day after Passover, they ate food produced in the land: unleavened bread and roasted grain. ¹²The manna stopped on that next day, when they ate food produced in the land. There was no longer any manna for the Israelites. So that year they ate the crops of the land of Canaan.

Commander of the LORD's heavenly force

¹³When Joshua was near Jericho, he looked up. He caught sight of a man standing in front of him with his sword drawn. Joshua went up and said to him, "Are you on our side or that of our enemies?"

ᶜMarch–April, Nisan ᵈOr Red Sea ᵉGilgal sounds like the Heb verb galal, "to roll away." ᶠMarch–April, Nisan

¹⁴He said, "Neither! I'm the commander of the LORD's heavenly force. Now I have arrived!"

Then Joshua fell flat on his face and worshipped. Joshua said to him, "What is my master saying to his servant?"

¹⁵The commander of the LORD's heavenly force said to Joshua, "Take your sandals off your feet because the place where you are standing is holy." So Joshua did this.

Instructions about Jericho

6 Now Jericho was closed up tightly because of the Israelites. No one went out or came in. ²The LORD said to Joshua, "Look. I have given Jericho and its king into your power, along with its mighty warriors. ³Circle the city with all the soldiers, going around the city one time. Do this for six days. ⁴Have seven priests carry seven trumpets made from rams' horns in front of the chest. On the seventh day, circle the city seven times, with the priests blowing the trumpets.

⁵"Have them blow a long blast on the ram's horn. As soon as you hear that trumpet blast, have all the people shout out a loud war cry. Then the city wall will collapse, and the people will rise up, attacking straight ahead."

Israel destroys Jericho

⁶So Joshua, Nun's son, called the priests. He said to them, "Lift up the covenant chest. Let seven priests carry seven trumpets made from rams' horns in front of the LORD's chest." ⁷He said to the people, "Go forward. Circle the city. Let the armed soldiers go in front of the LORD's chest." ⁸As soon as Joshua had spoken to the people, the seven priests carrying seven ram's horn trumpets moved forward in front of the LORD. They blew the trumpets. The LORD's covenant chest followed. ⁹The initial group of soldiers was going in front of the priests who were blowing the trumpets. The rear guard was coming behind the chest, with trumpets blowing continuously. ¹⁰Joshua ordered the people, "Don't shout. Don't let your voice be heard. Don't let a word come out of your mouth until the day I tell you, 'Shout!' Then shout!"

¹¹He made the LORD's chest circle the city, going around one time. They went back to the camp and stayed there overnight. ¹²Joshua got up early in the morning. The priests lifted up the LORD's chest. ¹³The seven priests carrying the seven trumpets made from rams' horns were going in front of the LORD's chest, blowing trumpets continuously. The armed soldiers were going in front of them. The rear guard was coming after the LORD's chest, blowing trumpets continuously. ¹⁴They circled the city one time on the second day. Then they went back to the camp. They did this for six days.

¹⁵On the seventh day, they got up at dawn. They circled the city in this way seven times. It was only on that day that

JERICHO

A town situated at an oasis in the Jordan Valley, just northwest of the Dead Sea, has gained a reputation for being one of the oldest cities in the world. The name *Jericho* is best known for its appearance in the conquest narrative of the book of Joshua. Its position on a major road from a ford of the Jordan to the highlands placed it directly in the path of the Israelites, and it was their first conquest after crossing the Jordan (Josh 6). In the NT, Jericho features most prominently in the Gospels in the story of Jesus restoring sight to the blind beggar(s). Only two references outside the book of Joshua, however, refer to the Israelites' conquest of the city (1 Kgs 16:34; Heb 11:30-31).

they circled the city seven times. [16]The seventh time, the priests blew the trumpets. Then Joshua said to the people, "Shout, because the LORD has given you the city! [17]The city and everything in it is to be utterly wiped out as something reserved for the LORD. Only Rahab the prostitute is to stay alive, along with everyone with her in her house. This is because she hid the messengers we sent. [18]But you, keep away from the things set aside for God so that you don't desire[g] and take some of the things reserved. That would turn the camp of Israel into a thing doomed to be utterly wiped out and bring calamity on it. [19]All silver and gold, along with bronze and iron equipment, are holy to the LORD. They must go into the LORD's treasury." [20]Then the people shouted. They blew the trumpets. As soon as the people heard the trumpet blast, they shouted a loud war cry. Then the wall collapsed. The people went up against the city, attacking straight ahead. They captured the city. [21]Without mercy, they wiped out everything in the city as something reserved for God—man and woman, young and old, cattle, sheep, and donkeys.

Consequences

[22]Joshua spoke to the two men who had scouted out the land. "Go to the prostitute's house. Bring out the woman from there, along with everyone related to her, exactly as you pledged to her." [23]So the young men who had been spies went and brought Rahab out, along with her father, her mother, her brothers, and everyone related to her. They brought her whole clan out and let them stay outside Israel's camp. [24]They burned the city and everything in it. But they put the silver and gold, along with the bronze and iron equipment, into the treasury of the LORD's house. [25]Joshua let Rahab the prostitute live, her family, and everyone related to her. So her family still lives among Israel today, because she hid the spies whom Joshua had sent to scout out Jericho.

[26]At that time Joshua made this decree:

"Anyone who starts to rebuild this city of Jericho will be cursed before the LORD.

Laying its foundations will cost them their oldest child.

Setting up its gates will cost them their youngest child."

[27]The LORD was with Joshua. News about him spread throughout the land.

Israel defeated at Ai

7 The Israelites did a disrespectful thing concerning the items reserved for God. Achan was the son of Carmi, grandson of Zabdi, great-grandson of Zerah. He was from the tribe of Judah. He took some of the things reserved for God. So the LORD was furious with the Israelites.

[2]Joshua sent men from Jericho to Ai, which is near Beth-aven to the east of Bethel. He said to them, "Go up. Scout out the land."

So the men went up and scouted out Ai. [3]They came back to Joshua and said to him, "There is no need for all of the people to go up. Two or three thousand men could go up and strike Ai. Don't make all of the people bother going there. There are just a few of them." [4]So about three thousand men from the people went up in that direction. But they fled from the men of Ai. [5]The men of Ai struck down approximately thirty-six of them. They chased them from outside the gate as far as Shebarim. They struck them down on the slope. Then the hearts of the people melted and turned to water.

Cause of Israel's defeat

[6]Joshua ripped open his clothes. He, along with the elders of Israel, lay flat on their faces before the LORD's chest until evening. They put dust on their heads. [7]Then Joshua said, "Oh no, LORD God! Why did you ever bring this people across the Jordan? Was it to hand us over to the power of the Amorites, to destroy us? If only we had been prepared to live on the other side of the Jordan! [8]Please forgive

[g]LXX; Heb wipe out as something reserved for God

me, LORD. What can I say now that Israel has retreated before its enemies? [9]The Canaanites and the whole population of the land will hear of it. They will surround us and make our name disappear from the earth. What will you do about your great name then?"

[10]The LORD said to Joshua, "Get up! Why do you lie flat on your face like this? [11]Israel has sinned. They have violated my covenant, which I commanded them to keep. They have taken some of the things reserved for me and put them with their own things. They have stolen and kept it a secret. [12]The Israelites can't stand up to their enemies. They retreat before their enemies because they themselves have become a doomed thing reserved for me. I will no longer be with you unless you destroy the things reserved for me that are present among you. [13]Go and make the people holy. Say, 'Get ready for tomorrow by making yourselves holy. This is what the LORD, the God of Israel, says: "Israel! Things reserved for me are present among you. You won't be able to stand up to your enemies until you remove from your presence the things reserved for me."' [14]In the morning, come forward tribe by tribe. Whichever tribe the LORD selects must come forward clan by clan. Whichever clan the LORD selects must come forward family by family. Whichever family the LORD selects will come forward by individual soldiers. [15]The person selected, who has the things reserved for God, must be put to death by burning. Burn everything that belongs to him too. This is because he has violated the LORD's covenant and has committed an outrage in Israel."

Achan discovered and punished

[16]Joshua got up early in the morning. He made Israel come forward tribe by tribe. The tribe of Judah was selected. [17]He made the clans of Judah come forward. He selected the clan of Zerah. He made the clan of Zerah come forward as individual soldiers. Zabdi was selected. [18]He made each soldier of his family come forward. Achan was selected. He was a son of Carmi, grandson of Zabdi, great-grandson of Zerah, and of the tribe of Judah. [19]Joshua said to Achan, "My son, give glory to the LORD the God of Israel. Tell me what you have done. Don't hide anything from me."

[20]Achan answered Joshua, "It's true. I've sinned against the LORD, the God of Israel. This is what I have done: [21]Among the booty I saw a single beautiful robe in the Babylonian style, two hundred shekels of silver, and a single gold bar weighing fifty shekels. I desired them and took them. Now they are hidden in the ground inside my tent, with the silver on the bottom."

[22]Then Joshua sent messengers. They ran to the tent. There it was, hidden in his tent, with the silver on the bottom. [23]They took the things from inside the tent. They brought them to Joshua and to all the Israelites and emptied them out before the LORD. [24]Then Joshua seized Achan, Zerah's son, along with the silver, the robe, the gold bar, his sons and daughters, his cattle, donkeys, flocks, tent, and everything that belonged to him. All Israel joined Joshua.

AI

A Canaanite town near Bethel (Gen 12:8; 13:3; Josh 7-8; Ezra 2:28; Neh 7:32; Jer 49:3). Biblical Ai today is almost universally identified with Khirbet et-Tell ("ruin of the tell"), which is located about nine miles northeast of Jerusalem. Ai is used as a reference point for the location of Abram's altar at the oak of Moreh. In the Bible the town is best known for the account in Joshua 7-8, where God orders Joshua to kill all the inhabitants of Ai except for the livestock and the spoils of the town.

They brought them up to Achor Valley. ²⁵Joshua said, "You have brought disaster to us! May the LORD bring disaster to you today!" Then all Israel stoned him. They burned them with fire and stoned them with stones. ²⁶They raised over him a great pile of stones that is still there today. Then the LORD turned away from his fury. So he named that place Achor Valley.ʰ It is still called that today.

Plan to capture Ai

8 The LORD said to Joshua, "Don't be afraid or terrified. Take the entire army with you. Start to go up to Ai. Look! I have given the king of Ai, his people, his city, and his land into your power. ²Do to Ai and its king what you did to Jericho and its king. But you may take its booty and cattle as plunder. Set your ambush behind the city."

³So Joshua and the whole army got ready to go up to Ai. Joshua chose thirty thousand brave soldiers. He sent them out by night. ⁴He commanded them, "Look. You are to ambush the city from behind. Don't move too far away from the city. Be ready, all of you. ⁵I will approach the city with all the people. When they come out against us the same way as before, we will flee from them. ⁶They will come out after us until we have drawn them away from the city. They will think, They are fleeing from us as before. So we will flee from them. ⁷But you will rise up from the ambush and take over the city. The LORD your God will give it into your power. ⁸As soon as you seize the city, set it on fire. Act according to the LORD's word. Indeed, I have given you an order!"

⁹Joshua sent them off, and they went to set the ambush. They stayed between Bethel and Ai, to the west of Ai. Joshua spent that night among the people. ¹⁰Joshua got up early in the morning and mustered the people. Then he and the elders of Israel went up in front of the people to Ai. ¹¹The entire army that was with him went up. They moved in close, in front of the city. Then they camped north of Ai, with the valley between them and Ai. ¹²He took about five thousand men and positioned them as an ambush between Bethel and Ai to the west of the city. ¹³The people positioned the main camp on the north side of the city and its rear guard on its west side. That night, Joshua went into the middle of the valley.

Israel's successful strategy

¹⁴As soon as the king of Ai saw this, he and all his troops, the men of the city, hurried out early in the morning to meet Israel in battle. They moved out to the battleground on the slopes down toward the Jordan.ⁱ He didn't know that there was an ambush set against him behind the city. ¹⁵Then Joshua and all Israel let themselves be beaten before them. They fled in the direction of the desert. ¹⁶Next, all the troops who were still in the city were called out to chase them. They chased after Joshua and so let themselves be drawn away from the city. ¹⁷No one who hadn't gone out after Israel was left in either Ai or Bethel. They left the city wide open and chased after Israel.

¹⁸The LORD said to Joshua, "Point the dagger in your hand toward Ai, because I will give it into your power." So Joshua pointed the dagger in his hand toward the city. ¹⁹The ambush quickly rose from its place. As soon as he reached out his hand, it charged. They entered the city and captured it. They set the city on fire at once. ²⁰Then the men of Ai turned around. They caught sight of the smoke of the city rising toward the sky. They had no chance to flee one way or the other. The troops who were fleeing toward the desert turned against the pursuit. ²¹Joshua and all Israel saw that the ambush had captured the city and that the smoke of the city was rising. So they turned and struck down the men of Ai. ²²When other Israelites came out of the city to confront them, the men of Ai were caught in the middle. Some Israelites were on one side of them and some on the other. The Israelites struck them down until there was no one left to escape. ²³But they seized the king of Ai alive and brought him to Joshua.

ʰOr *Calamity Valley* ⁱOr *the Arabah*

24Israel finished killing the entire population of Ai that had chased them out into the open wasteland. All of them were finished off without mercy. Then all Israel went back to Ai and struck it down without mercy. 25Twelve thousand men and women died that day, all the people of Ai. 26Joshua didn't pull back the hand that was stretched out holding a dagger until he had wiped out the whole population of Ai as something reserved for God. 27However, Israel did take the cattle and other booty of that city as plunder for themselves, in agreement with the command that the LORD had given Joshua. 28Then Joshua burned Ai. He made it a permanently deserted mound. That is still the case today. 29He hanged the king of Ai on a tree until evening. At sundown, Joshua gave an order, and they took his body down from the tree. They threw it down at the opening of the city gate. Then they raised over it a great pile of stones that is still there today.

Joshua reads the Instruction

30Then Joshua built an altar on Mount Ebal to the LORD, the God of Israel. 31This was exactly what Moses the LORD's servant had commanded the Israelites. It is what is written in the Instruction scroll from Moses: "an altar of crude stones against which no iron tool has swung."j On it they offered entirely burned offerings to the LORD and sacrificed well-being offerings. 32There, in the presence of the Israelites, Joshua wrote on the stones a copy of the Instruction from Moses, which Moses had written earlier. 33All Israel—with its elders, officers, and judges—were standing on either side of the chest. They were facing the levitical priests who carry the LORD's chest containing the covenant. They included both immigrants and full citizens. Half stood facing Mount Gerizim and half stood facing Mount Ebal. This was exactly what Moses the LORD's servant had initially commanded for the blessing of the Israelite people. 34Afterward, Joshua read aloud all the words of the Instruction, both blessing and curse, in agreement with everything written in the Instruction scroll. 35There wasn't a single word of all that Moses had commanded that Joshua failed to read aloud in the presence of the entire assembly of Israel. This assembly included the women and small children, along with the immigrants who lived among them.

The Gibeonites' trick

9 All the kings on the west side of the Jordan heard about this, including those in the highlands, the lowlands, and along the entire coast of the Mediterranean Sea toward Lebanon. They were Hittites and Amorites, Canaanites, Perizzites, Hivites, and Jebusites. 2They formed an alliance to fight Joshua and Israel. 3In contrast, when the population of Gibeon heard what Joshua had done to Jericho and Ai, 4they acted cleverly. They set out pretending to be messengers.k They took worn-out sacks for their donkeys and worn-out wineskins that were split and mended. 5They had worn-out, patched sandals on their feet and were wearing worn-out clothes. All the bread in their supplies was dry and crumbly.

6They went to Joshua at the camp at Gilgal. They said to him and to Israel, "We have come from a distant country. So now, make a treaty with us."

7Israel said to the Hivites, "Perhaps you live among us. How then could we make a treaty with you?"

8Then they said to Joshua, "We are your servants."

Joshua said to them, "Who are you? Where have you come from?"

9They said to him, "Your servants have come from a very distant country because of the reputation of the LORD your God. We have heard a report about him and everything he did in Egypt. 10We heard about everything he did to the two kings of the Amorites on the east side of the Jordan, Heshbon's King Sihon and Bashan's King Og, who was in Ashtaroth. 11Our elders and all the population of our land said to us, 'Take along supplies for the journey.

jDeut 27:5-6 kHeb uncertain

Go meet them and say to them, "We are your servants. So now make a treaty with us."' [12] This is our bread. On the day we left to come to you we took it warm from our houses as supplies. But now here it is, dried up and crumbly. [13] These wineskins were new when we filled them. But here they are, split open. These clothes and sandals of ours are worn out from the very long journey." [14] The Israelites[l] took some of their supplies, but they didn't ask for any decision from the LORD. [15] Joshua made peace with them. He made a treaty with them to protect their lives. The leaders of the community made a solemn pledge to them.

Israel discovers the trick

[16] Three days after the Israelites made a treaty with the Gibeonites, the Israelites heard that they were actually their neighbors and were living among them. [17] So on the third day the Israelites marched out and came to their cities: Gibeon, Chephirah, Beeroth, and Kiriath-jearim. [18] But the Israelites didn't strike at them. This was because the leaders of the community had made a solemn pledge to them by the LORD, the God of Israel. The entire community grumbled against the leaders. [19] Then all the leaders said to the whole community, "We have made a solemn pledge to them by the LORD, the God of Israel. So we can't touch them now. [20] This is what we'll do with them. We'll let them live so that wrath won't come down on us because of the solemn pledge that we made to them." [21] The leaders went on to say to them, "Let

them live." So they became woodcutters and water haulers for the whole community, exactly as the leaders had intended for them.

[22] Joshua called for the Gibeonites and spoke to them: "Why have you deceived us by saying, 'We live very far away from you,' when actually you live among us? [23] So now you are cursed. Some of you will always serve as woodcutters and water haulers for my God's house." [24] They answered Joshua, "Your servants had been told that the LORD your God had commanded his servant Moses to give you the entire land and to wipe out all its population on your account. So we feared for our very lives because of you and did this thing. [25] Now, here we are in your power. Do to us whatever seems good and proper to you." [26] So Joshua treated them in this way. He spared them from the power of the Israelites, and they didn't kill them. [27] That day Joshua assigned them as woodcutters and water haulers for the community and for the LORD's altar, located wherever God[m] would choose. That is still the case today.

Gibeonites under attack

10 Jerusalem's King Adoni-zedek heard that Joshua had captured Ai and had wiped it out as something reserved for God. Joshua did the same thing to Ai and its king that he had done to Jericho and its king. He also heard that the population of Gibeon had made peace with Israel and were living among them. [2] Adoni-zedek and his people[n] were very afraid, because Gibeon was a large city, like one of the royal cities. It was

[l] Or men [m] Or he [n] Or they

larger than Ai. All its men were soldiers. ³So Jerusalem's King Adoni-zedek sent word to Hebron's King Hoham, Jarmuth's King Piram, Lachish's King Japhia, and Eglon's King Debir: ⁴"Come up and help me. We will strike at Gibeon, because it has made peace with Joshua and with the Israelites." ⁵Then the five kings of the Amorites gathered. These were the kings of Jerusalem, Hebron, Jarmuth, Lachish, and Eglon. They went up with all their armies, camped against Gibeon, and attacked it. ⁶The people of Gibeon sent word to Joshua in the camp at Gilgal: "Don't desert your servants! Come to us quickly. Rescue us! Help us! All the Amorite kings from the highlands have assembled together against us." ⁷So Joshua went up from Gilgal with the entire army and all the bravest soldiers.

The LORD fights for Israel

⁸Then the LORD said to Joshua, "Don't be afraid of them. I have given them into your power. Not a single one of them can stand up against you." ⁹Joshua quickly attacked them, having come up overnight from Gilgal. ¹⁰Then the LORD threw them into a panic before Israel. Joshua struck a mighty blow against them at Gibeon. He chased them on the way up to Beth-horon and struck them down as far as Azekah and Makkedah. ¹¹When they were fleeing from Israel and were on the slope of Beth-horon, the LORD threw down large stones from the sky all the way to Azekah. So they died. More died from the hailstones than the Israelites killed with the sword.

¹²On the day the LORD gave the Amorites into the power of Israel, Joshua spoke to the LORD in the presence of the Israelites:

"Sun, stand still at Gibeon!
 and Moon, at the Aijalon Valley!"
¹³ The sun stood still
 and the moon stood motionless
 until a nation took revenge
 on its enemies.

Isn't this written in the Jashar scroll? So the sun stood motionless in the middle of the sky. For a whole day, it was in no hurry to go down. ¹⁴There hasn't been a day like it before or since, when the LORD responded

to a human voice. The LORD fought for Israel. ¹⁵Then Joshua along with all Israel came back to the camp at Gilgal.

Israel executes five kings

¹⁶Then those five kings fled and hid in the cave at Makkedah. ¹⁷It was reported to Joshua, "The five kings have been found, hidden in the cave at Makkedah."

¹⁸Joshua said, "Roll large stones over the mouth of the cave. Station some men by it to guard them, ¹⁹but don't you stay there. Chase after your enemies and attack them from the rear. Don't let them enter their cities, because the LORD your God has given them into your power." ²⁰Joshua and the Israelites finished dealing them a stunning blow until they were finished off. Some survivors among them escaped into the fortified cities. ²¹Then the whole people came back safely to Joshua in the camp at Makkedah. Not a single person threatened the Israelites.

²²Joshua said, "Open up the mouth of the cave. Bring those five kings out of the cave to me." ²³They did so. They brought the five kings out of the cave to him: the kings of Jerusalem, Hebron, Jarmuth, Lachish, and Eglon. ²⁴When they brought these kings out to Joshua, Joshua called for every Israelite. He said to the military commanders who had gone out with him, "Come forward. Put your feet on the necks of these kings." So they went forward and put their feet on their necks. ²⁵Then Joshua said to them, "Don't be afraid or terrified. Be brave and strong, because this is how the LORD will deal with all the enemies you fight." ²⁶Next, Joshua struck them down. He put them to death and then hanged them on five trees. They were hanging on the trees until evening. ²⁷At sundown, Joshua gave an order, and they took them down from the trees. They threw them into the cave where they had hidden themselves, and they set large stones over the mouth of the cave. The stones are still there to this very day.

Victories in the south

²⁸On that day, Joshua captured Makkedah. With a sword, he struck it and its king

without mercy. He wiped them out, treating everyone in the city as something reserved for God. He left no survivors. He did to the king of Makkedah exactly as he had done to the king of Jericho.

²⁹Then Joshua along with all Israel moved on from Makkedah to Libnah. They attacked Libnah. ³⁰The LORD also gave it and its king into the power of Israel. With a sword, he struck it and everyone in it without mercy. He left no survivors in it. He did to its king exactly as he had done to the king of Jericho.

³¹Joshua along with all Israel moved on from Libnah to Lachish. They camped near it and attacked it. ³²The LORD gave Lachish into the power of Israel. Joshua captured it on the second day. With a sword, he struck it and everyone in it without mercy, just exactly as he had done to Libnah. ³³Then Gezer's King Horam came up to help Lachish. But Joshua struck him and his people down, until no survivors were left.

³⁴Joshua along with all Israel moved on from Lachish to Eglon. They camped against it and attacked it. ³⁵They captured it on the same day and struck it down without mercy. On that day, he wiped out everyone in it as something reserved for God, just exactly as he had done to Lachish.

³⁶Joshua along with all Israel went up from Eglon to Hebron and attacked it. ³⁷They captured it and struck it down without mercy, along with its king, all its towns, and everyone in it. He left no survivors, just exactly as he had done to Eglon. He wiped out the city and everyone in it as something reserved for God.

³⁸Joshua along with all Israel turned back to Debir and attacked it. ³⁹He captured it along with its king and all its cities. They struck them down without mercy and wiped out everyone in it as something reserved for God. He left no survivors. Exactly as he had done to Hebron, so he did to Debir and its king—exactly as he had done to Libnah and its king.

⁴⁰So Joshua struck at the whole land: the highlands, the arid southern plains, the lowlands, the slopes, and all their kings. He left no survivors. He wiped out everything that breathed as something reserved for God, exactly as the LORD, the God of Israel, had commanded. ⁴¹Joshua struck them down from Kadesh-barnea to Gaza, and the whole land of Goshen as far as Gibeon. ⁴²Joshua captured all these kings and their land all at the same time. This was because the LORD, the God of Israel, fought for Israel. ⁴³Then Joshua along with all Israel came back to the camp at Gilgal.

Victories in the north

11 King Jabin of Hazor heard about this. So he sent word to Madon's King Jobab, to the king of Shimron, and to the king of Achshaph. ²He sent word to the kings from the north part of the highlands, in the desert plain south of Chinneroth, in the lowlands, and in Naphoth-dor on the west. ³He sent word to the Canaanites from east and west, to the Amorites, Hittites, Perizzites, and Jebusites in the highlands, and to the Hivites at the foot of Hermon in the land of Mizpah. ⁴They went out with all their battalions as a great army. They were as numerous as the grains of sand on the seashore. There were very many horses and chariots. ⁵All these kings came together. They came and camped together at the waters of Merom to fight against Israel.

⁶The LORD said to Joshua, "Don't be afraid of them. By this time tomorrow, I will make them all dead bodies in Israel's presence. Cripple their horses! Burn their chariots!"

⁷Then Joshua along with the entire army launched a surprise attack against them at the waters of Merom. ⁸The LORD gave them into Israel's power. They struck them down. They chased them as far as Great Sidon and Misrephoth-maim, then to the east as far as the Mizpeh Valley. They struck them down until no survivors were left. ⁹Joshua dealt with them exactly as the LORD had told him. He crippled their horses and burned their chariots.

¹⁰Joshua turned back at that time. He captured Hazor and struck down its king with the sword. Hazor had been the head of all those kingdoms in the past. ¹¹They struck down everyone there without mercy,

wiping them out as something reserved for God. Nothing that breathed was left. Hazor itself he burned. ¹²Joshua captured all these kings and their cities. He struck them down without mercy. He wiped them out as something reserved for God. This was exactly as Moses the LORD's servant had commanded. ¹³But Israel didn't burn any of the cities that still are standing on their mounds. Joshua burned only Hazor. ¹⁴The Israelites took all the valuable things from those cities and the cattle as plunder for themselves. But they struck down every person without mercy until they had wiped them out. They didn't let anything that breathed survive. ¹⁵What the LORD had commanded Moses his servant, Moses had commanded Joshua, and Joshua did exactly that. He didn't deviate a bit from any command that the LORD had given Moses.

Summary of Israel's victories

¹⁶So Joshua took this whole land: the highlands, the whole arid southern plain, the whole land of Goshen, the lowlands, the desert plain, and both the highlands and the lowlands of Israel. ¹⁷He took land stretching from Mount Halak, which goes up toward Seir, as far as Baal-gad at the foot of Mount Hermon in the Lebanon Valley. He captured all their kings. He struck them down and killed them. ¹⁸Joshua waged war against all these kings for a long time. ¹⁹There wasn't one city that made peace with the Israelites, except the Hivites who lived in Gibeon. They captured every single one in battle. ²⁰Their stubborn resistance

came from the LORD and led them to wage war against Israel. Israel was then able to wipe them out as something reserved for God, without showing them any mercy. This was exactly what the LORD had commanded Moses.

²¹At that time, Joshua went and wiped out the Anakim from the highlands. He wiped them out from Hebron, from Debir, and from Anab, from the whole highlands of Judah, and the whole highlands of Israel. Joshua wiped them out along with their cities as something reserved for God. ²²The Anakim no longer remained in the land of the Israelites. They survived only in Gaza, Gath, and Ashdod. ²³So Joshua took the whole land, exactly as the LORD had promised Moses. Joshua gave it as a legacy to Israel according to their tribal shares. Then the land had a rest from war.

Moses defeated two kings

12 The Israelites struck down these kings of the land and took over their land on the east side of the Jordan. This ran from the Arnon Valley as far as Mount Hermon and included the whole eastern part of the desert plain. ²First there was the Amorites' King Sihon, who lived in Heshbon. He ruled from Aroer by the rim of Arnon Valley and then from the middle of the valley as far as the Jabbok Valley, the border of the Ammonites. This was half of Gilead. ³He ruled the desert plain up to the east side of the Chinneroth Sea. This ran southward in the direction of Beth-jeshimoth at the foot of the Pisgah slopes as far as the

HAZOR

Tel Hazor is the site of an ancient city located in the Hule Valley, 8.5 mi. to the north of the Galilee Sea on the eastern foot of the upper Galilee ridge. Hazor is first mentioned in the Bible in the conquest narrative of Joshua, where it is referred to as "the head of all those kingdoms in the past" (Josh 11:10-13), and again in the prose version of Deborah's wars (Judg 4). Later, Hazor is mentioned among the cities that were built by king Solomon (1 Kgs 9:15), and again as one of the Israelite cities captured during the campaign of Tiglath-pileser, king of Assyria, in 732 BCE (2 Kgs 15:29).

east side of the desert plain (that is, the Dead Sea) and ⁴the territory next to it.º Then there was Bashan's King Og. He was one of the last of the Rephaim. He lived in Ashtaroth and Edrei. ⁵He ruled over Mount Hermon, Salecah, and all of Bashan as far as the border of the Geshurites and the Maacathites, and half of Gilead down to the border of Heshbon's King Sihon. ⁶Moses the LORD's servant and the Israelites struck them down. Moses the LORD's servant gave their land as property to the Reubenites, Gadites, and half the tribe of Manasseh.

Kings west of the Jordan

⁷Joshua and the Israelites struck down these kings of the land and took over their land on the west side of the Jordan. This ran from Baal-gad in the Lebanon Valley as far as Mount Halak, which goes up toward Seir. Joshua gave it to the tribes of Israel as shares of property. ⁸This was in the highlands, in the lowlands, in the desert plain, in the slopes, in the desert, and in the arid southern plain. The land belonged to Hittites, Amorites, Canaanites, Perizzites, Hivites, and Jebusites. They were:

⁹ the king of Jericho	one
the king of Ai (which is near Bethel)	one
¹⁰ the king of Jerusalem	one
the king of Hebron	one
¹¹ the king of Jarmuth	one
the king of Lachish	one
¹² the king of Eglon	one
the king of Gezer	one
¹³ the king of Debir	one
the king of Geder	one
¹⁴ the king of Hormah	one
the king of Arad	one
¹⁵ the king of Libnah	one
the king of Adullam	one
¹⁶ the king of Makkedah	one
the king of Bethel	one
¹⁷ the king of Tappuah	one
the king of Hepher	one
¹⁸ the king of Aphek	one
the king of Lasharon	one
¹⁹ the king of Madon	one
the king of Hazor	one
²⁰ the king of Shimron-meron	one
the king of Achshaph	one
²¹ the king of Taanach	one
the king of Megiddo	one
²² the king of Kedesh	one
the king of Jokneam in Carmel	one
²³ the king of Dor in Naphath-dor	one
the king of Goiim of Gilgal	one
²⁴ the king of Tirzah	one
Total of all kings:	thirty-one.

Land still unconquered

13 Now Joshua had reached old age. The LORD said to him, "You have reached old age, but much of the land remains to be taken over. ²This is the land that remains: All the districts of the Philistines and all those of the Geshurites. ³(The land stretching from the Shihor near Egypt northward as far as the Ekron territory is considered to be Canaanite. There are five rulers of the Philistines, for Gaza, Ashdod, Ashkelon, Gath, and Ekron.) The land of the Avvites ⁴in the south. The whole land of the Canaanites, along with Mearah, which belongs to the Sidonians, as far as Aphek and as far as the Amorite border. ⁵The land of the Gebalites and the whole Lebanon eastward, stretching from Baal-gad at the foot of Mount Hermon to Lebo-hamath.

⁶"I myself will remove the entire population of the highlands from Lebanon to Misrephoth-maim before the Israelites, that is, all the Sidonians. You have only to allot it to Israel as a legacy exactly as I commanded you. ⁷So now divide up this land as a legacy for the nine tribes and half the tribe of Manasseh. You will give it out from the Jordan to the Mediterranean Sea in the west. The Mediterranean Sea is the border."ᴾ

Land east of the Jordan

⁸As for the other half of the tribe of Manasseh,�q the Reubenites and Gadites together with it had already taken their legacy that Moses had given them on the

---

ºHeb lacks *next to it.* ᴾLXX; MT lacks *You will give it out from the Jordan to the Mediterranean Sea in the west. The Mediterranean Sea is the border.* qLXX; MT lacks *As for the other half of the tribe of Manasseh.*

east side of the Jordan. It was exactly what Moses the LORD's servant had given them. [9]It ran from Aroer by the rim of the Arnon Valley and the city in the middle of the valley through the whole Medeba plateau as far as Dibon. [10]It included all the cities of the Amorites' King Sihon, who ruled in Heshbon, as far as the Ammonite border. [11]It also included Gilead and the territory of the Geshurites and Maacathites, all Mount Hermon, and all Bashan as far as Salecah— [12]the entire kingdom of Og in Bashan, who ruled in Ashtaroth and in Edrei. He survived as the last of the Rephaim. Moses had struck down and removed them. [13]But the Israelites didn't remove the Geshurites or the Maacathites. So Geshur and Maacath still live among Israel today. [14]It was only to the tribe of Levi that he gave no legacy. Their legacy consists of the fire offerings for the LORD, the God of Israel, exactly as he had promised them.

For Reuben

[15]Moses provided for the clans of the Reubenite tribe. [16]Their territory ran from Aroer by the rim of the Arnon Valley and the city in the middle of the ravine, and the whole plateau as far as Medeba. [17]It included Heshbon and all its cities that are on the plateau: Dibon, Bamoth-baal, Beth-baal-meon, [18]Jahaz, Kedemoth, Mephaath, [19]Kiriathaim, Sibmah, the Zereth-shahar highlands, [20]Beth-peor, the slopes of Pisgah, and Beth-jeshimoth. [21]It included all

the cities of the plateau and the whole kingdom of Sihon king of the Amorites, who ruled in Heshbon. Moses had struck him down, along with Evi, Rekem, Zur, Hur, and Reba, the leaders of Midian. They had lived in the land as princes of Sihon. [22]In addition to those others slain, the Israelites killed the fortune-teller Balaam, Beor's son, with the sword. [23]The border of the people of Reuben was the Jordan and the territory next to it. This was the legacy of the people of Reuben—for their clans, their cities, and their settlements.

For Gad

[24]Moses provided for the clans of the Gadite tribe. [25]Their territory was Jazer, all the cities of Gilead, and half the land of the Ammonites as far as Aroer near Rabbah. [26]It also ran from Heshbon as far as Ramath-mizpeh and Betonim, and from Mahanaim as far as the territory of Lidebir. [27]In the valley were Beth-haram, Beth-nimrah, Succoth, and Zaphon. This was the rest of the kingdom of Sihon king of Heshbon. It included the Jordan and the territory next to it up to the tip of the Chinnereth Sea on the east side of the Jordan. [28]This was the legacy of the Gadites—for their clans, their cities, and their settlements.

For half of Manasseh

[29]Moses provided for half the tribe of Manasseh. It was for the clans in half the tribe of the people of Manasseh. [30]Their

GAD/GADITES

Gad is the seventh son of Jacob and ancestor of the tribe of Gad. Gad's mother, Zilpah, the maidservant of Leah, bore Gad on behalf of Leah. No actions of the man Gad are recorded; the Bible focuses exclusively on the tribe. Jacob's blessing suggests that Gad's history will be marked by violence (Gen 49:19). Moses' blessing on Gad also forecasts a violent future, but it adds the positive note that Gad will get "the commander's portion" and will take a leading role (Deut 33:20-21). Most of what we know about Gad we learn from Israel's entry and settlement stories, in which Gad plays a prominent role alongside Reuben.

territory ran from Mahanaim, all Bashan, the whole kingdom of Og king of Bashan, and all sixty of the tent villages of Jair that are in Bashan. ³¹Half of Gilead along with Ashtaroth and Edrei, cities of the kingdom of Og in Bashan, belonged to the people of Machir son of Manasseh. It belonged to the clans for half of the people of Machir.

³²Moses assigned these territories when he was in the Moab plains on the other side of the Jordan, east of Jericho. ³³But Moses gave no legacy to the tribe of Levi. The LORD God of Israel is their legacy, exactly as he promised them.

Dividing up Canaan

14 The Israelites received these inheritances in the land of Canaan. Eleazar the priest, Joshua son of Nun, and the heads of the families of the Israelite tribes assigned them. ²Their legacy was assigned by lot, exactly as the LORD had commanded the nine and a half tribes through Moses. ³In fact, Moses had given out the legacy of the two and a half tribes on the other side of the Jordan. But he gave no legacy among them to the Levites. ⁴The people of Joseph consisted of two tribes, Manasseh and Ephraim. The Levites weren't given any portion of the land, except cities to live in and pastureland for their cattle and flocks. ⁵The Israelites divided up the land exactly as the LORD had commanded Moses.

Caleb receives Hebron

⁶In Gilgal, the people of Judah approached Joshua. Caleb son of Jephunneh the Kenizzite said to him, "You know what the LORD said to Moses, man of God, about you and me when we were in Kadesh-barnea. ⁷I was 40 years old when Moses the LORD's servant sent me from Kadesh-barnea to scout out the land. I brought back a report to him of what I really thought. ⁸My companions who had gone up with me made the people's heart melt. But I remained loyal to the LORD my God. ⁹So Moses pledged on that day, 'The land on which you have walked will forever be a legacy for you and your children. This is because you remained loyal to the LORD my God.' ¹⁰Now look. The LORD has kept me alive, exactly as he promised. It is forty-five years since the LORD spoke about this to Moses. It was while Israel was journeying in the desert. Now look. Today I'm 85 years old. ¹¹I'm just as strong today as I was the day Moses sent me out. My strength then was as my strength is now, whether for war or for everyday activities. ¹²So now, give me this highland that the LORD promised me that day. True, the Anakim are there with large fortified cities, as you yourself heard that day. But if the LORD is with me, I should be able to remove them, exactly as the LORD promised."

¹³So Joshua blessed him. He gave Hebron to Caleb, Jephunneh's son, as a legacy. ¹⁴So Hebron still belongs to Caleb son of Jephunneh the Kenizzite as a legacy today. This was because he remained loyal to the LORD God of Israel. ¹⁵(Hebron used to be called Kiriath-arba. Arba had been the greatest of the Anakim.) Then the land rested from war.

Border of Judah

15 The land determined by lot for the clans of the Judahite tribe ran southward to the border of Edom. The Zin wasteland was the southern limit. ²Their south border ran from the end of the Dead Sea, from the bay that faces south. ³It went south from the ascent of Akrabbim, passed on to Zin, and went up south of Kadesh-barnea. It passed on to Hezron, went up to Addar, and turned toward Karka. ⁴It passed on to Azmon and went by the border^r of Egypt. The border ended at the sea. This will be their south border.

⁵The east border was the Dead Sea as far as the mouth of the Jordan.

The border on the north side ran from the bay of the sea at the mouth of the Jordan. ⁶The border went up to Beth-hoglah and passed north of Beth-arabah. The border went up to the Stone of Bohan (Reuben's son). ⁷The border went up to Debir

---

^r Or *Wadi*, traditionally Brook; LXX *their south border*; MT *your south border* from the Achor Valley, turning north to Gilgal. Gilgal was opposite the ascent of Adummim, which was south of the ravine. The border passed on to the waters of En-shemesh and ended at En-rogel. ⁸The border went up by the valley of Ben-Hinnom to the slope of the Jebusite city, Jerusalem, on the south. The border went up to the top of the mountain that is opposite the Hinnom Valley on the west, which is at the north end of the Rephaim Valley. ⁹The border turned from the top of the mountain to the waters of Nephtoah Spring and went to the cities of Mount Ephron. The border turned toward Baalah (that is, Kiriath-jearim). ¹⁰The border turned westward from Baalah to Mount Seir. It passed on to the slope of Mount Jearim on the north (that is, Chesalon), went down to Beth-shemesh, and passed by Timnah. ¹¹The border went to the slope of Ekron on the north. The border turned toward Shikkeron, passed on to Mount Baalah, and went to Jabneel. The border ended at the sea.

¹²The west border was the Mediterranean Sea and its shoreline. This was the border surrounding the clans of the Judahites.

Caleb and Achsah

¹³In agreement with the LORD's command to him, Joshua gave a portion among the Judahites to Caleb, Jephunneh's son. It was Kiriath-arba, that is, Hebron (Arba was the father of Anak). ¹⁴Caleb removed the three sons of Anak from there: Sheshai, Ahiman, and Talmai. They were the offspring of Anak. ¹⁵Then he went up from there against the population of Debir. Debir used to be called Kiriath-sepher. ¹⁶Caleb said, "I will give Achsah my daughter in marriage to whoever strikes Kiriath-sepher and captures it." ¹⁷So Othniel son of Kenaz, Caleb's brother, captured it, and Caleb gave him Achsah his daughter in marriage.

¹⁸Now when she arrived, she prodded Othniel into asking for a field from her father. After she got down off her donkey, Caleb asked her, "What do you want?" ¹⁹She said, "Give me a blessing. Since the land you've given me is in the arid southern plain, you should also give me springs of water." So he gave her the upper springs and the lower springs.

Cities of Judah

²⁰This is the legacy for the clans of the tribe of the people of Judah. ²¹The outlying cities of the tribe of the people of Judah ran down to the border of Edom.

In the arid southern plain: Kabzeel, Eder, Jagur, ²²Kinah, Dimonah, Adadah, ²³Kedesh, Hazor, Ithnan, ²⁴Ziph, Telem, Bealoth, ²⁵Hazor-hadattah, Kerioth-hezron (that is, Hazor), ²⁶Amam, Shema, Moladah, ²⁷Hazar-gaddah, Heshmon, Beth-pelet, ²⁸Hazar-shual, Beer-sheba and its dependent cities,ˢ ²⁹Baalah, Iim, Ezem, ³⁰Eltolad, Chesil, Hormah, ³¹Ziklag, Madmannah, Sansannah, ³²Lebaoth, Shilhim, Ain, and Rimmon. In total: twenty-nine cities and their surrounding areas.

³³In the lowlands: Eshtaol, Zorah, Ashnah, ³⁴Zanoah, En-gannim, Tappuah, Enam, ³⁵Jarmuth, Adullam, Socoh, Azekah, ³⁶Shaaraim, Adithaim, Gederah, and Gederothaim. In total: fourteen cities and their surrounding areas.

³⁷Zenan, Hadashah, Migdal-gad, ³⁸Dilan, Mizpeh, Jokthe-el, ³⁹Lachish, Bozkath, Eglon, ⁴⁰Cabbon, Lahmam, Chitlish, ⁴¹Gederoth, Beth-dagon, Naamah, and Makkedah. In total: sixteen cities and their surrounding areas.

⁴²Libnah, Ether, Ashan, ⁴³Iphtah, Ashnah, Nezib, ⁴⁴Keilah, Achzib, and Mareshah. In total: nine cities and their surrounding areas.

⁴⁵Ekron, its dependent cities and surrounding areas. ⁴⁶From Ekron toward the sea, everything that was near Ashdod and its surrounding areas. ⁴⁷Ashdod, its dependent cities and surrounding areas. Gaza, its dependent cities and surrounding areas as far as the border of Egypt and the Mediterranean Sea and its shoreline.

⁴⁸In the highlands: Shamir, Jattir, Socoh, ⁴⁹Dannah, Kiriath-sannah (that is, Debir), ⁵⁰Anab, Eshtemoh, Anim, ⁵¹Goshen, Holon,

---

ˢLXX and Neh 11:27; Heb *Biziothiah*

and Giloh. In total: eleven cities and their surrounding areas.

⁵²Arab, Dumah, Eshan, ⁵³Janim, Beth-tappuah, Aphekah, ⁵⁴Humtah, Kiriath-arba (that is, Hebron), and Zior. In total: nine cities and their surrounding areas.

⁵⁵Maon, Carmel, Ziph, Juttah, ⁵⁶Jezreel, Jokdeam, Zanoah, ⁵⁷Kain, Gibeah, and Timnah. In total: ten cities and their surrounding areas.

⁵⁸Halhul, Beth-zur, Gedor, ⁵⁹Maarath, Beth-anoth, and Eltekon. In total: six cities and their surrounding areas.

Tekoah, Ephrathah (that is, Bethlehem), Peor, Etam, Koulon, Tatam, Sores, Karem, Gallim, Bether, and Manahath. In total: eleven cities and their surrounding areas.ᵗ

⁶⁰Kiriath-baal (that is, Kiriath-jearim) and Rabbah. In total: two cities and their surrounding areas.

⁶¹In the desert: Beth-arabah, Middin, Secacah, ⁶²Nibshan (the Salt City), and En-gedi. In total: six cities and their surrounding areas.

⁶³But the people of Judah couldn't remove the Jebusites who lived in Jerusalem. So today the Jebusites still live along with the people of Judah in Jerusalem.

Ephraim

16 The land determined by lot for the people of Joseph went out from the Jordan near Jericho eastward to the waters of Jericho. It went up by the desert from Jericho to the Bethel highlands. ²It goes from Bethel to Luz and passes on to the border of the Archites at Ataroth. ³It goes down westward to the border of the Japhletites as far as the border of Lower Beth-horon and as far as Gezer. It ends at the sea. ⁴The people of Joseph, Manasseh and Ephraim, received their legacy.

⁵This was the territory for the clans of the people of Ephraim. The border of their legacy ran from Ataroth-adar on the east as far as Upper Beth-horon. ⁶The border goes to the sea. Michmethath is on the north. The border turns east of Taanath-shiloh and passes along beyond it east of Janoah.

⁷It goes down from Janoah to Ataroth and to Naarah, touches Jericho, and goes to the Jordan. ⁸From Tappuah the border goes westward by the Kanah Valley. It ends at the sea. This is the legacy for the clans of the Ephraimite tribe. ⁹It included cities set apart for the people of Ephraim within the legacy of the people of Manasseh, all the cities and their surrounding areas. ¹⁰But they didn't remove the Canaanites who lived in Gezer. So today the Canaanites, who were used for forced labor, still live within Ephraim.

Manasseh

17 Land was determined by lot for the tribe of Manasseh, who was actually Joseph's oldest son. Gilead and Bashan belonged to Machir, who was Manasseh's oldest son and Gilead's father. This was because he was a warrior. ²So an allotment took place for the rest of the clans of the people of Manasseh—for the people of Abiezer, Helek, Asriel, Shechem, Hepher, and Shemida. These were the sons of Manasseh the son of Joseph, the male descendants by their clans.

³Zelophehad was Hepher's son, Gilead's grandson, Machir's great-grandson and Manasseh's great-great-grandson. Zelophehad had no sons, only daughters, who were named Mahlah, Noah, Hoglah, Milcah, and Tirzah. ⁴The daughters approached Eleazar the priest, Joshua, Nun's son, and the leaders. They said, "The LORD commanded Moses to give us a legacy along with our male relatives." So in agreement with the LORD's command, they were given a legacy along with their uncles. ⁵Manasseh had ten parcels in addition to the land of Gilead and Bashan on the other side of the Jordan. ⁶This was because the daughters of Manasseh received a legacy along with his sons. The land of Gilead belonged to the rest of the people of Manasseh.

⁷The border of Manasseh ran from Asher to Michmethath, which is opposite Shechem. The border went south to the population of En-tappuah. ⁸The land

---

ᵗLXX; MT lacks *Tekoa, Ephrathah ... surrounding areas.*

of Tappuah belonged to Manasseh. But Tappuah itself belonged to the people of Ephraim, even though it was on the border of Manasseh. ⁹The border went down by the Kanah Valley. South of the ravine are those cities that belong to Ephraim, even though they are located among the cities of Manasseh. The border of Manasseh lay on the north side of the ravine and ended at the sea. ¹⁰What lay south of the border belonged to Ephraim, and what lay north of it belonged to Manasseh. The sea was its border. The territory bordered Asher on the north and Issachar on the east.

¹¹Belonging to Manasseh in Issachar and in Asher were Beth-shean and its dependent cities, Ibleam and its dependent cities, the population of Dor and its dependent cities, the population of En-dor and its dependent cities, the population of Taanach and its dependent cities, and the population of Megiddo and its dependent cities. (The third one is Naphath.)ᵘ ¹²The people of Manasseh couldn't take over these cities, and the Canaanites were determined to live in this land. ¹³When the Israelites grew strong, they subjected the Canaanites to hard labor but didn't remove them.

Future expansion for Joseph

¹⁴The tribe of Joseph spoke to Joshua: "Why have you only given us a single lot and a solitary parcel for a legacy? We are a numerous people whom the LORD has blessed so richly."

¹⁵Then Joshua said, "Yes, you are a numerous people. So go up to the forest and clear ground for yourselves there in the land of the Perizzites and Rephaim, because the Ephraimite highland is too small for you."

¹⁶The people of Joseph said, "The highland isn't enough for us. But all the Canaanites who live in the valley region have iron chariots, both those in Beth-shean and its dependent cities and those in the Jezreel Valley."

¹⁷Joshua then said to the house of Joseph, to Ephraim and to Manasseh, "You are a numerous people and possess great strength. You will have more than a single lot. ¹⁸The highland will belong to you. Because it is a forest, you can clear it. Its farthest limits will be yours. You will definitely remove the Canaanites, even though they have iron chariots and are strong."

Remainder of the land

18 The whole community of the Israelites assembled at Shiloh and set up the meeting tent there. The conquered land lay before them. ²Among the Israelites, seven tribes were left that had not yet received their legacy. ³Joshua said to the Israelites, "How long will you avoid going to take over the land that the LORD, the God of your ancestors, has given you? ⁴Pick out three men for each tribe. I will send them out, and they will go up and travel throughout the land. They will write a description of it as the basis for determining their legacy. Then they will come back to me. ⁵They will divide up the land among themselves into seven portions. Judah will stay on its territory to the south. The house of Joseph will stay on their territory to the north. ⁶But you will write a report in seven parts and bring the report back here to me. Then I will cast the lot for you here, before the LORD our God. ⁷However, there won't be a portion among you for the Levites because their legacy is the priesthood of the LORD. Gad, Reuben, and half the tribe of Manasseh have already received their legacy on the east side of the Jordan. Moses the LORD's servant gave it to them."

⁸When the men had prepared to go, Joshua gave orders to those going to write a description of the land. "Go and travel around the land, write about it, and return to me. I will cast the lot for you before the LORD here in Shiloh." ⁹So the men went and passed through the land and wrote about it in a document, city by city, in seven sections. They came back to Joshua in the camp at Shiloh. ¹⁰Then Joshua cast lots for them in Shiloh before the LORD. There Joshua divided up the shares of the land for the Israelites.

ᵘHeb uncertain

Border of Benjamin

[11] The lot for the clans of the Benjaminite tribe appeared first. The border of their allotment went out between the people of Judah and the people of Joseph. [12] Their border on the north side ran from the Jordan. The border went up to the slope of Jericho on the north. It went up westward in the highlands and ended at the wasteland of Beth-aven. [13] The border passed on from there to Luz, to the slope of Luz on the south (that is, Bethel). The border went down to Ataroth-adar on the mountain that is south of Lower Beth-horon. [14] The border turned and came around southward on the west side, running from the mountain that is opposite Beth-horon on the south. It ended at Kiriath-baal (that is, Kiriath-jearim), a city of the people of Judah. This was its west side.

[15] The south side ran from the limits of Kiriath-jearim. The border went out westward. It then proceeded to the waters of Nephtoah Spring. [16] The border went down to the foot of the mountain that is opposite the valley of the son of Hinnom, which is in the north part of the Rephaim Valley. It went down through the Hinnom Valley to the slope of the Jebusite city on the south. It then went down to En-rogel. [17] It turned northward. Then it went to En-shemesh and then to Geliloth, which is opposite the

ascent of Adummim. It went down to the Stone of Bohan (Reuben's son). [18] It passed on to the slope of Beth-arabah[v] on the north and went down into the desert plain. [19] The border passed on to the slope of Beth-hoglah on the north. The border ended at the north bay of the Dead Sea, at the southern mouth of the Jordan. This was the southern border. [20] The Jordan bordered it on the east side. This is the legacy of the Benjaminite clans according to its borders.

Cities of Benjamin

[21] The cities of the clans of the Benjaminite tribe are Jericho, Beth-hoglah, Emek-keziz, [22] Beth-arabah, Zemaraim, Bethel, [23] Avvim, Parah, Ophrah, [24] Chephar-ammoni, Ophni, and Geba. In total: twelve cities and their surrounding areas.

[25] Gibeon, Ramah, Beeroth, [26] Mizpeh, Chephirah, Mozah, [27] Rekem, Irpeel, Taralah, [28] Zela, Haeleph, the Jebusite city (that is, Jerusalem), Gibeath, and Kiriath. In total: fourteen cities and their surrounding areas. This is the legacy of the Benjaminite clans.

Simeon

19 The second lot fell to Simeon. The legacy of the clans of the Simeonite tribe lay inside the legacy of the people of Judah. [2] They had in their legacy: Beer-sheba,

---

[v] LXX and Josh 15:6; MT *slope opposite the desert plain*

BENJAMIN/BENJAMINITES

Benjamin was the youngest son of Jacob (Gen 35:18) and was the ancestor of the Israelite tribe that occupied the highland region between Ephraim and Judah. Although a minor tribe in terms of population and territory, Benjamin plays a prominent role in Israel's history and literature. The book of Joshua elaborates the campaigns waged against cities within Benjamin (Josh 2:1–10:15). Ehud, the first judge whose exploits are described in detail, is a Benjaminite (Judg 3:12-30), and Benjamin is at the center of the outrageous events of rape, murder, and war that conclude Judges (Judg 19–21). The tribe also figures significantly in the rise of the Israelite monarchy. A Benjaminite (Saul) becomes Israel's first king, another (Abner) facilitates the transference of the kingdom to David after Saul's death, and a third (Sheba) leads an insurrection against David.

Sheba, Moladah, ³Hazar-shual, Balah, Ezem, ⁴Eltolad, Bethul, Hormah, ⁵Ziklag, Beth-marcaboth, Hazar-susah, ⁶Beth-lebaoth, and Sharuhen. In total: thirteen cities and their surrounding areas. ⁷Ain, Rimmon, Ether, and Ashan. In total: four cities and their surrounding areas. ⁸In addition were all the areas that surround these cities as far as Baalath-beer and Ramah of the arid southern plain. This is the legacy of the clans of the Simeonite tribe. ⁹Some of the portion of the people of Judah belonged to the legacy of the people of Simeon. This was because the portion of the people of Judah was too large for them. So the people of Simeon received a legacy inside Judah's legacy.

Zebulun

¹⁰The lot turned up third for the clans of Zebulun. The border of their legacy ran as far as Sarid. ¹¹Their border went up westward to Maralah, touched Dabbesheth, and touched the ravine that is opposite Jokneam. ¹²It reversed from Sarid eastward toward the east to the border of Chisloth-tabor. It went to Daberath and then up to Japhia. ¹³From there it passed on the east side, running eastward to Gath-hepher and Eth-kazin. Going to Rimmon, it bent toward Neah. ¹⁴The border turned north of Hannathon and ended at the Iphtah-el Valley. ¹⁵They also owned Kattath, Nahalal, Shimron, Idalah, and Bethlehem; in total: twelve cities and their surrounding areas. ¹⁶These cities and their surrounding areas are the legacy of Zebulun's clans.

Issachar

¹⁷The lot went out fourth for the clans of Issachar. ¹⁸Their border ran toward Jezreel. They also owned Chesulloth, Shunem, ¹⁹Hapharaim, Shion, Anaharath, ²⁰Rabbith, Kishion, Ebez, ²¹Remeth, En-gannim, En-haddah, and Beth-pazzez. ²²The border touched Tabor, Shahazumah, and Beth-shemesh. Their border ended at the Jordan; in total: sixteen cities with their surrounding areas. ²³These cities and their surround-

ing areas are the legacy for the clans of the Issachar tribe.

Asher

²⁴The lot went out fifth for the clans of the tribe of Asher. ²⁵Their border included Helkath, Hali, Beten, Achshaph, ²⁶Allammelech, Amad, and Mishal. It touched Carmel on the west and Shihor-libnath. ²⁷The border reversed eastward to Beth-dagon. It touched Zebulun and the Iphtah-el Valley on the north, also Beth-emek and Neiel. It went to Cabul on the north, ²⁸as far as Great Sidon. They also owned Ebron, Rehob, Hammon, and Kanah. ²⁹The border turned around to Ramah as far as the fortified city of Tyre. The border turned around to Hosah and ended at the sea. They also owned Mahalab,ʷ Achzib, ³⁰Ummah, Aphek, and Rehob; in total: twenty-two cities and their surrounding areas. ³¹These cities and their surrounding areas are the legacy for the clans of the Asher tribe.

Naphtali

³²For the people of Naphtali, the lot went out sixth. For the clans of Naphtali ³³their border ran from Heleph, from the oak in Zaanannim and Adami-nekeb and Jabneel as far as Lakkum. It ended at the Jordan. ³⁴The border reversed westward to Aznoth-tabor. It went from there to Hukkok. It touched Zebulun on the south, Asher on the west, and Judah at the Jordan on the east. ³⁵They also owned the fortified cities Ziddim, Zer, Hammath, Rakkath, Chinnereth, ³⁶Adamah, Ramah, Hazor, ³⁷Kedesh, Edrei, En-hazor, ³⁸Iron, Migdal-el, Horem, Beth-anath, and Beth-shemesh; in total: nineteen cities and their surrounding areas. ³⁹These cities and their surrounding areas are the legacy for the clans of the Naphtali tribe.

Dan

⁴⁰The lot went out seventh for the clans of the Danite tribe. ⁴¹The territory of their legacy was Zorah, Eshtaol, Ir-shemesh, ⁴²Shaalabbin, Aijalon, Ithlah, ⁴³Elon, Tim-

ʷLXX; MT Mehebel

nah, Ekron, ⁴⁴Eltekeh, Gibbethon, Baalath, ⁴⁵Jehud, Bene-berak, Gath-rimmon, ⁴⁶Mejarkon, and Rakkon, along with the territory opposite Joppa. ⁴⁷But the territory of the people of Dan was lost to them. So the people of Dan went up and attacked Leshem and captured it. They struck it down without mercy. They took it over and settled it. Then they named Leshem as Dan, after the name of Dan their ancestor. ⁴⁸These cities and their surrounding areas are the legacy for the clans of the Danite tribe.

Legacy for Joshua

⁴⁹So when they finished assigning the borders of the land, the Israelites gave to Joshua, Nun's son, a legacy among them. ⁵⁰By the LORD's command, they gave him the city that he asked for. This was Timnathserah in the highlands of Ephraim. He built a city and lived in it. ⁵¹These are the legacies that Eleazar the priest, Joshua, Nun's son, and the heads of the families of the Israelite tribes assigned by lot at Shiloh. They did this before the LORD at the entrance of the meeting tent and finished dividing up the land.

Refuge cities

20 The LORD spoke to Joshua: ²"Say to the Israelites, 'Set up refuge cities for yourselves. I spoke to you about these through Moses. ³Anyone who kills by striking down someone unintentionally or by mistake may flee there. These places will be a refuge for you from any member of the victim's family seeking revenge. ⁴The killer will flee to one of these cities, stand at the entrance of the city gate, and explain their situation to the elders of that city. The elders are to let the killer into the city and provide a place of refuge for the killer to live with them. ⁵If a member of the victim's family follows, seeking revenge, they won't hand the killer over. This is because the killer struck down the neighbor by accident and hadn't been an enemy in the past. ⁶The killer will live in that city until there can be a trial before the community or˟ until the death of the one who is high priest at that time. Then the killer may return home, back to the city from which the flight began.'"

⁷So they set apart Kedesh in Galilee in the highlands of Naphtali, Shechem in the highlands of Ephraim, and Kiriatharba (that is, Hebron) in the highlands of Judah. ⁸On the other side of the Jordan east of Jericho, they set up Bezer in the wasteland on the plateau from the tribe of Reuben, Ramoth in Gilead from the tribe of Gad, and Golan in Bashan from the tribe of Manasseh. ⁹These cities were the ones designated for all the Israelites and for immigrants residing among them. Anyone who struck down a person by mistake could flee there and escape death at the hand of

˟Heb uncertain

CITY OF REFUGE

Cities of refuge were established in Israel to offer protection for those who had inadvertently killed another human being (Exod 21:12-14). The justice system of Israel's kinship system demanded a life for a life. The six cities designated in Joshua 20:8-9 were strategically located so that none lay outside a day's journey from any point in Israel.

The concept of asylum in the ancient Near East was generally associated with sanctuaries. The covenant scroll reflects this perspective through legislation that allows a killer to flee to a place appointed by God if the murder was not premeditated (Exod 21:12-14; Num 35:9-29; Deut 4:41-43; 19:1-13).

some member of the victim's family seeking revenge, until there could be a trial before the community.

Cities for the Levites

21 The heads of the levitical families approached Eleazar the priest, Joshua, Nun's son, and the heads of the families of the Israelite tribes. [2]They spoke to them at Shiloh in the land of Canaan: "The LORD gave a command through Moses to give us cities to live in and their pasturelands for our cattle." [3]So the Israelites gave the Levites the following cities and their pasturelands out of their own legacy. This was in agreement with the LORD's command.

[4]The lot went out for the clans of the Kohathites. The descendants of Aaron the priest from among the Levites acquired thirteen cities by lot from the tribes of Judah, Simeon, and Benjamin. [5]The rest of the descendants of Kohath acquired ten cities by lot from the clans of the tribes of Ephraim, Dan, and half of Manasseh. [6]The descendants of Gershon acquired thirteen cities by lot from the clans of the tribes of Issachar, Asher, Naphtali, and the half of Manasseh located in Bashan. [7]The descendants of Merari acquired twelve cities for their clans from the tribes of Reuben, Gad, and Zebulun. [8]So the Israelites gave these cities and their pasturelands to the Levites by lot, exactly as the LORD had commanded through Moses.

[9]They gave the following cities, identified here by name, from the tribe of the Judahites and the tribe of the Simeonites. [10]The cities belonged to the descendants of Aaron, one of the Kohathite clans of the Levites, because the lot had fallen to them first. [11]They gave them Kiriath-arba (that is, Hebron) in the highlands of Judah and the pastures around it. (Arba was the father of Anak.) [12]But they had already given the fields of the city and its surrounding areas to Caleb, Jephunneh's son, as his property. [13]To the descendants of Aaron the priest they gave: Hebron, the refuge city for a killer, and its pastures; Libnah and its pastures; [14]Jattir and its pastures; Eshtemoa and its pastures; [15]Holon and its pastures;

Debir and its pastures; [16]Ain and its pastures; Juttah and its pastures; and Beth-shemesh and its pastures. Total from these two tribes: nine cities. [17]From the tribe of Benjamin: Gibeon and its pastures, Geba and its pastures, [18]Anathoth and its pastures, and Almon and its pastures. In total: four cities. [19]This is the total of all the cities of the priests descended from Aaron: thirteen cities with their pastures.

[20]Other clans from the levitical descendants of Kohath still remained from among the descendants of Kohath. Some of their allotted cities were from the tribe of Ephraim. [21]They gave them: Shechem, the refuge city for a killer, and its pastures in the highlands of Ephraim; Gezer and its pastures; [22]Kibzaim and its pastures; and Beth-horon and its pastures; in total: four cities. [23]From the tribe of Dan: Elteke and its pastures, Gibbethon and its pastures, [24]Aijalon and its pastures, Gath-rimmon and its pastures; in total: four cities. [25]From half the tribe of Manasseh: Taanach and its pastures, and Gath-rimmon and its pastures; in total: two cities. [26]This is the total of all cities for the clans of the remaining descendants of Kohath: ten cities with their pastures.

[27]To the descendants of Gershon, one of the clans of the Levites, from half the tribe of Manasseh: Golan in Bashan, the refuge city for a killer, and its pastures; and Beeshterah and its pastures; in total: two cities. [28]From the tribe of Issachar: Kishion and its pastures, Daberath and its pastures, [29]Jarmuth and its pastures, En-gannim and its pastures; in total: four cities. [30]From the tribe of Asher: Mishal and its pastures, Abdon and its pastures, [31]Helkath and its pastures, and Rehob and its pastures; in total: four cities. [32]From the tribe of Naphtali: Kedesh in Galilee, the refuge city for the killer, and its pastures; Hammoth-dor and its pastures; and Kartan and its pastures; in total: three cities. [33]This is the total of all cities of the Gershonites for their clans: thirteen cities with their pastures.

[34]To the clans of the descendants of Merari, the rest of the Levites, from the

tribe of Zebulun: Jokneam and its pastures, Kartah and its pastures, [35]Dimnah and its pastures, Nahalal and its pastures; in total: four cities. [36]From the tribe of Reuben: Bezer and its pastures, Jahaz and its pastures, [37]Kedemoth and its pastures, and Mephaath and its pastures; in total: four cities.[y] [38]From the tribe of Gad: Ramoth in Gilead, the refuge city for a killer, and its pastures; Mahanaim and its pastures; [39]Heshbon and its pastures; Jazer and its pastures; in total: four cities. [40]As for the cities of the descendants of Merari for their clans, the remaining clans of the Levites, their total allotment was twelve cities.

[41]This is the total of all the cities of the Levites within the property of the Israelites: forty-eight cities with their pastures. [42]Each of these cities had its pastures around it. This was the case for all these cities.

Summary of the conquest

[43]The LORD gave to Israel all the land he had pledged to give to their ancestors. They took it over and settled there. [44]The LORD gave them rest from surrounding danger, exactly as he had pledged to their ancestors. Not one of all their enemies held out against them. The LORD gave all their enemies into their power. [45]Not one of all the good things that the LORD had promised to the house of Israel failed. Every promise was fulfilled.

Eastern tribes go home

22 Then Joshua summoned the Reubenites, the Gadites, and half the tribe of Manasseh. [2]He said to them, "You obeyed everything that Moses the LORD's servant commanded you. You have also obeyed me in everything that I have commanded you. [3]During these many years, you never once deserted your fellow Israelites. You faithfully obeyed the command of the LORD your God. [4]The LORD your God has now given rest to your fellow Israelites, exactly as he promised them. So turn around and go back home. Go to the land where you hold property, which Moses

the LORD's servant gave you on the other side of the Jordan. [5]Just be very careful to carry out the commandment and Instruction that Moses the LORD's servant commanded you. Love the LORD your God. Walk in all his ways and obey his commandments. Hold on to him and serve him with all your heart and being." [6]Then Joshua blessed them. He sent them away, and they went home.

[7]Moses had provided for half of the tribe of Manasseh in Bashan. But Joshua provided for the other half on the west side of the Jordan along with their fellow Israelites. When he sent them back home, Joshua also blessed them. [8]He said to them, "Return home with great wealth and many cattle, with silver, gold, bronze, and iron, and with much clothing. Divide the spoil taken from your enemies among your own people."

Disagreement about an altar

[9]So the people of Reuben, the people of Gad, and half the tribe of Manasseh went back. They left the Israelites at Shiloh, which is in the land of Canaan. They went to the land of Gilead, to the land that they owned. They had settled there at the LORD's command given by Moses. [10]They came to the districts[z] of the Jordan that are in the land of Canaan. The people of Reuben, the people of Gad, and half the tribe of Manasseh built an altar there by the Jordan, an altar that appeared to be immense. [11]Then the Israelites heard a report: "Look. The people of Reuben, the people of Gad, and half the tribe of Manasseh have built an altar at the far edge of the land of Canaan. It lies in the districts of the Jordan on the Israelite side!" [12]When the Israelites heard this, the entire Israelite community assembled at Shiloh to go up to war against them.

[13]Then the Israelites sent Phinehas son of Eleazar the priest to the people of Reuben, the people of Gad, and half the tribe of Manasseh in the land of Gilead. [14]They sent with him ten leaders, one leader from each important family among the tribes of Israel.

---

[y]LXX and 1 Chron 6:78-79 (Heb 6:63-64); some Heb manuscripts lack 21:36-37. [z]Heb *Geliloth*

Each was the head of an important family among the military units of Israel. [15]They came to the people of Reuben, the people of Gad, and half the tribe of Manasseh in the land of Gilead and spoke with them. [16]They said, "Here is what the LORD's entire community says: 'What's this disrespectful thing that you've done to the God of Israel? Today you've turned away from following the LORD by building yourselves an altar as an act of rebellion against the LORD. [17]Wasn't the offense of Peor enough for us? Even today we still haven't cleansed ourselves from that sin, when there was a plague on the LORD's community! [18]Today you are turning away from following the LORD. If you rebel against the LORD today, he will be angry with the entire community of Israel tomorrow. [19]If your own property is unclean land, then cross over into the land of the LORD's property and settle among us. That's where the dwelling of the LORD stands. But don't rebel against the LORD. And don't involve us in rebellion[a] by building an altar for yourselves other than the altar of the LORD our God. [20]Didn't Achan, Zerah's son, do such a disrespectful thing with the items reserved for God? Wrath came on the entire community of Israel. And he wasn't the only one to die for his crime.'"

[21]Then the people of Reuben, the people of Gad, and half the tribe of Manasseh answered the heads of the military units of Israel: [22]"The LORD is God of gods! The LORD is God of gods! He already knows, and now let Israel also know it! If we acted in rebellion or in disrespect against the LORD, don't spare us today. [23]If we've built ourselves an altar to turn away from following the LORD or to offer on it an entirely burned offering or gift offering, or to perform well-being sacrifices on it, let the LORD himself seek punishment. [24]No! The truth is we did this out of concern for what might happen. In the future your children might say to our children, 'What have you got to do with the LORD, the God of Israel? [25]The LORD has set the Jordan as a border

between us and you people of Reuben and Gad. You have no portion in the LORD!' So your children might make our children stop worshipping the LORD. [26]As a result we said, 'Let's protect ourselves by building an altar. It isn't to be for an entirely burned offering or for sacrifice.' [27]But it is to be a witness between us and you and between our descendants after us. It witnesses that we too perform the service of the LORD in his presence through our entirely burned offerings, sacrifices, and well-being offerings. So in the future your children could never say to our children, 'You have no portion in the LORD.' [28]We thought, If in the future they ever say this to us or to our descendants, we could say, 'Look at this replica of the altar of the LORD that our ancestors made. It isn't for entirely burned offerings or for sacrifice but to be a witness between us and you.' [29]God forbid that we should rebel against the LORD and turn away today from following the LORD by building an altar for an entirely burned offering, gift offering, or sacrifice, other than the altar of the LORD our God that stands before his dwelling!"

[30]Phinehas the priest, the leaders of the community, and the heads of the military units of Israel who were with him heard the words that the people of Reuben, Gad, and Manasseh spoke and approved them. [31]So Phinehas the son of Eleazar the priest said to the people of Reuben, Gad, and Manasseh, "Today we know that the LORD is among us, because you haven't done a disrespectful thing against the LORD. Now you've delivered the Israelites from the power of the LORD." [32]Then Phinehas the son of Eleazar the priest and the leaders left the people of Reuben and Gad in the land of Gilead and came back to the Israelites in the land of Canaan. They brought word back to them. [33]The Israelites agreed and blessed God. They no longer spoke of going to war against them to destroy the land where the people of Reuben and Gad were living. [34]The people of Reuben and Gad referred to the altar in this way: "It is a witness between us that the LORD is God."

---

[a]Or *rebel against us*

Joshua's word of warning

23 A long time passed. The LORD had given rest to Israel from all their surrounding enemies, and Joshua had grown very old. [2]Joshua summoned all Israel, their elders, their heads, their judges, and their officers. He said to them, "I've grown very old. [3]You've seen all that the LORD your God has done to all these nations because of you. It is the LORD your God who fights for you. [4]Look. I've allotted to you these remaining nations as a legacy for your tribes, along with all the nations I have destroyed. They stretch from the Jordan to the Mediterranean Sea. [5]The LORD your God will force them out before you and remove them from you. Then you will take over their land, exactly as the LORD your God has promised you. [6]Be very strong. Carefully obey everything written in the Instruction scroll from Moses. Don't deviate a bit from it either to the right or to the left. [7]Don't have anything to do with these nations that remain with you. Don't invoke the names of their gods or take oaths by them. Don't serve them or worship them. [8]Hold on to the LORD your God instead, exactly as you've done right up to today.

[9]"The LORD has removed great and powerful nations before you. To this day, no one has stood up to you. [10]A single one of you puts a thousand to flight. This is because the LORD your God fights for you, exactly as he promised you. [11]For your own sake, be very careful to love the LORD your God. [12]But if you should turn away and join the rest of these nations that remain with you, intermarry with them, and associate with each other, [13]then know for certain that the LORD your God won't keep on removing these nations before you. Instead, they will be a snare and a trap for you. They will be a whip on your sides and thorns in your eyes, until you vanish from this fertile land that the LORD your God has given you.

[14]"Look. I'm now walking on the road to death that all the earth must take. You know with all your heart and being that not a single one of all the good things that the LORD your God promised about you has failed. They were all fulfilled for you. Not a single one of them has failed. [15]But in the same way that every good thing that the LORD your God promised about you has been fulfilled, so the LORD could bring against you every bad thing as well. He could wipe you out from this fertile land that the LORD your God has given you. [16]If you violate the covenant of the LORD your God, which he commanded you to keep, and go on to serve other gods and worship them, then the LORD will be furious with you. You will quickly vanish from the fertile land that he has given you."

What God has done

24 Joshua gathered all the tribes of Israel at Shechem. He summoned the elders of Israel, its leaders, judges, and officers. They presented themselves before God. [2]Then Joshua said to the entire people, "This is what the LORD, the God of Israel, says: Long ago your ancestors lived on the other side of the Euphrates. They served other gods. Among them was Terah the father of Abraham and Nahor. [3]I took Abraham your ancestor from the other side of the Euphrates. I led him around through the whole land of Canaan. I added to his descendants and gave him Isaac. [4]To Isaac I gave Jacob and Esau. I gave Mount Seir to Esau to take over. But Jacob and his sons went down to Egypt. [5]Then I sent Moses and Aaron. I plagued Egypt with what I did to them. After that I brought you out. [6]I brought your ancestors out of Egypt, and you came to the sea. The Egyptians chased your ancestors with chariots and horses to the Reed Sea.[b] [7]Then they cried for help to the LORD. So he set darkness between you and the Egyptians. He brought the sea down on them, and it covered them. With your own eyes you saw what I did to the Egyptians. You lived in the desert for a long time.

[8]"Then I brought you into the land of the

[b] Or Red Sea

Amorites who lived on the other side of the Jordan. They attacked you, but I gave them into your power, and you took over their land. I wiped them out before you. [9]Then Moab's King Balak, Zippor's son, set out to attack Israel. He summoned Balaam, Beor's son, to curse you. [10]But I wasn't willing to listen to Balaam, so he actually blessed you. I rescued you from his power. [11]Then you crossed over the Jordan. You came to Jericho, and the citizens of Jericho attacked you. They were Amorites, Perizzites, Canaanites, Hittites, Girgashites, Hivites, and Jebusites. But I gave them into your power. [12]I sent the hornet[c] before you. It drove them out before you and did the same to the two kings of the Amorites. It wasn't your sword or bow that did this. [13]I gave you land on which you hadn't toiled and cities that you hadn't built. You settled in them and are enjoying produce from vineyards and olive groves that you didn't plant.

Challenge to be faithful

[14]"So now, revere the LORD. Serve him honestly and faithfully. Put aside the gods that your ancestors served beyond the Euphrates and in Egypt and serve the LORD. [15]But if it seems wrong in your opinion to serve the LORD, then choose today whom you will serve. Choose the gods whom your ancestors served beyond the Euphrates or the gods of the Amorites in whose land you live. But my family and I will serve the LORD."

[16]Then the people answered, "God forbid that we ever leave the LORD to serve other gods! [17]The LORD is our God. He is the one who brought us and our ancestors up from the land of Egypt, from the house of bondage. He has done these mighty signs in our sight. He has protected us the whole way we've gone and in all the nations through which we've passed. [18]The LORD has driven out all the nations before us, including the Amorites who lived in the land. We too will serve the LORD, because he is our God."

[19]Then Joshua said to the people, "You can't serve the LORD, because he is a holy God. He is a jealous God. He won't forgive your rebellion and your sins. [20]If you leave the LORD and serve foreign gods, then he will turn around and do you harm and finish you off, in spite of having done you good in the past."

[21]Then the people said to Joshua, "No! The LORD is the one we will serve."

[22]So Joshua said to the people, "You are witnesses against yourselves that you have chosen to serve the LORD."

[c] Heb uncertain

SHECHEM

Shechem ("shoulder") was one of the most prominent biblical locations, ca. 40 mi. north of Jerusalem. Shechem is strategically situated in Mount Ephraim in the pass between Mount Ebal and Mount Gerizim near modern Nablus. Joshua made a covenant and erected a standing stone at Shechem (Josh 24). Shechem was also an important site in the united and divided monarchies. Upon the death of Solomon, Rehoboam went to Shechem to try to claim the throne (1 Kgs 12:1). Jeroboam I refortified the site (1 Kgs 12:25). Archaeological excavations have found a casemate wall that belongs to this general period along with several private houses that attest to improved economic conditions. The city was destroyed in the raid of the Egyptian pharaoh Shishak, ca. 918 BCE (see 2 Chron 12:1-12).

They said, "We are witnesses!"

²³"So now put aside the foreign gods that are among you. Focus your hearts on the LORD, the God of Israel."

²⁴The people said to Joshua, "We will serve the LORD our God and will obey him."

Joshua makes a covenant

²⁵On that day Joshua made a covenant for the people and established just rule for them at Shechem. ²⁶Joshua wrote these words in God's Instruction scroll. Then he took a large stone and put it up there under the oak in the sanctuary of the LORD. ²⁷Joshua said to all the people, "This stone will serve here as a witness against us, because it has heard all the LORD's words that he spoke to us. It will serve as a witness against you in case you aren't true to your God." ²⁸Then Joshua sent the people away to each one's legacy.

Three important graves

²⁹After these events, Joshua, Nun's son, the LORD's servant, died. He was 110. ³⁰They buried him within the border of his own legacy, in Timnath-serah in the highlands of Ephraim north of Mount Gaash. ³¹Israel served the LORD all the days of Joshua and all the days of the elders who outlived Joshua. They had known every act the LORD had done for Israel.

³²The Israelites had brought up the bones of Joseph from Egypt. They buried them at Shechem in the portion of field that Jacob had purchased for one hundred qesitahs from the descendants of Hamor the father of Shechem. They became a legacy of the descendants of Joseph.

³³Eleazar son of Aaron died. They buried him at Gibeah, which belonged to his son Phinehas. It had been given to him in the highlands of Ephraim.

JUDGES

NAME

The title refers to this book's main characters, the judges. The Hebrew concept of "judge" differs somewhat, however, from our American use of the word. The biblical persons called judges were tribal or national leaders. Often they were military commanders. Sometimes they settled disputes or offered advice. They gained their leadership positions informally or by popular acclaim. Many judges displayed exceptional wisdom, unusual skill in organization, or personal charisma. Since Israel had no king or other central political figure, the judges played an important role in Israel's survival. They provided administrative and military leadership to a new, loosely organized nation.

CLASSIFICATION

Jews consider this book the second of the "former prophets." And, like the book of Joshua, it does exhibit a prophetic viewpoint. Christians, however, usually call this a historical book because it deals directly with the history of Israel and forms part of the epic historical work that includes most of Deuteronomy through 2 Kings.

AUTHOR

Who wrote the book of Judges? That is a complicated question. Scholars believe that the book grew over several centuries. We can recognize at least four major steps in that growth. First came the oral tradition. From the actual time of the judges up to about 950 BCE, people told stories about these leaders, passing the tales on from generation to generation. Between 950 and 800 BCE someone collected these stories and wrote them down. Around 615 BCE one or more writers, whom we call the first Deuteronomic historians, included these stories in a great history of Israel. After the destruction of Jerusalem in 587 BCE, another historian of the Deuteronomic school edited a final version.

So, who was the author of this book? Many people were. But the persons who did the most to put the book in the form we have today were the Deuteronomic historians. These were the same ones who prepared and edited the final version of Joshua. For convenience we call them (or him) D. Where possible we also try to distinguish the time period a particular passage comes from.

STYLE

The style of Judges varies because so many people contributed to it. We find earthiness and a sense of humor mixed with judgmental comments and dry connecting paragraphs. Still, throughout the book we can see one obvious formula repeated over and over. As given in the CEB, it can be summarized, "The Israelites did things the LORD saw as evil, and the LORD handed them over to . . . and the Israelites cried out to the LORD and the LORD sent them a deliverer . . . and the land had peace." With this formula one of the later editors tied his string of stories together and made a theological point all at the same time.

PURPOSE

The writers' purpose was, of course, to preserve Israel's history. But it was more than that. D and the others wanted to convey the lessons of history, to show the nation what it must do to survive and prosper. These writers wanted to encourage faithfulness and obedience in a people who could easily go astray. They wanted to warn the people of the consequences of disobedience and to remind them that God could be depended upon, no matter what the danger.

THE TIMES

What were the times like? Since the book grew over so many centuries we have to deal with several different times. First is the time of the judges themselves, 1200–1050 BCE. This was just after Joshua's conquest of Palestine and before Israel chose its first king. The time was a very unsettled one. Israel still had to fight to maintain its hold on the land. The nation was only loosely organized. It was surrounded by enemies, all trying to move into or regain land that Israel held. There was Ammon east of the Jordan, there was a Canaanite confederation in north-central Palestine, there were Philistines on the west, Moabites to the southeast, and Midianite nomads who ranged to the east and south of Israel.

Israel was frequently at war with these enemies. Unity among the tribes was essential. But Israel had no king. God was to be their only ruler. So, in times of special need, divinely inspired judges took on specific leadership tasks.

The religious situation under the judges was one of alternating faith and faithlessness. When they were faithful, the people depended upon God for protection and leadership. They recognized God's spirit working through the judges. The tribes periodically met to worship God at central sanctuaries, including Shiloh, Bethel, Gilgal, and Mizpah. Some individuals had home worship centers as well. Nonetheless, this was a primitive time. Faith and worship often went awry. Superstition ran high, and divination was a common practice. Idolatry crept in. Ethics were not the highest. We find many cases of sexual laxity, treachery, thievery, and violence here. Low morality was common and was sometimes approved or taken for granted.

The time of the seventh-century historian was a more organized one. But the writer felt that Israel had fallen into gross idolatry. So, the seventh-century writer's concern focuses on pagan influence and idol worship.

By the time of the exilic editor, Israel's land had been destroyed. The defeated Jews feared that God had rejected them or was powerless to help them. This editor used the stories of the judges to show that an all-powerful God will continue to fight for Israel if the people will only respond in obedience.

THEOLOGICAL PERSPECTIVE

The main theological points in Judges are the same as those in Joshua. The writer emphasizes God's power, desire to help Israel, and faithfulness in fulfilling promises, and the importance of obedience. If the people will obey, God will defend them and enable them to prosper. If they do not obey, disaster will befall them.

Here, as in Joshua, we encounter a problem with violence. These stories frequently show God to be an advocate of bloodshed. Why should the biblical writers portray God this way? One reason lies in human nature. It is very easy in time of war to assume that God hates the enemy as much as we do. Ancient peoples were no different from ourselves in that respect. They gleefully reported every detail of the foe's defeat and attributed it all to a vengeful God. Second, we must consider that early Israel may not yet have come to recognize God's love for all people. Very old stories tend to think of God's love for Israel alone. Third, a concern for preserving historical material or a reluctance to get into complex questions of God's character may have led a later, more sophisticated editor to let the ancient stories stand without revision or comment. A fourth possibility is that the writer saw God using the world as it is, not the world as we might wish it to be. In a violent world, God is shown moving in violent events toward long-term goals.

CONCLUSION

Judges, then, is not a simple book. It is an important one, though. It provides both vital historical information and a religious perspective on God's acts in history. This perspective is one that we need to consider in thinking through our own faith.

JUDGES

The tribes and their military conflicts

1 After Joshua's death, the Israelites asked the LORD, "Who should go up first to fight for us against the Canaanites?"

[2] The LORD said, "The tribe of Judah will go up. I've handed over the land to them."

[3] So the tribe of Judah said to the tribe of Simeon, their brothers, "Come up with us into our territory, and let's fight against the Canaanites. Then we'll go with you into your territory too." So Simeon went with them.

[4] When Judah went up, the LORD handed them the Canaanites and Perizzites. They defeated ten thousand men at Bezek. [5] There they found Adoni-bezek at Bezek, fought against him, and defeated the Canaanites and Perizzites. [6] Adoni-bezek fled, but they chased after him, captured him, and cut off his thumbs and big toes. [7] He said, "Seventy kings with severed thumbs and big toes used to pick up scraps under my table, so God has paid me back exactly for what I did." They brought him to Jerusalem, where he died. [8] The people of Judah fought against Jerusalem and captured it. They killed its people with their swords and set the city on fire.

[9] Afterward, the people of Judah went down to fight against the Canaanites who lived in the highlands, the southern plain,[a] and the western foothills.[b] [10] Judah moved against the Canaanites who lived in Hebron, known before as Kiriath-arba, and they defeated Sheshai, Ahiman, and Talmai. [11] From there they moved against those who lived in Debir, known before as Kiriath-sepher. [12] Caleb said, "I'll give my daughter Achsah as a wife to the one who defeats and captures Kiriath-sepher." [13] Othniel son of Kenaz, Caleb's younger brother, captured it; so Caleb gave him his daughter Achsah as a wife. [14] When she arrived, she convinced Othniel to ask her father for a certain piece of land. As she got down from her donkey, Caleb said to her, "What do you want?"

[15] Achsah said to Caleb, "Give me a gift. Since you've given me land in the southern plain, give me springs of water." So Caleb gave her the upper and lower springs.

[16] The descendants of Moses' father-in-law the Kenite went up with the people of Judah from Palm City into the Judean desert, which was in the southern plain near Arad. They went and lived with the Amalekites.[c] [17] Then the Judahites went with the Simeonites, their brothers, and they defeated the Canaanites who lived in Zephath, and they completely destroyed it. So the city was called Hormah.[d] [18] Judah also captured Gaza, Ashkelon, Ekron, and all their territories. [19] Thus the LORD was with the tribe of Judah, and they took possession of the highlands. However, they didn't drive out those who lived in the plain because they had iron chariots. [20] They gave Hebron to Caleb, just as Moses had commanded, and they drove out from there the three sons of Anak. [21] But the people of Benjamin didn't drive out the Jebusites who lived in Jerusalem. So the Jebusites still live with the people of Benjamin in Jerusalem today.

[22] In the same way, Joseph's household went up against Bethel, and the LORD was with them. [23] When they sent men to spy on Bethel, previously named Luz, [24] the spies saw a man coming out of the city, and they said to him, "Show us the way into the city, and we'll be loyal to you in return." [25] So he showed them the way into the city. They killed the city's people with their swords, but they let that man and all his relatives go. [26] The man went to the land of the Hittites and built a city. He named it Luz, which is still its name today.

[27] The tribe of Manasseh didn't drive out the people in Beth-shean, Taanach, Dor, Ibleam, Megiddo, or any of their villages. The Canaanites were determined to live in that land. [28] When Israel became stronger they forced the Canaanites to work for them, but they didn't completely drive them out. [29] The tribe of Ephraim didn't drive out the Canaanites living in Gezer, so the Canaanites kept on living there with them.

---

[a] Heb *negeb* [b] Heb *shephelah* [c] LXX (cf 1 Sam 15:6); MT *people* [d] Or *destruction*

³⁰The tribe of Zebulun didn't drive out the people living in Kitron or Nahalol. These Canaanites lived with them but were forced to work for them. ³¹The tribe of Asher didn't drive out the people living in Acco, Sidon, Ahlab, Achzib, Helbah, Aphik, or Rehob. ³²The people of Asher settled among the Canaanites in the land because they couldn't drive them out. ³³The tribe of Naphtali didn't drive out the people living in Beth-shemesh or Beth-anath but settled among the Canaanites in the land. The people living in Beth-shemesh and Beth-anath were forced to work for them.

³⁴The Amorites pushed the people of Dan back into the highlands because they wouldn't allow them to come down to the plain. ³⁵The Amorites were determined to live in Har-heres, Aijalon, and Shaalbim, but Joseph's household became strong, and the Amorites were forced to work for them. ³⁶The border of the Amorites ran from the Akrabbim pass, from Sela, and upward.

The LORD's messenger condemns

2 The LORD's messenger came up from Gilgal to Bochim and said, "I brought you up from Egypt and led you into the land that I had promised to your ancestors. I said, 'I will never break my covenant with you, ²and you are not to make a covenant with those who live in this land. You should break down their altars.' But you didn't obey me. What have you done? ³So now I tell you, I won't drive them out before you, but they'll be a problem^e for you, and their gods will be a trap for you." ⁴When the LORD's messenger spoke these words to all the Israelites, they raised their voices and cried out loud. ⁵So they named that place Bochim,^f and they offered a sacrifice to the LORD there.

Death of Joshua and his generation

⁶When Joshua dismissed the people, the Israelites each went to settle on their own family property in order to take possession of the land. ⁷The people served the LORD throughout the rest of Joshua's life and throughout the next generation of elders who outlived him, those who had seen all the great things that the LORD had done for Israel. ⁸Joshua, Nun's son and the LORD's servant, died when he was 110 years old. ⁹They buried him within the boundaries of his family property in

---

^eHeb uncertain   ^fOr *weepers* or *weeping*

JUDGE/JUDGES

The Hebrew words traditionally translated as "judge" have a much broader range of meaning than the English word, including judging, conducting foreign diplomacy, leading in battle, and ruling domestically. The term is also synonymous with "prince" (Isa 40:23), and the Hebrew words should often be translated as "govern" and "ruler."

The two lifelong national leaders, Moses and Joshua, appoint national deputies to handle all but the most difficult disputes (Exod 18:13-26; Josh 24:1). When the tribes have gone their separate ways, individuals emerge locally in times of crisis to deliver from foreign oppression (e.g., Judg 2:16; 3:9-10, 15) and govern (e.g., Judg 10:1-2; 12:7). The traditional translation *judges* began with the Greek translation of the book of Judges. Unfortunately it is still almost uniformly used for these savior-rulers, suggesting a very limited range of activities. Only one of these rulers, Deborah, is pictured as settling disputes (Judg 4:4-5), and this represents only one aspect of her work.

Timnath-heres in the highlands of Ephraim north of Mount Gaash. [10]When that whole generation had passed away, another generation came after them who didn't know the LORD or the things that he had done for Israel.

Israel's pattern of sin and punishment

[11]Then the Israelites did things that the LORD saw as evil: They served the Baals; [12]and they went away from the LORD, their ancestors' God, who had brought them out of the land of Egypt. They went after other gods from among the surrounding peoples, they worshipped them, and they angered the LORD. [13]They went away from the LORD and served Baal and the Astartes. [14]So the LORD became angry with Israel, and he handed them over to raiders who plundered them. He let them be defeated by their enemies around them, so that they were no longer able to stand up to them. [15]Whenever the Israelites marched out, the LORD's power worked against them, just as the LORD had warned them. And they were very distressed.

[16]Then the LORD raised up leaders[g] to rescue them from the power of these raiders. [17]But they wouldn't even obey their own leaders because they were unfaithful, following other gods and worshipping them. They quickly deviated from the way of their ancestors, who had obeyed the LORD's commands, and didn't follow their example.

[18]The LORD was moved by Israel's groaning under those who oppressed and crushed them. So the LORD would raise up leaders for them, and the LORD would be with the leader, and he would rescue Israel from the power of their enemies as long as that leader lived.

[19]But then when the leader died, they would once again act in ways that weren't as good as their ancestors', going after other gods, to serve them and to worship them. They wouldn't drop their bad practices or hardheaded ways. [20]So the LORD became angry with Israel and said, "Because this nation has violated my covenant that I re-quired of their ancestors and hasn't obeyed me, [21]I in turn will no longer drive out before them any of the nations that Joshua left when he died." [22]As a test for Israel, to see whether they would carefully walk in the LORD's ways just as their ancestors had done, [23]the LORD left these nations instead of driving them out immediately or handing them over to Joshua.

Nations remaining in the land

3 These are the nations that the LORD left to test all those Israelites who had no firsthand knowledge of the wars of Canaan. [2]They survived only to teach war to the generations of Israelites who had no firsthand knowledge of the earlier wars: [3]the five rulers of the Philistines, and all the Canaanites, Sidonians, and Hivites who lived in the highlands of Lebanon from Mount Baal-hermon to Lebo-hamath. [4]They were to be the test for Israel, to find out whether they would obey the LORD's commands, which he had made to their ancestors through Moses. [5]So the Israelites lived among the Canaanites, Hittites, Amorites, Perizzites, Hivites, and Jebusites. [6]But the Israelites intermarried with them and served their gods.

Othniel, the model judge

[7]The Israelites did things that the LORD saw as evil, and they forgot the LORD their God. They served the Baals and the Asherahs.[h] [8]The LORD became angry with Israel and gave them over to King Cushan-rishathaim of Aram-naharaim. The Israelites served Cushan-rishathaim eight years. [9]But then they cried out to the LORD. So the LORD raised up a deliverer for the Israelites, Othniel, Kenaz's son, Caleb's younger brother, who rescued them. [10]The LORD's spirit was in Othniel, and he led Israel. When he marched out for war, the LORD handed over Aram's King Cushan-rishathaim. Othniel overpowered Cushan-rishathaim, [11]and the land was peaceful for forty years, until Othniel, Kenaz's son, died.

[g]Or judges [h]Heb asherim; perhaps objects or a pole devoted to the goddess Asherah

Ehud

[12] The Israelites again did things that the LORD saw as evil, and the LORD put Moab's King Eglon in power over them, because they did these things that the LORD saw as evil. [13] He convinced the Ammonites and Amalekites to join him, defeated Israel, and took possession of Palm City. [14] So the Israelites served Moab's King Eglon eighteen years.

[15] Then the Israelites cried out to the LORD. So the LORD raised up a deliverer for them, Ehud, Gera's son, a Benjaminite, who was left-handed. The Israelites sent him to take their tribute payment to Moab's King Eglon. [16] Now Ehud made for himself a double-edged sword that was about a foot and a half long, and he strapped it on his right thigh under his clothes. [17] Then he presented the tribute payment to Moab's King Eglon, who was a very fat man. [18] When he had finished delivering the tribute payment, Ehud sent on their way the people who had carried it. [19] But he himself turned back at the carved stones near Gilgal, and he said, "I have a secret message for you, King."

So Eglon said, "Hush!" and all his attendants went out of his presence. [20] Ehud approached him while he was sitting alone in his cool second-story room, and he said, "I have a message from God for you." At that, Eglon got up from his throne. [21] Ehud reached with his left hand and grabbed the sword from his right thigh. He stabbed it into Eglon's stomach, [22] and even the handle went in after the blade. Since he did not pull the sword out of his stomach, the fat closed over the blade, and his guts spilled

out.[i] [23] Ehud slipped out to the porch, and closed and locked the doors of the second-story room behind him.

[24] After Ehud had slipped out, the king's servants came and found that the room's doors were locked. So they thought, He must be relieving himself in the cool chamber. [25] They waited so long that they were embarrassed, but he never opened the doors of the room. Then they used the key to open them, and there was their master lying dead on the ground!

[26] Ehud had gotten away while they were waiting and had passed the carved stones and escaped to Seirah. [27] When he arrived, he blew the ram's horn in the Ephraim highlands. So the Israelites went down from the highlands with Ehud leading them. [28] He told them, "Follow me, for the LORD has handed over your enemies the Moabites." So they followed him, and they took control of the crossing points of the Jordan in the direction of Moab, allowing no one to cross. [29] This time, they defeated the Moabites, about ten thousand big and strong men, and no one escaped. [30] Moab was brought down by the power of Israel on that day, and there was peace in the land for eighty years.

Shamgar

[31] After Ehud, Shamgar, Anath's son, struck down six hundred Philistines with an animal prod. He too rescued Israel.

Deborah, Barak, and Jael

4 After Ehud had died, the Israelites again did things that the LORD saw as evil. [2] So the LORD gave them over to King Jabin of Ca-

[i] Heb uncertain

SISERA

Sisera, the general of the Canaanite king Jabin's army, appears in Judges 4 and 5. Judges 4 offers a narrative account of the same events recorded in Judges 5 in poetic form. According to Judges 4:3, Sisera had cruelly oppressed the Israelites for 20 years before he met his match in Jael the wife of Heber the Kenite.

naan, who reigned in Hazor. The commander of his army was Sisera, and he was stationed in Harosheth-ha-goiim. [3] The Israelites cried out to the LORD because Sisera[j] had nine hundred iron chariots and had oppressed the Israelites cruelly for twenty years.

[4] Now Deborah, a prophet, the wife of Lappidoth,[k] was a leader of Israel at that time. [5] She would sit under Deborah's palm tree between Ramah and Bethel in the Ephraim highlands, and the Israelites would come to her to settle disputes. [6] She sent word to Barak, Abinoam's son, from Kedesh in Naphtali and said to him, "Hasn't the LORD, Israel's God, issued you a command? 'Go and assemble at Mount Tabor, taking ten thousand men from the people of Naphtali and Zebulun with you. [7] I'll lure Sisera, the commander of Jabin's army, to assemble with his chariots and troops against you at the Kishon River, and then I'll help you overpower him.'"

[8] Barak replied to her, "If you'll go with me, I'll go; but if not, I won't go."

[9] Deborah answered, "I'll definitely go with you. However, the path you're taking won't bring honor to you, because the LORD will hand over Sisera to a woman." Then Deborah got up and went with Barak to Kedesh. [10] He summoned Zebulun and Naphtali to Kedesh, and ten thousand men marched out behind him. Deborah marched out with him too.

[11] Now Heber the Kenite had moved away from the other Kenites, the descendants of Hobab, Moses' father-in-law, and had settled as far away as Elon-bezaanannim, which is near Kedesh.

[12] When it was reported to Sisera that Barak, Abinoam's son, had marched up to Mount Tabor, [13] Sisera summoned all of his nine hundred iron chariots and all of the soldiers who were with him from Harosheth-ha-goiim to the Kishon River. [14] Then Deborah said to Barak, "Get up! This is the day that the LORD has handed Sisera over to you. Hasn't the LORD gone out before you?" So Barak went down from Mount Tabor with ten thousand men behind him. [15] The LORD threw Sisera and all the chariots and army into a panic[l] before Barak; Sisera himself got down from his chariot and fled on foot. [16] Barak pursued the chariots and the army all the way back to Harosheth-ha-goiim, killing Sisera's entire army with the sword. No one survived.

[17] Meanwhile, Sisera had fled on foot to the tent of Jael, the wife of Heber the Kenite, because there was peace between Hazor's King Jabin and the family of Heber the Kenite. [18] Jael went out to meet Sisera and said to him, "Come in, sir, come in here. Don't be afraid." So he went with her into the tent, and she hid him under a blanket. [19] Sisera said to her, "Please give me a little water to drink. I'm thirsty." So she opened a jug of milk, gave him a drink, and hid him again. [20] Then he said to her, "Stand at the entrance to the tent. That way, if someone comes and asks you, 'Is there a man here?' you can say, 'No.'"

[21] But Jael, Heber's wife, picked up a tent stake and a hammer. While Sisera was sound asleep from exhaustion, she tiptoed to him. She drove the stake through his head and

---

[j] Or he   [k] Or a woman of torches   [l] MT adds before the edge of the sword.

JAEL

Jael plays a major role in the dramatic military victory recounted narratively in Judges 4 and poetically in the Song of Deborah in Judges 5. Deborah announces that the Lord "will hand over Sisera to a woman" (Judg 4:9). Jael is the woman to whom Deborah refers. The wife of Heber the Kenite, Jael, along with many other biblical heroines, is an outsider who courageously throws her lot in with Israel.

down into the ground, and he died. ²²Just then, Barak arrived after chasing Sisera. Jael went out to meet him and said, "Come and I'll show you the man you're after." So he went in with her, and there was Sisera, lying dead, with the stake through his head.

²³So on that day God brought down Canaan's King Jabin before the Israelites. ²⁴And the power of the Israelites grew greater and greater over Canaan's King Jabin until they defeated him completely.

Deborah's song

5 At that time, Deborah and Barak, Abinoam's son, sang:

² When hair is long in Israel,
　when people willingly offer themselves—
　　bless the LORD!

³ Hear, kings!
　Listen, rulers!
　I, to the LORD,
　I will sing.
　I will make music to the LORD,
　Israel's God.

⁴ LORD, when you set out from Seir,
　when you marched out from Edom's
　　fields, the land shook,
　the sky poured down,
　　the clouds poured down water.

⁵ The mountains quaked
　before the LORD, the one from Sinai,
　before the LORD, the God of Israel.

⁶ In the days of Shamgar, Anath's son,
　in the days of Jael, caravans ceased.

Those traveling by road
　kept to the backroads.

⁷ Villagers disappeared;
　they disappeared in Israel,
　until you,ᵐ Deborah, arose,
　until you arose as a mother in Israel.

⁸ When they chose new gods,
　then war came to the city gates.ⁿ
　Yet there wasn't a shield
　or spear to be seen
　among forty thousand in Israel!

⁹ My heart is with Israel's commanders,
　who willingly offered themselves
　　among the people—bless the LORD!

¹⁰ You who ride white donkeys,
　who sit on saddle blankets,ᵒ
　who walk along the road: tell of it.

¹¹ To the sound of instrumentsᵖ
　at the watering places,
　there they repeat the LORD's victories,
　his villagers' victories in Israel.

Then the LORD's people marched
　down to the city gates.

¹² "Wake up, wake up, Deborah!
　Wake up, wake up, sing a song!
　Arise, Barak!
　Capture your prisoners,
　Abinoam's son!"

¹³ Then those who remained
　marched down against royalty;
　the LORD's people marched down�q
　against warriors.

¹⁴ From Ephraim they set outʳ
　into the valley,ˢ
　after you, Benjamin, with your people!

ᵐOr I ⁿHeb uncertain ᵒHeb uncertain ᵖHeb uncertain qHeb adds *for me.* ʳOr *From Ephraim their root*
ˢLXX; MT *in Amalek*

DEBORAH

A judge and prophet. An Israelite leader, Deborah ("honeybee") is introduced in Judges 4:4 with a string of designations: "Deborah, a prophet, the wife of Lappidoth [or "a woman of torches"], was a leader of Israel at that time." She is the only female judge and the only named prophet in Judges and is also the only biblical individual called "a mother in Israel" (5:7).

From Machir commanders marched down,
　　and from Zebulun
　　　those carrying the official's staff.
15 The leaders of Issachar came
　　along with Deborah;
　　Issachar was attached to Barak,
　　and was sent into the valley behind him.
　　Among the clans of Reuben
　　there was deep soul-searching.
16 "Why did you stay back
　　among the sheep pens,
　　listening to the music for the flocks?"
　　For the clans of Reuben
　　there was deep soul-searching.
17 Gilead stayed on the other side
　　of the Jordan,
　　and Dan, why did he remain
　　with the ships?
　　Asher stayed by the seacoast,
　　camping at his harbors.
18 Zebulun is a people
　　that readily risked death;
　　Naphtali too in the high countryside.

19 Kings came and made war;
　　the kings of Canaan fought
　　　at Taanach by Megiddo's waters,
　　but they captured no spoils of silver.
20 The stars fought from the sky;
　　from their orbits
　　　they fought against Sisera.
21 The Kishon River swept them away;
　　the advancing river, the Kishon River.
　　March on, my life, with might!
22 Then the horses' hooves pounded
　　with the galloping,
　　　galloping of their stallions.

23 "Curse Meroz,"
　　says the LORD's messenger,
　　"curse its inhabitants bitterly,
　　because they didn't come
　　　to the LORD's aid,
　　to the LORD's aid against the warriors."
24 May Jael be blessed above all women;
　　may the wife of Heber the Kenite
　　be blessed above all
　　　tent-dwelling women.
25 He asked for water,
　　and she provided milk;
　　she presented him cream
　　　in a majestic bowl.
26 She reached out her hand for the stake,
　　her strong hand
　　　for the worker's hammer.
　　She struck Sisera;
　　she crushed his head;
　　she shattered and pierced his skull.
27 At her feet he sank, fell, and lay flat;
　　at her feet he sank, he fell;
　　where he sank, there he fell—dead.

28 Through the window she watched,
　　Sisera's mother looked longingly[t]
　　　through the lattice.
　　"Why is his chariot taking
　　so long to come?
　　Why are the hoofbeats
　　　of his chariot horses delayed?"
29 Her wisest attendants answer;
　　indeed, she replies to herself:
30 "Wouldn't they be finding
　　and dividing the loot?
　　A girl or two for each warrior;
　　loot of colored cloths for Sisera;
　　loot of colored, embroidered cloths;

[t] LXX; MT *cried*

SONG OF DEBORAH

　　The poem in Judges 5:2-30 (31) is commonly called the "Song of Deborah." Widely regarded as one of the oldest compositions in the OT, the song is characterized by repetitive style, vivid imagery, and a rapid montage of scenes. The related prose account in Judges 4, different in detail and emphasis, is judged by most to be later than the poem and at least partially dependent upon it.

two colored, embroidered cloths
as loot for every neck."

³¹ May all your enemies perish
like this, LORD!
But may your allies be like the sun,
rising in its strength.

And the land was peaceful for forty years.

Oppression by the Midianites

6 The Israelites did things that the LORD saw as evil, and the LORD handed them over to the Midianites for seven years. ²The power of the Midianites prevailed over Israel, and because of the Midianites, the Israelites used crevices and caves in the mountains as hidden strongholds. ³Whenever the Israelites planted seeds, the Midianites, Amalekites, and other easterners would invade. ⁴They would set up camp against the Israelites and destroy the land's crops as far as Gaza, leaving nothing to keep Israel alive, not even sheep, oxen, or donkeys. ⁵They would invade with their herds and tents, coming like a swarm of locusts, so that no one could count them or their camels. They came into the land to destroy it. ⁶So Israel became very weak on account of Midian, and the Israelites cried out to the LORD.

⁷This time when the Israelites cried out to the LORD because of Midian, ⁸the LORD sent them a prophet, who said to them, "The LORD, Israel's God, proclaims: I myself brought you up from Egypt, and I led you out of the house of slavery. ⁹I delivered you from the power of the Egyptians and from the power of all your oppressors. I drove them out before you and gave you their land. ¹⁰I told you, 'I am the LORD your God; you must not worship the gods of the Amorites, in whose land you are living.' But you have not obeyed me."

Gideon's commissioning

¹¹Then the LORD's messenger came and sat under the oak at Ophrah that belonged to Joash the Abiezrite. His son Gideon was threshing wheat in a winepress to hide it

from the Midianites. ¹²The LORD's messenger appeared to him and said, "The LORD is with you, mighty warrior!"

¹³But Gideon replied to him, "With all due respect, my Lord, if the LORD is with us, why has all this happened to us? Where are all his amazing works that our ancestors recounted to us, saying, 'Didn't the LORD bring us up from Egypt?' But now the LORD has abandoned us and allowed Midian to overpower us."

¹⁴Then the LORD turned to him and said, "You have strength, so go and rescue Israel from the power of Midian. Am I not personally sending you?"

¹⁵But again Gideon said to him, "With all due respect, my Lord, how can I rescue Israel? My clan is the weakest in Manasseh, and I'm the youngest in my household."

¹⁶The LORD replied, "Because I'm with you, you'll defeat the Midianites as if they were just one person."[u]

¹⁷Then Gideon said to him, "If I've gained your approval, please show me a sign that it's really you speaking with me. ¹⁸Don't leave here until I return, bring out my offering, and set it in front of you."

The Lord replied, "I'll stay until you return."

¹⁹So Gideon went and prepared a young goat and used an ephah[v] of flour for unleavened bread. He put the meat in a basket and the broth in a pot and brought them out to him under the oak and presented them. ²⁰Then God's messenger said to him, "Take the meat and the unleavened bread and set them on this rock, then pour out the broth." And he did so. ²¹The LORD's messenger reached out the tip of the staff that was in his hand and touched the meat and the unleavened bread. Fire came up from the rock and devoured the meat and the unleavened bread; and the LORD's messenger vanished before his eyes. ²²Then Gideon realized that it had been the LORD's messenger. Gideon exclaimed, "Oh no, LORD God! I have seen the LORD's messenger face-to-face!"

²³But the LORD said to him, "Peace! Don't be afraid! You won't die."

---

[u]Or *each and every one of them*   [v]An ephah is approximately twenty quarts.

²⁴So Gideon built an altar there to the LORD and called it "The LORD makes peace." It still stands today in Ophrah of the Abiezrites.

²⁵That night the LORD said to him, "Take your father's bull and a second bull seven years old. Break down your father's altar to Baal and cut down the Asherah[w] that is beside it. ²⁶Build an altar to the LORD your God in the proper way on top of this high ground. Then take the second bull and offer it as an entirely burned offering with the wood of the Asherah that you cut down." ²⁷So Gideon took ten of his servants and did just as the LORD had told him. But because he was too afraid of his household and the townspeople to do it during the day, he did it at night.

²⁸When the townspeople got up early in the morning, there was the altar to Baal broken down, with the asherah image that had been beside it cut down, and the second bull offered on the newly built altar! ²⁹They asked each other, "Who did this?" They searched and investigated, and finally they concluded, "Gideon, Joash's son, did this!" ³⁰The townspeople said to Joash, "Bring out your son for execution because he tore down the altar to Baal and cut down the Asherah that was beside it."

³¹But Joash replied to all who were lined up against him, "Will you make Baal's complaint for him? Will you come to his rescue? Anyone who argues for him will be killed before morning. If he is a god, let him argue for himself, because it was his altar that was torn down." ³²So on that day Gideon became known as Jerubbaal, meaning, "Let Baal argue with him," because he tore down his altar.

Gideon seeks a sign

³³Some time later, all the Midianites, Amalekites, and other easterners joined together, came over, and set up camp in the Jezreel Valley. ³⁴Then the LORD's spirit came over Gideon, and he sounded the horn and summoned the Abiezrites to follow him. ³⁵He sent messengers into all of Manasseh, and they were also summoned to follow him. Then he sent messengers into Asher, Zebulun, and Naphtali too, and they marched up to meet them.

³⁶But then Gideon said to God, "To see if you really intend to rescue Israel through me as you have declared, ³⁷I'm now putting a wool fleece on the threshing floor. If there is dew only on the fleece but all the ground is dry, then I'll know that you are going to rescue Israel through me, as you have

[w]Heb *asherim*; perhaps objects or a pole devoted to the goddess Asherah

GIDEON

The story of Gideon and his family is the fourth of six major stories told in the central section of the book of Judges (3:7–16:31). Gideon's position is pivotal in the book. The chieftains who precede him are exemplary characters who succeed in making the land "peaceful" (Judg 3:11, 30; 5:31). Gideon's story begins on a high note suggesting that he will rank not only with Othniel, Ehud, and Deborah but even with Abraham and Moses. His end, however, represents a nadir that places him instead with King Jeroboam, "because he made Israel sin too" (1 Kgs 14:16). After Gideon's death his son Abimelech only makes things worse. And the last two chieftains, Jephthah and Samson, follow him in his successes and especially his failures. The peacefulness brought by the first four chieftains will not appear again in the book. Thus Gideon experiences a turning point in his own life and represents a turning point in the book.

declared." [38]And that is what happened. When he got up early the next morning and squeezed the fleece, he wrung out enough dew from the fleece to fill a bowl with water.

[39]Then Gideon said to God, "Don't be angry with me, but let me speak just one more time. Please let me make just one more test with the fleece: now let only the fleece be dry and let dew be on all the ground." [40]And God did so that night. Only the fleece was dry, but there was dew on all the ground.

Battle with Midian

7Then Jerubbaal, that is, Gideon, and all of the people with him rose early and set up camp beside the Harod spring; Midian's camp was north of theirs, in the valley by the Moreh hill. [2]The LORD said to Gideon: "You have too many people on your side. If I were to hand Midian over to them, the Israelites might claim credit for themselves rather than for me, thinking, We saved ourselves. [3]So now, announce in the people's hearing, 'Anyone who is afraid or unsteady may return home from Gideon's mountain.'"[x] At this, twenty-two thousand people went home, and ten thousand were left.

[4]The LORD said to Gideon, "There are still too many people. Take them down to the water, and I will weed them out for you there. Whenever I tell you, 'This one will go with you,' he should go with you; but whenever I tell you, 'This one won't go with you,' he should not go." [5]So he took the people down to the water. And the LORD said to Gideon, "Set aside those who lap the water with their tongues, as a dog laps, from those who bend down on their knees to drink." [6]The number of men who lapped was three hundred, and all the rest of the people bent down on their knees to drink water, with their hands to their mouths.[y] [7]Then the LORD said to Gideon, "With the three hundred men who lapped I will rescue you and hand over the Midianites to you. Let everyone else go home." [8]So the people

gathered their supplies and trumpets,[z] and Gideon sent all the Israelites home, but kept the three hundred.

Now Midian's camp was below Gideon in the valley. [9]That night the LORD said to him, "Get up and attack the camp, because I've handed it over to you. [10]But if you're afraid to attack, go down to the camp with your servant Purah, [11]and you'll hear what they are saying. May you then get the courage to attack the camp." So he went down with his servant Purah to the outpost of the armies that were in the camp. [12]The Midianites, Amalekites, and other easterners were spread across the valley like a swarm of locusts; their camels were too many to count, like the grains of sand on the seashore.

[13]Just when Gideon arrived, there was a man telling his friend about a dream. He said, "Get this! I had a dream that a loaf of barley bread was rolling into the Midianite camp. It came to a tent and hit it, and the tent collapsed. In fact, it rolled the tent over upside down, so it fell flat."

[14]His friend replied, "Can this be anything other than the sword of the Israelite Gideon, Joash's son? God has handed over Midian and its entire camp to him!"

[15]When Gideon heard the telling of the dream and its meaning, he worshipped. Then he returned to the Israelite camp and said, "Get up! The LORD has handed over the Midianite camp to you." [16]He divided the three hundred men into three units and equipped every man with a trumpet and an empty jar, with a torch inside each jar. [17]"Now watch me," he ordered them, "and do what I do. When I get to the outpost of the camp, do just what I do. [18]When I blow the trumpet, along with all who are with me, then you blow the trumpets, all of you surrounding the whole camp. And then shout, 'For the LORD and for Gideon!'"

[19]Gideon and one hundred of his men moved to the outpost of the camp at the middle watch of the night, when they had just changed the guards. Then they blew the trumpets and smashed the jars that were in

---

[x]Or *Mount Gilead* [y]MT places the words *with their hands to their mouths* after the word *lapped*. [z]Or *the ones who lapped took the people's supplies and trumpets for themselves.*

their hands. ²⁰So the three units blew their trumpets and broke their jars, holding the torches with their left hands and blowing the trumpets in their right hands. And they called out, "A sword for the LORD and for Gideon!" ²¹Each man stood fast in his position around the camp, and the entire camp took off running, shouting, and fleeing. ²²When the three hundred trumpets sounded, the LORD turned the swords of fellow soldiers against each other throughout the whole camp. The camp fled as far as Beth-shittah toward Zererah, to the border of Abel-meholah, beside Tabbath.

²³The Israelites from Naphtali, Asher, and all of Manasseh were called out, and they chased after the Midianites. ²⁴Then Gideon sent messengers into all of the Ephraim highlands, saying, "Go down to meet the Midianites and take control of the Jordan's waters as far as Beth-barah." So all the Ephraimite men were called out, and they took control of the Jordan's waters as far as Beth-barah. ²⁵They also captured two Midianite officers, Oreb and Zeeb. They killed Oreb at Oreb's Rock, and killed Zeeb at Zeeb's Winepress. Then they went on chasing the Midianites, and they brought the heads of Oreb and Zeeb to Gideon on the other side of the Jordan.

Gideon's acts of vengeance

8 Then the Ephraimites said to him, "Why did you offend us this way by not calling us when you went to fight the Midianites?" And they argued with him fiercely.

²But he said to them, "What have I done now, compared to you? Aren't Ephraim's leftovers better than Abiezer's main harvest? ³God handed you the Midianite officers Oreb and Zeeb. What have I been able to do compared to you?" When he said this, their anger against him passed.

⁴Then Gideon came to the Jordan. As he and the three hundred men with him crossed over, they were exhausted but still giving chase. ⁵So he said to the people of Succoth, "Please give some loaves of bread to those who are on foot, because they're exhausted, but I'm chasing Zebah and Zalmunna, the kings of Midian."

⁶But the officials of Succoth replied, "Haven't you already almost gotten your hands on Zebah and Zalmunna? Why should we give food to your army now?"

⁷"Just for that," Gideon said, "when the LORD has handed over Zebah and Zalmunna to me, I'm going to beat your skin with desert thorns and briars!" ⁸From there he went up to Penuel and made the same request. And the people of Penuel responded in the same way the people of Succoth had. ⁹So he also told the people of Penuel, "When I return in victory,ᵃ I'll break down this tower!"

¹⁰Now Zebah and Zalmunna were in Karkor with their camp, about fifteen thousand men, all the ones who were left from the easterners' entire camp. One hundred twenty thousand armed men had fallen. ¹¹Gideon marched up the caravan roadᵇ east of Nobah and Jogbehah, and attacked the camp while it was off-guard. ¹²Zebah and Zalmunna fled, and he chased after them. He captured the two Midianite kings Zebah and Zalmunna and threw the entire army into panic.

¹³Then Gideon, Joash's son, returned from the battle by the Heres Pass. ¹⁴He captured a young man from the people of Succoth and interrogated him. He listed for Gideon the seventy-seven officials and elders of Succoth. ¹⁵So Gideon went to the people of Succoth and said, "Here are Zebah and Zalmunna! You made fun of me because of them by saying, 'Haven't you already almost gotten your hands on Zebah and Zalmunna? Why should we give food to your exhausted men now?'" ¹⁶Then he seized the city's elders, and he beatᶜ the people of Succoth with desert thorns and briars. ¹⁷He also broke down Penuel's tower, and killed the city's people.

¹⁸Then he asked Zebah and Zalmunna, "What kind of men were those whom you killed at Tabor?"

They replied, "They were just like you; each one looked like a king's son."

ᵃOr in peace ᵇOr the road of the tent dwellers ᶜCf 8:7, cf LXX; MT he taught a lesson to

¹⁹"They were my brothers," Gideon said, "my own mother's sons. As surely as the LORD lives, I promise that if you had let them live, I wouldn't kill you!" ²⁰So he ordered his oldest son Jether, "Stand up and kill them." But the young man didn't draw his sword because he was afraid, since he was still young.

²¹So Zebah and Zalmunna said, "You stand up and strike us yourself, because as they say, 'A man is measured by his strength!'" So Gideon stood up and killed Zebah and Zalmunna, and took the crescents that were on their camels' necks.

Gideon's request

²²Then the Israelites said to Gideon, "Rule over us, you and then your son and then your grandson, because you've rescued us from Midian's power."

²³Gideon replied to them, "I'm not the one who will rule over you, and my son won't rule over you either. The LORD rules over you." ²⁴But Gideon said to them, "May I make one request of you? Everyone give me the earrings from their loot"; the Midianites had worn gold earrings because they were Ishmaelites.

²⁵"We'll gladly give them," they replied. And they spread out a piece of cloth, and everyone pitched in the earrings from their loot. ²⁶The weight of the gold earrings that he requested was one thousand seven hundred shekels of gold, not counting the crescents, the pendants, and the purple robes worn by the Midianite kings, or the collars that were on their camels' necks. ²⁷Gideon fashioned a priestly vest^d out of it, and put it in his hometown of Ophrah. All Israel became unfaithful there because of it, and it became a trap for Gideon and his household.

²⁸So Midian was brought down before the Israelites and no longer raised its head. The land was peaceful for forty years during Gideon's time.

Gideon's death

²⁹Jerubbaal, Joash's son, went home to live with his own household. ³⁰Gideon had seventy sons of his own because he had many wives. ³¹His secondary wife who was in Shechem also bore him a son, and he named him Abimelech. ³²Gideon, Joash's son, died at a good old age and was buried in the tomb of his father Joash in Ophrah of the Abiezrites.

³³Right after Gideon died, the Israelites once again acted unfaithfully by worshipping the Baals, setting up Baal-berith as their god. ³⁴The people of Israel didn't remember the LORD their God, who had delivered them from the power of all their enemies on every side. ³⁵Nor did they act loyally toward the household of Jerubbaal, that is, Gideon, in return for all the good that he had done on Israel's behalf.

Abimelech becomes a king

9 Abimelech, Jerubbaal's son, went to his mother's brothers in Shechem. He spoke to them and to the entire clan of the household to which his mother belonged: ²"Ask all the leaders of Shechem, 'Which do you think is better to have ruling over you: seventy men—all of Jerubbaal's sons—or one man?' And remember that I'm your flesh and blood!"

³So his mother's brothers spoke all these words on his behalf to all the leaders of Shechem. They decided to follow Abimelech because they said, "He's our relative." ⁴They gave him seventy pieces of silver from the temple of Baal-berith, with which Abimelech hired worthless and reckless men, who became his posse. ⁵He went to his household in Ophrah and killed all seventy of his brothers, Jerubbaal's sons, on a single stone. Only Jotham the youngest of Jerubbaal's sons survived, because he had hidden himself. ⁶Then all the leaders of Shechem and all Beth-millo assembled and proceeded to make Abimelech king by the oak at the stone pillar^e in Shechem.

Jotham's fable

⁷When Jotham was told about this, he went and stood on the top of Mount Gerizim. He raised his voice and called out,

^d Heb ephod   ^e Heb uncertain

"Listen to me, you leaders of Shechem, so that God may listen to you!

[8]"Once the trees went out to anoint a king over themselves. So they said to the olive tree, 'Be our king!'

[9]"But the olive tree replied to them, 'Should I stop producing my oil, which is how gods and humans are honored, so that I can go to sway over the trees?'

[10]"So the trees said to the fig tree, 'You come and be king over us!'

[11]"The fig tree replied to them, 'Should I stop producing my sweetness and my delicious fruit, so that I can go to sway over the trees?'

[12]"Then the trees said to the vine, 'You come and be king over us!'

[13]"But the vine replied to them, 'Should I stop providing my wine that makes gods and humans happy, so that I can go to sway over the trees?'

[14]"Finally, all the trees said to the thornbush, 'You come and be king over us!'

[15]"And the thornbush replied to the trees, 'If you're acting faithfully in anointing me king over you, come and take shelter in my shade; but if not, let fire come out of the thornbush and burn up the cedars of Lebanon.'

[16]"So now, if you acted faithfully and innocently when you made Abimelech king, and if you've done right by Jerubbaal and his household, and have treated him as his actions deserve—[17]my father fought for you and risked his life to rescue you from Midian's power, [18]but today you've risen up against my father's household, killed his seventy sons on a single stone, and made Abimelech, his female servant's son, king over the leaders of Shechem, because he's your relative—[19]so if you've acted faithfully and innocently toward Jerubbaal and his household today, then be happy with Abimelech and let him be happy with you. [20]But if not, let fire come out from Abimelech and burn up the leaders of Shechem and Beth-millo; and let fire come out from the leaders of Shechem and Beth-millo and burn up Abimelech."

[21]Then Jotham ran away. He fled to Beer and stayed there for fear of his brother Abimelech.

Abimelech's monarchy fails

[22]Abimelech ruled over Israel for three years. [23]Then God stirred up ill will between Abimelech and the leaders of Shechem, and they acted like traitors toward Abimelech. [24]This occurred because of the violence done to Jerubbaal's seventy sons. Their blood came back on their brother Abimelech, who killed them, and on the leaders of Shechem, who supported him when he killed his brothers. [25]As an act against him, the leaders of Shechem set ambushes on the hilltops that robbed everyone who passed by them on the road. This was reported to Abimelech.

[26]Then Gaal, Ebed's son, and his relatives came passing through Shechem, and the leaders of Shechem shifted their allegiance to him. [27]They went out into the field, cut off clusters from their vineyards, trampled them out, and had a celebration. They entered their god's temple and ate, drank, and made fun of Abimelech. [28]Gaal, Ebed's son, said, "Who is Abimelech, and who are we of Shechem that we ought to serve him? Didn't this son of Jerubbaal and his deputy Zebul once serve the men of Hamor, Shechem's father? Why should we of all people serve him? [29]If only this people were under my command! I would push Abimelech aside! I[f] would tell Abimelech, 'Build up your army and march out for battle.'"

[30]When Zebul the city's ruler heard the words of Gaal, Ebed's son, he became angry. [31]He sent messengers to Abimelech at Arumah[g] to say, "Watch out! Gaal, Ebed's son, and his relatives have come to Shechem and are stirring up the city against you. [32]Now, you and the men who are with you: Get up tonight and set an ambush in the fields. [33]Then in the morning, at sunrise, rise early and rush on the city. Just as he and the men with him are marching out to face you, you can do to him whatever you wish."

[34]So Abimelech and all the men who were with him got up that night and set

[f]LXX; MT he   [g]Cf 9:41; Heb Tormah

an ambush around Shechem in four companies. [35]When Gaal, Ebed's son, came out and stood in the entrance of the city's gate, Abimelech and the men with him sprang up from the ambush. [36]Gaal saw the men and said to Zebul, "Look! People are coming down from the hilltops."

Zebul replied to him, "The shadows on the hills just look like persons to you."

[37]But Gaal spoke up again, "Look! People are coming down from Tabbur-erez, and one company is coming from the direction of Elon-meonenim."[h]

[38]Then Zebul replied to him, "Where's all your talk now, you who said, 'Who is Abimelech that we ought to serve him?' Aren't these the men you despised? Now march out and fight them!" [39]So Gaal marched out at the head of the leaders of Shechem and fought with Abimelech. [40]Abimelech routed him, and he ran away. Many fell wounded, all the way up to the entrance of the gate. [41]Afterward, Abimelech stayed in Arumah, and Zebul drove away Gaal and his relatives so they couldn't stay in Shechem.

[42]The next day, the men of Shechem went out into the fields. When it was reported to Abimelech, [43]he took his men, divided them into three companies, and set an ambush in the fields. As soon as he saw the men coming from the city, he sprang upon them and attacked them. [44]Abimelech and his company charged forward and took a position at the entrance of the city's gate, while the other two companies charged at all those in the fields and attacked them. [45]Abimelech fought against the city that entire day. He captured the city and killed its people. Then he leveled the city and scattered salt over it.

[46]When all the leaders in the Tower of Shechem heard about this, they entered the side rooms in the El-berith temple. [47]It was reported to Abimelech that all the leaders from the Tower of Shechem had gathered in one place. [48]So Abimelech and all the men who were with him went up on Mount Zalmon. He grabbed an ax, cut off a bundle of branches, and hoisted them onto his shoulder. Then he ordered the men who were with him, "Hurry up and do what you've seen me do!" [49]Each one of the men cut off a bundle as well and followed Abimelech. They piled them up against the side rooms and set fire to the side rooms above them. So all the people in the Tower of Shechem died too, about one thousand men and women.

[50]Then Abimelech moved on to Thebez, set up camp against it, and captured it. [51]But there was a strong tower inside the city. All the men and women and all the city's leaders had fled there, shut themselves inside, and climbed to the tower's roof. [52]Abimelech came to the tower to storm it. But when he approached the tower's entrance to set it on fire, [53]a woman dropped an upper millstone on Abimelech's head and cracked his skull. [54]He quickly cried out to the servant who carried his armor, "Draw your sword and kill me. Don't let it be said of me, 'A woman killed him.'" So his servant stabbed him, and he died. [55]When the Israelites saw that Abimelech was dead, they all went home.

[56]Thus God paid back Abimelech for the evil he had done to his father by killing his seventy brothers. [57]God also paid back the people of Shechem for their evil. The curse of Jotham, Jerubbaal's son, had come upon them.

Tola and Jair

10 After Abimelech, Tola son of Puah and grandson of Dodo, a man of Issachar, arose to rescue Israel. He lived in Shamir in the Ephraim highlands. [2]For twenty-three years he led Israel; then he died and was buried in Shamir.

[3]After Tola, Jair from Gilead arose, and he led Israel for twenty-two years. [4]He had thirty sons who were mounted on thirty donkeys and controlled thirty towns in the land of Gilead—these are still known as Havvoth-jair today. [5]When Jair died, he was buried in Kamon.

Israel's unfaithfulness and oppression by the Ammonites

[6]Then the Israelites again did things that the LORD saw as evil. They served the

---

[h]Or *the Diviners' Oak*

Baals and the Astartes, as well as the gods of Aram, Sidon, Moab, the Ammonites, and the Philistines. They went away from the LORD and didn't serve him. [7]The LORD became angry with Israel and handed them over to the Philistines and the Ammonites. [8]Starting that year and for the next eighteen years, they beat and bullied the Israelites, especially all the Israelites who lived on the east side of Jordan in the territory of the Ammonites in Gilead. [9]The Ammonites also crossed the Jordan to make raids into Judah, Benjamin, and the households of Ephraim. So Israel was greatly distressed.

[10]Then the Israelites cried out to the LORD, "We've sinned against you, for we went away from our God and served the Baals."

[11]The LORD replied to the Israelites, "When the Egyptians, Amorites, Ammonites, Philistines, [12]Sidonians, Amalekites, and Maonites oppressed you and you cried out to me, didn't I rescue you from their power? [13]But you have gone away from me and served other gods, so I won't rescue you anymore! [14]Go cry out to the gods you've chosen. Let them rescue you in the time of your distress."

[15]The Israelites responded to the LORD, "We've sinned. Do to us whatever you see as right, but please save us this time." [16]They put away the foreign gods from among them and served the LORD. And the LORD could no longer stand to see Israel suffer.

[17]The Ammonites called out their army and made camp in Gilead, while the Israelites gathered and set up their camp at Mizpah. [18]Gilead's rulers said to each other, "Whoever is willing to launch the attack against the Ammonites will become the leader over all those living in Gilead."

Rise of Jephthah

11 Now Jephthah the Gileadite was a mighty warrior. Gilead was his father, but he was a prostitute's son. [2]Gilead's wife gave birth to other sons for him, and when his wife's sons grew up, they drove Jephthah away. They told him, "You won't get an inheritance in our father's household be-

cause you're a different woman's son." [3]So Jephthah ran away from his brothers and lived in the land of Tob. Worthless men gathered around Jephthah and became his posse.

[4]Sometime afterward, the Ammonites made war against Israel. [5]And when the Ammonites attacked Israel, Gilead's elders went to bring Jephthah back from the land of Tob. [6]They said to him, "Come be our commander so we can fight against the Ammonites."

[7]But Jephthah replied to Gilead's elders, "Aren't you the ones who hated me and drove me away from my father's household? Why are you coming to me now when you're in trouble?"

[8]Gilead's elders answered Jephthah, "That may be, but now we're turning back to you, so come with us and fight the Ammonites. Then you'll become the leader over us and everyone who lives in Gilead."

[9]And Jephthah said to Gilead's elders, "If you bring me back to fight the Ammonites and the LORD gives them over to me, I alone will be your leader."

[10]Gilead's elders replied to him, "The LORD is our witness; we will surely do what you've said." [11]So Jephthah went with Gilead's elders, and the people made him leader and commander over them. At Mizpah before the LORD, Jephthah repeated everything he had said.

[12]Then Jephthah sent messengers to the Ammonite king, saying, "What is the problem between us that you've come against me to make war in my land?"

[13]The Ammonite king responded to Jephthah's messengers, "When the Israelites were coming up from Egypt, they seized my land from the Arnon to the Jabbok and all the way to the Jordan. Now give it back peacefully!"

[14]Then Jephthah again sent messengers to the Ammonite king [15]and said to him, "Jephthah states: Israel didn't seize the land of the Moabites or the land of the Ammonites. [16]When they were coming up from Egypt, the Israelites went through the desert to the Reed Sea[i] and came to Kadesh.

[i]Or Red Sea

[17] Then the Israelites sent messengers to the king of Edom, saying, 'Please allow us to pass through your land'; but the Edomite king refused. They sent the same request to the king of Moab, and he was unwilling. So the Israelites stayed at Kadesh.

[18] "Later they journeyed into the desert but went around the lands of Edom and Moab, arriving on the east side of the land of Moab and setting up camp on the other side of the Arnon. They never entered Moabite territory, because the Arnon was the boundary of Moab. [19] Then the Israelites sent messengers to Sihon king of the Amorites and king of Heshbon and said to him, 'Please allow us to pass through your land to our own place.' [20] Yet Sihon didn't trust the Israelites to pass through his territory. He assembled his entire army, set up camp at Jahaz, and went to war with the Israelites. [21] The LORD, Israel's God, handed over Sihon and his entire army to the Israelites, and they defeated Sihon. So the Israelites took possession of all the land of the Amorites who were living in that area. [22] They took possession of all the Amorite territory from the Arnon to the Jabbok and from the desert to the Jordan.

[23] "So now that the LORD, Israel's God, has driven out the Amorites before his people Israel, will you take possession of their land? [24] Shouldn't you possess what Chemosh your god has given you to possess? And shouldn't we possess everything that the LORD our God has given us to possess? [25] Do you now have a better case than Moab's King Balak, Zippor's son? Did he make an accusation against the Israelites or go to war with them? [26] Why didn't you take back this territory while the Israelites lived in Heshbon and its villages, in Aroer and its villages, and in all the towns along the branches of the Arnon for three hundred years? [27] I haven't sinned against you, but you're doing me wrong by making war against me. Let the LORD, who is the judge, decide today between the Israelites and the Ammonites!"

[28] But the Ammonite king refused to listen to the message that Jephthah sent to him.

Jephthah's promise

[29] Then the LORD's spirit came on Jephthah. He passed through Gilead and Manasseh, then through Mizpah in Gilead, and from there he crossed over to the Ammonites. [30] Jephthah made a solemn promise to the LORD: "If you will decisively hand over the Ammonites to me, [31] then whatever comes out the doors of my house to

JEPHTHAH

A male character in the book of Judges. The stories about Jephthah extend from Judges 10:6 to 12:7. Rather than trusting in God, Jephthah bargains with God using a vow to sacrifice the first thing he sees upon returning from successful battle. When Jephthah returns home to Mizpah, his unnamed daughter, rejoicing with drums and dancing, comes forth to meet him. In language reminiscent of Isaac and his near sacrifice (Gen 22:2), the narrator observes that she "was an only child; he had no other son or daughter except her" (11:34). Upon seeing her, Jephthah blames her for the predicament he himself has set up. He declares that he cannot turn back from his vow to the Lord. In her reply the daughter echoes the understanding of her father but asks that he give her two months to wander on the hills with her female friends, to lament her virginity. Jephthah grants the request. At the end of that period, the daughter returns, and Jephthah "did to her what he had promised" (11:39).

meet me when I return victorious from the Ammonites will be given over to the LORD. I will sacrifice it as an entirely burned offering." ³²Jephthah crossed over to fight the Ammonites, and the LORD handed them over to him. ³³It was an exceptionally great defeat; he defeated twenty towns from Aroer to the area of Minnith, and on as far as Abel-keramim. So the Ammonites were brought down before the Israelites.

³⁴But when Jephthah came to his house in Mizpah, it was his daughter who came out to meet him with tambourines and dancing! She was an only child; he had no other son or daughter except her. ³⁵When he saw her, he tore his clothes and said, "Oh no! My daughter! You have brought me to my knees! You are my agony! For I opened my mouth to the LORD, and I can't take it back."

³⁶But she replied to him, "My father, you've opened your mouth to the LORD, so you should do to me just what you've promised. After all, the LORD has carried out just punishment for you on your enemies the Ammonites." ³⁷Then she said to her father, "Let this one thing be done for me: hold off for two months and let me and my friends wander the hills in sadness, crying over the fact that I never had children."

³⁸"Go," he responded, and he sent her away for two months. She and her friends walked on the hills and cried because she would never have children.

³⁹When two months had passed, she returned to her father, and he did to her what he had promised. She had not known a man intimately. But she gave rise to a tradition in Israel where ⁴⁰for four days every year Israelite daughters would go away to recount the story of the Gileadite Jephthah's daughter.

Jephthah defeats the Ephraimites

12The Ephraimites were called up for battle and crossed over to Zaphon. They said to Jephthah, "Why did you cross over to fight the Ammonites and not call us to go with you? We're going to burn down your house over you!"

²Jephthah replied to them, "My people and I were in a great conflict with the Ammonites. But when I cried out to you, you

didn't rescue me from their power. ³When I saw that you weren't going to rescue me, I risked my own life and crossed over against the Ammonites, and the LORD handed them over to me. So why have you marched against me today to fight me?"

⁴So Jephthah gathered all the men of Gilead and fought the Ephraimites. The Gileadites defeated the Ephraimites, because they had said, "You are fugitives from Ephraim! Gilead stands within Ephraim and Manasseh."

⁵The Gileadites took control of the Jordan's crossing points into Ephraim. Whenever one of the Ephraimite fugitives said, "Let me cross," the Gileadites would ask him, "Are you an Ephraimite?" If he said, "No," ⁶they would tell him, "Then say *shibboleth*." But he would say, "*sibboleth*," because he couldn't pronounce it correctly. So they would seize him and kill him at the Jordan's crossing points. Forty-two thousand of the Ephraimites fell at that time.

⁷Jephthah led Israel for six years. Then Jephthah the Gileadite died and was buried in one of the towns in Gilead.

Ibzan, Elon, and Abdon

⁸After Jephthah, Ibzan from Bethlehem led Israel. ⁹He had thirty sons and thirty daughters. He married his thirty daughters to those outside his clan, and brought in thirty young women from outside for his sons. He led Israel for seven years. ¹⁰Then Ibzan died and was buried in Bethlehem.

¹¹After Ibzan, Elon from Zebulun led Israel; he did so for ten years. ¹²Then Elon the Zebulunite died and was buried in Aijalon in the land of Zebulun.

¹³After Elon, Abdon, Hillel's son from Pirathon, led Israel. ¹⁴He had forty sons and thirty grandsons mounted on seventy donkeys. He led Israel for eight years. ¹⁵Then Abdon, Hillel's son from Pirathon, died and was buried in Pirathon in the land of Ephraim, in the Amalekite highlands.

Samson's birth

13The Israelites again did things that the LORD saw as evil, and he handed them over to the Philistines for forty years.

²Now there was a certain man from Zorah, from the Danite clan, whose name was Manoah. His wife was unable to become pregnant and had not given birth to any children. ³The LORD's messenger appeared to the woman and said to her, "Even though you've been unable to become pregnant and haven't given birth, you are now pregnant and will give birth to a son! ⁴Now be careful not to drink wine or brandy or to eat anything that is ritually unclean, ⁵because you are pregnant and will give birth to a son. Don't allow a razor to shave his head, because the boy is going to be a nazirite for God from birth. He'll be the one who begins Israel's rescue from the power of the Philistines."

⁶Then the woman went and told her husband, "A man of God came to me, and he looked like God's messenger—very scary! I didn't ask him where he was from, and he didn't tell me his name. ⁷He said to me, 'You are pregnant and will give birth to a son, so don't drink wine or brandy or eat anything that is ritually unclean, because the boy is going to be a nazirite for God from birth until the day he dies.'"

⁸Manoah asked the LORD, "Please, my Lord," he said, "let the man of God whom you sent come back to us once more, so he can teach us how we should treat the boy who is to be born."

⁹God listened to Manoah, and God's messenger came once more to the woman. She was sitting in the field, but her husband Manoah wasn't with her. ¹⁰So the woman hurriedly ran and informed her husband. She said to him, "The man who came to me the other day has just appeared to me."

¹¹Manoah got up and followed his wife. He came to the man and said to him, "Are you the man who spoke to this woman?"

"I am," he replied.

¹²Manoah said, "Now when your words come true, what should be the rules for the boy and how he should act?"

¹³The LORD's messenger answered Manoah, "The woman should be careful to do everything that I told her. ¹⁴She must not consume anything that comes from the grapevine, drink wine or brandy, or eat anything that is ritually unclean. She must be careful to do everything I have commanded her."

¹⁵Manoah said to the LORD's messenger, "Please let us persuade you to stay so we can prepare a young goat for you."

¹⁶But the LORD's messenger replied to Manoah, "If you persuaded me to stay, I wouldn't eat your food. If you prepare an entirely burned offering, offer it to the LORD." Indeed, Manoah didn't know that he was the LORD's messenger. ¹⁷Manoah said to the LORD's messenger, "What's your name, so that we may honor you when your words come true?"

¹⁸The LORD's messenger responded to him, "Why do you ask my name? You couldn't understand it."

¹⁹So Manoah took a young goat and a grain offering and offered them on a rock to the LORD. While Manoah and his wife were looking, an amazing thing happened: ²⁰as the flame from the altar went up toward the sky, the LORD's messenger went up in the altar's flame. When Manoah and his wife saw this, they fell facedown on the ground. ²¹The LORD's messenger didn't reappear to Manoah or his wife, and Manoah then realized that it had been the LORD's messenger. ²²Manoah said to his wife, "We are certainly going to die, because we've seen God!"

²³But his wife replied to him, "If the LORD wanted to kill us, he wouldn't have accepted the entirely burned offering and grain offering from our hands. He wouldn't have shown us all these things or told us all of this now."

²⁴The woman gave birth to a son and named him Samson. The boy grew up, and the LORD blessed him. ²⁵The LORD's spirit began to move him when he was in Mahaneh-dan, between Zorah and Eshtaol.

Samson's marriage to a Philistine woman

14 Samson traveled down to Timnah. While he was in Timnah, a Philistine woman caught his eye. ²He went back home and told his father and mother, "A Philistine woman in Timnah caught my eye; now get her for me as a wife!"

³But his father and mother replied to

him, "Is there no woman among your own relatives or among all our people that you have to go get a wife from the uncircumcised Philistines?"

Yet Samson said to his father, "Get her for me, because she's the one I want!" ⁴His father and mother didn't know that the LORD was behind this. He was looking for an opening with the Philistines, because they were ruling over Israel at that time.

⁵Then Samson traveled down to Timnah with his father and mother. When he came to the vineyards in Timnah, suddenly a lone young lion came roaring to meet him. ⁶The LORD's spirit rushed over him, and he tore the lion apart with his bare hands as one might tear apart a young goat. But he didn't tell his father or mother what he had done. ⁷Then he traveled down and talked with the woman; she was the one Samson wanted.

⁸After a while, he came back again to marry her. He turned aside to look at the lion's remains, and there was a swarm of bees with honey inside the lion's skeleton. ⁹He scooped the honey into his hands, eating it as he continued along. When he got to his father and mother, he gave some to them, and they ate it too. But he didn't tell them that he had scooped the honey from the lion's skeleton.

¹⁰His father traveled down to the woman, and Samson put on a feast there, as was the custom for young men. ¹¹When the townspeople saw him, they selected thirty companions to be with him. ¹²Then Samson said to them, "Let me tell you a riddle. If you can figure it out and tell me the answer within the seven days of the feast, I'll give you thirty linen robes and thirty sets of clothes. ¹³But if you can't tell me the answer, then it's you who have to give me thirty linen robes and thirty sets of clothes."

So they replied to him, "Tell your riddle; let's hear it."

¹⁴He said to them,

"Out of the eater
    there came something to eat.
Out of the strong
    there came something sweet."

For three days they couldn't tell the answer to the riddle. ¹⁵On the fourthʲ day they said to Samson's wife, "Seduce your husband so he'll tell us the answer to the riddle, or else we'll set fire to you and your household. Were we invited here just to become poor?"

¹⁶So Samson's wife cried on his shoulder and said, "You hate me! You don't love me! You told a riddle to my people but didn't tell me the answer."

He replied to her, "Look, I haven't even told the answer to my father and mother. Why should I tell it to you?" ¹⁷But she cried on his shoulder for the rest of the seven days of the feast. Finally, on the seventh day, he told her the answer, for she had nagged him. And she told her people the answer to the riddle. ¹⁸So on the seventh day, before the sun set, the townspeople said to him,

"What's sweeter than honey?
    What's stronger than a lion?"

He replied to them,

"If you hadn't plowed with my heifer,
    you wouldn't have figured out my riddle!"

ʲLXX, Syr; MT *seventh*

LION

The lion (*Panthera leo* or *Felis leo*) that inhabited the ancient Near East and is now extinct there belongs to the family Felidae. The lion was one of the largest carnivores in the land. Biblical references suggest that the lion was prevalent both east and west of the Jordan. The lion was found in the mountains (Song 4:8), in the forests (Jer 12:8; Amos 3:4; Mic 5:8), in the thicket (Jer 4:7), near Bethel in Judah (1 Kgs 13), and near Timnah (Judg 14).

[19] Then the LORD's spirit rushed over him, and he went down to Ashkelon. He killed thirty of their men, stripped them of their gear, and gave the sets of clothes to the ones who had told the answer to the riddle. In anger, he went back up to his father's household. [20] And Samson's wife married one of those who had been his companions.

Samson attacks the Philistines

15 Later on, at the time of the wheat harvest, Samson went to visit his wife, bringing along a young goat. He said, "Let me go into my wife's bedroom."

But her father wouldn't allow him to go in. [2] Her father said, "I was so sure that you had completely rejected her that I gave her in marriage to one of your companions. Don't you think her younger sister is even better? Let her be your wife instead."

[3] Samson replied, "No one can blame me now for being ready to bring down trouble on the Philistines!"

[4] Then Samson went and caught three hundred foxes. He took torches, turned the foxes tail to tail, and put a torch between each pair of tails. [5] He lit the torches and released the foxes into the Philistines' grain fields. So he burned the stacked grain, standing grain, vineyards, and olive orchards.

[6] The Philistines inquired, "Who did this?"

So it was reported, "Samson the Timnite's son-in-law did it, because his father-in-law gave his wife in marriage to one of his companions." So the Philistines went up and burned her and her father to death.

[7] Samson then responded to them, "If this is how you act, then I won't stop until I get revenge on you!" [8] He struck them hard, taking their legs right out from under them.[k] Then he traveled down and stayed in a cave in the rock at Etam.

[9] The Philistines marched up, made camp in Judah, and released their forces on Lehi. [10] The people of Judah asked, "Why have you marched up against us?"

"We've marched up to take Samson prisoner," they replied, "and to do to him just what he did to us."

[11] So three thousand people from Judah traveled down to the cave in the rock at Etam and said to Samson, "Don't you realize that the Philistines rule over us? What have you done to us?"

But he told them, "I did to them just what they did to me."

[12] Then the people of Judah said to him, "We've come down to take you prisoner so we can turn you over to the Philistines."

Samson responded to them, "Just promise that you won't attack me yourselves."

[13] "We won't," they said to him. "We'll only take you prisoner so we can turn you over to them. We won't kill you." Then they tied him up with two new ropes, and brought him up from the rock.

[14] When Samson arrived at Lehi, the Philistines met him and came out shouting. The LORD's spirit rushed over him, the ropes on his arms became like burned-up linen, and the ties melted right off his hands. [15] He found a donkey's fresh jawbone, picked it up, and used it to attack one thousand men. [16] Samson said,

"With a donkey's jawbone,
    stacks on stacks!
With a donkey's jawbone,
    I've killed one thousand men."

[17] When he finished speaking, he tossed away the jawbone. So that place became known as Ramath-lehi.[l]

[18] Now Samson was very thirsty, so he called out to the LORD, "You are the one who allowed this great victory to be accomplished by your servant's hands. Am I now going to die of thirst and fall into the hands of the uncircumcised?" [19] So God split open the hollow rock in Lehi, and water flowed out of it. When Samson drank, his energy returned and he was recharged. Thus that place is still called by the name En-hakkore[m] in Lehi today.

[20] Samson led Israel for twenty years during the time of the Philistines.

Samson and the prostitute

16 One day Samson traveled to Gaza. While there, he saw a prostitute and

---

[k] Or struck them hip and thigh [l] Or Jawbone Hill [m] Or Caller's Spring

had sex with her. [2]The word spread[n] among the people of Gaza, "Samson has come here!" So they circled around and waited in ambush for him all night at the city gate. They kept quiet all night long, thinking, We'll kill him at the first light in the morning. [3]But Samson slept only half the night. He got up in the middle of the night, grabbed the doors of the city gate and the two gateposts, and pulled them up with the bar still across them. He put them on his shoulders and carried them up to the top of the hill that is beside Hebron.

Samson and Delilah

[4]Some time after this, in the Sorek Valley, Samson fell in love with a woman whose name was Delilah. [5]The rulers of the Philistines confronted her and said to her, "Seduce him and find out what gives him such great strength and what we can do to overpower him, so that we can tie him up and make him weak. Then we'll each pay you eleven hundred pieces of silver."

[6]So Delilah said to Samson, "Please tell me what gives you such great strength and how you can be tied up and made weak."

[7]Samson replied to her, "If someone ties me up with seven fresh bowstrings that aren't dried out, I'll become weak. I'll be like any other person." [8]So the rulers of the Philistines brought her seven fresh bowstrings that weren't dried out, and she tied him up with them.

[9]While an ambush was waiting for her signal in an inner room, she called out to him, "Samson, the Philistines are on you!" And he snapped the bowstrings like a thread of fiber snaps when it touches a flame. So the secret of his strength remained unknown.

[10]Then Delilah said to Samson, "You made a fool out of me and lied to me. Now please tell me how you can really be tied up!"

[11]He replied to her, "If someone ties me up with new ropes that haven't been used for work, I'll become weak. I'll be like any other person."

[12]So Delilah took new ropes and tied him up with them. Then she called out to him, "Samson, the Philistines are on you!" Once again, an ambush was waiting in an inner room. Yet he snapped them from his arms like thread.

[13]And Delilah said to Samson, "Up to now, you've made a fool out of me and lied to me. Tell me how you can be tied up!"

He responded to her, "If you weave the seven braids of my hair into the fabric on

[n]LXX; MT lacks *spread*.

DELILAH

A woman from the Valley of Sorek, beloved by the judge Samson (Judg 16:4). Unlike the former, unnamed, Philistine wife of Samson (Judg 14:1-20), Delilah bears a name but is not explicitly characterized as Philistine or Israelite. Bribed by the Philistines, Delilah tries to seduce Samson to make him reveal the secret of his superhuman strength. In return for obtaining this information, each of the Philistine lords promises her 1,100 pieces of silver (Judg 16:5). Three times her attempt fails because Samson lies to her when she coaxes him to divulge his weakness. Learning the truth at last, Delilah summons the Philistine lords, who this time carry with them the bribe money (Judg 16:18). Delilah makes Samson sleep in her lap so that his head can be shaven. When she calls again, "Samson, the Philistines are on you," Samson is not able to free himself since his strength has left him along with the loss of his hair (Judg 16:20). Betrayed and delivered by his mistress, he is overwhelmed by the Philistines (Judg 16:21).

a loom and pull it tight with a pin, then I'll become weak. I'll be like any other person."°

¹⁴So she got him to fall asleep, wove the seven braids of his hair into the fabric on a loom,ᵖ and pulled it tight with a pin. Then she called out to him, "Samson, the Philistines are on you!" He woke up from his sleep and pulled loose the pin, the loom, and the fabric.

¹⁵Delilah said to him, "How can you say, 'I love you,' when you won't trust me? Three times now you've made a fool out of me and not told me what gives you such great strength!" ¹⁶She nagged him with her words day after day and begged him until he became worn out to the point of death.

¹⁷So he told her his whole secret. He said to her, "No razor has ever touched my head, because I've been a nazirite for God from the time I was born. If my head is shaved, my strength will leave me, and I'll become weak. I'll be like every other person."

¹⁸When Delilah realized that he had told her his whole secret, she sent word to the rulers of the Philistines, "Come one more time, for he has told me his whole secret." The rulers of the Philistines came up to her and brought the silver with them.

¹⁹She got him to fall asleep with his head on her lap. Then she called a man and had him shave off the seven braids of Samson's hair. He began to weaken,�q and his strength left him. ²⁰She called out, "Samson, the Philistines are on you!"

He woke up from his sleep and thought, I'll escape just like the other times and shake myself free. But he didn't realize that the Lord had left him. ²¹So the Philistines captured him, put out his eyes, and took him down to Gaza. They bound him with bronze chains, and he worked the grinding mill in the prison.

²²But the hair on his head began to grow again right after it had been shaved.

Samson's death

²³The rulers of the Philistines gathered together to make a great sacrifice to their god Dagon and to hold a celebration. They cheered, "Our god has handed us Samson our enemy!" ²⁴When the people saw him, they praised their god, for they said, "Our god has handed us our enemy, the very one who devastated our land and killed so many of our people." ²⁵At the height of the celebration,ʳ they said, "Call for Samson so he can perform for us!" So they called Samson from the prison, and he performed in front of them. Then they had him stand between the pillars.

²⁶Samson said to the young man who led him by the hand, "Put me where I can feel the pillars that hold up the temple, so I can lean on them." ²⁷Now the temple was filled with men and women. All the rulers of the Philistines were there, and about three thousand more men and women were on the roof watching as Samson performed. ²⁸Then Samson called out to the Lord, "Lord God, please remember me! Make me strong just this once more, God, so I can have revenge on the Philistines, just one act of revenge for my two eyes."ˢ ²⁹Samson grabbed the two central pillars that held up the temple. He leaned against one with his right hand and the other with his left. ³⁰And Samson said, "Let me die with the Philistines!" He strained with all his might, and the temple collapsed on the rulers and all the people who were in it. So it turned out that he killed more people in his death than he did during his life.

³¹His brothers and his father's entire household traveled down, carried him back up, and buried him between Zorah and Eshtaol in the tomb of his father Manoah. He had led Israel for twenty years.

Micah's sanctuary and the Levite priest

17Once there was a man named Micah who lived in the Ephraim highlands. ²He said to his mother, "The eleven hundred pieces of silver that were taken from you led you to declare a curse and even to repeat it when I could hear. I have that

---

°LXX; MT lacks *and pull it . . . other person.* ᵖLXX; MT lacks *so she got him . . . on a loom.* qLXX; MT *she began to torment him.* ʳOr *When their hearts were glad* ˢor *so I can have revenge on the Philistines for one of my two eyes* silver. I'm the one who took it, and now I'll give it back to you."[t]

His mother replied, "May the LORD bless you, my son!" [3]When he gave the eleven hundred pieces of silver back to his mother, she said, "I wholeheartedly devote this silver to the LORD, to be made into a sculpted image and a molded image for my son." [4]So he gave the silver back to his mother, and she took two hundred pieces of silver and gave them to a silversmith, who used it for a sculpted image and a molded image. And they were placed in Micah's house. [5]This man Micah had his own sanctuary.[u] He made a priestly vest[v] and divine images[w] and appointed one of his sons to be his personal priest. [6]In those days there was no king in Israel; each person did what they thought to be right.

[7]Now there was a young man from Bethlehem in Judah, from the area of the Judahite clan. He was a Levite residing there as an immigrant. [8]The man left the town of Bethlehem in Judah to settle as an immigrant wherever he could find a place. He came to Micah's house in the Ephraim highlands while he was making his way.[x]

[9]"Where are you from?" Micah asked him.

He replied, "I'm a Levite from Bethlehem in Judah, and I'm looking to settle as an immigrant anywhere I can find a place."

[10]So Micah said to him, "Stay with me and be a father and a priest to me, and I'll give you ten pieces of silver a year, a set of clothes, and your basic needs."[y] [11]The Levite agreed to stay with him; and the young man became like one of his own sons. [12]Micah appointed the Levite so that the young man became his personal priest and lived in Micah's sanctuary. [13]And Micah said to himself, Now I know that the LORD will give me good things, because a Levite has become my priest.

Dan's search for a land

18 In those days there was no king in Israel. Also in those days the tribe of Dan was searching for a territory of their own to live in, since no permanent territory had been assigned to them among the tribes of Israel up to that point. [2]The Danites sent five men from their whole clan, strong men from Zorah and Eshtaol, to spy on the land and explore it. They told them, "Go explore the land." So they went into the Ephraim highland as far as Micah's house, and they spent the night there. [3]When they were in the area of Micah's house, they recognized the accent of the young Levite. They turned in there and said to him, "Who brought you here? What are you doing in these parts? What is there for you here?"

[4]"Micah has done a lot for me," he replied to them. "He hired me to be his personal priest."

[5]They said to him, "Ask for an answer from God so we can know whether we'll be successful on this trip we've taken."

[6]The priest replied to them, "Go in peace. The LORD is watching over you on this trip you've taken."

[7]So the five men journeyed on until they reached Laish. There they saw that its people were living without worry in the same way as the Sidonians, undisturbed and secure. Nobody held back anything in the land, so no one had to hoard.[z] Yet they lived far away from the Sidonians and had no dealings with anyone else.[a]

[8]When the men came back to their relatives at Zorah and Eshtaol, they asked them, "What did you find?"

[9]"Come on," they replied, "let's march up against them! Indeed, we've seen the land, and it's very good. Right now you're doing nothing! Don't hold back from going and taking possession of the land. [10]When you arrive, you'll come upon a secure people and a wide-open land, because God has given to you a place where nothing on earth is lacking." [11]At this, six hundred men from the Danite clan at Zorah and Eshtaol set out armed for battle. [12]They marched up and made camp at Kiriath-jearim in Judah. This is why the place west of Kiriath-jearim is still known as Dan's Camp today.

---

[t]The words *and now I'll give it back to you* are relocated from the end of 17:3 in Heb. [u]Or *god's house* [v]Heb *ephod* [w]Heb *terafim* [x]Or *to carry on his work* [y]Heb adds *and the Levite went.* [z]Heb uncertain [a]Or *with Aram*

[13]From there they crossed into the Ephraim highlands and came to Micah's house.

Dan acquires a levitical priest

[14]Then the five men who had gone to spy on the land around Laish reported to their relatives, "Did you know that there is a priestly vest, divine images, a sculpted image, and a molded image in these buildings? Now think about what you should do!" [15]So they turned in there and went to the young Levite's house in Micah's compound and greeted him. [16]While the six hundred Danites armed for battle stood at the entrance of the gate, [17]the five men who had gone to spy on the land moved up, went inside, and took the sculpted image, the priestly vest, the divine images, and the molded image. The priest was standing at the entrance of the gate with the six hundred men armed for battle [18]when these five entered Micah's sanctuary and took the sculpted image, the priestly vest, the divine images, and the molded image.

The priest said to them, "What are you doing?"

[19]"Shut up!" they said to him. "Put your hand over your mouth! Come with us and be a father and a priest for us. Would you rather be a priest for one man's household or a priest for a tribe and a clan in Israel?" [20]The priest was convinced, so he took the priestly vest, the divine images, and the sculpted image and went along with the people.

[21]They headed back on their way, but they put the children, the livestock, and the prized possessions in front of them. [22]After they had gone a good distance away from Micah's house, the men who were in the houses around Micah's home were summoned for battle and caught up to the Danites. [23]They called out to the Danites, who turned around and said to Micah, "Why have you summoned men for battle?"

[24]Micah replied, "You've taken my gods that I made, and the priest, and have gone off! What do I have left? How can you ask me what is wrong?"

[25]But the Danites said to him, "Don't raise your voice with us or else hotheaded men will attack you, and you and your household will lose your lives." [26]Then the

DAN/DANITES

1. The fifth son of Jacob through Rachel's servant Bilhah. The name, meaning "he has judged," is explained by the patriarch's birth story, during which Rachel interprets the birth of a son born through her servant Bilhah as a divine judgment on her behalf (Gen 30:3-6). The patriarchal narratives identify Dan as the first of the four sons born to the servants of Jacob's wives (the other sons are Naphtali, Gad, and Asher). See also Genesis 35:25; 46:23; Exodus 1:4.

2. The Israelite tribe that traced its descent through Dan. Tribal lists and traditions reflect the same grouping of Dan, Naphtali, Asher, and Gad (Num 13:12-15; Deut 33:20-25), although the absence of Gad in many cases indicates that the organizational scheme may have more to do with geography than genealogy. This is particularly apparent in Priestly literature, where tribal Dan is most commonly grouped only with Asher and Naphtali, the tribes that, with Dan, occupied the northernmost region of Israel (Num 1:38-39; 2:25-26; 7:66-71; 10:25; 26:42-43; cf. 1 Chron 12:35). An exception to this scheme is Dan's grouping with the Joseph tribes, Benjamin, and Naphtali (the children attributed to Rachel) in a list of tribal leaders from David's census (1 Chron 27:22 [Heb. 27:24]).

Danites went on their way. When Micah realized that they were too strong for him, he turned around and went home.

The Danites take possession of Laish

²⁷The Danites took along the things that Micah had made, as well as the priest who had been with him, and came to Laish, to a people who were undisturbed and secure. They killed the people and burned down the city. ²⁸No one was there to rescue them because the city was far away from Sidon and had no dealings with anyone else.ᵇ It was in the Beth-rehob Valley.

They rebuilt the city and settled in it. ²⁹They renamed the city Dan, after their ancestor Dan who had been one of Israel's sons; but in fact, the original name of the city was Laish. ³⁰The Danites set up the sculpted image for themselves, and Jonathan son of Gershom and grandson of Moses,ᶜ and his sons became priests for the Danite tribe until the land went into exile. ³¹They kept for themselves the sculpted image that Micah had made throughout the whole time that God's sanctuary was in Shiloh.

A Levite, a woman, and her father

19 In those days when there was no king in Israel, there was a certain Levite living as an immigrant in the far corners of the Ephraim highlands. He married a secondary wife from Bethlehem in Judah. ²In an act of unfaithfulness toward him, his secondary wife left him and went back to her father's household at Bethlehem in Judah. She stayed there four full months. ³Then her husband set out after her to convince her to come back. He had his servant and a couple of donkeys with him. She took him into her father's house, and when the young woman's father saw him, he was happy to welcome him. ⁴Since his father-in-law, the young woman's father, insisted, he stayed with him three days, eating, drinking, and spending the night there.

⁵On the fourth day, they got up early in the morning, and he got ready to set out. But the young woman's father said to his son-in-law, "Eat a little food to give you strength, and then you can go." ⁶So the two of them sat down and ate and drank together. The young woman's father said to the man, "Why not spend the night and enjoy yourself?" ⁷When the man got ready to set out, his father-in-law persuaded him, and he spent the night there again. ⁸On the fifth day, he got up early in the morning to set out, and the young woman's father said, "Have some food for strength." So the two of them ate, sitting around until late in the

ᵇOr with Aram ᶜOr Manasseh

GIBEAH

day. ⁹When the man got ready to set out with his secondary wife and servant, his father-in-law, the young woman's father, said, "Look, the day has turned to evening, so spend the night. Seriously, the day is over. Spend the night here and enjoy yourself. Then you can get up early tomorrow for your journey, and you can head home."

¹⁰But the man was unwilling to spend another night. He got up, set out, and went as far as the area of Jebus, that is, Jerusalem. He had a couple of saddled donkeys and his secondary wife with him. ¹¹When they were near Jebus, the day was totally gone. The servant said to his master, "Come on, let's turn into this Jebusite city and spend the night in it."

¹²But his master replied to him, "We won't turn into a city of foreigners who aren't Israelites. We'll travel on to Gibeah.

¹³"Come on," he said to his servant, "let's reach Gibeah or Ramah and spend the night in one of those places." ¹⁴So they traveled on, and the sun set when they were near Gibeah in Benjamin. ¹⁵They turned in to enter there, so they could spend the night in Gibeah, and he went and sat down in the city square. But no one offered to take them home to spend the night.

Rape and murder at Gibeah

¹⁶Then in the evening, an old man was coming home from his daily work in the fields. This man was from the Ephraim highlands and was an immigrant in Gibeah, the people of that place being Benjaminites. ¹⁷He looked up and saw the traveler in the city square. "Where are you heading and where have you come from?" the old man asked.

¹⁸"We're traveling from Bethlehem in Judah to the far corners of the Ephraim highlands," he replied to the old man. "That's where I'm from. I went to Bethlehem in Judah, and I'm heading to my home.ᵈ But no one has offered to take me in tonight. ¹⁹We've got our own straw and feed for our donkeys, plus food and wine to provide for me, the woman, and my servant with us. We don't need anything."

²⁰The old man answered, "You're welcome to stay with me,ᵉ but let me take care of all your needs. Just don't spend the night in the square." ²¹And he took him into his house. He mixed feed for the donkeys, and they washed their feet, ate, and drank.

²²While they were relaxing, suddenly the men of the city, a perverse bunch, surrounded the house and started pounding on the door. They said to the old man, the owner of the house, "Send out the man who came to your house, so we can have sex with him!"

²³The owner of the house went outside and said to them, "No, my friends, please don't commit such an evil act, given that this man has come to my home as a guest. Don't do this disgraceful thing! ²⁴Here's my daughter, the young woman, and his secondary wife. Let me send them out, and you can abuse them and do whatever you want to them. But don't do such a disgraceful thing to this man!" ²⁵But the men refused to listen to him.

ᵈLXX; MT *to the LORD's house* ᵉOr *Peace be with you*

SECONDARY WIFE

The term appears to mean a wife of lower status. Bilhah, Rachel's maid, is called both "wife" (Gen 30:4) and "secondary wife" (Gen 35:22). In Judges 19, an unnamed secondary wife's partner is called husband; the woman's father is called father-in-law. Secondary wives are named as mothers in genealogies more often than wives are (e.g., Gen 22:23-24; 36:12; Judg 8:31; 1 Chron 2:46, 48; 7:14).

So the Levite grabbed his secondary wife and sent her outside to them. They raped her and abused her all night long until morning. They finally let her go as dawn was breaking.

²⁶At daybreak, the woman came and collapsed at the door of the man's house where her husband was staying, where she lay until it was daylight. ²⁷When her husband got up in the morning, he opened the doors of the house and went outside to set out on his journey. And there was his secondary wife, lying at the entrance of the house, with her hands clutching the doorframe. ²⁸"Get up," he said to her, "let's go." But there was no response. So he laid her across a donkey, and the man set out for home. ²⁹When he got home, he picked up a knife, took his secondary wife, and chopped her, limb by limb, into twelve pieces. Then he sent them into all the areas of Israel. ³⁰Everyone who saw it said, "Has such a thing ever happened or been seen since the time when the Israelites came up from the land of Egypt until today? Think about it, decide what to do, and speak out!"

Civil war between the Benjaminites and the Israelites

20Then all the Israelites from Dan to Beer-sheba, as well as from the area of Gilead, marched out, and the group assembled as one body in the LORD's presence at Mizpah. ²The commanders of the people and of all the tribes of Israel took their place in the assembly of God's people, four hundred thousand foot soldiers armed with swords. ³And the Benjaminites got word that the Israelites had marched up to Mizpah.

The Israelites inquired, "Tell us how this evil act happened."

⁴So the Levite, the husband of the murdered woman, answered, "My secondary wife and I came to Gibeah of Benjamin to spend the night, ⁵and the leading citizens of Gibeah tried to attack me. They surrounded me in the house at night and were determined to kill me. They abused my secondary wife until she died. ⁶I took her, chopped her up, and sent her pieces into every part of Israel's territory, because they had committed a disgraceful act in Israel. ⁷All you Israelites, say what you think should be done here and now!"

⁸At this, all the people stood as one to say, "Not a single one of us is going home or returning to our house! ⁹This is what we're now going to do to Gibeah: We'll march up[f] against it as the lot determines. ¹⁰From all the tribes of Israel, we'll get ten men for every hundred, one hundred for every thousand, and one thousand for every ten thousand to take supplies for the troops who are going to pay back[g] Gibeah of Benjamin for the disgraceful act they've done in Israel." ¹¹So all the Israelites joined together and were united as one against the city.

¹²The Israelite tribes sent men throughout the whole tribe of Benjamin with this message: "What about this evil act that happened among you? ¹³Now hand over those perverse men in Gibeah so that we can execute them and remove the evil from Israel." But the Benjaminites refused to comply with the demand of their own relatives the Israelites. ¹⁴Instead, the Benjaminites from all the cities came together at Gibeah to march out for battle against the Israelites. ¹⁵On that day, the Benjaminites called up from their cities twenty-six thousand men armed with swords, not counting those living in Gibeah.[h] ¹⁶Out of this entire army, seven hundred specially chosen men were left-handed, and every one of them could sling a stone at a hair and not miss. ¹⁷Not counting Benjamin, the Israelites called up four hundred thousand men armed with swords, and every one of them was a trained warrior.

¹⁸Then the Israelites marched up to Bethel to ask for direction from God. They inquired, "Who should go up first to fight against the Benjaminites for us?"

And the LORD said, "Let the tribe of Judah be first."

---

[f]LXX; MT lacks *We'll march up.* [g]Cf LXX; Heb uncertain [h]LXX, Vulg, Syr; MT adds *seven hundred specially chosen men were called up.*

¹⁹So the next morning, the Israelites got up and camped near Gibeah. ²⁰They marched out to fight against the Benjaminites, lining up in battle formation against them at Gibeah. ²¹But the Benjaminites marched out from Gibeah and cut down twenty-two thousand Israelite men that day.

²³ᶦSo the Israelites went back up and wept before the LORD until evening. They asked the LORD, "Should we move in again to fight our relatives the Benjaminites?"

And the LORD replied, "March out against them."

²²The Israelite troops regrouped and lined up in battle formation again in the same place they had lined up the first day. ²⁴The Israelites moved in against the Benjaminites the second day. ²⁵But the Benjaminites marched out of Gibeah to meet them on that second day and cut down another eighteen thousand Israelite men, all of whom were armed with swords.

²⁶Then all the Israelite troops went back up to Bethel and wept, just sitting there in the LORD's presence. They fasted that whole day until evening. Then they offered entirely burned offerings and well-being sacrifices to the LORD. ²⁷Now in those days the chest containing God's covenant was there, ²⁸and Phinehas, Eleazar's son and Aaron's grandson, was in charge of ministering before it. The Israelites asked the LORD, "Should we march out once again to fight our relatives the Benjaminites or should we give up?"

And the LORD replied, "March up, for I'll hand them to you tomorrow."

²⁹So the Israelites set ambushes around Gibeah. ³⁰Three days later, the Israelites marched out against the Benjaminites. They lined up for battle against Gibeah as before. ³¹When the Benjaminites came out to meet them, they were drawn away from the city. They began to strike down some of the troops just like the last time, about thirty Israelites along the main roads, one of which goes up to Bethel and one to Gibeah, as well as in the open fields. ³²The Benjaminites thought, They're being wiped out

before us like the first time. But the Israelites had planned, We'll retreat and draw them away from the city toward the main roads. ³³The Israelites moved from their position and reformed their battle lines at Baal-tamar. Then the Israelites who had been set in ambush charged out from their positions west of Gibeah.ʲ ³⁴Ten thousand specially chosen men from all the Israelites came against Gibeah. The fighting was fierce, and the Benjaminites didn't realize that disaster was almost on them. ³⁵The LORD wiped out the Benjaminites before Israel. The Israelites slaughtered twenty-five thousand one hundred Benjaminite men that day, all of them armed with swords. ³⁶Then the Benjaminites saw that they had been defeated.

The Israelites had given ground to the Benjaminites because they relied on the ambush that they had set around Gibeah. ³⁷Indeed, those in the ambush had dashed swiftly into Gibeah and killed all the people in the city with their swords. ³⁸The plan between the main force of the Israelites and those in the ambush was that when they sent up a big cloud of smoke from the city, ³⁹the Israelites would turn around in battle. The Benjaminites had begun to defeat some of the Israelites and had killed about thirty men, thinking, They are definitely going to be wiped out before us, as in the first battle! ⁴⁰But then the column of smoke began to rise from the city. When the Benjaminites looked back, there was the entire city going up in smoke to the sky. ⁴¹The main force of the Israelites turned around, and the Benjaminites lost heart, because they recognized that disaster had fallen on them. ⁴²They turned back before the Israelites in the direction of the desert, but the fighting caught up with them, and those from the towns were slaughtering them there.ᵏ ⁴³They encircled the Benjaminites, chased them from Nohah,ˡ and trampled them to the east of Gibeah. ⁴⁴Eighteen thousand Benjaminites fell, all of whom were strong warriors. ⁴⁵When they turned back and fled toward the desert to the rock of Rimmon,

---

ᶦ20:22 and 20:23 are reversed. ʲHeb Geba ᵏHeb uncertain ˡLXX; MT *to a resting place* the Israelites picked off another five thousand men on the main roads. And when they caught up with them at Gidom, they struck down two thousand more.

⁴⁶All in all, the total number of Benjaminites who fell that day was twenty-five thousand men, all of whom were armed with swords and were strong warriors. ⁴⁷Six hundred men turned back and fled toward the desert to the rock of Rimmon. They stayed at the rock of Rimmon for four months. ⁴⁸But the Israelites turned their attention to the rest of the Benjaminites and massacred them entirely—the city, the people, even the animals, and everything else they found. They also burned down every city they came across.

Wives for the Benjaminites

21 The Israelites had made a pledge at Mizpah, declaring, "None of us will allow his daughter to marry a Benjaminite." ²But the people came to Bethel and sat there until evening before God, raising their voices and crying bitterly. ³"LORD, God of Israel," they said, "why has this happened among us that as of today one tribe will be missing from Israel?" ⁴And the next day, the people got up early and built an altar there. They offered entirely burned offerings and well-being sacrifices.

⁵Then the Israelites asked, "Were there any out of all the tribes of Israel who didn't march up to the assembly before the LORD?" Indeed, they had made a solemn pledge that anyone who didn't march up before the LORD at Mizpah would be put to death. ⁶The Israelites had a change of heart concerning their relatives the Benjaminites. They said, "Today one tribe has been cut off from Israel. ⁷What can we do to provide wives for the ones who are left, since we ourselves have made a pledge before the LORD not to allow our daughters to marry them?" ⁸So they asked, "Is there anyone from the tribes of Israel who didn't march up before the LORD at Mizpah?" There was! No one from Jabesh-gilead had come to the assembly at the camp. ⁹When the people's

attendance was taken, not one of those who lived in Jabesh-gilead had been there.

¹⁰The community dispatched twelve thousand warriors there with these orders: "Go kill all the people in Jabesh-gilead, including women and children. ¹¹Here's what you should do: Exterminate every man and every woman who has slept with a man." ¹²Among the people of Jabesh-gilead, they found four hundred young women who had not known a man intimately or slept with one, and they brought them to the camp at Shiloh in the land of Canaan. ¹³The whole community then sent word to the Benjaminites who were at the rock of Rimmon and offered them a truce.ᵐ ¹⁴So the Benjaminites returned at that time, and they gave them the women from Jabesh-gilead that they had allowed to live. Even so, there weren't enough for them.

¹⁵Since the people had a change of heart concerning the Benjaminites because the LORD had caused a rupture in the tribes of Israel, ¹⁶the community elders said, "What can we do to provide wives for the ones who are left, seeing that the Benjaminite women have been destroyed? ¹⁷There must be a surviving line for those who remain from Benjamin," they continued, "so that a tribe won't be erased from Israel. ¹⁸But we can't allow our daughters to marry them, for we Israelites have made this pledge: 'Let anyone who provides a wife for Benjamin be cursed!' ¹⁹However," they said, "the annual festival of the LORD is under way in Shiloh, which is north of Bethel, east of the main road that goes up from Bethel to Shechem, and south of Lebonah." ²⁰So they instructed the Benjaminites, "Go and hide like an ambush in the vineyards ²¹and watch. At the moment the women of Shiloh come out to participate in the dances, rush out from the vineyards. Each one of you, capture a wife for yourself from the women of Shiloh and go back to the land of Benjamin. ²²When their fathers or brothers come to us to object, we'll tell them, 'Do us a favor for their sake. We didn't capture enough women for every man during the

ᵐOr peace

battle, and this way you are not guilty because you didn't give them anything willingly.'" ²³And that is what the Benjaminites did. They took wives for their whole group from the dancers whom they abducted. They returned to their territory, rebuilt the cities, and lived in them. ²⁴Likewise, the

Israelites set out from there at that time, heading home to their respective tribes and clans. They all left there for their own territories.

²⁵In those days there was no king in Israel; each person did what they thought to be right.

RUTH

The book of Ruth is a historical short story. It is a love story of the conventional man-woman kind. But it is also a love story in a broader sense. This Old Testament book is a story of many good people who love and care for each other. And, beneath it all, this is a love story about God.

In Ruth, love and concern are everywhere. There is not an unkind person or a villain in the piece. There are only ordinary people showing love to family members and, beyond the family, to strangers. In this superb tale we meet unforgettable characters like Naomi, a grieving widow who looks after the interests of her daughters-in-law; Ruth, who leaves home and risks her safety to care for Naomi; and Boaz, who shows kindness to the foreigner, Ruth, and eventually marries her. Behind the scenes, guiding and protecting, we see a God whose love is stronger and broader than many humans may have suspected.

PURPOSE AND DATE

Ruth is intended to be both entertaining and instructive. One of the book's major purposes is to show that God wants people to live in self-giving love. But the author apparently had another, more specific, purpose: to deal with the problem of how Israel should relate to foreigners. Over and over the author reminds us that Ruth is from Moab, that she is a foreigner. Yet she and the other characters treat each other with love. In that light Ruth is a love story with wide social significance—a story of love between nations and groups, between people with differences who share the same parent-child relationship with God.

This second purpose probably arose from the historical situation in which the author lived. Both the language and content suggest that the story as it now stands comes from 450–250 BCE. This was a time after the exile when Nehemiah and others were trying very hard to preserve Israel's unity and purity by limiting the people's relationships with outsiders. They strictly enforced the traditional rule forbidding intermarriage with foreigners (Nehemiah 10:28-31). They emphasized the law in Deuteronomy 23:3 that forbids foreigners from fully entering the Israelite community. Some saw foreigners as evil, inferior, or both. To many, God seemed to be God of Israel alone. Ruth's author opposed this exclusivism. But instead of writing a diatribe, the author wrote a brilliantly gentle story—a story in which a loving Moabite woman marries an Israelite and eventually becomes the ancestress of Israel's greatest king.

The story itself may be a very old one. Its cultural details accurately reflect the Judges period. It contains many ancient words as well. So it seems likely that the author has taken a beloved old story and used it to make an effective point about a present situation.

While most commentators agree on the book's purpose, a few do not place the author in the post-exilic time period. Some scholars argue that much of the language could come from the monarchic period, and that concern for inclusiveness could have arisen before the exile. If this were the case, Ruth's date of composition could be set at the time of Jehoshaphat's reform in the second quarter of the ninth century BCE. However, these arguments do not seem compelling. Instead, the exilic setting still seems the more likely one.

THEOLOGY

God, in the book of Ruth, is a God who actively cares for people. However, God works in the shadows. Occasionally God's presence is noted directly. More often, though, we hear of God through the blessings and prayers of the story's characters.

The author assumes that God is behind the good things that happen—the famine's end, the "luck" that brings Ruth to Boaz's field, and so forth. We are led to feel that God is working toward good even when evil seems dominant.

In this story God acts most often through people. They are ordinary people in ordinary circumstances. Yet they are good people, good as God is good. They live in imitation of God and, in so doing, fulfill the plans of God.

The happy ending makes one final theological point: that God will reward righteous, godly living. This is no rigid legalism, however. The author suggests that happiness will eventually come to those who love and give. The greatest happiness comes to those who love and give beyond what is legally required.

PLACE IN THE CANON

Ruth was not originally part of the great Deuteronomic history that encompasses most of Deuteronomy through 2 Kings. In the Hebrew Bible, Ruth appears in the third section, among the Writings. Greek and Latin versions placed Ruth after Judges, probably because the story is set in the Judges period. Christian Bibles retain this later positioning.

Today, Jewish people read the book of Ruth during the Feast of Weeks, an ancient celebration of the grain harvest.

RUTH

The family in Moab

During the days when the judges ruled, there was a famine in the land. A man with his wife and two sons went from Bethlehem of Judah to dwell in the territory of Moab. ²The name of that man was Elimelech, the name of his wife was Naomi, and the names of his two sons were Mahlon and Chilion. They were Ephrathites from Bethlehem in Judah. They entered the territory of Moab and settled there.

³But Elimelech, Naomi's husband, died. Then only she was left, along with her two sons. ⁴They took wives for themselves, Moabite women; the name of the first was Orpah and the name of the second was Ruth. And they lived there for about ten years.

⁵But both of the sons, Mahlon and Chilion, also died. Only the woman was left, without her two children and without her husband.

⁶Then she arose along with her daughters-in-law to return from the field of Moab, because while in the territory of Moab she had heard that the LORD had paid attention to his people by providing food for them. ⁷She left the place where she had been, and her two daughters-in-law went with her. They went along the road to return to the land of Judah.

⁸Naomi said to her daughters-in-law, "Go, turn back, each of you to the household of your mother. May the LORD deal faithfully with you, just as you have done with the dead and with me. ⁹May the LORD provide for you so that you may find security, each woman in the household of her husband." Then she kissed them, and they lifted up their voices and wept.

¹⁰But they replied to her, "No, instead we will return with you, to your people."

¹¹Naomi replied, "Turn back, my daughters. Why would you go with me? Will there again be sons in my womb, that they would be husbands for you? ¹²Turn back, my daughters. Go. I am too old for a husband. If I were to say that I have hope, even if I had a husband tonight, and even more, if I were to bear sons—¹³would you wait until they grew up? Would you refrain from having a husband? No, my daughters. This is more bitter for me than for you, since the LORD's will has come out against me."

¹⁴Then they lifted up their voices and wept again. Orpah kissed her mother-in-law, but Ruth stayed with her. ¹⁵Naomi said, "Look, your sister-in-law is returning to her people and to her gods. Turn back after your sister-in-law."

¹⁶But Ruth replied, "Don't urge me to abandon you, to turn back from following after you. Wherever you go, I will go; and wherever you stay, I will stay. Your people will be my people, and your God will be my God. ¹⁷Wherever you die, I will die, and there I will be buried. May the LORD do this to me and more so if even death separates me from you." ¹⁸When Naomi saw that Ruth was determined to go with her, she stopped speaking to her about it.

¹⁹So both of them went along until they arrived at Bethlehem. When they arrived at Bethlehem, the whole town was excited on account of them, and the women of the town asked, "Can this be Naomi?"

NAOMI

Meaning "my pleasantness." An Ephrathite (Bethlehemite) woman whose story is central to the book of Ruth. Naomi's actions to save herself and her daughters-in-law ultimately lead to the birth of David and the preservation of the nation.

²⁰She replied to them, "Don't call me Naomi,^a but call me Mara,^b for the Almighty^c has made me very bitter. ²¹I went away full, but the LORD has returned me empty. Why would you call me Naomi, when the LORD has testified against me, and the Almighty has deemed me guilty?"

²²Thus Naomi returned. And Ruth the Moabite, her daughter-in-law, returned with her from the territory of Moab. They arrived in Bethlehem at the beginning of the barley harvest.

Gleaning in Bethlehem

2 Now Naomi had a respected relative, a man of worth, through her husband from the family of Elimelech. His name was Boaz. ²Ruth the Moabite said to Naomi, "Let me go to the field so that I may glean among the ears of grain behind someone in whose eyes I might find favor."

Naomi replied to her, "Go, my daughter." ³So she went; she arrived and she gleaned in the field behind the harvesters. By chance, it happened to be the portion of the field that belonged to Boaz, who was from the family of Elimelech.

⁴Just then Boaz arrived from Bethlehem. He said to the harvesters, "May the LORD be with you."

And they said to him, "May the LORD bless you."

⁵Boaz said to his young man, the one who was overseeing the harvesters, "To whom does this young woman belong?"

⁶The young man who was overseeing the harvesters answered, "She's a young Moabite woman, the one who returned with Naomi from the territory of Moab. ⁷She said, 'Please let me glean so that I might gather up grain from among the bundles behind the harvesters.' She arrived and has been on her feet from the morning until now, and has sat down for only a moment."^d

⁸Boaz said to Ruth, "Haven't you understood, my daughter? Don't go glean in another field; don't go anywhere else. Instead, stay here with my young women. ⁹Keep your eyes on the field that they are harvesting and go along after them. I've ordered the young men not to assault you. Whenever you are thirsty, go to the jugs and drink from what the young men have filled."

¹⁰Then she bowed down, face to the ground, and replied to him, "How is it that I've found favor in your eyes, that you notice me? I'm an immigrant." ¹¹Boaz responded to her, "Everything that you did for your mother-in-law after your husband's death has been reported fully to me: how you left behind your father, your mother, and the land of your birth, and came to a people you hadn't known beforehand. ¹²May the LORD reward you^e for your deed. May you receive a rich reward from the LORD, the God of Israel, under whose wings you've come to seek refuge." ¹³She said, "May I continue to find favor in your eyes, sir, because you've comforted me and because you've spoken kindly to your female servant—even though I'm not one of your female servants."

¹⁴At mealtime Boaz said to her, "Come over here, eat some of the bread, and dip

---

^aNaomi means *pleasant.*   ^bMara means *bitter.*   ^cHeb *El Shaddai* or *God of the Mountain*   ^dHeb uncertain   ^eLXX

RUTH

The Moabite daughter-in-law of Elimelech and Naomi, natives of Judah who search for food and a living in Moab, and the main character of the book of Ruth. Boaz married Ruth in fulfillment of the law of Levirate marriage (Deut 25:5-10). Their son, Obed, was the grandfather of David.

your piece in the vinegar." She sat alongside the harvesters, and he served roasted grain to her. She ate, was satisfied, and had leftovers. ¹⁵Then she got up to glean.

Boaz ordered his young men, "Let her glean between the bundles, and don't humiliate her. ¹⁶Also, pull out some from the bales for her and leave them behind for her to glean. And don't scold her."

¹⁷So she gleaned in the field until evening. Then she threshed what she had gleaned; it was about an ephah^f of barley. ¹⁸She picked it up and went into town. Her mother-in-law saw what she had gleaned. She brought out what she had left over after eating her fill and gave it to her. ¹⁹Her mother-in-law said to her, "Where did you glean today? Where did you work? May the one who noticed you be blessed."

She told her mother-in-law with whom she had worked and said, "The name of the man with whom I worked today is Boaz."

²⁰Naomi replied to her daughter-in-law, "May he be blessed by the LORD, who hasn't abandoned his faithfulness with the living or with the dead." Naomi said to her, "The man is one of our close relatives; he's one of our redeemers."

²¹Ruth the Moabite replied, "Furthermore, he said to me, 'Stay with my workers until they've finished all of my harvest.'"

²²Naomi said to Ruth her daughter-in-law, "It's good, my daughter, that you go out with his young women, so that men don't assault you in another field."

²³Thus she stayed with Boaz's young women, gleaning until the completion of the barley and wheat harvests. And she lived with her mother-in-law.

Encounter at the threshing floor

3 Naomi her mother-in-law said to her, "My daughter, shouldn't I seek security for you, so that things might go well for you? ²Now isn't Boaz, whose young women you were with, our relative? Tonight he will be winnowing barley at the threshing floor. ³You should bathe, put on some perfume, wear nice clothes, and then go down to the threshing floor. Don't make yourself known to the man until he has finished eating and drinking. ⁴When he lies down, notice the place where he is lying. Then go, uncover his feet, and lie down. And he will tell you what to do."

⁵Ruth replied to her, "I'll do everything you are telling me."

⁶So she went down to the threshing floor, and she did everything just as her mother-in-law had ordered.

⁷Boaz ate and drank, and he was in a good mood. He went over to lie down by the edge of the grain pile. Then she quietly approached, uncovered his legs, and lay down. ⁸During the middle of the night, the man shuddered and turned over—and there was a woman lying at his feet. ⁹"Who are you?" he asked.

She replied, "I'm Ruth your servant. Spread out your robe^g over your servant, because you are a redeemer."

¹⁰He said, "May you be blessed by the LORD, my daughter! You have acted even more faithfully than you did at first. You

^{f}An ephah is approximately twenty quarts of grain. ^{g}Or *wing;* cf 2:12; Ps 91:4

BOAZ

Boaz is a kinsman of Naomi's dead husband Elimelech (Ruth 2:1). He "redeems" (rescues) Naomi and her widowed daughter-in-law Ruth from poverty by marrying Ruth. Thus, Naomi can claim Ruth's child Obed as her dead husband's heir, keeping the family name and the family's property rights alive (see Lev 25).

haven't gone after rich or poor young men. [11]And now, my daughter, don't be afraid. I'll do for you everything you are asking. Indeed, my people—all who are at the gate—know that you are a woman of worth. [12]Now, although it's certainly true that I'm a redeemer, there's a redeemer who is a closer relative than I am. [13]Stay the night. And in the morning, if he'll redeem you—good, let him redeem. But if he doesn't want to redeem you, then—as the LORD lives—I myself will redeem you. Lie down until the morning."

[14]So she lay at his feet until morning. Then she got up before one person could recognize another, for he had said, "No one should know that the woman came to the threshing floor." [15]He said, "Bring the cloak that you have on and hold it out." She held it out, and he measured out six measures of barley and placed it upon her. Then she[h] went into town.

[16]She came to her mother-in-law, who said, "How are you, my daughter?"

So Ruth told her everything the man had done for her. [17]She said, "He gave me these six measures of barley, for he said to me, 'Don't go away empty-handed to your mother-in-law.'"

[18]"Sit tight, my daughter," Naomi replied, "until you know how it turns out. The man won't rest until he resolves the matter today."

A new family brings fulfillment

4 Meanwhile, Boaz went up to the gate and sat down there. Just then, the redeemer about whom Boaz had spoken was passing by. He said, "Sir, come over here and sit down." So he turned aside and sat down. [2]Then he took ten men from the town's elders and said, "Sit down here." And they sat down.

[3]Boaz said to the redeemer, "Naomi, who has returned from the field of Moab, is selling the portion of the field that belonged to our brother Elimelech. [4]I thought that I should let you know and say, 'Buy it, in the presence of those sitting here and in the presence of the elders of my people.' If you will redeem it, redeem it; but if you[i] won't redeem it, tell me so that I may know. There isn't anyone to redeem it except you, and I'm next in line after you."

He replied, "I will redeem it."

[5]Then Boaz said, "On the day when you buy the field from Naomi, you also buy[j] Ruth the Moabite, the wife of the dead man, in order to preserve the dead man's name for his inheritance."

[6]But the redeemer replied, "Then I can't redeem it for myself, without risking damage to my own inheritance. Redeem it for yourself. You can have my right of redemption, because I'm unable to act as redeemer."

[7]In Israel, in former times, this was the practice regarding redemption and exchange

[h]MT *he*; other Heb sources, Syr, Vulg *she* [i]MT *he*; LXX, Syr *you* [j]Vulg; MT *On the day that you buy the field from Naomi and from Ruth the Moabite*

LEVIRATE LAW

If a woman's husband dies before a son is born to the couple, it is the legally binding duty of the husband's brother to marry the widow and produce a son in his brother's name (Deut 25:5-10). If the brother-in-law does not wish to marry the widow, both parties consult with the elders, and the widow and her brother-in-law take part in a ceremony in which she removes his sandal, spits in his face, and renounces him as a man unwilling to establish a name for his brother in Israel. Once this ceremony is performed, the widow is free to marry outside her husband's family. This legal practice is the subject of Genesis 38 and, arguably, Ruth 4.

to confirm any such matter: a man would take off his sandal and give it to the other person. This was the process of making a transaction binding in Israel. [8]Then the redeemer said to Boaz, "Buy it for yourself," and he took off his sandal.

[9]Boaz announced to the elders and all the people, "Today you are witnesses that I've bought from the hand of Naomi all that belonged to Elimelech and all that belonged to Chilion and Mahlon. [10]And also Ruth the Moabite, the wife of Mahlon, I've bought to be my wife, to preserve the dead man's name for his inheritance so that the name of the dead man might not be cut off from his brothers or from the gate of his hometown—today you are witnesses."

[11]Then all the people who were at the gate and the elders said, "We are witnesses. May the LORD grant that the woman who is coming into your household be like Rachel and like Leah, both of whom built up the house of Israel. May you be fertile in Ephrathah and may you preserve a name in Bethlehem. [12]And may your household be like the household of Perez, whom Tamar bore to Judah—through the children that the LORD will give you from this young woman."

[13]So Boaz took Ruth, and she became his wife.

He was intimate with her, the LORD let her become pregnant, and she gave birth to a son. [14]The women said to Naomi, "May the LORD be blessed, who today hasn't left you without a redeemer. May his name be proclaimed in Israel. [15]He will restore your life and sustain you in your old age. Your daughter-in-law who loves you has given birth to him. She's better for you than seven sons." [16]Naomi took the child and held him to her breast, and she became his guardian. [17]The neighborhood women gave him a name, saying, "A son has been born to Naomi." They called his name Obed.[k] He became Jesse's father and David's grandfather.

[18]These are the generations of Perez: Perez became the father of Hezron, [19]Hezron the father of Ram, Ram the father of Amminadab, [20]Amminadab the father of Nahshon, Nahshon the father of Salmon, [21]Salmon the father of Boaz, Boaz the father of Obed, [22]Obed the father of Jesse, and Jesse the father of David.

[k]Obed means one who serves (God).

OBED

The son of Ruth and Boaz; the father of Jesse and grandfather of King David (Ruth 4:17, 22; 1 Chron 2:12). According to some, he was the "goel" or "next-of-kin" for Naomi and functioned as her son (Ruth 4:14-17). In the Levirate marriage, he was the son (or grandson) of Naomi's husband Elimelech (Ruth 4:3-9). In both genealogies of Jesus, in Matthew 1:5 and Luke 3:32, he was the son of Boaz. Because Obed is named a son of Naomi, he becomes both the son of Elimelech and the son of Boaz; both men were of Bethlehem, Judah. Through Obed, Moab entered the lineage of Jesus (Ruth 1:4; 4:6).

1 SAMUEL

The books of 1 and 2 Samuel highlight selected events in Israelite history from the end of the period of the judges (about 1025 BCE) until shortly before the death of King David (about 961 BCE). The opening three chapters of 1 Samuel tell of Samuel's miraculous birth and his entry into the priestly service. Samuel becomes the major transitional figure in early Israel who oversees the political move by the tribes of Israel from governance by judges to rule by kings.

Despite reservations, Samuel anoints Saul as Israel's first king. Although Saul manages to slow the Philistine aggression on Israelite territory, he lacks the military strength to defeat them. God turns against him (albeit for just causes) and turns in the direction of David. Saul is jealous and envious of David and plots his murder. This drives David into flight and hiding. As his relentless pursuit of David continues, Saul becomes increasingly unable to wage war successfully with the Philistines. Desperate for guidance, he turns to a deceased Samuel, by way of a medium, only to learn of his own impending death. The very next day, the Philistines rout Saul's army and wound the king. Saul falls on his own sword. First Samuel ends with an act of kindness by the men of Jabesh, when they stealthily remove the bodies of Saul and Jonathan from public display on the walls of Bethshan and provide appropriate burials.

THE PLACE OF THE BOOKS OF SAMUEL IN THE OLD TESTAMENT

Originally in early Hebrew manuscripts, 1 and 2 Samuel formed a single book on a single scroll. About the third or second century BCE, Greek versions of the Old Testament (known as the Septuagint) combined 1 and 2 Samuel with 1 and 2 Kings, and designated the entire collection as the books of Kingdoms. Exactly when these scrolls were first separated into four books in Hebrew is unclear, since the Greek and Latin versions, while combining them as books of the Kingdoms, divide them onto scrolls almost exactly as 1 and 2 Samuel and 1 and 2 Kings are divided and now appear in English translations. The division of 1 and 2 Samuel following the death of Saul is appropriate for two reasons. First, this split precedes the great reign of King David. Second, this division follows other Old Testament divisions. For example, the Pentateuch closes with the death of Moses rather than the more natural recapture of the promised land.

THE AUTHORSHIP OF 1 AND 2 SAMUEL

The title of the books reflects the name of their first major character, Samuel, rather than designating actual authorship. Also, the reference in 1 Chronicles

29:29 to records from Samuel, Nathan, and Gad probably refers to a set of documents, now lost, on which the books of Samuel are based, not to the Old Testament books themselves. Complicating matters further, we can hardly help noticing the duplications in these stories. (1) There are two accounts of how Saul becomes king (compare 1 Samuel 9:1–10:16 with 1 Samuel 10:17-27). (2) There are two accounts of how David enters Saul's service (compare 16:14-23 with 17:1-58). (3) There are two accounts of Saul's sin against God (compare 13:7b-15a with 15:1-35). In addition to these duplications, there are more general differences in points of view (pro-monarchy versus anti-monarchy). These factors seem to suggest that more than one writer's material has been combined into the present books of 1 and 2 Samuel. But who were these writers?

Most likely an anonymous author, or perhaps a group of authors, writing during the Babylonian Exile of the Jews (587–538 BCE), brought together several earlier sources and wrote a history of Israel from the settlement in Canaan (13th century BCE) until the deportation by the Neo-Babylonians (587 BCE). This author used different sources, both written and oral, which reflected different points of view or presented different accounts of the same incident.

Two reasons may be given why an ancient writer might have used stories that present different accounts of the same event. (1) Differences in factual details were less important than the overall theological message these different accounts presented. (2) The writer may have believed that each version contained some elements of truth. To have omitted one version would have resulted in a misrepresentation of the event. We must not fault the writer for using more than one account, nor should we judge his writing in light of our own standards of coherence and consistency today.

MAJOR THEOLOGICAL THEMES IN 1 AND 2 SAMUEL

Theological intentions outweigh factual accuracy in the history of Israel in 1 and 2 Samuel.

From the writer's point of view, Israel's entire history, from settlement to exile, is replete with apostasy. Using Deuteronomy 30:15-20 as his theological norm, the writer documents repeated instances where Israel worshiped other gods. Other than David, Hezekiah, and Josiah, few of Israel's and Judah's rulers upheld the first commandment: "You must have no other gods before me" (Exodus 20:3). The writer clearly blames the rulers of Judah and Israel for the exile. Israel's and Judah's kings committed evil in the sight of the Lord. And as the kings worshiped foreign gods, so did the general population. As the Lord of history, God will not long tolerate repeated violations of the commandments.

A second set of theological themes in 1 and 2 Samuel focuses on different forms of divine revelation. The writer interpreted Israel's history as displaying God's awesome presence, both for deliverance and for judgment. But in addition to this more general revelation for the nation, particular individuals also received God's word: Samuel (1 Samuel 3:1–4:1a), Nathan (2 Samuel 7:4-16), and David.

Through disclosures to these special persons, God's will was revealed to Israel and Judah.

God's covenant with David provides yet another theological theme of great importance in 1 and 2 Samuel. In 2 Samuel 7, Nathan tells David that the Lord does not desire a house (temple), but instead will build David a house (dynasty). In return for David's loyal and devoted service, God agrees to establish David as one of the world's great rulers, whose fame will reach foreign capitals; to provide David and his country peace and security; and to perpetuate the Davidic dynasty forever.

The Davidic covenant provided a theological justification for monarchy and quieted objections from conservative elements in the north. Kingship was now a legitimate institution. David was elevated to a theological stature comparable to that of figures such as Abraham and Moses.

A fifth theological theme in these two books is the nature of servanthood. What does it mean to be a true servant of the Lord? Judging from the stories and characters in 1 and 2 Samuel, three traits are essential: (1) obedience to God's word, (2) a sense of morality (even if imperfect in execution), and (3) a loyalty to God. Samuel and David both exhibited these qualities, as did many other Old Testament figures. Human perfection (freedom from sin) is not a prerequisite for servanthood, but consciousness of God's expectation does clearly distinguish God's person.

1 SAMUEL

Samuel's birth

1 Now there was a certain man from Ra-mathaim, a Zuphite[a] from the highlands of Ephraim, whose name was Elkanah. He was from the tribe of Ephraim, and he was the son of Jeroham son of Elihu son of Tohu son of Zuph. ²Elkanah had two wives, one named Hannah and the other named Peninnah. Peninnah had children, but Hannah didn't.

³Every year this man would leave his town to worship and sacrifice to the LORD of heavenly forces in Shiloh, where Eli's two sons Hophni and Phinehas were the LORD's priests. ⁴Whenever he sacrificed, Elkanah would give parts of the sacrifice to his wife Peninnah and to all her sons and daughters. ⁵But he would give only one part of it to Hannah, though he loved her, because the LORD had kept her from conceiving.[b] ⁶And because the LORD had kept Hannah from conceiving, her rival would make fun of her mercilessly, just to bother her. ⁷So that is what took place year after year. Whenever Hannah went to the Lord's house, Peninnah would make fun of her. Then she would cry and wouldn't eat anything.

⁸"Hannah, why are you crying?" her husband Elkanah would say to her. "Why won't you eat? Why are you[c] so sad? Aren't I worth more to you than ten sons?"

⁹One time, after eating and drinking in Shiloh, Hannah got up and presented herself before the LORD.[d] (Now Eli the priest was sitting in the chair by the doorpost of the LORD's temple.) ¹⁰Hannah was very upset and couldn't stop crying as she prayed to the LORD. ¹¹Then she made this promise: "LORD of heavenly forces, just look at your servant's pain and remember me! Don't forget your servant! Give her a boy! Then I'll give him to the LORD for his entire life. No razor will ever touch his head."

¹²As she kept praying before the LORD, Eli watched her mouth. ¹³Now Hannah was praying in her heart; her lips were moving, but her voice was silent, so Eli thought she was drunk.

¹⁴"How long will you act like a drunk? Sober up!" Eli told her.

¹⁵"No sir!" Hannah replied. "I'm just a very sad woman. I haven't had any wine or beer but have been pouring out my heart to the LORD. ¹⁶Don't think your servant is some good-for-nothing woman. This whole time I've been praying out of my great worry and trouble!"

¹⁷Eli responded, "Then go in peace. And may the God of Israel give you what you've asked from him."

¹⁸"Please think well of me, your servant," Hannah said. Then the woman went on her way, ate some food, and wasn't sad any longer.[e]

¹⁹They got up early the next morning and worshipped the LORD. Then they went back home to Ramah. Elkanah had sex with his wife Hannah, and the LORD remembered her. ²⁰So in the course of time, Hannah conceived and gave birth to a son. She named him Samuel, which means "I asked the LORD for him."[f]

Samuel's dedication

²¹When Elkanah and all his household went up to make the annual sacrifice and keep his solemn promise, ²²Hannah didn't go.

"I'll bring the boy when he is weaned," she told her husband, "so he can be presented to the LORD and stay there permanently. I will offer him as a nazirite forever."[g]

²³"Do what seems best to you," said her husband Elkanah. "Stay here until you've weaned him. But may the LORD bring to pass what you've[h] promised." So the woman stayed home and nursed her son until she had weaned him.

²⁴When he had been weaned and was still very young,[i] Hannah took him, along

---

ᵃLXX; MT *Ramathaim-zophim* ᵇHeb uncertain; Syr *But he would give a double portion to Hannah, because he loved her, though the LORD had kept her from conceiving.* ᶜOr *your heart* ᵈLXX; MT lacks *presented herself before the LORD.* ᵉLXX; MT lacks *sad.* ᶠSamuel means *God has heard* but here is connected to the Heb verb *to ask.* ᵍDSS (4QSamᵃ); MT lacks *I will offer . . . forever.* ʰLXX, DSS (4QSamᵃ); MT *he* ⁱOr *and the boy was a boy*; Heb uncertain with a three-year-old bull,[j] an ephah[k] of flour, and a jar of wine, and brought him to the LORD's house at Shiloh. [25]They slaughtered the bull, then brought the boy to Eli.

[26]"Excuse me, sir!" Hannah said. "As surely as you live, sir, I am the woman who stood here next to you, praying to the LORD. [27]I prayed for this boy, and the LORD gave me what I asked from him. [28]So now I give this boy back to the LORD. As long as he lives, he is given to the LORD."

Then they worshipped there before the LORD.[l]

Hannah's song

2 Then Hannah prayed:
My heart rejoices in the LORD.
  My strength[m] rises up in the LORD!
  My mouth mocks my enemies
    because I rejoice in your deliverance.
[2] No one is holy like the LORD—
  no, no one except you!
  There is no rock like our God!

[3] Don't go on and on, talking so proudly,
  spouting arrogance from your mouth,
  because the LORD is the God who knows,
    and he weighs every act.

[4] The bows of mighty warriors
  are shattered,
  but those who were stumbling
    now dress themselves in power!
[5] Those who were filled full
  now sell themselves for bread,
  but the ones who were starving
    are now fat from food!
  The woman who was barren
    has birthed seven children,
  but the mother with many sons
    has lost them all!
[6] The LORD!
  He brings death, gives life,
    takes down to the grave,[n]
    and raises up!
[7] The LORD!
  He makes poor, gives wealth,
    brings low, but also lifts up high!
[8] God raises the poor from the dust,
  lifts up the needy from the garbage pile.
  God sits them with officials,
    gives them the seat of honor!
  The pillars of the earth
    belong to the LORD;
  he set the world on top of them!
[9] God guards the feet of his faithful ones,
  but the wicked die in darkness

---

[j]LXX, DSS (4QSam[a]), Syr; MT *three bulls* [k]An ephah was approximately twenty quarts. [l]Some Heb manuscripts, Syr, Vulg; MT *he* (Eli?) *worshipped*; DSS (4QSam[a]) *and she* (Hannah) *left him there and worshipped the LORD.* [m]Or *my horn*; also in 2:10 [n]Heb *Sheol*

SAMUEL

Means "his name is El." Known primarily as a prophet, Samuel is presented in 1 Samuel as a fulfilling the roles of prophet, priest, and judge. Outside 1 Samuel, he is mentioned in the OT seven times in Chronicles (1 Chron 6:28 [Heb. 6:13], 33; 9:22; 11:3; 26:28; 29:29; 2 Chron 35:18), where he is remembered as the seer from David's reign (drawing on 1 Sam 9:9), and once each in Psalm 99:6 and Jeremiah 15:1, both of which refer to Samuel's role as intercessor from 1 Samuel 7. Three NT texts refer to Samuel in his role as a prophet (Acts 3:24; 13:20; Heb 11:32).

In the NT, Peter and John name Samuel as one of the prophets who had predicted "these days"—that is, the suffering and glorification of God's Messiah (Acts 3:24). The apostle Paul's summation of Israel's history in the synagogue in Antioch of Pisidia notes that God gave Israel judges "until the time of the prophet Samuel" (Acts 13:20).

because no one succeeds
  by strength alone.

¹⁰ The LORD!
  His enemies are terrified!
  God thunders against them
    from heaven!
  The LORD!
  He judges the far corners of the earth!

May God give strength to his king
  and raise high the strength
  of his anointed one.

¹¹ Then Elkanah went home to Ramah, but the boy served the LORD under Eli the priest.

Corruption of Eli's sons

¹² Now Eli's sons were despicable men who didn't know the LORD. ¹³ This was how the priest was supposed to act with the people: Whenever anyone made a sacrifice, while the meat was boiling, the priest's assistant would come with a three-pronged fork in hand. ¹⁴ He would thrust it into the cauldron or the pot.^o Whatever the fork brought up, the priest would take for himself. This is how it was done for all the Israelites who came to Shiloh.

¹⁵ But with Eli's sons,^p even before the fat was burned, the priest's assistant would come and say to the person offering the sacrifice, "Give the priest some meat to roast. He won't accept boiled meat from you."^q ¹⁶ If anyone said, "Let the fat be burned off first, as usual, then take whatever you

like for yourself," the assistant would reply, "No, hand it over now. If not, I'll take it by force." ¹⁷ The sin of these priestly assistants was very serious in the LORD's sight because they were disrespecting the Lord's own offering.

¹⁸ Now Samuel was serving the LORD. He was a young boy, clothed in a linen priestly vest.^r ¹⁹ His mother would make a small robe for him and take it to him every year when she went up with her husband to offer the annual sacrifice. ²⁰ Eli would bless Elkanah and his wife: "May the LORD replace^s the child of this woman that you gave back to the LORD." Then they would return home. ²¹ The LORD paid attention to Hannah, and she conceived and gave birth to three sons and two daughters. Meanwhile, the boy Samuel grew up in the LORD's service.

²² Eli was very old, but he heard everything his sons were doing to the Israelites, and how they had sex with the women who served at the meeting tent's entrance. ²³ Eli said to his sons, "Why are you doing these terrible things that I'm hearing about from everybody? ²⁴ No, my sons. Don't do this.^t The report I hear spreading among God's people isn't good. ²⁵ If someone sins against someone else, God can intercede; but if someone sins against the LORD, who will intercede then?" But they wouldn't obey their father because the LORD wanted to kill them. ²⁶ Meanwhile, the boy Samuel kept growing up and was more and more liked by both the LORD and the people.

HANNAH

Hannah was one of two wives of Elkanah, an Ephraimite (1 Sam 1:1–2). Hannah had no children, but Elkanah's other wife Peninnah did have children. During the annual pilgrimage to Shiloh, Hannah prayed at the shrine, promising that if God gave her a son she would give the son back to God. She then had a son whom she named Samuel. After she weaned him she took him to Eli the priest at Shiloh to fulfill her promise. On that occasion she sang the hymn known today as Hannah's Song (1 Sam 2:1–10).

²⁷Now a man of God came to Eli and said, "This is what the LORD says: I revealed myself very clearly to your father's household when they were slaves[u] in Egypt to the house of Pharaoh. ²⁸I chose your father from all of Israel's tribes to be my priest, to go up onto my altar, to burn incense, and to wear the priestly vest[v] in my presence. I also gave all of the Israelites' food offerings to your father's household. ²⁹Why then do you kick my sacrifices and my offerings—the very ones I commanded for my dwelling place? Why do you respect your sons more than me, getting fat off the best parts of every offering from my people Israel? ³⁰Because of all that, this is what the LORD, the God of Israel, declares: I had promised that your household and your father's household would serve me forever. But now—this is what the LORD declares: I'll do no such thing! No. I honor those who honor me, and whoever despises me will be cursed. ³¹The days are coming soon when I will eliminate both your children[w] and the children of your father's household. There won't be an old person left in your family tree. ³²You'll see trouble in my dwelling place, though all will go well for Israel.[x] But there will never be an old person in your family tree. ³³One of your descendants whom I don't eliminate from serving at my altar will cry his[y] eyes out and be full of grief. Any descendants in your household will die by the sword.[z] ³⁴And what happens to your two sons Hophni and Phinehas will be a sign for you: they will both die on the same day. ³⁵Then I will establish for myself a trustworthy priest who will act in accordance with my thoughts and desires. I will build a trustworthy household for him, and he will serve before my anointed one forever. ³⁶Anyone left from your household will come and beg him for a bit of silver or a loaf of bread, saying: 'Please appoint me to some priestly duty so I can have a scrap of bread to eat.'"

Samuel's call

3 Now the boy Samuel was serving the LORD under Eli. The LORD's word was rare at that time, and visions weren't widely known. ²One day Eli, whose eyes had grown so weak he was unable to see, was lying down in his room. ³God's lamp hadn't gone

[u]DSS (4QSamᵃ), LXX; MT lacks *slaves*.   [v]Heb *ephod*   [w]LXX; MT *arm* or *power*   [x]Heb uncertain; LXX and DSS (4QSamᵃ) omit 2:31b-32a.   [y]DSS (4QSamᵃ), LXX; MT *your*   [z]LXX, DSS (4QSamᵃ); MT *die by men* or *die as men*

ELI

Eli is the priest at Shiloh who raises Samuel to become priest in the place of his own sons Hophni and Phinehas. God finds Eli's family inadequate because these two sons treat the offerings made to God with disrespect and lie with the young women who come to work at the entrance to the sanctuary. Eli himself is unacceptable as a priest because he does not discipline his sons for their actions, and he benefits from their behavior regarding the meat for sacrifices (1 Sam 2:29). The judgment on the house of Eli is signaled by the deaths of both sons in a single day and the death of old Eli when he hears that the Philistines have captured the covenant chest (1 Sam 4:13-18). The priesthood at Shiloh is then replaced with Samuel, who lives at Ramah. Eli's line does continue in the genealogical structure in 1 Samuel. Abiathar, who carries the priestly vest for David, is the only survivor when Saul kills the priests at Nob (1 Sam 22:20). Abiathar is the son of Ahimelech, who is the son of Ahitub, called Ichabod's brother in 1 Samuel 14:3. Ichabod is the son of Phinehas, born as his mother hears of the death of her husband (1 Sam 4:21).

out yet, and Samuel was lying down in the LORD's temple, where God's chest[a] was.

[4] The LORD called to Samuel. "I'm here," he said.

[5] Samuel hurried to Eli and said, "I'm here. You called me?"

"I didn't call you," Eli replied. "Go lie down." So he did.

[6] Again the LORD called Samuel, so Samuel got up, went to Eli, and said, "I'm here. You called me?"

"I didn't call, my son," Eli replied. "Go and lie down."

([7] Now Samuel didn't yet know the LORD, and the LORD's word hadn't yet been revealed to him.)

[8] A third time the LORD called Samuel. He got up, went to Eli, and said, "I'm here. You called me?"

Then Eli realized that it was the LORD who was calling the boy. [9] So Eli said to Samuel, "Go and lie down. If he calls you, say, 'Speak, LORD. Your servant is listening.'" So Samuel went and lay down where he'd been.

[10] Then the LORD came and stood there, calling just as before, "Samuel, Samuel!"

Samuel said, "Speak. Your servant is listening."

[11] The LORD said to Samuel, "I am about to do something in Israel that will make the ears of all who hear it tingle! [12] On that day, I will bring to pass against Eli everything I said about his household—every last bit of it![b] [13] I told him that I would punish his family forever because of the wrongdoing he knew about—how his sons were cursing God,[c] but he wouldn't stop them. [14] Because of that I swore about Eli's household that his family's wrongdoing will never be reconciled by sacrifice or by offering."

[15] Samuel lay there until morning, then opened the doors of the LORD's house. Samuel was afraid to tell the vision to Eli. [16] But Eli called Samuel, saying: "Samuel, my son!"

"I'm here," Samuel said.

[17] "What did he say to you?" Eli asked. "Don't hide anything from me. May God deal harshly with you and worse still if you hide from me a single word from everything he said to you." [18] So Samuel told him everything and hid nothing from him.

"He is the LORD," Eli said. "He will do as he pleases."

[19] So Samuel grew up, and the LORD was with him, not allowing any of his words to fail. [20] All Israel from Dan to Beer-sheba knew that Samuel was trustworthy as the LORD's prophet. [21] The LORD continued to appear at Shiloh because the LORD revealed himself to Samuel at Shiloh through the LORD's own word. [1] And Samuel's word went out to all Israel.

The Philistines capture God's chest

In those days the Philistines gathered for war against Israel,[d] so Israel went out to engage the Philistines in war. Israel camped at Ebenezer, while the Philistines camped at Aphek. [2] The Philistines readied themselves to fight Israel. When the battle was joined, Israel was defeated by the Philistines, who killed about four thousand men on the battlefield. [3] When the troops returned to the camp, Israel's elders said, "Why did the LORD defeat us today before the Philistines? Let's bring the chest containing the LORD's covenant from Shiloh so it can go with us and save us from our enemies' power." [4] So the people sent to Shiloh and brought from there the chest containing the covenant of the LORD of heavenly forces, who sits enthroned on the winged heavenly creatures.[e] Eli's two sons Hophni and Phinehas were there with the chest containing God's covenant.

[5] When the chest containing the LORD's covenant entered the camp, all Israel let out such a loud shout that the ground shook. [6] When the Philistines heard the sound of that shout, they asked, "What is that loud shouting in the Hebrew camp about?" When they learned that the LORD's chest had come into the camp, [7] the Philistines were afraid and said, "A god has come into that camp! We're doomed," they said, "because nothing like this has ever happened before.

---

[a]Traditionally *ark* [b]Or *the beginning and the end* [c]LXX; MT *to themselves*, one of several intentional scribal corrections to avoid the phrase *cursing God* [d]LXX; MT lacks *In those days . . . against Israel.* [e]Heb *cherubim*

⁸We're doomed! Who will deliver us from the grip of these powerful deities? They are the same gods who struck the Egyptians in the desert with every kind of wound. ⁹Pull yourselves together and act like men, Philistines! Otherwise, you'll serve the Hebrews like they've been serving you. Act like men and fight!"

¹⁰So the Philistines fought. Israel was defeated, and everyone fled to their homes. It was a massive defeat: thirty thousand Israelite foot soldiers fell, ¹¹God's chest was taken, and Eli's two sons Hophni and Phinehas died.

¹²That very day, a Benjaminite ran from the battle to Shiloh. His clothes were torn, and dirt was on his head. ¹³When he got there, Eli was sitting in a chair beside the road, waiting because he was nervous about God's chest. The man arrived and gave the news to the city, and the whole city cried out. ¹⁴Eli heard the sound of the cry and said, "What's all this noise about?"

The man hurriedly went and told Eli the news. (¹⁵Now Eli was 98 years old, and his eyes stared straight ahead, unable to see.) ¹⁶The man told Eli, "I'm the one who just came from the battle. I fled from the battle today."

"What's the report, my son?" Eli asked.

¹⁷The messenger answered, "Israel has fled from the Philistines. The army has suf-fered a massive defeat. Also, your own two sons Hophni and Phinehas have died, and God's chest has been taken!" ¹⁸At the mention of God's chest, Eli fell backward off the chair beside the gate. His neck broke, and he died because he was an old man and overweight. Eli had judged Israel for forty years.

¹⁹Now Eli's daughter-in-law, Phinehas' wife, was pregnant and about to give birth. When she heard the news that God's chest had been captured and that her father-in-law and her husband had died, she doubled over and gave birth because her labor pains overwhelmed her. ²⁰As she was about to die, the women standing by helping her said, "Don't be afraid. You've given birth to a son!" But she didn't answer or pay them any attention. ²¹She named the boy Ichabod,[f] saying, "The glory has left Israel," referring to the capture of God's chest and the death of her father-in-law and her husband. ²²"The glory has left Israel because God's chest has been taken," she said.

God's chest among the Philistines

5 After the Philistines took God's chest, they brought it from Ebenezer to Ashdod. ²Then the Philistines took God's chest and brought it into Dagon's temple and set it next to Dagon. ³But when the citizens of Ashdod got up early the next morning,

[f]Meaning Where is the glory?

COVENANT CHEST

A sacred object kept in the covenant dwelling or the temple, indicating the presence of God in the midst of Israel. Nearly a third of all references to the chest are in the books of Samuel. Since the Chronicler uses the books of Samuel as a source, those designations of the chest reflect the ones used in 1 and 2 Samuel. Many scholars regard the reference in 1 Samuel 4:4 (see 2 Sam 6:2; 1 Chron 13:6) as the fullest and most ancient name for the chest: "the chest containing the covenant of the Lord of heavenly forces, who sits enthroned on the winged heavenly creatures." The chest represents the relationship between God and Israel as covenant partners. The tradition in Exodus, which includes the detailed description of God's instructions for and the fashioning of an elaborate gold-covered chest, refers to this sacred object solely as the "chest containing the covenant" (e.g., Exod 25:10-22).

there was Dagon, fallen facedown on the ground before the LORD's chest! So they took Dagon and set him back up where he belonged. ⁴But when they got up early the next morning, there was Dagon again, fallen facedown on the ground before the LORD's chest—and this time Dagon's head along with both his hands were cut off and lying on the doorstep! Only Dagon's bodyᵍ was left intact. ⁵That's why to this day Dagon's priests or anyone else who enters his temple in Ashdod doesn't step on the threshold.

⁶The LORD's hand was heavy on the people of Ashdod: God terrified them and struck them in Ashdod and its surroundings with tumors.ʰ ⁷When Ashdod's inhabitants saw what was happening, they said, "The chest of Israel's God must not stay here with us because his hand is hard against us and against our god Dagon."

⁸So they summoned all the Philistine rulers to a meeting and asked, "What should we do with the chest of Israel's God?" The people of Gath said, "Let the chest of Israel's God be moved to us." So they moved the chest of Israel's God to Gath.ⁱ ⁹But once they moved it, the LORD's hand came against the city, causing a huge panic. God struck the city's inhabitants, both young and old, and tumors broke out on them.

¹⁰Then they sent God's chest to Ekron, but as soon as God's chest entered Ekron, the inhabitants cried out, "Why have you moved the chest of Israel's God to us? In order to kill us and our people?"ʲ

¹¹So they summoned all the Philistine rulers to a meeting and said, "Send the chest of Israel's God away! Let it go back to its own home so it doesn't kill us and our people," because there was a deadly panic throughout the whole city. The hand of God was very heavy there. ¹²The people who didn't die were struck with tumors, and the screams of the city went all the way up to heaven.

God's chest is returned

6 The LORD's chest was in Philistine territory for seven months. ²The Philistines called for the priests and the diviners. "What should we do with the LORD's chest?" they asked. "Tell us how we should send it back to its own home."

³They replied, "If you are returning the chest of Israel's God, don't send it back empty, but be sure to return a guilt offering to him.ᵏ Then you will be healed, and it will become clear to you why God's hand hasn't left you alone."

⁴"What compensation offering should we return to him?" they asked.

The priests and diviners replied: "Five gold tumorsˡ and five gold mice,ᵐ matching

ᵍCf LXX ʰKethib; Qere *hemorrhoids* (cf Deut 28:27); also in 5:9, 12 ⁱLXX ʲDSS (4QSamᵃ), LXX ᵏOr *be sure to return it with a compensation offering.* ˡKethib; Qere *hemorrhoids* (cf Deut 28:27); also in 6:5; see note at 6:11. ᵐLXX lacks *and five gold mice.*

DAGON

A prominent ancient Near Eastern god described in the OT as the national god of the Philistines. The OT relates stories concerning temples of Dagon in Gaza (Samson's death, Judg 16), Ashdod (the capture of the covenant chest, 1 Sam 5:1-5), and Beth-shan (the display of Saul's head, 1 Chron 10:10, based on 1 Sam 31:9), none of which have been confirmed by archaeology. Sites named Beth-dagon in Judah and Asher (Josh 15:41; 19:27) suggest that other temples of Dagon once stood in those tribal territories. Theologically, the story in 1 Samuel 5 establishes the power of Israel's God over Dagon, as Dagon's statue is reported to have fallen over and broken into pieces in the presence of the covenant chest.

the number of the Philistine rulers, because the same plague came on all of you and your rulers. [5]You must make images of your tumors and the mice that have devastated the land. Honor Israel's God. Perhaps he will lighten the weight of his hand on you, your gods, and your land. [6]Why be stubborn like the Egyptians and Pharaoh? After God had dealt harshly with them, didn't they send the Israelites on their way? [7]So get a new cart ready along with two nursing cows that have never been yoked before. Harness the cows to the cart, but take any of their calves that are following back home. [8]Next, take the LORD's chest and put it in the cart. Set the gold items that you are giving God as a compensation offering in a box next to the chest. Then send it on its way. [9]Then watch what happens: If the cart goes up the road to its own territory toward Beth-shemesh, then Israel's God has brought this great disaster on us. If the cart goes another way, then we'll know that it wasn't God's hand that struck us. It happened to us randomly."

[10]The rulers[n] did just that. They took two nursing cows and harnessed them to the cart, penning their calves up at home. [11]They put the LORD's chest on the cart along with the box containing the gold mice and the images of their tumors.[o] [12]The cows went straight ahead, following the road to Beth-shemesh. They kept to one route, mooing as they went, without turning right or left. The Philistine rulers followed them as far as the territory of Beth-shemesh.

[13]Now the people of Beth-shemesh were harvesting wheat in the valley. When they looked up and saw the chest, they were overjoyed at the sight. [14]The cart entered the field belonging to Joshua of Beth-shemesh and stopped right by a large stone. They chopped up the wood of the cart and offered the cows as an entirely burned offering to the LORD. [15]The Levites unloaded the LORD's chest and the box that was with it that contained all the gold items, and they set them on the large stone. That very day the people of Beth-shemesh offered entirely burned offerings and made sacrifices to the LORD. [16]When the five Philistine rulers witnessed this, they went straight back to Ekron.

[17]These are the gold tumors that the Philistines returned as a compensation offering to the LORD: one for Ashdod, one for Gaza, one for Ashkelon, one for Gath, and one for Ekron. [18]The gold mice matched the number of Philistine cities belonging to the five rulers, from fortified cities to country villages. And the large stone[p] they set the LORD's chest on is a witness even now in the field that belongs to Joshua of Beth-shemesh.

[19]But God struck down some of the people from Beth-shemesh because they looked into the LORD's chest. God struck seventy people,[q] and the community grieved because the LORD had struck them so severely. [20]The people of Beth-shemesh said, "Who can stand before the LORD, this holy God? Where can he go that is away from us here?" [21]They sent messengers to the inhabitants of Kiriath-jearim. "The Philistines returned the LORD's chest!" they said. "Come down and take it back with you." [1]So the people of Kiriath-jearim came and took the LORD's chest. They brought it to Abinadab's house, which was on the hill. Then they dedicated Eleazar, Abinadab's son, to care for the LORD's chest.

Samuel leads Israel

[2]Now a long time passed—a total of twenty years—after the chest came to stay in Kiriath-jearim, and the whole house of Israel yearned for[r] the LORD.

[3]Then Samuel said to the whole house of Israel, "If you are turning to the LORD with all your heart, then get rid of all the foreign gods and the Astartes you have. Set your heart on the LORD! Worship him only! Then he will deliver you from the Philistines' power." [4]So the Israelites got rid of the Baals and the Astartes and worshipped the LORD only.

---

[n]See 6:12; MT *men*. [o]Or *hemorrhoids*; also in 6:17, the Qere form for the Hebrew written form of *tumors* used in 6:4-5 [p]LXX; [q]LXX; MT adds *fifty thousand people*. [r]Heb uncertain; LXX *searched for*

⁵Next Samuel said, "Assemble all Israel at Mizpah. I will pray to the LORD for you." ⁶So they assembled at Mizpah, and they drew water and poured it out in the LORD's presence. They fasted that same day and confessed, "We have sinned against the LORD." Samuel served as judge of the Israelites at Mizpah.

⁷When the Philistines heard that the Israelites had assembled at Mizpah, the Philistine rulers went up to attack Israel. When the Israelites learned of this, they were afraid of the Philistines. ⁸The Israelites said to Samuel, "Please don't stop praying to the LORD our God for us, so God will save us from the Philistines' power!" ⁹So Samuel took a suckling lamb and offered it as an entirely burned offering to the LORD. Samuel cried out in prayer to the LORD for Israel, and the LORD answered him.

¹⁰While Samuel was offering the entirely burned offering, the Philistines advanced to attack Israel. But the LORD thundered against the Philistines with a great blast on that very day, throwing the Philistines into such a panic that they were defeated by Israel. ¹¹The Israelite soldiers came out of Mizpah and pursued the Philistines. They struck them down until they reached a place just below Beth-car. ¹²Then Samuel took a stone and set it up between Mizpah and Jeshanah.ˢ He named it Ebenezer,ᵗ explaining, "The LORD helped us to this very point."

¹³So the Philistines were defeated, and they stopped coming into Israelite territory. The LORD's hand was against the Philistines throughout Samuel's life. ¹⁴The towns the Philistines had captured from Israel, from Ekron to Gath, were returned to Israel. Israel also recovered the territory around those two cities from the Philistines. And there was peace between Israel and the Amorites.

¹⁵Samuel served as Israel's judge his whole life. ¹⁶Each year he traveled between Bethel, Gilgal, and Mizpah, serving as Israel's judge in each of those locations. ¹⁷Then he would

return to Ramah because that's where his home was. In Ramah too he served as Israel's judge, and that is also where he built an altar to the LORD.

Israel demands a king

8 Now when Samuel got old, he appointed his sons to serve as Israel's judges. ²The name of his oldest son was Joel; the name of the second was Abijah. They served as judges in Beer-sheba. ³But Samuel's sons didn't follow in his footsteps. They tried to turn a profit, they accepted bribes, and they perverted justice.

⁴So all the Israelite elders got together and went to Samuel at Ramah. ⁵They said to him, "Listen. You are old now, and your sons don't follow in your footsteps. So appoint us a king to judge us like all the other nations have." ⁶It seemed very bad to Samuel when they said, "Give us a king to judge us," so he prayed to the LORD.

⁷The LORD answered Samuel, "Comply with the people's request—everything they ask of you—because they haven't rejected you. No, they've rejected me as king over them. ⁸They are doing to you only what they've been doing to meᵘ from the day I brought them out of Egypt to this very minute, abandoning me and worshipping other gods. ⁹So comply with their request, but give them a clear warning, telling them how the king will rule over them."ᵛ

¹⁰Then Samuel explained everything the LORD had said to the people who were asking for a king. ¹¹"This is how the king will rule over you," Samuel said:

"He will take your sons, and will use them for his chariots and his cavalry and as runners for his chariot. ¹²He will use them as his commanders of troops of one thousand and troops of fifty, or to do his plowing and his harvesting, or to make his weapons or parts for his chariots. ¹³He will take your daughters to be perfumers, cooks, or bakers. ¹⁴He will take your best fields, vineyards, and olive groves and give them to his servants. ¹⁵He will give one-tenth of your

---

ˢLXX, Syr; MT *Ha-shen* (the tooth)   ᵗMeaning *stone of help*   ᵘLXX; MT lacks *to me*.   ᵛOr *telling them the lawful practice of the king*; also in 8:11; cf 10:25.

grain and your vineyards to his officials and servants. [16]He will take your male and female servants, along with the best of your cattle[w] and donkeys, and make them do his work. [17]He will take one-tenth of your flocks, and then you yourselves will become his slaves! [18]When that day comes, you will cry out because of the king you chose for yourselves, but on that day the LORD won't answer you."

[w]LXX; MT *young men*

KING/KINGSHIP

Israel and its neighbors were often ruled by kings, but the beliefs and institutions surrounding the king and kingship varied widely.

Kingship was the main political organization in the ancient Near East. It was understood to be part of the basic fabric of the sociopolitical order, and the king was recognized as a shepherd appointed by the god(s) to run the society. The influence of kingship among Israel's neighbors is reflected in Deuteronomy 17:14, which predicts that the people may say, "Let's appoint a king over us, as all our neighboring nations have done" (cf. 1 Sam 8:5, 20).

The key Bible texts for understanding kingship are the laws of the king in Deuteronomy 17:14-20; the explanation of "how the king will rule over you" in 1 Samuel 8:11-17; the promise of an eternal dynasty to David in 2 Samuel 7:5-17; and the royal psalms. Like their ancient Near Eastern counterparts, the Israelite kings were responsible for military, judicial, religious, and state building projects.

One of the king's sons, usually but not always the oldest, often reigned after his father. In some cases, the "people of the land" decided who would reign (see 2 Kgs 11:14). Sometimes a foreign power removed a king and appointed his successor, but in such cases in Judah the successor was part of the royal Davidic family (e.g., 2 Kgs 24:15-17). In rare cases, there was a co-regency, where the successor began to reign before his father died (e.g., 2 Kgs 15:5).

The crown and the throne were the two most important objects associated with kingship. The crown was the main royal symbol, so a fallen or removed crown may represent lost kingship (e.g., Lam 5:16; Jer 13:18), but we have no idea what it looked like. To "sit on" the throne is equivalent to reigning (1 Kgs 1:13; 2:12; Jer 22:30). Only Solomon's throne is described in detail (1 Kgs 10:18-20; 2 Chron 9:17-19).

Kingship came to an end in 587 BCE, with the Babylonian capture of Jerusalem and destruction of the temple. Second Kings 25:7 and its parallels suggest that Zedekiah, the last king of Judah, was blinded, and his children were killed; 11 years earlier, King Jehoiachin had been exiled to Babylon. An attempt by Ishmael to restore the monarchy failed (2 Kgs 25:25). The very end of 2 Kings records the release of King Jehoiachin from prison in Babylon. It is unclear if there was an attempt to reestablish the Davidic monarchy after the return from exile.

¹⁹But the people refused to listen to Samuel and said, "No! There must be a king over us ²⁰so we can be like all the other nations. Our king will judge us and lead us and fight our battles."

²¹Samuel listened to everything the people said and repeated it directly to the LORD. ²²Then the LORD said to Samuel, "Comply with their request. Give them a king."

Samuel then told the Israelite people, "Go back, each of you, to your own hometown."

Saul chosen to lead Israel

9 There was a wealthy man from the tribe of Benjamin named Kish. He was the son of Abiel son of Zeror son of Becorath son of Aphiah, a Benjaminite. ²He had a son named Saul, who was a handsome young man. No one in Israel was more handsome than Saul, and he stood head and shoulders above everyone else.

³When the donkeys belonging to Saul's father Kish were lost, Kish said to his son Saul, "Take one of the servant boys with you and go look for the donkeys." ⁴So he traveled through the highlands of Ephraim and the land of Shalishah, but they didn't find anything. They traveled through the land of Shaalim, but still found nothing, so they crossed back into the land of Benjamin, but they still couldn't find the donkeys. ⁵When they came to the territory of Zuph, Saul said to the boy who was with him, "Let's go

back before my father stops worrying about the donkeys and starts worrying about us."

⁶But the boy said to him, "Listen, there's a man of God in this town. He's famous—everything he says actually happens! So let's go there. Maybe he'll be able to tell us which way we should go."

⁷Saul said to his young boy, "But if we go, what should we bring to the man? The food in our bags is all gone. We don't have any gift to offer the man of God. Do we have anything?"

⁸"Here," the boy answered Saul, "I've got a quarter-shekel of silver. I'll give that to the man of God so he tells us which way to go." (⁹Earlier in Israel, someone going to consult with God would say, "Let's go to the seer," because the people who are called prophets today were previously called seers.)

¹⁰Saul said to the boy, "Great idea! Let's go." So they went into the town where the man of God lived. ¹¹They were going up the hill to the town when they met some young women coming out to draw water. "Is the seer here?" they asked them.

¹²"He's just ahead of you," they answered. "Hurry up! He has just come to town because there is a sacrifice today for the people at the shrine. ¹³You'll find him as soon as you enter the town, before he goes up to the shrine to eat. The people won't eat until he gets there, because he must bless the sacrifice. Only after that can the invited

SHRINE

A structure used as a place of worship. In the times before Israel had a king, the Israelites established shrines throughout the land. There is much scholarly debate on their exact nature, but they were likely open-air raised platforms used for offerings and sacrifices. First Samuel 9:12-25 describes a sacrificial meal at such a shrine. Shrines contained other things that were necessary for ceremonies, such as the priestly vest and divine images in Judges 17:5. After the monarchy and the centralization of worship at the Jerusalem temple, all other shrines were outlawed. The reforms of Hezekiah and Josiah (2 Kgs 18:1-7; 23:4-25) included destruction of the shrines, reflecting the widespread, though unorthodox, continued popularity of local shrines throughout ancient Israel.

guests eat. Now get going because you'll find him momentarily."

¹⁴So Saul and the boy went up to the town, and as they entered it, suddenly Samuel came toward them on his way up to the shrine. ¹⁵Now the day before Saul came, the LORD had revealed the following to Samuel: ¹⁶"About this time tomorrow I will send you a man from the Benjaminite territory. You will anoint him as leader of my people Israel. He will save my people from the Philistines' power because I have seen the suffering of[x] my people, and their cry for help has reached me." ¹⁷When Samuel saw Saul, the LORD told him, "That's the man I told you about. That's the one who will rule[y] my people."

¹⁸Saul approached Samuel in the city gate and said, "Please tell me where the seer's house is."

¹⁹"I'm the seer," Samuel told Saul. "Go on ahead of me to the shrine. You can eat with me today. In the morning I'll send you on your way, and I will tell you everything you want to know. ²⁰As for the donkeys you lost three days ago, don't be worried about them because they've been found. Who owns all of Israel's treasures, anyway? Isn't it you and your whole family?"[z]

²¹"I'm a Benjaminite," Saul responded, "from the smallest Israelite tribe, and my family is the littlest of the families in the tribe of Benjamin. Why would you say something like that to me?"

²²Then Samuel took Saul and his young servant and brought them to the banquet room. He gave them an honored place among the invited guests. There were about thirty total. ²³Samuel said to the cook, "Serve the portion I gave you—the one I told you to set aside." ²⁴So the cook took the thigh and what was on it,[a] and put it in front of Saul. Samuel said, "Look, what had been reserved is now in front of you. Eat up, because it was set apart for you for this specific occasion, ever since I invited the guests."[b] So Saul ate with Samuel that day.

²⁵When they came back from the shrine to the town, a bed was made for Saul on the roof, and he slept.[c]

²⁶Near dawn, Samuel called to Saul on the roof, "Wake up! I will send you on your way." So Saul got up, and the two of them, he and Samuel, went outside. ²⁷As they were nearing the edge of town Samuel said, "Tell the boy to go on ahead of us" (the servant did so) "but you stop for a bit so I can tell you God's word."

Samuel anoints Saul as king

10Samuel took a small jar of oil and poured it over Saul's head and kissed him. "The LORD hereby anoints you leader of his people Israel," Samuel said. "You will rule the LORD's people and save them from the power of the enemies who surround them. And this will be the sign for you that the LORD has anointed you as leader of his very own possession:[d] ²When you leave me today, you will meet two men near Rachel's tomb at Zelzah on the border of Benjamin. They will tell you, 'The donkeys you went looking for have been found. Now your father has stopped thinking about the donkeys and is worried about you. He's asking: What should I do about my son?' ³Then, when you've gone on a bit farther, you will come to the oak at Tabor. Three men who are going to consult God at Bethel will meet up with you there, one carrying three young goats, one carrying three loaves of bread, and one carrying a jar of wine. ⁴They will ask how you're doing and will offer you sacrificial bread,[e] which you should accept. ⁵After that, you will come to Gibeath-elohim, which is a Philistine fort. When you enter the town, you will encounter a group of prophets coming down from the shrine preceded by harps, tambourines, flutes, and lyres. They will be caught up in a prophetic frenzy. ⁶Then the LORD's spirit will come over you, and you will be caught up in a prophetic frenzy right along with them; it will be like you've become a completely

---

[x]LXX; MT lacks *the suffering of.* [y]LXX; Heb uncertain, perhaps *restrain* or *gather (troops);* cf 10:1 [z]Or *But for whom does all Israel yearn if not for you and your whole family?* [a]Heb uncertain [b]Heb uncertain [c]LXX; MT *He (Samuel?) talked with Saul on the roof. Then they got up early.* [d]LXX; MT lacks *of his people Israel. . . . And this will be the sign for you that.* [e]LXX; DSS (4QSamᵃ) *uplifted bread* (see Num 18:11) ; MT *two of bread.*

different person. [7]Once these signs have happened to you, do whatever you would like to do, because God is with you. [8]Then go down to Gilgal ahead of me. I'll come down to meet you to offer entirely burned offerings and to make well-being sacrifices. Wait seven days until I get to you, then I'll tell you what you should do next."

[9]And just as Saul turned to leave Samuel's side, God gave him a different heart, and all these signs happened that very same day. [10]When Saul and the boy got to Gibeah, there was a group of prophets coming to meet him. God's spirit came over Saul, and he was caught up in a prophetic frenzy right along with them. [11]When all the people who had known Saul saw him prophesying with the prophets, they said to each other, "What's happened to Kish's son? Is Saul also one of the prophets?" [12]One of the locals then asked, "And who is their leader?"[f] So it became a proverb: "Is Saul also one of the prophets?" [13]When the prophetic frenzy was over, Saul went home.[g]

[14]Saul's uncle said to him and to his young servant, "Where did you go?"

"To look for the donkeys," Saul replied, "but when we couldn't find anything, we went to Samuel."

[15]"Please tell me what Samuel told you," Saul's uncle said.

[16]"He reassured us that the donkeys had been found," Saul answered. But Saul didn't tell his uncle what Samuel had said about the kingship.

Saul selected as king

[17]Samuel summoned the people to the LORD at Mizpah. [18]Then he told the Israelites: "This is what the LORD God of Israel says: I brought Israel up out of Egypt, and I delivered you from the Egyptians' power and from the power of all the kingdoms that oppressed you. [19]But today you've rejected your God who saved you from all your troubles and difficulties by saying, 'No! Appoint a king over us!' So now assemble yourselves before the LORD by your tribes and clans."

[20]Then Samuel brought all the Israelite tribes forward, and the tribe of Benjamin was selected. [21]Next Samuel brought the tribe of Benjamin forward by its families, and the family of Matri was selected. Samuel then brought the family of Matri forward, person by person,[h] and Saul, Kish's son, was selected. But when they looked for him, he wasn't to be found. [22]So they asked another question of the LORD: "Has the man come here yet?"

The LORD said, "Yes, he's hiding among the supplies." [23]They ran and retrieved Saul from there, and when he stood up in the middle of the people, he was head and shoulders taller than anyone else.

[24]"Can you see the one the LORD has chosen?" Samuel asked all the people. "He has no equal among the people."

Then the people shouted, "Long live the king!"

[25]Samuel then explained to the people how the monarchy should operate[i] and

---

[f]Or *father* [g]Correction; MT *Saul entered the shrine.* [h]LXX; MT lacks *Samuel then brought the family of Matri forward, person by person.* [i]Or *the lawful practices of the monarchy*

ANOINT

Anointing is the application of oil to a person or object by smearing, pouring, or sprinkling. Both the OT and NT refer to common, nonritual, cosmetic or hygienic anointing (see, e.g., Ruth 3:3; 2 Sam 12:20; Ezek 16:9; Amos 6:6; Ps 23:5; Matt 6:17; Luke 7:46). In most of its occurrences in the OT, *anoint* indicates the ritual application of oil to persons or objects to show or effect a change of identity or status.

wrote it in a scroll and placed it in the LORD's presence. Then Samuel sent every person back to their homes. ²⁶Saul also went back to his home in Gibeah. Along with him went courageous men whose hearts God had touched. ²⁷But some despicable people said, "How can this man save us?" They despised Saul and didn't bring him gifts, but Saul didn't say anything.

Saul delivers Jabesh-gilead

ʲNahash the Ammonite king had been severely oppressing the Gadites and the Reubenites. He gouged out everyone's right eye, thereby not allowing Israel to have a deliverer. There wasn't a single Israelite left across the Jordan River who hadn't had their right eye gouged out by the Ammonite king Nahash. But seven thousand people had escaped from the Ammonites' power and fled to Jabesh-gilead.

11 About a month later,ᵏ Nahash the Ammonite went up and laid siege to Jabesh-gilead. All the men of Jabesh said to Nahash, "Make a treaty with us, and we'll be your servants."

²"I will make a treaty with you on one condition: that everyone's right eye be gouged out!" Nahash the Ammonite said to them. "That's how I bring humiliation on all Israel."

³The elders of Jabesh replied to him, "Leave us alone for seven days so we can send messengers throughout Israel's territory. If there's no one to save us, then we'll surrender to you."

⁴When the messengers reached Gibeah where Saul lived, they reported the news directly to the people there. Then they all wept aloud. ⁵At just that moment, Saul was coming back from keeping the cattle in the fields. "What's wrong with everybody?" he asked. "Why are they crying?" Saul was then told what the men from Jabesh had said.

⁶God's spirit came over Saul when he heard those words, and he burned with anger. ⁷He took two oxen, cut them into pieces, and sent them by messengers throughout Israel's territory. "This is ex-

actly what will be done to the oxen of anyone who doesn't come to the aid of Saul and Samuel," he said. Great fear of the LORD came over the people, and they came to Saul completely unified.ˡ ⁸When Saul counted them at Bezek, the soldiers from Israel totaled three hundred thousand and those from Judah thirty thousand.

⁹The messengers who had come were then told, "Say this to the people of Jabesh-gilead: Tomorrow by the time the sun is hot, you will be saved." When the messengers returned and reported this to the people of Jabesh, they were overjoyed.

¹⁰Then the people of Jabesh told the Ammonites, "We will surrender to you tomorrow. Then you can do whatever you want to us."

¹¹The next day Saul organized his troops into three formations. They attacked the Ammonite camp during the morning watch and slaughtered them until the heat of the day. The survivors were so scattered that not even two of them could be found together.

¹²Then people asked Samuel, "Who was it who said, 'Will Saul rule over us?' Give us those people; we'll kill them!"

¹³But Saul said, "No one will be executed because today the LORD has saved Israel."

¹⁴"Let's go to Gilgal," Samuel told the people, "and renew the monarchy there." ¹⁵So everyone went to Gilgal, and there at Gilgal they made Saul king in the LORD's presence. They offered well-being sacrifices in the LORD's presence, and Saul and all the Israelites held a great celebration there.

Samuel's last speech

12 Samuel said to all Israel: "Listen: I have done everything you asked of me and have placed a king over you. ²The king will lead you now. I am old and gray, though my sons are still with you, and I've been your leader since I was young until now. ³So I'm here: Tell the truth about me in the presence of the LORD and his anointed. Have I ever stolen someone's ox? Have I ever taken someone's donkey? Have

---

ʲThis paragraph is found in DSS (4QSamᵃ) and is also attested in Josephus (*Ant.* 6.5.1 [68-71]), but is missing in MT. ᵏDSS (4QSamᵃ), LXX; MT lacks *About a month later.* ˡMT lacks *to Saul.*

I ever oppressed or mistreated anyone? Have I ever taken bribes from someone and looked the other way about something? Tell me the truth.[m] I will make it right."

⁴"You haven't oppressed or mistreated us, and you've never taken anything from anyone," the people answered.

⁵Samuel replied, "The LORD and his anointed one are witnesses against you today that you haven't found anything in my possession."

"Agreed," they said.

⁶Then Samuel told the people: "The witness[n] is indeed the LORD, who appointed Moses and Aaron and brought your ancestors up from the land of Egypt. ⁷So now stand here, and I will judge you in the LORD's presence because of all the LORD's righteous acts that he has done for you and your ancestors:

⁸"When Jacob entered Egypt, the Egyptians oppressed them.[o] So your ancestors cried out to the LORD. The LORD then sent Moses and Aaron, who brought your ancestors out of Egypt and settled them here. ⁹But your ancestors forgot the LORD their God, so he handed them over to Sisera the commander of Hazor's army, and to the Philistines, and to the Moabite king, all of whom fought against them. ¹⁰Then your ancestors cried out to the LORD and said: 'We have sinned because we have abandoned the LORD and have worshiped the Baals and the Astartes. But now deliver us from the power of our enemies, and we will worship you.' ¹¹So the LORD sent Jerubbaal, Barak,[p] Jephthah, and Samson,[q] and he delivered you from the power of your enemies on every side. And you lived safe and secure. ¹²But when you saw that Nahash the Ammonite king was coming against you, you said to me, 'No! There must be a king to rule over us.' But the LORD your God was already your king!

¹³"So now, here is the king you chose, the one you asked for. Yes, the LORD has put a king over you! ¹⁴If you will fear the LORD, worship him, obey him, and not rebel against the LORD's command, and if both you and the king who rules over you follow the LORD your God—all will be well. ¹⁵But if you don't obey the LORD and rebel against the LORD's command, then the LORD's power will go against you and your king to destroy you.[r]

¹⁶"So now take a stand! Look at this awesome thing the LORD is doing. ¹⁷Isn't the wheat harvest today? I will call upon the LORD to send thunder and rain. Then you will know and will see for yourselves what great evil you've done in the LORD's eyes by asking for a king."

¹⁸Samuel called upon the LORD, and God sent thunder and rain on that very day. Then all the people were in awe of the LORD and Samuel.

¹⁹All of them said to Samuel, "Please pray for us, your servants, to the LORD your God so we don't die because we have added to our many sins the evil of asking for a king."

²⁰But Samuel answered the people, "Don't be afraid. Yes, you've done all this evil; just don't turn back from following the LORD. Serve the LORD with all your heart. ²¹Don't turn aside to follow useless idols that can't help you or save you. They're absolutely useless! ²²For the sake of his reputation, the LORD won't abandon his people, because the LORD has decided to make you his very own people. ²³But me? I would never sin against the LORD by failing to pray for you. I will teach you what is good and right. ²⁴Just fear the LORD and serve him faithfully with all your heart. Look at what great things he has done for you! ²⁵But if you continue to do evil, then both you and your king will be destroyed."

Samuel rejects Saul's dynasty

13 Saul was 30 years old[s] when he became king, and he ruled over Israel forty-two years.[t] ²Saul selected three

---

[m]LXX: *witness.* [n]LXX; MT lacks *witness.* [o]LXX; MT lacks *the Egyptians oppressed them.* [p]LXX, Syr; MT *Bedan* [q]Syr (cf Targ), LXX[L] *Samson;* MT, LXX[AB] *Samuel* [r]LXX[L]; MT *against you and against your ancestors* [s]LXX[L]; Syr *twenty-one;* MT lacks a number; 13:1 is omitted in LXX[B]. [t]Part of the number is missing in MT (. . . *and two years*) and all ancient witnesses. Acts 13:21 says Saul ruled forty years, as does Josephus (*Ant.* 6.14.9 [378]), though Josephus also says Saul ruled twenty years (*Ant.* 10.8.4 [143]).

thousand men from Israel. Two thousand of those were with Saul at Michmash in the hills near Bethel, and one thousand were with Jonathan at Gibeah in Benjamin. He sent the remaining men home. ³Jonathan attacked the Philistine fort at Geba, and the Philistines heard about it. So Saul sounded the alarm[u] throughout the land and said, "Hebrews! Listen up!" ⁴When all Israel heard that Saul had attacked the Philistine fort and that Israel was hated by the Philistines, the troops were called to Saul's side at Gilgal. ⁵The Philistines also were gathered to fight against Israel. They brought thirty thousand chariots with them, six thousand cavalry, and as many soldiers as there is sand on the seashore to fight Israel.[v] They marched up and camped at Michmash, east of Beth-aven. ⁶When the Israelites saw that they were in trouble and that their troops were threatened, they hid in caves, in thickets, among rocks, in tunnels, and in cisterns. ⁷Some Hebrews even crossed the Jordan River, going into the land of Gad and Gilead.

Saul stayed at Gilgal, and the troops followed him anxiously. ⁸He waited seven days, the time appointed by Samuel, but Samuel didn't come to Gilgal, and his troops began to desert. ⁹So Saul ordered, "Bring me the entirely burned offering and the well-being sacrifices." Then he offered the entirely burned offering.

¹⁰The very moment Saul finished offering up the entirely burned offering, Samuel arrived. Saul went out to meet him and welcome him. ¹¹But Samuel said, "What have you done?"

"I saw that my troops were deserting," Saul replied. "You hadn't arrived by the appointed time, and the Philistines were gathering at Michmash. ¹²I thought, The Philistines are about to march against me at Gilgal and I haven't yet sought the LORD's favor. So I took control of myself[w] and offered the entirely burned offering."

¹³"How stupid of you to have broken the commands the LORD your God gave you!"

Samuel told Saul. "The LORD would have established your rule over Israel forever, ¹⁴but now your rule won't last. The LORD will search for a man following the Lord's own heart,[x] and the LORD will commission him as leader over God's people, because you didn't keep the LORD's command."

¹⁵Samuel got up and went on his way from Gilgal, but the rest of the people followed Saul to join the army, and they went from Gilgal[y] to Gibeah in Benjamin. Saul counted about six hundred men still with him. ¹⁶Saul, his son Jonathan, and the people who were with him were staying at Geba in Benjamin, while the Philistines camped at Michmash. ¹⁷Three raiding parties left the Philistine camp. One took the road to Ophrah toward the territory of Shual. ¹⁸Another took the road to Beth-horon, and the last took the border road that overlooks the Zeboim Valley toward the desert.

Philistine ironworking

¹⁹No metalworker was to be found anywhere in Israelite territory because the Philistines had said, "The Hebrews must not make swords and spears." ²⁰So every Israelite had to go down to the Philistines to sharpen their plowshares, mattocks, axes, and sickles. ²¹The cost was two-thirds of a shekel[z] for plowshares and mattocks, but one-third of a shekel for sharpening axes and for setting goads. ²²So on the day of the battle, no swords or spears were to be found in the possession of any of the troops with Saul and Jonathan, but Saul and his son Jonathan had them.

Jonathan leads Israel to victory

²³Now a group of Philistine soldiers had marched out to the pass at Michmash. **14** One day Jonathan, Saul's son, said to his young armor-bearer, "Come on! Let's go over to the Philistine fort on the opposite side." But he didn't tell his father. ²Saul was sitting on the outskirts of Gibeah under the pomegranate tree at Migron. He had about six hundred men with him,

[u]Heb *shofar*   [v]LXX; MT lacks *They brought, with them, and to fight Israel.*   [w]Or *forced myself*; Heb uncertain
[x]Or *a man loyal to the Lord*   [y]LXX; MT lacks much of this verse.   [z]Heb *pim*, which is two-thirds of a shekel

³including Ahijah, the son of Ahitub, who was Ichabod's brother and the son of Phinehas the son of Eli, who was the LORD's priest at Shiloh. He was wearing a priestly vest.ᵃ None of the troops knew that Jonathan had gone.

⁴There were two stone outcroppings in the pass where Jonathan planned on crossing over to the Philistine fort—one on each side. One of these was named Bozez; the other was named Seneh. ⁵One outcropping was on the north side, in front of Michmash, and the other was on the south side, in front of Geba. ⁶Jonathan said to his young armor-bearer, "Come on, let's go over to the fort of these uncircumcised men. Maybe the LORD will act on our behalf. After all, nothing can stop the LORD from saving, whether there are many soldiersᵇ or few."

⁷"Go ahead with whatever you're planning," his armor-bearer replied. "I'm with you, whatever you decide."

⁸"All right then," Jonathan said. "We'll go over to the men and show ourselves. ⁹If they say to us, 'Stay there until we get to you,' then we'll stay where we are and won't go up to them. ¹⁰But if they say, 'Come on up,' then we'll go up because that will be the sign that the LORD has handed them over to us."

¹¹So they showed themselves to the Philistine fort, and the Philistines said, "Look, the Hebrews are coming out of the holes they've been hiding in!" ¹²Then the troops in the fort yelled to Jonathan and his armor-bearer, "Come on up! We'll teach you a lesson!"

So Jonathan said to his armor-bearer, "Follow me, because the LORD has handed them over to Israel!" ¹³So Jonathan scrambled up on his hands and feet with his armor-bearer right behind him. The Philistines fell before Jonathan. His armor-bearer, coming behind him, would then finish them off. ¹⁴In the first attack, Jonathan and his armor-bearer killed about twenty men in an area of about half an acre.ᶜ ¹⁵Panic broke out in the camp, in the field, and among all the troops. Even those in the fort and the raiders shook with fear. The very ground shook! It was a terror from God.

¹⁶Now Saul's lookouts at Gibeah in Benjamin saw the Philistine camp running all over the place.ᵈ ¹⁷Saul said to the troops with him, "Take a count and see who is missing." So they counted, and Jonathan and his armor-bearer were gone. ¹⁸Saul said to Ahijah, "Bring the priestly vest!"ᵉ because at that time, Ahijah wore the priestly vest in Israel's presence.ᶠ ¹⁹As Saul was talking to the priest, the confusion in the Philistine camp continued to grow. Saul said to the priest, "Withdraw your hand."ᵍ

²⁰Then Saul called all his troops together, and they went into battle. The Philistines were completely confused; every soldier's sword was turned against his fellow soldier. ²¹Even those Hebrews who had earlier joined up with the Philistines and moved into their camp changed sides to be

---

ᵃHeb *ephod* ᵇMT lacks *soldiers.* ᶜHeb uncertain ᵈLXX ᵉLXX *ephod* ᶠLXX; MT *"Bring out God's chest!"* because at that time God's chest was with the Israelites; cf 14:3. ᵍThat is, from the priestly vest (Heb *ephod*) or from the Urim and Thummim contained therein

---

SAUL (SON OF KISH)

Means "one requested, asked for," likely a shortened form of a name meaning "requested of the Lord" and comparable to Shealtiel, "I requested [him] of God." Saul was the first king of Israel according to the book of Samuel. He was God's choice as king (1 Sam 9–11), but was rejected (1 Sam 13–15). Saul and David were rival rulers for a time (1 Sam 16–2 Sam 1).

with the Israelites who were with Saul and Jonathan. ²²Similarly, when all the Israelites who had been hiding in the highlands of Ephraim heard that the Philistines were on the run, they also joined the battle in hot pursuit of the Philistines. ²³The LORD saved Israel that day, and the fighting carried on beyond Beth-aven.

²⁴Now the Israelite soldiers were in a difficult situation that day because Saul had bound the troops by a solemn pledge: "Anyone who eats anything before evening when I have taken revenge on my enemies is doomed." So none of the army ate anything. ²⁵The troops[h] came across a honeycomb with honey on the ground. ²⁶But even when they came across the honeycomb with the honey still flowing, no one ate any of it because the troops were afraid of the solemn pledge. ²⁷But Jonathan hadn't heard his father make the people swear the pledge, so he dipped the end of the staff he was carrying into the honeycomb. When he ate some his eyes lit up. ²⁸Then one of the soldiers spoke up: "Your father bound the troops by a solemn pledge: 'Anyone who eats food today is doomed.' That's why the troops are exhausted."

²⁹Jonathan said, "My father has brought trouble to the land. Look how my eyes lit up when I tasted just a bit of that honey! ³⁰It would have been even better if the troops had eaten some of their enemies' plunder today when they found it! But now the Philistine defeat isn't as thorough as it might have been."

³¹That day, after they had fought the Philistines from Michmash to Aijalon, the troops were completely exhausted. ³²So the troops tore into the plunder, taking sheep, cattle, and calves. They slaughtered them right on the ground and devoured them with the blood still in them. ³³When it was reported to Saul, "The troops are sinning against the LORD by eating meat with blood in it," Saul said, "All of you are traitors! Roll a large stone over here right now.

³⁴Go among the troops and say to them, 'Everyone must bring their ox or sheep, and slaughter them here with me. Don't sin against the LORD by eating meat with blood still in it.'" So everyone brought whatever they had and slaughtered it there.[i] ³⁵And Saul built an altar to the LORD. It was the first altar he had built to the LORD.

³⁶"Let's go after the Philistines tonight and plunder them until morning," Saul said. "We won't leave them a single survivor!"

"Do whatever you think is best," the troops replied.

But the priest said, "Let's ask God first."

³⁷So Saul questioned God: "Should I go after the Philistines? Will you hand them over to Israel?" But God did not answer him that day.

³⁸Then Saul said, "All you officers in the army, come forward! Let's find out what sin was committed today. ³⁹As surely as the LORD lives—the one who has saved Israel—even if it's my own son Jonathan, that person will be executed." Not one of the soldiers answered him. ⁴⁰So Saul said to all Israel, "You be on one side, and my son Jonathan and I will be on the other."

"Do whatever you think is best," the troops said.

⁴¹Then Saul asked the LORD God of Israel, "Why haven't you answered your servant today? If the wrongdoing is mine or my son Jonathan's, respond with Urim, but if the wrongdoing belongs to your people Israel, respond with Thummim."[j] Jonathan and Saul were taken by lot, and the troops were cleared.

⁴²Then Saul said, "Decide between me and my son Jonathan."[k] And Jonathan was selected.

⁴³"Tell me what you've done," Saul said to Jonathan.

So Jonathan told him. "I only took a very small taste of honey on the end of my staff," he said. "And now I'm supposed to die?"

⁴⁴"May God deal harshly with me and worse still if you don't die today!"[l] Saul swore.

---

[h]MT *land*   [i]LXX; MT *brought their ox and slaughtered it there that night.*   [j]LXX, Vulg; MT *Saul asked the Lord God of Israel, "Give the right answer."* Urim and Thummim were sacred lots carried by the priest.   [k]LXX adds *Whoever the Lord selects will die. The army said to Saul, "Don't do this!" But Saul forced them, so they decided between him and Jonathan his son.*   [l]LXX; MT *if you don't die, Jonathan*

⁴⁵But the troops said to Saul, "Why should Jonathan die when he has won this great victory for Israel? No way! As surely as the LORD lives, not one hair off his head will fall to the ground, because he did this today with God's help." So the troops rescued Jonathan, and he wasn't executed.

⁴⁶Then Saul stopped chasing the Philistines, and the Philistines went back to their own country.

Saul's wars

⁴⁷Saul secured his kingship over Israel. He fought against his enemies on every side: against Moab, the Ammonites, Edom, the king of Zobah,ᵐ and the Philistines. Wherever he turned, he was victorious.ⁿ ⁴⁸He acted heroically, defeating the Amalekites and rescuing Israel from the power of any who had plundered them.

⁴⁹Saul's sons were Jonathan, Ishvi, and Malchishua. The names of his two daughters were Merab, the oldest, and Michal, the younger daughter. ⁵⁰The name of Saul's wife was Ahinoam, Ahimaaz's daughter. The name of his general was Abner, Ner's son, Saul's uncle. ⁵¹Kish, Saul's father, and Ner, Abner's father, were Abiel's sons.

⁵²There was fierce warfare against the Philistines throughout Saul's lifetime. So whenever Saul saw any strong or heroic man, he would add him to his troops.

Samuel rejects Saul's kingship

15 Samuel said to Saul, "The LORD sent me to anoint you king over his people Israel. Listen now to the LORD's words! ²This is what the LORD of heavenly forces says: I am going to punish the Amalekites for what they did to Israel: how they attacked the Israelites as they came up from Egypt. ³So go! Attack the Amalekites; put everything that belongs to them under the ban.° Spare no one. Kill men and women, children and infants, oxen and sheep, camels and donkeys."

⁴Saul called out the troops and counted them at Telaim: two hundred thousand foot soldiers and ten thousand more troops from Judah. ⁵Then Saul advanced on the Amalekite city and laid an ambush in the valley. ⁶Saul told the Kenites, "Get going! Leave the Amalekites immediately because you showed kindness to the Israelites when they came out of Egypt. Otherwise, I'll destroy you right along with them." So the Kenites left the Amalekites. ⁷Then Saul attacked the Amalekites from Havilah all the way to Shur, which is near Egypt. ⁸He captured Agag the Amalekite king alive, but Saul placed all the people under the ban, killing them with the sword. ⁹Saul and the troops spared Agag along with the best sheep, cattle, fattened calves,ᵖ lambs, and everything of value. They weren't willing to put them under the ban; but anything that was despised or of no value�q they placed under the ban.

¹⁰Then the LORD's word came to Samuel: ¹¹"I regret making Saul king because he has turned away from following me and hasn't done what I said." Samuel was upset at this, and he prayed to the LORD all night long.

¹²Samuel got up early in the morning to meet Saul, and was told, "Saul went to Carmel, where he is setting up a monument for himself. Then he left and went down to Gilgal."

¹³When Samuel reached Saul,ʳ Saul greeted him, "The LORD bless you! I have done what the LORD said."

¹⁴"Then what," Samuel asked, "is this bleating of sheep in my ears and mooing of cattle I hear?"

¹⁵"They were taken from the Amalekites," Saul said, "because the troops spared the best sheep and cattle in order to sacrifice them to the LORD your God. The rest was placed under the ban."

¹⁶Samuel then said to Saul, "Enough! Let me tell you what the LORD said to me last night."

"Tell me," Saul replied.

¹⁷Samuel said, "Even if you think you are

ᵐLXX, DSS (4QSamᵃ); MT *kings of Zobah* ⁿLXX °A technique of holy war that often involves total destruction, in which everything that is destroyed is dedicated to the deity who helps in the battle; also in 15:8-9, 15, 18, 20-21. ᵖLXX qLXX; Heb uncertain ʳLXX adds *he was offering entirely burned sacrifices to the LORD, the best of the plunder that he had taken from Amalek. As Samuel approached Saul.*

insignificant, aren't you the leader of Israel's tribes? The LORD anointed you king over Israel. [18]The LORD sent you on a mission, instructing you, 'Go, and put the sinful Amalekites under the ban. Fight against them until you've wiped them out.' [19]Why didn't you obey the LORD? You did evil in the LORD's eyes when you tore into the plunder!"

[20]"But I did obey the LORD!" Saul protested to Samuel. "I went on the mission the LORD sent me on. I captured Agag the Amalekite king, and I put the Amalekites under the ban. [21]Yes, the troops took sheep and cattle from the plunder—the very best items placed under the ban—but in order to sacrifice them to the LORD your God at Gilgal."

[22]Then Samuel replied,

"Does the LORD want
  entirely burned offerings and sacrifices
  as much as obedience to the LORD?
Listen to this:
  obeying is better than sacrificing,
  paying attention
    is better than fat from rams,
[23]because rebellion is as bad
  as the sin of divination;
  arrogance is like the evil of idolatry.[s]
Because you have rejected
  what the LORD said,
  he has rejected you as king."

[24]Saul said to Samuel, "I have sinned because I disobeyed the LORD's command and your instructions. I was afraid of the troops and obeyed them. [25]But now please forgive my sin! Come back with me, so I can worship the LORD."

[26]But Samuel said to Saul, "I can't[t] return with you because you have rejected what the LORD said, and the LORD has rejected you from being king over Israel."

[27]Samuel turned to leave, but Saul grabbed at the edge of his robe, and it ripped. [28]Then Samuel told him, "The LORD has ripped the kingdom of Israel from you today. He will give it to a friend of yours, someone who is more worthy than you. [29]What's more, the enduring one of Israel doesn't take back what he says and doesn't change his mind. He is not a human being who would change his mind."

[30]"I have sinned," Saul said, "but please honor me in front of my people's elders and before Israel, and come back with me so I can worship the LORD your God." [31]So Samuel went back with Saul, and Saul worshipped the LORD.

[32]"Bring me Agag the Amalekite king," Samuel said.

Agag came to him in chains, asking, "Would death have been as bitter as this is?"[u]

[33]Samuel said, "Just as your sword left women without their children, now your mother will be childless among women." Then Samuel cut Agag to pieces in the LORD's presence at Gilgal.

[34]Then Samuel went to Ramah, but Saul went up to his home in Gibeah. [35]Samuel never saw Saul again before he died, but he grieved over Saul. However, the LORD regretted making Saul king over Israel.

Samuel anoints David

16 The LORD said to Samuel, "How long are you going to grieve over Saul? I

[s]Sym, LXX[B]; MT *evil and idolatry* [t]Or *won't* [u]LXX; Heb uncertain

AGAG

King of the Amalekites. Samuel orders Saul to destroy Agag, the Amalekites, and all their possessions. But Saul and the Israelites spare Agag and the finest Amalekite possessions, supposedly to sacrifice them to God at Gilgal. God rejects Saul for his disobedience and regrets making Saul king over Israel. Samuel executes Agag (1 Sam 15).

have rejected him as king over Israel. Fill your horn with oil and get going. I'm sending you to Jesse of Bethlehem because I have found[v] my next king among his sons."

²"How can I do that?" Samuel asked. "When Saul hears of it he'll kill me!"

"Take a heifer with you," the LORD replied, "and say, 'I have come to make a sacrifice to the LORD.' ³Invite Jesse to the sacrifice, and I will make clear to you what you should do. You will anoint for me the person I point out to you."

⁴Samuel did what the LORD instructed. When he came to Bethlehem, the city elders came to meet him. They were shaking with fear. "Do you come in peace?" they asked.

⁵"Yes," Samuel answered. "I've come to make a sacrifice to the LORD. Now make yourselves holy, then come with me to the sacrifice." Samuel made Jesse and his sons holy and invited them to the sacrifice as well.

⁶When they arrived, Samuel looked at Eliab and thought, That must be the LORD's anointed right in front.

⁷But the LORD said to Samuel, "Have no regard for his appearance or stature, because I haven't selected him. God[w] doesn't look at things like humans do. Humans see only what is visible to the eyes, but the LORD sees into the heart."

⁸Next Jesse called for Abinadab, who presented himself to Samuel, but he said, "The LORD hasn't chosen this one either." ⁹So Jesse presented Shammah, but Samuel said, "No, the LORD hasn't chosen this one." ¹⁰Jesse presented seven of his sons to Samuel, but Samuel said to Jesse, "The LORD hasn't picked any of these." ¹¹Then Samuel asked Jesse, "Is that all of your boys?"

"There is still the youngest one," Jesse answered, "but he's out keeping the sheep."

"Send for him," Samuel told Jesse, "because we can't proceed until he gets here."[x]

¹²So Jesse sent and brought him in. He was reddish brown, had beautiful eyes, and was good-looking. The LORD said, "That's the one. Go anoint him." ¹³So Samuel took the horn of oil and anointed him right there in front of his brothers. The LORD's spirit came over David from that point forward.

Then Samuel left and went to Ramah.

David is introduced to Saul

¹⁴Now the LORD's spirit had departed from Saul, and an evil spirit from the LORD tormented him. ¹⁵Saul's servants said to him, "Look, an evil spirit from God is tormenting you. ¹⁶If our master just says the word, your servants will search for someone who knows how to play the lyre. The

---

[v]Or *seen*   [w]LXX; MT lacks *God*.   [x]MT; LXX *we won't sit down* (that is, to eat)

BETHLEHEM

A city in Judah 6 mi. south of Jerusalem, located on a spur running east from the watershed. Bethlehem is the setting for the book of Ruth and the birthplace of Ruth and Boaz's descendant David (ca. 1000 BCE). Samuel anointed David king in Bethlehem (1 Sam 16:1-13), and David made his home there (1 Sam 17:12, 15; 20:6, 28). The Philistines put a garrison in Bethlehem (2 Sam 23:14-16; 1 Chron 11:16-18) that remained until David established his capital in Jerusalem. David's grandson Rehoboam fortified Bethlehem (2 Chron 11:6). No traces of the wall have been found, but the excavations have not been complete or systematic.

Joseph and Mary were natives of Bethlehem, where they had a "house," according to Matthew (Matt 2:11). Luke concurs that Jesus was born in Bethlehem, "David's city" (Luke 2:4-7).

musician can play whenever the evil spirit from God is affecting you, and then you'll feel better."

[17] Saul said to his servants, "Find me a good musician and bring him to me."

[18] One of the servants responded, "I know that one of Jesse's sons from Bethlehem is a good musician. He's a strong man and heroic, a warrior who speaks well and is good-looking too. The LORD is with him."

[19] So Saul sent messengers to Jesse to say, "Send me your son David, the one who keeps the sheep."

[20] Jesse then took a donkey and loaded it with a homer of bread,[y] a jar of wine, and a young goat, and he sent it along with his son David to Saul. [21] That is how David came to Saul and entered his service. Saul liked David very much,[z] and David became his armor-bearer. [22] Saul sent a message to Jesse: "Please allow David to remain in my service because I am pleased with him."

[23] Whenever the evil spirit from God affected Saul, David would take the lyre and play it. Then Saul would relax and feel better, and the evil spirit would leave him alone.

David defeats Goliath

17 The Philistines assembled their troops for war at Socoh of Judah. They camped between Socoh and Azekah at Ephes-dammim. [2] Saul and the Israelite army assembled and camped in the Elah Valley, where they got organized to fight the Philistines. [3] The Philistines took positions on one hill while Israel took positions on the opposite hill. There was a valley between them.

[4] A champion named Goliath from Gath came out from the Philistine camp. He was more than nine feet tall.[a] [5] He had a bronze helmet on his head and wore bronze scale-armor weighing one hundred twenty-five pounds.[b] [6] He had bronze plates on his shins, and a bronze scimitar hung on his back. [7] His spear shaft[c] was as strong as the bar on a weaver's loom, and its iron head

weighed fifteen pounds.[d] His shield-bearer walked in front of him.

[8] He stopped and shouted to the Israelite troops, "Why have you come and taken up battle formations? I am the Philistine champion,[e] and you are Saul's servants. Isn't that right? Select one of your men, and let him come down against me. [9] If he is able to fight me and kill me, then we will become your slaves, but if I overcome him and kill him, then you will become our slaves and you will serve us. [10] I insult Israel's troops today!" The Philistine continued, "Give me an opponent, and we'll fight!" [11] When Saul and all Israel heard what the Philistine said, they were distressed and terrified.[f]

[12] Now David was Jesse's son, an Ephraimite from Bethlehem in Judah who had eight sons. By Saul's time, Jesse was already quite old and far along in age.[g] [13] Jesse's three oldest sons had gone with Saul to war. Their names were Eliab the oldest, Abinadab the second oldest, and Shammah the third oldest. [14] (David was the youngest.) These three older sons followed Saul, [15] but David went back and forth from Saul's side to shepherd his father's flock in Bethlehem.

[16] For forty days straight the Philistine came out and took his stand, both morning and evening. [17] Jesse said to his son David, "Please take your brothers an ephah[h] of this roasted grain and these ten loaves of bread. Deliver them quickly to your brothers in the camp. [18] And here, take these ten wedges of cheese to their unit commander. Find out how your brothers are doing and bring back some sign that they are okay. [19] They are with Saul and all the Israelite troops fighting the Philistines in the Elah Valley."

[20] So David got up early in the morning, left someone in charge of the flock, and loaded up and left, just as his father Jesse had instructed him. He reached the camp right when the army was taking up their battle formations and shouting the war cry. [21] Israel and the Philistines took

---

[y] LXX [z] Or *David liked Saul very much.* [a] LXX *over six feet tall* [b] Five thousand shekels [c] Qere, LXX, Syr (cf 2 Sam 21:19); Kethib *the point of his spear* [d] Six hundred shekels [e] MT *the Philistine* lacks *champion.* [f] The following verses are absent from LXX[B]: 17:12-31, 41, 48b, 50, 55-58. [g] LXX, Syr [h] One ephah is approximately twenty quarts.

up their battle formations opposite each other. [22]David left his things with an attendant and ran to the front line. When he arrived, he asked how his brothers were doing. [23]Right when David was speaking with them, Goliath, the Philistine champion from Gath, came forward from the Philistine ranks and said the same things he had said before. David listened. [24]When the Israelites saw Goliath, every one of them ran away terrified of him. ([25]Now the Israelite soldiers had been saying to each other: "Do you see this man who keeps coming out? How he comes to insult Israel? The king will reward with great riches whoever kills that man. The king will give his own daughter to him and make his household exempt from taxes[i] in Israel.")

[26]David asked the soldiers standing by him, "What will be done for the person who kills that Philistine over there and removes this insult from Israel? Who is that uncircumcised Philistine, anyway, that he can get away with insulting the army of the living God?"

[27]Then the troops repeated to him what they had been saying. "So that's what will be done for the man who kills him," they said.

[28]When David's oldest brother Eliab heard him talking to the soldiers, he got very mad at David. "Why did you come down here?" he said. "Who is watching those few sheep for you in the wilderness? I know how arrogant you are and your devious plan: you came down just to see the battle!"

[29]"What did I do wrong this time?" David replied. "It was just a question!"

[30]So David turned to someone else and asked the same thing, and the people said the same thing in reply. [31]The things David had said were overheard and reported to Saul, who sent for him.

[32]"Don't let anyone[j] lose courage because of this Philistine!" David told Saul. "I, your servant, will go out and fight him!"

[33]"You can't go out and fight this Philistine," Saul answered David. "You are still a boy. But he's been a warrior since he was a boy!"

[34]"Your servant has kept his father's sheep," David replied to Saul, "and if ever a lion or a bear came and carried off one of the flock, [35]I would go after it, strike it, and rescue the animal from its mouth. If it turned on me, I would grab it at its jaw, strike it, and kill it. [36]Your servant has fought both lions and bears. This uncircumcised Philistine will be just like one of them because he has insulted the army of the living God.

[37]"The LORD," David added, "who rescued me from the power of both lions and bears, will rescue me from the power of this Philistine."

"Go!" Saul replied to David. "And may the LORD be with you!"

[38]Then Saul dressed David in his own gear, putting a coat of armor on him and a bronze helmet on his head. [39]David strapped his sword on over the armor, but he couldn't walk around well because he'd never tried it before. "I can't walk in this," David told Saul, "because I've never tried it before." So he took them off. [40]He then grabbed his staff and chose five smooth stones from the streambed. He put them in

[i]Heb uncertain   [j]LXX *my master* (the king)

GOLIATH

Philistine champion defeated by David in single combat (1 Sam 17). Though Goliath is well armed and described as a giant who is nine feet tall, David defeats him with one stone and a sling. A giant named Goliath is also mentioned in 2 Samuel 21:19, but there he is reported to have been killed by Elhanan. Curiously, 1 Chronicles 20:5 says that Elhanan killed the giant Lahmi, the brother of Goliath.

the pocket of his shepherd's bag and with sling in hand went out to the Philistine.

⁴¹The Philistine got closer and closer to David, and his shield-bearer was in front of him. ⁴²When the Philistine looked David over, he sneered at David because he was just a boy; reddish brown and good-looking.

⁴³The Philistine asked David, "Am I some sort of dog that you come at me with sticks?" And he cursed David by his gods. ⁴⁴"Come here," he said to David, "and I'll feed your flesh to the wild birds and the wild animals!"

⁴⁵But David told the Philistine, "You are coming against me with sword, spear, and scimitar, but I come against you in the name of the LORD of heavenly forces, the God of Israel's army, the one you've insulted. ⁴⁶Today the LORD will hand you over to me. I will strike you down and cut off your head! Today I will feed your dead body and the dead bodies of the entire Philistine campᵏ to the wild birds and the wild animals. Then the whole world will know that there is a God on Israel's side. ⁴⁷And all those gathered here will know that the LORD doesn't save by means of sword and spear. The LORD owns this war, and he will hand all of you over to us."

⁴⁸The Philistine got up and moved closer to attack David, and David ran quickly to the front line to face him. ⁴⁹David put his hand in his bag and took out a stone. He slung it, and it hit the Philistine on his forehead. The stone penetrated his forehead, and he fell facedown on the ground. ⁵⁰And that's how David triumphed over the Philistine with just a sling and a stone, striking the Philistine down and killing him—and David didn't even have a sword! ⁵¹Then David ran and stood over the Philistine. He grabbed the Philistine's sword, drew it from its sheath, and finished him off. Then David cut off the Philistine's head with the sword.

When the Philistines saw that their hero was dead, they fled. ⁵²The soldiers from Israel and Judah jumped up with a shout and chased the Philistines all the way to Gathˡ and the gates of Ekron. The dead Philistines were littered along the Shaarim road all the way to Gath and Ekron. ⁵³When the Israelites came back from chasing the Philistines, they plundered their camp. ⁵⁴David took the head of the Philistine and brought it to Jerusalem, but he put the Philistine's weapons in his own tent.

⁵⁵Now when Saul saw David go out to meet the Philistine, he asked Abner the army general, "Abner, whose son is that boy?"

"As surely as you live, Your Majesty, I don't know," Abner answered.

⁵⁶"Then find out whose son that young man is," the king replied.

⁵⁷So when David came back from killing the Philistine, Abner sent for him and presented him to Saul. The Philistine's head was still in David's hand. ⁵⁸Saul said to him, "Whose son are you, my boy?"

"I'm the son of your servant Jesse from Bethlehem," David answered.

Jonathan and David

18 As soon as David had finished talking with Saul, Jonathan's lifeᵐ became bound up with David's life, and Jonathan loved David as much as himself.ⁿ ²From that point forward, Saul kept David in his serviceᵒ and wouldn't allow him to return to his father's household. ³And Jonathan and David made a covenant together because Jonathan loved David as much as himself. ⁴Jonathan took off the robe he was wearing and gave it to David, along with his armor, as well as his sword, his bow, and his belt. ⁵David went out and was successful in every mission Saul sent him to do. So Saul placed him in charge of the soldiers, and this pleased all the troops as well as Saul's servants.

Saul jealous of David

⁶After David came back from killing the Philistine, and as the troops returned home, women from all of Israel's towns came out to meet King Saulᵖ with singing

---

ᵏLXX; MT lacks *your dead body.* ˡLXX; MT *Gai* or *a valley* ᵐOr *soul*; also twice more in this verse and in 18:3 ⁿThe following verses are absent from LXXᴮ: 18:1-5, 10-11, 17-19, 29b-30. ᵒMT lacks *in his service.* ᵖMT; LXX *to meet David* and dancing, with tambourines, rejoicing, and musical instruments. [7] The women sang in celebration:

"Saul has killed his thousands,
 but David has killed
 his tens of thousands!"

[8] Saul burned with anger. This song annoyed him. "They've credited David with tens of thousands," he said, "but only credit me with thousands. What's next for him— the kingdom itself?" [9] So Saul kept a close eye on David from that point on.

[10] The next day an evil spirit from God came over Saul,[q] and he acted like he was in a prophetic frenzy in his house. So David played the lyre as he usually did. Saul had a spear in his hand, [11] and he threw it, thinking, I'll pin David to the wall. But David escaped from him two different times.

[12] Saul was afraid of David because the LORD was with David but no longer with Saul. [13] So Saul removed David from his service, placing him in command of a unit of one thousand men. David led the men out to war and back. [14] David was successful in everything he did because the LORD was with him. [15] Saul saw that he was very successful, and he was afraid of him. [16] Everyone in Israel and Judah loved David because he led them out in war and back again.

[17] Saul said to David, "Look, here is my oldest daughter Merab. I will give her to you in marriage on this condition: you must be my warrior and fight the LORD's battles." I won't raise my hand against him, Saul thought; let the Philistines do that!

[18] "I'm not worthy," David replied to Saul, "and neither is my family or my father's clan in Israel, to become the king's son-in-law." [19] And so when the time came for Saul's daughter Merab to be married to David, she was given to Adriel from Meholah instead.

[20] Now Saul's younger daughter Michal loved David. When this was reported to Saul, he was happy about it. [21] I'll give her to him, Saul thought; she'll cause him problems, and the Philistines will be against him. So Saul said to David a second time, "Become my son-in-law now."

[22] Saul instructed his servants, "Tell David in private: 'Look, the king likes you, and all his servants love you. You should become the king's son-in-law.'"

[23] Saul's servants whispered these things in David's ear. But David said, "Do you think it's a simple matter to become the king's son-in-law? I don't! I'm poor and insignificant."

[24] Saul's servants reported what David said, [25] and Saul replied, "Tell David this: 'The king doesn't want any bridal gift, just a hundred Philistine foreskins as vengeance on the king's enemies.'" (Saul was hoping that David would die at the hands of the Philistines.) [26] When the servants reported this to David, he was happy to become the king's son-in-law. Even before the allotted time had expired,[r] [27] David got up and went with his soldiers and killed one hundred Philistines.[s] David brought their foreskins and counted them out for the king so he could become the king's son-in-law. Then Saul gave his daughter Michal to him in marriage.

[28] When Saul knew for certain that the LORD was with David and that his daughter Michal loved him, [29] then Saul was even more afraid of David. Saul was David's enemy for the rest of his life.[t] [30] And whenever the Philistine commanders came out for battle, David would have more success than the rest of Saul's officers, so his fame spread widely.

David escapes Saul

19 Saul ordered his son Jonathan and all his servants to kill David, but Jonathan, Saul's son, liked David very much. [2] So Jonathan warned David, "My father Saul is trying to kill you. Be on guard tomorrow morning. Stay somewhere safe and hide. [3] I'll go out and stand by my father in the field where you'll be. I'll talk to my father about you, and I'll tell you whatever I find out."

[4] So Jonathan spoke highly about David to his father Saul, telling him, "The king shouldn't do anything wrong to his servant David, because he hasn't wronged you. In fact, his actions have helped you greatly.

[q] Or to Saul [r] Heb uncertain [s] LXX, cf 2 Sam 3:14; MT two hundred [t] Or Saul became David's constant enemy.

⁵He risked his own life when he killed that Philistine, and the LORD won a great victory for all Israel. You saw it and were happy about it. Why then would you do something wrong to an innocent person by killing David for no reason?"

⁶Saul listened to Jonathan and then swore, "As surely as the LORD lives, David won't be executed." ⁷So Jonathan summoned David and told him everything they had talked about. Then Jonathan brought David back to Saul, and David served Saul as he had previously.

⁸War broke out again. When David went out to fight the Philistines, he struck them with such force that they ran from him.

⁹Then an evil spirit from the LORD came over Saul.ᵘ He was sitting in his house with his spear in hand while David was playing music. ¹⁰Saul tried to pin David to the wall with his spear, but David escaped Saul. Saul drove the spear into the wall, but David fled and got away safely. That night ¹¹Saul sent messengers to David's house to keep watch on it and kill him in the morning. David's wife Michal warned him, "If you don't escape with your life tonight, you are a dead man tomorrow." ¹²So Michal lowered David through a window. He took off and ran, and he got away. ¹³Then Michal took the household's divine image and laid it in the bed, putting some goat's hair on its head and covering it with clothes.

¹⁴Saul sent messengers to arrest David, but she said, "He's sick."

¹⁵Saul sent the messengers back to check on David for themselves. "Bring him to me on his bed," he ordered, "so he can be executed." ¹⁶When the messengers arrived, they found the idol in the bed with the goat's hair on its head. ¹⁷Saul said to Michal, "Why could you betray me like this, letting my enemy go so that now he has escaped?"

Michal said to Saul, "David told me, 'Help me get away or I'll kill you!'"

¹⁸So David fled and escaped. When he reached Samuel at Ramah, he reported to him everything Saul had done to him. Then he and Samuel went to stay in the camps.ᵛ

¹⁹When Saul was told that David was in the camps at Ramah, ²⁰he sent messengers to arrest David. They saw a group of prophets in a prophetic frenzy, with Samuel standing there as their leader. God's spirit came over Saul's messengers, and they also fell into a prophetic frenzy. ²¹This was reported to Saul, and he sent different messengers, but they also fell into a prophetic frenzy. So Saul sent a third group of messengers, and they did the very same thing.

²²At that point, Saul went to Ramah himself. He came to the well at the threshing floor that was on the bare hill thereʷ and asked, "Where are Samuel and David?"

"In the camps at Ramah," he was told. ²³So Saul went to the camps at Ramah, and God's spirit came over him too. So as he traveled, he was in a prophetic frenzy until he reached the camps at Ramah. ²⁴He even took off all his clothes and fell into a prophetic frenzy in front of Samuel. He lay naked that whole day and night. That's why people say, "Is Saul also one of the prophets?"

Jonathan and David's friendship

20 David fled from the camps at Ramah. He came to Jonathan and asked, "What have I done? What is my crime? How have I wronged your father that he wants me dead?"

²Jonathan said to him, "No! You are not going to die! Listen: My father doesn't do anything big or small without telling me first. Why would my father hide this from me? It isn't true!"

³But David solemnly promised in response, "Your father knows full well that you like me. He probably said, 'Jonathan must not learn about this or he'll be upset.'ˣ But I promise you—on the LORD's life and yours!—that I am this close to death!"

⁴"What do you want me to do?" Jonathan said to David. "I'll do it."

⁵"Okay, listen," David answered Jonathan. "Tomorrow is the new moon, and I'm supposed to sit with the king at the feast. Instead, let me go and I'll hide in

---

ᵘOr *to Saul*   ᵛOr *Naioth,* also in 19:19, 22-23   ʷLXX; MT *the large well at Secu*   ˣLXX *or he'll tell David;* cf 20:34

the field until nighttime.^{y} ^{6}If your father takes note of my absence, tell him, 'David begged my permission to run down to his hometown Bethlehem, because there is an annual sacrifice there for his whole family.' ^{7}If Saul says 'Fine,' then I, your servant, am safe. But if he loses his temper, then you'll know for certain that he intends to harm me. ^{8}So be loyal to your servant, because you've brought your servant into a sacred covenant^z with you. If I'm guilty, then kill me myself; just don't take me back to your father."

^{9}"Enough!" Jonathan replied. "If I can determine for certain that my father intends to harm you, of course I'll tell you!"

^{10}"Who will tell me if your father responds harshly?" David asked Jonathan.

^{11}"Come on," Jonathan said to David. "Let's go into the field." So both of them went out into the field. ^{12}Then Jonathan told David, "I pledge by the LORD God of Israel that I will question my father by this time tomorrow or on the third day. If he seems favorable toward David, I will definitely send word and make sure you know. ^{13}But if my father intends to harm you, then may the LORD deal harshly with me, Jonathan, and worse still if I don't tell you right away so that you can escape safely. May the LORD be with you as he once was with my father. ^{14}If I remain alive, be loyal to me.^{a} But if I die, ^{15}don't ever stop being loyal to my household. Once the LORD has eliminated all of David's enemies from the earth, ^{16}if Jonathan's name is also eliminated, then the LORD will seek retribution from David!"^{b}

^{17}So Jonathan again made a pledge to David^c because he loved David as much as himself. ^{18}"Tomorrow is the festival of the new moon," Jonathan told David. "You will be missed because your seat will be empty. ^{19}The day after tomorrow, go all the way to the spot where you hid on the day of the incident, and stay close to that mound.^{d} ^{20}On

the third day I will shoot an arrow to the side of the mound as if aiming at a target.^{e} ^{21}Then I'll send the servant boy, saying, 'Go retrieve the arrow.' If I yell to the boy, 'Hey! The arrow is on this side of you. Get it!' then you can come out because it will be safe for you. There won't be any trouble—I make a pledge on the LORD's life. ^{22}But if I yell to the young man, 'Hey! The arrow is past you,' then run for it, because the LORD has sent you away. ^{23}Either way, the LORD is witness^f between us forever regarding the promise we made to each other." ^{24}So David hid himself in the field.

When the new moon came, the king sat at the feast to eat. ^{25}He took his customary seat by the wall. Jonathan sat opposite him^g while Abner sat beside Saul. David's seat was empty. ^{26}Saul didn't say anything that day because he thought, Perhaps David became unclean somehow. That must be it. ^{27}But on the next day, the second of the new moon, David's seat was still empty. Saul said to his son Jonathan, "Why hasn't Jesse's son come to the table,^{h} either yesterday or today?"

^{28}Jonathan answered Saul, "David begged my permission to go to Bethlehem. ^{29}He said, 'Please let me go because we have a family sacrifice there in town, and my brother has ordered me to be present. Please do me a favor and let me slip away so I can see my family.' That's why David hasn't been at the king's table."

^{30}At that, Saul got angry at Jonathan. "You son of a stubborn, rebellious woman!" he said. "Do you think I don't know how you've allied yourself with Jesse's son? Shame on you and on the mother who birthed you!^{i} ^{31}As long as Jesse's son lives on this earth, neither you nor your dynasty will be secure. Now have him brought to me because he's a dead man!"

^{32}But Jonathan answered his father Saul, "Why should David be executed? What has he done?"

[33] At that, Saul threw[j] his spear at Jonathan to strike him, and Jonathan realized that his father intended to kill David. [34] Jonathan got up from the table in a rage. He didn't eat anything on the second day of the new moon because he was worried about David and because his father had humiliated him.

[35] In the morning, Jonathan went out to the field for the meeting with David, and a young servant boy went with him. [36] He said to the boy, "Go quickly and retrieve the arrow that I shoot." So the boy ran off, and he shot an arrow beyond him. [37] When the boy got to the spot where Jonathan shot the arrow, Jonathan yelled to him, "Isn't the arrow past you?" [38] Jonathan yelled again to the boy, "Quick! Hurry up! Don't just stand there!" So Jonathan's servant boy gathered up the arrow and came back to his master. [39] The boy had no idea what had happened; only Jonathan and David knew. [40] Jonathan handed his weapons to the boy and told him, "Get going. Take these back to town."

[41] As soon as the boy was gone, David came out from behind the mound[k] and fell down, face on the ground, bowing low three times. The friends kissed each other, and cried with each other, but David cried hardest. [42][l] Then Jonathan said to David, "Go in peace because the two of us made a solemn pledge in the LORD's name when we said, 'The LORD is witness between us and between our descendants forever.'" Then David got up and left, but Jonathan went back to town.

David helped at Nob

21[m] David came to Nob where Ahimelech was priest. Ahimelech was shaking in fear when he met David. "Why are you alone? Why is no one with you?" he asked.

[2] David answered Ahimelech the priest, "The king has given me orders, but he instructed me, 'Don't let anyone know anything about the mission I'm sending you on or about your orders.' As for my troops, I told them to meet me at an undisclosed location. [3] Now what do you have here with you? Give me five loaves of bread or whatever you can find."

[4] "I don't have any regular bread on hand," the priest answered David, "just holy bread—but only if your troops have abstained from sexual activity."

[5] "Definitely," David answered the priest. "Whenever I go out to war, women are off-limits; that's our standard operating procedure. Even on regular missions, the men's gear is[n] kept holy. That's even more true today, with the mission holy along with the gear."[o] [6] So the priest gave David holy bread, because there was no other bread except the bread of the presence, which is removed from the LORD's presence and replaced by warm bread as soon as it is taken away.

[7] Now one of Saul's servants was there that day, detained in the LORD's presence. His name was Doeg. He was an Edomite and Saul's head shepherd.

[8] David asked Ahimelech, "Do you have a spear or sword on hand? I didn't bring my sword or gear with me because the king's mission was urgent."

---

[j] LXX; MT *pointed* [k] LXX; MT *beside the south* [l] 21:1 in Heb [m] 21:2 in Heb [n] MT; LXX *all the men are* [o] Heb uncertain

NOB

David flees from Saul to Nob, the city of priests, where he asks for and receives the bread of the presence and Goliath's sword from Saul's priest Ahimelech (1 Sam 21:1-9). These are important symbols of authority: holy bread and the sword of Israel's great enemy.

⁹The priest said, "The sword of Goliath, the Philistine you killed in the Elah Valley, is here wrapped in a cloth behind a priestly vest.ᵖ If you want it, take it, because there are no other swords here."

David said, "No sword is as good as that one! Give it to me!"

David pretends to be crazy

¹⁰So David got up and continued running from Saul. He went to Achish, Gath's king. ¹¹Achish's servants said to him, "Isn't that David, king of the land? He's the one people sing about in their dances,

'Saul has killed his thousands,
  but David has killed
    his tens of thousands!'"

¹²David took these words very seriously and became very frightened of Achish, Gath's king. ¹³So he changed the way he acted with them, pretending to be insane while he was with them.�q He scratched marks on the doors of the city gatesʳ and let spit run down his chin.

¹⁴"Can't you see he's crazy?" Achish asked his servants. "Why bring him to me? ¹⁵Am I short on insane people that you've brought this person to go crazy right in front of me? Do you really think I'm going to let this man enter my house?"

David gathers support

22David left Gath and escaped to Adullam's fortress.ˢ When David's siblings and all his extended family learned of this, they went to join him there. ²Everyone

who was in trouble, in debt, or in desperate circumstances gathered around David, and he became their leader. Approximately four hundred men joined him.

³From there David went to Mizpeh in Moab. He said to the Moabite king, "Please let my father and mother stay with you until I know what God will do to me." ⁴So David left his parents with the Moabite king, and they stayed with him the whole time David was in the fortress.

⁵Then the prophet Gad told David, "Don't stay in the fortress any longer. Leave now and go to the land of Judah." So David left and went to Hereth forest.

Saul kills the priests of Nob

⁶Saul learned that David and his soldiers had been located. Saul was sitting under the tamarisk tree on the hill at Gibeah, spear in hand, with all his servants waiting on him. ⁷He said to them, "Listen up, Benjaminites! Will Jesse's son give fields and vineyards to each and every one of you? Will he make each one of you commanders of units of one thousand men or commanders of units of one hundred? ⁸Is that why all of you have conspired against me? No one informed me when my son made a covenant with Jesse's son! Not one of you is concerned about me or informs me when my own son sets my servant against me in an ambush—but that's what has happened today!"

⁹Doeg the Edomite, who was standing with Saul's servants, responded, "I saw Jesse's son go to Ahimelech, Ahitub's son, at

ᵖDSS (4QSamᵇ); MT *behind the priestly vest* (Heb *ephod*) qOr *in their hand*; Heb uncertain ʳOr *with correction he spit on the doors of the city gate* or *he fell down at the doors of the city gate* (cf LXX). ˢCorrection; cf 22:4-5; MT *cave*

TAMARISK

A tall, shady tree with deep roots, particularly suitable to the sandy soil of the Sinai area, the Dead Sea, Israel, and Jordan. Various natural explanations for manna (Exod 16:14) have been connected with species of tamarisk, the closest of which may be a honey-like substance excreted from the tamarisk bush that is called "manna" by Bedouin.

Nob. ¹⁰Ahimelech questioned the LORD for David, and gave him provisions as well as the sword of Goliath the Philistine."

¹¹The king then sent for the priest Ahimelech, Ahitub's son, and all his extended family, who were the priests at Nob. All of them came to the king.

¹²"Listen here, son of Ahitub," Saul said. "Yes sir," he replied.

¹³Saul said to him, "Why have you conspired against me—you with Jesse's son—giving him food and a sword and questioning God for him so that he is now against me, waiting in ambush, which is what has happened today?"

¹⁴Ahimelech answered the king, "Out of all your servants, who is as trustworthy as David? He is the king's son-in-law, does whatever you ask, and is well respected in your house. ¹⁵Was that the first time I questioned God for him? Of course not! But please, the king shouldn't accuse me, his servant, or anyone in my father's household of any wrongdoing, because your servant knew nothing whatsoever about this matter."

¹⁶But the king said, "You will be executed, Ahimelech—you and all of your father's household!"

¹⁷The king ordered the guards waiting on him: "Go ahead and kill the LORD's priests because they've joined up with David too. They knew he was on the run but didn't inform me."

But the king's servants were unwilling to lift a hand to attack the LORD's priests.

¹⁸The king then ordered Doeg, "Doeg! You go attack the priests." So Doeg the Edomite went and attacked the priests, killing eighty-five men who wore the linen priestly vest[t] that day. ¹⁹He put the whole priestly city of Nob to the sword: men and women, children and infants, even oxen, donkeys, and sheep.

²⁰But one of the sons of Ahimelech, Ahitub's son, escaped. His name was Abiathar, and he fled to David. ²¹Abiathar reported to David that Saul had slaughtered the LORD's priests.

²²David told Abiathar, "That day, when Doeg the Edomite was there, I knew that he would tell Saul everything. I am to blame[u] for the deaths in your father's family. ²³Stay with me, and don't be afraid. The one who seeks my life now seeks yours too. But you'll be safe with me."

Saul chases David

23 David was told, "The Philistines are now attacking Keilah and looting the threshing floors!"

²David asked the LORD, "Should I go and fight these Philistines?"

"Go!" the LORD answered. "Fight the Philistines and save Keilah!"

³But David's men said to him, "Look how frightened we are here in Judah. It'll be worse if we go to Keilah against Philistine forces!"

⁴So David asked the LORD again, and the LORD reaffirmed, "Yes, go down to Keilah, because I will hand the Philistines over to you."

⁵Then David and his soldiers went to Keilah and fought the Philistines, driving off their cattle and defeating them decisively. And that's how David saved the residents of Keilah.

⁶Now after Abiathar, Ahimelech's son, fled to David, he had accompanied David to Keilah,[v] bringing a priestly vest[w] with him. ⁷When Saul was told that David had gone to Keilah, he said, "God has handed him over[x] to me now because he has trapped himself by entering a town with gates and bars!" ⁸So Saul called up all his troops for war, to go down to Keilah and attack David and his soldiers.

⁹When David learned that Saul was planning to harm him, he told the priest Abiathar, "Bring the priestly vest now."

¹⁰Then David said, "LORD God of Israel, I, your servant, have heard that Saul plans on coming to Keilah and will destroy the town because of me. ¹¹LORD God of Israel, will Saul come down as your servant has heard?[y] Please tell your servant."

---

[t]Heb *ephod* [u]LXX, Vulg; Heb uncertain [v]LXX; MT lacks *he had accompanied David to.* [w]Heb *ephod* [x]LXX, Targ; MT *made a stranger of him* [y]DSS (4QSam[b]), LXX; MT *LORD God of Israel, will the citizens of Keilah hand me over to him? Will Saul come down as your servant has heard?* Cf 23:12a.

"Yes, he will come down," the LORD answered.

¹²Next David asked, "Will the citizens of Keilah hand me and my soldiers over to Saul?"

"Yes, they will hand you over," the LORD replied.

¹³So David and his troops—approximately six hundred men—got up and left Keilah. They kept moving, going from one place to the next. When Saul was told that David had escaped from Keilah, he didn't go there.

¹⁴David lived in the fortresses in the wilderness and in the hills of the Ziph wilderness. Saul searched for him constantly, but God did not hand David over to Saul. ¹⁵While David was at Horesh in the Ziph wilderness he learned that Saul was looking to kill him. ¹⁶Saul's son Jonathan came to David at Horesh and encouraged him with God. ¹⁷Jonathan said to him, "Don't be afraid! My father Saul's hand won't touch you. You will be king over Israel, and I will be your second in command. Even my father Saul knows this." ¹⁸Then the two of them made a covenant before the LORD. David stayed at Horesh, but Jonathan went back home.

¹⁹Some Ziphites came to Saul at Gibeah. "David is hiding among us in the fortresses at Horesh on the hill of Hachilah, south of Jeshimon," they said. ²⁰"So whenever you want to come down, Your Majesty, do it! Leave it to us to hand him over to the king."

²¹"The LORD bless you because you have shown this kindness to me!" Saul said. ²²"Go now and get everything ready. Find out everything you can: where he stays, where he goes, who has seen him. I am told he is very shrewd. ²³Find out every hiding place he uses there and come back to me when you know for certain. I will then go with you. If David is in the area, I will hunt him down among any of Judah's clans!" ²⁴So they got up and left for Ziph ahead of Saul.

Meanwhile, David and his soldiers were in the Maon wilderness in the desert plain south of Jeshimon. ²⁵When Saul and his troops went looking for him, David was told about it, so he went down to a certain rock there and stayed in the Maon wilderness. When Saul heard that, he went into the Maon wilderness after David. ²⁶Saul was going around one side of a hill there while David and his soldiers were going around the other. David was hurrying to get away from Saul while Saul and his troops were trying to surround David and his soldiers in order to capture them. ²⁷But a messenger suddenly came to Saul. "Come quick!" he said. "The Philistines have invaded the land!" ²⁸So Saul broke off his pursuit of David and went to fight the Philistines. That's why that place is called Escape Rock. ²⁹ᶻThen David went from there and lived at the En-gedi fortresses.

David spares Saul's life

24 ᵃEven as Saul returned from pursuing the Philistines, he was informed that David was in the En-gedi wilderness. ²So Saul took three thousand men selected from all Israel and went to look for David and his soldiers near the rocks of the wild goats. ³He came to the sheep pens beside the road where there was a cave. Saul went into the cave to use the restroom.ᵇ Meanwhile, David and his soldiers were sitting in the very back of the cave.

⁴David's soldiers said to him, "This is the day the LORD spoke of when he promised you, 'I will hand your enemy over to you, and you can do to him whatever you think best.'" So David snuck up and cut off a corner of Saul's robe. ⁵But immediately David felt horrible that he had cut off a corner of Saul's robe.ᶜ

⁶"The LORD forbid," he told his men, "that I should do something like that to my master, the LORD's anointed, or lift my hand against him, because he's the LORD's anointed!" ⁷So David held his soldiers in check by what he said,ᵈ and he wouldn't allow them to attack Saul. Saul then left the cave and went on his way.

⁸Then David also went out of the cave and yelled after Saul, "My master the king!"

ᶻ24:1 in Heb ᵃ24:2 in Heb ᵇOr *to cover his feet* (a euphemism) ᶜLXX, Syr, Targ; MT lacks *robe*. ᵈHeb uncertain

Saul looked back, and David bowed low out of respect, nose to the ground.

[9] David said to Saul, "Why do you listen when people say, 'David wants to ruin you'? [10] Look! Today your own eyes have seen that the LORD handed you over to me in the cave. But I refused[e] to kill you. I spared you, saying, 'I won't lift a hand against my master because he is the LORD's anointed.' [11] Look here, my protector! See the corner of your robe in my hand? I cut off the corner of your robe but didn't kill you. So know now that I am not guilty of wrongdoing or rebellion. I haven't wronged you, but you are hunting me down, trying to kill me. [12] May the LORD judge between me and you! May the LORD take vengeance on you for me, but I won't lift a hand against you. [13] As the old proverb goes, 'Evil deeds come from evildoers!' but I won't lift a hand against you. [14] So who is Israel's king coming after? Who are you chasing? A dead dog? A single flea? [15] May the LORD be the judge and decide between you and me. May he see what has happened, argue my case, and vindicate me against you!"

[16] As soon as David finished saying all this to Saul, Saul said, "David, my son, is that your voice?" Then he broke down in tears, [17] telling David, "You are more righteous than I am because you have treated me generously, but I have treated you terribly. [18] Today you've told me the good you have done for me—how the LORD handed me over to you, but how you didn't kill me. [19] When someone finds an enemy, do they send the enemy away in peace? May the LORD repay you with good for what you have done for me today. [20] Now even I know that you will definitely become king, and Israel's kingdom will flourish in your hands. [21] Because of that, make a solemn pledge to me by the LORD that you won't kill off my descendants after I'm gone and that you won't destroy my name from my family lineage."

[22] David made a solemn pledge to Saul. Then Saul went back home, but David and his soldiers went up to the fortress.

Abigail saves David

25 Now Samuel died, and all Israel gathered to mourn for him. They buried him at his home in Ramah. David then left and went down to the Maon wilderness.[f]

[2] There was a man in Maon who did business in Carmel. He was a very important man and owned three thousand sheep and one thousand goats. At that time, he was shearing his sheep in Carmel. [3] The man's name was Nabal, and his wife's name was Abigail. She was an intelligent and attractive woman, but her husband was a hard man who did evil things. He was a Calebite.

[4] While in the wilderness, David heard that Nabal was shearing his sheep. [5] So David sent ten servants, telling them, "Go up to Carmel. When you get to Nabal, greet him for me. [6] Say this to him: 'Peace to you,[g] your household, and all that is yours! [7] I've heard that you are now shearing sheep. As you know, your shepherds were with us in the wilderness.[h] We didn't mistreat them. Moreover, the whole time they were at Carmel, nothing of theirs went missing. [8] Ask your servants; they will tell you the same. So please receive these young men favorably, because we've come on a special day. Please give whatever you have on hand to your servants and to your son David.'"

[9] When David's young men arrived, they said all this to Nabal on David's behalf. Then they waited. [10] But Nabal answered David's servants, "Who is David? Who is Jesse's son? There are all sorts of slaves running away from their masters these days. [11] Why should I take my bread, my water, and the meat I've butchered for my shearers and give it to people who came here from who knows where?" [12] So David's young servants turned around and went back the way they came. When they arrived, they reported every word of this to David.

[13] Then David said to his soldiers, "All of you, strap on your swords!" So each of them strapped on their swords, and David did the same. Nearly four hundred men went up with David. Two hundred men remained back with the supplies.

---

[e] LXX; MT *Some said* [f] LXX; MT *Paran* [g] Heb uncertain [h] LXX, Syr; MT lacks *in the wilderness*.

[14]One of Nabal's servants told his wife Abigail, "David sent messengers from the wilderness to greet our master, but he just yelled at them. [15]But the men were very good to us and didn't mistreat us. Nothing of ours went missing the whole time we were out with them in the fields. [16]In fact, the whole time we were with them, watching our sheep, they were a protective wall around us both night and day. [17]Think about that and see what you can do, because trouble is coming for our master and his whole household. But he's such a despicable person no one can speak to him."

[18]Abigail quickly took two hundred loaves of bread, two skins of wine, five sheep ready for cooking, five seahs[i] of roasted grain, one hundred raisin cakes, and two hundred fig cakes. She loaded all this on donkeys [19]and told her servants, "Go on ahead of me. I'll be right behind you." But she didn't tell her husband Nabal.

[20]As she was riding her donkey, going down a trail on the hillside, David and his soldiers appeared, descending toward her, and she met up with them. [21]David had just been saying, "What a waste of time—guarding all this man's stuff in the wilderness so that nothing of his went missing! He has repaid me evil instead of good! [22]May God deal harshly with me, David,[j] and worse still if I

leave alive even one single one who urinates on a wall[k] belonging to him come morning!"

[23]When Abigail saw David, she quickly got off her donkey and fell facedown before him, bowing low to the ground. [24]She fell at his feet and said, "Put the blame on me, my master! But please let me, your servant, speak to you directly. Please listen to what your servant has to say. [25]Please, my master, pay no attention to this despicable man Nabal. He's exactly what his name says he is! His name means fool,[l] and he is foolish![m] But I myself, your servant, didn't see the young men that you, my master, sent. [26]I pledge, my master, as surely as the LORD lives and as you live, that the LORD has held you back from bloodshed and taking vengeance into your own hands! But now let your enemies and those who seek to harm my master be exactly like Nabal! [27]Here is a gift, which your servant has brought to my master. Please let it be given to the young men who follow you, my master. [28]Please forgive any offense by your servant. The LORD will definitely make an enduring dynasty for my master because my master fights the LORD's battles, and nothing evil will be found in you throughout your lifetime. [29]If someone chases after you and tries to kill you, my master, then your life will be bound up securely in the bundle of

---

[i]One seah is approximately seven and a half quarts. [j]LXX; MT *with David's enemies* [k]Descriptive phrase meaning "a male"; also in 25:34 [l]Heb *nabal* [m]Heb *nebalah*

ABIGAIL

Possibly meaning "my (divine) father rejoices." She is the wife of Nabal the Carmelite, but later marries David and is the mother of David's son Chileab (2 Sam 3:3; Daniel in 1 Chron 3:1). In 1 Samuel 25 she appears wise, politically effective, and prophetic. Abigail's intelligence (v. 3), "good judgment" (v. 33), speaking, and hospitality contrast with the churlish Nabal (which means "fool"). She acts quickly to placate David's anger at Nabal. Through her speech, Abigail aligns herself with David while diffusing tension and averting violence. In a prophetic proclamation that anticipates Nathan's oracle in 2 Samuel 7:11, 16, Abigail assures David that God will make him "an enduring dynasty" (1 Sam 25:28). After God strikes Nabal dead, David sends messengers to Abigail, and she becomes his wife (1 Sam 25:42).

life[n] by the LORD your God, but he will fling away your enemies' lives as from the pouch of a sling. [30]When the LORD has done for my master all the good things he has promised you, and has installed you as Israel's leader, [31]don't let this be a blot or burden on my master's conscience, that you shed blood needlessly or that my master took vengeance into his own hands. When the LORD has done good things for my master, please remember your servant."

[32]David said to Abigail, "Bless the LORD God of Israel, who sent you to meet me today! [33]And bless you and your good judgment for preventing me from shedding blood and taking vengeance into my own hands today! [34]Otherwise, as surely as the LORD God of Israel lives—the one who kept me from hurting you—if you hadn't come quickly and met up with me, there wouldn't be one single one who urinates on a wall left come morning." [35]Then David accepted everything she had brought for him. "Return home in peace," he told her. "Be assured that I've heard your request and have agreed to it."

[36]When Abigail got back home to Nabal, he was throwing a party fit for a king in his house. Nabal was in a great mood and very drunk, so Abigail didn't tell him anything until daybreak. [37]In the morning, when Nabal was sober, his wife told him everything. Nabal's heart failed inside him, and he became like a stone. [38]About ten days later, the LORD struck Nabal, and he died.

[39]When David heard that Nabal was dead, he said, "Bless the LORD, who has rendered a verdict regarding Nabal's insult to me and who kept me, his servant, from doing something evil! The LORD has brought Nabal's evil down on his own head." Then David sent word to Abigail, saying that he would take her as his wife.

[40]When David's servants reached Abigail at Carmel, they said to her, "David has sent us to you so you can become his wife." [41]She bowed low to the ground and said, "I am your servant, ready to serve and wash the feet of my master's helpers." [42]Then Abigail got up quickly and rode on her donkey,

with five of her young women going with her. She followed David's messengers and became his wife.

[43]David also married Ahinoam from Jezreel, so both of them were his wives. [44]But Saul had given his daughter Michal, David's wife, to Palti, Laish's son, from Gallim.

David spares Saul's life a second time

26 The Ziphites came to Saul at Gibeah. "David is hiding on Hachilah's hill, which faces Jeshimon," they said. [2]So Saul got up and went down to the Ziph wilderness to look for David there. He had three thousand handpicked soldiers from Israel with him. [3]Saul camped on Hachilah's hill opposite Jeshimon beside the road, but David stayed in the wilderness. When David learned that Saul had come after him into the wilderness, [4]he sent spies and discovered that Saul had definitely arrived.

[5]So David got up and went to the place where Saul camped, and saw the place where Saul and Abner, Ner's son and Saul's general, were sleeping. Saul was sleeping inside the camp with the troops camped all around him. [6]David asked Ahimelech the Hittite and Joab's brother Abishai, Zeruiah's son, "Who will go down into the camp with me to Saul?"

"I'll go down with you," Abishai answered.

[7]So David and Abishai approached the troops at night and found Saul lying there, asleep in the camp, with his spear stuck in the ground by his head. Abner and the army were sleeping all around him.

[8]Abishai said to David, "God has handed your enemy over to you today! Let me pin him to the ground with my spear. One stroke is all I need! I won't need a second."

[9]But David said to Abishai, "Don't kill him! No one can lift a hand against the LORD's anointed and go unpunished. [10]As surely as the LORD lives," David continued, "it will be the LORD who will strike him down, or his day will come and he will die, or he'll fall in battle and be destroyed. [11]The LORD forbid that I lift my hand against the LORD's anointed! But go ahead and take the

---

[n]Or *bundle of the living*; Heb uncertain; perhaps a tied-up scroll (cf Exod 32:32-33; Ps 69:28; Isa 8:16)

spear by Saul's head and the water jug and let's go!" [12] So David took the spear and the water jug that were by Saul's head, and he and Abishai left. No one saw them, no one knew they were there, and no one woke up. All of them remained asleep because a deep sleep from the LORD had come over them. [13] David crossed over to the other side and stood on top of a hill with considerable distance between them. [14] Then David shouted to the army and to Abner, Ner's son, "Abner! Aren't you going to answer me?"

"Who are you to shout to the king?" Abner asked.

[15] David answered Abner, "You are a man, aren't you? And you have no equal in Israel, right? Then why haven't you kept watch over your master the king? One of the soldiers came to kill your master the king. [16] What you've done is terrible! As surely as the LORD lives, all of you are dead men because you didn't keep close watch over your master, the LORD's anointed. Have a look around! Where are the king's spear and the water jug that were by his head?"

[17] Saul recognized David's voice and said, "David, my son, is that your voice?"

David said, "Yes it is, my master the king. [18] Why," David continued, "is my master chasing me, his servant? What have I done and what wrong am I guilty of? [19] My master the king, please listen to what your servant has to say. If it is the LORD who has incited you against me, then let him accept an offering! But if human beings have done it, then let them be cursed before the LORD because they have now driven me off, keeping me from sharing in the LORD's inheritance. 'Go!' they tell me. 'Worship other gods!' [20] Don't let my blood spill on the ground apart from the LORD's presence, because the king of Israel has come out looking for a single flea[o] like someone hunting a partridge[p] in the mountains."

[21] Then Saul said, "I have sinned! David, my son, come back! Because you considered my life precious today, I won't harm you again. I have acted foolishly and have made a huge mistake."

[22] "Here is the king's spear," David answered. "Allow one of your servants to come over and get it. [23] Remember: The LORD rewards every person for their righteousness and loyalty, and I wasn't willing to lift a hand against the LORD's anointed, even though the LORD handed you over to me today. [24] And just as I considered your life valuable today, may the LORD consider my life valuable, and may he deliver me from all trouble."

[25] Then Saul said to David, "Bless you, David, my son! You will accomplish much and will certainly succeed." Then David went on his way, but Saul went back home.

David serves the Philistine Achish

27 David thought, One day I will be destroyed by Saul's power. The best thing for me to do is to escape to Philistine territory. Then Saul will give up looking for me in Israelite territory, and I will escape his power. [2] So David set out with his six hundred soldiers and went to Achish, Maoch's son and Gath's king. [3] David and his soldiers stayed there at Gath with Achish. Each man had his family with him, and David had his two wives, Ahinoam from Jezreel and Abigail, Nabal's widow from Carmel. [4] When Saul was told that David had fled to Gath, he didn't pursue him anymore.

[5] Then David said to Achish, "If you approve of me, please give me a place in one of the towns in the country so I can live there. Why should I, your servant, live in the capital city with you?" [6] So Achish gave the town of Ziklag to David at that time. That's why Ziklag has belonged to the kings of Judah until now. [7] David lived in the Philistine countryside for a total of one year and four months.

[8] David and his soldiers went out on raids against the Geshurites, the Girzites, and the Amalekites. They were the people who lived in the land from Telam[q] to Shur all the way to the land of Egypt. [9] When David attacked an area, he wouldn't leave anyone alive, man or woman. He would take the sheep, the cattle, the donkeys, the camels, and the clothes and would then

[o] Cf 24:14; LXX *my life*   [p] Or *a caller*, Heb sounds like verb *to shout* or *call* in 26:14.   [q] LXX; MT *from long ago*

go back to Achish. [10]When Achish asked, "Where did you raid today?"[r] David would say, "The southern plain of Judah," or "The southern plain of the Jerahmeelites," or "The southern plain of the Kenites." [11]David never spared a man or woman so they could be brought back alive to Gath. "Otherwise," he said, "they might talk about us, and say, 'David did this or that.'" So this was David's practice during the entire time he lived in the Philistine countryside.

[12]Achish trusted David, thinking, David has alienated himself so badly from his own people in Israel that he'll serve me forever.

28 At that time, the Philistines gathered their troops for war to fight against Israel. Achish said to David, "Count on you and your soldiers marching out with me in the army."

[2]"Excellent," David answered Achish. "Now you'll see for yourself what your servant can do."

"Excellent," Achish replied. "I will make you my permanent bodyguard."

Saul and the woman of En-dor

[3]Now Samuel had died, and all Israel mourned him and buried him in Ramah, his hometown. And Saul had banned all mediums and diviners from the land.

[4]The Philistines gathered their forces and advanced to camp at Shunem. Saul gathered all Israel, and they camped at Gilboa. [5]When Saul saw the Philistine army, he was so afraid that his heart beat wildly. [6]When Saul questioned the LORD, the LORD didn't answer him—not by dreams, not by the Urim, and not by the prophets. [7]So Saul said to his servants, "Find me a woman who communicates with ghosts! I'll then go to her and ask by using her techniques."[s]

"There is such a medium in En-dor," his servants replied.

[8]So Saul disguised himself, dressing in different clothes. Then he and two men set out, going to the woman at nighttime. "Please call up a ghost for me! Bring me the one I specify," Saul said.

[9]"Listen," the woman said to him, "you know what Saul has done, how he has banned all mediums and diviners from the land. What are you doing? Trying to get me killed?"

[10]But Saul promised to her by the LORD, "As surely as the LORD lives, you won't get into trouble for this."

[11]So the woman said, "Who do you want me to bring up for you?"

"Bring up Samuel," he said.

[12]When the woman saw Samuel, she screamed at Saul, "Why have you tricked me? You are Saul!"

[13]"Don't be afraid!" the king said to her. "What do you see?"

The woman said to Saul, "I see a god[t] coming up from the ground."

[14]"What does he look like?" Saul asked her.

"An old man is coming up," she said. "He's wrapped in a robe." Then Saul knew that it was Samuel, and he bowed low out of respect, nose to the ground.

[15]"Why have you disturbed me by bringing me up?" Samuel asked Saul.

"I'm in deep trouble!" Saul replied. "The Philistines are at war with me, and God has turned away from me and no longer answers me by prophets or by dreams. So I have called on you to tell me what I should do."

---

[r]DSS (4QSam[a]), LXX [s]Or *through her* or *by her* [t]Or *I see gods* or *I see divine figures*

EN-DOR

The exact location of En-dor is unknown. According to Joshua 17:11, En-dor is part of Manasseh's inheritance within or near the borders of Issachar. But Manassah was unable to take the city from the Canaanites. En-dor is the home of the medium who contacts Samuel for Saul (1 Sam 28:3-25).

[16]"Why do you ask me," Samuel said, "since the LORD has turned away from you and has become your enemy?[u] [17]The LORD has done to you[v] exactly what he spoke through me: The LORD has ripped the kingdom out of your hands and has given it to your friend David. [18]The LORD has done this very thing to you today because you didn't listen to the LORD's voice and didn't carry out his fierce anger against the Amalekites. [19]The LORD will now hand over both you and Israel to the Philistines. And come tomorrow, you and your sons will be with me![w] The LORD will hand Israel's army over to the Philistines."

[20]Saul immediately fell full length on the ground, utterly terrified at what Samuel had said. He was weak because he hadn't eaten anything all day or night. [21]The woman approached Saul, and after seeing how scared he was, she said, "Listen, your servant has obeyed you. I risked my life and did what you told me to do. [22]Now it's your turn to listen to me, your servant. Let me give you a bit of food. Eat it, then you'll have the strength to go on your way."

[23]But Saul refused. "I can't eat!" he said. But his servants and the woman urged him to do so, and so he did. He got up off the ground and sat on a couch. [24]The woman had a fattened calf in the house, and she quickly butchered it.[x] She took flour, kneaded it, and baked unleavened bread. [25]She served this to Saul and his servants, and they ate. They got up and left that very night.

David sent home from fighting Saul

29 The Philistines assembled all their forces at Aphek, and the Israelites camped by the spring in Jezreel. [2]As the Philistine rulers went out marching in units of hundreds and thousands, David and his soldiers were in the rear with Achish.

[3]"Who are these Hebrews?" the Philistine commanders asked.

"That's David," Achish told them, "the servant of Israel's King Saul. He's been with me a year or so now. I haven't found any-thing wrong with him from the day he defected until now."

[4]But the Philistine commanders were angry with Achish. "Send the man home!" they told Achish. "He can go back to the place you gave him, but he won't go with us into battle. Couldn't he turn against us in the middle of the fight? How better to please his former master than by taking the heads of our soldiers? [5]After all, this is the same David people sing about in their dances,

'Saul has killed his thousands,
  but David has killed
    his tens of thousands!'"

[6]So Achish summoned David and told him, "As surely as the LORD lives, you are an upstanding individual. I would very much like you to serve with me in the army because I haven't found anything wrong with you from the day you came to me until now. But the rulers don't approve of you. [7]So go back home now, and go in peace. Don't do anything to upset the Philistine rulers."

[8]"But what have I done?" David asked Achish. "What wrong have you found in me, your servant, from the day I came to you until now? Why shouldn't I go and fight the enemies of my master the king?"

[9]"I agree," Achish answered David. "I think you're as good as one of God's own messengers. Despite that, the Philistine commanders have ordered, 'He can't go into battle with us.' [10]So get up early in the morning, both you and your master's servants who came with you, and return to the place I gave you. Don't worry about this negative report, because you've done well before me.[y] Now get up early in the morning and leave as soon as it is light."

[11]So David and his soldiers got up early in the morning to go back to Philistine territory, but the Philistines went up to Jezreel.

The Amalekite raid on Ziklag

30 Three days later, David and his soldiers reached Ziklag. The Amalekites had raided the arid southern plain

[u]LXX *is with your neighbor;* cf 15:28; 28:17   [v]LXX; MT *The LORD himself has done just what*   [w]LXX *you and your sons will fall in battle.*   [x]Or *sacrificed it*   [y]LXX; MT lacks *and return to the place . . . done well before me.*

and Ziklag. They had attacked Ziklag and burned it down, [2] taking the women and everyone in the city prisoner, whether young or old.[z] They hadn't killed anyone but carried them off and went on their way. [3] When David and his soldiers got to the town and found it burned down, and their wives, their sons, and their daughters taken prisoner, [4] David and the troops with him broke into tears and cried until they could cry no more. [5] David's two wives had been captured as well: Ahinoam from Jezreel and Abigail, Nabal's widow from Carmel.

[6] David was in deep trouble because the troops were talking about stoning him. Each of the soldiers was deeply distressed about their sons and daughters. But David found strength in the LORD his God. [7] David said to the priest Abiathar, Ahimelech's son, "Bring the priestly vest[a] to me." So Abiathar brought it to David.

[8] Then David asked the LORD, "Should I go after this raiding party? Will I catch them?"

"Yes, go after them!" God answered. "You will definitely catch them and will succeed in the rescue!"

[9] So David set off with six hundred men. They came to the Besor ravine, where some stayed behind. [10] David and four hundred men continued the pursuit, while two hundred men stayed there, too exhausted to cross the Besor ravine.

[11] They found an Egyptian in the countryside and brought him to David. They gave him bread, and he ate, and they gave him water to drink. [12] They also gave him a piece of fig cake and two raisin cakes. He ate and regained his strength because he hadn't eaten any food or drunk any water for three days and nights.

[13] Then David asked him, "Whose slave are you? Where do you come from?"

"I'm an Egyptian servant boy," he said, "and the slave of an Amalekite. My master abandoned me when I got sick three days ago. [14] We had raided the arid southern plain belonging to the Cherethites, the territory belonging to Judah, and the southern plain of Caleb. We also burned Ziklag down."

[15] "Can you guide me to this raiding party?" David asked him.

"Make a pledge to me by God that you won't kill me or hand me over to my master," the boy said, "and I will guide you to the raiding party."

[16] So the boy led David to them, and he found them scattered all over the countryside, eating, drinking, and celebrating over the large amount of plunder they had taken from Philistine and Judean territory.

[17] David attacked them from twilight until evening of the next day. He killed them all.[b] No one escaped except four hundred young men who got on camels and fled. [18] David rescued everything that the Amalekites had taken, including his own two wives. [19] Nothing was missing from the plunder or anything that they had taken, neither old nor young, son nor daughter. David brought everything back. [20] David also captured all the sheep and cattle, which were driven in front of the other livestock. The troops said, "This is David's plunder!"

[21] David reached the two hundred men who were too exhausted to follow him and had stayed behind at the Besor ravine. They came out to greet him and the troops who were with him. When David approached them, he asked how they were doing. [22] But then all the evil and despicable individuals who had accompanied David said, "We won't share any of the plunder we rescued with them because they didn't go with us. Each of them can take his wife and children and go—but that's it."

[23] "Brothers!" David said. "Don't act that way with the things the LORD has given us. He has protected us and handed over to us the raiding party that had attacked us. [24] How could anyone agree with you on this plan? The share of those who went into battle and the share of those who stayed with the supplies will be divided equally." [25] So from that day forward, David made that a regulation and a law in Israel, which remains in place even now.

---

[z] LXX; MT lacks *and everyone in the city*.   [a] Heb *ephod*   [b] LXX; MT lacks *He killed them all*.

²⁶When David returned to Ziklag, he sent some of the plunder to the elders of Judah and to his friends. "Here is a gift for you from the plunder of the LORD's enemies," he said. ²⁷It went to those in Bethel, Ramoth of the arid southern plain, Jattir, ²⁸Aroer,ᶜ Siphmoth, Eshtemoa, ²⁹Racal, the towns of the Jerahmeelites, the towns of the Kenites, ³⁰Hormah, Bor-ashan, Athach, ³¹Hebron, and all the places where David and his soldiers had spent time.

Saul dies in the battle of Gilboa

31 When the Philistines attacked the Israelites, the Israelites ran away from the Philistines, and many fell dead on Mount Gilboa. ²The Philistines overtook Saul and his sons, and they killed his sons Jonathan, Abinadab, and Malchishua. ³The battle was fierce around Saul. When the archers located him, they wounded him badly.ᵈ

⁴Saul said to his armor-bearer, "Draw your sword and kill me with it! Otherwise, these uncircumcised men will come and kill me or torture me." But his armor-bearer refused because he was terrified. So Saul took the sword and impaled himself on it. ⁵When the armor-bearer saw that Saul was dead, he also impaled himself on his sword and died with Saul. ⁶So Saul, his three sons, his armor-bearer, and all his soldiers died together that day.

⁷When the Israelites across the valley and across the Jordan learned that the Israelite army had fled and that Saul and his sons were dead, they abandoned their towns and fled. So the Philistines came and occupied the towns.

⁸The next day, when the Philistines came to strip the dead, they found Saul and his three sons lying dead on Mount Gilboa. ⁹They cut off Saul's head and stripped off his armor, and then sent word throughout Philistine territory, carrying the good news to their gods' temples and to their people. ¹⁰They put Saul's armor in the temple of Astarte, and hung his body on the wall of Beth-shan.

¹¹But when all the people of Jabesh-gilead heard what the Philistines had done to Saul, ¹²the bravest of their men set out, traveled all night long, and took the bodies of Saul and his sons off the wall of Beth-shan. Then they went back to Jabesh, where they burned them. ¹³Then they took their bones and buried them under the tamarisk tree at Jabesh, and they fasted seven days.

ᶜLXX *Ararah* ᵈCorrection; LXX *wounded in the belly*

MOUNT GILBOA

Mount Gilboa is a ridge of limestone hills in the northern reaches of the central highlands extending into the eastern Jezreel Valley, rising 1,600 ft. above sea level, and is south of the Moreh hill. The main OT narrative concerning Mount Gilboa relates the battle between Israel and the Philistines who were encamped in the Jezreel Valley. Israel gathered on Mount Gilboa. Saul was defeated and his three sons died with him at the hands of the Philistines (1 Sam 28:1-4; 31:1-13). Saul's headless body was hung on the walls of Beth-shan about seven mi. away. David's lament (2 Sam 1:17-27, esp. 21) memorializes the death of Saul and Jonathan.

2 SAMUEL

See the introduction to 1 Samuel for information about authorship, place in the Bible, and major themes of 1 and 2 Samuel.

CONTENT OF 2 SAMUEL

Second Samuel is an account of David's reign, first over the southern tribes of Judah, then over the combined southern and northern tribes. David made his reputation as a great warrior by conquering not only the Philistines, but also the Syrians, the Amorites, the Amalekites, and many other neighboring tribes. At the height of his career, David controlled most of the territories from Syria (Aram) in the north to Elath in the south, and all the lands west and just east of the Jordan River. At no other time in her history would Israel's empire reach such broad limits!

But, for all David's accomplishments as a king and as a warrior, he seemed unable to manage his personal and domestic life with the same expertise. His adulterous affair with Bathsheba brought suffering and death to innocent persons. His mishandling of his sons Amnon and Absalom led to rebellion and to his temporary abdication of his royal throne in Jerusalem.

Even though David did quell Absalom's rebellion and regain his throne, the latter years of his reign seethed with internal political conflicts. He faced the difficult question of succession to his throne as well as subversive mistrust from many factions within the northern tribes. Second Samuel concludes with an act of contrition, when David erects an altar to God for having sinned in the taking of a census. This final act, however, connects the books of 1 and 2 Samuel to the book of 1 Kings, because the site of David's altar becomes the very site upon which King Solomon builds the famous temple.

The stories of the Hebrew monarchy continue in 1 and 2 Kings, where Solomon succeeds David as king of Israel. But the exciting stories of Samuel, Saul, and David and the early days of the Israelite monarchy come to an end. The books of 1 and 2 Samuel are unmatched in the Old Testament for their exciting action and for the pathos of real human experiences. These exciting days of early Israelite monarchy, energized by the personalities of Samuel, Saul, and David, are what 1 and 2 Samuel are all about.

2 SAMUEL

David learns of Saul's death

1 After Saul's death, when David had returned from defeating the Amalekites, he stayed in Ziklag two days. ²On the third day, a man showed up from Saul's camp with his clothes torn and dirt on his head. When he reached David, he fell to the ground, bowing low out of respect.

³"Where have you come from?" David asked him.

"I've escaped from the Israelite army!" he answered.

⁴"What's the report?" David asked him. "Tell me!"

The man answered, "The troops fled from the battle! Many of the soldiers have fallen and died. What's more, Saul and his son Jonathan have also died!"

⁵"How do you know," David asked the young man who brought the news, "that Saul and his son Jonathan are dead?"

⁶The young man who brought the news replied, "I just happened to be on Mount Gilboa and Saul was there, leaning on his spear, with chariots and horsemen closing in on him. ⁷He turned around and saw me, then he called to me. 'Yes, sir,' I answered. ⁸'Who are you?' he asked, and I told him, 'I'm an Amalekite.' ⁹He said to me, 'Please come over here and kill me, because convulsions have come over me but I'm still alive.'ᵃ ¹⁰So I went over to him and killed him, because I knew he couldn't survive after being wounded like that. I took the crown that was on his head and the bracelet that was on his arm, and I've brought them here to you, my master."

¹¹Then David grabbed his clothes and ripped them—and all his soldiers did the same. ¹²They mourned and cried and fasted until evening for Saul, his son Jonathan, the LORD's army, and the whole house of Israel, because they had died by the sword.

¹³"Where are you from?" David asked the young man who brought him the news.

"I'm the son of an immigrant," he answered. "An Amalekite."

¹⁴Then David said to him, "How is it that you weren't afraid to raise your hand and destroy the LORD's anointed?" ¹⁵Then David called for one of the young servants. "Come here!" he said. "Strike him down!" So the servant struck the Amalekite down, and he died.

¹⁶"Your blood is on your own head," David said to the Amalekite, "because your own mouth testified against you when you admitted, 'I killed the LORD's anointed.'"

David mourns Saul and Jonathan

¹⁷Then David sang this funeral songᵇ for Saul and his son Jonathan. ¹⁸David ordered everyone in Judah to learn the Song of the Bow.ᶜ (In fact, it is written in the scroll from Jashar.)

¹⁹ Oh, no, Israel! Your princeᵈ lies dead
    on your heights.ᵉ
  Look how the mighty warriors
    have fallen!
²⁰ Don't talk about it in Gath;
    don't bring news of it
    to Ashkelon's streets,
    or else the Philistines' daughters
    will rejoice;
  the daughters of the uncircumcised
    will celebrate.
²¹ You hills of Gilboa!
  Let there be no dew or rain on you,
    and no fields yielding grain offerings.ᶠ
  Because it was there
    that the mighty warrior'sᵍ shield
    was defiled—
    the shield of Saul!—
    never again anointed with oil.
²² Jonathan's bow never wavered
    from the blood of the slain,
    from the gore of the warriors.
    Never did Saul's sword return empty.

²³ Saul and Jonathan! So well loved,
    so dearly cherished!

ᵃSyr, Tg; Heb uncertain ᵇOr *lament* ᶜHeb lacks *Song.* ᵈOr *gazelle* or *splendor* or *splendid one* ᵉCorrection
ᶠHeb uncertain, perhaps *bountiful fields*; alternatively, with LXX ᴸ, *fields of death*, or with correction *and no springs from the deep* ᵍOr *warriors'* (plural)

In their lives and in their deaths
　　they were never separated.
They were faster than eagles,
　　stronger than lions!
24 Daughters of Israel, weep over Saul!
　　He dressed you in crimson with jewels;
　　he decorated your clothes
　　　　with gold jewelry.
25 Look how the mighty warriors
　　have fallen in the midst of battle!
　　Jonathan lies dead on your heights.
26 I grieve for you, my brother Jonathan!
　　You were so dear to me!
　　Your love was more amazing to me[h]
　　　　than the love of women.
27 Look how the mighty warriors
　　have fallen!
　　Look how the weapons of war
　　　　have been destroyed!

David made king in Hebron

2 Some time later, David questioned the LORD, "Should I go to one of the towns in Judah?"

"Yes, go," the LORD told him.

"Which one should I go to?" David asked.

"To Hebron," the LORD replied.

2 So David went there, along with his two wives: Ahinoam from Jezreel and Abigail, Nabal's widow, from Carmel. 3 David also took the soldiers who were with him, each with his family, and they lived in the towns around Hebron. 4 Then the people of Judah came to Hebron and anointed David king over the house of Judah.

When David was informed that it was the people of Jabesh-gilead who had buried Saul, 5 he sent messengers to the people of Jabesh-gilead. "The LORD bless you," he said to them, "for doing this loyal deed for your master Saul by burying him. 6 May the LORD now show you loyal love and faithfulness. I myself will also reward you because you did this. 7 So now take courage and be brave—yes, your master Saul is dead, but the house of Judah has anointed me king over them."

Israel's King Ishbosheth

8 Meanwhile, Abner, Ner's son, the commander of Saul's army, had taken Ishbosheth,[i] Saul's son, and brought him over to Mahanaim. 9 There he made him king over Gilead, the Geshurites,[j] Jezreel, Ephraim, and Benjamin—over all Israel. 10 Saul's son Ishbosheth was 40 years old when he became king over Israel, and he ruled for two years.

[h] Or your love (or care; cf 1 Sam 18:1, 3; 20:17) for me was more amazing [i] Ishbosheth means man of shame; shame (Heb bosheth) may be a deliberate alteration from Baal (cf Esh-baal, man of Baal in 1 Chron 8:33; 9:39; see also 2 Sam 4:4); one manuscript of LXX [L] reads Ishbaal. [j] Syr, Vulg; MT Ashurites or Assyrians; cf Tg, LXX [L], Judg 1:32 Asherites

ISHBOSHETH

The son of Saul who succeeded him as king over Israel (2 Sam 2:8). It is unlikely that Ishbosheth was 40 years old (2 Sam 2:10). Abner's placement of Ishbosheth ("man of shame") on the throne suggests that he was a minor. He was proclaimed king over "Gilead, the Geshurites, Jezreel, Ephraim, and Benjamin—over all Israel" (2 Sam 2:9), but the coronation took place in Transjordan (Mahanaim) because the Philistine's actually controlled those places. Further pressure by David's treaty with Geshur to his north (2 Sam 3:3) and overtures to Saul loyalists in Jabesh-gilead (2 Sam 2:4b-7) compelled Ishbosheth into a losing war with David, ended by Abner's assassination and then his own (recounted apologetically in 2 Sam 3–4). Ishbosheth's two-year reign during David's seven and one-half years in Hebron (2 Sam 2:11) may indicate that David became king over Judah while Saul was living.

The house of Judah, however, followed David. [11]The amount of time David ruled in Hebron over the house of Judah totaled seven and a half years.

Conflict between Judah and Israel

[12]Abner, Ner's son, along with the soldiers of Ishbosheth, Saul's son, left Mahanaim to go to Gibeon. [13]Joab, Zeruiah's son, and David's soldiers also came out and confronted them at the pool of Gibeon. One group sat on one side of the pool; the other sat on the opposite side of the pool. [14]Abner said to Joab, "Let's have the young men fight in a contest[k] before us."

"All right," Joab said, "let's do it." [15]So the men came forward and were counted as they passed by: twelve for Benjamin and Ishbosheth, Saul's son; and twelve of David's soldiers. [16]Each man grabbed his opponent by the head and stuck[l] his sword into his opponent's side so that they both fell dead together. That's why that place is called The Field of Daggers,[m] which is located in Gibeon. [17]A fierce battle took place that day, and Abner and the Israelite troops were defeated by David's soldiers.

[18]Now Zeruiah's three sons were present at the battle: Joab, Abishai, and Asahel. Asahel was as fast as a gazelle in an open field. [19]Asahel went after Abner, staying completely focused in his pursuit of Abner. [20]Abner looked behind him and said, "Is that you, Asahel?"

"Yes, it's me," Asahel answered.

[21]"Break off your pursuit!" Abner told him. "Fight one of the young warriors and take his gear for yourself!" But Asahel wouldn't stop chasing him.

[22]So Abner repeated himself to Asahel: "Stop chasing me. Why should I kill you? How could I look your brother Joab in the face?" [23]But Asahel wouldn't turn back, so Abner hit him in the stomach with the back end of his spear. But the spear went through Asahel's back. He fell down and died right there.

Everyone who came to the place where Asahel had fallen and died just stood there, [24]but Joab and Abishai went after Abner. The sun was setting when they came to the hill of Ammah, which faces Giah on the road to the Gibeon wilderness. [25]The Benjaminites rallied behind Abner, forming a single unit. Then they took their positions on the top of a hill. [26]Abner yelled down to Joab, "Must the sword keep killing forever? Don't you realize that this will end bitterly? How long before you order the troops to stop chasing their brothers?"

[27]"As surely as God lives," Joab replied, "if you hadn't just said that, the soldiers would have continued after their brothers until morning." [28]Joab blew the trumpet,[n] and all the soldiers stopped. They didn't pursue Israel anymore, nor did they continue to fight.

[29]Abner and his men then marched all night through the wilderness, crossing the Jordan River and marching all morning[o] until they got to Mahanaim. [30]Joab, meanwhile, returned from pursuing Abner and assembled the troops. Nineteen of David's soldiers were counted missing in addition to Asahel. [31]But David's soldiers had defeated the Benjaminites, killing three hundred sixty of Abner's soldiers. [32]They took Asahel and buried him in his father's

---

[k]Or *come forward and play* or *compete*   [l]Heb lacks *stuck*.   [m]Heb *Helkath-hazzurim*   [n]Heb *shofar*   [o]Heb uncertain

JOAB

Joab was David's nephew and chief military officer. Second Samuel 2–3 is a comprehensive introduction to Joab, including not only his exceptional military prowess but also his hardline violent tendencies and his hold over David—all of which are significant as the story of David's rule unfolds.

tomb in Bethlehem. Then Joab and his men marched all night. When daylight came, they were in Hebron.

3 The war between Saul's house and David's house was long and drawn out. David kept getting stronger, while Saul's house kept getting weaker.

David's family

[2] David's sons were born in Hebron. His oldest son was Amnon, by Ahinoam from Jezreel; [3] the second was Chileab, by Abigail, Nabal's widow from Carmel; the third was Absalom, by Maacah,[P] who was the daughter of Geshur's King Talmai; [4] the fourth was Adonijah, by Haggith; the fifth was Shephatiah, by Abital; [5] and the sixth was Ithream, by David's wife Eglah. These are David's sons that were born in Hebron.

Joab kills Abner

[6] Throughout the war between Saul's house and David's house, Abner was gaining power in Saul's house. [7] Now Saul had a secondary wife named Rizpah, Aiah's daughter. Ishbosheth[q] said to Abner, "Why have you had sex with my father's secondary wife?"

[8] Abner got very angry over what Ishbosheth had said.

"Am I some sort of dog's head?"[r] Abner asked. "I've been nothing but loyal to the house of your father Saul and to his broth-

ers and his friends. I haven't handed you over to David, but today you accuse me of doing something wrong with this woman. [9] May God deal harshly with me, Abner, and worse still if I don't do for David exactly what the LORD swore to him—[10] removing the kingdom from Saul's house and securing David's throne over Israel and over Judah, from Dan all the way to Beer-sheba!"

[11] Ishbosheth couldn't say a single word in reply to Abner because he was afraid of him.

[12] Abner sent messengers to represent him to David and to say, "Who will own the land?[s] Make a covenant with me, then I'll help bring all Israel over to your side."

[13] "Good!" David replied. "I will make a covenant with you, but on one condition: don't show yourself in my presence unless you bring Saul's daughter Michal when you come to see me."

[14] Then David sent messengers to Saul's son Ishbosheth. "Give me my wife Michal," he demanded. "I became engaged to her at the cost of one hundred Philistine foreskins."

[15] Ishbosheth then sent for Michal and took her from her husband Paltiel, Laish's son. [16] Her husband went with her all the way to Bahurim, crying as he followed her.

"Go home!" Abner told him. So he went home.

[17] Abner then sent word to Israel's elders. "You've wanted David to be your king for

[P] Or son of; also twice in 3:4   [q] Or he, supplied from 3:8; see note at 2:8 on Ishbosheth.   [r] LXX; MT adds that belongs to Judah.   [s] Heb uncertain; LXX lacks Who will own the land?

ABNER

Army commander under Saul (1 Sam 14:50) who brings David before the king (1 Sam 17:55-57). Abner even enjoys an esteemed place at Saul's table alongside David and the king's son Jonathan (1 Sam 20:25). He is also the king's bodyguard (1 Sam 26:13-25). Following the death of Saul on Mount Gilboa, Abner plays an instrumental role in elevating Ishbosheth as successor to the throne and establishing him at Mahanaim (2 Sam 2:8-9), far removed from David's territory in Hebron. After a rift develops between Abner and Ishbosheth (2 Sam 3:6-11), Abner promotes David's kingship. However, Joab kills Abner. The end of Abner signals the end of opposition to David's eventual kingship over Israel.

some time now," he said. [18] "It's time to act because the LORD has said about David: I will rescue my people Israel from the power of the Philistines and all their enemies through my servant David."

[19] Abner also spoke directly to the Benjaminites. He then went to inform David in person at Hebron regarding everything that all Israel and the house of Benjamin were willing to do.

[20] When Abner, along with twenty others, reached David at Hebron, David threw a celebration for Abner and his men. [21] Then Abner said to David, "Please let me get going so I can assemble all Israel for my master the king. Then they will make a covenant with you, and you will rule over everything your heart[t] desires." At that, David sent Abner off in peace.

[22] Right then, David's soldiers and Joab returned from a raid, bringing a great deal of loot with them. Abner was no longer with David in Hebron because David had sent him off in peace. [23] When Joab and all the troops with him returned, Joab was told that Abner, Ner's son, had come to the king and that David had sent him off in peace.

[24] Joab went to the king and asked, "What have you done? Abner came to you here! Why did you send him off? Now he's gotten away! [25] Don't you know the evil ways of Abner, Ner's son?[u] He came to trick you, to find out where you come and go, and to learn everything you do!"

[26] Joab left David and sent messengers after Abner. They brought him back from the well at Sirah, but David didn't know anything of this. [27] When Abner returned to Hebron, Joab took him aside next to[v] the gate to speak with him in private. But instead Joab stabbed Abner in the stomach, and he died for shedding the blood of Asahel, Joab's brother.

[28] When David heard about this later, he said, "I and my kingdom are forever innocent before the LORD concerning the shedding of the blood of Abner, Ner's son.

[29] May it fall upon the head of Joab and his entire family tree! May Joab's family never be without someone with a discharge or a skin disease,[w] someone who uses a crutch,[x] someone who dies by the sword, or someone who is hungry!"

[30] So that is how Joab and his brother Abishai murdered Abner, because he killed their brother Asahel in the battle at Gibeon.

[31] Then David ordered Joab and all the troops who were with him, "Tear your clothes and put on funeral clothes! Mourn for Abner!" King David himself walked behind the body. [32] They buried Abner in Hebron. The king wept loudly at Abner's grave. All the troops cried too. [33] Then the king sang this funeral song[y] for Abner:

"Should Abner have died like a fool dies?
[34] Your hands weren't bound,
   your feet weren't chained,
   but you have fallen
   like someone falls before the wicked."

Then the troops cried over Abner again. [35] Then all the soldiers came to urge David to eat something while it was still day, but David swore, "May God deal harshly with me and worse still if I eat bread or anything else before the sun goes down." [36] All the troops took notice of this and were pleased by it. Indeed, everything that the king did pleased them. [37] So on that day all the troops and all Israel knew that it wasn't the king's idea to kill Abner, Ner's son.

[38] The king told his soldiers, "Don't you know that a prince and a great man in Israel has fallen today? [39] And today, though I am the anointed king, I am weak. These men, Zeruiah's sons, are too strong for me.[z] May the LORD repay the one who does evil according to the evil they did!"

Ishbosheth murdered

4 When Ishbosheth,[a] Saul's son, heard that Abner had died in Hebron, he lost his courage,[b] and all Israel was alarmed. [2] Saul's son had two men who led the raiding parties—one was named Baanah and

---

[t] Or soul   [u] LXX; MT You know Abner, Ner's son.   [v] LXX; MT to the middle of   [w] Traditionally leprosy, a term used for several different skin diseases   [x] Or who holds a spindle   [y] Or lament   [z] Or more ruthless than me; DSS (4QSam[a]) lacks this clause.   [a] Heb lacks Ishbosheth; LXX, DSS (4QSam[a]) Mephibosheth; cf 4:4 and the note at 2 Sam 2:8.
[b] Or his hands grew weak

the other Rechab. Both were sons of Rimmon, a Benjaminite from Beeroth. (Beeroth was considered part of Benjamin. [3]The people of Beeroth had fled to Gittaim and even now live there as immigrants.)

[4]Now Saul's son Jonathan had a boy whose feet were crippled. He was only 5 years old when the news about Saul and Jonathan came from Jezreel, and so his nurse snatched him up and fled. But as she hurried to get away, he fell and was injured. His name was Mephibosheth.[c]

[5]Rechab and Baanah, the sons of Rimmon from Beeroth, set out and reached Ishbosheth's house at the heat of the day, right when he was lying down, taking an afternoon rest. [6]They went straight into his house, as if getting wheat,[d] and they stabbed him in the stomach. Then Rechab and his brother Baanah escaped. [7]They had entered the house while Ishbosheth was lying on the bed in his bedroom. After they stabbed him and killed him, they cut off his head, took it, and traveled all night through the wilderness.

[8]They brought Ishbosheth's head to David at Hebron. "Here is the head of Ishbosheth," they told the king, "the son of Saul your enemy, who wanted you dead. Today the LORD has avenged our master[e] the king on Saul and his descendants."

[9]David answered Rechab and his brother Baanah, the sons of Rimmon from Beeroth, "As surely as the LORD lives, who has rescued me[f] from all kinds of trouble," he told them, [10]"when someone told me Saul was dead back in Ziklag, thinking he was bringing good news, I grabbed him and killed him. That was the reward I gave him for his news! [11]What do you think I'll do when evil people kill a righteous person in his own house on his own bed? Why shouldn't I demand his blood from your hands and rid the earth of you both?"

[12]So David gave the order to his servants, and they killed Rechab and Baanah, cutting off their hands and feet and hanging them up by the pool at Hebron. But they took Ishbosheth's head and buried it in the grave of Abner at Hebron.

David becomes king of Israel and Judah

5 All the Israelite tribes came to David at Hebron and said, "Listen: We are your very own flesh and bone. [2]In the past, when Saul ruled over us, you were the one who led Israel out to war and back. What's more, the LORD told you, You will shepherd my people Israel, and you will be Israel's leader.

[3]So all the Israelite elders came to the king at Hebron. King David made a covenant with them at Hebron before the LORD, and they anointed David king over Israel.

[4]David was 30 years old when he became king, and he ruled for forty years. [5]He ruled over Judah for seven and a half years in Hebron. He ruled thirty-three years over all Israel and Judah in Jerusalem.

Jerusalem is captured

[6]The king and his troops marched on Jerusalem against the Jebusites, who inhabited the territory. The Jebusites said to David, "You'll never get us in here! Even the blind and the lame will beat you back!" "David will never enter here," they said to each other.[g] [7]But David did capture the fortress of Zion—which became David's City. [8]"On that day," David said, "whoever attacks the Jebusites should strike the windpipe because David hates the lame and the blind."[h] That is why people say, "The blind and the lame will not enter the temple."[i] [9]David occupied the fortress, so it was renamed David's City. David built a city around it from the earthen terraces[j] inward.[k] [10]David grew increasingly powerful, and the LORD of heavenly forces was with him.

[11]Tyre's King Hiram sent messengers to David with cedar logs, bricklayers, and carpenters to build David a palace. [12]Then David knew that the LORD had established him as king over Israel, and that his king-

---

[c]Called *Merib-baal* in 1 Chron 8:34; 9:40. See the note at 2 Sam 2:8. [d]Heb uncertain [e]Or *my master* [f]Or *my life* or *my soul* [g]Or *they thought*; Heb lacks *to each other.* [h]Or *take the water shaft against the lame and the blind who hate David;* Heb uncertain [i]Or *palace* [j]Heb *Millo* [k]DSS (4QSam[a]); MT lacks *city.*

ship was held in great honor for the sake of his people Israel. [13]After he left Hebron, David married more secondary wives in Jerusalem and fathered more sons and daughters. [14]The names of his children in Jerusalem were as follows: Shammua, Shobab, Nathan, Solomon, [15]Ibhar, Elishua, Nepheg, Japhia, [16]Elishama, Eliada, and Eliphelet.

David defeats the Philistines

[17]When the Philistines heard that David had been anointed king over Israel, they all marched up to find him, but David heard of it and went down to the fortress. [18]The Philistines arrived and spread out over the Rephaim Valley. [19]David asked the LORD, "Should I attack the Philistines? Will you hand them over to me?"

"Attack them," the LORD replied, "because I will definitely hand the Philistines over to you."

[20]So David arrived at Baal-perazim and defeated the Philistines there. He said, "The LORD has burst out against my enemies, the way water bursts out!" That is why that place is called Baal-perazim.[l] [21]The Philistines left their divine images behind, and David and his men carried them off.

[22]Once again the Philistines came up and spread out across the Rephaim Valley. [23]When David asked the LORD, God replied, "Don't attack them directly. Circle around behind them and come at them from in front of the balsam trees. [24]As soon as you hear the sound of marching in the tops of the trees, then attack, for God has attacked in front of you to defeat the Philistine army." [25]David followed God's orders exactly, and they defeated the Philistine army from Gibeon all the way to Gezer.

God's chest is brought to Jerusalem

6 Once again David assembled the select warriors of Israel, thirty thousand strong. [2]David and all the troops who were with him set out for Baalah, which is Kiriath-jearim of Judah,[m] to bring God's chest up from there—the chest that is called by the name[n] of the LORD of heavenly forces, who sits enthroned on the winged creatures. [3]They loaded God's chest on a new cart and carried it from Abinadab's house, which was on the hill. Uzzah and Ahio, Abinadab's sons, were driving the new cart. [4o]Uzzah was beside God's chest while Ahio was walking in front of it. [5]Meanwhile, David and the entire house of Israel celebrated in the LORD's presence with all their strength, with songs,[p] zithers, harps, tambourines, rattles, and cymbals.

[6]When they approached Nacon's threshing floor, Uzzah reached out to God's chest and grabbed it because the oxen had

---

[l]Baal-perazim means *the lord* (Heb *baal*) *of breaking out;* see note at 2 Sam 6:8. [m]DSS (4QSamª), 1 Chron 13:6; MT *from Baale-judah* [n]MT repeats *name,* but 1 Chron 13:6 omits one of these and LXX reads the first as *there.* [o]LXX, DSS (4QSamª), 1 Chron 13:7; MT repeats *they carried it from the house of Abinadab on the hill;* Uzzah has dropped out and must be restored. [p]LXX, DSS (4QSamª), 1 Chron 13:8; MT *with all sorts of pine instruments*

HEBRON

A geopolitically important city situated at the central high point of the Judean highlands (elevation 3,050 ft.). Hebron is one of the oldest continually occupied cities on earth. Roads ascending from the coastal plain to the west meet near Hebron with the main route connecting Jerusalem, 19 mi. to the north, and Beer-sheba, 23 mi. to the southwest. The city is associated with a number of well-known biblical figures. Abraham, Sarah, Isaac, Rebecca, Jacob, Leah, and Rachel all sojourned there; Caleb conquered and settled in Hebron; and David chose Hebron as his first royal city.

stumbled.[q] [7]The LORD became angry at Uzzah, and God struck him there because of his mistake,[r] and he died there next to God's chest. [8]Then David got angry because the LORD's anger lashed out against Uzzah, and so that place is called Perez-uzzah today.[s]

[9]David was frightened by the LORD that day. "How will I ever bring the LORD's chest to me?" he asked. [10]So David didn't take the chest away with him to David's City. Instead, he had it put in the house of Obed-edom, who was from Gath. [11]The LORD's chest stayed with Obed-edom's household in Gath for three months, and the LORD blessed Obed-edom's household and all that he had.

[12]King David was told, "The LORD has blessed Obed-edom's family and everything he has because of God's chest being there."[t] So David went and brought God's chest up from Obed-edom's house to David's City with celebration. [13]Whenever those bearing the chest advanced six steps, David sacrificed an ox and a fatling calf. [14]David, dressed in a linen priestly vest,[u] danced with all his strength before the LORD. [15]This is how David and the entire house of Israel brought up the LORD's chest with shouts and trumpet blasts.

[16]As the LORD's chest entered David's City, Saul's daughter Michal was watching from a window. She saw King David jumping and dancing before the LORD, and she lost all respect for him.[v]

[17]The LORD's chest was brought in and put in its place inside the tent that David had pitched for it. Then David offered entirely burned offerings in the LORD's presence in addition to well-being sacrifices. [18]When David finished offering the entirely burned offerings and the well-being sacrifices, he blessed the people in the name of the LORD of heavenly forces. [19]He distributed food among all the people of Israel— to the whole crowd, male and female—each receiving a loaf of bread, a date cake, and a raisin cake. Then all the people went back to their homes.

[20]David went home to bless his household, but Saul's daughter Michal came out to meet him. "How did Israel's king honor himself today?" she said. "By exposing himself in plain view of the female servants of his subjects like any indecent person would!"

[21]David replied to Michal, "I was celebrating before the LORD, who chose me over your father and his entire family, and who appointed me leader over the LORD's people, over Israel—and I will celebrate before the LORD again! [22]I may humiliate myself even more, and I may be humbled in my own eyes, but I will be honored by the female servants you are talking about!"

[23]Michal, Saul's daughter, had no children to the day she died.

God's promise to David

7When the king was settled in his palace,[w] and the LORD had given him rest from all his surrounding enemies, [2]the king said to the prophet Nathan, "Look! I'm living in a cedar palace, but God's chest is housed in a tent!"[x]

[3]Nathan said to the king, "Go ahead and do whatever you are thinking, because the LORD is with you."

[4]But that very night the LORD's word came to Nathan: [5]Go to my servant David and tell him: This is what the LORD says: You are not the one to build the temple for me to live in. [6]In fact, I haven't lived in a temple from the day I brought Israel out of Egypt until now. Instead, I have been traveling around in a tent and in a dwelling. [7]Throughout my traveling around with the Israelites, did I ever ask any of Israel's tribal leaders I appointed to shepherd my people: Why haven't you built me a cedar temple?

[8]So then, say this to my servant David: This is what the LORD of heavenly forces says: I took you from the pasture, from following the flock, to be leader over my

[q]Heb uncertain [r]Heb uncertain; LXX lacks this phrase; cf Targ, Syr, 1 Chron 13:10 *because he had placed his hand on the chest.* [s]*Perez-uzzah* means *Uzzah-outbreak;* cf 2 Sam 5:20. [t]Heb lacks *being there.* [u]Heb *ephod* [v]Or *despised him for it* [w]Or *house;* the same Heb word (*beth*) appears with different nuances (*house, temple, palace, dynasty, family*) in 7:2, 5, 6, 7, 11, 13, 16, 18, 19, 25-26, 27, 29. [x]Or *among curtains*

people Israel. [9]I've been with you wherever you've gone, and I've eliminated all your enemies before you. Now I will make your name great—like the name of the greatest people on earth. [10]I'm going to provide a place for my people Israel, and plant them so that they may live there and no longer be disturbed. Cruel people will no longer trouble them, as they had been earlier, [11]when I appointed leaders over my people Israel. And I will give you rest from all your enemies.

And the LORD declares to you that the LORD will make a dynasty for you. [12]When the time comes for you to die and you lie down with your ancestors, I will raise up your descendant—one of your very own children—to succeed you, and I will establish his kingdom. [13]He will build a temple for my name, and I will establish his royal throne forever. [14]I will be a father to him, and he will be a son to me. Whenever he does wrong, I will discipline him with a human rod, with blows from human beings. [15]But I will never take my faithful love away from him like I took it away from Saul, whom I set aside in favor of you. [16]Your dynasty and your kingdom will be secured forever before me.[y] Your throne will be established forever.

[17]Nathan reported all of these words and this entire vision to David.

David's prayer

[18]Then King David went and sat in the LORD's presence. He asked:

Who am I, LORD God, and of what significance is my family that you have brought me this far? [19]But even this was too small in your eyes, LORD God! Now you have also spoken about your servant's dynasty in the future and the generation to come,[z] LORD God!

[20]What more can David say to you? You know your servant, LORD God. [21]For the sake of your word and according to your own will, you have done this great thing so that your servant would know it.

[22]That is why you are so great, LORD God! No one can compare to you, no god except you, just as we have always heard with our own ears. [23]And who can compare to your people Israel? They are the one nation on earth that God redeemed as his own people, establishing his name by doing great and awesome things for them,[a] by driving out nations and their gods before your people, whom you redeemed from Egypt.[b] [24]You established your people Israel as your own people forever, and you, LORD, became their God.

[25]Now, LORD God, confirm forever the promise you have made about your servant and his dynasty. Do just as you have promised [26]so that your name will be great forever when people say, "The LORD of heavenly forces is Israel's God!" May your servant David's household be established before you, [27]because you, LORD of heavenly forces, Israel's God, have revealed to your servant that you will build a dynasty for him. That is why your servant has found the courage to pray this prayer to you.

[28]LORD God, you are truly God! Your words are trustworthy, and you have promised this good thing to your servant. [29]So now willingly bless your servant's dynasty so that it might continue forever before you, because you, LORD God, have promised. Let your servant's dynasty be blessed forever by your blessing.

David's wars

8 Some time later, David defeated the Philistines and subdued them. David captured Metheg-ammah from Philistine control.

[2]David also defeated the Moabites and made them lie on the ground, measuring them with a rope. He measured two rope lengths for those who were to be killed and one rope length for those who were to be spared. The Moabites became David's subjects and brought him tribute.

[3]Next David defeated Zobah's King Hadadezer, Rehob's son, as Hadadezer was on

[y]LXX (cf 7:26, 29); MT *you*   [z]Correction; Heb uncertain *this is the law of humankind*   [a]Or *you* (plural)   [b]LXX, 1 Chron 17:21; MT *for your land before your people whom you redeemed for yourself from Egypt, the nations and their gods*

his way to put[c] his monument along the Euphrates River.[d] [4]David captured one thousand chariots, seven hundred charioteers,[e] and twenty thousand foot soldiers. He cut the hamstrings of all but one hundred of the chariot horses. [5]When the Arameans of Damascus came to help Zobah's King Hadadezer, David killed twenty-two thousand of them. [6]David set up forts among the Arameans of Damascus. And the Arameans became David's subjects and brought him tribute. The LORD gave David victory wherever he went. [7]David took the gold shields carried by Hadadezer's servants and brought them to Jerusalem. [8]King David also took a large amount of bronze from Tebah[f] and Berothai, towns that belonged to Hadadezer.

[9]When Hamath's King Toi heard that David had defeated the entire army of Hadadezer, [10]he sent his son Joram to King David to wish him well and congratulate him on his battle and defeat of Hadadezer, because Toi was an enemy of Hadadezer. Joram brought silver, gold, and bronze objects with him. [11]King David dedicated these to the LORD, along with the silver and gold he had dedicated from all the nations that he had subdued: [12]Edom, Moab, the Ammonites, the Philistines, and Amalek, including the plunder of Zobah's King Hadadezer, Rehob's son.

[13]So David made a name for himself.[g] When he returned, he killed eighteen thousand Edomites[h] in the Salt Valley. [14]He set up forts in Edom,[i] and all the Edomites became David's subjects. The LORD gave David victory wherever he went.

David's administration

[15]David ruled over all Israel and maintained justice and righteousness for all his people. [16]Zeruiah's son Joab was in command of the army; Ahilud's son Jehoshaphat was recorder; [17]Ahitub's son Zadok and Ahimelech's son[j] Abiathar were priests; Seraiah was secretary; [18]Jehoiada's son Benaiah was in command of[k] the Cherethites and the Pelethites; and David's sons were priests.

David and Mephibosheth

9 David asked, "Is there anyone from Saul's family still alive that I could show faithful love for Jonathan's sake?" [2]There was a servant from Saul's household named Ziba, and he was summoned before David.

"Are you Ziba?" the king asked him.

"At your service!" he answered.

[3]The king asked, "Is there anyone left from Saul's family that I could show God's kindness to?"

"Yes," Ziba said to the king, "one of Jonathan's sons, whose feet are crippled."

[4]"Where is he?" the king asked.

"He is at the house of Ammiel's son Machir at Lo-debar," Ziba told the king.

[5]So King David had him brought from the house of Ammiel's son Machir at Lo-debar. [6]Mephibosheth, Jonathan's son and Saul's grandson, came to David, and he fell to the ground, bowing low out of respect.

"Mephibosheth?" David said.

"Yes," he replied. "I am at your service!"

[7]"Don't be afraid," David told him, "because I will certainly show you faithful love for the sake of your father Jonathan. I will restore to you all the fields of your grandfather Saul, and you will eat at my table always."

[8]Mephibosheth bowed low out of respect and said, "Who am I, your servant, that you should care about a dead dog like me?"

[9]Then David summoned Saul's servant Ziba and said to him, "I have given your master's grandson everything belonging to Saul and his family. [10]You will work the land for him—you, your sons, and your servants—and you will bring food into your master's house for them to eat.[l] But

---

[c]Or to restore [d]DSS(4QSam[a]), 1 Chron 18:3 [e]LXX, DSS(4QSam[a]), 1 Chron 18:4; MT seventeen hundred chariots [f]Some LXX manuscripts and 1 Chron 18:8; MT Betah [g]Or built a monument [h]LXX; MT he returned from killing eighteen thousand Arameans [i]Cf 1 Chron 18:13; MT repeats in all Edom he set up forts. [j]MT Abiathar's son Ahimelech; cf 1 Sam 22:20; 23:6; 30:7; 2 Sam 20:25 [k]Syr, Tg, Vulg, 1 Chron 18:17; MT lacks in command of. [l]LXX[L]; MT You will bring food for your master's son and he will eat it.

Mephibosheth, your master's grandson, will always be at my table." (Now Ziba had fifteen sons and twenty servants.)

[11]Then Ziba said to the king, "Your servant will do whatever my master the king commands."

So Mephibosheth ate at David's[m] table, like one of the king's own sons. [12]Mephibosheth had a young son named Mica. All who lived in Ziba's household became Mephibosheth's servants. [13]Mephibosheth lived in Jerusalem, because he always ate at the king's table. He was crippled in both feet.

War with the Ammonites and Arameans

10 Some time later, the king of the Ammonites died, and his son Hanun succeeded him as king. [2]David said, "I'll be loyal to Nahash's son Hanun, just as his father was loyal to me." So David sent his servants with condolences concerning Hanun's father.

But when David's servants arrived in Ammonite territory, [3]the Ammonite officials asked their master Hanun, "Do you really believe David is honoring your father because he has sent you condolences? Of course not! David has sent his servants to you to search the city, spy it out, and overthrow it." [4]So Hanun seized David's servants and shaved off their beards,[n] cut off half their garments, from their buttocks down, and sent them off.

[5]When this was reported to David, he sent men to meet them because they were completely ashamed. The king said, "Stay in Jericho until your beards have grown. Then you can come back."

[6]When the Ammonites realized that they had offended David, they sent for and hired the Arameans of Beth-rehob and the Arameans of Zobah, totaling twenty thousand foot soldiers; the king of Maacah with one thousand soldiers; and twelve thousand soldiers from Tob. [7]When David heard this, he sent Joab with the entire army of warriors. [8]The Ammonites marched out and formed a battle line at the entrance to the city. The Arameans of Zobah and Rehob

and the soldiers from Tob and Maacah remained in the countryside.

[9]When Joab saw that the battle would be fought on two fronts, he chose some of Israel's finest warriors and deployed them to meet the Arameans. [10]The rest of the army Joab placed under the command of his brother Abishai. When they took up their positions to meet the Ammonites, Joab said, [11]"If the Arameans prove too strong for me, you must help me, and if the Ammonites prove too strong for you, I'll help you. [12]Be brave! We must be courageous for the sake of our people and the cities of our God. The LORD will do what is good in his eyes."

[13]When Joab and the troops who were with him advanced into battle against the Arameans, they fled from him. [14]When the Ammonites saw that the Arameans had fled, they also fled from Abishai and retreated to the city. Then Joab returned from fighting the Ammonites and went to Jerusalem.

[15]The Arameans saw that they had been defeated by Israel, so they regrouped. [16]Hadadezer sent for Arameans from beyond the Euphrates River. They came to Helam with Shobach leading them as commander of Hadadezer's army. [17]When this was reported to David he gathered all Israel, crossed the Jordan, and went to Helam. The Arameans formed battle lines against David and fought with him. [18]But the Arameans fled before Israel, and David destroyed seven hundred of their chariots and forty thousand horsemen. David wounded their army commander Shobach, and he died there. [19]When all the kings who served Hadadezer saw that they were defeated by Israel, they made peace with Israel and became their subjects. Never again would the Arameans come to the aid of the Ammonites.

David and Bathsheba

11 In the spring,[o] when kings[p] go off to war, David sent Joab, along with his servants and all the Israelites, and they

---

[m]LXX; MT *my*   [n]LXX; MT *half their beard*   [o]Or *At the turn of the year*   [p]LXX, Tg, Vulg; MT *messengers*

destroyed the Ammonites, attacking the city of Rabbah. But David remained in Jerusalem.

²One evening, David got up from his couch and was pacing back and forth on the roof of the palace. From the roof he saw a woman bathing; the woman was very beautiful. ³David sent someone and inquired about the woman. The report came back: "Isn't this Eliam's daughter Bathsheba, the wife of Uriah the Hittite?" ⁴So David sent messengers to get her. When she came to him, he had sex with her. (Now she had been purifying herself after her monthly period.) Then she returned home. ⁵The woman conceived and sent word to David.

"I'm pregnant," she said.

⁶Then David sent a message to Joab: "Send me Uriah the Hittite." So Joab sent Uriah to David. ⁷When Uriah came to him, David asked about the welfare of Joab and the army and how the battle was going. ⁸Then David told Uriah, "Go down to your house and wash your feet."

Uriah left the palace, and a gift from the king was sent after him. ⁹However, Uriah slept at the palace entrance with all his master's servants. He didn't go down to his own house. ¹⁰David was told, "Uriah didn't go down to his own house," so David asked Uriah, "Haven't you just returned from a journey? Why didn't you go home?"

¹¹"The chest and Israel and Judah are all living in tents," Uriah told David. "And my master Joab and my master's troops are camping in the open field. How^q could I go home and eat, drink, and have sex with my wife? I swear on your very life,^r I will not do that!"

¹²Then David told Uriah, "Stay here one more day. Tomorrow I'll send you back." So Uriah stayed in Jerusalem that day. The next day ¹³David called for him, and he ate and drank, and David got him drunk. In the evening Uriah went out to sleep in the same place, alongside his master's servants, but he did not go down to his own home.

¹⁴The next morning David wrote a letter to Joab and sent it with Uriah. ¹⁵He wrote in the letter, "Place Uriah at the front of the fiercest battle, and then pull back from him so that he will be struck down and die."

¹⁶So as Joab was attacking the city, he put Uriah in the place where he knew there were strong warriors. ¹⁷When the city's soldiers came out and attacked Joab, some of the people from David's army fell. Uriah the Hittite was also killed. ¹⁸Joab sent a complete report of the battle to David.

¹⁹"When you have finished reporting all the news of the battle to the king," Joab instructed the messenger, ²⁰"if the king gets angry and asks you, 'Why did you go so close to the city to fight? didn't you know they would shoot from the wall? ²¹Who killed Jerubbaal's son Abimelech?^s didn't a woman throw an upper millstone on top of him from the wall so that he died in Thebez? Why did you go so close to the wall?' then say: 'Your servant Uriah the Hittite is dead too.'"

---

^qLXX^L; MT lacks *How.*   ^rOr *I swear on your life and your soul's life;* cf LXX   ^sLXX, Syr, Judg 7:1; MT *Jerub-besheth*

BATHSHEBA

Wife of Uriah and later of David; mother of Solomon. Listed as "the wife of Uriah" in the genealogy in Matthew 1:6. Bathsheba is identified in 2 Samuel 11:3 as the daughter of Eliam (Ammiel in 1 Chron 3:5) and wife of Uriah the Hittite, who served in David's army. David commits adultery with Bathsheba in 2 Samuel 11. In 1 Kings 1–2 Bathsheba is vocal and active in events that secure Solomon's accession to the throne over his older half-brother Adonijah.

Bathsheba is among five women included in the Gospel of Matthew's genealogy of Jesus (Matt 1:6).

²²So the messenger set off, and when he arrived he reported to David everything Joab sent him to say.

²³"The men overpowered us," the messenger told David. "They came out against us in the open field, but we fought against them[t] up to the entrance of the city gate. ²⁴Archers shot down on your servants from the wall. Some of the king's servants died. And your servant Uriah the Hittite is dead too."

²⁵David said to the messenger, "Say this to Joab: 'Don't be upset about this because the sword is that way: taking the life of this person or that person. Continue attacking the city and destroy it!' Encourage Joab!"

²⁶When Uriah's wife heard that her husband Uriah was dead, she mourned for her husband. ²⁷After the time of mourning was over, David sent for her and brought her back to his house. She became his wife and bore him a son.

But what David had done was evil in the LORD's eyes.

Nathan pronounces God's judgment

12 So the LORD sent Nathan to David. When Nathan arrived he said, "There were two men in the same city, one rich, one poor. ²The rich man had a lot of sheep and cattle, ³but the poor man had nothing—just one small ewe lamb that he had bought. He raised that lamb, and it grew up with him and his children. It would eat from his food and drink from his cup—even sleep in his arms! It was like a daughter to him.

⁴"Now a traveler came to visit the rich man, but he wasn't willing to take anything from his own flock or herd to prepare for the guest who had arrived. Instead, he took the poor man's ewe lamb and prepared it for the visitor."

⁵David got very angry at the man, and he said to Nathan, "As surely as the LORD lives, the one who did this is demonic![u] ⁶He must restore the ewe lamb seven times over[v] because he did this and because he had no compassion."

⁷"You are that man!" Nathan told David. "This is what the LORD God of Israel says: I anointed you king over Israel and delivered you from Saul's power. ⁸I gave your master's house[w] to you, and gave his wives into your embrace. I gave you the house[x] of Israel and Judah. If that was too little, I would have given even more. ⁹Why have you despised the LORD's word by doing what is evil in his eyes? You have struck down Uriah the Hittite with the sword and taken his wife as your own. You used the Ammonites to kill him. ¹⁰Because of that, because you despised me and took the wife of Uriah the Hittite as your own, the sword will never leave your own house.

¹¹"This is what the LORD says: I am making trouble come against you from inside your own family. Before your very eyes I will take your wives away and give them to your friend, and he will have sex with your wives in broad daylight. ¹²You did what you did secretly, but I will do what I am doing before all Israel in the light of day."

¹³"I've sinned against the LORD!" David said to Nathan.

"The LORD has removed your sin," Nathan replied to David. "You won't die. ¹⁴However, because you have utterly disrespected the LORD[y] by doing this, the son born to you will definitely die." ¹⁵Then Nathan went home.

Bathsheba's child dies

The LORD struck the child that Uriah's wife had borne for David, and he became very sick. ¹⁶David begged God for the boy. He fasted and spent the night sleeping on the ground. ¹⁷The senior servants of his house approached[z] him to lift him up off the ground, but he refused, and he wouldn't eat with them either.

¹⁸On the seventh day, the child died. David's servants were afraid to tell him that the child had died. "David wouldn't listen to us when we talked to him while the child was still alive," they said. "How can we tell

[t]Or we were upon them [u]Or as good as dead; MT a son of death [v]LXX; MT fourfold (cf Exod 22:1) [w]Syr daughters [x]Syr daughters [y]MT the LORD's enemies—a euphemism or ancient scribal correction (cf note at 1 Sam 25:22) [z]LXX[L], DSS(4QSam[a]); MT stood over

him the child has died? He'll do something terrible!"

[19] But when David saw his servants whispering, he realized the child had died.

"Is the child dead?" David asked his servants.

"Yes," they said, "he is dead."

[20] Then David rose from the ground, bathed, anointed himself, and changed his clothes. He entered the LORD's house and bowed down. Then he entered his own house. He requested food, which was brought to him, and he ate.

[21] "Why are you acting this way?" his servants asked. "When the child was alive, you fasted and cried and kept watch,[a] but now that the child is dead, you get up and eat food!"

[22] David replied, "While the child was alive I fasted and wept because I thought, Who knows? The LORD may have mercy on me and let the child live. [23] But he is dead now. Why should I fast? Can I bring him back again? No. I am going where he is, but he won't come back to me."

[24] Then David comforted his wife Bathsheba. He went to her and had sex with her. She gave birth to a son and named him Solomon.[b] The LORD loved him [25] and sent word by the prophet Nathan to name him Jedidiah[c] because of the LORD's grace.[d]

Defeat of the Ammonites

[26] Meanwhile, Joab fought the Ammonites at Rabbah and captured the royal city. [27] Joab then sent messengers to David, saying, "I have fought against Rabbah and captured the city's water supply.[e] [28] So gather the rest of the troops, attack the city, and capture it. Otherwise, I will capture the city myself, and it will be named after me."

[29] So David gathered all the troops, marched to Rabbah, fought against it, and captured it. [30] David took Milcom's[f] crown off his head. It weighed one kikkar of gold and was set with a valuable stone. It was placed on David's head. The amount of loot David took from the city was huge. [31] He brought out the people who were in the city and put them to work making bricks.

[a]LXX[L], OL; MT lacks *kept watch*.   [b]Qere; Kethib *he* (David) *named*   [c]*Jedidiah* means *Loved by the LORD*.
[d]Heb uncertain; some Heb and LXX manuscripts *by the LORD's word*   [e]Heb uncertain   [f]LXX; MT *their king's crown*

NATHAN

1. Nathan, son of David (2 Sam 5:14; 1 Chron 14:4) and elder brother of Solomon (1 Chron 3:5), whose name appears in the "day of the Lord" pronouncement in Zechariah 12:12 and who is included in Jesus' genealogy in Luke 3:31.

2. In Samuel–Kings, Nathan the prophet has three major appearances. He is first introduced in 2 Samuel 7:2, without any background information or genealogy. Nathan's next appearance is 2 Samuel 12, where he delivers a severe rebuke after the Bathsheba affair and the murder of Uriah. Nathan's final appearance is in 1 Kings 1, where he and Bathsheba orchestrate Solomon's anointing as the king of Israel.

3. Nathan of Zobah, father of Igal, one of David's mighty men (2 Sam 23:36), and brother of Joel, one of the heroes in 1 Chronicles 11:38.

4. Father of Azariah and Zabud (1 Kgs 4:5). Possibly the same Nathan as #1 or #2.

David demolished the city with saws, iron picks, and axes;[g] he did this to all the Ammonite cities. Then David and all the troops returned to Jerusalem.

Amnon rapes Tamar

13 Some time later, David's son Amnon fell in love with Tamar the beautiful sister of Absalom, who was also David's son. [2] Amnon was so upset over his half sister that he made himself sick. She was a virgin, and it seemed impossible in Amnon's view to do anything to her. [3] But Amnon had a friend named Jonadab, Shimeah's son, David's brother, who was a very clever man.

[4] "Prince," Jonadab said to him, "why are you so down, morning after morning? Tell me about it."

So Amnon told him, "I'm in love with Tamar, the sister of my brother Absalom."

[5] "Lie down on your bed and pretend to be sick," Jonadab said to him. "When your father comes to see you, tell him, 'Please let my sister Tamar come and give me some food to eat. Let her prepare the food in my sight so I can watch and eat from her own hand.'"

[6] So Amnon lay down and pretended to be sick. The king came to see him, and Amnon told the king, "Please let my sister Tamar come and make a couple of heart-shaped cakes in front of me so I can eat from her hand."

[7] David sent word to Tamar at the palace: "Please go to your brother Amnon's house and prepare some food for him."

[8] So Tamar went to her brother Amnon's house where he was lying down. She took dough, kneaded it, made heart-shaped cakes in front of him, and then cooked them. [9] She took the pan and served Amnon, but he refused to eat.

"Everyone leave me," Amnon said. So everyone left him. [10] Then Amnon said to Tamar, "Bring the food into the bedroom so I can eat from your hand." So Tamar took the heart-shaped cakes she had made and brought them to her brother Amnon in the bedroom. [11] When she served him the food, he grabbed her and said, "Come have sex with me, my sister."

[12] But she said to him, "No, my brother! Don't rape me. Such a thing shouldn't be done in Israel. Don't do this horrible thing. [13] Think about me—where could I hide my shame? And you—you would become like some fool in Israel! Please, just talk to the king! He won't keep me from marrying you."

[14] But Amnon refused to listen to her. He was stronger than she was, and so he raped her. [15] But then Amnon felt intense hatred for her. In fact, his hatred for her was greater than the love he had felt for her. So Amnon told her, "Get out of here!"

[16] "No, my brother!"[h] she said. "Sending me away would be worse than the wrong you've already done."

But Amnon wouldn't listen to her. [17] He summoned his young servant and said, "Get this woman out of my presence and lock the door after her." ([18] She was wearing a long-sleeved robe because that was what the virgin princesses wore as garments.)[i] So Amnon's servant put her out and locked the door after her.

[19] Tamar put ashes on her head and tore the long-sleeved robe she was wearing. She put her hand on her head and walked away, crying as she went.

[20] Her brother Absalom said to her, "Has your brother Amnon been with you? Keep quiet about it for now, sister; he's your brother. Don't let it bother you." So Tamar, a broken woman, lived in her brother Absalom's house.

[21] When King David heard about all this he got very angry, but he refused to punish his son Amnon because he loved him as his oldest child.[j] [22] Absalom never spoke to Amnon, good word or bad, because he hated him for raping his sister Tamar.

Absalom kills Amnon

[23] Two years later, Absalom was shearing sheep at Baal-hazor near Ephraim, and he

---

[g] Cf LXX[L], OL, Tg, 1 Chron 20:3 [h] Correction; Heb uncertain; cf LXX, Vulg [i] Heb uncertain [j] LXX, DSS(4QSam[a]); MT lacks *but he refused . . . oldest child.*

invited all the king's sons. [24]Absalom approached the king and said, "Your servant is shearing sheep. Would the king and his advisors please join me?"

[25]But the king said to Absalom, "No, my son. We shouldn't all go, or we would be a burden on you." Although Absalom urged him, the king wasn't willing to go, although he gave Absalom a blessing.

[26]Then Absalom said, "If you won't come, then let my brother Amnon go with us."

"Why should he go with you?" they asked him. [27]But Absalom urged him until he sent Amnon and all the other princes. Then Absalom made a banquet fit for a king.[k]

[28]Absalom commanded his servants, "Be on the lookout! When Amnon is happy with wine and I tell you to strike Amnon down, then kill him! Don't be afraid, because I myself am giving you the order. Be brave and strong men." [29]So Absalom's servants did to Amnon just what he had commanded. Then all the princes got up, jumped onto their mules, and fled.

[30]While they were on the way, the report came to David: "Absalom has killed all of the princes! Not one remains." [31]The king got up, tore his garments, and lay on the ground. All his servants stood near him, their garments torn as well. [32]But Jonadab, the son of David's brother Shimeah, said, "My master shouldn't think that all the young princes have been killed—only Amnon is dead. This has been Absalom's plan ever since the day Amnon raped his sister Tamar. [33]So don't let this bother

you, my master; don't think that all the princes are dead, because only Amnon is dead, [34]and Absalom has fled." Just then the young man on watch looked up and saw many people coming on the road behind him alongside the mountain. [35]Jonadab told the king, "Look, the princes are coming, just as I, your servant, said they would."

[36]When Jonadab finished speaking, the princes arrived. They broke into loud crying, and the king and his servants cried hard as well.

[37]Meanwhile, Absalom had fled and gone to Geshur's King Talmai, Ammihud's son. David mourned for his son a long time. [38]But Absalom, after fleeing to Geshur, stayed there for three years. [39]Then the king's desire to go out after Absalom faded away because he had gotten over Amnon's death.[l]

Absalom is restored

14 Now Joab, Zeruiah's son, could see that the king's mind was on Absalom. [2]So Joab sent someone to Tekoa and brought a wise woman from there. He said to her, "Pretend to be in mourning. Dress in mourning clothes. Don't anoint yourself with oil. Act like a woman who has spent a long time mourning over someone who has died. [3]Go to the king and speak to him as follows." Then Joab told her what to say.

[4]When the woman from Tekoa came to the king, she fell facedown, bowing low out of respect. "King, help me!" she said.

[5]"What is wrong?" the king asked her.

[k]LXX; MT lacks *Then Absalom . . . king.* [l]DSS(4QSam[a]), LXX; Heb uncertain

AMNON

The oldest son of David and Ahinoam (2 Sam 3:2). His name, ironically, means "faithful." Amnon rapes and discards his half-sister Tamar (2 Sam 13; a violation of laws in Exod 22:16; Lev 18:9-11; Deut 22:28-29; 27:22). David refuses to punish him, one of several stories of David's failure to hold himself and his family accountable to Israelite laws. In retribution Absalom, Tamar's full brother, orders his servants to kill Amnon.

"It's terrible!" she said. "I am a widow; my husband is dead. [6]Your servant had two sons, but the two of them fought in the field. No one could separate them, and one struck the other and killed him. [7]Now the entire clan has turned against your servant. They say, 'Hand over the one who killed his brother so we can execute him for murdering his brother, even though we would destroy the heir as well.' So they would snuff out the one ember I have left, leaving my husband without name or descendant on the earth."

[8]The king said to the woman, "Return home, and I will issue an order in your behalf."

[9]The woman of Tekoa said to the king, "My master and king, let the guilt be on me and on my father's household. The king and his throne are innocent."

[10]"If anyone speaks against you, bring him to me, and he will never trouble you again," the king replied.

[11]She said, "Please let the king remember the LORD your God so that the one seeking revenge doesn't add to the destruction and doesn't kill my son."

"As surely as the LORD lives," David said, "not one of your son's hairs will fall to the ground."

[12]Then the woman said, "May your female servant say something to my master the king?"

"Speak!" he said.

[13]The woman said, "Why have you planned the very same thing against God's people? In giving this order, the king has become guilty because the king hasn't restored his own banished son. [14]We all have to die—we're like water spilled out on the ground that can't be gathered up again. But God doesn't take life away; instead, he makes plans so those banished from him don't stay that way.[m]

[15n]"I have come to my master the king to talk about this because people have made me afraid. Your servant thought, I must speak with the king. Maybe the king will act on the request of his servant, [16]because the king will agree to deliver his servant from the power of anyone who would destroy both me and my son from the inheritance God gave. [17]Your servant thought, The word of my master the king will definitely comfort me, because my master the king is like one of God's messengers, understanding good and evil. May the LORD your God be with you!"

[18o]The king answered the woman, "I must ask you something—don't hide anything from me!"

The woman said, "Please, my master and king, speak."

[19]So the king said, "Has Joab put you up to this?"

The woman answered, "As surely as you live, my master and king, no one can deviate a bit from whatever my master and king says. Yes, it was your servant Joab who directed me, and it was Joab who told your female servant to say all these things. [20]Your servant Joab did this to change the way things look.[p] But my master's wisdom

---

[m]Heb uncertain   [n]14:15-17 may have originally followed 14:7.   [o]14:18 may have originally followed 14:14.
[p]Heb uncertain

TEKOA

A town on the edge of the Judean desert, located about 6 mi. southeast of Bethlehem and 10 mi. south of Jerusalem. To the east the land slopes down toward the Dead Sea in a series of desolate hills called the Tekoa wilderness (2 Chron 20:20). Seasonal sheep grazing is possible in this area, and to the west enough moisture falls during the rainy season to sustain some agriculture. The prophet Amos was from Tekoa (Amos 1:1), which was also the home for a wise woman of Tekoa (2 Sam 14:2).

is like the wisdom of one of God's own messengers—he knows everything that takes place in the land."

²¹So the king said to Joab, "All right then. I will do it. Go and bring back my boy Absalom."

²²Joab fell facedown, bowing low out of respect, and he blessed the king.

"Today your servant knows that you think well of me, my master and king," Joab said, "because the king has followed up on his servant's recommendation."

²³So Joab got up, went to Geshur, and brought Absalom back to Jerusalem.

²⁴The king said, "He must go straight to his own house. He must not see my face." So Absalom went straight to his own house and did not see the king.

²⁵No man throughout Israel was as praised for his good looks as Absalom. From the soles of his feet to the crown of his head there was nothing wrong with him. ²⁶When he shaved his head—he had to shave his head at the end of each year because his hair was so heavy that he had to shave it—the weight of the hair from his head was two hundred shekels by the royal weight. ²⁷Absalom had three sons and one daughter. The daughter's name was Tamar. She was a beautiful woman.

²⁸Absalom lived in Jerusalem two years without ever seeing the king's face. ²⁹Absalom called for Joab in order to send Joab to the king, but Joab refused to come. Absalom called for Joab a second time, but he still wouldn't come. ³⁰So Absalom said to his servants, "Look, Joab's property is next to mine. He has barley there. Go and set it on fire." So Absalom's servants set the property on fire. Then Joab's servants went to Joab with their clothes torn. "Absalom's servants set the property on fire," they said.�q

³¹So Joab went straight to Absalom's house and said to him, "Why have your servants set my property on fire?"

³²Absalom answered Joab, "Look, I sent you a message: Come here so I can send you

to the king to ask, 'Why have I returned from Geshur? I would be better off if I were still there!' Please let me see the king's face. If I'm guilty, then the king can kill me."

³³Joab went to the king and reported this to him. Then the king called for Absalom, and Absalom came to the king. He bowed low out of respect, nose to the ground before the king. Then the king kissed Absalom.

Absalom plots rebellion

15 Some time later, Absalom got a chariot and horses for his own use, along with fifty men to run ahead of him. ²Absalom would get up early and stand by the side of the road that went through the city gate. Whenever anyone had a lawsuit to bring before the king for judgment, Absalom would call to him, "What city are you from?" When the person said, "Your servant is from one of the tribes of Israel," ³then Absalom would say to him, "No doubt your claims are correct and valid, but the king won't listen to you. ⁴If only I were made a judge in the land," Absalom would continue, "then anyone with a lawsuit could come to me, and I would give them justice."

⁵Whenever anyone came near to Absalom, bowing low out of respect, he would reach his hand out, grab them, and kiss them. ⁶This is how Absalom treated every Israelite who came to the king seeking justice. This is how Absalom stole the hearts of the Israelites.

⁷At the end of fourʳ years, Absalom said to the king, "Please let me go to Hebron so I can fulfill a promise I made to the LORD. ⁸Your servant made this promise when I lived in Geshur, in Aram. I promised that if the LORD would bring me back to Jerusalem, then I would worship the LORD in Hebron."ˢ

⁹"Go in peace," the king said. So Absalom left and went to Hebron.

¹⁰But Absalom sent secret agents throughout the tribes of Israel with this message: "When you hear the sound of the

---

�q DSS (4QSamᶜ) LXX; MT lacks *Then Joab's servants . . . said.*   ʳ LXX, Syr, Vulg, Josephus; MT *forty*   ˢ LXX; MT lacks *in Hebron.*

trumpet, then say, 'Absalom has become king in Hebron!'" ¹¹Two hundred invited guests went with Absalom from Jerusalem. They were innocent and knew nothing of this matter when they went. ¹²While Absalom was offering the sacrifices, he summoned David's advisor Ahithophel, who was from Giloh, to come from his hometown. So the conspiracy grew stronger, and Absalom's following grew.

David flees from Jerusalem

¹³A messenger came to David, reporting, "The hearts of the Israelites have gone over to Absalom." ¹⁴Then David told all the servants who were with him in Jerusalem, "Come on! We have to run for it, or we won't be able to escape Absalom. Hurry, or he will catch up with us in no time, destroy us,ᵗ and attack the city with the sword." ¹⁵The king's servants said to him, "Your servants are ready to do whatever our master the king decides." ¹⁶So the king left, with his entire household following him, but he left ten secondary wives behind to take care of the palace.

¹⁷So the king left, with all his people following him, and they stopped at the last house. ¹⁸All the king's servants marched past him, as did all the Cherethites, all the Pelethites, and the six hundred Gittites who had followed him from Gath. ¹⁹The king said to Ittai the Gittite, "Why are you coming with us too? Go back! Stay with King Absalom.ᵘ You are a foreigner and an exile from your own country. ²⁰You just got here yesterday. So today should I make you wander around with us while I go wherever I have to go? No. Go back, and take your relatives with you. May the LORD show you loyal love and faithfulness."ᵛ

²¹But Ittai answered the king, "As surely as the LORD lives and as surely as my master the king lives, wherever my master the king may be, facing death or facing life, your servant will be there too."

²²"Okay then," David replied to Ittai. "Keep marching!"

So Ittai the Gittite and all of his men and all the little children with him marched past. ²³The whole countryside cried loudly as all the troops marched past. The king crossed the Kidron Valley, and all the troops passed by on the Olive roadʷ into the wilderness.

²⁴Zadok was there too, along with all the Levites carrying the chest containing God's covenant. They set God's chest down, and Abiathar offered sacrifices until all the troops had finished marching out of the city. ²⁵Then the king said to Zadok, "Carry God's chest back into the city. If the LORD thinks well of me, then he will bring me back and let me see it and its home again. ²⁶But if God says, 'I'm not pleased with you,' then I am ready. Let him do to me whatever pleases him."

²⁷"Do you understand?" the king said to the priest Zadok. "Go back to the city in safety—you and Abiatharˣ with your two

---

ᵗHeb uncertain; LXXᴸ *bring the city down on top of us* ᵘHeb lacks *Absalom.* ᵛLXX; MT lacks *may the Lord show you.* ʷLXXᴸ; MT lacks *Olive.* ˣCorrection; MT lacks *and Abiathar.*

ABSALOM

"(My) father is peace (or well-being)." Absalom was the third of the sons of David born in Hebron (2 Sam 3:3). Absalom plays a major role in the story of who will be king after David (2 Sam 9–20; 1 Kgs 1–2). Amnon, Absalom's half-brother, raped Absalom's sister Tamar. Absalom's revenge plan resulted in Amnon's death and Absalom's estrangement from David. Absalom later led a failed uprising against David. David ordered his commanders to protect Absalom (2 Sam 18:5), but Joab disregarded the order and killed Absalom.

sons, your son Ahimaaz and Abiathar's son Jonathan. [28]I will be waiting in the desert plains until you send word telling me what to do." [29]So Zadok and Abiathar took God's chest back to Jerusalem and stayed there.

[30]But David, his head covered, walked barefoot up the slope of the Mount of Olives crying. All the people who were with him covered their heads too and cried as they went up. [31]David was told that Ahithophel was also among the conspirators with Absalom, so he prayed, "Please, LORD, make Ahithophel's advice foolish."

David and Hushai

[32]When David came to the summit where people used to worship God, Hushai from Erek met him. Hushai's clothes were ripped, and dirt was on his head. [33]David said to him, "If you come with me, you will be a burden to me. [34]But if you return to the city and say to Absalom, 'King, I am your servant!'[y] Please spare my life! I was your father's servant in the past, but now I am your servant,' then you can help me by countering Ahithophel's advice. [35]The priests Zadok and Abiathar will be with you there. So report everything you hear in the king's palace to the priests Zadok and Abiathar. [36]Their two sons, Zadok's son Ahimaaz and Abiathar's son Jonathan, are also there. Use them to report to me everything you hear."

[37]So David's friend Hushai went into Jerusalem, just as Absalom was entering the city.

David and Ziba

16 When David had passed a short distance beyond the summit, Ziba, Mephibosheth's servant, met him with a pair of saddled donkeys loaded with two hundred loaves of bread, one hundred bunches of raisins, one hundred figs,[z] and a jar of wine. [2]"What is all this for?" the king asked Ziba.

"The donkeys are for the royal family to ride," Ziba explained. "The bread and summer fruit are for the young people to eat, and the wine is for those who get exhausted in the wilderness."

[3]"Where is your master's grandson?" the king asked.

"He is still in Jerusalem," Ziba answered the king, "because he thinks that the Israelites are now going to give his grandfather's kingdom back to him."

[4]"Look here," the king said to Ziba. "Everything that belonged to Mephibosheth now belongs to you."

Ziba said, "I bow out of respect! Please think well of me, my master and king."

Shimei curses David

[5]When King David came to Bahurim, a man from the same clan as Saul's family came out from there. His name was Shimei; he was Gera's son. He was cursing as he came out. [6]He threw rocks at David and at all of King David's servants, even though the entire army and all the warriors were on either side of him.

[7]This is what Shimei said as he cursed David: "Get out of here! Get out of here! You are a murderer! You are despicable! [8]The LORD has paid you back for all the blood of Saul's family, in whose place you rule, and the LORD has handed the kingdom over to your son Absalom. You are in this trouble because you are a murderer!"

[9]Zeruiah's son Abishai said to the king, "Why should this dead dog curse my master the king? Let me go over and cut his head off!"

[10]But the king said, "My problems aren't yours, you sons of Zeruiah. If he is cursing because the LORD told him to curse David, then who is to question, 'Why are you doing this?'"

[11]Then David addressed Abishai and all his servants: "Listen! My own son, one of my very own children, wants me dead. This Benjaminite can only feel the same—only more! Leave him alone. And let him curse, because the LORD told him to. [12]Perhaps the LORD will see my distress; perhaps the LORD will repay me with good for this cursing today."

[13]So David and his men kept walking, while Shimei went along on the hillside next to him, cursing as he went, throwing rocks and dirt at him. [14]The king and all the

---

[y]Correction, LXX; MT *King, I will be your servant.*   [z]Or *summer fruit*

people who were with him reached the Jordan River[a] exhausted, and he rested there.

Ahithophel's advice

[15] Now Absalom and all the Israelites entered Jerusalem, and Ahithophel was with him. [16] Then David's friend Hushai, who was from Erek, approached Absalom and said to him, "Long live the king! Long live the king!"

[17] But Absalom said to Hushai, "Is this how you show loyal love to your friend? Why didn't you go with him?"

[18] "No," Hushai replied to Absalom, "I will belong to the one chosen by the LORD, by this people, and by all Israel, and I will stay with him. [19] What's more, whom should I serve if not David's son? I served your father, and so I will serve you in the same way."

[20] Then Absalom said to Ahithophel, "Give your advice then. What should we do?"

[21] "Have sex with your father's secondary wives—the ones he left to take care of the palace," Ahithophel told Absalom. "Then all Israel will hear that you have alienated yourself from your father, and everyone who supports you will be encouraged."

[22] So they set up a tent for Absalom on the roof, and he had sex with his father's secondary wives in plain sight before all Israel. ([23] Now in those days, the advice Ahithophel gave was like asking for a word from God. That's why Ahithophel's advice was valued by both David and Absalom.)

17 Then Ahithophel said to Absalom, "Let me pick twelve thousand men, and I will go after David tonight. [2] I will attack him while he is tired and weak, and I will throw him into a panic. All the troops with him will run off. I promise to kill the king alone, [3] and I will bring all the people back to you like a bride comes back to her husband.[b] It's only one man's life you are seeking; everyone else can be at peace."

[4] This plan seemed excellent to Absalom and the Israelite elders.

Hushai's advice

[5] But Absalom said, "Call Hushai from Erek. Let's hear what he has to say as well."

[6] When Hushai from Erek arrived, Absalom said to him, "This is what Ahithophel has advised. Should we follow it or not? What do you say?"

[7] Hushai said to Absalom, "This time, the advice Ahithophel has given isn't right. [8] You know that your father and his men are warriors," he continued, "and they are as desperate as a wild bear robbed of her cubs. Your father is a seasoned fighter. He won't spend the night with his troops. [9] Even now he has probably hidden himself in one of the caves or some other place. When some of the troops[c] fall in the first attack, whoever hears it will say, 'The soldiers who follow Absalom have been defeated!' [10] Then even the bravest soldier, whose heart is like a lion's, will melt in fear because all Israel knows that your father is a warrior and that those who are with him are brave. [11] So I would advise that all the Israelites, from Dan to Beer-sheba—a group as countless as sand on the seashore—be summoned to join you, and that you yourself go into battle. [12] When we attack him wherever he might be, we will fall on him like dew that falls on the ground. No one will survive— not him and not one of the soldiers who are with him! [13] If he retreats into a city, all Israel will bring ropes to that city, and we will drag it into a valley until not even a pebble of it will be found."

[14] Then Absalom and everyone in Israel agreed, "The advice of Hushai from Erek is better than Ahithophel's advice." This was because the LORD had decided to counter Ahithophel's good advice so that the LORD could bring disaster on Absalom.

Hushai warns David

[15] Hushai told the priests Zadok and Abiathar, "Here is what Ahithophel advised Absalom and the Israelite elders, and here is what I advised. [16] Now send word immediately to David and tell him, 'Don't spend the night in the desert plains. You must cross over immediately. Otherwise, the king and all the troops who are with him will be swallowed up whole.'"

---

[a]LXX; MT lacks *at the Jordan River.*　[b]LXX; Heb uncertain　[c]LXX

[17]Jonathan and Ahimaaz were standing by at En-rogel. A female servant would come and report to them, and they would then travel and report to King David because they couldn't risk being seen entering the city. [18]But a boy saw them and reported it to Absalom. So the two of them left immediately and came to a man's house at Bahurim. He had a well in his courtyard, and they climbed down into it. [19]The man's wife took a covering and spread it over the well's opening, then scattered grain over it so no one would notice. [20]When Absalom's servants came to the woman at the house they demanded, "Where are Ahimaaz and Jonathan?"

The woman told them, "They crossed over the stream."[d] They looked for them but found nothing, so they returned to Jerusalem.

[21]After they had left, Jonathan and Ahimaaz climbed out of the well. They went and reported to King David, "Get up! Cross the water immediately because Ahithophel has made plans against you!" [22]So David and all the troops who were with him got up and crossed the Jordan River. By daybreak there was no one left who hadn't crossed the Jordan.

[23]Meanwhile, once Ahithophel saw that his advice hadn't been followed, he saddled his donkey and went home to his own town. He gave instructions to his household, then hanged himself and died. He was buried in his father's tomb.

[24]David had reached Mahanaim by the time Absalom and all the Israelites who were with him crossed the Jordan River. [25]Absalom had put Amasa in charge of the army instead of Joab. Amasa was the son of a man named Ithra, an Ishmaelite[e] who had married Abigail, who was Nahash's daughter and the sister of Zeruiah, Joab's mother. [26]Israel and Absalom camped in the territory of Gilead.

[27]When David arrived in Mahanaim, Nahash's son Shobi, who was from Rabbah of the Ammonites; Ammiel's son Machir, who was from Lo-debar; and Barzillai the Gileadite from Rogelim [28]brought couches, basins, and pottery, along with wheat, barley, flour, roasted grain, beans, lentils, [29]honey, curds, sheep, and cheese from the herd so that David and the troops who were with him could eat. They said, "The troops have grown hungry, tired, and thirsty in the wilderness."

Absalom's death

18 Then David gathered the troops who were with him and appointed unit commanders over thousands and hundreds. [2]David sent out the army—a third under Joab's command, a third under the command of Abishai, Zeruiah's son, and a third under the command of Ittai the Gittite. The king told the troops, "I will march out with you myself."

[3]But the troops replied, "No! You must not march out! If we flee, they won't care about us. Even if half of us die, they won't care about us. But you are worth ten thousand of us. It is much better if you support us from the city."

[4]The king said to them, "I will do whatever you think is best." So the king stood beside the gate as all the troops marched out by hundreds and thousands. [5]The king gave orders to Joab, Abishai, and Ittai: "For my sake, protect my boy Absalom." All the troops heard what the king ordered regarding Absalom to all the commanders.

[6]So the troops marched into the field to meet the Israelites. The battle was fought in the Ephraim forest. [7]The army of Israel was defeated there by David's soldiers. A great slaughter of twenty thousand men took place that day. [8]The battle spread out over the entire countryside, and the forest devoured more soldiers than the sword that day.

[9]Absalom came upon some of David's men. Absalom was riding on a mule, and the mule went under the tangled branches of a large oak tree. Absalom's head got caught in the tree. He was left hanging in midair while the mule under him kept on going. [10]One of the men saw this and reported to Joab, "I just saw Absalom hanging from an oak tree."

[d]Heb uncertain [e]LXX[A] and 1 Chron 2:17; MT *an Israelite*; LXX[M] *a Jezreelite*

¹¹Joab said to the man who told him, "You saw this? Why didn't you kill him on the spot? I would have given you ten pieces of silver and a belt."

¹²But the man said to Joab, "Even if I had a thousand pieces of silver in my hand, I wouldn't touch the king's son! We heard what the king commanded you, Abishai, and Ittai—'For my sake, take care of my boy Absalom.'ᶠ ¹³If I had taken Absalom's life behind the king's back then—though nothing is hidden from the king—you would have kept your distance from me."ᵍ

¹⁴Joab said, "I won't waste time like this with you!" He took three sticks in his hand and drove them into Absalom's chest while he was still alive in the oak. ¹⁵Then ten young armor-bearers of Joab surrounded Absalom, struck him, and killed him. ¹⁶Then Joab sounded the trumpet, and the troops stopped chasing the Israelites, because Joab held them back.

¹⁷They took Absalom and threw him into a big pit in the forest. They piled over him a huge heap of stones. Meanwhile, all the Israelites fled to their homes. ¹⁸When he was alive, Absalom had raised a large pillar for himself in the King's Valley because he said, "I have no son to carry on the memory of my name." He named the pillar after himself. It is called Absalom's Monument to this day.

David mourns for Absalom

¹⁹Then Zadok's son Ahimaaz said, "Please let me run and take the news to the king that the LORD has vindicated him against his enemies' power."

²⁰Joab said to him, "You aren't the one to bring the news today. You can bring news on another day, but not today, because the king's son is dead." ²¹Then Joab said to a Cushite, "Go tell the king what you have seen." The Cushite bowed low before Joab, then ran off.

²²But Zadok's son Ahimaaz again said to Joab, "I don't care what happens, just let me run after the Cushite too."

"Why do you want to go, son?" Joab asked. "You'll get no reward for going."ʰ

²³"I don't care what happens, I want to go," Ahimaaz said.ⁱ

So Joab said to him, "Run off then!"

Ahimaaz ran off, going by way of the plain, and passed the Cushite.

²⁴Now David was sitting between the two gates. The watchman on duty went up on the roof of the gate by the wall. He looked out and saw a man running alone. ²⁵The watchman called out and reported this to the king. The king said, "If he's alone, it's good news."

The man got nearer and nearer, ²⁶and the watchman saw another man running and called down to the gatekeeper, "There's another man running alone."

The king said, "That one must be bringing good news too."

²⁷The watchman said, "I can see that the first one runs like Zadok's son Ahimaaz."

"He's a good man," the king said, "and is coming with good news."

²⁸Ahimaaz called out to the king, "Peace!" then bowed low before the king, his nose to the ground. He said, "Bless the LORD your God, who has delivered up the men who raised their hands against my master the king."

²⁹The king said, "Is my boy Absalom okay?"

Ahimaaz said, "I saw a large crowd right when Joab, the king's servant, sent your servant off, but I don't know what it was about."

³⁰"Step aside and stand right here," the king said. So Ahimaaz stepped aside and waited.

³¹Then the Cushite arrived and said, "My master the king: Listen to this good news! The LORD has vindicated you this day against the power of all who rose up against you."

³²The king said to the Cushite, "Is my boy Absalom okay?"

The Cushite answered, "May the enemies of my master the king and all who rise up against you to hurt you end up like that young man."

³³ʲThe king trembled. He went up to the room over the gate and cried. As he went,

---

ᶠLXX, Vulg, Syr; Heb uncertain ᵍOr *Otherwise, I would have been dealing recklessly with my own life, because nothing is hidden from the king and you were stationed far from me*; Heb uncertain. ʰHeb uncertain ⁱLXX; MT lacks *Ahimaaz said*. ʲ19:1 in Heb he said, "Oh, my son Absalom! Oh, my son! My son Absalom! If only I had died instead of you! Oh, Absalom, my son! My son!"[k]

19 Joab was told that the king was crying and mourning Absalom. [2] So the victory that day was turned into mourning for all the troops because they heard that day that the king was grieving for his son. [3] So that day the troops crept back into the city like soldiers creep back ashamed after they've fled from battle. [4] The king covered his face and cried out in a loud voice, "Oh, my son Absalom! Oh, Absalom, my son! My son!"

[5] Joab came to the king inside and said, "Today you have humiliated all your servants who have saved your life today, not to mention the lives of your sons, your daughters, your wives, and your secondary wives, [6] by loving those who hate you and hating those who love you! Today you have announced that the commanders and their soldiers are nothing to you, because I know that if Absalom were alive today and the rest of us dead, that would be perfectly fine with you! [7] Now get up! Go out and encourage your followers! I swear to the LORD that if you don't go out there, not one man will stick with you tonight—and that will be more trouble for you than all the trouble that you've faced from your youth until now."

[8] So the king went and sat down in the city gate. All the troops were told that the king was sitting in the gate, so they came before the king.

David returns to Jerusalem

Meanwhile, the Israelites had fled to their homes. [9] Everyone was arguing throughout Israel's tribes, saying, "The king delivered us from our enemies' power, and he rescued us from the Philistines' power, but now he has fled from the land and from controlling his own kingdom.[l] [10] And Absalom, the one we anointed over us, is dead in battle. So why do you say nothing about bringing the king back?"

[11] When the things that all the Israelites were saying reached the king,[m] David sent a message to the priests Zadok and Abiathar: "Say the following to the elders of Judah: 'Why should you be the last to bring the king back to his palace?[n] [12] You are my relatives! You are my flesh and bones! Why should you be the last to bring the king back?' [13] And tell Amasa, 'Aren't you my flesh and bones too? May God deal harshly with me and worse still if you don't become commander of my army from now on instead of Joab!'"

[14] So he won over the hearts of everyone in Judah as though they were one person, and they sent word to the king: "Come back—you and all your servants." [15] So the king came back and arrived at the Jordan River. Judah came to Gilgal to meet the king and bring him across the Jordan.

[16] Gera's son Shimei, the Benjaminite from Bahurim, hurried down with the people of Judah to meet King David. [17] A thousand men from Benjamin were with him. Ziba too, the servant of Saul's house, along with his fifteen sons and twenty servants, rushed to the Jordan ahead of the king [18] to do the work of ferrying[o] over the king's household and to do whatever pleased him.

Gera's son Shimei fell down before the king when he crossed the Jordan. [19] He said to the king, "May my master not hold me guilty or remember your servant's wrongdoing that day my master the king left Jerusalem. Please forget about it, Your Majesty,[p] [20] because your servant knows that I have sinned. But look, I am the first person from the entire family of Joseph to come down today and meet my master the king."

[21] Zeruiah's son Abishai responded, "Shouldn't Shimei be put to death for that—for cursing the LORD's anointed?"

[22] But David said, "My problems aren't yours, you sons of Zeruiah. Why are you becoming my enemy today? Should anyone in Israel be put to death today? Don't I know that today I am again king over Israel?"

---

[k]19:2 in Heb [l]LXX; MT *from over Absalom* [m]LXX, OL; MT lacks *When . . . the king*, though a version of this clause appears in 19:12. [n]MT adds *The things that all the Israelites were saying reached the king in his home* (or *palace*). [o]LXX; MT *while the crossing was under way, to ferry* [p]19:18-19 Heb uncertain

²³Then the king told Shimei, "You will not die." And the king swore this to him.

²⁴Mephibosheth, Saul's grandson, also came down to meet the king. He hadn't taken care of his feet, trimmed his beard, or washed his clothes from the day the king left until the day he returned safely. ²⁵When he came from Jerusalem to meet the king, the king asked him, "Mephibosheth, why didn't you go with me?"

²⁶"My master and king," Mephibosheth answered, "my servant abandoned me! Because your servant is lame, I asked my servant, 'Saddle a donkey for me^q so I can ride and go to the king.' ²⁷So Ziba has slandered your servant to my master and king, but my master and king is a messenger of God. So do whatever seems best to you. ²⁸Even though all the members of my grandfather's family were nothing short of demonic^r toward my master and king, you still put your servant with those who eat at your table. So what right do I have to beg for still more from the king?"

²⁹"You don't need to talk any more about this," the king said to him. "I order you and Ziba to divide the property."

³⁰Mephibosheth said to the king, "Let him take all of it, since my master and king has come home safely."

³¹Now Barzillai the Gileadite had come down from Rogelim. He accompanied the king to the Jordan River to send him off there. ³²Barzillai was very old, 80 years of age. He had supported the king during his stay at Mahanaim because Barzillai was a very wealthy man.

³³The king said to Barzillai, "Come over the Jordan with me. I will provide for you at my side in Jerusalem."

³⁴But Barzillai said to the king, "How many years do I have left that I should go up with the king to Jerusalem? ³⁵I am now 80 years old. Do I know what is good or bad anymore? Can your servant taste what I eat or drink? Can I even hear the voices of men or women singers? Why should your servant be

a burden to my master and king? ³⁶Your servant will cross a short way over the Jordan with the king, but why should the king give me such a reward? ³⁷Let your servant return so I may die in my own town near the grave of my parents. But here is your servant Chimham. Let him cross over with my master and king, and treat him as you think best."

³⁸The king said, "Okay. Chimham will cross over with me, and I will treat him as I^s think best. And I will do for you anything you desire from me."

³⁹So all the people crossed over the Jordan River, and the king stayed behind.^t The king kissed Barzillai and blessed him, and then Barzillai went back to his home. ⁴⁰When the king crossed over to Gilgal, Chimham went with him. All the troops of Judah and half the troops of Israel escorted the king across.

⁴¹Then everyone in Israel came and said to the king, "Why did our relatives the people of Judah steal you away, and bring the king and his household across the Jordan River, along with all of his soldiers?"

⁴²Then all the people of Judah answered the Israelites, "Because the king is our relative! Why are you angry at us about this? Have we taken any of the king's food? Has he given us any gifts?"

⁴³But the Israelites answered the people of Judah, "We have ten shares in the monarchy! What's more, we are the oldest offspring, not you!^u So why have you disrespected us? Weren't we the first to talk about bringing back our king?"

But the words of the people of Judah were even harsher than the words of the Israelites.^v

Sheba's rebellion

20 Now a despicable man named Sheba, Bichri's son, from Benjamin, was also there. He sounded the trumpet and said:

"We don't care about David!
We have no stake in Jesse's son!
Go back to your homes, Israel!"

---

^qLXX, Syr, Vulg; MT *your servant said, I will saddle a donkey for myself* ^rOr *were doomed to death by my master the king*; MT *men of death* ^sLXX; MT *you* ^tLXX; MT *crossed over* ^uLXX, OL; MT *we have a greater claim on David than you do.* ^v19:39-43 Heb uncertain

²So all the Israelites left David to follow Bichri's son Sheba. But all the people of Judah stayed close to their king from the Jordan River all the way to Jerusalem.

³When David arrived at his palace in Jerusalem, the king took the ten secondary wives he had left to take care of the palace and put them in a house under guard. He provided for them, but he didn't have sex with them. They were confined until the day they died, and lived like widows.

⁴Then the king said to Amasa, "Call everyone in Judah here to me three days from now. You should be here too." ⁵So Amasa went to call Judah together, but he took longer than the allotted time.

⁶David told Abishai, "Bichri's son Sheba will cause more trouble for us than Absalom did. Take your master's servants and chase after him before he finds fortified cities and escapes from us." ⁷So Joab's men marched out after Sheba—this included the Cherethites, the Pelethites, and all the warriors. They marched out of Jerusalem to pursue Bichri's son Sheba.

⁸When they got to the great stone in Gibeon, Amasa came to meet them. Joab was dressed in his soldier's uniform. Over the tunic at his waist he wore a sword in its sheath. As Joab went forward it slipped out.

⁹"How are you, my brother?" Joab asked Amasa, and with his right hand he took hold of Amasa's beard as if to kiss him. ¹⁰But Amasa didn't notice the sword in Joab's hand. Joab struck him in the stomach with it so that Amasa's intestines spilled out on the ground. He died without Joab striking him a second time. Then Joab and his brother Abishai pursued Sheba, Bichri's son.

¹¹One of Joab's men stood by Amasa and said, "Whoever favors Joab, and whoever is for David, follow Joab!" ¹²Amasa was writhing in blood in the middle of the road, and the man saw that everyone was stopping. When he saw this, he dragged Amasa from the road into a field and threw a robe over him. ¹³Once Amasa was moved out of the road, everyone who followed Joab marched past in pursuit of Bichri's son Sheba.

¹⁴Sheba went through all the Israelite tribes up to Abel of Beth-maacah. All the Bichrites^w assembled and followed Sheba in. ¹⁵Then Joab's men arrived and attacked Sheba at Abel of Beth-maacah. They piled up a ramp against the city, and it stood against the outer wall.^x All of Joab's troops were hammering the wall, trying to bring it down.

¹⁶Then a wise woman called from the city, "Listen! Listen! Tell Joab to come over here, so I can talk to him."

¹⁷So Joab approached her, and the woman said, "Are you Joab?"

"I am," he answered.

"Pay close attention to the words of your female servant," she said.

"I'm listening," Joab replied.

¹⁸She said, "People used to say long ago: 'Ask your question at Abel,' and that settled the matter. ¹⁹I am one of the peaceful and faithful in Israel, but you are trying to kill a city that is one of Israel's mothers! Why would you annihilate the LORD's inheritance?"

²⁰Joab answered, "I would never, ever annihilate or destroy such a thing! ²¹That's not the issue. A man named Sheba, Bichri's son, who is from the Ephraim highlands, has rebelled against King David. Just hand him over, and I'll leave the city alone."

The woman said to Joab, "His head will be thrown over the wall to you!"

²²When the woman went to everyone with her wise counsel, they cut off the head of Sheba, Bichri's son, and threw it out to Joab. Then Joab sounded the trumpet, and his troops left the city, returning to their homes. But Joab returned to the king in Jerusalem.

David's officials

²³Now Joab was in command of Israel's army; Jehoiada's son Benaiah commanded the Cherethites and the Pelethites; ²⁴Adoram was in charge of the forced labor; Ahilud's son Jehoshaphat was the recorder; ²⁵Sheva was secretary; Zadok and Abiathar were priests; ²⁶and Ira from Jair was also a priest for David.

---

^w Cf LXX, Vulg; MT *Berites*   ^x Heb uncertain

Avenging the Gibeonites

21 There was a famine for three years in a row during David's rule. David asked the LORD about this, and the LORD said, "It is caused by Saul and his household, who are guilty of bloodshed because he killed the people of Gibeon." ²So the king called for the Gibeonites and spoke to them.

(Now the Gibeonites weren't Israelites but were survivors of the Amorites. The Israelites had sworn a solemn pledge to spare them, but Saul tried to eliminate them in his enthusiasm for the people of Israel and Judah.)

³David said to the Gibeonites, "What can I do for you? How can I fix matters so you can benefit from the LORD's inheritance?"

⁴The Gibeonites said to him, "We don't want any silver or gold from Saul or his family, and it isn't our right to have anyone in Israel killed."

"What do you want?"ʸ David asked. "I'll do it for you."

⁵"Okay then," they said to the king. "That man who opposed and oppressedᶻ us, who planned to destroy us, keeping us from having a place to live anywhere in Israel— ⁶hand over seven of his sons to us, and we will hang them before the LORD at Gibeonᵃ on the LORD's mountain."

"I will hand them over," the king said.

⁷But the king spared Mephibosheth, Jonathan's son and Saul's grandson, because of the LORD's solemn pledge that was between them—between David and Saul's son Jonathan. ⁸So the king took the two sons of Aiah's daughter Rizpah, Armoni and Mephibosheth, whom she had birthed for Saul; and the five sons of Saul's daughter Merab,ᵇ whom she birthed for Adriel, Barzillai's son, who was from Meholah, ⁹and he handed them over to the Gibeonites. They hanged them on the mountain before the LORD. The seven of them died at the same time. They were executed in the first days of the harvest, at the beginning of the barley harvest.

¹⁰Aiah's daughter Rizpah took funeral clothing and spread it out by herself on a rock. She stayed there from the beginning of the harvest until the rains poured down on the bodies from the sky, and she wouldn't let any birds of prey land on the bodies during the day or let wild animals come at nighttime. ¹¹When David was told what Aiah's daughter Rizpah, Saul's secondary wife, had done, ¹²he went and retrieved the bones of Saul and his son Jonathan from the citizens of Jabesh-gilead, who had stolen the bones from the public square in Beth-shan, where the Philistines had hanged them on the day the Philistines killed Saul at Gilboa. ¹³David brought the bones of Saul and his son Jonathan from there and collected the bones of the men who had been hanged by the Gibeonites. ¹⁴The bones of Saul and his son Jonathan were then buried in Zela, in Benjaminite territory, in the tomb of Saul's father Kish. Once everything the king had commanded was done, God responded to prayers for the land.

War with the Philistines

¹⁵Once again war broke out between the Philistines and Israel. David and the soldiers who were with him went down and fought the Philistines. When David grew tired, ¹⁶Ishbi-benob, a descendant of the Raphah,ᶜ planned on killing David.ᵈ The weight of his spear was three hundred shekels of bronze, and he was wearing new armor. ¹⁷But Zeruiah's son Abishai came to David's aid, striking the Philistine down and killing him. Then David's men swore a solemn pledge to him: "You will never march out to battle with us again! You must not snuff out Israel's lamp!"

¹⁸Some time later, another battle with the Philistines took place at Gob. Then Sibbecai from Hushah killed Saph, a descendant of the Raphah. ¹⁹There was yet another battle with the Philistines at Gob; and Elhanan, Jair's sonᵉ from Bethlehem,

---

ʸLXXᴸ, OL; MT *What are you saying?* ᶻLXXᴮ; MT *annihilated us* ᵃCorrection; cf LXX and 21:9; MT *at Gibeah of Saul, the LORD's chosen one* ᵇLXXᴸᴺ; MT *Michal* (but cf 2 Sam 6:23) ᶜOr *giants*; also in 21:18, 20, 22 ᵈLXX *Joash's son Dodo, a descendant of the Raphah* (see previous note), *captured David.* ᵉSee 1 Chron 20:5, LXXᴸᴹᴺ (cf 2 Sam 23:24); Heb *Jaare-oregim.*

killed Goliath from Gath, whose spear shaft was as strong as the bar on a weaver's loom. ²⁰In another battle at Gath, there was a huge[f] man who had six fingers on his hands and six toes on his feet, twenty-four in all. He too was descended from the Raphah. ²¹When he insulted Israel, Jonathan, who was the son of David's brother Shimei, killed him. ²²These four Philistines were descended from the Raphah in Gath, and they fell by the hands of David and his servants.

David's thanksgiving psalm

22 ^gDavid spoke the words of this song to the LORD after the LORD delivered him from the power of all his enemies and from Saul.

² He said:

The LORD is my solid rock,
  my fortress, my rescuer.
³ My God is my rock—
  I take refuge in him!—
he's my shield and
  my salvation's strength,
  my place of safety and my shelter.
  My savior! Save me from violence!
⁴ Because he is praiseworthy,[h]
  I cried out to the LORD,
  and I was saved from my enemies.
⁵ Death's waves were all around me;
  rivers of wickedness terrified me.
⁶ The cords of the grave[i] surrounded me;
  death's traps held me tight.
⁷ In my distress I cried out to the LORD;
  I cried out to my God.
God heard my voice from his temple;
  my cry for help reached his ears.

⁸ The earth rocked and shook;
  the sky's foundations trembled
  and reeled because of God's anger.
⁹ Smoke went up from God's nostrils;
  out of his mouth came a devouring fire;
  flaming coals blazed out in front of him!
¹⁰ God parted the skies and came down;
  thick darkness was beneath his feet.
¹¹ God mounted the heavenly creatures
  and flew;
  he was seen on the wind's wings.
¹² God made darkness his covering;
  water gathered in dense clouds!
¹³ Coals of fire blazed
  out of the brightness before him.
¹⁴ The LORD thundered from heaven;
  the Most High made his voice heard.
¹⁵ God shot arrows, scattering the enemy;
  he sent the lightning
  and whipped them into confusion.
¹⁶ The seabeds were exposed;
  the earth's foundations were laid bare
  at the LORD's rebuke,
  at the angry blast of air
  coming from his nostrils.

¹⁷ From on high God reached down
  and grabbed me;
  he took me out of deep waters.
¹⁸ God saved me from my powerful enemy,
  saved me from my foes,
  who were too much for me.
¹⁹ They came at me
  on the very day of my distress,
  but the LORD was my support.
²⁰ He brought me out to wide-open spaces;
  he pulled me out,
  because he is pleased with me.
²¹ The LORD rewarded me
  for my righteousness;
  he restored me
  because my hands are clean,
²² because I have kept the LORD's ways.
  I haven't acted wickedly against my God.
²³ All his rules are right in front of me;
  I haven't turned away
  from any of his laws.
²⁴ I have lived with integrity before him;
  I've kept myself from wrongdoing.
²⁵ And so the LORD restored me
  for my righteousness,
  because I am clean in his eyes.
²⁶ You deal faithfully with the faithful;
  you show integrity toward the one
  who has integrity.
²⁷ You are pure toward the pure,
  but toward the crooked, you are tricky.

---

[f]See 1 Chron 20:6; MT *a Midianite* or *a combative man.* [g]This poem also occurs in Psalm 18 with some variations. [h]Heb uncertain [i]Heb *Sheol*

²⁸ You are the one
who saves people who suffer,
but your eyes are against the proud.
You bring them down!
²⁹ You are my lamp, LORD;
the LORD illumines my darkness.
³⁰ With you I can charge into battle;
with my God I can leap over a wall.
³¹ God! His way is perfect;
the LORD's word is tried and true.
He is a shield for all who take refuge
in him.
³² Now really, who is divine
except the LORD?
And who is a rock except our God?
³³ Only God! My mighty fortress,
who makes my way^j perfect,
³⁴ who makes my step^k as sure as the deer's,
who lets me stand securely
on the heights,
³⁵ who trains my hands for war
so my arms can bend a bronze bow.
³⁶ You've given me
the shield of your salvation;
your help has made me great.
³⁷ You've let me walk fast and safe,
without even twisting an ankle.
³⁸ I chased my enemies and destroyed them!
I didn't come home until I finished
them off.
³⁹ I ate them up! I struck them down!
They couldn't get up;
they fell under my feet.
⁴⁰ You equipped me
with strength for war;
you brought my adversaries
down underneath me.
⁴¹ You made my enemies turn tail from me;
I destroyed my foes.
⁴² They looked around,
but there was no one to save them.
They looked to the LORD,
but he wouldn't answer them.
⁴³ I crushed them like dust on the ground;
I stomped on them,
trampled them like mud
dumped in the streets.

⁴⁴ You delivered me from struggles
with many people;
you appointed me the leader
of many nations.
Strangers come to serve me.
⁴⁵ Foreigners grovel before me;
after hearing about me, they obey me.
⁴⁶ Foreigners lose their nerve;
they come trembling
out of their fortresses.^l

⁴⁷ The LORD lives! Bless God, my rock!
Let my God, the rock of my salvation,
be lifted high!
⁴⁸ This is the God who avenges
on my behalf,
who subdues peoples before me,
⁴⁹ who rescues me from my enemies.
You lifted me high above my adversaries;
you delivered me from violent people.
⁵⁰ That's why I thank you, LORD,
in the presence of the nations.
That's why I sing praises to your name.
⁵¹ You are the one who gives
great victories to your king,
who shows faithful love
to your anointed one—
to David and to his descendants forever.

David's last words

23 These are David's last words:
This is the declaration
of Jesse's son David,
the declaration of a man raised high,
a man anointed by the God of Jacob,
a man favored
by the strong one of Israel.^m
² The LORD's spirit speaks through me;
his word is on my tongue.
³ Israel's God has spoken,
Israel's rock said to me:
"Whoever rules rightly over people,
whoever rules in the fear of God,
⁴ is like the light of sunrise
on a morning with no clouds,
like the bright gleam after the rain
that brings grass from the ground."
⁵ Yes, my house is this way with God!^n

---

^jQere; Kethib *his way* ^kQere; Kethib *his step* ^lOr *prisons* ^mOr *Israel's favorite singer* or *the favorite of Israel's songs* ^nOr *Yes, my house is surely with God!*

He has made an eternal covenant
  with me,
laid out and secure in every detail.
Yes, he provides every one of my victories
  and brings my every desire to pass.
⁶ But despicable people are like thorns,
  all of them good for nothing,
  because they can't be carried by hand.
⁷ No one can touch them,
  except with iron bar
  or the shaft of a spear.
They must be burned up with fire
  right on the spot!

David's warriors

⁸ These are the names of David's warriors: Jeshbaal° from Hachmonᵖ was chief of the Three.�q He raised his spearʳ against eight hundred, killing them on a single occasion.

⁹ Next in command was Eleazar, Dodo's son and Ahohi's grandson. He was among the three warriors with David when they insulted the Philistines who had gathered there for battle. The Israelites retreated, ¹⁰but he stood his ground and fought the Philistines until his hand was weary and stuck to the sword. But the LORD accomplished a great victory that day. The troops then returned to Eleazar, but only to plunder the dead.

¹¹Next in command was Agee's son Shammah, who was from Harar. The Philistines had gathered at Lehi, where there was a plot of land full of lentils. The troops fled from the Philistines, ¹²but Shammah took a position in the middle of the plot, defended it, and struck down the Philistines. The LORD accomplished a great victory.

¹³At harvesttime, three of the thirty chiefs went down and joined David at the fortressˢ of Adullam, while a force of Philistines were camped in the Rephaim Valley. ¹⁴At that time, David was in the fortress, and a Philistine fort was in Bethlehem. ¹⁵David had a craving and said, "If only someone could give me a drink of water from the well by the gate in Bethlehem." ¹⁶So the three warriors broke through the Philistine camp and drew water from the well by the gate in Bethlehem and brought it back to David. But he refused to drink it and poured it out to the LORD.

¹⁷"The LORD forbid that I should do that," he said. "Isn't this the blood of men who risked their lives?" So he refused to drink it.

These were the kinds of things the three warriors did.

¹⁸Now Zeruiah's son Abishai, the brother of Joab, was chief of the Thirty.ᵗ He raised his spear against three hundred men, killed them, and made a name for himself along with the Three. ¹⁹He was the most famous of the Thirty.ᵘ He became their commander, but he wasn't among the Three.

°LXXᴸ, OL; MT *Josheb-bashebeth*; cf 1 Chron 11:11 ᵖSee 1 Chron 11:11. qLXXᴸ, Vulg; cf 1 Chron 11:11; MT *chief of the officers* ʳCf 1 Chron 11:11; Heb uncertain ˢOr *cave*; cf 2 Sam 23:14 ᵗSome Heb manuscripts, Syr; MT *third* or *three* ᵘSyr; cf 1 Chron 11:25; MT *Wasn't he the most famous of the Three?*

URIAH

Means "The Lord is light (or fire)." A Hittite and an officer of David's army who died because of David's betrayal. He was named in a list of an elite group of officers in the Israelite army (2 Sam 23:24-39), and the fact that his house was near the king's house may indicate that he was a prominent member of the royal-military circles that antedated David's conquest of Jerusalem. He was on the battlefield against the Ammonites at Rabbah when David took advantage of his wife Bathsheba in his absence and, as a result, she became pregnant (2 Sam 11:1-5).

[20]Jehoiada's son Benaiah was a hero from Kabzeel who performed great deeds. He killed the two sons[v] of Ariel from Moab. He once went down into a pit and killed a lion on a snowy day. [21]He also killed a giant[w] Egyptian who had a spear in his hand.

[v]LXX; MT lacks sons. [w]MT handsome; cf 1 Chron 11:23

WELLS

Wells were highly valued and coveted throughout the ancient world. While spring water was preferred, well water was often necessary to sustain towns and villages (1 Sam 19:22; 2 Sam 23:15; John 4:6).

Wells in the biblical world were next to and within cities (Gen 24:11; 2 Sam 17:18) and in various topographical locations such as valleys (Gen 26:17-18) and fields (Gen 29:2). In the nomad's world of the wilderness, possession of wells was literally a life-and-death issue. Conflict over wells among nomadic peoples (Gen 26:20-21) has continued throughout time.

Moses' request for the Israelites to pass through Edom on their way to the land of promise includes a promise not to drink from any well in Edom (Num 20:17), and then he adds that any water the people or animals do consume will be purchased (Num 20:19; cf. Deut 2:27-28). The enormous value of water in the arid biblical lands comes into view in the request and in the denial by Edom.

In the biblical texts women usually perform the difficult task of drawing water from a well. Biblical writers display the qualities of individuals in stories involving wells. Eliezer arrives in Nahor seeking a wife for Isaac son of Abraham. Willingness to draw water for Eliezer and his camels is the sign of the right woman. Rebekah's actions reveal character. She is to be Isaac's wife (Gen 24:10-58). Moses draws water for the flocks of the priest of Midian after defending his daughters from shepherds, and Moses' marriage to Zipporah results (Exod 2:15-22). The account of Jesus and the Samaritan woman at the well (John 4:6-15) reveals the woman's desire for water she does not draw. The tedious and difficult task of drawing water is implied along with the revelation of her questionable character.

The word well can depict a cistern (2 Sam 17:18) or a pit. Oxen can fall into a pit (Luke 14:5). Often a pit was thought to reach the underworld (Pss 55:23 [Heb. 55:24]; 69:15 [Heb. 69:16]). In the ancient world wells were sometimes thought to be the home of spirits (see, e.g., Gen 16:14). In frightening imagery, the same term (here rendered as "shaft" in the CEB) is used in describing a bottomless pit with smoke pouring from the underworld, teeming with locusts rising to plague the earth (Rev 9:1-6).

Names of many places were based upon an event at a well. At Beer-sheba ("seven wells" or "well of seven"), Abraham requested King Abimelech to make an oath over seven lambs proclaiming Abraham's ownership of the well (Gen 21:30-31). Other sites include Beer-lahai-roi (Gen 16:14); Beer in Moab (Num 21:16); Beeroth in Sinai (Deut 10:6); Beer in Israel (Judg 9:21); Beeroth in Benjamin (Josh 9:17); and Beer-elim (Isa 15:8).

Benaiah went against him armed with a staff. He grabbed the spear out of the Egyptian's hand and killed him with his own spear. [22]These were the kinds of things Jehoiada's son Benaiah did. He made a name for himself along with the three warriors. [23]He was famous among the Thirty, but he didn't become one of the Three. David placed him in command of his own bodyguard.

[24]Among the Thirty were:
   Asahel, Joab's brother;
   Elhanan, Dodo's son
      from Bethlehem;
[25]Shammah from Harod;
   Elika from Harod;
[26]Helez from Pelet;
   Ira, Ikkesh's son from Tekoa;
[27]Abiezer from Anathoth;
   Mebunnai the Hushathite;
[28]Zalmon from Ahoh;
   Maharai from Netophah;
[29]Heleb, Baanah's son
      from Netophah;
   Ittai, Ribai's son
      from Gibeah in Benjamin;
[30]Benaiah from Pirathon;
   Hiddai from the Gaash ravines;
[31]Abi-albon from the desert plain;
   Azmaveth from Bahurim;
[32]Eliahba from Shaalbon;
   Jashen the Gizonite;[x]
   Jonathan, [33]Shammah's son[y]
      from Harar;
   Ahiam, Sharar's son from Harar;
[34]Eliphelet, Ahasbai's son from Maacah;
   Eliam, Ahithophel's son from Giloh;
[35]Hezro from Carmel;
   Paarai from Erab;
[36]Igal, Nathan's son from Zobah;
   Bani the Gadite;
[37]Zelek the Ammonite;
   Naharai from Beeroth, and the
      armor-bearer for Zeruiah's son Joab;
[38]Ira from Ither;
   Gaeb from Ither;
[39]and Uriah the Hittite—
   thirty-seven in all.

David's census

24 The LORD burned with anger against Israel again, and he incited David against them: Go and count the people of Israel and Judah.

[2]So the king said to Joab and the military commanders[z] who were with him, "Go throughout all the tribes of Israel, from Dan to Beer-sheba, and take a census of the people so I know how many people there are."

[3]Joab said to the king, "May the LORD your God increase the number of people a hundred times while the eyes of my master the king can still see it! But why does my master the king want to do this?"

[4]But the king's word overruled Joab and the military commanders. So Joab and the commanders left the king's presence to take a census of the Israelites. [5]They crossed the Jordan River and began from Aroer and from[a] the town that is in the middle of the valley of Gad, then on to Jazer. [6]They continued to Gilead and on to Kadesh in Hittite territory.[b] They came to Dan[c] and went around to Sidon. [7]They went to the fortress of Tyre and to all the towns of the Hivites and the Canaanites. They went out to Beer-sheba in the arid southern plain of Judah. [8]At the end of nine months and twenty days, after going through the entire country, they came back to Jerusalem. [9]Joab reported to the king the number of the people who had been counted: in Israel there were eight hundred thousand strong men who could handle a sword; in Judah the total was five hundred thousand men.

[10]But after this David felt terrible that he had counted the people. David said to the LORD, "I have sinned greatly in what I have done. Now, LORD, please take away the guilt of your servant because I have done something very foolish."

[11]When David got up the next morning, the LORD's word came to the prophet Gad, David's seer: [12]Go and tell David, This is what the LORD says: I'm offering you three punishments. Choose one of them, and that is what I will do to you.

[x]Cf 1 Chron 11:34; MT *Jashen's sons* [y]LXX; MT lacks *son*. [z]LXX and 2 Sam 24:4; MT *commander* [a]LXX; MT *camped in Aroer south of the city* [b]Hebrew uncertain; correction *on to the area beneath Hermon* [c]LXX[L]; MT *Dan-jaan*

¹³So Gad went to David and said to him, "Will three[d] years of famine come on your land? Or will you run from your enemies for three months while they chase you? Or will there be three days of plague in your land? Decide now what answer I should take back to the one who sent me."

¹⁴"I'm in deep trouble," David said to Gad. "Let's fall into the LORD's hands because his mercy is great, but don't let me fall into human hands."

¹⁵So the LORD sent a plague on Israel from that very morning until the allotted time. Seventy thousand people died, from Dan to Beer-sheba. ¹⁶But when the divine messenger stretched out his hand to destroy Jerusalem, the LORD regretted doing this disaster and said to the messenger who was destroying the people, "That's enough! Withdraw your hand." At that time the LORD's messenger was by the threshing floor of Araunah from Jebus.

¹⁷When David saw the messenger who was striking down the people, he said, "I'm the one who sinned! I'm the one who has done wrong. But these sheep—what have they done wrong? Turn your hand against me and my household."

¹⁸That same day Gad came to David and told him, "Go up and build an altar to the LORD on the threshing floor of Araunah from Jebus." ¹⁹So David went up, following Gad's instructions, just as the LORD had commanded.

²⁰Araunah looked up and saw the king and his servants approaching him. Araunah rushed out and bowed low before the king, his nose to the ground. ²¹Araunah said, "Why has my master and king come to his servant?"

David said, "To buy this threshing floor from you to build an altar to the LORD, so the plague among the people may come to an end."

²²Then Araunah said to David, "Take it for yourself, and may my master the king do what he thinks is best. Here are oxen for the entirely burned offering, and here are threshing boards and oxen yokes for wood. ²³All this, Your Majesty, Araunah gives to the king." Then he added, "May the LORD your God respond favorably to you!"

²⁴"No," the king said to Araunah. "I will buy them from you at a fair price. I won't offer up to the LORD my God entirely burned offerings that cost me nothing." So David bought the threshing floor and the oxen for fifty shekels of silver. ²⁵David built an altar there for the LORD and offered entirely burned offerings and well-being sacrifices. The LORD responded to the prayers for the land, and the plague against Israel came to an end.

---

[d]LXX, 1 Chron 21:12; MT *seven*

1 KINGS

See the introduction to 2 Kings for an introduction to historical writing in the Old Testament.

INTRODUCTION

The books of 1 and 2 Kings are part of a history of Israel that begins in Deuteronomy and runs through 2 Kings. The books of Joshua, Judges, 1 and 2 Samuel, and 1 and 2 Kings tell of Israel's settlement in Canaan, of the creation of the state of Israel, of the division of greater Israel into two kingdoms, and of the destruction of these kingdoms by Assyria and Babylon.

CONTENT OF FIRST AND SECOND KINGS

First and Second Kings were originally one book in Hebrew. The Septuagint (the oldest Greek translation of the Old Testament) put Kings together with Samuel and divided them into four books. The books of Samuel and Kings were later separated in both the Hebrew and Christian Bibles. In the Hebrew Bible, 1 and 2 Kings are included in the Former Prophets (Joshua, Judges, 1 and 2 Samuel, and 1 and 2 Kings).

First Kings begins in the last years of King David (around 962 BCE), and 2 Kings ends during the Babylonian Exile (in approximately 560 BCE).

In Kings the word *Israel* has three different meanings. During the reigns of David and Solomon, *Israel* refers to the covenant community (the original twelve tribes) that is united in the nation Israel. After the division of the nation, *Israel* refers to the Northern Kingdom and Judah refers to the Southern Kingdom. Even after the division and after the destruction of the Northern Kingdom, however, *Israel* or *the people of Israel* is often used to refer to all the chosen people, both south and north.

The history of the divided kingdoms is organized according to the careers of their kings. Each king is judged by whether he practices pure worship of God and whether the worship rituals are held in the Jerusalem temple. Most of the kings are condemned because they allow, or even encourage, the worship of foreign gods. Many of them also build shrines to God away from the temple, which draws the people away from the temple for worship.

THE CHRONOLOGY OF FIRST AND SECOND KINGS

The books of Kings do not give specific dates for the reign of each king. Rather, the reigns are coordinated with one another so that the years of one king are used to establish the years of another (see, for example, 1 Kings 15:25).

This method of dating is not always accurate. Differences exist between these dates and the dates figured by considering only the years of Judean kings or of Israelite kings. In addition, Assyrian and Babylonian documents mention Israelite and Judean kings. Dates from these records do not always match those given in Kings.

The coordinated system of dating used in Kings is not completely unreliable, but the dates must be compared to dates given in other historical sources. This is why various Old Testament commentaries do not all give the same dates for the kings of Judah and Israel.

THE WRITER OF FIRST AND SECOND KINGS

The books of Kings are the conclusion to the history of the people of Israel that begins in Deuteronomy. The writer or writers combined parts of many historical records within an interpretive framework to produce the document we have today.

There were possibly two major editions of this document. The first edition may have been written before the death of King Josiah of Judah in 609 BCE. The second edition may have been written around 550 BCE, after Judah's defeat by Babylon in 587 BCE and after many Jews were taken into exile in Babylonia, but before the fall of Babylon in 538 BCE. The later writer added material within the earlier structure and perspective. These historians may have been priests or prophets who had access to the records of Israel's history kept in the palace and the temple. The Jews may have taken some of these records with them when they went into exile.

The viewpoint of Kings is that God blesses those who are faithful to the covenant and punishes those who disobey the covenant. These actions are in accordance with the law that is spelled out in Deuteronomy. The writers emphasize that the people of Israel must be faithful to the covenant relationship. In practical terms, this means that the people must not worship other gods or contaminate their worship of God with foreign practices. All shrines outside of Jerusalem must be destroyed and all worship must be conducted in the temple in Jerusalem. In the books of Kings, all the Judean and Israelite kings are strictly judged by how they lived up to their covenant responsibilities. All idolatry and tolerance of foreign religious influences is condemned.

1 KINGS

David and Abishag

1 King David had become very old. His servants covered him with blankets, but he couldn't stay warm. ²They said to him, "Allow us to find a young woman for our master the king. She will serve the king and take care of him by lying beside our master the king and keeping him warm." ³So they looked in every corner of Israel until they found Abishag from Shunem. They brought her to the king. ⁴She was very beautiful. She cared for the king and served him, but the king didn't have sex with her.

Adonijah's rebellion

⁵Adonijah, Haggith's son, bragged about himself and said, "I'll rule as king myself." He got his own chariot and horses with fifty runners to go in front. ⁶Now Adonijah's father had never given him direction; he never questioned why Adonijah did what he did. He was very handsome and was born after Absalom. ⁷He took advice from Joab, Zeruiah's son, and from the priest Abiathar. They assisted Adonijah. ⁸But Zadok the priest, Jehoiada's son Benaiah, the prophet Nathan, Shimei and his friends, and David's veterans didn't join Adonijah. ⁹So Adonijah prepared lamb, oxen, and fattened cattle at the Stone of Zoheleth, next to En-rogel. He invited his brothers (the royal princes) and all the citizens of Judah who were the royal servants to come. ¹⁰But he didn't invite the prophet Nathan, Benaiah, David's veterans, or his brother Solomon.

¹¹Nathan said to Bathsheba, Solomon's mother, "Did you hear that Adonijah, Haggith's son, has become king, but our master David doesn't know about it? ¹²Let me give you some advice on how you and your son Solomon can survive this. ¹³Go to King David and say, 'Didn't my master the king swear to your servant, "Your son Solomon will certainly rule after me. He will sit on my throne"? Why then has Adonijah become king?' ¹⁴While you are speaking there with the king, I'll come along and support your words."

¹⁵So Bathsheba went to the king in his bedroom. The king was very old, and Abishag from Shunem was serving the king. ¹⁶Bathsheba bowed down on her face before the king.

The king asked, "What do you want?"

¹⁷She said to him, "Your Majesty, you swore by the LORD your God to your servant, 'Your son Solomon will certainly rule after me. He will sit on my throne.' ¹⁸But now, look, Adonijah has become king, and my master the king doesn't know about it. ¹⁹He has prepared large quantities of oxen, fattened cattle, and lamb. He has invited all the royal princes as well as Abiathar the priest and Joab the general. However, he didn't invite your servant Solomon. ²⁰As for you, my master the king, the eyes of all Israel are upon you to tell them who will follow you on the throne of my master the king. ²¹When my master the king lies down with his ancestors, then I and my son Solomon will become outlaws."

²²While she was still speaking with the king, the prophet Nathan arrived. ²³The king was informed, "The prophet Nathan is here." Then Nathan came in before the king and bowed his face to the ground. ²⁴He said, "My master the king, you must have said, 'Adonijah will become king after me and will sit on my throne.' ²⁵Indeed, today he went down and prepared oxen, fattened cattle, and lamb in large numbers. He invited all the royal princes, the generals, and Abiathar the priest. They are eating and drinking with him, and they said, 'Long live King Adonijah!' ²⁶Adonijah didn't invite me, your servant, Zadok the priest, Jehoiada's son Benaiah, or your servant Solomon. ²⁷If this message was from my master the king, you didn't make it known to your servant. Who should follow you on the throne of my master the king?"

²⁸King David answered, "Bring me Bathsheba." She came and stood before the king. ²⁹The king made a solemn pledge and said, "As surely as the LORD lives, who rescued me from every trouble, ³⁰regarding what I swore to you by the LORD, Israel's God, 'Your son Solomon will certainly succeed

me; he will sit on the throne after me'—I'll see that it happens today."

³¹Bathsheba bowed down with her face to the ground. She honored the king and said, "May my master King David live forever!"

³²King David said, "Bring me Zadok the priest, the prophet Nathan, and Benaiah, Jehoiada's son." They came to the king, ³³who said to them, "Take with you the servants of your masters. Put my son Solomon on my mule and bring him down to Gihon. ³⁴There Zadok the priest and the prophet Nathan will anoint him king over Israel. Blow the ram's horn and say, 'Long live King Solomon!' ³⁵You will follow him. He will enter and sit on my throne, and so he will succeed me as king. I have appointed him to become ruler over Israel and Judah."

³⁶Benaiah, Jehoiada's son, responded to the king, "Yes, may it happen as the LORD, the God of my king, says. ³⁷Just as the LORD was with my master the king, so may he be with Solomon. May his throne be even greater than the throne of my master King David." ³⁸Zadok the priest, the prophet Nathan, Jehoiada's son Benaiah, and the Cherethites and the Pelethites went down and put Solomon on King David's mule. They led him to Gihon. ³⁹Zadok the priest took the horn of oil from the tent and anointed Solomon. They blew the ram's horn, and all the people said, "Long live King Solomon!" ⁴⁰All the people followed

him playing flutes and celebrating. The ground shook at their noise.

⁴¹Adonijah and all his invited guests heard this when they had finished eating. When Joab heard the sound of the ram's horn, he said, "What's that noise coming from the city?" ⁴²While he was still speaking, Jonathan, Abiathar the priest's son, arrived. Adonijah said, "Come on in! You are an honest man and will bring a good report."

⁴³Jonathan replied to Adonijah, "No! Our master King David has made Solomon king! ⁴⁴To support him, the king sent along Zadok the priest; the prophet Nathan; Benaiah, Jehoiada's son; and the Cherethites and the Pelethites. They've put Solomon on the royal mule. ⁴⁵Zadok the priest and the prophet Nathan have anointed him king at Gihon. They went up from there celebrating so that the city was thrown into a commotion. That is the sound you heard. ⁴⁶There's more: Solomon has taken over the throne of the kingdom. ⁴⁷The royal attendants blessed our master King David: 'May your God make Solomon's name better than your name. May God elevate his throne above your throne.'"

The king then worshipped on his bed ⁴⁸and said, "Bless Israel's God, the LORD, who today has set my sonª on my throne, and has allowed my eyes to see it."

⁴⁹Trembling with fear, all of Adonijah's guests got up and fled, each going a different

ªHeb lacks *my son*; other versions have it or something similar.

ADONIJAH

David's fourth son, born in Hebron by his wife Haggith (2 Sam 3:4). First Kings 1–2 narrates Adonijah's failed bid to succeed David as king of Israel. Adonijah was heir apparent to David's throne, but his younger brother Solomon was a formidable rival. Solomon's mother Bathsheba and the prophet Nathan convince David to declare that Solomon should be anointed king (1 Kgs 1:32-35). Adonijah flees to the temple and refuses to come out without Solomon's promise to spare him. After David's death, Adonijah asks Solomon for David's secondary wife Abishag. Solomon interprets this as a subtle bid for kingship and has Adonijah killed.

way. ⁵⁰Adonijah was afraid of Solomon, so he got up and went to grab hold of the horns of the altar. ⁵¹Solomon was told, "Look! Adonijah is afraid of King Solomon and has grabbed the horns of the altar. He's saying, 'King Solomon must swear to me first that he won't execute his servant with the sword.'"

⁵²Solomon said, "If he shows himself to be an honorable person, then not a hair of his head will be harmed. But if any evil is found in him, he will die." ⁵³King Solomon sent word and had him brought down from the altar. He came and bowed down to King Solomon. Solomon said to him, "Go home!"

David's last words

2 David's time was coming to an end. So he commanded Solomon his son, ²"I'm following the path that the whole earth takes. Be strong and be a man. ³Guard what is owed to the LORD your God, walking in his ways and observing his laws, his commands, his judgments, and his testimonies, just as it is written in the Instruction from Moses. In this way you will succeed in whatever you do and wherever you go. ⁴So also the LORD will confirm the word he spoke to me: 'If your children will take care to walk before me faithfully, with all their heart and all their being, then one of your own children will never fail to be on the throne of Israel.' ⁵You should know what Joab, Zeruiah's son, has done to me and what he did to the two generals of Israel, Abner, Ner's son, and Amasa, Jether's son. He murdered them, spilling blood at peacetime and putting the blood of war on the belt around his waist and on the sandals on his feet. ⁶So act wisely: Don't allow him to die a peaceful death. ⁷As for Barzillai's sons from Gilead, show them kindness. Let them eat with you. When I was running away from your brother Absalom, they came to me. ⁸Now as for this Shimei, Gera's son—a Benjaminite from Bahurim—who is with you, he cursed me viciously when I went to Mahanaim. When he came down to meet me at the Jordan, I swore to him by the LORD, 'Surely I won't execute you with the sword.' ⁹But you don't need to excuse him.

You are wise and know what to do to him. Give him a violent death."

¹⁰Then David lay down with his ancestors and was buried in David's City. ¹¹He ruled over Israel forty years—seven years in Hebron and thirty-three years in Jerusalem.

Solomon secures his throne

¹²Solomon sat on the throne of his father David, and his royal power was well established. ¹³Adonijah, Haggith's son, went to Bathsheba, Solomon's mother. She said, "Are you coming in peace?"

He said, "Yes. ¹⁴I have something to say to you."

She said, "Say it."

¹⁵He said, "You know how the kingdom was mine. All Israel had appointed me as their king. Then suddenly the kingdom went to my brother as the LORD willed. ¹⁶Now I have just one request of you. Don't refuse me!"

She said to him, "Go on."

¹⁷Adonijah continued, "Ask King Solomon to let me marry Abishag from Shunem—he won't refuse you."

¹⁸Bathsheba said, "Okay; I'll speak to the king for you."

¹⁹So Bathsheba went to King Solomon to talk with him about Adonijah. The king stood up to meet her and bowed low to her. Then he returned to his throne and had a throne set up for the queen mother. She sat to his right. ²⁰She said, "I have just one small request for you. Don't refuse me."

The king said to her, "Mother, ask me. I won't refuse you."

²¹"Let Abishag from Shunem be married to your brother Adonijah," she said.

²²King Solomon replied to his mother, "Why ask only for Abishag from Shunem for Adonijah? Why not ask for the entire kingdom for him? After all, he is my older brother and has the support of Abiathar the priest and Joab, Zeruiah's son." ²³King Solomon swore by the LORD, "May God do to me as he sees fit! Adonijah has made this request at the cost of his life! ²⁴Now, as surely as the LORD lives—the one who supported me, put me on the throne of my father David, and provided a royal house

for me exactly as he promised—Adonijah will be executed today." ²⁵ So King Solomon sent Benaiah, Jehoiada's son. He attacked Adonijah, and Adonijah died.

²⁶ The king said to the priest Abiathar, "Go to your fields at Anathoth, because you are a condemned man. However, I won't kill you today because you carried the LORD's chest in front of my father David and because you shared in all my father's sufferings." ²⁷ So Solomon expelled Abiathar from the LORD's priesthood in order to fulfill the LORD's word that was spoken against Eli's family at Shiloh.

²⁸ Now the news reached Joab because he had supported Adonijah, though he hadn't supported Absalom. Joab ran to the LORD's tent and grabbed the horns of the altar. ²⁹ King Solomon was told that Joab had fled to the LORD's tent and was now beside the altar. So Solomon sent Benaiah, Jehoiada's son, instructing him, "Go. Attack Joab!"

³⁰ Benaiah came to the LORD's tent and said to Joab, "The king says, 'Come out!'"

Joab said, "No! I'd rather die here."

Benaiah sent a report back to the king: "This is what Joab said and how he answered me."

³¹ The king said to him, "Do as he said. Attack him and then bury him. In doing this, you will remove from me and from my father's royal house the guilt over the innocent blood that Joab shed. ³² May the LORD return that bloodguilt back on his own head for attacking the two men who were better and more righteous than he was. He murdered those two with the sword: Abner, Ner's son and Israel's general, and Amasa, Jether's son and Judah's general. But my father David didn't know about it. ³³ May the bloodguilt for their deaths return on Joab's head and on the head of his family line forever. But may the LORD's peace be on David, his family, and his royal house forever." ³⁴ So Benaiah, Jehoiada's son, went and attacked Joab and killed him.

Joab was buried at his home in the wilderness. ³⁵ In his place, the king gave leadership of the army to Benaiah, Jehoiada's son. The king put the priest Zadok in Abiathar's position. ³⁶ Then he sent for Shimei and said, "Build a house for yourself in Jerusalem and stay in the city. Don't leave to go anywhere else. ³⁷ If you try to leave, be advised that on the day you cross the Kidron Valley you will most certainly die. Your bloodguilt will be on your own head."

³⁸ Shimei said to the king, "This is a good idea. Your servant will do just what my master the king said." So Shimei stayed in Jerusalem for a long time.

³⁹ After three years, two of Shimei's servants fled to the king of Gath, Achish, Maacah's son. Shimei was informed, "Your servants are now in Gath." ⁴⁰ Shimei saddled his donkey and went to Achish in Gath to look for his servants. Shimei then brought his servants back from Gath. ⁴¹ Solomon was told that Shimei had left Jerusalem for Gath and then returned.

⁴² The king sent for Shimei and asked him, "Didn't I make you swear a solemn

ABIATHAR

Great-grandson of Eli and the only priest to survive Saul's command that all the priests in Nob be slaughtered (1 Sam 22:6-20). Abiathar fled to David's camp and took the priestly vest with him. His presence as David's priest from earliest times was crucial in swinging popular support to David. With David on his deathbed, Abiathar supported Adonijah instead of Solomon as David's successor. Solomon eventually found a reason to execute all of his rival's supporters except for Abiathar, whom he banished to Anathoth, outside Jerusalem (1 Kgs 2:13-46).

pledge by the LORD? And didn't I swear to you, 'If you try to leave and go anywhere, be advised that on that very day you will most certainly die'? You said to me, 'This is a good idea. I agree to it.' ⁴³Why didn't you keep your solemn promise to the LORD and the command that I gave you?" ⁴⁴The king said further, "You know quite well all the evil that you did to my father David. May the LORD return your evil on your own head. ⁴⁵However, may King Solomon be blessed and David's throne be secure before the LORD forever." ⁴⁶Then the king commanded Benaiah, Jehoiada's son, who went and attacked Shimei, and he died.

In these ways royal power was handed over to Solomon.

Solomon first meets God

3 Solomon became the son-in-law of Pharaoh, Egypt's king, when he married Pharaoh's daughter. He brought her to David's City until he finished building his royal palace, the LORD's temple, and the wall around Jerusalem. ²Unfortunately, the people were sacrificing at the shrines because a temple hadn't yet been built for the LORD's name in those days. ³Now Solomon loved the LORD by walking in the laws of his father David, with the exception that he also sacrificed and burned incense at the shrines.

⁴The king went to the great shrine at Gibeon in order to sacrifice there. He used to offer a thousand entirely burned offerings on that altar. ⁵The LORD appeared to Solomon at Gibeon in a dream at night. God said, "Ask whatever you wish, and I'll give it to you."

⁶Solomon responded, "You showed so much kindness to your servant my father David when he walked before you in truth, righteousness, and with a heart true to you. You've kept this great loyalty and kindness for him and have now given him a son to sit on his throne. ⁷And now, LORD my God, you have made me, your servant, king in my father David's place. But I'm young and inexperienced. I know next to nothing. ⁸But I'm here, your servant, in the middle of the people you have chosen, a large population

that can't be numbered or counted due to its vast size. ⁹Please give your servant a discerning mind in order to govern your people and to distinguish good from evil, because no one is able to govern this important people of yours without your help."

¹⁰It pleased the LORD that Solomon had made this request. ¹¹God said to him, "Because you have asked for this instead of requesting long life, wealth, or victory over your enemies—asking for discernment so as to acquire good judgment—¹²I will now do just what you said. Look, I hereby give you a wise and understanding mind. There has been no one like you before now, nor will there be anyone like you afterward. ¹³I now also give you what you didn't ask for: wealth and fame. There won't be a king like you as long as you live. ¹⁴And if you walk in my ways and obey my laws and commands, just as your father David did, then I will give you a very long life."

¹⁵Solomon awoke and realized it was a dream. He went to Jerusalem and stood before the chest containing the LORD's covenant. Then he offered entirely burned offerings and well-being sacrifices, and held a celebration for all his servants.

Solomon and the prostitutes

¹⁶Sometime later, two prostitutes came and stood before the king. ¹⁷One of them said, "Please, Your Majesty, listen: This woman and I have been living in the same house. I gave birth while she was there. ¹⁸This woman gave birth three days after I did. We stayed together. Apart from the two of us, there was no one else in the house. ¹⁹This woman's son died one night when she rolled over him. ²⁰She got up in the middle of the night and took my son from my side while I was asleep. She laid him on her chest and laid her dead son on mine. ²¹When I got up in the morning to nurse my son, he was dead! But when I looked more closely in the daylight, it turned out that it wasn't my son—not the baby I had birthed."

²²The other woman said, "No! My son is alive! Your son is the dead one."

But the first woman objected, "No! Your

son is dead! My son is alive!" In this way they argued back and forth in front of the king.

²³The king said, "This one says, 'My son is alive and your son is dead.' The other one says, 'No! Your son is dead and my son is alive.' ²⁴Get me a sword!" They brought a sword to the king. ²⁵Then the king said, "Cut the living child in two! Give half to one woman and half to the other woman."

²⁶Then the woman whose son was still alive said to the king, "Please, Your Majesty, give her the living child; please don't kill him," for she had great love for her son.

But the other woman said, "If I can't have him, neither will you. Cut the child in half."

²⁷Then the king answered, "Give the first woman the living newborn. Don't kill him. She is his mother."

²⁸All Israel heard about the judgment that the king made. Their respect for the king grew because they saw that God's wisdom was in him so he could execute justice.

Solomon's administration

4 King Solomon became king of all Israel. ²These were his officials: the priest Azariah, Zadok's son; ³the scribes Elihoreph and Ahijah, the sons of Shisha; Jehoshaphat, the recorder, Ahilud's son; ⁴the general Benaiah, Jehoiada's son; the priests Zadok and Abiathar; ⁵Azariah, Nathan's son, who was in charge of the officials; Zabud, Nathan's son, a priest and royal friend; ⁶Ahishar, who was in charge of the palace; and Adoniram, Abda's son, who was supervisor of the work gangs.

⁷Solomon had twelve officers over all Israel. They supplied the king and his palace with food. Each would provide the supplies for one month per year. ⁸Here are their names:

Ben-hur in the highlands of Ephraim;
⁹Ben-deker in Makaz, Shaalbim, Beth-shemesh, and Elon-bethhanan;
¹⁰Ben-hesed in Arubboth, who had Socoh and all the land of Hepher;
¹¹Ben-abinadab in all of Naphath-dor (Taphath, Solomon's daughter, was his wife);

¹²Baana, Ahilud's son, in Taanach, Megiddo, and all Beth-shean beside Zarethan and below Jezreel, from Beth-shean to Abel-meholah and over to the region opposite Jokmeam;
¹³Ben-geber in Ramoth-gilead, who controlled the villages of Jair, Manasseh's son, which were in Gilead, and who had the Argob region that was in Bashan—sixty large walled cities with bronze bars;
¹⁴Ahinadab, Iddo's son, in Mahanaim;
¹⁵Ahimaaz in Naphtali, who also took Solomon's daughter Basemath as his wife;
¹⁶Baana, Hushai's son, in Asher and Bealoth;
¹⁷Jehoshaphat, Paruah's son, in Issachar;
¹⁸Shimei, Ela's son, in Benjamin;
¹⁹Geber, Uri's son, in the land of Gilead, the land of the Amorite king Sihon and of King Og of Bashan;

and there was a single officer who was in the land of Judah.ᵇ

²⁰Judah and Israel grew numerous like the sand alongside the sea. They ate, drank, and celebrated.

²¹ᶜSolomon ruled over all the states from the Euphrates River through the Philistines' land and as far as the border of Egypt. These areas brought tribute to Solomon and served him all the days of his life. ²²Solomon's food requirements for a single day included thirty korsᵈ of refined flour; sixty kors of flour; ²³ten head of grain-fattened cattle; twenty head of pastured cattle; one hundred sheep; as well as deer, gazelles, roebucks, and the best of fowl. ²⁴He ruled over all the lands west of the Euphrates River, from Tiphsah to Gaza, and over all the kings west of the Euphrates. He had peace on all sides. ²⁵The people of Judah and Israel from Dan all the way to Beersheba lived securely under their vines and fig trees throughout the days of Solomon.

²⁶Solomon had forty thousand horse stalls for his chariots and twelve thousand additional horses. ²⁷The officials provided King Solomon and all who joined him at the royal table with monthly food rations.

ᵇLXX; MT lacks *of Judah*.　ᶜ5:1 in Heb　ᵈOne kor is possibly equal to fifty gallons.

They left out nothing. ²⁸Each brought their share of barley and straw for the horses and for the chariot horses, bringing it to its proper place. ²⁹And God gave Solomon wisdom and very great understanding—insight as long as the seashore itself. ³⁰Solomon's wisdom was greater than all the famous Easterners, greater even than all the wisdom of Egypt. ³¹He was wiser than anyone, more wise than Ethan the Ezrahite or Mahol's sons: Heman, Calcol, and Darda. His reputation was known throughout the region. ³²Solomon spoke three thousand proverbs and one thousand five songs. ³³He described the botany of trees, whether the cedar in Lebanon or the hyssop that grows out of the wall. He also described cattle, birds, anything that crawls on the ground, and fish. ³⁴People came from everywhere to listen to Solomon's wisdom; even the earth's kings who had heard about his wisdom came!

Wood and stone for the temple

5 ᵉBecause King Hiramᶠ of Tyre was loyal to David throughout his rule, Hiram sent his servants to Solomon when he heard that Solomon had become king after his father. ²Solomon sent the following message to Hiram: ³"You know that my father David wasn't able to build a temple for the name of the LORD my God. This was because of the enemies that fought him on all sides until the LORD put them under the soles of his feet. ⁴Now the LORD my God has given me peace on every side, without enemies or misfortune. ⁵So I'm planning to build a temple for the name of the LORD my God, just as the LORD indicated to my father David, 'I will give you a son to follow you on your throne. He will build the temple for my name.' ⁶Now give the order and have the cedars of Lebanon cut down for me. My servants will work with your servants. I'll pay your servants whatever price you set, because you know we have no one here who is skilled in cutting wood like the Sidonians."

⁷Hiram was thrilled when he heard Solomon's message. He said, "Today the LORD is blessed because he has given David a wise son who is in charge of this great people." ⁸Hiram sent word back to Solomon: "I have heard your message to me. I will do as you wish with the cedar and pinewood. ⁹My servants will bring the wood down the Lebanon Mountains to the sea. I'll make rafts out of them and float them on the sea to the place you specify. There I'll dismantle them, and you can carry them away. Now, as for what you must do for me in return, I ask you to provide for my royal house."

¹⁰So Hiram gave Solomon all the cedar and pinewood that he wanted. ¹¹In return, Solomon gave an annual gift to Hiram of twenty thousand korsᵍ of wheat to eat, and twenty thousand kors of pure oil for his palace use. ¹²Now the LORD made Solomon wise, just as he had promised. Solomon and Hiram made a covenant and had peace.

¹³King Solomon called up a work gang of thirty thousand workers from all over Israel. ¹⁴He sent ten thousand to work in Lebanon each month. Then they would spend two months at home. Adoniram was in charge of the work gang. ¹⁵Solomon had 70,000 laborers and 80,000 stonecutters in the highlands. ¹⁶This doesn't include Solomon's 3,300 supervisors in charge of the work, who had oversight over the laborers. ¹⁷At the king's command, they quarried huge stones of the finest quality in order to lay the temple's foundation with carefully cut stone. ¹⁸The craftsmen of Solomon and Hiram, along with those of Byblos, prepared the timber and the stones for the construction of the temple.

Solomon builds the temple

6 In the four hundred eightieth year after the Israelites left Egypt, in the month of Ziv, the second month,ʰ in the fourth year of Solomon's rule over Israel, he built the LORD's temple. ²The temple that King Solomon built for the LORD was ninety feet long, thirty feet wide, and forty-five

---

ᵉ5:15 in Heb ᶠChronicles spells the king's name *Huram*; for example, 2 Chron 2:3, 11-12; but cf 1 Chron 14:1 Kethib. ᵍOne kor is possibly equal to fifty gallons. ʰApril–May, Iyar; Ziv is a month from a Canaanite calendar.

feet high. ³The porch in front of the temple's main hall was thirty feet long. It ran across the whole width of the temple and extended fifteen feet in front of the temple. ⁴He made recessed and latticed windowsⁱ for the temple ⁵and built side rooms against the temple walls around both the main hall and the most holy place. ⁶The lower walls were seven and a half feet wide. At the second floor the walls were nine feet wide, and at the third floor they were ten and a half feet wide. He made niches around the outside of the temple so the beams wouldn't be inserted into the temple walls.ʲ ⁷When the temple was built, they did all the stone-cutting at the quarry. No hammers, axes, or any iron tools were heard in the temple during its construction. ⁸The door to the stairs was at the south side of the temple. Winding stairs went up to the second floor and from there to the third floor. ⁹He completed the temple with a roof of cedar beams and cross-planks.ᵏ ¹⁰Then he built the side rooms all around the temple. They were seven and a half feet high. He attached them to the temple with cedarwood.

¹¹The LORD's word came to Solomon, ¹²Regarding this temple that you are building: If you follow my laws, enact my regulations, and keep all my commands faithfully, then I will fulfill for you my promise that I made to your father David. ¹³I will live among the Israelites. I won't abandon my people Israel.

¹⁴So Solomon constructed the temple and completed it. ¹⁵He built the walls within the temple with cedar planks, paneled from the floor to the ceiling. He overlaid the floor of the temple with pine planks. ¹⁶At the back of the temple he built thirty feet of cedar panels from the floor to the ceiling. Solomon built the inner sanctuary, the most holy place. ¹⁷In front of this, the main hall was sixty feet. ¹⁸The cedar inside the temple was carved with gourds and blossoming flowers. The whole thing was cedar. No stone was seen. ¹⁹He set up the inner sanctuary inside the temple so that he could put the chest containing the LORD's covenant there. ²⁰The inner sanctuary was thirty feet in length, width, and height. Solomon overlaid it with pure gold and covered the altar with cedar.ˡ ²¹Solomon covered the temple's interior with pure gold. He placed gold chains in front of the inner sanctuary and covered it with gold. ²²He overlaid the whole temple inside with gold until the temple was completely covered. He covered the whole altar that was in the inner sanctuary with gold. ²³He made two winged creatures of olive wood for the inner sanctuary, each fifteen feet high. ²⁴The wings of the first winged creature were each seven and a half feet long. It was fifteen feet from the end of one wing to the end of the other. ²⁵The second winged creature also measured fifteen feet. Both winged creatures had identical measurements and form. ²⁶The height of both winged creatures was fifteen feet. ²⁷Solomon placed the winged creatures inside the temple. Their wings spread out so that the wing of the one touched one wall and the wing of the other touched the other wall. In the middle of the temple, the wings

---

ⁱHeb architectural and decorative terminology in 6:4-6 and elsewhere in chaps 6–7 is often uncertain.
ʲHeb uncertain; Heb lacks the beams. ᵏHeb uncertain ˡHeb uncertain

WINGED CREATURES

Also called "cherubim." Winged beings, part animal, part human (Ezek 10:14; 41:18-19), associated with transporting the Lord (2 Sam 22:11), the divine throne (Ezek 1; Rev 4:6-10), and sacred gardens (Gen 3:24; Ezek 28:14). Their images were carved on the covenant chest, the meeting tent (Exod 25:18-22; 26:1), and Solomon's temple (1 Kgs 6:23-28).

of the two winged creatures touched each other. ²⁸He covered the winged creatures with gold.

²⁹Solomon carved all the walls of the temple—inner and outer rooms—with engravings of winged creatures, palm trees, and blossoming flowers. ³⁰He also covered the floor of the temple with gold, in both the inner and the outer rooms. ³¹He made the doors of the inner sanctuary from olive wood and carved the doorframes with five recesses.ᵐ ³²He overlaid the two olive-wood doors with gold-plated carvings of winged creatures, palm trees, and blossoming flowers. ³³He made the door of the main hall with doorframes of olive wood with four recesses.ⁿ ³⁴The two doors of pinewood each pivoted on a socket. ³⁵Solomon carved winged creatures, palm trees, and blossoming flowers, and covered them with gold. ³⁶He built the inner courtyard with three rows of cut stone followed by one row of trimmed cedar.

³⁷Solomon laid the foundation of the LORD's temple in the fourth year in the month of Ziv.º ³⁸He finished the temple in all its details and measurements in the eleventh year during the eighth month, the month of Bul.ᴾ He built it in seven years.

Solomon builds palaces

7 Now as for Solomon's palace, it took thirteen years for him to complete its construction. ²He built the Forest of Lebanon Palace one hundred fifty feet in length, seventy-five feet in width, and forty-five feet in height. It had four rows of cedar columns with cedar engravings above the columns. ³The palace's cedar roof stood above forty-five beams resting on the columns, fifteen beams to each row. ⁴Three sets of window frames faced each other. ⁵All the doorframes were rectangular, facing each other in three sets. ⁶He made a porch with columns seventy-five feet long and forty-five feet wide. Another porch was in front of these with roofed columns in

front of them.�q ⁷He made the throne room the Hall of Justice, where he would judge. It was covered with cedar from the lower to the upper levels. ⁸The royal residence where Solomon lived was behind this hall. It had a similar design. Solomon also made a similar palace for his wife, Pharaoh's daughter. ⁹He built all these with the best stones cut to size, sawed with saws, back and front, from the foundation to the highest points and from the outer boundary to the great courtyard. ¹⁰The foundation was laid with large stones of high quality, some of fifteen feet and some of twelve feet. ¹¹Above them were high-quality stones cut to measure, as well as cedar. ¹²The surrounding great courtyard had three rows of cut stones and a row of trimmed cedar just like the inner courtyard of the LORD's temple and its porch.

Solomon's temple equipment

¹³Then King Solomon sent a message and brought Hiram from Tyre. ¹⁴Hiram's mother was a widow from the tribe of Naphtali. His father was a Tyrian skilled in bronze work. He was amazingly skillful in the techniques and knowledge for doing all kinds of work in bronze. He came to King Solomon and did all his work.

¹⁵Heʳ cast two bronze pillars. Each one was twenty-seven feet high and required a cord of eighteen feet to reach around it.ˢ ¹⁶He made two capitals of cast bronze for the tops of the columns. They were each seven and a half feet high. ¹⁷He made an intricate network of chains for the capitals on top of the columns, seven for each capital. ¹⁸He made the pillars and two rows of pomegranates for each network to adorn each of the capitals. ¹⁹The capitals on top of the columns in the porch were made like lilies, each six feet high. ²⁰Above the round-shaped part and next to the network were two hundred pomegranates. These were placed in rows around both of the capitals on top of the columns. ²¹He set up the columns at the temple's porch. He named the south column Jachin. The

---

ᵐHeb uncertain ⁿHeb uncertain ºApril–May, Iyar; Ziv is a month in the Canaanite calendar. ᴾOctober–November, Heshvan; Bul is a month in the Canaanite calendar. qHeb uncertain ʳOr *he*, either Solomon or Hiram; this ambiguity continues in the following verses, but cf 1 Kgs 7:1, 8, 13; 1 Kgs 7:40. ˢOr *the second*; cf Jer 52:21

north column he named Boaz. ²²After putting the lily shapes on top of the columns, he was finished with the columns.

²³He also made a tank of cast metal called the Sea. It was circular in shape, fifteen feet from rim to rim, seven and a half feet high, forty-five feet in circumference. ²⁴Under the rim were two rows of gourds completely encircling it, ten every eighteen inches, each cast in its mold. ²⁵The Sea rested on twelve oxen with their backs toward the center, three facing north, three facing west, three facing south, and three facing east. ²⁶The Sea was as thick as the width of a hand. Its rim was shaped like a cup or an open lily blossom. It could hold two thousand baths.ᵗ

²⁷He also made ten bronze stands. Each was six feet long, six feet wide, and four and a half feet high. ²⁸This is how each stand was made: There were panels connected between the legs. ²⁹Lions, bulls, and winged otherworldly creatures appeared on the panels between the legs. On the legs above and below the lions and bulls were wreaths on panels hanging off the stands. ³⁰There were four bronze wheels with bronze axles for each stand. There were four feet and supports cast for each basin with wreaths on their sides.ᵘ ³¹Inside the bowl was an opening eighteen inches deep. The opening was round, measuring twenty-seven inches, with engravings. The panels of the stands were square rather than round. ³²There were four wheels beneath the panels. The axles of the wheels were attached to the stand. Each wheel was twenty-seven inches in height. ³³The construction of the wheels resembled chariot wheels. The axles, rims, spokes, and hubs were all made of cast metal. ³⁴There was a handle on each of the four corners of every stand, projecting from the side of the stand. ³⁵The top of the stand had a band running around the perimeter that was nine inches deep. The stand had its own supports and panels. ³⁶On the surfaces of the supports and panels he carved winged otherworldly creatures, lions, and palm trees with wreaths everywhere.ᵛ ³⁷In this manner he made ten stands, each one cast in a single mold of the same size and shape.

³⁸He made ten bronze washbasins, each able to hold forty baths.ʷ Every washbasin was six feet across, and there was one for each of the ten stands. ³⁹He placed five stands on the south of the temple and five on the north of the temple. He placed the Sea at the southeast corner of the temple.

⁴⁰Hiram made the basins, shovels, and bowls.

And so Hiram finished his work on the LORD's temple for King Solomon:

⁴¹two columns;

  two circular capitals on top of the columns;

ᵗOne bath is approximately twenty quarts or five gallons. ᵘHeb uncertain ᵛHeb uncertain ʷOne bath is approximately twenty quarts or five gallons.

HIRAM

Two individuals in the OT—both Tyrians—are named Hiram.

1. As king of Tyre in the 10th century BCE (ca. 969–936) and a contemporary of David and Solomon, Hiram sent his envoys to David with material and labor for the building of his new royal palace (2 Sam 5:11; 1 Chron 14:1).

2. Hiram is described as a skilled artisan from Tyre who was responsible for the furnishing of Solomon's temple (1 Kgs 7:13-47; 2 Chron 2:13-16; 4:11-18). First Kings 7:14 describes him as skillful, intelligent, and knowledgeable in metalwork.

two networks, adorning the two circular capitals on top of the columns; ⁴²four hundred pomegranates for the two networks, with two rows of pomegranates for each network that adorned the two circular capitals on top of the columns;

⁴³ten stands with ten basins on them; ⁴⁴one Sea;

twelve oxen beneath the Sea;

⁴⁵and the pots, shovels, and bowls.

All the equipment that Hiram made for King Solomon for the LORD's temple was made from polished bronze. ⁴⁶The king cast it in clay molds in the Jordan Valley between Succoth and Zarethan. ⁴⁷Due to the very large number of objects, Solomon didn't even try to weigh the bronze.

⁴⁸Solomon also made all the equipment for the LORD's temple: the gold altar; the gold table for the bread of the presence; ⁴⁹the lampstands of pure gold, five on the right and five on the left in front of the inner sanctuary; the flowers, the lamps, and the tongs of gold; ⁵⁰the cups, wick trimmers, bowls, ladles, and censers of pure gold; and the gold sockets for the doors to the most holy place and for the doors to the main hall. ⁵¹When all King Solomon's work on the LORD's temple was finished, he brought the silver, gold, and all the objects his father David had dedicated and put them in the treasuries of the LORD's temple.

Solomon dedicates the temple

8 Then Solomon assembled Israel's elders, all the tribal leaders, and the chiefs of Israel's clans at Jerusalem to bring up the chest containing the LORD's covenant from David's City Zion. ²Everyone in Israel assembled before King Solomon in the seventh month, the month of Ethanim,ˣ during the festival. ³When all of Israel's elders had arrived, the priests picked up the chest. ⁴They brought the LORD's chest, the meeting tent, and all the holy equipment that was in the tent. The priests and the Levites brought them up, ⁵while King Solomon and the entire Israelite assem-

bly that had joined him before the chest sacrificed countless sheep and oxen. ⁶The priests brought the chest containing the LORD's covenant to its designated spot beneath the wings of the winged creatures in the inner sanctuary of the temple, the most holy place. ⁷The winged creatures spread their wings over the place where the chest rested, covering the chest and its carrying poles. ⁸The carrying poles were so long that their tips could be seen from the holy place in front of the inner sanctuary, though they weren't visible from outside. They are still there today. ⁹Nothing was in the chest except the two stone tablets Moses had placed there while at Horeb, where the LORD made a covenant with the Israelites after they left Egypt. ¹⁰When the priests left the holy place, the cloud filled the LORD's temple, ¹¹and the priests were unable to carry out their duties due to the cloud because the LORD's glory filled the LORD's temple.

¹²Then Solomon said, "The LORD said that he would live in a dark cloud, ¹³but I have indeed built you a lofty temple as a place where you can live forever." ¹⁴The king turned around, and while the entire assembly of Israel was standing there, he blessed them, ¹⁵saying, "Bless Israel's God, the LORD, who spoke directly to my father David and now has kept his promise: ¹⁶'From the day I brought my people Israel out of Egypt I haven't selected a city from any Israelite tribe as a site for the building of a temple for my name. But now I have chosen David to be over my people Israel.' ¹⁷My father David wanted to build a temple for the name of the LORD, Israel's God.

¹⁸"But the LORD said to my father David, 'It is very good that you thought to build a temple for my name. ¹⁹Nevertheless, you yourself won't build that temple. Instead, your very own son will build the temple for my name.' ²⁰The LORD has kept his promise—I have succeeded my father David on Israel's throne just as the LORD said, and I have built the temple for the name of the LORD, Israel's God. ²¹There I've placed the chest that contains the covenant that

---

ˣSeptember–October, Tishrei; Ethanim is a month from a Canaanite calendar.

the LORD made with our ancestors when he brought them out of Egypt."

²²Solomon stood before the LORD's altar in front of the entire Israelite assembly and, spreading out his hands toward the sky, ²³he said:

LORD God of Israel, there's no god like you in heaven above or on earth below. You keep the covenant and show loyalty to your servants who walk before you with all their heart. ²⁴This is the covenant you kept with your servant David, my father, which you promised him. Today, you have fulfilled what you promised. ²⁵So now, LORD, Israel's God, keep what you promised my father David, your servant, when you said to him, "You will never fail to have a successor sitting on Israel's throne as long as your descendants carefully walk before me just as you walked before me." ²⁶So now, God of Israel, may your promise to your servant David, my father, come true.

²⁷But how could God possibly live on earth? If heaven, even the highest heaven, can't contain you, how can this temple that I've built contain you? ²⁸LORD my God, listen to your servant's prayer and request, and hear the cry and prayer that your servant prays to you today. ²⁹Constantly watch over this temple, the place about which you said, "My name will be there," and listen to the prayer that your servant is praying toward^y this place. ³⁰Listen to the request of your servant and your people Israel when they pray toward this place. Listen from your heavenly dwelling place, and when you hear, forgive!

³¹If someone wrongs another and must make a solemn pledge asserting innocence before your altar in this temple,^z ³²then listen from heaven, act, and decide which of your servants is right. Condemn the guilty party, repaying them for their conduct, but justify the innocent

^y Or for, regarding; also used in several verses that follow ^z Heb uncertain person, repaying them for their righteousness.

[33] If your people Israel are defeated by an enemy because they have sinned against you, but then they change their hearts and lives, give thanks to your name, and ask for mercy before you at this temple, [34] then listen from heaven and forgive the sin of your people Israel. Return them to the land you gave their ancestors.

[35] When the sky holds back its rain because Israel has sinned against you, but they then pray toward this place, give thanks to your name, and turn away from their sin because you have punished them for it,[a] [36] then listen from heaven and forgive the sin of your servants, your people Israel. Teach them the best way for them to follow, and send rain on your land that you gave to your people as an inheritance.

[37] Whenever there is a famine or plague in the land; or whenever there is blight, mildew, locust, or grasshopper; or whenever someone's enemy attacks them in their cities;[b] or any plague or illness comes; [38] whatever prayer or petition is made by any individual or by all of your people Israel—because people will recognize their own pain and spread out their hands toward this temple— [39] then listen from heaven where you live. Forgive, act, and repay each person according to all their conduct, because you know their hearts. You alone know the human heart. [40] Do this so that they may revere you all the days they live on the land that you gave to our ancestors.

[41] Listen also to the immigrant who isn't from your people Israel but who comes from a distant country because of your reputation— [42] because they will hear of your great reputation, your great power, and your outstretched arm. When the immigrant comes and prays toward this temple, [43] then listen from heaven, where you live, and do everything the immigrant asks. Do this

so that all the people of the earth may know your reputation and revere you, as your people Israel do, and recognize that this temple I have built bears your name. [44] When your people go to war against their enemies, wherever you may send them, and they pray to the LORD toward the city you have chosen and toward this temple that I have built for your name, [45] then listen from heaven to their prayer and request and do what is right for them.

[46] When they sin against you (for there is no one who doesn't sin) and you become angry with them and hand them over to an enemy who takes them away as prisoners to enemy territory, whether distant or nearby, [47] if they change their heart in whatever land they are held captive, changing their lives and begging for your mercy,[c] saying, "We have sinned, we have done wrong, we have acted wickedly!" [48] and if they return to you with all their heart and all their being in the enemy territory where they've been taken captive, and pray to you, toward their land, which you gave their ancestors, toward the city you have chosen, and toward the temple I have built for your name, [49] then listen to their prayer and request from your heavenly dwelling place. Do what is right for them, [50] and forgive your people who have sinned against you. Forgive all their wrong that they have done against you. See to it that those who captured them show them mercy. [51] These are your people and your inheritance. You brought them out of Egypt, from the iron furnace.

[52] Open your eyes to your servant's request and to the request of your people Israel. Hear them whenever they cry out to you. [53] You set them apart from all the earth's peoples as your own inheritance, LORD, just as you promised through your servant Moses when you brought our ancestors out of Egypt.

[54] As soon as Solomon finished praying and making these requests to the LORD, he got up from before the LORD's altar, where

---

[a] Or answered them [b] LXX one of; MT in the land of their gates [c] Heb adds in the land they are held captive.

he had been kneeling with his hands spread out to heaven. [55]He stood up and blessed the whole Israelite assembly in a loud voice: [56]"May the LORD be blessed! He has given rest to his people Israel just as he promised. He hasn't neglected any part of the good promise he made through his servant Moses. [57]May the LORD our God be with us, just as he was with our ancestors. May he never leave us or abandon us. [58]May he draw our hearts to him to walk in all his ways and observe his commands, his laws, and his judgments that he gave our ancestors. [59]And may these words of mine that I have cried out before the LORD remain near to the LORD our God day and night so that he may do right by his servant and his people Israel for each day's need, [60]and so that all the earth's peoples may know that the LORD is God. There is no other God! [61]Now may you be committed to the LORD our God with all your heart by following his laws and observing his commands, just as you are doing right now."

[62]Then the king and all Israel with him sacrificed to the LORD. [63]Solomon offered well-being sacrifices to the LORD: twenty-two thousand oxen and one hundred twenty thousand sheep when the king and all Israel dedicated the LORD's temple. [64]On that day the king made holy the middle of the courtyard in front of the LORD's temple. He had to offer the entirely burned offerings, grain offerings, and the fat of well-being sacrifices there, because the bronze altar that was in the LORD's presence was too small to contain the entirely burned offerings, the grain offerings, and the fat of the well-being sacrifices. [65]At that time Solomon, together with all Israel, held a celebration. It was a large assembly from Lebo-hamath to the border of Egypt. They celebrated for seven days and then for another seven days in the presence of the LORD our God: fourteen days in all. [66]On the eighth day,[d] Solomon dismissed the people. They blessed the king and went back to their tents happy and pleased about

all the good that the LORD had done for his servant David and for his people Israel.

Solomon again meets God

9 Now once Solomon finished building the LORD's temple, the royal palace, and everything else he wanted to accomplish, [2]the LORD appeared to him a second time in the same way he had appeared to him at Gibeon. [3]The LORD said to him, "I have heard your prayer and your cry to me. I have set apart this temple that you built, to put my name there forever. My eyes and my heart will always be there. [4]As for you, if you walk before me just as your father David did, with complete dedication and honesty, and if you do all that I have commanded, and keep my regulations and case laws, [5]then I will establish your royal throne over Israel forever, just as I promised your father David, 'You will never fail to have a successor on the throne of Israel.' [6]However, if you or your sons turn away from following me and don't observe the commands and regulations that I gave you, and go to serve other gods, and worship them, [7]then I will remove Israel from the land I gave them and I will reject the temple that I dedicated for my name. Israel will become a joke, insulted by everyone. [8]Everyone who passes by this temple, so lofty now,[e] will be shocked and will whistle, wondering, Why has the LORD done such a thing to this land and this temple? [9]The answer will come: Because they deserted the LORD their God, who brought their ancestors out of Egypt's land. They embraced other gods, worshipping and serving them. That is why the LORD brought all this disaster on them."

Solomon's buildings and prosperity

[10]It took twenty years for Solomon to build the two structures, the LORD's temple and the royal palace. [11]King Hiram of Tyre gave Solomon all the cedar, pinewood, and gold that he wanted. Then King Solomon gave Hiram twenty towns in the region of Galilee. [12]Hiram went from Tyre to

[d]The second seven-day celebration (see 2 Chron 7:8-9); but contrast LXX. [e]Or *will become high*; OL, Syr, Tg *will become a ruin*

inspect the towns Solomon had given him. They didn't seem adequate in his view. [13] So Hiram remarked, "My brother, are these towns you've given me good for anything?" The cities are thus called the land of Cabul to this very day. [14] But Hiram sent the king one hundred twenty gold kikkars, nevertheless.

[15] This is the story of the labor gang that King Solomon put together to build the LORD's temple and his own palace, as well as the stepped structure, the wall of Jerusalem, Hazor, Megiddo, and Gezer: ([16] Pharaoh, Egypt's king, had attacked and captured Gezer, setting it on fire. He killed the Canaanites who lived in the city and gave it as a dowry to his daughter, Solomon's wife.) [17] Solomon built Gezer, Lower Beth-horon, [18] Baalath, and Tamar in the wilderness (within the land), [19] along with all the storage cities that belonged to Solomon, as well as the cities used for storing chariots and cavalry and whatever he wanted to build in Jerusalem, Lebanon, and throughout his kingdom. [20] Any non-Israelite people who remained of the Amorites, Hittites, Perizzites, Hivites, and Jebusites—[21] that is, the descendants of such people who were still in the land because the Israelites weren't able to wipe them out—Solomon forced into the labor gangs that are still in existence today. [22] However, Solomon didn't force the Israelites to work as slaves; instead, they became warriors, his servants, his leaders, his officers, and those in charge of his chariots and cavalry.

[23] These were the chief officers over Solomon's work: five hundred fifty had charge of the people who did the work. [24] When Pharaoh's daughter went up from David's City to the palace he had built for her, Solomon built the stepped structure. [25] Three times a year Solomon would offer entirely burned offerings and well-being sacrifices on the altar that he had built for the LORD. Along with this he would burn incense to the LORD. In this way, he completed the temple.[f] [26] King Solomon built a fleet near Eloth in Ezion-geber, on the coast of the Reed Sea[g] in the land of Edom. [27] Hiram sent his expert sailors on the fleet along with Solomon's workers. [28] They went to Ophir for four hundred twenty kikkars of gold, which they brought back to King Solomon.

Queen of Sheba

10 When the queen of Sheba heard reports about Solomon, due to the LORD's name,[h] she came to test him with riddles. [2] Accompanying her to Jerusalem was a huge entourage with camels carrying spices, a large amount of gold, and precious stones. After she arrived, she told Solomon everything that was on her mind. [3] Solomon answered all her questions; nothing was too difficult for him to answer. [4] When the queen of Sheba saw how wise Solomon was, the palace he had built, [5] the food on his table, the servants' quarters, the function and dress of his attendants, his cupbearers, and the entirely burned offerings that he offered at the LORD's temple, it took her breath away.

[6] "The report I heard about your deeds and wisdom when I was still at home is true," she said to the king. [7] "I didn't believe it until I came and saw it with my own eyes. In fact, the half of it wasn't even told to me! You have far more wisdom and wealth than I was told. [8] Your people and these servants who continually serve you and get to listen to your wisdom are truly happy! [9] Bless the LORD your God because he was pleased to place you on Israel's throne. Because the LORD loved Israel with an eternal love, the LORD made you king to uphold justice and righteousness."

[10] The queen gave the king one hundred twenty kikkars of gold, a great quantity of spice, and precious stones. Never again has so much spice come to Israel as when the queen of Sheba gave this gift to King Solomon. [11] Hiram's fleet went to Ophir and brought back gold, much almug wood, and precious stones. [12] The king used the almug wood to make parapets for the LORD's tem-

[f] Heb uncertain [g] Traditionally *Red Sea* [h] Heb uncertain

ple and for the royal palace as well as lyres and harps for the musicians. To this day, that much almug wood hasn't come into or been seen in Israel. [13]King Solomon gave the queen of Sheba everything she wanted and all that she had asked for, in addition to what he had already given her from his own personal funds. Then she and her servants returned to her homeland.

Solomon's wealth

[14]Solomon received an annual income of six hundred sixty-six kikkars of gold, [15]not including income from the traders, the merchants and their profits, all the Arabian kings, and the officials of the land. [16]King Solomon made two hundred body-sized shields of hammered gold, using fifteen pounds[i] of gold in each shield, [17]and three hundred small shields of hammered gold, using sixty ounces[j] of gold in each shield. The king placed these in the Forest of Lebanon Palace.

[18]The king also made a large ivory throne and covered it with pure gold. [19]Six steps led up to the throne, and the back of the throne was rounded at the top. Two lions stood beside the armrests on both sides of the throne. [20]Another twelve lions stood on both sides of the six steps. No other kingdom had anything like this. [21]All of King Solomon's drinking cups were made of gold, and all the items in the Forest of Lebanon Palace were made of pure gold, not silver, since even silver wasn't considered good enough in Solomon's time! [22]The royal fleet of Tarshish-style ships was at sea with Hiram's fleet, returning once every three years with gold, silver, ivory, monkeys, and peacocks.[k]

[23]King Solomon far exceeded all the earth's kings in wealth and wisdom, [24]and so the whole earth wanted an audience with Solomon in order to hear his God-given wisdom. [25]Year after year they came with tribute: objects of silver and gold, clothing, weapons, spices, horses, and mules.

[26]Solomon acquired more and more chariots and horses until he had fourteen hundred chariots and twelve thousand horses that he kept in chariot cities and with the king in Jerusalem. [27]In Jerusalem, the king made silver as common as stones and cedar as plentiful as sycamore trees that grow in the foothills. [28]Solomon's horses were imported from Egypt and Kue, purchased from Kue by the king's agents at the going price. [29]They would import a chariot from Egypt for six hundred pieces of silver and a horse for one hundred fifty, and then export them to all the Hittite and Aramean kings.

Solomon meets God a third time

11 In addition to Pharaoh's daughter, King Solomon loved many foreign women,

[i]Or *six hundred* (shekels) [j]*three manehs* [k]Heb uncertain

QUEEN OF SHEBA

The visit of an unnamed dignitary from Sheba, identified only by title, to the court of King Solomon bolsters the biblical perspective that Solomon oversaw a prosperous empire, which he ruled as a just king, renowned for his wisdom (1 Kgs 10:1-13; 2 Chron 9:1-12). The queen's acknowledgment of the God of Israel as the source of Solomon's wealth shows her as a foreigner who came to appreciate the power of God, a concept reiterated in the NT, where she is referred to as the queen of the South (Matt 12:42; Luke 11:31). The Islamic traditions (Qur'an 27:16-44) depict her in a similar light, as one who, in making the journey from southern Arabia, arrives at a spiritual destination.

including Moabites, Ammonites, Edomites, Sidonians, and Hittites. ²These came from the nations that the LORD had commanded the Israelites about: "Don't intermarry with them. They will definitely turn your heart toward their gods." Solomon clung to these women in love. ³He had seven hundred royal wives and three hundred secondary wives. They turned his heart. ⁴As Solomon grew old, his wives turned his heart after other gods. He wasn't committed to the LORD his God with all his heart as was his father David. ⁵Solomon followed Astarte the goddess of the Sidonians, and Milcom the detestable god of the Ammonites. ⁶Solomon did what was evil in the LORD's eyes and wasn't completely devoted to the LORD like his father David. ⁷On the hill east of Jerusalem, Solomon built a shrine to Chemosh the detestable god of Moab, and to Molech the detestable god of the Ammonites. ⁸He did the same for all his foreign wives, who burned incense and sacrificed to their gods. ⁹The LORD grew angry with Solomon, because his heart had turned away from being with the LORD, the God of Israel, who had appeared to him twice. ¹⁰The LORD had commanded Solomon about this very thing, that he shouldn't follow other gods. But Solomon didn't do what the LORD commanded.

¹¹The LORD said to Solomon, "Because you have done all this instead of keeping my covenant and my laws that I commanded you, I will most certainly tear the kingdom from you and give it to your servant. ¹²Even so, on account of your father David, I won't do it during your lifetime. I will tear the kingdom out of your son's hands. ¹³Moreover, I won't tear away the entire kingdom. I will give one tribe to your son on account of my servant David and on account of Jerusalem, which I have chosen."

Solomon and Hadad

¹⁴So the LORD raised up an opponent for Solomon: Hadad the Edomite from the royal line of Edom. ¹⁵When David was fighting against Edom, Joab the general had gone up to bury the Israelite dead, and he had killed every male in Edom. ¹⁶Joab and all the Israelites stayed there six months, until he had finished off every male in Edom. ¹⁷While still a youth, Hadad escaped to Egypt along with his father's Edomite officials. ¹⁸They set out from Midian and went to Paran. They took men with them from Paran and came to Egypt and to Pharaoh its king. Pharaoh assigned him a home, food, and land. ¹⁹Pharaoh was so delighted with Hadad that he gave him one of his wife's sisters for marriage, a sister of Queen Tahpenes. ²⁰This sister of Tahpenes bore Hadad a son, Genubath. Tahpenes weaned him in Pharaoh's house. So it was that Genubath was raised in Pharaoh's house, among Pharaoh's children. ²¹While in Egypt, Hadad heard that David had lain down with his ancestors and that Joab the general was also dead. Hadad said to Pharaoh, "Let me go to my homeland."

²²Pharaoh said to him, "What do you lack here with me that would make you want to go back to your homeland?"

Hadad said, "Nothing, but please let me go!"

Solomon and Rezon

²³God raised up another opponent for Solomon: Rezon, Eliada's son, who had escaped from Zobah's King Hadadezer. ²⁴Rezon recruited men and became leader of a band when David was killing them. They went to Damascus, stayed there, and ruled it. ²⁵Throughout Solomon's lifetime, Rezon was Israel's opponent and added to the problems caused by Hadad. Rezon hated Israel while he ruled as king of Aram.

Solomon and Jeroboam

²⁶Now Nebat's son Jeroboam was an Ephraimite from Zeredah. His mother's name was Zeruah; she was a widow. Although he was one of Solomon's own officials, Jeroboam fought against the king. ²⁷This is the story of why Jeroboam fought against the king:

Solomon had built the stepped structure and repaired the broken wall in his father David's City. ²⁸Now Jeroboam was a strong and honorable man. Solomon saw how well this youth did his work. So he appointed him over all the work gang of Joseph's house.

²⁹At that time, when Jeroboam left Jerusalem, Ahijah the prophet of Shiloh met him along the way. Ahijah was wearing a new garment. The two of them were alone in the country. ³⁰Ahijah tore his new garment into twelve pieces. ³¹He said to Jeroboam, "Take ten pieces, because Israel's God, the LORD, has said, 'Look, I am about to tear the kingdom from Solomon's hand. I will give you ten tribes. ³²But I will leave him one tribe on account of my servant David and on account of Jerusalem, the city I have chosen from all the tribes of Israel. ³³I am doing this because they have abandoned me[l] and worshipped the Sidonian goddess Astarte, the Moabite god Chemosh, and the Ammonite god Milcom. They haven't walked in my ways by doing what is right in my eyes—keeping my laws and judgments—as Solomon's father David did. ³⁴But I won't take the whole kingdom from his hand. I will keep him as ruler throughout his lifetime on account of my servant David, who did keep my commands and my laws. ³⁵I will take the kingdom from the hand of Solomon's son, and I will give you ten tribes. ³⁶I will give his son a single tribe so that my servant David will always have a lamp before me in Jerusalem, the city that I chose for myself to place my name. ³⁷But I will accept you, and you will rule over all that you could desire. You will be king of Israel. ³⁸If you listen to all that I command and walk in my ways, if you do what is right in my eyes, keeping my laws and my commands just as my servant David did, then I will be with you and I will build you a lasting dynasty just as I did for David. I will give you Israel. ³⁹I will humble David's descendants by means of all this, though not forever.'"

⁴⁰Then Solomon tried to kill Jeroboam. But Jeroboam fled to Egypt and its king Shishak. Jeroboam remained in Egypt until Solomon died.

Solomon's remaining days

⁴¹The rest of Solomon's deeds, including all that he did and all his wisdom, aren't they written in the official records of Solomon? ⁴²The amount of time Solomon ruled over all Israel in Jerusalem was forty years. ⁴³Then Solomon lay down with his ancestors. He was buried in his father David's City, and Rehoboam his son succeeded him as king.

How Rehoboam lost the kingdom

12 Rehoboam went to Shechem where all Israel had come to make him king. ²When Jeroboam, Nebat's son, heard the news, he returned from Egypt where he had fled from King Solomon. ³The people sent and called for Jeroboam, who along with the entire Israelite assembly went and said to Rehoboam, ⁴"Your father made our workload[m] very hard for us. If you will lessen the demands your father made of us and lighten the heavy workload he demanded from us, then we will serve you."

⁵He answered them, "Come back in three days." So the people left.

⁶King Rehoboam consulted the elders who had served his father Solomon when he was alive. "What do you advise?" Rehoboam asked. "How should I respond to these people?"

⁷"If you will be a servant to this people by answering them and speaking good words today," they replied, "then they will be your servants forever."

⁸But Rehoboam ignored the advice the elders gave him and instead sought the counsel of the young advisors who had grown up with him and now served him. ⁹"What do you advise?" he asked them. "How should we respond to these people who have said to me, 'Lighten the workload your father demanded of us'?"

¹⁰The young people who had grown up with him said to him, "This people said to you, 'Your father made our workload heavy; lighten it for us!' Now this is what you should say to them: 'My baby finger[n] is thicker than my father's entire waist! ¹¹So if my father

---

[l] LXX, Syr, Vulg *he has abandoned me*   [m] Or *our yoke*; also in the verses that follow   [n] Or *pinky finger*, perhaps a euphemism

made your workload heavy, I'll make it even heavier! If my father disciplined you with whips, I'll do it with scorpions!'"

¹²Jeroboam and all the people returned to Rehoboam on the third day, just as the king had specified when he said, "Come back to me in three days." ¹³The king then answered the people harshly. He ignored the elders' advice ¹⁴and instead followed the young people's advice. He said, "My father made your workload heavy, but I'll make it even heavier! My father disciplined you with whips, but I'll do it with scorpions!"

¹⁵The king didn't listen to the people because this turn of events came from the LORD so that he might keep the promise he delivered through Ahijah from Shiloh concerning Jeroboam, Nebat's son. ¹⁶When all Israel saw that the king wouldn't listen to them, the people answered the king:

"Why should we care about David?
We have no stake in Jesse's son!
Go back to your homes, Israel!
You better look
    after your own house now, David!"

Then the Israelites went back to their homes, ¹⁷and Rehoboam ruled over only the Israelites who lived in the cities of Judah.

¹⁸When King Rehoboam sent Adoram to them (he was the leader of the work gang), all Israel stoned him to death. King Rehoboam quickly got into his chariot and fled to Jerusalem. ¹⁹Israel has been in rebellion against the house of David to this day. ²⁰When all Israel heard that Jeroboam had returned, they sent for him. They called him to the assembly and crowned him king of all Israel.

Nothing was left to the house of David except the tribe of Judah. ²¹When Rehoboam arrived at Jerusalem, he assembled the whole house of Judah and the tribe of Benjamin—one hundred eighty thousand select warriors—to fight against the house of Israel and restore the kingdom for Rehoboam, Solomon's son. ²²But God's word came to Shemaiah the man of God, ²³"Tell Judah's King Rehoboam, Solomon's son, and all the house of Judah and Benjamin, and the rest of the people, ²⁴This is what the LORD says: Don't make war against your relatives the Israelites. Go home, every one of you, because this is my plan.'" When they heard the LORD's words, they went back home, just as the LORD had said.

Jeroboam I and the shrines

²⁵Jeroboam fortified Shechem at Mount Ephraim and lived there. From there he also fortified Penuel. ²⁶Jeroboam thought to himself, The kingdom is in danger of reverting to the house of David. ²⁷If these people continue to sacrifice at the LORD's temple in Jerusalem, they will again become loyal to their master Rehoboam, Judah's king, and they will kill me so they can return to Judah's King Rehoboam. ²⁸So the king asked for advice and then made two gold calves. He said to the people, "It's too far for you to go all the way up to Jerusalem. Look, Israel! Here are your gods who brought you out from the land of Egypt." ²⁹He put one calf in Bethel, and the other he placed in Dan. ³⁰This act was sinful. The people went to worship before the one calf at Bethel and before the other one as far

BETHEL AND DAN

Bethel was a town in Benjamin and Ephraim, mentioned more often in the Bible than any place other than Jerusalem. Dan was a town in Dan. Bethel was at the southern border of the northern kingdom and Dan was at the northern border. King Jeroboam's political strategy for consolidating his kingdom involved setting up worship sites at the southern and northern boundaries to prevent people from leaving the kingdom for worship (1 Kgs 12:26-33).

as Dan.° ³¹Jeroboam made shrines on the high places and appointed priests from all sorts of people, but none were Levites. ³²Jeroboam set a date for a celebration on the fifteenth day of the eighth month.ᵖ It was just like the celebration in Judah. He sacrificed on the altar. At Bethel he sacrificed to the calves he had made. There also he installed the priests for the shrines he had made. ³³On the fifteenth day of the eighth month—the time he alone had decided—Jeroboam went up�q to the altar he had built in Bethel. He made a celebration for the Israelites and offered sacrifices on the altar by burning them up.ʳ

Jeroboam I and the man of God

13 A man of God came from Judah by God's command to Bethel. Jeroboam was standing at the altar burning incense. ²By the LORD's word, the man of God cried out to the altar: "Altar! Altar! The LORD says this: Look! A son will be born to the house of David. His name will be Josiah. He will sacrifice on you, Altar, the very priests of the shrines who offer incense on you. They will burn human bones on you." ³At that time the man of God gave a sign: "This is the sign that the LORD mentioned: 'Look! The altar will be broken apart, and its ashes will spill out.'"

⁴When the king heard the word of the man of God and how he cried out to the altar at Bethel, Jeroboam stretched his hand from the altar and said, "Seize him!" But the hand that Jeroboam stretched out against the man of God grew stiff. Jeroboam wasn't able to bend it back to himself. ⁵The altar broke apart, and the ashes spilled out from the altar, just like the sign that the man of God gave by the LORD's word. ⁶The king said to the man of God, "Plead before the LORD your God and pray for me so that I can bend my hand back again." So the man of God pleaded before the LORD, and the king's hand returned to normal and was like it used to be. ⁷The king spoke to the man of God: "Come with me to the palace and refresh yourself. Let me give you a gift."

⁸The man of God said to the king, "Even if you gave me half your palace, I wouldn't go with you, nor would I eat food or drink water in this place. ⁹This is what God commanded me by the LORD's word: Don't eat food! Don't drink water! Don't return by the way you came!"

¹⁰So the man of God went by a different way. He didn't return by the way he came to Bethel. ¹¹Now there was an old prophet living in Bethel. His sons came and told him everything that the man of God had done that day at Bethel. They also told their father the words that he spoke to the king. ¹²"Which way did he go?" their father asked them. His sons had seen the way the man of God went when he came from Judah. ¹³The old prophet said to his sons, "Saddle

---

°Cf LXX; MT lacks *before the one at Bethel.* ᵖOctober–November qOr *offered sacrifices* ʳOr *went up on the altar to burn incense*

PROPHET

Prophets speak on behalf of the deity to the people, as the formula "This is what the Lord says" suggests, and, on occasion, they speak on behalf of an individual or the people as a whole to the deity. The term *prophet* does not necessarily mean someone who foretells the future; nor does it signify someone who "speaks forth," though prophets may, indeed, speak truth to various elements in Israelite society. Prophets appear in the books of Samuel and Kings, and several books focus on the words of prophets: Isaiah, Jeremiah, Ezekiel, and the 12 Minor Prophets.

my donkey." So they saddled his donkey, and he got on it. ¹⁴He went after the man of God and found him sitting underneath a terebinth tree. He said to him, "Are you the man of God who came from Judah?"

"I am," he replied.

¹⁵The old prophet then said to him, "Come home with me and eat some food."

¹⁶But the man of God answered, "I can't return or go with you, and I can't eat food or drink water with you in this place ¹⁷because of the message that came to me from the LORD's word: Don't eat food! Don't drink water! Don't return by the way you came!"

¹⁸The old prophet said to the man of God, "I'm also a prophet like you. A messenger spoke to me with the LORD's word, 'Bring him back with you to your house so that he may eat food and drink water.'"

But the old prophet was lying to him. ¹⁹So the man of God went back with the old prophet. He ate food in his home and drank water. ²⁰Then as they were sitting at the table, the LORD's word came to the prophet who had brought him back. ²¹He cried out to the man of God who had come from Judah:

"The LORD says this:

You rebelled against the LORD's word!

You didn't keep the command

that the LORD your God gave you!

²² You came back and ate food

and drank water in this place.

"But he had commanded you: 'Don't eat food! Don't drink water!' Now your body won't go to the grave of your ancestors."

²³After he ate food and drank, the old prophet saddled the donkey for the prophet he had brought back. ²⁴The man of God departed, and a lion found him on the road and killed him. His body was thrown down on the road. The donkey stood beside it, and the lion also stood beside the body. ²⁵Some people were traveling nearby, and they discovered the body thrown down on the road and the lion standing beside it. They entered the town where the old prophet lived and were talking about it. ²⁶The prophet who brought the man of God back from the road overheard. He thought: That's the man of God who rebelled against

the LORD's command. The LORD has given him to that lion that tore him apart, killing him in agreement with the LORD's word that was spoken to him.

²⁷The old prophet told his sons, "Saddle the donkey." They did so, ²⁸and he went and found the body thrown down on the road. The donkey and the lion were still standing beside the body. The lion hadn't eaten the body, nor had it torn the donkey apart. ²⁹The prophet lifted the body of the man of God and put it on the donkey. He brought it back, arriving in the old prophet's town to mourn and bury the man of God. ³⁰He placed the body in his own grave, and they mourned over him, "Oh, my brother!" ³¹After the old prophet buried him, he said to his sons, "When I die, bury me in the grave where the man of God is. Put my bones beside his bones. ³²The message he gave by the LORD's word concerning the altar of Bethel and all the shrines in the towns of Samaria will most certainly come true."

³³Even after this happened, Jeroboam didn't change his evil ways. Instead, he continued to appoint all sorts of people as priests of the shrines. Anyone who wanted to be a priest Jeroboam made a priest for the shrines. ³⁴In this way the house of Jeroboam acted sinfully, leading to its downfall and elimination from the earth.

Abijah's illness

14 At that time, Jeroboam's son Abijah became sick. ²Jeroboam said to his wife, "Please go with a disguise so no one will recognize you as Jeroboam's wife. Go to Shiloh where the prophet Ahijah is. He told me I would be king of this people. ³Take ten loaves of bread, cakes, and a bottle of honey with you. Go to him. He will tell you what will happen to the boy." ⁴Jeroboam's wife did precisely this. She left and went to Shiloh and came to Ahijah's house. Now Ahijah had become blind in his old age.

⁵The LORD said to Ahijah, "Look! Jeroboam's wife has come seeking a word from you about her son. He is sick. Say this and that to her. When she comes, she will be disguised."

[6]When Ahijah heard the sound of her feet coming through the doorway, he said, "Come in, Jeroboam's wife! Why have you disguised yourself? I have hard news for you. [7]Tell Jeroboam: This is what the LORD, Israel's God, says: When I lifted you up from among the people, I appointed you as a leader over my people Israel. [8]I tore the kingdom from David's house and gave it to you. But you haven't been like my servant David, who kept my commands and followed me with all his heart by doing only what is right in my eyes. [9]Instead, you have done more evil than any who were before you. You have made other gods and metal images to anger me. You have turned your back on me. [10]Therefore, I'm going to bring disaster on Jeroboam's house! Because of Jeroboam, I will eliminate everyone who urinates on a wall, whether slave or free. Then I will set fire to the house of Jeroboam, as one burns dung until it is gone. [11]Dogs will eat any of Jeroboam's family who die in town. Birds will eat those who die in the field. The LORD has spoken!

[12]"As for you, get up and go back home. When your feet enter the town, the boy will die. [13]All Israel will mourn for him and will bury him. Out of the whole line of Jeroboam, he alone will have a tomb, because only in him did Israel's God, the LORD, find something good. [14]For this reason the LORD will raise up a king over Israel who will eliminate the house of Jeroboam. This begins today. What's that? Even now![s] [15]The LORD will strike Israel so that it shakes like a reed in water. He will uproot Israel from this fertile land that he gave to their ancestors and their offspring, and he will scatter them across the Euphrates River, because they made the LORD angry by making their sacred poles.[t] [16]Because of the sins Jeroboam committed, and because he made Israel sin too, God will give Israel up."

[17]Then Jeroboam's wife left and went to Tirzah. When she stepped across the threshold of the house, the boy died. [18]All Israel buried him and mourned him in agreement with the LORD's word spoken through his servant the prophet Ahijah. [19]The rest of Jeroboam's deeds—how he fought and how he ruled—are written in the official records of Israel's kings. [20]Jeroboam ruled twenty-two years and he lay down with his ancestors. His son Nadab succeeded him as king.

Rehoboam rules Judah

[21]Rehoboam, Solomon's son, ruled over Judah. Rehoboam was 41 years old when he became king. He ruled for seventeen years in Jerusalem, the city the LORD chose from among all the tribes of Israel to set his name. Rehoboam's mother's name was Naamah from Ammon. [22]Judah did evil in the LORD's eyes. The sins they committed made the LORD angrier than anything their ancestors had done. [23]They also built shrines, standing stones, and sacred poles[u] on top of every high hill and under every green tree. [24]Moreover, the consecrated workers[v] in the land did detestable things, just like those nations that the LORD had removed among the Israelites.

[25]During King Rehoboam's fifth year, King Shishak of Egypt attacked Jerusalem. [26]He seized the treasures of the LORD's temple and the royal palace. He took everything, even all the gold shields that Solomon had made. [27]King Rehoboam replaced them with bronze shields and assigned them to the officers of the guard who protected the entrance to the royal palace. [28]Whenever the king entered the LORD's temple, the guards would carry the shields and then return them to the guardroom. [29]The rest of Rehoboam's deeds and all that he accomplished, aren't they written in the official records of Judah's kings? [30]There was continual warfare between Rehoboam and Jeroboam. [31]When Rehoboam died, he was buried with his ancestors in David's City. His mother's name was Naamah from Ammon. His son Abijam[w] succeeded him as king.

---

[s]Heb uncertain [t]Heb *asherim*, perhaps objects devoted to the goddess Asherah [u]Heb *asherim*, perhaps objects devoted to the goddess Asherah [v]Traditionally *cultic prostitutes* [w]Spelled *Abijah* in 2 Chron 12:16; LXX, Syr, Targ *Abijah* in 1 Kgs

KINGS OF ISRAEL AND JUDAH

ca. 1020–1000 BCE	King Saul
ca. 1000–960 BCE	King David
ca. 960–930 BCE	King Solomon

ca. 930–922 BCE DIVISION OF THE KINGDOM

Kings of Judah		Kings of Israel	
922–915	Rehoboam	922–901	Jeroboam I
915–913	Abijam		
913–873	Asa		
		901–900	Nadab
		900–877	Baasha
		877–876	Elah
		876	Zimri
		876–872	Tibni
		876–869	Omri
873–849	Jehoshaphat		
		869–850	Ahab
		850–849	Ahaziah
849–843	Jehoram	849–843	Joram
843–842	Ahaziah	843–815	Jehu
842–837	Athaliah		
837–800	Jehoash		
		815–802	Jehoahaz
800–783	Amaziah	802–786	Joash
		786–746	Jeroboam II
783–742	Azariah/Uzziah		
		746–745	Zechariah
		745	Shallum
		745–737	Menahem
742–735	Jotham		
		737–736	Pekahiah
735–715	Ahaz	736–732	Pekah
		732–724	Hoshea
		722 BCE	Fall of Samaria (capital of the Northern Kingdom) to Assyria
715–687	Hezekiah		
687–642	Manasseh		
642–640	Amon		
640–609	Josiah		
609	Jehoahaz		
609–598	Jehoiakim		
598–597	Jehoiachin		
597–587	Zedekiah		

Abijam rules Judah

15 Abijam[x] became king of Judah in the eighteenth year of King Jeroboam, Nebat's son. [2] He ruled for three years in Jerusalem. His mother's name was Maacah, and she was Abishalom's daughter. [3] Abijam followed all the sinful ways of his father before him. He didn't follow the LORD his God with all his heart like his ancestor David. [4] Even so, on account of David, the LORD his God gave Abijam a lamp in Jerusalem by supporting his son who succeeded him and by preserving Jerusalem. [5] This was because David did the right thing in the LORD's eyes. David didn't deviate from anything the LORD commanded him throughout his life—except in the matter of Uriah the Hittite. [6] There was war between Rehoboam and Jeroboam as long as Abijam lived. [7] The rest of Abijam's deeds and all that he did, aren't they written in the official records of Judah's kings? There was war between Abijam and Jeroboam. [8] Abijam lay down with his ancestors; he was buried in David's City. His son Asa succeeded him as king.

Asa rules Judah

[9] In the twentieth year of Israel's King Jeroboam, Asa became king of Judah. [10] He ruled in Jerusalem for forty-one years. His grandmother's[y] name was Maacah; she was Abishalom's daughter. [11] Asa did the right things in the LORD's eyes, just like his father David. [12] He removed the consecrated workers[z] from the land, and he did away with all the worthless idols that his predecessors had made. [13] He even removed his grandmother Maacah from the position of queen mother because she had made an image of Asherah. Asa cut down her image and burned it in the Kidron Valley. [14] Though the shrines weren't eliminated, nevertheless Asa remained committed with all his heart to the LORD throughout his life. [15] He brought into the LORD's temple the silver and gold equipment that he and his father had dedicated. [16] There was war between Asa and Israel's King Baasha throughout their lifetimes. [17] Israel's King Baasha attacked Judah and fortified Ramah to prevent Judah's King Asa from moving into that area.

[18] Asa took all the silver and gold that remained in the treasuries of the LORD's temple and the royal palace, and he gave them to his officials. Then King Asa sent them with the following message to Aram's King Ben-hadad, Tabrimmon's son and Hezion's grandson, who ruled from Damascus: [19] "Let's make a covenant similar to the one between our fathers. Since I have already sent you a gift of silver and gold, break your covenant with Israel's King Baasha so that he will leave me alone." [20] Ben-hadad agreed with King Asa and sent his army commanders against the cities of Israel, attacking Ijon, Dan, Abel-beth-maacah, and all Chinneroth, along with all the land of Naphtali. [21] As soon as Baasha learned this, he stopped building Ramah and stayed in Tirzah. [22] King Asa issued an order to every Judean without exception: all the people carried away the stone and timber that Baasha was using to build Ramah, and King Asa used it to build Geba of Benjamin and Mizpah. [23] The rest of Asa's deeds, his strength, and all that he did, as well as the towns that he built, aren't they written in the official records of Judah's kings? When he was old, Asa developed a severe foot disease. [24] He died and was buried with his ancestors in David's City.[a] His son Jehoshaphat succeeded him as king.

Nadab rules Israel

[25] Jeroboam's son Nadab became king of Israel in the second year of Judah's King Asa. He ruled over Israel for two years. [26] He did evil in the LORD's eyes by walking in the way of his father Jeroboam and the sin Jeroboam had caused Israel to commit. [27] Baasha, Ahijah's son from the house of Issachar, plotted against him and attacked him at Gibbethon, which belonged to the Philistines. Nadab and all Israel were laying siege against Gibbethon. [28] Baasha killed

---

[x] Spelled *Abijah* in 2 Chron 12   [y] Or *mother*; also in 15:13; cf 2 Chron 13:2   [z] Traditionally *cultic prostitutes*
[a] Heb adds *his father*.

Nadab in the third year of Judah's King Asa and ruled in Nadab's place.

²⁹When he became king, Baasha attacked the entire house of Jeroboam. He didn't allow any living person to survive in Jeroboam's family; he wiped them out according to the LORD's word spoken by the LORD's servant Ahijah of Shiloh. ³⁰This happened because of Jeroboam's sins that he committed and that he caused Israel to commit, and because he angered the LORD, Israel's God. ³¹The rest of Nadab's deeds and all that he did, aren't they written in the official records of Israel's kings? ³²There was war between Asa and Israel's King Baasha throughout their lifetimes.

Baasha rules Israel

³³In the third year of Judah's King Asa, Baasha, Ahijah's son, became king over all Israel. He ruled in Tirzah for twenty-four years. ³⁴He did evil in the LORD's eyes by walking in Jeroboam's ways and the sin he had caused Israel to commit.

16 The LORD's word came to Jehu, Hanani's son, against Baasha: ²I raised you up from the dust and made you a leader over my people Israel, but you walked in Jeroboam's ways, making my people Israel sin, making me angry with their sins. ³So look, I am about to set fire to Baasha and his household, and I will make your house like the house of Jeroboam, Nebat's son. ⁴Dogs will eat any of Baasha's family who die in town. Birds will eat any who die in the country.

⁵Now the rest of Baasha's deeds, what he did, and his powerful acts, aren't they written in the official records of Israel's kings? ⁶Baasha lay down with his ancestors and was buried in Tirzah. His son Elah succeeded him as king.

⁷But the LORD's word came through the prophet Jehu, Hanani's son, concerning Baasha and his house. It concerned everything evil in the LORD's eyes that Baasha had done, angering the Lord by his actions so that he would end up just like the house of Jeroboam. The message was also about how the Lord attacked Baasha.[b]

Elah rules Israel

⁸In the twenty-sixth year of Judah's King Asa, Elah, Baasha's son, became king over Israel. He ruled in Tirzah for two years. ⁹Zimri, his officer who led half the chariots, plotted against him. Elah was at Tirzah, getting drunk at the house of Arza, who had charge over the palace at Tirzah. ¹⁰Zimri came, attacked, and killed Elah in the twenty-seventh year of Judah's King Asa. Zimri succeeded him as king.

¹¹Once Zimri became king and sat on the throne, he attacked all of Baasha's house. He didn't spare anyone who urinates on a wall, whether relative or friend. ¹²Zimri destroyed the entire house of Baasha in agreement with the LORD's word that had been spoken by the prophet Jehu to Baasha. ¹³This happened because of all Baasha's sins, as well as the sins of his son Elah and because they caused Israel to sin. They angered Israel's God, the LORD, with their insignificant idols. ¹⁴The rest of Elah's deeds

---

[b]Or *and also about how he attacked him* or *and because Baasha had attacked Jeroboam*

AHAB

Ahab was king of northern Israel (ca. 869–850), succeeding his father Omri. He married Jezebel, daughter of King Ethbaal of Sidon. Jehu had Ahab's 70 sons in Samaria murdered (2 Kgs 10). Ahab's daughter (or sister) Athaliah ruled Judah prior to her murder (2 Kgs 8:26; 11:1-16, 20). Ahab holds the distinction of being northern Israel's worst king (1 Kgs 16:30, 33; 21:25; Mic 6:16).

and all that he did, aren't they written in the official records of Israel's kings?

Zimri rules Israel

¹⁵In the twenty-seventh year of Judah's King Asa, Zimri became king. He ruled in Tirzah for seven days. The army was camped at Gibbethon in Philistia. ¹⁶They heard the news: "Zimri has plotted against the king and killed him." Right then, in the camp, the whole Israelite army made their general Omri king of Israel. ¹⁷Omri and the entire army then went up from Gibbethon and laid siege to Tirzah. ¹⁸When Zimri saw that the city was captured, he went into the fort of the royal palace and burned it down on top of himself. So he died. ¹⁹This happened because of the sins Zimri had committed by doing evil in the LORD's eyes and by walking in Jeroboam's ways and the sin he had done by causing Israel to sin. ²⁰The rest of Zimri's deeds and the plot he carried out, aren't they written in the official records of Israel's kings?

Omri rules Israel

²¹At this time the people of Israel were split in two. One half of the people followed Tibni, Ginath's son, making him king; the other half followed Omri. ²²Omri's side was stronger than those who followed Tibni, Ginath's son. So Tibni died and Omri became king. ²³In the thirty-first year of Judah's King Asa, Omri became king of Israel. He ruled for twelve years, six of which were in Tirzah. ²⁴He bought the hill of Samaria from Shemer for two kikkars of silver. He fortified the hill and named the town that he built there after Shemer, the previous owner of the hill of Samaria. ²⁵Omri did evil in the LORD's eyes, more evil than anyone who preceded him. ²⁶He walked in all the ways and sins of Jeroboam, Nebat's son, because he caused Israel to sin. They angered Israel's God, the LORD, with their worthless idols. ²⁷The rest of Omri's deeds and his powerful acts, aren't they written in the official records of Israel's kings? ²⁸Omri lay down with his ancestors and was buried

in Samaria. His son Ahab succeeded him as king.

Ahab rules Israel

²⁹In the thirty-eighth year of Judah's King Asa, Ahab, Omri's son, became king of Israel. He ruled over Israel in Samaria for twenty-two years ³⁰and did evil in the LORD's eyes, more than anyone who preceded him. ³¹Ahab found it easy to walk in the sins of Jeroboam, Nebat's son. He married Jezebel the daughter of Ethbaal, who was the king of the Sidonians. He served and worshipped Baal. ³²He made an altar for Baal in the Baal temple he had constructed in Samaria. ³³Ahab also made a sacred pole^c and did more to anger the LORD, the God of Israel, than any of Israel's kings who preceded him. ³⁴During Ahab's time, Hiel from Bethel rebuilt Jericho. He set up its foundations at the cost of his oldest son Abiram. He hung its gates at the cost of his youngest son Segub. This fulfilled the LORD's word spoken through Joshua, Nun's son.

Elijah and the ravens

17 Elijah from Tishbe, who was one of the settlers in Gilead, said to Ahab, "As surely as the LORD lives, Israel's God, the one I serve, there will be neither dew nor rain these years unless I say so."

²Then the LORD's word came to Elijah: ³Go from here and turn east. Hide by the Cherith Brook that faces the Jordan River. ⁴You can drink from the brook. I have also ordered the ravens to provide for you there. ⁵Elijah went and did just what the LORD said. He stayed by the Cherith Brook that faced the Jordan River. ⁶The ravens brought bread and meat in the mornings and evenings. He drank from the Cherith Brook. ⁷After a while the brook dried up because there was no rain in the land.

Elijah and the widow from Zarephath

⁸The LORD's word came to Elijah: ⁹Get up and go to Zarephath near Sidon and stay there. I have ordered a widow there to

---

^cHeb *asherah*, perhaps an object devoted to the goddess Asherah

take care of you. [10]Elijah left and went to Zarephath. As he came to the town gate, he saw a widow collecting sticks. He called out to her, "Please get a little water for me in this cup so I can drink." [11]She went to get some water. He then said to her, "Please get me a piece of bread."

[12]"As surely as the LORD your God lives," she replied, "I don't have any food; only a handful of flour in a jar and a bit of oil in a bottle. Look at me. I'm collecting two sticks so that I can make some food for myself and my son. We'll eat the last of the food and then die."

[13]Elijah said to her, "Don't be afraid! Go and do what you said. Only make a little loaf of bread for me first. Then bring it to me. You can make something for yourself and your son after that. [14]This is what Israel's God, the LORD, says: The jar of flour won't decrease and the bottle of oil won't run out until the day the LORD sends rain on the earth." [15]The widow went and did what Elijah said. So the widow, Elijah, and the widow's household ate for many days. [16]The jar of flour didn't decrease nor did the bottle of oil run out, just as the LORD spoke through Elijah.

[17]After these things, the son of the widow, who was the matriarch of the household, became ill. His sickness got steadily worse until he wasn't breathing anymore. [18]She said to Elijah, "What's gone wrong between us, man of God? Have you come to me to call attention to my sin and kill my son?"

[19]Elijah replied, "Give your son to me." He took her son from her and carried him to the upper room where he was staying. Elijah laid him on his bed. [20]Elijah cried out to the LORD, "LORD my God, why is it that you have brought such evil upon the widow that I am staying with by killing her son?" [21]Then he stretched himself over the boy three times and cried out to the LORD, "LORD my God, please give this boy's life back to him." [22]The LORD listened to Elijah's voice and gave the boy his life back. And he lived. [23]Elijah brought the boy down from the upper room of the house and gave him to his mother. Elijah said, "Look, your son is alive!"

[24]"Now I know that you really are a man of God," the woman said to Elijah, "and that the LORD's word is truly in your mouth."

Elijah versus Baal's prophets

18 After many days, the LORD's word came to Elijah (it was the third year of the drought): Go! Appear before Ahab. I will then send rain on the earth. [2]So Elijah went to appear before Ahab.

Now the famine had become especially bad in Samaria. [3]Ahab had called Obadiah, who was in charge of the palace affairs. (Obadiah greatly feared the LORD. [4]When Jezebel killed the LORD's prophets, Obadiah took one hundred of them and hid them, fifty each in two caves. He supplied them with food and water.) [5]Ahab said to Obadiah, "Go throughout the land and check every spring of water and every brook. Perhaps we can find some grass to keep our horses and mules alive so we don't have to kill any of them." [6]To search, they divided the land between themselves. Ahab went one way by himself, while Obadiah went a different way by himself.

[7]While Obadiah was out searching, suddenly Elijah met up with him. When Obadiah saw him, he fell on his face. "My master!" he said. "Are you Elijah?"

[8]Elijah replied, "I am. Go and say to your master, 'Elijah is here!'"

[9]Then Obadiah said, "How have I sinned that you are handing me, your servant, over to Ahab so he can kill me? [10]As surely as the LORD your God lives, there's no nation or kingdom where my master Ahab hasn't looked for you. They would insist, 'He's not here,' but Ahab would make them swear that they couldn't find you. [11]And now you are commanding me: 'Go and say to your master, "Elijah is here"?' [12]But here's what will happen: As soon as I leave you, the LORD's spirit will carry you off somewhere—I don't know where—then I'll report to Ahab, but he won't be able to find you. Then he will kill me! But your servant has feared the LORD from my youth. [13]Wasn't my master told what I did when Jezebel killed the LORD's prophets? I hid one hundred of the LORD's prophets, fifty

each in two caves. I also supplied them with food and water. ¹⁴But even after all that, you tell me, 'Say to your master, "Elijah is here!"' Ahab will kill me!"

¹⁵Elijah said, "As surely as the LORD of heavenly forces lives, the one I serve, I will appear before Ahab today."

¹⁶So Obadiah went to meet Ahab. He told him what had happened. Then Ahab went to meet Elijah. ¹⁷When Ahab saw Elijah, Ahab said to him, "Is that you, the one who troubles Israel?"

¹⁸Elijah answered, "I haven't troubled Israel; you and your father's house have! You did as much when you deserted the LORD's commands and followed the Baals. ¹⁹Now send a message and gather all Israel to me at Mount Carmel. Gather the four hundred fifty prophets of Baal and the four hundred prophets of Asherah who eat at Jezebel's table."

²⁰Ahab sent the message to all the Israelites. He gathered the prophets at Mount Carmel. ²¹Elijah approached all the people and said, "How long will you hobble back and forth between two opinions? If the LORDᵈ is God, follow God. If Baal is God, follow Baal." The people gave no answer.

²²Elijah said to the people, "I am the last of the LORD's prophets, but Baal's prophets number four hundred fifty. ²³Give us two bulls. Let Baal's prophets choose one. Let them cut it apart and set it on the wood, but don't add fire. I'll prepare the other bull, put it on the wood, but won't add

fire. ²⁴Then all of you will call on the name of your god, and I will call on the name of the LORD. The god who answers with fire—that's the real God!"

All the people answered, "That's an excellent idea."

²⁵So Elijah said to the prophets of Baal, "Choose one of these bulls. Prepare it first since there are so many of you. Call on the name of your god, but don't add fire."

²⁶So they took one of the bulls that had been brought to them. They prepared it and called on Baal's name from morning to midday. They said, "Great Baal, answer us!" But there was no sound or answer. They performed a hopping dance around the altar that had been set up.

²⁷Around noon, Elijah started making fun of them: "Shout louder! Certainly he's a god! Perhaps he is lost in thought or wandering or traveling somewhere.ᵉ Or maybe he is asleep and must wake up!"

²⁸So the prophets of Baal cried with a louder voice and cut themselves with swords and knives as was their custom. Their blood flowed all over them. ²⁹As noon passed they went crazy with their ritual until it was time for the evening offering. Still there was no sound or answer, no response whatsoever.

³⁰Then Elijah said to all the people, "Come here!" All the people closed in, and he repaired the LORD's altar that had been damaged. ³¹Elijah took twelve stones, according to the number of the tribes of the

ᵈThe contrast between the LORD's divine name (*YHWH*) and Baal's name is crucial throughout this passage.
ᵉHeb uncertain

MOUNT CARMEL

Because of its abundant flora, Carmel, meaning "vineyard," "garden-land," or "fruitful" (Isa 10:18; 16:10), was used as a metaphor for beauty and fertility (Song 7:5; 2 Kgs 19:23; Isa 35:2; 37:24). Conversely, in the absence of flora during drought, Carmel was a metaphor for desolation (Isa 33:9). Mount Carmel was the meeting place between Elijah and the prophets of Baal and Asherah (1 Kgs 18:19-40) and later a sanctuary for Elijah (2 Kgs 2:25; 4:25).

sons of Jacob—to whom the LORD's word came: "Your name will be Israel." ³²He built the stones into an altar in the LORD's name, and he dug a trench around the altar big enough to hold two seahs[f] of dry grain. ³³He put the wood in order, butchered the bull, and placed the bull on the wood. "Fill four jars with water and pour it on the sacrifice and on the wood," he commanded. ³⁴"Do it a second time!" he said. So they did it a second time. "Do it a third time!" And so they did it a third time. ³⁵The water flowed around the altar, and even the trench filled with water. ³⁶At the time of the evening offering, the prophet Elijah drew near and prayed: "LORD, the God of Abraham, Isaac, and Israel, let it be known today that you are God in Israel and that I am your servant. I have done all these things at your instructions. ³⁷Answer me, LORD! Answer me so that this people will know that you, LORD, are the real God and that you can change their hearts."[g] ³⁸Then the LORD's fire fell; it consumed the sacrifice, the wood, the stones, and the dust. It even licked up the water in the trench!

³⁹All the people saw this and fell on their faces. "The LORD is the real God! The LORD is the real God!" they exclaimed.

⁴⁰Elijah said to them, "Seize Baal's prophets! Don't let any escape!" The people seized the prophets, and Elijah brought them to the Kishon Brook and killed them there. ⁴¹Elijah then said to Ahab, "Get up! Celebrate with food and drink because I hear the sound of a rainstorm coming." ⁴²So Ahab got up to celebrate with food and drink. But Elijah went up to the top of Mount Carmel. He bowed down to the ground and put his face between his knees. ⁴³He said to his assistant, "Please get up and look toward the sea."

So the assistant did so. He said, "I don't see anything."

Seven times Elijah said, "Do it again."

⁴⁴The seventh time the assistant said, "I see a small cloud the size of a human hand coming up from the sea."

Elijah said, "Go and tell Ahab, 'Pull your-self together, go down the mountain, and don't let the rain hold you back.'" ⁴⁵After a little while, the sky became dark with clouds, and a wind came up with a huge rainstorm. Ahab was already riding on his way to Jezreel, ⁴⁶but the LORD's power strengthened Elijah. He gathered up his clothes and ran in front of Ahab until he came to Jezreel.

Elijah runs to Mount Horeb

19 Ahab told Jezebel all that Elijah had done, how he had killed all Baal's prophets with the sword. ²Jezebel sent a messenger to Elijah with this message: "May the gods do whatever they want to me if by this time tomorrow I haven't made your life like the life of one of them."

³Elijah was terrified. He got up and ran for his life. He arrived at Beer-sheba in Judah and left his assistant there. ⁴He himself went farther on into the desert a day's journey. He finally sat down under a solitary broom bush. He longed for his own death: "It's more than enough, LORD! Take my life because I'm no better than my ancestors." ⁵He lay down and slept under the solitary broom bush.

Then suddenly a messenger tapped him and said to him, "Get up! Eat something!" ⁶Elijah opened his eyes and saw flatbread baked on glowing coals and a jar of water right by his head. He ate and drank, and then went back to sleep. ⁷The LORD's messenger returned a second time and tapped him. "Get up!" the messenger said. "Eat something, because you have a difficult road ahead of you." ⁸Elijah got up, ate and drank, and went refreshed by that food for forty days and nights until he arrived at Horeb, God's mountain. ⁹There he went into a cave and spent the night.

The LORD's word came to him and said, "Why are you here, Elijah?"

¹⁰Elijah replied, "I've been very passionate for the LORD God of heavenly forces because the Israelites have abandoned your covenant. They have torn down your altars, and they have murdered your prophets

---

[f] One seah is approximately seven and a half quarts. [g] Heb uncertain

with the sword. I'm the only one left, and now they want to take my life too!"

[11]The LORD said, "Go out and stand at the mountain before the LORD. The LORD is passing by." A very strong wind tore through the mountains and broke apart the stones before the LORD. But the LORD wasn't in the wind. After the wind, there was an earthquake. But the LORD wasn't in the earthquake. [12]After the earthquake, there was a fire. But the LORD wasn't in the fire. After the fire, there was a sound. Thin. Quiet. [13]When Elijah heard it, he wrapped his face in his coat. He went out and stood at the cave's entrance. A voice came to him and said, "Why are you here, Elijah?"

[14]He said, "I've been very passionate for the LORD God of heavenly forces because the Israelites have abandoned your covenant. They have torn down your altars, and they have murdered your prophets with the sword. I'm the only one left, and now they want to take my life too."

[15]The LORD said to him, "Go back through the desert to Damascus and anoint Hazael as king of Aram. [16]Also anoint Jehu, Nimshi's son, as king of Israel; and anoint Elisha from Abel-meholah, Shaphat's son, to succeed you as prophet. [17]Whoever escapes from the sword of Hazael, Jehu will kill. Whoever escapes from the sword of Jehu, Elisha will kill. [18]But I have preserved those who remain in Israel, totaling seven thousand—all those whose knees haven't bowed down to Baal and whose mouths haven't kissed him."

[19]So Elijah departed from there and found Elisha, Shaphat's son. He was plowing with twelve yoke of oxen before him. Elisha was with the twelfth yoke. Elijah met up with him and threw his coat on him. [20]Elisha immediately left the oxen and ran after Elijah. "Let me kiss my father and my mother," Elisha said, "then I will follow you."

Elijah replied, "Go! I'm not holding you back!" [21]Elisha turned back from following Elijah, took the pair of oxen, and slaughtered them. Then with equipment from the oxen, Elisha boiled the meat, gave it to the people, and they ate it. Then he got up, followed Elijah, and served him.

Ben-hadad's wars with Ahab

20King Ben-hadad of Aram brought together all his army along with thirty-two kings plus horses and chariots. He went up, surrounded Samaria, and made war against it. [2]He sent messengers to Ahab, Israel's king, inside Samaria. [3]The message said, "This is what Ben-hadad says: 'Your silver and your gold are mine. Your good-looking wives and children are mine.'"

[4]Israel's king answered, "Whatever you say, my master, great king. I am yours and so is everything I have."

[5]The messengers came back again: "This is what Ben-hadad says: 'I sent you the message: Give me your silver and gold, your wives and your sons. [6]However, at this time tomorrow I will send my officers to you, and they will search your palace and the houses of your officers. Everything that you find valuable they will seize and take away.'"

[7]Then Israel's king called all the elders of the land and he said, "Please know and understand the evil this man wants to do! He demanded from me my wives and sons, and my silver and gold; and I didn't refuse him."

[8]All of the elders and the people said to him, "Don't obey and don't give in!"

[9]So the king said to Ben-hadad's messengers, "Say to my master the king: 'Everything that you first ordered your servant, I will do. But I can't comply with this new command.'"

The messengers took this response to Ben-hadad, [10]who sent back this reply: "May the gods do whatever they want to me if there is even a handful of dust left in Samaria for the armies under me!"

[11]Then Israel's king replied, "The one who prepares for battle shouldn't brag like one returning from battle."

[12]When Ben-hadad heard this message, he and the other kings were drinking in their tents. Ben-hadad said to his officers, "Take your positions!" So they took up their positions against the city.

[13]Suddenly a prophet approached Israel's King Ahab. He said, "This is what the LORD says: Do you see that great army? Today I am handing it over to you. Then you will know that I am the LORD."

[14] Ahab said, "Who will do it?"

The prophet answered, "This is what the LORD says: The servants of the district officials will do it."

"Who should start the battle?" Ahab asked.

"You should," the prophet replied.

[15] So Ahab assembled the servants of the district officials. There were two hundred thirty-two of them. Next he assembled the entire Israelite army, seven thousand total. [16] At noon they marched for battle. Meanwhile, Ben-hadad and the thirty-two kings allied with him were getting drunk in their tents. [17] The servants of the district officials were at the head of the march. Ben-hadad sent for information and was told, "Some men have marched out of Samaria."

[18] He said, "If they have come out in peace, take them alive; if they have come out for war, take them alive as well." [19] So the servants of the district governors with the army behind them marched out from the city. [20] Each one struck down his opponent, so that the Arameans fled. Israel chased after them. Ben-hadad, Aram's king, escaped with some horses and chariots. [21] Israel's king went out and attacked the horses and chariots. He attacked the Arameans with a fierce assault.

[22] The prophet came to Israel's king and said to him, "Maintain your strength! Know and understand that at the turn of the coming year, Aram's king will attack you again." [23] The officers of Aram's king said to him, "Israel's god is a god of the mountains. That's why they were stronger than us. But if we fight them on the plains, we will certainly be stronger than they are. [24] This is what you need to do: Remove the kings from their military posts and appoint officials in their place. [25] Then raise another army like the one that was destroyed, with horses like those horses and chariots like those chariots. Then we will fight them on the plains, and we will certainly be stronger than they are." The king took their advice and followed it.

[26] So in the spring of the year, Ben-hadad assembled the Arameans and marched up to Aphek to fight with Israel. [27] Now the Israelites had already been assembled and provisioned, so they went to engage the Arameans. The Israelites camped before them like two small flocks of goats, but the Arameans filled the land.

[28] Then the man of God came forward and said to Israel's king, "This is what the LORD says: Because the Arameans said that the LORD is a god of the mountains but not a god of the valleys, I am handing this whole great army over to you. Then you will know that I am the LORD."

[29] The two armies camped opposite each other for seven days. On the seventh day, the battle began. The Israelites attacked and destroyed one hundred thousand Aramean foot soldiers in a single day. [30] Those who were left fled to Aphek, into the city where a wall fell on twenty-seven thousand more of them. But Ben-hadad escaped and hid in an inner room within the city.

[31] Ben-hadad's officers said to him, "Listen, we have heard that the kings of Israel

SAMARIA

The ancient city of Samaria, whose summit rose to a height of 1400 ft. above sea level, lay near the center of the northern kingdom of Israel at approximately 35 mi. north of Jerusalem. In the 9th century BCE, it became a capital city for the northern kingdom of Israel, until its defeat in 722. In the 5th century BCE, Samaria was an administrative capital for the Persian Empire. By the late 4th century BCE, a Samaritan temple existed on Mount Gerizim, and a deep schism existed between the Samaritans and the Jews. During the NT period, the city of Samaria was resurgent.

are merciful kings. Allow us to put mourning clothes on our bodies and cords around our heads. We will then go to Israel's king. Perhaps he will let you live." [32]So they put mourning clothes on their bodies and cords around their heads. They went to Israel's king and said, "Ben-hadad is your slave. He begs, 'Please let me live!'"

Israel's king said, "Is he still alive? He is my brother."

[33]Taking this as a good sign, Ben-hadad's men quickly accepted this statement.[h] "Yes, Ben-hadad is your brother!" they said.

"Go and get him," the king ordered. So Ben-hadad came to him, and the king received him into his chariot.

[34]Ben-hadad said to the king, "I will return the towns that my father took from your father. Furthermore, you can set up markets for yourself in Damascus just as my father did in Samaria."

The king replied,[i] "On the basis of this covenant, I will let you go." So he made a covenant with Ben-hadad and set him free.

[35]At the LORD's command a certain man who belonged to a prophetic group said to his friend: "Please strike me." But his friend refused to hit him. [36]So he said to his friend, "Because you didn't obey the LORD's voice, a lion will attack you as soon as you leave me." And as the friend left the prophet, a lion found him and attacked him. [37]Then the prophet found another man and said, "Please strike me." He hit the prophet, and the attack left a wound. [38]The prophet went and stood before the king by the road. He disguised himself by putting a bandage over his eyes. [39]When the king passed by, the prophet called out to the king, "Your servant was in the middle of the battle when someone brought a prisoner. 'Guard this man,' he said. 'If he escapes it will be your life for his—that, or you will owe me a kikkar of silver.' [40]Your servant got busy doing this and that, and the prisoner disappeared."

Israel's king replied, "It appears you have decided your own fate."

[41]The prophet quickly tore the bandage from over his eyes, and Israel's king recognized him as one of the prophets. [42]Then the prophet said to the king, "This is what the LORD says: Because you freed a man I condemned to die, it will be your life for his life, and your people for his people."

[43]So Israel's king went to his palace at Samaria, irritated and upset.

Naboth's vineyard

21 Now it happened sometime later that Naboth from Jezreel had a vineyard in Jezreel that was next to the palace of King Ahab of Samaria. [2]Ahab ordered Naboth, "Give me your vineyard so it can become my vegetable garden, because it is right next to my palace. In exchange for it, I'll give you an even better vineyard. Or if you prefer, I'll pay you the price in silver."

[3]Naboth responded to Ahab, "LORD forbid that I give you my family inheritance!"

[4]So Ahab went to his palace, irritated and upset at what Naboth[j] had said to him—because Naboth had said, "I won't give you my family inheritance!" Ahab lay down on his bed and turned his face away. He wouldn't eat anything.

[5]His wife Jezebel came to him. "Why are you upset and not eating any food?" she asked.

[6]He answered her, "I was talking to Naboth. I said, 'Sell me your vineyard. Or if you prefer, I'll give you another vineyard for it.' But he said, 'I won't give you my vineyard!'"

[7]Then his wife Jezebel said to him, "Aren't you the one who rules Israel? Get up! Eat some food and cheer up. I'll get Naboth's vineyard for you myself." [8]So she wrote letters in Ahab's name, putting his seal on them. She sent them to the elders and officials who lived in the same town as Naboth. [9]This is what she wrote in the letters: "Announce a fast and place Naboth at the head of the people. [10]Then bring in two liars in front of him and have them testify as follows: 'You cursed God and king!' Then take Naboth outside and stone him so he dies."

---

[h]Heb uncertain [i]Heb lacks *The king replied.* [j]Heb adds *from Jezreel;* also in 21:6-7, 15-16.

¹¹The elders and the officials who lived in Naboth's town did exactly as Jezebel specified in the letters that she had sent. ¹²They announced a fast and placed Naboth at the head of the people. ¹³Then the two liars came and sat in front of him. They testified against Naboth in front of the people, "Naboth cursed God and king!" So the people took Naboth outside the town and stoned him so that he died.

¹⁴It was then reported to Jezebel, "Naboth was stoned. He's dead." ¹⁵As soon as Jezebel heard that Naboth had been stoned to death, she said to Ahab, "Get up and take ownership of the vineyard of Naboth, which he had refused to sell to you. Naboth is no longer alive; he's dead." ¹⁶When Ahab heard that Naboth had died, he got up and went down to Naboth's vineyard to take ownership of it.

¹⁷The LORD's word came to Elijah from Tishbe: ¹⁸Get up and go down to meet Israel's King Ahab in Samaria. He is in Naboth's vineyard. He has gone down to take ownership of it.¹⁹Say the following to him: This is what the LORD says: So, you've murdered and are now taking ownership, are you? Then tell him: This is what the LORD says: In the same place where the dogs licked up Naboth's blood, they will lick up your own blood.

²⁰Ahab said to Elijah, "So you've found me, my old enemy!"

"I found you," Elijah said, "because you've enslaved yourself by doing evil in the LORD's eyes! ²¹So I am now bringing evil on you! I will burn until you are consumed, and I will eliminate everyone who urinates on a wall that belongs to Ahab, whether slave or free. ²²I will make your household like that of Jeroboam, Nebat's son, and like the household of Baasha, Ahijah's son, because of the way you've angered me and because you've made Israel sin. ²³As for Jezebel, the LORD says this: Dogs will devour Jezebel in the area of Jezreel. ²⁴Dogs will eat anyone of Ahab's family who dies in town, and birds will eat anyone who dies in the country."

(²⁵Truly there has never been anyone like Ahab who sold out by doing evil in the LORD's eyes—evil that his wife Jezebel led him to do. ²⁶Ahab's actions were deplorable. He followed after the worthless idols exactly like the Amorites had done—the very ones the LORD had removed before the Israelites.)

²⁷When Ahab heard these words, he tore his clothes and put mourning clothes on his body. He fasted, even slept in mourning clothes, and walked around depressed. ²⁸The LORD's word then came to Elijah from Tishbe: ²⁹Have you seen how Ahab has humbled himself before me? Because he has done so, I won't bring the evil during his lifetime. Instead, I will bring the evil on his household in the days of his son.

Jehoshaphat and Ahab

22 For three years there was no war between Aram and the Israelites. ²In the third year, Judah's King Jehoshaphat visited Israel's king. ³Israel's king said to his servants, "You know, don't you, that Ramoth-gilead is ours? But we aren't doing anything to take it back from the king of Aram." ⁴He said to Jehoshaphat, "Will you go with me into battle at Ramoth-gilead?"

NABOTH

Naboth lived in Jezreel during the reign of Ahab king of Israel and owned a vineyard adjacent to the royal palace (1 Kgs 21:1-2). Ahab wanted Naboth's land for a vegetable garden, offering a better vineyard or the value of the land in money. Naboth refused to sell his property, so the king's wife Jezebel plotted to kill Naboth and take possession of his land.

Jehoshaphat said to Israel's king, "I am with you, and my troops and my horses are united with yours. ⁵But," Jehoshapat said to Israel's king, "first let's see what the LORD has to say."

⁶So Israel's king gathered about four hundred prophets, and he asked them, "Should I go to war with Ramoth-gilead or not?"

"Attack!" the prophets answered. "The LORD will hand it over to the king."

⁷But Jehoshaphat said, "Isn't there any other prophet of the LORD whom we could ask?"

⁸"There is one other man who could ask the LORD for us," Israel's king told Jehoshaphat, "but I hate him because he never prophesies anything good about me, only bad. His name is Micaiah, Imlah's son."

"The king shouldn't speak like that!" Jehoshaphat said.

⁹So Israel's king called an officer and ordered, "Bring Micaiah, Imlah's son, right away."

¹⁰Now Israel's king and Judah's King Jehoshaphat were sitting on their thrones, dressed in their royal robes at the threshing floor beside the entrance to the gate of Samaria. All the prophets were prophesying in front of them. ¹¹Zedekiah, Chenaanah's son, made iron horns for himself and said, "This is what the LORD says: With these horns you will gore the Arameans until there's nothing left of them!"

¹²All the other prophets agreed: "Attack Ramoth-gilead and win! The LORD will hand it over to the king!"

¹³Meanwhile, the messenger who had gone to summon Micaiah said to him, "Listen, the prophets all agree that the king will succeed. You should say the same thing they say and prophesy success."

¹⁴But Micaiah answered, "As surely as the LORD lives, I will say only what the LORD tells me to say."

¹⁵When Micaiah arrived, the king asked him, "Micaiah, should we go to war with Ramoth-gilead or not?"

"Attack and win!" Micaiah answered. "The LORD will hand it over to the king!"

¹⁶But the king said, "How many times must I demand that you tell me the truth when you speak in the name of the LORD?"

¹⁷Then Micaiah replied, "I saw all Israel scattered on the hills like sheep without a shepherd! And then the LORD said: They have no master. Let them return safely to their own homes."

¹⁸Then Israel's king said to Jehoshaphat, "Didn't I tell you? He never prophesies anything good about me, only bad."

¹⁹Then Micaiah said, "Listen now to the LORD's word: I saw the LORD enthroned with all the heavenly forces stationed beside him, at his right and at his left. ²⁰The LORD said, 'Who will persuade Ahab so that he attacks Ramoth-gilead and dies there?' There were many suggestions ²¹until one particular spirit approached the LORD and said, 'I'll persuade him.' 'How?' the LORD asked. ²²'I will be a lying spirit in the mouth of all his prophets,' he said. The LORD agreed, 'You will succeed in persuading him! Go ahead!' ²³So now, since the LORD has placed a lying spirit in the mouths of every one of these prophets of yours, it is the LORD who has pronounced disaster against you!"

²⁴Zedekiah, Chenaanah's son, approached Micaiah and slapped him on the cheek. "Just how did the LORD's spirit leave me to speak to you?" he asked.

²⁵Micaiah answered, "You will find out on the day you try to hide in an inner room."

²⁶"Arrest him," ordered Israel's king, "and turn him over to Amon the city official and to Joash the king's son. ²⁷Tell them, 'The king says: Put this man in prison and feed him minimum rations of bread and water until I return safely.'"

²⁸"If you ever return safely," Micaiah replied, "then the LORD wasn't speaking through me." Then he added, "Pay attention, every last one of you!"

²⁹So Israel's king and Judah's King Jehoshaphat attacked Ramoth-gilead. ³⁰Israel's king said to Jehoshaphat, "I will disguise myself when we go into battle,ᵏ but you should wear your royal attire." When

---

ᵏLXX, Tg; MT *Disguise yourself and go*

Israel's king had disguised himself, they entered the battle.

[31] Meanwhile, Aram's king had commanded his thirty-two chariot officers, "Don't bother with anyone big or small. Fight only with Israel's king."

[32] As soon as the chariot officers saw Jehoshaphat, they assumed that he must be Israel's king, so they turned to attack him. But Jehoshaphat cried out for help. [33] When the chariot officers realized that he wasn't Israel's king, they stopped chasing him. [34] But someone randomly shot an arrow that struck Israel's king between the joints in his armor.[l]

"Turn around and get me out of the battle," the king told his chariot driver. "I've been hit!"

[35] While the battle raged all that day, the king stood propped up in the chariot facing the Arameans. But that evening he died after his blood had poured from his wound into the chariot. [36] When the sun set, a shout spread throughout the camp: "Retreat to your towns! Retreat to your land!" [37] Once the king had died, people came from Samaria and buried the king there. [38] They cleaned the chariot at the pool of Samaria. The dogs licked up the king's blood and the prostitutes bathed in it, just as the LORD had spoken.

Ahab's last days

[39] The rest of Ahab's deeds and all that he did—including the ivory palace he built and all the towns he constructed—aren't they written in the official records of Israel's kings? [40] Ahab lay down with his ancestors. His son Ahaziah succeeded him as king.

Jehoshaphat rules Judah

[41] Jehoshaphat, Asa's son, became king over Judah in the fourth year of Israel's

King Ahab. [42] Jehoshaphat was 35 years old when he became king, and he ruled for twenty-five years in Jerusalem. His mother's name was Azubah; she was Shilhi's daughter. [43] Jehoshapat walked in all the ways of his father Asa, not deviating from it. He did the right things in the LORD's eyes, with the exception that he didn't remove the shrines. The people continued to sacrifice and offer incense at them. [44] Jehoshaphat made peace with Israel's king. [45] The rest of Jehoshaphat's deeds, the great acts he did, and how he fought in battle, aren't they written in the official records of Judah's kings? [46] Additionally, Jehoshaphat purged the land of the consecrated workers[m] who remained from the days of Asa.

[47] Now Edom had no king; only a deputy was ruler. [48] Jehoshaphat built Tarshish-styled ships to go to Ophir for gold. But the fleet didn't go because it was wrecked at Ezion-geber. [49] Then Ahaziah, Ahab's son, said to Jehoshaphat, "Let my sailors go with your sailors on the ships." But Jehoshaphat didn't agree to this. [50] Jehoshaphat died and was buried with his ancestors in his ancestor David's City. His son Jehoram succeeded him as king.

Ahaziah rules Israel

[51] In the seventeenth year of Judah's King Jehoshaphat, Ahaziah, Ahab's son, became king over Israel in Samaria. He ruled over Israel for two years. [52] He did evil in the LORD's eyes. He walked in his father's ways and his mother's ways—that is, in the ways of Jeroboam, Nebat's son, who had caused Israel to sin. [53] Ahaziah served Baal and worshipped him. He angered the LORD, Israel's God, by doing all the same things his father had done.

---

[l] Heb uncertain   [m] Traditionally *cultic prostitutes*

2 KINGS

See the introduction to 1 Kings for information about the content, chronology, and writers of the books of Kings.

OLD TESTAMENT HISTORICAL NARRATIVE

In broad terms, history is an account of what has happened in the past. A narrative is a story that, in its simplest form, is a chronological account of more than one past event that also tells of causes and effects. Thus, some narratives can be history told as stories. Such stories are common in the Old Testament and are found in the books of First and Second Kings (for example, 1 Kings 19:1-21; 2 Kings 4:8-37).

Old Testament stories are different from other historical narratives, however, because they are sacred stories. These stories are told in the belief that all of life exists because of, and is subject to, God's will. In the Old Testament there is a recognition that some things are holy and others are not, but all life is held to be sacred. Old Testament historical narratives are told within the context of such faith. Because of this faith, Old Testament history is not just a list or report of events. Old Testament history describes events and people and also interprets them according to their causes and effects. God's will is seen as the ultimate source of all causes and effects in human history.

Old Testament historical narrative tells the story of Israel's life as a people who live in relationship to God. The chosen people are the particular subjects of these stories. The broader focus of these stories, though, is the relationship between God and all of creation. The result of this relationship is revelation. God is revealed to humankind. The Old Testament writers do not give us theological lectures about the nature and being of God. Rather, they tell us who God is by telling us how God acts.

The Old Testament writers do not try to convince us to believe their stories by giving us a lot of information about the setting or about the feelings and thoughts of the characters. Most of the time their narratives do not include many details. This reflects the fact that, in many cases, the stories were passed on by word of mouth for generations before they were written.

The goal of any narrative is communication. What the writer or speaker knows or sees must be communicated to the reader or listener. The result of narrative is that the readers or listeners see, recognize, and understand something, perhaps something with which they have had no personal experience. The writers of Old Testament stories seek such communication with their readers. Their stories are meant to communicate the same basic testimony: History is the will of a just God who knows us and cares about us. The writers want us to understand that our lives are contained in an order that is moving toward God's purposes.

Old Testament historical narratives witness to the fact that the world and everyone in it belong to God. They ask us to believe that we live in an ordered world that is moving toward a desired goal. The sacred stories of the Old Testament do not only offer the pleasure of a well-told story. They teach, encourage, and sustain the community of faith.

2 KINGS

Ahaziah's death

1 After Ahab died, Moab rebelled against Israel.

² Ahaziah fell out the window of his second-story room in Samaria and was hurt. He sent messengers, telling them, "Go to Ekron's god Baal-zebub, and ask if I will recover from this injury."

³ But the LORD's messenger said to Elijah from Tishbe, "Go, intercept the messengers of Samaria's king, and ask them, 'Is it because there's no God in Israel that you are going to question Ekron's god Baal-zebub? ⁴ This is what the LORD says: You will never get out of the bed you are lying in; you will die for sure!'" So Elijah set off.

⁵ The messengers returned to Ahaziah. He said to them, "Why have you come back?"

⁶ They said to him, "A man met us and said, 'Go back to the king who sent you. Say to him, This is what the LORD says: Is it because there's no God in Israel that you've come to question Ekron's god Baal-zebub? Because of this, you will never get out of the bed you are lying in; you will die for sure!'"

⁷ Ahaziah said to them, "Describe the man who met you and said these things."

⁸ They said to him, "He wore clothes made of hair[a] with a leather belt around his waist."

Ahaziah said, "That was Elijah from Tishbe."

⁹ So Ahaziah sent out a commander with fifty soldiers. The commander met up with Elijah while he was sitting on a hilltop. The commander said, "Man of God, the king says, 'Come down!'"

¹⁰ Elijah replied to the commander of the fifty soldiers, "If I really am a man of God, may fire come down from the sky and burn up you and your fifty soldiers." Then fire came down from the sky and burned up the commander and his fifty soldiers.

¹¹ Ahaziah then sent another commander with fifty soldiers. The commander said to Elijah, "Man of God, this is what the king says: 'Hurry and come down!'"

¹² Elijah said to them, "If I really am a man of God, may fire come down from the sky and burn up you and your fifty soldiers." Then God's fire came down from the sky and burned up the commander and his fifty soldiers.

¹³ For a third time Ahaziah sent a commander with fifty soldiers. So the third commander arrived. He kneeled before Elijah and begged him, "Man of God! Please have some regard for my life and the lives of these fifty soldiers who are your servants. ¹⁴ Look, fire came from the sky and burned up the two earlier commanders and their troops of fifty soldiers. Please have regard for my life."

¹⁵ Then the LORD's messenger said to Elijah, "Go down with him. Don't be afraid of him." So Elijah set out to go with him to the king.

¹⁶ Elijah said to the king: "This is what the LORD says: Why did you send messengers to question Ekron's god Baal-zebub? Is there no God in Israel whose word you could

---

[a] Or He was a hairy man.

ELIJAH

Elijah was an agent ("prophet") of the Lord who lived during the dynasty of Omri in the 9th century BCE and performed awesome and, at times, outrageous deeds (1 Kgs 17–19; 2 Kgs 1–2). These deeds verified that Elijah spoke for God and so authenticated the main theme of his story: sanction for toppling Omri's dynasty.

seek? Because of this, you won't ever get out of the bed you are lying in; you'll die for sure!" [17]So Ahaziah died in agreement with the LORD's word that Elijah had spoken.

Because Ahaziah had no son, Joram[b] became king after him in the second year of Judah's King Jehoram, who was Jehoshaphat's son. [18]The rest of Ahaziah's deeds, aren't they written in the official records of Israel's kings?

Elijah goes to heaven

2 Now the LORD was going to take Elijah up to heaven in a windstorm, and Elijah and Elisha were leaving Gilgal. [2]Elijah said to Elisha, "Stay here, because the LORD has sent me to Bethel."

But Elisha said, "As the LORD lives and as you live, I won't leave you." So they went down to Bethel.

[3]The group of prophets from Bethel came out to Elisha. These prophets said to Elisha, "Do you know that the LORD is going to take your master away from you today?"

Elisha said, "Yes, I know. Don't talk about it!"

[4]Elijah said, "Elisha, stay here, because the LORD has sent me to Jericho."

But Elisha said, "As the LORD lives and as you live, I won't leave you." So they went to Jericho.

[5]The group of prophets from Jericho approached Elisha and said to him, "Do you know that the LORD is going to take your master away from you today?"

He said, "Yes, I know. Don't talk about it!"

[6]Elijah said to Elisha, "Stay here, because the LORD has sent me to the Jordan."

But Elisha said, "As the LORD lives and as you live, I won't leave you." So both of them went on together. [7]Fifty members from the group of prophets also went along, but they stood at a distance. Both Elijah and Elisha stood beside the Jordan River. [8]Elijah then took his coat, rolled it up, and hit the water. Then the water was divided in two! Both of them crossed over on dry ground. [9]When they had crossed, Elijah said to Elisha,

"What do you want me to do for you before I'm taken away from you?"

Elisha said, "Let me have twice your spirit."

[10]Elijah said, "You've made a difficult request. If you can see me when I'm taken from you, then it will be yours. If you don't see me, it won't happen."

[11]They were walking along, talking, when suddenly a fiery chariot and fiery horses appeared and separated the two of them. Then Elijah went to heaven in a windstorm.

[12]Elisha was watching, and he cried out, "Oh, my father, my father! Israel's chariots and its riders!" When he could no longer see him, Elisha took hold of his clothes and ripped them in two.

Elisha succeeds Elijah

[13]Then Elisha picked up the coat that had fallen from Elijah. He went back and stood beside the banks of the Jordan River. [14]He took the coat that had fallen from Elijah and hit the water. He said, "Where is the LORD, Elijah's God?" And when he hit the water, it divided in two! Then Elisha crossed over.

[15]The group of prophets from Jericho saw him from a distance. They said, "Elijah's spirit has settled on Elisha!" So they came out to meet him, bowing down before him. [16]"Look," they told him, "there are fifty strong men among us, your servants. Please let them go and search for your master. Perhaps the LORD's spirit has picked him up and put him down on some mountain or in some valley."

Elisha said, "Don't send them." [17]They insisted until he became embarrassed and said, "Okay, send them." So they sent fifty men who searched for three days. But they couldn't find Elijah. [18]When these men returned to Elisha, who was staying in Jericho, he said to them, "Didn't I tell you not to go?"

[19]The citizens said to Elisha, "As you can see, sir, this city is in a good location, but the water is bad, and the land causes miscarriages."

---

[b]Heb *Jehoram*; the king's name is variously spelled in either long *Jehoram* or short *Joram* form.

²⁰He said, "Bring me a new bowl, and put some salt in it." They did so. ²¹Elisha then went out and threw salt into the spring. He said, "This is what the LORD has said: I have purified this water. It will no longer cause death and miscarriage." ²²The water has stayed pure right up to this very day, in agreement with the word that Elisha spoke.

Elisha and the bears

²³Elisha went up from there to Bethel. As he was going up the road, some young people came out of the city. They mocked him: "Get going, Baldy! Get going, Baldy!" ²⁴Turning around, Elisha looked at them and cursed them in the LORD's name. Then two bears came out of the woods and mangled forty-two of the youths. ²⁵From there Elisha went to Mount Carmel and then back to Samaria.

Moab's rebellion

3 Joram,ᶜ Ahab's son, became king of Israel in Samaria in the eighteenth year of Jehoshaphat, Judah's king. He ruled for twelve years. ²He did what was evil in the LORD's eyes, but he wasn't as bad as his father and mother. He removed the sacred pillar of Baal that his father had made. ³But he nevertheless clung to the sins that Jeroboam, Nebat's son, had caused Israel to commit. He didn't deviate from them.

⁴Now Moab's King Mesha kept sheep. He would pay Israel's king one hundred thousand lambs and the wool from one hundred thousand rams. ⁵But when Ahab

---

ᶜHeb *Jehoram* (also in 3:6); the king's name is variously spelled in either long *Jehoram* or short *Joram* form.

SALT

Salt, as a preservative and purifying agent, has both literal and metaphorical functions in the Bible. Salt was often a part of ritual observances. In Exodus 30:34-35 it is an ingredient in incense to be used in the temple (cf. Ezra 6:9; 7:21-22). Salt must be added to all offerings brought to the sanctuary (Ezek 43:24; Lev 2:13). The importance of salt as a preservative or cleanser may lie behind the story of Elisha in a town with bad water (2 Kgs 2:19-22), where he used salt to make the water wholesome. Although salt is often a preservative, it can also destroy or render a place uninhabitable or unusable (cf. Ezek 47:11; Jer 17:6). The OT refers to conquerors sowing the land with salt to destroy its fertility (Judg 9:45). God sometimes also treats the land of those who do not worship him with salt (Deut 29:22-28; Ps 107:33-34; Zeph 2:9).

These senses of salt are carried over into its metaphorical uses. Ezekiel 16:4 says infant Israel was not rubbed with salt to emphasize that only God's help allowed Israel to become a people. Numbers 18:19 refers to a "covenant of salt." In Numbers the covenant is between God and Aaron's descendants. In 2 Chronicles 13:5 God gives David and his descendants the kingship of Israel forever with a covenant of salt. These instances may reflect salt's use as a preservative; it perhaps was understood as making the covenant more permanent and secure (see Lev 2:13). The Gospels remember Jesus as referring to his disciples as "the salt of the earth" (Matt 5:13), but warning against the loss of their "saltiness" (see also Mark 9:49-50, where having "salt" in themselves allows them to be at peace with each other; Luke 14:34-35).

died, Moab's king rebelled against Israel's king. [6]So King Joram set out from Samaria at once. He prepared all Israel for war. [7]He sent word to Judah's King Jehoshaphat, "Moab's king has rebelled against me. Will you go with me to fight against Moab?"

Jehoshaphat responded, "Yes, I'll go. We'll fight as one: you and I, our troops and our horses."

[8]"Which road should we take?" Joram asked.

Jehoshaphat responded, "The road that goes through the Edomite wilderness."

[9]So Israel's and Judah's kings set out with the king of Edom. They marched around for seven days until there was no water left for the army or for the animals with them. [10]Israel's king said, "This is terrible! Has the LORD brought us three kings together only to hand us over to Moab?"

[11]Jehoshaphat said, "Isn't there any prophet of the LORD around, so we could question the LORD through him?"

One of the servants of Israel's king answered, "Elisha, Shaphat's son, is here. He used to pour water on Elijah's hands."

[12]Jehoshaphat said, "He has the LORD's word!" So Israel's king and Jehoshaphat and Edom's king went down to see Elisha.

[13]Elisha said to Israel's king, "What do we have to do with each other? Go to your father's or mother's prophets."

Then Israel's king said to him, "Don't say that, because it is the LORD who has brought us three kings together—but only to hand us over to Moab!"

[14]Elisha said, "I swear by the life of the LORD of heavenly forces, the one I stand before and serve, if I didn't care about Judah's King Jehoshaphat, I wouldn't notice you or even look at you! [15]Now bring me a musician." While the musician played, the LORD's power came over Elisha. [16]He said, "This is what the LORD says: This valley will be filled with pools.[d] [17]This is what the LORD says: You won't see any wind or rain, but that valley will be full of water. Then you'll be able to drink—you, your cattle, and your animals. [18]This is easy for the LORD to do. He will also hand Moab over to you. [19]You will then attack every fort and every grand city, cutting down all the good trees, stopping up all the springs, and ruining the good fields with stones."

[20]The next morning, at the time to offer the grain offering, water came flowing from the direction of Edom. The land filled up with water.

[21]Now all the Moabites had heard how these kings had come to fight against them. So all who were able to fight were summoned, and they took up positions along the border. [22]They got up early in the morning as the sun's rays shone on the water. The Moabites saw the water from a distance. It looked as red as blood. [23]They said, "It's blood! The kings must have fought each other and killed themselves! Now get the plunder, Moab!"

[24]But when they entered Israel's camp, the Israelites rose up and attacked the Moabites. The Moabites fled from them. Israel moved forward, striking the Moabites down as they went.[e] [25]Then the Israelites destroyed the Moabite cities. Each Israelite threw a stone on every piece of good land until it was covered. They stopped up every spring and cut down every good tree. Only Kir-hareseth remained with its stone wall intact,[f] but then stone throwers[g] surrounded it and attacked it.

[26]Moab's king saw that he was losing the battle. So he took seven hundred soldiers with him, each with sword in hand, to break through to Edom's king. But they failed. [27]Then he took his oldest son, who was to succeed him as king, and he offered him on the wall as an entirely burned offering. As a result, outrage was expressed by Israel. So they pulled back from Moab's king and returned to their own country.

A poor widow

4 Now there was a woman who had been married to a member of a group of prophets. She appealed to Elisha, saying, "My husband, your servant, is dead. You know how he feared the LORD. But now

---

[d]LXX, Vulg *Fill this valley with ditches.*   [e]Heb uncertain   [f]Heb uncertain   [g]Heb uncertain

someone he owed money to has come to take my two children away as slaves."

²Elisha said to her, "What can I do for you? Tell me what you still have left in the house."

She said, "Your servant has nothing at all in the house except a small jar of oil."

³He said, "Go out and borrow containers from all your neighbors. Get as many empty containers as possible. ⁴Then go in and close the door behind you and your sons. Pour oil into all those containers. Set each one aside when it's full."

⁵She left Elisha and closed the door behind her and her sons. They brought her containers as she kept on pouring. ⁶When she had filled the containers, she said to her son, "Bring me another container."

He said to her, "There aren't any more." Then the oil stopped flowing, ⁷and she reported this to the man of God.

He said, "Go! Sell the oil and pay your debts. You and your sons can live on what remains."

A rich woman

⁸One day Elisha went to Shunem. A rich woman lived there. She urged him to eat something, so whenever he passed by, he would stop in to eat some food. ⁹She said to her husband, "Look, I know that he is a holy man of God and he passes by regularly. ¹⁰Let's make a small room on the roof. We'll set up a bed, a table, a chair, and a lamp for him there. Then when he comes to us, he can stay there."

¹¹So one day Elisha came there, headed to the room on the roof, and lay down. ¹²He said to his servant Gehazi, "Call this Shunammite woman." Gehazi called her, and she stood before him. ¹³Elisha then said to Gehazi, "Say to her, 'Look, you've gone to all this trouble for us. What can I do for you? Is there anything I can say on your behalf to the king or to the commander of the army?'"

She said, "I'm content to live at home with my own people."

¹⁴Elisha asked, "So what can be done for her?"

Gehazi said, "Well, she doesn't have a son, and her husband is old."

¹⁵Elisha said, "Call her." So Gehazi called her, and she stood at the door. ¹⁶Elisha said, "About this time next year, you will be holding a son in your arms."

But she said, "No, man of God, sir; don't lie to your servant."

¹⁷But the woman conceived and gave birth to a son at about the same time the next year. This was what Elisha had promised her.

¹⁸The child grew up. One day he ran to his father, who was with the harvest workers. ¹⁹He said to his father, "Oh, my head! My head!"

The father said to a young man, "Carry him to his mother." ²⁰So he picked up the boy and brought him to his mother.

The boy sat on her lap until noon. Then he died. ²¹She went up and laid him down on the bed for the man of God. Then she went out and closed the door. ²²She called her husband and said, "Send me one of the young men and one of the donkeys so that I can hurry to the man of God and come back."

²³Her husband said, "Why are you going to him today? It's not a new moon or sabbath."

She said, "Don't worry about it." ²⁴She saddled the donkey, then said to her young servant, "Drive the donkey hard. Don't let me slow down unless I tell you." ²⁵So she went off and came to the man of God at Mount Carmel.

As soon as the man of God saw her from a distance, he said to Gehazi his servant, "Look, it's the Shunammite woman! ²⁶Run out to meet her and ask her, 'Are things okay with you, your husband, and your child?'"

She said, "Things are okay."

²⁷When she got to the man of God at the mountain, she grabbed his feet. Gehazi came up to push her away, but the man of God said, "Leave her alone! She is distraught, but the LORD has hidden the reason from me and hasn't told me why."

²⁸She said, "Did I ask you for a son, sir? Didn't I say, 'Don't raise my hopes'?"

²⁹Elisha said to Gehazi, "Get ready, take my staff, and go! If you encounter anyone, don't stop to greet them. If anyone greets you, don't reply. Put my staff on the boy's face."

³⁰But the boy's mother said, "I swear by

your life and by the LORD's life, I won't leave you!" So Elisha got up and followed her.

³¹Gehazi went on ahead of them. He set the staff on the young boy's face, but there was no sound or response. So he went back to meet Elisha and told him, "The boy didn't wake up."

³²Elisha came into the house and saw the boy lying dead on his bed. ³³He went in and closed the door behind the two of them. Then he prayed to the LORD. ³⁴He got up on the bed and lay down on top of the child, putting his mouth on the boy's mouth, his eyes on the boy's eyes, his hands on the boy's hands. And as he bent over him, the child's skin grew warm. ³⁵Then Elisha got down and paced back and forth in the house. Once again he got up on the bed and bent over the boy, at which point the boy sneezed[h] seven times and opened his eyes. ³⁶Elisha called for Gehazi and said, "Call the Shunammite woman." Gehazi called her, and she came to Elisha. He told her, "Pick up your son." ³⁷She came and fell at his feet,

[h]Or gasped; Heb uncertain

facedown on the ground. Then she picked up her son and left.

Miracles with food

³⁸When Elisha returned to Gilgal, there was a famine in the land. A group of prophets was sitting before him. He said to his servant, "Put on the big pot and cook some stew for the prophets." ³⁹So one of them went out to the field to gather plants; he found a wild vine and gathered wild gourds from it, filling his garment. He came and cut them up into the pot of stew, but no one knew what they were.

⁴⁰The stew was served to the men, but as they started to eat it, they cried out and said, "There is death in that pot, man of God!" They couldn't eat it.

⁴¹Elisha said, "Get some flour." He threw it into the pot and said, "Serve the people so they can eat." At that point, there was nothing bad left in the pot.

⁴²A man came from Baal-shalishah, bringing the man of God some bread from

STAFF

A variety of Hebrew and Greek words with a variety of functions are reflected in the CEB word "staff." In some cases (e.g., Zech 8:4; Heb 11:21), a staff is used by the elderly like a cane. Often, however, staffs function as walking sticks (e.g., 1 Sam 14:43). Shepherds used staffs (Mic 7:14) to negotiate difficult terrain, count their sheep (Lev 27:32), and hit their flock to guide them (cf. Num 22:27). This image is inverted in Psalm 23:4, where the Lord's staff "protect[s]" the individual. Staffs could be highly individualized and recognizable as belonging to a particular person (Gen 38:25).

Moses' staff turned into a snake (Exod 4:1-5), initiated plagues against Egypt, split the Reed Sea (Exod 14:16), and brought forth water from the rock (Num 20:2-13). It is thus twice called "the shepherd's rod from God" (Exod 4:20; 17:9). This suggests that a prophet's staff had magical powers and explains why Gehazi tried to use his master Elisha's staff to revive a dead child (2 Kgs 4:29-31). Staffs were typically made of dead wood from sturdy trees—hence the miraculous flowering staff of Aaron (Num 17:1-11 [Heb. 17:16-26]) and the image of Egypt compared to a "broken reed," which is both weak and sharp (e.g., 2 Kgs 18:21).

the early produce—twenty loaves of barley bread and fresh grain from his bag.[i] Elisha said, "Give it to the people so they can eat."

[43]His servant said, "How can I feed one hundred men with this?"

Elisha said, "Give it to the people so they can eat! This is what the LORD says: 'Eat and there will be leftovers.'" [44]So the servant gave the food to them. They ate and had leftovers, in agreement with the LORD's word.

Naaman is healed

5 Naaman, a general for the king of Aram, was a great man and highly regarded by his master, because through him the LORD had given victory to Aram. This man was a mighty warrior, but he had a skin disease.[j] [2]Now Aramean raiding parties had gone out and captured a young girl from the land of Israel. She served Naaman's wife.

[3]She said to her mistress, "I wish that my master could come before the prophet who lives in Samaria. He would cure him of his skin disease." [4]So Naaman went and told his master what the young girl from the land of Israel had said.

[5]Then Aram's king said, "Go ahead. I will send a letter to Israel's king."

So Naaman left. He took along ten kikkars of silver, six thousand shekels of gold, and ten changes of clothing. [6]He brought the letter to Israel's king. It read, "Along with this letter I'm sending you my servant Naaman so you can cure him of his skin disease."

[7]When the king of Israel read the letter, he ripped his clothes. He said, "What? Am I God to hand out death and life? But this king writes me, asking me to cure someone of his skin disease! You must realize that he wants to start a fight with me."

[8]When Elisha the man of God heard that Israel's king had ripped his clothes, he sent word to the king: "Why did you rip your clothes? Let the man come to me. Then he'll know that there's a prophet in Israel."

[9]Naaman arrived with his horses and chariots. He stopped at the door of Elisha's house. [10]Elisha sent out a messenger who said, "Go and wash seven times in the Jordan River. Then your skin will be restored and become clean."

[11]But Naaman went away in anger. He said, "I thought for sure that he'd come out, stand and call on the name of the LORD his God, wave his hand over the bad spot, and cure the skin disease. [12]Aren't the rivers in Damascus, the Abana[k] and the Pharpar, better than all Israel's waters? Couldn't I wash in them and get clean?" So he turned away and proceeded to leave in anger.

[13]Naaman's servants came up to him and spoke to him: "Our father, if the prophet had told you to do something difficult, wouldn't you have done it? All he said to you was, 'Wash and become clean.'" [14]So Naaman went down and bathed in the Jordan seven times, just as the man of God had said. His skin was restored like that of a young boy, and he became clean.

[15]He returned to the man of God with all his attendants. He came and stood before Elisha, saying, "Now I know for certain that there's no God anywhere on earth except in Israel. Please accept a gift from your servant."

[16]But Elisha said, "I swear by the life of the LORD I serve that I won't accept anything."

Naaman urged Elisha to accept something, but he still refused. [17]Then Naaman said, "If not, then let me, your servant, have two mule loads of earth. Your servant will never again offer entirely burned offerings or sacrifices to any other gods except the LORD. [18]But may the LORD forgive your servant for this one thing: When my master comes into Rimmon's temple to bow down there and is leaning on my arm, I must also bow down in Rimmon's temple. When I bow down in Rimmon's temple, may the LORD forgive your servant for doing that."

[19]Elisha said to him, "Go in peace."

But when Naaman had gone some distance from Elisha, [20]Gehazi (who was the servant of Elisha the man of God) thought, My master let this Aramean Naaman off the hook by not accepting the gift he brought!

[i]Or still on its stem [j]Traditionally leprosy, a kind of scale skin disease [k]Or Amana

As surely as the LORD lives, I'll go after him and accept something from him. [21]So Gehazi pursued Naaman.

Naaman saw him running after him, so he got down off his chariot to meet him. He said, "Is everything okay?"

[22]Gehazi answered, "Yes, but my master sent me to say, 'Two young men who are members of a group of prophets have just now come to me from the hills of Ephraim. Give them a kikkar of silver and two changes of clothing.'"

[23]Naaman said, "By all means, take two kikkars!" He encouraged Gehazi to accept them. He tied two kikkars of silver up in two bags, along with two changes of clothes. Naaman gave them to two of his servants, and they carried them in front of Gehazi. [24]When Gehazi arrived at the elevated fortress,[1] he took the items from them and stored them in his house. Then he sent the servants away, and they left. [25]Gehazi then went and stood before his master. Elisha said to Gehazi, "Where did you come from, Gehazi?"

"Your servant didn't go anywhere," Gehazi replied.

[26]Elisha said to him, "Wasn't my heart going along with you[m] when the man got off his chariot to meet you? Is this the time to accept silver, clothes, olive trees, vineyards, sheep, cattle, or male and female servants? [27]Naaman's skin disease will now cling to you and to your descendants forever!" And Gehazi left Elisha's presence, flaky like snow with skin disease.

An ax head floats

6 The members of the group of prophets said to Elisha, "Look, the place where we now live under your authority is too small for us. [2]Let's go to the Jordan River and each get a log from there. Then we can make a place to live there."

Elisha said, "Do it!"

[3]One of them said, "Please come with us, your servants."

Elisha said, "Okay, I'll go." [4]So he went with them. They came to the Jordan River

and began cutting down trees. [5]One of them was cutting down a tree when his ax head fell into the water. He cried out, "Oh, no! Master, it was a borrowed ax!"

[6]The man of God said, "Where did it fall?" He showed Elisha the place. Elisha then cut a piece of wood, threw it into the river there, and the ax head floated up. [7]"Lift it out," Elisha said. So the man then reached out and grabbed it.

Aramean attacks are stopped

[8]Aram's king was fighting against Israel. He took counsel with his officers, saying, "I'll camp at such-and-such a place."

[9]The man of God sent word to Israel's king: "Beware of passing by this place because the Arameans are going down there." [10]Then Israel's king sent word to the place the man of God had mentioned to him. Time after time, Elisha warned the king, and the king stayed on the alert.

[11]Aram's king was extremely upset about this. He called his officers and said to them, "Tell me! Who among us is siding with Israel's king?"

[12]One of his officers said, "No one, Your Majesty! It's Elisha the Israelite prophet who tells Israel's king the words that you speak in the privacy of your bedroom."

[13]He said, "Go and find out where he is. Then I will send men to capture him."

They told him, "He is in Dothan." [14]So the king sent horses and chariots there with a strong army. They came at night and surrounded the city.

[15]Elisha's servant got up early and went out. He saw an army with horses and chariots surrounding the city. His servant said to Elisha, "Oh, no! Master, what will we do?"

[16]"Don't be afraid," Elisha said, "because there are more of us than there are of them." [17]Then Elisha prayed, "LORD, please open his eyes that he may see." Then the LORD opened the servant's eyes, and he saw that the mountain was full of horses and fiery chariots surrounding Elisha. [18]The Arameans came toward him, so Elisha prayed to the LORD, "Strike this nation

---

[1]Or hillside; Heb uncertain   [m]LXX; MT lacks along with you.

with blindness." And the LORD struck them blind, just as Elisha asked. [19]Elisha said to them, "This isn't the right road or the right city. Follow me, and I'll lead you to the man you are looking for." But he took them to Samaria!

[20]When they arrived in Samaria, Elisha said, "LORD, open the eyes of these men so they can see." The LORD opened their eyes, and they saw that they were right in the middle of Samaria! [21]When he saw them, Israel's king said to Elisha, "Should I kill them, my father? Should I?"

[22]He said, "No, don't kill them. Did you capture them with your own sword or bow? Do you have the right to kill them?[n] Put food and water in front of them so they can eat and drink and return to their master." [23]So the king gave them a great feast, and they ate and drank. Then the king let them go, and they returned to their master. After that, Aramean raiding parties didn't come into Israel anymore.

Ben-hadad attacks Samaria

[24]Now it happened later that Aram's King Ben-hadad gathered all his forces and went up to attack Samaria. [25]The siege lasted so long that there was a great famine in Samaria. A donkey's head sold for eighty shekels of silver and a quarter kab of doves' dung[o] for five shekels. [26]Israel's king was passing by on the city wall when a woman appealed to him, "Help me, Your Majesty!"

[27]The king said, "No! May the LORD help you! Where can I find help for you? From the threshing floor or the winepress?" [28]But then the king asked her, "What's troubling you?"

She answered, "A woman said to me, 'Give up your son so we can eat him today; we'll eat my son tomorrow.' [29]So we cooked and ate my son. The next day I said to her, 'Hand over your son so we can eat him.' But she had hidden her son."

[30]When the king heard the woman's story, he ripped his clothes. And as he passed by along the wall, the people could

see that he was wearing mourning clothes underneath. [31]He said, "So may God do to me, and more, if the head of Elisha, Shaphat's son, remains on his shoulders today!"

[32]Elisha was sitting in his house, and the elders were sitting with him. The king sent a messenger on ahead, but before the man arrived, Elisha said to the elders, "Do you see that this murderer has sent someone to cut off my head? Watch for when the messenger comes, then close the door and hold it shut against him. The sound of his master's feet is right behind him, isn't it?"

[33]While Elisha was still speaking with them, the messenger[p] arrived and said, "Look, this disaster is the LORD's doing. Why should I trust the LORD any longer?"

7 Elisha said, "Hear the LORD's word! This is what the LORD says: At this time tomorrow a seah[q] of wheat flour will sell for a shekel at Samaria's gate, and two seahs of barley will sell for a shekel."

[2]Then the officer, the one the king leaned on for support, spoke to the man of God: "Come on! Even if the LORD should make windows in the sky, how could that happen?"

Elisha said, "You will see it with your own eyes, but you won't eat from it."

The siege is broken

[3]Now there were four men with skin disease[r] at the entrance to the city. They said to each other, "What are we doing sitting here until we die? [4]If we decide, 'Let's go into the city,' the famine is there, and we'll die in the city. But if we stay here, we'll die just the same. So let's go and surrender to the Aramean camp. If they let us live, we'll live. If they kill us, we'll die." [5]So they set out in the evening to the Aramean camp, and they came to the edge of the camp. But there was no one there because [6]the Lord had made the Aramean camp hear the sound of chariots, horses, and a strong army. They had said to each other, "Listen! Israel's king has hired the Hittite and Egyptian kings to come against us!" [7]So they had got up and fled in the evening, leaving their tents,

[n]Heb uncertain [o]Or *wild onions* or *carob pods* [p]Or perhaps *the king*; cf 7:2 [q]One seah is approximately seven and a half quarts. [r]Traditionally *leprosy*, a term used for several different skin diseases

horses, and donkeys. They left the camp exactly as it was and ran for their lives.

⁸So these men with skin disease came to the edge of the camp. They entered a tent where they ate and drank. They carried off some silver, gold, and garments, and they hid them. Then they returned and went into another tent. They took more things from there, went away, and hid them. ⁹But then they said to each other, "What we're doing isn't right. Today is a day of good news, but we're keeping quiet about it. If we wait until dawn, something bad will happen to us. Come on! Let's go and tell the palace." ¹⁰So they went and called out to the gatekeepers, telling them, "We went to the Aramean camp, and listen to this: No one was there, not even the sound of anyone! The only things there were tied-up horses and donkeys, and the tents left just as they were." ¹¹The gatekeepers shouted out the news, and it was reported within the palace.

¹²The king got up in the night. He said to his servants, "Let me tell you what the Arameans are doing to us. They know we are starving, so they've left the camp to hide in the fields. They are thinking, The Israelites will come out from the city, and then we'll capture them alive and invade the city."

¹³But one of his servants answered, "Please let some men take five of the horses that are left, and let's send them out to see what happens. They are in the same situation as the large number of Israelites who are left here; they are no better off than the large number of Israelites who've already perished."ˢ ¹⁴So they chose two chariots with their horses.

The king sent them after the Aramean army, saying, "Go and see!" ¹⁵So they went after the Arameans as far as the Jordan River. The road was filled the whole way with garments and equipment that the Arameans had thrown away in their rush. The messengers returned and reported this to the king.

¹⁶Then the people went out and looted the Aramean camp. And so it happened that a seah of wheat flour did sell for a shekel, and two seahs of barley sold for a shekel, in agreement with the LORD's word. ¹⁷But the king had put the officer whom he leaned on for support in charge of the city gate. The people trampled the officer at the gate, and he died. This was just what the man of God said when the king had come down to him. ¹⁸Because when the man of God said to the king, "At this time tomorrow two seahs of barley will sell for a shekel at Samaria's gate, and one seah of wheat flour will sell for a shekel," ¹⁹the officer had answered the man of God, "Come on! Even if the LORD should make windows in the sky, how could that happen?" Then Elisha had said, "You will see it with your own eyes, but you won't eat from it." ²⁰That's exactly what happened to him. The people trampled him at the city gate, and he died.

The woman from Shunem

8 Elisha spoke to the woman whose son he had brought back to life: "You and your household must go away and live wherever you can, because the LORD has called for a famine. It is coming to the land and will last seven years."

²So the woman went and did what the man of God asked. She and her household moved away, living in Philistia seven years. ³When seven years had passed, the woman returned from Philistia. She went to appeal to the king for her house and her farmland. ⁴The king was speaking to Gehazi, the man of God's servant, asking him, "Tell me about all the great things Elisha has done." ⁵So Gehazi was telling the king how Elisha had brought the dead to life. At that very moment, the woman whose son he had brought back to life began to appeal to the king for her house and her farmland.

Gehazi said, "Your Majesty, this is the woman herself! And this is her son, the one Elisha brought to life!"

⁶The king questioned the woman, and she told him her story. Then the king appointed an official to help her, saying,

ˢHeb uncertain

"Return everything that belongs to her, as well as everything that the farmland has produced, starting from the day she left the country until right now."

Hazael becomes king

[7]Now Elisha had gone to Damascus when Aram's King Ben-hadad became sick. The king was told, "The man of God has come all this way."

[8]So the king said to Hazael, "Take a gift with you and go to meet the man of God. Question the LORD through him: 'Will I recover from this sickness?'"

[9]So Hazael went out to meet Elisha. He took along forty camel-loads of Damascus' finest goods as a gift. He came and stood before Elisha and said, "Your son Ben-hadad, the king of Aram, sent me to you to ask, 'Will I recover from this sickness?'"

[10]Elisha said to him, "Go and tell him, 'You will definitely recover,' but actually the LORD has shown me that he will die." [11]Elisha stared straight at Hazael until he felt uneasy.[t] Then the man of God began to cry.

[12]Hazael said, "Master, why are you crying?"

"Because I know what violence you will do to the Israelites," Elisha said. "You will drive them from their forts with fire. You will kill their young men with the sword. You will smash their children and rip open their pregnant women."

[13]Hazael replied, "How could your servant, who is nothing but a dog, do such mighty things?"

Elisha said, "The LORD has shown me that you will be king over Aram." [14]Then Hazael left Elisha and returned to his master.

"What did Elisha say to you?" Ben-hadad asked.

"He told me that you will certainly live," Hazael replied. [15]But the next day he took a blanket, soaked it in water, and put it over Ben-hadad's face until he died. Hazael succeeded him as king.

Jehoram rules Judah

[16]In the fifth year of Israel's King Joram, Ahab's son Jehoram, the son of Judah's King Jehoshaphat, became king.[u] [17]He was 32 years old when he became king, and he ruled for eight years in Jerusalem. [18]He walked in the ways of Israel's kings, just as Ahab's dynasty had done, because he married Ahab's daughter. He did what was evil in the LORD's eyes. [19]Nevertheless, because of his servant David, the LORD wasn't willing to destroy Judah. The LORD had promised to preserve a lamp for David and his sons forever. [20]During Jehoram's rule Edom rebelled against Judah's power and appointed their own king. [21]Jehoram[v] along with all his chariots crossed over to Zair. He got up at night to attack the Edomites who had surrounded him and his chariot commanders,[w] but his army fled back home. [22]So Edom has been independent of Judah to this day. Libnah rebelled at the same time. [23]The rest of Jehoram's deeds and all that he accomplished, aren't they written in the official records of Judah's kings? [24]Jehoram died and was buried with his ancestors in David's City. His son Ahaziah succeeded him as king.

Ahaziah rules Judah

[25]Ahaziah, the son of Judah's king Jehoram, became king in the twelfth year of Israel's King Joram,[x] Ahab's son. [26]Ahaziah was 22 years old when he became king, and he ruled for one year in Jerusalem. His mother's name was Athaliah; she was the granddaughter of Israel's King Omri. [27]He walked in the ways of Ahab's dynasty, doing what was evil in the LORD's eyes, just as Ahab's dynasty had done, because he married into Ahab's family. [28]Ahaziah went with Joram, Ahab's son, to fight against Aram's King Hazael at Ramoth-gilead, where the Arameans wounded Joram. [29]King Joram returned to Jezreel to recover from the wounds the Arameans had given him at Ramah in his battle with Aram's King

[t]Heb uncertain   [u]LXX, Syr; MT includes *Jehoshaphat had been Judah's king*.   [v]Heb *Joram* (also in 8:23-24); the king's name is usually spelled in its long form *Jehoram* (cf 2 Chron 21:9).   [w]Heb uncertain   [x]Heb *Jehoram* (also in 8:29); the king's name is variously spelled in either long *Jehoram* or short *Joram* form.

Hazael. Then Judah's King Ahaziah, the son of Jehoram, went down to visit Joram, Ahab's son, at Jezreel because he had been wounded.

Jehu rules Israel

9 The prophet Elisha called to a member of the group of prophets, "Get ready, take this jug of oil with you, and go to Ramoth-gilead. ²When you arrive there, look for Jehu, Jehoshaphat's son and Nimshi's grandson. Go to him, then pull him away from his associates, taking him to a private room. ³Take the jug of oil and pour it on his head. Then say, 'This is what the LORD has said: I anoint you king of Israel.' Then open the door, and run out of there without stopping."

⁴So the young prophet went to Ramoth-gilead. ⁵He came in, and the military commanders were sitting right there. He said, "Commander, I have a word for you."

"For which one of us?" Jehu asked.

The young prophet said, "For you, Commander."

⁶So Jehu got up and went inside. The prophet then poured oil on his head and said to him, "This is what the LORD, Israel's God, says: I anoint you king over the LORD's people, over Israel. ⁷You will strike down your master Ahab's family. In this way I will take revenge for the violence done by Jezebel to my servants the prophets and to all the LORD's servants. ⁸Ahab's whole family will die. I will eliminate from Ahab everyone who urinates on a wall, whether slave or free, in Israel. ⁹I will make Ahab's dynasty like the dynasty of Jeroboam, Nebat's son, and like the dynasty of Baasha, Ahijah's son. ¹⁰And as for Jezebel: The dogs will devour her in the area of Jezreel. No one will bury her." Then the young prophet opened the door and ran.

¹¹Jehu went out to his master's officers. They said to him, "Is everything okay? Why did this fanatic come to you?"

Jehu said to them, "You know the man and the nonsense he talks."

¹²"That's a lie!" they said. "Come on, tell us!"

Jehu replied, "This is what he said to me: 'This is what the LORD says: I anoint you king of Israel.'"

¹³Then each man quickly took his cloak and put it beneath Jehu on the paved steps.ʸ They blew a trumpet and said, "Jehu has become king!"

Jehu kills his enemies

¹⁴Then Jehu, Jehoshaphat's son and Nimshi's grandson, plotted against Joram. Now Joram along with all of Israel had been guarding Ramoth-gilead against Aram's King Hazael, ¹⁵but King Joramᶻ had gone back to Jezreel to recover from wounds that the Arameans had given him when he fought Hazael. So Jehu said, "If this is the way you feel, then don't let anyone escape from the city to talk about it in Jezreel." ¹⁶Then Jehu got on a chariot and drove to Jezreel because Joram was resting there. Judah's King Ahaziah had also come to visit Joram.

¹⁷The guard standing on the tower at Jezreel saw a crowd of people coming with Jehu. He said, "I see a crowd of people."

Joram said, "Take a chariot driver. Send him out to meet them to ask, 'Do you come in peace?'" ¹⁸So the driver went to meet him and said, "The king asks, 'Do you come in peace?'"

Jehu replied, "What do you care about peace? Come around and follow me."

Meanwhile, the tower guard reported, "The messenger met them, but he isn't returning."

¹⁹The king sent a second driver. He came to them and said, "The king asks, 'Do you come in peace?'"

Jehu said, "What do you care about peace? Come around and follow me."

²⁰The tower guard reported, "The messenger met them, but he isn't returning. And the style of chariot driving is like Jehu, Nimshi's son. Jehu drives like a madman."

²¹Joram said, "Hitch up the chariot!" So they hitched up his chariot. Then Israel's

---

ʸHeb uncertain ᶻHeb *Jehoram* (also in 9:17, 21-24); the king's name is variously spelled in either long *Jehoram* or short *Joram* form.

King Joram and Judah's King Ahaziah—
each in his own chariot—went out to meet
Jehu. They happened to meet him at the
plot of ground that belonged to Naboth the
Jezreelite. [22] When Joram saw Jehu, he said, "Do
you come in peace, Jehu?"

He said, "How can there be peace as long
as the immoralities of your mother Jezebel
and her many acts of sorcery continue?"

[23] Then Joram turned his chariot around
and fled. He shouted to Ahaziah, "It's a
trap, Ahaziah!"

[24] Jehu took his bow and shot Joram
in the back. The arrow went through his
heart, and he fell down in his chariot.
[25] Jehu said to Bidkar his chariot officer,
"Pick him up, and throw him on the plot of
ground belonging to Naboth the Jezreelite. Remember how you and I were driving chariot teams behind his father Ahab
when the LORD spoke this prophecy about
him: [26] Yesterday I saw Naboth's blood and
his sons' blood, declares the LORD. I swear
that I will pay you back on this very plot of
ground, declares the LORD. Now pick him
up, and throw him on that plot of ground,
in agreement with the LORD's word."

[27] Judah's King Ahaziah saw this and fled
on the road to Beth-haggan. Jehu chased
after him. "Do the same to him!" he commanded. They shot him[a] in his chariot on
the way up to Gur, near Ibleam. Ahaziah
fled to Megiddo and died there. [28] His servants carried him back in a chariot to Jerusalem. He was buried in his tomb with
his ancestors in David's City. [29] Ahaziah had
become Judah's king in the eleventh year of
Ahab's son Joram.

[30] Jehu then went to Jezreel. When Jezebel heard of it, she put on her eye shadow
and arranged her hair. She looked down out
of the window. [31] When Jehu came through
the gate, she said, "Do you come in peace,
Zimri, you master murderer?"

[32] Jehu looked up to the window and
said, "Who's on my side? Anyone?" Two
or three high officials looked down at him.
[33] Then he said, "Throw her out!" So they
threw her out of the window. Some of her
blood splattered against the wall and on
the horses, and they trampled her. [34] Jehu
then went in to eat and drink. He said,
"Deal with this cursed woman and bury her.
She was, after all, a king's daughter." [35] They
went to bury her, but they couldn't find her

---

[a] LXX, Vulg; MT lacks *They shot him.*

JEZEBEL

1. As one of the most despised women in the OT, Jezebel has become
a symbol for uncontrolled female power and unrestrained sexuality, even
though the biblical text portrays her as a devoted spouse (1 Kgs 16:31–2 Kgs
9:37). She was the daughter of King Ethbaal of Tyre and Sidon, wife of the
reviled King Ahab of Israel (ca. 869–850 BCE), mother of Joram and Ahaziah, and possibly the sister-in-law to Queen Athaliah of Judah. Jezebel's
marriage to Ahab cemented the alliance between the Omride dynasty and
Phoenicia.

2. Jezebel is an epithet used in the NT for the Thyatiran prophetess accused by John of seducing his servants into practicing fornication and eating food sacrificed to idols (Rev 2:18-29). As in 2 Kings 9:22, this Jezebel is
labeled a whore because she serves other gods. By aligning this woman to
the Israelite queen, the author of Revelation shames her and associates her
with what is religiously unacceptable.

body. Only her skull was left, along with her hands and feet. [36]They went back and reported this to Jehu. He said, "This is the LORD's word spoken through his servant Elijah from Tishbe: Dogs will devour Jezebel's flesh in the area of Jezreel. [37]Jezebel's corpse will be like dung spread out in a field in that plot of land in Jezreel, so no one will be able to say, This was Jezebel.'"

Jehu kills Ahab's family

10 Now Ahab had seventy sons in Samaria. So Jehu wrote letters and sent them to Samaria, to the senior officers of the city,[b] the elders, and the guardians of Ahab's sons.[c] [2]The letters said: "Your master's sons are in your possession, along with horses and chariots, a fortified city, and weapons. Now when this letter reaches you, [3]look for the best and most capable of your master's sons. Place him on his father's throne. Then fight for your master's family."

[4]But they were frozen with fear. They said, "Not even two kings could resist him! How can we?" [5]So the palace administrator, the mayor, the elders, and the guardians sent a letter back to Jehu that read, "We are your servants. We will do whatever you tell us. We won't make anyone king. Do whatever seems right to you."

[6]Jehu wrote them a second letter: "If you are loyal to me and ready to obey me, take the heads of your master's sons and bring them to me at Jezreel at this time tomorrow."

Now the king's seventy sons were with the city leaders who were raising them. [7]So when the letter came to them, they took the king's sons and slaughtered all seventy of them. They placed their heads in baskets and sent them to Jehu at Jezreel.

[8]A messenger came and told Jehu, "They have brought the heads of the king's sons."

He responded, "Pile them in two stacks at the entrance of the gate where they will stay until morning." [9]In the morning he went out and stood there to address all the people. "You are innocent. I'm the one who plotted against my master and killed him, but who killed all these people? [10]Know this: Nothing that the LORD has said against Ahab's dynasty will fail to come true. The LORD has done what he said he would do, speaking through his servant Elijah." [11]Then Jehu struck down all those belonging to Ahab's family who were left in Jezreel, so that not one of his leaders, close acquaintances, or priests remained.

[12]Next Jehu set out for Samaria. Beth-eked of the Shepherds was on his way. [13]There Jehu met up with the brothers of Judah's King Ahaziah. "Who are you?" he asked.

"We're Ahaziah's relatives," they replied. "We've come down for a visit with the king's sons and the queen mother's sons."

[14]Jehu then commanded, "Take them alive!" His soldiers took them alive, then slaughtered them at the well of Beth-eked. There were forty-two of them, but not one was left.

Jehu kills Baal worshippers

[15]Jehu departed from there and encountered Rechab's son Jehonadab. Jehu greeted him, and asked, "Are you as committed to me as I am to you?"

Jehonadab responded, "Yes, I am."

"If so," said Jehu, "then give me your hand." So Jehonadab put out his hand, and Jehu pulled him up into the chariot.

[16]Jehu said, "Come with me and see my zeal for the LORD." So Jehu had Jehonadab ride with him in his chariot. [17]When Jehu arrived in Samaria, he killed all those belonging to Ahab who were left in Samaria until they were completely wiped out, in agreement with the LORD's word that was spoken to Elijah.

[18]Then Jehu gathered all the people, saying to them, "Ahab served Baal a little. Jehu will serve him a great deal! [19]So invite all of Baal's prophets, all his worshippers, and all his priests to come to me. Don't leave anyone out, because I have a great sacrifice planned for Baal. Anyone who doesn't show up won't survive." But Jehu was lying so that he could wipe out Baal's worshippers. [20]Jehu called for a holy assembly for

[b]Vulg, LXX; MT *Jezreel* [c]LXX; MT lacks *sons*.

Baal, and it was done. ²¹Jehu then sent word throughout Israel. All Baal's worshippers came. No one stayed away. They entered Baal's temple until it was packed from one end to the other. ²²Then Jehu said to the person in charge of the vestments, "Bring out the special clothes for all Baal's worshippers." So he brought out robes for them. ²³Then Jehu and Jehonadab, Rechab's son, entered Baal's temple. They said to Baal's worshippers, "Make sure there are no worshippers of the LORD here with you. There should be only Baal worshippers." ²⁴Then they went in to offer sacrifices and entirely burned offerings. But Jehu had stationed eighty soldiers outside and told them, "I'm handing these people over to you. Whoever lets even one of them escape will pay for it with his life." ²⁵So when Jehu finished offering the entirely burned offering, he said to the guards and the officers, "Go in and kill everyone! Don't let anyone escape!" They killed the Baal worshippers without mercy. The guards and the officers then disposed of the bodies and entered the inner part of Baal's temple. ²⁶They brought the sacred pillarᵈ out of Baal's temple and burned it. ²⁷They tore down Baal's sacred pillar and destroyed Baal's temple, turning it into a public restroom, which is what it still is today.

²⁸This is how Jehu eliminated Baal from Israel. ²⁹However, Jehu didn't deviate from the sins that Jeroboam, Nebat's son, had caused Israel to commit—specifically, the gold calves that were in Bethel and Dan.

Jehu rules Israel

³⁰The LORD said to Jehu: Because you've done well by doing what is right in my eyes, treating Ahab's family as I wished, your descendants will sit on Israel's throne for four generations. ³¹But Jehu wasn't careful to keep the LORD God of Israel's Instruction with all his heart. He didn't deviate from the sins that Jeroboam had caused Israel to commit.

³²In those days the LORD began to reduce Israel's size. Hazael struck them down in every region of Israel: ³³from the Jordan River eastward, throughout the land of Gilead (Gad, Reuben, and Manasseh), and from Aroer by the Arnon Valley (that is, Gilead) and Bashan.

³⁴The rest of Jehu's deeds, all that he accomplished, and all his powerful acts, aren't they written in the official records of Israel's kings? ³⁵Jehu lay down with his ancestors. He was buried in Samaria. His son Jehoahaz succeeded him as king. ³⁶Jehu had ruled over Israel for twenty-eight years in Samaria.

Queen Athaliah rules Judah

11When Athaliah, Ahaziah's mother, learned of her son's death, she immediately destroyed the entire royal family. ²But Jehosheba, King Jehoram'sᵉ daughter and Ahaziah's sister, secretly took Ahaziah's son Jehoashᶠ from the rest of the royal children who were about to be murdered and hidᵍ him in a bedroom along with his nurse. In this way Jehoash was hidden from Athaliah and wasn't murdered. ³He remained hidden with his nurse in the LORD's temple for six years while Athaliah ruled the country.

⁴But in the seventh year Jehoiada sent for the commanders of the Carites and of the guards and had them come to him at the LORD's temple. He made a covenant with them, and made them swear a solemn pledge in the LORD's temple. Then he showed them the king's son. ⁵He commanded them, "This is what you must do: A third of you coming on sabbath duty will guard the palace, ⁶a second third will be at the Sur Gate, and the final third will be at the gate behind the guards. You will take turns guarding the temple.ʰ ⁷You who are in the first two groups that usually go off duty on the Sabbath should also guard the LORD's temple to protect the king. ⁸Surround the king completely, each of you with your weapons drawn. Whoever comes near

---

ᵈLXX, Syr, Vulg; MT *pillars* ᵉHeb *Joram*; the king's name is usually spelled in its long form *Jehoram* (cf 2 Chron 22:11). ᶠHeb *Joash*; the king's name is variously spelled in either long *Jehoash* or short *Joash* forms. The latter is the form used in 2 Chron. ᵍSee 2 Chron 22:11; Heb lacks *hid*. ʰHeb uncertain your ranks must be killed. Stay near the king wherever he goes."

⁹The unit commanders did everything that Jehoiada the priest ordered. They each took charge of those men reporting for duty on the Sabbath as well as those going off duty on the Sabbath. They came to the priest Jehoiada. ¹⁰Then the priest gave the unit commanders King David's spears and shields, which were kept in the LORD's temple. ¹¹The guards, each with their weapons drawn, then took up positions near the temple and the altar, stretching from the south side of the temple to the north side to protect the king. Everyone was holding his weapons, surrounding the king. ¹²Jehoiada then brought out the king's son, crowned him, gave him the royal law,[i] and made him king and anointed him, as everyone applauded and cried out, "Long live the king!"

¹³When Athaliah heard the noise made by the guard and the people, she went to the people at the LORD's temple ¹⁴and saw the king standing by the royal pillar, as was the custom, with the commanders and trumpeters beside the king. All the people of the land were rejoicing and blowing trumpets. Athaliah ripped her clothes and screamed, "Treason! Treason!"

¹⁵Then the priest Jehoiada ordered the unit commanders who were in charge of the army: "Take her out under guard,"[j] he told them, "and kill anyone who follows her." This was because the priest had said, "She must not be executed in the LORD's temple." ¹⁶They arrested her when she reached the entrance of the Horse Gate at the royal palace. She was executed there.

¹⁷Jehoiada then made a covenant between the LORD, the king, and the people, that the people would belong to the LORD. The king and the people also made a covenant. ¹⁸Then all the people of the land went to Baal's temple and tore it down, smashing its altars and images into pieces. They executed Mattan, Baal's priest, in front of the altars. The priest Jehoiada posted guards at the LORD's temple. ¹⁹Then he took the

unit commanders, the Carites, the guards, and all the people of the land, and they led the king down from the LORD's temple, processing through the Guards' Gate to the palace, where the king sat upon the royal throne. ²⁰All the people of the land rejoiced, and the city was at peace now that Athaliah had been executed at the palace.

Jehoash rules Judah

²¹ᵏJehoash was 7 years old when he became king. ¹He[l] became king in Jehu's seventh year, and he ruled for forty years in Jerusalem. His mother's name was Zibiah; she was from Beer-sheba. ²Jehoash always did what was right in the LORD's eyes, because the priest Jehoiada was his teacher. ³However, the shrines were not removed. People kept sacrificing and burning incense at them. ⁴Jehoash said to the priests, "Collect all the currently available money relating to holy things that is brought to the temple—some is money people pay to redeem persons according to their assessed value. Collect all the money brought to the LORD's temple that people offer voluntarily.[m] ⁵The priests should take the money from their donors and use it to repair the temple wherever such a need for repair is discovered."

⁶But by the twenty-third year of King Jehoash, the priests still hadn't repaired the temple. ⁷So King Jehoash summoned Jehoiada the priest and the other priests together. "Why haven't you repaired the temple?" he asked them. "Stop taking money from your donors; instead, give it directly for temple repairs." ⁸The priests agreed that they wouldn't take any more money from the people nor be responsible for temple repairs. ⁹Then the priest Jehoiada took a box, made a hole in its lid, and placed it beside the altar, to the right as one enters the LORD's temple. The priests who stood watch at the door put all the money brought to the LORD's temple in the box. ¹⁰As soon as they saw that a large amount of money was in the box, the royal scribe and the high priest would come, count the money that

---

[i]Heb lacks *royal*.   [j]Heb uncertain   [k]12:1 in Heb   [l]12:2 in Heb   [m]Heb uncertain

was in the temple, and put it in a bag. [11]They would then hand over the money that had been counted[n] to those who supervised the work on the temple. These supervisors then paid money to those who worked on the LORD's temple: carpenters, builders, [12]masons, and stonecutters. The money was used to purchase wood and quarried stone to repair the LORD's temple and for every other cost involved in repairing it. [13]But the money that was brought to the LORD's temple was not used to make silver basins, wick trimmers, sprinkling bowls, trumpets, or any gold or silver object for the LORD's temple. [14]Instead, it was given directly to those who did the repair work; they used it to repair the LORD's temple. [15]There was no need to check on those who received the money and paid the workers, because they acted honestly. [16]Now as for the money for compensation and purification offerings, it wasn't brought to the LORD's temple. It belonged to the priests.

[17]About this same time, Aram's King Hazael came up, attacked Gath, and captured it. Next Hazael decided to march against Jerusalem. [18]Judah's King Jehoash took all the holy objects that had been dedicated by his ancestors—Judah's kings Jehoshaphat, Jehoram, and Ahaziah—along with the holy objects he himself had dedicated, as well as all the gold in the treasure rooms of the LORD's temple and the palace, and he sent them to Aram's King Hazael. Hazael then pulled back from Jerusalem.

[19]The rest of Jehoash's[o] deeds and all that he accomplished, aren't they written in the official records of Judah's kings? [20]Jehoash's officials plotted a conspiracy and killed him at Beth-millo on the road that goes down to Silla. [21]It was Jozacar son of Shimeath and Jehozabad son of Shomer, his officials, who struck him so that he died. He was buried with his ancestors in David's City. His son Amaziah succeeded him as king.

Jehoahaz rules Israel

13 Jehoahaz, Jehu's son, became king of Israel in Samaria in the twenty-third year of Judah's King Jehoash,[p] who was Ahaziah's son. He ruled for seventeen years. [2]He did what was evil in the LORD's eyes. He walked in the sins that Jeroboam, Nebat's son, had caused Israel to commit. He didn't deviate from them. [3]So the LORD was angry at Israel. Time after time God handed them over to Aram's king Hazael, and to Hazael's son Ben-hadad.

[4]But Jehoahaz sought the LORD's presence, and the LORD listened to him because he saw how badly Aram's king was oppressing Israel. [5]The LORD sent Israel a savior,

[n]Heb uncertain [o]Heb *Joash* (also in 13:20); the king's name is variously spelled in either long *Jehoash* or short *Joash* form. The latter is the form used in 2 Chron. [p]Heb *Joash* (also in 13:10); the king's name is variously spelled in either long *Jehoash* or short *Joash* form. The latter is the form used in 2 Chron.

ELISHA

Elisha was a legendary wonderworker of the 9th century BCE (1 Kgs 19:16-21; 2 Kgs 2:1–10:27; 13:14-21). Elisha succeeded Elijah, and their stories in the Bible were shaped together to support Jehu's usurpation of the Omride dynasty and founding of the longest-lasting dynasty in Israel, the house of Jehu or Nimshi (2 Kgs 9:2). As with Elijah, most of the tales about Elisha show him dealing with either kings or poor folk; two linked episodes involve a well-regarded woman of Shunem, and her tale too ends with reference to the king (2 Kgs 4:8-37; 8:1-6). Elisha was an Israelite, but his dealings with kings went well beyond political Israel to include Moab, Edom, and Syria.

and they escaped from Aram's power. Then the Israelites lived peacefully at home, just as they had in the past. ⁶But they didn't deviate from the sins that Jeroboam's dynasty had caused Israel to commit; they walked in them! Moreover, a sacred pole�q stood in Samaria. ⁷No, nothing was left of Jehoahaz's army except fifty chariot riders, ten chariots, and ten thousand foot soldiers, because Aram's king had decimated them, trampling them as if they were dirt. ⁸The rest of Jehoahaz's deeds, all that he accomplished, and all his powerful acts, aren't they written in the official records of Israel's kings? ⁹Jehoahaz lay down with his ancestors. He was buried in Samaria. His son Joash succeeded him as king.

Joash rules Israel

¹⁰Joash,ʳ Jehoahaz's son, became king of Israel in Samaria in the thirty-seventh year of Judah's King Jehoash. He ruled for sixteen years. ¹¹He did what was evil in the LORD's eyes. He didn't deviate from all the sins that Jeroboam, Nebat's son, had caused Israel to commit, but he walked in them! ¹²The rest of Joash's deeds, all that he accomplished, and his powerful acts—how he fought against Judah's King Amaziah—aren't they written in the official records of Israel's kings? ¹³Joash lay down with his ancestors, and Jeroboam followed him on the throne. Joash was buried in Samaria with the kings of Israel.

Elisha's last days

¹⁴Now Elisha became sick with the illness that would kill him. So Israel's King Joash went down to see him. Joash cried over Elisha, saying, "Oh, my father, my father! Israel's chariots and its riders!" ¹⁵Elisha told Joash, "Get a bow and some arrows." So he brought Elisha a bow and some arrows. ¹⁶Elisha then said to Israel's king, "Put your hand on the bow." So Joash put his hand on the bow. Elisha then put his hands over the king's hands ¹⁷and said, "Open the window to the east." The king did so. "Now shoot!" Elisha told him. Joash shot, then Elisha announced, "That's the LORD's rescue arrow! The rescue arrow against the Arameans! You will finish the Arameans off at Aphek." ¹⁸Then Elisha said, "Take the arrows!" so Joash took them. Elisha then said to Israel's king, "Hit the ground with them!" Joash hit the ground three times and stopped. ¹⁹The man of God became angry with him. He said, "If only you had struck five or six times, you would have finished the Arameans off. As it is, you will defeat them only three times."

²⁰So Elisha died, and he was buried.

Sometimes Moabite raiding parties used to come into the land each spring. ²¹Now it happened once that while a man was being buried, the people at the funeral suddenly saw a raiding party. They threw the body into Elisha's tomb and ran off. When the body touched Elisha's bones, the man came to life and stood up on his feet!

²²Aram's King Hazael had oppressed Israel throughout Jehoahaz's rule. ²³But the LORD was gracious to Israel and had compassion on them, turning back to them because of his covenant with Abraham, Isaac, and Jacob; he didn't want to destroy them or throw them out of his presence until now. ²⁴Aram's King Hazael died. His son Ben-hadad succeeded him as king. ²⁵Then Jehoahaz's son Joash recaptured from Hazael's son Ben-hadad those cities that Hazael had won in battle from Joash's father Jehoahaz. Joash attacked Ben-hadad three times and took back these Israelite cities.

Amaziah rules Judah

14 Amaziah, the son of Judah's King Jehoash,ˢ became king in the second year of Israel's King Joash, who was Jehoahaz's son. ²Amaziah was 25 years old when he became king, and he ruled for twenty-nine years in Jerusalem. His mother's name

---

�q Heb *asherah*, perhaps an object devoted to the goddess Asherah ʳ Heb *Jehoash* (also in 13:25); the king's name is variously spelled in either long *Jehoash* or short *Joash* form. The latter is the form used in 2 Chron.
ˢ Heb *Joash* (also in 14:3, 17, 23); the king's name is variously spelled in either long *Jehoash* or short *Joash* form. The latter is the form used in 2 Chron.

was Jehoaddin; she was from Jerusalem. ³He did what was right in the LORD's eyes, but not as well as his ancestor King David. He did everything his father Jehoash did. ⁴However, the shrines weren't removed. People kept sacrificing and burning incense at them. ⁵Once he had secured control over his kingdom, he executed the officials who had assassinated his father the king. ⁶However, he didn't kill the children of the murderers, because of what is written in the Instruction scroll from Moses, where the LORD commanded, *Parents shouldn't be executed because of what their children have done; neither should children be executed because of what their parents have done. Each person should be executed for their own guilty acts.*ᵗ

⁷Next Amaziah struck down ten thousand Edomites in the Salt Valley and captured Sela in battle. He renamed it Jokthe-el, which is what it is still called today. ⁸Then Amaziah sent messengers to Israel's King Joashᵘ son of Jehoahaz son of Israel's King Jehu, saying, "Come on! Let's go head-to-head."

⁹But Israel's King Joash responded to Judah's King Amaziah, "Once upon a time, a thistle in Lebanon sent a message to a cedar, 'Give your daughter to my son as a wife.' But then a wild beast in Lebanon came along and trampled the thistle. ¹⁰You have definitely defeated Edom and have now become conceited. Enjoy the honor, but stay home. Why invite disaster when both you and Judah will fall?"

¹¹But Amaziah wouldn't listen, so Israel's King Joash moved against him, and he

and Judah's King Amaziah went head-to-head in battle at Beth-shemesh in Judah. ¹²Judah was defeated by Israel, and everyone ran home. ¹³At Beth-shemesh, Israel's King Joash captured Judah's King Amaziah, Jehoash's son and Ahaziah's grandson. Joash then marched to Jerusalem and broke down six hundred feet of the Jerusalem wall from the Ephraim Gate to the Corner Gate. ¹⁴Joash took all the gold and silver, and all the objects he could find in the LORD's temple and the treasuries of the palace, along with some hostages and returned to Samaria. ¹⁵The rest of Joash's deeds and his powerful acts—how he fought against Judah's King Amaziah— aren't they written in the official records of Israel's kings? ¹⁶Joash lay down with his ancestors. He was buried in Samaria with the kings of Israel. His son Jeroboam succeeded him as king.

¹⁷Judah's King Amaziah, Jehoash's son, lived fifteen years after the death of Israel's King Joash, Jehoahaz's son. ¹⁸The rest of Amaziah's deeds, aren't they written in the official records of Judah's kings? ¹⁹Some people in Jerusalem plotted against him. When Amaziah fled to Lachish, they sent men after him to Lachish, and they murdered him there. ²⁰They carried him back on horses, and he was buried in Jerusalem with his ancestors in David's City.

²¹Then all the people of Judah took Azariah and made him king after his father Amaziah. He was 16 years old. ²²He rebuilt Elath, restoring it to Judah after King Amaziah had lain down with his ancestors.

ᵗDeut 24:16 ᵘHeb *Jehoash* (also in 14:9, 11, 13, 15, 16-17); the king's name is variously spelled in either long *Jehoash* or short *Joash* form. The latter is the form used in 2 Chron.

JEROBOAM II

King of Israel ca. 786–746 BCE. Fourth in the dynasty of Jehu and contemporary of kings Amaziah and Azariah (Uzziah) of Judah. The biblical historian offers a negative evaluation of Jeroboam II, consistent with that of the other kings of Israel, namely, that he followed in the sins of Jeroboam I (2 Kgs 14:24).

Jeroboam II rules Israel

[23] Jeroboam, the son of Israel's King Joash, became king in Samaria in the fifteenth year of Judah's King Amaziah, Jehoash's son. He ruled for forty-one years. [24] He did what was evil in the LORD's eyes. He didn't deviate from all the sins that Jeroboam, Nebat's son, had caused Israel to commit. [25] He reestablished Israel's border from Lebo-hamath to the Dead Sea. This was in agreement with the word that the LORD, the God of Israel, spoke through his servant the prophet Jonah, Amittai's son, who was from Gath-hepher. [26] The LORD saw how brutally Israel suffered, whether slave or free, with no one to help Israel. [27] But the LORD hadn't said he would erase Israel's name from under heaven, so he saved them through Jeroboam, Joash's son. [28] The rest of Jeroboam's deeds, all that he accomplished, and his powerful acts—how he fought and how he restored Damascus and Hamath to Judah in Israel[v]—aren't they written in the official records of Israel's kings? [29] Jeroboam lay down with his ancestors the kings of Israel. His son Zechariah succeeded him as king.

Azariah rules Judah

15 Azariah, Amaziah's son, became king of Judah in the twenty-seventh year of Israel's King Jeroboam. [2] He was 16 years old when he became king, and he ruled for fifty-two years in Jerusalem. His mother's name was Jecoliah; she was from Jerusalem. [3] He did what was right in the LORD's eyes, just as his father Amaziah had done. [4] However, the shrines weren't removed. People kept sacrificing and burning incense at them. [5] Now the LORD afflicted the king with a skin disease that he had until his dying day, so he lived in a separate house.[w] The king's son Jotham supervised the palace administration and governed the people of the land. [6] The rest of Azariah's deeds and all he accomplished, aren't they written in the official records of Judah's kings? [7] Azariah died and was buried with his ancestors in David's City. His son Jotham succeeded him as king.

Zechariah rules Israel

[8] Zechariah, Jeroboam's son, became king of Israel in Samaria in the thirty-eighth year of Judah's King Azariah. He ruled for six months. [9] He did what was evil in the LORD's eyes, just as his ancestors had done. He didn't deviate from the sins that Jeroboam, Nebat's son, had caused Israel to commit. [10] Shallum, Jabesh's son, plotted against Zechariah. He struck him down in public,[x] murdering him. Shallum then succeeded him as king. [11] The rest of Zechariah's deeds are written in the official records of Israel's kings. [12] This was exactly what the LORD spoke to Jehu: Your descendants will sit on Israel's throne for four generations. And that's exactly what happened.

Shallum rules Israel

[13] Shallum, Jabesh's son, became king in the thirty-ninth year of Judah's King Uzziah. He ruled for one month in Samaria. [14] Menahem, Gadi's son, went up from Tirzah and came to Samaria. He struck down Jabesh's son Shallum in Samaria, murdering him. Menahem then succeeded him as king. [15] The rest of Shallum's deeds and the conspiracy he plotted are written in the official records of Israel's kings.

Menahem rules Israel

[16] Menahem then moved from Tirzah and attacked Tiphsah, all its citizens, and its neighboring areas. Because they wouldn't surrender, he attacked and ripped open all its pregnant women. [17] Menahem, Gadi's son, became king of Israel in the thirty-ninth year of Judah's King Azariah. He ruled for ten years in Samaria. [18] He did what was evil in the LORD's eyes. Throughout his life, he didn't deviate from the sins that Jeroboam, Nebat's son, had caused Israel to commit. [19] When Assyria's King Tiglath-pileser[y] marched against the land, Menahem gave Tiglath-pileser one thousand silver kikkars in order to become his ally and to strengthen his hold on the kingdom. [20] Menahem taxed Israel for this money. All the wealthy people had to give fifty silver

---

[v] Heb uncertain   [w] Heb uncertain   [x] LXX *in Keblaam*; Heb uncertain   [y] Heb *Pul*

shekels each to Assyria's king. So Assyria's king went home and didn't stay there in the land. ²¹The rest of Menahem's deeds and all that he accomplished, aren't they written in the official records of Israel's kings? ²²Menahem lay down with his ancestors. His son Pekahiah succeeded him as king.

Pekahiah rules Israel

²³Pekahiah, Menahem's son, became king of Israel in the fiftieth year of Judah's King Azariah. He ruled for two years in Samaria. ²⁴He did what was evil in the LORD's eyes. He didn't deviate from the sins that Jeroboam, Nebat's son, had caused Israel to commit. ²⁵Pekah, Remaliah's son and Pekahiah's officer, plotted against him. Pekah struck Pekahiah in Samaria at the palace fortress, along with Argob and Arieh.ᶻ Pekah had fifty Gileadites with him. He murdered Pekahiah and succeeded him as king. ²⁶The rest of Pekahiah's deeds and all that he accomplished are written in the official records of Israel's kings.

Pekah rules Israel

²⁷Pekah, Remaliah's son, became king of Israel in the fifty-second year of Judah's King Azariah. Pekah ruled for twenty years in Samaria. ²⁸He did what was evil in the LORD's eyes. He didn't deviate from the sins that Jeroboam, Nebat's son, had caused Israel to commit. ²⁹In the days of Israel's King Pekah, Assyria's King Tiglath-pileser came and captured Ijon, Abel-beth-maacah, Janoah, Kedesh, and Hazor. He also captured Gilead, Galilee, and all the land of Naphtali. He sent the people into exile to Assyria. ³⁰Then Hoshea, Elah's son, plotted against Pekah, Remaliah's son. He struck Pekah down, murdering him. Hoshea became king after Pekah in the twentieth year of Uzziah's son Jotham. ³¹The rest of Pekah's kingship and all that he accomplished are written in the official records of Israel's kings.

Jotham rules Judah

³²Jotham, Uzziah's son, became king of Judah in the second year of Israel's King Pekah, Remaliah's son. ³³Jotham was 25 years old when he became king, and he ruled for sixteen years in Jerusalem. His mother's name was Jerusha; she was Zadok's daughter. ³⁴Jotham did what was right in the LORD's eyes, just as his father Uzziah had done. ³⁵However, he didn't remove the shrines. The people continued to sacrifice and burn incense at them. Jotham rebuilt the Upper Gate of the LORD's temple. ³⁶The rest of Jotham's deeds, aren't they written in the official records of Judah's kings? ³⁷It was in those days that the LORD began to send Aram's King Rezin and Pekah, Remaliah's son, against Judah. ³⁸Jotham died and was buried with his ancestors in David's City.ᵃ His son Ahaz succeeded him as king.

Ahaz rules Judah

16Ahaz, Jotham's son, became king of Judah in the seventeenth year of Pekah, Remaliah's son. ²Ahaz was 20 years old when he became king, and he ruled for sixteen years in Jerusalem. He didn't do what was right in the LORD's eyes, unlike his ancestor David. ³Instead, he walked in the ways of Israel's kings. He even burned his own son alive, imitating the detestable practices of the nations that the LORD had driven out before the Israelites. ⁴He also sacrificed and burned incense at the shrines on every hill and beneath every shady tree. ⁵Then Aram's King Rezin and Israel's King Pekah, Remaliah's son, came up to Jerusalem to fight. They surrounded Ahaz, but they weren't able to defeat him. ⁶At that time Aram's King Rezin recovered Elath for the Arameans, driving the Judeans out of Elath. The Edomitesᵇ came to Elath and settled there, and that's still the case now.

⁷Ahaz sent messengers to Assyria's King Tiglath-pileser, saying, "I'm your servant and your son. Come up and save me from the power of the kings of Aram and Israel. Both of them are attacking me!" ⁸And Ahaz took the silver and the gold that was in the LORD's temple and in the palace treasuries, and sent a gift to Assyria's king. ⁹The Assyrian king heard the request and marched

against Damascus. He captured it and sent its citizens into exile to Kir. He also killed Rezin.

¹⁰Then King Ahaz went to Damascus to meet up with Assyria's King Tiglath-pileser. King Ahaz noticed the altar that was in Damascus, and he sent the altar's plan and details for its construction to the priest Uriah. ¹¹Uriah built the altar, following the plans that King Ahaz had sent from Damascus; he had it finished before King Ahaz returned from Damascus.

¹²When the king arrived from Damascus, he inspected the altar. He came close to it, then went up on it, ¹³burning his entirely burned offering and grain offering, pouring out his drink offering, and sprinkling the blood of his well-being sacrifices on the altar. ¹⁴As for the bronze altar that used to stand before the LORD, Ahaz moved it away from the front of the temple where it had stood between the main altar and the LORD's temple. He put it on the north side of the new altar. ¹⁵Then King Ahaz ordered the priest Uriah, saying, "Burn the following sacrifices on the main altar:

in the morning, the entirely burned offering;

in the evening, the grain offering;

the king's entirely burned offering and his grain offering;

the entirely burned offering for all the people of the land, their grain offering, and their drink offerings.

"Sprinkle all the blood of the entirely burned offerings and all the blood of the sacrifices on it. I will use the bronze altar for seeking guidance."ᶜ ¹⁶Uriah the priest did everything that King Ahaz commanded. ¹⁷King Ahaz cut off the side panels from the stands and removed the basins from them. He took the Sea down from the bronze bulls that were under it and put it on a stone pavement. ¹⁸He also took away the sabbath canopy that had been built in the temple. He removed the royal entrance outside the LORD's temple. This was done because of the Assyrian king.

¹⁹The rest of Ahaz's deeds, aren't they written in the official records of Judah's kings? ²⁰Ahaz died and was buried with his ancestors in David's City. His son Hezekiah succeeded him as king.

Hoshea rules Israel

17 Hoshea, Elah's son, became king in Samaria in the twelfth year of Judah's king Ahaz. He ruled over Israel for nine years. ²He did what was evil in the LORD's eyes, but he wasn't as bad as the Israelite kings who preceded him. ³Assyria's King Shalmaneser marched against Hoshea, and Hoshea became Shalmaneser's servant, paying him tribute. ⁴But the Assyrian king discovered that Hoshea was a traitor, because Hoshea sent messengers to Egypt's King So. Hoshea stopped paying tribute to the Assyrian king as he had in previous

ᶜHeb uncertain

URIAH

Means "The Lord is light (or fire)." A priest in the reign of Ahaz of Judah and a contemporary of the prophet Isaiah. While in Damascus to meet Tiglath-pileser, king of Assyria, Ahaz sent Uriah detailed descriptions of the altar in Damascus (2 Kgs 16:10). Uriah built the altar before Ahaz returned from Damascus. When Ahaz arrived in Jerusalem, the king gave the priest instructions for the use of the altar (2 Kgs 16:15), and the priest "did everything that King Ahaz commanded" (2 Kgs 16:16). Apparently, this Uriah was one of the two "trusted people" whom Isaiah called on to witness an oracle against Damascus and Samaria (Isa 8:1-2). This is not the Uriah from 2 Samuel 11.

years, so the Assyrian king arrested him and put him in prison. [5]Then the Assyrian king invaded the whole country. He marched against Samaria and attacked it for three years. [6]In Hoshea's ninth year, the Assyrian king captured Samaria. He sent Israel into exile to Assyria, resettling them in Halah, in Gozan on the Habor River, and in the cities of the Medes.

The northern kingdom falls

[7]All this happened because the Israelites sinned against the LORD their God, who brought them up from the land of Egypt, out from under the power of Pharaoh, Egypt's king. They worshipped other gods. [8]They followed the practices of the nations that the LORD had removed before the Israelites, as well as the practices that the Israelite kings had done.[d] [9]The Israelites secretly did things against the LORD their God that weren't right. They built shrines in all their towns, from watchtowers to fortified cities. [10]They set up sacred pillars and sacred poles[e] on every high hill and beneath every green tree. [11]At every shrine they burned incense, just as the nations did that the LORD sent into exile before them. They did evil things that made the LORD angry. [12]They worshipped images about which the LORD had said, Don't do such things! [13]The LORD warned Israel and Judah through all the prophets and seers, telling them, Turn from your evil ways. Keep my commandments and my regulations in agreement with the entire Instruction that I commanded your ancestors and sent through my servants the prophets.

[14]But they wouldn't listen. They were stubborn like their ancestors who didn't trust the LORD their God. [15]They rejected his regulations and the covenant he had made with their ancestors, along with the warnings he had given them. They followed worthless images so that they too became worthless. And they imitated the neighboring nations that the LORD had forbidden them to imitate. [16]They deserted all the commandments of the LORD their God. They made themselves two metal idols cast in the shape of calves and made a sacred pole.[f] They bowed down to all the heavenly bodies. They served Baal. [17]They burned their sons and daughters alive. They practiced divination and sought omens. They gave themselves over to doing what was evil in the LORD's eyes and made him angry.

[18]So the LORD was very angry at Israel. He removed them from his presence. Only the tribe of Judah was spared. [19]But Judah didn't keep the commands of the LORD their God either. They followed the practices of Israel. [20]So the LORD rejected all of Israel's descendants. He punished them, and he handed them over to enemies who plundered them until he finally threw them out of his sight.

[21]When Israel broke away[g] from David's dynasty, they made Nebat's son Jeroboam the king. Jeroboam drove Israel away from the LORD. He caused them to commit great sin. [22]And the Israelites continued walking in all the sins that Jeroboam did. They didn't deviate from them, [23]and the LORD finally removed Israel from his presence. That was exactly what he had warned through all his servants the prophets. So Israel was exiled from its land to Assyria. And that's still how it is today.

New settlers in Samaria

[24]The Assyrian king brought people from Babylon, Cuth, Avva, Hamath, and Sepharvaim, resettling them in the cities of Samaria in place of the Israelites. These people took control of Samaria and settled in its cities. [25]But when they began to live there, they didn't worship the LORD, so the LORD sent lions against them, and the lions began to kill them. [26]Assyria's king was told about this: "The nations you sent into exile and resettled in the cities of Samaria don't know the religious practices of the local god. He's sent lions against them, and the lions are killing them because none of them know the religious practices of the local god."

---

[d]Heb uncertain [e]Heb *asherim*, perhaps objects devoted to the goddess Asherah [f]Heb *asherah*, perhaps an object devoted to the goddess Asherah [g]Or *When he* (God) *tore Israel away*

²⁷So Assyria's king commanded, "Return one of the priests that you exiled from there. He[h] should go back and live there. He should teach them the religious practices of the local god." ²⁸So one of the priests who had been exiled from Samaria went back. He lived in Bethel and taught the people how to worship the LORD.

²⁹But each nationality still made its own gods. They set them up in the houses that the people of Samaria had made at the shrines. Each nationality did this in whichever cities they lived. ³⁰The Babylonian people made the god Succoth-benoth, the Cuthean people made Nergal, and the people from Hamath made Ashima. ³¹The Avvites made Nibhaz and Tartak. The Sepharvites burned their children alive as a sacrifice to Adrammelech and Anammelech, the Sepharvite gods. ³²They also worshipped the LORD, but they appointed priests for the shrines from their whole population. These priests worked in the houses at the shrines. ³³So they worshipped the LORD, but they also served their own gods according to the religious practices of the nations from which they had been exiled.

³⁴They are still following their former religious practices to this very day. They don't really worship the LORD. Nor do they follow the regulations, the case laws, the Instruction, or the commandment that the LORD commanded the children of Jacob, whom he renamed Israel. ³⁵The LORD had made a covenant with them, commanding them, Don't worship other gods. Don't bow down to them or serve them. Don't sacrifice to them. ³⁶Instead, worship only the LORD. He's the one who brought you up from the land of Egypt with great strength and an outstretched arm. Bow down to him! Sacrifice to him! ³⁷You must carefully keep the regulations and case laws, the Instruction, and the commandment that he wrote for you. Don't worship other gods. ³⁸Don't forget the covenant that I made with you. Don't worship other gods. ³⁹Instead, worship only the LORD your God. He will rescue you from your enemies' power.

⁴⁰But they wouldn't listen. Instead, they continued doing their former religious practices. ⁴¹So these nations worship the LORD, but they also serve their idols. The children and the grandchildren are doing the very same thing their parents did. And that's how things still are today.

Hezekiah rules Judah

18 Hezekiah, Ahaz's son, became king of Judah in the third year of Israel's King Hoshea, Elah's son. ²He was 25 years old when he became king, and he ruled twenty-nine years in Jerusalem. His mother's name was Abi;[i] she was Zechariah's daughter.

[h]LXX, Vulg, Syr; MT *They* [i]Cf 2 Chron 29:1 *Abijah*

SAMARITANS

Sometimes used to designate all inhabitants of the northern kingdom of Israel or the later province of Samaria. The term first appears in 2 Kings 17:29 (usually translated "Samarians" or "people of Samaria" in English). More commonly, *Samaritans* refers to a Hebrew sect that focused on Mount Gerizim as their Holy Place and the first five books of the Hebrew scripture as the source of their doctrines. They understood their name as a reference to their being "keepers" of the Law, rather than as a geographical designation. Historically they lived primarily in the tribal regions of Ephraim and Manasseh in northern Palestine (Samaria). In the NT period, the Samaritans were frequent opponents of the forms of Judaism practiced in Jerusalem. Today they are mainly located on Mount Gerizim and in Holon, a suburb of Tel Aviv.

³Hezekiah did what was right in the LORD's eyes, just as his ancestor David had done. ⁴He removed the shrines. He smashed the sacred pillars and cut down the sacred pole.ʲ He crushed the bronze snake that Moses made, because up to that point the Israelites had been burning incense to it. (The snake was named Nehushtan.)

⁵Hezekiah trusted in the LORD, Israel's God. There was no one like him among all of Judah's kings—not before him and not after him. ⁶He clung to the LORD and never deviated from him. He kept the commandments that the LORD had commanded Moses. ⁷The LORD was with Hezekiah; he succeeded at everything he tried. He rebelled against Assyria's king and wouldn't serve him. ⁸He struck down the Philistines as far as Gaza and its territories, from watchtower to fortified city.

⁹Assyria's King Shalmaneser marched against Samaria and attacked it in the fourth year of King Hezekiah, which was the seventh year of Israel's King Hoshea, Elah's son. ¹⁰After three years the Assyrians captured the city. Samaria was captured in Hezekiah's sixth year, which was Hoshea's ninth year. ¹¹Assyria's king sent Israel into exile to Assyria. He settled them in Halah,

in Gozan on the Habor River, and in the cities of the Medes. ¹²All this happened because they wouldn't listen to the LORD their God. They broke his covenant—all that the LORD's servant Moses had commanded them. They didn't listen, and they didn't do it.

¹³Assyria's King Sennacherib marched against all of Judah's fortified cities and captured them in the fourteenth year of King Hezekiah. ¹⁴Judah's King Hezekiah sent a message to the Assyrian king at Lachish, saying, "I admit wrongdoing. Please withdraw from me, and I'll agree to whatever you demand from me." Assyria's king required Judah's King Hezekiah to pay him three hundred kikkars of silver and thirty kikkars of gold. ¹⁵So Hezekiah gave him all the silver that was in the LORD's temple and in the palace treasuries. ¹⁶At that time King Hezekiah had to strip down the doors and doorposts of the LORD's temple, which he had covered with gold. He gave all of it to the Assyrian king.

¹⁷Assryia's king sent his general, his chief officer, and his field commander from Lachish, together with a large army, to King Hezekiah at Jerusalem. They went up and arrived at Jerusalem. They stood at the water

ʲHeb *asherah*, perhaps an object devoted to the goddess Asherah

SCRIBE (OT)

A scribe was a member of a trained class of professionals who filled a variety of functions related to reading and writing in the governmental and religious administrations of ancient Near Eastern societies.

Most notably, scribes appear in the lists of officials included in the government bureaucracies of David and Solomon (2 Sam 8:16-18; 1 Kgs 4:1-6). A well-known illustration of how a scribe functioned within the royal court occurs in the description of King Josiah's reforms in 2 Kings 22. According to this text, a scribe, or "secretary," is called to read the newly discovered "Instruction scroll" before Josiah, initiating the king's religious reforms. Other descriptions of scribes in Samuel–Kings suggest that they functioned as international emissaries. For instance, 2 Kings depicts scribes as some of the emissaries that Hezekiah sent to the Assyrian king Sennacherib during his campaign against Judah (18:18, 37).

channel of the Upper Pool, which is on the road to the field where clothes are washed. ¹⁸Then they called for the king. Hilkiah's son Eliakim, who was the palace administrator, Shebna the secretary, and Asaph's son Joah the recorder went out to them.

¹⁹Then the field commander said to them, "Say to Hezekiah: This is what Assyria's Great King says: Why do you feel so confident? ²⁰Do you think that empty words are the same as good strategy and the strength to fight? Who are you trusting in that you now rebel against me? ²¹It appears that you are trusting in a staff—Egypt—that's nothing but a broken reed! It will stab the hand of anyone who leans on it! That's all that Pharaoh, Egypt's king, is to anyone who trusts in him. ²²Now suppose you say to me, 'We trust in the LORD our God.' Isn't he the one whose shrines and altars Hezekiah removed, telling Judah and Jerusalem, 'You must worship before this altar in Jerusalem'?

²³"So now make a wager with my master, Assyria's king. I'll give you two thousand horses if you can supply the riders! ²⁴How will you drive back even the least important official among my master's servants when you are relying on Egypt for chariots and riders? ²⁵What's more, do you think I've marched against this place to destroy it without the LORD's support? It was the LORD who told me, March against this land and destroy it!"

²⁶Hilkiah's son Eliakim, Shebna, and Joah said to the field commander, "Please speak to your servants in Aramaic because we understand it. Don't speak with us in Hebrew, because the people on the wall will hear it."

²⁷The field commander said to them, "Did my master send me to speak these words just to you and your master and not also to the men on the wall? They are the ones who will have to eat their dung and drink their urine along with you." ²⁸Then the field commander stood up and shouted in Hebrew at the top of his voice, saying, "Listen to the message of the great king, Assyria's king. ²⁹This is what the king says: Don't let Hezekiah lie to you. He won't be able to rescue you from the power of Assyria's king. ³⁰Don't let Hezekiah persuade you to trust the LORD by saying, 'The LORD will certainly rescue us. This city won't be handed over to Assyria's king.'

³¹"Don't listen to Hezekiah, because this is what Assyria's king says: Surrender to me and come out. Then each of you will eat from your own vine and fig tree, and drink water from your own well ³²until I come to take you to a land just like your land. It will be a land of grain and new wine, a land of bread and vineyards, a land of olive oil and honey. Then you will live and not die! Don't listen to Hezekiah, because he will mislead you by saying, 'The LORD will rescue us.' ³³Were any of the gods of the other nations able to rescue their lands from the power of Assyria's king? ³⁴Where are the gods of Hamath and Arpad? Where are the gods of Sepharvaim, Hena, and Ivvah? Have they rescued Samaria from my power? ³⁵Which one of any of the gods of those lands has rescued their country from my power? Why should the LORD rescue Jerusalem from my power?"

³⁶But the people kept quiet and didn't answer him with a single word, because King Hezekiah's command was, "Don't answer him!" ³⁷Hilkiah's son Eliakim, who was the palace administrator, Shebna the secretary, and Asaph's son Joah the recorder, came to Hezekiah with ripped clothes. They told him what the field commander had said.

Hezekiah and Isaiah

19 When King Hezekiah heard this, he ripped his clothes, covered himself with mourning clothes, and went to the LORD's temple. ²He sent Eliakim the palace administrator, Shebna the secretary, and the senior priests to the prophet Isaiah, Amoz's son. They were all wearing mourning clothes. ³They said to him, "This is what Hezekiah says: Today is a day of distress, punishment, and humiliation. It's as if children are ready to be born, but there's no strength to see it through. ⁴Perhaps the LORD your God has heard all the words of the field commander who was sent by his master, Assyria's king—how he insulted the living God—perhaps God will punish him for the words the LORD your God heard. Send up a prayer for those few people who still survive."

⁵When King Hezekiah's servants got to Isaiah, ⁶Isaiah said to them, "Say this to your master: 'This is what the LORD says: Don't be afraid at the words you heard, which the officers of Assyria's king have used to insult me. ⁷I'm about to put a spirit in him, so when he hears a rumor, he'll go back to his own country. Then I'll have him cut down by the sword in his own land.'"

⁸The field commander heard that the Assyrian king had left Lachish. So he went back to the king and found him attacking Libnah. ⁹Then the Assyrian king learned that Cush's King Tirhakah was on his way to fight against him. So he sent messengers to Hezekiah again, saying, ¹⁰"Say this to Judah's King Hezekiah: Don't let the God you trust in persuade you by saying, 'Jerusalem won't be handed over to the Assyrian king.' ¹¹You yourself have heard what Assyrian kings do to other countries, wiping them out. Is it likely that you will be saved? ¹²Did the gods of the nations destroyed by my fathers—Gozan, Haran, Rezeph, or the people of Eden in Telassar—save them? ¹³Where now is Hamath's king, Arpad's king, or the kings of Lair, Sepharvaim, Hena, or Ivvah?"ᵏ

Hezekiah's prayer

¹⁴Hezekiah took the letters from the messengers and read them. Then he went to the temple and spread them out before the LORD. ¹⁵Hezekiah prayed to the LORD, saying, "LORD God of Israel, you sit enthroned on the winged creatures. You alone are God over all the earth's kingdoms. You made both heaven and earth. ¹⁶LORD, turn your ear this way and hear! LORD, open your eyes and see! Listen to Sennacherib's words. He sent them to insult the living God! ¹⁷It's true, LORD, that the Assyrian kings have destroyed many nations and their lands. ¹⁸The Assyrians burned the gods of those nations with fire because they aren't real gods. They are only man-made creations of wood and stone. That's how the Assyrians could destroy them. ¹⁹So now, LORD our God, please save us from Sennacherib's power! Then all the earth's kingdoms will know that you, LORD, are the only true God."

²⁰Then Isaiah, Amoz's son, sent a message to Hezekiah: "This is what the LORD, Israel's God, says: I have heard your prayer about Assyria's King Sennacherib. ²¹This is the message that the LORD has spoken against him:

The young woman, Daughter Zion,
　despises you and mocks you;
　Daughter Jerusalem shakes her head
　behind your back.
²² Whom did you insult and ridicule?
　Against whom did you raise your voice
　and pridefully lift your eyes?
　It was against the holy one of Israel!
²³ You've insulted the Lord
　with your messengers;
　you said, 'I, with my many chariots,
　have gone up
　　to the highest mountains,
　to the farthest reaches of Lebanon.
　I have cut down its tallest cedars,
　the best of its pine trees.
　I have reached its most
　remote lodging place,
　its best forest.
²⁴ I have dug wells,
　have drunk waters in foreign lands.ˡ
　With my own feet, I dried up
　all of Egypt's streams.'
²⁵ Haven't you heard?
　I set this up long ago;
　I planned it in the distant past!
　Now I have made it happen,
　making fortified cities
　collapse into piles of rubble.
²⁶ Their citizens have lost their power.
　They are frightened and ashamed.
　They've become like plants in a field,
　tender green shoots,
　the grass on rooftops,
　burned up before it matures.

ᵏOr the king of the city of Sepharvaim or the king of the city of Sepharvaim, Hena, and Ivvah ˡHeb uncertain

²⁷ I know where you live,
  how you go out and come in,
  and how you rage against me.
²⁸ And because you rage against me
  and because your pride
  has reached my ears,
  I will put my hook in your nose,
  and my bit in your mouth.
  I will make you go back
  the same way you came.

²⁹"Now this will be the sign for you, Hezekiah: This year you will eat what grows by itself. Next year you will eat what grows from that. But in the third year, sow seed and harvest it; plant vineyards and eat their fruit. ³⁰The survivors of the house of Judah who have escaped will take root below and bear fruit above. ³¹Those who remain will go out from Jerusalem, and those who survive will go out from Mount Zion. The zeal of the LORD of heavenly forces^m will do this.

³²"Therefore, this is what the LORD says about Assyria's king: He won't enter this city. He won't shoot a single arrow there. He won't come near the city with a shield. He won't build a ramp to besiege it. ³³He will go back by the same way he came. He won't enter this city, declares the LORD. ³⁴I will defend this city and save it for my sake and for the sake of my servant David."

³⁵That night the LORD's messenger went out and struck down one hundred eighty-five thousand soldiers in the Assyrian camp. When people got up the next morning, there were dead bodies everywhere. ³⁶So Assyria's King Sennacherib departed, returning to Nineveh, where he stayed. ³⁷Later, while he was worshipping in the temple of his god Nisroch, his sons Adrammelech and Sharezer killed him with a sword. They then escaped to the land of Ararat. His son Esarhaddon succeeded him as king.

Hezekiah's illness

20 Around that same time, Hezekiah became deathly ill. The prophet Isaiah, Amoz's son, came to him and said, "This is what the LORD says: Put your af-fairs in order because you are about to die. You won't survive this."

²Hezekiah turned his face to the wall and prayed to the LORD, saying, ³"Please, LORD, remember how I have walked before you in truth and sincerity. I have done what is right in your eyes." Then Hezekiah cried and cried.

⁴Isaiah hadn't even left the middle courtyard of the palace when the LORD's word came to him: ⁵Turn around. Say to Hezekiah, my people's leader: This is what the LORD, the God of your ancestor David, says: I have heard your prayer and have seen your tears. So now I'm going to heal you. Three days from now you will be able to go up to the LORD's temple. ⁶I will add fifteen years to your life. I will rescue you and this city from the power of the Assyrian king. I will defend this city for my sake and for the sake of my servant David.

⁷Then Isaiah said, "Prepare a bandage made of figs." They did so and put it on the swelling, at which point Hezekiah started getting better.

⁸Hezekiah said to Isaiah, "What is the sign that the LORD will heal me and that I'll be able to go up to the LORD's temple in three days?"

⁹Isaiah said, "This will be your sign from the LORD that he will make his promise come true: Should the shadow go forward ten steps or back ten steps?"

¹⁰"It's easy for the shadow to go forward ten steps," Hezekiah said, "but not for the shadow to go back ten steps." ¹¹So the prophet Isaiah called on the LORD, who made the shadow go back ten steps, down the flight of stairs built by Ahaz.ⁿ

¹²At that time Merodach-baladan, son of Babylon's King Baladan, sent messengers to Hezekiah with letters and a gift. This was because he had heard that Hezekiah was sick. ¹³Hezekiah granted them an audience and showed them everything in his treasury—the silver, the gold, the spices, and the fine oil. He also showed them his stock of weaponry and everything in his storehouses. There wasn't a single thing in

---

^mQere, some Heb sources, and the parallel in Isa 32; Kethib lacks *of heavenly forces*. ⁿHeb uncertain

his palace or his whole kingdom that Hezekiah didn't show them. ¹⁴Then the prophet Isaiah came to King Hezekiah and said to him, "What did these men say? Where have they come from?"

Hezekiah said, "They came from a distant country: Babylon."

¹⁵"What have they seen in your palace?" Isaiah asked.

"They have seen everything in my palace," Hezekiah answered. "There's not a single thing in my storehouses that I haven't shown them."

¹⁶Then Isaiah said to Hezekiah, "Listen to the LORD's word: ¹⁷The days are nearly here when everything in your palace and all that your ancestors collected up to now will be carried off to Babylon. Not a single thing will be left, says the LORD. ¹⁸Some of your children, your very own offspring, will be taken away. They will become eunuchs in the palace of Babylon's king."

¹⁹Hezekiah said to Isaiah, "The LORD's word that you've spoken is good," because he thought: There will be peace and security in my lifetime.

²⁰The rest of Hezekiah's deeds and all his powerful acts—how he made the pool and the channel and brought water inside the city—aren't they written in the official records of Judah's kings? ²¹Hezekiah lay down with his ancestors. His son Manasseh succeeded him as king.

Manasseh rules Judah

21 Manasseh was 12 years old when he became king, and he ruled for fifty-five years in Jerusalem. His mother's name was Hephzibah. ²He did what was evil in the LORD's eyes, imitating the detestable practices of the nations that the LORD had driven out before the Israelites. ³He rebuilt the shrines that his father Hezekiah had destroyed, set up altars for Baal, and made a sacred pole,° just as Israel's King Ahab had done. He bowed down to all the stars in the sky and worshipped them. ⁴He even built altars in the two courtyards of the LORD's temple—the very place the LORD was speaking of when he said: "I will put my name in Jerusalem." ⁵Manasseh built altars for all the stars in the sky in both courtyards of the LORD's temple. ⁶He burned his own son alive, consulted sign readers and fortune-tellers, and used mediums and diviners. He did much evil in the LORD's eyes and made him angry.

⁷Manasseh set up the carved Asherah image he had made in the temple—the very temple the LORD had spoken about to David and his son Solomon, saying, In this temple and in Jerusalem, which I have chosen out of all Israel's tribes, I will put my name forever. ⁸I will never again remove Israel from the land I gave to their ancestors, provided they carefully do everything I have commanded them—keeping all the

°Heb *asherah*, perhaps a pole devoted to the goddess Asherah

MANASSEH

Manasseh son of Hezekiah became king of Judah at the age of 12 and reigned for longer than any other king in the history of ancient Israel. The Bible says he reigned for 55 years (2 Kgs 21:1), but that is difficult to reconcile with reigns of the other kings. What is undisputed is the portrayal of Manasseh as one of the most evil kings in the Bible, guilty of various acts of injustice and apostasy (2 Kgs 21:1-18; 2 Chron 33:1-9). In particular, he reintroduced "the detestable practices of the nations" (2 Kgs 21:2) that his father Hezekiah had purged, including necromancy, consulting with mediums and wizards, and even human sacrifice (2 Kgs 21:6). He provoked God's anger as no other king had done.

Instruction my servant Moses commanded them. ⁹But they wouldn't listen. Manasseh led them into doing even more evil than the nations the LORD had wiped out before the Israelites.

¹⁰The LORD spoke through his servants the prophets: ¹¹Judah's King Manasseh has done detestable things, things more evil than the Amorites had done before his time. He has caused Judah to sin with his images. ¹²Because of this, the LORD, Israel's God, has said: I'm about to bring on Jerusalem and Judah such a great disaster that the ears of anyone who hears about it will ring. ¹³I will stretch out over Jerusalem the same line that I used to measure Samaria and the same mason's level that I used on Ahab's family. I will wipe Jerusalem clean the same way someone wipes a plate clean, wiping it clean then turning it facedown. ¹⁴Whatever survives of my inheritance, I'll leave behind, handing them over to their enemies. They will be nothing but plunder and loot for every one of their enemies. ¹⁵This will happen because they have done what is evil in my eyes, making me angry from the day their ancestors left Egypt until this very moment.

¹⁶Manasseh spilled so much innocent blood that he filled up every corner of Jerusalem with it. And this doesn't include the sins he caused Judah to commit so that they did what was evil in the LORD's eyes. ¹⁷The rest of Manasseh's deeds, all that he accomplished, and the sin he committed, aren't they written in the official records of Judah's kings? ¹⁸Manasseh lay down with his ancestors. He was buried in his palace garden, the Uzza Garden. His son Amon succeeded him as king.

Amon rules Judah

¹⁹Amon was 22 years old when he became king, and he ruled for two years in Jerusalem. His mother's name was Meshullemeth; she was Haruz's daughter and was from Jotbah. ²⁰He did what was evil in the LORD's eyes, just as his father Manasseh had done. ²¹He walked in all the ways his father had walked. He worshipped the same worthless idols his father had worshipped, bowing down to them. ²²He deserted his ancestors' God, the LORD—he didn't walk in the LORD's way.

²³Amon's officials plotted against him and assassinated the king in his palace. ²⁴The people of the land then executed all those who had plotted against King Amon and made his son Josiah the next king. ²⁵The rest of Amon's deeds, aren't they written in the official records of Judah's kings? ²⁶He was buried in his tomb in the Uzza Garden. His son Josiah succeeded him as king.

Josiah rules Judah

22 Josiah was 8 years old when he became king, and he ruled for thirty-one years in Jerusalem. His mother's name was Jedidah; she was Adaiah's daughter and was from Bozkath. ²He did what was right in the LORD's eyes, and walked in the ways of his ancestor David—not deviating from it even a bit to the right or left.

³In the eighteenth year of King Josiah's rule, he sent the secretary Shaphan, Azaliah's son and Meshullam's grandson, to the LORD's temple with the following orders: ⁴"Go to the high priest Hilkiah. Have him carefully count^P the money that has been brought to the LORD's temple and that has been collected from the people by the doorkeepers. ⁵It should be given to the supervisors in charge of the LORD's temple, who in turn should pay it to those who are in the LORD's temple, repairing the temple—⁶the carpenters, the builders, and the masons. It should be used to pay for lumber and quarried stone to repair the temple. ⁷But there's no need to check on them regarding the money they receive, because they are honest workers."

⁸The high priest Hilkiah told Shaphan the secretary: "I have found the Instruction scroll in the LORD's temple." Then Hilkiah turned the scroll over to Shaphan, who read it.

⁹Shaphan the secretary then went to the king and reported this to him: "Your

^P Heb uncertain

officials have released the money that was found in the temple and have handed it over to those who supervise the work in the LORD's temple." [10]Then Shaphan the secretary told the king, "Hilkiah the priest has given me a scroll," and he read it out loud before the king.

[11]As soon as the king heard what the Instruction scroll said, he ripped his clothes. [12]The king ordered the priest Hilkiah, Shaphan's son Ahikam, Micaiah's son Achbor, Shaphan the secretary, and Asaiah the royal officer as follows: [13]"Go and ask the LORD on my behalf, and on behalf of the people, and on behalf of all Judah concerning the contents of this scroll that has been found. The LORD must be furious with us because our ancestors failed to obey the words of this scroll and do everything written in it about us."

[14]So Hilkiah the priest, Ahikam, Achbor, Shaphan, and Asaiah went to the prophetess Huldah. She was married to Shallum, Tikvah's son and Harhas' grandson, who was in charge of the wardrobe. She lived in Jerusalem in the second district. When they spoke to her, [15]she replied, "This is what the LORD, Israel's God, says: Tell this to the man who sent you to me: [16]This is what the LORD says: I am about to bring disaster on this place and its citizens—all the words in the scroll that Judah's king has read! [17]My anger burns against this place, never

to be quenched, because they've deserted me and have burned incense to other gods, angering me by everything they have done.[q] [18]But also say this to the king of Judah, who sent you to question the LORD: This is what the LORD, Israel's God, says about the message you've just heard: [19]Because your heart was broken and you submitted before the LORD when you heard what I said about this place and its citizens—that they will become a horror and a curse—and because you ripped your clothes and cried before me, I have listened to you, declares the LORD. [20]That's why I will gather you to your ancestors, and you will go to your grave in peace. You won't experience the disaster I am about to bring on this place."

Josiah's reform

When they reported Huldah's words to **23** the king, [1]the king sent a message, and all of Judah's and Jerusalem's elders gathered before him. [2]Then the king went up to the LORD's temple, together with all the people of Judah and all the citizens of Jerusalem, the priests and the prophets, and all the people, young and old alike. There the king read out loud all the words of the covenant scroll that had been found in the LORD's temple. [3]The king stood beside the pillar and made a covenant with the LORD that he would follow the LORD by keeping his commandments, his laws, and

[q]Or made

HULDAH

A prophet of Jerusalem and wife of Shallum (2 Kgs 22:14; 2 Chron 34:22), Huldah was consulted by the high priest Hilkiah and the officials of Josiah's court after the "Instruction scroll" was recovered from the temple (2 Kgs 22:8-13; 2 Chron 34:14-21). Her prophecy announced tragedy for the people of the kingdom, who had made offerings to idols, but offered a peaceful death to Josiah (2 Kgs 22:20; 2 Chron 34:28). The words of her prophecy encouraged the king to make a covenant to be obedient to the Instruction (2 Kgs 23:1-4; 2 Chron 34:29-33) and to initiate other religious reforms. Huldah's designation as a "prophetess" is shared by both Miriam (Exod 15:20) and Deborah (Judg 4:4).

his regulations with all his heart and all his being in order to fulfill the words of this covenant that were written in this scroll. All of the people accepted the covenant.

⁴The king then commanded the high priest Hilkiah, the second-order priests, and the doorkeepers to remove from the LORD's temple all the religious objects made for Baal, Asherah, and all the heavenly bodies. The king burned them outside Jerusalem in the Kidron fields and took the ashes to Bethel. ⁵He got rid of the pagan priests that the Judean kings had appointed to burn incense at the shrines in Judah's cities and the areas around Jerusalem. He did the same to those who burned incense to Baal, to the sun, to the moon, to the constellations, and to all the heavenly bodies. ⁶He removed the Asherah image^r from the LORD's temple, taking it to the Kidron Valley outside Jerusalem. There he burned it, ground it to dust, and threw the dust on the public graveyard. ⁷The king tore down the shrines for the consecrated workers^s that were in the LORD's temple, where women made woven coverings^t for Asherah.

⁸Then Josiah brought all the priests out of Judah's cities. From Geba to Beer-sheba, he defiled the shrines where the priests had been burning incense. He also tore down the shrines at the gates at the entrance to the gate of Joshua the city's governor, which were on the left as one entered the city gate. ⁹Although the priests of these shrines didn't go up on the LORD's altar in Jerusalem, they did eat unleavened bread with their fellow priests.

¹⁰Josiah defiled the Topheth in the Ben-hinnom Valley so no one could burn their child alive in honor of the god Molech. ¹¹He did away with the horses that Judah's kings had dedicated to the sun. They were kept at the entrance to the LORD's temple near a room in the annex^u that belonged to an official named Nathan-melech. Josiah set fire to the chariots that were dedicated to

the sun. ¹²The king also tore down the altars that were on the roof of Ahaz's upper story, which had been made by the Judean kings, and he did the same with the altars that Manasseh had built in the two courtyards of the LORD's temple. He broke them up there^v and threw their dust into the Kidron Valley. ¹³The king then defiled the shrines facing Jerusalem, south of the Mountain of Destruction. Solomon the king of Israel had built these for Ashtoreth, the monstrous Sidonian god, for Chemosh, the monstrous Moabite god, and for Milcom, the detestable Ammonite god. ¹⁴He smashed the sacred pillars and cut down the sacred poles,^w filling the places where they had been with human bones.

¹⁵Josiah also tore down the altar that was in Bethel. That was the shrine made by Jeroboam, Nebat's son, who caused Israel to sin. Josiah tore down that altar and its shrine. He burned the shrine, grinding it into dust. Then he burned its sacred pole.^x ¹⁶When Josiah turned around, he noticed tombs up on the hillside. So he ordered the bones to be taken out of the tombs. He then burned them on the altar, desecrating it. (This was in agreement with the word that the LORD announced by the man of God when Jeroboam stood by the altar at the festival.) Josiah then turned and saw the tomb of the man of God^y who had predicted these things. ¹⁷"What's this gravestone I see?" Josiah asked.

The people of the city replied, "That tomb belongs to the man of God who came from Judah and announced what you would do to the altar of Bethel."

¹⁸"Let it be," Josiah said. "No one should disturb his bones." So they left his bones untouched, along with the bones of the prophet who came from Samaria.

¹⁹Moreover, Josiah removed all the shrines on the high hills that the Israelite kings had constructed throughout the cities of Samaria. These had made the LORD angry.

---

^rHeb lacks *image*; perhaps a pole dedicated to the goddess. ^sTraditionally *cultic prostitutes* ^tHeb uncertain ^uHeb uncertain ^vCorrection; MT *removed them quickly* or *ran from there* ^wHeb *asherim*, perhaps objects devoted to the goddess Asherah ^xHeb *asherah*, perhaps an object devoted to the goddess Asherah ^yLXX; MT lacks *when Jeroboam stood by the altar at the festival. Josiah then turned and saw the tomb of the man of God.*

Josiah did to them just what he did at Bethel. [20]He actually slaughtered on those altars all the priests of the shrines who were there, and he burned human bones on them. Then Josiah returned to Jerusalem.

[21]The king commanded all the people, "Celebrate a Passover to the LORD your God following what is instructed in this scroll containing the covenant." [22]A Passover like this hadn't been celebrated since the days when the judges judged Israel; neither had it been celebrated during all the days of the Israelite and Judean kings. [23]But in the eighteenth year of King Josiah's rule, this Passover was celebrated to the LORD in Jerusalem.

[24]Josiah burned those who consulted dead spirits and the mediums, the household gods and the worthless idols—all the monstrous things that were seen in the land of Judah and in Jerusalem. In this way Josiah fulfilled the words of the Instruction written in the scroll that the priest Hilkiah found in the LORD's temple. [25]There's never been a king like Josiah, whether before or after him, who turned to the LORD with all his heart, all his being, and all his strength, in agreement with everything in the Instruction from Moses.

[26]Even so, the LORD didn't turn away from the great rage that burned against Judah on account of all that Manasseh had done to make him angry. [27]The LORD said, "I will remove Judah from my presence just as I removed Israel. I will reject this city, Jerusalem, which I chose, and this temple where I promised my name would reside."

[28]The rest of Josiah's deeds and all that he accomplished, aren't they written in the official records of Judah's kings? [29]In his days, the Egyptian king Pharaoh Neco marched against the Assyrian king at the Euphrates River. King Josiah marched out to intercept him. But when Neco encountered Josiah in Megiddo, he killed the king. [30]Josiah's servants took his body from Megiddo in a chariot. They brought him to Jerusalem and buried him in his own tomb. The people of the land took Jehoahaz, Josiah's son, anointed him, and made him king after his father.

Jehoahaz rules Judah

[31]Jehoahaz was 23 years old when he became king, and he ruled for three months in Jerusalem. His mother's name was Hamutal; she was Jeremiah's daughter and was from Libnah. [32]He did what was evil in the LORD's eyes, just as all his ancestors had done. [33]Pharaoh Neco made Jehoahaz a prisoner at Riblah in the land of Hamath, ending his rule in Jerusalem. Pharaoh Neco imposed a fine on the land totaling one hundred kikkars of silver and one kikkar of gold.

Jehoiakim rules Judah

[34]Pharaoh Neco made Eliakim, Josiah's son, king after his father Josiah. Neco changed Eliakim's name to Jehoiakim. Neco

MEGIDDO

A prominent mound, called Tel Megiddo in Hebrew and Tell el-Mutesellim in Arabic ("the tell of the governor"), marks the site of biblical Megiddo. The mound rises about 100 ft. above the surrounding plain, and its summit covers about 13 acres. Megiddo is located in the Jezreel Valley, where the narrow brook of Nahal Iron, which crosses the ridge of Mount Carmel, opens into the valley. The main highway from Egypt to Asia passed through Nahal Iron, and thus Megiddo controlled the highway. Three factors—the fertile valley, the ample supply of water, and its strategic position along the international highway—turned Meggido into one of the most important centers in the country.

took Jehoahaz away; he later died in Egypt.
[35] Jehoiakim gave Pharaoh the silver and gold, but he taxed the land in order to meet Pharaoh's financial demands. Each person was taxed appropriately. Jehoiakim exacted silver and the gold from the land's people in order to give it to Pharaoh Neco. [36] Jehoiakim was 25 years old when he became king, and he ruled for eleven years in Jerusalem. His mother's name was Zebidah; she was Pedaiah's daughter and was from Rumah. [37] He did what was evil in the LORD's eyes, just as all his ancestors had done.

24 In Jehoiakim's days, King Nebuchadnezzar of Babylon attacked. Jehoiakim had submitted to him for three years, but then Jehoiakim changed his mind and rebelled against him. [2] The LORD sent Chaldean, Aramean, Moabite, and Ammonite raiding parties against Jehoiakim, sending them against Judah in order to destroy it. This was in agreement with the word that the LORD had spoken through his servants the prophets. [3] Indeed, this happened to Judah because the LORD commanded them to be removed from his presence on account of all the sins that Manasseh had committed [4] and because of the innocent blood that he had spilled. Manasseh had filled Jerusalem with innocent blood, and the LORD didn't want to forgive that.

[5] The rest of Jehoiakim's deeds and all that he accomplished, aren't they written in the official records of Judah's kings? [6] Jehoiakim lay down with his ancestors. His son Jehoiachin succeeded him as king.

[7] The Egyptian king never left his country again because the Babylonian king had taken over all the territory that had previously belonged to him—from the border of Egypt to the Euphrates River.

Jehoiachin rules Judah

[8] Jehoiachin was 18 years old when he became king, and he ruled for three months in Jerusalem. His mother's name was Nehushta; she was Elnathan's daughter and was from Jerusalem. [9] He did what was evil in the LORD's eyes, just as all his ancestors had done. [10] At that time, the officers of Babylon's King Nebuchadnezzar attacked Jerusalem and laid siege to the city. [11] Babylon's King Nebuchadnezzar himself arrived at the city while his officers were blockading it. [12] Judah's King Jehoiachin, along with his mother, his servants, his officers,

NEBUCHADNEZZAR/ NEBUCHADREZZAR

There were two important kings of Babylon named Nebuchadnezzar, though only Nebuchadnezzar II is mentioned in the Bible.

1. Nebuchadnezzar I of the Second Dynasty of Isin ruled Babylon from 1125 to 1104 BCE. He kept Assyria at bay, but it was his successful campaign against Elam, in which he recovered the statue of Marduk, that made him great in the eyes of the Babylonians.

2. Nebuchadnezzar II, who ruled Babylon for 43 years (605–562 BCE), was the second ruler of the Neo-Babylonian dynasty founded by his father Nabopolassar (reigned 626–605). Nabopolassar had rebelled against Assyria, seized the Babylonian throne, and begun a long seesaw struggle to drive Assyria from Babylonian territory. In 2 Kings 24–25, Nebuchadnezzar II defeats Jehoiachin the king of Judah (598 BCE) and finally destroys Jerusalem in the reign of King Zedekiah (587 BCE).

and his officials, came out to surrender to the Babylonian king. The Babylonian king took Jehoiachin prisoner in the eighth year of Jehoiachin's rule.

[13]Nebuchadnezzar also took away all the treasures of the LORD's temple and of the royal palace. He cut into pieces all the gold objects that Israel's King Solomon had made for the LORD's temple, which is exactly what the LORD said would happen. [14]Then Nebuchadnezzar exiled all of Jerusalem: all the officials, all the military leaders—ten thousand exiles—as well as all the skilled workers and metalworkers. No one was left behind except the poorest of the land's people. [15]Nebuchadnezzar exiled Jehoiachin to Babylon; he also exiled the queen mother, the king's wives, the officials, and the land's elite leaders from Jerusalem to Babylon. [16]The Babylonian king also exiled seven thousand warriors—each one a hero trained for battle—as well as a thousand skilled workers and metalworkers to Babylon. [17]Then the Babylonian king made Mattaniah, Jehoiachin's uncle, succeed Jehoiachin as king. Nebuchadnezzar changed Mattaniah's name to Zedekiah.

Zedekiah rules Judah

[18]Zedekiah was 21 years old when he became king, and he ruled for eleven years in Jerusalem. His mother's name was Hamutal; she was Jeremiah's daughter and was from Libnah. [19]He did what was evil in the LORD's eyes, just as Jehoiakim had done. [20]It was precisely because the LORD

[z]LXX, cf Jer 52:7; MT lacks *fled.*

was angry with Jerusalem and Judah that he thrust them out of his presence.

The southern kingdom falls

Now Zedekiah rebelled against the Babylonian king. [1]So in the ninth year of Zedekiah's rule, on the tenth day of the tenth month, Babylon's King Nebuchadnezzar attacked Jerusalem with his entire army. He camped beside the city and built a siege wall all around it. [2]The city was under attack until King Zedekiah's eleventh year. [3]On the ninth day of the month, the famine in the city got so bad that no food remained for the common people. [4]Then the enemy broke into the city. All the soldiers fled[z] by night using the gate between the two walls near the King's Garden. The Chaldeans were surrounding the city, so the soldiers ran toward the desert plain. [5]But the Chaldean army chased King Zedekiah and caught up with him in the Jericho plains. His entire army deserted him. [6]So the Chaldeans captured the king and brought him back to the Babylonian king, who was at Riblah. There his punishment was determined. [7]Zedekiah's sons were slaughtered right before his eyes. Then he was blinded, put in bronze chains, and taken off to Babylon.

[8]On the seventh day of the fifth month in the nineteenth year of Babylon's King Nebuchadnezzar, Nebuzaradan arrived at Jerusalem. He was the commander of the guard and an official of the Babylonian king. [9]He burned down the LORD's temple, the royal palace, and all of Jerusalem's

CHALDEA/CHALDEANS

A region in Babylonia and its inhabitants. The designation *Chaldeans* is used in the Bible to refer to the last dynasty of Babylon (626–539 BCE), whose second king, Nebuchadnezzar II, conquered Jerusalem in 598 and 587, deporting many Judeans into exile in Babylon. The Chaldeans are mentioned in Isaiah 47–48; Jeremiah 50–51; Ezekiel 11:24; 16:29; 23:14-16; 2 Kings; Ezra; and Daniel.

houses. He burned down every important building. ¹⁰The whole Chaldean army under the commander of the guard tore down the walls surrounding Jerusalem. ¹¹Then Nebuzaradan the commander of the guard exiled the people who were left in the city, those who had already surrendered to Babylon's king, and the rest of the population. ¹²The commander of the guard left some of the land's poor people behind to work the vineyards and be farmers. ¹³The Chaldeans shattered the bronze columns, the stands, and the bronze Sea that were in the LORD's temple. They carried the bronze off to Babylon. ¹⁴They also took the pots, the shovels, the wick trimmers, the dishes, and all the bronze items that had been used in the temple. ¹⁵The commander of the guard took the fire pans and the sprinkling bowls, which were made of pure gold and pure silver. ¹⁶The bronze in all these objects—the two pillars, the Sea, and the stands that Solomon had made for the LORD's temple—was too heavy to weigh. ¹⁷Each pillar was twenty-seven feet high. The bronze capital on top of the first pillar was four and a half feet high. Decorative lattices and pomegranates, all made from bronze, were around the capital. And the second pillar was decorated with lattices just like the first.

¹⁸The commander of the guard also took away Seraiah the chief priest, Zephaniah the priest next in rank, and the three doorkeepers. ¹⁹Of those still left in the city, Nebuzaradan took away an officer who was in charge of the army and five royal advisors who were discovered in the city. He also took away the secretary of the officer responsible for drafting the land's people to fight, as well as sixty people who were discovered in the city. ²⁰Nebuzaradan the commander of the guard took all of these people and brought them to the Babylonian king at Riblah. ²¹The king of Babylon struck them down, killing them in Riblah in the land of Hamath.

So Judah was exiled from its land.

Gedaliah governs Judah

²²Babylon's King Nebuchadnezzar put Gedaliah, Ahikam's son and Shaphan's grandson, in charge of the people he had left behind in the land of Judah. ²³All the army officers and their soldiers heard that the Babylonian king had appointed Gedaliah as governor, so they came with their men to Gedaliah at Mizpah. The officers were Ishmael, Nethaniah's son; Johanan, Kareah's son; Seraiah, Tanhumeth's son who was a Netophathite; and Jaazaniah, Maacathite's son. ²⁴Gedaliah made a solemn pledge to them and their soldiers, telling them, "Don't be afraid of the Chaldean officials. Stay in the land and serve the Babylonian king, and things will go well for you."

²⁵But in the seventh month, Ishmael, Nethaniah's son and Elishama's grandson, who was from the royal family, came with ten soldiers, and they struck Gedaliah, and he died. They also killed the Judeans and the Chaldeans who were with him at Mizpah. ²⁶Then all the people, young and old, along with the army officers, departed for Egypt because they were afraid of the Chaldeans.

Jehoiachin in Babylon

²⁷In the year that Awil-merodach[a] became king of Babylon, he released Judah's King Jehoiachin from prison. This happened in the thirty-seventh year of the exile of King Jehoiachin, on the twenty-seventh day of the twelfth month. ²⁸Awil-merodach spoke kindly to Jehoiachin and seated him above the other kings who were with him in Babylon. ²⁹So Jehoiachin took off his prisoner clothes and ate regularly in the king's presence for the rest of his life. ³⁰At the king's command, a regular food allowance was given to him every day for the rest of his life.

---

[a] *Awil-merodach* means Man of Marduk in Akkadian.

1 CHRONICLES

The Hebrew title is "Events of the Days," that is, "Chronicles." The Hebrews put Chronicles at the end of their Bible because it was a later addition to all that had been said and written.

Following written histories and records of his people, the writer of Chronicles recast them with the fresh viewpoint and attitudes that experience had brought to Israel. He applied them to the needs of his times and of all times.

THE HISTORICAL PERIOD COVERED

The Chronicles cover the period of Judah's history as a kingdom. First, however, the books trace the background of world history from Adam to Jacob, the ancestor of Israel. They trace Jacob's descendants to the end of the reign of Israel's first king, Saul. The main story of Chronicles begins with the reign of David, about 1000 BCE, and continues to the last king, Zedekiah, and the fall of Jerusalem, 587 BCE. During these more than 400 years, the world political powers were Egypt, to the south of Judah, and Assyria, in the north, until 626 BCE, when Babylonia, to the east, replaced Assyria as a world power.

THE CHRONICLES' INTERPRETATION OF HISTORY

The Chronicler wrote his book with the conviction that God is the creator and controller of nature and the ruler over history. History, under God, is a matter of divine selection and of development by divine revelation. Through the generations, God prepared for and selected Israel as the chosen people. Of all Israel, God chose the tribe of Judah to be its leader (1 Chronicles 28:4). And in all Judah, God chose Jerusalem (2 Chronicles 6:6). From the descendants of Israel God chose David and his heirs to rule the people. God chose David's son, Solomon, to build a temple. Chronicles is a history of the temple.

Chronicles records the history of the kings of David's dynasty and of the people of Israel in relation to the temple and what it represents: God's rule and presence and purpose, the law and commandments, God's covenant with, and compassion for, the chosen people (and always the power of God's righteousness). For Chronicles, all that happened before Moses was pre-history. Moses, followed by Joshua, established Israel as a theocracy, a God-ruled people. The period of David followed by Solomon, who duplicated Moses and Joshua, was the fulfillment of God's kingdom on earth. The kings in David's line were God's stewards. When they were faithful, God blessed them. When they were unfaithful, God punished them. If they repented and returned to God, they were pardoned.

THE CHRONICLER'S PURPOSE

The Chronicler writes to inform his readers, through the story of their nation, how God's judgment works. He writes to urge them to be faithful worshipers at the temple, to keep the covenant, to obey the law and commandments, and to do what is right in the eyes of the Lord. He writes to warn them that what happened to their ancestors and to their nation as the result of faithlessness can happen again to them. He also writes to encourage them that, despite the Exile and the loss of their kingdom and David's dynasty of kings, there is yet hope for them. The people can sincerely hope for a renewal of those good days through faithfulness to God, who is faithful to them in return.

DATE

The date of composition of Chronicles is, as the work itself states, after the return from exile (538 BCE). First Chronicles mentions money coined not before 515 BCE (1 Chronicles 29:7). It takes David's lineage to the fifth generation after Zerubbabel, who was governor of Jerusalem under Darius at the end of the sixth century BCE (1 Chronicles 3:19-24). Scholars believe that Chronicles was written after Ezra-Nehemiah was written (as one book), but the book of Nehemiah records the high priests down to Jaddua, who was high priest at the time of Alexander of Macedonia (late fourth century BCE). Jaddua expressed goals and a zeal similar to those of the Chronicles, which uses the late Hebrew of that century. All this evidence indicates that the Chronicler wrote his work shortly after 350 BCE.

AUTHOR

The author does not name himself. Like Ezra-Nehemiah, Chronicles has a structure and a theology that emphasize counsel, covenant-making, purification of the land and people, and renewal of the temple ritual. This similarity is due to its author belonging to the same community and epoch. Nevertheless, there are marked differences in vocabulary and in attitudes toward non-Jews. The Chronicler places a strong emphasis, lacking in Ezra-Nehemiah, on the Levites, their importance and tasks. Because the author writes in levitical preaching style, and because he speaks more highly of the Levites than of the priests, many have thought the author may have been a Levite. The special place he gives to music among the Levites may mean he was also a musician.

ONE BOOK

Chronicles is one book with four sections: (1) the introduction, the genealogies (1 Chronicles 1–9); (2) the story of King David and plans for the temple (1 Chronicles 10–29); (3) the story of King Solomon and the building of the temple (2 Chronicles 1–9); and (4) the stories of the kings of Judah (2 Chronicles 10–36). The book was divided into 1 and 2 Chronicles simply because it was too long to go on one papyrus roll; each half fit neatly on one roll.

SOURCES

The Chronicler refers to a variety of sources. About half of the Chronicles' verses are quoted from 1 and 2 Samuel and 1 and 2 Kings. References to books of seers and prophets are to their appearances in Samuel and Kings (or, in one instance, in Isaiah). There being no division by chapters and books, the sections of a book were referred to by the persons storied in them, just as Paul, in Romans 11:2, refers to what was written in Elijah when he refers to 1 Kings 19:10. Genealogies from Genesis through 2 Kings are used, as well as military records and censuses, lists of Levites and of prominent families, local and family records and reminiscences, and oral tradition. The author uses the Psalms freely and phrases from the prophets. It is likely that a later editor has made some additions. This seems to be the case when references about priests are added that do not quite fit the text.

1 CHRONICLES

Adam to Israel

1 Adam, Seth, Enosh; [2]Kenan, Mahalalel, Jared; [3]Enoch, Methuselah, Lamech; [4]Noah; Noah's family:[a] Shem, Ham, and Japheth.

[5]Japheth's family: Gomer, Magog, Madai, Javan, Tubal, Meshech, and Tiras. [6]Gomer's family: Ashkenaz, Riphath,[b] and Togarmah.

[7]Javan's family: Elishah, Tarshish, Kittim, and Rodanim.

[8]Ham's family: Cush, Egypt, Put, and Canaan. [9]Cush's family: Seba, Havilah, Sabta, Raama, and Sabteca.

Raamah's family: Sheba and Dedan. [10]Cush was the father of Nimrod, the first warrior in the land.

[11]Egypt was the father of Ludim, Anamim, Lehabim, Naphtuhim, [12]Pathrusim, Casluhim, from whom the Philistines came, and Caphtorim.

[13]Canaan was the father of Sidon his oldest son, Heth, [14]the Jebusites, the Amorites, the Girgashites, [15]the Hivites, the Arkites, the Sinites, [16]the Arvadites, the Zemarites, and the Hamathites.

[17]Shem's family: Elam, Asshur, Arpachshad, Lud, and Aram.

Aram's family:[c] Uz, Hul, Gether, and Meshech.

[18]Arpachshad was Shelah's father, and Shelah was Eber's father. [19]Two sons were born to Eber: one was named Peleg,[d] because in his days the land was divided; and his brother's name was Joktan.

[20]Joktan was the father of Almodad, Sheleph, Hazarmaveth, Jerah, [21]Hadoram, Uzal, Diklah, [22]Ebal, Abimael, Sheba, [23]Ophir, Havilah, and Jobab. All these were Joktan's family.

[24]Shem, Arpachshad, Shelah; [25]Eber, Peleg, Reu; [26]Serug, Nahor, Terah; [27]and Abram, that is, Abraham.

[28]Abraham's family: Isaac and Ishmael. [29]These were their descendants.

Ishmael's oldest son was Nebaioth, then Kedar, Adbeel, Mibsam, [30]Mishma, Dumah, Massa, Hadad, Tema, [31]Jetur, Naphish, and Kedemah. This was Ishmael's family. [32]Abraham's secondary wife Keturah's family: she gave birth to Zimran, Jokshan, Medan, Midian, Ishbak, and Shuah.

Jokshan's family: Sheba and Dedan. [33]Midian's family: Ephah, Epher, Hanoch, Abida, and Eldaah. All these were members of Keturah's family.

[34]Abraham was Isaac's father. Isaac's family: Esau and Israel.

[35]Esau's family: Eliphaz, Reuel, Jeush, Jalam, and Korah.

[36]Eliphaz's family: Teman, Omar, Zephi, Gatam, Kenaz, Timna, and Amalek.

[37]Reuel's family: Nahath, Zerah, Shammah, and Mizzah.

[38]Seir's family: Lotan, Shobal, Zibeon, Anah, Dishon, Ezer, and Dishan.

[39]Lotan's family: Hori and Homam; Lotan's sister was Timna.

[40]Shobal's family: Alian, Manahath, Ebal, Shephi, and Onam.

Zibeon's family: Aiah and Anah.

[41]Anah's family: Dishon.

Dishon's family: Hamran, Eshban, Ithran, and Cheran.

[42]Ezer's family: Bilhan, Zaavan, and Jaakan.

Dishan's family:[e] Uz and Aran.

[43]These were the kings who ruled in the land of Edom before any king ruled over the Israelites: Bela, Beor's son, whose city was called Dinhabah. [44]When Bela died, Jobab, Zerah's son from Bozrah, succeeded him. [45]When Jobab died, Husham from the land of the Temanites succeeded him. [46]When Husham died, Hadad, Bedad's son who defeated Midian in the Moabite countryside, succeeded him; his city was called Avith. [47]When Hadad died, Samlah from Masrekah succeeded him. [48]When Samlah died, Shaul from Rehoboth on the river succeeded him.

[a]LXX; MT lacks *Noah's family.* [b]LXX; MT *Diphath* [c]LXX; MT lacks *Aram's family.* [d]Or *division* [e]Cf 1:38; or *Dishon's family*

⁴⁹When Shaul died, Baal-hanan, Achbor's son, succeeded him. ⁵⁰When Baal-hanan died, Hadad succeeded him; his city was called Pai. His wife's name was Mehetabel, Matred's daughter and Me-zahab's granddaughter. ⁵¹When Hadad died, Edom's tribal chiefs were: Chief Timna, Chief Aliah, Chief Jetheth, ⁵²Chief Oholibamah, Chief Elah, Chief Pinon, ⁵³Chief Kenaz, Chief Teman, Chief Mibzar, ⁵⁴Chief Magdiel, and Chief Iram. These were Edom's tribal chiefs.

2 This was Israel's family: Reuben, Simeon, Levi, Judah, Issachar, Zebulun, ²Dan, Joseph, Benjamin, Naphtali, Gad, and Asher.

Judah's line

³Judah's family: Er, Onan, and Shelah. These three were born to him with Bathshua the Canaanite. Although Er was Judah's oldest, the LORD considered him wicked and put him to death. ⁴His daughter-in-law Tamar bore him Perez and Zerah. Judah had five sons in all.

⁵Perez's family: Hezron and Hamul.

⁶Zerah's family: Zimri, Ethan, Heman, Calcol, and Darda[f]—five in all.

⁷Carmi's family: Achar, who made trouble for Israel by disobeying the law dedicating war spoils to God.

⁸Ethan's family: Azariah.

⁹Hezron's family, who were born to him: Jerahmeel, Ram, and Chelubai. ¹⁰Ram was the father of Amminadab, and Amminadab was the father of Nahshon, tribal chief of the Judeans. ¹¹Nahshon was the father of Salma, Salma was the father of Boaz, ¹²Boaz was the father of Obed, and Obed was the father of Jesse. ¹³Jesse was the father of Eliab his oldest son, Abinadab his second, Shimea his third, ¹⁴Nethanel his fourth, Raddai his fifth, ¹⁵Ozem his sixth, and David his seventh. ¹⁶Their sisters were Zeruiah and Abigail.

Zeruiah's family: Abishai, Joab, and Asahel—three in all. ¹⁷Abigail gave birth to Amasa, whose father was Jether the Ishmaelite.

¹⁸Caleb, Hezron's son, had children with his wife Azubah, and with Jerioth. These were her sons: Jesher, Shobab, and Ardon. ¹⁹After Azubah died, Caleb married Ephrath, who gave birth to Hur for him. ²⁰Hur was the father of Uri, and Uri was the father of Bezalel. ²¹Later, Hezron had sexual relations with the daughter of Machir, Gilead's father, whom he married when he was 60 years old, and she gave birth to Segub for him. ²²Segub was the father of Jair, who owned twenty-three towns in the land of Gilead, ²³but Geshur and Aram took Havvoth-jair from them, as well as Kenath and its villages, sixty towns.

All these were descendants of Machir, Gilead's father. ²⁴After Hezron's death, Caleb went to Ephrath.[g] Abijah, Hezron's wife, bore him Ashhur, Tekoa's father.

²⁵The family of Jerahmeel, Hezron's oldest son: Ram his oldest, Bunah, Oren, Ozem, and Ahijah. ²⁶Jerahmeel had another wife named Atarah; she was the mother of Onam.

²⁷The family of Ram, Jerahmeel's oldest son: Maaz, Jamin, and Eker.

²⁸Onam's family: Shammai and Jada.

Shammai's family: Nadab and Abishur. ²⁹Abishur's wife's name was Abihail, and she gave birth to Ahban and Molid for him.

³⁰Nadab's family: Seled and Appaim, but Seled died without children.

³¹Appaim's family: Ishi.

Ishi's family: Sheshan.

Sheshan's family: Ahlai.

³²The family of Jada, Shammai's brother: Jether and Jonathan, but Jether died without children.

³³Jonathan's family: Peleth and Zaza. These were Jerahmeel's descendants.

³⁴Sheshan had no sons, only daughters; but Sheshan had an Egyptian servant whose name was Jarha. ³⁵Sheshan gave his daughter in marriage to Jarha his servant, and she gave birth to Attai for him.

³⁶Attai was the father of Nathan, Nathan was the father of Zabad, ³⁷Zabad

---

was the father of Ephlal, Ephlal was the father of Obed, [38]Obed was the father of Jehu, Jehu was the father of Azariah, [39]Azariah was the father of Helez, Helez was the father of Eleasah, [40]Eleasah was the father of Sismai, Sismai was the father of Shallum, [41]Shallum was the father of Jekamiah, and Jekamiah was the father of Elishama.

[42]The family of Caleb, Jerahmeel's brother: Mesha his oldest son and Ziph's father; and his second son[h] Mareshah, Hebron's father.

[43]Hebron's family: Korah, Tappuah, Rekem, and Shema. [44]Shema was the father of Raham, Jorkeam's father; and Rekem was the father of Shammai.

[45]Shammai's son: Maon; Maon was Beth-zur's father. [46]Ephah, Caleb's secondary wife, gave birth to Haran, Moza, and Gazez. Haran was the father of Gazez. [47]Jahdai's family: Regem, Jotham, Geshan, Pelet, Ephah, and Shaaph. [48]Maacah, Caleb's secondary wife, gave birth to Sheber and Tirhanah. [49]She also gave birth to Shaaph, Madmannah's father; and to Sheva, Machbenah and Gibea's father. Caleb's daughter was Achsah. [50]These were Caleb's descendants.

The family of Hur, Ephrathah's oldest son: Shobal, Kiriath-jearim's father; [51]Salma, Bethlehem's father; and Hareph, Beth-gader's father.

[52]Shobal, Kiriath-jearim's father, had a family: Haroeh, and the ancestor of half of the Menuhoth.[i] [53]Kiriath-jearim's clans: the Ithrites, the Puthites, the Shumathites, and the Mishraites. From these came the Zorathites and the Eshtaolites. [54]The family of Salma, Bethlehem's father:[j] the Netophathites, Atroth-bethjoab, half of the Manahathites, and the Zorites. [55]The clans of the scribes who lived at Jabez: the Tirathites, the Shimeathites, and the Sucathites. They were Kenites who descended from Hammath, Bethrechab's father.

David's line

3This is David's family born to him in Hebron: the oldest Amnon, with Ahinoam the Jezreelite; the second Daniel, with Abigail the Carmelite; [2]the third Absalom son of Maacah, the daughter of Geshur's King Talmai; the fourth Adonijah, Haggith's son; [3]the fifth Shephatiah, with Abital; the sixth Ithream, with his wife Eglah. [4]Six were born to him in Hebron, where he reigned for seven and a half years. He also reigned in Jerusalem for thirty-three years. [5]These were born to him in Jerusalem: Shimea, Shobab, Nathan, and Solomon—four from Bath-shua, Ammiel's daughter; [6]Ibhar, Eli-shama, Eliphelet, [7]Nogah, Nepheg, Japhia, [8]Elishama, Eliada, and Eliphelet—nine in all. [9]This was all of David's family, except for his secondary wives' children. Tamar was their sister.

[10]The descendants[k] of Solomon: Rehoboam, his son Abijah, his son Asa, his son Jehoshaphat, [11]his son Joram, his son Ahaziah, his son Joash, [12]his son Amaziah, his son Azariah, his son Jotham, [13]his son Ahaz, his son Hezekiah, his son Manasseh, [14]his son Amon, and his son Josiah.

[15]Josiah's family: the oldest Johanan, the second Jehoiakim, the third Zedekiah, and the fourth Shallum.

[16]Jehoiakim's family: his son Jeconiah and his son Zedekiah.

[17]The family of Jeconiah the prisoner: Shealtiel his son; [18]Malchiram, Pedaiah, Shenazzar, Jekamiah, Hoshama, and Nedabiah.

[19]Pedaiah's family: Zerubbabel and Shimei.

Zerubbabel's family:[l] Meshullam, Hananiah, and their sister Shelomith; [20]Hashubah, Ohel, Berechiah, Hasadiah, and Jushab-hesed—these five also.

[21]Hananiah's family:[m] Pelatiah, Jeshaiah, Rephaiah's family, Arnan's family, Obadiah's family, and Shecaniah's family.

---

[h]Or *the family of* [i]Heb lacks *the ancestor of.* [j]Cf 2:51; Heb lacks *father.* [k]LXX, Syr; MT *son* [l]LXX, Syr; MT *son* [m]LXX, Syr, Tg; MT *son*

[22] Shecaniah's family: Shemaiah and his family, Hattush, Igal, Bariah, Neariah, and Shaphat—six in all.

[23] Neariah's family: Elioenai, Hizkiah, and Azrikam—three in all.

[24] Elioenai's family: Hodaviah, Eliashib, Pelaiah, Akkub, Johanan, Delaiah, and Anani—seven in all.

Judah's line

4 Judah's family: Perez, Hezron, Caleb,[n] Hur, and Shobal.

[2] Shobal's son Reaiah was Jahath's father, and Jahath was the father of Ahumai and Lahad. These were the Zorathite clans.

[3] This was Etam's family:[o] Jezreel, Ishma, and Idbash. Their sister's name was Hazzelelponi. [4] Penuel was Gedor's father, and Ezer was Hushah's father.

This was the family of Hur the oldest son of Ephrathah, Bethlehem's father: [5] Ashhur, Tekoa's father, had two wives, Helah and Naarah. [6] Naarah gave birth to Ahuzzam, Hepher, Temeni, and Haahashtari for him. This was Naarah's family.

[7] Helah's family: Zereth, Zohar,[p] and Ethnan. [8] Koz was the father of Anub, Hazzobebah, and the clans of Aharhel, Harum's son.

[9] Jabez was more honored than his brothers. His mother had named him Jabez, saying, "I bore him in pain."[q] [10] Jabez called on Israel's God: "If only you would greatly bless me and increase my territory. May your power go with me to keep me from trouble, so as not to cause me pain." And God granted his request.

[11] Chelub, Shuhah's brother, was the father of Mehir, who was Eshton's father. [12] Eshton was the father of Bethrapha, Paseah, and Tehinnah, Ir-nahash's father. These are the men of Recah.

[13] Kenaz's family: Othniel and Seraiah. Othniel's family: Hathath and Meonothai.[r] [14] Meonothai was the father of Ophrah. Seraiah was the father of Joab the father of Ge-harashim,[s] socalled because they were skilled workers. [15] The family of Caleb, Jephunneh's son: Iru, Elah, and Naam. This was Kenaz's family.[t]

[16] Jehallelel's family: Ziph, Ziphah, Tiria, and Asarel.

[17] Ezrah's family:[u] Jether, Mered, Epher, and Jalon. Jether was the father of[v] Miriam, Shammai, and Ishbah, Eshtemoa's father. [18] His Judean wife gave birth to Jered, Gedor's father; Heber, Soco's father; and Jekuthiel, Zanoah's father.

This is the family of Bithiah, Pharaoh's daughter, whom Mered married. [19] The family of his Judean wife,[w] the sister of Naham, Keilah's father the Garmite and Eshtemoa the Maacathite.

[20] Shimon's family: Amnon, Rinnah, Ben-hanan, and Tilon.

Ishi's family: Zoheth and Ben-zoheth.

[21] The family of Shelah, Judah's son: Er, Lecah's father; Laadah, Mareshah's father; the clans of the linen workers at Beth-ashbea; [22] Jokim; the men of Cozeba; Joash; and Saraph, who married into[x] Moab but returned to Bethlehem[y] (the records are ancient). [23] They were the potters who lived in Netaim and Gederah; they lived there with the king in his service.

Simeon's line

[24] Simeon's family: Nemuel, Jamin, Jarib, Zerah, Shaul, [25] his son Shallum, his son Mibsam, and his son Mishma. [26] Mishma's family: his son Hammuel, his son Zaccur, and his son Shimei. [27] Shimei had sixteen sons and six daughters; but his brothers didn't have many children, and none of their clans became as numerous as the Judeans.

[28] They lived in Beer-sheba, Moladah, Hazar-shual, [29] Bilhah, Ezem, Tolad, [30] Bethuel, Hormah, Ziklag, [31] Beth-marcaboth,

---

[n] Cf 1 Chron 2:19; MT *Carmi* [o] LXX; MT *father* [p] Qere, LXX; Kethib *Izhar* [q] Heb sounds like *Jabez*. [r] LXX, Vulg; MT lacks *Meonothai*. [s] Or *the valley of skilled workers* [t] Cf 4:13; MT *the family of Elah and Kenaz* [u] LXX, Vulg; MT *son* [v] LXX; MT *and she conceived* [w] LXX; MT *the wife of Hodiah* [x] Or *ruled over* [y] Cf Tg, Vulg; MT *Lehem returned*

Hazar-susim, Beth-biri, and Shaaraim. These were their towns until David became king. [32]Their villages were Etam, Ain, Rimmon, Tochen, and Ashan—five towns—[33]as well as all their villages around these towns as far as Baal. These were their settlements, and they kept their own family records:

[34]Meshobab, Jamlech, Joshah son of Amaziah, [35]Joel, Jehu son of Joshibiah son of Seraiah son of Asiel, [36]Elioenai, Jaakobah, Jeshohaiah, Asaiah, Adiel, Jesimiel, Benaiah, [37]and Ziza son of Shiphi son of Allon son of Jedaiah son of Shimri son of Shemaiah. [38]These mentioned by name were leaders in their clans, and their households increased greatly.

[39]They went to the entrance of Gedor, as far as the east side of the valley, to find pasture for their flocks. [40]They found fertile pasture, and the land was spacious, quiet, and peaceful; the people of Ham used to live there. [41]These whose names were recorded, however, came in the days of Judah's King Hezekiah, attacked their tents and the Meunim[z] found there, and completely destroyed them, as can be seen today. They settled in their place, because there was pasture there for their flocks. [42]Some of them, five hundred Simeonites, went to Mount Seir, led by Pelatiah, Neariah, Rephaiah, and Uzziel, Ishi's sons. [43]They struck down those who were left of the Amalekites and have lived there ever since.

Lines of Reuben, Gad, and East Manasseh

5 The family of Reuben, Israel's oldest son: he was actually the oldest, but when he dishonored his father's bed his birthright[a] was given to the family of Joseph, Israel's son, so Reuben isn't listed as the oldest in the records. [2]Although Judah became the strongest among his brothers and a leader came from him, the birthright belonged to Joseph.

[3]The family of Reuben, Israel's oldest son: Hanoch, Pallu, Hezron, and Carmi. [4]Joel's family: his son Shemaiah, his son Gog, his son Shimei, [5]his son Micah, his son Reaiah, his son Baal, [6]and his son Beerah, whom Assyria's King Tilgath-pilneser carried away into exile. He was a chief of the Reubenites. [7]His relatives, by their[b] clans when their genealogy was listed in the records, were: Jeiel the first; Zechariah; [8]and Bela, Azaz's son, Shema's grandson, and Joel's great-grandson.

They lived in Aroer, as far as Nebo and Baal-meon. [9]They also settled in the east as far as the edge of the desert that stretches to the Euphrates River, because their livestock had increased in the land of Gilead. [10]In Saul's days they waged war on the Hagrites, whom they defeated. So they lived in their tents throughout the entire region east of Gilead.

[11]Gad's family lived opposite them in the land of Bashan as far as Salecah: [12]Joel was the first, Shapham the second, and Janai governed[c] Bashan.

[13]Their relatives according to their households: Michael, Meshullam, Sheba, Jorai, Jacan, Zia, and Eber—seven in all. [14]This was the family of Abihail son of Huri son of Jaroah son of Gilead son of Michael son of Jeshishai son of Jahdo son of Buz. [15]Ahi, Abdiel's son and Guni's grandson, was the head of their household.

[16]They lived in Gilead, in Bashan and in its towns, and as far as the boundaries of all the open lands of Sharon. [17]They were all listed in the records in the days of Judah's King Jotham and Israel's King Jeroboam. [18]The Reubenites, the Gadites, and half the tribe of Manasseh were warriors who carried shield and sword, drew the bow, and were trained for war—44,760 ready for military service. [19]When they waged war on the Hagrites (the Jeturites, the Naphishites, and the Nodabites), [20]they received help against them. The Hagrites and all who were with them were handed over to them, because they cried out to God in battle. God granted their prayer because they trusted in him. [21]They seized their

[z]Qere; Kethib *Meinim*   [a]Or *oldest son's rights*   [b]LXX[L], Syr; MT *his*   [c]LXX, Tg; MT *Shaphatin*

livestock: 50,000 of their camels, 250,000 sheep and goats, 2,000 donkeys, and 100,000 captives. [22]Many died, because God fought the battle. They lived there in place of the inhabitants until the exile.

[23]The members of half the tribe of Manasseh lived in the land from Bashan to Baal-hermon, Senir, and Mount Hermon. They were very numerous.

[24]These were the heads of their households:

Epher, Ishi, Eliel, Azriel, Jeremiah, Hodaviah, and Jahdiel—mighty warriors, famous men, heads of their households.

[25]But they were unfaithful to the God of their ancestors and faithlessly followed the gods of the peoples of the land, whom God had destroyed before them. [26]As a result, Israel's God stirred up the spirit of Assyria's King Pul, otherwise known as Assyria's King Tilgath-pilneser, who led the Reubenites, the Gadites, and half the tribe of Manasseh into exile, and brought them to Halah, Habor, Hara, and the Gozan River, where they remain to this day.

High priests

6 [d]Levi's family: Gershom, Kohath, and Merari.

[2]Kohath's family: Amram, Izhar, Hebron, and Uzziel.

[3]Amram's family: Aaron, Moses, and Miriam.

Aaron's family: Nadab, Abihu, Eleazar, and Ithamar.

[4]Eleazar was the father of Phinehas, Phinehas of Abishua, [5]Abishua of Bukki, Bukki of Uzzi, [6]Uzzi of Zerahiah, Zerahiah of Meraioth, [7]Meraioth of Amariah, Amariah of Ahitub, [8]Ahitub of Zadok, Zadok of Ahimaaz, [9]Ahimaaz of Azariah, Azariah of Johanan, [10]and Johanan of Azariah. He was the one who served as priest in the temple that Solomon built in Jerusalem.

[11]Azariah was the father of Amariah, Amariah of Ahitub, [12]Ahitub of Zadok, Zadok of Shallum, [13]Shallum of Hilkiah,

Hilkiah of Azariah, [14]Azariah of Seraiah, and Seraiah of Jehozadak. [15]Jehozadak went away when the LORD caused Judah and Jerusalem to be exiled by Nebuchadnezzar.

Levites

[16e]Levi's family: Gershom, Kohath, and Merari.

[17]These are the names of Gershom's family: Libni and Shimei.

[18]Kohath's family: Amram, Izhar, Hebron, and Uzziel.

[19]Merari's family: Mahli and Mushi.

These are the Levites' clans according to their fathers:

[20]Of Gershom: his son Libni, his son Jahath, his son Zimmah, [21]his son Joah, his son Iddo, his son Zerah, and his son Jeatherai.

[22]Kohath's family: his son Amminadab, his son Korah, his son Assir, [23]his son Elkanah, his son Ebiasaph, his son Assir, [24]his son Tahath, his son Uriel, his son Uzziah, and his son Shaul.

[25]Elkanah's family: Amasai and Ahimoth, [26]his son Elkanah,[f] his son Zophai, his son Nahath, [27]his son Eliab, his son Jeroham, and his son Elkanah.

[28]Samuel's family: the oldest Joel,[g] and the second Abijah.

[29]Merari's family: Mahli, his son Libni, his son Shimei, his son Uzzah, [30]his son Shimea, his son Haggiah, and his son Asaiah.

Levitical singers

[31]David put the following in charge of the music in the LORD's house after the chest was placed there. [32]They ministered with song before the dwelling of the meeting tent, until Solomon built the LORD's temple in Jerusalem. They carried out their usual duties. [33]Those who served and their families were:

Kohath's family: Heman the singer, son of Joel son of Samuel [34]son of Elkanah son of Jeroham son of Eliel of Toah [35]son of Zuph son of Elkanah

---

[d]5:27 in Heb [e]6:1 in Heb [f]LXX; MT repeats *Elkanah*. [g]LXX, Syr; MT lacks *Joel*.

son of Mahath son of Amasai [36]son of Elkanah son of Joel son of Azariah son of Zephaniah [37]son of Tahath son of Assir son of Ebiasaph son of Korah [38]son of Izhar son of Kohath son of Levi son of Israel. [39]His relative was Asaph, who stood on his right, that is, Asaph son of Berechiah son of Shimea [40]son of Michael son of Baaseiah son of Malchijah [41]son of Ethni son of Zerah son of Adaiah [42]son of Ethan son of Zimmah son of Shimei [43]son of Jahath son of Gershom son of Levi.

[44]On the left were their relatives, Merari's family: Ethan son of Kishi son of Abdi son of Malluch [45]son of Hashabiah son of Amaziah son of Hilkiah [46]son of Amzi son of Bani son of Shemer [47]son of Mahli son of Mushi son of Merari son of Levi. [48]Their relatives the Levites were dedicated to all the services of the dwelling for God's house.

Priests from Aaron's line

[49]Aaron and his sons sacrificed on the altar for entirely burned offerings and on the altar for incense, doing all the work of the holiest place, to make reconciliation for Israel, just as Moses, God's servant, had commanded.

[50]This was Aaron's family: his son Eleazar, his son Phinehas, his son Abishua, [51]his son Bukki, his son Uzzi, his son Zerahiah, [52]his son Meraioth, his son Amariah, his son Ahitub, [53]his son Zadok, and his son Ahimaaz.

Levitical cities

[54]"These are the places they lived by their camps within their territory. To Aaron's family from the Kohathite clan, as chosen by lot, [55]they gave Hebron in the land of Judah with its surrounding pasturelands. [56]But the city's fields and its settlements they gave to Caleb, Jephunneh's son. [57]To Aaron's family they gave the refuge cities: Hebron, Libnah with its pasturelands, Jattir, Eshtemoa with its pasturelands,

[58]Hilen[h] with its pasturelands, Debir with its pasturelands, [59]Ashan with its pasturelands, Juttah with its pasturelands,[i] and Beth-shemesh with its pasturelands. [60]From Benjamin's tribe: Gibeon with its pasturelands,[j] Geba with its pasturelands, Alemeth with its pasturelands, and Anathoth with its pasturelands. They had thirteen towns within their clan.

[61]The remaining Kohathites were given ten towns by lot from the clan of half the tribe of Manasseh. [62]The Gershomites received by lot according to their clans thirteen towns from the tribes of Issachar, Asher, Naphtali, and Manasseh in Bashan. [63]The Merarites received by lot according to their clans twelve towns from the tribes of Reuben, Gad, and Zebulun. [64]In this way the Israelites gave the Levites the towns with their pasturelands. [65]They gave these towns, which they designated by name, by lot from the tribes of Judah, Simeon, and Benjamin.

[66]Some of the Kohathite clans had towns of their territory from the tribe of Ephraim. [67]They gave them refuge cities: Shechem with its pasturelands in the Ephraimite highlands, Gezer with its pasturelands, [68]Jokmeam with its pasturelands, Bethhoron with its pasturelands, [69]Aijalon with its pasturelands, Gath-rimmon with its pasturelands; [70]and from half the tribe of Manasseh, Taanach[k] with its pasturelands, and Bileam with its pasturelands, for the Kohathite clans who remained.

[71]To the Gershomites from the clan of half the tribe of Manasseh: Golan in Bashan with its pasturelands and Ashtaroth with its pasturelands; [72]from the tribe of Issachar: Kedesh with its pasturelands and Daberath with its pasturelands,[73]Ramoth with its pasturelands and Anem with its pasturelands; [74]from the tribe of Asher: Mashal with its pasturelands, Abdon with its pasturelands, and [75]Helkath[l] with its pasturelands and Rehob with its pasturelands; [76]and from the tribe of Naphtali: Kedesh in Galilee with its pasturelands,

[h]LXX, cf Josh 15:51; MT *Hilez* [i]LXX, Syr, cf Josh 21:16; MT lacks *Juttah.* [j]Cf Josh 21:17; MT lacks *Gibeon.*
[k]Cf Josh 21:25; MT *Aner* [l]Cf Josh 21:31; MT *Hukkok*

Hammon with its pasturelands, and Kiriathaim with its pasturelands. ⁷⁷To the remaining Merarites from the tribe of Zebulun: Jokneam with its pasturelands,ᵐ Rimmonⁿ with its pasturelands, Tabor with its pasturelands, and Nahalal with its pasturelands;ᵒ ⁷⁸on the other side of the Jordan at Jericho, on the east side of the Jordan, from the tribe of Reuben: Bezer in the desert with its pasturelands, Jahzah with its pasturelands, ⁷⁹Kedemoth with its pasturelands, and Mephaath with its pasturelands; ⁸⁰and from the tribe of Gad: Ramoth in Gilead with its pasturelands, Mahanaim with its pasturelands, ⁸¹Heshbon with its pasturelands, and Jazer with its pasturelands.

Issachar's line

7 Issachar's family: Tola, Puah, Jashub, and Shimron—four in all. ²Tola's family: Uzzi, Rephaiah, Jeriel, Jahmai, Ibsam, and Shemuel—the heads of their households in Tola's line, mighty warriors of their generations. In David's time they numbered 22,600. ³Uzzi's family: Izrahiah; and Izrahiah's family—Michael, Obadiah, Joel, and Isshiah—five in all, and all of them leaders. ⁴According to the family records of their households, they had 36,000 troops in the units of their fighting force, since they had many wives and children. ⁵Their relatives from all of Issachar's clans were 87,000 mighty warriors, all listed in the family records.

Lines of Benjamin and Naphtali

⁶Benjamin's family:ᵖ Bela, Becher, and Jediael—three in all. ⁷Bela's family: Ezbon, Uzzi, Uzziel, Jerimoth, and Iri—five heads of households, mighty warriors; 22,034 were listed in their family records. ⁸Becher's family: Zemirah, Joash, Eliezer, Elioenai, Omri, Jeremoth, Abijah, Anathoth, and Alemeth. These were all Becher's family. ⁹As listed in their

family records by generation, as heads of their households, mighty warriors, there were 22,200. ¹⁰Jediael's family: Bilhan.

Bilhan's family: Jeush, Benjamin, Ehud, Chenaanah, Zethan, Tarshish, and Ahishahar. ¹¹All these were Jediael's family, heads of their households, and mighty warriors. There were 17,200 ready for battle. ¹²The Shuppites and Huppites were Ir's family, and the Hushites were Aher's family.

¹³Naphtali's family: Jahziel, Guni, Jezer, and Shallum. These were Bilhah's family.

Manasseh's line

¹⁴Manasseh's family: Asriel, to whom his Aramean secondary wife gave birth. She gave birth to Machir, Gilead's father. ¹⁵Machir married Huppite and Shuppite women. His sister's name was Maacah. The second descendant's name was Zelophehad, who had only daughters. ¹⁶Machir's wife Maacah gave birth to a son and named him Peresh. His brother's name was Sheresh, and his sons were Ulam and Rekem. ¹⁷Ulam's family: Bedan.

This was the family of Gilead, Machir's son and Manasseh's grandson. ¹⁸His sister Hammolecheth gave birth to Ishhod, Abiezer, Mahlah, and Shemida.�q ¹⁹The members of Shemida's family were Ahian, Shechem, Likhi, and Aniam.

Ephraim's line

²⁰Ephraim's family: Shuthelah, his son Bered, his son Tahath, his son Eleadah, his son Tahath, ²¹his son Zabad, his son Shuthelah, and Ezer and Elead. The men of Gath, who were born in the land, killed them when they came down to take their cattle. ²²Ephraim their father mourned many days, and his brothers came to comfort him. ²³Ephraim had sex with his wife, and she conceived and gave birth to a son. He

---

ᵐCf Josh 21:34; MT lacks *Jokneam*. ⁿLXX; MT *Rimmono* ᵒCf Josh 21:35; MT lacks *Nahalal*. ᵖLXX; MT lacks *family*. qCf 7:19, Josh 17:2; MT lacks *and Shemida*.

named him Beriah, because misfortune had come to his house. [24] His daughter was Sheerah. She built both Lower and Upper Beth-horon and Uzzen-sheerah. [25] His son was Rephah, his son[r] Resheph, his son Telah, his son Tahan, [26] his son Ladan, his son Ammihud, his son Elishama, [27] his son Nun, and his son Joshua. [28] Their possessions and settlements were Bethel and its towns, to the east Naaran, and to the west Gezer and its towns, and Shechem and its towns as far as Ayyah and its towns. [29] Beth-shean and its towns, Taanach and its towns, Megiddo and its towns, and Dor and its towns were under Manassite authority. The family of Joseph, Israel's son, lived in them.

Asher's line

[30] Asher's family: Imnah, Ishvah, Ishvi, Beriah, and their sister Serah. [31] Beriah's family: Heber and Malchiel, who was Birzaith's father. [32] Heber was the father of Japhlet, Shomer, Hotham, and their sister Shua.

[33] Japhlet's family: Pasach, Bimhal, and Ashvath. This is Japhlet's family.

[34] Shemer's family: Ahi, Rohgah, Jehubbah, and Aram.

[35] His brother Helem's family: Zophah, Imna, Shelesh, and Amal.

[36] Zophah's family: Suah, Harnepher, Shual, Beri, Imrah, [37] Bezer, Hod, Shamma, Shilshah, Ithran, and Beera.

[38] Jether's family: Jephunneh, Pispa, and Ara.

[39] Ulla's family: Arah, Hanniel, and Rizia. [40] All these were Asher's family, heads of households, select mighty warriors, the heads of the princes. Those ready for battle listed in the records numbered 26,000.

Benjamin's line

8 Benjamin was the father of Bela his oldest son, Ashbel his second son, Aharah the third, [2] Nohah the fourth, and Rapha the fifth.

[3] Bela had a family: Addar, Gera, Abihud, [4] Abishua, Naaman, Ahoah, [5] Gera, Shephuphan, and Huram.

[6] This was Ehud's family. They were heads of households of the inhabitants of Geba, who were sent into exile to Manahath. [7] Gera[s] sent them into exile and was the father of Uzza and Ahihud.

[8] Shaharaim had children in the country of Moab after he divorced his wives Hushim and Baara. [9] He had children with his wife Hodesh: Jobab, Zibia, Mesha, Malcam, [10] Jeuz, Sachia, and Mirmah. These were his sons, heads of households. [11] He also had children with Hushim: Abitub and Elpaal.

[12] Elpaal's family: Eber, Misham, Shemed, who built Ono and Lod with its towns, [13] Beriah, and Shema. They were heads of households of the inhabitants of Aijalon, who drove out the inhabitants of Gath. [14] Their brothers[t] were Shashak and Jeremoth.

[15] Beriah's family: Zebadiah, Arad, Eder, [16] Michael, Ishpah, and Joha.

[17] Elpaal's family: Zebadiah, Meshullam, Hizki, Heber, [18] Ishmerai, Izliah, and Jobab.

[19] Shimei's family: Jakim, Zichri, Zabdi, [20] Elienai, Zillethai, Eliel, [21] Adaiah, Beraiah, and Shimrath.

[22] Shashak's family: Ishpan, Eber, Eliel, [23] Abdon, Zichri, Hanan, [24] Hananiah, Omri,[u] Elam, Anthothijah, [25] Iphdeiah, and Penuel.

[26] Jeroham's family: Shamsherai, Shehariah, Athaliah, [27] Jaareshiah, Elijah, and Zichri.

[28] These were the heads of households, in their generations. They were leaders who lived in Jerusalem. [29] Jeiel,[v] Gibeon's father, lived in Gibeon. His wife's name was Maacah; [30] his oldest son was Abdon, then Zur, Kish, Baal, Ner,[w] Nadab, [31] Gedor, Ahio, Zecher, and Mikloth. [32] Mikloth was the father of Shimeah. These also lived near their relatives in Jerusalem.[x]

---

[r]MT lacks *his son*.　[s]MT *Naaman, Ahijah, and Gera*　[t]LXX; MT *Ahio*　[u]LXX; MT lacks *Omri*.　[v]LXX; MT lacks *Jeiel*.
[w]LXX; MT lacks *Ner*.　[x]Syr; MT adds *with their relatives*.

33 Ner was the father of Kish, Kish was the father of Saul, and Saul was the father of Jonathan, Malchishua, Abinadab, and Esh-baal.

34 Jonathan's son was Merib-baal, and Merib-baal was Micah's father.

35 Micah's family: Pithon, Melech, Tarea, and Ahaz.

36 Ahaz was the father of Jehoaddah; Jehoaddah was the father of Alemeth, Azmaveth, and Zimri; and Zimri was the father of Moza. 37 Moza was the father of Binea; his son was Raphah, his son Eleasah, and his son Azel. 38 Azel had six sons, named Azrikam, his oldest,[y] Ishmael, Sheariah, Azariah,[z] Obadiah, and Hanan. All these were in Azel's family.

39 His brother Eshek's family: Ulam his oldest, Jeush the second, and Eliphelet the third. 40 Ulam's family were mighty warriors and archers, having many children and grandchildren—150 in all and all were Benjaminites.

9 So all Israel was listed in the official records of Israel's kings.

Restored Jerusalem community

Judah was carried into exile in Babylon because of their unfaithfulness. 2 The first to resettle their property in their towns were the Israelite people, the priests, the Levites, and the temple servants. 3 Those settling in Jerusalem included some from Judah, some from Benjamin, and some from Ephraim and Manasseh:

Judah and Benjamin

4 Uthai son of Ammihud son of Omri son of Imri son of Bani from the family of Perez, Judah's son.

5 From the Shilonites: Asaiah the oldest son and his family.

6 From Zerah's family: Jeuel and their relatives—690 in all.

7 From Benjamin's family: Sallu son of Meshullam son of Hodaviah son of Senaah;[a] 8 Ibneiah, Jeroham's son; Elah son of Uzzi son of Michri; Meshullam son of Shephatiah son of Reuel son of

Ibnijah; 9 and their relatives in their line of descent—956 in all. All of these were heads of their households.

Priests and Levites

10 From the priests: Jedaiah, Jehoiarib, Jachin, 11 and Azariah son of Hilkiah son of Meshullam son of Zadok son of Meraioth son of Ahitub the leader of God's house; 12 Adaiah son of Jeroham son of Pashhur son of Malchijah; Maasai son of Adiel son of Jahzerah son of Meshullam son of Meshillemith son of Immer; 13 and their relatives, heads of their households, 1,760 capable men for the religious work of God's house.

14 From the Levites: Shemaiah son of Hasshub son of Azrikam son of Hashabiah, from Merari's family; 15 Bakbakkar, Heresh, Galal, and Mattaniah son of Mica son of Zichri son of Asaph; 16 Obadiah son of Shemaiah son of Galal son of Jeduthun; and Berechiah son of Asa son of Elkanah, who lived in the settlements of the Netophathites.

Gatekeepers

17 The gatekeepers: Shallum, Akkub, Talmon, and Ahiman. Their brother Shallum was the leader, 18 stationed until now in the King's Gate on the east side. These were the gatekeepers belonging to the Levites' camp.

19 Shallum, Kore's son, Ebiasaph's grandson, and Korah's great-grandson, and his relatives belonging to his household, the Korahites, served as gatekeepers at the tent's entrances, as their ancestors had been gatekeepers at the entrance to the LORD's camp.

20 Phinehas, Eleazar's son, the LORD be with him, was their leader in former times.

21 Zechariah, Meshelemiah's son, was gatekeeper at the meeting tent's entrance.

22 All those selected as gatekeepers at the entrances were two hundred twelve. They were listed in the family records by their

settlements. David and Samuel the seer assigned them to their trusted position. [23]So they and their descendants were the gatekeepers guarding the LORD's house, that is, the tent.[b] [24]The gatekeepers were on the four sides: east, west, north, and south. [25]Their relatives came in from their settlements, from time to time, to assist them for a period of seven days. [26]Due to their trustworthiness, the four master gatekeepers, who were Levites, were in charge of the rooms and the treasuries of God's house. [27]They would spend the night patrolling God's house since they had guard duty and were responsible for unlocking it every morning. [28]Some of them were responsible for the worship objects; they counted them when they were brought in and taken out. [29]Others were appointed over the furniture, the holy equipment, the flour, wine, oil, incense, and spices. [30]Some of the priests blended the ointment for the spices; [31]and Mattithiah, one of the Levites, the oldest son of Shallum the Korahite, was entrusted with baking the flat cakes. [32]Also some of their Kohathite relatives were responsible for preparing the stacks of bread for each Sabbath. [33]The singers were the heads of the households of the Levites. They lived in temple rooms and were free from other service because they were on duty day and night. [34]These were the heads of the households of the Levites, according to descent. They lived in Jerusalem.

Saul's family

[35]Jeiel, Gibeon's father, lived in Gibeon. His wife's name was Maacah.

[36]His oldest son was Abdon, followed by Zur, Kish, Baal, Ner, Nadab, [37]Gedor, Ahio, Zechariah, and Mikloth. [38]Mikloth was the father of Shimeam. They too lived near their relatives in Jerusalem.[c] [39]Ner was the father of Kish, Kish of Saul, Saul of Jonathan, Malchishua, Abinadab, and Esh-baal.

[40]Jonathan's son was Merib-baal, and Merib-baal was the father of Micah. [41]Micah's family were Pithon, Melech, Tahrea, and Ahaz.[d] [42]Ahaz was the father of Jarah; and Jarah of Alemeth, Azmaveth, and Zimri.

Zimri was the father of Moza. [43]Moza was the father of Binea; Rephaiah was his son, Eleasah was his son, and Azel was his son. [44]Azel had six sons whose names were Azrikam, Bocheru, Ishmael, Sheariah, Obadiah, and Hanan. This was Azel's family.

Saul's death

10 When the Philistines attacked the Israelites, the Israelites ran away from the Philistines, and many fell dead on Mount Gilboa. [2]The Philistines overtook Saul and his sons, and they killed his sons Jonathan, Abinadab, and Malchishua. [3]The battle was fierce around Saul, and when the archers located him, he trembled in fear. [4]Saul said to his armor-bearer, "Draw your sword and kill me with it! Otherwise, these uncircumcised men will come and kill me or torture me." But his armor-bearer refused because he was terrified. So Saul took the sword and impaled himself on it. [5]When the armor-bearer saw that Saul was dead,

[b]Or house of the tent [c]Heb adds with their relatives. [d]Cf 8:35; MT lacks Ahaz.

BREAD OF THE PRESENCE

Sometimes translated as "showbread," the bread of the presence refers to the two stacks of six unleavened breads (symbolizing the 12 tribes of Israel) that were weekly placed by the high priest on the gold table in the temple in the vicinity of the covenant dwelling (Exod 35:13; 1 Kgs 7:48; 1 Chron 9:32; Num 4:7).

he also impaled himself on his sword and died with Saul. ⁶So Saul and his three sons died; his whole household died together. ⁷When all the Israelites who were in the valley saw that the army had run away and that Saul and his sons were dead, they abandoned their towns and fled. So the Philistines came to live in them.

⁸The next day when the Philistines came to strip the dead, they found Saul and his sons lying dead on Mount Gilboa. ⁹They stripped him, carried off his head and armor, and sent messengers throughout the land of the Philistines to spread the news to their idols and to the people. ¹⁰They placed his armor in their god's temple and displayed his skull on a pole in the temple of Dagon.

¹¹When all the people of Jabesh-gilead heard all that the Philistines had done to Saul, ¹²all their warriors arose and recovered the corpses of Saul and his sons. They brought them back to Jabesh, buried their bones under the oak in Jabesh, and fasted for seven days.

¹³Saul died because he was unfaithful to the LORD and hadn't followed the LORD's word. He even consulted a medium for guidance. ¹⁴He didn't consult the LORD, so the LORD killed him and gave the kingdom to David, Jesse's son.

All Israel makes David king

11 All the Israelites gathered around David at Hebron. "We're your own flesh and blood," they said. ²"In the past, even when Saul ruled over us, you were the one who led Israel. The LORD your God told you, 'You will shepherd my people Israel, and you will become a leader over my people Israel.'" ³So all of Israel's elders came to the king at Hebron, and David made a covenant with them before the LORD. They anointed David to make him king over Israel, just as the LORD had promised through Samuel.

David captures Jerusalem

⁴Then David and all Israel marched to Jerusalem, that is, Jebus, where the Jebusites lived. ⁵The people who lived in Jebus told David, "You'll never get in here!"

But David captured the mountain fortress of Zion, which became David's City. ⁶David had said, "The first one to kill a Jebusite will become commander in chief!" Joab, Zeruiah's son, was the first to attack and so became commander in chief. ⁷David occupied the fortress, so it was renamed David's City. ⁸He also built up the city on all sides, including its own foundations and the surrounding areas, while Joab restored the rest of the city. ⁹David grew increasingly powerful, and the LORD of heavenly forces was with him.

David and his warriors

¹⁰These are the commanders of David's warriors who continued to support him while he was king. Together with all Israel, they made him king, as the LORD had promised Israel. ¹¹This is the list of David's warriors:

Jashobeam, a Hacmonite, was commander of the Thirty. He raised his spear against eight hundred, killing them on a single occasion.

¹²Next in command came Eleazar, Dodo's son the Ahohite, who was one of the three warriors. ¹³He was with David at Pasdammim. The Philistines were gathered there for battle, where part of a field was full of barley. When the people ran away from the Philistines, ¹⁴he and David stood in the middle of the field, held their ground, and defeated the Philistines. So the LORD achieved a great victory.

¹⁵Three of the thirty commanders went down from the rock to David at the fortress[e] of Adullam, while the army of the Philistines camped in the Rephaim Valley. ¹⁶At that time David was in the fortress, and a Philistine fort was in Bethlehem. ¹⁷David had a craving and said, "If only someone could give me a drink of water from the well by the gate in Bethlehem." ¹⁸So the three warriors broke through the Philistine camp and drew water from the well by the gate in Bethlehem and brought

---

ᵉOr cave; cf 2 Sam 23:14

it back to David. But he refused to drink it and poured it out to the LORD.

¹⁹"God forbid that I should do that," he said. "Isn't this the blood of men who risked their lives?" So he refused to drink it. Since they had brought it at the risk of their lives, David refused to drink it.

These were the kinds of things the three warriors did.

²⁰Abishai, Joab's brother, was chief of the Thirty.ᶠ He raised his spear against the three hundred men he had slain, but he wasn't considered one of the Three. ²¹He was the most famous of the Thirty. He became their commander, but he wasn't among the Three.

²²Benaiah, Jehoiada's son from Kabzeel, was a hero who performed great deeds. He killed two of Moab's leaders,ᵍ and on a snowy day went down into a pit where he killed a lion. ²³He also killed an Egyptian seven and a half feet tall, who was holding a spear like a weaver's beam. Benaiah went down to him with a club, grabbed the spear from the Egyptian's hand, and killed him with it. ²⁴These were the exploits of Benaiah, Jehoiada's son; he wasn't considered one of the three warriors. ²⁵He was famous among the Thirty, but didn't become one of the Three. David placed him in command of his own bodyguard.

²⁶The mighty warriors:

Asahel, Joab's brother;
Elhanan, Dodo's son from Bethlehem;
²⁷Shammoth from Haror;
Helez from Pelon;
²⁸Ira, Ikkesh's son from Tekoa;
Abiezer from Anathoth;
²⁹Sibbecai the Hushathite;
Ilai from Ahoh;
³⁰Maharai from Netophah;
Heled, Baanah's son from Netophah;
³¹Ithai, Ribai's son
from Gibeah of the Benjaminites;
Benaiah from Pirathon;
³²Hurai from the Gaash ravines;
Abiel the Arbathite;
³³Azmaveth from Baharum;
Eliahba from Shaalbon;
³⁴Hashemʰ the Gizonite;
Jonathan, Shagee's son from Harar;
³⁵Ahiam, Sachar's son from Harar;
Eliphal, Ur's son;
³⁶Hepher the Mecherathite;
Ahijah the Pelonite;
³⁷Hezro from Carmel;
Naarai, Ezbai's son;
³⁸Joel, Nathan's brother;
Mibhar, Hagri's son;
³⁹Zelek the Ammonite;
Naharai from Beeroth, Zeruiah's son
and the armor-bearer for Joab;
⁴⁰Ira from Ither;
Gareb from Ither;
⁴¹Uriah the Hittite;
Zabad, Ahlai's son;
⁴²Adina son of Shiza the Reubenite,
a leader of the Reubenites,
and thirty with him;
⁴³Hanan, Maacah's son;
Joshaphat the Mithnite;
⁴⁴Uzzia the Ashterathite;

ᶠSyr; MT three ᵍHeb Ariel ʰMT the family of Hashem

PHILISTINES

A people located on the southern coastal strip of ancient Canaan during the Iron Age. According to the OT, the Philistines were organized in a confederation of five city-states (or Pentapolis), consisting of Ashdod, Ashkelon, Ekron, Gath, and Gaza, which were under the control of rulers referred to as "tyrants." The Philistines are presented as enemies of the Israelites, particularly during the period of the transition from a tribal to a monarchical society.

Shama and Jeiel
  the sons of Hotham the Aroerite;
⁴⁵Jediael, Shimri's son,
  and his brother Joha the Tizite;
⁴⁶Eliel the Mahavite;
  Jeribai and Joshaviah, Elnaam's sons;
  Ithmah the Moabite;
⁴⁷Eliel, Obed, and Jaasiel the
  Mezobaite.

David's desert army

12 The following persons came to David at Ziklag while he was banished from the presence of Saul, Kish's son. They were some of the warriors who helped him in battle, ²armed with bows, and they could use either hand to shoot arrows or sling stones. They were Saul's relatives from Benjamin:

³Ahiezer was the leader, then Joash, both Shemaah's sons from Gibeah; Jeziel and Pelet, Azmaveth's sons; Beracah; Jehu of Anathoth; ⁴Ishmaiah from Gibeon, a warrior in the Thirty and a leader over the Thirty;ⁱ Jeremiah; Jahaziel; Johanan; Jozabad from Gederah; ⁵ʲEluzai; Jerimoth; Bealiah; Shemariah; Shephatiah the Haruphite; ⁶Elkanah, Isshiah, Azarel, Joezer, and Jashobeam the Korahites; ⁷Joelah; and Zebadiah, Jeroham's son from Gedor.

⁸Some left Gad to join David at the desert fortress, brave warriors trained for battle, armed with shield and spear, who looked like lions and who were swift as gazelles on the mountains: ⁹Ezer the leader, Obadiah second, Eliab third, ¹⁰Mishmannah fourth, Jeremiah fifth, ¹¹Attai sixth, Eliel seventh, ¹²Johanan eighth, Elzabad ninth, ¹³Jeremiah tenth, Machbannai eleventh.

¹⁴These Gadites were military officers, the least of them ready to fight a hundred and the greatest a thousand. ¹⁵These are the ones who crossed the Jordan in the first month, when it was overflowing all its banks, and chased away everyone living in the valleys to the east and the west.

¹⁶Some Benjaminites and Judahites also came to David at the fortress. ¹⁷David went out to meet them and said to them, "If you've come to me with good intentions in order to help me, then we will join forces. But if you've come to betray me to my enemies, though I've done no wrong, then may our ancestors' God see it and punish you."

¹⁸Then a spirit took hold of Amasai, the leader of the Thirty:

David, we are yours;
  and on your side, Jesse's son!
May it go very well for you,
  and may it go well for whoever helps you!
Yes, your God has helped you.

Then David received them, and put them at the head of his troops.

¹⁹Some of the Manassites also joined David when he came with the Philistines for the battle against Saul. But heᵏ didn't help them, because after considering the matter, the Philistine rulers sent him away. "He'll rejoin his master Saul," they said, "and it will cost us our heads." ²⁰When he went to Ziklag some joined him from Manasseh: Adnah, Jozabad, Jediael, Michael, Jozabad, Elihu, and Zillethai, leaders of units of a thousand in Manasseh. ²¹They helped David against the raiding bands because they were all warriors and officers in the army. ²²Reinforcements came to David daily until there was an army as mighty as God's army.

²³These are the numbers of the commanders of those armed for battle who came to David in Hebron to make sure he took over Saul's kingdom, according to the LORD's word:

²⁴from Judah, carrying shield and spear,
  6,800 troops armed for battle;
²⁵from Simeon, mighty warriors, 7,100;
²⁶from Levi, 4,600;
²⁷also Jehoiada, leader of Aaron's line,
  and with him 3,700;
²⁸and Zadok, a young man, a mighty
  warrior, and 22 officers from his
  household;
²⁹from Benjamin, Saul's relatives, 3,000,
  most of whom had been loyal to
  Saul's household;
³⁰from Ephraim, 20,800, mighty warriors,
  famous in their households;

[31] from half the tribe of Manasseh, 18,000, designated by name to come and make David king;

[32] from Issachar, those who understood the times and what Israel should do, 200 chiefs, with all their relatives under their command;

[33] from Zebulun, 50,000 experienced troops, armed for battle with all the weapons of war, to help with undivided loyalty;

[34] from Naphtali, 1,000 officers, as well as 37,000 armed with shield and spear;

[35] from Dan, 28,600 armed for battle;

[36] from Asher, 40,000 experienced troops armed for battle;

[37] from the other side of the Jordan, the Reubenites, Gadites, and the other half of the tribe of Manasseh, 120,000 armed with all the weapons of war.

[38] All these men of war, armed[l] for battle, came to Hebron determined to make David king over all Israel, and all the rest of Israel were fully agreed to make David king. [39] They were there with David for three days, eating and drinking, while their relatives provided food for them. [40] Even their neighbors from as far away as Issachar, Zebulun, and Naphtali were bringing food by donkeys, camels, mules, and oxen. There was an abundance of flour, fig cakes, clusters of raisins, wine, oil, oxen, and sheep, because Israel was joyful.

David's first attempt to move the chest

13 After consulting with the captains of the units of a thousand and a hundred, in fact with every leader, [2] David said to the entire Israelite assembly: "If you approve, and if the LORD our God agrees, let's spread the word to the rest of our relatives in all the regions of Israel, including the priests and Levites in their cities with pasturelands. Let's ask them to join us [3] so that we may bring the chest of our God back to us, because we didn't look for it in Saul's days." [4] The whole assembly agreed to do so, because all the people thought it was the right thing to do.

[5] So David assembled all Israel, from the border[m] of Egypt to Lebo-hamath in order to bring up God's chest from Kiriath-jearim. [6] Then David and all Israel went up toward Baalah, to Kiriath-jearim, which belongs to Judah, to bring up from there the chest of God, the LORD, who sits enthroned on the winged creatures, where he is called by name.[n] [7] They moved God's chest on a new cart from Abinadab's house. Uzzah and Ahio were guiding the cart, [8] while David and all Israel celebrated in God's presence with all their strength, accompanied by songs, zithers, harps, tambourines, cymbals, and trumpets. [9] When they came to Chidon's threshing floor, Uzzah reached out to the chest and grabbed it because the oxen had stumbled. [10] But the LORD became angry with Uzzah and struck him because he had placed his hand on the chest. He died right there before God. [11] David was angry that the LORD lashed out at Uzzah; and so that place is still called Perez-uzzah today. [12] David was frightened by God that day. "How will I ever bring God's chest home to me?" he asked. [13] So David didn't take the chest away with him to David's City. Instead, he had it put in the house of Obed-edom the Gittite. [14] God's chest stayed with Obed-edom's household for three months, and the LORD blessed Obed-edom's household and all that he had.

David's kingship established in Jerusalem

14 Tyre's King Hiram sent messengers to David with cedar logs, bricklayers, and carpenters to build David a palace. [2] Then David knew that the LORD had established him as king over Israel, and that his kingship was held in great honor for the sake of his people Israel. [3] David married more secondary wives in Jerusalem and fathered more sons and daughters. [4] The names of his children in Jerusalem were as follows: Shammua, Shobab, Nathan, Solomon, [5] Ibhar, Elishua, Elpelet, [6] Nogah, Nepheg, Japhia, [7] Elishama, Beeliada, and Eliphelet.

[l] LXX; MT *helpers* [m] Heb *Shikhor, river*; cf Josh 15:4; 1 Kgs 8:65; 2 Chron 7:8 [n] Heb uncertain

David defeats the Philistines

⁸When the Philistines heard that David had been anointed king over all Israel, they all marched up to find him. David heard this and went out to confront them. ⁹The Philistines had invaded and were plundering the Rephaim Valley. ¹⁰David asked God for advice: "Should I attack the Philistines, and will you hand them over to me?"

The LORD answered, "Attack them, and I'll definitely hand them over to you."

¹¹So they marched up to Baal-perazim, and David defeated them there. "By my strength," David exclaimed, "God has burst out against my enemies, the way water bursts out." That's why the place is called Baal-perazim.° ¹²The Philistines left their divine images behind, and David ordered them burned.

¹³When the Philistines plundered the valley a second time, ¹⁴David again asked God's advice, but God answered, "Don't attack them directly. Circle around behind them and come at them from in front of the balsam trees. ¹⁵As soon as you hear the sound of marching in the tops of the trees, then attack, for God has attacked in front of you to defeat the Philistine army." ¹⁶David followed God's orders exactly, and they defeated the Philistine army from Gibeon all the way to Gezer. ¹⁷David's fame spread throughout all lands, and the LORD made all the nations fear him.

David prepares to bring the chest to Jerusalem

15 After he had built houses for himself in David's City, David prepared a place for God's chest and pitched a tent for it. ²David said, "Only the Levites may carry God's chest, because the LORD has chosen them to carry the LORD's chest and to minister to him forever."

³David assembled all Israel in Jerusalem to bring the LORD's chest to the place he had prepared for it. ⁴David also gathered Aaron's family and the Levites:

⁵Uriel, the leader of Kohath's family, and 120 of his relatives;

⁶Asaiah, the leader of Merari's family, and 220 of his relatives;

⁷Joel, the leader of Gershom's family, and 130 of his relatives;

⁸Shemaiah, the leader of Elizaphan's family, and 200 of his relatives;

⁹Eliel, the leader of Hebron's family, and 80 of his relatives;

¹⁰and Amminadab, the leader of Uzziel's family, and 112 of his relatives.

¹¹David called for the priests Zadok and Abiathar, and the Levites Uriel, Asaiah, Joel, Shemaiah, Eliel, and Amminadab. ¹²He said to them, "You are the household heads of the Levites. Make yourselves holy, you and your brothers, and then bring the chest of the LORD, Israel's God, to the place I've prepared for it. ¹³When you weren't with us the first time, the LORD our God burst out against us because we didn't ask his advice properly." ¹⁴So the priests and the Levites made themselves holy to bring up the chest of the LORD, Israel's God. ¹⁵The Levites carried God's chest with poles on their shoulders, just as Moses had commanded according to the LORD's word.

¹⁶Then David told the leaders of the Levites to appoint some of their relatives as singers to raise their voices joyfully, accompanied by musical instruments, including harps, lyres, and cymbals.

¹⁷So the Levites appointed Heman, Joel's son; and from his relatives, Asaph, Berechiah's son; and from their Merarite relatives, Ethan, Kushaiah's son; ¹⁸and second in rank with them their relatives: Zechariah, Jaaziel,ᴾ Shemiramoth, Jehiel, Unni, Eliab, Benaiah, Maaseiah, Mattithiah, Eliphelehu, Mikneiah, and Obed-edom and Jeiel the gatekeepers.

¹⁹The singers Heman, Asaph, and Ethan were to make music with bronze cymbals.

²⁰Zechariah, Aziel, Shemiramoth, Jehiel, Unni, Eliab, Maaseiah, and Benaiah were to play harps tuned to the Alamoth.

²¹Mattithiah, Eliphelehu, Mikneiah, Obed-edom, Jeiel, and Azaziah were to lead with lyres tuned to the Sheminith. ²²Chenaniah was leader of the Levites

---

°Or *master of outbursts* ᴾLXX; MT *Jaaziel's son*

who provided transportation,[q] because he was skilled at it.

[23]Berechiah and Elkanah were gatekeepers for the chest.

[24]The priests Shebaniah, Joshaphat, Nethanel, Amasai, Zechariah, Benaiah, and Eliezer were to blow the trumpets before God's chest. Obed-edom and Jehiah also were to be gatekeepers for the chest.

David brings the chest to Jerusalem

[25]Then David, along with Israel's elders and the captains of the thousands, went with rejoicing to bring up the chest containing the LORD's covenant from Obed-edom's house. [26]Since God had helped the Levites who were carrying the chest containing the LORD's covenant, they sacrificed seven bulls and seven rams. [27]David wore a fine-linen robe, as did the singers, all the Levites who were carrying the chest, and Chenaniah, the leader of transportation.[r] David also wore a linen priestly vest.[s] [28]So all Israel brought up the chest containing the LORD's covenant with shouts of joy, accompanied by the blast of the ram's horn, by trumpets and cymbals, and playing on harps and lyres. [29]As the chest containing the LORD's covenant entered David's City, Michal, Saul's daughter, looked out the window. When she saw King David leaping and dancing, she lost all respect for him.

16 They brought in God's chest and placed it inside the tent David had pitched for it. Then they brought entirely burned offerings and well-being sacrifices before God. [2]When David had finished offering the entirely burned offerings and the well-being sacrifices, he blessed the people in the LORD's name [3]and distributed a loaf of bread, a piece of meat,[t] and a raisin cake to every Israelite man and woman.

David establishes worship

[4]David appointed some of the Levites to serve before the LORD's chest in order to remember, to give thanks, and to praise the LORD, Israel's God: [5]Asaph was the leader, and Zechariah his assistant; also Jeiel, Shemiramoth, Jehiel, Mattithiah, Eliab, Benaiah, Obed-edom, and Jeiel with harps and lyres; Asaph sounding the cymbals; [6]and the priests Benaiah and Jahaziel blowing trumpets regularly before the chest containing God's covenant. [7]On the same day, for the first time, David ordered Asaph and his relatives to give thanks to the LORD.

David's song of praise

[8] Give thanks to the LORD,
    call on his name;
    make his deeds known to all people!
[9] Sing to God, sing praises to him;
    dwell on all his wondrous works!
[10] Give praise to God's holy name!
    Let the hearts rejoice
    of all those seeking the LORD!
[11] Pursue the LORD and his strength;
    seek his face always!
[12] Remember the wondrous works
    he has done,
    all his marvelous works,
    and the justice he declared—
[13] you who are the offspring of Israel,
    his servant,

---

[q]Heb uncertain   [r]MT adds *the singers.*   [s]Heb *ephod*   [t]Cf LXX, Syr, Vulg; Heb uncertain

DAVID

David means "beloved," probably the shortened form of a name meaning "Beloved of Yahweh" or "Yahweh is beloved." David was the second king of united Israel and the founder of the ruling dynasty of Judah, and he was considered a model of kingship. He is a main character in 1 Samuel 16–1, Kings 2, and 1 Chronicles 10–29.

and the children of Jacob,
  his chosen ones.
¹⁴ The LORD—he is our God.
  His justice is everywhere
    throughout the whole world.
¹⁵ God remembers[u] his covenant forever,
  the word he commanded
    to a thousand generations,
¹⁶ which he made with Abraham,
  the solemn pledge he swore to Isaac.
¹⁷ God set it up as binding law for Jacob,
  as an eternal covenant for Israel,
¹⁸ promising, "I hereby give you
  the land of Canaan
  as your allotted inheritance."
¹⁹ When they[v] were few in number—
  insignificant, just immigrants—
²⁰ wandering from nation to nation,
  from one kingdom to the next,
²¹ God didn't let anyone oppress them.
  God punished kings for their sake:
²² "Don't touch my anointed ones;
  don't harm my prophets!"
²³ Sing to the LORD, all the earth!
  Share the news of his saving work
    every single day!
²⁴ Declare God's glory among the nations;
  declare his wondrous works
    among all people
²⁵ because the LORD is great
  and so worthy of praise.
  He is awesome beyond all other gods
²⁶ because all the gods of the nations
  are just idols,
  but it is the LORD who created heaven!
²⁷ Greatness and grandeur
  are in front of him;
  strength and joy are in his place.
²⁸ Give to the LORD,
  all families of the nations—
  give to the LORD glory and power!
²⁹ Give to the LORD the glory due his name!
  Bring gifts! Enter his presence!
  Bow down to the LORD
    in his holy splendor!
³⁰ Tremble before him, all the earth!
  Yes, he set the world firmly in place;[w]
  it won't be shaken.

³¹ Let heaven celebrate!
  Let the earth rejoice!
  Let the nations say, "The LORD rules!"
³² Let the sea and everything in it roar!
  Let the countryside and
    everything in it celebrate!
³³ Then the trees of the forest
  will shout out joyfully
    before the LORD, because he is coming
    to establish justice on earth!
³⁴ Give thanks to the LORD
  because he is good,
  because his faithful love
    endures forever.
³⁵ Say: "Save us, God, our savior!
  Gather us! Deliver us from among
    the nations
  so we can give thanks
    to your holy name
  and rejoice in your praise."
³⁶ Bless the LORD, Israel's God,
  from forever in the past
    to forever always.
  And let all the people say, "Amen!"
    Praise the LORD!

³⁷ Then David placed Asaph and his relatives, together with Obed-edom and sixty-eight of his relatives, to minister there continually before the chest containing the LORD's covenant, following the routines required on each day. ³⁸ Obed-edom, Jeduthun's son, and Hosah served as gatekeepers. ³⁹ David also placed the priest Zadok and his other priestly relatives at the LORD's dwelling at the shrine in Gibeon. ⁴⁰ They were to offer continually, both morning and evening, entirely burned offerings to the LORD on the altar for entirely burned offerings, following the written requirements in the LORD's Instruction, which he had given Israel. ⁴¹ With them were Heman and Jeduthun and the rest of those chosen by name to give thanks to the LORD, because his faithful love lasts forever. ⁴² With them were also[x] the trumpets and the cymbals for the musicians and the instruments for God's songs. Jeduthun's family was at the gate. ⁴³ Then all of the people left for their

---

[u]LXX; MT *Remember*   [v]LXX, Vulg; MT *when you were*   [w]LXX; MT *the world is firmly established*   [x]LXX; MT adds *Heman and Jeduthun.*

homes. And David returned to bless his household.

God's promise to David

17 When David was settled into his palace,[y] he said to the prophet Nathan, "I'm living in a cedar palace while the chest containing the LORD's covenant is under curtains."

[2] Nathan replied, "Go ahead and do whatever you are thinking, because God is with you."

[3] But that very night God's word came to Nathan: [4] "Go to my servant David and tell him, This is what the LORD says: You are not the one to build the temple[z] for me to live in. [5] In fact, I haven't lived in a temple from the day I brought Israel out until this very day. I've been traveling from tent to tent and from dwelling to dwelling.[a] [6] Throughout my traveling with the Israelites, did I ever ask one of Israel's tribal leaders, whom I appointed to shepherd my people, Why haven't you built me a cedar temple?

[7] So then, say this to my servant David: This is what the LORD of heavenly forces says: I myself took you from the pasture, from following the flock, to be leader over my people Israel. [8] I've been with you wherever you've gone. I've eliminated all your enemies before you. Now I will make your name great—like the name of the greatest people on earth. [9] I'm going to provide a place for my people Israel, and plant them so that they may live there and no longer be disturbed. Cruel people will no longer trouble them as they did earlier, [10] when I appointed judges over my people Israel. I'll subdue all your enemies and make you great. As for a dynasty,[b] the LORD will build one for you! [11] When the time comes for you to die, I will raise up a descendant of yours after you, one of your own sons, to succeed you, and I will establish his kingship. [12] He is the one who will build me a temple, and I will establish his throne forever. [13] I will become his father and he will become my son, and I'll never withdraw my faithful

love from him as I did from the one before you. [14] I'll install him in my house and in my kingdom forever, and his throne will be established forever.

[15] Nathan faithfully reported all that he had seen and heard to David.

David's prayer

[16] Then King David went and sat in the LORD's presence. He asked:

Who am I, LORD God, and of what significance is my family that you have brought me this far? [17] But even this was too small in your eyes, God. You have spoken about the future of your servant's dynasty and have chosen me as an important person, LORD God.

[18] What more can I say to you for honoring your servant? You yourself know your servant. [19] LORD, for your servant's sake and according to your will, you have done this great thing in order to make all these great things known.

[20] LORD, no one can compare to you, no God except you, just as we have heard with our own ears.

[21] Who is like your people Israel, a unique nation on the earth, that God redeemed as his own people, establishing a name for yourself by doing great and awesome things, by driving out nations before your people whom you saved from Egypt? [22] You established your people Israel as your own people forever, and you, LORD, became their God.

[23] Now, LORD, confirm forever the promise you have made about your servant and his dynasty. Do as you have promised [24] so that it may be established and so that your name may be made great forever when people say, "The LORD of heavenly forces, the God of Israel, is Israel's God." May your servant David's household be established before you. [25] You, my God, have revealed to your servant that you will build him a dynasty. That is why your servant has found the courage to pray this prayer to

---

[y] Or, here and elsewhere in this chapter, *house*   [z] Or, here and elsewhere in this chapter, *house*   [a] MT lacks *to dwelling.*   [b] Or, here and elsewhere in this chapter, *house*

you. [26]LORD, you are truly God, and you promised this good thing to your servant. [27]So now willingly bless your servant's dynasty so that it might continue forever before you, because you, LORD God, have promised. Let your servant's dynasty be blessed forever by your blessing.

David's wars

18 Some time later, David defeated the Philistines, subdued them, and took Gath and its villages from Philistine control. [2]He also defeated Moab, enslaving them and requiring payment. [3]David defeated Zobah's King Hadadezer at Hamath, as he continued to establish his control along the Euphrates River. [4]David captured one thousand chariots from him, seven thousand cavalry, and twenty thousand foot soldiers. Then David cut the hamstrings of all but one hundred of the chariot horses. [5]When the Arameans of Damascus came to help Zobah's King Hadadezer, David killed twenty-two thousand of the Arameans. [6]David stationed soldiers[c] in Aram of Damascus, enslaved them, and required payment. The LORD gave David victory wherever he went.

[7]David took the gold shields carried by Hadadezer's servants and brought them to Jerusalem. [8]From Tibhath and Cun, Hadadezer's cities, David took large amounts of bronze, with which Solomon made the bronze basin,[d] the pillars, and the bronze equipment.

[9]When Hamath's King Tou heard that David had defeated the entire army of Zobah's King Hadadezer, [10]he sent his son Hadoram to King David to wish him well and to congratulate him over his battle and defeat of Hadadezer, because Tou was an enemy of Hadadezer. Hadoram brought with him all kinds of gold, silver, and bronze objects. [11]King David dedicated these to the LORD along with the silver and the gold he had taken from all these nations: Edom, Moab, the Ammonites, the Philistines, and Amalek. [12]Abishai, Zeruiah's son, struck down eighteen thousand Edomites in the Salt Valley. [13]He stationed soldiers in Edom, and all the Edomites became David's slaves. The LORD gave David victory wherever he went.

David's administration

[14]David ruled over all Israel and maintained justice and righteousness for all his people. [15]Zeruiah's son Joab was in command of the army; Ahilud's son Jehoshaphat was recorder; [16]Ahitub's son Zadok and Abiathar's son Ahimelech[e] were priests; Shavsha was secretary; [17]Jehoiada's son Benaiah was in command of the Cherethites and the Pelethites; and David's sons were the king's chief personal advisors.

War with the Ammonites and Arameans

19 Some time later, the Ammonite King Nahash died, and his son succeeded him as king. [2]"I'll be loyal to Nahash's son Hanun," David said, "because his father was

---

[c]Cf 2 Sam 8:6; Heb lacks *soldiers*.　[d]Or *sea*　[e]LXX, Syr; MT *Abimelech*

EUPHRATES RIVER

In the Bible, the Euphrates is one of the rivers of paradise (Gen 2:14). It formed the northeastern boundary of territory promised by the Lord to Israel (Gen 15:18; Deut 1:7; 11:24; Josh 1:4) and of the Israelite kingdom at its peak (2 Sam 8:3; 10:16; 1 Kgs 4:24; 1 Chron 18:3). The Euphrates and Egypt were used as idealized boundary markers of the kingdom God gave to Solomon (1 Kgs 3:13; 4:21). It is sometimes known simply as "the River" (Num 22:5) as in "the province Beyond the River" (Ezra 4:10-22; Neh 2:7-9).

loyal to me." So David sent messengers with condolences about his father's death.

But when David's servants arrived in the Ammonite territory to express his sympathy to Hanun, [3]the Ammonite leaders asked Hanun, "Do you really believe David is honoring your father because he has sent you condolences? Of course not! His servants have come to search the city, spy it out, and overthrow it!" [4]So Hanun took David's servants, shaved them, cut off half their garments from their buttocks down, and sent them off.

[5]When this was reported to David, he sent messengers to the men because they were completely ashamed. The king said, "Stay in Jericho until your beards have grown. Then you can come back."

[6]When the Ammonites realized that they had offended David, Hanun and the Ammonites sent one thousand kikkars of silver to hire chariots and cavalry for themselves from Aram-naharaim, Aram-maacah, and Zobah. [7]They hired thirty-two thousand chariots, as well as King Maacah and his army, who came and camped in front of Medeba, while the Ammonites left their cities and came together ready for battle. [8]When David heard this, he sent Joab and the entire army of warriors. [9]The Ammonites marched out and formed a battle line at the entrance to the city, while the kings who had come remained in the countryside.

[10]When Joab saw that the battle would be fought on two fronts, he chose some of Israel's finest warriors and deployed them to meet the Arameans. [11]The rest of the army Joab placed under the command of his brother Abishai. When they took up their positions to meet the Arameans, [12]Joab said, "If the Arameans prove too strong for me, you must help me, and if the Ammonites prove too strong for you, I'll help you. [13]Be brave! We must be courageous for the sake of our people and the cities of our God. The LORD will do what is good in his eyes."

[14]When Joab and the troops who were with him advanced into battle against the Arameans, they fled from him. [15]When the Ammonites saw that the Arameans had fled, they also fled from his brother Abishai and retreated into the city. So Joab returned to Jerusalem.

[16]The Arameans saw that they had been defeated by Israel. They sent out messengers to bring Aramean reinforcements from the other side of the river, with Shophach the commander of Hadadezer's army at their head. [17]Upon hearing this, David gathered all Israel and crossed the Jordan. David advanced and took up positions against the Arameans to meet them in battle. After initiating the battle, [18]the Arameans fled before Israel, and David killed seven thousand Aramean chariot drivers and forty thousand foot soldiers. Shophach the commander of their army was killed too. [19]When the servants of Hadadezer saw that they had been defeated by Israel, they made peace with David and served him. Never again would the Arameans come to the aid of the Ammonites.

Defeat of the Ammonites

20 In the spring, the time when kings go to war, Joab marched out with the army, destroyed the land of the Ammonites, and besieged Rabbah. David stayed in Jerusalem while Joab attacked Rabbah and overthrew it. [2]David took Milcom's[f] crown from his head. He found that it weighed one kikkar of gold and was set with a valuable stone. It was placed on David's head. The amount of loot David took from the city was huge. [3]After removing the people who were in the city, David demolished the city with saws, iron picks, and axes,[g] as he did to all the Ammonite cities. Then David and all his troops returned to Jerusalem.

War with the Philistines

[4]Once again war broke out at Gezer with the Philistines. At that time Sibbecai the Hushathite killed Sippai, one of the descendants of the Rephah,[h] and the Philistines were subdued. [5]In another war with the Philistines, Jair's son Elhanan killed Lahmi

---

[f]LXX, Vulg; MT *their king*   [g]Cf 2 Sam 12:31; MT *saws*   [h]Or *giants*; also in 20:6-7

the brother of Goliath the Gittite. The shaft of his spear was like a weaver's beam. ⁶At another war in Gath there was a huge man with six fingers on each hand and six toes on each foot, twenty-four in all, who was also descended from Raphah. ⁷When he taunted Israel, Jonathan the son of David's brother Shimea killed him. ⁸These were descended from the Raphah in Gath, and they fell by the hands of David and his servants.

David's census

21 A heavenly Adversaryⁱ arose against Israel and incited David to count Israel. ²So David told Joab and the leaders of the people, "Go throughout all the tribes of Israel, from Dan to Beer-sheba, and take a census of the people so I know how many people there are."

³But Joab replied, "May the LORD increase his people a hundred times! Sir, aren't you the king, and aren't they all your servants? Why do you want to do this? Why bring guilt on Israel?"

⁴But the king overruled Joab, who left and traveled throughout all Israel. When he returned to Jerusalem, ⁵he reported to David the total number: there were 1,100,000 men available for military service in all Israel, while Judah alone had 470,000. ⁶He didn't include Levi and Benjamin among them, because Joab disagreed with the king's order.

⁷God was offended by this census and punished Israel. ⁸Then David said to God, "I have sinned greatly in what I have done! Now please take away the guilt of your servant because I have done something very foolish."

⁹The LORD told Gad, David's seer: ¹⁰Go and tell David, This is what the LORD says: I'm offering you three punishments. Choose one of them, and that is what I will do to you.

¹¹When Gad came to David, he said to him, "This is what the LORD says: Take your choice: ¹²three years of famine, three months of fleeingʲ from your enemies while your enemies' sword overtakes you,

or three days of the LORD's sword, that is, plague in the land and the LORD's messenger bringing disaster in every part of Israel. Decide now what answer I should take back to the one who sent me."

¹³"I'm in deep trouble," David said to Gad. "I'd rather fall into the hands of the LORD, who is very merciful; don't let me fall into human hands." ¹⁴So the LORD sent a plague throughout Israel, and seventy thousand Israelites fell dead.

¹⁵Then God sent a messenger to Jerusalem to destroy it. But just as the messenger was about to destroy it, the LORD looked and changed his mind about the destruction. He said to the messenger who was destroying it, "That's enough! Withdraw your hand!" At that time the LORD's messenger was standing near the threshing floor of Ornan the Jebusite.

¹⁶When David looked up, he saw the LORD's messenger stationed between the earth and the sky with a drawn sword in his hand stretched out against Jerusalem. Then David and the elders, dressed in mourning clothes, fell on their faces; ¹⁷and David said to God, "Wasn't it I who ordered the numbering of the people? I'm the sinner, the one responsible for this evil. But these sheep— what have they done? LORD, my God, turn your hand against me and my household, but spare your people from the plague."

¹⁸The LORD's messenger ordered Gad to tell David that he should go up to the threshing floor of Ornan the Jebusite in order to set up an altar for the LORD. ¹⁹So David went up, following the instructions Gad had delivered in the LORD's name.

²⁰Ornan turned around and saw the king.ᵏ His four sons who were with him hid themselves, but Ornan continued threshing wheat. ²¹When David approached Ornan, Ornan looked up, recognized David, left the threshing floor, and bowed to David with his face to the ground. ²²David said to Ornan, "Give me the site of the threshing floor, charging me full price, so that I may build an altar to the LORD, and the plague among the people may come to an end."

ⁱHeb *satan* ʲLXX, cf 2 Sam 24:13; MT *being swept away* ᵏLXX, cf 2 Sam 24:20; MT *messenger*

[23] Ornan replied to David, "Take it for yourself, and may my master the king do what he thinks is best. I'll even provide the oxen for the entirely burned offerings, the threshing boards for wood, and the wheat for the grain offering—I'll provide everything!" [24] But King David said to Ornan, "No, I will buy them from you at a fair price. I won't offer to the LORD what belongs to you nor offer an entirely burned offering that costs me nothing." [25] Then David gave Ornan six hundred shekels of gold by weight for the site. [26] David built an altar there for the LORD and offered entirely burned offerings and well-being sacrifices. He called on the LORD, who answered him with fire from heaven on the altar of the entirely burned offering, consuming the entirely burned offering.[l] [27] Then the LORD commanded the messenger to return his sword to its sheath.

Location of the future temple

[28] At that time, after David saw that the LORD had answered him at the threshing floor of Ornan the Jebusite, he offered sacrifices there. [29] The LORD's dwelling that Moses had made in the desert and the altar for entirely burned offerings were then at the shrine in Gibeon, [30] but David couldn't go there to seek God because he feared the sword of the LORD's messenger.

22 Then David said, "This is where the LORD God's temple will be, along with Israel's altar for entirely burned offerings."

David prepares to build the temple

[2] David gave orders to gather the immigrants living in the land of Israel, and he appointed masons who would cut stones for building God's temple. [3] David also provided a huge amount of iron for nails for the doors of the gates and for the braces, so much bronze that it couldn't be weighed, [4] and innumerable cedar logs from the Sidonians and the Tyrians, who gave them to David. [5] David thought, My son Solomon is too inexperienced to build the LORD's temple. It must be great beyond compare in order to win fame and glory throughout all lands, so I myself will prepare things for him. So David made extensive preparations before his death.

Instructions to Solomon

[6] David sent for his son Solomon and instructed him to build a temple for the LORD, the God of Israel. [7] David said to Solomon, "My son,[m] I had intended to build a temple for the name of the LORD my God. [8] But the LORD told me: You've shed much blood and waged great wars. You won't build a temple for my name because you've spilled so much blood on the ground before me. [9] A son has just been born to you. He'll be a man of peace, and I'll give him peace with all his surrounding enemies. In fact, his name will be Solomon,[n] and I'll give Israel peace and quiet during his reign. [10] He will be the one to build a temple for my name. He'll become my son, and I'll become

[l] LXX; MT lacks *consuming the entirely burned offering.* [m] LXX, DSS; MT *his son* [n] *Solomon* sounds like *peace* in Heb.

THRESHING FLOOR

A threshing floor was an open space, often on or near the top of a hill, where grain would be threshed and winnowed. The open space allowed oxen or other draft animals to pull the threshing sledge over the grain and break the stalks from the heads of grain. In the winnowing process, the higher ground permitted the wind to blow the lighter straw and chaff a distance away while the heavier heads of grain fell to be gathered from the ground.

his father, and I'll establish his royal throne over Israel forever.

[11]"Now, my son, may the LORD be with you so that you may successfully build the temple of the LORD your God, as he promised you. [12]May the LORD be sure to give you insight and understanding so that when he appoints you over Israel, you will observe the Instruction from the LORD your God.[o] [13]Then, if you carefully follow the regulations and case laws that the LORD commanded Moses concerning Israel, you'll prosper. Be strong and brave. Don't be afraid or lose heart! [14]With great effort I've now provided for the LORD's temple one hundred thousand kikkars of gold, one million kikkars of silver, and so much bronze and iron that it can't be weighed, as well as wood and stone, though you may add to these. [15]You also have innumerable people to do the work: stonecutters, masons, and carpenters with every skill required for any task, [16]whether in gold, silver, bronze, or iron. So get to work, and may the LORD be with you."

Instructions to Israel's leaders

[17]Then David ordered all of Israel's leaders to help his son Solomon: [18]"The LORD your God is with you! He's given you peace on every side. He's placed under my power the land's people, so that the land is under the control of the LORD and his people. [19]Now then, dedicate yourselves to seeking the LORD your God. Get to work and build the sanctuary of the LORD God, so that the chest containing the LORD's covenant together with God's holy equipment may be brought into the temple built for the LORD's name."

David appoints the Levites

23 When David had grown old after a long life, he made his son Solomon king over Israel. [2]He then gathered together all Israel's leaders along with the priests and the Levites. [3]When the Levites were counted, the head count of every male 30 and older totaled 38,000. [4]Of these, there were 24,000 to supervise the work on the LORD's temple, 6,000 officers and judges, [5]4,000 gatekeepers, and 4,000 praising the LORD with instruments made[p] for offering praise. [6]Then David divided them into three groups named after Levi's family members: Gershon, Kohath, and Merari.

Gershonites

[7]The Gershonites included Ladan and Shimei.

[8]Ladan's family: Jehiel the first, Zetham, and Joel—three in all. [9]Jehiel's[q] family: Shelomith, Haziel, and Haran—three in all. These were the heads of the households of Ladan.

[10]Shimei's family: Jahath, Ziza,[r] Jeush, and Beriah. These four were Shimei's family: [11]Jahath was the first, and Ziza the second; since Jeush and Beriah didn't have many children, they became a single household.

Kohathites

[12]Kohath's family: Amram, Izhar, Hebron, and Uzziel—four in all.

[13]Amram's family: Aaron and Moses. Aaron, together with his sons, was set apart to make the holiest objects holy, to make offerings before the LORD, to serve him, and to give blessings in his name forever.

[14]As for Moses the man of God, his sons were considered to be Levites. [15]Moses' family: Gershom and Eliezer.

[16]Gershom's family: Shebuel the first.

[17]Eliezer's family: Rehabiah the first; Eliezer had no other sons, but Rehabiah had many children.

[18]Izhar's family: Shelomoth[s] the first.

[19]Hebron's family: Jeriah the first, Amariah the second, Jahaziel the third, and Jekameam the fourth.

[20]Uzziel's family: Micah the first and Isshiah the second.

Merarites

[21]Merari's family: Mahli and Mushi. Mahli's family: Eleazar and Kish.

---

[o]Heb uncertain   [p]LXX, Vulg; MT *I made*   [q]Cf 23:8, 10; MT *Shimei's*   [r]LXX; MT *Zina*   [s]LXX, Syr, Aram; MT *Shelomith*

²²Eleazar died without sons, but he did have daughters who married their relatives from Kish's family.

²³Mushi's family: Mahli, Eder, and Jeremoth—three in all.

²⁴These were the members of Levi's family according to their households. The household heads were registered, along with a listing of the names of each person 20 years old and above who carried out assigned tasks in the LORD's temple.

Levites' duties

²⁵David said, "Since the LORD, Israel's God, has given his people peace and has made his home in Jerusalem forever, ²⁶the Levites need no longer carry the dwelling or any of the equipment used in its service." ²⁷David's last instructions were to count the Levites 20 years old and above. ²⁸Their assignment was to be at the side of the Aaronites to serve in the LORD's temple, maintaining the courtyards and side rooms and cleansing all of the holy objects and doing whatever was needed in the service of God's temple. ²⁹They were responsible for the stacks of bread, the fine flour for grain offerings, the wafers of unleavened bread, the cakes made on the griddle, the offering mixed with oil, as well as all the measuring. ³⁰They were to be present every morning to thank and praise the LORD, and to do the same every evening. ³¹Whenever entirely burned offerings were offered to the LORD

for the sabbaths, the new moons, and festivals, a designated number were to serve in the LORD's presence continuously. ³²In this way they were to observe the instructions for the meeting tent, the instructions for the sanctuary, and the instructions for Aaron's family and relatives about serving in the LORD's temple.

Divisions of the priests

24 The divisions of the Aaronites: Aaron's family: Nadab, Abihu, Eleazar, and Ithamar.

²Nadab and Abihu died before their father did, without having sons, and so Eleazar and Ithamar served as priests. ³David, with the help of Zadok from Eleazar's family and Ahimelech from Ithamar's family, divided them according to their appointed duties. ⁴Since Eleazar's family was found to have more male heads than Ithamar's family, they divided them so that Eleazar's family had sixteen household heads and Ithamar's family had eight. ⁵They divided both groups by lots because there were holy leaders, even outstanding leaders, among both Eleazar's and Ithamar's descendants. ⁶Shemaiah, Nethanel's son, the levitical scribe, recorded their names in the presence of the king; the leaders; Zadok the priest; Ahimelech, Abiathar's son; and the household heads of the priests and Levites. One household was taken from Eleazar followed by one from Ithamar.

LOTS

Lots could be used for gambling (Job 6:27; Joel 3:3; Obad 1:11), but were also commonly used in the ancient Near East as a human means for determining the divine will. In Israel, lots were cast to determine guilt (Josh 7:14; 1 Sam 14:42; Jonah 1:7), to apportion land (Num 26:55; Josh 14:2), or to select which animals should be sacrificed (Lev 16:7-10). Various ranks of temple personnel were chosen by lot (1 Chron 24:5; 25:8; 26:13), as were assignments for temple provisions in time of need (Neh 10:34 [Heb. 10:35]; 11:1). The lot could be used to decide disputes in the lack of other evidence (Prov 18:18). Most notably, Israel resorted to the lot in order to choose its first king (1 Sam 10:20-21).

[7]The first lot fell to Jehoiarib,
the second to Jedaiah,
[8]the third to Harim,
the fourth to Seorim,
[9]the fifth to Malchijah,
the sixth to Mijamin,
[10]the seventh to Hakkoz,
the eighth to Abijah,
[11]the ninth to Jeshua,
the tenth to Shecaniah,
[12]the eleventh to Eliashib,
the twelfth to Jakim,
[13]the thirteenth to Huppah,
the fourteenth to Jeshebeab,
[14]the fifteenth to Bilgah,
the sixteenth to Immer,
[15]the seventeenth to Hezir,
the eighteenth to Happizzez,
[16]the nineteenth to Pethahiah,
the twentieth to Jehezkel,
[17]the twenty-first to Jachin,
the twenty-second to Gamul,
[18]the twenty-third to Delaiah,
and the twenty-fourth to Maaziah.

[19]These were to enter the LORD's temple according to their appointed duty and by the procedure established for them by their ancestor Aaron, just as the LORD God of Israel had instructed him.

Rest of the Levites

[20]The rest of the Levites included:
from Amram's family: Shubael;
from Shubael's family: Jehdeiah;
[21]from Rehabiah and his family: Isshiah the first;
[22]from the Izharites: Shelomoth;
from Shelomoth's family: Jahath;
[23]Hebron's family:[t] Jeriah the first,[u]
Amariah the second, Jahaziel the third, Jekameam the fourth;
[24]Uzziel's family: Micah;
from Micah's family: Shamir;
[25]Micah's brother Isshiah;
from Isshiah's family: Zechariah;
[26]Merari's family: Mahli, Mushi and his son Jaaziah's family;
[27]Merari's family by his son Jaaziah: Shoham, Zaccur, and Ibri;

[28]from Mahli: Eleazar, who had no sons;
[29]from Kish and his family: Jerahmeel;
[30]and Mushi's family: Mahli, Eder, and Jerimoth.

These were the Levites according to their households. [31]Both the household head and his youngest brother cast lots, just as their relatives, Aaron's descendants, had done in the presence of King David, Zadok, Ahimelech, and the heads of the priestly and levitical households.

Temple musicians

25 David and the army officers[v] set apart Asaph's family, Heman and Jeduthun, for service to prophesy[w] accompanied by lyres, harps, and cymbals.

This is the list of those who performed this special service:

[2]From Asaph's family: Zaccur, Joseph, Nethaniah, and Asarelah. Asaph's family was under Asaph's direction and prophesied by order of the king.

[3]From Jeduthun and his family: Gedaliah, Izri,[x] Jeshaiah, Shimei,[y] Hashabiah, and Mattithiah—six in all. They were under their father Jeduthun's direction, prophesying with the lyre and giving thanks and praise to the LORD.

[4]From Heman and his family: Bukkiah, Mattaniah, Uzziel, Shebuel, Jerimoth, Hananiah, Hanani, Eliathah, Giddalti, Romamti-ezer, Joshbekashah, Mallothi, Hothir, and Mahazioth.

[5]All these were the family of Heman the king's seer, according to God's promise to honor him. God gave Heman fourteen sons and three daughters. [6]They were all under their father's direction when singing in the LORD's temple with cymbals, harps, and lyres to provide service in God's temple, by order of the king.

As for Asaph, Jeduthun, and Heman, [7]the number of themselves and their relatives, who were trained in singing to the LORD and who were all skillful, was 288. [8]They cast lots for their assigned duties, small as well as great, teacher and pupil alike.

---

[t]LXX; MT *my sons* [u]Cf 1 Chron 23:19; MT lacks *Jeriah*. [v]Or *liturgical officers* [w]DSS, LXX, Vulg; MT *the prophets*
[x]Cf 25:11: MT *Zeri* [y]LXX, cf 25:17; MT lacks *Jeriah*.

⁹The first lot fell for Asaph to Joseph; the second to Gedaliah, his relatives, and his family, 12;

¹⁰the third to Zaccur, his family, and his relatives, 12;

¹¹the fourth to Izri, his family, and his relatives, 12;

¹²the fifth to Nethaniah, his family, and his relatives, 12;

¹³the sixth to Bukkiah, his family, and his relatives, 12;

¹⁴the seventh to Jesarelah, his family, and his relatives, 12;

¹⁵the eighth to Jeshaiah, his family, and his relatives, 12;

¹⁶the ninth to Mattaniah, his family, and his relatives, 12;

¹⁷the tenth to Shimei, his family, and his relatives, 12;

¹⁸the eleventh to Uzziel,ᶻ his family, and his relatives, 12;

¹⁹the twelfth to Hashabiah, his family, and his relatives, 12;

²⁰the thirteenth to Shubael, his family, and his relatives, 12;

²¹the fourteenth to Mattithiah, his family, and his relatives, 12;

²²the fifteenth to Jerimoth,ᵃ his family, and his relatives, 12;

²³the sixteenth to Hananiah, his family, and his relatives, 12;

²⁴the seventeenth to Joshbekashah, his family, and his relatives, 12;

²⁵the eighteenth to Hanani, his family, and his relatives, 12;

²⁶the nineteenth to Mallothi, his family, and his relatives, 12;

²⁷the twentieth to Eliathah, his family, and his relatives, 12;

²⁸the twenty-first to Hothir, his family, and his relatives, 12;

²⁹the twenty-second to Giddalti, his family, and his relatives, 12;

³⁰the twenty-third to Mahazioth, his family, and his relatives, 12;

³¹and the twenty-fourth to Romamti-ezer, his family, and his relatives, 12.

Gatekeepers

26 The divisions of the gatekeepers: from the Korahites: Meshelemiah, Kore's son, one of Ebiasaph'sᵇ family.

²Meshelemiah's family: Zechariah the oldest, Jediael the second, Zebadiah the third, Jathniel the fourth, ³Elam the fifth, Jehohanan the sixth, and Eliehoenai the seventh.

⁴Obed-edom's family: Shemaiah the oldest, Jehozabad the second, Joah the third, Sachar the fourth, Nethanel the fifth, ⁵Ammiel the sixth, Issachar the seventh, and Peullethai the eighth. God truly blessed him. ⁶To his son Shemaiah were born sons who ruled over their household, because they were valiant men. ⁷Shemaiah's family: Othni, Rephael, Obed, Elzabad, and his relatives, Elihu and Semachiah, who were valiant men. ⁸All these were members of Obed-edom's family, they, their sons, and their relatives. They were valiant and strong in their service, 62 men belonging to Obed-edom. ⁹Meshelemiah's family and relatives, valiant men, numbered 18.

¹⁰Hosah, one of Merari's family, also had a family: Shimri the first (though he wasn't the oldest, his father gave him that status), ¹¹Hilkiah the second, Tebaliah the third, and Zechariah the fourth. All of Hosah's family and relatives numbered 13.

¹²These were the divisions of the gatekeepers with their leaders, who were responsible to minister in the LORD's temple, along with their relatives. ¹³They cast lots for each gate in the same way, whether their household was small or large. ¹⁴The lot for the East Gate fell to Shelemiah. They then cast lots for his son Zechariah, a wise counselor, and his lot indicated the North Gate. ¹⁵Obed-edom was assigned the South Gate, and his sons were assigned the storehouses. ¹⁶Hosahᶜ was assigned the West Gate, that is, the chamberᵈ gate on the upper road.

The guards had the same task: ¹⁷eachᵉ day the East had six, the North four, and

---

ᶻLXX, Syr; MT *Azrael* ᵃCf 25:4; MT *Jeremoth* ᵇLXX; MT *Asaph* ᶜMT *Shuppim and Hosah* ᵈLXX; MT *Shallecheth* ᵉLXX; MT *Levites* the South four, with two at each of the storehouses. ¹⁸At the courtyard on the West, there were four at the road and two at the courtyard. ¹⁹These were the divisions of the gatekeepers from Korah's family and Merari's family.

²⁰Their fellow^f Levites were in charge of the treasuries of God's temple and the treasuries of the dedicated gifts: ²¹from Ladan's family, the family of the Gershonites belonging to Ladan, and the heads of the households belonging to Ladan the Gershonite: Jehieli. ²²Jehieli's family: Zetham and Joel his brother were in charge of the treasuries of the LORD's temple. ²³From the Amramites, Izharites, Hebronites, and Uzzielites: ²⁴Shebuel, a descendant of Gershom, Moses' son, was the chief officer in charge of the treasuries. ²⁵His relatives through Eliezer included his son Rehabiah, his son Jeshaiah, his son Joram, his son Zichri, and his son Shelomoth. ²⁶This Shelomoth and his relatives were in charge of all the treasuries of the gifts dedicated by King David, by the household leaders, by the commanders^g of the units of a thousand and a hundred, and by the army officers. ²⁷They had dedicated some of the valuable objects won in battle to repair the LORD's temple. ²⁸Everything that was dedicated by Samuel the seer, as well as by Saul, Kish's son; Abner, Ner's son; and Joab, Zeruiah's son—in fact, anything that had been dedicated—was under the supervision of Shelomoth^h and his relatives.

²⁹From the Izharites: Chenaniah and his family had responsibilities over Israel outside the temple as officials and judges. ³⁰From the Hebronites: Hashabiah and his relatives, 1,700 capable men, were put in charge of Israel west of the Jordan concerning all of the LORD's affairs and the king's service. ³¹From the Hebronites: Jerijah was the head of the Hebronites according to the family records of their households. In the fortieth year of David's rule, a search was made and capable men were found among them in Jazer in Gilead. ³²Jerijah's relatives,

capable men, were 2,700 heads of households. King David put them in charge of Reuben, Gad, and half the tribe of Manasseh concerning all of God's and the king's affairs.

Divisions of the military

27 This is the list of the Israelites, the heads of households, the commanders of units of a thousand and a hundred, and their officers. They served the king in every way their divisions required, and they were on duty for a month at a time through all the months of the year. Each division numbered 24,000.

²In charge of the first division for the first month was Jashobeam, Zabdiel's son. His division numbered 24,000. ³He was a Perezite and the head of all the army officers for the first month.

⁴In charge of the division for the second month was Dodai the Ahohite.ⁱ His division numbered 24,000.

⁵The third army commander for the third month was Benaiah the chief priest Jehoiada's son. His division numbered 24,000. ⁶This Benaiah was a warrior of the Thirty and in command of the Thirty. In command of his division was his son Ammizabad.

⁷The fourth for the fourth month was Asahel, Joab's brother, and after him his son Zebadiah. His division numbered 24,000.

⁸The fifth for the fifth month was the commander Shammoth the Zerahite.^j His division numbered 24,000.

⁹The sixth for the sixth month was Ira the Tekoite Ikkesh's son. His division numbered 24,000.

¹⁰The seventh for the seventh month was Helez the Pelonite from Ephraim's family. His division numbered 24,000.

¹¹The eighth for the eighth month was Sibbecai the Hushathite from the Zerahites. His division numbered 24,000.

¹²The ninth for the ninth month was Abiezer of Annathoth from the Benjaminites. His division numbered 24,000.

ᶠLXX; MT *Ahijah* ᵍLXX; MT *to the commanders* ʰLXX; MT *Shelomith* ⁱLXX; MT adds *and his division, and Mikloth the leader.* ʲCf 27:11, 13; MT *Izrahite*

¹³The tenth for the tenth month was Maharai the Netophathite from the Zerahites. His division numbered 24,000.

¹⁴The eleventh for the eleventh month was Benaiah the Pirathonite from Ephraim's family. His division numbered 24,000.

¹⁵The twelfth for the twelfth month was Heldai the Netophathite from Othniel. His division numbered 24,000.

Tribal leaders

¹⁶In charge of the tribes of Israel:

for the Reubenites—the leader was Eliezer, Zichri's son;

for the Simeonites—Shephatiah, Maacah's son;

¹⁷for the Levites—Hashabiah, Kemuel's son;

for Aaron—Zadok;

¹⁸for Judah—Eliab,ᵏ one of David's relatives;

for Issachar—Omri, Michael's son;

¹⁹for Zebulun—Ishmaiah, Obadiah's son;

for Naphtali—Jerimoth, Azriel's son;

²⁰for the Ephraimites—Hoshea, Azaziah's son;

for half the tribe of Manasseh—Joel, Pedaiah's son;

²¹for half the tribeˡ of Manasseh in Gilead—Iddo, Zechariah's son;

for Benjamin—Jaasiel, Abner's son;

²²for Dan—Azarel, Jeroham's son.

These were the leaders of the tribes of Israel. ²³But David didn't count those younger than 20 years of age, because the LORD had promised to make Israel as numerous as the stars in the sky. ²⁴Joab, Zeruiah's son, began to count them, but he never finished. Since Israel experienced wrath because of this, the number wasn't entered into the official records of King David.

Civil servants

²⁵In charge of the king's treasuries—Azmaveth, Adiel's son;

in charge of the treasuries in the country, cities, villages, and towers—Jonathan, Uzziah's son;

²⁶in charge of agricultural workers cultivating the fertile land—Ezri, Chelub's son;

²⁷in charge of the vineyards—Shimei the Ramathite;

in charge of the vineyard's produce for the wine cellars—Zabdi the Shiphmite;

²⁸in charge of the olive and sycamore trees in the western foothills—Baal-hanan the Gederite;

in charge of the stores of oil—Joash;

²⁹in charge of the cattle that grazed in Sharon—Shitrai the Sharonite;

in charge of the cattle in the valleys—Shaphat, Adlai's son;

³⁰in charge of the camels—Obil the Ishmaelite;

in charge of the female donkeys—Jehdeiah the Meronothite;

³¹in charge of the flocks of sheep and goats—Jaziz the Hagrite.

All these were stewards of King David's property.

Royal advisors

³²Jonathan, David's uncle, was a counselor, a man of understanding, and a scribe. Jehiel, Hachmoni's son, took care of the king's sons. ³³Ahithophel was the king's counselor, and Hushai the Archite was the king's political advisor.ᵐ ³⁴After Ahithophel came Benaiah's son Jehoiada, and Abiathar. Joab was commander of the king's army.

David addresses Israel's leaders

28 David assembled all of Israel's leaders in Jerusalem, the leaders of the tribes, the leaders of the divisions that served the king, the commanders of units of a thousand and a hundred, the officials in charge of all the property and livestock of the king and his sons, as well as the officers, warriors, and all the valiant men. ²Then King David stood up and said:

Listen to me, my relatives and my people. I wanted to build a temple as the permanent home for the chest containing the LORD's covenant, our God's footrest. But when I prepared to build

---

ᵏLXX; MT *Elihu* ˡLXX, Vulg; MT lacks *for half the tribe.* ᵐOr *friend* it, ³God said to me, You must not build a temple for my name, because you are a military man and you've shed blood. ⁴The LORD, the God of Israel, chose me from my whole household to become king over Israel forever. He chose Judah as leader, and within Judah's family, my household, and among my father's family he was pleased with me, making me king over all Israel. ⁵And from all the many sons the LORD has given me, he has chosen my son Solomon to sit on the throne of the LORD's kingdom over Israel. ⁶He said to me: Your son Solomon will build my temple and my courtyards, for I've chosen him to become my son even as I myself will become his father. ⁷I'll establish his kingdom forever if he remains committed to keeping my commands and case laws as he does now.

⁸So now, in the presence of all the LORD's assembly[n] and with God as our witness, carefully observe all the commands of the LORD your God, so that you may hold on to this good land and pass it on to your children forever. ⁹As for you, Solomon, my son, acknowledge your father's God and serve him with enthusiastic devotion, because the LORD searches every mind and understands the motive behind every thought. If you seek him, he will be found by you; but if you abandon him, he will reject you forever. ¹⁰Now then, since the LORD has chosen you to build a temple for him[o] as the sanctuary, work hard.

¹¹Then David gave his son Solomon the plan for the entrance hall, its buildings, treasuries, upper and inner rooms, and the room for the cover.[p] ¹²He provided all of the plans he had in mind: for the courtyards of the LORD's temple, and for all its surrounding rooms where the treasures of God's temple and the dedicated gifts would be stored; ¹³for the divisions of the priests and Levites, for all their responsibilities within the LORD's temple, and for all the equipment used in its service; ¹⁴for the weight of all the gold equipment used for every kind of service, and the weight of all the silver equipment used for every kind of service; ¹⁵for the weight of the gold lampstands and their gold lamps—the weight of gold for each lampstand with its lamps—and for the weight of each silver lampstand and its lamps depending on how each would be used; ¹⁶for the weight of gold for each table with the stacks of bread, and the silver for the silver tables; ¹⁷for the forks, bowls, and cups of pure gold; for the weight of each gold dish and the weight of each silver dish; ¹⁸for the weight of the incense altar made of refined gold; and for the construction of the chariot—with the gold winged creatures spreading their wings and covering the chest containing the LORD's covenant. ¹⁹All of this the LORD made clear to David[q] directly in a document, including the plan for all of the work.

²⁰"Be strong and courageous," David said to his son Solomon. "Get to work. Don't be afraid or discouraged, because the LORD God, my God, is with you. He'll neither let you down nor leave you before all the work for the service of the LORD's temple is done. ²¹Here are the divisions of the priests and the Levites who will perform all the service of God's temple. For all this work you will have willing and able workers with you to do it. The officials and all the people are ready to follow your instructions."

Offerings for building the temple

29 Then King David said to the whole assembly:

My son Solomon, the one whom God chose, is too inexperienced for this great task, since this temple won't be for humans but for the LORD God. ²Using every resource at my disposal, I've provided everything for my God's temple: gold for gold objects, silver for silver objects, bronze for bronze objects, iron for iron objects, lumber for wooden objects, carnelian stones for settings, antimony, colorful stones, every kind of precious

---

[n]LXX; MT *all Israel, the assembly of the LORD* [o]LXX; MT lacks *for him.* [p]Or *mercy seat* or perhaps *reconciliation cover* (Heb *kapporet*) [q]LXX; MT *to me*

stone, and a large amount of marble. ³What's more, because of my delight in my God's temple, I have dedicated my own private treasure of gold and silver to my God's temple, in addition to all that I've provided for the holy temple: "three thousand kikkars of gold from the gold of Ophir, seven thousand kikkars of refined silver for covering the walls of the rooms,ʳ ⁵gold for gold objects, and silver for silver objects, to be used for everything the skilled workers will make. Who else, then, will volunteer, dedicating themselves to the LORD today?

⁶Then the leaders of the households, the leaders of the tribes of Israel, and the commanders of the units of a thousand and a hundred, and the supervisors of the king's work volunteered ⁷to give five thousand kikkars and ten thousand darics of gold, ten thousand kikkars of silver, eighteen thousand kikkars of bronze, and one hundred thousand kikkars of iron for the work on God's temple. ⁸Anyone who had precious stones donated them to the treasury of the LORD's temple under the care of Je-

ʳOr houses

hiel the Gershonite. ⁹The people rejoiced at this response, because they had presented their offerings to the LORD so willingly and wholeheartedly. King David also rejoiced greatly.

¹⁰Then David blessed the LORD before the whole assembly:

Blessed are you, LORD,
  God of our ancestor Israel,
    forever and always.
¹¹To you, LORD,
  belong greatness and power,
  honor, splendor, and majesty,
    because everything in heaven
      and on earth belongs to you.
Yours, LORD, is the kingship,
  and you are honored as head of all.
¹²You are the source of wealth and honor,
  and you rule over all.
In your hand are strength and might,
  and it is in your power to magnify
    and strengthen all.
¹³And now, our God, we thank you
  and praise your glorious name.
¹⁴Who am I,
  and who are my people,

TEMPLE OF SOLOMON

King Solomon built the first permanent temple for the Lord in Jerusalem in the mid-10th century BCE, thus completing his father David's program of turning Jerusalem into the religious as well as political capital of the united kingdom of Israel and Judah. David began this process when he appointed two high priests in Jerusalem from rival priestly families from the different halves of his kingdom, and he furthered it when he brought into his new capital the covenant chest, the most revered cultic object of the earlier Israelite league. David sought divine permission to build a permanent temple to house the chest, the symbol of the Lord's presence, which would have completed his transformation of Jerusalem into the permanent religious center of his kingdom, but his plan was temporarily thwarted by Nathan's negative oracle (2 Sam 7). Though David was not allowed to build the temple, he may have begun collecting material for its construction, as the Chronicler claimed (1 Chron 22; 28–29). It was Solomon, however, who actually built the temple, beginning its construction in the second month of his fourth year and completing it in the eighth month of his eleventh year (1 Kgs 6:1, 37-38).

that we should be able to offer
so willingly?
Since everything comes from you,
we have given you
that which comes from your own hand.
[15] To be sure, we are like all our ancestors,
immigrants without permanent homes.
Our days are like a shadow on the ground,
and there's no hope.

[16] LORD, our God, all this abundance that we have provided to build you a temple for your holy name comes from your hand and belongs to you. [17] Since I know, my God, that you examine the mind and take delight in honesty, I have freely given all these things with the highest of motives. And now I've been delighted to see your people here offering so willingly to you.

[18] LORD, God of our ancestors Abraham, Isaac, and Israel, keep these thoughts in the mind of your people forever, and direct their hearts toward you. [19] As for Solomon my son, give him the wholehearted devotion to keep your commands, laws, and regulations—observing all of them—and to build the temple that I have prepared.

[20] Then David said to the whole assembly, "Bless the LORD your God," and the whole assembly blessed the LORD, the God of their ancestors, bowed down, and worshipped before the LORD and the king.

[21] On the very next day they offered sacrifices and entirely burned offerings to the LORD—a thousand bulls, a thousand rams, and a thousand lambs, along with their drink offerings—and many other sacrifices for all Israel's sake. [22] They ate and drank with great joy before the LORD that day and made David's son Solomon the king.[s] They anointed him[t] in the LORD's presence as prince, and Zadok as priest. [23] Thus Solomon sat on the LORD's throne as king, succeeding his father David, and he prospered. All Israel obeyed him, [24] and all the commanders and warriors, as well as all of King David's sons, submitted to King Solomon's authority. [25] Moreover, the LORD magnified Solomon before all Israel, giving him such royal majesty as no king before him[u] had enjoyed.

Summary of David's reign

[26] David, Jesse's son, was king over all Israel. [27] He reigned over Israel for forty years: seven years in Hebron and thirty-three in Jerusalem. [28] He died at a good old age, having enjoyed a full life, wealth, and honor; and his son Solomon followed him as king. [29] The account of King David from beginning to end is written in the records of Samuel the seer, Nathan the prophet, and Gad the visionary, [30] including everything concerning his powerful rule, and what happened to him, to Israel, and to all the kingdoms in other lands.

---

[s] LXX, Syr; MT adds *for the second time.*　[t] LXX; MT lacks *him.*　[u] LXX; MT adds *in Israel.*

2 CHRONICLES

See the introduction to 1 Chronicles for background information about the content, author, and dates of 2 Chronicles.

HISTORICAL AND RELIGIOUS SIGNIFICANCE

The Chronicler's use of his sources, so far as this can be checked, and the emphases of his writing show that he was a religious teacher rather than an historian. In rewriting the history of his people from Adam to Ezra (from David to Ezra in detail) he sought to show the divine origin, great antiquity, and permanent validity of the Jews' religious institutions and practices—so that all the world would know that God, the only God, was with them, protecting them, and helping them toward a divine destiny. He also wished to encourage his fellow Jews to believe in God's promises to David and Solomon and in their own future as the people of God. Above all, he wanted them to be obedient to the covenant law and to God's great prophets; because that is the only way they could realize their glorious destiny.

The Chronicler wrote and interpreted history, apologetic history, more so than any other Old Testament writer. Every piece of his work must be sifted critically if one's objective is the recovery of historical facts. Sometimes he offers supplementary material of historical value. The work is, of course, of great significance for a knowledge of the times in which he lived.

The writer's belief that true worship of God and absolute loyalty to God are the indispensable bases of national existence as the people of God is in line with the best emphases of the Old Testament. Some of the sermons and prayers of the book give expression to noble faith, and have influenced life and worship through the centuries (see, e.g., 1 Chronicles 29:10-19).

2 CHRONICLES

Solomon first meets God

1 Solomon, David's son, was securely established over his kingdom because the LORD his God was with him and made him very great. [2] Solomon summoned all Israel, including the officers of the army,[a] the judges, and every Israelite leader who was the head of a family. [3] Then Solomon, accompanied by the whole assembly, went to the shrine at Gibeon because that is where God's meeting tent was, the tent that the LORD's servant Moses had made in the wilderness. [4] Now David had already brought God's chest from Kiriath-jearim to the place he had prepared for it because he had pitched a tent for the chest in Jerusalem. [5] But the bronze altar that Bezalel, Uri's son and Hur's grandson, had made was there in front of the LORD's dwelling, so that is where Solomon and the assembly worshipped. [6] Solomon went there to the bronze altar in the LORD's presence at the meeting tent and offered a thousand entirely burned offerings upon it.

[7] That night God appeared to Solomon and said, "Ask whatever you wish, and I will give it to you."

[8] "You showed so much kindness to my father David," Solomon replied to God, "and you have made me king in his place. [9] Now, LORD God, let your promise to my father David be fulfilled because you have made me king over a people as numerous as the earth's dust. [10] Give me wisdom and knowledge so I can lead this people, because no one can govern this great people of yours without your help."

[11] God said to Solomon, "Since this is what you wish, and because you've asked for wisdom and knowledge to govern my people over whom I've made you king—rather than asking for wealth, riches, fame, victory over those who hate you, or even a long life—[12] your request for wisdom and knowledge is granted. But I will also give you wealth, riches, and fame beyond that of any king before you or after you." [13] Then Solomon went from[b] the shrine in Gibeon, from the meeting tent to Jerusalem where he ruled over Israel.

Solomon's wealth

[14] Solomon acquired more and more chariots and horses until he had fourteen hundred chariots and twelve thousand horses, which he stationed in chariot cities and

[a] Or officers over thousands and hundreds   [b] LXX, Vulg; MT to

---

SYCAMORE

The sycamore (or sycomore) fig (*Ficus sycomorus*). Old sycamore trees have massive trunks with clusters of small fig fruits growing through the bark of the trunk and branches. They are edible but not as delicious as the common fig. The young fruits are pollinated by certain wasps, some of which die inside and pollute the ripe fruit, so an ancient technique of cutting the young fruits was used to hasten their ripening and purity. As a "trimmer of sycamore trees," Amos performed this work (Amos 7:14). Luke 19:3-4 narrates how Zacchaeus, the short tax collector, climbed up a sycamore to see Jesus; the tree's low branches made it easy to climb. Sycamore timber is soft and white, unlike harder and reddish cedarwood, but was appreciated in Palestine where wood was in short supply (1 Kgs 10:27; Isa 9:10); in ancient Egypt the timber was important for sarcophagi. The frosting of sycamore fruits was a calamity (Ps 78:47).

with the king in Jerusalem. [15] In Jerusalem, the king made silver and gold as common as stones, and cedar as plentiful as sycamore trees that grow in the foothills. [16] Solomon's horses were imported from Egypt and Kue, purchased from Kue by the king's agents at the going price. [17] They would import a chariot from Egypt for six hundred pieces of silver and a horse for one hundred fifty, and then export them to all the Hittite and Aramean kings.

Solomon prepares to build the temple

2 [c] Solomon gave orders to build a temple for the LORD's name and to build a royal palace for himself. [2][d] To work in the highlands, Solomon drafted 70,000 laborers, 80,000 stonecutters, and 3,600 supervisors. [3] Solomon sent the following message to King Huram[e] of Tyre:

When my father David was building his palace, you sent him cedar logs. [4] Now as his son[f] I am about to build a temple in the name of the LORD my God. I will dedicate it to him to burn fragrant incense before him, to set out the bread that is regularly displayed, and to offer entirely burned offerings every morning and evening, on the sabbaths, the first of every month, and the festivals of the LORD our God, as Israel has been commanded to do forever. [5] The temple I am about to build must be magnificent, because our God is greater than all other gods. [6] But who is able to build such a temple when even the highest heaven can't contain God? And who am I that I should build this temple for God, except as a place to burn incense in his presence? [7] So now send me a craftsman skilled in gold, silver, bronze, and iron, as well as in purple, crimson, and violet yarn—someone also experienced as an engraver. He will work with my craftsmen in Judah and Jerusalem who were provided by my father David. [8] Also send me cedar, cypress, and sandalwood logs from Lebanon. I know your

servants know how to cut Lebanese timber, so my servants will work with your servants [9] to prepare plenty of timber for me, because the temple that I am about to build will be magnificent and amazing. [10] I will pay the woodcutters twenty thousand kors[g] of crushed wheat, twenty thousand kors of barley, twenty thousand baths[h] of wine, and twenty thousand baths of olive oil.

[11] Tyre's King Huram replied in a letter that he sent to Solomon:

The LORD must love his people Israel because he has made you their king! [12] Bless the LORD, Israel's God, who made heaven and earth. He gave King David a wise son who possesses the knowledge and understanding to build a temple for the LORD and a royal palace for himself. [13] I'm sending you a skilled and experienced craftsman, Huram-abi, [14] whose mother is from the tribe of Dan and whose father is from Tyre. He's skilled in working with gold, silver, bronze, iron, stone, and wood, as well as purple, violet, and crimson yarn, and fine linen. He can do any kind of engraving and make any design given to him with the assistance of your craftsmen and the craftsmen of my master, your father David. [15] So once my master sends the wheat, barley, olive oil, and wine he has promised, [16] we will cut as much timber as you need from Lebanon and bring it by raft on the sea to you at Joppa, where you can take it up to Jerusalem.

[17] Then Solomon counted all the immigrants in the land of Israel, as his father David had done, and the total was 153,600. [18] He made 70,000 of these immigrants laborers, 80,000 of them stonecutters in the highlands, and 3,600 of them supervisors to keep the people working.

Solomon builds the temple

3 Solomon began to build the LORD's temple in Jerusalem on Mount Mo-

---

[c] 1:18 in Heb　[d] 2:1 in Heb　[e] 1 Kings spells the king's name as Hiram.　[f] LXX; MT lacks *his son.*　[g] One kor is equivalent to a homer and is possibly equal to fifty gallons of grain.　[h] One bath is approximately twenty quarts or five gallons.

riah, where the Lord[i] had appeared to his father David, on the place David had prepared at the threshing floor of Ornan the Jebusite. [2] He began building in the second month[j] of the fourth year of his rule. [3] Solomon laid the foundations[k] for these structures in order to build the temple of God. The length according to the old standard of measurement was ninety feet and the width thirty feet. [4] Across the front of the temple[l] was a porch as long as the temple was and thirty feet wide, and thirty feet[m] high. He covered the inside walls with pure gold. [5] He paneled the walls of the main room with pine, covered them with fine gold, and decorated them with palm trees and chains. [6] He studded the room with precious stones for beauty; the gold was from Parvaim. [7] He covered the room, its beams, doorframes, walls, and doors with gold, and carved images of winged creatures on the walls. [8] Then he made the most holy place. It was as long as the temple was wide, thirty feet long and thirty feet wide. He covered it with six hundred kikkars of fine gold. [9] The gold nails weighed fifty shekels.[n] He also covered the upper rooms with gold.

[10] In the most holy place he formed two statues of winged creatures and covered them with gold. [11] Together the wingspan of these creatures was thirty feet. One of the first creature's wings was seven and a half feet long and touched the temple wall, while the other wing was seven and a half feet long, touching the wing of the other creature. [12] Similarly, one wing of the other creature was seven and a half feet long and touched the temple wall, while the other wing was seven and a half feet long and touched the other creature. [13] The wings of these creatures extended thirty feet. They stood on their feet facing the main room.

[14] Then he made the curtain out of fine linen and violet, purple, and crimson yarn, weaving winged creatures into it. [15] Then he made two columns in front of the temple, fifty-two and a half feet high, with a seven and a half foot cap on top of each. [16] Then he made chains like a necklace[o] and placed them on the tops of the columns. He made a hundred pomegranates and placed them into the chains. [17] Then he set up the pillars in front of the sanctuary, one on the south, the other on the north. The one on the south he named Jachin, and the one on the north he named Boaz.

Solomon's temple equipment

4 He[p] also made a bronze altar thirty feet long, thirty feet wide, and fifteen feet high. [2] Then he made a tank of cast metal called the Sea. It was circular in shape, fifteen feet from rim to rim, seven and a half feet high, and forty-five feet in circumference. [3] Under the rim were two rows of oxlike figures completely encircling it, ten every eighteen inches, each cast in its mold. [4] The Sea rested on twelve oxen with their backs toward the center, three facing north, three facing west, three facing south, and three facing east. [5] The Sea was as thick as the width of a hand. Its rim was shaped

---

[i] LXX; MT lacks *the Lord*.   [j] LXX; MT adds *on the second (day)*.   [k] Syr *the measurements*   [l] LXX; cf 1 Kgs 6:3   [m] LXX, Syr; MT *one hundred eighty feet*   [n] Or approximately thirty ounces   [o] Heb adds *in the inner room.*   [p] *Solomon* or *Huram*; this ambiguity with the pronoun continues in the following verses, but compare 2 Chron 3:1, 3; 4:11. If Huram is meant, this is a worker whose name is spelled Hiram in 1 Kgs 7:13-14.

JACHIN AND BOAZ

Jachin and Boaz, the two bronze pillars erected at the vestibule of the temple of Solomon, were each 27 ft. high and 18 ft. in circumference with capitals 7.5 ft. high on top (2 Kgs 7:15-16). The names appear only at 1 Kings 7:21 and 2 Chronicles 3:17.

like a cup or an open lily blossom. It could hold three thousand baths.[q] [6]He also made ten washbasins and put five on the south and five on the north. The items used for the entirely burned offerings were rinsed in these. The priests washed in the Sea. [7]He made ten gold lampstands as prescribed and put them in the sanctuary, five on the south and five on the north. [8]He also made ten tables and put them in the sanctuary, five on the south and five on the north, as well as a hundred gold bowls. [9]He made the courtyard of the priests and the great courtyard, with doors covered with bronze for the courtyard. [10]He placed the Sea at the southeast corner.

[11]Huram made the pots, the shovels, and the bowls. So Huram finished all his work on God's temple for King Solomon:

[12]two columns;

two circular capitals on top
of the columns;

two networks adorning the two
circular capitals on top of the columns;

[13]four hundred pomegranates for
the two networks, with two rows of
pomegranates for each network that
adorned the two circular capitals on
top of the columns;

[14]ten[r] stands with ten[s] basins on them;

[15]one Sea;

twelve oxen beneath the Sea;

[16]and the pots, the shovels,
and the meat forks.

All the things that Huram-abi made for King Solomon for the LORD's temple were made of polished bronze. [17]The king cast them in clay molds in the Jordan Valley between Succoth and Zarethan.[t] [18]Due to the very large number of objects, Solomon didn't even try to weigh the bronze. [19]Solomon also made all the equipment for God's temple: the gold altar; the tables for the bread of the presence; [20]the lampstands with their lamps, all of pure gold, to burn before the inner sanctuary as prescribed; [21]the flowers, the lamps, and the tongs of

pure gold; [22]and the wick trimmers, bowls, ladles, and censers of pure gold. As for the temple entrance, the inner doors to the most holy place as well as the doors to the main hall were made of gold.

5 When all of Solomon's work on the LORD's temple was finished, he brought the silver, gold, and all the objects his father David had dedicated and put them in the treasuries of God's temple.

Solomon dedicates the temple

[2]Then Solomon assembled Israel's elders, all the tribal leaders, and the clan chieftains of Israel at Jerusalem to bring up the chest containing the LORD's covenant from Zion, David's City. [3]Everyone in Israel assembled before the king in the seventh month,[u] during the festival. [4]When all Israel's elders had arrived, the Levites picked up the chest. [5]They brought the chest, the meeting tent, and all the holy objects that were in the tent. The priests and[v] the Levites brought them up, [6]while King Solomon and the entire Israelite assembly that had joined him before the chest sacrificed countless sheep and oxen. [7]The priests brought the chest containing the LORD's covenant to its designated spot beneath the wings of the winged creatures in the inner sanctuary of the temple, the most holy place. [8]The winged creatures spread their wings over the place where the chest rested, covering the chest and its carrying poles. [9]The carrying poles were so long that their tips could be seen from the holy place[w] in front of the inner sanctuary, though they weren't visible from outside. They are still there today. [10]Nothing was in the chest except the two stone tablets Moses placed there while at Horeb, where the LORD made a covenant with the Israelites after they left Egypt.

[11]Then the priests left the holy place. All the priests who were present had sanctified themselves, regardless of their divisions. [12]All the levitical musicians—Asaph, Heman, Jeduthun, and their families and

[q]One bath is approximately twenty quarts or five gallons.   [r]LXX and 1 Kgs 7:43; MT *he made*   [s]1 Kgs 7:43; MT *he made*   [t]With 1 Kgs 7:46; Heb *Zeredah*   [u]September–October, Tishrei   [v]LXX; MT *the levitical priests*   [w]LXX; MT *the chest*

relatives—were dressed in fine linen and stood east of the altar with cymbals, harps, and zithers, along with one hundred twenty priests blowing trumpets. [13] The trumpeters and singers joined together to praise and thank the LORD as one. Accompanied by trumpets, cymbals, and other musical instruments, they began to sing, praising the LORD:

Yes, God is good!

Yes, God's faithful love lasts forever!

Then a cloud filled the LORD's temple.[x] [14] The priests were unable to carry out their duties on account of the cloud because the LORD's glory filled God's temple.

6 Then Solomon said, "The LORD said that he would live in a dark cloud; [2] but God, I have built you a lofty temple—a place where you can live forever."

[3] The king turned around, and while the entire assembly of Israel was standing there, he blessed them, [4] saying:

Bless the LORD, the God of Israel, who spoke directly to my father David and now has kept his promise: [5] "From the day I brought my people out of the land of Egypt, I haven't selected a city from any Israelite tribe as a site for the building of a temple for my name. Neither have I chosen anyone as prince over my people Israel. [6] But now I have chosen Jerusalem as a place for my name, and David as prince over my people Israel."

[7] My father David wanted to build a temple for the name of the LORD, Israel's God. [8] But the LORD said to my father David: "It is very good that you thought to build a temple for my name. Nevertheless, [9] you yourself won't build that temple. Instead, your very own son will build the temple for my name." [10] The LORD has kept his promise—I have succeeded my father David on Israel's throne, just as the LORD said, and I have built the temple for the name of the LORD, Israel's God. [11] There I've placed the chest that contains the covenant that the LORD made with the Israelites. [12] Solomon stood before the LORD's altar

in front of the entire Israelite assembly and spread out his hands. [13] Now Solomon had made a bronze platform seven and a half feet long, seven and a half feet wide, and four and a half feet high, and he set it in the middle of the enclosure. He stood on it. Then, kneeling before the whole assembly of Israel and spreading his hands toward the sky, [14] he said:

LORD God of Israel, there is no god like you in heaven or on the earth. You keep the covenant and show loyalty to your servants who walk before you with all their heart. [15] This is the covenant you kept with your servant David my father, which you promised him. Today you have fulfilled what you promised.

[16] So now, LORD God of Israel, keep what you promised my father David your servant when you said to him, "You will never fail to have a successor sitting on Israel's throne as long as your descendants carefully walk according to my Instruction, just as you have walked before me." [17] So now, LORD God of Israel, may your promise to your servant David come true.

[18] But how could God possibly live on earth with people? If heaven, even the highest heaven, can't contain you, how can this temple that I have built contain you? [19] LORD, my God, listen to your servant's prayer and request, and hear the cry and prayer that I your servant pray to you. [20] Constantly watch over this temple, the place where you promised to put your name, and listen to the prayer your servant is praying concerning this place. [21] Listen to the request of your servant and your people Israel when they pray concerning this place. Listen from your heavenly dwelling place, and when you hear, forgive!

[22] If someone wrongs another and must take a solemn pledge asserting his innocence before your altar in this temple, [23] then listen from heaven, act, and decide which of your servants is right. Condemn the guilty party, repaying

them for their conduct, but justify the innocent person, repaying them for their righteousness.

²⁴If your people Israel are defeated by an enemy because they have sinned against you, but then they change their hearts, give thanks to your name, and ask for mercy in your presence at this temple, ²⁵then listen from heaven and forgive the sin of your people Israel. Return them to the land you gave to them and their ancestors.

²⁶When the sky holds back its rain because Israel has sinned against you, but they then pray concerning this place, give thanks to your name, and turn away from their sin because you have punished them for it,ʸ ²⁷then listen from heaven and forgive the sin of your servants, your people Israel. Teach them the best way for them to follow, and send rain on your land that you gave to your people as an inheritance.

²⁸Whenever there is a famine or plague in the land, or whenever there is blight, mildew, locusts, or grasshoppers, or whenever someone's enemies attack them in their cities, or any plague or illness comes, ²⁹whatever prayer or petition is made by any individual or by all of your people Israel—because people will recognize their own pain and suffering and spread out their hands toward this temple— ³⁰then listen from heaven where you live. Forgive, act, and repay each person according to all their conduct because you know their hearts. You alone know the human heart! ³¹Do this that they may revere you by following your ways all the days they live on the fertile land that you gave to our ancestors.

³²Listen also to the foreigner who isn't from your people Israel, but who comes from a distant country because of your great reputation, your great power, and your outstretched arm. When they come and pray toward this temple, ³³then listen from heaven where you live, and do everything the foreigner asks. Do this so that all the people of the earth may know your reputation and revere you, as your people Israel do, and recognize that this temple I have built bears your name.

³⁴When your people go to war against their enemies, wherever you may send them, and they pray to you toward this city that you have chosen and concerning this temple that I have built for your name, ³⁵then listen from heaven to their prayer and request and do what is right for them.

³⁶When they sin against you, for there is no one who doesn't sin, and you become angry with them and hand them over to an enemy who takes them away as prisoners to enemy territory, whether distant or nearby, ³⁷if they change their heart in whatever land they are held captive, turning back and begging for your mercy,ᶻ saying, "We have sinned, we have done wrong, and we have acted wickedly!" ³⁸and if they return to you with all their heart and all their being in the enemy territory where they've been taken captive, and pray concerning their land, which you gave to their ancestors, concerning the city you have chosen, and concerning this temple I have built for your name, ³⁹then listen to their prayer and request from your heavenly dwelling place. Do what is right for them, and forgive your people who have sinned against you.

⁴⁰Now, my God, may your eyes be open and your ears attentive to the prayers of this place. ⁴¹And now go, LORD God, to your resting place, you and your mighty chest. May your priests, LORD God, be clothed with salvation; may those loyal to you rejoice in what is good. ⁴²LORD God, don't reject your anointed one.ᵃ Remember your faithful loyalty to your servant David.

7 As soon as Solomon finished praying, fire came down from heaven and consumed the entirely burned offering and the sacrifices, while the LORD's glory filled the temple. ²The priests were unable to enter

---

ʸLXX, Vulg; MT *you have answered them*   ᶻMT adds *in the land they are held captive.*   ᵃLXX; MT *anointed ones* the LORD's temple because the LORD's glory had filled the LORD's temple. ³All the Israelites were watching when the fire fell. As the LORD's glory filled the temple, they knelt down on the pavement with their faces to the ground, worshipping and giving thanks to the LORD, saying, "Yes, God is good! Yes, God's faithful love lasts forever!"

⁴Then the king and all the people sacrificed to the LORD. ⁵King Solomon sacrificed twenty-two thousand oxen and one hundred twenty thousand sheep when the king and all the people dedicated God's temple. ⁶The priests stood at their posts, as did the Levites with the LORD's musical instruments, which King David had made for giving thanks to the LORD, saying, "Yes, God's faithful love lasts forever!" and which David had used when he gave praise. Across from them, the priests were blowing trumpets while all Israel was standing.

⁷Solomon also dedicated the middle of the courtyard in front of the LORD's temple. He had to offer the entirely burned offerings and the fat of the well-being sacrifices there because the bronze altar Solomon had made was too small to contain the entirely burned offerings, the grain offerings, and the pieces of fat.

⁸At that time Solomon, together with all Israel, celebrated the festival for seven days. It was a very large assembly that came from Lebo-hamath to the border[b] of Egypt. ⁹On the eighth day there was a gathering. They had dedicated the altar for seven days and celebrated the festival for another seven days. ¹⁰On the twenty-third day of the seventh month,[c] Solomon dismissed the people to their tents, happy and content because of the goodness the LORD had shown to David, to Solomon, and to his people Israel. ¹¹In this way, Solomon finished the LORD's temple and the royal palace. He successfully accomplished everything he intended for the LORD's temple and his own palace.

Solomon again meets God

¹²Then the LORD appeared to Solomon at night and said to him: I have heard your prayer and have chosen this place as my house of sacrifice. ¹³When I close the sky so that there is no rain or I order the locusts to consume the land or I send a plague against my people, ¹⁴if my people who belong to me will humbly pray, seek my face, and turn from their wicked ways, then I will hear from heaven, forgive their sin, and heal their land. ¹⁵From now on my eyes will be open and my ears will pay attention to the prayers offered in this place, ¹⁶because I have chosen this temple and declared it holy so that my name may be there forever. My eyes and my heart will always be there. ¹⁷As for you, if you will walk before me just as your father David did, doing all that I have commanded you and keeping my regulations and case laws, ¹⁸then I will establish your royal throne, just as I promised your father David: You will never fail to have a successor ruling in Israel. ¹⁹But if any of you ever turn away from and abandon the regulations and commands that I have given you, and go to serve other gods and worship them, ²⁰then I will uproot you[d] from my land that I gave you, and I will reject this temple that I made holy for my name. I will make it a joke, insulted by everyone. ²¹Everyone who passes by this temple—so lofty now—will be shocked and will wonder, Why has the LORD done such a thing to this land and temple? ²²The answer will come, Because they abandoned the LORD, the God of their ancestors, who brought them out of Egypt. They embraced other gods, worshipping and serving them. This is why God brought all this disaster on them.

Solomon's buildings and prosperity

8 After twenty years of building the LORD's temple and his royal palace, ²Solomon next rebuilt the cities Huram had given him, and he settled Israelites there.

³Solomon went to Hamath-zobah and seized it. ⁴He fortified Tadmor in the wilderness, along with all the storage cities he had built in Hamath. ⁵Solomon also built Upper Beth-horon and Lower Beth-horon as fortress cities with walls, gates, and

ᵇOr Wadi, traditionally Brook   ᶜSeptember–October, Tishrei   ᵈOr Israel (or them) crossbars; [6]Baalath; all the cities he used for storage; and all the cities used for chariots and cavalry—along with everything else he wanted to build in Jerusalem, Lebanon, and throughout his kingdom.

[7]Any non-Israelite people who remained of the Hittites, Amorites, Perizzites, Hivites, and Jebusites—[8]that is, the descendants of such people who were still in the land because the Israelites weren't able to destroy them—Solomon forced into the labor gangs that are still in existence today. [9]However, Solomon didn't force the Israelites to work as slaves; instead, they became warriors, chief officers, and the commanders of his chariots and cavalry. [10]And Solomon had two hundred fifty chief officers[e] who were in charge of the people.

[11]Solomon brought Pharaoh's daughter from David's City to a palace he had built for her, because he said, "My wife mustn't live in the palace of Israel's King David, because the places where the LORD's chest has been are holy."

[12]Then Solomon offered entirely burned offerings to the LORD on the LORD's altar that Solomon had built in front of the porch, [13]as each day required, according to the commandment of Moses for sabbaths, new moon festivals, and the three annual festivals—Unleavened Bread, Weeks, and Booths. [14]Just as his father David had ordered, Solomon set up the divisions of the priests for their services and the Levites to their posts for offering praise and ministering in front of the priests, doing what needed to be done each day; as well as the gatekeepers in their divisions at each gate, because this was what David the man of God had commanded. [15]They didn't deviate in any way from the king's commands concerning the priests, the Levites, or the treasuries. [16]All Solomon's work was carried out from the day the foundation of the LORD's temple was laid until its completion. Then the LORD's temple was completely finished.

[17]Then Solomon went to Ezion-geber and Eloth on the coast in the land of Edom.

[18]Huram had his servants bring ships to Solomon, along with crews of expert sailors. They went with Solomon's servants to Ophir and imported four hundred fifty kikkars of gold, which they brought back to King Solomon.

Queen of Sheba

9 When the queen of Sheba heard reports about Solomon, she came to Jerusalem to test Solomon with riddles. Accompanying her was a huge entourage, with camels carrying spices, large amounts of gold, and precious stones. After she arrived, she told Solomon everything that was on her mind. [2]Solomon answered all her questions; nothing was too difficult for him to answer. [3]When the queen of Sheba saw how wise Solomon was, the palace he had built, [4]the food on his table, his servants' quarters, the function and dress of his attendants, his cupbearers and their dress, and the entirely burned offerings he offered at the LORD's temple,[f] it took her breath away.

[5]"The report I heard about your deeds and wisdom when I was still at home is true," she said to the king. [6]"I didn't believe it until I came and saw it with my own eyes. In fact, the half of it wasn't told to me! You have far more than I was told. [7]Your people and these servants who continually serve you and get to listen to your wisdom are truly happy! [8]Bless the LORD your God because he was pleased to put you on the throne as king for the LORD your God. Because your God loved Israel and wanted to establish them forever, he has made you their king to uphold justice and righteousness."

[9]Then she gave the king one hundred twenty kikkars of gold, a great quantity of spices, and precious stones. Never again has such a quantity of spice come to Israel as when the queen of Sheba gave this gift to King Solomon.

[10]In addition, Huram's servants and the servants of Solomon, who had brought gold back from Ophir, also brought algum wood and precious stones. [11]The king made steps[g]

---

[e]Qere; Kethib *officers of the troops* [f]LXX, Syr, Vulg, 1 Kgs 10:5; MT *how he processed* (or *went up*) *to the* LORD's *temple.* [g]LXX, Vulg; Heb uncertain

for the LORD's temple and for the royal palace with the algum wood, as well as lyres and harps for the musicians. Never before had anything like them been seen in the land of Judah. [12]King Solomon gave the queen of Sheba everything she wanted, even more than she had brought the king. Then she and her servants returned to her homeland.

Solomon's wealth

[13]Solomon received an annual income of six hundred sixty-six kikkars of gold, [14]not including income from the traders and merchants. All the Arabian kings and the governors of the land also brought Solomon gold and silver. [15]King Solomon made two hundred body-sized shields of hammered gold, using fifteen pounds[h] of hammered gold in each shield; [16]and three hundred small shields of hammered gold, using seven and a half pounds[i] of hammered gold in each shield. The king placed these in the Forest of Lebanon Palace.

[17]The king also made a large ivory throne and covered it with pure gold. [18]Six steps led up to the throne, which had a gold footrest attached. Two lions stood beside the armrests on both sides of the throne. [19]Another twelve lions stood on both sides of the six steps. No other kingdom had anything like this.

[20]All King Solomon's drinking cups were made of gold, and all the items in the Forest of Lebanon Palace were made of pure gold, not silver, since even silver wasn't considered good enough in Solomon's time! [21]The royal fleet sailed to Tarshish with the servants of Huram, returning once every three years with gold, silver, ivory, monkeys, and peacocks.[j]

[22]King Solomon far exceeded all the earth's kings in wealth and wisdom, [23]and kings of every nation wanted an audience with Solomon in order to hear his God-given wisdom. [24]Year after year they came with tribute: objects of silver and gold, clothing, weapons, spices, horses, and mules.

[25]Solomon also had four thousand stalls for horses and chariots, together with twelve thousand horsemen that he kept in the chariot cities and with the king in Jerusalem. [26]He ruled all the kings from the Euphrates[k] to the Philistines' land and the border of Egypt. [27]In Jerusalem, the king made silver as common as stones and cedar as common as sycamore trees that grow in the foothills. [28]Solomon's horses were imported from Egypt and every land.

Solomon's remaining days

[29]The rest of Solomon's deeds, from beginning to end, aren't they written in the records of the prophet Nathan, the prophecies of Ahijah from Shiloh, and the visions of the seer Iddo concerning Jeroboam, Nebat's son? [30]Solomon ruled over all Israel in Jerusalem for forty years. [31]Solomon lay down with his ancestors and was buried in David's City with his father. His son Rehoboam succeeded him as king.

How Rehoboam lost the kingdom

10 Rehoboam went to Shechem, where all Israel had come to make him king. [2]When Jeroboam, Nebat's son, heard the news, he returned from Egypt where he had fled from King Solomon. [3]The people sent and called for Jeroboam, who along with all Israel came and said to Rehoboam, [4]"Your father made our workload[l] very heavy; if you will lessen the demands your father made of us and lighten the heavy workload he demanded from us, then we will serve you."

[5]He answered them, "Come back in three days." So the people left.

[6]King Rehoboam consulted the elders who had served his father Solomon when he was alive. "What do you advise?" Rehoboam asked. "How should I respond to these people?"

[7]"If you are kind to these people and try to please them by speaking gently with them," they replied, "they will be your servants forever."

[8]But Rehoboam ignored the advice the elders gave him and instead sought the counsel of the young advisors who had grown up with him and now served him.

---

[h]Or six hundred shekels [i]Or three hundred shekels [j]Or possibly apes; Heb uncertain [k]Or the river [l]Or our yoke

⁹"What do you advise?" he asked them. "How should we respond to these people who said to me, 'Lighten the workload your father demanded from us'?"

¹⁰The young people who had grown up with Rehoboam said to him, "This people said to you, 'Your father made our workload heavy. Lighten it for us!' Now this is what you should say to them, 'My baby[m] finger is thicker than my father's waist! ¹¹So if my father made your workload heavy, I'll make it even heavier! If my father disciplined you with whips, I'll do it with scorpions!'"

¹²Jeroboam and all the people returned to Rehoboam on the third day, just as the king had specified when he said, "Come back in three days." ¹³The king then answered the people harshly. He ignored the elders' advice, ¹⁴and instead followed the young people's advice. He said, "My father made your workload heavy, but I'll make it even heavier; my father disciplined you with whips, but I'll do it with scorpions!"

¹⁵The king didn't listen to the people because this turn of events came from God so that the LORD might keep his promise concerning Jeroboam, Nebat's son, which God delivered through Ahijah from Shiloh. ¹⁶When all Israel saw[n] that the king wouldn't listen to them, the people answered the king,

"Why should we care about David?
We have no stake in Jesse's son!
Go back to your homes, Israel!
You better look after
    your own house now, David!"

Then all Israel went back to their homes, ¹⁷and Rehoboam ruled over only the Israelites who lived in the cities of Judah.

¹⁸When King Rehoboam sent Hadoram to them (he was the leader of the work gang), the Israelites stoned him to death. King Rehoboam quickly got into his chariot and fled to Jerusalem. ¹⁹And so Israel has been in rebellion against David's dynasty to this day.

11 When Rehoboam arrived at Jerusalem, he assembled the house of Judah and Benjamin, one hundred eighty thousand select warriors, to fight against Israel and to restore the kingdom to Rehoboam. ²But the LORD's word came to Shemaiah the man of God: ³Tell Judah's King Rehoboam, Solomon's son, and all Israel in Judah and Benjamin, ⁴This is what the LORD says: Don't make war against your relatives. Go home, every one of you, because this is my plan. When they heard the LORD's words, they abandoned their attack against Jeroboam.

⁵Rehoboam lived in Jerusalem, but he built cities for Judah's defense ⁶in Bethlehem, Etam, Tekoa, ⁷Beth-zur, Soco, Adullam, ⁸Gath, Mareshah, Ziph, ⁹Adoraim, Lachish, Azekah, ¹⁰Zorah, Aijalon, and Hebron. These were the fortified cities in Judah and Benjamin. ¹¹He made the fortifications stronger, placed commanders in them, and supplied them with food, oil, and wine. ¹²He also stored shields and spears in each of the cities, making them very strong. This is how Judah and Benjamin remained under his control.

[m]Or pinky; perhaps a euphemism [n]Syr, OL, Tg; MT lacks saw.

REHOBOAM

Son of Solomon and the Ammonite woman Naamah (1 Kgs 14:21, 31) and grandson of David. Rehoboam is noted for precipitating the division of the kingdom of Israel. He retained the southern tribal areas of Benjamin and Judah under his control. These tribes survived as the kingdom of Judah until the Babylonian invasion and conquest in 587 BCE. Rehoboam lost the northern tribes, who formed their own union, Israel, which lasted until 722 BCE.

[13] The priests and the Levites from every region throughout all Israel sided with Rehoboam. [14] The Levites left their pastures and property to come to Judah and Jerusalem because Jeroboam and his sons had refused to let them serve as the LORD's priests, [15] having appointed his own priests for the shrines and the goat and calf idols he had made. [16] People from every tribe of Israel who had made up their minds to seek the LORD, Israel's God, came to Jerusalem to sacrifice to the LORD, the God of their ancestors. [17] They strengthened the kingdom of Judah and supported Rehoboam, Solomon's son, for three years by following the way of David and Solomon those three years.

[18] Rehoboam married Mahalath daughter of Jerimoth, David's son, and Abihail daughter of Eliab, Jesse's son. [19] The sons she bore him were Jeush, Shemariah, and Zaham. [20] Later he married Maacah, Absalom's daughter, who bore him Abijah, Attai, Ziza, and Shelomith. [21] Rehoboam loved Absalom's daughter Maacah more than all his wives and secondary wives. In all, he had eighteen wives and sixty secondary wives, twenty-eight sons, and sixty daughters. [22] Rehoboam named Abijah, Maacah's son, as his successor in order to make him king. [23] He wisely placed some of his sons in every region of Judah and Benjamin, in every fortified city, and gave them plenty of food and sought many wives for them.

12 But as soon as Rehoboam had secured his royal power, he, along with all Israel, abandoned the LORD's Instruction.

Rehoboam rules

[2] Egypt's King Shishak attacked Jerusalem in the fifth year of King Rehoboam because Israel had been unfaithful to the LORD. [3] Accompanying Shishak from Egypt were twelve hundred chariots, sixty thousand horses, and countless Libyan, Sukkite, and Cushite warriors. [4] He captured the fortified cities of Judah and came toward Jerusalem. [5] Then the prophet Shemaiah went to Rehoboam and the leaders of Judah who had gathered at Jerusalem because of Shishak, and told them, This is what the LORD says: Since you have abandoned me, now I am abandoning you to Shishak's power.

[6] Then the leaders of Israel and the king submitted. "The LORD is right," they said. [7] When the LORD saw that they had submitted, the LORD's word came to Shemaiah: Since they have submitted, I won't destroy them. I will deliver them in a little while, and I won't use Shishak to pour out my anger against Jerusalem. [8] Nevertheless, they will be subject to him so that they learn the difference between serving me and serving other nations.

[9] Egypt's King Shishak attacked Jerusalem and seized the treasures of the LORD's temple and the royal palace. He took everything, even the gold shields Solomon had made. [10] King Rehoboam replaced them with bronze shields and assigned them to the officers of the guard who protected the entrance to the royal palace. ([11] Whenever the king entered the LORD's temple, the guards would carry the shields and then return them to the guardroom.) [12] When Rehoboam submitted, the LORD was no longer angry with him, and total destruction was avoided. There were, after all, some good things still in Judah. [13] So King Rehoboam was securely established in Jerusalem. Rehoboam was 41

SHISHAK

The Egyptian king Shishak plays a pivotal role in the biblical accounts of the division of the kingdom after the death of King Solomon by harboring the fugitive rebel Jeroboam (1 Kgs 11:40) and attacking Judah (1 Kgs 14:25-26; 2 Chron 12:2-9). The biblical Shishak was Sheshonq I (or Shoshenq I), the first king of the 22nd Dynasty, who ruled Egypt 931–910 or 945–924 BCE.

years old when he became king, and he ruled seventeen years in Jerusalem, the city the LORD had chosen from all the tribes of Israel to put his name. His mother's name was Naamah from Ammon. [14]But Rehoboam did what was evil because he didn't set his heart on seeking the LORD. [15]The deeds of Rehoboam, from beginning to end, aren't they written in the records of the prophet Shemaiah and the seer Iddo, including the genealogical records? There was continual warfare between Rehoboam and Jeroboam. [16]Rehoboam lay down with his ancestors and was buried in David's City. His son Abijah° succeeded him as king.

Abijah rules Judah

13Abijah[p] became king over Judah in the eighteenth year of King Jeroboam. [2]He ruled for three years in Jerusalem. His mother's name was Micaiah; she was Uriel's daughter from Gibeah. When war broke out between Abijah and Jeroboam, [3]Abijah went to fight with an army of four hundred thousand select troops against Jeroboam's select forces numbering eight hundred thousand, who were arrayed in battle formation.

[4]Abijah stood on the heights of Mount Zemaraim in Ephraim's highlands and said: "Listen to me, Jeroboam and all Israel! [5]Surely you know that the LORD, Israel's God, made an unbreakable covenant[q] with David and his descendants that they would rule Israel forever. [6]It was Jeroboam, Nebat's son, the servant of Solomon, David's son, who rebelled against his master. [7]When some useless, worthless people joined his cause, they overpowered Rehoboam, Solomon's son, who was too young and timid to resist them. [8]And now do you intend to challenge the LORD's royal rule, entrusted to David's descendants? You may have a numerical advantage, as well as the gold calves Jeroboam made for you as gods. [9]But you've banished the LORD's priests, Aaron's sons, along with the Levites, so that you could appoint your own priests as other countries do. Now anyone who shows up with a young bull and seven rams can become a priest of these phony gods!

[10]"But us? The LORD is our God, and we haven't abandoned him. Aaron's descendants serve as the LORD's priests, assisted in the work by the Levites. [11]Every morning and every evening they offer entirely burned offerings and fragrant incense to the LORD, and set out bread in stacks upon a clean table. At night they light the lamps on the gold lampstand. Yes, while you are abandoning the LORD our God, we are doing what he requires. [12]Listen! God is on our side, at our head, along with his priests, who are ready to sound the battle trumpets against you. So, Israelites, don't fight against the LORD, the God of your ancestors, for you won't succeed!"

[13]Meanwhile, Jeroboam had sent troops around behind them for an ambush so that the main force was in front of Judah while the ambush was behind. [14]When Judah looked around and suddenly realized that they were surrounded, they cried out to the LORD while the priests sounded the trumpets [15]and raised the battle cry. When they raised the battle cry, God defeated Jeroboam and all Israel before Abijah and Judah. [16]So the Israelites fled before Judah, and God gave Judah the victory. [17]Abijah and his people struck them severely: five hundred thousand select warriors were killed. [18]Israel was subdued on that occasion, and Judah succeeded because they relied on the LORD, the God of their ancestors. [19]Abijah pursued Jeroboam and took these cities away from him: Bethel, Jeshanah, and Ephron,[r] along with their villages. [20]Jeroboam failed to regain power during the time of Abijah. The LORD finally struck him down, and he died. [21]Abijah, however, grew strong. He married fourteen wives; he had twenty-two sons and sixteen daughters. [22]The rest of Abijah's deeds, what he

---

°Spelled Abijam in 1 Kgs 14:31 [p]Spelled Abijam in 1 Kgs 15:1, 7-8 [q]Or *a covenant of salt* [r]Qere, LXX; Kethib *Ephrain*

did and what he said, are written in the account of the prophet Iddo. [1]Abijah lay
down with his ancestors and was buried in David's City. His son Asa succeeded
him as king.

Asa rules Judah

[s]In Asa's time, the land had peace for ten
years. [2t]Asa did what was right and good
in the LORD his God's eyes. [3]He removed
the foreign altars and shrines, smashed the
sacred pillars, cut down the sacred poles,[u]
[4]and urged Judah to seek the LORD, the
God of their ancestors, by doing what the
Instruction and the commandments required. [5]He also removed the shrines and
incense altars from all the cities of Judah
so that the kingdom was at peace under
him. [6]When the land was at peace, he built
fortified cities in Judah; there was no war
in those years because the LORD had given
him rest.

[7]"Let's build up these cities," Asa told
Judah. "We'll surround them with walls,
towers, gates, and crossbars while the land
is still ours, because we sought the LORD
our God and he sought us[v] and surrounded
us with rest." As a result, the people successfully completed their building projects.

Judah defeats Cush

[8]Asa had an army of three hundred
thousand Judeans armed with body-sized
shields and spears and another two hundred eighty thousand from Benjamin
armed with small shields and bows. All
were brave warriors. [9]Zerah the Cushite
marched against him with an army of one
million men and three hundred chariots.
When he got as far as Mareshah, [10]Asa
marched against him, setting up for battle
in a valley north[w] of Mareshah.

[11]Then Asa cried out to the LORD his
God, "LORD, only you can help the weak
against the powerful.[x] Help us, LORD our
God, because we rely on you and we have

marched against this multitude in your
name. You are the LORD our God. Don't let
a mere human stand against you!"

[12]So the LORD struck the Cushites before Asa and Judah, and the Cushites fled.
[13]Asa and his troops chased them as far as
Gerar. The Cushites fell until there were no
survivors. They were completely crushed by
the LORD and his army, who carried off a
huge amount of loot, [14]and attacked all the
cities surrounding Gerar who were terrified
of the LORD. They plundered all these cities
as well because there was a great amount
of loot in them. [15]They also attacked the
herdsmen's camps, taking many sheep and
camels before returning to Jerusalem.

15 When God's spirit came upon Azariah, Oded's son, [2]he confronted Asa:
"Listen to me, Asa and all Judah and Benjamin," he said. "The LORD is with you as long
as you are with him. If you seek him, he will
be found by you; but if you abandon him,
he will abandon you. [3]For a long time Israel
was without the true God, without a priest
to teach them, and without the Instruction.
[4]But in their time of trouble they turned to
the LORD, Israel's God. They sought him
and found him! [5]At that time, it wasn't safe
to travel because great turmoil affected all
the inhabitants of the area. [6]Nation was
crushed by nation and city by city, as God
troubled them with every kind of problem.
[7]But as for you, be brave and don't lose
heart, because your work will be rewarded!"

Asa's reforms

[8]As soon as Asa heard these words and
the prophecy of Azariah, Oded's son,[y] he
felt brave and removed the detestable
idols from all of Judah and Benjamin, as
well as from the cities he had captured in
Ephraim's highlands, and he repaired the
LORD's altar that stood before the LORD's
entrance hall. [9]Then Asa gathered all Judah
and Benjamin, along with those who were
living among them as immigrants from

---

[s]13:23 in Heb [t]14:1 in Heb [u]Heb *asherim*, perhaps objects devoted to the goddess Asherah; cf 1 Kgs
15:13 [v]LXX; MT lacks *and* and repeats *we sought.* [w]LXX; MT an otherwise unknown *Zephathah Valley*
[x]Heb uncertain; or *it is not with you to help between the many and the powerless.* [y]Cf Syr, Vulg; MT *and the
prophecy of the prophet Oded*

Ephraim, Manasseh, and Simeon, because many people from Israel had joined up with him when they saw that the LORD his God was with him. [10]They gathered in Jerusalem in the third month of the fifteenth year of Asa's rule. [11]On that day they sacrificed to the LORD part of the loot they had taken: seven hundred oxen and seven thousand sheep. [12]They made a covenant to seek the LORD, the God of their ancestors, with all their heart and all their being. [13]They agreed that anyone who refused to seek the LORD, Israel's God, would be put to death, whether young or old, male or female. [14]They swore this to the LORD with a loud voice, shouts of joy, and blasts from trumpets and horns. [15]All Judah was delighted with the solemn pledge because they had sworn it with all their hearts. When they enthusiastically sought God, he was found by them, and the LORD gave them peace on every side. [16]Asa the king even removed his grandmother Maacah from the position of queen mother because she had made an image of Asherah. Asa cut down her image, pulverized it, and burned it in the Kidron Valley. [17]Although the shrines weren't removed from Israel, Asa nevertheless remained committed with all his heart throughout his life. [18]He brought into God's temple the various silver and gold objects that he and his father had dedicated. [19]There was no war until the thirty-fifth year of Asa's rule.

Aram invades Judah

16 In the thirty-sixth year of Asa's rule, Israel's King Baasha attacked Judah and fortified Ramah to prevent Judah's King Asa from moving into that area. [2]Asa took silver and gold from the treasuries of the LORD's temple and the royal palace and sent them to Aram's King Ben-hadad, who ruled in Damascus, with the following message: [3]"Let's make a covenant similar to the one between our fathers. Since I have already sent you silver and gold, break your covenant with Israel's King Baasha so that he will leave me alone." [4]Ben-hadad agreed with King Asa and sent his army command-

ers against the cities of Israel, attacking Ijon, Dan, Abel-maim, and all the store-cities of Naphtali. [5]As soon as Baasha learned of this, he stopped building Ramah and abandoned his work. [6]Then King Asa had all Judah carry away the stone and timber that Baasha was using to build Ramah, and King Asa used it to build Geba and Mizpah. [7]At that time Hanani the seer came to Judah's King Asa and said to him, "Because you relied on Aram's king and not on the LORD your God, the army of Aram's king has slipped out of your grasp. [8]Weren't the Cushites and the Libyans a vast army with chariots and horsemen to spare? Still, when you relied on the LORD, he delivered them into your power, [9]because the LORD's eyes scan the whole world to strengthen those who are committed to him with all their hearts. Your foolishness means that you will have war on your hands from now on." [10]Asa was angry with the seer. Asa was so mad he threw Hanani in jail and took his anger out on some of the people.

Asa's disease and death

[11]The rest of Asa's deeds, from beginning to end, are written in the official records of Israel's and Judah's kings. [12]In the thirty-ninth year of his rule, Asa developed a severe foot disease. But even in his illness he refused to seek the LORD and consulted doctors instead. [13]In the forty-first year of his rule, Asa lay down with his ancestors. [14]He was buried in the tomb he had prepared for himself in David's City, and was laid on a bed filled with sweet spices and various kinds of perfume, with a huge fire made in his honor.

Jehoshaphat rules Judah

17 Asa's son Jehoshaphat succeeded him as king. Jehoshaphat strengthened his position against Israel [2]by stationing troops in the fortified cities of Judah and placing soldiers throughout the land of Judah and in the cities of Ephraim that his father Asa had captured. [3]The LORD was with Jehoshaphat because he followed the earlier ways of his father[z] by not seeking

Baal. ⁴Instead, he sought the God of his father, and unlike Israel, he followed God's commandments. ⁵The LORD gave him firm control over the kingdom, and all Judah brought Jehoshaphat tribute, so that he had abundant riches and honor. ⁶Jehoshaphat took pride in the LORD's ways and again removed the shrines and the sacred poles[a] from Judah.

⁷In the third year of his rule, Jehoshaphat sent his officials Ben-hail, Obadiah, Zechariah, Nethanel, and Micaiah to teach in the cities of Judah. ⁸They were accompanied by the Levites Shemaiah, Nethaniah, Zebadiah, Asahel, Shemiramoth, Jehonathan, Adonijah, Tobijah, and Tob-adonijah, and by the priests Elishama and Jehoram. ⁹They taught throughout Judah. They brought with them the LORD's Instruction scroll as they made their rounds to all the cities of Judah, teaching the people.

¹⁰All the kingdoms surrounding Judah were afraid of the LORD and didn't wage war against Jehoshaphat. ¹¹Some of the Philistines brought a load of silver as tribute to Jehoshaphat. The Arabians also brought flocks to Jehoshaphat: seventy-seven hundred rams and seventy-seven hundred goats. ¹²As Jehoshaphat grew increasingly powerful, he built fortresses and storage cities in Judah ¹³and had many supplies in the cities of Judah. He also had an army of mighty warriors in Jerusalem, ¹⁴registered by their clans as follows: Judah's officers over units of a thousand included Commander Adnah with three hundred thousand soldiers; ¹⁵next to him was Commander Jehohanan with two hundred eighty thousand soldiers; ¹⁶at his side was Amasiah, Zichri's son, who volunteered for the LORD with two hundred thousand soldiers. ¹⁷From Benjamin came a valiant warrior: Eliada, together with two hundred thousand armed with bow and shield; ¹⁸next to him was Jehozabad, together with one hundred eighty thousand soldiers. ¹⁹These were the individuals who served the king in addition to those the king placed in the fortified cities throughout Judah.

Jehoshaphat and Ahab

18 Even though Jehoshaphat already had great wealth and honor, he allied himself with Ahab through marriage. ²A few years later, while Jehoshaphat was visiting Ahab in Samaria, Ahab slaughtered many sheep and oxen for Jehoshaphat and those who were with him in order to persuade him to attack Ramoth-gilead. ³"Will you go with me to Ramoth-gilead?" Israel's King Ahab asked Judah's King Jehoshaphat.

Jehoshaphat replied, "I and my people will be united with you and your people in battle. ⁴But," Jehoshaphat said to Israel's king, "first, let's see what the LORD has to say." ⁵So Israel's king gathered four hundred prophets and asked them, "Should we go to war with Ramoth-gilead or not?"

"Attack!" the prophets answered. "God will hand it over to the king."

⁶But Jehoshaphat said, "Isn't there any other prophet of the LORD around whom we could ask?"

⁷"There's one other man who could ask the LORD for us," Israel's king told Jehoshaphat, "but I hate him because he never prophesies anything good about me, only bad. His name is Micaiah, Imlah's son."

"The king shouldn't speak like that!" Jehoshaphat said.

⁸So Israel's king called an officer and ordered, "Bring Micaiah, Imlah's son, right away."

⁹Now Israel's king and Judah's King Jehoshaphat were sitting on their thrones dressed in their royal robes at the threshing floor beside the entrance to the gate of Samaria. All the prophets were prophesying in front of them. ¹⁰Zedekiah, Chenaanah's son, made iron horns for himself and said, "This is what the LORD says: With these horns you will gore the Arameans until there's nothing left of them!"

¹¹The other prophets agreed: "Attack Ramoth-gilead and win! The LORD will hand it over to the king!"

¹²Meanwhile, the messenger who had gone to summon Micaiah said to him, "Listen, the prophets all agree that the king

[a]Heb *asherim*, perhaps objects devoted to the goddess Asherah

will succeed. You should say the same thing they say and prophesy success."

[13] But Micaiah answered, "As surely as the LORD lives, I will say only what God tells me to say."[b]

[14] When Micaiah arrived, the king asked him, "Micaiah, should we go to war with Ramoth-gilead or not?"

"Attack and win!" Micaiah answered. "The LORD will hand it over to the king."

[15] But the king said, "How many times must I demand that you tell me the truth when you speak in the LORD's name?"

[16] Then Micaiah replied, "I saw all Israel scattered on the hills like sheep without a shepherd! And then the LORD said: 'They have no master. Let them return safely to their own homes.'"

[17] Then Israel's king said to Jehoshaphat, "Didn't I tell you? He never prophesies anything good about me, only bad."

[18] Then Micaiah said, "Listen now to the LORD's word: I saw the LORD enthroned with all the heavenly forces stationed at his right and at his left. [19] The LORD said, 'Who will persuade Israel's King Ahab so that he attacks Ramoth-gilead and dies there?' There were several suggestions, [20] until one particular spirit approached the LORD and said, 'I will persuade him.' 'How?' the LORD asked. [21] 'I will be a lying spirit in the mouths of all his prophets,' he said. The LORD agreed: 'You will succeed in persuading him! Go ahead!' [22] So now, since the LORD placed a lying spirit in the mouths of these prophets of yours, it

is the LORD who has pronounced disaster against you!"

[23] Zedekiah, Chenaanah's son, approached Micaiah and slapped him on the cheek. "Just how did the LORD's spirit leave me to speak to you?" he asked.

[24] Micaiah answered, "You will find out on the day you try to hide in an inner room."

[25] "Arrest him," ordered Israel's king, "and turn him over to Amon the city governor and to Joash the king's son. [26] Tell them, 'The king says: Put this man in prison and feed him minimum rations of bread and water until I return safely.'"

[27] "If you ever return safely," Micaiah replied, "then the LORD wasn't speaking through me." Then he added, "Mark my words, every last one of you!"

[28] So Israel's king and Judah's King Jehoshaphat attacked Ramoth-gilead. [29] Israel's king said to Jehoshaphat, "I will disguise myself when we go into battle, but you should wear your royal attire." When the king of Israel had disguised himself, they entered the battle.

[30] Meanwhile, Aram's king had commanded his chariot officers, "Don't bother with anyone big or small. Fight only with Israel's king." [31] When the chariot officers saw Jehoshaphat, they assumed that he must be Israel's king, so they turned to attack him. But when Jehoshaphat cried out, the LORD helped him, and God lured them away from him. [32] When the chariot officers realized that he wasn't Israel's king, they stopped chasing him.

[b] LXX, 1 Kgs 22:14; MT omits *me*.

JEHOSHAPHAT

　　Son of Asa. He was the sixth king of the Davidic monarchy and the fourth king of Judah after the division of the kingdom in 922 BCE. His mother was Azubah the daughter of Shilhi (1 Kgs 22:41-42; 2 Chron 20:31). Jehoshaphat was 35 years old when he became king, and he ruled in Judah 25 years, from 873 to 849 BCE. He followed his father Asa, who had reigned in Jerusalem for 41 years (1 Kgs 15:10). Jehoshaphat ruled during the reigns of Omri, Ahab, Ahaziah, and Joram, kings of the northern kingdom of Israel.

³³Someone, however, randomly shot an arrow that struck Israel's king between the joints in his armor. "Turn around and get me out of the battle," the king told his chariot driver. "I've been hit!" ³⁴While the battle raged all that day, Israel's king stood propped up in his chariot facing the Arameans. But that evening he died, just as the sun was going down.

19 Upon the safe arrival of Judah's King Jehoshaphat to his palace in Jerusalem, ²Jehu son of Hanani the seer came out to meet him and said, "Why did you help the wicked? Why have you loved those who hate the LORD? This is why the LORD is angry with you. ³Nevertheless, there is some good to be found in you, in that you have removed the sacred poles^c from the land and set your mind to seek God."

Jehoshaphat's reforms

⁴Though Jehoshaphat lived in Jerusalem, he regularly went out among the people between Beer-sheba and Ephraim's highlands, and encouraged them to return to the LORD, the God of their ancestors. ⁵He appointed judges throughout the land in each of the fortified cities of Judah, ⁶instructing them, "Be careful when you pass judgment. You aren't dispensing justice by merely human standards but for the LORD, who is with you. ⁷Therefore, respect the LORD and act accordingly, because there can be no injustice, playing favorites, or taking bribes when it comes to the LORD our God."

⁸Jehoshaphat also appointed judges in Jerusalem from among the Levites, the priests, and the family heads of Israel to administer the LORD's Instruction and to settle disputes among those living^d in Jerusalem. ⁹He instructed them, "You must respect the LORD at all times, in truth, and with complete integrity. ¹⁰In any case that comes before you from a fellow citizen in an outlying town, whether it involves bloodshed or is an issue of instruction, commandment, regulations, or case laws,

you must warn them not to sin against the LORD, consequently making him angry with both you and your fellow citizen. Do this, and you won't sin. ¹¹Amariah the chief priest will be in charge of all religious matters, and Zebadiah, Ishmael's son, the leader of Judah's house, will be in charge of all civil matters. The Levites will serve as your officers of the court. Carry out your duties with confidence, and may the LORD be with those who do good."

Jehoshaphat's victory

20 Some time later, the Moabites and the Ammonites, along with some of the Meunites,^e attacked Jehoshaphat. ²Jehoshaphat was told, "A large army from beyond the sea, from Edom,^f is coming to attack you. They are already at Hazazon-tamar!" (that is, En-gedi). ³Frightened, Jehoshaphat decided to seek the LORD's help and proclaimed a fast for all Judah. ⁴People from all of Judah's cities came to ask the LORD for help. ⁵Then Jehoshaphat stood up in the congregation of Judah and Jerusalem in the LORD's temple in front of the new courtyard. ⁶"LORD, the God of our ancestors, you alone are God in heaven. You rule all the kingdoms of the nations. You are so powerful that no one can oppose you. ⁷You, our God, drove out the inhabitants of this land before your people Israel and gave this land to the descendants of your friend Abraham forever. ⁸They have lived in it and have built a sanctuary in honor of your name in it, saying, ⁹'If calamity, sword, flood,^g plague, or famine comes upon us, we will stand before this temple, before you, because your name is in this temple. We will cry out to you in our distress, and you will hear us and save us.' ¹⁰So look here! The Ammonites, the Moabites, and those from Mount Seir—the people you wouldn't let Israel invade when they came out of Egypt's land, so Israel avoided them and didn't destroy them—¹¹here they are, returning the favor by coming to drive us out of your possession that you gave to us!

---

^cHeb *asherot*, perhaps objects devoted to the goddess Asherah   ^dLXX, Vulg; MT *they returned to Jerusalem*
^eLXX; MT *Ammonites*   ^fOL; MT *Aram*   ^gLXX; MT *judgment*

¹²Our God, won't you punish them? We are powerless against this mighty army that is about to attack us. We don't know what to do, and so we are looking to you for help."

¹³All Judah was standing before the LORD, even their little ones, wives, and children. ¹⁴Then the LORD's spirit came upon Jahaziel son of Zechariah son of Benaiah son of Jeiel son of Mattaniah, a Levite of the line of Asaph, as he stood in the middle of the assembly.

¹⁵"Pay attention, all of Judah, every inhabitant of Jerusalem, and King Jehoshaphat," Jahaziel said. "This is what the LORD says to you: Don't be afraid or discouraged by this great army because the battle isn't yours. It belongs to God! ¹⁶March out against them tomorrow. Since they will be coming through the Ziz pass, meet them at the end of the valley that opens into the Jeruel wilderness. ¹⁷You don't need to fight this battle. Just take your places, stand ready, and watch how the LORD, who is with you, will deliver you, Judah and Jerusalem. Don't be afraid or discouraged! Go out tomorrow and face them. The LORD will be with you."

¹⁸Then Jehoshaphat bowed down with his face to the ground, and all Judah and the inhabitants of Jerusalem fell before the LORD in worship. ¹⁹Levites from the lines of Kohath and Korah stood up to loudly praise the LORD, the God of Israel.

²⁰Early the next morning they went into the Tekoa wilderness. When they were about to go out, Jehoshaphat stood and said, "Listen to me, Judah and every inhabitant of Jerusalem! Trust the LORD your God, and you will stand firm; trust his prophets and succeed!"

²¹After consulting with the people, Jehoshaphat appointed musicians to play for the LORD, praising his majestic holiness. They were to march out before the warriors, saying, "Give thanks to the LORD because his faithful love lasts forever!" ²²As they broke into joyful song and praise, the LORD launched a surprise attack against the Ammonites, the Moabites, and those from Mount Seir who were invading Judah, so that they were defeated. ²³The Ammonites and the Moabites turned on those from Mount Seir, completely destroying them. Once they had finished off the inhabitants of Seir, they helped to destroy each other!

²⁴When Judah arrived at the point overlooking the wilderness, all they could see were corpses lying all over the ground. There were no survivors. ²⁵When Jehoshaphat and his army came to take the loot, they found a great amount of cattle,ʰ goods, clothing,ⁱ and other valuables— much more than they could carry. In fact, there was so much it took three days to haul it away. ²⁶On the fourth day they assembled in Blessing Valley, where they blessed the LORD. That's why it is called Blessing Valley to this day. ²⁷Then everyone from Judah and Jerusalem, with Jehoshaphat at their head, joyfully returned home to Jerusalem because the LORD had given them reason to rejoice over their enemies. ²⁸They entered Jerusalem accompanied by harps, lutes, and trumpets, and they went to the LORD's temple.

²⁹The fear of God came on all the surrounding kingdoms when they heard how the LORD had fought against Israel's enemies. ³⁰As a result, Jehoshaphat's rule was peaceful because his God gave him rest on all sides.

Jehoshaphat's last days

³¹Jehoshaphat ruled over Judah. He was 35 years old when he became king, and he ruled for twenty-five years in Jerusalem. His mother's name was Azubah; she was Shilhi's daughter. ³²Jehoshaphat walked in the way of his father Asa and didn't turn aside from it, doing what was right in the LORD's eyes, ³³with the exception that he didn't remove the shrines. The people were still not committed with all their hearts to the God of their ancestors. ³⁴The rest of Jehoshaphat's deeds, from beginning to end, are written in the records of Jehu, Hanani's son, which are included in the records of Israel's kings.

ʰLXX; MT *among them*   ⁱVulg; MT *corpses*

³⁵Sometime later, Judah's King Jehoshaphat formed an alliance with Israel's King Ahaziah, which caused him to sin. ³⁶They agreed to build a fleet of Tarshish-styled ships, and they built them in Eziongeber. ³⁷Eliezer, Dodavahu's son from Mareshah, prophesied against Jehoshaphat: "Because you have formed an alliance with Ahaziah, the LORD will destroy what you have made." The ships were wrecked and couldn't sail to Tarshish.

21 Jehoshaphat died and was buried with his ancestors in David's City. His son Jehoram succeeded him as king.

Jehoram rules

²Jehoram's brothers, the other sons of Jehoshaphat, were Azariah, Jehiel, Zechariah, Azariah, Michael, and Shephatiah. All of these were the sons of Israel's King Jehoshaphat. ³Their father had given them many gifts of silver, gold, and other valuables, along with fortified cities in Judah, but he gave the kingdom to Jehoram because he was the oldest son.

⁴When Jehoram had taken control of his father's kingdom, he established his rule by killing all his brothers, along with some other leaders of Israel. ⁵Jehoram was 32 years old when he became king, and he ruled for eight years in Jerusalem. ⁶He walked in the ways of Israel's kings, just as Ahab's dynasty had done, because he married Ahab's daughter. He did what was evil in the LORD's eyes. ⁷Nevertheless, because of the covenant he had made with David, the LORD wasn't willing to destroy David's dynasty. He had promised to preserve a lamp for David and his sons forever. ⁸During Jehoram's rule, Edom rebelled against Judah's power and appointed its own king. ⁹Jehoram, along with all his chariots, crossed over to Zair.ʲ The Edomites, who had surrounded him, attacked at night, defeating himᵏ and his chariot officers. ¹⁰So Edom has been independent of Judah to this day. Libnah rebelled against Jehoram's rule at the same time because he had abandoned the LORD, the God of his ancestors.

¹¹As if that wasn't enough, Jehoram constructed shrines throughout Judah's highlands, encouraged Jerusalem's citizens to be unfaithful, and led Judah astray.

¹²A letter from the prophet Elijah came to Jehoram that read, "This is what the LORD, the God of your ancestor David, says: Because you haven't walked in the ways of your father Jehoshaphat or the ways of Judah's King Asa, ¹³but have walked in the ways of Israel's kings and have encouraged Judah and Jerusalem's citizens to be unfaithful, just as the house of Ahab did, and because you have even murdered your own brothers, your father's family, who were better than you, ¹⁴the LORD will now strike your family, your children, your wives, and all your possessions with a heavy blow. ¹⁵You yourself will become deathly ill with a chronic disease that will cause your intestines to fall out."

¹⁶Then the LORD made the Philistines and the Arabs, who lived near the Cushites, angry with Jehoram. ¹⁷They attacked Judah, broke down its defenses, and hauled off all the goods that were found in the royal palace, along with the king's children and wives. Only Jehoahaz, Jehoram's youngest son, was spared. ¹⁸After all this, the LORD struck Jehoram with an incurable intestinal disease. ¹⁹For almost two years he grew steadily worse, until two days before his death, when his intestines fell out, causing him to die in horrible pain. His people didn't make a fire in his honor as they had done for his ancestors. ²⁰He was 32 years old when he became king, and he ruled for eight years in Jerusalem. No one was sorry he died. He was buried in David's City but not in the royal cemetery.

22 The inhabitants of Jerusalem made his youngest son Ahaziah succeed him as king because the raiding party that had invaded the camp with the Arabs had killed all the older sons. So Ahaziah, Jehoram's son, became king of Judah.

Ahaziah rules

²Ahaziah was 22 years oldˡ when he became king, and he ruled for one year

---

ʲCorrection with 2 Kgs 8:21; MT *with his officers* ᵏOr *he defeated Edom* ˡLXX, Syr, 2 Kgs 8:26; MT 42 in Jerusalem. His mother's name was Athaliah; she was the granddaughter of Omri. [3]Ahaziah walked in the ways of Ahab's dynasty, encouraged in this wickedness by his mother. [4]He did what was evil in the LORD's eyes, just as Ahab's dynasty had done, because after his father's death they gave him advice that led to his downfall. [5]Ahaziah was following their advice when he went with Israel's King Joram,[m] Ahab's son, to fight against Aram's King Hazael at Ramoth-gilead, where the Arameans wounded Joram. [6]Joram returned to Jezreel to recover from the wounds he suffered at Ramah in his battle with Aram's King Hazael. Then Judah's King Ahaziah,[n] Jehoram's son, went down to visit Joram, Ahab's son, at Jezreel because he had been wounded. [7]But God used this visit to Joram to bring about Ahaziah's downfall. After his arrival, Ahaziah went with Joram to meet Jehu, Nimshi's son, whom the LORD had anointed to destroy Ahab's dynasty. [8]While Jehu was executing judgment on Ahab's dynasty, he discovered the princes of Judah, Ahaziah's nephews, serving Ahaziah, and Jehu killed them. [9]Jehu went looking for Ahaziah, who was captured while hiding in Samaria. He was then brought to Jehu and executed. He was given a decent burial, however, because people said, "He was the grandson of Jehoshaphat, who sought the LORD with all his heart."

There were now no members of Ahaziah's dynasty strong enough to rule the kingdom.

Queen Athaliah rules Judah

[10]When Athaliah, Ahaziah's mother, learned of her son's death, she immediately destroyed the entire royal family of Judah's dynasty. [11]But Jehoshabeath the king's daughter secretly took Ahaziah's son Jehoash[o] from the rest of the royal children who were about to be murdered, and hid him in a bedroom, along with his nurse. In this way Jehoshabeath, the daughter of King Jehoram, the wife of the priest Jehoiada and the sister of Ahaziah, hid Jehoash from Athaliah so she couldn't murder him. [12]He remained hidden with them in God's temple for six years while Athaliah ruled the country.

23 But in the seventh year Jehoiada boldly formed a conspiracy with the following unit commanders: Jeroham's son Azariah, Jehohanan's son Ishmael, Obed's son Azariah, Adaiah's son Maaseiah, and Zichri's son Elishaphat. [2]They went throughout Judah recruiting the Levites from all the cities of Judah, as well as the family heads of Israel, who then came to Jerusalem. [3]The entire assembly made a covenant with the king in God's temple. Jehoiada said, "Look! Here is the king's son. He must be king, just as the LORD promised about David's descendants. [4]This is what you must do: A third of you priests and Levites coming on sabbath duty will guard the gates, [5]another third will be at the royal palace, and another third will be at the Foundation Gate. Meanwhile, all the people will be in the courtyards of the LORD's temple. [6]Don't enter the LORD's temple, because only the priests or Levites on duty can do that. They are allowed to enter because they are holy, but the rest of the people must follow the LORD's requirements. [7]The Levites must surround the king, each with his weapons drawn. Whoever comes near your ranks must be killed; stay near the king wherever he goes."

[8]The Levites and all Judah did everything that the priest Jehoiada ordered. They each took charge of those men reporting for duty on the Sabbath, as well as those going off duty, since Jehoiada hadn't released any divisions from duty. [9]Then the priest Jehoiada gave the unit commanders King David's spears and large and small shields that were kept in God's temple. [10]He positioned all the people, each with their weapons drawn, near the altar and the temple, stretching from the south side of the

---

[m]Or *Jehoram* (also in 22:6-7); the king's name is variously spelled in either long *Jehoram* or short *Joram* form.
[n]LXX, Syr, Vulg; MT *Azariah*   [o]Or *Joash*; the king's name is variously spelled in either long *Jehoash* or short *Joash* form in 2 Kgs.

temple to the north side, so as to protect the king. [11]Then they brought out the king's son, crowned him, gave him the royal law,[p] and made him king. Jehoiada and his sons anointed him as everyone cried out, "Long live the king!"

[12]When Athaliah heard the noise made by the people running and cheering the king, she went to the people at the LORD's temple [13]and saw the king standing by the royal pillar at the entrance, with the commanders and trumpeters beside the king. All the people of the land were rejoicing and blowing trumpets, and singers accompanied by musical instruments were leading the praise. Athaliah ripped her clothes and screamed, "Treason! Treason!"

[14]Then the priest Jehoiada brought out the unit commanders who were in charge of the army. "Take her out under guard,"[q] he told them, "and kill anyone who follows her." This was because the priest had said, "She must not be executed in the LORD's temple." [15]They arrested her when she reached the entrance of the Horse Gate at the royal palace. She was executed there.

[16]Jehoiada then made a covenant between himself, all the people, and the king, that they would be the LORD's people. [17]Then all the people went to Baal's temple and tore it down, smashing its altars and images into pieces. They executed Baal's priest Mattan in front of the altars. [18]Jehoiada appointed the priests and[r] Levites in charge of the LORD's temple, and then appointed the divisions of the priests and Levites[s] that David had assigned to the LORD's temple to offer entirely burned sacrifices to the LORD, as written in the Instruction from Moses, with rejoicing and singing, just as David had ordered. [19]He posted guards at the gates of the LORD's temple so that no one who was unclean in any way could enter. [20]Then he took the unit commanders, the officials, the rulers of the people, and all the people of the land, and they led the king down from the LORD's

temple, processing through the Upper Gate to the palace, where the king sat upon the royal throne. [21]All the people of the land rejoiced, and the city was at peace now that Athaliah had been executed at the palace.

Jehoash rules

24 Jehoash[t] was 7 years old when he became king, and he ruled for forty years in Jerusalem. His mother's name was Zibiah; she was from Beer-sheba. [2]Jehoash did what was right in the LORD's eyes as long as Jehoiada the priest was alive. [3]Jehoiada had him marry two wives, and Jehoash fathered sons and daughters.

[4]Sometime later, Jehoash wanted to renovate the LORD's temple. [5]He gathered the priests and the Levites and said, "Go to the cities of Judah and collect the annual tax of silver due from all Israel for the upkeep of God's temple. Do it right away."

But the Levites procrastinated. [6]So the king summoned the chief priest Jehoiada and asked him, "Why haven't you required the Levites to bring in from Judah and Jerusalem the tax imposed by the LORD's servant Moses and the Israelite assembly for the covenant tent?" ([7]Now wicked Athaliah and her followers had broken into God's temple and used all the holy objects of the LORD's temple in their worship of the Baals.) [8]So at the king's command a box was made and placed outside the gate of the LORD's temple. [9]Then a proclamation was issued throughout Judah and Jerusalem requiring the people to bring to the LORD the tax that God's servant Moses had imposed on Israel in the wilderness. [10]This so pleased all the leaders and all the people that they gladly dropped their money in the box until it was full. [11]Whenever the box was brought by the Levites to the royal accountants, as soon as they saw that a large amount of money was in the box, the royal scribe and the representative of the high priest would come, empty the box, and return it to its place.

---

[p]Or *testimony*; MT lacks *royal*. [q]Heb uncertain [r]LXX; MT *levitical priests* [s]LXX; MT lacks *and then appointed the divisions of the priests and the Levites.* [t]Heb *Joash* (see 24:2, 4, 22, 24); the king's name is variously spelled in either long *Jehoash* or short *Joash* form in 2 Kgs.

This took place day after day, and a large amount of money was collected. ¹²The king and Jehoiada would give it to those in charge of the work on the LORD's temple who in turn hired masons and carpenters to renovate the LORD's temple, as well as metalworkers for the iron and bronze to repair the LORD's temple. ¹³The workers labored hard, and the restoration progressed smoothly under their control until they had brought God's temple back to its original state and reinforced it. ¹⁴As soon as they finished, they brought the remaining money to the king and Jehoiada. They used it to make equipment for the LORD's temple, including what was used for the service and the entirely burned offerings, pans, and other objects made of gold and silver. As long as Jehoiada lived, the entirely burned offerings were regularly offered in the LORD's temple.

¹⁵ Jehoiada grew old, and when he reached the age of 130, he died. ¹⁶He was buried among the kings in David's City because of his exemplary service to Israel, God, and God's temple.

¹⁷After Jehoiada's death, however, the leaders of Judah came and bowed before the king, and the king listened to them. ¹⁸They abandoned the temple of the LORD, their ancestors' God, and worshipped sacred poles[u] and idols. Anger came upon Judah and Jerusalem as a consequence of their sin, ¹⁹and though God sent prophets to them to bring them back to the LORD and to warn them, they refused to listen. ²⁰Then the spirit of God enwrapped Zechariah the son of the priest Jehoiada. Standing before the people, he told them, "This is what God says: Why do you defy the LORD's commands and keep yourselves from prospering? Because you have abandoned the LORD, he has abandoned you!" ²¹But the people plotted against Zechariah, and at the king's command stoned him to death in the courtyard of the LORD's temple. ²²King Jehoash failed to remember the loyalty that Jehoiada, Zechariah's father, had shown him and murdered Jehoida's son, who cried out as he lay dying, "May the LORD see and seek vengeance!"

²³That spring the Aramean army marched against Jehoash. They attacked Judah and Jerusalem, destroyed all the people's leaders, and sent all the loot to the king of Damascus. ²⁴Although the Aramean forces were relatively small, the LORD handed over to them a very large army, because the people of Judah had abandoned the LORD, their ancestors' God. Jehoash was justly punished. ²⁵The Arameans left him badly wounded, but his own officials plotted against him for murdering the son[v] of the priest Jehoiada. So they killed him in his bed. He died and was buried in David's City but not in the royal cemetery. ²⁶Those who plotted against him were the Ammonite Zabad, Shimeath's son, and the Moabite Jehozabad, Shimrith's son. ²⁷The list of Jehoash's sons, the many prophecies against him, and the account of his restoration of God's temple are written in the comments on the records of the kings. His son Amaziah succeeded him as king.

Amaziah rules

25 Amaziah was 25 years old when he became king, and he ruled for twenty-nine years in Jerusalem. His mother's name was Jehoaddan; she was from Jerusalem. ²He did what was right in the LORD's eyes but not with all his heart. ³Once he had secured control over his kingdom, he executed the officials who had assassinated his father the king. ⁴However, he didn't kill their children because of what is written in the Instruction scroll from Moses, where the LORD commanded, *Parents shouldn't be executed because of what their children have done; neither should children be executed because of what their parents have done. Each person should be executed for their own guilty acts.*[w]

⁵Amaziah gathered the people of Judah, organizing them into family units under captains of thousands and hundreds for all Judah and Benjamin. He summoned everyone 20 years old and older and found

---

[u]Heb *asherim*, perhaps objects devoted to the goddess Asherah [v]LXX, Vulg; MT *sons* [w]Deut 24:16

that there were three hundred thousand select troops, ready for service and able to handle spears and body-sized shields. [6]He also hired one hundred thousand warriors from Israel for one hundred kikkars of silver.

[7]But a man of God confronted him. "King," he said, "the troops from Israel must not go with you, because the LORD isn't on the side of Israel or any Ephraimite. [8]Should you go with them anyway, even if you fight fiercely, God will make you stumble before the enemy, because God has the ability to either help or make someone stumble."

[9]Amaziah asked the man of God, "What about the hundred kikkars I paid for the Israelite troops?"

"God can give you much more than that," the man of God replied.

[10]Amaziah released the Ephraimite troops who had joined him so they could go home, but this only infuriated them against Judah, and they left in a rage. [11]Amaziah courageously led his people to the Salt Valley, where they killed ten thousand people from Seir. [12]The Judean forces captured another ten thousand alive, brought them to the top of a cliff, and threw them off so that all were dashed to pieces. [13]Meanwhile, the troops Amaziah had released from fighting alongside him raided cities in Judah from Samaria to Beth-horon, killing three thousand people and carrying off a large amount of loot. [14]When Amaziah returned after defeating the Edomites, he brought the gods of the people of Seir. He set them up as his own gods, bowed down before them, and burned incense to them. [15]As a result, the LORD was angry with Amaziah and sent a prophet to him.

"Why do you seek the gods of this people?" the prophet asked. "They couldn't even deliver their own people from you!"

[16]"Since when do you give me advice?" Amaziah interrupted. "You better quit before you end up dead!"

So the prophet stopped, but not until he said, "I know God plans to destroy you because you've done this and because you've refused to listen to my advice."

[17]After Judah's King Amaziah consulted with his advisors, he sent a challenge to Israel's King Joash, Jehoahaz's son and Jehu's grandson. "Come on," he said, "let's go head-to-head!"

[18]Israel's King Joash sent the following reply to Judah's King Amaziah: "Once upon a time, a thistle in Lebanon sent a message to a cedar: 'Give your daughter to my son as a wife.' But then a wild beast in Lebanon came along and trampled the thistle. [19]Do you think that because you've defeated Edom, you can arrogantly seek even more? Stay home! Why invite disaster when both you and Judah will fall?" [20]But Amaziah wouldn't listen, because God intended to use this to destroy them since they had sought Edom's gods. [21]So Israel's King Joash moved against Judah's King Amaziah and went head-to-head in battle at Beth-shemesh in Judah. [22]Judah was defeated by Israel, and everyone ran home. [23]At Beth-shemesh, Israel's King Joash captured Judah's King Amaziah, Jehoash's[x] son and Ahaziah's[y] grandson. Joash brought him to Jerusalem and broke down six hundred feet of the Jerusalem wall from the Ephraim Gate to the Corner Gate. [24]Joash took[z] all the gold and silver, and all the objects he could find in God's temple in the care of Obed-edom, and in the treasuries of the palace, along with some hostages. Then he returned to Samaria.

[25]Judah's King Amaziah, Jehoash's son, lived fifteen years after the death of Israel's King Joash, Jehoahaz's son. [26]The rest of Amaziah's deeds, from beginning to end, aren't they written in the official records of Israel's and Judah's kings? [27]From the time Amaziah turned away from the LORD, some people conspired against him in Jerusalem. When Amaziah fled to Lachish, they sent men after him, and they murdered him in Lachish. [28]They carried him back on horses and he was buried with his ancestors in David's City.[a]

[x]Or *Joash* (see also 25:25); the king's name is variously spelled in either long *Jehoash* or short *Joash* form in 2 Kgs. [y]See 2 Kgs 14:13; MT *Jehoahaz*. [z]See 2 Kgs 14:14; Heb omits *took*. [a]LXX; MT *Judah*

Uzziah rules Judah

26 Then all the people of Judah took Uzziah,[b] who was 16 years old, and made him king after his father Amaziah. [2]He rebuilt Eloth, restoring it to Judah after King Amaziah had lain down with his ancestors.

[3]Uzziah was 16 years old when he became king, and he ruled for fifty-two years in Jerusalem. His mother's name was Jecoliah; she was from Jerusalem. [4]He did what was right in the LORD's eyes, just as his father Amaziah had done. [5]He sought God as long as Zechariah, who instructed him in the fear[c] of God, was alive. And as long as he sought the LORD, God gave him success. [6]He marched against the Philistines and broke down the walls of Gath, Jabneh, and Ashdod. Then he rebuilt towns near Ashdod and elsewhere among the Philistines. [7]God helped him against the Philistines, the Arabs who inhabited Gur,[d] and the Meunites. [8]The Meunites[e] paid taxes to Uzziah, whose fame spread even to Egypt because he had grown so powerful. [9]He built towers in Jerusalem, at the Corner Gate, the Valley Gate, and at the Angle, and reinforced them. [10]He also built towers in the wilderness and dug many wells for his large herds in the lowlands and the plain. He had many workers who tended his farms and vineyards, because he loved the soil. [11]Uzziah had a standing army equipped for combat whose units went to war according to the number determined by the scribe Jeiel and Maaseiah, an officer under the

[b]Uzziah is usually named Azariah in 2 Kgs 14:21; 15:1, 6-7. [c]LXX; MT *visions* [d]Tg; MT *Gur-baal* [e]LXX; MT *Ammonites*

UZZIAH

Means "The Lord is my strength." An early 8th-century king of Judah. Uzziah is also called Azariah ("the Lord is my help") nine times in the OT. The two names differ by a single consonant in Hebrew and are therefore much more similar than they appear in English. However, it has been suggested "Uzziah" was the king's throne name and "Azariah" his personal name, to which he reverted when disease forced him off the throne. This suggestion is based on the fact that the prophets use "Uzziah" exclusively (Isa 1:1; 6:1; 7:1; Hos 1:1; Amos 1:1; Zech 14:5).

The brief description of Azariah's reign in 2 Kings 15:1-7 portrays him as a basically righteous king except for his failure to take away the "shrines," but whom the Lord also struck with a skin disease that forced him to live in a "separate house," perhaps a euphemism for a sanatorium (2 Kgs 15:5). The very different version of Uzziah's reign in 2 Chronicles 26 is the result primarily of theological considerations. The Chronicler was compelled to account theologically for both Uzziah's longevity and his disease, which indicated opposite divine judgments, according to his worldview.

The accounts of Uzziah's reign in Kings and Chronicles agree in attributing to him a 52-year reign, beginning at age 16 (2 Kgs 15:2; 2 Chron 26:3). The reign of Uzziah appears to have been a relatively peaceful and prosperous time for Judah. This is largely because it overlapped with the reign of Jeroboam II of Israel, with whom Uzziah was at peace and by whom Judah was probably overshadowed if not dominated. An indication of Uzziah's success is the note in 2 Kings 14:22 that he rebuilt Elath and restored it to Judah.

authority of Hananiah, one of the king's officials. [12] The grand total of family heads in charge of these courageous warriors was twenty-six hundred. [13] They commanded an army of three hundred seven thousand five hundred. They formed a powerful force that could support the king against the enemy. [14] Uzziah supplied the entire force with shields, spears, helmets, armor, bows, and sling stones. [15] He set up clever devices in Jerusalem on the towers and corners of the wall designed to shoot arrows and large stones. And so Uzziah's fame spread far and wide, because he had received wonderful help until he became powerful.

[16] But as soon as he became powerful, he grew so arrogant that he acted corruptly. He was unfaithful to the LORD his God by entering the LORD's sanctuary to burn incense upon the incense altar. [17] The priest Azariah, accompanied by eighty other of the LORD's courageous priests, went in after him [18] and confronted King Uzziah.

"You have no right, Uzziah," he said, "to burn incense to the LORD! That privilege belongs to the priests, Aaron's descendants, who have been ordained to burn incense. Get out of this holy place because you have been unfaithful! The LORD God won't honor you for this."

[19] Then Uzziah, who already had a censer in his hand ready to burn the incense, became angry. While he was fuming at the priests, skin disease[f] erupted on his forehead in the presence of the priests before the incense altar in the LORD's temple. [20] When Azariah the chief priest and all the other priests turned and saw the skin disease on his forehead, they rushed him out of there. Uzziah also was anxious to leave because the LORD had afflicted him. [21] King Uzziah had skin disease until the day he died. He lived in a separate house,[g] diseased in his skin, because he was barred from the LORD's temple. His son Jotham supervised the palace administration and governed the people of the land. [22] The rest of Uzziah's deeds, from beginning to end, were written down by the prophet Isaiah, Amoz's son. [23] Uzziah died and was buried with his ancestors in a field belonging to the kings, because people said, "He had skin disease." His son Jotham succeeded him as king.

Jotham rules

27 Jotham was 25 years old when he became king, and he ruled for sixteen years in Jerusalem. His mother's name was Jerushah; she was Zadok's daughter. [2] Jotham did what was right in the LORD's eyes, just as his father Uzziah had done. Unlike Uzziah, Jotham didn't enter the LORD's temple. But the people continued their crooked practices. [3] Jotham rebuilt the Upper Gate of the LORD's temple and did extensive work on the wall of the elevated fortress.[h] [4] He built towns in Judah's highlands and fortresses and towers in the wooded areas. [5] He fought against the king of the Ammonites and defeated the Ammonites. They paid him one hundred kikkars of silver, ten thousand kors[i] of wheat, and ten thousand kors of barley that year and for the next two years. [6] Jotham was securely established because he maintained a faithful life before the LORD his God. [7] The rest of Jotham's deeds, including all his wars and accomplishments, are written in the official records of Israel's and Judah's kings. [8] He was 25 years old when he became king, and he ruled for sixteen years in Jerusalem. [9] Jotham lay down with his ancestors and was buried in David's City. His son Ahaz succeeded him as king.

Ahaz rules

28 Ahaz was 20 years old when he became king, and he ruled for sixteen years in Jerusalem. He didn't do what was right in the LORD's eyes, unlike his ancestor David. [2] Instead, he walked in the ways of Israel's kings, making images of the Baals [3] and burning incense in the Ben-hinnom Valley. He even burned his own sons alive,

---

[f] The precise meaning is uncertain; traditionally *leprosy*—a term used for several different skin diseases. Also in 26:21-20, 23. [g] Heb uncertain [h] Or *hillside;* Heb uncertain [i] One kor is equivalent to a homer and is possibly equal to fifty gallons of grain.

imitating the detestable practices of the nations the LORD had driven out before the Israelites. ⁴He also sacrificed and burned incense at the shrines on every hill and beneath every shady tree. ⁵So the LORD his God handed him over to Aram's king, who defeated him and carried off many prisoners, bringing them to Damascus. Ahaz was also handed over to Israel's king, who defeated him with a severe beating. ⁶In Judah, Pekah, Remaliah's son, killed one hundred twenty thousand warriors in the course of a single day because they had abandoned the LORD, God of their ancestors. ⁷An Ephraimite warrior named Zichri killed the king's son Maaseiah, the palace administrator Azrikam, and Elkanah, the king's second in command. ⁸The Israelites took captive two hundred thousand women, boys, and girls from their Judean relatives and seized enormous amounts of plunder, which they took back to Samaria.

⁹One of the LORD's prophets named Oded lived in Samaria. When the army arrived there, he went to meet them and said, "Don't you see that the LORD God of your ancestors was angry with Judah and let you defeat them? But look what you've done! Your merciless slaughter of them stinks to high heaven! ¹⁰And now you think you can enslave the men and women of Judah and Jerusalem? What about your own guilt before the LORD your God? ¹¹Listen to me! Send back the captives you took from your relatives, because the LORD is furious with you."

ʲLXX, Syr, Vulg; MT *kings*

¹²At this, some of the Ephraimite leaders—Johanan's son Azariah, Meshillemoth's son Berechiah, Shallum's son Jehizkiah, and Hadlai's son Amasa—confronted those returning from battle. ¹³"Don't bring the captives here," they told them. "Your plan will only add to our sin and guilt before the LORD. We're already guilty enough, and great anger is already directed at Israel." ¹⁴So the warriors released the captives and brought the loot before the officers and the whole assembly. ¹⁵Then people named for this task took charge of the captives and dressed everyone who was naked with items taken from the loot. They gave them clothing, sandals, food and drink, and bandaged their wounds. Everyone who couldn't walk they placed on donkeys, and they brought them to Jericho, Palm City, near their Judean relatives. Then they returned to Samaria.

¹⁶At that time King Ahaz sent for help from the king^ of Assyria. ¹⁷Once again, the Edomites had invaded Judah, defeating Judah and carrying off captives. ¹⁸The Philistines had raided the towns in the lowlands and the arid southern plain of Judah, capturing Beth-shemesh, Aijalon, and Gederoth, along with Soco and its surrounding villages, Timnah and its surrounding villages, and Gimzo and its surrounding villages, and occupying all of these cities. ¹⁹The LORD was humiliating Judah on account of Israel's King Ahaz, because he had exercised no restraint in Judah and had been utterly unfaithful to

TIGLATH-PILESER

Three Assyrian kings were named Tiglath-pileser: (1) Tiglath-pileser I (reigned 1114–1076 BCE), whose campaigns reached Lebanon; (2) Tiglath-pileser II (reigned 966–935 BCE), an insignificant king of whom little is known; and (3) Tiglath-pileser III (reigned 745–727 BCE), the only one of the three mentioned in the Bible, who in 733–732 conquered and annexed most of the northern kingdom of Israel, deporting significant elements of its population (2 Kgs 15:19, 29; 16:7, 10; 2 Chron 28:20).

the LORD. ²⁰Assyria's King Tiglath-pileser^k came to Ahaz, but he brought trouble, not support. ²¹Even though Ahaz took items from the LORD's temple, the royal palace, and the officials to buy off the king of Assyria, it was of no help.

²²It was during this troubled time that King Ahaz became even more unfaithful to the LORD ²³by sacrificing to the gods of Damascus, who had defeated him.

"Since the gods of Aram's kings are helping them," he said, "I'll sacrifice to them too, so that they will help me."

But they became the ruin of both him and all Israel. ²⁴Ahaz gathered the objects from God's temple, cut them up, shut the doors of the LORD's temple, and made himself altars on every corner in Jerusalem. ²⁵He made shrines in all the towns of Judah for burning incense to other gods. This made the LORD, the God of his ancestors, very angry.

²⁶The rest of Ahaz's deeds, from beginning to end, are written in the official records of Israel's and Judah's kings. ²⁷Ahaz lay down with his ancestors and was buried in the city, in Jerusalem, but not in the royal cemetery of Israel's kings. His son Hezekiah succeeded him as king.

Hezekiah rules

29 Hezekiah became king when he was 25 years old, and he ruled for twenty-nine years in Jerusalem. His mother's name was Abijah; she was Zechariah's daughter. ²He did what was right in the LORD's eyes, just as his ancestor David had done. ³In the very first year of his rule, during the first month, Hezekiah reopened the doors of the LORD's temple, having repaired them. ⁴Then he brought in the priests and Levites and assembled them in the eastern square.

⁵"Listen to me, you Levites!" he said. "Make yourselves holy so you can make holy the temple of the LORD God of your ancestors by removing from the sanctuary any impure thing. ⁶Our ancestors were unfaithful and did what was evil in the LORD our God's eyes. They abandoned him, they ignored the LORD's dwelling, and they defied him. ⁷They even closed the doors of the entrance hall, snuffed out the lamps, and stopped burning incense and offering entirely burned offerings in the sanctuary of the God of Israel. ⁸This angered the LORD so much that he made Judah and Jerusalem an object of terror and horror, something people hiss at, as you can see with your own eyes. ⁹That's why our ancestors died violent deaths, while our sons, daughters, and wives were taken captive. ¹⁰But now I intend to make a covenant with the LORD, Israel's God, so God will no longer be angry with us. ¹¹Don't be careless, my sons! The LORD has chosen you to stand in his presence to serve him, so that you can be his servants and burn incense to him."

¹²Then the following Levites got up:

from the descendants of the Kohathites: Mahath, Amasai's son, and Joel, Azariah's son;

from the descendants of Merari: Kish, Abdi's son, and Azariah, Jehallelel's son;

from the Gershonites: Joah, Zimmah's son, and Eden, Joah's son;

¹³from the descendants of Elizaphan: Shimri and Jeuel;

from the descendants of Asaph: Zechariah and Mattaniah;

¹⁴from the descendants of Heman: Jehuel and Shimei;

and from the descendants of Jeduthun: Shemaiah and Uzziel.

¹⁵These men gathered their relatives, made themselves holy, and went in to purify the LORD's temple by obeying the king's command as the LORD had told him. ¹⁶The priests went in to purify the inner portion of the LORD's temple. They brought out to the courtyard of the LORD's temple all the impurities they discovered inside. Then the Levites took them out to the Kidron Valley. ¹⁷They began to make things holy on the first day of the first month.^l On the eighth day of the month they reached the LORD's entrance hall. They made holy the LORD's

---

^k MT *Tilgath-pilneser*   ^l March–April, Nisan

temple for eight days, finishing on the sixteenth day of the first month.

¹⁸Then they went before King Hezekiah. "We have purified the LORD's entire temple," they said, "and the altar for the entirely burned offering together with all its equipment, and the table for the stacks of bread together with all its equipment. ¹⁹We have also restored and made holy all the items King Ahaz threw out during his rule in his unfaithfulness. They are now before the LORD's altar."

Hezekiah rededicates the temple

²⁰Early the next morning Hezekiah gathered the city leaders and went to the LORD's temple. ²¹They brought seven bulls, seven rams, and seven lambs, along with seven male goats, for a purification offering on behalf of the kingdom, the sanctuary, and Judah. Hezekiah ordered the priests, Aaron's sons, to offer them up on the LORD's altar. ²²When they slaughtered the bulls, the priests took the blood and splashed it against the altar. Next they slaughtered the rams and splashed their blood against the altar, and also slaughtered the lambs, splashing their blood against the altar as well. ²³Finally, they brought the goats for the purification offering before the king and the assembly. After laying their hands on them, ²⁴the priests slaughtered them and smeared the blood on the altar as a purification offering to take away the sin of all Israel, because the king had specifically ordered that the entirely burned sacrifice and the purification offering should be on behalf of all Israel. ²⁵Hezekiah had the Levites stand in the LORD's temple with cymbals, harps, and zithers, just as the LORD had ordered through David, the king's seer Gad, and the prophet Nathan. ²⁶While the Levites took their places holding David's instruments, and the priests their trumpets, ²⁷Hezekiah ordered the entirely burned offering to be offered up on the altar. As they began to offer the entirely burned offering, the LORD's song also began, accompanied by the trumpets and the other instruments

of Israel's King David. ²⁸The whole congregation worshipped with singing choirs and blaring trumpets until the end of the entirely burned offering. ²⁹After the entirely burned offering was complete, the king and all who were with him bowed down in worship. ³⁰Then King Hezekiah and the leaders ordered the Levites to praise the LORD by using the words of David and the seer Asaph. They did so joyously; then they bowed down in worship too.

³¹"Now that you have dedicated yourselves to the LORD," King Hezekiah told them, "bring sacrificial thank offerings to the LORD's temple." So the assembly brought sacrificial thank offerings, with some people volunteering to provide entirely burned offerings. ³²All in all, the congregation brought seventy bulls, a hundred rams, and two hundred lambs as entirely burned offerings for the LORD, ³³as well as six hundred bulls and three thousand sheep as holy offerings. ³⁴Unfortunately, there weren't enough priests to skin all these entirely burned offerings. So their relatives the Levites (who had been more conscientious about preparing themselves than the priests) stepped in and helped them until the work was done or additional priests had made themselves holy. ³⁵In addition to the wealth of entirely burned offerings, there was the fat of the well-being sacrifices and drink offerings accompanying the entirely burned offerings. In this way, the service of the LORD's temple was restored, ³⁶and Hezekiah and all the people rejoiced at what God had done for them, since it had happened so quickly.

Hezekiah's Passover

30Then Hezekiah sent word to all Israel and Judah, and wrote letters to Ephraim and Manasseh as well, inviting them to the LORD's temple in Jerusalem to celebrate the Passover of the LORD God of Israel. ²The king, his officials, and the entire Jerusalem congregation had decided to celebrate Passover in the second month.ᵐ ³They had been unable to celebrate it at the

---

ᵐApril–May, Iyar

usual time because the priests had failed to make themselves holy in sufficient numbers, and the people hadn't gathered at Jerusalem. ⁴Since the plan seemed good to the king and the entire congregation, ⁵they made arrangements to circulate an announcement throughout all Israel, from Beer-sheba to Dan, to come to Jerusalem to celebrate the Passover of the LORD God of Israel, because they hadn't often kept it as written. ⁶Under the authority of the king, runners took letters from the king and his officials throughout all Israel and Judah, which read:

> People of Israel! Return to the LORD, the God of Abraham, Isaac, and Israel, so that he may return to those of you who remain, who have escaped capture by the Assyrian kings. ⁷Don't be like your ancestors and relatives, who were unfaithful to the LORD, the God of their ancestors, so that he made them an object of horror as you can see for yourselves. ⁸So don't be stubborn like your ancestors. Surrender to the LORD! Come to God's sanctuary, which he has made holy forever, and serve the LORD your God so that he won't be angry with you any longer. ⁹When you return to the LORD, your relatives and your children will receive mercy from their captors and be allowed to return to this land. The LORD your God is merciful and compassionate. He won't withdraw his presence from you if you return to him.

¹⁰So the runners went from town to town in Ephraim and Manasseh, all the way to Zebulun. But they were laughed at and made fun of. ¹¹Even so, some people from Asher, Manasseh, and Zebulun were submissive and came to Jerusalem. ¹²Moreover, God's power was at work in Judah, unifying them to do what the king and his officials had ordered by the LORD's command.

¹³A huge crowd gathered in Jerusalem to celebrate the Festival of Unleavened Bread in the second month. A very large congregation gathered. ¹⁴First, they removed the altars in Jerusalem, and hauled off the incense altars and dumped them in the Kidron Valley. ¹⁵They slaughtered the Passover lambs on the fourteenth day of the second month. Ashamed of themselves, the priests and the Levites made themselves holy and brought entirely burned offerings to the LORD's temple. ¹⁶They now took their places as laid out in the Instruction from Moses the man of God, and the priests splashed the blood they received from the Levites against the altar. ¹⁷Since many in the congregation hadn't made themselves holy, the Levites slaughtered the Passover lambs, making them holy to the LORD for all who weren't ceremonially clean. ¹⁸This included most of those who had come from Ephraim, Manasseh, Issachar, and Zebulun—people who hadn't purified themselves and so hadn't eaten the Passover meal in the prescribed way. But Hezekiah prayed for them: "May the good LORD forgive ¹⁹everyone who has decided to seek the true God, the LORD, the God of their ancestors, even though they aren't ceremonially clean by sanctuary standards." ²⁰The LORD heard Hezekiah and healed the people. ²¹So the Israelites in Jerusalem joyfully celebrated the Festival of Unleavened Bread for seven days, with the Levites and the priests praising the LORD every day, accompanied by the LORD's mighty instruments. ²²Hezekiah congratulated all the Levites who had performed so skillfully for the LORD. They feasted throughout the seven days of the festival, sacrificing well-being offerings and praising the LORD, the God of their ancestors.

²³Then the whole congregation agreed to celebrate another seven days, which they joyfully did. ²⁴Judah's King Hezekiah contributed one thousand bulls and seven thousand sheep for the congregation, while the officials provided another thousand bulls and ten thousand sheep, and great numbers of priests made themselves holy. ²⁵Then the whole congregation of Judah rejoiced, as did the priests and the Levites, the whole congregation from Israel, the immigrants who had come from the land of Israel, and those who lived in Judah. ²⁶There was great joy in Jerusalem. Nothing like this had taken place in Jerusalem since the days of Israel's King Solomon,

David's son. [27]Then the levitical priests blessed the people, and their voice was heard when their prayer reached God's holy dwelling in heaven.

31 When all of these things were finished, all of the Israelites who were present went out to the cities of Judah, smashed the sacred pillars, cut down the sacred poles,[n] and completely destroyed the shrines and altars throughout Judah as well as Benjamin, Ephraim, and Manasseh. Then all the Israelites returned to their individual homes in their own cities.

Hezekiah's reform

[2]Hezekiah reappointed the priests and the Levites, each to their divisions and their tasks, to make entirely burned offerings and well-being sacrifices, to serve, to give thanks, and to offer praise in the gates of the LORD's camp. [3]As his portion, the king personally contributed the entirely burned offerings for the morning and evening sacrifices, as well as the entirely burned offerings for the Sabbaths, new moons, and festivals, as written in the LORD's Instruction. [4]He ordered the people living in Jerusalem to provide the required portion for the priests and the Levites so they could devote themselves to the LORD's Instruction. [5]As soon as the order was issued, the Israelites generously gave the best of their grain, new wine, oil, honey, and all their crops—a tenth of everything, a huge amount. [6]The people of Israel and Judah, living in the cities of Judah, also brought in a tenth of their herds and flocks and a tenth of the items that had been dedicated to the LORD their God, stacking it up in piles. [7]They began stacking up the piles in the third month[o] and finished them in the seventh.[p] [8]When Hezekiah and the officials saw the piles, they blessed the LORD and his people Israel.

[9]When Hezekiah asked the priests and Levites about the piles, [10]the chief priest Azariah, who was from Zadok's family, answered, "Ever since the people started bringing contributions to the LORD's temple we've had enough to eat with plenty to spare. The LORD has definitely blessed his people! There's a lot left over."

[11]So Hezekiah ordered them to prepare storerooms in the LORD's temple. When they finished preparing them, [12]the priests conscientiously brought in the contributions, the tenth-part gifts, and the dedicated things. Conaniah, a Levite, was put in charge, assisted by his brother Shimei, [13]while Jehiel, Azaziah, Nahath, Asahel, Jerimoth, Jozabad, Eliel, Ismachiah, Mahath, and Benaiah served as supervisors under them, as appointed by King Hezekiah and Azariah the official in charge of God's temple. [14]The Levite Kore, Imnah's son, who was keeper of the east gate, was in charge of the spontaneous gifts to God. He was responsible for distributing the contribution reserved for the LORD and the dedicated gifts. [15]Eden, Miniamin, Jeshua, Shemaiah, Amariah, and Shecaniah faithfully assisted him regarding[q] the priests by distributing the portions to their relatives, old and young alike, by divisions. [16]Additionally, they also distributed daily rations to those males, registered by genealogy, three years old and older, all who entered the LORD's temple to carry out their daily duties as their divisions required. [17]They also distributed to those priests registered by their families, and to Levites 20 years of age and older according to their divisional responsibilities. [18]The official genealogy included all their small children, their wives, their sons, and their daughters—the entire congregation—for they had faithfully made themselves holy. [19]As for Aaron's descendants, the priests who lived in the outskirts of the cities, men were assigned to distribute portions to every male among the priests and to every Levite listed in the genealogical records. [20]This is what Hezekiah did throughout all Judah, doing what the LORD his God considered good, right, and true. [21]Everything that Hezekiah began to do for the service of God's

---

[n]Heb *asherim,* perhaps objects devoted to the goddess Asherah   [o]May–June, Sivan   [p]September–October, Tishri   [q]Or *with the assistance of* cf LXX; MT *in the cities of*

temple, whether by the Instruction or the commands, in order to seek his God, he did successfully and with all his heart.

Sennacherib's invasion

32 After these things and these faithful acts, Assyria's King Sennacherib invaded Judah and attacked its fortified cities, intending to capture them. ²When Hezekiah realized that Sennacherib also planned on fighting Jerusalem, ³he consulted with his officials and soldiers about stopping up the springs outside the city, and they supported him. ⁴A large force gathered to stop up all the springs and the streams that flowed through the land. "Why should the kings of Assyria come and find plenty of water?" they asked. ⁵Hezekiah vigorously rebuilt all the broken sections of the wall, erected towers, constructed another wall outside the first, reinforced the terrace of David's City, and made a large supply of weapons and shields. ⁶He appointed military officers over the troops, assembled them in the square of the city gate, and spoke these words of encouragement: ⁷"Be brave and be strong! Don't let the king of Assyria and all those warriors he brings with him scare you or cause you dismay, because our forces are greater than his.ʳ ⁸All he has is human strength, but we have the LORD our God, who will help us fight our battles!"

The troops trusted Judah's King Hezekiah.

⁹After this Assyria's King Sennacherib, who was attacking Lachish with all his forces, sent his servants to Jerusalem with the following message for Judah's King Hezekiah and all the people of Judah who were in Jerusalem:

¹⁰This is what Assyria's King Sennacherib says: What makes you so confident that you stay put in Jerusalem while it is being attacked? ¹¹Obviously, Hezekiah has fooled you into surrendering yourselves to death by hunger and thirst when he says, "The LORD our God will rescue us from Assyria's king." ¹²Isn't this the same Hezekiah who got rid of his shrines and altars, and then demanded of Judah and Jerusalem, "You must worship and burn incense before only one altar"? ¹³Don't you know what I and my predecessors have done to the people of other nations? Were any of the gods of these other nations able to rescue their lands from my power? ¹⁴Which one of any of the gods of these nations that my predecessors destroyed was able to rescue them from my power? So why should your god be able to rescue you from my power? ¹⁵Don't let Hezekiah seduce you like fools. Don't believe him! No god of any other nation or kingdom has been able to rescue their people from me or from my predecessors. No, your gods won't rescue you from my power.

¹⁶The Assyrian king's servants continued to make fun of the LORD God and his servant Hezekiah. ¹⁷He wrote other letters insulting the LORD God of Israel, defying him

ʳOr there is greater power with us than with him

GIHON SPRING

Ancient Jerusalem's only permanent water source, located outside the fortified city in a cave in the Kidron Valley. Gihon was a siphon-type spring, fed by groundwater that sporadically "burst forth" through cracks in the cave's floor. Depending on the season of the year, Gihon may have provided enough water to supply about 2,500 people in a day.

Solomon's coronation occurred at this site (1 Kgs 1:33, 38, 45). See also 2 Chronicles 32:30; 33:14.

by saying, "Just as the gods of the nations in other countries couldn't rescue their people from my power, Hezekiah's god won't be able to rescue his people from my power." [18]Then they shouted loudly in Hebrew[s] at the people of Jerusalem gathered on the wall, in an attempt to frighten and demoralize them, in order to capture the city. [19]They spoke about the God of Jerusalem as though he were the work of human hands, like the gods of the other peoples of the earth. [20]King Hezekiah and the prophet Isaiah, Amoz's son, prayed about this, crying out to heaven. [21]Then the LORD sent a messenger who destroyed every warrior, leader, and officer in the camp of the Assyrian king. When Sennacherib went home in disgrace, he entered the temple of his god, and his own sons killed him with a sword. [22]This is how the LORD rescued Hezekiah and the citizens of Jerusalem from the power of Assyria's King Sennacherib, and all others, giving them rest[t] on all sides. [23]Many people brought offerings to the LORD in Jerusalem and costly gifts to Judah's King Hezekiah, who was highly regarded by all the nations from then on.

Hezekiah's illness

[24]Around that same time, Hezekiah became deathly ill and prayed to the LORD, who answered him with a miraculous sign. [25]But Hezekiah was too proud to respond appropriately to the kindness he had received, and he, along with Judah and Jerusalem, experienced anger. [26]However, Hezekiah and the citizens of Jerusalem humbled themselves in their pride, and so they didn't experience the LORD's anger for the rest of Hezekiah's reign.

[27]Hezekiah became very wealthy and greatly respected. He made storehouses for his silver, gold, precious stones, spices, shields, and other valuables. [28]He made barns to store the harvest of grain, wine, and olive oil; stalls for all kinds of cattle; and pens for flocks. [29]He acquired towns for himself and many flocks and herds because God had given him great wealth.

[30]Hezekiah was the one who blocked the upper outlet of the waters of the Gihon Spring, channeling them down to the west side of David's City. Hezekiah succeeded in all that he did, [31]even in the matter of the ambassadors sent from Babylonian officials to find out about the miraculous sign that occurred in the land, when God had abandoned him in order to test him and to discover what was in his heart.

[32]The rest of Hezekiah's deeds, including his faithfulness, are written in the vision of the prophet Isaiah, Amoz's son, in the records of Israel's and Judah's kings. [33]Hezekiah lay down with his ancestors and was buried in the upper area of the tombs of David's sons. All Judah and the inhabitants of Jerusalem honored him at his death. His son Manasseh succeeded him as king.

Manasseh rules

33 Manasseh was 12 years old when he became king, and he ruled for fifty-five years in Jerusalem. [2]He did what was evil in the LORD's eyes, imitating the detestable practices of the nations that the LORD had driven out before the Israelites. [3]He rebuilt the shrines that his father Hezekiah had destroyed, set up altars for the Baals, and made sacred poles.[u] He bowed down to all the stars in the sky and worshipped them. [4]He even built altars in the LORD's temple, the very place the LORD was speaking about when he said, "My name will remain in Jerusalem forever." [5]Manasseh built altars for all the stars in the sky in both courtyards of the LORD's temple. [6]He burned his own sons alive in the Ben-hinnom Valley, consulted sign readers, fortune-tellers, and sorcerers, and used mediums and diviners. He did much evil in the LORD's eyes and made him angry.

[7]Manasseh set up the carved image he had made in God's temple, the very temple God had spoken about to David and his son Solomon, saying: In this temple and in Jerusalem, which I have selected out of all Israel's tribes, I will put my name forever. [8]I will never again remove Israel from the fer-

---

[s]Or *the language of Judah*   [t]LXX; MT *he led them*   [u]Heb *asherot*, perhaps objects devoted to the goddess Asherah

tile land I gave to your ancestors, provided they carefully do everything I have commanded them—keeping all the Instruction, the regulations, and the case laws given through Moses. [9]In this way Manasseh led Judah and the residents of Jerusalem into doing even more evil than the nations that the LORD had wiped out before the Israelites.

[10]The LORD spoke to Manasseh and his people, but they wouldn't listen. [11]So the LORD brought the army commanders of Assyria's king against them. They captured Manasseh with hooks, bound him with bronze chains, and carried him off to Babylon. [12]During his distress, Manasseh made peace with the LORD his God, truly submitting himself to the God of his ancestors. [13]He prayed, and God was moved by his request. God listened to Manasseh's prayer and restored him to his rule in Jerusalem. Then Manasseh knew that the LORD was the true God.

[14]After this, Manasseh rebuilt the outer wall of David's City, west of the Gihon Spring in the valley, extending as far as the entrance of the Fish Gate, enclosing the elevated fortress[v] and greatly increasing its height. He also installed military commanders in all the fortified cities of Judah. [15]He removed the foreign gods and the idol from the LORD's temple, as well as all the altars he had built on the hill of the LORD's temple and in Jerusalem, dumping them outside the city. [16]He restored the LORD's altar, offered well-being sacrifices and thank offerings on it, and ordered the people of Judah to worship the LORD, Israel's God. [17]The people, however, still sacrificed at the shrines, but only to the LORD their God. [18]The rest of Manasseh's deeds, including his prayer to God and what the seers told him in the name of the LORD, Israel's God, are found in the records of Israel's kings. [19]Manasseh's prayer and its answer, all his sin and unfaithfulness, and the locations of the shrines, sacred poles,[w] and idols he set up before he submitted are written in the records of Hozai.[x] [20]Manasseh lay down with his ancestors and was buried in his palace. His son Amon succeeded him as king.

Amon rules

[21]Amon was 22 years old when he became king, and he ruled for two years in Jerusalem. [22]He did what was evil in the LORD's eyes, just as his father Manasseh had done. He sacrificed to all the idols his father had made and worshipped them. [23]But unlike his father Manasseh, Amon didn't submit before the LORD; instead, Amon increased his guilt. [24]His own officials plotted against him and killed him in his palace. [25]The people of the land then executed all those who had plotted against King Amon and made his son Josiah the next king.

Josiah rules

34 Josiah was 8 years old when he became king, and he ruled for thirty-one years in Jerusalem. [2]He did what was right in the LORD's eyes and walked in the ways of his ancestor David, not deviating from it even a bit to the right or left. [3]In the eighth year of his rule, while he was just a boy, he began to seek the God of his ancestor David, and in the twelfth year he began purifying Judah and Jerusalem of the shrines, the sacred poles,[y] idols, and images. [4]Under his supervision, the altars for the Baals were torn down, and the incense altars that were above them were smashed. He broke up the sacred poles, idols, and images, grinding them to dust and scattering them over the graves of those who had sacrificed to them. [5]He burned the bones of the priests on their altars, purifying Judah and Jerusalem. [6]In the cities of Manasseh, Ephraim, and Simeon, all the way up to Naphtali, he removed their temples,[z] [7]tore down the altars and sacred poles, ground the idols to dust, and smashed all the incense altars throughout the land of Israel. Then Josiah returned to Jerusalem.

---

[v]Or hillside; Heb uncertain [w]Heb asherim, perhaps objects devoted to the goddess Asherah [x]LXX the seers [y]Heb asherim, perhaps objects devoted to the goddess Asherah; also in 34:4, 7 [z]Heb uncertain

Josiah repairs the temple

[8]In the eighteenth year of his rule, after he had purified the land and the temple, Josiah sent Azaliah's son Shaphan, Maaseiah the mayor of the city, and Joahaz's son Joah the secretary to repair the LORD his God's temple. [9]When they came to the high priest Hilkiah, they delivered the money that had been collected in God's temple by the levitical gatekeepers from Manasseh, Ephraim, and the rest of Israel, as well as from Judah, Benjamin, and the residents of Jerusalem. [10]They handed it over to the supervisors[a] in charge of the LORD's temple, who in turn paid it to those working on, repairing, and restoring the LORD's temple. [11]They then gave it to the carpenters and the builders to pay for quarried stone and lumber for rafters and beams in the buildings the kings of Judah had neglected. [12]The men worked conscientiously under the supervision of Jahath and Obadiah, who were Levites descended from Merari, and Zechariah and Meshullam from the Kohathites. The Levites, all of whom were accomplished musicians, [13]were also in charge of the laborers and all the workers, no matter what their jobs, while some of the Levites served as scribes, officials, and guards.

The Instruction scroll

[14]While they were bringing out the money that had been brought into the LORD's temple, Hilkiah the priest found the Instruction scroll that the LORD had given through Moses. [15]Hilkiah told the secretary Shaphan, "I have found the Instruction scroll in the LORD's temple."

Then Hilkiah turned the scroll over to Shaphan, [16]who brought it to the king with this report: "Your servants are doing everything you've asked them to do. [17]They have released the money that was found in the LORD's temple and have handed it over to the supervisors and the workers." [18]Then the secretary Shaphan told the king, "The priest Hilkiah has given me a scroll," and he read it out loud before the king.

[19]As soon as the king heard what the Instruction scroll said, he ripped his clothes. [20]The king ordered Hilkiah, Shaphan's son Ahikam, Micah's son Abdon, the secretary Shaphan, and the royal officer Asaiah as follows: [21]"Go and ask the LORD on my behalf, and on behalf of those who still remain in Israel and Judah, concerning the contents of this scroll that has been found. The LORD must be furious with us because our ancestors failed to obey the LORD's word and do everything written in this scroll."

[22]So Hilkiah and the royal officials went to the prophetess Huldah. She was married to Shallum, Tokhath's son and Hasrah's grandson, who was in charge of the wardrobe. She lived in Jerusalem in the second district. When they spoke to her, [23]she replied, "This is what the LORD, Israel's God, says: Tell this to the man who sent you to me: [24]This is what the LORD says: I am about to bring disaster on this place and its citizens—all the curses written in the scroll that they have read to Judah's king. [25]My anger burns against this place, never to be quenched, because they've deserted me and have burned incense to other gods, angering me by everything they have done.[b]

[a]LXX, Vulg; MT supervisor [b]Or made; perhaps a reference to idols

JOSIAH

Josiah was king of Judah from 640 to 609 BCE; he was the son and successor of Amon, and his mother was Jedidah, daughter of Adaiah of Bozkath. Second Kings 22–23 reports that during the eighteenth year of his reign (622), he implemented reforms based on the Instruction scroll, which was found during a renovation of the temple.

²⁶But also say this to the king of Judah, who sent you to question the LORD: This is what the LORD, Israel's God, says about the message you've just heard: ²⁷Because your heart was broken and you submitted before the LORD when you heard what he said against this place and its citizens,ᶜ and because you ripped your clothes and cried before me, I have listened to you, declares the LORD. ²⁸I will gather you to your ancestors, and you will go to your grave in peace. You won't experience the disaster I am about to bring on this place and its citizens."

When they reported Huldah's words to the king, ²⁹the king sent a message and gathered together all the elders of Judah and Jerusalem. ³⁰Then the king went up to the LORD's temple, together with all the people of Judah and all the citizens of Jerusalem, the priests and the Levites, and all the people, young and old alike. There the king read out loud all the words of the covenant scroll that had been found in the LORD's temple. ³¹The king stood in his place and made a covenant with the LORD that he would follow the LORD by keeping his commandments, his instructions, and his regulations with all his heart and all his being, in order to fulfill the words of the covenant that were written in this scroll. ³²Then he made everyone found in Jerusalem and Benjamin join in a similar promise. The citizens of Jerusalem lived according to the covenant made with God, the God of their ancestors. ³³Josiah got rid of all the detestable idols from all the regions that belonged to the Israelites, and he made everyone who lived in Israel serve the LORD their God. As long as Josiah lived, they didn't turn away from following the LORD God of their ancestors.

Josiah's Passover

35 Then Josiah celebrated the LORD's Passover in Jerusalem. They slaughtered the Passover lambs on the fourteenth day of the first month.ᵈ ²He assigned the priests to their posts, encouraging them to fulfill their responsibilities in the LORD's temple.

³Next Josiah ordered the Levites, who were holy to the LORD and who instructed all Israel: "Put the holy chest in the temple built by Israel's King Solomon, David's son. You don't need to carry it around on your shoulders anymore. Now serve the LORD your God and his people Israel. ⁴Organize yourselves by families according to your divisions, as directed by Israel's King David and his son Solomon. ⁵Stand in the sanctuary, according to the family divisions of your relatives the laypeople, so that there can be Levites for each family division.ᵉ ⁶Slaughter the Passover lambs and prepare the holy sacrificesᶠ for your relatives in order to celebrate according to the LORD's word through Moses."

⁷On behalf of the laypeople, Josiah donated from his personal holdings thirty thousand lambs and young goats, and three thousand bulls, all for the Passover offerings. ⁸His officials also provided spontaneous gift offerings for the people, the priests, and the Levites. Hilkiah, Zechariah, and Jehiel, the ones in charge of God's temple, gave two thousand six hundred Passover lambs and three hundred bulls for the priests. ⁹Conaniah and his brothers Shemaiah and Nethanel, along with Hashabiah, Jeiel, and Jozabad, the leaders of the Levites, provided the Levites with five thousand lambs and five hundred bulls as Passover sacrifices. ¹⁰When everything was ready, the priests and the Levites took their places as the king had ordered. ¹¹Then they slaughtered the Passover lambs, and the priests splashed the bloodᵍ while the Levites skinned the animals. ¹²Next they divided the entirely burned offerings among the laypeople by their families to sacrifice to the LORD as written in the scroll from Moses, and they did the same with the bulls. ¹³They roasted the Passover lambs in the fire as instructed, cooked the holy offerings in pots, kettles, and pans, and brought them quickly to all the laypeople.

ᶜMT repeats *and because you humbled yourself before me.* ᵈMarch–April, Nisan ᵉHeb uncertain ᶠCorrection; cf 1 Esdr 1:6; MT *and sanctify yourselves* ᵍLXX; MT *from their hand*

¹⁴Next they prepared food for themselves and for the priests. Since the priests, Aaron's descendants, were busy offering up the entirely burned offerings and fat pieces until nighttime, the Levites prepared food for themselves and for the priests, Aaron's descendants. ¹⁵The Asaphite singers also remained at their stations as ordered by David, Asaph, Heman, and the king's seer Jeduthun, as did the guards at the various gates. They didn't need to leave their tasks because their fellow Levites prepared food for them. ¹⁶So on that day all of the LORD's service was prepared for celebrating Passover and offering up entirely burned offerings on the LORD's altar, just as King Josiah had ordered. ¹⁷The Israelites who were present celebrated the Passover at that time, and observed the Festival of Unleavened Bread for seven days. ¹⁸Not since the days of the prophet Samuel had such a Passover been celebrated in Israel. And no other king of Israel had celebrated a Passover like the one Josiah celebrated with the priests, the Levites, all the people of Judah and Israel who were present, and the residents of Jerusalem. ¹⁹This Passover was celebrated in the eighteenth year of Josiah's rule.

Josiah's death

²⁰After all of these things, when Josiah had finished restoring the temple, Egypt's King Neco marched against Carchemish by the Euphrates, and Josiah marched out against him. ²¹But Neco sent messengers to Josiah. "What do you want with me, king of Judah?" he asked. "I haven't come to attack you today. I'm after the dynasty that wars with me. God told me to hurry, and he is on my side. Get out of God's way, or he will destroy you."

²²But Josiah wouldn't turn back. Instead, he camouflaged himself in preparation for battle, refusing to listen to Neco's words from God's own mouth, and went to fight Neco on the plain of Megiddo. ²³When archers shot King Josiah, he said to his servants, "Take me away; I'm badly wounded!" ²⁴So his servants took him out of his chariot, placed him in another one, and brought him to Jerusalem, where he died and was buried in the tombs of his ancestors. All Judah and Jerusalem mourned for Josiah. ²⁵Jeremiah composed a funeral song[h] for Josiah, and to this day every singer, man or woman, continues to remember Josiah in their funeral songs. They are now traditional in Israel and are written down among the funeral songs.

²⁶The rest of Josiah's deeds, including his faithfulness in acting according to what is written in the LORD's Instruction, ²⁷and everything else he did, from beginning to end, are written in the official records of Israel's and Judah's kings.

Jehoahaz rules

36 The people of the land took Jehoahaz, Josiah's son, and made him the next king in Jerusalem. ²Jehoahaz was 23 years old when he became king, and he ruled for three months in Jerusalem. ³The king of Egypt removed him from office in Jerusalem. The Egyptian king imposed a

[h]Or lament, twice more in this verse

CARCHEMISH

A major city of northern Syria, located ca. 62 mi. northeast of Aleppo, near the major crossing of the upper Euphrates River. Carchemish is also mentioned in the Bible in 2 Chronicles 35:20 and Jeremiah 46:2 as the site of a famous battle in 605 BCE in which the Babylonian king Nebuchadnezzar defeated the waning forces of the Assyrians and their Egyptian allies, led by Pharaoh Neco II.

fine on the land totaling one hundred kikkars of silver and one kikkar of gold. ⁴Then the king of Egypt made Jehoahaz's brother Eliakim king of Judah and Jerusalem, and changed his name to Jehoiakim. Neco took his brother Jehoahaz prisoner and carried him off to Egypt.

Jehoiakim rules

⁵Jehoiakim was 25 years old when he became king, and he ruled for eleven years in Jerusalem. He did what was evil in the LORD's eyes. ⁶Babylon's King Nebuchadnezzar attacked him, bound him with bronze chains, and took him to Babylon. ⁷Nebuchadnezzar also took some equipment from the LORD's temple to Babylon and placed them in his own temple there. ⁸The rest of Jehoiakim's deeds, including his detestable practices and all that was charged against him, are written in the official records of Israel's and Judah's kings. His son Jehoiachin succeeded him as king.

Jehoiachin rules

⁹Jehoiachin was 18ⁱ years old when he became king, and he ruled for three monthsʲ in Jerusalem. He did what was evil in the LORD's eyes. ¹⁰In the springtime, King Nebuchadnezzar sent for him to be brought to Babylon, along with valuable equipment from the LORD's temple. Then

he made Zedekiah his uncle the next king of Judah and Jerusalem.

Zedekiah rules

¹¹Zedekiah was 21 years old when he became king, and he ruled for eleven years in Jerusalem. ¹²He did what was evil in the LORD his God's eyes and didn't submit before the prophet Jeremiah, who spoke for the LORD. ¹³Moreover, he rebelled against King Nebuchadnezzar, despite the solemn pledge Nebuchadnezzar had forced him to swear in God's name. He became stubborn and refused to turn back to the LORD, Israel's God. ¹⁴All the leaders of the priests and the people also grew increasingly unfaithful, following all the detestable practices of the nations. They polluted the LORD's temple that God had dedicated in Jerusalem. ¹⁵Time and time again, the LORD, the God of their ancestors, sent word to them through his messengers because he had compassion on his people and his dwelling. ¹⁶But they made fun of God's messengers, treating God's words with contempt and ridiculing God's prophets to such an extent that there was no hope of warding off the LORD's rising anger against his people.

Jerusalem destroyed

¹⁷So God brought the Babylonianᵏ king against them. The king killed their young

---

ⁱLXX, 2 Kgs 24:8; MT *eight*   ʲ2 Kgs 24:8; MT adds *and ten days.*   ᵏHeb *Chaldean*

BABYLON (OT)

City in southern Mesopotamia, located on a branch of the Euphrates, 59 mi. southwest of present-day Baghdad. Babylon rose to prominence early in the 2nd millennium BCE.

The OT contains more than 300 references to Babylon, the region of Babylonia, or its inhabitants, as well as 49 references to the ethnically precise term "Chaldeans." Because of its international and cultural significance, and its role later in destroying Jerusalem and deporting large portions of its citizens, Babylon came to carry theological significance in the Bible even beyond its obvious historical importance. The city itself came to symbolize ungodly power.

men with the sword in their temple's sanctuary, and showed no pity for young men or for virgins, for the old or for the feeble. God handed all of them over to him. [18] Then the king hauled everything off to Babylon, every item from God's temple, both large and small, including the treasures of the LORD's temple and those of the king and his officials. [19] Next the Babylonians burned God's temple down, demolished the walls of Jerusalem, and set fire to all its palaces, destroying everything of value. [20] Finally, he exiled to Babylon anyone who survived the killing so that they could be his slaves and the slaves of his children until Persia came to power. [21] This is how the LORD's word spoken by Jeremiah was carried out. The land finally enjoyed its sabbath rest.

For as long as it lay empty, it rested, until seventy years were completed.

Cyrus' decree

[22] In the first year of Persia's King Cyrus, to carry out the LORD's promise spoken through Jeremiah, the LORD moved Persia's King Cyrus to issue the following proclamation throughout his kingdom, along with a written decree:

[23] This is what Persia's King Cyrus says: The LORD, the God of heaven, has given me all the earth's kingdoms and has instructed me to build a temple for him at Jerusalem in Judah. Whoever among you belong to God's people, let them go up, and may the LORD their God be with them!

EZRA

Except for the books of Ezra and Nehemiah, our knowledge of the Israelite people in those formative years immediately following the Babylonian Exile would be virtually nil. We would know nothing of the return from the exile, almost nothing of the rebuilding of the temple and those who inspired this work, and nothing of the Samaritan opposition that began here, but lingered and festered for centuries afterward (see John 4:9).

We would have no information about the repopulation of Jerusalem and the reconstruction of the city walls. We would know nothing of the reforms under Nehemiah and Ezra, which rid the Israelite religion of pagan influences and protected it from foreign divinities. Most important, we would have no knowledge of Ezra's reading of the law to the people and of their acceptance of it as God's authoritative word, which, if our understanding of that event is correct, marks the true beginning both of Judaism as a religion and the formation of the Jewish Bible. The books of Ezra and Nehemiah, then, command a place of special honor among the books of the Bible.

THE ORIGIN OF THE BOOK

When first written, and for centuries afterward, Ezra and Nehemiah stood as one book, called Ezra. Not until the time of Origen (third century CE) do we have evidence that the book had been divided into two parts. The Book of Ezra/Nehemiah is related to the books of 1 and 2 Chronicles, which originally stood as one book, called The Chronicles. The relationship, in fact, is so close that many scholars believe all four of these books were originally one book. Additionally, the book of Ezra begins exactly where 2 Chronicles leaves off, even repeating the decree which ends that book (see 2 Chronicles 36:22-23 and Ezra 1:1-4).

THE AUTHOR

An ancient Jewish tradition says that Ezra himself was responsible for writing these four books, and modern scholarship finds much to commend that ancient belief. But there are also difficulties with this view. Most scholars call the author The Chronicler, preferring the awkwardness of that name to the uncertainty of the identification with Ezra.

WHO CAME FIRST—EZRA OR NEHEMIAH?

The careful reader of the books of Ezra and Nehemiah may well become confused. Events that at first glance seem to be connected with the story just read appear, upon closer reflection, to be related instead to a story told elsewhere in the book. Episodes are related out of chronological sequence, and similar types of action are told one after the other although the events themselves may have happened years, or even decades, apart.

One of the most baffling problems of chronology is whether Ezra or Nehemiah came to Jerusalem first. The present order of the material leaves the impression that Ezra did. Ezra left Babylonia in the seventh year of the reign of King Artaxerxes (Ezra 7:1, 6-7); thirteen years later Nehemiah returned to Jerusalem (Nehemiah 1:1; 2:1); the two men were there together for an undetermined length of time (Nehemiah 8:1, 9).

However, there are many indications that Nehemiah returned to Jerusalem before Ezra did. For example:

(1) When Nehemiah returned to Jerusalem, he found the city to be sparsely settled (Nehemiah 7:4), and he had to take measures to repopulate it (Nehemiah 11:1-2). By the time Ezra arrived, however, Jerusalem seems to have had a large number of people living in it (Ezra 10:1).

(2) Nehemiah had to rebuild the city wall after he arrived (Nehemiah 2:11-12, 16-17). In Ezra's day, the wall seems to have been already standing (Ezra 9:9).

(3) Nehemiah had to appoint people to act as temple treasurers (Nehemiah 13:13), whereas a group of priests was already acting in that capacity when Ezra first arrived (Ezra 8:33).

(4) Eliashib was the high priest at the time of Nehemiah (Nehemiah 3:1, 20), whereas Jehohanan, the son of Eliashib (or perhaps the grandson; see Nehemiah 12:10-11 and 13:28) seems to have been the high priest at the time of Ezra (Ezra 10:6).

(5) None of the persons who returned to Jerusalem with Ezra (Ezra 8:1-20), nor any of their children, are reported to have assisted Nehemiah in the rebuilding of the wall (Nehemiah 3:1-32). Nehemiah 2:17-18 gives the impression that all the people were eager to help. It seems especially incredible that those who returned with Ezra would not have helped in that project had they been there at the time the work was being done.

(6) Ezra left Babylon with the law book in his hand (Ezra 7:6, 14, 25). He was eager to teach the law to the people (Ezra 7:10), and he had full authority to command obedience to it (Ezra 7:25-26). Why, then, would he wait thirteen years, until Nehemiah arrived (Nehemiah 8:9), to do so? The more natural explanation is that Nehemiah had preceded Ezra to Jerusalem.

There are other reasons, too, for believing Nehemiah returned to Jerusalem before Ezra did, including supporting evidence from an archaeological find (discussed in the Introduction to Nehemiah). None of these arguments is conclusive, not even all of them together, but they certainly point in that direction.

But if Nehemiah actually preceded Ezra, why are we told that Ezra returned the seventh year of Artaxerxes, and Nehemiah the twentieth? The answer seems to lie in the fact that three Persian monarchs ruled under the name Artaxerxes. If we assume Nehemiah returned the twentieth year of Artaxerxes I (465–424 BCE), and Ezra the seventh year of Artaxerxes II (404–358 BCE), that would place Nehemiah's arrival in 445 and Ezra's in 397.

HISTORICAL BACKGROUND

The Babylonian Empire had only one great leader—its second king, Nebuchadnezzar. At Nebuchadnezzar's death in 562 BCE, there was no strong leader to take his place. Three weak kings later, Nabonidus came to the Babylonian throne. Though he reigned in name some sixteen years (555–539 BCE), his son, Belshazzar, was the actual ruler most of that time. In 539 Cyrus, the Persian king whose political shrewdness far outmatched that of either Nabonidus or Belshazzar, wrested the empire from their hands with hardly a drop of blood being shed.

Cyrus was a more enlightened ruler than the kings of Babylon had been. Nebuchadnezzar's policy, followed by all his successors, was to take the leaders of the conquered nations into exile in order to minimize the risk of insurrection. Cyrus's philosophy was different. He believed people are easiest to rule when they are happy, and they are happy when they are allowed to live in their own land and worship their own gods. Shortly after his takeover of the empire, therefore, Cyrus issued an edict allowing the exiles within his empire to return to their homelands and rebuild their temples. Among those enjoying this privilege were the exiles from Judah.

EZRA

Permission to return to Jerusalem

1 In the first year of King Cyrus of Persia's rule, to fulfill the Lord's word spoken by Jeremiah, the Lord stirred up the spirit of Persia's King Cyrus. The king issued a proclamation throughout his kingdom (it was also in writing) that stated:

² Persia's King Cyrus says: The Lord, the God of heaven, has given me all the kingdoms of the earth. He has commanded me to build him a house at Jerusalem in Judah. ³ If there are any of you who are from his people, may their God be with them! They may go up to Jerusalem in Judah and build the house of the Lord, the God of Israel—he is the God who is in Jerusalem. ⁴ And as for all those who remain in the various places where they are living, let the people of those places supply them with silver and gold, and with goods and livestock, together with spontaneous gifts for God's house in Jerusalem.ᵃ

Preparing to return

⁵ Then the heads of the families of Judah and Benjamin, and the priests and the Levites—everyone whose spirit God had stirred up—got ready to go up and build God's house in Jerusalem. ⁶ All their neighbors assisted them with silver equipment, with gold, with goods, livestock, and valuable gifts, in addition to all that was freely offered. ⁷ King Cyrus brought out the equipment of the Lord's house—those items that Nebuchadnezzar brought from Jerusalem and placed in the house of his gods. ⁸ Persia's King Cyrus handed them over to Mithredath the treasurer, who counted them out to Sheshbazzar the prince of Judah. ⁹ This was the count: thirty gold dishes, one thousand silver dishes, twenty-nine knives,ᵇ ¹⁰ thirty gold bowls, four hundred ten largerᶜ silver bowls, and one thousand other objects. ¹¹ The total of the gold and silver objects numbered five thousand four hundred. Sheshbazzar brought up all of these when the exiles went up from Babylonia to Jerusalem.

List of the returnees

2 These were the people of the province who went up from there—from among those captive exiles whom Babylon's King Nebuchadnezzar had deported to Babylonia. They returned to Jerusalem and Judah, all to their own towns. ² They came with Zerubbabel, Jeshua, Nehemiah, Seraiah, Reelaiah, Mordecai, Bilshan, Mispar, Bigvai, Rehum, and Baanah.

The number of the people of Israel

³ The family of Parosh	2,172
⁴ of Shephatiah	372
⁵ of Arah	775
⁶ of Pahath-moab, namely the family of Jeshua and Joab	2,812
⁷ of Elam	1,254
⁸ of Zattu	945
⁹ of Zaccai	760
¹⁰ of Bani	642
¹¹ of Bebai	623
¹² of Azgad	1,222
¹³ of Adonikam	666
¹⁴ of Bigvai	2,056
¹⁵ of Adin	454
¹⁶ of Ater, namely of Hezekiah	98
¹⁷ of Bezai	323
¹⁸ of Jorah	112
¹⁹ of Hashum	223
²⁰ of Gibbar	95
²¹ of Bethlehem	123
²² The people of Netophah	56
²³ of Anathoth	128
²⁴ The family of Azmaveth	42
²⁵ of Kiriatharim, Chephirah, and Beeroth	743
²⁶ of Ramah and Geba	621
²⁷ The people of Michmash	122
²⁸ of Bethel and Ai	223
²⁹ The family of Nebo	52
³⁰ of Magbish	156
³¹ of the other Elam	1,254
³² of Harim	320

ᵃHeb uncertain ᵇVulg; Heb uncertain ᶜHeb *double*

³³ of Lod, Hadid, and Ono   725
³⁴ of Jericho   345
³⁵ of Senaah   3,630

³⁶ *The priests*
The family of Jedaiah,
namely the house of Jeshua   973
³⁷ of Immer   1,052
³⁸ of Pashhur   1,247
³⁹ of Harim   1,017
⁴⁰ The Levites: the family
of Jeshua and Kadmiel—
the family of Hodaviah   74

⁴¹ *The singers*
The family of Asaph   128

⁴² *The family of the gatekeepers*
of Shallum, Ater, Talmon,
Akkub, Hatita, and Shobai   139 in all

⁴³ *The temple servants*
The family of Ziha, Hasupha,
Tabbaoth, ⁴⁴Keros, Siaha,
Padon, ⁴⁵Lebanah, Hagabah,
Akkub, ⁴⁶Hagab, Shamlai,
Hanan, ⁴⁷Giddel, Gahar,
Reaiah, ⁴⁸Rezin, Nekoda,
Gazzam, ⁴⁹Uzza, Paseah,
Besai, ⁵⁰Asnah, Meunim,
Nephisim, ⁵¹Bakbuk, Hakupha,
Harhur, ⁵²Bazluth, Mehida,

Harsha, ⁵³Barkos, Sisera,
Temah, ⁵⁴Neziah, and Hatipha

⁵⁵ *The family of Solomon's servants*
Sotai, Hassophereth, Peruda,
⁵⁶Jaalah, Darkon, Giddel,
⁵⁷Shephatiah, Hattil, Pochereth-
hazzebaim, and Ami.
⁵⁸ All of the temple servants and
the family of Solomon's servants   392

Exclusions
⁵⁹ The following came up from Tel-melah,
Tel-harsha, Cherub, Addan, and Immer,
but they were unable to demonstrate that
their family or their descent was from
Israel:
⁶⁰ the family of Delaiah, Tobiah,
and Nekoda,   652
⁶¹ and of the family of the priests:
the family of Habaiah, Hakkoz,
and Barzillai (who had married
one of the daughters of Barzillai
the Gileadite and was called by
their name).
⁶² They looked for their entries in the
genealogical records, but they were not
found there, so they were excluded from
the priesthood as unclean. ⁶³ The governor
ordered them not to eat of the most holy
food until a priest arose who could consult
Urim and Thummim.

PERSIA

The Persians were Iranian tribes who developed into a major empire. Their religion is commonly referred to as Zoroastrianism, after Zoroaster, the Greek form of Zarathustra, or as Mazdaism. This religion took shape among the Iranian tribes in Central Asia, and its oldest form is known from the Avesta sacred texts. The Persian Empire defeated the Babylonian Empire in 539 BCE, changing the ruling power over the Jerusalem area. In the OT, the Persian emperor Cyrus is praised as a victorious conqueror. According to Ezra, Cyrus was divinely inspired to rebuild the Jerusalem temple and allowed the exiles to go to Jerusalem and help in the building, notably those in Babylon (Ezra 1–2). Under a subsequent emperor, Darius, the original decree was allegedly found in Ecbatana (Ezra 6:2-12). Persian rule continued to around 330 BCE, when Alexander the Great defeated Persian forces and began the Hellenistic rule of the Palestine area.

Total

[64]The whole assembly together totaled 42,360, [65]not including their 7,337 male and female servants; they also had 200 male and female singers, [66]736 horses, 245 mules, [67]435 camels, and 6,720 donkeys.

Arrival in Jerusalem

[68]When they arrived at the LORD's house in Jerusalem, some of the heads of the families brought spontaneous gifts for the rebuilding of God's house on its site. [69]According to their means, they gave to the building fund 61,000 drachmen of gold, 5,000 manehs of silver, and 100 priestly robes.

[70]The priests, the Levites, some of the people, the singers, the gatekeepers, and the temple servants settled in their own towns, and all Israel in their towns.

Rebuilding the altar

3 When the seventh month[d] came and the Israelites were in their towns, the people gathered together as one in Jerusalem. [2]Then Jeshua, Jozadak's son along with his fellow priests, and Zerubbabel, Shealtiel's son along with his kin, started to rebuild the altar of Israel's God so that they might offer entirely burned offerings upon it as prescribed in the Instruction from Moses the man of God. [3]They set up the altar on its foundations,[e] because they were afraid of the neighboring peoples,[f] and they offered entirely burned offerings upon it to the LORD, both the morning and the evening offerings.

[4]They celebrated the Festival of Booths,

as prescribed. Every day they presented the number of entirely burned offerings required by ordinance for that day. [5]After this, they presented the continual burned offerings, the offerings at the new moons, and at all the sacred feasts of the LORD, and the offerings of everyone who brought a spontaneous gift to the LORD. [6]From the first day of the seventh month, they began to present entirely burned offerings to the LORD.

However, the foundation of the LORD's temple had not yet been laid. [7]So they gave money to the masons and carpenters; and food, drink, and oil to the Sidonians and the Tyrians to bring cedarwood by sea from Lebanon to Joppa, according to the authorization given them by Persia's King Cyrus.

Laying the foundations of God's house

[8]In the second month of the second year after their arrival at God's house in Jerusalem, Zerubbabel, Shealtiel's son, and Jeshua, Jozadak's son and the rest of their kin—the priests and the Levites and all who had come from the captivity to Jerusalem—made a beginning. They appointed Levites 20 years old and above to oversee the work on the LORD's house. [9]Then Jeshua with his sons and his kin, Kadmiel and his sons, Binnui and his sons, the sons of Judah, along with the sons of Henadad, the Levites, and their sons and kin, collaborated to supervise the workers in God's house.

[10]When the builders laid the foundation of the LORD's temple, the priests clothed in their vests and carrying their trumpets,

[d]September–October, Tishrei   [e]A technical word meaning *pedestals*   [f]Or *peoples of the lands*

SECOND TEMPLE PERIOD

The period (ca. 515 BCE–70 CE) after the Babylonian Exile, named for the temple rebuilt in Jerusalem under Zerubbabel the governor of Judah and Jeshua the high priest. The temple would have a number of transformations during this period, ultimately becoming a massive precinct under Herod the Great, until it was destroyed again (by the Romans) in 70 CE.

and the Levites the sons of Asaph with cymbals, arose to praise the LORD according to the directions of Israel's King David. [11]They praised and gave thanks to the LORD, singing responsively, "He is good, his graciousness for Israel lasts forever."

All of the people shouted with praise to the LORD because the foundation of the LORD's house had been laid. [12]But many of the older priests and Levites and heads of families, who had seen the first house, wept aloud when they saw the foundation of this house, although many others shouted loudly with joy. [13]No one could distinguish the sound of the joyful shout from the sound of the people's weeping, because the people rejoiced very loudly. The sound was heard at a great distance.

Facing opposition

4 When the enemies of Judah and Benjamin heard that the returned exiles were building a temple for the LORD, the God of Israel, [2]they came to Zerubbabel and the heads of the families and said to them, "Let's build with you, for we worship your God as you do, and we've been sacrificing to him ever since the days of Assyria's King Esarhaddon, who brought us here."

[3]But Zerubbabel, Joshua, and the rest of the heads of the families in Israel replied, "You'll have no part with us in building a house for our God. We alone will build because the LORD, the God of Israel, and Persia's King Cyrus commanded us."

[4]The neighboring peoples[g] discouraged the people of Judah, made them afraid to build, [5]and bribed officials to frustrate their plan. They did this throughout the rule of Persia's King Cyrus until the rule of Persia's King Darius.

Writing to King Artaxerxes

[6]In the rule of Ahasuerus, at the beginning of his rule, they composed an indictment against those who lived in Judah and Jerusalem. [7]In the days of Artaxerxes, Bishlam, Mithredath, Tabeel, and the rest of their associates wrote to Persia's King Artaxerxes. The letter was written in Aramaic and translated.[h] [8]Rehum the royal deputy and Shimshai the scribe wrote a letter concerning Jerusalem to King Artaxerxes as follows:

[9]From Rehum the royal deputy and Shimshai the scribe and the rest of their colleagues, the judges, the administrators, the officials, the Persians, the people of Erech, the Babylonians, the people of Susa (that is, the Elamites), [10]and the rest of the nations whom the great and famous Osnappar deported and settled in the cities of Samaria and in the rest of the province Beyond the River.

([11]This is a copy of the letter they sent to him.)

To King Artaxerxes from your servants, the people of the province Beyond the River. [12]May it be known to the king that the Jews who left you and came to us have arrived in Jerusalem. They are rebuilding the rebellious and wicked city; they are completing the walls and repairing the foundations. [13]May it be known to the king that if this city is rebuilt and the walls completed, they will not pay tribute or tax or dues, and the royal revenue will be reduced.

[g]Or peoples of the lands   [h]Heb adds in Aramaic, reporting that 4:8–6:18 is written in Aramaic.

BEYOND THE RIVER

The term "beyond the river" takes its reference from the Euphrates and could refer to the area east (1 Kgs 14:15) or west (Ezra 4:10) of the river depending on the location of the speaker. As reflected in Ezra, the term designated a satrapy that included Syria-Palestine during the Persian period.

[14]Since we receive our salary from the palace,[i] and since it is not fitting for us to witness the king's dishonor, we now send this letter[j] and inform the king [15]so that you may search the records of your ancestors. You will discover in the records that this is a rebellious city, harmful to kings and provinces, and that it has been in revolt over a long period of time. As a result, this city was laid waste. [16]We tell the king that if this city is rebuilt and its walls completed, you will then have no possession in the province Beyond the River.

Artaxerxes responds

[17]The king sent this answer:

Greetings to Rehum the royal deputy and Shimshai the scribe and the rest of their colleagues who live in Samaria and elsewhere in the province Beyond the River. [18]The entire letter that you sent to us has been read in translation for me. [19]I issued an order; they searched and discovered that this city has revolted against kings over a long period of time. There has been much rebellion and revolt there. [20]However, there have been mighty kings over Jerusalem who also ruled over the whole province Beyond the River. Tribute and taxes and dues were paid to them.

[21]Therefore, issue an order to stop these people: this city is not to be rebuilt until I make a decree. [22]Be sure to carry out this order! Why should danger grow and threaten the king?

[23]When the copy of King Artaxerxes' letter was read before Rehum and Shimshai the scribe and their colleagues, they hurried to Jerusalem to oppose the Jews and made them stop by force of arms.[k] [24]At that time the work on God's house in Jerusalem stopped and was suspended until the second year of the rule of Persia's King Darius.

Work on God's house continues

5 Then the prophet Haggai and the prophet Zechariah, Iddo's son, prophesied to the Jews who were in Judah and Jerusalem in the name of Israel's God who was over them. [2]Subsequently, Zerubbabel, Shealtiel's son, and Jeshua, Jozadak's son, began to rebuild God's house in Jerusalem. God's prophets were with them, helping them.

[3]At the same time, Tattenai, the governor of the province Beyond the River, and Shethar-bozenai and their colleagues came to them and spoke to them, asking, "Who authorized you to build this house and finish preparing[l] this building material?"[m] [4]They[n] also asked them, "What are the names of the people who are building this building?" [5]But their God looked after the elders of the Jews, and they didn't stop them until a report reached Darius and a letter with his response had arrived.

Writing to King Darius

[6]This is a copy of the letter that Tattenai, the governor of the province Beyond the River, and Shethar-bozenai and his colleagues the officials who were in the province Beyond the River sent to King Darius. [7]In the message they sent him, the following was written:

To King Darius, all peace! [8]Let the king know that we went to the province of Judah, to the house of the great God. It is being built with dressed stone and with timber set into the walls. This work makes good progress and prospers in their hands. [9]We asked those elders, "Who authorized you to build this house and to complete the preparation of this material?" [10]We also asked them their names so that we could write down the names of the leaders for your information.

[11]This was their reply to us: "We are the servants of the God of heaven and earth. We are rebuilding the house that was built many years ago, which a great king of Israel built and completed. [12]But because our ancestors angered the God of heaven, he gave them over into the power of Babylon's King Nebuchad-

---

[i]Or since we have salted the salt of the palace   [j]Heb lacks this letter.   [k]Or power and force   [l]Heb lacks preparing.
[m]Heb uncertain; so also 5:9   [n]LXX, Syr, Aram We

nezzar, the Chaldean, who destroyed this house and deported the people to Babylonia. [13]However, in the first year of his rule, Babylon's King Cyrus issued a decree to rebuild this house of God. [14]King Cyrus also took the gold and silver equipment from God's house out of the temple in Babylon (the ones that Nebuchadnezzar took from the temple in Jerusalem and placed in the temple in Babylon) and gave them to a man named Sheshbazzar, whom he had appointed governor. [15]Cyrus said to him, 'Take this equipment and go and put it in Jerusalem's temple, and let God's house be rebuilt on its original site.' [16]Then Sheshbazzar came and laid the foundations of God's house in Jerusalem. From then until now the rebuilding work has continued but is not yet complete."

[17]And now, if it seems good to the king, may a search be made in the royal archives in Babylon to see if King Cyrus had issued a decree to rebuild this house of God in Jerusalem. Then may the king be pleased to send us his decision about this matter.

Darius responds

6 Then King Darius made a decree, and they searched the archives where the documents were stored in Babylon. [2]But a scroll was found in Ecbatana, the capital of the province of Media, on which was written the following:

A memorandum—[3]In the first year of his rule, King Cyrus made a decree: Concerning God's house in Jerusalem: Let the house at the place where they offered sacrifices be rebuilt and let its foundations be retained. Its height will be ninety feet and its width ninety feet, [4]with three layers of dressed stones and one° layer of timber. The cost will be paid from the royal treasury. [5]In addition, the gold and silver equipment from God's house, which Nebuchadnezzar took out of the temple in Jerusalem and brought to Babylon, is to be restored, that is, brought back to Jerusalem and put in their proper place in God's house.

[6]Now you, Tattenai, governor of the province Beyond the River, Shethar-bozenai, and you, their colleagues, the officials in the province Beyond the River,

°LXX; Heb *new*

DARIUS

1. Darius I, the Great or the Conqueror (reigned 522–486 BCE). Work on rebuilding the temple began in the second year of Darius (520; Ezra 4:24). Simultaneously, the prophets Haggai and Zechariah (see also Isa 56–66) convinced the community, along with Zerubbabel the governor and Jeshua the high priest, to begin the work. When opponents petitioned Darius to stop the rebuilding efforts (Ezra 5:6-17), the king responded with Achaemenid resources to support the work (6:1-12).

2. Darius the Mede. This 62-year-old, according to the book of Daniel, ruled the Babylonian Empire upon the death of Belshazzar (Dan 5:30-31), ruled at least a year, and divided the empire into 120 satrapies (Dan 6:1). Babylonian, Persian, and Hellenistic sources all attribute the conquest of Babylon (539 BCE) to Cyrus the Persian. No Median king Darius is attested elsewhere, and attempts to identify him historically have failed to gain wide acceptance.

keep away! [7] Leave the work on this house of God alone. Let the governor of the Jews and the elders of the Jews rebuild this house of God on its original site.

[8] I also issue a decree about what you should do to help these elders of the Jews as they rebuild this house of God: The total cost is to be paid to these people, and without delay, from the royal revenue that is made up of the tribute of the province Beyond the River. [9] And whatever is needed—young bulls, rams, or sheep for entirely burned offerings to the God of heaven, wheat, salt, wine, or oil, as requested by the priests in Jerusalem—let that be given to them day by day without fail [10] so that they may offer pleasing sacrifices to the God of heaven and pray for the lives of the king and his sons.

[11] I also decree that if anyone disobeys this edict, a beam is to be pulled out of the house of the guilty party, and the guilty party will then be impaled upon it. The house will be turned into a trash heap. [12] May the God who has established his name there overthrow any king or people who try to change this order or to destroy God's house in Jerusalem. I, Darius, have decreed it; let it be done with all diligence.

God's house is completed and dedicated

[13] Then Tattenai, the governor of the province Beyond the River, Shethar-bozenai, and their colleagues carried out the order of King Darius with all diligence. [14] So the elders of the Jews built and prospered because of the prophesying of the prophet Haggai and Zechariah, Iddo's son. They finished building by the command of Israel's God and of Cyrus, Darius, and King Artaxerxes of Persia. [15] This house was completed on the third day of the month of Adar,[p] in the sixth year of the rule of King Darius.

[16] Then the Israelites, the priests and the Levites, and the rest of the returned exiles joyfully celebrated the dedication of this house of God. [17] At the dedication of this house of God, they offered one hundred bulls, two hundred rams, four hundred lambs, and as a purification offering for all Israel, twelve male goats, according to the number of the tribes of Israel. [18] They set the priests in their divisions and the Levites in their sections for the service of God in Jerusalem, as it is written in the scroll from Moses.

[19][q] On the fourteenth day of the first month,[r] the returned exiles celebrated the Passover. [20] All of the priests and the Levites had purified themselves; all of them were clean. They slaughtered the Passover animals for all the returned exiles, their fellow priests, and themselves. [21] The Israelites who had returned from exile, together with all those who had joined them by separating themselves from the pollutions of the nations of the land to worship the LORD, the God of Israel, ate the Passover meal.[s]

[22] They also joyfully celebrated the Festival of Unleavened Bread for seven days, because the LORD had made them joyful by changing the attitude of the king of Assyria toward them so that he assisted them in the work on the house of God, the God of Israel.

Introduction to Ezra

7 After this, in the rule of Persia's King Artaxerxes, Ezra son of Seraiah son of Azariah son of Hilkiah [2] son of Shallum son of Zadok son of Ahitub [3] son of Amariah son of Azariah son of Meraioth [4] son of Zerahiah son of Uzzi son of Bukki [5] son of Abishua son of Phinehas son of Eleazar son of Aaron the chief priest—[6] this Ezra came up from Babylon. He was a scribe skilled in the Instruction from Moses, which the LORD, the God of Israel, had given. Moreover, the king gave him everything he requested because the LORD his God's power was with him.

[7] Some of the Israelites and some of the priests and the Levites, the singers and gatekeepers and the temple servants also came up to Jerusalem in the seventh year of King Artaxerxes. [8] They reached Jerusalem in the fifth month, in the seventh year of

---

[p] February–March　[q] Heb resumes with this verse.　[r] March–April, Nisan　[s] Heb lacks *Passover meal.*

the king. [9]The journey from Babylon began on the first day of the first month, and they came to Jerusalem on the first day of the fifth month, for the gracious hand of his God was upon him. [10]Ezra had determined to study and perform the LORD's Instruction, and to teach law and justice in Israel.

Letter from Artaxerxes

[11]This is a copy of the letter that Artaxerxes gave to Ezra the priest and scribe, a scholar of the text of the LORD's commandments and his requirements for Israel:

[12t]Artaxerxes, king of kings, to Ezra the priest, the scribe of the Instruction from the God of heaven. Peace![u]

And now [13]I decree that any of the people of Israel or their priests or Levites in my kingdom who volunteer to go to Jerusalem with you may go. [14]You are sent by the king and his seven counselors to investigate Judah and Jerusalem according to the Instruction from your God, which is in your hand.

[15]You should bring the silver and gold that the king and his counselors have freely offered to the God of Israel, whose dwelling is in Jerusalem, [16]together with any of the silver and gold that you find in the entire province of Babylonia. You should also bring the spontaneous gifts of the people and the priests, given freely for God's house in Jerusalem. [17]With this money you will be careful to buy bulls, rams, and lambs, as well as their grain offerings and their drink offerings. And you will offer them on the altar of God's house in Jerusalem. [18]As long as it is God's will, you and your colleagues may do what you think best with the rest of the silver and gold. [19]You will deliver the equipment that has been given to you for the service of God's house to the God of Jerusalem. [20]If anything else is required for God's house that you are responsible to provide, you may provide it from the royal treasury.

[21]I, King Artaxerxes, decree to all of the treasurers in the province Beyond the River: Whatever Ezra the priest and scribe of the Instruction from the God of heaven requires of you, it must be provided precisely, [22]even up to one hundred kikkars of silver, one hundred kors of wheat, one hundred baths[v] of wine, one hundred baths of oil, and unlimited salt. [23]Whatever the God of heaven commands will be done carefully for the house of the God of heaven, or wrath will come upon the realm of the king and his

---

[t]7:12-26 is written in Aramaic. [u]Syr, Vulg 1 Esdr 8:9; Aram *Perfect* [v]One bath is approximately twenty quarts or five gallons.

EZRA

The story of Ezra is told in a first-person account (Ezra 7:27–8:34; 9:1-15) and a third-person account (Ezra 7:1-11; 8:35-36; 10:1-44; Neh 7:73b–8:18 [possibly also 9:1-5]). Ezra is called a priest and a "scribe of the Instruction from the God of heaven" (Ezra 7:12). Despite the genealogy connecting him to the high priestly line in Ezra 7:1-5, he was not a high priest. As a scribe he was no doubt an expert in the Instruction, but some have seen in this title an indication that he was a commissioner for Jewish affairs in the Persian government.

Ezra came to Jerusalem at the direction of the Persian king Artaxerxes in his seventh year of reign (458 BCE if this was Artaxerxes I; 397 BCE if it was Artaxerxes II).

heirs. [24]You must also know that it is illegal for you to charge tribute, custom, or dues on any of the priests and Levites, the singers, the doorkeepers, the temple servants, or other servants of this house of God.

[25]And you, Ezra, based on the divine wisdom that you have, appoint supervisors and judges to adjudicate among all the people in the province Beyond the River who know the laws of your God. You will also teach those who do not know them. [26]Let judgment be strictly carried out upon anyone who does not obey the Instruction from your God and the law of your king, including death, banishment, confiscation of property, or imprisonment.

Ezra prepares to leave

[27]Bless the LORD, the God of our ancestors, who has moved the king to glorify the LORD's house in Jerusalem, [28]and who has demonstrated his graciousness for me before the king and his counselors and all the king's mighty officers. I took courage because the LORD my God's power was with me. I gathered leaders from Israel to go up with me.

8 These are the heads of the families, and this is the genealogy of those who went up with me during the rule of King Artaxerxes:

[2]of the family of Phinehas, Gershom; of Ithamar, Daniel; of David, Hattush, [3]Shecaniah's son;[w] of Parosh, Zechariah and with him were registered 150 men;

[4]of Pahath-moab, Eliehoenai, Zerahiah's son and with him 200 men;

[5]of Zattu,[x] Shecaniah, Jahaziel's son and with him 300 men;

[6]of Adin, Ebed, Jonathan's son and with him 50 men;

[7]of Elam, Jeshaiah, Athaliah's son and with him 70 men;

[8]of Shephatiah, Zebadiah, Michael's son and with him 80 men;

[9]of Joab, Obadiah, Jehiel's son and with him 218 men;

---

[w]LXX and 1 Esdr 8:29; Heb *of the descendants of Shecaniah* [x]LXX and 1 Esdr 8:32; Heb lacks *of Zattu.*

ARTAXERXES

The name of three Persian kings.

1. Artaxerxes I Longimanus (465–424 BCE), son of Xerxes I. It is generally agreed that Nehemiah came to Jerusalem in the twentieth year of Artaxerxes I (445; Neh 2:1). Much more disputed is the date of Ezra's arrival. Ezra came to Jerusalem in the seventh year of an Artaxerxes (Ezra 7:7-8). If under Artaxerxes I, then Ezra came in 458; if under Artaxerxes II, Ezra arrived in 397. The principal argument in favor of Ezra's coming to Jerusalem in 458 is the order suggested by the books of Ezra and Nehemiah.

2. Artaxerxes II Mnemon (404–358 BCE). Those who favor a date for Ezra under Artaxerxes II note the mention of a wall (Ezra 9:9), possibly referring to the wall repaired by Nehemiah, and the fact that the high priest in the time of Nehemiah was Eliashib, while in the time of Ezra the high priest may have been Jehohanan, son of Eliashib (Ezra 10:6). Artaxerxes II worked to reconquer Egypt, which had revolted against Persia in 405.

3. Artaxerxes III Ochus (358–338 BCE). Under Artaxerxes III, Tennes, king of Sidon, revolted ca. 349, but the effect of this revolt on Israel cannot be measured.

¹⁰of Bani,ʸ Shelomith, Josiphiah's son and with him 160 men;

¹¹of Bebai, Zechariah, Bebai's son and with him 28 men;

¹²of Azgad, Johanan, Hakkatan's son and with them 110 men;

¹³of the last of Adonikam, namely Eliphelet, Jeuel, and Shemaiah and with them 60 men;

¹⁴of Bigvai, Uthai and Zaccur and with them were 70 men.

Voyage to Jerusalem

¹⁵I gathered them by the river that runs to Ahava, and there we camped for three days.

As I reviewed the people and the priests, I found no Levites there. ¹⁶So I called for Eliezer, Ariel, Shemaiah, Elnathan, Jarib, Elnathan, Nathan, Zechariah, and Meshullam, all leaders, together with Joiarib and Elnathan, who were wise. ¹⁷I sent themᶻ to Iddo, the leader at the place named Casiphia, telling them what to say to Iddo and his colleagues the temple servants at Casiphia, namely, to send us ministers for God's house. ¹⁸Because we were favored by God, they brought us Sherebiah, a skillful man of the family of Mahli, Levi's son and Israel's grandson, together with his sons and relatives so that there were eighteen in total. ¹⁹They also brought us Hashabiah and with him Jeshaiah of the family of Merari, together with his relatives and their sons so that there were twenty in total. ²⁰In addition, there were two hundred twenty temple servants whom David and the princes had appointed to serve the Levites. These were all recorded by name.

²¹Then I called for a fast there at the Ahava River so that we might submit before our God and ask of him a safe journey for ourselves, our children, and all our possessions. ²²I had been ashamed to ask the king for a group of soldiers and cavalry to help us in facing enemies on the way, because we had told the king, "The power of God favors all who seek him, but his fierce wrath is against all who abandon him." ²³So

we fasted and prayed to our God for this, and he responded to us.

²⁴Then I selected twelve of the leading priests, Sherebiah and Hashabiah and ten of their relatives with them. ²⁵I weighed out to them the silver and the gold and the equipment, the offering for the house of our God that the king, his counselors, his officials, and all Israel present there had offered. ²⁶I weighed out into their keeping six hundred fifty kikkars of silver, one hundred silver containers weighing a certain number of kikkars, one hundred kikkars of gold, ²⁷twenty gold bowls worth one thousand darics, and two containers of highly polished copper, which were as precious as gold. ²⁸I said to them, "You are holy to the LORD, and the equipment is holy; the silver and the gold are a spontaneous gift to the LORD, the God of your ancestors. ²⁹Guard them carefully until you weigh them out in Jerusalem before the officials of the priests, the Levites, and the heads of the families of Israel, within the rooms of the LORD's house." ³⁰So the priests and the Levites received the silver and the gold and the utensils as they were weighed out, in order to bring them to Jerusalem, to our God's house.

³¹Then we left the Ahava River on the twelfth day of the first monthᵃ to go to Jerusalem. The power of our God was with us; he saved us from the power of the enemy and ambushes along the way.

Finishing the journey

³²After arriving in Jerusalem, we rested there three days. ³³On the fourth day, the silver and the gold and the equipment were weighed out in our God's house into the care of the priest named Meremoth, Uriah's son, together with Eleazar, Phinehas' son; and the Levites, Jozabad, Jeshua's son, and Noadiah, Binnui's son. ³⁴Everything was counted and weighed, and the total weight was recorded.

³⁵At that time, those who had come from the captivity, the returned exiles, offered as entirely burned offerings to the

---

ʸLXX and 1 Esdr 8:36; Heb lacks *of Bani.*　ᶻKethib *I ordered them*　ᵃMarch–April, Nisan

God of Israel twelve bulls for all Israel, ninety-six rams, seventy-seven lambs, and twelve male goats as a purification offering. All this was an entirely burned offering to the LORD. [36] They also delivered the king's orders to the royal chief administrators and governors of the province Beyond the River, who supported the people and God's house.

Facing a communal problem

9 When these tasks were finished, the officials approached me and said, "The people of Israel, the priests, and the Levites haven't kept themselves separate from the peoples of the neighboring lands with their detestable practices; namely, the Canaanites, the Hittites, the Perizzites, the Jebusites, the Ammonites, the Moabites, the Egyptians, and the Amorites. [2] They've taken some of their daughters as wives for themselves and their sons, and the holy descendants have become mixed with the neighboring peoples.[b] Moreover, the officials and leaders have led the way in this unfaithfulness."

[3] When I heard this, I tore my clothes and cloak, pulled out hair from my head and beard, and sat down in shock. [4] Then all those who trembled at the words of the God of Israel gathered around me on account of the transgression of the returned exiles while I remained sitting in shock until the evening sacrifice.

Ezra prays

[5] At the time of the evening sacrifice, I ended my penitential acts. While still wearing[c] my torn clothes and cloak, I fell upon my knees, spread out my hands to the LORD my God, [6] and said,

"My God, I'm too ashamed to lift up my face to you. Our iniquities have risen higher than our heads, and our guilt has grown to the heavens. [7] "From the days of our ancestors to this day, we've been deep in guilt. On account of our iniquities we, our kings, and our priests have been handed over to the kings of the lands, to the sword, to captivity, to plundering, and to utter shame, as is now the case.

[8] "But now, for a brief while the LORD our God has shown favor in leaving us survivors and in giving us a stake in his holy place. Our God cheered us[d] and revived us for a little while in our slavery. [9] Even though we are slaves, our God hasn't abandoned us in our slavery. Instead, he's shown us his graciousness before Persia's kings by reviving us to set up our God's house, to repair its ruins, and to give us a wall in Judea and Jerusalem.

[10] "And now, our God, what will we say after this? We have abandoned your commandments, [11] which you commanded through your servants the prophets, saying: 'The land which you are about to enter to possess is a land polluted by the impurity of the neighboring peoples.[e] Their detestable practices have filled it with uncleanness from end to end. [12] So now, do not give your daughters to their sons in marriage, do not take their sons for your daughters to marry, and never seek their peace or prosperity. This is so

[b]Or *peoples of the lands* [c]Heb uncertain [d]Or *brightened our eyes* [e]Or *peoples of the lands*

HOLY PLACE

The larger of the two divisions of both the meeting tent and the temple, containing the lampstand(s) and the tables of the bread of the presence (cf. Exod 25–31; 35–40; 1 Kgs 6–7). "Holy place" is also used as a general term for the temple (e.g., Ezra 9:8), the inside of the temple (2 Chron 5:9), and even the temple grounds (Ezek 45:4).

you may be strong, and eat the good of the land, and leave it for an inheritance to your children forever.'

[13]"After all that has happened to us because of our evil deeds and our great guilt—although you, our God, have punished us less than our iniquities deserve and have allowed us to survive as we do—[14] will we once again break your commandments and intermarry with the peoples who practice these detestable things? Would you not be so angry with us that you leave us without remnant or survivor? [15] LORD, God of Israel, you are righteous, for we have survived and a few remain until now. Here we are before you in our guilt, though no one can face you because of this guilt."[f]

The community responds

10 While Ezra was praying and confessing, weeping and bowing down before God's house, a very large crowd of men, women, and children of Israel gathered around him. The people also wept in distress. [2] Then Shecaniah, Jehiel's son, from the family of Elam, spoke up and said to Ezra, "We've been unfaithful to our God by marrying foreign women from the neighboring peoples.[g] But even now, there is hope for Israel in spite of this. [3] Let's now make a covenant with our God to send away all these wives and their children, according to the advice of my master and of those who tremble at the commandment of our God. Let it be done according to the Instruction. [4] Get up, for it is your duty to deal with this matter; we will support you. Be strong and act." [5] So Ezra got up and made the leading priests, the Levites, and all Israel take a solemn pledge that they would do as had been said. So they took a solemn pledge.

The assembly decides

[6] Then Ezra got up from the area in front of God's house and went to the room of Jehohanan, Eliashib's son, where he spent[h] the night. He didn't eat food or drink water, for he was mourning because of the unfaithfulness of the exiles.

[7] An order was then circulated throughout Judah and Jerusalem that all the returned exiles should gather in Jerusalem. [8] All those who failed to appear within three days, as mandated by the officials and elders, would have all their property taken away. They would be separated from the congregation of the exiles. [9] So within three days, all the people of Judah and Benjamin gathered in Jerusalem. It was the twentieth day of the ninth month.[i] All of the people sat in the area in front of God's house, trembling because of this order and because of the heavy rain.

[10] Then Ezra the priest stood up and said to them, "You have been unfaithful by marrying foreign women and adding to Israel's guilt. [11] But now, make a confession to the LORD God of your ancestors and do his will. Separate yourselves from the neighboring peoples[j] and from the foreign wives."

[12] The whole assembly shouted in reply, "Yes. We must do as you have said. [13] But there are many people, and it's the rainy season; we can't continue to stand outside. Nor can this task be completed in a day or two because many of us have sinned in this matter. [14] Let our leaders represent the entire assembly. Let all in our towns who have taken foreign wives come at appointed times, along with the elders and judges of every town, until God's great anger at us on account of this matter be averted." [15] Only Jonathan, Asahel's son, and Jahzeiah, Tikvah's son, opposed this; Meshullam and Shabbethai the Levites supported them.

Resolving the issue

[16] Then the returned exiles did so. Ezra the priest chose[k] certain men, heads of families, each representing their family houses. Each of them was designated by name. On the first day of the tenth month[l] they sat down to examine the matter.

[f]Heb lacks *guilt*. [g]Or *peoples of the lands* [h]LXX, 1 Esdr 9:2; Heb *where he went* [i]November–December, Kislev [j]Or *peoples of the lands* [k]1 Esdr 9:16; Syr; Heb *And there were separated* [l]December–January, Tevet

[17]By the first day of the first month,[m] they had come to the end of all the men who had married foreign women.

[18]Of the family of priests, there were found the following who had married foreign women—of the family of Jeshua, Jozadak's son and his brothers: Maaseiah, Eliezer, Jarib, and Gedaliah. [19]They promised to send their wives away, and their compensation offering was a ram of the flock for their guilt.

[20]Of the family of Immer: Hanani and Zebadiah.

[21]Of the family of Harim: Maaseiah, Elijah, Shemaiah, Jehiel, and Uzziah.

[22]Of the family of Pashhur: Elioenai, Maaseiah, Ishmael, Nethanel, Jozabad, and Elasah.

[23]Of the Levites: Jozabad, Shimei, Kelaiah (that is, Kelita), Pethahiah, Judah, and Eliezer.

[24]Of the singers: Eliashib. Of the gatekeepers: Shallum, Telem, and Uri.

[25]Of Israel: of the family of Parosh: Ramiah, Izziah, Malchijah, Mijamin, Eleazar, Hashabiah,[n] and Benaiah.

[26]Of the family of Elam: Mattaniah, Zechariah, Jehiel, Abdi, Jeremoth, and Elijah.

[27]Of the family of Zattu: Elioenai, Eliashib, Mattaniah, Jeremoth, Zabad, and Aziza.

[28]Of the family of Bebai: Jehohanan, Hananiah, Zabbai, and Athlai.

[29]Of the family of Bani: Meshullam, Malluch, Adaiah, Jashub, Sheal, and Jeremoth.

[30]Of the family of Pahath-moab: Adna, Chelal, Benaiah, Maaseiah, Mattaniah, Bezalel, Binnui, and Manasseh.

[31]Of the family of Harim: Eliezer, Isshijah, Malchijah, Shemaiah, Shimeon, [32]Benjamin, Malluch, and Shemariah.

[33]Of the family of Hashum: Mattenai, Mattattah, Zabad, Eliphelet, Jeremai, Manasseh, and Shimei.

[34]Of the family of Bani: Maadai, Amram, Uel, [35]Benaiah, Bedeiah, Cheluhi, [36]Vaniah, Meremoth, Eliashib, [37]Mattaniah, Mattenai, and Jaasu.

[38]Of the family of Binnui:[o] Shimei, [39]Shelemiah, Nathan, Adaiah, [40]Machnadebai, Shashai, Sharai, [41]Azarel, Shelemiah, Shemariah, [42]Shallum, Amariah, and Joseph.

[43]Of the family of Nebu: Jeiel, Mattithiah, Zabad, Zebina, Jaddai, Joel, and Benaiah.

[44]All these men[p] had married foreign women, some of whom had borne children.[q]

---

[m]March–April, Nisan [n]1 Esdr 9:26; LXX, Heb Malchijah [o]LXX, Heb Bani, Binnui [p]Heb lacks men.
[q]Heb uncertain; 1 Esdr 9:36 they sent them away with their children.

NEHEMIAH

NEHEMIAH, THE MAN

Nehemiah has not claimed the attention through the centuries that Ezra has. Yet he, too, was a towering figure of his day, and is mentioned in two books of the Apocrypha. In fact, when ben Sira set out to "praise famous people," he mentioned the deeds of Nehemiah, but not those of Ezra (Sirach 44:1; 49:13).

A story about Nehemiah not in the Protestant Bible is found in 2 Maccabees 1:18-36, and 2 Maccabees 2:13 says Nehemiah founded a library and collected the books about the kings, the prophets, and the writings of David. This undoubtedly is a reference to the books of Samuel, Kings, and Psalms. Just as Ezra was responsible for preserving the Torah, Nehemiah preserved much of the rest of the Hebrew Bible. This is our only hint of such activity on the part of Nehemiah, however, and it is found in a book not considered to be historically reliable.

Like Ezra, Nehemiah has left us his memoirs, though scholars disagree on exactly how much and which portions of the book of Nehemiah come from Nehemiah himself. Nehemiah was a man of action, passionately devoted to living by the law of God. In the book that bears his name, we'll find Nehemiah building the city wall and putting into effect several religious reforms. In some ways he was a more likeable person than Ezra, but he, too, could be stern and demanding.

THE DATES OF NEHEMIAH AND EZRA

As noted in the introduction to the book of Ezra, one of the problems of Old Testament scholarship is trying to decide who returned to Jerusalem first—Ezra or Nehemiah. Probably Nehemiah did, and reasons for this are given in the introduction to Ezra. It was also stated there that archaeological evidence supported this claim. Here is that evidence.

In the fifth century BCE, there was a Jewish community on Elephantine Island in Egypt. Among the materials found there, left by this community, was a letter dated in the seventeenth year of Darius II, which would be 407 BCE. The letter is addressed to Delaiah and Shelemiah, sons of Sanballat, whom the letter identifies as the governor of Samaria. Since the letter was sent to the governor's sons, it is reasonable to assume that Sanballat was getting up in years, and had turned over to his sons the responsibility of governing the land.

This fits well with our belief that Nehemiah came to Jerusalem in 445 BCE, the twentieth year of Artaxerxes I (see Nehemiah 1:1; 2:1), for one of Nehemiah's most persistent foes was named Sanballat. And although Nehemiah never refers to him as governor, it is obvious that Sanballat was in a position of authority. He was a young and vigorous leader when Nehemiah was there.

Thirty-eight years later, in 407 (when the Elephantine letter was written), Sanballat was too old to govern, but kept the title of governor, and ruled through his sons.

The same letter refers to Jehohanan as the high priest at the time of the destruction of the Elephantine temple in 410 BCE. That information fits well with our belief that Ezra returned to Jerusalem not in the seventh year of Artaxerxes I but in the seventh year of Artaxerxes II, that is, in 397 BCE, because Ezra 10:6 indicates that Ezra "went to the room of Jehohanan, Eliashib's son, where he spent the night." Now, Eliashib was the high priest in 445 BCE, during the time of Nehemiah (Nehemiah 3:1, 20). If he had become high priest at a young age, he could have continued in that post for another thirty years or so. Then Jehohanan, his son, could have become high priest, and would have been in office at the time of the destruction of the Elephantine temple in 410 and when Ezra arrived in Jerusalem in 397. Thus the archaeological evidence fits the theory that Nehemiah preceded Ezra in returning to Jerusalem.

What leaves the question open, however, is the fact that archaeology is not infallible. Whereas the evidence cited above would support the conclusions to which we have come, other archaeological evidence indicates that there was a second Sanballat, who served as governor of Samaria during the reign of Artaxerxes II. If these are the Sanballat and the Artaxerxes referred to in the Book of Nehemiah, then Nehemiah came to Jerusalem not in 445 but in 384. And that reopens the possibility that Ezra preceded Nehemiah. It seems best, until more definite information can be obtained, to stay with the earlier dates.

NEHEMIAH

Loss of Jerusalem

1 These are the words of Nehemiah, Hacaliah's son.

In the month of Kislev,[a] in the twentieth year,[b] while I was in the fortress city of Susa, ²Hanani, one of my brothers, came with some other men from Judah. I asked them about the Jews who had escaped and survived the captivity, and about Jerusalem.

³They told me, "Those in the province who survived the captivity are in great trouble and shame! The wall around Jerusalem is broken down, and its gates have been destroyed by fire!"

Confession

⁴When I heard this news, I sat down and wept. I mourned for days, fasting and praying before the God of heaven. ⁵I said:

"LORD God of heaven, great and awesome God, you are the one who keeps covenant and is truly faithful to those who love you and keep your commandments. ⁶Let your ear be attentive and your eyes open to hear the prayer of your servant, which I now pray before you night and day for your servants, the people of Israel.

"I confess the sins of the people of Israel, which we have committed against you. Both I and my family have sinned. ⁷We have wronged you greatly. We haven't kept the commandments, the statutes, and the ordinances that you commanded your servant Moses.

⁸"Remember the word that you gave to your servant Moses when you said, 'If you are unfaithful, I will scatter you among the peoples. ⁹But if you return to me and keep my commandments by really doing them, then, even though your outcasts live[c] under distant skies, I will gather them from there and bring them to the place that I have chosen as a dwelling for my name.' ¹⁰They are your servants and your people. They are the ones whom you have redeemed by your great power and your strong hand.

¹¹"LORD, let your ear be attentive to the prayer of your servant and to the prayer of your servants who delight in honoring your name. Please give success to your servant today and grant him favor in the presence of this man!"

Cupbearer's plea

At that time, I was a cupbearer to the king.

2 ¹In the month of Nisan,[d] in the twentieth year of King Artaxerxes, the king was about to be served wine. I took the wine and gave it to the king. Since I had never seemed sad in his presence, ²the king asked me, "Why do you seem sad? Since you aren't sick, you must have a broken heart!"

I was very afraid ³and replied, "May the king live forever! Why shouldn't I seem sad when the city, the place of my family's graves, is in ruins and its gates destroyed by fire?"

⁴The king asked, "What is it that you need?"

I prayed to the God of heaven ⁵and replied, "If it pleases the king, and if your servant has found favor with you, please send me to Judah, to the city of my family's graves so that I may rebuild it."

⁶With the queen sitting beside him, the king asked me, "How long will you be away and when will you return?" So it pleased the king to send me, and I told him how long I would be gone.

⁷I also said to him, "If it pleases the king, may letters be given me addressed to the governors of the province Beyond the River to allow me to travel to Judah. ⁸May the king also issue a letter to Asaph the keeper of the king's forest, directing him to supply me with timber for the beams of the temple fortress gates, for the city wall, and for the house in which I will live."

The king gave me what I asked, for the gracious power of my God was with me.

Inspecting Jerusalem

⁹So I went to the governors of the province[e] Beyond the River and gave them the

---

[a]November–December   [b]Of Artaxerxes   [c]Heb lacks *live*.   [d]March–April   [e]Heb lacks *of the province*.

king's letters. The king had sent officers of the army and cavalry with me.

[10]When Sanballat the Horonite and Tobiah the Ammonite official heard this, they were very angry that someone had come to seek the welfare of the people of Israel.

[11]When I reached Jerusalem and had been there for three days, [12]I set out at night, taking only a few people with me. I didn't tell anyone what my God was prompting me to do for Jerusalem, and the only animal I took was the one I rode. [13]I went out by night through the Valley Gate past the Dragon's Spring to the Dung Gate so that I could inspect the walls of Jerusalem that had been broken down, as well as its gates, which had been destroyed by fire.

[14]Then I went on to the Spring Gate and to the King's Pool. Since there was no room for the animal on which I was riding to pass, [15]I went up by way of the valley by night and inspected the wall. Then I turned back and returned by entering through the Valley Gate.

Let's rebuild

[16]The officials didn't know where I had gone or what I was doing. I hadn't yet told the Jews, the priests, the officials, the officers, or the rest who were to do the work. [17]So I said to them, "You see the trouble that we're in: Jerusalem is in ruins, and its gates are destroyed by fire! Come, let's rebuild the wall of Jerusalem so that we won't continue to be in disgrace." [18]I told them that my God had taken care of me, and also told them what the king had said to me.

"Let's start rebuilding!" they said, and they eagerly began the work.[f]

[19]But when Sanballat the Horonite, Tobiah the Ammonite official, and Geshem the Arab heard about it, they mocked and made fun of us. "What are you doing?" they asked. "Are you rebelling against the king?"

[20]"The God of heaven will give us success!" I replied. "As God's servants, we will start building. But you will have no share, right, or claim in Jerusalem."

Rebuilding the gates and walls

3 Then Eliashib the high priest set to work with his fellow priests and built[g] the Sheep Gate. They dedicated it and set up its doors, then dedicated it as far as the Tower of the Hundred and as far as the Tower of Hananel.

[2]The people of Jericho built next to them, and Zaccur, Imri's son, built next to them. [3]The children of Hassenaah built the Fish Gate; they laid its beams and set up its doors, bolts, and bars. [4]Next to them Meremoth, Uriah's son and Hakkoz's grandson, made repairs. Meshullam, Berechiah's son and Meshezabel's grandson, made repairs next to them, and Zadok, Baana's son, made repairs next to them. [5]Next to them the people from Tekoa made repairs, but their officials wouldn't help with the work[h] of their supervisors.[i]

[6]Joiada, Paseah's son, and Meshullam, Besodeiah's son, repaired the Mishneh Gate;[j] they laid its beams and set up its doors, bolts, and bars. [7]Next to them repairs were

---

[f]Or they strengthened their hands for the good.   [g]Or rebuilt   [h]Or didn't bring their neck into the service of   [i]Or lords
[j]Or Old Gate

CUPBEARER

A wine taster and trusted royal adviser in Egyptian (Gen 40:1-23), Israelite (1 Kgs 10:5; 2 Chron 9:4), Assyrian, Persian (Neh 1:11b–2:1), and other ancient Near Eastern courts. At times, Jews held this prominent position in foreign lands. Nehemiah leveraged his position as cupbearer to the Persian ruler Artaxerxes to secure an appointment as governor of Judah during the period of post-exilic reconstruction.

made by Melatiah the Gibeonite, Jadon the Meronothite, and[k] the people of Gibeon and of Mizpah, who were ruled by the governor of the province Beyond the River.

[8] Uzziel, Harhaiah's son, one of the goldsmiths, made repairs next to them; and Hananiah, one of the perfumers, made repairs next to him. They restored Jerusalem as far as the Broad Wall. [9] Next to them Rephaiah, Hur's son, ruler of half the district of Jerusalem, made repairs. [10] Next to them Jedaiah, Harumaph's son, made repairs opposite his house, and Hattush, Hashabneiah's son, made repairs next to him.

[11] Malchijah, Harim's son, and Hasshub, Pahath-moab's son, repaired another section and the Tower of the Ovens. [12] Next to them Shallum, Hallohesh's son, ruler of half the district of Jerusalem, made repairs, along with his daughters.

[13] Hanun and the people of Zanoah repaired the Valley Gate; they built it and set up its doors, bolts, and bars. They also repaired fifteen hundred feet of the wall, as far as the Dung Gate.

[14] Malchiah, Rechab's son, ruler of the district of Beth-haccherem, repaired the Dung Gate. He rebuilt it and set up its doors, bolts, and bars.

[15] And Shallum, Col-hozeh's son, ruler of the Mizpah district, repaired the Spring Gate. He rebuilt and covered it, and set up its doors, bolts, and bars. He also built the wall of the Pool of Shelah of the King's Garden, as far as the stairs that go down from David's City.

[16] After him, Nehemiah, Azbuk's son, ruler of half the Beth-zur district, repaired from the point opposite David's tombs as far as the artificial pool and the Warriors' House. [17] After him, the Levites made repairs: Rehum, Bani's son, and next to him Hashabiah, ruler of half the district of Keilah, made repairs for his district. [18] After him, their relatives made repairs: Binnui,[l] Henadad's son, ruler of half the district of Keilah.

[19] Next to him, Ezer, Jeshua's son, ruler of Mizpah, repaired another section opposite the ascent to the armory at the Angle. [20] After him, Baruch, Zabbai's son, thoroughly repaired another section from the Angle to the door of the house of the high priest Eliashib. [21] After him, Meremoth, Uriah's son and Hakkoz's grandson, repaired another section from the door to the back of Eliashib's house.

[22] After him, the priests from the surrounding area made repairs. [23] After them, Benjamin and Hasshub made repairs opposite their house. After them, Azariah, Maaseiah's son and Ananiah's grandson, repaired beside his house. [24] After him, Binnui, Henadad's son, repaired another section from the house of Azariah to the Angle and to the corner. [25] Palal, Uzai's son, repaired[m] from the point opposite the Angle and the tower projecting from the upper house of the king at the court of the guard. After him, Pedaiah, Parosh's son, [26] and the temple servants living on Ophel made repairs[n] up to the point opposite the Water Gate to the east and the projecting tower. [27] After them, the people of Tekoa repaired another section opposite the great projecting tower as far as the wall of Ophel. [28] From the Horse Gate, the priests made repairs, each one opposite his own house.

[29] After them, Zadok, Immer's son, made repairs opposite his own house. After him, Shemaiah, Shecaniah's son, the keeper of the East Gate, made repairs. [30] After him, Hananiah, Shelemiah's son, and Hanun, Zalaph's sixth son, repaired another section. After them, Meshullam, Berechiah's son, made repairs opposite his own room.

[31] After him, Malchiah, one of the goldsmiths, made repairs as far as the house of the temple servants and the merchants, opposite the Parade Gate,[o] and as far as the upper room at the corner. [32] And between the upper room of the corner and the Sheep Gate, the goldsmiths and the merchants made repairs.

Opposition mounts

4 [p] When Sanballat heard that we were building the wall, he became angry and

---

[k] Syr; Heb lacks *and.* [l] Lxx, Syr; Heb *Bvvai* [m] Heb lacks *repaired.* [n] Heb lacks *made repairs.* [o] Or *Hammiphkad Gate* [p] 3:33 in Heb

raged. He mocked the Jews, [2]saying in the presence of his associates and the army of Samaria: "What are those feeble Jews doing? Will they restore things themselves? Will they offer sacrifices? Will they finish it in a day? Will they revive the stones from the piles of rubble, even though they are burned?"

[3]Tobiah the Ammonite, who was beside him, added: "If even a fox climbs on whatever they build, their wall of stones will crumble."

[4]Listen, God; we are despised! Turn their insults to us[q] back on their heads and make them like plunder in a captive land. [5]Don't forgive their iniquity or blot out their sins from your sight. They have thrown insults at the builders!

[6]We continued to build the wall. All of it was joined together, and it reached half of its intended height because the people were eager to work. [7][r]But when Sanballat, Tobiah, the Arabs, the Ammonites, and the people of Ashdod heard that the work on the walls was progressing and the gaps were being closed, they were very angry. [8]They plotted together to come and fight against Jerusalem and to create a disturbance in it. [9]So we prayed to our God and set a guard as protection against them day and night. [10]But in Judah it was said,

"The carrier's strength is failing, for there is too much rubble. We are unable to rebuild the wall!"

[11]Meanwhile, our enemies were saying: "Before they know or see anything, we can be in their midst and start to kill them. We'll stop the work!"

[12]Now the Jews who were living near them came and said to us again and again,[s] "You must return to us!"[t]

Armed guards protect the builders

[13]So I took up a position in the lowest parts of the space behind the wall in an open area.[u] Then I stationed the people by families, and they had their swords, spears, and bows. [14]After reviewing this, I stood up and said to the officials, the officers, and the rest of the people, "Don't be afraid of them! Remember that the LORD is great and awesome! Fight for your families, your sons, your daughters, your wives, and your houses!"

[15]Then our enemies heard that we had found out and that God had spoiled their plans. So we all returned to doing our own work on the wall. [16]But from that day on, only half of my workers continued in the construction, while the other half held the spears, shields, bows, and body armor. Meanwhile, the leaders positioned themselves[v] behind the whole house of Judah, [17]who were building the wall. The carriers did their work with a load in one hand and a weapon in the other. [18]The builders built with swords fastened in their belts, and the trumpeter stayed by my side.

[19]Then I said to the officials, the officers, and the rest of the people, "The work is very spread out, and we are far apart from each other along the wall. [20]When you hear the trumpet sound, come and gather where we are. Our God will fight for us!" [21]So we continued the work, with half of them holding spears from dawn until dusk.

[22]I also said to the people at that time, "Let every man and his servant spend the night in Jerusalem so that we can guard during the night and work during the day." [23]Neither I nor my relatives, nor my servants, nor my bodyguards took off our clothes, even when they sent for water.[w]

Internal unrest

5 Then there was a great protest of the people and their wives against their fellow Jews. [2]Some said, "With our sons and daughters we are many, and we all need grain to eat and stay alive."

[3]Others said, "We have to mortgage our fields, our vineyards, and our houses in order to get grain during the famine."

[4]Still others said, "We have had to borrow money against our fields and vineyards in order to pay the king's tax."

---

[q]Heb lacks *to us.* [r]4:1 in Heb [s]Or *ten times from all sides* [t]Heb uncertain [u]Heb uncertain [v]Heb lacks *positioned themselves.* [w]Heb uncertain

5 "We are of the same flesh and blood as our kin, and our children are the same as theirs. Yet we are just about to force our sons and daughters into slavery, and some of our daughters are already slaves! There is nothing we can do since our fields and vineyards now belong to others."

6 I was very angry when I heard their protest and these complaints. 7 After thinking it over, I brought charges against the officials and the officers. I told them, "You are all taking interest from your own people!" I also called for a large assembly in order to deal with them. 8 "To the best of our ability," I said to them, "we have bought back our Jewish kin who had been sold to other nations. But now you are selling your own kin, who must then be bought back by us!" At this they were silent, unable to offer a response.

9 So I continued, "What you are doing isn't good! Why don't you walk in the fear of our God? This will prevent the taunts of the nations that are our enemies! 10 I myself, along with my family and my servants, am lending them money and grain. But let's stop charging this interest! 11 Give it back to them, right now. Return their fields, their vineyards, their olive orchards, and their houses. And give back the interest on money, grain, wine, and oil that you are charging them."

12 They replied, "We'll return everything, and we won't charge anything else.x We'll do what you've asked."

So I called the priests and made them swear to do what they had promised. 13 I also shook out the fold of my robe, saying, "So may God shake out everyone from their house and property if they don't keep this promise. So may they be shaken out and emptied!"

The whole assembly said, "Amen," and praised the LORD. And the people did as they had promised.

Generous Governor Nehemiah

14 In addition, from the time that I was appointed to be their governor in the land of Judah (that is, from the twentieth to the thirty-second year of King Artaxerxes for a total of twelve years), neither I nor my family ate from the governor's food allowance. 15 The earlier governors who had come before me laid heavy burdens on the people. They took food and wine from them as well asy forty shekels of silver. Even their servants oppressed the people. But because I was God-fearing, I didn't behave in this way.

16 Instead, I devoted myself to the work on this wall. We acquired no land, and all my servants were gathered there for the work. 17 One hundred fifty Jews and officials, along with those who came to us from the surrounding nations, gathered around my table. 18 One ox, six choice sheep, and birds were prepared each day. Every ten days there was a large amount of wine. Yet even with this I didn't ask for the governor's food allowance because of the heavy burden the people had to carry.

19 Remember in my favor, my God, all that I've done for this people!

Nehemiah avoids his enemies

6 Now when Sanballat, Tobiah, Geshem the Arab, and the rest of our enemies heard that I had rebuilt the wall and that there were no gaps left in it (although I hadn't yet hung the doors in the gates), 2 Sanballat and Geshem sent me this message: "Come, let's meet together in one of the villagesz in the plain of Ono."

But they wanted to harm me, 3 so I sent messengers to tell them, "I'm doing important work, so I can't come down. Why should the work stop while I leave it to come down to you?"

4 They sent me a message like this four times, and every time I gave them a similar reply. 5 But the fifth time, Sanballat sent his servant to me in the same way, except that now he carried an open letter. 6 It stated:

It is reported among the nations and confirmed by Geshema that you and the Jews intend to rebel. This is why you are rebuilding the wall. According to these reports, you intend to become their

---

x Heb lacks *everything . . . anything else.*   y Heb uncertain   z LXX, Vulg; MT *at Hakkephirim*   a Or *Gashmu* king. [7]You have also appointed prophets to make this announcement about you in Jerusalem: There is a king in Judah! Now, the king will hear of these reports, so come; let's talk together.

[8]So I sent him this reply: "Nothing that you say has happened. You are simply inventing this."

[9]All of them were trying to make us afraid, saying, "They will be discouraged, and the work won't get finished." But now, God, strengthen me!

[10]Later I went to see Shemaiah, Delaiah's son and Mehetabel's grandson, who was confined to his house, and he said:

"Let's meet together in God's house,
    inside the temple itself.
Let's shut the doors of the temple,
    for they are coming to kill you;
    they are coming to kill you tonight!"

[11]But I replied, "Should someone like me run away? Who like me would go into the temple to save his life? I won't go in!" [12]Then I realized that God hadn't sent him at all but that he spoke this prophecy against me because Tobiah and Sanballat had hired him. [13]He was hired to frighten me and to make me sin by acting in this way. Then they could give me a bad name and discredit me. [14]My God, remember these deeds of Tobiah and Sanballat! Also remember Noadiah the prophetess and the rest of the prophets who have been trying to frighten me.

[15]So the wall was finished on the twenty-fifth day of the month of Elul.[b] It took fifty-two days. [16]When our enemies heard about this, all of the nations around us were afraid and their confidence was greatly shaken. They knew that this work was completed with the help of our God.

[17]In addition, in those days the officials of Judah sent many letters to Tobiah, and Tobiah's letters were coming to them. [18]Many in Judah were bound to him by solemn pledge because he was the son-in-law of Shecaniah, Arah's son, and his son Jehohanan had married the daughter of Meshullam, Berechiah's son. [19]They also

kept talking about his good deeds in my presence and then reported back to him what I said. In addition, Tobiah sent letters to intimidate me.

The wall is complete

7 When the wall had been built and I had hung the doors, the gatekeepers, singers, and Levites were appointed. [2]Then I put my brother Hanani and Hananiah the commander of the fortress in charge of Jerusalem. Hananiah was a faithful man who revered God more than many.

[3]I[c] said to them, "The gates of Jerusalem aren't to be opened during the hottest time of the day. While the gatekeepers[d] are still on duty, have them shut and bar the doors. Also, appoint guards from among those who live in Jerusalem. Station some at their watch posts and some in front of their own houses."

Nehemiah registers the families

[4]Now although the city was wide and large, only a few people were living within it, and no[e] houses had been rebuilt. [5]My God then prompted me to assemble the officials, the officers, and the people so that they could be registered by families. I found the record of the families who were the first to return, and I found the following written in it:

[6]These are the people of the province who returned from the captivity of those exiles whom Babylon's King Nebuchadnezzar had taken into exile. They all returned to Jerusalem and Judah, everyone to their own town.

[7]They came with Zerubbabel, Jeshua, Nehemiah, Azariah, Raamiah, Nahamani, Mordecai, Bilshan, Mispereth, Bigvai, Nehum, and Baanah.

The number of the people of Israel:

[8]The family of Parosh	2,172
[9]of Shephatiah	372
[10]of Arah	652
[11]of Pahath-moab, that is, of the descendants of Jeshua and Joab	2,818

[12] of Elam	1,254	[28] of Beth-azmaveth	42
[13] of Zattu	845	[29] of Kiriath-jearim, Chephirah,	
[14] of Zaccai	760	and Beeroth	743
[15] of Binnui	648	[30] of Ramah and Geba	621
[16] of Bebai	628	[31] of Michmas	122
[17] of Azgad	2,322	[32] of Bethel and Ai	123
[18] of Adonikam	667	[33] of the other Nebo	52
[19] of Bigvai	2,067	[34] the inhabitants of	
[20] of Adin	655	the other Elam	1,254
[21] of Ater, that is,		[35] of Harim	320
of the descendants of Hezekiah	98	[36] of Jericho	345
[22] of Hashum	328	[37] of Lod, Hadid, and Ono	721
[23] of Bezai	324	[38] of Senaah	3,930
[24] of Hariph	112	[39] The priests: the descendants	
[25] of Gibeon	95	of Jedaiah, that is, of the	
[26] The people of Bethlehem		house of Jeshua	973
and Netophah	188	[40] of Immer	1,052
[27] of Anathoth	128	[41] of Pashhur	1,247

URIM AND THUMMIM

Urim and *Thummim* are words of uncertain meaning. Some suspect that the terms come from the words for "light" and "truth" and in that way signal their obviously divinatory character. Others argue that they are formed from the roots for "curse" and "faultlessness," and thus signal two possible outcomes of using the Urim and Thummim to judge a person. Still others suggest that they denote the first and last letters of the alphabet, *alef* and *tav*, and therefore the instruments referred to with the name "Urim and Thummim" would actually be the letters of the Hebrew alphabet, from which the user would derive oracular meaning. None of these explanations have found sufficient following to obtain the status of anything approaching a consensus.

Though few in number, occurrences of the pair of terms (or of one of them singly) do provide some useful information. We learn where the Urim and Thummim are kept (in the breastpiece attached to the high priest's vest; Exod 28:30; Lev 8:8), that they can serve as a means of judgment exercised by the high priest (Exod 28:30), and that the judgment might be more than a simple yes or no answer (Num 27:21; Urim only). It may also be that the Urim and Thummim are only used by the high priest in the most holy place ("when he goes into the LORD's presence" in Exod 28:30; Num 27:21).

None of these passages tell us what the Urim and Thummim were or how their users consulted them. Scholars have made many suggestions, including sticks, dice, or colored stones. The 1st-century CE Jewish historian Josephus suggests that the Urim and Thummim were the 12 stones on or in the chest pendant of the high priest and that they simply shone to give a favorable response from God regarding a decision to march against enemies.

⁴²of Harim 1,017

⁴³The Levites: the descendants of Jeshua, that is, of Kadmiel, of the descendants of Hodaviah 74

⁴⁴The singers: the descendants of Asaph 148

⁴⁵The descendants of gatekeepers: of Shallum, Ater, Talmon, Akkub, Hatita, and Shobai 138

⁴⁶The temple servants: the descendants of Ziha, Hasupha, Tabbaoth, ⁴⁷Keros, Sia, Padon, ⁴⁸Lebanah, Hagabah, Shalmai, ⁴⁹Hanan, Giddel, Gahar, ⁵⁰Reaiah, Rezin, Nekoda, ⁵¹Gazzam, Uzza, Paseah, ⁵²Besai, Meunim, Nephushesim, ⁵³Bakbuk, Hakupha, Harhur, ⁵⁴Bazlith, Mehida, Harsha, ⁵⁵Barkos, Sisera, Temah, ⁵⁶Neziah, and Hatipha.

⁵⁷The descendants of Solomon's servants: Sotai, Sophereth, Perida, ⁵⁸Jaala, Darkon, Giddel, ⁵⁹Shephatiah, Hattil, Pochereth-hazzebaim, and Amon.

⁶⁰All of the temple servants and the descendants of Solomon's servants totaled 392.

⁶¹The following came up from Tel-Melah, Tel-harsha, Cherub, Addon, and Immer, but were unable to prove that their family or their descent was from Israel: ⁶²the descendants of Delaiah, Tobiah, and Nekoda, 642.

⁶³And of the priests: the descendants of Hobaiah, Hakkoz, and Barzillai (who had married one of the daughters of Barzillai the Gileadite and was called by his[f] name) ⁶⁴looked for their entries in the genealogical records, but they weren't found there, so they were excluded from the priesthood as unclean.

⁶⁵The governor ordered that they shouldn't eat of the most holy food until a priest arose who could consult Urim and Thummim.

⁶⁶The whole assembly together totaled 42,360. ⁶⁷This number doesn't include their 7,337 male and female servants; they also had 245 male and female singers, ⁶⁸736 horses, 245 mules,[g] ⁶⁹[h]435 camels, and 6,720 donkeys.

⁷⁰[i]Some of the heads of families made a donation for the work. The governor gave to the treasury 1,000 darics of gold, 50 bowls, and 530 priestly robes. ⁷¹Some of the heads of families gave 20,000 darics of gold and 2,200 manehs of silver to the treasury for the work. ⁷²The rest of the people gave 20,000 darics of gold, 2,000 manehs of silver, and 67 priestly robes.

⁷³So the priests, the Levites, the gatekeepers, the singers, some of the people, the temple servants, and all Israel settled in their towns.

Ezra reads the Instruction aloud

When the seventh month[j] came and the people of Israel were settled in their towns, **8** all the people gathered together in the area in front of the Water Gate. They asked Ezra the scribe to bring out the Instruction[k] scroll from Moses, according to which the LORD had instructed Israel.

²So on the first day of the seventh month, Ezra the priest brought the Instruction before the assembly. This assembly was made up of both men and women and anyone who could understand what they heard. ³Facing the area in front of the Water Gate, he read it aloud, from early morning until the middle of the day. He read it in the presence of the men and the women and those who could understand, and everyone listened attentively to the Instruction scroll.

⁴Ezra the scribe stood on a wooden platform that had been made for this purpose. And standing beside him were Mattithiah, Shema, Anaiah, Uriah, Hilkiah, and Maaseiah on his righthand side; while Pedaiah, Mishael, Malchijah, Hashum, Hashbaddanah, Zechariah, and Meshullam stood on his lefthand side.

⁵Standing above all of the people, Ezra the scribe opened the scroll in the sight of

---

[f]Or their [g]Ezra 2:66; MT lacks *they also . . . mules.* [h]7:68 in Heb [i]7:69 in Heb [j]September–October, Tishrei [k]Heb *Torah*

all of the people. And as he opened it, all of the people stood up. [6]Then Ezra blessed the LORD, the great God, and all of the people answered, "Amen! Amen!" while raising their hands. Then they bowed down and worshipped the LORD with their faces to the ground.

[7]The Levites—Joshua, Bani, Sherebiah, Jamin, Akkub, Shabbethai, Hodiah, Maaseiah, Kelita, Azariah, Jozabad, Hanan, and Pelaiah[l]—helped the people to understand the Instruction while the people remained in their places. [8]They read aloud from the scroll, the Instruction from God, explaining and interpreting it so the people could understand what they heard.

[9]Then Nehemiah the governor, Ezra the priest and scribe, and the Levites who taught the people said to all of the people, "This day is holy to the LORD your God. Don't mourn or weep." They said this[m] because all the people wept when they heard the words of the Instruction.

[10]"Go, eat rich food, and drink something sweet," he said to them, "and send portions of this to any who have nothing ready! This day is holy to our LORD. Don't be sad, because the joy from the LORD is your strength!"

[11]The Levites also calmed all of the people, saying, "Be quiet, for this day is holy. Don't be sad!" [12]Then all of the people went to eat and to drink, to send portions, and to have a great celebration, because they understood what had been said to them.

*The people celebrate
the Festival of Booths*

[13]On the second day, the heads of the families of all the people, along with the priests and the Levites, gathered together around Ezra the scribe in order to study the words of the Instruction. [14]And they found written in the Instruction that the LORD had commanded through Moses that the Israelites should live in booths during the festival of the seventh month.[n]

[15]They also found that they should make the following proclamation and announce it throughout their towns and in Jerusalem: "Go out to the hills and bring branches of olive, wild olive, myrtle, palm, and other leafy trees to make booths, as it is written."

[16]So the people went out and brought them, and made booths for themselves, each on the roofs of their houses or[o] their courtyards, in the courtyards of God's house, in the area by the Water Gate, or in the area by the Gate of Ephraim.

[17]The whole assembly of those who had returned from captivity made booths and lived in them. This was something that the people of Israel hadn't done since the days of Joshua,[p] Nun's son, and there was very great rejoicing.

[18]He read from God's Instruction scroll every day, from the first until the last day of the festival.[q] They kept the festival for seven days and held a solemn assembly on the eighth day, just as the Instruction required.

Remembering the LORD's mighty deeds

9On the twenty-fourth day of this month, the people of Israel were assembled. They fasted, wore funeral clothing,[r] and had dirt on their heads.[s] [2]After the Israelites separated themselves from all of the foreigners, they stood to confess their sins and the terrible behavior of their ancestors. [3]They stood in their place and read

---

[l]Vulg 1 Esdr 9:48; MT *and the Levites*   [m]Heb lacks *They said this.*   [n]September–October, Tishrei   [o]Or *and*   [p]Heb *Jeshua*   [q]Heb lacks *of the festival.*   [r]Or *sackcloth*   [s]Or *on them*

the Instruction scroll from the LORD their God for a quarter of the day. For another quarter of the day, they confessed and worshipped the LORD their God.

⁴On the stairs of the Levites stood Jeshua, Bani, Kadmiel, Shebaniah, Bunni, Sherebiah, Bani, and Chenani. They cried out with a loud voice to the LORD their God. ⁵Then the Levites—Jeshua, Kadmiel, Bani, Hashabneiah, Sherebiah, Hodiah, Shebaniah, and Pethahiah—said:

Stand up and bless the LORD your God.
From everlasting to everlasting
   bless your glorious name,
which is high above
   all blessing and praise.
⁶ You alone are the LORD.
You alone made heaven,
   even the heaven of heavens,
   with all their forces.
You made the earth and all that is on it,
   and the seas and all that is in them.
You preserve them all,
   and the heavenly forces worship you.
⁷ LORD God, you are the one
who chose Abram.
You brought him out
   of Ur of the Chaldeans
   and gave him the name Abraham.
⁸ You found him to be faithful before you,
   and you made a covenant with him.
You promised to give to his descendants
   the land of the Canaanites, the Hittites,
   the Amorites, the Perizzites,
   the Jebusites, and the Girgashites.
And you have kept your promise
   because you are righteous.

⁹ You saw the affliction
   of our ancestors in Egypt
   and heard their cry at the Reed Sea.ᵗ
¹⁰ You performed signs and wonders
   against Pharaoh,
   all his servants,
   and the people of his land.
You knew that they had acted arrogantly
   against our ancestors.
You made a name for yourself,
   a name that is famous even today.

¹¹ You divided the sea before them so that
   they went through it on dry land.
But you cast their pursuers
   into the depths,
   as a stone into the mighty waters.
¹² With a pillar of cloud you led them by day
   and with a column of lightning by night;
   they lit the way
   in which the people should go.
¹³ You came down upon Mount Sinai
   and spoke with them from heaven.
You gave them proper judgments
   and true Instruction,
   good statutes and commandments.
¹⁴ You made known to them
   your holy Sabbath,
   and gave them commandments,
   statutes, and Instruction
   through your servant Moses.
¹⁵ When they were hungry,
   you gave them bread from heaven;
   when they were thirsty, you brought
   water out of the rock for them.
You told them to go in to possess
   the land that you had sworn
   to give them.

¹⁶ But our ancestors acted arrogantly.
   They were stubborn and wouldn't
   obey your commandments.
¹⁷ They refused to obey,
   and didn't remember the wonders
   that you accomplished in their midst.
They acted arrogantly and decided
   to return to their slavery in Egypt.
But you are a God ready to forgive,
   merciful and compassionate,
   very patient, and truly faithful.
You didn't forsake them.
¹⁸ Even when they had cast
   an image of a calf for themselves,
   saying, "This is your God
   who brought you up out of Egypt,"
   and holding you in great contempt,
¹⁹ you, in your great mercy,
   didn't abandon them in the wilderness.
The column of cloud continued
   to guide them on their journey
   during the day,

ᵗOr Red Sea

and the column of lightning
lit their path during the night.
²⁰ You gave your good spirit to teach them.
You didn't withhold your manna
from them,
and you gave them water for their thirst.
²¹ You kept them alive for forty years—
they lacked nothing in the wilderness!
Their clothes didn't wear out,
and their feet didn't swell.

²² You gave them kingdoms and peoples,
and assigned to them every side.ᵘ
They took possession of the land
of King Sihon of Heshbon
and the land of King Og of Bashan.
²³ You multiplied their descendants
as the stars of heaven.
You brought them into the land
that you had told their ancestors
to enter and possess.
²⁴ So the descendants went in
and possessed the land.
Before them, you subdued the
Canaanites who inhabited the land.
You also handed over to them their
kings and the neighboring peoples,
to do with as they wished.
²⁵ They captured fortified cities
and productive land,
and took possession of houses filled
with all kinds of good things:
Excavated cisterns, vineyards,
olive orchards,
and a great many fruit trees.
They ate until they were satisfied
and grew fat,
and delighted themselves
in your great goodness.

²⁶ But they were disobedient,
rebelled against you,
and turned their back
on your Instruction.
They killed your prophets
who had warned them
so that they might return to you.
They held you in great contempt.
²⁷ Therefore, you handed them over

to the power of their enemies
who made them suffer.
But when they cried out to you
in their suffering,
you heard them from heaven.
Because you are merciful,
you gave them saviors who saved them
from the power of their enemies.
²⁸ But after they had rest from this, they
again started doing evil against you.
So you gave them over
to the power of their enemies
who ruled over them.
Yet when they turned and cried to you,
you heard from heaven
and rescued them many times
because of your great mercy.
²⁹ You also warned them
to return to your Instruction,
but they acted arrogantly
and didn't obey your commands.
They sinned against your judgments,
even though life comes
by keeping them.ᵛ
They turned a stubborn shoulder,
became headstrong,
and wouldn't obey.
³⁰ You were patient with them
for many years
and warned them by your spirit
through the prophets.
But they wouldn't listen,
so you handed them over
to the neighboring peoples.
³¹ In your great mercy, however,
you didn't make an end of them.
Neither did you forsake them,
because you are a merciful and
compassionate God.

³² Now, our God,
great and mighty and awesome God,
you are the one who faithfully
keeps the covenant.
Don't treat lightly all of the hardship
that has come upon us,
upon our kings, our officials,
our priests, our prophets,
our ancestors, and all your people,

ᵘHeb uncertain   ᵛ*Them* refers to judgments.

from the time of the kings of Assyria
    until today.
³³ You have been just in all
    that has happened to us;
    you have acted faithfully,
    and we have done wrong.
³⁴ Our kings, our officials, our priests,
    and our ancestors
    haven't kept your Instruction.
    They haven't heeded your
    commandments and the warnings
    that you gave them.
³⁵ Even in their own kingdom,
    surrounded by the great goodness
    that you gave to them,
    even in the wide and rich land
    that you gave them,
    they didn't serve you or turn
    from their wicked works.
³⁶ So now today we are slaves,
    slaves in the land
    that you gave to our ancestors
    to enjoy its fruit and its good gifts.
³⁷ Its produce profits the kings whom you
    have placed over us because of our sins.
    They have power over our bodies and
    do as they please with our livestock.
    We are in great distress.

Commitment to follow the Instruction

^{38w}Because of all this,^x we are making a
firm agreement in writing, with the names
of our officials, our Levites, and our priests
on the seal.

10^yUpon the seals are the names of
Governor Nehemiah, Hacaliah's son,
and Zedekiah;

² Seraiah, Azariah, Jeremiah,
³ Pashhur, Amariah, Malchijah,
⁴ Hattush, Shebaniah, Malluch,
⁵ Harim, Meremoth, Obadiah,
⁶ Daniel, Ginnethon, Baruch,
⁷ Meshullam, Abijah, Mijamin,
⁸ Maaziah, Bilgai, Shemaiah; these
are the priests.

⁹ The Levites: Jeshua, Azaniah's son;
Binnui of the descendants of Henadad;
Kadmiel; ¹⁰ and their associates:

Shebaniah, Hodiah, Kelita,
    Pelaiah, Hanan,
¹¹Mica, Rehob, Hashabiah,
¹²Zaccur, Sherebiah, Shebaniah,
¹³Hodiah, Bani, Beninu.
¹⁴The leaders of the people: Parosh,
Pahath-moab, Elam, Zattu, Bani,
¹⁵Bunni, Azgad, Bebai,
¹⁶Adonijah, Bigvai, Adin,
¹⁷Ater, Hezekiah, Azzur,
¹⁸Hodiah, Hashum, Bezai,
¹⁹Hariph, Anathoth, Nebai,
²⁰Magpiash, Meshullam, Hezir,
²¹Meshezabel, Zadok, Jaddua,
²²Pelatiah, Hanan, Anaiah,
²³Hoshea, Hananiah, Hasshub,
²⁴Hallohesh, Pilha, Shobek,
²⁵Rehum, Hashabnah, Maaseiah,
²⁶Ahiah, Hanan, Anan,
²⁷Malluch, Harim, Baanah.

²⁸The rest of the people, the priests,
the Levites, the gatekeepers, the singers, the temple servants, and all who have
separated themselves from the neighboring
peoples to follow the Instruction from God,
together with their wives, their sons, their
daughters, and all who have knowledge
and understanding. ²⁹They join with their
officials and relatives, and make a solemn
pledge to live by God's Instruction, which
was given by Moses, God's servant, and to
observe faithfully all the commandments,
judgments, and statutes of our LORD God.

³⁰ We won't give our daughters in mar-
riage to the neighboring peoples, nor take
their daughters in marriage for our sons.

³¹If the neighboring peoples bring
merchandise or any grain to sell on the
Sabbath, we won't buy it from them on
the Sabbath or on any holy day.

Every seventh year we won't plant
crops, and we will return anything held
in debt.

³²We pledge ourselves to keep the
commandment and pay one-third of a
shekel each year for the service of our
God's house, ³³for the stacks of bread
and the regular grain offering and the
regular entirely burned offering, for the

---

sabbaths and the new moons and the appointed festivals, for the holy offerings and the purification offerings to make reconcilation for Israel, and for all the work of our God's house.

³⁴We have also cast lots among the priests, the Levites, and the people so that we bring the wood offering into our God's house by families at the appointed times every year, to burn on the altar of the LORD our God, as it is written in the Instruction.

³⁵We will also bring the early produce of our soil and the early fruit from all trees every year to the LORD's house.

³⁶We will also bring the oldest offspring of our children and our cattle, as it is written in the Instruction, and the oldest males of our herds and flocks to our God's house, to the priests who serve in our God's house.

³⁷We will also bring the first of our dough, our contributions, the fruit of every tree, the wine, and the oil to the priests at the storerooms of our God's house. We will also bring one-tenth of the produce of our soil to the Levites, for it is the Levites who collect the tenth-part gifts in all the towns where we work.

³⁸A priest from the family of Aaron must be with the Levites when they collect the tenth-part gifts. Then the Levites must bring up one-tenth of the tenth-part gifts to our God's house, to the storerooms of the treasury. ³⁹The Israelites and the Levites must bring the contribution of grain, wine, and oil to the storerooms where the sanctuary equipment is kept, and where the priests on duty, the gatekeepers, and the singers reside. We won't neglect our God's house!

Inhabitants of Jerusalem

11 The leaders of the people lived in Jerusalem. The rest of the people cast lots to bring one out of ten to live in the holy city of Jerusalem, while the remaining nine stayed in the other towns. ²The people blessed those who agreed to live in Jerusalem.

³These are the leaders of the province who lived in Jerusalem; while the Israelites, the priests, the Levites, the temple servants, and the descendants of Solomon's servants lived in the towns of Judah on their own property in their towns. ⁴Some of the descendants of Judah and Benjamin settled in Jerusalem.

From the family of Judah: Athaiah son of Uzziah son of Zechariah son of Amariah son of Shephatiah son of Mahalalel of the family of Perez; ⁵and Maaseiah son of Baruch son of Col-hozeh son of Hazaiah son of Adaiah son of Joiarib son of Zechariah son of the Shilonite. ⁶All of the family of Perez who lived in Jerusalem totaled 468 courageous people.

⁷From the family of Benjamin: Sallu son of Meshullam son of Joed son of Pedaiah son of Kolaiah son of Maaseiah son of Ithiel son of Jeshaiah. ⁸And after him were Gabbai and Sallai: 928. ⁹Joel son of Zichri was their supervisor, and Judah son of Hassenuah was second in charge of the city.

¹⁰Of the priests: Jedaiah son of Joiarib, Jachin, ¹¹Seraiah son of Hilkiah son of Meshullam son of Zadok son of Meraioth son of Ahitub the officer of God's house, ¹²and their associates who carried out the work in the temple:ᶻ 822. There was also Adaiah son of Jeroham son of Pelaliah son of Amzi son of Zechariah son of Pashhur son of Malchijah, ¹³and his associates, heads of families: 242. There was also Amashsai son of Azarel son of Ahzai son of Meshillemoth son of Immer ¹⁴and their associates, for a total of 128 courageous people. Their supervisor was Zabdiel, Haggedolim's son.

¹⁵Of the Levites: Shemaiah son of Hasshub son of Azrikam son of Hashabiah son of Bunni; ¹⁶as well as Shabbethai and Jozabad, who were some of the leaders of the Levites in charge of the outside work on God's house; ¹⁷also Mattaniah son of Mica son of Zabdi son of Asaph the leader who began the thanksgiving with prayer, and Bakbukiah, who was the second among his associates; and Abda son of Shammua son of Galal

son of Jeduthun. [18]All the Levites in the holy city totaled 284. [19]The gatekeepers: Akkub, Talmon, and their associates who guarded the gates totaled 172. [20]The rest of Israel, the priests, and the Levites were in all the towns of Judah, each of them in their own property. [21]But the temple servants lived in Ophel, with Ziha and Gishpa in charge of them. [22]The supervisor of the Levites in Jerusalem was Uzzi son of Bani son of Hashabiah son of Mattaniah son of Mica, from the family of Asaph, who were the singers in charge of the work of God's house. [23]There was a command from the king setting out the daily requirements of the singers.

[24]Advising the king in all matters concerning the people was Pethahiah, Meshezabel's son, from the family of Zerah, Judah's son.

[25]As for the villages with their fields, some of the people of Judah lived in Kiriath-arba and its villages, in Dibon and its villages, in Jekabzeel and its villages, [26]in Jeshua, in Moladah and Beth-pelet, [27]in Hazarshual, in Beer-sheba and its villages, [28]in Ziklag, in Meconah and its villages, [29]in Enrimmon, Zorah, Jarmuth, [30]Zanoah, Adullam, and their villages, Lachish and its fields, and Azekah and its villages. So they settled from Beer-sheba to the Hinnom Valley.

[31]The people of Benjamin also lived from beyond Geba, at Michmash, Aija, Bethel and its villages, [32]Anathoth, Nob, Ananiah, [33]Hazor, Ramah, Gittaim, [34]Hadid, Zeboim, Neballat, [35]Lod, and Ono, the valley of artisans. [36]Some divisions of the Levites in Judah were joined to Benjamin.

12 These are the priests and the Levites who came up with Zerubbabel son of Shealtiel and Jeshua: Seraiah, Jeremiah, Ezra, [2]Amariah, Malluch, Hattush, [3]Shecaniah, Rehum, Meremoth, [4]Iddo, Ginnethon,[a] Abijah, [5]Mijamin, Maadiah, Bilgah, [6]Shemaiah, Joiarib, Jedaiah, [7]Sallu, Amok, Hilkiah, Jedaiah.

These were the leaders of the priests and of their associates in the days of Jeshua.

[8]The Levites: Jeshua, Binnui, Kadmiel, Sherebiah, Judah, and also Mattaniah, who was in charge of the thanksgiving songs along with his associates. [9]Bakbukiah and Unn and their associates stood opposite them in the service.

[10]Jeshua was the father of Joiakim, Joiakim the father of Eliashib, Eliashib the father of Joiada, [11]Joiada the father of Jonathan, and Jonathan the father of Jaddua.

[12]These were the heads of the priestly families in the days of Joiakim: of Seraiah, Meraiah; of Jeremiah, Hananiah; [13]of Ezra, Meshullam; of Amariah, Jehohanan; [14]of Malluch,[b] Jonathan; of Shebaniah, Joseph; [15]of Harim, Adna; of Meraioth, Helkai; [16]of Iddo, Zechariah; of Ginnethon, Meshullam; [17]of Abijah, Zichri; of Miniamin, of Moadiah, Piltai; [18]of Bilgah, Shammua; of Shemaiah, Jehonathan; [19]of Joiarib, Mattenai; of Jedaiah, Uzzi; [20]of Sallai, Kallai; of Amok, Eber; [21]of Hilkiah, Hashabiah; of Jedaiah, Nethanel.

[22]In the days of Eliashib, Joiada, Johanan, and Jaddua, the Levites and the priests were recorded as heads of families in the rule of[c] Darius the Persian. [23]The Levites who were heads of families were recorded in the official records until the time of Johanan, Eliashib's son. [24]These were the leaders of the Levites: Hashabiah, Sherebiah, and Jeshua, Kadmiel's son, and their associates who stood opposite them to praise and give thanks in turn according to the commandment of David, the man of God, namely, [25]Mattaniah, Bakbukiah, and Obadiah.

Meshullam, Talmon, and Akkub were gatekeepers standing guard by the storerooms of the gates. [26]These served in the days of Joiakim, Jeshua's son and Jozadak's grandson, and in the days of Governor Nehemiah and of Ezra the priest and scribe.

Dedication of the wall

[27]When it was time for the dedication of Jerusalem's wall, they sought out the Levites in all the places where they lived in order to bring them to Jerusalem to cele-

---

[a]Heb Ginnethoi [b]LXX; MT Malluchi [c]LXX, Vulg; MT upon

brate the dedication with joy, with thanks and singing, and with cymbals, harps, and lyres.

²⁸The singers also gathered together both from the region around Jerusalem and from the villages of the Netophathites, ²⁹also from Beth-hagilgal and from the region of Geba and Azmaveth, because the singers had built themselves villages around Jerusalem. ³⁰After the priests and the Levites purified themselves, they purified the people, the gates, and the wall.

³¹Then I[d] brought the leaders of Judah up onto the wall and organized two large groups to give thanks. The first group went in procession on the wall toward the right, in the direction of the Dung Gate. ³²Following them went Hoshaiah and half the officials of Judah, ³³along with Azariah, Ezra, Meshullam, ³⁴Judah, Benjamin, Shemaiah, and Jeremiah. ³⁵There were also some young priests with trumpets—Zechariah son of Jonathan son of Shemaiah son of Mattaniah son of Micaiah son of Zaccur son of Asaph—³⁶along with his associates Shemaiah, Azarel, Milalai, Gilalai, Maai, Nethanel, Judah, and Hanani. They brought[e] the musical instruments of David the man of God. Ezra the scribe went in front of them.

³⁷When they reached the Fountain Gate they went straight up by the stairs of David's City, on the ascent to the wall, past the house of David to the Water Gate on the east. ³⁸The second group went in procession to the left.[f] I followed them with half of the people along the wall past the Tower of the Ovens to the Broad Wall, ³⁹past the Gate of Ephraim and over the Mishneh Gate,[g] the Fish Gate, the Tower of Hananel, and the Tower of the Hundred as far as the Sheep Gate. They came to stop at the Gate of the Guard.

In God's house

⁴⁰Then both groups of those who gave thanks stood in God's house. I was there too along with the half of the officials who were with me. ⁴¹Also there were the priests Eliakim, Maaseiah, Miniamin, Micaiah, Elioenai, Zechariah, and Hananiah with trumpets. ⁴²Also there were Maaseiah, Shemaiah, Eleazar, Uzzi, Jehohanan, Malchijah, Elam, and Ezer. The singers sang with Jezrahiah as their leader.

⁴³They offered great sacrifices on that day and rejoiced, for God had made them rejoice with great joy. The women and children also rejoiced, and the sound of the joy in Jerusalem could be heard from far away.

⁴⁴On that day, people were appointed over the rooms for the things to be stored, the contributions, the early produce, and the tenth-part gifts. They were to gather into them the portions required by the Instruction for the priests and for the Levites from the fields belonging to the towns, for the people of Judah were delighted with the ministry of the priests and the Levites. ⁴⁵They performed the service of their God and the service of purification, as did the singers and the gatekeepers, according to the command of David and his son Solomon.

⁴⁶Long ago, in the days of David and Asaph, there was a leader of the singers, and there were songs of praise and thanks to God. ⁴⁷In the days of Zerubbabel and of Nehemiah all Israel gave the daily portions for the singers and the gatekeepers. They also set aside the portion for the Levites, and the Levites set aside the portion for the Aaronites.

Restoring the temple

13 On that day, when the scroll from Moses was being read to the people, they found written in it that no Ammonite or Moabite should ever enter God's assembly. ²This is because they hadn't met the Israelites with food and water but instead hired Balaam against them to curse them. Yet our God turned the curse into a blessing. ³When the people heard this law, they separated out from Israel all those of mixed descent.

⁴Now before this, however, Eliashib the priest, who was appointed to be in charge

of the storerooms of our God's house and who was related to Tobiah, [5]prepared a large room for Tobiah to use. This was the room where they had previously kept the grain offering, the incense, and the equipment, together with the tenth-part gifts of grain, wine, and oil. These items were for the Levites, singers, and gatekeepers as well as the portions for the priests.

[6]I wasn't in Jerusalem while this was happening because I had gone to Babylon's King Artaxerxes in the thirty-second year of the king. After some time, I asked the king's permission [7]and returned to Jerusalem. That was when I saw the wrong that Eliashib had done on behalf of Tobiah by preparing him a room in the courtyards of God's house. [8]I was very angry and threw all of Tobiah's household furniture out of the room. [9]Then I gave orders that the rooms be purified, and I put back the temple equipment, along with the grain offering and the incense.

[10]I also found out that the Levites hadn't been given their portions, so they and the singers who did the work had gone back to their fields. [11]So I scolded the officials, asking, "Why is God's house being neglected?" I gathered them together and set them in their stations.

[12]Then all Judah brought the tenth-part gifts of the grain, wine, and oil into the storehouses. [13]I appointed the priest Shelemiah, the scribe Zadok, and Pedaiah of the Levites to be in charge over the storehouses. I also appointed Hanan, Zaccur's son and Mattaniah's grandson, as their assistant. These men were considered trustworthy, and their task was to hand out shares to their colleagues.

[14]Remember me, my God, concerning this. Don't erase my good deeds that I have done for my God's house and for its services.

Keeping the Sabbath

[15]In those days I saw people in Judah using the winepresses on the Sabbath. They were also collecting piles of grain and loading them on donkeys, as well as wine, grapes, figs, and every kind of load, and then bringing them to Jerusalem on the Sabbath. I warned them at that time against selling food.

[16]In addition, people from Tyre who lived in the city were bringing in fish and all kinds of merchandise and selling them to the people of Judah on the Sabbath. This happened in Jerusalem itself!

[17]So I scolded the officials of Judah: "What is this evil thing that you are doing?" I asked. "You are making the Sabbath impure! [18]This is just what your ancestors did, and God brought all this evil upon us and upon this city. And now you are bringing

SABBATH (OT)

While the Sabbath eventually became a weekly holiday, characterized as a day of rest, this may not have been its original function. As the Mesopotamian parallel, the Shapattu festival, suggests, the Sabbath day originally marked the celebration of the full moon, and in many OT texts the word is used to mean the day of the full moon. While certain activities were prohibited on this particular day (in order to avoid provoking the gods' anger), it was not a day of general rest. Israel's Sabbath tradition may not have begun until the period of the exile, and it may have developed its full character over time. Parts of Genesis and Exodus (esp. Gen 2:2-3; Exod 16:22-30; 23:12-17), the Sabbath commandment in both versions of the Ten Commandments (Exod 20:8-11; Deut 5:12-15), and the book of Nehemiah (9:14; 10:31 [Heb. 10:32]; 13:15-22) are the most explicit witnesses to a new understanding of the Sabbath as a weekly observance.

more wrath upon Israel by making the Sabbath impure!"

¹⁹So when it began to grow dark at the gates of Jerusalem before the Sabbath, I gave orders that the doors should be shut. I also ordered that they shouldn't be reopened until after the Sabbath. To make sure that no load would come into the city[h] on the Sabbath, I stationed some of my own men at the gates. ²⁰Once or twice the traders and sellers of all kinds of merchandise spent the night outside Jerusalem. ²¹But I warned them: "Why are you spending the night by the wall? If you do that again, I will lay hands on you!" At that point, they stopped coming on the Sabbath. ²²I also commanded the Levites to purify themselves and to come and guard the gates in order to keep the Sabbath day holy.

Remember this also in my favor, my God, and spare me according to the greatness of your mercy.

Marrying foreign women

²³Also in those days I saw Jews who had married women of Ashdod, Ammon, and Moab. ²⁴Half of their children spoke the language of Ashdod or the language of various peoples; they couldn't speak the language of Judah.

---

[h]Heb lacks *the city.*

²⁵So I scolded them and cursed them, and beat some of them, and pulled out their hair. I also made them swear a solemn pledge in the name of God, saying, "You won't give your daughters to their sons in marriage, or take their daughters in marriage for your sons or yourselves. ²⁶Didn't Israel's King Solomon sin on account of such women? Among the many nations there was no king like him. He was well loved by his God, and God made him king over all Israel. Yet foreign wives led even him into sin! ²⁷Should we then listen to you and do all this great evil, acting unfaithfully toward our God by marrying foreign women?"

²⁸Now one of the sons of Joiada son of the high priest Eliashib was a son-in-law of Sanballat the Horonite. So I chased him away from me.

²⁹Remember them, my God, because they have defiled the priesthood and the covenant of the priests and the Levites!

³⁰So I purified them of everything foreign and established the services of the priests and Levites with specific duties for each person. ³¹I also provided for the wood offering at appointed times as well as for the early produce.

Remember me, my God, for good.

ESTHER

The book of Esther is intensely interesting and masterfully told. Esther must have been especially interesting to the Jews in exile during Persian rule. In the midst of the humiliation known only to a conquered people scattered throughout an alien empire, here is the story of a Jewish woman who became queen of that empire. And it is the story of a crafty Jewish man who turned the tables on the second most powerful person in the kingdom and eventually took that man's place as second in command. It is the story of the "divine reversal" of fortunes, God protecting the chosen people and bringing to ruin those who sought to harm them.

The book of Esther has been much beloved by Jews over the centuries. Scores of hand-copied texts have survived from the Middle Ages, more than any other book in the Old Testament. Medieval Jewish scholars produced more commentaries on Esther than on any other book in the Hebrew Bible except the books of Moses (Genesis through Deuteronomy). It was often said Esther ranked second in importance only to the Torah because it was the book that kept the Jews alive. It was a clarion call to fight back against enemy aggression. The Jews had been inspired by this call, not just during the days of the Persian Empire, but throughout the centuries. Some said Esther was even more important than the Torah, for Judaism could exist without the Torah, but it would have been exterminated without the book of Esther.

But this book, beloved though it is, has also been an embarrassment to sensitive Jews and Christians. Nowhere in its ten chapters is God ever mentioned. Nor are prayer, worship, or any of the great religious festivals mentioned. The great themes of the Old Testament are lacking—themes like the exodus from Egypt, the receiving of the Ten Commandments, and the making of the covenant. Even the great virtues taught in the rest of the Bible are missing. Instead, we have a story in which vengeance plays a primary role. Yet it is not entirely fair to characterize the book as secular.

GOD PLAYS AN IMPORTANT ROLE

We have mentioned the "divine reversal" of the fortunes of the characters in the story of Esther. The story is full of coincidences, quirks of fate, and little ironies that make for delightful reading. But when it is read on a different level, the book is a powerful statement about God's activity and the working out of the divine will even in those situations when God is silent and seems to be nowhere about. The fact that God is not mentioned in the story does not mean God was not active in the proceedings.

HISTORY OR SHORT STORY?

The book of Esther has been interpreted in three ways. Some think of it as a record of historical events that took place while the Jews were in exile and Ahasuerus was king. Whereas this is certainly possible, none of the events in the book can be verified by non-biblical sources, and many of them contradict what we know from our knowledge of history. Ahasuerus is the only character in the story whose historical reality is certain, and there is some disagreement even there as to which king is meant.

Most Old Testament scholars hold to a second possibility, namely that the book of Esther was written not as history but as a short story or a historical novel.

The third possibility is to regard Esther as a mythical story describing the conflict between the gods of Babylon and the gods of Elam. Esther could represent the Babylonian goddess Ishtar, and Mordecai the Babylonian god Marduk. Similarly, Haman and his wife, Zeresh, could represent the Elamite god Humman and his wife Seres, while Vashti, the deposed queen, could represent Mashti, the Elamite goddess.

Theoretically, any of the above interpretations of Esther is possible. A large majority of Old Testament scholars, however, favor the second interpretation. Esther is a short story, written to amuse, to instill a sense of pride into a defeated people, and to assure in an ever-so-subtle way that God does not leave the course of history in the hands of those who rely only upon the sword.

ESTHER

Queen Vashti

1 This is what happened back when Ahasuerus lived, the very Ahasuerus who ruled from India to Cush—one hundred twenty-seven provinces in all. ²At that time, Ahasuerus ruled the kingdom from his royal throne in the fortified part of Susa. ³In the third year of his rule he hosted a feast for all his officials and courtiers. The leaders of Persia and Media attended, along with his provincial officials and officers. ⁴He showed off the awesome riches of his kingdom and beautiful treasures as mirrors of how very great he was. The event lasted a long time—six whole months, to be exact! ⁵After that the king held a seven-day feast for everyone in the fortified part of Susa. Whether they were important people in the town or not, they all met in the walled garden of the royal palace. ⁶White linen curtains and purple hangings were held up by shining white and red-purple ropes tied to silver rings and marble posts. Gold and silver couches sat on a mosaic floor made of gleaming purple crystal, marble, and mother-of-pearl. ⁷They served the drinks in cups made of gold, and each cup was different. The king made sure there was plenty of royal wine. ⁸The rule about the drinks was "No limits!" The king had ordered everyone serving wine in the palace to offer as much as each guest wanted. ⁹At the same time, Queen Vashti held a feast for women in King Ahasuerus' palace.

¹⁰On the seventh day, when wine had put the king in high spirits, he gave an order to Mehuman, Biztha, Harbona, Bigtha, Abagtha, Zethar, and Carcas, the seven eunuchs who served King Ahasuerus personally. ¹¹They were to bring Queen Vashti before him wearing the royal crown. She was gorgeous, and he wanted to show off her beauty both to the general public and to his important guests. ¹²But Queen Vashti refused to come as the king had ordered through the eunuchs. The king was furious, his anger boiling inside. ¹³Now, when a need arose, the king would often talk with certain very smart people about the best way to handle it. They were people who knew both the kingdom's written laws and what judges had decided about cases in the past. ¹⁴The ones he talked with most often were Carshena, Shethar, Admatha, Tarshish, Meres, Marsena, and Memucan. They were seven very important people in Persia and Media who, as the kingdom's highest leaders, were in the king's inner circle. So the king said to them, ¹⁵"According to the law, what should I do with Queen Vashti since she didn't do what King Ahasuerus ordered her through the eunuchs?"

¹⁶Then Memucan spoke up in front of the king and the officials. "Queen Vashti," he said, "has done something wrong not just to the king himself. She has also done wrong to all the officials and the peoples in all the provinces of King Ahasuerus. ¹⁷This is the reason: News of what the queen did will reach all women, making them look down on their husbands. They will say, 'King Ahasuerus ordered servants to bring Queen Vashti before him, but she refused to come.' ¹⁸This very day, the im-

VASHTI

Esther's predecessor as queen (Esth 1:9–2:4). Vashti holds a banquet for the women, which echoes the king's lavish banquet for the men. King Ahasuerus commands her to leave the women's space for the men's, to show off her beauty. Her refusal, for reasons unstated, sets up Esther's entrance into the court and the story and emphasizes that the boundary between women's and men's space is a treacherous one.

portant women of Persia and Media who hear about the queen will tell the royal officials the same thing. There will be no end of put-downs and arguments. ¹⁹Now, if the king wishes, let him send out a royal order and have it written into the laws of Persia and Media, laws no one can ever change. It should say that Vashti will never again come before King Ahasuerus. It should also say that the king will give her royal place to someone better than she. ²⁰When the order becomes public through the whole empire, vast as it is, all women will treat their husbands properly. The rule should touch everyone, whether from an important family or not."

²¹The king liked the plan, as did the other men, and he did just what Memucan said. ²²He sent written orders to all the king's provinces. Each province received it written in its own alphabet and each people received it in its own language. It said that each husband should rule over his own house.

Finding a new queen

2 Sometime later when King Ahasuerus was less angry, he remembered Vashti, what she had done, and what he had decided about her. ²So his young male servants said, "Let the king have a search made for beautiful young women who haven't yet married. ³And let the king choose certain people in all the royal provinces to lead the search. Have them bring all the beautiful young women together to the fortified part of Susa, to the women's house, to the care of Hegai the king's eunuch in charge of the women so that he might provide beauty treatments for them. ⁴Let the young woman who pleases you the most

take Vashti's place as queen." The king liked the plan and implemented it.

⁵Now there was a Jew in the fortified part of Susa whose name was Mordecai, Jair's son. He came from the family line of Shimei and Kish; he was a Benjaminite. (⁶Benjaminites had been taken into exile away from Jerusalem along with the group, which included Judah's King Jeconiah, whom Babylon's King Nebuchadnezzar exiled to Babylon.) ⁷Mordecai had been a father to Hadassah (that is, Esther), though she was really his cousin, because she had neither father nor mother. The girl had a beautiful figure and was lovely to look at. When her parents died, Mordecai had taken her to be his daughter. ⁸When the king's order and his new law became public, many young women were gathered into the fortified part of Susa under the care of Hegai. Esther was also taken to the palace to the care of Hegai, the one in charge of the women. ⁹The young woman pleased him and won his kindness. He quickly began her beauty treatments and gave her carefully chosen foods. He also gave her seven servants selected from among the palace servants and moved her and her servants into the nicest rooms in the women's house. (¹⁰Esther hadn't told anyone her race and family background because Mordecai had ordered her not to.) ¹¹Each day found Mordecai pacing back and forth along the wall in front of the women's house to learn how Esther was doing and what they were doing with her. ¹²According to the rules for women, the moment for each young woman to go to King Ahasuerus came at the end of twelve months. (She had six months of treatment with pleasant-smelling creams and six

AHASUERUS

Likely the Persian king Xerxes I, who reigned 486–465 BCE. The most prominent appearance of Ahasuerus is in the book of Esther. In this story Ahasuerus is essentially a fictional version of a well-known historical figure. There is a brief mention of an Ahasuerus as the father of Darius the Mede in Daniel 9:1.

months with fragrant oils and other treatments for women.) [13]So this is how the young woman would go to the king: They gave her anything that she asked to take with her from the women's house to the palace. [14]In the evening she would go in, and the next morning she would return to the second women's house under the care of Shaashgaz. He was the king's eunuch in charge of the secondary wives. She would never go to the king again unless he was so pleased that he called for her by name. [15]Soon the moment came for Esther daughter of Mordecai's uncle Abihail, whom Mordecai had taken as his own daughter, to go to the king. But she asked for nothing except what Hegai the king's eunuch in charge of the women told her. (Esther

kept winning the favor of everyone who saw her.) [16]Esther was taken to King Ahasuerus, to his own palace, in the tenth month (that is, the month of Tevet)[a] in the seventh year of his rule. [17]The king loved Esther more than all the other women; she had won his love and his favor more than all the others. He placed the royal crown on her head and made her ruler in place of Vashti. [18]The king held a magnificent, lavish feast, "the feast of Esther," for all his officials and courtiers. He declared a public holiday[b] for the provinces and gave out gifts with royal generosity. [19]When they gathered the young women to the second women's house,[c] Mordecai was working for the king at the King's Gate. [20]Esther still wasn't tell-

[a]December–January [b]Or *remission of taxes* [c]Or *to the women's house a second time*

ESTHER

An orphan adopted by her cousin Mordecai, Esther appears in the book that bears her name as Mordecai's ward and as one of many virgin girls rounded up as potential replacements for the exiled Queen Vashti. Vashti's crime—refusing to appear before King Ahasuerus—and the unnerved response of the king's advisers (1:16-18) set off the gender dynamics of Esther's rise to the court and her actions there. She is singled out by the eunuch Hegai, who is in charge of the virgins' harem (2:8-9, 15). Mordecai instructed her not to reveal her Jewishness to the court (2:10, 20).

Esther's emergence as a character in her own right occurs only as she moves toward the strategic revelation of her ethnicity to Ahasuerus and to Mordecai's (and by extension, the Jews') mortal enemy Haman. Her initial incomprehension regarding Mordecai's act of public protest (4:4) suggests that Esther has lost touch with the concerns of her people. Interestingly, although the decree that the Jews be annihilated comes from the court, Mordecai hears it outside the King's Gate before Esther, tucked away under the court's wing, knows of it. She has in effect traded her identity as a Jew for an intimate knowledge of how to survive at the court itself. In her exchange with Mordecai, he tells her the status of their people and she tells him the laws of entry to the court (4:7, 11). The drama of Esther's character resides in her risky but successful efforts to regain her hidden Jewishness while staying close to power.

The initial name the narrator supplies to identify Esther is Hadassah (Esth 2:7), which means "myrtle." The common interpretation is that Hadassah was her given Hebrew name, but that she was subsequently known as Esther.

ing anyone her family background and race, just as Mordecai had ordered her. She continued to do what Mordecai said, just as she did when she was in his care.

Mordecai saves the king

²¹At that time, as Mordecai continued to work at the King's Gate, two royal eunuchs, Bigthan and Teresh, became angry with King Ahasuerus. They were among the guards protecting the doorway to the king, but they secretly planned to kill him. ²²When Mordecai got wind of it, he reported it to Queen Esther. She spoke to the king about it, saying the information came from Mordecai. ²³The matter was investigated and found to be true, so the two men were impaled on pointed poles.ᵈ A report about the event was written in the royal record with the king present.

Haman plans to destroy Mordecai

3 Sometime later, King Ahasuerus promoted Haman, Hammedatha the Agagite's son,ᵉ by promoting him above all the officials who worked with him. ²All the royal workers at the King's Gate would kneel and bow facedown to Haman because the king had so ordered. But Mordecai didn't kneel or bow down. ³So the royal workers at the King's Gate said to Mordecai, "Why don't you obey the king's order?" ⁴Day after day they questioned him, but he paid no attention to them. So they let Haman know about it just to see whether or not Mordecai's words would hold true.ᶠ (He

had told them that he was a Jew.) ⁵When Haman himself saw that Mordecai didn't kneel or bow down to him, he became very angry. ⁶But he decided not to kill only Mordecai, for people had told him Mordecai's race. Instead, he planned to wipe out all the Jews, Mordecai's people, throughout the whole kingdom of Ahasuerus. ⁷In the first month (that is, the month of Nisan)ᵍ in the twelfth year of the rule of King Ahasuerus, servants threw pur, namely, dice, in front of Haman to find the best day for his plan. They tried every day and every month, and the dice chose the thirteenthʰ day of the twelfth month (that is, the month of Adar).

⁸Then Haman said to King Ahasuerus, "A certain group of people exist in pockets among the other peoples in all the provinces of your kingdom. Their laws are different from those of everyone else, and they refuse to obey the king's laws. There's no good reason for the king to put up with them any longer. ⁹If the king wishes, let a written order be sent out to destroy them, and I will hand over ten thousand kikkars of silverⁱ to those in charge of the king's business. The silver can go into the king's treasuries."

¹⁰The king removed his royal ring from his finger and handed it to Haman, Hammedatha the Agagite's son, enemy of the Jews. ¹¹The king said to Haman, "Both the money and the people are under your power. Do as you like with them." ¹²So in the first month, on the thirteenth day, royal scribes were summoned to write down everything that

ᵈOr hanged the two men on gallows ᵉOr the braggart ᶠOr stand ᵍMarch–April ʰSee LXX and 3:13. ⁱA kikkar weighed approximately seventy-five pounds.

HAMAN

King Ahasuerus' highest adviser in the book of Esther. Haman is said to be an Agagite (Esth 3:1), which means that he was a descendant of the Amalekite's King Agag. Saul failed to execute Agag, and this disobedience (1 Sam 15:3, 9) resulted in Saul's losing his kingship (1 Sam 15:28-29). Haman's family history intersects with that of Mordecai and Esther, who were from the same family as Saul (Esth 2:5).

Haman ordered. The orders were for the king's rulers and the governors in charge of each province, as well as for the officials of each people. They wrote in the alphabet of each province and in the language of each people. They wrote in the name of King Ahasuerus and sealed the order with the king's royal ring. [13] Fast runners were to take the order to all the provinces of the king. The order commanded people to wipe out, kill, and destroy all the Jews, both young and old, even women and little children. This was to happen on a single day— the thirteenth day of the twelfth month (that is, the month of Adar).[j] They were also to seize their property. [14] A copy of the order was to become law in each province and to be posted in public for all peoples to read. The people were to be ready for this day to do as the order commanded. [15] Driven by the king's order, the runners left Susa just as the law became public in the fortified part of Susa. While the king and Haman sat down to have a drink, the city of Susa was in total shock.

A crisis for the Jews

4 When Mordecai learned what had been done, he tore his clothes, dressed in mourning clothes, and put ashes on his head. Then he went out into the heart of the city and cried out loudly and bitterly. [2] He went only as far as the King's Gate because it was against the law for anyone to pass through it wearing mourning clothes. [3] At the same time, in every province and place where the king's order and his new law arrived, a very great sadness came over the Jews. They gave up eating and spent whole days weeping and crying out loudly in pain. Many Jews lay on the ground in mourning clothes and ashes. [4] When Esther's female servants and eunuchs came and told her about Mordecai, the queen's whole body showed how upset she was. She sent everyday clothes for Mordecai to wear instead of mourning clothes, but he rejected them.

[5] Esther then sent for Hathach, one of the royal eunuchs whose job it was to wait on her. She ordered him to go to Mordecai and find out what was going on and why he was acting this way. [6] Hathach went out to Mordecai, to the city square in front of the King's Gate. [7] Mordecai told him everything that had happened to him. He spelled out the exact amount of silver that Haman promised to pay into the royal treasury. It was in exchange for the destruction of the Jews. [8] He also gave Hathach a copy of the law made public in Susa concerning the Jews' destruction so that Hathach could show it to Esther and report it to her. Through him Mordecai ordered her to go to the king to seek his kindness and his help for her people. [9] Hathach came back and told Esther what Mordecai had said.

[10] In reply Esther ordered Hathach to tell Mordecai: [11] "All the king's officials and the people in his provinces know that there's a single law in a case like this. Any man or woman who comes to the king in the inner courtyard without being called is to be put to death. Only the person to whom the king holds out the gold scepter may live. In my case, I haven't been called to come to the king for the past thirty days."

[12] When they told Mordecai Esther's words, [13] he had them respond to Esther: "Don't think for one minute that, unlike all the other Jews, you'll come out of this alive simply because you are in the palace. [14] In fact, if you don't speak up at this very important time, relief and rescue will appear for the Jews from another place, but you and your family will die. But who knows? Maybe it was for a moment like this that you came to be part of the royal family."

[15] Esther sent back this word to Mordecai: [16] "Go, gather all the Jews who are in Susa and tell them to give up eating to help me be brave. They aren't to eat or drink anything for three whole days, and I myself will do the same, along with my female servants. Then, even though it's against the law, I will go to the king; and if I am to die, then die I will." [17] So Mordecai left where he was and did exactly what Esther had ordered him.

Esther acts

5 Three days later, Esther put on royal clothes and stood in the inner courtyard of the palace, facing the palace itself. At that moment the king was inside sitting on his royal throne and facing the palace doorway. [2] When the king noticed Queen Esther standing in the entry court, he was pleased. The king held out to Esther the gold scepter in his hand, and she came forward and touched the scepter's tip.

[3] Then the king said to her, "What is it, Queen Esther? What do you want? I'll give you anything—even half the kingdom."

[4] Esther answered, "If the king wishes, please come today with Haman for the feast that I have prepared for him."

[5] "Hurry, get Haman," the king ordered, "so we can do what Esther says." So the king and Haman came to the feast that Esther had prepared. [6] As they sipped wine, the king asked, "Now what is it you wish? I'll give it to you. What do you want? I'll do anything—even give you half the kingdom."

[7] Esther answered, "This is my wish and this is what I want: [8] If I please the king, and if the king wishes to grant my wish and my desire, I'd like the king and Haman to come to another feast that I will prepare for them. Tomorrow I will answer the king's questions."

Haman boasts, complains, and acts

[9] That day Haman left Esther's place happy, his spirits high, but then he saw Mordecai in the King's Gate. Mordecai neither stood up nor seemed the least bit nervous around him, so Haman suddenly felt great rage toward Mordecai. [10] But Haman held himself back and went on home. He sent word that his friends and his wife Zeresh should join him there. [11] Haman boasted to them about his great wealth and his many sons. He told all about how the king had honored him by promoting him over the officials and high royal workers. [12] "Best of all," Haman said, "Queen Esther has invited no one else but me to join the king for food and drinks that she has prepared. In fact, I've been called to join the king at her place tomorrow! [13] But all this loses its meaning every time I see Mordecai the Jew sitting at the King's Gate."

[14] So his wife Zeresh and all his friends told him: "Have people prepare a pointed pole seventy-five feet high. In the morning, tell the king to have Mordecai impaled on it. Then you can go with the king to the feast in a happy mood." Haman liked the idea and had the pole prepared.

Honor for Mordecai

6 That same night, the king simply couldn't sleep. He had the official royal records brought in, and his young male servants began reading them to the king. [2] They came to the report about Mordecai informing on Bigthan and Teresh. (They were the two royal eunuchs among the guards protecting the king's doorway, who secretly planned to kill King Ahasuerus.) [3] "What was done to honor and reward Mordecai for this?" the king asked.

SCEPTER

A scepter is a royal staff or rod. As king, God possesses a scepter (e.g., Ps 60:7; Isa 30:31). The scepter represents royal power (Num 24:17), so Zechariah can say, "The scepter of Egypt will turn away," meaning it will become weak (Zech 10:11; cf. Ps 89:44 [Heb. 89:45]; Isa 14:5).

In the NT, *scepter* occurs in Heb 1:8-9 (quoting Ps 45:6-7 [Heb. 45:7-8]) in a string of quotations that apply to Christ, therefore associating him with the divine throne. The royal rod also appears three times in Revelation (2:27; 12:5; 19:15).

His young male servants replied, "Nothing was done for him, sir."

⁴"Who is that out in the courtyard?" the king asked. (Haman had just entered the outer courtyard of the palace. He had come to tell the king to impale Mordecai on the pole that he had set up for him.)

⁵The king's servants answered, "That's Haman standing out in the courtyard, sir." So the king said, "Have him come in."

⁶When Haman entered, the king asked him, "What should be done for the man whom the king really wants to honor?"

Haman thought to himself, Whom would the king really want to honor more than me? ⁷So Haman said to the king, "Here's what should be done for the man the king really wants to honor. ⁸Have servants bring out a royal robe that the king himself has worn and a horse on which the king himself has ridden. It should have a royal crest on its head. ⁹Then hand over the robe and the horse to another man, one of the king's officials. Have him personally robe^k the man whom the king really wants to honor and lead him on the horse through the city square. As he goes, have him shout, 'This is what the king does for the man he really wants to honor!'"

¹⁰Then the king said to Haman, "Hurry, take the robe and the horse just as you've said and do exactly that for Mordecai the Jew, who works at the King's Gate. Don't leave out a single thing you've said!"

¹¹So Haman took the robe and the horse and put the robe on Mordecai. He led him on horseback through the city square, shouting as he went, "This is what the king does for the man he really wants to honor!" ¹²Afterward, Mordecai returned to the King's Gate, while Haman hurried home feeling great shame, his head covered.

¹³Haman told his wife Zeresh and all his friends everything that had happened to him. Both his friends^l and his wife said to him, "You've already begun to lose out to Mordecai. If he is of Jewish birth, you'll not be able to win against him. You are surely going to lose out to him."

Haman's demise

¹⁴They were still discussing this with him when several royal eunuchs arrived. They quickly hurried Haman off to the feast that Esther had prepared. 7 ¹When the king and Haman came in for the banquet with Queen Esther, ²the king said to her, "This is the second day we've met for wine. What is your wish, Queen Esther? I'll give it to you. And what do you want? I'll do anything—even give you half the kingdom."

³Queen Esther answered, "If I please the king, and if the king wishes, give me my life—that's my wish—and the lives of my people too. That's my desire. ⁴We have been sold—I and my people—to be wiped out, killed, and destroyed. If we simply had been sold as male and female slaves, I would have said nothing. But no enemy can compensate the king for this kind of damage."

⁵King Ahasuerus said to Queen Esther, "Who is this person, and where is he? Who would dare do such a thing?"

⁶Esther replied, "A man who hates, an enemy—this wicked Haman!" Haman was overcome with terror in the presence of the king and queen. ⁷Furious, the king got up and left the banquet for the palace garden. But Haman stood up to beg Queen Esther for his life. He saw clearly that the king's mood meant a bad end for him.

⁸The king returned from the palace garden to the banquet room just as Haman was kneeling on the couch where Esther was reclining. "Will you even molest the queen while I am in the house?" the king said. The words had barely left the king's mouth before covering Haman's face with dread.^m

⁹Harbona, one of the eunuchs serving the king, said, "Sir, look! There's the stake that Haman made for Mordecai, the man who spoke up and did something good for the king. It's standing at Haman's house—seventy-five feet high."

"Impale him on it!" the king ordered. ¹⁰So they impaled Haman on the very pole that he had set up for Mordecai, and the king's anger went away.

---

^k LXX sing robe and lead, cf Heb plural verbs   ^l LXX; Heb wise ones   ^m Or the face of Haman was covered.

Esther acts again

8 That same day King Ahasuerus gave Queen Esther what Haman the enemy of the Jews owned. Mordecai himself came before the king because Esther had told the king that he was family to her. ²The king took off his royal ring, the one he had removed from Haman, and gave it to Mordecai. Esther put Mordecai in charge of what Haman had owned.

³Esther again spoke before the king. She bowed at his feet, wept, and begged him to treat her kindly. She wanted him to overturn the evil plot of Haman the Agagite—his secret plan directed against the Jews. ⁴The king held out the gold scepter to Esther, and she got up and stood before him. ⁵She said, "If the king wishes, and if I please him—that is, if the idea seems right to the king, and if he still sees me as a good person—then have people write something to call back the order—the order that put into effect the plan of Haman, Hammedatha the Agagite's son, that he wrote to destroy the Jews in all the royal provinces. ⁶How can I bear to watch the terrible evil about to sweep over my people? And how can I bear to watch others destroy my own family?"

Mordecai writes a new law

⁷King Ahasuerus said to Queen Esther and to Mordecai the Jew, "Look, I've given Esther everything Haman owned. And Haman himself my servants have impaled on the pole because he planned to attack the Jews. ⁸So you yourselves write to the Jews whatever you like in the name of the king and seal the letters with the king's royal ring. Anything written in the name of the king and sealed with the king's royal ring can't be called back." ⁹So that was when the royal scribes were summoned—on the twenty-third day of the third month (that is, the month of Sivan).ⁿ They wrote exactly what Mordecai ordered to the Jews, rulers, governors, and officials of the provinces from India to Cush—one hundred twenty-seven in all. They wrote in the alphabet of each province and in the language of each

people. ¹⁰They wrote in the name of King Ahasuerus and sealed the order with the king's royal ring. He sent letters with riders mounted on royal horses bred from mares known to run fast.° ¹¹The order allowed Jews in each town to join together and defend their lives. The Jews were free to wipe out, kill, and destroy every army of any people and province that attacked them, along with their women and children. They could also take and keep anything their attackers owned. ¹²The one day in all the provinces of King Ahasuerus on which they could do so was the thirteenth day of the twelfth month (that is, the month of Adar). ¹³A copy of the writing was to become law in each province and be on public display for all its peoples to read. The Jews were to be ready on this day to get back at their enemies. ¹⁴The riders mounted on royal horses left Susa, spurred on by the king's order, and the law also became public in the fortified part of Susa.

¹⁵Mordecai went out from the king's presence in a blue and white royal robe wearing a large gold crown and a white and red-purple coat. The city of Susa greeted him with shouts of joy. ¹⁶For the Jews it was a day of light, happiness, joy, and honor. ¹⁷In every province and in every town—wherever the king's order and his law arrived—for the Jews it was a day of happiness and joy. For them it meant feasts and a holiday. Many people in the land became Jews themselves, out of fear of the Jews.

The fateful day

9 It was on the thirteenth day of the twelfth month (that is, the month of Adar)ᴾ that the king's order and his law were to be enforced. On the very day that the enemies of the Jews hoped to overpower them, the tables were turned against them. The Jews overpowered their enemies instead. ²The Jews joined together in their towns in all the provinces of King Ahasuerus to defend themselves against those who tried to harm them. No one was able to stand in their way because everyone

ⁿMay–June   °Heb uncertain   ᴾFebruary–March

was afraid of the Jews. ³All the leaders of the provinces, rulers, governors, and those in charge of the king's business helped the Jews because they were afraid of Mordecai. ⁴Because Mordecai was very important in the palace, news about him was sweeping through the provinces. Indeed, Mordecai was becoming more and more important every day. ⁵The Jews put down all their enemies with sword blows, killing, and destruction. They did whatever they wanted with those who hated them. ⁶In the fortified part of Susa, the Jews killed five hundred people. ⁷They also killed Parshandatha, Dalphon, Aspatha, ⁸Poratha, Adalia, Aridatha, ⁹Parmashta, Arisai, Aridai, and Vaizatha. ¹⁰These were the ten sons of Haman, Hammedatha's son, the enemy of the Jews. But the Jews didn't lay a hand on anything their enemies owned. ¹¹That same day, a report concerning the number killed in the fortified part of Susa reached the king.

¹²So the king said to Queen Esther in the fortified part of Susa, "The Jews have killed five hundred people as well as the ten sons of Haman. What have they done in the rest of the royal provinces? What do you wish now? I'll give it to you. What is your desire? I'll do it this time too."

¹³Esther answered, "If the king wishes, let the Jews who are in Susa also have tomorrow to do what the law allows for today. And let them also impale the ten sons of Haman on pointed poles." ¹⁴The king ordered that this be done, and the law became public in Susa. They impaled the ten sons of Haman just as she said. ¹⁵The Jews in Susa joined together again, this time on the fourteenth day of the month of Adar. In Susa, they killed three hundred people,

but they didn't lay a hand on anything the people owned.

¹⁶The Jews out in the royal provinces also joined together to defend their lives. They put to rest the troubles with their enemies and killed those who hated them. The total was seventy-five thousand dead, but the Jews didn't lay a hand on anything their enemies owned. ¹⁷They acted on the thirteenth day of the month of Adar. Then on the fourteenth day they rested, making it a day of feasts and rejoicing. (¹⁸The Jews in Susa joined together for self-defense on the thirteenth and fourteenth days of the month. But they rested on the fifteenth day of the month and made it a day of feasts and joyous events.) ¹⁹That is why Jews who live in villages make the fourteenth day of the month of Adar a day of rejoicing and feasts, a holiday. It is a day on which they send gifts of food to each other.

The new holiday of Purim

²⁰Mordecai wrote these things down and sent letters to all the Jews in all the provinces, both near and far, of King Ahasuerus. ²¹He made it a rule that Jews keep the fourteenth and fifteenth days of the month of Adar as special days each and every year. ²²They are the days on which the Jews finally put to rest the troubles with their enemies. The month is the one when everything turned around for them from sadness to joy, and from sad, loud crying to a holiday. They are to make them days of feasts and joyous events, days to send food gifts to each other and money gifts to the poor. ²³The Jews agreed to continue what they had already begun to do—just what Mordecai had written to them. ²⁴Indeed, Haman, Hammedatha the Agagite's son, the enemy

PURIM

A festival in the Jewish liturgical calendar falling on the fourteenth day of the month of Adar. It commemorates the Jews' deliverance from Haman's genocidal plot through the actions of Esther and Mordecai.

of all the Jews, had planned to destroy the Jews. He had servants throw pur (that is, the dice) to find the best month and day to trouble greatly and destroy them. ²⁵But when Esther came before the king, his written order said: The wicked plan that Haman made against the Jews should turn back on him instead. So they impaled him and his sons on pointed poles. ²⁶That is why people call these days Purim, by using the ancient word *pur*. It all fit with what this letter said, with what they saw happen, and with what they themselves went through. ²⁷The Jews agreed that they, their children, grandchildren, and great-grandchildren, as well as all non-Jews who become Jews, should always keep these two days. They agreed to follow the written rules—and at the proper time too—every year. ²⁸So forever every family, province, and town remembers to keep these days. These days of Purim won't die out among the Jews. They will remember to keep them forever. ²⁹Queen Esther daughter of Abihail, along with Mordecai the Jew, wrote with her full royal power to show that this second letter about Purim was correct.�q ³⁰Letters conveying good wishes and words of friendship were sent to all the Jews throughout the

one hundred twenty-seven provinces in the kingdom of Ahasuerus. ³¹Their aim was to make sure that the Jews kept these days of Purim at the proper time, following the rule that Mordecai the Jew and Queen Esther had made. The rule fit well with what they themselves had agreed to do forever and with other things they did—like fasting and lamenting. ³²Esther's order made these features of Purim part of the law, so it was written down.

The fame of Mordecai

10 King Ahasuerus taxed the entire kingdom, including the islands of the Mediterranean. ²Now some may want to know about all the king's mighty, great deeds. They may also want a full report about how important Mordecai became after the king honored him. Are they not written in the official records of the kings of Media and Persia? ³Certainly, Mordecai the Jew was second only to King Ahasuerus in importance. The Jews also admired him greatly, and his many brothers and sisters were proud of him. He always wanted to do good things for his Jewish people and to speak up for all his family whenever they needed help.

�q Or *wrote a second time to show that this letter*

JOB

The moment you open the book of Job, you enter a mysterious world. Strange words and phrases bombard your senses. A shady character called the Adversary challenges God. An old man curses his sores and calls the Lord a variety of ancient names. When God speaks, it's not in any manner we recognize. The divine voice is heard over the roar of a whirling dust storm.

In spite of this alien nature—or perhaps because of it—the book of Job has a magnetic quality. Rabbi Kushner began his best-selling book *When Bad Things Happen to Good People* with an interpretation of Job. In so doing, he continued a millennia-old tradition: When people suffer, they turn to the experiences and wisdom found in this ancient book. In journeying with Job as he wrestles with cruel and unexplainable pain, people encounter God in a new and different way.

This same opportunity is open to us. If God is to speak to us in this manner, though, our eyes must first grow accustomed to the unfamiliar world of Job.

JOB: THE MAN AND THE LEGEND

Job was the central character in a popular story circulated in the ancient Middle East (the region around the Mediterranean Sea that included Egypt, the Sinai Peninsula, and Canaan). Job was a wealthy man living in Uz, which possibly was the ancient country of Edom, an area east of Palestine in the Syrian Desert. He was a semi-tragic figure in that he encountered intense—and undeserved—hardships. He lost possessions and health and became a social outcast. Throughout these sufferings, brought on as a result of a heavenly dispute, Job did not "curse God." In the end, consequently, his possessions, health, and status were restored.

The biblical writers were well acquainted with this story. References to Job were made by Ezekiel (14:14, 20) and James (5:11).

As was the custom in ancient Middle Eastern literature, the name signifies the nature and action of the character. *Job* has been traced to a variety of meanings stemming from both Hebrew and Arabic roots: "one who is at war with God"; "one born to be persecuted"; and "the repentant one" are possible interpretations.

HOW THE BOOK WAS WRITTEN

As Israel lived with its neighbors, it was natural that ideas and experiences of those countries found their way into Israelite culture. The Hebrew sages reflected on these impressions within the context of their faith in the Lord (Yahweh). The result was the Wisdom Literature found in the Old Testament. This literature is philosophical, with an emphasis upon teaching: Ecclesiastes, Proverbs, several psalms (1, 34, and 92, for example), and parts of other books.

Job is included in this wisdom tradition. In the early sixth century BCE, the Babylonians enslaved the citizens of Judah and deported the useful ones to Babylon. This period of biblical history, known as the Babylonian Exile, was traumatic, causing a crisis of faith for those who believed in God's providential care.

It was against this historical backdrop that the book of Job took its present form. A wise man/poet of Judah found the ancient legend to be an appropriate vehicle by which to examine faith in God in light of the national catastrophe. The tale he appropriated and edited may be found in the prose portions at the beginning and the end of the book (1:1–2:13; 42:7-17). The first part describes Job's sufferings and his virtuous character, while the last portion depicts the restoration of Job's fortunes. The poetic section in between reveals the poet's painful crisis of faith.

The exception to this is the section containing Elihu's speeches. These chapters (32–37) are viewed by many scholars as being foreign to the original poem.

THE THEME OF THE BOOK

It is popular to say that the central thrust of the book of Job is dealing with the question, "Why do the righteous suffer if there is a loving God?" This is actually, however, a sub-theme. The major motif instead is the larger question, "What is the nature of faith—how are we to relate to God?"

The poet verbalizes, through Job's friends, the popular theology of ancient Israel. Put simply, this theology is: Do good, and God will reward you; do evil, and God will punish you. This is the idea of divine retribution.

Job's replies to his friends, on the other hand, refute this simplistic theology. He stubbornly maintains his righteousness, asserting that his suffering cannot be based on anything he did. If Job is correct, then the theology of his friends— and of the ancient Hebrews, somewhat—has become bankrupt.

Stripped of such an easy view of faith and the world, how can one approach God? This theme is a reflection of the times in which the poet wrote. The nation was in shambles. The old principles and certainties had been turned upside down. Through the words of Job the poet searches for a faith that will discover God in the midst of fear and chaos.

THE STRUCTURE AND TEXT OF JOB

The bulk of the poetry section—the part sandwiched between the prose beginning and ending—consists of the dialogue between Job and three friends who come to console him: Eliphaz, Bildad, and Zophar. The conversation follows a set form: Eliphaz speaks, Job replies; Bildad speaks, Job replies; Zophar speaks, Job replies.

This forms a cycle of speeches, and there are three such cycles. (The third cycle, 22:1–27:23, is not complete, containing only the speeches of Eliphaz and Bildad, along with Job's replies.) Preceding and following this series of speeches, Job gives a pair of eloquent soliloquies regarding his suffering (3; 29–31).

A fourth friend, Elihu, follows Job's last soliloquy. Instead of conversing with Job, he makes a long series of speeches (32:6-37:24).

The poetry section concludes with the dialogue between God and Job. God makes two speeches, with Job responding to each. With this conversation the conflict is resolved, leading to the prose conclusion.

The Hebrew text of this poetry section is very poor in places. Translators in many instances had to make educated guesses regarding the meaning of a word or phrase. In addition, the third cycle of conversation between Job and his friends appears abrupt and illogical in places. This cycle contains fragments of other speeches.

TYPES OF LITERATURE FOUND IN JOB

Just as an epic novel may use different types of literature (adventure, romance, mystery), so does the book of Job. The poet, standing in the Hebrew wisdom tradition, employed different literary forms that were well recognized by his audience.

The first, and most obvious, was that of the narrative. In the prose sections the author adapted the ancient story of Job. This storytelling style was the basic vehicle by which God's interaction with the Hebrew people was transmitted.

The poem itself has the characteristics of a legal document. The dialogue between Job and his friends has the flavor of a debate. In addition, Job often appeals for a judge to decide between himself and the one who is responsible for his unjust treatment—God (e.g., 9:33). Finally, with the debate with his friends ended, Job calls for God to enter the courtroom and state the divine case against him.

The third major type of literature employed was the lament. Several of the psalms (such as 22, 39, 77, 88, 102) employ this form, wherein a sufferer expresses powerful emotions to God and cries out for help. The poet used this throughout his work, most poignantly in Job's two soliloquies.

A HINT ON READING THE BOOK OF JOB

To enter Job's world is to enter an environment alien to us. Consequently, while it is important to get a clear understanding of a passage, at times this is impossible. Ancient ways of looking at the world, corruptions in the text of Job, and uncertain Hebrew words and phrases assure us of this.

Using another instrument—your own experience—will help you deal with such a limitation. Read Job with one eye on his world and another on your own world. Read the book with an understanding of your own pain and the pain of those around you. Ask yourself if the words you find on Job's lips or on his friends' have ever been on your own.

The gap between Job's world and ours—made by the centuries that have passed since the poet first scratched on parchment—is enormous. Reading the book with your own experiences just under the surface will help bridge that gap. By doing this you will share the poet's wrestling with the Lord, and his ultimate victory will be yours as well.

JOB

Job's piety and life of bliss

1 A man in the land of Uz was named Job. That man was honest, a person of absolute integrity; he feared God and avoided evil. ²He had seven sons and three daughters, ³and owned seven thousand sheep, three thousand camels, five hundred pairs of oxen, five hundred female donkeys, and a vast number of servants, so that he was greater than all the people of the east. ⁴Each of his sons hosted a feast in his own house on his birthday. They invited their three sisters to eat and drink with them. ⁵When the days of the feast had been completed, Job would send word[a] and purify his children.[b] Getting up early in the morning, he prepared entirely burned offerings for each one of them, for Job thought, Perhaps my children have sinned and then cursed[c] God in their hearts. Job did this regularly.

Job's motives questioned

⁶One day the divine beings[d] came to present themselves before the LORD, and the Adversary[e] also came among them. ⁷The LORD said to the Adversary, "Where did you come from?"

The Adversary answered the LORD, "From wandering throughout the earth."

⁸The LORD said to the Adversary, "Have you thought about my servant Job; surely there is no one like him on earth, a man who is honest, who is of absolute integrity, who reveres God and avoids evil?"

⁹The Adversary answered the LORD, "Does Job revere God for nothing? ¹⁰Haven't you fenced him in—his house and all he has—and blessed the work of his hands so that his possessions extend throughout the earth? ¹¹But stretch out your hand and strike all he has. He will certainly curse you to your face."

¹²The LORD said to the Adversary, "Look, all he has is within your power; only don't stretch out your hand against him." So the Adversary left the LORD's presence.

Job passes the test

¹³One day Job's sons and daughters were eating and drinking wine in their oldest brother's house. ¹⁴A messenger came to Job and said: "The oxen were plowing, and the donkeys were grazing nearby ¹⁵when the Sabeans took them and killed the young men with swords. I alone escaped to tell you."

¹⁶While this messenger was speaking, another arrived and said: "A raging fire fell from the sky and burned up the sheep and devoured the young men. I alone escaped to tell you."

¹⁷While this messenger was speaking, another arrived and said: "Chaldeans set up three companies, raided the camels and took them, killing the young men with swords. I alone escaped to tell you."

¹⁸While this messenger was speaking, another arrived and said: "Your sons and your daughters were eating and drinking wine

---

[a]Heb lacks *word*. [b]Or *them* [c]Or *blessed*. The verb for *bless* is a euphemism for *curse* in 1:11; 2:5, 9; whereas in 1:10, 21 and 42:12 it has its usual meaning. [d]Or *children of God* [e]Heb *hassatan*

UZ

The homeland of Job, east of Israel but of an uncertain location (Job 1:1). One tradition places Uz in Edom. Lamentations 4:21 parallels Uz and Edom. Uz is listed in the Edomite genealogy (Gen 36:28) and several personal names in the book of Job are Edomite. Furthermore, there is an appendix to the book of Job in the Greek translation of the Old Testament placing the city between Idumea and Arabia, which supports an Edomite location.

in their oldest brother's house, ¹⁹when a strong wind came from the desert and struck the four corners of the house. It fell upon the young people, and they died. I alone escaped to tell you."

²⁰Job arose, tore his clothes, shaved his head, fell to the ground, and worshipped. ²¹He said: "Naked I came from my mother's womb; naked I will return there. The LORD has given; the LORD has taken; bless the LORD's name." ²²In all this, Job didn't sin or blame God.

Job's Adversary refuses to give up

2 One day the divine beings came to present themselves before the LORD. The Adversary also came among them to present himself before the LORD. ²The LORD said to the Adversary, "Where have you come from?"

The Adversary answered the LORD, "From wandering throughout the earth."

³The LORD said to the Adversary, "Have you thought about my servant Job, for there is no one like him on earth, a man

SATAN/THE ADVERSARY (OT)

In the OT *satan* is a Hebrew noun meaning "adversary" or "accuser." Although "the satan" is rendered in most English translations as "Satan," it should not be understood as a proper name. Proper names in Hebrew are not preceded by a definite article. Rather "the satan" refers to the role enacted by one of the heavenly beings. In the CEB it is translated "the Adversary."

In the OT, the satan, an adversary who opposes or obstructs another, can be either a human or divine being. The story about the upright and blameless Job presents a heavenly being as "the satan." When the sons of God, including the satan, go before the Lord (1:6), the satan's task becomes clear (1:8). The satan gathers information about Job not in opposition to the Lord, but as a member of the heavenly entourage. When the satan proposes to test Job, the Lord agrees.

It is important to note that the satan carries out the trials and tribulations he inflicts on Job only on the Lord's approval. However, the Lord casts some blame on the satan for Job's afflictions. He says to the satan, "You incited me to ruin him for no reason" (2:3).

The satan also appears in Zechariah 3 in a setting resembling a trial (3:1). Here the role of the satan appears to be like that of the satan in Job, who gathers intelligence about the behavior of people to be used in a kind of legal adversarial role. However, the Lord himself, who appears abruptly in the scene, cuts short the proceedings, rebuking the satan for his accusations (3:2). The satan appears to be rebuked because he is continuing to accuse Joshua when his guilt has been pardoned.

A final OT reference is made to a satan in 1 Chronicles 21:1, where it is mentioned that he "incited David to count Israel." This action angers the Lord, who punishes David. Significantly, the Lord still holds David, not the satan, responsible for his actions.

Satan as a personal enemy opposed to God's reign over creation does appear in later tradition, but the lines of development are obscure.

who is honest, who is of absolute integrity, who reveres God and avoids evil? He still holds on to his integrity, even though you incited me to ruin him for no reason."

⁴ The Adversary responded to the LORD, "Skin for skin—people will give up everything they have in exchange for their lives. ⁵ But stretch out your hand and strike his bones and flesh. Then he will definitely curse[f] you to your face."

⁶ The LORD answered the Adversary, "There he is—within your power; only preserve his life."

The test intensifies

⁷ The Adversary departed from the LORD's presence and struck Job with severe sores from the sole of his foot to the top of his head. ⁸ Job took a piece of broken pottery to scratch himself and sat down on a mound of ashes. ⁹ Job's wife said to him, "Are you still clinging to your integrity? Curse[g] God, and die."

¹⁰ Job said to her, "You're talking like a foolish woman. Will we receive good from God but not also receive bad?" In all this, Job didn't sin with his lips.

Job's three friends come to comfort him

¹¹ When Job's three friends heard about all this disaster that had happened to him, they came, each one from his home—Eliphaz from Teman, Bildad from Shuah, and Zophar from Naamah. They agreed to come so they could console and comfort him. ¹² When they looked up from a distance and didn't recognize him, they wept loudly. Each one tore his garment and scattered dust above his head toward the sky. ¹³ They sat with Job on the ground seven days and seven nights, not speaking a word to him, for they saw that he was in excruciating pain.

Job responds differently

3 Afterward, Job spoke up and cursed the day he was born.

² Job said:

³ Perish the day I was born,
    the night someone said,

"A boy has been conceived."
⁴ That day—let it be darkness;
    may God above ignore it,
    and light not shine on it.
⁵ May deepest darkness claim it
    and a cloud linger over it;
    may all that darkens the day terrify it.
⁶ May gloom seize that night;
    may it not be counted
      in the days of a year;
    may it not appear in the months.
⁷ May that night be childless;
    may no happy singing come in it.
⁸ May those who curse the day curse it,
    those with enough skill
      to awaken Leviathan.
⁹ May its evening stars stay dark;
    may it wait in vain for light;
    may it not see dawn's gleam,
¹⁰ because it didn't close the doors
    of my mother's womb,[h]
    didn't hide trouble from my eyes.

Job laments his misfortune

¹¹ Why didn't I die at birth,
    come forth from the womb and die?
¹² Why did knees receive me
    and breasts let me nurse?
¹³ For now I would be lying down quietly;
    I'd sleep; rest would be mine
¹⁴ with kings and earth's advisors,
    who rebuild ruins for themselves,
¹⁵ or with princes who have gold,
    who fill their houses with silver.
¹⁶ Or why wasn't I
    like a buried miscarried infant,
    like babies who never see light?
¹⁷ There the wicked rage no more;
    there the weak rest.
¹⁸ Prisoners are entirely at ease;
    they don't hear a boss's voice.
¹⁹ Both small and great are there;
    a servant is free from his masters.
²⁰ Why is light given to the hard worker,
    life to those bitter of soul,
²¹ those waiting in vain for death,
    who search for it
      more than for treasure,
²² who rejoice excitedly,

---

[f] Or *bless*   [g] Or *bless*   [h] Heb lacks *mother's.*

who are thrilled
    when they find a grave?
23 Why is light given[i] to the person
    whose way is hidden,
    whom God has fenced in?
24 My groans become my bread;
    my roars pour out like water.
25 Because I was afraid of something awful,
    and it arrived;
    what I dreaded came to me.
26 I had no ease, quiet, or rest,
    and trembling came.

Eliphaz tries to comfort Job

4 Then Eliphaz, a native of Teman,
responded:
2 If one tries to answer you,
    will you be annoyed?
    But who can hold words back?
3 Look, you've instructed many
    and given strength to drooping hands.
4 Your words have raised up the falling;
    you've steadied failing knees.
5 But now it comes to you,
    and you are dismayed;
    it has struck you,
    and you are frightened.
6 Isn't your religion
    the source of[j] your confidence;
    the integrity of your conduct,
    the source of your hope?

Sinners don't live long

7 Think! What innocent person
    has ever perished?
    When have those who do the right
    thing been destroyed?
8 As I've observed, those who plow sin
    and sow trouble will harvest it.
9 When God breathes deeply,
    they perish;
    by a breath of his nostril
    they are annihilated.
10 The roar of a lion and snarl
    of the king of beasts—
    yet the teeth of lions are shattered;
    11 the lion perishes without prey,
    and its cubs are scattered.

A frightening dream

12 But a word sneaked up on me;
    my ears caught a hint of it.
13 In profound thoughts, visions of night,
    when deep sleep falls on people,
    14 fear and dread struck me;
    all of my bones shook.
15 A breeze swept by my face;
    the hair of my skin bristled.
16 It stopped. I didn't recognize
    its visible form,
    although a figure was
    in front of my eyes.
    Silence! Then I heard a voice:
17 "Can a human be more righteous
    than God,
    a person purer than their maker?"

Its interpretation

18 If he doesn't trust his servants
    and levels a charge
    against his messengers,
19 how much less those who dwell
    in houses of clay,
    whose foundations are in dust,
    and who are crushed like a moth?
20 They are smashed
    between morning and evening;
    they perish forever
    without anyone knowing.
21 Isn't their tent cord pulled up?
    They die without wisdom.[k]

Life's problems

5 Call out. Will anyone answer you?
    To which holy one will you turn?
2 Surely anger can kill the foolish;
    fury can kill the simple.
3 I've seen the foolish take root
    and promptly curse their house.
4 Their children are far[l] from safety,
    crushed in the gate without a deliverer.
5 The hungry devour[m] their crops;
    it's taken even from the thorns,[n]
    and the thirsty pant after their yield.
6 Surely trouble doesn't come from dust,
    nor does distress sprout
    from the ground.

---

[i]Heb lacks *is light given*. [j]Heb lacks *the source*. [k]Some interpreters end the quotation here rather than 4:17.
[l]Or *May their children be far from safety*. [m]or *May the hungry devour their crops*. [n]Heb uncertain

⁷ Surely humans are born to distress,
just as sparks rise up.

The answer is God

⁸ But I would seek God,
put my case to God,
⁹ who does great things
beyond comprehension,
wonderful things without number;
¹⁰ who provides rain
over the earth's surface,
sends water to the open country,
¹¹ exalts the lowly,
raises mourners to victory;
¹² who frustrates the schemes of the clever
so that their hands achieve no success,
¹³ trapping the wise in their cleverness
so that the plans of the devious
don't succeed.
¹⁴ They encounter darkness during the day,
and at noon they fumble about
as at night.
¹⁵ Yet he rescues the orphan°
from the sword of their mouth,
the needy from the grip of the strong;
¹⁶ so the poor have hope
and violence shuts its mouth.

Divine favor

¹⁷ Look, happy is the person
whom God corrects;
so don't reject the Almighty's instruction.
¹⁸ He injures, but he binds up;
he strikes, but his hands heal.
¹⁹ From six adversities he will deliver you;
from seven harm won't touch you.
²⁰ In famine he will ransom you from death;
in war, from the power of the sword.
²¹ You will be hidden
from the tongue's sting,
and you won't fear destruction
when it comes.
²² You will laugh
at destruction and hunger;
you won't be afraid of wild beasts;
²³ for you will make an agreement with
the stones of the field;
and the beasts of the field
will be at peace with you.

²⁴ You will know that your tent is secure.
You will examine your home
and miss nothing.
²⁵ You will know that you'll have
many children.
Your offspring will be
like the grass of the earth.
²⁶ You will come to your grave in old age
as bundles of grain stacked up
at harvesttime.
²⁷ Look, we've searched this out, and so it is;
listen and find out for yourself.

Job defends his anger

6 Job responded:
² Oh, that my grief were actually weighed,
all of it were lifted up in scales;
³ for now it's heavier
than the sands of the sea;
therefore, my words are rash.ᵖ
⁴ The Almighty's arrows are in me;
my spirit drinks their poison,
and God's terrors are arrayed against me.
⁵ Does a donkey bray over grass
or an ox bellow over its fodder?
⁶ Is tasteless food eaten without salt,
or does egg white�q have taste?
⁷ I refuse to touch them;
they resemble food for the sick.

He wishes to die

⁸ Oh, that what I've requested would come
and God grant my hope;
⁹ that God be willing to crush me,
release his hand and cut me off.
¹⁰ I'd still take comfort,
relievedʳ even though in persistent pain;
for I've not denied
the words of the holy one.
¹¹ What is my strength, that I should hope;
my end, that my life should drag on?
¹² Is my strength that of rocks,
my flesh bronze?
¹³ I don't have a helper for myself;
success has been taken from me.

He accuses his friends

¹⁴ Are friends loyal to the one who despairs,ˢ
or do they stop fearing the Almighty?

°Heb lacks *orphan*. ᵖHeb uncertain �q Heb uncertain ʳHeb uncertain ˢHeb uncertain

15 My companions are treacherous
  like a stream in the desert,
  like channels that overrun
    their streambeds,
16 like those darkened by thawing ice,
  in which snow is obscured
17 but that stop flowing in dry times
  and vanish from their channels in heat.
18 Caravans turn aside from their paths;
  they go up into untamed areas
    and perish.
19 Caravans from Tema look;
  merchants from Sheba hope for it.
20 They are ashamed that they trusted;
  they arrive and are dismayed.
21 That's what you are like;[t]
  you see something awful and are afraid.

He appeals to his friends

22 Have I said, "Give me something?
  Offer a bribe from your wealth for me?
23 Rescue me from the hand of my enemy?
  Ransom me from
    the grip of the ruthless?"
24 Instruct me and I'll be quiet;
  inform me how I've erred.
25 How painful are truthful words,
  but what do your condemnations
    accomplish?
26 Do you intend to correct my words,
  to treat the words of a hopeless man
    as wind?
27 Would you even gamble over an orphan,
  barter away your friend?
28 Now look at me—
  would I lie to your face?
29 Turn! Don't be faithless.
  Turn now! I am righteous.
30 Is there wrong on my tongue,
  or can my mouth not
    recognize disaster?

The human condition

7 Isn't slavery everyone's condition
  on earth,
  our days like those of a hired worker?
2 Like a slave we pant for a shadow,
  await our task like a hired worker.

3 So I have inherited months of emptiness;
  nights of toil have been measured out
    for me.
4 If I lie down and think—
  When will I get up?—
  night drags on,[u] and restless thoughts
    fill me until dawn.
5 My flesh is covered with worms
  and crusted earth;
  my skin hardens and oozes.
6 My days are swifter
  than a weaver's shuttle;
  they reach their end without hope.[v]
7 Remember that my life is wind;
  my eyes won't see pleasure again.
8 The eye that sees me now
  will no longer look on me;
  your eyes will be on me,
    and I won't exist.
9 A cloud breaks apart and moves on—
  like the one who descends to the grave[w]
    and won't rise,
10 won't return home again,
  won't be recognized in town anymore.

Job wants to be left alone

11 But I won't keep quiet;
  I will speak in the adversity
    of my spirit,
  groan in the bitterness of my life.
12 Am I Sea[x] or the Sea Monster[y]
  that you place me under guard?
13 If I say, "My couch will comfort me,"
  my bed will diminish my murmuring.
14 You scare me with dreams,
  frighten me with visions.
15 I would choose strangling
  and death instead of my bones.
16 I reject life;[z] I don't want to live long;
  leave me alone,
    for my days are empty.

A parody of Psalm 8

17 What are human beings,
  that you exalt them,
  that you take note of them,
18 visit them each morning,
  test them every moment?

---

[t]Heb uncertain [u]Heb uncertain [v]Or *thread* [w]Heb *Sheol* [x]Heb *Yam*, a sea god [y]Heb *Tannin*, a sea dragon
[z]Heb lacks *life*.

19 Why not look away from me;
   let me alone until I swallow my spit?
20 If I sinned, what did I do to you,
   guardian of people?
   Why have you made me your target
   so that I'm a burden to myself?
21 Why not forgive my sin,
   overlook my iniquity?
   Then I would lie down in the dust;
   you would search hard for me,
   and I would not exist.

Bildad defends God

8 Bildad from Shuah responded:
2 How long will you mouth such things
   such that your utterances
   become a strong wind?
3 Does God pervert justice,
   or does the Almighty distort
   what is right?
4 If your children sinned against him,
   then he delivered them
   into the power of their rebellion.
5 If you will search eagerly for God,
   plead with the Almighty.
6 If you are pure and do the right thing,
   then surely he will become
   active on your behalf
   and reward your innocent dwelling.
7 Although your former state was ordinary,
   your future will be extraordinary.

Tradition

8 Ask a previous generation
   and verify the findings
   of your ancestors,
9 for we are only recently here
   and don't know
   because our days on earth
   are a shadow.

10 Won't they instruct you and tell you;
   will words not[a] proceed
   from their hearts?

Examples from nature

11 Does papyrus grow apart from a marsh?
   Does a reed flourish without water?
12 While still tender, uncut,
   it will wither before every other grass.
13 So are the paths of all who forget God.
   Hope perishes for the godless,
14 whose confidence is a fragile thing,[b]
   their trust, a spider's web.
15 He leans on its web, and it doesn't stand;
   grasps it, and it can't remain in place.
16 It's like a well-watered plant in the sun;
   its runners spread over its gardens.
17 Its roots are entwined over a pile of rocks,
   for it sees a home among stones.
18 If it's uprooted from its place,
   it lies, saying, "I can't see you."
19 Surely its way is a joy,
   for from the dust other plants[c] sprout.

God's faithfulness

20 Surely God won't reject integrity,
   won't strengthen the hand
   of the wicked.
21 He will still fill your mouth with joy,
   your lips with a victorious shout.
22 Those who hate you
   will be clothed with shame,
   and the tent of the wicked will vanish.

Hymnic praise

9 Job responded:
2 I know for certain that this is so;
   and how can anyone be innocent
   before God?

[a]Heb lacks *not*.   [b]Heb uncertain   [c]Heb lacks *plants*.

BILDAD

Bildad the Shuhite, Eliphaz, and Zophar are friends who gather to talk with Job in three cycles in the central poetic portion of the book. Bildad's speeches (Job 8; 18; 25) often support the view that only the wicked, not the righteous, suffer.

³ If one wants to contend with him,
  he won't answer one in a thousand.
⁴ He is wise[d] and powerful;
  who can resist him and prosper?
⁵ Who removes mountains,
  and they are unaware;
  who overthrows them in anger?
⁶ Who shakes the earth from its place,
  and its pillars shudder?
⁷ Who commands the sun,
  and it does not rise,
  even seals up the stars;
⁸ stretched out the heavens alone
  and trod on the waves of the Sea;[e]
⁹ made the Bear and Orion, Pleiades
  and the southern constellations;
¹⁰ does great and unsearchable things,
  wonders beyond number?

A mismatch
¹¹ If God goes by me, I can't see him;
  he glides past, and I can't perceive him.
¹² If he seizes, who can bring back?
  Who can say to him,
  "What are you doing?"
¹³ God won't retract his anger;
  the helpers of Rahab bow beneath him.
¹⁴ Yet I myself will answer him;
  I'll choose my words
  in a contest[f] with him.
¹⁵ Even if I'm innocent, I can't answer;
  I must plead for justice.
¹⁶ If I were to call and he answered me,
  I couldn't believe that he heard my voice.
¹⁷ Who bruises me with a tempest
  and multiplies my wounds for no reason?
¹⁸ He doesn't let me catch my breath,
  for he fills me with bitterness.
¹⁹ If the issue is strength—behold power!
  If justice—who calls God to meet me?

There is no justice
²⁰ If I'm innocent,
  my mouth condemns me;
  I have integrity;
  but God declares me perverse.
²¹ I'm blameless, yet don't know myself;
  I reject my life.
²² It's all the same;

therefore, I say God destroys
  the blameless and the sinners.
²³ If calamity suddenly kills,
  he mocks at the slaying[g] of innocents.
²⁴ The earth is handed over to the wicked;
  he covers the faces of its judges.
  If not God, then who does?

Job wants an arbitrator
²⁵ My days are swifter than a runner;
  they flee and don't experience good.
²⁶ They sweep by like ships made of reeds,
  as an eagle swoops on prey.
²⁷ If I say, "I'll forget my lament,
  put on a different face so I can smile,"
²⁸ I'm still afraid of all my suffering;
  I know that you
  won't declare me innocent.
²⁹ I myself am thought guilty;
  why have I tried so hard in vain?
³⁰ If I wash myself with snow,
  purify my hands with soap,
³¹ then you'll hurl me into a slimy pit
  so that my clothes detest me.
³² God is not a man like me—
  someone I could answer—
  so that we could come together in court.
³³ Oh, that[h] there were a mediator
  between us;
  he would lay his hand on both of us,
³⁴ remove his rod from me,
  so his fury wouldn't frighten me.
³⁵ Then I would speak—unafraid—
  for I'm not that way.

Complaint to God
10 I loathe my life; I will let loose
  my complaint;
  I will speak out of my own bitterness.
² I will say to God, Don't declare me guilty;
  tell me what you are accusing me
  of doing.
³ Does it seem good to you
  that you oppress me,
  that you reject the work of your hands
  and cause the purpose of sinners
  to shine?
⁴ Do you have physical eyes;
  do you see like a human?

---

[d]Or *wise in heart*; cf 37:24 [e]Heb *Yam*, a sea god [f]Heb lacks *in a contest*. [g]Heb uncertain [h]Or *There is no*

⁵ Are your days like those of a human,
    your years like years of a human,
 ⁶ that you search for my wrongdoing
    and seek my sin?
⁷ You know that I'm not guilty,
    yet no one delivers me from your power.

Creator
 ⁸ Your hands fashioned and made me;
    yet you want to destroy me utterly.
 ⁹ Remember that you made me from^i clay,
    and you will return me to dust.
¹⁰ Didn't you pour me out like milk,
    curdle me like cheese?
¹¹ You clothed me with skin and flesh,
    wove me from bones and sinews.
¹² Life and kindness you gave me,
    and you oversaw and preserved
      my breath.

No hiding place
¹³ These things you hid in your heart;
    I know this is the case with you.
¹⁴ If I sin and you observe me,
    you won't consider me innocent
      of wrongdoing.
¹⁵ If I were guilty, doom to me;
    I'm innocent, but can't lift my head,
      full of shame and facing my misery.

^i Or *like*   ^j Heb uncertain

¹⁶ I could boast like a lion,
    and you would hunt me;
    you would do awesome things
      to me again.
¹⁷ You continue to send your witnesses
    against me
    and increase your anger toward me,
      a swift army against me.^j

Death wish
¹⁸ Why did you let me emerge
    from the womb?
    I wish I had died
      without any eye seeing me.
¹⁹ Then I would be just as if I hadn't existed,
    taken from the belly to the grave.
²⁰ Aren't my few days coming to an end?
    Look away from me
    so I can brighten up a little
²¹ before I go and don't return
    to a land of deepest darkness,
²² a land whose light is like gloom,
    utter darkness and confusion,
    such that light shines like gloom.

Zophar's rebuke

11 Zophar from Naamah responded:
    ²Should all these words go unanswered
    or a wordy man be justified?

ZOPHAR

The name *Zophar* may come from a root meaning "to turn away." Zophar the Naamathite was one of Job's three friends who, after hearing of the disaster that had befallen him, traveled to Uz to console him (Job 2:11). Zophar is the third speaker in the three cycles of speeches offered by Job's friends (chaps. 11; 20—he offers no words in the third cycle). Zophar's speech presents a clear call for Job to repent, suggesting that he understands the cause of Job's affliction to be some form of sin in Job's life. In Job 11:13-14, Zophar attempts to convince Job to turn away from his sin and direct his heart to God. The speech of Zophar in chapter 20 judges Job more harshly. Interestingly, Zophar's words in 11:7-10 perhaps reflect some of the upcoming rebuke by God in chapter 38; it is likely these words reflect Zophar's reliance upon wisdom sayings. The conclusion of Job (42:7-9) suggests that it was Zophar (as well as Eliphaz and Bildad) who had turned Job's heart from God (speaking of him wrongly) and who needed to repent.

³ Will your idle talk silence everyone;
　　will you mock and not be put to shame?
⁴ You've said, "My teaching is pure,
　　and I'm clean in God's[k] eyes."

Divine secrecy
⁵ But oh, that God would speak,
　　open his lips against you
⁶ and tell you secrets of wisdom;
　　for sound insight has two sides.
　Know that God lets some of your sin
　　be forgotten.
⁷ Can you find the secret of God
　　or find the extent of the Almighty?
⁸ They are higher than the heavens—
　　what can you do?
　Deeper than the underworld[l]—
　　what can you know?
⁹ Its measurement is longer than the earth
　　and broader than the sea.
¹⁰ If God passes by, imprisons someone,
　　and calls a trial,
　　who can stop him?
¹¹ He knows worthless people,
　　sees sin, and certainly[m] takes note.
¹² A stupid person becomes intelligent
　　when a wild ass of a person
　　is born tame.[n]

Abiding hope
¹³ If you make your mind resolute
　　and spread your palms to him,
¹⁴ if you throw out the sin in your hands
　　and don't let injustice
　　dwell in your tents,
¹⁵ then you will lift up your face
　　without blemish;
　　you will be secure and not fear.
¹⁶ You will forget trouble;
　　you will remember it
　　as water that flows past.
¹⁷ A life span will rise brighter than noon;
　　darkness will be like morning.
¹⁸ You will be secure, for there is hope;
　　you will look around and rest safely.
¹⁹ You will lie down
　　without anyone to scare you;
　　many will beg for your favor.

²⁰ The eyes of the wicked will grow faint;
　　flight has vanished from them;
　　their hope is a dying gasp.

A living joke
12 Job responded:
² Surely you are the people,
　　and wisdom will die with you.
³ I am also intelligent;
　　I'm not inferior to you.
　Who isn't like these people?[o]
⁴ I'm a joke to friends
　　who called to God and he answered;
　　the innocent and blameless one is a joke,
⁵ a torch[p] of contempt to one who is idle,
　　a fixed point for slipping feet.

Proverbial wisdom
⁶ Raiders' tents are prosperous
　　and God's provokers secure,
　　who carry God in their hands.[q]
⁷ But ask Behemoth, and he will teach you,
　　the birds in the sky, and they will tell you;
⁸ or talk to earth, and it will teach you;
　　the fish of the sea will recount it for you.
⁹ Among all these, who hasn't known
　　that the LORD's hand did this?
¹⁰ In whose grasp is the life of every thing,
　　the breath of every person?
¹¹ Doesn't the ear test words
　　and the palate taste food?
¹² "In old age is wisdom;
　　understanding in a long life."

God's majesty
¹³ With him are wisdom and power;
　　counsel and understanding are his.
¹⁴ If he tears down, it can't be rebuilt;
　　if he ties a person up,
　　he can't be set free.
¹⁵ If he restricts water, they have drought;
　　if he lets it loose, it overturns the land.
¹⁶ With him are might and success;
　　the deceiver and the deceived are his.
¹⁷ He leads advisors away barefoot;
　　makes madmen of judges;
¹⁸ unties the belt of kings,
　　binds a garment around their loins;

---

[k]Or *your*　[l]Heb *Sheol*　[m]Or *does not*　[n]Or *a wild ass's colt can be born a man*　[o]Heb lacks *people.*　[p]Heb uncertain
[q]Heb uncertain

¹⁹ leads priests away barefoot;
   overthrows the well-established;
²⁰ silences the talk of trusted people;
   takes away elders' discernment;
²¹ pours contempt on royalty;
   loosens the belt of the strong;
²² discloses deep secrets of darkness,
   makes utter darkness enter the light;
²³ makes nations prominent
   and destroys them,
   expands nations and leads them astray;
²⁴ takes away the power to think
   from earth's leaders,
   making them wander
   in untraveled wastelands.
²⁵ They feel their way
   in the dark without light;
   he makes them stumble like drunks.

Self-defense

13 Look, my eye has seen it all;
   my ear has heard and understood it.
² Just as you know, I also know;
   I'm not inferior to you.
³ But I want to speak to the Almighty;
   I would gladly present my case to God.

Friends attacked

⁴ You, however, are plasterers of lies;
   ineffective healers, all of you.
⁵ Would that you were completely quiet;
   that would be your wisdom.
⁶ Hear my teaching
   and pay attention to the arguments
   of my lips.
⁷ Will you speak injustice for God,
   speak deceit on his behalf?
⁸ Will you be partial
   or contend for God?
⁹ Will it go well when he searches you,
   or can you fool him
   as you fool people?
¹⁰ He will certainly correct you
   if you've been secretly partial.
¹¹ Wouldn't his majesty scare you
   and dread of him fall on you?
¹² Your old sayings are proverbs
   made of ashes,
   your sayings defenses made of clay.

Job will speak out

¹³ Be quiet and I will speak,
   come what may.
¹⁴ For what reason will I take my flesh
   in my teeth,
   put my life in jeopardy?
¹⁵ He will slay me; I'm without hope;ʳ
   I will surely prove my way to his face.
¹⁶ Also this will be my vindication,
   that a godless person
   won't come before him.
¹⁷ Listen closely to my words
   so that my remarks will be in your ears.

Against God

¹⁸ Look, I have laid out my case;
   I know that I'm innocent.
¹⁹ Who would dare contend with me,
   for then I would be quiet and die.
²⁰ Only don't do two things to me,
   then I won't hide from your face.
²¹ Remove your hand far from me
   and don't terrify me with your anger.
²² Then call and I'll answer,
   or I'll speak and you can reply.
²³ How many are my offenses and sins?
   Inform me about my rebellions and sins.
²⁴ Why hide your face from me
   and consider me your enemy?
²⁵ Will you cause a wind-tossed leaf to
   tremble, or will you pursue dry straw?
²⁶ You even write bitter things about me,
   make me inherit
   my youthful indiscretions.
²⁷ You tie up my feet and restrict all actions;
   you stamp marks
   on the bottom of my feet.

Human destiny

²⁸ Surely a person wastes away like refuse,
   like clothing that a moth eats.

14 All of usˢ are born of women,
   have few days, and are full of turmoil.
² Like a flower, weᵗ bloom, then wither,
   flee like a shadow, and don't last.
(³ Yes, you open your eyes on this one;
   you bring me into trial against you.)
⁴ Who can make pure from impure?
   Nobody.

ʳOr *Though he slay me, yet I will trust him.*   ˢHeb *adam*   ᵗOr *he; also he in 14:5-6*

5 If our days are fixed,
  the number of our months with you,
  you set a statute and we can't exceed it.
6 Look away from us that we may rest,
  until we are satisfied
  like a worker at day's end.

Trees versus humans

7 Indeed there is hope for a tree.
  If it's cut down and still sprouting
  and its shoots don't fail,
8 if its roots age in the ground
  and its stump dies in the dust,
9 at the scent of water, it will bud
  and produce sprouts like a plant.
10 But a human dies and lies there;
  a person expires, and where is he?
11 Water vanishes from the sea;
  a river dries up completely.
12 But a human lies down and doesn't rise
  until the heavens cease;
  they don't get up and awaken from sleep.

Momentary hope

13 I wish you would hide me
  in the underworld,[u]
  conceal me until your anger passes,
  set a time for me, and remember me.
14 If people die, will they live again?
  All the days of my service I would wait
  until my restoration took place.
15 You would call, and I would answer you;
  you would long for your handiwork.
16 Though you now number my steps,
  you would not keep a record of my sin.

[u]Heb Sheol

17 My rebellion is sealed in a bag;
  you would cover my sin.

God crushes hope

18 But an eroding mountain breaks up,
  and rock is displaced.
19 Water wears away boulders;
  floods carry away soil;
  you destroy a people's hope.
20 You overpower them relentlessly,
  and they die;
  you change their appearance
  and send them away.
21 Their children achieve honor,
  and they don't know it;
  their children become insignificant,
  and they don't see it.
22 They only feel the pain of their body,
  and they mourn for themselves.

Job's intelligence questioned

15 Eliphaz answered:
2 Will the wise respond
  with windy knowledge
  and fill their belly with the east wind?
3 Will they argue with a word
  that has no benefit
  and with unprofitable words?
4 You are truly making religion ineffective
  and restraining meditation before God.
5 Your mouth multiplies your sins
  a thousand times;
  you opt for a clever tongue.
6 Your mouth condemns you, not I;
  your lips argue against you.

OLIVE/OLIVE TREE

The olive is perhaps the most important plant mentioned in the Bible. Olive trees typify the Holy Land and adjacent territories (cf. the description of the land of promise in Deut 8:8).

The olive tree is a medium-sized orchard tree with a lifespan of hundreds of years. Its knobby trunk may become massive and hollow with age while it still has leafy branches. When olive trees are felled, they sprout again (see Job 14:7-9), and the shoots may be seen around the base like children around a table (cf. Ps 128:3).

7 Were you born the first Adam,
   brought forth before the hills?
8 Did you listen in God's council;
   is wisdom limited to you?
9 What do you know that we don't know;
   what do you understand
      that isn't among us?
10 Both the graybeard and the aged
   are with us;
      those much older than your father.
11 Are God's comforts not enough for you,
   a word spoken gently with you?
12 Why has your mind seized you,
   why have your eyes flashed,
13 so that you return your breath to God
   and utter such words from your mouth?
14 What are humans
   that they might be pure,
      and those born of woman
      that they might be innocent?
15 If he doesn't trust his holy ones
   and the heavens aren't pure in his eyes,
16 how much less those who are
   abominable and corrupt,
      for they drink sin like water.

The wicked's downfall

17 Listen to me; I will argue with you;
   what I've seen, I will declare to you;
18 what the wise have told and have not
   concealed from their family,
19 to whom alone the earth was given
   and no stranger passed in their midst.
20 All the days of the wicked are painful;
   the number of years reserved
      for the hateful;
21 a sound of terror pierces^v their ears;
   when safe, raiders overtake them.
22 They can't count on turning away
   from darkness;
      they are destined for a sword.
23 They wander about for bread.
   "Where is it?"
      They know that their day of darkness
      is fixed.
24 Adversity and stress scare them,
   master them like a king ready to strike;
25 for they raise a fist against God
   and try to overpower the Almighty.

26 They run toward him aggressively,
   with a massive and strong shield.
27 They cover their face with grease
   and make their loins gross.
28 They lived in ruined cities,
   unoccupied houses that turn to rubble.
29 They won't get rich;
   their wealth won't last;
      their property won't extend
      over the earth.
30 They can't turn away from darkness;
   a flame will dry out their shoots,
      and they will be taken away
      by the wind from his mouth.
31 They shouldn't trust in what
   has no worth,
      for their reward will be worthless.
32 Before their branch is formed,
   before it is green,
33 like the vine,
   they will drop early grapes
      and cast off their blossoms
      like the olive.
34 The ruthless gang is barren,
   and fire consumes the tents of bribers.
35 They conceive toil
   and give birth to sorrow;
      their belly establishes deceit.

Job's response

16 Then Job answered:
   2 I've heard many things like these.
   All of you are sorry comforters.
3 Will windy talk ever cease;
   what bothers you that you must argue?
4 In your situation I could speak like you;
   I could put words together
      to oppose you,
      shake my head over you.
5 I could heap up words,
   strengthen you with my speech;
      my trembling lips
      would be held in check.
6 If I speak, my pain is not eased;
   if I hold back, what have I lost?

The innocent are God's targets

7 Now God has surely worn me out.
   You have destroyed my entire group,

---

^v Heb lacks *pierces*.

⁸ seized me, which became grounds
  for an accusation.ʷ
My leanness rises to bear witness
  against me.
⁹ His anger tears me and afflicts me;
  he slashes at me with his teeth.
My enemy pierces me with his eyes.
¹⁰ They open their mouths at me
  and strike my cheek in a taunt;
  they gang up on me.
¹¹ God delivers me to a criminal
  and forces me into the hands
  of the wicked.
¹² I was at rest, but he shattered me,
  seized me by the back of my neck,
  dashed me into pieces;
  he raised me up for his target.
¹³ His archers surround me;
  he cuts my kidneys open without pity
  and doesn't care,
  pours my gall on the ground,
¹⁴ bursts me open over and over,
  runs against me like a strong man.
¹⁵ I've sewed rough cloth over my skin
  and buried my dignity in the dust.
¹⁶ My face is red from crying,
  and dark gloom hangs on my eyelids.
¹⁷ But there is no violence in my hands,
  and my prayer is pure.

Lingering hope

¹⁸ Earth, don't cover my blood;
  let my outcry never cease.
¹⁹ Surely now my witness stands in heaven;
  my advocate is on high;
²⁰ my go-between, my friend.ˣ
While my eyes drip tears to God,
²¹ let him plead with God
  for a human being,
  like a person pleads for a friend.
²² A number of years will surely pass,
  and then I'll walk a path
  that I won't return.

Another lament

17 My spirit is broken,
  my days extinguished,
  the grave,ʸ mine.
² Surely mockers are with me,

and my eye looks on their rebellion.
³ Take my guarantee.
  Who else is willing
  to make an agreement?
⁴ You've closed their mind to insight;
  therefore, you won't be exalted.
⁵ He denounces his friends for gain,
  and his children's eyes fail.
⁶ He makes me a popular proverb;
  I'm like spit in people's faces.
⁷ My eye is weak from grief;
  my limbs like a shadow—all of them.
⁸ Those who do the right thing
  are amazed at this;
  the guiltless become troubled
  about the godless.
⁹ The innocent clings to his way;
  the one whose hands are clean
  grows stronger.
¹⁰ But you can bring all of them again,
  and I won't find
  a wise one among you.
¹¹ My days have passed;
  my goals are destroyed,
  my heart's desires.
¹² They turn night into day;
  light is near because of the darkness.
¹³ If I hope for the underworldᶻ
  as my dwelling,
  lay out my bed in darkness,
¹⁴ I've called corruption "my father,"
  the worm, "my mother and sister."
¹⁵ Where then is my hope?
  My hope—who can see it?
¹⁶ Will they go down with me
  to the underworld;ᵃ
  will we descend together to the dust?

Attack from a friend

18 Bildad from Shuah answered:
² How long?
  Would you all stop talking.
  Try to understand
  and then we can speak.
³ Why are we considered beasts,
  ignorant in your sight?
⁴ To you who tear yourself in rage—
  will earth be forsaken for your sake,
  a rock be dislodged from its place?

ʷHeb uncertain ˣGo-between and friend are plural in Heb. ʸOr graves ᶻHeb Sheol ᵃHeb Sheol

Evil people's fate

⁵ To be sure, the light of the wicked
      goes out;
   the blaze of their fire doesn't shine.
⁶ The light in their tent becomes dark,
   and their lamp above doesn't shine.
⁷ Their strong strides slow down;
   their plans trip themselves.
⁸ They are caught by their feet in a net;
   they walk on mesh.
⁹ A trap grabs them by the heel;
   a snare tightens on them.
¹⁰ A rope is hidden on the ground for them;
   a trap for them along the path.
¹¹ Terrors round about scare them;
   they follow their steps.
¹² Their offspring hunger;
   calamity is ready for their spouses.
¹³ It eats some of their skin.
   Death's firstborn consumes their limbs.
¹⁴ They are snatched from the safety
      of their tent;
   it parades them
      before the king of terrors.
¹⁵ Nothing they own remains in their tent;
   sulfur is scattered over their home.
¹⁶ Their roots dry out below;
   their branches wither above.
¹⁷ The memory of them will perish
      from the earth;
   they will achieve no recognition abroad.
¹⁸ They are thrust from light into darkness,
   banished from the world.
¹⁹ They have no offspring or descendants
      among their people,
   no survivor in their dwelling place.
²⁰ Their successors are appalled at what
      happens to them;
   their predecessors pull their hair.
²¹ These are surely the dwelling places
      of the evil;
   this is the place of the one
      who doesn't know God.

Failed friendship

19 Then Job responded:
   ² How long will you harass me
      and crush me with words?
³ These ten times you've humiliated me;
   shamelessly you insult me.

⁴ Have I really gone astray?
   If so, my error remains hidden
      inside me.
⁵ If you look down on me
   and use my disgrace to criticize me,
⁶ know then that God has wronged me
   and enclosed his net over me.

God's treatment of Job

⁷ If I cry "Violence!" I'm not answered;
   I shout—but there is no justice.
⁸ He walled up my path so I can't pass
   and put darkness on my trail,
⁹ stripped my honor from me,
   removed the crown from my head,
¹⁰ tore me down completely so that I'll
   die, and uprooted my hope like a tree.
¹¹ His anger burns against me;
   he considers me his enemy.
¹² His troops come as one
   and construct their siege ramp[b]
      against me;
   they camp around my tent.

Social ostracism

¹³ He has distanced my family from me;
   my acquaintances are also alienated
      from me.
¹⁴ My visitors have ceased;
   those who know me have forgotten me.
¹⁵ My guests and female servants
   think me a stranger;
   I'm a foreigner in their sight.
¹⁶ I call my servant, and he doesn't answer;
   I myself must beg him.
¹⁷ My breath stinks to my wife;
   I am odious to my children.
¹⁸ Even the young despise me;
   I get up, and they rail against me.
¹⁹ All my closest friends despise me;
   the ones I have loved turn against me.

Misery

²⁰ My bones cling to my skin and flesh;
   I have escaped by the skin of my teeth.
²¹ Pity me. Pity me. You're my friends.
   God's hand has truly struck me.
²² Why do you pursue me like God does,
   always hungry for my flesh?

---

[b]Or *their road*

Brief hope

23 Oh, that my words were written down,
 inscribed on a scroll
24 with an iron instrument and lead,
 forever engraved on stone.
25 But I know that my redeemer[c] is alive
 and afterward he'll rise upon the dust.
26 After my skin has been torn apart
 this way—
 then from my flesh[d] I'll see God,
 27 whom I'll see myself—
 my eyes see,[e] and not a stranger's.
 I am utterly dejected.

Warning

28 You say, "How will we pursue him
 so that the root of the matter can be
 found in him?"[f]
29 You ought to fear the sword yourselves,
 for wrath brings punishment
 by the sword.
 You should know that there is judgment.

Traditional belief

20 Zophar from Naamah said:
2 Therefore, my troubled thoughts
 make me turn back—
 because of my inner turmoil.
3 I hear teaching that insults me,
 but I am forced to answer based
 on my own understanding.[g]
4 Do you know this from long ago—
 from when humans were placed
 on earth—
 5 that the rejoicing of the wicked is short,
 the joy of the godless, brief?
6 Though their height reaches heaven
 and their heads touch the clouds,
7 they will perish forever like their dung;
 those who saw them will say,
 "Where are they?"
8 They will disappear like a dream,
 and none will find them,
 carried away like a nighttime vision.
9 The eye that saw them will do so no more;
 they won't be seen again at home.
10 Their children will repay the poor;
 their hands will give back their wealth.

11 Vigor filled their bones
 and now sleeps with them in the dust.
12 Though wickedness is sweet
 in their mouths,
 they hide it under their tongues;
13 they like it, won't let it go;
 they hold it in their cheeks.
14 Food turns their stomachs,
 becoming a cobra's poison inside.
15 They swallow wealth and vomit it;
 God dislodges it from their belly.
16 They suck cobra's poison;
 a viper's tongue kills them.
17 They won't experience streams,
 rivers of honey, and brooks of cream.
18 They won't receive the reward
 for their labor;
 they won't enjoy the wealth
 from their business.
19 They crushed and abandoned the poor;
 stole a house they didn't build;
20 didn't know contentment in their belly;
 couldn't escape with their treasure.
21 Nothing remained of their food,
 so their riches will not endure.
22 Even in their plenty,
 they are hard-pressed;
 all sorts of trouble come on them.
23 Let God[h] fill their belly,
 unleash his burning anger on them,
 rain punishing blows on them.
24 If they flee an iron weapon,
 a bronze bow pierces them.
25 They pull it out,
 but it sticks out from their backs;
 its shaft in their liver brings terror.
26 Complete darkness waits for their
 treasured possessions;
 fire that no one stoked consumes them;
 what's left in their tent is ruined.
27 Heaven exposes their guilt;
 earth opposes them.
28 Their household wealth
 will be carried off
 by rushing streams on the day
 of his anger.
29 This is a wicked person's lot from God,
 their heritage decreed by God.

[c]Or avenger [d]Or without my flesh or in my flesh [e]Or have seen [f]Heb manuscripts; MT in me [g]Heb uncertain
[h]Or him

Grant me a hearing

21 Then Job answered:
² Listen carefully to my remarks
   and let that comfort you.
³ Bear with me so I can speak, I myself;
   and after my reply you can mock.
⁴ Are my complaints against
   another human;
   why is my patience short?
⁵ Turn to me and be appalled;
   lay your hand over your mouth.
⁶ If I recall it, I'm scared;
   shaking seizes my body.

The success of the wicked

⁷ Why do the wicked live,
   grow old, and even become strong?
⁸ Their children are always with them,
   their offspring in their sight,
⁹ their houses safe from dread,
   God's punishing stick not upon them.
¹⁰ Their bull always breeds successfully;
   their cows give birth and never miscarry.
¹¹ They send forth their little ones like sheep;
   their infants bounce around.
¹² They raise drum and lyre,
   rejoice at the sound of a flute.
¹³ They spend their days contentedly,
   go down to the grave^i peacefully.
¹⁴ They say to God, "Turn away from us;
   we take no pleasure in
   knowing your ways;
¹⁵ who is the Almighty^j
   that we should serve him,
   and what can we gain if we meet him?"
¹⁶ Look, isn't their well-being the work
   of their own hands?
   A sinner's logic is beyond me.

Desired vindication

¹⁷ How often does the lamp
   of the wicked flicker
   or disaster come upon them,
   with its fury inflicting pain on them?
¹⁸ Let them be like straw in the wind,
   like dry grass stolen by a storm.
¹⁹ God stores up his punishment
   for his children.
   Let him destroy them so they know.

²⁰ Let their own eyes witness their doom.
   Let them drink
   from the Almighty's wrath.
²¹ What do they care about their household
   after they die,
   when their numbered days are cut off?

A common fate

²² Will they instruct God—
   he who judges the most powerful?
²³ Someone dies in wonderful health,
   completely comfortable and well,
²⁴ their buckets full of milk,
   their bones marrow-filled and sound.
²⁵ Another dies in bitter spirit,
   never having tasted the good things.
²⁶ They lie together in the dust
   and worms cover them.

Further disagreement

²⁷ Look, I know your thoughts;
   your plans harm me.
²⁸ You say, "Where is the official's house?
   Where is the tent,
   the dwelling of the wicked?"
²⁹ Haven't you asked travelers
   or paid attention to their reports?
³⁰ On the day of disaster
   the wicked are spared;
   on the day of fury they are rescued.
³¹ Who can criticize their behavior
   to their faces;
   they act, and who can avenge them?
³² They are carried to their graves;
   someone keeps guard over their tombs.
³³ The soil near the desert streambed
   is sweet to them;
   everyone marches after them—
   those before them, beyond counting.
³⁴ How empty is your comfort to me;
   only deceit remains in your responses.

Job's sins

22 Then Eliphaz from Teman answered:
² Can a human being
   be useful to God?
   Can an intelligent person bring profit?
³ Does the Almighty delight
   in your innocence?

---

^i Heb *Sheol* ^j Heb *Shaddai* or *Mountain One*

Does he gain
   when you perfect your ways?
⁴ Does he rebuke you for your piety,
   bring you in for judgment?
⁵ Isn't your wickedness massive,
   your iniquity endless?
⁶ You have taken payments from your
   family for no reason;
   stripped the naked, leaving no clothes;
  ⁷ denied water to the thirsty,
   withheld bread from the starving.
(⁸ The powerful own land;
   the favored live in it.)
⁹ You have sent widows away empty;
   crushed orphans' resources.
¹⁰ For this reason, snares surround you;
   sudden dread brings panic to you
  ¹¹ or a darkness that you can't see;
   rushing water will cover you.

God's activity

¹² Isn't God in the heights of heaven;
   see how high the topmost stars are?
¹³ You say: "What does God know?
   Can he judge through thick clouds?
¹⁴ Clouds conceal him so he can't see
   while he walks on heaven's rim."
¹⁵ Will you keep the ancient way
   traveled by sinful persons,
¹⁶ who were snatched prematurely
   when a river flooded their foundations,
¹⁷ who say to God, "Turn away from us;
   what can the Almighty do to us?"
¹⁸ Yet he filled their houses
   with good things;
   a sinner's logic is beyond me.
¹⁹ The righteous see and rejoice;
   the innocent mock them:

²⁰ our enemies are certainly cut off;
   fire will devour what's left of them.

Turn to God

²¹ Get along well with God and be at peace;
   from this something good
    will come to you.
²² Receive instruction from his mouth;
   put his words in your mind.
²³ If you return to the Almighty,ᵏ
   you will be restored;
   if you keep wrongdoing out
    of your tent.
²⁴ Lay your prized possession in the dust,
   your gold from Ophir on a rock
    in a desert streambed.
²⁵ The Almighty will be your
   prized possession,
   silver piled up for you.
²⁶ Then you will take pleasure
   in the Almighty;
   lift up your face to God.
²⁷ You will pray to him,
   and he will hear you;
   you will fulfill your solemn promises.
²⁸ If you decree something, it will stand;
   light will shine on your ways.
²⁹ When they're humbled, you will say:
   "Cheer up;
   God will rescue the lowly.
³⁰ He will deliver the guilty;
   they will be saved by your pure hands."

Grant me a trial

23 Job answered:
²Today my complaint is again bitter;ˡ
   my strength is weighed down
   because of my groaning.

ᵏHeb *Shaddai* or *Mountain One*; also in 22:25 and 24:1 ˡVulg, Syr, Tg; MT *my complaint is rebellious.*

ELIPHAZ

One of Job's three friends who argue with him about why he is suffering and whether God is just. Eliphaz is always listed first among the three friends, is the first to speak to Job in each of the three cycles (Job 4; 15; 22), and is the only one of the three friends whom God addresses directly (Job 42:7). He is called Eliphaz the Temanite, which connects him with the area of Edom.

3 Oh, that I could know how to find him—
   come to his dwelling place;
4 I would lay out my case before him,
   fill my mouth with arguments,
5 know the words
   with which he would answer,
   understand what he would say to me.
6 Would he contend with me
   through brute force?
   No, he would surely listen to me.
7 There those who do the right thing can
   argue with him;
   I could escape from my judge forever.

God's hiddenness

8 Look, I go east; he's not there,
   west, and don't discover him;
9 north in his activity,
   and I don't grasp him;
   he turns south, and I don't see.
10 Surely he knows my way;
   when he tests me,
   I will emerge as gold.
11 My feet have stayed right in his tracks.
   I have kept his way and not left it,
12 kept the commandments from his lips
   and not departed,
   valued the words from his mouth
   more than my food.

Dread

13 He is of one mind; who can reverse it?
   What he desires, he does.
14 He carries out what is decreed for me
   and can do many similar things with me.
15 Therefore, I am scared by his presence;
   I think and become afraid of him.
16 God has weakened my mind;
   the Almighty has frightened me.
17 Still I'm not annihilated by darkness;
   he has hidden deep darkness from me.

Absence of justice

24 Why doesn't the Almighty establish
   times for punishment?[m]
   Why can't those who know him
   see his days?
2 People move boundary stones,
   herd flocks they've stolen,

3 drive off an orphan's donkey,
   take a widow's ox as collateral,
4 thrust the poor out of the way,
   make the land's needy hide together.
5 They are like the wild donkeys
   in the desert;
   they go forth at dawn searching for prey;
   the wasteland is food for their young.
6 They gather their food in the field,
   glean in unproductive vineyards,
7 spend the night naked, unclothed,
   in the cold without a cover,
8 wet from mountain rains,
   with no refuge,
   huddled against a rock.
9 The orphan is stolen from the breast;
   the infant[n] of the poor
   is taken as collateral.
10 The poor go around naked,
   without clothes,
   carry bundles of grain while hungry,
11 crush olives between millstones,[o]
   tread winepresses, but remain thirsty.
12 From the city, the dying cry out;
   the throat of the mortally wounded
   screams, but God assigns no blame.

Sinners' conduct

13 They rebel against light,
   don't acknowledge its direction,
   don't dwell in its paths.
14 The murderer rises at twilight,
   kills the poor and needy;
   at night, they are like a thief.
15 The adulterer's eye watches for twilight,
   thinking, No eye can see me,
   and puts a mask over his face.
16 In the dark they break into houses;
   they shut themselves in by day;
   they don't know the light.
17 Deep darkness is morning to them
   because they recognize the horror
   of darkness.
18 They are scum on the water's surface;
   their portion of the land is cursed;
   no one walks down a path
   in the vineyards.
19 Drought and heat steal melted snow,
   just as the underworld[p] steals sinners.

---

[m]Heb lacks *for punishment.* [n]Reading Heb *we'ul (infant)* for *we'al (against)* [o]Heb uncertain [p]Heb *Sheol*

²⁰ The womb forgets them;
the worm consumes them;
they aren't remembered,
and so wickedness is shattered
like a tree.
²¹ They prey on the barren, the childless,
do nothing good for the widow.
²² They drag away the strong by force;
they may get up
but without guarantee of survival.
²³ They make themselves secure;
they are at ease.
His^q eyes are on their ways.

²⁴ They are exalted for a short time,
but no longer.
They are humbled then gathered in
like everyone else;
cut off like heads of grain.
²⁵ If this isn't so, who can prove me a liar
and make my words disappear?

Inferior humans

25 Bildad from Shuah replied:
² Supreme power and awe
belong to God;
he establishes peace on his heights.
³ Can his troops be counted?
On whom does his light not rise?
⁴ How can a person be innocent before God;
one born of a woman be pure?
⁵ If even the moon is not bright
and the stars not pure in his eyes,
⁶ how much less a human, a worm,
a person's child, a grub.

Sarcasm

26 Then Job said:
² How well you have helped the weak,
saved those with frail arms,
³ advised one lacking wisdom,
informed many with insight!
⁴ With whom have you spoken,^r
whose breath was expelled from you?

Truth about God

⁵ The dead writhe,
the inhabitants beneath the waters
as well.

⁶ The grave^s is naked before God;
the underworld^t lacks covering.
⁷ He stretched the North^u over chaos,
hung earth over nothing;
⁸ wrapped up water in his clouds,
yet they didn't burst out below;
⁹ hid the face of the full moon,^v
spreading his cloud over it;
¹⁰ traced a circle on the water's surface,
at the limit of light and darkness.
¹¹ Heaven's pillars shook,
terrified by his blast.
¹² By his power he stilled the Sea;
split Rahab with his cleverness.
¹³ Due to his wind, heaven became clear;
his hand split the fleeing serpent.
¹⁴ Look, these are only the outer fringe
of his ways;
we hear only a whispered word
about him.
Who can understand
his thunderous power?

Job rejects Bildad's argument

27 Then Job took up his topic again:
² As God lives,
who rejected my legal claim,
the Almighty, who made me bitter,
³ as long as breath is in me
and God's breath is in my nostrils—
⁴ my lips will utter no wickedness;
my tongue will mumble no deceit.
⁵ I will not agree that you are right.
Until my dying day,
I won't give up my integrity.
⁶ I will insist on my innocence,
never surrendering it;
my conscience will never blame me
for what I have done.^w

Job curses his enemies

⁷ Let my enemy be like the wicked,
my opposition like the vicious.
⁸ For what hope has the godless
when God cuts them off,
when he takes them away.
⁹ Will God hear their cries
when distress comes to them;

�q Or *God's*   ʳ Or *told words*   ˢ Heb *Sheol*   ᵗ Heb *Abaddon*   ᵘ Heb *Zaphon*   ᵛ Or *throne*; Heb uncertain   ʷ Or *for my days*

¹⁰ will they delight in the Almighty,
   call God at any time?

Job's view of his enemies' fate

¹¹ I will teach you God's power,
   not hide what pertains to the Almighty.
¹² Look, those of you
   who recognize this—
   why then this empty talk?
¹³ This is the wicked's portion with God,
   the inheritance that the ruthless
   receive from the Almighty.
¹⁴ If their children increase,
   they belong to the sword;
   their offspring
   won't have enough bread.
¹⁵ Their survivors will be buried
   with the dead;
   their widows won't weep.
¹⁶ If they store up silver like dust,
   amass clothing like clay,
¹⁷ they may amass,
   but the righteous will wear it;
   the innocent will divide the silver.
¹⁸ They built their houses like nests,
   like a hut made by a watchman.
¹⁹ They lie down rich, but no longer;
   open their eyes, but it's missing.
²⁰ Terrors overtake them like waters;
   a tempest snatches them by night;
²¹ an east wind lifts them,
   and they are gone,
   removes them from their places,
²² throws itself on them without mercy;
   they flee desperately from its force.
²³ It claps its hands over them,
   hisses at them from their place.

Expertise in mining

28 There is a sure source of silver,
   a place where gold is refined.
² Iron is taken from the earth;
   rock is smelted into copper.
³ Humans^x put an end to darkness,
   dig for ore to the farthest depths,
   into stone in utter darkness,
⁴ open a shaft away from any inhabitant,
   places forgotten by those on foot,
   apart from any human
   they hang and sway.
⁵ Earth—from it comes food—
   is turned over below ground as by fire.^y
⁶ Its rocks are the source for lapis lazuli;
   there is gold dust in it.
⁷ A path—
   no bird of prey knows it;
   a hawk's eye hasn't seen it;
⁸ proud beasts haven't trodden on it;
   a lion hasn't crossed over it.
⁹ Humans thrust their hands into flint,
   pull up mountains from their roots,
¹⁰ cut channels into rocks;
   their eyes see everything precious.
¹¹ They dam up the sources of rivers;
   hidden things come to light.

Wisdom's value

¹² But wisdom, where can it be found;
   where is the place of understanding?
¹³ Humankind doesn't know its value;
   it isn't found in the land of the living.
¹⁴ The Deep^z says, "It's not with me";
   the Sea^a says, "Not alongside me!"
¹⁵ It can't be bought with gold;
   its price can't be measured in silver,

^xOr *they* ^yHeb uncertain ^zHeb *Tehom*, a reference to a divine being in the grave or underworld ^aHeb *Yam*, a sea god

ABADDON

"Destruction." In the OT, it refers to the underworld (Job 26:6; 28:22; 31:12; Ps 88:11; Prov 15:11; 27:20). In the NT, it is personified as Apollyon, the angel of the bottomless pit who is the king over the demonic locusts of Revelation 9:3-11. In late Jewish literature it came to be known as the place in Sheol for the punishment of the wicked.

¹⁶ can't be weighed against gold
from Ophir,
with precious onyx or lapis lazuli.
¹⁷ Neither gold nor glass
can compare with it;
she can't be acquired with gold jewelry.
¹⁸ Coral and jasper shouldn't be mentioned;
the price of wisdom is more than rubies.
¹⁹ Cushite topaz won't compare with her;
she can't be set alongside pure gold.
²⁰ But wisdom, where does she come from?
Where is the place of understanding?
²¹ She's hidden from the eyes
of all the living,
concealed from birds of the sky.
²² Destruction^b and Death have said,
"We've heard a report of her."
²³ God understands her way;
he knows her place;
²⁴ for he looks to the ends of the earth
and surveys everything
beneath the heavens.
²⁵ In order to weigh the wind,
to prepare a measure for waters,
²⁶ when he made a decree for the rain,
a path for thunderbolts,
²⁷ then he observed it, spoke of it,
established it, searched it out,
²⁸ and said to humankind: "Look,
the fear of the LORD is wisdom;
turning from evil is understanding."

Job's previous blessing

29 Job took up his subject again:
² Oh, that life was like it used to be,
like days when God watched over me;
³ when his lamp shone on my head,
I walked by his light in the dark;
⁴ when I was in my prime;
when God's counsel was in my tent;
⁵ when the Almighty was with me,
my children around me;
⁶ when my steps were washed with cream
and a rock poured out
pools of oil for me.

Previous honor

⁷ When I went out to the city gate,
took my seat in the square,

⁸ the young saw me and drew back;
the old rose and stood;
⁹ princes restrained speech,
put their hand on their mouth;
¹⁰ the voices of officials were hushed,
their tongue stuck to their palate.

Job's implementation of justice

¹¹ Indeed, the ear that heard blessed me;
the eye that looked commended me,
¹² because I rescued the weak
who cried out,
the orphans who lacked help.
¹³ The blessing of the perishing reached me;
I made the widow's heart sing;
¹⁴ I put on justice, and it clothed me,
righteousness as my coat and turban;
¹⁵ I was eyes to the blind,
feet to the lame.
¹⁶ I was a father to the needy;
the case I didn't know, I examined.
¹⁷ I shattered the fangs of the wicked,
rescued prey from their teeth.

Job's expected blessing

¹⁸ I thought, I'll die in my nest,
multiply days like sand,^c
¹⁹ my roots opening to water,
dew lingering on my branches,
²⁰ my honor newly with me,
my bow ever successful in my hand.

Previous honor

²¹ People listened to me and waited,
were silent for my advice.
²² After my speech, they didn't respond.
My words fell gently on them;
²³ they waited for me as for rain,
opened their mouth as for spring rain.
²⁴ I smiled^d on them;
they couldn't believe it.
They never showed me disfavor.
²⁵ I decided their path, sat as chief.
I lived like a king with his troops,
like one who comforts mourners.

Mockers

30 But now
those younger than I mock me,

^bHeb *Abaddon* ^cHeb uncertain ^dOr *laughed at*

whose fathers I refused
　　to put beside my sheepdogs.
² Their strength, what's it to me,
　　their energy having perished?
³ Stiff from want and hunger,
　　those who gnaw dry ground,
　　yesterday's desolate waste,
⁴ who pluck off the leaves on a bush,
　　the root of the broom—
　　a shrub is their food.
⁵ People banish them from society,
　　shout at them as if to a thief;
⁶ so they live in scary ravines,
　　holes in the ground and rocks.
⁷ Among shrubs, they make sounds
　　like donkeys;
　　they are huddled together under a bush,
⁸ children of fools and the nameless,
　　whipped out of the land.

Specific mocking behavior

⁹ And now I'm their song;
　　I'm their cliché!
¹⁰ They detest me, keep their distance,
　　don't withhold spit from my face.
¹¹ Because he loosened my bowstring
　　and afflicted me,
　　they throw off restraint in my presence.
¹² On the right, upstarts^e rise
　　and target my feet,
　　build their siege ramps against me,
¹³ destroy my road, profit from my fall,
　　with no help.
¹⁴ They advance as if through
　　a destroyed wall;^f
　　they roll along beneath the ruin.
¹⁵ Terrors crash upon me;
　　they sweep away my honor like wind;
　　my safety disappears like a cloud.

Accusation against God

¹⁶ Now my life is poured out on me;
　　days of misery have seized me.
¹⁷ At night he bores my bones;
　　my gnawing pain won't rest.
¹⁸ With great force he grasps^g my clothing;^h
　　it binds me like the neck of my shirt.
¹⁹ He hurls me into mud;
　　I'm a cliché, like dust and ashes.

²⁰ I cry to you, and you don't answer;
　　I stand up, but you just look at me.
²¹ You are cruel to me,
　　attack me with the strength
　　of your hand.
²² You lift me to the wind
　　and make me ride;
　　you melt me in its roar.
²³ I know you will return me to death,
　　the house appointed for all the living.

Job's agony

²⁴ Surely he won't strike someone in ruins
　　if in distress he cries out to him,
²⁵ if I didn't weep for those
　　who have a difficult day
　　or my soul grieve for the needy;
²⁶ for I awaited good, but evil came;
　　I expected light, but gloom arrived.
²⁷ My insides, churning, are never quiet;
　　days of affliction confront me.
²⁸ I walk in the dark, lacking sunshine;
　　I rise in the assembly and cry out.
²⁹ I have become a brother to jackals,
　　a companion to young ostriches.
³⁰ My skin is charred;
　　my bones are scorched by the heat.
³¹ My lyre is for mourning,
　　my flute, a weeping sound.

Lust

31 I've made a covenant with my eyes;
　　how could I look at a virgin?
² What is God's portion for me^i from above,
　　the Almighty's inheritance
　　from on high?
³ Isn't it disaster for the wicked,
　　destruction for workers of iniquity?
⁴ Doesn't he see my ways,
　　count all my steps?

Deceit

⁵ If I have walked with frauds
　　or my feet have hurried to deceit,
⁶ let him weigh me on accurate scales;
　　let God know my integrity.
⁷ If my step has turned from the way,
　　if my heart has followed my eyes
　　or a blemish has clung to my hands,

---

^eHeb uncertain ^fOr *a wide opening* ^gLXX ^hHeb uncertain ^iHeb lacks *for me*.

⁸ then let me sow and another reap;
let my offspring be uprooted.

Adultery
⁹ If my heart has been drawn to a woman
and I have lurked
at my neighbor's door,
¹⁰ then may my wife grind for another
and others kneel over her;
¹¹ for that's a crime;
it's a punishable offense;
¹² indeed, it's a fire that consumes
to the underworld,^j
uprooting all my harvest.

Slaves
¹³ If I've rejected the just cause
of my male or female servant
when they contended with me,
¹⁴ what could I do when God rises;
when he requires an account,
what could I answer?
¹⁵ Didn't the one who made me in the belly
make them;
didn't the same one fashion us
in the womb?

The defenseless
¹⁶ If I have denied what the poor wanted,
made a widow's eyes tired,
¹⁷ eaten my morsel alone,
and not shared any with an orphan
(¹⁸ for from my youth
I raised the orphan as a father,
and from my mother's womb
I led the widow);^k
¹⁹ if I ever saw someone dying without
clothes, the needy naked;
²⁰ if they haven't blessed me fervently,^l
or if they weren't warmed
by the wool from my sheep;
²¹ if I have lifted my hand
against the orphans,
when I saw that I had help
in the city gate—
²² may my arm fall from my shoulder,
my forearm be broken
at the elbow—

²³ for God's calamity is terror to me;
I couldn't endure his splendor.

False worship
²⁴ If I've made gold my trust,
said to fine gold: "My security!"
²⁵ if I've rejoiced because
my wealth was great,
when my hand found plenty;
²⁶ if I've looked at the sun when it shone,
the moon, splendid as it moved;
²⁷ and my mind has been secretly enticed,
and threw a kiss with my hand,
²⁸ that also is a punishable offense,
because I would then be disloyal
to God above.

Other's misfortune
²⁹ If I have rejoiced over my foes' ruin
or was excited when evil found them,
³⁰ I didn't let my mouth sin
by asking for their life with a curse.
³¹ Surely those in my tent never said:
"Who has been filled by Job's food?"
³² A stranger didn't spend the night
in the street;
I opened my doors to the road.

Concealing sin
³³ If I have hidden my transgressions
like Adam,^m
concealing my offenses inside me
³⁴ because I feared the large crowd;
the clan's contempt frightened me;
I was quiet and didn't venture outside.

Sealing the solemn pledge
³⁵ Oh, that I had someone to hear me!
Here's my signature;ⁿ
let the Almighty respond,
and let my accuser write an indictment.
³⁶ Surely I would bear it on my shoulder,
tie it around me like a wreath.
³⁷ I would give him an account of my steps,
approach him like a prince.

Abuse of the land
³⁸ If my land has cried out against me,
its rows wept together;

^jHeb Abaddon   ^kHeb lacks orphan . . . widow.   ^lOr his loins   ^mOr like a human   ⁿHeb tau, the last letter of the Hebrew alphabet

³⁹ if I have eaten its yield without payment
and caused its owners grief,
⁴⁰ may briars grow instead of wheat,
poisonous weeds instead of barley.

Job's words are complete.

Introduction of Elihu

32 These three men stopped answering Job because he thought he was
righteous.^o ² Elihu son of Barachel the Buzite
from the clan of Ram was angry, angry with
Job because he considered himself more
righteous than God. ³ He was also angry with
his three friends because they hadn't found
an answer but nevertheless thought Job
wicked. ⁴ Elihu had waited while Job spoke,
for they were older than he. ⁵ When Elihu
saw that there had been no response in
the speeches of the three men, he became
very angry.

Elihu's justification for speaking

⁶ Elihu son of Barachel the Buzite said:
I'm young and you're old,
so I held back,
afraid to express my opinion to you.
⁷ I thought, Let days speak;
let multiple years make wisdom known.
⁸ But the spirit in a person,
the Almighty's breath,
gives understanding.
⁹ The advanced in days aren't wise;
the old don't understand what's right.
¹⁰ Therefore, I say: "Listen to me;
I'll state my view, even I."

¹¹ Look, I waited while you spoke,
listened while you reasoned,
while you searched for words.
¹² I was attentive to you,
but you offered no rebuke to Job,
no answer from you for his words.
¹³ Be careful you don't say,
"We've found wisdom;
God, not a person, will defeat him."
¹⁴ Now Job^p hasn't addressed me,
and I won't quote you to him.
¹⁵ They are troubled, no longer answer;
words now escape them.
¹⁶ I waited, but they didn't speak,
for they stood but answered no more.
¹⁷ I will answer. Indeed,
I will state^q my piece;
I too will declare my view,
¹⁸ for I'm full of words.
The spirit in my belly compels me.
¹⁹ Look, my belly is like unopened wine;
like new wineskins it will burst.
²⁰ I will speak and get relief;
I will open my lips and respond.
²¹ I won't be partial to anyone,
won't flatter a person;
²² for I don't know flattery;
otherwise my maker would quickly
whisk me away.

Elihu's appeal to be heard

33 But now, listen to me, Job;
pay attention to all my words.
² Notice that I am opening my mouth;
my tongue is speaking in my mouth.^r

^oOr *was righteous in his own eyes*   ^pOr *he*   ^qHeb lacks *will state.*   ^rOr *palate*

ELIHU

A man who responds to Job after Eliphaz, Bildad, and Zophar have finished their speeches. The Elihu material in Job 32–37 is generally considered to be a later insertion by an author who felt the three friends had not satisfactorily answered Job's complaint, a conclusion based on the fact that Job does not answer Elihu as he does the others, and Elihu is not among the friends God rebukes at the end of the book (Job 42:7-9). Elihu's arguments are similar to those of the three friends.

³ My words come from a virtuous heart;
  my lips speak knowledge clearly.
⁴ God's spirit made me;
  the Almighty's breath enlivens me.
⁵ If you are able, answer me;
  lay out your case^s before me
  and take a stand.
⁶ Notice that I'm just like you to God;
  I also was pinched from clay.
⁷ Surely fear of me shouldn't scare you;
  my pressure on you shouldn't be heavy.

The argument
⁸ You certainly said in my hearing;
  I heard the sound of your words:
⁹ "I'm pure, without sin;
  I'm innocent, without offense.
¹⁰ Notice that he invents arguments
  against me;
  he considers me his enemy,
¹¹ ties up my feet,
  watches all my paths."
¹² Now you're wrong about this;
  I'll answer you,
  for God is greater than anybody.
¹³ Why do you contend with him,
  saying that he doesn't answer
  all your words?^t
¹⁴ God speaks in one way,
  in two ways, but no one perceives it.
¹⁵ In the dream, a vision of the night,
  when deep sleep falls upon humans,
  during their slumber on a bed,
¹⁶ then he opens people's ears,
  scares them with warnings,
¹⁷ to turn them from a deed
  and to smother human pride.
¹⁸ He keeps one from the pit,
  a life from perishing by the sword.
¹⁹ Or a person may be disciplined by pain
  while in bed, bones ever aching
²⁰ until a person loathes food,
  an appetite rejects a delicacy;
²¹ the flesh wastes away, no longer visible;
  the bones, once hidden, protrude.
²² A life approaches the pit;
  its very being draws near
  the death dealers.
²³ Surely there's a messenger for this person,

a mediator, one out of a thousand
  to declare one's integrity to another
²⁴ so that God has compassion
  on that person and says,
  "Rescue this one from going down
  to the pit;
  I have found a ransom."
²⁵ That person's flesh is renewed
  like a child's;
  they regain their youth.
²⁶ They pray to God,
  and God is pleased with them;
  they behold God's presence
  with a joyful shout.
  God rewards a person's righteousness.
²⁷ They sing before people and say:
  "I have sinned, perverted justice,
  but didn't experience the
  consequences.
²⁸ He ransomed me from crossing
  into the pit;
  my life beholds light."
²⁹ Look, God does all this,
  twice, three times with persons
³⁰ to bring them back from the pit,
  to shine with life's light.
³¹ Listen, Job; hear me;
  be quiet, and I will speak.
³² If you have words, answer me;
  speak, for I want to be innocent.
³³ If not, you must hear me;
  be quiet, and I will teach you wisdom.

34 Elihu continued:
²Hear my words, wise ones;
  knowledgeable ones, listen to me,
³ for the ear tests words
  like the palate tastes food.
⁴ Let's choose for us what's right;
  let's determine among ourselves
  what's good;
⁵ for Job has said, "I'm innocent;
  God has denied my just cause;
⁶ because of my cause I'm thought a liar;
  my wound from an arrow is incurable,
  even though I didn't rebel."
⁷ Who is a man like Job?
  He drinks mockery like water
⁸ and travels a path with wrongdoers,

^sHeb lacks *your case.* ^tOr *his words*

walking with evil persons.
⁹ Indeed he said, "No one is rewarded
for delighting in God."
¹⁰ Therefore, intelligent ones, hear me;
far be it from God to do evil
and the Almighty to sin,
¹¹ for he repays people
based on what they do,
paying back everyone
according to their ways.
¹² Surely God doesn't act wickedly;
the Almighty doesn't distort justice.
¹³ Who placed earth in his care,
and who gave him dominion
over the entire world?
¹⁴ If he were to decide to do it—
to gather his spirit and breath
back to himself—
¹⁵ all flesh would die together,
and humans would return to dust.

¹⁶ But if you have understanding, hear this;
pay attention to the sound of my words.
¹⁷ Will one who hates justice rule;
will you condemn
the most righteous one?
¹⁸ Will you say to a king, "Worthless!"
to royalty, "Evil!"
¹⁹ Who shows no favor to princes
nor regards the rich over the poor,
for they are all the work of God's hands?
²⁰ In the middle of the night
they suddenly die;
people are shaken and pass away.
The mighty are removed,
not by a human hand.
²¹ God's eyes are on human ways,
and he sees all their steps.
²² There's no darkness, no deep darkness,
where evildoers can hide themselves;
²³ surely no time is set for a person
to appear before God in judgment.
²⁴ He shatters the mighty
without examining them;
makes others take their place.
²⁵ Thus he regards their deeds,
overturns them at night,
and they are crushed.
²⁶ He strikes them
because of their wickedness
at a place where people can see it.

²⁷ Because they turned from following him
and didn't value all his ways,
²⁸ causing the cry of the poor to reach him,
he hears the cry of the afflicted.
²⁹ Still, if he remains quiet,
who can condemn;
if he hides his face, who can see him?
³⁰ He prevents a lawless person from ruling,
from capturing people.

³¹ Has Job said to God,
"I have borne punishment;
I won't sin again?
³² You teach me what I can't see;
if I've sinned, I won't do it again."
³³ Will he repay you because you reject sin,
for you must choose, not I;
declare what you know.
³⁴ Smart people say to me,
the wise who hear me,
³⁵ "Job speaks without knowledge;
his words aren't astute."
³⁶ I wish Job would be tested to the limit
because he responds like evil people.
³⁷ He adds rebellion to his sin;
mocks us openly
and adds to his words against God.

Sin's impact

35 Elihu continued:
² Do you think it right?
You say, "I'm more just than God."
³ Yet you ask, "What does it benefit you?
What have I gained by avoiding sin?"
⁴ I'll answer you,
and your friends along with you.
⁵ Look at the heavens and see;
scan the clouds high over you.
⁶ If you've sinned,
how have you affected God?
Your offenses have multiplied;
what have you done to him?
⁷ If you are righteous,
what do you give to him?
Or what does he receive from your hand?
⁸ Your evil affects others like you,
and your righteousness affects
fellow human beings.
⁹ People cry out
because of heavy oppression;
shout under the power of the mighty.

¹⁰ But no one says, "Where is God my maker;
who gives songs in the night;
¹¹ who teaches us more
than the beasts of the earth,
makes us wiser
than the birds in the sky?"
¹² Then they cry out;
but he doesn't answer,
because of the pride of the wicked.
¹³ God certainly doesn't respond
to a deceitful cry;
the Almighty doesn't pay attention
to it.
¹⁴ Although you say that you don't see him,
the case is before him;
so wait anxiously for him.
¹⁵ Even though his anger is now held back,
a person doesn't know it's only delayed.^u
¹⁶ So Job mouths emptiness;
he piles up ignorant words.

Reason for continuing

36
Continuing, Elihu said,
² Wait a little while
so I can demonstrate for you
that there is still something more
to say about God.
³ I will draw from my broad knowledge,
attribute justice to my maker.
⁴ My words are certainly truthful;
one with total knowledge
is present with you.

Divine discipline

⁵ Look, God is mighty
and doesn't reject anyone;
he is mighty in strength and mind.
⁶ He doesn't let the wicked live,
but grants justice to the poor.
⁷ He doesn't avert his eyes
from the righteous;
he seats kings on thrones forever,
and they are lifted up.
⁸ If they are tied with ropes,
caught in cords of affliction,
⁹ he informs them about their offenses
and their grave sins.
¹⁰ He opens their ears with discipline
and commands them to turn from wrong.

¹¹ If they listen and serve,
they spend their days in plenty,
their years contentedly.
¹² But if they don't listen,
they perish by the sword,
breathe their last without understanding.
¹³ Those with impious hearts
become furious;
they don't cry out
even though he binds them.
¹⁴ They die young;
they are among the holy ones.
¹⁵ He saves the weak in their affliction,
opens their ears through oppression.
¹⁶ Surely he draws you up
from the brink of trouble
to a wide place without distress;
your table is set with rich food.
¹⁷ You are overly concerned
about the case of the wicked;
justice will be upheld in it.
¹⁸ Don't let them lure you with wealth;
don't let a huge bribe mislead you.
¹⁹ Will he arrange your rescue from distress
or from all your exertions of strength?
²⁰ Don't wish for the night
when people vanish from their place.
²¹ Take care; don't turn to evil
because you've chosen it over affliction.
²² Look, God is inaccessible due to his power;
who is a teacher like him?
²³ Who has repaid him for his action,
and who would ever say,
"You've done wrong"?
²⁴ Remember to praise his work
that all of us have seen.
²⁵ Every person has seen him;
people can observe at great distance.

God's control of the storm

²⁶ Look, God is exalted and unknowable;
the number of his years
is beyond counting.
²⁷ He draws up drops of water
that distill rain from his flood;
²⁸ the clouds pour moisture
and drip continually on humans.
²⁹ Even if one perceives a spreading cloud
and the thunder of his pavilion,^v

^uHeb uncertain   ^vOr *canopy*

³⁰ look how he spreads lightning across it
    and covers the seabed;
³¹ for by water[w] he judges peoples
    and gives food in abundance.
³² He conceals lightning in his palms
    and orders it to its target.
³³ His thunder announces it;
    even cattle proclaim its rising.

37 Oh, my mind is disturbed by this
    and is more troubled than usual.
² Listen closely to the rumble
    of his voice,
    the roar issuing from his mouth.
³ He looses it under the whole sky,
    his lightning on earth's edges.
⁴ After it, a voice roars;
    he thunders with a mighty voice,
    and no one can stop it
    when his voice is heard.
⁵ God roars with his wondrous voice;
    he does great things we can't know.
⁶ He says to the snow, "Fall to earth,"
    and to the downpour of rain,
    "Be a mighty shower."
⁷ He stamps the hand of every person
    so all can know his work.[x]
⁸ The wild beast enters its lair,
    lies down in its den.
⁹ The storm comes from its chamber,
    the cold from the north wind.
¹⁰ By God's breath ice forms;
    water's expanse becomes solid.
¹¹ He also fills clouds with moisture;
    his lightning scatters clouds.
¹² He overturns the circling clouds;[y]
    by his guidance they do[z] their work,
    doing everything he commands
    over the entire earth.
¹³ Whether for punishment, for his world,
    or for kindness,
    God makes it all happen.

¹⁴ Hear this, Job;
    stop and ponder God's mighty deeds.
¹⁵ Do you realize that when God
    commands them,
    his clouds produce lightning?

¹⁶ Do you understand the positioning
    of the clouds,
    the amazing deeds of one
    with perfect knowledge,
¹⁷ you whose clothes are hot
    when earth is calmed by the south wind?
¹⁸ Can you form the sky with him,
    hard like a mirror made of metal?
¹⁹ Tell us what we should say to him;
    we can't present our case
    due to darkness.
²⁰ Should someone inform him
    that I wish to speak,
    or would anyone say he wants
    to be devoured?

Divine splendor

²¹ For now, no one can look at the sun;
    it is bright in the sky;
    the wind has passed and cleared away
    the clouds.
²² From the north comes golden light,
    the awesome splendor of God.
²³ As for the Almighty, we can't find him—
    he is powerful and just,
    abundantly righteous—
    he won't respond.
²⁴ Therefore, people fear him;
    none of the wise[a] can see him.

The LORD answers from a whirlwind

38 Then the LORD answered Job from
    the whirlwind:
² Who is this darkening counsel
    with words lacking knowledge?
³ Prepare yourself like a man;
    I will interrogate you,
    and you will respond to me.

The establishing of order

⁴ Where were you
    when I laid the earth's foundations?
    Tell me if you know.
⁵ Who set its measurements?
    Surely you know.
    Who stretched a measuring tape on it?
⁶ On what were its footings sunk;
    who laid its cornerstone,

---

[w]Or them   [x]Or that everyone he has made can know it   [y]Heb uncertain   [z]Heb lacks they do.   [a]Or wise in heart; cf 9:4

7 while the morning stars sang in unison
   and all the divine beings shouted?
8 Who enclosed the Sea[b] behind doors
   when it burst forth from the womb,
9 when I made the clouds its garment,
   the dense clouds its wrap,
10 when I imposed[c] my limit for it,
    put on a bar and doors
11 and said, "You may come this far,
    no farther;
    here your proud waves stop"?

12 In your lifetime have you
    commanded the morning,
    informed the dawn of its place
13 so it would take hold of earth
    by its edges

and shake the wicked out of it?
14 Do you turn it over like clay for a seal,
    so it stands out
    like a colorful garment?
15 Light is withheld from the wicked,
    the uplifted arm broken.

The vast beyond
16 Have you gone to the sea's sources,
    walked in the chamber of the deep?
17 Have death's gates been revealed to you;
    can you see the gates of deep darkness?
18 Have you surveyed earth's expanses?
    Tell me if you know everything about it.
19 Where's the road to the place
    where light dwells;
    darkness, where's it located?

[b] Heb *Yam*, a sea god   [c] Heb uncertain

CREATION

The biblical concept of creation encompasses the entire world of nature, including humanity, and views this world as brought into being and sustained by God.

Genesis 1–3 is the most sustained biblical account of creation. When creation is described in other biblical literature, it is characterized as an integrated whole, and it plays a foundational role in the biblical story. The Psalms contain some of the most detailed accounts of creation outside of Genesis. Typically, psalmists describe God's establishment of larger cosmic orders as the foundation for God's establishment of the order of the historical sphere, so that cosmic orders are closely connected, for example, to the Law (Pss 19; 93), religious ritual (Ps 24), the exodus and settlement (Ps 136), the establishment of the Davidic dynasty (Ps 89), and the rebuilding of Zion (Ps 74). The praise of God at the heart of the Psalms is expressed not just by human beings but also by all members of creation (Pss 96–98; 145; 148; 150). When God delivers the climactic speech in the book of Job from the storm wind, God speaks about God's activity in all of creation, especially in those realms out of human reach (Job 38:1–42:6).

In his letter to the Romans, Paul describes the realm of nonhuman creation as sharing the fallen fate of humanity and its longing for redemption (Rom 8:18-25). When he says that "creation was subjected to frustration" (v. 20), that "the whole creation is groaning together and suffering labor pains" (v. 22), and that "the creation itself will be set free from slavery to decay and brought into the glorious freedom of God's children" (v. 21), Paul appears to make the claim that nonhuman nature together with human nature acquired a fatal defect as a result of human sin (Gen 3:14-19).

²⁰ Can you take it to its territory;
    do you know the paths to its house?
²¹ You know, for you were born then;
    you have lived such a long time!ᵈ
²² Have you gone to snow's storehouses,
    seen the storehouses of hail
²³ that I have reserved for a time
    of distress,
    for a day of battle and war?
²⁴ What is the way to the place
    where light is divided up;
    the east wind scattered over earth?

Meteorological facts

²⁵ Who cut a channel for the downpours
    and a way for blasts of thunder
²⁶ to bring water to uninhabited land,
    a desert with no human
²⁷ to saturate dry wasteland
    and make grass sprout?
²⁸ Has the rain a father
    who brought forth drops of dew?
²⁹ From whose belly does ice come;
    who gave birth to heaven's frost?
³⁰ Water hardens like stone;
    the surface of the deep thickens.
³¹ Can you bind Pleiades' chains
    or loosen the reins of Orion?
³² Can you guide the stars
    at their proper times,
    lead the Bear with her cubs?
³³ Do you know heaven's laws,
    or can you impose its rule on earth?
³⁴ Can you issue an order to the clouds
    so their abundant waters cover you?
³⁵ Can you send lightning so that it goes
    and then says to you, "I'm here"?
³⁶ Who put wisdom in remote places,
    or who gave understanding
    to a rooster?ᵉ
³⁷ Who is wise enough to count the clouds,
    and who can tilt heaven's
    water containers
³⁸ so that dust becomes mud
    and clods of dirt adhere?

Lion and raven

³⁹ Can you hunt prey for the lion
    or fill the cravings of lion cubs?

⁴⁰ They lie in their den,
    lie in ambush in their lair.
⁴¹ Who provides food for the raven
    when its young cry to God,
    move about without food?

Mountain goat and doe

39 Do you know when mountain goats
    give birth;
    do you observe the birthing of does?
² Can you count the months of pregnancy;
    do you know when they give birth?
³ They crouch, split open for their young,
    send forth their offspring.
⁴ Their young are healthy;
    they grow up in the open country,
    leave and never return.

Wild donkey

⁵ Who freed the wild donkey,
    loosed the ropes of the onager
⁶ to whom I gave the desert as home,
    his dwelling place in the salt flats?
⁷ He laughs at the clamor of the town,
    doesn't hear the driver's shout,
⁸ searches the hills for food
    and seeks any green sprout.

Wild ox

⁹ Will the wild ox agree to be your slave,
    or will it spend the night in your crib?
¹⁰ Can you bind it with a rope
    to a plowed row;
    will it plow the valley behind you?
¹¹ Will you trust it
    because its strength is great
    so that you can leave your work to it?
¹² Can you rely on it
    to bring back your grain
    to gather into your threshing floor?

Ostrich

¹³ The ostrich's wings flap joyously,
    but her wings and plumage
    are like a stork.
¹⁴ She leaves her eggs on the earth,
    lets them warm in the dust,
¹⁵ then forgets that a foot may crush them
    or a wild animal trample them.

ᵈOr *the number of your days is many*   ᵉHeb uncertain

¹⁶ She treats her young harshly
    as if they were not hers,
    without worrying that her labor
    might be in vain;
¹⁷ God didn't endow her with sense,
    didn't give her some good sense.
¹⁸ When she flaps her wings high,
    she laughs at horse and rider.

Horse
¹⁹ Did you give strength to the horse,
    clothe his neck with a mane,
²⁰ cause him to leap like a locust,
    his majestic snorting, a fright?
²¹ He^f paws in the valley, prances proudly,
    charges at battle weapons,
²² laughs at fear, unafraid.
    He doesn't turn away from the sword;
²³ a quiver of arrows flies by him,
    flashing spear and dagger.
²⁴ Excitedly, trembling,
    he swallows the ground;
    can't stand still at a trumpet's blast.
²⁵ At a trumpet's sound, he says, "Aha!"
    smells the battle from afar,
    hears^g officers' shouting
    and the battle cry.

^fOr *they* ^gHeb lacks *hears*.

Hawk and eagle
²⁶ Is it due to your understanding
    that the hawk flies,
    spreading its wings to the south?
²⁷ Or at your command
    does the eagle soar,
    the vulture build a nest on high?
²⁸ They dwell on
    an outcropping of rock,
    their fortress on rock's edge.
²⁹ From there they search for food;
    their eyes notice it from afar,
³⁰ and their young lap up blood;
    where carcasses lie, there they are.

The LORD speaks and Job answers
40 The LORD continued to respond
to Job:
² Will the one who disputes with the
    Almighty correct him?
    God's instructor must answer him.
³ Job responded to the LORD:
⁴ Look, I'm of little worth.
    What can I answer you?
    I'll put my hand over my mouth.
⁵ I have spoken once, I won't answer;
    twice, I won't do it again.

BEHEMOTH

The Behemoth of Job is related to ancient Near Eastern myth. However, the plain meaning of this text establishes that, like Job himself, Behemoth is one of God's beloved creatures (40:15): plant-eating (v. 15) with immense physical strength and sexual potency (vv. 16-17), enjoying primacy among God's creative acts (v. 19), and exhibiting a gentle quality, quietly living near playful animals in the reeds and "poplars of the stream" (vv. 20-22). These features have led many to identify Behemoth as a hippopotamus.

Given that God's speeches in Job 38-41 evoke the created order and its beloved creatures, perhaps this text does indeed celebrate one of the most extreme of the living animals. In later (non-biblical) Jewish tradition, however, Behemoth regains its mythic dimensions. Behemoth and Leviathan are identified as the unnamed "great sea animals" that God created on the fifth day (Gen 1:21). Behemoth is located in a desert lying east of the garden of Eden (1 Enoch 60:7-8). And in the rabbinic tradition, the two monsters become food for the righteous in the world to come.

A challenge from the LORD

⁶ The LORD answered Job
   from the whirlwind:
⁷ Prepare yourself like a man;
   I will interrogate you,
      and you will respond to me.
⁸ Would you question my justice,
   deem me guilty so you can be innocent?
⁹ Or do you have an arm like God;
   can you thunder with a voice like him?
¹⁰ Adorn yourself
   with splendor and majesty;
   clothe yourself with honor and esteem.
¹¹ Unleash your raging anger;
   look on all the proud and humble them.
¹² Look on all the proud and debase them;
   trample the wicked in their place.
¹³ Hide them together in the dust;
   bind their faces in a hidden place.
¹⁴ Then I, even I, will praise you,
   for your strong hand
      has delivered you.

Behemoth

¹⁵ Look at Behemoth,
   whom I made along with you;
   he eats grass like cattle.
¹⁶ Look, his strength is in his thighs,
   his power in stomach muscles.
¹⁷ He stiffens his tail like a cedar;
   the tendons in his thighs
   are tightly woven.
¹⁸ His bones are like bronze tubes,
   his limbs like iron bars.

ʰ40:25 in Heb

¹⁹ He is the first of God's acts;
   only his maker can come near him
      with a sword.
²⁰ Indeed, the hills bring him tribute,
   places where all the wild animals play.
²¹ He lies under the lotuses,
   under the cover of reed and marsh.
²² The lotuses screen him with shade;
   poplars of the stream surround him.
²³ If the river surges, he doesn't hurry;
   he is confident even though the Jordan
      gushes into his mouth.
²⁴ Can he be seized by his eyes?
   Can anyone pierce his nose by hooks?

Leviathan

41 ʰCan you draw out Leviathan
   with a hook,
      restrain his tongue with a rope?
² Can you put a cord through his nose,
   pierce his jaw with a barb?
³ Will he beg you at length
   or speak gentle words to you?
⁴ Will he make a pact with you
   so that you will take him
      as a permanent slave?
⁵ Can you play with him like a bird,
   put a leash on him for your girls?
⁶ Will merchants sell him;
   will they divide him among traders?
⁷ Can you fill his hide with darts,
   his head with a fishing spear?
⁸ Should you lay your hand on him,
   you would never remember the battle.

LEVIATHAN

This terrible serpent of the sea, slain by God at the beginning (Ps 74:14) and end of time (Isa 27:1), is mentioned by name only six times in the Bible (Job 3:8; 41:1; Pss 74:14; 104:26; Isa 27:1 [twice]).

The biblical Leviathan is not all bad. Job 41:1-34 depicts the monster as the Lord's playmate (see also Ps 104:25-26). In later Jewish literature Leviathan and its partner Behemoth are identified with "the great sea animals" that God created on the fifth day (Gen 1:21). After eons in hiding, they reemerge to become food for the righteous at the banquet at the end of time.

⁹ Such hopesⁱ would be delusional;
  surely the sight of him
    makes one stumble.
¹⁰ Nobody is fierce enough to rouse him;
  who then can stand before me?
¹¹ Who opposes me that I must repay?
  Everything under heaven is mine.
¹² I'm not awed by his limbs,
  his strength, and impressive form.
¹³ Who can remove his outer garment;
  who can come with a bridle for him?
¹⁴ Who can open the doors of his mouth,
  surrounded by frightening teeth?
¹⁵ His matching scales are his pride,
  closely locked and sealed.
¹⁶ One touches another;
  even air can't come between them.
¹⁷ Each clings to its pair;
  joined, they can't be separated.
¹⁸ His sneezes emit flashes of light;
  his eyes are like dawn's rays.
¹⁹ Shafts of fire shoot from his mouth;
  like fiery sparks they fly out.
²⁰ Smoke pours from his nostrils
  like a boiling pot over reeds.
²¹ His breath lights coals;
  a flame shoots from his mouth.
²² Power resides in his neck;
  violence dances before him.
²³ The folds of his flesh stick together;
  on him they are tough and unyielding.
²⁴ His heart is solid like a rock,
  hard like a lower millstone.
²⁵ The divine beings dread his rising;
  they withdraw before his thrashing.
²⁶ The sword that touches him
    won't prevail;
  neither will the dart, spear,
    nor javelin.
²⁷ He treats iron as straw,
  bronze as rotten wood.
²⁸ Arrows can't make him flee;
  slingstones he turns to straw.
²⁹ He treats a club like straw;
  he laughs at the lance's rattle.
³⁰ His abdomen is
  like jagged pottery shards;
  its sharp edges leave a trail in the mud.

³¹ He causes the depths
  to churn like a boiling pot,
  stirs up the sea like a pot of scented oils,
³² leaves a bright wake behind him;
  the frothy deep seems white-haired.
³³ None on earth can compare to him;
  he is made to be without fear.
³⁴ He looks on all the proud;
  he is king over all proud beasts.

Job's second response

42²Job answered the LORD:
²I know you can do anything;
  no plan of yours
    can be opposed successfully.
³ You said,^j "Who is this darkening counsel
    without knowledge?"
  I have indeed spoken about things
    I didn't understand,
  wonders beyond my comprehension.
⁴ You said,^k "Listen and I will speak;
  I will question you
    and you will inform me."
⁵ My ears had heard about you,
  but now my eyes have seen you.
⁶ Therefore, I relent^l and find comfort
  on dust and ashes.

Epilogue

⁷ After the LORD had spoken these words to Job, he said to Eliphaz from Teman, "I'm angry at you and your two friends because you haven't spoken about me correctly as did my servant Job. ⁸ So now, take seven bulls and seven rams, go to my servant Job, and prepare an entirely burned offering for yourselves. Job my servant will pray for you, and I will act favorably by not making fools of you because you didn't speak correctly, as did my servant Job."

⁹ Eliphaz from Teman, Bildad from Shuah, and Zophar from Naamah did what the LORD told them; and the LORD acted favorably toward Job. ¹⁰ Then the LORD changed Job's fortune when he prayed for his friends, and the LORD doubled all Job's earlier possessions. ¹¹ All his brothers, sisters, and acquaintances came to him

---

ⁱOr *his hopes* ^jHeb lacks *You said.* ^kHeb lacks *You said.* ^lThe verse is capable of several translations: *I despise* or *relent*, no direct object; *repent of* or *concerning dust and ashes.*

and ate food with him in his house. They comforted and consoled him concerning all the disaster the LORD had brought on him, and each one gave him a qesitah[m] and a gold ring. [12]Then the LORD blessed Job's latter days more than his former ones. He had fourteen thousand sheep, six thousand camels, one thousand yoke of oxen, and one thousand female donkeys. [13]He also had seven sons and three daughters. [14]He named one Jemimah,[n] a second Keziah,[o] and the third Keren-happuch.[p] [15]No women in all the land were as beautiful as Job's daughters; and their father gave an inheritance to them along with their brothers. [16]After this, Job lived 140 years and saw four generations of his children. [17]Then Job died, old and satisfied.

PSALMS

The core of the book of Psalms is the wonderful awareness of God's presence. The deepest yearnings of the soul for an intimate, personal, and right relationship with God are apparent. In those yearnings the broadest range of human emotion is evident. The psalmists are dealing with deepest despair and highest elation, profound grief and supreme joy, utmost sorrow and greatest gladness. But they are also dealing with profoundly important moral and ethical principles. Throughout these poems, we see the deepest respect for the law. It actually becomes the ethical ideal of the people of God's choosing.

At the same time the Psalms relate the story of the Israelite nation, its high moments of exultation and supreme glory and its grim days of calamity and national disaster. The episodes have a timeless quality about them, appropriate to any period of history, including the present. The glowing appeal of these stories is the almost continuous conquest of despair and the heart-warming victory of hope. As personal, devotional resources, these beautiful poems are deep springs of refreshment and renewal and marvelous sources of comfort.

PSALMS AND MUSIC

The book of Psalms is the Bible's prayerbook and hymnal. Each psalm is a lyric poem, and many of them were at one time set to music. The English word *psalm* is derived from the Greek *psalmos*, which meant the twanging or strumming of a stringed instrument. Verses 1-3 of Psalm 81 describe the degree to which music and poetry were related in Israel's early life:

> Rejoice out loud to God, our strength!
> Shout for joy to Jacob's God!
> Take up a song and strike the drum!
> Sweet lyre along with harp!
> Blow the horn on the new moon,
> at the full moon, for our day of celebration!

Among the very early Hebrew peoples, hymns and songs were memorized in religious training and during social activities of community life. In this way, their best-loved poetry was passed from generation to generation. Bible scholars generally believe that some of the present collection of psalms was accumulated by means of this oral tradition over a period of many centuries.

From the earliest periods in Israel's history, religious experiences were at the center of community life. Singing was a part of those activities. Psalms were sung during festivals, on national holidays and high holy days, and during pilgrimages to Jerusalem. As the Hebrews made their customary pilgrimages, they sang psalms of praise.

THE AUTHORSHIP OF THE PSALMS

Authorship of the Psalms is in dispute among biblical scholars, as is the question of by whom and when they were collected from the oral tradition. It is true that the Hebrew texts ascribe much of the poetry to David. Biblical scholars have suggested that some of the psalms attributed to David may be poems written by others for David or about him, or written using his literary style. Some scholarly opinion places authorship of many psalms much later in Israel's history, perhaps after the Babylonian captivity and up to the time of the Maccabean era. Recent evidence shows, however, that a number of the psalms may have been written or recorded at earlier dates than scholars had previously thought. In their original forms, many can be shown to date from the monarchical period of Saul, David, and Solomon.

Regardless of who wrote them, David is the central human figure in the Psalms.

PURPOSES OF THE PSALMS

The Psalms were put into their present arrangement sometime before the era of the Maccabees (165 BCE), probably 300–200 BCE. By the Christian era, the Psalter had been incorporated into the Hebrew Bible, and before too long thereafter into the earliest Christian Bibles as well. Two purposes seem to have been served by including the book of Psalms in the Bible: public worship and personal devotion. In the first instance, psalms have important liturgical uses in religious services. Introductory statements above the biblical text of a number of psalms include specific instructions for using the poem in worship or in celebration. Although the meaning of many of the words in those introductory statements is obscure, there is little doubt that they were directions given to the congregation to enable proper participation in the service. Within the text of a number of psalms, the word *selah* occurs repeatedly. It does not appear to have any literary significance and it has no known meaning in Hebrew. Some students of early music surmise that it may have been an instruction for singing, perhaps to indicate a pause in the liturgy or to allow the introduction of some special feature into the ritual.

A second purpose served by the Psalms was private, personal devotion. The twenty-third Psalm was evidently not used anywhere in liturgy among the people of Israel. But as a quiet, devotional, personal prayer it is incomparable. This and other psalms of comfort and confidence have shown unusual power in bringing people into a unique personal experience with the living God.

LITERARY STRUCTURE OF THE PSALMS

The reader's enjoyment and understanding of the Psalms will surely be enhanced by some understanding of their literary structure. We should remember that the individual psalms are poetry despite the fact that they do not appear to have any rhyme. The original Hebrew did not have rhyme either; it depended upon stress during recitation in order to achieve poetic quality. It might be helpful to try reading some psalms aloud, accenting certain words to assess the psalms as poetry.

As in all literature identified as poetry, psalms possess rhythm, meter, and a certain lyric quality. But these traits are not always evident. Translations have often sacrificed the original Hebrew metered stress and rhythm in order to achieve greater faithfulness in meaning.

Literary devices most commonly employed in the writing and the translating of the Psalms are word pictures (e.g., Psalm 104:3), figures of speech (e.g., 1:3), parallelisms (e.g., 13:4; 73:26; 116:3), and hyperbole (e.g., 14:4).

Many of the psalms, especially the laments, are written in a standard format. These psalms begin with a cry for help accompanied by a description of the cause of anguish. Often the cause is a false accusation, but it can also be threats of murder, terrible illness, mental distress, or even national calamities. A declaration of trust follows along with an expression of confidence that God will intervene. The final words of these poems are thanksgiving for deliverance (see, e.g., Psalm 3).

PSALMS

BOOK I
(Psalms 1–41)

Psalm 1

[1] The truly happy person
  doesn't follow wicked advice,
  doesn't stand on the road of sinners,
  and doesn't sit with the disrespectful.
[2] Instead of doing those things,
  these persons
    love the LORD's Instruction,
  and they recite God's Instruction
    day and night!
[3] They are like a tree
  replanted by streams of water,
    which bears fruit
    at just the right time
  and whose leaves don't fade.
    Whatever they do succeeds.

[4] That's not true for the wicked!
  They are like dust
    that the wind blows away.
[5] And that's why the wicked
  will have no standing
    in the court of justice—
  neither will sinners
    in the assembly of the righteous.
[6] The LORD is intimately acquainted
  with the way of the righteous,
  but the way of the wicked is destroyed.

Psalm 2

[1] Why do the nations rant?
  Why do the peoples rave uselessly?
[2] The earth's rulers take their stand;
  the leaders scheme together
    against the LORD and
    against his anointed one.
[3] "Come!" they say.
  "We will tear off their ropes
    and throw off their chains!"
[4] The one who rules in heaven laughs;
  my Lord makes fun of them.

[5] But then God speaks to them angrily;
  then he terrifies them with his fury:
[6] "I hereby appoint my king on Zion,
    my holy mountain!"

[7] I will announce the LORD's decision:
  He said to me, "You are my son,
    today I have become your father.
[8] Just ask me,
  and I will make the nations
    your possession;
  the far corners of the earth
    will be your property.
[9] You will smash them with an iron rod;
  you will shatter them like a pottery jar."

[10] So kings, wise up!
  Be warned, you rulers of the earth!
[11] Serve the LORD reverently—
  trembling, [12]kiss his feet[a]
    or else he will become angry,
  and your way will be destroyed
  because his anger ignites in an instant.

But all who take refuge in the LORD
  are truly happy!

Psalm 3

*A psalm of David,
when he fled from his son Absalom.*

[1] LORD, I have so many enemies!
  So many are standing against me.
[2] So many are talking about me:
  "Even God won't help him."   *Selah*[b]
[3] But you, LORD, are my shield!
  You are my glory!
  You are the one who restores me.
[4] I cry out loud to the LORD,
  and he answers me
    from his holy mountain.   *Selah*
[5] I lie down, sleep, and wake up
  because the LORD helps me.
[6] I won't be afraid of thousands of people
  surrounding me on all sides.

---

[a]Correction; Heb uncertain; MT *rejoice with trembling, kiss the son* (but with *son* in Aram, not Heb)   [b]Heb uncertain;
probably a musical term

⁷ Stand up, LORD!
   Save me, my God!
In fact, hit all my enemies on the jaw;
   shatter the teeth of the wicked!
⁸ Rescue comes from the LORD!
   May your blessing be on your people!
                   Selah

Psalm 4

*For the music leader. With stringed
instruments. A psalm of David.*

¹ Answer me when I cry out,
   my righteous God!
Set me free from my troubles!
   Have mercy on me!
   Listen to my prayer!

² How long, you people,
   will my reputation be insulted?
How long will you continue
   to love what is worthless
   and go after lies?   *Selah*
³ Know this: the LORD takes
   personal care of the faithful.
The LORD will hear me
   when I cry out to him.
⁴ So be afraid, and don't sin!
   Think hard about it in your bed
   and weep over it!   *Selah*
⁵ Bring righteous offerings,
   and trust the LORD!

⁶ Many people say,
   "We can't find goodness anywhere.
   The light of your face has left us, LORD!"ᶜ
⁷ But you have filled my heart
   with more joy
than when their wheat and wine
   are everywhere!
⁸ I will lie down and fall asleep in peace
   because you alone, LORD,
   let me live in safety.

Psalm 5

*For the music leader. For the flutes.
A psalm of David.*

¹ Hear my words, LORD!
   Consider my groans!

² Pay attention to the sound of my cries,
   my king and my God,
   because I am praying to you!
³ LORD, in the morning you hear my voice.
   In the morning I lay it all out before you.
   Then I wait expectantly.
⁴ Because you aren't a God
   who enjoys wickedness;
   evil doesn't live with you.
⁵ Arrogant people won't last long
   in your sight;
   you hate all evildoers;
⁶ you destroy liars.
   The LORD despises people who are
     violent and dishonest.

⁷ But me? I will enter your house
   because of your abundant, faithful love;
I will bow down at your holy temple,
   honoring you.
⁸ LORD, because of many enemies,
   please lead me in your righteousness.
Make your way clear,
   right in front of me.
⁹ Because there's no truth
   in my enemies' mouths,
   all they have inside them is destruction.
Their throats are open graves;
   their tongues slick with talk.
¹⁰ Condemn them, God!
   Let them fail by their own plans.
Throw them out for their many sins
   because they've rebelled against you.
¹¹ But let all who take refuge in you celebrate.
   Let them sing out loud forever!
Protect them
   so that all who love your name
   can rejoice in you.
¹² Because you, LORD, bless the righteous.
   You cover them with favor like a shield.

Psalm 6

*For the music leader. On stringed
instruments. According to the eighth.ᵈ
A psalm of David.*

¹ Please, LORD,
   don't punish me when you are angry;

ᶜCorrection; MT *Shine the light of your face on us, LORD!*   ᵈPerhaps a reference to an eight-string instrument;
also in Ps 12

don't discipline me when you are furious.
2 Have mercy on me, LORD,
   because I'm frail.
   Heal me, LORD,
   because my bones are shaking in terror!
3 My whole body[e] is completely terrified!
   But you, LORD! How long will this last?
4 Come back to me, LORD! Deliver me!
   Save me for the sake of your faithful love!
5 No one is going to praise you
   when they are dead.
   Who gives you thanks
   from the grave?[f]

6 I'm worn out from groaning.
   Every night, I drench my bed
   with tears;
   I soak my couch all the way through.
7 My vision fails because of my grief;
   it's weak because of all my distress.
8 Get away from me, all you evildoers,
   because the LORD has heard me crying!
9 The LORD has listened to my request.
   The LORD accepts my prayer.
10 All my enemies will be ashamed
   and completely terrified;
   they will be defeated
   and ashamed instantly.

Psalm 7

*A shiggayon[g] of David, which he sang
to the LORD about Cush, a Benjaminite.*
1 I take refuge in you, LORD, my God.
   Save me from all who chase me!
   Rescue me!
2 Otherwise, they will rip me apart,
   dragging me off with no chance of rescue.
3 LORD, my God, if I have done this—
   if my hands have done anything wrong,
4 if I have repaid a friend with evil
   or oppressed a foe for no reason—
5 then let my enemy
   not only chase but catch me,
   trampling my life into the ground,
   laying my reputation in the dirt. *Selah*
6 Get up, LORD; get angry!
   Stand up against the fury of my foes!

Wake up, my God;[h]
   you command that justice be done!
7 Let the assembled peoples surround you.
   Rule them from on high![i]
8 The LORD will judge the peoples.
   Establish justice for me, LORD,
   according to my righteousness
   and according to my integrity.
9 Please let the evil of the wicked be over,
   but set the righteous firmly in place
   because you, the righteous God,
   are the one who examines
   hearts and minds.

10 God is my shield;
   he saves those whose heart is right.
11 God is a righteous judge,
   a God who is angry at evil[j]
   every single day.
12 If someone doesn't change their ways,
   God will sharpen his sword,
   will bend his bow,
   will string an arrow.
13 God has deadly weapons in store
   for those who won't change;
   he gets his flaming arrows ready!

14 But look how the wicked hatch evil,
   conceive trouble, give birth to lies!
15 They make a pit, dig it all out,
   and then fall right into the hole
   that they've made!
16 The trouble they cause
   will come back on their own heads;
   the violence they commit
   will come down on their own skulls.
17 But I will thank the LORD
   for his righteousness;
   I will sing praises
   to the name of the LORD Most High.

Psalm 8

*For the music leader. According to
the Gittith.[k] A psalm of David.*
1 LORD, our Lord, how majestic
   is your name throughout the earth!

---

[e]Or *soul;* also in 6:4 [f]Heb *Sheol* [g]Perhaps *lament* [h]Or *for my sake* [i]Correction; MT *Come back to be exalted over them.* [j]Heb lacks *at evil.* [k]Perhaps the name of an instrument (Tg) or melody. LXX *About the winepresses;* or *About the Gittite;* also in Pss 81 and 84

You made your glory
　　higher than heaven!ˡ
² From the mouths of nursing babies
　　you have laid a strong foundation
　　because of your foes,
　　in order to stop vengeful enemies.
³ When I look up at your skies,
　　at what your fingers made—
　　the moon and the stars
　　that you set firmly in place—
　　⁴ what are human beings
　　　that you think about them;
　　what are human beings
　　　that you pay attention to them?
⁵ You've made them only slightly
　　less than divine,
　　crowning them with glory and grandeur.
⁶ You've let them rule over
　　your handiwork,
　　putting everything under their feet—
　　⁷ all sheep and all cattle,
　　the wild animals too,
　　⁸ the birds in the sky,
　　the fish of the ocean,
　　everything that travels
　　　the pathways of the sea.
⁹ LORD, our Lord, how majestic is your
　　name throughout the earth!

Psalm 9ᵐ

*For the music leader. According to
Muth-labben.ⁿ A psalm of David.*

א ¹ I will thank you, LORD, with all my heart;
　　I will talk about all your wonderful acts.
² I will celebrate and rejoice in you;
　　I will sing praises to your name,
　　Most High.

ב ³ When my enemies turn and retreat,
　　they fall down and die
　　　right in front of you
　　⁴ because you have established justice
　　for me and my claim,
　　because you rule from the throne,
　　establishing justice rightly.

ג ⁵ You've denounced the nations,
　　destroyed the wicked.
　　You've erased their names for all time.
⁶ Every enemy is wiped out,
　　like something ruined forever.
　　You've torn down their cities—
　　even the memory of them is dead.

ה ⁷ But the LORD rules forever!
　　He assumes his throne
　　for the sake of justice.
⁸ He will establish justice
　　in the world rightly;
　　he will judge all people fairly.

ו ⁹ The LORD is a safe place
　　for the oppressed—
　　a safe place in difficult times.
¹⁰ Those who know your name trust you
　　because you have not abandoned
　　any who seek you, LORD.

ז ¹¹ Sing praises to the LORD,
　　who lives in Zion!
　　Proclaim his mighty acts
　　among all people!
¹² Because the one
　　who avenges bloodshed
　　remembers those who suffer;
　　the LORD hasn't forgotten
　　their cries for help.

ח ¹³ Have mercy on me, LORD!
　　Just look how I suffer
　　because of those who hate me.
　　But you are the one
　　who brings me back
　　from the very gates of death
　　¹⁴ so I can declare all your praises,
　　so I can rejoice in your salvation
　　in the gates of Daughter Zion.

ט ¹⁵ The nations have fallen
　　into the hole they themselves made!
　　Their feet are caught
　　in the very net they themselves hid!
¹⁶ The LORD is famous for the justice
　　he has done;

ˡCorrection; Heb uncertain ᵐPs 9 is an alphabetic acrostic poem (cf Ps 119) in Heb, with successive letters of the alphabet beginning every few lines, with only a few exceptions. Only ten letters are found in Ps 9; the sequence may be continued in Ps 10, suggesting that Pss 9–10 are a single poem. ⁿOr *Almuth labben*; Heb uncertain, perhaps a reference to the melody; cf Pss 46:1; 48:14

it's his own doing that the wicked
    are trapped.   *Higgayon.*[o] *Selah*

[17] Let the wicked go straight to the grave,[P]
    the same for every nation
      that forgets God.

[18] Because the poor
    won't be forgotten forever,
    the hope of those who suffer
      won't be lost for all time.

[19] Get up, LORD! Don't let people prevail!
    Let the nations be judged before you.
[20] Strike them with fear, LORD.
    Let the nations know
      they are only human.   *Selah*

Psalm 10[q]

[1] Why do you stand so far away, LORD,
    hiding yourself in troubling times?
[2] Meanwhile, the wicked are proudly
    in hot pursuit of those who suffer.
    Let them get caught
    in the very same schemes
      they've thought up!

[3] The wicked brag
    about their body's[r] cravings;
    the greedy reject the LORD, cursing.
[4] At the peak of their wrath,
    the wicked don't seek God:
    There's no God—
      that's what they are always thinking.
[5] Their ways are always twisted.
    Your rules are too lofty for them.
    They snort at all their foes.
[6] They think to themselves,
    We'll never stumble.
    We'll never encounter any resistance.
[7] Their mouths are filled
    with curses, dishonesty, violence.
    Under their tongues lie
      troublemaking and wrongdoing.
[8] They wait in a place perfect for ambush;[s]
    from their hiding places
    they kill innocent people;
      their eyes spot those who are helpless.

[9] They lie in ambush
    in secret places,
    like a lion in its lair.
    They lie in ambush
    so they can seize those who suffer!
    They seize the poor, all right,
      dragging them off in their nets.
[10] Their helpless victims are crushed;
    they collapse, falling prey
      to the strength of the wicked.
[11] The wicked think to themselves:
    God has forgotten.
    God has hidden his face.
    God never sees anything!

[12] Get up, LORD!
    Get your fist ready, God!
    Don't forget the ones who suffer!
[13] Why do the wicked reject God?
    Why do they think to themselves
      that you won't find out?

[14] But you do see!
    You do see troublemaking and grief,
    and you do something about it!
    The helpless leave it all to you.
    You are the orphan's helper.

[15] Break the arms of those
    who are wicked and evil.
    Seek out their wickedness
      until there's no more to find.
[16] The LORD rules forever and always!
    The nations will vanish from his land.

[17] LORD, you listen to the desires
    of those who suffer.
    You steady their hearts;
    you listen closely to them,
[18] to establish justice
    for the orphan and the oppressed,
    so that people of the land
      will never again be terrified.

Psalm 11

For the music leader. Of David.

[1] I have taken refuge in the LORD.
    So how can you say to me,[t]
      "Flee to the hills like a bird

[o]Heb uncertain; or *recitation* (see Pss 1:2; 19:14) or *melody* (see Ps 92:3). [P]Heb *Sheol* [q]Pss 9 and 10 contain
part of an acrostic poem and might originally be one poem in Heb. [r]Or *soul's* [s]Heb uncertain [t]Or *my soul*

² because the wicked
have already bent their bows;
they've already strung their arrows;
they are ready to secretly shoot
those whose heart is right"?
³ When the very bottom of things falls out,
what can a righteous person
possibly accomplish?

⁴ But the LORD is in his holy temple.
The LORD! His throne is in heaven.
His eyes see—
his vision examines all of humanity.
⁵ The LORD examines
both the righteous and the wicked;
his very being[u] hates
anyone who loves violence.
⁶ God will rain fiery coals and sulfur
on the wicked;
their cups will be filled
with nothing but a scorching hot wind
⁷ because the LORD is righteous!
He loves righteous deeds.
Those whose heart is right
will see God's face.[v]

Psalm 12

For the music leader. According to the Sheminith.[w] A psalm of David.

¹ Help, LORD,
because the godly are all gone;
the faithful have completely disappeared
from the human race!
² Everyone tells lies to everyone else;
they talk with slick speech
and divided hearts.
³ Let the LORD cut off all slick-talking lips
and every tongue that brags and brags,
⁴ that says, "We're unbeatable
with our tongues!
Who could get the best of us
with lips like ours?"

⁵ But the LORD says,
"Because the poor are oppressed,
because of the groans of the needy,
I'm now standing up.

I will provide the help
they are gasping for."[x]
⁶ The LORD's promises are pure,
like silver that's been refined
in an oven,
purified seven times over!

⁷ You, LORD, will keep us,[y]
protecting us
from this generation forever.
⁸ The wicked roam all over the place,
while depravity is praised
by human beings.

Psalm 13

For the music leader. A song of David.

¹ How long will you forget me, LORD?
Forever?
How long will you hide your face
from me?
² How long will I be left to my own wits,
agony filling my heart? Daily?
How long will my enemy keep
defeating me?

³ Look at me!
Answer me, LORD my God!
Restore sight to my eyes!
Otherwise, I'll sleep the sleep of death,
⁴ and my enemy will say, "I won!"
My foes will rejoice over my downfall.

⁵ But I have trusted in your faithful love.
My heart will rejoice in your salvation.
⁶ Yes, I will sing to the LORD
because he has been good to me.

Psalm 14

For the music leader. Of David.

¹ Fools say in their hearts, There is no God.
They are corrupt and do evil things;
not one of them does anything good.

² The LORD looks down
from heaven on humans

---

[u]Or *soul* [v]Heb lacks *heart*, but see 11:2 and Pss 7:10; 32:11; 36:10. [w]Perhaps a reference to an eight-string instrument; also in Ps 6 [x]Heb uncertain [y]LXX; MT *keep them*

to see if anyone is wise,
to see if anyone seeks God,
³ but all of them have turned bad.
Everyone is corrupt.
No one does good—
not even one person!

⁴ Are they dumb, all these evildoers,
devouring my people
like they are eating bread
but never calling on the LORD?

⁵ Count on it:ᶻ they will be in utter panic
because God is with
the righteous generation.
⁶ You evildoers may humiliate
the plans of those who suffer,
but the LORD is their refuge.

⁷ Let Israel's salvation come out of Zion!
When the LORD changes
his people's circumstances
for the better,
Jacob will rejoice!
Israel will celebrate!

Psalm 15
A psalm of David.

¹ Who can live in your tent, LORD?
Who can dwell on your holy mountain?
² The person who
lives free of blame,
does what is right,
and speaks the truth sincerely;
³ who does no damage with their talk,
does no harm to a friend,
doesn't insult a neighbor;
⁴ someone who despises
those who act wickedly,
but who honors those
who honor the LORD;
someone who keeps their promise
even when it hurts;
⁵ someone who doesn't lend money
with interest,
who won't accept a bribe
against any innocent person.

Whoever does these things
will never stumble.

Psalm 16
A miktamᵃ of David.

¹ Protect me, God,
because I take refuge in you.
² I say to the LORD, "You are my Lord.
Apart from you, I have nothing good."
³ Now as for the "holy ones" in the land,
the "magnificent ones"
that I was so happy about;
⁴ let their suffering increase because
they hurried after a different god.ᵇ
I won't participate
in their blood offerings;
I won't let their names cross my lips.
⁵ You, LORD, are my portion, my cup;
you control my destiny.
⁶ The property lines have fallen
beautifully for me;
yes, I have a lovely home.

⁷ I will bless the LORD who advises me;
even at night I am instructed
in the depths of my mind.
⁸ I always put the LORD in front of me;
I will not stumble
because he is on my right side.
⁹ That's why my heart celebrates
and my mood is joyous;
yes, my whole body will rest in safety
¹⁰ because you won't abandon my lifeᶜ
to the grave;ᵈ
you won't let your faithful follower
see the pit.

¹¹ You teach me the way of life.
In your presence is total celebration.
Beautiful things are always
in your right hand.

Psalm 17
A prayer of David.

¹ Listen to what's right, LORD;
pay attention to my cry!

ᶻOr *There they will be*; cf 53:5 ᵃPerhaps *inscription* ᵇHeb uncertain in 16:3-4; Heb lacks *because* and *god* in 16:4.
ᶜOr *my soul* ᵈHeb *Sheol*

Listen closely to my prayer;
   it's spoken by lips that don't lie!
2 My justice comes from you;
   let your eyes see what is right!
3 You have examined my heart,
   testing me at night.
You've looked me over closely,
   but haven't found anything wrong.
   My mouth doesn't sin.
4 But these other people's deeds?
   I have avoided such violent ways
   by the command from your lips.
5 My steps are set firmly on your paths;
   my feet haven't slipped.

6 I cry out to you because you answer me.
   So tilt your ears toward me now—
   listen to what I'm saying!
7 Manifest your faithful love
   in amazing ways
because you are the one
   who saves those who take refuge in you,
   saving them from their attackers
   by your strong hand.
8 Watch me with the very pupil of your eye!
   Hide me in the protection of your wings,
   9 away from the wicked
      who are out to get me,
   away from my deadly enemies
      who are all around me!
10 They have no pity;[e]
   their mouths speak arrogantly.
11 They track me down—
   suddenly, they surround me!
   They make their plans
   to put me in the dirt.
12 They are like a lion eager to rip its prey;
   they are like a strong young lion
      lying in wait.

13 Get up, LORD!
   Confront them!
   Bring them down!
   Rescue my life from the wicked—
   use your sword!
14 Rescue me from these people—
   use your own hands, LORD!
   Rescue me from these people

whose only possession
   is their fleeting life.[f]
But fill the stomachs
   of your cherished ones;
   let their children be filled full
   so that they have leftovers
   enough for their babies.

15 But me? I will see your face
   in righteousness;
   when I awake, I will be filled full
   by seeing your image.

Psalm 18[g]

*For the music leader. Of David
the LORD's servant, who spoke the
words of this song to the LORD after
the LORD delivered him from the power
of all his enemies and from Saul.*

1 He said: I love you, LORD, my strength.
2 The LORD is my solid rock,
   my fortress, my rescuer.
My God is my rock—
I take refuge in him!—
   he's my shield,
   my salvation's strength,
   my place of safety.
3 Because he is praiseworthy,[h]
   I cried out to the LORD,
   and I was saved from my enemies.
4 Death's cords were wrapped around me;
   rivers of wickedness terrified me.
5 The cords of the grave[i] surrounded me;
   death's traps held me tight.
6 In my distress I cried out to the LORD;
   I called to my God for help.
God heard my voice from his temple;
   I called to him for help,
   and my call reached his ears.

7 The earth rocked and shook;
   the bases of the mountains
      trembled and reeled
   because of God's anger.
8 Smoke went up from God's nostrils;
   out of his mouth came a devouring fire;
   flaming coals blazed out in front of him!

---

[e]Heb uncertain [f]Heb uncertain [g]This poem also occurs in 2 Sam 22 with some variations. [h]Heb uncertain
[i]Heb *Sheol*

⁹ God parted the skies and came down;
     thick darkness was beneath his feet.
¹⁰ God mounted the heavenly creatures
     and flew;
     he soared on the wings of the wind.
¹¹ God made darkness cloak him;
     his covering was dark water
     and dense cloud.
¹² God's clouds went ahead
     of the brightness before him;
     hail and coals of fire went too.
¹³ The LORD thundered in heaven;
     the Most High made his voice heard
     with hail and coals of fire.
¹⁴ God shot his arrows,
     scattering the enemy;
     he sent the lightning and threw them
     into confusion.
¹⁵ The seabeds were exposed;
     the earth's foundations were laid bare
     at your rebuke, LORD,
     at the angry blast of air coming
     from your nostrils.

¹⁶ From on high God reached down
     and grabbed me;
     he took me out of all that water.
¹⁷ God saved me from my powerful enemy,
     saved me from my foes,
     who were too much for me.
¹⁸ They came at me on the very day
     of my distress,
     but the LORD was my support.
¹⁹ He brought me out to wide-open spaces;
     he pulled me out safe
     because he is pleased with me.
²⁰ The LORD rewarded me
     for my righteousness;
     he restored me
     because my hands are clean,
²¹ because I have kept the LORD's ways.
     I haven't acted wickedly
     against my God.
²² All his rules are right in front of me;
     I haven't turned away from
     any of his laws.
²³ I have lived with integrity before him;
     I've kept myself from wrongdoing.
²⁴ And so the LORD restored me
     for my righteousness
     because my hands are clean in his eyes.

²⁵ You deal faithfully with the faithful;
     you show integrity
     toward the one who has integrity.
²⁶ You are pure toward the pure,
     but toward the crooked, you are tricky.
²⁷ You are the one who saves
     people who suffer
     and brings down those with proud eyes.
²⁸ You are the one who lights my lamp—
     the LORD my God
     illumines my darkness.
²⁹ With you I can charge into battle;
     with my God I can leap over a wall.
³⁰ God! His way is perfect;
     the LORD's word is tried and true.
    He is a shield
     for all who take refuge in him.

³¹ Now really, who is divine except the LORD?
     And who is a rock but our God?
³² Only God! The God
     who equips me with strength
     and makes my way perfect,
³³ who makes my step as sure as the deer's,
     who lets me stand securely
     on the heights,
³⁴ who trains my hands for war
     so my arms can bend a bronze bow.
³⁵ You've given me the shield
     of your salvation;
     your strong hand has supported me;
     your help has made me great.
³⁶ You've let me walk fast and safe,
     without even twisting an ankle.
³⁷ I chased my enemies and caught them!
     I didn't come home
     until I finished them off.
³⁸ I struck them down;
     they couldn't get up again;
     they fell under my feet.
³⁹ You equipped me with strength for war;
     you brought my adversaries down
     underneath me.
⁴⁰ You made my enemies turn tail from me;
     I destroyed my foes.
⁴¹ They cried for help,
     but there was no one to save them.
    They cried for help to the LORD,
     but he wouldn't answer them.
⁴² I crushed them
     like dust blown away by the wind;

I threw them out
　　like mud dumped in the streets.
⁴³ You delivered me from struggles
　　with many people;
　　you appointed me the leader
　　　of many nations.
　　Strangers come to serve me.
⁴⁴ After hearing about me, they obey me;
　　foreigners grovel before me.
⁴⁵ Foreigners lose their nerve;
　　they come trembling
　　　out of their fortresses.^j

⁴⁶ The LORD lives! Bless God, my rock!
　　Let the God of my salvation be lifted high!
⁴⁷ This is the God who avenges on my behalf,
　　who subdues people before me,
⁴⁸ who delivers me from my enemies.
　　Yes, you lifted me high
　　above my adversaries;
　　　you delivered me from violent people.
⁴⁹ That's why I thank you, LORD,
　　in the presence of the nations.
　　That's why I sing praises to your name.
⁵⁰ You are the one who gives great victories
　　to your king,
　　who shows faithful love
　　　to your anointed one—
　　to David and to his descendants forever.

Psalm 19

For the music leader.
A psalm of David.

¹ Heaven is declaring God's glory;
　　the sky is proclaiming his handiwork.
² One day gushes the news to the next,
　　and one night informs another
　　what needs to be known.
³ Of course, there's no speech, no words—
　　their voices can't be heard—
⁴ but their sound^k extends
　　throughout the world;
　　their words reach the ends of the earth.

God has made a tent in heaven
　　for the sun.
⁵ The sun is like a groom
　　coming out of his honeymoon suite;

like a warrior,
　　it thrills at running its course.
⁶ It rises in one end of the sky;
　　its circuit is complete at the other.
　　Nothing escapes its heat.

⁷ The LORD's Instruction is perfect,
　　reviving one's very being.^l
　　The LORD's laws are faithful,
　　making naive people wise.
⁸ The LORD's regulations are right,
　　gladdening the heart.
　　The LORD's commands are pure,
　　giving light to the eyes.
⁹ Honoring the LORD is correct,
　　lasting forever.
　　The LORD's judgments are true.
　　All of these are righteous!
¹⁰ They are more desirable than gold—
　　than tons of pure gold!
　　They are sweeter than honey—
　　even dripping off the honeycomb!
¹¹ No doubt about it:
　　your servant is enlightened by them;
　　there is great reward in keeping them.
¹² But can anyone know
　　what they've accidentally done wrong?
　　Clear me of any unknown sin
¹³ and save your servant
　　from willful sins.
　　Don't let them rule me.
　　Then I'll be completely blameless;
　　I'll be innocent of great wrongdoing.

¹⁴ Let the words of my mouth
　　and the meditations of my heart
　　be pleasing to you,
　　LORD, my rock and my redeemer.

Psalm 20

For the music leader.
A psalm of David.

¹ I pray that the LORD answers you
　　whenever you are in trouble.
　　Let the name of Jacob's God protect you.
² Let God send help to you
　　from the sanctuary
　　and support you from Zion.

^jOr *prisons* 　^kLXX, Vulg, Sym; MT *line* or *string* 　^lOr *soul*

³ Let God recall your many grain offerings;
  let him savor your
    entirely burned offerings. *Selah*
⁴ Let God grant what is in your heart
  and fulfill all your plans.
⁵ Then we will rejoice
  that you've been helped.
  We will fly our flags
  in the name of our God.
  Let the LORD fulfill all your requests!

⁶ Now I know that the LORD saves
  his anointed one;
  God answers his anointed one
  from his heavenly sanctuary,
  answering with mighty acts
  of salvation
  achieved by his strong hand.
⁷ Some people trust in chariots,
  others in horses;
  but we praise the LORD's name.
⁸ They will collapse and fall,
  but we will stand up straight and strong.

⁹ LORD, save the king!
  Let him answer us when we cry out!

Psalm 21

For the music leader.
A psalm of David.

¹ The king celebrates your strength, LORD;
  look how happy he is
  about your saving help!
² You've given him what his heart desires;
  you haven't denied
  what his lips requested. *Selah*
³ You bring rich blessings right to him;
  you put a crown of pure gold
  on his head.
⁴ He asked you for life,
  and you gave it to him, all right—
  long days, forever and always!
⁵ The king's reputation is great
  because of your saving help;
  you've conferred on him
  glory and grandeur.
⁶ You grant him blessings forever;
  you make him happy
  with the joy of your presence.
⁷ Because the king trusts the LORD,

and because of the Most High's
  faithful love,
  he will not stumble.

⁸ Your hand will catch all your enemies;
  your strong hand will catch
  all who hate you.
⁹ When you appear, LORD,
  you will light them up
  like an oven on fire.
  God will eat them whole in his anger;
  fire will devour them.
¹⁰ You will destroy their offspring
  from the land;
  destroy their descendants
  from the human race.
¹¹ Because they sought to do you harm,
  they devised a wicked plan—
  but they will fail!
¹² Because you will make them turn and run
  when you aim your bow
  straight at their faces!

¹³ Be exalted, LORD, in your strength!
  We will sing and praise your power!

Psalm 22

For the music leader. According to the
"Doe of Dawn." A psalm of David.

¹ My God! My God,
  why have you left me all alone?
  Why are you so far from saving me—
  so far from my anguished groans?
² My God, I cry out during the day,
  but you don't answer;
  even at nighttime I don't stop.
³ You are the holy one, enthroned.
  You are Israel's praise.
⁴ Our ancestors trusted you—
  they trusted you and you rescued them;
⁵ they cried out to you
  and they were saved;
  they trusted you
  and they weren't ashamed.

⁶ But I'm just a worm, less than human;
  insulted by one person,
  despised by another.
⁷ All who see me make fun of me—
  they gape, shaking their heads:

⁸ "He committed himself to the LORD,
  so let God rescue him;
  let God deliver him
  because God likes him so much."
⁹ But you are the one who pulled me
  from the womb,
  placing me safely at my mother's breasts.
¹⁰ I was thrown on you from birth;
  you've been my God
  since I was in my mother's womb.
¹¹ Please don't be far from me,
  because trouble is near
  and there's no one to help.

¹² Many bulls surround me;
  mighty bulls from Bashan encircle me.
¹³ They open their mouths at me
  like a lion ripping and roaring!
¹⁴ I'm poured out like water.
  All my bones have fallen apart.
  My heart is like wax;
  it melts inside me.
¹⁵ My strength is dried up
  like a piece of broken pottery.
  My tongue sticks to the roof of my mouth;
  you've set me down in the dirt of death.
¹⁶ Dogs surround me;
  a pack of evil people
  circle me like a lion—
  oh, my poor hands and feet!
¹⁷ I can count all my bones!
  Meanwhile, they just stare at me,
  watching me.
¹⁸ They divvy up my garments
  among themselves;
  they cast lots for my clothes.

¹⁹ But you, LORD! Don't be far away!
  You are my strength!
  Come quick and help me!
²⁰ Deliver me[m] from the sword.
  Deliver my life from the power of the dog.
²¹ Save me from the mouth of the lion.
  From the horns of the wild oxen
  you have answered me!

²² I will declare your name
  to my brothers and sisters;

I will praise you in the very center
  of the congregation!
²³ All of you who revere the LORD—
  praise him!
  All of you who are Jacob's descendants—
  honor him!
  All of you who are all Israel's offspring—
  stand in awe of him!
²⁴ Because he didn't despise or detest
  the suffering of the one who suffered—
  he didn't hide his face from me.
  No, he listened when I cried out to him
  for help.

²⁵ I offer praise in the great congregation
  because of you;
  I will fulfill my promises
  in the presence of those who honor God.
²⁶ Let all those who are suffering
  eat and be full!
  Let all who seek the LORD praise him!
  I pray your hearts live forever!
²⁷ Every part of the earth
  will remember and come back
  to the LORD;
  every family among all the nations
  will worship you.
²⁸ Because the right to rule
  belongs to the LORD,
  he rules all nations.
²⁹ Indeed, all the earth's powerful
  will worship him;[n]
  all who are descending to the dust
  will kneel before him;
  my being also lives for him.[o]
³⁰ Future descendants will serve him;
  generations to come will be told
  about my Lord.
³¹ They will proclaim God's righteousness
  to those not yet born,
  telling them what God has done.

Psalm 23

A psalm of David.

¹ The LORD is my shepherd.
  I lack nothing.
² He lets me rest in grassy meadows;

---

[m]Or *my soul*; also in 22:29   [n]Correction; MT *All the earth's powerful have eaten and will worship.*   [o]Correction
with LXX; Heb uncertain

he leads me to restful waters;
³ he keeps me ᵖ alive.
He guides me in proper paths
  for the sake of his good name.

⁴ Even when I walk
  through the darkest valley,
  I fear no danger because you are with me.
Your rod and your staff—
  they protect me.

⁵ You set a table for me
  right in front of my enemies.
You bathe my head in oil;
  my cup is so full it spills over!
⁶ Yes, goodness and faithful love
  will pursue me all the days of my life,
  and I will live �q in the LORD's house
  as long as I live.

Psalm 24
A psalm of David.

¹ The earth is the LORD's
  and everything in it,
  the world and its inhabitants too.
² Because God is the one
  who established it on the seas;
  God set it firmly on the waters.

³ Who can ascend the LORD's mountain?
  Who can stand in his holy sanctuary?
⁴ Only the one with clean hands
  and a pure heart;
  the one who hasn't made
    false promises,
  the one who hasn't sworn dishonestly.
⁵ That kind of person receives blessings
    from the LORD
  and righteousness
    from the God who saves.
⁶ And that's how things are
  with the generation that seeks him—
  that seeks the face of Jacob's God.ʳ

                                              Selah

⁷ Mighty gates: lift up your heads!
  Ancient doors: rise up high!
    So the glorious king can enter!
⁸ Who is this glorious king?
  The LORD—strong and powerful!
  The LORD—powerful in battle!
⁹ Mighty gates: lift up your heads!
  Ancient doors: rise up high!
    So the glorious king can enter!
¹⁰ Who is this glorious king?
  The LORD of heavenly forces—
    he is the glorious king!   *Selah*

ᵖOr *my soul* �q LXX; MT *I will return* ʳLXX, Syr; MT *seek your face, Jacob*

VALLEY OF THE SHADOW/ DARK VALLEY

The term is familiar from its use in Psalm 23:4, where the CEB translates it as "darkest valley." Elsewhere it is translated "deepest darkness" (e.g., Ps 44:19 [Heb. 44:20]; Amos 5:8) or "darkness and deep gloom" (e.g., Ps 107:10, 14).

God's creative powers are described in terms of control over deep darkness (Job 12:22; 34:22; 38:17; Jer 13:16; Amos 5:8). The term often appears in contexts expressing hope (e.g., Isa 9:2 [Heb. 9:1], which promises that light will shine on those who live in "a pitch-dark land") or comfort (e.g., Jer 2:6, which speaks of the Lord guiding Israel "through the wilderness . . . in a land of drought and darkness"). The term may also express despair, however, and thus is a favorite of Job (16:16; 24:17), who wishes that the day of his birth would be turned into deep darkness (3:4) and hopes for the darkness of death (10:21-22).

Psalm 25
Of David.

א ¹ I offer my life† to you, LORD.

ב ² My God, I trust you.
Please don't let me be put to shame!
Don't let my enemies rejoice over me!

ג ³ For that matter,
don't let anyone who hopes in you
be put to shame;
instead, let those who are treacherous
without excuse be put to shame.

ד ⁴ Make your ways known to me, LORD;
teach me your paths.

ה ⁵ Lead me in your truth—teach it to me—
because you are the God who saves me.

ו I put my hope in you all day long.

ז ⁶ LORD, remember your compassion
and faithful love—
they are forever!

ח ⁷ But don't remember the sins
of my youth or my wrongdoing.
Remember me only
according to your faithful love
for the sake of your goodness, LORD.

ט ⁸ The LORD is good and does the right thing;
he teaches sinners which way
they should go.

י ⁹ God guides the weak to justice,
teaching them his way.

כ ¹⁰ All the LORD's paths
are loving and faithful
for those who keep his covenant
and laws.

ל ¹¹ Please, for the sake of your good name,
LORD, forgive my sins, which are many!

מ ¹² Where are the ones who honor the LORD?
God will teach them which path to take.

נ ¹³ They will live a good life,
and their descendants
will possess the land.

ס ¹⁴ The LORD counsels those who honor him;
he makes his covenant known to them.

ע ¹⁵ My eyes are always looking to the LORD
because he will free my feet
from the net.

פ ¹⁶ Turn to me, God, and have mercy on me
because I'm alone and suffering.

צ ¹⁷ My heart's troubles
keep getting bigger—
set me free from my distress!

¹⁸ Look at my suffering and trouble—
forgive all my sins!

ר ¹⁹ Look at how many enemies I have
and how violently they hate me!

ש ²⁰ Please protect my life! Deliver me!
Don't let me be put to shame
because I take refuge in you.

ת ²¹ Let integrity and virtue guard me
because I hope in you.

²² Please, God, save Israel
from all its troubles!

Psalm 26
Of David.

¹ Establish justice for me, LORD,
because I have walked with integrity.
I've trusted the LORD
without wavering.

² Examine me, LORD; put me to the test!
Purify ᵘ my mind ᵛ and my heart.

³ Because your faithful love
is right in front of me—
I walk in your truth!

⁴ I don't spend time with people
up to no good;
I don't keep company with liars.

⁵ I detest the company of evildoers,
and I don't sit with wicked people.

⁶ I wash my hands—they are innocent!
I walk all around your altar, LORD,

⁷ proclaiming out loud my thanks,
declaring all your wonderful deeds!

⁸ I love the beauty ʷ of your house, LORD;
I love the place where your glory resides.

⁹ Don't gather me ˣ up with the sinners,
taking my life along with violent people

¹⁰ in whose hands are evil schemes,
whose strong hands are full of bribes.

¹¹ But me? I walk with integrity.
Save me! Have mercy on me!

---

§Ps 25 is an alphabetic acrostic poem; see the note at Pss 9–10. †Or *soul*; also in 25:13, 20 ᵘLXX or *investigate* ᵛOr *kidneys* ʷLXX; MT *the dwelling of your house* ˣOr *my soul*

¹² My feet now stand on level ground.
     I will bless the LORD
       in the great congregation.

Psalm 27
Of David.

¹ The LORD is my light and my salvation.
     Should I fear anyone?
     The LORD is a fortress
       protecting my life.
     Should I be frightened of anything?

² When evildoers come at me
     trying to eat me up—
     it's they, my foes and my enemies,
     who stumble and fall!

³ If an army camps against me,
     my heart won't be afraid.
     If war comes up against me,
     I will continue to trust in this:

⁴ I have asked one thing from the LORD—
     it's all I seek:
       to live in the LORD's house
         all the days of my life,
       seeing the LORD's beauty
       and constantly adoring his temple.

⁵ Because he will shelter me
     in his own dwelling
       during troubling times;
     he will hide me in a secret place
       in his own tent;
     he will set me up high, safe on a rock.

⁶ Now my head is higher
     than the enemies surrounding me,
     and I will offer sacrifices in God's tent—
       sacrifices with shouts of joy!
     I will sing and praise the LORD.

⁷ LORD, listen to my voice when I cry out—
     have mercy on me and answer me!

⁸ Come, my heart says, seek God's face.^y
     LORD, I do seek your face!

⁹ Please don't hide it from me!
     Don't push your servant aside angrily—
       you have been my help!
     God who saves me,
       don't neglect me!
     Don't leave me all alone!

¹⁰ Even if my father and mother
     left me all alone,
     the LORD would take me in.

¹¹ LORD, teach me your way;
     because of my opponents,
     lead me on a good path.

¹² Don't give me over
     to the desires of my enemies,
     because false witnesses
       and violent accusers
     have taken their stand against me.

¹³ But I have sure faith
     that I will experience
       the LORD's goodness
     in the land of the living!

¹⁴ Hope in the LORD!
     Be strong! Let your heart take courage!
     Hope in the LORD!

Psalm 28
Of David.

¹ I cry out to you, LORD.
     You are my rock; don't refuse to hear me.
     If you won't talk to me,
       I'll be just like those
       going down to the pit.

² Listen to my request for mercy
     when I cry out to you,
     when I lift up my hands
       to your holy inner sanctuary.

³ Don't drag me off with the wicked
     and those who do evil;
     the type who talk nice to their friends
     while evil thoughts are in their hearts!

⁴ Pay them back for what they've done!
     Pay them back for their evil deeds!
     Pay them back for their handiwork!
     Give back to them
       exactly what they deserve!

⁵ Because they have no regard
     for what the LORD has done,
     no regard for his handiwork,
     God will tear them down
       and never rebuild!

⁶ Bless the LORD
     because he has listened
       to my request for mercy!

^yCorrection; MT *My heart says to/of you . . . see my face!*

⁷ The LORD is my strength and my shield.
    My heart trusts him.
    I was helped, my heart rejoiced,
        and I thank him with my song.
⁸ The LORD is his people's strength;
    he is a fortress of protection
        for his anointed one.
⁹ Save your people, God!
    Bless your possession!
    Shepherd them
        and carry them for all time!

Psalm 29
A psalm of David.

¹ You, divine beings! Give to the LORD—
    give to the LORD glory and power!
² Give to the LORD the glory due his name!
    Bow down to the LORD
        in holy splendor!

³ The LORD's voice is over the waters;
    the glorious God thunders;
        the LORD is over the mighty waters.
⁴ The LORD's voice is strong;
    the LORD's voice is majestic.
⁵ The LORD's voice breaks cedar trees—
    yes, the LORD shatters
        the cedars of Lebanon.
⁶ He makes Lebanon jump around
    like a young bull,
    makes Sirion jump around
        like a young wild ox.
⁷ The LORD's voice unleashes fiery flames;
⁸ the LORD's voice
    shakes the wilderness—
    yes, the LORD shakes
        the wilderness of Kadesh.
⁹ The LORD's voice convulses the oaks,
    strips the forests bare,
    but in his temple everyone shouts,
        "Glory!"
¹⁰ The LORD sits enthroned
    over the floodwaters;
    the LORD sits enthroned—king forever!

¹¹ Let the LORD give strength to his people!
    Let the LORD bless his people
        with peace!

Psalm 30
*A psalm. A song for the
temple dedication. Of David.*

¹ I exalt you, LORD,
    because you pulled me up;
    you didn't let my enemies
        celebrate over me.
² LORD, my God, I cried out to you for help,
    and you healed me.
³ LORD, you brought meᶻ up
    from the grave,ᵃ
    brought me back to life from among
        those going down to the pit.

⁴ You who are faithful to the LORD,
    sing praises to him;
    give thanks to his holy name!
⁵ His anger lasts for only a second,
    but his favor lasts a lifetime.
    Weeping may stay all night,
        but by morning, joy!

⁶ When I was comfortable, I said,
    "I will never stumble."
⁷ Because it pleased you, LORD,
    you made me a strong mountain.
    But then you hid your presence.
    I was terrified.
⁸ I cried out to you, LORD.
    I begged my Lord for mercy:
⁹ "What is to be gained by my spilled blood,
    by my going down into the pit?
    Does dust thank you?
    Does it proclaim your faithfulness?
¹⁰ LORD, listen and have mercy on me!
    LORD, be my helper!"

¹¹ You changed my mourning into dancing.
    You took off my funeral clothes
        and dressed me up in joy
¹² so that my whole being
    might sing praises to you and never stop.
    LORD, my God,
    I will give thanks to you forever.

Psalm 31
For the music leader. A psalm of David.

¹ I take refuge in you, LORD.
    Please never let me be put to shame.
    Rescue me by your righteousness!

ᶻOr *my soul* ᵃHeb *Sheol*

2 Listen closely to me!
   Deliver me quickly;
      be a rock that protects me;
      be a strong fortress that saves me!
3 You are definitely my rock
   and my fortress.
   Guide me and lead me
      for the sake of your good name!
4 Get me out of this net
   that's been set for me
   because you are my protective fortress.
5 I entrust my spirit into your hands;
   you, LORD, God of faithfulness—
   you have saved me.
6 I hate those who embrace
   what is completely worthless.
   I myself trust the LORD.
7 I rejoice and celebrate in your faithful love
   because you saw my suffering—
   you were intimately acquainted
      with my deep distress.
8 You didn't hand me over to the enemy,
   but set my feet in wide-open spaces.

9 Have mercy on me, LORD,
   because I'm depressed.
   My vision fails because of my grief,
   as do my spirit and my body.
10 My life is consumed with sadness;
   my years are consumed with groaning.
   Strength fails me because of my suffering;[b]
   my bones dry up.
11 I'm a joke to all my enemies,
   still worse to my neighbors.
   I scare my friends,
   and whoever sees me in the street
      runs away!
12 I am forgotten, like I'm dead,
   completely out of mind;
   I am like a piece of pottery, destroyed.
13 Yes, I've heard all the gossiping,
   terror all around;
   so many gang up together against me,
      they plan to take my life!

14 But me? I trust you, LORD!
   I affirm, "You are my God."
15 My future is in your hands.

Don't hand me over to my enemies,
   to all who are out to get me!
16 Shine your face on your servant;
   save me by your faithful love!
17 LORD, don't let me be put to shame
   because I have cried out to you.
   Let the wicked be put to shame;
   let them be silenced in death's domain![c]
18 Let their lying lips be shut up
   whenever they speak arrogantly
      against the righteous
      with pride and contempt!
19 How great is the goodness
   that you've reserved
      for those who honor you,
   that you commit to those
      who take refuge in you—
      in the sight of everyone!
20 You hide them
   in the shelter of your wings,[d]
   safe from human scheming.
   You conceal them in a shelter,
   safe from accusing tongues.

21 Bless the LORD,
   because he has wondrously revealed
   his faithful love to me
      when I was like a city under siege!
22 When I was panicked, I said,
   "I'm cut off from your eyes!"
   But you heard my request for mercy
   when I cried out to you for help.

23 All you who are faithful, love the LORD!
   The LORD protects those who are loyal,
      but he pays the proud back
      to the fullest degree.
24 All you who wait for the LORD,
   be strong and let your heart take courage.

Psalm 32
A maskil[e] of David.

1 The one whose wrongdoing is forgiven,
   whose sin is covered over,
      is truly happy!
2 The one the LORD
   doesn't consider guilty—

---

[b]LXX, Syr; MT *my sin*   [c]Heb *Sheol*   [d]Correction; see Ps 61:5; MT *in the hiding place of your face*.   [e]Perhaps
instruction; it also appears in Pss 42, 44–45, 52–55, 74, 78, 88–89, 142; cf 47:7; the root is used in Ps 32:8.

in whose spirit there is no dishonesty—
  that one is truly happy!

[3] When I kept quiet, my bones wore out;
  I was groaning all day long—
  every day, every night!—
[4] because your hand was heavy upon me.
  My energy was sapped as if in a
    summer drought.   *Selah*
[5] So I admitted my sin to you;
  I didn't conceal my guilt.
  "I'll confess my sins to the LORD,"
    is what I said.
  Then you removed the guilt of my sin.
        Selah

[6] That's why all the faithful should pray to
  you during troubled times,[f]
  so that a great flood of water
    won't reach them.
[7] You are my secret hideout!
  You protect me from trouble.
  You surround me with songs of rescue!
        Selah

[8] I will instruct you and teach you
  about the direction you should go.
  I'll advise you
    and keep my eye on you.
[9] Don't be like some senseless
  horse or mule,
  whose movement must be controlled
  with a bit and a bridle.[g]
  Don't be anything like that![h]
[10] The pain of the wicked is severe,
  but faithful love surrounds
    the one who trusts the LORD.
[11] You who are righteous,
  rejoice in the LORD and be glad!
  All you whose hearts are right,
    sing out in joy!

Psalm 33

[1] All you who are righteous,
  shout joyfully to the LORD!
  It's right for those who do right
    to praise God.
[2] Give thanks to the LORD with the lyre!

Sing praises to him
  with the ten-stringed harp!
[3] Sing to him a new song!
  Play your best with joyful shouts!
[4] Because the LORD's word is right,
  his every act is done in good faith.
[5] He loves righteousness and justice;
  the LORD's faithful love
    fills the whole earth.
[6] The skies were made
  by the LORD's word,
  all their starry multitude
    by the breath of his mouth.
[7] He gathered the ocean waters
  into a heap;
  he put the deep seas into storerooms.
[8] All the earth honors the LORD;
  all the earth's inhabitants
    stand in awe of him.
[9] Because when he spoke, it happened!
  When he commanded, there it was!

[10] The LORD overrules
  what the nations plan;
  he frustrates
    what the peoples intend to do.
[11] But the LORD's plan stands forever;
  what he intends to do lasts
    from one generation to the next.
[12] The nation whose God is the LORD,
  the people whom God has chosen
    as his possession,
  is truly happy!
[13] The LORD looks down from heaven;
  he sees every human being.
[14] From his dwelling place God observes
  all who live on earth.
[15] God is the one who made
  all their hearts,
  the one who knows everything they do.

[16] Kings aren't saved by the strength
  of their armies;
  warriors aren't rescued
    by how much power they have.
[17] A warhorse is a bad bet for victory;
  it can't save despite its great strength.
[18] But look here: the LORD's eyes watch
  all who honor him,
  all who wait for his faithful love,

---

[f]Correction; MT *at a time of finding only*　[g]Heb uncertain　[h]Heb uncertain

[19] to deliver their lives[i] from death
and keep them alive during a famine.

[20] We put our hope in the LORD.
He is our help and our shield.
[21] Our heart rejoices in God
because we trust his holy name.
[22] LORD, let your faithful love surround us
because we wait for you.

Psalm 34[j]

*Of David, when he pretended
to be crazy before Abimelech,
who banished him so that he left.*

א [1] I will bless the LORD at all times;
his praise will always be in my mouth.
ב [2] I[k] praise the LORD—
let the suffering listen and rejoice.
ג [3] Magnify the LORD with me!
Together let us lift his name up high!

ד [4] I sought the LORD and he answered me.
He delivered me from all my fears.
ה [5] Those who look to God will shine;
their faces are never ashamed.
ו [6] This suffering person cried out:
the LORD listened and saved him
from every trouble.
ח [7] On every side, the LORD's messenger
protects those who honor God;
and he delivers them.
ט [8] Taste and see how good the LORD is!
The one who takes refuge in him
is truly happy!
י [9] You who are the LORD's holy ones,
honor him,
because those who honor him
don't lack a thing.
כ [10] Even strong young lions
go without and get hungry,
but those who seek the LORD
lack no good thing.

ל [11] Come, children, listen to me.
Let me teach you
how to honor the LORD:
מ [12] Do you love life;

do you relish the chance
to enjoy good things?
נ [13] Then you must keep your tongue
from evil
and keep your lips from speaking lies!
ס [14] Turn away from evil! Do good!
Seek peace and go after it!

ע [15] The LORD's eyes watch the righteous,
his ears listen to their cries for help.
פ [16] But the LORD's face is set against
those who do evil,
to eliminate even the memory of them
from the earth.
צ [17] When the righteous cry out,
the LORD listens;
he delivers them from all their troubles.
ק [18] The LORD is close to the brokenhearted;
he saves those whose spirits are crushed.

ר [19] The righteous have many problems,
but the LORD delivers them
from every one.
ש [20] He protects all their bones;
not even one will be broken.
ת [21] But just one problem will kill the wicked,
and those who hate the righteous
will be held responsible.
[22] The LORD saves his servants' lives;
all those who take refuge in him
won't be held responsible for anything.

Psalm 35

Of David.

[1] LORD, argue with
those who argue with me;
fight with those who fight against me!
[2] Grab a shield and armor;
stand up and help me!
[3] Use your spear and ax
against those who are out to get me!
Say to me:[m] "I'm your salvation!"
[4] Let those who want me dead
be humiliated and put to shame.
Let those who intend to hurt me
be thoroughly frustrated and disgraced.
[5] Let them be like dust on the wind—

---

[i]Or *souls*; also in 33:20   [j]Ps 34 is an alphabetic acrostic poem; see the note at Pss 9–10 or Ps 111.   [k]Or *my soul*;
also in 34:22   [l]Correction   [m]Or *my soul*; also in 35:4, 7, 9, 12, 13, 17, 24

and let the LORD's messenger
  be the one who does the blowing!
⁶ Let their path be dark and slippery—
  and let the LORD's messenger
  be the one who does the chasing!
⁷ Because they hid their net for me
  for no reason,
  they dug a pit for me for no reason.
⁸ Let disaster come to them
  when they don't suspect it.
  Let the net they hid catch them instead!
  Let them fall into it—to their disaster!

⁹ But I will rejoice in the LORD;
  I will celebrate his salvation.
¹⁰ All my bones will say,
  "LORD, who could compare to you?
  You rescue the weak
    from those who overpower them;
    you rescue the weak and the needy
     from those who plunder them."

¹¹ Violent witnesses stand up.
  They question me about things
  I know nothing about.
¹² They pay me back evil for good,
  leaving me stricken with grief.
¹³ But when they were sick,
  I wore clothes for grieving,
  and I kept a strict fast.
  When my prayer came back unanswered,[n]
¹⁴ I would wander around
  like I was grieving a friend or a brother.
  I was weighed down, sad,
  like I was a mother in mourning.
¹⁵ But when I stumbled,
  they celebrated and gathered together—
  they gathered together against me!
  Strangers[o] I didn't know tore me
  to pieces and wouldn't quit.
¹⁶ They ridiculed me over and over again,
  like godless people would do,
  grinding their teeth at me.

¹⁷ How long, my Lord,
  will you watch this happen?
  Rescue me from their attacks;
  rescue my precious life
  from these predatory lions!

¹⁸ Then I will thank you
  in the great assembly;
  I will praise you
  in a huge crowd of people.
¹⁹ Don't let those who are my enemies
  without cause celebrate over me;
  don't let those who hate me
  for no reason
  wink at my demise.
²⁰ They don't speak the truth;
  instead, they plot false accusations
  against innocent people in the land.
²¹ They speak out against me,
  saying, "Yes! Oh, yes! We've seen it
  with our own eyes!"

²² But you've seen it too, LORD.
  Don't keep quiet about it.
  Please don't be far from me, my Lord.
²³ Wake up! Get up and do justice for me;
  argue my case, my Lord and my God!
²⁴ Establish justice for me
  according to your righteousness,
  LORD, my God.
  Don't let them celebrate over me.
²⁵ Don't let them say to themselves,
  Yes! Exactly what we wanted!
  Don't let them say, "We ate him up!"
²⁶ Let all those who celebrate my misfortune
  be disgraced and put to shame!
  Let those who exalt themselves over me
  be dressed up in shame and dishonor!
²⁷ But let those who want things
  to be set right for me
  shout for joy and celebrate!
  Let them constantly say,
  "The LORD is great—
  God wants his servant to be at peace."
²⁸ Then my tongue will talk
  all about your righteousness;
  it will talk
  about your praise all day long.

Psalm 36

*For the music leader.
Of the LORD's servant David.*
¹ I know the sinful utterance
  of the wicked:[p]
  No fear of God confronts their own eyes,

[n]Heb uncertain   [o]Correction   [p]Heb uncertain

[2] because in their own eyes
   they are slick with talk
about their guilt ever being
   found out and despised.[q]
[3] The words of their mouths
   are evil and dishonest.
They have stopped being wise
   and stopped doing good.
[4] They plot evil even while resting in bed!
   They commit themselves
   to a path that is no good.
   They don't reject what is evil.

[5] But your loyal love, LORD,
   extends to the skies;
   your faithfulness reaches the clouds.
[6] Your righteousness is
   like the strongest mountains;
   your justice is like the deepest sea.
   LORD, you save both humans
   and animals.
[7] Your faithful love is priceless, God!
   Humanity finds refuge
   in the shadow of your wings.
[8] They feast on the bounty of your house;
   you let them drink
   from your river of pure joy.
[9] Within you is the spring of life.
   In your light, we see light.

[10] Extend your faithful love
   to those who know you;
   extend your righteousness
   to those whose heart is right.
[11] Don't let the feet of arrogant people
   walk all over me;
   don't let the hands of the wicked
   drive me off.
[12] Look—right there is where
   the evildoers have fallen,
   pushed down, unable to get up!

Psalm 37[r]
Of David.

א [1] Don't get upset over evildoers;
   don't be jealous of those who do wrong,
[2] because they will fade fast, like grass;

they will wither like green vegetables.
ב [3] Trust the LORD and do good;
   live in the land, and farm faithfulness.
[4] Enjoy the LORD,
   and he will give what your heart asks.
ג [5] Commit your way to the LORD!
   Trust him! He will act
   [6] and will make your righteousness
   shine like the dawn,
   your justice like high noon.
ד [7] Be still before the LORD,
   and wait[s] for him.
   Don't get upset when
   someone gets ahead—
   someone who invents evil schemes.

ה [8] Let go of anger and leave rage behind!
   Don't get upset—it will only lead to evil.
[9] Because evildoers will be eliminated,
   but those who hope in the LORD—
   they will possess the land.
ו [10] In just a little while the wicked won't exist!
   If you go looking around their place,
   they won't be there.
[11] But the weak will inherit the land;
   they will enjoy a surplus of peace.
ז [12] The wicked plot against the righteous,
   grinding their teeth at them.
[13] But my Lord just laughs at them
   because he knows
   that their day is coming.
ח [14] The wicked draw their swords
   and bend their bows
   to bring down the weak and the needy,
   to slaughter those whose way is right.
[15] But the sword of the wicked
   will enter their own hearts!
   Their bows will be broken!

ט [16] Better is the little that the righteous have
   than the overabundant wealth
   of the wicked.[t]
[17] The arms of the wicked will be broken,
   but the LORD supports the righteous.
י [18] The LORD is intimately acquainted
   with the lives of the blameless;
   their heritage will last forever.
[19] They won't be ashamed in troubling times,

---

[q]Heb uncertain [r]Ps 37 is an alphabetic acrostic poem; see the note at Pss 9–10 or Ps 111. [s]Correction with LXX, Vulg [t]LXX, Vulg, Syr; MT *abundant wealth of many wicked*

and in a period of famine
they will eat their fill.
כ ²⁰ But the wicked will die,
the LORD's enemies will disappear—
disappear like the beauty
of a meadow—in smoke.
ל ²¹ The wicked borrow
and don't pay it back,
but the righteous are
generous and giving.
²² Those blessed by God
will possess the land,
but those cursed by God
will be cut off.

מ ²³ A person's steps are made secure
by the LORD
when they delight in his way.
²⁴ Though they trip up,
they won't be thrown down,
because the LORD holds their hand.
נ ²⁵ I was young and now I'm old,
but I have never seen
the righteous left all alone,
have never seen their children
begging for bread.
²⁶ They are always gracious and generous.
Their children are a blessing.

ס ²⁷ Turn away from evil! Do good!
Then you will live in the land forever.
²⁸ The LORD loves justice.
He will never leave his faithful all alone.
ע They are guarded forever,
but the children of the wicked
are eliminated.
²⁹ The righteous will possess the land;
they will live on it forever.

פ ³⁰ The mouths of the righteous
recite wisdom;
their tongues discuss justice.
³¹ The Instruction of their God
is in their hearts;
they don't miss a step.
צ ³² The wicked, on the other hand,
target the righteous,
seeking to kill them.
³³ But the LORD won't leave the righteous
to the power of the wicked,

and won't let the righteous
be found guilty when they are judged.

ק ³⁴ Hope in the LORD and keep his way!
He will lift you up
so you can possess the land.
When the wicked are eliminated,
you will see it for yourself!
ר ³⁵ I myself have seen
wicked powerful people,
exalting themselves like a stately cedar.ᵘ
³⁶ But when Iᵛ came back, they were gone!
I looked all over for them,
but they couldn't be found!

ש ³⁷ Observe those who have integrity
and watch those whose heart is right
because the future belongs
to persons of peace.
³⁸ But wrongdoers will be destroyed
all together;
the future of the wicked
will be cut short.
ת ³⁹ The salvation of the righteous
comes from the LORD;
he is their refuge in times of trouble.
⁴⁰ The LORD will help them
and rescue them—
rescue them from the wicked—
and he will save them
because they have taken refuge in him.

Psalm 38

A psalm of David.
For the memorial offering.

¹ Please, LORD, don't punish me
when you are mad;
don't discipline me
when you are furious.
² Your arrows have pierced me;
your fist has come down hard on me.
³ There's nothing in my body
that isn't broken
because of your rage;
there's no health in my bones
because of my sin.
⁴ My wrongdoings are
stacked higher than my head;

ᵘLXX ᵛLXX, Syr, Vulg

they are a weight
  that's way too heavy for me.
⁵ My wounds reek; they are all infected
  because of my stupidity.
⁶ I am hunched over, completely down;
  I wander around all day long, sad.
⁷ My insides are burning up;
  there's nothing in my body
    that isn't broken.
⁸ I'm worn out, completely crushed;
  I groan because of my miserable heart.

⁹ Everything I long for
  is laid out before you, my Lord;
  my sighs aren't hidden from you.
¹⁰ My heart pounds;
  my strength abandons me.
  Even the light of my eyes is gone.
¹¹ My loved ones and friends
  keep their distance
    from me in my sickness;
  those who were near me
    now stay far away.
¹² Those who want me dead lay traps;
  those who want me harmed
    utter threats,
  muttering lies all day long.
¹³ But I'm like someone who is deaf,
  who can't hear;
  like someone who can't speak,
    whose mouth won't open.
¹⁴ I've become like a person
  who doesn't hear what is being said,
  whose mouth has no good comeback.
¹⁵ But I wait for you, LORD!
  You will answer, my Lord, my God!
¹⁶ Because I prayed:
  "Don't let them celebrate over me
  or exalt themselves over me
    when my foot slips,"
¹⁷ because I'm very close to falling,
  and my pain is always with me.
¹⁸ Yes, I confess my wrongdoing;
  I'm worried about my sin.
¹⁹ But my mortal enemies are so strong;
  those who hate me for no reason
    seem countless.
²⁰ Those who give, repay good with evil;
  they oppose me for pursuing good.

²¹ Don't leave me all alone, LORD!
  Please, my God, don't be far from me!

²² Come quickly and help me,
  my Lord, my salvation!

Psalm 39

*For the music leader. To Jeduthun.
A psalm of David.*
¹ I promised I would watch my steps
  so as not to sin with my tongue;
  promised to keep my mouth shut
  as long as the wicked were
    in my presence.
² So I was completely quiet, silent.
  I kept my peace, but it did no good.
  My pain got worse.
³ My heart got hot inside me;
  while stewing over it, the fire burned.
  Then I spoke out with my tongue:
⁴ "Let me know my end, LORD.
  How many days do I have left?
  I want to know how brief my time is."
⁵ You've made my days so short;
  my lifetime is like nothing in your eyes.
    Yes, a human life
      is nothing but a puff of air!   *Selah*

⁶ Yes, people wander around like shadows;
  yes, they hustle and bustle,
    but pointlessly;
  they don't even know who will get
    the wealth they've amassed.
⁷ So now, Lord, what should I be waiting for?
  My hope is set on you.
⁸ Deliver me from all my sins;
  don't make me
    some foolish person's joke.
⁹ I am completely silent;
  I won't open my mouth
  because you have acted.
¹⁰ Get this plague of yours off me!
  I'm being destroyed by the blows
    from your fist.
¹¹ You discipline people for their sin,
  punishing them;
  like a moth, you ruin what they treasure.
  Yes, a human life is just a puff of air!
    Selah

¹² Hear my prayer, LORD!
  Listen closely to my cry for help!
  Please don't ignore my tears!

I'm just a foreigner—
　　an immigrant staying with you,
　　just like all my ancestors were.
¹³ Look away from me
　　so I can be happy again
　　before I pass away and am gone.

Psalm 40

For the music leader. Of David. A psalm.

¹ I put all my hope in the LORD.
　　He leaned down to me;
　　he listened to my cry for help.
² He lifted me out of the pit of death,
　　out of the mud and filth,
　　and set my feet on solid rock.
　　He steadied my legs.
³ He put a new song in my mouth,
　　a song of praise for our God.
　　Many people will learn of this
　　and be amazed;
　　they will trust the LORD.
⁴ Those who put their trust in the LORD,
　　who pay no attention to the proud
　　or to those who follow lies,
　　are truly happy!

⁵ You, LORD my God!
　　You've done so many things—
　　your wonderful deeds
　　and your plans for us—
　　no one can compare with you!
　　If I were to proclaim
　　and talk about all of them,
　　they would be too numerous to count!
⁶ You don't relish sacrifices or offerings;
　　you don't require
　　entirely burned offerings
　　or compensation offerings—
　　but you have given me ears!
⁷ So I said, "Here I come!
　　I'm inscribed in the written scroll.
⁸ I want to do your will, my God.
　　Your Instruction is deep within me."
⁹ I've told the good news
　　of your righteousness
　　in the great assembly.
　　I didn't hold anything back—
　　as you well know, LORD!

¹⁰ I didn't keep your righteousness
　　only to myself.
　　I declared your faithfulness
　　and your salvation.
　　I didn't hide your loyal love
　　and trustworthiness
　　from the great assembly.

¹¹ So now you, LORD—
　　don't hold back
　　any of your compassion from me.
　　Let your loyal love and faithfulness
　　always protect me,
¹² because countless evils surround me.
　　My wrongdoings
　　have caught up with me—
　　I can't see a thing!
　　There's more of them
　　than hairs on my head—
　　my courage leaves me.
¹³ Favor me, LORD, and deliver me!
　　LORD, come quickly and help me!
¹⁴ Let those who seek my life,
　　who want me dead,
　　be disgraced and put to shame.
　　Let those who want to do me harm
　　be thoroughly frustrated
　　and humiliated.
¹⁵ Let those who say to me, "Yes! Oh, yes!"ʷ
　　be destroyed by their shame.
¹⁶ But let all who seek you
　　celebrate and rejoice in you.
　　Let those who love your salvation
　　always say,
　　"The LORD is great!"
¹⁷ But me? I'm weak and needy.
　　Let my Lord think of me.
　　You are my help and my rescuer.
　　My God, don't wait any longer!

Psalm 41

For the music leader. A psalm of David.

¹ Those who pay close attention
　　to the poor are truly happy!
　　The LORD rescues them
　　during troubling times.
² The LORD protects them
　　and keeps them alive;

ʷSee Ps 35:21, 25.

they are widely regarded throughout
  the land as happy people.
You[x] won't hand them over to the will
  of their enemies.
[3] The LORD will strengthen them when
  they are lying in bed, sick.
You will completely transform the place
  where they lie ill.

[4] But me? I said,
  "LORD, have mercy on me!
  Heal me because I have sinned
  against you."
[5] My enemies speak maliciously about me:
  "When will he die
  and his name disappear?"
[6] Whenever they come to visit,
  they say nothing of value.
  Their hearts collect evil gossip;
  once they leave, they tell it to everybody.
[7] All of those who hate me talk about me,
  whispering to each other,
  plotting evil against me:
[8] "Some horrible thing
  has been poured into him;
  the next time he lies down,
  he won't get up."
[9] Even my good friend,
  the one I trusted,
  who shared my food,

has kicked me with his heel—a betrayer!
[10] But you, LORD, please have mercy on me
  and lift me up
  so I can pay them back!
[11] Then I'll know you are pleased with me
  because my enemy won't be shouting
  in triumph over me.
[12] You support me in my integrity;
  you put me in your presence forever.

[13] Bless the LORD, the God of Israel,
  from forever to forever!
  Amen and Amen!

BOOK II
(Psalms 42–72)

Psalm 42[y]
For the music leader.
A maskil[z] of the Korahites.

[1] Just like a deer that craves
    streams of water,
  my whole being[a] craves you, God.
[2] My whole being thirsts for God,
  for the living God.
  When will I come and see God's face?[b]
[3] My tears have been my food
  both day and night,

---

[x]LXX, Syr; Vulg *God won't* [y]Pss 42–43 form one single poem; cf the note at Pss 9–10. [z]Perhaps *instruction*
[a]Or *soul*; also in 42:2, 4, 5, 6, 11; 43:5 [b]Syr, Tg; MT *and appear before God?*

AMEN

A term of agreement, *amen* has passed from Hebrew to Greek to English and other languages in transliteration but is often untranslated. The Hebraic root indicates trustworthiness or firmness concerning what is said. Revelation 3:14 designates Christ himself as "the Amen, the faithful and true witness," with the implication that, in Christ, believers find authenticity and the incarnate ratification of God's covenant. First Corinthians 14:16 reveals that to say "amen" in the Christian assembly is to agree with something that has been spoken by another. This liturgical use of *amen* arose when no printed prayer books or hymnals existed, but congregational worship in synagogue and church had to actively involve all participants. Therefore, what an individual uttered in prayer or preaching was affirmed by the assembly; a congregational "amen" was one way of guaranteeing such participation.

as people constantly questioned me,
"Where's your God now?"

⁴ But I remember these things
as I bare my soul:
how I made my way
to the mighty one's abode,ᶜ
to God's own house,
with joyous shouts
and thanksgiving songs—
a huge crowd celebrating the festival!
⁵ Why, I ask myself, are you so depressed?
Why are you so upset inside?
Hope in God!
Because I will again give him thanks,
my saving presence and my God.

⁶ My whole being is depressed.
That's why I remember you
from the land of Jordan and Hermon,
from Mount Mizar.
⁷ Deep called to deep
at the noise of your waterfalls;
all your massive waves
surged over me.
⁸ By day the LORD commands
his faithful love;
by night his song is with me—
a prayer to the God of my life.

⁹ I will say to God, my solid rock,
"Why have you forgotten me?
Why do I have to walk around,
sad, oppressed by enemies?"
¹⁰ With my bones crushed,
my foes make fun of me,
constantly questioning me:
"Where's your God now?"

¹¹ Why, I ask myself, are you so depressed?
Why are you so upset inside?
Hope in God!
Because I will again give him thanks,
my saving presence and my God.

Psalm 43

¹ Establish justice for me, God!
Argue my case against ungodly people!

Rescue me from the dishonest
and unjust!
² Because you are my God,
my protective fortress!
Why have you rejected me?
Why do I have to walk around,
sad, oppressed by enemies?
³ Send your light and truth—
those will guide me!
Let them bring me
to your holy mountain,
to your dwelling place.
⁴ Let me come to God's altar—
let me come to God, my joy, my delight—
then I will give you thanks with the lyre,
God, my God!

⁵ Why, I ask myself, are you so depressed?
Why are you so upset inside?
Hope in God!
Because I will again give him thanks,
my saving presence and my God.

Psalm 44

For the music leader.
*A maskil*ᵈ *of the Korahites.*

¹ We have heard it, God, with our own ears;
our ancestors told us about it:
about the deeds you did in their days,
in days long past.
² You, by your own hand,
removed all the nations,
but you planted our ancestors.
You crushed all the peoples,
but you set our ancestors free.
³ No, not by their own swords
did they take possession of the land—
their own arms didn't save them.
No, it was your strong hand, your arm,
and the light of your face
because you were pleased with them.
⁴ It's you, God! You who are my king,
the one who orders salvation for Jacob.
⁵ We've pushed our foes away by your help;
we've trampled our enemies
by your name.
⁶ No, I won't trust in my bow;
my sword won't save me

ᶜHeb uncertain ᵈPerhaps *instruction*

⁷ because it's you who saved us
from our foes,
you who put those who hate us to shame.
⁸ So we glory in God at all times
and give thanks to your name forever.
Selah

⁹ But now you've rejected
and humiliated us.
You no longer accompany our armies.
¹⁰ You make us retreat from the enemy;
our adversaries plunder us.
¹¹ You've handed us over
like sheep for butchering;
you've scattered us among the nations.

¹² You've sold your people for nothing,
not even bothering to set a decent price.
¹³ You've made us a joke to all our neighbors;
we're mocked and ridiculed
by everyone around us.
¹⁴ You've made us a bad joke
to the nations,
something to be laughed at
by all peoples.
¹⁵ All day long my disgrace confronts me,
and shame covers my face
¹⁶ because of the voices of those
who make fun of me and bad-mouth me,
because of the enemy who is out
for revenge.

SWORD

In the Early Bronze Age, the sword was short and straight, a dagger. In the Middle Bronze Age the sword became broader and longer. Half the uses of *sword* occur in the prophets Isaiah, Jeremiah, and Ezekiel to announce God's imminent judgment on Israel/Judah or the nations (e.g., Jer 25:27-31; Ezek 23:25, 47). Another fourth occur in Joshua–Kings and Chronicles, mostly meaning a weapon to injure and kill. *Sword* may also connote guarding (Gen 3:24) or be used figuratively to describe violence generally (Gen 27:40). The 20 uses in Psalms occur in outcries to God to save from the sword (22:20) and to deliver from (17:13) or destroy the wicked by the sword (7:12). The wicked who live by the sword will die by the sword (Ps 37:14-15). Since military imagery for God is metaphorical and human use of the sword is descriptive, scripture's violent imagery does not endorse human use of the sword or violence. While God's defeat of Egypt may be viewed as a triumph of war (Exod 15:3), it was not achieved by the sword (Ps 44:3-6).

In Ephesians 6:17 *sword* is used metaphorically to describe the believers' spiritual armor to withstand evil. Echoing God's armor in the OT (Isa 11:4-5; 49:2; 52:7; 59:17), believers are instructed to "stand with the belt of truth around your waist, justice as your breastplate, and put shoes on your feet so that you are ready to spread the good news of peace. Above all, carry the shield of faith so that you can extinguish the flaming arrows of the evil one. Take the helmet of salvation and the sword of the Spirit, which is God's word" (Eph 6:14-17). The most important Gospel use of *sword* outside the Passion Narrative is Matthew 10:34: "I haven't come to bring peace but a sword." Luke clarifies by substituting *division* for *sword*, indicating that Jesus' statement does not mean military war (12:51).

In Luke 22:36, Jesus tells the disciples to sell their clothes to buy swords, but he is annoyed with them when they take him literally and produce two swords. Luke 22:38 (and Luke 6:27-38) suggest that Jesus was speaking metaphorically about swords.

¹⁷ All this has come upon us,
  but we haven't forgotten you
  or broken your covenant.
¹⁸ Our hearts haven't turned away,
  neither have our steps
   strayed from your way.
¹⁹ But you've crushed us in the place
  where jackals^e live,
  covering us with deepest darkness.
²⁰ If we had forgotten the name of our God
  or spread out our hands
  to some strange deity,
²¹ wouldn't God have discovered it?
  After all, God knows every secret
   of the heart.
²² No, God, it's because of you
  that we are getting killed every day—
  it's because of you that we are
   considered sheep ready for slaughter.

²³ Wake up! Why are you sleeping, Lord?
  Get up! Don't reject us forever!
²⁴ Why are you hiding your face,
  forgetting our suffering and oppression?
²⁵ Look: we're going down to the dust;
  our stomachs are flat on the ground!
²⁶ Stand up! Help us!
  Save us for the sake
   of your faithful love.

Psalm 45

*For the music leader. According to
"The Lilies." Of the Korahites.
A maskil.^f A love song.*
¹ A marvelous word has stirred my heart
  as I mention my works to the king.
  My tongue is the pen of a skillful scribe.

² You are the most handsome of men;
  grace has been poured out on your lips.
  No wonder God has blessed
   you forever!
³ Strap on your sword, great warrior,
  with your glory and grandeur.
⁴ Go and succeed in your grandeur!
  Ride out on behalf of truth,
   humility, and righteousness!
  Let your strong hand perform
   awesome deeds.^g
⁵ Let the peoples fall beneath you.
  May your sharp arrows pierce the
   hearts of the king's enemies.
⁶ Your divine throne
  is eternal and everlasting.
  Your royal scepter
  is a scepter of justice.
⁷ You love righteousness
  and hate wickedness.
  No wonder God, your God,
   has anointed you
  with the oil of joy
  more than all your companions!
⁸ All your clothes have the pleasing scent
  of myrrh, aloes, and cinnamon.
  The music of stringed instruments
   coming from ivory palaces
   entertains you.
⁹ The royal princess is standing
  in your precious jewels;^h
  the queen stands at your right,
   dressed in the gold of Ophir.

¹⁰ Listen, daughter; pay attention,
  and listen closely!
  Forget your people
  and your father's house.

---

^eOr *the sea monster(s)* ^fPerhaps *instruction* ^gHeb uncertain ^hSyr; MT *royal princess is among your precious ones.*

MYRRH

Used as an ingredient in certain perfumes, cosmetics, and medicines, myrrh is a reddish-colored resin obtained from a thorny bush that generally grows no more than nine ft. in height. Its precious nature and expense are reflected in its being given as a gift by Jacob to Pharaoh (Gen 43:11) and by the magi to the baby Jesus (Matt 2:11).

11 Let the king desire your beauty.
    Because he is your master,
       bow down to him now.
12 The city of Tyre, the wealthiest of all,
    will seek your favor with gifts,
       13 with riches of every sort
    for the royal princess, dressed in pearls,[i]
       her robe embroidered with gold.
14 In robes of many colors,
    she is led to the king.
    Her attendants,
       the young women servants
       following her,
    are presented to you as well.
15 As they enter the king's palace,
    they are led in with celebration and joy.

16 Your sons, great king,
    will succeed your fathers;[j]
    you will appoint them as princes
       throughout the land.
17 I will perpetuate your name
    from one generation to the next
    so the peoples will praise you
       forever and always.

Psalm 46

For the music leader. Of the Korahites.
    According to Alamoth.[k] A song.
1 God is our refuge and strength,
    a help always near
       in times of great trouble.
2 That's why we won't be afraid
    when the world falls apart,
    when the mountains crumble into the
       center of the sea,
3 when its waters roar and rage,
    when the mountains shake
       because of its surging waves.   *Selah*
4 There is a river whose streams
    gladden God's city,
    the holiest dwelling of the Most High.
5 God is in that city. It will never crumble.
    God will help it when morning dawns.
6 Nations roar; kingdoms crumble.
    God utters his voice; the earth melts.

7 The LORD of heavenly forces is with us!
    The God of Jacob is our place of safety.
                                              Selah

8 Come, see the LORD's deeds,
    what devastation he has imposed
       on the earth—
9 bringing wars to an end
    in every corner of the world,
    breaking the bow
       and shattering the spear,
    burning chariots with fire.
10 "That's enough!
    Now know that I am God!
    I am exalted among all nations;
    I am exalted throughout the world!

11 The LORD of heavenly forces is with us!
    The God of Jacob is our place of safety.
                                              Selah

Psalm 47

For the music leader.
A psalm of the Korahites.
1 Clap your hands, all you people!
    Shout joyfully to God
       with a joyous shout!
2 Because the LORD Most High
    is awesome,
    he is the great king of the whole world.
3 He subdues the nations under us,
    subdues all people beneath our feet.
4 He chooses our inheritance for us:
    the heights of Jacob, which he loves.
                                              Selah

5 God has gone up with a joyous shout—
    the LORD with the blast
       of the ram's horn.
6 Sing praises to God! Sing praises!
    Sing praises to our king! Sing praises
7 because God is king of the whole world!
    Sing praises with a song of instruction![l]

8 God is king over the nations.
    God sits on his holy throne.

[i]Correction; Heb lacks *for*; Heb uncertain in 45:12-13. [j]Heb lacks *great king*. [k]Heb uncertain; see note at Pss 9–10 or Ps 111. [l]Or *Sing praises with understanding* or *wisely* (cf LXX, Vulg); Heb *maskil*; see the note at Ps 32.

9 The leaders of all people are gathered
　with the people of Abraham's God
　because the earth's guardians
　　belong to God;
　　God is exalted beyond all.

Psalm 48

A song. A psalm of the Korahites.

1 In the city belonging to our God,
　the LORD is great
　　and so worthy of praise!
His holy mountain 2 is a beautiful summit,
　the joy of the whole world.
　Mount Zion, in the far north,
　　is the city of the great king.
3 God is in its fortifications,
　revealing himself as a place of safety.

4 Look: the kings assembled themselves,
　advancing all together—
5 when they saw it, they were stunned;
　they panicked and ran away frightened.
6 Trembling took hold of them right there—
　like a woman giving birth,
7 or like the east wind when it smashes
　the ships of Tarshish.
8 Just like we had heard,
　now we've seen it for ourselves
　in the city of
　　the LORD of heavenly forces,
　in the city of our God.
　　May God make it secure forever! *Selah*

9 We dwell on your faithful love, God,
　in your temple.
10 Your praise, God,
　just like your reputation,
　　extends to the far corners of the earth.
　　Your strong hand is filled
　　　with righteousness.
11 Let Mount Zion be glad;
　let the towns of Judah rejoice
　　because of your acts of justice!

12 Walk around Zion;
　go all the way around it;
　　count its towers.

13 Examine its defenses closely;
　tour its fortifications
　　so that you may tell future generations:
14 "This is God,
　our God, forever and always!
　He is the one who will lead us
　　even to the very end."[m]

Psalm 49

For the music leader.
A psalm of the Korahites.

1 Listen to this, all you people!
　Listen closely,
　　all you citizens of the world—
2 people of every kind,
　rich and poor alike!
3 My mouth speaks wisdom;
　my heart's meditation is full of insight.
4 I will pay close attention to a proverb;
　I will explain my riddle on the lyre.

5 Why should I be afraid in times of trouble,
　when the wrongdoing of my bullies
　　engulfs me—
6 those people who trust
　　in their fortunes
　　and boast of their fantastic wealth?
7 Wealth? It can't save a single person!
　It can't pay a life's ransom-price to God.
8 The price to save someone's life
　is too high—
　　wealth will never be enough—
9 no one can live forever
　　without experiencing the pit.

10 Everyone knows that the wise die too,
　just like foolish and stupid people do,
　　all of them leaving their fortunes
　　　to others.
11 Their graves[n] are their eternal homes,
　the place they live for all generations,
　　even if they had counties
　　　named after them!
12 People won't live any longer
　because of wealth;
　　they're just like the animals
　　　that pass away.

---

[m]LXX; Heb uncertain; Heb *al muth* (*unto death* or *against death*), but see the notes at Pss 9–10, 46—the words
might belong in the heading of Ps 49.　[n]Correction with LXX

¹³ That's how it goes
   for those who are foolish,
   as well as for those who follow their lead,
   pleased with their talk.
                              Selah

¹⁴ Like sheep, they're headed
   straight for the grave.°
   Death will be their shepherd—
   but those who do right in their hearts
   will rule over them come morning!—
   their forms wasting away in the grave
   rather than having
   some dignified residence.ᴾ
¹⁵ But God will save my life
   from the power of the grave,
   because he will take me.   *Selah*

¹⁶ Don't be overly impressed
   when someone becomes rich,
   their house swelling
   to fantastic proportions,
¹⁷ because when they die,
   they won't take any of it with them.
   Their fantastic things
   won't accompany them down under.
¹⁸ Though they consider themselves
   blessed during their lives,
   and even thank you
   when you deal well with them,�q
¹⁹ they too will join the ancestors
   who've gone ahead;
   they too will never see the light again.
²⁰ Wealthy people?
   They just don't understand;
   they're just like the animals
   that pass away.

Psalm 50

A psalm of Asaph.

¹ From the rising of the sun to where it sets,
   God, the LORD God, speaks,
   calling out to the earth.
² From Zion, perfect in beauty,
   God shines brightly.
³ Our God is coming;
   he won't keep quiet.
   A devouring fire is before him;
   a storm rages all around him.
⁴ God calls out to the skies above
   and to the earth
   in order to judge his people:
⁵ "Bring my faithful to me,
   those who made a covenant with me
   by sacrifice."
⁶ The skies proclaim his righteousness
   because God himself is the judge. *Selah*

⁷ "Listen, my people, I will now speak;
   Israel, I will now testify against you.
   I am God—your God!
⁸ I'm not punishing you for your sacrifices
   or for your entirely burned offerings,
   which are always before me.
⁹ I won't accept bulls from your house
   or goats from your corrals
¹⁰ because every forest animal
   already belongs to me,
   as do the cattle on a thousand hills.
¹¹ I know every mountain bird;
   even the insects in the fields are mine.
¹² Even if I were hungry, I wouldn't tell you
   because the whole world and
   everything in it already belong to me.

°Heb *Sheol*; also again in 49:7, 15 ᴾHeb uncertain in 49:13-14 qLXX, Syr

ASAPH

A Levite son of Berechiah from the Gershom clan (1 Chron 6:39 [Heb. 6:24]; 15:17). Asaph and his descendants became influential musicians in the religious life of Israel. He probably founded a school of singers and musicians who were called "the sons of Asaph" (Ezra 3:10) and played a prominent role in the worship and music of the postexilic community (1 Chron 25:1-2; 2 Chron 20:14; 29:13; Ezra 2:41; Neh 7:44; 11:22). Twelve psalms (Pss 50; 73–83) carry his name in their titles.

¹³ Do I eat bulls' meat?
   Do I drink goats' blood?
¹⁴ Offer God a sacrifice of thanksgiving!
   Fulfill the promises
     you made to the Most High!
¹⁵ Cry out to me whenever you are in trouble;
   I will deliver you,
     then you will honor me."

¹⁶ But to the wicked God says,
   "Why do you talk about my laws?
   Why do you even mention my covenant?
¹⁷ You hate discipline, and
   you toss my words behind your back.
¹⁸ You make friends with thieves whenever
   you see one;
   you spend your time with adulterers.
¹⁹ You set your mouth free to do evil,
   then harness your tongue to tell lies.
²⁰ You sit around,
   talking about your own siblings;
   you find fault with the children
     of your very own mother.
²¹ You've done these things
   and I've kept quiet.
   You thought I was just like you!
   But now I'm punishing you;
   I'm laying it all out,
     right in front of your face.
²² So consider this carefully,
   all you who forget God,
   or I'll rip you to pieces
     with no one to deliver you:
²³ The one who offers
   a sacrifice of thanksgiving
   is the one who honors me.

ʳHeb uncertain

And it is to the one who charts
   the correct path that I will show
   divine salvation."

Psalm 51

*For the music leader. A psalm of David,
when the prophet Nathan came to him
just after he had been with Bathsheba.*
¹ Have mercy on me, God,
   according to your faithful love!
   Wipe away my wrongdoings
   according to your great compassion!
² Wash me completely clean of my guilt;
   purify me from my sin!
³ Because I know my wrongdoings,
   my sin is always right in front of me.
⁴ I've sinned against you—you alone.
   I've committed evil in your sight.
   That's why you are justified
     when you render your verdict,
   completely correct
     when you issue your judgment.
⁵ Yes, I was born in guilt, in sin,
   from the moment my mother
     conceived me.
⁶ And yes, you want truth
   in the most hidden places;
   you teach me wisdom
     in the most secret space.ʳ

⁷ Purify me with hyssop
   and I will be clean;
   wash me and I will be whiter
     than snow.
⁸ Let me hear joy and celebration again;

SNOW

With the exception of Mount Hermon in the north, modern-day Israel does not experience snow on an annual basis. Occasionally, however, snow does fall on other mountainous regions, including the hills of Jerusalem. Psalm 147:16 acknowledges its presence in the environs of Jerusalem as one of the provisions of the Lord. Elsewhere, snow epitomizes spiritual purity and exemplifies the color white. Thus, Isaiah 1:18 and Psalm 51:7 use snow to illustrate the state of cleanness that results from the removal of sin's stain.

let the bones you crushed
  rejoice once more.
9 Hide your face from my sins;
  wipe away all my guilty deeds!
10 Create a clean heart for me, God;
  put a new, faithful spirit deep inside me!
11 Please don't throw me
  out of your presence;
  please don't take your holy spirit
    away from me.
12 Return the joy of your salvation to me
  and sustain me with a willing spirit.
13 Then I will teach wrongdoers your ways,
  and sinners will come back to you.

14 Deliver me from violence, God,
  God of my salvation,
  so that my tongue can sing
    of your righteousness.
15 Lord, open my lips,
  and my mouth will proclaim your praise.
16 You don't want sacrifices.
  If I gave an entirely burned offering,
  you wouldn't be pleased.
17 A broken spirit is my sacrifice, God.[s]
  You won't despise a heart, God,
    that is broken and crushed.
18 Do good things for Zion by your favor.
  Rebuild Jerusalem's walls.
19 Then you will again want
  sacrifices of righteousness—
  entirely burned offerings
  and complete offerings.
  Then bulls will again be sacrificed
    on your altar.

Psalm 52

*For the music leader. A maskil[t]
of David, when Doeg the Edomite
came and told Saul, "David has gone
to Ahimelech's house."*

1 Hey, powerful person!
  Why do you brag about evil?
  God's faithful love lasts all day long.
2 Your tongue devises destruction:
  it's like a sharpened razor,
  causing deception.

3 You love evil more than good;
  you love lying more than speaking
    what is right.   *Selah*
4 You love all destructive words;
  you love the deceiving tongue.

5 But God will take you down permanently;
  he will snatch you up,
  tear you out of your tent,
  and uproot you from the land
    of the living!   *Selah*
6 The righteous will see and be in awe;
  they will laugh at those people:
7 "Look at them! They didn't make God
  their refuge.
  Instead, they trusted in
    their own great wealth.
  They sought refuge in it—
    to their own destruction!"

8 But I am like a green olive tree
  in God's house;
  I trust in God's faithful love
    forever and always.
9 I will give thanks to you, God, forever,
  because you have acted.
In the presence of your faithful people,
  I will hope in your name
    because it's so good.

Psalm 53

*For the music leader,
according to the mahalath.
A maskil[u] of David.*

1 Fools say in their hearts,
  There's no God.
They are corrupt and do horrible deeds;
  not one of them does anything good.

2 God looks down from heaven
  on humans
  to see if anyone is wise,
  to see if anyone seeks God.
3 But all have turned away.
  Everyone is corrupt.
  No one does good—
  not even one person!

---

[s]Correction [t]Perhaps *instruction*; it also appears in Pss 42, 44–45, 52–55, 74, 78, 88–89, 142; cf 47:7; the root is used in Ps 32:8. [u]Perhaps *instruction*

⁴ Are they dumb—these evildoers—
    devouring my people
    like they are eating bread
    but never calling on God?

⁵ There, where there was nothing to fear,
    they will be in utter panic
    because God will scatter the bones
    of those who attacked you.
    You will put them to shame
    because God has rejected them.

⁶ Let Israel's salvation come out of Zion!
    When God changes
    his people's circumstances
        for the better,
    Jacob will rejoice;
    Israel will celebrate!

Psalm 54

For the music leader.
With stringed instruments.
*A maskil*ᵛ *of David,*
when the Ziphites came and said
to Saul, "Isn't David hiding among us?"

¹ God! Save me by your name;
    defend me by your might!
² God! Hear my prayer;
    listen to the words of my mouth!

³ The proud have come up against me;
    violent people want me dead.
    They pay no attention to God.   *Selah*

⁴ But look here: God is my helper;
    my Lord sustains my life.
⁵ He will bring disaster on my opponents.
    By your faithfulness, God,
        destroy them!

⁶ I will sacrifice to you freely;
    I will give thanks to your name, LORD,
    because it's so good,
        ⁷ and because God has delivered me
        from every distress.
    My eyes have seen
        my enemies' defeat.ʷ

Psalm 55

For the music leader. With stringed
*instruments. A maskil*ˣ *of David.*

¹ God, listen to my prayer;
    don't avoid my request!
² Pay attention! Answer me!
    I can't sit still while complaining.
    I'm beside myself
    ³ over the enemy's noise,
        at the wicked person's racket,
    because they bring disaster on me
    and harass me furiously.

⁴ My heart pounds in my chest
    because death's terrors have reached me.
⁵ Fear and trembling have come upon me;
    I'm shaking all over.
⁶ I say to myself,
    I wish I had wings like a dove!
    I'd fly away and rest.
⁷ I'd run so far away!
    I'd live in the desert.   *Selah*
⁸ I'd hurry to my hideout,
    far from the rushing wind and storm.

⁹ Baffle them, my Lord!
    Confuse their language
    because I see violence and conflict
        in the city.
¹⁰ Day and night they make their rounds
    on its walls,
    and evil and misery live inside it.
¹¹ Disaster lives inside it;
    oppression and fraud
        never leave the town square.

¹² It's not an enemy that is insulting me—
    I could handle that.
    It's not someone who hates me
        who is exalted over me—
    I could hide from them.
¹³ No. It's you, my equal,
    my close companion, my good friend!
¹⁴ It was so pleasant when
    together we entered God's house
        with the crowd.

¹⁵ Let death devastate my enemies;
    let them go to the graveʸ alive

ᵛPerhaps *instruction*; it also appears in Pss 42, 44–45, 52–55, 74, 78, 88–89, 142; cf 47:7; the root is used in Ps 32:8.   ʷHeb lacks *defeat*.   ˣPerhaps *instruction*   ʸHeb *Sheol*

because evil lives with them—
even inside them!

[16] But I call out to God,
and the LORD will rescue me.
[17] At evening, morning, and midday
I complain and moan
so that God will hear my voice.
[18] He saves me,[z] unharmed,
from my struggle,
though there are many
who are out to get me.
[19] God, who is enthroned
from ancient days,
will hear and humble them   *Selah*
because they don't change
and they don't worship God.

[20] My friend attacked his allies,
breaking his covenant.
[21] Though his talk
is smoother than butter,
war is in his heart;
though his words are more
silky than oil,
they are really drawn swords:
[22] "Cast your burden on the LORD—
he will support you!
God will never let the righteous
be shaken!"

[z]Or *my life* or *soul*   [a]Perhaps *inscription*

[23] But you, God, bring the wicked
down to the deepest pit.
Let bloodthirsty
and treacherous people
not live out even half their days.
But me? I trust in you!

Psalm 56

*For the music leader. According to
"The Silent Dove of Distant Places."
A miktam[a] of David, when the
Philistines seized him in Gath.*

[1] God, have mercy on me
because I'm being trampled.
All day long the enemy oppresses me.
[2] My attackers trample me all day long
because I have so many enemies.
Exalted one, [3]whenever I'm afraid,
I put my trust in you—
[4] in God, whose word I praise.
I trust in God; I won't be afraid.
What can mere flesh do to me?

[5] All day long they frustrate my pursuits;
all their thoughts are evil against me.
[6] They get together and set an ambush—
they are watching my steps,
hoping for my death.

GATH

One of the cities of the Philistine Pentapolis, Gath plays a particularly important role in the stories about King David. It appears first, however, in the book of Joshua, where it is listed as one of the cities where the Anakim, presumably a prehistoric race of giants, remained after the conquest. Later, the covenant chest was brought to Gath after it was captured by the Philistines (1 Sam 5:8-9). During his ministry, the prophet Samuel is supposed to have restored to Israel cities lying between Ekron and Gath on the border between Israel and Philistia (1 Sam 7:14). Gath's association with giants is continued in the story of David and Goliath (1 Sam 17), the latter a man of immense proportions from Philistine Gath. After the Israelites' rout of the Philistines subsequent to David's defeat of Goliath, the Israelites pursued the Philistines as far as Ekron and Gath (1 Sam 17:52), which is later the location of a series of anecdotes about the exploits of David's heroes in battle against fearsome Philistines (2 Sam 21:15-22; 1 Chron 20:4-8).

7 Don't rescue them for any reason!
  In wrath bring down the people, God!

8 You yourself have kept track of my misery.
  Put my tears into your bottle—
  aren't they on your scroll already?
9 Then my enemies will retreat
  when I cry out.
  I know this because God is mine.
10 God: whose word I praise.
   The LORD: whose word I praise.
11 I trust in God; I won't be afraid.
   What can anyone do to me?

12 I will fulfill my promises to you, God.
   I will present thanksgiving offerings
     to you
13 because you have saved my life
     from death,
   saved my feet from stumbling
     so that I can walk before God
     in the light of life.

Psalm 57

For the music leader. Do not destroy.
A miktam[b] of David, when he fled
from Saul into the cave.

1 Have mercy on me, God;
  have mercy on me
  because I[c] have taken refuge in you.
  I take refuge
  in the shadow of your wings
    until destruction passes by.
2 I call out to God Most High—
  to God, who comes through for me.
3 He sends orders from heaven
    and saves me,
  rebukes the one who tramples me.
                                Selah
  God sends his loyal love
    and faithfulness.

4 My life is in the middle of a pack of lions.
  I lie down
    among those who devour humans.
  Their teeth are spears and arrows;
    their tongues are sharpened swords.
5 Exalt yourself, God, higher than heaven!

  Let your glory be over all the earth!
6 They laid a net for my feet
    to bring me down;
  they dug a pit for me,
    but they fell into it instead!   *Selah*

7 My heart is unwavering, God—
  my heart is unwavering.
  I will sing and make music.
8 Wake up, my glory!
  Wake up, harp and lyre!
  I will wake the dawn itself!
9 I will give thanks to you,
  my Lord,
    among all the peoples;
  I will make music to you
    among the nations
10 because your faithful love
     is as high as heaven;
   your faithfulness reaches the clouds.
11 Exalt yourself, God, higher than heaven!
   Let your glory be over all the earth!

Psalm 58

For the music leader. Do not destroy.
A psalm of David, a miktam.[d]

1 Do you really speak what is right,
    you gods?
  Do you really judge humans fairly?
2 No: in your hearts you plan injustice;
  your hands do violence on the earth.

3 The wicked backslide from the womb;
  liars go astray from birth.
4 Their venom is like a snake's venom—
  like a deaf cobra's—
    one that shuts its ears
5 so it can't hear
    the snake charmer's voice
  or the spells of a skillful enchanter.

6 God, break their teeth out of their mouths!
  Tear out the lions' jawbones, LORD!
7 Let them dissolve like water flowing away.
  When they bend the bow,
    let their arrows be like headless shafts.[e]
8 Like the snail that dissolves into slime,
  like a woman's stillborn child,

b Perhaps *inscription*   c Or *my soul*   d Perhaps *inscription*   e Heb uncertain

let them never see the sun.
9 Before your pots feel the thorns,
   whether green or burned up,
   God will sweep them away!f

10 But the righteous will rejoice
    when they see vengeance done,
    when they wash their feet
    in the blood of the wicked.
11 Then it will be said:
    "Yes, there is a reward for the righteous!
    Yes, there is a God who judges people
    on the earth."

Psalm 59

*For the music leader. Do not destroy.
A miktam*g *of David, when Saul
sent men to watch the house
in order to kill him.*

1 Oh, my God, deliver me from my enemies;
   put me out of reach from those
   who rise up against me.
2 Deliver me from evildoers;
   save me from the bloodthirsty.
3 Look at how they lie in ambush
   for my life!
   Powerful people are attacking me,
   LORD—
   but not because of any error
   or sin of mine.
4 They run and take their stand—
   but not because of any fault of mine.

Get up when I cry out to you!
   Look at what's happening!
5 You are the LORD God of heavenly forces,
   the God of Israel!
   Wake up and punish all the nations!
   Grant no mercy to any wicked traitor!   *Selah*

6 They come back every evening,
   growling like dogs,
   prowling around the city.
7 See what they belch out with their mouths:
   swords are between their lips!
   Who can listen to them?h
8 But you, LORD, laugh at them.
   You mock all the nations.

9 I keep looking for you, my strength,
   because God is my stronghold.
10 My loving God will come to meet me.
    God will allow me to look down
    on my enemies.

11 Don't kill them,
    or my people might forget;
    instead, by your power
    shake them up and bring them down,
    you who are our shield and my Lord.
12 For the sin of their mouths,
    the words that they speak,
    let them be captured in their pride.
    For the curses and lies they repeat,
13 finish them off in anger;
    finish them off until they are gone!
    Then let it be known
    to the ends of the earth
    that God rules over Jacob.   *Selah*

14 They come back every evening,
    growling like dogs,
    prowling around the city.
15 They roam about for food,
    and if they don't get their fill,
    they stay all night.
16 But me? I will sing of your strength!
    In the morning I will shout out loud
    about your faithful love
    because you have been my stronghold,
    my shelter when I was distraught.
17 I will sing praises to you, my strength,
    because God is my stronghold,
    my loving God.

Psalm 60

*For the music leader. According to "Lily."
A testimony. A miktam*i *of David.
For instruction, when he went to war
with Aram-naharaim and Aram-sobah,
and when Joab returned and defeated
Edom, killing twelve thousand
in the Salt Valley.*

1 God, you have rejected us—
   shattered us.
   You've been so angry.
   Now restore us!

---

f Heb uncertain   g Perhaps *inscription*   h Heb uncertain   i Perhaps *inscription*

² You've made the ground quake,
  splitting it open.
  Now repair its cracks
  because it's shaking apart!
³ You've made your people suffer hardship;
  you've given us wine and we stagger.
⁴ Give a flag to those who honor you,
  so they can rally around it,
  safe from attack.ʲ   *Selah*
⁵ Save us by your power and answer us
  so that the people you love might
  be rescued.

⁶ God has spoken in his sanctuary:
  "I will celebrate as I divide up Shechem
  and portion out the Succoth Valley.
⁷ Gilead is mine;
  Manasseh is mine;
  Ephraim is my helmet;
  Judah is my scepter.
⁸ But Moab is my washbowl;
  I'll throw my shoe at Edom.
  I shout in triumph over Philistia!ᵏ
⁹ I wish someone would bring me
  to a fortified city!
  I wish someone would lead me to Edom!"

¹⁰ But you have rejected us, God,
  haven't you?
  God, you no longer accompany
  our armies.
¹¹ Give us help against the enemy;
  human help is worthless.
¹² With God we will triumph;
  he's the one who will trample
  our adversaries.

Psalm 61

*For the music leader,
with stringed instruments. Of David.*

¹ God, listen to my cry;
  pay attention to my prayer!
² When my heart is weak,
  I cry out to you
  from the very ends of the earth.
  Lead me to the rock
  that is higher than I am

³ because you have been my refuge,
  a tower of strength
  in the face of the enemy.
⁴ Please let me live in your tent forever!
  Please let me take refuge
  in the shelter of your wings!   *Selah*
⁵ Because you, God,
  have heard my promises;
  you've given meˡ the same possession
  as those who honor your name.

⁶ Add days to the king's life!
  Let his years extend
  for many generations!
⁷ Let him be enthroned forever before God!
  Make it so love and faithfulness
  watch over him!
⁸ Then I will sing praises
  to your name forever,
  and I will do what I promised
  every single day.

Psalm 62

*For the music leader. According to
Jeduthun. A psalm of David.*

¹ Only in God do Iᵐ find rest;
  my salvation comes from him.
² Only God is my rock and my salvation—
  my stronghold!—
  I won't be shaken anymore.

³ How long will all of you attack others;
  how long will you tear them downⁿ
  as if they were leaning walls
  or broken-down fences?
⁴ The only desire of this people
  is to bring others down low;
  they delight in deception.
  With their mouths they bless,
  but inside they are cursing.   *Selah*

⁵ Oh, Iᵒ must find rest in God only,
  because my hope comes from him!
⁶ Only God is my rock and my salvation—
  my stronghold!—I will not be shaken.
⁷ My deliverance and glory depend on God.
  God is my strong rock.
  My refuge is in God.

8 All you people: Trust in him at all times!
  Pour out your hearts before him!
  God is our refuge! *Selah*

9 Human beings are nothing but a breath.
  Human beings are nothing but lies.
  They don't even register on a scale;
  taken all together
    they are lighter than a breath!

10 Don't trust in violence;
  don't set false hopes in robbery.
  When wealth bears fruit,
  don't set your heart on it.

11 God has spoken one thing—
  make it two things—
  that I myself have heard:
  that strength belongs to God,

12 and faithful love comes from you,
    my Lord—
  and that you will repay
  everyone according to their deeds.

Psalm 63
A psalm of David,
when he was in the Judean desert.

1 God! My God! It's you—
  I search for you!
  My whole being[p] thirsts for you!
  My body desires you
    in a dry and tired land,
    no water anywhere.

2 Yes, I've seen you in the sanctuary;
  I've seen your power and glory.

3 My lips praise you
  because your faithful love
  is better than life itself!

4 So I will bless you as long as I'm alive;
  I will lift up my hands in your name.

5 I'm fully satisfied—
  as with a rich dinner.
  My mouth speaks praise
  with joy on my lips—

6 whenever I ponder you on my bed,
  whenever I meditate on you
    in the middle of the night—

7 because you've been a help to me
  and I shout for joy in the protection of
  your wings.

8 My whole being clings to you;
  your strong hand upholds me.

9 But what about those people
  who want to destroy me?
  Let them go into the bowels
    of the earth!

10 Let their blood flow by the sword!
  Let them be food for wild jackals!

11 But the king should rejoice in God;
  everyone who swears by God
    should give praise
    when the mouths of liars
    are shut for good.

Psalm 64
For the music leader. A psalm of David.

1 Listen to me when I complain, God!
  Protect my life from the enemy's terror!

2 Hide me from the secret plots
    of wicked people;
  hide me from the schemes of evildoers

3 who sharpen their tongues like swords.
  They aim their arrow—a cruel word—

4 from their hiding places
  so as to shoot an innocent person.
  They shoot without warning
    and without fear.

5 They encourage themselves
  with evil words.
  They plan on laying traps in secret.
  "Who will be able to see them?"
    they ask.

6 "Let someone try to expose our crimes!
  We've devised a perfect plot!
  It's deep within
    the human mind and heart."[q]

7 But God will shoot them with an arrow!
  Without warning,
    they will be wounded!

8 The LORD will make them trip
  over their own tongues;
  everyone who sees them
    will just shake their heads.

9 Then all people will honor God,
  will announce the act of God,
  will understand it was God's work.

[p]Or *my soul*; also in 63:5, 8   [q]Heb uncertain

¹⁰ Let the righteous rejoice in the LORD;
  let them take refuge in him;
  let everyone whose heart is
    in the right place give praise!

Psalm 65

For the music leader.
A psalm of David. A song.

¹ God of Zion, to you even silence is praise.
  Promises made to you are kept—
² you listen to prayer—
  and all living things come to you.
³ When wrongdoings become
  too much for me,
  you forgive our sins.
⁴ How happy is the one you choose
  to bring close,
  the one who lives in your courtyards!
We are filled full
  by the goodness of your house,
  by the holiness of your temple.

⁵ In righteousness you answer us,
  by your awesome deeds,
  God of our salvation—
you, who are the security
  of all the far edges of the earth,
  even the distant seas.
⁶ You establish the mountains
  by your strength;
  you are dressed in raw power.
⁷ You calm the roaring seas;
  calm the roaring waves,
  calm the noise of the nations.
⁸ Those who dwell on the far edges
  stand in awe of your acts.
You make the gateways
  of morning and evening sing for joy.
⁹ You visit the earth and make it abundant,
  enriching it greatly
  by God's stream, full of water.
You provide people with grain
  because that is what you've decided.
¹⁰ Drenching the earth's furrows,
  leveling its ridges,
  you soften it with rain showers;
  you bless its growth.
¹¹ You crown the year with your goodness;
  your paths overflow with rich food.
¹² Even the desert pastures drip with it,
  and the hills are dressed in pure joy.

¹³ The meadowlands are covered with flocks,
  the valleys decked out in grain—
  they shout for joy;
  they break out in song!

Psalm 66

For the music leader. A song. A psalm.

¹ Shout joyfully to God, all the earth!
² Sing praises to the glory of God's name!
  Make glorious his praise!
³ Say to God:
  "How awesome are your works!
  Because of your great strength,
    your enemies cringe before you.
⁴ All the earth worships you,
  sings praises to you,
  sings praises to your name!"   *Selah*

⁵ Come and see God's deeds;
  his works for human beings are awesome:
⁶ He turned the sea into dry land
  so they could cross the river on foot.
  Right there we rejoiced in him!
⁷ God rules with power forever;
  keeps a good eye on the nations.
  So don't let the rebellious
    exalt themselves.   *Selah*

⁸ All you nations, bless our God!
  Let the sound of his praise be heard!
⁹ God preserved us among the living;
  he didn't let our feet slip a bit.

¹⁰ But you, God, have tested us—
  you've refined us like silver,
¹¹ trapped us in a net,
  laid burdens on our backs,
¹² let other people run
  right over our heads—
we've been through fire and water.

But you brought us out to freedom!
¹³ So I'll enter your house
  with entirely burned offerings.
I'll keep the promises I made to you,
¹⁴ the ones my lips uttered,
  the ones my mouth spoke
  when I was in deep trouble.
¹⁵ I will offer the best burned offerings
  to you

along with the smoke of sacrificed rams.
I will offer both bulls and goats.   *Selah*

¹⁶ Come close and listen,
all you who honor God;
I will tell you what God has done for me:
¹⁷ My mouth cried out to him
with praise on my tongue.
¹⁸ If I had cherished evil in my heart,
my Lord would not have listened.
¹⁹ But God definitely listened.
He heard the sound of my prayer.
²⁰ Bless God! He didn't reject my prayer;
he didn't withhold
his faithful love from me.

Psalm 67

*For the music leader, with stringed
instruments. A psalm. A song.*

¹ Let God grant us grace and bless us;
let God make his face shine on us,   *Selah*
² so that your way becomes known
on earth,
so that your salvation becomes known
among all the nations.

³ Let the people thank you, God!
Let all the people thank you!
⁴ Let the people celebrate
and shout with joy
because you judge the nations fairly
and guide all nations on the earth.
                                                    Selah

⁵ Let the people thank you, God!
Let all the people thank you!

⁶ The earth has yielded its harvest.
God blesses us—our God blesses us!
⁷ Let God continue to bless us;
let the far ends of the earth honor him.

Psalm 68

*For the music leader. Of David.
A psalm. A song.*

¹ Let God rise up;
let his enemies scatter;
let those who hate him
run scared before him!

² Like smoke is driven away,
drive them away!
Like wax melting before fire,
let the wicked perish before God!
³ But let the righteous be glad
and celebrate before God.
Let them rejoice with gladness!
⁴ Sing to God! Sing praises to his name!
Exalt the one who rides the clouds!
The LORD is his name.
Celebrate before him!

⁵ Father of orphans and defender of widows
is God in his holy habitation.
⁶ God settles the lonely in their homes;
he sets prisoners free with happiness,ʳ
but the rebellious dwell
in a parched land.

⁷ When you went forth
before your people, God,
when you marched
through the wasteland,   *Selah*
⁸ the earth shook!
Yes, heaven poured down
before God, the one from Sinai—
before God, the God of Israel!
⁹ You showered down abundant rain, God;
when your inheritance grew weary,
you restored it yourself,
¹⁰ and your creatures settled in it.
In your goodness, God,
you provided for the poor.

¹¹ My Lord gives the command—
many messengers are
bringing good news:
¹² "The kings of armies are on the run!
The women back home divide the spoil.
¹³ Even if you lie down
among the sheepfolds,
there are wings of a dove
covered with silver;
its pinions covered in precious gold."ˢ
¹⁴ When the Almightyᵗ
scattered the kings there,
snow fell on Mount Zalmon.

¹⁵ Mighty mountain, Mount Bashan;
many-peaked mountain, Mount Bashan!

ʳOr *skillfully*; LXX, Vulg *with strength*; Heb uncertain ˢHeb uncertain ᵗHeb *Shaddai*

16 You many-peaked mountain:
   Why do you look with envy
   at the mountain
      God desired for his dwelling,
      the mountain
         where the LORD dwells forever?

17 God's chariots are twice ten thousand—
   countless thousands!
   My Lord came from Sinai[u]
      into the sanctuary.
18 You ascended the heights,
   leading away your captives,
   receiving tribute from people,
      even from those who rebel
      against the LORD God's dwelling there.
19 Bless the Lord!
   The God of our salvation
   supports us day after day!   Selah
20 Our God is the God of salvation,
   and escape from certain death
      comes through God my LORD.

21 Yes, God will shatter
   the heads of his enemies—
   the very skulls of those who walk in guilt.
22 My Lord has spoken:
   "From Bashan I will bring
   those people back.
   I will bring them back
      from the ocean's depths
23   so that you can wash your feet
      in their blood,
      so that your dogs' tongues
      can lap up their share of your enemies."

24 They saw your procession, God—
   the procession of my God,
   my king, into the sanctuary.
25 First came the singers,
   then the musicians;
   between them the young women
      were playing hand drums:
26 "Bless God in the great congregation;
   bless the LORD from Israel's fountain!"
27 There's Benjamin leading them,
   though he's little;
   then the princes of Judah,
   their speaker;

   then the princes of Zebulun
   and the princes of Naphtali.

28 Summon your strength, God!
   Show how strong you are, God,
   just as you've done for us before,
29   from your temple above Jerusalem,
   where kings bring you gifts.
30 Rebuke the wild animals of the marshland,
   the herd of bulls
      among the calves of the peoples.
   Trample those who delight in money;
   scatter the peoples
      who take pleasure in battles.
31 Let ambassadors come from Egypt;
   let Cush stretch out its hands to God.

32 Sing to God, all kingdoms of the earth!
   Sing praises to my Lord.   Selah
33 Sing to the one who rides through heaven,
   the most ancient heaven.
   Look! God sends forth his voice,
      his mighty voice.
34 Recognize how strong God is!
   His majesty extends over Israel;
   his strength is in the clouds.
35 You are awesome, God,
   in your sanctuaries—
      the God of Israel who gives strength
      and power to his people!

   Bless God!

Psalm 69

For the music leader.
According to "The Lilies." Of David.

1 Save me, God,
   because the waters have reached my neck!
2 I have sunk into deep mud.
   My feet can't touch the bottom!
   I have entered deep water;
   the flood has swept me up.
3 I am tired of crying.
   My throat is hoarse.
   My eyes are exhausted
      with waiting for my God.

4 More numerous than the hairs on my head
   are those who hate me for no reason.

---

u Correction; MT *My Lord was among them, the one from Sinai, in holiness.*

My treacherous enemies,
those who would destroy me,
are countless.
Must I now give back
what I didn't steal in the first place?
⁵ God, you know my foolishness;
my wrongdoings aren't hidden from you.

⁶ LORD God of heavenly forces!—
don't let those who hope in you
be put to shame because of me.
God of Israel!—
don't let those who seek you
be disgraced because of me.
⁷ I am insulted because of you.
Shame covers my face.
⁸ I have become a stranger
to my own brothers,
an immigrant to my mother's children.
⁹ Because passion for your house
has consumed me,
the insults of those who insult you
have fallen on me!
¹⁰ I wept while I fasted—
even for that I was insulted.
¹¹ When I wore funeral clothes,
people made fun of me.
¹² Those who sit at the city gate
muttered things about me;
drunkards made up rude songs.

¹³ But me? My prayer reaches you, LORD,
at just the right time.
God, in your great and faithful love,
answer me with your certain salvation!
¹⁴ Save me from the mud!
Don't let me drown!
Let me be saved from those who hate me
and from these watery depths!
¹⁵ Don't let me be swept away
by the floodwaters!
Don't let the abyss swallow me up!
Don't let the pit close its mouth over me!
¹⁶ Answer me, LORD,
for your faithful love is good!
Turn to me in your great compassion!
¹⁷ Don't hide your face from me,
your servant,
because I'm in deep trouble.
Answer me quickly!
¹⁸ Come close to me!

Redeem me!
Save me because of my enemies!

¹⁹ You know full well the insults
I've received;
you know my shame and my disgrace.
All my adversaries are right there
in front of you.
²⁰ Insults have broken my heart.
I'm sick about it.
I hoped for sympathy,
but there wasn't any;
I hoped for comforters,
but couldn't find any.
²¹ They gave me poison for food.
To quench my thirst
they gave me vinegar to drink.

²² Let the table before them become a trap,
their offerings a snare.
²³ Let their eyes grow too dim to see;
make their insides tremble constantly.
²⁴ Pour out your anger on them—
let your burning fury catch them.
²⁵ Let their camp be devastated;
let no one dwell in their tents.
²⁶ Because they go after those
you've already struck;
they talk about the pain
of those you've already pierced.
²⁷ Pile guilt on top of their guilt!
Don't let them come
into your righteousness!
²⁸ Let them be wiped out of the scroll of life!
Let them not be recorded
along with the righteous!
²⁹ And me? I'm afflicted.
I'm full of pain.
Let your salvation keep me safe, God!

³⁰ I will praise God's name with song;
I will magnify him with thanks
³¹ because that is more pleasing to the
LORD than an ox,
more pleasing than a young bull
with full horns and hooves.
³² Let the afflicted see it and be glad!
You who seek God—
let your hearts beat strong again
³³ because the LORD listens to the needy
and doesn't despise his captives.

³⁴ Let heaven and earth praise God,
   the oceans too, and all that moves
      within them!
³⁵ God will most certainly save Zion
   and will rebuild Judah's cities
      so that God's servants can live there
         and possess it.
³⁶ The offspring of God's servants
   will inherit Zion,
      and those who love God's name
         will dwell there.

Psalm 70

For the music leader. Of David.
For the memorial offering.

¹ Hurry, God, to deliver me;
   hurry, LORD, to help me!
² Let those who seek my life
   be ashamed and humiliated!
   Let them fall back and be disgraced—
      those people who delight
         in my downfall!
³ Let those who say, "Aha! Aha!"
   stop because of their shameful behavior.
⁴ But let all who seek you
   rejoice and be glad in you,
   and let those who love your saving help
      say again and again:
         "God is great!"
⁵ But me? I'm poor and needy.
   Hurry to me, God!
   You are my helper and my deliverer.
   Oh, LORD, don't delay!

Psalm 71

¹ I've taken refuge in you, LORD.
   Don't let me ever be put to shame!
² Deliver me and rescue me by your
      righteousness!
   Bend your ear toward me and save me!
³ Be my rock of refuge
   where I can always escape.
   You commanded that my life be saved
   because you are my rock and my fortress.

⁴ My God, rescue me
   from the power of the wicked;
   rescue me from the grip of the
      wrongdoer and the oppressor

⁵ because you are my hope, Lord.
   You, LORD, are the one I've trusted
      since childhood.
⁶ I've depended on you from birth—
   you cut the cord when I came
      from my mother's womb.
   My praise is always about you.
⁷ I've become an example to many people
   because you are my strong refuge.
⁸ My mouth is filled with your praise,
   glorifying you all day long.
⁹ Don't cast me off in old age.
   Don't abandon me when my strength
      is used up!
¹⁰ Yes, my enemies have been
   talking about me;
   those who stalk me plot together:
¹¹ "God has abandoned him!
   Pursue him!
   Grab him
      because no one will deliver him!"
¹² Don't be far from me, God!
   My God, hurry to help me!
¹³ Let my accusers be put to shame,
   completely finished off!
   Let those who seek my downfall
   be dressed in insults and disgrace!

¹⁴ But me? I will hope. Always.
   I will add to all your praise.
¹⁵ My mouth will repeat your righteous acts
   and your saving deeds all day long.
   I don't even know
      how many of those there are!
¹⁶ I will dwell on your mighty acts, my Lord.
   LORD, I will help others remember
      nothing but your righteous deeds.
¹⁷ You've taught me since my youth, God,
   and I'm still proclaiming
      your wondrous deeds!
¹⁸ So, even in my old age with gray hair,
   don't abandon me, God!
   Not until I tell generations
      about your mighty arm,
   tell all who are yet to come
      about your strength,
¹⁹ and about your ultimate
      righteousness, God,
   because you've done awesome things!
   Who can compare to you, God?

20 You, who have shown me
   many troubles and calamities,
   will revive me once more.ᵛ
   From the depths of the earth,
   you will raise me up one more time.
21 Please increase my honor
   and comfort me all around.
22 Then I'll give you thanks with a harp—
   I will thank you for your faithfulness,
      my God.
   I will make music for you with the lyre,
      holy one of Israel.
23 My lips will rejoice aloud
   when I make music for you;
   my whole being,ʷ which you saved,
      will do the same.
24 My tongue, also, will tell of your
      righteousness all day long,
   because those who seek my downfall
   have been put to shame and disgraced.

Psalm 72

Of Solomon.

1 God, give your judgments to the king.
   Give your righteousness to the king's son.
2 Let him judge your people
   with righteousness
   and your poor ones with justice.
3 Let the mountains bring peace
   to the people;
   let the hills bring righteousness.
4 Let the king bring justice
   to people who are poor;
   let him save the children
      of those who are needy,
   but let him crush oppressors!
5 Let the king liveˣ as long as the sun,
   as long as the moon,
   generation to generation.
6 Let him fall like rain upon fresh-cut grass,
   like showers that water the earth.
7 Let the righteous flourish
   throughout their lives,
   and let peace prosper
      until the moon is no more.
8 Let the king rule from sea to sea,
   from the river to the ends of the earth.
9 Let the desert dwellers
   bow low before him;
   let his enemies lick the dust.

10 Let the kings of Tarshish
   and the islands bring tribute;
   let the kings of Sheba and Seba
      present gifts.
11 Let all the kings bow down before him;
   let all the nations serve him.
12 Let it be so, because he delivers the
      needy who cry out,
   the poor, and those who have no helper.
13 He has compassion on the weak
      and the needy;
   he saves the lives of those
      who are in need.
14 He redeems their lives from oppression
      and violence;
   their blood is precious in his eyes.

15 Let the king live long!
   Let Sheba's gold be given to him!
   Let him be prayed for always!
   Let him be blessed all day long!
16 Let there be abundant grain in the land.
   Let it wave on the mountaintops.
   Let its fruit flourish like Lebanon.
   Let it thrive like grass on the land.
17 Let the king's name last forever.
   Let his name endure as long as the sun.
   Let all the nations be blessed
      through him and call him happy.

18 Bless the LORD God, the God of Israel—
   the only one who does wondrous things!
19 Bless God's glorious name forever;
   let his glory fill all the earth!
      Amen and Amen!

20 The prayers of David, Jesse's son,
   are ended.

BOOK III
(Psalms 73–89)

Psalm 73

A psalm of Asaph.

1 Truly God is good to Israel,
   to those who are have a pure heart.
2 But me? My feet had almost stumbled;
   my steps had nearly slipped

ᵛQere; Kethib *who have shown us . . . will revive us*   ʷOr soul   ˣLXX; MT *May they fear you.*

3 because I envied the arrogant;
    I observed how the wicked are well off:
4 They suffer no pain;
    their bodies are fit and strong.
5 They are never in trouble;
    they aren't weighed down
    like other people.
6 That's why they wear arrogance
    like a necklace,
    why violence covers them like clothes.
7 Their eyes bulge out from eating so well;
    their hearts overflow with delusions.
8 They scoff and talk so cruel;
    from their privileged positions
    they plan oppression.
9 Their mouths dare to speak
    against heaven!
    Their tongues roam the earth!
10 That's why people keep going back
    to them,
    keep approving what they say.[y]
11 And what they say is this:
    "How could God possibly know!
    Does the Most High know
    anything at all!"
12 Look at these wicked ones,
    always relaxed, piling up the wealth!

13 Meanwhile, I've kept my heart pure
    for no good reason;
    I've washed my hands
    to stay innocent for nothing.
14 I'm weighed down all day long.
    I'm punished every morning.
15 If I said, "I will talk about all this,"
    I would have been unfaithful
    to your children.
16 But when I tried to understand
    these things,
    it just seemed like hard work
17 until I entered God's sanctuary
    and understood what would happen
    to the wicked.
18 You will definitely put them
    on a slippery path;
    you will make them fall into ruin!
19 How quickly they are devastated,
    utterly destroyed by terrors!
20 As quickly as a dream departs
    from someone waking up, my Lord,

when you are stirred up,
    you make them disappear.[z]
21 When my heart was bitter,
    when I was all cut up inside,
22 I was stupid and ignorant.
    I acted like nothing but an animal
    toward you.
23 But I was still always with you!
    You held my strong hand!
24 You have guided me with your advice;
    later you will receive me with glory.
25 Do I have anyone else in heaven?
    There's nothing on earth I desire
    except you.
26 My body and my heart fail,
    but God is my heart's rock
    and my share forever.
27 Look! Those far from you die;
    you annihilate all those
    who are unfaithful to you.
28 But me? It's good for me to be near God.
    I have taken my refuge in you,
    my LORD God,
    so I can talk all about your works!

Psalm 74
A maskil[a] of Asaph.

1 God, why have you
    abandoned us forever?
    Why does your anger smolder
    at the sheep of your own pasture?
2 Remember your congregation
    that you took as your own long ago,
    that you redeemed to be the tribe
    of your own possession—
    remember Mount Zion,
    where you dwell.
3 March to the unending ruins,
    to all that the enemy destroyed
    in the sanctuary.

4 Your enemies roared
    in your own meeting place;
    they set up their own signs there!
5 It looked like axes raised
    against a thicket of trees.[b]

---

[y]Heb uncertain   [z]Heb uncertain   [a]Perhaps *instruction*; the root is used in Ps 32:8.   [b]Heb uncertain

⁶ And then all its carvings
  they hacked down with hatchet
    and pick.
⁷ They set fire to your sanctuary,
  burned it to the ground;
  they defiled the dwelling place
    of your name.
⁸ They said in their hearts,
  We'll kill all of them together!
  They burned all of God's meeting places
    in the land.
⁹ We don't see our own signs anymore.
  No prophet is left.
    And none of us know
      how long it will last.

¹⁰ How long, God, will foes insult you?
  Are enemies going to abuse
    your name forever?
¹¹ Why do you pull your hand back?
  Why do you hold your strong hand
    close to your chest?

¹² Yet God has been my king
  from ancient days—
  God, who makes salvation happen
    in the heart of the earth!
¹³ You split the sea with your power.
  You shattered the heads
    of the sea monsters on the water.
¹⁴ You crushed Leviathan's heads.
  You gave it to the desert dwellers
    for food!
¹⁵ You split open springs and streams;
  you made strong-flowing rivers
    dry right up.
¹⁶ The day belongs to you! The night too!
  You established both the moon
    and the sun.
¹⁷ You set all the boundaries of the earth
    in place.
  Summer and winter? You made them!

¹⁸ So remember this, LORD:
  how enemies have insulted you,
  how unbelieving fools
    have abused your name.
¹⁹ Don't deliver the life of your dove
  to wild animals!

Don't forget the lives
  of your afflicted people forever!
²⁰ Consider the covenant!
  Because the land's dark places
    are full of violence.
²¹ Don't let the oppressed live in shame.
  No, let the poor and needy
    praise your name!

²² God, rise up! Make your case!
  Remember how unbelieving fools
    insult you all day long.
²³ Don't forget the voices of your enemies,
  the racket of your adversaries
    that never quits.

Psalm 75

*For the music leader. Do not destroy.
A psalm of Asaph. A song.*
¹ We give thanks to you, God.
  Yes, we give thanks!
  Your name is near.
    Your marvelous deeds are declared.

² God says,ᶜ
  "When I decide the time is right,
  I will establish justice just so.
³ The earth and all its inhabitants will melt,
    but I will keep its pillars steady."   *Selah*

⁴ I said to the arrogant,
  "Don't be arrogant!"
To the wicked I said,
  "Don't exalt your strength!
⁵ Don't exalt your strength so highly.
  Don't speak so arrogantly
    against the rock."ᵈ
⁶ Because what exalts someone
  doesn't come from the east or west;
  it's not from the south either.
⁷ Rather it is God who is the judge.
  He brings this person down,
    but that person he lifts up.
⁸ Indeed, there's a cup in the LORD's hand
  full of foaming wine, mixed with spice.
  He will pour it out,
  and all of the earth's wicked people
    must drink it;
  they must drink every last drop!

ᶜHeb lacks *God says*.   ᵈLXX *against God*; MT *speak with an arrogant neck*

⁹ But I will rejoice[e] always;
  I will sing praises to Jacob's God!
¹⁰ God says:[f]
  "I will demolish every bit
     of the wicked's power,
  but the strength of the righteous
     will be lifted up."

Psalm 76

*For the music leader. With stringed
instruments. A psalm of Asaph. A song.*

¹ God is known in Judah;
   his name is great in Israel.
² His dwelling place became Salem;
   his habitation was Zion.
³ It was there that he broke
   the fiery shafts of the bow,
   the shield, the sword—
   even the battle itself!   *Selah*

⁴ You are ablaze with light,
   mightier than the mountains
     that give food.
⁵ The bravehearted lie plundered.
   They sank into deep lethargy.
   All the strong troops
     couldn't even lift their hands!
⁶ At your rebuke, Jacob's God,
   both chariot and horse
     were stopped dead-still.

⁷ You! You are awesome!
   Who can stand before you
     when you are angry?
⁸ You have announced judgment
     from heaven.
   The earth grew afraid and fell silent
⁹ when God rose up to establish justice,
   when God rose up to save
     all of the earth's poor.   *Selah*

¹⁰ Even human rage will turn to your praise
    when you dress yourself
    with whatever remains of your wrath.[g]
¹¹ Make promises to the LORD your God
    and keep them!
   Let all around him bring gifts
     to the awesome one.

¹² He breaks the spirit of princes.
   He is terrifying to all the kings
     of the earth.

Psalm 77

*For the music leader. According to
Jeduthun. Of Asaph. A psalm.*

¹ I cry out loud to God—
   out loud to God so that he can hear me!
² During the day when I'm in trouble
   I look for my Lord.
   At night my hands are still
     outstretched and don't grow numb;
   my whole being[h] refuses
     to be comforted.
³ I remember God and I moan.
   I complain, and my spirit grows tired.
                                    Selah

⁴ You've kept my eyelids from closing.
   I'm so upset I can't even speak.
⁵ I think about days long past;
   I remember years that seem an eternity
     in the past.
⁶ I meditate with my heart at night;[i]
   I complain,
     and my spirit keeps searching:
⁷ "Will my Lord reject me forever?
   Will he never be pleased again?
⁸ Has his faithful love
     come to a complete end?
   Is his promise over
     for future generations?
⁹ Has God forgotten how to be gracious?
   Has he angrily stopped
     up his compassion?"   *Selah*
¹⁰ It's my misfortune, I thought,
    that the strong hand of the Most High
     is different now.

¹¹ But I will remember the LORD's deeds;
    yes, I will remember your wondrous
     acts from times long past.
¹² I will meditate on all your works;
    I will ponder your deeds.
¹³ God, your way is holiness!
    Who is as great a god as you, God?
¹⁴ You are the God who works wonders;

---

[e]LXX; MT *I will declare*   [f]Heb lacks *God says.*   [g]Heb uncertain   [h]Or *soul*   [i]LXX; MT *I remember my song in the night.*

you have demonstrated your strength
   among all peoples.
¹⁵ With your mighty arm
   you redeemed your people;
   redeemed the children
      of Jacob and Joseph.   *Selah*

¹⁶ The waters saw you, God—
   the waters saw you and reeled!
   Even the deep depths shook!
¹⁷ The clouds poured water,
   the skies cracked thunder;
      your arrows were flying all around!
¹⁸ The crash of your thunder
   was in the swirling storm;
   lightning lit up the whole world;
   the earth shook and quaked.
¹⁹ Your way went straight through the sea;
   your pathways went right through the
      mighty waters.
      But your footprints left no trace!
²⁰ You led your people like sheep
   under the care of Moses and Aaron.

Psalm 78
A maskil^j of Asaph.

¹ Listen, my people, to my teaching;
   tilt your ears toward
      the words of my mouth.
² I will open my mouth with a proverb.
   I'll declare riddles
      from days long gone—
³ ones that we've heard
   and learned about,
   ones that our ancestors told us.
⁴ We won't hide them
   from their descendants;
   we'll tell the next generation
   all about the praise due the Lord
      and his strength—
   the wondrous works God has done.
⁵ He established a law for Jacob
   and set up Instruction for Israel,
   ordering our ancestors
      to teach them to their children.
⁶ This is so that the next generation
   and children not yet born
      will know these things,

and so they can rise up
   and tell their children
⁷ to put their hope in God—
   never forgetting God's deeds,
   but keeping God's commandments—
⁸ and so that they won't become like
      their ancestors:
   a rebellious, stubborn generation,
   a generation whose heart wasn't set firm
   and whose spirit wasn't faithful to God.

⁹ The children of Ephraim,
   armed with bows,
   retreated on the day of battle.
¹⁰ They didn't keep God's covenant;
   they refused to walk in his Instruction.
¹¹ They forgot God's deeds
   as well as the wondrous works
   he showed them.
¹² But God performed wonders
   in their ancestors' presence—
   in the land of Egypt, in the field of Zoan.
¹³ God split the sea and led them through,
   making the waters stand up like a wall.
¹⁴ God led them with the cloud by day;
   by the lightning all through the night.
¹⁵ God split rocks open in the wilderness,
   gave them plenty to drink—
   as if from the deep itself!
¹⁶ God made streams flow from the rock,
   made water run like rivers.

¹⁷ But they continued to sin against God,
   rebelling against the Most High
      in the desert.
¹⁸ They tested God in their hearts,
   demanded food for their stomachs.
¹⁹ They spoke against God!
   "Can God set a dinner table
      in the wilderness?" they asked.
²⁰ "True, God struck the rock
   and water gushed and streams flowed,
      but can he give bread too?
   Can he provide meat for his people?"
²¹ When the Lord heard this,
   he became furious.
   A fire was ignited against Jacob;
   wrath also burned against Israel
²² because they had no faith in God,

---

^jPerhaps *instruction*; the root is used in Ps 32:8.

because they didn't trust
   his saving power.

²³ God gave orders to the skies above,
   opened heaven's doors,
  ²⁴ and rained manna on them
    so they could eat.
   He gave them the very grain of heaven!

²⁵ Each person ate the bread
   of the powerful ones;^k
   God sent provisions to satisfy them.

²⁶ God set the east wind moving
   across the skies
   and drove the south wind
   by his strength.

²⁷ He rained meat on them
   as if it were dust in the air;
   he rained as many birds
   as the sand on the seashore!

²⁸ God brought the birds down
   in the center of their camp,
   all around their dwellings.

²⁹ So they ate and were completely satisfied;
   God gave them exactly
   what they had craved.

³⁰ But they didn't stop craving—
   even with the food still in their mouths!

³¹ So God's anger came up against them:
   he killed the most hearty of them;
   he cut down Israel's youth
   in their prime.

³² But in spite of all that, they kept sinning
   and had no faith
   in God's wondrous works.

³³ So God brought their days to an end,
   like a puff of air,
   and their years in total ruin.

³⁴ But whenever God killed them,
   they went after him!
   They would turn
   and earnestly search for God.

³⁵ They would remember that God
   was their rock,
   that the Most High was their redeemer.

³⁶ But they were just flattering him
   with lip service.
   They were lying to him
   with their tongues.

³⁷ Their hearts weren't firmly set on him;
   they weren't faithful to his covenant.

³⁸ But God, being compassionate,
   kept forgiving their sins,
   kept avoiding destruction;
   he took back his anger so many times,
   wouldn't stir up all his wrath!

³⁹ God kept remembering
   that they were just flesh,
   just breath that passes
   and doesn't come back.

⁴⁰ How often they rebelled
   against God in the wilderness
   and distressed him in the desert!

⁴¹ Time and time again they tested God,
   provoking the holy one of Israel.

⁴² They didn't remember God's power—
   the day when he saved them
   from the enemy;

⁴³ how God performed his signs in Egypt,
   his marvelous works in the field of Zoan.

⁴⁴ God turned their rivers into blood;
   they couldn't drink
   from their own streams.

⁴⁵ God sent swarms against them
   to eat them up,
   frogs to destroy them.

⁴⁶ God handed over their crops
   to caterpillars,
   their land's produce to locusts.

⁴⁷ God killed their vines with hail,
   their sycamore trees with frost.

⁴⁸ God delivered their cattle over to disease,^l
   their herds to plagues.

⁴⁹ God unleashed his burning anger
   against them—
   fury, indignation, distress,
   a troop of evil messengers.

⁵⁰ God blazed a path for his wrath.
   He didn't save them from death,
   but delivered their lives over to disease.

⁵¹ God struck down
   all of Egypt's oldest males;
   in Ham's tents,
   he struck their pride and joy.

⁵² God led his own people out like sheep,
   guiding them like a flock
   in the wilderness.

⁵³ God led them in safety—
   they were not afraid!

---

^kOr *everyone ate the bread from heaven;* Heb uncertain ^lCorrection; MT *to hailstones*

But the sea engulfed their enemies!
⁵⁴ God brought them to his holy territory,
    to the mountain that his own
        strong hand had acquired.
⁵⁵ God drove out the nations before them
    and apportioned property for them;
    he settled Israel's tribes in their tents.

⁵⁶ But they tested and defied
    the Most High God;
    they didn't pay attention to his warnings.
⁵⁷ They turned away, became faithless
    just like their ancestors;
    they twisted away like a defective bow.
⁵⁸ They angered God
    with their many shrines;
    they angered him with their idols.
⁵⁹ God heard and became enraged;
    he rejected Israel utterly.
⁶⁰ God abandoned the sanctuary at Shiloh,
    the tent where he had lived
        with humans.
⁶¹ God let his power be held captive,
    let his glory go to the enemy's hand.
⁶² God delivered his people up to the sword;
    he was enraged at his own possession.
⁶³ Fire devoured his young men,
    and his young women
        had no wedding songs.
⁶⁴ God's priests were killed by the sword,
    and his widows couldn't even cry.
⁶⁵ But then my Lord woke up—
    as if he'd been sleeping!
    Like a warrior shaking off wine,
⁶⁶ God beat back his foes;
    he made them an everlasting disgrace.

⁶⁷ God rejected the tent of Joseph
    and didn't choose the tribe of Ephraim.
⁶⁸ Instead, he chose the tribe of Judah,
    the mountain of Zion, which he loves.
⁶⁹ God built his sanctuary
    like the highest heaven
    and like the earth,
        which he established forever.
⁷⁰ And God chose David, his servant,
    taking him from the sheepfolds.
⁷¹ God brought him from shepherding
    nursing ewes
    to shepherd his people Jacob,
    to shepherd his inheritance, Israel.

⁷² David shepherded them
    with a heart of integrity;
    he led them with the skill of his hands.

Psalm 79
A psalm of Asaph.

¹ The nations have come
    into your inheritance, God!
    They've defiled your holy temple.
    They've made Jerusalem
        a bunch of ruins.
² They've left your servants' bodies
    as food for the birds;
    they've left the flesh of your faithful
    to the wild animals of the earth.
³ They've poured out the blood
    of the faithful
    like water all around Jerusalem,
    and there's no one left to bury them.
⁴ We've become a joke to our neighbors,
    nothing but objects of ridicule
    and disapproval to those around us.

⁵ How long will you rage, LORD? Forever?
    How long will your anger burn like fire?
⁶ Pour out your wrath on the nations
    who don't know you,
    on the kingdoms
    that haven't called on your name.
⁷ They've devoured Jacob
    and demolished his pasture.
⁸ Don't remember the iniquities
    of past generations;
    let your compassion hurry to meet us
    because we've been brought so low.
⁹ God of our salvation, help us
    for the glory of your name!
    Deliver us and cover our sins
    for the sake of your name!
¹⁰ Why should the nations say,
    "Where's their God now?"
    Let vengeance for the spilled blood
    of your servants
    be known among the nations
    before our very eyes!
¹¹ Let the prisoners' groaning reach you.
    With your powerful arm
    spare those who are destined to die.
¹² Pay back our neighbors seven times over,
    right where it hurts,
    for the insults they used on you, Lord.

¹³ We are, after all, your people
and the sheep of your very own pasture.
We will give you thanks forever;
we will proclaim your praises
from one generation to the next.

Psalm 80

For the music leader.
According to "Lotus Blossoms."
A testimony of Asaph. A psalm.

¹ Shepherd of Israel, listen!
You, the one who leads Joseph
as if he were a sheep.
You, who are enthroned
upon the winged heavenly creatures.
Show yourself ²before Ephraim,
Benjamin, and Manasseh!
Wake up your power!
Come to save us!
³ Restore us, God!
Make your face shine
so that we can be saved!

⁴ LORD God of heavenly forces,
how long will you fume
against your people's prayer?
⁵ You've fed them bread made of tears;
you've given them tears
to drink three times over!
⁶ You've put us at odds
with our neighbors;
our enemies make fun of us.
⁷ Restore us, God of heavenly forces!
Make your face shine
so that we can be saved!

⁸ You brought a vine out of Egypt.
You drove out the nations and planted it.
⁹ You cleared the ground for it;
then it planted its roots deep,
filling the land.
¹⁰ The mountains were covered by its shade;
the mighty cedars were covered
by its branches.
¹¹ It sent its branches all the way to the sea;
its shoots went
all the way to the Euphrates River.ᵐ
¹² So why have you now torn down its walls

so that all who come along
can pluck its fruit,
¹³ so that any boar from the forest
can tear it up,
so that the bugs can feed on it?

¹⁴ Please come back,
God of heavenly forces!
Look down from heaven and perceive it!
Attend to this vine,
¹⁵ this root that you planted
with your strong hand,
this son whom you secured
as your very own.
¹⁶ It is burned with fire. It is chopped down.
They die at the rebuke coming from you.
¹⁷ Let your hand be
with the one on your right side—
with the one whom you secured
as your own—
¹⁸ then we will not turn away from you!
Revive us so that we can call on your name.
¹⁹ Restore us, LORD God of heavenly forces!
Make your face shine
so that we can be saved!

Psalm 81

For the music leader.
According to the Gittith. Of Asaph.

¹ Rejoice out loud to God, our strength!
Shout for joy to Jacob's God!
² Take up a song and strike the drum!
Sweet lyre along with harp!
³ Blow the horn on the new moon,
at the full moon,
for our day of celebration!
⁴ Because this is the law for Israel;
this is a rule of Jacob's God.
⁵ He made it a decree for Joseph
when he went out
against the land of Egypt,
when I heard a language
I did not yet know:

⁶ "I lifted the burden off your shoulders;
your hands are free of the brick basket!
⁷ In distress you cried out,
so I rescued you.

ᵐOr *the Great River*

I answered you in the secret of thunder.
I tested you at the waters of Meribah. *Selah*

8 Listen, my people, I'm warning you!
If only you would listen to me, Israel.
9 There must be no foreign god among you.
You must not bow down
to any strange deity.
10 I am the LORD your God,
who brought you up from Egypt's land.
Open your mouth wide—I will fill it up!

11 But my people wouldn't listen
to my voice.
Israel simply wasn't agreeable toward me.
12 So I sent them off
to follow their willful hearts;
they followed their own advice.
13 How I wish my people would listen to me!
How I wish Israel would walk in my ways!
14 Then I would subdue their enemies
in a second;
I would turn my hand against their foes.
15 Those who hate the LORD
would grovel before me,
and their doom would last forever!
16 But I would feed you
with the finest wheat.
I would satisfy you with honey
from the rock."

Psalm 82
A psalm of Asaph.

1 God takes his stand in the divine council;
he gives judgment among the gods:
2 "How long will you judge unjustly
by granting favor to the wicked? *Selah*
3 Give justice to the lowly and the orphan;
maintain the right of the poor
and the destitute!
4 Rescue the lowly and the needy.
Deliver them
from the power of the wicked!
5 They don't know; they don't understand;
they wander around in the dark.
All the earth's foundations shake.

6 I hereby declare, "You are gods,
children of the Most High—all of you!

7 But you will die like mortals;
you will fall down like any prince."

8 Rise up, God! Judge the earth
because you hold all nations
in your possession!

Psalm 83
A song. A psalm of Asaph.

1 God, don't be silent!
Don't be quiet or sit still, God,
2 because—look!—
your enemies are growling;
those who hate you are acting arrogantly.
3 They concoct crafty plans
against your own people;
they plot against the people you favor.
4 "Come on," they say,
"let's wipe them out as a nation!
Let the name Israel
be remembered no more!"
5 They plot with a single-minded heart;
they make a covenant against you.
6 They are the clans
of Edom and the Ishmaelites,
Moab and the Hagrites,
7 Gebal, Ammon, Amalek,
Philistia along with the citizens of Tyre.
8 Assyria too has joined them—
they are the strong arm
for Lot's children. *Selah*

9 Do to them what you did to Midian,
to Sisera, and to Jabin
at the Kishon River.
10 They were destroyed at Endor;
they become fertilizer for the ground.
11 Make their officials like Oreb and Zeeb,
all their princes
like Zebah and Zalmunna—
12 those who said, "Let's take God's
pastures for ourselves."
13 My God, make them like tumbleweeds,
like chaff blown by wind.
14 Just like a fire consumes a forest,
just like flames set mountains ablaze,
15 pursue them with your storm,
terrify them with your hurricane.
16 Cover their faces with shame, LORD,
so that they might seek your name.

¹⁷ Let them be shamed
and terrified forever.
Let them die in disgrace.
¹⁸ Let them know that you—
your name is the LORD!—
you alone are Most High
over all the earth.

Psalm 84

*For the music leader. According to
the Gittith. Of the Korahites. A psalm.*
¹ How lovely is your dwelling place,
LORD of heavenly forces!
² My very being[n] longs, even yearns,
for the LORD's courtyards.
My heart and my body
will rejoice out loud to the living God!

³ Yes, the sparrow too
has found a home there;
the swallow has found herself a nest
where she can lay her young
beside your altars,
LORD of heavenly forces,
my king, my God!
⁴ Those who live in your house
are truly happy;
they praise you constantly.   *Selah*

⁵ Those who put their strength in you
are truly happy;
pilgrimage is in their hearts.
⁶ As they pass through the Baca Valley,[o]
they make it a spring of water.
Yes, the early rain covers it
with blessings.
⁷ They go from strength to strength,
until they see
the supreme God in Zion.[p]
⁸ LORD God of heavenly forces,
hear my prayer;
listen closely, Jacob's God!   *Selah*
⁹ Look at our shield, God;
pay close attention
to the face of your anointed one!

¹⁰ Better is a single day in your courtyards
than a thousand days anywhere else!

I would prefer to stand outside
the entrance of my God's house
than live comfortably
in the tents of the wicked!
¹¹ The LORD is a sun and shield;
God is favor and glory.
The LORD gives—doesn't withhold!—
good things
to those who walk with integrity.
¹² LORD of heavenly forces,
those who trust in you are truly happy!

Psalm 85

*For the music leader. Of the Korahites.
A psalm.*
¹ LORD, you've been kind to your land;
you've changed Jacob's circumstances
for the better.
² You've forgiven
your people's wrongdoing;
you've covered all their sins.   *Selah*
³ You've stopped being furious;
you've turned away
from your burning anger.
⁴ You, the God who can save us, restore us!
Stop being angry with us!
⁵ Will you be mad at us forever?
Will you prolong your anger
from one generation to the next?
⁶ Won't you bring us back to life again
so that your people can rejoice in you?
⁷ Show us your faithful love, LORD!
Give us your salvation!

⁸ Let me hear what the LORD God says,
because he speaks peace to his people
and to his faithful ones.
Don't let them return to foolish ways.
⁹ God's salvation is very close
to those who honor him
so that his glory can live in our land.
¹⁰ Faithful love and truth have met;
righteousness and peace have kissed.
¹¹ Truth springs up from the ground;
righteousness gazes down from heaven.
¹² Yes, the LORD gives what is good,
and our land yields its produce.
¹³ Righteousness walks before God,
making a road for his steps.

[n] Or *soul*   [o] LXX; Vulg *Valley of Tears*   [p] Correction; MT *the God of gods will be seen in Zion*

Psalm 86
A prayer of David.

¹ LORD, listen closely to me
and answer me,
because I am poor and in need.
² Guard my life because I am faithful.
Save your servant
who trusts in you—you! My God!
³ Have mercy on me, Lord,
because I cry out to you all day long.
⁴ Make your servant's life[q] happy again
because, my Lord, I offer my life to you,
⁵ because, my Lord,
you are good and forgiving,
full of faithful love
for all those who cry out to you.
⁶ Listen closely to my prayer, LORD;
pay close attention to the sound
of my requests for mercy.
⁷ Whenever I am in trouble,
I cry out to you,
because you will answer me.

⁸ My Lord! There is no one like you
among the gods!
There is nothing that can compare
to your works!
⁹ All the nations that you've made will come
and bow down before you, Lord;
they will glorify your name,
¹⁰ because you are awesome
and a wonder-worker.
You are God. Just you.

¹¹ Teach me your way, LORD,
so that I can walk in your truth.
Make my heart focused
only on honoring your name.
¹² I give thanks to you, my Lord, my God,
with all my heart,
and I will glorify your name forever,
¹³ because your faithful love toward me
is awesome
and because you've rescued my life
from the lowest part of hell.[r]

¹⁴ The arrogant rise up against me, God.
A gang of violent people want me dead.
They don't give a thought for you.

¹⁵ But you, my Lord,
are a God of compassion and mercy;
you are very patient
and full of faithful love.
¹⁶ Come back to me! Have mercy on me!
Give your servant your strength;
save this child of your servant!
¹⁷ Show me a sign of your goodness
so that those who hate me
will see it and be put to shame—
show a sign that you, LORD,
have helped me and comforted me.

Psalm 87
A psalm of the Korahites. A song.

¹ God's foundation is set
on the holy mountains.
² The LORD loves Zion's gates
more than all
of Jacob's houses combined.
³ Glorious things are said about you,
the city of God!   Selah
⁴ I count Rahab and Babel
among those who know me;
also Philistia and Tyre,
along with Cush—
each of these was born there.
⁵ And of Zion it is said:
"Each person was born in it,
but the one who will establish it
is the Most High."
⁶ The LORD makes a record
as he registers the peoples:
"Each one was born there."   Selah
⁷ And while they dance, people sing:
"The source of my life comes from you."

Psalm 88
A song. A psalm of the Korahites.
For the music leader. According to
"Mahalath Leannoth."[s] A maskil[t]
of Heman the Ezrahite.

¹ LORD, God of my salvation,
by day I cry out,
even at night, before you—
² let my prayer reach you!
Turn your ear to my outcry

[q]Or *soul*; also in 86:4*b*, 13 [r]Heb *Sheol* [s]Heb uncertain [t]Perhaps *instruction*; the root is used in Ps 32:8.

³ because my whole being[u]
    is filled with distress;
    my life is at the very brink of hell.[v]

⁴ I am considered as one of those
    plummeting into the pit.
    I am like those who are beyond help,
⁵ drifting among the dead,
    lying in the grave, like dead bodies—
    those you don't remember anymore,
    those who are cut off from your power.
⁶ You placed me down in the deepest pit,
    in places dark and deep.
⁷ Your anger smothers me;
    you subdue me with it,
    wave after wave.   *Selah*
⁸ You've made my friends distant.
    You've made me disgusting to them.
    I can't escape. I'm trapped!
⁹ My eyes are tired of looking
    at my suffering.
    I've been calling out
    to you every day, LORD—
    I've had my hands outstretched to you!

¹⁰ Do you work wonders for the dead?
    Do ghosts rise up and give you thanks?
       Selah

¹¹ Is your faithful love
    proclaimed in the grave,
    your faithfulness in the underworld?[w]
¹² Are your wonders known
    in the land of darkness,
    your righteousness
    in the land of oblivion?

¹³ But I cry out to you, LORD!
    My prayer meets you
    first thing in the morning!
¹⁴ Why do you reject my very being, LORD?
    Why do you hide your face from me?
¹⁵ Since I was young I've been afflicted,
    I've been dying.
    I've endured your terrors. I'm lifeless.
¹⁶ Your fiery anger has overwhelmed me;
    your terrors have destroyed me.
¹⁷ They surround me all day long like water;
    they engulf me completely.

¹⁸ You've made my loved ones
    and companions distant.
    My only friend is darkness.

Psalm 89
A maskil[x] of Ethan the Ezrahite.

¹ I will sing of the LORD's loyal love forever.
    I will proclaim your faithfulness
    with my own mouth
    from one generation to the next.
² That's why I say,
    "Your[y] loyal love is rightly built—forever!
    You establish your faithfulness
    in heaven."
³ You said,[z] "I made a covenant
    with my chosen one;
    I promised my servant David:
⁴ 'I will establish your offspring forever;
    I will build up your throne from one
    generation to the next.'"   *Selah*

⁵ Heaven thanks you
    for your wondrous acts, LORD—
    for your faithfulness too—
    in the assembly of the holy ones.
⁶ Is there any in the sky
    who could compare to the LORD?
    Who among the gods
    is equal to the LORD?
⁷ God is respected
    in the council of the holy ones;
    God is awesome and revered
    more than all those around him.
⁸ Who is like you,
    LORD God of heavenly forces?
    Mighty LORD, your faithfulness
    surrounds you!
⁹ You rule over the surging sea:
    When its waves rise up,
    it's you who makes them still.
¹⁰ It's you who crushed Rahab
    like a dead body;
    you scattered your enemies
    with your strong arm.
¹¹ Heaven is yours! The earth too!
    The world and all that fills it—
    you made all of it! North and south—
    you created them!

---

[u]Or *soul*, also in 88:14   [v]Heb *Sheol*   [w]Heb *Abaddon*   [x]Perhaps *instruction*; the root is used in Ps 32:8.   [y]Heb lacks *Your*.   [z]Heb lacks *You said.*

[12] The mountains Tabor and Hermon
    shout praises to your name.
[13] You have a powerful arm;
    your hand is strong;
    your strong hand is raised high!
[14] Your throne is built
    on righteousness and justice;
    loyal love and faithfulness
        stand in front of you.

[15] The people who know the celebratory
        shout are truly happy!
    They walk in the light of your presence,
        LORD!
[16] They rejoice in your name all day long
    and are uplifted by your righteousness
[17] because you are the splendor
        of their strength.
    By your favor you make us strong
[18] because our shield is the LORD's own;
    our king belongs to the holy one of Israel!

[19] Once you spoke in a vision
    to your faithful servants:
    I placed a crown on a strong man.
    I raised up someone specially chosen
        from the people.
[20] I discovered my servant David.
    I anointed him with my holy oil.

[21] My hand will sustain him—
    yes, my arm will strengthen him!
[22] No enemy will oppress him;
    no wicked person will make him suffer.
[23] I will crush all his foes in front of him.
    I will strike down all those who hate him.
[24] My faithfulness and my loyal love
    will be with him.
    He will be strengthened by my name.
[25] I will set his hand on the sea.
    I will set his strong hand on the rivers.
[26] He will cry out to me:
    "You are my father,
    my God, the rock of my salvation."
[27] Yes, I'll make him the one born first—
    I'll make him the high king
        of all earth's kings.
[28] I will always guard my loyal love
    toward him.
    My covenant with him will last forever.
[29] I will establish his dynasty for all time.
    His throne will last
        as long as heaven does.
[30] But if his children ever
    abandon my Instruction,
    stop following my rules—
[31] if they treat my statutes like dirt,
    stop keeping my commandments—
[32] then I will punish their sin with a stick,

MOUNT TABOR

Mount Tabor is a dome-shaped outcropping in lower Galilee rising to approximately 1,850 ft., lying about 11 mi. southwest of Tiberias and overlooking the Jezreel Valley at the intersection of the tribal territories of Zebulon, Issachar, and Naphtali.

The word *Tabor* occurs 12 times in the OT, with half of these instances referring to place-names other than the mountain: towns in tribal boundary lists that were near the mountain (Josh 19:12, 22, 34); a levitical city in Zebulon (1 Chron 6:77); a Transjordanian site (Judg 8:18); and an oak near Bethel (1 Sam 10:3). Mount Tabor itself figures prominently in the narrative of Deborah's victory over Sisera (Judg 4:6, 12, 14). The remaining three references are in poetic (Ps 89:12 [Heb. 89:13]) and prophetic (Jer 46:18; Hos 5:1) texts. The etymology of Tabor as a proper name is not completely certain, but some scholars suggest a possible Phoenician derivation from the name of a Semitic god who is known in Greek as Zeus Atabyros.

and I will punish their wrongdoing
  with a severe beating.
³³ But even then I won't withdraw
  my loyal love from him.
  I won't betray my faithfulness.
³⁴ I won't break my covenant.
  I won't renege on what crossed my lips.
³⁵ By my own holiness I've sworn one thing:
  I will not lie to David.
³⁶ His dynasty will last forever.
  His throne will be like the sun,
    always before me.
³⁷ It will be securely established forever;
  like the moon, a faithful witness
    in the sky.   *Selah*

³⁸ But you, God, have rejected
  and despised him.
  You've become infuriated
    with your anointed one.
³⁹ You've canceled the covenant
    with your servant.
  You've thrown his crown in the dirt.
⁴⁰ You've broken through all his walls.
  You've made his strongholds
    a pile of ruins.
⁴¹ All those who pass by plunder him.
  He's nothing but a joke to his neighbors.
⁴² You lifted high his foes' strong hand.
  You gave all his enemies
    reason to celebrate.
⁴³ Yes, you dulled the edge of his sword
  and didn't support him in battle.
⁴⁴ You've put an end to his splendor.
  You've thrown his throne to the ground.
⁴⁵ You've shortened the prime of his life.
  You've wrapped him up in shame. *Selah*

⁴⁶ How long will it last, LORD?
  Will you hide yourself forever?
  How long will your wrath burn like fire?
⁴⁷ Remember how short my life is!
  Have you created humans
    for no good reason?
⁴⁸ Who lives their life without seeing death?
  Who is ever rescued
    from the grip of the grave?^a   *Selah*
⁴⁹ Where now are your loving acts
  from long ago, my Lord—

the same ones you promised to David
  by your own faithfulness?
⁵⁰ Remember your servant's abuse, my Lord!
  Remember how I bear in my heart
    all the insults of the nations,^b
⁵¹ the ones your enemies, LORD, use—
    the ones they use to abuse
  every step your anointed one takes.

⁵² Bless the LORD forever!
  Amen and Amen!

BOOK IV
(Psalms 90–106)

Psalm 90
A prayer of Moses, the man of God.
¹ Lord, you have been our help,
    generation after generation.
² Before the mountains were born,
  before you birthed the earth
    and the inhabited world—
  from forever in the past
  to forever in the future, you are God.

³ You return people to dust,
  saying, "Go back, humans,"
⁴ because in your perspective
    a thousand years
  are like yesterday past,
  like a short period
    during the night watch.
⁵ You sweep humans away like a dream,
  like grass that is renewed
    in the morning.
⁶ True, in the morning it thrives, renewed,
  but come evening it withers, all dried up.
⁷ Yes, we are wasting away
    because of your wrath;
  we are paralyzed with fear
    on account of your rage.
⁸ You put our sins right in front of you,
  set our hidden faults
    in the light from your face.
⁹ Yes, all our days slip away
    because of your fury;
  we finish up our years with a whimper.

^aHeb *Sheol* ^bCorrection; MT *all of many peoples*

¹⁰ We live at best to be seventy years old,
    maybe eighty, if we're strong.
    But their duration brings
    hard work and trouble
    because they go by so quickly.
    And then we fly off.
¹¹ Who can comprehend
    the power of your anger?
    The honor that is due you
    corresponds to your wrath.
¹² Teach us to number our days
    so we can have a wise heart.

¹³ Come back to us, LORD!
    Please, quick!
    Have some compassion
    for your servants!
¹⁴ Fill us full every morning
    with your faithful love
    so we can rejoice and celebrate
    our whole life long.
¹⁵ Make us happy for the same amount of
    time that you afflicted us—
    for the same number of years that we
    saw only trouble.
¹⁶ Let your acts be seen by your servants;
    let your glory be seen by their children.
¹⁷ Let the kindness of the Lord our God
    be over us.
    Make the work of our hands last.
    Make the work of our hands last!

Psalm 91

¹ Living in the Most High's shelter,
    camping in the Almighty's[c] shade,
² I say to the LORD, "You are my refuge,
    my stronghold!
    You are my God—the one I trust!"

³ God will save you from the hunter's trap
    and from deadly sickness.
⁴ God will protect you with his pinions;
    you'll find refuge under his wings.
    His faithfulness is a protective shield.
⁵ Don't be afraid of terrors at night,
    arrows that fly in daylight,
⁶ or sickness that prowls in the dark,
    destruction that ravages at noontime.

⁷ Even if one thousand people
    fall dead next to you,
    ten thousand right beside you—
    it won't happen to you.
⁸ Just look with your eyes,
    and you will see the wicked punished.
⁹ Because you've made the LORD my refuge,
    the Most High, your place of residence—
    ¹⁰ no evil will happen to you;
        no disease will come close to your tent.
¹¹ Because he will order his messengers
    to help you,
    to protect you wherever you go.
¹² They will carry you with their own hands
    so you don't bruise your foot on a stone.
¹³ You'll march on top of lions and vipers;
    you'll trample young lions
    and serpents underfoot.

¹⁴ God says,[d]
    "Because you are devoted to me,
    I'll rescue you.
    I'll protect you
    because you know my name.
¹⁵ Whenever you cry out to me, I'll answer.
    I'll be with you in troubling times.
    I'll save you and glorify you.
¹⁶ I'll fill you full with old age.
    I'll show you my salvation."

Psalm 92

A psalm. A song for the Sabbath day.
¹ It is good to give thanks to the LORD,
    to sing praises to your name, Most High;
² to proclaim your loyal love
    in the morning,
    your faithfulness at nighttime
³ with the ten-stringed harp,
    with the melody of the lyre
⁴ because you've made me happy, LORD,
    by your acts.
    I sing with joy
    because of your handiwork.
⁵ How awesome are your works, LORD!
    Your thoughts are so deep!
⁶ Ignorant people don't know—
    fools don't understand this:
⁷ though the wicked spring up like grass

---

[c] Heb *Shaddai*   [d] Heb lacks *God says.*

and all evildoers seem to blossom,
they do so only to be destroyed forever.
⁸ But you, LORD, are exalted forever!

⁹ Look at your enemies, LORD!
Look at how your enemies die,
how all evildoers are scattered abroad!
¹⁰ But you've made me
as strong as a wild ox.
I'm soaked in precious ointment.
¹¹ My eyes have seen my enemies' defeat;
my ears have heard
the downfall of my evil foes.

¹² The righteous will spring up
like a palm tree.
They will grow strong
like a cedar of Lebanon.
¹³ Those who have been replanted
in the LORD's house
will spring up
in the courtyards of our God.
¹⁴ They will bear fruit
even when old and gray;
they will remain lush and fresh
¹⁵ in order to proclaim:
"The LORD is righteous.
He's my rock.
There's nothing unrighteous in him."

Psalm 93

¹ The LORD rules!
He is robed in majesty—
the LORD is robed,
clothed with strength.
Yes, he set the world firmly in place;ᵉ
it won't be shaken.
² Your throne is set firm
for a very long time.
You are eternal!

³ LORD, the floods have raised up—
the floods have raised up their voices;
the floods raise up a roar!
⁴ But mightier than the sound
of much water,
mightier than the sea's waves,
mighty on high is the LORD!

⁵ Your laws are so faithful.
Holiness decorates your house, LORD,
for all time.

Psalm 94

¹ LORD, avenging God—
avenging God, show yourself!
² Rise up, judge of the earth!
Pay back the arrogant
exactly what they deserve!
³ How long will the wicked—oh, LORD!—
how long will the wicked win?
⁴ They spew arrogant words;
all the evildoers are bragging.
⁵ They crush your own people, LORD!
They abuse your very own possession.
⁶ They kill widows and immigrants;
they murder orphans,
⁷ saying all the while,
"The LORD can't see it;
Jacob's God doesn't know
what's going on!"

⁸ You ignorant people better learn quickly.
You fools—
when will you get some sense?
⁹ The one who made the ear,
can't he hear?
The one who formed the eye,
can't he see?
¹⁰ The one who disciplines nations,
can't he punish?
The one who teaches humans,
doesn't he know?ᶠ
¹¹ The LORD does indeed
know human thoughts,
knows that they are nothing
but a puff of air.

¹² The people you discipline, LORD,
are truly happy—
the ones you teach
from your Instruction—
¹³ giving them relief from troubling times
until a pit is dug for the wicked.
¹⁴ The LORD will not reject his people;
he will not abandon
his very own possession.

ᵉLXX, Vulg; MT *the world is set firmly in place;* cf Ps 96:10   ᶠCorrection; MT *the one who teaches humans knowledge*

15 No, but justice will once again
  meet up with righteousness,
  and all whose heart is right
  will follow after.

16 Who will stand up for me
  against the wicked?
  Who will help me against evildoers?
17 If the LORD hadn't helped me,
  I[g] would live instantly in total silence.
18 Whenever I feel my foot slipping,
  your faithful love steadies me, LORD.
19 When my anxieties multiply,
  your comforting calms me down.

20 Can a wicked ruler be your ally;
  one who wreaks havoc
  by means of the law?
21 The wicked gang up
  against the lives of the righteous.
  They condemn innocent blood.
22 But the LORD is my fortress;
  my God is my rock of refuge.
23 He will repay them for their wickedness,
  completely destroy them
  because of their evil.
  Yes, the LORD our God
  will completely destroy them.

Psalm 95

1 Come, let's sing out loud to the LORD!
  Let's raise a joyful shout
  to the rock of our salvation!
2 Let's come before him with thanks!
  Let's shout songs of joy to him!
3 The LORD is a great God,
  the great king over all other gods.
4 The earth's depths are in his hands;
  the mountain heights belong to him;
5 the sea, which he made, is his
  along with the dry ground,
  which his own hands formed.

6 Come, let's worship and bow down!
  Let's kneel before the LORD, our maker!
7 He is our God,
  and we are the people of his pasture,
  the sheep in his hands.

If only you would listen to his voice
  right now!
8 "Don't harden your hearts
  like you did at Meribah,
  like you did when you were at Massah,
  in the wilderness,
9 when your ancestors tested me
  and scrutinized me,
  even though they had already seen
  my acts.
10 For forty years I despised that generation;
  I said, 'These people have twisted hearts.
  They don't know my ways.'
11 So in anger I swore:
  'They will never enter my place of rest!'"

Psalm 96

1 Sing to the LORD a new song!
  Sing to the LORD, all the earth!
2 Sing to the LORD! Bless his name!
  Share the news of his saving work
  every single day!
3 Declare God's glory among the nations;
  declare his wondrous works
  among all people
4 because the LORD is great
  and so worthy of praise.
  He is awesome beyond all other gods
5 because all the gods of the nations
  are just idols,
  but it is the LORD who created heaven!
6 Greatness and grandeur
  are in front of him;
  strength and beauty
  are in his sanctuary.

7 Give to the LORD,
  all families of the nations—
  give to the LORD glory and power!
8 Give to the LORD the glory due his name!
  Bring gifts!
  Enter his courtyards!
9 Bow down to the LORD
  in his holy splendor!
  Tremble before him, all the earth!

10 Tell the nations, "The LORD rules!
  Yes, he set the world firmly in place;[h]

---

[g]Or *soul*; also in 94:19, 21   [h]LXX, Vulg; MT *the world is firmly established*; cf Ps 93:1

it won't be shaken.
He will judge all people fairly."
[11] Let heaven celebrate! Let the earth rejoice!
Let the sea and everything in it roar!
[12] Let the countryside
and everything in it celebrate!
Then all the trees of the forest too
will shout out joyfully
[13] before the LORD because he is coming!
He is coming to establish justice
on the earth!
He will establish justice
in the world rightly.
He will establish justice
among all people fairly.

Psalm 97

[1] The LORD rules! Let the earth rejoice!
Let all the islands celebrate!
[2] Clouds and thick darkness
surround God.
His throne is built
on righteousness and justice.
[3] Fire proceeds before him,
burning up his enemies on every side.
[4] His lightning lights up the world;
the earth sees it and trembles!
[5] The mountains melt like wax
before the LORD,
before the Lord of the whole world!

[6] Heaven has proclaimed
God's righteousness,
and all nations have seen his glory.
[7] All those who worship images,
those who are proud of idols,
are put to shame.
All gods bow down to the Lord!
[8] Zion has heard and celebrates,
the towns[i] of Judah rejoice,
because of your acts of justice, LORD,
[9] because you, LORD, are the Most High
over all the earth,
because you are so superior
to all other gods.

[10] Those of you who love the LORD,
hate evil!

God guards the lives
of his faithful ones,
delivering them from
the power of the wicked.
[11] Light is planted like seed
for the righteous person;
joy too for those whose heart is right.
[12] Rejoice in the LORD, righteous ones!
Give thanks to his holy name!

Psalm 98
A psalm.

[1] Sing to the LORD a new song
because he has done wonderful things!
His own strong hand
and his own holy arm
have won the victory!
[2] The LORD has made his salvation
widely known;
he has revealed his righteousness
in the eyes of all the nations.
[3] God has remembered his loyal love
and faithfulness to the house of Israel;
every corner of the earth has seen
our God's salvation.

[4] Shout triumphantly to the LORD,
all the earth!
Be happy!
Rejoice out loud!
Sing your praises!
[5] Sing your praises to the LORD
with the lyre—
with the lyre and the sound of music.
[6] With trumpets and a horn blast,
shout triumphantly before the LORD,
the king!
[7] Let the sea and everything in it roar;
the world and all its inhabitants too.
[8] Let all the rivers clap their hands;
let the mountains rejoice out loud
altogether [9]before the LORD
because he is coming to establish
justice on the earth!
He will establish justice
in the world rightly;
he will establish justice
among all people fairly.

[i]Or *daughters*

Psalm 99

[1] The LORD rules—
    the nations shake!
    He sits enthroned on the winged
       heavenly creatures—
    the earth quakes!
[2] The LORD is great in Zion;
    he is exalted over all the nations.
[3] Let them thank your great
       and awesome name.
    He is holy!

[4] Strong king[j] who loves justice,
    you are the one
       who established what is fair.
    You worked justice and righteousness
       in Jacob.
[5] Magnify the LORD, our God!
    Bow low at his footstool!
    He is holy!
[6] Moses and Aaron were among his priests,
    Samuel too among those
       who called on his name.
    They cried out to the LORD,
    and he himself answered them—
[7] he spoke to them from a pillar of cloud.
    They kept the laws and the rules
    God gave to them.
[8] LORD our God, you answered them.
    To them you were a God who forgives
    but also the one who avenged
       their wrong deeds.
[9] Magnify the LORD our God!
    Bow low at his holy mountain
    because the LORD our God is holy!

Psalm 100

A psalm of thanks.

[1] Shout triumphantly to the LORD,
    all the earth!
[2] Serve the LORD with celebration!
    Come before him with shouts of joy!
[3] Know that the LORD is God—
    he made us; we belong to him.[k]
    We are his people,
    the sheep of his own pasture.
[4] Enter his gates with thanks;
    enter his courtyards with praise!

Thank him! Bless his name!
[5] Because the LORD is good,
    his loyal love lasts forever;
    his faithfulness lasts
       generation after generation.

Psalm 101

Of David. A psalm.

[1] Oh, let me sing
    about faithful love and justice!
    I want to sing my praises to you, LORD!
[2] I want to study the way of integrity—
    how long before it gets here?
    I will walk with a heart of integrity
    in my own house.
[3] I won't set my eyes on anything worthless.
    I hate wrongdoing;
    none of that will stick to me.
[4] A corrupt heart will be far from me.
    I won't be familiar with evil.
[5] I will destroy anyone
    who secretly tells lies about a neighbor.
    I can't stomach anyone
    who has proud eyes or an arrogant heart.
[6] My eyes focus on those
    who are faithful in the land,
    to have them close to me.
    The person who walks without blame
    will work for me.
[7] But the person who acts deceitfully
    won't stay in my house.
    The person who tells lies
    won't last for long before me.
[8] Every morning I will destroy
    all those who are wicked in the land
    in order to eliminate all evildoers
       from the LORD's city.

Psalm 102

*A prayer of an oppressed person,
when weak and pouring out grief
to the LORD.*

[1] LORD, hear my prayer!
    Let my cry reach you!
[2] Don't hide your face from me
    in my time of trouble!
    Listen to me!
    Answer me quickly as I cry out!

---

[j]Correction; MT *A king's strength*   [k]Qere; Kethib *and not we ourselves*

³ Because my days disappear like smoke,
  my bones are burned up
    as if in an oven;
⁴ my heart is smashed
  like dried-up grass.
  I even forget to eat my food
⁵ because of my intense groans.
  My bones are protruding from my skin.
⁶ I'm like some wild owl—
  like some screech owl in the desert.
⁷ I lie awake all night.
  I'm all alone like a bird on a roof.
⁸ All day long my enemies make fun of me;
  those who mock me
    curse using my name!
⁹ I've been eating ashes instead of bread.
  I've been mixing tears into my drinks
¹⁰ because of your anger and wrath,
  because you picked me up
    and threw me away.
¹¹ My days are like a shadow soon gone.
  I'm dried up like dead grass.

¹² But you, LORD, rule forever!
  Your fame lasts
    from one generation to the next!
¹³ You will stand up—
  you'll have compassion on Zion
    because it is time
      to have mercy on her—
  the time set for that has now come!
¹⁴ Your servants cherish Zion's stones;
  they show mercy even to her dirt.
¹⁵ The nations will honor the LORD's name;
  all the earth's rulers
    will honor your glory
¹⁶ because the LORD will rebuild Zion;
  he will be seen there in his glory.
¹⁷ God will turn
  to the prayer of the impoverished;
  he won't despise their prayers.

¹⁸ Let this be written down
  for the next generation
    so that people not yet created
      will praise the LORD:
¹⁹ The LORD looked down
  from his holy summit,
    surveyed the earth from heaven,

²⁰ to hear the prisoners' groans,
  to set free those condemned to death,
²¹ that the LORD's name
    may be declared in Zion
  and his praise declared in Jerusalem,
²² when all people
    are gathered together—
  all kingdoms—to serve the LORD.

²³ God broke my strength in midstride,
  cutting my days short.
²⁴ I said, "My God, don't take me away
  in the prime of life—
  your years go on
    from one generation to the next!
²⁵ You laid the earth's foundations long ago;
  the skies are your handiwork.
²⁶ These things will pass away,
  but you will last.
  All of these things will wear out
    like clothing;
  you change them like clothes,
    and they pass on.
²⁷ But you are the one!
  Your years never end!
²⁸ Let your servants' children live safe;
  let your servants' descendants live
    secure in your presence."

Psalm 103
Of David.

¹ Let my whole being¹ bless the LORD!
  Let everything inside me
    bless his holy name!
² Let my whole being bless the LORD
  and never forget all his good deeds:
³ how God forgives all your sins,
  heals all your sickness,
⁴ saves your life from the pit,
  crowns you with faithful love
    and compassion,
⁵ and satisfies you
  with plenty of good things
    so that your youth
      is made fresh like an eagle's.

⁶ The LORD works righteousness;
  does justice for all who are oppressed.

¹ Or *soul*; also in 103:2, 22

⁷ God made his ways known to Moses;
  made his deeds known to the Israelites.
⁸ The LORD is compassionate and merciful,
  very patient, and full of faithful love.
⁹ God won't always play the judge;
  he won't be angry forever.
¹⁰ He doesn't deal with us
  according to our sin
  or repay us according to our wrongdoing,
¹¹ because as high as heaven
  is above the earth,
  that's how large God's faithful love
  is for those who honor him.
¹² As far as east is from west—
  that's how far God has removed
  our sin from us.
¹³ Like a parent feels compassion
  for their children—
  that's how the LORD feels compassion
  for those who honor him.
¹⁴ Because God knows how we're made,
  God remembers we're just dust.

¹⁵ The days of a human life are like grass:
  they bloom like a wildflower;
¹⁶ but when the wind blows through it,
  it's gone;
  even the ground where it stood
  doesn't remember it.
¹⁷ But the LORD's faithful love is from
  forever ago to forever from now
  for those who honor him.
  And God's righteousness reaches
  to the grandchildren
¹⁸ of those who keep his covenant
  and remember to keep his commands.
¹⁹ The LORD has established his throne
  in heaven,
  and his kingdom rules over all.

²⁰ You divine messengers,
  bless the LORD!
  You who are mighty in power
  and keep his word,
  who obey everything he says,
  bless him!
²¹ All you heavenly forces,
  bless the LORD!
  All you who serve him and do his will,
  bless him!

²² All God's creatures,
  bless the LORD!
  Everywhere, throughout his kingdom,
  let my whole being
  bless the LORD!

Psalm 104

¹ Let my whole beingᵐ bless the LORD!
  LORD my God, how fantastic you are!
  You are clothed in glory and grandeur!
² You wear light like a robe;
  you open the skies like a curtain.
³ You build your lofty house on the waters;
  you make the clouds your chariot,
  going around on the wings of the wind.
⁴ You make the winds your messengers;
  you make fire and flame your ministers.
⁵ You established the earth
  on its foundations
  so that it will never ever fall.
⁶ You covered it with the watery deep
  like a piece of clothing;
  the waters were higher
  than the mountains!
⁷ But at your rebuke they ran away;
  they fled in fear
  at the sound of your thunder.
⁸ They flowed over the mountains,
  streaming down the valleys
  to the place you established for them.
⁹ You set a boundary they cannot cross
  so they'll never again cover the earth.

¹⁰ You put gushing springs
  into dry riverbeds.
  They flow between the mountains,
¹¹ providing water for every wild animal—
  the wild donkeys quench their thirst.
¹² Overhead, the birds in the sky
  make their home,
  chirping loudly in the trees.
¹³ From your lofty house,
  you water the mountains.
  The earth is filled full
  by the fruit of what you've done.
¹⁴ You make grass grow for cattle;
  you make plants for human farming
  in order to get food from the ground,

ᵐOr *soul*; also in 104:35

¹⁵ and wine,
   which cheers people's hearts,
along with oil,
   which makes the face shine,
and bread,
   which sustains the human heart.
¹⁶ The LORD's trees are well watered—
   the cedars of Lebanon,
   which God planted,
   ¹⁷ where the birds make their nests,
   where the stork has a home
      in the cypresses.
¹⁸ The high mountains
   belong to the mountain goats;
   the ridges are the refuge of badgers.
¹⁹ God made the moon for the seasons,
   and the sun too,
      which knows when to set.
²⁰ You bring on the darkness and it is night,
   when every forest animal prowls.
²¹ The young lions roar for their prey,
   seeking their food from God.
²² When the sun rises,
   they gather together
   and lie down in their dens.
²³ Then people go off to their work,
   to do their work until evening.

²⁴ LORD, you have done so many things!
   You made them all so wisely!
   The earth is full of your creations!
²⁵ And then there's the sea, wide and deep,
   with its countless creatures—
   living things both small and large.
²⁶ There go the ships on it,
   and Leviathan, which you made,
      plays in it!
²⁷ All your creations wait for you
   to give them their food on time.
²⁸ When you give it to them,
   they gather it up;
   when you open your hand,
      they are filled completely full!
²⁹ But when you hide your face,
   they are terrified;
   when you take away their breath,
   they die and return to dust.
³⁰ When you let loose your breath,
   they are created,
   and you make the surface of the
      ground brand-new again.

³¹ Let the LORD's glory last forever!
   Let the LORD rejoice in all he has made!
³² He has only to look at the earth,
   and it shakes.
   God just touches the mountains,
   and they erupt in smoke.

³³ I will sing to the LORD as long as I live;
   I will sing praises to my God
      while I'm still alive.
³⁴ Let my praise be pleasing to him;
   I'm rejoicing in the LORD!
³⁵ Let sinners be wiped clean from the earth;
   let the wicked be no more.
   But let my whole being bless the LORD!
   Praise the LORD!

Psalm 105

¹ Give thanks to the LORD;
   call upon his name;
   make his deeds known to all people!
² Sing to God;
   sing praises to the Lord;
   dwell on all his wondrous works!
³ Give praise to God's holy name!
   Let the hearts rejoice of all those
      seeking the LORD!
⁴ Pursue the LORD and his strength;
   seek his face always!
⁵ Remember the wondrous works
   he has done,
   all his marvelous works,
      and the justice he declared—
   ⁶ you who are the offspring of Abraham,
      his servant,
   and the children of Jacob,
      his chosen ones.

⁷ The LORD—he is our God.
   His justice is everywhere
      throughout the whole world.
⁸ God remembers his covenant forever,
   the word he commanded
      to a thousand generations,
   ⁹ which he made with Abraham,
      the solemn pledge he swore to Isaac.
¹⁰ God set it up as binding law for Jacob,
   as an eternal covenant for Israel,
   ¹¹ promising, "I hereby give you
      the land of Canaan
   as your allotted inheritance."

¹² When they were few in number—
     insignificant, just immigrants—
¹³ wandering from nation to nation,
     from one kingdom to the next,
¹⁴ God didn't let anyone oppress them.
     God punished kings for their sake:
¹⁵ "Don't touch my anointed ones;
     don't harm my prophets!"

¹⁶ When God called for a famine in the land,
     destroying every source of food,
¹⁷ he sent a man ahead of them,
     who was sold as a slave: it was Joseph.
¹⁸ Joseph's feet hurt in his shackles;
     his neck was in an iron collar,
¹⁹ until what he predicted
     actually happened,
     until what the LORD had said
     proved him true.ⁿ
²⁰ The king sent for Joseph
     and set him free;
     the ruler of many people released him.
²¹ The king made Joseph
     master of his house and ruler
     over everything he owned,
²² to make sure his princes acted
     according to his will,
     and to teach wisdom to his advisors.
²³ That's how Israel came to Egypt,
     how Jacob became an immigrant in the
     land of Ham.

²⁴ God made his people very fruitful,
     more powerful than their enemies,
²⁵ whose hearts God changed
     so they hated his people
     and dealt shrewdly with his servants.
²⁶ God sent Moses his servant
     and the one he chose, Aaron.
²⁷ They put God's signs on Egypt,ᵒ
     his marvelous works on the land of Ham.
²⁸ God sent darkness, and it became dark,
     but the Egyptians rejected his word.
²⁹ God turned their waters into blood
     and killed their fish.
³⁰ God made their land swarm with frogsᵖ—
     even in the bedrooms of their king!
³¹ God spoke, and the insects came—
     gnats throughout their whole country!

³² God turned their rain into hail
     along with lightning flashes
     throughout their land.
³³ God destroyed their vines
     and their fig trees;
     shattered the trees of their countryside.
³⁴ God spoke, and the locusts came—
     countless grasshoppers came!
³⁵ They devoured all the plants in their land;
     they devoured the fruit of their soil.
³⁶ God struck down all the oldest sons
     throughout their land;
     struck down their very pride and joy.
³⁷ Then God brought Israel out,
     filled with silver and gold;
     not one of its tribes stumbled.
³⁸ Egypt celebrated when they left,
     because the dread of Israel
     had come upon them.

³⁹ God spread out clouds as a covering;
     gave lightning to provide light at night.
⁴⁰ The people asked, and God brought quail;
     God filled them full
     with food from heaven.
⁴¹ God opened the rock
     and out gushed water—
     flowing like a river through the desert!
⁴² Because God remembered
     his holy promise
     to Abraham his servant,
⁴³ God brought his people
     out with rejoicing,
     his chosen ones with songs of joy.
⁴⁴ God gave them the lands
     of other nations;
     they inherited the wealth
     of many peoples—
⁴⁵ all so that they would keep his laws
     and observe his instructions.

Praise the LORD!

Psalm 106

¹ Praise the LORD!
     Give thanks to the LORD
     because he is good,
     because his faithful love endures forever.

ⁿHeb uncertain   ᵒCorrection; MT *they put on them the words of God's signs*   ᵖCorrection; DSS (11QPsᵃ) *their land swarmed with frogs*

2 Who could possibly repeat
    all of the LORD's mighty acts
    or publicly recount all his praise?

3 The people who uphold justice,
    who always do what is right,
    are truly happy!
4 Remember me, LORD, with the favor
    you show your people.
    Visit me with your saving help
        5 so I can experience the good things
            your chosen ones experience,
        so I can rejoice
            in the joy of your nation,
        so I can praise along
            with your possession.

6 We have sinned—
    right along with our ancestors.
    We've done what is wrong.
    We've acted wickedly.
7 Our ancestors in Egypt didn't
    understand your wondrous works.
    They didn't remember how much
    faithful love you have.
    So they rebelled by the sea—
        at the Reed Sea.q
8 But God saved them
    for the sake of his good name,
    to make known his mighty power.
9 God scolded the Reed Sea,
    and it dried right up;
    he led them through the deeps
    like they were a dry desert.
10 God saved them from hostile powers;
    he redeemed them
    from the power of the enemy.
11 But the waters covered over their foes—
    not one of them survived!
12 So our ancestors trusted God's words;
    they sang God's praise.

13 But how quickly they forgot
    what he had done!
    They wouldn't wait for his advice.
14 They were overcome with craving
    in the desert;
    they tested God in the wastelands.
15 God gave them what they asked for;
    he sent foodr to satisfy their appetites.

16 But then they were jealous of Moses
    in the camp,
    jealous too of Aaron,
        the LORD's holy one.
17 So the earth opened up,
    swallowing Dathan,
    and covering over Abiram's crowd.
18 Fire blazed throughout that whole group;
    flames burned up the wicked.

19 They made a calf at Horeb,
    bowing down to a metal idol.
20 They traded their glorious Gods
    for an image of a bull that eats grass.
21 They forgot the God who saved them—
    the one who had done
        great things in Egypt,
    22 wondrous works in the land of Ham,
        awesome deeds at the Reed Sea.
23 So God determined that he would
    destroy them—
    except for the fact that Moses,
        his chosen one,
    stood in the way, right in front of him,
    and turned God's destructive anger away.

24 But then they rejected the land
    that was so desirable.
    They didn't trust God's promise.
25 They muttered in their tents
    and wouldn't listen to the LORD's voice.
26 So God raised his hand against them,
    making them fall in the desert,
    27 scattering their offspring
        among the nations,
    casting them across many lands.

28 They joined themselves to Baal-peor
    and ate sacrifices offered to the dead.
29 They made God angry by what they did,
    so a plague broke out against them.
30 Then Phinehas stood up and prayed,
    and the plague was contained.
31 That's why Phinehas
    is considered righteous,
    generation after generation, forever.

32 But they angered God at Meribah's waters,
    and things went badly for Moses
        because of them,

qOr Red Sea; also in 106:9, 22   rLXX   sOr their Glory

33 because they made him bitter
so that he spoke rashly with his lips.

34 They didn't destroy the nations
as the LORD had ordered them to do.
35 Instead, they got mixed up
with the nations,
learning what they did
36 and serving those false gods,
which became a trap for them.
37 They sacrificed their own
sons and daughters to demons!
38 They shed innocent blood,
the blood of their own
sons and daughters—
the ones they sacrificed
to Canaan's false gods—
so the land was defiled by the bloodshed.
39 They made themselves unclean
by what they did;
they prostituted themselves
by their actions.

40 So the LORD's anger burned
against his people;
he despised his own possession.
41 God handed them over to the nations;
people who hated them
ruled over them.
42 Their enemies oppressed them,
and they were humbled
under their power.
43 God delivered them numerous times,
but they were determined to rebel,
and so they were brought down
by their own sin.
44 But God saw their distress
when he heard their loud cries.
45 God remembered his covenant
for their sake,
and because of how much
faithful love he has,
God changed his mind.
46 God allowed them to receive compassion
from all their captors.

47 LORD our God, save us!
Gather us back together
from among all the nations
so we can give thanks to your holy name
and rejoice in your praise!

48 Bless the LORD, the God of Israel,
from forever ago to forever from now!
And let all the people say, "Amen!"

Praise the LORD!

BOOK V
(Psalms 107–150)

Psalm 107

1 "Give thanks to the LORD
because he is good,
because his faithful love
lasts forever!"
2 That's what those who are redeemed
by the LORD say,
the ones God redeemed
from the power of their enemies,
3 the ones God gathered
from various countries,
from east and west, north and south.

4 Some of the redeemed had wandered
into the desert, into the wasteland.
They couldn't find their way
to a city or town.
5 They were hungry and thirsty;
their lives were slipping away.
6 So they cried out to the LORD
in their distress,
and God delivered them
from their desperate circumstances.
7 God led them straight
to human habitation.
8 Let them thank the LORD
for his faithful love
and his wondrous works for all people,
9 because God satisfied the one
who was parched with thirst,
and he filled up the hungry
with good things!

10 Some of the redeemed had been sitting
in darkness and deep gloom;
they were prisoners suffering in chains
11 because they had disobeyed
God's instructions
and rejected the Most High's plans.
12 So God humbled them with hard work.

They stumbled, and there was no one
   to help them.
¹³ So they cried out to the LORD
   in their distress,
   and God saved them
     from their desperate circumstances.
¹⁴ God brought them out
   from the darkness and deep gloom;
   he shattered their chains.
¹⁵ Let them thank the LORD
   for his faithful love
   and his wondrous works for all people,
¹⁶ because God has shattered
   bronze doors
   and split iron bars in two!

¹⁷ Some of the redeemed were fools
   because of their sinful ways.
   They suffered because of
     their wickedness.
¹⁸ They had absolutely no appetite
   for food;
   they had arrived at death's gates.
¹⁹ So they cried out to the LORD
   in their distress,
   and God saved them
     from their desperate circumstances.
²⁰ God gave the order and healed them;
   he rescued them from their pit.
²¹ Let them thank the LORD
   for his faithful love
   and his wondrous works for all people.
²² Let them offer thanksgiving sacrifices
   and declare what God has done
     in songs of joy!

²³ Some of the redeemed had gone out
   on the ocean in ships,
   making their living on the high seas.
²⁴ They saw what the LORD had made;
   they saw his wondrous works
     in the depths of the sea.
²⁵ God spoke and stirred up a storm
   that brought the waves up high.
²⁶ The waves went as high as the sky;
   they crashed down to the depths.
   The sailors' courage melted
     at this terrible situation.
²⁷ They staggered and stumbled around
   like they were drunk.
   None of their skill was of any help.

²⁸ So they cried out to the LORD
   in their distress,
   and God brought them out safe
     from their desperate circumstances.
²⁹ God quieted the storm to a whisper;
   the sea's waves were hushed.
³⁰ So they rejoiced because the waves
   had calmed down;
   then God led them to the harbor
     they were hoping for.
³¹ Let them thank the LORD
   for his faithful love
   and his wondrous works for all people.
³² Let them exalt God
   in the congregation of the people
   and praise God
     in the assembly of the elders.

³³ God turns rivers into desert,
   watery springs into thirsty ground,
³⁴ fruitful land into unproductive dirt,
   when its inhabitants are wicked.
³⁵ But God can also turn the desert
   into watery pools,
   thirsty ground into watery springs,
³⁶ where he settles the hungry.
   They even build a city and live there!
³⁷ They plant fields and vineyards
   and obtain a fruitful harvest.
³⁸ God blesses them,
   and they become many.
   God won't even let
     their cattle diminish.
³⁹ But when they do diminish—
   when they're brought down
     by oppression, trouble, and grief—
⁴⁰ God pours contempt on their leaders,
   making them wander aimlessly
     in the wastelands.
⁴¹ But God raises the needy
   from their suffering;
   he makes their families
     as numerous as sheep!

⁴² Those who do right see it and celebrate,
   but every wicked person
     shuts their mouth.
⁴³ Whoever is wise will pay attention
   to these things,
   carefully considering
     the LORD's faithful love.

Psalm 108[t]

A song. A psalm of David.

[1] My heart is unwavering, God.
　　I will sing and make music—
　　yes, with my whole being!
[2] Wake up, harp and lyre!
　　I will wake the dawn itself!
[3] I will give thanks to you, LORD,
　　among all the peoples;
　　I will make music to you
　　among the nations,
[4] because your faithful love
　　is higher than heaven;
　　your faithfulness reaches the clouds.
[5] Exalt yourself, God, higher than heaven!
　　Let your glory be over all the earth!
[6] Save me by your power and answer me
　　so that the people you love
　　might be rescued.

[7] God has spoken in his sanctuary:
　　"I will celebrate as I divide up Shechem
　　and portion out the Succoth Valley.
[8] Gilead is mine, Manasseh is mine;
　　Ephraim is my helmet,
　　Judah is my scepter.
[9] But Moab is my washbowl;
　　I'll throw my shoe at Edom.
　　I shout in triumph over Philistia!
[10] I wish someone would bring me
　　to a fortified city!
　　I wish someone would lead me to Edom!"

[11] But you have rejected us, God,
　　haven't you?
　　You, God, no longer accompany
　　our armies.
[12] Give us help against the enemy—
　　human help is worthless.
[13] With God we will triumph:
　　God is the one who will trample
　　our adversaries.

Psalm 109

To the leader. Of David. A psalm.

[1] God of my praise, don't keep quiet,
[2] because the mouths of wicked liars
　　have opened up against me,

talking about me with lying tongues.
[3] Hateful words surround me;
　　they attack me for no reason.
[4] Instead of returning my love,
　　they accuse me—
　　but I am at prayer.
[5] They repay me evil for good,
　　hatred in return for my love.

[6] "Appoint a wicked person to be
　　against this person," they say,
　　"an accuser to stand right next to him.
[7] When the sentence is passed,
　　let him be found guilty—
　　let his prayer be found sinful!
[8] Let his days be few;
　　let someone else assume his position.
[9] Let his children become orphans;
　　let his wife turn into a widow.
[10] Let his children wander aimlessly,
　　begging,
　　driven out of their ruined homes.
[11] Let a creditor seize everything he owns;
　　let strangers plunder his wealth.
[12] Let no one extend faithful love to him;
　　let no one have mercy on his orphans.
[13] Let his descendants be eliminated;
　　let their names be wiped out
　　in just one generation!
[14] Let his father's wrongdoing
　　be remembered before the LORD;
　　let his mother's sin never be wiped out.
[15] Let them be before the LORD always,
　　and let God eliminate the very memory
　　of them from the land.
[16] All because this person didn't remember
　　to demonstrate faithful love,
　　but chased after the poor and needy—
　　even the brokenhearted—
　　with deadly intent!
[17] Since he loved to curse,
　　let it come back on him!
　　Since he didn't care much for blessing,
　　let it be far away from him!
[18] Since he wore curses like a coat,
　　let them seep inside him like water,
　　seep into his bones like oil!
[19] Let them be like the clothes he wears,
　　like a belt that is always around him."

[t]Ps 108:1-5 parallels Ps 57:7-11; Ps 108:6-13 parallels Ps 60:5-12.

²⁰ But let all that be the reward my accusers
get from the LORD,
the reward for those
who speak evil against me!
²¹ But you, LORD, my Lord!—
act on my behalf
for the sake of your name;
deliver me
because your faithful love is so good;
²² because I am poor and needy,
and my heart is broken.
²³ Like a lengthening shadow,
I'm passing away;
I'm shaken off, like some locust.
²⁴ My legs are weak from fasting;
my body is skin and bones.
²⁵ I've become a joke to my accusers;
when they see me,
they just shake their heads.

²⁶ Help me, LORD my God!
Save me according to your faithful love!
²⁷ And let them know
that this is by your hand—
that you have done it, LORD!
²⁸ Let them curse—but you, bless me!
If they rise up, let them be disgraced,
but let your servant celebrate!
²⁹ Let my accusers be dressed in shame;
let them wear their disgrace like a coat.
³⁰ But I will give great thanks to the LORD
with my mouth;
among a great crowd I will praise God!
³¹ Because God stands
right next to the needy,
to save them from any
who would condemn them.

Psalm 110

Of David. A psalm.

¹ What the LORD says to my master:
"Sit right beside me
until I make your enemies
a footstool for your feet!"

² May the LORD make your mighty scepter
reach far from Zion!
Rule over your enemies!
³ Your people stand ready
on your day of battle.
"In holy grandeur,
from the dawn's womb, fight!^u
Your youthful strength
is like the dew itself."
⁴ The LORD has sworn a solemn pledge
and won't change his mind:
"You are a priest forever
in line with Melchizedek."^v
⁵ My master, by your strong hand,
God has crushed kings
on his day of wrath.^w

⁶ God brings the nations to justice,
piling the dead bodies,
crushing heads throughout the earth.
⁷ God drinks from a stream along the way,
then holds his head up high.^x

Psalm 111^y

א ¹ Praise the LORD!
ב 　I thank the LORD with all my heart
in the company of those who do right,
in the congregation.
ג ² The works of the LORD are magnificent;
ד 　they are treasured by all who desire them.
ה ³ God's deeds are majestic and glorious.
ו 　God's righteousness stands forever.
ז ⁴ God is famous for his wondrous works.
ח 　The LORD is
full of mercy and compassion.
ט ⁵ God gives food to those who honor him.
י 　God remembers his covenant forever.
כ ⁶ God proclaimed his powerful deeds
to his people
ל 　and gave them what had belonged
to other nations.
מ ⁷ God's handiwork is honesty and justice;
נ 　all God's rules are trustworthy—
ס ⁸ they are established always and forever:
ע 　they are fulfilled
with truth and right doing.
פ ⁹ God sent redemption for his people;
צ 　God commanded
that his covenant last forever.

---

^uCorrection; or *Go!;* MT *to you* ^vOr *a rightful king by my decree* ^wOr *My Lord (God), because of your (the king's) strong hand, has crushed* or *The LORD is above your strong hand, crushing kings* ^xHeb uncertain ^yPs 111 is an alphabetic acrostic poem; see the note at Pss 9–10.

ק   Holy and awesome is God's name!

ר   10 Fear of the LORD
         is where wisdom begins;
ש   sure knowledge
         is for all who keep God's laws.
ת   God's praise lasts forever!

Psalm 112[z]

א   1 Praise the LORD!
         Those who honor the LORD,
ב   who adore God's commandments,
         are truly happy!
ג   2 Their descendants will be strong
         throughout the land.
ד   The offspring of those who do right
         will be blessed;
ה   3 wealth and riches will be in their houses.
ו   Their righteousness stands forever.
ז   4 They shine in the dark
         for others who do right.
ח   They are merciful, compassionate,
         and righteous.
ט   5 Those who lend generously
         are good people—
י   as are those who conduct
         their affairs with justice.
כ   6 Yes, these sorts of people
         will never be shaken;
ל   the righteous
         will be remembered forever!
מ   7 They won't be frightened at bad news.

נ   Their hearts are steady,
         trusting in the LORD.
ס   8 Their hearts are firm; they aren't afraid.
ע   In the end, they will witness
         their enemies' defeat.
פ   9 They give freely to those in need.
צ   Their righteousness stands forever.
ק   Their strength increases gloriously.
ר   10 The wicked see all this and fume;
ש   they grind their teeth,
         but disappear to nothing.
ת   What the wicked want to see happen
         comes to nothing!

Psalm 113

1 Praise the LORD!
   You who serve the LORD—praise!
   Praise the LORD's name!
2 Let the LORD's name be blessed
   from now until forever from now!
3 From sunrise to sunset,
   let the LORD's name be praised!
4 The LORD is high over all the nations;
   God's glory is higher than the skies!

5 Who could possibly
   compare to the LORD our God?
   God rules from on high;
6 he has to come down
   to even see heaven and earth!
7 God lifts up the poor from the dirt

---

[z]Ps 112 is an alphabetic acrostic poem; see the note at Pss 9–10.

HALLELUJAH

This expression is a call to praise the Lord. In the NT the Greek equivalent occurs only in Revelation 19:1, 3, 4, 6, where it functions in hymns celebrating the victory of God.

The presence of *hallelujah* (translated in the CEB as "Praise the LORD") in a psalm usually helps to identify it as a hymn of praise, appropriate for worship in song (both praise and thanksgiving) led by Levites after the exile (suggested by the use of the verb in Chronicles). Earlier scholarship identified this verbal root as the core of the hymns of praise. It is difficult, however, to maintain that the cry "hallelujah" itself constituted the earliest indicator of hymns, since this form appears only in later parts of the psalter (books 4 and 5).

and raises up the needy
from the garbage pile
⁸ to seat them with leaders—
with the leaders of his own people!
⁹ God nests the once barren woman
at home—
now a joyful mother with children!

Praise the LORD!

Psalm 114

¹ When Israel came out of Egypt—
when the house of Jacob came out
from a people who spoke
a different language—
² Judah was God's sanctuary;
Israel was God's territory.

³ The sea saw it happen and ran away;
the Jordan River retreated!
⁴ The mountains leaped away like rams;
the hills leaped away like lambs!
⁵ Sea, why did you run away?
Jordan, why did you retreat?
⁶ Mountains, why did you leap away
like rams?
Hills, why did you leap away like lambs?

⁷ Earth: Tremble before the Lord!
Tremble before the God of Jacob,
⁸ the one who turned
that rock into a pool of water,
that flint stone into a spring of water!

Psalm 115

¹ Not to us, LORD, not to us—
no, but to your own name give glory
because of your loyal love
and faithfulness!

² Why do the nations say,
"Where's their God now?"
³ Our God is in heaven—
he can do whatever he wants!
⁴ Their idols are just silver and gold—
things made by human hands.
⁵ They have mouths, but they can't speak.
They have eyes, but they can't see.
⁶ They have ears, but they can't hear.
They have noses, but they can't smell.
⁷ They have hands, but they can't feel.
They have feet, but they can't walk.
They can't even make a noise
in their throats!
⁸ Let the people who made these idols

IDOLATRY

The worship of idols, or giving divine honors to human-made objects. Since ancient Israel and Judah were surrounded by nations (i.e., Egypt, Canaan, Syria, Assyria, Babylonia) that used cultic images in their religions, one of the most persistent themes in the OT is an attack on idolatry (Exod 20:4; Lev 19:4; 26:1; Deut 5:8; 27:15; and esp. the parodies in Jer 10:2-16; Isa 44:9-20; Ps 115:4-8). While the Gospels hardly mention the subject of idolatry, writings usually attributed to Paul are concerned with the issue. In Romans 1:25, Paul, without using the word *idolatry*, described it as worshiping and serving "the creation instead of the creator." Elsewhere, idolaters are grouped with the greedy, robbers, the sexually immoral, drunkards, and so on (1 Cor 5:9-11; Gal 5:19-21; Eph 5:3-5; note that in this last passage greed and idolatry are identified as one and the same thing; cf. Col 3:5-6).

The overall stance of the biblical witness seems to be that all "images" of God, whether made of wood, stone, precious metals, or even words, are incomplete, and thus none can claim exclusivity.

and all who trust in them
become just like them!

⁹ But you, Israel, trust in the LORD!
God is their help and shield.
¹⁰ Trust in the LORD, house of Aaron!
God is their help and shield.
¹¹ You who honor the LORD,
trust in the LORD!
God is their help and shield.
¹² The LORD remembers us and will bless us:
God will bless the house of Israel;
God will bless the house of Aaron;
¹³ God will bless those
who honor the LORD—
from the smallest to the greatest.

¹⁴ May the LORD add to your numbers—
both you and your children.
¹⁵ May you be blessed by the LORD,
the maker of heaven and earth!
¹⁶ The highest heaven
belongs to the LORD,
but he gave the earth to all people.
¹⁷ The dead don't praise the LORD,
nor do those who go down to silence.
¹⁸ But us? We will bless the LORD
from now until forever from now!

Praise the LORD!

Psalm 116

¹ I love the LORD because he hears
my requests for mercy.
² I'll call out to him as long as I live,
because he listens closely to me.
³ Death's ropes bound me;
the distress of the grave[a] found me—
I came face-to-face
with trouble and grief.
⁴ So I called on the LORD's name:
"LORD, please save me!"[b]

⁵ The LORD is merciful and righteous;
our God is compassionate.
⁶ The LORD protects simple folk;
he saves me
whenever I am brought down.

⁷ I tell myself, You can be at peace again,
because the LORD
has been good to you.
⁸ You, God, have delivered me from death,
my eyes from tears,
and my foot from stumbling,
⁹ so I'll walk before the LORD
in the land of the living.
¹⁰ I have remained faithful,
even when I said,
"I am suffering so badly!"
¹¹ even when I said, out of fear,
"Everyone is a liar!"

¹² What can I give back to the LORD
for all the good things
he has done for me?
¹³ I'll lift up the cup of salvation.
I'll call on the LORD's name.
¹⁴ I'll keep the promises
I made to the LORD
in the presence of all God's people.
¹⁵ The death of the LORD's faithful
is a costly loss in his eyes.

¹⁶ Oh yes, LORD,
I am definitely your servant!
I am your servant and the son
of your female servant—
you've freed me from my chains.
¹⁷ So I'll offer a sacrifice
of thanksgiving to you,
and I'll call on the LORD's name.
¹⁸ I'll keep the promises
I made to the LORD
in the presence of all God's people,
¹⁹ in the courtyards of the LORD's house,
which is in the center of Jerusalem.

Praise the LORD!

Psalm 117

¹ Praise the LORD, all you nations!
Worship him, all you peoples!
² Because God's faithful love toward us
is strong,
the LORD's faithfulness lasts forever!
Praise the LORD!

---

[a] Heb *Sheol*   [b] Or *my soul*; also in 116:7-8

Psalm 118

¹ Give thanks to the LORD
　　because he is good,
　　because his faithful love lasts forever.
² Let Israel say it:
　　"God's faithful love lasts forever!"
³ Let the house of Aaron say it:
　　"God's faithful love lasts forever!"
⁴ Let those who honor the LORD say it:
　　"God's faithful love lasts forever!"

⁵ In tight circumstances,
　　I cried out to the LORD.
　　The LORD answered me
　　with wide-open spaces.
⁶ The LORD is for me[c]—I won't be afraid.
　　What can anyone do to me?
⁷ The LORD is for me—as my helper.
　　I look in victory on those who hate me.
⁸ It's far better to take refuge in the LORD
　　than to trust any human.
⁹ It's far better to take refuge in the LORD
　　than to trust any human leader.
¹⁰ All the nations surrounded me,
　　but I cut them down[d]
　　in the LORD's name.
¹¹ Yes, they surrounded me
　　on every single side,
　　but I cut them down in the LORD's name.
¹² They surrounded me like bees,
　　but they were extinguished
　　like burning thorns.
　　I cut them down in the LORD's name!
¹³ I was pushed so hard[e] I nearly died,
　　but the LORD helped me.
¹⁴ The LORD was my strength
　　and protection;
　　he was my saving help!
¹⁵ The sounds of joyful songs and deliverance
　　are heard in the tents of the righteous:
　　"The LORD's strong hand is victorious!
¹⁶ The LORD's strong hand
　　is ready to strike!
　　The LORD's strong hand is victorious!"

¹⁷ I won't die—no, I will live
　　and declare what the LORD has done.

¹⁸ Yes, the LORD definitely disciplined me,
　　but he didn't hand me over to death.

¹⁹ Open the gates of righteousness for me
　　so I can come in
　　and give thanks to the LORD!
²⁰ This is the LORD's gate;
　　those who are righteous
　　enter through it.

²¹ I thank you because you answered me,
　　because you were my saving help.
²² The stone rejected by the builders
　　is now the main foundation stone!
²³ This has happened because of the LORD;
　　it is astounding in our sight!
²⁴ This is the day the LORD acted;
　　we will rejoice and celebrate in it!

²⁵ LORD, please save us!
　　LORD, please let us succeed!

²⁶ The one who enters in the LORD's name
　　is blessed;
　　we bless all of you
　　from the LORD's house.
²⁷ The LORD is God!
　　He has shined a light on us!
　　So lead the festival offering with ropes
　　all the way to the horns of the altar.[f]
²⁸ You are my God—I will give thanks to you!
　　You are my God—I will lift you up high!
²⁹ Give thanks to the LORD
　　because he is good,
　　because his faithful love lasts forever.

Psalm 119[g]

א ALEF

¹ Those whose way is blameless—
　　who walk in the LORD's Instruction—
　　are truly happy!
² Those who guard God's laws
　　are truly happy!
　　They seek God with all their hearts.
³ They don't even do anything wrong!

---

[c]LXX *with me* or *mine*; also in 118:7　[d]Heb uncertain; LXX, Vulg *drove* or *warded off*; also in 118:11-12　[e]LXX, Vulg, Syr; MT *you pushed me*　[f]Heb uncertain　[g]Ps 119 is an alphabetic acrostic poem (cf Pss 9–10, 111) in Heb, with each line of Heb within the marked sections beginning with the same letter of the alphabet.

They walk in God's ways.
[4] God, you have ordered that your decrees
   should be kept most carefully.
[5] How I wish my ways were strong
   when it comes to keeping your statutes!
[6] Then I wouldn't be ashamed
   when I examine all your commandments.
[7] I will give thanks to you
   with a heart that does right
   as I learn your righteous rules.
[8] I will keep your statutes.
   Please don't leave me all alone!

⊐ BET

[9] How can young people
   keep their paths pure?
   By guarding them
   according to what you've said.[h]
[10] I have sought you with all my heart.
   Don't let me stray
   from any of your commandments!
[11] I keep your word close, in my heart,
   so that I won't sin against you.
[12] You, LORD, are to be blessed!
   Teach me your statutes.
[13] I will declare out loud
   all the rules you have spoken.
[14] I rejoice in the content of your laws
   as if I were rejoicing over great wealth.
[15] I will think about your precepts
   and examine all your paths.
[16] I will delight in your statutes;
   I will not forget what you have said.

⌐ GIMEL

[17] Be good to your servant
   so I can go on living
   and keeping your word.
[18] Open my eyes so I can examine
   the wonders of your Instruction!
[19] I'm an immigrant in the land.
   Don't hide your commandments
   from me!
[20] I'm worn out by longing
   every minute for your rules!
[21] You rebuke the arrogant,
   accursed people
   who stray from your commandments.

[22] Take all their insults and contempt
   away from me
   because I've kept your laws!
[23] Even if rulers gather and scheme
   against me,
   your servant will contemplate
   your statutes!
[24] Yes, your laws are my joy—
   they are my most trusted advisors!

⊓ DALET

[25] My life is stuck in the dirt.
   Now make me live again
   according to your promise!
[26] I confessed my ways and you answered me.
   Now teach me your statutes!
[27] Help me understand
   what your precepts are about
   so I can contemplate
   your wondrous works!
[28] My spirit sags because of grief.
   Now raise me up
   according to your promise!
[29] Remove all false ways from me;
   show mercy to me
   by means of your Instruction.
[30] I've chosen the way of faithfulness;
   I'm set on your rules.
[31] I'm holding tight to your laws, LORD.
   Please don't let me be put to shame.
[32] I run the same path
   as your commandments
   because you give my heart insight.

⊓ HE

[33] LORD, teach me what your statutes
   are about,
   and I will guard every part of them.
[34] Help me understand
   so I can guard your Instruction
   and keep it with all my heart.
[35] Lead me on the trail
   of your commandments
   because that is what I want.
[36] Turn my heart to your laws,
   not to greedy gain.
[37] Turn my eyes away from looking at
   worthless things.
   Make me live by your way.

[h]LXX

³⁸ Confirm your promise to your servant—
   the promise that is
     for all those who honor you.
³⁹ Remove the insults that I dread
   because your rules are good.
⁴⁰ Look how I desire your precepts!
   Make me live by your righteousness.

ו WAW

⁴¹ LORD, let your faithful love come to me—
   let your salvation come to me
     according to your promise—
⁴² so I can have a response
   for those who mock me
   because I have trusted in your word!
⁴³ Please don't take your true word
   out of my mouth,
   because I have waited for your rules.
⁴⁴ I will always keep your Instruction,
   always and forever!
⁴⁵ I will walk around in wide-open spaces,
   because I have pursued your precepts.
⁴⁶ I will talk about your laws
   before rulers with no shame whatsoever.
⁴⁷ I will rejoice in your commandments
   because I love them.
⁴⁸ I will lift up my hands
   to your commandments
   because I love them,
   and I will contemplate all your statutes.

ז ZAYIN

⁴⁹ Remember your promise to your servant,
   for which you made me wait.
⁵⁰ My comfort during my suffering is this:
   your word gives me new life.
⁵¹ The arrogant make fun of me to no end,
   but I haven't deviated
     from your Instruction.
⁵² When I remember your ancient rules,
   I'm comforted, LORD.
⁵³ But I'm seized with anger
   because of the wicked—
   because of those who abandon
     your Instruction.
⁵⁴ Your statutes have been
   my songs of praise
   wherever I lived as an immigrant.
⁵⁵ LORD, I remember your name
   at nighttime,
   and I keep your Instruction.

⁵⁶ This has been my practice
   because I guard your precepts.

ח KHET

⁵⁷ The LORD is my possession.
   I promise to do what you have said.
⁵⁸ I've sought your favor with all my heart;
   have mercy on me
     according to your word.
⁵⁹ I've considered my ways and turned
   my feet back to your laws.
⁶⁰ I hurry to keep your commandments—
   I never put it off!
⁶¹ Though the wicked have surrounded me
   with their ropes,
   I haven't forgotten your Instruction.
⁶² I get up in the middle of the night
   to give thanks to you
   because of your righteous rules.
⁶³ I'm a friend to everyone who honors you
   and to all who keep your precepts.
⁶⁴ LORD, the world is full
   of your faithful love!
   Teach me your statutes!

ט TET

⁶⁵ You have treated your servant well,
   LORD, according to your promise.
⁶⁶ Teach me knowledge and good judgment
   because I've put my trust
     in your commandments.
⁶⁷ Before I suffered, I took the wrong way,
   but now I do what you say.
⁶⁸ You are good and you do good.
   Teach me your statutes!
⁶⁹ The arrogant cover me with their lies,
   but I guard your precepts
     with all my heart.
⁷⁰ Their hearts are unfeeling, like blubber,
   but I rejoice in your Instruction.
⁷¹ My suffering was good for me,
   because through it
     I learned your statutes.
⁷² The Instruction you've given me
   is better
   than thousands of pieces
     of gold and silver!

י YOD

⁷³ Your hands have made me
   and set me in place.

Help me understand
so I can learn your commandments.
⁷⁴ Then those who honor you
will see me and be glad
because I have waited for your promise.
⁷⁵ LORD, I know that your rules are right
and that you rightly made me suffer.
⁷⁶ Please let your faithful love comfort me,
according to what you've said
to your servant.
⁷⁷ Let your compassion come to me
so I can live again,
because your Instruction is my joy!
⁷⁸ But let the arrogant be ashamed
because they oppressed me with lies—
meanwhile, I will be contemplating
your precepts!
⁷⁹ Let the people who honor you
come back to me;
let those who know your precepts
return to me.
⁸⁰ Let my heart be blameless
in your statutes
so that I am not put to shame.

כ KAF
⁸¹ My whole being yearns
for your saving help!
I wait for your promise.
⁸² My eyes are worn out
looking for your word.
"When will you comfort me?" I ask,
⁸³ because I've become like a bottle
dried up by smoke,
though I haven't forgotten
your statutes.
⁸⁴ How much more time
does your servant have?
When will you bring my oppressors
to justice?
⁸⁵ The arrogant have dug pits for me—
those people who act
against your Instruction.
⁸⁶ All your commandments are true,
but people harass me for no reason.
Help me!
⁸⁷ They've almost wiped me
off the face of the earth!
Meanwhile, I haven't abandoned
your precepts!

⁸⁸ Make me live again
according to your faithful love
so I can keep the law you've given!

ל LAMED
⁸⁹ Your word, LORD,
stands firm in heaven forever!
⁹⁰ Your faithfulness extends
from one generation to the next!
You set the earth firmly in place,
and it is still there.
⁹¹ Your rules endure to this day
because everything serves you.
⁹² If your Instruction hadn't been
my delight,
I would have died
because of my suffering.
⁹³ I will never forget your precepts
because through them
you gave me life again.
⁹⁴ I'm yours—save me
because I've pursued your precepts!
⁹⁵ The wicked wait for me,
wanting to kill me,
but I'm studying your laws.
⁹⁶ I've seen that everything,
no matter how perfect, has a limit,ⁱ
but your commandment is boundless.

מ MEM
⁹⁷ I love your Instruction!
I think about it constantly.
⁹⁸ Your commandment makes me wiser
than my enemies
because it is always with me.
⁹⁹ I have greater insight than all my teachers
because I contemplate your laws.
¹⁰⁰ I have more understanding
than the elders
because I guard your precepts.
¹⁰¹ I haven't set my feet on any evil path
so I can make sure to keep your word.
¹⁰² I haven't deviated from any of your rules
because you are the one
who has taught me.
¹⁰³ Your word is so pleasing
to my taste buds—
it's sweeter than honey in my mouth!
¹⁰⁴ I'm studying your precepts—
that's why I hate every false path.

ⁱHeb uncertain

נ NUN

105 Your word is a lamp before my feet
and a light for my journey.
106 I have sworn, and I fully mean it:
I will keep your righteous rules.
107 I have been suffering so much—
LORD, make me live again
according to your promise.
108 Please, LORD, accept my
spontaneous gifts of praise.
Teach me your rules!
109 Though my life is constantly in danger,
I won't forget your Instruction.
110 Though the wicked have set a trap for me,
I won't stray from your precepts.
111 Your laws are my possession forever
because they are my heart's joy.
112 I have decided to keep your statutes
forever, every last one.

ס SAMEK

113 I hate fickle people,
but I love your Instruction.
114 You are my shelter and my shield—
I wait for your promise.
115 Get away from me, you evildoers;
I want to guard
my God's commandments!
116 Sustain me according to your word
so I can live!
Don't let me be put to shame
because of hope.
117 Support me so I can be saved
and so I can focus constantly
on your statutes.
118 You discard everyone who strays
from your statutes
because they are dishonest and false.
119 You dispose of all the wicked people on
earth like waste—
that's why I love your laws.
120 My body shudders because I fear you;
I'm in awe of your rules.

ע AYIN

121 I've done what is just and right.
Don't just hand me over
to my oppressors.
122 Guarantee good things for your servant.
Please don't let the arrogant oppress me.

123 My eyes are worn out
looking for your saving help—
looking for your word
that will set things right.
124 Act toward your servant
according to your faithful love.
Teach me your statutes!
125 I'm your servant!
Help me understand
so I can know your laws.
126 It is time for the LORD to do something!
Your Instruction has been broken.
127 But I love your commandments
more than gold,
even more than pure gold.
128 That's why I walk straight by every
single one of your precepts.
That's why I hate every false path.

פ PE

129 Your laws are wonderful!
That's why I guard them.
130 Access to your words[j] gives light,
giving simple folk understanding.
131 I open my mouth up wide, panting,
because I long for your commandments.
132 Come back to me and have mercy on me;
that's only right
for those who love your name.
133 Keep my steps steady by your word;
don't let any sin rule me.
134 Redeem me from the people
who oppress me
so I can keep your precepts.
135 Shine your face on your servant,
and teach me your statutes.
136 Rivers of tears stream from my eyes
because your Instruction isn't being kept.

צ TSADE

137 LORD, you are righteous,
and your rules are right.
138 The laws you commanded are righteous,
completely trustworthy.
139 Anger consumes me
because my enemies have forgotten
what you've said.
140 Your word has been tried and tested;
your servant loves your word!

---

j Vulg, Sym

¹⁴¹ I'm insignificant and unpopular,
　　but I don't forget your precepts.
¹⁴² Your righteousness lasts forever!
　　Your Instruction is true!
¹⁴³ Stress and strain
　　have caught up with me,
　　but your commandments are my joy!
¹⁴⁴ Your laws are righteous forever.
　　Help me understand so I can live!

צ QOF

¹⁴⁵ I cry out with all my heart:
　　"LORD, answer me
　　　so I can guard your statutes!"
¹⁴⁶ I cry out to you, "Save me
　　so I can keep your laws!"
¹⁴⁷ I meet the predawn light and cry for help.
　　I wait for your promise.
¹⁴⁸ My eyes encounter each hour of the night
　　as I think about your word.
¹⁴⁹ Listen to my voice,
　　according to your faithful love.
　　LORD, make me live again,
　　　according to your justice.
¹⁵⁰ The people who love to plot wicked
　　schemes are nearby,
　　but they are so far from your Instruction!
¹⁵¹ But you, LORD, are nearby too,
　　and all your commandments are true.
¹⁵² Long ago I learned from your laws
　　that you had established them forever.

ר RESH

¹⁵³ Look at my suffering and deliver me
　　because I haven't forgotten
　　　your Instruction.
¹⁵⁴ Argue my case and redeem me.
　　Make me live again by your word.

¹⁵⁵ Salvation is far from the wicked
　　because they haven't pursued
　　　your statutes.
¹⁵⁶ You have so much compassion, LORD—
　　make me live again,
　　according to your rules.
¹⁵⁷ My oppressors and enemies are many,
　　but I haven't turned away
　　　from your laws.
¹⁵⁸ I look on the faithless,
　　and I am disgusted
　　because they haven't kept your word.
¹⁵⁹ Look at how much I love your precepts.
　　Make me live again, LORD,
　　according to your faithful love!
¹⁶⁰ The first thing to know about your word
　　is that it is true
　　and that all your righteous rules
　　　last forever.

ש SIN AND ש SHIN

¹⁶¹ Rulers oppress me without cause,
　　but my heart honors what you've said.
¹⁶² I'm overjoyed at your word,
　　like someone who finds great treasure.
¹⁶³ I hate, I absolutely despise, what is false,
　　but I'm in love with your Instruction.
¹⁶⁴ I praise you seven times a day
　　for your righteous rules.
¹⁶⁵ The people who love your Instruction
　　enjoy peace—and lots of it.
　　There's no stumbling for them!
¹⁶⁶ LORD, I wait for your saving help.
　　I do what you've commanded.
¹⁶⁷ I keep your laws;
　　I love them so much!
¹⁶⁸ I keep your precepts and your laws
　　because all my ways are seen by you.

TORAH/INSTRUCTION

Torah is a Hebrew word meaning "instruction," "teaching," and "law." It is the OT's general term for God's commandments to Israel. It often refers to specific instructions, but it came to typify the literary corpus that contains those commandments (i.e., the first five books of the OT—Genesis, Exodus, Leviticus, Numbers, and Deuteronomy—otherwise known as the Pentateuch), as well as the divine will for Israel in general.

חTAV

169 Let my cry reach you, LORD;
    help me understand
        according to what you've said.
170 Let my request for grace
    come before you;
        deliver me according to your promise!
171 Let my lips overflow with praise
    because you've taught me
        your statutes.
172 Let my tongue declare your word,
    because all your commandments
        are righteous.
173 Let your power help me
    because I have chosen your precepts.
174 LORD, I long for your saving help!
    Your Instruction is my joy!
175 Let me live again so I can praise you!
    Let your rules help me!
176 I've wandered off like a sheep, lost.
    Find your servant
        because I haven't forgotten
            your commandments!

Psalm 120

A pilgrimage song.[k]

1 I cried out to the LORD
    when I was in trouble
        (and he answered me):
2 "LORD, deliver me[l] from lying lips
    and a dishonest tongue!"
3 What more will be given to you,
    what more will be done to you,
        you dishonest tongue?
4 Just this:[m] a warrior's sharpened arrows,
    coupled with burning coals
        from a wood[n] fire!

5 Oh, I'm doomed
    because I have been an immigrant
        in Meshech,
    because I've made my home
        among Kedar's tents.
6 I've lived far too long
    with people who hate peace.
7 I'm for peace,
    but when I speak, they are for war.

Psalm 121

A pilgrimage song.

1 I raise my eyes toward the mountains.
    Where will my help come from?
2 My help comes from the LORD,
    the maker of heaven and earth.
3 God won't let your foot slip.
    Your protector won't fall asleep
        on the job.
4 No! Israel's protector
    never sleeps or rests!
5 The LORD is your protector;
    the LORD is your shade
        right beside you.
6 The sun won't strike you during the day;
    neither will the moon at night.
7 The LORD will protect you from all evil;
    God will protect your very life.[o]
8 The LORD will protect you
    on your journeys—
        whether going or coming—
    from now until forever from now.

Psalm 122

A pilgrimage song. Of David.

1 I rejoiced with those who said to me,
    "Let's go to the LORD's house!"
2 Now our feet are standing
    in your gates, Jerusalem!

3 Jerusalem is built like a city
    joined together in unity.
4 That is where the tribes go up—
    the LORD's tribes!
    It is the law for Israel
        to give thanks
    there to the LORD's name,
5 because the thrones of justice
    are there—
    the thrones of the house of David!

6 Pray that Jerusalem has peace:
    "Let those who love you have rest.
7 Let there be peace on your walls;
    let there be rest on your fortifications."
8 For the sake of my family and friends,
    I say, "Peace be with you, Jerusalem."

---

[k] Or *song of ascents* or *song of going up* (that is, to Jerusalem); cf Ps 122:4. The heading is found in every psalm from Ps 120 to Ps 134. [l] Or *my soul*; also in 120:6 [m] Heb lacks *this*. [n] Or *the gorse* or *broom tree* [o] Or *your soul*

⁹ For the sake of the LORD
   our God's house
   I will pray for your good.

Psalm 123
A pilgrimage song.

¹ I raise my eyes to you—
   you who rule heaven.
² Just as the eyes of servants attend
   to their masters' hand,
   just as the eyes of a female servant
   attends to her mistress' hand—
   that's how our eyes attend
   to the LORD our God
   until he has mercy on us.

³ Have mercy on us, LORD! Have mercy
   because we've had
   more than enough shame.
⁴ We've had more than enough mockery
   from the self-confident,

---

   more than enough shame
   from the proud.

Psalm 124
A pilgrimage song. Of David.

¹ If the LORD hadn't been for us—
   let Israel now repeat!—
² if the LORD hadn't been for us,
   when those people attacked us
³ then they would have swallowed
   us up whole
   with their rage burning against us!
⁴ Then the waters would have drowned us;
   the torrent
   would have come over our necks;^P
⁵ then the raging waters
   would have come over our necks!

⁶ Bless the LORD
   because he didn't hand us over
   like food for our enemies' teeth!

---

^POr *soul*; also in 124:5, 7

ASCENT

The basic meaning is movement from a lower to a higher elevation. A path or mountain pass is referred to as an "ascent" (Num 34:4; Josh 15:3). Cities were usually built on an elevated location, hence, Judah "went up" to Timnah (Gen 38:12). The journey to Canaan from the desert or from Egypt is described as an ascent (Exod 13:18; 33:1). In both cases, movement is to a higher elevation, but in the biblical traditions, these moves also create a decisive increase in well-being and status. The verb is often used to describe the exodus, usually in the causative form with God as the subject (e.g., "This is your God who brought you up out of Egypt" [Neh 9:18]).

A similar sense applies to personal deliverance from danger.

The verb is often used in conjunction with sacrifice. The choice of this verb may relate to the elevation of the animal on the altar or the ascent of the smoke to God in heaven. The depiction of God dwelling in heaven is also assumed when persons are said to go "up" to God (e.g., Moses [Exod 24:1] and Elijah [2 Kgs 2:1]). The Greek verb is used in the NT to describe Jesus' ascension. Even God is said to have "gone up" after vanquishing chaos, in the language of divine enthronement (Ps 47:5 [Heb. 47:6]).

Finally, pilgrimages are described as "ascents," because they involve both a journey to a city and a "going up" to God. The designation (see footnotes) of Psalms 120–134 as songs of ascent reflects their use during pilgrimages.

7 We escaped like a bird
  from the hunters' trap;
  the trap was broken so we escaped!

8 Our help is in the name of the LORD,
  the maker of heaven and earth.

Psalm 125

A pilgrimage song.

1 The people who trust in the LORD
  are like Mount Zion:
  never shaken, lasting forever.
2 Mountains surround Jerusalem.
  That's how the LORD
   surrounds his people
  from now until forever from now!
3 The wicked rod won't remain
 in the land given to the righteous
  so that they don't use their hands
   to do anything wrong.q
4 LORD, do good to people who are good,
  to people whose hearts are right.
5 But as for those people
  who turn to their own twisted ways—
  may the LORD march them off
   with other evildoers!

Peace be on Israel!

Psalm 126

A pilgrimage song.

1 When the LORD changed Zion's
  circumstances for the better,
  it was like we had been dreaming.
2 Our mouths were suddenly filled
  with laughter;
  our tongues were filled
   with joyful shouts.
 It was even said, at that time,
  among the nations,
  "The LORD has done great things
   for them!"
3 Yes, the LORD has done great things for us,
  and we are overjoyed.

4 LORD, change our circumstances
  for the better,

like dry streams in the desert waste!
5 Let those who plant with tears
  reap the harvest with joyful shouts.
6 Let those who go out,
  crying and carrying their seed,
  come home with joyful shouts,
  carrying bales of grain!

Psalm 127

A pilgrimage song. Of Solomon.

1 Unless it is the LORD
  who builds the house,
  the builders' work is pointless.
 Unless it is the LORD
  who protects the city,
  the guard on duty is pointless.
2 It is pointless that you get up early
  and stay up late,
  eating the bread of hard labor
  because God gives sleep
   to those he loves.

3 No doubt about it:
  children are a gift from the LORD;
  the fruit of the womb
   is a divine reward.
4 The children born when one is young
  are like arrows
  in the hand of a warrior.
5 The person who fills a quiver
  full with them is truly happy!
  They won't be ashamed
  when arguing with their enemies
  in the gate.

Psalm 128

A pilgrimage song.

1 Everyone who honors the LORD,
  who walks in God's ways,
  is truly happy!
2 You will definitely enjoy
  what you've worked hard for—
  you'll be happy;
  and things will go well for you.
3 In your house, your wife will be
  like a vine full of fruit.

---

qHeb uncertain

All around your table,
  your children will be like olive trees,
  freshly planted.
⁴ That's how it goes for anyone
  who honors the LORD:
  they will be blessed!

⁵ May the LORD bless you from Zion.
  May you experience Jerusalem's
  goodness your whole life long.
⁶ And may you see your grandchildren.

Peace be on Israel!

Psalm 129
A pilgrimage song.

¹ From youth, people have constantly
  attacked me—
  let Israel now repeat!—
² from youth people have constantly
  attacked me—
  but they haven't beaten me!
³ They plowed my back like farmers;
  they made their furrows deep.
⁴ But the LORD is righteous—
  God cut me free
  from the ropes of the wicked!
⁵ Let everyone who hates Zion be ashamed,
  thoroughly frustrated.
⁶ Let them be like grass on a roof
  that dies before it can be pulled up,

ʳ Or *soul*; also in 132:6

⁷ which won't fill the reaper's hand
  or fill the harvester's arms.
⁸ Let no one who passes by say to them:
  "May the LORD's blessing be on you!
  We bless you in the LORD's name!"

Psalm 130
A pilgrimage song.

¹ I cry out to you from the depths, LORD—
² my Lord, listen to my voice!
  Let your ears pay close attention
  to my request for mercy!
³ If you kept track of sins, LORD—
  my Lord, who would stand a chance?
⁴ But forgiveness is with you—
  that's why you are honored.

⁵ I hope, LORD.
  My whole beingʳ hopes,
  and I wait for God's promise.
⁶ My whole being waits for my Lord—
  more than the night watch
  waits for morning;
  yes, more than the night watch
  waits for morning!

⁷ Israel, wait for the LORD!
  Because faithful love is with the LORD;
  because great redemption
  is with our God!
⁸ He is the one who will redeem Israel
  from all its sin.

PILGRIMAGE

A pilgrimage is a journey to a foreign or holy place. Pilgrimage to Zion, God's royal residence (Pss 46:4 [Heb. 46:5]; 76:2 [Heb. 76:3]), offers contact with the divine.

Exodus 23:14-17 lists three annual pilgrimage feasts—the Festival of Unleavened Bread, the Harvest Festival, and the Gathering Festival—during which Israelite males must appear before the Lord, presumably at local sanctuaries. In Deuteronomy 16:1-17, Passover has replaced Unleavened Bread and is celebrated in the temple; the Gathering Festival now receives its "booths" (possibly the tent camps of pilgrims to Jerusalem).

Psalm 131

A pilgrimage song. Of David.

¹ LORD, my heart isn't proud;
my eyes aren't conceited.
I don't get involved with things
too great or wonderful for me.
² No. But I have calmed and quieted myself[s]
like a weaned child on its mother;
I'm like the weaned child that is with me.

³ Israel, wait for the LORD—
from now until forever from now!

Psalm 132

A pilgrimage song.

¹ LORD, remember David—
all the ways he suffered
² and how he swore to the LORD,
how he promised
the strong one of Jacob:
³ "I won't enter my house,
won't get into my bed.
⁴ I won't let my eyes close,
won't let my eyelids sleep,
⁵ until I find a place for the LORD,
a dwelling place
for the strong one of Jacob."

⁶ Yes, we heard about it in Ephrathah;
we found it[t] in the fields of Jaar.
⁷ Let's enter God's dwelling place;
let's worship at the place
God rests his feet!
⁸ Get up, LORD, go to your residence—
you and your powerful covenant chest!
⁹ Let your priests be dressed
in righteousness;

let your faithful shout out with joy!
¹⁰ And for the sake of your servant David,
do not reject your anointed one.

¹¹ The LORD swore to David
a true promise that God won't take back:
"I will put one of your own children
on your throne.
¹² And if your children keep my covenant
and the laws that I will teach them,
then their children too
will rule on your throne forever."
¹³ Because the LORD chose Zion;
he wanted it for his home.
¹⁴ "This is my residence forever.
I will live here
because I wanted it for myself.[u]
¹⁵ I will most certainly
bless its food supply;
I will fill its needy full of food!
¹⁶ I will dress its priests in salvation,
and its faithful
will shout out loud with joy!
¹⁷ It is there that I will make David's
strength thrive.[v]
I will prepare a lamp
for my anointed one there.
¹⁸ I will dress his enemies in shame,
but the crown he wears will shine."

Psalm 133

A pilgrimage song. Of David.

¹ Look at how good and pleasing it is
when families[w] live together as one!
² It is like expensive oil
poured over the head,
running down onto the beard—

---

[s] Or *my soul*   [t] *It may refer to the covenant chest* (132:8*b*).   [u] Heb lacks *for myself*.   [v] Or *make a horn sprout*
[w] Or *brothers (and sisters)*; the term often encompasses extended family relationships.

MOUNT HERMON

The southernmost peak of the Anti-Lebanon Mountains, Hermon marked the northernmost reaches of Joshua's conquest (Josh 11:17; 12:1). It was also called Baal-hermon, reflecting its sacred nature to others also (Judg 3:3; 1 Chron 5:23).

Aaron's beard!—
which extended over the collar
of his robes.
³ It is like the dew on Mount Hermon
streaming down
onto the mountains of Zion,
because it is there that the LORD has
commanded the blessing:
everlasting life.

Psalm 134

A pilgrimage song.

¹ All you who serve the LORD:
bless the LORD right now!
All you who minister in the LORD's
house at night: bless God!
² Lift up your hands to the sanctuary
and bless the LORD!
³ May the LORD,
the maker of heaven and earth,
bless you from Zion.

Psalm 135

¹ Praise the LORD!
Praise the LORD's name!
All you who serve the LORD, praise God!
² All you who stand in the LORD's house—
who stand in the courtyards
of our God's temple—
³ praise the LORD,
because the LORD is good!
Sing praises to God's name
because it is beautiful!
⁴ Because the LORD chose Jacob as his own,
God chose Israel
as his treasured possession.

⁵ Yes, I know for certain
that the LORD is great—
I know our Lord is greater
than all other gods.
⁶ The LORD can do whatever he wants
in heaven or on earth,
in the seas and in every ocean depth.
⁷ God forms clouds at the far corners
of the earth.
God makes lightning for the rain.
God releases the wind
from its storeroom.

⁸ God struck down
the Egyptians' oldest offspring—
both human and animal!
⁹ God sent signs and wonders
into the very center of Egypt—
against Pharaoh and all his servants.
¹⁰ God struck down many nations
and killed mighty kings:
¹¹ Sihon the Amorite king,
Og the king of Bashan,
and all the Canaanite kings.
¹² Then God handed their land
over as an inheritance—
as an inheritance to Israel,
his own people.

¹³ LORD, your name is forever!
LORD, your fame extends
from one generation to the next!
¹⁴ The LORD gives justice to his people
and has compassion
on those who serve him.

¹⁵ The nations' idols
are just silver and gold—
things made by human hands.
¹⁶ They have mouths, but they can't speak.
They have eyes, but they can't see.
¹⁷ They have ears, but they can't listen.
No, there's no breath in their lungs!
¹⁸ Let the people who made these idols
and all who trust in them
become just like them!

¹⁹ House of Israel, bless the LORD!
House of Aaron, bless the LORD!
²⁰ House of Levi, bless the LORD!
You who honor the LORD,
bless the LORD!
²¹ Bless the LORD from Zion—
bless the one who lives in Jerusalem!

Praise the LORD!

Psalm 136

¹ Give thanks to the LORD
because he is good.
God's faithful love lasts forever!

² Give thanks to the God of all gods—
God's faithful love lasts forever.

³ Give thanks to the Lord of all lords—
 God's faithful love lasts forever.
⁴ Give thanks to the only one
 who makes great wonders—
 God's faithful love lasts forever.
⁵ Give thanks to the one
 who made the skies with skill—
 God's faithful love lasts forever.
⁶ Give thanks to the one
 who shaped the earth on the water—
 God's faithful love lasts forever.
⁷ Give thanks to the one
 who made the great lights—
 God's faithful love lasts forever.
⁸ The sun to rule the day—
 God's faithful love lasts forever.
⁹ The moon and the stars to rule the night—
 God's faithful love lasts forever!

¹⁰ Give thanks to the one who struck down
 the Egyptians' oldest offspring—
 God's faithful love lasts forever.
¹¹ Give thanks to the one
 who brought Israel out of there—
 God's faithful love lasts forever.
¹² With a strong hand
 and outstretched arm—
 God's faithful love lasts forever!

¹³ Give thanks to the one
 who split the Reed Seaˣ in two—
 God's faithful love lasts forever.
¹⁴ Give thanks to the one
 who brought Israel through—
 God's faithful love lasts forever.
¹⁵ And tossed Pharaoh and his army
 into the Reed Sea—
 God's faithful love lasts forever!

¹⁶ Give thanks to the one
 who led his people through the desert—
 God's faithful love lasts forever.
¹⁷ Give thanks to the one
 who struck down great kings—
 God's faithful love lasts forever.
¹⁸ And killed powerful kings—
 God's faithful love lasts forever.
¹⁹ Sihon, the Amorite king—
 God's faithful love lasts forever.

²⁰ Og, king of Bashan—
 God's faithful love lasts forever.
²¹ Handing their land over
 as an inheritance—
 God's faithful love lasts forever.
²² As an inheritance to Israel, his servant—
 God's faithful love lasts forever!
²³ God remembered us
 when we were humiliated—
 God's faithful love lasts forever.
²⁴ God rescued us from our enemies—
 God's faithful love lasts forever.
²⁵ God is the one who provides
 food for all living things—
 God's faithful love lasts forever!

²⁶ Give thanks to the God of heaven—
 God's faithful love lasts forever!

Psalm 137

¹ Alongside Babylon's streams,
 there we sat down,
 crying because we remembered Zion.
² We hung our lyres up
 in the trees there
³ because that's where
 our captors asked us to sing;
 our tormentors requested songs of joy:
 "Sing us a song about Zion!" they said.
⁴ But how could we possibly sing
 the LORD's song on foreign soil?

⁵ Jerusalem! If I forget you,
 let my strong hand wither!
⁶ Let my tongue stick
 to the roof of my mouth
 if I don't remember you,
 if I don't make Jerusalem my greatest joy.

⁷ LORD, remember what the Edomites did
 on Jerusalem's dark day:
 "Rip it down, rip it down!
 All the way to its foundations!"
 they yelled.
⁸ Daughter Babylon, you destroyer,ʸ
 a blessing on the one who pays you back
 the very deed you did to us!

ˣOr *Red Sea*; also in 136:15   ʸSym, Tg, Syr; MT *the devastated*

⁹ A blessing on the one
   who seizes your children
   and smashes them against the rock!

Psalm 138
Of David.

¹ I give thanks to you
   with all my heart, LORD.ᶻ
   I sing your praise before all other gods.
² I bow toward your holy temple
   and thank your name
   for your loyal love and faithfulness
      because you have made
      your name and word
   greater than everything else.ᵃ
³ On the day I cried out, you answered me.
   You encouraged me with inner strength.ᵇ

⁴ Let all the earth's rulers
   give thanks to you, LORD,
   when they hear what you say.
⁵ Let them sing about the LORD's ways
   because the LORD's glory is so great!
⁶ Even though the LORD is high,
   he can still see the lowly,
   but God keeps his distance
      from the arrogant.

⁷ Whenever I am in deep trouble,
   you make me live again;
   you send your power
      against my enemies' wrath;
   you save me with your strong hand.
⁸ The LORD will do all this for my sake.

   Your faithful love lasts forever, LORD!
   Don't let go of what your hands
   have made.

Psalm 139
For the music leader. Of David. A song.

¹ LORD, you have examined me.
   You know me.
² You know when I sit down
   and when I stand up.
   Even from far away,
      you comprehend my plans.

³ You study my traveling and resting.
   You are thoroughly familiar
      with all my ways.
⁴ There isn't a word on my tongue, LORD,
   that you don't already know completely.
⁵ You surround me—front and back.
   You put your hand on me.
⁶ That kind of knowledge
   is too much for me;
   it's so high above me
      that I can't fathom it.

⁷ Where could I go to get away
   from your spirit?
   Where could I go to escape
      your presence?
⁸ If I went up to heaven,
   you would be there.
   If I went down to the grave,ᶜ
      you would be there too!
⁹ If I could fly on the wings of dawn,
   stopping to rest only
      on the far side of the ocean—
¹⁰ even there your hand would guide me;
   even there your strong hand
      would hold me tight!
¹¹ If I said,
   "The darkness will definitely hide me;
   the light will become night
      around me,"
¹² even then the darkness
   isn't too dark for you!
   Nighttime would shine bright as day,
   because darkness is the same
      as light to you!

¹³ You are the one who created
   my innermost parts;
   you knit me together
      while I was still in my mother's womb.
¹⁴ I give thanks to you
   that I was marvelously set apart.
   Your works are wonderful—
      I know that very well.
¹⁵ My bones weren't hidden from you
   when I was being put together
      in a secret place,
   when I was being woven together
      in the deep parts of the earth.

ᶻLXX, Syr, Tg, DSS (11QPsᵃ); MT lacks *Lord*. ᵃCorrection; Heb uncertain ᵇHeb uncertain ᶜHeb *Sheol*

16 Your eyes saw my embryo,
and on your scroll every day was written
that was being formed for me,d
before any one of them
had yet happened.e
17 God, your plans are incomprehensible
to me!
Their total number is countless!
18 If I tried to count them—
they outnumber grains of sand!
If I came to the very end—
I'd still be with you.f

19 If only, God, you would kill the wicked!
If only murderers
would get away from me—
20 the people who talk about you,
but only for wicked schemes;
the people who are your enemies,
who use your name as if
it were of no significance.g
21 Don't I hate everyone who hates you?
Don't I despise those who attack you?
22 Yes, I hate them—through and through!
They've become my enemies too.

23 Examine me, God! Look at my heart!
Put me to the test!
Know my anxious thoughts!
24 Look to see if there is any idolatrous
wayh in me,
then lead me on the eternal path!

Psalm 140

For the music leader. A psalm of David.

1 Rescue me from evil people, LORD!
Guard me from violent people
2 who plot evil things in their hearts,
who pick fights every single day!
3 They sharpen their tongues like a snake's;
spider poisoni is on their lips.   *Selah*

4 Protect me from the power
of the wicked, LORD!
Guard me from violent people
who plot to trip me up!
5 Arrogant people have laid a trap
for me with ropes.

They've spread out a net
alongside the road.
They've set snares for me.   *Selah*

6 I tell the LORD, "You are my God!
Listen to my request for mercy, LORD!"
7 My LORD God, my strong saving help—
you've protected my head
on the day of battle.
8 LORD, don't give the wicked
what they want!
Don't allow their plans to succeed,
or they'll exalt themselves even more!j
   Selah

9 Let the heads of the people
surrounding me
be covered with the trouble
their own lips caused!k
10 Let burning coals fall on them!
Let them fall into deep pits
and never get out again!
11 Let no slanderer be safe in the land.
Let calamity hunt down violent people—
and quickly!l

12 I know that the LORD
will take up the case of the poor
and will do what is right for the needy.
13 Yes, the righteous will give thanks
to your name,
and those who do right
will live in your presence.

Psalm 141

A psalm of David.

1 I cry out to you, LORD:
Come to me—quickly!
Listen to my voice when I cry out to you!
2 Let my prayer stand before you
like incense;
let my uplifted hands
be like the evening offering.

3 Set a guard over my mouth, LORD;
keep close watch over the door
that is my lips.

---

dCorrection; Heb lacks *for me.*   eHeb uncertain   fCorrection   gHeb lacks *your name.*   hCorrection; cf Tg; LXX, Syr, Vulg *painful* or *wicked* or *hurtful way*   iLXX *snake poison*   jHeb uncertain   kHeb uncertain   lHeb uncertain

⁴ Don't let my heart turn aside to evil things
  so that I don't do wicked things
    with evildoers,
  so I don't taste their delicacies.

⁵ Instead, let the righteous discipline me;
  let the faithful correct me!
  Let my head never reject
    that kind of fine oil,
  because my prayers are always
    against the deeds of the wicked.ᵐ

⁶ Their leaders will fall from jagged cliffs,
  but my words will be heard
    because they are pleasing.ⁿ

⁷ Our bonesᵒ have been scattered
  at the mouth of the grave,ᵖ
  just like when the ground
    is broken up and plowed.�q

⁸ But my eyes are on you, my LORD God.
  I take refuge in you; don't let me die!

⁹ Protect me from the trap
    they've set for me;
  protect me from the snares
    of the evildoers.

¹⁰ Let the wicked fall into their own nets—
    all together!—
  but let me make it through safely.

Psalm 142

*A maskilʳ of David, when he was
in the cave. A prayer.*

¹ I cry out loud for help from the LORD.
  I beg out loud for mercy from the LORD.

² I pour out my concerns before God;
  I announce my distress to him.

³ When my spirit is weak inside me,
  you still know my way.
  But they've hidden a trap for me
    in the path I'm taking.

⁴ Look right beside me: See?
  No one pays attention to me.
  There's no escape for me.
  No one cares about my life.

⁵ I cry to you, LORD, for help.
  "You are my refuge," I say.

"You are all I have
  in the land of the living."

⁶ Pay close attention to my shouting,
  because I've been brought down so low!
  Deliver me from my oppressors
  because they're stronger than me.

⁷ Get me out of this prison
  so I can give thanks to your name.
  Then the righteous
  will gather all around me
  because of your good deeds to me.

Psalm 143

A psalm of David.

¹ Listen to my prayer, LORD!
  Because of your faithfulness,
    hear my requests for mercy!
  Because of your righteousness,
    answer me!

² Please don't bring your servant
  to judgment,
  because no living thing is righteous
    before you.

³ The enemy is chasing me,ˢ
  crushing my life in the dirt,
    forcing me to live in the dark
    like those who've been dead forever.

⁴ My spirit is weak inside me—
  inside, my mind is numb.

⁵ I remember the days long past;
  I meditate on all your deeds;
  I contemplate your handiwork.

⁶ I stretch out my hands to you;
  my whole being is like dry dirt,
    thirsting for you.ᵗ   *Selah*

⁷ Answer me, LORD—and quickly!
  My breath is fading.
  Don't hide your face from me
    or I'll be like those going down
    to the pit!

⁸ Tell me all about your faithful love
  come morning time,
  because I trust you.

ᵐHeb uncertain ⁿHeb uncertain ᵒLXX manuscripts, Syr *their bones*; DSS (11QPsᵃ) *my bones* ᵖHeb *Sheol* qHeb uncertain ʳPerhaps *instruction*; it also appears in Pss 42, 44–45, 52–55, 74, 78, 88–89, 142; cf 47:7; the root is used in Ps 32:8. ˢOr *my soul*; also in 143:6, 8, 11–12 ᵗHeb lacks *thirsting*.

Show me the way I should go,
  because I offer my life up to you.
⁹ Deliver me from my enemies, LORD!
  I seek protection from you.ᵘ
¹⁰ Teach me to do what pleases you,
  because you are my God.
  Guide me by your good spirit
    into good land.
¹¹ Make me live again, LORD,
  for your name's sake.
  Bring me out of distress
    because of your righteousness.
¹² Wipe out my enemies
  because of your faithful love.
  Destroy everyone who attacks me,
    because I am your servant.

Psalm 144
Of David.

¹ Bless the LORD, my rock,
  who taught my hands how to fight,
  who taught my fingers
    how to do battle!
² God is my loyal one, my fortress,
  my place of safety, my rescuer,
  my shield, in whom I take refuge,
    and the one who subdues
      people before me.

³ What are human beings, LORD,
  that you know them at all?
  What are human beings
    that you even consider them?
⁴ Humans are like a puff of air;
  their days go by like a shadow.

⁵ LORD, part your skies and come down!
  Touch the mountains so they smoke!
⁶ Flash lightning and scatter the enemy!
  Shoot your arrows and defeat them!
⁷ Stretch out your hand from above!
  Rescue me and deliver me
    from deep water,
  from the power of strangers,
    whose mouths speak lies,
⁸ and whose strong hand is
    a strong hand of deception!

⁹ I will sing a new song to you, God.
  I will sing praises to you
    on a ten-stringed harp,
¹⁰ to you—the one
  who gives saving help to rulers,
  and who rescues his servant David
    from the evil sword.
¹¹ Rescue me and deliver me
  from the power of strangers,
  whose mouths speak lies,
  and whose strong hand
    is a strong hand of deception,
¹² so thatᵛ our sons can grow up fully,
  in their youth, like plants;
  so that our daughters can be like pillars
    carved to decorate a palace;
¹³ so that our barns can be full,
  providing all kinds of food;
  so that our flocks can be
    in the thousands—
  even tens of thousands—in our fields;
¹⁴ so that our cattle can be loaded
  with calves;
  so that there won't be any breach
    in the walls,
  no exile, no outcries in our streets!

¹⁵ The people who have it like this
  are truly happy!
  The people whose God is the LORD
    are truly happy!

Psalm 145ʷ
Praise. Of David.

א ¹ I will lift you up high, my God,
    the true king.
  I will bless your name
    forever and always.
ב ² I will bless you every day.
  I will praise your name
    forever and always.
ג ³ The LORD is great
  and so worthy of praise!
  God's greatness can't be grasped.
ד ⁴ One generation will praise
  your works to the next one,
  proclaiming your mighty acts.

ᵘHeb uncertain; MT *to you I have hidden*   ᵛHeb uncertain   ʷPs 145 is an alphabetic acrostic poem; see the note
at Pss 9–10, 111, 119.

⁵ They will talk all about[x] the glorious
   splendor of your majesty;
   I will contemplate your wondrous works.
⁶ They will speak of the power
   of your awesome deeds;
   I will declare your great accomplishments.
⁷ They will rave in celebration
   of your abundant goodness;
   they will shout joyfully
      about your righteousness:
⁸ "The LORD is merciful
      and compassionate,
   very patient, and full of faithful love.
⁹ The LORD is good to everyone
      and everything;
   God's compassion extends,
      to all his handiwork!"
¹⁰ All that you have made
   gives thanks to you, LORD;
   all your faithful ones bless you!
¹¹ They speak of the glory of your kingdom;
   they talk all about your power,
¹² to inform all human beings
      about God's power
   and the majestic glory
      of God's kingdom.
¹³ Your kingdom is a kingship
      that lasts forever;
   your rule endures for all generations.
   The LORD is trustworthy
      in all that he says,
   faithful in all that he does.[y]
¹⁴ The LORD supports all who fall down,
   straightens up all who are bent low.
¹⁵ All eyes look to you, hoping,
   and you give them their food
      right on time,
¹⁶ opening your hand
   and satisfying the desire
      of every living thing.
¹⁷ The LORD is righteous in all his ways,
   faithful in all his deeds.
¹⁸ The LORD is close to everyone
   who calls out to him,
   to all who call out to him sincerely.
¹⁹ God shows favor to those who honor him,
   listening to their cries for help
      and saving them.

ש ²⁰ The LORD protects all who love him,
   but he destroys
      every wicked person.

ת ²¹ My mouth will proclaim
      the LORD's praise,
   and every living thing
      will bless God's holy name
      forever and always.

Psalm 146

¹ Praise the LORD!

   Let my whole being[z]
      praise the LORD!
² I will praise the LORD
   with all my life;
   I will sing praises to my God
      as long as I live.

³ Don't trust leaders;
   don't trust any human beings—
   there's no saving help with them!
⁴ Their breath leaves them,
   then they go back to the ground.
   On that very same day,
      their plans die too.

⁵ The person whose help
   is the God of Jacob—
   the person whose hope
   rests on the LORD their God—
      is truly happy!
⁶ God: the maker of heaven and earth,
   the sea, and all that is in them,
   God: who is faithful forever,
⁷ who gives justice to people
      who are oppressed,
   who gives bread to people
      who are starving!
   The LORD: who frees prisoners.
⁸ The LORD: who makes the blind see.
   The LORD: who straightens up
      those who are bent low.
   The LORD: who loves the righteous.
⁹ The LORD: who protects immigrants,
   who helps orphans and widows,
   but who makes the way of the wicked
      twist and turn!

---

[x] LXX, Syr, DSS (11QPs ᵃ); MT *and words of*   [y] LXX, DSS (11QPs ᵃ), Syr; MT lacks these lines, but they correspond
to the *nun* line in the alphabetic acrostic poem.   [z] Or *soul*

¹⁰ The LORD will rule forever!
  Zion, your God will rule
    from one generation to the next!

Praise the LORD!

Psalm 147

¹ Praise the LORD!
  Because it is good to sing praise
    to our God!
  Because it is a pleasure
    to make beautiful praise!

² The LORD rebuilds Jerusalem,
  gathering up Israel's exiles.
³ God heals the brokenhearted
  and bandages their wounds.
⁴ God counts the stars by number,
  giving each one a name.
⁵ Our Lord is great and so strong!
  God's knowledge can't be grasped!
⁶ The LORD helps the poor,
  but throws the wicked down on the dirt!

⁷ Sing to the LORD with thanks;
  sing praises to our God with a lyre!
⁸ God covers the skies with clouds;
  God makes rain for the earth;
  God makes the mountains
    sprout green grass.
⁹ God gives food to the animals—
  even to the baby ravens
    when they cry out.
¹⁰ God doesn't prize the strength of a horse;
  God doesn't treasure the legs of a runner.
¹¹ No. The LORD treasures the people
  who honor him,
    the people who wait for his faithful love.

¹² Worship the LORD, Jerusalem!
  Praise your God, Zion!
¹³ Because God secures the bars
  on your gates,
  God blesses the children
    you have there.
¹⁴ God establishes your borders peacefully.
  God fills you full
    with the very best wheat.

¹⁵ God issues his command to the earth—
  God's word speeds off fast!
¹⁶ God spreads snow like it was wool;
  God scatters frost like it was ashes;
¹⁷ God throws his hail down like crumbs—
  who can endure God's freezing cold?
¹⁸ Then God issues his word
  and melts it all away!
  God makes his winds blow;
    the water flows again.

¹⁹ God proclaims his word to Jacob;
  his statutes and rules to Israel.
²⁰ God hasn't done that
  with any other nation;
  those nations have no knowledge
    of God's rules.^a

Praise the LORD!

Psalm 148

¹ Praise the LORD!

Praise the LORD from heaven!
  Praise God on the heights!
² Praise God, all of you
  who are his messengers!
  Praise God, all of you
    who comprise his heavenly forces!
³ Sun and moon, praise God!
  All of you bright stars, praise God!
⁴ You highest heaven, praise God!
  Do the same, you waters
    that are above the sky!
⁵ Let all of these praise the LORD's name
  because God gave the command
    and they were created!
⁶ God set them in place
  always and forever.
  God made a law
    that will not be broken.

⁷ Praise the LORD from the earth,
  you sea monsters
    and all you ocean depths!
⁸ Do the same, fire and hail,
  snow and smoke,
    stormy wind that does what God says!

---

^aLXX, Tg, DSS (11QPs ^a) *God hasn't let those nations know his rules.*

⁹ Do the same, you mountains,
  every single hill,
  fruit trees, and every single cedar!
¹⁰ Do the same, you animals—
   wild or tame—
   you creatures that creep along
     and you birds that fly!
¹¹ Do the same, you kings of the earth
   and every single person,
   you princes and every single ruler
     on earth!
¹² Do the same, you young men—
   young women too!—
   you who are old together
     with you who are young!

¹³ Let all of these praise the LORD's name
   because only God's name
     is high over all.
   Only God's majesty
     is over earth and heaven.
¹⁴ God raised the strength[b] of his people,
   the praise of all his faithful ones—
     that's the Israelites,
     the people who are close to him.

Praise the LORD!

Psalm 149

¹ Praise the LORD!

  Sing to the LORD a new song;
    sing God's praise
    in the assembly of the faithful!
² Let Israel celebrate its maker;
   let Zion's children rejoice
     in their king!
³ Let them praise God's name
   with dance;
   let them sing God's praise
     with the drum and lyre!

⁴ Because the LORD is pleased
  with his people,
  God will beautify the poor
    with saving help.

⁵ Let the faithful celebrate with glory;
   let them shout for joy on their beds.[c]
⁶ Let the high praises of God
   be in their mouths
   and a double-edged sword
     in their hands,
⁷ to get revenge against the nations
   and punishment on the peoples,
⁸ binding their rulers in chains
   and their officials in iron shackles,
⁹ achieving the justice
   written against them.
That will be an honor
  for all God's faithful people.

Praise the LORD!

Psalm 150

¹ Praise the LORD!

  Praise God in his sanctuary!
    Praise God in his fortress, the sky!
² Praise God in his mighty acts!
   Praise God as suits
     his incredible greatness!
³ Praise God with the blast
   of the ram's horn!
   Praise God with lute and lyre!
⁴ Praise God with drum and dance!
   Praise God with strings and pipe!
⁵ Praise God with loud cymbals!
   Praise God with clashing cymbals!
⁶ Let every living thing
   praise the LORD!

Praise the LORD!

ᵇOr *horn* ᶜHeb uncertain

PROVERBS

The book of Proverbs presents a wide range of moral instructions, dressed in the literary styles of proverbial sayings and brief poems. The six sections of the book were written over many centuries, by many hands, and under vastly different circumstances. But beneath the watchful eye of post-exilic editors, these many diverse sayings were assembled, edited, and offered confidently as a guide to a happy, fulfilling, and prosperous life.

THE CONTENT OF PROVERBS

The range of ethical teachings is as broad as human experience itself. This anthology presents advice on conduct such as proper sexual behavior, industriousness, effective communication, loyalty, friendship, and abstinence from intoxicants.

Many sayings reflect a strong religious belief, encouraging faith and obedience to the Lord's will. Yet other sayings probe the mysteries of God's revelations in the world of nature or in human relationships. Some sayings reflect the regularity and predictability of the natural order. All these sayings are preserved precisely because they work well. They present a high standard of conduct. The writers are confident in their belief that God rewards the righteous person and punishes the evildoer.

Certainly the book of Proverbs is a manual of instruction, but it is also a profound synthesis of faith and human reason. For the sages who coined the proverbs and edited the sayings, there was no greater act of piety than learning and living out moral virtue. Moral knowledge was useful for conforming to God's will because it is exhibited in the natural and moral order.

STRUCTURE AND ORGANIZATION

The book of Proverbs can be divided into six sections, based on internal headings and clear changes in literary style and ethical/religious content: (1) Introduction (1:1–9:18); (2) The Proverbs of Solomon (10:1–22:16); (3) The Words of the Wise (22:17–24:22); (4) More Sayings of the Wise (24:23-34); (5) More Proverbs of Solomon (25:1–29:27); and (6) Four Appendixes (30:1–31:31). Analysis of these sections suggests to scholars that Proverbs is an anthology of materials that originally existed independently of one another. Variations in literary style alone indicate separate authors, different settings and dates, and distinct purposes.

AUTHORSHIP AND DATE

Tradition says the principal author of the book of Proverbs is King Solomon, the son of David, King of Israel. In part, this is because of the superscriptions in the book itself (1:1, 10:1, and 25:1). Also, the Bible says that Solomon composed three thousand proverbs and numerous songs and was wise in greater measure than the length of the seashore (1 Kings 4:29-34). While King Solomon may have written and collected thousands of proverbs (since he was probably responsible for promoting and nurturing the wisdom tradition in his royal court), the style, vocabulary, and theme of many sayings in chapters 1–9, 22:17–24:22, and 30–31 indicate authors and dates other than King Solomon. Yet because of the traditional association of Solomon with Israelite wisdom, the compilers of the Hebrew Bible honored Solomon with the superscription in 1:1.

Proverbial sayings came from three major centers: the Royal Wisdom School (founded by Solomon and nurtured during the monarchy), folk tradition, and the theological community. Still other sayings arose from anonymous individuals in ancient Israel and became part of an ever-increasing repository of collective knowledge. Also, we believe that a Hebrew sage borrowed substantial material from the Egyptian source known as *Instructions of Amenemope*. And from within the book of Proverbs, we have the materials ascribed to Agur (30:1) and Lemuel (31:1).

By their very nature as true and universal insight into human existence, the proverbs became the property of the entire community. The legacy of the book of Proverbs is not, therefore, a legacy of a particular scribe or king, but the legacy of the entire Israelite nation and its wisdom tradition.

Assigning dates to either individual sayings or the collections of sayings is difficult. There are few historical references, and the superscriptions that do exist reflect special patronage rather than actual authorship. Careful study of comparative wisdom literature from Egypt, Mesopotamia, and Ugarit has led Old Testament scholars to rethink earlier notions about the dating of certain literary forms and themes. A post-exilic date for Proverbs 1–9, for example, is no longer a necessary conclusion; there are parallel materials that are clearly from the tenth or ninth centuries BCE.

Although it is likely that most of the six sections of Proverbs were in existence by the latter part of the fourth century BCE, differences in the arrangement of certain sections of Proverbs in the Greek translation of the Old Testament suggest that the book itself was not finalized until the late Hellenistic period. It is also entirely possible that a few sayings were added during that late phase of development, as suggested by Aramaic and Greek loan words.

THEOLOGICAL THEMES IN PROVERBS

The book of Proverbs pivots on the axis of five major theological themes: (1) divine retribution, (2) the fear of the Lord, (3) moral conduct, (4) divine revelation, and (5) creation orders. Many other theological themes surface in Proverbs as well. From time to time, certain themes may even appear to contradict one another. There are repetitions of themes, comparisons, contrasts, analogies, puns, and so forth. But most of the proverbs relate to the five themes mentioned above.

Divine retribution is the idea that the Lord blesses (rewards) the person of faith and righteousness and punishes the apostate person and the evildoer. In Proverbs, divine retribution occurs through the operation of the moral order (11:8, 11). The law of act-consequence operates without exception: Evil acts bring their own punishment (1:8-19). Of course, this moral system of the universe is the creation of God, and as such it surely operates under God's will. But retribution, for the sages, does not require God to change the ordinary scheme of nature or intrude into history. Each human act contains the seeds of its own consequence; this is retribution for the sage.

The fear of the Lord is an expression used by the sage to refer to religious faith (1:7). In fact, for the sage, the ultimate level of human knowledge or wisdom brings a person to an acute consciousness of God's natural and social order. It is dangerous to ignore this "order" of things. But the benefits of wisdom are success and fulfillment. True respect for this sovereign moral order of the universe is known as the fear of the Lord.

Logically following from the notion of the fear of the Lord is a strongly rigid *moral code*. The ethical values displayed in Proverbs were encoded into the universe by God. Conformity yields success! Thus morality for the sage was measured by consequences; utility became the guide to what God expected. Specifically, the sages warn against association with evil companions (1:8-19), consorting with prostitutes (7:10-23), drunkenness (23:29-35), and so forth. They commend industry, proper communication, etiquette, honesty, friendship, and above all, the fear of the Lord.

Fourth, the sages perceived *divine revelation* in ways that were different from the concepts of revelation advanced by priests and prophets. The sages began theologically with general human experience in nature, and moved by analogy to the realm of human morality. They observed the orderly operations of nature: the regular seasons, gravity, growth, mating patterns, and so forth. By analogy, human interrelationships exhibited similar patterns of predictability, because the same divine laws that animated nature also structured human existence. The will of the Lord was clearly evident in the created order. Righteousness, loyalty, and prudence were God's moral expectations as preserved in experience.

Fifth, the *order of creation* for the sages marks the establishment of both a natural and a moral order. In contrast to the accounts in Genesis, it does not provide a historical framework for human sin and divine redemption. Creation here means regularity, predictability, causation, comprehensibility. Creation reflects the moral nature of the universe; the world and human existence are not indifferent moral concerns, precisely because God implanted a moral fabric within the scheme of the universe. To discover creation is to discover God's moral will. The notion of divine creation is a resounding affirmation of the meaning of human existence; life has value because God created it so.

PROVERBS

Purpose of Proverbs

1 The proverbs of Solomon, King David's
son, from Israel:

2 Their purpose is to teach wisdom
and discipline,
to help one understand wise sayings.
3 They provide insightful instruction,
which is righteous, just,
and full of integrity.
4 They make the naive mature,
the young knowledgeable and discreet.
5 The wise hear them and grow in wisdom;
those with understanding gain guidance.
6 They help one understand
proverbs and difficult sayings,
the words of the wise, and their puzzles.
7 Wisdom begins with the fear of the LORD,
but fools despise
wisdom and instruction.

Avoid evil associations

8 Listen, my son,
to your father's instruction;
don't neglect your mother's teaching;
9 for they are a graceful wreath
on your head,
and beads for your neck.
10 My son, don't let sinners entice you.
Don't go
11 when they say:
"Come with us.
Let's set up a deadly ambush.
Let's secretly wait for the innocent
just for fun.
12 Let's swallow up the living
like the grave[a]—

whole, like those who go down
into the pit.
13 We'll find all sorts of precious wealth;
we'll fill our houses with plunder.
14 Throw in your lot with us;
we'll share our money."
15 My son, don't go on the path with them;
keep your feet from their way,
16 because their feet run to evil;
they hurry to spill blood.
17 It's useless to cast a net
in the sight of a bird.
18 But these sinners set up a deadly ambush;
they lie in wait for their own lives.
19 These are the ways of all
who seek unjust gain;
it costs them their lives.

Listen to "Woman Wisdom"

20 Wisdom shouts in the street;
in the public square she raises her voice.
21 Above the noisy crowd, she calls out.
At the entrances of the city gates,
she has her say:
22 "How long will you clueless people
love your naïveté,
mockers hold their mocking dear,
and fools hate knowledge?
23 You should respond when I correct you.
Look, I'll pour out my spirit on you.
I'll reveal my words to you.
24 I invited you, but you rejected me;
I stretched out my hand to you,
but you paid no attention.
25 You ignored all my advice,
and you didn't want me to correct you.

[a]Heb *Sheol*

PROVERB

Readers of the Bible most often associate the word *proverb* with short, usually two-line sayings in Hebrew poetic parallel structure that provide basic insights into human relationships. These are frequent in the book of Proverbs as well as in other OT literature. The NT uses the term to refer to short stories as well as to sayings.

26 So I'll laugh at your disaster;
    I'll make fun of you
        when dread comes over you,
27 when terror hits you like a hurricane,
    and your disaster comes in
        like a tornado,
    when distress and oppression
        overcome you.
28 Then they will call me,
    but I won't answer;
    they will seek me, but won't find me
29 because they hated knowledge
    and didn't choose the fear of the LORD.
30 They didn't want my advice;
    they rejected all my corrections.
31 They will eat from the fruit of their way,
    and they'll be full of their own schemes.
32 The immature will die
    because they turn away;
    smugness will destroy fools.
33 Those who obey me will dwell securely,
    untroubled by the dread of harm."

Benefits of wisdom

2 My son, accept my words
    and store up my commands.
2 Turn your ear toward wisdom,
    and stretch your mind
        toward understanding.
3 Call out for insight,
    and cry aloud for understanding.
4 Seek it like silver;
    search for it like hidden treasure.
5 Then you will understand
    the fear of the LORD,
    and discover the knowledge of God.
6 The LORD gives wisdom;
    from his mouth come knowledge
        and understanding.
7 He reserves ability for those
    with integrity.
    He is a shield for those
        who live a blameless life.
8 He protects the paths of justice
    and guards the way of those
        who are loyal to him.
9 Then you will understand righteousness
    and justice,
    as well as integrity, every good course.
10 Wisdom will enter your mind,
    and knowledge will fill you with delight.

11 Discretion will guard you;
    understanding will protect you.
12 Wisdom will rescue you from the evil path,
    from people who twist their words.
13 They forsake the way of integrity
    and go on obscure paths.
14 They enjoy doing evil,
    rejoicing in their twisted evil.
15 Their paths are confused;
    they get lost on their way.
16 Wisdom will rescue you
    from the mysterious woman,
    from the foreign woman
        with her slick words.
17 She leaves behind the partner
    of her youth;
    she even forgets her covenant with God.
18 Her house sinks down to death,
    and her paths go down
        to the shadowy dead.
19 All those who go to her will never return;
    they will never again
        reach the ways of the living.
20 So you should stay on the path
    of good people,
    guarding the road of the righteous.
21 Those who have integrity
    will dwell in the land;
    the innocent will remain in it.
22 But the wicked will be cut off
    from the land,
    and the treacherous will be ripped up.

Trust in the LORD

3 My son, don't forget my instruction.
    Let your heart guard my commands,
2 because they will help you live
    a long time
    and provide you with well-being.
3 Don't let loyalty and faithfulness
    leave you.
    Bind them on your neck;
    write them on the tablet of your heart.
4 Then you will find favor and approval
    in the eyes of God and humanity.
5 Trust in the LORD with all your heart;
    don't rely on your own intelligence.
6 Know him in all your paths,
    and he will keep your ways straight.
7 Don't consider yourself wise.
    Fear the LORD and turn away from evil.

⁸ Then your body^b will be healthy
  and your bones strengthened.
⁹ Honor the LORD with your wealth
  and with the first of all your crops.
¹⁰ Then your barns will be filled
  with plenty,
  and your vats will burst with wine.
¹¹ Don't reject the instruction of the LORD,
  my son;
  don't despise his correction.
¹² The LORD loves those he corrects,
  just like a father who treats his son
  with favor.

Value of wisdom
¹³ Happy are those who find wisdom
  and those who gain understanding.
¹⁴ Her profit is better than silver,
  and her gain better than gold.
¹⁵ Her value exceeds pearls;
  all you desire can't compare with her.
¹⁶ In her right hand is a long life;
  in her left are wealth and honor.
¹⁷ Her ways are pleasant;
  all her paths are peaceful.
¹⁸ She is a tree of life
  to those who embrace her;
  those who hold her tight are happy.
¹⁹ The LORD laid the foundations
  of the earth with wisdom,
  establishing the heavens
  with understanding.
²⁰ With his knowledge,
  the watery depths burst open,
  and the skies drop dew.

Integrity of wisdom
²¹ My son, don't let them slip
  from your eyes;
  hold on to sound judgment
  and discretion.
²² They will be life for your whole being,
  and an ornament for your neck.
²³ Then you will walk safely on your path,
  and your foot won't stumble.
²⁴ If you lie down, you won't be terrified.
  When you lie down,
  your sleep will be pleasant.
²⁵ Don't fear sudden terror

or the ruin that comes to the wicked.
²⁶ The LORD will be your confidence;
  he will guard your feet
  from being snared.
²⁷ Don't withhold good
  from someone who deserves it,
  when it is in your power to do so.
²⁸ Don't say to your neighbor,
  "Go and come back;
  I'll give it to you tomorrow,"
  when you have it.
²⁹ Don't plan to harm your neighbor
  who trusts and lives near you.
³⁰ Don't accuse anyone without reason,
  when they haven't harmed you.
³¹ Don't envy violent people
  or choose any of their ways.
³² Devious people are detestable
  to the LORD,
  but the virtuous are his close friends.
³³ The LORD's curse is on
  the house of the wicked,
  but he blesses the home of the righteous.
³⁴ He mocks mockers,
  but he shows favor to the humble.
³⁵ The wise gain respect,
  but fools receive shame.

Love wisdom
4 Hear, children, fatherly instruction;
  pay attention to gain understanding.
² I'll teach you well.
  Don't abandon my instruction.
³ When I was a son to my father,
  tender and my mother's favorite,
⁴ he taught me and said to me:
  "Let your heart hold on to my words:
  Keep my commands and live.
⁵ Get wisdom; get understanding.
  Don't forget and don't turn away
  from my words.
⁶ Don't abandon her,
  and she will guard you.
  Love her, and she will protect you.
⁷ The beginning of wisdom:
  Get wisdom!
  Get understanding before anything else.
⁸ Highly esteem her, and she will exalt you.
  She will honor you if you embrace her.

^bHeb *navel*

⁹ She will place a graceful wreath
     on your head;
     she will give you a glorious crown."

Stay on the path of wisdom

¹⁰ Listen, my son, and take in my speech,
     then the years of your life will be many.
¹¹ I teach you the path of wisdom.
     I lead you in straight courses.
¹² When you walk, you won't be hindered;
     when you run, you won't stumble.
¹³ Hold on to instruction; don't slack off;
     protect it, for it is your life.
¹⁴ Don't go on the way of the wicked;
     don't walk on the path of evil people.
¹⁵ Avoid it! Don't turn onto it;
     stay off of it and keep going!
¹⁶ They don't sleep unless they do evil;
     they are robbed of sleep unless
       they make someone stumble.
¹⁷ They eat the bread of evil,
     and they drink the wine of violence.
¹⁸ The way of the righteous
     is like morning light
     that gets brighter and
       brighter till it is full day.
¹⁹ The path of the wicked
     is like deep darkness;
     they don't know where they will stumble.

Be careful about what you say

²⁰ My son, pay attention to my words.
     Bend your ear to my speech.
²¹ Don't let them slip from your sight.
     Guard them in your mind.
²² They are life to those who find them,
     and healing for their entire body.
²³ More than anything you guard,
     protect your mind, for life flows from it.
²⁴ Have nothing to do
     with a corrupt mouth;
     keep devious lips far from you.
²⁵ Focus your eyes straight ahead;
     keep your gaze on what
       is in front of you.
²⁶ Watch your feet on the way,
     and all your paths will be secure.
²⁷ Don't deviate a bit to the right or the left;
     turn your feet away from evil.

Avoid the mysterious woman

5 My son, pay attention to my wisdom.
     Bend your ear to what I know,
² so you might remain discreet,
     and your lips might guard knowledge.
³ The lips of a mysterious woman
     drip honey,
     and her tongue is smoother than oil,
⁴ but in the end she is bitter as gall,
     sharp as a double-edged sword.
⁵ Her feet go down to death;
     her steps lead to the grave.^c
⁶ She doesn't stay on the way of life.
     Her paths wander,
     but she doesn't know it.

⁷ Now children, listen to me,
     and don't deviate
     from the words of my mouth.
⁸ Stay on a path that is far from her;
     don't approach the entrance to her house.
⁹ Otherwise, you will give
     your strength to others,
     your years to a cruel person.
¹⁰ Otherwise, strangers
     will sap your strength,
     and your hard work will end up
       in a foreigner's house.
¹¹ You will groan at the end
     when your body and flesh are exhausted,
¹² and you say, "How I hated instruction!
     How my heart despised correction!
¹³ I didn't listen to the voice of my instructor.
     I didn't obey my teacher.
¹⁴ I'm on the brink of utter ruin
     in the assembled community."

¹⁵ Drink water from your own cistern,
     gushing water from your own well.
¹⁶ Should your fountains flood outside,
     streams of water in the public squares?
¹⁷ They are yours alone,
     not for you as well as strangers.
¹⁸ May your spring be blessed.
     Rejoice in the wife of your youth.
¹⁹ She is a lovely deer, a graceful doe.
     Let her breasts intoxicate you
     all the time;
     always be drunk on her love.

^cHeb *Sheol*

²⁰ Why, my son, should you lose
    your senses with a mysterious woman
    and embrace the breasts
      of a foreign female?

²¹ The LORD's eyes watch
    over every person's path,
    observing all their ways.
²² The wicked will be caught
    by their own evil acts,
    grabbed by the ropes of their own sin.
²³ Those without instruction will die,
    misled by their own stupidity.

Wise advice

6 My son, if you guarantee a loan
   for your neighbor
    or shake hands in agreement
      with a stranger,
² you will be trapped by your words;
    you will be caught by your words.
³ Do this, my son, to get out of it,
    for you have come under the control
      of your neighbor.
    So go, humble yourself,ᵈ
    and pester your neighbor.
⁴ Don't give sleep to your eyes
    or slumber to your eyelids.
⁵ Get yourself free like a gazelle
    from a hunter,
    like a bird from the hand of a fowler.
⁶ Go to the ant, you lazy person;
    observe its ways and grow wise.
⁷ The ant has no commander, officer,
    or ruler.
⁸ Even so, it gets its food in summer;
    gathers its provisions at harvest.
⁹ How long, lazy person, will you lie down?
    When will you rise from your sleep?
¹⁰ A little sleep, a little slumber,
    a little folding of the arms to lie down—
¹¹ and poverty will come on you
    like a prowler,
    destitution like a warrior.
¹² Worthless people and guilty people
    go around with crooked talk.
¹³ They wink their eyes,
    gesture with their feet,
    and point with their fingers.

¹⁴ Their hearts are corrupt
    and determined to do evil;
    they create controversies all the time.
¹⁵ Therefore, sudden disaster
    will come upon them;
    they will be quickly broken
      beyond healing.
¹⁶ There are six things that the LORD hates,
    seven things detestable to him:
    ¹⁷ snobbish eyes,
    a lying tongue,
    hands that spill innocent blood,
¹⁸ a heart set on wicked plans,
    feet that run quickly to evil,
¹⁹ a false witness who breathes lies,
    and one who causes conflicts
      among relatives.

Danger of adultery
²⁰ My son, keep your father's command;
    don't abandon your mother's instruction.
²¹ Bind them on your heart for all time;
    fasten them around your neck.
²² When you walk around,
    they will lead you;
    when you lie down,
      they will protect you;
    when you awake,
      they will occupy your attention.
²³ The commandment is a lamp
    and instruction a light;
    corrective teaching is the path of life.
²⁴ They guard you from the evil woman,
    from the flattering tongue
    of the foreign woman.
²⁵ Don't desire her beauty in secret;
    don't let her take you in
    with her eyelashes,
²⁶ for a prostitute costs a loaf of bread,ᵉ
    but a married woman
    hunts for a man's very life.
²⁷ Can a man scoop fire into his lap
    and his clothes not get burned?
²⁸ If a man walks on hot coals,
    don't his feet get burned?
²⁹ So is the man who approaches
    his neighbor's wife;
    anyone who touches her will be punished.
³⁰ People don't despise a thief if he steals
    to fill his starving stomach.

ᵈHeb uncertain ᵉHeb uncertain

³¹ But if he is caught,
  he must pay sevenfold;
  he must give all the riches of his house.
³² He who commits adultery is senseless.
  Doing so, he destroys himself.
³³ He is wounded and disgraced.
  His shame will never be wiped away.
³⁴ Jealousy makes a man rage;
  he'll show no mercy
    on his day of revenge.
³⁵ He won't accept compensation;
  he'll refuse even a large bribe.

Avoid loose women

7 My son, keep my words;
  store up my commands within you.
² Keep my commands and live,
  and my instruction
    like the pupil of your eye.
³ Bind them on your fingers;
  write them on the tablet of your heart.
⁴ Say to wisdom, "You are my sister";
  call understanding "friend,"
⁵ so she might guard you
  against the mysterious woman,
  from the foreign woman
    who flatters you.
⁶ When from the window of my house,
  from behind the screen, I gazed down,
⁷ I looked among the naive young men
  and noticed among the youth,
    one who had no sense.
⁸ He was crossing the street at her corner
  and walked down the path to her house
⁹ in the early evening,
  at the onset of night and darkness.
¹⁰ All of a sudden a woman approaches him,
  dressed like a prostitute
    and with a cunning mind.
¹¹ She is noisy and defiant;
  her feet don't stay long in her own house.
¹² She has one foot in the street,
  one foot in the public square.
  She lies in wait at every corner.
¹³ She grabs him and kisses him.
  Her face is brazen as she speaks to him:
¹⁴ "I've made a sacrifice of well-being;
  today I fulfilled my solemn promises.

¹⁵ So I've come out to meet you,
  seeking you, and I have found you.
¹⁶ I've spread my bed with luxurious covers,
  with colored linens from Egypt.
¹⁷ I've sprinkled my bed with myrrh,
  aloes, and cinnamon.
¹⁸ Come, let's drink deep of love
  until morning;
  let's savor our lovemaking.
¹⁹ For my husband isn't home;
  he's gone far away.
²⁰ He took a pouch of money with him;
  he won't come home till full moon."
²¹ She seduces him with all her talk.
  She entices him with her flattery.
²² He goes headlong after her,
  like an ox to the slaughter,
  like a deer leaping into a trap,[f]
²³ until an arrow pierces his liver,
  like a bird hurrying to the snare,
    not aware that it will cost him his life.
²⁴ Now children, listen to me,
  and pay attention to my speech.
²⁵ Don't turn your heart to her ways;
  don't wander down her paths.
²⁶ She has caused many corpses to fall;
  she has killed many people.
²⁷ Her house is a path to the grave,[g]
  going down to the chambers of death.

Wisdom's autobiography

8 Doesn't Wisdom cry out
  and Understanding shout?
² Atop the heights along the path,
  at the crossroads she takes her stand.
³ By the gate before the city,
  at the entrances she shouts:

⁴ I cry out to you, people;
  my voice goes out to all of humanity.
⁵ Understand skill, you who are naive.
  Take this to heart, you fools.
⁶ Listen, for I speak things that are correct;
  from my lips comes what is right.
⁷ My mouth utters the truth;
  my lips despise wickedness.
⁸ All the words of my mouth are righteous;
  nothing in them is twisted or crooked.

---

[f] Heb uncertain [g] Heb *Sheol*

9 All of them are straightforward
   to those who understand,
   and upright for the knowledgeable.
10 Take my instruction rather than silver,
   knowledge rather than choice gold.
11 Wisdom is better than pearls;
   nothing is more delightful than she.

12 I, Wisdom, dwell with prudence;
   I have found knowledge and discretion.
13 To fear the LORD is to hate evil.
   I hate pride and arrogance,
   the path of evil and corrupt speech.
14 I have advice and ability,
   as well as understanding and strength.
15 By me kings rule,
   and princes issue righteous decrees.
16 By me rulers govern,
   and officials judge righteously.[h]
17 I love those who love me;
   those who seek me will find me.
18 Riches and honor are with me,
   as well as enduring wealth
   and righteousness.

h Heb uncertain

SOPHIA

Wisdom, personified as a woman, is an important, if somewhat puzzling, construct in the OT. There, "Wisdom" is grammatically feminine in gender, as are most abstract concepts in the Hebrew language. One must distinguish whether the text is referring to Woman Wisdom, the character and patron of the sages, or the overall concept of knowledge, learning, and skill. Within Proverbs and elsewhere, both uses are found: at times, Woman Wisdom is speaking to those who scorn her, love her, or might be advised to seek her (Prov 1:20-33; 8:1-36; 9:1-6); in other places, the skill of the specially trained is meant (Exod 28:3; 31:3; 35:31; 1 Kgs 2:6; 4:29-34 [Heb. 5:9-14]; Prov 14:8; Isa 29:14).

The prologue (chapters 1–9) to the book of Proverbs features the literary figure of personified Wisdom. As a female figure of much public power and authority, it is perplexing to find her in the midst of writings that strongly reflect the gender ideologies of antiquity. While regular women were expected to occupy themselves with the world of the home and its management, Woman Wisdom can be found in public places where male leaders like prophets exhort the populace. She speaks authoritatively based on her "cosmic portfolio": she existed before creation, was a "model" for it, and was beside God during these acts, delighting in the created world, especially humanity (Prov 8). She uses harsh language and vows to laugh at all those who disregard her advice when the results of their own stupidity come to fruition. She eagerly invites young men to her side, to walk in her ways and dine at her table. Her language is often an exact duplicate of that of her social and theological "evil twin," Woman Folly, who can be either adulteress or foreigner (Prov 9:1-9 versus 9:13-18). Wisdom demonstrates the admirable traits found in the Good Woman (CEB, "competent wife") of Proverbs 31:10-31 but is comfortable and recognized in arenas normally inhabited by only one sex, serving, in effect, as a reliable mediator between them. In sum, she offers "the good life" and makes the sort of claims one usually finds attributed to Israel's (ostensibly masculine) God.

¹⁹ My fruit is better than gold,
  even fine gold;
  my crops are better than choice silver.
²⁰ I walk on the way of righteousness,
  on the paths of justice,
²¹ to provide for those who love me
  and to fill up their treasuries.

²² The LORD created me
  at the beginning of his way,
  before his deeds long in the past.
²³ I was formed in ancient times,
  at the beginning, before the earth was.
²⁴ When there were no watery depths,
  I was brought forth,
  when there were no springs
  flowing with water.
²⁵ Before the mountains were settled,
  before the hills, I was brought forth;
²⁶ before God[i] made the earth and the fields
  or the first of the dry land.
²⁷ I was there when he established
  the heavens,
  when he marked out the horizon
  on the deep sea,
²⁸ when he thickened the clouds above,
  when he secured the fountains
  of the deep,
²⁹ when he set a limit for the sea,
  so the water couldn't go beyond
  his command,
  when he marked out
  the earth's foundations.
³⁰ I was beside him as a master of crafts.[j]
  I was having fun,
  smiling before him all the time,
³¹ frolicking with his inhabited earth
  and delighting in the human race.

³² Now children, listen to me:
  Happy are those who keep to my ways!
³³ Listen to instruction, and be wise;
  don't avoid it.
³⁴ Happy are those who listen to me,
  watching daily at my doors,
  waiting at my doorposts.
³⁵ Those who find me find life;
  they gain favor from the LORD.
³⁶ Those who offend me injure themselves;
  all those who hate me love death.

"Woman Wisdom's" invitation

9 Wisdom built her house;
  she has carved out her seven pillars.
² She slaughtered her animals,
  mixed her wine,
  and set her table.
³ She sends out her female servants;
  she issues an invitation
  from the top of the city heights:
⁴ "Whoever is naive turn aside here,"
  she says to those who lack sense.
⁵ "Come, eat my food,
  and drink the wine I have mixed.
⁶ Abandon your simplistic ways and live;
  walk in the way of understanding."

Wise advice
⁷ Whoever instructs the cynic
  gets insulted;
  whoever corrects the wicked gets hurt.
⁸ Don't correct the impudent,
  or they will hate you;
  correct the wise, and they will love you.
⁹ Teach the wise,
  and they will become wiser;
  inform the righteous,
  and their learning will increase.
¹⁰ The beginning of wisdom
  is the fear of the LORD;
  the knowledge of the holy one
  is understanding.
¹¹ Through me your days will be many;
  years will be added to your life.
¹² If you are wise, it is to your benefit;
  if you are cynical,
  you will bear it all alone.

"Woman Folly's" invitation
¹³ Woman Folly is noisy;
  she's stupid and doesn't even know it.
¹⁴ She sits at the doorway of her house,
  on a seat at the city heights.
¹⁵ She invites those who pass by
  on the path,
  those going straight on their way.
¹⁶ "Whoever is naive, come in here,"
  she says to those who lack sense.
¹⁷ "Stolen water is sweet;
  food eaten in secret is pleasant."

[i]Heb lacks *God*. [j]Heb uncertain

[18] But they don't know that the dead
  are there;
  her guests are in the depths
    of the grave.[k]

Proverbs of Solomon

10 The proverbs of Solomon:
  A wise child makes a father glad,
  but a foolish child
    brings sorrow to his mother.
[2] The treasure of the wicked
    won't profit them,
  but righteousness rescues people
    from death.
[3] The LORD doesn't let the righteous starve,
  but he rejects the desires of the wicked.
[4] Laziness brings poverty;
  hard work makes one rich.
[5] A wise son harvests in the summer;
  a disgraceful son
    sleeps right through the harvest.
[6] Blessings cover the head of the righteous,
  but the mouth of the wicked
    conceals violence.
[7] The memory of the righteous
    is a blessing,
  but the name of the wicked rots.
[8] The skilled mind accepts commands,
  but a foolish talker is ruined.
[9] Those who walk in innocence
    walk with confidence,
  but those on crooked paths
    will be found out.
[10] Those who wink an eye bring trouble;
  those who speak foolishly are ruined.
[11] The mouth of the righteous
    is a fountain of life,

but the mouth of the wicked
  conceals violence.
[12] Hate stirs up conflict,
  but love covers all offenses.
[13] Wisdom is found on the lips
    of those who have understanding,
  but there is a rod for the back
    of those with no sense.
[14] The wise store up knowledge,
  but the mouth of a fool brings on ruin.
[15] The riches of the wealthy
    are their strong city;
  the ruin of the poor is their poverty.
[16] The wages of the righteous lead to life;
  the earnings of the wicked lead to sin.
[17] Those who heed instruction
    are on the way to life,
  but those who ignore correction
    lose their way.
[18] Lying lips conceal hate,
  and those who spread slander are fools.
[19] With lots of words comes wrongdoing,
  but the wise restrain their lips.
[20] The tongue of the righteous
    is choice silver,
  but the heart of the wicked lacks value.
[21] The lips of the righteous
    nourish many people,
  but fools who lack sense will die.
[22] The LORD's blessing
    makes a person rich,
  and no trouble is added to it.
[23] Fools enjoy vile deeds,
  but those with understanding
    take pleasure in wisdom.
[24] What the wicked dread
    will come on them,

[k] Heb *Sheol*

SOLOMON

The third king of Israel and son of David, Solomon reigned, according to the Bible, in the mid-10th century BCE and was a main character of 1 Kings and 2 Chronicles. The biblical stories about Solomon emphasize his wisdom, his connections with the building of the Jerusalem temple, and his efforts at centralizing political power in the monarchy. While the historicity of some of the stories about him is debatable, it seems clear that his reign marked a transition in the development of Israelite political life.

but what the righteous desire
will be given to them.
²⁵ After a whirlwind passes by,
the wicked are no more,
but the righteous stand firm forever.
²⁶ Like vinegar to the teeth
and smoke to the eyes,
so are lazy people
to those who authorize them.
²⁷ The fear of the LORD increases one's life,
but the years of the wicked
will be cut short.
²⁸ The expectations of the righteous
result in joy,
but the hopes of the wicked will perish.
²⁹ The path of the LORD is a refuge
for the innocent
and ruin for those who do evil.
³⁰ The righteous will never be shaken,
but the wicked won't dwell in the land.
³¹ The mouth of the righteous
flows with wisdom,
but the twisted tongue will be cut off.
³² The lips of the wise
know what is acceptable,
but the mouth of the wicked knows
only what is perverse.

11 The LORD detests dishonest scales,
but delights in an accurate weight.
² When pride comes, so does shame,
but wisdom brings humility.
³ Integrity guides the virtuous,
but dishonesty ruins the treacherous.
⁴ Riches don't help in the day of wrath,
but righteousness rescues from death.

⁵ The righteousness of the innocent
makes their path straight,
but the wicked fall in their wickedness.
⁶ Those who do right
are saved by their righteousness,
but the untrustworthy
are caught by their own desires.
⁷ When the wicked die,
their hope perishes.
Yes, any hope based
on money perishes.
⁸ The righteous are saved from distress,
and the wicked take their place.
⁹ The godless destroy their neighbors
by their words,
but the righteous are saved
by their knowledge.
¹⁰ When the righteous succeed,
a city rejoices;
when the wicked perish,
there are shouts of joy.
¹¹ A city is honored
by the blessing of the virtuous;
it is destroyed
by the words of the wicked.
¹² Whoever despises their neighbor
lacks sense;
a sensible person keeps quiet.
¹³ A slanderer walks around
revealing secrets,
but a trustworthy person
keeps a confidence.
¹⁴ Without guidance, a people will fall,
but there is victory
with many counselors.

BALANCES

Balances, or scales, were necessary in the world before coinage for each transaction in precious metals (especially silver and gold), since the sole way of determining their value was by weight. Throughout the Bronze and Iron Ages, balances were constructed of two pans, suspended by cords from a horizontal beam. The beam was suspended from its middle and either held by hand (in small balances or hand balances) or mounted on a vertical beam (in large balances). The OT does not detail the process of weighing but stresses its moral aspect. This is expressed by the terms "false balances" and "dishonest scales" as opposed to "fair scales" and "honest balances" (e.g., Amos 8:5; Prov 11:1; 16:11; Ezek 45:10).

¹⁵ Guaranteeing the debt of a stranger
  brings big trouble,
  but the one who refuses to shake hands
  will be secure.

¹⁶ A gracious woman gains honor;
  violent men gain only wealth.

¹⁷ Kind persons benefit themselves,
  but cruel people harm themselves.

¹⁸ The wicked earn false wages,
  but those who sow righteousness
  receive a true reward.

¹⁹ The righteous are headed toward life,
  but those who pursue evil,
  toward death.

²⁰ The LORD detests a crooked heart,
  but he favors those
  whose path is innocent.

²¹ The evil person will surely not
  go unpunished,
  but the children of the righteous
  will escape.

²² Like a gold ring in a pig's nose
  is a beautiful woman
  who lacks discretion.

²³ The desires of the righteous end up well,
  but the expectations of the wicked
  bring wrath.

²⁴ Those who give generously receive more,
  but those who are stingy with
  what is appropriate will grow needy.

²⁵ Generous persons will prosper;
  those who refresh others
  will themselves be refreshed.

²⁶ People curse those who hoard grain,
  but they bless thoseˡ who sell it.

²⁷ Those who look for good find favor,
  but those who seek evil—
  it will come to them.

²⁸ Those who trust in their wealth
  will wither,
  but the righteous will thrive
  like leafy trees.

²⁹ Those who trouble their family
  will inherit the wind.
  The fool will be servant to the wise.

³⁰ The fruit of the righteous is a tree of life,
  and the wise gather lives.ᵐ

³¹ If the righteous receive their due on earth,
  how much more the wicked and sinners?

12 Those who love discipline
  love knowledge,
  and those who hate correction are stupid.

² The LORD favors good people,
  but he condemns schemers.

³ No one is established by wicked acts,
  but the roots of the righteous
  can't be disturbed.

⁴ A strong woman is a crown
  to her husband,
  but a disgraceful woman
  is like rot in his bones.

⁵ The plans of the righteous are just,
  but the guidance of the wicked
  is deceptive.

⁶ The words of the wicked are a deathtrap,
  but the speech of those who do right
  rescues them.

⁷ The wicked are destroyed and are no more,
  but the family of the righteous
  will endure.

⁸ A person is praised for his insight,
  but a warped mind leads to contempt.

⁹ Better to be held in low regard
  and have a servant
  than to be conceited and lack food.

¹⁰ The righteous care about
  their livestock's needs,
  but even the compassion of the wicked
  is cruel.

¹¹ Those who work their land
  will have plenty to eat,
  but those who engage
  in empty pursuits have no sense.

¹² Desiring evil is a trap for the wicked,
  but the root of the righteous endures.ⁿ

¹³ The wicked are trapped
  by the transgressions of their lips,
  but the righteous escape from distress.

¹⁴ From the fruit of their speech,
  people are well satisfied;
  their work results in reward.

¹⁵ Fools see their own way as right,
  but the wise listen to advice.

¹⁶ Fools reveal their anger right away,
  but the shrewd hide their contempt.

¹⁷ Those who state the truth speak justly,
  but a false witness deceives.

¹⁸ Some chatter on like a stabbing sword,
  but a wise tongue heals.

ˡOr *the heads of those* ᵐOr LXX, Syr *violence takes lives away* ⁿOr *gives*

¹⁹ Truthful lips endure forever,
 but a lying tongue
  lasts only for a moment.
²⁰ Deceit is in the heart
 of those who plan evil,
 but there is joy
  for those who advise peace.
²¹ No harm happens to the righteous,
 but the wicked receive their fill of trouble.
²² The LORD detests false lips;
 he favors those who do what is true.
²³ The shrewd conceal their knowledge,
 but the heart of fools
  proclaims their stupidity.
²⁴ A hard worker is in charge,
 while a lazy one will be sentenced
  to hard labor.
²⁵ Anxiety leads to depression,
 but a good word encourages.
²⁶ The righteous offer guidance
 to their neighbors,^o
 but the path of the wicked
  makes them wander.
²⁷ The lazy don't roast^p their prey,
 but hard workers receive
  precious riches.
²⁸ The way of the righteous leads to life,
 but the detestable^q path leads to death.

13 A wise son listens to^r the discipline
 of his father,
 but a mocker doesn't listen
  to correction.
² People eat well from the fruit
 of their words,
 but the treacherous have an appetite
  only for violence.
³ People who watch their mouths
 guard their lives,
 but those who open their lips are ruined.
⁴ The lazy have strong desires
 but receive nothing;
 the appetite of the diligent is satisfied.
⁵ The righteous hate false words,
 but the wicked create disgust and scorn.
⁶ Righteousness guards the innocent
 on the path,
 but wickedness misleads sinners.
⁷ Some pretend to be rich but have nothing,

while others pretend to be poor,
 but have great riches.
⁸ Wealth can ransom a person's life,
 but the poor don't even receive threats.
⁹ The light of the righteous rejoices,
 but the lamp of the wicked goes out.
¹⁰ The empty-headed cause conflict
 out of pride;
 those who take advice are wise.
¹¹ Riches gotten quickly^s will dwindle,
 but those who acquire them
  gradually become wealthy.
¹² Hope delayed makes the heart sick;
 longing fulfilled is a tree of life.
¹³ Trouble will come on those
 who despise a word,
 but those who respect
  the commandment will be rewarded.
¹⁴ The teaching of the wise
 is a fountain of life,
 turning a person away from deathtraps.
¹⁵ Good insight brings favor,
 but the way of the faithless
  is their ruin.^t
¹⁶ The prudent all act intelligently,
 but fools display their stupidity.
¹⁷ Wicked messengers fall into trouble,
 but a reliable one brings healing.
¹⁸ Poverty and shame come to those
 who don't care about instruction;
 honor belongs to those
  who heed correction.
¹⁹ A desire fulfilled is pleasant,
 but fools find deviating
  from evil disgusting.
²⁰ Walk with wise people and become wise;
 befriend fools and get in trouble.
²¹ Trouble pursues sinners,
 but good things reward the righteous.
²² Good people leave their grandchildren
 an inheritance,
 but the wealth of sinners
  is stored up for the righteous.
²³ A poor person's land
 might produce much food,
 but it is unjustly swept away.
²⁴ Those who withhold the rod
 hate their children,

^oHeb uncertain ^pHeb uncertain ^qLXX; MT *the path of the trail* ^rHeb lacks *listens to.* ^sLXX; MT *from meaninglessness* ^tLXX, Syr, Vulg; MT *endures*

but the one who loves them
   applies discipline.
²⁵ The righteous eat their fill,
   but the wicked have empty stomachs.

14 A wise woman builds her house,
   while a foolish woman tears hers
    down with her own hands.
² Those who walk with integrity
   fear the LORD,
   but those who take a crooked path
    despise him.
³ Pride sprouts in the mouth of a fool,^u
   but the lips of the wise protect them.
⁴ When there are no oxen, the stall is clean,
   but when there is a strong bull,
    there is abundant produce.
⁵ A truthful witness doesn't lie,
   but a false witness spews lies.
⁶ A mocker searches for wisdom
   and gets none,
   but knowledge comes quickly
    to the intelligent.
⁷ Stay away from fools,
   for you won't learn wise speech there.
⁸ By their wisdom the prudent
   understand their way,
   but the stupidity of fools deceives them.
⁹ Fools mock a compensation offering,
   but favor is with those who do right.
¹⁰ The heart knows its own distress;
   another person can't share its joy.
¹¹ The house of the wicked is destroyed,
   but the tent flourishes
    for those who do right.
¹² There is a path that may seem straight
   to someone,
   but in the end it is a path to death.
¹³ The heart feels pain even in laughter,
   and in the end, joy turns to sorrow.
¹⁴ Rebellious hearts receive satisfaction
   from their ways;
   the good receive the due reward
    for their deeds.
¹⁵ The naive believe anything,
   but the prudent give thought
    to their steps.
¹⁶ The wise are careful and avoid evil,
   but fools become excited
    and overconfident.

¹⁷ Short-tempered people
   make stupid mistakes,
   and schemers are hated.
¹⁸ Stupidity is the lot of the naive,
   but the prudent are crowned
    with knowledge.
¹⁹ Evil people will bow down
   before the good;
   wicked people are at the gates
    of the righteous.
²⁰ Even their neighbors hate the poor,
   but many love the wealthy.
²¹ Those who despise their neighbors
   are sinners,
   but happy are those
    who are kind to the needy.
²² Don't those who plan evil go astray?
   Those who plan good
   receive loyalty and faithfulness.
²³ There is profit in hard work,
   but mere talk leads to poverty.
²⁴ Wealth is the crown of the wise,
   and the folly of fools is folly.
²⁵ A truthful witness saves lives,
   but a deceiver proclaims lies.
²⁶ In the fear of the LORD
   is strong confidence
   and refuge for one's children.
²⁷ The fear of the LORD is a fountain of life,
   turning people away from deathtraps.
²⁸ A king's glory is a large population,
   but a dwindling people is a ruler's ruin.
²⁹ Patience leads to abundant understanding,
   but impatience leads to stupid mistakes.
³⁰ A peaceful mind gives life to the body,
   but jealousy rots the bones.
³¹ Those who exploit the powerless
   anger their maker,
   while those who are kind to the poor
    honor God.
³² The wicked are thrown down
   by their own evil,
   but the righteous find refuge
    even in death.
³³ Wisdom resides
   in an understanding heart,
   but it's not^v known in fools.
³⁴ Righteousness dignifies a nation,
   but sin disgraces a people.

^uHeb uncertain   ^vLXX; MT lacks *not*.

³⁵ The king favors an insightful servant,
  but is furious at a shameful one.

15 A sensitive answer turns back wrath,
  but an offensive word stirs up anger.
² The tongue of the wise
  enhances knowledge,
  but the mouth of a fool
  gushes with stupidity.
³ The LORD's eyes are everywhere,
  keeping watch on evil and good people.
⁴ Wholesome speech is a tree of life,
  but dishonest talk breaks the spirit.
⁵ A fool doesn't like a father's instruction,
  but those who heed correction
  are mature.
⁶ Great treasure is in the house
  of the righteous,
  but the gain of the wicked brings trouble.
⁷ The lips of the wise spread knowledge,
  but the hearts of fools have none.
⁸ The LORD detests the sacrifices
  of the wicked,
  but favors the prayers
  of those who do right.
⁹ The LORD detests the path of the wicked,
  but loves those who pursue righteousness.
¹⁰ Discipline is severe for those
  who abandon the way;
  those who hate correction will die.
¹¹ The grave^w and the underworld^x lie open
  before the LORD;
  how much more the hearts
  of human beings!
¹² Mockers don't like those
  who correct them.
  They won't go to the wise.
¹³ A joyful heart brightens one's face,
  but a troubled heart breaks the spirit.
¹⁴ An understanding heart
  seeks knowledge;
  but fools feed on folly.
¹⁵ All the days of the needy are hard,
  but a happy heart has a continual feast.
¹⁶ Better a little with fear of the LORD
  than a great treasure with turmoil.
¹⁷ Better a meal of greens with love
  than a plump calf with hate.
¹⁸ Hotheads stir up conflict,
  but patient people calm down strife.

¹⁹ The path of the lazy
  is like a hedge of thorns,
  but the way of those who do right
  is a clear road.
²⁰ A wise child brings joy to a father,
  but fools despise their mothers.
²¹ Folly is joy to those who lack sense,
  but those with understanding
  walk straight ahead.
²² Plans fail with no counsel,
  but with many counselors they succeed.
²³ To give an appropriate answer is a joy;
  how good is a word at the right time!
²⁴ For those with insight,
  life is an upward path,
  avoiding the grave^y below.
²⁵ The LORD snatches away
  the arrogant one's house,
  but he preserves the widow's boundaries.
²⁶ The LORD detests evil plans,
  but gracious words are pure.
²⁷ Those who acquire things unjustly
  gain trouble for their house,
  but those who hate bribes will live.
²⁸ The righteous heart reflects
  before answering,
  but the wicked mouth blurts out evil.
²⁹ The LORD is far from the wicked,
  but he listens to the prayers
  of the righteous.
³⁰ Bright eyes give joy to the heart;
  good news strengthens the bones.
³¹ The ear that listens to life-giving correction
  dwells among the wise.
³² Those who refuse discipline
  despise themselves,
  but those who listen to correction
  gain understanding.
³³ The fear of the LORD is wise instruction,
  and humility comes before respect.

16 To people belong the plans
  of the heart,
  but the answer of the tongue
  comes from the LORD.
² All the ways of people
  are pure in their eyes,
  but the LORD tests the motives.
³ Commit your work to the LORD,
  and your plans will succeed.

^w Heb *Sheol*   ^x Heb *Abaddon*   ^y Heb *Sheol*

⁴ The LORD made everything for a purpose,
   even the wicked for an evil day.
⁵ The LORD detests all who are arrogant;
   they surely won't go unpunished.
⁶ Love and faithfulness reconcile guilt;
   the fear of the LORD turns away evil.
⁷ When people draw favor from the LORD,
   even their enemies are at peace
      with them.
⁸ Better a little with righteousness
   than great profits without justice.
⁹ People plan their path,
   but the LORD secures their steps.
¹⁰ A king's speech is like an oracle;
   in a judgment,
      one can't go against his words.
¹¹ Honest balances and scales
   are the LORD's;
   all the weights in the bag are his doing.
¹² Kings detest wicked deeds,
   for their thrones are founded
      on righteousness.
¹³ Kings favor those with righteous lips;
   they love words of integrity.
¹⁴ The king's anger is a messenger of death;
   the wise will calm him.
¹⁵ There's life in the light of the king's face.
   His favor is like a cloud
      that brings spring rain.
¹⁶ Acquiring wisdom
   is much better than gold,
   and acquiring understanding
      is better than silver.
¹⁷ The road of those who do right
   turns away from evil;
   those who protect their path
      guard their lives.
¹⁸ Pride comes before disaster,
   and arrogance before a fall.
¹⁹ Better to be humble with the needy
   than to divide plunder with the proud.
²⁰ Those with insight find prosperity;
   those who trust the LORD are blessed.
²¹ The skilled mind is called discerning,
   and pleasant speech enhances teaching.
²² One who has insight is a fountain of life,
   but the instruction of the foolish is folly.
²³ The mind of the wise
   makes their speech insightful
   and enhances the teaching of their lips.
²⁴ Pleasant words are flowing honey,

sweet to the taste
   and healing to the bones.
²⁵ There is a path that may seem straight
   to someone,
   but in the end it is the path of death.
²⁶ The appetite of workers labors for them,
   for their hunger presses them on.
²⁷ Worthless people dig up trouble;
   their lips are like a scorching fire.
²⁸ Destructive people produce conflict;
   gossips alienate close friends.
²⁹ Violent people entice their neighbors
   and walk them down a path
      that isn't good.
³⁰ Those who wink their eye
   plot destruction;
   those who purse their lips plan evil.
³¹ Gray hair is a crown of glory;
   it is found on the path of righteousness.
³² Better to be patient than a warrior,
   and better to have self-control
      than to capture a city.
³³ The dice are cast into the lap;
   all decisions are from the LORD.

17 Better a dry crust with quiet
   than a house full of feasting
      with quarrels.
² An insightful servant rules
   over a disgraceful son
   and will divide an inheritance
      with the brothers.
³ A crucible is for silver
   and a furnace for gold,
   but the LORD tests the heart.
⁴ An evildoer pays attention to guilty lips;
   a liar listens to a destructive tongue.
⁵ Those who mock the poor
   insult their maker;
   those who rejoice in disaster
      won't go unpunished.
⁶ Grandchildren are the crown
   of the elderly,
   and the glory of children is their parents.
⁷ Too much talking isn't right for a fool;
   even less so false speech
      for an honorable person.
⁸ A bribe seems magical in the eyes
   of those who give it,
   granting success to all who use it.
⁹ One who seeks love conceals an offense,
   but one who repeats it divides friends.

¹⁰ A rebuke goes deeper
to an understanding person
than a hundred lashes to a fool.
¹¹ Evil people seek only rebellion;
a cruel messenger
will be sent against them.
¹² Safer to meet a bear robbed of her cubs
than fools in their folly.
¹³ Evil will never depart from the house
of those who return evil for good.
¹⁴ The start of a quarrel is like
letting out water,
so drop the dispute before it breaks out.
¹⁵ Judging the righteous wicked
and the wicked righteous—
the LORD detests both of these.
¹⁶ Why should a fool have money
to pay for wisdom? He has no mind.
¹⁷ Friends love all the time,
and kinsfolk are born
for times of trouble.
¹⁸ One with no sense shakes hands on a deal,
securing a loan for a friend.
¹⁹ Those who love an offense love a quarrel;
those who build a high doorway
invite a collapse.
²⁰ Those with crooked hearts won't prosper,
and those with twisted tongues
will fall into trouble.
²¹ Having a fool for a son brings grief;
there's no joy for a scoundrel's father.
²² A joyful heart helps healing,
but a broken spirit dries up the bones.
²³ The wicked take secret bribes
to twist the way of justice.
²⁴ Wisdom is right in front of those
with understanding,
but the eyes of fools
are off to the edges of the earth.
²⁵ A foolish son is irritating to his father
and bitter to her who gave birth to him.
²⁶ It isn't good to punish the righteous,
to strike the honorable for their integrity.
²⁷ Wise are those who restrain their talking;
people with understanding
are coolheaded.
²⁸ Fools who keep quiet are deemed wise;
those who shut their lips are smart.

18 Unfriendly people look out
for themselves;
they bicker with sensible people.

² Fools find no pleasure in understanding,
but only in expressing their opinion.
³ When the wicked arrive, so does contempt;
with shame comes insult.
⁴ The words of a person's mouth
are deep waters,
a bubbling stream, a fountain of wisdom.
⁵ Favoring the wicked isn't good;
it denies justice to the righteous.
⁶ The lips of fools make accusations;
their mouths elicit beatings.
⁷ The mouth of fools is their ruin;
their lips are a trap for their lives.
⁸ The words of gossips are like choice snacks;
they go down to the inmost parts.
⁹ Those who are lazy in their work
are brothers to thugs.
¹⁰ The LORD's name is a strong tower;
the righteous run to it and find refuge.
¹¹ The riches of the wealthy are a strong city
and like a high wall in their imagination.
¹² Pride comes before a disaster,
but humility comes before respect.
¹³ Those who answer before they listen
are foolish and disgraceful.
¹⁴ The human spirit sustains a sick person,
but who can bear a broken spirit?
¹⁵ An understanding mind gains knowledge;
the ear of the wise seeks knowledge.
¹⁶ A gift opens the way
for access to important people.
¹⁷ The first person to testify seems innocent,
until the other comes
and cross-examines him.
¹⁸ The dice settle conflicts
and keep strong opponents apart.
¹⁹ An offended ally
is more formidable than a city;
such quarreling is like the bars of a castle.
²⁰ The stomach is satisfied
by the fruit of the mouth;
one's lips can earn a satisfying income.
²¹ Death and life
are in the power of the tongue;
those who love it will eat its fruit.
²² He who finds a wife finds what is good,
gaining favor from the LORD.
²³ The poor plead for help,
but the wealthy answer harshly.
²⁴ There are persons for companionship,
but then there are friends
who are more loyal than family.

19 Better to be poor
and walk in innocence
than to have dishonest lips and be a fool.

2 Ignorant desire isn't good;
rushing feet make mistakes.

3 People's own folly corrupts their way,
but their hearts rage against the LORD.

4 Riches increase one's friends,
but the poor lose their friends.

5 A false witness won't go unpunished,
and a liar won't escape.

6 Many seek favor from rulers;
everyone befriends a gift giver.

7 All the relatives of the poor hate them;
even more, their friends
stay far from them.
When they pursue them with words,
they aren't there.

8 Those who acquire good sense
love themselves;
those who keep understanding
find success.

9 False witnesses won't go unpunished,
and liars will perish.

10 Luxury isn't fitting for a fool;
even less so for a servant
to rule over princes.

11 Insightful people restrain their anger;
their glory is to ignore an offense.

12 A raging king roars like a lion;
his favor is like the dew on the grass.

13 A foolish son is a disaster to his father;
a contentious wife
is like constant dripping.

14 House and riches are an inheritance
from one's ancestors,
but an insightful wife is from the LORD.

15 Laziness brings on deep sleep;
a slacker goes hungry.

16 Those who keep the commandment
preserve their lives;
those who disregard their ways will die.

17 Those who are gracious to the poor
lend to the LORD,
and the Lord will fully repay them.

18 Discipline your children while there
is hope,
but don't plan to kill them.

19 Angry people must pay the penalty;
if you rescue them,
then you will have to do it again.

20 Listen to advice and accept instruction,
so you might grow wise in the future.

21 Many plans are in a person's mind,
but the LORD's purpose will succeed.

22 People long for trustworthiness;
it is better to be poor than a liar.

23 The fear of the LORD leads to life;
then one rests content,
untouched by harm.

24 Lazy people bury their hand in the bowl;
they won't even put it to their mouth.

25 Strike someone who scoffs,
and a naive person will become clever;
correct someone with understanding,
and they will gain knowledge.

26 Those who assault their father
and drive out their mother
are disgraceful children,
worthy of reproach.

27 If, my child, you stop listening
to discipline,
you will wander away from words
of knowledge.

28 A worthless witness mocks justice;
the wicked mouth gulps down trouble.

29 Punishments were made for mockers,
and blows for the backs of fools.

20 Wine is a mocker; beer a carouser.
Those it leads astray
won't become wise.

2 A king is as terrifying as a lion's growl.
Those who anger him may lose their life.

3 It is honorable to back off from a fight,
but fools jump right in.

4 The lazy don't plow during winter;
at harvest they look but find nothing.

5 Advice comes from the deep waters
of the heart;
those with understanding
can draw it out.

6 Many people will say that they are loyal,
but who can find a reliable person?

7 The righteous live with integrity;
happy are their children
who come after them.

8 A king who sits on his judgment throne
sifts out all evil with his eyes.

9 Who can say, "I'm innocent to the core;
I'm cleansed from my sin"?

10 False weights and measures—
the LORD detests them both.

¹¹ Even young people are known
   by their actions,
   whether their conduct is pure
   and upright.
¹² Ears to hear and eyes to see—
   the LORD made them both.
¹³ Don't love sleep or you will be poor;
   stay alert and you will have
   plenty to eat.
¹⁴ The buyer says, "Bad, bad,"
   but then goes away and brags.
¹⁵ Much gold and many pearls exist,
   but wise speech
   is the most precious jewel.
¹⁶ Take the garment of the person
   who secures a loan for a stranger;
   take his pledge for a foreigner.
¹⁷ Stolen bread is sweet,
   but afterward the mouth is full of gravel.
¹⁸ Plans are firmed up by advice;
   wage wars with good guidance.
¹⁹ Gossips reveal secrets;
   don't associate with those
   who talk too much.
²⁰ Those who curse their father or mother—
   their lamp will be snuffed out
   when it becomes dark.
²¹ Inheritance gained quickly at first
   won't bless later on.
²² Don't say, "I'll repay the evildoer!"
   Wait for the LORD,
   and he will save you.
²³ The LORD detests false weights;
   deceptive scales aren't right.
²⁴ A person's steps are from the LORD;
   how then can people understand
   their path?
²⁵ It is a snare to say rashly, "It is holy,"
   and only reflect after making the promise.
²⁶ A wise king sifts out the wicked,
   and runs them over with a wheel.
²⁷ The breath of a person
   is the lamp of the LORD,
   searching all the inmost parts.
²⁸ Kindness and faithfulness
   protect the king;
   he supports his throne by kindness.
²⁹ Strength is the glory of young men;
   gray hair is the splendor of old age.

³⁰ Blows and bruises remove evil;
   beatings cleanse the inner parts.

21 The king's heart is like channels of
   water in the hand of the LORD;
   he directs it wherever he wants.
² Everyone's path is straight
   in their own eyes,
   but the LORD weighs the heart.
³ Acting with righteousness and justice
   is more valued by the LORD
   than sacrifice.
⁴ Prideful eyes, an arrogant heart, and
   the lamp of the wicked are all sinful.
⁵ The plans of the diligent end up in profit,
   but those who hurry end up with loss.
⁶ Those who gain treasure with lies
   are like a drifting fog, leading to death.
⁷ The violence of the wicked
   will sweep them away,
   for they refuse to act with justice.
⁸ The ways of some people
   are twisted and strange,
   but the behavior of those who do right
   is pure.
⁹ Better to live on the edge of a roof
   than with a contentious woman
   in a large house.
¹⁰ Wicked people desire evil;
   their neighbors receive
   no mercy from them.
¹¹ When a mocker is punished,
   the naive person gains wisdom;
   when insight comes to the wise,
   knowledge increases.
¹² The righteous one observes
   the house of the wicked,
   turning the wicked toward trouble.
¹³ Those who close their ears
   to the cries of the poor
   will themselves call out
   but receive no answer.
¹⁴ A secret gift calms anger,
   and a hidden bribe
   removes^z furious wrath.
¹⁵ Acting justly is a joy to the righteous,
   but dreaded by those who do evil.
¹⁶ People who wander
   from the path of insight
   will rest in the company of the dead.

^z Heb lacks *removes.*

¹⁷ Those who love pleasure end up poor;
  lovers of wine and oil won't get rich.
¹⁸ The wicked are a ransom
    for the righteous;
  the treacherous will be punished[a]
    in the place of the virtuous.
¹⁹ Better to live in a wilderness
    than in a house
  with a contentious and angry woman.
²⁰ Precious treasure and oil
    stay in the home of the wise,
  but fools swallow them up.
²¹ Those who pursue righteousness
    and kindness
  will find life, righteousness, and honor.
²² A wise person fought a city of warriors
    and brought down the stronghold
    in which they felt safe.
²³ Those who guard their mouths
    and their tongues
  guard themselves from trouble.
²⁴ Incredibly proud—
    mockers are their name!
  Their conduct involves excessive pride.
²⁵ The desires of the lazy will kill them,
    because their hands refuse
    to do anything.
²⁶ The lazy desire things constantly,
    but the righteous give
    without holding back.
²⁷ The LORD detests
    the sacrifices of the wicked,
  especially when brought
    with devious motives.
²⁸ A lying witness will perish,
    but one who listens
    will testify successfully.
²⁹ The wicked person appears brash,
    but the virtuous
    think about the path ahead.
³⁰ No wisdom, understanding,
    or advice can stand up against the LORD.
³¹ A horse is made ready
    for the day of battle,
  but victory belongs to the LORD.

22 A good reputation
    is better than much wealth;
  high esteem
    is better than silver and gold.

² The rich and the poor
    have this in common:
  the LORD made them both.
³ Prudent people see trouble and hide,
    while the simpleminded
    go right to it and get punished.
⁴ The reward of humility
    and the fear of the LORD
  is wealth, honor, and life.
⁵ Thorns and nets are in the path
    of the crooked;
  those who guard their lives
    keep their distance.
⁶ Train children in the way they should go;
    when they grow old,
    they won't depart from it.
⁷ The wealthy rule over the poor;
    a borrower is a slave to a lender.
⁸ Those who sow injustice will harvest evil;
    the rod of their fury will come to an end.
⁹ Happy are generous people,
    because they give some of their food
    to the poor.
¹⁰ Remove the mocker
    and conflict disappears;
  judgment and shame also stop.
¹¹ Those who love a pure heart—
    their speech is gracious,
    and the king is their friend.
¹² The LORD's eyes protect knowledge,
    but he frustrates the words
    of the treacherous.
¹³ A lazy person says,
    "There's a lion in the street!
    I'll be killed in the town square!"
¹⁴ The mouth of a mysterious woman
    is a deep pit;
  those under the LORD's wrath
    will fall in it.
¹⁵ Folly is bound up in a child's heart;
    the rod of discipline removes it.
¹⁶ Oppressing the poor to get rich
    and giving to the wealthy
    lead only to poverty.

Thirty sayings of the wise
¹⁷ Turn your ear
    and hear the words of the wise;
  focus your mind on my knowledge.

---

[a] Heb lacks *will be punished*.

¹⁸ It will be pleasant
  if you keep the words in you,
  if you have them ready on your lips.
¹⁹ So that your trust will be in the LORD,
  I'm teaching you today—yes, you.
²⁰ Haven't I written for you thirty^b sayings
  full of advice and knowledge?
²¹ Their purpose is to teach you true,
    reliable words,
  so you can report back reliably
    to those who sent you.

²² Don't steal from the poor,
  because they are poor.
  Don't oppress the needy in the gate.
²³ The LORD will take up their case
  and press the life out of those
    who oppress them.^c

²⁴ Don't befriend people controlled by anger;
  don't associate with
    hot-tempered people;
  ²⁵ otherwise, you will learn their ways
  and become trapped.

²⁶ Don't shake hands to guarantee a loan.
²⁷ If you can't repay,
  why should they be able
    to take your bed from you?

²⁸ Don't remove an ancient boundary marker
  that your ancestors established.

²⁹ Do you see people who work skillfully?
  They will work for kings
  but not work for lowly people.

23 When you sit down
  to dine with a ruler,
  carefully consider what is in front of you.
² Place a knife at your throat
  to control your appetite.
³ Don't long for the ruler's delicacies;
  the food misleads.

⁴ Don't wear yourself out trying to get rich;
  be smart enough to stop.
⁵ When your eyes fly to wealth
  it is gone; it grows wings
  like an eagle and flies heavenward.

⁶ Don't eat food with stingy people;
  don't long for their delicacies,
  ⁷ because they are like
    a hair in the throat.^d
  They say to you, "Eat and drink!"
  but they don't mean it.
⁸ You will eat scraps and vomit them out.
  You will waste your pleasant words.
⁹ Don't speak in the ears of fools,
  for they will scorn your insightful words.

¹⁰ Don't remove an ancient
    boundary marker;
  don't invade the fields of orphans,
  ¹¹ for their redeemer is strong.
  He will bring charges against you.

¹² Bring your mind to instruction,
  your ear to knowledgeable sayings.

¹³ Don't withhold instruction
    from children;
  if you strike them with a rod,
    they won't die.
¹⁴ Strike them with a rod,
  and you will save their lives
    from the grave.^e

¹⁵ My child, if your heart is wise,
  then my heart too will be happy.
¹⁶ My inner being will rejoice
  when your lips speak with integrity.

¹⁷ Don't let your heart envy sinners,
  but fear the LORD constantly;
  ¹⁸ then you will have a future,
    and your hope won't be cut off.

¹⁹ Listen, my child, and be wise!
  Keep your mind straight on the path.
²⁰ Don't hang out with those
  who get drunk on wine
  or those who eat too much meat,
  ²¹ because drunks and gluttons
    will be impoverished;
  their stupor will clothe them in rags.

²² Listen to your father, who gave you life;
  don't despise your elderly mother.

^bHeb uncertain ^cHeb uncertain ^dLXX; Heb uncertain ^eHeb *Sheol*

²³ Buy truth and don't sell it;
   buy wisdom, instruction,
   and understanding.
²⁴ The father of the righteous
   will be very happy;
   the one who gives life to the wise
     will rejoice.
²⁵ Your father and your mother will rejoice;
   she who gave you birth will be happy.

²⁶ My child, give your mind to me
   and let your eyes keep to my path.
²⁷ A prostitute is a deep pit,
   and a foreign woman is a narrow well.
²⁸ Indeed, she ambushes like a robber
   and increases the number of the faithless.

²⁹ Who is suffering?
   Who is uneasy?
   Who has arguments?
   Who has complaints?
   Who has unnecessary wounds?
   Who has glazed eyes?—
   ³⁰ those who linger over wine;
     those who go looking for mixed wine.
³¹ Don't look at wine when it is red,
   when it sparkles in the cup,
   going down smoothly.
³² In the end, it bites like a snake
   and poisons like a viper.
³³ Your eyes will see strange things,
   and your heart will speak
   distorted words.
³⁴ You will be like one who lies down
   while out on the sea[f]
   or one who lies on top of a mast.
³⁵ "Though hit, I feel no pain;
   though beaten up,
     I don't know anything about it.
   When I wake up,
   I'll look for wine again!"

24 Don't envy evil people,
   and don't long to be with them.
² Their hearts are focused on violence,
   and their lips speak of trouble.

³ By wisdom a house is built;
   by understanding it is established.

⁴ By knowledge rooms are filled
   with all precious and pleasant wealth.
⁵ A wise person is mightier
   than a strong one;[g]
   a knowledgeable person
     than a powerful one.
⁶ You should make war with guidance;
   victory comes with many counselors.

⁷ Wisdom is beyond foolish people.
   They don't open their mouths in the gate.
⁸ Those who plot evil
   will be called master schemers.
⁹ The scheming of fools is sin;
   people detest mockers.

¹⁰ If you show yourself weak
   on a day of distress,
   your strength is too small.
¹¹ Rescue those being taken off to death;
   and from those staggering to the
     slaughter, don't hold back.
¹² If you say,
   "Look, we didn't know about it,"
   the one who weighs hearts—
     doesn't he understand?
   The one who protects your life—
     he knows.
   He makes people pay for their actions.

¹³ My child, eat honey, for it is good.
   The honeycomb is sweet in your mouth.
¹⁴ Know that wisdom is like that
   for your whole being.
   If you find it, there is a future.
   Your hope won't be cut off.

¹⁵ Wicked one, don't wait secretly
   at the home of the righteous.
   Don't destroy their dwelling.
¹⁶ The righteous may fall seven times
   but still get up,
   but the wicked will stumble into trouble.

¹⁷ When your enemies fall, don't rejoice.
   When they stumble,
     don't let your heart be glad,
¹⁸ or the LORD will see it and be displeased,
   and he will turn his anger from them.

---

[f] Or *in the heart of the sea* [g] LXX; MT *A wise man is strong*

¹⁹ Don't get fighting mad at evil people;
    don't be envious of the wicked.
²⁰ Indeed, there is no future for the evil;
    the lamp of the wicked will be put out.

²¹ Fear the LORD, my child,
    as well as the king.
  Don't associate with those
    who are rebellious.
²² Disaster comes suddenly from them.
    Who can know the ruin
      that both can bring?

More sayings of the wise

²³ These are also the sayings of the wise:

    Partiality in judgment isn't good.

²⁴ Those who say to the guilty,
    "You are innocent"—
  the people will curse them.
    Nations will condemn them.
²⁵ But it will go well for those
    who rebuke them.
  A rich blessing will come to them.
²⁶ Those who speak honestly
    are like those who kiss on the lips.

²⁷ Get your outside work done;
    make preparations in the field;
  then you can build your house.

²⁸ Don't be a witness against your neighbor
    without reason;
  don't deceive with your lips.
²⁹ Don't say, "I'll do to them
    what they did to me.
  I'll pay them back for their actions."

³⁰ I happened upon the field of a lazy person,
    by the vineyard of one with no sense.
³¹ Thorns grew all over it;
    weeds covered the ground,
  and the stone wall was falling down.
³² I observed this and took it to heart;
    I saw it and learned a lesson.
³³ "A little sleep, a little slumber,
    a little lying down with folded arms"—
³⁴ and poverty will come on you
    like a prowler,
  deprivation like a man with a shield.

More proverbs of Solomon

25 These are also proverbs of Solomon,
    copied by the men of Hezekiah, king
of Judah:

² It is the glory of God to hide something
    and the glory of kings
      to discover something.
³ Like the high heavens
    and the depths of the earth,
  so the mind of a king is unsearchable.

⁴ Remove the dross from the silver,
    and a vessel will come out for the refiner.
⁵ Remove the wicked
    from the king's presence,
  and his throne will be established
    in righteousness.

⁶ Don't exalt yourself
    in the presence of the king,
  or stand in the place
    of important people,
⁷ because it is better that he say to you,
    "Come up here,"
  than to be demoted before a ruler.

  What your eyes see,
⁸ don't be quick to quarrel over;
  what will you do in the future
    when your neighbor shames you?
⁹ Argue it out with your neighbor,
    and don't give away someone's secret.
¹⁰ Otherwise, the one who hears it
    will vilify you;
  the slander against you will never stop.

¹¹ Words spoken at the right time
    are like gold apples in a silver setting.
¹² Wise correction to an ear that listens
    is like a gold earring
      or jewelry of fine gold.

¹³ Like the coolness of snow
    on a harvest day
  are reliable messengers to those
    who send them;
  they restore the life of their master.
¹⁴ People who brag about a gift never given
    are like clouds and wind
      that produce no rain.

15 A commander can be persuaded
　　with patience,
　　and a tender tongue can break a bone.
16 If you find honey,
　　eat just the right amount;
　　otherwise, you'll get full and vomit it up.
17 Don't spend too much time
　　in your neighbor's house.
　　Otherwise, they'll get fed up with you
　　　and hate you.
18 People who testify falsely
　　against their neighbors
　　are like a club, sword,
　　and sharpened arrow.
19 Trusting a treacherous person
　　at a difficult time
　　is like having a bad tooth
　　or a wobbly foot.
20 Singing a song to a troubled heart
　　is like taking off a garment on a cold day
　　or putting vinegar on a wound.[h]
21 If your enemies are starving,
　　feed them some bread;
　　if they are thirsty,
　　give them water to drink.
22 By doing this, you will heap
　　burning coals on their heads,
　　and the LORD will reward you.
23 The north wind stirs up rain,
　　and a person who plots quietly
　　　provokes angry faces.
24 Better to live on the edge of a roof
　　than to share a house
　　with a contentious woman.
25 Good news from a distant land
　　is like cold water for a weary person.
26 A righteous person giving in to the wicked
　　is like a contaminated spring
　　or a polluted fountain.
27 Eating too much honey isn't good,
　　nor is it appropriate to seek honor.
28 A person without self-control
　　is like a breached city, one with no walls.

26 Like snow in the summer
　　or rain at harvest,
　　so honor isn't appropriate for a fool.
2 Like a darting sparrow,
　　like a flying swallow,
　　so an undeserved curse never arrives.

3 A whip for a horse, a bridle for a donkey,
　　and a rod for the back of fools.
4 Don't answer fools according to their folly,
　　or you will become like them yourself.
5 Answer fools according to their folly,
　　or they will deem themselves wise.
6 Sending messages with a fool
　　is like cutting off one's feet
　　or drinking down violence.
7 As legs dangle from a disabled person,
　　so does a proverb in the mouth of fools.
8 Like tying a stone in a sling,
　　so is giving respect to a fool.
9 Like a thorny bush in the hand of a drunk,
　　so is a proverb in the mouth of fools.
10 Like an archer who wounds
　　someone randomly,
　　so is one who hires a fool or a passerby.
11 Like a dog that returns to its vomit,
　　so a fool repeats foolish mistakes.
12 Do you see people
　　who consider themselves wise?
　　There is more hope for a fool
　　than for them.
13 A lazy person says,
　　"There's a lion in the path!
　　A lion in the plazas!"
14 As a door turns on its hinge,
　　so do lazy people in their beds.
15 Lazy people bury their hand into the bowl,
　　too tired to return it to their mouth.
16 Lazy people think they are wiser
　　than seven people who answer sensibly.

17 Like yanking the ears of a dog,
　　so is one who passes by and gets involved
　　in another person's fight.
18 Like a crazy person shooting deadly
　　flaming arrows
19 are those who deceive their neighbor
　　and say, "Hey, I was only joking!"
20 Without wood a fire goes out;
　　without gossips, conflict calms down.
21 Like adding charcoal to embers
　　or wood to fire,
　　quarrelsome people kindle strife.
22 The words of gossips
　　are like choice snacks;
　　they go down to the inmost parts.

hLXX; MT *vinegar on natron* (a detergent)

²³ Smooth[i] lips and an evil heart
  are like silver coating on clay.
²⁴ Hateful people mislead with their lips,
  keeping their deception within.
²⁵ Though they speak graciously,
  don't believe them,
  for seven horrible things
  are in their heart.
²⁶ They may cover their hatred
  with trickery,
  but their evil will be revealed in public.
²⁷ Those who dig a pit will fall in it;
  those who roll a stone
  will have it turn back on them.
²⁸ A lying tongue hates those it crushes;
  a flattering mouth causes destruction.

27 Don't brag about tomorrow,
  for you don't know
  what a day will bring.
² Let another person praise you,
  and not your own mouth;
  a stranger, and not your own lips.

[i]LXX; Heb uncertain [j]Heb uncertain

³ A stone is heavy and sand weighs much,
  but the nuisance of fools
  is heavier than both.
⁴ Wrath is cruel and anger is a flood,
  but who can withstand jealousy?
⁵ A public correction
  is better than hidden love.
⁶ Trustworthy are the bruises of a friend;
  excessive are the kisses of an enemy.
⁷ Someone who is full refuses honey,
  but anything bitter
  tastes sweet to a hungry person.
⁸ Like a bird wandering from its nest,
  so is one who wanders from home.
⁹ Oil and incense make the heart glad,
  and the sweetness of friends
  comes from their advice.[j]
¹⁰ Don't desert your friend
  or a friend of your family;
  don't go to your relative's house
  when disaster strikes.
  Better a neighbor nearby
  than a relative far away.

IRON

Iron is a metal with contradictory qualities. Iron ore is the most common of all metal ores. Iron can also be found in pure form, as meteoritic stones, containing some nickel, and these have been used to make objects of iron from earliest times. On the other hand, reduction of iron ore to pure metal is a complex process, requiring high temperatures and sophisticated techniques. Apart from that, in order to qualify for use as tools and weapons, the iron has to undergo complex treatment. But once that stage is reached, its qualities are unsurpassed by any other metal. These are the reasons why, on the one hand, iron did not become common until relatively late in human history, and on the other hand, it eventually became the most common metal for tools and weaponry. Together with other metals such as gold, silver, copper, and tin, iron was a symbol of wealth. At the same time, iron had a negative connotation, representing harshness and barrenness, as in the comparison of the heavens (Lev 26:19) and the earth (Deut 28:23) with iron, the equation of Egypt with an iron furnace (Deut 4:20), and the rod (scepter) of iron that symbolized the merciless ruler (e.g., Ps 2:9; Rev 2:27). Even though many of the implements of the temple were made of iron, the use of iron tools in the construction of the altar on Mount Ebal or of the temple in Jerusalem was forbidden (Deut 27:4-5; 1 Kgs 6:7).

¹¹ Be wise, my child,
and make my heart glad,
so I can answer those who insult me.
¹² Prudent people see evil and hide;
the simpleminded go right to it
and get punished.
¹³ Take the garment of the person
who secures a loan for a stranger;
take his pledge for a foreigner.
¹⁴ Greeting a neighbor with a loud voice
early in the morning
will be viewed as a curse.
¹⁵ The constant dripping on a rainy day
and a contentious woman are alike;
¹⁶ anyone who can control her
can control the wind
or pick up oil in his hand.
¹⁷ As iron sharpens iron,
so friends sharpen each other's faces.
¹⁸ Those who tend a fig tree will eat its fruit,
and those who look after their master
will be honored.
¹⁹ As water reflects the face,
so the heart reflects
one person to another.
²⁰ The grave^k and the underworld^l
are never satisfied;
and people's eyes are never satisfied.
²¹ A crucible is for silver
and a furnace for gold,
so are people in the presence
of someone who praises them.
²² Even if you grind fools in a mortar,
even grinding them along with the grain,
their folly won't be driven from them.
²³ Know your flock well;
pay attention to your herds,
²⁴ for no treasure lasts forever,
nor a crown generation after generation.
²⁵ When the grass goes away,
new growth appears,
and the plants of the hills are gathered,
²⁶ then the lambs will provide your clothes,
and the goats
will be the price of your fields.
²⁷ There will be enough goat's milk
for your food,
for the food of your house,
and to nourish your young women.

²⁸ The wicked run away even though
no one pursues them,
but the righteous
are as confident as a lion.
² When a land rebels,
there are many leaders;
but a person with understanding
brings order.
³ Poor people who oppress the needy
are rain that washes away food.
⁴ Those who abandon Instruction
praise the wicked,
but those who follow Instruction
battle them.
⁵ Evil people don't understand justice,
but those who seek the LORD
understand everything.
⁶ Better to be poor and walk in innocence
than to be on crooked paths and wealthy.
⁷ Intelligent children follow Instruction,
but those who befriend gluttons
shame their parents.
⁸ Those who become rich
through high interest rates
gather money for those
who are generous to the poor.
⁹ Those who turn their ears
from hearing Instruction—
even their prayers will be detested.
¹⁰ Whoever misleads those who do right
onto an evil path
will fall into their own pit,
but the blameless
will inherit good things.
¹¹ Rich people think they are wise,
but an insightful poor person
sees through them.
¹² When the righteous rejoice,
there is great respect,
but people hide when the wicked prosper.
¹³ Those who hide their sins won't succeed,
but those who confess
and give them up will receive mercy.
¹⁴ Happy are those
who are continually fearful,
but those whose hearts are hard
fall into trouble.
¹⁵ A wicked ruler over the poor
is like a growling lion or a prowling bear.

---

^k Heb *Sheol* ^l Heb *Abaddon*

¹⁶ A prince without understanding
  is a cruel oppressor,
  but one who hates unjust gain
  will live long.
¹⁷ If someone feels guilty about murder,
  don't hold them back
  from fleeing to the pit.
¹⁸ Those who walk in innocence
  will be saved,
  but those who go on twisted paths
  will fall into the grave.
¹⁹ Those who work the land
  will have plenty to eat,
  but those with worthless pursuits
  will have plenty of poverty.
²⁰ Reliable people
  will have abundant blessings,
  but those with get-rich-quick schemes
  won't go unpunished.
²¹ Those who show favoritism aren't good;
  people do wrong for a crust of bread.
²² The stingy try to get rich fast,
  unaware that loss will come to them.
²³ Those who correct someone will,
  in the end, find more favor
  than those with flattering tongues.
²⁴ Those who steal from their father
  and mother,
  and say, "It's not a crime,"
  are friends of vandals.
²⁵ Greedy people stir up conflict,
  but those who trust the LORD
  become prosperous.
²⁶ Those who trust in their own reasoning
  are fools,
  but those who walk in wisdom
  will be kept safe.
²⁷ Those who give to the poor
  will lack nothing,

but those who turn a blind eye
  will be greatly cursed.
²⁸ When the wicked rise up, people hide,
  but when they are destroyed,
  the righteous multiply.

29

One who stays stubborn
after many corrections
  will be suddenly broken, beyond healing.
² When the righteous become numerous,
  the people rejoice,
  but when the wicked dominate,
  the people moan.
³ A man who loves wisdom
  makes his father rejoice,
  but one who spends time
  with prostitutes destroys riches.
⁴ A king gives stability to the land by justice,
  but one who imposes heavy taxes
  tears it down.
⁵ People who flatter their friends
  spread out a net for their feet.
⁶ The wicked are snared by their own sin;^m
  the righteous sing and rejoice.
⁷ The righteous know the rights
  of the poor,
  but the wicked don't understand.
⁸ Mockers set a city on fire,
  but the wise turn back anger.
⁹ When the wise make a legal charge
  against the foolish,
  the fools shout, they laugh—
  there is no calm.
¹⁰ Murderous people hate the innocent,
  and they seek the lives of the virtuous.
¹¹ Fools show all their anger,
  but the wise hold it back.
¹² If a ruler listens to lies,
  those who serve him will be wicked.

^mTg, Syr; MT *In the sin of an evil man is a snare*

TAXES/TAXATION

The biblical traditions constantly engage and reflect the structures and daily realities of aristocratic-controlled empires. In empires, ruling elites claim taxes, tributes, rents, and forced labor by peasants. Taxation in the Bible does not benefit the common good. Rather, it supports the privileged lifestyle of elites.

¹³ The poor and their oppressors
　　have a common bond—
　　the LORD gives light to the eyes of both.
¹⁴ If a king judges the poor honestly,
　　his throne will be established forever.
¹⁵ The rod and correction lead to wisdom,
　　but children out of control
　　　shame their mothers.
¹⁶ When the wicked become numerous,
　　so do crimes;
　　the righteous will see their downfall.
¹⁷ Instruct your children;
　　they will give you peace of mind
　　and bring delight into your life.
¹⁸ When there's no vision,
　　the people get out of control,
　　but whoever obeys instruction is happy.
¹⁹ Servants aren't disciplined by words;
　　they might understand,
　　but they don't respond.
²⁰ Do you see people
　　who are quick to speak?
　　There is more hope for fools
　　　than for them.
²¹ Pamper servants from a young age,
　　and later on there will be trouble.
²² Angry people stir up conflict;
　　hotheads cause much offense.
²³ Pride lays people low,
　　but those of humble spirit gain honor.
²⁴ Those who share plunder with thieves
　　hate themselves;
　　even under oath, they don't testify.
²⁵ People are trapped by their fear of others;
　　those who trust the LORD are secure.
²⁶ Many seek access to the ruler,
　　but justice comes from the LORD.
²⁷ The unjust person is disgusting
　　to the righteous;
　　the straight path is disgusting
　　　to the wicked.

Words of Agur

30 The words of Agur, Jakeh's son, from
Massa.

　　The man declares: I'm tired, God;
　　I'm tired, God, and I'm exhausted.
² Actually, I'm too stupid to be human,
　　a man without understanding.
³ I haven't learned wisdom,
　　nor do I have knowledge of the holy one.

⁴ Who has gone up to heaven
　　and come down?
　　Who has gathered the wind
　　　by the handful?
　　Who has bound up the waters
　　　in a garment?
　　Who has established all the ends
　　　of the earth?
　　What is this person's name
　　and the name of this person's child—
　　　if you know it?

⁵ All God's words are tried and true;
　　a shield for those who take refuge in him.
⁶ Don't add to his words,
　　or he will correct you
　　and show you to be a liar.

⁷ Two things I ask of you;
　　don't keep them from me before I die:
⁸ Fraud and lies—
　　keep far from me!
　　Don't give me either poverty or wealth;
　　give me just the food I need.
⁹ Or I'll be full and deny you,
　　and say, "Who is the LORD?"
　　Or I'll be poor and steal,
　　and dishonor my God's name.

More sayings of the wise

¹⁰ Don't slander a servant to his master;
　　otherwise, the servant will curse you,
　　and you will be guilty.
¹¹ There are those who curse their father
　　and don't bless their mother.
¹² There are those who think they are clean,
　　but haven't washed off
　　　their own excrement.
¹³ There are those—
　　how arrogant are their eyes;
　　how their eyebrows are raised!
¹⁴ There are those whose teeth are swords;
　　their jaw is a butcher's knife,
　　ready to devour the needy from the earth,
　　and the poor from humanity.

¹⁵ The leech has two daughters: "Give, give!"
　　There are three things
　　　that are never satisfied,
　　four that never say, "Enough!":

¹⁶ the graveⁿ and a barren womb,
a land never filled with water,
and fire that doesn't say, "Enough!"

¹⁷ An eye that mocks a father
and rejects obedience to a mother,
may the ravens of the river valley
peck it out,
and the eagle's young eat it.
¹⁸ Three things are too wonderful for me,
four that I can't figure out:
¹⁹ the way of an eagle in the sky,
the way of a snake on the rock,
the way of a ship out on the open sea,
and the way of a man
with a young woman.

²⁰ This is the way of an adulterous woman:
she eats and wipes her mouth,
and she says, "I've done nothing wrong!"

²¹ At three things the earth trembles,
at four it can't bear up:
²² at a servant when he becomes king
and fools when they are full of food;
²³ at a detested woman
when she gets married
and a female servant
when she replaces her mistress.

²⁴ Four things are among
the smallest on earth,
but they are extremely wise:
²⁵ Ants as creatures aren't strong,
but they store away their food
in the summer.
²⁶ Badgers as creatures aren't powerful,
but they make their homes
in the rocks.

ⁿHeb *Sheol* ^oOr *where* or *or*

²⁷ Locusts don't have a king,
but they march together in ranks.
²⁸ You can catch lizards in your hand,
but they are in kings' palaces.

²⁹ There are three things
that are excellent in their stride,
four that are excellent as they walk:
³⁰ a lion, a warrior among beasts,
which doesn't back down
at anything;
³¹ the strut of a rooster or a male goat;
and a king with his army.

³² If you've been foolish and arrogant,
if you've been scheming,
put your hand to your mouth,
³³ because churning milk makes curds,
squeezing the nose brings blood,
and stirring up anger produces strife.

Words of King Lemuel

31 The words of King Lemuel of Massa,
which his mother taught him:
² No, my son!
No, son of my womb!
No, son of my solemn promises!
³ Don't give your strength to women,
your ways to those who wipe out kings.
⁴ It isn't for kings, Lemuel,
it isn't for kings to drink wine,
for rulers to crave^o strong drink.
⁵ Otherwise, they will drink
and forget the law,
and violate the rights of the needy.
⁶ Give strong drink
to those who are perishing
and wine to those
whose hearts are bitter.

LEMUEL

Means "belonging to God." Usually rendered as a proper name, *Lemuel* appears in Proverbs 31:1, 4 as the conveyor of his mother's wisdom. The Hebrew text calls him king of Massa, a land unknown except as a "descendant" of Ishmael (Gen 25:14). "Massa" could also mean "prophecy" or "oracle."

⁷ Let them drink and forget their poverty
  and no longer remember their toil.
⁸ Speak out on behalf of the voiceless,
  and for the rights of all
    who are vulnerable.^p
⁹ Speak out in order to judge
  with righteousness
  and to defend the needy and the poor.

The competent wife

¹⁰ A competent wife, how does one find her?
  Her value is far above pearls.
¹¹ Her husband entrusts his heart to her,
  and with her he will have all he needs.
¹² She brings him good and not trouble
  all the days of her life.
¹³ She seeks out wool and flax;
  she works joyfully with her hands.
¹⁴ She is like a fleet of merchant ships,
  bringing food from a distance.
¹⁵ She gets up while it is still night,
  providing food for her household,
  even some for her female servants.
¹⁶ She surveys a field and acquires it;
  from her own resources,
    she plants a vineyard.
¹⁷ She works energetically;
  her arms are powerful.
¹⁸ She realizes that her trading is successful;
  she doesn't put out her lamp at night.

¹⁹ She puts her hands to the spindle;
  her palms grasp the whorl.
²⁰ She reaches out to the needy;
  she stretches out her hands to the poor.
²¹ She doesn't fear for her household
  when it snows,
  because they are all dressed
  in warm^q clothes.
²² She makes bedspreads for herself;
  fine linen and purple are her clothing.
²³ Her husband is known in the city gates
  when he sits with the elders of the land.
²⁴ She makes garments and sells them;
  she supplies sashes to traders.
²⁵ Strength and honor are her clothing;
  she is confident about the future.
²⁶ Her mouth is full of wisdom;
  kindly teaching is on her tongue.
²⁷ She is vigilant over the activities
  of her household;
  she doesn't eat the food of laziness.
²⁸ Her children bless her;
  her husband praises her:
²⁹ "Many women act competently,
  but you surpass them all!"
³⁰ Charm is deceptive and beauty fleeting,
  but a woman who fears the LORD
  is to be praised.
³¹ Let her share in the results of her work;
  let her deeds praise her in the city gates.

^pOr *all children who are passing away*   ^qLXX; MT *the path of the trail*

ECCLESIASTES

The book of Ecclesiastes is one of the most fascinating books in the Old Testament. Yet, when one begins reading, one may well wonder exactly how such a book came to be included in the Bible. After all, the author does not believe in divine retribution. He feels that there is no real profit to be gained from work on earth. And even worse, divine revelation is altogether scarce—if available at all. This material differs radically from Proverbs and from most other books in the Old Testament.

Yet, for all of its differences, this small book contains some of the most intriguing reading in the Bible. The issues of doubt and pessimism it raises are issues that many persons confront day after day. The book truthfully concedes that goodness is not always rewarded tangibly, and evildoers are not always punished. Scarcely a thoughtful person has not wondered on occasion whether human existence has any real meaning or purpose. But the inclusion of Ecclesiastes within the Hebrew canon suggests that the content is worthy of examination.

THE AUTHOR OF THE BOOK

According to the superscription (1:1), the book belongs to *Qoheleth*, "David's son, king in Jerusalem." *Qoheleth* may be a personal name, or it may refer to an office or position such as a teacher. The word *Qoheleth* means one who speaks in an assembly, referring to a function rather than to a specific person. If the Hebrew word refers to a position rather than to a proper name, it should be translated as "the Teacher." When Martin Luther translated this book, he translated *Qoheleth* as the "preacher"; however, because of Qoheleth's theological skepticism, he can hardly be called a preacher.

Solomon was the only son of David to be king in Jerusalem; however, Solomon's name is never used in Ecclesiastes, and there are many indications that the book comes from a time much later than Solomon. It is most likely that Solomon is invoked because he was believed to have been the wisest king and the patron of wisdom.

What, really, do we know about Qoheleth? In terms of concrete biographical data, we know nothing. But judging from the style and content of his writing, this person had extensive training in the wisdom tradition and quite possibly was a sage himself. He quotes many traditional proverbs and occasionally adds his own peculiar words of skepticism. Also, in the conclusion, the final editors refer to Qoheleth as having taught knowledge and arranged proverbs with great care (12:9).

Here is a sage who has carefully weighed his real-life experience against his wisdom theology only to find the latter wanting. As the years pass, his pessimism deepens about the possibilities of human knowledge of God, including divine retribution. Finally, as he reaches his mature years, he submits his final legacy—his profound words of doubt—perfectly pointless. Everything is pointless!

For the most part, this book represents Qoheleth's memoirs. Perhaps the superscription (1:1) and the conclusion (12:9-14) belong to another writer, and various proverbs from the wisdom tradition may have been included. But the great majority of the book belongs to Qoheleth.

THE DATE OF THE BOOK

The date of Ecclesiastes is approximately 250 BCE. The book contains numerous Aramaic words from the post-exilic era, shows considerable influence from Greek philosophy, and displays a full knowledge (and rejection) of mature wisdom theology.

On the other hand, a scroll found at Qumran indicates the book was in use by the mid-second century BCE. There are no concrete historical allusions in the book that reflect its date. So most scholars concur in dating the book after 300 BCE but before 150 BCE.

THEOLOGICAL THEMES IN THE BOOK

Ecclesiastes lacks a clear pattern of thematic development or even of logical consistency. Most efforts to trace the development of a common theme (such as pointlessness) are futile. The book contains many tangents, overt contradictions, and repetitions. It is even difficult to prepare a basic outline of the book.

Qoheleth compiled this book over a number of years, and several themes have been examined and reexamined from different points of view. This technique gives the work a certain redundancy and even outright contradictoriness. Traditional proverbs are juxtaposed with pessimistic conclusions drawn from experience (1:14-18). Poems precede narratives (1:1-11; 3:1-15).

But the rough, uneven style of the book reflects Qoheleth's perception of the rough, uneven, undirected nature of human existence. It is pointless, he concludes, to try to understand the purpose and value of human existence. Instead, one should enjoy life as God gives it. Likewise, it is of no profit to try to discern a logical structure to his book. As Qoheleth advises persons to enjoy life and reap whatever benefits come along (2:24-26), so would he advise readers to examine his book, draw whatever lessons they may find appropriate, and not expect to solve the mysteries of human existence by studying the pages of his reflections.

The basic theological ideas in Qoheleth's book challenge the ideas in Proverbs, such as divine retribution, divine revelation communicated through the natural and moral order, wisdom as providing the way of understanding and succeeding in life, and our unique and exalted place in God's created order.

Qoheleth can find nothing in his experience to validate these ideas. Instead, he urges persons to enjoy life, accept their work as self-rewarding, and not expect complete understanding of God's ways. Morality—like faith—should be unconditional, that is, not based on anticipated rewards (or punishment). For life, even with all its perplexities, is still vastly superior to the alternative, death.

ECCLESIASTES

Opening motto

1 The words of the Teacher of the Assembly,[a] David's son, king in Jerusalem:

2 Perfectly pointless,[b] says the Teacher,
  perfectly pointless.
  Everything is pointless.

Some things are inevitable

3 What do people gain
  from all the hard work
  that they work so hard at under the sun?
4 A generation goes,
  and a generation comes,
  but the earth remains as it always has.
5 The sun rises, the sun sets;
  it returns panting to the place
  where it dawns.
6 The wind blows to the south,
  goes around to the north;
  around and around blows the wind;
  the wind returns to its rounds again.
7 All streams flow to the sea,
  but the sea is never full;
  to the place where the rivers flow,
  there they continue to flow.
8 All words[c] are tiring;
  no one is able to speak.
  The eye isn't satisfied with seeing,
  neither is the ear filled up by hearing.
9 Whatever has happened—
  that's what will happen again;
  whatever has occurred—
  that's what will occur again.
  There's nothing new under the sun.
10 People may say about something: "Look at this! It's new!" But it was already around for ages before us. 11 There's no remembrance of things in the past, nor of things to come in the future. Neither will there be any remembrance among those who come along in the future.

The Teacher's quest

12 I am the Teacher. I was king over Israel in Jerusalem.

13 I applied my mind to investigate and to explore by wisdom all that happens under heaven. It's an unhappy obsession that God has given to human beings. 14 When I observed all that happens under the sun, I realized that everything is pointless, a chasing after wind.

15 What's crooked can't be straightened;
  what isn't there can't be counted.

16 I said to myself, Look here, I have grown much wiser than any who ruled over Jerusalem before me. My mind has absorbed great wisdom and knowledge. 17 But when I set my mind to understand wisdom, and also to understand madness and folly, I realized that this too was just wind chasing.

---

[a]Or Gatherer or Convener or Assembler (Heb Qoheleth); see also 1:2, 12; 7:27; 12:8, 9, 10. [b]Or meaningless or vapor or puff of air (Heb hebel, which often occurs in the book) [c]Or things

WISDOM

Wisdom is a concept that finds expression in nearly every culture, in every time and place. Persons with particular insights into human motivations and interactions, those with exceptional abilities at artisanship and the crafting of words, and those with encyclopedic knowledge are called "wise." Society often identifies wise people and honors them, relying on them to teach others. Several books of the Bible represent wisdom traditions, including Proverbs, Job, and Ecclesiastes; other books depict wise persons or wisdom influences. In the NT, many of Jesus' sayings are examples of wisdom, and the Letters also include wisdom sayings.

[18] Remember:

In much wisdom is much aggravation;
the more knowledge, the more pain.

2 I said to myself,[d] Come, I will make you[e] experience pleasure; enjoy what is good! But this too was pointless! [2]Merriment, I thought, is madness; pleasure, of no use at all. [3]I tried cheering myself with wine and by embracing folly—with wisdom still guiding me—until I might see what is really worth doing in the few days that human beings have under heaven.

[4]I took on great projects: I built houses for myself, planted vineyards for myself. [5]I made gardens and parks for myself, planting every kind of fruit tree in them. [6]I made reservoirs for myself to water my lush groves. [7]I acquired male servants and female servants; I even had slaves born in my house. I also had great herds of cattle and sheep, more than any who preceded me in Jerusalem. [8]I amassed silver and gold for myself, the treasures of kings and provinces. I acquired male and female singers for myself, along with every human luxury, treasure chests galore![f] [9]So I became far greater than all who preceded me in Jerusalem. Moreover, my wisdom stood by me.

[10]I refrained from nothing that my eyes desired. I refused my heart no pleasure. Indeed, my heart found pleasure from the results of my hard work; that was the reward from all my hard work. [11]But when I surveyed all that my hands had done, and what I had worked so hard to achieve, I realized that it was pointless—a chasing after wind. Nothing is to be gained under the sun.

[12]My reflections then turned to wisdom, madness, and folly. What can the king's heir do but what has already been done? [13]I saw that wisdom is more beneficial than folly, as light is more beneficial than darkness.

[14] The wise have eyes in their head,
but fools walk around in darkness.

But I also realized that the same fate happens to both of them. [15]So I thought to myself, What happens to the fool will also happen to me. So why have I been so very wise? I said to myself, This too is pointless. [16]There is no eternal memory of the wise any more than the foolish,[g] because everyone is forgotten before long. How can the wise die just like the fool? [17]So I hated life, because the things that happen under the sun were troublesome to me. Definitely, everything is pointless—just wind chasing.

[d]Or *in my heart; mind* [e]Or *the self* (or *heart; mind*) [f]Or *many secondary wives* [g]Or *The wise and the foolish alike are never remembered.*

LIGHT AND DARKNESS (OT)

In ancient Near Eastern cultures, physical light and darkness were associated with the cycles of life, growth, decay, and death. The light from the heavens symbolized life, happiness, and prosperity, while darkness was an expression of chaos and death. The sun, moon, and stars were often deified and worshipped.

In the OT, light is the first manifestation of God's creative word (Gen 1:3-5). It is separated from darkness and declared by its creator to be good (1:4, 18). The light is associated with day and darkness with night. The appearance of God to people is often portrayed as light or fire or lightning, as in the exodus from Egypt (Exod 10:23; 13:21; Neh 9:12, 19; Pss 78:14; 104:2; 105:39; Dan 2:22). In the wisdom tradition, light and darkness are given their strongest ethical interpretation. Ecclesiastes 2:13 equates wisdom with light and folly with darkness. The wise person lives according to the light of God's Law (Ps 43:3; Prov 13:9) and is illuminated by God's presence.

¹⁸I hated the things I worked so hard for here under the sun, because I will have to leave them to someone who comes after me. ¹⁹And who knows whether that one will be wise or foolish? Either way, that person will have control over the results of all my hard work and wisdom here under the sun. That too is pointless. ²⁰I then gave myself up to despair, as I thought about all my laborious hard work under the sun, ²¹because sometimes those who have worked hard with wisdom, knowledge, and skill must leave the results of their hard work as a possession to those who haven't worked hard for it. This too is pointless—it's a terrible wrong. ²²I mean, What do people get for all their hard work and struggles under the sun? ²³All their days are pain, and their work is aggravation; even at night, their hearts don't find rest. This too is pointless.

²⁴There's nothing better for human beings than to eat, drink, and experience pleasure in their hard work. I also saw that this is from God's hand—²⁵Who can eat and find enjoyment otherwise?—²⁶because God gives wisdom, knowledge, and joy to those who please God. But to those who are offensive,ʰ God gives the task of hoarding and accumulating, but only so as to give it all to those who do please God. This too is pointless and a chasing after wind.

A season for everything

3 There's a season for everything
and a time for every matter
under the heavens:
² a time for giving birth
and a time for dying,
a time for planting and a time for
uprooting what was planted,
³ a time for killing and a time for healing,
a time for tearing down
and a time for building up,
⁴ a time for crying and a time for laughing,
a time for mourning
and a time for dancing,
⁵ a time for throwing stones
and a time for gathering stones,
a time for embracing
and a time for avoiding embraces,
⁶ a time for searching
and a time for losing,

ʰOr *to those who sin*

SHALOM

The concept has many meanings ranging from the basic notion of well-being, safety, and contentment to the more traditional understanding as freedom from warfare and violence.

People go or travel in safety (Gen 26:29) and can die in peace (Gen 15:15). *Shalom* expresses greeting and personal blessing (Gen 29:6; Num 6:26; 1 Sam 1:17; 25:6; 2 Sam 11:7), victory in warfare (2 Sam 8:10; after offering "peace" to a city, Deut 20), or the absence of war (1 Kgs 4:24).

The term comes to be used as "safety" in many contexts, suggesting protection from animal predators or human intruders (e.g., Pss 4:8; 29:11; 85:8; 122:7; Isa 9:7; 32:18; 54:13; Jer 12:12; Nah 1:15). When used in connection with treaty-making, however, it is clear that a more political meaning of peace is intended (Deut 2:26; 1 Sam 7:14). It can also be related to the practice of justice (Zech 8:16). *Shalom* is explicitly used in distinction to war in wisdom and prophetic literature (Eccl 3:8; Jer 12:12; Mic 3:5). The word is used increasingly as part of personal names in the post-exilic period (1 Chron 2:40; 4:25; Neh 3:12).

a time for keeping
and a time for throwing away,
⁷ a time for tearing
and a time for repairing,
a time for keeping silent
and a time for speaking,
⁸ a time for loving and a time for hating,
a time for war and a time for peace.

Hard work

⁹What do workers gain from all their hard work? ¹⁰I have observed the task that God has given human beings. ¹¹God has made everything fitting in its time, but has also placed eternity in their hearts, without enabling them to discover what God has done from beginning to end.

¹²I know that there's nothing better for them but to enjoy themselves and do what's good while they live. ¹³Moreover, this is the gift of God: that all people should eat, drink, and enjoy the results of their hard work. ¹⁴I know that whatever God does will last forever; it's impossible to add to it or take away from it. God has done this so that people are reverent before him.[i] ¹⁵Whatever happens has already happened, and whatever will happen has already happened before. And God looks after what is driven away.[j]

Enjoy what you do now

¹⁶I saw something else under the sun: in the place of justice, there was wickedness; and in the place of what was right, there was wickedness again! ¹⁷I thought to myself, God will judge both righteous and wicked people, because there's a time for every matter and every deed. ¹⁸I also thought, Where human beings are concerned, God tests them to show them that they are but animals ¹⁹because human beings and animals share the same fate. One dies just like the other—both have the same life-breath. Humans are no better off than animals because everything is pointless.

²⁰ All go to the same place:
all are from the dust;
all return to the dust.

²¹Who knows if a human being's life-breath rises upward while an animal's life-breath descends into the earth? ²²So I perceived that there was nothing better for human beings but to enjoy what they do because that's what they're allotted in life. Who, really, is able to see what will happen in the future?

Death is better than oppression

4 When I next observed all the oppressions that take place under the sun, I saw the tears of the oppressed—and they have no one to comfort them. Their oppressors wield power—but they have no one to comfort them. ²So I declare that the dead, who have already died, are more fortunate than the living, who are still alive. ³But happier than both are those who have never existed, who haven't witnessed the terrible things that happen under the sun.

Envy and loneliness

⁴I also observed that people work hard and become good at what they do only out of mutual envy. This too is pointless, just wind chasing.

⁵ Fools fold their hands
and eat their own flesh.
⁶ But better is resting with one handful
than working hard for two fistfuls
and chasing after wind.

⁷Next, I saw under the sun something else that was pointless: ⁸There are people who are utterly alone, with no companions, not even a child or a sibling. Yet they work hard without end, never satisfied with their wealth. So for whom am I working so hard and depriving myself of enjoyment? This too is pointless and a terrible obsession.

⁹Two are better than one because they have a good return for their hard work. ¹⁰If either should fall, one can pick up the other. But how miserable are those who fall and don't have a companion to help them up! ¹¹Also, if two lie down together, they can stay warm. But how can anyone stay warm alone? ¹²Also, one can be overpowered, but

[i]Or *to inspire awe before the divine* [j]Or *God seeks out what is pursued,* or *God seeks what has gone by,* or *God seeks the pursued;* Heb uncertain

two together can put up resistance. A three-ply cord doesn't easily snap.

[13] A poor but wise youth is better than an old and foolish king, who no longer listens to advice. [14] He emerged from prison to become king, even though during his rule a poor child[k] is born. [15] I saw all who live and walk under the sun following the next youth who would rise to take his place. [16] There was no counting the number of people he ruled, but those who came later aren't happy with him. This too is pointless and a chasing after wind.

Listen and speak carefully

5 Watch[l] your steps when you go to God's house. It's more acceptable to listen than to offer the fools' sacrifice—they have no idea that they're acting wrongly. [2] Don't[m] be quick with your mouth or say anything hastily before God, because God is in heaven, but you are on earth. Therefore, let your words be few.

[3] Remember:

Dreams come with many cares,
    and the voice of fools with many words.

[4] When you make a promise to God, fulfill it without delay because God has no pleasure in fools. Fulfill what you promise. [5] Better not to make a promise than to make a promise without fulfilling it. [6] Don't let your mouth make a sinner of you, and don't say to the messenger: "It was a mistake!" Otherwise, God may become angry at such talk and destroy what you have accomplished.

[7] Remember:

When dreams multiply,
    so do pointless thoughts
    and excessive speech.

Therefore, fear God.

Hoarding wealth

[8] If you witness the poor being oppressed or the violation of what is just and right in some territory, don't be surprised because a high official watches over another,

and yet others stand over them. [9] But the land's yield should be for everyone if the field is cultivated.[n] [10] The money lover isn't satisfied with money; neither is the lover of wealth satisfied with income. This too is pointless. [11] When good things flow, so do those who consume them. But what do owners benefit from such goods, except to feast their eyes on them? [12] Sweet is the worker's sleep, whether there's a lot or little to eat; but the excess of the wealthy won't let them sleep.

[13] I have seen a sickening tragedy under the sun: people hoard their wealth to their own detriment. [14] Then that wealth is lost in a bad business venture so that when they have children, they are left with nothing. [15] Just as they came from their mother's womb naked, naked they'll return, ending up just like they started. All their hard work produces nothing—nothing they can take with them. [16] This too is a sickening tragedy: they must pass on just as they arrived. What then do they gain from working so hard for wind? [17] What's more, they constantly eat in darkness, with much aggravation, grief, and anger.

[18] This is the one good thing I've seen: it's appropriate for people to eat, drink, and find enjoyment in all their hard work under the sun during the brief lifetime that God gives them because that's their lot in life. [19] Also, whenever God gives people wealth and riches and enables them to enjoy it, to accept their place in the world[o] and to find pleasure in their hard work—all this is God's gift. [20] Indeed, people shouldn't brood too much over the days of their lives because God gives an answer in their hearts' joy.

Controlled appetite

6 I saw a tragedy under the sun, and it weighs heavily upon humanity. [2] God may give some people plenty of wealth, riches, and glory so that they lack nothing they desire. But God doesn't enable them to

---

[k] Possibly the youth of 4:13; or *He emerged from prison to become king, even though he was born poor in the kingdom.*
[l] 4:17 in Heb [m] 5:1 in Heb [n] Correction; Heb uncertain; or *The land's advantage in everything is this: a king for a plowed field.* [o] Or *portion in life,* as in 5:18

enjoy it; instead, a stranger enjoys it. This is pointless and a sickening tragedy. ³Some people may have one hundred children and live a long life. But no matter how long they live, if they aren't content with life's good things, I say that even a stillborn child with no grave is better off than they are.ᴾ ⁴Because that child arrives pointlessly, then passes away in darkness. Darkness covers its name. ⁵It hasn't seen the sun or experienced anything. But it has more peace than those ⁶who live a thousand years twice over but don't enjoy life's good things. Isn't everyone heading to the same destination? ⁷All the hard work of humans is for the mouth, but the appetite is never full. ⁸What advantage do the wise have over the foolish? Or what do the poor gain by knowing how to conduct themselves before the living? ⁹It's better to enjoy what's at hand than to have an insatiable appetite. This too is pointless, just wind chasing.

¹⁰Whatever happens has already been designated, and human beings are fully known. They can't contend with the one who is stronger than they are. ¹¹Because the more words increase, the more everything is pointless. What do people gain by it? ¹²Because who knows what's good for human beings during life, during their brief pointless life, which will pass away like a shadow? Who can say what the future holds for people under the sun?

Wisdom is better than wealth

7 A good name is better than fine oil,
and the day of death
better than the birthday.
² It is better to go to a house in mourning
than to a house party,
because that is everyone's destiny;
and the living should take it to heart.
³ Aggravation is better than merriment
because a sad face may lead
to a glad heart.
⁴ The wise heart is in the house that mourns,
but the foolish heart
is in the house that rejoices.

⁵ It is better to obey the reprimand
of the wise
than to listen to the song of fools,
⁶ because the fool's merriment
is like nettles crackling under a kettle.
That too is pointless.
⁷ Oppression turns the wise into fools;
a bribe corrupts the heart.
⁸ The end of something
is better than its beginning.
Patience is better than arrogance.
⁹ Don't be too quick to get angry
because anger lives in the fool's heart.
¹⁰ Don't ask, "How is it that the former
days were better than these?"
because it isn't wise to ask this.
¹¹ Wisdom is as good as�q an inheritance—
an advantage for those who see the sun.
¹² Wisdom's protection is
like the protection of money;
the advantage of knowledge is that
wisdom preserves the lives
of its possessors.

Good times and bad

¹³ Consider God's work! Who can straighten what God has made crooked? ¹⁴When times are good, enjoy the good; when times are bad, consider: God has made the former as well as the latter so that people can't discover anything that will come to be after them.

¹⁵I have seen everything in my pointless lifetime: the righteous person may die in spite of their righteousness; then again, the wicked may live long in spite of their wickedness. ¹⁶Don't be too righteous or too wise, or you may be dumbfounded.ʳ ¹⁷Don't be too wicked and don't be a fool, or you may die before your time. ¹⁸It's good that you take hold of one of these without letting go of the other because the one who fears God will go forth with both.

¹⁹Wisdom makes a wise person stronger than ten rulers who are in a city. ²⁰Remember: there's no one on earth so righteous as to do good only and never make a mistake.ˢ ²¹Don't worry about all the things people

---

ᴾCorrection; Heb puts the lack of burial site with those who do not enjoy life's good things. qOr *Wisdom is good with* ʳOr *destroyed* ˢOr *and never sin* say, so you don't hear your servant cursing you. ²² After all, you know that you've often cursed others yourself!

Life is complicated

²³ I tested all of this by wisdom. I thought, I will be wise, but it eluded me.

²⁴ All that happens is elusive and utterly unfathomable. Who can grasp it? ²⁵ I turned my mind to know, to investigate, and to seek wisdom, along with an account of things, to know that wickedness is foolishness and folly is madness.

²⁶ I found one woman more bitter than death: she who is a trap, her heart a snare, her hands shackles. Anyone who pleases God escapes her, but a sinner is trapped by her. ²⁷ See, this is what I found, says the Teacher, examining one matter after another to account for things. ²⁸ But there's something that I constantly searched for but couldn't find: I found one man among a thousand, but I couldn't find a woman among any of these.^t

²⁹ See, this alone I found: God made human beings straightforward, but they search for many complications.

8 Who is wise? And who knows the meaning of anything?
A person's wisdom
  brightens the expression;
  it changes the hardness
  of someone's face.

Watch out for power

² Keep^u the king's command
  as you would keep a solemn pledge.
³ Don't be dismayed; leave his presence.
  Don't linger in a harmful situation
  because he can do whatever he wants!
⁴ Because the king's word has authority,
  no one can say to him,
  "What are you doing?"
⁵ Whoever keeps a command will meet no harm, and the wise heart knows the right time and the right way ⁶ because there's a right time and right way for every matter. But human misfortunes are overwhelming ⁷ because no one knows what will happen,

and no one can say when something might happen. ⁸ No one has control over the life-breath,^v to retain it, and there's no control over the day of death. There's no release from war, and wickedness won't deliver those who practice it.

⁹ I observed all of this as I paid attention to all that happens under the sun. Sometimes people exercise power over each other to their detriment. ¹⁰ Then I saw the wicked brought to their graves, with people processing from a holy place,^w while those who had lived honestly were neglected in the city. This too is pointless.

¹¹ The condemnation for wicked acts isn't carried out quickly; that's why people dare to do evil. ¹² Wrongdoers may commit a hundred crimes but still live long lives. But I also know that it will go well for those who fear God, for those who are reverent before God. ¹³ But it will not go well for the wicked; they won't live long at all because they aren't reverent before God. ¹⁴ Here's another thing that happens on earth that is pointless: the righteous get what the wicked deserve, and the wicked get what the righteous deserve. I say that this too is pointless.

Enjoy life

¹⁵ So I commend enjoyment because there's nothing better for people to do under the sun but to eat, drink, and be glad. This is what will accompany them in their hard work, during the lifetime that God gives under the sun.

¹⁶ Then I set my mind to know wisdom and to observe the business that happens on earth, even going without sleep day and night ¹⁷ I observed all the work of God—that no one can grasp what happens under the sun. Those who strive to know can't grasp it. Even the wise who are set on knowing are unable to grasp it.

Everyone faces the same fate

9 So I considered all of this carefully, examining all of it: The righteous and the wise and their deeds are in God's hand,

---

^t Heb uncertain   ^u Correction; Heb *I (say?) keep*   ^v Or *wind*   ^w Or *temple*

along with both love and hate. People don't know anything that's ahead of them. [2]Everything is the same for everyone. The same fate awaits the righteous and the wicked, the good and the bad,[x] the pure and the impure, those who sacrifice and those who don't sacrifice. The good person is like the wrongdoer; the same holds for those who make solemn pledges and those who are afraid to swear. [3]This is the sad thing about all that happens under the sun: the same fate awaits everyone. Moreover, the human heart is full of evil; people's minds are full of madness while they are alive, and afterward they die. [4]Whoever is among the living can be certain about this. A living dog is definitely better off than a dead lion, [5]because the living know that they will die. But the dead know nothing at all. There is no more reward for them; even the memory of them is lost. [6]Their love and their hate, as well as their zeal, are already long gone. They will never again have a stake in all that happens under the sun.

[7]Go, eat your food joyfully and drink your wine happily because God has already accepted what you do. [8]Let your garments always be white; don't run short of oil for your head. [9]Enjoy life with your dearly loved spouse all the days of your pointless life that God[y] gives you under the sun—all the days of your pointless life![z]—because that's your part to play[a] in this life and in your hard work under the sun. [10]Whatever you are capable of doing, do with all your might because there's no work, thought, knowledge, or wisdom in the grave,[b] which is where you are headed.

Listen to common wisdom, not fools

[11]I also observed under the sun that the race doesn't always go to the swift, nor the battle to the mighty, nor food to the wise, nor wealth to the intelligent, nor favor to the knowledgeable, because accidents can happen to anyone. [12]People most definitely don't know when their time will come. Like fish tragically caught in a net or like birds

trapped in a snare, so are human beings caught in a time of tragedy that suddenly falls to them.

[13]I also observed the following example of wisdom under the sun—it impressed me greatly: [14]There was a small town with only a few residents. A mighty king came against it, surrounded it, and waged a terrible war against it. [15]Now there lived in that town a poor but wise man who saved everyone by his wisdom. But no one remembered that poor man. [16]So I thought, Wisdom is better than might, but the wisdom of commoners is despised and their words aren't heeded.

[17]The calm words of the wise are better heeded than the racket caused by a ruler among fools.

[18]Wisdom is better than weapons of war, but one incompetent person destroys much good.

10 As dead flies spoil the perfumer's oil, so a little folly outweighs wisdom and honor.
[2] The mind of the wise
    tends toward the right,
    but the mind of the fool toward the left.
[3] Fools lack all sense
    even when they walk down the street;
    they show everyone that they are fools.
[4] If a ruler's temper rises against you,
    don't leave your post, because calmness
    alleviates great offenses.

[5]There's an evil that I have seen under the sun: the kind of mistake that comes from people in power. [6]Fools are appointed to high posts, while the rich sit in lowly positions. [7]I have seen slaves on horseback, while princes walk on foot like slaves.

[8] Whoever digs a pit may fall into it,
    and whoever breaks through a wall
    may be bitten by a snake.
[9] Whoever quarries stones
    may be injured by them;
    whoever splits logs
    may be endangered by them.
[10] If an ax is dull
    and one doesn't sharpen it first,
    then one must exert more force.
    It's profitable to be skillful and wise.

---

[x]LXX [y]Or *he* or *that are given you* [z]This phrase is missing in some LXX sources, Syr, and Tg. [a]Or *portion*
[b]Or *underworld*; Heb *Sheol*

¹¹ If a snake bites before it's charmed,
   then there's no profit
   for the snake charmer.

¹²Words from a wise person's mouth are beneficial, but fools are devoured by their own lips.

¹³Fools start out talking foolishness and end up speaking awful nonsense.

¹⁴Fools talk too much! No one knows what will happen; no one can say what will happen in the future.

¹⁵The hard work of fools tires them out because they don't even know the way to town!

¹⁶ Too bad for you, land,
   whose king is a boy
   and whose princes feast in the morning.

¹⁷ Happy is the land
   whose king is dignified
   and whose princes feast
     at the right time for energy,
     not for drunkenness.

¹⁸ Through laziness, the roof sags;
   through idle hands, the house leaks.

¹⁹ Feasts are made for laughter,
   wine cheers the living,
   and money answers everything.ᶜ

²⁰Don't curse a king even in private; don't curse the rich in your bedroom, because a bird could carry your voice; some winged creature could report what you said!

Take risks; life is short

11 Send your bread out on the water because, in the course of time, you may find it again. ²Give a portion to seven people, even to eight: you don't know what disaster may come upon the land. ³If clouds fill up, they will empty out rain on the earth. If a tree falls, whether to the south or to the north, wherever it falls, there it will lie. ⁴Those who watch the wind blow will never sow, and those who observe the clouds will never reap. ⁵Just as you don't understand what the life-breath does in the fetusᵈ inside a pregnant woman's womb, so you can't understand the work of God, who

ᶜOr *money is everyone's answer.*   ᵈCorrection with Tg; MT *like the bones*

FOOL/FOOLISHNESS

Foolishness has a range of meanings that include "folly," "vile thing," "outrage," and "stupidity." The noun is applied to the threatened rape of the Levite and the actual rape of his secondary wife (Judg 19:23-24; 20:6, 10), Dinah (Gen 34:7), and Tamar (2 Sam 13:12). In addition, it is frequently contrasted with wisdom, especially in the wisdom literature. As foolishness is contrasted with wisdom, the fool is contrasted with the sage. A fool is everything a sage is not—imprudent, stupid, lazy, perverse in speech, even wicked (see, e.g., Prov 1:7; 14:16; 19:1; Eccl 7:25). And as wisdom is understood as being given by God, the quintessential fool is the one who does not believe in God (Pss 14:1; 53:1).

In the NT, the word is also used in contrast to wisdom. For example, in Matthew, Jesus tells a parable of 10 virgins—five who are wise and five who are foolish (Matt 25:1-13). In his letters, Paul uses the word in a variety of ways, including as a rhetorical device. In 2 Corinthians 11:1, Paul mounts a defense of his own authority by asking the community to "put up with [him while he acts] like a fool." Then, he proceeds to speak as "a fool" by boasting of his credentials, the suffering he has endured, and the dangers he has braved (11:16–12:11). Both the Gospels and Paul use the epithet "fool" and "foolish" to rebuke those who stray from the right path (e.g., Matt 23:17; 2 Tim 3:9).

makes everything happen. [6]Scatter your seed in the morning, and in the evening don't be idle because you don't know which will succeed, this one or that, or whether both will be equally good.

[7]Sweet is the light, and it's pleasant for the eyes to see the sun. [8]Even those who live many years should take pleasure in them all. But they should be mindful that there will also be many dark days. Everything that happens is pointless.

[9]Rejoice, young person, while you are young! Your heart should make you happy in your prime. Follow your heart's inclinations and whatever your eyes see, but know this: God will call you to account for all of these things. [10]Remove anxiety from your heart, banish pain from your body, because youth and the dawn of life are pointless too.

Troubling days to come

12Remember your creator in your prime, before the days of trouble arrive,
    and those years, about which you'll say,
        "I take no pleasure in these"—
[2]before the sun and the light grow dark,
    the moon and the stars too,
    before the clouds return after the rain;
[3]on the day when the housekeepers
    tremble and the strong men stoop;
when the women who grind
    stop working because they're so few,
    and those who look
    through the windows grow dim;
[4]when the doors to the street are shut,
    when the sound of the mill fades,
    the sound of the bird rises,
    and all the singers come down low;
[5]when people are afraid of things above
    and of terrors along the way;
    when the almond tree blanches,
        the locust droops,
        and the caper-berry comes to nothing;[e]
when the human goes
    to the eternal abode,
    with mourners all around in the street;
[6]before the silver cord snaps
    and the gold bowl shatters;
    the jar is broken at the spring
        and the wheel is crushed at the pit;
[7]before dust returns to the earth
    as it was before
        and the life-breath returns to God
        who gave it.

Motto and conclusion

[8]Perfectly pointless, says the Teacher, everything is pointless.

[9]Additionally: Because the Teacher was wise, he constantly taught the people knowledge. He listened and investigated. He composed many proverbs. [10]The Teacher searched for pleasing words, and he wrote truthful words honestly.
[11]The words of the wise
    are like iron-tipped prods;
    the collected sayings of the masters
    are like nails fixed firmly
        by a shepherd.[f]
[12]Be careful, my child,
    of anything beyond them!
There's no end to the excessive production of scrolls. Studying too much wearies the body. [13]So this is the end of the matter; all has been heard. Worship God and keep God's commandments because this is what everyone must do. [14]God will definitely bring every deed to judgment, including every hidden thing, whether good or bad.

---

[e]Heb uncertain   [f]Or *fixed by one shepherd*

SONG OF SONGS

The Song of Songs is unlike any other book in the Bible and has evoked the broadest range of human reaction. Rabbi Akiva (1st century CE) is reported to have called this little book the *Holy of Holies*, referring to its special place in Hebrew life. Some readers have revered it as an allegory about Christ and his love for the church, while others have reacted negatively to its sensual, erotic imagery.

Some students of the Bible, both Jewish and Christian, condemn the book for the lack of a single reference to God in any verse. Yet others prize the work for its profound insight into love and human physical attraction. Imaginations have been taxed beyond their limits in an effort to identify the lovers and to untangle the seemingly disjointed sequence of love songs. But even with all of its mystery and ambiguities, Song of Songs was included in the canon. Today, it presents one of the most eloquent and moving tributes to love in all of literature.

THE NAME OF THE BOOK

In the Hebrew Bible, the book is entitled Song of Songs, and forms, along with four other shorter books, a group known as the Five Scrolls. These five books are read during the Jewish celebration of Passover. In the English translations of the Bible, the book is sometimes called Song of Solomon, whereas in Roman Catholic versions it is called Canticles.

THE DATE OF THE WRITING

A specific date for the Song is impossible to determine, because there are few reliable historical references in the book and because the songs seem to reflect more than a single author. Solomon's name appears six times in the book: 1:5; 3:7, 9, 11; 8:11-12. Most of the instances suggest Solomon's fame or even identify him as the beloved, but they do not actually identify him as the author.

Elsewhere, Tirzah, the tenth-century capital of the Northern Kingdom, is mentioned in parallel to Jerusalem (6:4). Perhaps, however, the most important evidence for dating the material is the appearance of foreign terms, such as a Persian word for garden in 4:12 and a Greek-derived word for a "canopied couch" in 3:9. Many of the words and syntactical elements in Song of Songs are unique in the Old Testament. In view of all these factors, most scholars cautiously assign a date for final composition to the fourth or third century BCE. This date allows for several songs that may date much earlier, possibly as far back as the tenth or ninth century, as suggested by the Tirzah-Jerusalem parallel.

THE AUTHOR OF THE BOOK

Likewise, it is not possible to identify the author of Song. The superscription (1:1) mentions Solomon; however, the Hebrew preposition used, taken by some scholars as indicating authorship, may actually have several other meanings: *for* Solomon, *to* Solomon, or *about* Solomon. Clearly, as the patron sage of wisdom in Israel, Solomon is the honoree, and is probably the pseudonymous lover and bridegroom. After all, the author of 1 Kings 4:32 refers to King Solomon as the composer of over one thousand songs. Finally, the book's inclusion in the Hebrew canon is generally attributed to its association with Solomon.

The book has the literary nature of an anthology rather than a continuous poetic narrative or hymn. There are too many logical inconsistencies, contradictions, and repetitions for the book to be from a single hand.

INTERPRETATIONS OF THE BOOK

Due to the numerous literary and thematic complications in Song of Songs, interpretations have been many and diverse. Basically, these different interpretations can be divided into five groups: allegorical, cultic, dramatic, liturgical, and secular.

The allegorical interpretation flourished among many Jews and early Christians, but has few adherents today. The rabbis saw the book as an expression of the intimate covenant relationship between God and Israel (see also Genesis 15:1; Jeremiah 31:31-34). Drawing on the motif of human marriage as symbolizing these covenants, early rabbis saw in the Song many images that had been developed by prophets such as Hosea and Jeremiah. Later, Christians such as Origen and Augustine saw the book as an allegory of Christ and his bride, the church. These multilevel interpretations disregarded the human aspect of love, opting instead to symbolize the entire book as meaningful only on another, more spiritual level.

The second major school of interpretation is the cultic school. According to these scholars, the Song of Songs is an adaptation of a pagan religious rite centering on the mythological dying/rising god motif, as found in Greece and Egypt. Still other scholars suggest that the book arose from the rituals found in early Canaanite nature/fertility myths. The sexual imagery in both (or either) liturgies celebrates a seasonal renewal of life and depicts the eager anticipation of the maiden for her lover's return. The springtime setting, the theme of the absentee lover, and the dancing rites (6:13) all support this interpretation.

A third interpretation relates Song of Songs to certain Greek tragedies. Some scholars identify two characters while other scholars find three roles—a king, his beloved, and a shepherd. A chorus serves as background. Some type of plot emerges that pits the king against a shepherd lad for the affections of a young maiden. The drama is incomplete because the dramatic struggle has been left out of the present book.

A fourth view sees Song of Songs as a series of Judean wedding songs, similar to certain songs and marriage celebrations among Syrian peasants. The bride and groom assume the identities of king and queen and celebrate the beauty of their physical natures in preparation for their wedding.

Finally, the book may be seen as a collection of secular love poetry, celebrating the eternal bliss of physical love. There is no hint of immorality here, no lusting, no eroticisms, and no adultery. Instead, what we find is a moving testimony to that fundamental yearning that moves the very souls of men and women, drawing them together in a moment of sheer yearning. Such a strong physical attraction lies at the heart of any loving relationship. But marriage is the context for this celebration, eliminating adultery or promiscuity as the setting.

THE CONTENT OF THE BOOK

These songs have been collected and edited much as an anthology. Many of them reflect a rural or pastoral setting; still other songs display signs of cult and ritual. Together, they form a collection of love songs and love poems that affirm the pure goodness of physical passion.

Absent from Song of Songs are the great theological traditions in the Old Testament, such as the covenants with Abraham, with Moses, and with David. There is not a single reference to the exodus, to the law, or to divine revelation. In fact, there is no mention of God at all. Retribution (or the absence thereof) occupies not a single line. Instead, we have in this book an affirmation of the uninhibited joy of physical love. This is nature at its best—unashamed, undefiled, and uncorrupted by society's norms.

SONG OF SONGS

1 The Song of Songs, which is for Solomon.

Mutual admiration

[Woman][a]

² If only he would give me
some of his kisses . . . .

Oh, your loving is sweeter than wine!
³ Your fragrance is sweet;
your very name is perfume.
That's why the young women love you.
⁴ Take me along with you; let's run!

My king has brought me
into his chambers, saying,
"Let's exult and rejoice in you.
Let's savor your loving more than wine.
No wonder they all love you!"

⁵ Dark am I, and lovely,
daughters of Jerusalem—
like the black tents
of the Kedar nomads,
like the curtains of Solomon's palace.
⁶ Don't stare at me because I'm darkened
by the sun's gaze.
My own brothers were angry with me.
They made me a caretaker
of the vineyards—
but I couldn't care for my own vineyard.

⁷ Tell me, you whom I love
with all my heart—
where do you pasture your flock,
where do you rest them at noon?—
so I don't wander around with the
flocks of your companions.

[Man]

⁸ If you don't know your way,
most beautiful of women,
then follow the tracks of the herds
and graze your little goats
by the tents of the shepherds.

⁹ I picture you, my dearest,
as a mare among Pharaoh's chariots!

¹⁰ Lovely are your cheeks,
adorned with ear hoops;
your neck, with beads.
¹¹ Let's make hoops of gold
beaded with silver for you!

[Woman]

¹² With my king close by,
my perfume filled the air.
¹³ A sachet of myrrh is my love to me,
lying all night between my breasts.
¹⁴ A cluster of henna flowers is my love to me
in the desert gardens of En-gedi.

[Man]

¹⁵ Look at you—so beautiful, my dearest!
Look at you—so beautiful!
Your eyes are doves!

[Woman]

¹⁶ Look at you—so beautiful, my love!
Yes, delightful!
Yes, our bed is lush and green!
¹⁷ The ceilings of our chambers are cedars;
our rafters, cypresses.

Love in bloom

[Woman]

2 I'm a rose of the Sharon plain,
a lily of the valleys.

[Man]

² Like a lily among thornbushes,
so is my dearest
among the young women.

[Woman]

³ Like an apple tree among the wild trees,
so is my lover among the young men.
In his shade I take pleasure in sitting,
and his fruit is sweet to my taste.
⁴ He has brought me to the house of wine;
his banner raised over me is love.

⁵ Sustain me with raisin cakes,
strengthen me with apples,
for I'm weak with love!

---

[a]Identification of speakers here and throughout the Song is hypothetical and in several cases uncertain.

⁶ His left arm is beneath my head,
　　his right embraces me.

⁷ Make a solemn pledge,
　　daughters of Jerusalem,
　　by the gazelles or the wild deer:
Don't rouse, don't arouse love
　　until it desires.

⁸ Listen! It's my lover: here he comes now,
　　leaping upon the mountains,
　　bounding over the hills.
⁹ My lover is like a gazelle
　　or a young stag.
Here he stands now,
　　outside our wall,
　　peering through the windows,
　　peeking through the lattices.

¹⁰ My lover spoke and said to me,
　　"Rise up, my dearest,
　　my fairest, and go.
¹¹ Here, the winter is past;
　　the rains have come and gone.
¹² Blossoms have appeared in the land;
　　the season of singing[b] has arrived,
　　and the sound of the turtledove is
　　heard in our land.
¹³ The green fruit is on the fig tree,

and the grapevines in bloom
　　are fragrant.
Rise up,[c] my dearest,
　　my fairest, and go.
¹⁴ My dove—in the rock crevices,
　　hidden in the cliff face—
　　let me catch sight of you;
　　let me hear your voice!
The sound of your voice is sweet,
　　and the sight of you is lovely."

¹⁵ Catch foxes for us—
　　those little foxes
　　that spoil vineyards,
　　now that our vineyards are in bloom!

¹⁶ I belong to my lover and he belongs to me—
　　the one grazing among the lilies.
¹⁷ Before the day breeze blows
　　and the shadows flee,
　　turn about, my love; be like a gazelle
　　or a young stag
　　upon the jagged mountains.[d]

The search

[Woman]

3 Upon my bed, night after night,
　　I looked for the one whom I love
　　with all my heart.

[b]Or *pruning*　[c]LXX and Kethib add *go*; but Qere, DSS, Vulg, Syr, and Tg lack the verb; cf 2:10.　[d]Or *upon the mountains of Bether*; cf 8:14 *mountains of spice*

FRANKINCENSE

A prized incense in the Near East and the Mediterranean prepared from the gum of several species of Boswellia (*Burseraceae*) trees and shrubs native to the Arabian peninsula (*Boswellia sacra*) and North Africa (*Boswellia papyrifera*, native to Ethiopia). The range of the frankincense tree in southern Arabia follows the rain shadow of the current southwest monsoon. To obtain its resin, a deep cut is made in the trunk of the tree; below it a narrow strip of bark is peeled off. The secreted milk-like juice hardens when exposed to the air, and within three months it is transformed into yellowish "tears" that are scraped off into baskets. Frankincense was used in the formula for sacred incense in the meeting tent (Exod 30:34), in combination with grain offerings (Lev 2:2), and with the bread offering (Lev 24:7). Its aromatic values are highlighted in references to sweet fragrances (Song 3:6; 4:6), and its high price and value as a kingly gift is demonstrated in its inclusion among the gifts of the magi to the infant Jesus (Matt 2:11).

I looked for him but couldn't find him.[e]

2 "I will rise now and go all around the city,
   through the streets and the squares.
I will look for the one whom I love
   with all my heart."
I looked for him but couldn't find him.

3 The guards found me,
   those who make their rounds in the city.
"The one whom I love with all my heart—
   have you seen him?"

4 No sooner did I depart from them
   than I found the one whom I love
   with all my heart.
I held on to him
   and now I won't let him go,
   until I've brought him
   to my mother's house,
   to the chamber of the one
   who conceived me.

5 I place you under oath,
   daughters of Jerusalem,
   by the gazelles or the wild deer:
   don't rouse, don't arouse love
   until it desires.

Visions of grandeur

6 Who is this,
   coming up from the wilderness,
   like pillars of smoke?
She is perfumed
   with myrrh and frankincense,
   selected from all
   the spice merchant's powders.

7 Picture Solomon's bed—
   sixty heroic men round about it,
   all from the heroes of Israel,
8 all of them skilled with the sword,
   expert in warfare,
   each with his sword ready at his thigh
   against terrors that come by night.
9 King Solomon made a canopied couch
   for himself
   from the trees of Lebanon.
10 Its pillars he made of silver,
   its covering, cloth of gold,
   its cushions, royal purple;
   its interior inlaid with love.

Daughters of Jerusalem, 11go forth!
Look, daughters of Zion—
   on King Solomon wearing the crown
   with which his mother crowned him
   on the day of his wedding,
   on the day of his heart's joy.

In praise of her
[Man]

4 Look at you—so beautiful, my dearest!
Look at you—so beautiful!
   Your eyes are doves
   behind the veil of your hair!
Your hair is like a flock of goats
   as they stream down Mount Gilead.
2 Your teeth are like newly shorn ewes
   as they come up
   from the washing pool—
   all of them perfectly matched,
   not one of them lacks its twin.
3 Like a crimson ribbon are your lips;
   when you smile, it is lovely.
Like a slice of pomegranate
   is the curve of your face
   behind the veil of your hair.
4 Like David's tower is your neck,
   splendidly built!
A thousand shields are hung upon it—
   all the weapons of the warriors.
5 Your two breasts are like two fawns,
   twins of a gazelle doe,
   that graze among the lilies.
6 Before the day breeze blows
   and the shadows flee,
   I will be off to the mountain of myrrh,
   to the hill of frankincense.
7 You are utterly beautiful, my dearest;
   there's not a single flaw in you.

Garden of delight
[Man]

8 Come down with me from Lebanon,
   my bride—
   if only you would come down
   with me from Lebanon.
Descend from the peak of Amana,
   from the peaks of Senir and Hermon,
   from the lions' dens,
   from the mountain lairs of leopards.

---

[e]LXX adds *I called him, but he didn't answer me;* cf 5:6.

⁹ You have captured my heart,
  my sister,ᶠ my bride!
  You have captured my heart
    with one glance from your eyes,
    with one strand of your necklace.
¹⁰ How beautiful is your loving,
  my sister, my bride!
  Your loving is so much better
    than wine,
  and your fragrance better
    than any perfume!
¹¹ Sweetness drops from your lips,
  my bride;
  honey and milk are under your tongue,
and the fragrance of your garments
  is like the fragrance of Lebanon.
¹² An enclosed garden is my sister,
  my bride;
  an enclosed pool, a sealed spring.
¹³ Your limbs are an orchard of pomegranates
  with all kinds of luscious fruit,
  henna, and spices:
  ¹⁴ nard and saffron,
    sweet cane and cinnamon,
    with all scented woods,
    myrrh, and aloes,
  with the very choicest perfumes!
¹⁵ You are a garden spring,
  a well of fresh water,
  streams from Lebanon.
¹⁶ Stir, north wind, and come,
  south wind!
  Blow upon my garden;
  let its perfumes flow!

ᶠ *Sister* here and below is a common term in ancient love poetry; it doesn't imply blood relation.

[Woman]
Let my love come to his garden;
  let him eat its luscious fruit!
[Man]
5 I have come to my garden, my sister,
  my bride!
I have gathered my myrrh and my spices.
I have eaten my honeycomb
  with my honey;
I have drunk my wine and my milk.
Eat, dear friends!
Drink and get drunk on love!

A missed encounter
[Woman]
² I was sleeping, but my heart was awake.
A sound! My love is knocking:
[Man]
"Open for me, my sister, my dearest,
  my dove, my perfect one!
  My head is soaked with dew,
  my hair, with the night mists."
[Woman]
³ "I have taken off my tunic—
  why should I put it on again?
I have bathed my feet—
  why should I get them dirty?"
⁴ My love put his hand in
  through the latch hole,
  and my body ached for him.
⁵ I rose; I went to open for my love,
  and my hands dripped myrrh,
  my fingers, liquid myrrh,
  over the handles of the lock.

NARD

An herb from the *Valerianaceae* family that grows in the Himalayan countries of Bhutan, Nepal, and Kashmir in India. The fragrant root and lower stems can be dried and used to make a perfumed ointment. In ancient times it was considered a very expensive luxury item. By including the detail that nard was contained in an alabaster flask, Mark (14:3) demonstrated the precious nature of the nard used by the woman to anoint Jesus' head (cf. John 12:3). Nard has an intense, warm, musky odor that is mentioned among "the very choicest perfumes" in the description of the woman's "limbs" in Song of Songs 4:14.

⁶ I went and opened for my love,
   but my love had turned, gone away.
I nearly died when he turned away.
I looked for him but couldn't find him.
   I called out to him,
     but he didn't answer me.
⁷ They found me—the guards
   who make their rounds in the city.
They struck me, bruised me.
They took my shawl away from me,
   those guards of the city walls!
⁸ I place you under oath,
   daughters of Jerusalem:
If you find my love,
   what should you tell him?
That I'm weak with love!

[Daughters of Jerusalem]

⁹ How is your lover different
   from any other lover,
   you who are the most beautiful
     of women?
How is your lover different
   from any other lover,
   that you make us swear a solemn pledge?

In praise of him
[Woman]

¹⁰ My lover is radiant and ruddy;
   he stands out among ten thousand!
¹¹ His head is finest gold;
   his wavy hair, black as a raven.
¹² His eyes are like doves
   by channels of water.
They are bathing in milk,
   sitting by brimming pools.
¹³ His cheeks are like fragrant plantings,
   towers of spices.
His lips are lilies
   dripping liquid myrrh.
¹⁴ His arms are gold cylinders
   studded with jewels.
His belly is smooth ivory
   encrusted with sapphires.
¹⁵ His thighs are pillars of whitest stone
   set on pedestals of gold.
His appearance—like Lebanon,
   stately, like the cedars.
¹⁶ His mouth is everything sweet,
   every bit of him desirable.

This is my love, this my dearest,
   daughters of Jerusalem!

[Daughters of Jerusalem]

6 Which way did your lover go,
   you who are the most beautiful
     of women?
Which way did your lover turn,
   that we may look for him
     along with you?

[Woman]

² My lover has gone down to his garden,
   to the fragrant plantings,
   to graze in the gardens,
   to gather the lilies.
³ I belong to my lover
   and my lover belongs to me—
   the one grazing among the lilies.

An overwhelming sight
[Man]

⁴ You are as beautiful,
   my dearest, as Tirzah,
   as lovely as Jerusalem,
   formidable as those lofty sights.
⁵ Turn your eyes away from me,
   for they overwhelm me!

Your hair is like a flock of goats
   as they stream down from Gilead.
⁶ Your teeth are like a flock of ewes
   as they come up
     from the washing pool—
   all of them perfectly matched,
   not one of them lacks its twin.
⁷ Like a slice of pomegranate
   is the curve of your face
   behind the veil of your hair.
⁸ There may be sixty queens
   and eighty secondary wives,
   young women beyond counting,
⁹ but my dove, my perfect one,
   is one of a kind.
To her mother she's the only one,
   radiant to the one who bore her.
Young women see her
   and declare her fortunate;
   queens and secondary wives praise her.

¹⁰ Who is this, gazing down
   like the morning star,
   beautiful as the full moon,
   radiant as the sun,
   formidable as those lofty sights?

Transported
[Man]

¹¹ To the nut grove I went down
　　to look upon the fresh growth
　　　in the valley,
　　to see whether the vine was in flower,
　　whether the pomegranates
　　　had bloomed.
¹² I hardly knew myself;
　　she had set me in an official's chariot!ᵍ

Graceful dancer
[Man]

¹³ ʰCome back, come back, Shulammite!ⁱ
　　Come back, come back,
　　　so we may admire you.
How you all admire the Shulammite
　　as she whirls between
　　　two circles of dancers!

7 How graceful are your sandaled feet,
　　willing woman!
The smooth curves of your thighs—
　　like fine jewelry,
　　the work of an artist's hands!
² Your navel, cupped like the full moon—
　　may it never lack spiced wine!
Your belly is a mound
　　of winnowed wheat
　　edged with lilies.
³ Your two breasts are like two fawns,
　　twins of a gazelle doe;
⁴ your neck, like a tower of ivory;
　　your eyes, pools in Heshbon,
　　by the gate of that lordly city.ʲ
Your profile is like the tower of Lebanon,
　　looking out toward Damascus.
⁵ Your head crowns you like Mount Carmel,
　　and your hair, braided in royal purple—
　　a king is bound by the tresses!
⁶ You are so beautiful, so lovely—
　　my love, delightful one!ᵏ
⁷ Your stately form
　　resembles a date palm,
　　and your breasts
　　are like clustered fruit.
⁸ I say, "I will climb the palm tree;

I will hold its fruit!"
May your breasts be now
　　like grape clusters,
and the scent of your breath like apples!
⁹ Your palate is like excellent wine . . .
[Woman]
. . . flowing smoothly for my love,
　　gliding through the lips and teeth.ˡ
¹⁰ I belong to my lover,
　　and his longing is only for me.

The ripeness of love
[Woman]

¹¹ Come, my love:
　　Let's go out to the field
　　and rest all night
　　　among the flowering henna.
¹² Let's set out early for the vineyards.
We will see if the vines have budded
　　and the blossoms opened,
　　see if the pomegranates have bloomed.
There I'll give my loving to you.

¹³ The mandrakes give off their scent,
　　and at our doorways
　　is every delicacy—
　　fresh or ripened—
my love, I have kept them
　　hidden for you.

Wishing
[Woman]

8 If only you were as my brother—
　　the one who nursed
　　at my mother's breast.
I would find you in the street
　　and kiss you,
　　and no one would shame me for it.
² I would lead you, I would bring you
　　to my mother's house;
　　she would teach me what to do.ᵐ
I would give you spiced wine to drink,
　　some of my fresh pomegranate juice.
³ His left arm is beneath my head,
　　and his right embraces me!

ᵍOr I hardly knew what happened; my passion set me in an official's chariot! LXX, Vulg Aminadab's chariots; Heb
uncertain　ʰ7:1 in Heb　ⁱA name or title for the woman　ʲOr by the gate of Bath-rabbim　ᵏWith Syr and Aquila
daughter of delights; MT love in delights or love with every charm　ˡLXX, Syr, Vulg; MT through the lips of those who
sleep; Heb uncertain　ᵐOr you would teach me; LXX, Syr to my mother's house, and to the chamber of the one who
conceived me (cf 3:4)

⁴ Make a solemn pledge,
  daughters of Jerusalem,
  never to rouse, never to arouse love
  until it desires.

Love, strong and invaluable
  [Daughters of Jerusalem]
⁵ Who is this coming up
  from the wilderness
  leaning against her lover?

[Woman]
Under the apple tree
I aroused you—
  there, where your mother
    labored with you,
  there where, laboring,
    she bore you.
⁶ Set me as a seal over your heart,
  as a seal upon your arm,
  for love is as strong as death,

VINE/VINEYARD

From earliest memory, vineyards have been essential to the life of the people of the Eastern Mediterranean; according to tradition, Noah planted a vineyard after the flood subsided (Gen 9:20). The centrality of the vineyard to the families of Israel made the vineyard a likely symbol for the nation of Israel and its people: "Israel is a growing vine that yields its fruit" (Hos 10:1; see also Ps 80:8-11; Isa 5:1-7; Jer 2:21). Christians adapted the vine imagery for their new community united with Jesus, as Jesus becomes the vine and his followers the branches that bear fruit (John 15:1-6).

Grapevines thrived in dry climates and provided much of the community's subsistence. The fruit was dried and stored for later consumption, used as a source of sugar, or pressed to make wine. Vineyards also provided food for the poor, widows, orphans, and sojourners, who were allowed to pick behind the harvesters (Lev 19:10; Deut 24:21). Extended family and friends helped pick and tread grapes during the short time between the fruit's ripening and rotting on the vine. Jesus' parable about an owner who goes out to hire more laborers up to the last moment may reflect such harvesttime pressures (Matt 20:1-16).

The vine was a metaphor for peace (Mic 4:4; Zech 3:10; cf. 2 Kgs 18:31; Isa 36:16) and prosperity (Ps 128). Prophets often turned to the image of the fruitless vine to illustrate religious and economic disorder (Isa 32:10-15; 34:4; Jer 8:13; Joel 1:11-12). Isaiah's "song of the vineyard" (Isa 5:1-7; 27:1-6) refers to unjust and unfaithful Israel as a vineyard bearing "rotten grapes" (Isa 5:2). Jesus adapts Isaiah's language for a parable of unfaithful vineyard workers who try to gain the vineyard for themselves (Matt 21:33-46; Mark 12:1-12; Luke 20:9-19). Burning or uprooting the vines is a metaphor for divine judgment (Ezek 15:1-7; 17:1-10). Harvesting and pressing the grapes serve as imagery for eschatological judgment, when an angel gathers "the clusters in the vineyard of the earth" and throws them into "the great wine-press of God's passionate anger" (Rev 14:18-20).

The fertility of the vine and imagery of luscious, juicy grapes might have inspired the poet(s) of the Song of Songs to use the vineyard and vine metaphorically to represent the woman's sexuality: "They made me a caretaker of the vineyards—but I couldn't care for my own vineyard" (Song 1:6b; see also 2:13; 6:11; 7:8, 12; 8:11-12).

passionate love unrelenting
   as the grave.[n]
Its darts are darts of fire—
   divine flame!
[7] Rushing waters can't quench love;
   rivers can't wash it away.
If someone gave
   all his estate in exchange for love,
   he would be laughed to utter shame.

       [The Woman's Brothers]

[8] Our sister is small;
   she has no breasts.
What will we do for our sister
   on the day that she is spoken for?
[9] If she is a city wall,
   then we will build a turret of silver
     on her.[o]
And if she is a door,
   then we will barricade her[p]
     with a panel of cedar.

       [Woman]

[10] I'm a city wall,
   and my breasts are the towers.
So now I'm in his eyes
   as one who brings peace.

       [Man]

[11] Solomon had a vineyard
   in Baal-hamon.
He gave charge of the vineyard
   to keepers;
   one would bring in exchange
     for its fruit
   a thousand pieces of silver.
[12] My vineyard, my very own,
   is before me.
You can have the thousand,
   Solomon[q]—
   with two hundred for those
     who tend the fruit!

[13] You who sit in the gardens,
   my companions are listening
   for your voice.
   Let me hear it!

       [Woman]

[14] "Take flight, my love,
   and be like a gazelle
   or a young stag
   on the mountains of spice!"

---

[n]Heb *Sheol*   [o]Or *on it (the city wall)*   [p]Or *it (the door)*   [q]Cf 1 Kgs 11:3

ISAIAH

ISAIAH 1–39

The prophet Isaiah was the son of Amoz, as the first verse in the book tells us. We know little or nothing about Isaiah's personal life. From reading Isaiah 6:1-8, some conclude that Isaiah was a priest in the temple before he was called to prophesy. Isaiah's name means *Yahweh gives salvation.*

Chapters 1–39 are a collection of prophecies from the ministry of Isaiah the prophet. The chapters after 39 in the book came from a later period, and were probably spoken and recorded by disciples of Isaiah the prophet.

Isaiah was a prophet of the Southern Kingdom (Judah). He directed his message to Judah, and especially Jerusalem, between 742 and 687 BCE. During this time, the Southern Kingdom was under the domination of Assyria, to the northeast. The Northern Kingdom (Israel) ceased to exist as an independent nation about 722 BCE, when it fell to the Assyrians.

The first 39 chapters of Isaiah are divided into six main parts: the prophet's memoirs (chapters 1–12), oracles concerning Judah and its neighbors (chapters 13–23), the Isaiah Apocalypse (chapters 24–27), oracles concerning Egypt (chapters 28–32), post-exilic oracles (chapters 33–35), and a historical appendix (chapters 36–39).

Throughout these chapters Isaiah preaches a message of social justice, faith in God, rewards for the obedient, and judgment on the unfaithful. With this message Isaiah stands in the tradition of his contemporaries (Hosea, Micah, and Amos).

ISAIAH 40–55

We know almost nothing about the prophet who wrote chapters 40–55 in the book of Isaiah. Because this prophet's words are included in the Old Testament book we call Isaiah and because he stands in the tradition of Isaiah, he has been given the name Second Isaiah. The messages of Isaiah and Second Isaiah are interrelated.

Whereas the prophet Isaiah lived and worked in Judah, Second Isaiah was a prophet of the Babylonian Exile. Although the book never states this explicitly, Second Isaiah probably ministered to the people while they were in exile in Babylon. The book contains many references to Babylon and to circumstances that existed there (see chapter 47, for example). In addition, the prophet speaks often of returning home to Judah. In fact, Second Isaiah's prophecies begin and end on that subject (see 40:3-5 and 55:12-13).

The Babylonian Exile began with the fall of Jerusalem in 587 BCE. The inhabitants were captured and taken to Babylon, where they lived until King Cyrus of Persia defeated Babylon in 539 BCE. Second Isaiah's prophecies were directed to those exiles, and were delivered shortly before their return to Judah in 538 BCE.

Second Isaiah has two main parts: oracles about God's activity in history (chapters 40–48), and prophecies about the future restoration of Judah (chapters 49–55).

The message of Second Isaiah's prophecies fits the historical circumstances of prophet and people well. The people are in exile. Cyrus is about to appear on the scene and release them, after fifty years of bondage in Babylon. In this context, the prophet preaches a message of trust in God and hope for an imminent return to their homeland.

ISAIAH 56–66

Chapters 56–66 form the third major portion of Isaiah. Many commentators maintain that this final section was written or compiled by yet a third prophet, a disciple of Second Isaiah in Jerusalem during the early years of the restoration. This unknown prophet is often called Third Isaiah.

Chapters 56–66 can be dated most probably sometime during the fourth century BCE. Five main characteristics suggest a late date for these prophecies. First, these chapters share many words and themes with the words of the prophets Haggai and Zechariah, who also lived and worked during the fourth century BCE. Second, spread throughout these chapters is an interest in the events surrounding the last days. In general, this is an interest of later biblical writers. Third, this prophet seems to take the content and themes of Second Isaiah and expand on them, adding his own interpretations. For example, the idea of making preparations to return to the homeland, central to the message of Second Isaiah, is taken up and altered slightly in chapters 56–66. There it is the persons inside the gates of Jerusalem who are to make preparations for those who are yet to return (not the exiles in Babylon, who are addressed in chapters 40–55). Fourth, the themes of worship and ritual, virtually absent in the prophecies of Second Isaiah, play a major role in the theology of chapters 56–66. And fifth, these final chapters emphasize the universality of the message of salvation, which is largely a later phenomenon in the Bible.

Chapters 60–62 form the heart of this prophet's message. The rest of the oracles in this third portion of Isaiah are a mixture of the prophet's own words and prophecies adapted from other places in the Bible.

ISAIAH

1 The vision about Judah and Jerusalem that Isaiah, Amoz's son, saw in the days of Judah's kings Uzziah, Jotham, Ahaz, and Hezekiah.

Rebels condemned

[2] Hear you heavens, and listen earth,
  for the LORD has spoken:
 I reared children; I raised them,
  and they turned against me!
[3] An ox knows its owner,
  and a donkey its master's feeding trough.
 But Israel doesn't know;
  my people don't behave intelligently.

[4] Doom! Sinful nation,
  people weighed down with crimes,
  evildoing offspring, corrupt children!
 They have abandoned the LORD,
  despised the holy one of Israel;
  they turned their backs on God.

[5] Why do you invite further beatings?
  Why continue to rebel?
 Everyone's head throbs,
  and everyone's heart fails.
[6] From head to toe, none are well—
  only bruises, cuts, and raw wounds,
  not treated, not bandaged,
  not soothed with oil.

[7] Your country is deserted,
  your cities burned with fire;
 your land—strangers are devouring it
  in plain sight.
 It's a wasteland, as when foreigners raid.
[8] Daughter Zion is left
  like a small shelter in a vineyard,
  like a hut in a cucumber field,
  like a city besieged.[a]
[9] If the LORD of heavenly forces
  had not spared a few of us,
 we would be like Sodom;
  we would resemble Gomorrah.

Hands filled with bloodshed

[10] Hear the LORD's word,
  you leaders of Sodom.

Listen to our God's teaching,
  people of Gomorrah!
[11] What should I think
  about all your sacrifices?
  says the LORD.
 I'm fed up with
  entirely burned offerings of rams
  and the fat of well-fed beasts.
 I don't want the blood of bulls,
  lambs, and goats.
[12] When you come to appear before me,
  who asked this from you,
  this trampling of my temple's courts?
[13] Stop bringing worthless offerings.
  Your incense repulses me.
 New moon, sabbath,
  and the calling of an assembly—
  I can't stand wickedness
  with celebration!
[14] I hate your new moons and your festivals.
  They've become a burden
  that I'm tired of bearing.
[15] When you extend your hands,
  I'll hide my eyes from you.
 Even when you pray for a long time,
  I won't listen.
 Your hands are stained with blood.
[16] Wash! Be clean!
  Remove your ugly deeds from my sight.
  Put an end to such evil;
[17] learn to do good.
 Seek justice:
  help the oppressed;[b]
  defend the orphan;
  plead for the widow.

[18] Come now, and let's settle this,
  says the LORD.
 Though your sins are like scarlet,
  they will be white as snow.
 If they are red as crimson,
  they will become like wool.
[19] If you agree and obey,
  you will eat the best food of the land.
[20] But if you refuse and rebel,
  you will be devoured by the sword.
 The LORD has said this.

---

[a]LXX, Vulg; MT *spared*   [b]LXX, Vulg; MT *lead the oppressor*

Zion will be redeemed

²¹ This faithful town
has become a prostitute!
She was full of justice;
righteousness lived in her—
but now murderers.
²² Your silver has become impure;
your beer is diluted with water.
²³ Your princes are rebels,
companions of thieves.
Everyone loves a bribe and pursues gifts.
They don't defend the orphan,
and the widow's cause
never reaches them.
²⁴ Therefore, says the
LORD God of heavenly forces,
the mighty one of Israel:
Doom! I will vent my anger
against my foes;
I will take it out on my enemies,
²⁵ and I will turn my hand against you.
I will refine your impurities as with lye,
and remove all your cinders.
²⁶ Then I will restore your judges
as in earlier times,
and your counselors
as at the beginning.
After this you will be called
Righteous City, Faithful Town.

²⁷ Zion will be redeemed by justice,
and those who change their lives
by righteousness.
²⁸ But God will shatter
rebels and sinners alike;
those who abandon the LORD
will be finished.
²⁹ You will be ashamed
of the oaks you once desired,
and embarrassed
by the gardens you once chose.
³⁰ You will be like an oak
with withering leaves,
like a garden without water.
³¹ The strong will be like dry twigs,
their deeds like sparks;
the two will burn together,
with no one to extinguish them.

The LORD's mountain

2 This is what Isaiah, Amoz's son, saw
concerning Judah and Jerusalem.
² In the days to come
the mountain of the LORD's house
will be the highest of the mountains.
It will be lifted above the hills;
peoples will stream to it.
³ Many nations will go and say,
"Come, let's go up
to the LORD's mountain,
to the house of Jacob's God
so that he may teach us his ways
and we may walk in God's paths."
Instruction will come from Zion;
the LORD's word from Jerusalem.
⁴ God will judge between the nations,
and settle disputes
of mighty nations.
Then they will beat
their swords into iron plows
and their spears into pruning tools.
Nation will not take up sword
against nation;
they will no longer learn
how to make war.

⁵ Come, house of Jacob,
let's walk by the LORD's light.

Everyone is brought low

⁶ You have abandoned your people,
house of Jacob.
They are full of sorcerers
from the east and fortune-tellers
like the Philistines;
they hold hands
with foreigners' children.ᶜ
⁷ Their land is full of silver and gold;
they have countless treasures.
Their land is filled with horses;
they have countless chariots.
⁸ Their land is filled with idols;
they worship their handiwork,
what their own fingers have made.

⁹ Humanity will be brought down;
each person laid low—
don't lift them up!ᵈ

ᶜHeb uncertain   ᵈOr *don't forgive them*

¹⁰ Go into the rocks,
and hide yourself in the dust
from the terror of the LORD,
from the splendor of God's majesty!
¹¹ People's proud gazing will be stopped
and humanity's arrogance
brought down;
the LORD alone will be exalted
on that day.

¹² The LORD of heavenly forces
has planned a day:
against all that is prideful and haughty;
against all that is lofty,
and it will be laid low;ᵉ
¹³ against all the cedars of Lebanon,
high and lofty;
against all the oaks of Bashan;
¹⁴ against all the high mountains;
against all the lofty hills;
¹⁵ against every tall tower;
against every fortified wall;
¹⁶ against all the ships of Tarshish;
against all the wonderful boats.ᶠ
¹⁷ People's pride will be brought down
and human arrogance humiliated.
The LORD alone will be exalted
on that day;
¹⁸ the idols will completely pass away.

¹⁹ Go into caves in the rocks
and holes in the dust
before the terror of the LORD
and the splendor of God's majesty,
when he arises to terrify the earth.
²⁰ On that day, people will toss
to the rodentsᵍ and to the bats
their idols of silver and idols of gold,
which they made for themselves
to worship.
²¹ They will hide in fissures of rocks
and in crevices of cliffs
before the terror of the LORD
and the splendor of God's majesty
when he arises to terrify the earth.

²² Quit admiring the human race,
who breathe through their nostrils.
Why should they be admired?

Your leaders mislead you

3 Now the LORD God of heavenly forces
is removing from Jerusalem and from
Judah every form of support:
all rations of food and water;
² soldier and warrior;
judge and prophet;
fortune-teller and elder;
³ commander and celebrity;
counselor, clever craftsman,
and cunning charmer.
⁴ I will make youths their commanders;
mischief makers will rule over them.
⁵ The people will oppress each other,
each one against the other,
neighbor against neighbor.
The young will bully the old,
the rogue, and the respectable.

⁶ Someone will seize a family member,
saying, "You have clothing!
You be our leader!
This mess will be your responsibility!"
⁷ Someone else will cry out on that day,
"I'm no healer!
I have neither food nor clothing
in my house!
Don't make me the leader
of the people!"

⁸ Yes, Jerusalem has stumbled
and Judah has fallen,
because the way they talk and act
in word and deed insults the LORD,
defying his brilliant glory.
⁹ Their bias in judgment gives them away;
like Sodom,
they display their sins in public.
Doom to them,
for they have done themselves in!
¹⁰ Tell the righteous how blessed they are;
they will eat the fruit of their labors.
¹¹ Doom to the wicked; they are evil.
What they have done
will be done to them.
¹² As for my people—oppressors strip them
and swindlersʰ rule them.
My people—your leaders mislead you
and confuse your paths.

ᵉLXX *and high* ᶠHeb uncertain ᵍHeb uncertain ʰLXX; MT *women*

[13] The LORD arises to accuse;
    he stands to judge the peoples.
[14] The LORD will enter into judgment
    with the elders and princes
    of his people:
  You yourselves have devoured
    the vineyard;
    the goods stolen from the poor
    are in your houses.
[15] How dare you crush my people
    and grind the faces of the poor?
    says the LORD God of heavenly forces.

[16] The LORD says:
  Because Zion's daughters
    applaud themselves,
    walking with their chins in the air,
    flirting with their eyes,
    tiptoeing as they walk, feet jingling—
[17] the Lord will shave the heads
    of Zion's daughters,
    and will expose their scalps.
[18] On that day, the LORD will remove:
    the splendid ankle chains; headbands
    and moon-shaped pendants;
[19] the earrings, bracelets, and veils;
[20] the hats, bangles, and sashes;
    the amulets and charms;
[21] the signet rings and nose rings;
[22] the robes and capes;
    the shawls and handbags;
[23] the mirrors and linen garments;
    the turbans and the veils.
[24] Instead of perfume
    there will be a disgusting odor;
    instead of a sash, a rope;
    instead of styled hair, shaved heads;
    instead of expensive clothes,
    rags as mourning clothes;
    instead of beauty, shame.[i]

[25] Your men will fall by the sword,
    your warriors in battle!
[26] Her gates will lament and mourn;
    desolate, she will sit on the ground.

4 Seven women will grab one man on that
day, saying, "We will eat our own bread
and wear our own clothes—only let us take
your name; take away our disgrace."

Zion's glorious future

[2] On that day, the LORD's branch will
become beautiful and glorious. The earth's
fruit will be the pride and splendor of Israel's survivors. [3] Whoever remains in Zion
and is left in Jerusalem will be called holy,
everyone who is on the list of those living
in Jerusalem. [4] When the Lord washes the
filth from Zion's daughters, and cleanses
Jerusalem's bloodguilt from within it by
means of a wind of judgment and a searing
wind, [5] then the LORD will create over the
whole site of Mount Zion and over its assembly a cloud by day and smoke and the
light of a blazing fire by night. Over all the
glory there will be a canopy, [6] which will be
a booth by day for shade from the heat and
a hiding place and shelter from a stormy
downpour.

Song of the vineyard

5 Let me sing for my loved one
  a love song for his vineyard.
  My loved one had a vineyard
    on a fertile hillside.
[2] He dug it,
    cleared away its stones,
    planted it with excellent vines,
    built a tower inside it,
    and dug out a wine vat in it.
  He expected it to grow good grapes—
    but it grew rotten grapes.
[3] So now, you who live in Jerusalem,
    you people of Judah,
    judge between me and my vineyard:
[4] What more was there to do
    for my vineyard
    that I haven't done for it?
  When I expected it to grow good grapes,
    why did it grow rotten grapes?
[5] Now let me tell you
    what I'm doing to my vineyard.
  I'm removing its hedge,
    so it will be destroyed.
  I'm breaking down its walls,
    so it will be trampled.
[6] I'll turn it into a ruin;
    it won't be pruned or hoed,
    and thorns and thistles will grow up.

---

[i] DSS (1QIsaᵃ); MT lacks *shame*.

I will command the clouds
  not to rain on it.
⁷ The vineyard of
  the LORD of heavenly forces
  is the house of Israel,
  and the people of Judah
  are the plantings
  in which God delighted.
  God expected justice,
  but there was bloodshed;
  righteousness,
  but there was a cry of distress!

Sayings of doom

⁸ Doom to those who acquire
  house after house,
  who annex field to field
  until there is no more space left
  and only you live alone in the land.
⁹ I heard the LORD of heavenly forces
  say this:ʲ
  Many houses will become total ruins,
  large, fine houses,
  with no one living in them.
¹⁰ Ten acres of vineyard
  will produce just one bath,ᵏ
  and a homer of seed
  will produce only an ephah.

¹¹ Doom to those who wake up
  early in the morning to run after beer,
  to those who stay up late, lit up by wine.
¹² They party with lyre and harp,
  tambourine, flute, and wine;
  but they ignore the LORD's work;
  they can't see what God is doing.

¹³ Therefore, my people go into exile
  since they didn't understand—
  their officials are dying of hunger;
  so many of them are dried up with thirst.
¹⁴ Therefore, the graveˡ opens wide its jaws,
  opens its mouth beyond all bounds,
  and the splendid multitudes
  will go down,
  with all their uproar and cheering.
¹⁵ Humanity will be humiliated;

each person laid low,
  the eyes of the exalted laid low.
¹⁶ But the LORD of heavenly forces
  will be exalted in justice,
  and the holy God will show himself
  holy in righteousness.
¹⁷ Lambs will graze as if in their pasture;
  young goatsᵐ will feed
  among the ruins of the rich.ⁿ

¹⁸ Doom to those who drag guilt
  along with cords of fraud,
  and haul sin as if with cart ropes,
¹⁹ who say, "God should hurry
  and work faster so we can see;
  let the plan of Israel's holy one come
  quickly, so we can understand it."

²⁰ Doom to those who call evil good
  and good evil,
  who present darkness as light
  and light as darkness,
  who make bitterness sweet
  and sweetness bitter.

²¹ Doom to those
  who consider themselves wise,
  who think of themselves as clever.

²² Doom to the wine-swigging warriors,
  mighty at mixing drinks,
²³ who spare the guilty for bribes,
  and rob the innocent of their rights.
²⁴ Therefore, as a tongue of fire
  devours stubble,
  and as hay shrivels in a flame,
  so their roots will rot,
  and their blossoms turn to dust,
  for they have rejected the teaching of
  the LORD of heavenly forces,
  and have despised the word
  of Israel's holy one.

God's powerful hand

²⁵ This is why the LORD's anger
  burned against the people:
  he extended his hand to strike them,

ʲHeb lacks *say this*. ᵏOne bath is approximately twenty quarts, the same as an ephah; one homer contains ten ephahs (or baths) of grain. ˡHeb *Sheol* ᵐOr *strangers* ⁿOr *Calves and young goats will feed on the ruins*; Heb uncertain

the mountains trembled,
and their corpses lay in the middle
of the streets like dung.
Even then God's anger didn't turn away;
God's hand was still extended.

26 God will raise a signal
to a nation from far away
and whistle to them
from the end of the earth—
now look—hurrying, swiftly they come!
27 Not one is tired; not one stumbles;
they don't rest or sleep;
no belt is loose; no sandal broken;
28 their arrows are sharp;
all their bows drawn;
their horses' hooves are like flint;
their wheels like the whirlwind.
29 Their roaring is like the lion;
they roar like young lions;
they growl, seize their prey,
and carry it off, with no one to rescue.
30 On that day, they will roar over it
like the roaring of the sea.
And if one looks toward the land,
there's darkness.
Tyre and the Nile
will be darkened by the clouds.°

The divine throne room

6 In the year of King Uzziah's death, I saw the Lord sitting on a high and exalted throne, the edges of his robe filling the temple. ²Winged creatures were stationed around him. Each had six wings: with two they veiled their faces, with two their feet, and with two they flew about. ³They shouted to each other, saying:

"Holy, holy, holy
is the LORD of heavenly forces!
All the earth is filled with God's glory!"

⁴The doorframe shook at the sound of their shouting, and the house was filled with smoke.

⁵I said, "Mourn for me; I'm ruined! I'm a man with unclean lips, and I live among a people with unclean lips. Yet I've seen the king, the LORD of heavenly forces!"

⁶Then one of the winged creatures flew

to me, holding a glowing coal that he had taken from the altar with tongs. ⁷He touched my mouth and said, "See, this has touched your lips. Your guilt has departed, and your sin is removed."

⁸Then I heard the Lord's voice saying, "Whom should I send, and who will go for us?"

I said, "I'm here; send me."

⁹God said, "Go and say to this people:
Listen intently, but don't understand;
look carefully, but don't comprehend.
10 Make the minds of this people dull.
Make their ears deaf
and their eyes blind,
so they can't see with their eyes
or hear with their ears,
or understand with their minds,
and turn, and be healed."

11 I said, "How long, Lord?"

And God said, "Until cities lie ruined with no one living in them, until there are houses without people and the land is left devastated." 12 The LORD will send the people far away, and the land will be completely abandoned. 13 Even if one-tenth remain there, they will be burned again, like a terebinth or an oak, which when it is cut down leaves a stump. Its stump is a holy seed.

Reassurance to King Ahaz

7 In the days of Ahaz (Jotham's son and grandson of Judah's King Uzziah), Aram's King Rezin and Israel's King Pekah (Remaliah's son) came up to attack Jerusalem, but they couldn't overpower it.

²When the house of David was told that Aram had become allies with Ephraim, their hearts and the hearts of their people shook as the trees of a forest shake when there is a wind. ³But the LORD said to Isaiah, "Go out to meet Ahaz, you and your son Shear-jashub,ᴾ at the end of the channel of the Upper Pool, by the road to the field where laundry is washed, ⁴and say to him, 'Be careful and stay calm. Don't fear, and don't lose heart over these two pieces of smoking torches, over the burning anger of Rezin, Aram, and Remaliah's son. ⁵Aram has planned evil against you with Ephraim

---

°Heb uncertain   ᴾOr *the remaining few will return*

and Remaliah's son, saying, [6]"Let's march up against Judah, tear it apart, capture it for ourselves, and install Tabeel's son as its king." [7]But the LORD God says: It won't happen; it won't take place. [8]The chief of Aram is Damascus; the chief of Damascus is Rezin (in sixty-five more years Ephraim will be shattered as a nation); [9]the chief of Ephraim is Samaria; and the chief of Samaria is the son of Remaliah. If you don't believe this, you can't be trusted.'"

The sign of Immanuel

[10]Again the LORD spoke to Ahaz: [11]"Ask a sign from the LORD your God. Make it as deep as the grave[q] or as high as heaven."

[12]But Ahaz said, "I won't ask; I won't test the LORD."

[13]Then Isaiah said, "Listen, house of David! Isn't it enough for you to be tiresome for people that you are also tiresome before my God? [14]Therefore, the Lord will give you a sign. The young woman is pregnant and is about to give birth to a son, and she will name him Immanuel.[r] [15]He will eat butter and honey, and learn to reject evil and choose good. [16]Before the boy learns to reject evil and choose good, the land of the two kings you dread will be abandoned. [17]The LORD will bring upon you, upon your people, and upon your families days unlike any that have come since the day Ephraim broke away from Judah—the king of Assyria."

The devastated land

[18]On that day, the LORD will whistle for the flies from the remotest streams of Egypt and for the bees that are in the land of Assyria. [19]They will come and settle in the steep ravines, in the cracks of the cliffs, in all the thornbushes, and in all the watering holes.

[20]On that day, the Lord will shave with a razor hired from beyond the Euphrates—with the king of Assyria—the head and the pubic hair, and will cut off the beard as well.

[21]On that day, one will raise a young cow and two sheep [22]and will eat butter because of the abundance of milk, for all who remain in the land will eat butter and honey.

[23]On that day, there will be thorns and thistles in every place where a thousand vines worth a thousand silver shekels once grew. [24]Only those with bows and arrows will go there, because the entire land will become thorns and thistles. [25]As for the hills that were once farmed with hoes, you won't go there for fear of the thorns and thistles. They will become places where cattle are turned loose and sheep wander.

Isaiah's testimonies

8 The LORD said to me, "Take a large tablet, and write on it in ordinary letters,[s] For Maher-shalal-hash-baz.[t] [2]Summon trusted people, Uriah the priest and Zechariah, Jeberechiah's son, to witness it."

[q]Heb *Sheol* [r]Or *God is with us* [s]Heb uncertain [t]Or *spoil hastens, plunder hurries*

AHAZ

Judean king from the 8th century BCE, under whom Judah became an Assyrian vassal. According to 2 Kings 16:2, Ahaz succeeded his father Jotham when he was 20 and reigned for 16 years, thought to be 735 to 715, although some prefer 743 to 727. Following standard formulas, 2 Kings 16 opens with the indictment that "He didn't do what was right in the LORD's eyes" (v. 2). Instead of emulating his ancestor David, Ahaz followed the northern kings and the pagan pre-Israelite inhabitants of the land by sacrificing his son and worshipping at unholy religious shrines (2 Kgs 16:3-4).

[3] I then had sex with the prophetess, and she became pregnant and gave birth to a son. Then the LORD said to me, "Name him Maher-shalal-hash-baz. [4] Before the boy knows how to say 'my father' and 'my mother,' the wealth of Damascus and the spoil of Samaria will be carried away before the king of Assyria."

[5] The LORD spoke again to me: [6] Since this people has rejected the waters of Shiloah that flow gently, and instead rejoices over[u] Rezin and Remaliah's son—[7] therefore, look, the Lord is raising up against them the powerful floodwaters of the Euphrates, the king of Assyria and all his glory. It will rise up over all its channels, overflowing all its banks, [8] and sweep into Judah, flooding, overflowing, and reaching up to the neck. But God is with us;[v] the span of his wings will cover the width of the land.

[9] Unite[w] yourselves, peoples,
and be shattered!
Listen, all distant places of the earth!
Prepare to be shattered!
Prepare to be shattered!
[10] Create a plan, but be frustrated!
Speak a word, but it won't stand,
for God is with us.[x]

[11] The LORD spoke to me, taking hold of me and warning me not to walk in the way of this people: [12] Don't call conspiracy all that this people calls conspiracy. Don't fear what they fear, and don't be terrified. [13] It is the LORD of heavenly forces whom you should hold sacred, whom you should fear, and whom you should hold in awe.

[14] God will become a sanctuary—
but he will be a stone to trip over
and a rock to stumble on
for the two houses of Israel;
a trap and a snare
for those living in Jerusalem.
[15] Many of them will stumble and fall,
and be broken, snared, and captured.

[16] Bind up the testimony; seal up the teaching among my disciples. [17] I will wait for the LORD, who has hidden his face from the house of Jacob, and I will hope in God.

[18] Look! I and the children the LORD gave me are signs and wonders in Israel from the LORD of heavenly forces, who lives on Mount Zion.

[19] If they say to you: "Consult the ghosts and the spirits that chirp and mutter. (Shouldn't a people consult its gods?) Consult the dead on behalf of the living [20] for instruction and for testimony"—they will surely say such things, but they will never see the dawn.[y]

[21] They will pass through the land,[z] dejected and hungry, and when they are hungry, they will be enraged and will curse their king and God. They will turn toward heaven [22] and look to the earth, but they will see only distress and darkness, random movement, and the anguish and doom of banishment.[a]

A great light

9 [b] Nonetheless, those who were in distress won't be exhausted. At an earlier time, God cursed the land of Zebulun and the land of Naphtali, but later he glorified the way of the sea, the far side of the Jordan, and the Galilee of the nations.[c]

[2] [d] The people walking in darkness
have seen a great light.
On those living in a pitch-dark land,
light has dawned.
[3] You have made the nation great;
you have increased its joy.
They rejoiced before you
as with joy at the harvest,
as those who divide plunder rejoice.
[4] As on the day of Midian,
you've shattered the yoke
that burdened them,
the staff on their shoulders,
and the rod of their oppressor.
[5] Because every boot
of the thundering warriors,
and every garment rolled in blood
will be burned, fuel for the fire.
[6] A child is born to us,
a son is given to us,
and authority will be on his shoulders.

[u] Or *melts before* [v] Heb *Immanuel* [w] Heb uncertain [x] Heb *Immanuel* [y] Heb uncertain for 8:19-20 [z] Or *it* [a] Heb uncertain for 8:21-22 [b] 8:23 in Heb [c] Heb uncertain [d] 9:1 in Heb

He will be named
Wonderful Counselor, Mighty God,
Eternal Father, Prince of Peace.
⁷ There will be vast authority
and endless peace
for David's throne and for his kingdom,
establishing and sustaining it
with justice and righteousness
now and forever.
The zeal of the LORD of heavenly forces
will do this.

God's hand still stretched out

⁸ The Lord sent a word against Jacob;
it fell upon Israel;
⁹ the people all knew it—
Ephraim and the one
who rules in Samaria.
But with a proud and arrogant heart
they said,
¹⁰ "Bricks have fallen,
but let's rebuild with stones.
Sycamores were cut down,
but let's replace them with cedars."
¹¹ So the LORD raised up their foes
against them,ᵉ
and stirred up their enemies—
¹² Aram from the east and the Philistines
from the west—
and they devoured Israel
with an open mouth.
Even then God's anger didn't turn away;
God's hand was still extended.

¹³ But the people didn't turn
to the one who struck them.
They didn't seek
the LORD of heavenly forces.
¹⁴ So the LORD cut off head and tail,
palm branch and reed
from Israel in one day.
¹⁵ (Elders and celebrities are the head;
prophets who teach lies are the tail.)
¹⁶ But this people's leaders
were misleading,
and those being led were confused.
¹⁷ So the Lord showed their youth no pity,
and showed their orphans and widows
no mercy;

for everyone was godless and evil;
every mouth spoke nonsense.
Even then God's anger didn't turn away;
God's hand was still extended.

¹⁸ Wickedness burned like fire,
devouring thorn and thistle.
It kindled the thickets of the forest;
they swirled in rising smoke.
¹⁹ The land was scorched by the rage of
the LORD of heavenly forces;
the people were like fuel for the fire.
Not one person pitied another:
²⁰ they consumed on the right,
but remained hungry;
devoured on the left,
and weren't satisfied.
They devoured the flesh
of their own children.ᶠ
²¹ Manasseh devoured Ephraim
and Ephraim Manasseh;
together they turned against Judah.
Even then God's anger didn't turn away;
God's hand was still extended.

Wicked laws

10 Doom to those
who pronounce wicked decrees,
and keep writing harmful laws
² to deprive the needy of their rights
and to rob the poor among my people
of justice;
to make widows their loot;
to steal from orphans!
³ What will you do
on the day of punishment
when disaster comes from far away?
To whom will you flee for help;
where will you stash your wealth?
⁴ How will you avoid
crouching among the prisoners
and falling among the slain?
Even so, God's anger hasn't turned away;
God's hand is still extended.

Assyria as God's punishing weapon

⁵ Doom to Assyria, rod of my anger,
in whose hand is the staff of my fury!
⁶ Against a godless nation I send him;

ᵉOr the enemies of Rezin ᶠOr arm

against an infuriating people
I direct him to seize spoil,
  to steal plunder,
and to trample them
  like mud in the streets.
⁷ But he has other plans;
  he schemes in secret;
  destruction is on his mind,
  extermination of nation after nation.
⁸ He says: Aren't my commanders all kings?
⁹ Isn't Calno like Carchemish?
  Isn't Hamath like Arpad?
  Isn't Samaria like Damascus?
¹⁰ Just as I took control
  of idolatrous kingdoms
  with more images
  than Jerusalem and Samaria,
¹¹ just as I did to Samaria
  and her false gods,
  won't I also do this to Jerusalem
  and her idols?
¹²But when the Lord has finished all this work on Mount Zion and in Jerusalem, he will punishᵍ the Assyrian king's arrogant actions and the boasting of his haughty eyes.
¹³ He said, "By my own strength
  I have achieved it,
  and by my wisdom, since I'm so clever.
  I disregarded national boundaries;
  I raided their treasures;
  I knocked down their rulers like a bull.
¹⁴ My hand found the wealth of the peoples
  as if it were in a nest.

Just as one gathers abandoned eggs,
  I have gathered the entire earth;
  no creature fluttered a wing
  or opened a mouth to chirp."
¹⁵ Will the ax glorify itself
  over the one who chops with it?
  Or will the saw magnify itself
  over its user?
As if a rod could wave the one who lifts it!
  As if a staff could lift up
  the one not made of wood!
¹⁶ Therefore,
  the LORD God of heavenly forces
  will make the well-fed people waste away;
  and among his officials,
  a blaze will burn like scorching fire.
¹⁷ The light of Israel will become a fire,
  its holy one a flame,
  which will burn and devour
  its thorns and thistles
  in a single day.
¹⁸ Its abundant forest and farmland
  will be finished completely,ʰ
  as when a sick person wastes away;
¹⁹ its forest's remaining trees
  will be no more than a child can count.

A few will return

²⁰On that day, what's left of Israel and the survivors of the house of Jacob will no longer depend on the one who beat them. Instead, they will faithfully depend on the

---

ᵍOr *I will punish* ʰSyr, Vulg *body and soul* (that is, *completely*); MT *he will finish*

ASSYRIA AND BABYLONIA

Two Mesopotamian kingdoms, both named after their capital cities, that exercised a profound cultural influence on Israel while destroying its political independence. Both kingdoms were located in what is now Iraq. Assyria predates the OT times, but it enters OT history mostly through the Neo-Assyrian Empire beginning around 934 BCE. Babylonia became the more dominant power throughout the 7th century and continued to hold sway over Judah and surrounding areas until its defeat by the Persian Empire in 539 BCE. Thus, for most of Israel's and Judah's monarchies, either Assyria or Babylonia represented the great imperial power of the world, with resources and armies far exceeding the strength of Israel or Judah.

LORD, the holy one of Israel. ²¹A few will return, what's left of Jacob, to the mighty God. ²²Although your people, Israel, were like the sand of the sea, only a few survivors will return. The end is announced, overflowing with justice. ²³Yes, destruction has been announced; the LORD God of heavenly forces will carry it out against the entire land.

²⁴Therefore, the LORD God of heavenly forces says: My people who live in Zion, don't fear Assyria, which strikes you with the rod and raises its staff against you as Egypt did. ²⁵In a very short time my fury will end, and my anger at the world will be finished.[i]

²⁶ Therefore, the LORD of heavenly forces
　　will crack a whip against Assyria,
　　as when he struck Midian
　　　at the rock of Oreb.
　　He will raise a rod over the sea,
　　　as he did in Egypt.
²⁷ On that day, God will remove
　　the burden from your shoulder
　　and destroy the yoke on your neck.[j]

The exalted laid low

　　He has gone up from Samaria,
²⁸ come against Aiath,
　　passed to Migron.
　　At Michmash he stored his equipment.
²⁹ They crossed at the pass:
　　"We'll camp at Geba!"
　　Ramah trembles; Gibeah of Saul has fled.
³⁰ Cry aloud, Daughter Gallim!
　　Listen, Laishah! Answer her, Anathoth!
³¹ Madmenah has flown.
　　Gebim's inhabitants sought refuge.
³² This very day he will stand at Nob
　　and shake his fist[k]
　　　at Daughter Zion's mountain,
　　the hill of Jerusalem!
³³ Look! The LORD God of heavenly forces
　　is chopping off the branches
　　　with terrible power.
　　The loftiest ones
　　　are about to be cut down
　　and the exalted laid low.

³⁴ He will strike down the forest thickets
　　with an ax,
　　and mighty Lebanon will fall.

A shoot from Jesse's stump

11 ¹ A shoot will grow up
　　from the stump of Jesse;
　　a branch will sprout[l] from his roots.
² The LORD's spirit will rest upon him,
　　a spirit of wisdom
　　　and understanding,
　　a spirit of planning and strength,
　　a spirit of knowledge
　　　and fear of the LORD.
³ He will delight in fearing the LORD.
　　He won't judge by appearances,
　　nor decide by hearsay.
⁴ He will judge the needy
　　with righteousness,
　　and decide with equity
　　　for those who suffer in the land.
　　He will strike the violent[m]
　　　with the rod of his mouth;
　　by the breath of his lips
　　　he will kill the wicked.
⁵ Righteousness will be
　　the belt around his hips,
　　and faithfulness
　　　the belt around his waist.
⁶ The wolf will live with the lamb,
　　and the leopard will lie down
　　　with the young goat;
　　the calf and the young lion
　　　will feed[n] together,
　　and a little child will lead them.
⁷ The cow and the bear will graze.
　　Their young will lie down together,
　　and a lion will eat straw like an ox.
⁸ A nursing child
　　will play over the snake's hole;
　　toddlers will reach
　　　right over the serpent's den.
⁹ They won't harm or destroy
　　anywhere on my holy mountain.
　　The earth will surely be filled
　　　with the knowledge of the LORD,
　　just as the water covers the sea.

---

[i]Heb uncertain　[j]Or and his yoke from your neck, and a yoke will be destroyed because of fatness　[k]Or wave his hand　[l]LXX, Vulg; MT bear fruit　[m]Or land　[n]Correction; MT and the calf

A signal to the peoples

¹⁰On that day, the root of Jesse will stand as a signal to the peoples. The nations will seek him out, and his dwelling will be glorious.

¹¹On that day, the Lord will extend his hand a second time to reclaim the survivors of God's people who are left from Assyria and from Egypt, from Pathros, Cush, Elam, Shinar, Hamath, and from the coastlands° of the sea.

¹² God will raise a signal for the nations
    and gather the outcast men of Israel.
    God will collect
      the dispersed women of Judah
      from the four corners of the earth.
¹³ Ephraim's jealousy will cease,
    and Judah's harassment
      will be eliminated.
    Ephraim won't be jealous of Judah,
    and Judah won't harass Ephraim.
¹⁴ But they will swoop down
    on the slopes of Philistia to the west;
    together they will plunder
      the people to the east.
    Edom and Moab will be under their power,
    and the Ammonites
      will be their subjects.
¹⁵The Lord will split the tongue of the Egyptian sea. God will wave a hand over the Euphrates with a powerfulᵖ wind and break it into seven streams so that it can be crossed in sandals. ¹⁶Then there will be a highway from Assyria for the survivors of God's people who are left from Assyria, just as there was for Israel on the day they went up from the land of Egypt.

°Or *islands* ᵖHeb uncertain

Hymn of trust

12 You will say on that day:
    "I thank you, Lord.
    Though you were angry with me,
      your anger turned away
      and you comforted me.
² God is indeed my salvation;
    I will trust and won't be afraid.
    Yah, the Lord, is my strength
      and my shield;
    he has become my salvation."

³ You will draw water with joy
    from the springs of salvation.
⁴ And you will say on that day:
    "Thank the Lord; call on God's name;
    proclaim God's deeds
      among the peoples;
    declare that God's name is exalted.
⁵ Sing to the Lord,
    who has done glorious things;
    proclaim this throughout all the earth."
⁶ Shout and sing for joy, city of Zion,
    because the holy one of Israel
    is great among you.

Babylon falls

13 An oracle about Babylon, which Isaiah, Amoz's son, saw.
² On a bare mountain raise a signal;
    cry aloud to them;
    wave a hand;
    let them enter the officials' gates.
³ I have commanded my holy ones;
    I have called my warriors,
    my proud, jubilant ones,
    to execute my wrath.

JESSE

David's father. He was from Bethlehem, presumably from the Ephrathah clan in the tribe of Judah (1 Chron 2:50), although the only genealogy in the OT with a clear connection from Judah to David is probably the Chronicler's composition (1 Chron 2:3-17; see also Matt 1:3-6; Luke 3:31-33). Jesse is also identified as the grandson of Ruth the Moabite (Ruth 4:17-22), which may be why David chose Moab as a refuge for his parents (1 Sam 22:3-4).

⁴ Listen!�q A roar on the mountains
　　like that of a great crowd.
　Listen! An uproar of kingdoms,
　　of nations coming together.
　The LORD of heavenly forces
　　is mustering an army for battle.
⁵ They are coming from a distant land,
　　from the faraway heavens,
　　the LORD and the instruments of his
　　fury, to destroy the whole land.

⁶ Wail, for the day of the LORD is near.
　　Like destruction from the Almightyʳ
　　it will come.
⁷ Then all hands will fall limp;
　　every human heart will melt,
⁸ and they will be terrified.
　Like a woman writhing in labor,
　　they will be seized by spasms and agony.
　They will look at each other aghast,
　　their faces blazing.

⁹ Look, the day of the LORD is coming
　　with cruel rage and burning anger,
　　making the earth a ruin,
　　and wiping out its sinners.

¹⁰ Heaven's stars and constellations
　　won't show their light.
　The sun will be dark when it rises;
　　the moon will no longer shine.
¹¹ I will bring disaster
　　upon the world for its evil,
　　and bring their own sin upon the wicked.
　I will end the pride of the insolent,
　　and the conceit of tyrants I will lay low.
¹² I will make humans scarcer than fine gold;
　　people rarer than the gold of Ophir.
¹³ I will rattle the heavens;
　　the earth will shake loose
　　　from its place—because of the rage
　　of the LORD of heavenly forces
　　on the day his anger burns.
¹⁴ They will be like hunted gazelles,
　　like sheep without a shepherd;
　　all will turn to their own people
　　and flee to their own lands.
¹⁵ Whoever is found will be stabbed;
　　whoever is caught will fall by the sword.
¹⁶ Their infants will be crushed
　　before their eyes;
　　their houses plundered,
　　their women raped.

�q Heb lacks Listen!　ʳ Heb Shaddai or Mountain One

DAY OF THE LORD

The origin of the phrase "the day of the Lord" is unclear, although it goes back at least as far as the prophet Amos (Amos 5:18, 20). It typically refers to a dramatic intervention of God in history, a judgment that will condemn God's enemies and save God's people. In Amos, however, many within Israel are disloyal, so the prophesied appearance of God will mean woe for them, too. Thereafter, "the day of the Lord" is darkness and judgment not for Israel's enemies only (Isa 13:6-9; 34:8-12; Jer 46:9-12; Ezek 30:1-9; Obad 15-18; Zeph 2:1-15), but also for faithless Israel (Isa 2:6–3:15; Ezek 7:19; Joel 1:1–2:17; Zeph 1:14-18). So proclamation of "the day of the Lord" more often serves to condemn and warn than to comfort, although it can do both (Zech 14:1-21; Mal 3:13–4:6).

Scholars dispute how literally the ancients understood the catastrophic prophecies associated with the day of the Lord. Isaiah 13:9-10 envisages stars and constellations going dark and the sun and moon not giving their light (cf. Joel 3:15). Such cosmic forecasts, whether they occur in the OT or the NT, can be understood either as poetic or factual.

[17] Look! I'm rousing the Medes against them;
  the Medes pay no mind to silver,
   no desire for gold.
[18] Their bows will smash youths;
  they will be merciless to newborns,
   pitiless to children.
[19] So Babylon, a jewel among kingdoms,
  the Chaldeans' splendor and pride,
  will be like Sodom and Gomorrah,
   destroyed by God.
[20] No one will ever resettle
  or live there for generations.
  No Arab will camp there;
   no shepherds will rest flocks there.
[21] Wildcats will rest there;
  houses will be filled with owls.
  Ostriches will live there,
   and goat demons will dance there.
[22] Hyenas will howl in its strongholds,
  and jackals in its luxurious palaces.
  Babylon's[s] time is coming soon;
   its days won't drag on.

Compassion for Jacob

14 The LORD will have compassion on Jacob, will again choose Israel, and will give them rest in their own land. Immigrants will join them, and attach themselves to the house of Jacob. [2] The peoples will take them and will bring them to their own place. The house of Israel will possess them as male and female slaves in the LORD's land, making captives of their captors and ruling their oppressors.

Mockery of a tyrant

[3] When the LORD has given you rest from pain and trouble and from the hard labor that you perform, [4] you will take up this taunt against the king of Babylon:
  How the oppressor[t] has ceased!
  How the flood[u] has receded!
[5] The LORD has broken
  the staff of the wicked,
  the rod of tyrants
   [6] that struck peoples in rage
  with ceaseless blows,
  that ruled nations with anger,
  with relentless aggression.

[7] All the earth rests quietly,
  then it breaks into song.
[8] Even the cypresses rejoice over you,
  the cedars of Lebanon:
  "Since you were laid low,
   no logger comes up against us!"

[9] The underworld[v] beneath
  becomes restless to greet your arrival.
  It awakens the ghosts,
  all the leaders of earth;
  it makes the kings of the nations
   rise from their thrones.
[10] All of them speak and say to you:
  "Even you've become weak like we are!
   You are the same as us!"
[11] Your majesty has been brought down
  to the underworld,[w]
  along with the sound of your harps.
  Under you is a bed of maggots,
   and worms are your blanket.

[12] How you've fallen from heaven,
  morning star, son of dawn!
  You are cut down to earth,
   helpless on your back!
[13] You said to yourself,
  I will climb up to heaven;
  above God's stars,
   I will raise my throne.
  I'll sit on the mount of assembly,
   on the heights of Zaphon.
[14] I'll go up to the cloud tops;
   I'll be like the Most High!
[15] But down to the underworld[x]
  you are brought,
   to the depths of the pit.

[16] Those who see you will stare at you;
  they will examine you closely:
  "Is this the man who rattled the earth,
   who shook kingdoms,
   [17] who made the world a wasteland
  and tore down its cities,
  and wouldn't let
   his prisoners go home?"
[18] All the kings of the nations
  lie down honored,
   all of them, each in his own tomb.

---

[s]Heb *Its* [t]Heb uncertain [u]DSS (1QIsa[a]), LXX, Syr, Tg; MT *fury* [v]Heb *Sheol* [w]Heb *Sheol* [x]Heb *Sheol*

¹⁹ But you are cast away
    from your own grave
    like a rejected branch,
    covered by the dead
    and those pierced by the sword—
    who go down to the stony pit—
    like a trampled corpse.
²⁰ You won't join them in burial,
    for you destroyed your own land;
    you killed your own people.
    Such evil offspring
    will never be mentioned again!
²¹Prepare a place to slaughter his sons
for the guilt of their father. Don't let them
arise to take over the earth or fill the world
with cities.

²²I will arise against them, says the
LORD of heavenly forces. I will cut off Babylon's renown and remnant, offshoot and
offspring. ²³I will make it the home of her-
ons, a swampland. I will sweep it away with
the broom of destruction, says the LORD of
heavenly forces.

Promise for oppressed Judah

²⁴ The LORD of heavenly forces
    has promised:
    As I intended, so it will be;
    and as I have planned,
    so it will happen:
²⁵ I will break Assyria in my land;
    on my mountains I will trample it
    and remove its yoke from my people;ʸ
    his burden will be taken
    from their shoulders.
²⁶ This is the plan that has been made
    for all the earth;
    this is the hand
    extended over all the nations.
²⁷ The LORD of heavenly forces
    has created a plan;
    who can stop it?
    God's hand is extended;
    who will stop it?

An oracle concerning the Philistines

²⁸This oracle came in the year of King
Ahaz's death:
²⁹ Don't rejoice, all you Philistines,
    that the rod that struck you is broken,

    because from the snake's root
        a viper will grow,
    and it will produce a winged creature.
³⁰ The oldest offspring of the poor
        will graze;
    their needy will lie down secure.
    But he will starve your offspring
        to death,
    and murder all who remain.
³¹ Wail, gate! Cry out, city!
    Melt in terror, all you Philistines!
    Smoke is coming from the north;
    there is no straggler in its ranks.ᶻ
³² What will one say
    to that nation's messengers?
    The LORD has founded Zion;
    the oppressed among God's people
        will find refuge there.

Concerning Moab

15 An oracle about Moab.
    Ar was devastated in a night;
    Moab is ruined!
    Kir was devastated in a night;
    Moab is ruined!
² Dibon has gone up to the temple,
    to the shrines to weep.ᵃ
    Moab wails over Nebo and over Medeba.
    Every head is shaved,
    every beard cut off.
³ In its streets they wear mourning clothes;
    on its rooftops and in its plazas,
    everyone wails and falls down weeping.
⁴ Heshbon and Elealeh cry out;
    as far as Jahaz their voice is heard.
    The armed men of Moab shout,
    spirits trembling.
⁵ My heart cries out for Moab.
    Its fugitives flee to Zoar,
    to Eglath-shelishiyah.ᵇ
    At the ascent of Luhith,
    each will go up with weeping.
    On the road to Horonaim,
    they will raise a piercing cry.
⁶ The waters of Nimrim are used up.
    Grass has withered;
    vegetation is dead;
    greenery is gone.
⁷ Therefore, they carry
    what they had stored up,

ʸOr them   ᶻHeb uncertain   ᵃHeb uncertain   ᵇHeb uncertain

all their provisions
　to the Valley of the Willows.
⁸ An outcry sounds
　within the borders of Moab,
　as far as Eglaim, a cry of distress,
　as far as Beer-elim, a cry of distress.
⁹ The waters of Dibon are full of blood.
　But I will bring still more upon Dibon:
　a lion for Moab's survivors,
　for the remaining few in the land.

16 Send lambs to the ruler of the land,ᶜ
　from Sela through the desert
　to the mountain of Daughter Zion.
² The daughters of Moab
　at the fords of the Arnon

ᶜHeb uncertain

are like orphaned birds
　pushed from the nest.
³ Consider carefully, act justly;
　at high noon
　provide your shade like night.
Hide the outcasts;
　keep the fugitives hidden.
⁴ Let the outcasts of Moab
　live among you.
Be a hiding place for them
　from the destroyer.
When the oppressor is no more,
　when destruction has ceased,
　when the trampler has vanished
　from the land,

HAIR

Semitic men are depicted in Egyptian art as having curly hair of moderate length. They would have favored the Mesopotamians, who described themselves as "the black-headed people" in reference to their typical hair color.

The norm was for men to cut or clip their hair periodically, though probably more often than Absalom, who reportedly cut his hair once each year (2 Sam 14:25-27). Persons who made nazirite vows demonstrated devotion to God by letting their hair and beards (for men) grow long, to be shaved when the votive period was completed (Num 6:5, 18), a practice that continued into the NT period (Acts 21:24). Some appear to have lived as lifelong nazirites: Samson's long hair was described as a sign of lifelong devotion (Judg 13:5) and a key to his superhuman strength (Judg 16:17-20). Priests were prohibited from shaving bald spots on their heads and from trimming the corners of their beards (Lev 21:5), perhaps to preserve a distinct appearance.

New Testament evidence suggests that women typically wore their hair long. The woman who anointed Jesus' feet with oil dried his feet with her hair (Luke 7:38). Paul reflected a belief that it was shameful for a woman to shave her head (1 Cor 11:5-6) and considered it a lesson of nature that men should maintain short hair rather than wearing it long, like women (1 Cor 11:14-15).

Sorrow or the changing of one's heart or life was expressed by shaving the head (Isa 15:2), pulling out the hair (Ezra 9:3), or imposing dust or ashes (Josh 7:6; Job 42:6; Ezek 27:30). Prophets used the image of shaving the hair as a metaphor for judgment. Isaiah predicted a time of baldness instead of "styled hair" (Isa 3:24) and predicted that Yahweh would shave the Israelites with an Assyrian razor (Isa 7:20). Ezekiel symbolically shaved his head and beard, dividing the hair as a sign of impending judgment (Ezek 5:1-4).

⁵ a throne will be established
  based on goodness,
    and someone will sit faithfully on it
      in David's dwelling^d—
  a judge who seeks justice
    and timely righteousness.

⁶ We have heard of Moab's pride,
  his great pride,
    his outrageous pride and arrogance,
      his empty boasting.
⁷ Therefore, let Moab wail;
  let everyone wail for Moab.
  Let them moan, utterly stricken,
    for the raisin cakes of Kir-hareseth.
⁸ The fields of Heshbon languish.
  The vines of Sibmah,
    whose honored grapes
      overpowered masters of nations,
  had reached as far as Jazer
    and strayed to the desert.
  Their tendrils spread out
    and crossed the sea.
⁹ Therefore,
  I will weep with Jazer's weeping
    for the vines of Sibmah.
  I will drench you with my tears,
    Heshbon and Elealeh.
  Cheers have fallen silent
    concerning your summer fruit
    and your grain harvest.
¹⁰ Joy and happiness have been harvested
    from the farmland,
  and in the vineyards no one sings,
    no one shouts.
  No treader crushes grapes
    in the wine vats;
  I have brought the cheers to an end.
¹¹ Therefore, my heart plays sadly
  like a harp for Moab,
    my inner being for Kir-heres.
¹² Even if Moab presents himself,
  and Moab wears himself out
    going to the shrine,
  and comes to his sanctuary to pray,
    he won't prevail.
¹³ This is the word that the LORD had spoken concerning Moab long ago. ¹⁴ But now

the LORD has said: In three years, like the years of a hired worker, the glory of Moab, with all its great multitude, will dwindle. The small remnant will be few and feeble.

Concerning Damascus and Ephraim

17 An oracle about Damascus.
  Look! Damascus is finished as a city;
    it will become a fallen ruin.
² The villages of Aroer
  are abandoned forever.^e
  They will be pastures for flocks,^f
    which will lie down undisturbed.
³ Ephraim's security will cease,
    as will Damascus' rule.
  What's left of Aram will resemble
    the glory of the Israelites,
  says the LORD of heavenly forces.

⁴ On that day, Jacob's glory will dwindle;
    his sleek body will waste away.
⁵ It will be as when harvesters gather grain.
    God will harvest armfuls at a time,
  like one who gathers grain
    in the Rephaim Valley.
⁶ Only remaining bits are left,
    like an olive tree that has been shaken:
  two or three olives on the highest branch;
    four or five on a fruitful twig,
  says the LORD God of Israel.

⁷ On that day, people will have regard
    for their maker,
  and their eyes will look
    to the holy one of Israel.
⁸ They will have no regard for altars,
    the work of their hands,
  or look to what their fingers made:
    sacred poles^g and incense stands.
⁹ On that day, their strong cities will be like those abandoned by the Hivites and the Amorites;^h abandoned because of the Israelites. They will be a wasteland,
¹⁰ because you forgot the God who saves you,
    and didn't remember the rock
      who shelters you.
  Therefore, plant your pleasant plants,
    and set out exotic sprouts;

---

^dOr *tent* ^eCf LXX; MT *The cities of Aroer are abandoned* ^fOr *For flocks they will be* ^gHeb *asherim*, possibly objects devoted to the goddess Asherah ^hLXX; MT *like the abandonment of the forest and the bough*

[11] make them grow the day you plant them,
  and make them bloom
    the morning you start them.
But the harvest will disappear on a day
  of sickness and incurable pain.

[12] Doom to the raging of many peoples;
  like the thundering seas they thunder.
  Doom to the roar of nations,
  like the roaring of mighty waters.
[13] Nations roar
  like the roaring of rushing waters.
But God will rebuke them,
  and they will flee far away,
  pursued like chaff
    by wind in the mountains,
  like tumbleweeds before a storm.
[14] In the evening, there is terror;
  but before morning it is gone.
This is the fate of those who loot us,
  the destiny of those who rob us.

Concerning Cush

18 Doom to the land of winged ships,
  beyond the rivers of Cush
[2] that sends messengers by sea,
  reed vessels on the water.
Go, swift messengers,

to a nation tall and clean-shaven,
  to a people feared near and far,
  a nation barbaric and oppressive,
  whose land the rivers divide.

[3] All you who inhabit the world,
  who live on earth,
  when a signal is raised on the
    mountains, you will see!
  When the trumpet blasts, you will hear!
[4] The LORD said to me:
  I will quietly watch from my own place,
  like the shimmering heat of sunshine,
  like a cloud's shade in the harvest heat.
[5] Before the harvest,
  when the bloom is finished,
  when the blossom is becoming
  a ripening fruit,
  God will cut the shoots
    with a pruning knife,
  and lop off the spreading branches.
[6] They will all be left to the mountain birds
  and to the beasts of the land.
The birds will eat them in summer,
  all the beasts of the land in winter.

[7] At that time, gifts will be brought
  to the LORD of heavenly forces

DAMASCUS

A city located ca. 150 mi. northeast of Jerusalem that became the capital of a powerful Aramean kingdom in the 10th to 8th centuries BCE. The city existed as a significant regional center into the Roman period. The Aramean kingdom centered in Damascus was one of the most dominant states in Syria-Palestine during the monarchical period, especially 900 to 730 BCE. The city appears in the NT as the location associated with the encounter of Saul of Tarsus with the risen Jesus. Damascus sits in one of the most fertile regions in Syria-Palestine and was known in the ancient world for its waters, gardens, and orchards (see 2 Kgs 5:12). Damascus had a powerful influence on Israel and Judah. The Umayyad Mosque in present-day Damascus, for example, likely stands on the ancient site of the temple of the god Hadad, after which Ahaz of Judah is said to have modeled an altar in Jerusalem (2 Kgs 16:10-16; cf. 2 Chron 28:22-23). The city often competed with Samaria for control of regions like Dan and Ramoth-Gilead and at times exercised political dominance over both Samaria and Jerusalem. At other times, Damascus was Israel's strongest ally against other foes.

from a tall and clean-shaven people
and from a people feared near and far,
a nation barbaric and oppressive,
whose land the rivers divide,
to the place of the name of
the LORD of heavenly forces,
to Mount Zion.

Concerning Egypt

19 An oracle about Egypt.
Look! The LORD is riding
upon a swift cloud,
and is coming to Egypt.
Egypt's idols will tremble before God;
the Egyptians' hearts will melt
within them.
² I will stir up Egyptian against Egyptian,
and they will fight,
one against another,
neighbor against neighbor,
city against city,
kingdom against kingdom.
³ Egypt's spirit will fail from within;
I will frustrate their plans.
They will consult the idols and spirits
and ghosts and fortune-tellers.
⁴ I will hand Egypt over to a harsh master;
a strong king will rule them,
says the LORD God of heavenly forces.

⁵ The waters of the sea will dry up;
the river will be parched and bare.
⁶ The rivers will stink;
the streams will shrink and dry;
reeds and rushes will decay.
⁷ Grass around the Nile,
the grass at the mouth of the Nile,

and all the sown land of the Nile
will dry up, blow away,
and be no more.
⁸ Those who fish will lament;
all who cast fishhooks in the Nile
will mourn,
and those who spread nets
on the water will pine away.
⁹ Workers with flax will be dismayed;
carders and weavers will grow pale.[i]
¹⁰ Makers of cloth will be crushed;
all who earn money
will become distressed.

¹¹ The officials of Tanis are fools;
the wisest of Pharaoh's counselors
give stupid advice.
How can you say to Pharaoh,
"I'm a wise person,
one of the ancient kings"?
¹² Where now are your wise ones?
Let them tell you,
let them inform you what
the LORD of heavenly forces
has planned concerning Egypt.
¹³ The officials of Tanis
have become fools;
the princes of Memphis are deluded;
the tribal chiefs have led Egypt astray.
¹⁴ The LORD has poured into them
a spirit of confusion.
They will make Egypt stumble
in everything it does,
just as a drunk stumbles in his vomit.
¹⁵ Neither head nor tail,
palm branch nor reed
will be able to do anything for Egypt.

[i] DSS (1QIsaᵃ)

CUSH

Cush, the ancestor of the nation that shares his name, appears in Genesis 10:6-9 and 1 Chronicles 1:8-10, where he is described as the eldest son of Noah's son Ham. He is presented as the ancestor of several significant North African tribes. In the Genesis account the major Mesopotamian kingdoms are also ascribed to his lineage. Cush is often conflated with modern Ethiopia, a land to the southeast of the biblical country.

Bless God's people

¹⁶On that day, the Egyptians will be like women and will tremble with terror before the hand that the LORD of heavenly forces will raise against them. ¹⁷Judah's land will become what the Egyptians dread; whenever anyone mentions it, they will be terrified because of the plans that the LORD of heavenly forces is making against them.

¹⁸On that day, there will be five cities in the land of Egypt that speak the language of Canaan and swear loyalty to the LORD of heavenly forces. One of them will be called "the city of the sun."ʲ

¹⁹On that day, there will be an altar to the LORD within the land of Egypt, and a standing stone for the LORD at its border. ²⁰It will be a sign and a witness to the LORD of heavenly forces in the land of Egypt. When they cry out to the LORD because of oppressors, God will send them a savior and defender to rescue them. ²¹The LORD will make himself known to the Egyptians; the Egyptians will know the LORD on that day. They will worship with sacrifices and offerings, making solemn promises to the LORD and fulfilling them. ²²The LORD will strike Egypt; striking and then healing. They will return to the LORD, who will hear their pleas and heal them.

²³On that day, there will be a highway from Egypt to Assyria. The Assyrians will come to Egypt, and the Egyptians to Assyria; and the Egyptians will worship with the Assyrians.

²⁴On that day, Israel will be the third along with Egypt and Assyria, a blessing at the center of the world. ²⁵The LORD of heavenly forces will pronounce this blessing: Bless Egypt my people, and Assyria my handiwork, and Israel my inheritance.

Isaiah naked and barefoot

20 In the year that Assyria's King Sargon sent his general to Ashdod, he fought against Ashdod and captured it. ²At that time the LORD had spoken through Isaiah, Amoz's son, "Go, take off the mourning clothes from your waist, and remove the shoes from your feet." And Isaiah did this, walking naked and barefoot.

³The LORD said, "Just as my servant Isaiah has walked naked and barefoot three years, as a sign and omen against Egypt and Cush, ⁴so will the king of Assyria lead the captives of Egypt and the exiles of Cush, both young and old, naked and barefoot, with buttocks bared, humiliating Egypt. ⁵They will be shattered and shamed because of Cush their hope, and because of Egypt their glory.

⁶"On that day, those who live on this coast will say, 'Look at those in whom we had hoped, to whom we fled for help and rescue from the king of Assyria. How then will we escape?'"

Fallen, fallen is Babylon

21 An oracle about the wilderness near the sea.

Like whirlwinds sweeping
  through the arid southern plain,
  it comes from the desert,
  from a fearsome land.
² A harsh vision was proclaimed to me:
  The betrayer betrays,
  and the destroyer destroys.
Go up, Elam! Lay siege, Media!
Put an end to all her groaning.
³ Therefore, I'm shaken to my core
  in anguish.
Pains have seized me
  like the pains of a woman in labor.
I'm too bent over to hear,
  too dismayed to see.
⁴ My heart pounds;
  convulsions overpower me.
He has turned my evening of pleasure
  into dread—
⁵ setting the table,
  spreading the cloth, eating, drinking.
"Arise, captains!
  Polish the shields."

⁶ The Lord said this to me:
  "Go, post a lookout
  to report what he sees.

ʲDSS (1QIsaᵃ), Tg, Vulg; Heb uncertain

[7] When he sees chariots, pairs of horsemen,
  donkey riders, camel riders,
  he should listen carefully,
  carefully, very carefully."

[8] Then the seer[k] called out:
  "Upon a watchtower, Lord,
  I'm standing all day;
  and upon my observation post
  I'm stationed throughout the night.
[9] Here they come:
  chariots, pairs of horsemen!"
One spoke up and said,
  "Fallen, fallen is Babylon,
  and all the images of her gods
  are shattered on the ground!"
[10] Oh, my downtrodden people,
  threshed on my threshing floor,
  what I heard from
  the LORD of heavenly forces,
  the God of Israel, I reported to you.

[k] DSS (1QIsaᵃ), Syr; MT *a lion* [l] LXX *Edom*

A mysterious dialogue
[11] An oracle about Dumah.[l]
Someone is calling to me from Seir:
  "Guard, how long is the night?
  Guard, how long is the night?"
[12] The guard said,
  "Morning has come, but it is still night.
  If you must inquire, inquire;
  come back again."

[13] An oracle about the desert.
  In the woods,
  in the desert where you camp,
  caravans of the Dedanites
[14] meet the thirsty with water;
  inhabitants of the land of Tema
  greet the refugees with bread.
[15] They have fled from swords,
  from the drawn sword,
  from the bent bow
  and from the intensity of battle.

KEDAR

Meaning "to be dark, darken." Kedar was the second of Ishmael's twelve sons (Gen 25:13; 1 Chr 1:29). The Kedarites were the tribal groups in northern Arabia that were regarded as Kedar's descendants according to the OT. They flourished from the 8th to the 5th centuries BCE and were important to the Assyrian, Neo-Babylonian, and Persian empires for dominating the trade routes that ran through northern Arabia to the Mediterranean and Egypt.

In the context of a more general proclamation of disaster for peoples in Arabia, Isaiah 21:16-17 predicts the economic and military decline of Kedar within a year. The date of the text, and so the historical situation envisioned, cannot be determined. Similarly, Jeremiah 49:28-29 proclaims that God has summoned King Nebuchadnezzar and the armies of Babylon to destroy Kedar, taking away their valuable flocks and herds and turning their territory into deserted wastelands. The language calls to mind the terror inspired by the surprise attack by military forces on small, unfortified villages and clusters of tents (vv. 29-30). The background for this text may be Babylon's attack on the Arabs in 599 to 598 BCE, when Nebuchadnezzar punished Kedar for not assisting him in an earlier campaign. The text underscores the importance of Kedar for the trade routes extending from Babylon to the Mediterranean and the interest of the Babylonian king in maintaining their cooperation for his military operations in the West.

¹⁶ So the Lord said to me: Within a year, according to the number of years for which a laborer is hired, all the glory of Kedar will end; ¹⁷ there will be few Kedarite archers remaining. The LORD God of Israel has spoken.

Jerusalemites rebuked

22 An oracle about the Valley of Vision.
What is wrong with you,
   that you have all gone
   up to the rooftops,
² you who are filled with noise,
   you roaring city, you party town?
Your dead weren't slaughtered
   by the sword;
   they didn't die in battle.
³ All your leaders escaped together
   but were captured
     without a single bow shot.
All your escapees were bound together,
   even though they fled far away.ᵐ
⁴ Therefore, I said, "Don't look at me;
   let me weep bitterly.
Don't try to comfort me
   about the destruction
     of my dearly loved people."
⁵ The LORD God of heavenly forces
   has a day of tumult and trampling
   and turmoil in the Valley of Vision,
   a breaking down of walls,
   a cry for help to the mountains.
⁶ Elam carried the quiver
   with chariots and horsemen,
   and Kir uncovered the shield.
⁷ Your finest valleys
   were filled with chariots,
   and horsemen doggedly
     guarded the gate.
⁸ Judah's covering has been stripped away.

On that day, you trusted the weapons
   in the Forest House.
⁹ You observed the many broken
   defenses in David's City,
   and you collected
   the waters of the lower pool.
¹⁰ You counted Jerusalem's houses,
   and you tore down houses
   to fortify the wall.

¹¹ You made a reservoir between the walls
   for the water of the earlier pool.
But you didn't trust its maker;
   you didn't consider the one
   who planned it long ago.

¹² The LORD God of heavenly forces
   called on that day
   for weeping and mourning,
   and shaven heads,
   and wearing of mourning clothes.
¹³ But instead there was
   fun and frivolity,
   killing of cattle
   and slaughtering of sheep,
   eating of meat and drinking of wine:
   "Eat and drink! Tomorrow we will die!"
¹⁴ But the LORD of heavenly forces
   has revealed in my hearing:
This iniquity won't
   be forgiven you until you die, says
   the LORD God of heavenly forces.

An administrator rebuked

¹⁵ The LORD God of heavenly forces says,
   Go now to this official, to Shebna,
   who is in charge of the house,
   and say to him:
¹⁶ What do you have here—
   and whom do you have here—
   that you have hewed out a tomb
   for yourself,
   you who cuts his grave on high and
   carves himself a home in the cliff?
¹⁷ The LORD is about to hurl you down,
   mighty man!

He is surely going to cover you
   with darkness;
¹⁸ he will indeed unroll your head wrapping,
   rolling it like a ball
   into the open country.
There you will die,
   with your glorious chariots,
   you disgrace to the house
   of your master!
¹⁹ I will thrust you from your monument;
   you will be pulled down
   from your platform.

ᵐHeb uncertain

²⁰ On that day, I will call my servant
  Eliakim, Hilkiah's son.
²¹ I will give him your robe
  and wrap him in your sash,
  and I will hand over to him
    your authority.
  He will be a father
  to the inhabitants of Jerusalem
  and to the house of Judah.
²² I will place the key to David's house
  on his shoulder;
  what he opens no one will close,
  and what he closes no one will open.
²³ I will fasten him securely like a tent peg,
  and he will be a throne of honor
    for his ancestors' house.

²⁴ All the honor of his household will hang on him, the offspring and the offshoots, every little dish, every bowl, every jar. ²⁵ On that day, says the LORD of heavenly forces, the peg that is fastened securely will give way; it will be cut down, and it will fall, and all the load hanging on it will be lost. The LORD has spoken.

Concerning Tyre

23 An oracle about Tyre.
  Wail, ships of Tarshish,
  because your port is destroyed!ⁿ
    When returning from Cyprus,
    they heard about it.
² Be still, inhabitants of the coast,
  traders of Sidon,
  whose messengers crossed
    over the sea,^o
³ over the mighty waters.
  The grain of Shihor, the Nile's harvest,
  was her income;
  she was the marketplace of nations.
⁴ Be ashamed, Sidon,
  because the sea has spoken;
  the fortress of the sea has said,
  "I haven't been in labor;
  I didn't give birth;
  I never raised young men
  or brought up young women."
⁵ When the Egyptians hear,
  they will be in anguish
  at the news about Tyre.

⁶ Cross over to Tarshish;
  wail, inhabitants of the coast.
⁷ Is this your triumphant town,
  whose origin is from ancient times,
  whose feet carried her to settle far away?
⁸ Who planned this concerning Tyre,
  the one who gives crowns,
  whose merchants were princes,
  whose traders were the honored
    of the earth?
⁹ The LORD of heavenly forces planned it,
  to defile the pride of all beauty,
  to shame all the honored of the earth.

¹⁰ Go through your own land,
  Daughter Tarshish,
  for the harbor^p is gone.
¹¹ God's hand is extended over the sea,
  shaking nations.
  The LORD gave the command to destroy
  Phoenicia's fortresses,
¹² saying, You will no longer celebrate,
  violated virgin Daughter Sidon.
  Get up and head to Cyprus;
  even there you will find no rest.
¹³ Look at the land of the Chaldeans,
  the people who are no more.
  Assyria destined it for wild animals:
  they raised up their siege towers,
  stripped its palaces,
  and made it a ruin.
¹⁴ Wail, ships of Tarshish,
  for your fortress is destroyed!

¹⁵ On that day, Tyre will be forgotten seventy years, the lifetime of one king. At the end of seventy years, Tyre will become like the prostitute in the song:
¹⁶ Take a harp, go around the city,
  forgotten prostitute.
    Play well, sing many songs,
    so they'll remember you.

¹⁷ At the end of seventy years, the LORD will visit Tyre. She will return to her trade and will prostitute herself with all the kingdoms on the earth. ¹⁸ Her profits and wages will be sacred to the LORD. They won't be stored or saved. Her profits will go to those living before the LORD, for plentiful food and elegant clothes.

ⁿHeb uncertain   ^oCorrection; MT *one crossing over the sea filled you*   ^pHeb uncertain

City of chaos falls

24 Look! The LORD will devastate the earth and destroy it,
will twist its face
and scatter its inhabitants.
² It will be the same for the people
and for the priest;
for the slave and for his master;
for the female servant
and for her mistress;
for the buyer and for the seller;
for the lender and for the borrower;
for the creditor and for the debtor.
³ The earth will be devastated,
totally devastated;
it will be destroyed, completely destroyed
because the LORD has said it would be so.

⁴ The earth dries up and wilts;
the world withers and wilts;
the heavens wither away
with the earth.
⁵ The earth lies polluted
under its inhabitants,
for they have disobeyed instruction,
swept aside law,
and broken the ancient covenant.
⁶ Therefore, a curse devours the earth;
its inhabitants suffer for their guilt.
Therefore, the earth's inhabitants dwindle;
very few are left.

⁷ The wine dries up;
the vine withers;
all the merry-hearted groan.
⁸ The joyous tambourines have ceased;
the roar of partyers has stopped;
the joyous harp has ceased.
⁹ No one drinks wine or sings;
beer is bitter to its drinkers.
¹⁰ The town is in chaos, broken;
every house is shut, without entrance.
¹¹ There is a cry for wine in the streets.
All joy has reached its dusk;
happiness is exiled from the earth.
¹² Ruin remains in the city,
and the gate is battered to wreckage.
¹³ It will be like this in the central part of
the land and among the peoples,
like an olive tree that has been shaken,
like remains from the grape harvest.

¹⁴ They raise their voice;
they sing with joy;
from the west they will shout
about the LORD's majesty.
¹⁵ Therefore, in the east honor the LORD;
in the islands of the sea,
the name of the LORD God of Israel!
¹⁶ From the ends of the earth
we have heard songs:
"Glory to the righteous one!"
But I say, "I waste away; I waste away;
I'm doomed!
Betrayers betray;
treacherously betrayers betray."

¹⁷ Terror, trench, and trap are upon you,
ruler of the earth!
¹⁸ Whoever flees from the sound of
terror will fall into the trench;
whoever climbs from the trench
will be caught in the trap.

Heaven's windows will open,
and the earth's foundations will quake.
¹⁹ The earth is shattering, shattering;
the earth is shaking, shaking;
the earth is teetering, tottering.
²⁰ The earth trembles like a drunk
and shudders like a hut;
its rebellion weighs heavy upon it;
it will fall, no more to rise.
²¹ On that day, the LORD will punish the
forces of heaven in heaven, and the kings of
the earth on earth. ²² They will be gathered
together like prisoners in a pit, shut into
a prison, and punished after many days.
²³ The moon will be diminished, and the sun
will fade, since the LORD of heavenly forces
will rule on Mount Zion and in Jerusalem,
glorious before his elders.

Rejoicing in God's salvation

25 LORD, you are my God.
I will exalt you;
I will praise your name,
for you have done wonderful things,
planned long ago, faithful and sure.
² You have turned the city into rubble,
the fortified town into a ruin,
the fortress of foreigners
into a city no more,
never to be rebuilt.

³ Therefore, strong people will glorify you;
    the towns of tyrant nations
    will fear you.
⁴ You have been a refuge for the poor,
    a refuge for the needy in distress,
    a hiding place from the storm,
    a shade from the heat.
When the breath of tyrants
    is like a winter^q storm
⁵ or like heat in the desert,
    you subdue the roar of foreigners.
Like heat shaded by a cloud,
    the tyrants' song falls silent.

⁶ On this mountain,
    the LORD of heavenly forces
    will prepare for all peoples
    a rich feast, a feast of choice wines,
    of select foods rich in flavor,
    of choice wines well refined.
⁷ He will swallow up on this mountain
    the veil that is veiling all peoples,
    the shroud enshrouding all nations.
⁸ He will swallow up death^r forever.
The LORD God will wipe tears
    from every face;
    he will remove his people's disgrace
    from off the whole earth,
    for the LORD has spoken.
⁹ They will say on that day,
    "Look! This is our God,
    for whom we have waited—
    and he has saved us!
This is the LORD,
    for whom we have waited;
    let's be glad
    and rejoice in his salvation!"
¹⁰ The LORD's hand will indeed rest
    on this mountain.

Moab will be trampled down
    as straw is trampled into manure.
¹¹ When in it they spread out their hands
    as swimmers spread out
    their hands to swim,
    God will lay low their pride,
    even by the efforts of their hands.
¹² The fortified towers of their^s walls
    will be thrown down,

will be leveled,
    will be brought down to the earth,
    to the dust.

Trusting in God forever

26 On that day, this song
    will be sung in the land of Judah:
    Ours is a strong city!
    God makes salvation
    its walls and ramparts.
² Open the gates
    and let a righteous nation enter,
    a nation that keeps faith.
³ Those with sound thoughts
    you will keep in peace,
    in peace because they trust in you.
⁴ Trust in the LORD forever,
    for the LORD is a rock for all ages.
⁵ He has thrown down
    those living on high,
    and he will level the lofty town,
    leveling it down to the earth;
    he will bring it down to dust.
⁶ The feet trample it,
    the feet of the poor,
    the steps of the needy.

⁷ The way of the righteous is level;
    you clear a path for the righteous.
⁸ In the path of your justice, LORD,
    we wait for you;
with all our being, we long
    for your name and your acclaim.
⁹ At night I long for you
    with my whole being;
    my spirit within me watches for you.
When your judgments
    are at work in the earth,
    those living in the world
    learn righteousness.
¹⁰ When the wicked are favored,
    they don't learn righteousness;
    even among those who do right
    they do wrong,
    and they fail to see the LORD's majesty.
¹¹ LORD, your hand is lifted up,
    but they don't see.
    Let them see and shrink back
    because of your zeal for your people;

---

^q Or wall ^r Heb Maveth ^s Or your

your burning anger
  that consumes your enemies.
[12] LORD, grant us peace,
  because all that we have done
    has been your doing.
[13] LORD our God, other masters
  besides you have ruled us,
    but we will profess your name alone.
[14] The dead don't live; ghosts don't rise.
  Indeed, you have punished
    and destroyed them,
    and abolished all memory of them.
[15] You've enlarged the nation, LORD.
  You've enlarged the nation;
    you are glorified.
  You've expanded
    all the land's boundaries.
[16] LORD, in distress they sought you out;
  they poured out prayers to you
    when you disciplined them.
[17] As a pregnant woman close to
    childbirth is in labor pains,
  crying out in her pangs,
    so were we because of you, LORD.
[18] We were pregnant, we writhed,
  but we gave birth to wind.
  We have achieved
    no victories on earth;
    the inhabitants of the earth never fall.

[19] Your dead will live,
  their[t] corpses will rise,
    and those who dwell in the dust
    will shout for joy.
  Your shadow is a shadow of light,
  but you will bring down
    the ghosts into the underworld.
[20] Go, my people, enter your rooms
  and shut your doors behind you.
  Take cover, for in a little while
    the fury will be over.
[21] Look! The LORD is going out
  from his place
    to bring the iniquity of the ruler
    of the earth down upon him.
  The earth will uncover its blood
    and will conceal its slain no longer.

Scattered people return

27 On that day, the LORD will take a
great sword, harsh and mighty, and
will punish Leviathan the fleeing serpent,
Leviathan the writhing serpent, and will kill
the dragon that is in the sea. [2] On that day:
  Sing about a delightful vineyard!
[3] I, the LORD, am its guardian.
  Every moment I water it;
    night and day I guard it from attack.
[4] I'm not angry,
  but if it yields thorns and thistles for me,
  I will march to battle against it;
    I will torch it completely.
[5] Or let them[u] cling to me for refuge;
  let them make peace with me;
  let them make peace with me.
[6] In coming days,[v]
  Jacob will take root;
  Israel will blossom and sprout
    and fill the whole world with produce.

[7] Did God strike Israel
    as he struck those who struck him?
  Was Israel killed
    as his killers were killed?[w]
[8] By frightening Jerusalem,
  by sending her away,[x]
  you contended with her,
  expelling with a fierce blast
    on the day of the east wind.
[9] By this Jacob's guilt is reconciled,
  and this was how his sins
    were finally removed:
  he made all the altar stones
    like shattered chalk,
  sacred poles[y] and incense altars
    that couldn't stand.

[10] The fortified city lies alone,
  a hut forsaken,
    abandoned like the desert.
  Calves graze there;
  they lie down there
    and feed on its boughs.
[11] When its branches are dry,
  they are broken.
  Women come and set fire to it.

---

[t] Or *my* [u] Or *it* [v] Or *those coming* [w] Heb uncertain [x] Heb uncertain [y] Heb *asherim*, perhaps objects devoted to the goddess Asherah

These people have no understanding;
　therefore, their maker
　　won't have compassion;
　the one who formed them
　　won't be gracious.

[12] On that day, the LORD will beat grain from the channel of the Euphrates up to the Valley of Egypt. You will be collected, Israelites, one by one. [13] On that day, a great trumpet will be played. Those who were lost in the land of Assyria and those who were scattered in the land of Egypt will come. They will bow to the LORD at his holy mountain in Jerusalem.

Judgment on Ephraim and Judah

28 Oh, the majestic garland of
　　　Ephraim's drunks
　and the fading flower
　　of its splendid beauty
　on the head that flows with perfume[z]
　of those hammered with wine.
[2] Look! The Lord has someone
　who is powerful and strong;
　like a hailstorm, a disastrous tempest,
　like a downpour of mighty,
　　overflowing waters,
　he can level them to the ground
　　with his hand.
[3] The majestic garland
　of Ephraim's drunks
　will be trampled underfoot.
[4] The withered flower,
　which is a thing of beauty[a]
　as it sits on the head
　of those bloated with fat,[b]
　will be like an early fig
　　before the summer harvest:
　whoever sees it
　swallows it as soon as it is in hand.
[5] On that day, the LORD of heavenly forces will be a splendid garland and a beautiful wreath for the people who survive, [6] and a spirit of justice for the one who sits in judgment, and a strength for those who repel the assault at the gate.
[7] These also stagger from wine
　and stumble from beer:
　priest and prophet stagger from beer;
　they are confused by wine;
　they stray on account of beer;
　they err when receiving visions;
　they stumble when making judgments.
[8] All the tables are covered with vomit;
　filth overruns the place.

[9] To whom will God teach knowledge?
　To whom will he explain the message?
　To those just weaned from milk?
　To those who have hardly
　　outgrown the breast?
[10] It is "tsav letsav, tsav lestav;
　qav leqav, qav leqav,"[c]
　a little of this, a little of that.
[11] With derisive speech and a foreign tongue,
　he will speak to this people.
[12] He has said to them,
　"This is the place of rest;
　give rest to the weary;
　this is the place of repose";
　but they refused to listen.
[13] So the LORD's word will be for them:
　"tsav letsav, tsav letsav;
　qav leqav, qav leqav,"
　a little of this, a little of that.
　So that they will go and stagger backward,
　they will be broken, snared,
　　and captured.

The covenant with death overturned
[14] Therefore, hear the LORD's word,
　you scoffers who rule this people
　　in Jerusalem.
[15] You said, "We've cut a deal with death;[d]
　with the underworld[e] we made a pact.
　When the overflowing flood
　　passes through, it won't reach us;
　for we have made lies our hiding place,
　and in falsehood we take shelter."
[16] Therefore, the LORD God says:
　Look! I'm laying in Zion a stone,
　a tested stone, a valuable cornerstone,
　a sure foundation:
　　the one who trusts won't tremble.
[17] I will make justice the measuring line
　and righteousness the plumb line.

---

[z] DSS (1QIsa[a])　[a] Heb uncertain　[b] Or *at the head of the fat valley*　[c] A Hebrew version of baby talk or gibberish
[d] Heb *Maveth*　[e] Heb *Sheol*

But hail will sweep away
the hiding place of lies,
and water will overflow the shelter.
[18] Your deal with death[f] will be dissolved,
and your pact with the grave[g]
won't stand.
...shing flood: when it passes through,
[19] Ever...be annihilated by it.
it will ...t passes through
for morn...,
by day and b...morning it will pass,

It will be nothing b...
understand the mess...or to
[20] The bed is too short to stre...
and the shroud is too narrow...t,
to cover oneself.

[21] Just as on Mount Perazim,
the LORD will rise up;
as in the Gibeon Valley he will rage
to do his deed—strange is his deed!—
And to work his work—
foreign is his work!
[22] So now stop your scoffing,
or your chains will be tightened,
because destruction has been ordered—
I have heard it!—

by the LORD God of heavenly forces
against the whole land.

Plowing and threshing

[23] Listen and hear my voice;
pay attention and hear my word:
[24] Does the plowman plow
without stopping for planting,
opening and harrowing their ground?
[25] When he has smoothed its surface,
doesn't he scatter fennel,[h]
and sow cumin,
and plant wheat and barley
in their places,
and spelt as a border?
[26] They are properly ordered;
their God directs them.[i]
[27] Fennel[j] isn't threshed
with a threshing sledge,
nor is a cart wheel rolled over cumin,
at fennel[k] is beaten with a staff,
[28] Bread...min with a rod.
...in is crushed,
but the t...esher[l]
doesn't thr...sh it forever.
He drives th...cart wheel over it;
he spreads it ...ut but doesn't crush it.
[29] This also comes fro...
the LORD of heaven...y forces,

[f]Heb Maveth [g]Heb Sheol [h]Or black cumin [i]Or waters them [j]Or black cumin [k]Or black cumin ...SS (1QIsa[a])

CORNERSTONE

An architectural term that has figurative meanings and messianic nuances in the NT (Matt 21:42; Mark 12:10-11; Luke 20:17; Acts 4:11; Eph 2:19-22; 1 Pet 2:6-7). Job 38:4-6 speaks of God laying the foundations of the earth, sinking the bases on the foundation, and laying the cornerstone. This usage implies that a cornerstone is a primary stone in the building's foundation. The same imagery is found in Isaiah 28:16; the Lord God is "laying in Zion a stone, a tested stone, a valuable cornerstone, a sure foundation." Many structures, including defensive walls around towns, were built of unhewn field stones with piers of hewn stones placed at intervals. This type of construction is referred to as pier-and-rubble construction. The corners of the structure are pier walls of hewn stone. The foundation course would have the largest cornerstone, to span both sides of the corner and provide a level base for upper courses. Thus the cornerstone was critical to the stability of the whole structure.

who gives wondrous counsel
and increases wisdom.

Ariel besieged but spared

29 Oh, Ariel, Ariel,
town where David encamped!
Year by year,
let the festivals come around—
² but I will oppress Ariel.
There will be mourning and lamentation;
she will be like an Ariel to me.
³ I will surround you like a wall,
and I will lay a siege against you
with assault towers,
and I will raise up siegeworks against you.
⁴ You will be brought down;
from the ground you will speak;
from low in the dust
your speech will come.
Your voice will be
like a ghost's from the earth;
from the dust your words will whisper.
⁵ But your many enemies
will be like fine dust,
the terrible horde like passing chaff.
Suddenly, in an instant,
⁶ the LORD of heavenly forces
will come to you
with thunder, earthquake,
and a mighty voice,
with whirlwind, tempest,
and flames of devouring fire.
⁷ The horde of nations
fighting against Ariel,
and all who make war on her
and her fortress and besiege her,
will be like a dream,
a vision of the night.
⁸ It will be like when
a hungry person dreams of eating
but wakes up and the mouth is empty.
Or when a thirsty person
dreams of drinking
but wakes up and has a dry throat.
So will it be for all the horde of nations
who fight against Mount Zion.

⁹ Be shocked and stunned;
blind yourselves; be blind!
Be drunk, but not on wine;
stagger, but not on account of beer!

¹⁰ The LORD has poured on you
a spirit of deep sleep,
and has shut your eyes, you prophets,
and covered your heads, you seers.
¹¹ This entire vision has become for you
like the words of a sealed scroll. When read
give it to one who can read, because it's
this," that one will say, "I can't given to
sealed." ¹² And when the read this," that
one who can't read, say
one will say, "I can't

The wisdom of the wise

¹³ The Lord people turn toward me
Since their mouths,
honor me with lip service
while their heart is distant from me,
and their fear of me is just a human
command that has been memorized,
¹⁴ I will go on doing amazing things
to these people,
shocking and startling things.
The wisdom of their wise will perish,
and the discernment of their
discerning will be hidden.
¹⁵ Doom to those who hide their plan deep,
away from the LORD,
whose deeds are in the dark,
who say, "Who sees us? Who knows us?"
¹⁶ You have everything backward!
Should the potter be thought of as clay?
Should what is made say of its maker,
"He didn't make me"?
Should what is shaped
say of the one who shaped it,
"He doesn't understand"?

¹⁷ In just a little while won't Lebanon
become farmland once again,
and the farmland be considered a forest?
¹⁸ On that day:
The deaf will hear
the words of a scroll and,
freed from dimness and darkness,
the eyes of the blind will see.
¹⁹ The poor will again find joy in the LORD,
and the neediest of people
will rejoice in the holy one of Israel.
²⁰ The tyrant will be no more,
the mocker will perish,
and all who plot evil will be eliminated:

²¹ all who incriminate others wrongly,
who entrap the judge in the gate,
and pointlessly postpone justice
for the innocent.

²² Therefore, proclaims the LORD,
the God of^m the house of Jacob,
who redeemed Abraham:
Jacob won't be ashamed now,
and his face won't grow pale now.
²³ When he sees his children among them,
the work of my hands,
proclaiming my name holy,
they will make holy the holy one of Jacob,
and stand in awe of Israel's God.
²⁴ Those who wander in spirit
will have understanding,
and those who grumble
will gain insight.

Help from Egypt is futile

30 Doom to you, rebellious children,
says the LORD,
who make a plan, which is not mine;
who weave a plot,ⁿ but not by my spirit,
piling up sin on sin;
² setting out to go down to Egypt
without consulting me,
taking refuge in Pharaoh's refuge
and hiding in Egypt's shadow.
³ Pharaoh's refuge will become your shame,
hiding in Egypt's shadow your disgrace.
⁴ Though their officials are in Zoan,
and their messengers reach Hanes,
⁵ all will become shamed
because of a people
who can't assist them.
They are no help; they are no profit;
rather, shame and disgrace.

⁶ An oracle about the beasts in the arid
southern plain.
Through a land of distress and danger,
lioness and roaring^o lion,
viper and flying serpent,
they will carry their wealth
on donkeys' shoulders
and their treasures on camels' humps
to a people who won't profit,

⁷ for Egypt's help is utterly worthless.
Therefore, I call her Rahab Who Sits Still.^p

⁸ Now go, write it before them on a tablet,
inscribe it on a scroll,
so in the future
it will endure as a witness.
⁹ These are rebellious people, lying children,
children unwilling
to hear the LORD's teaching,
¹⁰ who say to the seers, "Don't foresee,"
and to the visionaries,
"Don't report truthful visions;
tell us flattering things;
envision deceptions;
¹¹ get out of the way;
step off the path;
let's have no more 'holy one of Israel.'"

¹² Therefore, the holy one of Israel says:
Because you reject this word
and trust in oppression and cunning
and rely on them,
¹³ your sin will be like a crack in a high wall;
it bulges, about to fall:
suddenly, in an instant, it breaks!
¹⁴ Its breaking is like
the breaking of a storage jar
that is totally shattered.
No piece from among its fragments
will be large enough
to take fire from a hearth,
or to dip water from a cistern.

¹⁵ Therefore, the LORD God,
the holy one of Israel, says:
In return and rest you will be saved;
quietness and trust
will be your strength—
but you refused.
¹⁶ You said,
"No! We'll flee on horses"—
therefore, you will indeed flee—
"and we'll ride off;
on swift steeds we will ride"—
therefore, your pursuers will be swift.
¹⁷ One thousand will flee
at the threat of one,
and at the threat of five you will flee,

---

^mOr *to*   ⁿHeb uncertain   ^oOr *from them*   ^pOr *Rahab the silent*

until you are left like a flagstaff
  on a mountaintop,
  like a flag on a hill.
[18] Nonetheless, the LORD is waiting
  to be merciful to you,
  and will rise up to show you compassion.
  The LORD is a God of justice;
  happy are all who wait for him.

This is the way

[19] People in Zion, who live in Jerusalem,
you will weep no longer. God will certainly
be merciful to you. Hearing the sound of
your outcry, God will answer you. [20] Though
the Lord gives you the bread of distress
and the water of oppression, your teacher
will no longer hide, but you will see your
teacher. [21] If you stray to the right or the
left, you will hear a word that comes from
behind you: "This is the way; walk in it."
[22] You will defile your silver-plated idols and
your gold-covered priestly vest,[q] and you
will scatter them like menstrual rags. "Get
out," you will say to them.

[23] God will provide rain for the seed you
sow in the ground, and the food the ground
produces will be rich and abundant. On that
day, your cattle will graze in large pastures.
[24] The oxen and donkeys that are working
the ground will eat tasty feed spread for
them with shovel and fork.

[25] On every lofty mountain, and on every
high hill, streams will run with water on the
day of the great massacre, when the towers
fall. [26] The light of the moon will be like the
light of the sun, and the light of the sun will
be seven times brighter—like the light of
seven days—on the day that the LORD bandages the people's brokenness and heals
the wounds inflicted by his blows.

Assyria punished

[27] Look there!
  The LORD is coming from far away;
  his anger blazing, his smoke-cloud thick.
  His lips are full of fury;
  his tongue is like a devouring fire.
[28] His breath is like a raging river
  that reaches up to the neck,

to shake the nations
  with a sieve of destruction,
  and to put a misleading rein
  on the people's jaws.
[29] There will be singing for you
  as on the night
  that people celebrate a festival.
  The heart will be joyful as it is
  when one goes with a flute
  to the LORD's mountain,
  to the rock of Israel.
[30] The LORD will unleash his majestic voice
  and display his crushing arm
  in furious anger,
  with a flame of consuming fire,
  in stormy rain and hail.
[31] The LORD's voice will terrify Assyria;
  with a rod he will smite it.
[32] And every crack that is made
  in the foundation wall,
  which the LORD will bring down
  upon him,
  will be accompanied
  by timbrels and lyres.
  The LORD will raise his arm
  and fight against Assyria in battle.
[33] His place for burning[r]
  was arranged long ago;
  it is indeed made ready for a king.
  God has made its wood pile wide and deep,
  fire and wood in abundance.
  The breath of the LORD, like a stream
  of brimstone, ignites it.

Doom to those going to Egypt

31 Doom to those going down
  to Egypt for help!
  They rely on horses,
  trust in chariots because they are many,
  and on riders
  because they are very strong.
  But they don't look
  to the holy one of Israel;
  they don't seek the LORD.
[2] But God also knows how to bring disaster;
  he has not taken back his words.
  God will rise up
  against the house of evildoers
  and against the help
  of those who do wrong.

[q] *Correction*; Heb *ephod*   [r] Heb *Topheth*

³ Egypt is human and not divine;
  their horses are flesh and not spirit.
The LORD will extend his hand;
  the helper will stumble,
  those helped will fall,
  and they will all die together.

⁴ The LORD has said to me:
When the lion growls,
  the young lion, over its prey,
  though a band of shepherds
    is summoned against it,
  isn't scared off by their noise
  or frightened by their roar.
So the LORD of heavenly forces
  will go down
  to fight on Mount Zion
  and on her hill.
⁵ Like birds flying aloft,
  so the LORD of heavenly forces
  will shield Jerusalem:
  shielding and saving,
  sparing and rescuing.
⁶ People of Israel, return to the one
whom you have deeply betrayed! ⁷ On that
day, you will each reject the idols of silver
and the idols of gold, which you have sinfully made for yourselves.
⁸ Assyria will fall,
  but not by a human sword—
  a sword not made by humans
  will devour them.
They will flee before the sword;
  their young men
  will become forced laborers.
⁹ In horror they will flee
  from their stronghold;
  their officers will be terrified
    at the signal,
  says the LORD, whose fire is in Zion
  and whose oven is in Jerusalem.

Righteous rule

32 See here: A king rules
  to promote righteousness;
  rulers govern to promote justice,
² each like a shelter from the wind
  and a refuge from a storm,
  like streams of water in a wasteland,
  like the shade of a massive cliff
  in a worn-out land.

³ Then the eyes of those who can see
  will no longer be blind,
  the ears of those who can hear
    will listen,
⁴ the minds of the rash
  will know and comprehend,
  and the tongues of those who stammer
  will speak fluently and plainly.
⁵ Then a fool will no longer
  be called honorable,
  nor a villain considered respectable.
⁶ Fools speak folly;
  their minds devise wickedness,
  acting irreverently,
  speaking falsely of the LORD,
  leaving the hungry empty,
  and depriving the thirsty of drink.
⁷ As for the villain, his villainies are evil.
  He plans schemes
    to destroy the poor with lying words,
  even when the needy speak justly.
⁸ But an honorable person
  plans honorable things
  and stands up for what is honorable.

Warnings to the carefree

⁹ Women of leisure, stand up!
  Hear my voice!
  Carefree daughters, listen to my word!
¹⁰ In a little over a year,
  the carefree will shudder,
  because the grape harvest will fail;
  the vintage won't arrive.
¹¹ Tremble, all of you who are at ease;
  shudder, all of you who are secure!
  Strip yourselves, bare your skin,
  and tie mourning clothes
  around your waist,
¹² beating your breasts
  for the pleasant fields,
  for the fruitful vine,
¹³ for my people's soil
  growing barbs and thorns,
  for all the joyous houses
  in the jubilant town.
¹⁴ The palace will be deserted,
  the crowded city abandoned.
  Stronghold and watchtower
  will become empty fields forever,
  suited for the pleasure of wild donkeys,
  and a pasture for flocks—

¹⁵ until a spirit from on high
    is poured out on us,
    and the desert turns into farmland,
    and the farmland
    is considered a forest.
¹⁶ Then justice will reside in wild lands,
    and righteousness
    will abide in farmlands.
¹⁷ The fruit of righteousness will be peace,
    and the outcome of righteousness,
    calm and security forever.
¹⁸ Then my people will live
    in a peaceful dwelling,
    in secure homes,
    in carefree resting places.
¹⁹ Even if the forest fallsˢ
    and the humbled city is laid low,
²⁰ those who sow beside any stream
    will be happy,
    sending out ox and donkey to graze.

Judgment and hope for the righteous

33 Doom to the destroyer
        left undestroyed,
    you traitor whom none have betrayed:
    when you have finished destroying,
    you will be destroyed;
    and when you have stopped betraying,
    they will betray you.

² LORD, show us favor;
    we hope in you.
    Be our strength every morning,
    our salvation in times of distress.
³ At the noise, peoples fled;
    on account of your roar,
    nations scattered.
⁴ They gathered spoil like insects;
    they rushed upon it
    like a swarm of locusts.ᵗ
⁵ The LORD is exalted; he lives on high,
    filling Zion with
    justice and righteousness.
⁶ He will provide security
    during a lifetime:ᵘ
    a source of salvation,
    wisdom, and knowledge—
    fear of the LORD will be Zion's treasure.ᵛ

⁷ But then those in Arielʷ
    cried out in the streets;
    messengers of peace wept bitterly.
⁸ The highways were deserted;
    travelers left the road.
    The covenant was broken;
    solemn pledgesˣ were rejected;
    no one cared for humanity.
⁹ The land mourned; it wasted away;
    Lebanon was ashamed; it withered.
    Sharon became like the desert,
    and Bashan and Carmel
    were dropping their leaves.

¹⁰ Now I will arise, says the LORD.
    Now I will exalt myself;
    now I will stand tall.
¹¹ You conceive straw, give birth to stubble;
    your breath is a fire that devours you.
¹² Peoples will be burned to lime,
    thorns cut up and set ablaze.
¹³ You who are far away,
    hear what I have done;
    and you who are near,
    know my strength!

¹⁴ Sinners became terrified in Zion;
    trembling seized the godless:
    "Who among us can live
        with the devouring fire?
    Who among us can live
        with the everlasting blaze?"
¹⁵ The one who walks righteously
    and speaks truthfully,
    who rejects profit from extortion,
    who waves away a bribe
        instead of grabbing it,
    who won't listen to bloody plots,
    and who won't contemplate
        doing something evil.
¹⁶ He will live on the heights;
    fortresses in the cliffs will be his refuge.
    His food will be provided,
    his water guaranteed.
¹⁷ When you gaze upon a king in his glamour
    and look at the surrounding land,
¹⁸ in dismay you will think:
    Where is the one who counts?

ˢOr it will hail when the forest falls ᵗHeb uncertain ᵘOr your times ᵛOr his treasure ʷOr the valiant; Heb uncertain ˣCorrection; or cities; DSS (1QIsaᵃ) witnesses

Where is the one who weighs?
Where is the one who counts towers?

19 You will no longer see
the defiant people,
the people of speech
too obscure to understand,
who stammer
in an incomprehensible language.

20 Gaze upon Zion, our festival town.
Your eyes will see Jerusalem,
a carefree dwelling,
a tent that is not packed up,
whose stakes are never pulled up,
whose ropes won't snap.

21 The LORD's majesty will be there for us:
as a place of rivers, broad streams
where no boat will go,
no majestic ship will cross.

22 The LORD is our judge;
the LORD is our leader;
the LORD is our king—
he will deliver us.

23 Your ropes are loosened;
they can't hold the mast firmly;
they can't spread the sail.
Then abundant spoil will be divided;
even the lame will seize spoil.

24 And no inhabitant will say, "I'm sick."
The people living there
will be forgiven their sin.

Vengeance against Edom

34 Draw near, you nations, to hear;
and listen, you peoples.
Hear, earth and all who fill it,
world and all its offspring.

2 The LORD rages against all the nations,
and is angry with all their armies.
God is about to wipe them out
and has prepared them for slaughter.

3 Their dead will be cast out,
the stench of their corpses will rise,
and the mountains
will melt from their blood.

4 All the stars of heaven will dissolve,
the skies will roll up like a scroll,
and all the stars will fall,
like a leaf withering from a vine,
like fruit from a fig tree.

5 When my sword has drunk its fill
in the heavens,
it will descend upon Edom for judgment,
upon a people
I have doomed for destruction.

6 The LORD has a sword covered with blood;
it is soaked with fat
from the blood of lambs and goats,
from the kidney fat of rams,
for the LORD has a sacrifice in Bozrah,
a great slaughter in the land of Edom.

7 Wild oxen will fall with them,
steers with mighty bulls,
and their land will be drenched
with blood;
its soil soaked with fat.

8 The LORD has a day of vengeance,
a year of payback for Zion's cause.

9 Edom's streams will be turned into pitch,
its dust into sulfur,
and its land will become burning pitch.

10 Night and day won't be extinguished;
its smoke will go up forever.
From generation to generation
it will lie waste;
no one will ever pass through it again.

11 Screech owls and crows will possess it;
owls and ravens will live there.y
God will stretch over it
the measuring line of chaos
and the plummet stone of emptiness
over its officials.

12 No Kingdom There, they will call it,
and all its princes will disappear.

13 Thorns will grow up in its palaces,
weeds and brambles in its fortresses.
It will be a dwelling for jackals,
a home for ostriches.

14 Wildcats will meet hyenas,
the goat demon will call to his friends,
and there Lilithz will lurk
and find her resting place.

15 There the snake will nest and lay eggs
and brood and hatch in its shadow.
There too vultures will gather,
each with its mate.a

16 Consult the LORD's scroll and read:
Not one of these will be missing;
none will lack its mate.

---

ySpecies uncertain zName of a demon aSpecies uncertain

God's own mouth has commanded;
God's own spirit has gathered them.
[17] God has cast the lot for them;
God's hand allotted it to them
with the measuring line.
They will possess it forever;
they will live in it
from generation to generation.

Fertile wilderness

35 The desert and the dry land
will be glad;
the wilderness will rejoice
and blossom like the crocus.
[2] They will burst into bloom,
and rejoice with joy and singing.
They will receive the glory of Lebanon,
the splendor of Carmel and Sharon.
They will see the LORD's glory,
the splendor of our God.

[3] Strengthen the weak hands,
and support the unsteady knees.
[4] Say to those who are panicking:
"Be strong! Don't fear!
Here's your God,
coming with vengeance;
with divine retribution
God will come to save you."

[5] Then the eyes of the blind will be opened,
and the ears of the deaf will be cleared.
[6] Then the lame will leap like the deer,
and the tongue of the speechless
will sing.
Waters will spring up in the desert,
and streams in the wilderness.
[7] The burning sand will become a pool,
and the thirsty ground,
fountains of water.

[b] Heb uncertain   [c] Heb uncertain

The jackals' habitat, a pasture;[b]
grass will become reeds and rushes.
[8] A highway will be there.
It will be called The Holy Way.
The unclean won't travel on it,
but it will be for those walking
on that way.[c]
Even fools won't get lost on it;
[9] no lion will be there,
and no predator will go up on it.
None of these will be there;
only the redeemed will walk on it.
[10] The LORD's ransomed ones
will return and enter Zion with singing,
with everlasting joy upon their heads.
Happiness and joy will overwhelm them;
grief and groaning will flee away.

Sennacherib's message

36 Assyria's King Sennacherib marched
against all of Judah's fortified cities
and captured them in the fourteenth year
of King Hezekiah. [2] Assyria's king sent his
field commander from Lachish, together
with a large army, to King Hezekiah at Jerusalem. He stood at the water channel of the
Upper Pool, which is on the road to the field
where clothes are washed. [3] Hilkiah's son
Eliakim, who was the palace administrator,
Shebna the secretary, and Asaph's son Joah
the recorder went out to them.

[4] Then the field commander said to them,
"Say to Hezekiah: Assyria's Great King
says this: Why do you feel so confident?
[5] Do you think that empty words are the
same as good strategy and the strength to
fight? Who are you trusting that you now
rebel against me? [6] It appears that you are
trusting in a staff—Egypt—that's nothing
but a broken reed! It will stab the hand of

HEZEKIAH

An 8th-century BCE king of Judah. The information from the OT about
Hezekiah's reign is extensive and comes mainly from three major portions
of texts: 2 Kings 18–20; Isaiah 36–39; and 2 Chronicles 29–32.

anyone who leans on it! That's all that Pharaoh, Egypt's king, is to anyone who trusts in him. [7]Now suppose you say to me, 'We trust in the LORD our God.' Isn't he the one whose shrines and altars Hezekiah removed, telling Judah and Jerusalem, 'You must worship only at this altar'?

[8]"So now, make a wager with my master, Assyria's king. I'll give you two thousand horses if you can supply the riders! [9]How will you drive back even the least important official among my master's servants when you are relying on Egypt for chariots and riders? [10]What's more, do you think I've marched against this place to destroy it without the LORD's support? It was the LORD who told me, 'March against this land and destroy it!'"

[11]Eliakim, Shebna, and Joah said to the field commander, "Please speak to your servants in Aramaic, because we understand it. Don't speak with us in Hebrew,[d] because the people on the wall will hear it."

[12]The field commander said to them, "Did my master send me to speak these words just to you and your master and not also to the men on the wall? They are the ones who will have to eat their dung and drink their urine along with you." [13]Then the field commander stood up and shouted in Hebrew at the top of his voice: "Listen to the message of the great king, Assyria's king. [14]The king says this: Don't let Hezekiah lie to you. He won't be able to rescue you. [15]Don't let Hezekiah persuade you to trust the LORD by saying, 'The LORD will certainly rescue us. This city won't be handed over to Assyria's king.'

[16]"Don't listen to Hezekiah, because this

is what Assyria's king says: Surrender to me and come out. Then each of you will eat from your own vine and fig tree and drink water from your own well [17]until I come to take you to a land just like your land. It will be a land of grain and new wine, a land of bread and vineyards. [18]Don't let Hezekiah fool you by saying, 'The LORD will rescue us.' Did any of the other gods of the nations save their lands from the power of Assyria's king? [19]Where are the gods of Hamath and Arpad? Where are the gods of Sepharvaim? Did they rescue Samaria from my power? [20]Which one of the gods from those countries has rescued their land from my power? Will the LORD save Jerusalem from my power?"

[21]But they kept quiet and didn't answer him with a single word, because King Hezekiah's command was, "Don't answer him!" [22]Hilkiah's son Eliakim, who was the palace administrator, Shebna the secretary, and Asaph's son Joah the recorder came to Hezekiah with ripped clothes. They told him what the field commander had said.

Hezekiah and Isaiah

37 When King Hezekiah heard this, he ripped his clothes, covered himself with mourning clothes, and went to the LORD's temple. [2]He sent Eliakim the palace administrator, Shebna the secretary, and the senior priests to the prophet Isaiah, Amoz's son. They were all wearing mourning clothes. [3]They said to him, "Hezekiah says this: Today is a day of distress, punishment, and humiliation. It's as if children are ready to be born, but there's no strength to see it through. [4]Perhaps the LORD your God

[d]MT *Judean*, so also 36:13

SENNACHERIB

Sennacherib was the king of Assyria (704–681 BCE) who invaded Judah during the reign of Hezekiah. He was the son of Sargon II, king of Assyria (721–705 BCE). Second Kings 18–19 depicts Sennacherib's campaign against Jerusalem.

heard all the words of the field commander who was sent by his master, Assyria's king. He insulted the living God! Perhaps he will punish him for the words that the LORD your God has heard. Offer up a prayer for those few people who still survive."

⁵When King Hezekiah's servants got to Isaiah, ⁶Isaiah said to them, "Say this to your master: The LORD says this: Don't be afraid at the words you heard, which the officers of Assyria's king have used to insult me. ⁷I'm about to mislead him, so when he hears a rumor, he'll go back to his own country. Then I'll have him cut down by the sword in his own land."

⁸The field commander heard that the Assyrian king had left Lachish. So he went back to the king and found him attacking Libnah. ⁹Then the Assyrian king learned that Cush's King Tirhakah was on his way to fight against him. So he sent messengers to Hezekiah again: ¹⁰"Say this to Judah's King Hezekiah: Don't let the God you trust deceive you by saying, 'Jerusalem won't fall to the Assyrian king.' ¹¹You yourself have heard what Assyrian kings do to other countries, wiping them out. Is it likely that you will be saved? ¹²Did the gods of the nations that my ancestors destroyed save them, the gods of Gozan, Haran, Rezeph, or the people of Eden in Telassar? ¹³Where now is Hamath's king, Arpad's king, or the kings of Lair, Sepharvaim, Hena, or Ivvah?"ᵉ

Hezekiah prays

¹⁴Hezekiah took the letters from the messengers and read them. Then he went to the temple and spread them out before the LORD. ¹⁵Hezekiah prayed to the LORD: ¹⁶"LORD of heavenly forces, God of Israel: you sit enthroned on the winged creatures. You alone are God over all the earth's kingdoms. You made both heaven and earth. ¹⁷LORD, turn your ear this way and hear! LORD, open your eyes and see! Listen to Sennacherib's words. He sent them to insult the living God! ¹⁸It's true, LORD, that the Assyrian

kings have destroyed all the nations and their lands. ¹⁹The Assyrians burned the gods of those nations with fire because they aren't real gods. They are only man-made creations of wood and stone. That's how the Assyrians could destroy them. ²⁰So now, LORD our God, please save us from Sennacherib's power! Then all the earth's kingdoms will know that you alone are LORD."

²¹Then Isaiah, Amoz's son, sent a message to Hezekiah: The LORD God of Israel says this: Since you prayed to me about Assyria's King Sennacherib, ²²this is the message that the LORD has spoken against him:

The young woman, Daughter Zion,
  despises you and mocks you;
  Daughter Jerusalem shakes her head
    behind your back.
²³ Whom did you insult and ridicule?
  Against whom did you raise your voice
    and look on with disdain?
  It was against the holy one of Israel!
²⁴ With your servants,
  you've insulted the Lord;
  you said, "I, with my many chariots,
    have gone up to the highest mountains,
    to the farthest reaches of Lebanon.
  I have cut down its tallest cedars,
    the best of its pine trees.
  I have reached
    its most remote lodging place,
    its best forest.
²⁵ I have dug wells,
    have drunk water in foreign lands.ᶠ
  With my own feet,
    I dried up all of Egypt's streams."
²⁶ Haven't you heard?
  I set this up long ago;
    I planned it in the distant past!
  Now I have made it happen,
    making fortified cities
      collapse into piles of rubble.
²⁷ Their citizens have lost their power;
    they are frightened and dismayed.
  They've become like plants in a field,
    tender green shoots,
  the grass on rooftops,
    blasted by the east wind.

ᵉOr the king of the city of Sepharvaim; or the king of the city of Sepharvaim, Hena, and Ivvah   ᶠHeb uncertain; DSS (1QIsaᵃ) in foreign lands

28 I know where you are,
how you go out and come in,
and how you rage against me.
29 Because you rage against me
and because your pride
has reached my ears,
I will put my hook in your nose
and my bit in your mouth.
I will make you go back
the same way you came.

30 Now this will be the sign for you, Hezekiah: This year you will eat what grows by itself. Next year you will eat what grows from that. But in the third year, plant seed and harvest it; plant vineyards and eat their fruit. 31 The survivors of Judah's family who have escaped will put down roots and bear fruit above. 32 Those who remain will go out from Jerusalem, and those who survive will go out from Mount Zion. The zeal of the LORD of heavenly forces will do this.

33 Therefore, the LORD says this about Assyria's king: He won't enter this city. He won't shoot a single arrow here. He won't come near the city with a shield. He won't build a ramp to besiege it. 34 He'll go back by the same way he came. He won't enter this city, declares the LORD. 35 I will defend this city and save it for my sake and for the sake of my servant David.

36 The LORD's messenger went out and struck down one hundred eighty-five thousand soldiers in the Assyrian camp. When people got up the next morning, there were dead bodies everywhere. 37 So Assyria's King Sennacherib left and went back to Nineveh, where he stayed. 38 Later, while he was worshipping in the temple of his god Nisroch, his sons Adrammelech and Sharezer killed him with a sword. Then they escaped to the land of Ararat. His son Esarhaddon ruled after him.

Hezekiah's illness

38 At about that time Hezekiah became deathly sick. The prophet Isaiah, Amoz's son, came to him and said: "The LORD God says this: Put your affairs in order because you are about to die. You won't survive this."

2 Hezekiah turned his face to the wall and prayed to the LORD: 3 "Please, LORD, remember how I've walked before you in truth and sincerity. I've done what you consider to be good." Then Hezekiah cried and cried.

4 Then the LORD's word came to Isaiah: 5 "Go and say to Hezekiah: The LORD, the God of your ancestor David, says this: I have heard your prayer and have seen your tears. I will add fifteen years to your life. 6 I will rescue you and this city from the power of the Assyrian king. I will defend this city. 7 This will be your sign from the LORD that he will do what he promised: 8 once the shadow cast by the sun descends on the steps of Ahaz, I will make it back up ten steps." And the sun went back ten of the steps that it had already descended.

9 A composition by Judah's King Hezekiah when he was sick and then recovered from his sickness:
10 I thought, I must depart
in the prime of my life;
I have been relegated to the gates
of the underworld[g]
for the rest of my life.
11 I thought, I won't see the LORD.
The LORD is in the land of the living.
I won't look upon humans again
or be with the inhabitants of the world.
12 My lifetime is plucked up
and taken from me like a shepherd's tent.
My life is shriveled like woven cloth;
God cuts me off from the loom.
Between daybreak and nightfall
you carry out your verdict against me.
13 I cried out[h] until morning:
"Like a lion God crushes all my bones.
Between daybreak and nightfall
you carry out your verdict against me.
14 Like a swallow[i] I chirp;
I moan like a dove.
My eyes have grown weary
looking to heaven.
Lord, I'm overwhelmed; support me!"

15 What can I say?
God has spoken to me;
he himself has acted.

---

g Heb Sheol   h Or I lay down   i Heb uncertain

I will wander[j] my whole life
　　with a bitter spirit.
[16] The LORD Most High is
　　the one who gives life to every heart,
　　who gives life to the spirit![k]
[17] Look, he indeed exchanged my bitterness
　　for wholeness.[l]

You yourself have spared[m] my whole being
　　from the pit of destruction,
　　because you have cast all my sins
　　behind your back.
[18] The underworld[n] can't thank you,
　　nor can death[o] praise you;
　　those who go down to the pit
　　can't hope for your faithfulness.
[19] The living, the living can thank you,
　　as I do today.
　　Parents will tell children
　　about your faithfulness.
[20] The LORD has truly saved me,
　　and we will make music[p] at the LORD's
　　house all the days of our lives.

[21] Then Isaiah said, "Prepare a salve made from figs, put it on the swelling, and he'll get better."

[22] Hezekiah said to Isaiah, "What's the sign that I'll be able to go up to the LORD's temple?"

The Babylonian king's messengers

39 At that time, Babylon's King Merodach-baladan, Baladan's son, sent letters and a gift to Hezekiah, for he heard that he had been ill and had recovered. [2] Hezekiah was pleased, and he showed them his treasury—the silver and the gold, the spices and fine oil—and everything in his armory, all that was found in his storerooms. There wasn't a thing in his house or in all his realm that Hezekiah didn't show them.

[3] Then Isaiah the prophet came to King Hezekiah and said to him, "What did these men say? Where did they come from?"

Hezekiah replied, "They came to me from a distant land, from Babylon."

[4] So Isaiah said, "What did they see in your house?"

Hezekiah said, "They saw everything in my house. There was nothing in my storerooms that I didn't show them."

[5] Isaiah said to Hezekiah, "Hear the word of the LORD of heavenly forces: [6] Days are coming when all that is in your house, which your ancestors have stored up until this day, will be carried to Babylon. Nothing will be left, says the LORD. [7] Some of your sons, your own descendants whom you fathered, will be taken to become eunuchs in the king of Babylon's palace."

[8] Hezekiah said to Isaiah, "The LORD's word that you delivered is good," since he thought, That means there will be peace and security in my lifetime.

Comfort for God's people

40 Comfort, comfort my people!
　　says your God.
[2] Speak compassionately to Jerusalem,
　　and proclaim to her that her
　　compulsory service has ended,
　　that her penalty has been paid,
　　that she has received
　　from the LORD's hand
　　double for all her sins!

[3] A voice is crying out:
　"Clear the LORD's way in the desert!
　　Make a level highway in the wilderness
　　for our God!
[4] Every valley will be raised up,
　　and every mountain and hill
　　will be flattened.
　　Uneven ground will become level,
　　and rough terrain a valley plain.
[5] The LORD's glory will appear,
　　and all humanity will see it together;
　　the LORD's mouth has commanded it."

[6] A voice was saying:
　"Call out!"
And another[q] said,
　"What should I call out?"
All flesh is grass;

all its loyalty is
    like the flowers of the field.
7 The grass dries up
    and the flower withers
    when the LORD's breath blows on it.
    Surely the people are grass.
8 The grass dries up;
    the flower withers,
    but our God's word will exist forever.

9 Go up on a high mountain,
    messenger Zion!
Raise your voice and shout,
    messenger Jerusalem!
Raise it; don't be afraid;
    say to the cities of Judah,
    "Here is your God!"
10 Here is the LORD God,
    coming with strength,
    with a triumphant arm,
    bringing his reward with him
    and his payment before him.
11 Like a shepherd, God will tend the flock;
    he will gather lambs in his arms
    and lift them onto his lap.
    He will gently guide the nursing ewes.

The incomparable God
12 Who has measured the waters
    in the palm of a hand
    or gauged the heavens with a ruler
    or scooped the earth's dust up
    in a measuring cup
    or weighed the mountains on a scale
    and the hills in a balance?
13 Who directed the LORD's spirit
    and acted as God's advisor?
14 Whom did he consult for enlightenment?
    Who taught him the path of justice
    and knowledge
    and explained to him
    the way of understanding?
15 Look, the nations are like a drop
    in a bucket,
    and valued as dust on a scale.
    Look, God weighs the islands
    like fine dust.
16 Lebanon doesn't have enough fuel;
    its animals aren't enough
    for an entirely burned offering.

17 All the nations
    are like nothing before God.
    They are viewed as
    less than nothing and emptiness.

18 So to whom will you equate God;
    to what likeness will you compare him?
19 An idol? A craftsman pours it,
    a metalworker covers it with gold,
    and fashions silver chains.
20 The one who sets up an image
    chooses wood that won't rot[r]
    and then seeks a skilled artisan
    to set up an idol that won't move.
21 Don't you know? Haven't you heard?
    Wasn't it announced to you
    from the beginning?
    Haven't you understood
    since the earth was founded?
22 God inhabits the earth's horizon—
    its inhabitants are like locusts—
    stretches out the skies like a curtain
    and spreads it out like a tent for dwelling.
23 God makes dignitaries useless
    and the earth's judges into nothing.
24 Scarcely are they planted, scarcely sown,
    scarcely is their shoot rooted in the earth
    when God breathes on them,
    and they dry up;
    the windstorm
    carries them off like straw.
25 So to whom will you compare me,
    and who is my equal? says the holy one.

Power for the weary
26 Look up at the sky and consider:
    Who created these?
    The one who brings out
    their attendants one by one,
    summoning each of them by name.
Because of God's great strength
    and mighty power, not one is missing.
27 Why do you say, Jacob,
    and declare, Israel,
    "My way is hidden from the LORD
    my God ignores my predicament"?
28 Don't you know? Haven't you heard?
    The LORD is the everlasting God,
    the creator of the ends of the earth.

r Heb uncertain

He doesn't grow tired or weary.
His understanding
is beyond human reach,
²⁹ giving power to the tired
and reviving the exhausted.
³⁰ Youths will become tired and weary,
young men will certainly stumble;
³¹ but those who hope in the LORD
will renew their strength;
they will fly up on wings like eagles;
they will run and not be tired;
they will walk and not be weary.

Victor from the east

41 Be quiet before me, coastlands.
Let the nations renew their strength.
Let them approach and speak.
Let's draw near for a judgment.
² Who has awakened one from the east
and has authority to summon him
to serve—
giving him nations,
conquering kings,
making them like dust with his sword,
like scattered straw with his bow?
³ He pursues them and passes untouched,
needing no path for his feet.
⁴ Who has acted and who has done this,
calling upon generation after
generation since the beginning?
I, the LORD, was first,
and I will be the last!

⁵ The coastlands see and fear;
the ends of the earth tremble;
they draw near and arrive.
⁶ Each helps the other,
each saying to the other, "Take courage!"
⁷ The craftsman encourages
the metalworker;
the one who smoothes with the hammer
encourages the one who strikes the anvil,
saying of the welding, "That's good,"
and strengthening it with nails
so it won't move.

Israel as God's servant

⁸ But you, Israel my servant,
Jacob, whom I have chosen,
offspring of Abraham, whom I love,
⁹ you whom I took
from the ends of the earth

and called from its farthest corners,
saying to you, "You are my servant;
I chose you and didn't reject you":
¹⁰ Don't fear, because I am with you;
don't be afraid, for I am your God.
I will strengthen you,
I will surely help you;
I will hold you
with my righteous strong hand.
¹¹ All who rage against you
will be shamed and disgraced.
Those who contend with you
will be as nothing and will perish.
¹² You will look for your opponents,
and won't find them.
Those who fight you
will be of no account and will die.
¹³ I am the LORD your God,
who grasps your strong hand,
who says to you,
Don't fear; I will help you.
¹⁴ Don't fear, worm of Jacob,
people of Israel!
I will help you, says the LORD.
The holy one of Israel is your redeemer.
¹⁵ Look, I've made you
into a new threshing tool
with sharp teeth.
You will thresh mountains
and pulverize them;
you will reduce hills to straw.
¹⁶ When you winnow them,
the wind will carry them off;
the tempest will scatter them.
You will rejoice in the LORD
and take pride in the holy one of Israel.

¹⁷ The poor and the needy
seek water, and there is none;
their tongues are parched with thirst.
I, the LORD, will respond to them;
I, the God of Israel, won't abandon them.
¹⁸ I will open streams on treeless hilltops
and springs in valleys.
I will make the desert into ponds
and dry land into cascades of water.
¹⁹ I will plant in the desert cedar, acacia,
myrtle, and olive trees;
I will put in the wilderness cypress,
elm, and pine as well,
²⁰ so that they will see and know

and observe and comprehend
   that the LORD's hand has done this,
   and the holy one of Israel has created it.

Other gods challenged

²¹ Present your case, says the LORD.
   Bring forward your evidence,
      says Jacob's king.
²² Let the idols⁸ approach
   and tell us what will happen.
   The prior things—what are they?
   Announce them,
      and we'll think about them
   and know their significance.
   Or proclaim to us what is to come!
²³ Report things that will happen
   in the future,
      then we'll know that you are gods.
   Do good! Or do bad!
   Then we will all be afraid and fearful.
²⁴ Look! You are nobody,
   and your deeds are nothing.
   Whoever chooses you is disgusting.
²⁵ I woke up one from the north
   and he came;
      from the east, one who calls my name.
   He tramples governors like mud,
      as a potter treads clay.
²⁶ Who announced this from the start
      so that we would know;
   from an earlier time
      so we would say, "That's right"?
   Truly, no one announced it,
   no one proclaimed it,
   and no one heard your words.
²⁷ I first said it to Zion,
   "Look, here they are";
   to Jerusalem I now send a herald.
²⁸ But I look, and there's no one
   among them, no counselor;
   and when I ask,
   no one can answer.
²⁹ Look, all of them are frauds;
   their deeds amount to nothing;
   their images are a total delusion.

God's servant described

42 But here is my servant,
   the one I uphold;
   my chosen, who brings me delight.

I've put my spirit upon him;
   he will bring justice to the nations.
² He won't cry out or shout aloud
   or make his voice heard in public.
³ He won't break a bruised reed;
   he won't extinguish a faint wick,
   but he will surely bring justice.
⁴ He won't be extinguished or broken
   until he has established justice
   in the land.
   The coastlands await his teaching.

⁵ God the LORD says—
   the one who created the heavens,
   the one who stretched them out,
   the one who spread out the earth
      and its offspring,
   the one who gave breath to its people
   and life to those who walk on it—
⁶ I, the LORD, have called you
   for a good reason.
   I will grasp your hand and guard you,
   and give you as a covenant
      to the people,
   as a light to the nations,
⁷ to open blind eyes,
      to lead the prisoners from prison,
   and those who sit in darkness
      from the dungeon.
⁸ I am the LORD;
   that is my name;
   I don't hand out my glory to others
   or my praise to idols.
⁹ The things announced in the past—
   look—they've already happened,
   but I'm declaring new things.
   Before they even appear,
   I tell you about them.

Warrior and mother

¹⁰ Sing to the LORD a new song!
   Sing his praise
      from the ends of the earth!
   You who sail the sea and all that fills it,
      the coastlands and their residents.
¹¹ Let the desert and its towns shout aloud,
   the villages that Kedar inhabits.
   Let the cliff dwellers sing;
      from the top of the mountains
      let them shout.

⁸Or them

¹² Let them give the LORD glory
    and declare God's praise
        in the coastlands.
¹³ The LORD will go out like a soldier;
    like a warrior God will stir up rage.
    God will shout, will roar;
        over enemies he will prevail.
¹⁴ I've kept still for a very long time.
    I've been silent and restrained myself.
    Like a woman in labor I will moan;
        I will pant, I will gasp.
¹⁵ I will wither mountains and valleys,
    and I will dry up all their vegetation.
    I will turn rivers into deserts,ᵗ
        and I will dry up pools.
¹⁶ I will make the blind walk a road
    they don't know,
    and I will guide them
        in paths they don't know.
    But I will make darkness before them
    into light
    and rough places into level ground.
    These things I will do;
        I won't abandon them.

Blindness and deafness

¹⁷ Turned backward, utterly shamed
    are those who trust in idols,
    who say to a cast image,
        "You are our god!"
¹⁸ Hear, deaf ones,
    and blind ones, look and see!
¹⁹ Who is blind if not my servant
    and deaf like my messenger
        whom I send?
    Who is blind like the restored one,ᵘ
        blind like the servant of the LORD?
²⁰ You have seen many things,
    but don't keep watch.
    With ears open, you don't hear.ᵛ
²¹ The LORD desired
    for the sake of his righteousness
    to expand and glorify the Instruction.
²² But this is a people
    plundered and looted,
    everyone trapped in holes
        and hidden in dungeons.
    They have become plunder
    with no one to rescue,
    loot with no one to say, "Give it back."

²³ Which of you will listen to this,
    will pay attention and respond
        from now on?
²⁴ Who gave Jacob to the looter,
    and Israel to the plunderers?
    Wasn't it the LORD,
        the one we sinned against?
    They were not willing to walk
    in God's ways,
        and wouldn't listen to his teaching.
²⁵ So God poured out on Jacob
    the heat of his anger
    and the fury of battle.
    It scorched him, and he didn't know it;
    it burned him,
        but he didn't give it much thought.

Don't fear

43 But now, says the LORD—
    the one who created you, Jacob,
    the one who formed you, Israel:
    Don't fear, for I have redeemed you;
    I have called you by name; you are mine.
² When you pass through the waters,
    I will be with you;
    when through the rivers,
        they won't sweep over you.
    When you walk through the fire,
    you won't be scorched
        and flame won't burn you.
³ I am the LORD your God,
    the holy one of Israel, your savior.
    I have given Egypt as your ransom,
        Cush and Seba in your place.
⁴ Because you are precious in my eyes,
    you are honored, and I love you.
    I give people in your place,
        and nations in exchange for your life.
⁵ Don't fear,
    I am with you.
    From the east I'll bring your children;
    from the west I'll gather you.
⁶ I'll say to the north, "Give them back!"
    and to the south, "Don't detain them."
    Bring my sons from far away,
    and my daughters
        from the end of the earth,
⁷ everyone who is called by my name
    and whom I created for my glory,
    whom I have formed and made.

ᵗOr islands ᵘHeb Meshullam, possibly a proper name ᵛOr he does not hear

⁸ Bring out the blind people who have eyes,
  the deaf ones who have ears.
⁹ All the nations are gathered together;
  the peoples are assembled.
  Which of them announced this?
  Who predicted to us the past events?
  Let them bring their witnesses
  as a defense;
  let them hear and say, "It's true!"
¹⁰ You are my witnesses, says the LORD,
  my servant, whom I chose,
  so that you would know and believe me
  and understand that I am the one.
  Before me no god was formed;
  after me there has been no other.
¹¹ I, I am the LORD,
  and there is no savior besides me.
¹² I announced, I saved, I proclaimed,
  not some stranger among you.
  You are my witnesses, says the LORD,
  and I am God.
¹³ From the dawn of time, I am the one.
  No one can escape my power.
  I act, and who can undo it?

Don't remember

¹⁴ The LORD your redeemer,
  the holy one of Israel, says,
  For your sake,
  I have sent an army[w] to Babylon,
  and brought down all the bars,
  turning the Chaldeans' singing
  into a lament.[x]
¹⁵ I am the LORD, your holy one,
  Israel's creator, your king!
¹⁶ The LORD says—
  who makes a way in the sea
  and a path in the mighty waters,
¹⁷ who brings out chariot and horse,
  army and battalion;
  they will lie down together
  and will not rise;
  they will be extinguished,
  extinguished like a wick.
¹⁸ Don't remember the prior things;
  don't ponder ancient history.
¹⁹ Look! I'm doing a new thing;
  now it sprouts up; don't you recognize it?
  I'm making a way in the desert,
  paths[y] in the wilderness.

²⁰ The beasts of the field,
  the jackals and ostriches, will honor me,
  because I have put water in the desert
  and streams in the wilderness
  to give water to my people,
  my chosen ones,
²¹ this people whom I formed for myself,
  who will recount my praise.

²² But you didn't call out to me, Jacob;
  you were tired of me, Israel.
²³ You didn't bring me lambs
  for your entirely burned offering;
  you didn't honor me with your sacrifices.
  I didn't make you worship with offerings;
  I didn't weary you with frankincense.
²⁴ You didn't buy spices for me
  with your money,
  or satisfy me with
  the fat of your sacrifices.
  Instead, you have burdened me
  with your sins
  and wearied me with your evil actions.
²⁵ I, I am the one who wipes out
  your rebellious behavior for my sake.
  I won't remember your sin.
²⁶ Summon me, and let's go to trial together;
  you tell your story
  so that you may be vindicated!
²⁷ Your first ancestor sinned,
  and your officials rebelled against me.
²⁸ So I made the holy officials impure,
  handed over Jacob to destruction
  and Israel to abuse.

You are my witnesses

44 But now hear this, Jacob my servant,
  and Israel, whom I have chosen.
² The LORD your maker,
  who formed you in the womb
  and will help you, says:
  Don't fear, my servant Jacob,
  Jeshurun, whom I have chosen.
³ I will pour out water upon thirsty ground
  and streams upon dry land.
  I will pour out my spirit
  upon your descendants
  and my blessing upon your offspring.
⁴ They will spring up from among the reeds
  like willows by flowing streams.

[w]Heb lacks *an army.* [x]Heb uncertain [y]DSS (1QIsaᵃ); MT *streams*

⁵ This one will say, "I am the LORD's,"
  and that one will be named after Jacob.
Another will write on his hand,
  "The LORD's"
  and will take the name Israel.

⁶ The LORD, Israel's king and redeemer,
  the LORD of heavenly forces, says:
I am the first, and I am the last,
  and besides me there are no gods.
⁷ Who is like me?
  Let them speak up, explain it,
    and lay it out for me.
Who announced long ago what is to be?ᶻ
  Let them tell usᵃ what is to come.
⁸ Don't tremble; have no fear!
  Didn't I proclaim it?
  Didn't I inform you long ago?
You are my witnesses!
  Is there a God besides me?
  There is no other rock; I know of none.

Idol-makers mocked

⁹ Idol-makers are all as nothing;
  their playthings do no good.
Their promoters
  neither see nor know anything,
  so they ought to be ashamed.
¹⁰ Who would form a god or cast an idol
  that does no good?
¹¹ All its worshippers will be ashamed,
  and its artisans, who are only human.
They will all gather and stand,
  tremble and be ashamed together.
¹² A blacksmith with his tools
  works it over coals,
  and shapes it with hammers,
  and works it with his strong arm.
He even becomes hungry and weak.
  If he didn't drink water, he'd pass out.
¹³ A carpenter stretches out a string,
  marks it out with a stylus,
  fashions it with carving tools,
  and marks it with a compass.
He makes it into a human form,
  like a splendid human,
  to live in a temple.
¹⁴ He cuts down cedars for himself,
  or chooses a cypressᵇ or oak,

selecting from all the trees of the forest.
  He plants a pine,ᶜ
  and the rain makes it grow.
¹⁵ It becomes suitable to burn for humans,
  so he takes some of the wood
    and warms himself.
He kindles fire and bakes bread.
He fashions a god and worships it;
  he makes an idol and bows down to it.
¹⁶ Half of it he burns in the fire;
  on that half he roasts
    and eats meat, and he is satisfied.
He warms himself and says,
  "Ah, I'm warm, watching the fire!"
¹⁷ And the rest of it he makes into a god,
  into his idol,
  and he bows down, worships,
    and prays to it, saying,
  "Save me, for you are my god!"
¹⁸ They don't know or comprehend,
  for their eyes can't see
    and their minds can't comprehend.
¹⁹ He doesn't think,
  and has no knowledge or
    understanding to think:
Half of it I burned in the fire,
  and I baked bread on its coals,
    and roasted meat and ate.
Should I make the rest
  into something detestable?
  Should I bow down to a block of wood?
²⁰ He's feeding on ashes;
  his deluded mind has led him astray.
He can't save himself and say,
  "Isn't this thing in my hand a lie?"

Promises to Jacob and Jerusalem

²¹ Remember these things, Jacob;
  Israel, for you are my servant.
I formed you; you are my servant!
  I won't forget you, Israel.
²² I swept away your rebellions like a cloud,
  and your sins like fog.
Return to me,
  because I have redeemed you.

²³ Sing, heavens, for the LORD has acted;
  shout, depths of the earth!
Burst out with a ringing cry,

ᶻOr Since I placed an ancient people and coming things ᵃOr them ᵇSpecies uncertain ᶜSpecies uncertain

you mountains, forest,
and every tree in it.
The LORD has redeemed Jacob,
and will glorify himself through Israel.

²⁴ The LORD your redeemer
who formed you in the womb says:
I am the LORD, the maker of all,
who alone stretched out the heavens,
who spread out the earth by myself,
²⁵ who frustrates the omens of diviners
and makes a mockery of magicians,
who turns back the wise
and turns their knowledge into folly.
²⁶ But who confirms the word
of my[d] servant,
and fulfills the predictions
of my messengers;
who says about Jerusalem,
"It will be resettled";
and who says about the cities of Judah,
"They will be rebuilt,
and I will restore their ruins";
²⁷ who says to the ocean depths,
"Dry up; I will dry your streams";
²⁸ who says about Cyrus, "My shepherd—
he will do all that I want";
who says about Jerusalem,
"She will be rebuilt";
and who says about the temple,
"You will be founded once again."

Cyrus as God's anointed

45 The LORD says to his anointed,
to Cyrus,
whom I have grasped
by the strong hand,
to conquer nations before him,
disarming kings,
and opening doors before him,
so no gates will be shut:
² I myself will go before you,
and I will level mountains.
I will shatter bronze doors;
I will cut through iron bars.
³ I will give you hidden treasures
of secret riches,
so you will know that I am the LORD,
the God of Israel, who calls you by name.

⁴ For the sake of my servant Jacob
and Israel my chosen,
I called you by name.
I gave you an honored title,
though you didn't know me.
⁵ I am the LORD, and there is no other;
besides me there is no God.
I strengthen you—
though you don't know me—
⁶ so all will know, from the rising
of the sun to its setting,
that there is nothing apart from me.
I am the LORD; there's no other.
⁷ I form light and create darkness,
make prosperity and create doom;
I am the LORD, who does all these things.

⁸ Pour down, you heavens above,
and let the clouds flow
with righteousness.
Let the earth open for salvation
to bear fruit;
let righteousness sprout as well.
I, the LORD, have created these things.

Potter and clay

⁹ Doom to the one
who argues with the potter,[e]
as if he were just another clay pot!
Does the clay say to the potter,
"What are you making?"
or "Your work has no handles"?
¹⁰ Doom to one who says to a father,
"What have you fathered?"
and to a woman,
"With what are you in labor?"
¹¹ The LORD, the holy one of Israel
and its maker,[f] says:
Are you questioning me[g]
about my own children?
Are you telling me what to do
with the work of my hands?
¹² I myself made the earth,
and created humans upon it.
My own hands stretched out the heavens.
I commanded all their forces.
¹³ I have a right to awaken Cyrus;
I will smooth all his paths.
He will build my city

ᵈOr *his*; also in next line   ᵉOr *maker*   ᶠOr *potter*   ᵍOr *about future things ask me*

and set my exiles free,
    not for a price and not for a bribe,
    says the LORD of heavenly forces.

[14] The LORD says:
    Egypt will grow weary, Cush will be sold,[h]
    and the tall Sabeans
        will cross over to you.
    They will be yours,
        and after you they will go.
    In chains they will come;
    to you they will bow down.
    They will plead with you:
    "Truly God is with you;
        there's no other, no other God."
[15] Surely you are a god who hides himself,
    Israel's God and savior.

Idols contrasted with God

[16] They will all be shamed and disgraced;
    the makers of idols
        will end up disgraced together.
[17] Israel has been saved by the LORD
    of everlasting salvation.
    You won't be shamed,
        and you won't be disgraced
        forever and always.
[18] For this is what the LORD said,
    who created the heavens,
    who is God,
    who formed the earth and made it,
    who established it,
    who didn't create it a wasteland
        but formed it as a habitation:
    I, the LORD, and none other!
[19] I didn't speak in secret
    or in some land of darkness;
    I didn't say to the offspring of Jacob,

[h] Heb uncertain

"Seek me in chaos."
    I am the LORD, the one who speaks truth,
    who announces what is correct.
[20] Gather and come,
    draw near together,
    fugitives of the nations!
    Those who carry their wooden idols
    don't know;
    those who pray to a god who won't save.
[21] Announce! Approach! Confer together!
    Who proclaimed this from the beginning,
    announced it from long ago?
    Wasn't it I, the LORD?
    There's no other God except me,
    a righteous God and a savior;
    there's none besides me!
[22] Turn to me and be saved,
    all you ends of the earth,
    for I am God, and there's no other.
[23] I have sworn a solemn pledge;
    a word has left my mouth;
    it is reliable and won't fail.
    Surely every knee will bow
    and every tongue will confess;
[24] they will say, "Righteousness and
    strength come only from the LORD.
    All who are angry with him
    will come to shame.
[25] All the Israelites
    will be victorious and rejoice."

Babylon's idols can't compare

46 Bel crouches down; Nebo cowers.
    Their idols sit on animals, on beasts.
    The objects you once carried about
    are now borne as burdens
    by the weary animals.
[2] They crouch down and cower together.

CYRUS

Cyrus (II) the Great established the Persian Empire (559–ca. 530 BCE) during an important period in the history of the Jews and the development of Judaism. Ezra and Isaiah credit Cyrus with freeing the Judean exiles in Babylon and allowing them to return home (Ezra 1:1-8; Isa 45:1) to rebuild the temple at Jerusalem (Isa 44:28; Ezra 3:7; 4:3-5; 5:13-17; 6:3-5).

They aren't able to rescue the burden,
  but they themselves go into captivity.
³ Listen to me, house of Jacob,
  all that remains from the house of Israel
  who have been borne by me
    since pregnancy,
  whom I carried from the womb
⁴ until you grow old. I am the one,
  and until you turn gray
    I will support you.
I have done it,
  and I will continue to bear it;
  I will support and I will rescue.
⁵ To whom will you liken me
  and count me equal
  and compare me so that we are alike?
⁶ Those who pour out gold from a bag
  and weigh silver with a balance
  hire a metalworker; then he makes a god.
They bow down; they worship;
⁷ they carry the idol[i] on their
    shoulders and support it;
  they set it down, and it stands still,
  unable to move from its place.
If one cries out to it, it doesn't answer.
  It can't save people from their distress.

Remember past events
⁸ Remember this and take courage;
  take it to heart, you rebels.
⁹ Remember the prior things—
    from long ago;
  I am God, and there's no other.
  I am God! There's none like me,
¹⁰ who tells the end at the beginning,
  from ancient times things not yet done,
  saying, "My plan will stand;
  all that I decide I will do,"
¹¹ I call a bird of prey from the east,
  a man from a distant land for my plan.
  As surely as I have spoken,
    I'll make it happen;
  I have planned, and yes, I'll do it.
¹² Listen to me, you bullheaded people
  who are far from victory:
¹³ I'm bringing my victory near—it isn't far,
  and my salvation—it won't delay.
  I will establish salvation in Zion
  and grant my splendor to Israel.

Daughter Babylon dethroned
47 Go down and sit in the dust,
    virgin Daughter Babylon!
Sit on the ground without a throne,
  Daughter Chaldea,
  because they will no longer call you
    tender and pampered.
² Take the millstones and grind flour!
  Remove your veil, strip off your robe,
    expose your thighs,
    wade through the rivers!
³ Your nakedness will be exposed,
  and your disgrace will be seen.
I will take vengeance;
  no one will intervene.[j]
⁴ Our redeemer has spoken;
  the LORD of heavenly forces is his name,
  the holy one of Israel.

⁵ Sit silent and go into darkness,
  Daughter Chaldea,
  because they will no longer call you
    Queen of Kingdoms.
⁶ I was enraged with my people;
  I made my inheritance impure
  and put them under your power.
You took no pity on them.
  You made your yoke heavy
    even on the elderly.
⁷ You said, "I'm forever;
    I'm the eternal mistress."
  You didn't stop and think;
  you didn't consider the outcome.
⁸ So listen to this,
  luxuriant one who sits secure,
  who says in her heart,
  I'm utterly unique;
  I'll never sit as a widow;
  I'll never know childlessness:
⁹ Both of these will happen to you at once,
  on a single day:
  childlessness and widowhood
  will envelop you in full measure,
  despite your many sorceries,
  despite your very powerful spells.
¹⁰ You felt secure in your evil;
  you said, "No one sees me."
Your wisdom and knowledge
  spun you around.

ⁱOr it ^jSyr, cf Vulg; MT *I won't meet a man*

You thought to yourself,
    I and no one else.
[11] Now evil will come against you,
    something you won't anticipate.
A curse will fall upon you,
    something you won't be able to dispel.
Destruction will come upon you suddenly,
    something you won't foresee.

[12] Continue with your enchantments,
    and with your many spells,
    which you have practiced since childhood.
Maybe you will be able to succeed.
    Maybe you will inspire terror.
[13] You are weary from all your consultations;
    let the astrologers stand up and save you,
    those who gaze at the stars,
    and predict what will happen to you
        at each new moon.
[14] They are just like stubble;
    the fire burns them.
They won't save themselves
    from the powerful flames.
This is no warming ember
    or fire to sit beside.
[15] Those with whom you have
    wearied yourself are like this,
    those with whom you were
        in business from your youth:
each has wandered off on their own way;
    none will save you.

New things from now on

48 Listen to this, house of Jacob,
    who are known by the name of Israel,

---

[k] Or *came out from the waters of Judah*

---

descendants of Judah,[k]
    who swear by the LORD's name
    and invoke Israel's God
        dishonestly and unrighteously.

[2] They are known
    as residents of the holy city,
    those who depend
        upon the God of Israel—
    the LORD of heavenly forces
        is his name.
[3] Past things I announced long ago;
    from my mouth I proclaimed them.
    I acted suddenly, and they came about.
[4] Because I know that you are stubborn,
    your neck is made of iron,
    and your forehead is bronze.
[5] I informed you long ago;
    before they came about
    I proclaimed them to you
so you wouldn't say, "My idol did them;
    my wood statue and metal god
        commanded them."
[6] You've heard and seen all this—
    won't you admit it?
From now on I'll tell you new things,
    guarded secrets that you don't know.
[7] They are created now, not long ago;
    before today you hadn't heard of them,
    so you won't say,
        "I already knew them."
[8] You haven't heard, nor have you known;
    as in ages past your ears are closed,
    because I knew what a traitor you were;
    you were known as a rebel from birth.

ASTRONOMY/ASTROLOGY

The study of the sky, its inhabitants, and their impact upon people on the land below. In the biblical periods, while peasants read the sky as a seasonal, agricultural calendar, city experts (priests, scribes) read the regularities of the sky to set festal calendars and observe predictable social events (horoscopes) concerning societies, cities, and royalty (there were no horoscopes for individuals apart from royalty). These city experts, priests, and scribes were the astronomers/astrologers of the day in Mesopotamia and elsewhere in the Mediterranean world.

⁹ For the sake of my reputation
   I control my anger;
  for your sake
   I restrain my powerful radiance
  so as to not destroy you.
¹⁰ See, I have refined you, but not like silver;
   I have tested you[l]
  in the furnace of misery.
¹¹ For the sake of my reputation,
  for my own sake, I will act,
  for why will my name be made impure?
  I won't give my glory to another.

¹² Listen to me, Jacob;
  Israel, whom I called:
  I am the one;
  I am the first and I am the last.
¹³ My hand founded the earth;
  my strong hand spread out the heavens.
  When I call to them, they all stand up.
¹⁴ Gather yourselves, all of you, and listen.
  Who among you
   announced these things?
   "The LORD loves him.
   He will do what God wants with Babylon
   and with the descendants[m] of Chaldea."
¹⁵ I, I have spoken and told him
  the things that will happen to him;
  I will make him succeed.
¹⁶ Come close to me; listen to this:
  Since the very beginning
   I haven't spoken in secret.
  Whenever anything happens,
   I am there.
  (And now the LORD God
   has sent me with his spirit.)

¹⁷ The LORD your redeemer,
  the holy one of Israel, proclaims:
  I am the LORD your God
   who teaches you for your own good,
   who leads you in the way you should go.
¹⁸ If you would pay attention
  to my commands,
  your well-being would be like a river,
  and your righteousness
   like the waves of the sea.
¹⁹ Your offspring would be like the sand,
  and your descendants like its grains.

Their name would never be eliminated,
  never wiped out from before me.

²⁰ Go out from Babylon;
  flee from the Chaldeans!
Report this with a loud shout, proclaim it;
  broadcast it out to the end of the earth.
Say, "The LORD has redeemed
  his servant Jacob!"
²¹ They weren't thirsty when he led
  them through the deserts.
God made water flow
  from the rock for them;
  split the rock, and water flowed out.
²² There is no well-being,
  says the LORD, for the wicked.

The servant speaks up

49 Listen to me, coastlands;
  pay attention, peoples far away.
The LORD called me before my birth,
  called my name when
   I was in my mother's womb.
² He made my mouth like a sharp sword,
  and hid me in the shadow
   of God's own hand.
He made me a sharpened arrow,
  and concealed me in God's quiver,
³ saying to me, "You are my servant,
  Israel, in whom I show my glory."
⁴ But I said, "I have wearied myself in vain.
  I have used up my strength for nothing."
Nevertheless, the LORD
  will grant me justice;
  my reward is with my God.
⁵ And now the LORD has decided—
  the one who formed me
   from the womb as his servant—
  to restore Jacob to God,
  so that Israel might return to him.
Moreover, I'm honored
  in the LORD's eyes;
  my God has become my strength.
⁶ He said: It is not enough,
  since you are my servant,
  to raise up the tribes of Jacob
  and to bring back the survivors of Israel.
Hence, I will also appoint you
  as light to the nations

---

[l]Or I have chosen   [m]LXX; MT his arm

so that my salvation may reach
  to the end of the earth.

7 The LORD, redeemer of Israel
  and its holy one,
  says to one despised,
  rejected by nations,
  to the slave of rulers:
  Kings will see and stand up;
  commanders will bow down
  on account of the LORD, who is faithful,
  the holy one of Israel,
  who has chosen you.
8 The LORD said:
  At the right time, I answered you;
  on a day of salvation, I helped you.
  I have guarded you,
  and given you as a covenant to the
    people, to restore the land,
  and to reassign deserted properties,
9 saying to the prisoners, "Come out,"
  and to those in darkness,
    "Show yourselves."
  Along the roads animals[n] will graze;
  their pasture will be
  on every treeless hilltop.
10 They won't hunger or thirst;
  the burning heat and sun
  won't strike them,
  because one who has compassion
  for them will lead them
  and will guide them by springs of water.
11 I will turn all my mountains into roads;
  my highways will be built up.
12 Look! These will come from far away.
  Look! These from the north and west,
  and these from the southland.[o]

13 Sing, heavens! Rejoice, earth!
  Break out, mountains, with a song.
  The LORD has comforted his people,
  and taken pity on those who suffer.

Compassion for Zion

14 But Zion says,
  "The LORD has abandoned me;
  my Lord has forgotten me."
15 Can a woman forget her nursing child,
  fail to pity the child of her womb?

Even these may forget,
  but I won't forget you.
16 Look, on my palms I've inscribed you;
  your walls are before me continually.
17 Your builders[p] come quickly;
  those who destroy and demolish you
  will depart from you.
18 Look up all around and see:
  they are all gathered;
  they come to you.
  As surely as I live, says the LORD,
  you will put them all on like ornaments,
  bind them on like a bride.

19 As for your ruins and desolate places
  and destroyed land—
  you will soon be crowded with settlers,
  and those who swallowed you
  will be far away.
20 You will again hear the children
  who were born bereaved say,
  "The place is too crowded for me;
  make room for me to settle."
21 And you will think to yourself,
  Who bore me these?
  I was bereaved and desolate,
  exiled and sent off.
  So who raised these?
  I was left behind, I was alone;
  where were these?

22 The LORD God says:
  Look, I will raise my hand
  to the nations,
  and to the peoples
  I will lift up my signal.
  They will bring your sons in their arms,
  and will carry your daughters
  on their shoulders.
23 Kings will be your attendants,
  and their queens your nursemaids.
  With faces to the ground
  they will bow down to you;
  they will lick the dust from your feet.
  You will know that I am the LORD;
  the one who hopes in me
  won't be ashamed.
24 Can loot be taken from warriors?
  Can a tyrant's captives escape?

---

[n]Heb lacks *animals*.   [o]Heb *Sinim*   [p]Or *children*

²⁵ The LORD says:
Even the captives of warriors
    will be taken,
    and the tyrant's loot will escape.
I myself will oppose those
    who oppose you,
    and I myself will save your children.
²⁶ I will make your oppressors
    eat their own flesh;
    and as with wine, with their own
        blood they will be drunk,
    so that all flesh will know that
        I, the LORD, am your savior,
    and the mighty one of Jacob
        is your redeemer.

50 The LORD says:
Where's your mother's divorce decree,
    with which I sent her away?
Or to which lender did I sell you?
    On account of your sins you were sold;
    on account of your transgressions
        your mother was sent away.
² Why did I come and find no one?
    Why did I call when no one answered?
Is my hand too small to redeem you?^q
    Don't I have enough power to save?
With my rebuke I dry up the sea
    and make the rivers into wilderness.
Their fish stink from lack of water;
    they die of thirst.
³ I clothe the heavens with darkness
    and cover them with funeral clothing.

God's faithful servant
⁴ The LORD God
    gave me an educated tongue
    to know how to respond to the weary
    with a word that will awaken them
        in the morning.^r
    God awakens my ear
        in the morning to listen,
    as educated people do.
⁵ The LORD God opened my ear;
    I didn't rebel; I didn't turn my back.
⁶ Instead, I gave my body to attackers,
    and my cheeks to beard pluckers.
I didn't hide my face
    from insults and spitting.

⁷ The LORD God will help me;
    therefore, I haven't been insulted.
Therefore, I set my face like flint,
    and knew I wouldn't be ashamed.
⁸ The one who will declare me innocent
    is near.
    Who will argue with me?
Let's stand up together.
    Who will bring judgment against me?
    Let him approach me.
⁹ Look! The LORD God will help me.
    Who will condemn me?
Look, they will wear out like clothing;
    the moth will eat them.

¹⁰ Who among you fears the LORD?
    Who listens to the voice of his servant,
    who walks in darkness
        and has no light?
    They will trust in the LORD's name,
        and rely upon their God.
¹¹ Look! All of you are kindling fire,
    igniting torches.
Walk by the light of your fire,
    by the torches you have ignited.
This is what will happen
    to you by my hand:
    you will lie down in grief.

Look to Abraham and Sarah
51 Listen to me,
    you who look for righteousness,
    you who seek the LORD:
Look to the rock
    from which you were cut
    and to the quarry where you were dug.
² Look to Abraham your ancestor,
    and to Sarah, who gave you birth.
They were alone when I called them,
    but I blessed them
    and made them many.
³ The LORD will comfort Zion;
    he will comfort all her ruins.
He will make her desert like Eden
    and her wilderness
        like the LORD's garden.
Happiness and joy
    will be found in her—
    thanks and the sound of singing.

^qHeb lacks *you.* ^rHeb uncertain

Salvation endures forever

⁴ Pay attention to me, my people;
  listen to me, my nation,
    for teaching will go out from me,
    my justice, as a light to the nations.
⁵ I will quickly bring my victory.
  My salvation is on its way,
    and my arm will judge the peoples.
  The coastlands hope for me;
    they wait for my judgment.ˢ
⁶ Look up to the heavens,
    and gaze at the earth beneath.
  The heavens will disappear like smoke,
    the earth will wear out like clothing,
    and its inhabitants will die like gnats.
  But my salvation will endure forever,
    and my righteousness
      will be unbroken.
⁷ Listen to me,
    you who know what is right,
  people who carry my teaching
    in your heart:
  Don't fear human scorn,
    and don't be upset when they abuse you.
⁸ The moth will eat them
    as if they were clothing,
  and the worm will eat them like wool,
    but my righteousness is forever,
    and my salvation for all generations.

ˢOr *for my arm*

Awake, arm of the LORD

⁹ Awake, awake, put on strength,
    arm of the LORD.
  Awake as in times past,
    generations long ago.
  Aren't you the one who crushed Rahab,
    who pierced the dragon?
¹⁰ Didn't you dry up the sea,
    the waters of the great deep?
  And didn't you make
    the redeemed a road to cross
    through the depths of the sea,
  a road for the redeemed to pass?
¹¹ Then let those
    ransomed by the LORD return
  and come to Zion with singing
    and with everlasting joy
    upon their heads.
  Let happiness and joy overwhelm them;
    let grief and groaning flee.

¹² I, I am the one who comforts you.
  Why should you fear humans who will die,
    mortals who are treated like grass?
¹³ You forgot the LORD your maker,
    the one who stretched out the heavens
    and founded the earth.
  You were continually afraid,
    all day long,

SARAH

Sarah is the first matriarch in the Hebrew line. Her original name "Sarai" is an earlier form of Sarah, both meaning "princess." She is renamed at the time that the birth of her son Isaac is announced (Gen 17:15). Her husband is Abram (renamed Abraham in Gen 17:5). Sarah is the first of the line of Hebrew matriarchs who has difficulty bearing a child. She decides to do something about the problem and gives Hagar, variously described as her female servant and her slave, to Abraham to bear a child for her, a custom known from Mesopotamian sources. The plan does not turn out as Sarah apparently intends. Once Hagar is pregnant she becomes contemptuous of Sarah. Sarah blames Abraham, who gives her free rein to deal with Hagar. Sarah later gives birth to Isaac (Gen 17–21). She dies in Hebron, and Abraham buries her in Canaan in the cave of Machpelah. In Isaiah 51:2 she is described as the mother of the Hebrew people. In the NT Sarah is mentioned along with Abraham as an exemplar of faith (Heb 11:8-12).

on account of the oppressor's wrath—
a fear by which they intend
to destroy you.
Where now is the oppressor's wrath?
¹⁴ The imprisoned ones will soon be released;
they won't die in the pit
or even lack bread.
¹⁵ I am the LORD your God,
who stirs up the sea
so that its waves roar—
the LORD of heavenly forces is his name.
¹⁶ I put my words in your mouth
and hid you in the shadow of my hand,
stretching out^t the heavens,
founding the earth,
and saying to Zion, "You are my people."

Wake yourself, Jerusalem
¹⁷ Wake yourself, wake yourself!
Rise up, Jerusalem,
who drank the cup of wrath
from the LORD's hand.
You drank;
you drained the goblet of reeling.
¹⁸ There's no one to guide her
among all the children she bore;
there's no one to take her
by the hand among all the children
she raised.
¹⁹ These two things have happened to you—
Who will be sorry for you?^u—
destruction and devastation,
famine and sword—
who will comfort you?^v
²⁰ Your children passed out;
they lay at the head of every street
like antelope in a net,
filled with the LORD's wrath,
with the rebuke of your God.

²¹ Therefore, hear this, suffering one,
who is drunk, but not from wine.
²² The LORD, your Lord and your God,
who contends for his people, says:
Look, I have taken the cup of reeling,
the goblet of my wrath, from your hand.
You will no longer drink from it.
²³ I will put it
in the hand of your tormentors,

who said to you,
"Lie down so that we can walk on you.
Make your back like the ground,
like a street for those walking on it."

Awake, holy Zion
52 Awake, awake,
put on your strength, Zion!
Put on your splendid clothing,
Jerusalem, you holy city;
for the uncircumcised and unclean
will no longer come into you.
² Shake the dust off yourself;
rise up; sit enthroned, Jerusalem.
Loose the bonds from your neck,
captive Daughter Zion!

³ The LORD proclaims:
You were sold for nothing,
and you will be redeemed
without money.
⁴ The LORD God proclaims:
Long ago my people went down
to reside in Egypt.
Moreover, Assyria
has oppressed them without cause.
⁵ And now what have I here? says the LORD.
My people are taken away for nothing.
Their rulers wail, says the LORD,
and continually all day long
my name is despised.
⁶ Therefore, my people
will know my name on that day;
I'm the one who promises it; I'm here.

Your God rules
⁷ How beautiful upon the mountains
are the feet of a messenger
who proclaims peace,
who brings good news,
who proclaims salvation,
who says to Zion, "Your God rules!"
⁸ Listen! Your lookouts lift their voice;
they sing out together!
Right before their eyes they see
the LORD returning to Zion.

⁹ Break into song together,
you ruins of Jerusalem!

^tOr *planting* ^uDSS (1QIsaᵃ), LXX, Vulg; MT *How will I* ^vOr *how will I comfort you?*

The LORD has comforted his people and
  has redeemed Jerusalem.
¹⁰ The LORD has bared his holy arm
  in view of all the nations;
  all the ends of the earth have seen
    our God's victory.

¹¹ Depart! Depart! Go out from there!
  Unclean! Don't touch!
  Get out of that place; purify yourselves,
  carriers of the LORD's equipment!
¹² You won't go out in a rush,
  nor will you run away,
  because the one going before you
    is the LORD;
  your rear guard is the God of Israel.

Suffering servant
¹³ Look, my servant will succeed.
  He will be exalted and lifted very high.
¹⁴ Just as many were appalled by you,
  he too appeared disfigured, inhuman,
  his appearance unlike that of mortals.
¹⁵ But he will astonish^w many nations.
  Kings will be silenced because of him,
  because they will see
  what they haven't seen before;
  what they haven't heard before,
  they will ponder.

53 Who can believe what we have heard,
  and for whose sake has
  the LORD's arm^x been revealed?

---

^wOr *sprinkle* ^xOr *power*

SERVANT (OT)

Servants are persons under a superior for whom they perform tasks. They clearly are not chattel slaves. While a number of biblical terms may be translated as "servant," there is not always a clear distinction between who is a servant and who is a slave. The translation of either "servant" or "slave" depends on the specific context.

In the OT, servants look after the affairs of individuals; are part of extensive households; oversee laborers; serve in the military; advise the king; and assist in the temple. Conquered peoples are sometimes designated as servants of the king. The role of servants varies widely, but it is clear that these individuals are not in a restricted, permanent form of slavery. Indeed, many of them have the respect of the people they serve.

In a religious context, prominent individuals, kings, and prophets are designated as servants of God, a title that describes their humility, piety, and obedient performance of tasks given to them by God. Included among these are: Abraham (Gen 26:24; Ps 105:6); Moses (Exod 14:31; Num 11:11; Ps 105:26); Joshua (Judg 2:8); David (2 Sam 3:18; Ps 144:10); Hezekiah (2 Chron 32:16); Isaiah (Isa 20:3); Nebuchadnezzar (Jer 25:9); and Daniel (Dan 6:20).

The theme finds its most significant theological expression in the Servant Songs of Isaiah (Isa 40–55). Scholarship debates whether the servant is to be understood as a corporate or individual figure. While a number of the references clearly mean the nation of Israel as the servant, others are unclear and some portray the servant as an individual who will suffer on behalf of Israel (Isa 53). Both Judaism and Christianity adopted the Servant Songs as a model for understanding the suffering of righteous ones as having redemptive power for the larger community.

² He grew up like a young plant before us,ʸ
　　like a root from dry ground.
He possessed no splendid form
　　for us to see,
　　no desirable appearance.
³ He was despised and avoided by others;
　　a man who suffered,
　　who knew sickness well.
Like someone
　　from whom people hid their faces,
　　he was despised,
　　and we didn't think about him.

⁴ It was certainly our sickness
　　that he carried,
　　and our sufferings that he bore,
but we thought him afflicted,
　　struck down by God and tormented.
⁵ He was pierced because of our rebellions
　　and crushed because of our crimes.
He bore the punishment
　　that made us whole;
　　by his wounds we are healed.
⁶ Like sheep we had all wandered away,
　　each going its own way,
but the LORD let fall on him
　　all our crimes.

⁷ He was oppressed and tormented,
　　but didn't open his mouth.
Like a lamb being brought to slaughter,
　　like a ewe silent before her shearers,
　　he didn't open his mouth.

⁸ Due to an unjust ruling
　　he was taken away,
　　and his fate—who will think about it?
He was eliminated
　　from the land of the living,
　　struck dead
　　because of my people's rebellion.
⁹ His grave was among the wicked,
　　his tomb with evildoers,ᶻ
though he had done no violence,
　　and had spoken nothing false.

¹⁰ But the LORD wanted to crush him
　　and to make him suffer.
If his life is offeredᵃ as restitution,

he will see his offspring;
　　he will enjoy long life.
The LORD's plans will come
　　to fruition through him.
¹¹ After his deep anguish he will see light,ᵇ
　　and he will be satisfied.
Through his knowledge,
　　the righteous one, my servant,
　　will make many righteous,
　　and will bear their guilt.
¹² Therefore, I will give him a share
　　with the great,
and he will divide the spoil
　　with the strong,
in return for exposing his life to death
　　and being numbered with rebels,
though he carried the sin of many
　　and pleaded on behalf
　　of those who rebelled.

Sing, barren woman

54 Sing, barren woman
　　who has borne no child;
break forth into singing and cry out,
　　you who were never in labor,
for the children of the wife
　　who has been deserted
　　will be more numerous than the
　　children of the married,
　　says the LORD.
² Enlarge the site of your tent,
　　and stretch out the drapes
　　of your dwellings;
　　don't hold back.
Lengthen your tent ropes
　　and strengthen your stakes.
³ To the right and to the left
　　you will burst out,
and your children will possess
　　the nations' land
　　and settle their desolate cities.

⁴ Don't fear,
　　because you won't be ashamed;
don't be dismayed,
　　because you won't be disgraced.
You will forget the shame of your youth;
　　you'll no longer remember
　　the disgrace of your widowhood.

ʸOr him　ᶻCf Tg; MT *and with a rich one in his deaths*　ᵃOr *if you place his life*　ᵇDSS (1QIsaᵃ); MT lacks *light*.

5 The one marrying you
   is the one who made you—
   the LORD of heavenly forces is his name.
The one redeeming you
   is the holy one of Israel,
   the one called the God of all the earth.
6 As an abandoned
   and dejected woman
   the LORD has summoned you;
   as a young wife when she is rejected,
   says your God.
7 For a brief moment I abandoned you,
   but with great mercy
   I will bring you back.
8 In an outburst of rage,
   I hid my face from you for a moment,
   but with everlasting love
   I have consoled you,
   says your redeemer, the LORD.

9 These are like the days^c of Noah for me,
   when I promised that Noah's waters
   would never again cover the earth.
   Likewise I promise not to rage
   against you or rebuke you.
10 The mountains may shift,
   and the hills may be shaken,
   but my faithful love
   won't shift from you,
   and my covenant of peace
   won't be shaken,
   says the LORD, the one who pities you.

11 Suffering one, storm-tossed, uncomforted,
   look, I am setting your gemstones
   in silvery metal
   and your foundations with sapphires.

^c Or for the waters

12 I will make your towers of rubies,
   and your gates of beryl,
   and all your walls of precious jewels.
13 All your children will be disciples
   of the LORD—
   I will make peace abound
   for your children.
14 You will be firmly founded
   in righteousness.
   You will stay far from oppression
   because you won't fear,
   far from terror
   because it won't come near you.
15 If anyone attacks you,
   it's none of my doing.
   Whoever attacks you
   will fall because of you.
16 Look, I myself created the metalworker
   who blows the fire of coal
   and who produces a tool for his work.
   And I myself created the looter
   to destroy.
17 No weapon fashioned against
   you will succeed,
   and you may condemn every tongue
   that disputes with you.
This is the heritage of the LORD's servants,
   whose righteousness comes from me,
   says the LORD.

Invitation to the feast

55 All of you who are thirsty,
   come to the water!
Whoever has no money,
   come, buy food and eat!
Without money, at no cost,
   buy wine and milk!

NOAHIC COVENANT

A covenant established between God and Noah, as well as with Noah's descendants and all animals, following the flood (Gen 9:8-17). God promised never again to destroy the world by means of a flood and placed the rainbow in the clouds as a reminder of the covenant. Unlike most other covenants between God and humanity, the Noahic covenant did not impose any requirements on humans.

² Why spend money for what isn't food,
  and your earnings
    for what doesn't satisfy?
  Listen carefully to me
  and eat what is good;
    enjoy the richest of feasts.
³ Listen and come to me;
  listen, and you will live.
  I will make
  an everlasting covenant with you,
    my faithful loyalty to David.
⁴ Look, I made him a witness to the peoples,
  a prince and commander of peoples.
⁵ Look, you will call a nation
  you don't know,
  a nation you don't know will run to you
  because of the LORD your God,
  the holy one of Israel,
    who has glorified you.

⁶ Seek the LORD when he can still be found;
  call him while he is yet near.
⁷ Let the wicked abandon their ways
  and the sinful their schemes.
  Let them return to the LORD
  so that he may have mercy on them,
  to our God, because he is generous
    with forgiveness.
⁸ My plans aren't your plans,
  nor are your ways my ways,
  says the LORD.
⁹ Just as the heavens
  are higher than the earth,
  so are my ways higher than your ways,
  and my plans than your plans.
¹⁰ Just as the rain and the snow
  come down from the sky
  and don't return there
    without watering the earth,
  making it conceive and yield plants
  and providing seed to the sower
    and food to the eater,
¹¹ so is my word
  that comes from my mouth;
  it does not return to me empty.
  Instead, it does what I want,
  and accomplishes what I intend.
¹² Yes, you will go out with celebration,
  and you will be brought back in peace.

Even the mountains and the hills
  will burst into song before you;
  all the trees of the field
    will clap their hands.
¹³ In place of the thorn the cypress will grow;
  in place of the nettle the myrtle will grow.
  This will attest to the LORD's stature,
  an enduring reminder
    that won't be removed.

Keepers of God's Sabbath

56 The LORD says:
  Act justly and do what is righteous,
  because my salvation is coming soon,
  and my righteousness will be revealed.
² Happy is the one who does this,
  the person who holds it fast,
  who keeps the Sabbath,
    not making it impure,
  and avoids doing any evil.

³ Don't let the immigrant
  who has joined with the LORD say,
  "The LORD will exclude me
    from the people."
  And don't let the eunuch say,
    "I'm just a dry tree."
⁴ The LORD says:
  To the eunuchs who keep my sabbaths,
  choose what I desire,
  and remain loyal to my covenant.
⁵ In my temple and courts, I will give them
  a monument and a name
    better than sons and daughters.
  I will give to them an enduring name
  that won't be removed.
⁶ The immigrants who have joined me,[d]
  serving me and loving my name,[e]
  becoming my servants,[f]
  everyone who keeps the Sabbath
  without making it impure,
  and those who hold fast to my covenant:
⁷ I will bring them to my holy mountain,
  and bring them joy in my house of prayer.
  I will accept their entirely burned
  offerings and sacrifices on my altar.
  My house will be known as a house
    of prayer for all peoples,
⁸ says the LORD God,
  who gathers Israel's outcasts.

---

[d] Or *to the Lord*   [e] Or *serving him and loving the LORD name*   [f] Or *becoming his servants*

I will gather still others
to those I have already gathered.

Neglectful leaders

9 All you beasts of the field,
come and eat,
all you beasts of the forest!
10 The lookouts are blind;
they all lack sense.
They are all mute dogs that can't bark,
dreamers, loungers, loving to sleep.
11 But the dogs have monstrous appetites.
They never have enough.
They are shepherds
who don't understand.
All of them have turned to their own ways,
every last one greedy for profit.
12 "Come! I'll get some wine!

Let's drink beer!
Tomorrow will be like today,
or even much better."

57 The righteous person perishes,
and no one takes it to heart.
Loyal people are gathered together,
and no one understands
that because of evil
the righteous one passed away.
2 They will find peace;
those who walk in straight paths
will find rest on their burial beds.

Accusations against idolators

3 Come here, you children of sorcery,
offspring of adultery and prostitution!
4 Whom are you mocking?

EUNUCH

Although the term can designate a married royal official (Potiphar [Gen 39:1]), *eunuch* often suggests a castrated man attending female rulers (Jezebel [2 Kgs 9:30-32], Esther [Esth 4:4-5], Candace [Acts 8:27]) or overseeing the king's harem (Esth 2:14-15). The emasculated condition of eunuchs could include a range of physiological characteristics (defective, damaged, or dismembered testicles or penis) resulting from inherited nature ("eunuchs who have been eunuchs from birth"), imposed mutilation ("made eunuchs by other people"—often a casualty of war or slavery), or self-infliction (as with ascetics "who have made themselves eunuchs because of the kingdom of heaven") (see Matt 19:12).

While eunuchs could enjoy considerable political and economic influence (Acts 8:27), in ancient societies that placed a high premium on male virility, the eunuch embodied shame, impotence, and social deviance. Biblical law excludes men with damaged genitalia from the worshipping assembly in general (Deut 23:1) and the holy priesthood in particular (Lev 21:17-21).

Other traditions, however, paint a more positive picture. Isaiah envisions an honored and fruitful place for faithful eunuchs in the Lord's house (Isa 56:3-8); Jeremiah reports the noble efforts of Ebed-melech, an Ethiopian eunuch serving the king of Judah, to rescue Jeremiah from unjust imprisonment (Jer 38:7-13; 39:15-18); and Acts 8:26-40 recounts the baptism of a scripture-reading, God-fearing eunuch from Candace's Ethiopian court. In this latter text, the eunuch's prominent status as a chief financial officer is balanced by his apparent identification with the shorn and scorned figure from Isaiah 53:7-8 and his implied experience of being prohibited from participating in religious ceremonies ("What would keep me from being baptized?" [Acts 8:30-36]).

Against whom do you
open your mouth wide
and stick out your tongue?
Aren't you children of rebellion,
offspring of lies,
[5] who console yourselves with idols
under every green tree,
who slaughter children in the valleys,
under the rocky cliffs?
[6] You belong with the smooth talkers[g]
in the valley;
they, they are your lot.
For them you poured out a drink offering,
and presented a grain offering.
Should I condone these things?
[7] On a very high mountain
you made your bed.
You went up there to offer a sacrifice.
[8] Behind the door and the doorpost
you placed your symbols.
You abandoned me and lay down,
making room in your bed
and making deals for yourself
with them.[h]
You loved their bed;
you saw their nakedness.
[9] You went down to Molech[i] with oil,
and you slathered on your ointments;
you sent your messengers far away,
sent them down to the underworld.[j]
[10] Worn out by all your efforts,
yet you wouldn't say, "This is useless."
You found new strength;
therefore, you weren't tired.
[11] Whom did you dread and fear
so that you lied,
didn't remember me
or give me a thought?
Isn't it because I was silent
and closed my eyes
that you stopped fearing me?
[12] I will bring evidence about your
righteousness and your actions;
they won't help you.
[13] When you cry out,
let those things you've gathered save you!
The wind will lift them all;
one breath will take them away.
but those taking refuge in me

will inherit the land
and possess my holy mountain.

Peace for the remorseful

[14] It will be said:
"Survey, survey; build a road!
Remove barriers from my people's road!"
[15] The one who is high and lifted up,
who lives forever,
whose name is holy, says:
I live on high, in holiness,
and also with the crushed[k] and the lowly,
reviving the spirit of the lowly,
reviving the heart of those
who have been crushed.[l]
[16] I won't always accuse,
nor will I be enraged forever.
It is my own doing
that their spirit is exhausted—
I gave them breath!
[17] I was enraged about their illegal profits;
I struck them;
in rage I withdrew from them.
Yet they went on wandering
wherever they wanted.
[18] I have seen their ways,
but I will heal them.
I will guide them,
and reward them with comfort.
And for those who mourn,
[19] I will create reason for praise:[m]
utter prosperity to those far and near,
and I will heal them, says the LORD.
[20] But the wicked are like the churning sea
that can't keep still.
They churn up from their waters
muck and mud.
[21] There is no peace, says my God,
for the wicked.

Fasting from injustice

58 Shout loudly; don't hold back;
raise your voice like a trumpet!
Announce to my people their crime,
to the house of Jacob their sins.
[2] They seek me day after day,
desiring knowledge of my ways
like a nation that acted righteously,
that didn't abandon their God.

[g]Or *smooth things* [h]Heb uncertain [i]Or *the king* [j]Heb *Sheol* [k]Or *contrite* [l]Or *contrite* [m]Heb uncertain

They ask me for righteous judgments,
  wanting to be close to God.
³ "Why do we fast and you don't see;
  why afflict ourselves
    and you don't notice?"
Yet on your fast day
  you do whatever you want,
  and oppress all your workers.
⁴ You quarrel and brawl,
  and then you fast;
  you hit each other violently
    with your fists.
You shouldn't fast as you are doing today
  if you want to make
    your voice heard on high.
⁵ Is this the kind of fast I choose,
  a day of self-affliction,
  of bending one's head like a reed
  and of lying down
    in mourning clothing and ashes?
Is this what you call a fast,
  a day acceptable to the LORD?

⁶ Isn't this the fast I choose:
  releasing wicked restraints,
    untying the ropes of a yoke,
  setting free the mistreated,
  and breaking every yoke?
⁷ Isn't it sharing your bread
    with the hungry
  and bringing the homeless poor
    into your house,
  covering the naked when you see them,
  and not hiding from your own family?
⁸ Then your light
  will break out like the dawn,
  and you will be healed quickly.
Your own righteousness
  will walk before you,
  and the LORD's glory
    will be your rear guard.
⁹ Then you will call,
  and the LORD will answer;
  you will cry for help,
    and God will say, "I'm here."
If you remove the yoke from among you,
  the finger-pointing, the wicked speech;
¹⁰ if you open your heart to the hungry,
  and provide abundantly
    for those who are afflicted,
  your light will shine in the darkness,

and your gloom will be like the noon.
¹¹ The LORD will guide you continually
  and provide for you,
    even in parched places.
He will rescue your bones.
You will be like a watered garden,
  like a spring of water that won't run dry.
¹² They will rebuild ancient ruins
  on your account;
  the foundations of generations past
    you will restore.
You will be called Mender of Broken Walls,
  Restorer of Livable Streets.

¹³ If you stop trampling the Sabbath,
  stop doing whatever you want
    on my holy day,
  and consider the Sabbath a delight,
  sacred to the LORD, honored,
  and honor it
    instead of doing things your way,
  seeking what you want
    and doing business as usual,
¹⁴ then you will take delight in the LORD.
  I will let you ride on the heights
    of the earth;
  I will sustain you with the heritage
    of your ancestor Jacob.
The mouth of the LORD has spoken.

Alienation from God

59 Look! The LORD does not lack
  the power to save,
  nor are his ears too dull to hear,
² but your misdeeds have separated you
    from your God.
Your sins have hidden his face from you
  so that you aren't heard.
³ Your hands are stained with blood,
  and your fingers with guilt.
Your lips speak lies;
  your tongues mutter malice.
⁴ No one sues honestly;
  no one pleads truthfully.
By trusting in emptiness
  and speaking deceit,
  they conceive harm
    and give birth to malice.
⁵ They hatch adders' eggs,
  and weave spiderwebs.
Whoever eats their eggs will die.

Moreover, the crushed egg
  hatches a viper.
[6] Their webs can't serve as clothing;
  they can't cover themselves
    with their deeds.
Their deeds are deeds of malice,
  and the work of violence
    is in their hands.
[7] Their feet run to evil;
  they rush to shed innocent blood.
Their thoughts are thoughts of malice;
  desolation and destruction
    litter their highways.
[8] They don't know the way of peace;
  there's no justice in their paths.
They make their roads crooked;
  no one who walks in them knows peace.

Injustice obscures vision

[9] Because of all this, justice is far from us,
  and righteousness beyond our reach.
We expect light, and there is darkness;
  we await a gleam of light,
    but walk about in gloom.
[10] We grope along the wall like the blind;
  like those without eyes we grope.
We stumble at noonday
  as if it were twilight,
  and among the strong
    as if we were dying.
[11] All of us growl like bears,
  and like doves we moan.
We expect justice, but there is none;
  we await salvation, but it is far from us.
[12] Our rebellions are numerous
  in your presence;
  our sins testify against us.
Our rebellions are with us;
  we're aware of our guilt:
[13] defying and denying the LORD,
  turning away from our God,
  planning oppression and revolt,
  muttering lying words
    conceived in our minds.
[14] Justice is pushed aside;
  righteousness stands far off,
  because truth has stumbled
    in the public square,
  and honesty can't enter.
[15] Truth is missing;
  anyone turning from evil is plundered.

God will intervene

The LORD looked and was upset
  at the absence of justice.
[16] Seeing that there was no one,
  and astonished that
    no one would intervene,
  God's arm brought victory,
    upheld by righteousness,
[17] putting on righteousness as armor
  and a helmet of salvation on his head,
  putting on garments of vengeance,
  and wrapping himself in a cloak of zeal.
[18] God will repay according to their actions:
  wrath to his foes,
    retribution to enemies,
    retribution to the coastlands,
[19] so those in the west
  will fear the LORD's name,
  and those in the east
  will fear God's glory.
It will come like a rushing river
  that the LORD's wind drives on.
[20] A redeemer will come to Zion
  and to those in Jacob who stop rebelling,
    says the LORD.

[21] As for me, this is my covenant
  with them, says the LORD.
My spirit, which is upon you,
  and my words, which I have placed
    in your mouth
  won't depart from your mouth,
  nor from the mouths
    of your descendants,
  nor from the mouths
    of your descendants' children,
  says the LORD,
    forever and always.

Jerusalem's coming radiance

60 Arise! Shine! Your light has come;
  the LORD's glory has shone upon you.
[2] Though darkness covers the earth
  and gloom the nations,
  the LORD will shine upon you;
  God's glory will appear over you.
[3] Nations will come to your light
  and kings to your dawning radiance.

[4] Lift up your eyes and look all around:
  they are all gathered;
  they have come to you.

Your sons will come from far away,
and your daughters on caregivers' hips.
[5] Then you will see and be radiant;
your heart will tremble and open wide,
because the sea's abundance
will be turned over to you;
the nations' wealth will come to you.
[6] Countless camels will cover your land,
young camels from Midian and Ephah.
They will all come from Sheba,
carrying gold and incense,
proclaiming the LORD's praises.
[7] All Kedar's sheep will be gathered for you;
rams from Nebaioth
will be your offerings;
they will be accepted on my altar,
and I will glorify my splendid house.

[8] Who are these who fly like a cloud,
like doves to their shelters?
[9] I'm the hope of the coastlands.
Ships from Tarshish are in the lead
to bring your children from afar,
their silver and gold with them
for the name of the LORD your God
and for the holy one of Israel,
who has glorified you.
[10] Foreigners will rebuild your walls,
and their kings will serve you.
Though in my rage I struck you down,
in my favor I have consoled you.
[11] Your gates will be open continually;
day and night they won't close,
to bring to you the wealth of nations,
and their kings led in procession.
[12] The nation and the dynasty
that won't serve you will perish;
such nations will be devastated.
[13] Lebanon's glory will come upon you,
cypress, elm, and pine,
to glorify the site of my sanctuary,
and I will honor my royal footstool.
[14] The children of your tormenters
will come bending low to you;
all who despised you
will bow down at your feet.
They will call you The LORD's City,
Zion, of the holy one of Israel.
[15] Instead of being abandoned,

hated, and forbidden,
I will make you majestic forever,
a joy for all generations.
[16] You will suck the milk of nations,
and nurse at royal breasts.
You will know that I am the LORD,
your savior
and your redeemer,
the mighty one of Jacob.
[17] Instead of bronze I will bring gold;
instead of iron I will bring silver;
instead of wood, bronze;
and instead of stones, iron.
I will make peace your governor
and righteousness your taskmaster.
[18] Violence will no longer resound
throughout your land,
nor devastation or destruction
within your borders.
You will call your walls Salvation,
and your gates Praise.
[19] The sun will no longer
be your light by day,
nor will the moon shine for illumination
by night.[n]
The LORD will be your everlasting light;
your God will be your glory.
[20] Your sun will no longer set;
your moon will no longer wane.
The LORD will be
an everlasting light for you,
and your days of mourning will be ended.
[21] Your people will all be righteous;
they will possess the land forever.
They are the shoot that I planted,
the work of my hands, to glorify myself.
[22] The least will become a thousand,
and the smallest a powerful people.
I am the LORD; at the right moment,
I will hurry it along.

Joyful proclamations

61 The LORD God's spirit is upon me,
because the LORD has anointed me.
He has sent me
to bring good news to the poor,
to bind up the brokenhearted,
to proclaim release for captives,
and liberation for prisoners,

[n] Cf DSS (1QIsa[a]), LXX; MT lacks *by night*.

² to proclaim the year of the LORD's favor
and a day of vindication for our God,
to comfort all who mourn,
³ to provide for Zion's mourners,
to give them a crown in place of ashes,
oil of joy in place of mourning,
a mantle of praise
in place of discouragement.
They will be called Oaks of Righteousness,
planted by the LORD to glorify himself.
⁴ They will rebuild the ancient ruins;
they will restore formerly deserted places;
they will renew ruined cities,
places deserted in generations past.

⁵ Foreigners will stay
and shepherd your sheep,
and strangers will be
your farmers and vinedressers.
⁶ You will be called The Priests of the LORD;
Ministers of Our God,
they will say about you.
You will feed on the wealth of nations,
and fatten° yourself on their riches.
⁷ Instead of shame,
theirᵖ portion will be double;
instead of disgrace,
they will rejoice over their share.
They will possess a double portion
in their land;
everlasting joy will be theirs.
⁸ I, the LORD, love justice;
I hate robbery and dishonesty.�q
I will faithfully give them their wage,
and make with them
an enduring covenant.
⁹ Their offspring will be known
among the nations,
and their descendants
among the peoples.
All who see them will recognize
that they are a people
blessed by the LORD.

¹⁰ I surely rejoice in the LORD;
my heart is joyful because of my God,
because he has clothed me
with clothes of victory,
wrapped me in a robe of righteousness

like a bridegroom in a priestly crown,
and like a bride adorned in jewelry.
¹¹ As the earth puts out its growth,
and as a garden grows its seeds,
so the LORD God will grow righteousness
and praise before all the nations.

Jerusalem redeemed

62 For Zion's sake I won't keep silent,
and for Jerusalem's sake
I won't sit still
until her righteousness
shines out like a light,
and her salvation blazes like a torch.
² Nations will see your righteousness,
all kings your glory.
You will be called by a new name,
which the LORD's own mouth
will determine.
³ You will be a splendid garland
in the LORD's hand,
a royal turban in the palm
of God's hand.
⁴ You will no longer be called Abandoned,
and your land will no longer be called
Deserted.
Instead, you will be called
My Delight Is in Her,
and your land, Married.
Because the LORD delights in you,
your land will be cared for once again.
⁵ As a young man marries a young woman,
so your sons will marry you.
With the joy of a bridegroom
because of his bride,
so your God will rejoice because of you.

⁶ Upon your walls, Jerusalem,
I have appointed sentinels.
Continually, all day and all night,
they won't keep silent.
You who call on the LORD, don't rest,
⁷ and don't allow God to rest
until he establishes Jerusalem,
and makes it the praise of the earth.
⁸ The LORD has promised
with raised hand and strong arm:
I will never again give your grain
as food for your enemies.

°Heb uncertain ᵖOr *your* �q Heb manuscripts, LXX, Syr, Tg; MT *robbery with an entirely burned offering*

Foreigners won't drink your wine
for which you labored.
9 Those who harvest will eat it
and will praise the LORD;
those who gather will drink it
in my holy courtyards.

10 Pass through, pass through the gates;
prepare the way for the people!
Build, build the road;
clear away the stones!
Raise up a signal for the peoples.
11 This is what the LORD announced
to the earth's distant regions:
Say to Daughter Zion,
"Look! Your deliverer arrives,
bringing reward and payment!"
12 They will be called The Holy People,
Redeemed By the LORD.
And you will be called Sought After—
A City That Is Not Abandoned.

Vengeance against the nations

63 Who is this coming from Edom,
from Bozrah in bright red garments,
this splendidly dressed one,
striding[r] with great power?
It is I, proclaiming righteousness,
powerful to save!
2 Why is your clothing red,
and your garments like those
of one who stomps on grapes?
3 I have pressed out in the vat
by myself—from the peoples,
no one was with me.
I stomped on them in my anger,
trampled them in my wrath.
Their blood splashed on my garments,
and stained all my clothing,
4 because I intended a day of vengeance;
the year of my deliverance
had arrived.
5 I looked and found no helper;
I was astonished to find no supporter.
But my arm brought victory for me;
my wrath helped me.
6 I trampled down nations in my anger
and made them drunk on my wrath;
I spilled their blood on the ground.

Prayer of yearning

7 I will recount the LORD's faithful acts;
I will sing the LORD's praises,
because of all the LORD did for us,
for God's great favor
toward the house of Israel.
God treated them compassionately
and with deep affection.
8 God said, "Truly, they are my people,
children who won't do what is wrong."
God became their savior.
9 During all their distress,
God also was distressed,
so a messenger who served him
saved them.
In love and mercy God redeemed them,
lifting and carrying them
throughout earlier times.
10 But they rebelled,
and made God's holy spirit terribly sad,
so that he turned into their enemy—
he fought against them!

11 Then they remembered earlier times,
when he rescued his people.[s]
Where was the one
who drew them up from the sea,
the shepherd[t] of the flock?
Where was the one
who put within them his holy spirit;
12 the one who guided Moses' strong hand
with his glorious arm;
who split the water for them
to create an enduring reputation
for himself,
13 and who guided them through
the depths?
Like a horse in the desert,
they didn't stumble.
14 Like cattle descending to the valley,
the LORD's spirit brought them to rest.
In this way you led your people
and made for yourself
a glorious reputation.

15 Look down from heaven and see,
from your holy and glorious perch.
Where are your energy and your might,
your concern and your pity?
Don't hold back![u]

---

[r]Or stooping   [s]Or Moses, his people   [t]LXX, Tg; MT shepherds   [u]Heb uncertain

¹⁶ You are surely our father,
  even though Abraham doesn't know us,
  and Israel doesn't recognize us.
You, LORD, are our father;
  your reputation since long ago
  is that of our redeemer.
¹⁷ Why do you lead us astray, LORD,
  from your ways?
Why do you harden our heart
  so we don't fear you?
Return for the sake of your servants
  the tribes that are your heritage!
¹⁸ Why did the wicked
  bring down your holy place?^v

Why did our enemies
  trample your sanctuary?
¹⁹ For too long we have been
  like those you don't rule,
  like those not known by your name.

64 ^wIf only you would tear open
  the heavens and come down!
Mountains would quake before you
² like fire igniting brushwood
  or making water boil.
^xIf you would make your name known
  to your enemies,
  the nations would tremble
  in your presence.

^vCf LXX, Vulg; Heb uncertain ^w63:19*b* in Heb ^x64:1 in Heb

HOLY SPIRIT

The Hebrew and Greek words encompass a wide range of realities: divine energy and presence (e.g., Ps 51:11); the human core (e.g., Ps 77:6); breath (e.g., Isa 40:7); the waxing and waning of life itself (Job 34:14; Ezek 10:17); a disposition, as in "spirit of prostitution" (Hos 4:12); a demonic being (e.g., 1 Sam 16:16); and wind (e.g., Gen 1:2; Num 11:31; Ezek 11:1). Although Hebrew literature, for example, may play on the overlap between spirit and wind (Num 11:31) or breath and spirit (Isa 40:7), contemporary translators are compelled to choose one English word and, at best, to relegate the other to a footnote.

There existed no single technical term for the divine spirit in Israelite, Jewish, and Christian antiquity. The expression "holy spirit" occurs only three times—and with very different connotations—in the OT. In Psalm 51:11, the holy spirit ("your holy spirit") resides within the individual psalmist; in Isaiah 63:10-11, God's own holy spirit is saddened, but God has placed the holy spirit within the community of Israel. The spirit could, further, be identified in many ways: "spirit" without qualifiers (e.g., Num 11:17; Job 32:8; 1 Chron 12:18); "spirit of God" or "God's spirit" (e.g., Num 24:2; 2 Chron 15:1; Job 33:4); "spirit of wisdom" (e.g., Isa 11:2); "spirit of the LORD" or "the LORD's spirit" (e.g., Judg 6:34; 1 Sam 10:6; Mic 3:8); "good spirit" (Neh 9:20; Ps 143:10); "my [God's] spirit" (e.g., Isa 42:1; Ezek 39:29); and "extraordinary spirit" (e.g., Dan 5:12).

In early Jewish literature, the term *holy spirit* means a lot of different things. The Dead Sea Scrolls caution "not to defile your holy spirit," by which they mean not to forfeit one's integrity. They speak of the "spirit of holiness" that cleanses new members of the community. They refer to "spirits of holiness." Josephus and Philo tend to prefer the moniker "divine Spirit" for the Spirit in Israelite literature. In the NT, the expressions "Holy Spirit" and "Spirit of holiness" (Rom 1:4) occur alongside the more frequent use of the word *spirit* without qualifiers.

³ When you accomplished wonders
  beyond all our expectations;
  when you came down,
    mountains quaked before you.
⁴ From ancient times,
  no one has heard,
  no ear has perceived,
  no eye has seen any god but you
  who acts on behalf of
    those who wait for him!ʸ
⁵ You look after those who gladly do right;
  they will praise you for your ways.ᶻ
  But you were angry when we sinned;
  you hid yourself when we did wrong.ᵃ
⁶ We have all become like the unclean;
  all our righteous deeds
    are like a menstrual rag.
  All of us wither like a leaf;
    our sins, like the wind, carry us away.
⁷ No one calls on your name;
  no one bothers to hold on to you,
  for you have hidden yourself from us,
  and have handed us overᵇ to our sin.

⁸ But now, LORD, you are our father.
  We are the clay, and you are our potter.
  All of us are the work of your hand.
⁹ Don't rage so fiercely, LORD;
  don't hold our sins against us forever,
  but gaze now on your people, all of us:
¹⁰ Your holy cities
    have become a wilderness;
  Zion has become a wilderness,
    Jerusalem a wasteland.
¹¹ Our holy, glorious house,
  where our ancestors praised you,
  has gone up in flames;
  all that we treasured has become a ruin.
¹² After all this, will you hold back, LORD?
  Will you keep silent
    and torment us so terribly?

Judgment for idolators

65 I was ready to respond to those who
  didn't ask.
  I was ready to be found
    by those who didn't look for me.
  I said, "I'm here! I'm here!" to a nation
    that didn't call on my name.

² I extended my hands all day
  to a rebellious people
  walking in a way that isn't good,
  following their own plans;
³ people who provoke me
  to my face continually,
  sacrificing in gardens
  and burning incense on bricks,
⁴ who sit in tombs
  and spend the night among rocks;ᶜ
  who eat swine's flesh
  with broth of unclean meat
    in their bowls;
⁵ who say, "Keep to yourself!
  Keep away from me!
    I'm too holy for you."
  These people ignite my anger
    like a fire that burns all day.
⁶ Look, this stands written before me.
  I won't be silent, but I will repay;
  I will repay in full measure
⁷ your sins and the sins
    of your ancestors as well,
    says the LORD.
  Since they burned incense
    on the mountains,
  and mocked me in the hills,
  I will count out to them
    full payment for their actions.

⁸ The LORD proclaims:
  As new wine is found
    in the grape cluster,
  and someone says, "Don't destroy it,
    for there is a blessing in it,"
  so I will do for the sake of my servants
    and not destroy everything:
⁹ I will bring out offspring from Jacob,
  and from Judah, heirs to my mountains.
  My chosen ones will take possession;
    my servants will dwell there.
¹⁰ Sharon will become a pasture for sheep,
  and the Achor Valley
    a resting place for cattle,
  for my people who seek me.
¹¹ But you who abandon the LORD,
  who forget my holy mountain,
  who set a table
    for a god of good fortune,

ʸHeb uncertain ᶻHeb uncertain ᵃHeb uncertain ᵇLXX, cf Syr, Tg, Vulg; MT *melted* ᶜOr *in guarded places*

and fill cups of mixed wine
    for a god of fate:
¹² I will offer you to the sword.
    You will all bow down for slaughter,
    because I called and you didn't answer;
    I spoke and you wouldn't hear.
    You did what I considered evil,
    and chose what I didn't want.
¹³ Therefore, the LORD God says:
    Look, my servants will eat,
      but you will hunger.
    My servants will drink,
      but you will thirst.
    My servants will rejoice,
      but you will be ashamed.
¹⁴ My servants will sing
    with contented hearts,
    but you will cry out from heartache;
    with broken spirits you will wail.
¹⁵ You will leave your name behind
    for my chosen ones to curse:
    "May the LORD God kill you!
    May he call his servants
      by a different name!"
¹⁶ Those who pronounce
    a blessing in the land
    will do so by the God called Amen;
    those who make a solemn pledge
    in the land will do so
    by the God called Amen.ᵈ
    Past troubles will be forgotten
    and hidden from my sight.

New creation and new Jerusalem

¹⁷ Look! I'm creating
    a new heaven and a new earth:
    past events won't be remembered;
    they won't come to mind.
¹⁸ Be glad and rejoice forever
    in what I'm creating,
    because I'm creating Jerusalem as a joy
    and her people as a source of gladness.
¹⁹ I will rejoice in Jerusalem
    and be glad about my people.
    No one will ever hear the sound
    of weeping or crying in it again.
²⁰ No more will babies live only a few days,
    or the old fail to live out their days.
    The one who dies at a hundred
    will be like a young person,

and the one falling short of a hundred
    will seem cursed.
²¹ They will build houses and live in them;
    they will plant vineyards
    and eat their fruit.
²² They won't build for others to live in,
    nor plant for others to eat.
    Like the days of a tree
    will be the days of my people;
    my chosen will make full use
    of their handiwork.
²³ They won't labor in vain,
    nor bear children to a world of horrors,
    because they will be people
    blessed by the LORD,
    they along with their descendants.
²⁴ Before they call, I will answer;
    while they are still speaking, I will hear.
²⁵ Wolf and lamb will graze together,
    and the lion will eat straw like the ox,
    but the snake—its food will be dust.
    They won't hurt or destroy
    at any place on my holy mountain,
    says the LORD.

Where God may be found

66 The LORD says:
    Heaven is my throne,
    and earth is my footstool.
    So where could you build a house for me,
    and where could my resting place be?
² My hand made all these things
    and brought them into being,
    says the LORD.
    But here is where I will look:
    to the humble and contrite in spirit,
    who tremble at my word.

³ The one who slaughters an ox
    kills a person;
    the one who sacrifices a sheep
    breaks a dog's neck;
    the one who makes a grain offering
    offers swine's blood;
    the one who burns incense
    blesses an idol.
    All these have chosen their own ways,
    and prefer their detestable things.
⁴ So I too will choose to punish them,

ᵈOr so be it

to bring horrors upon them,
since I called and no one answered.
I spoke and no one heard,
   but they did evil in my eyes.
What I didn't want, they chose.

5 Listen to the LORD's word,
   you who tremble at his word:
Your family members,
   those who hate and exclude you
because of my name,
have said, "Let the LORD be glorified;
   let's see your joy."
But they will be ashamed.
6 The sound of an uproar from the city!
   A sound from the temple!
The sound of the LORD repaying his
   enemies what they have earned.

Mother Zion

7 Before she was in labor, she gave birth.
   Before her pangs came upon her,
      she delivered a boy.
8 Whoever heard of such a thing?
   Whoever saw such things as these?
Can a land come to birth in one day?
   Can a nation be born all at once?
Yet as soon as birth pangs came,
   Zion bore her children.
9 Will I open the womb
   and not bring to birth?
says the LORD.
Will I, who create life,
   close the womb? says your God.
10 Celebrate with Jerusalem;
   be happy with her,
all you who love her!

Rejoice with her in joy,
   all you who mourn over her,
11 so that you may nurse
      and be satisfied
from her comforting breasts,
   that you may drink and be refreshed
from her full breasts.
12 The LORD says:
Look, I'm extending prosperity
   to her like a river,
and the wealth of nations
   like an overflowing stream.
You will nurse
   and be carried on the hip
and bounced upon the knee.

13 As a mother comforts her child,
   so I will comfort you;
in Jerusalem you will be comforted.
14 When you see this,
   your heart will rejoice;
your entire being will flourish like grass.
The LORD's power will be known
   among his servants,
but his fury among his enemies.
15 The LORD will come with fire,
   God's chariots like a windstorm,
to repay in hot anger,
   to rebuke with fiery flames.
16 With fire and with sword
   the LORD will judge all humanity;
many will be slain by the LORD.
17 Those who became holy and purify themselves, following their leader into the gardens,e who eat pork, detestable animals, and mice, will meet their end together, says the LORD.

eHeb uncertain

LIBYA/LIBYANS

In antiquity, the term *Libya* was a general designation for much of northern Africa to the west of Egypt, a more extensive geographic domain than the modern nation of Libya. In the NT Simon of Cyrene was compelled to carry the cross for Jesus on his way to Golgotha (Matt 27:32). People from "the regions of Libya bordering Cyrene" were present at the event of Pentecost (Acts 2:10).

Worshippers gathered from the nations

¹⁸Because of their actions and thoughts, I'm coming to gather all nations and cultures. They will come to see my glory. ¹⁹I will put a sign on them, by sending out some of the survivors to the nations, to Tarshish, Libya, and Lydia, and to the archers of Cilicia and Greece—distant coastlands that haven't heard of my fame or seen my glory. They will declare my glory among the nations. ²⁰They will bring your family members from all nations as an offering to the LORD—on horses, in chariots, in wagons, on mules, and on camels—to my holy mountain Jerusalem, says the LORD, like Israelites bringing an offering in purified containers to the LORD's house. ²¹I will select some of them as priests and Levites, says the LORD.

²² As the new heavens
and the new earth that I'm making
will endure before me,
says the LORD,
so your descendants
and your name will endure.
²³ From month to month
and from Sabbath to Sabbath,
all humanity will come
to worship me, says the LORD.
²⁴ They will go out and see the corpses
of the people who rebelled against me,
where their worm never dies,
where their fire is never extinguished.
They will be a horror to everyone.

JEREMIAH

The prophetic ministry of Jeremiah began in 627 BCE, during the reign of the Judean king Josiah (640–609 BCE) when Jeremiah was only a youth. His ministry continued until around 580 BCE and ended in Egypt.

Jeremiah was one of the major prophets of ancient Israel. Much of his life and many of his words are recorded in the Old Testament book that bears his name. His personal story is interwoven with his prophecy and with the story of the people of Israel.

The years of Jeremiah's ministry were turbulent and tragic years for Israel. Jeremiah's prophecy must be seen against this background. He addressed specific circumstances in the life of Israel, and he delivered God's messages concerning these circumstances.

HISTORICAL BACKGROUND

After the death of King Solomon, the kingdom of Israel was divided into Israel in the north and Judah in the south. The Northern Kingdom was conquered by Assyria in 722 BCE.

When Assyria's power declined, King Josiah of Judah extended his power into parts of the Northern Kingdom. Josiah also initiated a religious reform in Judah. This reform sought to rid Israelite faith and practice of the pagan rituals that had been introduced in years past. Worship was purified and centralized into the temple in Jerusalem. Shrines and sanctuaries in outlying areas were closed.

Josiah's reign ended when he was killed in battle at Megiddo in 609 BCE. His son, Jehoahaz, took his place but was deposed by the Egyptians, who put Jehoahaz's brother, Jehoiakim (Eliakim), on the throne. The religious reforms of Josiah were soon forgotten.

During this time, Babylonia was becoming a world power. By 603 BCE, Jehoiakim and Judah were under Babylonian control. Jehoiakim tried to break away from Babylon in 601 BCE to establish Judah as an independent state once again.

In 598 BCE, the Babylonian army besieged Jerusalem. Jehoiakim was killed and his son, Jehoiachin, soon surrendered the city. Hundreds of Israelites were deported to Babylon, including the king, his court, priests, artisans, and other leading citizens. Zedekiah, the uncle of Jehoiachin, was made king under Babylonian control.

Judah rebelled in 588 BCE and Babylonian forces attacked Jerusalem. The city fell in 587 BCE after an eighteen-month siege. More Israelites were deported and the city was destroyed.

King Nebuchadnezzar of Babylon appointed Gedaliah, a member of a prominent Judean family, as provincial governor. Gedaliah was assassinated in 582 BCE by a zealous member of the Judean royal family. Fearing reprisals from the Babylonians for Gedaliah's death, some Israelites fled to Egypt. Jeremiah was forced to go with them. More captives were taken from Judah to Babylon, and the hardship of those left in Judah increased.

In 539 BCE, Persia defeated Babylonia. Cyrus, the Persian king, gave the exiled Israelites permission to return to Judah. Jeremiah did not live to see this return. His prophecy, however, helped pave the way for Israel's survival as a community of faith by dealing with Israel's disaster within the context of faith.

IMPORTANT DATES FOR THE BOOK OF JEREMIAH

722 BCE — Northern Kingdom absorbed by Assyria
687–642 BCE — Manasseh king of Judah
642–640 BCE — Amon king of Judah
640–609 BCE — Josiah king of Judah
627 BCE — Jeremiah called to prophesy
612 BCE — Babylonians conquer the Assyrian capital
609 BCE — Jehoahaz king of Judah, deposed by Egypt
609–598 BCE — Jehoiakim king of Judah
605 BCE — Babylonians defeat Egyptians and Assyrians at Carchemish; extend influence over Judah
601 BCE — Jehoiakim rebels against Babylon
598 BCE — Babylonian siege of Jerusalem; Jehoiakim killed
598 BCE — Jehoiachin king of Judah; Jerusalem surrenders; many Israelites deported to Babylon.
598–587 BCE — Zedekiah king of Judah
588–587 BCE — Judah rebels; Babylonian siege of Jerusalem; Jerusalem destroyed; more Israelites deported
587–582 BCE — Gedaliah governor of Judah
582 BCE — Gedaliah assassinated, Jeremiah forced into exile in Egypt
(Some dates are known precisely and others are only approximate. Historical sources frequently vary as much as a year or two in giving dates, and this situation is complicated by the fact that ancient systems of dating do not correspond to our present calendar.)

JEREMIAH THE MAN

Jeremiah was born into a priestly family sometime around 645 BCE. His father, Hilkiah, was a descendant of the priest Abiathar, who had been banished to his ancestral home in Anathoth by King Solomon. (See 1 Kings 2:26-27.)

Jeremiah was taught Israel's ancient traditions and the words of Israel's prophets. We do not know whether he received formal training as a priest.

At his call to prophesy, Jeremiah calls himself a child. This may or may not mean that he was a very young man. It may merely indicate that he felt himself too immature for the task God assigned to him. He must have been a relatively young man at the time, though, because his recorded ministry spanned forty-seven years.

At first Jeremiah tried to escape the claim of God's call. In later years, he expressed contempt for those people who embraced the office of prophet without appreciating the gravity of it. At times, Jeremiah hated his calling and longed to quit his duties as God's spokesman. He even confronted God with the terrible burdens he bore for God's sake. But he could not push God's word away.

To fulfill his duties, Jeremiah had to forgo a wife and children of his own. He had to suffer hatred, misunderstanding, and physical abuse. At times his life was threatened. His message of judgment against Israel often disagreed with popular belief and official theology.

Though Jeremiah is often remembered as a sorrowful and gloomy man, he also offered words of hope and comfort to Israel. He was commissioned by God not only to pluck up and to tear down but also to build and to plant.

JEREMIAH THE BOOK

The book of Jeremiah is a collection of different kinds of material. It contains prophetic oracles from Jeremiah's public preaching, prayers, stories about Jeremiah, vision reports, sermons, laments, and historical narratives. Some of the book is prose and some is poetry.

The collection was started during Jeremiah's ministry and was finished sometime after 560 BCE. Baruch, Jeremiah's friend and scribe, wrote much of the material in the collection. Jeremiah may have had other disciples or scribes who helped record his words and life.

The book has the following sections:

(1) Oracles Against Judah and Jerusalem, 1:1–25:14

(2) Biographical Narratives, chapters 26–29; 32–45

(3) Oracles of Consolation and Hope, chapters 30–31

(4) Oracles Against Foreign Nations, 25:15-38; chapters 46–51

(5) Historical Appendix, chapter 52

A WORD OF CAUTION

Keep in mind that the book of Jeremiah is the record of material that, for the most part, was originally spoken instead of written. These oracles, sermons, and laments were delivered over a period of approximately forty-seven years. Their present written order and relationships are not always in chronological order.

JEREMIAH

Introduction

1 These are the words of Jeremiah, Hilkiah's son, who was one of the priests from Anathoth in the land of Benjamin. ²The LORD's word came to Jeremiah in the thirteenth year of Judah's King Josiah, Amon's son, ³and throughout the rule of Judah's King Jehoiakim, Josiah's son, until the fifth month of the eleventh year of King Zedekiah, Josiah's son, when the people of Jerusalem were taken into exile.

Call of Jeremiah

⁴The LORD's word came to me:

⁵ "Before I created you in the womb
   I knew you;
   before you were born I set you apart;
   I made you a prophet to the nations."

⁶ "Ah, LORD God," I said,
   "I don't know how to speak
   because I'm only a child."

⁷ The LORD responded,
   "Don't say, 'I'm only a child.'
   Where I send you, you must go;
   what I tell you, you must say.

⁸ Don't be afraid of them,
   because I'm with you to rescue you,"
   declares the LORD.

⁹ Then the LORD stretched out his hand,
   touched my mouth, and said to me,
   "I'm putting my words in your mouth.

¹⁰ This very day I appoint you
   over nations and empires,
   to dig up and pull down,
   to destroy and demolish,
   to build and plant."

Jeremiah's mission confirmed

¹¹The LORD asked me, "What do you see, Jeremiah?"

I said, "A branch of an almond[a] tree."

¹²The LORD then said, "You are right, for I'm watching over[b] my word until it is fulfilled." ¹³The LORD asked me again, "What do you see?"

I said, "A pot boiling over from the north."

¹⁴The LORD said to me, "Trouble will erupt from the north against the people of this land."

¹⁵I'm calling for all the tribes of great nations from the north, says the LORD, and they will set up their rulers by the entrances of Jerusalem, on its walls, and in every city of Judah. ¹⁶I will declare my judgment against them for doing evil: for abandoning me, worshipping other gods, and trusting in the works of their hands. ¹⁷But you must prepare for battle and be ready to utter every word I command you. Don't be frightened before them, or I will frighten you before them. ¹⁸Today I have made you an armed city, an iron pillar, and a bronze wall against the entire land—the kings of Judah, its princes, its priests, and all its people. ¹⁹They will attack you, but they won't defeat you, because I am with you and will rescue you, declares the LORD.

God's people abandon their God

2 The LORD's word came to me:
²Go and proclaim
   to the people of Jerusalem,
The LORD proclaims:
I remember your first love,[c]
   your devotion as a young bride,
   how you followed me in the wilderness,
   in an unplanted land.

³ Israel was devoted to the LORD,
   the early produce of the harvest.
Whoever ate from it became guilty;
   disaster overtook them,
   declares the LORD.

⁴ Listen to the LORD's word,
   people of Judah,
   all you families of the Israelite household.
⁵ This is what the LORD says:
What wrong did your ancestors find in me
   that made them wander so far?
They pursued what was worthless
   and became worthless.

⁶ They didn't ask,
   "Where's the LORD who brought us up
   from the land of Egypt,
   who led us through the wilderness,

---

[a] Heb *shaqed* [b] Heb *shoqed* [c] Or *the love of your youth*

in a land of deserts and ravines,
in a land of drought and darkness,
in a land of no return,
where no one survives?"

⁷ I brought you into a land of plenty,
to enjoy its gifts and goodness,
but you ruined my land;
you disgraced my heritage.

⁸ The priests didn't ask,
"Where's the LORD?"
Those responsible for the Instruction
didn't know me;
the leaders rebelled against me;
the prophets spoke in the name of Baal,
going after what has no value.

⁹ That is why I will take you to court
and charge even your descendants,
declares the LORD.

¹⁰ Look to the west
as far as the shores of Cyprus
and to the east
as far as the land of Kedar.
Ask anyone there:
Has anything this odd ever taken place?

¹¹ Has a nation switched gods,
though they aren't really gods at all?
Yet my people have exchanged their glory
for what has no value.

¹² Be stunned at such a thing, you heavens;
shudder and quake,
declares the LORD.

¹³ My people have committed two crimes:
They have forsaken me,
the spring of living water.
And they have dug wells,
broken wells that can't hold water.

¹⁴ Is Israel a slave,
a servant by birth?
If not, why then has he become prey?

¹⁵ Lions roar at him; they growl.
They destroy his land
and make his towns desolate
until nothing is left.

¹⁶ As well, the people
of Memphis and Tahpanhes
lay open your scalp.

¹⁷ Haven't you brought this on yourself
by abandoning the LORD your God,
who has directed your paths?

¹⁸ So why take the path to Egypt
to drink water from the Nile?

Why travel the path to Assyria
to drink water from the Euphrates?

¹⁹ Your wrongdoing will punish you.
Your acts of unfaithfulness
will find you out.
Don't you understand how terribly bitter
it is to abandon the LORD your God
and not fear me?
declares the LORD of heavenly forces.

²⁰ Long ago I broke your yoke;
I shattered your chains.
But even then you said,
"I won't serve you."
On every high hill
and under every lush tree,
you have acted like a prostitute.

²¹ Yet it was I who planted you,
a precious vine of fine quality;
how could you turn into a wild vine
and become good for nothing?

²² Even though you scrub yourself
with soap or strong powder,
the stain of your sin is still before me,
declares the LORD God.

²³ How can you say,
"I'm not dirty;
I haven't gone after Baals."
Look what you have done in the valley;
consider what you have done there.
You are like a frenzied young camel,
racing around,

²⁴ a wild donkey in the wilderness,
lustfully sniffing the wind.
Who can restrain such passion?
Those who desire her need not give up;
with little effort they will find her in heat.

²⁵ Don't run about
until your feet are blistered
and your throat is parched.
But you say, "What's the use?
I have fallen in love with foreign gods,
and I must pursue them."

²⁶ As a thief is ashamed
when caught in his tracks,
so the people of Israel are ashamed—
their kings, officials,
priests, and prophets—

²⁷ when they say to a piece of wood,
"You are my father,"
and to a stone, "You gave me birth."
They have turned their backs to me
and not their faces.

Yet in their time of trouble they say,
   "Arise and save us!"
28 Where are the gods
   you have made for yourselves?
Let's see if they will come through
   for you in your time of trouble.
You have as many gods, Judah,
   as you have towns.
29 Why would you bring
   charges against me?
You have all rebelled against me,
   declares the LORD.
30 I have disciplined your children in vain;
   they have rejected my correction.
You have devoured your prophets
   like a hungry lion.
31 People of this generation,
   listen closely to the LORD's word:
Have I been a wasteland to Israel
   or a land of dense darkness?
Why then do my people say,
   "We have wandered far away;
   we'll come to you no longer"?
32 Does a young woman forget her jewelry
   or a bride her wedding dress?
Yet you have forgotten me
   days without end!
33 So skilled are you at pursuing lovers[d]
   that you instruct
      even the most wicked.[e]
34 Your garments are stained
   with the blood of the innocent poor,
   even though you didn't catch them
   breaking and entering.
Yet, despite all this,[f] 35 you still insist,
   "I'm innocent;
   as a result he will turn his anger
      away from me."
Because you claim not to have sinned,
   I will pass judgment against you.
36 You change sides so casually!
   But Egypt will shame you
   no less than Assyria.
37 From there you will go out
   with your hands on your heads,
   because the LORD has rejected
      those you rely on;
   they won't help you.

Jeremiah's summons to change

3 If a man divorces his wife,
   and after she leaves him
      marries another,
      can he return to her again?
Wouldn't such an act
   completely corrupt the land?
Yet you have prostituted yourself
   with many lovers.
Would you return to me?
   declares the LORD.
2 Look to the well-traveled paths[g] and see!
   Where haven't you committed adultery?
On the roadsides
   you sit in wait for lovers,
   like a nomad in the wilderness.
You have corrupted the land
   with your cheap and reckless behavior.
3 That's why the showers have failed
   and the spring rains have ceased.
Still you act like a brazen prostitute[h]
   who refuses to blush.
4 At the same time you say to me,
   "My father, my friend since youth,
   5 will you stay angry forever?
      Will you continue to be furious?"
This is what you say
   while you do as much evil
   as you possibly can.

6 During the rule of King Josiah, the LORD said to me: Have you noticed what unfaithful Israel has done? She's gone about looking for lovers on top of every high hill and under every lush tree. 7 I thought that after she had done all this she would return to me, but she didn't. Her disloyal sister Judah saw this. 8 She[i] also saw that I sent unfaithful Israel away with divorce papers because of all her acts of unfaithfulness; yet disloyal sister Judah was not afraid but kept on playing the prostitute. 9 She didn't think twice about corrupting the land and committing adultery with stone and tree. 10 Yet even after all this, disloyal sister Judah didn't return to me with all her heart but only insincerely, declares the LORD. 11 Then the LORD said to me: Unfaithful Israel is less guilty[j] than disloyal Judah.

---

[d] Or love [e] Or you have taught your ways to wicked women. [f] Heb uncertain [g] Or bare heights [h] Or You have a prostitute's forehead. [i] LXX, Syr; MT I [j] Or more righteous

¹²Go proclaim these words to the north and say:

Return, unfaithful Israel,
　declares the LORD.
I won't reject you,
　for I'm faithful,
　declares the LORD;
I won't stay angry forever.
¹³ Only acknowledge your wrongdoing:
　how you have rebelled
　against the LORD your God,
　and given yourself to strangers
　under every lush tree
　and haven't obeyed me,
　declares the LORD.
¹⁴ Return, rebellious children,
　declares the LORD,
　for I'm your husband.
I'll gather you—
　one from a city and two from a tribe—
　and bring you back to Zion.

¹⁵I will appoint shepherds with whom I'm pleased, and they will lead you with knowledge and understanding. ¹⁶And in those days, when your numbers have greatly increased in the land, declares the LORD, people will no longer talk about the LORD's covenant chest; they won't recall or remember it; they won't even miss it or try to build another one. ¹⁷At that time, they will call Jerusalem the LORD's throne, and all nations will gather there to honor the LORD's name. No longer will they follow their own willful and evil hearts. ¹⁸In those days the people of Judah and Israel will leave the north together for the land that I gave their ancestors as an inheritance.

¹⁹ I thought to myself,
　How wonderful it would be
　to treat you like children
　and give you a beautiful land,
　an inheritance unrivaled
　among the nations.
And I thought, You will call me father,
　and you won't turn away from me.
²⁰ But as a woman betrays her lover,
　so you, people of Israel,
　have betrayed me,
　declares the LORD.

²¹ A voice is heard
　on the well-traveled paths;ᵏ
　it's the crying and pleading
　of the people of Israel,
　who have lost their way
　and forgotten the LORD their God.
²² Return, rebellious children,
　and I will heal your rebellion.

"Here we are; we come to you,
　for you are the LORD our God.
²³ Surely what happens on the hillsˡ
　is a waste,
　as is the uproar on the mountains.
Only in the LORD our God
　is the salvation of Israel.
²⁴ From our youth, shameᵐ has devoured
　the fruit of our parents' labor—
　their flocks and herds,
　as well as their sons and daughters.
²⁵ Let's lie down in our shame.
　Let our dishonor cover us,
　for we have sinned
　against the LORD our God,
　both we and our ancestors,
　from our youth to this very day.
We have disobeyed the voice of the
　LORD our God."

4 If you return, Israel, return to me,
　declares the LORD.
　If you get rid of your disgusting idols
　from my presence
　and wander no more,
² and if you swear by the living God
　in truth, justice, and righteousness,
　then the nations
　will enjoy God's blessings;ⁿ
　they will boast about him.
³This is what the LORD says to the people of Judah and to the residents of Jerusalem:
Break up your hard rocky soil;
　don't plant among the thorns.
⁴ Dedicateᵒ yourselves to the LORD;
　don't be thick-skinned,ᵖ
　people of Judah
　and residents of Jerusalem,
　or else my anger will spread
　like a wildfire.

ᵏOr bare heights ˡLXX, Syr, Vulg; MT from the hills ᵐOr the shame ⁿOr bless themselves in him or be blessed by him or will bless themselves ᵒOr circumcise ᵖOr remove the foreskins of your hearts

It will burn, with no one to put it out,
because of your evil deeds.

Disaster approaches

5 Announce in Judah,
   in Jerusalem proclaim,
   sound the alarm throughout the land,
   cry out and say,
   "Gather together!
   Let's flee to the fortified towns!"
6 Set up a flag to Zion;
   take cover, don't just stand there!
   I'm bringing disaster from the north,
   massive devastation.
7 A lion bursts out of the thicket;
   a destroyer of nations advances.
   He's gone forth from his place
   to ravage your land,
   to wipe out your towns,
   until no one is left.
8 So put on funeral clothing.
   Weep and wail,
   for the LORD's fierce anger
   hasn't turned away from us.
9 On that day, declares the LORD,
   the courage of the king and his princes
   will fail,
   the priests will be stunned,
   and the prophets will be shocked.
10 Then I said, "LORD God, no!
   You have utterly deceived this people
   and Jerusalem
   by promising them peace
   even though the sword is at their throats."
11 At that time, this people and Jerusalem
   will be told:
   A blistering wind from the bare heights;
   it rages in the desert toward my people,
   not merely to winnow or cleanse.
12 This wind is too devastating for that.
   Now I, even I, will pronounce
   my sentence against them.
13 Look! He approaches like the clouds;
   his chariots advance like a tempest,
   his horses swifter than eagles.
   How horrible! We're doomed!
14 Cleanse your heart of evil, Jerusalem,
   that you may be saved.
   How long will you entertain
   your destructive ideas?
15 A voice declares from Dan;

someone proclaims disaster
from the highlands of Ephraim.
16 Warn the nations,
   proclaim it to Jerusalem!
   Armies are approaching
   from a far-away country,
   raising their war cries
   against the towns of Judah.
17 They hem her in
   like those guarding a field,
   because she has rebelled against me,
   declares the LORD.
18 Your own conduct, your own deeds
   have done this to you.
   This is your payment and how bitter it is,
   piercing into the depths of your heart.

Anguish over looming disaster

19 Oh, my suffering, my suffering!
   My pain is unbearable;
   my heart is in turmoil;
   it throbs nonstop.
   I can't be silent,
   because I hear the blast of the trumpet
   and the roar of the battle cry!
20 Disaster follows disaster;
   the whole land is ruined.
   Suddenly, my tents are destroyed,
   my shelter in a moment.
21 How long must I see the battle flags
   and hear the blast of the trumpet?
22 My people are foolish.
   They don't even know me!
   They are thoughtless children
   without understanding;
   they are skilled at doing wrong,
   inept at doing right.
23 I looked at the earth,
   and it was without shape or form;
   at the heavens
   and there was no light.
24 I looked at the mountains
   and they were quaking;
   all the hills were rocking
   back and forth.
25 I looked and there was no one left;
   every bird in the sky had taken flight.
26 I looked and the fertile land was a desert;
   all its towns were in ruins
   before the LORD,
   before his fury.

²⁷ The LORD proclaims:
 The whole earth will become a desolation,
 but I will not destroy it completely.
²⁸ Therefore, the earth will grieve
 and the heavens grow dark
 because I have declared my plan
 and will neither change my mind
 nor cancel the plan.
²⁹ As the horsemen and archers approach,
 the people take flight.
 They hide in the bushes
 and escape to the cliffs.
 Every city is deserted;
 no one remains.
³⁰ And you, devastated one,
 why dress up in scarlet,
 deck yourself in gold jewelry,
 and color your eyes with paint?
 In vain you get all decked out;
 your lovers have rejected you
 and now seek your life.
³¹ I hear the cry of a woman in labor,
 the distress of one delivering
 her first child.
 It is the cry of Daughter Zion,
 gasping for breath,
 her arms stretched out,
 and moaning,
 "I'm about to fall
 into the hands of murderers!"

Futile search for a good person

5 Search every street in Jerusalem,
 comb the squares,
 look far and wide
 for one person,
 even one who acts justly
 and seeks truth that I may pardon her!
² Even when making a pledge—
 "As the LORD lives"—
 they swear falsely.
³ LORD, don't you look for integrity?
 You have struck them down,
 but they didn't even cringe.
 You have crushed them,
 but they have ignored your discipline.
 They make their faces harder than rock
 and refuse to return.
⁴ Then I thought to myself,

 These are the poor
 who don't know better!
 They don't understand the LORD's way
 or the justice of their God.
⁵ Let me go and speak
 to the powerful people,
 for they will surely know the LORD's way
 and the justice of their God.
 But they too have broken their yoke
 and shattered the chains.
⁶ Therefore, a lion from the forest
 will attack them;
 a wolf from the desert will destroy them;
 a leopard prowling around their towns
 will tear to pieces
 anyone venturing out—
 because of their many crimes
 and countless acts of unfaithfulness.
⁷ How can I pardon you?
 Your children have forsaken me
 and swear by gods that are not gods.
 Although I could have satisfied them,
 they committed adultery,
 dashing off to the prostitution house.
⁸ They are lusty stallions roving about,
 snorting for another's wife.
⁹ The LORD declares:
 Shouldn't I confront these acts?
 Shouldn't I take revenge on such a
 nation?

Contempt for God

¹⁰ Climb through her vineyards
 and ravage them,
 although not completely.
 Prune back her branches,
 because they aren't the LORD's.
¹¹ The people of Israel and Judah
 have been utterly faithless to me,
 declares the LORD.
¹² They have lied about the LORD
 and said, "He'll do nothing!^q
 Disaster won't come upon us;
 we won't see war or famine."
¹³ The prophets are so much wind;
 the word isn't in them.
 Thus and so may it be done to them.
¹⁴Therefore, the LORD God of heavenly
forces proclaims:

^qOr not he

Because you have spoken this way,
I will put my words
in your mouth as a fire;
it will consume the people,
who are but kindling.

15 I am about to bring a distant nation
against you,
people of Israel,
declares the LORD.
It is an established nation,
an ancient nation,
a nation whose language
you don't know,
whose speech you won't understand.

16 Its weapons are deadly;ʳ
its warriors are many.

17 It will devour your harvest and food;
it will devour your sons and daughters;
it will devour your flocks and herds;
it will devour your vines and fig trees;
it will shatter your fortified towns
in which you trust—
with the sword!

18 Yet even in those days, declares the LORD, I won't completely destroy you. 19 And when they ask, "Why has the LORD our God done all these things to us?" you must reply, "Just as you have abandoned me and served foreign gods in your land, so you will serve strangers in a land not your own."

Shouldn't you fear me?

20 Declare this to the people of Jacob,
announce it in Judah:

21 Listen, you foolish and senseless people,
who have eyes but don't see
and ears but don't hear.

22 Shouldn't you fear me,
declares the LORD,
and tremble before me,
the one who set the shoreline
for the sea,
an ancient boundary that it can't pass?
Though its waves may rise and roar,
they can't pass the limits I have set.

23 And yet the people have stubborn
and rebellious hearts;
they turn and go their own way.

24 They don't say in their hearts,

Let's fear the LORD our God,
who provides rain in autumn and spring
and who assures us of a harvest
in its season.

25 Your wrongdoing has turned
these blessingsˢ away.
Your sin has robbed you of good.

26 Criminals are found among my people;
they set traps to catch people,
like hunters lying in wait.ᵗ

27 Like a cage full of birds,
so their houses are full of loot.
No wonder they are rich and powerful

28 and have grown fat and sleek!
To be sure, their evil deeds
exceed all limits,
and yet they prosper.
They are indifferent
to the plight of the orphan,
reluctant to defend the rights of the poor.

29 Shouldn't I punish such acts?
declares the LORD.
Shouldn't I repay that nation
for its deeds?

30 An awful, a terrible thing
has happened in the land:

31 The prophets prophesy falsely,
the priests rule at their sides,ᵘ
and my people love it this way!
But what will you do when the end comes?

Prepare for war

6 Escape, people of Benjamin,
get out of Jerusalem!
Blow the trumpet in Tekoa,
sound the alarm in Beth-haccherem;
for disaster looms from the north,
massive devastation.

2 You are like a lovely pasture,
Daughter Zion.ᵛ

3 Shepherds come to her with their flocks.
They pitch their tents around her
and graze in their place.

4 "Prepare for battle against her;
get ready; let's attack by noon!
Oh, no! Daylight is fading,
and the evening shadows lengthen.

5 Get ready, let's attack by night
and destroy her fortresses!"

ʳOr *Its quiver is like an open grave*　ˢHeb lacks *blessings.*　ᵗHeb uncertain　ᵘOr *by their hands*　ᵛHeb uncertain

6 The LORD of heavenly forces proclaims:
Cut down her trees,
  and build siege ramps against Jerusalem.
This city must be held accountable,[w]
  for there's nothing but oppression
    in her midst.
7 As a well brings forth fresh water,
  she brings forth evil.
Violence and destruction
  are heard within her;
  injury and wounds are ever before me.
8 Hear me out,[x] Jerusalem,
  or else I'll turn away from you
    and reduce you to ruins,
    a land unfit to live in.

Unresponsive people

9 This is what the LORD of heavenly forces
  says:
From top to bottom, let them harvest
  the remaining few in Israel.
    Pick clean every
    last grape on the vine!
10 To whom can I speak and warn?
  How can I get someone's attention?
  Their ears are shut tight,[y]
    so they won't hear.
They are ashamed of the LORD's word
  and take no pleasure in it.
11 But I'm filled with the LORD's rage
  and am tired of holding it in.

Pour it out on the children in the streets
  and on the youths gathered together;
husband with wife will be trapped,
  as will those old and gray.
12 Their homes will be turned over to others,
  their fields and wives as well.
I will stretch out my hand
  against the people of this land,
    declares the LORD.
13 From the least to the greatest,
  each is eager to profit;
from prophet to priest,
  each trades in dishonesty.
14 They treat the wound of my people
  as if it were nothing:
"All is well, all is well," they insist,
  when in fact nothing is well.

15 They should be ashamed
  of their detestable practices,
but they have no shame;
  they don't even blush!
Therefore, they will fall among the fallen
  and stumble when I bring disaster,
    declares the LORD.
16 The LORD proclaims:
Stop at the crossroads and look around;
  ask for the ancient paths.
Where is the good way?
Then walk in it
  and find a resting place for yourselves.
    But you[z] said, "We won't go!"
17 Still, I have appointed watchmen
  to warn you.
    But you[a] said, "We won't listen!"
18 Therefore, pay attention, nations;
  take notice, assembly,
    what is ahead of them.[b]
19 Pay attention, earth:
I'm bringing disaster upon my people,
  the fruit of their own devices,
because they have ignored my words
  and they have rejected my teaching.
20 What use to me is incense from Sheba
  or sweet cane from a faraway land?
Your entirely burned offerings
  won't buy your pardon;
  your sacrifices won't appease me.
21 Therefore, the LORD proclaims:
I'm putting obstacles before this people,
  and both parents and children
    will stumble over them;
  neighbor and friend alike will perish.

Panic-stricken Zion

22 The LORD proclaims:
An army is on the move
  from the northern regions;
a great nation is roused
  from the ends of the earth.
23 Equipped with bow and spear,
  they are cruel;
  they show no mercy.
Their horsemen sound
  like the roaring sea,
arrayed in battle formation
  against you, Daughter Zion.

---

[w]Heb uncertain   [x]Or *Accept correction*   [y]Or *uncircumcised*   [z]Or *they*   [a]Or *they*   [b]Heb uncertain

²⁴ We have heard reports of them
  and are panic-stricken;
  distress overwhelms us,
  pain like that of a woman in labor.
²⁵ Don't go out into the field!
  Don't walk on the road!
  The enemies' sword
    terrorizes at every turn.
²⁶ My people,
  put on funeral clothes
    and roll in ashes;
  weep and wail as for an only child,
    because the destroyer
    will suddenly descend upon us.

Prophet as tester

²⁷ I have made you a tester of metals,
  to examine my people[c]
  to know and prove their ways.
²⁸ They are tin[d] and iron;
  they are headstrong and rebellious.
  They live to slander.
  They act corruptly—every last one!
²⁹ The bellows roar;
  the lead is consumed.[e]
  Yet the refining fails;
  the impurities[f] remain.
³⁰ They are called "rejected silver,"
  for the LORD has rejected them.

The LORD's temple

7 Jeremiah received the LORD's word: ²Stand near the gate of the LORD's temple and proclaim there this message: Listen to the LORD's word, all you of Judah who enter these gates to worship the LORD. ³This is what the LORD of heavenly forces, the God of Israel, says: Improve your conduct and your actions, and I will dwell with you[g] in this place. ⁴Don't trust in lies: "This is the LORD's temple! The LORD's temple! The LORD's temple!" ⁵No, if you truly reform your ways and your actions; if you treat each other justly; ⁶if you stop taking advantage of the immigrant, orphan, or widow; if you don't shed the blood of the innocent in this place, or go after other gods to your own ruin, ⁷only then will I

dwell with you[h] in this place, in the land that I gave long ago to your ancestors for all time.

⁸And yet you trust in lies that will only hurt you. ⁹Will you steal and murder, commit adultery and perjury, sacrifice to Baal and go after other gods that you don't know, ¹⁰and then come and stand before me in this temple that bears my name, and say, "We are safe," only to keep on doing all these detestable things? ¹¹Do you regard this temple, which bears my name, as a hiding place for criminals? I can see what's going on here, declares the LORD. ¹²Just go to my sanctuary[i] in Shiloh, where I let my name dwell at first, and see what I did to it because of the evil of my people Israel. ¹³And now, because you have done all these things, declares the LORD, because you haven't listened when I spoke to you again and again or responded when I called you, ¹⁴I will do to this temple that bears my name and on which you rely, the place that I gave to you and your ancestors, just as I did to Shiloh. ¹⁵I will cast you out of my sight, just as I cast out the rest of your family, all the people of Ephraim.

¹⁶As for you, don't pray for these people, don't cry out or plead for them, and don't intercede with me, for I won't listen to you. ¹⁷Can't you see what they are doing in the towns of Judah and in the streets of Jerusalem? ¹⁸The children gather wood, the fathers light the fire, and the women knead dough to make sacrificial cakes for the queen of heaven. And to offend me all the more, they pour out drink offerings to foreign gods. ¹⁹But am I the one they are really offending? declares the LORD. Aren't they in fact humiliating themselves? ²⁰Therefore, this is what the LORD God says: I'm going to pour out my fierce anger on this place, on humans and beasts, on the trees of the field and the crops of the fertile land. It will burn and not go out.

²¹This is what the LORD of heavenly forces, the God of Israel, says: Add your entirely burned offerings to your sacrifices

and eat them yourselves! ²²On the day I brought your ancestors out of the land of Egypt, I didn't say a thing—I gave no instructions—about entirely burned offerings or sacrifices. ²³Rather, this is what I required of them: Obey me so that I may become your God and you may become my people. Follow the path I mark out for you so that it may go well with you. ²⁴But they didn't listen or pay attention. They followed their willful and evil hearts and went backward rather than forward. ²⁵From the moment your ancestors left the land of Egypt to this day, I have sent you all my servants the prophets—day after day. ²⁶But they didn't listen to me or pay attention; they were stubborn and did more harm than their ancestors. ²⁷When you tell them all this, they won't listen to you. When you call to them, they won't respond. ²⁸Therefore, say to them: This nation neither obeys the LORD its God nor accepts correction; truth has disappeared; it has vanished from their lips.

²⁹ Cut off your hair and cast it away;
    grieve on the well-traveled paths.

The LORD has rejected you
    and has cast off a generation
        that provokes his anger.

³⁰The people of Judah have done what displeases me, declares the LORD. They have corrupted the temple that bears my name by setting up their disgusting idols. ³¹They have built shrines at Topheth in the Ben-hinnom Valley to burn their sons and daughters in the fire, although I never commanded such a thing, nor did it ever cross my mind. ³²So now the time is coming, declares the LORD, when people will no longer speak of Topheth or the Ben-hinnom Valley, but the Carnage Valley. They will bury in Topheth until no space is left. ³³The corpses of this people will be food for birds and wild animals, with no one to drive them off. ³⁴I will silence the sound of joy and delight as well as the voice of bride and bridegroom in the towns of Judah and in the streets of Jerusalem, for the country will be reduced to a wasteland.

8 At that time, declares the LORD, the bones of the kings of Judah and its officers, the bones of the priests and the

SHILOH

A town mentioned in the Former Prophets, Jeremiah, and Psalms. In the book of Joshua, Shiloh functions as a sanctuary, repeatedly housing pan-Israelite gatherings. In Shiloh, Joshua completes the division of the land of promise among the tribes (Josh 18:1; 19:51), sets aside cities for the Levites (21:1-3), and announces to the Transjordanian tribes that they have fulfilled their military obligations and may return to their allotments (22:1-9). Shiloh housed the tent of meeting and the chest of the covenant. It derived its importance solely from the presence of these sacred objects and returned to obscurity when they were moved elsewhere.

A different understanding of Shiloh as a worship site is seen in Jeremiah 7:12 ("Just go to my sanctuary in Shiloh, where I let my name dwell at first, and see what I did to it because of the evil of my people Israel") and Psalm 78:60 ("God abandoned the sanctuary at Shiloh, the tent where he had lived with humans"). In both fragments, the location is initially favored by the Lord and abandoned not because the itinerant shrine simply moved on but as a punishment for the people's sins (see esp. Ps 78:56-58). Jeremiah explicitly links Shiloh and Jerusalem by repeatedly warning the latter that it will suffer the destruction that happened to the former (7:14; 26:6, 9).

prophets, and the bones of the people of Jerusalem will be taken from their graves [2] and exposed to the sun, the moon, and the whole heavenly forces, which they have loved and served and which they have followed, consulted, and worshipped. Their bones won't be gathered for reburial but will become like refuse lying on the ground. [3] The survivors of this evil nation will prefer death to life, wherever I have scattered them, declares the LORD of heavenly forces.

Depth of Judah's wrongdoing

[4] Say to them, The LORD proclaims:
   When people fall down, don't they get up?
   When they turn aside,
      don't they turn back?
[5] Why then does this people,
      rebellious Jerusalem,
   persistently turn away from me?
   They cling to deceit
   and refuse to return.
[6] I have listened carefully
   but haven't heard a word of truth
      from them.
   No one regrets their wrongdoing;
   no one says, "What have I done?"
   Everyone turns to their own course,
   like a stallion dashing
      into the thick of battle.
[7] Even the stork in the sky
   knows the seasons,
   and the dove, swallow,[j] and crane[k]
      return in due time.
      But my people
      don't know the LORD's ways.
[8] How can you say, "We are wise;
   we possess the LORD's Instruction,"

when the lying pen of the scribes
      has surely distorted it?
[9] The wise will be shamed and shocked
   when they are caught.
   Look, they have rejected
      the LORD's word;
   what kind of wisdom is that?
[10] Therefore, I will give their wives to others
   and their fields to their captors.
   From the least to the greatest,
      all are eager to profit.
   From prophet to priest,
      all trade in falsehood.
[11] They treat the wound of my people
      as if it were nothing:
   "All is well, all is well," they insist,
   when in fact nothing is well.
[12] They should be ashamed
      of their detestable practices,
   but they have no shame;
      they don't even blush!
   Therefore, they will fall among the fallen
   and stumble when disaster arrives,
      declares the LORD.
[13] I will put an end to them,[l]
      declares the LORD;
   there are no grapes on the vine,
      no figs on the tree,
      only withered leaves.
   They have squandered
   what I have given them![m]

A lament for God's people
[14] Why are we sitting here?
   Come, let's go to the fortified towns
   and meet our doom there.
   The LORD our God has doomed us
   by giving us poisoned water to drink,

[j]Heb uncertain   [k]Heb uncertain   [l]Heb uncertain   [m]Heb uncertain

BALM IN GILEAD

The aromatic ointment of an unidentified plant, known in ancient times for its medicinal qualities (Jer 46:11) and exported from Gilead to Egypt and Phoenicia (Ezek 27:17). Gilead's association with healing balm became well known in the African American spiritual based on Jeremiah's rhetorical question (Jer 8:22).

because we have sinned
   against the LORD!
¹⁵ We longed for relief,
   but received none;
   for a time of healing,
   but found only terror.
¹⁶ The snorting of their horses
   can be heard as far as Dan;
   the neighing of their stallions
   makes the whole land tremble.
They come to devour the land
   and everything in it,
   towns and people alike.
¹⁷ See, I'm sending serpents against you,
   vipers that you can't charm,
   and they will bite you,
   declares the LORD.
¹⁸ No healing,
   only grief;
   my heart is broken.ⁿ
¹⁹ Listen to the weeping of my people
   all across the land:
   "Isn't the LORD in Zion?
   Is her king no longer there?"
Why then did they anger me
   with their images,
   with pointless foreign gods?
²⁰ "The harvest is past,
   the summer has ended,
   yet we aren't saved."
²¹ Because my people are crushed,
   I am crushed;
   darkness and despair overwhelm me.

What to do with God's people
²² Is there no balm in Gilead?
   Is there no physician there?
   Why then have my people
   not been restored to health?

9 °If only my head were a spring of water,
   and my eyes a fountain of tears,
   I would weep day and night
   for the wounds of my people.
² ᵖIf only I could flee for shelter
   in the desert,
   to leave my people
   and forget them—
   for they are all adulterers,
   a bunch of crooks.

³ They bend their tongues like bows
   to spew out lies;
   they are renowned in the land,
   but not for truth.
They go from bad to worse.
They don't know me!
   declares the LORD.
⁴ Be wary of your friends!
   Don't trust your sibling!�q
Every sibling is a cheater,
   and every friend traffics in slander.
⁵ One cheats the other;
   no one tells the truth;
   they train themselves to lie;
   they wear themselves out
   by doing wrong.
⁶ You live in a world of deceit,
   and in their deceit
   they refuse to know me,ʳ
   declares the LORD.
⁷ Therefore, the LORD of heavenly forces
   proclaims:
I'm going to refine and test them,
   for what else can I do with my people?
⁸ Their tongue is a lethal arrow;
   their words are deceitful.
They wish their neighbors well,
   but in their hearts plot their ruin.
⁹ Shouldn't I punish them for this?
   declares the LORD;
   shouldn't I avenge such a nation?
¹⁰ I will weep and wail for the mountains,
   and lament for the grazing lands
   in the wilderness.
They are dried up and deserted;
   no sound of the flocks is heard;
   no sign of birds or animals is seen;
   all have vanished.
¹¹ I will reduce Jerusalem to ruins,
   a den for wild dogs.
I will make the towns of Judah a
   wasteland, without inhabitant.
¹² Who is wise enough to understand this?
   Who has been taught by the LORD
   and can therefore explain it?
Why has the land been reduced to rubble
   and laid waste like a desert,
   with no one passing through?
¹³ The LORD says: It is because they have

ⁿHeb uncertain °8:23 in Heb ᵖ9:1 in Heb qOr *brother* ʳHeb uncertain abandoned my Instruction that I gave them, and haven't obeyed or followed it. [14]Instead, they have followed their own willful hearts and have gone after the Baals, as their ancestors taught them. [15]Therefore, this is what the LORD of heavenly forces, the God of Israel, says: I'm going to feed this people bitter food and give them poison to drink. [16]I will scatter them among nations about whom neither they nor their ancestors have ever heard. I will pursue them with the sword until all are gone.

[17] The LORD of heavenly forces proclaims:
Pay attention!
Summon the women who mourn,
  let them come;
send for those best trained,
  let them come.
[18] Hurry!
Let them weep for us
  so that our eyes fill up with tears
  and water streams down.
[19] The sound of sobbing
  is heard from Zion:
"We're devastated!
We're so ashamed!
We have to leave the land
  and abandon our homes!"
[20] Women, hear the LORD's word.
Listen closely to the word
  from his mouth:
  teach your daughters to mourn;
  teach each other to grieve.
[21] Death has climbed through our windows;
  it has entered our fortresses
    to eliminate children from the streets,
    the youth from the squares.
[22] Declare what the LORD says:
Dead bodies will lie
  like dung on the fields,
  like bundles of grain after the harvest,
  with no one to pick them up.
[23] The LORD proclaims:
  the learned should not boast
    of their knowledge,
    nor warriors boast of their might,
    nor the rich boast of their wealth.
[24] No, those who boast should boast in this:
  that they understand and know me.
I am the LORD who acts with kindness,
  justice, and righteousness in the world,

and I delight in these things,
  declares the LORD.
[25] The time is coming, declares the LORD, when I will deal with everyone who is physically circumcised: [26]whether they are Egyptians or Judeans, Edomites or Ammonites, Moabites or the desert dwellers who cut the hair on their foreheads. All these nations are really uncircumcised; even the people of Israel are uncircumcised in heart.

Living God or human handiwork

10 Listen to the word that the LORD has spoken to you, people of Israel!
[2] The LORD proclaims:
Don't follow the ways of the nations
  or be troubled by signs in the sky,
    even though the nations
    are troubled by them.
[3] The rituals of the nations are hollow:
  a tree from the forest
    is chopped down
    and shaped by the craftsman's tools.
[4] It's overlaid with silver and gold,
  and fastened securely
    with hammer and nails
    so it won't fall over.
[5] They are no different than a scarecrow
  in a cucumber patch:
  they can't speak;
  they must be carried
    because they can't walk.
Don't be afraid of them,
  because they can't do harm or good.
[6] LORD, no one is like you!
You are great,
  and great is your mighty name.
[7] Who wouldn't fear you,
  king of the nations?
That is your due;
  among all the wise of the nations
  and in all their countries,
    there is no one like you!
[8] But they are both foolish and silly;
  they offer nothing
    because they are mere wood.
[9] Covered with silver from Tarshish
  and gold from Uphaz,
    they are the work of a craftsman
    and the hands of a goldsmith.
Clothed in blue and purple,

all of them nothing more than the
work of artisans.
¹⁰ But the LORD is the true God!
He's the living God
and the everlasting king!
When he's angry, the earth quakes;
the nations can't endure his rage.
¹¹ Tell them this: The gods who didn't
make the heavens and the earth will perish
from the earth and from under the heavens.ˢ
¹² But God made the earth by his might;
he shaped the world by his wisdom,
crafted the skies by his knowledge.
¹³ At the sound of his voice,
the heavenly waters roar.
He raises the clouds
from the ends of the earth.
He sends the lightning with the rain,
the wind from his treasuries.
¹⁴ Everyone is too foolish to understand;
every goldsmith is dishonored
by his idols,
for their images are shams;
they aren't alive.
¹⁵ They are a delusion, a charade;
at the appointed time
they will vanish!
¹⁶ Jacob's portion is utterly different
because God has formed all things,
including Israel, his very own people—
the LORD of heavenly forces
is his name!

Get ready for exile!

¹⁷ Pack your bags and get ready to leave,
you who live under siege.ᵗ

ˢ10:11 is written in Aramaic. ᵗHeb uncertain ᵘOr *find it*

¹⁸ The LORD proclaims:
I'm going to eject those who live
in the land at this time;
I will badger them until they leave.ᵘ

¹⁹ How terrible for me, due to my injury;
my wound is terrible.
Yet I said to myself:
This is my sickness,
and I must bear it.
²⁰ But now my tent is destroyed;
all its ropes are cut,
and my children are gone for good.
There's no one left
to set up my tent frame
and to attach the fabric.
²¹ The shepherd kings have lost their senses
and don't seek answers from the LORD.
That is why they have failed
and their flock is scattered.
²² Listen! The sound is getting louder,
a mighty uproar
from the land of the north;
it will reduce the towns of Judah to ruins,
a den for wild dogs.
²³ I know, LORD, that our lives
are not our own,
that we're not able to direct our paths.
²⁴ So correct me, LORD, but with justice,
not in your anger,
or else you will reduce me to nothing.
²⁵ Pour out your wrath on the nations
that ignore you
and on the people
who don't call on you,

EXILE

The biblical exilic period begins with the Babylonian deportations of the people of Judah in the early years of the 6th century BCE. While Assyria, beginning with Tiglath-pileser III (745–727 BCE), had deported many people from the northern kingdom in the 8th century—including 27,290 from Samaria alone according to the claims of Sargon II—those exiles disappeared from history. The Judean exile, in contrast, played a profound role in shaping the literature and theology of the OT, and those who returned from exile were the primary leaders in the post-exilic community.

since they have devoured Jacob;
   they have devoured him completely
      and ruined his country.

Judah's broken covenant with God

11 Jeremiah received the LORD's word: [2]Listen to the terms of this covenant and proclaim them to the people of Judah and the citizens of Jerusalem. [3]Say to them: This is what the LORD, the God of Israel, says: Cursed are those who don't heed the terms of this covenant [4]that I commanded your ancestors when I bought them out of the land of Egypt, that iron crucible, saying, Obey me and observe all that I instruct you. Then you will be my people and I, even I, will be your God. [5]I will fulfill my solemn pledge that I made to your ancestors to give them a land full of milk and honey, as is the case today.

And I replied, "As you say, LORD!"

[6]The LORD said to me: Announce all these words in the towns of Judah and on the streets of Jerusalem: Obey the terms of this covenant and perform them. [7]I repeatedly and tirelessly warned your ancestors when I brought them out of the land of Egypt to this very day, saying, Obey me. [8]But they didn't listen or pay attention; they followed their own willful ambitions. So I brought upon them all the punishments I prescribed for violating this covenant—for refusing to obey.

[9]The LORD said to me: A conspiracy is taking place among the people of Judah and residents of Jerusalem. [10]They have returned to the sins of their ancestors who refused to obey my words. They too are following other gods and serving them. The people of Israel and the people of Judah have broken my covenant that I made with their ancestors.

[11]Therefore, the LORD proclaims: I will bring upon them a disaster from which they won't be able to escape. They will cry out to me, but I won't listen to them. [12]Then the people of Judah and those living in Jerusalem will call upon the gods they worship,[v] but they won't save them when

disaster strikes. [13]You have as many gods as you have towns, Judah, and you have as many shameful altars for worshipping Baal as you have streets in Jerusalem.

[14]As for you, don't pray for these people, don't cry out or plead for them, for I won't listen when they cry out to me on account of their distress.

[15] What are my loved ones doing
      in my temple
   while working out
      their many evil schemes?
   Can sacred offerings cancel your sin
      so that you revel in your evil deeds?[w]
[16] The LORD named you,
   "A blossoming olive tree,
      fair and fruitful";
      but with the blast of a powerful storm
      he will set it ablaze,
      until its branches
      are completely consumed.[x]

[17]The LORD of heavenly forces who planted you has announced disaster for you, because the people of Israel and Judah have done evil and made me angry by worshipping Baal.

Jeremiah's lament

[18] The LORD informed me and I knew.
      Then he helped me see
         what they were up to.
[19] I was like a young lamb
      led to the slaughter;
      I didn't realize that they were planning
         their schemes against me:
   "Let's destroy the tree with its fruit;
      let's cut him off from the land
         of the living
      so that even any knowledge of him
         will be wiped out."
[20] LORD of heavenly forces, righteous judge,
      who tests the heart and mind,
         let me see your revenge upon them,
         because I have committed
            my case to you.

[21]This is what the LORD says concerning the men from Anathoth who seek your life and say, "Don't prophesy in the LORD's name or else you will die at our hands."

---

[v]Or to whom they burn incense [w]Heb uncertain [x]Vulg; MT broken

²²Therefore, the LORD of heavenly forces proclaims, I'm going to punish them. Their young men will die in war, and their sons and daughters will die by famine. ²³No one will be left because I will bring disaster upon the men of Anathoth when their time comes.

12

If I took you to court, LORD, you would win.
But I still have questions
   about your justice.
Why do guilty persons enjoy success?
Why are evildoers so happy?
² You plant them, and they take root;
   they flourish and bear fruit.
You are always on their lips
   but far from their hearts.
³ Yet you, LORD, you know me.
   You see me.
You can tell that I love you.ʸ
   So drag them away
   and butcher them like sheep.
   Prepare them for the slaughterhouse.
⁴ How long will the land mourn
   and the grass in the fields dry up?
The animals and birds are swept away
   due to the evil of those in the land.
The people say,
   "God doesn't see what we're up to!"

⁵ If you have raced with people
   and are worn out,
   how will you compete with horses?
If you fall down in an open field,ᶻ
   how will you survive in the forest
     along the Jordan?
⁶ Even your relatives, your very family,
   are planning to trap you.
   They are out to get you.
   So don't trust them,
     even if they appear to be on your side.

God's lament over Judah's destruction

⁷ I have abandoned my house;
   I have deserted my inheritance.
I have given the one I love
   into the power of her enemies.
⁸ My inheritance has turned against me
   like a lion in the forest;
   she growls at me;
     therefore, I have rejected her.

⁹ My inheritance has become
   like a bird of prey,
     surrounded and attacked.ᵃ
Go, gather all the wild animals
   for the feast.
¹⁰ Many shepherds have destroyed
   my vineyard;
   they have trampled down my field;
   they have reduced my treasured field
     to a desolate wilderness.
¹¹ They have devastated her;
   desolate, she cries out to me in distress:
   "The whole land is desolate,
     and no one seems to care."
¹² Over all the desert roads
   destroyers march;
   for the sword of the LORD devours
   from one end of the land to the other;
   no one is safe.
¹³ They have sown wheat and reaped weeds;
   they have worn themselves out
   for nothing.
They will be ashamed of theirᵇ harvest
   on account of the LORD's fierce anger.

¹⁴The LORD proclaims: The evil nations have seized the landᶜ that I gave my people Israel. I'm going to dig them up from their own lands, and I will dig up the people of Judah from among them. ¹⁵And after I have dug them up, I will again have compassion on them and restore their inheritance and their land. ¹⁶And then, if they will learn the ways of my people, to make a solemn pledge in my name, "As the LORD lives," just as they once taught my people to swear to Baal, then they will be built up in the midst of my people. ¹⁷But if they don't listen, I will dig up that nation; yes, I will dig up and destroy, declares the LORD.

Jeremiah's symbolic acts

13

The LORD proclaimed to me: Go and buy a linen undergarment. Wear it for a while without washing it. ²So I bought a linen undergarment, as the LORD told me, and I put it on. ³The LORD spoke to me again: ⁴Take the undergarment that you are wearing and go at once to the Euphrates and put it under a rock. ⁵So I went and

---

ʸOr You test my heart.   ᶻOr If you are at ease only when in a peaceful land   ᵃHeb uncertain   ᵇOr your   ᶜOr inheritance buried it at the Euphrates,[d] as the LORD instructed. [6]After a long time, the LORD said to me: Return to the Euphrates and dig up the undergarment that I commanded you to bury there. [7]So I went to the Euphrates and I dug up the linen undergarment from the place I had buried it. But it was ruined and good for nothing.

[8]Then the LORD's word came to me: [9]The LORD proclaims: In the same way I will ruin the brazen pride of Judah and Jerusalem! [10]Instead of listening to me, this wicked people follow their own willful hearts and pursue other gods, worshipping and serving them. They will become like this linen garment—good for nothing! [11]Just as a linen undergarment clings to the body, so I created the people of Israel and Judah to cling to me, declares the LORD, to be my people for my honor, praise, and grandeur. But they wouldn't obey.

[12]So deliver this word to them: The LORD the God of Israel proclaims: Every wine jug should be filled with wine. And they will answer you, "Don't we already know that? Obviously every wine jug should be filled with wine!" [13]Then you should say to them: The LORD proclaims: I'm going to fill everyone who lives in this country with wine that makes them drunk, including the kings on David's throne, the priests, the prophets, and all those living in Jerusalem. [14]And I will shatter every one of them, even parents and children, declares the LORD. I won't take pity; I won't have compassion; I will show no mercy when I destroy them.

[15] Listen closely, don't be arrogant,
  for the LORD has spoken.
[16] Honor the LORD your God,
  before it's too late,
  before you stumble
    on the mountain paths
    in the evening shadows.
  Then you will hope for light,
    only to find darkness and gloom.
[17] If you are too proud to listen,
  I will go off alone
    and cry my eyes out.
  I will weep uncontrollably

because the LORD's flock
  will be dragged off into exile.
[18] Tell the king and the queen mother:
  Come down from your lofty place,
    because your glorious crowns
    will soon be removed
    from your heads.
[19] The towns of the arid southern plain
  will be surrounded;
  no one will get in or out;
  all Judah will be taken into exile;
    everyone will be led away.

[20] Lift up your eyes
  and see who is approaching
    from the north.
  Where is the flock entrusted to you,
    your beautiful flock?
[21] What will you say when he appoints
    someone as head over you:
    your defenders, your trusted allies?[e]
  Won't pain grip you
    like that of a woman in labor?
[22] And when you ask yourself,
    Why have all these things
    happened to me?
    it is because of your many sins
    that you have been stripped
    and violated.
[23] Can a Cushite change his skin
  or a leopard its spots?
  Neither can you do good
    when doing evil comes so naturally.
[24] So I will scatter you[f] like straw
    that is blown away by the desert winds.
[25] This is the future
    that I have prepared for you,
    declares the LORD,
  because you have forgotten me
    and trusted in lies.
[26] I myself will pull up your skirt
    over your face
    and expose your shame.
[27] I have seen your adultery and lust,
    your disgusting idols
    and shameless prostitution
    on the hills and in the fields.
  How terrible for you, Jerusalem!
  How long will you remain dirty?

[d]Heb *Perath* [e]Heb uncertain [f]Or *them*

Destruction on the horizon

14 The LORD's word to Jeremiah concerning the droughts:

² Judah mourns;
  her gates wither away.
The people fall to the ground in sorrow,
  as sobs of Jerusalem ascend.
³ The rich send their servants for water,
  but the wells run dry.
They return with empty jars,
  ashamed, bewildered, and in despair.
⁴ Because the ground is cracked
  due to lack of rain,
  the farmers too are ashamed;
  they cover their heads.
⁵ Even the doe in the field
  abandons her newborn,
  for there's no grass.
⁶ The wild donkeys stand
  on the well-traveled paths,
  panting like thirsty dogs;
  they go blind
  since there's nothing to eat.

⁷ Even though our sins testify against us,
  help us, LORD, for your name's sake.
We have turned away from you
  and sinned against you time and again.
⁸ You are the hope of Israel,
  its savior in times of trouble.
Why are you like a stranger in the land,
  like a tourist spending only the night?
⁹ Why are you like one taken by surprise,
  like a warrior unable to act?
Yet you are in our midst, LORD;
  we are called by your name.
  Don't give up on us.

¹⁰ This is what the LORD proclaims about
  this people:
Since they have loved to wander off
  and haven't restrained themselves,
  I^g won't accept them.
Now I will recall their wrongdoing
  and punish their sin.

¹¹ The LORD said to me: Don't pray for the safety of these people. ¹² When they fast, I won't pay attention to their pleas, and when they offer entirely burned offerings and grain offerings, I won't accept them. Instead, I will devour them with war, famine, and disease.

¹³ I replied, "LORD God, the prophets are telling them: 'You won't see war or famine, for I will give you lasting peace in this place.'"

¹⁴ Then the LORD said to me: The prophets are telling lies in my name. I haven't sent them. I haven't commanded them. I haven't spoken to them. They are prophesying to you false visions, worthless predictions, and deceit they have made up on their own. ¹⁵ Therefore, this is what the LORD proclaims concerning the prophets who are speaking in my name when I didn't send them, and who are telling you that war or famine will never come to this land: Those very prophets will die in war and by famine! ¹⁶ And the people they are prophesying to will be thrown into the streets of Jerusalem, victims of famine and war. There will be no one to bury them or their wives and children. I will pour out on them their own wickedness.

¹⁷ So deliver this word to them:
  My eyes well up with tears;
  I can't stop weeping—day and night,
  because my virgin daughter, my people,
    has suffered a crushing blow
    and is mortally wounded.
¹⁸ If I go into the fields,
  I see only the slain in battle.
If I enter the city,
  I see only those suffering from famine.
Even both prophet and priest
  wander about aimlessly in ignorance.
¹⁹ Have you completely rejected Judah?
  Do you hate Zion?
  Why then have you
    mortally wounded us?
We look for peace,
  but nothing good comes of it;
for a time of healing,
  only to be terrorized.
²⁰ We acknowledge our sin, LORD,
  the wrongdoing of our ancestors,
  because we have sinned against you.
²¹ For your name's sake, don't reject us,
  don't scorn your glorious throne.

^g Or *the Lord*

Remember your covenant with us;
  don't break it.
²² Can any of the false gods of the nations
  make it rain?
  Can the sky by itself bring showers?
  Aren't you the LORD, our God?
  You are our hope,
    since only you can do such things.

Lamenting Jerusalem's dire circumstances

15 The LORD said to me: Even if Moses and Samuel stood before me, I wouldn't change my mind about these people. Send them away from me. Let them go! ²And if they say, "Go where?" tell them, This is what the LORD proclaims:

Those marked for death—to death,
  those marked for war—to war,
  those marked for famine—to famine,
  and those marked for exile—to exile.

³I will appoint over them four agents[h] of death, declares the LORD: soldiers to kill, dogs to drag off, and vultures and wild animals to devour and destroy. ⁴Because of what Judah's King Manasseh, Hezekiah's son, has done in Jerusalem, I will make them an object of horror to all nations on earth.

⁵ Who will pity you, Jerusalem?
  Who will shed tears over you?
  Who will stop and ask how you're doing?
⁶ You have deserted me,
    declares the LORD.
  You have turned your back on me.
  So I will turn my hand against you
    and destroy you.
  I'm tired of holding back.
⁷ I will winnow them
    with a winnowing fork
    at the gates of their country.
  I will bereave and destroy my people
    because they haven't changed their ways.
⁸ Their widows will outnumber
    the sand on the shore.
  I will bring a destroyer in broad daylight
    against the mothers of young men.[i]
  Suddenly I will bring distress
    and terror upon them.
⁹ The mother of seven

will grow weak and gasp for air;
  her sun will set while it is yet day;
  she will be ashamed and disgraced.
  I will deliver the survivors to the sword,
  to the power of their enemies,
    declares the LORD.

¹⁰I wish I had never been born! I have become a source of conflict and dissension in my own country. Even though I haven't lent or borrowed, still everyone curses me.

¹¹ The LORD said:

Haven't I taken care of you?
  Haven't I helped you with your enemies
    in time of trouble and distress?[j]
¹² Can a person shatter iron,
  iron from the north, or bronze?
¹³ Your wealth and belongings
  I will deliver as plunder,
  without a fee,
  because of all your sins
    throughout your territory.
¹⁴ I will make you serve your enemies
  in a land you don't know,
  for my anger blazes like a fire
  that won't go out.

¹⁵ You understand, LORD!
  Remember me and act on my behalf.
  Bring judgment on those
    who torment me.
  In your mercy, spare my life.[k]
  Consider how I'm insulted
    on your account.
¹⁶ When your words turned up,
  I feasted on them;
  and they became my joy,
    the delight of my heart,
  because I belong to you,
  LORD God of heavenly forces.
¹⁷ I didn't join the festive occasions;
  I took no delight in them.
  I sat alone
    because your hand was upon me
    and you had filled me with curses.
¹⁸ Why am I always in pain?
  Why is my wound incurable,
    so far beyond healing?
  You have become for me as unreliable
    as a spring gone dry!

---

[h]Or *families* [i]Heb uncertain [j]Heb uncertain [k]Heb uncertain

¹⁹ Therefore, the LORD proclaims:
If you return to me, I will take you back
   and let you stand before me.
If you utter what is worthwhile,
   not what is worthless,
   you will be my spokesman.
They will turn to you,
   not you to them!
²⁰ I will make you a sturdy bronze wall
   against these people.
They will attack you,
   but they won't triumph,
   because I am with you
   to protect and rescue you,
      declares the LORD.
²¹ I will rescue you
   from the hand of the wicked;
I will redeem you
   from the grasp of the violent.

Loss of hope

16 The LORD's word came to me: ² Don't marry or have children in this place. ³ This is what the LORD proclaims concerning children who are born in this place and their mothers and fathers who give birth to them in this place:
⁴ They will die of horrible diseases.
   No one will mourn for them
      or bury them.
They will be like refuse
   lying on the ground.
They will die from the sword
   and by famine,
   and their corpses will be food
      for birds and wild animals.
⁵ This is what the LORD says:
Don't enter a house
   where there is mourning;
   don't grieve or lament for them,
   for I have taken away my blessing,
      kindness, and mercy from this people,
         declares the LORD.
⁶ From the least to the greatest,
   all will die in this land,
   and there will be no funerals
      or time of mourning.
No one will gash themselves in grief
   or shave their heads in sorrow.

⁷ No one will bring food^l for the mourner
   as comfort for the dead.
No one will offer a cup of consolation
   for the loss of father or mother.
⁸ Don't enter a house where there is feasting and sit down to eat and drink. ⁹ This is what the LORD of heavenly forces, the God of Israel, proclaims:

Before your very eyes and in your own lifetime, I will silence in this place the sounds of joy and gladness and the voices of the bridegroom and the bride.

¹⁰ When you proclaim all these things to the people, and they ask you, "Why has the LORD pronounced such massive devastation against us? What have we done wrong? How have we sinned against the LORD our God?" ¹¹ then you should tell them: It's because your ancestors have deserted me and followed other gods, declares the LORD. They have served and worshipped them, while abandoning me and refusing to keep my Instruction. ¹² And you, you have acted worse than your ancestors, each of you following your own willful, evil hearts and paying no attention to me. ¹³ So I will banish you from this land to a place that neither you nor your ancestors have known, and there you will serve other gods day and night, for I will show you no mercy.

¹⁴ But the time is coming, declares the LORD, when no one will say, "As the LORD lives who brought up the Israelites from the land of Egypt"; ¹⁵ instead, they will say, "As the LORD lives who brought up the Israelites from the land of the north and from all the lands where he has banished them." I will bring them back to the land that I gave to their ancestors.

¹⁶ I'm going to send hordes of fishermen to catch them, declares the LORD. Afterward I will send a party of hunters to hunt them down on every mountain, hill, and cave. ¹⁷ I am watching their every move; not one is hidden from me. Nor is their sin concealed from my sight. ¹⁸ I will initially pay them back double for their evil and sin, because they have corrupted my land with their disgusting, lifeless idols and have

---

^l LXX; Heb *break for them*

filled my inheritance with their detestable
practices.

¹⁹ LORD, you are my strength
and my stronghold;
you are my refuge in time of trouble.
The nations will flock to you
from the ends of the earth,
and they will say:
"Our ancestors have inherited utter lies,
things that are hollow and useless."
²⁰ Can humans make their own gods?
If so, they are not gods at all!
²¹ Therefore, I will teach them;
this time I will teach them
my power and my might.
They will understand that I am the LORD.

17 Judah's sin is engraved
with an iron pen.
It's etched with a diamond point
on the tablets of their hearts
and on the horns of their altars.
² Their children remember their altars
and sacred poles^m
by the lush trees and high hills.

³ Because you have committed such sins
throughout your country,
I will give to your enemies
my mountain in the land,
as well as your wealth
and all that you treasure.^n
⁴ You will lose the inheritance
that I gave you.
I will make you slaves of your enemies
in a land you don't know,
for my anger blazes like a fire
that won't go out.

⁵ The LORD proclaims:
Cursed are those who trust
in mere humans,
who depend on human strength
and turn their hearts from the LORD.
⁶ They will be like a desert shrub
that doesn't know when relief comes.
They will live in the parched places
of the wilderness,
in a barren land where no one survives.

⁷ Happy are those who trust in the LORD,
who rely on the LORD.
⁸ They will be like trees
planted by the streams,
whose roots reach down to the water.
They won't fear drought when it comes;
their leaves will remain green.
They won't be stressed
in the time of drought
or fail to bear fruit.

⁹ The most cunning heart—
it's beyond help.
Who can figure it out?
¹⁰ I, the LORD, probe the heart
and discern hidden motives,
to give everyone what they deserve,
the consequences of their deeds.

¹¹ Like a partridge gathering a brood
that is not its own,
so are those who acquire
their wealth corruptly.
By midlife it will be gone;
afterward they will look like fools.

¹² Splendid and exalted throne,
the place of our sanctuary
from the beginning!
¹³ LORD, the hope of Israel,
all who forsake you will suffer disgrace;
those who turn away from you^o
in the land
will be written off,^p
for they have abandoned the LORD,
the fountain of living water.

¹⁴ Heal me, LORD, and I'll be healed.
Save me and I'll be saved,
for you are my heart's desire.
¹⁵ See how they harass me:
"Where's the LORD's word?
Let it come now!"
¹⁶ Yet I didn't urge you to bring disaster;^q
I didn't want the calamity to happen.
You know what comes out of my mouth;
it's always before you.
¹⁷ Don't terrorize me;
you are my refuge in time of disaster.

---

^mHeb *asherim*; perhaps objects devoted to the worship of Asherah   ^nHeb uncertain   ^oOr *me*   ^pHeb uncertain
^qLXX; Heb uncertain

¹⁸ Let my tormentors be disgraced,
    but not me;
  let them be terrorized, but not me.
  Bring on them the time of disaster,
    as they deserve; destroy them repeatedly.

¹⁹The LORD proclaimed to me: Go and stand by the People's Gate where Judah's kings go in and out, and then by all the gates of Jerusalem, ²⁰and say to them: Listen to the LORD's word, you kings of Judah, all you people of Judah, and anyone living in Jerusalem who passes through these gates. ²¹The LORD says: Be on guard not to carry a load on the Sabbath day or conduct business at the gates of Jerusalem. ²²Don't carry a load from your houses or do any kind of work on the Sabbath day. Rather, keep the Sabbath day holy as I commanded your ancestors, ²³although they didn't listen or pay attention. They were stubborn and wouldn't obey or accept correction. ²⁴If you are careful to obey me, declares the LORD, and don't conduct business at the gates of this city on the Sabbath day, if you keep the Sabbath day holy by not working, ²⁵then through the gates of this city will come kings who occupy the throne of David and their officers, all riding on chariots and horses. They will be accompanied by the people of Judah and those living in Jerusalem. And this city will always be inhabited. ²⁶Others will come from the towns of Judah and Benjamin, from all around Jerusalem, and from the western foothills, the highlands, and the arid southern plain—they will come bringing entirely burned offerings, sacrifices, grain offerings, incense, and thanksgiving offerings to the LORD's temple. ²⁷But if you don't obey me by keeping the Sabbath day holy, if you carry your loads and conduct your business at the gates of Jerusalem as usual, then I will set fire to those gates that will completely engulf the fortresses of Jerusalem; it will not be put out.

God the potter

18 Jeremiah received the LORD's word: ²Go down to the potter's house, and I'll give you instructions about what to do there. ³So I went down to the potter's house; he was working on the potter's wheel. ⁴But the piece he was making was flawed while still in his hands, so the potter started on another, as seemed best to him. ⁵Then the LORD's word came to me: ⁶House of Israel, can't I deal with you like this potter, declares the LORD? Like clay in the potter's hand, so are you in mine, house of Israel! ⁷At any time I may announce that I will dig up, pull down, and destroy a nation or kingdom; ⁸but if that nation I warned turns from its evil, then I'll relent and not carry out the harm I intended for it. ⁹At the same time, I may announce that I will build and plant a nation or kingdom; ¹⁰but if that nation displeases and disobeys me, then I'll relent and not carry out the good I intended for it. ¹¹Now say to the people of Judah and those living in Jerusalem: This is what the LORD says: I am a potter preparing a disaster for you; I'm working out a plan against you. So each one of you, turn from your evil ways; reform your ways and your actions. ¹²But they said, "What's the use! We will follow our own plans and act according to our own willful, evil hearts."

¹³ Therefore, the LORD proclaims:
  Ask among the nations:
    Have you ever heard anything like this?
    Virgin Israel has done
    the most horrible thing.
¹⁴ Does the snow on the mountains of
  Lebanon ever melt entirely
    off their rocky cliffs?
  Do the cool mountain streams
    ever dry up?ʳ
¹⁵ Yet my people have forgotten me;
    they have offered sacrifices to a lie.
  And so they have stumbled along the way,
    even along the ancient paths.
  They have taken side roads,
    not the main roads.ˢ
¹⁶ They have ruined their country
    and brought utter shame on it.
  All who pass by are shocked
    and shake their heads.
¹⁷ Like a strong east wind,
    I will scatter them before their enemy.

ʳHeb uncertain; or be dug up   ˢHeb uncertain

When disaster strikes them,
  I will show them my back,
  not my face.

¹⁸Then they said, "Come, let's unite against Jeremiah, for the priest's instruction won't fail, nor will the sage's counsel, nor the prophet's word. Come, let's silence him and pay no attention to his words."

¹⁹ Pay attention to me, LORD;
  listen to what my enemies are saying.

²⁰ Should evil be returned for good?
  Yet they have set traps for me.
  Remember that I stood before you,
    begging you to be merciful
    and not to punish them.

²¹ Enough! Let their children starve;
  let them die by the sword.
  Let their wives be barren widows;
  let their men be slaughtered
  and their youth struck down in battle.

²² Let screams be heard from their homes
  when you suddenly bring armies
    against them.
  They have dug a pit to capture me,
    set traps for my feet.

²³ But you, LORD, you know
  all their sinister plots to kill me.
  Don't overlook their wrongdoing;
    don't cleanse their sin from before you.
  May they stumble before you;
    when you become angry,
    do something about them.

Broken beyond repair

19 The LORD proclaims: Go buy a clay jar from a potter in the presence of the elders of the people and the priests. ²Then go out to the Ben-hinnom Valley at the entrance of the gate called Broken Pots and proclaim there the words I will tell you. ³Listen to the LORD's word, you kings of Judah and those of you living in Jerusalem: This is what the LORD of heavenly forces, the God of Israel, says: I'm going to bring such disaster upon this place that it will shock all who hear of it. ⁴They have deserted me and degraded this place into a shrine for other gods, which neither they nor their ancestors nor Judah's kings have ever known. And they have filled this place with the blood of the innocent. ⁵Yes, they have built shrines to Baal, to burn their sons and daughters in the fire, although I never commanded or ordered such a thing, nor did it ever cross my mind.

⁶So now the time is coming, declares the LORD, when people will no longer call this place Topheth or Ben-hinnom Valley but Carnage Valley. ⁷I will foil the plans of Judah and Jerusalem in this place and will have them fall in battle before their enemies, before those who seek their lives. I will give their corpses as food to the birds and the wild animals. ⁸I will make this city something that sounds horrible; all who pass by it will be shocked at its pain. ⁹And when their enemies lay siege to the city, seeking their lives, they will resort in desperation to eating the flesh of their sons and daughters, and to devouring the flesh of their neighbors.

¹⁰Then you should shatter the clay jar in the sight of the people who are with you, ¹¹and you should say to them: This is what the LORD of heavenly forces says: Just as one smashes the potter's piece beyond repair, so I will smash this people and this city. And they will bury the dead in Topheth until there's no room left. ¹²That is what I will do to this place and its residents, declares the LORD: I will make this city like Topheth. ¹³The houses of Jerusalem and those of Judah's kings will become as foul as Topheth—all the houses on whose roofs they made offerings to the heavenly force and poured out drink offerings to other gods.

¹⁴When Jeremiah returned from Topheth where the LORD had sent him to prophesy, he stood in the court of the LORD's temple and said to all the people: ¹⁵The LORD of heavenly forces, the God of Israel, proclaims: I am about to bring upon this city and its surrounding towns every disaster that I have pronounced against them, because they have been stubborn and wouldn't obey my words.

20 When the priest Pashhur, Immer's son, the officer in charge of the LORD's temple, heard Jeremiah prophesying these words, ²he beat the prophet and detained him in confinement at the upper Benjamin Gate in the LORD's temple. ³The next day, when Pashhur released Jeremiah from confinement, Jeremiah said to him, "The LORD has changed your name from Pashhur to Panic Lurks Everywhere. ⁴The LORD proclaims: I'm going to strike panic into your heart and into the hearts of your friends. You will watch as they fall in battle to their enemies. I will hand over all Judah to the king of Babylon, who will exile some to Babylon and slaughter others. ⁵I will hand over all the wealth of this city, all its goods and valuables, including the treasures of the kings of Judah, to their enemies, who will ransack and pillage and carry it all off to Babylon. ⁶And you, Pashhur, and all those in your household, will go into captivity. You will be deported to Babylon where you will die. There you will be buried with all your friends to whom you prophesied falsely."

Total despair

⁷ LORD, you enticed me, and I was taken in.
  You were too strong for me,
    and you prevailed.
  Now I'm laughed at all the time;
    everyone mocks me.
⁸ Every time I open my mouth, I cry out
  and say, "Violence and destruction!"
  The LORD's word has brought me
    nothing but insult and injury, constantly.
⁹ I thought, I'll forget him;
  I'll no longer speak in his name.
  But there's an intense fire in my heart,
    trapped in my bones.
  I'm drained trying to contain it;
    I'm unable to do it.
¹⁰ I hear many whispering—
  "Panic Lurks Everywhere!—
    proclaim, yes, let's proclaim it ourselves!"
  All my friends are waiting
    for me to stumble:
  "Perhaps he can be enticed.
    Then we'll prevail against him
      and get our revenge on him!"
¹¹ But the LORD is with me
  like a strong defender.
  Therefore, my oppressors
    will stumble and not prevail.

They will be disgraced
  by their own failures.
  Their dishonor will never be forgotten.
¹² The LORD of heavenly forces
  tests the righteous
  and discerns the heart and the mind.
  Let me see your retribution upon them,
  for I have committed my case to you.
¹³ Sing to the LORD,
  praise the LORD,
    for he has rescued the needy
    from the clutches of evildoers.
¹⁴ Cursed be the day that I was born.
  May the day my mother
    gave birth to me not be blessed.
¹⁵ Cursed be the one
  who delivered the news to my father,
  "You have a son!"—
    filling him with joy.
¹⁶ May the bearer of that news
  be like the cities
  that the LORD destroyed without mercy.
  May he hear screams in the morning,
    and the battle cries at noon,
¹⁷ because he didn't kill me in the womb
  and let my mother become my grave,
    her womb pregnant forever.
¹⁸ Why was I ever born
  when all I see is suffering and misery,
    and my days are filled with shame?

Verdict against king and city

21 Jeremiah received the LORD's word when King Zedekiah sent Pashhur, Malchiah's son, and the priest Zephaniah, Maaseiah's son, to him with an appeal: ²"Speak to the LORD on our behalf because Babylon's King Nebuchadnezzar[t] is attacking us. Perhaps the LORD will perform one of his mighty deeds and force him to withdraw from us."

³Jeremiah answered them: This is what you should tell Zedekiah: ⁴The LORD, the God of Israel, says: I'm going to turn your own weapons against you, yes, the weapons you are using to fight the king of Babylon and the Babylonians[u] who have surrounded you! I will round them up in the center of the city. ⁵Then I myself will fight against

you with an outstretched hand and strong arm in fierce anger and rage. ⁶I will strike down those within this city—both people and animals—and they will die of a terrible plague. ⁷Afterward, declares the LORD, I will deliver Judah's King Zedekiah, his servants, and those in this city who have survived plague, war, and famine to Babylon's King Nebuchadnezzar[v] and to their enemies who seek to do them harm. He will put them to the sword without pity, mercy, or compassion.

⁸This is what you should tell this people: The LORD says: I'm setting before you the way of life and the way of death. ⁹Whoever stays in the city will die by the sword, famine, and disease. But whoever leaves the city and surrenders to the Babylonians[w] will live; yes, their lives will be spared. ¹⁰I have set my face against this city for harm and not for good, declares the LORD; it will be delivered to the king of Babylon, who will set it on fire.

Judah: Hear the LORD's word

¹¹House of Judah!
This is what the LORD says:
¹²House of David! The LORD proclaims:
Begin each morning
by administering justice,
rescue from their oppressor
those who have been robbed,
or else my anger
will spread like a wildfire,
with no one to put it out,
because of your evil deeds.
¹³I am against you,
you who live in the valley,[x]
like a rock of the plain,
declares the LORD,
and who say, "Who will come down
to attack us?
Who will breach our fortresses?"
¹⁴I will punish you
based on what you have done,
declares the LORD.
I will set your[y] forests on fire;
the flames will engulf
everything around you.[z]

Oracles against the kings

22 The LORD proclaims: Go down to the palace of the king of Judah and declare this message: ²Listen to the LORD's word, king of Judah, you who sit on David's throne—you and your attendants, and all those who go through these gates. ³The LORD proclaims: Do what is just and right; rescue the oppressed from the power of the oppressor. Don't exploit or mistreat the refugee, the orphan, and the widow. Don't spill the blood of the innocent in this place. ⁴If you obey this command, then through the gates of this palace will come kings who occupy the throne of David, riding on chariots and horses along with their entourage and subjects. ⁵But if you ignore these words, I swear by myself, declares the LORD, that this palace will become a ruin. ⁶The LORD proclaims concerning the palace of the king of Judah:

Though you are like Gilead to me,
like the summit of Lebanon,
I will turn you into a desert—
uninhabited cities.
⁷I will summon destroyers against you,
who will use their weapons
to cut down your finest cedars
and hurl them into the fire.
⁸People from many nations will pass by this city and ask each other: "Why has the LORD treated that great city like this?" ⁹And the answer will be, "Because they abandoned the covenant with the LORD their God and worshipped and served other gods."
¹⁰Don't weep or lament for the dead king.[a]
Weep instead for the one
who has gone away,
for he will never return
to see his native soil.
¹¹This is what the LORD says about Shallum son of Judah's King Josiah, who succeeded his father Josiah as king but who is now gone from this place: He will never return! ¹²He will die where he's been exiled and never see this land again.
¹³How terrible for Jehoiakim,
who builds his house with corruption
and his upper chambers with injustice,

---

[v]Heb *Nebuchadrezzar* [w]Heb *Chaldeans* [x]Heb uncertain [y]Or *its* [z]Or *it* [a]Heb lacks *king*.

working his countrymen for nothing,
refusing to give them their wages.
[14] He says, "I'll build myself a grand palace,
with huge upper chambers,
ornate windows,
cedar paneling,
and rich red decor."
[15] Is this what makes you a king,
having more cedar than anyone else?
Didn't your father eat and drink
and still do what was just and right?
Then it went well for him!
[16] He defended the rights
of the poor and needy;
then it went well.
Isn't that what it means to know me?
declares the LORD.
[17] But you set your eyes and heart
on nothing but unjust gain;
you spill the blood of the innocent;
you practice cruelty;
you oppress your subjects.
[18] Therefore, this is what the LORD says
to Jehoiakim son of Judah's King Josiah:
They won't grieve for him, saying,
"My brother, my sister!"
They won't grieve for him, saying,
"My master, my majesty!"
[19] They will give him a donkey's burial,
dragging him outside
the gates of Jerusalem
and dumping him there.
[20] Go up to Lebanon and cry out,
lift up your voice in Bashan,
cry out from Abarim,
because all your lovers
have been ravished.
[21] I spoke to you
when you felt safe and secure,
but you said, "I won't listen."
You have been that way since your youth:
not listening to a word I say.
[22] Your shepherds will be tossed to the wind,
your lovers taken off to exile.
Then you will be embarrassed
and humiliated
by all your wickedness.
[23] You who live in Lebanon,

nestled in cedar,
who will pity you[b]
when you are overcome in pain,
like that of childbirth?
[24] As surely as I live, declares the LORD,
even if Coniah,[c] King Jehoiakim's son from
Judah were a signet ring on my right hand,
I would still remove you from there. [25] I
would hand you over to those who seek to
kill you, those you dread, even Babylon's
King Nebuchadnezzar and his army.[d] [26] I will
banish you and your mother who bore you
to a land far from your native soil, and there
the two of you will die. [27] You[e] will never return to the land you[f] long to go back to.
[28] Is this man Coniah
merely a defiled and broken pottery jar
that no one wants?
Why then have he and his children
been hurled out
and cast into an unfamiliar land?
[29] Land, land, land,
hear the LORD's word:
[30] The LORD proclaims:
Mark this man as childless;
he will not prosper during his lifetime.
None of his children
will sit on David's throne
and rule again in Judah.

Promise of restoration

23 Watch out, you shepherds who destroy and scatter the sheep of my
pasture, declares the LORD. [2] This is what
the LORD, the God of Israel, proclaims
about the shepherds who "tend to" my
people: You are the ones who have scattered my flock and driven them away. You
haven't attended to their needs, so I will
take revenge on you for the terrible things
you have done to them, declares the LORD.
[3] I myself will gather the few remaining
sheep from all the countries where I have
driven them. I will bring them back to their
pasture, and they will be fruitful and multiply. [4] I will place over them shepherds who
care for them. Then they will no longer be
afraid or dread harm, nor will any be missing, declares the LORD.

[b]Heb uncertain [c]Cf *Jeconiah* in Jer 24:1 [d]Or *the Babylonians* [e]Or *They* [f]Or *they*

Promise of a righteous and just king

5 The time is coming, declares the LORD, when I will raise up a righteous descendant[g] from David's line, and he will rule as a wise king. He will do what is just and right in the land. 6 During his lifetime, Judah will be saved and Israel will live in safety. And his name will be The LORD Is Our Righteousness.[h]

7 So the time is coming, declares the LORD, when no one will say, "As the LORD lives who brought up the Israelites from the land of Egypt." 8 Instead, they will say, "As the LORD lives who brought up the descendants of the people of Israel from the land of the north and from all the lands where he[i] has banished them so that they can live in their own land."

Oracles against the prophets

9 As for the prophets:
  My heart inside me is broken;
    my body aches.[j]
  I stagger like a drunk
    who has had too much wine to drink,
    because of the LORD
    and because of God's holy words.
10 Because the country teems
    with adulterers,
  because of them,[k]
    yes, because their might isn't right
    and their way is evil,
    the land dries up,
    and the grazing areas in the
      wilderness wither.[l]
11 Both prophet and priest are godless;
  I even find their evil in my temple,
    declares the LORD.
12 Therefore, they will find themselves
    on slippery ground
  and will be thrust into darkness,
    where they will collapse.
  I will bring disaster upon them,
    when their time comes,
    declares the LORD.
13 In the prophets of Samaria
  I saw something shocking:
  They prophesied by Baal
    and led astray my people Israel.

14 In the prophets of Jerusalem
  I saw something horrible:
  They commit adultery and tell lies.
  They encourage evildoers
    so that no one turns
    from their wickedness.
In my eyes,
  they are no better than Sodom;
    its people are like Gomorrah.
15 Therefore, this is what the LORD of heavenly forces proclaims concerning the prophets:
  I'm going to feed them bitter food
    and give them poison to drink.
  Wickedness has spread from the
    prophets of Jerusalem
    throughout the land.

16 The LORD proclaims:
  Don't listen to the prophets
    who are speaking to you;
    they are deceiving you.
  Their visions come from their own hearts,
    not from the LORD's mouth.
17 They keep saying to those
    who scorn God's message,
  "All will go well for you,"
    and to those who follow
    their own willful hearts,
  "Nothing bad will happen to you."
18 But who has stood in the LORD's council
    to listen to God's word?
  Who has paid attention
    to his word and announced it?
19 Look! The LORD's angry storm breaks out;
    it whirls around the heads of the wicked.
20 The LORD's fierce anger
    won't turn back
    until it accomplishes
    all that he has planned.
  In the days to come,
    you will understand what this means.

21 I didn't send the prophets,
    yet they ran anyway.
  I didn't speak to them,
    yet they prophesied anyway.
22 If they had stood in my council,

---

[g]Or branch [h]Or of Our Righteousness, possibly a play on the name Zedekiah [i]Or I [j]Heb uncertain; or my bones shake [k]LXX; MT a curse [l]Heb uncertain

they would have proclaimed
my words to my people;
  they would have turned them
  from their evil ways and deeds.
²³ The LORD declares, Am I a God
  who is only nearby and not far off?
²⁴ Can people hide themselves
  in secret places
so I might not see them?
  Don't I fill heaven and earth?

²⁵ I have heard the prophets prophesying lies in my name. They claim, "I've had a dream; I've had a dream!" ²⁶ How long will deceitful prophecies dominate the minds of the prophets? Those prophets are treacherous. ²⁷ They scheme to make my people forget me by their dreams that people tell each other, just as their ancestors forgot me because of Baal. ²⁸ Let the prophet who has a dream declare it, but let the one who has my word proclaim it faithfully.

What a difference
  between straw and wheat!
  declares the LORD.
²⁹ Isn't my word like fire
  and like a hammer that shatters rock?
  declares the LORD.
³⁰ Therefore, I'm against the prophets
  who steal my words from each other,
  declares the LORD.
³¹ I'm against the prophets
  who carelessly deliver oracles,ᵐ
  declares the LORD.

³² I'm against the prophets
  who dream up lies
  and then proclaim them,
    declares the LORD.
With their reckless lies,
  they lead my people astray.
I didn't send them;
  I didn't commission them.
They are completely useless
  to these people,
    declares the LORD.

³³ When these people or a prophet or a priest asks you, "What is the LORD's message?"ⁿ say to them, "What message? I will cast you off, declares the LORD." ³⁴ I will punish anyone, including prophet or priest, who says, "This is the LORD's message." ³⁵ This is what you should ask each other: "What has the LORD said?" "What has the LORD declared?" ³⁶ But you are no longer to mention the LORD's message, because everyone thinks they have received a message from the LORD. You destroy the very word of the living God, the LORD of heavenly forces, our God. ³⁷ So this is what you should say to the prophet: "What has the LORD said to you?" "What has the LORD declared?" ³⁸ But if you insist on saying, "This is the LORD's message," the LORD says to you: Because you have made this claim—this is the LORD's message—when I told you not to proclaim the LORD's mes-

ᵐHeb uncertain ⁿOr *burden*

GOMORRAH

One of the cities in "the entire valley" destroyed by God (Gen 19:24-25); information in Genesis indicates that Gomorrah was located in the Jordan Valley in the Dead Sea area (Gen 13:10).

In Genesis 14, King Birsha of Gomorrah joins other cities in the area in an unsuccessful revolt against Chedorlaomer of Elam. Gomorrah is later destroyed after God sends two divine messengers to Sodom to find out if the wickedness of these cities is as great as he has heard (Gen 18:16-21). Sodom and Gomorrah are mentioned frequently in both the OT and NT as paradigms of wickedness (Jer 23:14) and examples of God's punishment (Isa 13:19; Matt 10:15; 2 Pet 2:6).

sage, [39]I will lift you up° and cast you out of my presence, together with the city that I gave to your ancestors. [40]I will make you an object of disgrace and enduring shame that no one will ever forget.

Good and bad figs

24 After Babylon's King Nebuchadnezzar had deported Judah's King Jeconiah, King Jehoiakim's son, and the Judean officials, as well as the craftsmen and metalworkers from Jerusalem to Babylon, the LORD showed me two baskets of figs set in front of the LORD's temple. [2]One basket was filled with fresh and ripe figs; the other basket was filled with rotten figs—too rotten to eat. [3]And the LORD asked me: "What do you see, Jeremiah?"

I replied: "Figs! Some good ones and others very bad—so bad that they can't be eaten."

[4]Then the LORD said to me: [5]The LORD, the God of Israel, proclaims: Just as with these good figs, I will treat kindly the Judean exiles that I have sent from this place to Babylon. [6]I regard them as good, and I will bring them back to this land. I will build them up and not pull them down; I will plant them and not dig them up. [7]I will give them a heart to know me, for I am the LORD. They will be my people, and I will be their God, for they will return to me with all their heart. [8]And just like the rotten figs that are so bad that they can't be eaten, the LORD says, I will do to Judah's King Zedekiah and his officials, as well as the remaining few in Jerusalem and those who are living in Egypt. [9]I will make them an object of horror and evil to all the kingdoms of the earth. Wherever I scatter them, they will be disgraced and insulted, mocked and cursed. [10]I will send the sword, famine, and disease against them until they vanish from the fertile land that I gave to their ancestors.

A summary of Jeremiah's message

25 Jeremiah received the LORD's word concerning all the people of Judah in the fourth year of Judah's King Jehoiakim, Josiah's son. This was the first year of Babylon's King Nebuchadnezzar. [2]The prophet Jeremiah addressed all the people of Judah and all those living in Jerusalem. [3]From the thirteenth year of Judah's King Josiah, Amon's son, to this very day— twenty-three years—the LORD's word has come to me. I have delivered it to you repeatedly, although you wouldn't listen. [4]In fact, the LORD has tirelessly sent you all his servants, the prophets, but you wouldn't listen or pay attention. [5]They said, "Each one of you, turn from your evil ways and deeds and live in the fertile land that the LORD gave you and your ancestors for all time. [6]Don't follow or worship other gods and don't anger me by what you make with your hands. Then I won't bring disaster upon you." [7]But you wouldn't listen to me, making me angry by what you do and bringing disaster upon yourselves, declares the LORD.

[8]Therefore, this is what the LORD of heavenly forces says: Because you haven't listened to my words, [9]I am going to muster all the tribes of the north and my servant King Nebuchadnezzar of Babylon, declares the LORD, and I will bring them against this country and its residents as well as against all the surrounding nations. I will completely destroy them and will make them an object of horror, shock, and ruins for all time. [10]I will silence the sounds of joy and laughter and the voices of the bride and the bridegroom. Yes, I will silence the millstones and snuff out the lamplight. [11]This whole country will be reduced to a wasteland, and these nations will serve the king of Babylon for seventy years. [12]When the seventy years are over, I will punish the king of Babylon and his nation for their wrongdoing, declares the LORD. I will reduce the land of the Babylonians to a wasteland for all time. [13]I will unleash upon that land everything I decree, all that is written in this scroll, which Jeremiah prophesied against all the nations. [14]Yes, many great nations and powerful kings will

°LXX, Syr, Vulg; MT *forget you*

enslave them, and I will pay them back in full for what they have done and made with their hands.

¹⁵This is what the LORD, God of Israel, said to me: Take this seething cup of wine from my hand and make all the nations gulp it down where I'm sending you. ¹⁶They will drink and stagger about half-crazed because of the sword that I am sending against them.

¹⁷So I took the cup from the LORD's hand, and I made all the nations drink from it where the LORD had sent me: ¹⁸Jerusalem and the towns of Judah, its kings and officials. This was to make them a wasteland, an object of horror, shock, and cursing, as it is today; ¹⁹Pharaoh, Egypt's king, his attendants and officials, and all his people, ²⁰including the foreignersᵖ living there; all the kings of the land of Uz; all the kings of the land of the Philistines— Ashkelon, Gaza, Ekron, and what's left of Ashdod; ²¹Edom, Moab, and the Ammonites; ²²all the kings of Tyre and Sidon, and the kings of the coastlands across the sea; ²³Dedan, Tema, Buz, and all those who cut the hair of their foreheads;�q ²⁴all the kings of Arabia and the nomadic tribes,ʳ ²⁵all the kings of Zimri,ˢ Elam, and Media; ²⁶all the kings of the north, those nearby and those faraway, one after another, all the empires on the earth will drink from this cup.ᵗ And after them the king of Sheshachᵘ will drink from it.

²⁷Then say to them: The LORD of heavenly forces, the God of Israel, proclaims: Drink this seething cup of wine and get drunk. Vomit and collapse and don't get up again because of the sword that I'm thrusting into you. ²⁸If they refuse to take the cup in your hand and drink from it, tell them: This is what the LORD of heavenly forces says: You must drink! ²⁹Look! I'm bringing disaster upon the city that bears my name; how then will you escape unpunished? You will not! I'm summoning the sword against everyone on earth, declares the LORD of heavenly forces.

³⁰Now prophesy all these things
and say to them:
The LORD roars on high;
from his holy place he thunders.
He roars fiercely against his flock,
like the shouting of those
who tread on grapes,
against everyone on earth.
³¹The uproar is heard far and wide,
because the LORD is bringing
a lawsuit against the nations.
He's entering into judgment
with all people,
sentencing the guilty to death,
declares the LORD.
³²The LORD of heavenly forces proclaims:
Look! Disaster travels
from nation to nation.
A terrible storm comes
from the far ends of the earth.
³³At that time, those struck down by the LORD will fill the earth. And no one will mourn for them or prepare their bodies for burial. They will become like refuse lying on the ground.
³⁴Wail, you shepherds, cry out.
Roll in the dust, you masters of the flock!
The day of your slaughter has arrived.
You will fall and shatter like a fragile vase.
³⁵The shepherds have no place to hide;
the masters of the flock can't escape.
³⁶Hear the cry of the shepherds
and the sobbing of the masters
of the flock,
because the LORD
is ravaging their pasture.
³⁷There's an eerie silence
in the peaceful meadows,
because of the LORD's fierce anger.
³⁸The lion is on the prowl,
and the land is reduced to nothing,
because of the fierce sword,ᵛ
because of his fierce anger.

Jeremiah arrested and sentenced to death

26 Early in the rule of Judah's King Jehoiakim, Josiah's son, this word

---

ᵖHeb uncertain �q Heb uncertain ʳHeb uncertain ˢHeb uncertain ᵗHeb lacks *will drink from this cup.* ᵘ*Sheshach* is a name for Babylon. ᵛLXX, Heb manuscripts; Heb uncertain came from the LORD: ²The LORD proclaims: Stand in the temple courtyard and speak to all the people of the towns of Judah who have come to the temple to worship. Tell them everything I command you; leave nothing out. ³Perhaps they will listen and each will turn from their evil ways. If they do, I will relent and not carry out the harm I have in mind for them because of the wrong they have done. ⁴So tell them, The LORD proclaims: If you don't listen to me or follow the Instruction I have set before you— ⁵if you don't listen to the words of the prophets that I have sent to you time and again, though you haven't listened, ⁶then I will make this temple a ruin like Shiloh, and this city I will make a curse before all nations on earth.

⁷The priests, the prophets, and all the people heard Jeremiah declare these words in the LORD's temple. ⁸And when Jeremiah finished saying everything the LORD told him to say, the priests and the prophets and all the people seized him and said, "You must die! ⁹Why do you prophesy in the LORD's name that 'this temple will become a ruin like Shiloh, and this city will be destroyed and left without inhabitant'?" Then all the people joined ranks against Jeremiah in the LORD's temple.

¹⁰When the officials of Judah heard these things, they went up from the royal palace to the LORD's temple and took their places at the entrance of the New Gate of the LORD's temple. ¹¹The priests and the prophets said to the officials and all the people: "This man deserves to die for prophesying against this city as you have all heard firsthand."

¹²Jeremiah said to all the officials and to all the people, "The LORD sent me to prophesy to this temple and this city everything you have heard. ¹³So now transform your ways and actions. Obey the LORD your God, and the LORD may relent and not carry out the harm that he's pronounced against you. ¹⁴But me? I'm in your hands. Do whatever you would like to me. ¹⁵Only know for certain that if you sentence me to death, you and the people of this city will be guilty of

killing an innocent man. The LORD has in fact sent me to speak everything I have said to you."

¹⁶Then the officials and all the people said to the priests and the prophets, "This man doesn't deserve to die, for he has spoken to us in the name of the LORD our God."

¹⁷A few of the community elders got up and addressed the whole crowd: ¹⁸"Micah of Moresheth, who prophesied during the rule of Judah's Hezekiah, said to all the people of Judah, 'The LORD of heavenly forces proclaims:

Zion will be plowed down like a field,
Jerusalem will become piles of rubble,
and the temple mount will become
    an overgrown mound.'

¹⁹"Did King Hezekiah or anyone else in Judah execute him? Didn't he instead fear the LORD and plead for his mercy? Then the LORD relented of the harm that he had pronounced against them. We are about to commit a huge mistake that will cost us our lives."

²⁰There was another man who prophesied in the LORD's name: Uriah, Shemaiah's son from Kiriath-jearim. He prophesied the same things that Jeremiah did about this city and against this land. ²¹When King Jehoiakim and all his warriors and officials heard his words, the king sought to kill him. Uriah heard of this and fled in fear to Egypt. ²²But King Jehoiakim dispatched Elnathan, Achbor's son, and others to Egypt. ²³They brought Uriah back from Egypt to the king who had him killed, and his body was thrown into the common burial ground.

²⁴But Ahikam, Shaphan's son, protected Jeremiah and wouldn't let the people execute him.

Submit to the king of Babylon and live

27 Early in the rule of Judah's King Zedekiah,ʷ Josiah's son, this word came to Jeremiah from the LORD: ²This is what the LORD said to me: Make a yoke of straps and bars and wear it on your neck. ³Then send wordˣ to the kings of Edom, Moab, Ammon, Tyre, and Sidon through

---

ʷHeb manuscripts, Syr; MT *Jehoiakim* ˣOr *them* (the yokes) their representatives who have come to Jerusalem to Judah's King Zedekiah. ⁴Tell them to say to their masters: The Lord of heavenly forces, the God of Israel, proclaims: Say this to your masters:

⁵By my great power and outstretched arm, I have made the earth and the people and animals that are on it. I can give it to anyone I please. ⁶Now I hand over all these countries to my servant King Nebuchadnezzar of Babylon. I even give him the wild animals as subjects. ⁷All nations will serve him, his son and grandson, until the time for his land arrives; then many nations and great kings will conquer him.

⁸As for the nation or country that won't serve Babylon's King Nebuchadnezzar and won't put its neck under his yoke, I will punish it with sword, famine, and disease until I have destroyed it by his hand, declares the Lord. ⁹As for you, don't listen to your prophets, diviners, dreamers,ʸ mediums, or your sorcerers who say to you, "Don't serve the king of Babylon." ¹⁰They are lying to you, and their lies will lead to banishment from your land. I will drive you out, and you will perish. ¹¹But any nation that puts its neck under the yoke of the king of Babylon and serves him, I will let stay in its land to till it and live on it, declares the Lord.

¹²I delivered the same message to Judah's King Zedekiah: If you want to live, put your necks under the yoke of the king of Babylon and serve him and his people. ¹³Why should you and your people die by sword, famine, and disease, as the Lord pronounced against any nation that won't serve the king of Babylon? ¹⁴Pay no attention to the words of the prophets who encourage you not to serve the king of Babylon, for they are lying to you. ¹⁵I haven't sent these prophets, declares the Lord; they are prophesying falsely in my name. If you listen to them, I will drive you out, and you will perish, both you and your prophets!

¹⁶Then I spoke to the priests and all this people: This is what the Lord says: Don't listen to the words of the prophets who are prophesying to you, "In a short while,

the temple equipment will be brought back from Babylon." They are prophesying a lie to you. ¹⁷Don't listen to them; serve the king of Babylon and live. Otherwise, this city will be reduced to ruin. ¹⁸If they are really prophets and have the Lord's word, let them intercede with the Lord of heavenly forces not to let the equipment left in the Lord's temple and in the royal palace of Judah and Jerusalem be carted off to Babylon.

¹⁹This is what the Lord of heavenly forces proclaims about the pillars, the Sea, the stands, and the rest of the equipment left in this city, ²⁰which Babylon's King Nebuchadnezzar didn't plunder when he deported Jeconiah the son of Judah's King Jehoiakim from Jerusalem to Babylon, along with all the officials of Judah and Jerusalem. ²¹Yes, this is what the Lord of heavenly forces, the God of Israel, proclaims about the equipment that is left in the Lord's temple and in the royal palace in Judah, and in Jerusalem: ²²They will be carted off to Babylon where they will remain until the day I come looking for them, declares the Lord; then I will bring them back and restore them to this place.

Prophet against prophet

28 That same year, early in the rule of Judah's King Zedekiah, in the fifth month of his fourth year, the prophet Hananiah, Azzur's son from Gibeon, spoke to me in the Lord's temple before the priests and all the people. ²He said: "The Lord of heavenly forces, the God of Israel, proclaims: I have broken the yoke of the king of Babylon. ³In two years I will restore to this place all of the temple equipment that Babylon's King Nebuchadnezzar carted off to Babylon. ⁴I will also restore to this place Judah's King Jeconiah, Jehoiakim's son, along with all the exiles from Judah who were deported to Babylon, for I will break the yoke of the king of Babylon, declares the Lord."

⁵Then the prophet Jeremiah responded to Hananiah in the presence of the priests and all the people who were standing in the Lord's temple. ⁶The prophet Jeremiah

ʸOr dreams

said: "Indeed. May the LORD do just as you have said! May the LORD fulfill the words that you have prophesied and bring back from Babylon the equipment of the LORD's temple and all the exiles to this place. [7]However, listen closely to what I have to say to you and all the people: [8]The prophets who came before you and me long ago prophesied war, disaster, and disease against many lands and great kingdoms. [9]So the prophet who prophesies peace is recognized as one who is actually sent by the LORD only when that prophet's message is fulfilled."

[10]Then the prophet Hananiah took hold of the yoke that was on the prophet Jeremiah's neck and broke it. [11]He said before all the people, "This is what the LORD says: Just as this yoke has been broken, I will break the yoke of Babylon's King Nebuchadnezzar from the neck of all the nations within two years." Then the prophet Jeremiah walked away.

[12]Sometime after Hananiah had broken the yoke that was on Jeremiah's neck, the LORD told him: [13]Go, say to Hananiah, The LORD proclaims: You have broken a wooden yoke,[z] but I[a] will replace it with an iron one. [14]The LORD of heavenly forces, the God of Israel, proclaims: I will put iron yokes on the necks of all these nations, and they will serve Babylon's King Nebuchadnezzar; even the wild animals will be subject to him! [15]Then the prophet Jeremiah said to the prophet Hananiah: "Listen, Hananiah! The LORD hasn't sent you. All you are doing is persuading these people to believe a lie.

[16]Therefore, the LORD proclaims: I'm going to send you somewhere—right off the face of the earth! Before the year ends, you will die since you have incited rebellion against the LORD." [17]The prophet Hananiah died in the seventh month[b] of that year.

Disturbing hope: Settle down in Babylon

29 The prophet Jeremiah sent a letter from Jerusalem to the few surviving elders among the exiles, to the priests and the prophets, and to all the people Nebuchadnezzar had taken to Babylon from Jerusalem. [2]The letter was sent after King Jeconiah, the queen mother, the court officials, the government leaders of Judah and Jerusalem, and the craftsmen and smiths had left Jerusalem. [3]It was delivered to Babylon by Elasah, Shaphan's son, and Gemariah, Hilkiah's son—two men dispatched to Babylon's King Nebuchadnezzar by King Zedekiah.

[4]The LORD of heavenly forces, the God of Israel, proclaims to all the exiles I have carried off from Jerusalem to Babylon: [5]Build houses and settle down; cultivate gardens and eat what they produce. [6]Get married and have children; then help your sons find wives and your daughters find husbands in order that they too may have children. Increase in number there so that you don't dwindle away. [7]Promote the welfare of the city where I have sent you into exile. Pray to the LORD for it, because your future depends on its welfare.

[z]Or yokes [a]Heb uncertain [b]September–October, Tishrei

HANANIAH

Means "Yahweh has been gracious."

1. A false prophet from Gibeon who predicted Nebuchadnezzar's defeat, which he symbolized through breaking the yoke that Jeremiah wore (Jer 28).

2. Father of Zedekiah, an official in Jerusalem (Jer 36:12).

3. Grandfather of Irijah, who arrested and charged Jeremiah for desertion (Jer 37:13).

⁸The LORD of heavenly forces, the God of Israel, proclaims: Don't let the prophets and diviners in your midst mislead you. Don't pay attention to your dreams. ⁹They are prophesying lies to you in my name. I didn't send them, declares the LORD.

¹⁰The LORD proclaims: When Babylon's seventy years are up, I will come and fulfill my gracious promise to bring you back to this place. ¹¹I know the plans I have in mind for you, declares the LORD; they are plans for peace, not disaster, to give you a future filled with hope. ¹²When you call me and come and pray to me, I will listen to you. ¹³When you search for me, yes, search for me with all your heart, you will find me. ¹⁴I will be present for you, declares the LORD, and I will end your captivity. I will gather you from all the nations and places where I have scattered you, and I will bring you home after your long exile,ᶜ declares the LORD.

¹⁵Yet you say, The LORD has raised up prophets for us in Babylon:

¹⁶This is what the LORD proclaims concerning the king sitting on David's throne and all the people who live in this city, that is, those among you who didn't go into exile: ¹⁷The LORD of heavenly forces proclaims: I'm going to send the sword, famine, and disease against them. I will make them like rotten figs that are too spoiled to eat. ¹⁸I will pursue them with the sword, famine, and disease; and I will make them an object of horror to all nations on earth and an object of cursing, scorn, shock, and disgrace among all the countries where I have scattered them, ¹⁹because they wouldn't listen to my words, declares the LORD, which I sent them time and again through my servants the prophets. Theyᵈ wouldn't listen, declares the LORD.

²⁰But now, all you exiles I deported from Jerusalem to Babylon, listen to the LORD's word. ²¹This is what the LORD of heavenly forces, the God of Israel, proclaims concerning Ahab, Kolaiah's son, and Zedekiah, Maaseiah's son, who are prophesying lies in your name: I will hand them over to Babylon's King Nebuchadnezzar, and he will slay them before your very eyes. ²²Because of them, all the Judean exiles in Babylon will use this curse: "The LORD make you like Zedekiah and Ahab, who were burned alive by the king of Babylon." ²³They committed a horrible scandal in Israel—adultery with their neighbors' wives and deceit spoken in my name, with which I had nothing to do. Yet I'm still aware of it and am witness to it, declares the LORD.

²⁴Tell Shemaiah the Nehelamite, ²⁵This is what the LORD of heavenly forces, the God of Israel, proclaims: ᵉYou sent letters on your own accord to all the people in Jerusalem, to the priest Zephaniah, Maaseiah's son, and to the rest of the priests. ²⁶You said to Zephaniah:ᶠ The LORD has appointed you priest in charge of the LORD's temple instead of Jehoiada. You are responsible for putting every madman who prophesies into stocks and neck irons. ²⁷So why haven't you threatened Jeremiah of Anathoth, who pretends to be a prophet among you? ²⁸He has sent a letter telling those of us in Babylon: "You are going to be there a long time, so build houses and settle down, plant gardens and eat what they produce."

²⁹The priest Zephaniah read this letter to the prophet Jeremiah. ³⁰Then the LORD's word came to Jeremiah: ³¹Send word to all the exiles: The LORD proclaims concerning Shemaiah the Nehelamite: Because Shemaiah prophesied to you when I didn't send him, and because he convinced you to believe a lie, ³²I will punish Shemaiah the Nehelamite and his descendants, declares the LORD. Not one member of this people will be around to see the good that I have in store for my people, declares the LORD, for he incited rebellion against me.

THE SCROLL OF COMFORT

Healing and restoration for my people

30 Jeremiah received the LORD's word: ²The LORD, the God of Israel, pro-

---

ᶜOr *I will restore you to the place from which I exiled you.* ᵈSyr; MT *you* ᵉOr *because you sent* ᶠHeb lacks *You said to Zephaniah.*

claims: Write down in a scroll all the words I have spoken to you. ³ The time is coming, declares the LORD, when I will bring back my people Israel and Judah from captivity,ᵍ says the LORD. I will bring them home to the land that I gave to their ancestors, and they will possess it. ⁴ Here are the words that the LORD spoke concerning Israel and Judah:

⁵ The LORD proclaims:
Iʰ hear screams of panic and terror;
  no one is safe.
⁶ Ask and see:
  Can men bear children?
  Then why do I see every man
    bent over in pain,ⁱ as if he's in labor?
  Why have all turned pale?
⁷ That day is awful, beyond words.
  A time of unspeakable pain
    for my people Jacob.
  But they will be delivered from it.

⁸ At that time, I will break the yoke off theirʲ necks and remove theirᵏ shackles. Foreigners will no longer enslave them, declares the LORD of heavenly forces. ⁹ They will serve the LORD their God and the king whom I will raise up for them from David's family.

¹⁰ So don't be afraid, my servant Jacob,
  declares the LORD,
    Don't lose hope, Israel.
  I will deliver you from faraway places
  and your children
    from the land of their exile.
    My people Jacob
      will again be safe and sound,
      with no one harassing them.
¹¹ I am with you and will rescue you,
  declares the LORD.
  I will put an end to all the nations
  where I have scattered you.
  But I won't put an end to you.
  I won't let you remain unpunished:
    I will discipline you as you deserve.

¹² This is what the LORD says:
  Your injury is incurable;
  your illness is grave.
¹³ No one comes to your aid;

no one attends to your wound;
  your disease is incurable.
¹⁴ All your lovers disregard you;
  they write you off as a lost cause,
  because I have dealt harshly with you
    as an enemy would,
  because your guilt is great
    and your sins are many.
¹⁵ Why cry out for relief from your pain?
  Your wound is incurable.
  I have done these things to you,
  because your guilt is great
    and your sins are many.

¹⁶ Yet all who ravage you will be ravaged;
  all who oppress you will go into exile.
  Those who rob you will be robbed,
  and all who plunder you
    will be plundered.
¹⁷ I will restore your health,
  and I will heal your wounds,
    declares the LORD,
  because you were labeled an outcast,
    "Zion, the lost cause."

¹⁸ The LORD proclaims:
  I will restore Jacob's tents
  and have pity on their birthplace.
  Their city will be rebuilt on its ruins
  and the palace in its rightful place.
¹⁹ There will be laughter
  and songs of thanks.
  I will add to their numbers
  so they don't dwindle away.
  I will honor them
  so they aren't humiliated.
²⁰ Their children will thrive
  as they did long ago,
  and their community will be
  established before me.
  I will punish their oppressors.
²¹ They will have their own leader;
  their ruler will come from among them.
  I will let him approach me,
  and he will draw near.
  Who would dare approach me
  unless I let them come?
    declares the LORD.
²² You will be my people,
  and I will be your God.

ᵍOr restore the fortunes   ʰOr We   ⁱOr with his hands on his groin   ʲOr your   ᵏOr your

²³ Look! The LORD's anger breaks out
  like a violent storm,
  a fierce wind that strikes
  the heads of the wicked.
²⁴ The LORD's fierce anger won't turn back
  until God's^l purposes
  are entirely accomplished.
In the days to come,
  you will understand what this means.

31 At that time, declares the LORD,
  I will be the God of all the families
  of Israel,
  and they will be my people.

² The LORD proclaims:
The people who survived the sword
  found grace in the wilderness.
As Israel searched for a place of rest,
³ the LORD appeared to them^m
  from a distance:^{n}
I have loved you with a love
  that lasts forever.
  And so with unfailing love,
  I have drawn you to myself.^{o}
⁴ Again, I will build you up,
  and you will be rebuilt, virgin Israel.
  Again, you will play your tambourines
  and dance with joy.
⁵ Again, you will plant vineyards
  on the hills of Samaria;
  farmers will plant
  and then enjoy the harvests.
⁶ The time will come when
  the watchmen shout from
  the highlands of Ephraim:
"Get ready! We're going up to Zion
  to the LORD our God!"
⁷ The LORD proclaims:
Sing joyfully for the people of Jacob;
  shout for the leading nation.
Raise your voices with praise
  and call out:
  "The LORD has saved his people,^{p}
  the remaining few in Israel!"

⁸ I'm going to bring them back
  from the north;
  I will gather them
  from the ends of the earth.

Among them will be
  the blind and the disabled,
  expectant mothers and those in labor;
  a great throng will return here.
⁹ With tears of joy they will come;
  while they pray, I will bring them back.
I will lead them by quiet streams
  and on smooth paths
  so they don't stumble.
I will be Israel's father,
  Ephraim will be my oldest child.

¹⁰ Listen to the LORD's word, you nations,
  and announce it to the distant islands:
The one who scattered Israel
  will gather them
  and keep them safe,
  as a shepherd his flock.
¹¹ The LORD will rescue the people of Jacob
  and deliver them from the power
  of those stronger than they are.
¹² They will come shouting for joy
  on the hills of Zion,
  jubilant over the LORD's gifts:
  grain, wine, oil, flocks, and herds.
Their lives will be like a lush garden;
  they will grieve no more.
¹³ Then the young women will dance for joy;
  the young and old men will join in.
I will turn their mourning into laughter
  and their sadness into joy;
  I will comfort them.
¹⁴ I will lavish the priests with abundance
  and shower my people with my gifts,
  declares the LORD.

¹⁵ The LORD proclaims:
A voice is heard in Ramah,
  weeping and wailing.
It's Rachel crying for her children;
  she refuses to be consoled,
  because her children are no more.
¹⁶ The LORD proclaims:
Keep your voice from crying
  and your eyes from weeping,
  because your endurance will be rewarded,
  declares the LORD.
They will return
  from the land of their enemy!

¹Or *his* or *its*   ᵐOr *to me*   ⁿOr *a long time ago*   ᵒHeb lacks *myself.*   ᵖLXX; MT *Save your people, LORD*

¹⁷ There's hope for your future,
    declares the LORD.
      Your children will return home!

¹⁸ I hear, yes, I hear Ephraim lamenting:
    "You disciplined me,
      and I learned my lesson,
    even though I was as stubborn as a mule.
    Bring me back, let me return,
      because you are the LORD my God.

¹⁹ After I turned away from you,
    I regretted it;
    I realized what I had done,
      and I have hit myself^q—
    I was humiliated and disgraced,
      and I have carried this disgrace
    since I was young."

²⁰ Isn't Ephraim my much-loved child?
    Don't I utterly adore him?
    Even when I scold him,
    I still hold him dear.
    I yearn for him and love him deeply,
      declares the LORD.

²¹ Set up markers,
    put up signs;
    think about the road you have traveled,
      the path you have taken.
    Return, virgin Israel;
      return to these towns of yours.

²² How long will you hem and haw,
    my rebellious daughter?
    The LORD has created
      something new on earth:
    Virgin Israel will once again
      embrace her God!^r

²³ The LORD of heavenly forces, the
God of Israel, proclaims: When I bring my
people^s back from captivity, they will once
again utter these words in the land and
towns of Judah:
    The LORD bless you,
      righteous dwelling place,
      holy mountain.

²⁴ Those who live in Judah and its towns
will dwell together with farmers and shepherds. ²⁵ I will strengthen the weary and
renew those who are weak.

²⁶ Then I woke up and looked around.
What a pleasant sleep I had!

²⁷ The time is coming, declares the LORD,
when I will plant seeds in Israel and Judah,
and both people and animals will spring up.
²⁸ Just as I watched over them to dig up and
pull down, to overthrow, destroy, and bring
harm, so I will watch over them to build and
plant, declares the LORD. ²⁹ In those days,
people will no longer say:
    Sour grapes eaten by parents
      leave a bitter taste
      in the mouths of their children.

³⁰ Because everyone will die
      for their own sins:
    whoever eats sour grapes
    will have a bitter taste
      in their own mouths.

³¹ The time is coming, declares the LORD,
when I will make a new covenant with the
people of Israel and Judah. ³² It won't be
like the covenant I made with their ancestors when I took them by the hand to
lead them out of the land of Egypt. They
broke that covenant with me even though I
was their husband, declares the LORD.
³³ No, this is the covenant that I will make
with the people of Israel after that time, declares the LORD. I will put my Instructions
within them and engrave them on their
hearts. I will be their God, and they will be
my people. ³⁴ They will no longer need to
teach each other to say, "Know the LORD!"
because they will all know me, from the
least of them to the greatest, declares the
LORD; for I will forgive their wrongdoing
and never again remember their sins.

³⁵ The LORD proclaims:
    The one who established the sun
      to light up the day
      and ordered^t the moon and stars
        to light up the night,
    who stirs up the sea
      into crashing waves,
    whose name is
      the LORD of heavenly forces:
³⁶ If the created order should vanish
    from my sight,
    declares the LORD,

---

^q Or struck my thigh   ^r Or a woman surrounds a man   ^s Or them   ^t Or orders of

only then would Israel's descendants
ever stop being a nation
before me.
[37] The LORD proclaims:
If the heavens above could be measured
and the foundation of the earth below
could be fathomed,
only then would I reject
Israel's descendants
for what they have done,
declares the LORD.
[38] The time is coming, declares the LORD,
when the city will be rebuilt for the LORD
from the Tower of Hananel to the Corner
Gate. [39] Its boundaries will extend to the
Gareb Hill and around to Goah. [40] The entire
valley defiled by corpses and ashes, and all
the fields as far as the Kidron Valley and the
Horse Gate on the east, all this will be set
apart for the LORD. And the city will never
again be dug up or overthrown.

Nothing is too hard for the LORD

32 Jeremiah received the LORD's word
in the tenth year of Judah's King
Zedekiah, which was the eighteenth year
of Nebuchadnezzar's rule. [2] At that time,
the army of the Babylonian king had surrounded Jerusalem, and the prophet Jeremiah was confined to the prison quarters
in the palace of Judah's king. [3] Judah's King
Zedekiah had Jeremiah sent there after
questioning him: "Why do you prophesy,
'This is what the LORD says: I'm handing
this city over to the king of Babylon, and he
will occupy it; [4] and Judah's King Zedekiah
will be captured and handed over to the
king of Babylon; he will speak to the king
of Babylon personally and see him with
his very own eyes. [5] And Zedekiah will be
carried off to Babylon to live out his days
until I punish him, declares the LORD. If
you make war against the Babylonians, you
will fail.'"

[6] Jeremiah said, The LORD's word came
to me: [7] Your cousin Hanamel, Shallum's
son, is on his way to see you; and when he
arrives, he will tell you: "Buy my field in
Anathoth, for by law you are next in line
to purchase it." [8] And just as the LORD had
said, my cousin Hanamel showed up at the
prison quarters and told me, "Buy my field
in Anathoth in the land of Benjamin, for
you are next in line and have a family obligation to purchase it." Then I was sure this
was the LORD's doing.

[9] So I bought the field in Anathoth from
my cousin Hanamel, and weighed out for
him seventeen shekels of silver. [10] I signed
the deed, sealed it, had it witnessed, and
weighed out the silver on the scales. [11] Then
I took the deed of purchase—the sealed
copy, with its terms and conditions, and
the unsealed copy—[12] and gave it to Baruch,
Neriah's son and Mahseiah's grandson, before my cousin Hanamel and the witnesses
named in the deed, as well as before all the
Judeans who were present in the prison
quarters. [13] I charged Baruch before all of
them: [14] "The LORD of heavenly forces, the
God of Israel, proclaims: Take these documents—this sealed deed of purchase along
with the unsealed one—and put them into
a clay container so they will last a long time.
[15] The LORD of heavenly forces, the God of
Israel, proclaims: Houses, fields, and vineyards will again be bought in this land."

[16] After I had given the documents to Baruch, Neriah's son, I prayed to the LORD:
[17] LORD God, you created heaven and earth
by your great power and outstretched arm;
nothing is too hard for you! [18] You act with
mercy toward thousands upon thousands,
but you also bring the consequences of the
fathers' sins on their children after them.
Great and mighty God, whose name is the
LORD of heavenly forces, [19] marvelous are
your purposes, and mighty are your deeds.
You are aware of all the ways of humanity,
and you reward us for how we live and what
we do even now. [20] You have performed
signs and wonders in the land of Egypt as
you do to this very day in Israel and everywhere else. That's why you are so renowned.
[21] With a strong hand, an outstretched arm,
and with awesome power, yes, with signs
and wonders, you brought your people Israel out of the land of Egypt. [22] You gave
them this land that you promised to their
ancestors, a land full of milk and honey.
[23] They entered and took possession of it,
but they didn't obey you or follow your In-

struction. In fact, they didn't do anything you commanded them. So you brought upon them this disaster. ²⁴Now the siege ramps are in place to take the city. And the Babylonians are about to capture it by war, famine, and disease. What you have pronounced is now happening, as you can see. ²⁵So why tell me, LORD God, Buy the field for money and make sure there are witnesses, when the city is under Babylonian control?

²⁶Then the LORD's word came to Jeremiah: ²⁷I am the LORD, the God of all living things! Is anything too hard for me? ²⁸Therefore, the LORD proclaims: I'm handing this city over to the Babylonians and King Nebuchadnezzar, who will capture it. ²⁹They will enter the city, set it on fire, and burn it down—including the houses on whose roofs offerings have been made to Baal and drink offerings to other gods, which made me especially angry. ³⁰The people of Israel and Judah have done nothing but evil in my eyes since their youth; the people of Israel and Judah have done nothing but anger me by the work of their hands, declares the LORD. ³¹This city has enraged me from the day it was built to this very day, and so it must be removed from my sight—³²because of all the evil done by the people of Israel and Judah to make me angry—they, their kings and officials, their priests and prophets, the men of Judah, and those who live in Jerusalem. ³³They turned their backs to me and not their faces; and though I taught them over and over, they wouldn't accept my correction. ³⁴They set up their disgusting idols in the temple that bears my name and violated it; ³⁵and they built shrines to Baal in the Ben-hinnon Valley, where they sacrifice their sons and daughters to Molech, though I never commanded them—nor did it even cross my mind—that they should do such detestable things, leading Judah to sin. ³⁶You have been saying, "This city will be handed over to the king of Babylon through sword, famine, and disease." But this is what the LORD, the God of Israel, says: ³⁷I will gather them from all the countries where I have scattered them in my fierce anger and rage. I will bring them back to this place to live securely. ³⁸They will be my people, and I will be their God. ³⁹I will give them one heart and one mind so that they may worship me all the days of their lives, for their own good and for the good of their children after them. ⁴⁰I will make an everlasting covenant with them, never to stop treating them graciously. I will put into their hearts a sense of awe for me so that they won't turn away from me. ⁴¹I will rejoice in treating them graciously, and I will plant them in this land faithfully and with all my heart and being.

⁴²The LORD proclaims: Just as I brought this great disaster on this people, so I will bring on them all the good I promised them. ⁴³Fields will be bought in this land, a land you have said is bleak and uninhabited and in the possession of the Babylonians. ⁴⁴Fields will be bought, and deeds will be signed, sealed, and witnessed in the land of Benjamin and in the outlying areas of Jerusalem, in the towns of Judah and in the highlands, in the towns of the western foothills and the arid southern plain; for I will bring them back from their captivity, declares the LORD.

Restoration of Judah and Israel

33 While he was still confined to the prison quarters, the LORD's word came to Jeremiah a second time: ²The LORD proclaims, the LORD who made the earth,ᵘ who formed and established it, whose name is the LORD: ³Call to me and I will answer and reveal to you wondrous secrets that you haven't known.

⁴This is what the LORD, the God of Israel, proclaims about the houses of this city and the palaces of the kings of Judah that were torn down to defend against the siege ramps and weapons ⁵of the invading Babylonians.ᵛ They will be filled with the corpses of those slain in my fierce anger. I hid my face from the people of this city because of all their evil deeds, ⁶but now I

ᵘLXX *the earth*; MT *it* ᵛHeb uncertain

will heal and mend them. I will make them whole and bless them[w] with an abundance of peace and security. [7]I will bring back the captives of Judah and Israel, and I will rebuild them as they were at first. [8]I will cleanse them of all the wrongdoing they committed against me, and I will forgive them for all of their guilt and rebellion. [9]Then this city[x] will bring me great joy, praise, and renown before all nations on earth, when they hear of all the good I provide for them. They will be in total awe at all the good and prosperity I provide for them.

[10]The LORD proclaims: You have said about this place, "It is a wasteland, without humans or animals." Yet in the ravaged and uninhabited towns of Judah and the streets of Jerusalem, [11]the sounds of joy and laughter and the voices of the bride and the bridegroom will again be heard. So will the voices of those who say, as thank offerings are brought to the LORD's temple, "Give thanks to the LORD of heavenly forces, for the LORD is good and his kindness lasts forever." I will bring back the captives of this land as they were before, says the LORD.

[12]The LORD of heavenly forces proclaims: This wasteland, without humans or animals—and all its towns—will again become pastures for shepherds to care for their flocks. [13]Shepherds will again count their flocks in the towns of the highlands, the western foothills and the arid southern plain, in the land of Benjamin, as well as in the outlying areas of Jerusalem and the towns of Judah, says the LORD.

[14]The time is coming, declares the LORD, when I will fulfill my gracious promise with the people of Israel and Judah. [15]In those days and at that time, I will raise up a righteous branch from David's line, who will do what is just and right in the land. [16]In those days, Judah will be saved and Jerusalem will live in safety. And this is what he will be called: The LORD Is Our Righteousness. [17]The LORD proclaims: David will always have one of his descendants sit on the throne of the house of Israel. [18]And the levitical priests will always have someone in my presence to make entirely burned offerings and grain offerings, and to present sacrifices.

[19]Then the LORD's word came to Jeremiah: [20]This is what the LORD says: If one could break my covenant with the day and my covenant with the night so that they wouldn't come at their proper time, [21]only then could my covenant with my servant David and my covenant with the levitical priests who minister before me be broken; only then would David no longer have a descendant to rule on his throne. [22]And just as the stars in the sky can't be numbered and the sand on the shore can't be counted, so I will increase the descendants of my servant David and the Levites who minister before me.

[23]Then the LORD's word came to Jeremiah: [24]Aren't you aware of what people are saying: "The LORD has rejected the two families that he had chosen"? They are insulting my people as if they no longer belong to me.[y] [25]The LORD proclaims: I would no sooner break my covenant with day and night or the laws of heaven and earth [26]than I would reject the descendants of Jacob and my servant David and his descendants as rulers for the children of Abraham, Isaac, and Jacob. I will restore the captives and have compassion on them.

Lessons on obedience and disobedience

34 Jeremiah received the LORD's word when Babylon's King Nebuchadnezzar and his army, and all the countries and people he ruled, were attacking Jerusalem and all its towns. [2]The LORD, the God of Israel, proclaims, Go and speak to Judah's King Zedekiah and say to him: The LORD proclaims, I'm handing this city over to the king of Babylon, and he will burn it down. [3]You won't escape but will be captured and handed over to him. You will see the king of Babylon with your very own eyes and speak to him personally, and you will be taken to Babylon. [4]Even so, hear the LORD's word,

---

[w]Heb uncertain [x]Or it [y]Heb uncertain

King Zedekiah of Judah: This is what the LORD proclaims about you: You won't die in battle; [5]you will die a peaceful death. As burial incense was burned to honor your ancestors, the kings who came before you, so it will be burned to honor you as people mourn, "Oh, master!" I myself promise this, declares the LORD.

[6]The prophet Jeremiah delivered this message to Judah's King Zedekiah in Jerusalem [7]when the army of the king of Babylon was attacking Jerusalem and all the remaining Judean towns, Lachish and Azekah—the only fortified towns still standing in Judah.

[8]Jeremiah received the LORD's word after King Zedekiah had made a covenant with all the people in Jerusalem to proclaim liberty for their slaves: [9]everyone was to free their male and female Hebrew slaves and no longer hold a Judean brother or sister in bondage. [10]So all the officials and people who entered into this covenant agreed to free their male and female slaves and no longer hold them in bondage; they obeyed the king's command[z] and let them

[z]Heb lacks the king's command.

go. [11]But afterward they broke their promise, took back the men and women they had freed, and enslaved them again.

[12]Then the LORD's word came to Jeremiah: [13]The LORD, the God of Israel, proclaims: I made a covenant with your ancestors when I brought them out of the land of Egypt, out of the house of slavery. [14]I said that every seventh year each of you must free any Hebrews who have been sold to you. After they have served you for six years, you must set them free. But your ancestors didn't obey or pay any attention to me. [15]Recently you turned about and did what was right in my sight; each of you proclaimed liberty for the other and made a covenant before me in the temple that bears my name. [16]But then you went back on your word and made my name impure; each of you reclaimed the men and women you had set free and forced them to be your slaves again.

[17]Therefore, the LORD proclaims: Since you have defied me by not setting your fellow citizens free, I'm setting you free,

JUDEA

The Greek form of the term *Judah* (Lat. *Iudaea*), the Jewish territory in the southern land of Israel, in the area surrounding Jerusalem. Following the conquest and destruction of the kingdom of Judah (named after the southern core tribe that derived its name from Judah, Jacob's son) in 587 BCE, the Babylonians established an administrative entity, which was much smaller than the occupied kingdom, called the "land of Judah" (Jer 39:10; 40:11-12; 43:4), under Gedaliah, who governed for a short time from Mizpah.

The territorial extension of Judea was, generally, from Beth-horon and Bethel in the north to Beth-zur and En-gedi in the south, and from Emmaus and Modein in the west to the Jordan River and Dead Sea in the east. The mostly mountainous region was approximately 1,080 sq. mi. and included part of the Jordan Valley and Judean desert in the east. The population of the province included those from a low social stratum left behind by Nebuchadnezzar II after the fall of the Southern Kingdom (2 Kgs 25:22; Jer 40:7-12; Ezek 33:23-24) and the returnees from the Babylonian exile, especially in the times of Zerubbabel, Ezra, and Nehemiah (Ezra 2; 7-8; Neh 7).

declares the LORD, free to die by the sword, disease, and famine! And I will make you an object of horror for all nations on earth. [18]I will make those who disregarded my covenant, violating its terms that they agreed to in my presence, like the calf they cut in two and then walked between the halves of its carcass. [19]The officials of Judah and Jerusalem, the eunuchs and priests, and all the people who passed through the pieces of the calf [20]I will hand over to their enemies who seek to kill them. And their corpses will become food for birds and wild animals. [21]I will hand over Judah's King Zedekiah and his officials to their enemies who seek to kill them: namely, the army of Babylon's king, which has just withdrawn from you. [22]I'm about to issue orders, declares the LORD, that the army of Babylon return to this city. They will wage war against it, capture it, and burn it down along with other Judean cities. I will make Judah a wasteland, without inhabitants.

35 Jeremiah received the LORD's word during the rule of Judah's King Jehoiakim, Josiah's son: [2]Go to the Rechabite family and invite them to come to one of the rooms of the LORD's temple. When they arrive, offer them some wine to drink. [3]So I took Jaazaniah, Jeremiah's son and Habazziniah's grandson, and his brothers and all his sons, and the whole Rechabite family. [4]I brought them to the room in the LORD's temple assigned to the sons of Hanan, Igdaliah's son, the man of God. The room was next to the one used by the chief officers and right above the room of Maaseiah, Shallum's son, the temple doorkeeper.[a] [5]Then I set bowls full of wine before the Rechabites, along with several cups, and I said to them, "Have some."

[6]But they refused: "We don't drink wine because our ancestor Jonadab, Rechab's son, commanded us, 'You and your children are never to drink wine; [7]nor are you to build or own houses or plant gardens and vineyards; rather, you are always to dwell in tents so you may live a long time in the fertile land you pass through.' [8]We have obeyed everything our ancestor Jonadab, Rechab's son, commanded us. No one in our household, including our wives and children, has ever had wine. [9]And we haven't built houses to live in or had vineyards, fields, or crops. [10]We have lived in tents and done everything our ancestor Jonadab commanded us. [11]But when Babylon's King Nebuchadnezzar invaded the country, we said, 'We better go to Jerusalem to escape the Babylonian and Aramean armies.' That's why we're here in Jerusalem."

[12]Then the LORD's word came to Jeremiah: [13]The LORD of heavenly forces, the God of Israel, proclaims: Go and tell the people of Judah and those who live in Jerusalem: Can't you learn a lesson about what it means to obey me? declares the LORD. [14]Jonadab, Rechab's son, commanded his descendants not to drink wine, and to this very day they have not drunk wine, obeying their ancestor's instruction. But I have spoken to you again and again, and you haven't listened to me. [15]I have sent you all my servants, the prophets, time and again, saying, "Each of you, turn from your evil ways and reform your actions; don't worship or serve other gods. Then you may live in the fertile land I gave to you and your ancestors." But you haven't paid attention or listened to me. [16]The descendants of Jonadab, Rechab's son, have thoroughly obeyed their ancestor, but this people has not listened to me. [17]Therefore, this is what the LORD of heavenly forces, the God of Israel, says: I'm going to bring upon the people of Judah and all those who live in Jerusalem the disaster I pronounced against them, because they wouldn't listen to me or respond when I called.

[18]Then Jeremiah said to the Rechabite family: The LORD of heavenly forces, the God of Israel, proclaims: Because you have obeyed all Jonadab's instructions and you have done everything he commanded you, [19]the LORD of heavenly forces, the God of Israel proclaims: Jonadab, Rechab's son, will always have a descendant that stands before me.

---

[a]Or *keeper of the threshold*

Enduring word of God

36 In the fourth year of Judah's King Jehoiakim, Josiah's son, this word came to Jeremiah from the LORD: ²Take a scroll and write in it all the words I have spoken to you concerning Israel, Judah, and all the nations from the time of Josiah until today. ³Perhaps when the people of Judah hear about every disaster I intend to bring upon them, they will turn from their evil ways, and I will forgive their wrongdoing and sins. ⁴So Jeremiah sent for Baruch, Neriah's son. As Jeremiah dictated all the words that the LORD had spoken to him, Baruch wrote them in the scroll. ⁵Then Jeremiah told Baruch, "I'm confined here and can't go to the LORD's temple. ⁶So you go to the temple on the next day of fasting, and read the LORD's words from the scroll that I have dictated to you. Read them so that all the people in the temple can hear them, as well as all the Judeans who have come from their towns. ⁷If they turn from their evil ways, perhaps the LORD will hear their prayers. The LORD has threatened them with fierce anger." ⁸Baruch, Neriah's son, did everything the prophet Jeremiah instructed him: he read all the LORD's words from the scroll in the temple.

⁹In the ninth month of the fifth year of Judah's King Jehoiakim, Josiah's son, all the people in Jerusalem and all those who had come from Judean towns observed a fast for the LORD in Jerusalem. ¹⁰Then Baruch read Jeremiah's words from the scroll to all the people in the LORD's temple; he read them in the chamber of Gemariah, Shaphan the scribe's son, in the upper courtyard near the entrance of the New Gate of the LORD's temple. ¹¹When Micaiah, Gemariah's son and Shaphan's grandson, heard all the LORD's words from the scroll, ¹²he went down to the scribes' chamber in the royal palace. There he found all the officials meeting together: Elishama the scribe; Delaiah, Shemaiah's son; Elnathan, Achbor's son; Gemariah, Shaphan's son; Zedekiah, Hananiah's son, and all the other officials. ¹³Micaiah told them all the words he heard Baruch read from the scroll before the people.

¹⁴Then all the officials sent Jehudi, Nethaniah's son and Shelemiah's grandson, and Cushi's great-grandson, to Baruch: "Take the scroll you read to the people and come with me."

So Baruch, Neriah's son, took the scroll and went to the officials. ¹⁵They said to him, "Sit down and read it to us." So Baruch read it to them. ¹⁶When they heard all its words, they were alarmed and said to Baruch: "We must at once report all this to the king!" ¹⁷Then they asked Baruch, "Tell us, how did you write all these words? Did they come from Jeremiah?"

¹⁸Baruch replied, "He dictated all the words to me, and I wrote them with ink in the scroll."

¹⁹The officials then said to Baruch, "You and Jeremiah had better go and hide. And don't let anyone know where you are."

²⁰After leaving the scroll in the room of Elishama the scribe, they went to the king's court and told him everything. ²¹The king sent Jehudi to take the scroll, and he retrieved it from the room of Elishama the scribe. Then Jehudi read it to the king and all his royal officials who were standing next to the king. ²²Now it was the ninth month,ᵇ and the king was staying in the winterized part of the palace with the firepot burning near him. ²³And whenever Jehudi read three or four columns of the scroll, the king would cut them off with a scribe's knife and throw them into the firepot until the whole scroll was burned up. ²⁴Neither the king nor any of his attendants who heard all these words were alarmed or tore their clothes. ²⁵Elnathan, Delaiah, and Gemariah begged the king not to burn the scroll, but he wouldn't listen to them.

²⁶The king commanded Jerahmeel, the king's son, along with Seraiah, Azriel's son, and Shelemiah, Abdeel's son, to arrest the scribe Baruch and the prophet Jeremiah. But the LORD hid them.

²⁷The LORD's word came to Jeremiah after the king had burned the scroll

ᵇNovember–December, Kislev

containing the words written by Baruch at Jeremiah's dictation: ²⁸Get another scroll and write in it all the words that were in the first scroll that Judah's King Jehoiakim burned. ²⁹Then say to Judah's King Jehoiakim: The LORD proclaims: You burned that scroll because it declared that the king of Babylon will come and destroy this land and eliminate every sign of life from it. ³⁰Therefore, this is what the LORD proclaims about Judah's King Jehoiakim: He won't have any heirs to occupy the throne of David, and his dead body will be cast out and exposed to the heat of the day and the frost of the night. ³¹I will punish him and his family and his attendants for their wrongdoing. I will bring upon them, as well as the residents of Jerusalem and the people of Judah, every disaster I pronounced against them. But they wouldn't listen.

³²So Jeremiah took another scroll and gave it to the scribe Baruch, Neriah's son, who wrote at Jeremiah's dictation all the words in the scroll burned in the fire by Judah's King Jehoiakim. Many similar words were added to them.

Jeremiah falsely accused and imprisoned

37 Babylon's King Nebuchadnezzar appointed Zedekiah, Josiah's son, to succeed Coniah, Jehoiakim's son, as king of Judah. ²Neither Zedekiah, his attendants, nor the people of the land listened to the LORD's words spoken by the prophet Jeremiah.

³Nevertheless, King Zedekiah sent Jehucal, Shelemiah's son, and the priest Zephaniah, Maaseiah's son, to Jeremiah the prophet with this plea: "Please pray for us to the LORD our God." (⁴Now Jeremiah hadn't been imprisoned yet, so he was free to come and go among the people. ⁵Pharaoh's army had recentlyᶜ set out from Egypt; when the Babylonians who were attacking Jerusalem learned of the Egyptian advance, they withdrew from Jerusalem.)

⁶Then the LORD's word came to Jeremiah the prophet: ⁷The LORD, the God of Israel, proclaims: Tell the king of Judah who sent his emissaries to seek advice from me: "Pharaoh's army that came to assist you is heading back to Egypt. ⁸The Babylonians will return and attack this city. They will capture it and burn it down."

⁹The LORD proclaims: Don't let yourself be deceived into thinking that the Babylonians will withdraw for good.ᵈ They won't! ¹⁰Even if you were to crush the entire Babylonian army that's attacking you and only the wounded in their tents remained, they would rise up and burn this city down.

¹¹Now when the Babylonian army had withdrawn from Jerusalem due to Pharaoh's advance, ¹²Jeremiah set out for the land of Benjamin to secure his share of the family property.ᵉ ¹³He got as far as the Benjamin Gate in Jerusalem when the guard there named Irijah, Shelemiah's son and Hananiah's grandson, arrested the prophet Jeremiah, saying, "You are deserting to the Babylonians."

¹⁴"That's a lie," Jeremiah replied. "I'm not deserting to the Babylonians." But Irijah wouldn't listen to him. He arrested Jeremiah and brought him to the officials, ¹⁵who were furious with him. They beat him and threw him into the house of the scribe Jonathan, which had been turned into a prison. ¹⁶So Jeremiah was put in a cistern, which was like a dungeon, where he remained a long time.

¹⁷Later King Zedekiah sent for him and questioned Jeremiah secretly in the palace: "Is there a word from the LORD?"

"There is," Jeremiah replied. "You are going to be handed over to the king of Babylon." ¹⁸Then Jeremiah asked King Zedekiah, "What have I done wrong to you or your attendants or this people that you should throw me into prison? ¹⁹Where are your prophets now who prophesied that the king of Babylon wouldn't attack you and this land? ²⁰Now, my master and king, I beg you, don't send me back to the house of Jonathan the scribe, or I'll die there." ²¹So King Zedekiah gave orders that Jeremiah be held in the prison quarters

---

ᶜHeb lacks *recently.*   ᵈHeb lacks *for good.*   ᵉHeb uncertain and that he receive a loaf of bread daily from the street vendors[f]—until all the bread in the city was gone. So Jeremiah remained in the prison quarters.

38 Shephatiah, Mattan's son; Gedaliah, Pashhur's son; Jucal, Shelemiah's son; and Pashhur, Malchiah's son heard what Jeremiah had been telling the people: [2]The LORD proclaims: Whoever stays in this city will die by the sword, famine, and disease. But whoever surrenders to the Babylonians will live; yes, their lives will be spared. [3]The LORD proclaims: This city will certainly be handed over to the army of Babylon's king, who will capture it.

[4]Then the officials said to the king: "This man must be put to death! By saying such things, he is discouraging the few remaining troops left in the city, as well as all the people. This man doesn't seek their welfare but their ruin!"

[5]"He's in your hands," King Zedekiah said, "for the king can do nothing to stop you." [6]So they seized Jeremiah, threw him into the cistern of the royal prince Malchiah, within the prison quarters, and lowered him down by ropes. Now there wasn't any water in the cistern, only mud, and Jeremiah began to sink into the mud.

[7]Ebed-melech the Cushite, a court official in the royal palace, got word that they had thrown Jeremiah into the cistern. Since the king was sitting at the Benjamin Gate, [8]Ebed-melech left the palace and said to the king: [9]"My master the king, these men have made a terrible mistake in treating the prophet Jeremiah the way they have; they have thrown him into the cistern where he will die of starvation, for there's no bread left in the city."

[10]Then the king commanded Ebed-melech the Cushite, "Take thirty men from here and take Jeremiah the prophet out of the cistern before he dies." [11]So Ebed-melech took the men and returned to the palace, to an underground supply room, where he found some old rags and scraps of clothing. Ebed-melech lowered them down the cistern by the ropes [12]and called to Jeremiah, "Put these old rags and scraps of clothing under your arms and hold on to the ropes." When Jeremiah did this, [13]they pulled him up by the ropes and got him out of the cistern. After that Jeremiah remained in the prison quarters.

[14]King Zedekiah ordered that the prophet Jeremiah be brought to him at the third entrance of the LORD's temple, where the king said to Jeremiah, "I want to ask you something, and don't hide anything from me."

[15]Jeremiah replied, "If I do, you'll kill me! And if I tell you what to do, you won't listen to me!"

[16]So King Zedekiah swore to Jeremiah behind closed doors, "As the LORD lives, who has given us this life, I won't put you to death and I won't hand you over to those who seek to kill you."

[17]So Jeremiah said to Zedekiah: "The LORD of heavenly forces, the God of Israel, proclaims: If you surrender to the officers of the king of Babylon, you and your family will

[f]Or from the street of the bakers

EBED-MELECH

Ebed-melech ("servant of the king") was an Ethiopian eunuch who served in King Zedekiah's court. Ebed-melech rescued Jeremiah from his cistern prison (Jer 38:7-13), resulting in a promise from God of survival when the kingdom of Judah fell (Jer 39:15-18). With Mesopotamian origins, the title "servant of the king" within the royal court often referred to a paid position of service. The Assyrians developed the title Ebed-melech into a proper name for important members of the court.

live, and this city will not be burned down. ¹⁸ If you don't surrender to the officers of the king of Babylon, the city will be handed over to the Babylonians, who will burn it down, and you won't escape from them."

¹⁹ King Zedekiah said to Jeremiah, "I'm afraid that I will fall into the hands of the Judeans who have defected to the Babylonians, and they will torture me."

²⁰ "That won't happen," Jeremiah replied, "if you obey the LORD, whose message I bring. You will survive, and all will go well for you. ²¹ But if you refuse to surrender, this is what the LORD has shown me: ²² All the women left in the palace of the king of Judah will be led out to the officers of the king of Babylon. And they will say:

'Your trusted friends have betrayed you;
    they have deceived you;
now that your feet are stuck in the mud,
    they are nowhere to be found.'

²³ "All your wives and children will be led out to the Babylonians, and you yourself won't escape from them. The king of Babylon will capture you, and this city will be burned down."

²⁴ Zedekiah said to Jeremiah, "No one is to know about these matters or else you will die. ²⁵ If the officials find out that we met, and they come and say to you, 'Tell us what you said to the king. Don't hide anything from us; otherwise, we'll kill you. So what did the king say to you?' ²⁶ you should say to them, 'I was begging the king not to send me back to the house of Jonathan to die there.'"

²⁷ Then all the officials approached Jeremiah to question him. And he responded exactly as the king had instructed him. So they stopped interrogating him because the conversation between the king and Jeremiah[g] hadn't been overheard. ²⁸ Jeremiah remained in the prison quarters until Jerusalem was captured.

Fall of Jerusalem

39 In the ninth year and the tenth month of Judah's King Zedekiah, Babylon's King Nebuchadnezzar and his entire army came against Jerusalem and surrounded it. ² In the eleventh year of Zedekiah, on the ninth day of the fourth month, they broke through the city walls. ³ Then all the commanding officers of the king of Babylon—Nergal-sharezer, Samgar-nebo,[h] Sarsechim the chief officer, Nergal-sharezer the field commander—entered it and took their places at the middle gate with the rest of the officials of the king of Babylon.

⁴ When Judah's King Zedekiah and his troops saw them, they tried to escape at night through the royal gardens and the gate between the two walls, toward the desert plain. ⁵ But the Babylonian[i] army chased them down and caught Zedekiah in the plains of Jericho. They arrested him and brought him before Babylon's King Nebuchadnezzar at Riblah in the land of Hamath. There the king put him on trial. ⁶ The king of Babylon slaughtered Zedekiah's children at Riblah before his very own eyes, and the king of Babylon slaughtered all the officials of Judah. ⁷ Then he gouged out Zedekiah's eyes, bound him in chains, and dragged him off to Babylon.

⁸ The Babylonians burned down the royal palace and the houses of the people, and they destroyed the Jerusalem walls. ⁹ Nebuzaradan the captain of the special guard rounded up the rest of the people who were left in the city, including those who had defected to the Babylonians, and deported them to Babylon. ¹⁰ But Nebuzaradan the captain of the special guard left some of the poorest people in the land of Judah. He gave them vineyards and fields at that time.

¹¹ Babylon's King Nebuchadnezzar gave orders concerning Jeremiah to Nebuzaradan the captain of the special guard: ¹² "Find Jeremiah and look after him; don't harm him but do whatever he asks from you." ¹³ So Nebuzaradan the captain of the special guard, Nebushazban the chief officer, Nergal-sharezer the field commander, and all the commanders of the king of Bab-

---

^g Heb lacks *between the king and Jeremiah*. ^h Or *Nergal-sharezer the Simmagir* ⁱ Heb *Chaldean* and hereafter through Jeremiah

ylon [14] sent orders[j] to release Jeremiah from the prison quarters. They entrusted him to Gedaliah, Ahikam's son and Shaphan's grandson, so that Jeremiah could move about freely[k] among the people.

[15] The LORD's word came to Jeremiah when he was still confined to the prison quarters: [16] Go and say to Ebed-melech the Cushite that the LORD of heavenly forces, the God of Israel, proclaims: I'm about to fulfill my words concerning this city, for harm and not for good. You will witness it for yourself on that day. [17] But on that day, declares the LORD:

I will rescue you;
　you won't be handed over
　　to those you dread.
[18] I will defend you;
　you won't die in battle.
You will escape with your life,
　because you have trusted in me,
　　declares the LORD.

Jeremiah's release

40 Jeremiah received the LORD's word after Nebuzaradan the captain of the special guard had released him from Ramah. He had been bound in chains there along with all the other detainees from Jerusalem and Judah who were being sent off to Babylon. [2] The captain of the special guard located Jeremiah and said to him, "The LORD your God declared that a great disaster would overtake this place. [3] Now the LORD has made it happen. He has done just as he warned because all of you have sinned against the LORD and haven't obeyed him. That's why this has happened to you. [4] But I'm setting you free from the chains on your hands. If you would like, come with me to Babylon, and I'll take care of you. If you would rather not come with me, that's fine too. Now, the whole land lies before you; go wherever you want. [5] If you decide to remain here,[l] stay with Gedaliah, Ahikam's son and Shaphan's grandson— the Babylonian appointee in charge of the cities of Judah. Stay with him and the people he rules or go wherever you want."

Then the captain of the special guard gave him ample provisions and let him go. [6] Jeremiah went to Gedaliah, Ahikam's son at Mizpah, and he stayed with him and the people who remained in the land.

Gedaliah's provisional government

[7] Some of the army officers and their troops were still hiding out in the countryside when they heard that the king of Babylon had appointed Gedaliah, Ahikam's son, over the region, responsible for the men, women, and children who were the poorest in the land and who hadn't been deported to Babylon. [8] So they went out to meet Gedaliah at Mizpah: Ishmael, Nethaniah's son; Johanan and Jonathan, Kareah's sons; Seraiah son of Tanhumeth; the sons of Ephai the Netophathite; Jezaniah son of the Maacathite; and their troops. [9] Gedaliah, Ahikam's son and Shaphan's grandson, firmly assured them all: "Don't be afraid of serving the Babylonians. Remain in the land, serve the king of Babylon, and all will go well for you. [10] But me? I will stay at Mizpah so I can speak on your behalf when the Babylonians arrive. But you? Settle down in the towns you have taken; harvest the grapes, the summer fruits and figs, and then store them in your containers."

[11] In the same way, all the Judeans living in Moab, Ammon, Edom, and in other countries heard that the king of Babylon had left a few people in the land and that he had put Gedaliah, Ahikam's son and Shaphan's grandson, in charge of them. [12] So they left the places where they had been scattered and returned to the land, to Gedaliah at Mizpah. There they gathered large amounts of grapes and summer fruits.

[13] Johanan, Kareah's son, and all the army officers in the countryside approached Gedaliah at Mizpah [14] and said to him, "Are you aware that King Baalis of Ammon has sent Ishmael, Nethaniah's son, to kill you?" But Gedaliah, Ahikam's son, wouldn't believe them. [15] Still Johanan, Kareah's son, met with Gedaliah secretly at Mizpah and said to him, "Let me go and kill Ishmael,

[j] Heb lacks orders.　[k] Heb uncertain　[l] Heb uncertain

Nethaniah's son; no one needs to knows about this matter. Otherwise, he'll kill you, and all the Judeans who have gathered around you will be scattered, and the few who are left will perish."

[16] But Gedaliah son of Ahikam told Johanan, Kareah's son, "Don't do such a thing, for what you are saying about Ishmael is wrong."

Mutiny and murder

41 In the seventh month,[m] Ishmael, Nethaniah's son and Elishama's grandson, who was from a royal family and who was one of the chief officers of the king, came with ten men to Gedaliah, Ahikam's son, at Mizpah. While they were eating a meal together, [2] Ishmael, Nethaniah's son, and the ten men got up and struck down Gedaliah, Ahikam's son and Shaphan's grandson, with the sword. They murdered him because he had been appointed over the region by the king of Babylon. [3] Ishmael also murdered all the Judeans who had rallied around Gedaliah at Mizpah as well as the Babylonian soldiers who were posted there.

[4] The day after Gedaliah was killed, before anyone knew of it, [5] eighty men with shaved beards, torn clothes, and gashed bodies arrived from Shechem, Shiloh, and Samaria. They were bringing grain offerings and incense to present at the LORD's temple. [6] Ishmael, Nethaniah's son, left Mizpah to meet them, weeping as he went. When he reached them, he said, "Come to Gedaliah, Ahikam's son!" [7] When they arrived in the middle of the town, Ishmael, Nethaniah's son, and the men with him slaughtered them and threw their bodies[n] into a cistern.

[8] But there were ten men among them who begged Ishmael, "Don't kill us; we have wheat, barley, oil, and honey hidden in a field." So he stopped and didn't kill them along with the rest.

([9] Now the cistern that Ishmael used to discard the bodies of the men he had killed because of their association with Gedaliah[o] was the one that King Asa had made to defend against Israel's King Baasha. Ishmael, Nethaniah's son, filled it with the dead.)

[10] Ishmael captured the rest of the people who were at Mizpah, including the daughters of the king and all those assigned to Gedaliah, Ahikam's son, at Mizpah by Nebuzaradan the captain of the special guard. Then Ishmael, Nethaniah's son, set out to cross over to the Ammonites with the hostages.

[11] Johanan, Kareah's son, and all the army officers at his side heard of the terrible acts committed by Ishmael, Nethaniah's son.

[m] September–October, Tishrei   [n] Heb lacks *and threw their bodies; cf* 41:9.   [o] Or *by the hand of Gedaliah*

CISTERN

A pit or well used for water storage, vital for survival in the arid Palestine region. Cisterns were generally bulbous or pear-shaped cavities of varying sizes, normally chiseled (Deut 6:11; Neh 9:25; 2 Chron 26:10) into limestone bedrock for the primary purpose of water storage. Archaeologists have excavated numerous Palestinian cisterns of both plastered and unplastered types. Jeremiah 2:13 uses the metaphor that "they have dug wells [cisterns], broken wells that can't hold water" to describe the emptiness of idolatry. "Cistern" seems to be an erotic metaphor in Proverbs 5:15. The Covenant Code legislated the covering of cisterns to guard against animals falling in (Exod 21:33-34). Cisterns were sometimes equipped with wheels to facilitate water-drawing (Eccl 12:6). Grain storage and refuse pits are among the secondary uses of cisterns that archaeology has validated. They were also occasionally used as prisons (Gen 37:20-29; Jer 37:16; 38:6-13).

¹²So they mustered all their forces and went to fight him. They found Ishmael, Nethaniah's son, at the great pool in Gibeon. ¹³When all those taken by Ishmael at Mizpah saw Johanan, Kareah's son, and all his army officers with him, they were delighted. ¹⁴They rallied around Johanan, Kareah's son, and returned home with him. ¹⁵But Ishmael, Nethaniah's son, and eight of his men eluded Johanan and went to the Ammonites.

¹⁶Then Johanan, Kareah's son, and all the army officers with him took the small group they had rescued in Gibeon, including the soldiers, women, children, and commanding officers that Ishmael, Nethaniah's son, had captured at Mizpah after killing Gedaliah, Ahikam's son. ¹⁷They set out for Egypt, stopping on the way at Geruth Chimham near Bethlehem, ¹⁸because they were afraid of what the Babylonians would do when they found out that Ishmael, Nethaniah's son, had killed Gedaliah, Ahikam's son, whom the king of Babylon had appointed over the region.

Don't go to Egypt!

42 Then all the army officers, including Johanan, Kareah's son, and Jezaniah, Hoshaiah's son, and the rest of the people, from the least to the greatest, approached ²Jeremiah the prophet and said to him, "We have something to ask you: Please pray to the LORD your God for us, this small group, for as you can see we were once many but now are very few. ³May the LORD your God show us where we should go and what we should do."

⁴The prophet Jeremiah replied, "Yes, I'll pray to the LORD your God as you have asked. And I'll tell you whatever the LORD says; I won't hide anything from you."

⁵Then they said to Jeremiah, "May the LORD be a true and faithful witness against us if we fail to do everything that the LORD your God tells us through you. ⁶Whether we like it or not, we will obey all that the LORD our God says. We will obey the LORD our God, to whom we're sending you, so it may go well for us."

⁷Ten days later Jeremiah received the LORD's word. ⁸So he called Johanan, Kareah's son, and all the army officers with him and the rest of the people, from the least to the greatest, ⁹and he said to them: You have sent me to present your plea to the LORD, and this is what the LORD, the God of Israel, says: ¹⁰If you live in this land, I will build you up and not pull you down. I will plant you and not dig you up because I grieve over the disaster I have brought upon you. ¹¹You don't have to be afraid of the king of Babylon, whom you now fear. You don't have to be afraid of him anymore, declares the LORD, for I will be with you to save you and rescue you from his hand. ¹²I will be merciful to you, and he will be merciful and return you to your land.

¹³But if you say, "We won't live in this land," you will disobey the LORD your God. ¹⁴And if you insist, "No, we're going to live in Egypt, where there's no war, battle alarms, or hunger, and there we will stay," ¹⁵then listen to the LORD's word, you remaining Judeans. The LORD of heavenly forces, the God of Israel, proclaims: If you are determined to go to Egypt and you then go and live there, ¹⁶then the war you fear will seize you in the land of Egypt; and the famine you dread will hunt you down in Egypt, and there you will die. ¹⁷Every one of you who is determined to go and live in Egypt will die by the sword, famine, and disease. No one will escape the disaster that I will bring upon them there.

¹⁸The LORD of heavenly forces, the God of Israel, proclaims: Just as my fierce anger was poured out on the people of Jerusalem, so it will be poured out on you if you go to Egypt. You will become an object of cursing, scorn, shock, and disgrace. And you will never see this place again. ¹⁹You who survive from Judah, the LORD has told you: Don't go to Egypt. Know without a doubt that I have warned you this day. ²⁰You are putting your lives at risk[p] by sending me to the LORD your God, saying, "Pray for us to the LORD our God; tell us everything the LORD our God says, and we'll do it." ²¹Today

---

[p]Or to do evil

I have told you, but you still haven't obeyed all that the LORD your God has sent me to tell you. ²²So know without a doubt that you will die by war, famine, and disease in the place you yearn to go and live.

Off to Egypt with Jeremiah and Baruch

43 When Jeremiah finished telling the people all the words of the LORD their God—he didn't omit anything the LORD sent him to convey—²Azariah, Hoshaiah's son, and Johanan, Kareah's son, and all the arrogant men said to Jeremiah, "You're lying to us! The LORD our God didn't send you to tell us not to go to Egypt to live. ³It's Baruch, Neriah's son, who put you up to it so that we end up in the hands of the Babylonians, who will either kill us or deport us to Babylon."

⁴So Johanan, Kareah's son, and all the army officers and the rest of the people disobeyed the LORD's command to stay in the land of Judah. ⁵Johanan, Kareah's son, and all the army officers took the remaining Judeans who had returned to the land of Judah after being scattered among the nations—⁶men, women, children, the king's daughters, everyone Nebuzaradan the captain of the special guard had left with Gedaliah, Ahikam's son and Shaphan's grandson, including Jeremiah the prophet and Baruch, Neriah's son. ⁷They went to the land of Egypt, as far as Tahpanhes, for they wouldn't obey the LORD.

⁸The LORD's word came to Jeremiah in Tahpanhes: ⁹Take some large stones and set them in the clay pavement^q in front of Pharaoh's palace in Tahpanhes while the people of Judah are watching. ¹⁰After that, say to the people: The LORD of heavenly forces, the God of Israel, proclaims: I'm sending for my servant King Nebuchadnezzar of Babylon, who^r will set his throne over these stones and will spread his canopy over them. ¹¹He will come and ravage the land of Egypt:

those marked for disaster, to disaster,
and those marked for exile, to exile.
and those marked for war, to war.

¹²He will set on fire^s the temples of the Egyptian gods. He will burn them down and carry off their gods. He will wrap the land of Egypt around himself, just as a shepherd wraps^t his garment around himself, and he will move on unharmed.^{u} ¹³He will shatter the sacred pillars in the temple of the sun in Egypt and burn down the temples of the Egyptian gods.

Jeremiah's final words to Judeans in Egypt

44 Jeremiah received the LORD's word for the Judeans living in the land of Egypt, those living in Migdol, Tahpanhes, and Memphis and in the land of Pathros. ²The LORD of heavenly forces, the God of Israel, proclaims: You have seen the disaster I brought on Jerusalem and the towns of Judah. They are now a wasteland with no one left ³because of their evil ways. They have angered me by making offerings and worshipping other gods that neither they nor you nor your ancestors knew. ⁴Yet time and again I sent you all my servants the prophets, saying, "Don't do these detestable things that I hate." ⁵But they wouldn't

---

^{q}Heb uncertain ^{r}LXX; MT *I* ^{s}LXX, Syr; MT *I will set on fire* ^{t}Or *picks clean* ^{u}Heb uncertain

BARUCH

The son of Neriah was Jeremiah's scribe and a member of a prominent Judean family. Baruch appears only in the book of Jeremiah (32:12-16; 36; 43:1-7; 45). He served Jeremiah by performing standard scribal duties: certifying land transactions, writing down the prophet's words, and presenting Jeremiah's divine oracles to the people and the royal court.

listen or pay attention or turn from their evil ways. They continued making offerings to other gods. [6]So my fierce anger poured out and blazed against the towns of Judah and the streets of Jerusalem. And they were reduced to an utter wasteland, as they are today.

[7]Now the LORD of heavenly forces, the God of Israel, proclaims: Why are you committing this huge mistake that will cost you your lives? Every man, woman, child, and infant will be eliminated from the midst of Judah, and no one will be left. [8]Why do you anger me by what you do: by burning incense to other gods in the land of Egypt where you have come to live? You will be eliminated and become an object of cursing and disgrace among all the nations of the earth. [9]Have you forgotten the sins of your ancestors and the sins of the kings of Judah and their wives?[v] Have you forgotten the sins that you and your wives committed in the land of Judah and in the streets of Jerusalem? [10]To this day you[w] haven't shown any sorrow for what you have done. And you haven't revered me or followed my Instruction and my laws that I set before you and your ancestors.

[11]Therefore, the LORD of heavenly forces, the God of Israel, proclaims: I'm determined to bring disaster on you, to eliminate all of Judah. [12]I will take the few remaining Judeans who were determined to go to the land of Egypt to live. They will all perish there. They will fall by the sword and perish due to famine. The least to the greatest will die by the sword and by famine. They will become an object of cursing, scorn, contempt, and disgrace. [13]I will punish those who live in the land of Egypt, just as I punished Jerusalem with war, famine, and disease. [14]From the few remaining in Judah, no fugitive or survivor who came to live here in the land of Egypt will be able to return to the land of Judah. Even though they want to return and live there, they won't be able to return, except for some fugitives.

[15]Then all the men who knew that their wives had made offerings to other gods, along with the great crowd of women who were present, as well as the people living in Pathros in the land of Egypt, all answered Jeremiah: [16]"We're not going to listen to a word you have said to us in the LORD's name! [17]No, we're going to do exactly what we want: We're going to burn incense to the queen of heaven and pour out drink offerings to her, as we and our ancestors, our kings and our officials, have done in the towns of Judah and in the streets of Jerusalem. Then we had plenty to eat and we were thriving; we didn't have any troubles. [18]But ever since we stopped burning incense to the queen of heaven and pouring drink offerings to her, we have been destroyed by the sword and by famine."

[19]And the women added,[x] "Do you think that we burn incense to the queen of heaven and pour drink offerings to her without our

[v]Heb *his wives*   [w]Or *they*   [x]Syr; MT lacks *and the women added*.

QUEEN OF HEAVEN

According to Jeremiah 7:16-20 and 44:15-25, some ancient Israelites burned incense, poured out libations, and baked cakes to honor a goddess known only as the Queen of Heaven. In exchange, according to the queen's followers, she made available plenty of food and kept them safe from enemy attack. It is particularly women, moreover, who seem devoted to the Queen of Heaven; thus they become, in Jeremiah 44:25, the object of Jeremiah's special scorn. The Queen of Heaven may be a goddess of Israel's neighbors, such as Astarte or Ishtar.

husbands' support when we make cakes in her image and pour drink offerings to her?"

²⁰Jeremiah said to all the people, men and women alike, in fact everyone who had spoken this way: ²¹"Do you really think the LORD was unaware of what you were up to in the towns of Judah and the streets of Jerusalem? Don't you think the LORD knew that you and your ancestors were making offerings to other gods[y]—along with your kings and officials, and the people of the land? ²²It got so bad that the LORD could no longer bear your evil and shameless acts; it was at that point that your land was reduced to an utter wasteland and a curse, as it is today. ²³The current dire situation occurred because you made offerings to other gods[z] and sinned against the LORD—because you wouldn't obey the LORD or follow the LORD's instruction, laws, or warnings."

²⁴Then Jeremiah said to all the people, including the women: Listen to the LORD's word, all you Judeans in the land of Egypt. ²⁵The LORD of heavenly forces, the God of Israel, proclaims: You and your wives have done exactly what you said you would do. You said, "We will definitely fulfill our promise to burn incense to the queen of heaven and pour out drink offerings to her." Go ahead and keep your promises! ²⁶But listen to the LORD's word, all you Judeans who live in the land of Egypt. I swear by my great name, says the LORD, that no one from Judah living in Egypt will utter my name again, even in the solemn pledge: "As surely as the LORD God lives." ²⁷I'm watching over them for harm and not for good. Everyone from Judah who is living in the land of Egypt will die by the sword and by famine, until all are gone. ²⁸Those who actually survive war and return from Egypt to the land of Judah will be very few. Then the few remaining Judeans living in Egypt will know for certain whose word is true—mine or theirs! ²⁹And this will be a sign for you, declares the LORD: I will punish you here so that you know my threats against you will surely be fulfilled. ³⁰The LORD proclaims: I will hand Pharaoh Hophra, Egypt's king,

over to his enemies who seek to kill him, just as I delivered Judah's King Zedekiah over to his enemy King Nebuchadnezzar of Babylon, who sought to kill him.

A final word for Baruch

45 In the fourth year of Judah's King Jehoiakim, Josiah's son, Baruch was writing in a scroll the words that Jeremiah was dictating to him. Jeremiah the prophet told Baruch, Neriah's son: ²This is what the LORD the God of Israel proclaims about you, Baruch: ³You have said, "I can't take it anymore! The LORD has added sorrow to my pain. I'm worn out from groaning and can find no rest." ⁴This is what you should say to him: "The LORD proclaims: I'm breaking down everything I have built up. I'm digging up that which I have planted—the entire land. ⁵You seek great things for yourself, but don't bother. I'm bringing disaster on all humanity, declares the LORD, but wherever you go I will let you escape with your life."

ORACLES CONCERNING THE NATIONS

46 This is what the LORD told the prophet Jeremiah concerning the nations.

Prophecy against Egypt

²About Egypt! A message for the army of Pharaoh Neco, Egypt's king, which was defeated by Babylon's Nebuchadnezzar at Carchemish near the Euphrates River in the fourth year of Judah's King Jehoiakim, Josiah's son:

³ Grab your shields
    and prepare for war!
⁴ Saddle the horses;
    mount the stallions!
Take your positions
    with helmets on!
Polish your spears;
    put on your armor!
⁵ Why do I see them terrified,
    retreating in haste?

---

[y]Heb lacks *to other gods.*   [z]Heb lacks *to other gods.*

Their soldiers are crushed,
  running for cover,
  and they don't turn back.
Panic lurks at every turn,
  declares the LORD.
⁶ The swift can't flee;
  the mighty can't escape.
Up north by the Euphrates River,
  they stagger and fall.

⁷ Who is this that rises like the Nile,
  whose banks overflow?^a
⁸ It's Egypt that rises like the Nile,
  whose banks overflow,^b
  who declares, "I will arise
  and cover the earth
  and destroy cities and inhabitants."
⁹ Charge, you horses;
  advance, you chariots!
Attack, you soldiers
  with your shield in hand,
  you people of Cush and Put^c
  with your bow drawn,
  you archers from Lud.

¹⁰ But that day belongs to the
  LORD God of heavenly forces;
  it's a day of reckoning,
  settling scores with enemies.
The sword will devour
  until it has had its fill of blood.
The LORD God of heavenly forces
  is preparing a sacrifice in the north
  by the Euphrates River.
¹¹ Go up to Gilead and seek balm,
  virgin Daughter Egypt.
You search out remedies in vain,
  for your disease is incurable.
¹² Nations hear of your shame;
  the earth is filled with your sobs.
Soldier stumbles over soldier;
  together they go down.
¹³This is the word that the LORD spoke
to the prophet Jeremiah about the military
offensive of Babylon's King Nebuchadnezzar against the land of Egypt:
¹⁴ Tell Egypt, warn Migdol,
  alert Memphis and Tahpanhes!

Say: "Brace yourselves for what's coming.
  War is breaking out from every side!"
¹⁵ Why have your mighty fallen?
  Why haven't they stood their ground?
  Because the LORD
  has struck them down.
¹⁶ He's tripped them up;
  they fall over each other and say,
  "Let's get out of here
  and go home to our people,
  where we were born,
  far away from the oppressor's sword."^d
¹⁷ There they call Pharaoh, Egypt's king,
  Loudmouth—Nothing But Hot Air!
¹⁸ As I live, declares the king,
  whose name is
  the LORD of heavenly forces,
  one is coming
  just as surely as Tabor is
  in the mountains
  and Carmel is by the sea.^e
¹⁹ Get what you need for deportation,
  you inhabitants of Egypt.^f
Memphis will be reduced to a wasteland,
  a ruin with no one left.
²⁰ Egypt is a beautiful, yes, beautiful heifer,
  but a horsefly from the north
  is coming to bite her.^g
²¹ Even her mercenaries
  are like well-fed calves;
  they too will retreat and run for cover;
  they won't survive.
The day of disaster
  has come to haunt them,
  the time of their punishment.
²² Like the sound of a snake hissing
  as it slithers away
  is Egypt^h as armies approach in force;
  they come against her with axes,
  like woodcutters.
²³ They destroy her dense forest,
  though it is vast,
  because they outnumber locusts
  and can't be counted,
  declares the LORD.
²⁴ Daughter Egypt will be humiliated,
  handed over to people from the north.
²⁵This is what the LORD of heavenly
forces, the God of Israel, proclaims: I'm

---

^aOr *like rivers whose waters roar*   ^bOr *like rivers whose waters roar*   ^cTraditionally *Ethiopia and Libya*
^dHeb uncertain   ^eHeb uncertain   ^fOr *inhabitant, Daughter Egypt*   ^gHeb uncertain   ^hHeb lacks *is Egypt*.

going to punish Amon of Thebes, Egypt and its gods and kings, as well as Pharaoh and all who rely on him. ²⁶I will hand them over to those who seek to kill them, namely Babylon's King Nebuchadnezzar and his servants. But afterward Egypt will dwell like it did a long time ago, declares the LORD.

²⁷ But don't be afraid,
  my servant Judah;
  don't lose heart, Israel.
I will deliver you from a faraway place
  and your children
    from the land of their exile.
My people Jacob will again
  be safe and sound,
  with no one harassing them.
²⁸ So don't be afraid, my servant Jacob,
  declares the LORD.
I'm with you;
I will put an end to all the nations
  where I have scattered you.
But I won't put an end to you.
I won't let you avoid punishment;
I will discipline you as you deserve.

ⁱOr *a helper*

Prophecy against Philistia

47 The LORD's word to the prophet Jeremiah concerning the Philistines before Pharaoh conquered Gaza.

² The LORD proclaims:
  Waters are rising from the north
    and turning into a raging flood.
  They will engulf the land
    and everything in it,
    the towns and those living in them.
  The people cry out;
    all who live there scream.
³ At the pounding of the stallions' hooves,
    at the deafening roar
      of the chariots' wheels,
    parents abandon children,
      so paralyzed are they with fear.
⁴ Because the time is coming
    for the Philistines' destruction,
    for cutting off from Tyre and Sidon
      anyone who might try to save Gaza,ⁱ
    because the LORD will destroy
      the Philistines,
    the few left from the island of Caphtor.

ASHKELON

Biblical Ashkelon is a large semicircular 150-acre tell facing the Mediterranean Sea next to the modern city of Ashkelon. Ashkelon is best known in the Bible as one of the Philistine Pentapolis cities, a league of five Philistine centers mentioned in Joshua 13:3.

In the Bible, Ashkelon is infamous as the city where Samson killed 30 men to procure their clothes as payment for a wager he had lost to the Philistines (Judg 14:10-19). It was also one of the Philistine cities struck by a plague following the Philistine capture of the covenant chest (1 Sam 6:4, 17). During the final centuries of the Iron Age, Ashkelon was a center for wine production, as testified by the discovery of an architectural complex that included at least three workrooms and the remains of plastered platforms, vats, and basins. The end of Iron Age Ashkelon is marked by its devastation by Nebuchadnezzer in 604 BCE and the exile of the last Philistine king, Aga, an event documented in the Babylonian Chronicle and reflected in the biblical prophecy (Jer 25:20; 47:5, 7; Amos 1:8; Zeph 2:4, 7; Zech 9:5). Archaeological excavations have uncovered physical evidence of Nebuchadnezzer's campaign and Ashkelon's demise, indicated by the massive destruction of the city, including the ruins of a public marketplace.

5 Mourning[j] will come upon Gaza;
    silence will cover Ashkelon,
        the few left in their valley.
How long will you gash yourselves
    in grief?[k]
6 You sword of the LORD,
    how long until you are silent?
Return to your sheath;
    rest and be still!
7 How can you be silent
    when the LORD has directed you[l]
        to attack Ashkelon and the coast line?

Prophecy against Moab

48 Concerning Moab:
    The LORD of heavenly forces,
    the God of Israel, proclaims:
How awful for Nebo;
    it lies in ruins.
Kirathaim is captured and shamed;
    the fortress is disgraced,
        reduced to rubble.
2 No one sings Moab's praise any longer!
    In Heshbon they are hatching
        a plot against her:
"Come, let's bring down the nation!"
You too, madmen, will be silenced;
    the sword will pursue you.

3 Listen to the cries for help
    from Horonaim:
        "Destruction and massive devastation!"
4 Moab is shattered;
    its young cry for help.
5 On the way up to Luhith,
    there is uncontrollable weeping.
On the way down to Horonaim,
    they hear sobs of anguish.
6 Run for your lives!
    Be like Aroer[m] in the desert.
7 Because you have relied
    on your own strength
        and treasures,
    you also will be captured.
Chemosh will go into exile,
    together with his priests and officials.
8 The destroyer will sweep
    through every town;
        no town will escape.
The valleys will be ravaged;
    the plateaus will be destroyed,
        because the LORD
            has declared it so.
9 Give wings to Moab,
    and it would fly away[n]
        because its towns lie in ruins,
            with no one left in them.

[j]Or *baldness* [k]Heb lacks *in grief.* [l]Or *it* [m]Heb uncertain [n]Heb uncertain

MOAB

1. The son of Lot by one of his daughters according to the etiological account in Genesis 19:30-38. The Ammonites are descended from Lot by his other daughter and are related to Moab.

2. Moab refers to a geographic region and more particularly to the plateau areas east of the Dead Sea. Moab also refers to the nation-state in that same region during the Iron Age, with political antecedents that may reach back into the Late Bronze Age. The designation *Moabite*, therefore, can refer either to someone living in the area of Moab or to someone attached to the political entity of Moab. In spite of the ancestral accounts that recognize a certain kinship between Israel and Moab, the dominant reaction in the OT to Moabite religion and culture is negative. In Deuteronomy 23:3-6 Moabites and Ammonites are forbidden entry into the assembly of Israel. Historical reasons are cited for this prohibition. This negative view of Moab continues into the post-exilic period.

¹⁰ Cursed is the one who is halfhearted
   in doing the LORD's work.
   Cursed is the one who restrains
   the sword from bloodshed.

¹¹ From early on Moab has been at ease,
   like wine° left to settle on its sediment.
   It hasn't been poured into jars;
      nor has Moab been taken into exile.
   Therefore, its taste is still pleasant,
      and its aroma is the same.
¹² But the time is coming, declares the
LORD, when I will send to him someone to
spill it—to pour out his wine and to smash
his jars. ¹³ And Moab will be put to shame
on account of Chemosh, just as the people
of Israel were put to shame on account of
Bethel, in which they trusted.ᴾ
¹⁴ How can you claim,
   "We're soldiers; we're war heroes"?
¹⁵ Moab is doomed;
   its towns will surrender;�q
   its elite forces will go down in defeat,
      declares the king whose name
      is the LORD of heavenly forces.
¹⁶ Moab's destruction is near;
   its downfall approaches rapidly.
¹⁷ Grieve for this nation,
   you neighbors of Moab,
   all you who know his name.
   Proclaim how its mighty scepter
      and magnificent staff are shattered!

¹⁸ Come down from your lofty place
   and sit in the dust,ʳ
   you inhabitants of Daughter Dibon;ˢ
   because Moab's destroyer
      has arrived to level your fortresses.
¹⁹ Stand by the roads and watch,
   you inhabitants of Aroer.
   Ask the men who flee
      and the women who run off,
   "What's happened?"
²⁰ Moab is shamed and shocked;
   weep and wail!
   Tell it by the Arnon River:
      Moab's been destroyed!

²¹ Judgment has come
   to the towns of the plateau—
      to Holon, Jahzah, and Mephaath,
²² to Dibon, Nebo, and Beth-diblathaim,
²³ to Kiriathaim, Beth-gamul,
   and Beth-meon,
²⁴ to Kerioth and Bozrah,
   to all the towns of Moab, far and near.

²⁵ Moab's horn is cut off;
   its arm is broken,
   declares the LORD.
²⁶ Get Moab drunk,
   because it has exalted itself
   above the LORD.
   Moab will collapse in its vomit
   and become the butt of every joke.
²⁷ Wasn't Israel the butt of your jokes?
   Didn't you shake your head
      as if they were thieves
      caught in the act?
²⁸ Leave your towns, head for the cliffs,
   you people of Moab.
   Hide like a dove
   that nests in the mouth of a cave.

²⁹ We have heard of Moab's pride:
   arrogant, puffed up, exalted,
      high and mighty, boastful!
³⁰ I myself know about its arrogance,
   declares the LORD,
   the idle talk, the empty deeds.
³¹ But I'll still wail for Moab;
   I'll cry out for all Moab;
      I'llᵗ sob for the people of Kir-heres.
³² I'll weep for you, vine of Sibmah,
   more than I would for Jazer.
   Though your branches extended to the sea
   and reached the coast of Jazer,
      now the destroyer has come
      to harvest your grapes
      and summer fruits.
³³ Joy and gladness have been taken
   from the orchards and farms of Moab.
   I have stopped making wine
   in the presses.
   No one shouts with joy
   while treading the grapes.

°Heb lacks *like wine.*   ᴾOr *And Moab will be ashamed of Chemosh just as the people of Israel were ashamed of
Bethel, in which they trusted.*   qHeb uncertain   ʳOr *thirst*   ˢHeb uncertain, or *residing Daughter Dibon*
ᵗOr *He*

Though there are shouts,
they are not shouts of joy!^u

³⁴ Screams are heard from Heshbon
to Elealeh and Jahaz;
their cries resound from Zoar
to Horonaim and Eglath-shelishiyah.
Even the waters of Nimrim
are dried up.

³⁵ I'll put an end to Moab,
declares the LORD,
for making offerings on the shrines,
and worshipping their gods.

³⁶ Therefore, my heart wails for Moab
like a mournful^v flute
that plays the dirge;
my heart wails for the people
of Kir-heres,
like a mournful flute.
Their abundance is now gone.

³⁷ Every head is shaved,
every beard is cut off,
every hand is slashed,
and everyone wears
mourning clothes.

³⁸ On every housetop of Moab
and in all its streets,
there's nothing but mourning.
I have shattered Moab
like a pottery vessel no one wants,
declares the LORD.

³⁹ How it's shattered! Go wail!
How Moab turns away!
What shame!
Moab has become the butt of every joke,
horrific to all its neighbors.

⁴⁰ The LORD proclaims:
Look! One who soars like an eagle
and spreads its wings over Moab.

⁴¹ The towns will be captured;
the strongholds will be seized.
On that day,
the heart of every soldier from Moab
will be like that of a woman
in the throes of labor.

⁴² Moab will be destroyed once and for all
because it has exalted itself
above the LORD.

⁴³ Terror, traps, and trackers^w
are upon you, people of Moab,
declares the LORD.

⁴⁴ Those who flee from terror
will fall into a pit;
those who escape the pit
will be captured by the trap.
I will bring upon Moab
the year of its punishment,
declares the LORD.

⁴⁵ In Heshbon tired refugees seek shelter.
But fire is raging in Heshbon,
flames from the house^x of Sihon.
It has burned up part of Moab,
including the leader
of this rebellious nation.^y

⁴⁶ How terrible for you, Moab;
the people of Chemosh have perished.
Your sons have been carried off;
your daughters
have been taken captive.

⁴⁷ But in the days to come
I'll bring back Moab from captivity,
declares the LORD.
Such is the judgment on Moab.

Prophecy against the Ammonites

49 Concerning the Ammonites,
the LORD proclaims:
Doesn't Israel have children?
Aren't there heirs to his land?
Why then has Milcom taken over Gad?
Why have his people
settled in its towns?

² Therefore, the time is coming,
declares the LORD,
when I will sound the battle alarm
against Rabbah,
the capital city of the Ammonites.
The city will be demolished,
and its neighboring villages
will be burned to the ground.
Then Israel will repossess
the land seized by its captors,
says the LORD.

³ Weep, you people of Heshbon;
Ai has been destroyed.
Wail, you daughters of Rabbah;
put on funeral clothing,

^uHeb uncertain   ^vHeb lacks *mournful*.   ^wOr *terror, pit, and trap*   ^xHeb manuscripts; MT *from among*   ^yHeb uncertain

cry your eyes out,
  run for shelter.[z]
Milcom will surely go into exile,
  together with his priests and ministers.

[4] Why do you brag about your strength?
  Your strength is exhausted,[a]
    you rebellious daughter.
You trust in your treasures,
  never imagining who would attack you.
[5] I'm the one who will terrify you
  from every side,
  declares the LORD of heavenly forces.
Every one of you will be scattered about;
  no one will gather those who fled.
[6] Afterward, though, I will bring back
  the Ammonites from captivity,
  declares the LORD.

Prophecy against Edom

[7] Concerning Edom,
  the LORD of heavenly forces proclaims:
Is wisdom no longer in Teman?
  Has good sense vanished
    from the perceptive?
  Are they no longer wise?
[8] Turn, flee, and run for cover,
  you inhabitants of Dedan.
I'm bringing disaster on Esau:
  its day of reckoning.
[9] If workers would come to you
  to pick grapes,
  they would at least leave
    a few on the vine.
If thieves would come in the night,
  they would take only what they needed.
[10] But me? I will strip Esau bare.
  I will expose his hiding places,
    and he will find no place to take cover.
His offspring, family, and acquaintances
  will perish,
  and there will be no one left to say,[b]
[11] "Leave me your orphans,
  and I'll look after them;
    trust your widows into my care."
[12] The LORD proclaims: If the innocent
must drink the cup, why do you expect to
escape punishment? You won't! You will

drink it! [13] I myself swear, declares the
LORD, that Bozrah will become an object of
horror and scorn, a wasteland and a curse.
And all of its towns will lie in ruins forever.
[14] I have heard a report from the LORD
  that a messenger is sent
    among the nations:
Join forces and come against her;
  prepare for war!
[15] I'm about to cut you down to size
  before the nations;
  you will be scorned by everyone.
[16] The terror you have inflicted on others
  has deceived you,
    as has your own pride.
Though you live in a fortress
  and occupy the high ground;
  though you nest on high like the eagles,
  I will bring you down,
    declares the LORD.
[17] Then Edom will become a wasteland.
  All who pass by will be shocked
    by its injuries.
[18] It will be like the destruction
  of Sodom and Gomorrah
  and their surrounding towns,
    says the LORD.
No one will live there;
  no human will dwell in it.
[19] Like a lion coming up
  from the jungle of the Jordan
    to a well-watered meadow,[c]
  so I will suddenly chase down Edom
    and single out its choicest of rams.[d]
Who is like me?
  Who can direct me?
  What shepherd can withstand me?
[20] Therefore, listen to the counsel
  that the LORD has for Edom
  and the plans he's devised
    against the people of Teman:
  The little ones of the flock
    will be dragged off,
  as their pasture watches
    in utter disbelief.[e]
[21] The earth quakes
  as the Edomites go down;
  their screams echo
    as far as the Reed Sea.[f]

---

[z]Heb uncertain; or *run back and forth in the sheepfolds* [a]Heb uncertain [b]LXX; MT *and there will (or he will) be no more* [c]Heb uncertain [d]Heb uncertain [e]Heb uncertain [f]Or *Red Sea*

²² Look! One who mounts up
 and soars like an eagle,
 who swoops down and spreads
  his wings over Bozrah.
 On that day, the heart
 of every soldier from Edom
 will be like that of a woman
  in the throes of labor.

Prophecy against Damascus

²³ Concerning Damascus:
 Hamath and Arpad lose heart
 when they hear the bad news.
 They are trembling with fear,
  like the raging sea,
 which can't become quiet.
²⁴ Damascus staggers about;
  she tries to flee,
 but panic overwhelms her.
 She's gripped by anguish and pain,
  like a woman in labor.
²⁵ Forsaken^g is the renowned city,
  city of my delight.
²⁶ Yes, her young men will fall in the streets,

and her soldiers will be silent
  on that day,
 declares the LORD of heavenly forces.
²⁷ I will set fire to the walls of Damascus;
  it will burn up the fortresses
  of Ben-hadad.

Prophecy against Kedar and Hazor

²⁸ Concerning Kedar and the kingdoms
of Hazor, which Babylon's King Nebuchadnezzar defeated, the LORD proclaims:
 Get ready to attack Kedar;
  destroy the people from the east!
²⁹ Seize^h their tents and their flocks,
  their belongings and all their goods.
 Take off with their camels
  and shout as you go:
  "Panic Lurks Everywhere!"
³⁰ Run away; take cover,
  you people of Hazor,
  declares the LORD.
 Babylon's King Nebuchadnezzar
  has taken counsel and devised a plan
  against you.

^gVulg; MT *Not forsaken*   ^hOr *They will seize . . . they will take off*

ELAM

Elam is the name of several individuals and of a nation.

1. The ancestor of the nation Elam (Gen 10:22; 1 Chron 1:17).

2. An early Benjaminite (1 Chron 8:24), perhaps to be identified with Elam (3) below.

3. One or two ancestors of a group of returning exiles (Ezra 2:7, 31; 8:7; 10:2; Neh 7:12, 34). Though the text mentions "the other Elam" (Ezra 2:31; Neh 7:34), it gives precisely the same number of returnees from this Elam as from the first (Ezra 2:7; Neh 7:12), possibly suggesting this is the same individual and the same group of returnees.

4. A leader of the people (Neh 10:14).

5. A priest (Neh 12:42).

6. A priestly gatekeeper appointed by David (1 Chron 26:3).

7. Elam, located in the southwestern corner of Iran north of the Persian Gulf, was a major power during the late 3rd millennium through the first half of the 1st millennium BCE, but the area controlled by the Elamites differed considerably from period to period.

³¹ Get ready to attack a nation
    that feels safe and secure,
    declares the LORD,
    one without barred gates
    that lives by itself.
³² Their camels will become plunder;
    their many cattle will be pillaged.
 I will scatter to the winds those
    who are clean-shaven,ⁱ
    and I will bring disaster on them
    from every side,
    declares the LORD.
³³ Hazor will become a den for wild dogs,
    a wilderness forever.
 No one will live there;
    no human will dwell in it.

Prophecy against Elam

³⁴ This is what the LORD told the prophet
Jeremiah concerning Elam at the beginning
of the rule of Judah's King Zedekiah. ³⁵ The
LORD of heavenly forces proclaims:
    I'm going to break the bow of Elam,
    the backbone of its military might.
³⁶ I will bring against Elam four winds
    from the four corners of heaven,
    and I will scatter them to the winds.
 Those banished from Elam
    will migrate to every nation.
³⁷ I will terrify Elam before their enemies,
    before those who seek to kill them.
 I will bring disaster upon them,
    my fierce anger,
    declares the LORD.
 I will send the sword to attack them
    until I have destroyed them all.
³⁸ I will establish my rule in Elam
    and dispose of its king and officials,
    declares the LORD.
³⁹ But in the days to come
    I will bring back the captives of Elam,
    declares the LORD.

Prophecy against Babylon

50 This is what the LORD said concerning Babylon and the land of the Babylonians through the prophet Jeremiah:
² Tell the nations;
    proclaim it far and wide!

Set up a flag;
    proclaim it far and wide!
Hold nothing back;
    just shout it:
"Babylon is captured;
    Bel is shamed;
Marduk is panic-stricken.
    Her images are shamed;
    her idols are panic-stricken."
³ A nation from the north
    has risen up against her.
It will decimate her land,
    and no one will live in it.
    Every living thing will flee.

⁴ In those days and at that time,
    declares the LORD,
    the people of Israel and Judah
    will come out of Babylonʲ together;
    with weeping they will leave
    as they seek the LORD their God.
⁵ They will search for Zion,
    turning their faces toward it.
 They will comeᵏ and
    unite with the LORD,
    in an everlasting covenant
    that will never be forgotten.
⁶ My people were lost sheep;
    their shepherds led them astray;
 they deserted them on the mountains,
    where they wandered off among
    the hills,
    forgetting their resting place.
⁷ All who found them devoured them;
    and their attackers said,
    "It's not our fault,
    because they have sinned against
    the LORD,
    the true pasture,ˡ
    the hope of their ancestors—
    the LORD."
⁸ Now wander far from Babylon.
    Get out of that country.
 Like rams of the flock,
    lead the way home.
⁹ I'm stirring up against Babylon
    a coalition of mighty nations.
 It will mobilize in the north,
    and from there she will be captured.

ⁱOr *those who have temples that are shaved* ʲHeb lacks *of Babylon.* ᵏHeb uncertain ˡOr *righteous dwelling place*

Their arrows are like
  those of an expert archer
  who does not return empty-handed.
¹⁰ Babylon will be defeated;
  its attackers will carry off
    all that they want,
    declares the LORD.

¹¹ Sure, you gloat and rejoice,
  you plunderers of my possession.
  Sure, you dance around like a calf
  and neigh like a stallion.
¹² But Mother Babylonᵐ will be humiliated;
  the one who bore you will be disgraced.
  She will become the least of the nations:
  a wilderness, a desert, and parched land.
¹³ Because of the LORD's anger,
  no one will live there;
    she will be reduced to total ruin.
  All who pass by Babylon will be shocked;
  they will gasp at all her injuries.
¹⁴ Take up your positions around Babylon,
  all you archers;
  now shoot at her;
    save none of your arrows,
    because she's sinned
    against the LORD.
¹⁵ Raise a victory shout
  against her on every side!
  She's surrendered;
    her towers have collapsed;
    her walls are destroyed.
  This is the LORD's retribution;
  now pay her back:
    do to her what she's done to others!
¹⁶ Cut Babylon off from those who plant
  and those who harvest the crops,
    because of its ruthless sword.ⁿ
  Now return, all of you, to your people;
  flee to your homeland!

¹⁷ Israelites are scattered sheep,
  driven away by lions.
  First the king of Assyria devoured them,
  and now Babylon's King
    Nebuchadnezzar has ravaged them.ᵒ
¹⁸ Therefore, the LORD of heavenly forces,
the God of Israel, proclaims:

I'm going to punish the king of Babylon
  and his land,
  just as I punished the king of Assyria.
¹⁹ But I will restore Israel to their pasture;
  they will graze on Carmel and Bashan;
  they will eat their fill
    in the highlands of Ephraim and Gilead.
²⁰ In those days and at that time,
  declares the LORD,
  if one searches for the sin of Israel,
    they will find nothing;
  if one seeks out
  the wrongdoing of Judah,
    they will look in vain.
    I will forgive those I have spared.

²¹ Attack the land of Merathaim;ᵖ
  crush those living in Pekod.
  Ruin and destroy them,
    declares the LORD;
  do all I have commanded you.
²² There's the sound of war in the land
  and enormous devastation.
²³ How the hammer of the whole earth
  has been broken and shattered
  into pieces!
  How Babylon has become a wasteland
  among the nations!
²⁴ You set a trap for others, Babylon,�q
  but you yourself were caught
  in it unaware;
    you have been found and captured
    because you have defied the LORD.
²⁵ The LORD has opened his arsenal
  and brought out his brutal weapons.
  The LORD God of heavenly forces
  has a job to do
  in the land of the Babylonians.
²⁶ Come against her from every side;
  throw open her granaries;
  pile her up like stalks of grain;
  totally destroy her;
  leave nothing intact.
²⁷ Destroy all her bulls;
  prepare them for slaughter.
  How terrible for them!
  Their time has come,
  the day of reckoning.

ᵐOr *your mother* ⁿHeb uncertain ᵒOr *gnawed their bones* ᵖOr *Double rebellion* qOr *I set a trap for you, Babylon, and you were*

²⁸ A voice of fugitives and refugees,
    from the land of Babylon,
    declaring in Zion
      the retribution of the LORD our God
      because of what has been done
      to his temple.

²⁹ Send the archers against Babylon,
    all who draw the bow!
  Surround her
    and let no one escape.
  Pay her back for her deeds;
    do to her what she's done to others.
  She has acted arrogantly
    toward the LORD,
    the holy one of Israel!

³⁰ Therefore, her soldiers will fall
  in the streets;
    all her warriors will be silenced
    on that day,
      declares the LORD.

³¹ I'm against you, you arrogant one!
    declares the LORD God
    of heavenly forces.
  Your day has come,
    your time of reckoning.

³² The arrogant one will stumble and fall,
    and no one will help her up.
  I'll set your cities on fire,
    and it will consume all that's around her.

³³ The LORD of heavenly forces proclaims:
  The people of Israel were oppressed,
    together with the people of Judah.
  Their captors held them
    and refused to let them go.

³⁴ Yet their redeemer is strong;
    the LORD of heavenly forces is his name.
  He will surely defend their cause
    and give them rest in the land.
  But he will unsettle
    the people of Babylon.

³⁵ A sword against Babylon and its people,
    declares the LORD,
    along with its officials and sages.

³⁶ A sword against its diviners
    so that they become fools.
  A sword against its warriors
    so that they are terrified.

³⁷ A sword against its horses
    and chariots,
    and the mercenaries[r] in its midst
      so that they lose courage.[s]
  A sword against its treasures
    so that they are looted.

³⁸ A sword[t] against the water supplies
    so that they dry up.
  It is truly the land of idols,
    idols about which they have gone
    utterly mad!

³⁹ Therefore, Babylon
    will become a ghost town,
    a place for desert animals,
    hyenas, and ravenous birds.[u]
  No one will live there again;
    no one will make it their home.

⁴⁰ Just as God destroyed Sodom
    and Gomorrah and their neighbors,
      declares the LORD,
    so no one will live in Babylon
    or settle there again.

⁴¹ Look! An army is on the move
    from the northern regions.
  A powerful nation
    and many kings are coming
    from the ends of the earth.

⁴² Equipped with bow and spear,
    they are cruel
    and show no mercy.
  Their horsemen sound
    like the roaring sea,
    arrayed in battle formation against you,
    Daughter Babylon.

⁴³ The king of Babylon has heard
    reports of them
    and is panic-stricken;
    distress overwhelms him,
    pain like that of a woman in labor.

⁴⁴ Like a lion coming up from
    the jungle of the Jordan
    to a well-watered meadow,[v]
    so I will suddenly chase down Babylon
    and single out its choicest of rams.
  Who is like me?
    Who can direct me?
    What shepherd can withstand me?

ʳOr foreigners   ˢOr become like women   ᵗOr drought or A drought   ᵘHeb uncertain   ᵛHeb uncertain

45 Therefore, listen to the counsel
   that the LORD has for Babylon
   and the plans he's devised
      against the land of Babylon:
   The little ones of the flock
      will be dragged off,
   as their pasture watches
   in utter disbelief.^w
46 The earth quakes
   at the sound of Babylon's capture;
      its screams echo
      throughout the world.

51 The LORD proclaims:
   I'm stirring up a violent wind
   against Babylon
   and those who live in Leb-qamai.^x
2 I will send mercenaries^y to Babylon
   who will sift her and clear out her land.
   They will surround her
      on the day of disaster.
3 Let the archers draw their bows;
   let them prepare their armor.
   Show no mercy to her young men;
      wipe out her entire company!
4 They will fall wounded
   in the land of Babylon,
      struck down in her streets.
5 God, the LORD of heavenly forces,
   hasn't abandoned Israel and Judah,
      even though they live
      in a land filled with guilt
      before the holy one of Israel.
6 Escape from Babylon;
   each of you run for your lives!
   Don't perish because of her guilt,
      because this is the time
   for the LORD's retribution,
      a day of reckoning
      for all that Babylon^z has done.

7 Babylon was a gold cup
   in the LORD's hand;
      it made the whole earth drunk.
   The nations drank her wine
      and went mad.
8 But suddenly Babylon fell
   and shattered into pieces.

Wail for her!
   Bring medicine for her pain;
      perhaps she will recover.
9 We tried to cure Babylon,
   but she was beyond help.
   Let's depart from her
      and return to your own country,
      each of you.
   Her punishment reaches to heaven
      and extends to the clouds.
10 The LORD has come to our defense,
      so let's declare in Zion
      what the LORD our God has done!

11 Sharpen your arrows;
      prepare your shields.
   The LORD is stirring up
      the spirit of kings from Media.
   He intends to destroy Babylon;
      this is the LORD's retribution,
      a day of reckoning for his temple.
12 Set up a flag on the walls of Babylon,
      fortify the guards,
      post watchmen,
      prepare an ambush,
      because the LORD has a plan
      against the inhabitants of Babylon.
   He will accomplish it,
      just as he said he would.
13 You live beside a great river,
      and you are rich in treasures.
   But your time has come;
      your cruelty has caught up with you.^a
14 The LORD of heavenly forces
   has sworn by his own name:
      I'm going to fill your cities^b
      with soldiers like a swarm of locusts;
      they will celebrate their victory over you.

15 God made the earth by his might,
      shaped the world by his wisdom,
      and crafted the skies by his knowledge.
16 At the sound of God's voice,
      the heavenly waters roar.
      God raises the clouds
      from the ends of the earth.
   He makes lightning for the rain
      and sends the wind from his treasuries.

^wHeb uncertain ^xOr *the inhabitants of Leb qamai*, a reference to Chaldea (Babylonia); or *those who rise up against me* ^yOr *foreigners* ^zOr *she* or *it* ^aHeb uncertain ^bHeb lacks *cities*.

¹⁷ Everyone is too foolish to understand;
  every smith is shamed by his idols,
    for their images are shams;
      they aren't alive.
¹⁸ They are a delusion, a charade;
  at the appointed time they will be ruined!
¹⁹ But the portion of Jacob
  is utterly different,
    for he has formed all things,
      including his very own tribe;
        the LORD of heavenly forces
      is his name!

²⁰ You are my hammer,
  my weapon of war.
With you I will crush the nations.
With you I will destroy kingdoms.
²¹ With you I will crush horse and rider.
  With you I will crush chariot and driver.
²² With you I will crush men and women.
  With you I will crush old and young.
  With you I will crush
    young men and young women.
²³ With you I will crush
    shepherds and flocks.
  With you I will crush farmers and oxen.
  With you I will crush
    governors and officials.

²⁴ I will repay Babylon and all its inhabitants
  for the terrible things
    they have done to Zion in your sight,
      declares the LORD.
²⁵ I'm against you,
  you mountain of destruction,
    declares the LORD,
  you destroyer of the whole earth!
I will reach out against you;
  I will topple you from your heights;
  I will turn you into a rubbish heap.
²⁶ They will never remove a cornerstone
  or a foundation stone from you.
You will be a wasteland forever,
  declares the LORD.

²⁷ Set up a flag in the land;
  sound the alarm among the nations!
Prepare them for war against her;
  summon kingdoms against her—

Ararat, Minni, and Ashkenaz.
Appoint a commander against her;
  call up the troops,
    like swarms of locusts!
²⁸ Prepare the nations for war against her,
  the kings of Media,
    its governors, all its officials,
    and all the countries they rule.

²⁹ The earth quakes and trembles
  because the LORD's plans
    against Babylon are fulfilled:
      to reduce Babylon to a wasteland,
        with no one left in it.
³⁰ Babylon's warriors quit fighting;
  they hide in their fortifications.
Their strength is worn out;
  their courage is gone!
Babylon's houses are burned down,
  and its gates are smashed.
³¹ Courier joins courier,
  messenger joins messenger
    to relate the news
      to the king of Babylon
    that his entire city has fallen.
³² The river crossings are blocked;
  the marshes are on fire;
  the soldiers are terrified.
³³ The LORD of heavenly forces, the God
of Israel, proclaims:
  Daughter Babylon is like a threshing floor
    ready to be trampled down.
  In a little while her harvest will come.

³⁴ Babylon's King Nebuchadnezzar
  has eaten us alive;
    he's drained us of strength;
      he's left us for dead.^c
He's gobbled us up
  like a great sea monster;
    he's filled his belly with our treasures;
    and he's spit us out.
³⁵ May Babylon be violated
  as our bodies were,
    say the inhabitants of Zion.
May our blood be on the Babylonians,
  say those from Jerusalem.
³⁶ Therefore, the LORD proclaims:
  I'm going to defend your cause;

^cOr *He's made us an empty container.*

I'll turn the tables on your attacker.
I'll dry up her sea;
I'll shut up her springs.
[37] Babylon will become a heap of ruins,
a den of wild dogs, a wasteland
with no one left in it.
[38] Like lions they will roar together;
they will growl like lions' cubs.
[39] They are ready to devour,
so I'll prepare the feast
and mix the drinks!
But after their noisy drunkenness,
they will fall fast asleep.
They will sleep forever,
never to get up,
declares the LORD.
[40] I'll lead them off
like lambs for slaughter,
like rams and goats.

[41] How Sheshach[d] has been defeated,
the pride of the whole earth
taken captive!
How Babylon has become a wasteland
among the nations!
[42] The sea has risen over Babylon;
its pounding waves overwhelm her.
[43] Her towns are devastated;
her land is scorched and barren,
a place where no one lives
or dares to pass through.
[44] I will punish Bel in Babylon;
I will force him to vomit
what he's consumed.
Then nations will no longer
stream to him,
and Babylon's walls will collapse!

[45] Get out of Babylon, my people!
Run for your lives
from the LORD's fierce anger.
[46] Don't be distracted or frightened
by the rumors you hear in the land.
Sometimes you hear one thing
and another time something else:
rumors of violence and uprisings.
[47] The time is coming
when I will deal with Babylon's idols;

the whole land will be disgraced,
and her wounded will fall
in her midst.
[48] Then all creation will rejoice over Babylon,
because out of the north
destroying armies will come
to attack her,
declares the LORD.
[49] Babylon must fall
for the dead in Israel,
as the dead of all the earth
have fallen to Babylon.

[50] You survivors of war,
leave now; don't delay!
Remember the LORD,
from a faraway land.
Keep Jerusalem alive in your hearts.

[51] We're humiliated by their taunts;
we're disgraced that strangers
have violated the sacred places
of the LORD's temple.

[52] The time is coming,
declares the LORD,
when I will deal with her idols,
and the wounded in her land will groan.
[53] Even if Babylon scales the heavens
and strengthens its towering defenses,
the destroying armies will still come
against her, at my command,
declares the LORD.
[54] Listen to the cries for help from Babylon,
signs of massive devastation in the land,
declares the LORD.
[55] The LORD is destroying Babylon
and silencing her outcry,
whose roar is like the crushing waves,
a deafening crash.
[56] He certainly comes against her;
the destroyer comes against Babylon.
Her warriors are captured;
their bows are broken.
The LORD is an exacting God
who repays in full.
[57] I'll make her leaders and sages drunk,
her governors, officials,
and warriors as well.

[d]Sheshach is a name for Babylon.

They will sleep forever, never to get up,
  declares the king,
    whose name is
    the LORD of heavenly forces.
58 The LORD of heavenly forces proclaims:
  Babylon's massive walls will come down,
    down to the ground;
  and its high gates will be burned
    to the ground.

People labor in vain;
  nations toil for nothing but ashes!

59 This is what the prophet Jeremiah instructed the staff officer[e] Seraiah, Neriah's son and Mahseiah's grandson, when Seraiah went to Babylon with Judah's King Zedekiah in the fourth year of his rule. 60 Jeremiah wrote down in a single scroll all the disasters that would happen to Babylon—all these things concerning Babylon. 61 Jeremiah said to Seraiah: When you get to Babylon, see to it that you read all these words. 62 Then say, "LORD, you declared that this place will be destroyed and nothing will remain in it—neither human nor animal; that it will forever be a wasteland!" 63 When you finish reading the scroll, tie a stone to it and throw it into the Euphrates River. 64 Then say, "In the same way, Babylon will sink and never rise again because of the disaster I'm bringing against it."

Jeremiah's words end here.

Rule of Zedekiah and the fall of Jerusalem

52 Zedekiah was 21 years old when he became king, and he ruled for eleven years in Jerusalem. His mother's name was Hamutal; she was a daughter of Jeremiah from Libnah. 2 He did evil in the LORD's eyes just as Jehoiachin had done. 3 It was because the LORD was angry against Jerusalem and Judah that he thrust them out of his presence. Zedekiah rebelled against the king of Babylon.

4 In the ninth year, the tenth month, and the tenth day of the month, Babylon's King Nebuchadnezzar attacked Jerusalem with all of his army. He camped beside the city and built a siege wall around it. 5 The city was under siege until the eleventh year of King Zedekiah. 6 On the ninth day of the fourth month, the famine in the city reached a point that no food remained for the people. 7 The enemy entered the city, and all the soldiers fled by night along the gate between the two walls by the royal gardens. So the Babylonians surrounded the city while the soldiers fled toward the desert plain. 8 However, the Babylonian army chased down Zedekiah and caught him in the plains of Jericho. (His entire army had fled from him.) 9 They arrested the king and brought him before the king of Babylon at Riblah in the land of Hamath. And he pronounced sentence on him. 10 The king of Babylon slaughtered Zedekiah's children before his very own eyes, and he slaughtered all Judah's officers at Riblah. 11 Then he gouged out Zedekiah's eyes and bound him in chains. The king of Babylon dragged him off to Babylon and put him in prison, where he remained until he died.

12 In the tenth day of the fifth month, which was the nineteenth year of Babylon's King Nebuchadnezzar, Nebuzaradan commander of the guard came to Jerusalem on behalf of his king. 13 He burned down the LORD's temple, the royal palace, all the houses of Jerusalem, and all the important buildings. 14 The entire Babylonian army and the commander of the guard destroyed the walls surrounding Jerusalem. 15 Nebuzaradan commander of the guard deported some of the poorest people, the rest of the people left in the city, a few skilled workers, and those who had joined the king of Babylon. 16 But Nebuzaradan commander of the guard left some of the poor to tend the vineyards and till the land.

17 The Babylonians broke apart the bronze columns, the stands, and the bronze Sea in the LORD's temple. They carried the bronze to Babylon. 18 They took the pots, the shovels, the wick trimmers, the sprinkling bowls, the incense dishes, and all the bronze equipment used for the temple

---

[e] Or *officer of rest*, often translated as *quartermaster*

services. [19]The commander of the guard took whatever gold or silver he could find as well: the small bowls, the fire pans, the sprinkling bowls, the pots, the lampstands, the basins, and the offering bowls. [20]There was too much bronze to be weighed: two columns, the bronze Sea and the twelve bronze bulls that held it up, and the stands, all of which Solomon had made for the LORD's temple. [21]Each column was about twenty-seven feet high and eighteen feet around. They were hollow, but the bronze was about three inches thick. [22]Each had a capital of bronze above it that towered seven and a half feet high, and each had an ornate design of bronze pomegranates around it. The second

ZEDEKIAH

The twentieth and final king of Judah (r. 598-587 BCE). Zedekiah was placed on the throne after Nebuchadnezzar had deported the palace officials who served under Jehoiachin, together with the leading citizens of Judah, the professional people, and thousands of skilled workers. When Zedekiah ascended the throne, Judah became a tributary to Babylon. As a vassal of Nebuchadnezzar, Zedekiah was compelled to pay an annual tribute and take an oath of allegiance to the king of Babylon (Ezek 17:13-14). However, incited by the prophets who were taken to Babylon (Jer 29:8-9) and by the nobles who formed part of the anti-Babylonian forces in Judah, Zedekiah eventually violated his oath of allegiance and rebelled against Babylon.

Zedekiah's rebellion caused Nebuchadnezzar to invade Judah. The Babylonian army conquered all Judean cities except Lachish and Azekah, two fortified cities in the western plains (Jer 34:7). In addition, the Babylonians besieged Jerusalem. The siege of the city lasted eighteen months. During the siege, Zedekiah sent a delegation to Jeremiah asking the prophet to pray for Jerusalem (Jer 37:3). Jeremiah responded with an oracle declaring that the Babylonians would return and destroy the city (Jer 37:6-10). In his last meeting with Jeremiah, Zedekiah again sought the prophet's advice. Jeremiah advised Zedekiah to surrender. Zedekiah was willing to surrender, but he was afraid of the pro-Egyptian (Jer 37:5; Ezek 17:15) and the pro-Babylonian groups within his government (Jer 38:14-28).

In the eleventh year of Zedekiah's reign, the Babylonian army entered Jerusalem (Jer 39:1-3). Zedekiah, members of his family, and a few of his military officers who had survived the invasion of Jerusalem fled the city by night (2 Kgs 25:4; Jer 39:4). The Babylonian army pursued the king and his entourage and captured them on the road to Jericho. Zedekiah was taken to Nebuchadnezzar.

Nebuchadnezzar passed judgment on Zedekiah. Zedekiah's sons were killed before him and his own eyes were put out. Zedekiah was bound in chains and taken captive to Babylon (2 Kgs 25:1-7; Jer 32:4-5; 34:2-3; 39:1-7; 52:4-11). A month after Zedekiah's capture, Nebuzaradan, the commander of Nebuchadnezzar's army, entered Jerusalem. He plundered the temple, burned the king's palace and all the houses of Jerusalem, and tore down the walls of Jerusalem (2 Kgs 25:8-10; Jer 39:8).

column was the same, also with pomegranates. [23]There were ninety-six pomegranates on the sides, a total of one hundred pomegranates around the ornate design.

[24]The commander of the guard also took Seraiah the high priest, Zephaniah the deputy priest, and the three doorkeepers. [25]From the city, he took a eunuch who was appointed over the army and the seven royal advisors who remained in the city. He also took the scribe of the commander of the army in charge of military conscription and sixty military personnel[f] who were found in the city. [26]Nebuzaradan the commander of the guard took them and brought them to the king of Babylon at Riblah. [27]The king of Babylon struck them and put them to death at Riblah in the land of Hamath. And Judah went away from its land into exile.

[28]This is the number of people whom Nebuchadnezzar deported: In the seventh year, 3,023 Judeans. [29]In the eighteenth year of Nebuchadnezzar, he took 832 people from Jerusalem. [30]In the twenty-third year of Nebuchadnezzar, he dispatched Nebuzaradan commander of the guard, who deported 745 Judeans. Altogether, 4,600 were taken captive.

[31]Judah's King Jehoiachin had been in exile for thirty-seven years when Awil-merodach[g] became king in Babylon. He took note of Jehoiachin's plight and released him from prison on the twenty-fifth day of the twelfth month[h] of that very year. [32]Awil-merodach treated Jehoiachin kindly and gave him a throne higher than those of the other kings with him in Babylon. [33]So Jehoiachin discarded his prison clothes and ate his meals at the king's table for the rest of his life. [34]The Babylonian king provided him daily provisions for the rest of his life, right up until he died.

[f]Or *from the people of the land* [g]Or *Evil-merodach* [h]February–March, Adar

LAMENTATIONS

The book of Lamentations is a series of five poems that mourn the ruin of Jerusalem and the suffering of her people. These poems were written in response to the destruction of the city by the Babylonians in 587 BCE. Hundreds of people, including the king and his court, were either killed or forcibly deported to Babylon. Details of the siege and its aftermath are found in the books of Jeremiah and 2 Kings. The book of Lamentations records the emotional, psychological, and religious impact of this loss on the people of Israel.

The five poems express the people's grief and sorrow and their horror at what happened to them and to their homeland. The poems also acknowledge God as the power behind Israel's downfall. They ask, What is the meaning of this tragedy?

THE AUTHOR OF LAMENTATIONS

Both Jewish and Christian tradition at one time named Jeremiah as this author. This view was, in part, based on 2 Chronicles 35:25. However, the general view today is that Chronicles refers to laments Jeremiah wrote that are not in the book of Lamentations. We do not know the name of the author (or authors) of Lamentations.

The events described in Lamentations are seen from the perspective of someone living in Judah between 587 and 538 BCE, when the exiles were given permission to return to Judah. These were harsh years for Judah, a time of economic hardship and spiritual reassessment. The people struggled to feed themselves and to come to terms with what had happened to them. The poems of Lamentations were composed over a period of years during this time.

All the poems were probably written or adapted for use in public worship services on days of fasting and mourning. In particular, these poems would have been used at the annual service held in remembrance of Jerusalem's destruction. An editor (who may or may not have been the author) collected the poems and put them in order. Perhaps these laments were once part of a larger collection of worship materials.

THE FORM OF THE POEMS

The five poems in Lamentations are laments, as the title suggests. Such poems are common in the Old Testament, since one-third of the Old Testament is poetry. Psalms, Proverbs, Song of Songs, Lamentations, Obadiah, Micah, Nahum, Habakkuk, and Zephaniah are almost entirely poetry. The greater parts of Job, Isaiah, Hosea, Joel, and Amos are poetry, and Jeremiah is about one-half poetry.

Four of the five laments (chapters 1-4) are acrostic poems. In an acrostic poem, each of the twenty-two letters of the Hebrew alphabet appears in order at the beginning of each line or stanza. In English, we would compose an acrostic poem with the first line beginning with A, the second with B, the third with C, and so on. Such a form helps someone in memorizing a poem. This form also helps its writer express the completeness of grief and despair or of hope and faith. It lets the poet express "everything from A to Z," so to speak. Lamentations 5 is not an acrostic poem, but it does have twenty-two lines.

Laments express the sorrow or despair of individuals (for example, Jeremiah 11:18–12:6) and of whole communities (for example, Lamentations 5). Sometimes a community is personified as an individual (for example, Lamentations 1:18-19). Having one voice speak for the community expresses the tragedy on a personal level for each member of that community.

Laments are written in response to a disaster or the threat of a disaster. They usually have these parts:

(1) The situation of the lamenter is described.

(2) Sin is confessed.

(3) God is called on to act on behalf of the lamenter.

(4) Faith in God is affirmed.

(5) God is praised.

Funeral laments, often accompanied by music, are composed for the dead (see for example, 2 Samuel 1:18-27). The dead are eulogized, their passing is mourned, or, in the case of an enemy, a death is celebrated. Funeral laments also offer consolation to those who are grieving. The poems of lamentations mourn for the people of Israel individually and as a community.

LAMENTATIONS IN THE CHURCH

By the end of the second century BCE, Lamentations was included in the part of the Hebrew Scripture known as the Writings. After its inclusion in the Hebrew Bible, it became part of the Christian Old Testament.

Because the poems of Lamentations are regarded as sacred scripture by both Christians and Jews, the poems became more than a defeated community's remembrance and reflection. The poems provide expressions of sorrow that have been and will be used by other mourners and others who are reflecting on how God relates to what happens in this world.

In Jewish tradition and practice, Lamentations is read during the public mourning in the Hebrew month of Ab (July/August). This mourning commemorates the fall of Jerusalem in 587 BCE.

In Christian congregations, Lamentations is traditionally read during Holy Week to reflect on the sufferings of Jesus before his crucifixion.

LAMENTATIONS[a]

Jerusalem's suffering

א 1 Oh, no!
She sits alone,
  the city that was once full of people.
Once great among nations,
  she has become like a widow.
Once a queen over provinces,
  she has become a slave.

ב 2 She weeps bitterly in the night,
  her tears on her cheek.
None of her lovers comfort her.
  All her friends lied to her;
they have become her enemies.

ג 3 Judah was exiled after suffering
  and hard service.
She lives among the nations;
  she finds no rest.
All who were chasing her caught her—
  right in the middle of her distress.

ד 4 Zion's roads are in mourning;
  no one comes to the festivals.
All her gates are deserted.
  Her priests are groaning,
her young women grieving. She is bitter.

ה 5 Her adversaries have become rulers;
  her enemies relax.
Certainly the LORD caused her grief
  because of her many wrong acts.
Her children have gone away,
  captive before the enemy.

ו 6 Daughter Zion lost all her glory.
Her officials are like deer
  that can't find pasture.
They have gone away, frail,
  before the hunter.

ז 7 While suffering and homeless,
  Jerusalem remembers all her treasures
  from days long past.

When her people fell by the enemy's hand,
  there was no one to help her.
Enemies saw her, laughed at her defeat.

ח 8 Jerusalem has sinned greatly;
  therefore, she's become a joke.[b]
All who honored her now detest her,
  for they've seen her naked.
Even she groans and turns away.

ט 9 Her uncleanness shows on her clothing;
  she didn't consider
  what would happen to her.
She's gone down shockingly;
  she has no comforter.
"LORD, look at my suffering—
  the enemy has definitely triumphed!"

י 10 The enemy grabbed all her treasures.
She watched nations
  enter her sanctuary—
nations that you, God,[c] commanded:
  They must not enter your assembly.

כ 11 All her people are groaning,
  seeking bread.
They give up their most precious things
  for food to survive.
"LORD, look and take notice:
  I am most certainly despised."

ל 12 Is this nothing to all you who pass by?[d]
Look around: Is there any suffering like
  the suffering inflicted on me,
the grief that the LORD caused
  on the day of his fierce anger?

מ 13 From above he sent fire into my bones;
  he trampled them.
He spread a net for my feet;
  he forced me backward.
He left me devastated, constantly sick.

נ 14 My steps[e] are being watched;[f]
  by his hand they are tripped up.

---

[a]Four of the five chaps of Lamentations are alphabetically structured (acrostic) poems. Each verse in chaps 1, 2, and 4 begins with a consecutive letter of the Hebrew alphabet. Chap 3 is a triple acrostic: three verses in a row use the same letter before moving to the next letter. The acrostic form is not used in chap 5, though it does contain twenty-two verses, the same number as chaps 1, 2, and 4. [b]Or *she's become unclean.* [c]Heb lacks *God.* [d]Heb uncertain [e]Correction; or *my wrong acts* [f]Or *a yoke is bound to my wrong acts*; Heb uncertain

His yoke is on my neck;
  he makes my strength fail.
My Lord has handed me over
  to people I can't resist.

ס ¹⁵ My Lord has despised
  my mighty warriors.
He called a feast for me—
  in order to crush my young men!
My Lord has stomped on the winepress
  of the young woman Daughter Judah.

ע ¹⁶ Because of all these things I'm crying.
  My eyes, my own eyes pour water
because a comforter who might
  encourage me is nowhere near.
My children are destroyed because the
  enemy was so strong.

פ ¹⁷ Zion spreads out her hands;
  she has no comforter.
The LORD commanded Jacob's enemies
  to surround him.
Jerusalem is just a piece of garbage
  to them.

צ ¹⁸ The LORD is right,
  because I disobeyed his word.
Listen, all you people;
  look at my suffering.
My young women and young men
  have gone away as prisoners.

ק ¹⁹ I called to my lovers,
  but they deceived me.
My priests and my elders
  have perished in the city;
they were looking for food to survive.

ר ²⁰ Pay attention, LORD, for I am in trouble.
  My stomach is churning;
my heart is pounding inside me
  because I am so bitter.
In the streets the sword kills;
  in the house it is like death.

ש ²¹ People heard that I was groaning,
  that I had no comforter.
All my enemies heard about my distress;

they were thrilled
  that you had done this.
Bring the day you have announced
  so they become like me!

ת ²² Let all their evil come before you.
  Then injure them like you've injured me
  because of all my wrong acts;
my groans are many, my heart is sick.

God's anger toward Jerusalem

2 Oh, no!
  In anger, my Lord put Daughter Zion
א   under a cloud;ᵍ
  he threw Israel's glory from heaven
    down to earth.
  On that day of wrath,
    he didn't consider his own footstool.

ב ² Showing no compassion, my Lord
  devoured each of Jacob's meadows;
in his wrath he tore down the walled cities
  of Daughter Judah.
The kingdom and its officials,
  he forced to the ground, shamed.

ג ³ In his burning rage,
  he cut off each of Israel's horns;
right in front of the enemy,
  he withdrew his strong hand;
he burned against Jacob
  like a flaming fire that ate up everything
    nearby.

ד ⁴ He bent his bow as an enemy would;
  his strong hand was poised
    like an adversary.
He killed every precious thing in sight;
  he poured out his wrath
    like fire on Daughter Zion's tent.

ה ⁵ My Lord has become like an enemy.
  He devoured Israel;
he devoured all her palaces;
  he made ruins of her city walls.
In Daughter Judah
  he multiplied mourning
    along with more mourning!

ᵍHeb uncertain

ו ⁶ He wrecked his own booth like a garden;
he destroyed his place for festivals.
The LORD made Zion forget
both festival and sabbath;
in his fierce rage, he scorned
both monarch and priest.

ז ⁷ My Lord rejected his altar,
he abandoned his sanctuary;
he handed Zion's palace walls
over to enemies.
They shouted in the LORD's own house
as if it were a festival day.

ח ⁸ The LORD planned to destroy
Daughter Zion's wall.
He stretched out a measuring line,
didn't stop himself from devouring.
He made barricades and walls wither—
together they wasted away.

ט ⁹ Zion's gates sank into the ground;
he broke and shattered her bars;
her king and her officials are now
among the nations.
There is no Instruction!^h
Even her prophets couldn't find
a vision from the LORD.

י ¹⁰ Daughter Zion's elders
sit on the ground and mourn.
They throw dust on their heads;
they put on mourning clothes.
Jerusalem's young women bow
their heads all the way to the ground.

כ ¹¹ My eyes are worn out from weeping;
my stomach is churning.
My insides are poured on the ground
because the daughter of my people
is shattered,
because children and babies
are fainting in the city streets.

ל ¹² They say to their mothers,
"Where are grain and wine?"
while fainting like the wounded
in the city streets,

while their lives are draining away
at their own mothers' breasts.

מ ¹³ What can I testify about you,
Daughter Jerusalem?ⁱ
To what could I compare you?
With what could I equate you?
How can I comfort you,
young woman Daughter Zion?
Your hurt is as vast as the sea.
Who can heal you?

נ ¹⁴ Your prophets gave you worthless
and empty visions.
They didn't reveal your sin
so as to prevent your captivity.
Instead, they showed you
worthless and incorrect prophecies.

ס ¹⁵ All who pass by on the road
clap their hands about you;
they whistle, shaking their heads
at Daughter Jerusalem:
"Could this be the city called Perfect
Beauty, the Joy of All the Earth?"

פ ¹⁶ All your enemies open wide their mouths
against you;
they whistle, grinding their teeth.
They say, "We have devoured!
This is definitely the day
we've been waiting for.
We've seen it come to pass."

ע ¹⁷ The LORD did what he had planned.
He accomplished the word
that he had commanded long ago.
He ripped down,
showing no compassion.
He made the enemy rejoice over you;
he raised up your adversaries' horn.

צ ¹⁸ Cry out to my Lord from the heart,^j
you wall of Daughter Zion;
make your^k tears run down like a flood
all day and night.
Don't relax at all;
don't rest your eyes a moment.

^hHeb *Torah* ⁱOr *How can I warn you?* or *To what could I liken you?*; Heb uncertain ^jCorrection; or *their heart cried out to my Lord* ^kHeb lacks *your*.

ק ¹⁹ Get up and cry out at nighttime,
    at the start of the night shift;
    pour out your heart
    before my Lord like water.
Lift your hands up to him
    for the life of your children—
the ones who are fainting from hunger
    on every street corner.

ר ²⁰ LORD, look and see to whom
    you have done this!
Should women eat their own offspring,
    their own beautiful babies?
Should priest and prophet be killed
    in my Lord's own sanctuary?

ש ²¹ Young and old alike
    lie on the ground in the streets;

my young women and young men
    fall dead by the sword.
On the day of your anger, you killed;
    you slaughtered,
    showing no compassion.

ת ²² You invited—as if to a festival!—
    terrors[l] from every side.
On the day of the LORD's anger,
    no one escaped, not one survived.
The children that I nurtured,
    that I raised myself,
    my enemy finished them off.

An individual's complaint

3 I am someone[m] who saw
    the suffering caused
    by God's[n] angry rod.

---

[l]Correction; or *my attackers*   [m]Or *the man*; also in 3:27, 35, 39   [n]Or *his*

ZION

In both the OT and the NT, the term *Zion* is used in various ways: as a name for the city of Jerusalem or occasionally Judah, as a name for a particular part of Jerusalem, as a name for the inhabitants of the city, and as the name of the entire people of God.

Most often in the Bible, the term *Zion* refers to the city of Jerusalem and its environs or part of the city or to the country of which the city is capital. In both the OT and the NT, Zion is always used as a proper name. In the OT, Zion is used over 150 times, often with an addition or parallel (Daughter Zion, Mount Zion, Zion = Jerusalem). More than half of its occurrences can be found in the books of Isaiah and Psalms.

Zion is frequently used as a description of the place of the Lord's seat or throne. Zion is where Israelites go to worship or praise God. The temple itself is referred to as Zion, and that is where the Lord lives and is enthroned (Ps 9). In expansion of its geographical usage, Zion often refers to the entire city of Jerusalem.

In the NT, *Zion* is used seven times—five times in relation to texts from the OT. Matthew 21:5 and John 12:15 (cf. Isa 62:11; Zech 9:9) refer to Daughter Zion. Romans 9:33 (Isa 8:14-15; 28:16) and 1 Peter 2:6 (Isa 28:16) refer to a stone in Zion. Romans 11:26 (Ps 14:7; Isa 59:20) refers to salvation coming from Zion. The two remaining occurrences are found in Hebrews 12:22, which refers to "Mount Zion, the city of the living God"; and Revelation 14:1, which depicts the Lamb standing on Mount Zion. In Revelation, Mount Zion becomes the place of eschatological preservation.

א ² He drove me away, forced me to walk
   in darkness, not light.
³ He turned his hand even against me,
   over and over again, all day long.

ב ⁴ He wore out my flesh and my skin;
   he broke my bones.
⁵ He besieged me, surrounding me
   with bitterness and weariness.
⁶ He made me live in dark places
   like those who've been dead
   a long time.

ג ⁷ He walled me in so I couldn't escape;
   he made my chains heavy.
⁸ Even though I call out and cry for help,
   he silences my prayer.
⁹ He walled in my paths with stonework;
   he made my routes crooked.

ד ¹⁰ He is a bear lurking for me,
   a lion in hiding.
¹¹ He took me from my path°
   and tore me apart;
   he made me desolate.
¹² He drew back his bow, made me
   a shooting target for arrows.

ה ¹³ He shot the arrows of his quiver
   into my inside parts.
¹⁴ I have become a joke to all my people,
   the object of their song of ridicule
   all day long.
¹⁵ He saturated me with grief,
   made me choke on bitterness.

ו ¹⁶ He crushed my teeth into the gravel;
   he pressed me down into the ashes.
¹⁷ I'veᴾ rejected peace;
   I've forgotten what is good.
¹⁸ I thought: My future is gone,
   as well as my hope from the LORD.

ז ¹⁹ The memory of my suffering and
   homelessness is bitterness and poison.
²⁰ I�q can't help but remember
   and am depressed.

²¹ I call all this to mind—
   therefore, I will wait.

ח ²² Certainly the faithful love
   of the LORD hasn't ended;ʳ
   certainly God's compassion isn't through!
²³ They are renewed every morning.
   Great is your faithfulness.
²⁴ I think:ˢ The LORD is my portion!
   Therefore, I'll wait for him.

ט ²⁵ The LORD is good to those who hope in
   him, to the personᵗ who seeks him.
²⁶ It's good to wait in silence
   for the LORD's deliverance.
²⁷ It's good for a man to carry a yoke
   in his youth.
²⁸ He should sit alone and be silent
   when God lays it on him.
²⁹ He should put his mouth in the dirt—
   perhaps there is hope.
³⁰ He should offer his cheek for a blow;
   he should be filled with shame.

כ ³¹ My Lord definitelyᵘ won't reject forever.
³² Although he has caused grief,
   he will show compassion in measure
   with his covenant loyalty.
³³ He definitely doesn't enjoy affliction,ᵛ
   making humans suffer.

ל ³⁴ Now crushing underfoot
   all the earth's prisoners,
³⁵ denying someone justice
   before the Most High,
³⁶ subverting a person's lawsuit—
   doesn't my Lord see all this?

מ ³⁷ Who ever spoke and it happened if my
   Lord hadn't commanded the same?
³⁸ From the mouth of the Most High
   evil things don't come,
   but rather good!
³⁹ Why then
   does any living person complain;
   why should anyone complain
   about their sins?

°Heb uncertain ᴾOr my spirit; also in 3:20, 24, 25, 51, 58   qOr My spirit can't help but remember and is depressed
ʳTg, Syr, and other ancient sources; MT we aren't finished. ˢOr My spirit thinks ᵗOr spirit ᵘOr Because my Lord
won't reject forever ᵛHeb He does not afflict from his heart.

נ ⁴⁰ We must search and examine our ways;
we must return to the LORD.
⁴¹ We should lift up our hearts and hands
to God in heaven.
⁴² We are the ones who did wrong;
we rebelled.
But you, God, have not forgiven.

ס ⁴³ You wrapped yourself up in wrath
and hunted us;
you killed, showing no compassion.
⁴⁴ You wrapped yourself up in a cloud;
prayers can't make it through!
⁴⁵ You made us trash and garbage
in front of all other people.

פ ⁴⁶ All our enemies have opened
their mouths against us.
⁴⁷ Terror and trap have come upon us,
catastrophe and collapse!
⁴⁸ Streams of water pour from my eyes
because of the destruction of the
daughter of my people.

ע ⁴⁹ My eyes flow and don't stop.
There is no relief
⁵⁰ until the LORD looks down
from the heavens and notices.
⁵¹ My eyes hurt me[w] because of what's
happened to my city's daughters.

צ ⁵² My enemies hunted me down like a bird,
relentlessly, for no reason.
⁵³ They caught me alive in a pit
and threw stones at me;
⁵⁴ water flowed over my head.
I thought: I'm finished.

ק ⁵⁵ I call on your name, LORD,
from the depths of the pit.
⁵⁶ Hear my voice. Don't close your ear[x]
to my need for relief,
to my cry for help.[y]
⁵⁷ Come near to me on the day I call to you.
Say to me, "Don't be afraid."

ר ⁵⁸ My Lord! Plead my desperate case;[z]
redeem my life.

⁵⁹ LORD, look at my mistreatment;
judge my cause.
⁶⁰ Look at all of my enemies' vengeance,
all of their scheming against me.

ש ⁶¹ Hear their jeering, LORD,
all of their scheming against me,
⁶² the speech of those
who rise up against me,
their incessant gossiping about me.
⁶³ Whether sitting or standing,
look at how I am the object
of their song of ridicule.

ת ⁶⁴ Pay them back fully, LORD,
according to what they have done.
⁶⁵ Give them a tortured mind—
put your curse on them!
⁶⁶ Angrily hunt them down; wipe them out
from under the LORD's heaven.

The people's suffering

4 Oh, no!
Gold is tarnished;[a]
א   even the purest gold is changed.
Sacred jewels are scattered
on every street corner.

ב ² Zion's precious children,
once valued as pure gold—
oh no!—now they are worth no more
than clay pots made by a potter.

ג ³ Even jackals offer the breast;
they nurse their young.
But the daughter of my people
has become cruel,
like desert ostriches.

ד ⁴ The baby's tongue sticks to the roof
of its mouth, thirsty.
Children ask for bread, beg for it—
but there is no bread.

ה ⁵ Those who once ate gourmet food
now tremble in the streets.
Those who wore
the finest purple clothes
now cling to piles of garbage.

ו ⁶ Greater was the punishment[b]
   of the daughter of my people
   than Sodom's penalty,[c]
   which was quickly overthrown
   without any hand-wringing.[d]

ז ⁷ Her nazirites were purer than snow;
   they were more dazzling than milk.
   Their limbs were redder than coral;
   their bodies were sapphire.

ח ⁸ But their appearance grew darker
      than soot;
   they weren't recognized in the streets.
   Their skin shriveled on their bones;
   it became dry like wood.

ט ⁹ Things were better for those stabbed
      by the sword
   than for those stabbed by famine—
   those who bled away, pierced,
   lacking food from the field.

י ¹⁰ The hands of loving women
    boiled their own children

to become their food during
   the destruction of the daughter of
   my people.

כ ¹¹ The LORD let loose his fury;
   he poured out his fierce anger.
   He started a fire in Zion;
   it licked up its foundations.

ל ¹² The earth's rulers didn't believe it—
   neither did any who inhabit the world—
   that either enemy or adversary
   could enter Jerusalem's gates.

מ ¹³ It was because of her prophets' sins,
   her priests' iniquities,
   those who shed righteous blood
   in the middle of the city.

נ ¹⁴ People wandered blindly in the streets,
   polluted with blood.
   No one would even touch their clothing.

ס ¹⁵ "Go away! Unclean!" was shouted at them,
   "Go away! Away! Don't touch!"

[b]Or *iniquity* [c]Or *sin* [d]Heb uncertain

PURPLE

In the ancient world, purple goods were typically made with a dye extracted from sea snails. Because of the difficult and lengthy production process, purple dye was very expensive, making purple cloth a luxury item. In the OT, the manufacture of purple textiles is often associated with Phoenicia in general and the city of Tyre in particular (2 Chron 2:14; Ezek 27:16). As a status symbol, purple cloth was often connected with royalty (Judg 8:26; Esth 1:6; Song 3:10) and honor (Esth 8:15; Dan 5:16, 29). It is high praise to say that the wife in Proverbs 31:21-22 can provide such goods to her family.

Purple is also associated with luxury and royalty in the NT. When the Roman soldiers mock Jesus as a king, they place a purple robe on him (Mark 15:17, 20; John 19:2, 5). In the parable of the rich man and Lazarus, the wealth of the rich man is illustrated by his purple robes (Luke 16:19). In Revelation, the woman representing Rome is dressed in purple and scarlet (Rev 17:4; 18:16), but after her destruction the merchants mourn because Rome is no longer able to buy imported goods, such as purple cloth (Rev 18:11-12). Paul's first convert in Europe is Lydia, "a dealer in purple cloth" (Acts 16:14). This suggests that she was a person of some wealth, which is consistent with the fact that she may have hosted a church in her house (Acts 16:40).

So they fled and wandered around.
The nations said,
"They can't stay here anymore."

ב ¹⁶ It was the LORD's presence
that scattered them;[e]
he no longer notices them.
They didn't honor the priests' presence;
they didn't favor the elders.

ע ¹⁷ Our eyes continually failed,
looking for some help,
but for nothing.

[e]Heb uncertain

From our watchtower we watched
for a nation that doesn't save.

צ ¹⁸ Our steps were tracked;
we could no longer walk in our streets.
Our end had drawn near;
our days were done—
our end had definitely come.

ק ¹⁹ Our hunters were faster
than airborne eagles.
They chased us up the mountains;
they ambushed us in the wilderness.

DANCING

Dancing and music form important elements of Israelite religious worship. Both singers and dancers praise God (Ps 87:7). As well, dance includes musical accompaniment (Pss 149:3; 150:4). For example, David's procession to bring the covenant chest of God to Jerusalem includes singing, dancing, and music (2 Sam 6; 1 Chron 15). As part of this procession, David wears a linen vest and dances "with all his strength before the LORD" (2 Sam 6:14). David's wife Michal admonishes him for what she perceives as shameless behavior, but he rebukes her (2 Sam 6:20-22).

Dance may be employed in idolatrous worship. For instance, Joshua hears what he assumes is the noise of warfare when he and Moses return from Mount Sinai. Instead, he and Moses find the Israelites singing and dancing as they worship the gold calf (Exod 32:17-19). Also, in a contest at Mount Carmel, Elijah makes fun of the prophets of Baal who limp about the altar as they pray to Baal to answer them (1 Kgs 18:21, 26).

Dancing is the opposite of mourning. For example, Ecclesiastes contrasts weeping and mourning with laughing and dancing (Eccl 3:4). In a psalm of thanksgiving, the psalmist exclaims, "You changed my mourning into dancing" (Ps 30:11 [Heb. 30:12]). Conversely, in a communal lament the people ask the Lord to remember the calamities that have befallen them and complain, "Our dancing has changed into lamentation" (Lam 5:15).

Instances of dancing in the NT do not involve religious worship. Yet, as in the OT, dancing involves rejoicing and festivity. For instance, in the parable of the prodigal son, as the elder son approaches home, he hears singing and dancing in celebration of the younger son's return (Luke 15:25). Also, at the birthday party of Herod Antipas, his stepdaughter, the daughter of Herodias, dances for him and his guests (Matt 14:6; Mark 6:22). Her performance leads to a rash vow by Herod and the beheading of John the Baptist (Matt 14:6-11; Mark 6:22-28).

ר ²⁰ The LORD's chosen one,
  the very breath in our lungs,
  was caught in their traps—
  the one we used to talk about, saying,
  Under his protection we will live
  among the nations."

ש ²¹ Rejoice and be happy, Daughter Edom,
  you who live in the land of Uz.
  But this cup will pass over to you too.
  You will get drunk on it.
  You will be stripped naked.

ת ²² Your punishmentᶠ is over, Daughter Zion;
  God won't expose you anymore.
  But he will attend to your punishment,
  Daughter Edom; he will expose your sins.

The people's complaint

5 LORD, consider what has become of us;
  take notice of our disgrace.
  Look at it!
² Our property has been turned
  over to strangers;
   our houses belong to foreigners.
³ We have become orphans,
  having no father;
  our mothers are like widows.
⁴ We drink our own water—
  but for a price;
  we gather our own wood—
  but pay for it.
⁵ Our hunters have been at our necks;ᵍ
  we are worn out, but have no rest.
⁶ We held out a hand to Egypt
  and to Assyria, to get sufficient food.
⁷ Our fathers have sinned
  and are gone,
  but we are burdened
  with their iniquities.

⁸ Slaves rule over us;
  there is no one to rescue us
  from their power.
⁹ We get our bread at the risk of our lives
  because of the desert heat.ʰ
¹⁰ Our skin is as hot as an oven
  because of the burning heat of famine.
¹¹ Women have been raped in Zion,
  young women in Judah's cities.
¹² Officials have been hung up
  by their hands;
  elders have been shown no respect.
¹³ Young men have carried grinding stones;
  boys have stumbled
  under loads of wood.
¹⁴ Elders have left the city gate;
  young people stop their music.
¹⁵ Joy has left our heart;
  our dancing has changed
  into lamentation.
¹⁶ The crown has fallen off our head.
  We are doomed
  because we have sinned.
¹⁷ Because of all this our heart is sick;
  because of these things
  our glance is dark.
¹⁸ Mount Zion, now deserted—
  only jackals walk on it now!
¹⁹ But you, LORD, will rule forever;
  your throne lasts from one generation
  to the next.
²⁰ Why do you forget us continually;
  why do you abandon us
  for such a long time?
²¹ Return us, LORD, to yourself.
  Please let us return!ⁱ
  Give us new days,
  like those long ago—
²² unless you have completely rejected us,
  or have become too angry with us.ʲ

ᶠOr *iniquity* ᵍHeb uncertain ʰOr *sword;* Heb uncertain ⁱOr *and we will return* or *so that we can return* ʲOr *But instead you have completely rejected us, become too angry with us,* or *Because if you have completely rejected us, have become too angry with us.*

EZEKIEL

Ezekiel was a prophet of Israel whose ministry and words are recorded in the book that bears his name. His call to prophesy came in 593 BCE when he was living in exile in Babylonia. He fulfilled his prophetic duties in exile and probably never returned to his homeland.

The events of 598 BCE, when King Jehoiachin was deposed and deported by Nebuchadnezzar, had thrown Israel into a crisis that was both political and spiritual. With their humiliation and defeat at the hands of the Babylonians the people of Israel began to question God's power to control events in history. They also questioned God's faithfulness to the promises made to Israel in the past.

Ezekiel dealt with these disturbing questions. His prophecies answered these questions according to God's power, justice, and mercy. Ezekiel's prophecy showed the people of Israel how to understand what had happened to them and how to find their way into the future as God's chosen people.

EZEKIEL THE BOOK

The book of Ezekiel is a collection of prophetic speeches and vision reports. Ezekiel's speeches (also called oracles) are announcements (through the prophet) of God's word for Israel. Ezekiel announces judgment and punishment for Israel's sins. He also announces God's promises of restoration and salvation for the people.

The collection of Ezekiel's prophecies may be divided into three major sections. Chapters 1–24 are mainly announcements of judgment against Jerusalem from 593 BCE (the time of Ezekiel's call to prophecy) to 587 BCE (the destruction of Jerusalem). Chapters 25–32 announce judgment against foreign nations from approximately 587–585 BCE (except 29:17-21, from 571 BCE). Chapters 33–48 are prophecies about the future restoration of Israel, which come after 587 BCE.

Ezekiel's prophecies were collected and preserved, either orally or in writing. This was probably first done by Ezekiel himself and a group of his followers. This collection was eventually organized and edited into the form we know today.

EZEKIEL THE MAN

Ezekiel was born into a priestly family and may have been trained for the priesthood. He was probably taken from Jerusalem to Babylon in 598 BCE along with other temple priests. We do not know how old he was at the time, but he may have been a young adult. As far as we know he spent the rest of his life in Babylonia.

Once in Babylon, Ezekiel settled with other exiles in a village away from the capital and lived in humble circumstances. His wife went with him into exile. She died in Babylonia, leaving Ezekiel numb and speechless with grief.

The spectacular vision in which Ezekiel was called to prophesy (see Ezekiel 1:1–3:15) reflects the strength and turbulence of his prophetic ministry. The power and thunder of God's might echo in Ezekiel's life and words. Ezekiel showed self-discipline and strong emotion as he fulfilled the duties God set before him. He was stern and passionate in his commitment to proclaim and to act out God's word for Israel.

Ezekiel suffered misunderstanding and sometimes outright hostility for the message he brought. His actions at times may have seemed bizarre to his fellow exiles. Even his wife's death and the great loss he felt were used by God as part of his message. He shared physically and emotionally in the despair and hardship of exiled Israelites.

Ezekiel was more than just a "fellow sufferer," however. His message about Israel's sin and its consequences helped the people of Israel make sense out of what had happened to them. Ezekiel provided answers to the inevitable questions of "Why?" and "Where do we go from here?"

EZEKIEL

First vision

¶ In the thirtieth year, on the fifth day of the fourth month, I was with the exiles at the Chebar River when the heavens opened and I saw visions of God. ²(It happened on the fifth day of the month, in the fifth year after King Jehoiachin's deportation. ³The LORD's word burst in on the priest Ezekiel, Buzi's son, in the land of Babylon at the Chebar River. There the LORD's power overcame him.)

⁴As I watched, suddenly a driving storm came out of the north, a great cloud flashing fire, with brightness all around. At its center, in the middle of the fire, there was something like gleaming amber. ⁵And inside that were forms of four living creatures. This was what they looked like: Each had the form of a human being, ⁶though each had four faces and four wings. ⁷Their feet looked like proper feet, but the soles of their feet were like calves' hooves, and they shone like burnished bronze. ⁸Human hands were under their wings on all four sides. All four creatures had faces and wings, and ⁹their wings touched each other's wings. When they moved, they each went straight ahead without turning. ¹⁰As for the form of their faces: each of the four had a human face, with a lion's face on the right and a bull's face on the left, and also an eagle's face. ¹¹The pairs of wingsᵃ that stretched out overhead touched each other, while the other pairs covered their bodies. ¹²Each moved straight ahead wherever the wind propelled them; they moved without turning. ¹³Regarding the creatures' forms: they looked like blazing coals, like torches. Fire darted about between the creatures and illuminated them, and lightning flashed from the fire. ¹⁴The creatures looked like lightning streaking back and forth.

¹⁵As I looked at the creatures, suddenly there was a wheel on the earth corresponding to all four faces of the creatures. ¹⁶The appearance and composition of the wheels were like sparkling topaz. There was one shape for all four of them, as if one wheel were inside another. ¹⁷When they moved in any of the four directions, they moved without swerving. ¹⁸Their rims were tall and terrifying, because all four of them were filled with eyes all around. ¹⁹When the creatures moved, the wheels moved next to them. Whenever the creatures rose above the earth, the wheels also rose up. ²⁰Wherever the wind would appear to go, the wind would make them go there too. The wheels rose up beside them, because the spiritᵇ of the creatures was in the wheels. ²¹When they moved, the wheelsᶜ moved; when they stood still, the wheels stood still; and when they rose above the earth, the wheels rose up along with them, because the spiritᵈ of the creatures was in the wheels.

²²The shape above the heads of the creaturesᵉ was a dome; it was like glittering ice stretched out over their heads. ²³Just below the dome, their outstretched wings touched each other. They each also had two wings to cover their bodies. ²⁴Then I heard the sound of their wings when they moved forward. It was like the sound of mighty waters, like the sound of the Almighty,ᶠ like the sound of tumult or the sound of an army camp. When they stood still, their wings came to rest. ²⁵Then there was a sound from above the dome over their heads. They stood still, and their wings came to rest.

²⁶Above the dome over their heads, there appeared something like lapis lazuli in the form of a throne. Above the form of the throne there was a form that looked like a human being. ²⁷Above what looked like his waist, I saw something like gleaming amber, something like fire enclosing it all around. Below what looked like his waist, I saw something that appeared to be fire. Its brightness shone all around. ²⁸Just as a rainbow lights up a cloud on a rainy day, so its brightness shone all around. This was how the form of the LORD's glory appeared. When I saw it, I fell on my face. I heard the sound of someone speaking.

ᵃLXX; MT adds *and their faces.* ᵇOr *wind* ᶜOr *they* ᵈOr *wind* ᵉLXX; MT *creature* ᶠHeb *Shaddai* or *Mountain One*

Ezekiel's commissioning

2 The voice said to me: Human one, stand on your feet, and I'll speak to you. [2]As he spoke to me, a wind[g] came to me and stood me on my feet, and I heard someone addressing me. [3]He said to me: Human one, I'm sending you to the Israelites, a traitorous and rebellious people. They and their ancestors have been rebelling against me to this very day. [4]I'm sending you to their hardheaded and hard-hearted descendants, and you will say to them: The LORD God proclaims. [5]Whether they listen or whether they refuse, since they are a household of rebels, they will know that a prophet has been among them.

[6]And as for you, human one, don't be afraid of them or their words. Don't be

[g]Or *spirit*

VISION

A mystical revelatory experience involving a visual dimension. The OT describes both waking visions and night visions. Visions often include auditory components and are usually, but not always, associated with prophetic activity or apocalyptic revelation. Visions occur throughout the OT, though in the NT most are clustered in Acts and Revelation.

Various Hebrew and Greek words translated "vision" encompass a range of meanings and literary forms. God establishes the covenant with Abraham through a vision that includes both a conversation and a dream (Gen 15:1-21). In a night vision Daniel receives the interpretation of Nebuchadnezzar's dream (2:17-45). The Hebrew word can serve as a generic introduction to prophetic books (Isa 1:1; Obad 1; Nah 1:1) or units (2 Sam 7:17; 1 Chron 17:15; Ezek 7:13; Hab 2:2-3), even as it applies to visions generally (e.g., 1 Sam 3:1; Ps 89:19; Lam 2:9; Hos 12:10). Visions may convey messages from God, introduce the seer to mysteries such as heavenly beings and places (1 Kgs 22:19-23; Isa 6; Ezek 40–48; Amos 9:1-10; Revelation includes visions of the risen Jesus, the heavenly court, and the New Jerusalem), provide images that require interpretation (Ezek 1; Amos 7–8), or even require participation on the part of the visionary (Ezek 8:1-18; Rev 10:8-10). Some visions rely upon wordplay (Jer 1:11-12; Amos 8:1-3).

Visions are especially important in Acts. Peter's Pentecost sermon alludes to Joel's prophecy concerning visions and dreams in the last days (Joel 2:28-32 [Heb. 3:1-5]; Acts 2:17-21). Through a visionary encounter with the risen Jesus, Saul turns from one who harasses the church into its most prominent missionary to the Gentiles (Acts 9:1-9; 22:1-21; 26:2-23). A vision also convinces Peter to evangelize the Gentile Cornelius (10:9-16; 11:1-18). The effectiveness of these visions depends upon complementary visions received by Ananias (9:10-19) and Cornelius (10:1-8). Paul appeals to his visionary and apocalyptic experiences in defending his authority (2 Cor 12:1-10; Gal 1:11-17).

Among the Synoptic Gospels, Matthew alone describes Jesus' transformation as a vision (17:9). Both biblical apocalypses, Daniel and Revelation, narrate sequences of visions.

afraid! You possess thistles and thorns that subdue scorpions.[h] Don't be afraid of their words or shrink from their presence, because they are a household of rebels. [7]You'll speak my words to them whether they listen or whether they refuse. They are just a household[i] of rebels!

[8]As for you, human one, listen to what I say to you. Don't become rebellious like that household of rebels. Open your mouth and eat what I give you. [9]Then I looked, and there in a hand stretched out to me was a scroll. [10]He spread it open in front of me, and it was filled with writing on both sides, songs of mourning, lamentation, and doom.

3 Then he said to me: Human one, eat this thing that you've found. Eat this scroll and go, speak to the house of Israel. [2]So I opened my mouth, and he fed me the scroll. [3]He said to me: Human one, feed your belly and fill your stomach with this scroll that I give you. So I ate it, and in my mouth it became as sweet as honey.

[4]Then he said to me: Human one, go! Go to the house of Israel and speak my words to them. [5]You aren't being sent to a people whose language and speech are difficult and obscure but to the house of Israel. [6]No, not to many peoples who speak difficult and obscure languages, whose words you wouldn't understand. If I did send you to them, they would listen to you. [7]But the house of Israel—they will refuse to listen to you because they refuse to listen to me. The whole house of Israel is hardheaded and hard-hearted too. [8]I've now hardened your face so that you can meet them head-on. [9]I've made your forehead like a diamond, harder than stone. Don't be afraid of them or shrink away from them, because they are a household of rebels.

[10]He said to me: Human one, listen closely, and take to heart every word I say to you. [11]Then go to the exiles, to your people's children. Whether they listen or not, speak to them and say: The LORD God proclaims! [12]Then a wind lifted me up, and I heard behind me a great quaking sound from his place. Blessed is the LORD's glory! [13]The sound was the creatures' wings beating against each other and the sound of the wheels beside them; it was a great rumbling noise. [14]Then the wind picked me up and took me away. With the LORD's power pressing down against me I went away, bitter and deeply angry, [15]and I came to the exiles who lived beside the Chebar River at Tel-abib. I stayed there among them for seven desolate days.

[16]At the end of the seven days, the LORD's word came to me: [17]Human one, I've made you a lookout for the house of Israel. When you hear a word from me, deliver my warning. [18]If I declare that the wicked will die but you don't warn them, if you say nothing to warn them from their wicked ways so that they might live, they will die because of their guilt, but I will hold you accountable for their deaths. [19]If you do warn the wicked and they don't turn from their wickedness or their wicked ways, they will die because of their guilt, but you will save your life.

[20]Or suppose righteous people turn away from doing the right thing. If they act dishonestly, and I make them stumble because of it, they will die because you didn't warn them of their sin. Their righteous deeds won't be remembered, and I will hold you accountable for their deaths. [21]But if you do warn the righteous not to sin, and they don't sin, they will be declared righteous. Their lives will be preserved because they heeded the warning, and you will save your life.

[22]The LORD's power overcame me, and he said to me: Get up! Go out to the valley, and I'll speak to you there. [23]So I got up and went out to the valley. Suddenly, the LORD's glory stood there, like the glory that I had seen at the Chebar River, and I fell on my face. [24]When a wind came to me and stood me on my feet, he spoke to me and said: Go, shut yourself up inside your house. [25]Look at you, human one! They've now put cords on you and bound you up so that you can't go out among them. [26]I'll make your tongue stick to the roof of your mouth and take away your ability to speak.

---

[h]Or thistles and thorns are with you, and you sit on scorpions. [i]LXX, Syr, Tg; MT lacks household.

You won't be able to correct them, because they are a household of rebels. ²⁷But whenever I speak to you, I'll open your mouth, and you will say to them: The LORD God proclaims. Those who hear will understand, but those who refuse will not. They are just a household of rebels.

Jerusalem's siege

4 You, human one, take a brick. Put it in front of you and draw the city of Jerusalem on it. ²Prepare the siege: Build a wall, construct ramps, set up army camps, and place battering rams all around. ³Take an iron plate and set it up as an iron wall between you and the city. Face it directly. When it is under siege like this, press hard against it. This is a sign for the house of Israel.

⁴Now, lie on your left side, and set the guilt of the house of Israel on it. For the length of time that you lie on your side, you will bear their punishment. ⁵I appoint to you three hundred ninety days, one day for each year of their guilt. So you will bear the punishment of the house of Israel. ⁶When you have completed these days, lie on your right side to bear the guilt of the house of Judah. I appoint forty days to you, one day for each year. ⁷With your arm stretched out, face the siege of Jerusalem directly and prophesy against it. ⁸I've now bound you with cords so that you can't turn from one side to the other until you have completed the days of your siege.

⁹You, gather some wheat and barley, beans and lentils, and millet and spelt. Put them in a bowl and make your bread from them. Eat it during the three hundred ninety days that you lie on your side. ¹⁰At fixed times you will eat your food by weight, fourteen ounces a day.ʲ ¹¹You will also ration your water by measure, drinking a sixth of a hinᵏ at fixed times each day. ¹²Eat it like barley bread, and bake it on human excrement while they watch. ¹³The LORD says: In this same way the Israelites will eat their unclean bread among the nations where I am scattering them.

¹⁴And I said: "Ah, LORD God! I've never been unclean! From my childhood until now I've never eaten anything that wasn't properly slaughtered,ˡ and no unclean meat has ever entered my mouth!"

¹⁵He answered me: "Then I'll let you use cow dung instead of human excrement. You can make your bread over that."

¹⁶Then he said to me: Human one, I'm destroying the food supply in Jerusalem. They will anxiously ration and eat their food, and in dismay they will dole out and drink their water. ¹⁷When their food and water dwindles away, everyone will be horrified, and they will waste away because of their guilt.

5 You, human one, take a sharp sword. Use it like a razor and shave your head and beard. Then use scales to divide the hair. ²At the end of the siege, burn one-third of it in the city. Strike another third with the sword left and right. Then scatter one-third to the wind and let looseᵐ the sword after it. ³From that third, take a few strands and hide them in your garment. ⁴From that hair, take yet another batch and throw it into the fire and burn it up. From there, fire will spread to the whole house of Israel.

⁵The LORD God proclaims: This is Jerusalem! I have set her in the middle of the nations and surrounding countries. ⁶But she rebelled against my case laws and my regulations with greater treachery than these nations and surrounding countries, who also rejected my case laws and didn't follow my regulations. ⁷Therefore, the LORD God proclaims: You have become more turbulent than these nations around you because you haven't obeyed my regulations or followed my case laws. You haven't even followed the case laws of the nations around you! ⁸So now the LORD God proclaims: I myself am now against you! I will impose the case law penalties on you in the sight of the nations. ⁹Because of you, I will do what I've never done before and will never do again—all because of your

---

ʲOr twenty shekels ᵏA hin is approximately one pint. ˡOr what died of itself or was torn by wild beasts ᵐOr I will let loose detestable practices. [10]Therefore, parents among you will eat their children, and children will eat their parents. I will impose penalties from case laws on you and scatter all that is left of you to the winds. [11]Therefore, as surely as I live, this is what the LORD God says: Because you made my sanctuary unclean with all your disgusting practices and detestable things, I myself will shave you. I will not shed a tear. You will have no compassion, even from me. [12]One-third of you will die of plague and waste away by famine among you. One-third will fall by the sword all around you. And one-third I will scatter to all the winds, letting loose a sword to pursue them. [13]My anger will be complete. I will exhaust my wrath against them and take my revenge. Then they will know that I, the LORD, have spoken against them in my zeal and consumed them in my wrath. [14]I will turn you into a desolation to the ridicule of the nations all around you, in the sight of all who pass by. [15]You will become an object of ridicule, a mockery, and a horrifying lesson to the nations all around you, when I impose penalties from case laws against you in anger, wrath, and overflowing fury. I, the LORD, have spoken. [16]When I launch my deadly arrows of famine against you, I have released them for your destruction! I will add to your famine and completely cut off your food supply. [17]I will send famine and wild animals against you, and they will leave you childless. Plague and bloodshed will come to you, and I will bring the sword against you. I, the LORD, have spoken.

Against the mountains of Israel

6 The LORD's word came to me: [2]Human one, face Israel's mountains, and prophesy to them. [3]Say:

Hear the LORD God's word,
mountains of Israel!
The LORD God proclaims
to the mountains and hills,
to the valleys and their deepest ravines:
I'm about to bring a sword against you
and destroy your shrines.
[4]Your altars will be destroyed,
your incense altars broken.

And I'll make your slain
fall in front of your idols.
[5]I'll throw the Israelites' corpses
in front of their idols,
and I'll scatter your bones
all around your altars.
[6]Wherever you live,
cities will be in ruins,
shrines made desolate,
turned into utter ruin.
Your altars will be punished
and then broken down.
Your idols will be demolished,
your incense altars shattered,
and all your works wiped out.
[7]The slain will fall among you,
and you will know that I am the LORD.

[8]But I will spare a few.
Some of you will escape
the nations' swords
when you are scattered
throughout the lands.
[9]Your fugitives will remember me
in the nations
to which they've been banished,
how I was crushed
when their roving hearts
turned away from me,
and their roving eyes
went after their idols.
They will loathe themselves
for their treacherous acts
and detestable practices,
[10]and they will know that I am the LORD.
Not in vain have I threatened
to bring this evil against them.

[11]The LORD God proclaims: Clap your hands, stamp your feet, and cry "Horror" over all the detestable practices of the house of Israel. They will fall by the sword, famine, and plague. [12]Whoever is far off will die of plague, whoever is nearby will fall to the sword, and whoever finds refuge will die of famine. I'll satisfy my wrath against them! [13]They will know that I am the LORD when their slain appear among their idols and around their altars, wherever they offered up pleasing aromas for all their idols, on every high hill and mountaintop, and under every lofty tree and leafy oak.

¹⁴Wherever they live, I will direct my power against them. I will turn the land into a greater wasteland than the Riblah desert. Then they will know that I am the LORD.

The end

7 The LORD's word came to me: ²You, human one, this is what the LORD God proclaims to the land of Israel:

An end! The end has come
  to the four corners of the earth!
³ Even now the end is upon you!
I'll send my anger against you,
  I'll judge you according to your ways,
    and I'll turn
      all your detestable practices against you.
⁴ I won't shed a tear for you
  or show any pity.
    Instead, I'll turn your ways against you,
    and your detestable practices
      will stay with you.
Then you will know that I am the LORD.

⁵The LORD God proclaims:
Disaster! A singular disaster!
  Look, it comes!
⁶ The end has come!
  Oh, yes, it has come!
    It has come to you! Look, it's here!
⁷ You who live on the earth,
  you are finally caught in your own trap!
    The time has come; the day draws near.
    On the hills panic, not glory.
⁸ And now it's near!
Against you I will pour out my wrath,
  and my anger will be satisfied.
I'll judge you according to your ways,
  and turn all your detestable practices
    against you.
⁹ I won't shed a tear or show any pity
  when I turn your ways against you,
    and your detestable practices
      stay with you.
Then you will know that I, the LORD,
  am the one who strikes you!

¹⁰ Look, the day! Look, it comes!
  Doom has arrived! The staff blossoms,
    and pride springs up!

¹¹ Violence rises up as a wicked master.ⁿ
  It isn't from others
    or their armies or their violence.
    It hasn't loomed up because of them.
¹² The time is coming! The day draws near!
  No buyer should rejoice,
    and no seller should mourn,
    because wrath overcomes
      the whole crowd.
¹³ The seller will never get back
    what was sold,
      even if both of them survive.
The vision concerns the whole crowd.
  It won't be revoked.
    And the guilty ones—
      they won't even be able
        to hang on to their lives.
¹⁴ They have blown the horn,
  and everything is ready,
    but no one goes to battle,
    because my wrath
      overcomes the whole crowd.
¹⁵ Outside, the sword!
  Inside, plague and famine!
    Whoever is out in the field
      will die by the sword.
    Whoever is in the city,
      plague and famine will consume them.
¹⁶ And those who flee?
  They will turn up on the hills
    like valley doves,
      all of them moaning, those guilty ones.
¹⁷ Every hand will hang limp;
  urine will run down every leg.
¹⁸ They will put on mourning clothes,
  and horror will cover them.
    On every face, shame;
      on all their heads, baldness.
¹⁹ They will hurl their silver into the street,
  and their gold will seem unclean.
    Their silver and their gold
      won't deliver them
        on the day of the LORD's anger.
    They won't satisfy their appetites
      or fill their bellies.
    Their guilt will bring them down.

²⁰ From their beautiful ornament,
  in which they took pride,

ⁿOr *wicked staff*

they have made horrible
and detestable images!
Therefore, I've declared it
an unclean thing for them.
²¹ I'll hand it over to foreigners
as loot taken in war,
to the earth's wicked ones as plunder—
they will defile it!
²² When I hide my face from my people,
foreigners will defile my treasured place.
Violent intruders will invade it;
they will defile it!

²³ Make a chain!
The earth is full of perverted justice,
the city full of violence.
²⁴ I'll bring up the cruelest nations,
and they will seize their houses.
I'll break their proud strength,
and their sanctuaries will be defiled.

²⁵ Disaster! It has come!
They seek peace, but there is none.
²⁶ One disaster comes after another,
and rumor follows rumor.

They seek a vision from the prophet.
Instruction disappears from the priest,
and counsel from the elders.
²⁷ The king will go into mourning,
the prince will clothe himself in despair,
and the hands of the land's people
will tremble.
When I do to them as they have done
and judge them by their own justice,
they will know that I am the LORD.

Temple vision

8 In the sixth year, on the fifth day of the sixth month, I was sitting in my house, and Judah's elders were sitting with me, when the LORD God's power overcame me. ² I looked, and there was a form that looked like fire. Below what looked like his waist was fire, but above his waist it looked like gold, like gleaming amber. ³ He stretched out the form of a hand and picked me up by the hair of my head. A wind lifted me up between earth and heaven, and in a divine vision it brought me to Jerusalem, to the north-facing entrance of the gate to the inner court. That was where the pedestal was for the outrageous image that incites outrage. ⁴ There I saw the glory of Israel's God, exactly like what I had seen in the valley. ⁵ He said to me: Human one, look toward the north. So I looked north, and there, north of the altar gate, was this outrageous image in the entrance. ⁶ He said to me: Human one, do you see what they are doing, the terribly detestable practices that the house of Israel is doing here that drive me far from my sanctuary? Yet you will see even more detestable practices than these.

⁷ Then he brought me to the court entrance. When I looked, I saw a hole in the wall. ⁸ He said to me: Human one, dig through the wall. So I dug through the wall, and I discovered a doorway. ⁹ And he said to me: Go in and see what wicked and detestable things they are doing in there. ¹⁰ So I went in and looked, and I saw every form of loathsome beasts and creeping things and all the idols of the house of Israel engraved on the walls all around. ¹¹ The seventy elders of the house of Israel were standing in front of them, and all of them were holding censers in their hands. Jaazaniah, Shaphan's son, was standing right there with them, and the scent of the incense cloud rose up. ¹² He said to me: Human one, do you see what the elders of the house of Israel are doing in the dark, every one of them in their rooms full of sculptured images? They say, "The LORD doesn't see us; the LORD has abandoned the land." ¹³ He said to me: You will see them performing even more detestable practices. ¹⁴ He brought me to the entrance of the north gate of the temple, where women were sitting and performing the Tammuz lament.

¹⁵ He said to me: Human one, do you see? Yet you will see even more detestable practices than these. ¹⁶ He brought me to the inner court of the LORD's temple. There, at the entrance to the LORD's temple, between the porch and the altar, were twenty-five men facing toward the east with their backs to the LORD's temple. They were bowing to the sun in the east. ¹⁷ He said to me: Do you see, human one? Isn't it enough that the house of Judah has observed here all these

detestable things? They have filled the land with violence, and they continue to provoke my fury. Look at them! They even put the branch to their noses! ¹⁸ I will certainly respond with wrath. I won't spare or pity anyone. Even though they call out loudly to me in my hearing, I won't listen to them.

9 Then in my hearing he called out loudly: Draw near, you guardians of the city, and bring your weapons of destruction! ²Suddenly, six men came from the Upper Gate that faces north. All of them were holding weapons of destruction. Among them was another man who was dressed in linen and had a writing case at his side. When they came in and stood beside the bronze altar, ³the glory of Israel's God rose from above the winged creatures° where he had been and moved toward the temple's threshold. The LORD called to the man who was dressed in linen with the writing case at his side: ⁴Go through the city, through Jerusalem, and mark the foreheads of those who sigh and groan because of all the detestable practices that have been conducted in it. ⁵To the others he said in my hearing: Go through the city after him, and attack. Spare no one! Be merciless! ⁶Kill them all, old men, young men and women, babies and mothers. Only don't touch anyone who has the mark. Begin at my sanctuary. So they began with the men, the elders in front of the temple. ⁷He said to them: Make the temple unclean! Fill the courts with the slain! Go! And they went out and attacked the city.

⁸While they were attacking, I was left alone. I fell on my face, and I cried out, "Oh, LORD God! When you pour out your wrath on Jerusalem, will you destroy all that is left of Israel?"

⁹He said to me: "Judah and the house of Israel are very, very guilty. The land is filled with blood, and the city is full of injustice. They have said, 'The LORD has forsaken the land; the LORD sees nothing.'¹⁰ I most definitely won't spare or pity anyone! I will hold them accountable for their ways."

¹¹Just then the man who was dressed in linen with the writing case at his side

returned and said, "I've done just as you commanded."

10 At that moment I saw a form of a throne in the dome above the heads of the winged creatures. It appeared above them, and it looked like lapis lazuli. ²He said to the man clothed in linen: Go in between the wheels under the winged creatures.ᴾ Fill your hands with fiery coals from between the winged creatures, and scatter them over the city. As I watched, he went in. ³Now the winged creatures were standing to the right of the temple when the man went in, and the cloud filled the inner courtyard. ⁴Then the LORD's glory rose from above the winged creaturesᑫ and moved toward the temple's threshold. The temple was filled with the cloud, and the courtyard was filled with the brightness of the LORD's glory. ⁵The sound of the winged creatures' wings could be heard as far as the outer courtyard. It was like the sound of God Almightyʳ when he speaks. ⁶When he instructed the man clothed in linen to take fire from between the winged creatures and their wheels, the man went and stood next to the wheel. ⁷Then one of the winged creatures stretched a hand between the winged creatures into the fire that was between them, and he drew out some of it and set it in the palm of the one clothed in linen. He took it and went out. ⁸It appeared that the winged creatures had the form of a human hand under their wings.

⁹Suddenly, I saw four wheels next to the winged creatures. There was a wheel next to each winged creature, and the appearance of the wheels was like sparkling topaz. ¹⁰It appeared that there was one shape for all four of them, as if one wheel were inside another. ¹¹When they moved in any of the four directions, they moved without swerving. Whichever way the leading one faced, they moved in that direction without swerving. ¹²Their whole body—backs, hands, and wings—as well as their wheels, all four of them, were covered with eyes all around. ¹³It was these wheels that were called "the wheels" in my hearing. ¹⁴Each winged

creature had four faces. The first face was that of a winged creature, the second face was that of a human being, the third that of a lion, and the fourth that of an eagle. ¹⁵The winged creatures rose up, the same creatures that I had seen at the Chebar River. ¹⁶When the winged creatures moved, the wheels moved beside them. When the winged creatures lifted their wings to ascend above the earth, the wheels remained beside them without swerving. ¹⁷When they stood still, the wheels stood still; when they rose up, they rose up with them, because the spirit^s of the living creatures was in them. ¹⁸Then the LORD's glory went out from above the temple's threshold and it stood over the winged creatures. ¹⁹While I watched, the winged creatures raised their wings and rose from the ground to leave, with their wheels beside them. They stopped at the entrance to the east gate of the temple, and the glory of Israel's God was up above them. ²⁰These were the same living creatures that I saw underneath Israel's God at the Chebar River, and I realized that they were winged creatures. ²¹Each had four faces and four wings, with the form of a human hand under their wings. ²²The forms of their faces were the same faces that I saw at the Chebar River. Their appearance was also the same. All four of them moved straight ahead.

11A wind lifted me up and brought me to the east gate of the LORD's temple. There at the entrance to the gate were twenty-five men, and I saw that two officials of the people, Jaazaniah, Azzur's son, and Pelatiah, Benaiah's son, were with them.

²He said to me: Human one, these men devise evil plans and give wicked advice in this city. ³They are the ones who say, "The nearest relatives aren't building houses.^t The city is the cooking pot, and we are the meat." ⁴Therefore, prophesy against them, human one, prophesy! ⁵The LORD's spirit took hold of me, and he said to me: Say, This is what the LORD God proclaims: So you have said, house of Israel! But I know what you really mean. ⁶You continue to commit murder in this city, and you fill its streets with the slain.

⁷Therefore, the LORD God proclaims: The city is the cooking pot, and the ones you have slain in it are the meat. But you will be taken out of it. ⁸You fear the sword, so I will bring the sword against you. This is what the LORD God says! ⁹I will lead you out of the city, hand you over to foreigners, and execute judgments against you. ¹⁰You will fall by the sword! At Israel's borders I will judge you, and you will know that I am the LORD. ¹¹The city won't be your cooking pot, and you won't be the meat in it. At Israel's borders, I will judge you. ¹²You will know

---

^sOr *wind* ^tOr *it is not time to build houses*

WHEEL

The wheel was known and used in the ancient Near East as early as the 4th millennium BCE. Twenty-five of the 35 uses of *wheel* in the Bible appear in Ezekiel, mostly in Ezekiel 1 and 10. Although ambiguity in the description and uncertainty regarding the function of the wheels in the Ezekiel visions call for caution on the part of the interpreter, current consensus seems to understand Ezekiel's "wheels" as depicting the wheels of a sacred chariot or cart.

Texts other than Ezekiel that clearly refer to chariot wheels include Exodus 14:25, which references the Egyptian chariot wheels, and Nahum 3:2. Proverbs 20:26 associates a wheel with the threshing process, perhaps the wheel of a threshing cart (see also Isa 28:27).

that I am the LORD, whose regulations you didn't observe and whose case laws you didn't follow. Instead, you followed the case laws of the nations around you.

¹³While I was prophesying, Benaiah's son Pelatiah dropped dead. I fell on my face, and I wailed and said, "Oh, LORD God! Are you finishing off even the Israelites who are left?"

¹⁴The LORD's word came to me: ¹⁵Human one, when the people living in Jerusalem said, "They've gone far from the LORD, and we've been given the land as an inheritance," they were talking about your family, your nearest relatives, the whole house of Israel, all of it.

¹⁶Therefore, say, The LORD God proclaims: Even though I made them go far away among the nations and caused them to scatter throughout the earth, I've provided some sanctuary for them in the countries to which they've gone.

¹⁷Therefore, say, The LORD God proclaims: I will gather you from the nations, assemble you from the countries where you were scattered, and I will give you Israel's fertile land. ¹⁸They will enter the land, and they will remove from it all its disgusting and detestable things. ¹⁹I will give them a single heart, and I will put a new spirit in them. I will remove the stony hearts from their bodies and give them hearts of flesh ²⁰so that they may follow my regulations and carefully observe my case laws. They will be my people, and I will be their God. ²¹As for those whose hearts continue to go after their disgusting and detestable things, I will hold them accountable for their ways. This is what the LORD God says!

²²Then the winged creatures raised their wings. The wheels were next to them, and the glory of Israel's God was above them. ²³The LORD's glory ascended from the middle of the city, and it stopped at the mountain east of the city. ²⁴And a wind lifted me up and brought me to the exiles in Chaldea, through a vision with a divine wind.ᵘ When the vision I had seen left me, ²⁵I spoke to the exiles about everything the LORD had shown to me.

Baggage for exile

12 The LORD's word came to me: ²Human one, you live in a household of rebels. They have eyes to see but they don't see, ears to hear but they don't hear, because they are a household of rebels. ³But you, human one, prepare a backpack for going into exile. In the daytime while they watch, go into exile; while they watch, go out from your place to another. Even though they are a household of rebels, perhaps they will understand. ⁴In the daytime while they watch, carry your backpack as if for exile. At twilight while they watch, go out like those who are led out to exile. ⁵While they watch, dig a hole through the wall and take your backpack out through it. ⁶While they watch, shoulder your backpack and carry it out in the dark. Cover your face so that you can't see the land, because I'm making you a sign for the house of Israel. ⁷So I did as I was commanded. I carried out my backpack like an exile's backpack in the daytime. At night I dug a hole through the wall with my hands. In the darkness, I shouldered my backpack and carried it out while they watched.

⁸In the morning, the LORD's word came to me: ⁹Human one, has the house of Israel, that household of rebels, asked you, "What are you doing?" ¹⁰Say to them, The LORD God proclaims: This concerns the prince in Jerusalem, along with the entire house of Israel in it.ᵛ ¹¹Say: I'm your sign. Just as I have done, so it will be done to them. They will go into captivity in exile. ¹²Their prince will shoulder his backpack at night and go out. They will dig through the wall to lead him out through it, and he will cover his face so that his eyes won't see the land. ¹³But I will spread my net over him, catch him in my trap, and bring him to Babylon, to the land of the Chaldeans. He won't see it, but he will die there. ¹⁴As for all those who are in league with him, I will scatter his helpers and all his troops to the winds and let the sword loose after them. ¹⁵They will know that I am the LORD when I disperse them among the nations and scatter them

ᵘOr spirit   ᵛOr them

throughout the lands. ¹⁶But I will preserve a few of their number from the sword, famine, and plague, so that they may confess all their detestable practices among the nations where they go. Then they will know that I am the LORD.

¹⁷The LORD's word came to me: ¹⁸Human one, eat your bread in trembling, and drink your water in anxious agitation. ¹⁹Say to the land's people, The LORD God proclaims to those living in Jerusalem regarding Israel's fertile land: As they anxiously eat up their bread and drink up their water in dismay, the land will be emptied of everything in it because of the violence of all who live there. ²⁰The inhabited cities will be laid waste, the land left desolate, and you will know that I am the LORD.

Fulfillment of prophecy

²¹The LORD's word came to me: ²²Human one, what is this proverb of your people concerning Israel's fertile land? They say, "The days go by, and every vision vanishes." ²³Therefore, say to them, The LORD God proclaims: I'll put an end to this proverb! It will never again be uttered in Israel. Tell them instead: The days are coming soon for the fulfillment of every vision. ²⁴Never again will there be any worthless vision or deceptive divination in the house of Israel. ²⁵I am the LORD! The word that I speak is the word that I will speak! It will happen and be delayed no longer. In your own days, household of rebels, I speak a word and make it happen. This is what the LORD God says!

²⁶The LORD's word came to me: ²⁷Human one, the house of Israel is now saying, "The vision that he sees is for distant days; he prophesies about future times." ²⁸Therefore, say to them, The LORD God proclaims: It will be delayed no longer. Every word of mine that I've spoken is certain, and it will happen. This is what the LORD God says.

Against the prophets

13 The LORD's word came to me: ²Human one, prophesy to Israel's prophets who prophesy from their own imaginations. Say, Hear the LORD's word! ³The LORD God proclaims: Doom to the foolish prophets who follow their own whims but see nothing. ⁴Israel, your prophets have been like jackals among ruins. ⁵You haven't gone up into the breach or reinforced the wall of the house of Israel, so that it might withstand the battle on the day of the LORD. ⁶They saw worthless visions and performed deceptive divinations. Even though the LORD didn't send them, they said, "This is what the LORD says" and expected their word to stand. ⁷Didn't you see worthless visions? And didn't you report deceptive divinations and say, "This is what the LORD says," even though I didn't speak?

⁸Therefore, the LORD God proclaims: Because you spoke worthless things and had false visions, I'm against you. This is what the LORD God says! ⁹I'll wield my power against the prophets, those seers of nothingness and diviners of lies. They won't be included in my people's council, or recorded in the house of Israel's official records, or enter Israel's fertile land. Then you will know that I am the LORD.

¹⁰Without a doubt, they led my people astray, saying "Peace" when there was no peace, and "He is building a wall" when they were the ones who laid on the plaster. ¹¹Say to those who laid on the plaster that it will fall. When the flooding rains appear and I send hailstones, it will collapse, and the storm winds will break it apart. ¹²The wall will certainly fall. Won't it be said about you, "Where is your plaster now?"

¹³Therefore, the LORD God proclaims: In my fury I will make a storm wind break out, and in my anger there will be flooding rains and hailstones in consuming wrath. ¹⁴I will tear down the wall on which you laid plaster. I will raze it to the ground and expose its foundation. When it falls, you will be destroyed with it, and you will know that I am the LORD. ¹⁵I will exhaust my fury on the wall and on those who laid plaster on it. Then I will say to you, "Where is the wall?"ʷ and "Where are those who plastered it,

---

ʷSyr, cf 13:12; MT *There is no wall.*

[16] those prophets of Israel who prophesied to Jerusalem and envisioned peace when there was no peace?" This is what the LORD God says!

[17] You, human one, face the daughters of your people, those women who prophesy from their imaginations. Prophesy against them [18] and say, The LORD God proclaims: Doom to the women who sew bands on every wrist and make veils for heads of all sizes to entrap human lives. Will you ensnare my people's lives but preserve your own? [19] When you degrade me to my people for handfuls of barley and bread crumbs, you mislead my gullible people, and you bring about the death of those who shouldn't die and keep alive those who shouldn't live.

[20] Therefore, the LORD God proclaims: I'm against the bands that you use to trap human lives.[x] I will tear them from your arms, and I will set free the lives that you've trapped like birds. [21] I will tear off your veils and snatch my people out of your clutches. They will be prey in your clutches no longer. Then you will know that I am the LORD. [22] You hurt the righteous with slander—I didn't wound them!—and you strengthened the hands of the wicked so that they survived without changing their evil ways! [23] Therefore, you will no longer see empty visions or perform divinations. I will rescue my people from your clutches, and you will know that I am the LORD.

False devotion

14 When some of the elders of the house of Israel came to sit in my presence, [2] the LORD's word came to me: [3] Human one, these men decide on their own to set up their idols, so the cause of their downfall is right in front of them. Why should I allow them to ask me anything? [4] Therefore, speak to them and tell them, The LORD God proclaims: If anyone from the house of Israel decides on his own to set up his idols and puts the cause of his downfall right in front him, but then comes to the prophet, I, the LORD, will require an answer from him

through his many idols. [5] So I'll seize the hearts of the house of Israel, whose idols have made them all strangers to me.

[6] Therefore, say to the house of Israel, The LORD God proclaims: Come back! Turn away from your idols and from all your detestable practices. Turn away! [7] Or anyone of the house of Israel or any immigrant in Israel who becomes estranged from me by deciding on their own to set up their idols and puts the cause of their downfall right in front of them, but then comes to the prophet to ask me something through him, I, the LORD, will require an answer. [8] I will confront that one. I will set them up as a sign and an object lesson, and I will cut them off from my people. Then you will know that I am the LORD.

[9] As for the prophet who was seduced into speaking a word, even though it was I, the LORD, who seduced that prophet, I will use my power against him and cut him off completely from my people Israel. [10] The prophet and the inquirer alike will bear their guilt, [11] so that the house of Israel won't stray away from me again or make themselves impure with any of their sins. They will be my people, and I will be their God. This is what the LORD God says!

Failed request

[12] The LORD's word came to me: [13] Human one, suppose a land sins against me by acting faithlessly, so that I use my power against it, break off its food supply, let famine run rampant, and eliminate both humans and animals. [14] If these three men, Noah, Daniel, and Job, lived there, their lives alone would be saved because they were righteous. This is what the LORD God says. [15] Or suppose I allow wild animals to roam through the land, and it becomes so wild that no one can live there or even travel through it on account of the wild animals. [16] If these three men lived there, as surely as I live, proclaims the LORD God, they wouldn't be able to rescue even their sons or daughters. They alone would be rescued, but the land would become a ruin.

---

[x] LXX; MT adds *like birds.*

¹⁷Or suppose I bring a sword against that land and command the sword to pass through and eliminate both humans and animals. ¹⁸If these three men lived there, as surely as I live, proclaims the LORD God, they wouldn't be able to rescue even their sons or daughters. They alone would be rescued. ¹⁹Or suppose I send a plague against that land and pour out my fury on it. With great bloodshed I would eliminate both humans and animals. ²⁰If Noah, Daniel, and Job lived there, as surely as I live, proclaims the LORD God, they wouldn't be able to rescue either sons or daughters. But they would save their lives because they were righteous.

²¹The LORD God proclaims: How much more if I send all four of these terrible acts of judgment—sword, famine, wild animals, and plague—against Jerusalem, to eliminate both humans and animals? ²²Yet a few survivors will be left. Sons and daughters will be brought out to you. When you see their ways and their deeds, you will be consoled for the evil that I inflicted on Jerusalem, for all that I brought against it. ²³Seeing their ways and their deeds will bring you some consolation, because then you will understand what I've done, and that I didn't do any of these things without cause. This is what the LORD God says.

The vine's wood

15 The LORD's word came to me: ²Human one, how is the vine's wood better than the wood of all the trees in the forest? ³Can you make anything useful from its wood? Can you make a peg from it and hang objects on it? ⁴If not, can it be used as firewood? Fire would consume its two ends, but its middle part would only get charred. So is it useful for anything? ⁵Look, even when it was whole, it was worthless. Now that the fire has consumed it, and it is charred, it's even more useless.

⁶Therefore, the LORD God proclaims: Of all the trees in the forest, I have decreed that the vine's wood is destined to be consumed by fire. So also have I decreed for those who live in Jerusalem, ⁷and I have confronted them. They may try to go out from the fire, but the fire will consume them. You will know that I am the LORD, because I confronted them. ⁸I will turn the land into a ruin because they acted faithlessly, proclaims the LORD God.

Jerusalem's unfaithfulness

16 The LORD's word came to me: ²Human one, show Jerusalem her detestable practices. ³Say, The LORD God proclaims to Jerusalem: By origin and birth you are from the land of Canaan. Your father was an Amorite, your mother a Hittite. ⁴This is how you were treated on the day you were born: Your umbilical cord wasn't cut, you weren't washed clean with water or rubbed with salt, and you weren't wrapped in blankets. ⁵No one took pity or cared enough to do any of these things for you. You were despised on the day of your birth and thrown out on the open field. ⁶When I happened to come by, I saw you flailing about in your blood. I said to you while you were still bloody, "Live!" ⁷I helped you to flourish like a young plant in the field, and you grew tall and became wonderfully endowed. Your breasts were firm, your hair beautifully thick. And you were completely naked.

⁸When I passed by you, I realized that you were ready for love. So I spread my cloak over you and covered your nakedness. I made a solemn promise and entered into a covenant with you, and you became mine. This is what the LORD God says. ⁹Then I washed you with water, rinsed off your blood, and poured oil on you. ¹⁰I clothed you with colorful garments, put fine sandals on you, wrapped your head in linen, and covered you with jewels. ¹¹I adorned you with fine jewelry, and put bracelets on your wrists and a necklace around your neck. ¹²I put a ring in your nose, earrings in your ears, and a beautiful crown on your head. ¹³I adorned you with gold and silver, and your garments were made of the finest linen and brocade. You ate the finest flour, honey, and oil. You became very beautiful, fit for royalty. ¹⁴Among the nations you were famous for your beauty. It was perfect because of the splendor that I had given you. This is what the LORD God says.

¹⁵But you trusted in your beauty and traded on your fame. At every opportunity, you seduced all who came by. ¹⁶You took some of your clothing to make colorful shrines and prostituted yourself in them. ¹⁷You took the beautiful gold and silver jewelry that I had given to you, and you made male images for yourself and prostituted yourself with them. ¹⁸You took your fine garments and clothed them. You set my oil and incense before them. ¹⁹You set my food that I had given you to eat—fine wheat, oil, and honey—before them as a pleasing aroma. This is what the LORD God says. ²⁰You took your sons and daughters, which you had borne to me, and you sacrificed these to them so they could consume them. Was this promiscuity of yours a small thing? ²¹You slaughtered my sons and placed them in the fire for them! ²²In all your detestable practices and promiscuities, you didn't remember the days of your infancy when you lay completely naked, flailing about in your blood.

²³After all your wickedness—doom, doom to you, proclaims the LORD God—²⁴you built a pavilion for yourself and set up platforms in every square. ²⁵At every crossroad you built your platform and degraded your beauty by spreading your legs to all comers. And so you encouraged even more promiscuity. ²⁶You prostituted yourself with the Egyptians, your neighbors with the large sexual organs, and as you added to your seductions, you provoked me to anger. ²⁷So I used my power against you, cut off your allowance, and gave you up to the passions of the Philistine women who had been confounded by your infamous ways and had rejected you. ²⁸Still not satisfied, you prostituted yourself to the Assyrians, but they weren't enough for you either. ²⁹So you prostituted yourself with the Babylonians, the land of traders, but again you weren't satisfied. ³⁰How sick was your heart—the LORD God proclaims—that you could do all these things, the deeds of a hardened prostitute. ³¹But you weren't like an ordinary prostitute! When you built your pavilion

at the head of every street and made your platform in every square, you refused to be paid. ³²You are like an adulterous wife: you take in strangers instead of your husband. ³³Ordinary prostitutes are given gifts, but you gave your gifts to all your lovers. From every direction you even bribed them to come to you for your sexual favors. ³⁴As a prostitute, you were more perverse than other women. No one approached you for sexual favors, but you yourself gave gifts instead of receiving them. You are perversion itself! ³⁵Therefore, you prostitute, hear the LORD's word!

³⁶The LORD God proclaims: You were in a constant state of arousalʸ and exposed yourself when you acted like a prostitute with your lovers and with the idols to which you gave your children's blood. ³⁷Therefore, I will now gather all of your lovers whom you pleased, the ones you loved and the ones you rejected. I will gather them against you from all around, and I will expose you to them. They will see it all. ³⁸I will convict you of adultery and murder, and I will hand you over in bloody fury and zeal. ³⁹I will hand you over to them, and they will tear down your pavilion and destroy your platforms. They will strip you of your garments, take your beautiful jewels, and they will leave you completely naked. ⁴⁰They will bring an army against you, pelt you with stones, and slaughter you with their swords. ⁴¹They will burn down your houses and execute judgments against you in the sight of many women. I will bring an end to your prostitution; indeed, you will never again give payment. ⁴²When I've satisfied my anger, and my rage has turned away from you, I will be calm and no longer angry. ⁴³Because you didn't remember your youthful days, and infuriated me with all these things, I will hold you accountable for what you've done. This is what the LORD God says.

Have you not added bad reputation to all your detestable acts? ⁴⁴Now everyone who speaks in proverbs will say this about you: "Like mother, like daughter." ⁴⁵You are your mother's daughter! She loathed her

ʸHeb uncertain

husband and also her children. You are just like your sisters too! They also loathed their husbands and children. Your mother was a Hittite, and your father was an Amorite. ⁴⁶Your older sister is Samaria, who lives with her daughters in the north. Your younger sister is Sodom, who lives with her daughters in the south. ⁴⁷You didn't follow in their ways or engage in their detestable practices in any small way. You were far more destructive. ⁴⁸As surely as I live, says the Lord God, not even your sister Sodom and her daughters did what you and your daughters have done! ⁴⁹This is the sin of your sister Sodom: She and her daughters were proud, had plenty to eat, and enjoyed peace and prosperity; but she didn't help the poor and the needy. ⁵⁰They became haughty and did detestable things in front of me, and I turned away from them as soon as I saw it.

⁵¹Samaria didn't sin even half as much as you did. You've so outstripped her in multiplying your detestable practices, with all the detestable things you've done, that you've even made your sisters seem innocent. ⁵²Bear your disgrace, which has actually improved your sisters' position. Because your sins and detestable acts were greater than theirs, they are now more righteous than you. Be ashamed, and bear the disgrace of making your sisters righteous! ⁵³I will improve the circumstances of Sodom and her daughters and the circumstances of Samaria and her daughters. And what's left of your fortune will go to them, ⁵⁴so that you will bear your disgrace and be humiliated by all that you've done to make them feel better. ⁵⁵Then your sister Sodom and her daughters will return to their former state, and your sister Samaria and her daughters will return to their former state. You and your daughters will return to your former state, ⁵⁶but you will no longer talk about your sister Sodom as in your haughty days ⁵⁷before your wickedness was exposed. You are now the reproach of all the daughters of Edomᶻ and all those around her, including the daughters of the Philistines. They mock

you on every side. ⁵⁸You alone must bear your bad reputation and your detestable ways. This is what the Lord says.

⁵⁹The Lord God proclaims: I will do to you just as you have done, despising solemn pledges and breaking covenants. ⁶⁰Nevertheless, I will remember my covenant with you when you were young, and I will establish an everlasting covenant with you. ⁶¹And you will remember your ways and be ashamed, when in spite of your covenant Iᵃ take your big sisters and little sisters from you and give them back to you as daughters. ⁶²I myself will establish my covenant with you, and you will know that I am the Lord. ⁶³Then you will remember and be ashamed, and you won't even open your mouth because of your shame, after I've forgiven you for all that you've done. This is what the Lord God says.

Transplanted cedar

17 The Lord's word came to me: ²Human one, compose a riddle and a parable about the house of Israel. ³Say, The Lord God proclaims: The great eagle with great wings, long feathers, and full, colorful plumage came to Lebanon and took the top branch of the cedar. ⁴He plucked a twig from the cedar's crown, brought it to the land of traders, and set it down in a city of merchants. ⁵He took a native seed and planted it in a prepared field, placing it like a willow beside plentiful water. ⁶It grew and became a low-spreading vine. Its foliage turned toward him, and its roots developed under him. And so it became a vine, and it produced branches and sent out its shoots.

⁷Now there was another great eagle with great wings and much plumage. This vine bent its roots and turned its branches toward him so that it might draw more water from him than from its own bed, ⁸a good field with plentiful water where it was planted to grow branches, bear fruit, and become a splendid vine. ⁹Say, The Lord God proclaims: Will it thrive? Won't he tear out its roots, strip its fruit, and cause all the

leaves of its branches to wither? It will dry up, and no one will need a strong arm or a mighty army to uproot it. ¹⁰Though it is planted, will it thrive? When the east wind touches it, won't it completely wither? On the bed in which it was planted, it will wither away.

¹¹The LORD's word came to me: ¹²Say now to the rebellious household: Don't you know what these things mean? Say: The king of Babylon came to Jerusalem and carried its king and its officers away with him to Babylon. ¹³Then he took a prince from the royal line, made an agreement with him, and made him take a solemn pledge of loyalty. He also took away the land's officials. ¹⁴Thus it would be a lowly kingdom, not asserting its own interests but observing the agreement so that it would survive. ¹⁵But the prince rebelled against him and sent messengers to Egypt to supply him with horses and a great army. Can such a person succeed? Can one who does these things escape? Can he overturn the agreement and escape capture? ¹⁶As surely as I live, says the LORD God, he will die in Babylon, in the place of the king who gave him the authority to rule, whose solemn pledge he scorned and whose agreement he overturned. ¹⁷Pharaoh won't help him. There will be no strong force or mighty army in battle when siege ramps are set

up and towers are built to eliminate many lives. ¹⁸He scorned the solemn pledge and overturned the agreement! Even though he made a promise, he did all these things, and he won't escape capture. ¹⁹So now the LORD God proclaims: As surely as I live, it was my solemn pledge that he scorned and my agreement that he overturned, and I will hold him accountable. ²⁰I will spread my net over him, and he will be caught in my trap. I will bring him to Babylon, and I myself will enter into judgment with him there for rebelling against me. ²¹All his elite fighters[b] along with all his troops will fall by the sword, and those who are left will be scattered to the winds. Then you will know that I, the LORD, have spoken.

²²The LORD God proclaims: I myself will take one of the top branches from the tall cedar. I will pluck a tender shoot from its crown, and I myself will plant it on a very high and lofty mountain. ²³On Israel's mountainous highlands I will plant it, and it will send out branches and bear fruit. It will grow into a mighty cedar. Birds of every kind will nest in it and find shelter in the shade of its boughs. ²⁴Then all the trees in the countryside will know that I, the LORD, bring down the tall tree and raise up the lowly tree, and make the green tree wither and the dry tree bloom. I, the LORD, have spoken, and I will do it.

---

[b]LXX, Syr, Tg; MT *his fugitives*

CEDAR

Like pines, cedars have needlelike leaves clustered on short branch shoots. Cedars of Lebanon probably never grew within the bounds of present-day Israel but were abundant on the high Lebanon mountain ridge to the north.

Historically, the cedar of Lebanon was one of the most important building materials in the Near East. The most famous cedar building, although not the largest, was the temple built by Solomon (1 Kgs 6). In addition, Solomon built a magnificent home for himself entirely out of cedar (1 Kgs 7) that took 13 years to complete, six more years than the temple. Earlier, David had built a house out of cedar (2 Sam 7:2). While cedar wood is fragrant and attractive, its chief value lies in being the only tree in the region abundant and large enough for big buildings.

Sins of parents and children

18 The LORD's word came to me: [2]What do you mean by this proverb of yours about the land of Israel: "When parents eat unripe grapes, the children's teeth suffer"? [3]As surely as I live, says the LORD God, no longer will you use this proverb in Israel! [4]All lives are mine; the life of the parent and the life of the child belong to me. Only the one who sins will die.

[5]People are declared innocent when they act justly and responsibly. [6]They don't eat on the hills or give their attention to the idols of the house of Israel. They don't defile the wives of their neighbors or approach menstruating women. [7]They don't cheat anyone, but fulfill their obligations. They don't rob others, but give food to the hungry and clothes to the naked. [8]They don't impose interest or take profit. They refrain from evil and settle cases between people fairly. [9]They follow my regulations, keep my case laws, and act faithfully. Such people are innocent, and they will live, proclaims the LORD God.

[10]But suppose one of them has a violent child who sheds blood or does any one of these things, [11]even though his parents didn't do any of them. He eats on the mountains, defiles his neighbor's wife, [12]oppresses the poor and needy, robs others and doesn't fulfill his obligations, pays attention to the idols and does detestable things, [13]and takes interest and profit. Should he live? He should not. He engaged in all these detestable practices. He will surely die, and his blood will be on him.

[14]But suppose he has a child who sees all the sins that his father committed. He becomes alarmed and doesn't do them. [15]He doesn't eat on the mountains or pay attention to the idols of the house of Israel. He doesn't defile his neighbor's wife. [16]He doesn't cheat anyone, either by seizing collateral for loans or committing robbery. He gives his food to the hungry and clothes to the naked. [17]He refrains from oppressing the poor by taking neither interest nor profit. He observes my case laws and follows my regulations. He won't die because of his father's guilt. He will surely live. [18]As

for his father: If he exploited the weak or committed robbery, or did anything else that wasn't good for the people, he will die because of his own guilt.

[19]You will say, "Why doesn't the child bear his parent's guilt?" The child has acted justly and responsibly. The child kept all my regulations and observed them. The child will surely live. [20]Only the one who sins will die. A child won't bear a parent's guilt, and a parent won't bear a child's guilt. Those who do right will be declared innocent, and the wicked will be declared guilty.

[21]But if the wicked turn away from all the sins that they have committed, keep all my regulations, and act justly and responsibly, they will surely live and not die. [22]None of the sins that they committed will be held against them, but they will live because they do the right things. [23]Do I take pleasure in the death of the wicked? says the LORD God. Certainly not! If they change their ways, they will live.

[24]If those who do the right thing turn from righteousness and engage in the same detestable practices that the wicked committed, can they do these things and live? None of their righteous deeds will be remembered. They will die because of their treacheries and sins. [25]But you say, "My Lord's way doesn't measure up." Listen, house of Israel, is it my ways that don't measure up? Isn't it your ways that don't measure up? [26]When those who do the right thing turn from their responsible ways and act maliciously, they will die because of it. For their malicious acts they will die. [27]And when the wicked turn from their wicked deeds and act justly and responsibly, they will preserve their lives. [28]When they become alarmed and turn away from all their sins, they will surely live; they won't die. [29]Yet the house of Israel says, "My Lord's way doesn't measure up." Is it my ways that don't measure up? Isn't it your ways that don't measure up, house of Israel? [30]Therefore, I will judge each of you according to your ways, house of Israel. This is what the LORD God says. Turn, turn away from all your sins. Don't let them be sinful obstacles for you. [31]Abandon all of

your repeated sins. Make yourselves a new heart and a new spirit. Why should you die, house of Israel? ³²I most certainly don't want anyone to die! This is what the LORD God says. Change your ways, and live!

A mother's sons

19 You, raise a lament for Israel's princes. ²Say:

What a lioness among lionesses
    was your mother!
She bedded down among the strong
    young lions and reared her cubs.
³ She singled out one of her cubs
    and he became a strong young lion;
he learned to tear flesh
    and devour humans.
⁴ When the nations heard about him,
    they caught him in their trap
and carried him with hooks
    to the land of Egypt.
⁵ When she realized that she waited in vain,
    her hope faded.
So she took another of her cubs
    and set him up as a strong young lion.
⁶ He went on the prowl with the other lions
    and became a strong young lion.
He learned to tear flesh
    and devour humans;
⁷ he ravagedᶜ their widows
    and laid waste to their cities.
When the earth and everything in it
    became horrified by the sound
    of his raging,
⁸ the nations from the surrounding regions
    allied against him.
They cast their nets over him
    and caught him in their trap.
⁹ They put a collar on him
    and brought him with hooks.
They brought him with nets
    to the king of Babylon
so that his voice would no longer be
    heard on the mountains of Israel.

The proud mother

¹⁰ Your mother was like a vine in a vineyardᵈ
    planted beside the waters;
she bore lush fruit and foliage
    because of the plentiful water,
¹¹ and she produced mighty branches,
    fit for rulers' scepters.
She grew tall, and her crown
    went up between the clouds.
Because of her height and thick growth,
    she became conspicuous.
¹² So she was struck down in anger,
    thrown down to the ground.
The east wind dried her out
    and destroyed her fruit;
it sapped the branch of its strength,
    and fire consumed it.
¹³ So now she is planted in the desert,
    in a parched and thirsty land,
¹⁴ and fire has gone out from her branch
    and consumed her foliage and fruit,
leaving her no strong branch
    or ruler's scepter.

This is a lamentation, and it will serve as a lamentation.

History of rebellion

20 In the seventh year, on the tenth day of the fifth month, some of Israel's elders came to inquire of the LORD. As they were sitting with me, ²the LORD's word came to me: ³Human one, speak to Israel's elders and say to them, The LORD God proclaims: Have you come to petition me? As surely as I live, I reject your petitions. This is what the LORD God says! ⁴Will you judge them, human one, will you judge them? Then expose to them the detestable practices of their ancestors. ⁵Say to them, The LORD God proclaims: On the day I chose Israel, I swore a solemn pledge to the descendants of Jacob's household. When I made myself known to them in the land of Egypt, I swore a solemn pledge: I am the LORD your God. ⁶On that day I swore that I would lead them out of the land of Egypt to a land that I would show them, a land full of milk and honey, the most splendid of all lands. ⁷And I said to them, Every one of you must cast away your disgusting things. Don't let yourselves be defiled by Egypt's idols. I am the LORD your God. ⁸But they rebelled against me and refused to listen to me. No one cast off their disgusting things

ᶜOr knew   ᵈOr in your blood

or abandoned their Egyptian idols. So I declared that I would pour out my wrath on them and satisfy my anger against them in the land of Egypt. ⁹But I acted for my name's sake, so that it wouldn't be degraded in the sight of the nations among whom they lived, and in whose sight I made it known that I would lead them out of the land of Egypt.

¹⁰So I led them out of the land of Egypt and brought them into the desert. ¹¹I gave them my regulations and made known to them my case laws, which bring life to all who observe them. ¹²I also gave them my sabbaths as a sign between us that I, the LORD, have set them apart for my purpose.ᵉ ¹³But the house of Israel rebelled against me in the desert. They didn't follow my regulations and rejected my case laws, which bring life to all who observe them. They completely degraded my sabbaths. So I declared that I would pour out my anger against them and destroy them in the desert. ¹⁴But instead, I acted for the sake of my name so that it wouldn't be degraded in the sight of the nations who saw me lead them out of Egypt. ¹⁵So in the desert I swore another solemn pledge, that I wouldn't bring them to the land that I had given to them, a land full of milk and honey, a land more splendid than any other, ¹⁶because they rejected my case laws, didn't follow my regulations, and degraded my sabbaths. They had their hearts set on their idols.

¹⁷But I had too much compassion to destroy them, so I didn't put an end to them in the desert.

¹⁸In the desert, I said to their children, Don't follow your parents' regulations or observe their case laws or become defiled by their idols. ¹⁹I am the LORD your God! Follow my regulations! Observe my case laws and do them! ²⁰Make my sabbaths holy, and let them be a sign between us that I am the LORD your God. ²¹But the children rebelled against me. They didn't follow my regulations or observe my case laws, which bring life to all who observe them. They also degraded my sabbaths. So I declared that I would pour out my wrath on them and satisfy my anger against them in the desert. ²²But I restrained myself and acted for the sake of my name so that it wouldn't be diminished in the sight of the nations who saw me lead them out of Egypt. ²³And I swore yet another solemn pledge in the desert, that I would disperse them among the nations and scatter them throughout the earth, ²⁴because they didn't observe my case laws, they rejected my regulations, and they degraded my sabbaths while they kept looking to their parents' idols. ²⁵I also issued regulations that were not good and case laws by which they could not live. ²⁶I defiled them with their very gifts when they offered up all their oldest children. They were supposed to be so horrified that they would acknowledge that I am the LORD.

ᵉOr *to make them holy*

FIRE

Both in the OT and the NT, fire is part of everyday life. On the one hand, fire is a useful, beneficial element providing light and warmth (Isa 44:15-16; Acts 28:2) and heat for cooking (Exod 12:8; Jer 7:18) or the work of craftsmen (Ezek 22:20). On the other hand, fire has a destructive quality and is therefore employed in war (Judg 20:48; Jer 21:10) and sometimes, though seldom, as a means of execution (Gen 38:24; Lev 20:14; 21:9; Josh 7:15). It may also refer to the scorching heat of the sun (Joel 1:19; Amos 7:4). In a figurative sense or as a metaphor it describes feelings such as extreme pain (Ps 39:3), passion of love (Song 8:6), wickedness (Isa 9:18), or anger (Zeph 3:8).

²⁷Therefore, human one, speak to the house of Israel and say to them, The LORD God proclaims: Yet again your ancestors defamed me by rebelling against me! ²⁸I brought them into the land that I swore to give to them. But when they saw all the high hills and lofty trees, there they made their sacrifices: irksome offerings here, pleasing aromas there, and drink offerings elsewhere! ²⁹I said to them, What shrine are you going to now? So it's called Shrine[f] to this very day.

³⁰So now say to the house of Israel, The LORD God proclaims: Will you defile yourselves as your ancestors did, and will you prostitute yourself after their disgusting things? ³¹When you offer up your gifts and make your children pass through the fire, you defile yourselves with all your idols to this very day. Should I let you seek me out, house of Israel? This is what the LORD God says: As surely as I live, I won't let you seek me. ³²What is in your minds will never happen! You've been saying, "Let's be like the nations and the clans of the lands in the service of wood and stone." ³³This is what the LORD God says: As surely as I live, with a strong hand, an outstretched arm, and with wrath poured out, I will be your king! ³⁴I will lead you out from the peoples and gather you from the countries where you've been scattered—yes, with a strong hand and an outstretched arm and with wrath poured out! ³⁵I will march you out to the wilderness nations, and there I will judge you face-to-face. ³⁶Just as I judged your ancestors in the desert of the land of Egypt, so will I judge you. This is what the LORD God says. ³⁷I will make you walk under the rod, and I will bring you into the covenant bond. ³⁸I will remove from among you those who rebel and transgress against me. I will lead them out from the land where they lived as immigrants, but they won't enter Israel's fertile land. Then you will know that I am the LORD.

³⁹But to you, house of Israel, the LORD God proclaims: Go ahead and serve your idols, all of you! But afterward, if any of you are left to listen to me,[g] you will no longer make my holy name impure with your gifts or your idols! ⁴⁰On my holy mountain, on the high mountain in Israel, the whole house of Israel will serve me there—every one of them in the land! This is what the LORD God says. There I will accept them, and there I will ask for their offerings, their finest gifts, and all their holy things. ⁴¹When I bring you out from the nations and gather you from the countries where you are scattered, I will accept you as a pleasing aroma. Through you I will be made holy in the sight of the nations. ⁴²Then you will know that I am the LORD, when I bring you to Israel's fertile land, to the land that I swore to give to your ancestors. ⁴³There you will remember how your ways and all your wicked deeds defiled you, and you will loathe yourselves for all the wicked things that you've done. ⁴⁴Then, house of Israel, you will know that I am the LORD, when I deal with you for the sake of my name and not according to your wicked ways and ruinous deeds. This is what the LORD God says.

Fire in the southern plain

⁴⁵[h]The LORD's word came to me: ⁴⁶Human one, face Teman, preach against the south, and prophesy against the thicket in the arid southern plain. ⁴⁷Say to the thicket in the arid southern plain: Hear the LORD God's word. This is what the LORD God says: I'm about to set a fire in you, and it will consume every green and every dry tree in you. Its blazing flame won't be put out, and everything from south to north will be scorched. ⁴⁸Everyone will see that I, the LORD, have set it on fire. It won't be quenched. ⁴⁹Then I said, "Oh, LORD God! They say about me, 'Isn't he one for making metaphors?'"

The sword

21 ¹[i]The LORD's word came to me: ²Human one, face Jerusalem, preach against their sanctuary, and prophesy against Israel's fertile land. ³Say to Israel's fertile land,

---

[f]Heb sounds like *Where are you going?* [g]Heb uncertain [h]21:1 in Heb [i]21:6 in Heb

The LORD proclaims: I'm now against you! I will draw my sword from its sheath and cut off both the righteous and the wicked from you. ⁴In order to cut off the righteous and wicked from you, my sword will go out from its sheath against everyone from south to north. ⁵And everyone will know that I, the LORD, have taken my sword out of its sheath. It won't be put away again.

⁶You, human one, groan in their sight; groan bitterly with trembling knees. ⁷If they ask you why you're groaning, say to them, "Because of the news." When it comes, every heart will despair, every hand will hang lifeless, every spirit will be listless, and urine will run down every leg. It's coming! It will happen! This is what the LORD God says.

The sword dance

⁸The LORD's word came to me: ⁹Human one, prophesy! Say, The Lord proclaims! Say:
A sword! A sharp and polished sword!
¹⁰ For utter slaughter it is sharpened,
    polished to flash like lightning.
Let's not rejoice,
    because no one will escape the purge.ʲ
¹¹ He appoints it for polishing,
    to seize in the hand.
The sword is sharpened,
    it is polished;
it is ready for the destroyer's hand.
¹² Human one, cry aloud, and wail,
    for it comes against my people,
    against all of Israel's princes,
    handed over to the sword
        along with my people.
Therefore, strike your thigh.
¹³ He's testing.
When even the rod rejects,
    will it not certainly happen?ᵏ
This is what the LORD God says.

¹⁴ And you, human one, prophesy!
    Strike hand to hand.
Let the sword strike twice,
    three times!
It's a deadly sword,
    a great deadly sword.
It whirls around them

¹⁵ to make hearts shudder,
    to make many stumble and fall.
I've set the slaughtering sword
    against all their gates.
Oh! It's crafted to flash like lightning,
    polished for slaughter!
¹⁶ Stab again and again! Plunge right,
    plunge left, wherever your edge goes.
¹⁷ It is I who strike hand to hand!
    I'll satisfy my wrath!
    I, the LORD, have spoken.

Guilt remembered

¹⁸The LORD's word came to me: ¹⁹You, human one, mark two roads for the coming of the sword of the king of Babylon. They should diverge from a single country. Where the road to the city begins, set up a sign, ²⁰and point out the way for the sword to come: "To Rabbah of the Ammonites" or "To Judah in its stronghold Jerusalem." ²¹The king of Babylon stands at the fork in the road where the two roads begin and performs his divinations. He shakes the arrows, consults the divine images, and inspects the liver. ²²On his right side appeared the omen for Jerusalem: to put battering rams in place, to proclaim war and raise the alarm, to place battering rams against the gates, and to set up siege ramps and build towers. ²³It seems to them like a lying divination, because solemn pledges had been sworn to them. But he will remind them of their guilt, and they will be captured.

²⁴So the LORD God proclaims: Now that you have remembered your guilt and your treacheries are exposed, your sins can be seen in everything you do. Because you have brought your guilt to light, you will be captured! ²⁵But you vile, wicked prince of Israel whose day has come, the time of final punishment, ²⁶this is what the LORD God says: Remove the turban, take off the crown! Nothing will be as it was. Bring down the exalted, and exalt the lowly. ²⁷A ruin, ruin, ruin, I'll make it! Such a thing has never happened! Even before the rightful judge comes, I've handed it over to him.

ʲHeb uncertain ᵏHeb uncertain

Avenging Ammon's disgrace

²⁸You, human one, prophesy and say, The LORD God proclaims to the Ammonites concerning their disgrace. Say, Sword! Sword unsheathed for slaughter, burnished, battle-ready,[1] flashing like lightning: ²⁹False visions and lying divinations set you against the necks of vile, wicked men whose day had come, the time of final punishment. ³⁰Return it to its sheath. In the place where you were created, in the land of your origin, I will judge you. ³¹I will pour out my wrath against you. With a raging fire I will blow against you, and I will hand you over to those who burn and forge destruction. ³²Fire will consume you, your blood will sink into the earth, and you will no longer be remembered. I, the LORD, have spoken.

Bloody city

22 The LORD's word came to me: ²You, human one, will you judge? Will you judge the bloody city? Then explain all her detestable practices to her. ³Say, The LORD God proclaims: City, self-destructive blood-letter, self-defiling idol maker: ⁴All the blood that you've shed is your punishment, and all the idols that you've made are your defilement. This is how you've shortened your days and hastened the end[m] of your years! For this reason I've given you over to the ridicule of nations and the derision of every land. ⁵Those from near and far will mock your infamous name and great chaos. ⁶Look, Israel's princes, every one of them, have joined forces to shed blood in you. ⁷In you they treat father and mother with contempt. In you they oppress immigrants and deny the rights of orphans and widows. ⁸You despise my holy things and degrade my sabbaths. ⁹In you slanderers show up to shed blood. In you they eat on the mountains. In you they do obscene things. ¹⁰In you a father's nakedness is uncovered. In you menstruating women are violated. ¹¹Every man engages in detestable practices with his neighbor's wife, every man defiles his daughter-in-law with obscene acts, and every man violates his sister, his own father's daughter. ¹²In you they take bribes to shed blood. You collect interest and fees, you profit by extorting your neighbor, and you neglect even me! This is what the LORD God says.

¹³I now strike my hands over your ill-gotten gain and blood that's been shed in you. ¹⁴Will your strength and courage endure when I deal with you? I am the LORD: I speak, and I act! ¹⁵I will scatter you among the nations and disperse you throughout the lands, and so I will remove your uncleanness from you. ¹⁶When you are degraded[n] like this in the sight of the nations, then you will know that I am the LORD.

¹⁷The LORD's word came to me: ¹⁸Human one, the house of Israel has become a waste product for me. They are all copper, tin, iron, and lead. In the furnace, they've become the waste product of silver. ¹⁹So this is what the LORD God says: Because you've all become a waste product, I'm now gathering you into the middle of Jerusalem. ²⁰Just as silver, copper, iron, lead, and tin are collected and placed in a furnace to fan the flames under them and melt them down, so in my anger and rage I will collect you, put you in, and melt you down. ²¹I will gather you, fan the flames of my wrath under you, and melt you down in the middle of it. ²²As silver is melted in a furnace, so you will be melted in it. You will know that I, the LORD, have poured out my rage on you.

²³The LORD's word came to me: ²⁴Human one, say to her, You are an unclean land without rain on the day of reckoning. ²⁵The conspiracy of princes[o] in her is like a roaring lion ripping up prey. They've piled up wealth and precious goods and made many widows in her. ²⁶Her priests have done violence to my instructions and made my holy things impure. They have not clearly separated the holy from the ordinary, and they have not taught the difference between unclean and clean things. They've disregarded my sabbaths. So I've been degraded among them. ²⁷The officials in her are like wolves ripping up prey. They shed blood and destroy lives for unjust riches. ²⁸Her prophets

---

[1]Or *to take in the hand*   [m]LXX, Syr; Vulg *time*; MT *until*   [n]MT adds *in you*.   [o]LXX; MT *prophets*

have whitewashed everything for them, seeing false visions and making wrong predictions for them, saying, "This is what the LORD God says," when the LORD hasn't spoken. ²⁹The important people of the land have practiced extortion and have committed robbery. They've oppressed the poor and mistreated the immigrant. They've oppressed and denied justice. ³⁰I looked for anyone to repair the wall and stand in the gap for me on behalf of the land, so I wouldn't have to destroy it. But I couldn't find anyone. ³¹So I've poured out my anger on them. With my furious fire I've finished them off. I've held them accountable. This is what the LORD God proclaims.

Two sisters

23 The LORD's word came to me: ²Human one, there were two women, daughters of one woman. ³When they were girls in Egypt, they began to prostitute themselves by allowing their young and nubile breasts to be touched and fondled. ⁴The older sister was named Oholah, and the younger sister was named Oholibah. They became mine and gave birth to sons and daughters. Now Oholah is Samaria, and Oholibah is Jerusalem. ⁵But Oholah became unfaithful to me and lusted after her lovers the Assyrians: ⁶warriors dressed in fine blue cloth, governors and officers, charioteers and horsemen, all of them the most handsome of men. ⁷She sought them out to seduce them, all of them men of the highest rank of Assyria. She defiled herself by everyone she lusted after and also by all their idols. ⁸But she never gave up her promiscuities with the Egyptians, who had slept with her in her girlhood and fondled her nubile breasts, and who continued to seduce her. ⁹Therefore, I handed her over to her lovers, to the Assyrians for whom she lusted. ¹⁰They stripped her naked, took her sons and daughters, and killed her with the sword. And she became notorious among women for the punishments they enacted against her.

¹¹Her sister Oholibah saw it, and she proceeded to outdo her sister in her lust and in her seductions. ¹²She lusted after the Assyrians, governors and officers, warriors richly clothed, charioteers and horsemen, all of them the most handsome of men. ¹³I saw that she too defiled herself. Both had the same tendencies, ¹⁴but she was even more promiscuous. She saw men carved in wall reliefs, images of Chaldeans outlined in vermilion, ¹⁵wearing only loincloths around their hips and flowing headbands on their heads. All of them had the appearance of warriors of the third rank, the likeness of Babylonians whose native land is Chaldea. ¹⁶Aroused just by looking at them, she sent messengers to them in Chaldea. ¹⁷The Babylonians came to her to lie down and make love with her, defiling her with their seductions. But once she had defiled herself with them, she recoiled from them in disgust. ¹⁸When her seductions became known and her nakedness exposed, I recoiled from her just as I had recoiled from her sister. ¹⁹But she added to her promiscuities, bringing to mind her youthful days when she was a prostitute in the land of Egypt. ²⁰She lusted after their male consorts, whose sexual organs were like those of donkeys, and whose ejaculation was like that of horses. ²¹She relived the wicked days of her youth, when the Egyptians touched and fondled her young and nubile breasts.

²²So Oholibah, the LORD God proclaims: I'm now inciting your lovers against you, all those from whom you recoiled, and I will bring them against you from all around— ²³Babylonians and all the Chaldeans, Pekod and Shoa and Koa, all the Assyrians with them, the most handsome young men, all of them governors and officers, career officers and conscripts, all of them on horseback. ²⁴They will come against you with weapons,^p chariots, and wagons, and with a great army, with shield, buckler, and helmet; and they will surround you. I will hand your punishment over to them, and they will judge you according to their laws. ²⁵I will direct my passion against you, and they will deal with you in wrath. They will

cut off your nose and ears, and those who are left will fall by the sword. They will seize your sons and daughters, and those who are left will be burned with fire. ²⁶They will strip your clothing from you and remove your beautiful crown. ²⁷That's how I will put an end to your lewdness and your Egyptian-styled promiscuity. Never again will you stare at them, and you won't remember Egypt anymore. ²⁸The LORD God proclaims: I'm now handing you over to those whom you hate and from whom you recoil. ²⁹They will deal hatefully with you: They will seize your pay and leave you completely naked. Your promiscuity, betrayal, and seductions will be exposed. ³⁰This will be done to you because you sold yourself to the nations and became defiled by their idols. ³¹You followed in your sister's path, so I have put her cup into your hand.

³²The LORD God proclaims:
Deep and wide is your sister's cup. Drink!
Appointed for abuse and scorn,
it overflows.
³³You will be filled with drunken sadness.
A cup of devastation and dismay
is the cup of your sister Samaria.
³⁴Drink it, drain it dry,
break it into pieces,
and tear off your breasts,
for I have spoken.
This is what the LORD God says.

³⁵So now the LORD God proclaims: Because you forgot me and turned your back on me, you alone will bear the consequences of your betrayal and promiscuities.

³⁶Then the LORD said to me, Human one, judge Oholah and Oholibah, and make known their detestable practices to them. ³⁷They committed adultery, so now blood

OHOLAH AND OHOLIBAH

Symbolic names of Samaria and Jerusalem, cities represented as unfaithful wives of the Lord, in Ezekiel 23. The metaphor of cities as women wedded to patron gods was already in use in ancient Near Eastern literature before Hosea and Jeremiah described "wives" of the Lord who are punished for their unfaithfulness. Ezekiel, however, pushes this metaphor much further. In chapter 16, without resorting to a symbolic name, the prophet is told to announce Jerusalem's status as an abandoned infant whom God first rescued and then, in her adulthood, wedded, bathed, and dressed. But trusting in her own beauty, she has consorted with idols and foreign countries, engaging in worse abominations than her "sisters," Samaria and Sodom. God will punish her violently in the hope of eliciting her repentance.

When the metaphor recurs in Ezekiel 23, the lack of emotional engagement is striking. Here God allegorically retells the story of both Samaria and Jerusalem, who begin as young women in Egypt. Samaria (Oholah) is graphically described as lusting after the Assyrian warriors and being given into their hands, where she is killed. Though Jerusalem (Oholibah) sees this, she extends her favors to the Babylonians. God's violent punishment is described in gruesome detail. Following this, accusations and judgments against both cities are reviewed. Both are stoned, their children killed, and their houses burned, in order that women in the land will take warning. Unlike chapter 16, this chapter offers no hope of reconciliation but relates the death of both sister cities. The metaphor dies with the wives, and Ezekiel 40–48 describes Jerusalem as an inanimate city belonging to God.

is on their hands. They committed adultery with their idols, and they even took their children whom they had borne to me and offered them up to be consumed for them. ³⁸They also did this to me: On the same day, they made my sanctuary unclean and made my sabbaths impure. ³⁹When they slaughtered their children for their idols, they came into my sanctuary and made it impure on that very same day. They actually did this inside my temple. ⁴⁰They even sent for men who came from a great distance. No sooner than a messenger was sent, they arrived! For these men you bathed, you painted your eyes, and you put on your jewelry. ⁴¹You took your place on a splendid couch with a richly set table in front of it, and you set my incense and my oil on it. ⁴²The sound of a noisy crowd was around her. Men from the common multitude, drinkers of wine, were brought from the desert. They put bracelets on their wrists and beautiful crowns on their heads. ⁴³Then I thought, For a foolish woman they become adulterers! Incited by her seduction, they prostitute themselves—for her!�q ⁴⁴They come as if coming to a prostitute, first to Oholah, and then to Oholibah, those traitorous women. ⁴⁵But men who do the right thing will judge them, and they will be punished as adulterers and murderers, because they are in fact adulterers, and blood is on their hands.

⁴⁶The LORD God proclaims: Bring up an assembly against them, and decree terror and plunder for them. ⁴⁷Let the assembly stone them! Let them carve them up with their swords, slay their sons and daughters, and burn their houses with fire! ⁴⁸So I will put an end to betrayal in the land. Taking warning, no woman will betray as you have done. ⁴⁹You will be held accountable for your betrayals, and you will bear the sins of your idols. Then you will know that I am the LORD God.

The useless pot

24 In the ninth year, on the tenth day of the tenth month, the LORD's word came to me: ²Human one, write down today's date, because today the king of Babylon has set up camp at Jerusalem—today! ³Compose a parable for the rebels' household and say to them, The LORD God proclaims:

Put on the pot, set it on,
   and fill it with water.
⁴ Add meat to it,
   every good piece.
With shoulder and thigh,
   the meatiest bones, fill it up.
⁵ Take the flock's best animal;
   arrange the woodʳ beneath it.
Bring it to a rolling boil,
   and cook its bones in it.

⁶The LORD God proclaims: Horror! You bloody city, you corroded pot; pot whose corrosion can't be removed! Empty it piece by piece. She is rejectedˢ ⁷because her blood is still with her. She didn't pour it out on the ground so that it could be covered with dirt, but she spread it out on a bare rock. ⁸In order to arouse wrath, to guarantee vengeance, I will spread her blood on a bare rock, never to be covered.

⁹So now the LORD God proclaims:
Horror! You bloody city!
   I myself will add fuel to the fire!
¹⁰ Pile on the wood, light the fire,
   and cook the meat.
Season it well
   and let the bones be charred.
¹¹ Let the pot stand empty on its coals
   until it's so hot that its copper glows,
   its impurities melt in it,
   and its corrosion is consumed.
¹² It's a worthless task.
   Even by fire its great corrosion
   isn't removed.

¹³ How your betrayals defile you! I cleansed you, but you didn't come clean from your impurities. You won't be clean again until I have exhausted my anger against you. ¹⁴I, the LORD, have spoken! It's coming, and I'll do it. I won't relent or have any pity or compassion. Your punishments will fit your ways and your deeds! This is what the LORD God says.

�q Heb uncertain   ʳ Or *bones*   ˢ Or *the lot did not fall to her*

Ezekiel's wife dies

[15]The LORD's word came to me: [16]Human one, I am about to take the delight of your eyes away from you in a single stroke. Don't mourn or weep. Don't even let your tears well up. [17]Sigh inwardly; be deathly still. Don't perform mourning rites, but bind on your turban and put your shoes on your feet. And don't cover your upper lip or eat in human company.

[18]I spoke with the people in the morning, and by evening my wife was dead. The next morning I did as I was commanded. [19]The people asked, "Won't you tell us what your actions mean for us?"

[20]So I said to them, The LORD's word came to me: [21]Say to the house of Israel, the LORD God proclaims: I'm about to make my sanctuary impure, the pride of your strength, the delight of your eyes. Your heart's desire, the sons and daughters you left behind, will fall by the sword. [22]You will do as I have done. You will neither cover your upper lip nor eat in human company. [23]Your turbans will be on your heads, your sandals on your feet. You won't mourn or weep. You will waste away in your guilt, all of you groaning to each other. [24]Ezekiel is your sign. You will do everything that he has done. When this happens, you will know that I am the LORD God.

[25]And you, human one: On the day that I take from them their proud stronghold— their crowning joy, the delight of their eyes—and their sons and daughters, whose fate weighs on them, [26]on that day, a refugee will come to you so that you yourself will hear the news. [27]On that day your mouth will be opened to the refugee, and you will speak and no longer be silent. You will be their sign, and they will know that I am the LORD.

Against the neighboring nations

25 The LORD's word came to me: [2]Human one, face the Ammonites and prophesy against them. [3]Say to the Ammonites: Hear the LORD God's word! The LORD God proclaims: You laughed when my sanctuary was degraded, when Israel's fertile land was laid waste, and when the house of Judah went into exile; [4]therefore, I'm handing you over to people in the east for them to take possession. They will set up their encampments against you, establish residence, devour your fruit, and drink your milk. [5]I'll make Rabbah into pastureland for camels and Ammon a resting place for flocks. Then you will know that I am the LORD.

[6]The LORD God proclaims: Because you clapped your hands and stamped your feet when you rejoiced with utter contempt for Israel's fertile land, [7]I'm about to overpower you. Nations will plunder you. I will cut you off from the peoples, remove you from the lands, and utterly destroy you. Then you will know that I am the LORD.

AMMON/AMMONITES

A tribal people living east of the Jordan River. A reflection of their history is preserved in the name Amman, the modern capital of Jordan. In the OT the ancestor of the Ammonites is Ben-ammi, a product of an incestuous union between Lot and his younger daughter (Gen 19:30-38). The Ammonites play a role in the biblical accounts of wilderness wandering and settlement in the promised land. Indeed, they are noted periodically throughout the historical and prophetic books, though less so in references to the post-exilic period. Both Saul and David fight against the Ammonites (1 Sam 11:1-13; 2 Sam 10:1–11:25; 12:26-31). Saul was able to muster an army and defeat the Ammonites led by Nahash, and David's forces captured the Ammonite capital.

⁸The LORD God proclaims: Because Moab and Seir say, "Aha! The house of Judah has become like all the nations," ⁹I'll open up the flank of Moab from the cities at its border, the land's splendid cities, Beth-jeshimoth, Baal-meon, and Kiriathaim. ¹⁰I'll hand it over, along with the Ammonites, to people in the east for them to take possession. And so Ammon will no longer be remembered among the nations. ¹¹I'll execute judgments in Moab, and they will know that I am the LORD.

¹²The LORD God proclaims: Edom acted with excessive force against the house of Judah. The Judeans were guilty, but Edom's vengeance was excessive. ¹³So the LORD God now proclaims: I'll overpower Edom, eliminate all living creatures, and make it a wasteland from Teman to Dedan. They will fall by the sword. ¹⁴I will execute my vengeance in Edom through my people Israel's power. They will act in Edom according to my anger and fury, and they will know my vengeance. This is what the LORD God says.

¹⁵The LORD God proclaims: When the Philistines set out to right the wrongs done to them, they enacted revenge with utter contempt and old hatreds. ¹⁶So now the LORD God proclaims: I will overpower the Philistines, eliminate the Cherethites, and obliterate all who are left along the coastline. ¹⁷I will act against them with great vengeance and with wrathful punishments. When I execute my vengeance against them, they will know that I am the LORD.

Against Tyre

26 In the eleventh year, on the first day of the month, the LORD's word came to me:

² Human one,
  because Tyre laughed at Jerusalem:
"The gate of the peoples is broken,
  she lies open before me,
  she is destroyed, but I will succeed!"

³The LORD God now proclaims:
Tyre, I'm now against you!
  Just as the sea hurls up its waves,
I will bring many nations
  up against you.
⁴ When they destroy the walls of Tyre
  and throw down its towers,
I will scrape off all its dirt
  and make it into a bare rock,
⁵ a place for drying nets
  in the middle of the sea.
I have spoken!
This is what the LORD God says.
It will become prey for the nations,
⁶ and its towns around it
  will be put to the sword.
  Then they will know
    that I am the LORD.

⁷ The LORD God proclaims:
I'm bringing Nebuchadrezzar
  against Tyre,
  the king of Babylon from the north,
  the greatest of all kings,
  with horses, chariots, and charioteers,
  an assembly, a great army.
⁸ The towns around you
  he will destroy with the sword.
  Then he will build towers against you,
  erect siege ramps against you,
  and set up shields.
⁹ He will pound his battering ram
  against your walls;
  with crowbars he will tear down
  your towers.
¹⁰ The dust from all his horses
  will cover you
  when he enters your gates
  as one who enters a breached city.
  Your walls will quake
  at the thundering of the charioteers
  and chariot wheels.
¹¹ His horses' hooves will trample
  all your courtyards;
  he will cut down your people
  with the sword,
  and the monuments to your strength
  he will bring down^t to the ground.
¹² They will destroy your wealth,
  plunder your goods,
  tear down your walls,
  and raze your fine houses.

---

^t LXX; MT *it will fall*

Your stone, lumber, and rubble
   they will dump into the sea.

¹³ I will bring an end
   to your cacophonous songs;
   the sound of your lyres
   will never be heard again.
¹⁴ I will make you into a bare rock,
   a place for drying nets,
   and you will never be rebuilt.
   I, the LORD, have spoken.
   This is what the LORD God says.

A lament for Tyre

¹⁵ The LORD God proclaims to Tyre: Won't the coastlands quake at the news of your downfall, when the wounded groan, and when the slaughter in your midst goes on and on? ¹⁶ All the princes of the sea will come down from their thrones, remove their royal robes, and strip off their fine garments. They will be clothed only in terror as they sit on the ground. They will be so terrified, they won't stop shuddering because of you. ¹⁷ They will sing a lament for you, and they will say:

How you have perished,
   queen of the sea,
   city once praised,
   who once dominated the sea,
   she and her rulers,
   who spread their terror abroad,
   every one of them.
¹⁸ Now the wastelands tremble
   on the day of your fall.
   Your expulsion horrifies
   the islands of the sea.

¹⁹ The LORD God proclaims: When I turn you into ruins like uninhabitable cities, when the deep sea washes over you and the raging seas cover you, ²⁰ I will lead you down into the pit, to the everlasting people. I will install you in the world below,^u in the everlasting ruins, with those who go down to the pit. And so you will neither rule nor radiate splendor in the land of the living.

^u Or *the land of the lowest places*

TYRE

An important Phoenician island city just off the coast of southern Lebanon, about 50 mi. south of Beirut. References to Tyre also appear some 40 times in the OT, often in contexts of condemning materialism and pride. In any case, Tyre, "queen of the seas," represents one of the most significant historical sites of the entire Mediterranean coast; as the prophet Ezekiel acknowledged, "Your territory is in the depths of the sea, and it's your builders who made you beautiful" (Ezek 27:4).

The Tyrian "golden age" was the 10th century BCE, with the accession of Hiram I to the throne (ca. 980). Friend to both Kings David and Solomon of Israel, this king apparently built no fewer than three lavish temples in Tyre. A later king, Ethbaal I (ca. 878–847 BCE) succeeded in reestablishing his dominion over the entire southern territory of Phoenicia; Jezebel, his daughter, was married to King Ahab of Israel.

Condemnatory references to Tyre are found in Joel 3:4-8 (Heb. 4:4-8); Amos 1:9-10; and Zechariah 9:2-4. Tyre is accused of social sin (enslaving peoples) in Amos and Joel and of ostentatious wealth in Zechariah. In Isaiah 23, and especially in Ezekiel 26–28, Tyre infamously symbolizes proud, willful opposition to the God of Israel, and its inevitable doom is celebrated at length.

²¹I will terrify you, and you will disappear. You will be sought but never found again. This is what the LORD God says.

Tyre, the ship of state

27 The LORD's word came to me: ²You, human one, sing a lament for Tyre. ³Say this about Tyre, who sits enthroned at the entrance to the sea, the people's agent for trade throughout the coastlands. The LORD God proclaims:

Tyre, you say,
    "I'm perfectly beautiful!"
⁴ But your territory is
    in the depths of the sea,
and it's your builders
    who made you beautiful.
⁵ For you they made your deck
    of cypress from Senir.
To make your mast,
    they took cedar from Lebanon.
⁶ For your oars,
    they used the oaks of Bashan.
They made your hull, inlaid with ivory,
    of boxwood from the coasts of Cyprus.
⁷ Fine embroidered linen from Egypt
    was your sail;
    it became your emblem.
Your awning was made of blue and
    purple cloth from the coasts of Elishah.

⁸The princes of Sidon and Arvad were your oarsmen. Your own wise men were in you as your helmsmen. ⁹The elders and wise men of Gebal were in you, patching up your leaks. Every seagoing ship and its sailors came to do business with you. ¹⁰Paras, Lud, and Put were the warriors in your army. By hanging their shields and helmets on you, they made you radiant. ¹¹The men of Arvad and Helech were stationed on your walls all around; the men of Gamad were in your towers. They hung their weapons on your walls all around. They were the ones who completed your beauty.

¹²Tarshish was your procurer of great wealth. For your wares, they exchanged silver, iron, tin, and lead. ¹³Javan, Tubal, and Meshech were your agents in human trafficking. They gave you bronze vessels

for these wares of yours. ¹⁴Beth-togarmah traded horses, warhorses, and mules for your wares. ¹⁵Islanders from Rhodesᵛ were your agents. By contract they procured ebony and ivory for you from many coastlands. ¹⁶Aram was your agent for many products. They traded turquoise, purple cloth, colorful brocades, linen, coral, and rubies for your wares. ¹⁷Judah and the land of Israel were your agents, trading the finest wheat,ʷ millet,ˣ honey, oil, and balm for your wares. ¹⁸For many of your finished products, Damascus traded out of its great wealth the wine of Helbon and white wool. ¹⁹Vedan and Javan from the region of Uzal traded with you. They exchanged wrought iron, cinnamon, and spices for your wares. ²⁰Dedan was your agent for saddle blankets. ²¹Arabia and all the princes of Kedar traded for you. They procured lambs, rams, and goats for you. ²²They were your agents in Sheba and Raamah. For your wares they exchanged the finest spices, every kind of precious stone, and gold. ²³Haran, Canneh, and Eden were your agents,ʸ and also Assyria and Chilmad. ²⁴They procured fine finished goods for you, garments of purple and brocade, and plush carpets rolled up and securely tied with ropes, among your acquisitions. ²⁵The ships of Tarshish carried your goods.

You were filled to capacity
    and heavily laden
    in the middle of the sea.
²⁶ Your oarsmen brought you out
    onto the high seas;
    an east wind sank you
    into the sea's depths.
²⁷ Your goods, your wares, your wealth,
    your sailors, your helmsmen,
    those patching your leaks,
    your merchants, all your warriors in you,
    and all the company that is with you—
    they also sank into the sea's depth
    on the day of your demise.
²⁸ At your helmsmen's cries for help,
    the troubled waters seethe.
²⁹ Those entrusted with the oars
    desert their posts.

ᵛHeb *Dedan* ʷOr *wheat from Minnith* ˣHeb uncertain ʸLXX; MT adds *Sheba*.

All sailors and helmsmen
  seek footing on the shore.
³⁰ Loudly they cry,
  bitterly they wail,
  and they put dust on their heads
  and cover themselves with ashes.
³¹ They cut off all their hair
  and put on mourning clothes.
  In despair they weep for you,
  and bitterly perform the mourning rites.
³² In their lamentation
  they raise a lament for you;
  they sing lamentions over you:
    "Who was like Tyre,
      silenced in the middle of the sea?"

³³ When your wares came out from the seas,
  you satisfied many people.
  Your abundant wealth and merchandise
    enriched the kings of the earth.
³⁴ Now you are shattered by the seas;
  your cargoes,
    as well as everyone in your company,
    are sunk into the water's depths.
³⁵ Now the inhabitants of the coastlands
  shudder on account of you.
  And as for their kings,
    their hair stands on end;
    their faces betray their horror.
³⁶ The merchants for the peoples
  hiss because of you.
  You have become a terror;
    from now on you are nothing.

Prince of Tyre

28 The LORD's word came to me: ²Human one, say to the prince of Tyre, The LORD God proclaims: In your arrogance, you say, "I am God, and as God I rule the seas!" Though you claim to have the mind of a god, you are mortal, not divine. ³You are certainly wiser than Daniel; no secrets are hidden from you. ⁴By your wisdom and discernment, you made yourself rich, and you filled your storehouses with silver and gold. ⁵Through your shrewd trading you multiplied your riches. But then you became proud of your riches. ⁶So now the LORD God proclaims: Because you claim to have the mind of a god, ⁷I'll bring foreigners, the most ruthless na-

tions, against you. They will let loose their swords against your fine wisdom, and they will degrade your splendor. ⁸They will hurl you to destruction, and you will die, murdered, on the high seas. ⁹When you face your murderers, will you still say, "I'm God"? In your killers' hands, you are mortal, not divine. ¹⁰You will die as the uncircumcised do, at the hands of foreigners. I have spoken. This is what the LORD God has said.

¹¹The LORD's word came to me: ¹²Human one, sing a lament for the king of Tyre. Say to him, The LORD God proclaims: You were full of wisdom and beauty, the image of perfection. ¹³You were in Eden, God's garden. You were covered with gold and every precious stone: carnelian, topaz, and moonstone; beryl, onyx, and jasper; lapis lazuli, turquoise, and emerald. On the day that you were created, finely crafted pendants and engravings were prepared. ¹⁴You, a winged creature, were installed as a guardian. I placed you in God's holy mountain where you walked among the stones of fire. ¹⁵From the day you were created until injustice was found in you, your ways were assured. ¹⁶But because of your trade, your oppressive business practices piled up, and you became impure. So I expelled you from God's mountain. I removed you, winged creature, guardian, from among the stones of fire. ¹⁷You exalted yourself because of your beauty and corrupted your wisdom for the sake of your splendor. I will cast you down to the earth in the sight of kings, and I will make a spectacle of you. ¹⁸Because of your corrupt trade, which surpassed your many other sins, you made your sanctuaries impure. Therefore, I will bring fire from your midst. When it has consumed you, I will turn you into dust on the earth in the sight of all who see you. ¹⁹Everyone among the peoples who knows you will be appalled because of you. You will become a terror. From that time on, you will be nothing.

Against Sidon

²⁰The LORD's word came to me: ²¹Human one, face Sidon, prophesy against it, ²²and say, The LORD God proclaims: I'm against

you, Sidon, and I will manifest my glory in you. When I've executed judgment against it and through it have manifested my holiness, they will know that I am the LORD. ²³ I will hurl plague against it, and blood will run in its streets. When the sword comes against it from all sides, the slain will fall within it. Then they will know that I am the LORD. ²⁴The house of Israel will no longer suffer from the pricking thorn or painful briar of any of its neighbors who hold it in contempt. And they will know that I am the LORD God.

²⁵The LORD God proclaims: When I gather the house of Israel from the peoples among whom they've scattered, and I demonstrate my holiness through them in the sight of the nations, they will live on their fertile land, which I gave to my servant Jacob. ²⁶They will live on it in safety. They will build houses, plant vineyards, and live in safety. When I execute judgments against all who hold them in contempt on every side, they will know that I, the LORD, am their God.

Against Egypt

29 In the tenth year, on the twelfth day of the tenth month, the LORD's word came to me: ²Human one, face Pha-

raoh, Egypt's king, and prophesy against him and against all of Egypt. ³Speak and say, The LORD God proclaims:

I'm against you, Pharaoh, Egypt's king,
  great crocodile lurking
    in the Nile's canals,
  who says, "The Nile is all mine;
    I made it for myself!"
⁴ I will set hooks in your jaws;
  I will make the fish
    from the Nile's canals
    cling to your scales.
I will drag you out of the Nile's canals,
  and also all the fish
    from the Nile's canals
    clinging to your scales.
⁵ I will fling you out into the desert,
  and also all the fish
    from the Nile's canals.
You will fall on the open ground,
  and won't be gathered or retrieved.

I've given you to the beasts of the earth
  and the birds in the sky for food.
⁶ Everyone living in Egypt
  will know that I am the LORD.
Because they were a flimsy crutch for the house of Israel—⁷when they took you

SIDON

Sidon and Tyre, the twin Phoenician cities (Jer 25:22; 27:3; 47:4; 1 Chron 22:4; Matt 11:21-22; 15:21; Mark 3:8; 7:24, 31; Luke 6:17; 10:13-14; Acts 12:20) 25 and 50 mi. south of Beirut, were for many centuries independent of each other. Sidon was considered from the classical period onward to be the most ancient and the most prominent of the Canaanite/Phoenician coastal cities. Sidon is mentioned in the OT as the "oldest son" of Canaan (Gen 10:15; 1 Chron 1:13). The terms *Sidon* and *Sidonians* were not only used in a narrow sense of the city itself and its inhabitants but also included at times the whole of Phoenicia (Judg 10:12; 18:7; 1 Kgs 5:6; 11:1, 5; 16:31; 2 Kgs 23:13; Ezek 32:30). Early use of the names in this wider sense indicates a period in antiquity when Sidon was powerful enough to impose her rule and her name upon large areas outside the city. *Sidonian* and *Phoenician* were at times synonymous.

Sidon's dominant position among the Phoenician coastal cities during this period seems clear. In biblical accounts (Deut 3:9; Josh 13:6; Judg 3:3; 10:12; 18:7) it is Sidon, not Tyre, that appears as a powerful city.

in hand, you would splinter and make their shoulders sore; when they leaned on you, you would break, bringing them to their knees— [8]now the LORD God proclaims: I'm bringing a sword against you, and I will cut off from you human and beast. [9]The land of Egypt will be turned into a wasteland and ruins. Then they will know that I am the LORD.

Because you[z] said, "The Nile is mine; I made it," [10]I'm against you and against the Nile's canals. I will make the land of Egypt into an utter ruin, a wasteland, from Migdol to Syene and as far as its boundary with Cush. [11]No foot, animal or human, will walk across it, and it won't be inhabited for forty years. [12]I will make the land of Egypt the most desolate of wastelands and its cities the most devastated of ruined cities. It will be a wasteland for forty years, and the Egyptians will be scattered among the nations and dispersed throughout the lands.

[13]The LORD God proclaims: At the end of forty years, I will gather the Egyptians from among the nations where they are scattered. [14]I will improve their circumstances and bring them back to the land of Pathros, the land of their origin. Egypt will be a lowly kingdom there. [15]Out of all the kingdoms, it will be the lowliest. It will never again exalt itself over the nations, and I will make it small to keep it from ruling the nations. [16]The house of Israel will never again bring guilt on itself by faithlessly turning to Egypt for help, for they will know that I am the LORD God.

[17]In the twenty-seventh year, on the first day of the first month, the LORD's word came to me: [18]Human one, Babylon's King Nebuchadrezzar made his army labor very hard against Tyre. Every head was scraped bald, and every shoulder was rubbed raw, yet he got nothing from Tyre for himself or for his army for any of his efforts against it. [19]So now the LORD God proclaims: I'm going to give the land of Egypt to Babylon's King Nebuchadnezzar. He will carry off its wealth, he will plunder and loot it, and it will be the wages for his army. [20]I will give him the land of Egypt as payment for his laboring for me. This is what the LORD God says.

[21]On that day I will give new strength[a] to the house of Israel, and I will open your mouth among them. Then they will know that I am the LORD.

30

The LORD's word came to me: [2]Human one, prophesy and say, The LORD God proclaims:

> Howl! Horror for the day!

[3] The day is coming,
>   the day of the LORD comes,
>   a day of clouds:
>   the nations' time has come.

[4] A sword will come into Egypt,
>   and trembling will overcome Cush,
>   when the slain fall in Egypt,
>   its wealth carried away,
>   and its foundations razed.

[5] Cush, Put, and Lud,
>   all Arabia and Cub,
>   and the people from
>   the allied country[b] with them
>   will fall by the sword.

[6] The LORD proclaims:
>   When Egypt's helpers fall,
>   its proud strength will decline.

---

[z]Or he [a]Or make a horn sprout [b]Or land of the covenant

From Migdol to Syene
    they will fall by the sword.
        This is what the LORD God says.

⁷Of all the lands laid waste, it will be the most desolate; of all cities, the most ruined. ⁸They will know that I am the LORD. On the day that I set fire to Egypt and all its helpers are broken, ⁹messengers in ships will go out from me to startle the complacent Cushites. Anguish will overcome them on Egypt's day. It's certainly coming.

¹⁰The LORD God proclaims:
    I will bring an end to the hordes of Egypt
        through the power
        of Babylon's King Nebuchadrezzar.
¹¹He and his people with him,
        the most terrible of the nations,
        will be brought in to destroy the land.
    They will draw their swords against Egypt
        and fill the land with the slain.
¹²I will dry up the Nile canals;
        I will sell the land to evildoers.
    With the help of foreigners
        I will lay waste to the land
        and everything in it.
        I, the LORD, have spoken.

¹³The LORD God proclaims:
    I will destroy the idols
        and bring an end to the images
        in Memphis.
    Never again will there be
        a prince from the land of Egypt;
        so I will kindle fear in the land of Egypt.
¹⁴I will turn Pathros into a desolation,
        set fire to Zoan,
        and execute judgments in Thebes.
¹⁵I will pour out my anger on Pelusium,
        the stronghold of Egypt,
        and I will cut down pompous Thebes.
¹⁶I will set Egypt on fire;
        Pelusium will writhe in travail,
        Thebes will be split open,
        Memphis assaulted in broad daylight.
¹⁷The elite troops of On and Pi-beseth
        will fall by the sword,
        and the cities themselves
        will go into captivity.
¹⁸At Tehaphnehes the day will go dark when I break Egypt's yoke and bring an end to its proud strength. A cloud will cover it,

and the towns around it will go into captivity. ¹⁹I will execute judgments in Egypt, and they will know that I am the LORD.

²⁰In the eleventh year, on the first day of the seventh month, the LORD's word came to me: ²¹Human one, I've broken the arm of Pharaoh, Egypt's king, and it hasn't been set so that it might heal, nor has it been braced or wrapped up so that it might be strong enough to grasp a sword. ²²So now the LORD God proclaims: I'm against Pharaoh, and I will break his arms, both the sound one and the broken one, and I'll make the sword fall out of his hand. ²³I will scatter the Egyptians among the nations and disperse them throughout the earth. ²⁴I will strengthen the arms of the king of Babylon, and I will put my sword into his hand. When I break the arms of Pharaoh, he will groan like a dying man in his presence. ²⁵I will strengthen the arms of the king of Babylon, but the arms of Pharaoh will fall. They will know that I am the LORD, when I put my sword into the hand of the king of Babylon and he uses it against the land of Egypt. ²⁶When I scatter the Egyptians among the nations and disperse them throughout the earth, they will know that I am the LORD.

Egypt is not Assyria

31 In the eleventh year, on the first day of the third month, the LORD's word came to me: ²Human one, say to Pharaoh, Egypt's king, and his troops:
    With whom do you compare
        in your greatness?
³ Consider Assyria, a cedar of Lebanon:
        beautiful branches, dense shade,
            towering height;
        indeed, its top went up
            between the clouds.
⁴ Waters nourished it; the deep raised it up,
        because its streams flowed around
            the place where it was planted.
    From there, water trickled down
        to all the other trees of the field.
⁵ And so it became higher than
        all the trees of the field.
    Its branches became abundant;
        its boughs grew long.

Because of the plentiful water,
  it grew freely.
[6] All the birds in the sky
  made nests in its branches;
  all the beasts of the field
  gave birth under its boughs,
  and in its shade,
  every great nation lived.

[7] It became beautiful in its greatness
  and in its lush foliage,
  because it took root in plentiful water.
[8] No cedar was its equal in God's garden.
  The fir trees didn't have anything
  like its branches,
  and the plane trees had nothing
  like its boughs.

GARDEN OF EDEN

Most readers of the Bible associate Eden with Genesis 2–3, but it is important to note that the word occurs in several other places in the OT: Isaiah 51:3; Ezekiel 28:13; 31:9, 16, 18; 36:35; Joel 2:3. One key to understanding Eden is the description of its location in Genesis 2:10-14. The Garden is characterized by four rivers that flow from it: the Pishon, Gihon, Tigris, and Euphrates. It is significant that no single geographic location can be identified as the origin of all these rivers. The fact that the rivers are four in number points to the universal reach of Eden, for classical Mesopotamian sources frequently divide the world into four quadrants and the living waters of the earth are thought to emerge from a sacred center. And because the sources of rivers tend to be found in mountainous regions, it is likely that Eden was thought of as a cosmic mountain. The mountainous character of the Garden of God is made explicit in another Eden tradition found in the Bible: Ezekiel's famous oracle against the king of Tyre (28:11-19, esp. v. 14). We also know from Psalm 24:2-3 that there was an intimate connection between the founding of the world on top of mythic waters and the establishment of the temple. For an Israelite reader, it was a commonplace to associate Eden with the sacred center of Jerusalem.

It is striking to note that kings in Mesopotamia often described themselves as great gardeners. Given the symbolic lineage between Zion and Eden it is not surprising that recent excavations in Jerusalem have revealed that tremendous care was put into its irrigation systems such that it could be a location of an abundant variety of trees and other ornamental vegetation. The lushness of Zion was meant to show the abundance of Eden.

In Ezekiel 47:1-12, the prophet is taken in a vision to the entrance of the temple. There he is witness to an extraordinary miracle: waters issue from the threshold of the building and begin to make their way out of the city of Jerusalem. As they head toward the region of the Dead Sea and the vast desert that surrounds it, the waters gradually grow in strength and slowly turn this barren desert into a luxuriant garden. This return of the wilderness to an Edenic state is picked up by the author of Revelation in the very last chapter of the Christian Bible (Rev 22:1-2). In this vision, all of creation will be returned to the paradisiacal state in which it was made through the mediation of God's appointed dwelling place in Jerusalem.

None of the trees in God's garden
could compare to it in its beauty.
⁹ As for its beauty—I made it so,
with its abundant foliage.
All the trees of Eden envied it,
all that were in God's garden.

¹⁰ So now the LORD God proclaims:
Consider the fate of those who tower high!
When it allowed its branches to reach up
among the clouds,
it became arrogant.
¹¹ So I handed it over
to the most powerful nation,
who continually
acted treacherously against it.
I banished it!
¹² Foreigners, the worst of the nations,
cut it down
and left it to lie among the hills.
All its branches fell among the valleys,
and its boughs were broken off
in the earth's deep ravines.
All the earth's peoples departed
from its shade and abandoned it.
¹³ On its trunk roost all the birds in the sky,
and on its boughs lie
all the beasts of the field.
¹⁴ All this has happened so that no other
well-watered tree would tower high or allow
its branches to reach among the clouds.
Nor would their leaders achieve the towering stature of such well-watered trees. Certainly, all of them are consigned to death,
to the world below,ᶜ among human beings
who go down to the pit.
¹⁵ The LORD God proclaims: On the day
that it went down to the underworld,ᵈ I
caused mourning. I blocked off the deep
sea against it. I dried up its rivers and restrained the mighty waters. I made Lebanon go into mourning for it, and all the
trees of the field languished on its account.
¹⁶ When it was felled, the nations quaked at
the sound. When I cast it down into the underworld, with those who go down to the
pit, all the trees of Eden were comforted in
the world below, the choicest and the best
of Lebanon, all the trees that depended on

water. ¹⁷ His allies,ᵉ those among the nations who lived under his shade, these also
went down with him to the underworld, to
those who are slain by the sword.

¹⁸ Are you like any of these in glory or
greatness among Eden's trees? Then you
too will go down with Eden's trees to the
world below. You will lie among the uncircumcised, with those who are slain by the
sword. This is Pharaoh and his entire horde.
This is what the LORD God says.

Egypt the crocodile

32 In the twelfth year, on the first day
of the twelfth month, the LORD's
word came to me: ²Human one, sing a lament for Pharaoh, Egypt's king. Say to him:
You consider yourself a young lion
among the nations,
but you are like the sea monster!
You thrash about in your rivers,
you roil the waters with your feet,
and you muddy yourᶠ rivers.
³ The LORD God proclaims:
In the company of many peoples
I will spread my net over you,
and I will haul you up in my dragnet.
⁴ I will cast you out on the earth
and throw you on the open ground.
I will cause all the birds in the sky
to settle on you,
and all the beasts of the earth
to devour you.
⁵ Your flesh I will set upon the mountains,
and I will fill the valleys
with your gore.
⁶ With your blood I will soak
your irrigated land,ᵍ
and the streambeds
will be filled with you.
⁷ When you are snuffed out,
I will cover the sky,
and I will darken the stars.
I will cover the sun with a cloud,
and the moon won't radiate its light.
⁸ As for the shining lights of the heavens,
I will make them dark over you,
and set darkness over your land.
This is what the LORD God says.

ᶜOr *the land of the lowest places* ᵈHeb *Sheol* ᵉOr *his arms* ᶠLXX; MT *their* ᵍMT adds *to the mountains.*

⁹ I will trouble the hearts of many peoples
  when I bring about your destruction
  with nations from lands you didn't know.
¹⁰ I will make many peoples appalled
  because of you.
  Their kings will shudder violently
    on your account
  when I brandish my sword before them.
  They will tremble for their lives
    again and again
  on the day of your downfall.

¹¹The LORD God proclaims: The sword of the king of Babylon is coming against you! ¹²I will make your hordes fall by the swords of mighty men, the most terrifying of the nations, all of them. They will bring an end to Egypt's pride, and all of its hordes will be destroyed. ¹³I will remove all its livestock from beside the plentiful waters so that neither human foot nor livestock's hoof will trouble it again. ¹⁴At that time, I will allow the waters to run clear, and make its rivers flow like oil. This is what the LORD God says. ¹⁵When I turn the land of Egypt into a wasteland and the land is deprived of all that fills it, and when I strike down those who live there, then they will know that I am the LORD. ¹⁶This is a lament, and it will be sung as a lament. The daughters of the nations will lament for Egypt, and they will also lament for Egypt's hordes. This is what the LORD God says.

¹⁷In the twelfth year, on the fifteenth day of the first month,[h] the LORD's word came to me: ¹⁸Human one, mourn for Egypt's hordes. Send Egypt down
  with the mighty nations subject[i] to it,
  to the world below,[j]
  among those who go down to the pit.
¹⁹ Whom do you surpass in beauty?
  Go down and take your bed
    with the uncircumcised,
²⁰ among those who fall
    slain by the sword.
  A sword is appointed, and all his hordes will carry him off. ²¹The mighty chieftains, those who once came to his aid, will speak to him from the middle of the underworld,[k]

for the uncircumcised have gone down and have lain down, slain by the sword.

Vanished glory
²² Assyria is there, and all its assembly
    round about his grave,
  all of them slain, fallen by the sword,
²³ who were assigned graves
    in the deepest region of the pit.
  His assembly surrounded his grave,
    all of them slain, fallen by the sword,
  who caused terror
    in the land of the living.

²⁴ Elam is there, her entire horde
    round about her grave,
  all of them slain, fallen by the sword,
  who went down uncircumcised
    to the world below,[l]
  who caused terror
    in the land of the living.
  They bore their shame
    like those who go down to the pit.
²⁵ Among the slain they made a bed for her,
    with all her hordes
    round about her grave,
  all of them uncircumcised,
    slain by the sword,
  for they caused terror
    in the land of the living.
  They bore their shame
    like those who go down to the pit;
  in the midst of the slain
    she[m] was placed.

²⁶ Meshech and Tubal are there,
    and all their hordes around their graves,
  all of them uncircumcised,
    slain by the sword,
  for they caused terror
    in the land of the living.
²⁷They don't lie with the mighty men fallen among the uncircumcised. When they went down to the underworld[n] with their weapons of war, they put their swords under their heads and their shields[o] over their bones. The terror of the mighty men is in the land of the living.

---

[h]LXX; MT lacks *the first month*. [i]Or *daughter nations* [j]Or *the land of the lowest places* [k]Heb *Sheol* [l]Or *the land of the lowest places* [m]Or *he* [n]Heb *Sheol* [o]Or *sin*

²⁸But you, you will be broken among the uncircumcised, and you will lie with those who are slain by the sword.

²⁹ Edom is there, its kings and all its princes,
　who, though strong,
　　were put with those slain
　　by the sword.
　They lie with the uncircumcised,
　like those who go down to the pit.

³⁰ All the princes of the north are there,
　and all the Sidonians
　　who went down with the slain;
　　in spite of the terror of their strength,
　　they were disgraced.
　They lie uncircumcised with
　　those slain by the sword.
　They bore their shame
　like those who go down to the pit.

³¹ When Pharaoh sees them,
　he will be sorry for all his hordes
　　who are slain by the sword—
　　Pharaoh and all his army.
　This is what the LORD God says,
³² Though it was I who put his terror
　　in the land of the living,
　he will be laid out
　　among the uncircumcised,
　　with those slain by the sword,
　　Pharaoh and all his horde.
　This is what the LORD God says.

The lookout

33 The LORD's word came to me: ²Human one, speak to your people and say to them: Suppose I bring a sword against a country, and the people of the land take a certain person from their assembly and make him their lookout. ³When he sees the sword coming against the land, he blows the trumpet and warns the people. ⁴If they hear the sound of the trumpet but don't heed the warning, when the sword comes and they are taken away, they are responsible for their blood. ⁵They heard the sound of the trumpet but didn't heed the warning, so their blood is on them. If they had paid attention to the warning, they would have saved their lives. ⁶If the lookout sees the sword coming but doesn't blow the trumpet to warn the people, when the sword comes and takes away any of them, they are taken away in their sin, but I'll hold the lookout responsible for their blood.

⁷You, human one, I've made you a lookout for the house of Israel. Whenever you hear me speaking, you must give them warning from me. ⁸If I pronounce a death sentence on wicked people, and you don't warn them to turn from their way, they will die in their guilt, but I will hold you responsible for their blood. ⁹But suppose you do warn the wicked of their ways so that they might turn from them. If they don't turn from their ways, they will die in their guilt, but you will save your life.

¹⁰You, human one, say to the house of Israel: This is what all of you are saying: "How our transgressions and our sins weigh on us! We waste away because of them. How can we live?" ¹¹Say to them, This is what the LORD God says: As surely as I live, do I take pleasure in the death of the wicked? If the wicked turn from their ways, they will live. Turn, completely turn from your wicked ways! Why should you die, house of Israel?

¹²You, human one, say to your people: The righteousness of the righteous doesn't rescue them when they begin to sin. Nor does the wickedness of the wicked make them stumble if they turn from their wickedness. If the righteous sin, their righteousness won't protect them. ¹³Even if I've told the righteous they will live, none of their righteous deeds will be remembered if they trust in their righteousness and do wrong. They will die because of their evil deeds. ¹⁴And even if I have pronounced a death sentence on the wicked, if they turn from sin and do what is just and right—¹⁵if they return pledges, make restitution for robbery, and walk in life-giving regulations in order not to sin—they will live and not die. ¹⁶None of the sins they've committed will be remembered against them. They've done what is just and right, and they will live.

¹⁷Yet your people say, "My Lord's way doesn't measure up." Isn't it their ways that don't measure up? ¹⁸When the righteous turn from their righteousness to do wrong, they will die because of it. ¹⁹And when the

wicked turn from their wickedness to do what is just and right, it is for that reason they will live. ²⁰Yet you say, "My Lord's way doesn't measure up." I judge each one of you according to your ways, house of Israel!

News from Jerusalem

²¹In the twelfth year, on the fifth day of the tenth month of our exile, a survivor from Jerusalem came to me and reported, "The city has fallen!" ²²The LORD's power was with me in the evening before the survivor arrived, and just before he arrived in the morning, God opened my mouth. So my mouth was opened, and I was no longer speechless.

²³The LORD's word came to me: ²⁴Human one, those who live among those ruins in Israel's fertile land are saying, "Abraham was just one man, and he inherited the land. We are many, so certainly the land has been given to us as an inheritance."

²⁵So say to them, The LORD God proclaims: You eat with the blood, you lift your eyes to the idols, and you shed blood. Should you inherit the land? ²⁶You live by the sword, you observe detestable practices, and every one of you commits adultery.ᴾ Should you inherit the land?

²⁷Say to them, The LORD God proclaims: As surely as I live, those in the ruins will fall by the sword, those in the countryside I will give to the wild beasts to consume, and those in the strongholds and caves will die of plague. ²⁸I will make the land an uninhabitable waste. Its proud strength will come to an end, and Israel's highlands will become so deserted that no one will cross through them. ²⁹They will know that I am the LORD when I make the land an uninhabitable waste because of all their detestable practices.

A fickle audience

³⁰As for you, human one, your people talk about you beside the walls and in their doorways. One by one, they say to each other, "Let's go hear what sort of message has come from the LORD." ³¹So they come

to you as people do, and they sit before you as my people. They listen to your words, but they refuse to do them. Though they speak of their longing�q for me, they act out of their own interests and opinions. ³²To them you are like a singer of love songs with a lovely voice and skilled technique. They listen to your words, but no one does them. ³³When this comes—and it is certainly coming—they will know that a prophet has been among them.

The good shepherd

34²The LORD's word came to me: ²Human one, prophesy against Israel's shepherds. Prophesy and say to them, The LORD God proclaims to the shepherds: Doom to Israel's shepherds who tended themselves! Shouldn't shepherds tend the flock? ³You drink the milk, you wear the wool, and you slaughter the fat animals, but you don't tend the flock. ⁴You don't strengthen the weak, heal the sick, bind up the injured, bring back the strays, or seek out the lost; but instead you use force to rule them with injustice. ⁵Without a shepherd, my flock was scattered; and when it was scattered, it became food for all the wild animals. ⁶My flock strayed on all the mountains and on every high hill throughout all the earth. My flock was scattered, and there was no one to look for them or find them. ⁷So now shepherds, hear the LORD's word! ⁸This is what the LORD God says: As surely as I live, without a shepherd, my flock became prey. My flock became food for all the wild animals. My shepherds didn't seek out my flock. They tended themselves, but they didn't tend my flock.

⁹So, shepherds, hear the LORD's word! ¹⁰The LORD God proclaims: I'm against the shepherds! I will hold them accountable for my flock, and I will put an end to their tending the flock. The shepherds will no longer tend them, because I will rescue my flock from their mouths, and they will no longer be their food.

¹¹The LORD God proclaims: I myself will search for my flock and seek them out.

ᴾOr *defiles his neighbor's wife*   qOr *love songs*

¹²As a shepherd seeks out the flock when some in the flock have been scattered, so will I seek out my flock. I will rescue them from all the places where they were scat-tered during the time of clouds and thick darkness. ¹³I will gather and lead them out from the countries and peoples, and I will bring them to their own fertile land. I will

SHEPHERD

Biblical references to shepherding reflect the agricultural environment of the ancient Near East, in which sheep and goats (domesticated from 7000 BCE or earlier) were a primary source of food, wool, and hides. Accordingly, livestock constituted a significant component of wealth (see Gen 26:12-14; 1 Sam 25:2; Job 42:12; Ps 144:13).

In scripture, the antiquity of shepherding is evident from the fact that Abel "cared for the flocks" (Gen 4:2-4), and that Abraham, Isaac, and especially Jacob (Gen 30:37-43) shared this role. But the biblical portrait of the shep-herd is indebted above all to David, who in youth cared for the family flock (1 Sam 16:11; 17:34); hence the terms of God's commission: "You will shepherd my people Israel, and you will be Israel's leader" (2 Sam 5:2; cf. Ps 78:70-71). Likewise, the Davidic psalms characterize the life of faith in pastoral imagery: "The LORD is my shepherd. I lack nothing" (Ps 23:1; cf. 28:9; 68:10). Such metaphors are a staple feature of Israel's worship: "He is our God," declares Psalm 95:7, "and we are the people of his pasture, the sheep in his hands" (similarly Pss 79:13; 100:3; 119:176).

Later prophets frequently denounce national leaders as unfaithful shep-herds who abuse the flocks in their care (Isa 56:11; Jer 12:10; 23:1-2; 50:6; Ezek 34:2-10; Zech 10:2-3). This forms the background for Jesus' bold an-nouncement: "I am the good shepherd. The good shepherd lays down his life for the sheep" (John 10:11; cf. 10:14). His words run counter to the appar-ently low reputation of shepherds in his day, which also accounts for the un-usual choice of shepherds as the first to learn of Jesus' birth (Luke 2:8-20). Jesus reiterates prophetic language by characterizing previous leaders as "thieves and outlaws" (John 10:8) and God's people as lost sheep (Mark 6:34; Luke 15:4-7), with himself as their true shepherd (Matt 15:24; 25:32; Mark 14:27; cf. Matt 2:6). According to John 10:16, this ministry also embraces those outside ethnic Israel: "I have other sheep that don't belong to this sheep pen. I must lead them too. They will listen to my voice and there will be one flock, with one shepherd."

In similar terms, Jesus commissions Peter to care for his followers: "Feed my lambs. . . . Take care of my sheep" (John 21:15-17); and the early church continues to use shepherding language both for Jesus (Heb 13:20; 1 Pet 2:25) and for those who pastor in his name (Acts 20:28; 1 Pet 5:2-4). Scrip-ture's last word on this theme, however, points back to Jesus and the eternal destiny of the saints: "The Lamb who is in the midst of the throne will shep-herd them. He will lead them to the springs of life-giving water, and God will wipe away every tear from their eyes" (Rev 7:17).

feed them on Israel's highlands, along the riverbeds, and in all the inhabited places. ¹⁴I will feed them in good pasture, and their sheepfold will be there, on Israel's lofty highlands. On Israel's highlands, they will lie down in a secure fold and feed on green pastures. ¹⁵I myself will feed my flock and make them lie down. This is what the LORD God says. ¹⁶I will seek out the lost, bring back the strays, bind up the wounded, and strengthen the weak. But the fat and the strong I will destroy, because I will tend my sheepʳ with justice.

¹⁷As for you, my flock, the LORD God proclaims: I will judge between the rams and the bucks among the sheep and the goats. ¹⁸Is feeding in good pasture or drinking clear water such a trivial thing that you should trample and muddy what is left with your feet? ¹⁹But now my flock must feed on what your feet have trampled and drink water that your feet have muddied.

²⁰So the LORD God proclaims to them: I will judge between the fat and the lean sheep. ²¹You shove with shoulder and flank, and with your horns you ram all the weak sheep until you've scattered them outside. ²²But I will rescue my flock so that they will never again be prey. I will even judge between the sheep! ²³I will appoint for them a single shepherd, and he will feed them. My servant David will feed them. He will be their shepherd. ²⁴I, the LORD, will be their God, and my servant David will be their prince. I, the LORD, have spoken. ²⁵I will make a covenant of peace for them, and I will banish the wild animals from the land. Then they will safely live in the desert and sleep in the forest. ²⁶I will give them and those around my hill a blessing by sending the rain in its season. They will be rains of blessing. ²⁷The trees in the field will bear fruit, and the earth will yield its harvest. They will be safe on their fertile land, and they will know that I am the LORD when I break the bars of their yoke and deliver them from those who enslaved them. ²⁸The nations will no longer prey on them, and wild animals will no longer devour them.

They will live in safety, with no one to trouble them. ²⁹I will establish for them a place famous for what it grows. No longer will they experience famine in the land, nor will they bear the disgrace of the nations. ³⁰They will know that I, the LORD their God, am with them, and they, the house of Israel, are my people. This is what the LORD God says. ³¹You are my flock, the flock of my pasture. You are human, and I am your God. This is what the LORD God says.

Against Edom

35 The LORD's word came to me: ²Human one, face Mount Seir, and prophesy against it. ³Say to it, The LORD God proclaims:

I'm against you, Mount Seir!
I will use my power against you.
I will make you into a desolate wasteland,
⁴I will turn your cities into ruins,
and you will become a desolation.
Then you will know that I am the LORD.

⁵Because you nursed an ancient grudge, you handed the Israelites over to the sword in the time of their distress, during their final punishment. ⁶So now the LORD God proclaims: As surely as I live, I will prepare you for blood, and blood will pursue you. Because you don't hate bloodshed, bloodshed will pursue you. ⁷I will turn Mount Seir into a desolate wasteland, when I cut off from it both passerby and homecomer. ⁸I will fill its highlands—your hills and your valleys, and all your ravines—with its slain. Those who are slain by the sword will fall on them. ⁹I will turn you into an eternal desolation. Your cities won't be inhabited, and you will know that I am the LORD.

¹⁰You said, "These two nations and these two territories are mine. We will take possession of them even if the LORD is there." ¹¹Therefore, the LORD God proclaims: As surely as I live, I will act according to the anger and zeal you displayed when you dealt with them so hatefully. When I judge you, I will make myself known to them, ¹²and you will know that I am the LORD. I've heard the lies and libels that you uttered

ʳOr them

against Israel's highlands when you said, "They are laid waste. They've been given to us to consume." [13]With your mouths you exalted yourselves against me and spoke your words against me. I myself heard it!

[14]The LORD God proclaims: As the whole world rejoices, I will turn you into a desolation. [15]Just as you rejoiced over the house of Israel's inheritance because it became desolate, so I will deal with you. Mount Seir, you will become a desolation, with all of Edom, all of it. Then they will know that I am the LORD.

Mountains of Israel

36 You, human one, prophesy to Israel's mountains and say, Hear the LORD's word, mountains of Israel! [2]The LORD God proclaims: The enemy mocked you and said, "The ancient heights belong to us." [3]Therefore, prophesy and say, The LORD God proclaims: When the surviving nations pressed in and ravaged you from all around to lay claim to you, you became an object of the people's slander and derision. [4]Hear the LORD God's word, mountains of Israel! The LORD God proclaims to the mountains and the hills, the watercourses and the valleys, the desolate ruins and the abandoned cities that were contemptuously looted by the surviving nations all around you.

[5]So now, says the LORD God, I will speak in my fiery passion against the surviving nations and against Edom, all those who gleefully and spitefully took my land for themselves as a possession only for plunder.[s] [6]Prophesy concerning Israel's fertile land, and say to the mountains and to the hills, to the ravines and to the valleys, The LORD God proclaims: Because you endured the ridicule of the nations, my passion and fury lead me to speak. [7]So now the LORD God proclaims: I myself swear that the nations round about you will themselves suffer ridicule. [8]But you, mountains of Israel, will extend your branches and bear your fruit for my people Israel, because they will come home very soon. [9]Look, I'm here for you, and I will turn to-

ward you, and you will be farmed and sown. [10]I will populate you with human beings, the whole house of Israel, all of them. The cities will be inhabited, the ruins rebuilt. [11]When I make people and animals increase on you, they will multiply and be fruitful. I will cause you to be inhabited as you were before. I will do more good for you than in the beginning, and you will know that I am the LORD. [12]I will let people walk through you, my people Israel! They will lay claim to you, you will be their inheritance, and you will no longer deprive them of anything.

[13]The LORD God proclaims: Because people say, "You are a devourer of human beings" and "You are depriving your nation," [14]therefore, you will no longer devour human beings or deprive your nation of anything. This is what the LORD God says. [15]You won't have to listen anymore to the taunts of the nations or endure the scorn of the peoples. And you will no longer deprive your nation of anything. This is what the LORD God says.

A new heart

[16]The LORD's word came to me: [17]Human one, when the house of Israel lived on their fertile land, they polluted it with their ways and deeds. Their ways before me were polluted like the blood of menstruation, [18]and so I poured out my fury on them for all the blood they had poured out on the land and for all the defilement of their idols. [19]When I scattered them to the nations and dispersed them into other lands, I judged them according to their ways and deeds. [20]But then when they entered the other nations, they degraded my holy name because it was said of them, "These are the LORD's people, yet they had to leave his land." [21]So I had compassion on my holy name, which the house of Israel degraded among the nations where they had gone.

[22]Therefore, say to the house of Israel, The LORD God proclaims: House of Israel, I'm not acting for your sake but for the sake of my holy name, which you degraded among the nations where you have gone.

[s]MT adds *to drive it out.*

²³I will make my great name holy, which was degraded among the nations when you dishonored it among them. Then the nations will know that I am the LORD. This is what the LORD God says.

When I make myself holy among you in their sight, ²⁴I will take you from the nations, I will gather you from all the countries, and I will bring you to your own fertile land. ²⁵I will sprinkle clean water on you, and you will be cleansed of all your pollution. I will cleanse you of all your idols. ²⁶I will give you a new heart and put a new spirit in you. I will remove your stony heart from your body and replace it with a living one, ²⁷and I will give you my spirit so that you may walk according to my regulations and carefully observe my case laws. ²⁸Then you will live in the land that I gave to your ancestors, you will be my people, and I will be your God. ²⁹I will save you from all your uncleanness, and I will summon the grain and make it grow abundantly so that you won't endure famine. ³⁰I will make abundant the orchards' fruit and the fields' produce so that you will never again endure the shame of famine among the nations. ³¹Then you will remember your evil ways and no-good deeds, and you will feel disgust for yourselves because of your sinful and detestable practices. ³²Not for your sake do I act. This is what the LORD God proclaims. Let that be known to you! Be ashamed and be humiliated because of all your ways, house of Israel.

³³The LORD God proclaims: On the day that I cleanse you of all your guilt, I will cause the cities to be inhabited, and the ruins will be rebuilt. ³⁴The desolate land will be farmed, and it won't be like it was when it seemed a wasteland to all who passed by. ³⁵They will say, "This land, which was a desolation, has become like the garden of Eden." And the cities that were ruined, ravaged, and razed are now fortified and inhabited. ³⁶The surviving nations around you will know that I, the LORD, have rebuilt what was torn down and have planted what was made desolate. I, the LORD, have spoken, and I will do it.

³⁷The LORD God proclaims: I will also allow the house of Israel to ask me to do this for them: that I increase them like a human flock. ³⁸Like the holy flock, like the flock of Jerusalem at its festivals, the ruined cities will be filled with a human flock. Then they will know that I am the LORD.

Valley of dry bones

37 The LORD's power overcame me, and while I was in the LORD's spirit, he led me out and set me down in the middle of a certain valley. It was full of bones. ²He led me through them all around, and I saw that there were a great many of them on the valley floor, and they were very dry.

³He asked me, "Human one, can these bones live again?"

I said, "LORD God, only you know."

⁴He said to me, "Prophesy over these bones, and say to them, Dry bones, hear the LORD's word! ⁵The LORD God proclaims to these bones: I am about to put breath in you, and you will live again. ⁶I will put sinews on you, place flesh on you, and cover you with skin. When I put breath in you, and you come to life, you will know that I am the LORD."

⁷I prophesied just as I was commanded. There was a great noise as I was prophesying, then a great quaking, and the bones came together, bone by bone. ⁸When I looked, suddenly there were sinews on them. The flesh appeared, and then they were covered over with skin. But there was still no breath in them.

⁹He said to me, "Prophesy to the breath; prophesy, human one! Say to the breath, The LORD God proclaims: Come from the four winds, breath! Breathe into these dead bodies and let them live."

¹⁰I prophesied just as he commanded me. When the breath entered them, they came to life and stood on their feet, an extraordinarily large company.

¹¹He said to me, "Human one, these bones are the entire house of Israel. They say, 'Our bones are dried up, and our hope has perished. We are completely finished.' ¹²So now, prophesy and say to them, The LORD God proclaims: I'm opening your graves! I will raise you up from your graves,

my people, and I will bring you to Israel's fertile land. [13]You will know that I am the LORD, when I open your graves and raise you up from your graves, my people. [14]I will put my breath[t] in you, and you will live. I will plant you on your fertile land, and you will know that I am the LORD. I've spoken, and I will do it. This is what the LORD says."

Divided kingdom united

[15]The LORD's word came to me: [16]You, human one, take a stick, and write on it, "Belonging to Judah and to the Israelites associated with him." Take another stick and write on it, "Stick of Ephraim belonging to Joseph and everyone of the house of Israel associated with him." [17]Join them to each other to make a single stick so that they become one stick in your hand. [18]When your people ask you, "Why won't you tell us what these sticks mean to you?" [19]say to them, The LORD God proclaims: I'm taking Joseph's stick, which has been in Ephraim's hand, and the tribes of Israel associated with him, and I'm putting it with Judah's stick, and I'm making them into a single stick so that they will be one stick in my hand. [20]When the two sticks that you've written on are in your hand in their sight, [21]speak to them, This is what the LORD God says: I will take the Israelites from among the nations where they've gone, I will gather them from all around, and I will bring them to their fertile land. [22]I will make them into a single nation in the land on Israel's highlands. There will be just one king for all of them. They will no longer be two nations, and they will no longer be divided into two kingdoms. [23]They will no longer defile themselves with their idols or their worthless things or with any of their rebellions. I will deliver them from all the places where they sinned, and I will cleanse them. They will be my people, and I will be their God. [24]My servant David will be king over them. There will be just one shepherd for all of them. They will follow my case laws and carefully observe my regulations. [25]They will live on the land that I gave to my servant Jacob, where their ancestors lived. They will live on it, they and their children and their grandchildren, forever. My servant David will be their prince forever. [26]I will make a covenant of peace for them. It will be their covenant forever. I will grant it to them and allow them to increase. I will set my sanctuary among them forever. [27]My dwelling will be with them, and I will be their God, and they will be my people. [28]The nations will know that I, the LORD, make Israel holy, when my sanctuary is among them forever.

Attack of Gog

38

[2]The LORD's word came to me: Human one, face Gog in the land of Magog, chief prince of Meshech and Tubal. Prophesy concerning him [3]and say, The LORD God proclaims: I challenge you, Gog, chief prince of Meshech and Tubal! [4]I will turn you about, set hooks in your jaws, and lead you out, you and all your army, horses and riders, handsomely dressed, all of them, a great assembly, with buckler and shield, all of them wielding swords. [5]Persia, Cush, and Put are with you,[u] all of them equipped with shield and helmet. [6]Gomer and all his troops, Beth-togarmah from the far north and all his troops; many peoples are with you. [7]Stand ready and be prepared, you and all your assembly. You will watch out for those who gather against you.

[8]After many days you will be called out. In future years you will enter a country that has been freed from the sword, a gathering from many peoples on the mountains of Israel, which had become a perpetual ruin. This country was brought out from the peoples, and all of them live securely. [9]You will invade like a sudden storm. You and all your troops, and the many peoples with you, will be like clouds covering the earth.

[10]The LORD God proclaims: On that day, thoughts will come into your mind, and you will devise an evil plan. [11]You will say, "I will go up against the open country and come against a quiet people who all live securely without walls, bars, or doors [12]to take

---

[t]Or *spirit*   [u]Cf 38:6; MT *them*

plunder and seize loot, to use my[v] power against the resettled waste places, against a people gathered from the nations, who are acquiring goods and cattle, and who live at the center[w] of the earth." [13]Sheba and Dedan and the merchants and officials of Tarshish will say to you, "Have you come to take plunder and seize loot? Have you assembled your army to take silver and gold, to take goods and cattle, to engage in great looting?"

[14]So now, prophesy, human one, and say to Gog, The LORD God proclaims: Isn't that what you will decide to do[x] on that day, when my people Israel live securely? [15]You will come up from your place from the far north, you and many peoples with you, all of them riding horses, a great assembly, a mighty army. [16]You will go up against my people Israel like a cloud covering the earth. But when this happens in future days, I will be the one who brings you up against my land, so that the nations may know me, Gog, when through you I show my holiness in their sight!

[17]The LORD God proclaims: Are you the one about whom I spoke in former times through my servants, Israel's prophets, the ones who prophesied for years in those days to bring you against them? [18]On that day, the day when Gog comes against Israel's fertile land, my wrath will be aroused. This is what the LORD God says. [19]In my jealousy and blazing anger I declare: On that day, a great quaking will come over Israel's fertile land. [20]The fish of the sea, the birds in the sky, the beasts of the field, all

the creatures crawling on the ground, and every living human being will quake in my presence. Mountains will be thrown down and cliffs will crumble; every wall will fall to the ground. [21]I will summon a sword against Gog on all my mountains. This is what the LORD God says! The swords of the warriors will be against each other, [22]and I will enter into judgment with him, with plague and blood. I will pour out flooding rain, hailstones, fire, and sulfur on him, on all his troops, and on the many peoples with him. [23]So I will display my greatness, show my holiness, and make myself known in the sight of many nations. And they will know that I am the LORD.

39 You, human one, prophesy about Gog and say, The LORD God proclaims: I challenge you, Gog, chief prince of Meshech and Tubal! [2]I will turn you about, drag you out, and bring you out of the far north, and I will bring you to Israel's mountains. [3]I will strike your bow from your left hand, and make your arrows fall from your right. [4]You will fall on Israel's mountains, you, all your troops, and the peoples who are with you. I will give you to the birds of prey, to every kind of bird and wild animal as food. [5]You will fall on the open field, for I have spoken! This is what the LORD God says! [6]I will send fire on Magog and on those who live securely in the coastlands, and they will know that I am the LORD. [7]I will make known my holy name among my people Israel. They will never again degrade my holy name, and the nations will know that I, the LORD, am holy in Israel. [8]Look,

[v]LXX; MT *your*　[w]Or *navel*　[x]Or *you will know*

GOG AND MAGOG

Gog from the land of Magog first appears in Ezekiel 38–39 as the archetypal evil force rising up in the final age, marshaling all the enemies of Israel to attack this peaceful and defenseless people. The Lord defeats Gog and his hordes, establishing the promised covenant of peace (Ezek 34:25; 37:26). Gog and Magog also appear in Revelation 20:7-10, where Magog has become a general, fighting alongside Gog.

it has come! It has happened! This is what the LORD God says. This is the day that I spoke about.

⁹Those who live in Israel's cities will go out and kindle a fire with the weapons—shield and buckler, bow and arrow, spear and lance. They will burn them with fire for seven years. ¹⁰They won't gather wood from the field or chop down trees from the forest, because they will be able to keep the fire burning with the weapons. So they will take plunder and seize loot. This is what the LORD says.

¹¹On that day, I will assign Gog a place for burial in Israel in the Travelers' Valley east of the sea. It will block the travelers' way, because Gog and all of his horde will be buried there. It will be called Hamon-gogʸ Valley. ¹²For seven months, the house of Israel will bury them in order to cleanse the land. ¹³All the people of the land will take part in the burial, so they will make a name for themselves on the day that I glorify myself. This is what the LORD God says. ¹⁴They will appoint people who will continually cross through the land and buryᶻ the human remains that are left on the surface of the ground in order to purify it. They will begin their search at the end of seven months. ¹⁵As the travelers cross through the land, when they see a human bone, they will set up a marker next to it until the gravediggers bury it in Hamon-gog Valley ¹⁶(the name of the city is Hamonah). So they will purify the land.

¹⁷And you, human one, the LORD God proclaims: Say to the birds of prey, to every kind of bird and every wild animal: Assemble and come! Come together from all around for the sacrifice that I make for you, a great sacrifice on Israel's mountains! You will eat flesh and drink blood. ¹⁸You will eat the flesh of warriors and drink the blood of the princes of the earth: rams, lambs, goats, bulls, all fattened animals from Bashan. ¹⁹Gorge yourselves on their fat, and get drunk on their blood, from the sacrifice that I have made for you. ²⁰Satisfy yourselves at my table with horses and riders,

mighty men and every warrior. This is what the LORD God says! ²¹When I glorify myself among the nations, all the nations will understand the judgments that I executed and the power that I used among them. ²²And the house of Israel will know that I, the LORD, am their God, from that day on. ²³The nations will know that the house of Israel went into exile because of their guilt. Because they rebelled against me, I hid my face from them. When I handed them over to their enemies, all of them fell by the sword. ²⁴I dealt with them according to their uncleanness and their transgressions and hid my face from them.

²⁵So the LORD God proclaims: Now I will bring back the captives of Jacob. I will have compassion on the whole house of Israel and defend my holy name. ²⁶They will forget their humiliation and all their rebellions against me when they live securely on their fertile land with no one to frighten them. ²⁷When I bring them back from the peoples and gather them from the lands of their enemies, I will be made holy through them in the sight of the many nations. ²⁸They will know that I am the LORD their God when, after I made them go into exile among the nations, I gathered them to their land. I won't leave any of them behind. ²⁹When I pour my Spirit upon the house of Israel, I won't hide my face from them again. This is what the LORD God says.

Vision of restoration

40 In the beginning of the twenty-fifth year of our exile, on the tenth day of the month, exactly fourteen years after the city was struck down, on that very day, the LORD's power was on me, and he took me there. ²In God's visions, he brought me to the land of Israel and set me down on a very high mountain, where there was a city structure to the south. ³When he brought me there, I saw a man standing in the gate. He appeared to be bronze, and he had a linen cord and a measuring rod in his hand. ⁴The man spoke to me, "Human one, look and listen well, and take seriously every-

ʸOr horde of Gog ᶻLXX; MT adds the travelers.

thing I show you, because you were brought here so that these things could be revealed to you. Describe everything you see to the house of Israel."

Temple compound

⁵Now there was an outer wall that went all the way around the temple compound. The measuring rod in the man's hand was ten and a half feet[a] (based on a standard eighteen inches[b] plus three inches[c]). When he measured the wall's height and width it was ten and a half feet high and ten and a half feet wide. ⁶He entered the gate facing east. He went up its steps, and he measured the plaza[d] at the gate. It was ten and a half feet wide: the plaza was ten and a half feet wide. ⁷The rooms were ten and a half feet long and ten and a half feet wide, with a space of seven and a half feet between them. The plaza next to the porch at the gate opposite the temple was ten and a half feet. ⁸He measured the porch of the gate opposite the temple: it was ten and a half feet. ⁹Then he measured the porch of the gate: it was twelve feet,[e] and its arches were three feet. The porch of the gate was opposite the temple. ¹⁰Inside the east gate, there were three rooms on each side. Each was the same size, and the arches on each side were the same size also. ¹¹Then he measured the width of the gate opening, which was fifteen feet, and the gate's length, which was nineteen and a half feet. ¹²A border running along the front of the rooms on each side was eighteen inches wide, and each of the rooms was nine feet square. ¹³He measured the gate through the room openings that faced each other. From the outer ceiling edge of one room to the outer ceiling edge of the other, the gate was thirty-seven and a half feet wide. ¹⁴Next he made out the perimeter of the hallway, defined by the arches inside the gate: it was ninety feet. ¹⁵It was seventy-five feet from the front of the outer gate to the front of the inner porch of the gate. ¹⁶Inside the gate, all of the rooms and their arches had closed windows; there were also niches inside the porch all the way around. The arches were decorated with palm trees.

¹⁷Then he brought me to the outer courtyard, which consisted of chambers and a pavement all the way around. Thirty chambers came up to the pavement, ¹⁸and the pavement came up to the facades of the gates along their entire length. That was the lower pavement. ¹⁹When he measured the width from the inside of the lower gate to the outer edge of the inner courtyard, it was one hundred fifty feet.

After he measured the east gate, he measured the north gate, ²⁰the one facing north at the outer courtyard. He measured its length and width, ²¹its three inner rooms on each side, its arches, and its porch. Its measurements were the same as the first gate: seventy-five feet long and thirty-seven and a half feet wide. ²²The windows, porch, and palm decorations had the same measurements as those of the east gate. Seven steps led up to the entrance, and the porch was at the other end. ²³There were also gates to the inner courtyard opposite the north and east gates. When he measured from gate to gate, it was one hundred fifty feet.

²⁴Then he had me walk toward the south, where there was a gate facing south. He measured its arches and porch using the same measurements. ²⁵Its windows and its porch all around were like the others, and the gate also was seventy-five feet long and thirty-seven and a half feet wide. ²⁶Its stairway had seven steps, and its porch was at the other end. On its arches, one on either side, were palm decorations. ²⁷There was a gate to the inner courtyard on the south. When he measured from gate to gate on the south side, it was one hundred fifty feet.

---

[a]Heb *shesh ammoth ba'ammah* traditionally *six long cubits*, which is defined as six times a standard *ammah* of eighteen inches plus a *topha* (traditionally *handbreadth*) of three inches. So the measuring rod has six segments of twenty-one inches each, which equals ten and a half feet. It is unclear whether the measurements with the rod continue past 40:8, when standard *ammah* appear, though the longer *ammah* do continue briefly in 43:13-17 for the altar. [b]Or *a standard cubit* [c]Or *a handbreadth* [d]Or *threshold*; Heb architectural and decorative terminology in Ezek 40–48 is often uncertain. [e]Or *eight cubits*

²⁸When he brought me to the inner courtyard by way of the south gate, he took the same measurements of the south gate. ²⁹Its rooms, arches, and porch, as well as its windows and porch all the way around, measured the same as the others. It was seventy-five feet long and thirty-seven and a half feet wide. ³⁰There were porches all around, thirty-seven and a half feet long and seven and a half feet wide. ³¹Its porch faced the outer courtyard. Palms decorated its arches, and its stairway had eight steps.

³²Then he brought me to the inner courtyard on the east side, and again he took the same measurements of the gate. ³³Its rooms, arches, and porch measured the same as the others, as well as its windows and porch all the way around. It was seventy-five feet long and thirty-seven and a half feet wide. ³⁴Its porch faced the outer courtyard. Palm trees decorated its arches on both sides, and its stairway had eight steps. ³⁵Then he brought me to the north gate and took the same measurements of the ³⁶rooms, arches, and porch, and also its windows all around. It was seventy-five feet long and thirty-seven and a half feet wide. ³⁷Its porchᶠ faced the outer courtyard. Palm trees decorated its arches on both sides, and its stairway had eight steps.

³⁸At that gate, there was a room with an entrance in the arches for washing the entirely burned offering, ³⁹and inside the porch on each side of the gate were two tables where the entirely burned offerings, the purification offerings, and the compensation offerings were slaughtered. ⁴⁰Outside, two pairs of tables flanked the entrance of the north gate at both ends, at the steps on one end and the porch on the other. ⁴¹There were four tables on each side of the gate, eight tables in all, for preparing the animal offerings. ⁴²The four tables that were used for the entirely burned offering as well as for the communal sacrifices were made of hewn stone. Each was twenty-seven inches square and eighteen inches high. Equipment used in the ritual slaughter was set on them. ⁴³Hooks,ᵍ three inches wide, were

securely fixed all the way around. The tables were for the flesh of the offerings.

⁴⁴Outside the inner gate there were twoʰ chambers in the inner courtyard. The one beside the north gate faced south, and the one beside the east gate faced north. ⁴⁵He spoke to me: "The chamber facing south is for the priests who keep watch over the temple, ⁴⁶and the chamber facing north is for the priests who keep watch over the altar. Of all the Levites, only the Zadokites may draw near to serve the LORD." ⁴⁷Then he measured the courtyard. It was square, one hundred fifty feet long and one hundred fifty feet wide. The altar was in front of the temple.

The temple

⁴⁸Then he brought me to the porch of the temple and measured its arches. They were seven and a half feet on each side, and the width of the gate was four and a half feet on each side. ⁴⁹The porch was thirty feet long and eighteen feet wide. Steps led up into the porch, and there were columns for the arches, one on each side.

41 He brought me to the main hall, and he measured the arches. They were nine feet deep on both sides, so that was also the depth of the tent. ²The entrance was fifteen feet wide, and the facades on either side of the entrance were seven and a half feet. When he measured its length, it was sixty feet, and its width was thirty feet. ³Then he went into the inner room, and he measured the arches on both sides of the entrance; they were each three feet. The entrance was nine feet wide, and its depth was ten and a half feet. ⁴When he measured the length of the inner room, it was thirty feet, and the width of the side adjoining the main hall was also thirty feet. He said to me, "This is the most holy place."

⁵When he measured the wall of the temple, it was nine feet, and the side chambers that went all the way around the temple were six feet. ⁶Now these side chambers adjoined each other, thirty chambers in three stories. The side chambers had a ledge in

---

ᶠLXX; MT *arches* ᵍHeb uncertain ʰLXX; MT *singing*

the temple wall all the way around to serve as supports, but these supports were not inserted into the temple wall itself. [7] A wide ramp ascended stage by stage to the side chambers all the way around the temple. In this way, the ascent stage by stage all around the temple added to the temple's width. One ascended from the foundation to the top by way of the middle story. [8] Then I looked at the temple: Its roof all around rested on the side chambers. Each raised section was ten and a half feet, and the indentations between them were nine feet.[i] [9] The width of the outer wall of the side chambers was seven and a half feet. The space left free between the temple's side chambers and [10] the other chambers was thirty feet wide all the way around the temple. [11] There were two entrances from the side chambers to the free space, one facing north, the other facing south. And the width of the place that was left free was seven and a half feet all the way around. [12] The structure facing the yard on the west was one hundred five feet wide. The structure's wall was seven and a half feet wide all the way around, and its length was one hundred thirty-five feet.

[13] Then he measured the temple. It was one hundred fifty feet long. The yard, the structure, and its walls were also one hundred fifty feet. [14] The area in front of the house and the yard to the east was one hundred fifty feet also. [15] Then he measured the length of the structure along the side of the yard, including its promenades on both sides: one hundred fifty feet.

Now the interior of the main hall as well as the porches in the courtyard [16] were paneled all around, including the ceilings,[j] closed windows, and its three courses of promenades adjoined the ceiling. From the ground up to the windows was covered. [17] Above the entrance, from the interior to the exterior of the temple, and on every interior and exterior wall, [18] there were carved winged creatures and palm trees. The palm trees were positioned between the winged creatures, and each winged creature had

two faces. [19] A human face turned toward one palm tree, and the face of a lion turned toward another. They were carved on the temple all the way around. [20] From the ground to above the entrance, the walls of the main hall were carved with winged creatures and palm trees. [21] In the main hall itself, there were square doorposts in front of the holy place, where there was the appearance of [22] the altar. It was four and a half feet high and three feet wide. It was made of wood, and its corners, base, and sides were also wood. He said to me, "This is the table that stands before the LORD."

[23] The main hall and the holy place each had two doors, [24] and each door had two turning panels, two for one door and two for the other. [25] Like the walls, the doors of the main hall were carved with winged creatures and palm trees. A single luxuriant[k] tree stood outside, in front of the porch, [26] while closed windows and palm trees decorated both sides of the facade of the porch, the temple's side chambers, and the beams.

Chambers and promenades

42 Then he led me north to the outer courtyard and brought me into the set of chambers opposite the yard and the structure to the north. [2] The length of the facade at the north entrance was one hundred fifty feet, its depth seventy-five feet. [3] It was next to the twenty chambers that belonged to the inner courtyard and next to the pavement of the outer courtyard, and it had three courses of promenades. [4] In front of the chambers there was a passage fifteen feet wide, and to the inside, a passage eighteen inches wide. The entrance to the chambers was on the north. [5] The upper chambers were smaller, because the promenades took up more space from them than from the first and second stories. [6] This was because the promenades were arranged in three levels, but they didn't have columns like those in the courtyards. For this reason, the top story was narrower than the first and second stories. [7] A stone wall ran parallel to the chambers facing the outer

---

[i] Heb uncertain   [j] Or *thresholds*   [k] Heb uncertain

courtyard. It was seventy-five feet long, [8] the same length, seventy-five feet, as the chambers facing the outer courtyard. Those facing the temple were one hundred fifty feet. [9.10] These chambers were entered from the outer courtyard at the end of the courtyard wall, because the entrance was at the end of the chambers at the east. South of the yard and the building, there were more chambers with a passage [11] in front of them. The design of the chambers resembled the ones to the north in length and width, as well as in all their exits. The arrangement of the entrances [12] to the chambers on the south side was identical as well. One entered from the east at the beginning of the corresponding wall.

[13] Then he said to me, "The north and south chambers that face the building and the yard are the holy chambers where the priests eat the offerings that have been brought to the LORD. They are most holy. Here they will place the most holy things, the grain offering, the purification offering, and the compensation offering. The place is holy. [14] When the priests enter, they won't go out of the sanctuary to the outer courtyard. There they will place the priestly vests that they wore when they were ministering, because these garments are also holy. They will put on other garments when they go out to the people's area."

[15] When he finished making the interior measurements of the temple, he led me out toward the east gate, and he measured all the way around. [16] He used the same measuring rod on all four sides. He measured the east side, seven hundred fifty feet; [17] the north side, seven hundred fifty feet; and [18] the south side, seven hundred fifty feet. [19] He turned to the west side, seven hundred fifty feet. [20] On all four sides he measured the wall all the way around. Its length was seven hundred fifty feet, and its width seven hundred fifty feet. So he made a division between the holy and the ordinary.

Return of the divine glory

43 Then he led me to the east gate, [2] where the glory of Israel's God was coming in from the east. Its sound was like the sound of a mighty flood, and the earth was lit up with his glory. [3] What appeared when I looked was like what I had seen when he[l] came to destroy the city, and also like what I saw at the Chebar River, and I fell on my face. [4] Then the LORD's glory came into the temple by way of the east gate. [5] A wind picked me up and brought me to the inner courtyard, and there the LORD's glory filled the temple. [6] A man was standing next to me, but the voice that I heard came from inside the temple. [7] He said to me, Human one, this is the place for my throne and the place for the soles of my feet, where I will dwell among the Israelites forever. The house of Israel will never again defile my holy name, neither they nor their kings, with their disloyalties[m] and with their kings' corpses at the shrines. [8] When they set their plazas[n] with mine and their doorposts next to mine, the wall was between us. They defiled my holy name with their detestable practices, so I consumed them in my anger. [9] Now let them remove their disloyalties and their kings' corpses from me, and I will dwell among them forever.

[10] You, human one, describe the temple to the house of Israel. Let them be humiliated because of their guilt when they think about its design. [11] When they feel humiliated by all that they have done, make known to them the shape of the temple and its adornment, its exits and its entrances, its entire plan and all of its regulations.[o] Write them down in their sight so that they may observe all of its entire plan and all its regulations and perform them. [12] These are the instructions for the temple: the top of the mountain, as well as its boundaries all around, are most holy. These are the instructions for the temple.

The altar

[13] These are the dimensions of the altar, according to a twenty-one-inch unit of measure.[p] The base is twenty-one inches high and twenty-one inches wide, with an outer curb measuring one and a half

[l] Vulg; MT *I*   [m] Or *prostitution*   [n] Or *thresholds*   [o] LXX; MT adds *and all of its structures and all of its instructions.*
[p] Heb *ammah ammah*, traditionally *a long cubit*

inches all around. This is the altar's height. ¹⁴From the base at ground level to the lower ledge is forty-two inches; the lower ledge is twenty-one inches wide. The distance from the lower to the upper ledge is seven feet; the upper ledge is twenty-one inches wide. ¹⁵The hearth is seven feet high, with four horns projecting upward from the hearth. ¹⁶The hearth is twenty-one feet square; each side is equal to the others. ¹⁷The ledge around the hearth is twenty-four and a half feet long by twenty-four and a half feet wide, a square. Its outer rim is ten and a half inches, and its base all around is twenty-one inches. Its ramp faces east.

Purification of the altar

¹⁸He said to me, Human one, the LORD God proclaims: These are the regulations established for the altar on the day when it is prepared for making entirely burned offerings and dashing blood on it. ¹⁹You will provide a young bull as a purification offering to the levitical priests who are descendants of Zadok, the ones who may draw near to minster to me. This is what the LORD God says. ²⁰You will take some of its blood and set it on the four horns of the altar and on the four sides of the ledge and on the curb all around. So you will purify it and purge it. ²¹Then you will take the bull selected as the purification offering, and the priests will burn it in a designated place of the temple outside of the sanctuary. ²²On the second day, you will present a flawless male goat as a purification offering. The priests will purify the altar just as they purified the altar with the bull. ²³When you have completed the purification, you will present a flawless bull from the herd and a flawless ram from the flock. ²⁴You will present them to the LORD. The priests will throw salt on them and offer them as entirely burned offerings to the LORD. ²⁵Daily, for seven days, you will present a male goat for a purification offering. You will also present a bull from the herd and a ram from the flock, both flawless. ²⁶For seven days the priests will purge the altar in order to purify it and to dedicate it. ²⁷When the seven days are completed, the priests will offer your entirely burned offerings and your well-being sacrifices on the altar from the eighth day on, and I will accept you with pleasure. This is what the LORD God says.

The closed gate

44 He brought me back to the outer sanctuary gate that faces east. It was closed. ²The LORD said to me, This gate remains closed. It shouldn't be opened. No one should come in through it because the LORD, Israel's God, has entered through it. It will remain closed. ³As for the prince, he may sit in it to eat bread in the LORD's presence. He may come in and go out by way of the gate's porch.

Foreigners, Levites, Zadokites

⁴Then he brought me by way of the north gate to the front of the temple. I looked, and suddenly the LORD's glory filled the LORD's temple, and I fell on my face. ⁵Then the LORD said to me: Human one, pay close attention! Use your eyes and ears and listen to all that I say to you concerning the regulations of the LORD's temple and all its instructions. Pay close attention to the access to the temple through all the sanctuary portals.�q ⁶Speak to the rebels, to the house of Israel, The LORD God proclaims: Enough of your detestable practices, house of Israel! ⁷You made my temple unclean because you brought into my sanctuary foreigners who were physically and spiritually uncircumcised. When you offered my food of fat and blood to me, youʳ broke my covenant with all your detestable practices. ⁸You didn't keep charge of my holy things. On the contrary, you appointed themˢ to keep charge in my sanctuary for you.

⁹The LORD God proclaims: Foreigners who are spiritually and physically uncircumcised must not enter my sanctuary; that is, all foreigners among the Israelites. ¹⁰But the Levites, who went far from me when Israel went astray, who went astray from me after their idols, will bear their

guilt. [11]They will keep charge in my sanctuary, and they will oversee the temple gates and keep charge of the temple. They will slaughter the entirely burned offerings and the sacrifices for the people, and they will stand before them to minister to them. [12]Because they ministered to them before their idols, they brought about the downfall of the house of Israel. For that reason I made a solemn pledge against them—this is what the LORD God says—and they will bear their guilt. [13]They won't approach me to officiate for me as priests or approach any of my holy things or the most holy place. Though they will bear their humiliation and the consequences of their detestable practices, [14]I will appoint them to keep charge of the temple, all its work, and all that is done in it.

[15]As for the priests of the levitical family of Zadok who did keep charge of my sanctuary when the Israelites strayed away from me, they will draw near to me to serve me. They will stand in my presence to present fat and blood to me. This is what the LORD God says. [16]They will come into my sanctuary, and they will approach my table to minister to me. They will keep my charge. [17]When they come through the gates to the inner courtyard, they will wear linen garments. They won't wear any wool when they minister at the gates of the inner courtyard or in the temple. [18]They will have linen turbans on their heads and linen undergarments around their waists. They won't wear anything that makes them sweat. [19]When they go out to the outer courtyard to the people, they will remove the garments in which they were ministering. They will lay them aside in the holy chambers and wear other clothing. They must not transfer holiness to the people through their clothing. [20]They must neither shave their heads nor let their hair grow long, but they will trim the hair on their heads. [21]None of the priests should drink wine when they come into the inner courtyard. [22]They must not marry widows or divorced women, but only Israelite virgins. Priests may, however, marry the widows of other priests. [23]They must teach my people the difference between the holy and the ordinary, and show them the difference between clean and unclean. [24]They must execute judgments according to my case laws in cases of civil conflict. They must observe my instructions and my regulations regarding all my festivals. They must keep my sabbaths holy. [25]In order to avoid uncleanness, they must not approach the dead. They may, however, become unclean for their father or mother, son or daughter, brother or unmarried sister. [26]Once the priest is clean again, he must count off seven days. [27]On the day that he comes into the holy place, the inner courtyard, to minister in the holy place, he will present his purification offering. This is what the LORD God says. [28]As for their inheritance, I am their inheritance. They won't be given family property in Israel; I am their family property. [29]They will eat the grain offerings, the purification offerings, and the compensation offerings. Every dedicated thing in Israel belongs to them. [30]The best of the early produce of every kind, and every contribution, all of them, belong to the priests. You will give the best of your bread dough to the priest so that a blessing may come to rest on your household. [31]The priests must not eat any bird or animal that dies naturally or is torn apart by prey.

The holy portion

45 When you distribute the land as an inheritance, you will set aside a holy portion of land for the LORD. It will be 7.1 miles long and 5.68 miles[t] wide. It will be holy throughout the entire area. [2]Out of this portion, an area seven hundred fifty feet by seven hundred fifty feet square will be for the sanctuary. All around it will be an open space seventy-five feet wide. [3]Beginning with this measurement, you will measure out an area 7.1 miles long and 2.84 miles wide. The sanctuary, the most holy place, will lie on it. [4]It is holy, set apart from the land, and it belongs to the priests who draw near to minister in the LORD's

[t]LXX *twenty thousand* (*pechon*, standard cubit); MT *ten thousand* (*ammah*); see note at Ezek 40:5.

sanctuary. It will be a place for their houses, and a holy place for the sanctuary. ⁵The area 7.1 miles long and 2.84 miles wide will be for the Levites who minister in the temple. Twenty chambers are theirs as their property. ⁶As the property for the city, you will set aside an area 1.42 miles wide and 7.1 miles long next to the holy portion. It will be for the whole house of Israel. ⁷The territory for the prince will be on both sides of the holy portion and the city property, alongside the holy portion and alongside the city property, from their western boundaries westward and from their eastern boundaries eastward. Its length will equal one tribal portion, from the western border to the eastern border. ⁸The land will be his property in Israel, and my princes will no longer oppress my people. They will give the land to the house of Israel according to their tribes.

⁹The LORD God proclaims: Enough, princes of Israel! Turn aside from violence and oppression. Establish justice and righteousness. Cease your evictions of my people! This is what the LORD God says: ¹⁰You must use fair scales, a fair ephah,ᵘ and a fair bath.ᵛ ¹¹The ephah and the bath must be the same size. Both should be calibrated to the homer: each will contain one-tenth of a homer. ¹²The shekel must weigh twenty gerahs. Twenty shekels, twenty-five shekels, and fifteen shekels will equal one maneh for you.

Sacrificial offerings and gifts

¹³These are your prescribed contributions: one-sixth of an ephah for each homer of wheat, and one-sixth of an ephah for each homer of barley; ¹⁴a regular amount of oil,ʷ one-tenth of a bath for each korˣ (each korʸ contains ten baths); ¹⁵and one sheep from the flock for every two hundred from Israel's pastureland, for grain offerings, for entirely burned offerings, and for well-being sacrifices to make reconciliation for them. This is what the LORD God says. ¹⁶All the people will make this contribution on behalf of the prince in Israel. ¹⁷The prince will be responsible for the entirely burned offerings, grain offerings, and drink offerings for the festivals, new moons, and sabbaths, all the appointed festivals of the house of Israel. He will offer the purification offering, the grain offering, the entirely burned offering, and the well-being sacrifice to make reconciliation on behalf of the house of Israel.

Festivals

¹⁸The LORD God proclaims: On the first day of the first month,ᶻ you will take a flawless young bull from the herd, and you will purify the sanctuary. ¹⁹The priest will take some of the blood from the purification offering, and he will set it on the doorposts of the temple and on the four corners of the ledge of the altar and on the doorposts of the gate to the inner courtyard.

ᵘOne ephah is approximately twenty quarts of grain. ᵛOne bath is approximately twenty quarts of liquid.
ʷSyr, Tg; MT adds *a bath of oil.* ˣMT adds *each homer contains ten baths.* ʸVulg; MT *homer* ᶻMarch–April, Nisan

SANCTUARY

Places inhabited by or significant to deities. Sanctuaries took many forms, from locations marked by natural features in the landscape to a portable tent to the temple in Jerusalem and the temples of the Greco-Roman world, with a diversity of shrines besides. Most sanctuaries shared at least two basic features: (1) they were holy and required some kind of purification before one could enter and (2) they were divided into sections that were more and less holy.

²⁰You will do the same on the seventh day of the month for anyone who sins through inadvertence or ignorance. So you will purge the temple. ²¹Your Passover will be on the fourteenth day of the first month. Unleavened bread will be eaten during the seven days of the festival. ²²On that day, the prince will provide a young bull as the purification offering for himself and for the people of the land. ²³For the seven days of the festival, he will provide seven flawless bulls and seven flawless rams, one for each day of the festival, as the entirely burned offering for the LORD, and, for the purification offering, one male goat for each day. ²⁴He will also provide the grain offerings, one ephahᵃ for each bull, and one ephah for each ram, with one hinᵇ of oil for each ephah. ²⁵For the festival that begins on the fifteenth day of the seventh month,ᶜ he will make the same provisions for the purification offerings, entirely burned offerings, grain offerings, and oil, for all seven days of the festival.

Sabbaths and gift offerings

46 The LORD God proclaims: The east-facing gate of the inner courtyard will remain closed for the six days of the workweek. But on the Sabbath and on the day of the new moon it will be opened, ²and the prince will come in from outside by way of the porch of the gate and stand at the gate's doorposts. The priests will present the prince's entirely burned offerings and well-being sacrifices, and then he will bow down on the threshold of the gate and go out. The gate won't be closed until evening ³so that the people of the land may bow in the presence of the LORD on sabbaths and new moons at the opening of that gate. ⁴On the Sabbath day, the prince will offer to the LORD an entirely burned offering of six flawless lambs and a flawless ram, ⁵a grain offering of one ephah for the ram, and a grain offering at his discretion for the lambs, with one hin of oil for each ephah. ⁶For the day of the new moon, the offering will be a

flawless young bull from the herd, six lambs, and a flawless ram, ⁷and he will provide a grain offering of one ephah each for the bull and the ram, and for the lambs as much as he likes, with one hin of oil for each ephah. ⁸When the prince enters, he comes in by way of the porch of the gate and goes out in the same direction. ⁹When the people of the land come into the LORD's presence for the festivals, those who enter through the north gate to worship should go out through the south, and those who come in through the south gate should go out through the north gate. They shouldn't turn around and go out the same way they came in. Instead, they should go out the opposite gate. ¹⁰The prince should accompany them: when they come in, he comes in, and when they go out, he goes out. ¹¹At the festivals and appointed gatherings, the grain offering is one ephah for each bull, one ephah for each ram, and whatever one is able to give for each lamb, with one hin of oil for each ephah.

¹²Whenever the prince makes a spontaneous gift to the LORD, whether it is an entirely burned offering or a well-being sacrifice, the gate facing east will be opened for him, and he will present his entirely burned offering and well-being sacrifices, just as he does on the Sabbath day. When he leaves, the gate will be closed after he has gone out.

Daily offerings

¹³As a daily entirely burned offering for the LORD, you will provide a flawless year-old lamb. You will make the offering every morning. ¹⁴You will provide a grain offering along with it every morning, one-sixth of an ephah along with one-third of a hin of oil to moisten the choice flour. This is a permanent and perpetual regulation for the grain offering to the LORD. ¹⁵So the lamb, the grain offering, and the oil are provided every morning as a perpetual entirely burned offering.

Royal land grants

¹⁶The LORD God proclaims: When the prince gives a gift to each of his sons, it be-

---

ᵃOne ephah is approximately twenty quarts of grain.   ᵇOne hin is approximately equal to one pint.
ᶜSeptember–October, Tishrei

comes their inheritance. It becomes their family property as an inheritance. ¹⁷And if he gives one of his servants a gift from his inheritance, it will belong to the servant only until the year of release, and then it will revert to the prince. It is his children's inheritance; it belongs to them. ¹⁸The prince won't take the people's inheritance by evicting them from their family property. He will bequeath only his own property to his sons, lest any of my people be deprived of their rightful property.

Kitchens

¹⁹Then he brought me through the passage beside the gate next to the priests' quarters, the holy chambers facing north. There was a place hidden away on the western side. ²⁰He said to me, "Rather than taking these offerings out into the outer courtyard and transferring holiness to the people, this is the place where the priests will boil the compensation offerings and the purification offerings, and where they will bake the grain offerings."

²¹Then he took me to the outer courtyard, and he had me pass through its four corners, and I saw that there were additional courtyards in each of the corners. ²²In all four corners of the courtyard, these courtyards were constructed to handle smoke. All four were the same size, sixty feet long by forty-five feet wide. ²³All four had stone masonry all the way around, and hearths were built under this masonry all the way around. ²⁴He said to me, "These are the kitchens where those who minister in the temple cook the people's sacrifices."

The river

47 When he brought me back to the temple's entrance, I noticed that water was flowing toward the east from under the temple's threshold (the temple faced east). The water was going out from under the temple's facade toward the south, south of the altar. ²He led me out through the north gate and around the outside to the outer east gate, where the water flowed out under

the facade on the south side. ³With the line in his hand, the man went out toward the east. When he measured off fifteen hundred feet, he made me cross the water; it was ankle-deep. ⁴He measured off another fifteen hundred feet and made me cross the water; it was knee-deep. He measured off another fifteen hundred feet and made me cross the water, and it was waist-high. ⁵When he measured off another fifteen hundred feet, it had become a river that I couldn't cross. The water was high, deep enough for swimming but too high to cross. ⁶He said to me, "Human one, do you see?" Then he led me back to the edge of the river. ⁷When I went back, I saw very many trees on both banks of the river. ⁸He said to me, "These waters go out to the eastern region, flow down the steep slopes,ᵈ and go into the Dead Sea.ᵉ When the flowing waters enter the sea, its water becomes fresh. ⁹Wherever the river flows, every living thing that moves will thrive. There will be great schools of fish, because when these waters enter the sea, it will be fresh. Wherever the river flows, everything will live. ¹⁰People will stand fishing beside it, from En-gedi to En-eglayim, and it will become a place for spreading nets. It will be like the Mediterranean Sea,ᶠ having all kinds of fish in it. ¹¹Its marshes and swamps won't be made fresh (they are left for salt), ¹²but on both banks of the river will grow up all kinds of fruit-bearing trees. Their leaves won't wither, and their fruitfulness won't wane. They will produce fruit in every month, because their water comes from the sanctuary. Their fruit will be for eating, their leaves for healing."

¹³The LORD God proclaims: Theseᵍ are the boundaries of the portions of land that will be distributed as an inheritance to the twelve tribes of Israel. Joseph will receive two portions. ¹⁴What I swore to give to your ancestors, you will distribute as an inheritance equally. This land is given to you as an inheritance. ¹⁵This is the boundary of the land. The northern limit begins at the Mediterranean Sea and goes in the direction of Hethlon toward Lebo-hamath, Zedad,ʰ

ᵈOr *Arabah* ᵉOr *sea* ᶠOr *great sea* ᵍLXX, Tg, Vulg; Heb uncertain ʰLXX; MT transposes *Hamath* and *Zedad*.

16Berothah, Sibraim (which is between the boundary of Damascus and the boundary of Hamath), and Hazer-hatticon (that is on the boundary of Hauran). 17So the boundary from the Mediterranean Sea[i] to Hazar-enon will run north of the boundary of Damascus, with the boundary of Hamath to the north. This is the northern limit. 18For the eastern limit, you will measure continuously between Hauran and Damascus and between Gilead and the land of Israel, along the Jordan River as far as the Dead Sea.[j] This is the eastern limit. 19The southern limit runs from Tamar to the waters of Meribath-kadesh and from there along the border[k] of Egypt to the Mediterranean Sea. This is the southern limit. 20For the western limit, the Mediterranean Sea is the boundary up to Lebo-hamath. This is the western limit. 21You will apportion this land among yourselves according to the tribes of Israel. 22When you distribute the land as an inheritance, the immigrants who reside with you and raise families among you are considered full citizens along with the Israelites. They will receive an inheritance along with you among the tribes of Israel. 23You will assign the immigrants' inheritance with the tribe with

whom they reside. This is what the LORD God says.

48 These are the tribes' names: Beginning at the north, along the Hethlon road from Lebo-hamath to Hazar-enon, the boundary of Damascus with Hamath to the north, from the eastern border to the western border: Dan, one portion. 2Along the boundary of Dan from the eastern border to the western border: Asher, one portion. 3Along the boundary of Asher from the eastern border to the western border: Naphtali, one portion. 4Along the boundary of Naphtali from the eastern border to the western border: Manasseh, one portion. 5Along the boundary of Manasseh from the eastern border to the western border: Ephraim, one portion. 6Along the boundary of Ephraim from the eastern border to the western border: Reuben, one portion. 7Along the boundary of Reuben from the eastern border to the western border: Judah, one portion.

8Along the boundary of Judah from the eastern border to the western border will be the portion that you will set aside, 7.1 miles wide and the length of a tribal portion from the eastern border to the western border. The sanctuary is in its center. 9The portion

[i]Or *the sea* [j]Or *eastern sea* [k]Or *Wadi*; traditionally *Brook*

MEDITERRANEAN SEA

Also known as the Great Sea or the Western Sea. When referenced in the Bible, the Mediterranean Sea is usually identified as the ideal western boundary of the land of Israel (e.g., Num 34:6; Deut 11:24; 34:2; Josh 15:12). In truth, for most of its history Israel had no control of cities along the Mediterranean coast, and references to seagoing activity by Israel's tribes are both rare and obscure (Gen 49:13; Judg 5:17). For the most part, the coast was occupied by the Philistines in the south and the Phoenicians in the north. The Mediterranean Sea, referred to as simply "the sea" in Joshua 16:8, was distinguished from the Dead Sea on Israel's eastern border not only by its greater size but also in that it was teeming with life (Ezek 47:8-10). It was also noted as the home of great sea monsters (Gen 1:21) and a place of violent and dangerous storms (Jon 1:4). The vast collection of salt waters that was the Mediterranean Sea remained an ongoing symbol of the forces of death-dealing chaos (Dan 7:2).

that you will set aside for the LORD will be 7.1 miles long and 5.68 miles[l] wide. [10]These measurements define the holy portion for the priests: along the north, a length of 7.1 miles; along the west, a width of 2.84 miles; along the east, a width of 2.84 miles; and along the south, a length of 7.1 miles. The LORD's sanctuary is in its center. [11]This holy area is for the Zadokite priests who kept my charge and didn't stray as the Levites did when the house of Israel strayed away from me. [12]It belongs to them as a most special portion of the land, a most holy place, up to the border of the Levites. [13]The Levites' allotment is next to the boundary of the priests, a length of 7.1 miles and a width of 2.84 miles. The entire length is 7.1 miles and the width 2.84 miles. [14]None of it will be sold, exchanged, or transferred. It is the choicest land, because it is holy to the LORD. [15]The remaining area, 1.42 miles wide and 7.1 miles long, is for ordinary use for the city, for residences, and for pastures. The city will be in the middle of it. [16]It measures 1.28 miles on its northern border, 1.28 miles on its southern border, 1.28 miles on its eastern border, and 1.28 miles on its western border. [17]There will be pastures for the city, three hundred seventy-five feet on the north side, three hundred seventy-five feet on the south side, three hundred seventy-five feet on the east side, and three hundred seventy-five feet on the west side. [18]The remaining area alongside the holy portion is 2.84 miles on the east and 2.84 miles on the west. These areas that adjoin the holy portion will produce the food for the city's workers. [19]The city's workers from every tribe of Israel will farm it. [20]The entire portion that you will set aside is 7.1 miles by 7.1 miles, a square; it includes the holy portion in addition to the city property. [21]What is left on both sides of the holy portion and the city property belongs to the prince. The land from the edge of the portion of 7.1 miles, to the eastern boundary, and on the western edge of the 7.1 miles to the western boundary, belongs to the prince. It corresponds to one tribal portion. The holy portion and the temple sanctuary are in the middle of it, [22]but what belongs to the prince is separate from both the levitical property and the city property. The prince's territory will be between the boundary of Judah and the boundary of Benjamin.

[23]Now for the rest of the tribes: From the eastern border to the western border: Benjamin, one portion. [24]Along the boundary of Benjamin from the eastern border to the western border: Simeon, one portion. [25]Along the boundary of Simeon from the eastern border to the western border: Issachar, one portion. [26]Along the boundary of Issachar from the eastern border to the western border: Zebulun, one portion. [27]Along the boundary of Zebulun from the eastern border to the western border: Gad, one portion. [28]Along the boundary of Gad to the southern border, the boundary will run from Tamar to the waters of Meribath-kadesh and from there to the border of Egypt[m] and to the Mediterranean Sea.[n] [29]This is the land that you will distribute as an inheritance for the tribes of Israel. These are their portions. This is what the LORD God says.

[30]These are the city exits. The north side is measured at 1.28 miles. [31]The gates of the city go by the names of the tribes of Israel. There are three gates on the north side: one gate for Reuben, one gate for Judah, and one gate for Levi. [32]There are three gates on the east side along its 1.28 miles: one gate for Joseph, one gate for Benjamin, and one gate for Dan. [33]There are three gates on the south side measuring 1.28 miles: one gate for Simeon, one gate for Issachar, and one gate for Zebulun. [34]There are three gates on the west side along its 1.28 miles: one gate for Gad, one gate for Asher, and one gate for Naphtali. [35]The circumference of the city is 5.1 miles. As of today, the name of the city is The LORD Is There.

---

[l]Cf LXX and Ezek 45:1; MT *ten thousand ammah* equals 2.84 miles.   [m]Or *Wadi*; traditionally *Brook*, MT lacks *of Egypt*.   [n]Or *Great Sea*

DANIEL

Like Ezekiel, Daniel was an exile caught up in the struggle between mighty Babylon and tiny Judah.

The book of Daniel tells of events in Daniel's life as an exile and tells of visions that came to Daniel from God. The overall perspective of these visions and stories is that underlying all earthly reality is God's reality. That is, both history and time are subject to God's control; and no one—king, captive, or peasant, those who are wise or are unknowing, angelic prince or human being—can escape the influence of God's dominion.

DANIEL THE BOOK

The book of Daniel is a collection of stories and vision reports. Chapters 1–6 are stories about Daniel and his friends in Babylon. Chapters 7–12 tell of Daniel's visions.

Part of the book was written in Hebrew, the language of Israel (Daniel 1:1–2:4a and 8:1–12:13). The rest of the book was written in Aramaic (Daniel 2:4b–7:28), which was the international language of Daniel's day.

The stories and visions in the Aramaic chapters demonstrate that God is Lord of all peoples and that God's power is greater than the power of any earthly ruler. The Hebrew chapters place Daniel and his friends in Babylon and tell how world events will affect Jerusalem and God's chosen people.

The book contains stories told by Daniel and stories told about him. Daniel 7:1 says that Daniel himself wrote an account of one of his visions. Daniel may have written others or he may have dictated these accounts to a scribe. The Israelites took their sacred writings with them into exile and they continued in Babylon to practice their scribal traditions of recording history (for example, Jeremiah 52), prophecy (for example, Ezekiel 20), and hymns (for example, Psalm 137).

These stories and vision reports could have been recorded in part during Daniel's lifetime and then collected and arranged in their present form after his death.

HISTORICAL CIRCUMSTANCES

Who wrote the book of Daniel and when it was written are matters of dispute. Many of the earliest Jewish and Christian interpreters of Daniel believed Daniel to have been a prophet and accepted the book as scripture that came from the Babylonian Exile.

Later interpreters came to believe that the book of Daniel was written during the Maccabean period, which was the second century BCE (approximately 170–165) in Palestine. They concluded that Daniel best reflects the conflict of that time between the Jews and the Greek tyrant Antiochus IV Epiphanes. In this case, the book of Daniel would have been written by someone using Daniel's name and holding him up as an example of a pious and wise man from the past. This would make the book of Daniel prophecy "after the fact." The purpose of such prophecy would have been to instruct and encourage the Jews in their struggle against Greek oppression.

Whenever Daniel was written, it is obvious that the book came out of a community under stress. In the face of warfare and oppression, the community of God's people naturally would ask "What does all this mean?" In answering this question, Daniel offers God's people a particular way to look at the world. Daniel's perspective is that all reality, both earthly and heavenly, is under God's dominion. Therefore, God's people may face the world and the future with confidence.

DANIEL THE MAN

What we know of Daniel's personal background comes from Daniel 1:3-4.

Daniel was from an honored and privileged Israelite family. This may be one of the reasons that he was taken to Babylon in 605 BCE. In 598 and 587 BCE the Babylonians also took many Israelite leaders and artisans into exile. When he went to live in Babylon, Daniel was probably in his late teens. He was a well-educated, intelligent, and handsome young man.

Like most upper-class Israelite boys of his time, Daniel's education probably began at home, where he was taught the history of his people and of God's covenant with Israel. He was probably also instructed in the ethical conduct of life as well as in reading and writing.

During his time in Babylon, Daniel learned the Babylonian language and script and was probably taught Babylonian history as well. He became an able administrator in the governments of Babylon and Persia and led a prosperous life.

The Israelites brought their sacred writings with them into exile, and Daniel continued to study them. He also observed the personal rituals of his faith, such as prayer, meditation, and fasting.

Daniel knew about dreams and about their interpretation. He had visions from God concerning great mysteries. He was a man of courage and conviction. Though he knew how to flourish in a pagan society, he also continued to live out his faith in God.

Indeed, the fundamental fact about Daniel is his reliance on God. Daniel was an outstanding man who is renowned to later generations for his wisdom and courage. Yet, it is to God that Daniel gave the praise and credit for all his accomplishments.

DANIEL

Jerusalem taken by the Babylonians

1 In the third year of the rule of Judah's King Jehoiakim, Babylon's King Nebuchadnezzar came to Jerusalem and attacked it. [2] The Lord handed Judah's King Jehoiakim over to Nebuchadnezzar, along with some of the equipment from God's house. Nebuchadnezzar took these to Shinar, to his own god's temple, putting them in his god's treasury.

Training for royal service

[3] Nebuchadnezzar instructed his highest official Ashpenaz to choose royal descendants and members of the ruling class from the Israelites—[4] good-looking young men without defects, skilled in all wisdom, possessing knowledge, conversant with learning, and capable of serving in the king's palace. Ashpenaz was to teach them the Chaldean language and its literature. [5] The king assigned these young men daily allotments from his own food and from the royal wine. Ashpenaz was to teach them for three years so that at the end of that time they could serve before the king. [6] Among these young men from the Judeans were Daniel, Hananiah, Mishael, and Azariah. [7] But the chief official gave them new names. He named Daniel "Belteshazzar," Hananiah "Shadrach," Mishael "Meshach," and Azariah "Abednego."

Test

[8] Daniel decided that he wouldn't pollute himself with the king's rations or the royal wine, and he appealed to the chief official in hopes that he wouldn't have to do so. [9] Now God had established faithful loyalty between Daniel and the chief official; [10] but the chief official said to Daniel, "I'm afraid of my master, the king, who has mandated what you are to eat and drink. What will happen if he sees your faces looking thinner than the other young men in your group? The king will have my head because of you!"

[11] So Daniel spoke to the guard whom the chief official had appointed over Daniel, Hananiah, Mishael, and Azariah: [12] "Why not test your servants for ten days? You could give us a diet of vegetables to eat and

DANIEL

Means "God is my judge." Elsewhere in the OT we hear of an outstandingly righteous man named Daniel (Ezek 14:14, 20). Evidently he was thought of as an ancient Gentile righteous man, because he is mentioned in the same breath with Job and Noah. In Ezekiel 28:3 this legendary Daniel is praised for his wisdom. Scholars generally regard Ezekiel's wise and righteous Daniel as the literary ancestor of the hero of the late OT book.

Even farther back in the ancestry of our Daniel is the king Dnil (or Danel or even Daniel) of Canaanite legend. We know him from the fragmentary Tale of Aqhat, a text found in the rich trove of ca. 14th cent. BCE epigraphic remains from Ugarit (Ras Shamra, on the Mediterranean coast of Syria). Aqhat, Daniel's son by his wife, Danatiya, is conceived with a kiss after the rain and fertility god Baal intercedes with the high god El on Daniel's behalf. Baal bases his plea for Daniel upon the man's piety (manifested in daily oblations to the gods) and upon his justice. From antiquity, therefore, a Daniel existed who revered deity, showed wisdom and discretion, and led the community with justice.

water to drink. [13]Then compare our appearance to the appearance of the young men who eat the king's food. Then deal with your servants according to what you see."

[14]The guard decided to go along with their plan and tested them for ten days. [15]At the end of ten days they looked better and healthier than all the young men who were eating the king's food. [16]So the guard kept taking away their rations and the wine they were supposed to drink and gave them vegetables instead. [17]And God gave knowledge, mastery of all literature, and wisdom to these four men. Daniel himself gained understanding of every type of vision and dream.

Result of the training

[18]When the time came to review the young men as the king had ordered, the chief official brought them before Nebuchadnezzar. [19]When the king spoke with them, he found no one as good as Daniel, Hananiah, Mishael, and Azariah. So they took their place in the king's service. [20]Whenever the king consulted them about any aspect of wisdom and understanding, he found them head and shoulders above all the dream interpreters and enchanters in his entire kingdom. [21]And Daniel stayed in the king's service until the first year of King Cyrus.

An impossible challenge

2 In the second year of Nebuchadnezzar's rule, he had many dreams. The dreams made him anxious, but he kept sleeping. [2]The king summoned the dream interpreters, enchanters, diviners, and Chaldeans to explain his dreams to him. They came and stood before the king.

[3]Then the king said to them: "I had a dream, and I'm anxious to know its meaning."

[4]The Chaldeans answered the king in Aramaic:[a] "Long live the king! Tell your servants the dream, and we will explain its meaning."

[5]The king answered the Chaldeans: "My decision is final: If you can't tell me the dream and its meaning, you will be torn limb from limb, and your houses will be turned into trash dumps. [6]But if you do explain the dream and its meaning, you'll receive generous gifts and glorious honor from me. So explain to me the dream as well as its meaning."

[7]They answered him again: "The king must tell his servants the dream. We will then explain the meaning."

[8]The king replied: "Now I definitely know you are stalling for time, because you see that my decision is final [9]and that if you can't tell me the dream, your fate is certain. You've conspired to make false and lying speeches before me until the situation changes. Tell me the dream now! Then I'll know you can explain its meaning to me."

[10]The Chaldeans answered the king: "No one on earth can do what the king is asking! No king or ruler, no matter how great, has ever asked such a thing of any dream interpreter, enchanter, or Chaldean. [11]What the king is asking is impossible! No one could declare the dream to the king but the gods, who don't live among mere humans."

[a]The book switches into Aramaic at this point, returning to Hebrew in 8:1.

ARAMAIC

Aramaic describes a cluster of closely related dialects that first appeared ca. the 9th century BCE and have continued in use down to today. Aramaic is used in both the OT (Gen 31:47; Jer 10:11; Ezra 4:8–6:18; 7:12-26; Dan 2:4–7:28) and the NT (Mark 5:41; 7:34; 15:34; Matt 27:46; 1 Cor 16:22). An Aramaism is an expression in Greek or Hebrew that has been influenced by a typical phrase in Aramaic, showing an author's awareness of both languages.

¹²At this, the king exploded in a furious rage and ordered that all Babylon's sages be wiped out. ¹³So the command went out: The sages were to be killed. Daniel and his friends too were hunted down; they were to be killed as well.

God reveals the mystery

¹⁴Then Daniel, with wisdom and sound judgment, responded to Arioch the king's chief executioner, who had gone out to kill Babylon's sages. ¹⁵He said to Arioch the king's royal officer, "Why is the king's command so unreasonable?" After Arioch explained the situation to Daniel, ¹⁶Daniel went and asked the king to give him some time so he could explain the dream's meaning to him. ¹⁷Then Daniel went to his house and explained the situation to his friends Hananiah, Mishael, and Azariah ¹⁸so that they would ask the God of heaven for help about this mystery, in hopes that Daniel and his friends wouldn't die with the rest of Babylon's sages. ¹⁹Then, in a vision by night, the mystery was revealed to Daniel! Daniel praised the God of heaven:

²⁰ God's name be praised
   from age to eternal age!
   Wisdom and might are his!
²¹ God is the one who changes
   times and eras,
   who dethrones one king,
   only to establish another,
   who grants wisdom to the wise and
   knowledge to those with insight.
²² God is the one who uncovers
   what lies deeply hidden;
   he knows what hides in darkness;
   light lives with him!
²³ I acknowledge and praise you,
   my fathers' God!
   You've given me wisdom and might,
   and now you've made known to me
   what we asked of you:
   you've made known to us
   the king's demand.

Daniel recounts the dream

²⁴So Daniel went to Arioch, the man the king had appointed to wipe out Babylon's sages. Daniel said to him, "Don't wipe out the sages of Babylon! Bring me before the king, and I will explain the dream's meaning to him." ²⁵Wasting no time, Arioch brought Daniel before the king, telling him, "I have found someone from the Judean exiles who will tell the dream's meaning to the king."

²⁶In reply the king said to Daniel (whose name was Belteshazzar), "Can you really tell me the dream that I saw, as well as its meaning?"

²⁷Daniel answered the king, "Sages, enchanters, dream interpreters, and diviners can't explain to the king the mystery he seeks. ²⁸But there is a God in heaven, a revealer of mysteries, who has shown King Nebuchadnezzar what will happen in the days to come! Now this was your dream—this was the vision in your head as you lay in your bed:

²⁹"As you lay in bed, Your Majesty, your thoughts turned to what will happen in the future. The revealer of mysteries has revealed to you what will happen. ³⁰Now this mystery was revealed to me, not because I have more wisdom than any other living person but so that the dream's meaning might be made known to the king, and so that you might know the thoughts of your own mind.

³¹"Your Majesty, you were looking, and there, rising before you, was a single, massive statue. This statue was huge, shining with dazzling light, and was awesome to see. ³²The statue's head was made of pure gold; its chest and arms were made from silver; its abdomen and hips were made of bronze. ³³Its legs were of iron, and its feet were a mixture of iron and clay. ³⁴You observed this until a stone was cut, but not by hands; and it smashed the statue's feet of iron and clay and shattered them. ³⁵Then all the parts shattered simultaneously—iron, clay, bronze, silver, and gold. They became like chaff, left on summer threshing floors. The wind lifted them away until no trace of them remained. But the stone that smashed the statue became a mighty mountain, and it filled the entire earth.

The dream's meaning: four future rulers

³⁶"This was the dream. Now we will tell the king its meaning: ³⁷You, Your Majesty, are the king of kings. The God of heaven has

given kingship, power, might, and glory to you! [38]God has delivered into your care human beings, wild creatures, and birds in the sky—wherever they live—and has made you ruler of all of them. You are the gold head. [39]But in your place, another kingdom will arise, one inferior to yours, and then a third, bronze kingdom will rule over all the earth. [40]Then will come a fourth kingdom, mighty like iron. Just as iron shatters and crushes everything; so like an iron that smashes, it will shatter and crush all these others. [41]As for the feet and toes that you saw, which were a mixture of potter's clay and iron, that signifies a divided kingdom; but it will possess some of the unyielding strength of iron. Even so, you saw the iron mixed with earthy clay [42]so that the toes were made from a mixture of iron and clay. Part of the kingdom will be mighty, but part of it will be fragile. [43]Just as you saw the iron mixed with earthy clay, they will join together by intermarrying, but they will not bond to each other, just as iron does not fuse with clay.

[44]"But in the days of those kings, the God of heaven will raise up an everlasting kingdom that will be indestructible. Its rule will never pass to another people. It will shatter other kingdoms. It will put an end to all of them. It will stand firm forever, [45]just like you saw when the stone, which was cut from the mountain, but not by hands, shattered the iron, bronze, clay, silver, and gold. A great God has revealed to the king what will happen in the future. The dream is certain. Its meaning can be trusted."

Nebuchadnezzar honors Daniel

[46]Then King Nebuchadnezzar bowed low and honored Daniel. The king ordered that grain and incense offerings be made to Daniel. [47]The king declared to Daniel, "No doubt about it: your God is God of gods, Lord of kings, and a revealer of mysteries because you were able to reveal this mystery!" [48]Then the king exalted Daniel and lavished gifts on him, making him ruler over all the province of Babylon and chief minister over all Babylon's sages. [49]At Daniel's urging, the king appointed Shadrach, Meshach, and Abednego to administer the province of Babylon, but Daniel himself remained at the royal court.

Gold statue

3 King Nebuchadnezzar made a gold statue. It was ninety feet high and nine feet wide. He set it up in the Dura Valley in the province of Babylon. [2]King Nebuchadnezzar then ordered the chief administrators, ministers, governors, counselors, treasurers, judges, magistrates, and all the provincial officials to assemble and come for the dedication of the statue that he had set up. [3]So the chief administrators, ministers, governors, counselors, treasurers, judges, magistrates, and all the provincial officials assembled for the dedication of the statue that King Nebuchadnezzar had set up. They stood in front of the statue the king had set up. [4]The herald proclaimed loudly: "Peoples, nations, and languages! This is what you must do: [5]When you hear the sound of the horn, pipe, zither, lyre, harp, flute, and every kind of instrument, you must bow down and worship the gold statue that King Nebuchadnezzar has set up. [6]Anyone who will not bow down and worship will be immediately thrown into a furnace of flaming fire." [7]So because of this order as soon as they heard the sound of the horn, pipe, zither, lyre, harp, flute,[b] and every kind of instrument, all the peoples, nations, and languages bowed down and worshipped the gold statue that King Nebuchadnezzar had set up.

Plot against Shadrach, Meshach, and Abednego

[8]At that moment some Chaldeans came forward, seizing a chance to attack the Jews. [9]They said to King Nebuchadnezzar: "Long live the king! [10]Your Majesty, you gave a command that everyone who hears the sound of the horn, pipe, zither, lyre, harp, flute, and every kind of instrument should bow down and worship the gold

[b]Identification of the instruments is not certain; several of the Aramaic terms are Greek loanwords.

statue. [11]Anyone who wouldn't bow and worship would be thrown into a furnace of flaming fire. [12]Now there are some Jews, ones you appointed to administer the province of Babylon—specifically, Shadrach, Meshach, and Abednego—who have ignored your command. They don't serve your gods, and they don't worship the gold statue you've set up."

[13]In a violent rage Nebuchadnezzar ordered them to bring Shadrach, Meshach, and Abednego. They were brought before the king.

[14]Nebuchadnezzar said to them: "Shadrach, Meshach, and Abednego: Is it true that you don't serve my gods or worship the gold statue I've set up? [15]If you are now ready to do so, bow down and worship the gold statue I've made when you hear the sound of horn, pipe, zither, lyre, harp, flute, and every kind of instrument. But if you won't worship it, you will be thrown straight into the furnace of flaming fire. Then what god will rescue you from my power?"

[16]Shadrach, Meshach, and Abednego answered King Nebuchadnezzar: "We don't need to answer your question. [17]If our God—the one we serve—is able to rescue us from the furnace of flaming fire and from your power, Your Majesty, then let him rescue us.[c] [18]But if he doesn't, know this for certain, Your Majesty: we will never serve your gods or worship the gold statue you've set up."

Inside the furnace

[19]Nebuchadnezzar was filled with rage, and his face twisted beyond recognition because of Shadrach, Meshach, and Abednego. In response he commanded that the furnace be heated to seven times its normal heat. [20]He told some of the strongest men in his army to bind Shadrach, Meshach, and Abednego and throw them into the furnace of flaming fire. [21]So Shadrach, Meshach, and Abednego were bound, still dressed in all their clothes, and thrown into the furnace of flaming fire. ([22]Now the king's command had been rash, and the furnace was heated to such an extreme that the fire's flame killed the very men who carried Shadrach, Meshach, and Abednego to it.) [23]So these three men, Shadrach, Meshach, and Abednego, fell, bound, into the furnace of flaming fire.

[24]Then King Nebuchadnezzar jumped up in shock and said to his associates, "Didn't we throw three men, bound, into the fire?"

They answered the king, "Certainly, Your Majesty."

[25]He replied, "Look! I see four men, unbound, walking around inside the fire, and they aren't hurt! And the fourth one looks like one of the gods." [26]Nebuchadnezzar went near the opening of the furnace of flaming fire and said, "Shadrach, Meshach, and Abednego, servants of the Most High God, come out! Come here!" Then Shadrach, Meshach, and Abednego came out of the fire. [27]The chief administrators, ministers, governors, and the king's associates crowded around to look at them. The fire hadn't done anything to them: their hair wasn't singed; their garments looked the same as before; they didn't even smell like fire!

Nebuchadnezzar praises God

[28]Nebuchadnezzar declared: "May the God of Shadrach, Meshach, and Abednego be praised! He sent his messenger[d] to rescue his servants who trusted him. They ignored the king's order, sacrificing their bodies, because they wouldn't serve or worship any god but their God. [29]I now issue a decree to every people, nation, and language: whoever speaks disrespectfully about Shadrach, Meshach, and Abednego's God will be torn limb from limb and their house made a trash heap, because there is no other god who can rescue like this." [30]Then the king made Shadrach, Meshach, and Abednego prosperous in the province of Babylon.

Nebuchadnezzar's testimony

4 [e]King Nebuchadnezzar's message to all the peoples, nations, and languages in-

[c]Or he will deliver us [d]Or angel [e]3:31 in Aram

habiting the entire earth: "I wish you much peace. [2]I'm delighted to share the signs and miracles that the Most High God has worked in my life.

[3] His signs are superb!
His miracles so powerful!
His kingdom is everlasting.
His rule is for all time.

[4]"While I, Nebuchadnezzar, was safe in my house, content in my palace, [5]I had a terrifying dream. My thoughts while I was lying in bed and the vision in my mind overwhelmed me. [6]I ordered all Babylon's sages to come before me, so they might tell me the dream's meaning. [7]So the dream interpreters, enchanters, Chaldeans, and diviners came. I told them the dream, but they couldn't interpret it for me. [8]Daniel, who is called Belteshazzar after the name of my god, was the last to come before me. In him is the breath[g] of the holy gods! I told Daniel the dream:

Nebuchadnezzar's dream

[9]"Belteshazzar, chief of the dream interpreters, I know the breath of the holy gods is in you, and no mystery is too difficult for you. Tell me the meaning of the visions I had in my dream. [10]In my mind, as I lay in bed, I saw a vision:

At the center of the earth
was a towering tree.
[11]The tree grew in size and strength;
it was as high as the sky;
it could be seen
from every corner of the earth.
[12]Its leaves were beautiful,
its fruit abundant;
it had enough food for everyone.
Wild animals took shade under it;
birds nested in its branches.
All living things lived off that tree.

[13]"In my mind, as I lay in bed, I saw another vision: A holy watcher came down from heaven. [14]He proclaimed loudly:

'Cut down the tree
and shear off its branches!
Strip its leaves and scatter its fruit!

The creatures should flee
from its shelter;
the birds should take flight
from its branches.
[15]But leave its deepest root in the earth,
bound with iron and bronze
in the field grass.
Dew from heaven is to wash it,
and it must live with the animals
in the earth's vegetation.
[16]Its[h] human mind is to be changed:
it will be given the mind of an animal.
Seven periods of time will pass over it.
[17]This sentence is by the watchers' decree;
this decision is the holy ones' word
so that all who live might know
that the Most High
dominates human kingship.
The Most High gives kingship
to anyone he wants
and sets over it the lowest of people.'

[18]"This is the dream that I, King Nebuchadnezzar, had. So now Belteshazzar, tell me the meaning because all the sages in my kingdom were unable to interpret it for me. But you are able to do it because the breath of the holy gods is in you."

Daniel interprets the visions

[19]Daniel, who was called Belteshazzar, was shocked for a bit. What he thought about frightened him.

The king declared, "Don't let the dream and its meaning scare you, Belteshazzar."

Then Belteshazzar answered, "Sir, I wish the dream to be for those who hate you and its meaning to be for your enemies! [20]The tree you saw that grew in size and strength, that was as high as the sky, that could be seen from every corner of the earth, [21]with its beautiful leaves and its abundant fruit, and that had enough food for everyone, with wild animals living under it and birds nesting in its branches—[22]Your Majesty, that tree is you! You have grown large and become powerful. Your greatness is as high as the sky; your rule extends to the edge of the earth!

[f]4:1 in Aram [g]Or *spirit*; also in 4:9, 18 [h]Throughout 4:15-16 and later in this chap, *it* and *its* could also be translated *he* and *his*.

²³"Your Majesty, the holy watcher you saw coming down from heaven, who said, 'Cut down the tree and destroy it, but leave its deepest root in the earth, bound with iron and bronze in the field grass, dew from heaven is to wash it, and it must live with the wild animals until seven periods of time pass over it'— ²⁴Your Majesty, this is the dream's meaning: It is the sentence of the Most High, delivered to my master the king. ²⁵You will be driven away from other humans and will live with the wild animals. You will eat grass like cattle and will be washed by dew from heaven. Seven periods of time will pass over you, until you acknowledge that the Most High dominates human kingship, giving it to anyone he wants. ²⁶And when he said to leave the deepest root of the tree—that means your kingship will again be yours, once you acknowledge that heaven rules all. ²⁷Therefore, Your Majesty, please accept my advice: remove your sins by doing what is right; remove your wrongdoing by showing mercy to the poor. Then your safety will be long lasting."

Visions come true

²⁸All this happened to King Nebuchadnezzar. ²⁹Twelve months later, he was walking on the roof of the royal palace in Babylon. ³⁰The king declared, "Isn't this Babylon, the magnificent city that I built as the royal house by my own mighty strength and for my own majestic glory?"

³¹These words hadn't even left the king's mouth when a voice came from heaven: "You, King Nebuchadnezzar, are now informed: Kingship is taken away from you. ³²You will be driven away from other humans and will live with the wild animals. You will eat grass like cattle, and seven periods of time will pass over you until you acknowledge that the Most High dominates human kingship, giving it to anyone he wants."

³³Nebuchadnezzar's sentence was immediately carried out. He was driven away from other humans and ate grass like cattle. Dew from heaven washed his body until

he grew hair like eagles' feathers and claws like a bird.

Nebuchadnezzar is restored

³⁴"At the end of that time, I, Nebuchadnezzar, raised my eyes to heaven. My reason returned to me, and I praised the Most High. I worshipped and glorified the one who lives forever because his rule is everlasting; his kingdom is for all time. ³⁵All of earth's inhabitants are nothing in comparison. The Most High does whatever he wants with heaven's forces and with earth's inhabitants. No one can contain his power or say to him, 'What do you think you are doing?' ³⁶So at that moment my reason returned to me. My honor and splendor came back to me for the glory of my kingdom. My associates and my princes wanted to be with me again. Not only was I reinstated over my kingdom, I received more power than ever before.

³⁷"Now I, Nebuchadnezzar, worship, magnify, and glorify the king of heaven. All his works are truth, all his paths are justice, and he is able to humble all who walk in pride."

Belshazzar's party

5 King Belshazzar threw a huge party for a thousand of his princes, and he drank a lot of wine in front of them. ²While he was under the wine's influence, Belshazzar commanded that the gold and silver equipment that his father Nebuchadnezzar had taken from Jerusalem's temple be brought to the party so that the king, his princes, his consorts, and his secondary wives could drink wine out of them. ³So the goldⁱ equipment that had been carried out of the temple, God's house in Jerusalem, was brought in; and the king, his princes, his consorts, and his secondary wives drank out of it. ⁴They drank a lot of wine; and they praised the gods of gold, silver, bronze, iron, wood, and stone.

Writing on the wall

⁵Right then the fingers of a human hand appeared and wrote on the plaster of the

---

ⁱVulg, Theodotion add *silver*.

king's palace wall in the light of the lamp. The king saw the hand that wrote. [6]The king's mood changed immediately, and he was deeply disturbed. He felt weak, and his knees were shaking. [7]The king yelled, calling for the enchanters, the Chaldeans, and the diviners.

The king told these sages of Babylon: "Anyone who can read this writing and tell me its meaning will wear royal robes, will have a gold chain around his neck, and will rule the kingdom as third in command."

[8]Then all the king's sages arrived, but they couldn't read the writing or interpret it for the king. [9]At that point King Belshazzar was really frightened. All the color drained from his face, and his princes were also very worried.

[10]Upon hearing the commotion coming from the king and his princes, the queen entered the banqueting hall and declared, "Long live the king! Don't be so disturbed. Don't be so frightened. [11]There is a man in your kingdom who has the breath[j] of holy gods in him! When your father was alive, this man was shown to possess illumination, insight, and wisdom like the very wisdom of the gods.[k] Your father King Nebuchadnezzar appointed this man as chief over the dream interpreters, enchanters, Chaldeans, and diviners. Yes, your father did this [12]because this man—Daniel, the one the king named Belteshazzar—possesses an extraordinary spirit, knowledge, and insight into the meaning of dreams. He can explain ambiguities and resolve mysteries. Now in light of all that, summon Daniel! He will explain the meaning of this thing."

[13]So Daniel was brought before the king. The king said to him, "So you are Daniel, the Daniel from the exiles that my father the king brought from Judah? [14]I have heard that the breath of the gods is in you and that you possess illumination, insight, and extraordinary wisdom. [15]Now, the sages and the dream interpreters were brought before me to read this writing and interpret it for me, but they couldn't explain its meaning. [16]But I've heard that you can explain meanings and solve mysteries. So if you can read this writing and interpret it for me, you will wear royal robes, have a gold chain around your neck, and will rule the kingdom as third in command."

Daniel interprets the writing

[17]Daniel answered the king: "Keep your gifts. Give the rewards to someone else. But I will still read the writing to the king and interpret it for him. [18]Listen, Your Majesty: The Most High God gave kingship, power, glory, and majesty to your father Nebuchadnezzar. [19]Because of the power God gave Nebuchadnezzar, all peoples, nations, and languages were terrified of him. He did whatever he wanted, whenever he wanted: killing or sparing, exalting or humbling. [20]But when he became arrogant, acting in stubborn pride, he was pulled off his royal throne and the glory was taken from him. [21]He was driven away from other humans, and his mind became like an animal's. He lived with wild donkeys, he ate grass like cattle, and dew from heaven washed his body until he realized that the Most High God dominates human kingship and sets over it anyone he wants.

[j]Or *spirit*; also in 5:14   [k]Or *wisdom of God*

BELSHAZZAR

In Daniel 5:2, 11, 13, 18, 22, Belshazzar ("Bel protect the king") is the son of the Neo-Babylonian king Nebuchadnezzar, but cuneiform documents and inscriptions state that Belshazzar was the son of the last Neo-Babylonian ruler, Nabonidus.

[22] "But you who are his son, Belshazzar, you haven't submitted, even though you've known all this. [23] Instead, you've set yourself up against the Lord of heaven! The equipment of God's house was brought to you; and you, your princes, your consorts, and your secondary wives drank wine out of it, all the while praising the gods of silver, gold, bronze, iron, wood, and stone—gods who can't see, hear, or know anything. But you didn't glorify the true God who holds your very breath in his hand and who owns every road you take.

[24] "That's why this hand was sent from God and why this message was written down. [25] This is what was written down:

MENE, MENE, TEKEL, and PARSIN.[l]

[26] "This is the meaning of the word MENE: God has numbered[m] the days of your rule. It's over! [27] TEKEL means that you've been weighed[n] on the scales, and you don't measure up. [28] PERES[o] means your kingship is divided[p] and given to the Medes and the Persians."[q]

[29] Then Belshazzar commanded that Daniel be dressed in a purple robe, have a gold chain around his neck, and be officially appointed as third in command in the kingdom.

[30] That very same night, Belshazzar the Chaldean king was killed. [31] Darius the Mede received the kingdom at the age of 62.

Plot against Daniel

6 Darius decided to appoint one hundred twenty chief administrators throughout the kingdom, [2] and to set over them three main officers to whom they would report so that the king wouldn't have to be bothered with too much.[r] One of these main officers was Daniel. [3] Because of his extraordinary spirit, Daniel soon surpassed the other officers and the chief administrators—so much so that the king had plans to set him over the entire kingdom. [4] As a result, the other officers and the chief administrators tried to find some problem with Daniel's work for the kingdom. But they couldn't find any problem or corruption at all because Daniel was trustworthy. He wasn't guilty of any negligence or corruption.

[5] So these men said, "We won't find any fault in Daniel, unless we can find something to use against him from his religious practice."[s]

[6] So these officers and chief administrators ganged together and went to the king. They said to him, "Long live King Darius! [7] All the officers of the kingdom, the ministers, the chief administrators, the royal associates, and the governors advise the king to issue an edict and enforce a law, that for thirty days anyone who says prayers to any god or human being except you, Your Majesty, will be thrown into a pit of lions. [8] Now, Your Majesty, issue the law and sign the document so that it cannot be changed, as per the law of Media and Persia, which cannot be annulled." [9] Because of this, King

---

[l]Aram *Upharsin* [m]Aram *menah*, which is a wordplay with *Mene* [n]Aram *teqal*, which is a wordplay with *Tekel* [o]The singular form of the plural *Parsin* in 5:25 [p]Aram *peras*, which is a wordplay with *Parsin* [q]Aram *Paras*, another wordplay with *Parsin* [r]Aram uncertain [s]Or *in the Instruction of his God*

MENE, MENE, TEKEL, AND PARSIN

These are the famous words written by "the fingers of a human hand . . . on the plaster of the king's palace wall" (Dan 5:5-28) that terrified the putative last Babylonian king, Belshazzar. In Daniel 5:24-28, the Jewish sage and riddle-solver Daniel, brought into the banquet at the insistence of the queen (vv. 10-12), uses puns in order to create an oracle of judgment against the king.

Darius signed the document containing the law.

Daniel prays

[10]When Daniel learned that the document had been signed, he went to his house. Now his upper room had open windows that faced Jerusalem. Daniel knelt down, prayed, and praised his God three times that day, just like he always did. [11]Just then these men, all ganged together, came upon Daniel praying and seeking mercy from his God. [12]They then went and talked to the king about the law: "Your Majesty! Didn't you sign a law, that for thirty days any person who prays to any god or human being besides you, Your Majesty, would be thrown into a pit of lions?"

The king replied, "The decision is absolutely firm in accordance with the law of Media and Persia, which cannot be annulled."

[13]So they said to the king, "One of the Judean exiles, Daniel, has ignored you, Your Majesty, as well as the law you signed. He says his prayers three times a day!"

[14]When the king heard this report, he was very unhappy. He decided to rescue Daniel and did everything he could do to save Daniel before the sun went down. [15]But these men, all ganged together, came and said to the king, "You must realize, Your Majesty, that the law of Media and Persia, including every law and edict the king has issued, cannot be changed."

Daniel in the lions' pit

[16]So the king gave the order, and they brought Daniel and hurled him into the pit of lions.

The king said to Daniel: "Your God—the one you serve so consistently—will rescue you."[t]

[17]A single stone was brought and placed over the entrance to the pit. The king sealed it with his own ring and with those of his princes so that Daniel's situation couldn't be changed. [18]The king then went home to his palace and fasted through the night. No pleasures[u] were brought to him, and he couldn't

sleep. [19]At dawn, at the first sign of light, the king rose and rushed to the lions' pit.

[20]As he approached it, he called out to Daniel, worried: "Daniel, servant of the living God! Was your God—the one you serve so consistently—able to rescue you from the lions?"

[21]Then Daniel answered the king: "Long live the king! [22]My God sent his messenger, who shut the lions' mouths. They haven't touched me because I was judged innocent before my God. I haven't done anything wrong to you either, Your Majesty."

[23]The king was thrilled. He commanded that Daniel be brought up out of the pit, and Daniel was lifted out. Not a scratch was found on him, because he trusted in his God. [24]The king then ordered that the men who had accused Daniel be brought and thrown into the lions' pit—including their wives and children. They hadn't even reached the bottom of the pit before the lions overpowered them, crushing all their bones.

New decree

[25]Then King Darius wrote the following decree:

To all the peoples, nations, and languages inhabiting the entire earth: I wish you much peace. [26]I now issue this command: In every region of my kingdom, all people must fear and revere Daniel's God because:

He is the living God.
God stands firm forever.
His kingship is indestructible.
God's rule will last until the end of time.
[27]He is rescuer and savior;
God performs signs and miracles
in heaven and on earth.
Here's the proof:
He rescued Daniel from the lions' power.
[28]And so Daniel was made prosperous during the rule of Darius and during the rule of Cyrus the Persian.

Daniel's vision: four beasts

7In the first year of Babylon's King Belshazzar, Daniel had a dream—a vision

---

[t]Or *May your God—the one you serve so consistently—rescue you.* [u]Aram uncertain

in his head as he lay on his bed. He wrote the dream down. Here is the beginning of the account:

[2] I am Daniel. In the vision I had during the night I saw the four winds of heaven churning the great sea. [3] Four giant beasts emerged from the sea, each different from the others. [4] The first was like a lion with eagle's wings. I observed it until its wings were pulled off, and it was lifted up from the ground. It was then set on two feet, like a human being, and it received a human mind. [5] Then I saw another beast, a second one, like a bear. It was raised on one side. It had three ribs in its mouth between its teeth. It was told: "Get up! Devour much flesh!" [6] I kept watching, and suddenly there was another beast, this one like a leopard. On its back it had four wings like bird wings. This beast had four heads. Authority was given to it.

[7] After this, as I continued to watch this night vision, I saw a fourth beast, terrifying and hideous, with extraordinary power and with massive iron teeth. As it ate and crushed, its feet smashed whatever was left over. It was different from all the other beasts before it, and it had ten horns. [8] I was staring at the horns when, suddenly, another small horn came up between them. Three of the earlier horns were ripped out

to make room for it. On this new horn were eyes like human eyes and a mouth that bragged and bragged.

Throne of fire and the human figure

[9] As I was watching,
   thrones were raised up.
The ancient one took his seat.
   His clothes were white like snow;
   his hair was like a lamb's wool.
   His throne was made of flame;
   its wheels were blazing fire.
[10] A river of fire flowed out
   from his presence;
   thousands upon thousands served him;
   ten thousand times ten thousand
   stood ready to serve him!
The court sat in session;
   the scrolls were opened.

[11] I kept watching. I watched from the moment the horn started bragging until the beast was killed and its body was destroyed, handed over to be burned with fire. [12] Then the authority of the remaining beasts was brought to an end, but they were given an extension among the living for a set time and season.

[13] As I continued to watch this night vision of mine, I suddenly saw
   one like a human being[v]
   coming with the heavenly clouds.

[v] Aram *kebar enash* (*like a son of man*) is an idiom that means *like a human being;* cf also 8:17; 10:16, 18 for Heb approximations.

APOCALYPTICISM

A cluster of religious ideas, some of which were found in texts like Daniel and Revelation. Apocalypticism is frequently seen as being about the end times, with well-defined characteristics: (1) hope for a better world, with a belief that God's kingdom will break into history, which then leads to history's end; (2) dualism (contrast between the present evil age and a glorious future); (3) exotic symbolism (e.g., Dan 7); (4) an expectation for a dramatic transformation of this sinful age into the coming of a heavenly kingdom; (5) a sectarian ethos—suggested by the stark contrast between the present evil age and the glorious future—in which communities cut themselves off from wider society and await a divine reordering of the world; (6) the imminent end of this world; and (7) a deterministic view of history.

He came to the ancient one
and was presented before him.
[14] Rule, glory, and kingship
were given to him;
all peoples, nations, and languages
will serve him.
His rule is an everlasting one—
it will never pass away!—
his kingship is indestructible.

Beasts interpreted

[15] Now this caused me, Daniel, to worry.[w]
My visions disturbed me greatly. [16] So I
went to one of the servants who was standing ready nearby. I asked him for the truth
about all this.

He spoke to me and explained to me
the meaning of these things. [17] "These four
giant beasts are four kings that will rise up
from the earth, [18] but the holy ones of the
Most High will receive the kingship. They
will hold the kingship securely forever and
always."

[19] Next I wanted greater clarity about
the fourth beast, the one that was different
from all the others and utterly terrifying
with its iron teeth and bronze claws. As it
ate and crushed, its feet smashed whatever
was left over. [20] I wanted greater clarity
about the ten horns on its head, and the
other horn that came up, along with the
three that fell out to make room for it—but
especially about the horn that had eyes and
a mouth that bragged, and that seemed
more important than the others. [21] As I
watched, this same horn waged war against
the holy ones and defeated them, [22] until
the Ancient One came. Then judgment was
given in favor of the holy ones of the Most
High. The set time arrived, and the holy
ones held the kingship securely.

[23] This is what he said:

"The fourth beast means
that there will be a fourth kingship
on the earth.
It will be different
from all the other kingships.
It will devour the entire earth,
trample it, crush it.

[24] The ten horns mean
that from this kingship
will rise ten kings,
and after them will rise yet another.
He will be different
from the previous ones.
He will defeat three kings.
[25] He will say things against the Most High
and will exhaust the holy ones
of the Most High.
He will try to change times set by law.
And for a period of time,
periods of time,
and half a period of time,
they will be delivered into his power.
[26] Then the court will sit in session.
His rule will be taken away—
ruined and wiped out for all time.
[27] The kingship, authority, and power
of all kingdoms under heaven
will be given to the people,
the holy ones of the Most High.
Their kingship is an everlasting one;
every authority will serve them
and obey."
[28] The account ends here.

Now as for how I, Daniel, felt about this:
My thoughts disturbed me greatly. My
mood darkened considerably, and I kept
thinking about this matter.

Vision of a ram and a goat

8 In the third year of King Belshazzar's
rule, a vision came to me, Daniel, some
time after the earlier vision I had. [2] I saw this
vision, and as I experienced it I was in the
walled city of Susa in the province of Elam,[x]
by the Ulai canal. [3] When I lifted my eyes, I
suddenly saw a ram with two horns standing in front of the canal. Both horns were
high, but one was higher than the other.
The higher one came up after the other
one. [4] I saw the ram goring west, north, and
south. No animal could resist the ram, and
no one could stop it, rescuing others from
its power. The ram did whatever it pleased.
It became powerful.

[5] I was trying to understand this when
suddenly a he-goat came from the west,

---

[w] Or *my spirit was distressed in its sheath*; Aram uncertain   [x] Some LXX sources; MT repeats *I had this vision before
I was by the Ulai canal.*

crossing the entire earth but not touching the ground. Between this goat's eyes was a horn that was a sight to see. [6]The he-goat came to the ram that had two horns, the one I'd seen standing in front of the canal. The he-goat charged the ram in powerful anger. [7]I saw the he-goat approach the ram. It was enraged at the ram and attacked it, shattering the ram's two horns. The ram couldn't resist the he-goat. The he-goat threw the ram on the ground and trampled on it. No one could rescue the ram from the he-goat's power.

[8]The he-goat became even greater, but at the height of its power, its large horn snapped. In its place, four horns, each a sight to see, came up toward the four winds of heaven. [9]A single, very small horn came out of one of the four horns. It grew bigger and bigger, stretching toward the south, the east, and the beautiful country. [10]It grew as high as the heavenly forces, until it finally threw some of them and some of the stars down to the earth. Then it trampled on them. [11]It grew as high as the very leader of those forces, taking the daily sacrifice away from him[y] and overturning his holy place. [12]In an act of rebellion, another force will take control of the daily sacrifice. It will throw truth to the ground and will succeed in everything it does.[z]

How long?

[13]I then heard a certain holy one speaking. A second holy one said to the first one: "How long will this vision last—the one concerning the daily sacrifice, the desolating rebellion, and the handing over of the sanctuary and its forces to be trampled?"

[14]He said to me, "For two thousand three hundred evenings and mornings. Then the sanctuary will be restored."

Vision interpreted

[15]Now I, Daniel, needed help understanding the vision I saw. Suddenly standing in front of me was someone who looked like a man. [16]I then heard a human voice coming out of the center of the Ulai canal. It called out: "Gabriel, help this person understand what he has seen."

[17]Gabriel approached me, and I was terrified when he came. I fell with my face to the ground. Gabriel said to me, "Know this, human one: the vision is for the end time." [18]As soon as he said this to me, I fell into a trance. My face was still on the ground. Then Gabriel touched me and set me up on my feet.

[19]He said, "Now, I am going to tell you what will happen during the time of doom that is coming, because at the appointed time there will be an end. [20]The two-horned ram you saw represents the kings of Media and Persia. [21]The long-haired he-goat is the king of Greece, and the big horn between its eyes is the first king. [22]The horn that snapped so that four came up in its place means that four kingdoms will come from one nation, but these four won't have the strength of the first one.

[23]When their kingship nears its end
    and their sins[a] are almost complete,
        a king will step forward.
    He will be stern
        and a master of deception.
[24]At the height of his power,[b]
        he will wreak unbelievable destructions.

---

[y]Or *the daily sacrifice was taken away from him.* [z]Heb uncertain [a]LXX; MT *rebels* [b]LXX *His power will grow strong, but not by his own power,* perhaps influenced by 8:22.

GABRIEL

Angel named twice in Daniel (8:16; 9:21) and twice in Luke (1:19, 26). According to several second temple Jewish documents, Gabriel was one of the archangels, along with Michael (Dan 10:13, 21; 12:1; Jude 9; Rev 12:7), Raphael, and others.

He will succeed in all he does.
He will destroy both the mighty
    and the people of the holy ones.
²⁵ Along with his cunning,
    he will succeed by using deceit.
In his own mind, he will be great.
    In a time of peace,
he will bring destruction on many,
    opposing even the supreme leader.
But he will be broken—
    and not by a human hand.
²⁶ Now this vision of evening and morning,
which has been announced, is true. But you
must seal it up, because it is for days far in
the future."

²⁷ Then I, Daniel, was overwhelmed and
felt sick for days. When I finally got up and
went about the king's business, I remained
troubled by the vision and couldn't understand it.

Daniel's prayer

9 In the first year of Darius' rule—Darius,
who was Ahasuerus' son, a Median by
birth and who ruled the Chaldean kingdom—²I, Daniel, pondered the scrolls, specifically the number of years that it would
take to complete Jerusalem's desolation according to the LORD's word to the prophet
Jeremiah. It was seventy years. ³I then
turned my face to my Lord God, asking for
an answer with prayer and pleading, and
with fasting, mourning clothes, and ashes.
⁴As I prayed to the LORD my God, I made
this confession:

Please, my Lord—you are the great
and awesome God, the one who keeps the
covenant, and truly faithful to all who
love him and keep his commands: ⁵We
have sinned and done wrong. We have
brought guilt on ourselves and rebelled,
ignoring your commands and your laws.
⁶We haven't listened to your servants,
the prophets, who spoke in your name
to our kings, our leaders, our parents,
and to all the land's people. ⁷Righteousness belongs to you, my Lord! But we
are ashamed this day—we, the people
of Judah, the inhabitants of Jerusalem,
all Israel whether near or far, in whatever country where you've driven them
because of their unfaithfulness when
they broke faith with you. ⁸LORD, we
are ashamed—we, our kings, our leaders, and our parents who sinned against
you. ⁹Compassion and deep forgiveness
belong to my Lord, our God, because we
rebelled against him. ¹⁰We didn't listen
to the voice of the LORD our God by following the teachings he gave us through
his servants, the prophets. ¹¹All Israel
broke your Instruction and turned away,
ignoring your voice. Then the curse that
was sworn long ago—the one written in
the Instruction from Moses, God's servant—swept over us because we sinned
against God. ¹²God confirmed the words
he spoke against us and against our rulers, bringing great trouble on us. What
happened in Jerusalem hasn't happened
anywhere else in the entire world! ¹³All
this trouble came upon us, exactly as it
was written in the Instruction of Moses,
but we didn't try to reconcile with the
LORD our God by turning from our
wrongdoing or by finding wisdom in

DESOLATING MONSTROSITY

This phrase is from Daniel 9:27; 11:31; and 12:11; with a parallel in 8:13.
The phrase in Greek appears in Matthew 24:15 and Mark 13:14. Most scholars believe that the desolating monstrosity refers to the destructive work of
the Seleucid king Antiochus IV Epiphanes. He forced idolatrous practices on
the people and desecrated the temple in Jerusalem by placing an altar to
Zeus on the altar of entirely burned offerings. Swine, which are unclean according to levitical law, were offered as sacrifices on this pagan altar.

your faithfulness. [14]So the LORD oversaw the great trouble and brought it on us, because the LORD our God has been right in every move he's made, but we haven't listened to his voice.

[15]"But now, my Lord, our God—you who brought your people out of Egypt with a strong hand, making a name for yourself even to this day: We have sinned and done the wrong thing." [16]My Lord, please! In line with your many righteous acts, please turn your raging anger from Jerusalem, which is your city, your own holy mountain. Because of our sins and the wrongdoing of our parents, both Jerusalem and your people have become a disgrace to all our neighbors.

[17]"But now, our God, listen to your servant's prayer and pleas for help. Shine your face on your ruined sanctuary, for your own sake, my Lord. [18]Open your ears, my God, and listen! Open your eyes and look at our devastation. Look at the city called by your name! We pray our prayers for help to you, not because of any righteous acts of ours but because of your great compassion. [19]My Lord, listen! My Lord, forgive! My Lord, pay attention and act! Don't delay! My God, do all this for your own sake, because your city and your people are called by your name.

Seventy weeks

[20]While I was still speaking, praying, and confessing my sin and the sins of my people Israel—while I was still praying my prayer for help to the LORD my God about my God's holy mountain—[21]while I was still speaking this prayer, the man Gabriel approached me at the time of the evening

offering. This was the same Gabriel I had seen in my earlier vision. He was weary with exhaustion.[c]

[22]He explained as he spoke with me: "Daniel, here's why I've come: to give you insight and understanding. [23]When you began making your requests, a word went out, and I've come to tell it to you because you are greatly treasured. So now understand this word and grasp the meaning of this vision! [24]Seventy weeks are appointed for your people and for your holy city to complete the rebellion, to end sins, to cover over wrongdoing, to bring eternal righteousness, to seal up prophetic vision, and to anoint the most holy place.

[25]"So you must know and gain wisdom about this: There will be seven weeks from the moment the word went out to restore and rebuild Jerusalem until a leader is anointed. And for sixty-two weeks the city will be rebuilt with a courtyard and a moat. But in difficult times, [26]after the sixty-two weeks, an anointed one will be eliminated. No one will support him.[d] The army of a future leader will destroy the city and the sanctuary. His[e] end will come in a flood, but devastations will be decreed until the end of the war.[f] [27]For one week, he will make a strong covenant with many people. For a half-week, he will stop both sacrifices and offerings. In their place[g] will be the desolating monstrosities until the decreed destruction sweeps over the devastator."

Vision of a man

10 In the third year of Persia's King Cyrus, a message was revealed to Daniel, who was called Belteshazzar. The message was true: there would be a great

---

[c]Or *approached me in swift flight at the time of the evening offering;* Heb uncertain   [d]Or *and will have nothing* or *and will disappear;* Heb uncertain   [e]Or *Its* (the army's)   [f]Heb uncertain   [g]Correction *on the wing;* Heb uncertain

APOCALYPSE

The Greek term *apocalypse* means "revelation" or "disclosure." An apocalypse consists of visions, auditions, and dreams, whereby the divine world and its secrets are uncovered, revealed, or opened up to the seer.

conflict. Daniel understood the message, having discerned the meaning of the vision.

²During that time, I, Daniel, had been mourning for three weeks. ³I didn't eat any rich foods. Neither meat nor wine passed my lips, and I didn't clean up at all until the three weeks were up. ⁴Then, on the twenty-fourth day of the first month, as I was on the bank of the great Tigris River, ⁵I looked up and suddenly saw a man clothed in linen in front of me. He had a brilliant gold belt around his waist, ⁶and his body was like topaz. His face was like a flash of lightning, and his eyes were like burning torches. His arms and feet looked like polished bronze. When he spoke, it sounded like the roar of a crowd. ⁷Only I, Daniel, saw this vision. The other people who were with me didn't see it. Despite that, they were terrified and ran away to hide.

⁸So I was left alone to see this great vision all by myself. All my strength left me. My energy was sapped, and I couldn't stay strong. ⁹Then I heard the sound of the man's words. When I heard it, I fell into a trance with my face on the ground. ¹⁰But then a hand touched me, lifting me up to my hands and knees.

¹¹The man said to me, "Daniel, you are greatly treasured. Now grasp the meaning of what I'm saying to you. And stand up, because I've been sent to you."

As he said this to me, I stood up, shaking. ¹²Then the man said to me, "Don't be afraid, Daniel, because from the day you first set your mind to understand things and to humble yourself before your God, your words were heard. I've come because of your words! ¹³For twenty-one days the leader of the Persian kingdom blocked my way. But then Michael, one of the highest leaders, came to help me. I left Michael there with the leader of the Persian kingdom.ʰ ¹⁴But I've come to help you understand what will happen to your people in the future, because there is another vision concerning that time."

¹⁵While he said this to me, I turned my face to the ground and kept quiet. ¹⁶But then someone who looked like a human beingⁱ touched my lips. Then I opened my mouth and spoke, saying to the person standing in front of me: "My lord, the vision bothered me deeply, and I couldn't stay strong during it. ¹⁷So how can I, my lord's servant, speak with you, my lord? Even now there's no strength in me, and I can barely breathe."

¹⁸The one who looked like a human being touched me again and gave me strength. ¹⁹He said, "Don't be afraid. You are greatly treasured. All will be well with you. Be strong!"

As he spoke to me, I suddenly felt strong. Then I said: "My lord can go on, because you've made me strong."

²⁰Then he said: "Do you know why I have come to you? Now I must go back to fight the leader of Persia. As I leave, the leader of Greece will come! ²¹But I will tell you what

---

ʰLXX; Heb after I was detained there with the kings of Persia   ⁱHeb bene adam (a son of a man) is an idiom that means human being; cf 7:13.

TIGRIS RIVER

The Tigris River, 1,150 mi. long, arises in the Taurus Mountains of eastern Turkey and flows in a southeasterly direction through northern Iraq, the heartland of ancient Assyria. Near Baghdad in central Iraq it takes up a roughly parallel course with the Euphrates River as it flows through the territory of ancient Babylon and then ancient Sumer. The Tigris is mentioned twice in the OT. According to Genesis 2:14, the Tigris, which passed east of Assyria, was one of the four rivers flowing out of Eden. Daniel is standing on the banks of the Tigris when he receives the final revelation of the book (Dan 10:4).

is written in the Scroll of Truth. No one stands strong with me against these leaders except your leader Michael.

A vast empire divided

11 "In the first year of Darius the Mede's rule, I took my stand to strengthen and protect him." ²I will now tell you the truth. Persia will have three more kings, but the fourth will be richer than all of them. Once he has become strong through his great riches, he will disturb everyone, including the Greek kingdom. ³Then a warrior-king will come forward, ruling over a vast empire and doing whatever he wants. ⁴But even as he takes control, his kingdom will be broken, divided to the four winds of heaven. It won't pass to his descendants. No one will rule like he did because his kingdom will be uprooted. It will belong to others, not to these.

South and north

⁵"Then the southern king will gain power, but one of his princes will overpower him, ruling in his place. His empire will be vast. ⁶After some years, they will make an agreement together. The southern king's daughter will go to the northern king to finalize the agreement, but she won't retain her great power. Neither will his power remain in place. In those times she will be handed over, along with her escort, the one who fathered her, and the one who strengthened her.ʲ

⁷"A branch from her roots will rise up in his place. Attacking the army, he will enter the walled fortress of the northern king. He will fight with them, and he will conquer. ⁸He will even carry off their gods to Egypt, along with their statues and their silver and gold equipment. For years he will avoid the northern king. ⁹Then the northern king will attack the kingdom of the southern king, but will return to his own land. ¹⁰His sons will get ready for war, gathering massive forces. Their attack will be like an overwhelming flood. And they will attack again, taking the battle as far as his walled fortress.

¹¹"The southern king, in a bitter rage, will come out to battle the northern king.

He will muster a huge army, but the army will be handed over to his enemy. ¹²When the army is carried off, he will become confident. He will kill tens of thousands, but he will not stand strong. ¹³The northern king will then muster another army—this one bigger than the first. After some years have passed, he will attack with a large and well-equipped army. ¹⁴In those times, many will oppose the southern king. Violent persons from among your people also will rise up to support the vision, but they will fail.

¹⁵"When the northern king attacks, he will throw up a siege ramp and occupy a walled city. The southern forces will not be able to resist—not even its elite forces. No one will be strong enough to resist. ¹⁶The one who comes to attack will do whatever he wants; no one will be able to oppose him. He will take his place in the beautiful country, and he will hand out destruction. ¹⁷He will decide to occupy his entire kingdom by force. He will make an agreement with him and will give him a wife, intending to destroy him,ᵏ but it won't succeed and it won't happen.ˡ ¹⁸He will turn his face to the coastlands, capturing many people. A commander will put an end to his disgrace,ᵐ even though he won't repay that disgrace. ¹⁹Then he will turn his attention to the walled fortresses of his own country but will stumble, fall, and disappear.

²⁰"In his place one will arise who will send his agent to exact a kingdom's glory, but in a few days he will be broken, though not by anger and not by war. ²¹A worthless person will arise in his place. Royal majesty will not have been given to him, but he will come in a time of security and seize the kingdom by deceitful means. ²²Forces will be completely swept away and broken before him. The same is true for the leader of the covenant. ²³From the moment they make an agreement with him, he will act deceitfully. He will gain power at the expense of a small nation. ²⁴He will come into a province's richest places untroubled and will do what his fathers and grandfathers never could. He will hand out plunder,

---

ʲHeb uncertain   ᵏDSS; MT *her* or *it* (the kingdom)   ˡHeb adds *for him*.   ᵐHeb adds *for him*.

spoil, and wealth to them. He will make plans against fortresses, but only for a time.

²⁵"Then with a large army he will gather his strength and courage against the southern king. The southern king, with a large and super powerful army, will prepare for war, but he won't endure because they will make plans against him. ²⁶Those who eat the king's provisions will destroy him. His army will be overrun. Many will die.

²⁷"These two kings, with their minds set on evil, will sit at one table, telling lies, but with no success because the end will come at the set time. ²⁸He will return to his country with great wealth and set his mind against a holy covenant. He will do what he wants and then return to his country. ²⁹At the set time he will again battle against the south, but the second time will be different from the first. ³⁰Kittim ships will fight against him, and he will retreat in fear. He will rage against a holy covenant and will do what he wants. Then he will pay special attention to those who violate a holy covenant. ³¹His forces will come and make the sanctuary fortress impure. They will stop the daily sacrifice and set up a desolating monstrosity. ³²By deceitful means he will corrupt those who violate a covenant, but the people who acknowledge their God will stand strong and will act.

³³"The people's teachers will help many understand, but for a time they will fall by sword and by flame, by captivity and by plunder. ³⁴When they fall, they will receive a little help, but many will join them with deceitful plans. ³⁵Some of the teachers too will fall in order that they might be refined, purified, and cleansed—until an end time, because it is still not yet the set time.

An end to the arrogant king

³⁶"The king will do whatever he wants. He will exalt himself, making himself greater than any god. He will say unbelievable things against the God of gods. He will succeed until the doom is completed, because what is decreed must take place. ³⁷He will give no thought to the gods of his fathers, nor to the god cherished by women. He will give no thought to any god, because he will make himself greater than all of them. ³⁸In their place, he will worship a god of walled fortresses. With gold and silver, rare stones and precious things, he will worship a god his fathers did not acknowledge. ³⁹He will deal with walled fortresses with the help of a foreign god. He will heap rewards on those who support him, making them rule over many and dividing up the land for a price. ⁴⁰At the end time, the southern king will attack him. The northern king will storm against him with chariots and horses and many ships. He will invade countries, sweeping over them like a flood. ⁴¹He will invade the beautiful country, and tens of thousands will die. But Edom, Moab, and the best of the Ammonites will escape from his hand. ⁴²He will extend his power into other countries. Even Egypt won't escape. ⁴³He will take control of Egypt's hidden treasures of gold, silver, and all its precious things. Libyans and Cushites will follow at his feet. ⁴⁴But reports from the east and north will alarm him, and in a great rage he will set off to devastate and destroy many. ⁴⁵He will pitch his royal tents between the sea and the beautiful holy mountain. But he will come to his end, and no one will help him.

ANTIOCHUS

Antiochus IV Epiphanes (175–164 BCE) was the son of Antiochus III. Seleucus IV (187–175) had a rather undistinguished reign before the throne was taken by his brother Antiochus IV Epiphanes. This figure is infamous in history because of his attempt to suppress Judaism in Judah, and he features prominently in Jewish literature.

Eternal life or eternal disgrace

12 "At that time, Michael the great leader who guards your people will take his stand. It will be a difficult time—nothing like it has ever happened since nations first appeared. But at that time every one of your people who is found written in the scroll will be rescued. [2]Many of those who sleep in the dusty land[n] will wake up—some to eternal life, others to shame and eternal disgrace. [3]Those skilled in wisdom[o] will shine like the sky. Those who lead many to righteousness will shine like the stars forever and always. [4]But you, Daniel, must keep these words secret! Seal the scroll until the end time! Many will stray far, but knowledge will increase."

Waiting for the end time

[5]I, Daniel, looked and suddenly saw two other figures—one standing on each side of the stream. [6]One said to the man clothed in white linen, who was farther upstream: "When will these astonishing things be over?"

[7]I heard the man clothed in white linen, who was farther upstream, swear by the one who lives forever as he raised both hands to heaven: "For one set time, two set times, and half a set time. When the breaking of the holy people's power is over, all these things will be over."

[8]I heard it, but I didn't understand it. "My lord," I said, "what will happen after all this?"

[9]He said, "Get going now, Daniel, because these words must remain secret and sealed up until the end time. [10]Many will purify, cleanse, and refine themselves, but the wicked will act wickedly. None of the wicked will understand, but those skilled in wisdom will understand. [11]There will be one thousand two hundred ninety days from the time the daily sacrifice is stopped to the setting up of the desolating monstrosity. [12]Happy is the one who waits and reaches one thousand three hundred thirty-five days. [13]Now as for you, go on to the end. You will rest and will stand to receive your reward at the end of days.

[n]Or *earthy soil* or *dust of the earth*   [o]See 1:4; or *The teachers*; see 11:33, 35; also in 12:10.

RESURRECTION (OT)

The concept of resurrection of the dead did not develop until after 587 BCE. The First Temple period (ca. 950–587 BCE) gives us no proof of a conception of resurrection nor of any other afterlife like paradise (i.e., a reward for good behavior on earth). It could be that there was no idea of the afterlife at all, but that would make the Hebrews unique among world cultures and especially out of place in the ancient Near East, where elaborate ideas about postmortem existence and even more elaborate funeral rituals were everywhere part of literature, myth, and social life.

Two persons in the OT—Enoch (Gen 5) and Elijah (2 Kgs 2)—can be said to have achieved a beatific afterlife, in that they were assumed bodily into heaven without dying. Nothing suggests that this was viewed as a common fate of humanity.

The doctrine of resurrection is first clearly shown in biblical writing in Daniel 12, which can be dated a bit more than a century and a half before Jesus was born (approximately 168 BCE is a well-established date for the composition of the visions at the end of Daniel). Resurrection may be generally defined as the doctrine that after death the body will be reconstituted and revivified by God as a reward for the righteous and faithful. But resurrection is central to Christianity in a way that it is not to any of the other 1st-century sects of Judaism.

HOSEA

Hosea is the first of the twelve books known as the Minor Prophets. His name occurs in the title and in the heading. The name Hosea (also spelled Hoshea) does appear in other places in the Hebrew Scriptures (see 2 Kings 15:30; 1 Chronicles 27:20). He is identified as the son of Beeri. We know very little about him except that he was probably fairly young when he began his ministry, as he was of marriageable age. His career spanned nearly a quarter of a century of Israel's most difficult history.

HISTORICAL CIRCUMSTANCES

Hosea's work began during the peaceful years of Jeroboam II (786–746 BCE) and concluded sometime around the time of the horrendous defeat of Israel by the Assyrians in 722 BCE.

Even Israel's peaceful years were disrupted both by internal and external developments. Internally Jeroboam's own son Zechariah (746–745 BCE) succeeded to the throne. Within six months Shallum ben Jabesh gained the throne by assassinating Zechariah. The internal politics of Israel quickly became marred by conspiracy and murder. Shallum was himself assassinated within a month by Menahem (745–737 BCE; see 2 Kings 15:8-17). Given the fact of Assyrian expansion and the grave threat that expansion posed for Israel, Menahem expediently decided to become a vassal state to the Assyrian ruler Tiglath-pileser III. Israel had to pay an enormous tax as tribute to the Assyrians (see 2 Kings 15:19). The palace intrigue continued with the rapid accession of Pekahiah (737–736 BCE). Pekah ben Remaliah (736–732) then seized the throne. He very soon attempted to form an alliance against the detested Assyrians. Israel attempted to force her southern sister nation, Judah, into the alliance by means of a war. The Syro-Ephraimitic war forms a part of the backdrop against which Hosea must be read.

The Assyrian ruler Tiglath-pileser attacked the rebellious nations. Israel's king, Hoshea ben Elah (732–724 BCE) surrendered. Later on he attempted to secure aid from Egypt (see Hosea 9:3; 11:5). Under the onslaught of Assyria, Damascus/Syria collapsed in 732; Israel in 722; and Egypt in 664.

In Assyria, Shalmaneser (727–722 BCE) succeeded Tiglath-pileser. Hoshea, the king of Israel, foolishly withheld the payment required from vassal states. Angered by the challenge, the Assyrians made Hoshea Shalmaneser's captive (Hosea 13:10). The capital city was besieged; Israel's armies were soundly defeated. Hosea depicts the collapse of all Samaria/Israel (Hosea 13:16).

THE MESSAGE OF HOSEA

Hosea used various metaphors to describe the relationship that existed between God and Israel as the people of God. The most frequently used metaphor is that of the unfaithful wife as a prostitute; Hosea is saying that the people of God are not being true to their covenant with God. Throughout Hosea's work he shows familiarity with major centers of Israel's land: Samaria (7:1; 8:5; 10:5, 7), Bethel (called also insultingly Beth-Aven; 4:15; 5:8; 10:5; 12:4), and Gilgal (4:15; 9:15; 12:11).

The book can be easily divided into two major sections. The first part centers on the prophet's experience with marriage and family (chapters 1–4). The second part consists of loosely joined material that defies simple attempts to organize or outline it (chapters 5–14).

HOSEA

1 The LORD's word that came to Hosea, Beeri's son, in the days of Judah's Kings Uzziah, Jotham, Ahaz, and Hezekiah, and in the days of Israel's King Jeroboam, Joash's son.

God commands Hosea to marry

² When the LORD first spoke through Hosea, the LORD said to him, "Go, marry a prostitute and have children of prostitution, for the people of the land commit great prostitution by deserting the LORD." ³ So Hosea went and took Gomer, Diblaim's daughter, and she became pregnant and bore him a son. ⁴ The LORD said to him, "Name him Jezreel; for in a little while I will punish the house of Jehu for the blood of Jezreel, and I will destroy the kingdom of the house of Israel. ⁵ On that day I will break the bow of Israel in the Jezreel Valley." ⁶ Gomer became pregnant again and gave birth to a daughter. Then the LORD said to Hosea, "Name her No Compassion, because I will no longer have compassion on the house of Israel or forgive them. ⁷ But I will have compassion on the house of Judah. I, the LORD their God, will save them; I will not save them by bow, or by sword, or by war, or by horses, or by horsemen." ⁸ When Gomer finished nursing No Compassion, she became pregnant and gave birth to a son. ⁹ Then the LORD said, "Name him Not My People because you are not my people, and I am not your God."^a

Hope for the future

^{10b} Yet the number of the people of Israel will be like the sand of the sea, which can be neither measured nor numbered; and in the place where it was said to them, "You are not my people," it will be said to them, "Children of the living God." ¹¹ The people of Judah and the people of Israel will be gathered together, and they will choose one head. They will become fruitful in the land.^c The day will be a wonderful one for Jezreel.

Proclamation of wrongdoing

2 ^d Say to your brother, My People, and to your sister, Compassion:

² Level a charge against your mother;
   plead with her!
   She is not my wife,
      and I am not her husband.
   Let her remove prostitution
      from her presence,
      and adultery from between
      her breasts,
³ or else I will strip her naked
      and expose her
      as on the day she was born.
   I will make her like a desert,
      and turn her into a dry land,
      and make her die of thirst.

^a Or *I am not yours.*   ^b 1:10-11=Heb 2:12   ^c Or *They will go up from the land.*   ^d 2:1-23=Heb 2:3-25

GOMER

1. Gomer the daughter of Diblaim was the wife of the prophet Hosea. Gomer is taken by the prophet as a living sign and becomes the mother of three symbolic children: Jezreel, "No Compassion," and "Not My People" (Hos 1:3-9).

2. Oldest son of Japheth, grandson of Noah, and the father of Ashkenaz, Riphath, and Togarmah according to the Table of Nations (Gen 10:2-3; cf. 1 Chron 1:5-6). Ezekiel names "Gomer and all his troops" among the nations to be defeated as part of God's judgment on King Gog of Magog (Ezek 38:2-6).

4 I will also have no compassion
    on her children
      because they are
        children of prostitution.
5 Their mother has played the prostitute;
    she who conceived them
      has behaved shamefully.
  She said, "I will seek out my lovers;
    they give me my bread and my water,
      my wool and my linen cloth,
        my oil and my drink."

Divine correction

6 Therefore, I will line her path
    with thorns;
  and I will build a wall against her,
    so that she can't find her paths.
7 She will go after her lovers,
    but she won't catch up with them;
  she will seek them,
    but she won't find them.
  Then she will say,
    "I will return to my first husband,
      for I had it better then than now."
8 She didn't know that I gave her
    the corn, the new wine,
      and the fresh oil,
  and that I gave her much silver,
    and gold that they used for Baal.
9 So now I will take back
    my corn in its time,
      and my wine in its season;
  and I will take away my wool
    and my linen cloth,
  which were to cover her nakedness.
10 Now I will uncover her nakedness
    in plain view of her lovers,
      and no one will rescue her from me.

11 I will end all her religious celebrations,
    her festivals, her new moons,
      her Sabbath days,
  and all her sacred seasons.
12 I will destroy her vines and her fig trees,
    of which she said,
      "These are my pay,
        which my lovers have given to me."
  I will change them into a forest,
    and the wild animals will eat them.
13 I will punish her for the days
    dedicated to the Baals,
  when she offered sweet-smelling
    sacrifices to them
  and dressed herself up
    with rings and jewelry,
  and went after her lovers,
    and forgot me, says the LORD.

Promises:
restoration and covenant love

14 Therefore, I will charm her,
    and bring her into the desert,
      and speak tenderly to her heart.
15 From there I will give her vineyards,
    and make the Achor Valley
      a door of hope.
  There she will respond to me
    as in the days of her youth,
      like the time when she came out of
        the land of Egypt.

16 On that day, says the LORD, you will call me, "My husband," and no longer will you call me, "My Lord." 17 I will take away the names of the Baals from her mouth, and they will not be mentioned by name anymore. 18 On that day, I will make a covenant

CERTIFICATE OF DIVORCE

According to the deuteronomic law code (Deut 24:1, 3), a husband "writes up divorce papers, hands them to her, and sends her out of his house." The content of the writ is not specified, although it possibly included the formula "She is not my wife, and I am not her husband" (Hos 2:2 [Heb. 2:4]). In both testaments, the husband alone gives a certificate of divorce. It is not known if this was always the practice or required in all cases.

for them with the wild animals, the birds in
the sky, and the creeping creatures of the
fertile ground. I will do away with the bow,
the sword, and war from the land; I will
make you lie down in safety.

¹⁹ I will take you for my wife forever;
   I will take you for my wife in
      righteousness and in justice,
      in devoted love, and in mercy.
²⁰ I will take you for my wife in faithfulness;
   and you will know the LORD.

²¹ On that day I will answer, says the LORD.
   I will answer the heavens
      and they will answer the earth.
²² The earth will answer the corn,
   the new wine, and the fresh oil,
      and they will answer Jezreel;
²³ I will sow him for myself in the land;
   and I will have compassion on
      No Compassion,
   and I will say to Not My People,
      "You are my people";
   and he will say, "You are my God."

The lesson of infidelity

3 Then the LORD said to me again, "Go,
make love to a woman who has a lover
and is involved in adultery, just as the LORD
loves the people of Israel, though they turn
to other gods and love raisin cakes." ² So I
bought her for fifteen pieces of silver, a large
amount of barley, and a portion of wine.^e
³ I said to her, "You must stay with me for
many days; you won't act like a prostitute;
you won't have sex with a man, nor I with
you." ⁴ Similarly, the Israelites will remain
many days without king or prince, without
sacrifice or sacred standing stone, without
a priestly vest or household divine images.
⁵ Afterward the Israelites will return and
seek the LORD their God and David their
king; they will come trembling to the LORD
and to the LORD's goodness in the latter days.

Israel's sins and coming punishment

4 Hear the LORD's word,
   people of Israel;

for the LORD has a dispute
   with the inhabitants of the land.
There's no faithful love or loyalty,
   and no knowledge of God in the land.
² Swearing, lying, murder,
   together with stealing and adultery
   are common;
   bloody crime followed by bloody crime.
³ Therefore, the earth itself becomes sick,
   and all who live on it grow weak;
   together with the wild animals
   and the birds in the sky,
   even the fish of the sea are dying.
⁴ Yet let no one protest,
   and let no one complain.

   Listen, priest,
   I am angry with your people.^f
⁵ You will stumble by day;
   and at nighttime so will your prophet,
   and I will destroy your mother.
⁶ My people are destroyed
   from lack of knowledge.
   Since you have rejected knowledge,
   so I will reject you
      from serving me as a priest.
   Since you have forgotten the
      Instruction of your God,
   so also I will forget your children.
⁷ The more they increased,
   the more they sinned against me;
   they exchanged their glory for shame.
⁸ They feed on the sin of my people;
   they set their hearts on evil things.
⁹ The priest will be just like the people;
   I will punish them for their ways,
   and judge them for their deeds.
¹⁰ They will eat but not be satisfied;
   they will have sex like prostitutes,
   but they will not have children,
   because they have rejected the LORD
   to devote themselves
      to ¹¹false religious practices.

Description of Israel's idolatry
   Wine and new wine
   destroy understanding.
¹² My people take advice
   from a piece of wood,

and their divining rod
  gives them predictions.
  A spirit of prostitution
  has led them astray;
  they have left God to follow
  other gods.
13 They offer sacrifices on mountaintops,
  and make entirely burned offerings
  on hills;
  they offer sacrifices
  under various green trees,
  because their shade is pleasant.
  Therefore, your daughters
  act like prostitutes,
  and your daughters-in-law
  commit adultery.
14 I will not punish your daughters
  because they act like prostitutes,
  nor your daughters-in-law
  because they commit adultery;
  for the men themselves visit prostitutes,
  and offer sacrifices
  with consecrated workers at temples;
  so now the people without sense
  must come to ruin.
15 Israel, even though you act
  like a prostitute,
  don't let Judah become guilty.
  Don't enter into Gilgal,
  or go up to Beth-aven,
  and don't swear, "As the LORD lives."
16 Like a stubborn cow Israel is stubborn.
  Now the LORD will tend them,g
  as the LORD tends a lamb in a pasture.
17 Ephraim is associated with idols—
  let him alone!
18 Though they have stopped drinking,
  they continue to behave
  like prostitutes;
  indeed, they "love";
  shame is their pride.
19 The wind has wrapped her in its wings;
  they will be ashamed of their sacrifices.

Judgment on Israel and Judah

5 Hear this, priests!
  Pay attention, house of Israel!
  Listen, house of the king!
  The judgment concerns you because
  you have been a trap at Mizpah,

and a net spread out upon Tabor.
2 In their wicked condition,
  they have sunk deep into corruption;
  I will correct them through judgment.
3 I know Ephraim;
  Israel doesn't escape my eye;
  for now Ephraim
  you have acted like a prostitute;
  Israel is defiled.
4 Their deeds don't allow them
  to return to their God,
  because the spirit of prostitution
  is within them,
  and they don't know the LORD.
5 Israel's pride is a witness against him;
  both Israel and Ephraim stagger
  because of their guilt;
  Judah staggers with them.
6 With their sheep and their cattle
  they will go
  to seek the LORD,
  but they will not find him;
  he has withdrawn from them.
7 They have acted faithlessly
  against the LORD;
  for their children have produced
  illegitimate children.
  Now the new moon will devour themh
  along with their fields.
8 Blow a horn in Gibeah;
  blow a trumpet in Ramah.
  Sound the warning at Beth-aven:
  "Look behind you, Benjamin!"
9 Ephraim will become a horrible place
  on the Judgment Day.
  Against the tribes of Israel
  I will certainly announce
  what is to take place.
10 The princes of Judah act like raiders
  who steal the land;
  I will pour out my anger
  like water upon them.
11 Ephraim is under pressure
  from its enemies;
  Ephraim's rights aren't protected.
  This is because Ephraim chose to
  pursue worthless things.
12 Therefore, I am like a moth to Ephraim,
  and like decay to the house of Judah.

gOr her hHeb uncertain

13 When Ephraim saw his sickness,
and Judah his wound,
then Ephraim went to Assyria,
and Ephraim sent for the great king.
But he could not heal them;
nor could he cure their wound.
14 I am like a lion to Ephraim,
like a young lion
to the house of Judah.
I am the one who tears the prey
and goes forth;
no one can snatch it from me.
15 I will leave so that I can return
to my place
until they pay for their deeds,
until they seek me.
In their distress,
they will beg for my favor:

6 "Come, let's return to the LORD;
for it is he who has injured us
and will heal us;
he has struck us down,
but he will bind us up.
2 After two days he will revive us;
on the third day he will raise us up,
so that we may live before him.
3 Let's know, let's press on
to know the LORD;
whose appearing
is as certain as the dawn;
who will come to us like the showers,
like the spring rains
that give drink to the earth."

Infidelity and divine retribution

4 Ephraim, what will I do with you?
Judah, what will I do with you?
Your love is like a morning cloud,
like the dew that vanishes quickly.
5 Therefore, I have attacked them
by the prophets,
I have killed them
by the words of my mouth,
and my judgment goes forth
like a light.
6 I desire faithful love
and not sacrifice,
the knowledge of God
instead of entirely burned offerings.

7 But like Adam[i]
they broke the covenant;
then they acted in bad faith
against me.
8 Gilead is a city of wicked people,
tracked with blood.
9 As robbers lie in wait for someone,
so the priests are in league
with each other;
they murder on the road to Shechem;
they have done evil things.
10 In the house of Israel I have seen
something horrible;
Ephraim acts like a prostitute;
Israel is defiled.
11 For you also, Judah,
a harvest is appointed,
when I would improve the
circumstances of my people.

7 When I would heal Israel,
the evil acts of Ephraim are exposed,
and the wicked deeds of Samaria;
for they deceive and steal,
a thief breaks in;
a group of bandits raid outside.
2 But they don't consider
within their hearts
that I remember all their wickedness.
Now their deeds show who they are,
right in front of my face.
3 By their wickedness
they make the king glad,
and give joy to the officials
with their lies.
4 They all act like adulterers;
they are like a heated oven,
whose baker doesn't need
to stoke the fire,
from the kneading of the dough
until it is leavened.
5 On the day of our king,
the officials became sick with the
heat of wine;
he stretched out his hand to those
who mocked him.
6 They approach like a hot oven,
their hearts burning.
Throughout the night,
their anger smolders;

---

[i]Or at Adam

in the morning, it continues
    to burn like a flaming fire.
[7] All of them are hot as an oven;
    they devour their rulers.
All their kings have fallen;
    none of them call upon me.
[8] Ephraim mixes himself
    among the people;
    Ephraim is like flatbread that is
    cooked on only one side.
[9] Strangers have eaten up his strength,
    yet he doesn't know it;
gray hairs are sprinkled
    here and there upon him,
    yet he doesn't know it.
[10] Israel's pride is a witness against him;
    yet they don't return
    to the LORD their God,
    or seek him because of all this.

Foolishness and God's wrath

[11] Ephraim has become like a dove,
    silly and without common sense;
    they call upon Egypt; they go to Assyria.
[12] As they go, I will spread my net over them;
    like birds in the sky,
    I will bring them down;

I will judge them according to the
    report made to their assembly.
[13] Doom to them,
    for they have strayed from me;
    destruction will be their lot
    because they have rebelled
    against me.
I would redeem them,
    but they speak lies against me.
[14] They don't cry to me from the heart,
    but they sob upon their beds;
they fight[j] over grain and wine;
    they resist me.
[15] It was I who gave them their strength,
    yet they plot evil against me.
[16] They return,
    but not to the Most High;[k]
    they have become like a worthless bow;
    their officials will fall by the sword
    because of the rage of their tongues;
    in Egypt they will make fun of them.[l]

Divine proclamation about Israel's idolatry

8 Put a trumpet to your lips!
    It's as if a bird of prey has flown over
    the LORD's house,

[j]Or cut themselves [k]Heb uncertain [l]Or they will be scorned in the land of Egypt.

OVEN

The dome-shaped oven used by the Israelites for baking bread (Exod 8:3; cf. Lev 11:35) was made of clay and straw, with broken pottery used as further insulating material, and was sometimes sunk into the earth. Sticks and straw were used to kindle a fire inside the oven at the bottom of the dome (Matt 6:30), and when the fire had been reduced to hot coals the loaves were affixed to the interior walls of the oven for baking. Each household had its own oven, as the description of famine in Leviticus 26:26 illustrates: when grain is scarce, a single oven will suffice to bake bread for 10 households. Bread baked in ovens could be leavened (Hos 7:4-7) or unleavened (Lev 2:4; 7:9).

The heat of an oven was proverbial, and could serve as an image of coming catastrophe (Mal 4:1 [Heb. 3:19]). Hosea uses a heated oven as a metaphor for hotheaded wicked people (7:4-7). In Lamentations 5:10, the effect of famine on the exiles is compared to the effect of the heat that blackened the interior of an oven's dome: "Our skin is as hot as an oven because of the burning heat of famine."

because they have broken my covenant,
  and have not kept my Instruction.
2 Israel cries to me,
  "My God, we know you!"
3 Israel has turned away from the good;
  the enemy will pursue him.
4 They set up kings, but not through me;
  they chose princes,
    but without my knowledge.
  With silver and gold they crafted idols
    for their own destruction.
5 Your calf is rejected, Samaria.
  My anger burns against them.
  How long will they remain guilty?
6 The calf is from Israel,
  a person made it;
  it is not God.
  The calf of Samaria will be smashed.
7 Because they sow the wind,
  they will get the whirlwind.
  Standing grain, but no fresh growth;
  it will yield no meal;
  if it were to yield,
    strangers would devour it.

Bargains, apostasy, and coming punishment

8 Israel is swallowed up;
  among the nations, they are now
    like a useless jar.
9 They have gone up to Assyria,
  a wild ass wandering alone;
  Ephraim has hired lovers.
10 Though they have bargained
  with the nations,
  I will now gather them up.
  They will soon be diminished
    due to the burden of kings and princes.
11 When Ephraim added more altars
  to take away sin,
    they became altars to him for sinning.
12 Even though I write out for him
  a large number of my instructions,
    they are regarded as strange.
13 Though they offer choice sacrifices,[m]
  though they eat flesh,
  the LORD doesn't accept them.
  Now he will remember
    their wickedness

and punish their sins;
  they will return to Egypt.
14 Israel has forgotten his maker,
  and built palaces;
  and Judah has multiplied walled cities;
  but I will send a fire upon his cities,
  and it will devour his fortresses.

Arrival of divine judgment

9 Don't rejoice, Israel!
  Don't celebrate as other nations do;
  for as whores you have gone away
    from your God.
  You have loved a prostitute's pay
    on all threshing floors of grain.
2 Threshing floor and wine vat
  won't feed them;
  the new wine will fail them.
3 They won't remain
  in the land of the LORD;
  but Ephraim will return to Egypt,
  and in Assyria
    they will eat unclean food.
4 They won't pour wine
  as an offering to the LORD;
  their sacrifices won't please him.
  Such sacrifices will be like food
  for those who touch the dead;
  all who eat of it will be unclean;
  their bread will be
    for their hunger alone;
  it will not come
    to the LORD's house.
5 What will you do
  on the day of appointed festival,
  on the day of the LORD's festival?
6 Even if they escape destruction,
  Egypt will gather them,
  Memphis will bury them.
  Briars will possess
    their precious things of silver;[n]
  thorns will be in their tents.
7 The days of punishment have come;
  the days of judgment have arrived;
  Israel cries,
  "The prophet is a fool,
    the spiritual man is mad!"
  Because of your great wickedness,
  your rejection of me is great.

---

[m]Correction; Heb uncertain   [n]Or *the proud glory pertaining to their silver*; Heb uncertain

Tragic consequences

⁸ The prophet is God's watchman
  looking over Ephraim,
  yet a hunter's trap is set,
  covering all his ways,
  and rejection is in his God's house.
⁹ They have corrupted themselves terribly
  as in the days of Gibeah;
  he will remember their wickedness;
  he will punish their sins.

¹⁰ Like grapes in the wilderness,
  I found Israel.
  In its first season,
  like the first fruit on the fig tree,
  I saw your ancestors.
  But they came to Baal-peor,
  and worshipped a thing of shame;
  they became detestable
  like the thing they loved.°
¹¹ Ephraim's glory will fly away like a bird—
  no birth, no pregnancy, no conception!
¹² Though they bring up children,
  I will make them childless
  until no one is left.
  Doom to them indeed when I leave them!
¹³ When I looked toward Tyre, Ephraim
  was planted in a lovely meadow;
  but now Ephraim must lead out his
  children for slaughter.
¹⁴ Give them, LORD—
  what will you give them?
  Give them a womb that miscarries
  and breasts that are dried up.
¹⁵ Every wickedness of theirs
  began at Gilgal;
  there I came to hate them.
  Because of the wickedness
  of their deeds
  I will drive them out of my house.

° Heb uncertain

I will love them no more;
  all their officials are rebels.
¹⁶ Ephraim is sick,
  their root is dried up,
  they will bear no fruit.
  Even though they give birth,
  I will put to death
  their much-loved little ones.
¹⁷ Because they haven't listened to him,
  my God will reject them;
  they will wander among the nations.

The folly of Israel's idolatry

10 Israel is a growing vine
   that yields its fruit.
  The more his fruit increased,
  the more altars he built;
  the richer his land became,
  the more he set up
  sacred standing stones.
² Their heart is false;
  now they must bear their guilt.
  The LORD will break down their altars
  and destroy their standing stones.
³ For now they will say:
  "We have no king,
  because we don't love the LORD.
  What then could a king do for us?"
⁴ They have spoken empty words,
  swearing falsely
  when making covenants;
  so judgment springs up
  like poisonous weeds
  in the furrows of the field.
⁵ The inhabitants of Samaria shake
  because of the calf of Beth-aven.
  Its people will mourn over it,
  just as its idolatrous priests
  who rejoiced over its glory
  that is now gone.

MESOPOTAMIA

The vast land between the Tigris and the Euphrates Rivers, the region from which international powers ruled the ancient world, including Assyria and Babylonia in the 1st millennium BCE.

Shame and punishment

⁶ To Assyria it will be carried
     as a gift for the great king.
Ephraim will be put to shame;
     Israel will be ashamed of his own idol.
⁷ Samaria will be cut off;
     her king is like a chip of wood
        on the surface of the water.
⁸ The sin of Israel, the shrines of Aven
     will be torn down.
Thorn and thistle will sprout up
     on their altars.
They will say to the mountains,
     "Cover us,"
to the hills, "Fall on us."
⁹ Since the days of Gibeah,
     you have sinned, Israel;
        there they have continued.
Will not war overtake them in Gibeah?
¹⁰ I will come and punish them;
     nations will be gathered against them
        when they are punished
        for their double crime.
¹¹ Ephraim was a trained cow
     that loved to pull a plow;
I spared her fair neck;
     but I will make Ephraim
        break through the ground;
Judah will plow;
     Jacob will turn the soil for himself.
¹² Sow for yourselves righteousness;
     reap faithful love;
break up your unplanted ground,
     for it is time to seek the LORD,
     that he may come
     and rain righteousness upon you.
¹³ You have plowed wickedness,
     you have reaped depravity,
     you have eaten the fruit of lies,
because you have trusted in your way
     and in your many warriors.
¹⁴ Therefore, the noise of war
     will rise against your people;
all your fortresses will be destroyed,
     as Shalman destroyed Beth-arbel
     on the day of battle,
     when mothers were dashed
        into pieces with their children.
¹⁵ It will indeed happen to you, Bethel,
     because of your great wickedness.

At dawn, the king of Israel
     will be cut off completely.

Divine love

11 When Israel was a child, I loved him,
     and out of Egypt I called my son.
² The more I called them,
     the further they went from me;
     they kept sacrificing to the Baals,
     and they burned incense to idols.
³ Yet it was I who taught Ephraim to walk;
     I took them up in my arms,
     but they did not know
        that I healed them.
⁴ I led them
     with bands of human kindness,
     with cords of love.
I treated them like those
     who lift infants to their cheeks;
     I bent down to them and fed them.

Divine frustration

⁵ They will return to the land of Egypt,
     and Assyria will be their king,
     because they have refused
        to return to me.
⁶ The sword will strike wildly
     in their cities;
     it will consume the bars of their gates
     and will take everything
        because of their schemes.
⁷ My people are bent on turning
     away from me;
     and though they cry out
        to the Most High,ᴾ
     he will not raise them up.

Divine compassion

⁸ How can I give you up, Ephraim?
     How can I hand you over, Israel?
How can I make you like Admah?
     How can I treat you like Zeboiim?
My heart winces within me;
     my compassion
        grows warm and tender.

Israel's and Judah's responses

⁹ I won't act on the heat of my anger;
     I won't return to destroy Ephraim;

ᴾHeb uncertain

for I am God and not a human being,
the holy one in your midst;
I won't come in harsh judgment.
¹⁰ They will walk after the LORD,
who roars like a lion.
When he roars,
his children will come trembling
from the west.
¹¹ They will come trembling like a bird,
and like a dove
from the land of Assyria;
and I will return them to their homes,
says the LORD.
¹² �q Ephraim has surrounded me with lies,
the house of Israel with faithless acts;
but Judah still walks with God,
and is faithful to the holy one.

God's charge against Judah

12 ʳEphraim herds the wind,
and pursues the east wind
all day long;
they multiply lies and violence;
they make a treaty with Assyria,
and oil is carried to Egypt.
² The LORD has a charge against Judah,
and will punish Jacob
according to his ways,
and respond to him
according to his deeds.
³ From the womb he tried to be
the oldest of twin brothers;
as an adult he struggled with God.
⁴ He struggled with the messenger
and survived;
he wept and sought his favor;
he met him at Bethel,
and there he spoke with him.
⁵ The LORD God of heavenly forces,
the LORD is his name!
⁶ But you! Return to your God
with faithful love and justice,
and wait continually for your God.

⁷ He is a merchant;
the means to cheat are in his hands;
he loves to take advantage of others.
⁸ Ephraim has said,
"I'm rich,

I've gained wealth for myself;
in all of my gain
no offense has been found in me
that would be sin."
⁹ I am the LORD your God
from the land of Egypt;
I will make you live in tents again,
as in former days.
¹⁰ I spoke to the prophets;
and I multiplied visions,
and through them I uttered parables.
¹¹ In Gilead there is wickedness;
they will surely come to nothing.
In Gilgal they sacrifice bulls,
so their altars will be
like piles of stones
on the rows of the field.
¹² Jacob fled to the land of Aram;
there Israel served for a wife,
and for a wife he kept watch
over livestock.
¹³ By a prophet the LORD
brought Israel up from Egypt,
and by a prophet he was guarded.
¹⁴ Ephraim has given bitter offense;
so the LORD will bring his crimes
down on him
and pay him back for his wrongdoing.

Infidelity despite divine goodness

13 When Ephraim spoke,
there was excitement;
he was praised in Israel;
but he became guilty through Baal
and died.
² And now they keep on sinning;
they have made metal images,
idols of silver,
as a result of their skill,
all of them the work of craftsmen.
"Sacrifice to these," they say.
People are kissing calves!
³ Therefore, they will be
like the morning mist,
like the dew that passes away early,
like husks that swirl
from the threshing floor,
or like smoke from a window.
⁴ Yet I have been the LORD your God
ever since the land of Egypt;

and you will know no other gods but me;
　　there is no savior besides me.
[5] I knew you in the wilderness,
　　in the land of no rain.
[6] When I fed them, they were satisfied;
　　and their hearts became proud;
　　therefore, they forgot me.

Consequences of infidelity

[7] So I will become like a lion to them;
　　like a leopard I will lurk beside the road.
[8] I will fall upon them
　　like a bear robbed of her cubs,
　　　and I will tear open
　　　　the covering of their hearts.
　I will devour them like a lion,
　　as a wild animal would eat them.
[9] I will destroy you, Israel;
　　for you didn't realize
　　　that I could help you.
[10] Where is your king now,
　　so that he can save you?
　Where in all your cities are your judges,
　　of whom you said,
　　"Give me a king and rulers"?
[11] I gave you a king in my anger,
　　and I took him away in my wrath.
[12] Ephraim's wickedness is bound up;
　　his sin is kept in store.
[13] The pangs of a woman in childbirth
　　come for him,
　　　but he is not aware
　　　　of the time to be born;

for at the proper time
　he doesn't present himself
　　at the mouth of the womb.
[14] Will I ransom them
　　from the power of the grave[s]
　Will I redeem them
　　from death's hold?
Death, where are your diseases?
　Grave,[t] where is your destruction?
　Compassion is hidden from my eyes.
[15] Although he may flourish among rushes,
　　the east wind will come—
　the breath of God
　　rising from the wilderness;
　and his spring will dry up;
　　his fountain will be dried up.
　It will strip his household
　　of every cherished possession.
[16] [u]Samaria will be desolate,
　　because she has rebelled
　　　against her God;
　by the sword they will fall—
　　their babies will be dashed,
　　and their pregnant women
　　　ripped open.

A plea: Return to God

14 [v]Return, Israel, to the LORD your God;
　you have stumbled
　　because of your wickedness.
[2] Prepare to speak
　　and return to the LORD;
　　say to the LORD,

[s]Heb *Sheol* [t]Heb *Sheol* [u]14:1 in Heb [v]14:2 in Heb

IDOL

From the Greek word for "image." Idols were an indigenous part of ancient Near Eastern religions. Israel was surrounded by nations where a variety of deities were represented by anthropomorphic (human-like) and theriomorphic (animal-like) images. Idols were also common in later Greco-Roman religion. That people actually believed these images themselves were gods is unlikely. For the most part, biblical scholars have assumed that this common practice of representing god(s) with images was taboo in ancient Israel and Judah from their earliest beginnings. However, since the 1980s there has been a wealth of publications on Israelite religion that have seriously challenged this long-held assumption.

"Forgive all wickedness;
  and receive the good.
Instead of bulls,
  let us offer what we can say:
³ Assyria won't save us;
  we won't ride upon horses;
  we will no longer say, 'Our God,'
  to the work of our hands.
  In you the orphan finds compassion."

Divine promise of healing

⁴ I will heal their faithlessness;
  I will love them freely,
  for my anger has turned from them.
⁵ I will be like the dew to Israel;
  he will blossom like the lily;
  he will cast out his roots
  like the forests of Lebanon.ʷ
⁶ His branches will spread out;
  his beauty will be like the olive tree,
  and his fragrance
  like that of Lebanon.

⁷ They will again live
  beneath my shadow,
  they will flourish like a garden;
  they will blossom like the vine,
  their fragrance will be
  like the wine of Lebanon.
⁸ Ephraim, what do idols
  have to do with me?
  It is I who answer
  and look after you.
  I am like a green cypress tree;
  your fruit comes from me.

Be careful

⁹ Whoever is wise
  understands these things.
  Whoever observes
  carefully knows them.
  Truly, the LORD's ways are right,
  and the righteous
  will walk in them,
  but evildoers will stumble in them.

ʷOr like Lebanon

JOEL

The immediate cause for the book of Joel is a devastating plague of locusts that threatens to destroy the land and the economy. Like other prophets, Joel takes his cue from real events in the life of the nation. He goes further than the event by interpreting the importance or the meaning of the event to his contemporaries. For Joel the overwhelming swarms of locusts suggest not only an act of God but also the future activity of God in the life of the nation.

JOEL, THE MAN

We know very little about Joel himself. His name, meaning "Yahweh is God," is not an unusual name, as it occurs elsewhere in the Old Testament (for example, 1 Samuel 8:2; Ezra 10:43). He is the son of Pethuel. His home may have been in the territory traditionally associated with Reuben (see 1 Chronicles 5:4).

Joel is familiar with worship procedures and priests, and himself may well have been a temple prophet. In this sense he shares similar views with Haggai and Zechariah. He shows a familiarity with Jerusalem and the surrounding country.

DATE OF THE WRITING

The date of writing is one of the critical questions in interpreting Joel. Since some of his words are parallels with other prophets (some 20 verses), either those prophets quoted from him, or he quoted from them. Since there is no mention of national sins that would warrant punishment from God and no mention of large menacing empires (neither Assyria nor Babylon is mentioned), scholars conclude that Joel's work comes at a relatively late time. At least one allusion is to scattered people (3:2), thus implying the Babylonian Exile is an historical era already past. Therefore, this work fits best sometime in the fifth century BCE.

THE MESSAGE OF JOEL

A careful reading of Joel shows that the prophet takes the rich traditions of his predecessors and reinterprets them for the present moment. Joel stands at a time when the old traditions of the prophets were giving way to newer apocalyptic thinking. In large measure, he reinterprets the traditional prophetic message with a new freshness for his listeners. Joel seeks the meaning of a current crisis while straining to see the horizon of God's future. Just as Joel would not arbitrarily do away with tradition, he would not eliminate formal worship services.

One of the central elements in Joel's work is the Day of the Lord, mentioned no fewer than five times (see 1:15; 2:1, 11, 31; 3:14). No one can escape from its inevitable disaster. But there is still room for hope, since the opportunity for repentance is always present. God's intention is not merely judgment and punishment, because God always yearns for repentance and acknowledgment by the chosen people.

JOEL

Song of lament

1 The LORD's word that came to Joel, Pethuel's son:

² Hear this, elders;
   pay attention, everyone in the land!
Has anything like this ever happened
   in your days,
   or in the days of your ancestors?ᵃ
³ Tell it to your children,
   and have your children
      tell their children,
   and their children tell their children.
⁴ What the cutting locust left,
   the swarming locust has eaten.
What the swarming locust left,
   the hopping locust has eaten.
And what the hopping locust left,
   the devouring locust has eaten.ᵇ
⁵ Wake up, you who drink too much,
   and weep.
Scream over the sweet wine,
   all you wine drinkers,
   because it is snatched
      from your mouth;
⁶ because a nation,
   powerful and beyond number,
   has invaded my land.

Its teeth are like lions' teeth;
   its fangs are like those of a lioness.
⁷ It has destroyed my vines,
   splintered my fig trees,
   stripped off their bark
      and thrown it down;
   their branches have turned white.
⁸ Lament like a woman
   dressed in funeral clothing,
   one who has lost
      the husband of her youth.
⁹ The grain offering and the drink offering
   are gone from the LORD's temple.
The priests
   and the LORD's ministers mourn.
¹⁰ The fields are devastated,
   the ground mourns;
   for the grain is destroyed,

the new wine dries up,
   the olive oil fails.
¹¹ Be shocked, you farmers;
   howl, you vinedressers,
   over the wheat and the barley,
   for the crops of the field are destroyed.
¹² The grapevine is dried up;
   the fig tree withers.
Pomegranate, palm, and apple—
   all the trees of the field are dried up.
Joy fades away from the people.ᶜ

Call to mourn

¹³ Dress for a funeral and grieve,
   you priests;
   lament, ministers of the altar.
Come, spend the night in funeral
   clothing, servants of my God,
because the grain offering
   and the drink offering
   have gone from the temple
      of your God.
¹⁴ Demand a fast,
   request a special assembly.
Gather the elders
   and all the land's people
   to the temple of the LORD your God,
   and cry out to the LORD.

Time of suffering

¹⁵ What a terrible day!
   The day of the LORD is near;
   it comes like chaos
      from the Almighty.ᵈ
¹⁶ Isn't the food cut off
   right before our eyes?
Aren't joy and gladness
   also gone from our God's house?
¹⁷ The grain shrivels under the shovels;ᵉ
   the barns are empty.
The granaries are in ruin
   because the grain has dried up.
¹⁸ How the animals groan!
   Herds of cattle are in distress
   because there is no pasture for them;
   even the flocks of sheep pant.

ᵃOr *your fathers* ᵇThe Heb uses several different words for *locust*; none of the meanings are identical. ᶜOr *from the sons of men*; cf 2:1 Heb *the people of the land* ᵈHeb *Shaddai* ᵉHeb uncertain

The prophet's prayer

¹⁹ To you, LORD, I cry,
 for fire has completely destroyed
  the pastures of the wilderness;
 and flames have burned
  all the trees of the field.
²⁰ Even the field's wild animals cry to you
 because the streams have dried up;
 the fire has completely destroyed
  the meadows of the wilderness.

Announcement of alarm and peril

2 Blow the horn in Zion;
 give a shout on my holy mountain!
Let all the people of the land tremble,
 for the day of the LORD is coming.
It is near—
² a day of darkness and no light,
 a day of clouds and thick darkness!
Like blackness spread out
 upon the mountains,
 a great and powerful army^f comes,
 unlike any that has ever come
  before them,

or will come after them
 in centuries ahead.
³ In front of them a fire consumes;
 and behind them a flame burns.
Land ahead of them
 is like Eden's garden,
but they leave behind them
 a barren wasteland;
 nothing escapes them.
⁴ They resemble horses,
 and like warhorses they charge,
⁵ like the rumbling of chariots.
They leap on the mountaintops—
 like the crackling of a fire's flame,
 devouring the stubble;
like a powerful army
 ready for battle.
⁶ In their presence,
 peoples shake with fear,
 all faces turn red with worry.
⁷ Like warriors they charge;
 like soldiers they climb the wall.
Each keeps to their own path;
 they didn't change their course.

---

^fOr *a great and strong people*

FIG TREE/FIGS

One staple of the ancient diet that provided a sweet accompaniment to other foods was the fig (*Ficus carica*). Cultivated at least since the Early Bronze Age (ca. 3000 BCE), the tree could take root in rocky soil and within seven years bear fruit for as many as 50 years. Place-names associated with fig trees (Bethphage = "house of unripe figs"; possibly Bethany = "house of figs" [Mark 11:1]) testify to their importance to the economy. The fig tree's pride in its flavor is chronicled playfully in its refusal to rule the other trees in Jotham's parable (Judg 9:10-11). In fact, newly ripened figs were so loved that Isaiah describes the zest with which they were eaten (Isa 28:4). Other prophets use the fig as an analogy for Israel (Hos 9:10; Amos 8:1-2; Nah 3:12). The budding or barren fig tree is a symbol of fruitfulness in some of Jesus' parables (Matt 24:32; Mark 13:28; Luke 13:6-9; 21:29-30). The fig tree begins to put on its leaves in spring and is quite lush by summer, when its shade is a relief from the sun (John 1:48-50). It is also paired with the grapevine as a symbol of prosperity and peace for the farmer (Mic 4:4). Fig cakes served as rations for soldiers that could be carried on campaign or stored for later consumption in camp (1 Sam 25:18; 30:12). Figs were also used medicinally as a poultice for boils (2 Kgs 20:7).

8 They don't crowd each other;
  each keeps to their own path.
Even if they fall among the weapons,
  they won't stop.
9 They rush upon the city;
  they run upon the walls.
They climb into the houses;
  they enter through the windows
    like thieves.
10 The earth quakes before them;
  the heavens shake.
The sun and the moon are darkened;
  the stars have stopped shining,
11 because the LORD utters his voice
  at the head of his army.
How numerous are his troops!
  Mighty are those who obey his word.
The day of the LORD is great;
  it stirs up great fear—
    who can endure it?

Change your hearts

12 Yet even now, says the LORD,
  return to me with all your hearts,
  with fasting, with weeping,
    and with sorrow;
13 tear your hearts
  and not your clothing.
Return to the LORD your God,
  for he is merciful and compassionate,
  very patient, full of faithful love,
    and ready to forgive.
14 Who knows whether he will have
  a change of heart
  and leave a blessing behind him,
  a grain offering and a drink offering
    for the LORD your God?
15 Blow the horn in Zion;
  demand a fast;
  request a special assembly.
16 Gather the people;
  prepare a holy meeting;
  assemble the elders;
  gather the children,
    even nursing infants.
Let the groom leave his room
  and the bride her chamber.
17 Between the porch and the altar
  let the priests,
    the LORD's ministers, weep.

Let them say, "Have mercy, LORD,
  on your people,
  and don't make your inheritance
    a disgrace,
  an example of failure
    among the nations.
Why should they say
  among the peoples,
    'Where is their God?'"

Words of compassion and promise

18 Then the LORD became passionate about this land,[g] and had pity on his people.
19 The LORD responded to the people:
See, I am sending you
  the corn, new wine, and fresh oil,
  and you will be fully satisfied by it;
and I will no longer make you
  a disgrace among the nations.
20 I will remove the northern army
  far from you
  and drive it into a dried-up
    and desolate land,
  its front into the eastern sea,
  and its rear into the western sea.
Its stench will rise up;
  its stink will come to the surface.
The LORD is about to do great things!
21 Don't fear, fertile land;
  rejoice and be glad,
  for the LORD is
    about to do great things!
22 Don't be afraid, animals of the field,
  for the meadows of the wilderness
    will turn green;
  the tree will bear its fruit;
  the fig tree and grapevine
    will give their full yield.
23 Children of Zion,
  rejoice and be glad
  in the LORD your God,
because he will give you the early rain
  as a sign of righteousness;
he will pour down abundant rain
  for you,
  the early and the late rain,
    as before.[h]
24 The threshing floors
  will be full of grain;

---

g Or then the LORD became jealous for his land   h Or at the first

the vats will overflow with new wine
and fresh oil.
²⁵ I will repay you for the years
that the cutting locust,
the swarming locust, the hopping
locust, and the devouring locust
have eaten—
my great army,
which I sent against you.
²⁶ You will eat abundantly
and be satisfied,
and you will praise the name
of the LORD your God,
who has done wonders for you;
and my people will never again
be put to shame.
²⁷ You will know
that I am in the midst of Israel,
and that I am the LORD your God—
no other exists;
never again will my people
be put to shame.
²⁸ After that I will pour out my spirit
upon everyone;
your sons and your daughters
will prophesy,
your old men will dream dreams,
and your young men
will see visions.
²⁹ In those days, I will also pour out my
spirit on the male and female slaves.
³⁰ I will give signs in the heavens and on
the earth—blood and fire and columns of
smoke. ³¹ The sun will be turned to dark-

ness, and the moon to blood before the
great and dreadful day of the LORD comes.
³² But everyone who calls on the LORD's
name will be saved; for on Mount Zion and
in Jerusalem there will be security, as the
LORD has promised; and in Jerusalem, the
LORD will summon those who survive.

Judgment on the nations

3 Truly, in those days and in that time, I
will bring back to Judah and Jerusalem
those who were sent away. ² I will gather
all the nations, and I will bring them to
the Jehoshaphat Valley. There I will enter
into judgment with them in support of my
people and my possession, Israel, which
they have scattered among the nations. They
have divided my land, ³ and have cast lots for
my people. They have traded boys for prostitutes, and sold girls for wine, which they
drank down. ⁴ What are you to me, Tyre and
Sidon, and all the regions of Philistia? Are
you paying me back for something? If you
are paying me back, then in a flash I will
turn your deeds back upon your own heads.
⁵ You have taken my silver and my gold,
and have carried my rich treasures into
your temples. ⁶ You have sold the people
of Judah and Jerusalem to the Greeks, removing them far from their own border.
⁷ But now I am calling them from the places
where you have sold them, and I will repay
you for your deeds. ⁸ I will sell your sons
and your daughters as a possession of the

HOLY WAR

The practice of warfare as a religious activity. Unlike *crusade* or *jihad*,
which signify human struggles to achieve what is thought to be divine will,
"holy war" describes the military activity of God in which humans could
sometimes assist in a secondary fashion. Modern readers often experience
discomfort with the idea of divinely directed warfare. However, we should remember that Israel was always threatened by the loss of its land and spent
much of its history under the domination of militarily superior foreign rulers. Menaced by outside forces that were politically and technically superior,
Israel's faith that its God had the power to give victory in battle must have
been essential for national survival.

people of Judah, and they will sell them to the Sabeans, to a nation far away; for the LORD has spoken.

Declaration of war

⁹ Announce this among the nations:
　Prepare a holy war,
　　wake up the warriors;
　let all the soldiers draw near,
　　let them come up!
¹⁰ Beat the iron tips of your plows
　　into swords
　　　and your pruning tools into spears;
　　let the weakling say, "I am mighty."
¹¹ Come quickly,
　　all you surrounding nations;
　gather yourselves there;
　bring your mighty ones, LORD.
¹² Let the nations prepare themselves,
　　and come up
　　　to the Jehoshaphat Valley;
　　for there I will sit to judge
　　all the surrounding nations.
¹³ Cut with the sickle,
　　for the harvest is ripe.
　Go and crush grapes,
　　for the winepress is full.
　The jars overflow with wine,
　　for their wickedness is great.
¹⁴ Crowd after crowd
　　fills the valley of judgment,
　for the day of the LORD is near
　　in the valley of judgment.
¹⁵ The sun and the moon are darkened;
　　the stars have ceased shining.

Salvation for God's people

¹⁶ The LORD roars from Zion,
　　and utters his voice from Jerusalem;
　　the heavens and the earth quake.
　But the LORD is a refuge for his people,
　　a shelter for the people of Israel.
¹⁷ So you will know
　　that I am the LORD your God,
　　settle down in Zion,
　　　my holy mountain.
　Jerusalem will be holy,
　　and never again
　　　will strangers pass through it.
¹⁸ In that day
　　the mountains will drip sweet wine,
　　the hills will flow with milk,
　　and all the streambeds of Judah
　　　will flow with water;
　a spring will come forth
　　from the LORD's house
　　and water the Shittim Valley.
¹⁹ Egypt will become desolate
　　and Edom a desolate wilderness.
　This is because of the violence
　　done to the people of Judah,
　in whose land they have shed
　　innocent blood.
²⁰ But Judah will be inhabited forever,
　　and Jerusalem for all generations.
²¹ I will forgive their bloodguilt,
　　which I had not forgiven.
　I will act on their account;
　　I will not pardon the guilty.

　The LORD dwells in Zion.

AMOS

The prophet Amos is the third of the twelve minor prophets in the canon. Chronologically, however, he is the first of the writing prophets. His work occurs during the long and prosperous reign of Jeroboam II, around 786–746 BCE.

THE MESSAGE OF AMOS

Other prophetic books describe the sights of military collapse, natural catastrophe, economic disaster, and foreign intrigue. Amos, however, ministers during a time remarkably free from external stress. Other prophets have to make sense of disaster, both natural and political. Amos finds himself speaking an urgent word to a complacent people who have long since grown wealthy, spiritually negligent, and morally insensitive. Amos describes the voice of God raging against a nation complacent in the false security of ritual and ignorant of the divine will. Power and wealth, luxury and licentiousness have yielded abuses of justice and oppression of the poor.

The people Amos addresses are prideful (Amos 6:13-14) and comfortable with abundant wealth (Amos 3:15; 5:11; 6:4-6). Sinfulness is not restricted to the male population. Women too are addicted to wine (Amos 4:1). Injustice prevails, and it takes the prophet to name the sin for what it is. The poor are oppressed, sold into slavery (Amos 2:6-8; 5:11), and have no recourse through the legal system because the judges themselves are as corrupt as the surrounding culture (Amos 5:12).

The tragedy is that even though the prophet speaks, entrenched and vested interests will adamantly ignore the divine will for the nation (Amos 7:10-14). Amos speaks a word from God to a people who have lost the sensitivity to the demands of God for their personal and corporate lives.

Amos, like other individuals summoned by God into God's work, is called against his will and quite without his asking for the responsibility. However, Amos is overwhelmed by the reality of God and the urgency of God's will for Israel. He can do nothing else but obey (Amos 3:8). The result of Amos' faithfulness is this great prophetic work of social justice.

AMOS

Introduction

These are the words of Amos, one of the shepherds of Tekoa. He perceived these things concerning Israel two years before the earthquake, in the days of Judah's King Uzziah and in the days of Israel's King Jeroboam, Joash's son.

Proclamation of divine judgment

2 He said:

The LORD roars from Zion.
  He shouts from Jerusalem;
  the pastures of the shepherds wither,
  and the top of Carmel dries up.

A word to Damascus

3 The LORD proclaims:

For three crimes of Damascus,
  and for four,
    I won't hold back the punishment,
  because they have harvested Gilead
  with sharp iron tools.
4 I will send down fire
  on the house of Hazael;
  it will devour
    the palaces of Ben-hadad.
5 I will break the fortified
  gates of Damascus,
  and eliminate the people
    from the Aven Valley,
  including the one who rules
    from Beth-eden;
  the people of Aram will be forced
    to live in Kir,
              says the LORD.

A word to Gaza and Ashdod

6 The LORD proclaims:

For three crimes of Gaza,
  and for four,
    I won't hold back the punishment,
  because they rounded up
    entire communities,
    to hand them over to Edom.
7 I will send down a fire
  on the wall of Gaza;
  it will devour Gaza's palaces.
8 I will eliminate
  the people from Ashdod,

  the one who rules from Ashkelon.
I will turn my hand against Ekron,
  and the Philistines who remain
    will perish,
              says the LORD God.

A word to Tyre

9 The LORD proclaims:

For three crimes of Tyre,
  and for four,
    I won't hold back the punishment,
  because they have delivered up
  entire communities over to Edom,
  and neglected
    their covenantal obligations.
10 So I will send a fire on the wall of Tyre;
  it will devour their palaces.

A word to Edom

11 The LORD proclaims:

For three crimes of Edom,
  and for four,
    I won't hold back the punishment,
  because he chased after his brother
  with the sword,
  denied all compassion,
  kept his anger alive,
  and fueled his wrath forever.
12 So I will send a fire on Teman;
  it will devour
    the fortresses of Bozrah.

A word to Ammon

13 The LORD proclaims:

For three crimes of the Ammonites,
  and for four,
    I won't hold back the punishment,
  because they have ripped open
  pregnant women in Gilead
  in order to possess more land.
14 So I will start a fire
  at the wall of Rabbah;
  the fire will devour its palaces,
  with a war cry on the day of battle,
  with strong wind
  on the day of the storm.
15 Then their king will be taken away,
  he and his officials together,
              says the LORD.

A word to Moab

2 The LORD proclaims:
  For three crimes of Moab,
    and for four,
    I won't hold back the punishment,
  because he burned to lime
    the bones of the king of Edom.
[2] So I will send down a fire on Moab;
  it will devour the palaces of Kerioth.
  Moab will die in a great uproar,
    with a war cry,
    with the sound of the ram's horn.
[3] I will remove their judge from them
  and slay all their officials with him,
                    says the LORD.

A word to Judah

[4] The LORD proclaims:
  For three crimes of Judah,
    and for four,
    I won't hold back the punishment,
  because they have rejected the
    Instruction of the LORD,
    and haven't kept his laws.
  They have been led off the right path by
    the same lies
  after which their ancestors walked.
[5] So I will send a fire on Judah,
    and it will devour the palaces
      of Jerusalem.

A word to Israel

[6] The LORD proclaims:
  For three crimes of Israel,
    and for four,
    I won't hold back the punishment,
  because they have sold the innocent
    for silver,
    and those in need
      for a pair of sandals.
[7] They crush the head of the poor
    into the dust of the earth,
    and push the afflicted out of the way.
  Father and son have intercourse
    with the same young woman,
    degrading my holy name.
[8] They stretch out beside every altar
    on garments taken in loan;
  in the house of their god they drink
    wine bought with fines they imposed.

[9] Yet I destroyed the Amorite
    before them,
  whose height was as tall as cedar trees,
    and whose strength
      was as strong as oak trees.
  I destroyed his fruit above
    and his roots below.
[10] Also I brought you up
    out of the land of Egypt,
    and led you forty years
      in the wilderness,
  to lay claim to the land of the Amorite.
[11] I raised up some of your children
    to be prophets
    and some of your youth
      to be nazirites.
  Isn't this so, people of Israel?
                    says the LORD.

[12] But you made the nazirites drink wine,
    and commanded the prophets,
    saying, "You won't prophesy."
[13] So now I will oppress you,
    just like a cart is weighed down[a]
    when it is full of harvested grain.
[14] Fast runners will find no refuge;
    the strong will lose their strength;
    the mighty will be unable
      to save their lives.
[15] Those who shoot the bow won't survive.
    Fast runners won't escape;
    those who ride horses
      won't save themselves.
[16] The bravest warrior
    will flee away naked in that day,
                    says the LORD.

Words of doom for Israel

3 Hear this word that the LORD has spoken
  against you, people of Israel, against the
whole family that I brought out of the land
of Egypt:
[2] You only have I loved so deeply
    of all the families of the earth.
  Therefore, I will punish you
    for all your wrongdoing.
[3] Will two people walk together
    unless they have agreed to do so?[b]
[4] Does a lion roar in the forest
    when it has no prey?

---

[a]Heb uncertain   [b]Or *Will two walk together unless they have agreed?*

Does a young lion cry out from its den
  if it has caught nothing?
[5] Will a bird fall into a trap
  on the ground
  when there is no bait for it?
Will a trap spring up from the ground
  when it has taken nothing?
[6] If a ram's horn is blown in a city,
  won't people tremble?
If disaster falls on a city,
  is it the LORD who has done it?
[7] Surely the LORD God does nothing
  without revealing his secret
  to his servants the prophets.

[8] A lion has roared;
  who will not fear?
The LORD God has spoken;
  who can but prophesy?
[9] Proclaim it to the palaces of Ashdod
  and to the palaces
  in the land of Egypt.
Say, "Gather yourselves
  on Mount Samaria,
  and see the great turmoil in the city,
  and what violent deeds are inside it."
[10] They don't know how to do right,
                says the LORD—

^cHeb uncertain

those who store up violence and
  robbery in their palaces.
[11] Therefore, the LORD my God proclaims:
  An enemy will surround the land;
  he will bring you down
  from your protected places,
  and your palaces will be robbed.

[12] The LORD proclaims:
Just as the shepherd rescues two legs or
the piece of an ear from the mouth of the
lion, so will the people of Israel be rescued.
Those who live in Samaria will escape with
the corner of a bed, and those in Damascus
with a piece of a couch.^c
[13] Hear this and speak
  against the house of Jacob,
  says the LORD God,
  the God of heavenly forces:
[14] On the day I punish the crimes of Israel,
  I will also visit the altars of Bethel;
  the horns of the altar will be cut off
  and will fall to the ground.
[15] I will tear down the winter house
  as well as the summer house;
  the houses of ivory will perish;
  the great houses will be swept away,
              says the LORD.

ALTAR

A place for sacrifice. Offerings were sacrificed at the altar, and the people of God joined in celebrating the divine pleasure in this sacred and communal meal, a feast that they also shared with each other. The Hebrew word for *altar*, derived from the root meaning "to slaughter," suggests that originally the altar was the place where the slaughter of animals for sacrifice occurred (Gen 22:9). In the Bible, however, animals are never sacrificed on the altar, but offerings of things not slaughtered (grain, wine, incense) are made on altars. Three types of material were used for building altars: earth, stone, and metal. The law on altars in Exodus 20:24-26 stipulates three conditions: (a) they are to be built of earth or stone; (b) if from stone, it must be un-worked; (c) altars are to be built without steps. No OT laws mention altars made of metal, but there were two in the covenant dwelling (Exod 27:1-8; 30:1-5; 37:25-28; 38:1-7) and later in the temple. In the NT, Revelation speaks of a heavenly altar in the heavenly sanctuary (Rev 6:9; 8:3-5).

Judgment on Israel's elite

4 Hear this word, you cows of Bashan,
　　who are on Mount Samaria,
　　who cheat the weak,
　　who crush the needy,
　　who say to their husbands,
　　"Bring drinks, so we can get drunk!"
² The LORD God has solemnly promised
　　by his holiness:
　　The days are surely coming upon you,
　　when they will take you away
　　　with hooks,
　　even the last one of you
　　　with fishhooks.
³ You will go out through the broken wall,
　　each one after another;
　　and you will be flung out
　　　into Harmon,
　　　　　　says the LORD.

A divine taunt

⁴ Come to Bethel—and commit a crime;
　　multiply crimes at Gilgal.
　Bring your sacrifices every morning,
　　your tenth-part gifts every three days.
⁵ Offer a thanksgiving sacrifice
　　of leavened bread,
　　and publicize your gifts to the LORD;
　　for so you love to do,
　　　people of Israel!
　　　　　　says the LORD God.

Israel's stubbornness

⁶ I have sent a famine in all your cities,
　　and not provided enough bread
　　　in all your places,
　　yet you didn't return to me,
　　　　　　says the LORD.
⁷ I also withheld rain from you
　　when there were still three months
　　　to the harvest.
　I allowed no rain to fall on one city,
　　no rain to fall on another city.
　One field was rained on,
　　and the field dried up
　　　where it didn't rain.
⁸ So two or three thirsty towns went to
　　one city to drink water,
　　and weren't satisfied;
　　yet you didn't return to me,
　　　　　　says the LORD.

⁹ I struck you with disease and mildew.
　I destroyed your gardens
　　and your vineyards.
　The locust devoured your fig trees
　　and your olive trees;
　yet you didn't return to me,
　　　　　　says the LORD.

¹⁰ I sent a plague against you
　　like the one in Egypt.
　I killed your young men with the sword.
　I carried away your horses.
　I made the stink of your camp
　　go up into your nostrils;
　yet you didn't return to me,
　　　　　　says the LORD.

¹¹ I destroyed some of you,
　　as when God destroyed
　　　Sodom and Gomorrah.
　You were like a burning coal
　　plucked out of the fire;
　yet you didn't return to me,
　　　　　　says the LORD.

¹² Truly, Israel,
　　I will act in this way toward you;
　　therefore, I will do this to you.
　　Prepare to meet your God, Israel!

¹³ The one who forms the mountains,
　　creates the wind,
　　makes known his thoughts
　　　to humankind,
　makes the morning darkness,
　　and moves over the heights
　　　of the earth—
　the LORD, the God of heavenly forces
　　is his name!

A song of lament

5 Hear this word—a funeral song—that I
　am lifting up against you, house of Israel:
² Fallen, no more to rise,
　　is virgin Israel,
　　deserted on her land,
　　with no one to raise her up.
³ The LORD God proclaims:
　　The city that marched out
　　　one thousand people
　　will have one hundred left,
　　and the city that marched out

one hundred will have ten left
in the house of Israel.

Words of encouragement

4 The LORD proclaims
to the house of Israel:
Seek me and live.
5 But don't seek Bethel,
don't enter into Gilgal,
or cross over to Beer-sheba;
for Gilgal will go into exile,
and Bethel will come to nothing.
6 Seek the LORD and live,
or else God might rush like a fire
against the house of Joseph.
The fire will burn up Bethel,
with no one to put it out.

Words of doom

7 Doom to you
who turn justice into poison,
and throw righteousness
to the ground!

8 The one who made
the Pleiades and Orion,
and turns deep darkness
into the morning,
and darkens the day into night;
who summons the waters of the sea,
and pours them out
on the surface of the earth—
this one's name is the LORD—
9 who causes destruction to flash out
against the strong,
so that destruction comes
upon the fortress.

10 They hate the one who judges
at the city gate,
and they reject the one
who speaks the truth.
11 Truly, because you crush the weak,
and because you tax their grain,
you have built houses of carved stone,
but you won't live in them;
you have planted pleasant vineyards,
but you won't drink their wine.
12 I know how many are your crimes,
and how numerous are your sins—
afflicting the righteous,
taking money on the side,
turning away the poor who seek help.
13 Therefore, the one who is wise
will keep silent in that time;
it is an evil time.

Words of inspiration

14 Seek good and not evil,
that you may live;
and so the LORD,
the God of heavenly forces,
will be with you just as you have said.
15 Hate evil, love good,
and establish justice at the city gate.
Perhaps the LORD God of heavenly forces
will be gracious to what is left of Joseph.

Divine wrath anticipated

16 Truly, the LORD proclaims,
the God of heavenly forces, the Lord:
Crying will be heard in all the squares.
In all the streets they will say,
"Oh no! Oh no!"
They will call upon the farmers to wail,
and those skilled in mourning to lament.
17 In all the vineyards
there will be bitter crying because
I will pass through your midst,
says the LORD.

SAKKUTH AND KAIWAN

Assyrian gods mentioned only in Amos 5:26. The name "Sakkuth" perfectly matches the consonants of a well-known star deity from a variety of Mesopotamian locations. Kaiwan has been identified with the star god Saturn. The pair of names has appeared together in star deity texts. Amos thus proclaims that those who carry detestable Assyrian idols in cult processionals will be lifted up and carried into exile.

A statement of divine disgust

18 Doom to those who desire
     the day of the LORD!
     Why do you want the day of the LORD?
   It is darkness, not light;
19 as if someone fled from a lion,
     and was met by a bear;
   or sought refuge in a house,
     rested a hand against the wall,
     and was bitten by a snake.
20 Isn't the day of the LORD darkness,
     not light;
     all dark with no brightness in it?

21 I hate, I reject your festivals;
     I don't enjoy your joyous assemblies.
22 If you bring me your entirely burned
     offerings and gifts of food—
     I won't be pleased;
   I won't even look at your offerings
     of well-fed animals.

23 Take away the noise of your songs;
     I won't listen to the melody
     of your harps.
24 But let justice roll down like waters,
     and righteousness
     like an ever-flowing stream.

25 Did you bring me sacrifices and offerings
     during the forty years in the wilderness,
     house of Israel?
26 You will take up Sakkuth your king,
     and Kaiwan your star-god,
     your images,
     which you made for yourselves.
27 Therefore, I will take you away
     beyond Damascus, says the LORD,
     whose name is
     the God of heavenly forces.

Warnings to the self-satisfied

6 Doom to those resting
   comfortably in Zion
     and those trusting in Mount Samaria,
   the chiefs of the nations,
     to whom the house of Israel comes!
2 Cross over to Calneh and see;
     from there go to Hamath the great;
     then go down to Gath
     of the Philistines.
   Are you better than these kingdoms?

Or is your territory greater
     than their territory?

3 Doom to those who ignore the evil day
     and make violent rule draw near:
4 who lie on beds of ivory,
     stretch out on their couches,
     eat lambs from the flock,
     and bull calves from the stall;
5 who sing idle songs
     to the sound of the harp,
     and, like David, compose tunes
     on musical instruments;
6 who drink bowls of wine,
     put the best of oils on themselves,
     but who aren't grieved
     over the ruin of Joseph!
7 Therefore, they will now
     be the first to be taken away,
     and the feast of those who lounged
     at the table will pass away.

8 The LORD God has solemnly sworn,
     says the LORD,
     the God of heavenly forces:
   I reject the pride of Jacob.
   I hate his fortresses.
   I will hand over the city
     and all that is in it.
9 If ten people remain in one house,
     then they will die.
10 If a relative,
     someone who burns the dead,
     picks up the body to bring it out
     of the house,
   and says to someone
     inside the house,
   "Is anyone else with you?"
     the answer will be, "No."
   Then the relative will say,
     "Hush! We mustn't mention
     the name of the LORD."
11 Look, the LORD is giving an order;
     he will shatter the great house into bits
     and the little house into pieces.
12 Do horses run on rocks?
     Does one plow the sea with oxen?
   But you have turned justice
     into poison
     and the fruit of righteousness
     into bitterness—

[13] you who rejoice in Lo-debar,
who say, "Haven't we by our own strength
taken Karnaim for ourselves?"
[14] Indeed, I will raise up against you
a nation, house of Israel,
says the LORD God of heavenly forces,
and they will oppress you from
Lebo-hamath to the desert ravine.

A vision of locusts

7 This is what the LORD God showed me:
The LORD God was forming locusts at
the time the late grass began to sprout. (It
was the late grass after the king's harvest.)
[2] When they had finished eating the green
plants of the land, I said,

"LORD God, please forgive!
How can Jacob survive?
He is so small!"
[3] The LORD relented concerning this:
"It won't take place,"
says the LORD.

A vision of fire

[4] This is what the LORD God showed me:
The LORD God was calling for judgment
with fire, and it devoured the great deep
and was eating up part of the land. [5] Then
I said,

"LORD God, I beg you, stop!
How can Jacob survive?
He is so small!"
[6] The LORD relented concerning this:
"This also won't take place,"
says the LORD God.

[d] Or *was*; the verb is implied.

A vision of a plumb line

[7] This is what the LORD showed me: The
LORD was standing by a wall, with a plumb
line in his hand. [8] The LORD said to me,
"Amos, what do you see?"

"A plumb line," I said.

Then the LORD said,
"See, I am setting a plumb line
in the middle of my people Israel.
I will never again forgive them.
[9] The shrines of Isaac will be made desolate,
and the holy places of Israel
will be laid waste,
and I will rise against the house of
Jeroboam with the sword."

Exchange between Amaziah, Jeroboam, and Amos

[10] Then Amaziah, the priest of Bethel,
reported to Israel's King Jeroboam, "Amos
has plotted against you within the house
of Israel. The land isn't able to cope with
everything that he is saying. [11] Amos has
said, 'Jeroboam will die by the sword, and
Israel will be forced out of its land.'"

[12] Amaziah said to Amos, "You who see
things, go, run away to the land of Judah,
eat your bread there, and prophesy there;
[13] but never again prophesy at Bethel, for it
is the king's holy place and his royal house."

[14] Amos answered Amaziah, "I am[d] not
a prophet, nor am I a prophet's son; but I
am a shepherd, and a trimmer of sycamore
trees. [15] But the LORD took me from shepherding the flock, and the LORD said to me,
'Go, prophesy to my people Israel.'

PLUMB LINE

A string with a stone or metal weight (plumb bob) attached, used by a
builder to determine whether a stone or mud-brick wall is vertical. As a tool
used to measure straightness, the plumb line serves as a metaphor for the
moral assessment of Israel's kings (Manasseh in 2 Kgs 21:13), of the nation's
adherence to the covenant (Amos 7:7-8), and of the justice and righteousness expected of the people (Isa 28:17).

16 "Now then hear the LORD's word.
    You say, 'Don't prophesy against Israel,
        and don't preach
        against the house of Isaac.'
17 "Therefore, the LORD proclaims:
    'Your wife will become a prostitute
        in the city,
    and your sons and your daughters
        will fall by the sword,
    and your land will be measured
        and divided up;
    you yourself will die in an unclean land,
    and Israel will surely be taken away
        from its land.'"

A vision of summer fruit

8 This is what the LORD God showed me:
a basket of summer fruit. ²He said,
"Amos, what do you see?"
    I said, "A basket of summer fruit."
    Then the LORD said to me,
    "The end has come upon my people Israel;
        I will never again forgive them.
³ On that day, the people
    will wail the temple songs,"
    says the LORD God;
    "there will be many corpses,
    thrown about everywhere.ᵉ
    Silence."

Judgment on oppressors
and hypocrites

⁴ Hear this, you who trample
    on the needy and destroy
    the poor of the land, ⁵saying,
    "When will the new moon
        be over so that we may sell grain,
    and the Sabbath
        so that we may offer wheat for sale,
    make the ephah smaller,
        enlarge the shekel,
    and deceive with false balances,
⁶ in order to buy the needy for silver
    and the helpless for sandals,
    and sell garbage as grain?"

⁷ The LORD has sworn
    by the pride of Jacob:
    Surely I will never forget
    what they have done.

⁸ Will not the land tremble on this account,
    and all who live in it mourn,
    as it rises and overflows like the Nile,
        and then falls again,
    like the River of Egypt?ᶠ

⁹ On that day, says the LORD God,
    I will make the sun go down at noon,
    and I will darken the earth
        in broad daylight.
¹⁰ I will turn your feasts into sad affairs
    and all your singing into a funeral song;
    I will make people
        wear mourning clothes
        and shave their heads;
    I will make it like the loss
        of an only child,
    and the end of it like a bitter day.
¹¹ The days are surely coming,
    says the LORD God,
    when I will send hunger and thirst
        on the land;
    neither a hunger for bread,
        nor a thirst for water,
    but of hearing the LORD's words.
¹² They will wander from sea to sea,
    and from north to east;
    they will roam all around,
        seeking the LORD's word,
    but they won't find it.
¹³ On that day the beautiful young women
    and the young men
        will faint with thirst.
¹⁴ Those who swear by the guilt of Samaria,
    and say, "As your god lives, Dan,"
    and, "As the way of Beer-sheba lives"—
    even they will fall and never rise again.

Description of Israel's fate

9 I saw the Lord standing beside the
altar, and the Lord said:
    Strike the pillars
        until the foundations shake,
    shatter them on the heads
        of all the people.
    With the sword,
        I will kill the last of them;
    not one of them will flee,
        not one of them will escape.
² If they dig through into the underworld,ᵍ

ᵉHeb uncertain ᶠHeb uncertain ᵍHeb Sheol

from there my hand will take them.
If they climb up to the heavens,
   from there I will bring them down.
3 If they hide themselves
   on the top of Carmel,
   I will search for them there
     and remove them.
If they hide from my sight
   at the bottom of the sea,
   I will give an order to the sea serpent,
     and it will bite them.
4 If they are forced from their homes
   before their enemies,
   there I will give an order to the sword,
     and it will kill them.
I will fix my eyes on them
   for harm and not for good.

A divine confession

5 The LORD, God of heavenly forces,
   touches the earth and it melts,
   and all who live in it are sick to death.
All of it[h] rises up like the Nile
   and sinks again, like the Nile of Egypt.
6 It is the LORD who builds
   his upper rooms in the heavens
   and establishes his residence
     upon the earth;
who summons the waters of the sea,
   and pours them out
     upon the face of the earth—
     the LORD is his name.

Divine address to the Israelites

7 Aren't you like the Cushites to me,
   people of Israel?
            says the LORD.
Haven't I brought Israel up
   from the land of Egypt,
   and the Philistines from Caphtor
   and the Arameans from Kir?
8 Look, the LORD God is eyeing
   the sinful kingdom,
   and I will destroy it
   from the face of the earth.
However, I won't destroy fully
   the house of Jacob,
         says the LORD.

Warning to the house of Israel

9 Look, I am giving orders,
   and I will shake the house of Israel
     among all the nations
as one sifts dirt with a screen,
   but no pebble will fall to the ground.
10 All the sinners of my people
   will die by the sword,
   those who say,
   "Evil won't overtake or meet us."

Divine promise of restoration

11 On that day I will raise up
   the meeting tent of David
     that has fallen,
   and repair its broken places.
   I will raise up its ruins,
   and I will rebuild it
     like a long time ago;
12 so that they may possess
   what is left of Edom,
   as well as all the nations
   who are called by my name,
     says the LORD who will do this.
13 The days are surely coming,
   says the LORD,
   when the one who plows
   will overtake the one who gathers,
   when the one who crushes grapes
   will overtake the one
     who sows the seed.
The mountains will drip wine,
   and all the hills will flow with it.
14 I will improve the circumstances
   of my people Israel;
   they will rebuild the ruined cities
     and inhabit them.
They will plant vineyards
   and drink their wine;
and they will make gardens
   and eat their fruit.
15 I will plant them upon their land,
   and they will never again
     be plucked up
out of the land
   that I have given them,
     says the LORD your God.

[h] Or the earth

OBADIAH

The prophecy of Obadiah consists of merely twenty-one verses, making it the shortest book in the Old Testament. The work focuses on the historic enemy Edom and its reprehensible attitude and behavior during the final collapse of Jerusalem.

The name Obadiah means *servant of the Lord*. Twelve individuals share this name in the Old Testament (e.g., 1 Kings 18:3; 1 Chronicles 3:21; Ezra 8:9; Nehemiah 10:5). Other than Obadiah's name we know nothing specific about him. Unlike other prophets, he lists no dates of his work, no family identity, no occupation, and no home territory.

HISTORICAL CIRCUMSTANCES

What can we deduce from Obadiah's work? He speaks of the dreadful events that occurred when Jerusalem finally fell to the Babylonians in 587 BCE. Obadiah makes many references to other prophetic works, especially Jeremiah 49:7-22. One possibility is that the work is in part a collection of material assembled from various prophetic works that Obadiah re-presented and reinterpreted to his people. Since the work does focus on a single theme of God's justice and judgment, scholars think that it is the work of one writer who used other material. While we cannot date Obadiah to a specific year, it appears to have been written while the prophet and his people languished in exile in Babylon.

The prophet's attitude parallels that of another exile, who wrote Psalm 137. The last three verses of Psalm 137 are rarely read in Christian worship services. The soul-deep anger, the graphic expression of hate, a yearned-for day when an enemy will have to pay for what was done to innocent people are simply too strong for most of us. But shallow piety and sentimentality were not an option for the pained exiles. The memories ran too deep. We have a record of how deeply the people of God yearned for a day of vindication. The Bible does not blink or flinch at even the harshest of human realities.

THE MESSAGE OF OBADIAH

Since the book concentrates on the long-hated Edomites' doom, why is it included in the Bible? It seems to have small spiritual insight or message. It speaks not a word about sin, mercy, or righteousness. Like the author of Psalm 137, Obadiah believed in the higher values and aspirations of life and of the nation. He had seen all that he held highest and dearest thoroughly demolished, while a hated enemy only scoffed and then participated in the looting and killing. Obadiah went into exile with his blood boiling, remembering the taunts of the conquerors. But then the scoffing words would not be the last words.

The higher values of life are God's, and they cannot be destroyed. Not only will God have the last word against Edom, God will have the last word in the lives of all nations. On Obadiah's experience, or one very much like it, another psalmist reflected, "those who go out, crying and carrying their seed, come home with joyful shouts" (Psalm 126:6).

OBADIAH

Edom falls

¹ The vision of Obadiah.

The LORD God proclaims
concerning Edom:
We have heard a message
from the LORD—
a messenger has been sent
among the nations:
"Rise up! Let us rise against her
for battle!"
² Look now, I will make you of little
importance among the nations;
you will be totally despised.
³ Your proud heart has tricked you—
you who live in the cracks of the rock,
whose dwelling is high above.
You who say in your heart,
"Who will bring me
down to the ground?"
⁴ Though you soar like the eagle,
though your nest is set
among the stars,
I will bring you down from there,
says the LORD.

Edom is robbed

⁵ If thieves approach you,
if robbers by night—
how you've been devastated!—
wouldn't they steal
only what they wanted?
If those who gather grapes came to you,
wouldn't they leave some grapes?
⁶ How Esau has been looted,
his treasures taken away!
⁷ All those who were your allies
have driven you to the border.
Those who were on your side
tricked you
and triumphed over you.
They are setting your own bread
as a trap under you,ᵃ
but you don't see it coming.
⁸ Won't I on that day, says the LORD,
destroy the wise from Edom
and understanding from Mount Esau?
⁹ Your warriors will be shattered, Teman,

and everyone from Mount Esau
will be eliminated.

Edom's misdeeds

¹⁰ Because of the slaughter and violence
done to your brother Jacob,
shame will cover you,
and you will be destroyed forever.
¹¹ You stood nearby,
strangers carried off his wealth,
and foreigners entered his gates
and cast lots for Jerusalem;
you too were like one of them.
¹² But you should have taken no pleasure
over your brother
on the day of his misery;
you shouldn't have rejoiced
over the people of Judah
on the day of their devastation;
you shouldn't have bragged
on their day of hardship.
¹³ You shouldn't have entered
the gate of my people
on the day of their defeat;
you shouldn't have even looked
on his suffering
on the day of his disaster;
you shouldn't have stolen
his possessions
on the day of his distress.
¹⁴ You shouldn't have waited on the roads
to destroy his escapees;
you shouldn't have handed over
his survivors
on the day of defeat.
¹⁵ The day of the LORD is near
against all the nations.
As you have done,
so it will be done to you;
your actions will make you suffer!
¹⁶ Just as you have drunk
on my holy mountain,
so will all the nations
around you drink;
they will drink and swallow quickly,
and they will be like they've never
been before.

ᵃHeb uncertain

Edom's punishers

¹⁷ But on Mount Zion
   there will be those who escape,
      and it will be holy;
   and the house of Jacob will drive out
      those who drove them out.
¹⁸ The house of Jacob will be a fire,
   the house of Joseph a flame,
   and the house of Esau straw;
      they will burn them up completely,
   and there will be no one left
      of the house of Esau,
         for the LORD has spoken.
¹⁹ Those of the arid southern plain
   will possess Mount Esau,
and those of the western foothills,
   the land of the Philistines;
they will possess the land of Ephraim
   and the land of Samaria,
   and Benjamin will possess Gilead.
²⁰ Those who remain of the Israelites
   will possess the land of the
      Canaanites as far as Zarephath;
and those left from Jerusalem
   and who are now living in Sepharad
   will possess the cities
      of the arid southern plain.
²¹ The deliverers will go up to Mount Zion
   to rule Mount Esau,
   and the kingdom will be the LORD's.

The book of Jonah is unique. No other book contains such remarkable circumstances, miraculous rescues, human traits, peculiar reversals, or surprises. Because the book is unique, and because it contains what is one of the most quickly recognized stories in the Old Testament, it evokes more discussion and argument than many other books.

In contrast to other prophetic works that are collections of oracles, Jonah contains only one oracle (Jonah 3:4). With the exception of Amos, all the other prophets pronounce their oracles to their own people, in their home territory. Jonah must travel to the heart of the nation to which this oracle is proclaimed.

In Israel's tradition, many of those called to prophesy hesitated and argued with God about the task. Moses argued that he could not speak well (Exodus 3–4). Elijah resisted God's summons to further work, citing his lack of support (1 Kings 19:4-18). Jeremiah argued that he was too young to do such work (Jeremiah 1). But in each of these instances, the prophet finally succumbed to the will of God.

In Jonah's story, the reluctant prophet does a good deal more than resist with an argument. Jonah actually denies his God's claim and attempts to flee from God's presence. The entire first half of the story is of Jonah's refusal.

The name Jonah does occur in earlier tradition. Second Kings 14:25 lists the name as a prophet, the son of Amittai of the region of Gath-hepher. A careful reading of the episode in Kings shows the prophet's concern for the expansion of national boundaries, with no further concern for God's will for the king, the social order, or the nation's behavior. He gives evidence of the same attitude of which the prophet Jonah is guilty.

THE NATURE OF THE BOOK

The story itself overflows with peculiar and spectacular phenomena. Had the writer been concerned primarily with a historically reliable series of events, the story would take on a different character. As it is, the story is replete with storytelling devices. The story is a parable.

HISTORICAL CIRCUMSTANCES

Determining the date of the book's composition is very difficult. Since the book is essentially a parable, it could have been composed at any time. Another book in the Old Testament, the book of Ruth, shares a similar ambiguity with regard to its date.

In Jonah, the major city Nineveh, to which the prophet is to travel, is referred to as a place in the remote past. The author also refers to the words of two post-exilic prophets (Jonah 3:8, 10 build on Jeremiah 18:8, and Jonah 3:9 quotes Joel 2:14), which gives evidence of a late date for the book's composition.

THE PURPOSE OF THE BOOK

Jonah's outrage that his prophecy has been frustrated suggests that the purpose may center on the issue of unfulfilled prophecy. However, if Jonah 4:11 is the point toward which the entire book moves, then unfulfilled prophecy is too narrow a theme.

Through sensitive and human representation of foreigners, this book forces listeners to reconsider the meaning of God's sovereignty. Against a popularly held prejudice that relished God's punishment of enemies, Jonah lifts up the truth of God's compassion. God's care and compassion are equal to God's wrath and judgment.

In this work Jonah presents the possibility of repentance. The important question is not whether Nineveh could or would repent, but whether or not Israel could or would repent from a narrow, nationalistic view of God.

JONAH

Commissioning of a reluctant prophet

1 The LORD's word came to Jonah, Amittai's son: ²"Get up and go to Nineveh, that great city, and cry out against it, for their evil has come to my attention."

³So Jonah got up—to flee to Tarshish from the LORD! He went down to Joppa and found a ship headed for Tarshish. He paid the fare and went aboard to go with them to Tarshish, away from the LORD. ⁴But the LORD hurled a great wind upon the sea, so that there was a great storm on the sea; the ship looked like it might be broken to pieces. ⁵The sailors were terrified, and each one cried out to his god. They hurled the cargo that was in the ship into the sea to make it lighter.

Now Jonah had gone down into the hold of the vessel to lie down and was deep in sleep. ⁶The ship's officer came and said to him, "How can you possibly be sleeping so deeply? Get up! Call on your god! Perhaps the god will give some thought to us so that we won't perish."

⁷Meanwhile, the sailors said to each other, "Come on, let's cast lots so that we might learn who is to blame for this evil that's happening to us." They cast lots, and the lot fell on Jonah. ⁸So they said to him, "Tell us, since you're the cause of this evil happening to us: What do you do and where are you from? What's your country and of what people are you?"

⁹He said to them, "I'm a Hebrew. I worship the LORD, the God of heaven—who made the sea and the dry land."

¹⁰Then the men were terrified and said to him, "What have you done?" (The men knew that Jonah was fleeing from the LORD, because he had told them.)

¹¹They said to him, "What will we do about you so that the sea will become calm around us?" (The sea was continuing to rage.) ¹²He said to them, "Pick me up and hurl me into the sea! Then the sea will become calm around you. I know it's my fault that this great storm has come upon you."

¹³The men rowed to reach dry land, but they couldn't manage it because the sea continued to rage against them. ¹⁴So they called on the LORD, saying, "Please, LORD, don't let us perish on account of this man's life, and don't blame us for innocent blood! You are the LORD: whatever you want, you can do." ¹⁵Then they picked up Jonah and hurled him into the sea, and the sea ceased its raging. ¹⁶The men worshipped the LORD with a profound reverence; they offered a sacrifice to the LORD and made solemn promises.

No escape for the prophet

¹⁷ᵃMeanwhile, the LORD provided a great fish to swallow Jonah. Jonah was in the belly of the fish for three days and three nights.

2 Jonah prayed to the LORD his God from the belly of the fish:
² "I called out to the LORD in my distress,
    and he answered me.
    From the belly of the underworldᵇ
      I cried out for help;
    you have heard my voice.
³ You had cast me into the depths
    in the heart of the seas,
      and the flood surrounds me.

ᵃ2:1 in Heb ᵇHeb *Sheol*

All your strong waves and rushing
  water passed over me.
[4] So I said, 'I have been driven
  away from your sight.
  Will I ever again look
    on your holy temple?
[5] Waters have grasped me
  to the point of death;
  the deep surrounds me.
Seaweed is wrapped around my head
  [6] at the base
  of the undersea[c] mountains.
I have sunk down to the underworld;
  its bars held me with no end in sight.
  But you brought me out of the pit.'
[7] When my endurance[d] was weakening,
  I remembered the LORD,
  and my prayer came to you,
  to your holy temple.
[8] Those deceived by worthless things
  lose their chance for mercy.[e]
[9] But me, I will offer a sacrifice to you
  with a voice of thanks.
  That which I have promised, I will pay.
  Deliverance belongs to the LORD!"

[10] Then the LORD spoke to the fish, and it vomited Jonah onto the dry land.

Nineveh hears God's word

3 The LORD's word came to Jonah a second time: [2] "Get up and go to Nineveh, that great city, and declare against it the proclamation that I am commanding you." [3] And Jonah got up and went to Nineveh, according to the LORD's word. (Now Nineveh was indeed an enormous city, a three days' walk across.)

[4] Jonah started into the city, walking one day, and he cried out, "Just forty days more and Nineveh will be overthrown!" [5] And the people of Nineveh believed God. They proclaimed a fast and put on mourning clothes, from the greatest of them to the least significant.

[6] When word of it reached the king of Nineveh, he got up from his throne, stripped himself of his robe, covered himself with mourning clothes, and sat in ashes. [7] Then he announced, "In Nineveh, by decree of the king and his officials: Neither human

[c]Heb lacks undersea. [d]Endurance here renders the same Heb word as life in 1:14 and death in 2:5. [e]Heb uncertain

NINEVEH

A major city in northern Mesopotamia during the Bronze and Iron Ages and the capital of Assyria at the height of the Neo-Assyrian Empire. In the wake of its destruction in 612 BCE, the city experienced sudden reversal of political fortune, from extreme wealth and power to abject ruin.

Nineveh lay on the east bank of the Tigris River, directly across from modern Mosul on the west bank of the Tigris. The ancient city was surrounded by a roughly rectangular double wall, approximately 1.25 mi. wide and 3 mi. long. Nineveh was truly a "great city" (Jon 1:2).

The 7th-century prophets Nahum and Zephaniah proclaim the fall of Nineveh. The post-exilic book of Jonah tells the story of Jonah son of Amittai, commissioned by the Lord to prophesy against Nineveh. The OT thus presents two images of Nineveh: the arrogant city that deservedly suffers divine punishment and the repentant city that God spares.

The image of Nineveh as a repentant city surfaces in Luke 11:32 (cf. Matt 12:41). The saying reasons that, since the Ninevites changed their ways at the proclamation of Jonah, they are qualified to condemn the recalcitrant generation of Jesus on Judgment Day.

nor animal, cattle nor flock, will taste anything! No grazing and no drinking water! [8]Let humans and animals alike put on mourning clothes, and let them call upon God forcefully! And let all persons stop their evil behavior and the violence that's under their control!" [9]He thought, Who knows? God may see this and turn from his wrath, so that we might not perish.[f]

[10]God saw what they were doing—that they had ceased their evil behavior. So God stopped planning to destroy them, and he didn't do it.

Jonah balks at God's mercy

4 But Jonah thought this was utterly wrong, and he became angry. [2]He prayed to the LORD, "Come on, LORD! Wasn't this precisely my point when I was back in my own land? This is why I fled to Tarshish earlier! I know that you are a merciful and compassionate God, very patient, full of faithful love, and willing not to destroy. [3]At this point, LORD, you may as well take my life from me, because it would be better for me to die than to live."

[4]The LORD responded, "Is your anger a good thing?" [5]But Jonah went out from the city and sat down east of the city. There he made himself a hut and sat under it, in the shade, to see what would happen to the city.

[6]Then the LORD God provided a shrub,[g] and it grew up over Jonah, providing shade for his head and saving him from his misery. Jonah was very happy about the shrub. [7]But God provided a worm the next day at dawn, and it attacked the shrub so that it died. [8]Then as the sun rose God provided a dry east wind, and the sun beat down on Jonah's head so that he became faint. He begged that he might die, saying, "It's better for me to die than to live."

[9]God said to Jonah, "Is your anger about the shrub a good thing?"

Jonah said, "Yes, my anger is good— even to the point of death!"

[10]But the LORD said, "You 'pitied' the shrub, for which you didn't work and which you didn't raise; it grew in a night and perished in a night. [11]Yet for my part, can't I pity Nineveh, that great city, in which there are more than one hundred twenty thousand people who can't tell their right hand from their left, and also many animals?

---

[f]Heb lacks *For he thought*. [g]Botanists disagree about whether Heb *qiqayon* refers to a climbing gourd plant, a castor bean plant, or some other shrub.

MICAH

MICAH THE BOOK

Micah's prophetic ministry happened in the eighth century BCE, when the states of Israel and Judah were confronted with overwhelming foreign military powers. Internally, Israel was in chaos with betrayal and murder the order of the day within the ruling families. Economic and social injustices were the norm, and pagan worship was tolerated and openly practiced. Micah saw the destruction of Israel and foresaw the destruction of Judah. He gave reasons for these events and linked the present, past, and future of Israel and Judah with God's will and power.

In the midst of destruction and uncertainty, Micah focused on the need for divinely ordained justice and true worship in the lives of God's people. He also proclaimed that a time would come when all would be made right by God. Such a time will come because God's ultimate will is not for destruction but for restoration and relationship with all peoples.

MICAH THE MAN

Micah was from the village of Moresheth (perhaps the same as Moresheth-gath) in the region of broad valleys and rolling hills that runs from north to south between the coastal plain and the central highlands of Judah. In biblical times this area was heavily forested and was also under cultivation. Groves of olives and sycamore figs as well as vineyards were tended here. The chalky hills on the western side of the central valley provided raw materials for the pottery industry.

The region is crossed by many valleys running both north-south and east-west. These valleys were well-traveled military and trade routes from the coast into the hill country and from Jerusalem and Samaria into southern Judah. Since Moresheth is on the western edge of the central north-south valley, Micah could observe the comings and goings of travelers (and of invading armies) and hear news from Jerusalem and Israel.

Micah may have been a farmer or a tradesman before his call to prophesy took him to Jerusalem. He identified with the common people of Judah. The rulers of Judah come under sharp attack in his prophecies because they were mistreating the people.

Tekoa, the hometown of the prophet Amos, was not far from Moresheth, and Micah may have heard of the prophecies of Amos in Israel. Micah may also have been in Jerusalem at times and heard the preaching of Isaiah. His calls for justice within Israelite society echo the concern for justice expressed by Amos. His preaching, like that of Isaiah, influenced King Hezekiah of Judah.

Micah may have returned to his home and resumed his life there once his prophetic duties were completed. He was not connected to the priesthood or the royalty, and he had no official standing in the community in Jerusalem that he was called to address. He was apparently a man of humble origins with a gift for eloquent speech and a willingness to respond to God's call.

MICAH THE BOOK

The book of Micah is a collection of prophecies organized around the themes of punishment and hope. Micah's prophecies were first spoken, then written. He perhaps had followers who copied his words onto scrolls. This material was then organized and recopied and an introduction was added. The book went through many copies and possible revisions before it came to its present form. As a result, some of Micah's prophecies may have been lost or left out.

Micah himself may have written down some of his prophecies. The ability to read was apparently common in ancient Israel, but it was not until the Assyrian period that writing also became a common skill. So, although Micah was a farmer or tradesman rather than a scribe or priest, he still could probably read and write.

The book of Micah contains two major sections (chapters 1–5 and 6–7) which are each divided into prophecies of punishment (chapters 1–3 and 6–7:6) and prophecies of hope (chapters 4–5 and 7:7–20). None of the prophecies are dated, apart from the general dates given in 1:1.

MICAH

The LORD is coming!

1 The LORD's word that came to Micah of Moresheth in the days of Judah's Kings Jotham, Ahaz, and Hezekiah, which he saw concerning Samaria and Jerusalem:

² Listen, all you peoples!
  Pay attention, earth, and all that fills it!
  May the LORD God
  be a witness against you,
    the Lord from his holy temple.
³ Look! The LORD is coming out
  from his place;
  he will go down and tread
    on the shrines of the earth.
⁴ Then the mountains will melt under him;
  the valleys will split apart,
    like wax yielding to the fire,
    like waters poured down a slope.
⁵ All this is for the crime of Jacob
  and the sins of the house of Israel.
  Who is responsible
    for the crime of Jacob?ᵃ
  Isn't it Samaria?
  Who is responsible
    forᵇ the shrines of Judah?
  Isn't it Jerusalem?
⁶ So I will make Samaria
  a pile of rubble in the open field,

a place for planting vineyards.
  I will pour her stones into the valley;
    her foundations I will lay bare.
⁷ All her images will be beaten to pieces;
  all her wages will be burned;
  I will make all her idols worthless.
  Since she gathered them
    from the wages of a prostitute,
    they will again become
    wages of a prostitute.
⁸ On account of this, I will cry out and howl;
  I will go about barefoot and stripped.
  I will cry out like the jackals,
    and mourn like the ostriches.

Destruction looms

⁹ Indeed, Zion has been weakened
  by her wounds!
  It has come as far as Judah;
  he has struck as far as the gate
    of my people,
    as far as Jerusalem.
¹⁰ In Gath tell it not; no need to weep there!ᶜ
  In Beth-le-aphrah,
    roll yourself in the dust!
¹¹ Pass by (for your sake),ᵈ
  inhabitants of Shaphir!
  In nakedness and shame

ᵃHeb lacks *responsible for.* ᵇHeb lacks *responsible for.* ᶜHeb lacks *there.* ᵈ*You* (plural)

MICAH

1. Resident of the highlands in Ephraim, who stole from and later returned to his mother 1,100 silver shekels. Micah's mother made an idol out of silver for his shrine. Micah placed his son as priest over the shrine, then later replaced him with a Levite from Bethlehem in Judah (Judg 17:1–18:4).

2. Son of Joel and a descendant of Reuben (1 Chron 5:5).

3. Son of Merib-baal (Mephibosheth in 2 Sam 9:12), descendant of Jonathan and Saul (1 Chron 8:33-35; 9:40-41).

4. A Levite and the elder son of Uzziel during Solomon's reign and David's last days (1 Chron 23:20; 24:24-25).

5. Father of Abdon (2 Chron 34:20). Called Micaiah in 2 Kings 22:12.

6. A prophet (Mic 1:1).

she will not go out,
  inhabitants of Zaanan.
The cry of Beth-ezel
  will take away from you[e]
  any place to stand.
¹² How she longs for good,
  inhabitants of Maroth!
  Calamity has come down from the LORD
  to the gate of Jerusalem.
¹³ Harness the horses to the chariot,
  inhabitants of Lachish!
  It was the beginning of sin
  for Daughter Zion;
  the crimes of Israel
  have been found in you.
¹⁴ Therefore, you will give good-bye gifts
  to Moresheth-gath;
  the houses of Achzib have become
  a deception for the kings of Israel.
¹⁵ Again I will bring to you
  the one who conquers,
  inhabitants of Mareshah;
  the glory of Israel
  will come as far as Adullam.
¹⁶ Make yourself bald and cut off your hair
  because of your cherished children!
  Make yourself as bald as the vulture,
  for they have gone from you into exile.

Oppressors will themselves be ruined

2 Doom to those who devise wickedness,
  to those who plan evil
  when they are in bed.
  By the light of morning they do it,
  for they are very powerful.
² They covet fields and seize them,
  houses and take them away.
  They oppress a householder
  and those in his house,
  a man and his estate.
³ Therefore, the LORD proclaims:
  I myself am devising an evil
  against this family
  from which you will not be able
  to remove your necks!
  You will no longer be able
  to go about arrogantly,
  for it will be an evil time.
⁴ On that day, a taunt will be raised
  against you;

someone will wail bitterly:
  "We are utterly destroyed!
  He exchanges the portion
  of my people;
  he removes what belongs to me;
  he gives away our fields to a rebel."
⁵ Therefore, you will have no one
  to set boundary lines
  by lot in the LORD's assembly.

Leaders unwilling to hear God's word

⁶ "They mustn't preach!" so they preach.
  "They mustn't preach of such things!
  Disgrace won't overtake us."
⁷ (Should this be said, house of Jacob?)
  "Is the LORD's patience cut short?
  Are these his deeds?"
  Don't my words help
  the one who behaves righteously?
⁸ But yesterday, my people,
  the LORD rose up as an enemy.[f]
  You strip off the glorious clothes[g]
  from trusting passersby,
  those who reject war.
⁹ You drive out the women of my people,
  each from her cherished house;
  from their young children
  you take away my splendor forever.
¹⁰ Rise up and go! This can't be
  the resting place;
  because of its uncleanness,
  it destroys and the destruction
  is horrific.
¹¹ If someone were to go about inspired
  and say deceitfully:
  "I will preach to you
  for wine and liquor,"
  such a one would be
  the preacher for this people!

The false prophet's "peace" will be destruction

¹² I'll surely gather Jacob—all of you!
  I'll surely assemble you,
  those who are left of Israel!
  I'll put them together
  like sheep in Bozrah,[h]
  like a flock in its pen,
  noisy with people.

---

[e]*You* (feminine singular) [f]Heb lacks *the LORD.* [g]Heb uncertain [h]See Isa 34:6; 63:1.

¹³ The one who breaks out
will go before them;
they will break out
and pass through the gate;
they will leave by it.
They will pass on,
their king before them,
the LORD at their head.

Micah justifies the coming destruction

3 But I said:
Hear, leaders of Jacob,
rulers of the house of Israel!
Isn't it your job to know justice?—
² you who hate good and love evil,
who tear the skin off them,
and the flesh off their bones,
³ who devour the flesh of my people,
tear off their skin,
break their bones in pieces,
and spread them out as if in a pot,
like meat in a kettle.
⁴ Then they will cry out to the LORD,
but he won't answer them.
He will hide his face from them
at that time,
because of their evil deeds.
⁵ The LORD proclaims
concerning the prophets,
those who lead my people astray,
those who chew with their teeth
and then proclaim "Peace!"
but stir up war against the one
who puts nothing in their mouths:
⁶ Therefore, it will become night for you,
without vision, only darkness
without divination!
The sun will set on the prophets;
the day will be dark upon them.
⁷ Those seeing visions will be ashamed,
and the diviners disgraced;
they will all cover their upper lips,[i]
for there will be no answer from God.
⁸ But me! I am filled with power,
with the spirit of the LORD,
with justice and might,
to declare to Jacob his wrongdoing
and to Israel his sin!
⁹ Hear this, leaders of the house of Jacob,
rulers of the house of Israel,

you who reject justice
and make crooked all that is straight,
¹⁰ who build Zion with bloodshed
and Jerusalem with injustice!
¹¹ Her officials give justice for a bribe,
and her priests teach for hire.
Her prophets offer divination for silver,
yet they rely on the LORD, saying,
"Isn't the LORD in our midst?
Evil won't come upon us!"
¹² Therefore, because of you,
Zion will be plowed like a field,
Jerusalem will become piles of rubble,
and the temple mount will become
an overgrown mound.

A peaceable world

4 But in the days to come,
the mountain of the LORD's house
will be the highest of the mountains;
it will be lifted above the hills;
peoples will stream to it.
² Many nations will go and say:
"Come, let's go up
to the mountain of the LORD,
to the house of Jacob's God,
so that he may teach us his ways
and we may walk in God's paths!"
Instruction will come from Zion
and the LORD's word from Jerusalem.
³ God will judge between the nations
and settle disputes of mighty nations,
which are far away.
They will beat their swords
into iron plows
and their spears into pruning tools.
Nation will not take up sword
against nation;
they will no longer learn
how to make war.
⁴ All will sit underneath
their own grapevines,
under their own fig trees.
There will be no one to terrify them;
for the mouth of the LORD of
heavenly forces has spoken.

An assertion of enduring loyalty

⁵ Each of the peoples walks
in the name of their own god;

ⁱOr *mustache* or *beard*

but as for us, we will walk
  in the name of the LORD our God
    forever and always.

Dominion in Zion

6 On that day, says the LORD,
  I will gather the lame;
  I will assemble those
    who were driven away
    and those whom I have harmed.
7 I will make the lame into survivors,
  those driven away into a mighty nation.
The LORD will rule over them
  on Mount Zion
    from now on and forever.
8 As for you, Tower of Eder,[j]
  hill of Daughter Zion,
  as for you it will come,
    the former dominion will come,
    the royal power
      belonging to Daughter Zion.

God is in control

9 Now why do you cry out so loudly?
  Isn't the king in you?
  Or has your counselor perished,
    so that pain has seized you
    like that of a woman in labor?
10 Writhe and scream, Daughter Zion,
  like a woman in labor!
    Now you will leave the city
    and dwell in the open field;
    you will go to Babylon.
  There you will be rescued;
    there the LORD will redeem you
      from the power of your enemies.
11 Now many nations
  may gather against you;
    they say, "Let her be defiled,"
    or "Let our eyes look with desire
    at Zion."
12 But they don't know
  the plans of the LORD;
    they can't understand his scheme,
    namely, that he will bring them
    like grain to the threshing floor!
13 Arise and thresh, Daughter Zion,
  for I will make your horn out of iron;
    your hooves I will make out of bronze.

You will crush many peoples;
  you will dedicate their ill-gotten gains
    to the LORD,
  their wealth to the LORD
    of all the earth.

Call to arms; the future is secure

5 [k]Now muster your troops,
  Daughter Troop![l]
  They have laid siege against us;
    with a rod they will strike the cheek
    of the judge of Israel.
2 As for you, Bethlehem of Ephrathah,
  though you are the least significant
    of Judah's forces,
  one who is to be a ruler in Israel
    on my behalf will come out from you.
  His origin is from remote times,
    from ancient days.
3 Therefore, he will give them up
  until the time when
    she who is in labor gives birth.
  The rest of his kin will return
    to the people of Israel.
4 He will stand and shepherd his flock[m]
  in the strength of the LORD,
  in the majesty of the name
    of the LORD his God.
  They will dwell secure,
    because he will surely become great
    throughout the earth;
5 he will become one of peace.[n]
When Assyria invades our land
  and treads down our fortresses,
    then we will raise up against him
    seven shepherds and
    eight human princes.
6 They will shepherd the land of Assyria
  with the sword,
    the land of Nimrod
    with the drawn sword.
He will rescue us from Assyria
  when he invades our land
    and treads within our territory.
7 Then the few remaining in Jacob
  will be amid many peoples
    like dew from the LORD,
    like spring showers upon the grass,
  which does not hope for humans
    or wait for human ones.

[j]Or *tower of the flock*   [k]4:14 in Heb   [l]Heb uncertain   [m]Heb lacks *his flock*.   [n]Or *this will ensure peace.*

8 Then the few remaining in Jacob
  will be among the nations,
    amid many peoples,
  like a lion among the creatures
    of the forest,
  like a young lion among flocks
  of sheep, which when it passes by,
    tramples and tears to pieces
    with no one to deliver.
9 Your hand will be lifted over your foes;
  all your enemies will be cut off.

Doom for Israel's enemies

10 On that day—says the LORD—
  I will cut down your horses
    in your midst;
  I will destroy your chariots!
11 I will cut down the cities of your land;
  I will tear down your defenses!
12 I will demolish the sorceries you perform;
  you will have no more diviners!
13 I will cut down your images
  and your sacred pillars in your midst.
  You will no longer bow down
    to the works of your hands!
14 I will tear down your sacred poles[o]
    in your midst;
  I will destroy your cities!
15 I will exact vengeance in anger
    and in wrath
      on the nations that don't obey!

God's dispute with Israel

6 Hear what the LORD is saying:
  Arise, lay out the lawsuit
    before the mountains;
    let the hills hear your voice!
2 Hear, mountains, the lawsuit
  of the LORD!
    Hear, eternal foundations
    of the earth!
  The LORD has a lawsuit against his people;
    with Israel he will argue.
3 "My people, what did I ever do to you?
  How have I wearied you? Answer me!
4 I brought you up out of the land of Egypt;
  I redeemed you
    from the house of slavery.

I sent Moses, Aaron, and Miriam
  before you.
5 My people, remember what
  Moab's King Balak had planned,
  and how Balaam, Beor's son,
    answered him!
  Remember everything[p]
    from Shittim to Gilgal,
  that you might learn to recognize
    the righteous acts of the LORD!"

What does the LORD require?

6 With what should I approach the LORD
  and bow down before God on high?
  Should I come before him
  with entirely burned offerings,
    with year-old calves?
7 Will the LORD be pleased
  with thousands of rams,
  with many torrents of oil?
  Should I give my oldest child for my crime;
    the fruit of my body
    for the sin of my spirit?
8 He has told you, human one,
  what is good and
    what the LORD requires from you:
    to do justice, embrace faithful love,
      and walk humbly with your God.

Punishment is near

9 The voice of the LORD calls out to the city;
    wisdom appears
      when one fears your name.[q]
    Hear, tribe, and who appointed her![r]
10 Are the treasures of wickedness
    still in the house of wickedness,
    while the shorted basket[s] is denounced?[t]
11 Can I approve wicked scales
    and a bag of false weights
12 in a city[u] whose wealthy
    are full of violence
  and whose inhabitants speak falsehood
    with lying tongues in their mouths?
13 So I have made you sick by striking you!
  I have struck you because of your sins.
14 You devour, but you aren't satisfied;
  a gnawing emptiness is within you.
  You put something aside,
  but you don't keep it safe.

---

[o]Heb asherim   [p]Heb lacks everything.   [q]Heb uncertain   [r]Heb uncertain   [s]Or ephah, approximately twenty quarts of grain   [t]Heb uncertain   [u]Heb lacks in a city.

That which you do try to keep safe,
  I will give to the sword.
¹⁵ You sow, but you don't gather.
  You tread down olives,
    but you don't anoint with oil;
    you tread grapes, but don't drink wine.
¹⁶ Yet you^v have kept the policies of Omri,
  all the practices of the house of Ahab;
  you have followed their counsels.
  Therefore, I will make you
    a sign of destruction,
    your^w inhabitants an object of hissing!
  You must bear the reproach of my people.

The prophet laments

7 I'm doomed!
  I've become like one who,
    even after the summer fruit
    has been gathered,
    after the ripened fruits
    have been collected,
    has no cluster of grapes to eat,
    no ripe fig that I might desire.
² Faithful ones have perished
  from the land;
    there is no righteous one
    among humanity.
  All of them lie in wait for bloodshed;
    they hunt each other with nets.
³ Their hands are skilled at doing evil.
  Official and judge alike ask for a bribe;
    the powerful speak however they like;
    this is how they conspire.
⁴ The good among them are like a briar;
    those who do the right thing are
    like a thorny thicket.
    (A day for your lookouts!^x
    Your punishment has arrived.
    The confusion of the wicked^y is nearby.)
⁵ Don't rely on a friend;
    put no trust in a companion;
    guard the doors of your mouth
    from her who lies in your embrace.
⁶ Son disrespects father;
    a daughter rises up against her mother,
    a daughter-in-law against
    her mother-in-law;
    the enemies of a man
    are those of his own household.

⁷ But me! I will keep watch for the LORD;
  I will wait for the God of my salvation;
  my God will hear me.

Zion speaks

⁸ Do not rejoice^z over me, my enemy,
  because when I fall, I will rise;
    if I sit in darkness,
    the LORD is my light.
⁹ I must bear the raging of the LORD,
  for I have sinned against him,
    until he decides my case
    and provides justice for me.
  He will bring me out into the light;
    I will see
    by means of his righteousness.
¹⁰ Then my enemy will see;
    shame will cover her who said to me:
    "Where is the LORD your God?"
  My eyes will see her ruin;^a
    now she will become something
    to be trampled,
    like mud in the streets.

Micah responds to Zion

¹¹ A day for the building of your walls!
  On that day, the boundary
    will be distant.
¹² On that day, they will come to you
    from Assyria and the cities of Egypt,
    from Egypt to the River,
    from sea to sea,
    and from mountain to mountain.
¹³ And the earth will become desolate
    because of her inhabitants,
    because of the fruit of their actions.

Micah intercedes for the people

¹⁴ Shepherd your people with your staff,
    the sheep of your inheritance,
    those dwelling alone in a forest
    in the midst of Carmel.
  Let them graze in Bashan and Gilead,
    as a long time ago.

God agrees

¹⁵ As in the days when you came
    out of the land of Egypt,
    I will show Israel wonderful things.

^vOr *he* ^wOr *her* ^xHeb uncertain ^yHeb lacks *the wicked.* ^z*Rejoice* (feminine singular) ^aHeb lacks *ruin.*

The prophet continues

16 Nations will see and be ashamed
  of all their strength;
    they will cover their mouths;
    their ears will be deaf.
17 They will lick dust like the snake,
    like things that crawl on the ground.
  They will come trembling from their
    strongholds to the LORD our God;
    they will dread and fear you!
18 Who is a God like you,
    pardoning iniquity,
  overlooking the sin of the few
    remaining for his inheritance?
  He doesn't hold on to his anger forever;
    he delights in faithful love.
19 He will once again have compassion on us;
    he will tread down our iniquities.
  You will hurl all our sins
    into the depths of the sea.
20 You will provide faithfulness to Jacob,
    faithful love to Abraham,
  as you swore to our ancestors
    a long time ago.

NAHUM

The ministry of the prophet Nahum came at a time when Judah had hopes of gaining her independence from her Assyrian overlords. Nahum foresaw Assyria's ruin, and his prophecies celebrate the destruction of the Assyrian capital of Nineveh.

Nahum had other reasons to be confident of Judah's future. King Josiah had begun a series of religious reforms in 622 BCE that were designed to rid Judah of the influence of foreign cults and bring Israelite life more firmly under the rule of God's law. Thus, Nahum spoke to the people of Jerusalem when forces for positive change were at work for the people of Israel.

NAHUM THE MAN

The record of Nahum's prophecies contains little personal information about him. He is said to have received a vision, that is, the word of God received through revelation and inspiration. This vision was an oracle. The Hebrew word used here for an oracle means "a burden." Nahum received this oracle about Nineveh which he then announced to the people of Israel.

An oracle is the revealed word of God, and the term *burden* is also used by other prophets to refer to a word concerning punishment and disaster (see Jeremiah 23:33-40). This meaning may come from the belief that the message of a prophet is a burden placed by God on the prophet. The prophet is then to place the burden of God's condemnation on the nation or individual receiving the message.

Nahum probably delivered his prophecies in Jerusalem, perhaps even in the temple itself. Since all of the prophecies recorded in the book that bears his name concern the fall of Nineveh, he was probably active in his prophetic ministry shortly before 612 BCE. He was called from his home in the countryside to come to the capital city of Jerusalem to speak words of disaster for Nineveh, which were in turn words of hope for Israel.

NAHUM THE BOOK

Nahum is the only prophetic book in the Old Testament that is called a scroll (1:1). This perhaps indicates that Nahum's prophecies were collected and recorded on a scroll in their present form soon after he spoke them. Nahum's prophecies may have been used in temple services of prayer and worship.

The book of Nahum is included in the section of the Old Testament known as the Latter Prophets: Isaiah, Jeremiah, Ezekiel, and the twelve Minor Prophets (Hosea through Malachi). This part of the Old Testament was essentially complete by the end of the fifth century BCE and was recognized as scripture by 200 BCE.

NAHUM

1 An oracle about Nineveh: the scroll containing the vision of Nahum the Elkoshite.

Power of the creator

2 The LORD is a jealous and vengeful God;
  the LORD is vengeful
    and strong in wrath.
The LORD is vengeful against his foes;
  he rages against his enemies.
3 The LORD is very patient
  but great in power;
    the LORD punishes.
His way is in whirlwind and storm;
  clouds are the dust of his feet.
4 He can blast the sea and make it dry up;
  he can dry up all the rivers.
Bashan and Carmel wither;
  the bud of Lebanon withers.
5 The mountains quake because of him;
  the hills melt away.
The earth heaves before him—
  the world and all who dwell in it.
6 Who can stand before his indignation?
  Who can confront the heat of his fury?
His wrath pours out like fire;
  the rocks are shattered
    because of him.
7 The LORD is good,
  a haven in a day of distress.
He acknowledges those
  who take refuge in him.
8 With a rushing flood,
  he will utterly destroy her^a place
    and pursue his enemies into darkness.

A challenge to God's enemies

9 What are you plotting
  against the LORD?
He is one who can annihilate!
  Distress will not arise twice.
10 They are tangled up like thorns,
  like drunkards in their cups.
They are consumed like stubble
  that is entirely dried up.
11 From you^b goes out
  one who plots evil against the LORD—
    a worthless counselor!

Reassurance for God's people

12 The LORD proclaims:
Though once they were a healthy
  and numerous force,
    they have been cut off
      and have disappeared.
I have afflicted you;
  I won't afflict you further, Zion.^c
13 Now I will break off his yoke from you
  and tear off your chains.

---

^a _her_; likely Nineveh ^b _you_ (feminine singular); likely Nineveh ^c Heb lacks _Zion_.

ELKOSH

The expression "Nahum the Elkoshite" suggests that Elkosh was Nahum's birthplace. The location of Elkosh is not known with any certainty. The four most common possibilities are: (1) Al-Kush, a village about 25 mi. north of Mosul in present-day Iraq—an old Turkish tradition, based mainly on similarity of name and an apparent familiarity with Assyria reflected in the book; (2) Elcesi, a village in Galilee, a view promoted by Eusebius and Jerome; (3) Capernaum, on the northern shore of the Sea of Galilee, based on the proposal that "Capernaum" comes from Hebrew for "village of Nahum"; (4) A Judaean location near Beit Jibrin, southwest of Jerusalem; a view that dates as early as the mid 4th cent. CE. The fourth view appears to be the most viable option and enjoys widespread support.

Assyrian king's future doom

14 The LORD has commanded
　concerning you:
　　You will have no children
　　　to carry on your name.
　I will remove carved idol and cast
　　image from the house of your gods;
　I will make your grave,
　　for you are worthless.
15 d Look, on the mountains: the feet of a
　messenger who announces peace!
　　Celebrate your festivals, Judah!
　　Fulfill your solemn promises!
　The worthless one
　　will never again invade you;
　he has been completely cut off.

A city under attack

2 A scatterer has come up against you.
　Guard the ramparts, watch the road,
　　protect your groin,
　　　save your e strength!
2 The LORD will restore
　the pride of Jacob,
　　indeed, the pride of Israel,
　because ravagers have destroyed
　　them and spoiled their branches.
3 The shields of his warriors are red;
　his soldiers are dressed in crimson.
　The ironwork of the chariots
　　flashes like fire

on the day he has prepared;
　the horses quiver.
4 The chariots race wildly
　through the streets;
　they rush back and forth
　　through the squares.
They look like flaming torches;
　they dart like bolts of lightning.
5 He musters his officers;
　they stumble as they press forward.
They hurry to the city wall,
　and the portable shield is set up.
6 The gates of the rivers are opened;
　the palace melts.
7 It is decreed:f
　She is sent into exile, carried away,
　while her female servants moan
　　like doves, beating their breasts.
8 Nineveh has been like a pool of water.
　Such are its waters,g
　and others are fleeing.
　"Stop, stop!"—but no one
　　can turn them back.
9 Plunder silver! Plunder gold!
　There is no end to the supplies,
　an abundance of precious objects!
10 Destruction and devastation;
　the city is laid waste!
　The heart grows faint and knees buckle;
　there is anguish in every groin;
　all the faces grow pale.

---

d 2:1 in Heb　e Heb lacks *your.*　f Heb uncertain　g Heb uncertain

CHARIOT

　　Two- or four-wheeled horse-drawn vehicle, used in both civilian and military contexts, primarily to transport passengers. Domesticated donkeys and horses were used to pull carts or chariots as early as the 3rd millennium BCE. During the Iron Age chariots and horses determined military superiority. Although both Israel and the military powers that dominated them possessed chariots, the Neo-Assyrian and Neo-Babylonian empires excelled in chariotry. Armies adapted chariots to be swift, mobile archery platforms and troop transports. As armies began to rely on cavalries, chariots became a less efficient weapon because of the expense of building them and the difficulty of maneuvering them in battle against mounted troops. In nonmilitary contexts, royalty, governmental officials, and the wealthy employed chariots to travel to their destinations.

Cruel Nineveh will be destroyed

¹¹ Where is the lions' den,
  the meadow of the young lions,
    where lion, lioness, even lion cub go
    about with no one to terrify them?
¹² The lion has torn enough prey
    for his cubs and strangled enough
    for his lionesses;
  he has filled his lairs with prey,
    his dens with torn flesh.
¹³ Look! I am against you, proclaims
    the LORD of heavenly forces.
  I will burn your[h] chariots in smoke;
    the sword will devour
    your young lions;
  I will cut off your prey from the earth,
    the voice of your messengers
    will never again be heard!

3 Doom, city of bloodshed—all deceit,
    full of plunder: prey cannot get away.
² Cracking whip and rumbling wheel,
    galloping horse and careening chariot!
³ Charging cavalry, flashing sword,
    and glittering spear;
  countless slain, masses of corpses,
    endless dead bodies—they stumble
    over their dead bodies!
⁴ Because of the many whorings
  of the whore,
    the lovely graces
    of the mistress of sorceries,
    the one who sells nations
    by means of her whorings
    and peoples
    by means of her sorceries:
⁵ Look! I am against you, proclaims
    the LORD of heavenly forces.
  I will lift your skirts over your face;
  I will show nations your nakedness
    and kingdoms your dishonor.
⁶ I will throw disgusting things at you;
  I will treat you with contempt
    and make you a spectacle.
⁷ Then all who look at you
  will recoil from you and say,
    "Nineveh has been devastated!
  Who will lament for her?"
  Where could I possibly
    seek comforters for you?

⁸ Are you better than Thebes,
    situated by the Nile,
    waters surrounding her,
    whose fortress is sea
    and whose city wall is waters?
⁹ Cush[i] and Egypt constituted
  her strength, without limit;
    Put and the Libyans were her[j] help.
¹⁰ Yet even she was destined for exile;
    she went into captivity.
  Indeed, her infants were dashed
    to pieces at the head of every street.
    They cast lots for her officials;
    all of her powerful citizens
    were bound in chains.
¹¹ Yes, even you will become drunk;
    you will have to hide!
    Even you will have to seek refuge
    from the enemy!
¹² All your fortifications
  are fig trees with ripe fruit;
    when the trees are shaken, the fruit
    falls into the mouth of the eater.
¹³ Look, your people are women
  in your midst.
    The gates of your land have been flung
    wide open to your enemies.
    Fire consumes the bars of your gates.
¹⁴ Draw water for yourself
  to prepare for siege!
    Strengthen your fortifications!
    Tread the clay, trample the mortar,
    grab the brick mold!
¹⁵ Fire will consume you there;
    the sword will cut you down;
    like the locust it will consume you.
  Multiply like the locust;
    multiply like the grasshopper!
¹⁶ You boasted more traders
    than the heavens have stars.
    The locust sheds its skin
    and flies away.
¹⁷ Your guards are like grasshoppers,
    your marshals
    like swarms of cicadas
    that encamp on stone fences
    on a chilly day;
  when the sun rises, they take flight;
    no one knows where they have gone.

---

[h]Or *her* [i]Traditionally *Ethiopia* [j]LXX; MT *your*

¹⁸ Your shepherds have fallen asleep,
    king of Assyria!
  Your officials are lying down.
Your people are scattered
  across the mountains;
    there is no one to gather them.

¹⁹ There is no remedy for your injury;
    your wound is grievous.
  All who hear the news about you
    clap their hands over you.
  Who has not suffered
    from your continual cruelty?

HABAKKUK

The prophet Habakkuk is one of the Latter Prophets of the Old Testament. He lived during the last quarter of the seventh century BCE in Judah. His prophecies focus on how God, the righteous, and the wicked relate to one another. He concludes that God is just and all-powerful; therefore, the righteous may look forward to divine vindication and the wicked to divine punishment.

HABAKKUK THE MAN

The book of Habakkuk gives no personal information about him. The dates and circumstances of his prophetic ministry must be determined from references in the book. The prophet Habakkuk probably lived during the time of the end of the Assyrian Empire and delivered his prophecies around 625–612 BCE. The wicked whom the prophet Habakkuk condemns are probably the Assyrians.

Habakkuk is identified as a prophet, that is, as one who is called. He was called by God to receive an oracle, which was God's word to the people. This word concerns God's dealings with the righteous and with the wicked. Habakkuk may have been a member of a group of prophets who were part of the staff, so to speak, in the temple. It was Habakkuk's duty to receive the words that God gave him and then to pass on these oracles to the people.

HABAKKUK THE BOOK

The book of Habakkuk is a collection of different types of prophetic messages. Verses 1:2–2:5 are a dialogue between the prophet and God concerning divine justice. Verses 2:6-20 are a collection of announcements of woe against the wicked. Chapter 3 is a hymn of praise and confession of faith in God.

Habakkuk may have spoken his prophecies in the temple in Jerusalem, perhaps even during worship services in the temple. His prophecies (in particular the hymn in chapter 3) were likely used many times as part of the worship ritual.

HABAKKUK

1 The oracle that Habakkuk the prophet saw.

The prophet complains

² LORD, how long will I call for help
and you not listen?
I cry out to you, "Violence!"
but you don't deliver us.
³ Why do you show me injustice
and look at anguish
so that devastation and violence
are before me?
There is strife, and conflict abounds.
⁴ The Instruction is ineffective.
Justice does not endure
because the wicked
surround the righteous.
Justice becomes warped.

The LORD responds

⁵ Look among the nations and watch!
Be astonished and stare
because something is happening
in your days
that you wouldn't believe even if told.
⁶ I am about to rouse the Chaldeans,
that bitter and impetuous nation,
which travels throughout the earth
to possess dwelling places
it does not own.
⁷ The Chaldean is dreadful and fearful.
He makes his own justice and dignity.ᵃ
⁸ His horses are faster than leopards;
they are quicker than
wolves of the evening.
His horsemen charge forward;
his horsemen come from far away.
They fly in to devour, swiftly,
like an eagle.ᵇ
⁹ They come for violence,
the horde with all their faces
set toward the desert.ᶜ
He takes captives like sand.
¹⁰ He makes fun of kings;
rulers are ridiculous to him.
He laughs at every fortress,
then he piles up dirt and takes it.

¹¹ He passes through like the wind
and invades;
but he will be held guilty,
the one whose strength is his god.

The prophet questions the LORD

¹² LORD, aren't you ancient,
my God, my holy one?
Don't let us die.ᵈ
LORD, you put the Chaldean here
for judgment.
Rock, you established him as a rebuke.
¹³ Your eyes are too pure to look on evil;
you are unable to look at disaster.
Why would you look at the treacherous
or keep silent when the wicked
swallows one who is more righteous?
¹⁴ You made humans like the fish of the sea,
like creeping things
with no one to rule over them.
¹⁵ The Chaldean brings all of them up
with a fishhook.
He drags them away with a net;
he collects them in his fishing net,
then he rejoices and celebrates.
¹⁶ Therefore, he sacrifices to his net;
he burns incense to his fishing nets,
because due to them
his portion grows fat
and his food becomes luxurious.
¹⁷ Should he continue to empty his net
and continue to slay nations
without sparing them?

2 I will take my post;
I will position myself on the fortress.
I will keep watch to see
what the Lord says to me
and how heᵉ will respond
to my complaint.

The LORD responds

² Then the LORD answered me and said,
Write a vision,
and make it plain upon a tablet
so that a runner can read it.ᶠ
³ There is still a vision
for the appointed time;

ᵃOr *his justice and dignity come from him* ᵇOr *vulture* ᶜHeb uncertain ᵈHeb uncertain ᵉSyr *he*; MT *I*
ᶠOr *a reader can run with it*

it testifies to the end;
it does not deceive.[g]
If it delays, wait for it;
for it is surely coming; it will not be late.
[4] Some people's desires are truly audacious;[h]
they don't do the right thing.
But the righteous person
will live honestly.
[5] Moreover, wine betrays an arrogant man.
He doesn't rest.
He opens his jaws[i] like the grave;[j]
like death, he is never satisfied.
He gathers all nations to himself
and collects all peoples for himself.
[6] Won't everyone tell parables about him
or mocking poems concerning him?
They will say:
Doom to the one who multiplies
what doesn't belong to him
and who increases his own burden.
How long?
[7] Won't they suddenly rise up to bite you?
Those who frighten you will awaken;
you will become plunder for them.
[8] Since you yourself
have plundered many nations,
all the rest of the peoples
will plunder you
because of the human bloodshed
and the violence done to the earth,
to every village,
and to all its inhabitants.

[9] Doom to the one making evil gain
for his own house,
for putting his own nest up high,
for delivering himself
from the grasp of calamity.
[10] You plan shame for your own house,
cutting off many peoples
and sinning against your own life.
[11] A stone will cry out from a village wall,
and a tree branch will respond.
[12] Pity the one building a city
with bloodshed
and founding a village with injustice.
[13] Look, isn't this from the LORD
of heavenly forces?

Peoples grow weary from making just
enough fire;
nations become tired for nothing.[k]
[14] But the land will be full of the knowledge
of the LORD's glory,
just as water covers the sea.

[15] Doom to the one
who makes his companions drunk,
pouring out your wrath
in order to see them naked.[l]
[16] You have drunk your fill of dishonor
rather than glory.
So drink and stagger.[m]
The cup of the LORD's strong hand
will come around to you;
disgrace will engulf you.
[17] Because of the violence done to Lebanon,
he will overwhelm you;
the destruction of animals
will terrify you,
as will human bloodshed and violence
throughout the land, the villages,
and all their inhabitants.[n]

[18] Of what value is an idol,
when its potter carves it,
or a cast image that has been shaped?
It is a teacher of lies,
for the potter trusts the pottery,
though it is incapable of speaking.
[19] Doom to the one saying to the tree,
"Wake up!"
or "Get up" to the silent stone.
Does it teach?
Look, it is overlaid with gold and silver,
but there is no breath within it.
[20] But the LORD is in his holy temple.
Let all the earth be silent before him.

The LORD's victory

3 The prayer of Habakkuk the prophet,
according to Shigionoth:
[2] LORD, I have heard your reputation.
I have seen your work.
Over time, revive it.
Over time, make it known.
Though angry, remember compassion.

---

[g]Heb uncertain; antecedants to pronouns in 2:3-6 are uncertain. [h]Heb uncertain [i]Or *throat* [j]Heb *Sheol*
[k]Heb uncertain [l]Heb uncertain [m]DSS, LXX; MT *uncircumcised* [n]Heb uncertain

³ God comes from Teman
and the holy one
from the mountain of Paran.   *Selah*
His majesty covers the heavens
and his praise fills the earth.
⁴ His radiance is like the sunlight,
with rays flashing from his hand.
That is the hiding place of his power.
⁵ Pestilence walks in front of him.
Plague marches at his feet.
⁶ He stops and measures the earth.
He looks and sets out
against the nations.
The everlasting mountains collapse;
the eternal hills bow down;
the eternal paths belong to him.
⁷ I saw the tents of Cushan under duress.
The curtains of the land of Midian
were quaking.

⁸ Was the Lord raging
against the rivers?
Or was your anger directed
against the rivers?
Or was your fury directed
against the sea
when you rode on your horses
or rode your chariots to victory?
⁹ You raise up your empty bow,
uttering curses for the arrows.°   *Selah*
With rivers you split open the earth.
¹⁰ The mountains see you and writhe.
A flood of water rushes through.
The deep utters its voice;
it raises its hands aloft.ᵖ

¹¹ Sun and moon stand still
high above.
With the light, your arrows shoot,
your spear at the flash of lightning.
¹² In fury, you stride the earth;
in anger you tread the nations.
¹³ You go out to save your people.
For the salvation of your anointed
you smashed the head
of the house of wickedness,
laying bare the foundation
up to the neck.   *Selah*
¹⁴ You pierce the head of his warrior
with his own spear.
His warriors are driven off,
those who take delight
in oppressing us,�q
those who take pleasure
in secretly devouring the poor.
¹⁵ You make your horses
tread on the sea;
turbulent waters foam.

The prophet responds
¹⁶ I hear and my insides tremble.
My lips quiver at the sound.
Rottenness enters my bones.
I tremble while I stand,ʳ
while I wait for the day of distress
to come against the people
who attack us.
¹⁷ Though the fig tree doesn't bloom,
and there's no produce on the vine;
though the olive crop withers,
and the fields don't provide food;

°Heb uncertain   ᵖHeb uncertain   qOr *me*   ʳOr *I tremble beneath me.*

CUSHAN

The term *Cushan* occurs once in the psalm-like prayer of Habakkuk 3:7. Habakkuk describes an appearance of God that comes from the desert regions far to the south toward Judah. In v. 7 the term *Cushan* is paralleled with the term *Midian*. When terms appear in this parallel arrangement in Hebrew poetry, it means that they are similar or identical. Thus Cushan may be understood as a sub-tribal group of Midian, an area east of the Jordan River and associated with the wilderness wanderings after the exodus from Egypt.

though the sheep is cut off from the pen,
 and there is no cattle in the stalls;
¹⁸ I will rejoice in the LORD.
 I will rejoice in the God
 of my deliverance.

¹⁹ The LORD God is my strength.
 He will set my feet like the deer.
 He will let me walk upon the heights.^s

To the director, with stringed instruments

---

^sOr *my heights*

ZEPHANIAH

Zephaniah's prophetic ministry came during the reign of King Josiah of Judah (640–609 BCE). Josiah began a program of religious reform in 622 BCE in connection with his efforts to get out from under the influence of Assyria and to rid Judah of foreign gods (see 2 Kings 22–23). The worship of foreign gods in Judah was a symbol of the power of other nations over Judah and was a violation of the covenant on which Israel was founded. While repairs were being made in the temple a book of the law was found and brought to the king. Josiah based much of his reform on this book, which is now part of the book of Deuteronomy. Pagan cults were prohibited and worship services were limited to the temple in Jerusalem.

Josiah aimed to purify Israelite faith and stop the practice of combining worship of God with worship of foreign gods. The kings who came before Josiah, Manasseh (687–642 BCE) and Amon (642–640 BCE), had allowed pagan cults to flourish openly in Judah.

Zephaniah's prophecies probably came before the reforms of 622 BCE. His words may have encouraged Josiah in his reform efforts.

ZEPHANIAH THE MAN

Zephaniah was apparently a descendant of King Hezekiah of Judah (715–687 BCE). He lived in Jerusalem and probably associated with the upper classes in the city, those with power and wealth. Despite these connections, Zephaniah condemned the powerful officials and merchants in Israelite society who abused their positions and those who were indifferent to God. He declared that God would punish sinners, both in Israel and in foreign countries.

Beyond punishment, Zephaniah saw that God intended to renew the people of Israel and to draw them together as God's people once more.

ZEPHANIAH THE BOOK

Like other prophetic books, Zephaniah is a collection of prophetic messages that were spoken before they were written. Verses 1:2–2:3 are a prophetic message of doom that focuses on Judah and Jerusalem. Zephaniah 2:4-15 is a collection of oracles against foreign nations. Zephaniah 3:1-13 tells of the sins and coming punishment of Jerusalem. The conclusion, Zephaniah 3:14-20, is an announcement of salvation for the people of Israel.

ZEPHANIAH

1 The LORD's word that came to Zephaniah, Cushi's son, Gedaliah's grandson, Amariah's great-grandson, and Hezekiah's great-great-grandson in the days of Judah's King Josiah, Amon's son.

Judgment on the world and Judah

2 I will wipe out everything
   from the earth, says the LORD.
   3 I will destroy humanity
      and the beasts;
   I will destroy the birds in the sky
      and the fish in the sea.
   I will make the wicked
      into a heap of ruins;
   I will eliminate humanity
      from the earth, says the LORD.

4 I will stretch out my hand
   against Judah
      and against all the inhabitants
         of Jerusalem.
   I will eliminate what's left of Baal
      from this place
      and the names of the priests
         of foreign gods,[a]
   5 those bowing down to the
         forces of heaven on the rooftops,
      those swearing by the LORD along
         with those swearing by Milcom,
   6 those turning away from the LORD,
      those who don't seek the LORD
         and don't pursue him.

The day of the LORD

7 Hush before the LORD God,
   for the day of the LORD is near!
   The LORD has established a sacrifice;
      he has made holy those
         he has summoned.
8 On the day of the LORD's sacrifice,
   I will punish the princes, the king's sons,
      and all those wearing foreign clothes.
9 I will punish the one leaping
   on the threshold on that day,
      those filling the house of their master
         with violence and deceit.
10 On that day—says the LORD—
   an outcry will resound
      from the Fish Gate,
   wailing from the second quarter,
      a loud crash from the hills.
11 The ones who grind the grain[b] will wail;
   all the merchants will be silenced.
   I will eliminate all those
      weighing out silver.
12 At that time,
   I will search Jerusalem with lamps;
   I will punish the men growing fat
      on the sediment in their wine,
   those saying to themselves,
      The LORD won't do good or evil.

[a] Or the name of the priests of foreign gods along with the priests   [b] Or keeper of the mortar

---

ZEPHANIAH

1. Son of Maaseiah, a priest during the reign of Zedekiah, who sent Zephaniah to inquire of the prophet Jeremiah concerning the Babylonian crisis (Jer 21:1; 29:25-29; 37:3). After the destruction of Jerusalem, Zephaniah was put to death by the Babylonians (2 Kgs 25:18-21; Jer 52:24-27).

2. A Kohathite (1 Chron 6:36 [Heb. 6:21]).

3. A prophet in Jerusalem during the reign of Josiah king of Judah (Zeph 1:1), and a contemporary of Jeremiah.

4. Father of Josiah, a priest who returned from the Babylonian Exile (Zech 6:10, 14).

¹³ Their wealth will be looted
  and their houses destroyed.
They will rebuild houses,
  but not live in them;
they will plant vineyards,
  but not drink the wine.
¹⁴ The great day of the LORD is near;
  it is near and coming very quickly.
The sound of the day of the LORD
  is bitter.
  A warrior screams there.
¹⁵ That day is a day of fury,
  a day of distress and anxiety,
  a day of desolation and devastation,
  a day of darkness and gloominess,
  a day of clouds and deep darkness,
¹⁶ a day for blowing the trumpet
  and alarm against their invincible cities
  and against their high towers.
¹⁷ I will make humanity suffer;
  they will walk like the blind
  because they sinned against the LORD.
Their blood will be poured out like dust
  and their intestines like manure.
¹⁸ Moreover, their silver and their gold
  won't be able to deliver them
  on the day of the LORD's fury.
His jealousy will devour
  the entire land with fire;
  he will make an end,
  a truly horrible one,
  for all the inhabitants of the land.

2 Gather together and assemble yourselves,
  shameless nation,
² before the decision is made—
  the day vanishes like chaff^c—
  before the burning anger
  of the LORD comes against you,
  before the day of the LORD's anger
  comes against you.
³ Seek the LORD, all you humble
  of the land who practice his justice;
  seek righteousness;
  seek humility.
  Maybe you will be hidden
  on the day of the LORD's anger.

Oracles against foreign nations
⁴ Gaza will certainly be abandoned;
  and Ashkelon destroyed.

Ashdod will be driven out at noon;
  Ekron will be uprooted.
⁵ Doom, inhabitants of the seacoast,
  nation of Cretans.
The LORD's word is against you,
Canaan, land of the Philistines.
I will exterminate you,
  leaving no inhabitant.
⁶ The seacoast will become pastureland,
  with wells for shepherds
  and pens for the flocks.
⁷ The coast will belong to the
  survivors from the house of Judah;
  they will pasture beside the sea;^d
  in the houses of Ashkelon
    they will lie down in the evening.
The LORD their God will visit them
  and restore their possessions.

⁸ I have heard the taunting of Moab
  and the defamation
    of the Ammonites;
  they taunted my people
  and enlarged their borders.
⁹ Therefore, as I live—
  says the LORD of heavenly forces,
    the God of Israel—
  Moab will become like Sodom
  and the Ammonites like Gomorrah:
  a plot of weeds, salt pits,
  and devastation forever.
The few remaining from my people
  will plunder them;
  the rest of my nation will possess them.
¹⁰ This will happen on account of their pride,
  because they taunted and boasted
  over the people
  of the LORD of heavenly forces.
¹¹ The LORD will terrify them;
  he will make all the gods
  of the earth disappear.
  All the coastlands of the nations
    will bow down to the LORD,
    each one in its own place.

¹² Moreover, you too, Cushites,
  will be pierced by my sword.
¹³ He will stretch out his hand
  against the north
  and will cause Assyria to perish.

---

^cHeb uncertain   ^dOr *they will pasture by them.*

Let him make Nineveh a desolation,
  a desolate place like the wilderness.
¹⁴ Flocks will lie down in its midst,
  every living thing of the nation.
Moreover, the owl and the porcupine
  will spend the night on its columns.
A bird's call will resound from the window.
Desolation will be on the sill,
  for the cedar will be stripped bare.
¹⁵ This is the jubilant city,
  the one dwelling securely,
  the one saying in her heart,
    I, and no one else, will endure forever.
How she has become a desolation,
  a resting place for the wild animals.
All those who pass through her
  hiss and shake their fist.

Judgment against Jerusalem

3 Doom, obstinate one,
  the defiled one,
    the violent city.
² She listened to no voice;
  she accepted no discipline.
She didn't trust in the LORD,
  nor did she draw near to her God.
³ The princes in her midst are roaring lions.
  Her judges are wolves of the evening;
  they leave nothing for the morning.
⁴ Her prophets are reckless,
  men of treachery.
  Her priests pollute that which is holy;
  they do violence to the Instruction.
⁵ The LORD is righteous in her midst.
He does nothing unjust.
  Morning by morning he renders justice,

but the unrighteous one
  knows no shame.
⁶ I will cut off nations;
  their towers will be destroyed;
  I will devastate their streets.
  No one will pass through.
  Their cities will be laid waste.
  There will be no person,
    no inhabitant left.
⁷ I said, "Surely, she will fear me;
  she will take instruction
  so that her habitation won't be cut off^e
  because of everything I did to her."
However, they rose early
  to corrupt their deeds.
⁸ Therefore, wait for me, says the LORD,
  wait for the day
  when I rise up as a witness,^f
  when I decide to gather nations,
    to collect kingdoms,
  to pour out my indignation upon them,
    all the heat of my anger.
In the fire of my jealousy,
  all the earth will be devoured.

Restoration of the nations and Jerusalem

⁹ Then I will change the speech
  of the peoples into pure speech,
  that all of them will call on
    the name of the LORD
    and will serve him as one.^g
¹⁰ From beyond the rivers of Cush,
  my daughter, my dispersed ones,
  will bring me offerings.
¹¹ On that day, you won't be ashamed
  of all your deeds

^eHeb uncertain ^fLXX; MT *it* ^gOr *with one shoulder*

DAUGHTER ZION

A phrase that serves to personify Zion and, by extension, Jerusalem, in a particularly personal, tender, and—at times—vulnerable way. This term of endearment appears twenty-six times in the OT and on six occasions appears in parallel with its synonym "Daughter Jerusalem" (2 Kgs 19:21; Isa 37:22; Lam 2:13; Mic 4:8; Zeph 3:14; Zech 9:9). "Daughter Zion" appears most frequently in one of two formulations: in reference either to circumstances of real or impending distress or to redemption and a promising future.

with which you sinned against me;
  then I will remove from your midst
    those boasting with pride.
No longer will you be haughty
  on my holy mountain,
[12] but I will cause a humble and powerless
  people to remain in your midst;
    they will seek refuge
      in the name of the LORD.
[13] The few remaining from Israel
  won't commit injustice;
    they won't tell lies;
  a deceitful tongue
    won't be found on their lips.
  They will graze and lie down;
    no one will make them afraid.

[14] Rejoice, Daughter Zion! Shout, Israel!
  Rejoice and exult with all your heart,
    Daughter Jerusalem.
[15] The LORD has removed your judgment;
  he has turned away your enemy.
The LORD, the king of Israel,
  is in your midst;
    you will no longer fear evil.

[16] On that day,
  it will be said to Jerusalem:
    Don't fear, Zion.
    Don't let your hands fall.
[17] The LORD your God is in your midst—
  a warrior bringing victory.
He will create calm with his love;
  he will rejoice over you with singing.
[18] I will remove from you those worried
  about the appointed feasts.[h]
    They have been a burden for her,
      a reproach.
[19] Watch what I am about to do
  to all your oppressors at that time.
    I will deliver the lame;
    I will gather the outcast.
  I will change their shame into praise
    and fame throughout the earth.
[20] At that time, I will bring all of you back,
  at the time when I gather you.
    I will give you fame and praise
      among all the neighboring peoples
  when I restore your possessions and
    you can see them[i]—says the LORD.

HAGGAI

HISTORICAL BACKGROUND

Haggai's prophetic ministry came in 520 BCE when the people of Judah were struggling to recover from their long years of domination by Babylon. After Persia defeated Babylon in 539 BCE, King Cyrus of Persia gave permission for exiles to return to their homelands. He restored the worship of the various sects in the empire and allowed the returning Jewish exiles to rebuild the temple in Jerusalem.

In 538 BCE, some of the Jewish Babylonian exiles returned to Jerusalem, though many stayed behind and continued their lives in Babylon. The people who went back to Jerusalem found the city still in ruins from the siege of 587 BCE. The temple had been used to some extent during the intervening years but it was basically in ruins, too.

This split between civil authority and religious authority was new for Israel. In the past, the church and state had been one under the ultimate authority of God. The king had led the people on God's behalf. Now political and military power were no longer associated with religious power, because foreigners held the final civil authority.

In this situation it was especially important to restore the temple and maintain the religious structures, because this meant nothing less than the preservation and future of the people of Israel.

Cyrus died in 530 BCE and was succeeded by his son, Cambyses, who committed suicide in 522 BCE. Darius I then took the Persian throne and faced restlessness and rebellion in his vast empire. This may have seemed to Haggai to be a sign of the end of foreign rule over Judah. During the Babylonian Exile, the prophets Ezekiel and Second Isaiah had proclaimed that God would reestablish God's people in Judah and God's rule on the throne in Zion. With Zerubbabel, a descendant of David, already installed as governor, the time was right for Haggai to declare that God's house must be rebuilt in preparation for the coming of a new era.

HAGGAI THE MAN

The book of Haggai gives no personal information about him. He is simply called the prophet, one who is called. Jewish tradition states that he was known as a prophet in Babylon during the exile, so he may have been among those returning to Judah in the years 538–520 BCE. Along with the prophet Zechariah, he became the major force in Jerusalem behind the restoration of the temple. Serious reconstruction work was begun in 520 BCE, and the new temple was completed in 515 BCE.

Haggai combined the concerns of prophet and priest. His prophecy brings together the method and inspiration of the prophet and the institutional concerns of the priest. Under the circumstances of his day, the temple and the proper worship of God were the keys to renewal and regeneration for the Israelite people. The symbols and ritual of their faith had to be maintained as part of their identity as God's chosen people.

HAGGAI THE BOOK

The record of Haggai's prophecies is a collection of addresses that are dated from the sixth to the ninth months of 520 BCE. The collection also contains information about the results of Haggai's oracles. Haggai himself or an editor/scribe collected and organized the prophet's words.

The book of Haggai is the shortest of the three prophetic books (Haggai, Zechariah, and Malachi) that come from after the Babylonian Exile. The books of Ezra and Nehemiah also deal with this time in Israel's history.

HAGGAI

The challenge to rebuild

1 The LORD's word came through Haggai the prophet in the second year of King Darius, in the sixth month on the first day of the month, to Judah's governor Zerubbabel, Shealtiel's son, and to the high priest Joshua, Jehozadak's son:

² This is what the LORD
  of heavenly forces says:

These people say, "The time hasn't come,
  the time to rebuild the LORD's house."

³ Then the LORD's word came through Haggai the prophet:

⁴ Is it time for you to dwell
  in your own paneled houses
  while this house lies in ruins?

⁵ So now, this is what
  the LORD of heavenly forces says:
  Take your ways to heart.

⁶ You have sown much,
  but it has brought little.
You eat, but there's not enough to satisfy.
You drink, but not enough to get drunk.
There is clothing, but not enough
  to keep warm.
Anyone earning wages puts those
  wages into a bag with holes.

⁷ This is what the LORD
  of heavenly forces says:
  Take your ways to heart.

⁸ Go up to the highlands
  and bring back wood.
Rebuild the temple
  so that I may enjoy it

and that I may be honored,
  says the LORD.

⁹ You expect a surplus,
  but look how it shrinks.
You bring it home, and I blow it away,
  says the LORD of heavenly forces,
  because my house lies in ruins.
But all of you hurry to your own houses.

¹⁰ Therefore, the skies above you
  have withheld the dew,
  and the earth has withheld
  its produce because of you.

¹¹ I have called for drought on the earth,
  on the mountains, on the grain,
  on the wine, on the olive oil,
  on that which comes forth
  from the fertile ground,
  on humanity, on beasts,
  and upon everything that
  handles produce.

¹² Zerubbabel, Shealtiel's son, and the high priest Joshua, Jehozadak's son, along with all who remained among the people, listened to the voice of the LORD God and to the words of Haggai the prophet because the LORD their God sent him. Then the people feared the LORD.

¹³ Then Haggai, the LORD's messenger, gave the LORD's message to the people:
  I am with you, says the LORD.

¹⁴ The LORD moved the spirit of Judah's governor Zerubbabel, Shealtiel's son, and the spirit of the high priest Joshua, Jehozadak's son, and the spirit of all the rest of the

ZERUBBABEL

Zerubbabel was a Jewish governor of Judah in the early post-exilic period under Persian rule (beginning no later than 520 BCE) and a major leader in the reconstruction of Jewish life after exile. His name (common in Babylonia) implies that Zerubbabel was born in Babylon. He is a main character in the books of Haggai, Zechariah, Ezra, and Nehemiah.

Zerubbabel appears in Jesus' genealogies. Both Matthew (1:12-13) and Luke (3:27) record him as Shealtiel's son (albeit with a transliterated version of the name) but with different grandfathers (Jechoniah in Matthew; Neri in Luke).

people. Then they came and did work on the house of the LORD of heavenly forces, their God, ¹⁵ on the twenty-fourth day of the sixth month in the second year of Darius the king.

Encouraging the people

2 On the twenty-first day of the seventh month, the LORD's word came through Haggai the prophet: ²Say to Judah's governor Zerubbabel, Shealtiel's son, and to the chief priest Joshua, Jehozadak's son, and to the rest of the people:

³ Who among you is left who saw
this house in its former glory?
How does it look to you now?
Doesn't it appear as nothing to you?
⁴ So now, be strong, Zerubbabel,
says the LORD.
Be strong, High Priest Joshua,
Jehozadak's son,
and be strong, all you people of the land,
says the LORD.
Work, for I am with you,
says the LORD of heavenly forces.
⁵ As with our agreement
when you came out of Egypt,
my spirit stands in your midst.
Don't fear.
⁶ This is what the LORD
of heavenly forces says:
In just a little while,
I will make the heavens, the earth,
the sea, and the dry land quake.
⁷ I will make all the nations quake.
The wealth of all the nations will come.
I will fill this house with glory,
says the LORD of heavenly forces.
⁸ The silver and the gold belong to me,
says the LORD of heavenly forces.
⁹ This house will be more glorious
than its predecessor,
says the LORD of heavenly forces.
I will provide prosperity in this place,
says the LORD of heavenly forces.

Cleansing the work

¹⁰ On the twenty-fourth day of the ninth month in the second year of Darius, the LORD's word came to Haggai the prophet:

¹¹ This is what the LORD
of heavenly forces says:
Go ahead and ask the priests for a ruling:
¹² "If someone lifts holy meat
into the hem of one's garment
and that hem touches bread,
stew, wine, oil, or any kind of food,
will it be made holy?"
And the priests responded, "No."
¹³ Haggai said,
"If an unclean person touches any of
these things, will it become unclean?"
And the priests responded,
"It will be unclean."
¹⁴ Then Haggai responded:
Thus has this people and this nation
become to me, says the LORD,
and everything that they do
with their hands.
Whatever they offer is unclean.
¹⁵ So now, take it to heart
from this day forward.
Before stone was placed on stone
in the LORD's temple,
¹⁶ when one came to the granary
for twenty measures,
there were only ten;
and when one came to the wine vat
for fifty measures,
there were only twenty.
¹⁷ I struck you—
everything you do with your hands—
with blight and mildew and hail;
but you didn't return to me.ᵃ
¹⁸ So take it to heart from this day forward,
from the twenty-fourth day
of the ninth month.
Take it to heart from the day when
the foundation for the LORD's
temple was laid.
¹⁹ Is the seed yet in the granary—
or the vine, the fig tree,
or the pomegranate—
or has the olive tree not borne fruit?
From this day forward, I will bless you.

Royal expectations

²⁰ And the LORD's word came to Haggai a second time on the twenty-fourth of the month, saying:

ᵃ Or but you weren't with me.

²¹ Speak to Judah's governor Zerubbabel:
  I am about to make the heavens
    and the earth quake.
²² I will overthrow the thrones
    of the kingdoms;
  I will destroy the strength
    of the nations.ᵇ
  I will overthrow
    chariot and rider;
  horses and riders will fall.

Each one will fall
  by the sword of his companion.
²³ On that day,
    says the LORD of heavenly forces:
  I will take you,
    Zerubbabel, Shealtiel's son, my servant,
    says the LORD;
  I will make you like a signet ring
    because I have chosen you,
    says the LORD of heavenly forces.

ᵇOr of the kingdoms of the nations

ZECHARIAH

The prophets Zechariah and Haggai were both leaders in reconstruction of the temple in Jerusalem, which had been in ruins since 587 BCE. Zechariah's prophecies deal with the temple and its ritual. They are based on the traditions that name Zion and Jerusalem as the places God has chosen to dwell in the midst of the people. Zechariah says that the completion of the temple will be part of a new age of salvation for the chosen people in God's kingdom.

ZECHARIAH THE MAN

Though not all of Zechariah's family history is clear, he was probably, like Ezekiel, a prophet from a priestly family. He was born in exile in Babylon and came to Jerusalem sometime between 538 and 520 BCE.

Zechariah's prophecies show the influence of both priestly and prophetic concerns in his life. As a member of a priestly family, Zechariah would have been taught the precepts of the law, particularly those relating to the priestly duties of sacrifice and ritual. He would have learned how to judge and give opinions in cases involving questions of religious or ritual procedure.

The law and memories of the temple, its rituals of worship and sacrifice, were handed on to him through his family and the other priests and teachers in exile. The law and the temple were probably an important part of his life even though he lived far from Jerusalem.

Zechariah may have also listened to the prophetic preaching of Ezekiel and Second Isaiah, who were among the Jewish exiles in Babylon. Some of the prophecies of Zechariah and of Ezekiel express a similar concern for the temple, its rituals, and its maintenance.

Zechariah was also a visionary prophet who called his people to return to God in preparation for the coming of God's kingdom.

ZECHARIAH THE BOOK

The book of Zechariah is a collection of vision reports and prophetic oracles that may be divided into four sections:

(1) Zechariah 1:1-6 is an introduction.

(2) Zechariah 1:7–6:15 is a series of eight vision reports.

(3) Zechariah 7:1–8:23 is a collection of prophetic oracles concerning ethical living.

(4) Zechariah 9:1–14:21 is a collection of oracles condemning other nations and proclaiming God's plans for and actions in history.

This final section is probably from a time later than Zechariah's time, likely from the end of the fourth and beginning of the third centuries BCE. These later prophecies are from unknown prophets who could be called Zechariah's spiritual disciples. They elaborate on themes found in chapters 1–8 concerning the future of God's people and of the world.

The record of Zechariah's prophecies from chapters 1–8 probably existed as an independent collection until the record of chapters 9–14 was added in the editorial process which brought the book to its final form.

HISTORICAL BACKGROUND

The historical setting and circumstances for Zechariah's prophecy are the same as those of the prophet Haggai. Zechariah moved from Babylon into a discouraging situation in Jerusalem. The territory available to the Israelites had shrunk to an area around Jerusalem about twenty-five miles from north to south. The population was somewhere around 20,000, which was less than half of what it had been before 587 BCE.

Many exiles chose to stay in Babylon because, after three generations there, it was the only home they had known. Many of them were well established in business there as well. Those who did return faced many hardships. The city of Jerusalem was still in ruins. Farmers had endured a series of unsuccessful seasons that left many people destitute.

There was conflict among the people as well. Those who returned from exile saw themselves as the remnant of the true Israel in whom the hopes of the nation rested. Some of those who had stayed in Judah resented the newcomers and their claims to their ancestral land.

There was also conflict between the Israelites and the Samaritans, their neighbors in what had been the northern kingdom of Israel. The Samaritan aristocracy wanted to claim Judah as their territory. They may also have been among the group of people from the old territory of Israel whose offers to help with the rebuilding of the temple were rejected by the leaders in Jerusalem (see Ezra 4:1-3). This rejection increased hostilities between the people in Judah and those in Israel.

There were also religious differences to settle. The returning exiles were ready to rebuild the temple and claim the prophetic promises of restoration and renewal for God's people. The people who had stayed behind had, in many cases, either abandoned their faith in favor of pagan cults or had mixed worship of God with worship of idols.

In 538 BCE, the Persian king had promised the returnees help in rebuilding the temple, but this aid never materialized. Indeed, as the years went on and the throne of Persia changed hands, the authorization given to rebuild the temple was misplaced in the Persian archives. Added to this was the evidence that

Persian power over Judah gave no sign of weakening. The people began to wonder about the reality of the promises of restoration. They became preoccupied with their struggles to survive in a hostile situation, and their concern with the temple faded.

Into this discouraging situation the prophets Haggai and Zechariah stepped with their bold calls for the people of Israel to throw off their doubt and apathy and get to work doing God's will.

ZECHARIAH

The people change

1 In the eighth month in the second year of Darius, the LORD's word came to Zechariah the prophet, Berechiah's son and Iddo's grandson:

2 The LORD was terribly angry
with your ancestors.
3 But you must say to the people,
The LORD of heavenly forces proclaims:
Return to me,
says the LORD of heavenly forces,
and I will return to you,
says the LORD of heavenly forces.
4 Don't be like your ancestors to whom
the former prophets preached:
The LORD of heavenly forces proclaims:
Turn from your evil ways
and your evil deeds.
But they didn't listen;
they didn't draw near to me.
5 So where are your ancestors?
Do the prophets live forever?
6 In fact, didn't my words and laws,
which I gave to my servants,
the prophets,
pursue your ancestors?
And then the people changed their hearts,
and they said,
The LORD of heavenly forces
has treated us according to
what we have done,[a]
exactly as he planned.

First night vision

7 On the twenty-fourth day of the eleventh month (the month of Shebat[b]) in the second year of Darius, the LORD's word came to Zechariah the prophet, Berechiah's son and Iddo's grandson:
8 Tonight I looked and saw a man
riding on a red horse,
which was standing
among the myrtle trees in the valley;
and behind him were red, sorrel,
and white horses.
9 I said, "What are these, sir?"
The messenger speaking with me said,
"I will show you what they are."
10 The man standing
among the myrtles responded,
"These are the ones the LORD sent
to patrol the earth."
11 Then they responded
to the LORD's messenger,
who was standing among the myrtles,
"We have patrolled the earth.
The whole earth is peaceful and quiet."
12 Then the LORD's messenger,
who was speaking with me, said:
"LORD of heavenly forces,
how long will you withhold
compassion from Jerusalem
and the cities of Judah,
with whom you have been angry
these seventy years?"
13 The LORD responded to the messenger
who was speaking with me
with kind and compassionate words.
14 The messenger speaking with me
called out,
"This is what
the LORD of heavenly forces says:
I care passionately
about Jerusalem and Zion.

[a]Or *our ways and our actions* [b]January–February

¹⁵ And I am exceedingly angry
 with those carefree nations.
 Though I was somewhat angry,
  they added to the violence."
¹⁶ Therefore, this is what the LORD says:
 I have returned to Jerusalem
  with compassion.
 My house will be built in it,
 says the LORD of heavenly forces.
 Let a measuring line
  be stretched over Jerusalem.
¹⁷ "Call out again,
 The LORD of heavenly forces proclaims:
 My cities will again
  overflow with prosperity.
 The LORD will again
  show compassion to Zion
 and will again choose Jerusalem."

Second night vision

¹⁸ Then I looked up and saw four horns.
¹⁹ I said to the messenger speaking
  with me,
  "What are these?"
 He said to me,
  "These are the horns that scattered
  Judah, Israel, and Jerusalem."
²⁰ Then the LORD showed me
  four metalworkers.
²¹ I said,
  "What are they coming to do?"
 And he said,
  "These are the horns that scattered
  Judah so that no one could raise
  his head.
 The metalworkers have come to terrify
  them and to destroy the horns of the
  nations, those who were attacking
  the land of Judah with[d] their horns
  to scatter it."

Third night vision

2[c] Then I looked up and saw a man.
 In his hand was a measuring line.
² I said, "Where are you going?"
 He said to me,
 "To measure Jerusalem to see how
  wide and long it will be."

³ As I watched, the messenger speaking
 with me went ahead and another
 messenger came to meet him.
⁴ He said to him,
 "Run! Say to this young man:
 Jerusalem will be inhabited
  like open fields
  because of the throngs
  of people and cattle inside it.
⁵ But I will be a wall of fire around it,
 says the LORD,
 and I will be glorious inside it.
⁶ Look out; look out!
 Flee from the land of the north,
 says the LORD,
 for I will scatter you like the four winds
  of heaven, says the LORD.
⁷ Look out, Zion.
 Flee, you who dwell
 with Daughter Babylon!
⁸ The LORD of heavenly forces proclaims
 (after his glory sent me)[f]
 concerning the nations
  plundering you:
 Those who strike you
  strike the pupil of my eye.
⁹ But look, I am about to raise my hand
  against them;
 they will become prey
  to their own slaves,
 so you will know that the LORD of
  heavenly forces sent me.
¹⁰ Rejoice and be glad, Daughter Zion,
 because I am about to come
 and dwell among you,
 says the LORD.
¹¹ Many nations will be joined
 to the LORD on that day.
 They will become my people,
 and I will dwell among you
 so you will know that
  the LORD of heavenly forces
  sent me to you."
¹² The LORD will possess Judah as his
  inheritance upon the holy land;
 he will again choose Jerusalem.
¹³ Be silent, everyone, in the LORD's
  presence, because he has moved
  from his holy habitation!

[c]2:1 in Heb [d]Or *those lifting their horns toward Judah* [e]2:5 in Heb [f]Heb uncertain

Fourth night vision

3 Then the LORD showed me the high
priest Joshua, standing before the
messenger from the LORD,
    and the Adversary[g] was standing by
    his right side to accuse him.
² And the LORD said to the Adversary:
    "The LORD rebukes you, Adversary.
    The LORD, the one choosing Jerusalem,
    rebukes you.
    Is this one not a log
    snatched from the fire?"
³ Joshua was wearing filthy clothes
    and standing before the messenger.
⁴ He responded
    to those standing before him,
    "Take off his filthy clothes."
And he said to Joshua,
    "Look, I have removed your guilt
    from you.
    Put on priestly robes."
⁵ He[h] said, "Put a clean turban
    upon his head."
    So they put the clean turban
    upon his head,
    and they dressed him in garments
    while the LORD's messenger stood by.
⁶ Then the LORD's messenger
    admonished Joshua:
⁷ "The LORD of heavenly forces proclaims:
    If you will walk in my paths,
    if you will keep my charge,
    then you will lead my house
    and guard my courts,
    and I will allow you to walk
    among those standing here.
⁸ Now listen, High Priest Joshua,
    you and your companions
    sitting before you—
    for these men are a sign—
    look, I am about to bring
    my servant, Branch.
⁹ See this stone
    that I have put before Joshua.
    Upon one stone,
    there are seven facets.
    I am about to engrave
    an inscription on it,
    says the LORD of heavenly forces.

I will remove the guilt of that land
    in one day.
¹⁰ On that day,
    says the LORD of heavenly forces,
    everyone will invite their neighbors
    to sit beneath their vines
    and the fig trees."

Fifth night vision

4 The messenger speaking with me returned and woke me like one who awakens someone who is asleep.
² Then he said to me, "What do you see?"
    I said, "I see a lampstand
    made entirely of gold.
    It has a bowl on top.
    The bowl has seven lamps on top
    and seven metal pipes
    for those lamps.
³ It has two olive trees
    beside the lampstand,
    one to the right of its bowl
    and one to the left."
⁴ I responded to the messenger speaking
    with me,
    "What are these, sir?"
⁵ The messenger responded to me:
    "Don't you know what these are?"
    I said, "No, sir. I don't."
⁶ He answered me:
    "This is the LORD's word to Zerubbabel:
    Neither by power, nor by strength,
    but by my spirit,
    says the LORD of heavenly forces."
⁷ Who are you, great mountain?
    Before Zerubbabel
    you will become a plain.
    He will present the capstone
    to shouts of great gratitude.
⁸ The LORD's word came to me:
⁹ The hands of Zerubbabel laid the
    foundation of this house,
    and his hands will finish it
    so that you will know
    that the LORD of heavenly forces
    has sent me to you.
¹⁰ Those who despise a time
    of little things will rejoice

---

g Heb *hassatan*; cf Job 1:6   h Or I

when they see the plumb line[i]
  in Zerubbabel's hand.
These are the seven eyes of the LORD,
  surveying the entire earth.

[11] I responded to him,
  "What are these two olive trees
  on the right and left sides
  of the lampstand?"
[12] Then I responded a second time,
  "What are these two olive branches
  that empty out golden oil
  through the two gold pipes?"
[13] He said to me,
  "Don't you know what these are?"
  I said, "No, sir."
[14] He said,
  "These are the two anointed ones[j]
  standing beside the LORD
  of all the earth."

Sixth night vision

5 I looked up again and saw a flying scroll.
  [2] And he said to me, "What do you see?"
  I said, "I see a flying scroll, thirty feet long
  and fifteen feet wide."
[3] He said to me,
  "This is the curse
  going out across all the land.
  Anyone stealing will be purged
  according to what's on one side
  of the scroll,[k]
  and anyone swearing lies[l]
  will be purged according to
  what's on the other side.
[4] I sent it out,
  says the LORD of heavenly forces.
  It will come to the house of the thief
  and the one swearing lies
  in my name.
  It will lodge in their house and
  destroy the wood and stones
  of that house."

Seventh night vision

[5] Then the messenger speaking with me
came forward and said,
  "Look up and see what's approaching."
  [6] I said, "What's this?"

He said, "This is the basket[m]
  that is going out.
  This is how it appears[n]
  throughout the entire land."[o]
[7] Then a lead cover was lifted,
  showing a woman sitting
  in the middle of the basket.
[8] He said, "This is wickedness."
  He shoved her back into the basket,
  and he put the lead stone
  over its opening.
[9] I looked up again and saw two women
  going out.
  There was a wind in their wings;
  their wings were like
  the wings of a stork.
  They carried the basket
  between the earth and the sky.
[10] I said to the messenger
  speaking with me,
  "Where are they taking the basket?"
[11] He said to me,
  "To build a house for it
  in the land of Shinar.
  It will be firmly placed there
  on its base."

Eighth night vision

6 I looked up again
  and saw four chariots coming out
  from between two mountains;
  the mountains were made of bronze.
  [2] The first chariot had red horses,
  and the second chariot had black horses.
  [3] The third chariot had white horses,
  and the fourth chariot
  had horses that were heavily spotted.
[4] I responded and said to the messenger
  speaking with me,
  "What are these, sir?"
[5] The messenger answered and said to me,
  "These are the four winds of heaven
  that are going out
  after presenting themselves
  to the LORD of all the earth.
[6] The one with the black horses
  is going to the north country;
  the white ones are going to the west;[p]

---

[i]Or stone, tin [j]Or sons of oil [k]Heb lacks of the scroll. [l]Heb lacks lies. [m]Heb ephah, a basket measuring approximately twenty quarts [n]Or their eye [o]Heb uncertain [p]Or after them

and the spotted ones are going south."
⁷ Then the powerful ones approached,
   intent on going to patrol the earth.
He said, "Go! Patrol the earth!"
   So they patrolled the earth.
⁸ Then he called out and said to me,
   "Look, the ones going north
   have provided rest for my spirit
   in the north."

⁹ The LORD's word came to me:
¹⁰ Take silver and gold^q from the exiles
   who came from Babylon,
   from Heldai, from Tobijah,
   and from Jedaiah.
   As for you, go that same day to the
   house of Josiah son of Zephaniah.
¹¹ Take silver and gold and make a crown.^r
   Place it on the head of the
   high priest Joshua, Jehozadak's son.
¹² Say to him,
   "The LORD of heavenly forces proclaims:
   Here is a man.
   His name is Branch, and he will
   branch out from his place;
   he will build the LORD's temple.
¹³ He will build the LORD's temple.
   He will be majestic;
   he will sit and rule on his throne.
   There will be a priest on his throne,
   and the two of them
   will share a peaceable plan.
¹⁴ The crown will be a memorial
   in the LORD's temple
   for Helem, Tobijah, Jedaiah,
   and for Hen, Zephaniah's son.
¹⁵ People from far away will come
   and build the LORD's temple
   so you might know that
   the LORD of heavenly forces
   has sent me to you.
   It will happen if you truly obey
   the voice of the LORD your God."

Answering the Bethel delegation

7 In the fourth year of Darius the king, the LORD's word came to Zechariah on the fourth day of the ninth month, Kislev.^s

² The people of^t Bethel sent Sharezer and Regem-Melech,^u along with his men, to seek the LORD's favor, ³ saying to the priests who were in the house of the LORD of heavenly forces and to the prophets: "Should I weep in the fifth month and abstain as I have done for a number of years?"

⁴ Then the word of the LORD of heavenly forces came to me: ⁵ Say to all the land's people and to the priests: When you fasted and lamented in the fifth month and the seventh month for these past seventy years, did you fast for me? ⁶ When you ate and drank, weren't you the ones eating and drinking? ⁷ Weren't these the words that the LORD proclaimed through the former prophets when Jerusalem was dwelling quietly along with the surrounding cities, and when the arid southern plain and the western foothills were inhabited?

⁸ The LORD's word came to Zechariah:
⁹ The LORD of heavenly forces proclaims:
   Make just and faithful decisions; show kindness and compassion to each other! ¹⁰ Don't oppress the widow, the orphan, the stranger, and the poor; don't plan evil against each other! ¹¹ But they refused to pay attention. They turned a cold shoulder and stopped listening.

¹² They steeled their hearts against hearing the Instruction and the words that the LORD of heavenly forces sent by his spirit through the earlier prophets. As a result, the LORD of heavenly forces became enraged.

¹³ So just as he called and they didn't listen, when they called, I didn't listen, says the LORD of heavenly forces. ¹⁴ I scattered them throughout the nations whom they didn't know. The land was devastated behind them, with no one leaving or returning. They turned a delightful land into a wasteland.

8 The word from the LORD of heavenly forces came to me:^v

² The LORD of heavenly forces proclaims: I care passionately about Zion; I burn with passion for her. ³ The LORD proclaims:

^q Heb lacks *silver and gold*; cf 6:11.   ^r LXX; Heb *crowns*, so also 6:14   ^s November–December   ^t Heb lacks *the people of.*   ^u Heb uncertain   ^v Heb lacks *to me.*

I have returned to Zion; I will settle in Jerusalem. Jerusalem will be called the city of truth; the mountain of the LORD of heavenly forces will be the holy mountain.

⁴ The LORD of heavenly forces proclaims:

Old men and old women will again dwell in the plazas of Jerusalem. Each of them will have a staff in their hand because of their great age. ⁵The city will be full of boys and girls playing in its plazas.

⁶ The LORD of heavenly forces proclaims:

Even though it may seem to be a miracle for the few remaining among this people in these days, should it seem to be a miracle for me? says the LORD of heavenly forces.

⁷ The LORD of heavenly forces proclaims:

I'm about to deliver my people from the land of the east and the land of the west. ⁸I'll bring them back so they will dwell in Jerusalem. They will be my people, and I will be their God—in truth and in righteousness.

⁹ The LORD of heavenly forces proclaims:

Be strong, you who are now hearing these words from the mouths of the prophets spoken on the day when the foundations for the house of the LORD of heavenly forces were laid. ¹⁰Before this time, there were no wages for people or animals; there was no relief from distress about going out or coming in, because I set everyone against their own neighbor. ¹¹But now, unlike those earlier days, I'll be with the few remaining among this people, says the LORD of heavenly forces.

¹² The seed is healthy:

the vine will give its fruit.
The land will give its produce;
the heavens will give its dew.

FESTIVALS AND FASTS

Both festivals (feasts) and fasts were occasions for religious rites in response to events, whether favorable or unfavorable. While there were spontaneous times for celebration and grief, there were also set times for communal observances. Reconciliation Day falls into both categories in that it is termed a festival as well as a fast.

Pilgrimage festivals were times when men were to appear before God at the sanctuary with an offering (Exod 23:14-17; 34:18, 22-23; Deut 16:1-17). The first of the pilgrimage holidays is the "Festival of Unleavened Bread." The second is the "Harvest Festival" or "Festival of Weeks." The third is the "Gathering Festival" or "Festival of Booths" at the last harvest.

A second category of lists, commonly attributed to priestly sources, finds expression in Leviticus 23 and Numbers 28–29. The two provide fuller enumerations that also incorporate the three pilgrimage festivals of the shorter summaries; they also date most of the festivals to specific times. They use a system of numbered, not named, months, with the sequence beginning in the spring. Later traditions added other feasts, but the basic ones endured into NT times and beyond.

Two kinds of communal fasts are connected with specific dates. The first is Reconciliation Day, which became associated with fasting. The only other dated fasts figure in the book of Zechariah. Zechariah 7:3, 5; 8:19 mention a fast in the fifth month, the month in which Babylonians destroyed Jerusalem and the temple in 587 BCE (2 Kgs 25:8). Zechariah 8:19 makes reference to other fasts in the fourth, seventh, and tenth months.

I will give the remnant of
  this people all these things.
¹³ Just as you were a curse
  among the nations,
  house of Judah and house of Israel,
  so now I will deliver you;
    you will be a blessing.
  Don't fear, but be strong.
¹⁴ The LORD of heavenly forces proclaims:
Just as I planned evil against you when your ancestors angered me, says the LORD of heavenly forces, and did not relent, ¹⁵so now I have changed course and again plan to do good to Jerusalem and the house of Judah. Don't be afraid.

¹⁶ These are the things you should do: Speak the truth to each other; make truthful, just, and peaceable decisions within your gates. ¹⁷Don't plan evil for each other. Don't adore swearing falsely, for all of these are things that I hate, says the LORD.

¹⁸ The word of the LORD of heavenly forces
  came to me:
¹⁹ The LORD of heavenly forces proclaims:
The fasts of the fourth, fifth, seventh, and tenth months will become times of joy and gladness, pleasant feasts for the house of Judah. Love truth and peace!

²⁰ The LORD of heavenly forces proclaims:
Peoples will still come, the inhabitants of many cities. ²¹The inhabitants of one city will go to another saying, "Let's go and seek the favor of the LORD, and look for the LORD of heavenly forces. I'm going too." ²²Many peoples and mighty nations will come to seek the LORD of heavenly forces in Jerusalem and to seek the favor of the LORD.

²³ The LORD of heavenly forces proclaims:
In those days ten men from nations with entirely different languages will grab hold of a Judean's clothes and say, "Let's go with you, for we have heard that God is with you."

Fate of the nations

9 A pronouncement. The LORD's word is
  against the land of Hadrach,
  and Damascus is its resting place,
  for the city of Aram^w and all the tribes
  of Israel belong to the LORD.

² Hamath also borders on it.
Tyre and Sidon, indeed,
  each is exceedingly wise.
³ Tyre built a fortress for herself.
She piled up silver like dust
  and gold like mud in the streets,
⁴ but the LORD will take
  her possessions away
  and knock her wealth into the sea.
She will be devoured with fire.

⁵ Ashkelon will look and be afraid.
  Gaza will writhe in agony,
    and also Ekron,
      because her hope has dried up.
The king will perish from Gaza;
  Ashkelon won't be inhabited.
⁶ An illegitimate child will dwell in Ashdod;
  I will eliminate
  the pride of the Philistines.
⁷ I will remove bloody food from his mouth
  and pieces of unclean food
    from between his teeth.
He will be a survivor
  who belongs to our God.
  He will be like a chieftain in Judah;
  Ekron will be like a Jebusite.
⁸ I will encamp before my house as a guard
  against anyone departing or returning.
  A slave driver will no longer
    pass through against them,
    for I have seen you^x with my eyes.

Joy and protection
for Judah and Ephraim

⁹ Rejoice greatly, Daughter Zion.
  Sing aloud, Daughter Jerusalem.
Look, your king will come to you.
  He is righteous and victorious.
  He is humble and riding on an ass,
    on a colt, the offspring of a donkey.
¹⁰ He^y will cut off the chariot from Ephraim
    and the warhorse from Jerusalem.
The bow used in battle will be cut off;
  he will speak peace to the nations.
His rule will stretch from sea to sea,
  and from the river
    to the ends of the earth.
¹¹ Moreover,^z by the blood of your covenant,

---

^w Or *eyes of humanity*   ^x Heb lacks *you.*   ^y LXX; MT *I*   ^z Heb uncertain

I will release your prisoners
    from the waterless pit.
[12] Return to the stronghold,
    prisoners of hope.
    Moreover, declare today
      that I will return double to you.
[13] Indeed, I myself will bend Judah as a bow;
    I will fill it with Ephraim.
Zion, I will rouse your sons
    against your sons.
Greece, I will make you
    like a warrior's sword.
[14] The LORD will appear above them;
    his arrow will go forth like lightning.
The LORD God will blow the horn;
    he will march forth on the stormy
      winds of the south.
[15] The LORD of heavenly forces
    will protect them.
They will devour and subdue
    like sling stones.[a]
They will drink,
    mumbling like one having wine.
They will be filled like a bowl,
    like the corners of the altar.
[16] The LORD their God will deliver them
    on that day as the flock of his people;
    they will be the jewels
    in a crown dotting his land.

[a]Heb uncertain   [b]Heb lacks *of them.*

[17] What is his goodness,
    and what is his beauty?
Grain will make his young men flourish;
    so too wine his young women.

Fate of Judah and Ephraim

10 Ask the LORD for rain when it is time
    for the spring rain.
    The LORD is the one
      who makes the thunderstorms.
    He gives them rain showers.
    He gives vegetation in the field
      to each of them.[b]
[2] The household divine images
    speak idolatry, and diviners see lies.
They interpret dreams falsely
    and provide empty comfort.
Therefore, they wander like sheep,
    but they are oppressed
    because there is no shepherd.
[3] My anger burns hot
    against the shepherds;
    I will punish the goats.
The LORD of heavenly forces
    will take care of his splendor,
    the house of Judah.
He will make them
    like his majestic horse in battle.
[4] The cornerstone, the tent peg,

EPHRAIM

Ephraim is the second son of Joseph and the ancestor of the Israelite tribe that inhabited the central highlands of Palestine. The tribes of Ephraim and Manasseh thus traced their descent not to Jacob's sons but to grandsons of Jacob who were born to Joseph in Egypt (Gen 41:50-52; 46:20). The anomaly is resolved through the story of Jacob's blessing of the two sons (Gen 48:1-22), which has been rendered to explain, first, Ephraim and Manasseh's tribal status; second, Ephraim's ascendancy over Manasseh; and third, the legitimacy of the tribes' possession of Shechem.

Ephraim occupied the country situated in the southern region of the central highlands of Israel. The "Ephraim highlands" was a distinct geographical region in early Israel (e.g., Josh 17:15; Judg 3:27; 4:5; 1 Sam 1:1; 9:4; 2 Chron 13:4). The area is topographically diverse and receives sufficient rainfall, which, along with good soil, created the conditions for an agricultural economy based on herding, raising grains, and cultivating olives.

and the bow used in battle
will come from Judah.
Every oppressor
will leave Judah simultaneously.
5 Judah will be like warriors,
trampling through the muddy streets
during battle.
They will do battle
because the LORD is with them.
All the cavalry will be ashamed.
6 I will strengthen the house of Judah
and deliver the house of Joseph.
I will bring them back[c] because I have
compassion on them.
They will be as though
I hadn't rejected them,
for I am the LORD their God;
I will respond to them.

7 Ephraim will be like a warrior.
They will be as glad
as if they were drinking wine.
Their children will watch and be glad.
Their hearts will rejoice in the LORD.
8 I will whistle for them and gather them,
because I have ransomed them.
They will be as numerous
as they were previously.
9 Though I sowed them
among the peoples,
they will remember me
in the distant places
where they are living with
their children until they return.
10 I will bring them back
from the land of Egypt;
I will collect them from Assyria.
I will bring them to the land
of Gilead and Lebanon
until there is no more room for them.
11 They[d] will pass through the sea of distress
and strike the sea with waves.[e]
All the depths of the river will dry up.
The pride of Assyria
will be brought down;
the scepter of Egypt will turn away.
12 I will strengthen them in the LORD,
and they will walk in his name,
says the LORD.

11 Open your doors, Lebanon,
so that fire will devour your cedars.
2 Scream, cypress, for the cedar has fallen;
those majestic ones
have been devastated.
Scream, oaks of Bashan,
for the deep forest has fallen.
3 The sound of screaming
appears among the shepherds
because their majesty
has been devastated.
The sound of roaring can be heard
among the young lions
because the pride of the Jordan
has been devastated.

The shepherd's two staffs

4 This is what the LORD my God says:
Shepherd the flock
intended for slaughter.
5 Those who buy them will kill them,
but they will go unpunished.
Those who sell them will say,
"Blessed is the LORD,
for I have become rich."
And their own shepherds
won't spare them.
6 In fact, I will no longer spare
the inhabitants of the land,
says the LORD.
But look what I am about to bring
upon humanity,
upon each of them by their neighbor's
hand and by the hand of their king:
They will beat the land to pieces,
but I won't rescue anyone
from their hand.
7 So I shepherded the flock
intended for slaughter,
the afflicted of the flock.[f]
I took two staffs for myself.
I named one Delight;
the other I named Harmony.
I shepherded the flock.
8 I removed three shepherds in one month
when I grew impatient with them.
Moreover, they detested me.
9 Then I said, "I won't shepherd you.
Let the dying die,

---

[c]Or *I will restore them* [d]LXX; MT *he* [e]Heb uncertain [f]Heb uncertain

and let what is to be removed
be removed.
Let those who are left
devour the flesh of their neighbor."

[10] Then I took the staff Delight,
and I chopped it up
in order to break my covenant
that I had made with all the peoples.
[11] It was broken on that day.
As a result, the afflicted[g] of the flock
knew that it was the LORD's word.
[12] And I said to them,
"If it appears good to you,
give me my wages;
but if not, then stop."
So they weighed out my wages,
thirty shekels of silver.
[13] The LORD said to me,
"Put it in the treasury.[h]
They value me
at too magnificent a price."
So I took the thirty shekels[i] of silver
and put them in the treasury
of the LORD's house.

[14] Then I chopped up
my second staff Harmony,
to break the alliance
between Judah and Israel.
[15] Then the LORD said to me,
"Take for yourself again the equipment
of a foolish shepherd,
[16] because I am about to appoint
a shepherd in the land.
He won't tend to those
who have been removed.
He won't seek the young
or heal the broken.
He won't sustain the one standing.
Instead, he will devour the flesh
of the fat ones,
even tearing off their hooves.
[17] Doom, foolish shepherd
who forsakes the flock.
A sword will strike[j] his arm
and his right eye.
His arm will wither completely;
his right eye will become blind."

Jerusalem on that day

12 A pronouncement.
The LORD's word against Israel,
an utterance of the LORD
who stretches out the heavens,
who establishes the earth,
and who fashions the spirit
of humanity within it:
[2] I am about to make Jerusalem a cup
that will stagger
all the surrounding nations.
There will be a siege against Judah
and against Jerusalem.

[3] On that day I will make Jerusalem
into a heavy stone[k] for all the peoples.
All who carry it will hurt themselves;
nevertheless, the nations of the earth
will conspire against it.

[4] On that day, says the LORD, I will strike
every horse with confusion
and its rider with madness.
I will keep my eyes open
for the house of Judah;
I will strike blind
every horse of the peoples.
[5] The chieftains of Judah will say to
themselves, We are strong;
the inhabitants of Jerusalem will say,
The LORD their God of heavenly forces
is strong.[l]

[6] On that day I will place
the chieftains of Judah like a pot
on a wood fire and like a burning torch
among the bundles of grain.
They will devour all the surrounding
nations to the right and the left.
Jerusalem will dwell again in its place,
in Jerusalem.
[7] The LORD will first deliver
the tents of Judah
so that the splendor of David's house
and the splendor
of Jerusalem's inhabitants
won't overshadow Judah.

[8] On that day the LORD will protect
the inhabitants of Jerusalem.

---

[g]Cf Zech 11:7   [h]Syr; MT *to the potter*   [i]Heb lacks *shekels*.   [j]Heb lacks *will strike*.   [k]Heb uncertain   [l]Heb uncertain

Anyone among them who stumbles
    on that day will become like David,
    and David's house will become like God,
    like the LORD's messenger
        in front of them.

9 On that day I intend to destroy all the
    nations who come against Jerusalem,
10 but I will pour out a spirit of grace
    and mercy on David's house
    and on the inhabitants of Jerusalem.
They will look to me concerning
    the one whom they pierced;
    they will mourn over him
        like the mourning for an only child.
    They will mourn bitterly over him
    like the bitter mourning
        over the death of[m] an oldest child.

11 On that day, the mourning in Jerusalem
    will be as great
        as the mourning of Hadad-Rimmon
        in the Megiddo Valley.
12 The land will mourn,
    each of the clans by itself:
    the clan of David's house by themselves,
        and their women by themselves;
        the clan of Nathan's house
            by themselves,
        and their women by themselves;
13 the clan of Levi's house by themselves,
        and their women by themselves;
        and the Shimeites' clan by themselves,
        and their women by themselves;
14 and all the remaining clans,
    each clan by itself,
        and their women by themselves.

13 On that day, a fountain will open
    to cleanse[n] the sin and impurity of
    David's house and the inhabitants of
    Jerusalem.

2 On that day,
    says the LORD of heavenly forces,
    I will eliminate the names of the idols
        from the land;
    they will no longer be remembered.
Moreover, I will remove the prophets
    and the sinful spirit from the land.

3 If anyone again prophesies,
    then that person's
        birth father and mother will say,
    "You won't live, for you have told a lie
        in the name of the LORD."
That person's own birth father and
    mother will stab him
    when he prophesies.

4 On that day each of the prophets
    will be ashamed of his vision
    when he prophesies
    and won't put on a shaggy coat
        in order to deceive.
5 Each will say, "I'm not a prophet.
    I'm a man who works the ground,
        for the soil has been my occupation
        since I was young."
6 Someone will say to him,
    "What are these wounds
        between your hands?"
    And he will say, "These happened
        when I was hit in my friends' home."

7 Sword, arise against my shepherd,
    against the man responsible for[o]
        my community,
        says the LORD of heavenly forces!
    Strike the shepherd
        in order to scatter the flock!
    I will turn my hand
        against the little ones.
8 Throughout all the land, says the LORD,
    two-thirds will be cut off and die;
    but one-third will be left in it.
9 I will put the third part into the fire.
    I will refine them
        like one refines silver;
    I will test them like one tests gold.
They will call on my name,
    and I will respond to them.
I will say, "They are my people."
    And they will say,
    "The LORD is our God."

The day of the LORD

14 A day is coming
    that belongs to the LORD,
    when that which has been plundered
    from you will be divided among you.

[m]Heb lacks *the death of.*   [n]Heb lacks *to cleanse.*   [o]Heb lacks *responsible for.*

² I will gather all the nations to Jerusalem
  for the battle,
    the city will be captured,
    the houses will be plundered,
    and the women will be raped.
  Half of the city will go forth into exile,
    but what is left of the people
      won't be eliminated from the city.
³ The LORD will go out and fight
  against those nations
  as when he fights on a day of battle.
⁴ On that day he will stand upon
  the Mount of Olives,
  to the east of Jerusalem.
  The Mount of Olives will be split
    in half by a very large valley
    running from east to west.
  Half of the mountain will move north,
    and the other half will move south.
⁵ You will flee
  through the valley of my mountain,
    because the valley of the mountains
    will reach to Azal.
  You will flee just as you fled
    from the earthquake in the days
    of Judah's King Uzziah.
  The LORD my God will come,
    and all the holy ones with him.ᵖ
⁶ On that day, there will be no light.
  Splendid things will disappear.�q
⁷ On one day known to the LORD,
  there will be neither day nor night,
  but at evening time there will be light.
⁸ On that day, running water will flow
  out from Jerusalem,
  half of it to the Dead Seaʳ

and half of it to the Mediterranean;ˢ
  this will happen
  during the summer and the fall.
⁹ The LORD will become king
  over all the land.
  On that day the LORD will be one,
  and the LORD's name will be one.
¹⁰ The entire land will become
  like the desertᵗ
  from Geba to Rimmon,
  south of Jerusalem.
  Jerusalem will be high up
  and firmly in place
  from the Benjamin Gate
    to the place of the former gate,
    to the Corner Gate, and from the
    Hananel Tower to the king's wine vats.
¹¹ People will dwell in it;
  it will never again be destroyed.
  Jerusalem will dwell securely.
¹² This will be the plague with which the
    LORD will strike all the peoples who
    swarmed against Jerusalem:
  their flesh will rot,
    even while standing on their feet;
    their eyes will rot in their sockets;
  and their tongues will rot
    in their mouths.
¹³ On that day, a great panic brought on
  by the LORD will fall upon them;
  they will all grasp at the hand
    of their neighbors;
  neighbors will attack each other.
¹⁴ Even Judah will fight in Jerusalem.
  The wealth of all the surrounding
  nations will be collected:

ᵖOr you qHeb uncertain ʳOr eastern sea ˢOr western sea ᵗHeb Arabah

DEAD SEA

The Jordan River's terminal basin, a narrow, land-locked, salty lake lying below sea level near the southern end of the Syrian Rift Valley. Originally called the Salt Sea, the Hebrew expression "Dead Sea" does not occur in the Bible. Modern translations like the CEB render "Dead Sea" in place of more literal Hebrew wording. Post-exilic prophets knew it as the "eastern sea," distinguishing it from the "western sea," the Mediterranean (Joel 2:20).

The NT lacks any explicit reference to the Dead Sea.

gold, silver, and a great abundance of garments.

[15] This[u] plague will also affect the horses, mules, camels, donkeys, and any cattle in those camps during this plague.

[16] All those left from all the nations who attacked Jerusalem will go up annually to pay homage to the king, the LORD of heavenly forces, and to celebrate the Festival of Booths.

[17] Whoever among the families of the earth doesn't go up to Jerusalem to pay homage to the king, the LORD of heavenly forces, upon them no rain will fall.

[18] And if the family of Egypt doesn't go up and doesn't present itself, then no rain[v] will fall on them. There will[w] be a plague like the one with which the LORD struck the na-

tions that didn't go up to celebrate the Festival of Booths.

[19] This would be the sin of Egypt and the sin of all the nations who don't go up to celebrate the Festival of Booths.

[20] On that day, *Holy to the LORD* will be inscribed[x] on the bells of the horses, and the pots in the LORD's house will be holy[y] like the bowls before the altar.

[21] Every pot in Jerusalem and in Judah will be holy to the LORD of heavenly forces. All those who sacrifice will come. They will take some of the pots and cook with them. There will no longer be any merchants[z] in the house of the LORD of heavenly forces on that day.

---

[u]Heb lacks *this*, cf 14:12.   [v]Heb lacks *rain*.   [w]Or *will not*.   [x]Heb lacks *inscribed*.   [y]Heb lacks *holy*.   [z]Heb *Canaanite*

MALACHI

The book of Malachi comes from a time when many Jews in Judah were disillusioned with their fate and lax in their faith. The abundant life they had expected after the completion of the second temple in 515 BCE had not come about. In the face of this disappointment, many of them, including priests, turned away from their religious and moral obligations. The prophecies of Malachi confront the people with their shortcomings and call on them to renew their commitment to God.

HISTORICAL BACKGROUND

Malachi comes from the time between the completion of the second temple in 515 BCE and the arrival of Nehemiah in Jerusalem in 445 BCE. Judah was still a province of Persia under the administration of a Persian governor (the Israelite governor, Zerubbabel, was no longer in power). Despite the high hopes the returning exiles brought to Jerusalem from Babylon, even the rebuilding of the temple did not guarantee harmony and prosperity in Judah. There were still many difficulties to be faced and overcome if the people of Israel were to survive as a distinct community.

Both Malachi and Nehemiah tell of the problems that threatened to destroy the Jewish community. Though the temple ritual was maintained, there was a general feeling in the community that there was no real profit from practicing the faith. People neglected the Sabbath and made it a day for business. Businessmen cheated their employees and their customers. Jewish men divorced their Jewish wives to marry foreign women who had no loyalty to Jewish faith.

Economic conditions became so bad that some poor people had to sell themselves and their children into slavery to pay their debts and taxes. During the Babylonian Exile, agricultural production in Judah was greatly reduced. There were no large estates and much of the marginal lands went unused. The farms that remained in the highlands were small and not very productive. When the exiles returned to Judah, repairs were begun on the agricultural terraces and other farming installations, but progress was slow and crops were poor.

Proper tithes were not paid to the temple so that priests had to leave their positions in the temple to earn a living elsewhere. Priests even offered improper sacrifices in the temple and perverted the law in cases which were brought before them. With such corrupt leadership, public morality was breaking down.

MALACHI THE MAN

Little is known about the prophet whose words are recorded in the book of Malachi. The Hebrew word *Malachi* means "my messenger," and it probably is not the personal name of the prophet. Rather, the name of the book of Malachi may have been taken from Malachi 3:1 where "my messenger" is the one who prepares the way for the coming of God. The prophet may have identified himself as such a messenger or those who recorded his prophecies may have identified him in this way.

Most Old Testament prophetic books give few details about the life or background of the prophets, but the book of Malachi gives even less information than most. What we know about Malachi as a person must come from his prophetic announcements. Malachi was a man who believed that both morality and ritual were important in the life of God's people. He was able to grasp the depth and power of God's feelings for the people of Israel, from fierce anger and judgment to love and care. He was a man of courage who accepted God's call to be a messenger. This call put him at odds with the leaders of his community, his neighbors, and perhaps even his friends. Though he must have faced hostility at times, he fulfilled his duties as God's messenger.

MALACHI THE BOOK

The central message of Malachi's prophecies is that the people of Israel must remain faithful to their covenant with God. This means that they must obey the requirements of the covenant that are given to Israel in the Instruction from Moses. Only through obedience can they find life and peace.

Malachi's prophecies may be divided into the following sections:

(1) Introduction, 1:1

(2) Proclamation of God's Love for Israel, 1:2-5

(3) Condemnation of Priests, 1:6–2:9

(4) Condemnation of Divorce, 2:10-16

(5) Declaration That God Is Just, 2:17–3:5

(6) Declaration That Proper Tithes Must Be Paid, 3:6-12

(7) Announcement That God Will Reward the Faithful and Punish the Wicked, 3:13–4:3

(8) A Call for Obedience and a Promise of Guidance, 4:4-6

Each major section of the book uses a series of questions and answers. This style of prophecy has been called a "prophetic dispute" in which questions are asked (either from God's, the prophet's, or the people's point of view) and then answered by the prophet (see also Isaiah 40:12-17; Micah 2:6-11; Haggai 1:4-6; 2:3-5 for other examples of this form).

These disputes put questions before the people so that they will think about their situation from God's perspective and see themselves in a new light.

MALACHI

1 A pronouncement. The LORD's word to Israel through Malachi.[a]

Love of Jacob

² I have loved you, says the LORD;
  but you say, "How have you loved us?"
Wasn't Esau Jacob's brother?
          says the LORD.
I loved Jacob, ³but I rejected Esau.
I turned Esau's mountains into desolation,
  his inheritance into a wilderness
      for jackals.
⁴ Edom may say, "We are beaten down,
  but we will rebuild the ruins";
  but the LORD of heavenly forces
    proclaims:
They may build,
  but I will tear them down.
They will call themselves
  a wicked territory,
    the people against whom
    the LORD rages forever.
⁵ Your eyes will see it and you will say,

"May the LORD be great
  beyond the borders of Israel."

Honoring the LORD

⁶ A son honors a father,
  and a servant honors his master.
But if I'm a father, where is my honor?
  Or if I'm a master, where is my respect?
      says the LORD of heavenly forces
  to you priests who despise my name.
So you say,
  "How have we despised your name?"
⁷ By approaching my altar
  with polluted food.
But you say, "How have we polluted it[b]?"
  When you say,
    "The table of the LORD
    can be despised."
⁸ If you bring a blind animal to sacrifice,
  isn't that evil?
If you bring a lame or sick one,
  isn't that evil?
Would you bring it to your governor?

[a]Or *my messenger* [b]Gk; Heb *you*

LORD OF HEAVENLY FORCES

The divine epithet "LORD [God] of heavenly forces" occurs more than 200 times in the OT, making it the most common designation for God in the OT. By far, most of its occurrences are in the prophetic books, and it does not appear at all in Genesis through Joshua. A number of passages associate it directly with the Lord, noting "the LORD of heavenly forces is his name" (Isa 47:4; 48:2; 51:15; 54:5; Jer 10:16; 31:35; 50:34; 51:19; Amos 5:27). The variety of usages suggests a range of possible meanings.

The phrase is commonly associated with the concept of the Lord as commander of the armies (forces) of Israel, as in 1 Samuel 17:45. Tradition also associates the Lord with the covenant chest and the shrine at Shiloh (1 Sam 1:3, 11). Thus the Lord is referred to as "the LORD of heavenly forces, who sits enthroned on the winged heavenly creatures" (1 Sam 4:4; 2 Sam 6:2; Isa 37:16). The Lord could also be depicted as the head of the heavenly bodies, including sun, moon, and stars, and of the members of his heavenly forces, from which prophetic authority may be claimed (1 Kgs 22:19; Jer 23:18, 22; Amos 3:7). Also counted among the heavenly forces were the angels who gave the Lord praise (Ps 148:2).

Would he be pleased with it or accept you?
     says the LORD of heavenly forces.

⁹ So now ask God to be gracious to us.
After what you have done,
   will he accept you?
     says the LORD of heavenly forces.
¹⁰ Who among you will shut
   the doors of the temple^c
     so that you don't burn something
     on my altar in vain?
I take no delight in you,
     says the LORD of heavenly forces.
I won't accept a grain offering
   from your hand.

¹¹ Nevertheless, from sunrise to sunset,
   my name will be great
     among the nations.
Incense and a pure grain offering will be
   offered everywhere in my name,
     because my name is great
     among the nations,
     says the LORD of heavenly forces.
¹² But you make my name impure
   when you say,
   "The table of the LORD is polluted.
   Its fruit, its food, is despised."
¹³ But you say, "How tedious!"
   and you groan about it,
     says the LORD of heavenly forces.
You permit what is stolen, lame, or sick
   to be brought for a sacrifice,^d
     and you bring the grain offering.
Should I accept such from your hands?
         says the LORD.
¹⁴ I will curse the cheater
   who has a healthy^e male in his flock,
   but who promises and sacrifices
     to the LORD that which is corrupt.
I am truly a great king,
     says the LORD of heavenly forces,
   and my name is feared
     among the nations.

2 But now, this command is for you,
   priests:
² If you don't listen,
   or don't intend to glorify my name,
     says the LORD of heavenly forces,

then I will send a curse among you.
I will curse your blessings,
   and I mean really curse them,
     because none of you intend to do it.
³ I am about to denounce your offspring;
I will scatter feces on your faces,
   the feces of your festivals.
Then I will lift you up to me,^f
⁴ and you will know that I have sent
   this command to you
     so that my covenant with Levi
     can continue to exist,
     says the LORD of heavenly forces.
⁵ My covenant with him involved
   life and peace, which I gave him,
     and also fear so that he honored me.
     He was in awe of my name.
⁶ True Instruction was in his mouth;
   injustice wasn't found on his lips.
He walked with me in peace
   and did the right thing;
     he made many turn from iniquity.
⁷ The lips of the priest
   should guard knowledge;
     everyone^g should seek Instruction
     from his mouth,
     for he is the messenger from
     the LORD of heavenly forces.
⁸ But you have turned from the path.
   You have caused many to stumble
     by your instruction.
   You have corrupted
     the covenant of Levi,
     says the LORD of heavenly forces.
⁹ Moreover, I have made you despised
   and humiliated in the view
   of all the people,
     since none of you keep my ways
     or show respect for Instruction.

Judah's dishonesty

¹⁰ Isn't there one father for all of us,
   one God who created us?
Why does everyone cheat each other
   to make the covenant
   of our ancestors impure?
¹¹ Judah cheated—
   a detestable thing was done
   in Israel and Jerusalem.

---

^cHeb lacks *of the temple*.   ^dHeb lacks *for a sacrifice*.   ^eHeb lacks *healthy*.   ^fHeb uncertain; MT *He will carry you to it.*   ^gOr *they*

Judah made the LORD's
   holy place impure, which God loved,
   and married the daughter
     of a foreign god.
[12] May the LORD eliminate anyone
   who does so from the tents of Jacob,
   anyone awaking, testifying,[h]
   and making an offering
     to the LORD of heavenly forces.
[13] You should do this as well:
   cover the altar of the LORD
   with tears, weeping, and groaning
   because there is still no divine favor
     for your offering
     or favorable regard
     for anything from your hand.
[14] But you say, "Why?"
   Because the LORD testifies about you
   and the wife of your youth
     against whom you cheated.
   She is your partner,
     the wife of your covenant.
[15] Didn't he make her[i] the one[j]
  and the remnant of his spirit?[k]
   What is the one?
   The one seeking godly offspring.
   You should guard your own spirit.
     Don't cheat on the wife of your youth
[16] because he hates divorce,
     says the LORD God of Israel,
   and he also hates the one covering
   his garment with violence,[l]
     says the LORD of heavenly forces.
   Guard your own life, and don't cheat.

Purifying judgment
[17] You have made the LORD tired
   with your words.
   You say, "How have we made him tired?"
   When you say:
   "Anyone doing evil is good in the
     LORD's eyes,"
   or "He delights in those doing evil,"[m]
   or "Where is the God of justice?"

3 Look, I am sending my messenger
  who will clear the path before me;
   suddenly the LORD whom you are
   seeking will come to his temple.

The messenger of the covenant
   in whom you take delight is coming,
     says the LORD of heavenly forces.
[2] Who can endure the day of his coming?
   Who can withstand his appearance?
   He is like the refiner's fire
     or the cleaner's soap.
[3] He will sit as a refiner
   and a purifier of silver.
   He will purify the Levites
   and refine them like gold and silver.
   They will belong to the LORD,
     presenting a righteous offering.
[4] The offering of Judah and Jerusalem
  will be pleasing to the LORD
   as in ancient days
   and in former years.
[5] I will draw near to you for judgment.
  I will be quick to testify
   against the sorcerers,
   the adulterers, those swearing falsely,
   against those who cheat
   the day laborers out of their wages
   as well as oppress the widow
     and the orphan,
   and against those
   who brush aside the foreigner
   and do not revere me,
     says the LORD of heavenly forces.
[6] I am the LORD, and I do not change;
  and you, children of Jacob,
   have not perished.

Return to the LORD
[7] Ever since the time of your ancestors,
   you have deviated from my laws
   and have not kept them.
  Return to me
   and I will return to you,
     says the LORD of heavenly forces.
  But you say,
   "How should we return?"
[8] Should a person deceive God?
   Yet you deceive me.
  But you say,
   "How have we deceived you?"
  With your tenth-part gifts and offerings.
[9] You are being cursed with a curse,

[h]Heb uncertain [i]Heb lacks *her.* [j]Heb uncertain; *her* refers to the *wife* in Mal 2:14. [k]Heb uncertain
[l]Heb uncertain [m]Or *them*

and you, the entire nation,
are robbing me.
[10] Bring the whole tenth-part
to the storage house so there
might be food in my house.
Please test me in this,
       says the LORD of heavenly forces.
See whether I do not open all the
windows of the heavens for you
and empty out a blessing
until there is enough.[n]
[11] I will threaten the one
who wants to devour you
so that it doesn't spoil the fruit
of your fertile land,
and so that the vine doesn't abort
its fruit in your field,
       says the LORD of heavenly forces.
[12] All the nations
will consider you fortunate,
for you will be a desirable land,
       says the LORD of heavenly forces.

[13] You have spoken harshly about me,
              says the LORD;
but you say,
   "What have we spoken about you?"
[14] You said,
   "Serving God is useless.
What do we gain
by keeping his obligation
or by walking around as mourners
before the LORD of heavenly forces?
[15] So now we consider
the arrogant fortunate.

Moreover, those doing evil
are built up;
they test God and escape."

The scroll of remembrance
[16] Then those revering the LORD,
each and every one,
spoke among themselves.
The LORD paid attention
and listened to them.
Then a scroll of remembrance
was written before the LORD
about those revering the LORD,
the ones meditating on his name.
[17] On the day that I am preparing,
       says the LORD of heavenly forces,
they will be my special possession.
I will spare them just as parents
spare a child who serves them.
[18] You will again distinguish
between the righteous
and the wicked,
between those serving God
and those not serving him.

The day of the LORD
4 [o]Look, the day is coming,
   burning like an oven.
All the arrogant ones and
all those doing evil
will become straw.
The coming day will burn them,
       says the LORD of heavenly forces,
leaving them
neither root nor branch.

[n]Or *Until what is required is lacking.*   [o]3:19 in Heb

BOOK

In antiquity a book generally took the form of scrolls that had been attached end to end. In the Roman period, wooden tablets that had been laced together also came into use. Known as a codex, this proved to be easier to use than unrolling a long scroll. By the early Christian era, sheets of papyrus or leather parchment emerged to replace the wooden tablets. Such papyri and parchments were bound together, making a collection of writings much lighter and more manageable. Most of the early Christian documents that survive from the 2nd and 3rd centuries were constructed in the form of a codex.

² But the sun of righteousness will rise
on those revering my name;
healing will be in its wings
so that you will go forth and jump
about like calves in the stall.
³ You will crush the wicked;
they will be like dust
beneath the soles of your feet
on the day that I am preparing,
says the LORD of heavenly forces.
⁴ Remember the Instruction from Moses,
my servant,

to whom I gave Instruction
and rules for all Israel at Horeb.
⁵ Look, I am sending
Elijah the prophet to you,
before the great and terrifying
day of the LORD arrives.
⁶ Turn the hearts of the parents
to the children
and the hearts of the children
to their parents.
Otherwise, I will come and
strike the land with a curse.

NEW TESTAMENT

NEW TESTAMENT

MATTHEW

THEME

Jesus, the divine-human Christ, gathers together the people of the kingdom of heaven.

INTRODUCTION

The most important thing to know about the Gospel according to Matthew is that it is a book of good news about Jesus the Christ. A history book, a book of teachings, a manual for Christian disciples—Matthew is all of these. But above all it proclaims that Jesus is Emmanuel, God with us (1:23); that Jesus is the Christ, the Son of the living God (16:16). Matthew is the first of four such books in the New Testament. We call the first three of these Synoptic Gospels because they give us parallel accounts of the life and teachings of Jesus and his death and resurrection.

STRUCTURE

Matthew has been called "The Teacher's Gospel," because nowhere else are the teachings of Jesus so helpfully and memorably arranged for teachers. Chapters 3 through 25 are divided into five "books," calling to mind the first five books of the Old Testament, which are called the five books of Moses, and also the division of the book of Psalms into five books. The narrative from the Gospel of Mark forms the basic structure of the Gospel of Matthew (chapters 3–4, 8–9, 11–12, 14–17, 19–23). Into this arrangement Matthew introduces five blocks of teachings or sayings of Jesus that serve as commentaries on the unfolding story of Jesus' ministry (chapters 5–7, 10, 13, 18, and 24–25). In each book Matthew recounts a sequence of events in the ministry of Jesus, followed by a collection of sayings, parables, or instructions appropriate to what is happening in Jesus' own life, and in the life of the first-century church for which Matthew wrote.

The genealogy, preparations for Jesus' coming, and the stories of his birth and infancy introduce the Gospel (chapters 1–2). The passion narrative and the resurrection stories conclude the Gospel (chapters 27–28). All the material in the first two chapters is unique to Matthew. (Luke's genealogy differs from Matthew's in significant ways.) The passion-resurrection narrative almost certainly circulated among early Christians, first as oral tradition, and perhaps even before Mark's Gospel as a written document.

Against the skyline of Matthew's Gospel a number of towering peaks rise up from which the whole Gospel takes its special meaning. Five in particular provide the distinctive character of this work.

THE CHRIST

At the very beginning, Joseph learns from an angel who Jesus is and why he is coming: "you will call him Jesus, because he will save his people from their sins. . . . And they will call him, Emmanuel. (*Emmanuel* means, 'God with us')" (Matthew 1:21, 23).

Peter's confession, "You are the Christ" (Matthew 16:16), puts into words the faith out of which Matthew speaks. Christ is from the Greek *christos*, meaning God's "anointed" or "chosen one," sometimes called *messiah* from the Jewish word for the one who was to rule at the end of the age.

At the end of the episode where Peter fails to walk on the water and Jesus pulls him into the boat, Matthew writes, "Then those in the boat worshipped Jesus and said, 'You must be God's Son!'" (14:33). The word *worshipped* and the designation *God's Son* convey the understanding of Jesus as the Christ. The same word is used at the very end of the Gospel on the mountain in Galilee when the risen Christ appears to the disciples: "When they saw him, they worshipped him" (28:17). The identification of Jesus with the Christ of God puts the God's authority on everything that Jesus says and does in the Gospel.

FULFILLMENT OF PROPHECY

More than any of the other Gospel writers, Matthew establishes that Jesus fulfilled prophecy from the Hebrew Scriptures. Matthew brings more than sixty quotations from the Old Testament into his Gospel, anchoring the good news of the coming of the Christ deeply in Jewish hopes and expectations. Jesus says in the Sermon on the Mount that he has come to fulfill the Law and the Prophets, not to do away with them (5:17). A close study of the way Matthew uses scripture reveals that frequently he bends prophecy to accord with events happening to Jesus. And one strongly suspects that he sometimes bends the report of what takes place to make it agree with prophecy. One can see this most vividly in 21:2-7, the story of the triumphal entry into Jerusalem, where the story seems to have Jesus riding two beasts into the Holy City because the prophecy appears that way in Zechariah 9:9. But whatever distortions may lie in Matthew's use of the Old Testament, the effect of his vision is to weave an unbreakable strand around Jesus and his Jewish predecessors, biding them in faith, hope, and covenant.

APOCALYPTIC

The stress the evangelist puts on the apocalyptic Christ is unmistakable. Apocalyptic faith believes that at the heavenly-appointed time God will overthrow the ruler of this present age of darkness and evil and will establish the eternal rule of blessedness. Matthew identifies Jesus the Christ with this figure of Jewish apocalyptic expectation. For Matthew the center of history lies in the future day of judgment, of which Matthew gives us glimpses in Chapters 24–25. Throughout the Gospel are recurring references to darkness, where there will be weeping and grinding of teeth (e.g., 25:30). The heavy news of Matthew's Gospel to the church for which it was written is that the apocalypse is coming soon. Says John the Baptist, "The ax is already at the root of the trees" (3:10).

THE CHURCH

Matthew leaves no doubt that Jesus the risen Lord is present in the community of believers. At the heart of the chapter on church discipline and administration, Jesus promises, "For where two or three are gathered in my name, I'm there with them" (18:20). At his final appearance to his disciples Jesus promises to those who have taken up God's mission, "I myself will be with you every day until the end of this present age" (28:20). Matthew is the only one of the four evangelists to use the Greek word *ekklesia*, meaning church—a people who are called out of society to a life in covenant with one another and with their risen Lord. In fact, chapter 18 is a manual of discipline for church members living between the appearing of Christ and the day of judgment.

ETHICAL RIGHTEOUSNESS

The Gospel of Matthew might well be called a summons to righteousness. Among the Beatitudes is this blessing, "Happy are people who are hungry and thirsty for righteousness" (5:6), and the more explicit "Happy are people whose lives are harassed because they are righteous" (5:10). Later in the Sermon on the Mount Jesus commands, "desire first and foremost God's kingdom and God's righteousness" (6:33). Righteousness means being faithful to the covenant that binds the church (the new Israel) to God. It means being right with God. Throughout the Gospel, Matthew stresses the importance of ethical obedience to the higher righteousness (e.g., 5:20). It was to fulfill all righteousness that Jesus was baptized (3:15).

SETTING

We do not know who wrote (compiled) this Gospel. It is improbable that Matthew the tax collector and disciple could be the author, although his memories could be scattered through these pages. Of some things we may be sure. This Gospel is the work of a Jewish Christian, one who brings the faith and traditions of Israel to the new covenant. The book was prepared for a congregation (or congregations) of Jewish Christians in a time of controversy between the followers of Christ and the Jewish priestly establishment of the late first century. Sometime between the fall of Jerusalem to the Romans in 70 CE and the end of the century, Christians were expelled from the synagogues. The intensity of the conflict between Jesus and the scribes and Pharisees, apparent in this Gospel, may indeed reflect the conflict between Jews and Christians in the bitter years between 70 and 100. Apocalyptic fervor was strong in northern Palestine. This invites the speculation that Matthew may have been written for Christians in one or more of the cities of Syria. One cannot be more precise as to date and location. What is beyond any question is that this Gospel comes out of the crucible of the first century when the followers of Christ faced both persecution and apocalyptic judgment. The Gospel prepared for them has not ceased to be good news for us, their descendants in the crucible of the twenty-first century.

MATTHEW

Genealogy of Jesus

1 A record of the ancestors of Jesus Christ, son of David, son of Abraham:
2 Abraham was the father of Isaac.
Isaac was the father of Jacob.
Jacob was the father of Judah and his brothers.
3 Judah was the father of Perez and Zerah, whose mother was Tamar.
Perez was the father of Hezron.
Hezron was the father of Aram.
4 Aram was the father of Amminadab.
Amminadab was the father of Nahshon.
Nahshon was the father of Salmon.
5 Salmon was the father of Boaz, whose mother was Rahab.
Boaz was the father of Obed, whose mother was Ruth.
Obed was the father of Jesse.
6 Jesse was the father of David the king.
David was the father of Solomon, whose mother had been the wife of Uriah.
7 Solomon was the father of Rehoboam.
Rehoboam was the father of Abijah.
Abijah was the father of Asaph.
8 Asaph was the father of Jehoshaphat.
Jehoshaphat was the father of Joram.
Joram was the father of Uzziah.
9 Uzziah was the father of Jotham.
Jotham was the father of Ahaz.
Ahaz was the father of Hezekiah.
10 Hezekiah was the father of Manasseh.
Manasseh was the father of Amos.
Amos was the father of Josiah.
11 Josiah was the father of Jechoniah and his brothers.
This was at the time of the exile to Babylon.
12 After the exile to Babylon: Jechoniah was the father of Shealtiel.
Shealtiel was the father of Zerubbabel.
13 Zerubbabel was the father of Abiud.
Abiud was the father of Eliakim.
Eliakim was the father of Azor.
14 Azor was the father of Zadok.
Zadok was the father of Achim.
Achim was the father of Eliud.
15 Eliud was the father of Eleazar.
Eleazar was the father of Matthan.
Matthan was the father of Jacob.
16 Jacob was the father of Joseph, the husband of Mary—of whom Jesus was born, who is called the Christ.
17 So there were fourteen generations from Abraham to David, fourteen generations from David to the exile to Babylon, and fourteen generations from the exile to Babylon to the Christ.

SON OF DAVID

In the OT, the phrase "David's son" primarily refers to Solomon (2 Chron 1:1; 13:6; 35:3; Prov 1:1; cf. Eccl 1:1) or a descendant of David (2 Chron 11:18; cf. Matt 1:20; Luke 3:31). It later became a title referring to the royal Messiah, stemming from the promise God made to David regarding the eternal reign of David's offspring (2 Sam 7:12-16).

In the NT, the title "Son of David" is applied to Jesus, exclusively in Matthew, Mark, and Luke (e.g., Matt 1:1; 9:27; 12:23; 20:30-31; see also Luke 1:32; John 7:42; Rom 1:3). Jesus never explicitly claimed to be the Son of David, perhaps because the title had nationalistic and militaristic overtones. The title refers to Jesus' earthly life and is subordinated to other christological titles, especially "Christ" and "God's Son."

Birth of Jesus

[18]This is how the birth of Jesus Christ took place. When Mary his mother was engaged to Joseph, before they were married, she became pregnant by the Holy Spirit. [19]Joseph her husband was a righteous man. Because he didn't want to humiliate her, he decided to call off their engagement quietly. [20]As he was thinking about this, an angel from the Lord appeared to him in a dream and said, "Joseph son of David, don't be afraid to take Mary as your wife, because the child she carries was conceived by the Holy Spirit. [21]She will give birth to a son, and you will call him Jesus, because he will save his people from their sins." [22]Now all of this took place so that what the Lord had spoken through the prophet would be fulfilled:

[23] Look! A virgin will become pregnant
    and give birth to a son,
        And they will call him, Emmanuel.[a]
    (Emmanuel means "God with us.")

[24]When Joseph woke up, he did just as an angel from God commanded and took Mary as his wife. [25]But he didn't have sexual rela-

tions with her until she gave birth to a son. Joseph called him Jesus.

Coming of the magi

2 After Jesus was born in Bethlehem in the territory of Judea during the rule of King Herod, magi came from the east to Jerusalem. [2]They asked, "Where is the newborn king of the Jews? We've seen his star in the east, and we've come to honor him."

[3]When King Herod heard this, he was troubled, and everyone in Jerusalem was troubled with him. [4]He gathered all the chief priests and the legal experts and asked them where the Christ was to be born. [5]They said, "In Bethlehem of Judea, for this is what the prophet wrote:

[6] You, Bethlehem, land of Judah,
    by no means are you least
        among the rulers of Judah,
    because from you will come
        one who governs,
    who will shepherd my people Israel."[b]

[7]Then Herod secretly called for the magi and found out from them the time when the star had first appeared. [8]He sent them to Beth-

[a]Isa 7:14   [b]Mic 5:2; 2 Sam 5:2

JOSEPH (NT)

1. The NT Gospels refer to Joseph the husband of Mary 19 times by name. Eleven appear in Matthew (1:16, 18, 19, 20, 24, 25; 2:13, 14, 19, 21, 22), none in Mark (omitted from Mark 6:3, for example), six in Luke (1:27; 2:4, 16, 39; 3:23; 4:22), and two in John (1:45; 6:42). All but four references appear in the stories about Jesus' birth in Matthew and Luke. Of the four remaining references, one occurs in Luke's genealogy (3:23), and three come from the crowds in Nazareth and Capernaum (Luke 4:22 and John 6:42) and from Philip (John 1:45). These three instances identify Jesus as "Joseph's son."

2. Joseph is one of the brothers of Jesus, along with James, Simon, and Judas (Matt 13:55).

3. One of the women present at the crucifixion of Jesus is called "Mary the mother of James and Joseph" (Matt 27:56).

4. Joseph of Arimathea is known for his request to Pilate to bury Jesus' body. In Matthew 27:57-60 and John 19:38-42, Joseph's wealth had not prevented him from becoming a disciple of Jesus even though Jesus had spoken of the difficulties of the rich in entering God's kingdom (Matt 19:16-26).

lehem, saying, "Go and search carefully for the child. When you've found him, report to me so that I too may go and honor him." [9]When they heard the king, they went; and look, the star they had seen in the east went ahead of them until it stood over the place where the child was. [10]When they saw the star, they were filled with joy. [11]They entered the house and saw the child with Mary his mother. Falling to their knees, they honored him. Then they opened their treasure chests and presented him with gifts of gold, frankincense, and myrrh. [12]Because they were warned in a dream not to return to Herod, they went back to their own country by another route.

Escape to Egypt

[13]When the magi had departed, an angel from the Lord appeared to Joseph in a dream and said, "Get up. Take the child and his mother and escape to Egypt. Stay there until I tell you, for Herod will soon search for the child in order to kill him." [14]Joseph got up and, during the night, took the child and his mother to Egypt. [15]He stayed there until Herod died. This fulfilled what the Lord had spoken through the prophet: *I have called my son out of Egypt.*[c]

Murder of the Bethlehem children

[16]When Herod knew the magi had fooled him, he grew very angry. He sent soldiers to kill all the children in Bethlehem and in all the surrounding territory who were two years old and younger, according to the time that he had learned from the magi. [17]This fulfilled the word spoken through Jeremiah the prophet:

[c]Hos 11:1

STAR OF BETHLEHEM

Magi, Zoroastrian priests, observed this star as it rose (Matt 2:2b). To relate a newly rising star to a king in Israel, the star would have to appear in the constellation governing the "land of Israel" (Matt 2:20-21), that is, the Roman province of Syro-Palestine. This constellation was Aries, the springtime constellation, the first-created, celestial Lamb of God. Further, spring marked the onset of the dry season, offering the possibility of night travel.

In antiquity, only royalty and entire peoples had relevant horoscopes. Earth, sea, and sky formed a single social environment. Astronomers/astrologers could read the sky, understood to be analogous to reading books. Their readings announced what was occurring among people in the regions over which the celestial entities had their impact.

For modern astronomers and their computer simulations, this star was either a nova or a conjunction of planets (usually Jupiter, Saturn, and Mars in 6 BCE) or a comet (5 BCE). The magi in the story followed a star that moved and stopped and moved (acting like the column and cloud in Num 9:17). Such motion fits comets and planets when hidden for a time behind the moon or sun. Comets often were interpreted to mean political disturbance, notably for kings and people in the regions over which they appeared. The appearance of a comet over Judea would mean trouble or regime change for the local king, in this case Herod (Matt 2:3). The most famous comet of the period, much celebrated and depicted on countless Roman coins, was the star of Julius Caesar that announced that the recently deceased Caesar had become a god, and his son Augustus, a son of a god.

¹⁸*A voice was heard in Ramah,*
weeping and much grieving.
Rachel weeping for her children,
and she did not want to be comforted,
because they were no more.^d

Return from Egypt

¹⁹After King Herod died, an angel from the Lord appeared in a dream to Joseph in Egypt. ²⁰"Get up," the angel said, "and take the child and his mother and go to the land of Israel. Those who were trying to kill the child are dead." ²¹Joseph got up, took the child and his mother, and went to the land of Israel. ²²But when he heard that Archelaus ruled over Judea in place of his father Herod, Joseph was afraid to go there. Having been warned in a dream, he went to the area of Galilee. ²³He settled in a city called Nazareth so that what was spoken through the prophets might be fulfilled: He will be called a Nazarene.

Ministry of John the Baptist

3 In those days John the Baptist appeared in the desert of Judea announcing, ²"Change your hearts and lives! Here comes the kingdom of heaven!" ³He was the one of whom Isaiah the prophet spoke when he said:

The voice of one shouting in the wilderness,
   "Prepare the way for the Lord;
   make his paths straight."^e

⁴John wore clothes made of camel's hair, with a leather belt around his waist. He ate locusts and wild honey.

⁵People from Jerusalem, throughout Judea, and all around the Jordan River came to him. ⁶As they confessed their sins, he baptized them in the Jordan River. ⁷Many Pharisees and Sadducees came to be baptized by John. He said to them, "You children of snakes! Who warned you to escape from the angry judgment that is coming soon? ⁸Produce fruit that shows you have changed your hearts and lives. ⁹And don't even think about saying to yourselves, Abraham is our father. I tell you that God is able to raise up Abraham's children from these stones. ¹⁰The ax is already at the root of the trees. Therefore, every tree that doesn't produce good fruit will be chopped down and tossed into the fire. ¹¹I baptize with water those of you who have changed your hearts and lives. The one who is coming after me is stronger than I am. I'm not worthy to carry his sandals. He will baptize you with the Holy Spirit and with fire. ¹²The shovel he uses to sift the wheat from the husks is in his hands. He will clean out his threshing area and bring the wheat into his barn. But he will burn the husks with a fire that can't be put out."

Baptism of Jesus

¹³At that time Jesus came from Galilee to the Jordan River so that John would baptize him. ¹⁴John tried to stop him and

^dJer 31:15   ^eIsa 40:3

JORDAN RIVER

The Jordan River rises at the foot of Mount Hermon, the highest point in the southern Levant. The river's headwaters flow through the Huleh Valley and the Galilee Sea before eventually emptying into the Dead Sea. The Jordan is somewhat unique in Palestine, as it is one of relatively few perennially flowing rivers. The Jordan formed a significant barrier to travel and commerce in biblical times, was a boundary of several Israelite tribes during the Iron Age (and of Judea in later periods), and remains a political boundary today. Because it served as a boundary in ancient Israel, the river evokes images of entering into the promised land.

said, "I need to be baptized by you, yet you come to me?"

¹⁵Jesus answered, "Allow me to be baptized now. This is necessary to fulfill all righteousness."

So John agreed to baptize Jesus. ¹⁶When Jesus was baptized, he immediately came up out of the water. Heaven was opened to him, and he saw the Spirit of God coming down like a dove and resting on him. ¹⁷A voice from heaven said, "This is my Son whom I dearly love; I find happiness in him."

Temptation of Jesus

4 Then the Spirit led Jesus up into the wilderness so that the devil might tempt him. ²After Jesus had fasted for forty days and forty nights, he was starving. ³The tempter came to him and said, "Since you are God's Son, command these stones to become bread."

⁴Jesus replied, "It's written, *People won't live only by bread, but by every word spoken by God.*"ᶠ

⁵After that the devil brought him into the holy city and stood him at the highest point of the temple. He said to him, ⁶"Since you are God's Son, throw yourself down; for it is written, *I will command my angels concerning you, and they will take you up in their hands so that you won't hit your foot on a stone.*"ᵍ

⁷Jesus replied, "Again it's written, *Don't test the Lord your God.*"ʰ

⁸Then the devil brought him to a very high mountain and showed him all the kingdoms of the world and their glory. ⁹He said, "I'll give you all these if you bow down and worship me."

¹⁰Jesus responded, "Go away, Satan, because it's written, *You will worship the Lord your God and serve only him.*"ⁱ ¹¹The devil left him, and angels came and took care of him.

Move to Galilee

¹²Now when Jesus heard that John was arrested, he went to Galilee. ¹³He left Nazareth and settled in Capernaum, which lies alongside the sea in the area of Zebulun and Naphtali. ¹⁴This fulfilled what Isaiah the prophet said:

¹⁵ *Land of Zebulun and land of Naphtali,*
    alongside the sea, across the Jordan,
    Galilee of the Gentiles,
¹⁶ *the people who lived in the dark*
    have seen a great light,
    and a light has come upon those
    who lived in the region
    *and in shadow of death.*ʲ

¹⁷From that time Jesus began to announce, "Change your hearts and lives! Here comes the kingdom of heaven!"

Calling of the first disciples

¹⁸As Jesus walked alongside the Galilee Sea, he saw two brothers, Simon, who is called Peter, and Andrew, throwing fishing nets into the sea, because they were fishermen. ¹⁹"Come, follow me," he said, "and I'll show you how to fish for people." ²⁰Right away, they left their nets and followed him. ²¹Continuing on, he saw another set of brothers, James the son of Zebedee and his brother John. They were in a boat with Zebedee their father repairing their nets. Jesus called them and ²²immediately they left the boat and their father and followed him.

ᶠDeut 8:3 ᵍPs 91:11-12 ʰDeut 6:16 ⁱDeut 6:13 ʲIsa 9:1-2

SYRIA

Syria in biblical times was roughly equivalent to the present-day state of Syria, covering an area from the northeastern Mediterranean coast and the nearby mountains as far eastward as the Euphrates River. Many different states and civilizations existed in this region during biblical times.

Ministry to the crowds

[23]Jesus traveled throughout Galilee, teaching in their synagogues. He announced the good news of the kingdom and healed every disease and sickness among the people. [24]News about him spread throughout Syria. People brought to him all those who had various kinds of diseases, those in pain, those possessed by demons, those with epilepsy, and those who were paralyzed, and he healed them. [25]Large crowds followed him from Galilee, the Decapolis, Jerusalem, Judea, and from the areas beyond the Jordan River. [1]Now when Jesus saw the crowds, he went up a mountain. He sat down and his disciples came to him. [2]He taught them, saying:

Happy people

[3]"Happy are people who are hopeless, because the kingdom of heaven is theirs.

[4]"Happy are people who grieve, because they will be made glad.

[5]"Happy are people who are humble, because they will inherit the earth.

[6]"Happy are people who are hungry and thirsty for righteousness, because they will be fed until they are full.

[7]"Happy are people who show mercy, because they will receive mercy.

[8]"Happy are people who have pure hearts, because they will see God.

[9]"Happy are people who make peace, because they will be called God's children.

[10]"Happy are people whose lives are harassed because they are righteous, because the kingdom of heaven is theirs.

[11]"Happy are you when people insult you and harass you and speak all kinds of bad and false things about you, all because of me. [12]Be full of joy and be glad, because you have a great reward in heaven. In the same way, people harassed the prophets who came before you.

Salt and light

[13]"You are the salt of the earth. But if salt loses its saltiness, how will it become salty again? It's good for nothing except to be thrown away and trampled under people's feet. [14]You are the light of the world. A city on top of a hill can't be hidden. [15]Neither do people light a lamp and put it under a basket. Instead, they put it on top of a lampstand, and it shines on all who are in the house. [16]In the same way, let your light shine before people, so they can see the good things you do and praise your Father who is in heaven.

Jesus and the Law

[17]"Don't even begin to think that I have come to do away with the Law and the Prophets. I haven't come to do away with them but to fulfill them. [18]I say to you very seriously that as long as heaven and earth exist, neither the smallest letter nor even the smallest stroke of a pen will be erased from the Law until everything there becomes a reality. [19]Therefore, whoever ignores one of the least of these commands and teaches others to do the same will be called the lowest in the kingdom of heaven. But whoever keeps these commands and teaches people to keep them will be called great in the kingdom of heaven. [20]I say to you that unless your righteousness is greater than the righteousness of the legal experts and the Pharisees, you will never enter the kingdom of heaven.

ZEBEDEE

The name means "gift of the Lord." Zebedee was the father of two core members of the Twelve, James and John. He is mentioned solely in the Gospels and in relation to these two sons (Matt 4:21; 10:2; 20:20; 26:37; 27:56; Mark 1:19-20; 3:17; 10:35; Luke 5:10; John 21:2). He was a fisherman from the Capernaum area (Matt 4:12-22) with a boat (owned or leased) and hired hands (Mark 1:20).

Law of murder

[21]"You have heard that it was said to those who lived long ago, *Don't commit murder*,[k] and all who commit murder will be in danger of judgment. [22]But I say to you that everyone who is angry with their brother or sister will be in danger of judgment. If they say to their brother or sister, 'You idiot,' they will be in danger of being condemned by the governing council. And if they say, 'You fool,' they will be in danger of fiery hell. [23]Therefore, if you bring your gift to the altar and there remember that your brother or sister has something against you, [24]leave your gift at the altar and go. First make things right with your brother or sister and then come back and offer your gift. [25]Be sure to make friends quickly with your opponents while you are with them on the way to court. Otherwise, they will haul you before the judge, the judge will turn you over to the officer of the court, and you will be thrown into prison. [26]I say to you in all seriousness that you won't get out of there until you've paid the very last penny.

Law of adultery

[27]"You have heard that it was said, *Don't commit adultery*.[l] [28]But I say to you that every man who looks at a woman lustfully has already committed adultery in his heart. [29]And if your right eye causes you to fall into sin, tear it out and throw it away. It's better that you lose a part of your body than that your whole body be thrown into hell. [30]And if your right hand causes you to fall into sin, chop it off and throw it away. It's better that you lose a part of your body than that your whole body go into hell.

Law of divorce

[31]"It was said, 'Whoever divorces his wife must *give her a divorce certificate*.'[m] [32]But I say to you that whoever divorces his wife except for sexual unfaithfulness forces her to commit adultery. And whoever marries a divorced woman commits adultery.

Law of solemn pledges

[33]"Again you have heard that it was said to those who lived long ago: *Don't make a false solemn pledge, but you should follow through on what you have pledged to the Lord*.[n] [34]But I say to you that you must not pledge at all. You must not pledge by heaven, because it's God's throne. [35]You must not pledge by the earth, because it's God's footstool. You must not pledge by Jerusalem, because it's the city of the great king. [36]And you must not pledge by your head, because you can't turn one hair white or black. [37]Let your *yes* mean yes, and your *no* mean no. Anything more than this comes from the evil one.

Law of retaliation

[38]"You have heard that it was said, *An eye for an eye and a tooth for a tooth*.[o] [39]But I say to you that you must not oppose those who want to hurt you. If people slap you on your right cheek, you must turn the left cheek to them as well. [40]When they wish to haul you to court and take your shirt, let them have your coat too. [41]When they force you to go one mile, go with them two. [42]Give to those who ask, and don't refuse those who wish to borrow from you.

Law of love

[43]"You have heard that it was said, *You must love your neighbor*[p] and hate your enemy. [44]But I say to you, love your enemies and pray for those who harass you [45]so that you will be acting as children of your Father who is in heaven. He makes the sun rise on both the evil and the good and sends rain on both the righteous and the unrighteous. [46]If you love only those who love you, what reward do you have? Don't even the tax collectors do the same? [47]And if you greet only your brothers and sisters, what more are you doing? Don't even the Gentiles do the same? [48]Therefore, just as your heavenly Father is complete in showing love to everyone, so also you must be complete.

---

[k]Exod 20:13 [l]Exod 20:14; Deut 5:18 [m]Deut 24:1 [n]Lev 19:12; Num 30:2; Deut 23:21 [o]Exod 21:24; Lev 24:20; Deut 19:21 [p]Lev 19:18

Showy religion

6 "Be careful that you don't practice your religion in front of people to draw their attention. If you do, you will have no reward from your Father who is in heaven.

[2] "Whenever you give to the poor, don't blow your trumpet as the hypocrites do in the synagogues and in the streets so that they may get praise from people. I assure you, that's the only reward they'll get. [3] But when you give to the poor, don't let your left hand know what your right hand is doing [4] so that you may give to the poor in secret. Your Father who sees what you do in secret will reward you.

Showy prayer

[5] "When you pray, don't be like hypocrites. They love to pray standing in the synagogues and on the street corners so that people will see them. I assure you, that's the only reward they'll get. [6] But when you pray, go to your room, shut the door, and pray to your Father who is present in that secret place. Your Father who sees what you do in secret will reward you.

Proper prayer

[7] "When you pray, don't pour out a flood of empty words, as the Gentiles do. They think that by saying many words they'll be heard. [8] Don't be like them, because your Father knows what you need before you ask. [9] Pray like this:

Our Father who is in heaven,
    uphold the holiness of your name.
[10] Bring in your kingdom
    so that your will is done on earth
    as it's done in heaven.
[11] Give us the bread we need for today.
[12] Forgive us for the ways
    we have wronged you,
    just as we also forgive those
    who have wronged us.
[13] And don't lead us into temptation,
    but rescue us from the evil one.

SERMON ON THE MOUNT

The "Sermon on the Mount" is the traditional name for a section of Matthew's Gospel (Matt 5–7) that presents the teaching of Jesus on matters of discipleship.

The name "Sermon on the Mount" derives from Matthew 5:1, which says that Jesus delivered this teaching to his disciples on a mountain. About half the material in the Sermon on the Mount finds parallel in a section of Luke's Gospel in which Jesus instructs a multitude of people "on a large area of level ground" (Luke 6:17); this portion of Luke's Gospel is accordingly called the Sermon on the Plain (Luke 6:20-49).

The Sermon on the Mount contains material that has been extremely influential on the Christian religion and on secular civilization in areas where Christianity has flourished. It is here that one finds the beatitudes (Matt 5:3-12), the Golden Rule (Matt 7:12), and the Lord's Prayer (Matt 6:9-13). Here Jesus speaks of the humble inheriting the earth (Matt 5:5) and identifies his followers as "the salt of the earth" (Matt 5:13). He taught, "If people slap you on your right cheek, you must turn the left cheek to them as well" (Matt 5:39); and "When they force you to go one mile, go with them two" (5:41). He refers to wolves "dressed like sheep" (Matt 7:15), serving "two masters" (Matt 6:24), collecting "treasures for yourselves in heaven" (Matt 6:20), and throwing "your pearls in front of pigs" (Matt 7:6).

[14]"If you forgive others their sins, your heavenly Father will also forgive you. [15]But if you don't forgive others, neither will your Father forgive your sins.

Showy fasting

[16]"And when you fast, don't put on a sad face like the hypocrites. They distort their faces so people will know they are fasting. I assure you that they have their reward. [17]When you fast, brush your hair and wash your face. [18]Then you won't look like you are fasting to people, but only to your Father who is present in that secret place. Your Father who sees in secret will reward you.

Earthly and heavenly treasures

[19]"Stop collecting treasures for your own benefit on earth, where moth and rust eat them and where thieves break in and steal them. [20]Instead, collect treasures for yourselves in heaven, where moth and rust don't eat them and where thieves don't break in and steal them. [21]Where your treasure is, there your heart will be also.

Seeing and serving

[22]"The eye is the lamp of the body. Therefore, if your eye is healthy, your whole body will be full of light. [23]But if your eye is bad, your whole body will be full of darkness. If then the light in you is darkness, how terrible that darkness will be! [24]No one can serve two masters. Either you will hate the one and love the other, or you will be loyal to the one and have contempt for the other. You cannot serve God and wealth.

Worry about necessities

[25]"Therefore, I say to you, don't worry about your life, what you'll eat or what you'll drink, or about your body, what you'll wear. Isn't life more than food and the body more than clothes? [26]Look at the birds in the sky. They don't sow seed or harvest grain or gather crops into barns. Yet your heavenly Father feeds them. Aren't you worth much more than they are? [27]Who among you by worrying can add a single moment to your life? [28]And why do you worry about clothes? Notice how the lilies in the field grow. They don't wear themselves out with work, and they don't spin cloth. [29]But I say to you that even Solomon in all of his splendor wasn't dressed like one of these. [30]If God dresses grass in the field so beautifully, even though it's alive today and tomorrow it's thrown into the furnace, won't God do much more for you, you people of weak faith? [31]Therefore, don't worry and say, 'What are we going to eat?' or 'What are we going to drink?' or 'What are we going to wear?' [32]Gentiles long for all these things. Your heavenly Father knows that you need them. [33]Instead, desire first and foremost God's kingdom and God's righteousness, and all these things will be given to you as well. [34]Therefore, stop worrying about tomorrow, because tomorrow will worry about itself. Each day has enough trouble of its own.

Judging

7"Don't judge, so that you won't be judged. [2]You'll receive the same judgment you give. Whatever you deal out will be dealt out to you. [3]Why do you see the splinter that's in your brother's or sister's eye, but don't notice the log in your own eye? [4]How can you say to your brother or sister, 'Let me take the splinter out of your eye,' when there's a log in your eye? [5]You deceive yourself! First take the log out of your eye, and then you'll see clearly to take the splinter out of your brother's or sister's eye. [6]Don't give holy things to dogs, and don't throw your pearls in front of pigs. They will stomp on the pearls, then turn around and attack you.

Asking, seeking, knocking

[7]"Ask, and you will receive. Search, and you will find. Knock, and the door will be opened to you. [8]For everyone who asks, receives. Whoever seeks, finds. And to everyone who knocks, the door is opened. [9]Who among you will give your children a stone when they ask for bread? [10]Or give them a snake when they ask for fish? [11]If you who are evil know how to give good gifts to your children, how much more will your heavenly Father give good things to

PARABLES IN MATTHEW, MARK, & LUKE

Parable	Luke	Matthew	Mark
Patches and wineskins	Luke 5:36-39	Matt 9:16-17	Mark 2:21-22
The blind leading the blind	Luke 6:39-40	Matt 15:14b	
The log in your own eye	Luke 6:41-42	Matt 7:3-5	
Producing good fruit	Luke 6:43-45	Matt 7:16-20	
The two builders/building on a solid foundation	Luke 6:46-49	Matt 7:24-27	
The riddle of the children	Luke 7:31-35	Matt 11:16-19	
The two debtors	Luke 7:41-43		
Seed and the soil/the farmer	Luke 8:4-8	Matt 13:3-9	Mark 4:3-9
The lamp	Luke 8:16-17	Matt 5:14-16	Mark 4:21-22
The good Samaritan	Luke 10:30-35		
The shameless neighbor	Luke 11:5-8		
The kingdom divided against itself	Luke 11:17a	Matt 12:25a	Mark 3:24
The house divided against itself	Luke 11:17b	Matt 12:25b	Mark 3:25
The return of the unclean spirit	Luke 11:24-26	Matt 12:43-45	
The rich fool	Luke 12:16-21		
The returning master	Luke 12:36-38		
The thief in the night/the watchful owner	Luke 12:39-40	Matt 24:43-44	
The good and wicked servants	Luke 12:42-46	Matt 24:45-51	(Mark 13:33-37)
Going before a judge	Luke 12:58-59	Matt 5:25-26	
The barren fig tree	Luke 13:6-9	(Matt 21:20-22)	(Mark 11:20-25)
The mustard seed	Luke 13:18-19	Matt 13:31-32	Mark 4:30-32
The yeast	Luke 13:20-21	Matt 13:33	
The narrow gate	Luke 13:24-30		
The best seats at the table	Luke 14:7-11		
The large dinner/wedding party	Luke 14:16-24	Matt 22:1-14	
The fool at work	Luke 14:28-30		
The fool at war	Luke 14:31-32		
The lost sheep	Luke 15:3-7	Matt 18:12-14	
The lost coin	Luke 15:8-10		
The prodigal son	Luke 15:11-32		
The dishonest manager	Luke 16:1-9		
The rich man and Lazarus	Luke 16:19-31		
The servant who serves without reward	Luke 17:7-10		
The unjust judge and the persistent widow	Luke 18:1-8		
The Pharisee and the tax collector	Luke 18:9-14		
The valuable coins	Luke 19:11-27	Matt 25:14-30	
The tenant farmers	Luke 20:9-18	Matt 21:33-44	Mark 12:1-11
The fig tree in bloom	Luke 21:29-31	Matt 24:32-33	Mark 13:28-29
The weeds		Matt 13:24-30	
The hidden treasure and the pearl		Matt 13:44-46	
The net		Matt 13:47-48	
The owner of a house		Matt 13:52	
What can contaminate		Matt 15:10-11	Mark 7:14-15
The unforgiving servant		Matt 18:23-35	
The workers in the vineyard		Matt 20:1-16	
The two sons		Matt 21:28-32	
The bridesmaids		Matt 25:1-13	
The seed growing by itself			Mark 4:26-29
The watchful servants			Mark 13:33-37

those who ask him. [12]Therefore, you should treat people in the same way that you want people to treat you; this is the Law and the Prophets.

Narrow gate

[13]"Go in through the narrow gate. The gate that leads to destruction is broad and the road wide, so many people enter through it. [14]But the gate that leads to life is narrow and the road difficult, so few people find it.

Tree and fruit

[15]"Watch out for false prophets. They come to you dressed like sheep, but inside they are vicious wolves. [16]You will know them by their fruit. Do people get bunches of grapes from thorny weeds, or do they get figs from thistles? [17]In the same way, every good tree produces good fruit, and every rotten tree produces bad fruit. [18]A good tree can't produce bad fruit. And a rotten tree can't produce good fruit. [19]Every tree that doesn't produce good fruit is chopped down and thrown into the fire. [20]Therefore, you will know them by their fruit.

Entrance requirements

[21]"Not everybody who says to me, 'Lord, Lord,' will get into the kingdom of heaven. Only those who do the will of my Father who is in heaven will enter. [22]On the Judgment Day, many people will say to me, 'Lord, Lord, didn't we prophesy in your name and expel demons in your name and do lots of miracles in your name?' [23]Then I'll tell them, 'I've never known you. Get away from me, you people who do wrong.'

Two foundations

[24]"Everybody who hears these words of mine and puts them into practice is like a wise builder who built a house on bedrock. [25]The rain fell, the floods came, and the wind blew and beat against that house. It didn't fall because it was firmly set on bedrock. [26]But everybody who hears these words of mine and doesn't put them into practice will be like a fool who built a house on sand. [27]The rain fell, the floods came, and the wind blew and beat against that house. It fell and was completely destroyed."

Crowd's response

[28]When Jesus finished these words, the crowds were amazed at his teaching [29]because he was teaching them like someone with authority and not like their legal experts.

A man with a skin disease

8 Now when Jesus had come down from the mountain, large crowds followed him. [2]A man with a skin disease came, kneeled before him, and said, "Lord, if you want, you can make me clean." [3]Jesus reached out his hand and touched him, saying, "I do want to. Become clean." Instantly his skin disease was cleansed. [4]Jesus said to him, "Don't say anything to anyone. Instead, go and show yourself to the priest and offer the gift that Moses commanded. This will be a testimony to them."

Healing of the centurion's servant

[5]When Jesus went to Capernaum, a centurion approached, [6]pleading with him, "Lord, my servant is flat on his back at home, paralyzed, and his suffering is awful."

[7]Jesus responded, "I'll come and heal him."

[8]But the centurion replied, "Lord, I don't deserve to have you come under my roof. Just say the word and my servant will be healed. [9]I'm a man under authority, with soldiers under me. I say to one, 'Go,' and he goes, and to another, 'Come,' and he comes. I say to my servant, 'Do this,' and the servant does it."

[10]When Jesus heard this, he was impressed and said to the people following him, "I say to you with all seriousness that even in Israel I haven't found faith like this. [11]I say to you that there are many who will come from east and west and sit down to eat with Abraham and Isaac and Jacob in the kingdom of heaven. [12]But the children of the kingdom will be thrown outside into the darkness. People there will be weeping and grinding their teeth." [13]Jesus said to the centurion, "Go; it will be done for you just as you have believed." And his servant was healed that very moment.

Healing of many people

[14] Jesus went home with Peter and saw Peter's mother-in-law lying in bed with a fever. [15] He touched her hand, and the fever left her. Then she got up and served them. [16] That evening people brought to Jesus many who were demon-possessed. He threw the spirits out with just a word. He healed everyone who was sick. [17] This happened so that what Isaiah the prophet said would be fulfilled: *He is the one who took our illnesses and carried away our diseases.*[q]

Discussions about following

[18] Now when Jesus saw the crowd, he ordered his disciples to go over to the other side of the lake. [19] A legal expert came and said to him, "Teacher, I'll follow you wherever you go."

[20] Jesus replied, "Foxes have dens, and the birds in the sky have nests, but the Human One[r] has no place to lay his head."

[21] Another man, one of his disciples, said to him, "Lord, first let me go and bury my father."

[22] But Jesus said to him, "Follow me, and let the dead bury their own dead."

Calming a storm

[23] When Jesus got into a boat, his disciples followed him. [24] A huge storm arose on the lake so that waves were sloshing over the boat. But Jesus was asleep. [25] They came and woke him, saying, "Lord, rescue us! We're going to drown!"

[26] He said to them, "Why are you afraid, you people of weak faith?" Then he got up and gave orders to the winds and the lake, and there was a great calm.

[27] The people were amazed and said, "What kind of person is this? Even the winds and the lake obey him!"

Jesus frees demon-possessed men

[28] When Jesus arrived on the other side of the lake in the country of the Gadarenes, two men who were demon-possessed came from among the tombs to meet him. They were so violent that nobody could travel on that road. [29] They cried out, "What are you going to do with us, Son of God? Have you come to torture us before the time of judgment?" [30] Far off in the distance a large herd of pigs was feeding. [31] The demons pleaded with him, "If you throw us out, send us into the herd of pigs."

[32] Then he said to the demons, "Go away," and they came out and went into the pigs. The whole herd rushed down the cliff into the lake and drowned. [33] Those who tended the pigs ran into the city and told everything that had happened to the demon-possessed men. [34] Then the whole city came out and met Jesus. When they saw him, they pleaded with him to leave their region.

[q] Isa 53:4   [r] Or *Son of Man*

CENTURION

A centurion was a ranking officer in the Roman army, usually the commander over a company of 100 men or fewer. The word appears in the NT 25 times. The centurion functioned like a master sergeant, with responsibilities for training and discipline, and in his duties to the tribune he functioned more like a captain. Usually the centurion had as much experience as any soldier in the army, had endured assignments all over the empire, and could have filled such diverse assignments as general oversight of building projects, posting to duty in mines and quarries, functioning as a tax collector, or acting as an umpire in boundary disputes. In the NT, centurions serve as lead officers in security patrols or execution squads.

Healing of a man who was paralyzed

9 Boarding a boat, Jesus crossed to the other side of the lake and went to his own city. [2]People brought to him a man who was paralyzed, lying on a cot. When Jesus saw their faith, he said to the man who was paralyzed, "Be encouraged, my child, your sins are forgiven."

[3]Some legal experts said among themselves, "This man is insulting God."

[4]But Jesus knew what they were thinking and said, "Why do you fill your minds with evil things? [5]Which is easier—to say, 'Your sins are forgiven,' or to say, 'Get up and walk'? [6]But so you will know that the Human One[s] has authority on the earth to forgive sins"—he said to the man who was paralyzed—"Get up, take your cot, and go home." [7]The man got up and went home. [8]When the crowds saw what had happened, they were afraid and praised God, who had given such authority to human beings.

Calling of Matthew

[9]As Jesus continued on from there, he saw a man named Matthew sitting at a kiosk for collecting taxes. He said to him, "Follow me," and he got up and followed him. [10]As Jesus sat down to eat in Matthew's house, many tax collectors and sinners joined Jesus and his disciples at the table.

[11]But when the Pharisees saw this, they said to his disciples, "Why does your teacher eat with tax collectors and sinners?"

[12]When Jesus heard it, he said, "Healthy people don't need a doctor, but sick people do. [13]Go and learn what this means: *I want mercy and not sacrifice*.[t] I didn't come to call righteous people, but sinners."

Question about fasting

[14]At that time John's disciples came and asked Jesus, "Why do we and the Pharisees frequently fast, but your disciples never fast?"

[15]Jesus responded, "The wedding guests can't mourn while the groom is still with them, can they? But the days will come when the groom will be taken away from them, and then they'll fast.

[16]"No one sews a piece of new, unshrunk cloth on old clothes because the patch tears away the cloth and makes a worse tear. [17]No one pours new wine into old wineskins. If they did, the wineskins would burst, the wine would spill, and the wineskins would be ruined. Instead, people pour new wine into new wineskins so that both are kept safe."

A ruler's daughter and the woman who touched Jesus' clothes

[18]While Jesus was speaking to them, a ruler came and knelt in front of him, saying, "My daughter has just died. But come and place your hand on her, and she'll live." [19]So Jesus and his disciples got up and went with him. [20]Then a woman who had been bleeding for twelve years came up behind Jesus and touched the hem of his clothes. [21]She thought, If I only touch his robe I'll be healed.

[22]When Jesus turned and saw her, he said, "Be encouraged, daughter. Your faith

[s]Or *Son of Man* [t]Hos 6:6

TAX COLLECTOR

A "tax" or (preferably) "toll" collector was usually stationed at a "toll booth" and was responsible for collecting the toll, tariff, or customs duty on transported goods. Other tax collectors secured payments for farm production. Generally, many people hated and despised toll collectors since they were able to exploit the toll collection system to their own advantage. This negative attitude is present in the Gospels, where tax collectors are frequently grouped with "sinners."

has healed you." And the woman was healed from that time on.

²³When Jesus went into the ruler's house, he saw the flute players and the distressed crowd. ²⁴He said, "Go away, because the little girl isn't dead but is asleep"; but they laughed at him. ²⁵After he had sent the crowd away, Jesus went in and touched her hand, and the little girl rose up. ²⁶News about this spread throughout that whole region.

Healing of two blind men

²⁷As Jesus departed, two blind men followed him, crying out, "Show us mercy, Son of David."

²⁸When he came into the house, the blind men approached him. Jesus said to them, "Do you believe I can do this?"

"Yes, Lord," they replied.

²⁹Then Jesus touched their eyes and said, "It will happen for you just as you have believed." ³⁰Their eyes were opened. Then Jesus sternly warned them, "Make sure nobody knows about this." ³¹But they went out and spread the word about him throughout that whole region.

Healing of a man unable to speak

³²As they were leaving, people brought to him a man who was demon-possessed and unable to speak. ³³When Jesus had thrown out the demon, the man who couldn't speak began to talk. The crowds were amazed and said, "Nothing like this has ever been seen in Israel."

³⁴But the Pharisees said, "He throws out demons with the authority of the ruler of demons."

Compassion

³⁵Jesus traveled among all the cities and villages, teaching in their synagogues, announcing the good news of the kingdom, and healing every disease and every sickness. ³⁶Now when Jesus saw the crowds, he had compassion for them because they were troubled and helpless, like sheep without a shepherd. ³⁷Then he said to his disciples, "The size of the harvest is bigger than you can imagine, but there are few workers. ³⁸Therefore, plead with the Lord of the harvest to send out workers for his harvest."

Mission of the Twelve

10He called his twelve disciples and gave them authority over unclean spirits to throw them out and to heal every disease and every sickness. ²Here are the names of the twelve apostles: first, Simon, who is called Peter; and Andrew his brother; James the son of Zebedee; and John his brother; ³Philip; and Bartholomew; Thomas; and Matthew the tax collector; James the son of Alphaeus; and Thaddaeus; ⁴Simon the Cananaean;ᵘ and Judas, who betrayed Jesus.

Commissioning of the Twelve

⁵Jesus sent these twelve out and commanded them, "Don't go among the Gentiles or into a Samaritan city. ⁶Go instead to the

ᵘOr zealot

THADDAEUS

One of the 12 disciples of Jesus according to Matthew 10:3 and Mark 3:18, but Luke lists "Judas the son of James" in his place (Luke 6:16; Acts 1:13). If all three Gospels refer to the same disciple, it is likely that his given name was Judas, as attested in Luke, but that he became known by his nickname Thaddaeus in Matthew and Mark, in order to be differentiated from Judas Iscariot the traitor. He might then be the disciple "Judas (not Judas Iscariot)" who asked Jesus at the Last Supper why he would reveal himself to the disciples but not to the world (John 14:22).

lost sheep, the people of Israel. [7]As you go, make this announcement: 'The kingdom of heaven has come near.' [8]Heal the sick, raise the dead, cleanse those with skin diseases, and throw out demons. You received without having to pay. Therefore, give without demanding payment. [9]Workers deserve to be fed, so don't gather gold or silver or copper coins for your money belts to take on your trips. [10]Don't take a backpack for the road or two shirts or sandals or a walking stick. [11]Whatever city or village you go into, find somebody in it who is worthy and stay there until you go on your way. [12]When you go into a house, say, 'Peace!' [13]If the house is worthy, give it your blessing of peace. But if the house isn't worthy, take back your blessing. [14]If anyone refuses to welcome you or listen to your words, shake the dust off your feet as you leave that house or city. [15]I assure you that it will be more bearable for the land of Sodom and Gomorrah on Judgment Day than it will be for that city.

Response to harassment

[16]"Look, I'm sending you as sheep among wolves. Therefore, be wise as snakes and innocent as doves. [17]Watch out for people— because they will hand you over to councils and they will beat you in their synagogues. [18]They will haul you in front of governors and even kings because of me so that you may give your testimony to them and to the Gentiles. [19]Whenever they hand you over, don't worry about how to speak or what you will say, because what you can say will be given to you at that moment. [20]You aren't doing the talking, but the Spirit of my Father is doing the talking through you.

[21]Brothers and sisters will hand each other over to be executed. A father will turn his child in. Children will defy their parents and have them executed. [22]Everyone will hate you on account of my name. But whoever stands firm until the end will be saved. [23]Whenever they harass you in one city, escape to the next, because I assure that you will not go through all the cities of Israel before the Human One[v] comes.

[24]"Disciples aren't greater than their teacher, and slaves aren't greater than their master. [25]It's enough for disciples to be like their teacher and slaves like their master. If they have called the head of the house Beelzebul, it's certain that they will call the members of his household by even worse names.

Whom to fear

[26]"Therefore, don't be afraid of those people because nothing is hidden that won't be revealed, and nothing secret that won't be brought out into the open. [27]What I say to you in the darkness, tell in the light; and what you hear whispered, announce from the rooftops. [28]Don't be afraid of those who kill the body but can't kill the soul. Instead, be afraid of the one who can destroy both body and soul in hell. [29]Aren't two sparrows sold for a small coin? But not one of them will fall to the ground without your Father knowing about it already. [30]Even the hairs of your head are all counted. [31]Don't be afraid. You are worth more than many sparrows.

Confessing Christ to people

[32]"Therefore, everyone who acknowledges me before people, I also will acknowledge

[v]Or Son of Man

BARTHOLOMEW

In the Synoptic Gospels (Matt 10:3; Mark 3:18; Luke 6:14) and Acts (Acts 1:13) Bartholomew is one of the Twelve, associated with either Philip or Matthew. Bartholomew is never mentioned in the Gospel of John. Bartholomew is usually identified with Nathanael of Cana (John 21:2; see also 1:45).

before my Father who is in heaven. ³³But everyone who denies me before people, I also will deny before my Father who is in heaven.

Trouble in the family

³⁴"Don't think that I've come to bring peace to the earth. I haven't come to bring peace but a sword. ³⁵I've come to turn a man *against his father, a daughter against her mother, and a daughter-in-law against her mother-in-law.* ³⁶*People's enemies are members of their own households.*^w

³⁷"Those who love father or mother more than me aren't worthy of me. Those who love son or daughter more than me aren't worthy of me. ³⁸Those who don't pick up their crosses and follow me aren't worthy of me. ³⁹Those who find their lives will lose them, and those who lose their lives because of me will find them.

Rewards

⁴⁰"Those who receive you are also receiving me, and those who receive me are receiving the one who sent me. ⁴¹Those who receive a prophet as a prophet will receive a prophet's reward. Those who receive a righteous person as a righteous person will receive a righteous person's reward. ⁴²I assure you that everybody who gives even a cup of cold water to these little ones because they are my disciples will certainly be rewarded."

Ministry to the people

11 When Jesus finished teaching his twelve disciples, he went on from there to teach and preach in their cities.

Question from John the Baptist

²Now when John heard in prison about the things the Christ was doing, he sent word by his disciples to Jesus, asking, ³"Are you the one who is to come, or should we look for another?"

⁴Jesus responded, "Go, report to John what you hear and see. ⁵*Those who were blind are able to see.* Those who were crippled are walking. People with skin diseases are cleansed. Those *who were deaf now hear.* Those who were dead are raised up. *The poor have good news proclaimed to them.*^x ⁶Happy are those who don't stumble and fall because of me."

^wMic 7:6   ^xIsa 35:5-6; 61:1

JOHN

1. John 1:42; 21:15-17 refers to Peter as "Simon, son of John," while Matthew 16:17 identifies Peter's father as Jonah.

2. A member of the Jerusalem high council (Acts 4:6) who is otherwise unknown. Some manuscripts read "Jonathan" instead, probably identifying this person with the son of Annas, who succeeded Caiaphas to the high priesthood in 36 CE.

3. John, the late 1st-century Christian prophet and teacher in Asia Minor, who identifies himself as the author of Revelation (Rev 1:1, 4, 9; 22:8), came to be identified with John the son of Zebedee (see John #5) in the 2nd century.

4. John the Baptist figures prominently in the Gospels and Acts. He provides the context for the ministry of Jesus.

5. John the son of Zebedee, one of the 12 disciples, is traditionally held to be the author of five NT writings: the Gospel, Letters, and Revelation of John.

Appeal of John's ministry

[7]When John's disciples had gone, Jesus spoke to the crowds about John: "What did you go out to the wilderness to see? A stalk blowing in the wind? [8]What did you go out to see? A man dressed up in refined clothes? Look, those who wear refined clothes are in royal palaces. [9]What did you go out to see? A prophet? Yes, I tell you, and more than a prophet. [10]He is the one of whom it is written: *Look, I'm sending my messenger before you, who will prepare your way before you.*[y]

Significance of John's ministry

[11]"I assure you that no one who has ever been born is greater than John the Baptist. Yet whoever is least in the kingdom of heaven is greater than he. [12]From the days of John the Baptist until now the kingdom of heaven is violently attacked as violent people seize it. [13]All the Prophets and the Law prophesied until John came. [14]If you are willing to accept it, he is Elijah who is to come. [15]Let the person who has ears, hear.

This generation

[16]"To what will I compare this generation? It is like a child sitting in the marketplaces calling out to others, [17]'We played the flute for you and you didn't dance. We sang a funeral song and you didn't mourn.' [18]For John came neither eating nor drinking, and they say, 'He has a demon.' [19]Yet the Human One[z] came eating and drinking, and they say, 'Look, a glutton and a drunk, a friend of tax collectors and sinners.' But wisdom is proved to be right by her works."

Condemnation of Bethsaida and Capernaum

[20]Then he began to scold the cities where he had done his greatest miracles because they didn't change their hearts and lives. [21]"How terrible it will be for you, Chorazin! How terrible it will be for you, Bethsaida! For if the miracles done among you had been done in Tyre and Sidon, they would have changed their hearts and lives and

put on funeral clothes and ashes a long time ago. [22]But I say to you that Tyre and Sidon will be better off on Judgment Day than you. [23]And you, Capernaum, will you be honored by being raised up to heaven? No, you will be thrown down to the place of the dead. After all, if the miracles that were done among you had been done in Sodom, it would still be here today. [24]But I say to you that it will be better for the land of Sodom on the Judgment Day than it will be for you."

The Father and the Son

[25]At that time Jesus said, "I praise you, Father, Lord of heaven and earth, because you've hidden these things from the wise and intelligent and have shown them to babies. [26]Indeed, Father, this brings you happiness.

[27]"My Father has handed all things over to me. No one knows the Son except the Father. And nobody knows the Father except the Son and anyone to whom the Son wants to reveal him.

[28]"Come to me, all you who are struggling hard and carrying heavy loads, and I will give you rest. [29]Put on my yoke, and learn from me. I'm gentle and humble. And you will find rest for yourselves. [30]My yoke is easy to bear, and my burden is light."

Working on the Sabbath

12 At that time Jesus went through the wheat fields on the Sabbath. His disciples were hungry so they were picking heads of wheat and eating them. [2]When the Pharisees saw this, they said to him, "Look, your disciples are breaking the Sabbath law." [3]But he said to them, "Haven't you read what David did when he and those with him were hungry? [4]He went into God's house and broke the law by eating the bread of the presence, which only the priests were allowed to eat. [5]Or haven't you read in the Law that on the Sabbath the priests in the temple treat the Sabbath as any other day and are still innocent? [6]But I tell you that

[y]Mal 3:1 [z]Or *Son of Man*

something greater than the temple is here. [7] If you had known what this means, *I want mercy and not sacrifice,*[a] you wouldn't have condemned the innocent. [8] The Human One[b] is Lord of the Sabbath."

Healing on the Sabbath

[9] Jesus left that place and went into their synagogue. [10] A man with a withered hand was there. Wanting to bring charges against Jesus, they asked, "Does the Law allow a person to heal on the Sabbath?"

[11] Jesus replied, "Who among you has a sheep that falls into a pit on the Sabbath and will not take hold of it and pull it out? [12] How much more valuable is a person than a sheep! So the Law allows a person to do what is good on the Sabbath." [13] Then Jesus said to the man, "Stretch out your hand." So he did and it was made healthy, just like the other one. [14] The Pharisees went out and met in order to find a way to destroy Jesus.

Healing the crowd

[15] Jesus knew what they intended to do, so he went away from there. Large crowds followed him, and he healed them all. [16] But he ordered them not to spread the word about him, [17] so that what was spoken through Isaiah the prophet might be fulfilled:

[18] *Look, my Servant whom I chose,*
  the one I love,
    in whom I find great pleasure.
  I'll put my Spirit upon him,
    and he'll announce judgment
    to the Gentiles.
[19] *He won't argue or shout,*
    and nobody will hear his voice
    in the streets.
[20] *He won't break a bent stalk,*
    and he won't snuff out a smoldering wick,
    until he makes justice win.
[21] *And the Gentiles will put their hope*
  in his name.[c]

[22] They brought to Jesus a demon-possessed man who was blind and unable

---

[a] Hos 6:6 [b] Or *Son of Man* [c] Isa 42:1-4

SABBATH (NT)

The NT reveals that on the Sabbath, the congregation assembled in the synagogue to read from the scriptures, a practice Jesus participated in and that Paul and his associates continued as part of their missionary efforts among Jews (Acts 13:14-15; 18:4). Prior to the destruction of the temple in 70 CE, the Sabbath revolved around both the sacrificial worship at the temple and the study of scripture in the synagogue. The most characteristic feature of the NT accounts of the Sabbath is Jesus' controversies with the Pharisees about the Sabbath, especially with regard to Jesus' healing on the Sabbath. Jesus considered the Sabbath as the appropriate day for healings, while his opponents categorized them as labor and thus judged that the healings had their proper place on one of the six workdays (Luke 13:14). Especially in Matthew and Luke (e.g., Luke 13:18), the healings are linked to the impending nearness of God's kingdom, which was also foreshadowed in the holiness of the Sabbath day.

While Jewish Christians kept observing the Sabbath as long as they also remained within the community of the synagogue, Sunday quickly became the day Christians came together to celebrate Christ's resurrection. The significance of what was called the Lord's day is attested already in texts from the 1st century CE.

to speak. Jesus healed him so that he could both speak and see. ²³All the crowds were amazed and said, "This man couldn't be the Son of David, could he?"

²⁴When the Pharisees heard, they said, "This man throws out demons only by the authority of Beelzebul, the ruler of the demons."

²⁵Because Jesus knew what they were thinking, he replied, "Every kingdom involved in civil war becomes a wasteland. Every city or house torn apart by divisions will collapse. ²⁶If Satan throws out Satan, he is at war with himself. How then can his kingdom endure? ²⁷And if I throw out demons by the authority of Beelzebul, then by whose authority do your followers throw them out? Therefore, they will be your judges. ²⁸But if I throw out demons by the power of God's Spirit, then God's kingdom has already overtaken you. ²⁹Can people go into a house that belongs to a strong man and steal his possessions, unless they first tie up the strong man? Then they can rob his house. ³⁰Whoever isn't with me is against me, and whoever doesn't gather with me scatters.

Insulting the Holy Spirit

³¹"Therefore, I tell you that people will be forgiven for every sin and insult to God. But insulting the Holy Spirit won't be forgiven. ³²And whoever speaks a word against the Human One[d] will be forgiven. But whoever speaks against the Holy Spirit won't be forgiven, not in this age or in the age that is coming.

Trees and fruits

³³"Either consider the tree good and its fruit good, or consider the tree rotten and its fruit rotten. A tree is known by its fruit. ³⁴Children of snakes! How can you speak good things while you are evil? What fills the heart comes out of the mouth. ³⁵Good people bring out good things from their good treasure. But evil people bring out evil things from their evil treasure. ³⁶I tell you that people will have to answer on Judgment Day for every useless word they

speak. ³⁷By your words you will be either judged innocent or condemned as guilty."

Request for a sign

³⁸At that time some of the legal experts and the Pharisees requested of Jesus, "Teacher, we would like to see a sign from you."

³⁹But he replied, "An evil and unfaithful generation searches for a sign, but it won't receive any sign except Jonah's sign. ⁴⁰Just as *Jonah was in the whale's belly for three days and three nights,*[e] so the Human One[f] will be in the heart of the earth for three days and three nights. ⁴¹The citizens of Nineveh will stand up at the judgment with this generation and condemn it as guilty, because they changed their hearts and lives in response to Jonah's preaching. And look, someone greater than Jonah is here. ⁴²The queen of the South will be raised up by God at the judgment with this generation and condemn it because she came from a distant land to hear Solomon's wisdom. And look, someone greater than Solomon is here.

Unclean spirit seeking a home

⁴³"When an unclean spirit leaves a person, it wanders through dry places looking for a place to rest. But it doesn't find any. ⁴⁴Then it says, 'I'll go back to the house I left.' When it arrives, it finds the place vacant, cleaned up, and decorated. ⁴⁵Then it goes and brings with it seven other spirits more evil than itself. They go in and make their home there. That person is worse off at the end than at the beginning. This is the way it will be also for this evil generation."

Jesus' family

⁴⁶While Jesus was speaking to the crowds, his mother and brothers stood outside trying to speak with him. ⁴⁷Someone said to him, "Look, your mother and brothers are outside wanting to speak with you."

⁴⁸Jesus replied, "Who is my mother? Who are my brothers?" ⁴⁹He stretched out his hand toward his disciples and said, "Look,

---

[d]Or *Son of Man* [e]Jonah 1:17 [f]Or *Son of Man*

here are my mother and my brothers. [50] Whoever does the will of my Father who is in heaven is my brother, sister, and mother."

Setting for the parables

13 That day Jesus went out of the house and sat down beside the lake. [2] Such large crowds gathered around him that he climbed into a boat and sat down. The whole crowd was standing on the shore.

Parable of the soils

[3] He said many things to them in parables: "A farmer went out to scatter seed. [4] As he was scattering seed, some fell on the path, and birds came and ate it. [5] Other seed fell on rocky ground where the soil was shallow. They sprouted immediately because the soil wasn't deep. [6] But when the sun came up, it scorched the plants, and they dried up because they had no roots. [7] Other seed fell among thorny plants. The thorny plants grew and choked them. [8] Other seed fell on good soil and bore fruit, in one case a yield of one hundred to one, in another case a yield of sixty to one, and in another case a yield of thirty to one. [9] Everyone who has ears should pay attention."

Why Jesus speaks in parables

[10] Jesus' disciples came and said to him, "Why do you use parables when you speak to the crowds?"

[11] Jesus replied, "Because they haven't received the secrets of the kingdom of heaven, but you have. [12] For those who have will receive more and they will have more than enough. But as for those who don't have, even the little they have will be taken away from them. [13] This is why I speak to the crowds in parables: although they see, they don't really see; and although they hear, they don't really hear or understand. [14] What Isaiah prophesied has become completely true for them:

You will hear, to be sure,
  but never understand;
  and you will certainly see but never
    recognize what you are seeing.

[15] *For this people's senses*
  have become calloused,
  and they've become hard of hearing,
  and they've shut their eyes
    so that they won't see with their eyes
    or hear with their ears
    or understand with their minds,
  and change their hearts and lives
    that I may heal them.[g]

[16] "Happy are your eyes because they see. Happy are your ears because they hear. [17] I assure you that many prophets and righteous people wanted to see what you see and hear what you hear, but they didn't.

Explanation of the parable of the farmer

[18] "Consider then the parable of the farmer. [19] Whenever people hear the word about the kingdom and don't understand it, the evil one comes and carries off what was planted in their hearts. This is the seed that was sown on the path. [20] As for the seed that was spread on rocky ground, this refers to people who hear the word and immediately receive it joyfully. [21] Because they have no roots, they last for only a little while. When they experience distress or abuse because of the word, they immediately fall away. [22] As for the seed that was spread among thorny plants, this refers to those who hear the word, but the worries of this life and the false appeal of wealth choke the word, and it bears no fruit. [23] As for what was planted on good soil, this refers to those who hear and understand, and bear fruit and produce—in one case a yield of one hundred to one, in another case a yield of sixty to one, and in another case a yield of thirty to one."

Parable of the weeds

[24] Jesus told them another parable: "The kingdom of heaven is like someone who planted good seed in his field. [25] While people were sleeping, an enemy came and planted weeds among the wheat and went away. [26] When the stalks sprouted and bore grain, then the weeds also appeared. [27] "The servants of the landowner came

[g] Isa 6:9-10

and said to him, 'Master, didn't you plant good seed in your field? Then how is it that it has weeds?'

²⁸"'An enemy has done this,' he answered.

"The servants said to him, 'Do you want us to go and gather them?'

²⁹"But the landowner said, 'No, because if you gather the weeds, you'll pull up the wheat along with them. ³⁰Let both grow side by side until the harvest. And at harvesttime I'll say to the harvesters, "First gather the weeds and tie them together in bundles to be burned. But bring the wheat into my barn."'"

Parable of the mustard seed

³¹He told another parable to them: "The kingdom of heaven is like a mustard seed that someone took and planted in his field. ³²It's the smallest of all seeds. But when it's grown, it's the largest of all vegetable plants. It becomes a tree so that the birds in the sky come and nest in its branches."

Parable of the yeast

³³He told them another parable: "The kingdom of heaven is like yeast, which a woman took and hid in a bushel of wheat flour until the yeast had worked its way through all the dough."

Purpose of parables to the crowds

³⁴Jesus said all these things to the crowds in parables, and he spoke to them only in parables. ³⁵This was to fulfill what the prophet spoke:

I'll speak in parables;
    I'll declare what has been hidden
        since the beginning of the world.ʰ

Explanation of the parable of the weeds

³⁶Jesus left the crowds and went into the house. His disciples came to him and said, "Explain to us the parable of the weeds in the field."

³⁷Jesus replied, "The one who plants the good seed is the Human One.ⁱ ³⁸The field is the world. And the good seeds are the followers of the kingdom. But the weeds are the followers of the evil one. ³⁹The enemy who planted them is the devil. The harvest is the end of the present age. The harvesters are the angels. ⁴⁰Just as people gather weeds and burn them in the fire, so it will be at the end of the present age. ⁴¹The Human Oneʲ will send his angels, and they will gather out of his kingdom all things that cause people to fall away and all people who sin. ⁴²He will throw them into a burning furnace. People there will be weeping and grinding their teeth. ⁴³Then the righteous will shine like the sun in their Father's kingdom. Those who have ears should hear."

Parable of the treasure

⁴⁴"The kingdom of heaven is like a treasure that somebody hid in a field, which someone else found and covered up. Full of joy, the finder sold everything and bought that field.

Parable of the merchant

⁴⁵"Again, the kingdom of heaven is like a merchant in search of fine pearls. ⁴⁶When he found one very precious pearl, he went and sold all that he owned and bought it.

Parable of the net

⁴⁷"Again, the kingdom of heaven is like a net that people threw into the lake and gathered all kinds of fish. ⁴⁸When it was full, they pulled it to the shore, where they sat down and put the good fish together into containers. But the bad fish they threw away. ⁴⁹That's the way it will be at the end of the present age. The angels will go out and separate the evil people from the righteous people, ⁵⁰and will throw the evil ones into a burning furnace. People there will be weeping and grinding their teeth.

Treasures new and old

⁵¹"Have you understood all these things?" Jesus asked.

They said to him, "Yes."

⁵²Then he said to them, "Therefore, every legal expert who has been trained as a disciple for the kingdom of heaven is like the

ʰPs 78:2 ⁱOr *Son of Man* ʲOr *Son of Man*

head of a household who brings old and new things out of their treasure chest."

Jesus in his hometown

53 When Jesus finished these parables, he departed. 54 When he came to his hometown, he taught the people in their synagogue. They were surprised and said, "Where did he get this wisdom? Where did he get the power to work miracles? 55 Isn't he the carpenter's son? Isn't his mother named Mary? Aren't James, Joseph, Simon, and Judas his brothers? 56 And his sisters, aren't they here with us? Where did this man get all this?" 57 They were repulsed by him and fell into sin.

But Jesus said to them, "Prophets are honored everywhere except in their own hometowns and in their own households." 58 He was unable to do many miracles there because of their disbelief.

Death of John the Baptist

14 At that time Herod the ruler[k] heard the news about Jesus. 2 He said to his servants, "This is John the Baptist. He's been raised from the dead. This is why these miraculous powers are at work through him." 3 Herod had arrested John, bound him, and

[k]Or *tetrarch*, which refers to a prince over a small region

put him in prison because of Herodias, the wife of Herod's brother Philip. 4 "That's because John told Herod, "It's against the law for you to marry her."

5 Although Herod wanted to kill him, he feared the crowd because they thought John was a prophet. 6 But at Herod's birthday party Herodias' daughter danced in front of the guests and thrilled Herod. 7 Then he swore to give her anything she asked.

8 At her mother's urging, the girl said, "Give me the head of John the Baptist here on a plate." 9 Although the king was upset, because of his solemn pledge and his guests he commanded that they give it to her. 10 Then he had John beheaded in prison. 11 They brought his head on a plate and gave it to the young woman, and she brought it to her mother. 12 But John's disciples came and took his body and buried it. Then they went and told Jesus what had happened.

Feeding the five thousand

13 When Jesus heard about John, he withdrew in a boat to a deserted place by himself. When the crowds learned this, they followed him on foot from the cities. 14 When Jesus arrived and saw a large crowd, he had compassion for them and

HERODIAS

Daughter of Bernice and Aristobulus, Herodias was of combined Hasmonean and Idumean descent, presumably born between 16 and 7 BCE in Judea. She divorced her first husband, with whom she had a daughter, and married Herod Antipas, her husband's half-brother and tetrarch over Galilee and Perea.

Herodias is mentioned in the Gospels for two related reasons: John the Baptist apparently criticized her marriage with Herod Antipas (Matt 14:3-4; Mark 6:17-18; Luke 3:19), and in Matthew and Mark she is presented as the one who inspired her daughter to ask Herod for John's head (Matt 14:8; Mark 6:24). Outside the NT, the most important source of information for her life is Flavius Josephus, who mentions both her marriages, but identifies her first husband as Herod (called Philip according to Matt 14:3 and Mark 6:17) and calls her daughter Salome (but Herodias according to Mark 6:22).

healed those who were sick. [15]That evening his disciples came and said to him, "This is an isolated place and it's getting late. Send the crowds away so they can go into the villages and buy food for themselves."

[16]But Jesus said to them, "There's no need to send them away. You give them something to eat."

[17]They replied, "We have nothing here except five loaves of bread and two fish."

[18]He said, "Bring them here to me." [19]He ordered the crowds to sit down on the grass. He took the five loaves of bread and the two fish, looked up to heaven, blessed them and broke the loaves apart and gave them to his disciples. Then the disciples gave them to the crowds. [20]Everyone ate until they were full, and they filled twelve baskets with the leftovers. [21]About five thousand men plus women and children had eaten.

Walking on the water

[22]Right then, Jesus made the disciples get into the boat and go ahead to the other side of the lake while he dismissed the crowds. [23]When he sent them away, he went up onto a mountain by himself to pray. Evening came and he was alone. [24]Meanwhile, the boat, fighting a strong headwind, was being battered by the waves and was already far away from land. [25]Very early in the morning he came to his disciples, walking on the lake. [26]When the disciples saw him walking on the lake, they were terrified and said, "It's a ghost!" They were so frightened they screamed.

[27]Just then Jesus spoke to them, "Be encouraged! It's me. Don't be afraid."

[28]Peter replied, "Lord, if it's you, order me to come to you on the water."

[29]And Jesus said, "Come."

Then Peter got out of the boat and was walking on the water toward Jesus. [30]But when Peter saw the strong wind, he became frightened. As he began to sink, he shouted, "Lord, rescue me!"

[31]Jesus immediately reached out and grabbed him, saying, "You man of weak faith! Why did you begin to have doubts?"

[32]When they got into the boat, the wind settled down.

[33]Then those in the boat worshipped Jesus and said, "You must be God's Son!"

Healing the sick

[34]When they had crossed the lake, they landed at Gennesaret. [35]When the people who lived in that place recognized him, they sent word throughout that whole region, and they brought to him everyone who was sick. [36]Then they begged him that they might just touch the edge of his clothes. Everyone who touched him was cured.

Rules from the elders

15 Then Pharisees and legal experts came to Jesus from Jerusalem and said, [2]"Why are your disciples breaking the elders' rules handed down to us? They don't ritually purify their hands by washing before they eat."

[3]Jesus replied, "Why do you break the command of God by keeping the rules handed down to you? [4]For God said, *Honor your father and your mother,*[l] and *The person who speaks against father or mother will certainly be put to death.*[m] [5]But you say, 'If you tell your father or mother, "Everything I'm expected to contribute to you I'm giving to God as a gift," then you don't have to honor your father.' [6]So you do away with God's Law for the sake of the rules that have been handed down to you. [7]Hypocrites! Isaiah really knew what he was talking about when he prophesied about you, [8]*This people honors me with their lips, but their hearts are far away from me.* [9]*Their worship of me is empty since they teach instructions that are human rules.*"[n]

[10]Jesus called the crowd near and said to them, "Listen and understand. [11]It's not what goes into the mouth that contaminates a person in God's sight. It's what comes out of the mouth that contaminates the person."

[12]Then the disciples came and said to him, "Do you know that the Pharisees were offended by what you just said?"

[l]Exod 20:12; Deut 5:16   [m]Exod 21:17; Lev 20:9   [n]Isa 29:13

¹³Jesus replied, "Every plant that my heavenly Father didn't plant will be pulled up. ¹⁴Leave the Pharisees alone. They are blind people who are guides to blind people. But if a blind person leads another blind person, they will both fall into a ditch."

¹⁵Then Peter spoke up, "Explain this riddle to us."

¹⁶Jesus said, "Don't you understand yet? ¹⁷Don't you know that everything that goes into the mouth enters the stomach and goes out into the sewer? ¹⁸But what goes out of the mouth comes from the heart. And that's what contaminates a person in God's sight. ¹⁹Out of the heart come evil thoughts, murders, adultery, sexual sins, thefts, false testimonies, and insults. ²⁰These contaminate a person in God's sight. But eating without washing hands doesn't contaminate in God's sight."

Canaanite woman

²¹From there, Jesus went to the regions of Tyre and Sidon. ²²A Canaanite woman from those territories came out and shouted, "Show me mercy, Son of David. My daughter is suffering terribly from demon possession." ²³But he didn't respond to her at all.

His disciples came and urged him, "Send her away; she keeps shouting out after us."

²⁴Jesus replied, "I've been sent only to the lost sheep, the people of Israel."

²⁵But she knelt before him and said, "Lord, help me."

²⁶He replied, "It is not good to take the children's bread and toss it to dogs."

²⁷She said, "Yes, Lord. But even the dogs eat the crumbs that fall off their masters' table."

²⁸Jesus answered, "Woman, you have great faith. It will be just as you wish." And right then her daughter was healed.

Healing of many people

²⁹Jesus moved on from there along the shore of the Galilee Sea. He went up a mountain and sat down. ³⁰Large crowds came to him, including those who were paralyzed, blind, injured, and unable to speak, and many others. They laid them at his feet, and he healed them. ³¹So the crowd was amazed when they saw those who had been unable to speak talking, and the paralyzed cured, and the injured walking, and the blind seeing. And they praised the God of Israel.

Feeding the four thousand

³²Now Jesus called his disciples and said, "I feel sorry for the crowd because they have been with me for three days and have nothing to eat. I don't want to send them away hungry for fear they won't have enough strength to travel."

³³His disciples replied, "Where are we going to get enough food in this wilderness to satisfy such a big crowd?"

³⁴Jesus said, "How much bread do you have?"

They responded, "Seven loaves and a few fish."

³⁵He told the crowd to sit on the ground. ³⁶He took the seven loaves of bread and the fish. After he gave thanks, he broke them into pieces and gave them to the disciples, and the disciples gave them to the crowds. ³⁷Everyone ate until they were full. The disciples collected seven baskets full of leftovers. ³⁸Four thousand men ate, plus women and children. ³⁹After dismissing the crowds, Jesus got into the boat and came to the region of Magadan.

Demand for a sign

16 The Pharisees and Sadducees came to Jesus. In order to test him they asked him to show them a sign from heaven.

²But he replied, "At evening you say, 'It will be nice weather because the sky is bright red.' ³And in the morning you say, 'There will be bad weather today because the sky is cloudy.' You know how to make sense of the sky's appearance. But you are unable to recognize the signs that point to what the time is. ⁴An evil and unfaithful generation searches for a sign. But it won't receive any sign except Jonah's sign." Then he left them and went away.

Yeast of the Pharisees and Sadducees

⁵When the disciples arrived on the other side of the lake, they had forgotten to bring

bread. [6]Jesus said to them, "Watch out and be on your guard for the yeast of the Pharisees and Sadducees."

[7]They discussed this among themselves and said, "We didn't bring any bread."

[8]Jesus knew what they were discussing and said, "You people of weak faith! Why are you discussing among yourselves the fact that you don't have any bread? [9]Don't you understand yet? Don't you remember the five loaves that fed the five thousand and how many baskets of leftovers you gathered? [10]And the seven loaves that fed the four thousand and how many large baskets of leftovers you gathered? [11]Don't you know that I wasn't talking about bread? But be on your guard for the yeast of the Pharisees and Sadducees." [12]Then they understood that he wasn't telling them to be on their guard for yeast used in making bread. No, he was telling them to watch out for the teaching of the Pharisees and Sadducees.

Peter's declaration about Jesus

[13]Now when Jesus came to the area of Caesarea Philippi, he asked his disciples, "Who do people say the Human One[o] is?"

[14]They replied, "Some say John the Baptist, others Elijah, and still others Jeremiah or one of the other prophets."

[15]He said, "And what about you? Who do you say that I am?"

[16]Simon Peter said, "You are the Christ, the Son of the living God."

[17]Then Jesus replied, "Happy are you, Simon son of Jonah, because no human has shown this to you. Rather my Father who is in heaven has shown you. [18]I tell you that you are Peter.[p] And I'll build my church on this rock. The gates of the underworld won't be able to stand against it. [19]I'll give you the keys of the kingdom of heaven. Anything you fasten on earth will be fastened in heaven. Anything you loosen on earth will be loosened in heaven." [20]Then he ordered the disciples not to tell anybody that he was the Christ.

First prediction of Jesus' death and resurrection

[21]From that time Jesus began to show his disciples that he had to go to Jerusalem and suffer many things from the elders, chief priests, and legal experts, and that he had to be killed and raised on the third day. [22]Then Peter took hold of Jesus and, scolding him, began to correct him: "God forbid, Lord! This won't happen to you." [23]But he turned to Peter and said, "Get behind me, Satan. You are a stone that could make me stumble, for you are not thinking God's thoughts but human thoughts."

Saving and losing life

[24]Then Jesus said to his disciples, "All who want to come after me must say no to themselves, take up their cross, and follow me. [25]All who want to save their lives will lose them. But all who lose their lives because of me will find them. [26]Why would people gain the whole world but lose their lives? What will people give in exchange for their lives? [27]For the Human One[q] is about to come with the majesty of his Father with

[o]Or *Son of Man*   [p]Peter means *rock*.   [q]Or *Son of Man*

CAESAREA PHILIPPI

Caesarea Philippi is mentioned twice in the NT: Matthew 16:13 and Mark 8:27. Both texts identify the place as the setting for Peter's confession of Jesus as the Messiah. Today the site is known as *Banias*, an Arabic word derived from the Greek *Panias*. The site is 33 mi. north of the Sea of Galilee at the southwestern extremity of Mount Hermon. The Hermon River, one of the sources of the Jordan, emerges from a prominent cave at the site.

his angels. And then he will repay each one for what that person has done. [28]I assure you that some standing here won't die before they see the Human One[r] coming in his kingdom."

Jesus' transformation

17 Six days later Jesus took Peter, James, and John his brother, and brought them to the top of a very high mountain. [2]He was transformed in front of them. His face shone like the sun, and his clothes became as white as light.

[3]Moses and Elijah appeared to them, talking with Jesus. [4]Peter reacted to all of this by saying to Jesus, "Lord, it's good that we're here. If you want, I'll make three shrines: one for you, one for Moses, and one for Elijah."

[5]While he was still speaking, look, a bright cloud overshadowed them. A voice from the cloud said, "This is my Son whom I dearly love. I am very pleased with him. Listen to him!" [6]Hearing this, the disciples fell on their faces, filled with awe.

[7]But Jesus came and touched them. "Get up," he said. "Don't be afraid." [8]When they looked up, they saw no one except Jesus.

[9]As they were coming down the mountain, Jesus commanded them, "Don't tell anybody about the vision until the Human One[s] is raised from the dead."

[10]The disciples asked, "Then why do the legal experts say that Elijah must first come?"

[11]Jesus responded, "Elijah does come first and will restore all things. [12]In fact, I tell you that Elijah has already come, and they didn't know him. But they did to him whatever they wanted. In the same way the Human One[t] is also going to suffer at their hands." [13]Then the disciples realized he was telling them about John the Baptist.

Healing of a boy who was demon-possessed

[14]When they came to the crowd, a man met Jesus. He knelt before him, [15]saying, "Lord, show mercy to my son. He is epileptic and suffers terribly, for he often falls into the fire or the water. [16]I brought him to your disciples, but they couldn't heal him."

[17]Jesus answered, "You faithless and crooked generation, how long will I be with you? How long will I put up with you? Bring the boy here to me." [18]Then Jesus spoke harshly to the demon. And it came out of the child, who was healed from that time on.

[19]Then the disciples came to Jesus in private and said, "Why couldn't we throw the demon out?"

[20]"Because you have little faith," he said. "I assure you that if you have faith the size of a mustard seed, you could say to this mountain, 'Go from here to there,' and it will go. There will be nothing that you can't do."[u]

Second prediction of Jesus' death and resurrection

[22]When the disciples came together in Galilee, Jesus said to them, "The Human One[v] is about to be delivered over into human hands. [23]They will kill him. But he will be raised on the third day." And they were heartbroken.

Paying the temple tax

[24]When they came to Capernaum, the people who collected the half-shekel temple tax came to Peter and said, "Doesn't your teacher pay the temple tax?"

[25]"Yes," he said.

But when they came into the house, Jesus spoke to Peter first. "What do you think, Simon? From whom do earthly kings collect taxes, from their children or from strangers?"

[26]"From strangers," he said.

Jesus said to him, "Then the children don't have to pay. [27]But just so we don't offend them, go to the lake, throw out a fishing line and hook, and take the first fish you catch. When you open its mouth, you will find a shekel coin. Take it and pay the tax for both of us."

Greatest in the kingdom

18 At that time the disciples came to Jesus and asked, "Who is the greatest in the kingdom of heaven?"

[2]Then he called a little child over to sit

---

[r]Or *Son of Man*   [s]Or *Son of Man*   [t]Or *Son of Man*   [u]17:21 is omitted in most critical editions of the Gk New Testament *This kind doesn't come out except through prayer and fasting.*   [v]Or *Son of Man*

among the disciples, [3]and said, "I assure you that if you don't turn your lives around and become like this little child, you will definitely not enter the kingdom of heaven. [4]Those who humble themselves like this little child will be the greatest in the kingdom of heaven. [5]Whoever welcomes one such child in my name welcomes me.

Falling into sin

[6]"As for whoever causes these little ones who believe in me to trip and fall into sin, it would be better for them to have a huge stone hung around their necks and be drowned in the bottom of the lake. [7]How terrible it is for the world because of the things that cause people to trip and fall into sin! Such things have to happen, but how terrible it is for the person who causes those things to happen! [8]If your hand or your foot causes you to fall into sin, chop it off and throw it away. It's better to enter into life crippled or lame than to be thrown into the eternal fire with two hands or two feet. [9]If your eye causes you to fall into sin, tear it out and throw it away. It's better to enter into life with one eye than to be cast into a burning hell with two eyes.

Parable of the lost sheep

[10]"Be careful that you don't look down on one of these little ones. I say to you that their angels in heaven are always looking into the face of my Father who is in heaven.[w] [12]What do you think? If someone had one hundred sheep and one of them wandered off, wouldn't he leave the ninety-nine on the hillsides and go in search for the one that wandered off? [13]If he finds it, I assure you that he is happier about having that one sheep than about the ninety-nine who didn't wander off. [14]In the same way, my Father who is in heaven doesn't want to lose one of these little ones.

Sinning brother or sister

[15]"If your brother or sister sins against you, go and correct them when you are alone

together. If they listen to you, then you've won over your brother or sister. [16]But if they won't listen, take with you one or two others so that *every word may be established by the mouth of two or three witnesses.*[x] [17]But if they still won't pay attention, report it to the church. If they won't pay attention even to the church, treat them as you would a Gentile and tax collector. [18]I assure you that whatever you fasten on earth will be fastened in heaven. And whatever you loosen on earth will be loosened in heaven. [19]Again I assure you that if two of you agree on earth about anything you ask, then my Father who is in heaven will do it for you. [20]For where two or three are gathered in my name, I'm there with them."

Parable of the unforgiving servant

[21]Then Peter said to Jesus, "Lord, how many times should I forgive my brother or sister who sins against me? Should I forgive as many as seven times?"

[22]Jesus said, "Not just seven times, but rather as many as seventy-seven times.[y] [23]Therefore, the kingdom of heaven is like a king who wanted to settle accounts with his servants. [24]When he began to settle accounts, they brought to him a servant who owed him ten thousand bags of gold.[z] [25]Because the servant didn't have enough to pay it back, the master ordered that he should be sold, along with his wife and children and everything he had, and that the proceeds should be used as payment. [26]But the servant fell down, kneeled before him, and said, 'Please, be patient with me, and I'll pay you back.' [27]The master had compassion on that servant, released him, and forgave the loan.

[28]"When that servant went out, he found one of his fellow servants who owed him one hundred coins.[a] He grabbed him around the throat and said, 'Pay me back what you owe me.'

[29]"Then his fellow servant fell down and begged him, 'Be patient with me, and I'll pay you back.' [30]But he refused. Instead,

---

[w]18:11 is omitted in most critical editions of the Gk New Testament *For the Human One has come to save the lost.*
[x]Deut 19:15 [y]Or *seventy times seven* [z]Or *ten thousand talanta,* an amount equal to the wages for sixty million days [a]Or *one hundred denaria,* an amount equal to the wages for one hundred days

he threw him into prison until he paid back his debt.

[31]"When his fellow servants saw what happened, they were deeply offended. They came and told their master all that happened. [32]His master called the first servant and said, 'You wicked servant! I forgave you all that debt because you appealed to me. [33]Shouldn't you also have mercy on your fellow servant, just as I had mercy on you?' [34]His master was furious and handed him over to the guard responsible for punishing prisoners, until he had paid the whole debt. [35]"My heavenly Father will also do the same to you if you don't forgive your brother or sister from your heart."

Teaching about divorce

19 When Jesus finished saying these things, he left Galilee and came to the area of Judea on the east side of the Jordan. [2]Large crowds followed him, and he healed them. [3]Some Pharisees came to him. In order to test him, they said, "Does the Law allow a man to divorce his wife for just any reason?"

[4]Jesus answered, "Haven't you read that at the beginning the creator *made them male and female?*[b] [5]And God said, 'Because of this a man should leave his father and mother and be joined together with his wife, and the two will be one flesh.'[c] [6]So they are no longer two but one flesh. Therefore, humans must not pull apart what God has put together."

[7]The Pharisees said to him, "Then why did Moses command us to *give a divorce certificate and divorce her?*[d]

[8]Jesus replied, "Moses allowed you to divorce your wives because your hearts are unyielding. But it wasn't that way from the beginning. [9]I say to you that whoever divorces his wife, except for sexual unfaithfulness, and marries another woman commits adultery."

[10]His disciples said to him, "If that's the way things are between a man and his wife, then it's better not to marry."

[11]He replied, "Not everybody can accept this teaching, but only those who have received the ability to accept it. [12]For there are eunuchs who have been eunuchs from birth. And there are eunuchs who have been made eunuchs by other people. And there are eunuchs who have made themselves eunuchs because of the kingdom of heaven. Those who can accept it should accept it."

Jesus blesses children

[13]Some people brought children to Jesus so that he would place his hands on them

[b]Gen 1:27; 5:2   [c]Gen 2:24   [d]Deut 24:1

KINGDOM OF HEAVEN/ GOD'S KINGDOM

The OT and the NT portray God as king of the universe, the fundamental force behind everything. The biblical phrases "kingdom of God" and "kingdom of heaven" focus on God's role in shaping human experience. The promise of the kingdom is that people will at last come to realize divine justice and peace in all that they do. Jesus made God's kingdom the center of his preaching and activity, and this idea has been essential for the development of Christian life and theology. Views of the coming and present kingdom of God influenced the ethical behavior of the earliest Christians and gave them the hope and strength to spread the message of the transformative power of God's action in the created world.

and pray. But the disciples scolded them. [14]"Allow the children to come to me," Jesus said. "Don't forbid them, because the kingdom of heaven belongs to people like these children." [15]Then he blessed the children and went away from there.

A rich man's question

[16]A man approached him and said, "Teacher, what good thing must I do to have eternal life?"

[17]Jesus said, "Why do you ask me about what is good? There's only one who is good. If you want to enter eternal life, keep the commandments."

[18]The man said, "Which ones?"

Then Jesus said, *"Don't commit murder. Don't commit adultery. Don't steal. Don't give false testimony.* [19]*Honor your father and mother,*[e] *and love your neighbor as you love yourself."*[f]

[20]The young man replied, "I've kept all these. What am I still missing?"

[21]Jesus said, "If you want to be complete, go, sell what you own, and give the money to the poor. Then you will have treasure in heaven. And come follow me."

[22]But when the young man heard this, he went away saddened, because he had many possessions.

Teaching about giving up things

[23]Then Jesus said to his disciples, "I assure you that it will be very hard for a rich person to enter the kingdom of heaven. [24]In fact, it's easier for a camel to squeeze through the eye of a needle than for a rich person to enter God's kingdom."

[25]When his disciples heard this, they were stunned. "Then who can be saved?" they asked.

[26]Jesus looked at them carefully and said, "It's impossible for human beings. But all things are possible for God."

[27]Then Peter replied, "Look, we've left everything and followed you. What will we have?"

[28]Jesus said to them, "I assure you who have followed me that, when everything is made new, when the Human One[g] sits on his magnificent throne, you also will sit on twelve thrones overseeing the twelve tribes of Israel. [29]And all who have left houses, brothers, sisters, father, mother, children, or farms because of my name will receive one hundred times more and will inherit eternal life. [30]But many who are first will be last. And many who are last will be first.

Workers in the vineyard

20 "The kingdom of heaven is like a landowner who went out early in the morning to hire workers for his vineyard. [2]After he agreed with the workers to pay them a denarion,[h] he sent them into his vineyard.

[3]"Then he went out around nine in the morning and saw others standing around the marketplace doing nothing. [4]He said to them, 'You also go into the vineyard, and I'll pay you whatever is right.' [5]And they went.

"Again around noon and then at three in the afternoon, he did the same thing. [6]Around five in the afternoon he went and found others standing around, and he said to them, 'Why are you just standing around here doing nothing all day long?'

[7]"'Because nobody has hired us,' they replied.

"He responded, 'You also go into the vineyard.'

[8]"When evening came, the owner of the vineyard said to his manager, 'Call the workers and give them their wages, beginning with the last ones hired and moving on finally to the first.' [9]When those who were hired at five in the afternoon came, each one received a denarion. [10]Now when those hired first came, they thought they would receive more. But each of them also received a denarion. [11]When they received it, they grumbled against the landowner, [12]'These who were hired last worked one hour, and they received the same pay as we did even though we had to work the whole day in the hot sun.'

[13]"But he replied to one of them, 'Friend, I did you no wrong. Didn't I agree to pay you a denarion? [14]Take what belongs to you and

[e]Exod 20:12-16; Deut 5:16-20   [f]Lev 19:18   [g]Or *Son of Man*   [h]A denarion was a typical day's wage.

go. I want to give to this one who was hired last the same as I give to you. [15]Don't I have the right to do what I want with what belongs to me? Or are you resentful because I'm generous?' [16]So those who are last will be first. And those who are first will be last."

Jesus predicts his death and resurrection

[17]As Jesus was going up to Jerusalem, he took the Twelve aside by themselves on the road. He told them, [18]"Look, we are going up to Jerusalem. The Human One[i] will be handed over to the chief priests and legal experts. They will condemn him to death. [19]They will hand him over to the Gentiles to be ridiculed, tortured, and crucified. But he will be raised on the third day."

Request from James and John's mother

[20]Then the mother of Zebedee's sons came to Jesus along with her sons. Bowing before him, she asked a favor of him.

[21]"What do you want?" he asked.

She responded, "Say that these two sons of mine will sit, one on your right hand and one on your left, in your kingdom."

[22]Jesus replied, "You don't know what you're asking! Can you drink from the cup that I'm about to drink from?"

They said to him, "We can."

[23]He said to them, "You will drink from my cup, but to sit at my right or left hand isn't mine to give. It belongs to those for whom my Father prepared it."

[24]Now when the other ten disciples heard about this, they became angry with the two brothers. [25]But Jesus called them over and said, "You know that those who rule the Gentiles show off their authority over them and their high-ranking officials order them around. [26]But that's not the way it will be with you. Whoever wants to be great among you will be your servant. [27]Whoever wants to be first among you will be your slave—[28]just as the Human One[j] didn't come to be served but rather to serve and to give his life to liberate many people."

Healing of two blind men

[29]As Jesus and his disciples were going out of Jericho a large crowd followed him. [30]When two blind men sitting along the road heard that Jesus was passing by, they shouted, "Show us mercy, Lord, Son of David!"

[31]Now the crowd scolded them and told them to be quiet. But they shouted even louder, "Show us mercy, Lord, Son of David!"

[32]Jesus stopped in his tracks and called to them. "What do you want me to do for you?" he asked.

[33]"Lord, we want to see," they replied.

[34]Jesus had compassion on them and touched their eyes. Immediately they were able to see, and they followed him.

Entry into Jerusalem

21 When they approached Jerusalem and came to Bethphage on the Mount of Olives, Jesus gave two disciples a task. [2]He said to them, "Go into the village over there. As soon as you enter, you will find a donkey tied up and a colt with it. Untie them and bring them to me. [3]If anybody says anything to you, say that the Lord needs it." He sent them off right away. [4]Now this happened to fulfill what

[i]Or Son of Man   [j]Or Son of Man

COURT OF THE GENTILES

The area of the Jerusalem temple where Gentiles who conducted themselves reverently were permitted to enter. It was an open area surrounded by porches or cloisters. This court was the location of the merchants and the moneychangers Jesus drove from the temple.

the prophet said, [5]*Say to Daughter Zion,* *"Look, your king is coming to you, humble and riding on a donkey, and on a colt the donkey's offspring."*[k] [6]The disciples went and did just as Jesus had ordered them. [7]They brought the donkey and the colt and laid their clothes on them. Then he sat on them.

[8]Now a large crowd spread their clothes on the road. Others cut palm branches off the trees and spread them on the road. [9]The crowds in front of him and behind him shouted, *"Hosanna to the Son of David! Blessings on the one who comes in the name of the Lord!*[l] *Hosanna in the highest!"* [10]And when Jesus entered Jerusalem, the whole city was stirred up. "Who is this?" they asked. [11]The crowds answered, "It's the prophet Jesus from Nazareth in Galilee."

Cleansing the temple

[12]Then Jesus went into the temple and threw out all those who were selling and buying there. He pushed over the tables used for currency exchange and the chairs of those who sold doves. [13]He said to them, "It's written, *My house will be called a house of prayer.*[m] But you've made it a hideout for crooks."

[14]People who were blind and lame came to Jesus in the temple, and he healed them. [15]But when the chief priests and legal experts saw the amazing things he was doing and the children shouting in the temple, *"Hosanna to the Son of David!"* they were angry. [16]They said to Jesus, "Do you hear what these children are saying?"

"Yes," he answered. "Haven't you ever read, *From the mouths of babies and infants you've arranged praise for yourself?*[n] [17]Then he left them and went out of the city to Bethany and spent the night there.

Cursing the fig tree

[18]Early in the morning as Jesus was returning to the city, he was hungry. [19]He saw a fig tree along the road, but when he came to it, he found nothing except leaves. Then he said to it, "You'll never again bear fruit!" The fig tree dried up at once.

[20]When the disciples saw it, they were amazed. "How did the fig tree dry up so fast?" they asked.

[21]Jesus responded, "I assure you that if you have faith and don't doubt, you will not only do what was done to the fig tree. You will even say to this mountain, 'Be lifted up and thrown into the lake.' And it will happen. [22]If you have faith, you will receive whatever you pray for."

Jesus' authority questioned

[23]When Jesus entered the temple, the chief priests and elders of the people came to him as he was teaching. They asked, "What kind of authority do you have for doing these things? Who gave you this authority?"

[24]Jesus replied, "I have a question for you. If you tell me the answer, I'll tell you what kind of authority I have to do these things. [25]Where did John get his authority to baptize? Did he get it from heaven or from humans?"

They argued among themselves, "If we say 'from heaven,' he'll say to us, 'Then why didn't you believe him?' [26]But we can't say 'from humans' because we're afraid of the crowd, since everyone thinks John was a prophet." [27]Then they replied, "We don't know."

Jesus also said to them, "Neither will I tell you what kind of authority I have to do these things.

Parable of two sons

[28]"What do you think? A man had two sons. Now he came to the first and said, 'Son, go and work in the vineyard today.'

[29]"'No, I don't want to,' he replied. But later he changed his mind and went.

[30]"The father said the same thing to the other son, who replied, 'Yes, sir.' But he didn't go.

[31]"Which one of these two did his father's will?"

They said, "The first one."

Jesus said to them, "I assure you that tax collectors and prostitutes are entering

[k]Isa 62:11; Zech 9:9 [l]Ps. 118:26 [m]Isa 56:7; Jer 7:11 [n]Ps 8:3 LXX

God's kingdom ahead of you. ³²For John came to you on the righteous road, and you didn't believe him. But tax collectors and prostitutes believed him. Yet even after you saw this, you didn't change your hearts and lives and you didn't believe him.

Parable of the tenant farmers

³³"Listen to another parable. There was a landowner who planted a vineyard. He put a fence around it, dug a winepress in it, and built a tower. Then he rented it to tenant farmers and took a trip. ³⁴When it was time for harvest, he sent his servants to the tenant farmers to collect his fruit. ³⁵But the tenant farmers grabbed his servants. They beat some of them, and some of them they killed. Some of them they stoned to death.

³⁶"Again he sent other servants, more than the first group. They treated them in the same way. ³⁷Finally he sent his son to them. 'They will respect my son,' he said.

³⁸"But when the tenant farmers saw the son, they said to each other, 'This is the heir. Come on, let's kill him and we'll have his inheritance.' ³⁹They grabbed him, threw him out of the vineyard, and killed him.

⁴⁰"When the owner of the vineyard comes, what will he do to those tenant farmers?"

⁴¹They said, "He will totally destroy those wicked farmers and rent the vineyard to other tenant farmers who will give him the fruit when it's ready."

⁴²Jesus said to them, "Haven't you ever read in the scriptures, *The stone that the builders rejected has become the cornerstone. The Lord has done this, and it's amazing in our eyes?*⁰ ⁴³Therefore, I tell you that God's kingdom will be taken away from you and will be given to a people who produce its fruit. ⁴⁴Whoever falls on this stone will be crushed. And the stone will crush the person it falls on."

⁴⁵Now when the chief priests and the Pharisees heard the parable, they knew Jesus was talking about them. ⁴⁶They were trying to arrest him, but they feared the crowds, who thought he was a prophet.

Parable of the wedding party

22 Jesus responded by speaking again in parables: ²"The kingdom of heaven is like a king who prepared a wedding party for his son. ³He sent his servants to call those invited to the wedding party. But they didn't want to come. ⁴Again he sent other servants and said to them, 'Tell those who have been invited, "Look, the meal is all prepared. I've butchered the oxen and the fattened cattle. Now everything's ready. Come to the wedding party!"' ⁵But they paid no attention and went away—some to their fields, others to their businesses. ⁶The rest of them grabbed his servants, abused them, and killed them.

⁷"The king was angry. He sent his soldiers to destroy those murderers and set their city on fire. ⁸Then he said to his servants, 'The wedding party is prepared, but those who were invited weren't worthy. ⁹Therefore, go to the roads on the edge of town and invite everyone you find to the wedding party.'

¹⁰"Then those servants went to the roads and gathered everyone they found, both evil and good. The wedding party was full of guests. ¹¹Now when the king came in and saw the guests, he spotted a man who wasn't wearing wedding clothes. ¹²He said to him, 'Friend, how did you get in here without wedding clothes?' But he was speechless. ¹³Then the king said to his servants, 'Tie his hands and feet and throw him out into the farthest darkness. People there will be weeping and grinding their teeth.'

¹⁴"Many people are invited, but few people are chosen."

Question about taxes

¹⁵Then the Pharisees met together to find a way to trap Jesus in his words. ¹⁶They sent their disciples, along with the supporters of Herod, to him. "Teacher," they said, "we know that you are genuine and that you teach God's way as it really is. We know that you are not swayed by people's opinions, because you don't show favoritism.

¹⁷So tell us what you think: Does the Law allow people to pay taxes to Caesar or not?"

¹⁸Knowing their evil motives, Jesus replied, "Why do you test me, you hypocrites? ¹⁹Show me the coin used to pay the tax." And they brought him a denarion. ²⁰"Whose image and inscription is this?" he asked.

²¹"Caesar's," they replied.

Then he said, "Give to Caesar what belongs to Caesar and to God what belongs to God." ²²When they heard this they were astonished, and they departed.

Question about resurrection

²³That same day Sadducees, who deny that there is a resurrection, came to Jesus. ²⁴They asked, "Teacher, Moses said, *If a man who doesn't have children dies, his brother must marry his wife and produce children for his brother.*ᴾ ²⁵Now there were seven brothers among us. The first one married, then died. Because he had no children he left his widow to his brother. ²⁶The same thing happened with the second brother and the third, and in fact with all seven brothers.

²⁷Finally, the woman died. ²⁸At the resurrection, which of the seven brothers will be her husband? They were all married to her."

²⁹Jesus responded, "You are wrong because you don't know either the scriptures or God's power. ³⁰At the resurrection people won't marry nor will they be given in marriage. Instead, they will be like angels from God. ³¹As for the resurrection of the dead, haven't you read what God told you, ³²*I'm the God of Abraham, the God of Isaac, and the God of Jacob?*�q He isn't the God of the dead but of the living." ³³Now when the crowd heard this, they were astonished at his teaching.

Great commandment

³⁴When the Pharisees heard that Jesus had left the Sadducees speechless, they met together. ³⁵One of them, a legal expert, tested him. ³⁶"Teacher, what is the greatest commandment in the Law?"

³⁷He replied, "*You must love the Lord your God with all your heart, with all your being,*ʳ and with all your mind. ³⁸This is the first and greatest commandment. ³⁹And the

ᴾDeut 25:5 qExod 3:6, 15-16 ʳDeut 6:5

SADDUCEES

A religious and social party that played a dominant role in the history of the high priesthood, the temple, and Jewish Law during Jesus' time. The Sadducees are mentioned several times in the NT as among Jesus' adversaries, together with the Pharisees (e.g., Matt 3:7; 16:1, 6, 11). The Sadducees did not believe in the resurrection of the body or in the persistence of the soul after death (Matt 22:23-33; Mark 12:18-27). Sadducean high priests led the harassment of Jesus and other early Christian leaders. Joseph Caiaphas (who was the governing high priest ca. 18–36 CE) arrested Jesus. One of the accusations with which Jesus was charged was his threat to destroy the temple (Matt 26:3, 57-68; Mark 14:53-65). The Sadducees, including Caiaphas and Annas the Elder, arrested and flogged Peter and the apostles when the apostles preached and healed in the name of Jesus at the temple mount (Acts 4:1-22; 5:12-40). According to Acts, after Paul was arrested at the temple mount for allowing a Gentile to enter the temple's sacred precinct, he was brought before the Sanhedrin, which consisted of Sadducees and Pharisees (who debated the theological problem of resurrection instead of accusing Paul; Acts 22:30–23:10).

second is like it: *You must love your neighbor as you love yourself.*[s] [40]All the Law and the Prophets depend on these two commands."

Question about David's son

[41]Now as the Pharisees were gathering, Jesus asked them, [42]"What do you think about the Christ? Whose son is he?"

"David's son," they replied.

[43]He said, "Then how is it that David, inspired by the Holy Spirit, called him Lord when he said, [44]*The Lord said to my lord, 'Sit at my right side until I turn your enemies into your footstool'?*[t] [45]If David calls him Lord, how can he be David's son?" [46]Nobody was able to answer him. And from that day forward nobody dared to ask him anything.

Ways of the legal experts and the Pharisees

23 Then Jesus spoke to the crowds and his disciples, [2]"The legal experts and the Pharisees sit on Moses' seat. [3]Therefore, you must take care to do everything they say. But don't do what they do. [4]For they tie together heavy packs that are impossible to carry. They put them on the shoulders of others, but are unwilling to lift a finger to move them. [5]Everything they do, they do to be noticed by others. They make extra-wide prayer bands for their arms and long tassels for their clothes. [6]They love to sit in places of honor at banquets. [7]They love to

be greeted with honor in the markets and to be addressed as 'Rabbi.'

[8]"But you shouldn't be called *Rabbi*, because you have one teacher, and all of you are brothers and sisters. [9]Don't call anybody on earth your father, because you have one Father, who is heavenly. [10]Don't be called *teacher*, because Christ is your one teacher. [11]But the one who is greatest among you will be your servant. [12]All who lift themselves up will be brought low. But all who make themselves low will be lifted up.

Condemnation of the legal experts and the Pharisees

[13]"How terrible it will be for you legal experts and Pharisees! Hypocrites! You shut people out of the kingdom of heaven. You don't enter yourselves, and you won't allow those who want to enter to do so.[u]

[15]"How terrible it will be for you, legal experts and Pharisees! Hypocrites! You travel over sea and land to make one convert. But when they've been converted, they become twice the child of hell you are.

[16]"How terrible it will be for you blind guides who say, 'If people swear by the temple, it's nothing. But if people swear by the gold in the temple, they are obligated to do what they swore.' [17]You foolish and blind people! Which is greater, the gold or the temple that makes the gold holy? [18]You say, 'If people swear by the altar, it's nothing.

[s]Lev 19:18 [t]Ps 110:1 [u]Most critical editions of the Gk New Testament omit 23:14 *How terrible it will be for you legal experts and Pharisees! Hypocrites! You eat up widows' houses and make a show of praying long prayers. Therefore, you will receive greater judgment.*

ABEL

The second son of Adam and Eve (Gen 4:2), Abel appears in the OT only as the brother killed by Cain because God preferred Abel's offering to Cain's (Gen 4:1-16). Commentators connect the name Abel with the Hebrew noun meaning "vapor, breath" (e.g., Isa 57:13; Ps 144:4), which would show Abel's ephemeral life, underscored by the absence of any mention of offspring. In Matthew 23:35 (Luke 11:51) Abel is the prototype of the murdered innocent. In Hebrews 11:4 he is shown as the first man of faith, recognized as such by God's acceptance of his offering.

But if they swear by the gift on the altar, they are obligated to do what they swore.' ¹⁹You blind people! Which is greater, the gift or the altar that makes the gift holy? ²⁰Therefore, those who swear by the altar swear by it and by everything that's on it. ²¹Those who swear by the temple swear by it and by everything that's part of it. ²²Those who swear by heaven swear by God's throne and by the one who sits on it.

²³"How terrible it will be for you legal experts and Pharisees! Hypocrites! You give to God a tenth of mint, dill, and cumin, but you forget about the more important matters of the Law: justice, peace, and faith. You ought to give a tenth but without forgetting about those more important matters. ²⁴You blind guides! You filter out an ant but swallow a camel.

²⁵"How terrible it will be for you legal experts and Pharisees! Hypocrites! You clean the outside of the cup and plate, but inside they are full of violence and pleasure seeking. ²⁶Blind Pharisee! First clean the inside of the cup so that the outside of the cup will be clean too.

²⁷"How terrible it will be for you legal experts and Pharisees! Hypocrites! You are like whitewashed tombs. They look beautiful on the outside. But inside they are full of dead bones and all kinds of filth. ²⁸In the same way you look righteous to people. But inside you are full of pretense and rebellion.

²⁹"How terrible it will be for you legal experts and Pharisees! Hypocrites! You build tombs for the prophets and decorate the graves of the righteous. ³⁰You say, 'If we had lived in our ancestors' days, we wouldn't have joined them in killing the prophets.' ³¹You testify against yourselves that you are children of those who murdered the prophets. ³²Go ahead, complete what your ancestors did. ³³You snakes! You children of snakes! How will you be able to escape the judgment of hell? ³⁴Therefore, look, I'm sending you prophets, wise people, and legal experts. Some of them you will kill and crucify. And some you will beat in your synagogues and chase from

city to city. ³⁵Therefore, upon you will come all the righteous blood that has been poured out on the earth, from the blood of that righteous man Abel to the blood of Zechariah the son of Barachiah, whom you killed between the temple and the altar. ³⁶I assure you that all these things will come upon this generation.

Crying over Jerusalem

³⁷"Jerusalem, Jerusalem! You who kill the prophets and stone those who were sent to you. How often I wanted to gather your people together, just as a hen gathers her chicks under her wings. But you didn't want that. ³⁸Look, your house is left to you deserted. ³⁹I tell you, you won't see me until you say, *Blessings on the one who comes in the Lord's name.*"ᵛ

The temple's fate

24 Now Jesus left the temple and was going away. His disciples came to point out to him the temple buildings. ²He responded, "Do you see all these things? I assure that no stone will be left on another. Everything will be demolished."

Beginning of troubles

³Now while Jesus was sitting on the Mount of Olives, the disciples came to him privately and said, "Tell us, when will these things happen? What will be the sign of your coming and the end of the age?"

⁴Jesus replied, "Watch out that no one deceives you. ⁵Many will come in my name, saying, 'I'm the Christ.' They will deceive many people. ⁶You will hear about wars and reports of wars. Don't be alarmed. These things must happen, but this isn't the end yet. ⁷Nations and kingdoms will fight against each other, and there will be famines and earthquakes in all sorts of places. ⁸But all these things are just the beginning of the sufferings associated with the end. ⁹They will arrest you, abuse you, and they will kill you. All nations will hate you on account of my name. ¹⁰At that time many will fall away. They will betray each other and

ᵛPs 118:26

hate each other. ¹¹Many false prophets will appear and deceive many people. ¹²Because disobedience will expand, the love of many will grow cold. ¹³But the one who endures to the end will be delivered. ¹⁴This gospel of the kingdom will be proclaimed throughout the world as a testimony to all the nations. Then the end will come.

The great suffering

¹⁵"When you see the disgusting and destructive thing that Daniel talked about standing in the holy place (the reader should understand this), ¹⁶then those in Judea must escape to the mountains. ¹⁷Those on the roof shouldn't come down to grab things from their houses. ¹⁸Those in the field shouldn't come back to grab their clothes. ¹⁹How terrible it will be at

that time for women who are pregnant and for women who are nursing their children. ²⁰Pray that it doesn't happen in winter or on the Sabbath day. ²¹There will be great suffering such as the world has never before seen and will never again see. ²²If that time weren't shortened, nobody would be rescued. But for the sake of the ones whom God chose, that time will be cut short.

²³"Then if somebody says to you, 'Look, here's the Christ,' or 'He's over here,' don't believe it. ²⁴False christs and false prophets will appear, and they will offer great signs and wonders in order to deceive, if possible, even those whom God has chosen. ²⁵Look, I've told you ahead of time. ²⁶So if they say to you, 'Look, he's in the desert,' don't go out. And if they say, 'Look, he's in the rooms deep inside the house,' don't be-

MOUNT OF OLIVES

A ridge with three crests, approximately two mi. long, located across the Kidron Valley from Jerusalem. With the highest point reaching approximately 2,700 ft., it stands just over 100 ft. above the temple mount in Jerusalem to the east and about 4,000 ft. above the Dead Sea to the west, thus providing dramatic views of the surrounding area. In biblical times, it supported a plentiful stand of olive trees, from which it received its name.

The name Mount of Olives appears only three times in the OT (Zech 14:4 twice and 2 Sam 15:30). References to the Mount of Olives in the NT are limited to the Jesus-tradition reported in the Gospels and Acts. Jesus' familiarity with the mount is evident from his lodging with friends in Bethany (e.g., Mark 11:11; 14:3), located on the ridge of the mount. During Jesus' final week teaching in the temple, "he spent each night on the Mount of Olives" (Luke 21:37). It is from the Mount of Olives that Jesus sends two disciples to prepare for his entry into Jerusalem, and his triumphal entry would have begun from Bethphage on its summit (Matt 21:1-11; Mark 11:1-10; Luke 19:29-40 read "Bethphage and Bethany"; see John 12:12-15). Luke adds that, on the way down the Mount of Olives, Jesus wept over the city (19:41-44). The site of ancient Bethany is probably to be identified with the modern village el-Azariyeh, but the exact location of Bethphage is contested; presumably, it was along the ridge nearer the summit. According to Matthew 24 and Mark 13, Jesus warned of the coming destruction of the temple while seated with his disciples on the Mount of Olives.

Luke also locates the ascension of Jesus on the Mount of Olives (Luke 24:50-51; Acts 1:9-12).

lieve it. [27] Just as the lightning flashes from the east to the west, so it will be with the coming of the Human One.[w] [28] The vultures gather wherever there's a dead body.

Coming of the Human One

[29] "Now immediately after the suffering of that time the sun will become dark, and the moon won't give its light. The stars will fall from the sky and the planets and other heavenly bodies will be shaken. [30] Then the sign of the Human One[x] will appear in the sky. At that time all the tribes of the earth will be full of sadness, and they will see *the Human One[y] coming in the heavenly clouds[z]* with power and great splendor. [31] He will send his angels with the sound of a great trumpet, and they will gather his chosen ones from the four corners of the earth, from one end of the sky to the other.

A lesson from the fig tree

[32] "Learn this parable from the fig tree. After its branch becomes tender and it sprouts new leaves, you know that summer is near. [33] In the same way, when you see all these things, you know that the Human One[a] is near, at the door. [34] I assure you that this generation won't pass away until all these things happen. [35] Heaven and earth will pass away, but my words will certainly not pass away.

Day and hour

[36] "But nobody knows when that day or hour will come, not the heavenly angels and not the Son. Only the Father knows. [37] As it was in the time of Noah, so it will be at the coming of the Human One.[b] [38] In those days before the flood, people were eating and drinking, marrying and giving in marriage, until the day Noah entered the ark. [39] They didn't know what was happening until the flood came and swept them all away. The coming of the Human One[c] will be like that. [40] At that time there will be two men in the field. One will be taken and the other left. [41] Two women will be grinding at

the mill. One will be taken and the other left. [42] Therefore, stay alert! You don't know what day the Lord is coming. [43] But you understand that if the head of the house knew at what time the thief would come, he would keep alert and wouldn't allow the thief to break into his house. [44] Therefore, you also should be prepared, because the Human One[d] will come at a time you don't know.

Faithful and unfaithful servants

[45] "Who then are the faithful and wise servants whom their master puts in charge of giving food at the right time to those who live in his house? [46] Happy are those servants whom the master finds fulfilling their responsibilities when he comes. [47] I assure you that he will put them in charge of all his possessions. [48] But suppose those bad servants should say to themselves, My master won't come until later. [49] And suppose they began to beat their fellow servants and to eat and drink with the drunks? [50] The master of those servants will come on a day when they are not expecting him, at a time they couldn't predict. [51] He will cut them in pieces and put them in a place with the hypocrites. People there will be weeping and grinding their teeth.

Parable of the ten young bridesmaids

25 "At that time the kingdom of heaven will be like ten young bridesmaids who took their lamps and went out to meet the groom. [2] Now five of them were wise, and the other five were foolish. [3] The foolish ones took their lamps but didn't bring oil for them. [4] But the wise ones took their lamps and also brought containers of oil.

[5] "When the groom was late in coming, they all became drowsy and went to sleep. [6] But at midnight there was a cry, 'Look, the groom! Come out to meet him.'

[7] "Then all those bridesmaids got up and prepared their lamps. [8] But the foolish bridesmaids said to the wise ones, 'Give us some of your oil, because our lamps have gone out.'

---

[w] Or *Son of Man*   [x] Or *Son of Man*   [y] Or *Son of Man*   [z] Dan 7:13 *I suddenly saw one like a human being* (Aram *kebar enash*) *coming with the heavenly clouds.*   [a] Or *Son of Man*   [b] Or *Son of Man*   [c] Or *Son of Man*   [d] Or *Son of Man*

⁹"But the wise bridesmaids replied, 'No, because if we share with you, there won't be enough for our lamps and yours. We have a better idea. You go to those who sell oil and buy some for yourselves.' ¹⁰But while they were gone to buy oil, the groom came. Those who were ready went with him into the wedding. Then the door was shut.

¹¹"Later the other bridesmaids came and said, 'Lord, lord, open the door for us.'

¹²"But he replied, 'I tell you the truth, I don't know you.'

¹³"Therefore, keep alert, because you don't know the day or the hour.

Parable of the valuable coins

¹⁴"The kingdom of heaven is like a man who was leaving on a trip. He called his servants and handed his possessions over to them. ¹⁵To one he gave five valuable coins,ᵉ and to another he gave two, and to another he gave one. He gave to each servant according to that servant's ability. Then he left on his journey.

¹⁶"After the man left, the servant who had five valuable coins took them and went to work doing business with them. He gained five more. ¹⁷In the same way, the one who had two valuable coins gained two more. ¹⁸But the servant who had received the one valuable coin dug a hole in the ground and buried his master's money.

¹⁹"Now after a long time the master of those servants returned and settled accounts with them. ²⁰The one who had received five valuable coins came forward with five additional coins. He said, 'Master, you gave me five valuable coins. Look, I've gained five more.'

²¹"His master replied, 'Excellent! You are a good and faithful servant! You've been faithful over a little. I'll put you in charge of much. Come, celebrate with me.'

²²"The second servant also came forward and said, 'Master, you gave me two valuable coins. Look, I've gained two more.'

²³"His master replied, 'Well done! You are a good and faithful servant. You've been faithful over a little. I'll put you in charge of much. Come, celebrate with me.'

²⁴"Now the one who had received one valuable coin came and said, 'Master, I knew that you are a hard man. You harvest grain where you haven't sown. You gather crops where you haven't spread seed. ²⁵So I was afraid. And I hid my valuable coin in the ground. Here, you have what's yours.'

²⁶"His master replied, 'You evil and lazy servant! You knew that I harvest grain where I haven't sown and that I gather crops where I haven't spread seed? ²⁷In that case, you should have turned my money over to the bankers so that when I returned, you could give me what belonged to me with interest. ²⁸Therefore, take from him the valuable coin and give it to the one who has ten coins. ²⁹Those who have much will receive more, and they will have more than they need. But as for those who don't have much, even the little bit they have will be taken away from them. ³⁰Now take the worthless servant and throw him outside into the darkness.'

"People there will be weeping and grinding their teeth.

Judgment of the nations

³¹"Now when the Human Oneᶠ comes in his majesty and all his angels are with him, he will sit on his majestic throne. ³²All the nations will be gathered in front of him. He will separate them from each other, just as a shepherd separates the sheep from the goats. ³³He will put the sheep on his right side. But the goats he will put on his left.

³⁴"Then the king will say to those on his right, 'Come, you who will receive good things from my Father. Inherit the kingdom that was prepared for you before the world began. ³⁵I was hungry and you gave me food to eat. I was thirsty and you gave me a drink. I was a stranger and you welcomed me. ³⁶I was naked and you gave me clothes to wear. I was sick and you took care of me. I was in prison and you visited me.'

³⁷"Then those who are righteous will reply to him, 'Lord, when did we see you hungry and feed you, or thirsty and give you a drink? ³⁸When did we see you as a

ᵉOr talantas (talents) ᶠOr Son of Man

stranger and welcome you, or naked and give you clothes to wear? ^{39}When did we see you sick or in prison and visit you?'

^{40}"Then the king will reply to them, 'I assure you that when you have done it for one of the least of these brothers and sisters of mine, you have done it for me.'

^{41}"Then he will say to those on his left, 'Get away from me, you who will receive terrible things. Go into the unending fire that has been prepared for the devil and his angels. ^{42}I was hungry and you didn't give me food to eat. I was thirsty and you didn't give me anything to drink. ^{43}I was a stranger and you didn't welcome me. I was naked and you didn't give me clothes to wear. I was sick and in prison, and you didn't visit me.'

^{44}"Then they will reply, 'Lord, when did we see you hungry or thirsty or a stranger or naked or sick or in prison and didn't do anything to help you?' ^{45}Then he will answer, 'I assure you that when you haven't done it for one of the least of these, you haven't done it for me.' ^{46}And they will go away into eternal punishment. But the righteous ones will go into eternal life."

Plot to kill Jesus

26 When Jesus finished speaking all these words, he said to his disciples, ^{2}"You know that the Passover is two days from now. And the Human One^g will be handed over to be crucified."

^{3}Then the chief priests and elders of the people gathered in the courtyard of Caiaphas the high priest. ^{4}They were plotting to arrest Jesus by cunning tricks and to kill him. ^{5}But they agreed that it shouldn't happen during the feast so there wouldn't be an uproar among the people.

A woman pouring perfume on Jesus

^{6}When Jesus was at Bethany visiting the house of Simon, who had a skin disease, ^{7}a woman came to him with a vase made of alabaster containing very expensive perfume. She poured it on Jesus' head while he was sitting at dinner. ^{8}Now when the

disciples saw it they were angry and said, "Why this waste? ^{9}This perfume could have been sold for a lot of money and given to the poor."

^{10}But Jesus knew what they were thinking. He said, "Why do you make trouble for the woman? She's done a good thing for me. ^{11}You always have the poor with you, but you won't always have me. ^{12}By pouring this perfume over my body she's prepared me to be buried. ^{13}I tell you the truth that wherever in the whole world this good news is announced, what she's done will also be told in memory of her."

Judas betrays Jesus

^{14}Then one of the Twelve, who was called Judas Iscariot, went to the chief priests ^{15}and said, "What will you give me if I turn Jesus over to you?" They paid him thirty pieces of silver. ^{16}From that time on he was looking for an opportunity to turn him in.

Passover with the disciples

^{17}On the first day of the Festival of Unleavened Bread, the disciples came to Jesus and said, "Where do you want us to prepare for you to eat the Passover meal?"

^{18}He replied, "Go into the city, to a certain man, and say, 'The teacher says, "My time is near. I'm going to celebrate the Passover with my disciples at your house."'" ^{19}The disciples did just as Jesus instructed them. They prepared the Passover.

^{20}That evening he took his place at the table with the twelve disciples. ^{21}As they were eating he said, "I assure you that one of you will betray me."

^{22}Deeply saddened, each one said to him, "I'm not the one, am I, Lord?"

^{23}He replied, "The one who will betray me is the one who dips his hand with me into this bowl. ^{24}The Human One^h goes to his death just as it is written about him. But how terrible it is for that person who betrays the Human One!^{i} It would have been better for him if he had never been born."

^{25}Now Judas, who would betray him, replied, "It's not me, is it, Rabbi?"

Jesus answered, "You said it."

^{g}Or Son of Man ^{h}Or Son of Man ^{i}Or Son of Man

Last supper

²⁶While they were eating, Jesus took bread, blessed it, broke it, and gave it to the disciples and said, "Take and eat. This is my body." ²⁷He took a cup, gave thanks, and gave it to them, saying, "Drink from this, all of you. ²⁸This is my blood of the covenant, which is poured out for many so that their sins may be forgiven. ²⁹I tell you, I won't drink wine again until that day when I drink it in a new way with you in my Father's kingdom." ³⁰Then, after singing songs of praise, they went to the Mount of Olives.

Predictions about disciples leaving Jesus

³¹Then Jesus said to his disciples, "Tonight you will all fall away because of me. This is because it is written, *I will hit the shepherd, and the sheep of the flock will go off in all directions.*ʲ ³²But after I'm raised up, I'll go before you to Galilee."

³³Peter replied, "If everyone else stumbles because of you, I'll never stumble."

³⁴Jesus said to him, "I assure you that, before the rooster crows tonight, you will deny me three times."

³⁵Peter said, "Even if I must die alongside you, I won't deny you." All the disciples said the same thing.

ʲZech 13:7 ᵏOr *Son of Man*

Jesus in prayer

³⁶Then Jesus went with his disciples to a place called Gethsemane. He said to the disciples, "Stay here while I go and pray over there." ³⁷When he took Peter and Zebedee's two sons, he began to feel sad and anxious. ³⁸Then he said to them, "I'm very sad. It's as if I'm dying. Stay here and keep alert with me." ³⁹Then he went a short distance farther and fell on his face and prayed, "My Father, if it's possible, take this cup of suffering away from me. However—not what I want but what you want."

⁴⁰He came back to the disciples and found them sleeping. He said to Peter, "Couldn't you stay alert one hour with me? ⁴¹Stay alert and pray so that you won't give in to temptation. The spirit is eager, but the flesh is weak." ⁴²A second time he went away and prayed, "My Father, if it's not possible that this cup be taken away unless I drink it, then let it be what you want."

⁴³Again he came and found them sleeping. Their eyes were heavy with sleep. ⁴⁴But he left them and again went and prayed the same words for the third time. ⁴⁵Then he came to his disciples and said to them, "Will you sleep and rest all night? Look, the time has come for the Human Oneᵏ to be betrayed into the hands of sinners. ⁴⁶Get up. Let's go. Look, here comes my betrayer."

GETHSEMANE

An olive orchard located within the Mount of Olives. In the Gospel tradition, there is only one reference to Gethsemane (Mark 14:32 //Matt 26:36). It is the site of Jesus' agonizing prayer, Judas' betrayal, and Jesus' arrest. Both Mark and Matthew refer to it as "a place" or "plot of land." Luke prefers a broader reference, the "Mount of Olives" (22:39; compare Mark 14:26), perhaps as an allusion to this "mount" as a traditional place of mourning. John refers to Judas' betrayal and Jesus' arrest scene occurring in "a garden" (across the Kidron Valley) without any other specific designation (John 18:1). The phrase "garden of Gethsemane" is derived from combining the account from Matthew and Mark with that of John. Apparently, it was a place Jesus visited frequently (Luke 22:39), which may explain why Judas knew where to find him (John 18:2).

Arrest

⁴⁷While Jesus was still speaking, Judas, one of the Twelve, came. With him was a large crowd carrying swords and clubs. They had been sent by the chief priests and elders of the people. ⁴⁸His betrayer had given them a sign: "Arrest the man I kiss." ⁴⁹Just then he came to Jesus and said, "Hello, Rabbi." Then he kissed him.

⁵⁰But Jesus said to him, "Friend, do what you came to do." Then they came and grabbed Jesus and arrested him. ⁵¹One of those with Jesus reached for his sword. Striking the high priest's slave, he cut off his ear. ⁵²Then Jesus said to him, "Put the sword back into its place. All those who use the sword will die by the sword. ⁵³Or do you think that I'm not able to ask my Father and he will send to me more than twelve battle groups^l of angels right away? ⁵⁴But if I did that, how would the scriptures be fulfilled that say this must happen?" ⁵⁵Then Jesus said to the crowds, "Have you come with swords and clubs to arrest me, like a thief? Day after day, I sat in the temple teaching, but you didn't arrest me. ⁵⁶But all this has happened so that what the prophets said in the scriptures might be fulfilled." Then all the disciples left Jesus and ran away.

Jesus before the council

⁵⁷Those who arrested Jesus led him to Caiaphas the high priest. The legal experts and the elders had gathered there. ⁵⁸Peter followed him from a distance until he came to the high priest's courtyard. He entered that area and sat outside with the officers to see how it would turn out.

⁵⁹The chief priests and the whole council were looking for false testimony against Jesus so that they could put him to death. ⁶⁰They didn't find anything they could use from the many false witnesses who were willing to come forward. But finally they found two ⁶¹who said, "This man said, 'I can destroy God's temple and rebuild it in three days.'"

⁶²Then the high priest stood and said to Jesus, "Aren't you going to respond to the testimony these people have brought against you?" ⁶³But Jesus was silent.

The high priest said, "By the living God, I demand that you tell us whether you are the Christ, God's Son."

⁶⁴"You said it," Jesus replied. "But I say to you that from now on you'll see *the Human One^m sitting on the right side of the Almightyⁿ and coming on the heavenly clouds.*"^o

⁶⁵Then the high priest tore his clothes and said, "He's insulting God! Why do we need any more witnesses? Look, you've heard his insult against God. ⁶⁶What do you think?"

And they answered, "He deserves to die!" ⁶⁷Then they spit in his face and beat him. They hit him ⁶⁸and said, "Prophesy for us, Christ! Who hit you?"

Peter's denial

⁶⁹Meanwhile, Peter was sitting outside in the courtyard. A servant woman came and said to him, "You were also with Jesus the Galilean."

⁷⁰But he denied it in front of all of them, saying, "I don't know what you are talking about."

⁷¹When he went over to the gate, another woman saw him and said to those who were there, "This man was with Jesus, the man from Nazareth."

⁷²With a solemn pledge, he denied it again, saying, "I don't know the man."

⁷³A short time later those standing there came and said to Peter, "You must be one of them. The way you talk gives you away."

⁷⁴Then he cursed and swore, "I don't know the man!" At that very moment the rooster crowed. ⁷⁵Peter remembered Jesus' words, "Before the rooster crows you will deny me three times." And Peter went out and cried uncontrollably.

Jesus before Pilate

27Early in the morning all the chief priests and the elders of the people reached the decision to have Jesus put to death. ²They bound him, led him away, and turned him over to Pilate the governor.

---

^lOr *legions* (of the Roman army, about five thousand soldiers each)   ^mOr *Son of Man*   ⁿOr *the Power*   ^oDan 7:13

Judas' death

³When Judas, who betrayed Jesus, saw that Jesus was condemned to die, he felt deep regret. He returned the thirty pieces of silver to the chief priests and elders, and ⁴said, "I did wrong because I betrayed an innocent man."

But they said, "What is that to us? That's your problem." ⁵Judas threw the silver pieces into the temple and left. Then he went and hanged himself.

⁶The chief priests picked up the silver pieces and said, "According to the Law it's not right to put this money in the treasury. Since it was used to pay for someone's life, it's unclean." ⁷So they decided to use it to buy the potter's field where strangers could be buried. ⁸That's why that field is called "Field of Blood" to this very day. ⁹This fulfilled the words of Jeremiah the prophet: *And I took the thirty pieces of silver, the price for the one whose price had been set by some of the Israelites,* ¹⁰*and I gave them for the potter's field, as the Lord commanded me.*ᵖ

Questioned by Pilate

¹¹Jesus was brought before the governor. The governor said, "Are you the king of the Jews?"

Jesus replied, "That's what you say." ¹²But he didn't answer when the chief priests and elders accused him.

¹³Then Pilate said, "Don't you hear the testimony they bring against you?" ¹⁴But he didn't answer, not even a single word. So the governor was greatly amazed.

Death sentence

¹⁵It was customary during the festival for the governor to release to the crowd one prisoner, whomever they might choose. ¹⁶At that time there was a well-known prisoner named Jesus Barabbas. ¹⁷When the crowd had come together, Pilate asked them, "Whom would you like me to release to you, Jesus Barabbas or Jesus who is called Christ?" ¹⁸He knew that the leaders of the people had handed him over because of jealousy.

¹⁹While he was serving as judge, his wife sent this message to him, "Leave that righteous man alone. I've suffered much today in a dream because of him."

²⁰But the chief priests and the elders persuaded the crowds to ask for Barabbas and kill Jesus. ²¹The governor said, "Which of the two do you want me to release to you?"

"Barabbas," they replied.

²²Pilate said, "Then what should I do with Jesus who is called Christ?"

They all said, "Crucify him!"

²³But he said, "Why? What wrong has he done?"

They shouted even louder, "Crucify him!"

²⁴Pilate saw that he was getting nowhere and that a riot was starting. So he took water and washed his hands in front of the crowd. "I'm innocent of this man's blood," he said. "It's your problem."

²⁵All the people replied, "Let his blood be on us and on our children." ²⁶Then he released Barabbas to them. He had Jesus whipped, then handed him over to be crucified.

Soldiers mocking Jesus

²⁷The governor's soldiers took Jesus into the governor's house, and they gathered the whole company�q of soldiers around him. ²⁸They stripped him and put a red military coat on him. ²⁹They twisted together a crown of thorns and put it on his head. They put a stick in his right hand. Then they bowed down in front of him and mocked him, saying, "Hey! King of the Jews!" ³⁰After they spit on him, they took the stick and struck his head again and again. ³¹When they finished mocking him, they stripped him of the military coat and put his own clothes back on him. They led him away to crucify him.

Crucifixion

³²As they were going out, they found Simon, a man from Cyrene. They forced him to carry his cross. ³³When they came to a place called Golgotha, which means Skull Place, ³⁴they gave Jesus wine mixed with vinegar to drink. But after tasting

ᵖZech 11:12-13; Jer 32:6-9 qOr *cohort* (approximately six hundred soldiers) it, he didn't want to drink it. ³⁵After they crucified him, they divided up his clothes among them by drawing lots. ³⁶They sat there, guarding him. ³⁷They placed above his head the charge against him. It read, "This is Jesus, the king of the Jews." ³⁸They crucified with him two outlaws, one on his right side and one on his left.

³⁹Those who were walking by insulted Jesus, shaking their heads ⁴⁰and saying, "So you were going to destroy the temple and rebuild it in three days, were you? Save yourself! If you are God's Son, come down from the cross."

⁴¹In the same way, the chief priests, along with the legal experts and the elders, were making fun of him, saying, ⁴²"He saved others, but he can't save himself. He's the king of Israel, so let him come down from the cross now. Then we'll believe in him. ⁴³He trusts in God, so let God deliver him now if he wants to. He said, 'I'm God's Son.'" ⁴⁴The outlaws who were crucified with him insulted him in the same way.

Death

⁴⁵From noon until three in the afternoon the whole earth was dark. ⁴⁶At about three Jesus cried out with a loud shout, *"Eli, Eli, lama sabachthani,"* which means, "My God, my God, why have you left me?"ʳ

⁴⁷After hearing him, some standing there said, "He's calling Elijah." ⁴⁸One of them ran over, took a sponge full of vin-

ʳPs 22:1

egar, and put it on a pole. He offered it to Jesus to drink.

⁴⁹But the rest of them said, "Let's see if Elijah will come and save him."

⁵⁰Again Jesus cried out with a loud shout. Then he died.

⁵¹Look, the curtain of the sanctuary was torn in two from top to bottom. The earth shook, the rocks split, ⁵²and the bodies of many holy people who had died were raised. ⁵³After Jesus' resurrection they came out of their graves and went into the holy city where they appeared to many people. ⁵⁴When the centurion and those with him who were guarding Jesus saw the earthquake and what had just happened, they were filled with awe and said, "This was certainly God's Son."

⁵⁵Many women were watching from a distance. They had followed Jesus from Galilee to serve him. ⁵⁶Among them were Mary Magdalene, Mary the mother of James and Joseph, and the mother of Zebedee's sons.

Burial

⁵⁷That evening a man named Joseph came. He was a rich man from Arimathea who had become a disciple of Jesus. ⁵⁸He came to Pilate and asked for Jesus' body. Pilate gave him permission to take it. ⁵⁹Joseph took the body, wrapped it in a clean linen cloth, ⁶⁰and laid it in his own new tomb, which he had carved out of the rock.

ELI, ELI, LAMA SABACHTHANI

In Matthew 27:46 and Mark 15:34, Jesus' last words from the cross. Both versions can be rendered as "My God, my God, why have you left me?" Both are Greek transliterations of the first four words of Psalm 22, but in Aramaic—the language Jesus spoke—rather than in Hebrew, the language in which Psalm 22 was written. Matthew changed Mark's word for "my God" to one that sounded more like "Elijah" (see Matt 27:47-49).

After he rolled a large stone at the door of the tomb, he went away. ⁶¹Mary Magdalene and the other Mary were there, sitting in front of the tomb.

Guard at the tomb

⁶²The next day, which was the day after Preparation Day, the chief priests and the Pharisees gathered before Pilate.

⁶³They said, "Sir, we remember that while that deceiver was still alive he said, 'After three days I will arise.' ⁶⁴Therefore, order the grave to be sealed until the third day. Otherwise, his disciples may come and steal the body and tell the people, 'He's been raised from the dead.' This last deception will be worse than the first."

⁶⁵Pilate replied, "You have soldiers for

RESURRECTION (NT)

Paul is the first Christian writer to describe what resurrection was, apparently from descriptions of the risen Christ, which came to him in a visionary experience ("a revelation from Jesus Christ" [Gal 1:11-12]). Paul claims that our flesh will be transformed into another kind of body (1 Cor 15:42-44). He calls the physical, fleshly body, in which we live our earthly lives, a natural body that is left behind. The resurrected body is an immortal and incorruptible body or spiritual body. Paul calls this process a "transformation" in several related ways (Rom 12:2; 1 Cor 15:51-52; 2 Cor 3:18; Phil 3:21). Paul understands this process to have begun with the resurrection of Christ and to continue until the end of history, when the dead will be raised immortal and changed. Faith in Christ begins a process of transformation that will end in the resurrection of believers, and this explains Paul's terminology of being "in Christ."

The Gospels' interpretation of resurrection does not in every way correspond to Paul's description. Mark, the earliest Gospel, has no description of Jesus' resurrection, instead presenting us with an empty tomb, which signifies the mystery of Easter (Mark 16:1-8). The later Gospels expand the story of the empty tomb but do not describe the actual resurrection. Instead the Gospels stress Jesus' humanity and messiahship. So he is fully human and appears in human form, arguably even in fleshly form, after his resurrection, as he eats, walks, and talks, and in these ways is indistinguishable from ordinary humans (Matt 28:9-10, 17-20; Luke 24:13-48; John 20:14-29; 21:1-24).

In Luke, the ascension is a separate process, not included within the resurrection itself but placed temporally at the end of the post-resurrection appearances. The story is narrated twice by Luke—once at the end of the Gospel (24:51) and again at the beginning of the Acts of the Apostles (1:9-11), also written by Luke.

Throughout the Gospels, several other aspects of resurrection become clear. The term *resurrection*, for example, appears frequently in Paul but infrequently in the Gospels. There, it is explicitly part of Jesus' polemic with the Pharisees. Against the Sadducees (who are characterized as not believing in resurrection, neither as a spirit nor as an angel [Acts 23:8]), the Pharisees do believe in resurrection. Conflicts with Pharisees and Sadducees are an opportunity for the evangelists to specify what they mean by *resurrection*.

guard duty. Go and make it as secure as you know how." ⁶⁶Then they went and secured the tomb by sealing the stone and posting the guard.

Resurrection

28 After the Sabbath, at dawn on the first day of the week, Mary Magdalene and the other Mary came to look at the tomb. ²Look, there was a great earthquake, for an angel from the Lord came down from heaven. Coming to the stone, he rolled it away and sat on it. ³Now his face was like lightning and his clothes as white as snow. ⁴The guards were so terrified of him that they shook with fear and became like dead men. ⁵But the angel said to the women, "Don't be afraid. I know that you are looking for Jesus who was crucified. ⁶He isn't here, because he's been raised from the dead, just as he said. Come, see the place where they laid him. ⁷Now hurry, go and tell his disciples, 'He's been raised from the dead. He's going on ahead of you to Galilee. You will see him there.' I've given the message to you."

⁸With great fear and excitement, they hurried away from the tomb and ran to tell his disciples. ⁹But Jesus met them and greeted them. They came and grabbed his feet and worshipped him. ¹⁰Then Jesus said to them, "Don't be afraid. Go and tell my brothers that I am going into Galilee. They will see me there."

Guards' report

¹¹Now as the women were on their way, some of the guards came into the city and told the chief priests everything that had happened. ¹²They met with the elders and decided to give a large sum of money to the soldiers. ¹³They told them, "Say that Jesus' disciples came at night and stole his body while you were sleeping. ¹⁴And if the governor hears about this, we will take care of it with him so you will have nothing to worry about." ¹⁵So the soldiers took the money and did as they were told. And this report has spread throughout all Judea to this very day.

Commissioning of the disciples

¹⁶Now the eleven disciples went to Galilee, to the mountain where Jesus told them to go. ¹⁷When they saw him, they worshipped him, but some doubted. ¹⁸Jesus came near and spoke to them, "I've received all authority in heaven and on earth. ¹⁹Therefore, go and make disciples of all nations, baptizing them in the name of the Father and of the Son and of the Holy Spirit, ²⁰teaching them to obey everything that I've commanded you. Look, I myself will be with you every day until the end of this present age."

MARK

THEME

Jesus, the mighty Son of God concealed in human form, accomplishes his redemptive work for all people through a ministry of sacrificial service and through death on a cross.

AUTHORSHIP, DATE, PLACE OF WRITING

We do not know who wrote the Gospel of Mark. According to Eusebius (fourth century), Papias, a bishop of the second century, reported the tradition that Mark was composed by (John) Mark based upon the recollections of Peter. It does not seem likely today that this tradition is reliable. Mark does not have the character of an eyewitness piece of work; it is, rather, based on oral traditions circulating in the Markan church. The author remains anonymous, though he must also be given credit for having created the Gospel as a type of literature, since Mark was the first to be written.

The customary date for Mark is around 70 CE, at about the time of the Jewish revolt against Rome. No one really knows and the Gospel does not say, but internal indications point to a time when conditions were severe for some Christian communities. And Mark also seems to be aware of the destruction of the temple in 70 CE (see 13:2).

Rome is given in early sources as the traditional site of writing, but the Gospel itself does not say where it originated. Other places have been suggested, such as Syria, Egypt, or Asia Minor. We cannot know for sure, though a reasonable case can still be made for the Roman location. For example, the persecution of Christians at Rome under the lunatic emperor Nero in the sixties could be the source of certain problems reflected in Mark.

PURPOSE OF THE GOSPEL

Why the Gospel was written has to be inferred. Certainly Mark wished to set out the Gospel as he understood it. Beyond that, he likely meant to address the situation posed by hard times for the Christian community. Mark looks at his time apocalyptically. He sees that the suffering now inflicted on the Christians is not accidental but points to the time of the end, when the faithful will experience tribulation.

Other related problems appear, such as false messiahs and false prophets in the church (13:6, 22), coming to terms with the destruction of the Jerusalem temple (13:1-2), accomplishing the universal mission of the church (13:10), and enduring to the end (13:11-13).

We might further suppose that Mark—probably not consciously—was responding to the situation in the church when the tradition about Jesus was growing dramatically and probably getting out of bounds. What Mark did was to take a large slice of the oral tradition about Jesus and commit it to writing. In this way he fixed its form forever. In a sense Mark represents the initial effort towards the formation of a canon.

THE SYNOPTIC PROBLEM

The first three Gospels are called "Synoptic" Gospels because of their broad similarity. Following a long period of debate, scholarship concluded that this similarity was not accidental, that Mark was written first and then used independently by both Matthew and Luke. In addition, Matthew and Luke had a second source, which we do not any longer possess, but from which they drew substantial material. This source is called "Q." It contains the non-Markan material common to Matthew and Luke.

So Mark was written first and served as a source for both Matthew and Luke. The author of Mark, then, even though anonymous, has greatly influenced Christian history and literature. He was certainly a creative figure and, as the church came to recognize, composed a work of inspiration.

STYLE AND SOURCES

Mark's style of writing is elementary, even rough. Though his Greek is correct, he writes in a popular fashion, in the way of oral storytelling. His language is not complex and he obviously did not intend to produce a work of high literary merit. Characteristic of his style is the coordinating sentence—lots of "and's" coupled with modest use of subordinating clauses.

There is a sense of urgency; Mark likes to say "immediately," "right away," and "at once." Yet Mark's thought is also very subtle, and his theological intention is not always easy to grasp.

As to sources, it is not so apparent that Mark had any beyond the oral material that lay at hand in his community. There has been some success in identifying a collection of miracle stories, perhaps a collection of parables and of Scripture proof-texts. Certainly also the narrative of the crucifixion had attained some fixed form before Mark set pen to papyrus, but for the most part Mark had no models to emulate.

MAJOR THEMES IN MARK

"Here comes God's kingdom!" (1:15) points to the major Markan theme. Mark takes up the message of Jesus and renews it for his own time and situation.

The kingdom in Mark is to be understood apocalyptically; the end approaches and brings with it struggle and hostility. Mark's community sees itself passing through the final hours of tribulation. Suffering is inevitable and must precede the time of the end.

At the same time the apocalyptic outlook carries certain implications for discipleship, another of Mark's major concerns. Through the portrayal of the historical disciples, Mark implements his own view. The picture of the disciples is largely negative; they repeatedly fail to understand Jesus or even to remain loyal to him. In the end they abandon him to his fate in the world. One of them denies him; another betrays him. This picture is so powerful in the Gospel that it cannot be accidental. Mark is evidently campaigning for his own view of discipleship—perhaps against others in his community—a view that insists that following Jesus, who was crucified, necessarily entails the possibility of suffering and sacrifice.

It is also apparent from the internal evidence of the Gospel that Mark's community has separated from Judaism. It is probably a community that has its own roots in Judaism, but has become of mixed Gentile-Jewish-Christian character. Such issues as Sabbath observance, ritual regulations, and the value of the law generally can be seen as having already been determined in Mark's community. These debates with Judaism are not so bitter as, say, in Matthew; in fact, it seems that they are already settled for Mark and his community. What we are hearing in the Gospel are the echoes of those controversies.

Mark also contains the silence-theme, better known as the "messianic secret." A feature of Mark is that Jesus commands those whom he has healed to be silent, and he commands others (including demons) not to disclose his identity. This peculiarity of Mark has been long recognized, but there has been no unanimity as to its meaning.

The silence commands are actually of three types: (1) commands to demons (1:25); (2) commands to be silent about healings (1:44-45; 5:43; 7:36-37; 8:26); and (3) commands to be silent about Jesus' identity (1:34; 3:11-12; 8:30). The first—the only clear example—is the oldest of all the types and perhaps even became the inspiration for the others. Originally these commands were simply part of the commanding word of the exorcist by which he gained control over the demons; they had nothing to do with Jesus' identity or with suppression of Jesus' reputation as a healer.

The other two show Mark's handiwork. Jesus urges those whom he has healed to say nothing—there is one exception in 5:19-20—though he is often unsuccessful. At the same time there are many healings in which no injunction to silence is given. Mark is probably trying to put some restraints on the picture of Jesus as a miracle worker. There is no doubt for Mark that Jesus does mighty deeds; yet at the same time there is much more to the story of Jesus. In particular, there is the message of the cross, which unveils the true meaning of Jesus. So it is the paradoxical portrayal of Jesus as the powerful yet suffering one that is underlying the peculiar mixture of silence and openness in Mark.

The identity sayings are similarly motivated. Jesus is shown as not wishing it known who he is, except at the moment of his own self-disclosure (14:62). Caesarea Philippi is the key scene here (8:27-33). Jesus publicly disclaims any messianic titles until they are given the appropriate meaning—that is, until the suffering role becomes apparent.

MARK

Beginning of good news

1 The beginning of the good news about Jesus Christ, God's Son, [2]happened just as it was written about in the prophecy of Isaiah:

Look, I am sending my messenger
    before you.
He will prepare your way,
[3] a voice shouting in the wilderness:
    "Prepare the way for the Lord;
    make his paths straight."[a]

John's preaching

[4]John the Baptist was in the wilderness calling for people to be baptized to show that they were changing their hearts and lives and wanted God to forgive their sins. [5]Everyone in Judea and all the people of Jerusalem went out to the Jordan River and were being baptized by John as they confessed their sins. [6]John wore clothes made of camel's hair, with a leather belt around his waist. He ate locusts and wild honey. [7]He announced, "One stronger than I am is coming after me. I'm not even worthy to bend over and loosen the strap of his sandals. [8]I baptize you with water, but he will baptize you with the Holy Spirit."

Jesus is baptized and tempted

[9]About that time, Jesus came from Nazareth of Galilee, and John baptized him in the Jordan River. [10]While he was coming up out of the water, Jesus saw heaven splitting open and the Spirit, like a dove, coming down on him. [11]And there was a voice from heaven: "You are my Son, whom I dearly love; in you I find happiness."

[12]At once the Spirit forced Jesus out into the wilderness. [13]He was in the wilderness for forty days, tempted by Satan. He was among the wild animals, and the angels took care of him.

Jesus' message

[14]After John was arrested, Jesus came into Galilee announcing God's good news, [15]saying, "Now is the time! Here comes God's kingdom! Change your hearts and lives, and trust this good news!"

Jesus calls disciples

[16]As Jesus passed alongside the Galilee Sea, he saw two brothers, Simon and Andrew, throwing fishing nets into the sea, for they were fishermen. [17]"Come, follow me," he said, "and I'll show you how to fish for people." [18]Right away, they left their nets and followed him. [19]After going a little farther, he saw James and John, Zebedee's sons, in their boat repairing the fishing nets. [20]At that very moment he called them. They followed him, leaving their father Zebedee in the boat with the hired workers.

Jesus throws a demon out

[21]Jesus and his followers went into Capernaum. Immediately on the Sabbath Jesus entered the synagogue and started teaching. [22]The people were amazed by his teaching, for he was teaching them with authority, not like the legal experts. [23]Suddenly, there in the synagogue, a person with an evil spirit screamed, [24]"What have you to do with us, Jesus of Nazareth? Have you come to destroy us? I know who you are. You are the holy one from God."

[25]"Silence!" Jesus said, speaking harshly to the demon. "Come out of him!" [26]The unclean spirit shook him and screamed, then it came out.

[27]Everyone was shaken and questioned among themselves, "What's this? A new teaching with authority! He even commands unclean spirits and they obey him!" [28]Right away the news about him spread throughout the entire region of Galilee.

Jesus heals Simon's mother-in-law

[29]After leaving the synagogue, Jesus, James, and John went home with Simon and Andrew. [30]Simon's mother-in-law was in bed, sick with a fever, and they told Jesus

---

[a]Isa 40:3; Mal 3:1; Exod 23:20

about her at once. [31]He went to her, took her by the hand, and raised her up. The fever left her, and she served them.

Jesus' ministry spreads

[32]That evening, at sunset, people brought to Jesus those who were sick or demon-possessed. [33]The whole town gathered near the door. [34]He healed many who were sick with all kinds of diseases, and he threw out many demons. But he didn't let the demons speak, because they recognized him.

[35]Early in the morning, well before sunrise, Jesus rose and went to a deserted place where he could be alone in prayer. [36]Simon and those with him tracked him down. [37]When they found him, they told him, "Everyone's looking for you!"

[38]He replied, "Let's head in the other direction, to the nearby villages, so that I can preach there too. That's why I've come." [39]He traveled throughout Galilee, preaching in their synagogues and throwing out demons.

A man with a skin disease

[40]A man with a skin disease approached Jesus, fell to his knees, and begged, "If you want, you can make me clean."

[41]Incensed,[b] Jesus reached out his hand, touched him, and said, "I do want to. Be clean." [42]Instantly, the skin disease left him, and he was clean. [43]Sternly, Jesus sent him away, [44]saying, "Don't say anything to anyone. Instead, go and show yourself to the priest and offer the sacrifice for your cleansing that Moses commanded. This will be a testimony to them." [45]Instead, he went out and started talking freely and spreading the news so that Jesus wasn't able to enter a town openly. He remained outside in deserted places, but people came to him from everywhere.

Healing and forgiveness

2 After a few days, Jesus went back to Capernaum, and people heard that he was at home. [2]So many gathered that there was no longer space, not even near the door. Jesus was speaking the word to them. [3]Some people arrived, and four of them were bringing to him a man who was paralyzed. [4]They couldn't carry him through the crowd, so they tore off part of the roof above where Jesus was. When they had made an opening, they lowered the mat on which the paralyzed man was lying. [5]When Jesus saw their faith, he said to the paralytic, "Child, your sins are forgiven!"

[6]Some legal experts were sitting there, muttering among themselves, [7]"Why does he speak this way? He's insulting God. Only the one God can forgive sins."

[8]Jesus immediately recognized what they were discussing, and he said to them, "Why do you fill your minds with these questions? [9]Which is easier—to say to a paralyzed person, 'Your sins are forgiven,' or to say, 'Get up, take up your bed, and walk'? [10]But so you will know that the Human One[c] has authority on the earth to forgive sins"—he

[b]Most critical editions of the Gk New Testament read *filled with compassion.*   [c]Or *Son of Man*

GOSPELS

said to the man who was paralyzed, [11]"Get up, take your mat, and go home."

[12]Jesus raised him up, and right away he picked up his mat and walked out in front of everybody. They were all amazed and praised God, saying, "We've never seen anything like this!"

Eating with sinners

[13]Jesus went out beside the lake again. The whole crowd came to him, and he began to teach them. [14]As he continued along, he saw Levi, Alphaeus' son, sitting at a kiosk for collecting taxes. Jesus said to him, "Follow me." Levi got up and followed him.

[15]Jesus sat down to eat at Levi's house. Many tax collectors and sinners were eating with Jesus and his disciples. Indeed, many of them had become his followers. [16]When some of the legal experts from among the Pharisees saw that he was eating with sinners and tax collectors, they asked his disciples, "Why is he eating with sinners and tax collectors?"

[17]When Jesus heard it, he said to them, "Healthy people don't need a doctor, but sick people do. I didn't come to call righteous people, but sinners."

When to fast

[18]John's disciples and the Pharisees had a habit of fasting. Some people asked Jesus, "Why do John's disciples and the Pharisees' disciples fast, but yours don't?"

[19]Jesus said, "The wedding guests can't fast while the groom is with them, can they? As long as they have the groom with them, they can't fast. [20]But the days will

SCRIBE/LEGAL EXPERT (NT)

In the early Jewish and NT eras, a scribe was an elite scholar who specialized in the teaching and interpretation of religious texts, particularly the Instruction or Torah. There are numerous references to scribes (CEB "legal experts") in the NT. The Gospels frequently pair scribes with Pharisees, especially in Jesus' indictment: "How terrible it will be for you legal experts [scribes] and Pharisees! Hypocrites!" (Matt 23:13-33; Luke 11:39-52). It is possible that the pairing of these groups in the Gospels derives from similarities in their theological beliefs, such as belief in resurrection. Several other NT passages present scribes as questioning Jesus' actions and authority (e.g., Mark 2:13-17; 11:27-28). The frequent references to scribes in these indictments no doubt reflect the Gospel writers' efforts to depict Jesus as deeply divided against the scribes in the interpretation of the Instruction. These depictions, which are particularly prominent in Matthew, should be understood as having a specific location within the early church's rivalry with rabbinic Judaism.

Several NT texts give us glimpses of the social status held by scribes during the Second Temple Period. For instance, Mark 12:38-40 describes scribes as those who walk around in long robes expecting to be greeted in marketplaces and given good seats in synagogues and banquets (see also Matt 23:5-7). The description of scribes in this passage suggests that scribes held a high social status within Jewish society. The high social status of scribes can also be inferred from their position within the Sanhedrin, the main governing body of Judaism during the Second Temple Period (Acts 4:6).

come when the groom will be taken away from them, and then they will fast.

²¹"No one sews a piece of new, unshrunk cloth on old clothes; otherwise, the patch tears away from it, the new from the old, and makes a worse tear. ²²No one pours new wine into old leather wineskins; otherwise, the wine would burst the wineskins and the wine would be lost and the wineskins destroyed. But new wine is for new wineskins."

Scripture and the Sabbath

²³Jesus went through the wheat fields on the Sabbath. As the disciples made their way, they were picking the heads of wheat. ²⁴The Pharisees said to Jesus, "Look! Why are they breaking the Sabbath law?"

²⁵He said to them, "Haven't you ever read what David did when he was in need, when he and those with him were hungry? ²⁶During the time when Abiathar was high priest, David went into God's house and ate the bread of the presence, which only the priests were allowed to eat. He also gave bread to those who were with him." ²⁷Then he said, "The Sabbath was created for humans; humans weren't created for the Sabbath. ²⁸This is why the Human One[d] is Lord even over the Sabbath."

Healing on the Sabbath

3 Jesus returned to the synagogue. A man with a withered hand was there. ²Wanting to bring charges against Jesus, they were watching Jesus closely to see if he would heal on the Sabbath. ³He said to the man with the withered hand, "Step up where people can see you." ⁴Then he said to them, "Is it legal on the Sabbath to do good

or to do evil, to save life or to kill?" But they said nothing. ⁵Looking around at them with anger, deeply grieved at their unyielding hearts, he said to the man, "Stretch out your hand." So he did, and his hand was made healthy. ⁶At that, the Pharisees got together with the supporters of Herod to plan how to destroy Jesus.

Healing and throwing demons out

⁷Jesus left with his disciples and went to the lake. A large crowd followed him because they had heard what he was doing. They were from Galilee, ⁸Judea, Jerusalem, Idumea, beyond the Jordan, and the area surrounding Tyre and Sidon. ⁹Jesus told his disciples to get a small boat ready for him so the crowd wouldn't crush him. ¹⁰He had healed so many people that everyone who was sick pushed forward so that they could touch him. ¹¹Whenever the evil spirits saw him, they fell down at his feet and shouted, "You are God's Son!" ¹²But he strictly ordered them not to reveal who he was.

Jesus appoints twelve apostles

¹³Jesus went up on a mountain and called those he wanted, and they came to him. ¹⁴He appointed twelve and called them apostles. He appointed them to be with him, to be sent out to preach, ¹⁵and to have authority to throw out demons. ¹⁶He appointed twelve: Peter, a name he gave Simon; ¹⁷James and John, Zebedee's sons, whom he nicknamed Boanerges, which means "sons of Thunder"; ¹⁸and Andrew; Philip; Bartholomew; Matthew; Thomas; James, Alphaeus' son; Thaddaeus; Simon the Cananaean;[e] ¹⁹and Judas Iscariot, who betrayed Jesus.

---

[d]Or *Son of Man* [e]Or *zealot*

BOANERGES

A Heb. or Aram. term of uncertain etymology ascribed to James and John by Jesus (Mark 3:17). The narrator renders the word into Greek as "sons of thunder," suggesting that they either spoke boldly and vigorously, had experienced a sudden awakening, or perhaps even had survived a lightning strike.

Misunderstandings about Jesus

²⁰Jesus entered a house. A crowd gathered again so that it was impossible for him and his followers even to eat. ²¹When his family heard what was happening, they came to take control of him. They were saying, "He's out of his mind!"

²²The legal experts came down from Jerusalem. Over and over they charged, "He's possessed by Beelzebul. He throws out demons with the authority of the ruler of demons."

²³When Jesus called them together he spoke to them in a parable: "How can Satan throw Satan out? ²⁴A kingdom involved in civil war will collapse. ²⁵And a house torn apart by divisions will collapse. ²⁶If Satan rebels against himself and is divided, then he can't endure. He's done for. ²⁷No one gets into the house of a strong person and steals anything without first tying up the strong person. Only then can the house be burglarized. ²⁸I assure you that human beings will be forgiven for everything, for all sins and insults of every kind. ²⁹But whoever insults the Holy Spirit will never be forgiven. That person is guilty of a sin with consequences that last forever." ³⁰He said this because the legal experts were saying, "He's possessed by an evil spirit."

³¹His mother and brothers arrived. They stood outside and sent word to him, calling for him. ³²A crowd was seated around him, and those sent to him said, "Look, your mother, brothers, and sisters are outside looking for you."

³³He replied, "Who is my mother? Who are my brothers?" ³⁴Looking around at those seated around him in a circle, he said, "Look, here are my mother and my brothers. ³⁵Whoever does God's will is my brother, sister, and mother."

Parable of the soils

4 Jesus began to teach beside the lake again. Such a large crowd gathered that he climbed into a boat there on the lake. He sat in the boat while the whole crowd was nearby on the shore. ²He said many things to them in parables. While teaching them, he said, ³"Listen to this! A farmer went out to scatter seed. ⁴As he was scattering seed, some fell on the path; and the birds came and ate it. ⁵Other seed fell on rocky ground where the soil was shallow. They sprouted immediately because the soil wasn't deep. ⁶When the sun came up, it scorched the plants; and they dried up because they had no roots. ⁷Other seed fell among thorny plants. The thorny plants grew and choked the seeds, and they produced nothing. ⁸Other seed fell into good soil and bore fruit. Upon growing and increasing, the seed produced in one case a yield of thirty to one, in another case a yield of sixty to one, and in another case a yield of one hundred to one." ⁹He said, "Whoever has ears to listen should pay attention!"

Jesus explains his parable

¹⁰When they were alone, the people around Jesus, along with the Twelve, asked him about the parables. ¹¹He said to them, "The secret of God's kingdom has been given to you, but to those who are outside everything comes in parables. ¹²This is so that they can look and see but have no insight, and they can hear but not understand. Otherwise, they might turn their lives around and be forgiven.

¹³"Don't you understand this parable? Then how will you understand all the parables? ¹⁴The farmer scatters the word. ¹⁵This is the meaning of the seed that fell on the path: When the word is scattered and people hear it, right away Satan comes and steals the word that was planted in them. ¹⁶Here's the meaning of the seed that fell on rocky ground: When people hear the word, they immediately receive it joyfully. ¹⁷Because they have no roots, they last for only a little while. When they experience distress or abuse because of the word, they immediately fall away. ¹⁸Others are like the seed scattered among the thorny plants. These are the ones who have heard the word; ¹⁹but the worries of this life, the false appeal of wealth, and the desire for more things break in and choke the word, and it bears no fruit. ²⁰The seed scattered on good soil are those who hear the word and embrace it. They bear fruit, in one case a yield

of thirty to one, in another case sixty to one, and in another case one hundred to one."

Parables about lamps and measures

²¹Jesus said to them, "Does anyone bring in a lamp in order to put it under a basket or a bed? Shouldn't it be placed on a lampstand? ²²Everything hidden will be revealed, and everything secret will come out into the open. ²³Whoever has ears to listen should pay attention!"

²⁴He said to them, "Listen carefully! God will evaluate you with the same standard you use to evaluate others. Indeed, you will receive even more. ²⁵Those who have will receive more, but as for those who don't have, even what they don't have will be taken away from them."

More parables about God's kingdom

²⁶Then Jesus said, "This is what God's kingdom is like. It's as though someone scatters seed on the ground, ²⁷then sleeps and wakes night and day. The seed sprouts and grows, but the farmer doesn't know how. ²⁸The earth produces crops all by itself, first the stalk, then the head, then the full head of grain. ²⁹Whenever the crop is ready, the farmer goes out to cut the grain because it's harvesttime."

³⁰He continued, "What's a good image for God's kingdom? What parable can I use to explain it? ³¹Consider a mustard seed. When scattered on the ground, it's the smallest of all the seeds on the earth; ³²but when it's planted, it grows and becomes the largest of all vegetable plants. It produces such large branches that the birds in the sky are able to nest in its shade."

³³With many such parables he continued to give them the word, as much as they were able to hear. ³⁴He spoke to them only in parables, then explained everything to his disciples when he was alone with them.

Jesus stops a storm

³⁵Later that day, when evening came, Jesus said to them, "Let's cross over to the other side of the lake." ³⁶They left the crowd and took him in the boat just as he was. Other boats followed along. ³⁷Gale-force winds arose, and waves crashed against the boat so that the boat was swamped. ³⁸But Jesus was in the rear of the boat, sleeping on a pillow. They woke him up and said, "Teacher, don't you care that we're drowning?"

³⁹He got up and gave orders to the wind, and he said to the lake, "Silence! Be still!" The wind settled down and there was a great calm. ⁴⁰Jesus asked them, "Why are you frightened? Don't you have faith yet?"

⁴¹Overcome with awe, they said to each other, "Who then is this? Even the wind and the sea obey him!"

Jesus frees a demon-possessed man

5 Jesus and his disciples came to the other side of the lake, to the region of the Gerasenes. ²As soon as Jesus got out

---

MUSTARD

The smallness of the mustard seed is used in Jesus' teaching to depict God's kingdom (Matt 13:31-32; Mark 4:30-32; Luke 13:18-19) and faith (Matt 17:20; Luke 17:6). Proverbially known as the smallest of seeds in the ancient Mediterranean world (mentioned in both Hellenistic and Jewish sources), its diameter is about 0.1 in. But the plant can normally grow six ft. high. When conditions are favorable, a height of 15 ft. is attainable, with the main stem as thick as a human arm. This is sufficient to hold the weight of small birds that come to eat its aromatic seeds, which have been used since ancient times as a spice.

of the boat, a man possessed by an evil spirit came out of the tombs. ³This man lived among the tombs, and no one was ever strong enough to restrain him, even with a chain. ⁴He had been secured many times with leg irons and chains, but he broke the chains and smashed the leg irons. No one was tough enough to control him. ⁵Night and day in the tombs and the hills, he would howl and cut himself with stones. ⁶When he saw Jesus from far away, he ran and knelt before him, ⁷shouting, "What have you to do with me, Jesus, Son of the Most High God? Swear to God that you won't torture me!"

⁸He said this because Jesus had already commanded him, "Unclean spirit, come out of the man!"

⁹Jesus asked him, "What is your name?"

He responded, "Legion is my name, because we are many." ¹⁰They pleaded with Jesus not to send them out of that region. ¹¹A large herd of pigs was feeding on the hillside. ¹²"Send us into the pigs!" they begged. "Let us go into the pigs!" ¹³Jesus gave them permission, so the unclean spirits left the man and went into the pigs. Then the herd of about two thousand pigs rushed down the cliff into the lake and drowned.

¹⁴Those who tended the pigs ran away and told the story in the city and in the countryside. People came to see what had happened. ¹⁵They came to Jesus and saw the man who used to be demon-possessed. They saw the very man who had been filled with many demons sitting there fully dressed and completely sane, and they were filled with awe. ¹⁶Those who had actually seen what had happened to the demon-possessed man told the others about the pigs. ¹⁷Then they pleaded with Jesus to leave their region.

¹⁸While he was climbing into the boat, the one who had been demon-possessed pleaded with Jesus to let him come along as one of his disciples. ¹⁹But Jesus wouldn't allow it. "Go home to your own people," Jesus said, "and tell them what the Lord has done for you and how he has shown you mercy." ²⁰The man went away and began to proclaim in the Ten Cities all that Jesus had done for him, and everyone was amazed.

Jesus heals two people

²¹Jesus crossed the lake again, and on the other side a large crowd gathered around him on the shore. ²²Jairus, one of the synagogue leaders, came forward. When he saw Jesus, he fell at his feet ²³and pleaded with him, "My daughter is about to die. Please, come and place your hands on her so that she can be healed and live." ²⁴So Jesus went with him.

A swarm of people were following Jesus, crowding in on him. ²⁵A woman was there who had been bleeding for twelve years. ²⁶She had suffered a lot under the care of many doctors, and had spent everything she had without getting any better. In fact, she had gotten worse. ²⁷Because she had heard about Jesus, she came up behind him in the crowd and touched his clothes. ²⁸She was thinking, If I can just touch his clothes, I'll be healed. ²⁹Her bleeding stopped immediately, and she sensed in her body that her illness had been healed.

³⁰At that very moment, Jesus recognized that power had gone out from him. He turned around in the crowd and said, "Who touched my clothes?"

LEGION

The fundamental unit of the much-vaunted ancient Roman army. The number, size, and structure of the legion changed somewhat throughout Roman history. In the early 1st century CE, the Roman army would have had 25 such legions stationed throughout the empire. Biblical references to legion are limited to just four, and these only in the NT, all of which are figurative.

[31] His disciples said to him, "Don't you see the crowd pressing against you? Yet you ask, 'Who touched me?'" [32] But Jesus looked around carefully to see who had done it.

[33] The woman, full of fear and trembling, came forward. Knowing what had happened to her, she fell down in front of Jesus and told him the whole truth. [34] He responded, "Daughter, your faith has healed you; go in peace, healed from your disease."

[35] While Jesus was still speaking with her, messengers came from the synagogue leader's house, saying to Jairus, "Your daughter has died. Why bother the teacher any longer?"

[36] But Jesus overheard their report and said to the synagogue leader, "Don't be afraid; just keep trusting." [37] He didn't allow anyone to follow him except Peter, James, and John, James' brother. [38] They came to the synagogue leader's house, and he saw a commotion, with people crying and wailing loudly. [39] He went in and said to them, "What's all this commotion and crying about? The child isn't dead. She's only sleeping." [40] They laughed at him, but he threw them all out. Then, taking the child's parents and his disciples with him, he went to the room where the child was. [41] Taking her hand, he said to her, "*Talitha koum*," which means, "Young woman, get up." [42] Suddenly the young woman got up and began to walk around. She was 12 years old. They were shocked! [43] He gave them strict orders that no one should know what had happened. Then he told them to give her something to eat.

Jesus in his hometown

6 Jesus left that place and came to his hometown. His disciples followed him. [2] On the Sabbath, he began to teach in the synagogue. Many who heard him were surprised. "Where did this man get all this? What's this wisdom he's been given? What about the powerful acts accomplished through him? [3] Isn't this the carpenter? Isn't he Mary's son and the brother of James, Joses, Judas, and Simon? Aren't his sisters here with us?" They were repulsed by him and fell into sin.

[4] Jesus said to them, "Prophets are honored everywhere except in their own hometowns, among their relatives, and in their own households." [5] He was unable to do any miracles there, except that he placed his hands on a few sick people and healed them. [6] He was appalled by their disbelief.

Sending out the disciples

Then Jesus traveled through the surrounding villages teaching.

[7] He called for the Twelve and sent them out in pairs. He gave them authority over unclean spirits. [8] He instructed them to take nothing for the journey except a walking stick—no bread, no bags, and no money in their belts. [9] He told them to wear sandals but not to put on two shirts. [10] He said, "Whatever house you enter, remain there until you leave that place. [11] If a place doesn't welcome you or listen to you, as you leave, shake the dust off your feet as a witness against them." [12] So they went out and proclaimed that people should change their hearts and lives. [13] They cast out many demons, and they anointed many sick people with olive oil and healed them.

Death of John the Baptist

[14] Herod the king heard about these things, because the name of Jesus had become well-known. Some were saying, "John the Baptist has been raised from the dead, and this is why miraculous powers are at work through him." [15] Others were saying, "He is Elijah." Still others were saying, "He is a prophet like one of the ancient prophets." [16] But when Herod heard these rumors, he said, "John, whom I beheaded, has been raised to life."

[17] He said this because Herod himself had arranged to have John arrested and put in prison because of Herodias, the wife of Herod's brother Philip. Herod had married her, [18] but John told Herod, "It's against the law for you to marry your brother's wife!" [19] So Herodias had it in for John. She wanted to kill him, but she couldn't. [20] This was because Herod respected John. He regarded him as a righteous and holy person, so he protected him. John's words greatly

confused Herod, yet he enjoyed listening to him.

²¹Finally, the time was right. It was on one of Herod's birthdays, when he had prepared a feast for his high-ranking officials and military officers and Galilee's leading residents. ²²Herod's daughter Herodias[f] came in and danced, thrilling Herod and his dinner guests. The king said to the young woman, "Ask me whatever you wish, and I will give it to you." ²³Then he swore to her, "Whatever you ask I will give to you, even as much as half of my kingdom."

²⁴She left the banquet hall and said to her mother, "What should I ask for?"

"John the Baptist's head," Herodias replied.

²⁵Hurrying back to the ruler, she made her request: "I want you to give me John the Baptist's head on a plate, right this minute." ²⁶Although the king was upset, because of his solemn pledge and his guests, he didn't want to refuse her. ²⁷So he ordered a guard to bring John's head. The guard went to the prison, cut off John's head, ²⁸brought his head on a plate, and gave it to the young woman, and she gave it to her mother. ²⁹When John's disciples heard what had happened, they came and took his dead body and laid it in a tomb.

Jesus feeds five thousand people

³⁰The apostles returned to Jesus and told him everything they had done and taught.

³¹Many people were coming and going, so there was no time to eat. He said to the apostles, "Come by yourselves to a secluded place and rest for a while." ³²They departed in a boat by themselves for a deserted place.

³³Many people saw them leaving and recognized them, so they ran ahead from all the cities and arrived before them. ³⁴When Jesus arrived and saw a large crowd, he had compassion on them because they were like sheep without a shepherd. Then he began to teach them many things.

³⁵Late in the day, his disciples came to him and said, "This is an isolated place, and it's already late in the day. ³⁶Send them away so that they can go to the surrounding countryside and villages and buy something to eat for themselves."

³⁷He replied, "You give them something to eat."

But they said to him, "Should we go off and buy bread worth almost eight months' pay[g] and give it to them to eat?"

³⁸He said to them, "How much bread do you have? Take a look."

After checking, they said, "Five loaves of bread and two fish."

³⁹He directed the disciples to seat all the people in groups as though they were having a banquet on the green grass. ⁴⁰They sat down in groups of hundreds and fifties. ⁴¹He took the five loaves and the two fish, looked up to heaven, blessed them, broke the loaves

[f] Or *the daughter of Herodias herself*; Gk uncertain   [g] Or *two hundred denaria*; a denarion was a typical day's wage.

HEROD AND FAMILY

The Idumean dynasty that played a powerful role in Judean affairs from 37 BCE to 100 CE and provided Rome with a number of client rulers. Herod the Great was born in the late 70s BCE and was appointed governor of Galilee at the age of 25. In 37 BCE Herod began his long reign as king of the Jews. In 20–19, Herod began construction on a remodeled Jerusalem temple with Greek influences, to serve as a symbol of his rule and power. Herod the Great died ca. 4 BCE. His son Archelaus became ruler after a succession contested by his brothers, and he assumed the name Herod as well for his reign from 4 BCE to 6 CE. His brother Antipas and Herod the Great's great-grandson Agrippa II were also influential leaders in the region.

into pieces, and gave them to his disciples to set before the people. He also divided the two fish among them all. [42]Everyone ate until they were full. [43]They filled twelve baskets with the leftover pieces of bread and fish. [44]About five thousand had eaten.

Jesus walks on water

[45]Right then, Jesus made his disciples get into a boat and go ahead to the other side of the lake, toward Bethsaida, while he dismissed the crowd. [46]After saying goodbye to them, Jesus went up onto a mountain to pray. [47]Evening came and the boat was in the middle of the lake, but he was alone on the land. [48]He saw his disciples struggling. They were trying to row forward, but the wind was blowing against them. Very early in the morning, he came to them, walking on the lake. He intended to pass by them. [49]When they saw him walking on the lake, they thought he was a ghost and they screamed. [50]Seeing him was terrifying to all of them. Just then he spoke to them, "Be encouraged! It's me. Don't be afraid." [51]He got into the boat, and the wind settled down. His disciples were so baffled they were beside themselves. [52]That's because they hadn't understood about the loaves. Their hearts had been changed so that they resisted God's ways.

Healings at Gennesaret

[53]When Jesus and his disciples had crossed the lake, they landed at Gennesaret, anchored the boat, [54]and came ashore. People immediately recognized Jesus [55]and ran around that whole region bringing sick people on their mats to wherever they heard he was. [56]Wherever he went—villages, cities, or farming communities—they would place the sick in the marketplaces and beg him to allow them to touch even the hem of his clothing. Everyone who touched him was healed.

What contaminates a life?

7 The Pharisees and some legal experts from Jerusalem gathered around Jesus.

[2]They saw some of his disciples eating food with unclean hands. (They were eating without first ritually purifying their hands through washing. [3]The Pharisees and all the Jews don't eat without first washing their hands carefully. This is a way of observing the rules handed down by the elders. [4]Upon returning from the marketplace, they don't eat without first immersing themselves. They observe many other rules that have been handed down, such as the washing of cups, jugs, pans, and sleeping mats.) [5]So the Pharisees and legal experts asked Jesus, "Why are your disciples not living according to the rules handed down by the elders but instead eat food with ritually unclean hands?"

[6]He replied, "Isaiah really knew what he was talking about when he prophesied about you hypocrites. He wrote,

This people honors me with their lips,
  but their hearts are far away from me.
[7] *Their worship of me is empty*
  since they teach instructions that are
    human words.[h]

[8]You ignore God's commandment while holding on to rules created by humans and handed down to you." [9]Jesus continued, "Clearly, you are experts at rejecting God's commandment in order to establish these rules. [10]Moses said, *Honor your father and your mother,*[i] and *The person who speaks against father or mother will certainly be put to death.*[j] [11]But you say, 'If you tell your father or mother, "Everything I'm expected to contribute to you is *corban* (that is, a gift I'm giving to God)," [12]then you are no longer required to care for your father or mother.' [13]In this way you do away with God's word in favor of the rules handed down to you, which you pass on to others. And you do a lot of other things just like that."

[14]Then Jesus called the crowd again and said, "Listen to me, all of you, and understand. [15]Nothing outside of a person can enter and contaminate a person in God's sight; rather, the things that come out of a person contaminate the person."[k]

---

[h]Isa 29:13 [i]Exod 20:12; Deut 5:16 [j]Exod 21:17; Lev 20:9 [k]7:16 is omitted in most critical editions of the Gk New Testament *Whoever has ears to listen should pay attention!*

¹⁷After leaving the crowd, he entered a house where his disciples asked him about that riddle. ¹⁸He said to them, "Don't you understand either? Don't you know that nothing from the outside that enters a person has the power to contaminate? ¹⁹That's because it doesn't enter into the heart but into the stomach, and it goes out into the sewer." By saying this, Jesus declared that no food could contaminate a person in God's sight. ²⁰"It's what comes out of a person that contaminates someone in God's sight," he said. ²¹"It's from the inside, from the human heart, that evil thoughts come: sexual sins, thefts, murders, ²²adultery, greed, evil actions, deceit, unrestrained immorality, envy, insults, arrogance, and foolishness. ²³All these evil things come from the inside and contaminate a person in God's sight."

An immigrant's daughter is delivered

²⁴Jesus left that place and went into the region of Tyre. He didn't want anyone to know that he had entered a house, but he couldn't hide. ²⁵In fact, a woman whose young daughter was possessed by an unclean spirit heard about him right away. She came and fell at his feet. ²⁶The woman was Greek, Syrophoenician by birth. She begged Jesus to throw the demon out of her daughter. ²⁷He responded, "The children have to be fed first. It isn't right to take the children's bread and toss it to the dogs."

²⁸But she answered, "Lord, even the dogs under the table eat the children's crumbs."

²⁹"Good answer!" he said. "Go on home. The demon has already left your daughter." ³⁰When she returned to her house, she found the child lying on the bed and the demon gone.

A deaf man is healed

³¹After leaving the region of Tyre, Jesus went through Sidon toward the Galilee Sea through the region of the Ten Cities. ³²Some people brought to him a man who was deaf and could hardly speak, and they begged him to place his hand on the man for healing. ³³Jesus took him away from the crowd by himself and put his fingers in the man's ears. Then he spit and touched the man's tongue. ³⁴Looking into heaven, Jesus sighed deeply and said, *"Ephphatha,"* which means, "Open up." ³⁵At once, his ears opened, his twisted tongue was released, and he began to speak clearly.

³⁶Jesus gave the people strict orders not to tell anyone. But the more he tried to silence them, the more eagerly they shared the news. ³⁷People were overcome with wonder, saying, "He does everything well! He even makes the deaf to hear and gives speech to those who can't speak."

Jesus feeds four thousand people

8 In those days there was another large crowd with nothing to eat. Jesus called his disciples and told them, ²"I feel sorry for the crowd because they have been with me for three days and have nothing to eat. ³If I send them away hungry to their homes, they won't have enough strength to travel, for some have come a long distance."

⁴His disciples responded, "How can anyone get enough food in this wilderness to satisfy these people?"

⁵Jesus asked, "How much bread do you have?"

They said, "Seven loaves."

⁶He told the crowd to sit on the ground. He took the seven loaves, gave thanks, broke them apart, and gave them to his disciples to distribute; and they gave the bread to the crowd. ⁷They also had a few fish. He said a blessing over them, then gave them to the disciples to hand out also. ⁸They ate until they were full. They collected seven baskets full of leftovers. ⁹This was a crowd of about four thousand people! Jesus sent them away, ¹⁰then got into a boat with his disciples and went over to the region of Dalmanutha.

Looking for proof

¹¹The Pharisees showed up and began to argue with Jesus. To test him, they asked for a sign from heaven. ¹²With an impatient sigh, Jesus said, "Why does this generation look for a sign? I assure you that no sign will be given to it." ¹³Leaving them, he got back in the boat and crossed to the other side of the lake.

Understanding about the bread

[14] Jesus' disciples had forgotten to bring any bread, so they had only one loaf with them in the boat. [15] He gave them strict orders: "Watch out and be on your guard for the yeast of the Pharisees as well as the yeast of Herod." [16] The disciples discussed this among themselves, "He said this because we have no bread."

[17] Jesus knew what they were discussing and said, "Why are you talking about the fact that you don't have any bread? Don't you grasp what has happened? Don't you understand? Are your hearts so resistant to what God is doing? [18] Don't you have eyes? Why can't you see? Don't you have ears? Why can't you hear? Don't you remember? [19] When I broke five loaves of bread for those five thousand people, how many baskets full of leftovers did you gather?"

They answered, "Twelve."

[20] "And when I broke seven loaves of bread for those four thousand people, how many baskets full of leftovers did you gather?"

They answered, "Seven."

[21] Jesus said to them, "And you still don't understand?"

A blind man is healed

[22] Jesus and his disciples came to Bethsaida. Some people brought a blind man to Jesus and begged him to touch and heal him. [23] Taking the blind man's hand, Jesus led him out of the village. After spitting on his eyes and laying his hands on the man, he asked him, "Do you see anything?"

[24] The man looked up and said, "I see people. They look like trees, only they are walking around."

[25] Then Jesus placed his hands on the man's eyes again. He looked with his eyes wide open, his sight was restored, and he could see everything clearly. [26] Then Jesus sent him home, saying, "Don't go into the village!"

Jesus predicts his death

[27] Jesus and his disciples went into the villages near Caesarea Philippi. On the way he asked his disciples, "Who do people say that I am?"

[28] They told him, "Some say John the Baptist, others Elijah, and still others one of the prophets."

[29] He asked them, "And what about you? Who do you say that I am?"

Peter answered, "You are the Christ." [30] Jesus ordered them not to tell anyone about him.

[31] Then Jesus began to teach his disciples: "The Human One[l] must suffer many things and be rejected by the elders, chief priests, and the legal experts, and be killed, and then, after three days, rise from the dead." [32] He said this plainly. But Peter took hold of Jesus and, scolding him, began to correct him. [33] Jesus turned and looked at his disciples, then sternly corrected Peter: "Get behind me, Satan. You are not thinking God's thoughts but human thoughts."

[34] After calling the crowd together with his disciples, Jesus said to them, "All who want to come after me must say no to

[l] Or *Son of Man*

PETER (THE APOSTLE)

The most prominent disciple of Jesus, Peter is mentioned more than 200 times in the NT. His name was Simon (in Matt 4:18) or Simeon (in Acts 15:14; 2 Pet 1:1). He is also called "bar Jonah" or "son of Jonah" (Matt 16:17) or "son of John" (John 1:42). Jesus nicknamed him "Peter" (Mark 3:16), meaning "rock," which is "Cephas" in Aramaic; Paul ordinarily uses the Aramaic (1 Cor 1:12; Gal 1:18). He is a major character in the book of Acts, and he is also known as the author of two letters in the NT, which bear his name.

themselves, take up their cross, and follow me. [35]All who want to save their lives will lose them. But all who lose their lives because of me and because of the good news will save them. [36]Why would people gain the whole world but lose their lives? [37]What will people give in exchange for their lives? [38]Whoever is ashamed of me and my words in this unfaithful and sinful generation, the Human One[m] will be ashamed of that person when he comes in the Father's glory with the holy angels." [1]Jesus continued, "I assure you that some standing here won't die before they see God's kingdom arrive in power."

Jesus transformed

[2]Six days later Jesus took Peter, James, and John, and brought them to the top of a very high mountain where they were alone. He was transformed in front of them, [3]and his clothes were amazingly bright, brighter than if they had been bleached white. [4]Elijah and Moses appeared and were talking with Jesus. [5]Peter reacted to all of this by saying to Jesus, "Rabbi, it's good that we're here. Let's make three shrines—one for you, one for Moses, and one for Elijah." [6]He said this because he didn't know how to respond, for the three of them were terrified. [7]Then a cloud overshadowed them, and a voice spoke from the cloud, "This is my Son, whom I dearly love. Listen to him!" [8]Suddenly, looking around, they no longer saw anyone with them except Jesus.

[9]As they were coming down the mountain, he ordered them not to tell anyone what they had seen until after the Human One[n] had risen from the dead. [10]So they kept it to themselves, wondering, "What's this 'rising from the dead'?" [11]They asked Jesus, "Why do the legal experts say that Elijah must come first?"

[12]He answered, "Elijah does come first to restore all things. Why was it written that the Human One[o] would suffer many things and be rejected? [13]In fact, I tell you that Elijah has come, but they did to him whatever they wanted, just as it was written about him."

A demon-possessed boy

[14]When Jesus, Peter, James, and John approached the other disciples, they saw a large crowd surrounding them and legal experts arguing with them. [15]Suddenly the whole crowd caught sight of Jesus. They ran to greet him, overcome with excitement. [16]Jesus asked them, "What are you arguing about?"

[17]Someone from the crowd responded, "Teacher, I brought my son to you, since he has a spirit that doesn't allow him to speak. [18]Wherever it overpowers him, it throws him into a fit. He foams at the mouth, grinds his teeth, and stiffens up. So I spoke to your disciples to see if they could throw it out, but they couldn't."

[19]Jesus answered them, "You faithless generation, how long will I be with you? How long will I put up with you? Bring him to me."

[20]They brought him. When the spirit saw Jesus, it immediately threw the boy into a fit. He fell on the ground and rolled around, foaming at the mouth. [21]Jesus asked his father, "How long has this been going on?"

---

[m]Or *Son of Man*   [n]Or *Son of Man*   [o]Or *Son of Man*

HELL

In the NT, *hell* occurs as punishment after death. There are three contexts: (1) sin leads there (Matt 5:22), to unquenched fire (Matt 5:29-30; Mark 9:43-48); (2) disciples must fear the one who can throw or destroy them there (Matt 10:28; Luke 12:5); and (3) some legal experts and Pharisees and their converts are destined there (Matt 23:15, 33).

He said, "Since he was a child. ²²It has often thrown him into a fire or into water trying to kill him. If you can do anything, help us! Show us compassion!"

²³Jesus said to him, "'If you can do anything'? All things are possible for the one who has faith."

²⁴At that the boy's father cried out, "I have faith; help my lack of faith!"

²⁵Noticing that the crowd had surged together, Jesus spoke harshly to the unclean spirit, "Mute and deaf spirit, I command you to come out of him and never enter him again." ²⁶After screaming and shaking the boy horribly, the spirit came out. The boy seemed to be dead; in fact, several people said that he had died. ²⁷But Jesus took his hand, lifted him up, and he arose.

²⁸After Jesus went into a house, his disciples asked him privately, "Why couldn't we throw this spirit out?"

²⁹Jesus answered, "Throwing this kind of spirit out requires prayer."

Jesus predicts his death

³⁰From there Jesus and his followers went through Galilee, but he didn't want anyone to know it. ³¹This was because he was teaching his disciples, "The Human One[p] will be delivered into human hands. They will kill him. Three days after he is killed he will rise up." ³²But they didn't understand this kind of talk, and they were afraid to ask him.

³³They entered Capernaum. When they had come into a house, he asked them, "What were you arguing about during the journey?" ³⁴They didn't respond, since on the way they had been debating with each other about who was the greatest. ³⁵He sat down, called the Twelve, and said to them, "Whoever wants to be first must be least of all and the servant of all." ³⁶Jesus reached for a little child, placed him among the Twelve, and embraced him. Then he said, ³⁷"Whoever welcomes one of these children in my name welcomes me; and whoever welcomes me isn't actually welcoming me but rather the one who sent me."

Recognize your allies

³⁸John said to Jesus, "Teacher, we saw someone throwing demons out in your name, and we tried to stop him because he wasn't following us."

³⁹Jesus replied, "Don't stop him. No one who does powerful acts in my name can quickly turn around and curse me. ⁴⁰Whoever isn't against us is for us. ⁴¹I assure you that whoever gives you a cup of water to drink because you belong to Christ will certainly be rewarded.

⁴²"As for whoever causes these little ones who believe in me to trip and fall into sin, it would be better for them to have a huge stone hung around their necks and to be thrown into the lake. ⁴³If your hand causes you to fall into sin, chop it off. It's better for you to enter into life crippled than to go away with two hands into the fire of hell, which can't be put out.[q] ⁴⁵If your foot causes you to fall into sin, chop it off. It's better for you to enter life lame than to be thrown into hell with two feet.[r] ⁴⁷If your eye causes you to fall into sin, tear it out. It's better for you to enter God's kingdom with one eye than to be thrown into hell with two. ⁴⁸That's a place where worms don't die and the fire never goes out.[s] ⁴⁹Everyone will be salted with fire. ⁵⁰Salt is good; but if salt loses its saltiness, how will it become salty again? Maintain salt among yourselves and keep peace with each other."

Divorce and remarriage

10 Jesus left that place and went beyond the Jordan and into the region of Judea. Crowds gathered around him again and, as usual, he taught them. ²Some Pharisees came and, trying to test him, they asked, "Does the Law allow a man to divorce his wife?"

³Jesus answered, "What did Moses command you?"

---

[p]Or Son of Man   [q]9:44 is omitted in most critical editions of the Gk New Testament where worms don't die and the fire never goes out.   [r]9:46 is omitted in most critical editions of the Gk New Testament where worms don't die and the fire never goes out.   [s]Isa 66:24

⁴They said, "Moses allowed a man to write a divorce certificate and to divorce his wife."

⁵Jesus said to them, "He wrote this commandment for you because of your unyielding hearts. ⁶At the beginning of creation, *God made them male and female.*[t] ⁷*Because of this, a man should leave his father and mother and be joined together with his wife,* ⁸*and the two will be one flesh.*[u] So they are no longer two but one flesh. ⁹Therefore, humans must not pull apart what God has put together."

¹⁰Inside the house, the disciples asked him again about this. ¹¹He said to them, "Whoever divorces his wife and marries another commits adultery against her; ¹²and if a wife divorces her husband and marries another, she commits adultery."

Jesus blesses children

¹³People were bringing children to Jesus so that he would bless them. But the disciples scolded them. ¹⁴When Jesus saw this, he grew angry and said to them, "Allow the children to come to me. Don't forbid them, because God's kingdom belongs to people like these children. ¹⁵I assure you that whoever doesn't welcome God's kingdom like a child will never enter it." ¹⁶Then he hugged the children and blessed them.

A rich man's question

¹⁷As Jesus continued down the road, a man ran up, knelt before him, and asked, "Good Teacher, what must I do to obtain eternal life?"

¹⁸Jesus replied, "Why do you call me good? No one is good except the one God. ¹⁹You know the commandments: *Don't com-*

mit murder. Don't commit adultery. Don't steal. Don't give false testimony. Don't cheat. *Honor your father and mother.*"[v]

²⁰"Teacher," he responded, "I've kept all of these things since I was a boy."

²¹Jesus looked at him carefully and loved him. He said, "You are lacking one thing. Go, sell what you own, and give the money to the poor. Then you will have treasure in heaven. And come, follow me." ²²But the man was dismayed at this statement and went away saddened, because he had many possessions.

²³Looking around, Jesus said to his disciples, "It will be very hard for the wealthy to enter God's kingdom!" ²⁴His words startled the disciples, so Jesus told them again, "Children, it's difficult to enter God's kingdom! ²⁵It's easier for a camel to squeeze through the eye of a needle than for a rich person to enter God's kingdom."

²⁶They were shocked even more and said to each other, "Then who can be saved?"

²⁷Jesus looked at them carefully and said, "It's impossible with human beings, but not with God. All things are possible for God."

²⁸Peter said to him, "Look, we've left everything and followed you."

²⁹Jesus said, "I assure you that anyone who has left house, brothers, sisters, mother, father, children, or farms because of me and because of the good news ³⁰will receive one hundred times as much now in this life—houses, brothers, sisters, mothers, children, and farms (with harassment)—and in the coming age, eternal life. ³¹But many who are first will be last. And many who are last will be first."

[t]Gen 1:27 [u]Gen 2:24 [v]Exod 12:16; Deut 16:20

BARTIMAEUS

The name means "son of Timaeus." A blind beggar Jesus healed as he was leaving Jericho (Mark 10:46-52). Thereafter, Bartimaeus follows Jesus, presumably into Jerusalem. Similar stories are found in Matthew 20:29-34, which mentions two anonymous blind men healed upon leaving Jericho, and in Luke 18:35-43, wherein Jesus heals one blind man upon entering Jericho.

Jesus predicts his death and resurrection

³²Jesus and his disciples were on the road, going up to Jerusalem, with Jesus in the lead. The disciples were amazed while the others following behind were afraid. Taking the Twelve aside again, he told them what was about to happen to him. ³³"Look!" he said. "We're going up to Jerusalem. The Human One^w will be handed over to the chief priests and the legal experts. They will condemn him to death and hand him over to the Gentiles. ³⁴They will ridicule him, spit on him, torture him, and kill him. After three days, he will rise up."

A request from James and John

³⁵James and John, Zebedee's sons, came to Jesus and said, "Teacher, we want you to do for us whatever we ask."

³⁶"What do you want me to do for you?" he asked.

³⁷They said, "Allow one of us to sit on your right and the other on your left when you enter your glory."

³⁸Jesus replied, "You don't know what you're asking! Can you drink the cup I drink or receive the baptism I receive?"

³⁹"We can," they answered.

Jesus said, "You will drink the cup I drink and receive the baptism I receive, ⁴⁰but to sit at my right or left hand isn't mine to give. It belongs to those for whom it has been prepared."

⁴¹Now when the other ten disciples heard about this, they became angry with James and John. ⁴²Jesus called them over and said, "You know that the ones who are considered the rulers by the Gentiles show off their authority over them and their high-ranking officials order them around. ⁴³But that's not the way it will be with you. Whoever wants to be great among you will be your servant. ⁴⁴Whoever wants to be first among you will be the slave of all, ⁴⁵for the Human One^x didn't come to be served but rather to serve and to give his life to liberate many people."

Healing of blind Bartimaeus

⁴⁶Jesus and his followers came into Jericho. As Jesus was leaving Jericho, together with his disciples and a sizable crowd, a blind beggar named Bartimaeus, Timaeus' son, was sitting beside the road. ⁴⁷When he heard that Jesus of Nazareth was there, he began to shout, "Jesus, Son of David, show me mercy!" ⁴⁸Many scolded him, telling him to be quiet, but he shouted even louder, "Son of David, show me mercy!"

⁴⁹Jesus stopped and said, "Call him forward."

They called the blind man, "Be encouraged! Get up! He's calling you."

⁵⁰Throwing his coat to the side, he jumped up and came to Jesus.

⁵¹Jesus asked him, "What do you want me to do for you?"

The blind man said, "Teacher, I want to see."

⁵²Jesus said, "Go, your faith has healed you." At once he was able to see, and he began to follow Jesus on the way.

Jesus enters Jerusalem

11 When Jesus and his followers approached Jerusalem, they came to Bethphage and Bethany at the Mount of Olives. Jesus gave two disciples a task, ²saying to them, "Go into the village over there. As soon as you enter it, you will find tied up there a colt that no one has ridden. Untie it and bring it here. ³If anyone says to you, 'Why are you doing this?' say, 'Its master needs it, and he will send it back right away.'"

⁴They went and found a colt tied to a gate outside on the street, and they untied it. ⁵Some people standing around said to them, "What are you doing, untying the colt?" ⁶They told them just what Jesus said, and they left them alone. ⁷They brought the colt to Jesus and threw their clothes upon it, and he sat on it. ⁸Many people spread out their clothes on the road while others spread branches cut from the fields. ⁹Those in front of him and those following were shouting, "*Hosanna! Blessings on the one who comes in the name of the Lord!*^y ¹⁰Blessings on the coming kingdom of our ancestor David!

---

^w Or *Son of Man*   ^x Or *Son of Man*   ^y Ps 118:26

Hosanna in the highest!" ¹¹Jesus entered Jerusalem and went into the temple. After he looked around at everything, because it was already late in the evening, he returned to Bethany with the Twelve.

Fig tree and the temple

¹²The next day, after leaving Bethany, Jesus was hungry. ¹³From far away, he noticed a fig tree in leaf, so he went to see if he could find anything on it. When he came to it, he found nothing except leaves, since it wasn't the season for figs. ¹⁴So he said to it, "No one will ever again eat your fruit!" His disciples heard this.

¹⁵They came into Jerusalem. After entering the temple, he threw out those who were selling and buying there. He pushed over the tables used for currency exchange and the chairs of those who sold doves. ¹⁶He didn't allow anyone to carry anything through the temple. ¹⁷He taught them, "Hasn't it been written, *My house will be called a house of prayer for all nations?*ᶻ But you've turned it into *a hideout for crooks.*"ᵃ ¹⁸The chief priests and legal experts heard this and tried to find a way to destroy him. They regarded him as dangerous because the whole crowd was enthralled at his teaching. ¹⁹When it was evening, Jesus and his disciples went outside the city.

Power, prayer, and forgiveness

²⁰Early in the morning, as Jesus and his disciples were walking along, they saw the fig tree withered from the root up. ²¹Peter remembered and said to Jesus, "Rabbi, look how the fig tree you cursed has dried up."

²²Jesus responded to them, "Have faith in God! ²³I assure you that whoever says to this mountain, 'Be lifted up and thrown into the sea'—and doesn't waver but believes that what is said will really happen—it will happen. ²⁴Therefore I say to you, whatever you pray and ask for, believe that you will receive it, and it will be so for you. ²⁵And whenever you stand up to pray, if you have something against anyone, forgive so that your Father in heaven may forgive you your wrongdoings."ᵇ

Controversy over authority

²⁷Jesus and his disciples entered Jerusalem again. As Jesus was walking around the temple, the chief priests, legal experts, and elders came to him. ²⁸They asked, "What kind of authority do you have for doing these things? Who gave you this authority to do them?"

²⁹Jesus said to them, "I have a question for you. Give me an answer, then I'll tell you what kind of authority I have to do these things. ³⁰Was John's baptism of heavenly or of human origin? Answer me."

³¹They argued among themselves, "If we say, 'It's of heavenly origin,' he'll say, 'Then why didn't you believe him?' ³²But we can't say, 'It's of earthly origin.'" They said this because they were afraid of the crowd, because they all thought John was a prophet. ³³They answered Jesus, "We don't know."

ᶻIsa 56:7 ᵃJer 7:11 ᵇ11:26 is omitted in most critical editions of the Gk New Testament *And if you don't forgive, neither will your Father in heaven forgive you your wrongdoings.*

HOSANNA

From Psalm 118:25-26, meaning "save now." Mark's paraphrase, "Hosanna! Blessings on the one who comes in the name of the Lord!" (Mark 11:9), thus represents the first part of each verse of Psalm 118:25-26. The expression "hosanna" evoked kingly associations, and Psalm 118 was connected to the recognition of David as Israel's rightful king. The Davidic orientation of Psalm 118 fits with the crowd's paraphrase: "Blessings on the coming kingdom of our ancestor David!" (Mark 11:10).

Jesus replied, "Neither will I tell you what kind of authority I have to do these things."

Parable of the tenant farmers

12 Jesus spoke to them in parables. "A man planted a vineyard, put a fence around it, dug a pit for the winepress, and built a tower. Then he rented it to tenant farmers and took a trip. [2] When it was time, he sent a servant to collect from the tenants his share of the fruit of the vineyard. [3] But they grabbed the servant, beat him, and sent him away empty-handed. [4] Again the landowner sent another servant to them, but they struck him on the head and treated him disgracefully. [5] He sent another one; that one they killed. The landlord sent many other servants, but the tenants beat some and killed others. [6] Now the landowner had one son whom he loved dearly. He sent him last, thinking, They will respect my son. [7] But those tenant farmers said to each other, 'This is the heir. Let's kill him, and the inheritance will be ours.' [8] They grabbed him, killed him, and threw him out of the vineyard.

[9] "So what will the owner of the vineyard do? He will come and destroy those tenants and give the vineyard to others. [10] Haven't you read this scripture, *The stone that the builders rejected has become the cornerstone.* [11] *The Lord has done this, and it's amazing in our eyes?*"[c]

[12] They wanted to arrest Jesus because they knew that he had told the parable

[c]Ps 118:22-23　[d]Deut 25:5; Gen 38:8

against them. But they were afraid of the crowd, so they left him and went away.

A question about taxes

[13] They sent some of the Pharisees and supporters of Herod to trap him in his words. [14] They came to him and said, "Teacher, we know that you're genuine and you don't worry about what people think. You don't show favoritism but teach God's way as it really is. Does the Law allow people to pay taxes to Caesar or not? Should we pay taxes or not?"

[15] Since Jesus recognized their deceit, he said to them, "Why are you testing me? Bring me a coin. Show it to me." [16] And they brought one. He said to them, "Whose image and inscription is this?"

"Caesar's," they replied.

[17] Jesus said to them, "Give to Caesar what belongs to Caesar and to God what belongs to God." His reply left them overcome with wonder.

A question about the resurrection

[18] Sadducees, who deny that there is a resurrection, came to Jesus and asked, [19] "Teacher, Moses wrote for us that *if a man's brother dies,* leaving a widow *but no children, the brother must marry the widow and raise up children for his brother.*[d] [20] Now there were seven brothers. The first one married a woman; when he died, he left no children. [21] The second married her and died without leaving any children. The third did

CAESAR

Originally the personal name of the Roman dictator Gaius Julius, who was murdered in 44 BCE. Caesar was taken up as the family name of his adopted heir Octavian (Augustus) and thereafter came to designate each successive Roman emperor. Caesar appears in the NT, particularly the Gospels and Acts, often in contrast to the rule of God or Jesus (e.g., Matt 22:17-21). Emperors established laws, judged cases, functioned as the final court of appeals, and served as the high priests of the Augustan system of Roman religion.

the same. ²²None of the seven left any children. Finally, the woman died. ²³At the resurrection, when they all rise up, whose wife will she be? All seven were married to her."

²⁴Jesus said to them, "Isn't this the reason you are wrong, because you don't know either the scriptures or God's power? ²⁵When people rise from the dead, they won't marry nor will they be given in marriage. Instead, they will be like God's angels. ²⁶As for the resurrection from the dead, haven't you read in the scroll from Moses, in the passage about the burning bush, how God said to Moses, *I am the God of Abraham, the God of Isaac, and the God of Jacob?*ᵉ ²⁷He isn't the God of the dead but of the living. You are seriously mistaken."

God's most important command

²⁸One of the legal experts heard their dispute and saw how well Jesus answered them. He came over and asked him, "Which commandment is the most important of all?"

²⁹Jesus replied, "The most important one is *Israel, listen! Our God is the one Lord,* ³⁰*and you must love the Lord your God with all your heart, with all your being, with all your mind, and with all your strength.*ᶠ ³¹The second is this, *You will love your neighbor as yourself.*ᵍ No other commandment is greater than these."

³²The legal expert said to him, "Well said, Teacher. You have truthfully said that God is one and there is no other besides him. ³³And to love God with all of the heart, a full understanding, and all of one's strength, and to love one's neighbor as oneself is much more important than all kinds of entirely burned offerings and sacrifices."

³⁴When Jesus saw that he had answered with wisdom, he said to him, "You aren't far from God's kingdom." After that, no one dared to ask him any more questions.

Jesus corrects the legal experts

³⁵While Jesus was teaching in the temple, he said, "Why do the legal experts say that the Christ is David's son? ³⁶David himself, inspired by the Holy Spirit, said, *The Lord said to my lord, 'Sit at my right side until I turn your enemies into your footstool.'*ʰ ³⁷David himself calls him 'Lord,' so how can he be David's son?" The large crowd listened to him with delight.

³⁸As he was teaching, he said, "Watch out for the legal experts. They like to walk around in long robes. They want to be greeted with honor in the markets. ³⁹They long for places of honor in the synagogues and at banquets. ⁴⁰They are the ones who cheat widows out of their homes, and to show off they say long prayers. They will be judged most harshly."

A poor widow's contribution

⁴¹Jesus sat across from the collection box for the temple treasury and observed how the crowd gave their money. Many rich people were throwing in lots of money. ⁴²One poor widow came forward and put in two small copper coins worth a penny.ⁱ ⁴³Jesus called his disciples to him and said, "I assure you that this poor widow has put in more than everyone who's been putting money in the treasury. ⁴⁴All of them are giving out of their spare change. But she from her hopeless poverty has given everything she had, even what she needed to live on."

The temple's fate

13 As Jesus left the temple, one of his disciples said to him, "Teacher, look! What awesome stones and buildings!"

²Jesus responded, "Do you see these enormous buildings? Not even one stone will be left upon another. All will be demolished."

³Jesus was sitting on the Mount of Olives across from the temple. Peter, James, John, and Andrew asked him privately, ⁴"Tell us, when will these things happen? What sign will show that all these things are about to come to an end?"

Keep watch!

⁵Jesus said, "Watch out that no one deceives you. ⁶Many people will come in my

---

ᵉExod 3:6, 15-16 ᶠDeut 6:4-5 ᵍLev 19:18 ʰPs 110:1   ⁱOr two *lepta* (the smallest Greek copper coin, each worth 1/128 of a single day's pay), that is, a *kodrantes* (the smallest Roman coin, equal in value to two *lepta*) name, saying, 'I'm the one!' They will deceive many people. [7]When you hear of wars and reports of wars, don't be alarmed. These things must happen, but this isn't the end yet. [8]Nations and kingdoms will fight against each other, and there will be earthquakes and famines in all sorts of places. These things are just the beginning of the sufferings associated with the end.

[9]"Watch out for yourselves. People will hand you over to the councils. You will be beaten in the synagogues. You will stand before governors and kings because of me so that you can testify before them. [10]First, the good news must be proclaimed to all the nations. [11]When they haul you in and hand you over, don't worry ahead of time about what to answer or say. Instead, say whatever is given to you at that moment, for you aren't doing the speaking but the Holy Spirit is. [12]Brothers and sisters will hand each other over to death. A father will turn in his children. Children will rise up against their parents and have them executed. [13]Everyone will hate you because of my name. But whoever stands firm until the end will be saved.

[14]"When you see the disgusting and destructive thing standing where it shouldn't be (the reader should understand this), then those in Judea must escape to the mountains. [15]Those on the roof shouldn't come down or enter their houses to grab anything. [16]Those in the field shouldn't come back to grab their clothes. [17]How terrible it will be at that time for women who are pregnant and for women who are nursing their children. [18]Pray that it doesn't happen in winter. [19]In those days there will be great suffering such as the world has never before seen and will never again see. [20]If the Lord hadn't shortened that time, no one would be rescued. But for the sake of the chosen ones, the ones whom God chose, he has cut short the time.

[21]"Then if someone says to you, 'Look, here's the Christ,' or 'There he is,' don't believe it. [22]False christs and false prophets will appear, and they will offer signs and wonders in order to deceive, if possible, those whom God has chosen. [23]But you, watch out! I've told you everything ahead of time.

[24]"In those days, after the suffering of that time, the sun will become dark, and the moon won't give its light. [25]The stars will fall from the sky, and the planets and other heavenly bodies will be shaken. [26]Then they will see the Human One[j] coming in the clouds with great power and splendor. [27]Then he will send the angels and gather together his chosen people from the four corners of the earth, from the end of the earth to the end of heaven.

A lesson from the fig tree

[28]"Learn this parable from the fig tree. After its branch becomes tender and it

[j]Or Son of Man

ANDREW

Andrew is first mentioned in Mark's Gospel as the brother of Simon Peter (Mark 1:16). He appears 12 times in the NT, four times in the Gospels and Acts among the lists of apostles (Mark 3:18; Matt 10:2; Luke 6:14; Acts 1:13), and always among the first four names in these lists (Peter, Andrew, James, and John). Among the Gospels, Mark and John give Andrew the most attention. In Mark's Gospel, Andrew is one of the first disciples to be called by Jesus along with Peter (1:16-18), is present when Jesus cures Peter's mother-in-law (1:29-31), and is among the few (Peter, James, and John) to hear Jesus predict the destruction of the temple (13:3-4).

sprouts new leaves, you know that summer is near. ²⁹In the same way, when you see these things happening, you know that he's near, at the door. ³⁰I assure you that this generation won't pass away until all these things happen. ³¹Heaven and earth will pass away, but my words will certainly not pass away.

³²"But nobody knows when that day or hour will come, not the angels in heaven and not the Son. Only the Father knows. ³³Watch out! Stay alert! You don't know when the time is coming. ³⁴It is as if someone took a trip, left the household behind, and put the servants in charge, giving each one a job to do, and told the doorkeeper to stay alert. ³⁵Therefore, stay alert! You don't know when the head of the household will come, whether in the evening or at midnight, or when the rooster crows in the early morning or at daybreak. ³⁶Don't let him show up when you weren't expecting and find you sleeping. ³⁷What I say to you, I say to all: Stay alert!"

Preparation for burial

14 It was two days before Passover and the Festival of Unleavened Bread. The chief priests and legal experts through cunning tricks were searching for a way to arrest Jesus and kill him. ²But they agreed that it shouldn't happen during the festival; otherwise, there would be an uproar among the people.

³Jesus was at Bethany visiting the house of Simon, who had a skin disease. During dinner, a woman came in with a vase made of alabaster and containing very expensive perfume of pure nard. She broke open the vase and poured the perfume on his head. ⁴Some grew angry. They said to each other, "Why waste the perfume? ⁵This perfume could have been sold for almost a year's pay^k and the money given to the poor." And they scolded her.

⁶Jesus said, "Leave her alone. Why do you make trouble for her? She has done a good thing for me. ⁷You always have the poor with you; and whenever you want, you can do something good for them. But you won't always have me. ⁸She has done what she could. She has anointed my body ahead of time for burial. ⁹I tell you the truth that, wherever in the whole world the good news is announced, what she's done will also be told in memory of her."

Passover meal

¹⁰Judas Iscariot, one of the Twelve, went to the chief priests to give Jesus up to them. ¹¹When they heard it, they were delighted and promised to give him money. So he started looking for an opportunity to turn him in.

¹²On the first day of the Festival of Unleavened Bread, when the Passover lamb was sacrificed, the disciples said to Jesus, "Where do you want us to prepare for you to eat the Passover meal?"

¹³He sent two of his disciples and said to them, "Go into the city. A man carrying a water jar will meet you. Follow him. ¹⁴Wherever he enters, say to the owner of the house, 'The teacher asks, "Where is my guest room where I can eat the Passover meal with my disciples?"' ¹⁵He will show you a large room upstairs already furnished. Prepare for us there." ¹⁶The disciples left, came into the city, found everything just as he had told them, and they prepared the Passover meal.

¹⁷That evening, Jesus arrived with the Twelve. ¹⁸During the meal, Jesus said, "I assure you that one of you will betray me— someone eating with me."

¹⁹Deeply saddened, they asked him, one by one, "It's not me, is it?"

²⁰Jesus answered, "It's one of the Twelve, one who is dipping bread with me into this bowl. ²¹The Human One^l goes to his death just as it is written about him. But how terrible it is for that person who betrays the Human One!^m It would have been better for him if he had never been born."

²²While they were eating, Jesus took bread, blessed it, broke it, and gave it to them, and said, "Take; this is my body." ²³He took a cup, gave thanks, and gave it to them, and they all drank from it. ²⁴He said

---

^k Or *three hundred denaria*; a denarion was equivalent to a day's pay.   ^l Or *Son of Man*   ^m Or *Son of Man* to them, "This is my blood of the covenant, which is poured out for many. ²⁵I assure you that I won't drink wine again until that day when I drink it in a new way in God's kingdom." ²⁶After singing songs of praise, they went out to the Mount of Olives.

Predictions about disciples leaving Jesus

²⁷Jesus said to them, "You will all falter in your faithfulness to me. It is written, *I will hit the shepherd, and the sheep will go off in all directions.*ⁿ ²⁸But after I'm raised up, I will go before you to Galilee."

²⁹Peter said to him, "Even if everyone else stumbles, I won't."

³⁰But Jesus said to him, "I assure you that on this very night, before the rooster crows twice, you will deny me three times."

³¹But Peter insisted, "If I must die alongside you, I won't deny you." And they all said the same thing.

Jesus in prayer

³²Jesus and his disciples came to a place called Gethsemane. Jesus said to them, "Sit here while I pray." ³³He took Peter, James, and John along with him. He began to feel despair and was anxious. ³⁴He said to them, "I'm very sad. It's as if I'm dying. Stay here and keep alert." ³⁵Then he went a short distance farther and fell to the ground. He prayed that, if possible, he might be spared the time of suffering. ³⁶He said, "Abba, Father, for you all things are possible. Take this cup of suffering away from me. However—not what I want but what you want."

³⁷He came and found them sleeping. He said to Peter, "Simon, are you asleep? Couldn't you stay alert for one hour? ³⁸Stay alert and pray so that you won't give in to temptation. The spirit is eager, but the flesh is weak."

³⁹Again, he left them and prayed, repeating the same words. ⁴⁰And, again, when he came back, he found them sleeping, for they couldn't keep their eyes open, and they didn't know how to respond to him. ⁴¹He came a third time and said to them, "Will you sleep and rest all night? That's enough! The time has come for the Human One° to be betrayed into the hands of sinners. ⁴²Get up! Let's go! Look, here comes my betrayer."

Arrest

⁴³Suddenly, while Jesus was still speaking, Judas, one of the Twelve, came with a

ⁿZech 13:7 °Or *Son of Man*

SANHEDRIN

In the NT often a designation for the supreme Jewish council in Jerusalem in the Second Temple Period. In the Jewish trial of Jesus, the Gospels mention the Sanhedrin consisting of the chief priests, scribes, and elders who call witnesses, pass a sentence, and insist before Pilate, the Roman governor, that Jesus should be executed (Matt 26:59; Mark 14:55; 15:1; Luke 22:66; 23:50-51; John 11:47).

It continues to be disputed whether the Sanhedrin had the jurisdiction for capital cases and the right to execute offenders. As Roman governors kept capital cases under their own jurisdiction, most scholars assume that when Judea was under direct Roman rule, the Sanhedrin could pass death sentences only in exceptional cases: when Gentiles contravened the ban, inscribed on the wall that divided the Court of the Gentiles from the temple courts, not to trespass beyond the gates leading into the temple, and perhaps for other clearly religious offenses.

mob carrying swords and clubs. They had been sent by the chief priests, legal experts, and elders. [44]His betrayer had given them a sign: "Arrest the man I kiss, and take him away under guard."

[45]As soon as he got there, Judas said to Jesus, "Rabbi!" Then he kissed him. [46]Then they came and grabbed Jesus and arrested him.

[47]One of the bystanders drew a sword and struck the high priest's slave and cut off his ear. [48]Jesus responded, "Have you come with swords and clubs to arrest me, like an outlaw? [49]Day after day, I was with you, teaching in the temple, but you didn't arrest me. But let the scriptures be fulfilled." [50]And all his disciples left him and ran away. [51]One young man, a disciple, was wearing nothing but a linen cloth. They grabbed him, [52]but he left the linen cloth behind and ran away naked.

A hearing before the Sanhedrin

[53]They led Jesus away to the high priest, and all the chief priests, elders, and legal experts gathered. [54]Peter followed him from a distance, right into the high priest's courtyard. He was sitting with the guards, warming himself by the fire. [55]The chief priests and the whole Sanhedrin were looking for testimony against Jesus in order to put him to death, but they couldn't find any. [56]Many brought false testimony against him, but they contradicted each other. [57]Some stood to offer false witness against him, saying, [58]"We heard him saying, 'I will destroy this temple, constructed by humans, and within three days I will build another, one not made by humans.'" [59]But their testimonies didn't agree even on this point.

[60]Then the high priest stood up in the middle of the gathering and examined Jesus. "Aren't you going to respond to the testimony these people have brought against you?" [61]But Jesus was silent and didn't answer. Again, the high priest asked, "Are you the Christ, the Son of the blessed one?"

[62]Jesus said, "I am. And you will see the Human One[p] sitting on the right side of the Almighty[q] and coming on the heavenly clouds."

[63]Then the high priest tore his clothes and said, "Why do we need any more witnesses? [64]You've heard his insult against God. What do you think?"

They all condemned him. "He deserves to die!"

[65]Some began to spit on him. Some covered his face and hit him, saying, "Prophesy!" Then the guards took him and beat him.

[p]Or *Son of Man* [q]Or *the Power*

COVENANT (NT)

The concerns of covenant are embedded in the theological thinking of the NT. Luke 1:72 declares that Jesus came because God "remembered his holy covenant," and the Gospel of Mark casts Jesus' death in light of OT covenant: "my blood of the covenant . . . is poured out for many" (Mark 14:24). According to the Gospels, Jesus came to fulfill the covenant. The reference to "pouring out" and to "many" suggests a link with Isa 53 and thus ultimately with the "covenant to the people" in Isaiah 42:6; 49:8. The Jesus covenant will benefit the world more spectacularly than the previous versions of the covenant did.

Apostles such as Paul saw themselves as "ministers of a new covenant," whose novelty lies in its being "not based on what is written but on the Spirit" (2 Cor 3:6). Hebrews develops the notion of the new covenant most systematically (see esp. Heb 8–9).

Peter denies Jesus

⁶⁶ Meanwhile, Peter was below in the courtyard. A woman, one of the high priest's servants, approached ⁶⁷ and saw Peter warming himself by the fire. She stared at him and said, "You were also with the Nazarene, Jesus."

⁶⁸ But he denied it, saying, "I don't know what you're talking about. I don't understand what you're saying." And he went outside into the outer courtyard. A rooster crowed.

⁶⁹ The female servant saw him and began a second time to say to those standing around, "This man is one of them." ⁷⁰ But he denied it again.

A short time later, those standing around again said to Peter, "You must be one of them, because you are also a Galilean."

⁷¹ But he cursed and swore, "I don't know this man you're talking about." ⁷² At that very moment, a rooster crowed a second time. Peter remembered what Jesus told him, "Before a rooster crows twice, you will deny me three times." And he broke down, sobbing.

Trial before Pilate

15 At daybreak, the chief priests—with the elders, legal experts, and the whole Sanhedrin—formed a plan. They bound Jesus, led him away, and turned him over to Pilate. ² Pilate questioned him, "Are you the king of the Jews?"

Jesus replied, "That's what you say." ³ The chief priests were accusing him of many things.

⁴ Pilate asked him again, "Aren't you going to answer? What about all these accusations?" ⁵ But Jesus gave no more answers, so that Pilate marveled.

⁶ During the festival, Pilate released one prisoner to them, whomever they requested. ⁷ A man named Barabbas was locked up with the rebels who had committed murder during an uprising. ⁸ The crowd pushed forward and asked Pilate to release someone, as he regularly did. ⁹ Pilate answered them, "Do you want me to release to you the king of the Jews?" ¹⁰ He knew that the chief priests had handed him over because of jealousy. ¹¹ But the chief priests stirred up the crowd to have him release Barabbas to them instead. ¹² Pilate replied, "Then what do you want me to do with the one you call king of the Jews?"

¹³ They shouted back, "Crucify him!"

¹⁴ Pilate said to them, "Why? What wrong has he done?"

They shouted even louder, "Crucify him!"

¹⁵ Pilate wanted to satisfy the crowd, so he released Barabbas to them. He had Jesus whipped, then handed him over to be crucified.

Jesus is tortured and killed

¹⁶ The soldiers led Jesus away into the courtyard of the palace known as the governor's headquarters,ʳ and they called together the whole company of soldiers.ˢ ¹⁷ They dressed him up in a purple robe and twisted together a crown of thorns and put it on him. ¹⁸ They saluted him, "Hey! King of the Jews!" ¹⁹ Again and again, they struck his head with a stick. They spit on him and knelt before him to honor him. ²⁰ When they finished mocking him, they stripped him of the purple robe and put his own clothes back on him. Then they led him out to crucify him.

ʳ Or *praetorium*　ˢ Or *cohort* (approximately six hundred soldiers)

SALOME

Mark lists Salome as the third of the three women who witnessed the crucifixion (15:40) and who came to the empty tomb (16:1). Matthew identifies "the mother of Zebedee's sons" as the third witness (27:56), leading some commentators to conclude that Salome was this woman's name.

²¹Simon, a man from Cyrene, Alexander and Rufus' father, was coming in from the countryside. They forced him to carry his cross.

²²They brought Jesus to the place called Golgotha, which means Skull Place. ²³They tried to give him wine mixed with myrrh, but he didn't take it. ²⁴They crucified him. They divided up his clothes, drawing lots for them to determine who would take what. ²⁵It was nine in the morning when they crucified him. ²⁶The notice of the formal charge against him was written, "The king of the Jews." ²⁷They crucified two outlaws with him, one on his right and one on his left.ᵗ

²⁹People walking by insulted him, shaking their heads and saying, "Ha! So you were going to destroy the temple and rebuild it in three days, were you? ³⁰Save yourself and come down from that cross!"

³¹In the same way, the chief priests were making fun of him among themselves, together with the legal experts. "He saved others," they said, "but he can't save himself. ³²Let the Christ, the king of Israel, come down from the cross. Then we'll see and believe." Even those who had been crucified with Jesus insulted him.

³³From noon until three in the afternoon the whole earth was dark. ³⁴At three, Jesus cried out with a loud shout, "*Eloi, eloi,* *lama sabachthani*," which means, "My God, my God, why have you left me?"

³⁵After hearing him, some standing there said, "Look! He's calling Elijah!" ³⁶Someone ran, filled a sponge with sour wine, and put it on a pole. He offered it to Jesus to drink, saying, "Let's see if Elijah will come to take him down." ³⁷But Jesus let out a loud cry and died.

³⁸The curtain of the sanctuary was torn in two from top to bottom. ³⁹When the centurion, who stood facing Jesus, saw how he died, he said, "This man was certainly God's Son."

⁴⁰Some women were watching from a distance, including Mary Magdalene and Mary the mother of James (the younger one) and Joses, and Salome. ⁴¹When Jesus was in Galilee, these women had followed and supported him, along with many other women who had come to Jerusalem with him.

Jesus' burial

⁴²Since it was late in the afternoon on Preparation Day, just before the Sabbath, ⁴³Joseph from Arimathea dared to approach Pilate and ask for Jesus' body. (Joseph was a prominent council member who also eagerly anticipated the coming of God's kingdom.) ⁴⁴Pilate wondered if Jesus was already dead. He called the centurion and asked him whether Jesus had already died.

ᵗ15:28 is omitted in most critical editions of the Gk New Testament *The scripture was fulfilled, which says, He was numbered among criminals.*

PREPARATION DAY

The day when Jews made special arrangements to observe the Sabbath. Because the Sabbath was a day of complete rest, food had to be cooked, clothing prepared, and travel concluded before it began. To avoid profaning the Sabbath, work ceased before sunset on Friday and was prohibited until after sunset on Saturday.

According to the Gospels, Jesus was crucified on a Preparation Day. Matthew, Mark, and Luke say people were preparing for the Sabbath (Matt 27:62; Mark 15:42; Luke 23:54), but John says they were preparing for the festival of Passover, a special Sabbath (John 19:14, 31, 42).

⁴⁵When he learned from the centurion that Jesus was dead, Pilate gave the dead body to Joseph. ⁴⁶He bought a linen cloth, took Jesus down from the cross, wrapped him in the cloth, and laid him in a tomb that had been carved out of rock. He rolled a stone against the entrance to the tomb. ⁴⁷Mary Magdalene and Mary the mother of Joses saw where he was buried.

Empty tomb

16 When the Sabbath was over, Mary Magdalene, Mary the mother of James, and Salome bought spices so that they could go and anoint Jesus' dead body. ²Very early on the first day of the week, just after sunrise, they came to the tomb. ³They were saying to each other, "Who's going to roll the stone away from the entrance for us?" ⁴When they looked up, they saw that the stone had been rolled away. (And it was a very large stone!) ⁵Going into the tomb, they saw a young man in a white robe seated on the right side; and they were startled.

⁶But he said to them, "Don't be alarmed! You are looking for Jesus of Nazareth, who was crucified.ᵘ He has been raised. He isn't here. Look, here's the place where they laid him. ⁷Go, tell his disciples, especially Peter, that he is going ahead of you into Galilee. You will see him there, just as he told you." ⁸Overcome with terror and dread, they fled from the tomb. They said nothing to anyone, because they were afraid.ᵛ

Endings Added Later

[⁹They promptly reported all of the young man's instructions to those who were with Peter. Afterward, through the work of his disciples, Jesus sent out, from the east to the west, the sacred and undying message of eternal salvation. Amen.]

[[⁹After Jesus rose up early on the first day of the week, he appeared first to Mary Magdalene, from whom he had cast out seven demons. ¹⁰She went and

---

ᵘOr *the Crucified One*   ᵛIn most critical editions of the Gk New Testament, the Gospel of Mark ends at 16:8.

KING OF THE JEWS

In Matthew's account of Jesus' birth, magi come from the east seeking the "newborn king of the Jews" (Matt 2:2). Herod, client king of Judea (who is not really a king or a Jew), seeks to kill this potential rival in an act of brutality that defines the sort of "king" he is (Matt 2:16). In contrast, Matthew says that Jesus is the Christ and son of David (Matt 1:1), whose throne is established forever (2 Sam 7:16), in fulfillment of the prophecy (Mic 5:2) that a ruler will come from Bethlehem to shepherd Israel (Matt 2:6). For Matthew, Jesus is the true king who inaugurates the kingdom of heaven (4:17, 23) and fulfills the Jewish Law and the Prophets (5:17-20).

All four Gospels record that Pontius Pilate asks Jesus if he is "king of the Jews" (Matt 27:11; Mark 15:2; Luke 23:3; John 18:33). Jesus does not answer this charge, because his accusers do not understand who he is or what kind of kingdom he represents (in John 18:36-37 Jesus clarifies that his kingdom "doesn't originate from this world"). The mocking soldiers hail him as "king of the Jews" (Matt 27:29; Mark 15:18; Luke 23:37; John 19:3) and give him a "crown" made of thorns (Matt 27:29; Mark 15:17; John 19:2). Jesus is crucified with the title "king of the Jews" over his head (Matt 27:37; Mark 15:26; Luke 23:38; John 19:19, 21), an indication that his crime is insurrection against Rome.

reported to the ones who had been with him, who were mourning and weeping. [11]But even after they heard the news, they didn't believe that Jesus was alive and that Mary had seen him.

[12]After that he appeared in a different form to two of them who were walking along in the countryside. [13]When they returned, they reported it to the others, but they didn't believe them. [14]Finally he appeared to the eleven while they were eating. Jesus criticized their unbelief and stubbornness because they didn't believe those who saw him after he was raised up. [15]He said to them, "Go into the whole world and proclaim the good news to every creature. [16]Whoever believes and is baptized will be saved, but whoever doesn't believe will be condemned. [17]These signs will be associated with those who believe: they will throw out demons in my name. They will speak in new languages. [18]They will pick up snakes with their hands. If they drink anything poisonous, it will not hurt them. They will place their hands on the sick, and they will get well."

[19]After the Lord Jesus spoke to them, he was lifted up into heaven and sat down on the right side of God. [20]But they went out and proclaimed the message everywhere. The Lord worked with them, confirming the word by the signs associated with them.]]

LUKE

THEME

The Christian church is the true people of God, called into being by God through the ministry, death, and resurrection of Jesus of Nazareth and empowered by God for a redemptive mission to all the earth; it is not a perversion of Judaism or a subversive society promoting rebellion against the Roman government.

THE RELATIONSHIPS AMONG THE GOSPELS

Why does our Bible have four accounts of the life of Jesus? In Luke you will find much of what is in Matthew and Mark and a little of what is recorded in John. Perhaps your own experience may give you part of the reason. Think of an occasion when some important news event took place in which you had a keen interest. So significant was that event that each television and radio station was reporting what it had observed and learned about it. You found yourself turning from station to station to secure more data or the latest information. One reporter may have had information not known by another. So it is with the accounts of the life of Jesus.

Each writer brought his own background, conversations, observations, and concern to the written account. They had certain people in mind to whom they wanted to make a witness and they had certain convictions about Jesus that they wanted to convey. Placing the accounts together makes a more comprehensive picture of who Jesus was as well as what Jesus taught and did.

THE WRITER OF THE GOSPEL

The author of the Gospel of Luke does not identify himself. The Gospel was originally anonymous, but ancient tradition says that the author is Paul's companion "Luke, the dearly loved physician" (Colossians 4:14). This writer, whom we call Luke, was writing as a non-Jew and was probably the only non-Jewish writer of a Gospel. Through the Gospel and the book of Acts he wanted to let the world know that Christ was for all persons—not just for Jews.

When you pick up this Gospel, remember that you are looking at the first part of a two-part work. The book of Acts is the second section. Both books appear to have been written by the same author and are addressed to the same unknown individual, Theophilus. At the outset of the Gospel, Luke refers to other accounts "of the events that have been fulfilled among us" (1:1). He says he wants to write an "orderly account" (1:3).

In his introduction to Acts, Luke states that in the Gospel he dealt with all that Jesus "did and taught" until "the day when he was taken up" (Acts 1:1-2). Acts is a sequel to Luke and presents what happened after Jesus' ascension through the acts of the apostles and the activity of the Holy Spirit.

THE CONTENT OF LUKE

The writer never identifies himself as a physician, but this designation is consistent with the concerns revealed in this Gospel. Persons appear to be more important than systems and structures. The extensive account of Jesus' travels through Samaria and his attitude toward Samaritans illustrate these concerns. The prominence Luke gives to women in his narratives is another illustration. Although Luke states his purpose to be the writing of an orderly account of what has been heard from eyewitnesses, he seems to have been even more interested in writing an orderly account of the nature and compassion of Jesus.

Luke begins at the very beginning. He tells us more about the events surrounding the birth of Jesus than any of the other Gospel writers. These impressive events are to underline the spiritual importance of the personhood of Jesus. Luke introduces us to John the Baptist and includes the account of his baptizing Jesus with a description which again underlines the spiritual significance of Jesus. To strengthen his case, Luke provides a genealogy that traces the ancestry of Jesus back to David, Abraham, Noah, and Adam—a line of spiritual heroes from the beginning of creation.

The narration of the ministry of Jesus begins in the synagogue in his home town, Nazareth. It moves out from there to surrounding areas until ultimately it ends in Jerusalem. Basically Luke describes three phases of ministry and witness: in the area of Galilee (4:1–9:50), on the way to Jerusalem (9:51–19:44), and in or near Jerusalem (19:45–21:38). The larger portion of the narrative relates to the ministry on the way to Jerusalem. Especially in this portion do we see Jesus encountering many different types of persons, responding to each one in ways appropriate to his or her needs.

The language of this Gospel is distinctive. The Greek in which it was written is some of the best in the New Testament, suggesting that the writer had formal education, possibly training as a physician. Another characteristic is that Luke records most of the sayings of Jesus as short, pithy statements.

This Gospel (and the book of Acts) give more attention to the Holy Spirit than do Matthew or Mark. There are seventeen references to the Spirit in Luke (compared with twelve in Matthew, six in Mark), and there are fifty-seven references in Acts. The presence and work of the Holy Spirit are prominent especially in the beginning of both books. In Luke the Spirit is related to the stories of Zechariah, Gabriel, Mary, Elizabeth, and Simeon. Acts begins with the story of Pentecost. From Luke's perspective Jesus and the church lived and ministered through the empowerment of the Holy Spirit. Thus it is not surprising to discover that the prayer and devotional experiences of Jesus occupy an important place in Luke.

Among the materials Luke includes that are not in the other Gospels are five miracle events; sixteen parables, including that of the good Samaritan; and special events such as the story of Zacchaeus, the trial before Herod, the thief on the cross, and the walk to Emmaus.

No one knows the exact date of the writing of this Gospel. The earliest projected date is about 75 CE, but most Bible scholars place its writing later, in the 80s or 90s. It would have been about the same time as Matthew, and after Mark, since it includes much of Mark.

LUKE

Luke's purpose

1 Many people have already applied themselves to the task of compiling an account of the events that have been fulfilled among us. ²They used what the original eyewitnesses and servants of the word handed down to us. ³Now, after having investigated everything carefully from the beginning, I have also decided to write a carefully ordered account for you, most honorable Theophilus. ⁴I want you to have confidence in the soundness of the instruction you have received.

John the Baptist's birth foretold

⁵During the rule of King Herod of Judea there was a priest named Zechariah who belonged to the priestly division of Abijah. His wife Elizabeth was a descendant of Aaron. ⁶They were both righteous before God, blameless in their observance of all the Lord's commandments and regulations. ⁷They had no children because Elizabeth was unable to become pregnant and they both were very old. ⁸One day Zechariah was serving as a priest before God because his priestly division was on duty. ⁹Following the customs of priestly service, he was chosen by lottery to go into the Lord's sanctuary and burn incense. ¹⁰All the people who gathered to worship were praying outside during this hour of incense offering. ¹¹An angel from the Lord appeared to him, standing to the right of the altar of incense. ¹²When Zechariah saw the angel, he was startled and overcome with fear.

¹³The angel said, "Don't be afraid, Zechariah. Your prayers have been heard. Your wife Elizabeth will give birth to your son and you must name him John. ¹⁴He will be a joy and delight to you, and many people will rejoice at his birth, ¹⁵for he will be great in the Lord's eyes. He must not drink wine and liquor. He will be filled with the Holy Spirit even before his birth. ¹⁶He will bring many Israelites back to the Lord their God. ¹⁷He will go forth before the Lord, equipped with the spirit and power of Elijah. He will turn the hearts of fathers[a] back to their children, and he will turn the disobedient to righteous patterns of thinking. He will make ready a people prepared for the Lord."

¹⁸Zechariah said to the angel, "How can I be sure of this? My wife and I are very old."

¹⁹The angel replied, "I am Gabriel. I stand in God's presence. I was sent to speak to you and to bring this good news to you. ²⁰Know this: What I have spoken will come true at the proper time. But because you didn't believe, you will remain silent, unable to speak until the day when these things happen."

²¹Meanwhile, the people were waiting for Zechariah, and they wondered why he was in the sanctuary for such a long time. ²²When he came out, he was unable to speak to them. They realized he had seen a vision in the temple, for he gestured to them and couldn't speak. ²³When he completed the days of his priestly service, he returned home. ²⁴Afterward, his wife Elizabeth became pregnant. She kept to herself for five months, saying, ²⁵"This is the Lord's doing. He has shown his favor to me by removing my disgrace among other people."

Jesus' birth foretold

²⁶When Elizabeth was six months pregnant, God sent the angel Gabriel to Nazareth, a city in Galilee, ²⁷to a virgin who was engaged to a man named Joseph, a descendant of David's house. The virgin's name was Mary. ²⁸When the angel came to her, he said, "Rejoice, favored one! The Lord is with you!" ²⁹She was confused by these words and wondered what kind of greeting this might be. ³⁰The angel said, "Don't be afraid, Mary. God is honoring you. ³¹Look! You will conceive and give birth to a son, and you will name him Jesus. ³²He will be great and he will be called the Son of the Most High. The Lord God will give him the throne of David his father. ³³He will rule over Jacob's house forever, and there will be no end to his kingdom."

---

[a]Or parents

³⁴Then Mary said to the angel, "How will this happen since I haven't had sexual relations with a man?"

³⁵The angel replied, "The Holy Spirit will come over you and the power of the Most High will overshadow you. Therefore, the one who is to be born will be holy. He will be called God's Son. ³⁶Look, even in her old age, your relative Elizabeth has conceived a son. This woman who was labeled 'unable to conceive' is now six months pregnant. ³⁷Nothing is impossible for God."

³⁸Then Mary said, "I am the Lord's servant. Let it be with me just as you have said." Then the angel left her.

Mary visits Elizabeth

³⁹Mary got up and hurried to a city in the Judean highlands. ⁴⁰She entered Zechariah's home and greeted Elizabeth. ⁴¹When Elizabeth heard Mary's greeting, the child leaped in her womb, and Elizabeth was filled with the Holy Spirit. ⁴²With a loud voice she blurted out, "God has blessed you above all women, and he has blessed the child you carry. ⁴³Why do I have this honor, that the mother of my Lord should come to me? ⁴⁴As soon as I heard your greeting, the baby in my womb jumped for joy. ⁴⁵Happy is she who believed that the Lord would fulfill the promises he made to her."

Mary praises God

⁴⁶Mary said,

"With all my heart I glorify the Lord!
⁴⁷ In the depths of who I am
    I rejoice in God my savior.
⁴⁸ He has looked with favor
    on the low status of his servant.
Look! From now on, everyone
    will consider me highly favored
⁴⁹ because the mighty one
    has done great things for me.
Holy is his name.
⁵⁰ He shows mercy to everyone,
    from one generation to the next,
    who honors him as God.
⁵¹ He has shown strength with his arm.
    He has scattered those with arrogant
    thoughts and proud inclinations.
⁵² He has pulled the powerful
    down from their thrones
    and lifted up the lowly.
⁵³ He has filled the hungry with good things
    and sent the rich away empty-handed.
⁵⁴ He has come to the aid
    of his servant Israel,
    remembering his mercy,
⁵⁵ just as he promised to our ancestors,
    to Abraham and to Abraham's
    descendants forever."

⁵⁶Mary stayed with Elizabeth about three months, and then returned to her home.

THEOPHILUS

The individual to whom the author of Luke–Acts addresses and presumably dedicates both volumes of his work (Luke 1:3; Acts 1:1). Since the time of the 3rd cent. CE, it has been popular to interpret the name according to its etymology as "lover of God" or perhaps "beloved of God," and to understand Luke–Acts to be written for all who love God. But there is little basis for this. The name Theophilus is attested in both pagan and Jewish circles from the 3rd cent. BCE, and the honorific "most honorable" was a widely used form of address for individuals of rank from imperial freedman to governors. Theophilus was therefore almost certainly a ranking Roman official. That he was also a Christian convert is implied in Luke 1:4. He may also have provided financial underwriting for the two volumes. Apart from his mention in Luke–Acts, this Theophilus is unknown.

57When the time came for Elizabeth to have her child, she gave birth to a boy. 58Her neighbors and relatives celebrated with her because they had heard that the Lord had shown her great mercy. 59On the eighth day, it came time to circumcise the child. They wanted to name him Zechariah because that was his father's name. 60But his mother replied, "No, his name will be John."

61They said to her, "None of your relatives have that name." 62Then they began gesturing to his father to see what he wanted to call him.

63After asking for a tablet, he surprised everyone by writing, "His name is John." 64At that moment, Zechariah was able to speak again, and he began praising God.

65All their neighbors were filled with awe, and everyone throughout the Judean highlands talked about what had happened. 66All who heard about this considered it carefully. They said, "What then will this child be?" Indeed, the Lord's power was with him.

Zechariah's prophecy

67John's father Zechariah was filled with the Holy Spirit and prophesied,

68 "Bless the Lord God of Israel
      because he has come to help
      and has delivered his people.
69 He has raised up a mighty savior for us
      in his servant David's house,
70 just as he said through the mouths
      of his holy prophets long ago.
71 He has brought salvation
      from our enemies
      and from the power
      of all those who hate us.
72 He has shown the mercy promised
      to our ancestors,
      and remembered his holy covenant,
73 the solemn pledge he made
      to our ancestor Abraham.
He has granted 74 that we would be rescued
      from the power of our enemies
      so that we could serve him without fear,
75 in holiness and righteousness
      in God's eyes,
      for as long as we live.

76 You, child, will be called a prophet
      of the Most High,
      for you will go before the Lord
      to prepare his way.
77 You will tell his people how to be saved
      through the forgiveness of their sins.
78 Because of our God's deep compassion,
      the dawn from heaven will break upon us,
79 to give light to those
      who are sitting in darkness
      and in the shadow of death,
      to guide us on the path of peace."
80The child grew up, becoming strong in character. He was in the wilderness until he began his public ministry to Israel.

Jesus' birth

2 In those days Caesar Augustus declared that everyone throughout the empire should be enrolled in the tax lists. 2This first enrollment occurred when Quirinius governed Syria. 3Everyone went to their own cities to be enrolled. 4Since Joseph belonged to David's house and family line, he went up from the city of Nazareth in Galilee to David's city, called Bethlehem, in Judea. 5He went to be enrolled together with Mary, who was promised to him in marriage and who was pregnant. 6While they were there, the time came for Mary to have her baby. 7She gave birth to her first-born child, a son, wrapped him snugly, and laid him in a manger, because there was no place for them in the guestroom.

Announcement to shepherds

8Nearby shepherds were living in the fields, guarding their sheep at night. 9The Lord's angel stood before them, the Lord's glory shone around them, and they were terrified.

10The angel said, "Don't be afraid! Look! I bring good news to you—wonderful, joyous news for all people. 11Your savior is born today in David's city. He is Christ the Lord. 12This is a sign for you: you will find a newborn baby wrapped snugly and lying in a manger." 13Suddenly a great assembly of the heavenly forces was with the angel praising God. They said, 14"Glory to God in heaven, and on earth peace among those whom he favors."

[15]When the angels returned to heaven, the shepherds said to each other, "Let's go right now to Bethlehem and see what's happened. Let's confirm what the Lord has revealed to us." [16]They went quickly and found Mary and Joseph, and the baby lying in the manger. [17]When they saw this, they reported what they had been told about this child. [18]Everyone who heard it was amazed at what the shepherds told them. [19]Mary committed these things to memory and considered them carefully. [20]The shepherds returned home, glorifying and praising God for all they had heard and seen. Everything happened just as they had been told.

Jesus' circumcision, naming, and temple presentation

[21]When eight days had passed, Jesus' parents circumcised him and gave him the name Jesus. This was the name given to him by the angel before he was conceived. [22]When the time came for their ritual cleansing, in accordance with the Law from Moses, they brought Jesus up to Jerusalem to present him to the Lord. ([23]It's written in the Law of the Lord, "Every firstborn male will be dedicated to the Lord.") [24]They offered a sacrifice in keeping with what's

[b]Lev 12:8; 5:11 LXX

stated in the Law of the Lord, *A pair of turtledoves or two young pigeons.*[b]

Simeon's response to Jesus

[25]A man named Simeon was in Jerusalem. He was righteous and devout. He eagerly anticipated the restoration of Israel, and the Holy Spirit rested on him. [26]The Holy Spirit revealed to him that he wouldn't die before he had seen the Lord's Christ. [27]Led by the Spirit, he went into the temple area. Meanwhile, Jesus' parents brought the child to the temple so that they could do what was customary under the Law. [28]Simeon took Jesus in his arms and praised God. He said,

[29] "Now, master, let your servant go in
    peace according to your word,
[30] because my eyes have seen your
    salvation.
[31] You prepared this salvation in the
    presence of all peoples.
[32] It's a light for revelation to the Gentiles
    and a glory for your people Israel."

[33]His father and mother were amazed by what was said about him. [34]Simeon blessed them and said to Mary his mother, "This boy is assigned to be the cause of the falling and rising of many in Israel and to be a sign that generates opposition [35]so that the

ZECHARIAH (NT)

The father of John the Baptist and priest from the clan of Abijah during the reign of Herod the Great and Caesar Augustus (Luke 1:5; 3:2; see 1 Chron 24:10). Zechariah's wife was Elizabeth, the elderly woman whose womb God miraculously opened in order to bear the prophet John the Baptist, forerunner of Jesus Christ (Luke 1:5-7). Zechariah is depicted as an active priest whose division cares for the temple for part of the year (Luke 1:8-10). Chosen by lot to burn incense in the temple, Zechariah is confronted by the angel from the Lord who presages the birth and ministry of John (Luke 1:11-17). Because of his unbelief, the angel strikes Zechariah mute until the child is born and named John (Luke 1:18-25, 57-66). Immediately upon naming his son, Zechariah is filled with the Holy Spirit, and his mouth opens to prophesy a song of praise to the Lord for raising up John as a prophet of the Most High (Luke 1:64, 67-79).

inner thoughts of many will be revealed. And a sword will pierce your innermost being too."

Anna's response to Jesus

³⁶There was also a prophet, Anna the daughter of Phanuel, who belonged to the tribe of Asher. She was very old. After she married, she lived with her husband for seven years. ³⁷She was now an 84-year-old widow. She never left the temple area but worshipped God with fasting and prayer night and day. ³⁸She approached at that very moment and began to praise God and to speak about Jesus to everyone who was looking forward to the redemption of Jerusalem.

Jesus as a child in Nazareth

³⁹When Mary and Joseph had completed everything required by the Law of the Lord, they returned to their hometown, Nazareth in Galilee. ⁴⁰The child grew up and became strong. He was filled with wisdom, and God's favor was on him.

Jesus in the temple at Passover

⁴¹Each year his parents went to Jerusalem for the Passover Festival. ⁴²When he was 12 years old, they went up to Jerusalem according to their custom. ⁴³After the festival was over, they were returning home, but the boy Jesus stayed behind in Jerusalem. His parents didn't know it. ⁴⁴Supposing that he was among their band of travelers, they journeyed on for a full day while looking for him among their family and friends. ⁴⁵When they didn't find Jesus, they returned to Jerusalem to look for him. ⁴⁶After three days they found him in the temple. He was sitting among the teachers, listening to them and putting questions to them. ⁴⁷Everyone who heard him was amazed by his understanding and his answers. ⁴⁸When his parents saw him, they were shocked.

His mother said, "Child, why have you treated us like this? Listen! Your father and I have been worried. We've been looking for you!"

⁴⁹Jesus replied, "Why were you looking for me? Didn't you know that it was necessary for me to be in my Father's house?" ⁵⁰But they didn't understand what he said to them.

⁵¹Jesus went down to Nazareth with them and was obedient to them. His mother cherished every word in her heart. ⁵²Jesus matured in wisdom and years, and in favor with God and with people.

John the Baptist's message

3 In the fifteenth year of the rule of the emperor Tiberius—when Pontius Pilate

---

ANNA

1. Anna's story is told as a parallel to Simeon's (Luke 2:36-38). They both praise God because they recognize Jesus as the Christ, but Anna's words are not included. Anna is described as a prophet, like Miriam or Deborah in the OT or like others in Acts who fulfill the prophecy of Joel (Acts 2:17). Luke depicts her as pious, devoted to God, worshipping daily at the temple, praying, and fasting. She is very old, either 84 or widowed for 84 years (thus 105, if she was married at 14, as was customary). The latter is more likely. This characterization is like that of Elizabeth and Zechariah (Luke 1:6-7). Pious, celibate widows like Anna were important in the early church (see 1 Tim 5:3-16).

2. According to the post-biblical Christian tradition, Anna (or Anne) is the mother of Mary, and so the grandmother of Jesus.

was governor over Judea and Herod was ruler[c] over Galilee, his brother Philip was ruler[d] over Ituraea and Trachonitis, and Lysanias was ruler[e] over Abilene, [2]during the high priesthood of Annas and Caiaphas— God's word came to John son of Zechariah in the wilderness. [3]John went throughout the region of the Jordan River, calling for people to be baptized to show that they were changing their hearts and lives and wanted God to forgive their sins. [4]This is just as it was written in the scroll of the words of Isaiah the prophet,

A voice crying out in the wilderness:
  "Prepare the way for the Lord;
    make his paths straight.
[5] Every valley will be filled,

and every mountain and hill will be leveled.
  The crooked will be made straight
    and the rough places made smooth.
[6] All humanity will see God's salvation."[f]

[7]Then John said to the crowds who came to be baptized by him, "You children of snakes! Who warned you to escape from the angry judgment that is coming soon? [8]Produce fruit that shows you have changed your hearts and lives. And don't even think about saying to yourselves, Abraham is our father. I tell you that God is able to raise up Abraham's children from these stones. [9]The ax is already at the root of the trees. Therefore, every tree that doesn't produce good fruit will be chopped down and tossed into the fire."

[c]Or tetrarch   [d]Or tetrarch   [e]Or tetrarch   [f]Isa 40:3-5

WAY

In both the OT and the NT, way has both literal and figurative meanings. It indicates a road or path (e.g., Gen 38:21; 2 Sam 18:23; Matt 2:12; Luke 10:31) or denotes direction toward something. In the OT, way also commonly refers to God's deliverance of Israel: God "makes a way in the sea" (Isa 43:16; cf. Ps 77:19; Isa 51:10).

Way also has a number of metaphorical uses. God's customary actions or habits are referred to as God's "ways" (e.g., Exod 33:13; Pss 119:3; 128:1; Isa 42:24; Mark 6:52). God's ways are beyond human understanding (e.g., Job 26:14; Rom 11:33) and contrast with human ways (i.e., "my ways" vs. "your ways" [Isa 55:8-9]). However, God's ways are also made available to humans in following the Instruction. God's commandments are known as "the path the LORD your God commanded you to take" (Deut 13:5; cf. Exod 32:8). Isaiah 30:21 advises, "This is the way; walk in it." Following the logic of the metaphor, those who do not live according to God's Instruction or wisdom "turn from the path" (Deut 9:12; cf. Deut 11:28; Job 31:7) or "stumble" (Jer 18:15).

In the NT, way often appears in a direct quotation of the OT. John the Baptist is described as "the voice of one shouting in the wilderness, 'Prepare the way for the Lord'" (Matt 3:3//Isa 40:3; cf. Matt 11:10//Mal 3:1; Acts 2:28//Ps 16:11). The OT quotation communicates that the "way for the Lord" that has been known to Israel before is present in the person of Jesus.

Acts uses "the Way" as a description or name for the early Christian church (Acts 9:2; 18:25-26; 19:9, 23; 22:4; 24:14, 22). Because it is also called "God's way" (Acts 18:26), it seems that Acts also claims that "the way" God showed people in the Jewish scriptures is now embodied in those who follow Jesus.

[10]The crowds asked him, "What then should we do?"

[11]He answered, "Whoever has two shirts must share with the one who has none, and whoever has food must do the same."

[12]Even tax collectors came to be baptized. They said to him, "Teacher, what should we do?"

[13]He replied, "Collect no more than you are authorized to collect."

[14]Soldiers asked, "What about us? What should we do?"

He answered, "Don't cheat or harass anyone, and be satisfied with your pay."

Responses to John

[15]The people were filled with expectation, and everyone wondered whether John might be the Christ. [16]John replied to them all, "I baptize you with water, but the one who is more powerful than me is coming. I'm not worthy to loosen the strap of his sandals. He will baptize you with the Holy Spirit and fire. [17]The shovel he uses to sift the wheat from the husks is in his hands. He will clean out his threshing area and bring the wheat into his barn. But he will burn the husks with a fire that can't be put out." [18]With many other words John appealed to them, proclaiming good news to the people.

[19]But Herod the ruler had been criticized harshly by John because of Herodias, Herod's brother's wife, and because of all the evil he had done. [20]He added this to the list of his evil deeds: he locked John up in prison.

Jesus' baptism

[21]When everyone was being baptized, Jesus also was baptized. While he was praying, heaven was opened [22]and the Holy Spirit came down on him in bodily form like a dove. And there was a voice from heaven: "You are my Son, whom I dearly love; in you I find happiness."

Jesus' genealogy

[23]Jesus was about 30 years old when he began his ministry. People supposed that he was the son of Joseph son of Heli [24]son of Matthat son of Levi son of Melchi son of Jannai son of Joseph [25]son of Mattathias son of Amos son of Nahum son of Esli son of Naggai [26]son of Maath son of Mattathias son of Semein son of Josech son of Joda [27]son of Joanan son of Rhesa son of Zerubbabel son of Shealtiel son of Neri [28]son of Melchi son of Addi son of Cosam son of Elmadam son of Er [29]son of Joshua son of Eliezer son of Jorim son of Matthat son of Levi [30]son of Simeon son of Judah son of Joseph son of Jonam son of Eliakim [31]son of Melea son of Menna son of Mattatha son of Nathan son of David [32]son of Jesse son of Obed son of Boaz son of Sala son of Nahshon [33]son of Amminadab son of Admin son of Arni son of Hezron son of Perez son of Judah [34]son of Jacob son of Isaac son of Abraham son of Terah son of Nahor [35]son of Serug son of Reu son of Peleg son of Eber son of Shelah [36]son of Cainan son of Arphaxad son of Shem son of Noah son of Lamech [37]son of Methuselah son of Enoch son of Jared son of Mahalalel son of Cainan [38]son of Enos son of Seth son of Adam son of God.

Jesus' temptation

4 Jesus returned from the Jordan River full of the Holy Spirit, and was led by the Spirit into the wilderness. [2]There he was tempted for forty days by the devil. He ate nothing during those days and afterward Jesus was starving. [3]The devil said to him, "Since you are God's Son, command this stone to become a loaf of bread."

[4]Jesus replied, "It's written, *People won't live only by bread.*"[g]

[5]Next the devil led him to a high place and showed him in a single instant all the kingdoms of the world. [6]The devil said, "I will give you this whole domain and the glory of all these kingdoms. It's been entrusted to me and I can give it to anyone I want. [7]Therefore, if you will worship me, it will all be yours."

[8]Jesus answered, "It's written, *You will worship the Lord your God and serve only him.*"[h]

[g]Deut 8:3 [h]Deut 6:13

[9]The devil brought him into Jerusalem and stood him at the highest point of the temple. He said to him, "Since you are God's Son, throw yourself down from here; [10]for it's written: *He will command his angels concerning you, to protect you* [11]and *they will take you up in their hands so that you won't hit your foot on a stone.*"[i]

[12]Jesus answered, "It's been said, *Don't test the Lord your God.*"[j] [13]After finishing every temptation, the devil departed from him until the next opportunity.

Jesus announces good news to the poor

[14]Jesus returned in the power of the Spirit to Galilee, and news about him spread throughout the whole countryside. [15]He taught in their synagogues and was praised by everyone.

[16]Jesus went to Nazareth, where he had been raised. On the Sabbath he went to the synagogue as he normally did and stood up to read. [17]The synagogue assistant gave him the scroll from the prophet Isaiah. He unrolled the scroll and found the place where it was written:

[18] *The Spirit of the Lord is upon me,*
   because the Lord has anointed me.
He has sent me to preach good news
   to the poor,
     to proclaim release to the prisoners
     and recovery of sight to the blind,
   to liberate the oppressed,
[19] *and to proclaim the year of the Lord's favor.*[k]

[20]He rolled up the scroll, gave it back to the synagogue assistant, and sat down. Every eye in the synagogue was fixed on him. [21]He began to explain to them, "Today, this scripture has been fulfilled just as you heard it."

[22]Everyone was raving about Jesus, so impressed were they by the gracious words flowing from his lips. They said, "This is Joseph's son, isn't it?"

[23]Then Jesus said to them, "Undoubtedly, you will quote this saying to me: 'Doctor, heal yourself. Do here in your hometown what we've heard you did in Capernaum.'"

[24]He said, "I assure you that no prophet is welcome in the prophet's hometown. [25]And I can assure you that there were many widows in Israel during Elijah's time, when it didn't rain for three and a half years and there was a great food shortage in the land. [26]Yet Elijah was sent to none of them but only to a widow in the city of Zarephath in the region of Sidon. [27]There were also many persons with skin diseases in Israel during the time of the prophet Elisha, but none of them were cleansed. Instead, Naaman the Syrian was cleansed."

[28]When they heard this, everyone in the synagogue was filled with anger. [29]They rose up and ran him out of town. They led him to the crest of the hill on which their town had been built so that they could throw him off the cliff. [30]But he passed through the crowd and went on his way.

Jesus in Capernaum

[31]Jesus went down to the city of Capernaum in Galilee and taught the people each Sabbath. [32]They were amazed by his teaching because he delivered his message with authority.

[33]A man in the synagogue had the spirit of an unclean demon. He screamed, [34]"Hey! What have you to do with us, Jesus of Nazareth? Have you come to destroy us? I know who you are. You are the holy one from God."

[35]"Silence!" Jesus said, speaking harshly to the demon. "Come out of him!" The demon threw the man down before them, then came out of him without harming him.

[36]They were all shaken and said to each other, "What kind of word is this, that he can command unclean spirits with authority and power, and they leave?" [37]Reports about him spread everywhere in the surrounding region.

[38]After leaving the synagogue, Jesus went home with Simon. Simon's mother-in-law was sick with a high fever, and the family asked Jesus to help her. [39]He bent over her and spoke harshly to the fever, and it left her. She got up at once and served them.

[40]When the sun was setting, everyone

---

[i]Ps 91:11-12   [j]Deut 6:16   [k]Isa 61:1-2; 58:6

In the NT Satan becomes an opponent of God's intentions for humankind. Satan becomes more identifiable as a personified figure as well, but only fleeting glimpses are given of his identity. *Satan* occurs 35 times in the NT. However, other names are used often interchangeably, such as the devil or "Beelzebul" (Matt 10:25; 12:24, 27; Mark 3:22; Luke 11:15, 18, 19). He is also designated as "the tempter" (Matt 4:3; 1 Thess 3:5), "the evil one" (Matt 13:19; 1 John 5:18), "the accuser" (Rev 12:10), "the ruler of demons" (Matt 9:34; 12:24; Mark 3:22; Luke 11:15), "this world's ruler" (John 12:31; 16:11), and "a destructive spiritual power" (Eph 2:2).

Mark 1:12-13 is a short account of how the Spirit drove Jesus into the desert for 40 days where he was tempted by Satan. In a longer account in Matthew (4:1-11), the devil, "the tempter," tries to entice Jesus to show himself as God's Son. A similar account occurs in Luke 4:1-13. Here Satan, who is performing the role of testing faith, appears to have some connection to "the satan" (the Adversary) who tests Job. The texts are not clear, however, about whether God condones Satan's role or whether Satan is acting independently. When Peter tries to persuade Jesus not to go to Jerusalem, Jesus responds, "Get behind me, Satan. You are a stone that could make me stumble, for you are not thinking God's thoughts but human thoughts" (Matt 16:23; see also Mark 8:33). Here Peter's actions attempting to lead Jesus astray are likened to those of Satan, who tempted him in the wilderness.

Satan also enters into individuals such as Judas Iscariot, who schemes to have Jesus turned over to the authorities (Luke 22:3; John 13:27); and into Ananias, who lies to the Holy Spirit about the sale of a piece of property (Acts 5:3). Luke 22:31, in which Jesus says to Simon Peter, "Satan has asserted the right to sift you all like wheat," suggests that Satan may be acting here with God's approval.

While it is possible to draw lines of connection between these references in the Gospels to the heavenly being in the OT who acts as God's adversary (*satan*), other passages suggest relationships with the fallen angels noted in the Second Temple literature. In these stories the demons enter the world when the angels engage in sexual activity with "human daughters" (Gen 6:4).

Satan is also associated with the demons who are presented in the Gospels as causing physical and psychological disabilities. Luke 10 speaks about the 72 who return to Jesus after he sent them out to prepare the way for him. They have been curing the sick, announcing that "God's kingdom has come upon you." When they return they say, "Lord, even the demons submit themselves to us in your name" (10:17). Jesus responds by saying that he observed Satan falling "from heaven like lightning" (10:18). Paul's reference to Satan in Acts 26:18 when he speaks of opening the eyes of the Gentiles so that they may "turn from darkness to light and from the power of Satan to God" suggests a dualistic concept. Here Satan is reminiscent of Belial, who leads the army of darkness, and this reference resonates with 2 Corinthians 6:15, where the contrast between the believer and unbeliever is paralleled by the distinction between Christ and Belial.

brought to Jesus relatives and acquaintances with all kinds of diseases. Placing his hands on each of them, he healed them. [41]Demons also came out of many people. They screamed, "You are God's Son." But he spoke harshly to them and wouldn't allow them to speak because they recognized that he was the Christ. [42]When daybreak arrived, Jesus went to a deserted place. The crowds were looking for him. When they found him, they tried to keep him from leaving them. [43]But he said to them, "I must preach the good news of God's kingdom in other cities too, for this is why I was sent." [44]So he continued preaching in the Judean synagogues.

Jesus calls disciples

5 One day Jesus was standing beside Lake Gennesaret when the crowd pressed in around him to hear God's word. [2]Jesus saw two boats sitting by the lake. The fishermen had gone ashore and were washing their nets. [3]Jesus boarded one of the boats, the one that belonged to Simon, then asked him to row out a little distance from the shore. Jesus sat down and taught the crowds from the boat. [4]When he finished speaking to the crowds, he said to Simon, "Row out farther, into the deep water, and drop your nets for a catch."

[5]Simon replied, "Master, we've worked hard all night and caught nothing. But because you say so, I'll drop the nets."

[6]So they dropped the nets and their catch was so huge that their nets were splitting. [7]They signaled for their partners in the other boat to come and help them. They filled both boats so full that they were about to sink. [8]When Simon Peter saw the catch, he fell at Jesus' knees and said, "Leave me, Lord, for I'm a sinner!" [9]Peter and those with him were overcome with amazement because of the number of fish they caught. [10]James and John, Zebedee's sons, were Simon's partners and they were amazed too.

Jesus said to Simon, "Don't be afraid. From now on, you will be fishing for people." [11]As soon as they brought the boats to the shore, they left everything and followed Jesus.

A man with a skin disease

[12]Jesus was in one of the towns where there was also a man covered with a skin disease. When he saw Jesus, he fell on his face and begged, "Lord, if you want, you can make me clean."

Apostles Identified in Matthew, Mark, Luke/Acts, John, and Paul

Matthew	Mark	Luke/Acts	John	Paul
1. Simon Peter	1. Simon Peter	1. Simon Peter	1. Simon Peter	1. Simon Peter
2. Andrew	3. James	2. Andrew	2. Andrew	19. James brother
3. James	4. John	3. James	3–4. "the sons of	of Jesus
4. John	2. Andrew	4. John	Zebedee"	(Gal 1:19)
5. Philip	5. Philip	5. Philip	5. Philip	20. Andronicus
6. Bartholomew	6. Bartholomew	6. Bartholomew		(Rom 16:7)
7. Thomas	8. Matthew	8. Matthew		21. Junia
8. Matthew	7. Thomas	7. Thomas	7. Thomas	(Rom 16:7)
9. James son of	9. James son of	9. James son of		22. Paul
Alphaeus	Alphaeus	Alphaeus		(1 Cor 9:1, etc.)
10. Thaddaeus	10. Thaddaeus			
11. Simon the	11. Simon the	11. Simon the		1 Cor 15:7 indicates
Cananaean	Cananaean	Zealot		that Paul knew of
12. Judas Iscariot	12. Judas Iscariot	12. Judas Iscariot	12. Judas Iscariot	more than 12 apostles.
13. *Lebbaeus* for	14. Levi son of	15. Judas son of	15. Judas (not	
Thaddaeus in	Alphaeus	James	Judas Iscariot)	
some MSS		16. Matthias	17. Nathanael	
			18. The Beloved	
			Disciple	

¹³Jesus reached out his hand, touched him, and said, "I do want to. Be clean." Instantly, the skin disease left him. ¹⁴Jesus ordered him not to tell anyone. "Instead," Jesus said, "go and show yourself to the priest and make an offering for your cleansing, as Moses instructed. This will be a testimony to them." ¹⁵News of him spread even more and huge crowds gathered to listen and to be healed from their illnesses. ¹⁶But Jesus would withdraw to deserted places for prayer.

Jesus heals a paralyzed man

¹⁷One day when Jesus was teaching, Pharisees and legal experts were sitting nearby. They had come from every village in Galilee and Judea, and from Jerusalem. Now the power of the Lord was with Jesus to heal. ¹⁸Some men were bringing a man who was paralyzed, lying on a cot. They wanted to carry him in and place him before Jesus, ¹⁹but they couldn't reach him because of the crowd. So they took him up on the roof and lowered him—cot and all—through the roof tiles into the crowded room in front of Jesus. ²⁰When Jesus saw their faith, he said, "Friend, your sins are forgiven."

²¹The legal experts and Pharisees began to mutter among themselves, "Who is this who insults God? Only God can forgive sins!"

²²Jesus recognized what they were discussing and responded, "Why do you fill your minds with these questions? ²³Which is easier—to say, 'Your sins are forgiven,' or to say, 'Get up and walk'? ²⁴But so that you will know that the Human One^l has authority on the earth to forgive sins"—Jesus now spoke to the man who was paralyzed, "I say to you, get up, take your cot, and go home." ²⁵Right away, the man stood before them, picked up his cot, and went home, praising God.

²⁶All the people were beside themselves with wonder. Filled with awe, they glorified God, saying, "We've seen unimaginable things today."

Jesus calls a tax collector

²⁷Afterward, Jesus went out and saw a tax collector named Levi sitting at a kiosk for collecting taxes. Jesus said to him, "Follow me."

²⁸Levi got up, left everything behind, and followed him. ²⁹Then Levi threw a great banquet for Jesus in his home. A large number of tax collectors and others sat down to eat with them. ³⁰The Pharisees and their legal experts grumbled against his disciples. They said, "Why do you eat and drink with tax collectors and sinners?"

³¹Jesus answered, "Healthy people don't need a doctor, but sick people do. ³²I didn't come to call righteous people but sinners to change their hearts and lives."

The old and the new

³³Some people said to Jesus, "The disciples of John fast often and pray frequently. The disciples of the Pharisees do the same, but your disciples are always eating and drinking."

³⁴Jesus replied, "You can't make the wedding guests fast while the groom is with them, can you? ³⁵The days will come when the groom will be taken from them, and then they will fast."

³⁶Then he told them a parable. "No one tears a patch from a new garment to patch an old garment. Otherwise, the new garment would be ruined, and the new patch wouldn't match the old garment. ³⁷Nobody pours new wine into old wineskins. If they did, the new wine would burst the wineskins, the wine would spill, and the wineskins would be ruined. ³⁸Instead, new wine must be put into new wineskins. ³⁹No one who drinks a well-aged wine wants new wine, but says, 'The well-aged wine is better.'"

Activities on the Sabbath

6 One Sabbath, as Jesus was going through the wheat fields, his disciples were picking the heads of wheat, rubbing them in their hands, and eating them. ²Some Pharisees said, "Why are you breaking the Sabbath law?"

^lOr *Son of Man*

³Jesus replied, "Haven't you read what David and his companions did when they were hungry? ⁴He broke the Law by going into God's house and eating the bread of the presence, which only the priests can eat. He also gave some of the bread to his companions." ⁵Then he said to them, "The Human One^m is Lord of the Sabbath."

⁶On another Sabbath, Jesus entered a synagogue to teach. A man was there whose right hand was withered. ⁷The legal experts and the Pharisees were watching him closely to see if he would heal on the Sabbath. They were looking for a reason to bring charges against him. ⁸Jesus knew their thoughts, so he said to the man with the withered hand, "Get up and stand in front of everyone." He got up and stood there. ⁹Jesus said to the legal experts and Pharisees, "Here's a question for you: Is it legal on the Sabbath to do good or to do evil, to save life or to destroy it?" ¹⁰Looking around at them all, he said to the man, "Stretch out your hand." So he did and his hand was made healthy. ¹¹They were furious and began talking with each other about what to do to Jesus.

Jesus chooses apostles

¹²During that time, Jesus went out to the mountain to pray, and he prayed to God all night long. ¹³At daybreak, he called together his disciples. He chose twelve of them whom he called apostles: ¹⁴Simon, whom he named Peter; his brother Andrew; James; John; Philip; Bartholomew; ¹⁵Matthew; Thomas; James the son of Alphaeus; Simon, who was called a zealot; ¹⁶Judas the son of James; and Judas Iscariot, who became a traitor.

Jesus' popularity increases

¹⁷Jesus came down from the mountain with them and stood on a large area of level ground. A great company of his disciples and a huge crowd of people from all around Judea and Jerusalem and the area around Tyre and Sidon joined him there. ¹⁸They came to hear him and to be healed from their diseases, and those bothered by unclean spirits were healed. ¹⁹The whole crowd wanted to touch him, because power was going out from him and he was healing everyone.

Happy people and doomed people

²⁰Jesus raised his eyes to his disciples and said:

"Happy are you who are poor,
because God's kingdom is yours.
²¹ Happy are you who hunger now,
because you will be satisfied.
Happy are you who weep now,
because you will laugh.
²²Happy are you when people hate you, reject you, insult you, and condemn your name as evil because of the Human One.^n ²³Rejoice when that happens! Leap for joy because you have a great reward in heaven. Their ancestors did the same things to the prophets.
²⁴ But how terrible for you who are rich,
because you have already received
your comfort.

^mOr Son of Man ^nOr Son of Man

SERMON ON THE PLAIN

"Sermon on the Plain" is the traditional designation given to a section of Luke's Gospel (Luke 6:20-49) that parallels the better-known Sermon on the Mount found in the Gospel of Matthew (Matt 5–7). The name derives from Luke 6:17, which indicates that Jesus spoke to his disciples and a great crowd of people "on a large area of level ground" (cf. Matt 5:1, which indicates that similar teaching was presented to the disciples on a mountain).

25 How terrible for you who have plenty now,
       because you will be hungry.
    How terrible for you who laugh now,
       because you will mourn and weep.
26 How terrible for you when all speak well
       of you.
    Their ancestors did the same things to
       the false prophets.

Behaving as God's children

27 "But I say to you who are willing to hear: Love your enemies. Do good to those who hate you. 28 Bless those who curse you. Pray for those who mistreat you. 29 If someone slaps you on the cheek, offer the other one as well. If someone takes your coat, don't withhold your shirt either. 30 Give to everyone who asks and don't demand your things back from those who take them. 31 Treat people in the same way that you want them to treat you.

32 "If you love those who love you, why should you be commended? Even sinners love those who love them. 33 If you do good to those who do good to you, why should you be commended? Even sinners do that. 34 If you lend to those from whom you expect repayment, why should you be commended? Even sinners lend to sinners expecting to be paid back in full. 35 Instead, love your enemies, do good, and lend expecting nothing in return. If you do, you will have a great reward. You will be acting the way children of the Most High act, for he is kind to ungrateful and wicked people. 36 Be compassionate just as your Father is compassionate.

37 "Don't judge, and you won't be judged. Don't condemn, and you won't be condemned. Forgive, and you will be forgiven. 38 Give, and it will be given to you. A good portion—packed down, firmly shaken, and overflowing—will fall into your lap. The portion you give will determine the portion you receive in return."

Avoiding self-deception

39 Jesus also told them a riddle. "A blind person can't lead another blind person, right? Won't they both fall into a ditch? 40 Disciples aren't greater than their teacher, but whoever is fully prepared will be like their teacher. 41 Why do you see the splinter in your brother's or sister's eye but don't notice the log in your own eye? 42 How can you say to your brother or sister, 'Brother, Sister, let me take the splinter out of your eye,' when you don't see the log in your own eye? You deceive yourselves! First take the log out of your eye, and then you will see clearly to take the splinter out of your brother's or sister's eye.

43 "A good tree doesn't produce bad fruit, nor does a bad tree produce good fruit. 44 Each tree is known by its own fruit. People don't gather figs from thorny plants, nor do they pick grapes from prickly bushes. 45 A good person produces good from the good treasury of the inner self, while an evil person produces evil from the evil treasury of the inner self. The inner self overflows with words that are spoken.

46 "Why do you call me 'Lord, Lord' and don't do what I say? 47 I'll show what it's like when someone comes to me, hears my words, and puts them into practice. 48 It's like a person building a house by digging deep and laying the foundation on bedrock. When the flood came, the rising water smashed against that house, but the water couldn't shake the house because it was well built. 49 But those who don't put into practice what they hear are like a person who built a house without a foundation. The floodwater smashed against it and it collapsed instantly. It was completely destroyed."

A servant is healed

7 After Jesus finished presenting all his words among the people, he entered Capernaum. 2 A centurion had a servant who was very important to him, but the servant was ill and about to die. 3 When the centurion heard about Jesus, he sent some Jewish elders to Jesus to ask him to come and heal his servant. 4 When they came to Jesus, they earnestly pleaded with Jesus. "He deserves to have you do this for him," they said. 5 "He loves our people and he built our synagogue for us."

6 Jesus went with them. He had almost

reached the house when the centurion sent friends to say to Jesus, "Lord, don't be bothered. I don't deserve to have you come under my roof. ⁷In fact, I didn't even consider myself worthy to come to you. Just say the word and my servant will be healed. ⁸I'm also a man appointed under authority, with soldiers under me. I say to one, 'Go,' and he goes, and to another, 'Come,' and he comes. I say to my servant, 'Do this,' and the servant does it."

⁹When Jesus heard these words, he was impressed with the centurion. He turned to the crowd following him and said, "I tell you, even in Israel I haven't found faith like this." ¹⁰When the centurion's friends returned to his house, they found the servant restored to health.

Jesus raises a widow's son

¹¹A little later Jesus went to a city called Nain. His disciples and a great crowd traveled with him. ¹²As he approached the city gate, a dead man was being carried out. He was his mother's only son, and she was a widow. A large crowd from the city was with her. ¹³When he saw her, the Lord had compassion for her and said, "Don't cry." ¹⁴He stepped forward and touched the stretcher on which the dead man was being carried. Those carrying him stood still. Jesus said, "Young man, I say to you, get up." ¹⁵The dead man sat up and began to speak, and Jesus gave him to his mother.

¹⁶Awestruck, everyone praised God. "A great prophet has appeared among us," they said. "God has come to help his people." ¹⁷This news about Jesus spread throughout Judea and the surrounding region.

John the Baptist and Jesus

¹⁸John's disciples informed him about all these things. John called two of his disciples ¹⁹and sent them to the Lord. They were to ask him, "Are you the one who is coming, or should we look for someone else?"

²⁰When they reached Jesus, they said, "John the Baptist sent us to you. He asks, 'Are you the one who is coming, or should we look for someone else?'"

²¹Right then, Jesus healed many of their diseases, illnesses, and evil spirits, and he gave sight to a number of blind people. ²²Then he replied to John's disciples, "Go, report to John what you have seen and heard. *Those who were blind are able to see. Those who were crippled now walk.* People with skin diseases are cleansed. *Those who were deaf now hear. Those who were dead are raised up. And good news is preached to the poor.*ᵒ ²³Happy is anyone who doesn't stumble along the way because of me."

²⁴After John's messengers were gone, Jesus spoke to the crowds about John. "What did you go out into the wilderness to see? A stalk blowing in the wind? ²⁵What did you go out to see? A man dressed up in refined clothes? Look, those who dress in fashionable clothes and live in luxury are in royal palaces. ²⁶What did you go out to

ᵒIsa 35:5-6; 61:1

CAPERNAUM

Capernaum was the center of Jesus' Galilean ministry (Matt 4:13; 8:5; 17:24; Mark 2:1; 9:33; Luke 4:23, 31; 7:1; John 2:12; 4:46; 6:17, 24, 59). Located on the northwest shore of the Sea of Galilee, the place was also known as "Tal Hum" in Arabic (the "Hill of Hum"), and "Kefar Nahum" in Hebrew (the "Village of Nahum"). Though there is archaeological evidence (pottery shards) of human activity here as early as the 3rd millennium BCE, the town reached its peak during the late Roman and Byzantine periods, with an estimated size of 13 acres and a population of ca. 1,500 people.

see? A prophet? Yes, I tell you, and more than a prophet. ²⁷He is the one of whom it's written: *Look, I'm sending my messenger before you, who will prepare your way before you.*ᴾ ²⁸I tell you that no greater human being has ever been born than John. Yet whoever is least in God's kingdom is greater than he." ²⁹Everyone who heard this, including the tax collectors, acknowledged God's justice because they had been baptized by John. ³⁰But the Pharisees and legal experts rejected God's will for themselves because they hadn't been baptized by John.

³¹"To what will I compare the people of this generation?" Jesus asked. "What are they like? ³²They are like children sitting in the marketplace calling out to each other, 'We played the flute for you and you didn't dance. We sang a funeral song and you didn't cry.' ³³John the Baptist came neither eating bread nor drinking wine, and you say, 'He has a demon.' ³⁴Yet the Human Oneq came eating and drinking, and you say, 'Look, a glutton and a drunk, a friend of tax collectors and sinners.' ³⁵But wisdom is proved to be right by all her descendants."

Forgiveness and gratitude

³⁶One of the Pharisees invited Jesus to eat with him. After he entered the Pharisee's home, he took his place at the table. ³⁷Meanwhile, a woman from the city, a sinner, discovered that Jesus was dining in the Pharisee's house. She brought perfumed oil in a vase made of alabaster. ³⁸Standing behind him at his feet and crying, she began to wet his feet with her tears. She wiped them with her hair, kissed them, and poured the oil on them. ³⁹When the Pharisee who had invited Jesus saw what was happening, he said to himself, If this man were a prophet, he would know what kind of woman is touching him. He would know that she is a sinner.

⁴⁰Jesus replied, "Simon, I have something to say to you."

"Teacher, speak," he said.

⁴¹"A certain lender had two debtors. One owed enough money to pay five hundred people for a day's work.ʳ The other owed enough money for fifty. ⁴²When they couldn't pay, the lender forgave the debts of them both. Which of them will love him more?"

⁴³Simon replied, "I suppose the one who had the largest debt canceled."

Jesus said, "You have judged correctly."

⁴⁴Jesus turned to the woman and said to Simon, "Do you see this woman? When I entered your home, you didn't give me water for my feet, but she wet my feet with tears and wiped them with her hair. ⁴⁵You didn't greet me with a kiss, but she hasn't stopped kissing my feet since I came in. ⁴⁶You didn't anoint my head with oil, but she has poured perfumed oil on my feet. ⁴⁷This is why I tell you that her many sins have been forgiven; so she has shown great love. The one who is forgiven little loves little."

⁴⁸Then Jesus said to her, "Your sins are forgiven."

⁴⁹The other table guests began to say among themselves, "Who is this person that even forgives sins?"

⁵⁰Jesus said to the woman, "Your faith has saved you. Go in peace."

Women who followed Jesus

8 Soon afterward, Jesus traveled through the cities and villages, preaching and proclaiming the good news of God's kingdom. The Twelve were with him, ²along with some women who had been healed of evil spirits and sicknesses. Among them were Mary Magdalene (from whom seven demons had been thrown out), ³Joanna (the wife of Herod's servant Chuza), Susanna, and many others who provided for them out of their resources.

Parable of the soils

⁴When a great crowd was gathering and people were coming to Jesus from one city after another, he spoke to them in a parable: ⁵"A farmer went out to scatter his seed. As he was scattering it, some fell on the path where it was crushed, and the birds in the sky came and ate it. ⁶Other seed fell on rock. As it grew, it dried up because it

---

ᴾMal 3:1 q*Or Son of Man* r*Or five hundred denaria*

had no moisture. [7]Other seed fell among thorny plants. The thorns grew with the plants and choked them. [8]Still other seed landed on good soil. When it grew, it produced one hundred times more grain than was scattered." As he said this, he called out, "Everyone who has ears should pay attention."

[9]His disciples asked him what this parable meant. [10]He said, "You have been given the mysteries of God's kingdom, but these mysteries come to everyone else in parables so that *when they see, they can't see, and when they hear, they can't understand.*[s]

[11]"The parable means this: The seed is God's word. [12]The seed on the path are those who hear, but then the devil comes and steals the word from their hearts so that they won't believe and be saved. [13]The seed on the rock are those who receive the word joyfully when they hear it, but they have no root. They believe for a while but fall away when they are tempted. [14]As for the seed that fell among thorny plants, these are the ones who, as they go about their lives, are choked by the concerns, riches, and pleasures of life, and their fruit never matures. [15]The seed that fell on good soil are those who hear the word and commit themselves to it with a good and upright heart. Through their resolve, they bear fruit.

Sharing the light

[16]"No one lights a lamp and then covers it with a bowl or puts it under a bed. Instead, they put it on top of a lampstand so that those who enter can see the light. [17]Nothing is hidden that won't be exposed. Nor is anything concealed that won't be made known and brought to the light. [18]Therefore, listen carefully. Those who have will receive more, but as for those who don't have, even what they seem to have will be taken away from them."

Jesus' family

[19]Jesus' mother and brothers came to him but were unable to reach him because of the crowd. [20]Someone told him, "Your mother and brothers are standing outside, wanting to see you."

[21]He replied, "My mother and brothers are those who listen to God's word and do it."

Jesus calms the sea

[22]One day Jesus and his disciples boarded a boat. He said to them, "Let's cross over to the other side of the lake." So they set sail. [23]While they were sailing, he fell asleep. Gale-force winds swept down on the lake. The boat was filling up with water and they were in danger. [24]So they went and woke Jesus, shouting, "Master, Master, we're going to drown!" But he got up and gave orders to the wind and the violent waves. The storm died down and it was calm.

[25]He said to his disciples, "Where is your faith?"

Filled with awe and wonder, they said to each other, "Who is this? He commands even the winds and the water, and they obey him!"

Jesus frees a demon-possessed man

[26]Jesus and his disciples sailed to the Gerasenes' land, which is across the lake from Galilee. [27]As soon as Jesus got out of the boat, a certain man met him. The man was from the city and was possessed by demons. For a long time, he had lived among the tombs, naked and homeless. [28]When he saw Jesus, he shrieked and fell down before him. Then he shouted, "What have you to do with me, Jesus, Son of the Most High God? I beg you, don't torture me!" [29]He said this because Jesus had already commanded the unclean spirit to come out of the man. Many times it had taken possession of him, so he would be bound with leg irons and chains and placed under guard. But he would break his restraints, and the demon would force him into the wilderness.

[30]Jesus asked him, "What is your name?"

"Legion," he replied, because many demons had entered him. [31]They pleaded with him not to order them to go back into the abyss.[t] [32]A large herd of pigs was feeding on the hillside. The demons begged Jesus to

[s]Isa 6:9   [t]Or *underworld*

let them go into the pigs. Jesus gave them permission, [33] and the demons left the man and entered the pigs. The herd rushed down the cliff into the lake and drowned.

[34] When those who tended the pigs saw what happened, they ran away and told the story in the city and in the countryside. [35] People came to see what had happened. They came to Jesus and found the man from whom the demons had gone. He was sitting at Jesus' feet, fully dressed and completely sane. They were filled with awe. [36] Those people who had actually seen what had happened told them how the demon-possessed man had been delivered. [37] Then everyone gathered from the region of the Gerasenes asked Jesus to leave their area because they were overcome with fear. So he got into the boat and returned across the lake. [38] The man from whom the demons had gone begged to come along with Jesus as one of his disciples. Jesus sent him away, saying, [39] "Return home and tell the story of what God has done for you." So he went throughout the city proclaiming what Jesus had done for him.

Jesus heals two women

[40] When Jesus returned, the crowd welcomed him, for they had been waiting for him. [41] A man named Jairus, who was a synagogue leader, came and fell at Jesus' feet. He pleaded with Jesus to come to his house [42] because his only daughter, a twelve-year-old, was dying.

As Jesus moved forward, he faced smothering crowds. [43] A woman was there who had been bleeding for twelve years. She had spent her entire livelihood on doctors, but no one could heal her. [44] She came up behind him and touched the hem of his clothes, and at once her bleeding stopped.

[45] "Who touched me?" Jesus asked.

When everyone denied it, Peter said, "Master, the crowds are surrounding you and pressing in on you!"

[46] But Jesus said, "Someone touched me. I know that power has gone out from me."

[47] When the woman saw that she couldn't escape notice, she came trembling and fell before Jesus. In front of everyone, she explained why she had touched him and how she had been immediately healed.

[48] "Daughter, your faith has healed you," Jesus said. "Go in peace."

[49] While Jesus was still speaking, someone came from the synagogue leader's house, saying to Jairus, "Your daughter has died. Don't bother the teacher any longer."

[50] When Jesus heard this, he responded, "Don't be afraid; just keep trusting, and she will be healed."

[51] When he came to the house, he didn't allow anyone to enter with him except Peter, John, and James, and the child's father and mother. [52] They were all crying and mourning for her, but Jesus said, "Don't cry. She isn't dead. She's only sleeping."

[53] They laughed at him because they knew she was dead.

[54] Taking her hand, Jesus called out, "Child, get up." [55] Her life returned and she got up at once. He directed them to give her something to eat. [56] Her parents were beside themselves with joy, but he ordered them to tell no one what had happened.

The Twelve sent out

9 Jesus called the Twelve together and he gave them power and authority over all demons and to heal sicknesses. [2] He sent them out to proclaim God's kingdom and to heal the sick. [3] He told them, "Take nothing for the journey—no walking stick, no bag, no bread, no money, not even an extra shirt. [4] Whatever house you enter, remain there until you leave that place. [5] Wherever they don't welcome you, as you leave that city, shake the dust off your feet as a witness against them." [6] They departed and went through the villages proclaiming the good news and healing people everywhere.

Herod's confusion

[7] Herod the ruler[u] heard about everything that was happening. He was confused because some people were saying that John had been raised from the dead, [8] others

---

[u] Or tetrarch

that Elijah had appeared, and still others that one of the ancient prophets had come back to life. [9]Herod said, "I beheaded John, so now who am I hearing about?" Herod wanted to see him.

Jesus feeds the five thousand

[10]When the apostles returned, they described for Jesus what they had done. Taking them with him, Jesus withdrew privately to a city called Bethsaida. [11]When the crowds figured it out, they followed him. He welcomed them, spoke to them about God's kingdom, and healed those who were sick.

[12]When the day was almost over, the Twelve came to him and said, "Send the crowd away so that they can go to the nearby villages and countryside and find lodging and food, because we are in a deserted place."

[13]He replied, "You give them something to eat."

But they said, "We have no more than five loaves of bread and two fish—unless we go and buy food for all these people." [14](They said this because about five thousand men were present.)

Jesus said to his disciples, "Seat them in groups of about fifty." [15]They did so, and everyone was seated. [16]He took the five loaves and the two fish, looked up to heaven, blessed them, and broke them and gave them to the disciples to set before the crowd. [17]Everyone ate until they were full, and the disciples filled twelve baskets with the leftovers.

Following Christ

[18]Once when Jesus was praying by himself, the disciples joined him, and he asked them, "Who do the crowds say that I am?"

[19]They answered, "John the Baptist, others Elijah, and still others that one of the ancient prophets has come back to life."

[20]He asked them, "And what about you? Who do you say that I am?"

Peter answered, "The Christ sent from God."

[21]Jesus gave them strict orders not to tell this to anyone. [22]He said, "The Human One[v] must suffer many things and be rejected—by the elders, chief priests, and the legal experts—and be killed and be raised on the third day."

[23]Jesus said to everyone, "All who want to come after me must say no to themselves, take up their cross daily, and follow me. [24]All who want to save their lives will lose them. But all who lose their lives because of me will save them. [25]What advantage do people have if they gain the whole world for themselves yet perish or lose their lives? [26]Whoever is ashamed of me and my words, the Human One[w] will be ashamed of that person when he comes in his glory and in the glory of the Father and of the holy angels. [27]I assure you that some standing here won't die before they see God's kingdom."

Jesus transformed

[28]About eight days after Jesus said these things, he took Peter, John, and James, and went up on a mountain to pray. [29]As he was praying, the appearance of his face changed and his clothes flashed white like lightning. [30]Two men, Moses and Elijah, were talking with him. [31]They were clothed with heavenly splendor and spoke about Jesus' departure, which he would achieve in Jerusalem. [32]Peter and those with him were almost overcome by sleep, but they managed to stay awake and saw his glory as well as the two men with him.

[33]As the two men were about to leave Jesus, Peter said to him, "Master, it's good that we're here. We should construct three shrines: one for you, one for Moses, and one for Elijah"—but he didn't know what he was saying. [34]Peter was still speaking when a cloud overshadowed them. As they entered the cloud, they were overcome with awe.

[35]Then a voice from the cloud said, "This is my Son, my chosen one. Listen to him!" [36]Even as the voice spoke, Jesus was found alone. They were speechless and at the time told no one what they had seen.

[v]Or Son of Man [w]Or Son of Man

Miracle Stories in the Gospels

A. Miracles Performed Directly on Persons

1. Exorcisms
#1 Throwing Out the Demon in the Synagogue in Capernaum

| | Mark 1:21-28 | Luke 4:31-37 | ——— |

#2 Demon-possessed Man/Men in the Country of the Gadarenes

| Matt 8:28-34 | Mark 5:1-20 | Luke 8:26-39 | ——— |

#3 The Syrophoenician (Canaanite) Woman

| Matt 15:21-28 | Mark 7:24-30 | ——— | ——— |

2. Exorcisms/Healings
#4 The Demon-possessed Man Who Couldn't Speak

| Matt 9:32-34 | ——— | Luke 11:14-15 | ——— |

#5 On Collusion with Satan

| Matt 12:22-30 | (cf. Mark 3:22-27) | Luke 11:14-22 | ——— |

#6 Jesus Heals a Boy Possessed by a Demon

| Matt 17:14-21 | Mark 9:14-29 | Luke 9:37-43a | ——— |

3. Healings
#7 Jesus Heals a Deaf Man (and Many Others)

| ——— | Mark 7:31-37 | ——— | ——— |

#8 A Blind Man Is Healed at Bethsaida

| ——— | Mark 8:22-26 | ——— | ——— |

#9 Cleansing of the Man with a Skin Disease

| Matt 8:1-4 | Mark 1:40-45 | Luke 5:12-16 | ——— |

#10 The Centurion of Capernaum

| Matt 8:5-13 | ——— | Luke 7:1-10 | John 4:46b-54 |

#11 The Healing of Peter's Mother-in-law

| Matt 8:14-15 | Mark 1:29-31 | Luke 4:38-39 | ——— |

#12 The Healing of the Man Who Was Paralyzed

| Matt 9:1-8 | Mark 2:1-12 | Luke 5:17-26 | ——— |

#13 (Jairus' Daughter and) the Bleeding Woman

| Matt 9:18-26 | Mark 5:21-43 | Luke 8:40-56 | ——— |

#14 Two Blind Men

| Matt 9:27-31 | (cf. Mark 10:46-52) | (cf. Luke 18:35-43) | ——— |

#15 Healing the Withered Hand

| Matt 12:9-14 | Mark 3:1-6 | Luke 6:6-11 | ——— |

#16 The Healing of the Blind Man/Men

| Matt 20:29-34 | Mark 10:46-52 | Luke 18:35-43 | ——— |

#17 The Healing of the Disabled Woman on the Sabbath

| ——— | ——— | Luke 13:10-17 | ——— |

Miracle Stories in the Gospels

#18 The Healing of the Man with Swelling
Luke 14:1-6

#19 The Cleansing of the Ten Men with Skin Diseases
Luke 17:11-19

#20 The Healing at the Pool
John 5:2-47

#21 Jesus Heals the Man Born Blind
John 9:1-41

#22 Jesus Heals a Slave's Ear
Luke 22:50-51

4. Raising the Dead

#23 Jairus' Daughter (and the Bleeding Woman)
Matt 9:18-26   Mark 5:21-43   Luke 8:40-56

#24 The Widow's Son at Nain
Luke 7:11-17

#25 The Raising of Lazarus
John 11:1-44

B. Miracles Performed on Nature

5. Sea Miracles

#26 Calming the Storm
Matt 8:23-27   Mark 4:35-41   Luke 8:22-25

#27 Walking on the Water
Matt 14:22-33   Mark 6:45-52   John 6:16-21

6. Miraculous Provision

#28 Five Thousand Are Fed
Matt 14:13-21   Mark 6:32-44   Luke 9:10b-17   John 6:1-15

#29 Four Thousand Are Fed
Matt 15:32-39   Mark 8:1-10

#30 Payment of the Temple Tax
Matt 17:24-27

#31 The Miraculous Catch of Fish
Matt 4:18-22   Mark 1:16-20   Luke 5:1-11   (cf. John 21:1-11)

#32 The Wedding at Cana
John 2:1-11

7. Curse Miracles

#33 The Cursing of the Fig Tree; the Fig Tree Is Withered
Matt 21:18-19   Mark 11:12-14
Matt 21:20-22   Mark 11:20-26

Jesus heals a boy

³⁷The next day, when Jesus, Peter, John, and James had come down from the mountain, a large crowd met Jesus. ³⁸A man from the crowd shouted, "Teacher, I beg you to take a look at my son, my only child. ³⁹Look, a spirit seizes him and, without any warning, he screams. It shakes him and causes him to foam at the mouth. It tortures him and rarely leaves him alone. ⁴⁰I begged your disciples to throw it out, but they couldn't."

⁴¹Jesus answered, "You faithless and crooked generation, how long will I be with you and put up with you? Bring your son here." ⁴²While he was coming, the demon threw him down and shook him violently. Jesus spoke harshly to the unclean spirit, healed the child, and gave him back to his father. ⁴³Everyone was overwhelmed by God's greatness.

Jesus warns about his arrest

While everyone was marveling at everything he was doing, Jesus said to his disciples, ⁴⁴"Take these words to heart: the Human One˟ is about to be delivered into human hands." ⁴⁵They didn't understand this statement. Its meaning was hidden from them so they couldn't grasp it. And they were afraid to ask him about it.

Jesus corrects the disciples

⁴⁶An argument arose among the disciples about which of them was the greatest. ⁴⁷Aware of their deepest thoughts, Jesus took a little child and had the child stand beside him. ⁴⁸Jesus said to his disciples, "Whoever welcomes this child in my name welcomes me. Whoever welcomes me, welcomes the one who sent me. Whoever is least among you all is the greatest."

⁴⁹John replied, "Master, we saw someone throwing demons out in your name, and we tried to stop him because he isn't in our group of followers."

⁵⁰But Jesus replied, "Don't stop him, because whoever isn't against you is for you."

Jesus sets out for Jerusalem

⁵¹As the time approached when Jesus was to be taken up into heaven, he determined to go to Jerusalem. ⁵²He sent messengers on ahead of him. Along the way, they entered a Samaritan village to prepare for his arrival, ⁵³but the Samaritan villagers refused to welcome him because he was determined to go to Jerusalem. ⁵⁴When the disciples James and John saw this, they said, "Lord, do you want us to call fire down from heaven to consume them?" ⁵⁵But Jesus turned and spoke sternly to them, ⁵⁶and they went on to another village.

Following Jesus

⁵⁷As Jesus and his disciples traveled along the road, someone said to him, "I will follow you wherever you go."

⁵⁸Jesus replied, "Foxes have dens and the birds in the sky have nests, but the Human Oneʸ has no place to lay his head."

⁵⁹Then Jesus said to someone else, "Follow me."

He replied, "Lord, first let me go and bury my father."

⁶⁰Jesus said to him, "Let the dead bury their own dead. But you go and spread the news of God's kingdom."

⁶¹Someone else said to Jesus, "I will follow you, Lord, but first let me say good-bye to those in my house."

⁶²Jesus said to him, "No one who puts a hand on the plow and looks back is fit for God's kingdom."

Seventy-two sent out

10 After these things, the Lord commissioned seventy-two others and sent them on ahead in pairs to every city and place he was about to go. ²He said to them, "The harvest is bigger than you can imagine, but there are few workers. Therefore, plead with the Lord of the harvest to send out workers for his harvest. ³Go! Be warned, though, that I'm sending you out as lambs among wolves. ⁴Carry no wallet, no bag, and no sandals. Don't even greet anyone along the way. ⁵Whenever you

˟Or Son of Man ʸOr Son of Man

enter a house, first say, 'May peace be on this house.' [6]If anyone there shares God's peace, then your peace will rest on that person. If not, your blessing will return to you. [7]Remain in this house, eating and drinking whatever they set before you, for workers deserve their pay. Don't move from house to house. [8]Whenever you enter a city and its people welcome you, eat what they set before you. [9]Heal the sick who are there, and say to them, 'God's kingdom has come upon you.' [10]Whenever you enter a city and the people don't welcome you, go out into the streets and say, [11]'As a complaint against you, we brush off the dust of your city that has collected on our feet. But know this: God's kingdom has come to you.' [12]I assure you that Sodom will be better off on Judgment Day than that city.

Judgment against cities that reject Jesus

[13]"How terrible it will be for you, Chorazin. How terrible it will be for you, Bethsaida. If the miracles done among you had been done in Tyre and Sidon, they would have changed their hearts and lives long ago. They would have sat around in funeral clothes and ashes. [14]But Tyre and Sidon will be better off at the judgment than you. [15]And you, Capernaum, will you be honored by being raised up to heaven? No, you will be cast down to the place of the dead. [16]Whoever listens to you listens to me. Whoever rejects you rejects me. Whoever rejects me rejects the one who sent me."

The seventy-two return

[17]The seventy-two returned joyously, saying, "Lord, even the demons submit themselves to us in your name."

[18]Jesus replied, "I saw Satan fall from heaven like lightning. [19]Look, I have given you authority to crush snakes and scorpions underfoot. I have given you authority over all the power of the enemy. Nothing will harm you. [20]Nevertheless, don't rejoice because the spirits submit to you. Rejoice instead that your names are written in heaven."

[21]At that very moment, Jesus overflowed with joy from the Holy Spirit and said, "I praise you, Father, Lord of heaven and earth, because you've hidden these things from the wise and intelligent and shown them to babies. Indeed, Father, this brings you happiness. [22]My Father has handed all things over to me. No one knows who the Son is except the Father, or who the Father is except the Son and anyone to whom the Son wants to reveal him." [23]Turning to the disciples, he said privately, "Happy are the eyes that see what you see. [24]I assure you that many prophets and kings wanted to see what you see and hear what you hear, but they didn't."

Loving your neighbor

[25]A legal expert stood up to test Jesus. "Teacher," he said, "what must I do to gain eternal life?"

[26]Jesus replied, "What is written in the Law? How do you interpret it?"

[27]He responded, "*You must love the Lord*

THE GOOD SAMARITAN

Jesus gives the parable of the good Samaritan (Luke 10:30-36). The parable would have astonished Jesus' audience because of strong tensions between Jews and Samaritans. Jesus' answer illustrates that everyone is a neighbor and that we should act neighborly to all who need us. While this parable addresses the command to love one's neighbor (Luke 10:27b), the story that follows, Mary and Martha's interaction with Jesus (Luke 10:38-42), teaches how to fulfill the command to love God (Luke 10:27a).

your God with all your heart, with all your being, with all your strength, and with all your mind, and love your neighbor as yourself."[z]

²⁸ Jesus said to him, "You have answered correctly. Do this and you will live."

²⁹ But the legal expert wanted to prove that he was right, so he said to Jesus, "And who is my neighbor?"

³⁰ Jesus replied, "A man went down from Jerusalem to Jericho. He encountered thieves, who stripped him naked, beat him up, and left him near death. ³¹ Now it just so happened that a priest was also going down the same road. When he saw the injured man, he crossed over to the other side of the road and went on his way. ³² Likewise, a Levite came by that spot, saw the injured man, and crossed over to the other side of the road and went on his way. ³³ A Samaritan, who was on a journey, came to where the man was. But when he saw him, he was moved with compassion. ³⁴ The Samaritan went to him and bandaged his wounds, tending them with oil and wine. Then he placed the wounded man on his own donkey, took him to an inn, and took care of him. ³⁵ The next day, he took two full days' worth of wages and gave them to the innkeeper. He said, 'Take care of him, and when I return, I will pay you back for any additional costs.' ³⁶ What do you think? Which one of these three was a neighbor to the man who encountered thieves?"

³⁷ Then the legal expert said, "The one who demonstrated mercy toward him."

Jesus told him, "Go and do likewise."

Jesus visits Martha and Mary

³⁸ While Jesus and his disciples were traveling, Jesus entered a village where a woman named Martha welcomed him as a guest. ³⁹ She had a sister named Mary, who sat at the Lord's feet and listened to his message. ⁴⁰ By contrast, Martha was preoccupied with getting everything ready for their meal. So Martha came to him and said, "Lord, don't you care that my sister has left me to prepare the table all by myself? Tell her to help me."

⁴¹ The Lord answered, "Martha, Martha, you are worried and distracted by many things. ⁴² One thing is necessary. Mary has chosen the better part. It won't be taken away from her."

Teaching the disciples to pray

11 Jesus was praying in a certain place. When he finished, one of his disciples said, "Lord, teach us to pray, just as John taught his disciples."

² Jesus told them, "When you pray, say:
'Father, uphold the holiness of your name.
Bring in your kingdom.
³ Give us the bread we need for today.
⁴ Forgive us our sins,
    for we also forgive everyone who has
    wronged us.
And don't lead us into temptation.'"

⁵ He also said to them, "Imagine that one of you has a friend and you go to that friend in the middle of the night. Imagine saying, 'Friend, loan me three loaves of bread ⁶ because a friend of mine on a journey has arrived and I have nothing to set before him.' ⁷ Imagine further that he answers from within the house, 'Don't bother me. The door is already locked, and my children and I are in bed. I can't get up to give you anything.' ⁸ I assure you, even if he wouldn't get up and help because of his friendship, he will get up and give his friend whatever he needs because of his friend's brashness. ⁹ And I tell you: Ask and you will receive. Seek and you will find. Knock and the door will be opened to you. ¹⁰ Everyone who asks, receives. Whoever seeks, finds. To everyone who knocks, the door is opened.

¹¹ "Which father among you would give a snake to your child if the child asked for a fish? ¹² If a child asked for an egg, what father would give the child a scorpion? ¹³ If you who are evil know how to give good gifts to your children, how much more will the heavenly Father give the Holy Spirit to those who ask him?"

Controversy over Beelzebul

¹⁴ Jesus was throwing out a demon that causes muteness. When the demon was

gone, the man who couldn't speak began to talk. The crowds were amazed. [15]But some of them said, "He throws out demons with the authority of Beelzebul, the ruler of demons." [16]Others were testing him, seeking a sign from heaven.

[17]Because Jesus knew what they were thinking, he said to them, "Every kingdom involved in civil war becomes a wasteland, and a house torn apart by divisions will collapse. [18]If Satan is at war with himself, how will his kingdom endure? I ask this because you say that I throw out demons by the authority of Beelzebul. [19]If I throw out demons by the authority of Beelzebul, then by whose authority do your followers throw them out? Therefore, they will be your judges. [20]But if I throw out demons by the power[a] of God, then God's kingdom has already overtaken you. [21]When a strong man, fully armed, guards his own palace, his possessions are secure. [22]But as soon as a stronger one attacks and overpowers him, the stronger one takes away the armor he had trusted and divides the stolen goods.

[23]"Whoever isn't with me is against me, and whoever doesn't gather with me, scatters. [24]When an unclean spirit leaves a person, it wanders through dry places looking for a place to rest. But it doesn't find any. Then it says, 'I'll go back to the house I left.' [25]When it arrives, it finds the house cleaned up and decorated. [26]Then it goes and brings with it seven other spirits more evil than itself. They go in and make their home there. That person is worse off at the end than at the beginning."

[a]Or *finger*   [b]Or *Son of Man*

On seeking signs

[27]While Jesus was saying these things, a certain woman in the crowd spoke up: "Happy is the mother who gave birth to you and who nursed you."

[28]But he said, "Happy rather are those who hear God's word and put it into practice."

[29]When the crowds grew, Jesus said, "This generation is an evil generation. It looks for a sign, but no sign will be given to it except Jonah's sign. [30]Just as Jonah became a sign to the people of Nineveh, so the Human One[b] will be a sign to this generation. [31]The queen of the South will rise up at the judgment with the people of this generation and condemn them, because she came from a distant land to hear Solomon's wisdom. And look, someone greater than Solomon is here. [32]The people of Nineveh will rise up at the judgment with this generation and condemn it, because they changed their hearts and lives in response to Jonah's preaching—and one greater than Jonah is here.

[33]"People don't light a lamp and then put it in a closet or under a basket. Rather, they place the lamp on a lampstand so that those who enter the house can see the light. [34]Your eye is the lamp of your body. When your eye is healthy, your whole body is full of light. But when your eye is bad, your whole body is full of darkness. [35]Therefore, see to it that the light in you isn't darkness. [36]If your whole body is full of light—with no part darkened—then it will be as full of light as when a lamp shines brightly on you."

BEELZEBUL

Jesus' opponents refer to him, and also to the ruler or prince of demons, as "Beelzebul" (Matt 10:25; 12:24, 27; Mark 3:22; Luke 11:15, 18-19), with the claim that Beelzebul was his means of exorcising demons. The name means "lord of the flies" and was the name of a Philistine god (2 Kgs 1:3).

Jesus condemns Pharisees and legal experts

³⁷While Jesus was speaking, a Pharisee invited him to share a meal with him, so Jesus went and took his place at the table. ³⁸When the Pharisee saw that Jesus didn't ritually purify his hands by washing before the meal, he was astonished.

³⁹The Lord said to him, "Now, you Pharisees clean the outside of the cup and platter, but your insides are stuffed with greed and wickedness. ⁴⁰Foolish people! Didn't the one who made the outside also make the inside? ⁴¹Therefore, give to those in need from the core of who you are and you will be clean all over.

⁴²"How terrible for you Pharisees! You give a tenth of your mint, rue, and garden herbs of all kinds, while neglecting justice and love for God. These you ought to have done without neglecting the others.

⁴³"How terrible for you Pharisees! You love the most prominent seats in the synagogues and respectful greetings in the marketplaces.

⁴⁴"How terrible for you! You are like unmarked graves, and people walk on them without recognizing it."

⁴⁵One of the legal experts responded, "Teacher, when you say these things, you are insulting us too."

⁴⁶Jesus said, "How terrible for you legal experts too! You load people down with impossible burdens and you refuse to lift a single finger to help them.

⁴⁷"How terrible for you! You built memorials to the prophets, whom your ancestors killed. ⁴⁸In this way, you testify that you approve of your ancestors' deeds. They killed the prophets, and you build memorials! ⁴⁹Therefore, God's wisdom has said, 'I will send prophets and apostles to them and they will harass and kill some of them.' ⁵⁰As a result, this generation will be charged with the murder of all the prophets since the beginning of time. ⁵¹This includes the murder of every prophet—from Abel to Zechariah—who was killed between the altar and the holy place. Yes, I'm telling you, this generation will be charged with it.

⁵²"How terrible for you legal experts! You snatched away the key of knowledge. You didn't enter yourselves, and you stood in the way of those who were entering."

⁵³As he left there, the legal experts and Pharisees began to resent him deeply and to ask him pointed questions about many things. ⁵⁴They plotted against him, trying to trap him in his words.

Warnings to Jesus' friends

12When a crowd of thousands upon thousands had gathered so that they were crushing each other, Jesus began to speak first to his disciples: "Watch out for the yeast of the Pharisees—I mean, the mismatch between their hearts and lives. ²Nothing is hidden that won't be revealed, and nothing is secret that won't be brought out into the open. ³Therefore, whatever you have said in the darkness will be heard in the light, and whatever you have whispered in the rooms deep inside the house will be announced from the rooftops.

⁴"I tell you, my friends, don't be terrified by those who can kill the body but after that can do nothing more. ⁵I'll show you whom you should fear: fear the one who, after you have been killed, has the authority to throw you into hell. Indeed, I tell you, that's the one you should fear. ⁶Aren't five sparrows sold for two small coins?ᶜ Yet not one of them is overlooked by God. ⁷Even the hairs on your head are all counted. Don't be afraid. You are worth more than many sparrows.

Acknowledging the Human One

⁸"I tell you, everyone who acknowledges me before humans, the Human Oneᵈ will acknowledge before God's angels. ⁹But the one who rejects me before others will be rejected before God's angels. ¹⁰Anyone who speaks a word against the Human Oneᵉ will be forgiven, but whoever insults the Holy Spirit won't be forgiven. ¹¹When they bring you before the synagogues, rulers, and authorities, don't worry about how to defend yourself or what you should say. ¹²The Holy

---

ᶜOr two assaria—that is, 1/8 of a day's wage   ᵈOr Son of Man   ᵉOr Son of Man

Spirit will tell you at that very moment what you must say."

Warning against greed

[13]Someone from the crowd said to him, "Teacher, tell my brother to divide the inheritance with me."

[14]Jesus said to him, "Man, who appointed me as judge or referee between you and your brother?"

[15]Then Jesus said to them, "Watch out! Guard yourself against all kinds of greed. After all, one's life isn't determined by one's possessions, even when someone is very wealthy." [16]Then he told them a parable: "A certain rich man's land produced a bountiful crop. [17]He said to himself, What will I do? I have no place to store my harvest! [18]Then he thought, Here's what I'll do. I'll tear down my barns and build bigger ones. That's where I'll store all my grain and goods. [19]I'll say to myself, You have stored up plenty of goods, enough for several years. Take it easy! Eat, drink, and enjoy yourself. [20]But God said to him, 'Fool, tonight you will die. Now who will get the things you have prepared for yourself?' [21]This is the way it will be for those who hoard things for themselves and aren't rich toward God."

Warning about worry

[22]Then Jesus said to his disciples, "Therefore, I say to you, don't worry about your life, what you will eat, or about your body, what you will wear. [23]There is more to life than food and more to the body than clothing. [24]Consider the ravens: they neither plant nor harvest, they have no silo or barn, yet God feeds them. You are worth so much more than birds! [25]Who among you by worrying can add a single moment to your life?[f] [26]If you can't do such a small thing, why worry about the rest? [27]Notice how the lilies grow. They don't wear themselves out with work, and they don't spin cloth. But I say to you that even Solomon in all his splendor wasn't dressed like one of these. [28]If God dresses grass in the field so

beautifully, even though it's alive today and tomorrow it's thrown into the furnace, how much more will God do for you, you people of weak faith! [29]Don't chase after what you will eat and what you will drink. Stop worrying. [30]All the nations of the world long for these things. Your Father knows that you need them. [31]Instead, desire his kingdom and these things will be given to you as well.

[32]"Don't be afraid, little flock, because your Father delights in giving you the kingdom. [33]Sell your possessions and give to those in need. Make for yourselves wallets that don't wear out—a treasure in heaven that never runs out. No thief comes near there, and no moth destroys. [34]Where your treasure is, there your heart will be too.

Warning about being prepared

[35]"Be dressed for service and keep your lamps lit. [36]Be like people waiting for their master to come home from a wedding celebration, who can immediately open the door for him when he arrives and knocks on the door. [37]Happy are those servants whom the master finds waiting up when he arrives. I assure you that, when he arrives, he will dress himself to serve, seat them at the table as honored guests, and wait on them. [38]Happy are those whom he finds alert, even if he comes at midnight or just before dawn.[g] [39]But know this, if the homeowner had known what time the thief was coming, he wouldn't have allowed his home to be broken into. [40]You also must be ready, because the Human One[h] is coming at a time when you don't expect him."

[41]Peter said, "Lord, are you telling this parable for us or for everyone?"

[42]The Lord replied, "Who are the faithful and wise managers whom the master will put in charge of his household servants, to give them their food at the proper time? [43]Happy are the servants whom the master finds fulfilling their responsibilities when he comes. [44]I assure you that the master will put them in charge of all his possessions.

[45]"But suppose that these servants

---

[f]Or eighteen inches to your height   [g]Or in the second or third watch   [h]Or Son of Man

should say to themselves, My master is taking his time about coming. And suppose they began to beat the servants, both men and women, and to eat, drink, and get drunk. ⁴⁶The master of those servants would come on a day when they weren't expecting him, at a time they couldn't predict. The master will cut them into pieces and assign them a place with the unfaithful. ⁴⁷That servant who knew his master's will but didn't prepare for it or act on it will be beaten severely. ⁴⁸The one who didn't know the master's will but who did things deserving punishment will be beaten only a little. Much will be demanded from everyone who has been given much, and from the one who has been entrusted with much, even more will be asked.

Conflicts brought by Jesus

⁴⁹"I came to cast fire upon the earth. How I wish that it was already ablaze! ⁵⁰I have a baptism I must experience! How I am distressed until it's completed! ⁵¹Do you think that I have come to bring peace to the earth? No, I tell you, I have come instead to bring division. ⁵²From now on, a household of five will be divided—three against two and two against three. ⁵³Father will square off against son and son against father; mother against daughter and daughter against mother; and mother-in-law against daughter-in-law and daughter-in-law against mother-in-law."

Learning and practicing good judgment

⁵⁴Jesus also said to the crowds, "When you see a cloud forming in the west, you immediately say, 'It's going to rain.' And indeed it does. ⁵⁵And when a south wind blows, you say, 'A heat wave is coming.' And it does. ⁵⁶Hypocrites! You know how to interpret conditions on earth and in the sky. How is it that you don't know how to interpret the present time? ⁵⁷And why don't you judge for yourselves what is right? ⁵⁸As you are going to court with your accuser, make your best effort to reach a settlement along the way. Otherwise, your accuser may

bring you before the judge, and the judge hand you over to the officer, and the officer throw you into prison. ⁵⁹I tell you, you won't get out of there until you have paid the very last cent."ⁱ

Demand for genuine change

13 Some who were present on that occasion told Jesus about the Galileans whom Pilate had killed while they were offering sacrifices. ²He replied, "Do you think the suffering of these Galileans proves that they were more sinful than all the other Galileans? ³No, I tell you, but unless you change your hearts and lives, you will die just as they did. ⁴What about those eighteen people who were killed when the tower of Siloam fell on them? Do you think that they were more guilty of wrongdoing than everyone else who lives in Jerusalem? ⁵No, I tell you, but unless you change your hearts and lives, you will die just as they did."

⁶Jesus told this parable: "A man owned a fig tree planted in his vineyard. He came looking for fruit on it and found none. ⁷He said to his gardener, 'Look, I've come looking for fruit on this fig tree for the past three years, and I've never found any. Cut it down! Why should it continue depleting the soil's nutrients?' ⁸The gardener responded, 'Lord, give it one more year, and I will dig around it and give it fertilizer. ⁹Maybe it will produce fruit next year; if not, then you can cut it down.'"

Healing on a Sabbath

¹⁰Jesus was teaching in one of the synagogues on the Sabbath. ¹¹A woman was there who had been disabled by a spirit for eighteen years. She was bent over and couldn't stand up straight. ¹²When he saw her, Jesus called her to him and said, "Woman, you are set free from your sickness." ¹³He placed his hands on her and she straightened up at once and praised God.

¹⁴The synagogue leader, incensed that Jesus had healed on the Sabbath, responded, "There are six days during which work is permitted. Come and be healed on those days, not on the Sabbath day."

ⁱOr *leptos* (1/128 of a day's wages)

[15] The Lord replied, "Hypocrites! Don't each of you on the Sabbath untie your ox or donkey from its stall and lead it out to get a drink? [16] Then isn't it necessary that this woman, a daughter of Abraham, bound by Satan for eighteen long years, be set free from her bondage on the Sabbath day?" [17] When he said these things, all his opponents were put to shame, but all those in the crowd rejoiced at all the extraordinary things he was doing.

Growth of God's kingdom

[18] Jesus asked, "What is God's kingdom like? To what can I compare it? [19] It's like a mustard seed that someone took and planted in a garden. It grew and developed into a tree and the birds in the sky nested in its branches."

[20] Again he said, "To what can I compare God's kingdom? [21] It's like yeast, which a woman took and hid in a bushel of wheat flour until the yeast had worked its way through the whole."

Who will be saved?

[22] Jesus traveled through cities and villages, teaching and making his way to Jerusalem. [23] Someone said to him, "Lord, will only a few be saved?"

Jesus said to them, [24] "Make every effort to enter through the narrow gate. Many, I tell you, will try to enter and won't be able to. [25] Once the owner of the house gets up

[j] Ps 6:9 LXX

and shuts the door, then you will stand outside and knock on the door, saying, 'Lord, open the door for us.' He will reply, 'I don't know you or where you are from.' [26] Then you will begin to say, 'We ate and drank in your presence, and you taught in our streets.' [27] He will respond, 'I don't know you or where you are from. *Go away from me, all you evildoers!*'[j] [28] There will be weeping and grinding of teeth when you see Abraham, Isaac, Jacob, and all the prophets in God's kingdom, but you yourselves will be thrown out. [29] People will come from east and west, north and south, and sit down to eat in God's kingdom. [30] Look! Those who are last will be first and those who are first will be last."

Sorrow for Jerusalem

[31] At that time, some Pharisees approached Jesus and said, "Go! Get away from here, because Herod wants to kill you."

[32] Jesus said to them, "Go, tell that fox, 'Look, I'm throwing out demons and healing people today and tomorrow, and on the third day I will complete my work. [33] However, it's necessary for me to travel today, tomorrow, and the next day because it's impossible for a prophet to be killed outside of Jerusalem.'

[34] "Jerusalem, Jerusalem, you who kill the prophets and stone those who were sent to you! How often I have wanted to gather your people just as a hen gathers her

SILOAM

A water reservoir or pool in the southeast corner of ancient Jerusalem that is fed by the Gihon ("Gushing") Spring, later known as the Virgin's Fountain. The name seems to be derived from a Hebrew term meaning "aqueduct" or "(water) channel."

In NT times, a "pool of Siloam" was a popular feature in Jerusalem. It may have been in this large pool that Jesus told a blind man to immerse himself (John 9:7, 11). Luke 13:4 refers to an otherwise unknown incident in which 12 people "were killed when the tower of Siloam fell on them." It is reasonable to consider this tower as an architectural feature associated with the pool.

chicks under her wings. But you didn't want that. [35]Look, your house is abandoned. I tell you, you won't see me until the time comes when you say, *Blessings on the one who comes in the Lord's name.*[k]

Healing on the Sabbath

14 One Sabbath, when Jesus went to share a meal in the home of one of the leaders of the Pharisees, they were watching him closely. [2]A man suffering from an abnormal swelling of the body was there. [3]Jesus asked the lawyers and Pharisees, "Does the Law allow healing on the Sabbath or not?" [4]But they said nothing. Jesus took hold of the sick man, cured him, and then let him go. [5]He said to them, "Suppose your child or ox fell into a ditch on the Sabbath day. Wouldn't you immediately pull it out?" [6]But they had no response.

Lessons on humility and generosity

[7]When Jesus noticed how the guests sought out the best seats at the table, he told them a parable. [8]"When someone invites you to a wedding celebration, don't take your seat in the place of honor. Someone more highly regarded than you could have been invited by your host. [9]The host who invited both of you will come and say to you, 'Give your seat to this other person.' Embarrassed, you will take your seat in the least important place. [10]Instead, when you receive an invitation, go and sit in the least important place. When your host approaches you, he will say, 'Friend, move up here to a better seat.' Then you will be honored in the presence of all your fellow guests. [11]All who lift themselves up will be brought low, and those who make themselves low will be lifted up."

[12]Then Jesus said to the person who had invited him, "When you host a lunch or dinner, don't invite your friends, your brothers and sisters, your relatives, or rich neighbors. If you do, they will invite you in return and that will be your reward. [13]Instead, when you give a banquet, invite the poor, crippled, lame, and blind. [14]And you

will be blessed because they can't repay you. Instead, you will be repaid when the just are resurrected."

[15]When one of the dinner guests heard Jesus' remarks, he said to Jesus, "Happy are those who will feast in God's kingdom."

[16]Jesus replied, "A certain man hosted a large dinner and invited many people. [17]When it was time for the dinner to begin, he sent his servant to tell the invited guests, 'Come! The dinner is now ready.' [18]One by one, they all began to make excuses. The first one told him, 'I bought a farm and must go and see it. Please excuse me.' [19]Another said, 'I bought five teams of oxen, and I'm going to check on them. Please excuse me.' [20]Another said, 'I just got married, so I can't come.' [21]When he returned, the servant reported these excuses to his master. The master of the house became angry and said to his servant, 'Go quickly to the city's streets, the busy ones and the side streets, and bring the poor, crippled, blind, and lame.' [22]The servant said, 'Master, your instructions have been followed and there is still room.' [23]The master said to the servant, 'Go to the highways and back alleys and urge people to come in so that my house will be filled. [24]I tell you, not one of those who were invited will taste my dinner.'"

Discipleship's demands

[25]Large crowds were traveling with Jesus. Turning to them, he said, [26]"Whoever comes to me and doesn't hate father and mother, spouse and children, and brothers and sisters—yes, even one's own life—cannot be my disciple. [27]Whoever doesn't carry their own cross and follow me cannot be my disciple.

[28]"If one of you wanted to build a tower, wouldn't you first sit down and calculate the cost, to determine whether you have enough money to complete it? [29]Otherwise, when you have laid the foundation but couldn't finish the tower, all who see it will begin to belittle you. [30]They will say, 'Here's the person who began construc-

tion and couldn't complete it!' ³¹Or what king would go to war against another king without first sitting down to consider whether his ten thousand soldiers could go up against the twenty thousand coming against him? ³²And if he didn't think he could win, he would send a representative to discuss terms of peace while his enemy was still a long way off. ³³In the same way, none of you who are unwilling to give up all of your possessions can be my disciple.

³⁴"Salt is good. But if salt loses its flavor, how will it become salty again? ³⁵It has no value, neither for the soil nor for the manure pile. People throw it away. Whoever has ears to hear should pay attention."

Occasions for celebration

15 All the tax collectors and sinners were gathering around Jesus to listen to him. ²The Pharisees and legal experts were grumbling, saying, "This man welcomes sinners and eats with them."

³Jesus told them this parable: ⁴"Suppose someone among you had one hundred sheep and lost one of them. Wouldn't he leave the other ninety-nine in the pasture and search for the lost one until he finds it? ⁵And when he finds it, he is thrilled and places it on his shoulders. ⁶When he arrives home, he calls together his friends and neighbors, saying to them, 'Celebrate with me because I've found my lost sheep.' ⁷In the same way, I tell you, there will be more joy in heaven over one sinner who changes both heart and life than over ninety-nine righteous people who have no need to change their hearts and lives.

⁸"Or what woman, if she owns ten silver coins and loses one of them, won't light a lamp and sweep the house, searching her home carefully until she finds it? ⁹When she finds it, she calls together her friends and neighbors, saying, 'Celebrate with me because I've found my lost coin.' ¹⁰In the same way, I tell you, joy breaks out in the presence of God's angels over one sinner who changes both heart and life."

¹¹Jesus said, "A certain man had two sons. ¹²The younger son said to his father, 'Father, give me my share of the inheri-

tance.' Then the father divided his estate between them. ¹³Soon afterward, the younger son gathered everything together and took a trip to a land far away. There, he wasted his wealth through extravagant living.

¹⁴"When he had used up his resources, a severe food shortage arose in that country and he began to be in need. ¹⁵He hired himself out to one of the citizens of that country, who sent him into his fields to feed pigs. ¹⁶He longed to eat his fill from what the pigs ate, but no one gave him anything. ¹⁷When he came to his senses, he said, 'How many of my father's hired hands have more than enough food, but I'm starving to death! ¹⁸I will get up and go to my father, and say to him, "Father, I have sinned against heaven and against you. ¹⁹I no longer deserve to be called your son. Take me on as one of your hired hands." ' ²⁰So he got up and went to his father.

"While he was still a long way off, his father saw him and was moved with compassion. His father ran to him, hugged him, and kissed him. ²¹Then his son said, 'Father, I have sinned against heaven and against you. I no longer deserve to be called your son.' ²²But the father said to his servants, 'Quickly, bring out the best robe and put it on him! Put a ring on his finger and sandals on his feet! ²³Fetch the fattened calf and slaughter it. We must celebrate with feasting ²⁴because this son of mine was dead and has come back to life! He was lost and is found!' And they began to celebrate.

²⁵"Now his older son was in the field. Coming in from the field, he approached the house and heard music and dancing. ²⁶He called one of the servants and asked what was going on. ²⁷The servant replied, 'Your brother has arrived, and your father has slaughtered the fattened calf because he received his son back safe and sound.' ²⁸Then the older son was furious and didn't want to enter in, but his father came out and begged him. ²⁹He answered his father, 'Look, I've served you all these years, and I never disobeyed your instruction. Yet you've never given me as much as a young goat so I could celebrate with my friends. ³⁰But when this son of yours returned,

after gobbling up your estate on prostitutes, you slaughtered the fattened calf for him.' ³¹Then his father said, 'Son, you are always with me, and everything I have is yours. ³²But we had to celebrate and be glad because this brother of yours was dead and is alive. He was lost and is found.'"

Faithfulness with money

16 Jesus also said to the disciples, "A certain rich man heard that his household manager was wasting his estate. ²He called the manager in and said to him, 'What is this I hear about you? Give me a report of your administration because you can no longer serve as my manager.'

³"The household manager said to himself, What will I do now that my master is firing me as his manager? I'm not strong enough to dig and too proud to beg. ⁴I know what I'll do so that, when I am removed from my management position, people will welcome me into their houses.

⁵"One by one, the manager sent for each person who owed his master money. He said to the first, 'How much do you owe my master?' ⁶He said, 'Nine hundred gallons of olive oil.'ˡ The manager said to him, 'Take your contract, sit down quickly, and write four hundred fifty gallons.' ⁷Then the manager said to another, 'How much do you owe?' He said, 'One thousand bushels of wheat.'ᵐ He said, 'Take your contract and write eight hundred.'

⁸"The master commended the dishonest manager because he acted cleverly. People who belong to this world are more clever in dealing with their peers than are people who belong to the light. ⁹I tell you, use worldly wealth to make friends for yourselves so that when it's gone, you will be welcomed into the eternal homes.

¹⁰"Whoever is faithful with little is also faithful with much, and the one who is dishonest with little is also dishonest with much. ¹¹If you haven't been faithful with worldly wealth, who will trust you with true riches? ¹²If you haven't been faithful with someone else's property, who will give you your own? ¹³No household servant can serve two masters. Either you will hate the one and love the other, or you will be loyal to the one and have contempt for the other. You cannot serve God and wealth."

Jesus responds to Pharisees

¹⁴The Pharisees, who were money-lovers, heard all this and sneered at Jesus. ¹⁵He said to them, "You are the ones who justify yourselves before other people, but God knows your hearts. What is highly valued by people is deeply offensive to God. ¹⁶Until John, there was only the Law and the Prophets. Since then, the good news of God's kingdom is preached, and everyone is urged to enter it. ¹⁷It's easier for heaven and earth to pass away than for the smallest stroke of a pen in the Law to drop out. ¹⁸Any man who divorces his wife and marries another commits adultery, and a man who marries a woman divorced from her husband commits adultery.

¹⁹"There was a certain rich man who clothed himself in purple and fine linen, and who feasted luxuriously every day. ²⁰At his gate lay a certain poor man named Lazarus who was covered with sores. ²¹Lazarus longed to eat the crumbs that fell from the

---

ˡOr one hundred jugs (approximately nine gallons each)　ᵐOr eighty measures (ten to twelve bushels each)

ABRAHAM'S SIDE

The expression occurs only in Luke 16:22. It represents the blessed state of the righteous who join the patriarchs in paradise after death. Transport to Abraham's side or bosom may come from the ancient idea of being gathered to one's ancestors (Gen 25:8).

rich man's table. Instead, dogs would come and lick his sores.

²²"The poor man died and was carried by angels to Abraham's side. The rich man also died and was buried. ²³While being tormented in the place of the dead, he looked up and saw Abraham at a distance with Lazarus at his side. ²⁴He shouted, 'Father Abraham, have mercy on me. Send Lazarus to dip the tip of his finger in water and cool my tongue, because I'm suffering in this flame.' ²⁵But Abraham said, 'Child, remember that during your lifetime you received good things, whereas Lazarus received terrible things. Now Lazarus is being comforted and you are in great pain. ²⁶Moreover, a great crevasse has been fixed between us and you. Those who wish to cross over from here to you cannot. Neither can anyone cross from there to us.'

²⁷"The rich man said, 'Then I beg you, Father, send Lazarus to my father's house. ²⁸I have five brothers. He needs to warn them so that they don't come to this place of agony.' ²⁹Abraham replied, 'They have Moses and the Prophets. They must listen to them.' ³⁰The rich man said, 'No, Father Abraham! But if someone from the dead goes to them, they will change their hearts and lives.' ³¹Abraham said, 'If they don't listen to Moses and the Prophets, then neither will they be persuaded if someone rises from the dead.'"

Faithful service

17 Jesus said to his disciples, "Things that cause people to trip and fall into sin must happen, but how terrible it is for the person through whom they happen. ²It would be better for them to be thrown into a lake with a large stone hung around their neck than to cause one of these little ones to trip and fall into sin. ³Watch yourselves! If your brother or sister sins, warn them to stop. If they change their hearts and lives, forgive them. ⁴Even if someone sins against you seven times in one day and returns to you seven times and says, 'I am changing my ways,' you must forgive that person."

⁵The apostles said to the Lord, "Increase our faith!"

⁶The Lord replied, "If you had faith the size of a mustard seed, you could say to this mulberry tree, 'Be uprooted and planted in the sea,' and it would obey you.

⁷"Would any of you say to your servant, who had just come in from the field after plowing or tending sheep, 'Come! Sit down for dinner'? ⁸Wouldn't you say instead, 'Fix my dinner. Put on the clothes of a table servant and wait on me while I eat and drink. After that, you can eat and drink'? ⁹You won't thank the servant because the servant did what you asked, will you? ¹⁰In the same way, when you have done everything required of you, you should say, 'We servants deserve no special praise. We have only done our duty.'"

Jesus heals a Samaritan

¹¹On the way to Jerusalem, Jesus traveled along the border between Samaria and Galilee. ¹²As he entered a village, ten men with skin diseases approached him. Keeping their distance from him, ¹³they raised their voices and said, "Jesus, Master, show us mercy!"

¹⁴When Jesus saw them, he said, "Go, show yourselves to the priests." As they left, they were cleansed. ¹⁵One of them, when he saw that he had been healed, returned and praised God with a loud voice. ¹⁶He fell on his face at Jesus' feet and thanked him. He was a Samaritan. ¹⁷Jesus replied, "Weren't ten cleansed? Where are the other nine? ¹⁸No one returned to praise God except this foreigner?" ¹⁹Then Jesus said to him, "Get up and go. Your faith has healed you."

The kingdom is coming

²⁰Pharisees asked Jesus when God's kingdom was coming. He replied, "God's kingdom isn't coming with signs that are easily noticed. ²¹Nor will people say, 'Look, here it is!' or 'There it is!' Don't you see? God's kingdom is already among you."

²²Then Jesus said to the disciples, "The time will come when you will long to see one of the days of the Human One,ⁿ and

ⁿOr Son of Man

you won't see it. ²³People will say to you, 'Look there!' or 'Look here!' Don't leave or go chasing after them. ²⁴The Human One° will appear on his day in the same way that a flash of lightning lights up the sky from one end to the other. ²⁵However, first he must suffer many things and be rejected by this generation.

²⁶"As it was in the days of Noah, so it will be during the days of the Human One.ᴾ ²⁷People were eating, drinking, marrying, and being given in marriage until the day Noah entered the ark and the flood came and destroyed them all. ²⁸Likewise in the days of Lot, people were eating, drinking, buying, selling, planting, and building. ²⁹But on the day Lot left Sodom, fire and sulfur rained down from heaven and destroyed them all. ³⁰That's the way it will be on the day the Human One𐞥 is revealed. ³¹On that day, those on the roof, whose possessions are in the house, shouldn't come down to grab them. Likewise, those in the field shouldn't turn back. ³²Remember Lot's wife! ³³Whoever tries to preserve their life will lose it, but whoever loses their life will preserve it. ³⁴I tell you, on that night two people will be in the same bed: one will be taken and the other left. ³⁵Two women will be grinding grain together: one will be taken and the other left."ʳ

³⁷The disciples asked, "Where, Lord?"

Jesus said, "The vultures gather wherever there's a dead body."

Justice for the faithful

18 Jesus was telling them a parable about their need to pray continuously and not to be discouraged. ²He said, "In a certain city there was a judge who neither feared God nor respected people. ³In that city there was a widow who kept coming to him, asking, 'Give me justice in this case against my adversary.' ⁴For a while he refused but finally said to himself, I don't fear God or respect people, ⁵but I will give this widow justice because she keeps bothering me. Otherwise, there will be no end to her coming here and embarrassing me." ⁶The Lord said, "Listen to what the unjust judge says. ⁷Won't God provide justice to his chosen people who cry out to him day and night? Will he be slow to help them? ⁸I tell you, he will give them justice quickly. But when the Human Oneˢ comes, will he find faithfulness on earth?"

The Pharisee and the tax collector

⁹Jesus told this parable to certain people who had convinced themselves that they were righteous and who looked on everyone else with disgust: ¹⁰"Two people went up to the temple to pray. One was a Pharisee and the other a tax collector. ¹¹The Pharisee stood and prayed about himself

---

°Or *Son of Man* ᴾOr *Son of Man* 𐞥Or *Son of Man* ʳCritical editions of the Gk New Testament do not include 17:36 *Two will be in a field: one will be taken and the other left.* ˢOr *Son of Man*

GALILEE/GALILEANS

1. The term *Galilee* refers to a district generically (e.g., Josh 20:7), on the west side of the Galilee Sea.

2. A Galilean is a resident or native of Galilee. Jesus is once identified as "Jesus the Galilean" (Matt 26:69). The original core of Jesus' disciples are twice called Galileans (Acts 1:11; 2:7) and could be so identified by their accents (Matt 26:73; cf. Mark 14:70; Luke 22:59). Since in Jesus' lifetime Galilee fell under the jurisdiction of Herod Antipas, in Luke Pilate transfers Jesus to him upon learning that Jesus is from Galilee (Luke 23:6-7).

with these words, 'God, I thank you that I'm not like everyone else—crooks, evildoers, adulterers—or even like this tax collector. [12]I fast twice a week. I give a tenth of everything I receive.' [13]But the tax collector stood at a distance. He wouldn't even lift his eyes to look toward heaven. Rather, he struck his chest and said, 'God, show mercy to me, a sinner.' [14]I tell you, this person went down to his home justified rather than the Pharisee. All who lift themselves up will be brought low, and those who make themselves low will be lifted up."

Jesus blesses children

[15]People were bringing babies to Jesus so that he would bless them. When the disciples saw this, they scolded them. [16]Then Jesus called them to him and said, "Allow the children to come to me. Don't forbid them, because God's kingdom belongs to people like these children. [17]I assure you that whoever doesn't welcome God's kingdom like a child will never enter it."

[t]Deut 5:16-20; Exod 20:12-16

A rich man's question

[18]A certain ruler asked Jesus, "Good Teacher, what must I do to obtain eternal life?"

[19]Jesus replied, "Why do you call me good? No one is good except the one God. [20]You know the commandments: *Don't commit adultery. Don't murder. Don't steal. Don't give false testimony. Honor your father and mother.*"[t]

[21]Then the ruler said, "I've kept all of these things since I was a boy."

[22]When Jesus heard this, he said, "There's one more thing. Sell everything you own and distribute the money to the poor. Then you will have treasure in heaven. And come, follow me." [23]When he heard these words, the man became sad because he was extremely rich.

[24]When Jesus saw this, he said, "It's very hard for the wealthy to enter God's kingdom! [25]It's easier for a camel to squeeze through the eye of a needle than for a rich person to enter God's kingdom."

Jesus' Favorite Places

1. Nazareth
Matthew 2:23; 4:13; 21:11; Mark 1:24; 10:47; 16:6; Luke 1:26; 2:4, 39, 51; 4:16, 34; 18:37; John 1:45-46; Acts 10:38

2. Capernaum
Matthew 4:13; 8:5; 11:23; 17:24; Mark 1:21; 2:1; 9:33; Luke 4:23, 31; 7:1; 10:15; John 2:12; 4:46; 6:17, 24, 59

3. Cana
John 2:1, 11; 4:46; 21:2

4. Nain
Luke 7:11

5. Gergesa or Gerasenes' land
Mark 5:1; Luke 8:26, 37

6. Sea of Galilee (C2)
Matthew 4:13, 15, 18; 8:24, 26-27, 32; 13:1, 47; 14:25-26; 15:29; 16:5; 17:27; 18:6; 21:21; Mark 1:16; 2:13; 3:7; 4:1, 39, 41; 5:1, 13, 21; 6:47-49; 7:31; 9:42; 11:23; Luke 8:22-25; 17:2; John 6:1, 16-19, 22-25; 21:1, 7

7. Tyre and Sidon (B1)
Matthew 11:21-22; 15:21; Mark 3:8; 7:24, 31; Luke 4:26; 6:17; 10:13-14

8. Caesarea Philippi (C1)
Matthew 16:13; Mark 8:27

9. Samaria (B4)
Luke 17:11; John 4:4-5

10. Jericho (C4)
Matthew 20:29; Mark 10:46; Luke 10:30; 18:35; 19:1

²⁶Those who heard this said, "Then who can be saved?"

²⁷Jesus replied, "What is impossible for humans is possible for God."

²⁸Peter said, "Look, we left everything we own and followed you."

²⁹Jesus said to them, "I assure you that anyone who has left house, husband, wife, brothers, sisters, parents, or children because of God's kingdom ³⁰will receive many times more in this age and eternal life in the coming age."

Jesus predicts his death and resurrection

³¹Jesus took the Twelve aside and said, "Look, we're going up to Jerusalem, and everything written about the Human One[u] by the prophets will be accomplished. ³²He will be handed over to the Gentiles. He will be ridiculed, mistreated, and spit on. ³³After torturing him, they will kill him. On the third day, he will rise up." ³⁴But the Twelve understood none of these words. The meaning of this message was hidden from them and they didn't grasp what he was saying.

A blind man is healed

³⁵As Jesus came to Jericho, a certain blind man was sitting beside the road begging. ³⁶When the man heard the crowd passing by, he asked what was happening. ³⁷They told him, "Jesus the Nazarene is passing by."

³⁸The blind man shouted, "Jesus, Son of David, show me mercy." ³⁹Those leading the procession scolded him, telling him to be quiet, but he shouted even louder, "Son of David, show me mercy."

⁴⁰Jesus stopped and called for the man to be brought to him. When he was present Jesus asked, ⁴¹"What do you want me to do for you?"

He said, "Lord, I want to see."

⁴²Jesus said to him, "Receive your sight! Your faith has healed you." ⁴³At once he was able to see, and he began to follow Jesus, praising God. When all the people saw it, they praised God too.

A rich tax collector

19 Jesus entered Jericho and was passing through town. ²A man there named Zacchaeus, a ruler among tax collectors, was rich. ³He was trying to see who Jesus was, but, being a short man, he couldn't because of the crowd. ⁴So he ran ahead and climbed up a sycamore tree so he could see Jesus, who was about to pass that way. ⁵When Jesus came to that spot, he looked up and said, "Zacchaeus, come down at once. I must stay in your home today." ⁶So Zacchaeus came down at once, happy to welcome Jesus.

⁷Everyone who saw this grumbled, saying, "He has gone to be the guest of a sinner."

⁸Zacchaeus stopped and said to the Lord, "Look, Lord, I give half of my possessions to the poor. And if I have cheated anyone, I repay them four times as much."

⁹Jesus said to him, "Today, salvation has come to this household because he too is a son of Abraham. ¹⁰The Human One[v] came to seek and save the lost."

Faithful service

¹¹As they listened to this, Jesus told them another parable because he was near Jerusalem and they thought God's kingdom would appear right away. ¹²He said, "A certain man who was born into royalty went to a distant land to receive his kingdom and then return. ¹³He called together ten servants and gave each of them money worth four months' wages.[w] He said, 'Do business with this until I return.' ¹⁴His citizens hated him, so they sent a representative after him who said, 'We don't want this man to be our king.' ¹⁵After receiving his kingdom, he returned and called the servants to whom he had given the money to find out how much they had earned. ¹⁶The first servant came forward and said, 'Your money has earned a return of one thousand percent.' ¹⁷The king replied, 'Excellent! You are a good servant. Because you have been faithful in a small matter, you will have authority over ten cities.'

¹⁸"The second servant came and said,

---

[u]Or Son of Man [v]Or Son of Man [w]Or he divided ten minas among them

'Master, your money has made a return of five hundred percent.' ¹⁹To this one, the king said, 'You will have authority over five cities.'

²⁰"Another servant came and said, 'Master, here is your money. I wrapped it up in a scarf for safekeeping. ²¹I was afraid of you because you are a stern man. You withdraw what you haven't deposited and you harvest what you haven't planted.' ²²The king replied, 'I will judge you by the words of your own mouth, you worthless servant! You knew, did you, that I'm a stern man, withdrawing what I didn't deposit, and harvesting what I didn't plant? ²³Why then didn't you put my money in the bank? Then when I arrived, at least I could have gotten it back with interest.'

²⁴"He said to his attendants, 'Take his money and give it to the one who has ten times as much.' ²⁵'But Master,' they said, 'he already has ten times as much!' ²⁶He replied, 'I say to you that everyone who has will be given more, but from those who have nothing, even what they have will be taken away. ²⁷As for my enemies who don't want me as their king, bring them here and slaughter them before me.'"

²⁸After Jesus said this, he continued on ahead, going up to Jerusalem.

Procession into Jerusalem

²⁹As Jesus came to Bethphage and Bethany on the Mount of Olives, he gave two disciples a task. ³⁰He said, "Go into the village over there. When you enter it, you will find tied up there a colt that no one has ever ridden. Untie it and bring it here. ³¹If someone asks, 'Why are you untying it?' just say, 'Its master needs it.'" ³²Those who had been sent found it exactly as he had said.

³³As they were untying the colt, its owners said to them, "Why are you untying the colt?"

³⁴They replied, "Its master needs it." ³⁵They brought it to Jesus, threw their clothes on the colt, and lifted Jesus onto it. ³⁶As Jesus rode along, they spread their clothes on the road.

³⁷As Jesus approached the road leading down from the Mount of Olives, the whole throng of his disciples began rejoicing. They praised God with a loud voice because of all the mighty things they had seen. ³⁸They said,

> "Blessings on the king who comes in the name of the Lord.
> Peace in heaven and glory in the highest heavens."

³⁹Some of the Pharisees from the crowd said to Jesus, "Teacher, scold your disciples! Tell them to stop!"

⁴⁰He answered, "I tell you, if they were silent, the stones would shout."

Jesus predicts Jerusalem's destruction

⁴¹As Jesus came to the city and observed it, he wept over it. ⁴²He said, "If only you knew on this of all days the things that lead to peace. But now they are hidden from your eyes. ⁴³The time will come when your enemies will build fortifications around you, encircle you, and attack you from all sides. ⁴⁴They will crush you completely, you and the people within you. They won't leave one stone on top of another within you, because you didn't recognize the time of your gracious visit from God."

Jesus clears the temple

⁴⁵When Jesus entered the temple, he threw out those who were selling things there. ⁴⁶He said to them, "It's written, *My house will be a house of prayer, but you have made it a hideout for crooks.*"ˣ

⁴⁷Jesus was teaching daily in the temple. The chief priests, the legal experts, and the foremost leaders among the people were seeking to kill him. ⁴⁸However, they couldn't find a way to do it because all the people were enthralled with what they heard.

Controversy over authority

20 On one of the days when Jesus was teaching the people in the temple and proclaiming the good news, the chief priests, legal experts, and elders approached him. ²They said, "Tell us: What kind of authority do you have for doing these things? Who gave you this authority?"

ˣIsa 56:7; Jer 7:11

³He replied, "I have a question for you. Tell me: ⁴Was John's baptism of heavenly or of human origin?"

⁵They discussed among themselves, "If we say, 'It's of heavenly origin,' he'll say, 'Why didn't you believe him?' ⁶But if we say, 'It's of human origin,' all the people will stone us to death because they are convinced that John was a prophet." ⁷They answered that they didn't know where it came from.

⁸Then Jesus replied, "Neither will I tell you what kind of authority I have to do these things."

Parable of the tenant farmers

⁹Jesus told the people this parable: "A certain man planted a vineyard, rented it to tenant farmers, and went on a trip for a long time. ¹⁰When it was time, he sent a servant to collect from the tenants his share of the fruit of the vineyard. But the tenants sent him away, beaten and empty-handed. ¹¹The man sent another servant. But they beat him, treated him disgracefully, and sent him away empty-handed as well. ¹²He sent a third servant. They wounded this servant and threw him out. ¹³The owner of the vineyard said, 'What should I do? I'll send my son, whom I love dearly. Perhaps they will respect him.' ¹⁴But when they saw him, they said to each other, 'This is the heir. Let's kill him so the inheritance will be ours.' ¹⁵They threw him out of the vineyard and killed him. What will the owner of the vineyard do to them? ¹⁶He will come and destroy those tenants and give the vineyard to others."

When the people heard this, they said, "May this never happen!"

¹⁷Staring at them, Jesus said, "Then what is the meaning of this text of scripture: *The stone that the builders rejected has become the cornerstone?*ʸ ¹⁸Everyone who falls on that stone will be crushed. And the stone will crush the person it falls on." ¹⁹The legal experts and chief priests wanted to arrest him right then because they knew he had told this parable against them. But they feared the people.

An attempt to trap Jesus

²⁰The legal experts and chief priests were watching Jesus closely and sent spies who pretended to be sincere. They wanted to trap him in his words so they could hand him over to the jurisdiction and authority of the governor. ²¹They asked him, "Teacher, we know that you are correct in what you say and teach. You don't show favoritism but teach God's way as it really is. ²²Does the Law allow people to pay taxes to Caesar or not?"

²³Since Jesus recognized their deception, he said to them, ²⁴"Show me a coin.ᶻ Whose image and inscription does it have on it?"

"Caesar's," they replied.

²⁵He said to them, "Give to Caesar what belongs to Caesar and to God what belongs to God." ²⁶They couldn't trap him in his words in front of the people. Astonished by his answer, they were speechless.

Question about the resurrection

²⁷Some Sadducees, who deny that there's a resurrection, came to Jesus and asked, ²⁸"Teacher, Moses wrote for us that *if a man's brother dies* leaving a widow *but no children, the brother must marry the widow and raise up children for his brother.*ᵃ ²⁹Now there were seven brothers. The first man married a woman and then died childless. ³⁰The second ³¹and then the third brother married her. Eventually all seven married her, and they all died without leaving any children. ³²Finally, the woman died too. ³³In the resurrection, whose wife will she be? All seven were married to her."

³⁴Jesus said to them, "People who belong to this age marry and are given in marriage. ³⁵But those who are considered worthy to participate in that age, that is, in the age of the resurrection from the dead, won't marry nor will they be given in marriage. ³⁶They can no longer die, because they are like angels and are God's children since they share in the resurrection. ³⁷Even Moses demonstrated that the dead are raised—in the passage about the burning bush, when he speaks of the Lord as *the God*

ʸPs 118:22 ᶻOr *denarion* ᵃDeut 25:5; Gen 38:8

of Abraham, the God of Isaac, and the God of Jacob.[b] [38]He isn't the God of the dead but of the living. To him they are all alive."

[39]Some of the legal experts responded, "Teacher, you have answered well." [40]No one dared to ask him anything else.

[41]Jesus said to them, "Why do they say that the Christ is David's son? [42]David himself says in the scroll of Psalms, *The Lord said to my lord, 'Sit at my right side* [43]*until I make your enemies a footstool for your feet.'*[c] [44]Since David calls him 'Lord,' how can he be David's son?"

Jesus condemns the legal experts

[45]In the presence of all the people, Jesus said to his disciples, [46]"Watch out for the legal experts. They like to walk around in long robes. They love being greeted with honor in the markets. They long for the places of honor in the synagogues and at banquets. [47]They are the ones who cheat widows out of their homes, and to show off they say long prayers. They will be judged most harshly."

A poor widow's offering

21 Looking up, Jesus saw rich people throwing their gifts into the collec-tion box for the temple treasury. [2]He also saw a poor widow throw in two small copper coins worth a penny.[d] [3]He said, "I assure you that this poor widow has put in more than them all. [4]All of them are giving out of their spare change. But she from her hopeless poverty has given everything she had to live on."

The temple's fate

[5]Some people were talking about the temple, how it was decorated with beautiful stones and ornaments dedicated to God. Jesus said, [6]"As for the things you are admiring, the time is coming when not even one stone will be left upon another. All will be demolished."

[7]They asked him, "Teacher, when will these things happen? What sign will show that these things are about to happen?"

[8]Jesus said, "Watch out that you aren't deceived. Many will come in my name, saying, 'I'm the one!' and 'It's time!' Don't follow them. [9]When you hear of wars and rebellions, don't be alarmed. These things must happen first, but the end won't happen immediately."

[10]Then Jesus said to them, "Nations and kingdoms will fight against each other.

[b]Exod 3:6, 15-16 [c]Ps 110:1 [d]Or *two lepta*

JERUSALEM TEMPLE

In its long history Israel built numerous sanctuaries and temples for its God, but the most important were the three temples built on the same site in Jerusalem. The first was built by Solomon in the mid-10th century BCE. This temple continued with minor and major repairs and alterations until it was looted in 598 BCE, and then utterly destroyed in 587. The second temple was built by Zerubbabel, the Persian-appointed governor of Judea, on the site of the ruins of the first temple between 520 and 515 BCE. This temple stood until Herod the Great tore it down ca. 20 BCE in order to make way for his new temple. Herod rebuilt the temple proper in only a year and six months, but his work on the larger temple precincts, which he massively enlarged and adorned with elaborate structures, lasted eight and a half years. Work continued on the complex well after Herod's reign, until ca. 63 CE, during the reign of Herod Agrippa II and the procuratorship of Albinus. Herod's temple was destroyed in 70 CE when the Romans sacked Jerusalem at the end of the Jewish War.

¹¹There will be great earthquakes and wide-scale food shortages and epidemics. There will also be terrifying sights and great signs in the sky. ¹²But before all this occurs, they will take you into custody and harass you because of your faith. They will hand you over to synagogues and prisons, and you will be brought before kings and governors because of my name. ¹³This will provide you with an opportunity to testify. ¹⁴Make up your minds not to prepare your defense in advance. ¹⁵I'll give you words and wisdom that none of your opponents will be able to counter or contradict. ¹⁶You will be betrayed by your parents, brothers and sisters, relatives, and friends. They will execute some of you. ¹⁷Everyone will hate you because of my name. ¹⁸Still, not a hair on your heads will be lost. ¹⁹By holding fast, you will gain your lives.

²⁰"When you see Jerusalem surrounded by armies, then you will know that its destruction is close at hand. ²¹At that time, those in Judea must flee to the mountains, those in the city must escape, and those in the countryside must not enter the city. ²²These are the days of punishment, when everything written will find its fulfillment. ²³How terrible it will be at that time for women who are pregnant or for women who are nursing their children. There will be great agony on the earth and angry judgment on this people. ²⁴They will fall by the edge of the sword and be taken away as captives among all nations. Jerusalem will be plundered by Gentiles until the times of the Gentiles are concluded.

²⁵"There will be signs in the sun, moon, and stars. On the earth, there will be dismay among nations in their confusion over the roaring of the sea and surging waves. ²⁶The planets and other heavenly bodies will be shaken, causing people to faint from fear and foreboding of what is coming upon the world. ²⁷Then they will see the Human One[e] coming on a cloud with power and great splendor. ²⁸Now when these things begin to happen, stand up straight and raise your heads, because your redemption is near."

A lesson from the fig tree

²⁹Jesus told them a parable: "Look at the fig tree and all the trees. ³⁰When they sprout leaves, you can see for yourselves and know that summer is near. ³¹In the same way, when you see these things happening, you know that God's kingdom is near. ³²I assure you that this generation won't pass away until everything has happened. ³³Heaven and earth will pass away, but my words will certainly not pass away.

³⁴"Take care that your hearts aren't dulled by drinking parties, drunkenness, and the anxieties of day-to-day life. Don't let that day fall upon you unexpectedly, ³⁵like a trap. It will come upon everyone who lives on the face of the whole earth. ³⁶Stay alert at all times, praying that you are strong enough to escape everything that is about to happen and to stand before the Human One."[f]

³⁷Every day Jesus was teaching in the temple, but he spent each night on the Mount of Olives. ³⁸All the people rose early in the morning to hear him in the temple area.

Plot to kill Jesus

22 The Festival of Unleavened Bread, which is called Passover, was approaching. ²The chief priests and the legal experts were looking for a way to kill Jesus, because they were afraid of the people. ³Then Satan entered Judas, called Iscariot, who was one of the Twelve. ⁴He went out and discussed with the chief priests and the officers of the temple guard how he could hand Jesus over to them. ⁵They were delighted and arranged payment for him. ⁶He agreed and began looking for an opportunity to hand Jesus over to them—a time when the crowds would be absent.

Disciples prepare for the Passover

⁷The Day of Unleavened Bread arrived, when the Passover had to be sacrificed. ⁸Jesus sent Peter and John with this task: "Go and prepare for us to eat the Passover meal."

⁹They said to him, "Where do you want us to prepare it?"

[e]Or Son of Man   [f]Or Son of Man

¹⁰Jesus replied, "When you go into the city, a man carrying a water jar will meet you. Follow him to the house he enters. ¹¹Say to the owner of the house, 'The teacher says to you, "Where is the guestroom where I can eat the Passover meal with my disciples?"' ¹²He will show you a large upstairs room, already furnished. Make preparations there." ¹³They went and found everything just as he had told them, and they prepared the Passover meal.

The Passover meal

¹⁴When the time came, Jesus took his place at the table, and the apostles joined him. ¹⁵He said to them, "I have earnestly desired to eat this Passover with you before I suffer. ¹⁶I tell you, I won't eat it until it is fulfilled in God's kingdom." ¹⁷After taking a cup and giving thanks, he said, "Take this and share it among yourselves. ¹⁸I tell you that from now on I won't drink from the fruit of the vine until God's kingdom has come." ¹⁹After taking the bread and giving thanks, he broke it and gave it to them, saying, "This is my body, which is given for you. Do this in remembrance of me." ²⁰In the same way, he took the cup after the meal and said, "This cup is the new covenant by my blood, which is poured out for you.

²¹"But look! My betrayer is with me; his hand is on this table. ²²The Human One^g goes just as it has been determined. But how terrible it is for that person who betrays him." ²³They began to argue among themselves about which of them it could possibly be who would do this.

^g Or *Son of Man*

UPPER ROOM

A room in an upper story of a private house or multiunit housing. In Mark 14:12-16 (cf. Matt 26:17-19; Luke 22:7-13), two disciples enter Jerusalem to prepare a Passover meal in an upstairs room (Mark 14:15; Luke 22:12) where Jesus and the Twelve will eat their final meal together. The room is described as large and furnished, possibly indicating couches spread out for guests to recline at a banquet. The house was probably a two-story private urban home, where second-floor rooms were often used as living areas or dining rooms while first-floor rooms might be workspaces, living areas, or shops.

Acts uses a different Greek word for an upper-story room. After the 11 male apostles witness Jesus' ascension, they return to Jerusalem and gather in an upper room (Act 1:13). Shown to be united and in prayer (v. 14), Jesus' followers regroup during this transition stage as they await the Holy Spirit (1:5, 8; cf. 1:21-26). The women's presence correlates with recent archaeological studies arguing that household space was not clearly divided by gender. The diverse group assembled suggests the inclusiveness of the early church and its leaders. This may be the same upper room where the disciples ate the Passover meal (see also Acts 2:1; 12:12).

In Acts 9:36-43, Tabitha, a disciple and benefactor, is laid in a room upstairs after her death, where Peter prays for her. "Then he called God's holy people, including the widows, and presented her alive to them." Later in Acts, Eutychus falls out of a window from the third story of an apartment house where Paul is meeting with others to break bread and preach (Acts 20:7-12).

The disciples debate greatness

²⁴An argument broke out among the disciples over which one of them should be regarded as the greatest.

²⁵But Jesus said to them, "The kings of the Gentiles rule over their subjects, and those in authority over them are called 'friends of the people.' ²⁶But that's not the way it will be with you. Instead, the greatest among you must become like a person of lower status and the leader like a servant. ²⁷So which one is greater, the one who is seated at the table or the one who serves at the table? Isn't it the one who is seated at the table? But I am among you as one who serves.

²⁸"You are the ones who have continued with me in my trials. ²⁹And I confer royal power on you just as my Father granted royal power to me. ³⁰Thus you will eat and drink at my table in my kingdom, and you will sit on thrones overseeing the twelve tribes of Israel.

Peter's denial predicted

³¹"Simon, Simon, look! Satan has asserted the right to sift you all like wheat. ³²However, I have prayed for you that your faith won't fail. When you have returned, strengthen your brothers and sisters."

³³Peter responded, "Lord, I'm ready to go with you, both to prison and to death!"

³⁴Jesus replied, "I tell you, Peter, the rooster won't crow today before you have denied three times that you know me."

Call for preparedness

³⁵Jesus said to them, "When I sent you out without a wallet, bag, or sandals, you didn't lack anything, did you?"

They said, "Nothing."

³⁶Then he said to them, "But now, whoever has a wallet must take it, and likewise a bag. And those who don't own a sword must sell their clothes and buy one. ³⁷I tell you that this scripture must be fulfilled in relation to me: *And he was counted among criminals.*[h] Indeed, what's written about me is nearing completion."

³⁸They said to him, "Lord, look, here are two swords."

He replied, "Enough of that!"

Jesus in prayer

³⁹Jesus left and made his way to the Mount of Olives, as was his custom, and the disciples followed him. ⁴⁰When he arrived, he said to them, "Pray that you won't give in to temptation." ⁴¹He withdrew from them about a stone's throw, knelt down, and prayed. ⁴²He said, "Father, if it's your will, take this cup of suffering away from me. However, not my will but your will must be done." ⁴³Then a heavenly angel appeared to him and strengthened him. ⁴⁴He was in anguish and prayed even more earnestly. His sweat became like drops of blood falling on the ground. ⁴⁵When he got up from praying, he went to the disciples. He found them asleep, overcome by grief. ⁴⁶He said to them, "Why are you sleeping? Get up and pray so that you won't give in to temptation."

Jesus' arrest

⁴⁷While Jesus was still speaking, a crowd appeared, and the one called Judas, one of the Twelve, was leading them. He approached Jesus to kiss him.

⁴⁸Jesus said to him, "Judas, would you betray the Human One[i] with a kiss?"

⁴⁹When those around him recognized what was about to happen, they said, "Lord, should we fight with our swords?" ⁵⁰One of them struck the high priest's servant, cutting off his right ear.

⁵¹Jesus responded, "Stop! No more of this!" He touched the slave's ear and healed him.

⁵²Then Jesus said to the chief priests, the officers of the temple guard, and the elders who had come to get him, "Have you come with swords and clubs to arrest me, as though I were a thief? ⁵³Day after day I was with you in the temple, but you didn't arrest me. But this is your time, when darkness rules."

Peter denies knowing Jesus

⁵⁴After they arrested Jesus, they led him away and brought him to the high priest's

^hIsa 53:12 ⁱOr *Son of Man*

house. Peter followed from a distance. ⁵⁵When they lit a fire in the middle of the courtyard and sat down together, Peter sat among them.

⁵⁶Then a servant woman saw him sitting in the firelight. She stared at him and said, "This man was with him too."

⁵⁷But Peter denied it, saying, "Woman, I don't know him!"

⁵⁸A little while later, someone else saw him and said, "You are one of them too."

But Peter said, "Man, I'm not!"

⁵⁹An hour or so later, someone else insisted, "This man must have been with him, because he is a Galilean too."

⁶⁰Peter responded, "Man, I don't know what you are talking about!" At that very moment, while he was still speaking, a rooster crowed. ⁶¹The Lord turned and looked straight at Peter, and Peter remembered the Lord's words: "Before a rooster crows today, you will deny me three times." ⁶²And Peter went out and cried uncontrollably.

Jesus taunted

⁶³The men who were holding Jesus in custody taunted him while they beat him. ⁶⁴They blindfolded him and asked him repeatedly, "Prophesy! Who hit you?" ⁶⁵Insulting him, they said many other horrible things against him.

Jesus before the Jerusalem leadership

⁶⁶As morning came, the elders of the people, both chief priests and legal experts, came together, and Jesus was brought before their council.

⁶⁷They said, "If you are the Christ, tell us!"

He answered, "If I tell you, you won't believe. ⁶⁸And if I ask you a question, you won't answer. ⁶⁹But from now on, *the Human One*ʲ *will be seated on the right side of the power of God.*"ᵏ

⁷⁰They all said, "Are you God's Son, then?"

He replied, "You say that I am."

⁷¹Then they said, "Why do we need further testimony? We've heard it from his own lips."

Jesus before Pilate

23 The whole assembly got up and led Jesus to Pilate and ²began to accuse him. They said, "We have found this man misleading our people, opposing the payment of taxes to Caesar, and claiming that he is the Christ, a king."

³Pilate asked him, "Are you the king of the Jews?"

Jesus replied, "That's what you say."

⁴Then Pilate said to the chief priests and the crowds, "I find no legal basis for action against this man."

⁵But they objected strenuously, saying, "He agitates the people with his teaching throughout Judea—starting from Galilee all the way here."

Jesus before Herod

⁶Hearing this, Pilate asked if the man was a Galilean. ⁷When he learned that Jesus was from Herod's district, Pilate sent him to Herod, who was also in Jerusalem at that time. ⁸Herod was very glad to see Jesus, for he had heard about Jesus and had wanted to see him for quite some time. He was hoping to see Jesus perform some sign. ⁹Herod questioned Jesus at length, but Jesus didn't respond to him. ¹⁰The chief priests and the legal experts were there, fiercely accusing Jesus. ¹¹Herod and his soldiers treated Jesus with contempt. Herod mocked him by dressing Jesus in elegant clothes and sent him back to Pilate. ¹²Pilate and Herod became friends with each other that day. Before this, they had been enemies.

Jesus and Barabbas

¹³Then Pilate called together the chief priests, the rulers, and the people. ¹⁴He said to them, "You brought this man before me as one who was misleading the people. I have questioned him in your presence and found nothing in this man's conduct that provides a legal basis for the charges you have brought against him. ¹⁵Neither did Herod, because Herod returned him to us. He's done nothing that deserves death.

¹⁶Therefore, I'll have him whipped, then let him go."[1]

¹⁸But with one voice they shouted, "Away with this man! Release Barabbas to us." (¹⁹Barabbas had been thrown into prison because of a riot that had occurred in the city, and for murder.)

²⁰Pilate addressed them again because he wanted to release Jesus.

²¹They kept shouting out, "Crucify him! Crucify him!"

²²For the third time, Pilate said to them, "Why? What wrong has he done? I've found no legal basis for the death penalty in his case. Therefore, I will have him whipped, then let him go."

²³But they were adamant, shouting their demand that Jesus be crucified. Their voices won out. ²⁴Pilate issued his decision to grant their request. ²⁵He released the one they asked for, who had been thrown into prison because of a riot and murder. But he handed Jesus over to their will.

On the way to the cross

²⁶As they led Jesus away, they grabbed Simon, a man from Cyrene, who was coming in from the countryside. They put the cross on his back and made him carry it behind Jesus. ²⁷A huge crowd of people followed Jesus, including women, who were mourning and wailing for him. ²⁸Jesus turned to the women and said, "Daughters of Jerusalem, don't cry for me. Rather, cry for yourselves and your children. ²⁹The time will come when they will say, 'Happy are those who are unable to become pregnant, the wombs that never gave birth, and the breasts that never nursed a child.' ³⁰Then *they will say to the mountains, 'Fall on us,' and to the hills, 'Cover us.'*[m] ³¹If they do these things when the tree is green, what will happen when it is dry?"

Jesus on the cross

³²They also led two other criminals to be executed with Jesus. ³³When they arrived

---

[1]Critical editions of the Gk New Testament do not include 23:17 *He had to release one prisoner for them because of the festival.* [m]Hos 10:8

BARABBAS

This enigmatic character appears in Jesus' Roman trial in all four Gospels (Matt 27; Mark 15; Luke 23; John 18): Pilate offers to release one prisoner as part of a Passover amnesty; the Jewish crowd, stirred up by the chief priests, chooses Barabbas rather than Jesus.

The Gospels are our only sources of information about Barabbas. Mark 15:7 ambiguously states that Barabbas was "locked up with the rebels who had committed murder during an uprising"; Matthew 27:16 simply calls him "a well-known prisoner"; and Luke 23:19 heightens his insurrectionary activity, implicating him in an uprising and murder. Finally, John 18:40 describes him as an outlaw or political activist.

A complicating factor is that there is no firm evidence for a Passover amnesty in 1st cent. Judea. The evangelists are unclear about the details: John thinks it was a Jewish custom; Matthew and Mark link it to the Roman governor. Perhaps Barabbas was tried on the same day as Jesus but was released, either because the charges were found to be groundless, or as an isolated act of clemency. Christian tradition, reflecting on the injustice of Barabbas's release and Jesus' crucifixion, provided the link between the two men.

at the place called The Skull, they crucified him, along with the criminals, one on his right and the other on his left. [34]Jesus said, "Father, forgive them, for they don't know what they're doing." They drew lots as a way of dividing up his clothing.

[35]The people were standing around watching, but the leaders sneered at him, saying, "He saved others. Let him save himself if he really is the Christ sent from God, the chosen one."

[36]The soldiers also mocked him. They came up to him, offering him sour wine [37]and saying, "If you really are the king of the Jews, save yourself." [38]Above his head was a notice of the formal charge against him. It read "This is the king of the Jews."

[39]One of the criminals hanging next to Jesus insulted him: "Aren't you the Christ? Save yourself and us!"

[40]Responding, the other criminal spoke harshly to him, "Don't you fear God, seeing that you've also been sentenced to die? [41]We are rightly condemned, for we are receiving the appropriate sentence for what we did. But this man has done nothing wrong." [42]Then he said, "Jesus, remember me when you come into your kingdom."

[43]Jesus replied, "I assure you that today you will be with me in paradise."

Jesus' death

[44]It was now about noon, and darkness covered the whole earth until about three o'clock, [45]while the sun stopped shining. Then the curtain in the sanctuary tore down the middle. [46]Crying out in a loud voice, Jesus said, "Father, *into your hands I entrust my life*."[n] After he said this, he breathed for the last time.

[47]When the centurion saw what happened, he praised God, saying, "It's really

[n]Ps 31:5

SEVEN WORDS FROM THE CROSS

Sometimes called the "seven last words" of Jesus, this is a traditional set of seven sayings created by combining the four accounts of the crucifixion. None of the sayings appear in all four Gospels, and most occur only in one. No single account contains all seven sayings.

According to the traditional order, the seven words are: (1) Jesus' prayer for those who are crucifying him: "Father, forgive them, for they don't know what they're doing" (Luke 23:34). (2) Jesus' promise to the repentant criminal who is being crucified beside him: "I assure you that today you will be with me in paradise" (Luke 23:43). (3) Jesus' words to his mother Mary and to the beloved disciple: "Woman, here is your son. . . . Here is your mother" (John 19:26-27). (4) Jesus' cry of abandonment (Matt 27:46; Mark 15:34), translated by the evangelists: "My God, my God, why have you left me?" The cry mirrors the opening words of Psalm 22 (v. 1 [Heb. 22:2]), a fact that has given rise to much debate over whether Jesus spoke the words in despair or in hope. (5) "I am thirsty" (John 19:28). (6) "It is completed" (John 19:30; cf. John 17:4). (7) "Father, into your hands I entrust my life" (Luke 23:46). This final phrase is a quotation from a psalm expressing trust in God's deliverance (Ps 31:5 [Heb. 31:6]).

true: this man was righteous." ⁴⁸All the crowds who had come together to see this event returned to their homes beating their chests after seeing what had happened. ⁴⁹And everyone who knew him, including the women who had followed him from Galilee, stood at a distance observing these things.

Jesus' burial

⁵⁰Now there was a man named Joseph who was a member of the council. He was a good and righteous man. ⁵¹He hadn't agreed with the plan and actions of the council. He was from the Jewish city of Arimathea and eagerly anticipated God's kingdom. ⁵²This man went to Pilate and asked for Jesus' body. ⁵³Taking it down, he wrapped it in a linen cloth and laid it in a tomb carved out of the rock, in which no one had ever been buried. ⁵⁴It was the Preparation Day for the Sabbath, and the Sabbath was quickly approaching. ⁵⁵The women who had come with Jesus from Galilee followed Joseph. They saw the tomb and how Jesus' body was laid in it, ⁵⁶then they went away and prepared fragrant spices and perfumed oils. They rested on the Sabbath, in keeping with the commandment.

The empty tomb

24 Very early in the morning on the first day of the week, the women went to the tomb, bringing the fragrant spices they had prepared. ²They found the stone rolled away from the tomb, ³but when they went in, they didn't find the body of the Lord Jesus. ⁴They didn't know what to make of this. Suddenly, two men were standing beside them in gleaming bright clothing. ⁵The women were frightened and bowed their faces toward the ground, but the men said to them, "Why do you look for the living among the dead? ⁶He isn't here, but has been raised. Remember what he told you while he was still in Galilee, ⁷that the Human One° must be handed over to sinners, be crucified, and on the third day rise again." ⁸Then they remembered his words.

⁹When they returned from the tomb, they reported all these things to the eleven and all the others. ¹⁰It was Mary Magdalene, Joanna, Mary the mother of James, and the other women with them who told these things to the apostles. ¹¹Their words struck the apostles as nonsense, and they didn't believe the women. ¹²But Peter ran to the tomb. When he bent over to look inside, he saw only the linen cloth. Then he returned home, wondering what had happened.

Encounter on the Emmaus road

¹³On that same day, two disciples were traveling to a village called Emmaus, about seven miles from Jerusalem. ¹⁴They were talking to each other about everything that had happened. ¹⁵While they were discussing these things, Jesus himself arrived and joined them on their journey. ¹⁶They were prevented from recognizing him.

¹⁷He said to them, "What are you talking about as you walk along?" They stopped, their faces downcast.

¹⁸The one named Cleopas replied, "Are you the only visitor to Jerusalem who is unaware of the things that have taken place there over the last few days?"

¹⁹He said to them, "What things?"

They said to him, "The things about Jesus of Nazareth. Because of his powerful deeds and words, he was recognized by God and all the people as a prophet. ²⁰But our chief priests and our leaders handed him over to be sentenced to death, and they crucified him. ²¹We had hoped he was the one who would redeem Israel. All these things happened three days ago. ²²But there's more: Some women from our group have left us stunned. They went to the tomb early this morning ²³and didn't find his body. They came to us saying that they had even seen a vision of angels who told them he is alive. ²⁴Some of those who were with us went to the tomb and found things just as the women said. They didn't see him."

²⁵Then Jesus said to them, "You foolish people! Your dull minds keep you from believing all that the prophets talked about.

°Or Son of Man

²⁶Wasn't it necessary for the Christ to suffer these things and then enter into his glory?" ²⁷Then he interpreted for them the things written about himself in all the scriptures, starting with Moses and going through all the Prophets.

²⁸When they came to Emmaus, he acted as if he was going on ahead. ²⁹But they urged him, saying, "Stay with us. It's nearly evening, and the day is almost over." So he went in to stay with them. ³⁰After he took his seat at the table with them, he took the bread, blessed and broke it, and gave it to them. ³¹Their eyes were opened and they recognized him, but he disappeared from their sight. ³²They said to each other, "Weren't our hearts on fire when he spoke to us along the road and when he explained the scriptures for us?"

³³They got up right then and returned to Jerusalem. They found the eleven and their companions gathered together. ³⁴They were saying to each other, "The Lord really has risen! He appeared to Simon!" ³⁵Then the two disciples described what had happened along the road and how Jesus was made known to them as he broke the bread.

Jesus appears to the disciples

³⁶While they were saying these things, Jesus himself stood among them and said, "Peace be with you!" ³⁷They were terrified and afraid. They thought they were seeing a ghost.

³⁸He said to them, "Why are you startled? Why are doubts arising in your hearts? ³⁹Look at my hands and my feet. It's really me! Touch me and see, for a ghost doesn't have flesh and bones like you see I have." ⁴⁰As he said this, he showed them his hands and feet. ⁴¹Because they were wondering and questioning in the midst of their happiness, he said to them, "Do you have anything to eat?" ⁴²They gave him a piece of baked fish. ⁴³Taking it, he ate it in front of them.

MARY

The name Mary, derived from the Hebrew *Miriam*, is the name of several NT women.

1. Mary the mother of Jesus.

2. Mary Magdalene is one of the best-known disciples of Jesus, and she appears in all four Gospels. The name by which she is known indicates her association with Magdala, most likely the city by that name located on the northwestern shore of the Galilee Sea.

3. Mary of Bethany was the sister of Martha (Luke 10:38-42; John 11:1-37; 12:1-3) and Lazarus (John 11:1-3, 19, 32) who lived in Bethany.

4. Mary the mother of James and Joseph/Joses was a witness to the empty tomb and the angelic announcement of Jesus' resurrection (Matt 27:55-56; 28:1-10; Mark 15:40-41, 47; 16:1-8; Luke 24:1-10).

5. Mary the mother of John Mark was a member of the Jesus movement, most likely a widow, in whose home the community of faith regularly gathered for meetings and prayer (Acts 12:12-16). Mary "was John's mother; he was also known as Mark" (Acts 12:12).

6. Mary the wife of Clopas was a follower, perhaps a relative, of Jesus (John 19:25).

⁴⁴Jesus said to them, "These are my words that I spoke to you while I was still with you—that everything written about me in the Law from Moses, the Prophets, and the Psalms must be fulfilled." ⁴⁵Then he opened their minds to understand the scriptures. ⁴⁶He said to them, "This is what is written: the Christ will suffer and rise from the dead on the third day, ⁴⁷and a change of heart and life for the forgiveness of sins must be preached in his name to all nations, beginning from Jerusalem. ⁴⁸You are witnesses of these things. ⁴⁹Look, I'm sending to you what my Father promised, but you are to stay in the city until you have been furnished with heavenly power."

Ascension of Jesus

⁵⁰He led them out as far as Bethany, where he lifted his hands and blessed them. ⁵¹As he blessed them, he left them and was taken up to heaven. ⁵²They worshipped him and returned to Jerusalem overwhelmed with joy. ⁵³And they were continuously in the temple praising God.

JOHN

THEME

Jesus is the heaven-sent Son of God and the giver of eternal life to all who believe in him.

INTRODUCTION

The early church symbol for the Gospel of John is the eagle. According to the church scholar Jerome (349–420 CE), each New Testament Gospel can be identified with one of the faces of the four creatures in the vision of Ezekiel (see Ezekiel 1 and 10). One of the four, the eagle, was thought to best represent the Gospel of John. An eagle soars in the heights with majestic patterns of flight. So John's Gospel soars to heaven and swoops back to earth, telling the story of Jesus the Christ.

THE UNIQUENESS OF JOHN'S GOSPEL

John is the odd one out of the four New Testament Gospels. The first three Gospels are very similar in content. In fact, Matthew, Mark, and Luke are so similar that the earliest must have been used in composing the other two. But the Gospel of John is very different from these other Gospels. For example, in John's Gospel Jesus offers no parables; he does not give a long sermon (compare Matthew 5–7; Luke 6:20-49); he does not give brief sayings and teachings (such as Mark 2:27; 3:28-29); all miracles are signs of his identity (and not simply acts of mercy).

John is also unique in its use of opposites or contrasts. The Gospel constantly contrasts light and darkness; Jesus and the disciples with the Jewish leaders; and so forth. Embedded in these contrasts is a strong use of symbolism. The Gospel's use of symbolism is not meant to suggest that things did not really happen as presented. Rather, the use of symbolism is an attempt to help the reader penetrate deeper into the greater significance and meaning of events.

How can the uniqueness of John's Gospel be explained? People, geography, times, and intended purpose influence the writing of any document. These influences are important for understanding the uniqueness of John's Gospel.

THE PEOPLE BEHIND JOHN'S GOSPEL

The earliest reference to the writer of this Gospel is from the church leader Irenaeus (ca. 130–203 CE). He states that this Gospel was written in Ephesus by

John, the disciple of Jesus. Irenaeus received this information from his teacher, Polycarp (ca. 70–155 CE), who knew John the apostle personally. But this information must be taken with some caution, because early church writers have not always been proven correct.

Perhaps the writer left his masked signature in the Gospel narrative. The Gospel contains several references to a dearly loved disciple who is present at important points in the story but is never named (see 13:23-25; 18:15-16; 20:2-10). According to John 21:20-25, this disciple is the author of this Gospel.

However, things are not that simple. A good analysis of the text indicates different styles of writing and word choice. This implies editing and revision by different individuals. The final edition that we find in our New Testament was probably completed between 80 and 100 CE.

This brings up an intriguing question. Were the writer of John and his disciples aware of the other Gospels during these stages of development? Certainly as an eyewitness, the writer of John would have drawn from the same basic pool of information that influenced the other Gospel writers. But it is more likely that John and his disciples never knew the other Gospels in their finished state as we know them today. If they did know the other Gospels, it was probably in some form of a rough draft.

THE STRUCTURE OF JOHN'S GOSPEL

John is a carefully finished account of Jesus' life. Material was chosen and organized with care to announce a central theme: Eternal life comes through Jesus Christ, and this is God's purpose for humanity. This is accomplished in two ways: First, Jesus is directly related to four major Jewish festivals. Second, signs play a very important role, pointing to the central message. For example, there are signs of turning water into wine (2:1-11), healing the sick (4:43-54), feeding the five thousand (6:1-15), and raising Lazarus from the dead (11:1-44). All of these signs point to eternal life through Christ. At the end of the Gospel, the reader is assured that Jesus did additional signs, which the disciples witnessed (20:30). The Gospel also has an introductory section, which attempts to prepare the minds of the readers, and a concluding chapter that challenges believers and disciples to follow Jesus (21:22).

THE PURPOSE OF JOHN'S GOSPEL

This is by far the most important aspect of the Gospel. What was the intention of those behind this writing? It seems quite clear that the Gospel is meant to help the reader understand the identity of Jesus as the Christ and the Son of God and to initiate response to him (see 20:31). But what else can we know about the purpose of John's Gospel?

As noted above, this Gospel is written for early church believers. On the one hand, tradition tells us that John the apostle was involved with a particular congregation or church in Ephesus. Perhaps he was associated with several congregations in and outside of this city. But more than likely one community was his home congregation. This particular congregation was the setting for the formation of John's Gospel. Like all other New Testament documents, John was written with a particular living church situation in mind. On the other hand, through this one congregation, the Gospel addresses all humanity and the church universal. This is the complete audience to whom the message is directed. But with the help of this particular congregation, we can better hear what John is saying about Jesus the Christ.

The social structures of the first century make some useful suggestions about church congregations. Beyond the Gentile/Jewish distinction, a church in Asia Minor would have been composed of two groups of believers: Jewish Christians and Hellenistic or Greek-influenced Christians. The Jewish believers would have tended to see Christ through the Jewish Torah, or Instruction. The Hellenistic Christians would have tended to see Christ through Greek philosophy, culture, and wisdom. It would follow that Jewish converts would have had difficulty accepting Jesus as more than a man (that is, divine). The Hellenistic Christians would have had difficulty thinking of Jesus as less than divine (that is, human) because of the influence of Greek philosophy.

In the middle of these social groups, John's purpose emerges. He seeks to present a very balanced Christ who is more than human as fully God, and yet not less than God, despite having become fully human. Christ is the true mediator of God and humankind. John then goes on to use Jesus' teachings about love and unity to encourage the congregation(s) to seek oneness in Christ (chapters 13–17). This is John's deeper theological purpose.

JOHN AND RELATED NEW TESTAMENT WRITINGS

The apostle behind the Gospel also influenced the three letters of John and the book of Revelation. The tension noted above between Jewish Christians and Greek or Gentile Christians is probably behind the issues evident in these later writings. The first letter, for example, refers to an antichrist withdrawing from the community (1 John 2:18-19). The second letter speaks of deceivers who have gone out into the world but will not acknowledge Jesus Christ as having come in the flesh; such a person is "the deceiver and the antichrist" (2 John v. 7). In the third letter, Diotrephes the troublemaker is referred to as one "who likes to put himself first, [and] doesn't welcome us" (3 John v. 9). The letters of John and the book of Revelation indicate serious problems among John's followers. They confirm a continued need for a well-balanced, well-organized, and carefully presented witness to Jesus the Christ.

A FINAL WORD

Such is the uniqueness of John's Gospel. Knowing a little about the people behind this writing and its plan and purpose should help us soar on its wings to the heights of heaven and swoop back to earth for a better understanding of Jesus the Christ.

JOHN

Story of the Word

1 In the beginning was the Word
and the Word was with God
and the Word was God.

² The Word was with God in the beginning.

³ Everything came into being
through the Word,
and without the Word
nothing came into being.
What came into being
⁴ through the Word was life,[a]
and the life was the light for all people.

⁵ The light shines in the darkness,
and the darkness doesn't
extinguish the light.

⁶ A man named John was sent from God. ⁷ He came as a witness to testify concerning the light, so that through him everyone would believe in the light. ⁸ He himself wasn't the light, but his mission was to testify concerning the light.

⁹ The true light that shines on all people
was coming into the world.

¹⁰ The light was in the world,
and the world came into being
through the light,
but the world didn't recognize the light.

¹¹ The light came to his own people,
and his own people didn't welcome him.

¹² But those who did welcome him,
those who believed in his name,
he authorized to become God's children,

¹³ born not from blood
nor from human desire or passion,
but born from God.

¹⁴ The Word became flesh
and made his home among us.
We have seen his glory,
glory like that of a father's only son,
full of grace and truth.

¹⁵ John testified about him, crying out, "This is the one of whom I said, 'He who comes after me is greater than me because he existed before me.'"

¹⁶ From his fullness we have all received
grace upon grace;

¹⁷ as the Law was given through Moses,
so grace and truth came into being
through Jesus Christ.

¹⁸ No one has ever seen God.
God the only Son,
who is at the Father's side,
has made God known.

John's witness

¹⁹ This is John's testimony when the Jewish leaders in Jerusalem sent priests and Levites to ask him, "Who are you?"

²⁰ John confessed (he didn't deny but confessed), "I'm not the Christ."

²¹ They asked him, "Then who are you? Are you Elijah?"

John said, "I'm not."

"Are you the prophet?"

John answered, "No."

²² They asked, "Who are you? We need to give an answer to those who sent us. What do you say about yourself?"

²³ John replied,

"I am a voice crying out in the wilderness,
Make the Lord's path straight,[b]
just as the prophet Isaiah said."

²⁴ Those sent by the Pharisees ²⁵ asked, "Why do you baptize if you aren't the Christ, nor Elijah, nor the prophet?"

²⁶ John answered, "I baptize with water. Someone greater stands among you, whom you don't recognize. ²⁷ He comes after me, but I'm not worthy to untie his sandal straps." ²⁸ This encounter took place across the Jordan in Bethany where John was baptizing.

²⁹ The next day John saw Jesus coming toward him and said, "Look! The Lamb of God who takes away the sin of the world! ³⁰ This is the one about whom I said, 'He who comes after me is really greater than me because he existed before me.' ³¹ Even I didn't recognize him, but I came baptizing with water so that he might be made known to Israel." ³² John testified, "I saw the Spirit coming down from heaven like a

---

[a]Or Everything came into being through the Word, / and without the Word / nothing came into being that came into being. In the Word was life   [b]Isa 40:3

dove, and it rested on him. ³³Even I didn't recognize him, but the one who sent me to baptize with water said to me, 'The one on whom you see the Spirit coming down and resting is the one who baptizes with the Holy Spirit.' ³⁴I have seen and testified that this one is God's Son."

Jesus calls disciples

³⁵The next day John was standing again with two of his disciples. ³⁶When he saw Jesus walking along he said, "Look! The Lamb of God!" ³⁷The two disciples heard what he said, and they followed Jesus.

³⁸When Jesus turned and saw them following, he asked, "What are you looking for?"

They said, "Rabbi (which is translated *Teacher*), where are you staying?"

³⁹He replied, "Come and see." So they went and saw where he was staying, and they remained with him that day. It was about four o'clock in the afternoon.

⁴⁰One of the two disciples who heard what John said and followed Jesus was Andrew, the brother of Simon Peter. ⁴¹He first found his own brother Simon and said to him, "We have found the Messiah" (which is translated *Christ*^c). ⁴²He led him to Jesus. Jesus looked at him and said, "You are Simon, son of John. You will be called Cephas" (which is translated *Peter*).

⁴³The next day Jesus wanted to go into Galilee, and he found Philip. Jesus said to him, "Follow me." ⁴⁴Philip was from Bethsaida, the hometown of Andrew and Peter.

⁴⁵Philip found Nathanael and said to him, "We have found the one Moses wrote about in the Law and the Prophets: Jesus, Joseph's son, from Nazareth."

⁴⁶Nathanael responded, "Can anything from Nazareth be good?"

Philip said, "Come and see."

⁴⁷Jesus saw Nathanael coming toward him and said about him, "Here is a genuine Israelite in whom there is no deceit."

⁴⁸Nathanael asked him, "How do you know me?"

Jesus answered, "Before Philip called you, I saw you under the fig tree."

⁴⁹Nathanael replied, "Rabbi, you are God's Son. You are the king of Israel."

⁵⁰Jesus answered, "Do you believe because I told you that I saw you under the fig tree? You will see greater things than these! ⁵¹I assure you that you will see heaven open and God's angels going up to heaven and down to earth on the Human One."^d

Wedding at Cana

2 On the third day there was a wedding in Cana of Galilee. Jesus' mother was there, and ²Jesus and his disciples were also invited to the celebration. ³When the wine ran out, Jesus' mother said to him, "They don't have any wine."

⁴Jesus replied, "Woman, what does that have to do with me? My time hasn't come yet."

⁵His mother told the servants, "Do whatever he tells you." ⁶Nearby were six stone water jars used for the Jewish cleansing ritual, each able to hold about twenty or thirty gallons.

^cOr Anointed One   ^dOr Son of Man

RABBI

Throughout rabbinic literature, *rabbi* means "master" and "teacher of disciples." As such, a rabbi serves as a metaphorical father. These meanings are still in use in the modern era. *Rabbi* derives from the Hebrew term meaning "mighty," "great," or "numerous." In the NT, *rabbi* is explained as "teacher" in Matthew 23:8 and John 1:38 (cf. John 20:16). The term *rabbi* is transliterated frequently in Mark, Matthew, and John but is absent from Luke. In almost every NT citation, the term *rabbi* refers to Jesus.

⁷Jesus said to the servants, "Fill the jars with water," and they filled them to the brim. ⁸Then he told them, "Now draw some from them and take it to the headwaiter," and they did. ⁹The headwaiter tasted the water that had become wine. He didn't know where it came from, though the servants who had drawn the water knew.

The headwaiter called the groom ¹⁰and said, "Everyone serves the good wine first. They bring out the second-rate wine only when the guests are drinking freely. You kept the good wine until now." ¹¹This was the first miraculous sign that Jesus did in Cana of Galilee. He revealed his glory, and his disciples believed in him.

¹²After this, Jesus and his mother, his brothers, and his disciples went down to Capernaum and stayed there for a few days.

Jesus in Jerusalem at Passover

¹³It was nearly time for the Jewish Passover, and Jesus went up to Jerusalem. ¹⁴He found in the temple those who were selling cattle, sheep, and doves, as well as those involved in exchanging currency sitting there. ¹⁵He made a whip from ropes and chased them all out of the temple, including the cattle and the sheep. He scattered the coins and overturned the tables of those who exchanged currency. ¹⁶He said to the dove

ᵉPs 69:9

sellers, "Get these things out of here! Don't make my Father's house a place of business." ¹⁷His disciples remembered that it is written, *Passion for your house consumes me.*ᵉ

¹⁸Then the Jewish leaders asked him, "By what authority are you doing these things? What miraculous sign will you show us?"

¹⁹Jesus answered, "Destroy this temple and in three days I'll raise it up."

²⁰The Jewish leaders replied, "It took forty-six years to build this temple, and you will raise it up in three days?" ²¹But the temple Jesus was talking about was his body. ²²After he was raised from the dead, his disciples remembered what he had said, and they believed the scripture and the word that Jesus had spoken.

²³While Jesus was in Jerusalem for the Passover Festival, many believed in his name because they saw the miraculous signs that he did. ²⁴But Jesus didn't trust himself to them because he knew all people. ²⁵He didn't need anyone to tell him about human nature, for he knew what human nature was.

Jesus and Nicodemus

3 There was a Pharisee named Nicodemus, a Jewish leader. ²He came to Jesus at night and said to him, "Rabbi, we know that you are a teacher who has come from

CANA

A city of Galilee. In the NT, Cana is mentioned only in the Gospel of John (2:1-11; 4:46; 21:2). Its name probably comes from the Hebrew for "reed." The location of Cana of Galilee is uncertain. Ancient pilgrim literature primarily lists two locations. One of these, Kefr Kenna, is just 4 mi. from Nazareth and on the road to Capernaum and Bethsaida. This location suggests the site arose as a conveniently accessible location for pilgrims. On the other hand, the other site, Khirbet Qana, is 8 mi. northwest of Nazareth on the north side of the Bet Netofa Valley. Initial results of an archaeological excavation at Khirbet Qana support the site's identification as Cana of Galilee. The excavation has revealed an active settlement at the location from the Hellenistic through the early Arab periods. Especially notable is a cave that matches the description of a veneration cave in pilgrim accounts of Cana.

God, for no one could do these miraculous signs that you do unless God is with him."

³Jesus answered, "I assure you, unless someone is born anew,[f] it's not possible to see God's kingdom."

⁴Nicodemus asked, "How is it possible for an adult to be born? It's impossible to enter the mother's womb for a second time and be born, isn't it?"

⁵Jesus answered, "I assure you, unless someone is born of water and the Spirit, it's not possible to enter God's kingdom. ⁶Whatever is born of the flesh is flesh, and whatever is born of the Spirit is spirit. ⁷Don't be surprised that I said to you, 'You must be born anew.' ⁸God's Spirit[g] blows wherever it wishes. You hear its sound, but you don't know where it comes from or where it is going. It's the same with everyone who is born of the Spirit."

⁹Nicodemus said, "How are these things possible?"

¹⁰"Jesus answered, "You are a teacher of Israel and you don't know these things? ¹¹I assure you that we speak about what we know and testify about what we have seen, but you don't receive our testimony. ¹²If I have told you about earthly things and you don't believe, how will you believe if I tell you about heavenly things? ¹³No one has gone up to heaven except the one who came down from heaven, the Human One.[h] ¹⁴Just as Moses lifted up the snake in the wilderness, so must the Human One[i] be lifted up ¹⁵so that everyone who believes in him will have eternal life. ¹⁶God so loved the world that he gave his only Son, so that everyone who believes in him won't perish but will have eternal life. ¹⁷God didn't send his Son into the world to judge the world, but that the world might be saved through him. ¹⁸Whoever believes in him isn't judged; whoever doesn't believe in him is already judged, because they don't believe in the name of God's only Son.

¹⁹"This is the basis for judgment: The light came into the world, and people loved darkness more than the light, for their actions are evil. ²⁰All who do wicked things hate the light and don't come to the light for fear that their actions will be exposed to the light. ²¹Whoever does the truth comes to the light so that it can be seen that their actions were done in God."

John's final witness

²²After this Jesus and his disciples went into Judea, where he spent some time with them and was baptizing. ²³John was baptizing at Aenon near Salem because there was a lot of water there, and people were coming to him and being baptized. (²⁴John hadn't yet been thrown into prison.)

²⁵A debate started between John's disciples and a certain Jew about cleansing rituals. ²⁶They came to John and said, "Rabbi, look! The man who was with you across the Jordan, the one about whom you testified, is baptizing and everyone is flocking to him."

²⁷John replied, "No one can receive anything unless it is given from heaven. ²⁸You yourselves can testify that I said that I'm not the Christ but that I'm the one sent before him. ²⁹The groom is the one who is getting married. The friend of the groom stands close by and, when he hears him, is overjoyed at the groom's voice. Therefore, my joy is now complete. ³⁰He must increase and I must decrease. ³¹The one who comes from above is above all things. The one who is from the earth belongs to the earth and speaks as one from the earth. The one who comes from heaven is above all things. ³²He testifies to what he has seen and heard, but no one accepts his testimony. ³³Whoever accepts his testimony confirms that God is true. ³⁴The one whom God sent speaks God's words because God gives the Spirit generously. ³⁵The Father loves the Son and gives everything into his hands. ³⁶Whoever believes in the Son has eternal life. Whoever doesn't believe in the Son won't see life, but the angry judgment of God remains on them."

Jesus leaves Judea

4 Jesus learned that the Pharisees had heard that he was making more disciples

---

[f] Or from above [g] Or wind [h] Or Son of Man [i] Or Son of Man

and baptizing more than John (²although Jesus' disciples were baptizing, not Jesus himself). ³Therefore, he left Judea and went back to Galilee.

Jesus in Samaria

⁴Jesus had to go through Samaria. ⁵He came to a Samaritan city called Sychar, which was near the land Jacob had given to his son Joseph. ⁶Jacob's well was there. Jesus was tired from his journey, so he sat down at the well. It was about noon.

⁷A Samaritan woman came to the well to draw water. Jesus said to her, "Give me some water to drink." ⁸His disciples had gone into the city to buy him some food.

⁹The Samaritan woman asked, "Why do you, a Jewish man, ask for something to drink from me, a Samaritan woman?" (Jews and Samaritans didn't associate with each other.)

¹⁰Jesus responded, "If you recognized God's gift and who is saying to you, 'Give me some water to drink,' you would be asking him and he would give you living water."

¹¹The woman said to him, "Sir, you don't have a bucket and the well is deep. Where would you get this living water? ¹²You aren't greater than our father Jacob, are you? He gave this well to us, and he drank from it himself, as did his sons and his livestock."

¹³Jesus answered, "Everyone who drinks this water will be thirsty again, ¹⁴but whoever drinks from the water that I will give will never be thirsty again. The water that I give will become in those who drink it a spring of water that bubbles up into eternal life."

¹⁵The woman said to him, "Sir, give me this water, so that I will never be thirsty and will never need to come here to draw water!"

¹⁶Jesus said to her, "Go, get your husband, and come back here."

¹⁷The woman replied, "I don't have a husband."

"You are right to say, 'I don't have a husband,'" Jesus answered. ¹⁸"You've had five husbands, and the man you are with now isn't your husband. You've spoken the truth."

¹⁹The woman said, "Sir, I see that you are a prophet. ²⁰Our ancestors worshipped on this mountain, but you and your people say that it is necessary to worship in Jerusalem."

²¹Jesus said to her, "Believe me, woman,

SAMARITAN WOMAN

A woman of Samaria who meets Jesus at a well near the city of Sychar, has an extended personal and theological discussion with him, and bears witness to his identity as prophet and Messiah before her townspeople. John 4:7-26 represents the longest and most evenly balanced dialogue between Jesus and an individual in the canonical Gospels. The Samaritan woman holds her own (speaking roughly as much as Jesus) and is a worthy conversation partner on two matters of theological substance. First, she questions Jesus' offer of "living water" with reference to scriptural traditions surrounding ancestor Jacob (4:11-12). Second, she initiates discussion about the proper central place for worshiping God, a major dividing point between Samaritans and Jews (4:19-20). Although in both cases Jesus corrects the woman's misunderstanding, she consistently exhibits an open and receptive heart to match her sharp and inquisitive mind. As a result of her testimony—a high vocation in the Fourth Gospel (1:6-9, 15, 19-34, 40-46)—"many Samaritans . . . believed in Jesus," and many others were prompted to hear his "word" for themselves and to profess him as "truly the savior of the world" (4:39-42).

the time is coming when you and your people will worship the Father neither on this mountain nor in Jerusalem. ²²You and your people worship what you don't know; we worship what we know because salvation is from the Jews. ²³But the time is coming—and is here!—when true worshippers will worship in spirit and truth. The Father looks for those who worship him this way. ²⁴God is spirit, and it is necessary to worship God in spirit and truth."

²⁵The woman said, "I know that the Messiah is coming, the one who is called the Christ. When he comes, he will teach everything to us."

²⁶Jesus said to her, "I Am—the one who speaks with you."^j

²⁷Just then, Jesus' disciples arrived and were shocked that he was talking with a woman. But no one asked, "What do you want?" or "Why are you talking with her?" ²⁸The woman put down her water jar and went into the city. She said to the people, ²⁹"Come and see a man who has told me everything I've done! Could this man be the Christ?" ³⁰They left the city and were on their way to see Jesus.

³¹In the meantime the disciples spoke to Jesus, saying, "Rabbi, eat."

³²Jesus said to them, "I have food to eat that you don't know about."

³³The disciples asked each other, "Has someone brought him food?"

³⁴Jesus said to them, "I am fed by doing the will of the one who sent me and by completing his work. ³⁵Don't you have a saying, 'Four more months and then it's time for harvest'? Look, I tell you: open your eyes and notice that the fields are already ripe for the harvest. ³⁶Those who harvest are receiving their pay and gathering fruit for eternal life so that those who sow and those who harvest can celebrate together. ³⁷This is a true saying, that one sows and another harvests. ³⁸I have sent you to harvest what you didn't work hard for; others worked hard, and you will share in their hard work."

³⁹Many Samaritans in that city believed in Jesus because of the woman's word when she testified, "He told me everything I've ever done." ⁴⁰So when the Samaritans came to Jesus, they asked him to stay with them, and he stayed there two days. ⁴¹Many more believed because of his word, ⁴²and they said to the woman, "We no longer believe because of what you said, for we have heard for ourselves and know that this one is truly the savior of the world."

Jesus arrives in Galilee

⁴³After two days Jesus left for Galilee. (⁴⁴Jesus himself had testified that prophets have no honor in their own country.) ⁴⁵When he came to Galilee, the Galileans welcomed him because they had seen all the things he had done in Jerusalem during the festival, for they also had been at the festival.

Jesus' second miraculous sign in Galilee

⁴⁶He returned to Cana in Galilee where he had turned the water into wine. In Capernaum there was a certain royal official whose son was sick. ⁴⁷When he heard that Jesus was coming from Judea to Galilee, he went out to meet him and asked Jesus if he would come and heal his son, for his son was about to die. ⁴⁸Jesus said to him, "Unless you see miraculous signs and wonders, you won't believe."

⁴⁹The royal official said to him, "Lord, come before my son dies."

⁵⁰Jesus replied, "Go home. Your son lives." The man believed the word that Jesus spoke to him and set out for his home.

⁵¹While he was on his way, his servants were already coming to meet him. They said, "Your son lives!" ⁵²So he asked them at what time his son had started to get better. And they said, "The fever left him yesterday at about one o'clock in the afternoon." ⁵³Then the father realized that this was the hour when Jesus had said to him, "Your son lives." And he and his entire household believed in Jesus. ⁵⁴This was the second miraculous sign Jesus did while going from Judea to Galilee.

^jOr It is I, the one who speaks with you.

Sabbath healing

5 After this there was a Jewish festival, and Jesus went up to Jerusalem. ²In Jerusalem near the Sheep Gate in the north city wall is a pool with the Aramaic name Bethsaida. It had five covered porches, ³and a crowd of people who were sick, blind, lame, and paralyzed sat there.ᵏ ⁵A certain man was there who had been sick for thirty-eight years. ⁶When Jesus saw him lying there, knowing that he had already been there a long time, he asked him, "Do you want to get well?"

⁷The sick man answered him, "Sir,ˡ I don't have anyone who can put me in the water when it is stirred up. When I'm trying to get to it, someone else has gotten in ahead of me."

⁸Jesus said to him, "Get up! Pick up your mat and walk." ⁹Immediately the man was well, and he picked up his mat and walked. Now that day was the Sabbath.

¹⁰The Jewish leaders said to the man who had been healed, "It's the Sabbath; you aren't allowed to carry your mat."

¹¹He answered, "The man who made me well said to me, 'Pick up your mat and walk.'"

¹²They inquired, "Who is this man who said to you, 'Pick it up and walk'?" ¹³The man who had been cured didn't know who it was, because Jesus had slipped away from the crowd gathered there.

¹⁴Later Jesus found him in the temple and said, "See! You have been made well.

Don't sin anymore in case something worse happens to you." ¹⁵The man went and proclaimed to the Jewish leaders that Jesus was the man who had made him well.

¹⁶As a result, the Jewish leaders were harassing Jesus, since he had done these things on the Sabbath. ¹⁷Jesus replied, "My Father is still working, and I am working too." ¹⁸For this reason the Jewish leaders wanted even more to kill him—not only because he was doing away with the Sabbath but also because he called God his own Father, thereby making himself equal with God.

Work of the Father and the Son

¹⁹Jesus responded to the Jewish leaders, "I assure you that the Son can't do anything by himself except what he sees the Father doing. Whatever the Father does, the Son does likewise. ²⁰The Father loves the Son and shows him everything that he does. He will show him greater works than these so that you will marvel. ²¹As the Father raises the dead and gives life, so too does the Son give life to whomever he wishes. ²²The Father doesn't judge anyone, but he has given all judgment to the Son ²³so that everyone will honor the Son just as they honor the Father. Whoever doesn't honor the Son doesn't honor the Father who sent him.

²⁴"I assure you that whoever hears my word and believes in the one who sent me has eternal life and won't come under judgment but has passed from death into life.

ᵏCritical editions of the Gk New Testament do not include the following addition *waiting for the water to move.*
ˡ *Sometimes an angel would come down to the pool and stir up the water. Then the first one going into the water after it had been stirred up was cured of any sickness.* ˡOr *Lord*

BETHSAIDA/BETHESDA

Two large pools with five colonnades in Jerusalem at the end of the Second Temple Period, located north of the temple compound. Excavations have revealed that a health rite took place there during the Roman period. The lower of the two pools was probably used for washing sheep, which were then sold for sacrifices at the nearby temple. The name *Bethesda* continues to survive as a symbol of healing to this day.

²⁵"I assure you that the time is coming—and is here!—when the dead will hear the voice of God's Son, and those who hear it will live. ²⁶Just as the Father has life in himself, so he has granted the Son to have life in himself. ²⁷He gives the Son authority to judge, because he is the Human One.[m] ²⁸Don't be surprised by this, because the time is coming when all who are in their graves will hear his voice. ²⁹Those who did good things will come out into the resurrection of life, and those who did wicked things into the resurrection of judgment. ³⁰I can't do anything by myself. Whatever I hear, I judge, and my judgment is just. I don't seek my own will but the will of the one who sent me.

Witnesses to Jesus

³¹"If I testify about myself, my testimony isn't true. ³²There is someone else who testifies about me, and I know his testimony about me is true. ³³You sent a delegation to John, and he testified to the truth. ³⁴Although I don't accept human testimony, I say these things so that you can be saved. ³⁵John was a burning and shining lamp, and, at least for a while, you were willing to celebrate in his light.

³⁶"I have a witness greater than John's testimony. The Father has given me works to do so that I might complete them. These works I do testify about me that the Father sent me. ³⁷And the Father who sent me testifies about me. You have never even heard his voice or seen his form, ³⁸and you don't have his word dwelling with you because you don't believe the one whom he has sent. ³⁹Examine the scriptures, since you think that in them you have eternal life. They also testify about me, ⁴⁰yet you don't want to come to me so that you can have life.

⁴¹"I don't accept praise from people, ⁴²but I know you, that you don't have God's love in you. ⁴³I have come in my Father's name, and you don't receive me. If others come in their own name, you receive them. ⁴⁴How can you believe when you receive praise from each other but don't seek the praise that comes from the only God?

⁴⁵"Don't think that I will accuse you before the Father. Your accuser is Moses, the one in whom your hope rests. ⁴⁶If you believed Moses, you would believe me, because Moses wrote about me. ⁴⁷If you don't believe the writings of Moses, how will you believe my words?"

Feeding of the five thousand

6 After this Jesus went across the Galilee Sea (that is, the Tiberias Sea). ²A large crowd followed him, because they had seen the miraculous signs he had done among the sick. ³Jesus went up a mountain and sat there with his disciples. ⁴It was nearly time for Passover, the Jewish festival.

⁵Jesus looked up and saw the large crowd coming toward him. He asked Philip, "Where will we buy food to feed these people?" ⁶Jesus said this to test him, for he already knew what he was going to do.

⁷Philip replied, "More than a half year's salary[n] worth of food wouldn't be enough for each person to have even a little bit."

⁸One of his disciples, Andrew, Simon Peter's brother, said, ⁹"A youth here has five barley loaves and two fish. But what good is that for a crowd like this?"

¹⁰Jesus said, "Have the people sit down." There was plenty of grass there. They sat down, about five thousand of them. ¹¹Then Jesus took the bread. When he had given thanks, he distributed it to those who were sitting there. He did the same with the fish, each getting as much as they wanted. ¹²When they had plenty to eat, he said to his disciples, "Gather up the leftover pieces, so that nothing will be wasted." ¹³So they gathered them and filled twelve baskets with the pieces of the five barley loaves that had been left over by those who had eaten.

¹⁴When the people saw that he had done a miraculous sign, they said, "This is truly the prophet who is coming into the world." ¹⁵Jesus understood that they were about to come and force him to be their king, so he took refuge again, alone on a mountain.

---

[m]Or Son of Man [n]Or two hundred denaria

Jesus walks on water

¹⁶When evening came, Jesus' disciples went down to the lake. ¹⁷They got into a boat and were crossing the lake to Capernaum. It was already getting dark and Jesus hadn't come to them yet. ¹⁸The water was getting rough because a strong wind was blowing. ¹⁹When the wind had driven them out for about three or four miles, they saw Jesus walking on the water. He was approaching the boat and they were afraid. ²⁰He said to them, "I Am.° Don't be afraid." ²¹Then they wanted to take him into the boat, and just then the boat reached the land where they had been heading.

²²The next day the crowd that remained on the other side of the lake realized that only one boat had been there. They knew Jesus hadn't gone with his disciples, but that the disciples had gone alone. ²³Some boats came from Tiberias, near the place where they had eaten the bread over which the Lord had given thanks. ²⁴When the crowd saw that neither Jesus nor his disciples were there, they got into the boats and came to Capernaum looking for Jesus. ²⁵When they found him on the other side of the lake, they asked him, "Rabbi, when did you get here?"

Bread of life

²⁶Jesus replied, "I assure you that you are looking for me not because you saw miraculous signs but because you ate all the food you wanted. ²⁷Don't work for the food that doesn't last but for the food that endures for eternal life, which the Human One^P will give you. God the Father has confirmed him as his agent to give life."

²⁸They asked, "What must we do in order to accomplish what God requires?"

²⁹Jesus replied, "This is what God re-

°Or *It is I.*   ^POr *Son of Man*

GALILEE SEA

The Galilee Sea is a freshwater lake located in northern Palestine. At its greatest length, the present-day lake stretches approximately 13 mi.; at its widest point, it is approximately seven mi. across. Its primary source is the Jordan River, which flows into it from Mount Hermon to the north and exits to the south toward the Dead Sea, though it is also filled by other streams and springs.

By the early 1st century CE, the coast of the lake was dotted with villages and small cities. On the western coast stood Capernaum, Ginnesar, Magdala (also known as Taricheae), and Hammath, famous for its hot springs. Around 20 CE, Herod Antipas built his capital city Tiberias on the lakeside, naming it after the current emperor. Another city, perhaps Philoteria, was located at Beth-yerah on the southern shore. The southeastern portion of the lake adjoined the Decapolis, an administrative district within the province of Syria, and the Decapolis city of Hippos stood directly across the lake from Tiberias. The northeastern portion of the lake, including Bethsaida, was included within the territory of the Herodian king Philip. Territorial boundaries changed throughout the 1st century; at the time of the first Jewish Revolt, for example, Tiberias, Magdala, and the former territory of Philip belonged to Agrippa II. The area west of the lake was predominantly Jewish; that to its east was mostly Gentile. Thus Jesus would have encountered Gentiles in his travels around the lake.

quires, that you believe in him whom God sent."

³⁰They asked, "What miraculous sign will you do, that we can see and believe you? What will you do? ³¹Our ancestors ate manna in the wilderness, just as it is written, *He gave them bread from heaven to eat.*"�q

³²Jesus told them, "I assure you, it wasn't Moses who gave the bread from heaven to you, but my Father gives you the true bread from heaven. ³³The bread of God is the one who comes down from heaven and gives life to the world."

³⁴They said, "Sir,ʳ give us this bread all the time!"

³⁵Jesus replied, "I am the bread of life. Whoever comes to me will never go hungry, and whoever believes in me will never be thirsty. ³⁶But I told you that you have seen me and still don't believe. ³⁷Everyone whom the Father gives to me will come to me, and I won't send away anyone who comes to me. ³⁸I have come down from heaven not to do my will, but the will of him who sent me. ³⁹This is the will of the one who sent me, that I won't lose anything he has given me, but I will raise it up at the last day. ⁴⁰This is my Father's will: that all who see the Son and believe in him will have eternal life, and I will raise them up at the last day."

⁴¹The Jewish opposition grumbled about him because he said, "I am the bread that came down from heaven."

⁴²They asked, "Isn't this Jesus, Joseph's son, whose mother and father we know? How can he now say, 'I have come down from heaven'?"

⁴³Jesus responded, "Don't grumble among yourselves. ⁴⁴No one can come to me unless they are drawn to me by the Father who sent me, and I will raise them up at the last day. ⁴⁵It is written in the Prophets, And they *will all be taught by God.*ˢ Everyone who has listened to the Father and learned from him comes to me. ⁴⁶No one has seen the Father except the one who is from God. He has seen the Father. ⁴⁷I assure you, whoever believes has eternal life. ⁴⁸I am the bread of life. ⁴⁹Your ancestors ate manna in the wil-

derness and they died. ⁵⁰This is the bread that comes down from heaven so that whoever eats from it will never die. ⁵¹I am the living bread that came down from heaven. Whoever eats this bread will live forever, and the bread that I will give for the life of the world is my flesh."

⁵²Then the Jews debated among themselves, asking, "How can this man give us his flesh to eat?"

⁵³Jesus said to them, "I assure you, unless you eat the flesh of the Human Oneᵗ and drink his blood, you have no life in you. ⁵⁴Whoever eats my flesh and drinks my blood has eternal life, and I will raise them up at the last day. ⁵⁵My flesh is true food and my blood is true drink. ⁵⁶Whoever eats my flesh and drinks my blood remains in me and I in them. ⁵⁷As the living Father sent me, and I live because of the Father, so whoever eats me lives because of me. ⁵⁸This is the bread that came down from heaven. It isn't like the bread your ancestors ate, and then they died. Whoever eats this bread will live forever." ⁵⁹Jesus said these things while he was teaching in the synagogue in Capernaum.

⁶⁰Many of his disciples who heard this said, "This message is harsh. Who can hear it?"

⁶¹Jesus knew that the disciples were grumbling about this and he said to them, "Does this offend you? ⁶²What if you were to see the Human Oneᵘ going up where he was before? ⁶³The Spirit is the one who gives life and the flesh doesn't help at all. The words I have spoken to you are spirit and life. ⁶⁴Yet some of you don't believe." Jesus knew from the beginning who wouldn't believe and the one who would betray him. ⁶⁵He said, "For this reason I said to you that none can come to me unless the Father enables them to do so." ⁶⁶At this, many of his disciples turned away and no longer accompanied him.

⁶⁷Jesus asked the Twelve, "Do you also want to leave?"

⁶⁸Simon Peter answered, "Lord, where would we go? You have the words of eternal

---

�q Ps 78:24   ʳ Or Lord   ˢ Isa 54:13   ᵗ Or Son of Man   ᵘ Or Son of Man life. ⁶⁹We believe and know that you are God's holy one."

⁷⁰Jesus replied, "Didn't I choose you twelve? Yet one of you is a devil." ⁷¹He was speaking of Judas, Simon Iscariot's son, for he, one of the Twelve, was going to betray him.

Jesus goes to Jerusalem

7After this Jesus traveled throughout Galilee. He didn't want to travel in Judea, because the Jewish authorities wanted to kill him. ²When it was almost time for the Jewish Festival of Booths, ³Jesus' brothers said to him, "Leave Galilee. Go to Judea so that your disciples can see the amazing works that you do. ⁴Those who want to be known publicly don't do things secretly. Since you can do these things, show yourself to the world." ⁵His brothers said this because even they didn't believe in him.

⁶Jesus replied, "For you, anytime is fine. But my time hasn't come yet. ⁷The world can't hate you. It hates me, though, because I testify that its works are evil. ⁸You go up to the festival. I'm not going to this one because my time hasn't yet come." ⁹Having said this, he stayed in Galilee. ¹⁰However, after his brothers left for the festival, he went too—not openly but in secret.

¹¹The Jewish leaders were looking for Jesus at the festival. They kept asking, "Where is he?" ¹²The crowds were murmuring about him. "He's a good man," some said, but others were saying, "No, he tricks the people." ¹³No one spoke about him publicly, though, for fear of the Jewish authorities.

Jesus teaches in the temple

¹⁴Halfway through the festival, Jesus went up to the temple and started to teach. ¹⁵Astonished, the Jewish leaders asked, "He's never been taught! How has he mastered the Law?"

¹⁶Jesus responded, "My teaching isn't mine but comes from the one who sent me. ¹⁷Whoever wants to do God's will can tell whether my teaching is from God or whether I speak on my own. ¹⁸Those who speak on their own seek glory for themselves. Those who seek the glory of him who sent me are people of truth; there's no falsehood in them. ¹⁹Didn't Moses give you the Law? Yet none of you keep the Law. Why do you want to kill me?"

²⁰The crowd answered, "You have a demon. Who wants to kill you?"

²¹Jesus replied, "I did one work, and you were all astonished. ²²Because Moses gave you the commandment about circumcision

NICODEMUS

Nicodemus appears only in the Gospel of John (John 3:1-10; 7:45-52; 19:38-42). In Nicodemus's first appearance, he engages Jesus in debate. Jesus speaks to Nicodemus metaphorically. Nicodemus's words indicate that he has not understood the metaphor (John 3:9). Yet Nicodemus's initial approach to Jesus shows understanding. He calls Jesus "Rabbi" and "a teacher who has come from God" (John 3:2). Both the appellation of rabbi and the notion that Jesus is sent from God are important to John's presentation of Jesus (e.g., John 1:38, 49; 4:31; 6:41-42; 8:4).

Nicodemus's later appearances may suggest a growing understanding of Jesus. In Nicodemus's second appearance (John 7:45-52), he defends Jesus, saying the Law requires that the Pharisees give Jesus a fair hearing.

Finally, Nicodemus brings a great quantity of spices and helps Joseph of Arimathea bury Jesus (John 19:38-42).

(although it wasn't Moses but the patriarchs), you circumcise a man on the Sabbath. ²³If a man can be circumcised on the Sabbath without breaking Moses' Law, why are you angry with me because I made an entire man well on the Sabbath? ²⁴Don't judge according to appearances. Judge with right judgment."

²⁵Some people from Jerusalem said, "Isn't he the one they want to kill? ²⁶Here he is, speaking in public, yet they aren't saying anything to him. Could it be that our leaders actually think he is the Christ? ²⁷We know where he is from, but when the Christ comes, no one will know where he is from."

²⁸While Jesus was teaching in the temple, he exclaimed, "You know me and where I am from. I haven't come on my own. The one who sent me is true, and you don't know him. ²⁹I know him because I am from him and he sent me." ³⁰So they wanted to seize Jesus, but they couldn't because his time hadn't yet come.

³¹Many from that crowd believed in Jesus. They said, "When the Christ comes, will he do more miraculous signs than this man does?" ³²The Pharisees heard the crowd whispering such things about Jesus, and the chief priests and Pharisees sent guards to arrest him.

³³Therefore, Jesus said, "I'm still with you for a little while before I go to the one who sent me. ³⁴You will look for me, but you won't find me, and where I am you can't come."

³⁵The Jewish opposition asked each other, "Where does he intend to go that we can't find him? Surely he doesn't intend to go where our people have been scattered and are living among the Greeks! He isn't going to teach the Greeks, is he? ³⁶What does he mean when he says, 'You will look for me, but you won't find me, and where I am you can't come'?"

³⁷On the last and most important day of the festival, Jesus stood up and shouted,

"All who are thirsty should come to me!
³⁸ All who believe in me should drink!

As the scriptures said concerning me,ᵛ
Rivers of living water will flow out
from within him."

³⁹Jesus said this concerning the Spirit. Those who believed in him would soon receive the Spirit, but they hadn't experienced the Spirit yet since Jesus hadn't yet been glorified.

⁴⁰When some in the crowd heard these words, they said, "This man is truly the prophet." ⁴¹Others said, "He's the Christ." But others said, "The Christ can't come from Galilee, can he? ⁴²Didn't the scripture say that the Christ comes from David's family and from Bethlehem, David's village?" ⁴³So the crowd was divided over Jesus. ⁴⁴Some wanted to arrest him, but no one grabbed him.

⁴⁵The guards returned to the chief priests and Pharisees, who asked, "Why didn't you bring him?"

⁴⁶The guards answered, "No one has ever spoken the way he does."

⁴⁷The Pharisees replied, "Have you too been deceived? ⁴⁸Have any of the leaders believed in him? Has any Pharisee? ⁴⁹No, only this crowd, which doesn't know the Law. And they are under God's curse!"

⁵⁰Nicodemus, who was one of them and had come to Jesus earlier, said, ⁵¹"Our Law doesn't judge someone without first hearing him and learning what he is doing, does it?"

⁵²They answered him, "You are not from Galilee too, are you? Look it up and you will see that the prophet doesn't come from Galilee."

Pharisees test Jesus

⁵³They each went to their own homes, **8** And Jesus went to the Mount of Olives. ²Early in the morning he returned to the temple. All the people gathered around him, and he sat down and taught them. ³The legal experts and Pharisees brought a woman caught in adultery. Placing her

---

ᵛOr Whoever is thirsty should come to me and drink. Whoever believes in me, just as the scriptures said, rivers of living water will flow out from within them.

in the center of the group, ⁴they said to Jesus, "Teacher, this woman was caught in the act of committing adultery. ⁵In the Law, Moses commanded us to stone women like this. What do you say?" ⁶They said this to test him, because they wanted a reason to bring an accusation against him. Jesus bent down and wrote on the ground with his finger.

⁷They continued to question him, so he stood up and replied, "Whoever hasn't sinned should throw the first stone." ⁸Bending down again, he wrote on the ground. ⁹Those who heard him went away, one by one, beginning with the elders. Finally, only Jesus and the woman were left in the middle of the crowd. ¹⁰Jesus stood up and said to her, "Woman, where are they? Is there no one to condemn you?"

¹¹She said, "No one, sir."ʷ

Jesus said, "Neither do I condemn you. Go, and from now on, don't sin anymore."ˣ

Jesus continues to teach in the temple

¹²Jesus spoke to the people again, saying, "I am the light of the world. Whoever follows me won't walk in darkness but will have the light of life."

¹³Then the Pharisees said to him, "Because you are testifying about yourself, your testimony isn't valid."

¹⁴Jesus replied, "Even if I testify about myself, my testimony is true, since I know where I came from and where I'm going. You don't know where I come from or where I'm going. ¹⁵You judge according to human standards, but I judge no one. ¹⁶Even if I do judge, my judgment is truthful, because I'm not alone. My judgments come from me and from the Father who sent me. ¹⁷In your Law it is written that the witness of two people is true. ¹⁸I am one witness concerning myself, and the Father who sent me is the other."

¹⁹They asked him, "Where is your Father?"

Jesus answered, "You don't know me and you don't know my Father. If you knew me, you would also know my Father." ²⁰He spoke these words while he was teaching in the temple area known as the treasury. No one arrested him, because his time hadn't yet come.

²¹Jesus continued, "I'm going away. You will look for me, and you will die in your sin. Where I'm going, you can't come."

²²The Jewish leaders said, "He isn't going to kill himself, is he? Is that why he said, 'Where I'm going, you can't come'?"

²³He said to them, "You are from below; I'm from above. You are from this world; I'm not from this world. ²⁴This is why I told you that you would die in your sins. If you don't believe that I Am, you will die in your sins."

²⁵"Who are you?" they asked.

Jesus replied, "I'm exactly who I have claimed to be from the beginning. ²⁶I have many things to say in judgment concerning you. The one who sent me is true, and what I have heard from him I tell the world." ²⁷They didn't know he was speaking about his Father. ²⁸So Jesus said to them, "When the Human Oneʸ is lifted up,ᶻ then you will know that I Am.ᵃ Then you will know that I do nothing on my own, but I say just what the Father has taught me. ²⁹He who sent me is with me. He doesn't leave me by myself, because I always do what makes him happy." ³⁰While Jesus was saying these things, many people came to believe in him.

Children of Abraham

³¹Jesus said to the Jews who believed in him, "You are truly my disciples if you remain faithful to my teaching. ³²Then you will know the truth, and the truth will set you free."

³³They responded, "We are Abraham's children; we've never been anyone's slaves. How can you say that we will be set free?"

³⁴Jesus answered, "I assure you that everyone who sins is a slave to sin. ³⁵A slave

isn't a permanent member of the household, but a son is. [36]Therefore, if the Son makes you free, you really will be free. [37]I know that you are Abraham's children, yet you want to kill me because you don't welcome my teaching. [38]I'm telling you what I've seen when I am with the Father, but you are doing what you've heard from your father."

[39]They replied, "Our father is Abraham."

Jesus responded, "If you were Abraham's children, you would do Abraham's works. [40]Instead, you want to kill me, though I am the one who has spoken the truth I heard from God. Abraham didn't do this. [41]You are doing your father's works."

They said, "Our ancestry isn't in question! The only Father we have is God!"

[42]Jesus replied, "If God were your Father, you would love me, for I came from God. Here I am. I haven't come on my own. God sent me. [43]Why don't you understand what I'm saying? It's because you can't really hear my words. [44]Your father is the devil. You are his children, and you want to do what your father wants. He was a murderer from the beginning. He has never stood for the truth, because there's no truth in him. Whenever that liar speaks, he speaks according to his own nature, because he's a liar and the father of liars. [45]Because I speak the truth, you don't believe me. [46]Who among you can show I'm guilty of sin? Since I speak the truth, why don't you believe me? [47]God's children listen to God's words. You don't listen to me because you aren't God's children."

[48]The Jewish opposition answered, "We were right to say that you are a Samaritan and have a demon, weren't we?"

[49]"I don't have a demon," Jesus replied. "But I honor my Father and you dishonor me. [50]I'm not trying to bring glory to myself. There's one who is seeking to glorify me, and he's the judge. [51]I assure you that whoever keeps my word will never die."

Abraham and Jesus

[52]The Jewish opposition said to Jesus, "Now we know that you have a demon. Abraham and the prophets died, yet you say, 'Whoever keeps my word will never die.' [53]Are you greater than our father Abraham? He died and the prophets died, so who do you make yourself out to be?"

[54]Jesus answered, "If I glorify myself, my glory is meaningless. My Father, who you say is your God, is the one who glorifies me. [55]You don't know him, but I do. If I said I didn't know him, I would be like you, a liar. But I do know him, and I keep his word. [56]Your father Abraham was overjoyed that he would see my day. He saw it and was happy."

[57]"You aren't even 50 years old!" the Jewish opposition replied. "How can you say that you have seen Abraham?"

[58]"I assure you," Jesus replied, "before Abraham was, I Am." [59]So they picked up stones to throw at him, but Jesus hid himself and left the temple.

Jesus heals a blind man

9 As Jesus walked along, he saw a man who was blind from birth. [2]Jesus' disciples asked, "Rabbi, who sinned so that he was born blind, this man or his parents?"

[3]Jesus answered, "Neither he nor his parents. This happened so that God's mighty works might be displayed in him. [4]While it's daytime, we must do the works of him who sent me. Night is coming when no one can work. [5]While I am in the world, I am the light of the world." [6]After he said this, he spit on the ground, made mud with the saliva, and smeared the mud on the man's eyes. [7]Jesus said to him, "Go, wash in the pool of Siloam" (this word means *sent*). So the man went away and washed. When he returned, he could see.

Disagreement about the healing

[8]The man's neighbors and those who used to see him when he was a beggar said, "Isn't this the man who used to sit and beg?"

[9]Some said, "It is," and others said, "No, it's someone who looks like him."

But the man said, "Yes, it's me!"

[10]So they asked him, "How are you now able to see?"

[11]He answered, "The man they call Jesus made mud, smeared it on my eyes, and said,

'Go to the Pool of Siloam and wash.' So I went and washed, and then I could see."

[12] They asked, "Where is this man?"

He replied, "I don't know."

[13] Then they led the man who had been born blind to the Pharisees. [14] Now Jesus made the mud and smeared it on the man's eyes on a Sabbath day. [15] So Pharisees also asked him how he was able to see.

The man told them, "He put mud on my eyes, I washed, and now I see."

[16] Some Pharisees said, "This man isn't from God, because he breaks the Sabbath law." Others said, "How can a sinner do miraculous signs like these?" So they were divided. [17] Some of the Pharisees questioned the man who had been born blind again: "What do you have to say about him, since he healed your eyes?"

He replied, "He's a prophet."

Conflict over the healing

[18] The Jewish leaders didn't believe the man had been blind and received his sight until they called for his parents. [19] The Jewish leaders asked them, "Is this your son? Are you saying he was born blind? How can he now see?"

[20] His parents answered, "We know he is our son. We know he was born blind. [21] But we don't know how he now sees, and we don't know who healed his eyes. Ask him. He's old enough to speak for himself." [22] His parents said this because they feared the Jewish authorities. This is because the Jewish authorities had already decided that whoever confessed Jesus to be the Christ would be expelled from the synagogue. [23] That's why his parents said, "He's old enough. Ask him."

[24] Therefore, they called a second time for the man who had been born blind and said to him, "Give glory to God. We know this man is a sinner."

[25] The man answered, "I don't know whether he's a sinner. Here's what I do know: I was blind and now I see."

[26] They questioned him: "What did he do to you? How did he heal your eyes?"

[27] He replied, "I already told you, and you didn't listen. Why do you want to hear it again? Do you want to become his disciples too?"

[28] They insulted him: "You are his disciple, but we are Moses' disciples. [29] We know that God spoke to Moses, but we don't know where this man is from."

[30] The man answered, "This is incredible! You don't know where he is from, yet he healed my eyes! [31] We know that God doesn't listen to sinners. God listens to anyone who is devout and does God's will. [32] No one has ever heard of a healing of the eyes of someone born blind. [33] If this man wasn't from God, he couldn't do this."

[34] They responded, "You were born completely in sin! How is it that you dare to teach us?" Then they expelled him.

Jesus finds the man born blind

[35] Jesus heard they had expelled the man born blind. Finding him, Jesus said, "Do you believe in the Human One?"[b]

[36] He answered, "Who is he, sir?[c] I want to believe in him."

[37] Jesus said, "You have seen him. In fact, he is the one speaking with you."

[38] The man said, "Lord,[d] I believe." And he worshipped Jesus.

Jesus teaches the Pharisees

[39] Jesus said, "I have come into the world to exercise judgment so that those who don't see can see and those who see will become blind."

[40] Some Pharisees who were with him heard what he said and asked, "Surely we aren't blind, are we?"

[41] Jesus said to them, "If you were blind, you wouldn't have any sin, but now that you say, 'We see,' your sin remains.

10 I assure you that whoever doesn't enter into the sheep pen through the gate but climbs over the wall is a thief and an outlaw. [2] The one who enters through the gate is the shepherd of the sheep. [3] The guard at the gate opens the gate for him, and the sheep listen to his voice. He calls

[b] Or Son of Man   [c] Or Lord   [d] Or Sir

his own sheep by name and leads them out. ⁴Whenever he has gathered all of his sheep, he goes before them and they follow him, because they know his voice. ⁵They won't follow a stranger but will run away because they don't know the stranger's voice." ⁶Those who heard Jesus use this analogy didn't understand what he was saying.

I am the gate

⁷So Jesus spoke again, "I assure you that I am the gate of the sheep. ⁸All who came before me were thieves and outlaws, but the sheep didn't listen to them. ⁹I am the gate. Whoever enters through me will be saved. They will come in and go out and find pasture. ¹⁰The thief enters only to steal, kill, and destroy. I came so that they could have life—indeed, so that they could live life to the fullest.

I am the good shepherd

¹¹"I am the good shepherd. The good shepherd lays down his life for the sheep. ¹²When the hired hand sees the wolf coming, he leaves the sheep and runs away. That's because he isn't the shepherd; the sheep aren't really his. So the wolf attacks the sheep and scatters them. ¹³He's only a hired hand and the sheep don't matter to him.

¹⁴"I am the good shepherd. I know my own sheep and they know me, ¹⁵just as the Father knows me and I know the Father. I give up my life for the sheep. ¹⁶I have other sheep that don't belong to this sheep pen. I must lead them too. They will listen to my voice and there will be one flock, with one shepherd.

¹⁷"This is why the Father loves me: I give up my life so that I can take it up again. ¹⁸No one takes it from me, but I give it up because I want to. I have the right to give it up, and I have the right to take it up again. I received this commandment from my Father."

¹⁹There was another division among the Jews because of Jesus' words. ²⁰Many of them said, "He has a demon and has lost his mind. Why listen to him?" ²¹Others said, "These aren't the words of someone who has a demon. Can a demon heal the eyes of people who are blind?"

Jesus at the Festival of Dedication

²²The time came for the Festival of Dedication[e] in Jerusalem. It was winter, ²³and Jesus was in the temple, walking in the covered porch named for Solomon. ²⁴The Jewish opposition circled around him and asked, "How long will you test our patience? If you are the Christ, tell us plainly."

²⁵Jesus answered, "I have told you, but you don't believe. The works I do in my Father's name testify about me, ²⁶but you don't believe because you don't belong to my sheep. ²⁷My sheep listen to my voice. I know them and they follow me. ²⁸I give them eternal life. They will never die, and

[e]Hanukkah

HANUKKAH

The Hebrew title for the Jewish celebration known as the Festival of Dedication. Commemorated for eight days beginning on the twenty-fifth of the month of Kislev (Nov–Dec), Hanukkah celebrates the victory of the Judeans over the oppressive and genocidal policies of the Seleucid king Antiochus IV Epiphanes. Antiochus, for reasons still unclear to modern scholarship, forbade the practice of Judaism and desecrated the Jerusalem temple. A group of Judean rebels under the leadership of Judas Maccabee retook the temple on the twenty-fifth of Kislev in 165 or 164 BCE and purified the temple of the desecrations committed by Antiochus.

no one will snatch them from my hand. [29]My Father, who has given them to me, is greater than all, and no one is able to snatch them from my Father's hand. [30]I and the Father are one."

[31]Again the Jewish opposition picked up stones in order to stone him. [32]Jesus responded, "I have shown you many good works from the Father. For which of those works do you stone me?"

[33]The Jewish opposition answered, "We don't stone you for a good work but for insulting God. You are human, yet you make yourself out to be God."

[34]Jesus replied, "Isn't it written in your Law, *I have said, you are gods*?[f] [35]Scripture calls those to whom God's word came *gods*, and scripture can't be abolished. [36]So how can you say that the one whom the Father has made holy and sent into the world insults God because he said, 'I am God's Son'? [37]If I don't do the works of my Father, don't believe me. [38]But if I do them, and you don't believe me, believe the works so that you can know and recognize that the Father is in me and I am in the Father." [39]Again, they wanted to arrest him, but he escaped from them.

Jesus at the Jordan

[40]Jesus went back across the Jordan to the place where John had baptized at first, and he stayed there. [41]Many people came to him. "John didn't do any miraculous signs," they said, "but everything John said about this man was true." [42]Many believed in Jesus there.

Lazarus is ill

11 A certain man, Lazarus, was ill. He was from Bethany, the village of Mary and her sister Martha. ([2]This was the Mary who anointed the Lord with fragrant oil and wiped his feet with her hair. Her brother Lazarus was ill.) [3]So the sisters sent word to Jesus, saying, "Lord, the one whom you love is ill."

[4]When he heard this, Jesus said, "This illness isn't fatal. It's for the glory of God so that God's Son can be glorified through it." [5]Jesus loved Martha, her sister, and Lazarus. [6]When he heard that Lazarus was ill, he stayed where he was. After two days, [7]he said to his disciples, "Let's return to Judea again."

[8]The disciples replied, "Rabbi, the Jewish opposition wants to stone you, but you want to go back?"

[9]Jesus answered, "Aren't there twelve hours in the day? Whoever walks in the day doesn't stumble because they see the light of the world. [10]But whoever walks in the night does stumble because the light isn't in them."

[11]He continued, "Our friend Lazarus is sleeping, but I am going in order to wake him up."

[12]The disciples said, "Lord, if he's sleep-

[f]Ps 82:6

MARTHA

According to Luke, the sister of Mary (10:38-42); according to John, the sister of Mary and Lazarus (11:1–12:11). The Fourth Gospel associates the siblings with Bethany and describes them as persons whom Jesus loved (John 11:5). Whereas both Gospels mention Martha's work, Luke's portrayal of the sisters is often read as an affirmation of Mary, who prioritizes learning at the feet of Jesus, and as a rebuke of Martha, who "was preoccupied with getting everything ready for their meal" (10:39-40). In contrast to Luke, John attributes to Martha an extensive dialogue with Jesus that sets the stage for Jesus to reveal his identity and Martha to give her confession of faith (11:27).

ing, he will get well." [13]They thought Jesus meant that Lazarus was in a deep sleep, but Jesus had spoken about Lazarus' death.

[14]Jesus told them plainly, "Lazarus has died. [15]For your sakes, I'm glad I wasn't there so that you can believe. Let's go to him."

[16]Then Thomas (the one called Didymus) said to the other disciples, "Let us go too so that we may die with Jesus."

Jesus with Martha and Mary

[17]When Jesus arrived, he found that Lazarus had already been in the tomb for four days. [18]Bethany was a little less than two miles from Jerusalem. [19]Many Jews had come to comfort Martha and Mary after their brother's death. [20]When Martha heard that Jesus was coming, she went to meet him, while Mary remained in the house. [21]Martha said to Jesus, "Lord, if you had been here, my brother wouldn't have died. [22]Even now I know that whatever you ask God, God will give you."

[23]Jesus told her, "Your brother will rise again."

[24]Martha replied, "I know that he will rise in the resurrection on the last day."

[25]Jesus said to her, "I am the resurrection and the life. Whoever believes in me will live, even though they die. [26]Everyone who lives and believes in me will never die. Do you believe this?"

[27]She replied, "Yes, Lord, I believe that you are the Christ, God's Son, the one who is coming into the world."

[28]After she said this, she went and spoke privately to her sister Mary, "The teacher is here and he's calling for you." [29]When Mary heard this, she got up quickly and went to Jesus. [30]He hadn't entered the village but was still in the place where Martha had met him. [31]When the Jews who were comforting Mary in the house saw her get up quickly and leave, they followed her. They assumed she was going to mourn at the tomb.

[32]When Mary arrived where Jesus was and saw him, she fell at his feet and said, "Lord, if you had been here, my brother wouldn't have died."

[33]When Jesus saw her crying and the Jews who had come with her crying also, he was deeply disturbed and troubled. [34]He asked, "Where have you laid him?"

They replied, "Lord, come and see."

[35]Jesus began to cry. [36]The Jews said, "See how much he loved him!" [37]But some of them said, "He healed the eyes of the man born blind. Couldn't he have kept Lazarus from dying?"

Jesus at Lazarus' tomb

[38]Jesus was deeply disturbed again when he came to the tomb. It was a cave, and a stone covered the entrance. [39]Jesus said, "Remove the stone."

Martha, the sister of the dead man, said, "Lord, the smell will be awful! He's been dead four days."

[40]Jesus replied, "Didn't I tell you that if you believe, you will see God's glory?" [41]So they removed the stone. Jesus looked up and said, "Father, thank you for hearing me. [42]I know you always hear me. I say this for the benefit of the crowd standing here

BETHANY

The ministries of Jesus and John the Baptist are associated with two places named Bethany.

1. Bethany near Jerusalem appears several times in the NT. Bethany was on the Mount of Olives (Mark 11:1), 1.75 mi. from Jerusalem (John 11:18).

2. The Gospel of John refers to the place where John the Baptist conducted his ministry as "across the Jordan in Bethany" (John 1:28).

so that they will believe that you sent me." [43]Having said this, Jesus shouted with a loud voice, "Lazarus, come out!" [44]The dead man came out, his feet bound and his hands tied, and his face covered with a cloth. Jesus said to them, "Untie him and let him go."

[45]Therefore, many of the Jews who came with Mary and saw what Jesus did believed in him. [46]But some of them went to the Pharisees and told them what Jesus had done.

Caiaphas prophesies

[47]Then the chief priests and Pharisees called together the council[g] and said, "What are we going to do? This man is doing many miraculous signs! [48]If we let him go on like this, everyone will believe in him. Then the Romans will come and take away both our temple and our people."

[49]One of them, Caiaphas, who was high priest that year, told them, "You don't know anything! [50]You don't see that it is better for you that one man die for the people rather than the whole nation be destroyed." [51]He didn't say this on his own. As high priest that year, he prophesied that Jesus would soon die for the nation—[52]and not only for the nation. Jesus would also die so that God's children scattered everywhere would be gathered together as one. [53]From that day on they plotted to kill him.

The Passover draws near

[54]Therefore, Jesus was no longer active in public ministry among the Jewish leaders. Instead, he left Jerusalem and went to a place near the wilderness, to a city called Ephraim, where he stayed with his disciples.

[55]It was almost time for the Jewish Passover, and many people went from the countryside up to Jerusalem to purify themselves through ritual washing before the Passover. [56]They were looking for Jesus. As they spoke to each other in the temple, they said, "What do you think? He won't come to the festival, will he?" [57]The chief priests and Pharisees had given orders that anyone who knew where he was should report it, so they could arrest him.

Mary anoints Jesus' feet

12 Six days before Passover, Jesus came to Bethany, home of Lazarus, whom Jesus had raised from the dead. [2]Lazarus and his sisters hosted a dinner for him. Martha served and Lazarus was among those who joined him at the table. [3]Then Mary took an extraordinary amount, almost three-quarters of a pound,[h] of very expensive perfume made of pure nard. She anointed Jesus' feet with it, then wiped his feet dry with her hair. The house was filled with the aroma of the perfume. [4]Judas Iscariot, one of his disciples (the one who was about to betray him), complained, [5]"This perfume was worth a year's wages![i] Why wasn't it sold and the money given to the poor?" ([6]He said this not because he cared about the poor but because he was a thief. He carried the money bag and would take what was in it.)

[7]Then Jesus said, "Leave her alone. This perfume was to be used in preparation for my burial, and this is how she has used it. [8]You will always have the poor among you, but you won't always have me."

[9]Many Jews learned that he was there. They came not only because of Jesus but also to see Lazarus, whom he had raised from the dead. [10]The chief priests decided that they would kill Lazarus too. [11]It was because of Lazarus that many of the Jews had deserted them and come to believe in Jesus.

Jesus enters Jerusalem

[12]The next day the great crowd that had come for the festival heard that Jesus was coming to Jerusalem. [13]They took palm branches and went out to meet him. They shouted,

> "Hosanna!
> Blessings on the one who comes
>   in the name of the Lord![j]
> Blessings on the king of Israel!"

[14]Jesus found a young donkey and sat on it, just as it is written,

> [15]Don't be afraid, Daughter Zion.
>   Look! Your king is coming,
>   sitting on a donkey's colt.[k]

[g]Or *Sanhedrin* [h]Or *a litra*, a Roman pound, approximately twelve ounces [i]Or *three hundred denaria* [j]Ps 118:26
[k]Zech 9:9

¹⁶His disciples didn't understand these things at first. After he was glorified, they remembered that these things had been written about him and that they had done these things to him.

¹⁷The crowd who had been with him when he called Lazarus out of the tomb and raised him from the dead were testifying about him. ¹⁸That's why the crowd came to meet him, because they had heard about this miraculous sign that he had done. ¹⁹Therefore, the Pharisees said to each other, "See! You've accomplished nothing! Look! The whole world is following him!"

Jesus teaches about his death

²⁰Some Greeks were among those who had come up to worship at the festival. ²¹They came to Philip, who was from Bethsaida in Galilee, and made a request: "Sir, we want to see Jesus." ²²Philip told Andrew, and Andrew and Philip told Jesus.

²³Jesus replied, "The time has come for the Human One[l] to be glorified. ²⁴I assure you that unless a grain of wheat falls into the earth and dies, it can only be a single seed. But if it dies, it bears much fruit. ²⁵Those who love their lives will lose them, and those who hate their lives in this world will keep them forever. ²⁶Whoever serves

me must follow me. Wherever I am, there my servant will also be. My Father will honor whoever serves me.

²⁷"Now *I am deeply troubled*.[m] What should I say? 'Father, save me from this time'? No, for this is the reason I have come to this time. ²⁸Father, glorify your name!"

Then a voice came from heaven, "I have glorified it, and I will glorify it again."

²⁹The crowd standing there heard and said, "It's thunder." Others said, "An angel spoke to him."

³⁰Jesus replied, "This voice wasn't for my benefit but for yours. ³¹Now is the time for judgment of this world. Now this world's ruler will be thrown out. ³²When I am lifted up[n] from the earth, I will draw everyone to me." (³³He said this to show how he was going to die.)

³⁴The crowd responded, "We have heard from the Law that the Christ remains forever. How can you say that the Human One[o] must be lifted up? Who is this Human One?"[p]

³⁵Jesus replied, "The light is with you for only a little while. Walk while you have the light so that darkness doesn't overtake you. Those who walk in the darkness don't know where they are going. ³⁶As long as you have the light, believe in the light so that you

[l]Or *Son of Man* [m]Ps 6:2 [n]Or *exalted* [o]Or *Son of Man* [p]Or *Son of Man*

LAZARUS

Two men in the NT are named Lazarus.

1. Lazarus, the poor man in the parable of the rich man (Luke 16:19-31), is the only named character in any of Jesus' parables.

2. Lazarus of Bethany is a character unique to John's Gospel (John 11:1–12:11). Lazarus is from the village of Bethany and is the brother of Mary and Martha (John 11:1-2), whose interactions with Jesus constitute the bulk of this story (11:20-40). When Lazarus becomes sick, the sisters send word to Jesus (11:3), believing he will heal their brother (11:21, 32). Jesus' intentional delay (11:4-7) sets up the astonishing miracle of Lazarus's resurrection (11:43-44), which occurs after Lazarus has been dead four days (11:17, 39).

might become people whose lives are determined by the light." After Jesus said these things, he went away and hid from them.

Fulfillment of prophecy

[37] Jesus had done many miraculous signs before the people, but they didn't believe in him. [38] This was to fulfill the word of the prophet Isaiah:

Lord, who has believed through our message?
　To whom is the arm of the Lord
　　fully revealed?[q]

[39] Isaiah explains why they couldn't believe:
[40] He made their eyes blind
　and closed their minds
　so that they might not see with their eyes,
　understand with their minds,
　and turn their lives around—
　and I would heal them.[r]

[41] Isaiah said these things because he saw Jesus' glory; he spoke about Jesus. [42] Even so, many leaders believed in him, but they wouldn't acknowledge their faith because they feared that the Pharisees would expel them from the synagogue. [43] They believed, but they loved human praise more than God's glory.

Summary of Jesus' teaching

[44] Jesus shouted, "Whoever believes in me doesn't believe in me but in the one who sent me. [45] Whoever sees me sees the one who sent me. [46] I have come as a light into the world so that everyone who believes in me won't live in darkness. [47] If people hear my words and don't keep them, I don't judge them. I didn't come to judge the world but to save it. [48] Whoever rejects me and doesn't receive my words will be judged at the last day by the word I have spoken. [49] I don't speak on my own, but the Father who sent me commanded me regarding what I should speak and say. [50] I know that his commandment is eternal life. Therefore, whatever I say is just as the Father has said to me."

Foot washing

13 Before the Festival of Passover, Jesus knew that his time had come to leave this world and go to the Father. Having loved his own who were in the world, he loved them fully.

[2] Jesus and his disciples were sharing the evening meal. The devil had already provoked Judas, Simon Iscariot's son, to betray Jesus. [3] Jesus knew the Father had given everything into his hands and that he had come from God and was returning to God. [4] So he got up from the table and took off his robes. Picking up a linen towel, he tied it around his waist. [5] Then he poured water into a washbasin and began to wash the disciples' feet, drying them with the towel he was wearing. [6] When Jesus came to Simon Peter, Peter said to him, "Lord, are you going to wash my feet?"

[7] Jesus replied, "You don't understand what I'm doing now, but you will understand later."

[8] "No!" Peter said. "You will never wash my feet!"

Jesus replied, "Unless I wash you, you won't have a place with me."

[9] Simon Peter said, "Lord, not only my feet but also my hands and my head!"

[10] Jesus responded, "Those who have bathed need only to have their feet washed, because they are completely clean. You disciples are clean, but not every one of you." [11] He knew who would betray him. That's why he said, "Not every one of you is clean."

[12] After he washed the disciples' feet, he put on his robes and returned to his place at the table. He said to them, "Do you know what I've done for you? [13] You call me 'Teacher' and 'Lord,' and you speak correctly, because I am. [14] If I, your Lord and teacher, have washed your feet, you too must wash each other's feet. [15] I have given you an example: Just as I have done, you also must do. [16] I assure you, servants aren't greater than their master, nor are those who are sent greater than the one who sent them. [17] Since you know these things, you will be happy if you do them. [18] I'm not speaking about all of you. I know those whom I've chosen. But this is to fulfill the scripture, The one who eats my bread has turned against me.[s]

[q] Isa 53:1　[r] Isa 6:10　[s] Ps 41:9

[19]"I'm telling you this now, before it happens, so that when it does happen you will believe that I Am. [20]I assure you that whoever receives someone I send receives me, and whoever receives me receives the one who sent me."

Announcement of the betrayal

[21]After he said these things, Jesus was deeply disturbed and testified, "I assure you, one of you will betray me."

[22]His disciples looked at each other, confused about which of them he was talking about. [23]One of the disciples, the one whom Jesus loved, was at Jesus' side. [24]Simon Peter nodded at him to get him to ask Jesus who he was talking about. [25]Leaning back toward Jesus, this disciple asked, "Lord, who is it?"

[26]Jesus answered, "It's the one to whom I will give this piece of bread once I have dipped into the bowl." Then he dipped the piece of bread and gave it to Judas, Simon Iscariot's son. [27]After Judas took the bread, Satan entered into him. Jesus told him, "What you are about to do, do quickly." [28]No one sitting at the table understood why Jesus said this to him. [29]Some thought that, since Judas kept the money bag, Jesus told him, "Go, buy what we need for the feast," or that he should give something to the poor. [30]So when Judas took the bread, he left immediately. And it was night.

[t]Or *Son of Man* [u]Or *Son of Man*

Love commandment

[31]When Judas was gone, Jesus said, "Now the Human One[t] has been glorified, and God has been glorified in him. [32]If God has been glorified in him, God will also glorify the Human One[u] in himself and will glorify him immediately. [33]Little children, I'm with you for a little while longer. You will look for me—but, just as I told the Jewish leaders, I also tell you now—'Where I'm going, you can't come.'

[34]"I give you a new commandment: Love each other. Just as I have loved you, so you also must love each other. [35]This is how everyone will know that you are my disciples, when you love each other."

Announcement of Peter's denial

[36]Simon Peter said to Jesus, "Lord, where are you going?"

Jesus answered, "Where I am going, you can't follow me now, but you will follow later." [37]Peter asked, "Lord, why can't I follow you now? I'll give up my life for you." [38]Jesus replied, "Will you give up your life for me? I assure you that you will deny me three times before the rooster crows.

The way, the truth, and the life

14 "Don't be troubled. Trust in God. Trust also in me. [2]My Father's house has room to spare. If that weren't the case, would I have told you that I'm going to prepare a place for you? [3]When I go to prepare a

FOOT WASHING

Biblical and Greco-Roman hospitality required hosts to provide water for washing guests' feet (Gen 18:4; Luke 7:44). Typically, the washing was done either by a slave (1 Sam 25:41) or by the guests themselves.

Exodus 30:17-20 requires priests to wash their feet before approaching the altar, and acting "with unwashed feet" came to suggest inadequate preparation.

In John 13:4-20, Jesus washes his disciples' feet, an act without recorded parallel in antiquity, where superiors did not willingly wash the feet of inferiors.

place for you, I will return and take you to be with me so that where I am you will be too. [4]You know the way to the place I'm going."

[5]Thomas asked, "Lord, we don't know where you are going. How can we know the way?"

[6]Jesus answered, "I am the way, the truth, and the life. No one comes to the Father except through me. [7]If you have really known me, you will also know the Father. From now on you know him and have seen him."

[8]Philip said, "Lord, show us the Father; that will be enough for us."

[9]Jesus replied, "Don't you know me, Philip, even after I have been with you all this time? Whoever has seen me has seen the Father. How can you say, 'Show us the Father'? [10]Don't you believe that I am in the Father and the Father is in me? The words I have spoken to you I don't speak on my own. The Father who dwells in me does his works. [11]Trust me when I say that I am in the Father and the Father is in me, or at least believe on account of the works themselves. [12]I assure you that whoever believes in me will do the works that I do. They will do even greater works than these because I am going to the Father. [13]I will do whatever you ask for in my name, so that the Father can be glorified in the Son. [14]When you ask me for anything in my name, I will do it.

I won't leave you as orphans

[15]"If you love me, you will keep my commandments. [16]I will ask the Father, and he will send another Companion,[v] who will be with you forever. [17]This Companion is the Spirit of Truth, whom the world can't receive because it neither sees him nor recognizes him. You know him, because he lives with you and will be with you.

[18]"I won't leave you as orphans. I will come to you. [19]Soon the world will no longer see me, but you will see me. Because I live, you will live too. [20]On that day you will know that I am in my Father, you are in me, and I am in you. [21]Whoever has my commandments and keeps them loves me. Whoever loves me will be loved by my Father, and I will love them and reveal myself to them."

[22]Judas (not Judas Iscariot) asked, "Lord, why are you about to reveal yourself to us and not to the world?"

[23]Jesus answered, "Whoever loves me will keep my word. My Father will love them, and we will come to them and make our home with them. [24]Whoever doesn't love me doesn't keep my words. The word that you hear isn't mine. It is the word of the Father who sent me.

[25]"I have spoken these things to you while I am with you. [26]The Companion,[w] the Holy Spirit, whom the Father will send in my name, will teach you everything and will remind you of everything I told you.

[27]"Peace I leave with you. My peace I give you. I give to you not as the world gives. Don't be troubled or afraid. [28]You have heard me tell you, 'I'm going away and returning to you.' If you loved me, you would be happy that I am going to the Father, because the Father is greater than

---

[v]Or *Advocate* [w]Or *Advocate*

ORPHAN

The OT use of this term does not distinguish between the loss of both parents and the loss of the father. Orphaned children were given special consideration, and a collection was given every third year for their care (Deut 14:28-29; 24:19-21; 26:12; 27:19). God is the father of the orphan and protector of widows (Pss 10:14; 68:5). God oversees justice and fairness for them (Deut 10:18; Ps 10:18). The NT mandates the care of orphans as a hallmark of religious faith and practice (Jas 1:27). Paul likens his separation from the Thessalonians to being orphaned (1 Thess 2:17).

me. [29]I have told you before it happens so that when it happens you will believe. [30]I won't say much more to you because this world's ruler is coming. He has nothing on me. [31]Rather, he comes so that the world will know that I love the Father and do just as the Father has commanded me. Get up. We're leaving this place.

I am the true vine

15 [1]"I am the true vine, and my Father is the vineyard keeper. [2]He removes any of my branches that don't produce fruit, and he trims any branch that produces fruit so that it will produce even more fruit. [3]You are already trimmed because of the word I have spoken to you. [4]Remain in me, and I will remain in you. A branch can't produce fruit by itself, but must remain in the vine. Likewise, you can't produce fruit unless you remain in me. [5]I am the vine; you are the branches. If you remain in me and I in you, then you will produce much fruit. Without me, you can't do anything. [6]If you don't remain in me, you will be like a branch that is thrown out and dries up. Those branches are gathered up, thrown into a fire, and burned. [7]If you remain in me and my words remain in you, ask for whatever you want and it will be done for you. [8]My Father is glorified when you produce much fruit and in this way prove that you are my disciples.

Love each other

[9]"As the Father loved me, I too have loved you. Remain in my love. [10]If you keep my commandments, you will remain in my love, just as I kept my Father's commandments and remain in his love. [11]I have said these things to you so that my joy will be in you and your joy will be complete. [12]This is my commandment: love each other just as I have loved you. [13]No one has greater love than to give up one's life for one's friends. [14]You are my friends if you do what I command you. [15]I don't call you servants any longer, because servants don't know what their master is doing. Instead, I call you friends, because everything I heard from my Father I have made known to you. [16]You didn't choose me, but I chose you and appointed you so that you could go and produce fruit and so that your fruit could last. As a result, whatever you ask the Father in my name, he will give you. [17]I give you these commandments so that you can love each other.

If the world hates you

[18]"If the world hates you, know that it hated me first. [19]If you belonged to the world, the world would love you as its own. However, I have chosen you out of the world, and you don't belong to the world. This is why the world hates you. [20]Remember what I told you, 'Servants aren't greater than their master.' If the world harassed me, it will harass you too. If it kept my word, it will also keep yours. [21]The world will do all these things to you on account of my name, because it doesn't know the one who sent me.

PARACLETE/COMPANION

The word *paraclete* means "someone called in assistance" or "advocate." The word does not occur in the OT and is found in the NT only in John 14:16, 26; 15:26-27; 16:7-11, translated as "Companion" (1 John 2:1, "advocate"). In the Gospel of John it is Jesus' name for the Holy Spirit, whom the Father (or Jesus) will send to the disciples to be Jesus' presence in the world after his return to the Father. In 1 John it describes Jesus' role in relation to the sinner. Biblical scholars and theologians use *paraclete* as a technical term for the spiritual form that Jesus' presence will take in and among the Johannine community after his death and resurrection, to comfort and counsel them (John 14:16).

[22]"If I hadn't come and spoken to the people of this world, they wouldn't be sinners. But now they have no excuse for their sin. [23]Whoever hates me also hates the Father. [24]If I hadn't done works among them that no one else had done, they wouldn't be sinners. But now they have seen and hated both me and my Father. [25]This fulfills the word written in their Law, *They hated me without a reason.*[x]

[26]"When the Companion[y] comes, whom I will send from the Father—the Spirit of Truth who proceeds from the Father—he will testify about me. [27]You will testify too, because you have been with me from the beginning. [1]I have said these things to you so that you won't fall away. [2]They will expel you from the synagogue. The time is coming when those who kill you will think that they are doing a service to God. [3]They will do these things because they don't know the Father or me. [4]But I have said these things to you so that when their time comes, you will remember that I told you about them.

I go away

"I didn't say these things to you from the beginning, because I was with you. [5]But now I go away to the one who sent me. None of you ask me, 'Where are you going?' [6]Yet because I have said these things to you, you are filled with sorrow. [7]I assure you that it is better for you that I go away. If I don't go away, the Companion[z] won't come to you. But if I go, I will send him to you. [8]When he comes, he will show the world it was wrong about sin, righteousness, and judgment. [9]He will show the world it was wrong about sin because they don't believe in me. [10]He will show the world it was wrong about righteousness because I'm going to the Father and you won't see me anymore. [11]He will show the world it was wrong about judgment because this world's ruler stands condemned.

I still have many things to say

[12]"I have much more to say to you, but you can't handle it now. [13]However, when the Spirit of Truth comes, he will guide you in all truth. He won't speak on his own, but will say whatever he hears and will proclaim to you what is to come. [14]He will glorify me, because he will take what is mine and proclaim it to you. [15]Everything that the Father has is mine. That's why I said that the Spirit takes what is mine and will proclaim it to you. [16]Soon you won't be able to see me; soon after that, you will see me."

I will see you again

[17]Some of Jesus' disciples said to each other, "What does he mean: 'Soon you won't see me, and soon after that you will see me' and 'Because I'm going to the Father'? [18]What does he mean by 'soon'? We don't understand what he's talking about."

[19]Jesus knew they wanted to ask him, so he said, "Are you trying to find out from each other what I meant when I said, 'Soon you won't see me, and soon after that you will see me'? [20]I assure you that you will cry and lament, and the world will be happy. You will be sorrowful, but your sorrow will turn into joy. [21]When a woman gives birth, she has pain because her time has come. But when the child is born, she no longer remembers her distress because of her joy that a child has been born into the world. [22]In the same way, you have sorrow now; but I will see you again, and you will be overjoyed. No one takes away your joy. [23]In that day, you won't ask me anything. I assure you that the Father will give you whatever you ask in my name. [24]Up to now, you have asked nothing in my name. Ask and you will receive so that your joy will be complete.

I have conquered the world

[25]"I've been using figures of speech with you. The time is coming when I will no longer speak to you in such analogies. Instead, I will tell you plainly about the Father. [26]In that day you will ask in my name. I'm not saying that I will ask the Father on your behalf. [27]The Father himself loves you, because you have loved me and believed that I

[x]Pss 35:19; 69:4   [y]Or *Advocate*   [z]Or *Advocate*

came from God. [28]I left the Father and came into the world. I tell you again: I am leaving the world and returning to the Father."

[29]His disciples said, "See! Now you speak plainly; you aren't using figures of speech. [30]Now we know that you know everything and you don't need anyone to ask you. Because of this we believe you have come from God."

[31]Jesus replied, "Now you believe? [32]Look! A time is coming—and is here!—when each of you will be scattered to your own homes and you will leave me alone. I'm not really alone, for the Father is with me. [33]I've said these things to you so that you will have peace in me. In the world you have distress. But be encouraged! I have conquered the world."

Jesus prays

17 When Jesus finished saying these things, he looked up to heaven and said, "Father, the time has come. Glorify your Son, so that the Son can glorify you. [2]You gave him authority over everyone so that he could give eternal life to everyone you gave him. [3]This is eternal life: to know you, the only true God, and Jesus Christ whom you sent. [4]I have glorified you on earth by finishing the work you gave me to do. [5]Now, Father, glorify me in your presence with the glory I shared with you before the world was created.

[6]"I have revealed your name to the people you gave me from this world. They were yours and you gave them to me, and they have kept your word. [7]Now they know that everything you have given me comes from you. [8]This is because I gave them the words that you gave me, and they received them. They truly understood that I came from you, and they believed that you sent me.

[9]"I'm praying for them. I'm not praying for the world but for those you gave me, because they are yours. [10]Everything that is mine is yours and everything that is yours is mine; I have been glorified in them. [11]I'm no longer in the world, but they are in the world, even as I'm coming to you. Holy Father, watch over them in your name, the name you gave me, that they will be one just

as we are one. [12]When I was with them, I watched over them in your name, the name you gave to me, and I kept them safe. None of them were lost, except the one who was destined for destruction, so that scripture would be fulfilled. [13]Now I'm coming to you and I say these things while I'm in the world so that they can share completely in my joy. [14]I gave your word to them and the world hated them, because they don't belong to this world, just as I don't belong to this world. [15]I'm not asking that you take them out of this world but that you keep them safe from the evil one. [16]They don't belong to this world, just as I don't belong to this world. [17]Make them holy in the truth; your word is truth. [18]As you sent me into the world, so I have sent them into the world. [19]I made myself holy on their behalf so that they also would be made holy in the truth.

[20]"I'm not praying only for them but also for those who believe in me because of their word. [21]I pray they will be one, Father, just as you are in me and I am in you. I pray that they also will be in us, so that the world will believe that you sent me. [22]I've given them the glory that you gave me so that they can be one just as we are one. [23]I'm in them and you are in me so that they will be made perfectly one. Then the world will know that you sent me and that you have loved them just as you loved me.

[24]"Father, I want those you gave me to be with me where I am. Then they can see my glory, which you gave me because you loved me before the creation of the world.

[25]"Righteous Father, even the world didn't know you, but I've known you, and these believers know that you sent me. [26]I've made your name known to them and will continue to make it known so that your love for me will be in them, and I myself will be in them."

Arrest in the garden

18 After he said these things, Jesus went out with his disciples and crossed over to the other side of the Kidron Valley. He and his disciples entered a garden there. [2]Judas, his betrayer, also knew the place because Jesus often gathered there with his disciples. ³Judas brought a company of soldiersª and some guards from the chief priests and Pharisees. They came there carrying lanterns, torches, and weapons. ⁴Jesus knew everything that was to happen to him, so he went out and asked, "Who are you looking for?"

⁵They answered, "Jesus the Nazarene."

He said to them, "I Am."ᵇ (Judas, his betrayer, was standing with them.) ⁶When he said, "I Am," they shrank back and fell to the ground. ⁷He asked them again, "Who are you looking for?"

They said, "Jesus the Nazarene."

⁸Jesus answered, "I told you, 'I Am.'ᶜ If you are looking for me, then let these people go." ⁹This was so that the word he had spoken might be fulfilled: "I didn't lose anyone of those whom you gave me."

¹⁰Then Simon Peter, who had a sword,

ªOr *cohort* (approximately six hundred soldiers)   ᵇOr *It is I*   ᶜOr *It is I*

JUDAS

Judas is the Greek name for the Hebrew patriarch Judah. In the NT, references to the patriarch (e.g., Matt 1:2; Luke 3:33) or to the traditional tribal territory of Judah (more or less synonymous with "Judea" [e.g., Luke 1:39]) appear in the Greek as *Judas*, but are usually translated as *Judah* in English.

1. The brother of Jesus and/or James. According to several sources, Jesus had a brother named Judas (e.g., Mark 6:1-6).

2. According to some sources, the disciple of Jesus identified as "Thomas" in the canonical Gospels was actually named Judas. The suggestion makes sense, as the word *Thomas* is an epithet meaning "twin" (e.g., John 11:16).

3. Yet another disciple named Judas is identified by the Gospels of Luke and John. Thaddaeus in the list of the Twelve in Matthew and Mark is replaced in Luke's list by "Judas the son of James" (Luke 6:16; also Acts 1:13). The Gospel of John also refers to a disciple named Judas, present at the Last Supper, who is described as "Judas (not Judas Iscariot)" (John 14:22).

4. Judas Barsabbas, representative of the Jerusalem church, is mentioned in Acts at the decision of the Jerusalem Council to send two leading figures of the Jerusalem church as emissaries to Antioch with Paul and Barnabas. The men are identified as "Judas Barsabbas and Silas" (Acts 15:22). They are also described as prophets (15:32).

5. Judas was the owner of a house in Damascus. According to the Acts account of Paul's call by God, after being blinded on the road to Damascus, Paul takes refuge in the Damascus house of a man named Judas who lives on Straight Street (Acts 9:11).

6. Judas the Galilean (Acts 5:37) was a revolutionary around the time Judea was brought under direct Roman rule and subjected to a census in 6 CE.

7. Judas Iscariot was one of Jesus' inner circle of 12 disciples (Matt 10:4; Mark 3:19; Luke 6:16; John 6:71). All the Gospels agree he played some role in Jesus' arrest, but the details about him differ widely.

drew it and struck the high priest's servant, cutting off his right ear. (The servant's name was Malchus.) ¹¹Jesus told Peter, "Put your sword away! Am I not to drink the cup the Father has given me?" ¹²Then the company of soldiers, the commander, and the guards from the Jewish leaders took Jesus into custody. They bound him ¹³and led him first to Annas. He was the father-in-law of Caiaphas, the high priest that year. (¹⁴Caiaphas was the one who had advised the Jewish leaders that it was better for one person to die for the people.)

Peter denies Jesus

¹⁵Simon Peter and another disciple followed Jesus. Because this other disciple was known to the high priest, he went with Jesus into the high priest's courtyard. ¹⁶However, Peter stood outside near the gate. Then the other disciple (the one known to the high priest) came out and spoke to the woman stationed at the gate, and she brought Peter in. ¹⁷The servant woman stationed at the gate asked Peter, "Aren't you one of this man's disciples?"

"I'm not," he replied. ¹⁸The servants and the guards had made a fire because it was cold. They were standing around it, warming themselves. Peter joined them there, standing by the fire and warming himself.

Jesus testifies

¹⁹Meanwhile, the chief priest questioned Jesus about his disciples and his teaching. ²⁰Jesus answered, "I've spoken openly to the world. I've always taught in synagogues and in the temple, where all the Jews gather. I've said nothing in private. ²¹Why

ask me? Ask those who heard what I told them. They know what I said."

²²After Jesus spoke, one of the guards standing there slapped Jesus in the face. "Is that how you would answer the high priest?" he asked.

²³Jesus replied, "If I speak wrongly, testify about what was wrong. But if I speak correctly, why do you strike me?" ²⁴Then Annas sent him, bound, to Caiaphas the high priest.

Peter denies Jesus again

²⁵Meanwhile, Simon Peter was still standing with the guards, warming himself. They asked, "Aren't you one of his disciples?"

Peter denied it, saying, "I'm not."

²⁶A servant of the high priest, a relative of the one whose ear Peter had cut off, said to him, "Didn't I see you in the garden with him?" ²⁷Peter denied it again, and immediately a rooster crowed.

Trial before Pilate

²⁸The Jewish leaders led Jesus from Caiaphas to the Roman governor's palace.ᵈ It was early in the morning. So that they could eat the Passover, the Jewish leaders wouldn't enter the palace; entering the palace would have made them ritually impure.

²⁹So Pilate went out to them and asked, "What charge do you bring against this man?"

³⁰They answered, "If he had done nothing wrong, we wouldn't have handed him over to you."

³¹Pilate responded, "Take him yourselves and judge him according to your Law."

The Jewish leaders replied, "The Law

ᵈOr praetorium

CAIAPHAS

Joseph Caiaphas was the Jewish high priest who interrogated Jesus and handed him over to Pilate. The longest-serving high priest of the 1st century CE, Caiaphas was deposed in 37. We hear no more about him, although a tomb found to the south of Jerusalem in 1990 may have been his final resting place.

doesn't allow us to kill anyone." ([32]This was so that Jesus' word might be fulfilled when he indicated how he was going to die.)

Pilate questions Jesus

[33]Pilate went back into the palace. He summoned Jesus and asked, "Are you the king of the Jews?"

[34]Jesus answered, "Do you say this on your own or have others spoken to you about me?"

[35]Pilate responded, "I'm not a Jew, am I? Your nation and its chief priests handed you over to me. What have you done?"

[36]Jesus replied, "My kingdom doesn't originate from this world. If it did, my guards would fight so that I wouldn't have been arrested by the Jewish leaders. My kingdom isn't from here."

[37]"So you are a king?" Pilate said.

Jesus answered, "You say that I am a king. I was born and came into the world for this reason: to testify to the truth. Whoever accepts the truth listens to my voice."

[38]"What is truth?" Pilate asked.

Release of Barabbas

After Pilate said this, he returned to the Jewish leaders and said, "I find no grounds for any charge against him. [39]You have a custom that I release one prisoner for you at Passover. Do you want me to release for you the king of the Jews?"

[40]They shouted, "Not this man! Give us Barabbas!" (Barabbas was an outlaw.)

Jesus is whipped and mocked as king

19 Then Pilate had Jesus taken and whipped. [2]The soldiers twisted together a crown of thorns and put it on his head, and dressed him in a purple robe. [3]Over and over they went up to him and said, "Greetings, king of the Jews!" And they slapped him in the face.

[4]Pilate came out of the palace again and said to the Jewish leaders, "Look! I'm bringing him out to you to let you know that I find no grounds for a charge against him." [5]When Jesus came out, wearing the crown of thorns and the purple robe, Pilate said to them, "Here's the man."

[6]When the chief priests and their deputies saw him, they shouted out, "Crucify, crucify!"

Pilate told them, "You take him and crucify him. I don't find any grounds for a charge against him."

[7]The Jewish leaders replied, "We have a Law, and according to this Law he ought to die because he made himself out to be God's Son."

Pilate questions Jesus again

[8]When Pilate heard this word, he was even more afraid. [9]He went back into the residence and spoke to Jesus, "Where are

GOLGOTHA

Luke calls the place of Christ's crucifixion simply "Skull" (Luke 23:33), but the three other evangelists give both this Greek name and its Semitic equivalent *Golgotha* (Matt 27:33; Mark 15:22; John 19:17). The site may have received its name because of a topographical feature such as holes reminiscent of a pair of eyes. This interpretation is followed by those that connect the location of Jesus' crucifixion to a cliff that resembles a skull and the burial site to a nearby rock-cut tomb outside the Old City near the Damascus Gate. But a more generic explanation is also possible. The Arabic term *ras* ("head") is frequently applied to a ridge jutting out from a range. The site traditionally identified as Gologtha was in fact a section of poor rock left projecting from the east wall of the quarry beneath the Holy Sepulchre.

you from?" Jesus didn't answer. [10]So Pilate said, "You won't speak to me? Don't you know that I have authority to release you and also to crucify you?"

[11]Jesus replied, "You would have no authority over me if it had not been given to you from above. That's why the one who handed me over to you has the greater sin." [12]From that moment on, Pilate wanted to release Jesus.

However, the Jewish leaders cried out, saying, "If you release this man, you aren't a friend of the emperor! Anyone who makes himself out to be a king opposes the emperor!"

[13]When Pilate heard these words, he led Jesus out and seated him on the judge's bench at the place called Stone Pavement (in Aramaic, *Gabbatha*). [14]It was about noon on the Preparation Day for the Passover. Pilate said to the Jewish leaders, "Here's your king."

[15]The Jewish leaders cried out, "Take him away! Take him away! Crucify him!"

Pilate responded, "What? Do you want me to crucify your king?"

"We have no king except the emperor," the chief priests answered. [16]Then Pilate handed Jesus over to be crucified.

Crucifixion

The soldiers took Jesus prisoner. [17]Carrying his cross by himself, he went out to a place called Skull Place (in Aramaic, *Golgotha*). [18]That's where they crucified him—and two others with him, one on each side and Jesus in the middle. [19]Pilate had a public notice written and posted on the cross. It read "Jesus the Nazarene, the king of the Jews." [20]Many of the Jews read this sign, for the place where Jesus was crucified was near the city and it was written in Aramaic, Latin, and Greek. [21]Therefore, the Jewish chief priests complained to Pilate, "Don't write, 'The king of the Jews' but 'This man said, "I am the king of the Jews."'"

[22]Pilate answered, "What I've written, I've written."

[23]When the soldiers crucified Jesus, they took his clothes and his sandals, and divided them into four shares, one for each soldier. His shirt was seamless, woven as one piece from the top to the bottom. [24]They said to each other, "Let's not tear it. Let's cast lots to see who will get it." This was to fulfill the scripture,

They divided my clothes among themselves,
 and they cast lots for my clothing.[e]

That's what the soldiers did.

[25]Jesus' mother and his mother's sister, Mary the wife of Clopas, and Mary Magdalene stood near the cross. [26]When Jesus saw his mother and the disciple whom he loved standing nearby, he said to his mother, "Woman, here is your son." [27]Then he said to the disciple, "Here is your mother." And from that time on, this disciple took her into his home.

[28]After this, knowing that everything was already completed, in order to fulfill the scripture, Jesus said, "I am thirsty." [29]A jar full of sour wine was nearby, so the soldiers soaked a sponge in it, placed it on a hyssop branch, and held it up to his lips. [30]When he had received the sour wine, Jesus said, "It is completed." Bowing his head, he gave up his life.

[e]Ps 22:18

CROWN OF THORNS

According to the Gospels, the soldiers carrying out Jesus' crucifixion "twisted together a crown of thorns and put it on his head" (John 19:22). The crown, meant to resemble the laurel wreath worn by Caesar, is part of the mockery of Jesus. This mockery includes a purple cloak, a reed (symbolizing the scepter), and personal address as a so-called king (Mark 15:17-19; John 19:2-3).

Witness at the cross

³¹It was the Preparation Day and the Jewish leaders didn't want the bodies to remain on the cross on the Sabbath, especially since that Sabbath was an important day. So they asked Pilate to have the legs of those crucified broken and the bodies taken down. ³²Therefore, the soldiers came and broke the legs of the two men who were crucified with Jesus. ³³When they came to Jesus, they saw that he was already dead so they didn't break his legs. ³⁴However, one of the soldiers pierced his side with a spear, and immediately blood and water came out. ³⁵The one who saw this has testified, and his testimony is true. He knows that he speaks the truth, and he has testified so that you also can believe. ³⁶These things happened to fulfill the scripture, *They won't break any of his bones.*[f] ³⁷And another scripture says, *They will look at him whom they have pierced.*[g]

Jesus' body is buried

³⁸After this Joseph of Arimathea asked Pilate if he could take away the body of Jesus. Joseph was a disciple of Jesus, but a secret one because he feared the Jewish authorities. Pilate gave him permission, so he came and took the body away.

³⁹Nicodemus, the one who at first had come to Jesus at night, was there too. He brought a mixture of myrrh and aloe, nearly seventy-five pounds in all.[h] ⁴⁰Following Jewish burial customs, they took Jesus' body and wrapped it, with the spices, in linen cloths. ⁴¹There was a garden in the place where Jesus was crucified, and in the garden was a new tomb in which no one had ever been laid. ⁴²Because it was the Jewish Preparation Day and the tomb was nearby, they laid Jesus in it.

Empty tomb

20 Early in the morning of the first day of the week, while it was still dark, Mary Magdalene came to the tomb and saw that the stone had been taken away from the tomb. ²She ran to Simon Peter and the other disciple, the one whom Jesus loved, and said, "They have taken the Lord from the tomb, and we don't know where they've put him." ³Peter and the other disciple left to go to the tomb. ⁴They were running together, but the other disciple ran faster than Peter and was the first to arrive at the tomb. ⁵Bending down to take a look, he saw the linen cloths lying there, but he didn't go in. ⁶Following him, Simon Peter entered the

[f]Exod 12:46 [g]Zech 12:10 [h]*Or one hundred litra*; that is, one hundred Roman pounds

NAIL

Nails were rare in antiquity, where construction usually used holes and pegs to attach boards. In those few instances in which iron nails are mentioned in the construction process, the context is the decoration of the Jerusalem temple (1 Chron 22:3; 2 Chron 3:9), often relating to the extravagance of affixing gold foil or plates to the inner walls of the temple. Fifty shekels of gold were then used to overlay the heads of these small iron nails (perhaps the size of tacks). Both Jeremiah and Isaiah refer to the fashioning of idols using iron nails or clasps to fasten them together (Isa 41:7; Jer 10:4). To deal with the demands of heavier tasks, the Romans invented forged iron nails and the claw hammer to remove them. Long iron nails (7.5 in. in one recovered example) would have been used and probably reused when possible for crucifixion (John 20:25; cf. Col 2:14). Arms were nailed above the wrist, the legs bent, and a nail driven through the heel bones to pin the lower torso to the cross.

tomb and saw the linen cloths lying there. [7] He also saw the face cloth that had been on Jesus' head. It wasn't with the other clothes but was folded up in its own place. [8] Then the other disciple, the one who arrived at the tomb first, also went inside. He saw and believed. [9] They didn't yet understand the scripture that Jesus must rise from the dead. [10] Then the disciples returned to the place where they were staying.

Jesus appears to Mary

[11] Mary stood outside near the tomb, crying. As she cried, she bent down to look into the tomb. [12] She saw two angels dressed in white, seated where the body of Jesus had been, one at the head and one at the foot. [13] The angels asked her, "Woman, why are you crying?"

She replied, "They have taken away my Lord, and I don't know where they've put him." [14] As soon as she had said this, she turned around and saw Jesus standing there, but she didn't know it was Jesus.

[15] Jesus said to her, "Woman, why are you crying? Who are you looking for?"

Thinking he was the gardener, she replied, "Sir, if you have carried him away, tell me where you have put him and I will get him."

[16] Jesus said to her, "Mary."

She turned and said to him in Aramaic, "Rabbouni" (which means *Teacher*).

[17] Jesus said to her, "Don't hold on to me, for I haven't yet gone up to my Father. Go to my brothers and sisters and tell them, 'I'm going up to my Father and your Father, to my God and your God.'"

[18] Mary Magdalene left and announced to the disciples, "I've seen the Lord." Then she told them what he said to her.

Jesus appears to the disciples

[19] It was still the first day of the week. That evening, while the disciples were behind closed doors because they were afraid of the Jewish authorities, Jesus came and stood among them. He said, "Peace be with you." [20] After he said this, he showed them his hands and his side. When the disciples

saw the Lord, they were filled with joy. [21] Jesus said to them again, "Peace be with you. As the Father sent me, so I am sending you." [22] Then he breathed on them and said, "Receive the Holy Spirit. [23] If you forgive anyone's sins, they are forgiven; if you don't forgive them, they aren't forgiven."

Jesus appears to Thomas and the disciples

[24] Thomas, the one called Didymus,[i] one of the Twelve, wasn't with the disciples when Jesus came. [25] The other disciples told him, "We've seen the Lord!"

But he replied, "Unless I see the nail marks in his hands, put my finger in the wounds left by the nails, and put my hand into his side, I won't believe."

[26] After eight days his disciples were again in a house and Thomas was with them. Even though the doors were locked, Jesus entered and stood among them. He said, "Peace be with you." [27] Then he said to Thomas, "Put your finger here. Look at my hands. Put your hand into my side. No more disbelief. Believe!"

[28] Thomas responded to Jesus, "My Lord and my God!"

[29] Jesus replied, "Do you believe because you see me? Happy are those who don't see and yet believe."

[30] Then Jesus did many other miraculous signs in his disciples' presence, signs that aren't recorded in this scroll. [31] But these things are written so that you will believe that Jesus is the Christ, God's Son, and that believing, you will have life in his name.

Jesus appears again to the disciples

21 Later, Jesus himself appeared again to his disciples at the Sea of Tiberias. This is how it happened: [2] Simon Peter, Thomas (called Didymus[j]), Nathanael from Cana in Galilee, Zebedee's sons, and two other disciples were together. [3] Simon Peter told them, "I'm going fishing."

They said, "We'll go with you." They set out in a boat, but throughout the night they caught nothing. [4] Early in the morning,

---

[i] Or *the twin*   [j] Or *the twin*

Jesus stood on the shore, but the disciples didn't realize it was Jesus.

[5] Jesus called to them, "Children, have you caught anything to eat?"

They answered him, "No."

[6] He said, "Cast your net on the right side of the boat and you will find some."

So they did, and there were so many fish that they couldn't haul in the net. [7] Then the disciple whom Jesus loved said to Peter, "It's the Lord!" When Simon Peter heard it was the Lord, he wrapped his coat around himself (for he was naked) and jumped into the water. [8] The other disciples followed in the boat, dragging the net full of fish, for they weren't far from shore, only about one hundred yards.

[9] When they landed, they saw a fire there, with fish on it, and some bread. [10] Jesus said to them, "Bring some of the fish that you've just caught." [11] Simon Peter got up and pulled the net to shore. It was full of large fish, one hundred fifty-three of them. Yet the net hadn't torn, even with so many fish. [12] Jesus said to them, "Come and have breakfast." None of the disciples could bring themselves to ask him, "Who are you?" They knew it was the Lord. [13] Jesus came, took the bread, and gave it to them. He did the same with the fish. [14] This was now the third time Jesus appeared to his disciples after he was raised from the dead.

Jesus and Peter

[15] When they finished eating, Jesus asked Simon Peter, "Simon son of John, do you love me more than these?"

Simon replied, "Yes, Lord, you know I love you."

Jesus said to him, "Feed my lambs." [16] Jesus asked a second time, "Simon son of John, do you love me?"

Simon replied, "Yes, Lord, you know I love you."

Jesus said to him, "Take care of my sheep." [17] He asked a third time, "Simon son of John, do you love me?"

Peter was sad that Jesus asked him a third time, "Do you love me?" He replied, "Lord, you know everything; you know I love you."

Jesus said to him, "Feed my sheep. [18] I assure you that when you were younger you tied your own belt and walked around wherever you wanted. When you grow old,

THOMAS

One of the 12 disciples of Jesus (Matt 10:3; Mark 3:18; Luke 6:15; Acts 1:13), often referred to as "doubting Thomas" because of his initial refusal to believe in Jesus' resurrection (John 20:25). "Thomas" is a Greek transliteration of the Aramaic and Hebrew words for "twin." It is not clear whether it is a proper name or a nickname. Some Syriac manuscripts call him "Judas Thomas" in place of "Judas, not Iscariot" (John 14:22), who is listed as "Judas son of James" in Luke 6:16 and Acts 1:13. This may suggest that "Thomas" was understood as a nickname for Judas son of James in Syriac-speaking churches. In the Gospel of John, he is specified three times as "Thomas who was called Didymus" meaning "Thomas the Twin" (John 11:16; 20:24; 21:2). This may suggest that he was better known as "Didymus" in Greek-speaking churches.

Thomas is mentioned in all four Gospels, but stories in which Thomas figures as a character appear only in the Gospel of John. Thomas might be slow to believe, but his searching mind is rewarded with a spiritual insight to Jesus' divine identity, even as Jesus blesses those who believe without the benefit of seeing (John 20:29).

you will stretch out your hands and another will tie your belt and lead you where you don't want to go." [19] He said this to show the kind of death by which Peter would glorify God. After saying this, Jesus said to Peter, "Follow me."

Jesus and the disciple whom he loved

[20] Peter turned around and saw the disciple whom Jesus loved following them. This was the one who had leaned against Jesus at the meal and asked him, "Lord, who is going to betray you?" [21] When Peter saw this disciple, he said to Jesus, "Lord, what about him?"

[22] Jesus replied, "If I want him to remain until I come, what difference does that make to you? You must follow me." [23] Therefore, the word spread among the brothers and sisters that this disciple wouldn't die. However, Jesus didn't say he wouldn't die, but only, "If I want him to remain until I come, what difference does that make to you?" [24] This is the disciple who testifies concerning these things and who wrote them down. We know that his testimony is true. [25] Jesus did many other things as well. If all of them were recorded, I imagine the world itself wouldn't have enough room for the scrolls that would be written.

BELOVED DISCIPLE

"Beloved Disciple" is an abbreviated form of "the disciple whom Jesus loved," a phrase that appears in some form five times in John (13:23; 19:26; 20:2; 21:7, 20). Based on the reference to the disciple's testifying and writing about "these things" (21:24), ancient writers typically associated the traditional author of the Gospel, John the son of Zebedee, with the Beloved Disciple. However, few scholars would make this connection now. Beyond the traditional approach, there have been multiple suggestions regarding the Beloved Disciple's identity. Possible candidates proposed include Lazarus, Andrew, Philip, Nathanael, Thomas, the rich young ruler, and even Judas Iscariot. A few scholars have even proposed Mary Magdalene as the disciple in question.

THEME

The universal church came into existence through the heroic, Spirit-filled witnessing of Jesus' disciples to Jews and Gentiles concerning the power of God, which is redemptively acting in the world through the crucified and resurrected Jesus.

INTRODUCTION

Acts is a sequel to the Gospel witness of the life and work of Jesus. Acts is the only book that continues the narrative of the work of Jesus through the church and the apostles. Originally the book was part of a larger corpus of material (see Acts 1:1). When the New Testament canon was formed the first volume, the Gospel of Luke, was placed with the three other Gospels. Acts was placed following the Fourth Gospel. Its placement indicates its function as it links the life of Jesus with the letters of Paul.

THE AUTHOR OF ACTS

The author of the book of Acts is the same as the author of the Gospel of Luke, who has traditionally been identified as Luke, the beloved physician (see 2 Timothy 4:11; Colossians 4:14; Philemon verse 24, which all mention Luke). The book is addressed to Theophilus, which in Greek means "lover of God." Therefore, the work could easily have been intended for a single reader's eye.

On the other hand, the tone of the work is clearly apologetic. The book could have been a work intended to place the Christian faith and church in a positive light before the Roman authorities. Theophilus could have been a patron of the early Christian movement, or Theophilus may have been the author's name for any reader of Luke and Acts. All attempts at identification of the book's original audience are matters of conjecture, since we simply cannot ascertain beyond doubt the individual or individuals to whom the work is addressed. One thing is certain, however. The work is read by Christians as a stirring account of the initial moments in the life of the Christian movement.

THE DATE OF ACTS

Any attempt to date the writing is equally frustrating. No evidence in the book itself gives specific years. The tone of defense and apologetic imply a time when the church was under stress, possibly persecution. A good number of episodes in the book of Acts give strong encouragement to those under stress. But a specific date simply cannot be determined. Scholars do conclude that the work was written sometime late in the first century.

THE PURPOSE OF ACTS

The overriding purpose of Acts is the edification of Christian believers. The beginning of Luke, which was originally connected directly to Acts, implies that the author thought that a corrective with respect to doctrine or tradition was necessary (Luke 1:3). Since much of the second half of the work centers on the trial and defense of Paul, the purpose could well have been to defend Paul as a representative of all Christianity. One scholar suggests that the book is an attempt to recover the reputation of Paul.

Certainly a reading of Acts gives a different perspective from what Paul's own letters reveal. In Acts, the great apostle strides across the Mediterranean—in sharp contrast to the beleaguered preacher and struggling apostle portrayed in the letters.

Throughout the work divine guidance is emphasized. The reason is quite clear. The early church's expansion could not be the result merely of individuals who wanted to direct the fortunes of the believing community. The expansion had to be the result of God's own intention and direction. This in turn gives justification for the mission to the Gentiles. Perhaps no other single purpose is as clear or important in Acts as defending the legitimacy of the Gentile mission.

THE THEOLOGY OF ACTS

Theological concerns to which the writer addresses himself include the expected return of Jesus. Christians felt that Jesus' return was imminent. At any moment all of history could come to its grand conclusion with the return of Jesus. The delay of the return posed a special problem for the early church. Indeed, Acts begins with a scene intended to dispel sky-gazing expectation (1:11).

The book of Acts contains no systematic presentation of major topics in Christian thinking. At no time is any complete treatise presented regarding God, Jesus, the church, or even the Holy Spirit. Throughout the work passages can be found in which these issues are mentioned. But any organized formulation of theological issues is largely accidental.

The work of the Holy Spirit does occupy a major place in Acts. However, the work of the Spirit is varied and never fits into categories or systems. Some readers may want to find in these pages the Holy Spirit working with pure spontaneity. Indeed, there are moments of spontaneity and ecstasy. However, a good deal of the Holy Spirit's work is challenging, confrontational, directive, and stern. The early church struggled long and hard, not only within itself but with its Lord as well, with regard to the mission to those outside the Law. At every important point in the church's history the Holy Spirit prevails and the church reaches out to its ultimate destination: a universal gospel.

HOW TO READ ACTS

Modern readers will face certain difficulties when reading Acts. The reason for this is quite simple: Acts is an ancient book and uses ancient customs and conventions. Miracles, for instance, are sprinkled throughout the work—people are healed, both through a touch and by the mere passing of Peter's shadow. A young boy is brought back to life by the apostle Paul. A poisonous snake can do no harm to Paul on Malta. Prisoners are released from prison by earthquake and angels— for the ancient Israelites these incidents are not unusual at all.

Such stories are central in Christian thinking. But for modern readers they are difficult. We must remember to consider the abiding human experience that these peculiar images or categories address. We will be a good deal closer to understanding the Bible if we can allow the ancient methods to express something that is true in human nature and in God's work with the creation. We must resist the temptation to rationalize everything away for scientific or logical reasons.

Similarly, ancient historical methods include speeches or sermons that were not verbatim reports. Composite speeches were common in the ancient world. Again, the writer is not concerned solely with strict reporting of events and statements. Luke's concern is the meaning of events and beliefs contained in the sermons. Another ancient convention is that of using a specific incident as representative of a larger phenomenon. For instance, there were many more encounters between Christians and Samaritans than the single incident reported by Luke. However, the intention is accomplished. The reader will understand that single events stand for widespread occurrences.

At times the writer does not quote the Hebrew Scriptures exactly. For some readers such incidents are errors and thereby call into question the authority of the Bible. Such a perspective, however, is shortsighted. The writer did not have at his disposal fine libraries with multiple volumes that were cross-indexed. He had only the material at hand, recollections saved through storytelling, his own reminiscences, and the memorized Scriptures. Again, ancient readers would not have balked at slight misquotations of Scripture.

The same insight should be kept in mind with respect to details that appear either contradictory or incredible. Luke's purpose was not to present a seamless weave of exact history. We can almost see his excitement grow as he tells the dramatic story of how the church grew from a few frightened souls to the victorious faith that reached even Rome itself!

Finally, we must remember that Luke's purpose was to tell the story of the movement of Christianity beyond the bounds of race, tradition, and culture. Therefore, if we attempt to make this work serve as an anvil on which to work out systematic theological formulations, we overstep Luke's intention.

THE MEANING OF ACTS

The development of the book of Acts underscores its purpose. Beginning in Jerusalem with a handful of believers, the gospel moves steadily outward. It travels first from Jerusalem to the Gentile world. Then it moves from Aramaic-speaking converts to Gentile converts. Through the work of Peter and Paul the gospel makes its way to the masses of people populating the entire known world.

When we ask the question, What is the book of Acts about? The answer might well be that Acts is about the inevitable work of God to spread the gospel of Christ to every corner of the world.

ACTS OF THE APOSTLES

The risen Jesus with his disciples

1 Theophilus, the first scroll I wrote concerned everything Jesus did and taught from the beginning, ²right up to the day when he was taken up into heaven. Before he was taken up, working in the power of the Holy Spirit, Jesus instructed the apostles he had chosen. ³After his suffering, he showed them that he was alive with many convincing proofs. He appeared to them over a period of forty days, speaking to them about God's kingdom. ⁴While they were eating together, he ordered them not to leave Jerusalem but to wait for what the Father had promised. He said, "This is what you heard from me: ⁵John baptized with water, but in only a few days you will be baptized with the Holy Spirit."

⁶As a result, those who had gathered together asked Jesus, "Lord, are you going to restore the kingdom to Israel now?"

⁷Jesus replied, "It isn't for you to know the times or seasons that the Father has set by his own authority. ⁸Rather, you will receive power when the Holy Spirit has come upon you, and you will be my witnesses in Jerusalem, in all Judea and Samaria, and to the end of the earth."

⁹After Jesus said these things, as they were watching, he was lifted up and a cloud took him out of their sight. ¹⁰While he was going away and as they were staring toward heaven, suddenly two men in white robes stood next to them. ¹¹They said, "Galileans, why are you standing here, looking toward heaven? This Jesus, who was taken up from you into heaven, will come in the same way that you saw him go into heaven."

Jesus' followers in Jerusalem

¹²Then they returned to Jerusalem from the Mount of Olives, which is near Jerusalem—a sabbath day's journey away. ¹³When they entered the city, they went to the upstairs room where they were staying. Peter, John, James, and Andrew; Philip and Thomas; Bartholomew and Matthew; James, Alphaeus' son; Simon the zealot; and Judas, James' son—¹⁴all were united in their devotion to prayer, along with some women, including Mary the mother of Jesus, and his brothers.

A replacement for Judas

¹⁵During this time, the family of believers was a company of about one hundred

SABBATH DAY'S JOURNEY

The distance a Jew could travel on the Sabbath according to scribal interpretation. Dating rabbinic materials is difficult, so what this distance was at particular times is hard to establish.

The Bible prohibits travel on the Sabbath: "you should . . . not leave your place on the seventh day" (Exod 16:29). Later interpreters argued that "your place" meant "your town" and that a town's boundaries extended 1,000 cubits (1,500 ft., Num 35:5). Thus, *the Damascus Document* from Qumran (dated to ca. 100 BCE) says that an individual could not travel over 1,000 cubits beyond one's town. By 200 CE, the rabbis argued that one could travel 2,000 cubits, since one could travel 1,000 cubits outside the town and return.

The only author to use this phrase in the Bible is Luke, who says that the distance from Jerusalem to the Mount of Olives was "a sabbath's day journey" (Acts 1:12). Jesus alluded to the limited ability to travel on the Sabbath by suggesting that flight on the Sabbath would be difficult (Matt 24:20).

twenty persons. Peter stood among them and said, [16]"Brothers and sisters, the scripture that the Holy Spirit announced beforehand through David had to be fulfilled. This was the scripture concerning Judas, who became a guide for those who arrested Jesus. [17]This happened even though he was one of us and received a share of this ministry." ([18]In fact, he bought a field with the payment he received for his injustice. Falling headfirst, he burst open in the middle and all his intestines spilled out. [19]This became known to everyone living in Jerusalem, so they called that field in their own language Hakeldama, or "Field of Blood.") [20]"It is written in the Psalms scroll,

Let his home become deserted and
  let there be no one living in it;[a]

and

  Give his position of leadership to another.[b]

[21]"Therefore, we must select one of those who have accompanied us during the whole time the Lord Jesus lived among us, [22]beginning from the baptism of John until the day when Jesus was taken from us. This person must become along with us a witness to his resurrection." [23]So they nominated two: Joseph called Barsabbas, who was also known as Justus, and Matthias.

[24]They prayed, "Lord, you know everyone's deepest thoughts and desires. Show us clearly which one you have chosen from among these two [25]to take the place of this ministry and apostleship, from which Judas turned away to go to his own place." [26]When they cast lots, the lot fell

[a]Ps 69:25 [b]Ps 109:8

on Matthias. He was added to the eleven apostles.

Pentecost

2 When Pentecost Day arrived, they were all together in one place. [2]Suddenly a sound from heaven like the howling of a fierce wind filled the entire house where they were sitting. [3]They saw what seemed to be individual flames of fire alighting on each one of them. [4]They were all filled with the Holy Spirit and began to speak in other languages as the Spirit enabled them to speak.

[5]There were pious Jews from every nation under heaven living in Jerusalem. [6]When they heard this sound, a crowd gathered. They were mystified because everyone heard them speaking in their native languages. [7]They were surprised and amazed, saying, "Look, aren't all the people who are speaking Galileans, every one of them? [8]How then can each of us hear them speaking in our native language? [9]Parthians, Medes, and Elamites; as well as residents of Mesopotamia, Judea, and Cappadocia, Pontus and Asia, [10]Phrygia and Pamphylia, Egypt and the regions of Libya bordering Cyrene; and visitors from Rome (both Jews and converts to Judaism), [11]Cretans and Arabs—we hear them declaring the mighty works of God in our own languages!" [12]They were all surprised and bewildered. Some asked each other, "What does this mean?" [13]Others jeered at them, saying, "They're full of new wine!"

KOINONIA

The Greek noun translated in the NT as "fellowship, participation, sharing, or contribution." The term is absent from the Gospels, but in Acts 2:42 it appears to be an essential part of the early church. *Koinonia* is typically a Pauline theme (thirteen of the nineteen occurrences), where fellowship means that with Christ (1 Cor 1:9; 10:16; Phil 3:10), the Holy Spirit (2 Cor 13:13; Phil 2:1), or the gospel (Phil 1:5; Phlm 6). Elsewhere, it also refers to participating in the collection for Jerusalem's poor (Rom 15:26; 2 Cor 8:4; 9:13).

¹⁴Peter stood with the other eleven apostles. He raised his voice and declared, "Judeans and everyone living in Jerusalem! Know this! Listen carefully to my words! ¹⁵These people aren't drunk, as you suspect; after all, it's only nine o'clock in the morning! ¹⁶Rather, this is what was spoken through the prophet Joel:

¹⁷ In the last days, God says,
I will pour out my Spirit on all people.
Your sons and daughters will prophesy.
Your young will see visions.
Your elders will dream dreams.
¹⁸ Even upon my servants, men and women,
I will pour out my Spirit in those days,
and they will prophesy.

¹⁹ I will cause wonders to occur in the
heavens above
and signs on the earth below,
blood and fire and a cloud of smoke.
²⁰ The sun will be changed into darkness,
and the moon will be changed into blood,
before the great and spectacular day
of the Lord comes.
²¹ And everyone who calls on the name
of the Lord will be saved.ᶜ

²²"Fellow Israelites, listen to these words! Jesus the Nazarene was a man whose credentials God proved to you through miracles, wonders, and signs, which God performed through him among you. You yourselves know this. ²³In accordance with God's es-

ᶜJoel 2:28-32

PENTECOST

Meaning "fiftieth (day)," a Greek name for the Festival of Weeks described in the holiday lists in Exodus 23:14-17; 34:18, 22-24; Leviticus 23; Numbers 28–29; and Deuteronomy 16. The name was used by Greek writers for the second of the three pilgrimage festivals stipulated in the OT because of the procedure arranged for determining its date. Both Leviticus 23:15-16 (part of the Holiness Code) and Deuteronomy 16:9-10 say that one should count seven complete weeks from an event occurring in the first month around the time of Passover and Unleavened Bread (the waving of the bundle in Lev 23:15; putting the sickle to the standing grain in Deut 16:9), with the next or fiftieth day being the date of the festival. Because neither of these events is assigned to a specific date, the Pentateuch prescribes no exact time for the Festival of Weeks/Pentecost; as a result, there was, at least in the Second Temple period, disagreement about when it was to be celebrated. The festival marked the beginning of the wheat harvest (Exod 34:22) and was to be the occasion for a number of offerings (Lev 23:17-19; Num 28:26-31), including two loaves made from wheat flour and "baked with leaven" (Lev 23:17). It was a day for a holy convocation, and labor was prohibited (Lev 23:21; Num 28:26). It was a popular holiday.

The most famous NT reference to the holiday is in Acts 2, where the Holy Spirit was poured out on Jesus' first followers on Pentecost Day (see v. 1). On that day, in obedience to the Instruction, large numbers of Jews from many parts of the world had gathered in Jerusalem for the pilgrimage holiday and thus provided a worldwide audience that could understand the message the disciples were suddenly and miraculously speaking in their several languages (vv. 8-11).

tablished plan and foreknowledge, he was betrayed. You, with the help of wicked men, had Jesus killed by nailing him to a cross. [24]God raised him up! God freed him from death's dreadful grip, since it was impossible for death to hang on to him. [25]David says about him,

> I foresaw that the Lord was always with me;
>   because he is at my right hand
>   I won't be shaken.
> [26] Therefore, my heart was glad
>   and my tongue rejoiced.
> Moreover, my body will live in hope,
>   [27] because you won't abandon me
>   to the grave,
>   nor permit your holy one
>   to experience decay.
> [28] You have shown me the paths of life;
>   your presence will fill me with happiness.[d]

[29]"Brothers and sisters, I can speak confidently about the patriarch David. He died and was buried, and his tomb is with us to this very day. [30]Because he was a prophet, he knew that God promised him with a solemn pledge to seat one of his descendants on his throne. [31]Having seen this beforehand, David spoke about the resurrection of Christ, that *he wasn't abandoned to the grave, nor did his body experience decay.*[e] [32]This Jesus, God raised up. We are all witnesses to that fact. [33]He was exalted to God's right side and received from the Father the promised Holy Spirit. He poured out this Spirit, and you are seeing and hearing the results of his having done so. [34]David didn't ascend into heaven. Yet he says,

> The Lord said to my Lord,
>   'Sit at my right side,
> [35] until I make your enemies
>   a footstool for your feet.'[f]

[36]"Therefore, let all Israel know beyond question that God has made this Jesus, whom you crucified, both Lord and Christ."

[37]When the crowd heard this, they were deeply troubled. They said to Peter and the other apostles, "Brothers, what should we do?"

[38]Peter replied, "Change your hearts and lives. Each of you must be baptized in the name of Jesus Christ for the forgiveness of your sins. Then you will receive the gift of the Holy Spirit. [39]This promise is for you, your children, and for all who are far away—as many as the Lord our God invites." [40]With many other words he testified to them and encouraged them, saying, "Be saved from this perverse generation." [41]Those who accepted Peter's message were baptized. God brought about three thousand people into the community on that day.

Community of believers

[42]The believers devoted themselves to the apostles' teaching, to the community, to their shared meals, and to their prayers. [43]A sense of awe came over everyone. God performed many wonders and signs through the apostles. [44]All the believers were united and shared everything. [45]They would sell pieces of property and possessions and distribute the proceeds to everyone who needed them. [46]Every day, they met together in the temple and ate in their homes. They shared food with gladness and simplicity. [47]They praised God and demonstrated God's goodness to everyone. The Lord added daily to the community those who were being saved.

Healing of a crippled man

3 Peter and John were going up to the temple at three o'clock in the afternoon, the established prayer time. [2]Meanwhile, a man crippled since birth was being carried in. Every day, people would place him at the temple gate known as the Beautiful Gate so he could ask for money from those entering the temple. [3]When he saw Peter and John about to enter, he began to ask them for a gift. [4]Peter and John stared at him. Peter said, "Look at us!" [5]So the man gazed at them, expecting to receive something from them. [6]Peter said, "I don't have any money, but I will give you what I do have. In the name of Jesus Christ the Nazarene, rise up and walk!" [7]Then he grasped the man's right hand and raised him up. At once his feet

---

[d]Ps 16:8-11　[e]Ps 16:10　[f]Ps 110:1

and ankles became strong. [8]Jumping up, he began to walk around. He entered the temple with them, walking, leaping, and praising God. [9]All the people saw him walking and praising God. [10]They recognized him as the same one who used to sit at the temple's Beautiful Gate asking for money. They were filled with amazement and surprise at what had happened to him.

[11]While the healed man clung to Peter and John, all the people rushed toward them at Solomon's Porch, completely amazed. [12]Seeing this, Peter addressed the people: "You Israelites, why are you amazed at this? Why are you staring at us as if we made him walk by our own power or piety? [13]The God of Abraham, Isaac, and Jacob—the God of our ancestors—has glorified his servant Jesus. This is the one you handed over and denied in Pilate's presence, even though he had already decided to release him. [14]You rejected the holy and righteous one, and asked that a murderer be released to you instead. [15]You killed the author of life, the very one whom God raised from the dead. We are witnesses of this. [16]His name itself has made this man strong. That is, because of faith in Jesus' name, God has strengthened this man whom you see and know. The faith that comes through Jesus gave him complete health right before your eyes.

[17]"Brothers and sisters, I know you acted in ignorance. So did your rulers. [18]But this is how God fulfilled what he foretold through all the prophets: that his Christ would suffer. [19]Change your hearts and lives! Turn back to God so that your sins may be wiped away. [20]Then the Lord will provide a season of relief from the distress of this age and he will send Jesus, whom he handpicked to be your Christ. [21]Jesus must remain in heaven until the restoration of all things, about which God spoke long ago through his holy prophets. [22]Moses said, *The Lord your God will raise up from your own people a prophet like me. Listen to whatever he tells you.* [23]*Whoever doesn't listen to that prophet will be totally cut off from the people.*[g] [24]All the prophets who spoke—from Sam-

uel forward—announced these days. [25]You are the heirs of the prophets and the covenant that God made with your ancestors when he told Abraham, *Through your descendants, all the families on earth will be blessed.*[h] [26]After God raised his servant, he sent him to you first—to bless you by enabling each of you to turn from your evil ways."

Peter and John questioned

4 While Peter and John were speaking to the people, the priests, the captain of the temple guard, and the Sadducees confronted them. [2]They were incensed that the apostles were teaching the people and announcing that the resurrection of the dead was happening because of Jesus. [3]They seized Peter and John and put them in prison until the next day. (It was already evening.) [4]Many who heard the word became believers, and their number grew to about five thousand.

[5]The next day the leaders, elders, and legal experts gathered in Jerusalem, [6]along with Annas the high priest, Caiaphas, John, Alexander, and others from the high priest's family. [7]They had Peter and John brought before them and asked, "By what power or in what name did you do this?"

[8]Then Peter, inspired by the Holy Spirit, answered, "Leaders of the people and elders, [9]are we being examined today because something good was done for a sick person, a good deed that healed him? [10]If so, then you and all the people of Israel need to know that this man stands healthy before you because of the name of Jesus Christ the Nazarene—whom you crucified but whom God raised from the dead. [11]This Jesus is the stone you builders rejected; he has become the cornerstone! [12]Salvation can be found in no one else. Throughout the whole world, no other name has been given among humans through which we must be saved."

[13]The council was caught by surprise by the confidence with which Peter and John spoke. After all, they understood that these apostles were uneducated and inexperi-

---

[g]Deut 18:15, 19   [h]Gen 22:18; 26:4

enced. They also recognized that they had been followers of Jesus. [14]However, since the healed man was standing with Peter and John before their own eyes, they had no rebuttal. [15]After ordering them to wait outside, the council members began to confer with each other. [16]"What should we do with these men? Everyone living in Jerusalem is aware of the sign performed through them. It's obvious to everyone and we can't deny it. [17]To keep it from spreading further among the people, we need to warn them not to speak to anyone in this name." [18]When they called Peter and John back, they demanded that they stop all speaking and teaching in the name of Jesus.

[19]Peter and John responded, "It's up to you to determine whether it's right before God to obey you rather than God. [20]As for us, we can't stop speaking about what we have seen and heard." [21]They threatened them further, then released them. Because of public support for Peter and John, they couldn't find a way to punish them. Everyone was praising God for what had happened, [22]because the man who had experienced this sign of healing was over 40 years old.

The believers pray

[23]After their release, Peter and John returned to the brothers and sisters and reported everything the chief priests and elders had said. [24]They listened, then lifted their voices in unison to God, "Master, you are the one who created the heaven, the earth, the sea, and everything in them. [25]You are the one who spoke by the Holy Spirit through our ancestor David, your servant:

Why did the Gentiles rage,
    and the peoples plot in vain?
[26] *The kings of the earth took their stand*
    and the rulers gathered together as one
    against the Lord and against his Christ.[i]
[27]Indeed, both Herod and Pontius Pilate, with Gentiles and Israelites, did gather in this city against your holy servant Jesus, whom you anointed. [28]They did what your

power and plan had already determined would happen. [29]Now, Lord, take note of their threats and enable your servants to speak your word with complete confidence. [30]Stretch out your hand to bring healing and enable signs and wonders to be performed through the name of Jesus, your holy servant." [31]After they prayed, the place where they were gathered was shaken. They were all filled with the Holy Spirit and began speaking God's word with confidence.

Sharing among the believers

[32]The community of believers was one in heart and mind. None of them would say, "This is mine!" about any of their possessions, but held everything in common. [33]The apostles continued to bear powerful witness to the resurrection of the Lord Jesus, and an abundance of grace was at work among them all. [34]There were no needy persons among them. Those who owned properties or houses would sell them, bring the proceeds from the sales, [35]and place them in the care and under the authority of the apostles. Then it was distributed to anyone who was in need.

[36]Joseph, whom the apostles nicknamed Barnabas (that is, "one who encourages"), was a Levite from Cyprus. [37]He owned a field, sold it, brought the money, and placed it in the care and under the authority of the apostles.

Pretenders of sharing

5 However, a man named Ananias, along with his wife Sapphira, sold a piece of property. [2]With his wife's knowledge, he withheld some of the proceeds from the sale. He brought the rest and placed it in the care and under the authority of the apostles. [3]Peter asked, "Ananias, how is it that Satan has influenced you to lie to the Holy Spirit by withholding some of the proceeds from the sale of your land? [4]Wasn't that property yours to keep? After you sold it, wasn't the money yours to do with whatever you wanted? What made you think of such a thing? You haven't lied to other

[i]Or *anointed one*; Ps 2:1-2

people but to God!" [5]When Ananias heard these words, he dropped dead. Everyone who heard this conversation was terrified. [6]Some young men stood up, wrapped up his body, carried him out, and buried him.

[7]About three hours later, his wife entered, but she didn't know what had happened to her husband. [8]Peter asked her, "Tell me, did you and your husband receive this price for the field?"

She responded, "Yes, that's the amount."

[9]He replied, "How could you scheme with each other to challenge the Lord's Spirit? Look! The feet of those who buried your husband are at the door. They will carry you out too." [10]At that very moment, she dropped dead at his feet. When the young men entered and found her dead, they carried her out and buried her with her husband. [11]Trepidation and dread seized the whole church and all who heard what had happened.

Responses to the church

[12]The apostles performed many signs and wonders among the people. They would come together regularly at Solomon's Porch. [13]No one from outside the church dared to join them, even though the people spoke highly of them. [14]Indeed, more and more believers in the Lord, large numbers of both men and women, were added to the church. [15]As a result, they would even bring the sick out into the main streets and lay them on cots and mats so that at least Peter's shadow could fall on some of them as he passed by. [16]Even large numbers of persons from towns around Jerusalem would gather, bringing the sick and those harassed by unclean spirits. Everyone was healed.

The Jerusalem Council harasses the apostles

[17]The high priest, together with his allies, the Sadducees, was overcome with jealousy. [18]They seized the apostles and made a public show of putting them in prison. [19]An angel from the Lord opened the prison doors during the night and led them out. The angel told them, [20]"Go, take your place in the temple, and tell the people everything about this new life." [21]Early in the morning, they went into the temple as they had been told and began to teach.

When the high priest and his colleagues gathered, they convened the Jerusalem Council, that is, the full assembly of Israel's elders. They sent word to the prison to have the apostles brought before them. [22]However, the guards didn't find them in the prison. They returned and reported, [23]"We found the prison locked and wellsecured, with guards standing at the doors, but when we opened the doors we found no one inside!" [24]When they received this news, the captain of the temple guard and the chief priests were baffled and wondered what might be happening. [25]Just then, someone arrived and announced, "Look! The people you put in prison are standing in the temple and teaching the people!" [26]Then the captain left with his guards and brought the apostles back. They didn't use force because they were afraid the people would stone them.

[27]The apostles were brought before the council where the high priest confronted them: [28]"In no uncertain terms, we demanded that you not teach in this name. And look at you! You have filled Jerusalem with your teaching. And you are determined to hold us responsible for this man's death."

[29]Peter and the apostles replied, "We must obey God rather than humans! [30]The God of our ancestors raised Jesus from the dead—whom you killed by hanging him on a tree. [31]God has exalted Jesus to his right side as leader and savior so that he could enable Israel to change its heart and life and to find forgiveness for sins. [32]We are witnesses of such things, as is the Holy Spirit, whom God has given to those who obey him."

[33]When the council members heard this, they became furious and wanted to kill the apostles. [34]One council member, a Pharisee and teacher of the Law named Gamaliel, well-respected by all the people, stood up and ordered that the men be taken outside for a few moments. [35]He said, "Fellow Israelites, consider carefully what you intend to

do to these people. ³⁶Some time ago, Theudas appeared, claiming to be somebody, and some four hundred men joined him. After he was killed, all of his followers scattered, and nothing came of that. ³⁷Afterward, at the time of the census, Judas the Galilean appeared and got some people to follow him in a revolt. He was killed too, and all his followers scattered far and wide. ³⁸Here's my recommendation in this case: Distance yourselves from these men. Let them go! If their plan or activity is of human origin, it will end in ruin. ³⁹If it originates with God, you won't be able to stop them. Instead, you would actually find yourselves fighting God!" The council was convinced by his reasoning. ⁴⁰After calling the apostles back, they had them beaten. They ordered them not to speak in the name of Jesus, then let them go. ⁴¹The apostles left the council rejoicing because they had been regarded as worthy to suffer disgrace for the sake of the name. ⁴²Every day they continued to teach and proclaim the good news that Jesus is the Christ, both in the temple and in houses.

Selection of seven to serve

6 About that time, while the number of disciples continued to increase, a complaint arose. Greek-speaking disciples accused the Aramaic-speaking disciples because their widows were being overlooked in the daily food service. ²The Twelve called a meeting of all the disciples and said, "It isn't right for us to set aside proclamation of God's word in order to serve tables. ³Brothers and sisters, carefully choose seven well-respected men from among you. They must be well-respected and endowed by the Spirit with exceptional wisdom. We will put them in charge of this concern. ⁴As for us, we will devote ourselves to prayer and the service of proclaiming the word." ⁵This proposal pleased the entire community. They selected Stephen, a man endowed by the Holy Spirit with exceptional faith, Philip, Prochorus, Nicanor, Timon, Parmenas, and Nicolaus from Antioch, a convert to Judaism. ⁶The community presented these seven to the apostles, who prayed and laid their hands on them. ⁷God's word continued to grow. The number of disciples

STEPHEN

One of the seven Hellenists (Greek-speaking Jews) and the first martyr in Luke's depiction of the early Jesus movement in Jerusalem. As one of the seven (Acts 6:5), Stephen is initially appointed to resolve an internal problem (the neglect of Greek-speaking Jewish widows in the daily distribution of food [6:1]). His work extends, however, beyond "[serving] tables" (6:2) and includes the performance of "great wonders and signs" (6:8), a feat evoking both the work of the apostles in the earlier part of Acts (2:43; 5:12; cf. 4:30) and ultimately that of Moses (Deut 7:19; 11:3; 28:46; 29:2-3; cf. Stephen's speech [7:36]). Though the narrative does not indicate the reception of Stephen's deeds, the powerful force of his words (6:10) leads to an external problem, because members of the Synagogue of Former Slaves, with whom Stephen has disputed (6:9), bring him before the Jerusalem Council (6:12) on the false charge of blasphemy against Moses and God (6:11), that is, speaking words against "this holy place" (the temple, 6:13-14), the Law (6:13), and the "customary practices" of Moses (6:14). Thereafter, and repeatedly, his words (including a long speech) are met with outright rejection (7:54, 57), with the result that he is stoned to death (7:58), the levitical punishment for blasphemy (Lev 24:16), and buried by devout men (8:2).

in Jerusalem increased significantly. Even a large group of priests embraced the faith.

Arrest and murder of Stephen

[8]Stephen, who stood out among the believers for the way God's grace was at work in his life and for his exceptional endowment with divine power, was doing great wonders and signs among the people. [9]Opposition arose from some who belonged to the so-called Synagogue of Former Slaves. Members from Cyrene, Alexandria, Cilicia, and Asia entered into debate with Stephen. [10]However, they couldn't resist the wisdom the Spirit gave him as he spoke. [11]Then they secretly enticed some people to claim, "We heard him insult Moses and God." [12]They stirred up the people, the elders, and the legal experts. They caught Stephen, dragged him away, and brought him before the Jerusalem Council. [13]Before the council, they presented false witnesses who testified, "This man never stops speaking against this holy place and the Law. [14]In fact, we heard him say that this man Jesus of Nazareth will destroy this place and alter the customary practices Moses gave us." [15]Everyone seated in the council stared at Stephen, and they saw that his face was radiant, just like an angel's.

7 The high priest asked, "Are these accusations true?"

[2]Stephen responded, "Brothers and fathers, listen to me. Our glorious God appeared to our ancestor Abraham while he was still in Mesopotamia, before he settled in Haran. [3]God told him, 'Leave your homeland and kin, and go to the land that I will show you.'[j] [4]So Abraham left the land of the Chaldeans and settled in Haran. After Abraham's father died, God had him resettle in this land where you now live. [5]God didn't give him an inheritance here, not even a square foot of land. However, God did promise to give the land as his possession to him and to his descendants, even though Abraham had no child. [6]God put it this way: *His descendants will be strangers in a land that belongs to others, who will enslave them and abuse them for four hundred years.*[k] [7]*And I will condemn the nation they serve as slaves,* God said, *and afterward they will leave*[l] that land and serve me in this place. [8]God gave him the covenant confirmed through circumcision. Accordingly, eight days after Isaac's birth, Abraham circumcised him. Isaac did the same with Jacob, and Jacob with the twelve patriarchs.

[9]"Because the patriarchs were jealous of Joseph, they sold him into slavery in Egypt. God was with him, however, [10]and rescued him from all his troubles. The grace and wisdom he gave Joseph were recognized by Pharaoh, king of Egypt, who appointed him ruler over Egypt and over his whole palace. [11]A famine came upon all Egypt and Canaan, and great hardship came with it. Our ancestors had nothing to eat. [12]When Jacob heard there was grain in Egypt, he sent our ancestors there for the first time. [13]During their second visit, Joseph told his brothers who he was, and Pharaoh learned

[j]Gen 12:1   [k]Gen 15:13   [l]Gen 15:14

NAZARETH

A village in the Roman district of Galilee identified in the NT as the home of Joseph, Mary, and Jesus (Matt 2:23; Luke 2:4, 39, 51). Located in lower Galilee, Nazareth is approximately midway between the Mediterranean Sea to the west and the southern tip of the Galilee Sea to the east. Situated on a ridge overlooking the Jezreel Valley, Nazareth had a commanding view of the large basin to the south and was in close proximity to Sepphoris, the capital of Galilee, and to a major highway three mi. to the north.

about Joseph's family. ¹⁴Joseph sent for his father Jacob and all his relatives—seventy-five in all—and invited them to live with him. ¹⁵So Jacob went down to Egypt, where he and our ancestors died. ¹⁶Their bodies were brought back to Shechem and placed in the tomb that Abraham had purchased for a certain sum of money from Hamor's children, who lived in Shechem.

¹⁷"When it was time for God to keep the promise he made to Abraham, the number of our people in Egypt had greatly expanded. ¹⁸But then *another king rose to power over Egypt who didn't know anything about Joseph.*ᵐ ¹⁹He exploited our people and abused our ancestors. He even forced them to abandon their newly born babies so they would die. ²⁰That's when Moses was born. He was highly favored by God, and for three months his parents cared for him in their home. ²¹After he was abandoned, Pharaoh's daughter adopted and cared for him as though he were her own son. ²²Moses learned everything Egyptian wisdom had to offer, and he was a man of powerful words and deeds.

²³"When Moses was 40 years old, he decided to visit his family, the Israelites. ²⁴He saw one of them being wronged so he came to his rescue and evened the score by killing the Egyptian. ²⁵He expected his own kin to understand that God was using him to rescue them, but they didn't. ²⁶The next day he came upon some Israelites who were caught up in an argument. He tried to make peace between them by saying, 'You are brothers! Why are you harming each other?' ²⁷The one who started the fight against his neighbor pushed Moses aside and said, *'Who appointed you as our leader and judge?* ²⁸*Are you planning to kill me like you killed that Egyptian yesterday?'*ᵐ ²⁹When Moses heard this, he fled to Midian, where he lived as an immigrant and had two sons.

³⁰"Forty years later, an angel appeared to Moses in the flame of a burning bush in the wilderness near Mount Sinai. ³¹Enthralled by the sight, Moses approached to get a closer look and he heard the Lord's voice:

³²*'I am the God of your ancestors, the God of Abraham, Isaac, and Jacob.'*ᵒ Trembling with fear, Moses didn't dare to investigate any further. ³³The Lord continued, *'Remove the sandals from your feet, for the place where you are standing is holy ground.* ³⁴*I have clearly seen the oppression my people have experienced in Egypt, and I have heard their groaning. I have come down to rescue them. Come! I am sending you to Egypt.'*ᵖ

³⁵"This is the same Moses whom they rejected when they asked, 'Who appointed you as our leader and judge?' This is the Moses whom God sent as leader and deliverer. God did this with the help of the angel who appeared before him in the bush. ³⁶This man led them out after he performed wonders and signs in Egypt at the Red Sea and for forty years in the wilderness. ³⁷This is the Moses who told the Israelites, *'God will raise up for you a prophet like me from your own people.'*�q ³⁸This is the one who was in the assembly in the wilderness with our ancestors and with the angel who spoke to him on Mount Sinai. He is the one who received life-giving words to give to us. ³⁹He's also the one whom our ancestors refused to obey. Instead, they pushed him aside and, in their thoughts and desires, returned to Egypt. ⁴⁰They told Aaron, *'Make us gods that will lead us. As for this Moses who led us out of Egypt, we don't know what's happened to him!'*ʳ ⁴¹That's when they made an idol in the shape of a calf, offered a sacrifice to it, and began to celebrate what they had made with their own hands. ⁴²So God turned away from them and handed them over to worship the stars in the sky, just as it is written in the scroll of the Prophets:

Did you bring sacrifices and offerings to me
for forty years in the wilderness,
house of Israel?
⁴³No! Instead, you took
the tent of Moloch with you,
and the star of your god Rephan,
the images that you made
in order to worship them.
Therefore, I will send you far away,
farther than Babylon.ˢ

ᵐExod 1:8 ⁿExod 2:14 ᵒExod 3:6 ᵖExod 3:5, 7 qDeut 18:15 ʳExod 32:1 ˢAmos 5:25-27

⁴⁴"The tent of testimony was with our ancestors in the wilderness. Moses built it just as he had been instructed by the one who spoke to him and according to the pattern he had seen. ⁴⁵In time, when they had received the tent, our ancestors carried it with them when, under Joshua's leadership, they took possession of the land from the nations whom God expelled. This tent remained in the land until the time of David. ⁴⁶God approved of David, who asked that he might provide a dwelling place for the God of Jacob.ᵗ ⁴⁷But it was Solomon who actually built a house for God. ⁴⁸However, the Most High doesn't live in houses built by human hands. As the prophet says,

⁴⁹ Heaven is my throne,
     and the earth is my footstool.
   'What kind of house will you build for me,'
     says the Lord,
     'or where is my resting place?
⁵⁰ Didn't I make all these things
     with my own hand?'ᵘ

⁵¹"You stubborn people! In your thoughts and hearing, you are like those who have had no part in God's covenant! You continuously set yourself against the Holy Spirit, just like your ancestors did. ⁵²Was there a single prophet your ancestors didn't harass? They even killed those who predicted the coming of the righteous one, and you've betrayed and murdered him! ⁵³You received the Law given by angels, but you haven't kept it."

⁵⁴Once the council members heard these words, they were enraged and began to grind their teeth at Stephen. ⁵⁵But Stephen, enabled by the Holy Spirit, stared into heaven and saw God's majesty and Jesus standing at God's right side. ⁵⁶He exclaimed, "Look! I can see heaven on display and the Human Oneᵛ standing at God's right side!" ⁵⁷At this, they shrieked and covered their ears. Together, they charged at him, ⁵⁸threw him out of the city, and began to stone him. The witnesses placed their coats in the care of a young man named Saul. ⁵⁹As they battered him with stones, Stephen prayed, "Lord Jesus, accept my life!" ⁶⁰Falling to his knees, he shouted, "Lord, don't hold this sin against them!" Then he died. ¹Saul was in full agreement with Stephen's murder.

8

The church scatters

At that time, the church in Jerusalem began to be subjected to vicious harassment. Everyone except the apostles was scattered throughout the regions of Judea and Samaria. ²Some pious men buried Stephen and deeply grieved over him. ³Saul began to wreak havoc against the church. Entering one house after another, he would drag off both men and women and throw them into prison.

Philip in Samaria

⁴Those who had been scattered moved on, preaching the good news along the way. ⁵Philip went down to a city in Samariaʷ and began to preach Christ to them. ⁶The crowds were united by what they heard Philip say and the signs they saw him perform, and they gave him their undivided attention. ⁷With loud shrieks, unclean spirits came out of many people, and many who were paralyzed or crippled were healed. ⁸There was great rejoicing in that city.

⁹Before Philip's arrival, a certain man named Simon had practiced sorcery in that city and baffled the people of Samaria. He claimed to be a great person. ¹⁰Everyone, from the least to the greatest, gave him their undivided attention and referred to him as "the power of God called Great." ¹¹He had their attention because he had baffled them with sorcery for a long time. ¹²After they came to believe Philip, who preached the good news about God's kingdom and the name of Jesus Christ, both men and women were baptized. ¹³Even Simon himself came to believe and was baptized. Afterward, he became one of Philip's supporters. As he saw firsthand the signs and great miracles that were happening, he was astonished. ¹⁴When word reached the apostles in

---

ᵗCritical editions of the Gk New Testament read *house of Jacob*.   ᵘIsa 66:1-2   ᵛOr *Son of Man*   ʷOr *the city of Samaria*

Jerusalem that Samaria had accepted God's word, they commissioned Peter and John to go to Samaria. [15]Peter and John went down to Samaria where they prayed that the new believers would receive the Holy Spirit. ([16]This was because the Holy Spirit had not yet fallen on any of them; they had only been baptized in the name of the Lord Jesus.) [17]So Peter and John laid their hands on them, and they received the Holy Spirit.

[18]When Simon perceived that the Spirit was given through the laying on of the apostles' hands, he offered them money. [19]He said, "Give me this authority too so that anyone on whom I lay my hands will receive the Holy Spirit."

[20]Peter responded, "May your money be condemned to hell along with you because you believed you could buy God's gift with money! [21]You can have no part or share in God's word because your heart isn't right with God. [22]Therefore, change your heart and life! Turn from your wickedness! Plead with the Lord in the hope that your wicked intent can be forgiven, [23]for I see that your bitterness has poisoned you and evil has you in chains."

[24]Simon replied, "All of you, please, plead

to the Lord for me so that nothing of what you have said will happen to me!" [25]After the apostles had testified and proclaimed the Lord's word, they returned to Jerusalem, preaching the good news to many Samaritan villages along the way.

Philip and the Ethiopian eunuch

[26]An angel from the Lord spoke to Philip, "At noon, take[x] the road that leads from Jerusalem to Gaza." (This is a desert road.) [27]So he did. Meanwhile, an Ethiopian man was on his way home from Jerusalem, where he had come to worship. He was a eunuch and an official responsible for the entire treasury of Candace. (Candace is the title given to the Ethiopian queen.) [28]He was reading the prophet Isaiah while sitting in his carriage. [29]The Spirit told Philip, "Approach this carriage and stay with it."

[30]Running up to the carriage, Philip heard the man reading the prophet Isaiah. He asked, "Do you really understand what you are reading?"

[31]The man replied, "Without someone to guide me, how could I?" Then he invited Philip to climb up and sit with him. [32]This was the passage of scripture he was reading:

[x]Or travel south along

CAESAREA MARITIMA

Midway between Haifa and Tel Aviv stand the remains of a port city built by Herod the Great. The city became the political center of the Roman and Byzantine province called Palestina Prima. The 15 biblical references to the city all occur in the book of Acts. Caesarea also became the center of ecclesiastical administration during the Byzantine period, eclipsing even Jerusalem until the latter was designated as a patriarchate in the 5th century.

Caesarea played a significant role in the development of early Christianity. Philip came from Jerusalem to evangelize the city (Acts 8:40). Cornelius, the first Gentile convert, was a centurion stationed at Caesarea. Peter came from Joppa to baptize him (Acts 10). Cornelius's conversion started the process that transformed Christianity into a world religion with an identity distinct from Judaism. Paul passed through the city several times (e.g., Acts 9:30; 18:22; 21:8). He was imprisoned there for two years before being sent to Rome for trial (Acts 23–26).

Like a sheep he was led to the slaughter
and like a lamb before its shearer is silent
so he didn't open his mouth.
[33] In his humiliation
justice was taken away from him.
Who can tell the story of his descendants
because his life was taken from the earth?[y]

[34] The eunuch asked Philip, "Tell me, about whom does the prophet say this? Is he talking about himself or someone else?" [35] Starting with that passage, Philip proclaimed the good news about Jesus to him. [36] As they went down the road, they came to some water.

The eunuch said, "Look! Water! What would keep me from being baptized?"[z] [38] He ordered that the carriage halt. Both Philip and the eunuch went down to the water, where Philip baptized him. [39] When they came up out of the water, the Lord's Spirit suddenly took Philip away. The eunuch never saw him again but went on his way rejoicing. [40] Philip found himself in Azotus. He traveled through that area, preaching the good news in all the cities until he reached Caesarea.

Saul encounters the risen Jesus

9 Meanwhile, Saul was still spewing out murderous threats against the Lord's disciples. He went to the high priest, [2] seeking letters to the synagogues in Damascus. If he found persons who belonged to the Way, whether men or women, these letters would authorize him to take them as prisoners to Jerusalem. [3] During the journey, as he approached Damascus, suddenly a light from heaven encircled him. [4] He fell to the ground and heard a voice asking him, "Saul, Saul, why are you harassing me?"

[5] Saul asked, "Who are you, Lord?"

"I am Jesus, whom you are harassing," came the reply. [6] "Now get up and enter the city. You will be told what you must do."

[7] Those traveling with him stood there speechless; they heard the voice but saw no one. [8] After they picked Saul up from the ground, he opened his eyes but he couldn't see. So they led him by the hand into Damascus. [9] For three days he was blind and neither ate nor drank anything.

[10] In Damascus there was a certain disciple named Ananias. The Lord spoke to him in a vision, "Ananias!"

He answered, "Yes, Lord."

[11] The Lord instructed him, "Go to Judas' house on Straight Street and ask for a man from Tarsus named Saul. He is praying. [12] In a vision he has seen a man named Ananias enter and put his hands on him to restore his sight."

[13] Ananias countered, "Lord, I have heard many reports about this man. People say he has done horrible things to your holy people in Jerusalem. [14] He's here with authority from the chief priests to arrest everyone who calls on your name."

[15] The Lord replied, "Go! This man is the agent I have chosen to carry my name before Gentiles, kings, and Israelites. [16] I will show him how much he must suffer for the sake of my name."

[17] Ananias went to the house. He placed his hands on Saul and said, "Brother Saul,

[y] Isa 53:7-8 [z] Critical editions of the Gk New Testament do not include 8:37 *Philip said to him, "If you believe with all your heart, you can be." The eunuch answered, "I believe that Jesus Christ is God's Son."*

DORCAS

The Greek name of Tabitha. She was brought back to life by Peter (Acts 9:36-43). Called a disciple, she was probably a woman of some financial means and significant status in the Christian communities because "Her life overflowed with good works and compassionate acts on behalf of those in need" (9:36), especially among widows, for whom she provided clothing (9:39).

the Lord sent me—Jesus, who appeared to you on the way as you were coming here. He sent me so that you could see again and be filled with the Holy Spirit." [18]Instantly, flakes fell from Saul's eyes and he could see again. He got up and was baptized. [19]After eating, he regained his strength.

He stayed with the disciples in Damascus for several days. [20]Right away, he began to preach about Jesus in the synagogues. "He is God's Son," he declared.

[21]Everyone who heard him was baffled. They questioned each other, "Isn't he the one who was wreaking havoc among those in Jerusalem who called on this name? Hadn't he come here to take those same people as prisoners to the chief priests?" [22]But Saul grew stronger and stronger. He confused the Jews who lived in Damascus by proving that Jesus is the Christ.

[23]After this had gone on for some time, the Jews hatched a plot to kill Saul. [24]However, he found out about their scheme. They were keeping watch at the city gates around the clock so they could assassinate him. [25]But his disciples took him by night and lowered him in a basket through an opening in the city wall.

[26]When Saul arrived in Jerusalem, he tried to join the disciples, but they were all afraid of him. They didn't believe he was really a disciple. [27]Then Barnabas brought Saul to the apostles and told them the story about how Saul saw the Lord on the way and that the Lord had spoken to Saul. He also told them about the confidence with which Saul had preached in the name of Jesus in Damascus. [28]After this, Saul moved freely among the disciples in Jerusalem and was speaking with confidence in the name of the Lord. [29]He got into debates with the Greek-speaking Jews as well, but they tried to kill him. [30]When the family of believers learned about this, they escorted him down to Caesarea and sent him off to Tarsus.

[31]Then the church throughout Judea, Galilee, and Samaria enjoyed a time of peace. God strengthened the church, and its life was marked by reverence for the Lord. Encouraged by the Holy Spirit, the church continued to grow in numbers.

Peter heals and raises the dead

[32]As Peter toured the whole region, he went to visit God's holy people in Lydda. [33]There he found a man named Aeneas who was paralyzed and had been confined to his bed for eight years. [34]Peter said to him, "Aeneas, Jesus Christ heals you! Get up and make your bed." At once he got up. [35]Everyone who lived in Lydda and Sharon saw him and turned to the Lord.

[36]In Joppa there was a disciple named Tabitha (in Greek her name is Dorcas). Her life overflowed with good works and compassionate acts on behalf of those in need. [37]About that time, though, she became so ill that she died. After they washed her body, they laid her in an upstairs room. [38]Since Lydda was near Joppa, when the disciples heard that Peter was there, they sent two people to Peter. They urged, "Please come right away!" [39]Peter went with them. Upon his arrival, he was taken to the upstairs room. All the widows stood beside him, crying as they showed the tunics and other clothing Dorcas made when she was alive.

[40]Peter sent everyone out of the room, then knelt and prayed. He turned to the body and said, "Tabitha, get up!" She opened her eyes, saw Peter, and sat up. [41]He gave her his hand and raised her up. Then he called God's holy people, including the widows, and presented her alive to them. [42]The news spread throughout Joppa, and many put their faith in the Lord. [43]Peter stayed for some time in Joppa with a certain tanner named Simon.

Peter, Cornelius, and the Gentiles

10 There was a man in Caesarea named Cornelius, a centurion in the Italian Company.[a] [2]He and his whole household were pious, Gentile God-worshippers. He gave generously to those in need among the Jewish people and prayed to God constantly. [3]One day at nearly three o'clock in the afternoon, he clearly saw an angel from

[a]Or *cohort* (approximately six hundred soldiers)

God in a vision. The angel came to him and said, "Cornelius!"

⁴Startled, he stared at the angel and replied, "What is it, Lord?"

The angel said, "Your prayers and your compassionate acts are like a memorial offering to God. ⁵Send messengers to Joppa at once and summon a certain Simon, the one known as Peter. ⁶He is a guest of Simon the tanner, whose house is near the seacoast." ⁷When the angel who was speaking to him had gone, Cornelius summoned two of his household servants along with a pious soldier from his personal staff. ⁸He explained everything to them, then sent them to Joppa.

⁹At noon on the following day, as their journey brought them close to the city, Peter went up on the roof to pray. ¹⁰He became hungry and wanted to eat. While others were preparing the meal, he had a visionary experience. ¹¹He saw heaven opened up and something like a large linen sheet being lowered to the earth by its four corners. ¹²Inside the sheet were all kinds of four-legged animals, reptiles, and wild birds.ᵇ ¹³A voice told him, "Get up, Peter! Kill and eat!"

¹⁴Peter exclaimed, "Absolutely not, Lord! I have never eaten anything impure or unclean."

¹⁵The voice spoke a second time, "Never consider unclean what God has made pure." ¹⁶This happened three times, then the object was suddenly pulled back into heaven.

¹⁷Peter was bewildered about the meaning of the vision. Just then, the messengers sent by Cornelius discovered the whereabouts of Simon's house and arrived at the gate. ¹⁸Calling out, they inquired whether the Simon known as Peter was a guest there.

¹⁹While Peter was brooding over the vision, the Spirit interrupted him, "Look! Three people are looking for you. ²⁰Go downstairs. Don't ask questions; just go with them because I have sent them."

²¹So Peter went downstairs and told them, "I'm the one you are looking for. Why have you come?"

²²They replied, "We've come on behalf of Cornelius, a centurion and righteous man, a God-worshipper who is well-respected by all Jewish people. A holy angel directed him to summon you to his house and to hear what you have to say." ²³Peter invited them into the house as his guests.

The next day he got up and went with them, together with some of the believers from Joppa. ²⁴They arrived in Caesarea the following day. Anticipating their arrival, Cornelius had gathered his relatives and close friends. ²⁵As Peter entered the house, Cornelius met him and fell at his feet in order to honor him. ²⁶But Peter lifted him up, saying, "Get up! Like you, I'm just a human." ²⁷As they continued to talk, Peter went inside and found a large gathering of people. ²⁸He said to them, "You all realize that it is forbidden for a Jew to associate or visit with outsiders. However, God has shown me that I should never call a person impure or unclean. ²⁹For this reason, when you sent for me, I came without objection. I want to know, then, why you sent for me."

³⁰Cornelius answered, "Four days ago at this same time, three o'clock in the afternoon, I was praying at home. Suddenly a man in radiant clothing stood before me. ³¹He said, 'Cornelius, God has heard your prayers, and your compassionate acts are like a memorial offering to him. ³²Therefore, send someone to Joppa and summon Simon, who is known as Peter. He is a guest in the home of Simon the tanner, located near the seacoast.' ³³I sent for you right away, and you were kind enough to come. Now, here we are, gathered in the presence of God to listen to everything the Lord has directed you to say."

³⁴Peter said, "I really am learning that God doesn't show partiality to one group of people over another. ³⁵Rather, in every nation, whoever worships him and does what is right is acceptable to him. ³⁶This is the message of peace he sent to the Israelites by proclaiming the good news through Jesus Christ: He is Lord of all! ³⁷You know what happened throughout Judea, beginning in

ᵇOr birds in the sky

Galilee after the baptism John preached. [38]You know about Jesus of Nazareth, whom God anointed with the Holy Spirit and endowed with power. Jesus traveled around doing good and healing everyone oppressed by the devil because God was with him. [39]We are witnesses of everything he did, both in Judea and in Jerusalem. They killed him by hanging him on a tree, [40]but God raised him up on the third day and allowed him to be seen, [41]not by everyone but by us. We are witnesses whom God chose beforehand, who ate and drank with him after God raised him from the dead. [42]He commanded us to preach to the people and to testify that he is the one whom God appointed as judge of the living and the dead. [43]All the prophets testify about him that everyone who believes in him receives forgiveness of sins through his name."

[44]While Peter was still speaking, the Holy Spirit fell on everyone who heard the word. [45]The circumcised believers who had come with Peter were astonished that the gift of the Holy Spirit had been poured out even on the Gentiles. [46]They heard them speaking in other languages and praising God. Peter asked, [47]"These people have received the Holy Spirit just as we have. Surely no one can stop them from being baptized with water, can they?" [48]He directed that they be baptized in the name of Jesus Christ. Then they invited Peter to stay for several days.

Jerusalem church questions Peter

11 The apostles and the brothers and sisters throughout Judea heard that even the Gentiles had welcomed God's word. [2]When Peter went up to Jerusalem, the circumcised believers criticized him. [3]They accused him, "You went into the home of the uncircumcised and ate with them!"

[4]Step-by-step, Peter explained what had happened. [5]"I was in the city of Joppa praying when I had a visionary experience. In my vision, I saw something like a large linen sheet being lowered from heaven by its four corners. It came all the way down to me.

[6]As I stared at it, wondering what it was, I saw four-legged animals—including wild beasts—as well as reptiles and wild birds.[c] [7]I heard a voice say, 'Get up, Peter! Kill and eat!' [8]I responded, 'Absolutely not, Lord! Nothing impure or unclean has ever entered my mouth.' [9]The voice from heaven spoke a second time, 'Never consider unclean what God has made pure.' [10]This happened three times, then everything was pulled back into heaven. [11]At that moment three men who had been sent to me from Caesarea arrived at the house where we were staying. [12]The Spirit told me to go with them even though they were Gentiles. These six brothers also went with me, and we entered that man's house. [13]He reported to us how he had seen an angel standing in his house and saying, 'Send to Joppa and summon Simon, who is known as Peter. [14]He will tell you how you and your entire household can be saved.' [15]When I began to speak, the Holy Spirit fell on them, just as the Spirit fell on us in the beginning. [16]I remembered the Lord's words: 'John will baptize with water, but you will be baptized with the Holy Spirit.' [17]If God gave them the same gift he gave us who believed in the Lord Jesus Christ, then who am I? Could I stand in God's way?"

[18]Once the apostles and other believers heard this, they calmed down. They praised God and concluded, "So then God has enabled Gentiles to change their hearts and lives so that they might have new life."

The Antioch church

[19]Now those who were scattered as a result of the trouble that occurred because of Stephen traveled as far as Phoenicia, Cyprus, and Antioch. They proclaimed the word only to Jews. [20]Among them were some people from Cyprus and Cyrene. They entered Antioch and began to proclaim the good news about the Lord Jesus also to Gentiles. [21]The Lord's power was with them, and a large number came to believe and turned to the Lord.

[22]When the church in Jerusalem heard about this, they sent Barnabas to Antioch.

[c]Or birds in the sky

²³When he arrived and saw evidence of God's grace, he was overjoyed and encouraged everyone to remain fully committed to the Lord. ²⁴Barnabas responded in this way because he was a good man, whom the Holy Spirit had endowed with exceptional faith. A considerable number of people were added to the Lord. ²⁵Barnabas went to Tarsus in search of Saul. ²⁶When he found him, he brought him to Antioch. They were there for a whole year, meeting with the church and teaching large numbers of people. It was in Antioch where the disciples were first labeled "Christians."

²⁷About that time, some prophets came down from Jerusalem to Antioch. ²⁸One of them, Agabus, stood up and, inspired by the Spirit, predicted that a severe famine would overtake the entire Roman world. (This occurred during Claudius' rule.) ²⁹The disciples decided they would send support to the brothers and sisters in Judea, with everyone contributing to this ministry according to each person's abundance. ³⁰They

sent Barnabas and Saul to take this gift to the elders.

Herod imprisons Peter

12 About that time King Herod began to harass some who belonged to the church. ²He had James, John's brother, killed with a sword. ³When he saw that this pleased the Jews, he arrested Peter as well. This happened during the Festival of Unleavened Bread. ⁴He put Peter in prison, handing him over to four squads of soldiers, sixteen in all, who guarded him. He planned to charge him publicly after the Passover. ⁵While Peter was held in prison, the church offered earnest prayer to God for him.

⁶The night before Herod was going to bring Peter's case forward, Peter was asleep between two soldiers and bound with two chains, with soldiers guarding the prison entrance. ⁷Suddenly an angel from the Lord appeared and a light shone in the prison cell. After nudging Peter on his side

SYRIAN ANTIOCH

Antioch was the name of at least 16 cities in the Greco-Roman period, five of which were located in Syria. The NT mentions Antioch of Pisidia (Acts 13) and Antioch of Syria (Acts 6; 11; 13–15; 18; Gal 2; 2 Tim 3). The latter is also known as the Syrian Antioch or Antioch on the Orontes. It was the third-largest city in the Greco-Roman world behind Rome and Alexandria (Egypt). The city of Antioch is mentioned several times in the NT. The disciples chose seven men, including Stephen and Nicolaus from Antioch, to serve Greek-speaking Jews (Acts 6:5). Some Christians fleeing harassment in Jerusalem, following the stoning of Stephen, traveled as far as Phoenicia, Cyprus, and Antioch. In Antioch some of these refugees preached only to the Jews while others, originally from Cyprus and Cyrene, preached to Greek-speaking Gentiles as well (Acts 11:19–21). This activity resulted in many new converts. When news of this growth reached the Jerusalem leaders, they dispatched Barnabas to assess the situation (Acts 11:22). Finding things in good order, Barnabas then traveled to Tarsus and brought Paul, a native of that city, back to Antioch (Acts 11:25-26).

The term "Christian" was first used at Antioch to describe the followers of Christ (Acts 11:26). The Christians of Antioch collected funds for Judean famine relief and sent them with Paul and Barnabas to Jerusalem (Acts 11:27-30).

to awaken him, the angel raised him up and said, "Quick! Get up!" The chains fell from his wrists. [8]The angel continued, "Get dressed. Put on your sandals." Peter did as he was told. The angel said, "Put on your coat and follow me." [9]Following the angel, Peter left the prison. However, he didn't realize the angel had actually done all this. He thought he was seeing a vision. [10]They passed the first and second guards and came to the iron gate leading to the city. It opened for them by itself. After leaving the prison, they proceeded the length of one street, when abruptly the angel was gone.

[11]At that, Peter came to his senses and remarked, "Now I'm certain that the Lord sent his angel and rescued me from Herod and from everything the Jewish people expected." [12]Realizing this, he made his way to Mary's house. (Mary was John's mother; he was also known as Mark.) Many believers had gathered there and were praying. [13]When Peter knocked at the outer gate, a female servant named Rhoda went to answer. [14]She was so overcome with joy when she recognized Peter's voice that she didn't open the gate. Instead, she ran back in and announced that Peter was standing at the gate.

[15]"You've lost your mind!" they responded. She stuck by her story with such determination that they began to say, "It must be his guardian angel." [16]Meanwhile, Peter remained outside, knocking at the gate. They finally opened the gate and saw him there, and they were astounded.

[17]He gestured with his hand to quiet them down, then recounted how the Lord led him out of prison. He said, "Tell this to James and the brothers and sisters." Then he left for another place.

[18]The next morning the soldiers were flustered about what had happened to Peter. [19]Herod called for a thorough search. When Peter didn't turn up, Herod interrogated the guards and had them executed. Afterward, Herod left Judea in order to spend some time in Caesarea.

[20]Herod had been furious with the people of Tyre and Sidon for some time. They made a pact to approach him together, since their region depended on the king's realm for its food supply. They persuaded Blastus, the king's personal attendant, to join their cause, then appealed for an end to hostilities. [21]On the scheduled day Herod dressed himself in royal attire, seated himself on the throne, and gave a speech to the people. [22]Those assembled kept shouting, over and over, "This is a god's voice, not the voice of a mere human!" [23]Immediately an angel from the Lord struck Herod down, because he didn't give the honor to God. He was eaten by worms and died.

[24]God's word continued to grow and increase. [25]Barnabas and Saul returned to Antioch from Jerusalem[d] after completing their mission, bringing with them John, who was also known as Mark.

Barnabas and Saul sent to minister

13 The church at Antioch included prophets and teachers: Barnabas, Simeon (nicknamed Niger), Lucius from Cyrene, Manaen (a childhood friend of Herod the ruler), and Saul. [2]As they were worshipping the Lord and fasting, the Holy Spirit said, "Appoint Barnabas and Saul to the work I have called them to undertake." [3]After they fasted and prayed, they laid their hands on these two and sent them off.

Serving in Cyprus

[4]After the Holy Spirit sent them on their way, they went down to Seleucia. From there they sailed to Cyprus. [5]In Salamis they proclaimed God's word in the Jewish synagogues. John was with them as their assistant. [6]They traveled throughout the island until they arrived at Paphos. There they found a certain man named Bar-Jesus, a Jew who was a false prophet and practiced sorcery. [7]He kept company with the governor of that province, an intelligent man named Sergius Paulus. The governor sent for Barnabas and Saul since he wanted to hear God's word. [8]But Elymas the sorcerer[e] (for that's what people understood his

[d]Critical editions of the Gk New Testament read returned to Jerusalem. [e]Or magician (Gk magos)

name meant) opposed them, trying to steer the governor away from the faith. [9]Empowered by the Holy Spirit, Saul, also known as Paul, glared at Bar-Jesus and [10]said, "You are a deceiver and trickster! You devil! You attack anything that is right! Will you never stop twisting the straight ways of the Lord into crooked paths? [11]Listen! The Lord's power is set against you. You will be blind for a while, unable even to see the daylight." At once, Bar-Jesus' eyes were darkened, and he began to grope about for someone to lead him around by the hand. [12]When the governor saw what had taken place, he came to believe, for he was astonished by the teaching about the Lord.

Paul and Barnabas in Pisidian Antioch

[13]Paul and his companions sailed from Paphos to Perga in Pamphylia. John deserted them there and returned to Jerusalem. [14]They went on from Perga and arrived at Antioch in Pisidia. On the Sabbath, they entered and found seats in the synagogue there. [15]After the reading of the Law and the Prophets, the synagogue leaders invited them, "Brothers, if one of you has a sermon for the people, please speak."

[16]Standing up, Paul gestured with his hand and said, "Fellow Israelites and Gentile God-worshippers, please listen to me. [17]The God of this people Israel chose our ancestors. God made them a great people while they lived as strangers in the land of Egypt. With his great power, he led them out of that country. [18]For about forty years,

God put up with them in the wilderness. [19]God conquered seven nations in the land of Canaan and gave the Israelites their land as an inheritance. [20]This happened over a period of about four hundred fifty years.

"After this, he gave them judges until the time of the prophet Samuel. [21]The Israelites requested a king, so God gave them Saul, Kish's son, from the tribe of Benjamin, and he served as their king for forty years. [22]After God removed him, he raised up David to be their king. God testified concerning him, 'I have found David, Jesse's son, *a man who shares my desires.*[f] Whatever my will is, he will do.' [23]From this man's descendants, God brought to Israel a savior, Jesus, just as he promised. [24]Before Jesus' appearance, John proclaimed to all the Israelites a baptism to show they were changing their hearts and lives. [25]As John was completing his mission, he said, 'Who do you think I am? I'm not the one you think I am, but he is coming after me. I'm not worthy to loosen his sandals.'

[26]"Brothers, children of Abraham's family, and you Gentile God-worshippers, the message about this salvation has been sent to us. [27]The people in Jerusalem and their leaders didn't recognize Jesus. By condemning him they fulfilled the words of the prophets that are read every Sabbath. [28]Even though they didn't find a single legal basis for the death penalty, they asked Pilate to have him executed. [29]When they finished doing everything that had been written about him, they took him down

[f]Tg 1 Sam 13:14

PROCONSUL

The title for a Roman official who governed a province. Paul and Barnabas encountered a proconsul named Sergius Paulus, who became a Christian believer (Acts 13:7-12). Gallio, proconsul of Achaia, refused to try Paul when Jews who opposed Paul's teachings brought him before the tribunal (Acts 18:12-17). Paul escaped being brought before the proconsul in Ephesus after silversmiths of the shrines of Artemis fomented a riot in opposition to Paul's teaching that silver idols were not really gods (Acts 19:23-41).

from the cross[g] and laid him in a tomb. [30]But God raised him from the dead! [31]He appeared over many days to those who had traveled with him from Galilee to Jerusalem. They are now his witnesses to the people.

[32]"We proclaim to you the good news. What God promised to our ancestors, [33]he has fulfilled for us, their children, by raising up Jesus. As it was written in the second psalm, *You are my son; today I have become your father.*[h]

[34]"God raised Jesus from the dead, never again to be subjected to death's decay. Therefore, God said, *I will give to you the holy and firm promises I made to David.*[i] [35]In another place it is said, *You will not let your holy one experience death's decay.*[j] [36]David served God's purpose in his own generation, then he died and was buried with his ancestors. He experienced death's decay, [37]but the one whom God has raised up didn't experience death's decay.

[38]"Therefore, brothers and sisters, know this: Through Jesus we proclaim forgiveness of sins to you. From all those sins from which you couldn't be put in right relationship with God through Moses' Law, [39]through Jesus everyone who believes is put in right relationship with God. [40]Take care that the prophets' words don't apply to you:

[41] *Look, you scoffers,*
     marvel and die.

   I'm going to do work in your day —
     a work you won't believe
     even if someone told you."[k]

[42]As Paul and Barnabas were leaving the synagogue, the people urged them to speak about these things again on the next Sabbath. [43]When the people in the synagogue were dismissed, many Jews and devout converts to Judaism accompanied Paul and Barnabas, who urged them to remain faithful to the message of God's grace.

[44]On the next Sabbath, almost everyone in the city gathered to hear the Lord's word. [45]When the Jews saw the crowds, they were overcome with jealousy. They ar-

gued against what Paul was saying by slandering him. [46]Speaking courageously, Paul and Barnabas said, "We had to speak God's word to you first. Since you reject it and show that you are unworthy to receive eternal life, we will turn to the Gentiles. [47]This is what the Lord commanded us:

   I have made you a light for the Gentiles,
     so that you could bring salvation
     to the end of the earth."[l]

[48]When the Gentiles heard this, they rejoiced and honored the Lord's word. Everyone who was appointed for eternal life believed, [49]and the Lord's word was broadcast throughout the entire region. [50]However, the Jews provoked the prominent women among the Gentile God-worshippers, as well as the city's leaders. They instigated others to harass Paul and Barnabas, and threw them out of their district. [51]Paul and Barnabas shook the dust from their feet and went to Iconium. [52]Because of the abundant presence of the Holy Spirit in their lives, the disciples were overflowing with happiness.

Paul and Barnabas in Iconium

14 The same thing happened in Iconium. Paul and Barnabas entered the Jewish synagogue and spoke as they had before. As a result, a huge number of Jews and Greeks believed. [2]However, the Jews who rejected the faith stirred up the Gentiles, poisoning their minds against the brothers. [3]Nevertheless, Paul and Barnabas stayed there for quite some time, confidently speaking about the Lord. And the Lord confirmed the word about his grace by the signs and wonders he enabled them to perform. [4]The people of the city were divided—some siding with the Jews, others with the Lord's messengers. [5]Then some Gentiles and Jews, including their leaders, hatched a plot to mistreat and stone Paul and Barnabas. [6]When they learned of it, these two messengers fled to the Lycaonian cities of Lystra and Derbe and the surrounding area, [7]where they continued to proclaim the good news.

---

[g]Or tree   [h]Ps 2:7   [i]Isa 55:3   [j]Ps 16:10   [k]Hab 1:5   [l]Isa 49:6

PAUL'S MINISTRY & WRITING

Event	Approximate dates (CE)	Related passages
Jesus' crucifixion	30	
Paul's call	34	Gal 1:15-16
Paul's ministry in Arabia/Nabatea	34–37	Gal 1:17
Paul's escape from Damascus ruled by an ethnarch, presumably Aretas IV of Nabatea	37/38	2 Cor 11:32-33
First trip to Jerusalem (two-week stay)	37/38	Gal 1:18
Mission in Syria and Cilicia (Paul's home province)	38–47	Gal 1:21
Second trip to Jerusalem; council endorses Paul's Gentile mission	47 (between 46 and 48)	Gal 2:1-10
Edict of Claudius expelling Jews from Jerusalem	49	Acts 18:2
First mission in Europe (Philippi, Thessalonica, and Athens)	48–50	Acts 15:36–17:34
Ministry in Corinth	fall 50–summer 52	Acts 18:1-11
Arraignment before proconsul Gallio	summer/fall 52	Acts 18:12-17
Paul writes 1 Thessalonians	summer/fall 52	
Paul in Ephesus	fall 52–56	
Lost letter written to Corinth	52	1 Cor 5:9
Paul writes 1 Corinthians	53	
Letter from Ephesus and Macedonia collected in fragmentary form in 2 Corinthians	54–57	
Paul writes Galatians	55	
Imprisonment	late 55 into early 56	2 Cor 1:8-11
Philippian correspondence from prison, probably in Ephesus	56	
Philemon possibly written during imprisonment	56	
The "painful letter" to Corinth	56	2 Cor 2:3-4
Reconciling letter to Corinthians from Macedonia	fall 56	2 Cor 1:1–2:13; 7:5-16
Circular letter to churches in Achaia urging completion of offering	fall 56	2 Cor 9
Paul winters in Corinth preparing the offering and delegation for delivery to Jerusalem	56–57	
Paul departs with delegation for Jerusalem with offering for the "poor among God's people" and final visit to Jerusalem	spring 57	Acts 21:15–23:31; Rom 15:25-33
Arrest, imprisonment, and transfer to Rome	57–59	Acts 25:4–28:16
Execution	60–64	Acts of Paul 10:1-7

Healing a crippled man in Lystra

[8] In Lystra there was a certain man who lacked strength in his legs. He had been crippled since birth and had never walked. Sitting there, he [9] heard Paul speaking. Paul stared at him and saw that he believed he could be healed.

[10] Raising his voice, Paul said, "Stand up straight on your feet!" He jumped up and began to walk.

[11] Seeing what Paul had done, the crowd shouted in the Lycaonian language, "The gods have taken human form and come down to visit us!" [12] They referred to Barnabas as Zeus and to Paul as Hermes, since Paul was the main speaker. [13] The priest of Zeus, whose temple was located just outside the city, brought bulls and wreaths to the city gates. Along with the crowds, he wanted to offer sacrifices to them.

[14] When the Lord's messengers Barnabas and Paul found out about this, they tore their clothes in protest and rushed out into the crowd. They shouted, [15] "People, what are you doing? We are humans too, just like you! We are proclaiming the good news to you: turn to the living God and away from such worthless things. He *made the heaven, the earth, the sea, and everything in them.*[m] [16] In the past, he permitted every nation to go its own way. [17] Nevertheless, he hasn't left himself without a witness. He has blessed you by giving you rain from above as well as seasonal harvests, and satisfying you with food and happiness." [18] Even with these words, they barely kept the crowds from sacrificing to them.

[19] Jews from Antioch and Iconium arrived and won the crowds over. They stoned Paul and dragged him out of the city, supposing he was dead. [20] When the disciples surrounded him, he got up and entered the city again. The following day he left with Barnabas for Derbe.

Returning to Antioch

[21] Paul and Barnabas proclaimed the good news to the people in Derbe and made many disciples. Then they returned to Lystra, Iconium, and Antioch, where [22] they strengthened the disciples and urged them to remain firm in the faith. They told them, "If we are to enter God's kingdom, we must pass through many troubles." [23] They appointed elders for each church. With prayer and fasting, they committed these elders to the Lord, in whom they had placed their trust.

[24] After Paul and Barnabas traveled through Pisidia, they came to Pamphylia. [25] They proclaimed the word in Perga, then went down to Attalia. [26] From there they sailed to Antioch, where they had been entrusted by God's grace to the work they had now completed. [27] On their arrival, they gathered the church together and reported everything that God had accomplished through their activity, and how God had opened a door of faith for the Gentiles. [28] They stayed with the disciples a long time.

The Jerusalem Council

15 Some people came down from Judea teaching the family of believers, "Unless you are circumcised according to the custom we've received from Moses, you can't be saved." [2] Paul and Barnabas took sides against these Judeans and argued strongly against their position.

The church at Antioch appointed Paul, Barnabas, and several others from Antioch to go up to Jerusalem to set this question before the apostles and the elders. [3] The church sent this delegation on their way. They traveled through Phoenicia and Samaria, telling stories about the conversion of the Gentiles to everyone. Their reports thrilled the brothers and sisters. [4] When they arrived in Jerusalem, the church, the apostles, and the elders all welcomed them. They gave a full report of what God had accomplished through their activity. [5] Some believers from among the Pharisees stood up and claimed, "The Gentiles must be circumcised. They must be required to keep the Law from Moses."

[6] The apostles and the elders gathered to consider this matter. [7] After much debate,

Peter stood and addressed them, "Fellow believers, you know that, early on, God chose me from among you as the one through whom the Gentiles would hear the word of the gospel and come to believe. [8]God, who knows people's deepest thoughts and desires, confirmed this by giving them the Holy Spirit, just as he did to us. [9]He made no distinction between us and them, but purified their deepest thoughts and desires through faith. [10]Why then are you now challenging God by placing a burden on the shoulders of these disciples that neither we nor our ancestors could bear? [11]On the contrary, we believe that we and they are saved in the same way, by the grace of the Lord Jesus."

[12]The entire assembly fell quiet as they listened to Barnabas and Paul describe all the signs and wonders God did among the Gentiles through their activity. [13]When Barnabas and Paul also fell silent, James responded, "Fellow believers, listen to me. [14]Simon reported how, in his kindness, God came to the Gentiles in the first place, to raise up from them a people of God. [15]The prophets' words agree with this; as it is written,

[16] After this I will return,
    and I will rebuild David's fallen tent;
    I will rebuild what has been torn down.
    I will restore it
[17] so that the rest of humanity
    will seek the Lord,
    even all the Gentiles who belong to me.
The Lord says this,
    the one who does these things[n]

[18] known from earliest times.

[19]"Therefore, I conclude that we shouldn't create problems for Gentiles who turn to God. [20]Instead, we should write a letter, telling them to avoid the pollution associated with idols, sexual immorality, eating meat from strangled animals, and consuming blood. [21]After all, Moses has been proclaimed in every city for a long time, and is read aloud every Sabbath in every synagogue."

Letter to the Gentile believers

[22]The apostles and the elders, along with the entire church, agreed to send some delegates chosen from among themselves to Antioch, together with Paul and Barnabas. They selected Judas Barsabbas and Silas, who were leaders among the brothers and sisters. [23]They were to carry this letter:

The apostles and the elders, to the Gentile brothers and sisters in Antioch, Syria, and Cilicia. Greetings! [24]We've heard that some of our number have disturbed you with unsettling words we didn't authorize. [25]We reached a united decision to select some delegates and send them to you along with our dear friends Barnabas and Paul. [26]These people have devoted their lives to the name of our Lord Jesus Christ. [27]Therefore, we are sending Judas and Silas. They will confirm what we have written. [28]The Holy Spirit has led us to the decision that no burden should be placed on you other than these essentials: [29]refuse food offered to idols, blood, the meat

[n]Amos 9:11-12

CYPRUS

Paul visited this Mediterranean island during a missionary journey (Acts 13:4), as did Barnabas and John Mark after parting ways with Paul over a disagreement about retaining John Mark in their work (see Acts 15:39). Cyprus is the third-largest island in the Mediterranean Sea. It is located approximately 60 mi. west of Syria, 45 mi. south of Turkey, and some 250 mi. north of Egypt.

from strangled animals, and sexual immorality. You will do well to avoid such things. Farewell.

³⁰When Barnabas, Paul, and the delegates were sent on their way, they went down to Antioch. They gathered the believers and delivered the letter. ³¹The people read it, delighted with its encouraging message. ³²Judas and Silas were prophets, and they said many things that encouraged and strengthened the brothers and sisters. ³³Judas and Silas stayed there awhile, then were sent back with a blessing of peace from the brothers and sisters to those who first sent them.° ³⁵Paul and Barnabas stayed in Antioch, where, together with many others, they taught and proclaimed the good news of the Lord's word.

Paul and Barnabas part company

³⁶Some time later, Paul said to Barnabas, "Let's go back and visit all the brothers and sisters in every city where we preached the Lord's word. Let's see how they are doing." ³⁷Barnabas wanted to take John Mark with them. ³⁸Paul insisted that they shouldn't take him along, since he had deserted them in Pamphylia and hadn't continued with them in their work. ³⁹Their argument became so intense that they went their separate ways. Barnabas took Mark and sailed to Cyprus. ⁴⁰Paul chose Silas and left, entrusted by the brothers and sisters to the Lord's grace. ⁴¹He traveled through Syria and Cilicia, strengthening the churches.

Paul adds Timothy

16 Paul reached Derbe, and then Lystra, where there was a disciple named Timothy. He was the son of a believing Jewish woman and a Greek father. ²The brothers and sisters in Lystra and Iconium spoke well of him. ³Paul wanted to take Timothy with him, so he circumcised him. This was because of the Jews who lived in those areas, for they all knew Timothy's father was Greek. ⁴As Paul and his companions traveled through the cities, they instructed Gentile believers to keep the regulations put in place by the apostles and elders in Jerusalem. ⁵So the churches were strengthened in the faith and every day their numbers flourished.

Vision of the Macedonian

⁶Paul and his companions traveled throughout the regions of Phrygia and Galatia because the Holy Spirit kept them from speaking the word in the province of Asia. ⁷When they approached the province

°Critical editions of the Gk New Testament do not include 15:34 *Silas decided to remain there.*

LYDIA/LYDIANS

1. A region in western Asia Minor (modern Turkey), centered in the lower Hermus and Cayster valleys, which is named after its non-Semitic inhabitants (seemingly Indo-European), Iron Age people called the Lydians. At least since the 8th century BCE, Lydia's capital was Sardis (modern Sart), positioned in the center of the Hermus' fertile plain, near the highway leading from the interior to the Aegean coast. The Lydians were the first to mint gold and silver coins (ca. 600 BCE).

2. According to the account in Acts 16:13-40, Lydia was Paul's first convert to the Way in Europe. A woman from Thyatira, she was a dealer in purple fabric. Her trade and the use of her personal name (unusual for a Greco-Roman woman) suggest that Lydia enjoyed high social status among free persons and merchants.

of Mysia, they tried to enter the province of Bithynia, but the Spirit of Jesus wouldn't let them. [8]Passing by Mysia, they went down to Troas instead. [9]A vision of a man from Macedonia came to Paul during the night. He stood urging Paul, "Come over to Macedonia and help us!" [10]Immediately after he saw the vision, we prepared to leave for the province of Macedonia, concluding that God had called us to proclaim the good news to them.

Lydia's conversion

[11]We sailed from Troas straight for Samothrace and came to Neapolis the following day. [12]From there we went to Philippi, a city of Macedonia's first district and a Roman colony. We stayed in that city several days. [13]On the Sabbath we went outside the city gate to the riverbank, where we thought there might be a place for prayer. We sat down and began to talk with the women who had gathered. [14]One of those women was Lydia, a Gentile God-worshipper from the city of Thyatira, a dealer in purple cloth. As she listened, the Lord enabled her to embrace Paul's message. [15]Once she and her household were baptized, she urged, "Now that you have decided that I am a believer in the Lord, come and stay in my house." And she persuaded us.

Paul and Silas in prison

[16]One day, when we were on the way to the place for prayer, we met a slave woman. She had a spirit that enabled her to predict the future. She made a lot of money for her owners through fortune-telling. [17]She began following Paul and us, shouting, "These people are servants of the Most High God! They are proclaiming a way of salvation to you!" [18]She did this for many days.

This annoyed Paul so much that he finally turned and said to the spirit, "In the name of Jesus Christ, I command you to leave her!" It left her at that very moment.

[19]Her owners realized that their hope for making money was gone. They grabbed Paul and Silas and dragged them before the officials in the city center. [20]When her owners approached the legal authorities, they said, "These people are causing an uproar in our city. They are Jews [21]who promote customs that we Romans can't accept or practice." [22]The crowd joined in the attacks against Paul and Silas, so the authorities ordered that they be stripped of their clothes and beaten with a rod. [23]When Paul and Silas had been severely beaten, the authorities threw them into prison and ordered the jailer to secure them with great care. [24]When he received these instructions, he threw them into the innermost cell and secured their feet in stocks.

[25]Around midnight Paul and Silas were praying and singing hymns to God, and the other prisoners were listening to them. [26]All at once there was such a violent earthquake that it shook the prison's foundations. The doors flew open and everyone's chains came loose. [27]When the jailer awoke and saw the open doors of the prison, he thought the prisoners had escaped, so he drew his sword and was about to kill himself. [28]But Paul shouted loudly, "Don't harm yourself! We're all here!"

[29]The jailer called for some lights, rushed in, and fell trembling before Paul and Silas.

THYATIRA

Thyatira (modern Akhisar), a city of ancient Lydia, was at the junction of the roads between Pergamum and Sardis. It is approximately 50 mi. northeast of ancient Smyrna (modern Izmir), 40 mi. southwest of Pergamum (modern Bergama), and 40 mi. from the Aegean Sea. Thyatira's vulnerable position on an open plain made it an easy victim for repeated military conquests throughout its history. The city is mentioned in Acts 16:14 (cf. 16:15, 40) and Revelation 1:11; 2:18-29.

³⁰He led them outside and asked, "Honorable masters, what must I do to be rescued?" ³¹They replied, "Believe in the Lord Jesus, and you will be saved—you and your entire household." ³²They spoke the Lord's word to him and everyone else in his house. ³³Right then, in the middle of the night, the jailer welcomed them and washed their wounds. He and everyone in his household were immediately baptized. ³⁴He brought them into his home and gave them a meal. He was overjoyed because he and everyone in his household had come to believe in God.

³⁵The next morning the legal authorities sent the police to the jailer with the order "Release those people." ³⁶So the jailer reported this to Paul, informing him, "The authorities sent word that you both are to be released. You can leave now. Go in peace."

³⁷Paul told the police, "Even though we are Roman citizens, they beat us publicly without first finding us guilty of a crime, and they threw us into prison. And now they want to send us away secretly? No way! They themselves will have to come and escort us out." ³⁸The police reported this to the legal authorities, who were alarmed to learn that Paul and Silas were Roman citizens. ³⁹They came and consoled Paul and Silas, escorting them out of prison and begging them to leave the city.

⁴⁰Paul and Silas left the prison and made their way to Lydia's house where they encouraged the brothers and sisters. Then they left Philippi.

More troubles for Paul

17 Paul and Silas journeyed through Amphipolis and Apollonia, then came to Thessalonica, where there was a Jewish synagogue. ²As was Paul's custom, he entered the synagogue and for three Sabbaths interacted with them on the basis of the scriptures. ³Through his interpretation of the scriptures, he demonstrated that the Christ had to suffer and rise from the dead. He declared, "This Jesus whom I proclaim to you is the Christ." ⁴Some were convinced and joined Paul and Silas, including a larger number of Greek God-worshippers and quite a few prominent women.

⁵But the Jews became jealous and brought along some thugs who were hanging out in the marketplace. They formed a mob and started a riot in the city. They attacked Jason's house, intending to bring Paul and Silas before the people. ⁶When they didn't find them, they dragged Jason and some believers before the city officials. They were shouting, "These people who have been disturbing the peace throughout the empire have also come here. ⁷What is more, Jason has welcomed them into his home. Every one of them does what is contrary to Caesar's decrees by naming someone else as king: Jesus." ⁸This provoked the crowd and the city officials even more. ⁹After Jason and the others posted bail, they released them.

¹⁰As soon as it was dark, the brothers and sisters sent Paul and Silas on to Beroea. When they arrived, they went to the Jewish synagogue. ¹¹The Beroean Jews were more honorable than those in Thessalonica. This was evident in the great eagerness with which they accepted the word and examined the scriptures each day to see whether Paul and Silas' teaching was true. ¹²Many came to believe, including a

SILAS/SILVANUS

A delegate from the Jerusalem church to report to the church at Antioch the results of the Jerusalem conference (Acts 15:22-35). After Paul's split with Barnabas, Silas becomes one of Paul's missionary companions (Acts 15:40–18:5), working in Philippi (Acts 16:16-28); Thessalonica; Beroea, where Silas stays behind with Timothy when Paul departs (Acts 17:1-15); and Corinth (Acts 18:5; 2 Cor 1:19).

number of reputable Greek women and many Greek men.

[13] The Jews from Thessalonica learned that Paul also proclaimed God's word in Beroea, so they went there too and were upsetting and disturbing the crowds. [14] The brothers and sisters sent Paul away to the seacoast at once, but Silas and Timothy remained at Beroea. [15] Those who escorted Paul led him as far as Athens, then returned with instructions for Silas and Timothy to come to him as quickly as possible.

[16] While Paul waited for them in Athens, he was deeply distressed to find that the city was flooded with idols. [17] He began to interact with the Jews and Gentile God-worshippers in the synagogue. He also addressed whoever happened to be in the marketplace each day. [18] Certain Epicurean and Stoic philosophers engaged him in discussion too. Some said, "What an amateur! What's he trying to say?" Others remarked, "He seems to be a proclaimer of foreign gods." (They said this because he was preaching the good news about Jesus and the resurrection.) [19] They took him into custody and brought him to the council on Mars Hill. "What is this new teaching? Can we learn what you are talking about? [20] You've told us some strange things and we want to know what they mean." ([21] They said this because all Athenians as well as the foreigners who live in Athens used to spend their time doing nothing but talking about or listening to the newest thing.)

[22] Paul stood up in the middle of the council on Mars Hill and said, "People of Athens, I see that you are very religious in every way. [23] As I was walking through town and carefully observing your objects of worship, I even found an altar with this inscription: 'To an unknown God.' What you worship as unknown, I now proclaim to you. [24] God, who made the world and everything in it, is Lord of heaven and earth. He doesn't live in temples made with human hands. [25] Nor is God served by human hands, as though he needed something, since he is the one who gives life, breath, and everything else. [26] From one person God created every human nation to live on the whole earth, having determined their appointed times and the boundaries of their lands. [27] God made the nations so they would seek him, perhaps even reach out to him and find him. In fact, God isn't far away from any of us. [28] In God we live, move, and exist. As some of your own poets said, 'We are his offspring.'

[29] "Therefore, as God's offspring, we have no need to imagine that the divine being is like a gold, silver, or stone image made by human skill and thought. [30] God overlooks ignorance of these things in times past, but now directs everyone everywhere to change their hearts and lives. [31] This is because God has set a day when he intends to judge the world justly by a man he has appointed. God has given proof of this to everyone by raising him from the dead."

[32] When they heard about the resurrection from the dead, some began to ridicule Paul. However, others said, "We'll hear from you about this again." [33] At that, Paul left the council. [34] Some people joined him and came to believe, including Dionysius, a member of the council on Mars Hill, a woman named Damaris, and several others.

ATHENS

The city of Athens and its immediate territory of Attica lie at the south end of the mainland of Greece. Paul arrived in Athens by sea from Macedonia, presumably arriving at Piraeus, the port. According to the book of Acts, the city itself was "flooded with idols" (17:16). This reflects the way the city was dominated by the acropolis, which contained a number of sanctuaries, but most notably the Parthenon, the main temple to Athena, the patron deity of the city.

Paul in Corinth

18 After this, Paul left Athens and went to Corinth. [2] There he found a Jew named Aquila, a native of Pontus. He had recently come from Italy with his wife Priscilla because Claudius had ordered all Jews to leave Rome. Paul visited with them. [3] Because they practiced the same trade, he stayed and worked with them. They all worked with leather. [4] Every Sabbath he interacted with people in the synagogue, trying to convince both Jews and Greeks. [5] Once Silas and Timothy arrived from Macedonia, Paul devoted himself fully to the word, testifying to the Jews that Jesus was the Christ. [6] When they opposed and slandered him, he shook the dust from his clothes in protest and said to them, "You are responsible for your own fates! I'm innocent! From now on I'll go to the Gentiles!" [7] He left the synagogue and went next door to the home of Titius Justus, a Gentile God-worshipper. [8] Crispus, the synagogue leader, and his entire household came to believe in the Lord. Many Corinthians believed and were baptized after listening to Paul.

[9] One night the Lord said to Paul in a vision, "Don't be afraid. Continue speaking. Don't be silent. [10] I'm with you and no one who attacks you will harm you, for I have many people in this city." [11] So he stayed there for eighteen months, teaching God's word among them.

[12] Now when Gallio was the governor of the province of Achaia, the Jews united in their opposition against Paul and brought him before the court. [13] "This man is persuading others to worship God unlawfully," they declared.

[14] Just as Paul was about to speak, Gallio said to the Jews, "If there had been some sort of injury or criminal behavior, I would have reason to accept your complaint. [15] However, since these are squabbles about a message, names, and your own Law, deal with them yourselves. I have no desire to sit in judgment over such things." [16] He expelled them from the court, [17] but everyone seized Sosthenes, the synagogue leader, and gave him a beating in the presence of the governor. None of this mattered to Gallio.

[18] After Paul stayed in Corinth for some time, he said good-bye to the brothers and sisters. At the Corinthian seaport of Cenchreae he had his head shaved, since he had made a solemn promise. Then, accompanied by Priscilla and Aquila, he sailed away to Syria. [19] After they arrived in Ephesus, he left Priscilla and Aquila and entered the synagogue and interacted with the Jews. [20] They asked him to stay longer, but he declined. [21] As he said farewell to them, though, he added, "God willing, I will return." Then he sailed off from Ephesus. [22] He arrived in Caesarea, went up to Jerusalem and greeted the church, and then went down to Antioch.

[23] After some time there he left and traveled from place to place in the region of Galatia and the district of Phrygia, strengthening all the disciples.

AQUILA AND PRISCILLA

A married couple; business and missionary associates of the apostle Paul.

Priscilla (the diminutive form used in Acts 18:2, 18, 19, 26) or *Prisca* (Rom 16:3; 1 Cor 16:19; 2 Tim 4:19) is cited before her husband in five of the seven NT references, probably signaling her more prominent role in the early church. Both bear Latin names, and Aquila is identified as a Jewish "native of Pontus" (Acts 18:2). The Pauline Letters and Acts sketch the couple's work and travels across the eastern Mediterranean world, based in Rome, Corinth, and Ephesus.

Apollos and his ministry

24 Meanwhile, a certain Jew named Apollos arrived in Ephesus. He was a native of Alexandria and was well-educated and effective in his use of the scriptures. 25 He had been instructed in the way of the Lord and spoke as one stirred up by the Spirit. He taught accurately the things about Jesus, even though he was aware only of the baptism John proclaimed and practiced. 26 He began speaking with confidence in the synagogue. When Priscilla and Aquila heard him, they received him into their circle of friends and explained to him God's way more accurately. 27 When he wanted to travel to Achaia, the brothers and sisters encouraged him and wrote to the disciples so they would open their homes to him. Once he arrived, he was of great help to those who had come to believe through grace. 28 He would vigorously defeat Jewish arguments in public debate, using the scriptures to prove that Jesus was the Christ.

Paul in Ephesus

19 While Apollos was in Corinth, Paul took a route through the interior and came to Ephesus, where he found some disciples. 2 He asked them, "Did you receive the Holy Spirit when you came to believe?"

They replied, "We've not even heard that there is a Holy Spirit."

3 Then he said, "What baptism did you receive, then?"

They answered, "John's baptism."

4 Paul explained, "John baptized with a baptism by which people showed they were changing their hearts and lives. It was a baptism that told people about the one who was coming after him. This is the one in whom they were to believe. This one is Jesus." 5 After they listened to Paul, they were baptized in the name of the Lord Jesus. 6 When Paul placed his hands on them, the Holy Spirit came on them, and they began speaking in other languages and prophesying. 7 Altogether, there were about twelve people.

8 Paul went to the synagogue and spoke confidently for the next three months. He interacted with those present and offered convincing arguments concerning the nature of God's kingdom. 9 Some people had closed their minds, though. They refused to believe and publicly slandered the Way. As a result, Paul left them, took the disciples with him, and continued his daily interactions in Tyrannus' lecture hall. 10 This went on for two years, so that everyone living in the province of Asia—both Jews and Greeks—heard the Lord's word.

11 God was doing unusual miracles through Paul. 12 Even the small towels and aprons that had touched his skin were taken to the

ASIA

In the time of Paul, the Roman province of Asia was bounded on the north by Bithynia and Pontus, on the south by Lycia and Pamphylia, and on the east by Galatia. There were also some very significant and well-established Jewish communities in Asia. We have evidence that at least some of these communities were involved in the lives of their cities, and they clearly had an impact on the development of early Christianity in the province.

According to Acts, Paul was active in the province of Asia (Acts 13:1–16:10; 18:19–19:41; 20:6-38). The NT Letters of Colossians, Philemon, and Ephesians give us information about Christian communities in Asia. Believers in Asia are mentioned in a number of other NT documents (Rom 16:5; 1 Cor 16:19; 2 Cor 1:8; 2 Tim 1:15; 1 Pet 1:1; cf. 1 Cor 15:32; 16:8; 1 Tim 1:3; 2 Tim 1:18; 4:12).

sick, and their diseases were cured and the evil spirits left them.

¹³There were some Jews who traveled around throwing out evil spirits. They tried to use the power of the name of the Lord Jesus against some people with evil spirits. They said, "In the name of the Jesus whom Paul preaches, I command you!" ¹⁴The seven sons of Sceva, a Jewish chief priest, were doing this.

¹⁵The evil spirit replied, "I know Jesus and I'm familiar with Paul, but who are you?" ¹⁶The person who had an evil spirit jumped on them and overpowered them all with such force that they ran out of that house naked and wounded. ¹⁷This became known to the Jews and Greeks living in Ephesus. Everyone was seized with fear and they held the name of the Lord Jesus in the highest regard.

¹⁸Many of those who had come to believe came, confessing their past practices. ¹⁹This included a number of people who practiced sorcery. They collected their sorcery texts and burned them publicly. The value of those materials was calculated at more than someone might make if they worked for one hundred sixty-five years.ᴾ ²⁰In this way the Lord's word grew abundantly and strengthened powerfully.

²¹Once these things had come to an end, Paul, guided by the Spirit, decided to return to Jerusalem, taking a route that would carry him through the provinces of Macedonia and Achaia. He said, "After I have been there, I must visit Rome as well." ²²He sent two of his assistants, Timothy and Erastus, to Macedonia, while he remained awhile in the province of Asia.

²³At that time a great disturbance erupted about the Way. ²⁴There was a silversmith named Demetrius. He made silver models of Artemis' temple, and his business generated a lot of profit for the craftspeople. ²⁵He called a meeting with these craftspeople and others working in related trades and said, "Friends, you know that we make an easy living from this business. ²⁶And you can see and hear that this Paul

has convinced and misled a lot of people, not only in Ephesus but also throughout most of the province of Asia. He says that gods made by human hands aren't really gods. ²⁷This poses a danger not only by discrediting our trade but also by completely dishonoring the great goddess Artemis. The whole province of Asia—indeed, the entire civilized world—worships her, but her splendor will soon be extinguished."

²⁸Once they heard this, they were beside themselves with anger and began to shout, "Great is Artemis of the Ephesians!"

²⁹The city was thrown into turmoil. They rushed as one into the theater. They seized Gaius and Aristarchus, Paul's traveling companions from the province of Macedonia. ³⁰Paul wanted to appear before the assembly, but the disciples wouldn't allow him. ³¹Even some officials of the province of Asia, who were Paul's friends, sent word to him, urging him not to risk going into the theater. ³²Meanwhile, the assembly was in a state of confusion. Some shouted one thing, others shouted something else, and most of the crowd didn't know why they had gathered. ³³The Jews sent Alexander to the front, and some of the crowd directed their words toward him. He gestured that he wanted to offer a defense before the assembly, ³⁴but when they realized he was a Jew, they all shouted in unison, "Great is Artemis of the Ephesians!" This continued for about two hours.

³⁵The city manager brought order to the crowd and said, "People of Ephesus, doesn't everyone know that the city of Ephesus is guardian of the temple of the great Artemis and of her image, which fell from heaven? ³⁶Therefore, since these facts are undeniable, you must calm down. Don't be reckless. ³⁷The men you brought here have neither robbed the temple nor slandered our goddess. ³⁸Therefore, if Demetrius and the craftspeople with him have a charge against anyone, the courts are in session and governors are available. They can press charges against each other there. ³⁹Additional disputes can be resolved in a legal

---

ᴾOr *fifty thousand silver drachmen* (a drachme is equivalent in value to a denarion, a typical day's wage).

assembly. [40]As for us, we are in danger of being charged with rioting today, since we can't justify this unruly gathering." [41]After he said this, he dismissed the assembly.

Paul visits Macedonia and Greece

20 When the riot was over, Paul sent for the disciples, encouraged them, said good-bye, and left for the province of Macedonia. [2]He traveled through that region with a message of encouragement. When he came to Greece, [3]he stayed for three months. Because the Jews hatched a plot against Paul as he was about to sail for Syria, he decided instead to return through Macedonia. [4]He was accompanied by Sopater, Pyrrhus' son from Beroea, Aristarchus and Secundus from Thessalonica, Gaius from Derbe, Timothy, and Tychicus and Trophimus from the province of Asia. [5]They went on ahead and waited for us in Troas. [6]We sailed from Philippi after the Festival of Unleavened Bread and met them five days later in Troas, where we stayed for a week.

Meeting with believers in Troas

[7]On the first day of the week, as we gathered together for a meal, Paul was holding a discussion with them. Since he was leaving the next day, he continued talking until midnight. [8]There were many lamps in the upstairs room where we had gathered. [9]A young man named Eutychus was sitting in the window. He was sinking into a deep sleep as Paul talked on and on. When he was sound asleep, he fell from the third floor and died. [10]Paul went down, fell on him and embraced him, then said, "Don't be alarmed. He's alive!" [11]Then Paul went back upstairs and ate. He talked for a long time—right up until daybreak—then he left. [12]They took the young man away alive, and they were greatly comforted.

Farewell to the Ephesian leaders

[13]We went on to the ship and sailed for Assos, where we intended to take Paul on board. Paul had arranged this, since he intended to make his way there by land.

PHILIPPI

Philippi is in eastern Macedonia (northern Greece) on the Via Egnatia overlooking an inland plain to the east of Mount Pangaeus/Pangaion. Philippi is named for Philip II, king of Macedonia (359–336 BCE) and father of Alexander the Great. Philip named the city "Philippi" after himself when the citizens asked for his help against the Thracians. Around 49–50 CE, the apostle Paul started the first church in ancient Greece at Philippi (Acts 16:11-40) following his Macedonian vision at Troas (Acts 16:8-10). Although he was shamefully treated at Philippi (1 Thess 2:2), he nevertheless had a significant ministry in the city and spoke affectionately about the church and his ministry among them (Phil 4:10-20). His converts at Philippi included Lydia, in whose house he began the church (Acts 16:14-15); the jailer and his family (Acts 16:27-34); Epaphroditus (Phil 2:25-30); Euodia and Syntyche, who were at odds with each other after Paul's departure (Phil 4:2); Clement; and others who served with Paul and Silas at Philippi (Phil 4:3).

The Philippian church contributed substantially to Paul's missionary activity (Phil 4:15-18) and became very dear to him. He visited here at least one more time (Acts 20:1-6; 1 Cor 16:5-6; 2 Cor 2:13; 7:5), and on that visit he may have gone west to Illyricum (Rom 15:19). He may have written his letter(s) to the leaders of the church at Philippi (ca. 55–56 CE) from Ephesus or later while he was at Rome (ca. 60 CE).

¹⁴When he met us at Assos, we took him aboard and went on to Mitylene. ¹⁵The next day we sailed from there and arrived opposite Chios. On the day after, we sailed to Samos, and on the following day we came to Miletus. ¹⁶Paul had decided to sail past Ephesus so that he wouldn't need to spend too much time in the province of Asia. He was hurrying to reach Jerusalem, if possible, by Pentecost Day.

¹⁷From Miletus he sent a message to Ephesus calling for the church's elders to meet him. ¹⁸When they arrived, he said to them, "You know how I lived among you the whole time I was with you, beginning with the first day I arrived in the province of Asia. ¹⁹I served the Lord with great humility and with tears in the midst of trials that came upon me because of the Jews' schemes. ²⁰You know I held back nothing that would be helpful so that I could proclaim to you and teach you both publicly and privately in your homes. ²¹You know I have testified to both Jews and Greeks that they must change their hearts and lives as they turn to God and have faith in our Lord Jesus. ²²Now, compelled by the Spirit, I'm going to Jerusalem. I don't know what will happen to me there. ²³What I do know is that the Holy Spirit testifies to me from city to city that prisons and troubles await me. ²⁴But nothing, not even my life, is more important than my completing my mission. This is nothing other than the ministry I received from the Lord Jesus: to testify about the good news of God's grace.

²⁵"I know that none of you will see me again—you among whom I traveled and proclaimed the kingdom. ²⁶Therefore, today I testify to you that I'm not responsible for anyone's fate. ²⁷I haven't avoided proclaiming the entire plan of God to you. ²⁸Watch yourselves and the whole flock, in which the Holy Spirit has placed you as supervisors, to shepherd God's church, which he obtained with the death of his own Son.�q ²⁹I know that, after my departure, savage wolves will come in among you and won't spare the flock. ³⁰Some of your own people

will distort the word in order to lure followers after them. ³¹Stay alert! Remember that for three years I constantly and tearfully warned each one of you. I never stopped warning you! ³²Now I entrust you to God and the message of his grace, which is able to build you up and give you an inheritance among all whom God has made holy. ³³I haven't craved anyone's silver, gold, or clothing. ³⁴You yourselves know that I have provided for my own needs and for those of my companions with my own hands. ³⁵In everything I have shown you that, by working hard, we must help the weak. In this way we remember the Lord Jesus' words: 'It is more blessed to give than to receive.'"

³⁶After he said these things, he knelt down with all of them to pray. ³⁷They cried uncontrollably as everyone embraced and kissed Paul. ³⁸They were especially grieved by his statement that they would never see him again. Then they accompanied him to the ship.

Paul travels to Jerusalem

21 After we tore ourselves away from them, we set sail on a straight course to Cos, reaching Rhodes the next day, and then Patara. ²We found a ship crossing over to Phoenicia, boarded, and put out to sea. ³We spotted Cyprus, but passed by it on our left. We sailed on to the province of Syria and landed in Tyre, where the ship was to unload its cargo. ⁴We found the disciples there and stayed with them for a week. Compelled by the Spirit, they kept telling Paul not to go to Jerusalem. ⁵When our time had come to an end, we departed. All of them, including women and children, accompanied us out of town where we knelt on the beach and prayed. ⁶We said good-bye to each other, then we boarded the ship and they returned to their homes.

⁷Continuing our voyage, we sailed from Tyre and arrived in Ptolemais. We greeted the brothers and sisters there and spent a day with them. ⁸The next day we left and came to Caesarea. We went to the house of Philip the evangelist, one of the Seven, and

�q Or with the death of his own, or with his own death

stayed with him. [9]He had four unmarried daughters who were involved in the work of prophecy. [10]After staying there for several days, a prophet named Agabus came down from Judea. [11]He came to us, took Paul's belt, tied his own feet and hands, and said, "This is what the Holy Spirit says: 'In Jerusalem the Jews will bind the man who owns this belt, and they will hand him over to the Gentiles.'" [12]When we heard this, we and the local believers urged Paul not to go up to Jerusalem.

[13]Paul replied, "Why are you doing this? Why are you weeping and breaking my heart? I'm ready not only to be arrested but even to die in Jerusalem for the sake of the name of the Lord Jesus."

[14]Since we couldn't talk him out of it, the only thing we could say was, "The Lord's will be done."

[15]After this, we got ready and made our way up to Jerusalem. [16]Some of the disciples from Caesarea accompanied us and led us to Mnason's home, where we were guests. He was from Cyprus and had been a disciple a long time. [17]When we arrived in Jerusalem, the brothers and sisters welcomed us warmly.

Meeting the Jerusalem church leaders

[18]On the next day Paul and the rest of us went to see James. All of the elders were present. [19]After greeting them, he gave them a detailed report of what God had done among the Gentiles through his ministry. [20]Those who heard this praised God. Then they said to him, "Brother, you see how many thousands of Jews have become believers, and all of them keep the Law passionately. [21]They have been informed that you teach all the Jews who live among the Gentiles to reject Moses, telling them not to circumcise their children nor to live according to our customs. [22]What about this? Without a doubt, they will hear that you have arrived. [23]You must therefore do what we tell you. Four men among us have made a solemn promise. [24]Take them with you, go through the purification ritual with them, and pay the cost of having their heads shaved. Everyone will know there is nothing to those reports about you but that you too live a life in keeping with the Law. [25]As for the Gentile believers, we wrote a letter about what we decided, that they avoid food offered to idols, blood, the meat from strangled animals, and sexual immorality." [26]The following day Paul took the men with him and went through the purification ritual with them. He entered the temple and publicly announced the completion of the days of purification, when the offering would be presented for each one of them.

Paul seized by the people

[27]When the seven days of purification were almost over, the Jews from the province of Asia saw Paul in the temple. Grabbing him, they threw the whole crowd into confusion by shouting, [28]"Fellow Israelites! Help! This is the man who teaches everyone everywhere against our people, the Law, and this place. Not only that, he has even brought Greeks into the temple and defiled this holy place." ([29]They said this because they had seen Trophimus the Ephesian in the city with him earlier, and they assumed Paul had brought him into the temple.) [30]The entire city was stirred up. The people came rushing, seized Paul, and dragged him out of the temple. Immediately the gates were closed. [31]While they were trying to

TRIBUNE

A high-ranking military officer (Acts 24:22; 25:23). The official whom Paul encounters while in Jerusalem (Acts 21:31-40; 22:22-30; 23:10-22) appears to be a *tribunus militum*, a Roman military commander in charge of a cohort (approximately 600 soldiers). The CEB uses the term "commander."

kill him, a report reached the commander of a company of soldiers that all Jerusalem was in a state of confusion. [32]Without a moment's hesitation, he took some soldiers and officers and ran down to the mob. When the mob saw the commander and his soldiers, they stopped beating Paul. [33]When the commander arrived, he arrested Paul and ordered him to be bound with two chains. Only then did he begin to ask who Paul was and what he had done.

[34]Some in the crowd shouted one thing, others shouted something else. Because of the commotion, he couldn't learn the truth, so he ordered that Paul be taken to the military headquarters. [35]When Paul reached the steps, he had to be carried by the soldiers in order to protect him from the violence of the crowd. [36]The mob that followed kept screaming, "Away with him!"

[37]As Paul was about to be taken into the military headquarters, he asked the commander, "May I speak with you?"

He answered, "Do you know Greek? [38]Aren't you the Egyptian who started a revolt and led four thousand terrorists into the desert some time ago?"

[39]Paul replied, "I'm a Jew from Tarsus in Cilicia, a citizen of an important city. Please, let me speak to the people." [40]With the commander's permission, Paul stood on the steps and gestured to the people. When they were quiet, he addressed them in Aramaic.

Paul's defense before his accusers

22"Brothers and fathers, listen now to my defense." [2]When they heard him address them in Aramaic, they became even more quiet. [3]Paul continued, "I'm a Jew, born in Tarsus in Cilicia but raised in this city. Under Gamaliel's instruction, I was trained in the strict interpretation of our ancestral Law. I am passionately loyal to God, just like you who are gathered here today. [4]I harassed those who followed this Way to their death, arresting and delivering both men and women into prison. [5]The high priest and the whole Jerusalem Council can testify about me. I received letters from them, addressed to our associates in Damascus, then went there to bring those who were arrested to Jerusalem so they could be punished.

[6]"During that journey, about noon, as I approached Damascus, suddenly a bright light from heaven encircled me. [7]I fell to the ground and heard a voice asking me, 'Saul, Saul, why are you harassing me?' [8]I answered, 'Who are you, Lord?' 'I am Jesus the Nazarene, whom you are harassing,' he replied. [9]My traveling companions saw the light, but they didn't hear the voice of

TARSUS

A major port city on the river Cydnus near the Mediterranean Sea, directly north of the eastern tip of Cyprus. Paul's hometown was Tarsus (Acts 9:11, 30; 11:25; 21:39; 22:3). Tarsus stands at the intersection of the fertile plain of East Cilicia and the Taurus Mountains to the north that extend to the sea. Its strategic location at a crossroads between north and south, east and west, and on a harbor miles from the sea made Tarsus safe from pirates and storms, promoted trade and commerce, and encouraged vigorous cultural exchanges. The road to the north ran through a rugged mountain pass, the Cilician Gates, linking it to Syria at the top of the Fertile Crescent and offering a place where Hellenistic and Semitic cultures could meet. Vigorous cultural and commercial exchanges took place over the sea-lanes to Alexandria, Egypt, in the south and to Rome and Greece to the west. It still stands on the site in modern Turkey that it has occupied for over 5,000 years.

the one who spoke to me. ¹⁰I asked, 'What should I do, Lord?' 'Get up,' the Lord replied, 'and go into Damascus. There you will be told everything you have been appointed to do.' ¹¹I couldn't see because of the brightness of that light, so my companions led me by the hand into Damascus.

¹²"There was a certain man named Ananias. According to the standards of the Law, he was a pious man who enjoyed the respect of all the Jews living there. ¹³He came and stood beside me. 'Brother Saul, receive your sight!' he said. Instantly, I regained my sight and I could see him. ¹⁴He said, 'The God of our ancestors has selected you to know his will, to see the righteous one, and to hear his voice. ¹⁵You will be his witness to everyone concerning what you have seen and heard. ¹⁶What are you waiting for? Get up, be baptized, and wash away your sins as you call on his name.'

¹⁷"When I returned to Jerusalem and was praying in the temple, I had a visionary experience. ¹⁸I saw the Lord speaking to me. 'Hurry!' he said. 'Leave Jerusalem at once because they won't accept your testimony about me.' ¹⁹I responded, 'Lord, these people know I used to go from one synagogue to the next, beating those who believe in you and throwing them into prison. ²⁰When Stephen your witness was being killed, I stood there giving my approval, even watching the clothes that belonged to those who were killing him.' ²¹Then the Lord said to me, 'Go! I will send you far away to the Gentiles.'"

²²The crowd listened to Paul until he said this. Then they shouted, "Away with this man! He's not fit to live!" ²³As they were screaming, throwing off their garments, and flinging dust into the air, ²⁴the commander directed that Paul be taken into the military headquarters. He ordered that Paul be questioned under the whip so that he could find out why they were shouting at him like this.

²⁵As they were stretching him out and tying him down with straps, Paul said to the centurion standing there, "Can you legally whip a Roman citizen who hasn't been found guilty in court?"

²⁶When the centurion heard this, he went to the commander and reported it. He asked, "What are you about to do? This man is a Roman citizen!"

²⁷The commander went to Paul and demanded, "Tell me! Are you a Roman citizen?" He said, "Yes."

²⁸The commander replied, "It cost me a lot of money to buy my citizenship."

Paul said, "I'm a citizen by birth." ²⁹At once those who were about to examine him stepped away. The commander was alarmed when he realized he had bound a Roman citizen.

Paul appears before the Jewish council

³⁰The commander still wanted to know the truth about why Paul was being accused by the Jews. Therefore, the next day he ordered the chief priests and the entire Jerusalem Council to assemble. Then he took Paul out of prison and had him stand before them.

23 Paul stared at the council and said, "Brothers, I have lived my life with an altogether clear conscience right up to this very day." ²The high priest Ananias ordered those standing beside Paul to strike him in the mouth. ³Then Paul said to him, "God is about to strike you, you whitewashed wall! You sit and judge me according to the Law, yet disobey the Law by ordering that I be struck."

⁴Those standing near him asked, "You dare to insult God's high priest?"

⁵Paul replied, "Brothers, I wasn't aware that he was the high priest. It is written, *You will not speak evil about a ruler of your people.*"ʳ

⁶Knowing that some of them were Sadducees and the others Pharisees, Paul exclaimed in the council, "Brothers, I'm a Pharisee and a descendant of Pharisees. I am on trial because of my hope in the resurrection of the dead!"

⁷These words aroused a dispute between the Pharisees and Sadducees, and

the assembly was divided. [8]This is because Sadducees say that there's no resurrection, angel, or spirit, but Pharisees affirm them all. [9]Council members were shouting loudly. Some Pharisees who were legal experts stood up and insisted forcefully, "We find nothing wrong with this man! What if a spirit or angel has spoken to him?" [10]The dispute became so heated that the commander feared they might tear Paul to pieces. He ordered soldiers to go down and remove him by force from their midst. Then they took him back to the military headquarters.

[11]The following night the Lord stood near Paul and said, "Be encouraged! Just as you have testified about me in Jerusalem, so too you must testify in Rome."

A murder plot discovered

[12]The next morning some Jewish leaders formulated a plot and solemnly promised that they wouldn't eat or drink until they had killed Paul. [13]More than forty people were involved in the conspiracy. [14]They went to the chief priests and elders and said, "We have solemnly promised to eat nothing until we have killed Paul. [15]You and the council must explain to the commander that you need Paul brought down to you. Pretend that you want to examine his case more closely. We're prepared to kill him before he arrives."

[16]Paul's sister had a son who heard about the ambush and he came to the military headquarters and reported it to Paul. [17]Paul called for one of the centurions and said, "Take this young man to the commander because he has something to report to him." [18]He took him to the commander and said, "The prisoner Paul asked me to bring this young man to you. He has something to tell you."

[19]The commander took him by the hand and withdrew to a place where they could speak privately. He asked, "What do you have to report to me?"

[20]He replied, "The Jewish leaders have conspired to ask that you bring Paul down to the council tomorrow. They will pretend that they want to investigate his case more closely. [21]Don't fall for it! More than forty of them are waiting to ambush him. They have solemnly promised not to eat or drink until they have killed him. They are ready now, awaiting your consent."

[22]The commander dismissed the young man, ordering him, "Don't tell anyone that you brought this to my attention."

[23]The commander called two centurions and said, "Prepare two hundred soldiers, seventy horsemen, and two hundred spearmen to leave for Caesarea at nine o'clock tonight. [24]Have horses ready for Paul to ride, so they may take him safely to Governor Felix." [25]He wrote the following letter:

PHARISEES

The Greek term occurs for the first time in the NT (more than 90 times) and is also used by the 1st-century CE Jewish historian Josephus (44 times). The term is not found in other early Jewish texts, or in the writings of Greco-Roman authors who refer to the Jews. The Pharisees were a Jewish sect in the time of the NT; Paul was a Pharisee. The Pharisees are repeatedly described as people who transmit, preserve, and develop the tradition of the Instruction from Moses in its written and oral form. Their understanding of tradition evidently was nonexclusive, which explains their interest in Jesus: they are prepared to listen to Jesus as long as he can demonstrate the continuity between his teaching and the Instruction tradition. Pharisees were known for their piety and their strict adherence to the Instruction.

[26]Claudius Lysias, to the most honorable Governor Felix: Greetings. [27]This man was seized by the Jews and was almost killed by them. I was nearby with a unit of soldiers, and I rescued him when I discovered that he was a Roman citizen. [28]I wanted to find out why they were accusing him, so I brought him to their council. [29]I discovered that they were accusing him about questions related to their Law. I found no charge deserving of death or imprisonment. [30]When I was informed of a conspiracy against his life, I sent him to you at once and ordered his accusers to bring their case against him before you.

[31]Following their orders, the soldiers took Paul during the night and brought him to Antipatris. [32]The following day they let the horsemen continue on with Paul while they returned to the military headquarters in Jerusalem. [33]The horsemen entered Caesarea, delivered the letter to the governor, and brought Paul before him. [34]After he read the letter, he asked Paul about his home province. When he learned that he was from Cilicia, [35]the governor said, "I will hear your case when your accusers arrive." Then he ordered that Paul be kept in custody in Herod's palace.

Paul's trial before Felix

24 Five days later the high priest Ananias came down with some elders and a lawyer named Tertullus. They pressed charges against Paul before the governor. [2]After the governor summoned Paul, Tertullus began to make his case against him. He declared, "Under your leadership, we have experienced substantial peace, and your administration has brought reforms to our nation. [3]Always and everywhere, most honorable Felix, we acknowledge this with deep gratitude. [4]I don't want to take too much of your time, so I ask that you listen with your usual courtesy to our brief statement of the facts. [5]We have found this man to be a troublemaker who stirs up riots among all the Jews throughout the empire. He's a ringleader of the Nazarene faction [6]and even tried to defile the temple. That's when we arrested him.[s] [8]By examining him yourself, you will be able to verify the allegations we are bringing against him." [9]The Jews reinforced the action against Paul, affirming the truth of these accusations.

[10]The governor nodded at Paul, giving him permission to speak.

He responded, "I know that you have been judge over this nation for many years, so I gladly offer my own defense. [11]You can verify that I went up to worship in Jerusalem no more than twelve days ago. [12]They didn't find me arguing with anyone in the temple or stirring up a crowd, whether in the synagogue or anywhere else in the city. [13]Nor can they prove to you the allegations they are now bringing against me. [14]I do admit this to you, that I am a follower of the Way, which they call a faction. Accordingly, I worship the God of our ancestors and believe everything set out in the Law and written in the Prophets. [15]The hope I have in God I also share with my accusers, that there will be a resurrection of both the righteous and the unrighteous. [16]On account of this, I have committed myself to maintaining a clear conscience before God and with all people. [17]After an absence of several years, I came to Jerusalem to bring gifts for the poor of my nation and to offer sacrifices. [18]When they found me in the temple, I was ritually pure. There was no crowd and no disturbance. [19]But there were some Jews from the province of Asia. They should be here making their accusations, if indeed they have something against me. [20]In their absence, have these people who are here declare what crime they found when I stood before the Jerusalem Council. [21]Perhaps it concerns this one statement that I blurted out when I was with them: 'I am on trial before you today because of the resurrection of the dead.'"

[s]Critical editions of the Gk New Testament do not include *We wanted to put him on trial according to our Law,* [7]*but Lysias the commander arrived and took him from our hands with great force.* [8]*Then he ordered his accusers to appear before you.*

[22]Felix, who had an accurate understanding of the Way, adjourned the meeting. He said, "When Lysias the commander arrives from Jerusalem, I will decide this case." [23]He arranged for a centurion to guard Paul. He was to give Paul some freedom, and his friends were not to be hindered in their efforts to provide for him.

Paul in custody

[24]After several days, Felix came with his wife Drusilla, who was Jewish, and summoned Paul. He listened to him talk about faith in Christ Jesus. [25]When he spoke about upright behavior, self-control, and the coming judgment, Felix became fearful and said, "Go away for now! When I have time, I'll send for you." [26]At the same time, he was hoping that Paul would offer him some money, so he often sent for him and talked with him.

[27]When two years had passed, Felix was succeeded by Porcius Festus. Since Felix wanted to grant a favor to the Jews, he left Paul in prison.

Paul appeals to Caesar

25 Three days after arriving in the province, Festus went up to Jerusalem from Caesarea. [2]The chief priests and Jewish leaders presented their case against Paul. Appealing to him, [3]they asked as a favor from Festus that he summon Paul to Jerusalem. They were planning to ambush and kill him along the way. [4]But Festus responded by keeping Paul in Caesarea, since he was to return there very soon himself. [5]"Some of your leaders can come down with me," he said. "If he's done anything wrong, they can bring charges against him."

[6]He stayed with them for no more than eight or ten days, then went down to Caesarea. The following day he took his seat in the court and ordered that Paul be brought in. [7]When he arrived, many Jews who had come down from Jerusalem surrounded him. They brought serious charges against him, but they couldn't prove them. [8]In his own defense, Paul said, "I've done nothing wrong against the Jewish Law, against the temple, or against Caesar."

[9]Festus, wanting to put the Jews in his debt, asked Paul, "Are you willing to go up to Jerusalem to stand trial before me concerning these things?"

[10]Paul replied, "I'm standing before Caesar's court. I ought to be tried here. I have done nothing wrong to the Jews, as you well know. [11]If I'm guilty and have done something that deserves death, then I won't try to avoid death. But if there is nothing to their accusations against me, no one has the authority to hand me over to them. I appeal to Caesar!"

[12]After Festus conferred with his advisors, he responded, "You have appealed to Caesar. To Caesar you will go."

ROMAN EMPIRE

By the 1st century CE, Rome's empire extended from Britain in the northwest, through (present-day) France and Spain, across Europe to Turkey and Syria in the east, and to the south along North Africa. Rome ruled an estimated 60–65 million people of diverse ethnicities and cultures. The empire was hierarchical with vast differences in power and wealth. For the small number of ruling elite, both in Rome and the provinces, life was quite comfortable. For the majority who were not the elite, it was at best livable and at worst miserable. There was no middle class, little opportunity to improve one's lot, and few safety nets in adversity. Instances of *Rome* in the NT usually refer to the Roman Empire.

King Agrippa informed about Paul

¹³After several days had passed, King Agrippa and Bernice arrived in Caesarea to welcome Festus. ¹⁴Since they were staying there for many days, Festus discussed the case against Paul with the king. He said, "There is a man whom Felix left in prison. ¹⁵When I was in Jerusalem, the Jewish chief priests and elders brought charges against him and requested a guilty verdict in his case. ¹⁶I told them it is contrary to Roman practice to hand someone over before they have faced their accusers and had opportunity to offer a defense against the charges. ¹⁷When they came here, I didn't put them off. The very next day I took my seat in the court and ordered that the man be brought before me. ¹⁸When the accusers took the floor, they didn't charge him with any of the crimes I had expected. ¹⁹Instead, they quibbled with him about their own religion and about some dead man named Jesus, who Paul claimed was alive. ²⁰Since I had no idea how to investigate these matters, I asked if he would be willing to go to Jerusalem to stand trial there on these issues. ²¹However, Paul appealed that he be held in custody pending a decision from His Majesty the emperor, so I ordered that he be held until I could send him to Caesar."

²²Agrippa said to Festus, "I want to hear the man myself."

"Tomorrow," Festus replied, "you will hear him."

²³The next day Agrippa and Bernice came with great fanfare. They entered the auditorium with the military commanders and the city's most prominent men. Festus then ordered that Paul be brought in. ²⁴Festus said, "King Agrippa and everyone present with us: You see this man! The entire Jewish community, both here and in Jerusalem, has appealed to me concerning him. They've been calling for his immediate death. ²⁵I've found that he has done nothing deserving death. When he appealed to His Majesty, I decided to send him to Rome. ²⁶I have nothing definite to write to our lord emperor. Therefore, I've brought him before all of you, and especially before you, King Agrippa, so that after this inves-

tigation, I might have something to write. ²⁷After all, it would be foolish to send a prisoner without specifying the charges against him."

Paul's defense before Agrippa

26 Agrippa said to Paul, "You may speak for yourself."

So Paul gestured with his hand and began his defense. ²"King Agrippa, I consider myself especially fortunate that I stand before you today as I offer my defense concerning all the accusations the Jews have brought against me. ³This is because you understand well all the Jewish customs and controversies. Therefore, I ask you to listen to me patiently. ⁴Every Jew knows the way of life I have followed since my youth because, from the beginning, I was among my people and in Jerusalem. ⁵They have known me for a long time. If they wanted to, they could testify that I followed the way of life set out by the most exacting group of our religion. I am a Pharisee. ⁶Today I am standing trial because of the hope in the promise God gave our ancestors. ⁷This is the promise our twelve tribes hope to receive as they earnestly worship night and day. The Jews are accusing me, King Agrippa, because of this hope! ⁸Why is it inconceivable to you that God raises the dead?

⁹"I really thought that I ought to oppose the name of Jesus the Nazarene in every way possible. ¹⁰And that's exactly what I did in Jerusalem. I locked up many of God's holy people in prison under the authority of the chief priests. When they were condemned to death, I voted against them. ¹¹In one synagogue after another—indeed, in all the synagogues—I would often torture them, compelling them to slander God. My rage bordered on the hysterical as I pursued them, even to foreign cities.

¹²"On one such journey, I was going to Damascus with the full authority of the chief priests. ¹³While on the road at midday, King Agrippa, I saw a light from heaven shining around me and my traveling companions. That light was brighter than the sun. ¹⁴We all fell to the ground, and I heard a voice that said to me in Aramaic, 'Saul,

Saul, why are you harassing me? It's hard for you to kick against a spear.'ᵗ ¹⁵Then I said, 'Who are you, Lord?' The Lord replied, 'I am Jesus, whom you are harassing. ¹⁶Get up! Stand on your feet! I have appeared to you for this purpose: to appoint you as my servant and witness of what you have seen and what I will show you. ¹⁷I will rescue you from your own people and from the Gentiles. I am sending you ¹⁸to open their eyes. Then they can turn from darkness to light and from the power of Satan to God,

ᵗOr goads

SYNAGOGUE

A Jewish community, a gathering of people, the area or building in which the people gather, or all three. In particular, the synagogue was (and is) an assembly drawn together for religious worship and study, with an emphasis on the public reading and explication of scripture.

All four of the canonical Gospels report that Jesus taught in synagogues (Matt 4:23; 13:54; Mark 1:21; Luke 4:16; 6:6; John 6:59; 18:20) and that he also healed there (Matt 4:23; Mark 1:23-27). Luke's Gospel introduces Jesus' ministry with the pronouncement—in the synagogue in Nazareth—that he has come to fulfill the prophet Isaiah (Luke 4:16-21).

According to Acts, Paul went to the synagogues in all the towns he visited to try to persuade Jews (and Gentile converts to Judaism) to follow Jesus as the Christ (e.g., Acts 9:20; 13:5, 14-16; 14:1; 17:1-2, 10, 17; 18:4, 7-8, 19; 19:8). Even though Paul's own letters do not confirm this practice (indeed, Paul says he went to the Gentiles, not Jews), Acts provides literary evidence of the many synagogues throughout the Mediterranean area in the 1st century, their function as a central gathering place for Jews (including sojourners like Paul), and the attendance of Gentile seekers.

In the 1st–2nd centuries CE, the growing tension between Jews who believed Jesus was the Christ and those who did not sometimes took place in the context of the synagogue. For example, while one leader of the synagogue was receptive to Jesus (Mark 5:22-24, 35-42; cf. Matt 9:18-19, 23-25), another questioned his authority (Luke 13:10-14). The book of Acts describes both positive and negative responses to the gospel message preached in synagogues (Acts 13:42-50; 14:1-2; 17:1-9; 19:8-10).

By the time the Gospel of John was written (late 1st century), evidence of a rift within the synagogues becomes greater, as John refers to adversaries of Jesus collectively as "the Jewish authorities" and reports that those who proclaim Jesus to be the Messiah risk being expelled from the synagogue (John 9:22; 12:42; 16:2). In the book of Revelation, the author bitterly claims that the people "who say they are Jews (though they are not)" are "from Satan's synagogue" (2:9; 3:9). These conflicts within and around the synagogue need to be understood as disagreements among 1st-century Jews who were grappling with great complexity of belief and not as a condemnation of Jews or Judaism.

and receive forgiveness of sins and a place among those who are made holy by faith in me.'

¹⁹"So, King Agrippa, I wasn't disobedient to that heavenly vision. ²⁰Instead, I proclaimed first to those in Damascus and Jerusalem, then to the whole region of Judea and to the Gentiles. My message was that they should change their hearts and lives and turn to God, and that they should demonstrate this change in their behavior. ²¹Because of this, some Jews seized me in the temple and tried to murder me. ²²God has helped me up to this very day. Therefore, I stand here and bear witness to the lowly and the great. I'm saying nothing more than what the Prophets and Moses declared would happen: ²³that the Christ would suffer and that, as the first to rise from the dead, he would proclaim light both to my people and to the Gentiles."

²⁴At this point in Paul's defense, Festus declared with a loud voice, "You've lost your mind, Paul! Too much learning is driving you mad!"

²⁵But Paul replied, "I'm not mad, most honorable Festus! I'm speaking what is sound and true. ²⁶King Agrippa knows about these things, and I have been speaking openly to him. I'm certain that none of these things have escaped his attention. This didn't happen secretly or in some out-of-the-way place. ²⁷King Agrippa, do you believe the prophets? I know you do."

²⁸Agrippa said to Paul, "Are you trying to convince me that, in such a short time, you've made me a Christian?"

²⁹Paul responded, "Whether it is a short or a long time, I pray to God that not only you but also all who are listening to me today will become like me, except for these chains."

³⁰The king stood up, as did the governor, Bernice, and those sitting with them. ³¹As they left, they were saying to each other, "This man is doing nothing that deserves death or imprisonment."

³²Agrippa said to Festus, "This man could have been released if he hadn't appealed to Caesar."

Paul's voyage to Rome

27When it was determined that we were to sail to Italy, Paul and some other prisoners were placed in the custody of a centurion named Julius of the Imperial Company.ᵘ ²We boarded a ship from Adramyttium that was about to sail for ports along the coast of the province of Asia. So we put out to sea. Aristarchus, a Macedonian from Thessalonica, came with us. ³The next day we landed in Sidon. Julius treated Paul kindly and permitted him to go to some friends so they could take care of him. ⁴From there we sailed off. We passed Cyprus, using the island to shelter us from the headwinds. ⁵We sailed across the open sea off the coast of Cilicia and Pamphylia, and landed in Myra in Lycia. ⁶There the centurion found an Alexandrian ship headed for Italy and put us on board. ⁷After many days of slow and difficult sailing, we arrived off the coast of Cnidus. The wind wouldn't allow us to go farther, so we sailed under the shelter of Crete off Salmone. ⁸We sailed along the coast only with difficulty until we came to a place called Good Harbors,ᵛ near the city of Lasea.

⁹Much time had been lost, and the voyage was now dangerous since the Day of Reconciliation had already passed. Paul warned them, ¹⁰"Men, I see that our voyage will suffer damage and great loss, not only for the cargo and ship but also for our lives." ¹¹But the centurion was persuaded more by the ship's pilot and captain than by Paul's advice. ¹²Since the harbor was unsuitable for spending the winter, the majority supported a plan to put out to sea from there. They thought they might reach Phoenix in Crete and spend the winter in its harbor, which faced southwest and northwest.

¹³When a gentle south wind began to blow, they thought they could carry out their plan. They pulled up anchor and sailed closely along the coast of Crete. ¹⁴Before long, a hurricane-strength wind known as a northeaster swept down from Crete. ¹⁵The ship was caught in the storm and couldn't be turned into the wind. So we gave in to

---

ᵘOr *cohort* (approximately six hundred soldiers) ᵛOr *Fair Havens* it, and it carried us along. ¹⁶After sailing under the shelter of an island called Cauda, we were able to control the lifeboat only with difficulty. ¹⁷They brought the lifeboat aboard, then began to wrap the ship with cables to hold it together. Fearing they might run aground on the sandbars of the Gulf of Syrtis, they lowered the anchor and let the ship be carried along. ¹⁸We were so battered by the violent storm that the next day the men began throwing cargo overboard. ¹⁹On the third day, they picked up the ship's gear and hurled it into the sea. ²⁰When neither the sun nor the moon appeared for many days and the raging storm continued to pound us, all hope of our being saved from this peril faded.

²¹For a long time no one had eaten. Paul stood up among them and said, "Men, you should have complied with my instructions not to sail from Crete. Then we would have avoided this damage and loss. ²²Now I urge you to be encouraged. Not one of your lives will be lost, though we will lose the ship. ²³Last night an angel from the God to whom I belong and whom I worship stood beside me. ²⁴The angel said, 'Don't be afraid, Paul! You must stand before Caesar! Indeed, God has also graciously given you everyone sailing with you.' ²⁵Be encouraged, men! I have faith in God that it will be exactly as he told me. ²⁶However, we must run aground on some island."

²⁷On the fourteenth night, we were being carried across the Adriatic Sea. Around midnight the sailors began to suspect that land was near. ²⁸They dropped a weighted line to take soundings and found the water to be about one hundred twenty feet deep.

After proceeding a little farther, we took soundings again and found the water to be about ninety feet deep. ²⁹Afraid that we might run aground somewhere on the rocks, they hurled out four anchors from the stern and began to pray for daylight. ³⁰The sailors tried to abandon the ship by lowering the lifeboat into the sea, pretending they were going to lower anchors from the bow. ³¹Paul said to the centurion and his soldiers, "Unless they stay in the ship, you can't be saved from peril." ³²The soldiers then cut the ropes to the lifeboat and let it drift away.

³³Just before daybreak, Paul urged everyone to eat. He said, "This is the fourteenth day you've lived in suspense, and you've not had even a bite to eat. ³⁴I urge you to take some food. Your health depends on it. None of you will lose a single hair from his head." ³⁵After he said these things, he took bread, gave thanks to God in front of them all, then broke it and began to eat. ³⁶Everyone was encouraged and took some food. (³⁷In all, there were two hundred seventy-six of us on the ship.) ³⁸When they had eaten as much as they wanted, they lightened the ship by throwing the grain into the sea.

³⁹In the morning light they saw a bay with a sandy beach. They didn't know what land it was, but they thought they might possibly be able to run the ship aground. ⁴⁰They cut the anchors loose and left them in the sea. At the same time, they untied the ropes that ran back to the rudders. They raised the foresail to catch the wind and made for the beach. ⁴¹But they struck a sandbar and the ship ran aground. The bow was stuck and wouldn't move, and the

MALTA

Malta is an island near the narrowest point of the Mediterranean Sea. It is 18 mi. by 8 mi. and lies 50 mi. south of Sicily and 190 mi. east of Tunisia. The fact that the storm in Acts 27 ends with shipwreck on Malta is no surprise, archaeologically. The archaeological museum on Gozo (an island in the Maltese chain) has a room dedicated to Roman shipwrecks. Many anchor bars and other items have been found in bays around the islands.

stern was broken into pieces by the force of the waves. ⁴²The soldiers decided to kill the prisoners to keep them from swimming to shore and escaping. ⁴³However, the centurion wanted to save Paul, so he stopped them from carrying out their plan. He ordered those who could swim to jump overboard first and head for land. ⁴⁴He ordered the rest to grab hold of planks or debris from the ship. In this way, everyone reached land safely.

On the Island of Malta

28 After reaching land safely, we learned that the island was called Malta. ²The islanders showed us extraordinary kindness. Because it was rainy and cold, they built a fire and welcomed all of us. ³Paul gathered a bunch of dry sticks and put them on the fire. As he did, a poisonous snake, driven out by the heat, latched on to his hand. ⁴When the islanders saw the snake hanging from his hand, they said to each other, "This man must be a murderer! He was rescued from the sea, but the goddess Justice hasn't let him live!" ⁵Paul shook the snake into the fire and suffered no harm. ⁶They expected him to swell up with fever or suddenly drop dead. After waiting a long time and seeing nothing unusual happen to him, they changed their minds and began to claim that he was a god.

⁷Publius, the island's most prominent person, owned a large estate in that area. He welcomed us warmly into his home as his guests for three days. ⁸Publius' father was bedridden, sick with a fever and dysentery. Paul went to see him and prayed. He placed his hand on him and healed him. ⁹Once this happened, the rest of the sick on the island came to him and were healed. ¹⁰They honored us in many ways. When we were getting ready to sail again, they supplied us with what we needed.

Paul makes it to Rome

¹¹After three months we put out to sea in a ship that had spent the winter at the island. It was an Alexandrian ship with carvings of the twin gods Castor and Pollux as its figurehead. ¹²We landed in Syracuse where we stayed three days. ¹³From there we sailed to Rhegium. After one day a south wind came up, and we arrived on the second day in Puteoli. ¹⁴There we found brothers and sisters who urged us to stay with them for a week. In this way we came to Rome. ¹⁵When the brothers and sisters there heard about us, they came as far as the Forum of Appius and the Three Taverns to meet us. When Paul saw them, he gave thanks to God and was encouraged. ¹⁶When we entered Rome, Paul was permitted to live by himself, with a soldier guarding him.

Paul meets Jewish leaders in Rome

¹⁷Three days later, Paul called the Jewish leaders together. When they gathered, he said, "Brothers, although I have done nothing against our people or the customs of our ancestors, I'm a prisoner from Jerusalem. They handed me over to the Romans, ¹⁸who intended to release me after they examined me, because they couldn't find any reason for putting me to death. ¹⁹When the Jews objected, I was forced to appeal to Caesar. Don't think I appealed to Caesar because I had any reason to bring charges against my nation. ²⁰This is why I asked to see you and speak with you: it's because of the hope of Israel that I am bound with this chain."

²¹They responded, "We haven't received any letters about you from Judea, nor have any of our brothers come and reported or said anything bad about you. ²²But we think it's important to hear what you think, for we know that people everywhere are speaking against this faction."

²³On the day scheduled for this purpose, many people came to the place where he was staying. From morning until evening, he explained and testified concerning God's kingdom and tried to convince them about Jesus through appealing to the Law from Moses and the Prophets. ²⁴Some were persuaded by what he said, but others refused to believe. ²⁵They disagreed with each other and were starting to leave when Paul made one more statement: "The Holy Spirit spoke

correctly when he said to your ancestors through Isaiah the prophet,

²⁶ *Go to this people and say:*
   You will hear, to be sure,
      but never understand;
   and you will certainly see but never
      recognize what you are seeing.
²⁷ *This people's senses have become calloused,*
   and they've become hard of hearing,
   and they've shut their eyes
      so that they won't see with their eyes
      or hear with their ears
      or understand with their minds,
and change their hearts and lives
   *that I may heal them.*ʷ

²⁸"Therefore, be certain of this: God's salvation has been sent to the Gentiles. They will listen!"ˣ

Paul's ministry in Rome

³⁰Paul lived in his own rented quarters for two full years and welcomed everyone who came to see him. ³¹Unhindered and with complete confidence, he continued to preach God's kingdom and to teach about the Lord Jesus Christ.

ʷIsa 6:9-10 ˣCritical editions of the Gk New Testament do not include 28:29 *After he said this, the Jews left, debating among themselves.*

ROMANS

THEME

The gospel is the power of God for salvation for everyone who has faith.

INTRODUCTION

Paul's letter to the Romans was probably written from Corinth in the winter of 56–57 CE. In the letter itself, Paul mentions his host, Gaius of Corinth (16:23), and recommends Phoebe, from the nearby town of Cenchreae (16:1). Thus we can conclude that the letter was written during the three-month period that Paul spent in or around Corinth. This period was just prior to Paul's departure to deliver the Jerusalem offering.

THE MESSAGE

The letter to the Romans contains a carefully formulated statement of Paul's total message, a message that appears in pieces, often illogically arranged, in his other letters.

The key to the contents of the letter is Romans 1:16-17. The subject of the letter is the good news about God's Son (1:3), which has power to bring salvation to everyone (Jew and Gentile) who responds in faith.

"Salvation" means one's becoming righteous (that is, being put into a right relationship with God) through God's righteousness (that is, God's faithful, loving, redeeming activity in Jesus Christ). The good news reveals to people this redemptive activity and the salvation offered to them, if they respond in faith.

Paul's starting point is that people are not in right relationship with God (1:18–3:20). The gospel reveals, first of all, the tragic plight of the human race; humankind's guilt before God.

The Gentiles (1:18-32) cannot plead ignorance of God, because they have seen, in the wonders of creation, God's everlasting power. But they did not receive this knowledge and act on it; they refused to recognize and worship God as God. They worshiped what was created instead of the Creator, and they stand under God's wrath.

The Jews (2:1–3:20) also have knowledge of God. In addition to the revelation in nature, they have the Law of Moses and the scriptures. But many Jews indulge in the same things they condemn in the Gentiles. God requires inner dedication and inner goodness rather than outer correctness. So the Jews too stand under God's judgment.

In short, all people are sinners. They have rebelled against God, who is revealed in various ways: in the created order, in their consciences (2:15), and in the scriptures. All live under the power of sin (3:9) and are guilty before God.

But God has provided in Jesus Christ a way for the guilty, alienated people to come into right relationship with himself (3:21-31). This way is not by earning acceptance through obedience to the Law, which no one can keep and which serves to reveal one's sin rather than to break its power (3:20). It is the way of faith is God's gracious, saving work in Jesus Christ. God does for people what they cannot do for themselves and asks only for their grateful response. Their freedom and new relationship flow from Christ Jesus' sacrificial death, which God made a means of taking away sin and guilt. Since the new relationship comes from God's act, gratitude, not boasting in human achievement, is the appropriate attitude of the believer. The consequences of trust in God's saving act in Jesus Christ are far-reaching (5:1–8:39). Believers have a new status before God. They enjoy the divine favor, have peace, and are reconciled. They have a new spirit. They rejoice in their hope and their sufferings. They have a new knowledge: that suffering has blessed results. They have a new self: the Holy Spirit and God's love within. They are participants in a new humanity. They are freed from the realm of sin and death, introduced by Adam, to a new order of right relations with God and new life, introduced by Jesus Christ.

They have a new kind of life under a new master. They no longer serve sin and the Law and earn suffering and death as their pay, but they experience a new quality of existence, serve God and righteousness, and receive the gift of eternal life. They at last escape the power of sin, which has the Law as its agent and the body as its host, and are introduced to life in the Spirit, a life pleasing to God, as is fitting for the children of God. As children of God they are heirs of a glorious future, which no hostile power in the universe can stop.

Who is going to participate in this glorious future? Will it include both Jews and Gentiles (chapters 9–11)? The hard fact, according to Romans, is that most Jews have rejected the good news. Does this mean that God is going to fail to bring about salvation of the chosen people? Emphatically, no! The rejection by the majority of the Jews is to be seen in the light of the divine selectivity that has always been at work in Israel, by which God preserved a faithful remnant, a remnant useful for God's purpose of salvation for all (9:1-29). But Jewish rejection can also be attributed to the Jews' free choice: having heard the gospel of salvation by faith in Jesus Christ, they preferred salvation by works (9:32; 10:3). Their zeal for God was misguided (10:2). They stand condemned (10:21).

Yet God brings good results out of people's evil decisions. Jewish rejection led to the preaching of the gospel to the Gentiles, and that in turn will lead to the ultimate salvation of the Jews. When the Jews see the Gentiles becoming heirs of the promises made to Abraham, they will want to be included too and will turn to Christ in faith. Thus God's merciful plan for both Jews and Gentiles will be accomplished (11:11-32).

The new life in Christ determines the character of one's existence in the church and in the world (12:1–15:13). Right relations with God and others require total surrender of one's self to God and learning to do God's will.

God's will is that we love one another in the church (12:3-13), and even our enemies (12:14-21), and live as responsible citizens of the state (13:1-10). Love, further, requires consideration of those who believe differently than we do (14:1–15:13). The Christian is not to be pleased but to please God and neighbor (14:3; 15:1-2). "Walking in love" (14:15) glorifies God and builds up the church. By such conduct people who live in the day wait for the coming of the Day of the Lord (13:11-14).

THE FORM OF THE ORIGINAL LETTER

Although there are many textual variants related to the final chapters of Romans, it now appears certain that Paul's original letter contained sixteen chapters. The only portions that may not stem from Paul are the closing benediction (16:25-27) and the warning against heretics that breaks up the sequence of greetings (16:17-20). Thus it is essential to take the material from the final chapters into account in considering the purpose and character of Romans.

THE NATURE AND PURPOSE OF ROMANS

Paul dictated this letter to solicit help from the Roman house churches in the planning and logistical support for a mission to Spain (see 15:24, 28). The theological argument is designed to unify the competitive house churches in Rome so they will be willing and able to cooperate in this effort. The power of the gospel (1:16) to achieve the unification of all nations (15:7-13) provides the imperative for this mission and therefore stands at the heart of Romans.

ROMANS

Greeting

1 From Paul, a slave of Christ Jesus, called to be an apostle and set apart for God's good news. [2-3] God promised this good news about his Son ahead of time through his prophets in the holy scriptures. His Son was descended from David. [4] He was publicly identified as God's Son with power through his resurrection from the dead, which was based on the Spirit of holiness. This Son is Jesus Christ our Lord. [5] Through him we have received God's grace and our appointment to be apostles. This was to bring all Gentiles to faithful obedience for his name's sake. [6] You who are called by Jesus Christ are also included among these Gentiles.

[7] To those in Rome who are dearly loved by God and called to be God's people.

Grace to you and peace from God our Father and the Lord Jesus Christ.

Thanksgiving and Paul's plans to visit

[8] First of all, I thank my God through Jesus Christ for all of you, because the news about your faithfulness is being spread throughout the whole world. [9] I serve God in my spirit by preaching the good news about God's Son, and God is my witness that I continually mention you [10] in all my prayers. I'm always asking that somehow, by God's will, I might succeed in visiting you at last. [11] I really want to see you to pass along some spiritual gift to you so that you can be strengthened. [12] What I mean is that we can mutually encourage each other while I am with you. We can be encouraged by the faithfulness we find in each other, both your faithfulness and mine.

[13] I want you to know, brothers and sisters, that I planned to visit you many times, although I have been prevented from coming until now. I want to harvest some fruit among you, just as I have done among the other Gentiles. [14] I have a responsibility both to Greeks and to those who don't speak Greek, both to the wise and to the foolish.

God's righteousness is revealed

[15] That's why I'm ready to preach the gospel also to you who are in Rome. [16] I'm not ashamed of the gospel: it is God's own power for salvation to all who have faith in God, to the Jew first and also to the Greek. [17] God's righteousness is being revealed in the gospel, from faithfulness[a] for faith,[b] as it is written, *The righteous person will live by faith.*[c]

Gentiles are without excuse

[18] God's wrath is being revealed from heaven against all the ungodly behavior and the injustice of human beings who silence the truth with injustice. [19] This is because what is known about God should be plain to them because God made it plain to them. [20] Ever since the creation of the world, God's invisible qualities—God's eternal power and divine nature—have been clearly seen, because they are understood through the things God has made. So humans are without excuse. [21] Although they knew God, they didn't honor God as God or thank him. Instead, their reasoning became pointless, and their foolish hearts were darkened. [22] While they were claiming to be wise, they made fools of themselves. [23] They exchanged the glory of the immortal God for images that look like mortal humans: birds, animals, and reptiles. [24] So God abandoned them to their hearts' desires, which led to the moral corruption of degrading their own bodies with each other. [25] They traded God's truth for a lie, and they worshipped and served the creation instead of the creator, who is blessed forever. Amen.

[26] That's why God abandoned them to degrading lust. Their females traded natural sexual relations for unnatural sexual relations. [27] Also, in the same way, the males traded natural sexual relations with females, and burned with lust for each other.

---

[a] Or faith [b] Or faithfulness [c] Hab 2:4

Males performed shameful actions with males, and they were paid back with the penalty they deserved for their mistake in their own bodies. ²⁸Since they didn't think it was worthwhile to acknowledge God, God abandoned them to a defective mind to do inappropriate things. ²⁹So they were filled with all injustice, wicked behavior, greed, and evil behavior. They are full of jealousy, murder, fighting, deception, and malice. They are gossips, ³⁰they slander people, and they hate God. They are rude and proud, and they brag. They invent ways to be evil, and they are disobedient to their parents. ³¹They are without understanding, disloyal, without affection, and without mercy. ³²Though they know God's decision that those who persist in such practices deserve death, they not only keep doing these things but also approve others who practice them.

Jews are without excuse

2 So every single one of you who judge others is without any excuse. You condemn yourself when you judge another person because the one who is judging is doing the same things. ²We know that God's judgment agrees with the truth, and

^dPs 62:12; Prov 24:12

his judgment is against those who do these kinds of things. ³If you judge those who do these kinds of things while you do the same things yourself, think about this: Do you believe that you will escape God's judgment? ⁴Or do you have contempt for the riches of God's generosity, tolerance, and patience? Don't you realize that God's kindness is supposed to lead you to change your heart and life? ⁵You are storing up wrath for yourself because of your stubbornness and your heart that refuses to change. God's just judgment will be revealed on the day of wrath. ⁶*God will repay everyone based on their works.*^d ⁷On the one hand, he will give eternal life to those who look for glory, honor, and immortality based on their patient good work. ⁸But on the other hand, there will be wrath and anger for those who obey wickedness instead of the truth because they are acting out of selfishness and disobedience. ⁹There will be trouble and distress for every human being who does evil, for the Jew first and also for the Greek. ¹⁰But there will be glory, honor, and peace for everyone who does what is good, for the Jew first and also for the Greek. ¹¹God does not have favorites.

PAUL (THE APOSTLE)

Aside from Jesus, no one shaped the development of early Christianity more than Paul. Even though he was the foremost advocate of the Gentile mission, an eloquent interpreter of a Jewish Messiah for a Hellenistic world, and a visionary whose journeys carried him through Asia Minor and beyond, he undoubtedly would have been surprised that his occasional letters would one day become scripture alongside the Law and the Prophets.

The themes at the core of Paul's gospel were Israel's traditions, scriptures, morality, God, and a crucified Jewish Messiah whose life, death, and resurrection expanded the people of God to include believing "pagans," inaugurating a new age that would soon be brought to a grand and even revolutionary conclusion with Jesus' return. This vision gave Paul's mission urgency and his letters the intensity characteristic of a time of crisis. In a great apocalyptic drama, converts lived out their faith within a community of care and hope as well as sectarian rivalry. In Paul's letters we witness that conflict and a theology in the making.

[12]Those who have sinned outside the Law will also die outside the Law, and those who have sinned under the Law will be judged by the Law. [13]It isn't the ones who hear the Law who are righteous in God's eyes. It is the ones who do what the Law says who will be treated as righteous. [14]Gentiles don't have the Law. But when they instinctively do what the Law requires they are a Law in themselves, though they don't have the Law. [15]They show the proof of the Law written on their hearts, and their consciences affirm it. Their conflicting thoughts will accuse them, or even make a defense for them, [16]on the day when, according to my gospel, God will judge the hidden truth about human beings through Christ Jesus.

Jews will be judged as well

[17]But,

if you call yourself a Jew;
if you rely on the Law;
if you brag about your relationship to God;
[18]if you know the will of God;
if you are taught by the Law
    so that you can figure out
    the things that really matter;
[19]if you have persuaded yourself that
    you are:
    a guide for the blind;
    a light to those who are in darkness;
    [20]an educator of the foolish;
    a teacher of infants (since you have
        the full content of knowledge and
        truth in the Law);

[e]Isa 52:5 LXX

[21]then why don't you who are teaching others teach yourself? If you preach, "No stealing," do you steal? [22]If you say, "No adultery," do you commit adultery? If you hate idols, do you rob temples? [23]If you brag about the Law, do you shame God by breaking the Law? [24]As it is written: *The name of God is discredited by the Gentiles because of you.*[e]

[25]Circumcision is an advantage if you do what the Law says. But if you are a person who breaks the Law, your status of being circumcised has changed into not being circumcised. [26]So if the person who isn't circumcised keeps the Law, won't his status of not being circumcised be counted as if he were circumcised? [27]The one who isn't physically circumcised but keeps the Law will judge you. You became a lawbreaker after you had the written Law and circumcision. [28]It isn't the Jew who maintains outward appearances who will receive praise from God, and it isn't people who are outwardly circumcised on their bodies. [29]Instead, it is the person who is a Jew inside, who is circumcised in spirit, not literally. That person's praise doesn't come from people but from God.

God's faithfulness and justice

3 So what's the advantage of being a Jew? Or what's the benefit of circumcision? [2]Plenty in every way. First of all, the Jews were trusted with God's revelations. [3]What does it matter, then, if some weren't

JEW/JEWS

Originally meaning someone from the tribe of Judah. That tribe gave its name to the southern kingdom, whose capital was Jerusalem. After the destruction of the northern kingdom by the Assyrians in 722 BCE, the traditions of Israel were preserved by the southern kingdom. In the Hellenistic period, the favored self-designation of Jews was "Israel," so *Jew* may have originated as a term used by outsiders. Over time, Jewish writers also referred to themselves at Jews.

faithful? Their lack of faith won't cancel God's faithfulness, will it? [4]Absolutely not! God must be true, even if every human being is a liar, as it is written:

So that it can show
  that you are right in your words;
  and you will triumph when you are judged.[f]

[5]But if our lack of righteousness confirms God's justice, what will we say? That God, who brings wrath upon us, isn't just (I'm speaking rhetorically)? [6]Absolutely not! If God weren't just, how could he judge the world? [7]But if God's truth is demonstrated by my lie and it increases his glory, why am I still judged as a sinner? [8]Why not say, "Let's do evil things so that good things will come out of it"? (Some people who slander us accuse us of saying that, but these people deserve criticism.)

All are under the power of sin

[9]So what are we saying? Are we better off? Not at all. We have already stated the charge: both Jews and Greeks are all under the power of sin. [10]As it is written,

There is no righteous person, not even one.
[11] There is no one who understands.
  There is no one who looks for God.
[12] They all turned away.
  They have become worthless together.
  There is no one who shows kindness.
  There is not even one.[g]
[13] Their throat is a grave
  that has been opened.
  They are deceitful with their tongues,
  and the poison of vipers is under their lips.[h]
[14] Their mouths are full of cursing
  and bitterness.[i]
[15] Their feet are quick to shed blood;
[16] destruction and misery are in their ways;
[17] and they don't know the way of peace.[j]
[18] There is no fear of God
  in their view of the world.[k]

[19]Now we know that whatever the Law says, it speaks to those who are under the Law, in order to shut every mouth and make it so the whole world has to answer to God. [20]It follows that no human being will be treated as righteous in his presence by doing what the Law says, because the knowledge of sin comes through the Law.

God's righteousness through faithfulness of Christ

[21]But now God's righteousness has been revealed apart from the Law, which is confirmed by the Law and the Prophets. [22]God's righteousness comes through the faithfulness of Jesus Christ for all who have faith in him. There's no distinction. [23]All have sinned and fall short of God's glory, [24]but all are treated as righteous freely by his grace because of a ransom that was paid by Christ Jesus. [25]Through his faithfulness, God displayed Jesus as the place of sacrifice where mercy is found by means of his blood. He did this to demonstrate his righteousness in passing over sins that happened before, [26]during the time of God's patient tolerance. He also did this to demonstrate that he is righteous in the present time, and to treat the one who has faith in Jesus as righteous.

[27]What happens to our bragging? It's thrown out. With which law? With what we have accomplished under the Law? [28]No, not at all, but through the law of faith. We consider that a person is treated as righteous by faith, apart from what is accomplished under the Law. [29]Or is God the God of Jews only? Isn't God the God of Gentiles also? Yes, God is also the God of Gentiles. [30]Since God is one, then the one who makes the circumcised righteous by faith will also make the one who isn't circumcised righteous through faith. [31]Do we then cancel the Law through this faith? Absolutely not! Instead, we confirm the Law.

Abraham's faith was credited as righteousness

4 So what are we going to say? Are we going to find that Abraham is our ancestor on the basis of genealogy? [2]Because if Abraham was made righteous because of his actions, he would have had a reason to brag, but not in front of God. [3]What does the scripture say? Abraham had faith in God,

[f]Ps 51:4 [g]Ps 14:1-3 [h]Ps 5:9 [i]Ps 10:7 [j]Isa 59:7-8 [k]Ps 36:1

and it was credited to him as righteousness.[l]
[4]Workers' salaries aren't credited to them on
the basis of an employer's grace but rather
on the basis of what they deserve. [5]But faith
is credited as righteousness to those who
don't work, because they have faith in God
who makes the ungodly righteous. [6]In the
same way, David also pronounces a blessing
on the person to whom God credits righteousness apart from actions:

[7] Happy are those whose actions
    outside the Law are forgiven,
    and whose sins are covered.
[8] Happy are those whose sin isn't counted
    against them by the Lord.[m]

[9]Is this state of happiness only for the
circumcised or is it also for those who aren't
circumcised? We say, "Faith was credited to
Abraham as righteousness." [10]So how was
it credited? When he was circumcised, or
when he wasn't circumcised? In fact, it was
credited while he still wasn't circumcised,
not after he was circumcised. [11]He received
the sign of circumcision as a seal of the righteousness that comes from the faith he had
while he still wasn't circumcised. It happened this way so that Abraham could be

the ancestor of all those people who aren't
circumcised, who have faith in God, and so
are counted as righteous. [12]He could also be
the ancestor of those circumcised people,
who aren't only circumcised but who also
walk in the path of faith, like our ancestor
Abraham did while he wasn't circumcised.

Abraham's promise is received through faith

[13]The promise to Abraham and to his
descendants, that he would inherit the
world, didn't come through the Law but
through the righteousness that comes from
faith. [14]If they inherit because of the Law,
then faith has no effect and the promise
has been canceled. [15]The Law brings about
wrath. But when there isn't any law, there
isn't any violation of the law. [16]That's why
the inheritance comes through faith, so
that it will be on the basis of God's grace.
In that way, the promise is secure for all
of Abraham's descendants, not just for
those who are related by Law but also for
those who are related by the faith of Abraham, who is the father of all of us. [17]As it
is written: *I have appointed you to be the*

[l]Gen 15:6 [m]Ps 32:1-2

INHERITANCE

Property and rights that transfer to an heir or heirs following the death of
the owner. In the OT, individual property rights can be traced to the traditions
about the division of the land of Israel among the 12 tribes. The tribal divisions were to be distributed so that each clan, lineage, and individual household shared in that inheritance. New Testament inheritance texts should be
read against the background of the OT and Jewish traditions about Abraham.
The promise of "inheriting the land," generally understood in Judaism as a
reference to the literal land of Canaan, was commonly broadened to "inheriting the world," and sometimes spiritualized to refer to heaven or the
recreated "new heavens and new earth."

While a few passages reflect the literal practice of inheritance (Luke 12:13;
Mark 12:1-12; Matt 21:33-46; Luke 20:9-19; Gal 4:1-2; cf. Heb 9:15-22), most
refer to figurative, end-time ideas of salvation. Often associated with inheritance are the concepts of "election"/"choosing," believers as "sojourners,"
and God's promise that "I will be their/your God/father, and they/you will be
my people/children" (Gen 17:8; Exod 6:7-8; Jer 31:33; Ezek 37:23).

father of many nations.[n] So Abraham is our father in the eyes of God in whom he had faith, the God who gives life to the dead and calls things that don't exist into existence. [18]When it was beyond hope, he had faith in the hope that he would become the father of many nations, in keeping with the promise God spoke to him: *That's how many descendants you will have.*[o] [19]Without losing faith, Abraham, who was nearly 100 years old, took into account his own body, which was as good as dead, and Sarah's womb, which was dead. [20]He didn't hesitate with a lack of faith in God's promise, but he grew strong in faith and gave glory to God. [21]He was fully convinced that God was able to do what he promised. [22]Therefore, it was credited to him as righteousness.

[23]But the scripture that says *it was credited to him*[p] wasn't written only for Abraham's sake. [24]It was written also for our sake, because it is going to be credited to us too. It will be credited to those of us who have faith in the one who raised Jesus our Lord from the dead. [25]He was handed over because of our mistakes, and he was raised to meet the requirements of righteousness for us.

Therefore, we have peace with God

5 Therefore, since we have been made righteous through his faithfulness[q] combined with our faith, we have peace with God through our Lord Jesus Christ. [2]We have access by faith into this grace in which we stand through him, and we boast in the hope of God's glory. [3]But not only that! We even take pride in our problems, because we know that trouble produces endurance, [4]endurance produces character, and character produces hope. [5]This hope doesn't put us to shame, because the love of God has

[n]Gen 17:5   [o]Gen 15:5   [p]Gen 15:6   [q]Or *faith*

DEATH

The writers of the OT (especially the psalmists) used the language of death not just to describe the physical end of life but also as a metaphor for distress and anguish.

The Gospel writers use the term *death* to refer to the literal end of biological life. The evangelists have variant notions about the rituals of death; for example, Jesus advises his followers to let the dead bury their own dead (Matt 8:22; Luke 9:60) but commends the woman who anoints him prior to his own death (Mark 14:3-9; Matt 26:6-13; Luke 7:36-50; John 12:1-8). In five instances, people are resuscitated from death (Mark 5:21-43; Matt 9:18-26; Luke 8:40-56; Luke 7:11-17; John 11:1-44; Acts 9:36-43; Acts 20:9-12), but there is no reason to believe that their physical resuscitations would be permanent.

Paul uses the concept of death theologically in both literal and metaphorical senses. In the literal sense, death is not a natural part of creation and is the result of sin; Jesus saves humankind from sin and, therefore, death is overcome in the afterlife (see Rom 4:25; 5:12; 6:23; 1 Cor 15:26). In his comparison of Jesus and Adam, Paul argues that the first created human was, because of disobedience, earthly, perishable, dishonorable, weak, and physical; Christ, on the other hand, is heavenly, imperishable, glorious, powerful, and spiritual. Jesus, according to Paul, is the "last Adam" who overcomes death (1 Cor 15:42-49). Paul assures his followers that "those who are dead in Christ will rise" first (1 Thess 4:16-17).

been poured out in our hearts through the Holy Spirit, who has been given to us.

⁶While we were still weak, at the right moment, Christ died for ungodly people. ⁷It isn't often that someone will die for a righteous person, though maybe someone might dare to die for a good person. ⁸But God shows his love for us, because while we were still sinners Christ died for us. ⁹So, now that we have been made righteous by his blood, we can be even more certain that we will be saved from God's wrath through him. ¹⁰If we were reconciled to God through the death of his Son while we were still enemies, now that we have been reconciled, how much more certain is it that we will be saved by his life? ¹¹And not only that: we even take pride in God through our Lord Jesus Christ, the one through whom we now have a restored relationship with God.

Grace now rules

¹²So, in the same way that sin entered the world through one person, and death came through sin, so death spread to all human beings with the result that all sinned. ¹³Although sin was in the world, since there was no Law, it wasn't taken into account until the Law came. ¹⁴But death ruled from Adam until Moses, even over those who didn't sin in the same way Adam did—Adam was a type of the one who was coming.

¹⁵But the free gift of Christ isn't like Adam's failure. If many people died through what one person did wrong, God's grace is multiplied even more for many people with the gift—of the one person Jesus Christ—that comes through grace. ¹⁶The gift isn't like the consequences of one person's sin. The judgment that came from one person's sin led to punishment, but the free gift that came out of many failures led to the verdict of acquittal. ¹⁷If death ruled because of one person's failure, those who receive the multiplied grace and the gift of righteousness will even more certainly rule in life through the one person Jesus Christ.

¹⁸So now the righteous requirements necessary for life are met for everyone through the righteous act of one person, just as judg-ment fell on everyone through the failure of one person. ¹⁹Many people were made righteous through the obedience of one person, just as many people were made sinners through the disobedience of one person. ²⁰The Law stepped in to amplify the failure, but where sin increased, grace multiplied even more. ²¹The result is that grace will rule through God's righteousness, leading to eternal life through Jesus Christ our Lord, just as sin ruled in death.

Our new life in Christ

6 So what are we going to say? Should we continue sinning so grace will multiply? ²Absolutely not! All of us died to sin. How can we still live in it? ³Or don't you know that all who were baptized into Christ Jesus were baptized into his death? ⁴Therefore, we were buried together with him through baptism into his death, so that just as Christ was raised from the dead through the glory of the Father, we too can walk in newness of life. ⁵If we were united together in a death like his, we will also be united together in a resurrection like his. ⁶This is what we know: the person that we used to be was crucified with him in order to get rid of the corpse that had been controlled by sin. That way we wouldn't be slaves to sin anymore, ⁷because a person who has died has been freed from sin's power. ⁸But if we died with Christ, we have faith that we will also live with him. ⁹We know that Christ has been raised from the dead and he will never die again. Death no longer has power over him. ¹⁰He died to sin once and for all with his death, but he lives for God with his life. ¹¹In the same way, you also should consider yourselves dead to sin but alive for God in Christ Jesus.

¹²So then, don't let sin rule your body, so that you do what it wants. ¹³Don't offer parts of your body to sin, to be used as weapons to do wrong. Instead, present yourselves to God as people who have been brought back to life from the dead, and offer all the parts of your body to God to be used as weapons to do right. ¹⁴Sin will have no power over you, because you aren't under Law but under grace.

Freedom from sin

[15] So what? Should we sin because we aren't under Law but under grace? Absolutely not! [16] Don't you know that if you offer yourselves to someone as obedient slaves, that you are slaves of the one whom you obey? That's true whether you serve as slaves of sin, which leads to death, or as slaves of the kind of obedience that leads to righteousness. [17] But thank God that although you used to be slaves of sin, you gave wholehearted obedience to the teaching that was handed down to you, which provides a pattern. [18] Now that you have been set free from sin, you have become slaves of righteousness. [19] (I'm speaking with ordinary metaphors because of your limitations.) Once, you offered the parts of your body to be used as slaves to impurity and to lawless behavior that leads to still more lawless behavior. Now, you should present the parts of your body as slaves to righteousness, which makes your lives holy. [20] When you were slaves of sin, you were free from the control of righteousness. [21] What consequences did you get from doing things that you are now ashamed of? The outcome of those things is death. [22] But now that you have been set free from sin and become slaves to God, you have the consequence of a holy life, and the outcome is eternal life. [23] The wages that sin pays are death, but God's gift is eternal life in Christ Jesus our Lord.

Freedom from the Law

7 Brothers and sisters, I'm talking to you as people who know the Law. Don't you know that the Law has power over someone only as long as he or she lives? [2] A married woman is united with her husband under the Law while he is alive. But if her husband dies, she is released from the Law concerning her husband. [3] So then, if she lives with another man while her husband is alive, she's committing adultery. But if her husband dies, she's free from the Law, so she won't be committing adultery if she marries someone else. [4] Therefore, my brothers and sisters, you also died with respect to the Law through the body of Christ, so that you could be united with someone else. You are united with the one who was raised from the dead so that we can bear fruit for God. [5] When we were self-centered, the sinful passions aroused through the Law were at work in all the parts of our body, so that we bore fruit for death. [6] But now we have been released from the Law. We have died with respect to the thing that controlled us, so that we can be slaves in the new life under the Spirit, not in the old life under the written Law.

The function of the Law

[7] So what are we going to say? That the Law is sin? Absolutely not! But I wouldn't have known sin except through the Law. I wouldn't have known the desire for what others have if the Law had not said, *Don't desire to take what others have.*[r] [8] But sin seized the opportunity and used this commandment to produce all kinds of desires in me. Sin is dead without the Law. [9] I used to be alive without the Law, but when the commandment came, sin sprang to life, [10] and I died. So the commandment that was intended to give life brought death. [11] Sin seized the opportunity through the commandment, deceived me, and killed me. [12] So the Law itself is holy, and the commandment is holy, righteous, and good.

Living under the Law

[13] So did something good bring death to me? Absolutely not! But sin caused my death through something good so that sin would be exposed as sin. That way sin would become even more thoroughly sinful through the commandment. [14] We know that the Law is spiritual, but I'm made of flesh and blood, and I'm sold as a slave to sin. [15] I don't know what I'm doing, because I don't do what I want to do. Instead, I do the thing that I hate. [16] But if I'm doing the thing that I don't want to do, I'm agreeing that the Law is right. [17] But now I'm not the one doing it anymore. Instead, it's sin that

[r] Exod 20:17; Deut 5:21

lives in me. [18]I know that good doesn't live in me—that is, in my body. The desire to do good is inside of me, but I can't do it. [19]I don't do the good that I want to do, but I do the evil that I don't want to do. [20]But if I do the very thing that I don't want to do, then I'm not the one doing it anymore. Instead, it is sin that lives in me that is doing it.

[21]So I find that, as a rule, when I want to do what is good, evil is right there with me. [22]I gladly agree with the Law on the inside, [23]but I see a different law at work in my body. It wages a war against the law of my mind and takes me prisoner with the law of sin that is in my body. [24]I'm a miserable human being. Who will deliver me from this dead corpse? [25]Thank God through Jesus Christ our Lord! So then I'm a slave to God's Law in my mind, but I'm a slave to sin's law in my body.

Set free by the Spirit

8 So now there isn't any condemnation for those who are in Christ Jesus. [2]The law of the Spirit of life in Christ Jesus has set you free from the law of sin and death. [3]God has done what was impossible for the Law, since it was weak because of selfishness. God condemned sin in the body by sending his own Son to deal with sin in the same body as humans, who are controlled by sin. [4]He did this so that the righteous requirement of the Law might be fulfilled in us. Now the way we live is based on the Spirit, not based on selfishness. [5]People whose lives are based on selfishness think about selfish things, but people whose lives are based on the Spirit think about things

that are related to the Spirit. [6]The attitude that comes from selfishness leads to death, but the attitude that comes from the Spirit leads to life and peace. [7]So the attitude that comes from selfishness is hostile to God. It doesn't submit to God's Law, because it can't. [8]People who are self-centered aren't able to please God.

[9]But you aren't self-centered. Instead you are in the Spirit, if in fact God's Spirit lives in you. If anyone doesn't have the Spirit of Christ, they don't belong to him. [10]If Christ is in you, the Spirit is your life because of God's righteousness, but the body is dead because of sin. [11]If the Spirit of the one who raised Jesus from the dead lives in you, the one who raised Christ from the dead will give life to your human bodies also, through his Spirit that lives in you.

[12]So then, brothers and sisters, we have an obligation, but it isn't an obligation to ourselves to live our lives on the basis of selfishness. [13]If you live on the basis of selfishness, you are going to die. But if by the Spirit you put to death the actions of the body, you will live. [14]All who are led by God's Spirit are God's sons and daughters. [15]You didn't receive a spirit of slavery to lead you back again into fear, but you received a Spirit that shows you are adopted as his children. With this Spirit, we cry, "Abba, Father." [16]The same Spirit agrees with our spirit, that we are God's children. [17]But if we are children, we are also heirs. We are God's heirs and fellow heirs with Christ, if we really suffer with him so that we can also be glorified with him.

ABBA

The transliterated Aramaic word *Abba* appears three times in the NT, always as an address to God and always with the translation "father." Paul attributes the cry "Abba, Father!" to the Spirit in the hearts of believing communities, interpreting it as evidence of their adoption as God's children and heirs (Rom 8:15; Gal 4:6). Mark 14:36 attributes this cry to Jesus—before Jesus' arrest, he pleads: "Abba, Father, for you all things are possible. Take this cup of suffering away from me. However—not what I want but what you want."

Our suffering and our hope

¹⁸I believe that the present suffering is nothing compared to the coming glory that is going to be revealed to us. ¹⁹The whole creation waits breathless with anticipation for the revelation of God's sons and daughters. ²⁰Creation was subjected to frustration, not by its own choice—it was the choice of the one who subjected it—but in the hope ²¹that the creation itself will be set free from slavery to decay and brought into the glorious freedom of God's children. ²²We know that the whole creation is groaning together and suffering labor pains up until now. ²³And it's not only the creation. We ourselves who have the Spirit as the first crop of the harvest also groan inside as we wait to be adopted and for our bodies to be set free. ²⁴We were saved in hope. If we see what we hope for, that isn't hope. Who hopes for what they already see? ²⁵But if we hope for what we don't see, we wait for it with patience.

²⁶In the same way, the Spirit comes to help our weakness. We don't know what we should pray, but the Spirit himself pleads our case with unexpressed groans. ²⁷The one who searches hearts knows how the Spirit thinks, because he pleads for the saints, consistent with God's will. ²⁸We know that God works all things together for good for the ones who love God, for those who are called according to his purpose. ²⁹We know this because God knew them in advance, and he decided in advance that they would be conformed to the image of his Son. That way his Son would be the first of many brothers and sisters. ³⁰Those who God decided in advance would be conformed to his Son, he also called. Those whom he called, he also made righteous. Those whom he made righteous, he also glorified.

³¹So what are we going to say about these things? If God is for us, who is against us? ³²He didn't spare his own Son but gave him up for us all. Won't he also freely give us all things with him?

³³Who will bring a charge against God's elect people? It is God who acquits them. ³⁴Who is going to convict them? It is Christ Jesus who died, even more, who was raised, and who also is at God's right side. It is Christ Jesus who also pleads our case for us.

³⁵Who will separate us from Christ's love? Will we be separated by trouble, or distress, or harassment, or famine, or nakedness, or danger, or sword? ³⁶As it is written,

We are being put to death all day long for your sake.

We are treated like sheep for slaughter.^s

³⁷But in all these things we win a sweeping victory through the one who loved us. ³⁸I'm convinced that nothing can separate us from God's love in Christ Jesus our Lord: not death or life, not angels or rulers, not present things or future things, not powers ³⁹or height or depth, or any other thing that is created.

The tragedy of Israel's unbelief

9 I'm speaking the truth in Christ—I'm not lying, as my conscience assures me with the Holy Spirit: ²I have great sadness and constant pain in my heart. ³I wish I could be cursed, cut off from Christ if it helped my brothers and sisters, who are my flesh-and-blood relatives. ⁴They are Israelites. The adoption as God's children, the glory, the covenants, the giving of the Law, the worship, and the promises belong to them. ⁵The Jewish ancestors are theirs, and the Christ descended from those ancestors. He is the one who rules over all things, who is God, and who is blessed forever. Amen.

Israel and God's choice

⁶But it's not as though God's word has failed. Not all who are descended from Israel are part of Israel. ⁷Not all of Abraham's children are called Abraham's descendants, but instead *your descendants will be named through Isaac.*^t ⁸That means it isn't the natural children who are God's children, but it is the children from the promise who are counted as descendants. ⁹The words in the promise were: *A year from now I will return, and Sarah will have a son.*^u

^sPs 44:22 ^tGen 21:12 ^uGen 18:10, 14

¹⁰Not only that, but also Rebecca conceived children with one man, our ancestor Isaac. ¹¹When they hadn't been born yet and when they hadn't yet done anything good or bad, it was shown that God's purpose would continue because it was based on his choice. ¹²It wasn't because of what was done but because of God's call. This was said to her: *The older child will be a slave to the younger one.*ᵛ ¹³As it is written, *I loved Jacob, but I hated Esau.*ʷ

¹⁴So what are we going to say? Isn't this unfair on God's part? Absolutely not! ¹⁵He says to Moses, *I'll have mercy on whomever I choose to have mercy, and I'll show compassion to whomever I choose to show compassion.*ˣ ¹⁶So then, it doesn't depend on a person's desire or effort. It depends entirely on God, who shows mercy. ¹⁷Scripture says to Pharaoh, *I have put you in this position for this very thing: so I can show my power in you and so that my name can be spread through the entire earth.*ʸ ¹⁸So then, God has mercy on whomever he wants to, but he makes resistant whomever he wants to.

¹⁹So you are going to say to me, "Then why does he still blame people? Who has ever resisted his will?" ²⁰You are only a human being. Who do you think you are to talk back to God? *Does the clay say to the potter, "Why did you make me like this?"*ᶻ ²¹Doesn't the potter have the power over the clay to make one pot for special purposes and another for garbage from the same lump of clay? ²²What if God very patiently puts up with pots made for wrath that were designed for destruction, because he wanted to show his wrath and to make his power known? ²³What if he did this to make the wealth of his glory known toward pots made for mercy, which he prepared in advance for glory? ²⁴We are the ones God has called. We don't come only from the Jews but we also come from the Gentiles. ²⁵As it says also in Hosea,

I will call "my people" those
*   who aren't my people,*
and the one who isn't well loved,
*I will call "loved one."*ᵃ

²⁶And in the place where it was said to them,
*   "You aren't my people,"*
*   there they will be called*
*   "the living God's children."*ᵇ
²⁷But Isaiah cries out for Israel,
Though the number of Israel's children
*   will be like the sand of the sea,*
*   only a remaining part will be saved,*
²⁸ *because the Lord does what he says*
*   completely and quickly.*ᶜ
²⁹As Isaiah prophesied,
If the Lord of the heavenly forces
*   had not left descendants for us,*
we would have been like Sodom,
*and we would have become like Gomorrah.*ᵈ

Israel and God's righteousness

³⁰So what are we going to say? Gentiles who weren't striving for righteousness achieved righteousness, the righteousness that comes from faith. ³¹But though Israel was striving for a Law of righteousness, they didn't arrive. ³²Why? It's because they didn't go for it by faith but they went for it as if it could be reached by doing something. They have tripped over a stumbling block. ³³As it is written:

Look! I'm putting a stumbling block in Zion,
*   which is a rock that offends people.*
And the one who has faith in him
*   will not be put to shame.*ᵉ

10 Brothers and sisters, my heart's desire is for Israel's salvation. That's my prayer to God for them. ²I can vouch for them: they are enthusiastic about God. However, it isn't informed by knowledge. ³They don't submit to God's righteousness because they don't understand his righteousness, and they try to establish their own righteousness. ⁴Christ is the goal of the Law, which leads to righteousness for all who have faith in God.

⁵Moses writes about the righteousness that comes from the Law: *The person who does these things will live by them.*ᶠ ⁶But the righteousness that comes from faith talks like this: *Don't say in your heart, "Who will*

go up into heaven?"[g] (that is, to bring Christ down) [7]or "Who will go down into the region below?"[h] (that is, to bring Christ up from the dead). [8]But what does it say? *The word is near you, in your mouth and in your heart*[i] (that is, the message of faith that we preach). [9]Because if you confess with your mouth "Jesus is Lord" and in your heart you have faith that God raised him from the dead, you will be saved. [10]Trusting with the heart leads to righteousness, and confessing with the mouth leads to salvation. [11]The scripture says, *All who have faith in him won't be put to shame.*[j] [12]There is no distinction between Jew and Greek, because the same Lord is Lord of all, who gives richly to all who call on him. [13]*All who call on the Lord's name will be saved.*[k]

[14]So how can they call on someone they don't have faith in? And how can they have faith in someone they haven't heard of? And how can they hear without a preacher? [15]And how can they preach unless they are sent? As it is written, *How beautiful are the feet of those who announce the good news.*[l]

[16]But everyone hasn't obeyed the good news. As Isaiah says, *Lord, who has had faith in our message?*[m] [17]So, faith comes from listening, but it's listening by means of Christ's message. [18]But I ask you, didn't they hear it? Definitely! *Their voice has gone out into the entire earth, and their message has gone out to the corners of the inhabited world.*[n] [19]But I ask you again, didn't Israel understand? First, Moses says, *I will make you jealous of those who aren't a people, of a people without understanding.*[o] [20]And Isaiah even dares to say, *I was found by those who didn't look for me; I revealed myself to those who didn't ask for me.*[p] [21]But he says about Israel, *All day long I stretched out my hands to a disobedient and contrary people.*[q]

Israel and God's faithfulness

11 So I ask you, has God rejected his people? Absolutely not! I'm an Israelite, a descendant of Abraham, from the tribe of Benjamin. [2]God hasn't rejected

his people, whom he knew in advance. Or don't you know what the scripture says in the case of Elijah, when he pleads with God against Israel? [3]*Lord, they have killed your prophets, and they have torn down your altars. I'm the only one left, and they are trying to take my life.*[r] [4]But what is God's reply to him? *I have kept for myself seven thousand people who haven't bowed their knees to Baal.*[s] [5]So also in the present time there is a remaining group by the choice of God's grace. [6]But if it is by grace, it isn't by what's done anymore. If it were, God's grace wouldn't be grace.

[7]So what? Israel didn't find what it was looking for. Those who were chosen found it, but the others were resistant. [8]As it is written, *God gave them a dull spirit, so that their eyes would not see and their ears not hear, right up until the present day.*[t] [9]And David says,

> *Their table should become a pitfall*
>   *and a trap,*
>   *a stumbling block and payback to them for*
>   *what they have done.*
> [10]*Their eyes should be darkened*
>   *so they can't see,*
>   *and their backs always bent.*[u]

[11]So I'm asking you: They haven't stumbled so that they've fallen permanently, have they? Absolutely not! But salvation has come to the Gentiles by their failure, in order to make Israel jealous. [12]But if their failure brings riches to the world, and their defeat brings riches to the Gentiles, how much more will come from the completion of their number! [13]I'm speaking to you Gentiles. Considering that I'm an apostle to the Gentiles, I publicize my own ministry [14]in the hope that somehow I might make my own people jealous and save some of them. [15]If their rejection has brought about a close relationship between God and the world, how can their acceptance mean anything less than life from the dead?

[16]But if part of a batch of dough is offered to God as holy, the whole batch of dough is holy too. If a root is holy, the branches

---

[g]Deut 9:4; 30:12 [h]Deut 30:13 [i]Deut 30:14 [j]Isa 28:16 [k]Joel 2:32 [l]Isa 52:7; Nah 1:15 [m]Isa 53:1 [n]Ps 19:4
[o]Deut 32:21 [p]Isa 65:1 [q]Isa 65:2 [r]1 Kgs 19:10, 14 [s]1 Kgs 19:18 [t]Deut 29:4; Isa 29:10 [u]Ps 69:22-23

will be holy too. [17]If some of the branches were broken off, and you were a wild olive branch, and you were grafted in among the other branches and shared the root that produces the rich oil of the olive tree, [18]then don't brag like you're better than the other branches. If you do brag, be careful: it's not you that sustains the root, but it's the root that sustains you. [19]You will say then, "Branches were broken off so that I could be grafted in." [20]Fine. They were broken off because they weren't faithful, but you stand only by your faithfulness.[v] So don't think in a proud way; instead be afraid. [21]If God didn't spare the natural branches, he won't spare you either. [22]So look at God's kindness and harshness. It's harshness toward those who fell, but it's God's kindness for you, provided you continue in his kindness; otherwise, you could be cut off too. [23]And even those who were cut off will be grafted back in if they don't continue to be unfaithful, because God is able to graft them in again. [24]If you were naturally part of a wild olive tree and you were cut off from it, and then, contrary to nature, you were grafted into the cultivated olive tree, won't these natural branches stand an even better chance of being grafted back onto their own olive tree?

All Israel will be saved

[25]I don't want you to be unaware of this secret,[w] brothers and sisters. That way you won't think too highly of yourselves. A part of Israel has become resistant until the full number of the Gentiles comes in. [26]In this way, all Israel will be saved, as it is written:

The deliverer will come from Zion.
    He will remove ungodly behavior
        from Jacob.
[27] This is my covenant with them,
    when I take away their sins.[x]

[28]According to the gospel, they are enemies for your sake, but according to God's choice, they are loved for the sake of their ancestors. [29]God's gifts and calling can't be taken back. [30]Once you were disobedient to God, but now you have mercy because they

were disobedient. [31]In the same way, they have also been disobedient because of the mercy that you received, so now they can receive mercy too. [32]God has locked up all people in disobedience, in order to have mercy on all of them.

[33]God's riches, wisdom, and knowledge are so deep! They are as mysterious as his judgments, and they are as hard to track as his paths!

[34] Who has known the Lord's mind?
    Or who has been his mentor?[y]
[35] Or who has given him a gift
    and has been paid back by him?[z]
[36] All things are from him and through him and for him.

    May the glory be to him forever. Amen.

Living sacrifice and transformed lives

12 So, brothers and sisters, because of God's mercies, I encourage you to present your bodies as a living sacrifice that is holy and pleasing to God. This is your appropriate priestly service. [2]Don't be conformed to the patterns of this world, but be transformed by the renewing of your minds so that you can figure out what God's will is—what is good and pleasing and mature.

Transformed relationships

[3]Because of the grace that God gave me, I can say to each one of you: don't think of yourself more highly than you ought to think. Instead, be reasonable since God has measured out a portion of faith to each one of you. [4]We have many parts in one body, but the parts don't all have the same function. [5]In the same way, though there are many of us, we are one body in Christ, and individually we belong to each other. [6]We have different gifts that are consistent with God's grace that has been given to us. If your gift is prophecy, you should prophesy in proportion to your faith. [7]If your gift is service, devote yourself to serving. If your gift is teaching, devote yourself to teaching. [8]If your gift is encouragement, devote yourself to encouraging. The one giving should do it with no strings attached. The

[v]Or faith [w]Or mystery [x]Isa 59:20-21; 27:9; Jer 31:33-34 [y]Isa 40:13 [z]Job 41:11

leader should lead with passion. The one showing mercy should be cheerful.

⁹Love should be shown without pretending. Hate evil, and hold on to what is good. ¹⁰Love each other like the members of your family. Be the best at showing honor to each other. ¹¹Don't hesitate to be enthusiastic—be on fire in the Spirit as you serve the Lord! ¹²Be happy in your hope, stand your ground when you're in trouble, and devote yourselves to prayer. ¹³Contribute to the needs of God's people, and welcome strangers into your home. ¹⁴Bless people who harass you—bless and don't curse them. ¹⁵Be happy with those who are happy, and cry with those who are crying. ¹⁶Consider everyone as equal, and don't think that you're better than anyone else. Instead, associate with people who have no status. Don't think that you're so smart. ¹⁷Don't pay back anyone for their evil actions with evil actions, but show respect for what everyone else believes is good.

¹⁸If possible, to the best of your ability, live at peace with all people. ¹⁹Don't try to get revenge for yourselves, my dear friends, but leave room for God's wrath. It is written, *Revenge belongs to me; I will pay it back, says the Lord.*ᵃ ²⁰Instead, *If your enemy is hungry, feed him; if he is thirsty, give him a drink. By doing this, you will pile burning coals of fire upon his head.*ᵇ ²¹Don't be defeated by evil, but defeat evil with good.

13 Every person should place themselves under the authority of the government. There isn't any authority unless it comes from God, and the authorities that are there have been put in place by God. ²So anyone who opposes the authority is standing against what God has established. People who take this kind of stand will get punished. ³The authorities don't frighten people who are doing the right thing. Rather, they frighten people who are doing wrong. Would you rather not be afraid of authority? Do what's right, and you will receive its approval. ⁴It is God's servant given for your benefit. But if you do what's wrong, be afraid because it doesn't have weapons

to enforce the law for nothing. It is God's servant put in place to carry out his punishment on those who do what is wrong. ⁵That is why it is necessary to place yourself under the government's authority, not only to avoid God's punishment but also for the sake of your conscience. ⁶You should also pay taxes for the same reason, because the authorities are God's assistants, concerned with this very thing. ⁷So pay everyone what you owe them. Pay the taxes you owe, pay the duties you are charged, give respect to those you should respect, and honor those you should honor.

⁸Don't be in debt to anyone, except for the obligation to love each other. Whoever loves another person has fulfilled the Law. ⁹The commandments, *Don't commit adultery, don't murder, don't steal, don't desire what others have,*ᶜ and any other commandments, are all summed up in one word: *You must love your neighbor as yourself.*ᵈ ¹⁰Love doesn't do anything wrong to a neighbor; therefore, love is what fulfills the Law.

The day is near

¹¹As you do all this, you know what time it is. The hour has already come for you to wake up from your sleep. Now our salvation is nearer than when we first had faith. ¹²The night is almost over, and the day is near. So let's get rid of the actions that belong to the darkness and put on the weapons of light. ¹³Let's behave appropriately as people who live in the day, not in partying and getting drunk, not in sleeping around and obscene behavior, not in fighting and obsession. ¹⁴Instead, dress yourself with the Lord Jesus Christ, and don't plan to indulge your selfish desires.

Welcoming each other like Christ

14 Welcome the person who is weak in faith—but not in order to argue about differences of opinion. ²One person believes in eating everything, while the weak person eats only vegetables. ³Those who eat must not look down on the ones who don't, and the ones who don't eat must

ᵃDeut 32:35   ᵇProv 25:21-22   ᶜExod 20:13-15, 17; Deut 5:17-19, 21   ᵈLev 19:18

not judge the ones who do, because God has accepted them. ⁴Who are you to judge someone else's servants? They stand or fall before their own Lord (and they will stand, because the Lord has the power to make them stand). ⁵One person considers some days to be more sacred than others, while another person considers all days to be the same. Each person must have their own convictions. ⁶Someone who thinks that a day is sacred, thinks that way for the Lord. Those who eat, eat for the Lord, because they thank God. And those who don't eat, don't eat for the Lord, and they thank the Lord too. ⁷We don't live for ourselves and we don't die for ourselves. ⁸If we live, we live for the Lord, and if we die, we die for the Lord. Therefore, whether we live or die, we belong to God. ⁹This is why Christ died and lived: so that he might be Lord of both the dead and the living. ¹⁰But why do you judge your brother or sister? Or why do you look down on your brother or sister? We all will stand in front of the judgment seat of God. ¹¹Because it is written,

As I live, says the Lord,
    every knee will bow to me,
    and every tongue will give praise to God.ᵉ

¹²So then, each of us will give an account of ourselves to God.

¹³So stop judging each other. Instead, this is what you should decide: never put a stumbling block or obstacle in the way of your brother or sister. ¹⁴I know and I'm convinced in the Lord Jesus that nothing is wrong to eat in itself. But if someone thinks something is wrong to eat, it becomes wrong for that person. ¹⁵If your brother or sister is upset by your food, you are no longer walking in love. Don't let your food destroy someone for whom Christ died. ¹⁶And don't let something you consider to be good be criticized as wrong. ¹⁷God's kingdom isn't about eating food and drinking but about righteousness, peace, and joy in the Holy Spirit. ¹⁸Whoever serves Christ this way pleases God and gets human approval.

¹⁹So let's strive for the things that bring peace and the things that build each other up. ²⁰Don't destroy what God has done because of food. All food is acceptable, but it's a bad thing if it trips someone else. ²¹It's a good thing not to eat meat or drink wine or to do anything that trips your brother or sister. ²²Keep the belief that you have to yourself—it's between you and God. People

ᵉIsa 45:23

CHRIST

Most frequently used in the NT to refer to Jesus (531 times). Christ is a transliteration of a Greek adjective meaning "anointed (with oil or ointment)" and often used to mean "anointed one." Christ is used approximately forty-five times in the Greek translation of the OT to translate the Hebrew word for "messiah," which means—as does the Greek word—"anointed (by oil)." The Hebrew term is used for the anointing of kings, but also (rarely) for that of priests or prophets. The term *Christ* early became a typical designation for Jesus, so much so that it functioned as a proper name for him, thus "an apostle of Jesus Christ" (e.g., 1 Pet 1:1). Since the 1st century, followers of Jesus have been labeled "Christian" (Acts 11:26).

The term bore no religious significance in secular Greek. Its importance in the NT stems from Jewish texts, where it referred to the fulfillment of God's promises regarding the eternal rule of a king from the line of David. Each of the NT writers employs the term *Christ* for Jesus.

are blessed who don't convict themselves by the things they approve. ²³But those who have doubts are convicted if they go ahead and eat, because they aren't acting on the basis of faith. Everything that isn't based on faith is sin.

15 We who are powerful need to be patient with the weakness of those who don't have power, and not please ourselves. ²Each of us should please our neighbors for their good in order to build them up. ³Christ didn't please himself, but, as it is written, *The insults of those who insulted you fell on me.*ᶠ ⁴Whatever was written in the past was written for our instruction so that we could have hope through endurance and through the encouragement of the scriptures. ⁵May the God of endurance and encouragement give you the same attitude toward each other, similar to Christ Jesus' attitude. ⁶That way you can glorify the God and Father of our Lord Jesus Christ together with one voice.

⁷So welcome each other, in the same way that Christ also welcomed you, for God's glory. ⁸I'm saying that Christ became a servant of those who are circumcised for the sake of God's truth, in order to confirm the promises given to the ancestors, ⁹and so that the Gentiles could glorify God for his mercy. As it is written,

Because of this I will confess you
  among the Gentiles,
  *and I will sing praises to your name.*ᵍ
¹⁰And again, it says,
*Rejoice, Gentiles, with his people.*ʰ
¹¹And again,
Praise the Lord, all you Gentiles,
  *and all the people should sing his praises.*ⁱ
¹²And again, Isaiah says,
There will be a root of Jesse,
  who will also rise to rule the Gentiles.
  *The Gentiles will place their hope in him.*ʲ
¹³May the God of hope fill you with all joy and peace in faith so that you overflow with hope by the power of the Holy Spirit.

Paul's ministry to the Gentiles

¹⁴My brothers and sisters, I myself am convinced that you yourselves are full of goodness, filled with all knowledge, and are able to teach each other. ¹⁵But I've written to you in a sort of daring way, partly to remind you of what you already know. I'm writing to you in this way because of the grace that was given to me by God. ¹⁶It helps me to be a minister of Christ Jesus to the Gentiles. I'm working as a priest of God's gospel so that the offering of the Gentiles can be acceptable and made holy by the Holy Spirit. ¹⁷So in Christ Jesus I brag about things that have to do with God. ¹⁸I don't dare speak about anything except what Christ has done through me to bring about the obedience of the Gentiles. He did it by what I've said and what I've done, ¹⁹by the power of signs and wonders, and by the power of God's Spirit. So I've completed the circuit of preaching Christ's gospel from Jerusalem all the way around to Illyricum. ²⁰In this way, I have a goal to preach the gospel where they haven't heard of Christ yet, so that I won't be building on someone else's foundation. ²¹Instead, as it's written, *Those who hadn't been told about him will see, and those who hadn't heard will understand.*ᵏ

Travel plans to visit Rome

²²That's why I've been stopped so many times from coming to see you. ²³But now, since I don't have any place to work in these regions anymore, and since I've wanted to come to see you for many years, ²⁴I'll visit you when I go to Spain. I hope to see you while I'm passing through. And I hope you will send me on my way there, after I have first been reenergized by some time in your company.

²⁵But now I'm going to Jerusalem, to serve God's people. ²⁶Macedonia and Achaia have been happy to make a contribution for the poor among God's people in Jerusalem. ²⁷They were happy to do this, and they are actually in debt to God's people in Jerusalem. If the Gentiles got a share of the Jewish people's spiritual resources, they ought to minister to them with ma-

terial resources. [28]So then after I have finished this job and have safely delivered the final amount of the Gentiles' offering to them, I will leave for Spain, visiting you on the way. [29]And I know that when I come to you I will come with the fullest blessing of Christ.

[30]Brothers and sisters, I urge you, through our Lord Jesus Christ and through the love of the Spirit, to join me in my struggles in your prayers to God for me. [31]Pray that I will be rescued from the people in Judea who don't believe. Also, pray that my service for Jerusalem will be acceptable to God's people there [32]so that I can come to you with joy by God's will and be reenergized with your company. [33]May the God of peace be with you all. Amen.

Introduction to Phoebe

16 I'm introducing our sister Phoebe to you, who is a servant[l] of the church in Cenchreae. [2]Welcome her in the Lord in a way that is worthy of God's people, and give her whatever she needs from you, because she herself has been a sponsor of many people, myself included.

Greetings to Roman Christians

[3]Say hello to Prisca and Aquila, my co-workers in Christ Jesus, [4]who risked their own necks for my life. I'm not the only one who thanks God for them, but all the churches of the Gentiles do the same. [5]Also say hello to the church that meets in their house. Say hello to Epaenetus, my dear friend, who was the first convert[m] in Asia for Christ. [6]Say hello to Mary, who has worked very hard for you. [7]Say hello to Andronicus and Junia, my relatives and my fellow prisoners. They are prominent among the apostles, and they were in Christ before me. [8]Say hello to Ampliatus, my dear friend in the Lord. [9]Say hello to Urbanus, our co-worker in Christ, and my dear friend Stachys. [10]Say hello to Apelles, who is tried and true in Christ. Say hello to the members of the household of Aristobulus. [11]Say hello to my relative Herodion. Say hello to the members of the household of Narcissus who are in the Lord. [12]Say hello to Tryphaena and Tryphosa, who are workers for the Lord. Say hello to my dear friend Persis, who has worked hard in the Lord. [13]Say hello to Rufus, who is an outstanding believer,

[l]Or deacon   [m]Or is the firstfruits

JUNIA

Junia was a Jewish Christian female whom Paul called a "prominent" apostle. She was imprisoned with him presumably because of their gospel ministry (Rom 16:7). Since the 12th cent., scholars have usually claimed that Paul was speaking of a male called Junias because they believed a woman could not be an apostle. However, no evidence exists that such a male name existed, while the name Junia is supported by at least 250 sources. Commentators before the 12th cent. believed Paul was speaking of a woman, for instance, the 4th cent. scholar John Chrysostom said of her in his commentary on Romans 16:5, "Oh, how great is the devotion of this woman, that she should be counted worthy of the appellation of apostle!" She is probably the wife of Andronicus (Rom 16:7) and may have belonged to the closed group of apostles who were appointed directly by the risen Christ in a limited period following his resurrection (compare 1 Cor 15:7). Paul states that she was "in Christ" before he was, which points to her being appointed an apostle before Paul and may have given her additional status in his eyes (compare 1 Cor 15:8).

along with his mother and mine. [14] Say hello to Asyncritus, Phlegon, Hermes, Patrobas, Hermas, and the brothers and sisters who are with them. [15] Say hello to Philologus and Julia, Nereus and his sister, and Olympas, and all the saints who are with them. [16] Say hello to each other with a holy kiss. All the churches of Christ say hello to you.

Warning against divisions

[17] Brothers and sisters, I urge you to watch out for people who create divisions and problems against the teaching that you learned. Keep away from them. [18] People like that aren't serving the Lord. They are serving their own feelings. They deceive the hearts of innocent people with smooth talk and flattery. [19] The news of your obedience has reached everybody, so I'm happy for you. But I want you to be wise about what's good, and innocent about what's evil. [20] The God of peace will soon crush Satan[n] under your feet. The grace of our Lord Jesus Christ be with you.

Greetings from Paul's coworkers

[21] Timothy my coworker says hello to you, and Lucius, Jason, and Sosipater, my relatives. [22] I'm Tertius, and I'm writing this letter to you in the Lord—hello! [23] Gaius, who is host to me and to the whole church, says hello to you. Erastus the city treasurer says hello to you, along with our brother Quartus.[o]

Final prayer

[25] May the glory be to God who can strengthen you with my good news and the message that I preach about Jesus Christ. He can strengthen you with the announcement of the secret[p] that was kept quiet for a long time. [26] Now that secret is revealed through what the prophets wrote. It is made known to the Gentiles[q] in order to lead to their faithful obedience based on the command of the eternal God. [27] May the glory be to God, who alone is wise! May the glory be to him through Jesus Christ forever! Amen.

[n] Or *the Adversary* [o] Critical editions of the Gk New Testament do not include 16:24 *The grace of our Lord Jesus Christ be with you.* [p] Or *mystery* [q] Or *all the Gentiles*

PHOEBE

A female resident of Cenchreae (a seaport east of Corinth), Phoebe was the apparent deliverer of Paul's letter to the Romans. In commending her to that church (Rom 16:1-2), Paul urged them to welcome her and help her with whatever she might need. This possibly involved assisting her in advance planning for Paul's intended visit to Rome and subsequent mission to Spain.

1 CORINTHIANS

THEME

How to grow from babyhood to maturity in Christ (3:1)

THE CITY OF CORINTH

Corinth was a Greek city that was less than fifty miles west of Athens. It was also a port city that provided access to the Mediterranean Sea and, by way of a short two-mile canal, the Aegean Sea. As a port city, Corinth would have been very cosmopolitan, bursting with activity. Interesting people, new trends and ideas, plenty of employment opportunities, cultural activities, and athletic contests contributed to life in Corinth. As in any port city of the Roman Empire in the first century, there also would have been a certain amount of crime, licentiousness, and sexual promiscuity evident.

Corinth also had a strong Jewish population. So it is not surprising that in Corinth Paul met two Jewish converts, Aquila and Priscilla (Acts 18:1-3; 1 Corinthians 16:19), who had been exiled from Rome because of the emperor Claudius's edict, probably issued about 49 CE.

PAUL IN CORINTH

The one clear piece of evidence that helps us date Paul's activities with the Corinthian Christians is the dates of the Roman proconsul in Corinth, Gallio. According to Acts 18:1-18, Paul's preaching in the Jewish synagogue brought him into serious conflict with the local Jews. Paul was told in a vision to stay in Corinth despite the tension, and he stayed a year and six months (Acts 18:11). The Jews finally brought a lawsuit against Paul (Acts 18:12-17) and Paul was brought before the local Roman governor, Gallio.

An inscription found at an archaeological excavation in Delphi shows that Gallio was proconsul in either 51–52 or 52–53 CE. Assuming Paul was in Corinth for almost two years, and considering Gallio's dates as proconsul, Paul must have founded the church in Corinth between the years 51 and 53 CE (see also 1 Corinthians 3:5-15).

THE CORINTHIAN CHURCH

The Christian community was composed of numerous house churches. These cells of Christians included both Gentiles (Acts 18:6) and Jews (1 Corinthians

1:22-24). Sometimes Paul refers to these individual cells in his writings (see, for example, 1 Corinthians 1:16; 16:19). On other occasions, Paul seems to address all the cell groups as the church, suggesting that on occasion all got together—perhaps to hear one of Paul's letters (Romans 16:23; 1 Corinthians 14:23). The number of Christian converts was not great. Hence, we could estimate that in a city the size of Corinth (which probably had a population of about 100,000), there were perhaps only about fifty to one hundred converts when Paul wrote his letters. If we very roughly estimate ten persons to a house church, Paul was writing to about five to ten house churches.

THE SOCIAL SETTING

The first Corinthian house churches experienced social tensions. First, there were tensions between Jews and Gentiles. Many of the Jews felt that their religious heritage was important for any who believed Jesus of Nazareth was the expected messiah. Hence they had to become Jews before they could become Christians! (See Paul's letter to the Galatians.) But Paul merely emphasizes that Christ is everything and Jewish practices are no longer valid for a right relationship with God.

There were also tensions between the social classes. The Christian faith brought together people from various backgrounds and social classes. It was a Roman custom to rank people at communal meals according to social standing in the community. Thus when house churches in Corinth held communal meals, Roman customs highlighted social stratification. It is not surprising then to find Paul addressing such problems (read 1 Corinthians 11:17-34 with this tension in mind).

There were also tensions over leadership (1 Corinthians 1:12-13; 3:4-9). With many house churches that rarely would have gathered in one place, competition and jostling for superiority would have been a natural development—as is sometimes evident in churches today!

Finally, there were apparently tensions with pagan religious groups in the city. Because the Corinthians attributed great importance to knowledge or wisdom (Greek *gnosis*), many scholars have argued that Gnosticism influenced the believers of Corinth (1 Corinthians 1:5, 20-22; 3:18-19; 8:1). Although the source of this influence is not clear, there does appear to be a tension between a pagan-type knowledge and Christian wisdom. Perhaps a stronger indication of a Gnostic social tension between Christian believers and pagan religions is a question Paul was asked to address: Should believers eat foods dedicated to the gods of pagan religions (1 Corinthians 8:1-13)?

THE MESSAGE OF 1 CORINTHIANS

Paul wrote 1 Corinthians from Ephesus (1 Corinthians 16:8) in 53 or 54 CE. It had not been long since his departure when Paul received a report from "Chloe's people" (1 Corinthians 1:11) of tensions, rivalries, and confusion over behavior and beliefs. Paul's response was the New Testament letter entitled 1 Corinthians.

First, Paul emphasizes the resurrection of Christ. Because of Paul's experience on the Damascus road (Acts 9:1-22), he knows Christ is alive. His summary of the gospel to the Christians at the city of Corinth emphasizes that Christ was raised on the third day and appeared to many, and appeared also to Paul himself (1 Corinthians 15:3-8). Because Christ is alive, those who are in Christ are a new creation (2 Corinthians 5:17). The theme of Christ's resurrection emanates from every thought and idea Paul communicates—it leaps from every line of his letters. It is the driving force behind his enthusiasm, his excitement, and his energetic communication of the Christian faith.

Second, Paul emphasizes the work of the Holy Spirit. The Spirit of God is the Spirit of the resurrected and living Christ. Paul deeply and profoundly experiences the Spirit of the living Christ in all his missionary activity following his experience on the Damascus road. He understands the Spirit as the practical experience of Christ working in all of the Christian life. There is no Christian activity without the Spirit (1 Corinthians 12:7-31). This same Spirit not only works within all Christian activity but also gives gifts to individuals for the upbuilding of the community.

For Paul, these two Christian truths cannot be disputed. The living Christ and the work of the Spirit are two necessities of the Christian's faith that will even rescue and reconstitute the fussing Corinthian believers. These two experiential truths are emphasized again and again throughout the Corinthian correspondence. In fact, all the other issues that Paul addresses in his letters to Corinth assume these two intensely practical beliefs.

1 CORINTHIANS

Greeting

1 From Paul, called by God's will to be an apostle of Jesus Christ, and from Sosthenes our brother.

2 To God's church that is in Corinth:

To those who have been made holy to God in Christ Jesus, who are called to be God's people.

Together with all those who call upon the name of our Lord Jesus Christ in every place—he's their Lord and ours!

3 Grace to you and peace from God our Father and the Lord Jesus Christ.

Thanksgiving for the Corinthians

4 I thank my God always for you, because of God's grace that was given to you in Christ Jesus. 5 That is, you were made rich through him in everything: in all your communication and every kind of knowledge, 6 in the same way that the testimony about Christ was confirmed with you. 7 The result is that you aren't missing any spiritual gift while you wait for our Lord Jesus Christ to be revealed. 8 He will also confirm your testimony about Christ until the end so that you will be blameless on the day of our Lord Jesus Christ. 9 God is faithful, and you were called by him to partnership with his Son, Jesus Christ our Lord.

Rival groups in Corinth

10 Now I encourage you, brothers and sisters, in the name of our Lord Jesus Christ: Agree with each other and don't be divided into rival groups. Instead, be restored with the same mind and the same purpose. 11 My brothers and sisters, Chloe's people gave me some information about you, that you're fighting with each other. 12 What I mean is this: that each one of you says, "I belong to Paul," "I belong to Apollos," "I belong to Cephas," "I belong to Christ." 13 Has Christ been divided? Was Paul crucified for you, or were you baptized in Paul's name? 14 Thank God that I didn't baptize any of you, except Crispus and Gaius, 15 so that nobody can say that you were baptized in my name! 16 Oh, I baptized the house of Stephanas too. Otherwise, I don't know if I baptized anyone else. 17 Christ didn't send me to baptize but to preach the good news. And Christ didn't send me to preach the good news with clever words so that Christ's cross won't be emptied of its meaning.

Human wisdom versus the cross

18 The message of the cross is foolishness to those who are being destroyed. But it is the power of God for those of us who are being saved. 19 It is written in scripture: *I will destroy the wisdom of the wise, and I will reject the intelligence of the intelligent.*[a] 20 Where are the wise? Where are the legal experts? Where are today's debaters? Hasn't God made the wisdom of the world foolish? 21 In God's wisdom, he determined that the world wouldn't come to know him through its wisdom. Instead, God was pleased to save those who believe through

[a] Isa 29:14

CHLOE

Chloe is mentioned only in 1 Corinthians 1:11 in a reference to Chloe's people. Chloe was likely a wealthy businesswoman from Ephesus whose "people" were probably business agents (perhaps freed persons or slaves) acting for her. Those agents brought upsetting news of the Corinthian church to Paul, notably about serious splits (1:10-17; 3:4-23), theological misunderstandings (1:18–3:3; 4:8-13), and immorality (5:1–6:20).

the foolishness of preaching. [22]Jews ask for signs, and Greeks look for wisdom, [23]but we preach Christ crucified, which is a scandal to Jews and foolishness to Gentiles. [24]But to those who are called—both Jews and Greeks—Christ is God's power and God's wisdom. [25]This is because the foolishness of God is wiser than human wisdom, and the weakness of God is stronger than human strength.

[26]Look at your situation when you were called, brothers and sisters! By ordinary human standards not many were wise, not many were powerful, not many were from the upper class. [27]But God chose what the world considers foolish to shame the wise. God chose what the world considers weak to shame the strong. [28]And God chose what the world considers low-class and low-life—what is considered to be nothing—to reduce what is considered to be something to nothing. [29]So no human being can brag in God's presence. [30]It is because of God that you are in Christ Jesus. He became wisdom from God for us. This means that he made us righteous and holy, and he delivered us. [31]This is consistent with what was written: *The one who brags should brag in the Lord!*[b]

2 When I came to you, brothers and sisters, I didn't come preaching God's secrets to you like I was an expert in speech or wisdom. [2]I had made up my mind not to think about anything while I was with you except Jesus Christ, and to preach him as crucified. [3]I stood in front of you

[b]Jer 9:24

CRUCIFIXION

Crucifixion was a form of execution practiced in late antiquity, whereby a person was tied or nailed to a pole or cross and left to hang. Crucifixion was practiced in the eastern Mediterranean long before the Romans adopted the practice. It was practiced by Persians, Assyrians, Scythians, and Thracians. Alexander the Great is said to have crucified. Jewish authorities practiced crucifixion. In time the Romans adopted this form of execution, primarily for murderous or rebellious slaves. The major difference between Jewish crucifixion and Roman crucifixion is that in the case of the former the bodies were taken down and buried, at least if they had been crucified in lands inhabited by Jews.

According to the Gospels, Jesus was taken down from the cross the very day he was crucified. To hasten the deaths of the two men crucified with Jesus, their legs were broken. In 1968 an ossuary was found at Giv'at ha-Mivtar, just north of Jerusalem (i.e., ossuary no. 4), which contained three skeletons. One of the skeletons was of a man who had been crucified, and an iron spike still transfixed the right heel bone. Fragments of wood at both ends of the spike were present. Moreover, the man's legs had been broken. The skeleton of the crucified man has been dated to the late 20s CE, when Judea and Samaria were administered by the Roman prefect Pontius Pilate. The crucified remains prove that Pilate permitted crucified Jewish criminals proper burial (as the Gospels say was the case for Jesus of Nazareth) and—if the broken leg bones are relevant—allowed them to be buried before sundown, contrary to normal Roman practice but in keeping with Jewish law and sensitivities.

with weakness, fear, and a lot of shaking. [4]My message and my preaching weren't presented with convincing wise words but with a demonstration of the Spirit and of power. [5]I did this so that your faith might not depend on the wisdom of people but on the power of God.

Definition of wisdom

[6]What we say is wisdom to people who are mature. It isn't a wisdom that comes from the present day or from today's leaders who are being reduced to nothing. [7]We talk about God's wisdom, which has been hidden as a secret. God determined this wisdom in advance, before time began, for our glory. [8]It is a wisdom that none of the present-day rulers have understood, because if they did understand it, they would never have crucified the Lord of glory! [9]But this is precisely what is written: *God has prepared things for those who love him that no eye has seen, or ear has heard, or that haven't crossed the mind of any human being.*[c] [10]God has revealed these things to us through the Spirit. The Spirit searches everything, including the depths of God. [11]Who knows a person's depths except their own spirit

that lives in them? In the same way, no one has known the depths of God except God's Spirit. [12]We haven't received the world's spirit but God's Spirit so that we can know the things given to us by God. [13]These are the things we are talking about—not with words taught by human wisdom but with words taught by the Spirit—we are interpreting spiritual things to spiritual people. [14]But people who are unspiritual don't accept the things from God's Spirit. They are foolishness to them and can't be understood, because they can only be comprehended in a spiritual way. [15]Spiritual people comprehend everything, but they themselves aren't understood by anyone. [16]*Who has known the mind of the Lord, who will advise him?*[d] But we have the mind of Christ.

Wisdom applied to divisions in the church

3 Brothers and sisters, I couldn't talk to you like spiritual people but like unspiritual people, like babies in Christ. [2]I gave you milk to drink instead of solid food, because you weren't up to it yet. [3]Now you are still not up to it because you are still unspiritual. When jealousy and fighting exist

[c]Isa 64:4 [d]Isa 40:13

APOLLOS

According to Luke, Apollos was a Jew and "a native of Alexandria . . . well-educated and effective in his use of the scriptures" (Acts 18:24). Having received instruction in "the way of the Lord," Luke states that he "spoke as one stirred up by the Spirit" and "taught accurately the things about Jesus" (Acts 18:25). This zeal and rhetorical proficiency impressed the Ephesians, who commended him to Corinth, where he exercised a similar influence over that community (Acts 18:27–19:1). Luke's statement that Apollos was deficient in the Holy Spirit makes him clearly subordinate to Paul (Acts 18:25c-26; cf. 19:1-7). This demotion may reflect Apollos's popularity, a fact that Paul himself recognized (1 Cor 1:12; 3:4, 21-22). Because of Apollos's reputation in Corinth, Paul validates his work as a fellow servant of God and a "mentor," but ultimately elevates himself to the role of the Corinthians' father (1 Cor 3:5-15; 4:14-16). Even so, Paul's closing remarks demonstrate that while he and Apollos were in Ephesus together, the two worked independently (1 Cor 16:12).

between you, aren't you unspiritual and living by human standards? ⁴When someone says, "I belong to Paul," and someone else says, "I belong to Apollos," aren't you acting like people without the Spirit? ⁵After all, what is Apollos? What is Paul? They are servants who helped you to believe. Each one had a role given to them by the Lord: ⁶I planted, Apollos watered, but God made it grow. ⁷Because of this, neither the one who plants nor the one who waters is anything, but the only one who is anything is God who makes it grow. ⁸The one who plants and the one who waters work together, but each one will receive their own reward for their own labor. ⁹We are God's coworkers, and you are God's field, God's building.

¹⁰I laid a foundation like a wise master builder according to God's grace that was given to me, but someone else is building on top of it. Each person needs to pay attention to the way they build on it. ¹¹No one can lay any other foundation besides the one that is already laid, which is Jesus Christ. ¹²So, whether someone builds on top of the foundation with gold, silver, precious stones, wood, grass, or hay, ¹³each one's work will be clearly shown. The day will make it clear, because it will be revealed with fire—the fire will test the quality of each one's work. ¹⁴If anyone's work survives, they'll get a reward. ¹⁵But if anyone's work goes up in flames, they'll lose it. However, they themselves will be saved as if they had gone through a fire. ¹⁶Don't you know that you are God's temple and God's

Spirit lives in you? ¹⁷If someone destroys God's temple, God will destroy that person, because God's temple is holy, which is what you are.

¹⁸Don't fool yourself. If some of you think they are worldly-wise, then they should become foolish so that they can become wise. ¹⁹This world's wisdom is foolishness to God. As it's written, *He catches the wise in their cleverness.*ᵉ ²⁰And also, *The Lord knows that the thoughts of the wise are silly.*ᶠ ²¹So then, no one should brag about human beings. Everything belongs to you—²²Paul, Apollos, Cephas, the world, life, death, things in the present, things in the future—everything belongs to you, ²³but you belong to Christ, and Christ belongs to God.

Paul's role as an apostle

4 So a person should think about us this way—as servants of Christ and managers of God's secrets. ²In this kind of situation, what is expected of a manager is that they prove to be faithful. ³I couldn't care less if I'm judged by you or by any human court; I don't even judge myself. ⁴I'm not aware of anything against me, but that doesn't make me innocent, because the Lord is the one who judges me. ⁵So don't judge anything before the right time—wait until the Lord comes. He will bring things that are hidden in the dark to light, and he will make people's motivations public. Then there will be recognition for each person from God.

⁶Brothers and sisters, I have applied

ᵉJob 5:13   ᶠPs 94:11

APOSTLE

Used in the NT both as a general designation for someone authorized to act on behalf of another, or sent with a commission, and as a title for particular founding figures and church leaders. Of the more than 80 appearances of the term, the majority are found in Luke–Acts and in letters attributed to Paul (34 each). In Luke–Acts, *apostle* is used almost exclusively of the Twelve (usually the group as a whole), both during the time of Jesus and (with Matthias replacing Judas) after the resurrection.

these things to myself and Apollos for your benefit. I've done this so that you can learn what it means not to go beyond what has been written and so none of you will become arrogant by supporting one of us against the other. [7]Who says that you are better than anyone else? What do you have that you didn't receive? And if you received it, then why are you bragging as if you didn't receive it? [8]You've been filled already! You've become rich already! You rule like kings without us! I wish you did rule so that we could be kings with you! [9]I suppose that God has shown that we apostles are at the end of the line. We are like prisoners sentenced to death, because we have become a spectacle in the world, both to angels and to humans. [10]We are fools for Christ, but you are wise through Christ! We are weak, but you are strong! You are honored, but we are dishonored! [11]Up to this very moment we are hungry, thirsty, wearing rags, abused, and homeless. [12]We work hard with our own hands. When we are insulted, we respond with a blessing; when we are harassed, we put up with it; [13]when our reputation is attacked, we are encouraging. We have become the scum of the earth, the waste that runs off everything, up to the present time.

[14]I'm not writing these things to make you ashamed but to warn you, since you are my loved children. [15]You may have ten thousand mentors in Christ, but you don't have many fathers. I gave birth to you in Christ Jesus through the gospel, [16]so I encourage you to follow my example. [17]This is why I've sent Timothy to you; he's my loved and trusted child in the Lord; he'll remind you about my way of life in Christ Jesus. He'll teach the same way as I teach everywhere in every church. [18]Some have become arrogant as if I'm not coming to see you. [19]But, if the Lord is willing, I'll come to you soon. Then I won't focus on what these arrogant people say, but I'll find out what power they possess. [20]God's kingdom isn't about words but about power. [21]Which do you want? Should I come to you with a big stick to punish you, or with love and a gentle spirit?

Confronting sexual immorality in the church

5Everyone has heard that there is sexual immorality among you. This is a type of immorality that isn't even heard of among the Gentiles—a man is having sex with his father's wife! [2]And you're proud of yourselves instead of being so upset that the one who did this thing is expelled from your community. [3]Though I'm absent physically, I'm present in the spirit and I've already judged the man who did this as if I were present. [4]When you meet together in the name of our Lord Jesus, I'll be present in spirit with the power of our Lord Jesus. [5]At that time we need to hand this man over to Satan to destroy his human weakness so that his spirit might be saved on the day of the Lord.

[6]Your bragging isn't good! Don't you know that a tiny grain of yeast makes a whole batch of dough rise? [7]Clean out the old yeast so you can be a new batch of dough, given that you're supposed to be unleavened bread. Christ our Passover lamb has been sacrificed, [8]so let's celebrate the feast with the unleavened bread of honesty and truth, not with old yeast or with the yeast of evil and wickedness.

[9]I wrote to you in my earlier letter not to associate with sexually immoral people. [10]But I wasn't talking about the sexually immoral people in the outside world by any means—or the greedy, or the swindlers, or people who worship false gods—otherwise, you would have to leave the world entirely! [11]But now I'm writing to you not to associate with anyone who calls themselves "brother" or "sister" who is sexually immoral, greedy, someone who worships false gods, an abusive person, a drunk, or a swindler. Don't even eat with anyone like this. [12]What do I care about judging outsiders? Isn't it your job to judge insiders? [13]God will judge outsiders. *Expel the evil one from among you!*[8]

[8]Deut 17:7; 19:19; 22:21, 24; 24:7

Confronting lawsuits in the church

6 When someone in your assembly has a legal case against another member, do they dare to take it to court to be judged by people who aren't just, instead of by God's people? [2]Or don't you know that God's people will judge the world? If the world is to be judged by you, are you incompetent to judge trivial cases? [3]Don't you know that we will judge angels? Why not ordinary things? [4]So then if you have ordinary lawsuits, do you appoint people as judges who aren't respected by the church? [5]I'm saying this because you should be ashamed of yourselves! Isn't there one person among you who is wise enough to pass judgment between believers? [6]But instead, does a brother or sister have a lawsuit against another brother or sister, and do they do this in front of unbelievers? [7]The fact that you have lawsuits against each

other means that you've already lost your case. Why not be wronged instead? Why not be cheated? [8]But instead you are doing wrong and cheating—and you're doing it to your own brothers and sisters.

[9]Don't you know that people who are unjust won't inherit God's kingdom? Don't be deceived. Those who are sexually immoral, those who worship false gods, adulterers, both participants in same-sex intercourse,[h] [10]thieves, the greedy, drunks, abusive people, and swindlers won't inherit God's kingdom. [11]That is what some of you used to be! But you were washed clean, you were made holy to God, and you were made right with God in the name of the Lord Jesus Christ and in the Spirit of our God.

Avoid sexual immorality

[12]I have the freedom to do anything, but not everything is helpful. I have the

[h]Or submissive and dominant male sexual partners

LEAVEN

An agent that causes fermentation. In biblical times it was often a piece of fermented dough left from a previous batch. In some passages there is reference to baking that did (Hos 7:4) or did not (Gen 19:3; Judg 6:19-21; 1 Sam 28:24) involve yeast. But a more frequent usage has to do with the absence of yeast on festival occasions. The legislation for Passover and the Festival of Unleavened Bread says that no yeast was to be consumed or found in the houses of the Israelites (Exod 12:8, 15, 17-20, 34, 39; 13:3, 6-7; 23:15; 34:18). Deuteronomy 16:3 calls unleavened bread "bread symbolizing misery" and notes that baking bread without leaven was related to Israel's hasty departure from Egypt.

The word took on a figurative meaning in the NT and rabbinic literature. Leaven is something small that works its way entirely through something larger (see 1 Cor 5:6; Gal 5:9). It could convey a positive meaning. In Matthew 13:33 (cf. Luke 13:20-21) Jesus tells a short parable: "The kingdom of heaven is like yeast, which a woman took and hid in a bushel of wheat flour until the yeast had worked its way through all the dough." But there are also several instances of negative connotations. Matthew 16:6 quotes Jesus as warning his disciples: "Watch out and be on your guard for the yeast of the Pharisees and Sadducees" (see also vv. 11-12; Mark 8:15); in Luke 12:1 this becomes "the yeast of the Pharisees—I mean, the mismatch between their hearts and lives."

freedom to do anything, but I won't be controlled by anything. [13]Food is for the stomach and the stomach is for food, and yet God will do away with both. The body isn't for sexual immorality but for the Lord, and the Lord is for the body. [14]God has raised the Lord and will raise us through his power. [15]Don't you know that your bodies are parts of Christ? So then, should I take parts of Christ and make them a part of someone who is sleeping around?[i] No way! [16]Don't you know that anyone who is joined to someone who is sleeping around is one body with that person? The scripture says, *The two will become one flesh.*[j] [17]The one who is joined to the Lord is one spirit with him. [18]Avoid sexual immorality! Every sin that a person can do is committed outside the body, except those who engage in sexual immorality commit sin against their own bodies. [19]Or don't you know that your body is a temple of the Holy Spirit who is in you? Don't you know that you have the Holy Spirit from God, and you don't belong to yourselves? [20]You have been bought and paid for, so honor God with your body.

Marriage and celibacy

7 Now, about what you wrote: "It's good for a man not to have sex with a woman." [2]Each man should have his own wife, and each woman should have her own husband because of sexual immorality. [3]The husband should meet his wife's sexual needs, and the wife should do the same for her husband. [4]The wife doesn't have authority over her own body, but the husband does. Likewise, the husband doesn't have authority over his own body, but the wife does. [5]Don't refuse to meet each other's needs unless you both agree for a short period of time to devote yourselves to prayer. Then come back together again so that Satan might not tempt you because of your lack of self-control. [6]I'm saying this to give you permission; it's not a command. [7]I wish all people were like me, but each has a particular gift from God: one has this gift, and another has that one.

[8]I'm telling those who are single and widows that it's good for them to stay single like me. [9]But if they can't control themselves, they should get married, because it's better to marry than to burn with passion. [10]I'm passing on the Lord's command to those who are married: A wife shouldn't leave her husband, [11]but if she does leave him, then she should stay single or be reconciled to her husband. And a man shouldn't divorce his wife.

[12]I'm telling everyone else (the Lord didn't say this specifically): If a believer has a wife who doesn't believe, and she agrees to live with him, then he shouldn't divorce her. [13]If a woman has a husband who doesn't believe and he agrees to live with her, then

[i]Or *a prostitute;* commonly, women who sell their bodies to multiple sex partners but includes those who are sexually immoral [j]Gen 2:24

MARRIAGE

In the NT, marriage represents the cornerstone of the household. Closely related to concepts of kinship and family, marriage has important social, economic, and spiritual dimensions. Men interact publicly with each other as married heads of households. The husband's authority over his wife is closely tied to ownership of property. He has exclusive sexual access to his wife; children born in the household belong to him. As in the OT, metaphorical references to marriage in the NT explore the nature of the community's relationship with God. In the NT, however, human marriage is also at times forsaken as a sign of the dawning of God's kingdom.

she shouldn't divorce him. ¹⁴The husband who doesn't believe belongs to God because of his wife, and the wife who doesn't believe belongs to God because of her husband. Otherwise, your children would be contaminated by the world, but now they are spiritually set apart. ¹⁵But if a spouse who doesn't believe chooses to leave, then let them leave. The brother or sister isn't tied down in these circumstances. God has called you to peace. ¹⁶How do you know as a wife if you will save your husband? Or how do you know as a husband if you will save your wife?

¹⁷Nevertheless, each person should live the kind of life that the Lord assigned when he called each one. This is what I teach in all the churches. ¹⁸If someone was circumcised when called, he shouldn't try to reverse it. If someone wasn't circumcised when he was called, he shouldn't be circumcised. ¹⁹Circumcision is nothing; not being circumcised is nothing. What matters is keeping God's commandments. ²⁰Each person should stay in the situation they were in when they were called. ²¹If you were a slave when you were called, don't let it bother you. But if you are actually able to be free, take advantage of the opportunity. ²²Anyone who was a slave when they were called by the Lord has the status of being the Lord's free person. In the same way, anyone who was a free person when they were called is Christ's slave. ²³You were bought and paid for. Don't become slaves of people. ²⁴So then, brothers and sisters, each of you should stay with God in the situation you were in when you were called.

²⁵I don't have a command from the Lord about people who have never been married,ᵏ but I'll give you my opinion as someone you can trust because of the Lord's mercy. ²⁶So I think this advice is good because of the present crisis: Stay as you are. ²⁷If you are married, don't get a divorce. If you are divorced, don't try to find a spouse. ²⁸But if you do marry, you haven't sinned; and if someone who hasn't been married gets married, they haven't sinned. But married

people will have a hard time, and I'm trying to spare you that. ²⁹This is what I'm saying, brothers and sisters: The time has drawn short. From now on, those who have wives should be like people who don't have them. ³⁰Those who are sad should be like people who aren't crying. Those who are happy should be like people who aren't happy. Those who buy something should be like people who don't have possessions. ³¹Those who use the world should be like people who aren't preoccupied with it, because this world in its present form is passing away.

³²I want you to be free from concerns. A man who isn't married is concerned about the Lord's concerns—how he can please the Lord. ³³But a married man is concerned about the world's concerns—how he can please his wife. ³⁴His attention is divided. A woman who isn't married or who is a virgin is concerned about the Lord's concerns so that she can be dedicated to God in both body and spirit. But a married woman is concerned about the world's concerns—how she can please her husband. ³⁵I'm saying this for your own advantage. It's not to restrict you but rather to promote effective and consistent service to the Lord without distraction.

³⁶If someone thinks he is acting inappropriately toward an unmarried woman whom he knows, and if he has strong feelings and it seems like the right thing to do, he should do what he wants—he's not sinning—they should get married. ³⁷But if a man stands firm in his decision, and doesn't feel the pressure, but has his own will under control, he does right if he decides in his own heart not to marry the woman. ³⁸Therefore, the one who marries the unmarried woman does right, and the one who doesn't get married will do even better. ³⁹A woman is obligated to stay in her marriage as long as her husband is alive. But if her husband dies, she is free to marry whomever she wants, only it should be a believer in the Lord. ⁴⁰But in my opinion, she will be happier if she stays the way she is. And I think that I have God's Spirit too.

ᵏOr virgins

Meat sacrificed to false gods

8 Now concerning meat that has been sacrificed to a false god: We know that we all have knowledge. Knowledge makes people arrogant, but love builds people up. ²If anyone thinks they know something, they don't yet know as much as they should know. ³But if someone loves God, then they are known by God.

⁴So concerning the actual food involved in these sacrifices to false gods, we know that a false god isn't anything in this world, and that there is no God except for the one God. ⁵Granted, there are so-called "gods," in heaven and on the earth, as there are many gods and many lords. ⁶However, for us believers,

There is one God the Father.
　All things come from him,
　　and we belong to him.
And there is one Lord Jesus Christ.
　All things exist through him,
　　and we live through him.

⁷But not everybody knows this. Some are eating this food as though it really is food sacrificed to a real idol, because they were used to idol worship until now. Their conscience is weak because it has been damaged. ⁸Food won't bring us close to God. We're not missing out if we don't eat, and we don't have any advantage if we do eat. ⁹But watch out or else this freedom of yours might be a problem for those who are weak. ¹⁰Suppose someone sees you (the person who has knowledge) eating in an idol's temple. Won't the person with a weak conscience be encouraged to eat the meat sacrificed to false gods? ¹¹The weak brother or sister for whom Christ died is destroyed by your knowledge. ¹²You sin against Christ if you sin against your brothers and sisters and hurt their weak consciences this way. ¹³This is why, if food causes the downfall of my brother or sister, I won't eat meat ever again, or else I may cause my brother or sister to fall.

Waiving rights for the gospel

9 Am I not free? Am I not an apostle? Haven't I seen Jesus our Lord? Aren't you my work in the Lord? ²If I'm not an apostle to others, at least I am to you! You are the seal that shows I'm an apostle. ³This is my defense against those who criticize me. ⁴Don't we have the right to eat and drink? ⁵Don't we have the right to travel with a wife who believes like the rest of the apostles, the Lord's brothers, and Cephas?

SLAVERY

Slavery is not simply owning a human being as property (chattel), the equivalent of forced labor, the denial of civil rights, or the loss of freedom. Its distinctiveness lies in the permanent and violent domination of persons alienated from birth who live in a general state of dishonor. This preliminary definition from historical sociology offers a useful model of slavery as "social death."

In the OT, the Hebrews experienced slavery in Egypt, and this is the consistent framework for understanding the limits to be placed on slavery. Slavery was usually the result of a debt and was rarely related to race. The Roman Empire in the NT used slaves gathered from conquest throughout the known world, and slaves were common in all levels of the economy and society. Paul frequently uses slavery as a metaphor, calling himself a "slave of Christ Jesus," an apostolic designation (Rom 1:1; Phil 1:1; Gal 1:10; see 1 Cor 9:16-18), and "a slave to all people," a commonplace way of describing servant leadership (1 Cor 9:19-23; see 2 Cor 4:5).

[6] Or is it only I and Barnabas who don't have the right to not work for our living? [7] Who joins the army and pays their own way? Who plants a vineyard and doesn't eat its fruit? Who shepherds a flock and doesn't drink its milk? [8] I'm not saying these things just based on common sense, am I? Doesn't the Law itself say these things? [9] In Moses' Law it's written: *You will not muzzle the ox when it is threshing.*[l] Is God worried about oxen, [10] or did he say this entirely for our sake? It was written for our sake because the one who plows and the one who threshes should each do so with the hope of sharing the produce. [11] If we sowed spiritual things in you, is it so much to ask to harvest some material things from you?

[12] If others have these rights over you, don't we deserve them all the more? However, we haven't made use of this right, but we put up with everything so we don't put any obstacle in the way of the gospel of Christ. [13] Don't you know that those who serve in the temple get to eat food from the temple, and those who serve at the altar share part of what is sacrificed on the altar? [14] In the same way, the Lord commanded that those who preach the gospel should get their living from the gospel. [15] But I haven't taken advantage of this. And I'm not writing this so that it will be done for me. It's better for me to die than to lose my right to brag about this! [16] If I preach the gospel, I have no reason to brag, since I'm obligated to do it. I'm in trouble if I don't preach the gospel. [17] If I do this voluntarily, I get rewarded for it. But if I'm forced to do it, then I've been charged with a responsibility. [18] What reward do I get? That when I preach, I offer the good news free of charge. That's why I don't use the rights to which I'm entitled through the gospel.

[19] Although I'm free from all people, I make myself a slave to all people, to recruit more of them. [20] I act like a Jew to the Jews, so I can recruit Jews. I act like I'm under the Law to those under the Law, so I can recruit those who are under the Law (though I myself am not under the Law). [21] I act like I'm outside the Law to those who are outside the Law, so I can recruit those outside the Law (though I'm not outside the law of God but rather under the law of Christ). [22] I act weak to the weak, so I can recruit the weak. I have become all things to all people, so I could save some by all possible means. [23] All the things I do are for the sake of the gospel, so I can be a partner with it.

[24] Don't you know that all the runners in the stadium run, but only one gets the prize? So run to win. [25] Everyone who competes practices self-discipline in everything. The runners do this to get a crown of leaves that shrivel up and die, but we do it to receive a crown that never dies. [26] So now this is how I run—not without a clear goal in sight. I fight like a boxer in the ring, not like someone who is shadowboxing. [27] Rather, I'm landing punches on my own body and subduing it like a slave. I do this to be sure that I myself won't be disqualified after preaching to others.

Warning from the wilderness generation

10 Brothers and sisters, I want you to be sure of the fact that our ancestors were all under the cloud and they all went through the sea. [2] All were baptized into Moses in the cloud and in the sea. [3] All ate the same spiritual food, [4] and all drank the same spiritual drink. They drank from a spiritual rock that followed them, and the rock was Christ. [5] However, God was unhappy with most of them, and they were struck down in the wilderness. [6] These things were examples for us, so we won't crave evil things like they did. [7] Don't worship false gods like some of them did, as it is written, *The people sat down to eat and drink and they got up to play.*[m] [8] Let's not practice sexual immorality, like some of them did, and twenty-three thousand died in one day. [9] Let's not test Christ, like some of them did, and were killed by the snakes. [10] Let's not grumble, like some of them did, and were killed by the destroyer. [11] These things happened to them as an example and

---

[l] Deut 25:4   [m] Exod 32:6

were written as a warning for us to whom the end of time has come. [12]So those who think they are standing need to watch out or else they may fall. [13]No temptation has seized you that isn't common for people. But God is faithful. He won't allow you to be tempted beyond your abilities. Instead, with the temptation, God will also supply a way out so that you will be able to endure it.

Avoid false gods to glorify God

[14]So then, my dear friends, run away from the worship of false gods! [15]I'm talking to you like you are sensible people. Think about what I'm saying. [16]Isn't the cup of blessing that we bless a sharing in the blood of Christ? Isn't the loaf of bread that we break a sharing in the body of Christ? [17]Since there is one loaf of bread, we who are many are one body, because we all share the one loaf of bread. [18]Look at the people of Israel. Don't those who eat the sacrifices share from the altar? [19]What am I saying then? That food sacrificed to a false god is anything, or that a false god is anything? [20]No, but this kind of sacrifice is sacrificed to demons and not to God. I don't want you to be sharing in demons. [21]You can't drink the cup of the Lord and the cup of demons; you can't participate in the table of the Lord and the table of demons. [22]Or should we make the Lord jealous? We aren't stronger than he is, are we?

[23]Everything is permitted, but everything isn't beneficial. Everything is permitted, but everything doesn't build others up. [24]No one should look out for their own advantage, but they should look out for each other. [25]Eat everything that is sold in the marketplace, without asking questions about it because of your conscience. [26]*The earth and all that is in it belong to the Lord.*[n] [27]If an unbeliever invites you to eat with them and you want to go, eat whatever is served, without asking questions because of your conscience. [28]But if someone says to you, "This meat was sacrificed in a temple," then don't eat it for the sake of the one who told you and for the sake of conscience.

[29]Now when I say "conscience" I don't mean yours but the other person's. Why should my freedom be judged by someone else's conscience? [30]If I participate with gratitude, why should I be blamed for food I thank God for? [31]So, whether you eat or drink or whatever you do, you should do it all for God's glory. [32]Don't offend either Jews or Greeks, or God's church. [33]This is the same thing that I do. I please everyone in everything I do. I don't look out for my own advantage, but I look out for many people so that they can be saved. [1]Follow my example, just like I follow Christ's.

Appropriate dress in worship

[2]I praise you because you remember all my instructions, and you hold on to the traditions exactly as I handed them on to you. [3]Now I want you to know that the head of every man is Christ, and the head of the woman is the man, and the head of Christ is God. [4]Every man who prays or prophesies with his head covered shames his head.

[5]Every woman who prays or prophesies with her head uncovered disgraces her head. It is the same thing as having her head shaved. [6]If a woman doesn't cover her head, then she should have her hair cut off. If it is disgraceful for a woman to have short hair or to be shaved, then she should keep her head covered. [7]A man shouldn't have his head covered, because he is the image and glory of God; but the woman is man's glory. [8]Man didn't have his origin from woman, but woman from man; [9]and man wasn't created for the sake of the woman, but the woman for the sake of the man. [10]Because of this a woman should have authority over her head, because of the angels. [11]However, woman isn't independent from man, and man isn't independent from woman in the Lord. [12]As woman came from man so also man comes from woman. But everything comes from God. [13]Judge for yourselves: Is it appropriate for a woman to pray to God with her head uncovered? [14]Doesn't nature itself teach you that if a man has long hair, it is a disgrace to him; [15]but if a woman has

[n]Ps 24:1

long hair, it is her glory? This is because her long hair is given to her for a covering. ¹⁶But if someone wants to argue about this, we don't have such a custom, nor do God's churches.

The community meal

¹⁷Now I don't praise you as I give the following instruction because when you meet together, it does more harm than good. ¹⁸First of all, when you meet together as a church, I hear that there are divisions among you, and I partly believe it. ¹⁹It's necessary that there are groups among you, to make it clear who is genuine. ²⁰So when you get together in one place, it isn't to eat the Lord's meal. ²¹Each of you goes ahead and eats a private meal. One person goes hungry while another is drunk. ²²Don't you have houses to eat and drink in? Or do you look down on God's churches and humiliate those who have nothing? What can I say to you? Will I praise you? No, I don't praise you in this.

²³I received a tradition from the Lord, which I also handed on to you: on the night on which he was betrayed, the Lord Jesus took bread. ²⁴After giving thanks, he broke it and said, "This is my body, which is for you; do this to remember me." ²⁵He did the same thing with the cup, after they had eaten, saying, "This cup is the new covenant in my blood. Every time you drink it, do this to remember me." ²⁶Every time you eat this bread and drink this cup, you broadcast the death of the Lord until he comes.

²⁷This is why those who eat the bread or drink the cup of the Lord inappropriately will be guilty of the Lord's body and blood. ²⁸Each individual should test himself or herself, and eat from the bread and drink from the cup in that way. ²⁹Those who eat and drink without correctly understanding the body are eating and drinking their own judgment. ³⁰Because of this, many of you are weak and sick, and quite a few have died. ³¹But if we had judged ourselves, we wouldn't be judged. ³²However, we are disciplined by the Lord when we are judged

so that we won't be judged and condemned along with the whole world. ³³For these reasons, my brothers and sisters, when you get together to eat, wait for each other. ³⁴If some of you are hungry, they should eat at home so that getting together doesn't lead to judgment. I will give directions about the other things when I come.

Spiritual gifts

12Brothers and sisters, I don't want you to be ignorant about spiritual gifts. ²You know that when you were Gentiles you were often misled by false gods that can't even speak. ³So I want to make it clear to you that no one says, "Jesus is cursed!" when speaking by God's Spirit, and no one can say, "Jesus is Lord," except by the Holy Spirit. ⁴There are different spiritual gifts but the same Spirit; ⁵and there are different ministries and the same Lord; ⁶and there are different activities but the same God who produces all of them in everyone. ⁷A demonstration of the Spirit is given to each person for the common good. ⁸A word of wisdom is given by the Spirit to one person, a word of knowledge to another according to the same Spirit, ⁹faith to still another by the same Spirit, gifts of healing to another in the one Spirit, ¹⁰performance of miracles to another, prophecy to another, the ability to tell spirits apart to another, different kinds of tongues° to another, and the interpretation of the tongues to another. ¹¹All these things are produced by the one and same Spirit who gives what he wants to each person.

¹²Christ is just like the human body—a body is a unit and has many parts; and all the parts of the body are one body, even though there are many. ¹³We were all baptized by one Spirit into one body, whether Jew or Greek, or slave or free, and we all were given one Spirit to drink. ¹⁴Certainly the body isn't one part but many. ¹⁵If the foot says, "I'm not part of the body because I'm not a hand," does that mean it's not part of the body? ¹⁶If the ear says, "I'm not part of the body because I'm not an eye,"

°Or *ecstatic speech* or *languages* could be used for *tongues* or *tongue* throughout chaps 12–14.

does that mean it's not part of the body? [17] If the whole body were an eye, what would happen to the hearing? And if the whole body were an ear, what would happen to the sense of smell? [18] But as it is, God has placed each one of the parts in the body just like he wanted. [19] If all were one and the same body part, what would happen to the body? [20] But as it is, there are many parts but one body. [21] So the eye can't say to the hand, "I don't need you," or in turn, the head can't say to the feet, "I don't need you." [22] Instead, the parts of the body that people think are the weakest are the most necessary. [23] The parts of the body that we think are less honorable are the ones we honor the most. The private parts of our body that aren't presentable are the ones that are given the most dignity. [24] The parts of our body that are presentable don't need this. But God has put the body together, giving greater honor to the part with less honor [25] so that there won't be division in the body and so the parts might have mutual concern for each other. [26] If one part suffers, all the parts suffer with it; if one part gets the glory, all the parts celebrate with it. [27] You are the body of Christ and parts of each other. [28] In the church, God has appointed first apostles, second prophets, third teachers, then miracles, then gifts of healing, the ability to help others, leadership skills, different kinds of tongues. [29] All aren't apostles, are they? All aren't prophets, are they? All aren't teachers, are they? All don't perform miracles, do they? [30] All don't have gifts of healing, do they? All don't speak in different tongues, do they? All don't interpret, do they? [31] Use your ambition to try to get the greater gifts. And I'm going to show you an even better way.

Love: the universal spiritual gift

13 If I speak in tongues of human beings and of angels but I don't have love, I'm a clanging gong or a clashing cymbal. [2] If I have the gift of prophecy and I know all the mysteries and everything else, and if I have such complete faith that I can move mountains but I don't have love, I'm nothing. [3] If I give away everything that I have

and hand over my own body to feel good about what I've done but I don't have love, I receive no benefit whatsoever.

[4] Love is patient, love is kind, it isn't jealous, it doesn't brag, it isn't arrogant, [5] it isn't rude, it doesn't seek its own advantage, it isn't irritable, it doesn't keep a record of complaints, [6] it isn't happy with injustice, but it is happy with the truth. [7] Love puts up with all things, trusts in all things, hopes for all things, endures all things.

[8] Love never fails. As for prophecies, they will be brought to an end. As for tongues, they will stop. As for knowledge, it will be brought to an end. [9] We know in part and we prophesy in part; [10] but when the perfect comes, what is partial will be brought to an end. [11] When I was a child, I used to speak like a child, reason like a child, think like a child. But now that I have become a man, I've put an end to childish things. [12] Now we see a reflection in a mirror; then we will see face-to-face. Now I know partially, but then I will know completely in the same way that I have been completely known. [13] Now faith, hope, and love remain—these three things—and the greatest of these is love.

Spiritual gifts and church order

14 Pursue love, and use your ambition to try to get spiritual gifts but especially so that you might prophesy. [2] This is because those who speak in a tongue don't speak to people but to God; no one understands it—they speak mysteries by the Spirit. [3] Those who prophesy speak to people, building them up, and giving them encouragement and comfort. [4] People who speak in a tongue build up themselves; those who prophesy build up the church. [5] I wish that all of you spoke in tongues, but I'd rather you could prophesy. Those who prophesy are more important than those who speak in tongues, unless they are able to interpret them so that the church might be built up. [6] After all, brothers and sisters, if I come to you speaking in tongues, how will I help you unless I speak to you with a revelation, some knowledge, a prophecy, or a teaching? [7] Likewise, things that aren't alive like a harp or a lyre can make a sound, but if there aren't different notes in the sounds they make, how will the tune from the harp or the lyre be recognized? ⁸And if a trumpet call is unrecognizable, then who will prepare for battle? ⁹It's the same way with you: If you don't use language that is easy to understand when you speak in a tongue, then how will anyone understand what is said? ¹⁰It will be as if you are speaking into the air! There are probably many language families in the world, and none of them are without meaning. ¹¹So if I don't know the meaning of the language, then I will be like a foreigner to those who speak it, and they will be like foreigners to me. ¹²The same holds true for you: since you are ambitious for spiritual gifts, use your ambition to try to work toward being the best at building up the church.

¹³Therefore, those who speak in a tongue should pray to be able to interpret. ¹⁴If I pray in a tongue, my spirit prays but my mind isn't productive. ¹⁵What should I do? I'll pray in the Spirit, but I'll pray with my mind too; I'll sing a psalm in the Spirit, but I'll sing the psalm with my mind too. ¹⁶After all, if you praise God in the Spirit, how will the people who aren't trained in that language say "Amen!" to your thanksgiving, when they don't know what you are saying? ¹⁷You may offer a beautiful prayer of thanksgiving, but the other person is not being built up. ¹⁸I thank God that I speak in tongues more than all of you. ¹⁹But in the church I'd rather speak five words in my right mind than speak thousands of words in a tongue so that I can teach others.

²⁰Brothers and sisters, don't be like children in the way you think. Well, be babies when it comes to evil, but be adults in your thinking. ²¹In the Law it is written: *I will speak to this people with foreign languages and foreigners' lips, but they will not even listen to me this way,*ᵖ says the Lord. ²²So then, tongues are a sign for those who don't believe, not for those who believe. But prophecy is a sign for believers, not for those who don't believe. ²³So suppose that the whole church is meeting and everyone is speaking in tongues. If people come in who are outsiders or unbelievers, won't they say that you are out of your minds? ²⁴But if everyone is prophesying when an unbeliever or outsider comes in, they are tested by all and called to account by all. ²⁵The secrets of their hearts are brought to light. When that happens, they will fall on their faces and worship God, proclaiming out loud that truly God is among you!

²⁶What is the outcome of this, brothers and sisters? When you meet together, each one has a psalm, a teaching, a revelation, a tongue, or an interpretation. All these things must be done to build up the church. ²⁷If some speak in a tongue, then let two or at most three speak, one at a time, and someone must interpret. ²⁸However, if there is no interpreter, then they should keep quiet in the meeting. They should speak privately to themselves and to God. ²⁹In the case of prophets, let two or three speak and have the rest evaluate what is said. ³⁰And if some revelation comes to someone else who is sitting down, the first one should be quiet. ³¹You can all prophesy one at a time so that everyone can learn and be encouraged. ³²The spirits of prophets are under the control of the prophets. ³³God isn't a God of disorder but of peace. Like in all the churches of God's people, ³⁴the women should be quiet during the meeting. They are not allowed to talk. Instead, they need to get under control, just as the Law says. ³⁵If they want to learn something, they should ask their husbands at home. It is disgraceful for a woman to talk during the meeting.

³⁶Did the word of God originate with you? Has it come only to you? ³⁷If anyone thinks that they are prophets or "spiritual people," then let them recognize that what I'm writing to you is the Lord's command. ³⁸If someone doesn't recognize this, they aren't recognized. ³⁹So then, brothers and sisters, use your ambition to try to get the gift of prophecy, but don't prevent speaking in tongues. ⁴⁰Everything should be done with dignity and in proper order.

ᵖIsa 28:11-12

The resurrection

15 Brothers and sisters, I want to call your attention to the good news that I preached to you, which you also received and in which you stand. ²You are being saved through it if you hold on to the message I preached to you, unless somehow you believed it for nothing. ³I passed on to you as most important what I also received: Christ died for our sins in line with the scriptures, ⁴he was buried, and he rose on the third day in line with the scriptures. ⁵He appeared to Cephas, then to the Twelve, ⁶and then he appeared to more than five hundred brothers and sisters at once—most of them are still alive to this day, though some have died. ⁷Then he appeared to James, then to all the apostles, ⁸and last of all he appeared to me, as if I were born at the wrong time. ⁹I'm the least important of the apostles. I don't deserve to be called an apostle, because I harassed God's church. ¹⁰I am what I am by God's grace, and God's grace hasn't been for nothing. In fact, I have worked harder than all the others—that is, it wasn't me but the grace of God that is with me. ¹¹So then, whether you heard the message from me or them, this is what we preach and this is what you have believed.

¹²So if the message that is preached says that Christ has been raised from the dead, then how can some of you say, "There's no resurrection of the dead"? ¹³If there's no resurrection of the dead, then Christ hasn't been raised either. ¹⁴If Christ hasn't been raised, then our preaching is useless and your faith is useless. ¹⁵We are found to be false witnesses about God, because we testified against God that he raised Christ, when he didn't raise him if it's the case that the dead aren't raised. ¹⁶If the dead aren't raised, then Christ hasn't been raised either. ¹⁷If Christ hasn't been raised, then your faith is worthless; you are still in your sins, ¹⁸and what's more, those who have died in Christ are gone forever. ¹⁹If we have a hope in Christ only in this life, then we deserve to be pitied more than anyone else.

²⁰But in fact Christ has been raised from the dead. He's the first crop of the harvest[q] of those who have died. ²¹Since death came through a human being, the resurrection of the dead came through one too. ²²In the same way that everyone dies in Adam, so also everyone will be given life in Christ. ²³Each event will happen in the right order: Christ, the first crop of the harvest,[r] then those who belong to Christ at his coming, ²⁴and then the end, when Christ hands over the kingdom to God the Father, when he brings every form of rule, every authority and power to an end. ²⁵It is necessary for him to rule until *he puts all enemies under his feet.*[s] ²⁶Death is the last enemy to be brought to an end, ²⁷since he has brought everything under control under his feet. When it says that everything has been brought under his control, this clearly means everything except for the one who placed everything under his control. ²⁸But when all things have been brought under his control, then the Son himself will also be under the control of the one who gave him control over everything so that God may be all in all.

²⁹Otherwise, what are those who are getting baptized for the dead doing? If the

---

[q]Or *firstfruits* [r]Or *firstfruits* [s]Ps 110:1

SECOND ADAM

Paul calls Jesus the "last Adam" in 1 Corinthians 15:45. He contrasts the first Adam, created as a living being (Gen 2:7), with the last Adam, who "became a spirit that gives life." Paul states that in the first Adam all die, while "everyone will be given life in Christ" (1 Cor 15:22).

dead aren't raised, then why are they being baptized for them? ³⁰And what about us? Why are we in danger all day every day? ³¹Brothers and sisters, I swear by the pride I have in you in Christ Jesus our Lord, I'm facing death every day. ³²From a human point of view, what good does it do me if I fought wild animals in Ephesus? If the dead aren't raised, *let's eat and drink because tomorrow we'll die.*ᵗ ³³Don't be deceived, bad company corrupts good character. ³⁴Sober up by acting like you should and don't sin. Some of you are ignorant about God—I say this because you should be ashamed of yourselves!

³⁵But someone will say, "How are the dead raised? What kind of body will they have when they come back?" ³⁶Look, fool! When you put a seed into the ground, it doesn't come back to life unless it dies. ³⁷What you put in the ground doesn't have the shape that it will have, but it's a bare grain of wheat or some other seed. ³⁸God gives it the sort of shape that he chooses, and he gives each of the seeds its own shape. ³⁹All flesh isn't alike. Humans have one kind of flesh, animals have another kind of flesh, birds have another kind of flesh, and fish have another kind. ⁴⁰There are heavenly bodies and earthly bodies. The heavenly bodies have one kind of glory, and the earthly bodies have another kind of glory. ⁴¹The sun has one kind of glory, the moon has another kind of glory, and the stars have another kind of glory (but one star is different from another star in its glory). ⁴²It's the same with the resurrection of the dead: a rotting body is put into the ground, but what is raised won't ever decay. ⁴³It's degraded when it's put into the ground, but it's raised in glory. It's weak when it's put into the ground, but it's raised in power. ⁴⁴It's a physical body when it's put into the ground, but it's raised as a spiritual body.

If there's a physical body, there's also a spiritual body. ⁴⁵So it is also written, *The first human, Adam, became a living person,*ᵘ and the last Adam became a spirit that gives

life. ⁴⁶But the physical body comes first, not the spiritual one—the spiritual body comes afterward. ⁴⁷The first human was from the earth made from dust; the second human is from heaven. ⁴⁸The nature of the person made of dust is shared by people who are made of dust, and the nature of the heavenly person is shared by heavenly people. ⁴⁹We will look likeᵛ the heavenly person in the same way as we have looked like the person made from dust.

⁵⁰This is what I'm saying, brothers and sisters: Flesh and blood can't inherit God's kingdom. Something that rots can't inherit something that doesn't decay. ⁵¹Listen, I'm telling you a secret: All of us won't die, but we will all be changed—⁵²in an instant, in the blink of an eye, at the final trumpet. The trumpet will blast, and the dead will be raised with bodies that won't decay, and we will be changed. ⁵³It's necessary for this rotting body to be clothed with what can't decay, and for the body that is dying to be clothed in what can't die. ⁵⁴And when the rotting body has been clothed in what can't decay, and the dying body has been clothed in what can't die, then this statement in scripture will happen:

*Death has been swallowed up by a victory.*ʷ
⁵⁵ *Where is your victory, Death?*
    *Where is your sting, Death?*ˣ

(⁵⁶Death's sting is sin, and the power of sin is the Law.) ⁵⁷Thanks be to God, who gives us this victory through our Lord Jesus Christ! ⁵⁸As a result of all this, my loved brothers and sisters, you must stand firm, unshakable, excelling in the work of the Lord as always, because you know that your labor isn't going to be for nothing in the Lord.

Collection for Jerusalem

16 Concerning the collection of money for God's people: You should do what I have directed the churches in Galatia to do. ²On the first day of the week, each of you should set aside whatever you can afford from what you earn so that the collection won't be delayed until I come. ³Then

---

ᵗIsa 22:13 ᵘGen 2:7 ᵛOr *bear the image of* ʷIsa 25:8 ˣHos 13:14

when I get there, I'll send whomever you approve to Jerusalem with letters of recommendation to bring your gift. [4] If it seems right for me to go too, they'll travel with me.

Plans to visit

[5] I'll come to you after I go through Macedonia, and because I'm going through Macedonia, [6] I may stay with you or even spend the winter there in Corinth so that you can send me on my way to wherever I'm off to next. [7] I don't want to make a quick visit to you, since I hope to spend some time with you if the Lord lets it happen. [8] I'll stay here in Ephesus until the Festival of Pentecost. [9] In spite of the fact that there are many opponents, a big and productive opportunity has opened up for my mission here.

[10] If Timothy comes to you, be sure that he has no reason to be afraid while he's with you, because he does the work of the Lord just like I do. [11] So don't let anyone disrespect him, but send him on in peace so he can join me. I'm waiting for him along with the brothers and sisters. [12] Concerning Apollos our brother: I strongly encouraged him to visit you with the brothers and sisters, but he didn't want to go now. He'll come when he has an opportunity.

Final greeting

[13] Stay awake, stand firm in your faith, be brave, be strong. [14] Everything should be done in love.

[15] Brothers and sisters, I encourage you to do something else. You know that the people in Stephanas' household were the first crop of the harvest to come from the mission to Achaia. They have dedicated themselves to the service of God's people. [16] So accept the authority of people like them and of anyone who cooperates and works hard. [17] I'm so happy that Stephanas, Fortunatus, and Achaicus have arrived; they've made up for my missing you. [18] Indeed they've provided my spirit and yours with a much-needed rest. Therefore, give them proper recognition.

[19] The churches in the province of Asia greet you. Aquila and Prisca greet you warmly in the Lord, together with the church that meets in their house. [20] All the brothers and sisters greet you. You in turn should greet each other with a holy kiss. [21] Here is my greeting in my own handwriting—Paul.

[22] A curse on anyone who doesn't love the Lord. Come, Lord! [23] The grace of the Lord Jesus be with you. [24] My love is with all of you in Christ Jesus.

MARANATHA

The Gk. transliteration of the Aram. expression "Come, Lord!" or "Our Lord has come." Paul used the term in his closing words to the Corinthian congregation (1 Cor 16:22) to encourage them that Jesus would be returning within their lifetimes.

2 CORINTHIANS

THEME

The nature of Christian ministry

THE IMPORTANCE OF THE CORINTHIAN LETTERS

In Paul's day, Corinth must have been an exciting and very modern place. The problems and difficulties of the first Christians in that fast-paced city of Corinth remain very real issues today. Questions of wisdom, Christian knowledge, lifestyles, death, love, marriage, worship, suffering, and so forth remain very serious issues for believers of all ages. Because Paul boldly addresses these Christian concerns, the Corinthian correspondence is a major help in working through these ever-present Christian issues. Here, perhaps more than anywhere else, Paul achieves a profound balance between doctrinal statement and practical Christian living.

THE TIME AND OCCASION FOR 2 CORINTHIANS

Second Corinthians is more difficult to date than 1 Corinthians, because 2 Corinthians appears to be made up of more than one letter, each reflecting different occasions and circumstances (many scholars argue that chapters 1–9 and 10–13 are two separate letters). But, even if there is more than one letter contained in 2 Corinthians, Paul was writing not long after his 1 Corinthians letter. Probably about one year later, that is, 54 or 55 CE, Paul met with Titus in Macedonia and was greatly encouraged because of what he heard about the believers at Corinth (2 Corinthians 7:5-9). This news may have led Paul to dash off a letter telling of his care for the Corinthian believers (chapters 1–9). It was perhaps a little later that Paul received some disturbing news and wrote again, attacking the false apostles (2 Corinthians 11:13).

For the most part, Paul's letters are courteous and considerate. They attempt to address the down-to-earth concrete situations and problems with which the various Christian communities of the Mediterranean world struggled. But at times Paul does become less than gentle with his new converts. He refers to the Galatians as being foolish and bewitched (Galatians 3:1; his emotion is also expressed in Galatians 4:19). He affectionately refers to the Christians at Thessalonica as children in need of nursing (1 Thessalonians 2:7-8; see also 3:7-8). And to the Corinthians he speaks of his hardship and anxiety for all the churches that have made him indignant about their fall from the true gospel (2 Corinthians 11:21-29).

THE NUMBER OF CORINTHIAN LETTERS

How many letters did Paul write to the Corinthians? The question has been raised by Paul's own statements. In 1 Corinthians he refers to his "earlier letter" (1 Corinthians 5:9-11), suggesting that 1 Corinthians is not his first letter. Because of the immorality theme of this previous letter (1 Corinthians 5:9), at least a portion of it could be identified with the same theme found in a section of 2 Corinthians (2 Corinthians 6:14–7:1). If this previous letter is contained in 2 Corinthians, then it follows that 2 Corinthians is composed of several letters from Paul to the Corinthian churches.

If shorter communications of Paul have been blended into this letter, they probably were combined to make them available for all the cell house churches. Over time, these letters would have been viewed as one document. Regardless of how many letters make up 2 Corinthians, the letter brings us teachings, explanations, and directives from Paul to the church at Corinth.

PAUL'S OPPONENTS AT CORINTH AND THE GOSPEL

In 1 Corinthians, Paul addresses a host of problems that are unlikely to all come from one group of people or even from a single house church. He discusses many problems of sexual relationships (1 Corinthians 5:1-13), marriage (7:1-16), spiritual wisdom (2:6-16), death (chapter 15), and so forth. Paul's first letter more accurately reflects various tensions, disagreements, and opinions from any number of groups (including Gnostic groups) that affected the young house churches on occasion.

In 2 Corinthians, Paul does refer specifically to some opponents who are causing trouble and undermining his authority in Corinth (2 Corinthians 10–13). He sarcastically calls these people "super-apostles" (11:5; 12:11). They apparently were claiming that Paul's speech lacked authority and power (11:6); that Paul did not perform signs and wonders (12:12); and that his personal finances were suspect (11:7-9; 12:13-18). Paul aggressively defends the legitimacy and integrity of his apostolic activity in chapters 10 through 13.

Paul's correspondence always addresses and responds to real-life situations. Frequently Paul's letters are profound and theological (2 Corinthians 10:10). But this is because Paul attempts to encourage believers to live in thankful response to God's grace in Christ from their particular station in life. This was certainly the situation throughout his sometimes stormy relationship with the believers at Corinth. The Corinthian letters have always been and remain today a wonderful example of ministry for laity and pastors.

2 CORINTHIANS

Greeting

1 From Paul, an apostle of Christ Jesus by God's will, and Timothy our brother. To God's church that is in Corinth, along with all of God's people throughout Achaia.

2 Grace to you and peace from God our Father and from our Lord Jesus Christ.

God's comfort in trouble

3 May the God and Father of our Lord Jesus Christ be blessed! He is the compassionate Father and God of all comfort. 4 He's the one who comforts us in all our trouble so that we can comfort other people who are in every kind of trouble. We offer the same comfort that we ourselves received from God. 5 That is because we receive so much comfort through Christ in the same way that we share so many of Christ's sufferings. 6 So if we have trouble, it is to bring you comfort and salvation. If we are comforted, it is to bring you comfort from the experience of endurance while you go through the same sufferings that we also suffer. 7 Our hope for you is certain, because we know that as you are partners in suffering, so also you are partners in comfort.

8 Brothers and sisters, we don't want you to be unaware of the troubles that we went through in Asia. We were weighed down with a load of suffering that was so far beyond our strength that we were afraid we might not survive. 9 It certainly seemed to us as if we had gotten the death penalty. This was so that we would have confidence in God, who raises the dead, instead of ourselves. 10 God rescued us from a terrible death, and he will rescue us. We have set our hope on him that he will rescue us again, 11 since you are helping with your prayer for us. Then many people can thank God on our behalf for the gift that was given to us through the prayers of many people.

Paul explains his change of plans

12 We have conducted ourselves with godly sincerity and pure motives in the world, and especially toward you. This is why we are confident, and our conscience confirms this. We didn't act with human wisdom but we relied on the grace of God. 13 We don't write anything to you except what you can read and also understand. I hope that you will understand totally 14 since you have already understood us partly. Understand that in the day of our Lord Jesus, we will make you proud as you will also make us proud.

15 Because I was sure of this, I wanted to visit you first so that you could have a second opportunity to see me. 16 I wanted to visit you on my way to Macedonia, and then come to you again on my way back from Macedonia, at which point I was hoping you would help me on my way to Judea.

17 So I wasn't unreliable when I planned to do this, was I? Or do I make decisions with a substandard human process so that I say "Yes, yes" and "No, no" at the same time? 18 But as God is faithful, our message to you isn't both yes and no. 19 God's Son, Jesus Christ, is the one who was preached

CORINTH

City commanding the isthmus linking the Peloponnese to mainland Greece. Paul worked with Prisca (Priscilla) and Aquila for 18 months while founding the church there (50–52 CE [Acts 18:1-18]). He made two subsequent visits (2 Cor 12:14; 13:1), on the second of which he wrote Romans. He wrote a series of letters to the community, at least two of which have been lost (1 Cor 5:9; 2 Cor 2:4).

among you by us—through me, Silvanus, and Timothy—he wasn't yes and no. In him it is always yes. ²⁰All of God's promises have their yes in him. That is why we say Amen through him to the glory of God.

²¹God is the one who establishes us with you in Christ and who anointed us. ²²God also sealed us and gave the Spirit as a down payment in our hearts. ²³I call on God as my witness—I didn't come again to Corinth because I wanted to spare you. ²⁴It isn't that we are trying to control your faith, but we are working with you for your happiness, because you stand firm in your faith.

2 So I decided that, for my own sake, I wouldn't visit you again while I was upset. ²If I make you sad, who will be there to make me glad when you are sad because of me?

Paul's former letter

³That's why I wrote this very thing to you, so that when I came I wouldn't be made sad by the ones who ought to make

MACEDONIA

The Roman province of Macedonia lay in the northern part of Greece and extended beyond the historic kingdom of Macedonia, from the Adriatic east to Thrace. To the north were the provinces of Illyricum and Moesia. Southward it took in the area of Thessaly (and the mountainous range around Olympus). To the southwest of Macedonia was the region of Epirus, and to the south the province of Achaia.

In the NT Paul was invited to "come over to Macedonia" in a dream, while he was at Troas in northwestern Anatolia (Acts 16:9-10). He arrived in the province at Neapolis (the modern Kavala opposite the island of Thasos), the harbor for the main Roman colony of Philippi (Acts 16:11). At Philippi, Paul established a church whose members included Lydia from Thyatira (Acts 16:14). After Paul and Silas had been arrested, beaten, and imprisoned (Acts 16:19-40), the pair headed west along the line of the Roman road passing through the cities of Amphipolis and Apollonia (Acts 17:1). They then arrived at the major seaport of Thessalonica, where there was a Jewish community (Acts 17). There was an uproar in response to their preaching in the city. Paul and Silas were sent west to Beroea (Acts 17:10). Paul was sent off by sea to Athens while Timothy and Silas remained in the city (Acts 17:14).

Timothy and Erastus were sent to Macedonia from the province of Asia (Acts 19:21-22); Paul followed on, traveling through Macedonia and continuing down to Greece (the province of Achaia) (Acts 20:1-3). He then returned through Macedonia accompanied by several Macedonians, Sopater son of Pyrrhus from Beroea, and Aristarchus and Secundus from Thessalonica (Acts 20:3-6). Aristarchus and another Macedonian, Gaius—clearly Roman in origin—had accompanied Paul in Ephesus (Acts 19:29). It was perhaps during this second visit to northern Greece that Paul found himself at Illyricum on the Adriatic (Rom 15:19). His departure from Philippi (Acts 20:6) may perhaps be dated to the Passover of 57 CE.

Two major churches were established in Macedonia: at Philippi and Thessalonica. They were the recipients of three NT Epistles.

me happy. I have confidence in you, that my happiness means your happiness. [4]I wrote to you in tears, with a very troubled and anxious heart. I didn't write to make you sad but so you would know the overwhelming love that I have for you.

[5]But if someone has made anyone sad, that person hasn't hurt me but all of you to some degree (not to exaggerate). [6]The punishment handed out by the majority is enough for this person. [7]This is why you should try your best to forgive and to comfort this person now instead, so that this person isn't overwhelmed by too much sorrow. [8]So I encourage you to show your love for this person.

[9]This is another reason why I wrote you. I wanted to test you and see if you are obedient in everything. [10]If you forgive anyone for anything, I do too. And whatever I've forgiven (if I've forgiven anything), I did it for you in the presence of Christ. [11]This is so that we won't be taken advantage of by Satan, because we are well aware of his schemes.

Paul's ministry

[12]When I came to Troas to preach Christ's gospel, the Lord gave me an opportunity to preach. [13]But I was worried because I couldn't find my brother Titus there. So I said good-bye to them and went on to Macedonia.

[14]But thank God, who is always leading us around through Christ as if we were in a parade. He releases the fragrance of the knowledge of him everywhere through us. [15]We smell like the aroma of Christ's of-

fering to God, both to those who are being saved and to those who are on the road to destruction. [16]We smell like a contagious dead person to those who are dying, but we smell like the fountain of life to those who are being saved.

Who is qualified for this kind of ministry? [17]We aren't like so many people who hustle the word of God to make a profit. We are speaking through Christ in the presence of God, as those who are sincere and as those who are sent from God.

3 Are we starting to commend ourselves again? We don't need letters of introduction to you or from you like other people, do we? [2]You are our letter, written on our hearts, known and read by everyone. [3]You show that you are Christ's letter, delivered by us. You weren't written with ink but with the Spirit of the living God. You weren't written on tablets of stone but on tablets of human hearts.

[4]This is the confidence that we have through Christ in the presence of God. [5]It isn't that we ourselves are qualified to claim that anything came from us. No, our qualification is from God. [6]He has qualified us as ministers of a new covenant, not based on what is written but on the Spirit, because what is written kills, but the Spirit gives life.

Ministers of the new covenant

[7]The ministry that brought death was carved in letters on stone tablets. It came with such glory that the Israelites couldn't look for long at Moses' face because his face was shining with glory, even though it was a fading glory. [8]Won't the ministry of the

NEW TESTAMENT

Commonly refers to the 27 books comprising the second portion of the Christian scriptures, the first portion being the OT. The Greek phrase (1 Cor 11:25; 2 Cor 3:6; Heb 8:8, 13; 9:15) has a variant translation of "new covenant" in reference to the covenant of Jeremiah 31:31-34. The transfer of the language from "covenant" to a body of writings reflects Paul's use of "old covenant" to refer to the writings of the Mosaic covenant (e.g., 2 Cor 3:14).

Spirit be much more glorious? [9]If the ministry that brought condemnation has glory, how much more glorious is the ministry that brings righteousness? [10]In fact, what was glorious isn't glorious now, because of the glory that is brighter. [11]If the glory that fades away was glorious, how much more glorious is the one that lasts!

[12]So, since we have such a hope, we act with great confidence. [13]We aren't like Moses, who used to put a veil over his face so that the Israelites couldn't watch the end of what was fading away. [14]But their minds were closed. Right up to the present day the same veil remains when the old covenant is read. The veil is not removed because it is taken away by Christ. [15]Even today, whenever Moses is read, a veil lies over their hearts. [16]But whenever someone turns back to the Lord, the veil is removed. [17]The Lord is the Spirit, and where the Lord's Spirit is, there is freedom. [18]All of us are looking with unveiled faces at the glory of the Lord as if we were looking in a mirror. We are being transformed into that same image from one degree of glory to the next degree of glory. This comes from the Lord, who is the Spirit.

4 This is why we don't get discouraged, given that we received this ministry in the same way that we received God's mercy. [2]Instead, we reject secrecy and shameful actions. We don't use deception, and we don't tamper with God's word. Instead, we commend ourselves to everyone's conscience in the sight of God by the public announcement of the truth. [3]And even if our gospel is veiled, it is veiled to those who are on the road to destruction. [4]The god of this age has blinded the minds of those who don't have faith so they couldn't see the light of the gospel that reveals Christ's glory. Christ is the image of God.

[5]We don't preach about ourselves. Instead, we preach about Jesus Christ as Lord, and we describe ourselves as your slaves for Jesus' sake. [6]God said that light should shine out of the darkness. He is the same one who shone in our hearts to give us the light of the knowledge of God's glory in the face of Jesus Christ.

Physical bodies and eternal glory

[7]But we have this treasure in clay pots so that the awesome power belongs to God and doesn't come from us. [8]We are experiencing all kinds of trouble, but we aren't crushed. We are confused, but we aren't depressed. [9]We are harassed, but we aren't abandoned. We are knocked down, but we aren't knocked out.

[10]We always carry Jesus' death around in our bodies so that Jesus' life can also be seen in our bodies. [11]We who are alive are always being handed over to death for Jesus' sake so that Jesus' life can also be seen in our bodies that are dying. [12]So death is at work in us, but life is at work in you.

[13]We have the same faithful spirit as what is written in scripture: *I had faith, and so I spoke.*[a] We also have faith, and so we also speak. [14]We do this because we know that the one who raised the Lord Jesus will also raise us with Jesus, and he will bring us into his presence along with you. [15]All these things are for your benefit. As grace increases to benefit more and more people, it will cause gratitude to increase, which results in God's glory.

[16]So we aren't depressed. But even if our bodies are breaking down on the outside, the person that we are on the inside is being renewed every day. [17]Our temporary minor problems are producing an eternal stockpile of glory for us that is beyond all comparison. [18]We don't focus on the things that can be seen but on the things that can't be seen. The things that can be seen don't last, but the things that can't be seen are eternal.

5 We know that if the tent that we live in on earth is torn down, we have a building from God. It's a house that isn't handmade, which is eternal and located in heaven. [2]We groan while we live in this residence. We really want to dress ourselves

[a]Ps 116:10 (115:1 LXX)

with our building from heaven—[3]since we assume that when we take off this tent, we won't find out that we are naked. [4]Yes, while we are in this tent we groan, because we are weighed down. We want to be dressed not undressed, so that what is dying can be swallowed up by life. [5]Now the one who prepared us for this very thing is God, and God gave us the Spirit as a down payment for our home.

[6]So we are always confident, because we know that while we are living in the body, we are away from our home with the Lord. [7]We live by faith and not by sight. [8]We are confident, and we would prefer to leave the body and to be at home with the Lord. [9]So our goal is to be acceptable to him, whether we are at home or away from home. [10]We all must appear before Christ in court so that each person can be paid back for the things that were done while in the body, whether they were good or bad.

Ministry of reconciliation

[11]So we try to persuade people, since we know what it means to fear the Lord. We are well known by God, and I hope that in your heart we are well known by you as well. [12]We aren't trying to commend ourselves to you again. Instead, we are giving you an opportunity to be proud of us so that you could answer those who take pride in superficial appearance, and not in what is in the heart.

[13]If we are crazy, it's for God's sake. If we are rational, it's for your sake. [14]The love of Christ controls us, because we have concluded this: one died for the sake of all; therefore, all died. [15]He died for the sake of all so that those who are alive should live not for themselves but for the one who died for them and was raised.

[16]So then, from this point on we won't recognize people by human standards. Even though we used to know Christ by

TENT

Portable dwelling used by nomads, shepherds, and armies. The structure consisted of poles held upright and connected with cords stretched between them and grounded with wooden pegs hammered into the ground using a wooden mallet. Hand-woven goat's hair, animal skins, or other materials served as covering for the roof and sides (Judg 4:21; Song 1:5; Isa 40:22; 54:2; Jer 10:20).

After settling in Canaan, the Israelites generally lived in houses, although soldiers camped in tents during military expeditions (1 Sam 29:1). *Tent* sometimes was used to refer to the more permanent "home" (1 Kgs 8:66). Prior to the construction of the Jerusalem temple, the Israelites utilized a movable sanctuary called the "meeting tent" or simply the "tent" (Exod 33:7-11).

In the NT, *tent* often has this OT concept of tent in view. For example, Hebrews 8–9, in which approximately half the NT occurrences of the term are located, compares the earthly tent constructed by Moses and the true or heavenly tent (see also Acts 7:43-44). The NT also speaks of tents as the portable dwellings of the ancestors Abraham, Isaac, and Jacob (Heb 11:9) and metaphorically as the "fallen tent" or house/kingdom of David (Acts 15:16). In 2 Corinthians 5:1-5 the apostle Paul contrasts the metaphorical "tent that we live in on earth" that the Corinthians live in now with the "building from heaven" with which God will clothe them and for which the Spirit was sent as a guarantee.

human standards, that isn't how we know him now. [17]So then, if anyone is in Christ, that person is part of the new creation. The old things have gone away, and look, new things have arrived!

[18]All of these new things are from God, who reconciled us to himself through Christ and who gave us the ministry of reconciliation. [19]In other words, God was reconciling the world to himself through Christ, by not counting people's sins against them. He has trusted us with this message of reconciliation.

[20]So we are ambassadors who represent Christ. God is negotiating with you through us. We beg you as Christ's representatives, "Be reconciled to God!" [21]God caused the one who didn't know sin to be sin for our sake so that through him we could become the righteousness of God.

6 Since we work together with him, we are also begging you not to receive the grace of God in vain. [2]He says, *I listened to you at the right time, and I helped you on the day of salvation.*[b] Look, now is the right time! Look, now is the day of salvation!

[3]We don't give anyone any reason to be offended about anything so that our ministry won't be criticized. [4]Instead, we commend ourselves as ministers of God in every way. We did this with our great endurance through problems, disasters, and stressful situations. [5]We went through beatings, imprisonments, and riots. We experienced hard work, sleepless nights, and hunger. [6]We displayed purity, knowledge, patience, and generosity. We served with the Holy Spirit, genuine love, [7]telling the truth, and God's power. We carried the weapons of righteousness in our right hand and our left hand. [8]We were treated with honor and dishonor and with verbal abuse and good evaluation. We were seen as both fake and real, [9]as unknown and well known, as dying—and look, we are alive! We were seen as punished but not killed, [10]as going through pain but always happy, as poor but making many rich, and as having nothing but owning everything.

Call to relationship and holiness

[11]Corinthians, we have spoken openly to you, and our hearts are wide open. [12]There are no limits to the affection that we feel for you. You are the ones who placed boundaries on your affection for us. [13]But as a fair trade—I'm talking to you like you are children—open your hearts wide too.

[14]Don't be tied up as equal partners with people who don't believe. What does righteousness share with that which is outside the Law? What relationship does light have with darkness? [15]What harmony does Christ have with Satan?[c] What does a believer have in common with someone who doesn't believe? [16]What agreement can there be between God's temple and idols? Because we are the temple of the living God. Just as God said, *I live with them, and I will move among them. I will be their God, and they will be my people.*[d] [17]Therefore, *come out from among them and be separated, says the Lord. Don't touch what is unclean. Then I will welcome you.*[e] [18]*I will be a father to you, and you will be my sons and daughters, says the Lord Almighty.*[f] [1]My dear friends, since we have these promises, let's cleanse ourselves from anything that contaminates our body or spirit so that we make our holiness complete in the fear of God.

[2]Make room in your hearts for us. We didn't do anything wrong to anyone. We didn't ruin anyone. We didn't take advantage of anyone. [3]I'm not saying this to make you feel guilty. I've already said that you are in our hearts so that we die and live together with you. [4]I have every confidence in you. I'm terribly proud of you. I'm filled with encouragement. I'm overwhelmed with happiness while in the middle of our problems.

Titus' good report

[5]Even after we arrived in Macedonia, we couldn't rest physically. We were surrounded by problems. There was external conflict, and there were internal fears. [6]However, God comforts people who are discouraged, and he comforted us by Titus' arrival. [7]We

---

[b]Isa 49:8 [c]Or *Beliah* [d]Lev 26:11-12 [e]Isa 52:11; Ezek 20:34, 41 [f]2 Sam 7:14

weren't comforted only by his arrival but also by the comfort he had received from you. He told us about your desire to see me, how you were sorry, and about your concern for me, so that I was even happier.

⁸Even though my letter hurt you, I don't regret it. Well—I did regret it just a bit because I see that that letter made you sad, though only for a short time. ⁹Now I'm glad—not because you were sad but because you were made sad enough to change your hearts and lives. You felt godly sadness so that no one was harmed by us in any way. ¹⁰Godly sadness produces a changed heart and life that leads to salvation and leaves no regrets, but sorrow under the influence of the world produces death. ¹¹Look at what this very experience of godly sadness has produced in you: such enthusiasm, what a desire to clear yourselves of blame, such indignation, what fear, what purpose, such concern, what justice! In everything you have shown yourselves to be innocent in the matter.

¹²So although I wrote to you, it wasn't for the sake of the one who did wrong, or for the sake of the one who was wronged, but to show you your own enthusiasm for us in the sight of God. ¹³Because of this we have been encouraged. And in addition to our own encouragement, we were even more pleased at how happy Titus was. His mind has been put at rest by all of you. ¹⁴If I've bragged about you to him in any way, I haven't been embarrassed. Instead, our bragging to Titus has also been proven to be true, just like everything we said to you was true. ¹⁵His devotion to you is growing even more as he remembers how all of you were obedient when you welcomed him with fear and trembling. ¹⁶I'm happy, because I can completely depend on you.

Encouragement to give generously

8 Brothers and sisters, we want to let you know about the grace of God that was given to the churches of Macedonia. ²While they were being tested by many problems, their extra amount of happiness and their extreme poverty resulted in a surplus of rich generosity. ³I assure you that they gave what they could afford and even more than they could afford, and they did it voluntarily. ⁴They urgently begged us for the privilege^g of sharing in this service for the saints. ⁵They even exceeded our expectations, because they gave themselves to the Lord first and to us, consistent with God's will. ⁶As a result, we challenged Titus to finish this work of grace with you the way he had started it.

⁷Be the best in this work of grace in the same way that you are the best in everything, such as faith, speech, knowledge, total commitment, and the love we inspired in you. ⁸I'm not giving an order, but by mentioning the commitment of others, I'm trying to prove the authenticity of your love also. ⁹You know the grace of our Lord Jesus Christ. Although he was rich, he became poor for our sakes, so that you could become rich through his poverty.

^{g}Or grace

TITUS

Titus was a traveling companion of Paul by the time of the visit to Jerusalem recorded in Galatians 2:1 (identified as either Acts 11:27-30; 12:25; or 15:1-29). From a Gentile background (Gal 2:3), possibly in Antioch, he may have come to faith in Christ through Paul (Titus 1:4). He accompanied Paul for some years on his travels. Paul speaks of him with great affection as "my brother" (2 Cor 2:13) and "my partner and coworker" (2 Cor 8:23), terms that Paul rarely or never uses for others.

[10]I'm giving you my opinion about this. It's to your advantage to do this, since you not only started to do it last year but you wanted to do it too. [11]Now finish the job as well so that you finish it with as much enthusiasm as you started, given what you can afford. [12]A gift is appreciated because of what a person can afford, not because of what that person can't afford, if it's apparent that it's done willingly. [13]It isn't that we want others to have financial ease and you financial difficulties, but it's a matter of equality. [14]At the present moment, your surplus can fill their deficit so that in the future their surplus can fill your deficit. In this way there is equality. [15]As it is written, *The one who gathered more didn't have too much, and the one who gathered less didn't have too little.*[h]

Plans for the Collection

[16]But thank God, who put the same commitment that I have for you in Titus' heart. [17]Not only has he accepted our challenge but he's on his way to see you voluntarily, and he's excited. [18]We are sending the brother who is famous in all the churches because of his work for the gospel along with him. [19]In addition to this, he is chosen by the churches to be our traveling companion in this work of grace, which we are taking care of for the sake of the glory of the Lord himself, and to show our desire to help. [20]We are trying to avoid being blamed by anyone for the way we take care of this large amount of money. [21]We care about doing the right thing, not only in the Lord's eyes but also in the eyes of other people.

[22]We are sending our brother with them. We have tested his commitment in many ways and many times. Now he's even more committed, because he has so much confidence in you. [23]If there is any question about Titus, he is my partner and co-worker among you. If there is any question about our brothers, they are the churches' apostles and an honor to Christ. [24]So show them the proof of your love and the reason we are so proud of you, in such a way that the churches can see it.

9 It's unnecessary for me to write to you about this service for God's people. [2]I know about your willingness to help. I brag about you to the Macedonians, saying, "Greece has been ready since last year," and your enthusiasm has motivated most of them.

[3]But I'm sending the brothers so that our bragging about you in this case won't be empty words, and so that you can be prepared, just as I keep telling them you will be. [4]If some Macedonians should come with me and find out that you aren't ready, we (not to mention you) would be embarrassed as far as this project goes.

[5]This is why I thought it was necessary to encourage the brothers to go to you ahead of time and arrange in advance the generous gift you have already promised. I want it to be a real gift from you. I don't want you to feel like you are being forced to give

[h]Exod 16:18

THE COLLECTION

Paul organized a large ecumenical collection for the poor in the Jerusalem churches in various Christian communities under his control between 48 and 57 CE. His various references to this ambitious venture indicate that it was not just an "ordinary" fund-raising project (1 Cor 16:1-4; 2 Cor 8-9; Gal 2:10; Rom 15:25-27). The collection was important for building the church, because it was a concrete expression of the unity between Jewish and Gentile Christians.

anything. [6]What I mean is this: the one who sows a small number of seeds will also reap a small crop, and the one who sows a generous amount of seeds will also reap a generous crop.

[7]Everyone should give whatever they have decided in their heart. They shouldn't give with hesitation or because of pressure. God loves a cheerful giver. [8]God has the power to provide you with more than enough of every kind of grace. That way, you will have everything you need always and in everything to provide more than enough for every kind of good work. [9]As it is written, *He scattered everywhere; he gave to the needy; his righteousness remains forever.*[i]

[10]The one who supplies seed for planting and bread for eating will supply and multiply your seed and will increase your crop, which is righteousness. [11]You will be made rich in every way so that you can be generous in every way. Such generosity produces thanksgiving to God through us. [12]Your ministry of this service to God's people isn't only fully meeting their needs but it is also multiplying in many expressions of thanksgiving to God. [13]They will give honor to God for your obedience to your confession of Christ's gospel. They will do this because this service provides evidence of your obedience, and because of your generosity in sharing with them and with everyone. [14]They will also pray for you, and they will care deeply for you because of the outstanding grace that God has given to you. [15]Thank God for his gift that words can't describe!

Paul's personal request for obedience

10 [1]I, Paul, make a personal request to you with the gentleness and kindness of Christ. I'm shy when I'm with you, but I'm bossy when I'm away from you! [2]I beg you that when I'm with you in person, I won't have to boss you around. I'm afraid that I may have to use that kind of behavior with those people who think we live by human standards. [3]Although we live in the world, we don't fight our battles with human methods. [4]Our weapons that we fight with aren't human, but instead they are powered by God for the destruction of fortresses. They destroy arguments, [5]and every defense that is raised up to oppose the knowledge of God. They capture every thought to make it obedient to Christ. [6]Once your obedience is complete, we are ready to punish any disobedience.

[7]Look at what is right in front of you! If anyone is sure about belonging to Christ, that person should think again. We belong to Christ just like that person. [8]Even if I went on to brag about our authority, I wouldn't be ashamed of it. The Lord gave us that authority to build you up and not to destroy you.

[9]I don't want it to seem like I'm trying to intimidate you with my letters. [10]I know what some people are saying: "His letters are severe and powerful, but in person he is weak and his speech is worth nothing." [11]These people need to think about this—that when we are with you, our actions will show that we are the same as the words we wrote when we were away from you. [12]We won't dare to place ourselves in the same league or to compare ourselves with some of those who are promoting themselves. When they measure themselves by themselves, and compare themselves with themselves, they have no understanding.

[13]We won't take pride in anything more than what is appropriate. Let's look at the boundaries of our work area that God has assigned to us. It's an area that includes you. [14]We aren't going out of bounds, as if our work area doesn't extend as far as you. We were the first ones to travel as far as Corinth with the gospel of Christ. [15]We don't take pride in what other people do outside of our boundaries. We hope that our work will be extended even more by you as your faith grows, until it expands fully (within the boundaries, of course). [16]We hope that our work grows even to the point of the gospel being preached in places beyond Corinth, without bragging about

[i]Ps 112:9

what has already been done in another person's work area. [17]But, *the one who brags should brag in the Lord.*[j] [18]It isn't the person who promotes himself or herself who is approved but the person whom the Lord commends.

Confrontation of the super-apostles

11 I hope that you will put up with me while I act like a fool. Well, in fact, you are putting up with me! [2]I'm deeply concerned about you with the same concern that God has. As your father, I promised you in marriage to one husband. I promised to present you as an innocent virgin to Christ himself. [3]But I'm afraid that your minds might be seduced in the same way as the snake deceived Eve with his devious tricks. You might be unable to focus completely on a genuine and innocent commitment to Christ.

[4]If a person comes and preaches some other Jesus than the one we preached, or if you receive a different Spirit than the one you had received, or a different gospel than the one you embraced, you put up with it so easily! [5]I don't consider myself as second-rate in any way compared to the "super-apostles." [6]But even if I'm uneducated in public speaking, I'm not uneducated in knowledge. We have shown this to you in every way and in everything we have done. [7]Did I commit a sin by humbling myself to give you an advantage because I preached the gospel of God to you free of

charge? [8]I robbed other churches by taking a salary from them in order to serve you! [9]While I was with you, I didn't burden any of you even though I needed things. The believers who came from Macedonia gave me everything I needed. I kept myself from being a financial drain on you in any way, and I will continue to keep myself from being a burden.

[10]Since Christ's truth is in me, I won't stop telling the entire area of Greece that I'm proud of what I did. [11]Why? Is it because I don't love you? God knows that I do! [12]But I'm going to continue to do what I'm doing. I want to contradict the claims of the people who want to be treated like they are the same as us because of what they brag about. [13]Such people are false apostles and dishonest workers who disguise themselves as apostles of Christ. [14]And no wonder! Even Satan disguises himself as an angel of light. [15]It is no great surprise then that his servants also disguise themselves as servants of righteousness. Their end will be what their actions deserve.

Paul defends himself

[16]I repeat, no one should take me for a fool. But if you do, then allow me to be a fool so that I can brag like a fool for a bit. [17]I'm not saying what I'm saying because the Lord tells me to. I'm saying it like I'm a fool. I'm putting my confidence in this business of bragging. [18]Since so many people are bragging based on human standards,

[j]Jer 9:24

SUPER-APOSTLES

"False apostles" and "super-apostles" are the derogatory terms Paul uses to characterize his rival missionaries in Corinth (2 Cor 11:5, 13; 12:11). Paul's sharp critique provides the only clues about them: they appear to have boasted of their Jewish heritage (2 Cor 11:22) and ability to perform miracles (2 Cor 12:12 ; see 10:12; 11:18). They also criticized Paul for his inferior speaking and his refusal to accept the Corinthians' financial support (2 Cor 10:10; 11:5-11; 12:13). Paul denounces these missionaries as ministers of Satan for proclaiming "another Jesus" and a "different gospel" (11:4, 13-14).

that is how I'm going to brag too. [19]Because you, who are so wise, are happy to put up with fools. [20]You put up with it if someone enslaves you, if someone exploits you, if someone takes advantage of you, if someone places themselves over you, or if someone hits you in the face. [21]I'm ashamed to say that we have been weak in comparison! But in whatever they challenge me, I challenge them (I'm speaking foolishly).

[22]Are they Hebrews? So am I. Are they Israelites? So am I. Are they descendants of Abraham? So am I. [23]Are they ministers of Christ? I'm speaking like a crazy person. What I've done goes well beyond what they've done. I've worked much harder. I've been imprisoned much more often. I've been beaten more times than I can count. I've faced death many times. [24]I received the "forty lashes minus one" from the Jews five times. [25]I was beaten with rods three times. I was stoned once. I was shipwrecked three times. I spent a day and a night on the open sea. [26]I've been on many journeys. I faced dangers from rivers, robbers, my people, and Gentiles. I faced dangers in the city, in the desert, on the sea, and from false brothers and sisters. [27]I faced these dangers with hard work and heavy labor, many sleepless nights, hunger and thirst, often without food, and in the cold without enough clothes.

[28]Besides all the other things I could mention, there's my daily stress because I'm concerned about all the churches. [29]Who is weak without me being weak? Who is led astray without me being furious about it? [30]If it's necessary to brag, I'll brag about my

GREECE

Greece forms the southern part of the Balkans. To the east of the mainland lies the Aegean Sea, and to the west is the Adriatic. The mainland stretches from Macedonia in the north down to Attica in the south; to the west, joined to the mainland by the narrow isthmus of Corinth, is the Peloponnese. Greece itself contains a large number of islands, such as Euboia, which lies just off the coast of the mainland.

Greece figures in the OT only in oracles in response to persecution of Jews under Greek rule. Daniel denigrates the "king of Greece" (whom some scholars think refers to Alexander the Great) as a long-haired goat (Dan 8:21). And Zechariah sees the day when Zion's king will come and defeat "Greece," a possible reference to war between Greece and Persia (Zech 9:13).

Greece is the setting for parts of the NT. Paul arrived in the province of Achaia after leaving Macedonia. His first stop was Athens. From there Paul moved to Corinth, the administrative heart of the Roman province. Paul may have traveled in northwestern Greece after a second visit to Macedonia (Acts 20:1; see also 19:21) before traveling to Greece (presumably the province of Achaia as distinct from Macedonia), where he stayed for three months (Acts 20:2-3). It may have been at this point that he reached Illyricum (Rom 15:19), the province created by Augustus on the Adriatic coast. If so, Paul is likely to have crossed over from Macedonia along the Egnatian Way, which linked Macedonia (and the eastern provinces) with the Adriatic. From the Adriatic he would have been able to take a ship down the west coast of Greece, down the Corinthian Gulf, passing colonies like Patras and arriving at Lechaeum, the harbor of Corinth.

weaknesses. ³¹The God and Father of the Lord Jesus, the one who is blessed forever, knows that I'm not lying. ³²At Damascus the governor under King Aretas was guarding the city of Damascus in order to capture me, ³³but I got away from him by being lowered in a basket through a window in the city wall.

Paul's visions and revelations from the Lord

12 It is necessary to brag, not that it does any good. I'll move on to visions and revelations from the Lord. ²I know a man in Christ who was caught up into the third heaven fourteen years ago. I don't know whether it was in the body or out of the body. God knows. ³⁻⁴I know that this man was caught up into paradise and that he heard unspeakable words that were things no one is allowed to repeat. I don't know whether it was in the body or apart from the body. God knows. ⁵I'll brag about this man, but I won't brag about myself, except to brag about my weaknesses.

⁶If I did want to brag, I wouldn't make a fool of myself because I'd tell the truth. I'm holding back from bragging so that no one will give me any more credit than what anyone sees or hears about me. ⁷I was given a thorn in my body because of the outstanding revelations I've received so that I wouldn't be conceited. It's a messenger from Satan sent to torment me so that I wouldn't be conceited.

⁸I pleaded with the Lord three times for it to leave me alone. ⁹He said to me, "My grace is enough for you, because power is made perfect in weakness." So I'll gladly spend my time bragging about my weaknesses so that Christ's power can rest on me. ¹⁰Therefore, I'm all right with weaknesses, insults, disasters, harassments, and stressful situations for the sake of Christ, because when I'm weak, then I'm strong.

¹¹I've become a fool! You made me do it. Actually, I should have been commended by you. I'm not inferior to the super-apostles in any way, even though I'm a nonentity. ¹²The signs of an apostle were performed among you with continuous endurance through signs, wonders, and miracles. ¹³How were you treated worse than the other churches, except that I myself wasn't a financial burden on you? Forgive me for this wrong!

Paul's plans to visit and a warning

¹⁴Look, I'm ready to visit you a third time, and I won't be a burden on you. I don't want your things; I want you. It isn't the children's responsibility to save up for their parents but parents for children. ¹⁵I will very gladly spend and be spent for your sake. If I love you more, will you love me less?

¹⁶We all know that I didn't place a burden on you, but in spite of that you think I'm a con artist who fooled you with a trick. ¹⁷I haven't taken advantage of you through any of the people I sent to you, have I? ¹⁸I strongly encouraged Titus to go to you and sent the brother with him. Titus didn't take advantage of you, did he? Didn't we live by the same Spirit? Didn't we walk in the same footsteps?

¹⁹Have you been thinking up to now that we are defending ourselves to you? Actually, we are speaking in the sight of God and in Christ. Dear friends, everything is meant to build you up. ²⁰I'm afraid that maybe when I come you will be different from the way I want you to be, and that I'll be different from the way you want me to be. I'm afraid that there might be fighting, obsession, losing your temper, competitive opposition, backstabbing, gossip, conceit, and disorderly conduct. ²¹I'm afraid that when I come again, my God may embarrass me in front of you. I might have to go into mourning over all the people who have sinned before and haven't changed their hearts and lives from what they used to practice: moral corruption, sexual immorality, and doing whatever feels good.

13 This is the third time that I'm coming to visit you. Every matter is settled on the evidence of two or three witnesses. ²When I was with you on my second visit, I already warned those who continued to sin. Now I'm repeating that warning to all the rest of you while I'm at a safe distance: if I come again, I won't spare anyone. ³Since you are demanding proof that Christ speaks through me, Christ isn't weak in dealing with you but shows his power among you. ⁴Certainly he was crucified because of weakness, but he lives by the power of God. Certainly we also are weak in him, but we will live together with him, because of God's power that is directed toward you.

⁵Examine yourselves to see if you are in the faith. Test yourselves. Don't you understand that Jesus Christ is in you? Unless, of course, you fail the test. ⁶But I hope that you will realize that we don't fail the test. ⁷We pray to God that you don't do anything wrong, not because we want to appear to pass the test but so that you might do the right thing, even if we appear to fail.

⁸We can't do anything against the truth but only to help the truth. ⁹We are happy when we are weak but you are strong. We pray for this: that you will be made complete. ¹⁰This is why I'm writing these things while I'm away. I'm writing so that I won't need to act harshly when I'm with you by using the authority that the Lord gave me. He gave it to me so that I could build you up, not tear you down.

Final greeting

¹¹Finally, brothers and sisters, good-bye. Put things in order, respond to my encouragement, be in harmony with each other, and live in peace—and the God of love and peace will be with you.

¹²Say hello to each other with a holy kiss.^k All of God's people say hello to you.

¹³The grace of the Lord Jesus Christ, the love of God, and the fellowship of the Holy Spirit be with you all.

---

^k2 Cor 13:12-13 is in some versions equivalent to 13:12-14.

GALATIANS

THEME

The gospel of the right relationship with God by faith in Jesus Christ—and not by obedience to the requirements of the Law—is the one and only divine gospel.

THE NATURE OF THE LETTER

Galatians presents one of the most spiritually vibrant and concise introductions to the Christian faith in the New Testament. In only a few chapters Paul brings readers examples of his most mature thought. Galatians opens with his defense of his apostleship (1:11–2:10) and his vision for the Gentile mission (2:11-18). Moving to his mystical understanding of being crucified with Christ and living in Christ (2:19-21), he then concentrates on his central concept of justification by faith (3:1–4:28) and the revelation that there is neither Jew nor Greek, male nor female, slave nor free since all are one in Christ (3:26-29). He completes the letter with a moving definition of Christian freedom and the role of the Holy Spirit in daily life (5:1–6:16).

In Galatians Paul reveals his concern for the truth of the gospel and the spiritual health of the congregations in Galatia. Skipping over his customary words of praise to a church community, he goes right to the heart of the problem. He begins the very first chapter with a strong reprimand: "I'm amazed that you are so quickly deserting the one who called you" (1:6), and continues throughout the letter to express his feelings openly. He condemns those who oppose his ministry (1:8-9), sarcastically hopes that those who favor circumcision will castrate themselves (5:12), defends his own ministry against all critics (1:11–2:21), uses personal examples to persuade his readers (2:20; 4:12-14, 19-20; 6:11), and ends with a testy challenge to his enemies to leave him (and the Galatians) alone in the future (6:17).

Galatians is partially modeled on a type of ancient Greek literature known as an apologetic letter, which can be traced back at least to the fourth century BCE. In the ancient world an "apology" was a formal defense in which an author argued against opponents in a fairly predictable form. Paul probably read numerous examples when he studied in Jerusalem (Acts 22:3). Throughout Galatians the outline of such a form is clearly visible: the introduction (1:6-11), the statement of the facts (1:12–2:14), the major proposition (2:15-21), the proof (3:1–4:31), and the giving of practical advice (5:16–6:10).

It is also possible to see in Galatians how much Paul was influenced by the training he received as a rabbi and a Pharisee. In Galatians he admits rather proudly that he was first in his class in rabbinic studies (1:14). In Chapters 3 and 4 of Galatians he employs arguments to show that Jesus is the Christ predicted in the Old Testament. This type of argument was common in the Judaism he studied in the first century but is foreign to modern readers.

THE AUTHOR

Bible scholars generally agree that the apostle Paul is certainly the author of Galatians. The very first word in the text is his name, and the argument and style are similar to those in his other authentic letters, especially the much longer letter to the Romans.

THE GALATIANS

The churches of Galatia (1:2) were located somewhere in Asia Minor (now modern Turkey). At various times in history the word *Galatia* referred to regions either in the central or the southern part of that area, and it is difficult to know how Paul defined the term. Scholars who think that the letter went to congregations in the Roman province in the south suppose that Paul visited them when he traveled to other nearby cities (Acts 13:14–14:23; 16:1-6; 18:23). References elsewhere in the New Testament provide very little concrete information about where Galatia was (Acts 16:6; 18:23; 1 Corinthians 16:1; 2 Timothy 4:10; 1 Peter 1:1). The itineraries given for Paul's travels in Acts are notoriously difficult to coordinate with the information provided in Galatians 1 and 2.

THE OCCASION

The Christians in Galatia were under pressure to abandon the message of faith that Paul had given to them on a previous visit (1:9; 4:13-20). The opponents with whom Paul is so angry were probably Jewish-Christian missionaries (possibly from Jerusalem, as 2:1-21 seems to imply) who came to Galatia after Paul founded the churches there. Their mission was to bring the Galatians' faith in line with a Christianity that still observed the major principles of the Torah and the traditions of Judaism. In Paul's view they were perverting the gospel of Christ. The opponents taught a number of things that Paul rejected: that Christians still had to be circumcised to believe in Jesus Christ (2:1-6); that they had to depend on works of the law to be saved (3:1–4:28); and that they had to keep ritual observances of the Jewish calendar (4:10) in order to be true believers in God. Paul argues that they must return to the true gospel that he taught them, that they must not exchange the truth for a lie (2:14) or trade their new-found freedom for slavery (4:8-9). Instead they must believe in God's promise in the Old Testament, visible especially in the life of Abraham and fulfilled in Christ, so that they will live life by faith and faith alone.

THE DATE

Galatians was probably written during one of Paul's later missionary tours (see Acts 15:36–18:22; 18:24–21:17) between the years 50 and 55 CE. It is likely that he composed it after he finished the letters to the church in Corinth and just before he began his longer letter to the Romans. Church tradition says that he wrote it while he was in the city of Ephesus (see 1 Corinthians 16:8; Acts 19:1-10), but it could have been sent from Macedonia, Antioch, Corinth, or even Rome.

GALATIANS

Greeting

1 From Paul, an apostle who is not sent from human authority or commissioned through human agency, but sent through Jesus Christ and God the Father who raised him from the dead; ²and from all the brothers and sisters with me.

To the churches in Galatia.

³Grace and peace to you from God the Father and the Lord Jesus Christ. ⁴He gave himself for our sins, so he could deliver us from this present evil age, according to the will of our God and Father. ⁵To God be the glory forever and always! Amen.

The gospel challenged in Galatia

⁶I'm amazed that you are so quickly deserting the one who called you by the grace of Christ to follow another gospel. ⁷It's not really another gospel, but certain people are confusing you and they want to change the gospel of Christ. ⁸However, even if we ourselves or a heavenly angel should ever preach anything different from what we preached to you, they should be under a curse. ⁹I'm repeating what we've said before: if anyone preaches something different from what you received, they should be under a curse!

Paul's leadership

¹⁰Am I trying to win over human beings or God? Or am I trying to please people? If I were still trying to please people, I wouldn't be Christ's slave. ¹¹Brothers and sisters, I want you to know that the gospel I preached isn't human in origin. ¹²I didn't receive it or learn it from a human. It came through a revelation from Jesus Christ.

¹³You heard about my previous life in Judaism, how severely I harassed God's church and tried to destroy it. ¹⁴I advanced in Judaism beyond many of my peers, because I was much more militant about the traditions of my ancestors. ¹⁵But God had set me apart from birth and called me through his grace. He was pleased ¹⁶to reveal his Son to me, so that I might preach about him to the Gentiles. I didn't immediately consult with any human being. ¹⁷I didn't go up to Jerusalem to see the men who were apostles before me either, but I went away into Arabia and I returned again to Damascus. ¹⁸Then after three years I went up to Jerusalem to visit Cephas and stayed with him fifteen days. ¹⁹But I didn't see any other of the apostles except James the brother of the Lord. ²⁰Before God, I'm not lying about the things that I'm writing to you! ²¹Then I went into the regions of Syria and Cilicia, ²²but I wasn't known personally by the Christian churches in Judea. ²³They only heard a report about me: "The man who used to harass us now preaches the faith that he once tried to destroy." ²⁴So they were glorifying God because of me.

Confirmation of Paul's leadership

2 Then after fourteen years I went up to Jerusalem again with Barnabas, and I took Titus along also. ²I went there because of a revelation, and I laid out the gospel that I preach to the Gentiles for them. But I did it privately with the influential leaders to make sure that I wouldn't be working or that I hadn't worked for nothing.

GALATIA

The Roman province of Galatia lies in central Anatolia or modern Turkey. To the west was the province of Asia, to the southwest Lycia and Pamphylia, to the south Cilicia, to the east Cappadocia, and to the north Bithynia and Pontus.

³However, not even Titus, who was with me and who was a Greek, was required to be circumcised. ⁴But false brothers and sisters, who were brought in secretly, slipped in to spy on our freedom, which we have in Christ Jesus, and to make us slaves. ⁵We didn't give in and submit to them for a single moment, so that the truth of the gospel would continue to be with you.

⁶The influential leaders didn't add anything to what I was preaching—and whatever they were makes no difference to me, because God doesn't show favoritism. ⁷But on the contrary, they saw that I had been given the responsibility to preach the gospel to the people who aren't circumcised, just as Peter had been to the circumcised. ⁸The one who empowered Peter to become an apostle to the circumcised empowered me also to be one to the Gentiles. ⁹James, Cephas, and John, who are considered to be key leaders, shook hands with me and Barnabas as equals when they recognized the grace that was given to me. So it was agreed that we would go to the Gentiles, while they continue to go to the people who were circumcised. ¹⁰They asked only that we would remember the poor, which was certainly something I was willing to do.

The Jewish-Gentile controversy

¹¹But when Cephas came to Antioch, I opposed him to his face, because he was wrong. ¹²He had been eating with the Gentiles before certain people came from James. But when they came, he began to back out and separate himself, because he was afraid of the people who promoted circumcision. ¹³And the rest of the Jews also joined him in this hypocrisy so that even Barnabas got carried away with them in their hypocrisy. ¹⁴But when I saw that they weren't acting consistently with the truth of the gospel, I said to Cephas in front of everyone, "If you, though you're a Jew, live like a Gentile and not like a Jew, how can you require the Gentiles to live like Jews?"

¹⁵We are born Jews—we're not Gentile sinners. ¹⁶However, we know that a person isn't made righteous by the works of the Law but rather through the faithfulness of Jesus Christ. We ourselves believed in Christ Jesus so that we could be made righteous by the faithfulness of Christ and not by the works of the Law—because no one will be made righteous by the works of the Law. ¹⁷But if it is discovered that we ourselves are sinners while we are trying to be made righteous in Christ, then is Christ a servant of sin? Absolutely not! ¹⁸If I rebuild the very things that I tore down, I show that I myself am breaking the Law. ¹⁹I died to the Law through the Law, so that I could live for God. ²⁰I have been crucified with Christ and I no longer live, but Christ lives in me. And the life that I now live in my body, I live by faith, indeed, by the faithfulness of God's Son, who loved

BARNABAS

Also named Joseph, a prominent apostle and associate of Paul in Antioch of Syria, Cyprus, and Asia Minor (see esp. Acts 4–15 and Gal 2:1-10). Speculation about Barnabas persisted for centuries beyond the NT era. Among the church fathers, Tertullian attributed the book of Hebrews to Barnabas, and Clement of Alexandria credited him with the so-called *Epistle of Barnabas*, written, however, in the 2nd cent., well after Barnabas's time. Later sources further embellish Barnabas's career, identifying him, variously, as one of the seventy(-two) disciples commissioned by Jesus in Luke 10:1, the founder of the church at Rome, and the chief apostle to Cyprus, where he was martyred and buried.

me and gave himself for me. [21]I don't ignore the grace of God, because if we become righteous through the Law, then Christ died for no purpose.

Works versus the Spirit

3 You irrational Galatians! Who put a spell on you? Jesus Christ was put on display as crucified before your eyes! [2]I just want to know this from you: Did you receive the Spirit by doing the works of the Law or by believing what you heard? [3]Are you so irrational? After you started with the Spirit, are you now finishing up with your own human effort? [4]Did you experience so much for nothing? I wonder if it really was for nothing. [5]So does the one providing you with the Spirit and working miracles among you do this by you doing the works of the Law or by you believing what you heard?

Abraham: an example of righteousness

[6]Understand that in the same way that Abraham *believed God and it was credited to him as righteousness,*[a] [7]those who believe are the children of Abraham. [8]But when it saw ahead of time that God would make the Gentiles righteous on the basis of faith, scripture preached the gospel in advance to Abraham: *All the Gentiles will be blessed in you.*[b] [9]Therefore, those who believe are blessed together with Abraham who believed.

[10]All those who rely on the works of the Law are under a curse, because it is written, *Everyone is cursed who does not keep on doing all the things that have been written in the Law scroll.*[c] [11]But since no one is made righteous by the Law as far as God is concerned, it is clear that *the righteous one will live on the basis of faith.*[d] [12]The Law isn't based on faith; rather, *the one doing these things will live by them.*[e] [13]Christ redeemed us from the curse of the Law by becoming a curse for us—because it is written, *Everyone who is hung on a tree is cursed.*[f] [14]He redeemed us so that the blessing of Abraham would come to the Gentiles through Christ Jesus,

and that we would receive the promise of the Spirit through faith.

[15]Brothers and sisters, I'll use an example from human experience. No one ignores or makes additions to a validated will. [16]The promises were made to Abraham and to his descendant. It doesn't say, "and to the descendants," as if referring to many rather than just one. It says, "and to your descendant," who is Christ. [17]I'm saying this: the Law, which came four hundred thirty years later, doesn't invalidate the agreement that was previously validated by God so that it cancels the promise. [18]If the inheritance were based upon the Law, it would no longer be from the promise. But God has given it graciously to Abraham through a promise.

The Law's origin and purpose

[19]So why was the Law given? It was added because of offenses, until the descendant would come to whom the promise had been made. It was put in place through angels by the hand of a mediator. [20]Now the mediator does not take one side; but God is one. [21]So, is the Law against the promises of God? Absolutely not! If a Law had been given that was able to give life, then righteousness would in fact have come from the Law. [22]But scripture locked up all things under sin, so that the promise based on the faithfulness of Jesus Christ might be given to those who have faith. [23]Before faith came, we were guarded under the Law, locked up until faith that was coming would be revealed, [24]so that the Law became our custodian until Christ so that we might be made righteous by faith.

God's children are heirs in Christ

[25]But now that faith has come, we are no longer under a custodian. [26]You are all God's children through faith in Christ Jesus. [27]All of you who were baptized into Christ have clothed yourselves with Christ. [28]There is neither Jew nor Greek; there is neither slave nor free; nor is there male and female, for you are all

---

[a]Gen 15:6 [b]Gen 12:3 [c]Deut 27:26 [d]Hab 2:4 [e]Lev 18:5 [f]Deut 21:23

one in Christ Jesus. ²⁹Now if you belong to Christ, then indeed you are Abraham's descendants, heirs according to the promise.

4 I'm saying that as long as the heirs are minors, they are no different from slaves, though they really are the owners of everything. ²However, they are placed under trustees and guardians until the date set by the parents. ³In the same way, when we were minors, we were also enslaved by this world's system. ⁴But when the fulfillment of the time came, God sent his Son, born through a woman, and born under the Law. ⁵This was so he could redeem those under the Law so that we could be adopted. ⁶Because you are sons and daughters, God sent the Spirit of his Son into our hearts, crying, "Abba, Father!" ⁷Therefore, you are no longer a slave but a son or daughter, and if you are his child, then you are also an heir through God.

Paul's concern for the Galatians

⁸At the time, when you didn't know God, you were enslaved by things that aren't gods by nature. ⁹But now, after knowing God (or rather, being known by God), how can you turn back again to the weak and worthless world system? Do you want to be slaves to it again? ¹⁰You observe religious days and months and seasons and years. ¹¹I'm afraid for you! Perhaps my hard work for you has been for nothing.

¹²I beg you to be like me, brothers and sisters, because I have become like you!

You haven't wronged me. ¹³You know that I first preached the gospel to you because of an illness. ¹⁴Though my poor health burdened you, you didn't look down on me or reject me, but you welcomed me as if I were an angel from God, or as if I were Christ Jesus! ¹⁵Where then is the great attitude that you had? I swear that, if possible, you would have dug out your eyes and given them to me. ¹⁶So then, have I become your enemy by telling you the truth? ¹⁷They are so concerned about you, though not with good intentions. Rather, they want to shut you out so that you would run after them. ¹⁸However, it's always good to have people concerned about you with good intentions, and not just when I'm there with you. ¹⁹My little children, I'm going through labor pains again until Christ is formed in you. ²⁰But I wish I could be with you now and change how I sound, because I'm at a loss about you.

Slave versus free

²¹Tell me—those of you who want to be under the Law—don't you listen to the Law? ²²It's written that Abraham had two sons, one by the slave woman and one by the free woman. ²³The son by the slave woman was conceived the normal way, but the son by the free woman was conceived through a promise. ²⁴These things are an allegory: the women are two covenants. One is from Mount Sinai, which gives birth to slave children; this is Hagar. ²⁵Hagar is

HAGAR

Hagar's story is found in the OT in Genesis 16:1-16 and 21:8-21. She was Sarai's Egyptian servant. In the NT, Hagar appears in Galatians 4:21-31. She is the only named woman in the book of Galatians. Paul used her and the "free woman," that is, Sarah, in an allegory to represent the Judaizing Christians who were slaves to the Law and the Gentile Christians who were free children through the promise. Hagar was equated with Mount Sinai and the earthly Jerusalem, but the free woman Sarah was Jerusalem from above. Paul wanted to refute the claims of those who insisted that circumcision and obedience to the Law were required for becoming a Christian.

Mount Sinai in Arabia, and she corresponds to the present-day Jerusalem, because the city is in slavery with her children. ²⁶But the Jerusalem that is above is free, and she is our mother. ²⁷It's written:

Rejoice, barren woman,
   you who have not given birth.
Break out with a shout,
   you who have not suffered labor pains;
because the woman who has been deserted
   will have many more children
   than the woman who has a husband.^g

²⁸Brothers and sisters, you are children of the promise like Isaac. ²⁹But just as it was then, so it is now also: the one who was conceived the normal way harassed the one who was conceived by the Spirit. ³⁰But what does the scripture say? *Throw out the slave woman and her son, because the slave woman's son won't share the inheritance with the free woman's son.*^h ³¹Therefore, brothers and sisters, we aren't the slave woman's children, but we are the free woman's

5 children. ¹Christ has set us free for freedom. Therefore, stand firm and don't submit to the bondage of slavery again.

Arguments against being circumcised

²Look, I, Paul, am telling you that if you have yourselves circumcised, having Christ won't help you. ³Again I swear to every man who has himself circumcised that he is re-

quired to do the whole Law. ⁴You people who are trying to be made righteous by the Law have been estranged from Christ. You have fallen away from grace! ⁵We eagerly wait for the hope of righteousness through the Spirit by faith. ⁶Being circumcised or not being circumcised doesn't matter in Christ Jesus, but faith working through love does matter.

⁷You were running well—who stopped you from obeying the truth? ⁸This line of reasoning doesn't come from the one who calls you. ⁹A little yeast works through the whole lump of dough. ¹⁰I'm convinced about you in the Lord that you won't think any other way. But the one who is confusing you will pay the penalty, whoever that may be. ¹¹Brothers and sisters, if I'm still preaching circumcision, why am I still being harassed? In that case, the offense of the cross would be canceled. ¹²I wish that the ones who are upsetting you would castrate themselves!

¹³You were called to freedom, brothers and sisters; only don't let this freedom be an opportunity to indulge your selfish impulses, but serve each other through love. ¹⁴All the Law has been fulfilled in a single statement: *Love your neighbor as yourself.*ⁱ ¹⁵But if you bite and devour each other, be careful that you don't get eaten up by each other!

^gIsa 54:1 ^hGen 21:10 ⁱLev 19:18

CIRCUMCISION

An operation performed on males—infants, children, and adults—to remove all or a portion of the foreskin. The OT requires the circumcision of every Hebrew male on the eighth day after birth (Gen 17:10-11; Lev 12:2-3), every slave of an Israelite (Gen 17:12-13; Exod 12:44), and immigrants who resided permanently within Israel if they desired to celebrate and eat the Passover (Exod 12:48).

Circumcision was not practiced exclusively by the Israelites. The prophet Jeremiah (9:25-26) lists "Egyptians [and] Judeans, Edomites [and] Ammonites, Moabites [and] the desert dwellers who cut the hair on their foreheads" as being circumcised.

Two different ways of living

[16]I say be guided by the Spirit and you won't carry out your selfish desires. [17]A person's selfish desires are set against the Spirit, and the Spirit is set against one's selfish desires. They are opposed to each other, so you shouldn't do whatever you want to do. [18]But if you are being led by the Spirit, you aren't under the Law. [19]The actions that are produced by selfish motives are obvious, since they include sexual immorality, moral corruption, doing whatever feels good, [20]idolatry, drug use and casting spells, hate, fighting, obsession, losing your temper, competitive opposition, conflict, selfishness, group rivalry, [21]jealousy, drunkenness, partying, and other things like that. I warn you as I have already warned you, that those who do these kinds of things won't inherit God's kingdom.

[22]But the fruit of the Spirit is love, joy, peace, patience, kindness, goodness, faithfulness, [23]gentleness, and self-control. There is no law against things like this. [24]Those who belong to Christ Jesus have crucified self with its passions and its desires.

[25]If we live by the Spirit, let's follow the Spirit. [26]Let's not become arrogant, make each other angry, or be jealous of each other.

Caring and sharing

6 Brothers and sisters, if a person is caught doing something wrong, you who are spiritual should restore someone like this with a spirit of gentleness. Watch out for yourselves so you won't be tempted too. [2]Carry each other's burdens and so you will fulfill the law of Christ. [3]If anyone thinks they are important when they aren't, they're fooling themselves. [4]Each person should test their own work and be happy with doing a good job and not compare themselves with others. [5]Each person will have to carry their own load.

[6]Those who are taught the word should share all good things with their teacher. [7]Make no mistake, God is not mocked. A person will harvest what they plant. [8]Those who plant only for their own benefit will harvest devastation from their selfishness, but those who plant for the benefit of the Spirit will harvest eternal life from the Spirit. [9]Let's not get tired of doing good, because in time we'll have a harvest if we don't give up. [10]So then, let's work for the good of all whenever we have an opportunity, and especially for those in the household of faith.

Final greeting

[11]Look at the large letters I'm making with my own handwriting! [12]Whoever wants to look good by human standards will try to get you to be circumcised, but only so they won't be harassed for the cross of Christ. [13]Those who are circumcised don't observe the Law themselves, but they want you to be circumcised, so they can boast about your physical body.[j]

[14]But as for me, God forbid that I should boast about anything except for the cross of our Lord Jesus Christ. The world has been crucified to me through him, and I have been crucified to the world. [15]Being circumcised or not being circumcised doesn't mean anything. What matters is a new creation. [16]May peace and mercy be on whoever follows this rule and on God's Israel.

[17]From now on, no one should bother me because I bear the marks of Jesus on my body.

[18]Brothers and sisters, may the grace of our Lord Jesus Christ be with your spirit. Amen.

---

[j]In Gk the word traditionally rendered as *flesh* is rendered here as *physical body*, but it has a wide range of meaning. Gal 5:13-25; 6:8, 12 contain nine close occurrences of the same word in Gk, but it is rendered as *selfish* in regard to impulses, desires, motives, or benefit, and *human standards* in 6:12.

EPHESIANS

THEME

It is God's purpose to unite the universe in Christ and the church.

WHO WROTE EPHESIANS?

For over 150 years there has been a continuous, sustained debate about the real author of Ephesians. Some scholars take what the letter says at face value and assume that because Paul is mentioned by name in 1:1 and 3:1 that the apostle Paul must be the author. Many others argue that the style, content, and perspective of the letter show that someone other than Paul wrote it.

All serious students of Ephesians agree that the letter presents difficult problems. The content differs particularly from Romans and Galatians and clearly has different major themes. Whereas justification by faith, freedom from the law, and the question of circumcision are primary issues in Romans and Galatians, they are not important in Ephesians. Ephesians also has unbearably long and complex sentences. Although Paul sometimes uses a lengthy style in his uncontested letters (see Romans 1:1-7, which is one sentence), generally he does not, and certainly not page after page.

The author of Ephesians also indicates a reverential attitude toward the apostles, which differs considerably from that in Galatians 1 and 2, and many scholars are convinced that Paul could not have changed his mind so much in a relatively short time.

Those who think that Paul wrote Ephesians argue that it is not unusual for authors to change their style if they are writing at different times in their lives for different readers. In addition, they point to themes in Ephesians that are found throughout Paul's letters. In their opinion, Paul's style may differ in Ephesians because he is older and because he is quoting more Christian hymns and Old Testament passages.

While these arguments are worth considering, it is most likely, as most scholars argue, that Paul did not write Ephesians. The long, ponderous style is different from his writings anywhere else in the New Testament. The attitude toward the apostles is also very revealing. In Galatians 1:16 Paul says that he did not have to confer with other apostles to receive revelation from God, and refers to them as of only reputed importance, who added nothing to him (2:6).

In Ephesians, however, the apostles are people who should be honored. Although the Spirit has revealed the mystery to God's holy apostles and prophets

(3:5), and the church was built on them (2:20), the author implies that they were people who received a blessing from God in the past and that he himself was not one of them. It is also unlikely that Paul would call himself a "holy" apostle. In 1 Corinthians 15:8-10 he refers to himself instead as one born at the wrong time, as the least important of the apostles.

It is best to assume that Ephesians was written not during Paul's lifetime but much later, when the church was an established institution that revered the apostles as figures of the past. It is most likely that Ephesians was written by an unknown Christian who borrowed Paul's name. Perhaps he was a student of Paul's or, more probably, an admirer who respected his memory as a "holy apostle."

In the ancient world it was not unusual for a writer to assume another's name if he thought that the author's ideas were similar to his. It is likely that the New Testament books of James and Jude were written the same way, utilizing the names of apostles to make sure that the letters were widely read.

In a final sense, it is not critically important who wrote Ephesians. The author of Hebrews is also unknown, but all Christians realize that it contains Christian truth. In a similar way, Ephesians has a great deal to teach us about Christ's church, the unity of his body, and the way Christians should act.

TO WHOM WAS THE LETTER WRITTEN?

We cannot be certain where the original readers of Ephesians lived. The oldest and most reliable copies of Ephesians do not contain any reference at all to those in Ephesus. It is possible, as is often suggested, that Ephesians was a "circular letter" that left the name of the recipients blank and was sent around to many different churches in one area. Although we cannot be certain, it is likely that the letter was sent to congregations throughout western Asia Minor (modern Turkey).

WHY WAS THE LETTER WRITTEN?

In a strict sense, Ephesians is not a letter but a style of writing called rhetoric in the ancient world. Rhetoric was delivered in speeches or written in tracts to influence the thought and conduct of a general audience. Unlike Paul's letters, Ephesians is not directed toward incidents in a specific church but is written very generally to build the Christian church as a whole (chapters 1–3) and tell the readers how they should act (chapters 4–6).

The author's writing indicates that his readers are aware of a popular philosophy called Gnosticism. He appears to be worried that they may be influenced by it so much that they might lose their faith in Christ. Gnosticism was a philosophy that prided itself on the knowledge (*gnosis* in Greek) of those who believed in it. In one popular form of the belief system, followers believed that only they could understand the secret plan (see 3:3) of God. They thought that there was a whole series of planets and beings in different levels of heaven that controlled human destiny. Sometimes they were spiritual powers (*archons* in Greek, 2:2), ages (*aeons*, see 3:9), or rulers and powers (3:10). The goal of philosophy and religion, in the Gnostics' opinion, was to return the divine spark that dwells in every human being to the fullness of God (3:19), so that all divine things could be all in all.

The writer of Ephesians counters this kind of thinking with the Christian belief that through Christ, God has overcome all heavenly beings, real or unreal. All things will rest in God, who brings the love that surpasses all knowledge.

Ephesians is written to Gentiles, that is, to people who were not born as Jews (see 3:1, 8). The writer refers to them as aliens and strangers (2:12), those who were once far off (2:13, 17), in order to show them that in Christ their status has been changed and they are now part of the one body of Christ (2:14-18), fellow citizens in God's household (2:19).

WHEN WAS EPHESIANS WRITTEN?

Ephesians was written sometime between Paul's death in 64–67 CE (the exact year is not known) and the end of the first century. Since reference is made to it in a letter written about 96 CE by Clement, an early bishop of Rome, it is often assumed that Ephesians was completed sometime around 90 CE.

EPHESIANS

Greeting

1 From Paul, an apostle of Christ Jesus by God's will.

To the holy and faithful people in Christ Jesus in Ephesus.[a]

[2]Grace and peace to you from God our Father and our Lord Jesus Christ.

The believers' blessings

[3]Bless the God and Father of our Lord Jesus Christ! He has blessed us in Christ with every spiritual blessing that comes from heaven. [4]God chose us in Christ to be holy and blameless in God's presence before the creation of the world. [5]God destined us to be his adopted children through Jesus Christ because of his love. This was according to his goodwill and plan [6]and to honor his glorious grace that he has given to us freely through the Son whom he loves. [7]We have been ransomed through his Son's blood, and we have forgiveness for our failures based on his overflowing grace, [8]which he poured over us with wisdom and understanding. [9]God revealed his hidden design[b] to us, which is according to his goodwill and the plan that he intended to accomplish through his Son. [10]This is what God planned for the climax of all times:[c] to bring all things together in Christ, the things in heaven along with the things on earth. [11]We have also received an inheritance in Christ. We were destined by the plan of God, who accomplishes everything according to his design. [12]We are called to be an honor to God's glory because we were the first to hope in Christ. [13]You too heard the word of truth in Christ, which is the good news of your salvation. You were sealed with the promised Holy Spirit because you believed in Christ. [14]The Holy Spirit is the down payment on our inheritance, which is applied toward our redemption as God's own people, resulting in the honor of God's glory.

Paul's prayer for the Ephesians

[15]Since I heard about your faith in the Lord Jesus and your love for all God's people, this is the reason that [16]I don't stop giving thanks to God for you when I remember you in my prayers. [17]I pray that the God of our Lord Jesus Christ, the Father of glory, will give you a spirit of wisdom and revelation that makes God known to you. [18]I pray that the eyes of your heart will have enough light to see what is the hope of God's call, what is the richness of God's glorious inheritance among believers, [19]and what is the overwhelming greatness of God's power that is working among us believers. This power is conferred by the energy of God's powerful strength. [20]God's power was at work in Christ when God raised him from the dead and sat him at God's right side in the heavens, [21]far above every ruler and authority and power and angelic power, any power that might

---

[a]The location of Ephesus was added in some later manuscripts, probably to make the opening of this letter similar to the others in the collection of Paul's letters. [b]Or *mystery* [c]Or *the fullness of times*

EPHESUS

As the capital of the Roman province of Asia, Ephesus benefitted from its strategic location, banking, and commerce. It was situated at the mouth of the Cayster River, near modern Selçuk on the western coast of Turkey. Ephesus's known history begins in the 10th century BCE. Paul ministered in Ephesus for about three years (Acts 19:8-10; 20:31) and wrote letters to Corinth from that city.

be named not only now but in the future. [22]God put everything under Christ's feet and made him head of everything in the church, [23]which is his body. His body, the church, is the fullness of Christ, who fills everything in every way.

Saved from sin to life

2 At one time you were like a dead person because of the things you did wrong and your offenses against God. [2]You used to live like people of this world. You followed the rule of a destructive spiritual power. This is the spirit of disobedience to God's will that is now at work in persons whose lives are characterized by disobedience. [3]At one time you were like those persons. All of you used to do whatever felt good and whatever you thought you wanted so that you were children headed for punishment just like everyone else.

[4-5]However, God is rich in mercy. He brought us to life with Christ while we were dead as a result of those things that we did wrong. He did this because of the great love that he has for us. You are saved by God's grace! [6]And God raised us up and seated us in the heavens with Christ Jesus. [7]God did this to show future generations the greatness of his grace by the goodness that God has shown us in Christ Jesus.

[8]You are saved by God's grace because of your faith.[d] This salvation is God's gift. It's not something you possessed. [9]It's not something you did that you can be proud

of. [10]Instead, we are God's accomplishment, created in Christ Jesus to do good things. God planned for these good things to be the way that we live our lives.

The reconciliation of God's people

[11]So remember that once you were Gentiles by physical descent, who were called "uncircumcised" by Jews who are physically circumcised. [12]At that time you were without Christ. You were aliens rather than citizens of Israel, and strangers to the covenants of God's promise. In this world you had no hope and no God. [13]But now, thanks to Christ Jesus, you who once were so far away have been brought near by the blood of Christ.

[14]Christ is our peace. He made both Jews and Gentiles into one group. With his body, he broke down the barrier of hatred that divided us. [15]He canceled the detailed rules of the Law so that he could create one new person out of the two groups, making peace. [16]He reconciled them both as one body to God by the cross, which ended the hostility to God.

[17]When he came, he announced the good news of peace to you who were far away from God and to those who were near. [18]We both have access to the Father through Christ by the one Spirit. [19]So now you are no longer strangers and aliens. Rather, you are fellow citizens with God's people, and you belong to God's household. [20]As God's household, you are built on the foundation of the

[d]Or through his faithfulness

SALVATION

The most fundamental meaning of *salvation* in scripture is that God delivers people from a bad situation and restores them to wholeness. Behind the OT salvation language lies the worldview in which the exodus from Egyptian bondage, followed by entry into the land of promise, forms the most important model for how God delivers a people. In the NT salvation is God's project of rescue and restoration effected through Jesus Christ as the climax of Israel's story and the culmination of creation itself. Salvation is God's gift of life affecting every aspect of existence.

apostles and prophets with Christ Jesus himself as the cornerstone. [21] The whole building is joined together in him, and it grows up into a temple that is dedicated to the Lord. [22] Christ is building you into a place where God lives through the Spirit.

Paul, apostle to the Gentiles

3 This is why I, Paul, am a prisoner of Christ for you Gentiles.

[2] You've heard, of course, about the responsibility to distribute God's grace, which God gave to me for you, right? [3] God showed me his secret plan[e] in a revelation, as I mentioned briefly before ([4] when you read this, you'll understand my insight into the secret plan[f] about Christ). [5] Earlier generations didn't know this hidden plan that God has now revealed to his holy apostles and prophets through the Spirit. [6] This plan is that the Gentiles would be coheirs and parts of the same body, and that they would share with the Jews in the promises of God in Christ Jesus through the gospel. [7] I became a servant of the gospel because of the grace that God showed me through the exercise of his power.

[8] God gave his grace to me, the least of all God's people, to preach the good news about the immeasurable riches of Christ to the Gentiles. [9] God sent me to reveal the secret plan[g] that had been hidden since the beginning of time by God, who created everything. [10] God's purpose is now to show the rulers and powers in the heavens the many different varieties of his wisdom through the church. [11] This was consistent with the plan he had from the beginning of time that he accomplished through Christ Jesus our Lord. [12] In Christ we have bold and confident access to God through faith in him.[h] [13] So then, I ask you not to become discouraged by what I'm suffering for you, which is your glory.

Paul's prayer for the Ephesians

[14] This is why I kneel before the Father. [15] Every ethnic group in heaven or on earth is recognized by him. [16] I ask that he will strengthen you in your inner selves from the riches of his glory through the Spirit. [17] I ask that Christ will live in your hearts through faith. As a result of having strong roots in love, [18] I ask that you'll have the power to grasp love's width and length, height and depth, together with all believers. [19] I ask that you'll know the love of Christ that is beyond knowledge so that you will be filled entirely with the fullness of God.

[20] Glory to God, who is able to do far beyond all that we could ask or imagine by his power at work within us; [21] glory to him in the church and in Christ Jesus for all generations, forever and always. Amen.

Unity of the body of Christ

4 Therefore, as a prisoner for the Lord, I encourage you to live as people worthy of the call you received from God. [2] Conduct yourselves with all humility, gentleness, and patience. Accept each other with love, [3] and make an effort to preserve the unity of the Spirit with the peace that ties you together. [4] You are one body and one spirit, just as God also called you in one hope. [5] There is one Lord, one faith, one baptism, [6] and one God and Father of all, who is over all, through all, and in all.

[7] God has given his grace to each one of us measured out by the gift that is given by Christ. [8] That's why scripture says, *When he climbed up to the heights, he captured prisoners, and he gave gifts to people.*[i]

[9] What does the phrase "he climbed up" mean if it doesn't mean that he had first gone down into the lower regions, the earth? [10] The one who went down is the same one who climbed up above all the heavens so that he might fill everything.

[11] He gave some apostles, some prophets, some evangelists, and some pastors and teachers. [12] His purpose was to equip God's people for the work of serving and building up the body of Christ [13] until we all reach the unity of faith and knowledge of God's Son. God's goal is for us to become mature adults—to be fully grown, measured by the

---

[e] Or *mystery* [f] Or *mystery* [g] Or *mystery* [h] Or *through his faithfulness* [i] Ps 68:18

standard of the fullness of Christ. [14]As a result, we aren't supposed to be infants any longer who can be tossed and blown around by every wind that comes from teaching with deceitful scheming and the tricks people play to deliberately mislead others. [15]Instead, by speaking the truth with love, let's grow in every way into Christ, [16]who is the head. The whole body grows from him, as it is joined and held together by all the supporting ligaments. The body makes itself grow in that it builds itself up with love as each one does its part.

The old and new life

[17]So I'm telling you this, and I insist on it in the Lord: you shouldn't live your life like the Gentiles anymore. They base their lives on pointless thinking, [18]and they are in the dark in their reasoning. They are disconnected from God's life because of their ignorance and their closed hearts. [19]They are people who lack all sense of right and wrong, and who have turned themselves over to doing whatever feels good and to practicing every sort of corruption along with greed.

[20]But you didn't learn that sort of thing from Christ. [21]Since you really listened to him and you were taught how the truth is in Jesus, [22]change the former way of life that was part of the person you once were, corrupted by deceitful desires. [23]Instead, renew the thinking in your mind by the Spirit [24]and clothe yourself with the new person created according to God's image in justice and true holiness.

[25]Therefore, after you have gotten rid of lying, *Each of you must tell the truth to your neighbor*[j] because we are parts of each other in the same body. [26]*Be angry without sinning.*[k] Don't let the sun set on your anger. [27]Don't provide an opportunity for the devil. [28]Thieves should no longer steal. Instead, they should go to work, using their hands to do good so that they will have something to share with whoever is in need.

[29]Don't let any foul words come out of your mouth. Only say what is helpful when it is needed for building up the community so that it benefits those who hear what you say. [30]Don't make the Holy Spirit of God unhappy—you were sealed by him for the day of redemption. [31]Put aside all bitterness, losing your temper, anger, shouting, and slander, along with every other evil. [32]Be kind, compassionate, and forgiving to each other, in the same way God forgave you in Christ.

5 Therefore, imitate God like dearly loved children. [2]Live your life with love, following the example of Christ, who loved us and gave himself for us. He was a sacrificial offering that smelled sweet to God.

[3]Sexual immorality, and any kind of impurity or greed, shouldn't even be mentioned among you, which is right for holy persons. [4]Obscene language, silly talk, or vulgar jokes aren't acceptable for believers. Instead, there should be thanksgiving. [5]Because you know for sure that persons who are sexually immoral, impure, or greedy—which happens when things become gods—those persons won't inherit the kingdom of Christ and God.

Be children of light

[6]Nobody should deceive you with stupid ideas. God's anger comes down on those who are disobedient because of this kind of thing. [7]So you shouldn't have anything to do with them. [8]You were once darkness, but now you are light in the Lord, so live your life as children of light. [9]Light produces fruit that consists of every sort of goodness, justice, and truth. [10]Therefore, test everything to see what's pleasing to the Lord, [11]and don't participate in the unfruitful actions of darkness. Instead, you should reveal the truth about them. [12]It's embarrassing to even talk about what certain persons do in secret. [13]But everything exposed to the light is revealed by the light. [14]Everything that is revealed by the light is light. Therefore, it says, *Wake up, sleeper!*[l] *Get up from the dead,*[m] *and Christ will shine on you.*[n]

[j]Zech 8:16 [k]Ps 4:4 [l]Isa 26:19; 51:17; 52:1; 60:1 [m]Isa 26:19 [n]Isa 60:1

Be filled with the Spirit

[15]So be careful to live your life wisely, not foolishly. [16]Take advantage of every opportunity because these are evil times. [17]Because of this, don't be ignorant, but understand the Lord's will. [18]Don't get drunk on wine, which produces depravity. Instead, be filled with the Spirit in the following ways: [19]speak to each other with psalms, hymns, and spiritual songs; sing and make music to the Lord in your hearts; [20]always give thanks to God the Father for everything in the name of our Lord Jesus Christ; [21]and submit to each other out of respect for Christ. [22]For example, wives should submit to their husbands as if to the Lord. [23]A husband is the head of his wife like Christ is head of the church, that is, the savior of the body. [24]So wives submit to their husbands in everything like the church submits to Christ. [25]As for husbands, love your wives just like Christ loved the church and gave himself for her. [26]He did this to make her holy by washing her in a bath of water with the word. [27]He did this to present himself with a splendid church, one without any sort of stain or wrinkle on her clothes, but rather one that is holy and blameless. [28]That's how husbands ought to love their wives—in the same way as they do their own bodies. Anyone who loves his wife loves himself. [29]No one ever hates his own body, but feeds it and takes care of it just like Christ does for the church [30]because we are parts of his body. [31]*This is why a man will leave his father and mother and be united with his wife, and the two of them will be one body.*[o] [32]Marriage is a significant allegory,[p] and I'm applying it to Christ and the church. [33]In any case, as for you individually, each one of you should love his wife as himself, and wives should respect[q] their husbands.

6 As for children, obey your parents in the Lord, because it is right. [2]The commandment *Honor your father and mother* is the first one with a promise attached: [3]*so that things will go well for you, and you will live for a long time in the land.*[r] [4]As for parents, don't provoke your children to anger, but raise them with discipline and instruction about the Lord.

[5]As for slaves, obey your human masters with fear and trembling and with sincere devotion to Christ. [6]Don't work to make yourself look good and try to flatter people, but act like slaves of Christ carrying out God's will from the heart. [7]Serve your own-

[o]Gen 2:24   [p]Or *mystery*   [q]Or *fear*   [r]Exod 20:12; Deut 5:16

LIGHT AND DARKNESS (NT)

Light and darkness continue in the NT as a metaphor for knowledge or ignorance of God. Light and darkness are also metaphors for human lives attuned either to God or to the world and the powers of evil. The ways of the nations can be described as darkness (Rom 2:19), but the completion of the apocalyptic process will result in the recognition of the light by all nations (Rev 21:24).

Although Jesus is the "light of the world" in John's Gospel, the other Gospels insist that the community of believers is also a source of illumination as they "walk in the light" (Matt 5:14-16//Luke 8:16-17; Matt 10:27//Luke 12:3; Matt 6:22-23//Luke 11:33-36; see 1 John 1:7). The followers of Jesus are referred to as "people who belong to/whose lives are determined by the light" and "children of light" (Luke 16:8; John 12:36; Eph 5:8; 1 Thess 5:5).

Conversion is described as the movement from darkness to light (2 Cor 4:6; Acts 26:18; 1 Pet 2:9), and those who separate themselves from darkness show it in a new way of life (Eph 5:8-11).

ers enthusiastically, as though you were serving the Lord and not human beings. [8]You know that the Lord will reward every person who does what is right, whether that person is a slave or a free person. [9]As for masters, treat your slaves in the same way. Stop threatening them, because you know that both you and your slaves have a master in heaven. He doesn't distinguish between people on the basis of status.

Put on the armor of God

[10]Finally, be strengthened by the Lord and his powerful strength. [11]Put on God's armor so that you can make a stand against the tricks of the devil. [12]We aren't fighting against human enemies but against rulers, authorities, forces of cosmic darkness, and spiritual powers of evil in the heavens. [13]Therefore, pick up the full armor of God so that you can stand your ground on the evil day and after you have done everything possible to still stand. [14]So stand with the belt of truth around your waist, justice as your breastplate, [15]and put shoes on your feet so that you are ready to spread the good news of peace. [16]Above all, carry the shield of faith so that you can extinguish the flaming arrows of the evil one. [17]Take the helmet of salvation and the sword of the Spirit, which is God's word.

[18]Offer prayers and petitions in the Spirit all the time. Stay alert by hanging in there and praying for all believers. [19]As for me, pray that when I open my mouth, I'll get a message that confidently makes this secret plan[s] of the gospel known. [20]I'm an ambassador in chains for the sake of the gospel. Pray so that the Lord will give me the confidence to say what I have to say.

Final greeting

[21]Tychicus, my loved brother and faithful servant of the Lord, can inform you about my situation and what I'm doing. [22]I've sent him for this reason—so that you will know about us. He can reassure you.

[23]May there be peace with the brothers and sisters as well as love with the faith that comes from God the Father and the Lord Jesus Christ. [24]May grace be with all those who love our Lord Jesus Christ forever.

[s]Or mystery

ARMOR OF GOD

The armor of God is a rare feature of the larger biblical tradition of divine warfare (e.g., Exod 14–15; Deut 32–33; Pss 18; 68; Hab 3). Isaiah 59:17 is the earliest biblical instance of God wearing armor. God fights against a violent society where no one intervenes on behalf of vulnerable victims.

Paul transformed this idea, bringing human actions into the sphere of God's warfare. In 1 Thessalonians 5:8, Paul transfers God's breastplate and helmet onto the Thessalonians themselves. In Ephesians 6:10-17 believers are to put on God's armor for struggle, not against human enemies, but against the diabolical powers that control that society (2:1-3; 6:12). Added to Isaiah's breastplate and helmet are a belt of truth, footwear of the good news of peace, a shield of faith, and the sword of the Spirit, God's word (vv. 14-17). The Pauline view of the church as the body of the Christ who is himself at war with the powers (1 Cor 15:24-26) but who kills with his own death on the cross (Eph 2:16), accounts for the transfer of the divine armor to believers. With the emphasis on peace (6:15), the armor becomes, ironically, a metaphor for the battle against war and violence.

THEME

The progress of the gospel

THE CHURCH AT PHILIPPI

According to the book of Acts, Paul founded the church at Philippi on his second missionary journey, probably in 50 CE. He crossed over the Aegean Sea—from Troas in the province of Asia (modern western Turkey) to Neapolis in Macedonia and on to the nearby Philippi—in response to a nighttime vision at Troas (Acts 16:9-10). Silas, Timothy, and possibly Luke (Acts 16:10) were with him.

Philippi, the most important city of the first district of Macedonia in Paul's time (Acts 16:12), had been built (or rebuilt) about the middle of the fourth century BCE by Philip II of Macedon, the father of Alexander the Great. The city had become part of the Roman Empire after Rome's defeat of the Macedonians in 168 BCE. After 42 BCE it was enlarged by Mark Antony and Octavian (Augustus), settled with Roman colonists, made a Roman colony governed by "Italian law," and blessed with all the privileges Rome bestowed on citizens who lived in its colonies.

The city, located in a fertile area fed by copious springs and with gold and silver mines nearby, lay astride the main road connecting Rome with Byzantium in the East. The inhabitants were mostly Romans and Macedonian Greeks, with some Jews as well.

The religions of the city were many, centering in the worship of Roman, Greek, and Thracian gods and goddesses, deities from Phrygia and Egypt, and Yahweh of the Jews.

Whether there was a Jewish synagogue at Philippi is uncertain. Acts refers to a place for prayer by the side of a river, where some women had gathered (Acts 16:13). Since Jewish synagogues were sometimes built close to water for convenience for ritual washings, a small synagogue may have stood there.

The first convert at Philippi was a Gentile woman called Lydia (Acts 16:14). Apparently Lydia was a seller at Philippi (and elsewhere) of purple-dyed cloth, made at Thyatira in Lydia (south-central Asia Minor). It may be that the name Lydia means simply *the Lydian*, and that she had an unknown personal name. She offered her home to the missionaries as a place of residence and as the gathering place of the fledgling church (Acts 16:15, 40).

Women seem to have had a prominent part in the life and work of the Philippian church, even in the proclamation of the gospel (Philippians 4:3). This accords with the general status of women in Macedonia, where they played an unusually important role in the political, religious, and social life of the province.

How long the missionaries stayed in Philippi is unknown, probably a few weeks. The membership, besides Lydia and her household, included the converted jailer and his family (Acts 16:27-34), Epaphroditus (Philippians 2:25), Euodia, Syntyche, and Clement (Philippians 4:2-3). The names indicate that the church was largely Gentile.

Paul's mission at Philippi ended because he performed an exorcism that cost the local slave owners money and led to Paul's hearing before the magistrates and a subsequent beating and imprisonment (Acts 16:16-24). The charge was that the Jewish missionaries were troublemakers who were unlawfully promoting un-Roman customs (Acts 16:20-21). Paul might have revealed his Roman citizenship in order to escape beating and imprisonment without a proper trial before the proconsul of the province, but he did not do so. He may have wished to embarrass the local magistrates and thereby gain a more favorable position for the church (Acts 16:35-39).

Through the missionaries a vigorous church was raised up at Philippi, one that Paul trusted implicitly and one that made a unique contribution to his subsequent ministry (Philippians 1:5, 7; 4:14-16).

PLACE AND DATE OF WRITING

Acts records only three of Paul's prison experiences: at Philippi (16:23-40); at Caesarea (23:35; 24:23, 27); and at Rome (28:16, 20). But Paul speaks of more imprisonments than his opponents had experienced (2 Corinthians 11:23); and Clement, a Roman Christian, wrote that Paul was in prison seven times. Many modern scholars have argued that to the three in Acts we should add one in Ephesus and perhaps one in Corinth.

The arguments for an imprisonment in Corinth are weak, but one at Ephesus is quite possible. First Corinthians 15:32, Acts 20:17-19, 2 Corinthians 1:8-10, and Philippians and Philemon offer support for such a conclusion.

If Paul was in prison in Ephesus (about 55 CE), this city's relative closeness to Philippi helps us understand Paul's many exchanges with the Philippian church while he was confined. These exchanges are: News of Paul's arrest reached Philippi (Philippians 1:13-14); the Philippians sent a gift by Epaphroditus to aid him (2:25; 4:18); news of Epaphroditus's illness is carried back to Philippi (2:26); word comes to Paul and Epaphroditus concerning the Philippians' distress over Epaphroditus's illness (2:26); Paul hopes to send Timothy to Philippi and to receive a report back from him (2:19) and to go to Philippi himself (2:24).

If Paul had written the letter to the Philippians from Rome or Caesarea, so many exchanges with the Philippians while he was in prison seem difficult or unlikely. Journeys between Ephesus and Philippi could be made in about a week, whereas trips between Rome and Philippi (some 800 miles) and Caesarea, which is even farther from Philippi, would require a month or more.

Other arguments exist for Ephesus as the place of origin. There was a praetorium (the governor's residence) at Ephesus (Philippians 1:13), and those of Caesar's household (4:22) could mean slaves and freedmen in the governor's service there. Also, the language, style, issues addressed, and concepts of Philippians bear some similarities to those in 1 and 2 Corinthians, letters written at Ephesus or shortly thereafter.

Scholars who argue for Rome or Caesarea as the place of writing of Philippians point out that the Ephesian imprisonment is only hypothetical. The two-year period Paul was in prison both in Caesarea (Acts 24:27) and Rome (Acts 28:30) allows plenty of time for the exchanges with the Philippians noted above. Furthermore, the references in Philippians to the praetorium and Caesar's household connect more naturally with Rome or Caesarea (Acts 23:35). The best evidence for Rome as the place of origin is the fact that in Philippians Paul seems to be awaiting a final life-or-death decision (1:20-26; 2:23). He would not have expected a final decision at Ephesus or Caesarea, since, as a Roman citizen, he had the right of appeal to Caesar's court in Rome.

At present, equally good reasons can be cited in support of Ephesus, Rome, or Caesarea. Fortunately, the exact place of origin is not crucial to an understanding of the message of Philippians.

THE UNITY OF THE LETTER

There is considerable roughness in the flow of thought in the letter. The sudden outburst in 3:2-3 is surprising. Also, 3:1 seems to connect logically with 4:4, making the intervening material appear intrusive. The farewell and benediction of 4:4-9 could well end the letter. But a long section about Epaphroditus and the Philippians' gift, which would appropriately appear near the beginning of the letter (or at least in connection with 2:19-30), is tacked on. And why doesn't 2:19-30, with its practical concerns, come at the end, according to Paul's usual practice?

Many scholars have concluded that two or three letters were combined into our present letter by someone later than Paul. Their reasons are, in part, the roughness noted above; the likelihood that Paul wrote more than one letter to his favorite church; the fact that 2 Corinthians appears to have been compiled by a later editor from at least two letters addressed to the Corinthians; and a reference by the second-century Christian martyr Polycarp to "letters" written by Paul to the Philippians.

Various attempts, not always agreeing in details, have been made to identify these letters. The hypothesis of two letters usually assigns to the first letter 3:2–4:23 and to the second 1:1–3:1. The hypothesis of three letters goes as follows: letter one 4:10-20; letter two 1:1–3:1; 4:2-9, 21-23; and letter three 3:2–4:1.

Many scholars argue for the unity of the letter we have. They point out that Paul was writing an informal letter, not a logical treatise. He may have been interrupted in his dictation and begun again without careful consideration of logical sequence. Such breaks in logical sequence appear in other letters he wrote (for example, Romans 16:17-20; 2 Corinthians 2:14-16). Furthermore, why would a later editor arrange the supposed letters in the illogical fashion we find here? And what happened to the original openings and conclusions of the previous letters?

Since scholars have not agreed on the question of the letter's unity, it is best to study the letter as it now is, rather than to try to rearrange its "original" parts for chronological consideration.

THE PURPOSES OF THE LETTER

(1) The letter informs the Philippians of Paul's present situation and his prospects for the future (1:12-26; 2:24).

(2) It thanks the Philippians for their gift (1:5; 4:10-20).

(3) It insures a good reception for Epaphroditus, who was returning with the letter (2:25-30).

(4) It prepares the way for the coming of Timothy (2:19-23).

(5) It assists the Philippians in solving certain problems in the church—persecution by opponents (probably Gentiles and Jews, and possibly legalistic or Gnostic Christians) (1:28-30; 3:2-19) and dissension among members (1:27; 2:2-3; 4:2-3)—and encourages them to move on toward Christian maturity (3:12-21).

PHILIPPIANS

Greeting

1 From Paul and Timothy, slaves of Christ Jesus.

To all those in Philippi who are God's people in Christ Jesus, along with your supervisors[a] and servants.[b] ²May the grace and peace from God our Father and the Lord Jesus Christ be with you.

Thanksgiving and prayer

³I thank my God every time I mention you in my prayers. ⁴I'm thankful for all of you every time I pray, and it's always a prayer full of joy. ⁵I'm glad because of the way you have been my partners in the ministry of the gospel from the time you first believed it until now. ⁶I'm sure about this: the one who started a good work in you will stay with you to complete the job by the day of Christ Jesus. ⁷I have good reason to think this way about all of you because I keep you in my heart. You are all my partners in God's grace, both during my time in prison and in the defense and support of the gospel. ⁸God is my witness that I feel affection for all of you with the compassion of Christ Jesus.

⁹This is my prayer: that your love might become even more and more rich with knowledge and all kinds of insight. ¹⁰I pray this so that you will be able to decide what really matters and so you will be sincere and blameless on the day of Christ. ¹¹I pray that you will then be filled with the fruit of righteousness, which comes from Jesus Christ, in order to give glory and praise to God.

Priority of the gospel

¹²Brothers and sisters, I want you to know that the things that have happened to me have actually advanced the gospel. ¹³The whole Praetorian Guard and everyone else knows that I'm in prison for Christ. ¹⁴Most of the brothers and sisters have had more confidence through the Lord to speak the word boldly and bravely because of my jail time. ¹⁵Some certainly preach Christ with jealous and competitive motives, but others preach with good motives. ¹⁶They are motivated by love, because they know that I'm put here to give a defense of the gospel; ¹⁷the others preach Christ because of their selfish ambition. They are insincere, hoping to cause me more pain while I'm in prison.

¹⁸What do I think about this? Just this: since Christ is proclaimed in every possible way, whether from dishonest or true motives, I'm glad and I'll continue to be glad. ¹⁹I'm glad because I know that this will result in my release through your prayers and the help of the Spirit of Jesus Christ. ²⁰It is my expectation and hope that I won't be put to shame in anything. Rather, I hope with daring courage that Christ's greatness will be seen in my body, now as always, whether I live or die. ²¹Because for me, living serves Christ and dying is even better. ²²If I continue to live in this world, I get results from my work. ²³But I don't know

[a]Or overseers, bishops [b]Or deacons

PRAETORIAN GUARD

The title originally described the select group of legionaries who guarded the praetor (commander) of a Roman army. The praetor's location was the praetorium, a structure in the center of the camp; the term came to be applied to a governor's residence (Matt 27:27; Mark 15:16; John 18:28, 33; 19:9). Philippians 1:13 refers to the Praetorian Guard, suggesting that some guardsmen became devotees of Jesus.

what I prefer. I'm torn between the two because I want to leave this life and be with Christ, which is far better. [24]However, it's more important for me to stay in this world for your sake. [25]I'm sure of this: I will stay alive and remain with all of you to help your progress and the joy of your faith, [26]and to increase your pride in Christ Jesus through my presence when I visit you again.

Live worthy of the gospel

[27]Most important, live together in a manner worthy of Christ's gospel. Do this, whether I come and see you or I'm absent and hear about you. Do this so that you stand firm, united in one spirit and mind as you struggle together to remain faithful to the gospel. [28]That way, you won't be afraid of anything your enemies do. Your faithfulness and courage are a sign of their coming destruction and your salvation, which is from God. [29]God has generously granted you the privilege, not only of believing in Christ but also of suffering for Christ's sake. [30]You are having the same struggle that you saw me face and now hear that I'm still facing.

Imitate Christ

2 Therefore, if there is any encouragement in Christ, any comfort in love, any sharing in the Spirit, any sympathy, [2]complete my joy by thinking the same way, having the same love, being united, and agreeing with each other. [3]Don't do anything for selfish

purposes, but with humility think of others as better than yourselves. [4]Instead of each person watching out for their own good, watch out for what is better for others. [5]Adopt the attitude that was in Christ Jesus:

[6]Though he was in the form of God,
    he did not consider being equal
    with God something to exploit.
[7]But he emptied himself
    by taking the form of a slave
    and by becoming like human beings.
When he found himself
    in the form of a human,
[8]he humbled himself by becoming
    obedient to the point of death,
    even death on a cross.
[9]Therefore, God highly honored him
    and gave him a name above all names,
[10]so that at the name of Jesus everyone
    in heaven, on earth,
    and under the earth might bow
[11]and every tongue confess that
    Jesus Christ is Lord,
    to the glory of God the Father.

Carry out your salvation

[12]Therefore, my loved ones, just as you always obey me, not just when I am present but now even more while I am away, carry out your own salvation with fear and trembling. [13]God is the one who enables you both to want and to actually live out his good purposes. [14]Do everything without grumbling and arguing [15]so that you may

EPAPHRODITUS

A leader in Paul's assembly at Philippi who was sent by the assembly (Phil 2:25, 30) to take gifts to Paul when he was in prison (Phil 4:18). Presumably the carrier of the letter to the Philippians (cf. Phil 2:25, 28), Epaphroditus was also sent back to the assembly to show them that he had recovered from his grave illness (Phil 2:26-28). Paul does not describe the nature of the illness, but Epaphroditus's willingness to serve as the assembly's proxy, even nearly dying (Phil 2:30), both emulates Christ's action of obedience "to the point of death" (Phil 2:8) and illustrates the mindset (Phil 2:5) the Philippians were being called to embrace.

be blameless and pure, innocent children of God surrounded by people who are crooked and corrupt. Among these people you shine like stars in the world ¹⁶because you hold on to the word of life. This will allow me to say on the day of Christ that I haven't run for nothing or worked for nothing. ¹⁷But even if I am poured out like a drink offering upon the altar of service for your faith, I am glad. I'm glad with all of you. ¹⁸You should be glad about this in the same way. Be glad with me!

Sending Timothy and Epaphroditus

¹⁹I hope in the Lord Jesus to send Timothy to see you soon so that I may be encouraged by hearing about you. ²⁰I have no one like him. He is a person who genuinely cares about your well-being. ²¹All the others put their own business ahead of Jesus Christ's business. ²²You know his character, how he labors with me for the gospel like a son works with his father. ²³So he is the one that I hope to send as soon as I find out how things turn out here for me. ²⁴I trust in the Lord that I also will visit you soon.

²⁵I think it is also necessary to send Epaphroditus to you. He is my brother, coworker, and fellow soldier; and he is your representative who serves my needs. ²⁶He misses you all, and he was upset because you heard he was sick. ²⁷In fact, he was so sick that he nearly died. But God had mercy on him—and not just on him but also on me, because his death would have caused me great sorrow. ²⁸Therefore, I am sending him immediately so that when you see him again you can be glad and I won't worry. ²⁹So welcome him in the Lord with great joy and show great respect for people like him. ³⁰He risked his life and almost died for the work of Christ, and he did this to make up for the help you couldn't give me.

Values and priorities

3 So then, my brothers and sisters, be glad in the Lord. It's no trouble for me to repeat the same things to you because they will help keep you on track. ²Watch out for the "dogs." Watch out for people who do evil things. Watch out for those who insist on circumcision, which is really mutilation. ³We are the circumcision. We are the ones who serve by God's Spirit and who boast in Christ Jesus. We don't put our confidence in rituals performed on the body, ⁴though I have good reason to have this kind of confidence. If anyone else has reason to put their confidence in physical advantages, I have even more:

⁵I was circumcised on the eighth day.

I am from the people of Israel and the tribe of Benjamin.

I am a Hebrew of the Hebrews.

With respect to observing the Law, I'm a Pharisee.

⁶With respect to devotion to the faith, I harassed the church.

With respect to righteousness under the Law, I'm blameless.

⁷These things were my assets, but I wrote them off as a loss for the sake of Christ. ⁸But even beyond that, I consider everything a loss in comparison with the superior value of knowing Christ Jesus my Lord. I have lost everything for him, but what I lost I think of as sewer trash, so that I might gain Christ ⁹and be found in him. In Christ I have a righteousness that is not my own and that does not come from the Law but rather from the faithfulness of Christ. It is the righteousness of God that is based on faith. ¹⁰The righteousness that I have comes from knowing Christ, the power of his resurrection, and the participation in his sufferings. It includes being conformed to his death ¹¹so that I may perhaps reach the goal of the resurrection of the dead.

¹²It's not that I have already reached this goal or have already been perfected, but I pursue it, so that I may grab hold of it because Christ grabbed hold of me for just this purpose. ¹³Brothers and sisters, I myself don't think I've reached it, but I do this one thing: I forget about the things behind me and reach out for the things ahead of me. ¹⁴The goal I pursue is the prize of God's upward call in Christ Jesus. ¹⁵So all of us who are spiritually mature should think this way, and if anyone thinks differently,

God will reveal it to him or her. [16]Only let's live in a way that is consistent with whatever level we have reached.

Imitate Paul

[17]Brothers and sisters, become imitators of me and watch those who live this way—you can use us as models. [18]As I have told you many times and now say with deep sadness, many people live as enemies of the cross. [19]Their lives end with destruction. Their god is their stomach, and they take pride in their disgrace because their thoughts focus on earthly things. [20]Our citizenship is in heaven. We look forward to a savior that comes from there—the Lord Jesus Christ. [21]He will transform our humble bodies so that they are like his glorious body, by the power that also makes him able to subject all things to himself.

Stand firm in the Lord

4 Therefore, my brothers and sisters whom I love and miss, who are my joy and crown, stand firm in the Lord.

Loved ones, [2]I urge Euodia and I urge Syntyche to come to an agreement in the Lord. [3]Yes, and I'm also asking you, loyal friend, to help these women who have struggled together with me in the ministry of the gospel, along with Clement and the rest of my coworkers whose names are in the scroll of life.

[4]Be glad in the Lord always! Again I say, be glad! [5]Let your gentleness show in your treatment of all people. The Lord is near. [6]Don't be anxious about anything; rather, bring up all of your requests to God in your prayers and petitions, along with giving thanks. [7]Then the peace of God that exceeds all understanding will keep your hearts and minds safe in Christ Jesus.

[8]From now on, brothers and sisters, if anything is excellent and if anything is admirable, focus your thoughts on these things: all that is true, all that is holy, all that is just, all that is pure, all that is lovely, and all that is worthy of praise. [9]Practice these things: whatever you learned, received, heard, or saw in us. The God of peace will be with you.

Paul's thanks for gifts

[10]I was very glad in the Lord because now at last you have shown concern for me again. (Of course you were always concerned but had no way to show it.) [11]I'm not saying this because I need anything, for I have learned how to be content in any circumstance. [12]I know the experience of being in need and of having more than enough; I have learned the secret to being content in any and every circumstance, whether full or hungry or whether having plenty or being poor. [13]I can endure all these things through the power of the one who gives me strength. [14]Still, you have done well to share my distress.

[15]You Philippians know from the time of my first mission work in Macedonia how no church shared in supporting my ministry except you. [16]You sent contributions repeatedly to take care of my needs even while I was in Thessalonica. [17]I'm not hoping for a gift, but I am hoping for a profit that accumulates in your account. [18]I now have plenty and it is more than enough. I am full to overflowing because I received

EUODIA

Paul urges this Christian woman to agree with fellow believer Syntyche so that they can live in harmony in the church in Philippi (Phil 4:2), continuing the tradition of women leaders in the church in Philippi (cf. Acts 16:40). Euodia and Syntyche are included in the group of "coworkers" having previously helped Paul in his evangelistic endeavors (Phil 4:3).

the gifts that you sent from Epaphroditus. Those gifts give off a fragrant aroma, an acceptable sacrifice that pleases God. [19]My God will meet your every need out of his riches in the glory that is found in Christ Jesus. [20]Let glory be given to God our Father forever and always. Amen.

Final greeting

[21]Greet all God's people in Christ Jesus. The brothers and sisters with me send you their greeting. [22]All God's people here, especially those in Caesar's household, send you their greeting. [23]The grace of the Lord Jesus Christ be with your spirits.

COLOSSIANS

THEME

The supremacy and all-sufficiency of Christ in the salvation of believers

THE CHURCH AT COLOSSAE

From the fifth century BCE, Colossae (in the Lycus River valley of central Asia Minor, some 100 miles east of Ephesus) was a populous wool-working and cloth-dyeing center. It lay near the cities of Hierapolis and Laodicea. The three cities, all prosperous, vied with one another in the textile and wool-dyeing industry. They are mentioned together in Colossians 4:13.

The church at Colossae was founded by Epaphras (1:7). He was a Colossian (4:12) who may have been converted by Paul during his long ministry at Ephesus (Acts 19:10) and who represented Paul (Colossians 1:7) in the evangelization of the three cities of the Lycus valley (4:12-13). Epaphras was in prison with Paul at the time of the writing of this letter (Philemon v. 23). He was the source of Paul's information about the situation in the church at Colossae (Colossians 1:8).

Philemon, Paul's convert (Philemon v. 19)—also probably at Ephesus—was the owner of the slave Onesimus (Philemon v. 15; Colossians 4:9). Philemon was a prominent member of the church at Colossae. His house was large enough to accommodate the meetings of the Christian church (Philemon v. 2) and to have a guest room for Paul (Philemon v. 22).

PAUL'S PURPOSE IN WRITING TO THE COLOSSIANS

Paul had never been to Colossae (Colossians 1:4, 9), but he felt a responsibility for the church there. Not only had a convert of his founded the church, probably under his direction (1:7), but he knew himself to be God's apostle and priest to the whole Gentile world (Romans 15:16; Colossians 1:24-29). The church at Colossae lay in his special area of evangelization (Romans 15:19-20; 2 Corinthians 10:13-18). Undoubtedly, when Epaphras described its needs to Paul, he resolved to help by writing this letter.

Several purposes are apparent.

(1) Some people, whether members of the church or not, were advocating a philosophy and foolish deception (2:8) that threatened to undermine the truth about Jesus Christ long preached by the church and the way of

salvation taught by Paul. The philosophy involved the worship of angelic, cosmic powers (2:8, 18, 20) in addition to Christ. These were celestial spirits who apparently were regarded as God's agents in governing the movements of the heavenly bodies. Thus the spirits in some respects controlled human destiny, as astrological thought holds. Their worshipers observed feast days, special seasons, and certain practices to honor and perhaps appease these spirits (2:16-23).

Apparently it was taught that all these powers, along with Christ, constituted God's fullness, that is, the full range of God's attributes and manifestations. Allegiance to Christ was not enough to guarantee salvation. The ruling powers also had to be recognized and pacified.

This philosophy stressed special visions offering secret knowledge of ultimate reality and the way of salvation. Paul thought that such knowledge led to pretensions and self-congratulation (2:18).

The heresy seems to have been a mixture of elements from several sources: Judaism (perhaps like that found in the Dead Sea Scrolls); early Gnosticism and Hellenistic astrology and pagan mystery cults. Paul felt that glorifying and pacifying astral powers debased Christ and introduced practices that were a threat to Christian freedom.

(2) Paul meant by the letter to introduce Tychicus, the carrier of the letter, who was to encourage the Colossians in the true way of salvation and inform them about Paul's circumstances (4:7-8).

(3) Paul wanted to ensure a good reception for Onesimus, the converted runaway slave, who was returning in company with Tychicus to his master at Colossae (4:9).

(4) Epaphras, the founder of the church, apparently was under attack by the heretic philosophers and needed Paul's support. This letter would enhance his standing with the Colossian church (4:12-13).

(5) Paul meant to prepare the way for the visit of Mark (4:10); and also to urge Archippus, possibly Philemon's son or a resident in Philemon's house (Philemon vv. 1-2), to carry out some responsibility entrusted to him in the Lord's service (4:17). Since Epaphras was in prison with Paul, it may be that Archippus was to carry on Epaphras's pastoral responsibilities.

(6) Finally, Paul seems to wish to establish his authority and teaching firmly in the Gentile churches, both those founded directly by him and those raised up by his followers (1:7, 23-29; 4:16).

AUTHORSHIP, PLACE, AND DATE

Two positions are widely held today on the question of authorship.
The first says that Paul, as the letter clearly claims (1:1, 23; 4:18), was the author.

As was frequent with Paul (1 Corinthians 16:21; Galatians 6:11; Colossians 4:18; 2 Thessalonians 3:17), he added an authentication in his own handwriting.

In Colossians there is some variation in language, style, and theology from Paul's other letters, due to the special circumstances under which Colossians was written. But the similarities to the other letters are greater than the dissimilarities.

Furthermore, strong ties with the letter to Philemon, unquestionably written by Paul, argue for Paul's authorship of Colossians. The two letters have the same senders (Paul and Timothy), greetings from many of the same persons (Aristarchus, Mark, Epaphras, Luke, Demas), and the mention of Archippus. The letters seem to have been written at about the same time and carried to Colossae by Tychicus and Onesimus.

The second option is that a disciple of Paul wrote the letter to the Colossians in Paul's name.

Many facts argue that Paul was not the author. A few are: the use of many words not found elsewhere in Paul's letters; the absence of Paul's characteristic ideas (righteousness, justification by faith alone, the purpose and function of the law); the highly speculative view of Christ, especially in 1:15-20; and the strong emphasis on apostolic tradition as a way of counteracting heresy.

Possibly a disciple of Paul, one who was thoroughly familiar with Paul's language and thoughts, used his master's authority as a way of meeting heresy sometime after Paul's death.

If the letter was written by Paul, the place was Ephesus, Rome, or Caesarea. The date was about 55-62 CE. If a disciple wrote it, the time was after Paul's death, possibly 70-90 CE, and the place is unknown.

COLOSSIANS

Greeting

1 From Paul, an apostle of Christ Jesus by God's will, and Timothy our brother. ²To the holy and faithful brothers and sisters in Christ in Colossae.

Grace and peace to you from God our Father.

Thanksgiving and prayer for the Colossians

³We always give thanks to God, the Father of our Lord Jesus Christ, when we pray for you. ⁴We've done this since we heard of your faith in Christ Jesus and your love for all God's people. ⁵You have this faith and love because of the hope reserved for you in heaven. You previously heard about this hope through the true message, the good news, ⁶which has come to you. This message has been bearing fruit and growing among you since the day you heard and truly understood God's grace, in the same way that it is bearing fruit and grow-ing in the whole world. ⁷You learned it from Epaphras, who is the fellow slave we love and Christ's faithful minister for your sake. ⁸He informed us of your love in the Spirit.

⁹Because of this, since the day we heard about you, we haven't stopped praying for you and asking for you to be filled with the knowledge of God's will, with all wisdom and spiritual understanding. ¹⁰We're pray-ing this so that you can live lives that are worthy of the Lord and pleasing to him in every way: by producing fruit in every good work and growing in the knowledge of God; ¹¹by being strengthened through his glori-ous might so that you endure everything and have patience; ¹²and by giving thanks with joy to the Father. He made it so you could take part in the inheritance, in light granted to God's holy people. ¹³He rescued us from the control of darkness and trans-ferred us into the kingdom of the Son he loves. ¹⁴He set us free through the Son and forgave our sins.

HEAD

The head as the upper part of the body (Gen 28:11, 18; 40:16-17). People bowed their heads in worship or prayer (Gen 24:26, 48; Ps 5:7), and kings (1 Sam 10:1; 2 Kgs 9:3, 6) and priests (Exod 29:7; Lev 21:10) were installed by anointing their heads with oil. Mourners put dust or ashes on their heads (2 Sam 13:19; Job 42:6), people covered their heads in shame (Jer 14:3-4), and mockers wagged their heads (2 Kgs 19:21; Ps 64:8). Lifting one's head showed pride (Judg 8:28; Job 10:15), unless it was God who lifted it (Pss 3:3 [CEB "restores"]; 27:6). People's evil deeds were said to return upon their heads (Josh 2:19 [CEB "take the blame"]; 1 Sam 25:39). The head was also considered to be the seat of a person's intellect (Dan 4:5, 10, 13 [CEB "mind"]); and a "head" was one person counted in a census.

In the NT, *head* likewise occurs most frequently in a literal sense (Matt 5:36; 10:30; Mark 12:4; John 13:9), including references to Jesus' head (Matt 8:20; 26:7; 27:29; Mark 14:3; Luke 7:46; 9:58; John 19:2, 30); and Revela-tion features several references to the heads of various apocalyptic figures (e.g., 4:4; 9:7, 17, 19). In keeping with OT usage, the expression figura-tively refers to leadership or authority in Paul's writings. Hence Paul calls Christ the head of the church (1 Cor 11:3; Eph 1:22; 4:15-16; 5:23; Col 1:18; 2:10, 19).

Hymn about Christ's work

[15] The Son is the image of the invisible God,
the one who is first over all creation,[a]

[16] Because all things were created by him:
both in the heavens and on the earth,
the things that are visible
and the things that are invisible.
Whether they are thrones or powers,
or rulers or authorities,
all things were created
through him and for him.

[17] He existed before all things,
and all things are held together in him.

[18] He is the head of the body, the church,
who is the beginning,
the one who is firstborn
from among the dead[b]
so that he might occupy
the first place in everything.

[19] Because all the fullness of God
was pleased to live in him,

[20] and he reconciled all things to himself
through him—
whether things on earth
or in the heavens.
He brought peace
through the blood of his cross.

[21] Once you were alienated from God and you were enemies with him in your minds, which was shown by your evil actions. [22] But now he has reconciled you by his physical body through death, to present you before God as a people who are holy, faultless, and without blame. [23] But you need to remain well established and rooted in faith and not shift away from the hope given in the good news that you heard. This message has been preached throughout all creation under heaven. And I, Paul, became a servant of this good news.

Paul's service for the church

[24] Now I'm happy to be suffering for you. I'm completing what is missing from Christ's sufferings with my own body. I'm doing this for the sake of his body, which is the church. [25] I became a servant of the church by God's commission, which was given to me for you, in order to complete God's word. [26] I'm completing it with a secret plan[c] that has been hidden for ages and generations but which has now been revealed to his holy people. [27] God wanted to make the glorious riches of this secret plan[d] known among the Gentiles, which is Christ living in you, the hope of glory. [28] This is what we preach as we warn and teach every person with all wisdom so that we might present each one mature in Christ. [29] I work hard and struggle for this goal with his energy, which works in me powerfully.

[2] I want you to know how much I struggle for you, for those in Laodicea, and for all who haven't known me personally. [2] My goal is that their hearts would be encouraged and united together in love so that they might have all the riches of assurance that come with understanding, so that they might have the knowledge of the secret plan[e] of God, namely Christ. [3] All the treasures of wisdom and knowledge are hidden in him. [4] I'm telling you this so that no one deceives you with convincing arguments, [5] because even though I am absent physically, I'm with you in spirit. I'm happy to see the discipline and stability of your faith in Christ.

Error threatening the church

[6] So live in Christ Jesus the Lord in the same way as you received him. [7] Be rooted and built up in him, be established in faith, and overflow with thanksgiving just as you were taught. [8] See to it that nobody enslaves you with philosophy and foolish deception, which conform to human traditions and the way the world thinks and acts rather than Christ. [9] All the fullness of deity lives in Christ's body. [10] And you have been filled by him, who is the head of every ruler and authority. [11] You were also circumcised by him. This wasn't performed by human hands—the whole body

---

[a] Or firstborn of all creation [b] Or first over the dead [c] Or mystery [d] Or mystery [e] Or mystery

was removed through this circumcision by Christ. [12]You were buried with him through baptism and raised with him through faith in the power of God, who raised him from the dead. [13]When you were dead because of the things you had done wrong and because your body wasn't circumcised, God made you alive with Christ and forgave all the things you had done wrong. [14]He destroyed the record of the debt we owed, with its requirements that worked against us. He canceled it by nailing it to the cross. [15]When he disarmed the rulers and authorities, he exposed them to public disgrace by leading them in a triumphal parade.

[16]So don't let anyone judge you about eating or drinking or about a festival, a new moon observance, or sabbaths. [17]These religious practices are only a shadow of what was coming—the body that cast the shadow is Christ. [18]Don't let anyone who wants to practice harsh self-denial and worship angels rob you of the prize. They go into detail about what they have seen in visions and have become unjustifiably arrogant by their selfish way of thinking. [19]They don't stay connected to the head. The head nourishes and supports the whole body through the joints and ligaments, so the body grows with a growth that is from God.

[20]If you died with Christ to the way the world thinks and acts, why do you submit to rules and regulations as though you were living in the world? [21]"Don't handle!" "Don't taste!" "Don't touch!" [22]All these things cease to exist when they are used. Such rules are human commandments and teachings. [23]They look like they are wise with this self-made religion and their self-denial by the harsh treatment of the body, but they are no help against indulging in selfish immoral behavior.

Your life hidden in Christ

3 Therefore, if you were raised with Christ, look for the things that are above where Christ is sitting at God's right side. [2]Think about the things above and not things on earth. [3]You died, and your life is hidden with Christ in God. [4]When Christ, who is your life, is revealed, then you also will be revealed with him in glory.

[5]So put to death the parts of your life that belong to the earth, such as sexual immorality, moral corruption, lust, evil desire, and greed (which is idolatry). [6]The wrath of God is coming upon disobedient people because of these things. [7]You used to live this way, when you were alive to these things. [8]But now set aside these things, such as

LAODICEA

Laodicea or its inhabitants are mentioned six times in the NT (Col 2:1; 4:13, 15, 16; Rev 1:11; 3:14). The passages in Colossians convey the depth and sincerity of Paul's concern for Christian congregations located in the Lycus Valley. The passages in Revelation contain a message from Christ scolding the Christians in Laodicea for their halfhearted efforts and lack of total commitment to the faith.

The city most probably was founded in the middle of the 3rd cent. BCE by the Syrian king Antiochus II (reigned 261–246 BCE). He named it in honor of his first wife, Laodice. It stood on a plateau about 6 mi. south of Hierapolis, approximately 10 mi. west of Colossae, and approximately 100 mi. east of Ephesus. It replaced two earlier settlements, Diospolis and Rhoas. It was originally intended to serve as a Seleucid stronghold against foreign invaders. Laodicea became a major thoroughfare for people traveling to and from Ephesus in the west or Pergamum and Sardis in the north.

anger, rage, malice, slander, and obscene language. [9]Don't lie to each other. Take off the old human nature with its practices [10]and put on the new nature, which is renewed in knowledge by conforming to the image of the one who created it. [11]In this image there is neither Greek nor Jew, circumcised nor uncircumcised, barbarian, Scythian, slave nor free, but Christ is all things and in all people.

[12]Therefore, as God's choice, holy and loved, put on compassion, kindness, humility, gentleness, and patience. [13]Be tolerant with each other and, if someone has a complaint against anyone, forgive each other. As the Lord forgave you, so also forgive each other. [14]And over all these things put on love, which is the perfect bond of unity. [15]The peace of Christ must control your hearts—a peace into which you were called in one body. And be thankful people. [16]The word of Christ must live in you richly. Teach and warn each other with all wisdom by singing psalms, hymns, and spiritual songs. Sing to God with gratitude in your hearts. [17]Whatever you do, whether in speech or action, do it all in the name of the Lord Jesus and give thanks to God the Father through him.

[18]Wives, submit to your husbands in a way that is appropriate in the Lord. [19]Husbands, love your wives and don't be harsh with them. [20]Children, obey your parents in everything, because this pleases the Lord. [21]Parents, don't provoke your children in a way that ends up discouraging them.

[22]Slaves, obey your masters on earth in everything. Don't just obey like people pleasers when they are watching. Instead, obey with the single motivation of fearing the Lord. [23]Whatever you do, do it from the heart for the Lord and not for people. [24]You know that you will receive an inheritance as a reward. You serve the Lord Christ. [25]But evildoers will receive their reward for their evil actions. There is no discrimination.

4 Masters, be just and fair to your slaves, knowing that you yourselves have a master in heaven.

[2]Keep on praying and guard your prayers with thanksgiving. [3]At the same time, pray for us also. Pray that God would open a door for the word so we can preach the secret plan[f] of Christ—which is why I'm in

---

[f]Or *mystery*

COLOSSAE

Access from the Aegean coast into the interior of Asia Minor (modern Turkey) was provided by river valleys. One of the most important was the Meander, running east from near Ephesus. About 100 mi. upstream it was joined by the river Lycus, whose valley provided the most accessible route to the central plateau and served as a major artery of east-west communication during the Greek and Roman periods. The fertile Lycus Valley also encouraged settlement and supported three prominent cities—Laodicea and Hierapolis, with Colossae a further 10 mi. upstream.

Four or five centuries before the time of the NT, Colossae had been populous, large and wealthy, its wealth due both to its position on the main road from Ephesus and Sardis to the Euphrates and its wool industry. But by the early years of the Roman Empire, its significance had been much reduced, in contrast to Laodicea (an administrative and financial center) and Hierapolis (famous for its hot mineral springs). Christianity was established there by Epaphras, a native of Colossae (Col 1:7; 4:12).

chains. [4]Pray that I might be able to make it as clear as I ought to when I preach. [5]Act wisely toward outsiders, making the most of the opportunity. [6]Your speech should always be gracious and sprinkled with insight so that you may know how to respond to every person.

Final greeting

[7]Tychicus, our dearly loved brother, faithful minister, and fellow slave in the Lord, will inform you about everything that has happened to me. [8]This is why I sent him to you, so that you'll know all about us and so he can encourage your hearts. [9]I sent him with Onesimus, our faithful and dearly loved brother, who is one of you. They will let you know about everything here.

[10]Aristarchus, my fellow prisoner, says hello to you. So does Mark, Barnabas' cousin (you received instructions about him; if he comes to you, welcome him). [11]Jesus, called Justus, also says hello. These are my only fellow workers for God's kingdom who are Jewish converts. They have been an encouragement to me. [12]Epaphras, who is one of you, says hello. He's a slave of Christ Jesus who always wrestles for you in prayers so that you will stand firm and be fully mature and complete in the entire will of God. [13]I can vouch for him that he has worked hard for you and for those in Laodicea and Hierapolis. [14]Luke, the dearly loved physician, and Demas say hello.

[15]Say hello to the brothers and sisters in Laodicea, along with Nympha and the church that meets in her house. [16]After this letter has been read to you publicly, make sure that the church in Laodicea reads it and that you read the one from Laodicea. [17]And tell Archippus, "See to it that you complete the ministry that you received in the Lord."

[18]I, Paul, am writing this greeting personally. Remember that I'm in prison. Grace be with you.

1 THESSALONIANS

THEME

Your new Christian faith and experience are valid; go on to maturity in Christ.

THE CHURCH AT THESSALONICA

Thessalonica, modern Thessaloniki, located at the head of the Thermaic Gulf of the Aegean Sea in Macedonia, was founded about 315 BCE by Cassander, a general in Alexander the Great's army. He named the city after his wife, the daughter of Philip II and half-sister of Alexander.

In 146 BCE, when Macedonia became a Roman province, the city became the capital of the new province. Its location on the Via Egnatia, the famous East-West road, plus its harbor facilities, made it a prosperous trade and political center.

Many religions (advocating the worship of Greek, Roman, and oriental gods, and even Yahweh of the Jews) vied for acceptance and loyalty among the cosmopolitan populace. The Jewish population there was a considerable one. In the Roman period a civic cult praised Roman rulers (especially Julius Caesar and Augustus) and prominent patrons of Rome and exalted the goddess Roma.

The location of the synagogue where Paul preached is unknown. It may have been near an agora (marketplace) close to the harbor area.

Paul, Silvanus (Silas), and Timothy came into this politically and religiously charged atmosphere on Paul's second missionary journey (Acts 17:1-9), after a disastrous experience in Philippi (Acts 16:11-40; 1 Thessalonians 2:2). Paul preached in the synagogue for three Sabbaths and evidently remained in the city for some time thereafter. He was there long enough to have worked intensively at his trade (1 Thessalonians 2:9) and to have received financial help more than once from the Philippians (Philippians 4:16). We may guess that he and his companions were there for two or three months.

Paul argued in the synagogue that the Old Testament predicts the coming of a suffering messiah and that Jesus of Nazareth fulfilled this expectation (Acts 17:3). Some Jews and also many god-fearing Gentiles were convinced, including a number of influential women. The Gentiles, male and female, were attracted to Judaism by its worship of one God and its high religious and ethical teaching. However, they did not accept the full yoke of the Jewish law (circumcision, Sabbath observance, and the food laws). They were excellent prospects for Paul's law-free gospel about Jesus.

Paul's proclamation about the present and coming rule of Jesus Christ provoked unbelieving and jealous Jews to twist a religious affirmation into a political charge of disloyalty to Caesar and into mob action directed against Paul, his companions, and their host Jason. When Paul and his associates could not be found, Jason and other Christians were brought before the city authorities and forced to put up money to guarantee the good conduct of their guests. For the good of all, Paul and his companions immediately left the city by night. The infant church was thus put in a precarious position almost from birth.

When Paul arrived at Athens, after a mission in Beroea (Acts 17:10-15), he sent Timothy back to Thessalonica to assist the infant congregation and to bring him word of its condition (1 Thessalonians 3:1-5). Paul then crossed over to Corinth and began preaching there. Later Timothy brought a letter to him from the Thessalonians, inquiring about some important matters, to which Paul responded in 1 Thessalonians, chapters 4–5.

First Thessalonians is Paul's joyful reaction to the news of the fidelity of the Thessalonians in spite of their sufferings. It is also Paul's attempt to guide the Thessalonians to a fuller Christian life. It is a pastoral letter.

THE PROBLEMS IN THE CHURCH AT THESSALONICA

(1) Persecution by fellow townspeople, probably spearheaded by the unbelieving Jews who had forced Paul from the city (Acts 17:5; 1 Thessalonians 2:14-16; 3:3-4).

(2) Doubts about the integrity of the missionaries, spread probably by the hostile Jews (2:1).

(3) Confusion about the validity of their new faith and experience in the light of Jewish attacks (1:4-10); about the Christian view of the future (the fate of Christians who have died before the coming of Christ, the time of Christ's coming, and Christian activity meanwhile—4:13–5:11); and about the place of suffering in the life of Christians (3:3-4).

(4) Sexual irregularities (4:3-8), idleness and troublemaking (4:11-12), and quarreling (5:13).

DATE AND PLACE OF WRITING

This letter is probably the earliest of the preserved letters of Paul. It dates to 50 or 51 CE and was written by Paul from Corinth.

1 THESSALONIANS

Greeting

1 From Paul, Silvanus, and Timothy.
To the Thessalonians' church that is in God the Father and the Lord Jesus Christ.

Grace and peace to all of you.

Thanksgiving to God

[2] We always thank God for all of you when we mention you constantly in our prayers. [3] This is because we remember your work that comes from faith,[a] your effort that comes from love, and your perseverance that comes from hope in our Lord Jesus Christ in the presence of our God and Father. [4] Brothers and sisters, you are loved by God, and we know that he has chosen you. [5] We know this because our good news didn't come to you just in speech but also with power and the Holy Spirit and with deep conviction. You know as well as we do what kind of people we were when we were with you, which was for your sake. [6] You became imitators of us and of the Lord when you accepted the message that came from the Holy Spirit with joy in spite of great suffering. [7] As a result you became an example to all the believers in Macedonia and Achaia. [8] The message about the Lord rang out from you, not only in Macedonia and Achaia but in every place. The news about your faithfulness to God has spread so that we don't even need to mention it. [9] People tell us about what sort of welcome we had from you and how you turned to God from idols. As a result, you are serving[b] the living and true God, [10] and you are waiting for his Son from heaven. His Son is Jesus, who is the one he raised from the dead and who is the one who will rescue us from the coming wrath.

Paul's ministry in Thessalonica

2 As you yourselves know, brothers and sisters, our visit with you wasn't a waste of time. [2] On the contrary, we had the courage through God to speak God's good news in spite of a lot of opposition, although we had already suffered and were publicly insulted in Philippi, as you know. [3] Our appeal isn't based on false information, the wrong motives, or deception. [4] Rather, we have been examined and approved by God to be trusted with the good news, and that's exactly how we speak. We aren't trying to please people, but we are trying to please God, who continues to examine our hearts. [5] As you know, we never used flattery, and God is our

[a] Or faithfulness [b] Or to become slaves of

THESSALONICA

Thessalonica, modern Thessaloniki or Salonika, was founded by Cassander (one of Alexander the Great's successors) in 315 BCE on important trade routes. Thessalonica became the capital of the second district of Macedonia and the seat of the Roman governor. In 146 it became the capital of the reorganized province of Macedonia.

Once Paul reached Thessalonica he engaged in a brief ministry before being driven out by Jewish opposition (Acts 17:1-13; cf. 1 Thess 1:8-9). The response to his message was the establishment of a strong church. After Timothy's report that the new congregation remained strong despite harassment, Paul wrote 1 Thessalonians. The city is mentioned elsewhere in the NT in Acts 20:4; 27:2; Philippians 4:16; and 2 Timothy 4:10.

witness that we didn't have greedy motives. [6] We didn't ask for special treatment from people—not from you or from others— [7] although we could have thrown our weight around as Christ's apostles. Instead, we were gentle with you like a nursing mother caring for her own children. [8] We were glad to share not only God's good news with you but also our very lives because we cared for you so much. [9] You remember, brothers and sisters, our efforts and hard work. We preached God's good news to you, while we worked night and day so we wouldn't be a burden on any of you. [10] You and God are witnesses of how holy, just, and blameless we were toward you believers. [11] Likewise, you know how we treated each of you like a father treats his own children. [12] We appealed to you, encouraged you, and pleaded with you to live lives worthy of the God who is calling you into his own kingdom and glory.

How the Thessalonians received God's message

[13] We also thank God constantly for this: when you accepted God's word that you heard from us, you welcomed it for what it truly is. Instead of accepting it as a human message, you accepted it as God's message, and it continues to work in you who are believers. [14] Brothers and sisters, you be-came imitators of the churches of God in Judea, which are in Christ Jesus. This was because you also suffered the same things from your own people as they did from the Jews. [15] They killed both the Lord Jesus and the prophets and drove us out. They don't please God, and they are hostile to the en-tire human race [16] when they try to stop us from speaking to the Gentiles so they can be saved. Their sins are constantly pushing the limit.[c] God's wrath has caught up with them in the end.

Paul's desire to visit

[17] Brothers and sisters, we were separated from you for a while physically but not in our hearts. We made every effort in our desire to see you again face-to-face. [18] We wanted to come to you—I, Paul, tried over and over again—and Satan stopped us. [19] What is our hope, joy, or crown that we can brag about in front of our Lord Jesus when he comes? Isn't it all of you? [20] You are our glory and joy!

3 So when we couldn't stand it any longer, we thought it was a good idea to stay on in Athens by ourselves, [2] and we sent you Timothy, who is our brother and God's co-worker in the good news about Christ. We sent him to strengthen and encourage you in your faithfulness. [3] We didn't want any of you

---

[c] Or *They constantly fill up the measure of their sin.*

SATAN (PAUL'S LETTERS)

In Paul's letters Satan appears as an adversary. Paul says in 1 Thessa-lonians 2:18 that he and his associates wanted to return to Thessalonica on many occasions "and Satan stopped us." Paul exhorts the Corinthians not to be "taken advantage of by Satan, because we are well aware of his schemes" (2 Cor 2:11). Sexual immorality is understood to be surrendering to the temptations of Satan (1 Cor 7:5), and Paul instructs that a man who is living with his father's wife should be handed "over to Satan to destroy his human weakness so that his spirit might be saved on the day of the Lord" (1 Cor 5:5; see 1 Tim 1:20; 5:15). Paul also says, "I was given a thorn in my body. . . . It's a messenger from Satan sent to torment me so that I wouldn't be conceited" (2 Cor 12:7). Whether this is a physical illness or an opponent is not clear.

to be shaken by these problems. You know very well that we were meant to go through this. ⁴In fact, when we were with you, we kept on predicting that we were going to face problems exactly like what happened, as you know. ⁵That's why I sent Timothy to find out about your faithfulness when I couldn't stand it anymore. I was worried that the tempter might have tempted you so that our work would have been a waste of time.

Paul's prayer for the Thessalonians

⁶Now Timothy has returned to us from you and has given us good news about your faithfulness and love! He says that you always have good memories about us and that you want to see us as much as we want to see you. ⁷Because of this, brothers and sisters, we were encouraged in all our distress and trouble through your faithfulness. ⁸For now we are alive if you are standing your ground in the Lord. ⁹How can we thank God enough for you, given all the joy we have because of you before our God? ¹⁰Night and day, we pray more than ever to see all of you in person and to complete whatever you still need for your faith. ¹¹Now may our God and Father himself guide us on our way back to you. ¹²May the Lord cause you to increase and enrich your love for each other and for everyone in the same way as we also love you. ¹³May the love cause your hearts to be strengthened, to be blameless in holiness before our God and Father when our Lord Jesus comes with all his people. Amen.

Living that pleases God

4 So then, brothers and sisters, we ask and encourage you in the Lord Jesus to keep living the way you already are and even do better in how you live and please God—just as you learned from us. ²You know the instructions we gave you through the Lord Jesus. ³God's will is that your lives are dedicated to him.ᵈ This means that you stay away from sexual immorality ⁴and learn how to control your own body in a pureᵉ and respectable way. ⁵Don't be controlled by your sexual urges like the Gentiles who don't know God. ⁶No one should mistreat or take advantage of their brother or sister in this issue. The Lord punishes people for all these things, as we told you before and sternly warned you. ⁷God didn't call us to be immoral but to be dedicated to him.ᶠ ⁸Therefore, whoever rejects these instructions isn't rejecting a human authority. They are rejecting God, who gives his Holy Spirit to you.

⁹You don't need us to write about loving your brothers and sisters because God has already taught you to love each other. ¹⁰In fact, you are doing loving deeds for all the brothers and sisters throughout Macedonia. Now we encourage you, brothers and sisters, to do so even more. ¹¹Aim to live quietly, mind your own business, and earn your own living, just as I told you. ¹²That way you'll behave appropriately toward outsiders, and you won't be in need.

Believers who have died

¹³Brothers and sisters, we want you to know about people who have diedᵍ so that you won't mourn like others who don't have any hope. ¹⁴Since we believe that Jesus died and rose, so we also believe that God will bring with him those who

---

ᵈOr holy, sanctified ᵉOr holy, sanctified ᶠOr holy, sanctified ᵍOr fallen asleep

---

SECOND COMING

A belief held by many Christians that at the conclusion of history Jesus will return bodily and start God's new kingdom on a newly constituted earth. The most explicit NT sources for this belief are 1 Thessalonians 4:16-17 and Revelation 1:7.

have died in Jesus. [15]What we are saying is a message from the Lord: we who are alive and still around at the Lord's coming definitely won't go ahead of those who have died. [16]This is because the Lord himself will come down from heaven with the signal of a shout by the head angel and a blast on God's trumpet. First, those who are dead in Christ will rise. [17]Then, we who are living and still around will be taken up together with them in the clouds to meet with the Lord in the air. That way we will always be with the Lord. [18]So encourage each other with these words.

The Lord's coming

5 We don't need to write to you about the timing and dates, brothers and sisters. [2]You know very well that the day of the Lord is going to come like a thief in the night. [3]When they are saying, "There is peace and security," at that time sudden destruction will attack them, like labor pains start with a pregnant woman, and they definitely won't escape. [4]But you aren't in darkness, brothers and sisters, so the day won't catch you by surprise like a thief. [5]All of you are children of light and children of the day. We don't belong to night or darkness. [6]So then, let's not sleep like the others, but let's stay awake and stay sober. [7]People who sleep sleep at night, and people who get drunk get drunk at night. [8]Since we belong to the day, let's stay sober, wearing faithfulness and love as a piece of armor that protects our body[h] and the hope of salvation as a helmet. [9]God didn't intend for us to suffer his wrath but rather to possess salvation through our Lord Jesus Christ. [10]Jesus died for us so that, whether we are awake or asleep, we will live together with him. [11]So continue encouraging each other and building each other up, just like you are doing already.

Final instructions and blessing

[12]Brothers and sisters, we ask you to respect those who are working with you, leading you, and instructing you. [13]Think of them highly with love because of their work. Live in peace with each other. [14]Brothers and sisters, we urge you to warn those who are disorderly. Comfort the discouraged. Help the weak. Be patient with everyone. [15]Make sure no one repays a wrong with a wrong, but always pursue the good for each other and everyone else. [16]Rejoice always. [17]Pray continually. [18]Give thanks in every situation because this is God's will for you in Christ Jesus. [19]Don't suppress the Spirit. [20]Don't brush off Spirit-inspired messages, [21]but examine everything carefully and hang on to what is good. [22]Avoid every kind of evil. [23]Now, may the God of peace himself cause you to be completely dedicated to him; and may your spirit, soul, and body be kept intact and blameless at our Lord Jesus Christ's coming. [24]The one who is calling you is faithful and will do this.

Final greeting

[25]Brothers and sisters, pray for us. [26]Greet all the brothers and sisters with a holy kiss. [27]By the Lord's authority, I order all of you to have this letter read aloud to all the brothers and sisters. [28]The grace of our Lord Jesus Christ be with all of you.

[h]Or breastplate

2 THESSALONIANS

THEME

The truth about the second coming of Christ

INTRODUCTION

On the church at Thessalonica and the problems addressed by Paul in 1 Thessalonians, see the introduction to 1 Thessalonians.

THE OCCASION AND PURPOSE OF THE LETTER

The letter indicates that reports had come to Paul about problems in the church at Thessalonica (3:11), mainly concerning the persecution the church was experiencing, probably from both Jews and Gentiles (1:4-8).

Another problem centered in wrong ideas some Thessalonians had about the coming of Christ. Someone evidently claimed Paul as the authority for the false view that the day of the Lord has already come (2:2). The practical result of this mistaken view was that some people had quit their daily work. Thus there was a great deal of idleness and meddling in other people's affairs (3:6, 11). Paul had faced the problem of lazy spongers when he was at Thessalonica (3:10), but his instructions went unheeded. Indeed, the situation was much worse.

We can only guess who was teaching church members at Thessalonica that the day of the Lord had arrived.

There were church members at Corinth who believed that they were enjoying the kingdom of God already (1 Corinthians 4:8). A clear statement in 2 Timothy 2:18 attributes to two false teachers in the church the view that the resurrection is already past. Such a position was held by Gnostic heretics of the late first and second centuries and may have appeared in embryonic form in the church as early as the time of Paul. It held that the only resurrection there ever will be is release of the spirit from the bondage of flesh, which occurs in baptism and new birth.

Or had the Thessalonians taken too realistically Paul's statement in 1 Thessalonians 5:5, 8 that they were children of the day and we belong to the day, as if the day had already broken in? In addition, did the severity of suffering suggest to them that the end-time birth pangs of the new order (see Isaiah 66:7-9) were actually being felt?

It is even possible that a forged letter, claiming Paul's authorship and authority for the view that the day of the Lord had arrived, was circulating at Thessalonica

(2:2). Such a letter would make necessary Paul's repudiation of it and the reference to his handwriting as a way of authenticating his letters in the future (3:17).

Whatever the exact cause of the confusion, Paul wrote this letter to straighten out the Thessalonians on the significance, time, and consequence of the coming of Christ for present living.

AUTHORSHIP, DATE, AND PLACE OF WRITING

It is difficult to explain why we have two letters to the Thessalonians that are so alike and yet so different.

Second Thessalonians covers many of the same subjects as 1 Thessalonians: notably, thanksgiving for the readers' steadfastness in persecution; a declaration of God's judgment on their persecutors; prayers for their establishment in every good work and word; teaching about the end-time events and about appropriate Christian conduct in the time before the end; and emphasis on Paul's and his associates' authority and on traditional church teaching. And much of the language is the same in the two letters.

But there are marked differences. First Thessalonians is warm in tone and filled with personal data; 2 Thessalonians is colder, more formal, and authoritarian. The first letter stresses the unpredictability and suddenness of the coming of Christ; the second offers signs by which one can predict that coming. The second gives information about the lawless one—a kind of speculation about the future that is unparalleled anywhere in the letters of Paul.

Under what circumstances would Paul and his associates write two letters to the Thessalonians so alike, so different, and so close together in time?

Many scholars believe that within a few months of the writing of 1 Thessalonians the missionaries, then at Corinth, received new reports about the situation at Thessalonica (3:11). The church members there had not wavered in loyalty to Christ because of persecutions and afflictions (1:4). But serious controversy about the time of the coming of Christ had arisen, provoked by revelations claimed by false teachers and possibly by a letter falsely attributed to Paul. The false teaching that the day of the Lord had already come had led to serious moral consequences in the church. The missionaries wrote to correct the new situation, which was yet not wholly new. The date of writing of 2 Thessalonians then would be 50 or 51 CE.

Other scholars believe that a disciple of Paul (perhaps between 75 and 90 CE) used 1 Thessalonians as a source of material for a rebuttal of the claim made in the Christian church of that time that Paul believed that the day of the Lord had already arrived. This rebuttal is our 2 Thessalonians. Because of his imitation of Paul's language and ideas, the letters are similar; and because of his later date, situation, and purpose, the letters are different.

The most satisfactory view is probably the first.

2 THESSALONIANS

Greeting

1 From Paul, Silvanus, and Timothy:
To the church of the Thessalonians,
which is in God our Father, and in the
Lord Jesus Christ.
²Grace and peace to all of you from God
our Father and the Lord Jesus Christ.

Thanksgiving and encouragement

³Brothers and sisters, we must always
thank God for you. This is only right because your faithfulness is growing by leaps
and bounds, and the love that all of you
have for each other is increasing. ⁴That's
why we ourselves are bragging about you
in God's churches. We tell about your endurance and faithfulness in all the harass-
ments and trouble that you have put up
with. ⁵This shows that God's judgment is
right, and that you will be considered worthy of God's kingdom for which you are suffering. ⁶After all, it's right for God to pay
back the ones making trouble for you with
trouble ⁷and to pay back you who are having trouble with relief along with us. This
payback will come when the Lord Jesus
is revealed from heaven with his powerful angels. ⁸He will give justice with blazing fire to those who don't recognize God

and don't obey the good news of our Lord
Jesus. ⁹They will pay the penalty of eternal
destruction away from the Lord's presence
and away from his mighty glory. ¹⁰This will
happen when he comes on that day to receive honor from his holy people and to be
admired by everyone who has believed—
and our testimony to you was believed.

¹¹We are constantly praying for you for
this: that our God will make you worthy of
his calling and accomplish every good desire and faithful work by his power. ¹²Then
the name of our Lord Jesus will be honored
by you, and you will be honored by him,
consistent with the grace of our God and
the Lord Jesus Christ.

Day of the Lord

2 Brothers and sisters, we have a request
for you concerning our Lord Jesus
Christ's coming and when we are gathered
together to be with him. ²We don't want
you to be easily confused in your mind or
upset if you hear that the day of the Lord is
already here, whether you hear it through
some spirit, a message, or a letter supposedly from us. ³Don't let anyone deceive you
in any way. That day won't come unless the
rebellion comes first and the person who

TIMOTHY

In the NT, Timothy is a close associate of the apostle Paul. In the Acts of
the Apostles, Timothy figures prominently in Paul's second and third missionary journeys. He remains with Silas in Beroea with a plan to go on to
Athens to meet Paul (Acts 17:14-15). Acts 18:5 reports that he arrives in
Corinth. Paul sends him to Macedonia with Erastus (Acts 19:22), and Timothy later travels with Paul through Macedonia and Greece and is with him
in Corinth on the eve of his journey to Jerusalem (Acts 20:4; Rom 16:21). As
related in Paul's letters, Timothy serves as Paul's representative.

Timothy appears frequently in the Pauline Letters, where he is referred to
as Paul's "coworker," a term frequently used for Paul's fellow missionaries
(Rom 16:21; 1 Thess 3:2), as well as his "brother" (i.e., in the faith, 2 Cor 1:1;
Col 1:1; 1 Thess 3:2; Phlm v. 1); "son" (Phil 2:22); "true child in the faith"
(1 Tim 1:2); and "dear child" (2 Tim 1:2).

is lawless is revealed, who is headed for destruction. [4]He is the opponent of every so-called god or object of worship and promotes himself over them. So he sits in God's temple, displaying himself to show that he is God. [5]You remember that I used to tell you these things while I was with you, don't you? [6]Now you know what holds him back so that he can be revealed when his time comes. [7]The hidden plan to live without any law is at work now, but it will be secret only until the one who is holding it back is out of the way. [8]Then the person who is lawless will be revealed. The Lord Jesus will destroy him with the breath from his mouth. When the Lord comes, his appearance will put an end to him. [9]When the person who is lawless comes, it will happen through Satan's effort, with all kinds of fake power, signs, and wonders. [10]It will happen with every sort of wicked deception of those who are heading toward destruction because they have refused to love the truth that would allow them to be saved. [11]This is why God will send them an influence that will mislead them so that they will believe the lie. [12]The result will be that everyone will be judged who is not convinced by the truth but is happy with injustice.

Prayer of thanks and encouragement

[13]But we always must thank God for you, brothers and sisters who are loved by God. This is because he chose you from the beginning to be the first crop of the harvest. This brought salvation, through your dedication to God by the Spirit and through your belief in the truth. [14]God called all of you through our good news so you could possess the honor of our Lord Jesus Christ. [15]So then, brothers and sisters, stand firm and hold on to the traditions we taught you, whether we taught you in person or through our letter. [16]Our Lord Jesus Christ himself and God our Father loved us and through grace gave us eternal comfort and a good hope. [17]May he encourage your hearts and give you strength in every good thing you do or say.

Prayer request

3 Finally, brothers and sisters, pray for us so that the Lord's message will spread quickly and be honored, just like it happened with you. [2]Pray too that we will be rescued from inappropriate and evil people since everyone that we meet won't respond with faith. [3]But the Lord is faithful and will give you strength and protect you from the evil one. [4]We are confident about you in the Lord—that you are doing and will keep doing what we tell you to do. [5]May the Lord lead your hearts to express God's love and Christ's endurance.

Discipline for the undisciplined

[6]Brothers and sisters, we command you in the name of our Lord Jesus Christ to stay away from every brother or sister who lives an undisciplined life that is not in line with the traditions that you received from us. [7]You yourselves know how you need to imitate us because we were not undisciplined when we were with you. [8]We didn't eat anyone's food without paying for it. Instead,

PAROUSIA

Parousia is used widely in the NT (e.g., Matt 24:3; 1 Cor 15:23; 1 Thess 5:23; 2 Thess 2:1; 2 Pet 1:16; 1 John 2:28; cf. Jas 5:7). In these passages it refers to the presence of Christ coming on the clouds of heaven (Mark 13:26) and is sometimes called the "second coming" of Christ. Nevertheless, the ambiguity of the word should be noted, as when expectation of a public coming when "Every eye will see him" (Rev 1:7) allowed for the possibility of the presence of Christ in other modes of experience, whether in worship or the lives of the apostles and ministers (Gal 2:20). See also "Second Coming" on page 1427.

we worked night and day with effort and hard work so that we would not impose on you. ⁹We did this to give you an example to imitate, not because we didn't have a right to insist on financial support. ¹⁰Even when we were with you we were giving you this command: "If anyone doesn't want to work, they shouldn't eat." ¹¹We hear that some of you are living an undisciplined life. They aren't working, but they are meddling in other people's business. ¹²By the Lord Jesus Christ, we command and encourage such people to work quietly and put their own food on the table. ¹³Brothers and sisters, don't get discouraged in doing what is right. ¹⁴Take note of anyone who doesn't obey what we have said in this letter. Don't associate with them so they will be ashamed of themselves. ¹⁵Don't treat them like enemies, but warn them like you would do for a brother or sister.

Final greeting

¹⁶May the Lord of peace himself give you peace always in every way. The Lord be with all of you. ¹⁷I, Paul, am writing this greeting with my own hand. This verifies that the letter is from me, as in every letter of mine. This is how I write. ¹⁸The grace of our Lord Jesus Christ be with all of you.

1 TIMOTHY

THEME

Timothy's role in preserving the true faith and life of the church from the false instruction and way of life of heretical teachers

INTRODUCTION

First Timothy belongs with 2 Timothy and Titus to a subgroup of the letters ascribed to Paul that is known as the Pastoral Letters. These writings contain instructions and warnings concerning the work of pastors in Christian churches.

In many respects these books are more like church manuals than personal letters. This is especially true of 1 Timothy, where personal information is almost entirely lacking. Since most of the material in these manuals would surely have been known already to Paul's long-time associates Timothy and Titus, it is likely that the books were written more for the benefit of church members than for the leaders mentioned—though the latter, of course, were included.

A hint that church members as well as leaders were addressed appears in the benedictions of these writings, where the "you" is plural in the Greek. Further, the center of interest in all three is the problems of faith and conduct of church members and how to meet these problems with the help of accredited leaders.

These books contain many crisp, salty sayings and instructions for the church. They do not probe the depths or scale the heights of life in Christ and the church as the other letters ascribed to Paul do, but their practical morality and wise counsel offer help to churches tempted to stray from historic Christianity into false beliefs and practices. Their keynote is: At all costs keep the faith delivered to you by the apostle Paul!

AUTHORSHIP OF THE PASTORAL LETTERS

All three of the letters clearly claim Paul as their author, either directly or indirectly. From the late second century until the nineteenth century, the church believed that Paul wrote them. Today, however, most scholars think that the letters were written by someone else in Paul's name sometime after Paul's death.

There are many striking differences in language, style, and theology between the Pastorals and Paul's certainly genuine letters that make it difficult to defend Paul's direct authorship of these letters. Further, the situation of the church reflected in the Pastorals is not that of a time before Paul's death. It is too advanced. Timothy and Titus appear as supervisors or bishops who appoint elders, discipline them, guard the church morally and doctrinally, and serve as a pattern for church members. This episcopal role did not come into being until the second century.

It should be noted that it was a recognized practice in antiquity for a disciple to write in the name of his teacher and to ascribe his insights to his honored master. This involved no dishonesty. And the person or persons who brought these letters together may well have assembled Paul's own notes to serve the needs of the church after the apostle's death.

THE VALUE OF 1 TIMOTHY

First Timothy, a handbook of church administration and discipline, is not filled with sublime and inspiring passages. The author did not blaze new trails in Christian thought, but rather sought to consolidate, conserve, and protect the conquests already made by the church. This is no small achievement, even if it is less dramatic than pioneering work.

Of lasting value are the following:

Loyalty to the truth and the preservation of a good conscience (1:5, 19; 3:9)—instead of succumbing to attractive, erroneous novelties which gratify the senses—belong to the essence of Christianity, as Christian martyrs later demonstrated.

The spiritual and moral requirements for church officials, set forth here, offer generally valid guidelines for every age.

The Christian teacher, as an example to those who are taught (1:16; 4:12-16), exhibits Christianity as truth incarnate.

The emphasis on the goodness of the created order and the human right to enjoy it (4:3-5) opposes recurring asceticism in Christian thought and life.

1 TIMOTHY

Greeting

1 From Paul, who is an apostle of Jesus Christ by the command of God our savior and of Christ Jesus our hope. [2] To Timothy, my true child in the faith. Grace, mercy, and peace from God the Father and from Christ Jesus our Lord.

Timothy's purpose in Ephesus

[3] When I left for Macedonia, I asked you to stay behind in Ephesus so that you could instruct certain individuals not to spread wrong teaching. [4] They shouldn't pay attention to myths and endless genealogies. Their teaching only causes useless guessing games instead of faithfulness to God's way of doing things. [5] The goal of instruction is love from a pure heart, a good conscience, and a sincere faith. [6] Because they missed this goal, some people have been distracted by talk that doesn't mean anything. [7] They want to be teachers of Law without understanding either what they are saying or what they are talking about with such confidence. [8] Now we know that the Law is good if used appropriately. [9] We understand this: the Law isn't established for a righteous person but for people who live without laws and without obeying any authority. They are the ungodly and the sinners. They are people who are not spiritual, and nothing is sacred to them. They kill their fathers and mothers, and murder others. [10] They are people who are sexually unfaithful, and people who have intercourse with the same sex. They are kidnappers,[a] liars, individuals who give false testimonies in court, and those who do anything else that is opposed to sound teaching. [11] Sound teaching agrees with the glorious gospel of the blessed God that has been trusted to me.

Thanksgiving

[12] I thank Christ Jesus our Lord, who has given me strength because he considered me faithful. So he appointed me to ministry [13] even though I used to speak against him, attack his people, and I was proud. But I was shown mercy because I acted in ignorance and without faith. [14] Our Lord's favor poured all over me along with the faithfulness and love that are in Christ Jesus. [15] This saying is reliable and deserves full acceptance: "Christ Jesus came into the world to save sinners"—and I'm the biggest sinner of all. [16] But this is why I was shown mercy, so that Christ Jesus could show his endless patience to me first of all. So I'm an example for those who are going to believe in him for eternal life. [17] Now to the king of the ages, to the immortal, invisible, and only God, may honor and glory be given to him forever and always! Amen.

[a] Or slave dealers

PASTORAL LETTERS

The "Pastoral Letters" is a name for the collection of letters that includes 1 and 2 Timothy and Titus. Timothy and Titus serve as exemplary figures with whom the reader identifies, because the letters are from an older pastor (Paul) to younger pastors (Timothy and Titus). The letters' preoccupations include church order ("how you should behave in God's household. It is the church" [1 Tim 3:15; see also 5:3-22]), preservation of apostolic teaching (1 Tim 1:3-10; 3:14–4:10; 6:3-5, 20; 2 Tim 1:11-12; Titus 1:10-16), and the church's reputation (1 Tim 2:1-2; 5:14; 6:1-12; Titus 2:1-10).

Importance of faith and a good conscience

[18]Timothy, my child, I'm giving you these instructions based on the prophecies that were once made about you. So if you follow them, you can wage a good war [19]because you have faith and a good conscience. Some people have ruined their faith because they refused to listen to their conscience, [20]such as Hymenaeus and Alexander. I've handed them over to Satan so that they can be taught not to speak against God.

Prayer for everyone

2 First of all, then, I ask that requests, prayers, petitions, and thanksgiving be made for all people. [2]Pray for kings and everyone who is in authority so that we can live a quiet and peaceful life in complete godliness and dignity. [3]This is right and it pleases God our savior, [4]who wants all people to be saved and to come to a knowledge of the truth. [5]There is one God and one mediator between God and humanity, the human Christ Jesus, [6]who gave himself as a payment to set all people free. This was a testimony that was given at the right time. [7]I was appointed to be a preacher and apostle of this testimony—I'm telling the truth and I'm not lying! I'm a teacher of the Gentiles in faith and truth.

Instructions for men and women

[8]Therefore, I want men to pray everywhere by lifting up hands that are holy, without anger or argument. [9]In the same way, I want women to enhance their appearance with clothing that is modest and sensible, not with elaborate hairstyles, gold, pearls, or expensive clothes. [10]They should make themselves attractive by doing good, which is appropriate for women who claim to honor God.

[11]A wife[b] should learn quietly with complete submission. [12]I don't allow a wife[c] to teach or to control her husband.[d] Instead, she should be a quiet listener. [13]Adam was formed first, and then Eve. [14]Adam wasn't deceived, but rather his wife[e] became the one who stepped over the line because she was completely deceived. [15]But a wife[f] will be brought safely through childbirth,[g] if they both continue in faith, love, and holiness, together with self-control.

Supervisors in God's household

3 This saying is reliable: if anyone has a goal to be a supervisor[h] in the church, they want a good thing. [2]So the church's supervisor must be without fault. They should be faithful to their spouse, sober, modest, and honest. They should show hospitality and be skilled at teaching. [3]They shouldn't be addicted to alcohol or be a bully. Instead, they should be gentle, peaceable, and not greedy. [4]They should manage their own household well—they should see that their children are obedient with complete respect, [5]because if they don't know how to manage their own household, how can they take care of God's church? [6]They shouldn't be new believers so that they won't become proud and fall under the devil's spell. [7]They should also have a good reputation with those outside the church so that they won't be embarrassed and fall into the devil's trap.

Servants in God's household

[8]In the same way, servants[i] in the church should be dignified, not two-faced, heavy drinkers, or greedy for money. [9]They should hold on to the faith that has been revealed with a clear conscience. [10]They should also be tested and then serve if they are without fault. [11]In the same way, women who are servants[j] in the church should be dignified and not gossip. They should be sober and faithful in everything they do. [12]Servants[k] must be faithful to their spouse and manage their children and their own households well. [13]Those who have served well gain a good standing and considerable confidence in the faith that is in Christ Jesus.

---

[b]Or a woman   [c]Or a woman   [d]Or a man   [e]Or the woman   [f]Or a woman   [g]Or saved through childbearing
[h]Or bishop, overseer   [i]Or deacons   [j]Or wives, omit who are servants   [k]Or deacons

Leading God's household

¹⁴I hope to come to you quickly. But I'm writing these things to you so that ¹⁵if I'm delayed, you'll know how you should behave in God's household. It is the church of the living God and the backbone and support of the truth. ¹⁶Without question, the mystery of godliness is great: he was revealed as a human, declared righteous by the Spirit, seen by angels, preached throughout the nations, believed in around the world, and taken up in glory.

4 The Spirit clearly says that in latter times some people will turn away from the faith. They will pay attention to spirits that deceive and to the teaching of demons. ²They will be controlled by the pretense of lying, and their own consciences will be seared. ³They will prohibit marriage and eating foods that God created—and he intended them to be accepted with thanksgiving by those who are faithful and have come to know the truth. ⁴Everything that has been created by God is good, and nothing that is received with thanksgiving should be rejected. ⁵These things are made holy by God's word and prayer. ⁶If you point these things out to the believers, you will be a good servant of Christ Jesus who has been trained by the words of faith and the good teaching that you've carefully followed. ⁷But stay away from the godless myths that are passed down from the older women.

Practices of spiritual leadership

Train yourself for a holy life! ⁸While physical training has some value, training in holy living is useful for everything. It has promise for this life now and the life to come. ⁹This saying is reliable and deserves complete acceptance. ¹⁰We work and struggle for this: "Our hope is set on the living God, who is the savior of all people, especially those who believe." ¹¹Command these things. Teach them. ¹²Don't let anyone look down on you because you are young. Instead, set an example for the believers through your speech, behavior, love, faith, and by being sexually pure. ¹³Until I arrive, pay attention to public reading, preaching, and teaching. ¹⁴Don't neglect the spiritual gift in you that was given through prophecy

SERVANT (NT)

In the NT, individuals continue to understand themselves as God's servants (Luke 1:38; Jas 1:1; Titus 1:1), and with the advent of Christianity, servants of Christ (Rom 1:1; Gal 1:10; Phil 1:1). A translation of either "servant" or "slave" depends on the context.

A more specific term for servant in the NT is sometimes translated as "deacon," which in ancient Greek denotes a table server, messenger, or minister. The earliest evidence for the term in early Christianity is found in Paul. Although commonly associated with the office of deacon (1 Tim 3:8-13), the majority of occurrences are less specific. Paul refers to himself and others as servants of the gospel, God, and Christ (1 Cor 3:5; 2 Cor 11:23). As servants of God, these emissaries are entrusted with the gospel (2 Cor 3:5) and have earned the right to be heard (2 Cor 6:4). On the other hand, some people are of Satan who oppose the servants of righteousness (2 Cor 11:14-15). Apart from individuals, Paul calls Christ the servant of the circumcision (Rom 15:8), but not of sin (Gal 2:17). Government is also the servant of God (Rom 13:4). There is early evidence that this became a more specific title for a local church office during Paul's lifetime (Rom 16:1; Phil 1:1), but the exact role of this position is unclear.

when the elders laid hands on you. [15]Practice these things, and live by them so that your progress will be visible to all. [16]Focus on working on your own development and on what you teach. If you do this, you will save yourself and those who hear you.

Caring for God's family

5 Don't correct an older man, but encourage him like he's your father; treat younger men like your brothers, [2]treat older women like your mother, and treat younger women like your sisters with appropriate respect.

[3]Take care of widows who are truly needy. [4]But if a particular widow has children or grandchildren, they should first learn to respect their own family and repay their parents, because this pleases God. [5]A widow who is truly needy and all alone puts her hope in God and keeps on going with requests and prayers, night and day. [6]But a widow who tries to live a life of luxury is dead even while she is alive. [7]Teach these things so that the families[1] will be without fault. [8]But if someone doesn't provide for their own family, and especially for a member of their household, they have denied the faith. They are worse than those who have no faith.

[9]Put a widow on the list who is older than 60 years old and who was faithful to her husband. [10]She should have a reputation for doing good: raising children, providing hospitality to strangers, washing the feet of the saints, helping those in distress, and dedicating herself to every kind of good thing. [11]But don't accept younger widows for the list. When their physical desires distract them from Christ, they will want to get married. [12]Then they will be judged for setting aside their earlier commitment. [13]Also, they learn to be lazy by going from house to house. They are not only lazy, but they also become gossips and busybodies, talking about things they shouldn't. [14]So I want younger widows to marry, have children, and manage their homes so that they won't give the enemy any reason to slander us. ([15]Some have already turned away to follow Satan.) [16]If any woman who is a believer has widows in her family, she should take care of them and not burden the church, so that it can help other widows who are truly needy.

Instructions for elders

[17]Elders who lead well should be paid double, especially those who work with public speaking and teaching. [18]The scripture says, *Don't put a muzzle on an ox while it treads grain,*[m] and *Workers deserve their pay.*[n] [19]Don't accept an accusation made against an elder unless it is confirmed by two or three witnesses. [20]Discipline those who are sinning in front of everyone so that all the others will be afraid. [21]I charge you before God and Christ Jesus and the elect angels to follow these practices without bias, and without playing favorites. [22]Don't rush to commission anyone to leadership, and don't participate in the sins of others. Keep yourself morally pure.

[23]Don't drink water anymore, but use a

---

[1]Or *they*   [m]Deut 25:4   [n]Luke 10:7

HOSPITALITY

The ancient custom of hospitality revolved around welcoming and assisting strangers or travelers. By extending hospitality to a traveler, the host committed himself or herself to provide the guest with provisions and protection while the guest remained in the region. Hosts and guests often forged long-term, reciprocal relationships, which are commonly referred to as guest-friendships.

little wine because of your stomach problems and your frequent illnesses. [24]The sins of some people are obvious, and the sins are judged before the people must face judgment, but the sins of other people show up later. [25]In the same way, the good that people do is also obvious and can't be hidden.

Conduct of Christian slaves

6 Those who are under the bondage of slavery should consider their own masters as worthy of full respect so that God's name and our teaching won't get a bad reputation. [2]And those who have masters who are believers shouldn't look down on them because they are brothers. Instead, they should serve them more faithfully, because the people who benefit from your good service are believers who are loved. Teach and encourage these things.

Warning about false teachers

[3]If anyone teaches anything different and doesn't agree with sound teaching about our Lord Jesus Christ and teaching that is consistent with godliness, [4]that person is conceited. They don't understand anything but have a sick obsession with debates and arguments. This creates jealousy, conflict, verbal abuse, and evil suspicions. [5]There is constant bickering between people whose minds are ruined and who have been robbed of the truth. They think that godliness is a way to make money! [6]Actually, godliness is a great source of profit when it is combined with being happy with what you already have. [7]We didn't bring anything into the world and so we can't take anything out of it: [8]we'll be happy with food and clothing. [9]But people who are trying to get rich fall into temptation. They are trapped by many stupid and harmful pas-

PONTIUS PILATE

The Roman prefect of Judea (26–37 CE) who crucified Jesus of Nazareth. Pilate's main role was to maintain law and order in a territory subjugated only twenty years earlier. He commanded only auxiliary troops (five infantry cohorts and one cavalry regiment), but in difficult circumstances could call upon the legions under the neighboring and more powerful Syrian legate. Like earlier governors, Pilate made his capital in the predominantly Gentile coastal city of Caesarea Maritima. Most troops were stationed here, while smaller garrisons were dispersed throughout the province, including a permanent cohort in Jerusalem. During festivals, Pilate arrived in the holy city with reinforcements (though the heightened military presence often created friction).

Pilate possessed supreme magisterial power in the region. Whether, or to what extent, local courts had the right of capital punishment is disputed. Quite possibly they could execute for infringements against the Jewish Law while Pilate concerned himself with matters of national security. As governor, he also had financial duties.

What became of Pilate is unknown. Where history finished, Christian imagination began, and Pilate's life was a popular topic in both apocryphal literature and legend. While the Eastern church, dwelling on his proclamation of Jesus' innocence, regarded him favorably (he is a saint in the Ethopian Orthodox Church; his feast date is June 25th), the Western church saw him as the enemy of Christ and delighted in devising ingenious and gruesome ends for him.

sions that plunge people into ruin and destruction. [10]The love of money is the root of all kinds of evil. Some have wandered away from the faith and have impaled themselves with a lot of pain because they made money their goal.

[11]But as for you, man of God, run away from all these things. Instead, pursue righteousness, holy living, faithfulness, love, endurance, and gentleness. [12]Compete in the good fight of faith. Grab hold of eternal life—you were called to it, and you made a good confession of it in the presence of many witnesses. [13]I command you in the presence of God, who gives life to all things, and Christ Jesus, who made the good confession when testifying before Pontius Pilate. [14]Obey this order without fault or failure until the appearance of our Lord Jesus Christ. [15]The timing of this appearance is revealed by God alone, who is the blessed and only master, the King of kings and Lord of lords. [16]He alone has immortality and lives in light that no one can come near. No human being has ever seen or is able to see him. Honor and eternal power belong to him. Amen.

Wealth of good works

[17]Tell people who are rich at this time not to become egotistical and not to place their hope on their finances, which are uncertain. Instead, they need to hope in God, who richly provides everything for our enjoyment. [18]Tell them to do good, to be rich in the good things they do, to be generous, and to share with others. [19]When they do these things, they will save a treasure for themselves that is a good foundation for the future. That way they can take hold of what is truly life.

Protect the tradition

[20]Timothy, protect what has been given to you in trust. Avoid godless and pointless discussions and the contradictory claims of so-called "knowledge." [21]When some people adopted this false knowledge, they missed the goal of faith.

May grace be with you all.

2 TIMOTHY

THEME

Be loyal to me and my gospel, and you will be rewarded with eternal life.

AUTHORSHIP

See the introduction to 1 Timothy.

INTRODUCTION

First Timothy and Titus are manuals of church administration. Second Timothy is much more personal and is something of a last will and testament. Literary testaments (the instructions of a dying patriarch to his children) were common in Judaism at the time. So here Paul, facing his hour of death (4:6-8), instructs his dear child Timothy (1:2; 2:1) how to carry on after his departure. If Timothy follows these instructions, he will escape the dangers that threaten him and the people under his care.

HIGH POINTS IN 2 TIMOTHY

The intimate personal bond between Paul and Timothy is everywhere evident in the letter. Timothy is called "my dear child" (1:2); Paul knows about his family (1:5); Paul participated in his ordination to the work of ministry (1:6); Paul had been his teacher (1:13); and Paul prays constantly for him (1:3). Paul wants to strengthen the bond of personal loyalty that his imprisonment might weaken (1:8). The close relationship between Paul and Timothy is also evident in Philippians 2:19-24.

The purpose of strengthening the bond is so Timothy will be fully loyal to Paul's gospel in the face of the heresy that is facing the church (possibly that of the late-first-century heretic Marcion). Timothy's opposition to the false teachers will cost him much suffering. He must be willing, as his teacher has been (1:8, 16; 2:9), to suffer for the gospel.

The nature of Paul's gospel comes to clear focus in 2:8. It centers on Jesus as the fulfillment of Israel's history and hopes (the Messiah from the line of David, a real human person), who died and rose from the dead, as the mighty Son of God and inaugurator of the salvation of the New Age. His resurrection is the promise of the resurrection of all believers, contrary to the teaching of the heretics (2 Timothy 2:17-18).

How Timothy is to deal with false teaching is treated in considerable detail:

(1) Timothy and his people should avoid senseless controversy and the false teachers who engage in it (2:14, 16, 23; 3:5). They should be kind, patient, and gentle (2:24-25).

(2) He must be a good interpreter of Christian truth himself (2:15).

(3) He and his people must live righteously and associate with those others who live in the same manner (2:22).

(4) They must realize that God's church is basically unshakable, because God knows and cares about them (2:19).

(5) They must realize that the church is a mixed community, with good and bad members, and that individual and group discipline is constantly needed (2:20-21).

(6) They must keep in mind what hour it is on God's clock—the time of great evil and suffering before the end, when God's people must defend the truth and persevere in righteousness, according to the teachings of the Holy Scriptures (3:1–4:8).

2 TIMOTHY

Greeting

1 From Paul, an apostle of Christ Jesus by God's will, to promote the promise of life that is in Christ Jesus.

²To Timothy, my dear child.

Grace, mercy, and peace from God the Father and Christ Jesus our Lord.

Thanksgiving and prayer

³I'm grateful to God, whom I serve with a good conscience as my ancestors did. I constantly remember you in my prayers day and night. ⁴When I remember your tears, I long to see you so that I can be filled with happiness. ⁵I'm reminded of your authentic faith, which first lived in your grandmother Lois and your mother Eunice. I'm sure that this faith is also inside you. ⁶Because of this, I'm reminding you to revive God's gift that is in you through the laying on of my hands. ⁷God didn't give us a spirit that is timid but one that is powerful, loving, and self-controlled.

Don't be ashamed of the testimony

⁸So don't be ashamed of the testimony about the Lord or of me, his prisoner. Instead, share the suffering for the good news, depending on God's power. ⁹God is the one who saved and called us with a holy calling. This wasn't based on what we have done, but it was based on his own purpose and grace that he gave us in Christ Jesus before time began. ¹⁰Now his grace is revealed through the appearance of our savior, Christ Jesus. He destroyed death and brought life and immortality into clear focus through the good news. ¹¹I was ap-pointed a messenger, apostle, and teacher of this good news. ¹²This is also why I'm suffering the way I do, but I'm not ashamed. I know the one in whom I've placed my trust. I'm convinced that God is powerful enough to protect what he has placed in my trust until that day. ¹³Hold on to the pattern of sound teaching that you heard from me with the faith and love that are in Christ Jesus. ¹⁴Protect this good thing that has been placed in your trust through the Holy Spirit who lives in us.

¹⁵You know that everyone in Asia has turned away from me, including Phygelus and Hermogenes. ¹⁶May the Lord show mercy to Onesiphorus' household, because he supported me many times and he wasn't ashamed of my imprisonment. ¹⁷After I arrived in Rome, he quickly looked for me and found me. ¹⁸May the Lord allow him to find his mercy on that day (and you know very well how much he served me in Ephesus).

Pass on the message and share suffering

2 So, my child, draw your strength from the grace that is in Christ Jesus. ²Take the things you heard me say in front of many other witnesses and pass them on to faithful people who are also capable of teaching others.

³Accept your share of suffering like a good soldier of Christ Jesus. ⁴Nobody who serves in the military gets tied up with civilian matters, so that they can please the one who recruited them. ⁵Also in the same way, athletes don't win unless they follow the rules. ⁶A hardworking farmer should

EUNICE

Eunice, whose name means "good victory," was the mother of Timothy, one of Paul's closest friends and coworkers. She was from Lystra or Derbe in Galatia and had been converted to faith in Christ from Judaism, although she was apparently married to a Gentile (2 Tim 1:5; Acts 16:1, 3).

get the first share of the crop. [7]Think about what I'm saying; the Lord will give you understanding about everything.

[8]Remember Jesus Christ, who was raised from the dead and descended from David. This is my good news. [9]This is the reason I'm suffering to the point that I'm in prison like a common criminal. But God's word cannot be imprisoned. [10]This is why I endure everything for the sake of those who are chosen by God so that they too may experience salvation in Christ Jesus with eternal glory. [11]This saying is reliable:

"If we have died together,
we will also live together.
[12] If we endure, we will also rule together.
If we deny him, he will also deny us.
[13] If we are disloyal, he stays faithful"
because he can't be anything else
than what he is.

Speak, instruct, and act correctly

[14]Remind them of these things and warn them in the sight of God not to engage in battles over words that aren't helpful and only destroy those who hear them. [15]Make an effort to present yourself to God as a tried-and-true worker, who doesn't need to be ashamed but is one who interprets the message of truth correctly. [16]Avoid their godless discussions, because they will lead many people into ungodly behavior, [17]and their ideas will spread like an infection. This includes Hymenaeus and Philetus, [18]who have deviated from the truth by claiming that the resurrection has already happened. This has undermined some people's faith.

[19]God's solid foundation is still standing with this sign: *The Lord knows the people who belong to him,*[a] and *Everyone who confesses the Lord's name must avoid wickedness.*[b] [20]In a mansion, there aren't just gold and silver bowls but also some bowls that are made of wood and clay. Some are meant for special uses, some for garbage.[c] [21]So if anyone washes filth off themselves, they will be set apart as a "special bowl." They will be useful to the owner of the mansion for every sort of good work.

Avoid conflict with opponents

[22]Run away from adolescent cravings. Instead, pursue righteousness, faith, love, and peace together with those who confess the Lord with a clean heart. [23]Avoid foolish and thoughtless discussions, since you know that they produce conflicts. [24]God's slave shouldn't be argumentative but should be kind toward all people, able to teach, patient, [25]and should correct opponents with gentleness. Perhaps God will change their mind and give them a knowledge of the truth. [26]They may come to their senses and escape from the devil's trap that holds them captive to do his will.

Avoid people like this

3 Understand that the last days will be dangerous times. [2]People will be selfish and love money. They will be the kind of people who brag and who are proud. They will slander others, and they will be disobedient to their parents. They will be ungrateful, unholy, [3]unloving, contrary, and critical. They will be without self-control and brutal, and they won't love what is good. [4]They will be people who are disloyal, reckless, and conceited. They will love pleasure instead of loving God. [5]They will look like they are religious but deny God's power. Avoid people like this. [6]Some will slither into households and control immature women who are burdened with sins and driven by all kinds of desires. [7]These women are always learning, but they can never arrive at an understanding of the truth. [8]These people oppose the truth in the same way that Jannes and Jambres opposed Moses. Their minds are corrupt and their faith is counterfeit. [9]But they won't get very far. Their foolishness will become obvious to everyone like those others.

Take Paul as your model

[10]But you have paid attention to my teaching, conduct, purpose, faithfulness, patience, love, and endurance. [11]You have seen me experience physical abuse and ordeals in places such as Antioch, Iconium,

[a]Num 16:5 LXX [b]Possibly modeled on Isa 26:13 [c]Or *dishonorable purposes*

and Lystra. I put up with all sorts of abuse, and the Lord rescued me from it all! [12]In fact, anyone who wants to live a holy life in Christ Jesus will be harassed. [13]But evil people and swindlers will grow even worse, as they deceive others while being deceived themselves.

[14]But you must continue with the things you have learned and found convincing. You know who taught you. [15]Since childhood you have known the holy scriptures that help you to be wise in a way that leads to salvation through faith that is in Christ Jesus. [16]Every scripture is inspired by God and is useful for teaching, for showing mistakes, for correcting, and for training character, [17]so that the person who belongs to God can be equipped to do everything that is good.

Timothy's commission and Paul's departure

4 I'm giving you this commission in the presence of God and of Christ Jesus, who is coming to judge the living and the dead, and by his appearance and his kingdom. [2]Preach the word. Be ready to do it whether it is convenient or inconvenient. Correct, confront, and encourage with patience and instruction. [3]There will come a time when people will not tolerate sound teaching. They will collect teachers who say what they want to hear because they are self-centered. [4]They will turn their back on the truth and turn to myths. [5]But you must keep control of yourself in all circumstances. Endure suffering, do the work of a preacher of the good news, and carry out your service fully.

[6]I'm already being poured out like a sacrifice to God, and the time of my death is near. [7]I have fought the good fight, finished the race, and kept the faith. [8]At last the champion's wreath that is awarded for righteousness[d] is waiting for me. The Lord, who is the righteous[e] judge, is going to give it to me on that day. He's giving it not only to me but also to all those who have set their heart on waiting for his appearance.

Final instructions

[9]Do your best to come to me quickly. [10]Demas has fallen in love with the present world and has deserted me and has gone to Thessalonica. Crescens has gone to Galatia, and Titus has gone to Dalmatia. [11]Only Luke is with me. Get Mark, and bring him with you. He has been a big help to me in the ministry. [12]I sent Tychicus to Ephesus. [13]When you come, bring along the coat I left with Carpus in Troas. Also bring the scrolls and especially the parchments. [14]Alexander, the craftsman who works with metal, has really hurt me. The Lord will pay him back for what he has done. [15]But watch out for him, because he opposes our teaching.

[16]No one took my side at my first court

[d]Or justice [e]Or just

JANNES AND JAMBRES

Names assigned by tradition to Pharaoh's magicians who opposed Moses and Aaron (Exod 7:11-12, 22). Their behavior is cited as a warning to believers (2 Tim 3:8-9). The two brother magicians appear frequently in Jewish, Christian, and pagan sources. In Jewish literature, the two are prominent in legends about the birth and early years of Moses, as assistants or sons of Balaam, and magicians of Pharaoh. In some traditions they perish at the Red Sea, while in others they accompany Israel in the "diverse crowd" (Exod 12:38) to head up the gold calf rebellion at Sinai (Exod 32). A third tradition has them executed with Balaam and the kings of Midian (compare Num 31:8).

hearing. Everyone deserted me. I hope that God doesn't hold it against them! [17]But the Lord stood by me and gave me strength, so that the entire message would be preached through me and so all the nations could hear it. I was also rescued from the lion's mouth! [18]The Lord will rescue me from every evil action and will save me for his heavenly kingdom. To him be the glory forever and always. Amen.

Final greetings

[19]Say hello to Prisca and Aquila and the household of Onesiphorus. [20]Erastus stayed in Corinth, and I left Trophimus in Miletus because of his illness. [21]Try hard to come to me before winter. Eubulus, Pudens, Linus, Claudia, and all the brothers and sisters say hello.

[22]The Lord be with your spirit. Grace be with you all.

PRISCA/PRISCILLA

A prominent woman in the early church, Prisca (Rom 16:3; 1 Cor 16:19; 2 Tim 4:19), or Priscilla (Acts 18:2, 18-19, 26), is always paired with her husband Aquila. The couple traveled both independently and with Paul, spreading the gospel to Rome, Ephesus, and Corinth. Paul particularly honored their mutual sacrifice and work in establishing "all the churches of the Gentiles" (Rom 16:3-4; cf. 1 Cor 16:19). Priscilla and Aquila supported themselves by working with leather, which was easily transportable and suitable to evangelistic shoptalk with customers. Although a physically demanding occupation, there is no reason to doubt Priscilla's full participation with her husband (Acts 18:2-3). During their sojourns in major cities, they hosted a house church in their residence (Rom 16:5; 1 Cor 16:19). As one who "explained to [Apollos] God's way more accurately," Priscilla is the only woman in Acts depicted as an authoritative teacher (Acts 18:24-26).

THEME

Teach Christians in Crete to think straight and live right, because that is what God expects from those who have experienced God's boundless generosity in Jesus Christ and are the heirs of eternal life.

AUTHORSHIP

See the introduction to 1 Timothy.

INTRODUCTION

The letter to Titus is more similar in its contents to 1 Timothy than to 2 Timothy. The latter contains the last will and testament of a father in the faith to his son in the gospel, while the others deal with church order and discipline. First Timothy offers fuller instructions than Titus does.

Titus, like Timothy, was a trusted companion of Paul and emissary to his churches. He was the spearhead of Paul's movement to free Christians from the Law from Moses. Paul made him a test case before the church in Jerusalem and won acceptance of Titus as an uncircumcised Gentile Christian (Galatians 2:1-5). He was a gifted and skillful person, to judge from his part in the successful reconciliation of the rebellious Corinthian church to Paul (2 Corinthians 7:6-16) and his effective service in collecting the offering for the church in Jerusalem (2 Corinthians 8:6, 16, 23).

The letter to Titus represents this Christian leader as head of the church in Crete by Paul's appointment (1:5). His task was to organize and discipline the church there—in an admittedly disorderly place (1:12). We hear of him last on a mission to Dalmatia (2 Timothy 4:10), a territory now in Croatia.

The greeting to the letter shows that Titus was one of Paul's converts: "my true child in a common faith" (1:4).

HIGH POINTS IN TITUS

This brief letter is full of charm and help for effective Christian living. Its setting is interesting. An old apostle is writing to a son in the gospel (1:4) to assist him in carrying out his mission in a tough spot (Crete). The son was living and working among people who were notorious as "liars, wild animals, and lazy gluttons" (1:12). The nature of the counsel offered indicates that the church members there were undisciplined, quarrelsome, insubordinate, and indolent in their Christian service. Their way of life was not markedly different from that of their heathen neighbors. And false teachers were destroying whatever foundations of Christian understanding and living had been laid down when they were first evangelized.

Titus's task is to improve the understanding of Christian truth and the level of Christian living and service in the Cretan church. To do this he must teach them healthy doctrine (1:9), as opposed to the teachings of the heretics. Healthy doctrine teaches that:

(1) God wills the salvation of all people from their "ungodly lives and the desires of this world" (2:12).

(2) This salvation is both present ("he saved us"; 3:5) and future ("hope for eternal life"; 3:7) and consists in rebirth and renewal in the Holy Spirit, effected in baptism, through Jesus Christ's act of redemption (2:14; 3:5-6).

(3) One who has been saved and awaits final salvation lives a "sensible, ethical, and godly" life in this world (2:12). Specifically, this means these qualities: temperance, self-control, honesty, hospitality, kindness, submission to authority, and mutual helpfulness. Those who live this way will "make the teaching about God our savior attractive in every way" (2:10).

(4) Christians live in hope of the coming triumph of Christ (2:13) and of eternal life (1:2; 3:7).

TITUS

Greeting

1 From Paul, a slave of God and an apostle of Jesus Christ. I'm sent to bring about the faith of God's chosen people and a knowledge of the truth that agrees with godliness. ²Their faith and this knowledge are based on the hope of eternal life that God, who doesn't lie, promised before time began. ³God revealed his message at the appropriate time through preaching, and I was trusted with preaching this message by the command of God our savior.

⁴To Titus, my true child in a common faith.

Grace and peace from God the Father and Christ Jesus our savior.

Appointing elders

⁵The reason I left you behind in Crete was to organize whatever needs to be done and to appoint elders in each city, as I told you. ⁶Elders should be without fault. They should be faithful to their spouse,ª and have faithful children who can't be accused of self-indulgence or rebelliousness. ⁷This is because supervisorsᵇ should be without fault as God's managers: they shouldn't be stubborn, irritable, addicted to alcohol, a bully, or greedy. ⁸Instead, they should show hospitality, love what is good, and be reasonable, ethical, godly, and self-controlled.

⁹They must pay attention to the reliable message as it has been taught to them so that they can encourage people with healthy instruction and refute those who speak against it.

Correcting rebellious people

¹⁰In fact, there are many who are rebellious people, loudmouths, and deceivers, especially some of those who are Jewish believers.ᶜ ¹¹They must be silenced because they upset entire households. They teach what they shouldn't to make money dishonestly. ¹²Someone who is one of their own prophets said, "People from Crete are always liars, wild animals, and lazy gluttons." ¹³This statement is true. Because of this, correct them firmly, so that they can be healthy in their faith. ¹⁴They shouldn't pay attention to Jewish myths and commands from people who reject the truth. ¹⁵Everything is clean to those who are clean, but nothing is clean to those who are corrupt and without faith. Instead, their mind and conscience are corrupted. ¹⁶They claim to know God, but they deny God by the things that they do. They are detestable, disobedient, and disqualified to do anything good.

Teaching all people how to be godly

2 But you should talk in a way that is consistent with sound teaching. ²Tell the

---

ªOr *they should be a one-woman man.* ᵇOr *overseers, bishops* ᶜOr *from the circumcision*

CRETE

Crete is a large Greek island in the Mediterranean Sea. It is in the southern part of the Aegean Sea and separates the Aegean from the Libyan Sea. The Minoans, made famous through the excavation of Knossos, inhabited the island during the second millennium BCE. OT references to Caphtor (Deut 2:23; Jer 47:4; Amos 9:7) have been linked to Crete. Paul sailed along the southern side of Crete on his way to Rome (Acts 27:7-16). A series of Christian communities was established on the island during the 1st century CE, and these formed the context for the letter to Titus.

older men to be sober, dignified, sensible, and healthy in respect to their faith, love, and patience.

[3]Likewise, tell the older women to be reverent in their behavior, teaching what is good, rather than being gossips or addicted to heavy drinking. [4]That way they can mentor young women to love their husbands and children, [5]and to be sensible, morally pure, working at home, kind and submissive to their own husbands, so that God's word won't be ridiculed. [6]Likewise, encourage the younger men to be sensible [7]in every way. Offer yourself as a role model of good actions. Show integrity, seriousness, [8]and a sound message that is above criticism when you teach, so that any opponent will be ashamed because they won't find anything bad to say about us.

[9]Tell slaves to submit to their own masters and please them in everything they do. They shouldn't talk back [10]or steal. Instead, they should show that they are completely reliable in everything so that they might make the teaching about God our savior attractive in every way.

[11]The grace of God has appeared, bringing salvation to all people. [12]It educates us so that we can live sensible, ethical, and godly lives right now by rejecting ungodly lives and the desires of this world. [13]At the same time we wait for the blessed hope and the glorious appearance of our great God and savior Jesus Christ. [14]He gave himself for us in order to rescue us from every kind of lawless behavior, and cleanse a special people for himself who are eager to do good actions.

[15]Talk about these things. Encourage and correct with complete authority. Don't let anyone disrespect you. [1]Remind **3** them to submit to rulers and authorities. They should be obedient and ready to do every good thing. [2]They shouldn't speak disrespectfully about anyone, but they should be peaceful, kind, and show complete courtesy toward everyone. [3]We were once foolish, disobedient, deceived, and slaves to our desires and various pleasures too. We were spending our lives in evil behavior and jealousy. We were disgusting, and we hated other people. [4]But "when God our savior's kindness and love appeared, [5]he saved us because of his mercy, not because of righteous things we had done. He did it through the washing of new birth and the renewing by the Holy Spirit, [6]which God poured out upon us generously through Jesus Christ our savior. [7]So, since we have been made righteous by his grace, we can inherit the hope for eternal life." [8]This saying is reliable. And I want you to insist on these things, so that those who have come to believe in God might give careful attention to doing good. These things are good and useful for everyone.

Final instructions and greetings

[9]Avoid stupid controversies, genealogies, and fights about the Law, because they are useless and worthless. [10]After a first and second warning, have nothing more to do with a person who causes conflict, [11]because you know that someone like this is twisted and sinful—so they condemn themselves.

[12]When I send Artemas or Tychicus to you, try to come to me in Nicopolis, because I've decided to spend the winter there. [13]Help Zenas the lawyer and Apollos on their journey with enthusiasm so that they won't need anything. [14]But our people should also learn to devote themselves to doing good in order to meet pressing needs so they aren't unproductive.

[15]Everyone with me greets you; greet those who love us faithfully.

Grace be with all of you.

PHILEMON

THEME

Paul's appeal to Philemon for Christian forgiveness

INTRODUCTION

The letter to Philemon is a personal letter written by Paul. The immediate reason for the letter is that an escaped slave, Onesimus, is now a trusted helper for the imprisoned apostle. Paul writes to the slave's owner, Philemon, with a remarkable request. Paul wants Philemon not only to refrain from punishing the escaped slave but also to receive him back graciously. At least one interpreter suggests that Paul implies even more than this. According to this interpretation, Paul wants Philemon to release Onesimus from slavery altogether so that Onesimus can stay with Paul as his trusted assistant during the very trying period of Paul's own imprisonment. Most interpreters do not subscribe to such a radical interpretation.

Paul writes the letter while in prison (verse 1), probably the period of house arrest in Rome sometime during the years 61–63 CE. His other letters are addressed to churches (Romans 1:7; 1 Corinthians 1:2; 2 Corinthians 1:1; Galatians 1:2; Ephesians 1:1; Philippians 1:1; Colossians 1:2; 1 Thessalonians 1:1; 2 Thessalonians 1:1). The Pastoral Epistles, which were written ostensibly to individuals, were also intended for a wider reading.

All of Paul's letters are written to specific congregations or specific individuals who are wrestling with difficulties or stresses that have come up during the course of normal personal and corporate life together. Paul writes as a pastor attempting to bring every facet of life into the perspective of the work of God through Christ.

Modern readers will at once be struck by Paul's seeming lack of concern for the reprehensible but socially acceptable standard of slavery. Why doesn't the apostle address the issue?

The first reason Paul does not attack the institution of slavery is that slavery had long since become a major part of the Roman Empire's culture. In fact, slavery had become a predominant means of labor. Roman practice included slaves in nearly every aspect of labor, from the most menial tasks to the higher responsibilities. Wealthy people would often have a large number of slaves who would care for every detail of family life. Slaves were frequently artists, painters, architects, librarians, even doctors. Slavery was intertwined with every aspect of culture. In short, slavery was a fact of life as readily accepted as Roman rule itself.

This is not to suggest that slavery in the Roman practice was a positive institution. A slave had no rights. Indeed, a slave was little more than another object in the owner's inventory of possessions to be considered along with wagons, cattle, and household goods. The slave's entire life lay within the authority of the owner. Marriage was not a right. Punishments were entirely up to the owner; there was no recourse for the slave. Punishments varied. Frequently slaves were branded on the forehead, or forced to carry a *furca*—a V-shaped instrument of torture. Occasionally slaves were the playthings of cruel owners and were forced to fight animals in an arena. One incident gives stark evidence of how precarious the slave's life could be. A record exists of how one slave was crucified for no more reason than for the master's own pleasure. No more reason was required!

Had the Christian movement arbitrarily attacked the detestable institution, the church could easily have become the target of immeasurable censure and attack by a threatened society and government. A more subtle reason can be discerned as well. The moral implications of slavery include poor self-esteem, identity as something other than fully human, and a coarseness of soul that renders any vulnerability or compassion impossible. The Christian movement hardly stood by with nothing to say. Indeed, the movement was a radically transforming movement, but not in public and immediately social manifestations. Rather, the movement emphasized the change that occurred within the human soul with respect to identity, self-esteem, and community. Jesus' teachings include respect for every human life (Matthew 6:26). Many of Jesus' parables dealt with the importance of one. Recall the parables of the lost sheep and the woman who had lost one coin (Luke 15:3-10).

Paul himself refuses to see slaves as anything but people. They are certainly not mere property (Philemon v. 10). Granted, slaves still have certain responsibilities to their masters, but by the same token Christian masters also have responsibilities toward their slaves (Ephesians 6:9; Colossians 4:1).

In Paul's thinking, the distinction between slave and free man or woman—so strongly marked in society—has begun to fade (1 Corinthians 12:13). To the Galatians Paul asserts, "There is neither Jew nor Greek; there is neither slave nor free; nor is there male and female, for you are all one in Christ Jesus" (Galatians 3:28).

It appears almost incredible to the modern reader, but Paul sees the social and cultural institution as a given, and as such an appropriate place in which the Christian gospel should be lived out (1 Corinthians 7:21-24). He also charges, "As for slaves, obey your human masters . . . but act like slaves of Christ carrying out God's will from the heart" (Ephesians 6:5-6).

Paul's extraordinary request depends not only upon Philemon's own Christian convictions but also upon the relationship that the two men have. Paul himself characterizes the relationship in warm terms—"dearly loved coworker" (verse 1), "partner" (verse 17)—and in his request for a guest room (verse 22). This closeness comes as no surprise, since Philemon had been converted to

Christianity through Paul's ministry in Ephesus. According to Acts, Paul spent more time ministering in Ephesus than anywhere else (Acts 19). He would have known this church more intimately than any other. From the evidence in this letter, we see that Philemon had assumed a major leadership role in the church, so he and Paul would have undoubtedly worked together (verses 5, 7). The church may have even met in Philemon's home (verse 2).

PHILEMON

Greeting

[1] From Paul, who is a prisoner for the cause of Christ Jesus, and our brother Timothy.

To Philemon our dearly loved coworker, [2] Apphia our sister, Archippus our fellow soldier, and the church that meets in your house.

[3] May the grace and peace from God our Father and the Lord Jesus Christ be with you.

Paul's prayer for Philemon

[4] Philemon, I thank my God every time I mention you in my prayers [5] because I've heard of your love and faithfulness, which you have both for the Lord Jesus and for all God's people. [6] I pray that your partnership in the faith might become effective by an understanding of all that is good among us in Christ. [7] I have great joy and encouragement because of your love, since the hearts of God's people are refreshed by your actions, my brother.

Paul's appeal for Onesimus

[8] Therefore, though I have enough confidence in Christ to command you to do the right thing, [9] I would rather appeal to you through love. I, Paul—an old man, and now also a prisoner for Christ Jesus—[10] appeal to you for my child Onesimus. I became his father in the faith during my time in prison. [11] He was useless to you before, but now he is useful to both of us. [12] I'm sending him back to you, which is like sending you my own heart. [13] I considered keeping him with me so that he might serve me in your place during my time in prison because of the gospel. [14] However, I didn't want to do anything without your consent so that your act of kindness would occur willingly and not under pressure. [15] Maybe this is the reason that Onesimus was separated from you for a while so that you might have him back forever—[16] no longer as a slave but more than a slave—that is, as a dearly loved brother. He is especially a dearly loved brother to me. How much more can he become a brother to you, personally and spiritually in the Lord!

[17] So, if you really consider me a partner, welcome Onesimus as if you were welcoming me. [18] If he has harmed you in any way or owes you money, charge it to my account. [19] I, Paul, will pay it back to you (I'm writing this with my own hand). Of course, I won't mention that you owe me your life.

[20] Yes, brother, I want this favor from

ONESIMUS

1. In the letter to Philemon, Paul refers to himself as having become father to one of his colleagues in the gospel, Onesimus, while Paul was in prison (Phlm 10). Onesimus was Philemon's slave. The traditional interpretation that Onesimus is a fugitive slave has been challenged in some recent scholarship but remains the dominant scholarly and popular interpretation.

2. Colossians mentions a "faithful and dearly loved brother" called Onesimus (Col 4:9) whom Paul had sent to Colossae and who was apparently himself a Colossian. This seems to be the same Onesimus from the letter to Philemon.

3. Ignatius, a 1st-century bishop of Antioch, writes of an Onesimus, bishop of Ephesus, "a man of indescribable charity and your bishop here on earth."

you in the Lord! Refresh my heart in Christ. [21] I'm writing to you, confident of your obedience and knowing that you will do more than what I ask. [22] Also, one more thing—prepare a guest room for me. I hope that I will be released from prison to be with you because of your prayers.

Final greeting

[23] Epaphras, who is in prison with me for the cause of Christ Jesus, greets you, [24] as well as my coworkers Mark, Aristarchus, Demas, and Luke.

[25] May the grace of the Lord Jesus Christ be with your spirit.

HEBREWS

THEME

Jesus, the eternal Son of God, by his completely effective priestly work, offers all people perfect cleansing from their sins and admittance to the presence of the living God.

INTRODUCTION

Hebrews is unique in the New Testament. It has the richest vocabulary, the most eloquent Greek, and the style of the Jewish rabbis. It quotes the Old Testament most frequently and at greatest length. It has the most severe warning and the warmest encouragement for Christians.

Hebrews is about Jesus Christ, what he has done and what he is. It is a message of hope, a promise of eternal fellowship with God, conditioned only on our response. It is about God's greatness, righteousness, grace, and love inviting us to respond. Hebrews is a book of action, of persevering movement toward God into God's presence.

AUTHORSHIP

We do not know who wrote the letter. Shortly after it was written, no one knew. People guessed. We are still guessing.

Some have guessed that Paul wrote the letter. Saying Paul wrote it helped to get Hebrews accepted when Christians were deciding what to include in the New Testament. It was not written by Paul, however. The style, vocabulary, and emphases are not Paul's. Others have guessed it was Barnabas because he encouraged people (Acts 4:36) as Hebrews does. Some have guessed Priscilla because she and her husband, Aquila, instructed a man named Apollos in the gospel (Acts 18:26). Many have guessed Apollos himself, an eloquent man, well versed in the Old Testament (Acts 18:24), and a leading preacher (1 Corinthians 1:12).

Proof of authorship is not needed to appreciate the value of what has been written. Whoever wrote the letter to the Hebrews was gifted in speech, as well as in vocabulary and style. This anonymous writer knew the contemporary culture and literature. He or she knew how Jewish rabbis taught. Greek was the universal language of the time, and the author knew how Greek authors wrote. From the Old Testament the writer drew symbols and illustrations to press home a message of warning and encouragement for the Christians.

THE AUDIENCE

We do not know to whom the message was sent or where they lived. Again, there have been many guesses such as somewhere in Italy, in Judea, in Egypt. Someone added on the title "To the Hebrews" because the author refers extensively to Hebrew stories and worship in the Old Testament.

All Christians, however, whether of Jewish or pagan background, were accustomed to "search the Scriptures," that is, the Old Testament, to read what it said about the Messiah, Christ. All we know is that the letter was addressed to Christians who needed encouragement. It tells us that they were at one time new and joyful Christians. They have had troubles, however, maybe ridicule or persecution that has disheartened them. They have become lax in the practice of their faith.

DATE

We know Hebrews was written by 90 CE, because it was quoted in both Rome and Alexandria by that date. We cannot tell if it was earlier than 90, except that Timothy, evidently the Apostle Paul's young friend, was still active (13:23).

LITERARY STYLE

Was Hebrews a letter? We do not know even that. It begins with no greetings and no address and has no signature. The last chapter reads like the closing of a letter from a Christian leader with words of counsel, a benediction, a postscript with news about coming with Timothy, and with the phrase "grace be with all of you" (13:25).

The previous parts (twelve chapters in our Bible) read like a lecture or sermon. Was it a sermon—or several short sermons—which someone sent to a group of Christians, attaching a personal note? Was it a tract?

One thing we do know. Hebrews is a masterpiece, a beautiful and intense expression of faith and hope applicable to all Christians.

THE TRIPLE THEME OF HEBREWS

There is a triple theme in Hebrews: (1) movement from the inadequate to the adequate, from the imperfect to the perfect, to God; (2) the supreme sufficiency of Christ alone to make that movement possible; and (3) warning and encouragement to persevere in that Christ-enabled movement.

THE LOGIC OF HEBREWS

(1) The assumption is that the business of life, and the desire of all people, is access to God. Everlasting separation from God is the ultimate tragedy.

(2) The problem is that sin and indifferent neglect of faith prevent fellowship with God.

(3) The need is to break through sin's wall of separation.

(4) The solution is Christ. Through Christ we can be forgiven. Through Christ we gain access to God.

(5) The responsibility is ours to accept forgiveness and to move toward communion with God through faithfulness to Christ, who opens up the way.

THE MESSAGE OF HEBREWS

Hebrews is a warning against the neglect of what God has offered in Christ. Rejecting Christ means rejecting God, God's Word, God's Spirit, God's grace. It is a warning against drifting off into the inadequacies of pre-Christian Judaism, into exotic cults, into immorality, or into mere indifference and neglect. But Hebrews is also an encouragement to endure suffering, to persevere in faithfulness to Christ. It is an assurance that God's promise is unfailing and that Christ is the supreme and only adequate means of our inheriting that promise. That promise is salvation, purification, perfection, "rest" in God's presence forever.

The warnings and encouragement interweave with illustrations and arguments that point out Christ's superiority as God's one appointed means of salvation.

CHRIST IN HEBREWS IS OUR HIGH PRIEST

Hebrews calls Christ a high priest because, like a priest, he offers a sacrifice on behalf of people. Hebrews uses a story from Genesis (14:17-20) to illustrate Christ's high priesthood. Melchizedek was a priest-king who blessed Abraham, ancestor of the Israelites. Melchizedek was not an Israelite. The story mentions no lineage, birth, or death of Melchizedek. Christ, says Hebrews, is like that (6:20). Using contrast, Hebrews shows that Christ is the only effective priest for our salvation (7:11, 16, 22; 9:13-14, 23).

THE OLD TESTAMENT IN HEBREWS

When people became Christians, they inherited the Jewish faith based on the Jewish interpretation of the Old Testament at the time of Jesus. Christians studied the Old Testament and knew it well. The book of Hebrews shows how Jesus fulfilled the religious hope and faith of the Old Testament.

HEBREWS

The Son is God's ultimate messenger

1 In the past, God spoke through the prophets to our ancestors in many times and many ways. [2] In these final days, though, he spoke to us through a Son. God made his Son the heir of everything and created the world through him. [3] The Son is the light of God's glory and the imprint of God's being. He maintains everything with his powerful message. After he carried out the cleansing of people from their sins, he sat down at the right side of the highest majesty. [4] And the Son became so much greater than the other messengers, such as angels, that he received a more important title than theirs.

Speaking to the Son and angels

[5] After all, when did God ever say to any of the angels:

You are my Son.
   Today I have become your Father?[a]

Or, even,

I will be his Father,
   and he will be my Son?[b]

[6] But then, when he brought his firstborn into the world, he said,

All of God's angels must worship him.[c]

[7] He talks about the angels:

He's the one who uses the spirits
   for his messengers
   and who uses flames of fire as ministers.[d]

[8] But he says to his Son,

God, your throne is forever
   and your kingdom's scepter
      is a rod of justice.
[9] You loved righteousness
   and hated lawless behavior.
   That is why God, your God,
   has anointed you with oil
      instead of your companions.[e]

[10] And he says,

You, Lord, laid the earth's foundations
   in the beginning,
   and the heavens are made by your hands.
[11] They will pass away,
   but you remain.

They will all wear out like old clothes.
[12] You will fold them up like a coat.
They will be changed
   like a person changes clothes,
   but you stay the same,
   and the years of your life
      won't come to an end.[f]

[13] When has he ever said to any of the angels,

Sit at my right side
   until I put your enemies
      under your feet like a footstool?[g]

[14] Aren't all the angels ministering spirits who are sent to serve those who are going to inherit salvation?

Listen to the Son's message

2 This is why it's necessary for us to pay more attention to what we have heard, or else we may drift away from it. [2] If the message that was spoken by angels was reliable, and every offense and act of disobedience received an appropriate consequence, [3] how will we escape if we ignore such a great salvation? It was first announced through the Lord, and then it was confirmed by those who heard him. [4] God also vouched for their message with signs, amazing things, various miracles, and gifts from the Holy Spirit, which were handed out the way he wanted.

Jesus is the enthroned human being

[5] God didn't put the world that is coming (the world we are talking about) under the angels' control. [6] Instead, someone declared somewhere,

What is humanity
   that you think about them?
   Or what are the human beings
      that you care about them?
[7] For a while you made them lower
   than angels.
   You crowned the human beings
      with glory and honor.
[8] You put everything under their control.[h]

---

[a] Ps 2:7   [b] 2 Sam 7:14; 1 Chron 17:13   [c] Deut 32:43 and Ps 97:7 LXX   [d] Ps 104:4   [e] Ps 45:6-7   [f] Ps 102:25-27
[g] Ps 110:1   [h] Ps 8:4-6

When he puts everything under their control, he doesn't leave anything out of control. But right now, we don't see everything under their control yet. [9]However, we do see the one who was made lower in order than the angels for a little while—it's Jesus! He's the one who is now crowned with glory and honor because of the suffering of his death. He suffered death so that he could taste death for everyone through God's grace.

Qualified to be a high priest

[10]It was appropriate for God, for whom and through whom everything exists, to use experiences of suffering to make perfect the pioneer of salvation. This salvation belongs to many sons and daughters whom he's leading to glory. [11]This is because the one who makes people holy and the people who are being made holy all come from one source. That is why Jesus isn't ashamed to call them brothers and sisters when he says,

[12] *I will publicly announce your name*
to my brothers and sisters.
I will praise you in the middle
of the assembly.[i]

[13]He also says,
I will rely on him.[j]
And also,
Here I am with the children
whom God has given to me.[k]

[14]Therefore, since the children share in flesh and blood, he also shared the same things in the same way. He did this to destroy the one who holds the power over death—the devil—by dying. [15]He set free those who were held in slavery their entire lives by their fear of death. [16]Of course, he isn't trying to help angels, but rather he's helping Abraham's descendants. [17]Therefore, he had to be made like his brothers and sisters in every way. This was so that he could become a merciful and faithful high priest in things relating to God, in order to wipe away the sins of the people. [18]He's able to help those who are being tempted, since he himself experienced suffering when he was tempted.

We are Jesus' house

3 Therefore, brothers and sisters who are partners in the heavenly calling, think about Jesus, the apostle and high priest of our confession. [2]Jesus was faithful to the one who appointed him just like Moses was faithful in God's house. [3]But he deserves greater glory than Moses in the same way that the builder of the house deserves more honor than the house itself. [4]Every house is built by someone, but God is the builder of everything. [5]Moses was faithful in all God's house as a servant in order to affirm the things that would be spoken later. [6]But Jesus was faithful over God's house as a Son. We are his house if we hold on to the confidence and the pride that our hope gives us.

Respond to Jesus' voice now

[7]So, as the Holy Spirit says,
Today, if you hear his voice,
[8] *don't have stubborn hearts*
as they did in the rebellion,
on the day when they tested me
in the desert.
[9] *That is where your ancestors*
challenged and tested me,
though they had seen my work
for forty years.
[10] *So I was angry with them.*
I said, "Their hearts always go off course,
and they don't know my ways."
[11] *Because of my anger I swore:*
"They will never enter my rest!"[l]

[12]Watch out, brothers and sisters, so that none of you have an evil, unfaithful heart that abandons the living God. [13]Instead, encourage each other every day, as long as it's called "today," so that none of you become insensitive to God because of sin's deception. [14]We are partners with Christ, but only if we hold on to the confidence we had in the beginning until the end.

[15]When it says,
Today, if you hear his voice,
don't have stubborn hearts
as they did in the rebellion.[m]
[16]Who was it who rebelled when they heard his voice? Wasn't it all of those who were

---

[i]Ps 22:22   [j]Isa 8:17 LXX   [k]Isa 8:18   [l]Ps 95:7-11   [m]Ps 95:7-8

brought out of Egypt by Moses? [17]And with whom was God angry for forty years? Wasn't it with the ones who sinned, whose bodies fell in the desert? [18]And against whom did he swear that they would never enter his rest, if not against the ones who were disobedient? [19]We see that they couldn't enter because of their lack of faith.

Enter the rest

4 Therefore, since the promise that we can enter into rest is still open, let's be careful so that none of you will appear to miss it. [2]We also had the good news preached to us, just as the Israelites did. However, the message they heard didn't help them because they weren't united in faith with the ones who listened to it. [3]We who have faith are entering the rest. As God said,

And because of my anger I swore:
"They will never enter into my rest!" [n]

And yet God's works were completed at the foundation of the world. [4]Then somewhere he said this about the seventh day of creation: *God rested on the seventh day from all his works.* [o] [5]But again, in the passage above, God said, *They will never enter my rest!* [p] [6]Therefore, it's left open for some to enter it, and the ones who had the good news preached to them before didn't enter because of disobedience. [7]Just as it says in the passage above, God designates a certain day as "today," when he says through David much later,

Today, if you hear his voice,
don't have stubborn hearts. [q]

[8]If Joshua gave the Israelites rest, God wouldn't have spoken about another day later on. [9]So you see that a sabbath rest is left open for God's people. [10]The one who entered God's rest also rested from his works, just as God rested from his own.

First summary of the message

[11]Therefore, let's make every effort to enter that rest so that no one will fall by following the same example of disobedience, [12]because God's word is living, active, and sharper than any two-edged sword. It pene-

trates to the point that it separates the soul from the spirit and the joints from the marrow. It's able to judge the heart's thoughts and intentions. [13]No creature is hidden from it, but rather everything is naked and exposed to the eyes of the one to whom we have to give an answer.

[14]Also, let's hold on to the confession since we have a great high priest who passed through the heavens, who is Jesus, God's Son; [15]because we don't have a high priest who can't sympathize with our weaknesses but instead one who was tempted in every way that we are, except without sin. [16]Finally, let's draw near to the throne of favor with confidence so that we can receive mercy and find grace when we need help.

Introduction to a deeper teaching

5 Every high priest is taken from the people and put in charge of things that relate to God for their sake, in order to offer gifts and sacrifices for sins. [2]The high priest is able to deal gently with the ignorant and those who are misled since he himself is prone to weakness. [3]Because of his weakness, he must offer sacrifices for his own sins as well as for the people. [4]No one takes this honor for themselves but takes it only when they are called by God, just like Aaron.

[5]In the same way Christ also didn't promote himself to become high priest. Instead, it was the one who said to him,

You are my Son.
Today I have become your Father,
[6]as he also says in another place,
You are a priest forever,
according to the order of Melchizedek. [r]

[7]During his days on earth, Christ offered prayers and requests with loud cries and tears as his sacrifices to the one who was able to save him from death. He was heard because of his godly devotion. [8]Although he was a Son, he learned obedience from what he suffered. [9]After he had been made perfect, he became the source of eternal salvation for everyone who obeys him. [10]He was appointed by God to be a high priest according to the order of Melchizedek.

[n]Ps 95:11 [o]Gen 2:2 [p]Ps 95:11 [q]Ps 95:7-8 [r]Ps 110:4

[11]We have a lot to say about this topic, and it's difficult to explain, because you have been lazy and you haven't been listening. [12]Although you should have been teachers by now, you need someone to teach you an introduction to the basics about God's message. You have come to the place where you need milk instead of solid food. [13]Everyone who lives on milk is not used to the word of righteousness, because they are babies. [14]But solid food is for the mature, whose senses are trained by practice to distinguish between good and evil.

Let's press on to maturity

6 So let's press on to maturity, by moving on from the basics about Christ's word. Let's not lay a foundation of turning away from dead works, of faith in God, [2]of teaching about ritual ways to wash with water, laying on of hands, the resurrection from the dead, and eternal judgment—all over again. [3]We're going to press on, if God allows it.

[4]Because it's impossible to restore people to changed hearts and lives who turn away once they have seen the light, tasted the heavenly gift, become partners with the Holy Spirit, [5]and tasted God's good word and the powers of the coming age. [6]They are crucifying God's Son all over again and exposing him to public shame. [7]The ground receives a blessing from God when it drinks up the rain that regularly comes and falls on it and yields a useful crop for those people for whom it is being farmed. [8]But if it produces thorns and thistles, it's useless and close to being cursed. It ends up being burned.

Make your hope sure

[9]But we are convinced of better things in your case, brothers and sisters, even though we are talking this way—things that go together with salvation. [10]God isn't unjust so that he forgets your efforts and the love you have shown for his name's sake when you served and continue to serve

VEIL OF THE TEMPLE

In Zerubbabel's and Herod's temples, a curtain or veil blocked the entrance into the shrine. Another elaborately decorated curtain hung inside the massive doors that led from the open vestibule into the central nave. These curtains have a precedent in the curtain and screen of the meeting tent (Exod 26:31-37).

Solomon's temple had wooden doors between the shrine and the nave (1 Kgs 6:31) and between the nave and the vestibule (1 Kgs 6:33-34), but no curtains are mentioned. Second Chronicles 3:14 mentions a curtain, not a door, before the shrine, but this may reflect the layout of the Second Temple. But many scholars think that a curtain hung behind the doors into the shrine to veil the shrine when the doors were open (see 1 Kings 8:8, which suggests that a curtain blocked a direct view of the chest from the open doorway, but the gap between the doorway and the ends of the curtain permitted a view of the ends of the long poles).

The NT claims that the curtain between the nave and the shrine was mysteriously torn from top to bottom at the time of Jesus' crucifixion (Matt 27:51; Mark 15:38; Luke 23:45), indicating that access into the presence of God had been provided for all the followers of Jesus by his self-sacrifice (Heb 6:19; 10:20).

God's holy people. [11]But we desperately want each of you to show the same effort to make your hope sure until the end. [12]This is so you won't be lazy but follow the example of the ones who inherit the promises through faith and patience.

Our hope in Jesus' priesthood

[13]When God gave Abraham his promise, he swore by himself since he couldn't swear by anyone greater. [14]He said, *I will certainly bless you and multiply your descendants.*[s] [15]So Abraham obtained the promise by showing patience. [16]People pledge by something greater than themselves. A solemn pledge guarantees what they say and shuts down any argument. [17]When God wanted to further demonstrate to the heirs of the promise that his purpose doesn't change, he guaranteed it with a solemn pledge. [18]So these are two things that don't change, because it's impossible for God to lie. He did this so that we, who have taken refuge in him, can be encouraged to grasp the hope that is lying in front of us. [19]This hope, which is a safe and secure anchor for our whole being, enters the sanctuary behind the curtain. [20]That's where Jesus went in advance and entered for us, since he became a high priest according to the order of Melchizedek. [1]This Melchizedek, who was king of Salem and priest of the Most High God, met Abraham as he returned from the defeat of the kings, and Melchizedek blessed him. [2]Abraham gave a tenth of everything to him. His name means first "king of righteousness," and then "king of Salem," that is, "king of peace." [3]He is without father or mother or any family. He has no beginning or end of life, but he's like God's Son and remains a priest for all time.

A priest like Melchizedek

[4]See how great Melchizedek was! Abraham, the father of the people, gave him a tenth of everything he captured. [5]The descendants of Levi who receive the office of priest have a commandment under the Law to collect a tenth of everything from the people who are their brothers and sisters, though they also are descended from Abraham. [6]But Melchizedek, who isn't related to them, received a tenth of everything from Abraham and blessed the one who had received the promises. [7]Without question, the less important person is blessed by the more important person. [8]In addition, in one case a tenth is received by people who die, and in the other case, the tenth is received by someone who continues to live, according to the record. [9]It could be said that Levi, who received a tenth, paid a tenth through Abraham [10]because he was still in his ancestor's body when Abraham paid the tenth to Melchizedek.

[11]So if perfection came through the levitical office of priest (for the people received the Law under the priests), why was there still a need to speak about raising up another priest according to the order of Melchizedek rather than one according to the order of Aaron? [12]When the order of the priest changes, there has to be a change in the Law as well. [13]The person we are talking about belongs to another tribe, and no one ever served at the altar from that

[s]Gen 22:17

SALEM

1. The city of King Melchizedek (Gen 14:18), long associated with Jerusalem. In the NT, Salem is understood as a symbolic name for Jerusalem.

2. A city situated west of the Jordan River, south of the Galilee Sea. The city is mentioned in John 3:23 in association with Aenon, where John the Baptist was baptizing in the Judean countryside (John 3:22).

tribe. [14]It's clear that our Lord came from the tribe of Judah, but Moses never said anything about priests from that tribe. [15]And it's even clearer if another priest appears who is like Melchizedek. [16]He has become a priest by the power of a life that can't be destroyed, rather than a legal requirement about physical descent. [17]This is confirmed:

You are a priest forever,
    according to the order of Melchizedek.[t]

Able to save completely

[18]On the one hand, an earlier command is set aside because it was weak and useless [19](because the Law made nothing perfect). On the other hand, a better hope is introduced, through which we draw near to God. [20]And this was not done without a solemn pledge! The others have become priests without a solemn pledge, [21]but this priest was affirmed with a solemn pledge by the one who said,

The Lord has made a solemn pledge
    and will not change his mind:
You are a priest forever.[u]

[22]As a result, Jesus has become the guarantee of a better covenant. [23]The others who became priests are numerous because death prevented them from continuing to serve. [24]In contrast, he holds the office of priest permanently because he continues to serve forever. [25]This is why he can completely save those who are approaching God through him, because he always lives to speak with God for them.

[26]It's appropriate for us to have this kind of high priest: holy, innocent, incorrupt, separate from sinners, and raised high above the heavens. [27]He doesn't need to offer sacrifices every day like the other high priests, first for their own sins and then for the sins of the people. He did this once for all when he offered himself. [28]The Law appoints people who are prone to weakness as high priests, but the content of the solemn pledge, which came after the Law, appointed a Son who has been made perfect forever.

Meeting tents, sacrifices, and covenants

8 Now the main point of what we are saying is this: We have this kind of high priest. He sat down at the right side of the throne of the majesty in the heavens. [2]He's serving as a priest in the holy place, which is the true meeting tent that God, not any human being, set up. [3]Every high priest is appointed to offer gifts and sacrifices. So it's necessary for this high priest also to have something to offer. [4]If he was located on earth, he wouldn't be a priest because there are already others who offer gifts based on the Law. [5]They serve in a place that is a copy and shadow of the heavenly meeting tent. This is indicated when Moses was warned by God when he was about to set up the meeting tent: *See that you follow the pattern that I showed you on the mountain in every detail.*[v] [6]But now, Jesus has received a superior priestly service just as he arranged a better covenant that is enacted with better promises.

[7]If the first covenant had been without fault, it wouldn't have made sense to

---

[t]Ps 110:4 [u]Ps 110:4 [v]Exod 25:40

MEETING TENT

The portable tent sanctuary constructed by the people of Israel in the Sinai desert according to instructions given by God to Moses on Mount Sinai after God's conclusion of a covenant with Israel (Exod 25–31; 35–40). Together with its religious leaders and its rituals, the meeting tent is the model of OT worship.

expect a second. [8]But God did find fault with them, since he says,

> Look, the days are coming, says the Lord,
>> when I will make a covenant
>> with the house of Israel,
>> and I will make a new covenant
>> with the house of Judah.
> [9]It will not be like the covenant
>> that I made with their ancestors
>> on the day I took them by the hand
>> to lead them out of the land of Egypt,
>> because they did not continue
>>> to keep my covenant,
>> and I lost interest in them, says the Lord.
> [10]This is the covenant that I will make
>> with the house of Israel
>> after those days, says the Lord.
> I will place my laws in their minds,
>> and write them on their hearts.
> I will be their God,
>> and they will be my people.
> [11]And each person
>> won't ever teach a neighbor
>> or their brother or sister, saying,
>> "Know the Lord,"
>> because they will all know me,
>>> from the least important of them
>>> to the most important;
> [12]because I will be lenient
>> toward their unjust actions,
>> and I won't remember
>> their sins anymore.[w]

[13]When it says new, it makes the first obsolete. And if something is old and outdated, it's close to disappearing.

[w]Jer 31:31-34   [x]Heb *cherubim*

Christ's service in the heavenly meeting tent

9 So then the first covenant had regulations for the priests' service and the holy place on earth. [2]They pitched the first tent called the holy place. It contained the lampstand, the table, and the loaves of bread presented to God. [3]There was a tent behind the second curtain called the holy of holies. [4]It had the gold altar for incense and the chest containing the covenant, which was covered with gold on all sides. In the chest there was a gold jar containing manna, Aaron's rod that budded, and the stone tablets of the covenant. [5]Above the chest there were magnificent winged creatures[x] casting their shadow over the seat of the chest, where sin is taken care of. Right now we can't talk about these things in detail. [6]When these things have been prepared in this way, priests enter the first tent all the time as they perform their service. [7]But only the high priest enters the second tent once a year. He never does this without blood, which he offers for himself and for the sins the people committed in ignorance. [8]With this, the Holy Spirit is showing that the way into the holy place hadn't been revealed yet while the first tent was standing. [9]This is a symbol for the present time. It shows that the gifts and sacrifices that are being offered can't perfect the conscience of the one who is serving. [10]These are superficial regulations that are only about food, drink, and various ritual ways

OLD TESTAMENT

The Christian name for the *Tanakh,* in contrast to the New Testament. Both terms are based on the "new covenant" and a perceived "old covenant" (Jer 31:31; Luke 22:20; 1 Cor 11:25). The OT is not a single canon, but has different formulations according to different branches of Christianity. The OT for Catholic and Eastern Orthodox churches was based on the Septuagint, the Greek translation of the Jewish Scriptures, and thus it contains books such as Judith. The Protestant OT is based on the Hebrew Jewish Scriptures and does not contain such Greek books.

to wash with water. They are regulations that have been imposed until the time of the new order.

[11]But Christ has appeared as the high priest of the good things that have happened. He passed through the greater and more perfect meeting tent, which isn't made by human hands (that is, it's not a part of this world). [12]He entered the holy of holies once for all by his own blood, not by the blood of goats or calves, securing our deliverance for all time. [13]If the blood of goats and bulls and the sprinkled ashes of cows made spiritually contaminated people holy and clean, [14]how much more will the blood of Jesus wash our consciences clean from dead works in order to serve the living God? He offered himself to God through the eternal Spirit as a sacrifice without any flaw.

Christ's death and the new covenant

[15]This is why he's the mediator of a new covenant (which is a will): so that those who are called might receive the promise of the eternal inheritance on the basis of his death. His death occurred to set them free from the offenses committed under the first covenant. [16]When there is a will, you need to confirm the death of the one who made the will. [17]This is because a will takes effect only after a death, since it's not in force while the one who made the will is alive. [18]So not even the first covenant was put into effect without blood. [19]Moses took the blood of calves and goats, along with water, scarlet wool, and hyssop, and sprinkled both the Law scroll itself and all the people after he had proclaimed every command of the Law to all the people. [20]While he did it, he said, *This is the blood of the covenant that God established for you.*[y] [21]And in the same way he sprinkled the meeting tent and also all the equipment that would be used in the priests' service with blood. [22]Almost everything is cleansed by blood, according to the Law's regulations, and there is no forgiveness without blood being shed.

[23]So it was necessary for the copies of the heavenly things to be cleansed with these sacrifices, but the heavenly things had to be cleansed with better sacrifices than these. [24]Christ didn't enter the holy place (which is a copy of the true holy place) made by human hands, but into heaven itself, so that he now appears in God's presence for us. [25]He didn't enter to offer himself over and over again, like the high priest enters the earthly holy place every year with blood that isn't his. [26]If that were so, then Jesus would have to suffer many times since the foundation of the world. Instead, he has now appeared once at the end of the ages to get rid of sin by sacrificing himself. [27]People are destined to die once and then face judgment. [28]In the same way, Christ was also offered once to take on himself the sins of many people. He will appear a second time, not to take away sin but to save those who are eagerly waiting for him.

Christ's once-for-all sacrifice

10 The Law is a shadow of the good things that are coming, not the real things themselves. It never can perfect the ones who are trying to draw near to God through the same sacrifices that are offered continually every year. [2]Otherwise, wouldn't they have stopped being offered? If the people carrying out their religious duties had been completely cleansed once, no one would have been aware of sin anymore. [3]Instead, these sacrifices are a reminder of sin every year, [4]because it's impossible for the blood of bulls and goats to take away sins.

[5]Therefore, when he comes into the world he says,

You didn't want a sacrifice or an offering,
  but you prepared a body for me;
[6] *you weren't pleased with entirely burned*
  offerings or a sin offering.
[7] *So then I said,*
"Look, I've come to do your will, God.
This has been written about me
  in the scroll."[z]

[8]He says above, *You didn't want* and *you weren't pleased with a sacrifice or an offering*

or *with entirely burned offerings or a purification offering,*[a] which are offered because the Law requires them. [9]Then he said, *Look, I've come to do your will.*[b] He puts an end to the first to establish the second. [10]We have been made holy by God's will through the offering of Jesus Christ's body once for all.

[11]Every priest stands every day serving and offering the same sacrifices over and over, sacrifices that can never take away sins. [12]But when this priest offered one sacrifice for sins for all time, he sat down at the right side of God. [13]Since then, he's waiting until his enemies are made into a footstool for his feet, [14]because he perfected the people who are being made holy with one offering for all time.

[15]The Holy Spirit affirms this when saying,

[16] *This is the covenant*
 that I will make with them.
 After these days, says the Lord,
 I will place my laws in their hearts
 and write them on their minds.
[17] *And I won't remember their sins*
 and their lawless behavior anymore.[c]

[18]When there is forgiveness for these things, there is no longer an offering for sin.

Second summary of the message

[19]Brothers and sisters, we have confidence that we can enter the holy of holies by means of Jesus' blood, [20]through a new and living way that he opened up for us through the curtain, which is his body, [21]and we have a great high priest over God's house.

[22]Therefore, let's draw near with a genuine heart with the certainty that our faith gives us, since our hearts are sprinkled clean from an evil conscience and our bodies are washed with pure water.

[23]Let's hold on to the confession of our hope without wavering, because the one who made the promises is reliable.

[24]And let us consider each other carefully for the purpose of sparking love and good deeds. [25]Don't stop meeting together with other believers, which some people have gotten into the habit of doing. In-

stead, encourage each other, especially as you see the day drawing near.

Judgment for intentional sin

[26]If we make the decision to sin after we receive the knowledge of the truth, there isn't a sacrifice for sins left any longer. [27]There's only a scary expectation of judgment and of a burning fire that's going to devour God's opponents. [28]When someone rejected the Law from Moses, they were put to death without mercy on the basis of the testimony of two or three witnesses. [29]How much worse punishment do you think is deserved by the person who walks all over God's Son, who acts as if the blood of the covenant that made us holy is just ordinary blood, and who insults the Spirit of grace? [30]We know the one who said,

Judgment is mine; I will pay people back.[d]

And he also said,

The Lord will judge his people.[e]
[31]It's scary to fall into the hands of the living God!

Confidence and faith to endure

[32]But remember the earlier days, after you saw the light. You stood your ground while you were suffering from an enormous amount of pressure. [33]Sometimes you were exposed to insults and abuse in public. Other times you became partners with those who were treated that way. [34]You even showed sympathy toward people in prison and accepted the confiscation of your possessions with joy, since you knew that you had better and lasting possessions. [35]So don't throw away your confidence—it brings a great reward. [36]You need to endure so that you can receive the promises after you do God's will.

[37] *In a little while longer,*
 the one who is coming will come
 and won't delay;
[38] *but my righteous one will live by faith,*
 and my whole being won't be pleased
 with anyone who shrinks back.[f]
[39]But we aren't the sort of people who timidly draw back and end up being de-

---

[a]Ps 40:6   [b]Ps 40:7-8   [c]Jer 31:33-34   [d]Deut 32:35   [e]Deut 32:36; Ps 135:14   [f]Hab 2:3-4

stroyed. We're the sort of people who have faith so that our whole beings are preserved.

Description of faith

11 Faith is the reality of what we hope for, the proof of what we don't see. [2]The elders in the past were approved because they showed faith.

Acts of faith by God's people

[3]By faith we understand that the universe has been created by a word from God so that the visible came into existence from the invisible.

[4]By faith Abel offered a better sacrifice to God than Cain, which showed that he was righteous, since God gave approval to him for his gift. Though he died, he's still speaking through faith.

[5]By faith Enoch was taken up so that he didn't see death, and *he wasn't found because God took him up.*[g] He was given approval for having pleased God before he was taken up. [6]It's impossible to please God without faith because the one who draws near to God must believe that he exists and that he rewards people who try to find him.

[7]By faith Noah responded with godly fear when he was warned about events he hadn't seen yet. He built an ark to deliver his household. With his faith, he criticized the world and became an heir of the righteousness that comes from faith.

[8]By faith Abraham obeyed when he was called to go out to a place that he was going to receive as an inheritance. He went out without knowing where he was going.

[9]By faith he lived in the land he had been promised as a stranger. He lived in tents along with Isaac and Jacob, who were coheirs of the same promise. [10]He was looking forward to a city that has foundations, whose architect and builder is God.

[11]By faith even Sarah received the ability to have a child, though she herself was barren and past the age for having children, because she believed that the one who promised was faithful. [12]So descendants were born from one man (and he was as good as dead). They were as many as the number of the stars in the sky and as countless as the grains of sand on the seashore. [13]All of these people died in faith without receiving the promises, but they saw the promises from a distance and welcomed them. They confessed that they were strangers and immigrants on earth. [14]People who say this kind of thing make it clear that they are looking for a homeland. [15]If they had been thinking about the country that they had left, they would have had the opportunity to return to it. [16]But at this point in time, they are longing for a better country, that is, a heavenly one. Therefore, God isn't ashamed to be called their God— he has prepared a city for them.

[g]Gen 5:24

NOAH

Noah is the hero of the flood story in Genesis 6:5–9:28 and thus is arguably the central character of the primeval history (Gen 1–11). Isaiah 54:9 mentions the covenant with Noah as an example of God's steadfast love, and Ezekiel 14:14, 20 depict Noah (together with Daniel and Job) as an exceptionally righteous person whose prayer might change the fortune of an entire nation. Since Isaiah and Ezekiel seem to presuppose that their readers were familiar with Noah as a literary character, it is safe to assume that the Noah tradition was known widely in the exilic and early post-exilic periods. There are no extra-biblical references to Noah, and the name does not occur in the Mesopotamian flood traditions.

¹⁷By faith Abraham offered Isaac when he was tested. The one who received the promises was offering his only son. ¹⁸He had been told concerning him, *Your legitimate descendants will come from Isaac.*^h ¹⁹He figured that God could even raise him from the dead. So in a way he did receive him back from the dead.

²⁰By faith Isaac also blessed Jacob and Esau concerning their future.

²¹By faith Jacob blessed each of Joseph's sons as he was dying and *bowed in worship over the head of his staff.*ⁱ

²²By faith Joseph recalled the exodus of the Israelites at the end of his life, and gave instructions about burying his bones.

²³By faith Moses was hidden by his parents for three months when he was born, because they saw that the child was beautiful and they weren't afraid of the king's orders.

²⁴By faith Moses refused to be called the son of Pharaoh's daughter when he was grown up. ²⁵He chose to be mistreated with God's people instead of having the temporary pleasures of sin. ²⁶He thought that the abuses he suffered for Christ were more valuable than the treasures of Egypt, since he was looking forward to the reward.

²⁷By faith he left Egypt without being afraid of the king's anger. He kept on going as if he could see what is invisible.

²⁸By faith he kept the Passover and the sprinkling of blood, in order that the destroyer could not touch their firstborn children.

²⁹By faith they crossed the Red Sea as if they were on dry land, but when the Egyptians tried it, they were drowned.

³⁰By faith Jericho's walls fell after the people marched around them for seven days.

³¹By faith Rahab the prostitute wasn't killed with the disobedient because she welcomed the spies in peace.

³²What more can I say? I would run out of time if I told you about Gideon, Barak, Samson, Jephthah, David, Samuel, and the prophets. ³³Through faith they conquered kingdoms, brought about justice, realized promises, shut the mouths of lions, ³⁴put out raging fires, escaped from the edge of the sword, found strength in weakness, were mighty in war, and routed foreign armies. ³⁵Women received back their dead by resurrection. Others were tortured and refused to be released so they could gain a better resurrection.

³⁶But others experienced public shame by being taunted and whipped; they were even put in chains and in prison. ³⁷They were stoned to death, they were cut in two, and they died by being murdered with swords. They went around wearing the skins of sheep and goats, needy, oppressed, and mistreated. ³⁸The world didn't deserve them. They wandered around in deserts, mountains, caves, and holes in the ground.

³⁹All these people didn't receive what was promised, though they were given approval for their faith. ⁴⁰God provided something better for us so they wouldn't be made perfect without us.

Let's also run the race

12 So then let's also run the race that is laid out in front of us, since we have such a great cloud of witnesses surrounding us. Let's throw off any extra baggage, get rid of the sin that trips us up, ²and fix our eyes on Jesus, faith's pioneer and perfecter. He endured the cross, ignoring the shame, for the sake of the joy that was laid out in front of him, and sat down at the right side of God's throne.

Run the race with discipline

³Think about the one who endured such opposition from sinners so that you won't be discouraged and you won't give up. ⁴In your struggle against sin, you haven't resisted yet to the point of shedding blood, ⁵and you have forgotten the encouragement that addresses you as sons and daughters:

My child, don't make light
of the Lord's discipline
or give up when you are corrected by him,

[6] because the Lord disciplines
whomever he loves,
    and he punishes every son or daughter
    whom he accepts.[j]
[7] Bear hardship for the sake of discipline. God is treating you like sons and daughters! What child isn't disciplined by his or her father? [8] But if you don't experience discipline, which happens to all children, then you are illegitimate and not real sons and daughters. [9] What's more, we had human parents who disciplined us, and we respected them for it. How much more should we submit to the Father of spirits and live? [10] Our human parents disciplined us for a little while, as it seemed best to them, but God does it for our benefit so that we can share his holiness. [11] No discipline is fun while it lasts, but it seems painful at the time. Later, however, it yields the peaceful fruit of righteousness for those who have been trained by it.

[12] So strengthen your drooping hands and weak knees! [13] Make straight paths for your feet so that if any part is lame, it will be healed rather than injured more seriously. [14] Pursue the goal of peace along with everyone—and holiness as well, because no one will see the Lord without it. [15] Make sure that no one misses out on God's grace. Make sure that no root of bitterness grows up that might cause trouble and pollute many people. [16] Make sure that no one becomes sexually immoral or ungodly like Esau. He sold his inheritance as the oldest son for one meal. [17] You know that afterward, when he wanted to inherit the blessing, he was rejected because he couldn't find a way to change his heart and life, though he looked for it with tears.

Priestly service in heavenly Jerusalem

[18] You haven't drawn near to something that can be touched: a burning fire, darkness, shadow, a whirlwind, [19] a blast of a trumpet, and a sound of words that made the ones who heard it beg that there wouldn't be one more word. [20] They couldn't stand the command, If even a wild animal touches the mountain, it must be stoned.[k] [21] The sight was so frightening that Moses said, "I'm terrified and shaking!"

[22] But you have drawn near to Mount Zion, the city of the living God, heavenly Jerusalem, to countless angels in a festival gathering, [23] to the assembly of God's firstborn children who are registered in heaven, to God the judge of all, to the spirits of the righteous who have been made perfect, [24] to Jesus the mediator of the new covenant, and to the sprinkled blood that speaks better than Abel's blood.

[25] See to it that you don't resist the one who is speaking. If the people didn't escape when they refused to listen to the one who warned them on earth, how will we escape if we reject the one who is warning from heaven? [26] His voice shook the earth then, but now he has made a promise: Still once more I will shake not only the earth but heaven also.[l] [27] The words "still once more" reveal the removal of what is shaken—the things that are part of this creation—so that what isn't shaken will remain. [28] Therefore, since we are receiving a kingdom that can't be shaken, let's continue to express our gratitude.[m] With this gratitude, let's serve[n] in a way that is pleasing to God with respect and awe, [29] because our God really is a consuming fire.

Our acts of service and sacrifice

13 Keep loving each other like family. [2] Don't neglect to open up your homes to guests, because by doing this some have been hosts to angels without knowing it. [3] Remember prisoners as if you were in prison with them, and people who are mistreated as if you were in their place. [4] Marriage must be honored in every respect, with no cheating on the relationship, because God will judge the sexually immoral person and the person who commits adultery. [5] Your way of life should be free from the love of money, and you should be content with what you have. After all, he has

---

[j] Prov 3:11-12   [k] Exod 19:12-13   [l] Exod 19:18   [m] Or hold on to grace   [n] Or offer priestly service

said, *I will never leave you or abandon you.*[o]

[6] This is why we can confidently say,

The Lord is my helper,
and I won't be afraid.
What can people do to me?[p]

[7] Remember your leaders who spoke God's word to you. Imitate their faith as you consider the way their lives turned out. [8] Jesus Christ is the same yesterday, today, and forever!

[9] Don't be misled by the many strange teachings out there. It's a good thing for the heart to be strengthened by grace rather than by food. Food doesn't help those who live in this context. [10] We have an altar, and those who serve as priests in the meeting tent don't have the right to eat from it. [11] The blood of the animals is carried into the holy of holies by the high priest as an offering for sin, and their bodies are burned outside the camp. [12] And so Jesus also suffered outside the city gate to make the people holy with his own blood.

[13] So now, let's go to him outside the camp, bearing his shame. [14] We don't have a permanent city here, but rather we are looking for the city that is still to come.

[15] So let's continually offer up a sacrifice of praise through him, which is the fruit from our lips that confess his name. [16] Don't forget to do good and to share what you have because God is pleased with these kinds of sacrifices.

Closing greeting and blessing

[17] Rely on your leaders and defer to them, because they watch over your whole being as people who are going to be held responsible for you. They need to be able to do this with pleasure and not with complaints about you, because that wouldn't help you. [18] Pray for us. We're sure that we have a good conscience, and we want to do the right thing in every way. [19] I'm particularly asking you to do this so that I can be returned to you quickly.

[20] May the God of peace,
who brought back
the great shepherd of the sheep,
our Lord Jesus,
from the dead by the blood
of the eternal covenant,
[21] equip you with every good thing
to do his will,
by developing in us what pleases him
through Jesus Christ.
To him be the glory forever and always.
Amen.

[22] I urge you, brothers and sisters, to put up with this message of encouragement, since I've only written a short letter to you! [23] You should know that our brother Timothy has been set free. If he comes soon, we will travel together to see you.

[24] Greet your leaders and all of God's holy people. The group from Italy greets you. [25] May grace be with all of you.

[o] Deut 31:6; Gen 28:15 [p] Ps 118:6

JAMES

THEME

Correct belief, inner feelings, and pious confessions are not enough. The kind of religion approved by God includes righteous conduct and acts of mercy.

THE NATURE OF JAMES

James is the first of the books of the New Testament that are traditionally referred to as "the Catholic Epistles." "Catholic" means "general" and refers to the fact that these letters were written to general audiences rather than specific congregations. Along with 1 and 2 Peter; 1, 2, and 3 John; and Jude, James was written toward the end of the first century CE or the beginning of the second century. At that time, the church was establishing itself as an institution and struggling to help its members establish a consistent code of ethics.

Strictly speaking, James is a homily. It is not a letter, since it is not written to any congregation by name. It is not addressed to particular problems as are 1 and 2 Corinthians, Galatians, and Romans. Rather, it deals with these general Christian concerns:

- The danger of double-mindedness (1:8; 4:8)
- The danger of pride (1:9-10, 21; 2:1-7, 13; 3:1; 4:13-17)
- Endurance in a time of trial (1:2-4, 12-15)
- Maintaining equality between the rich and the poor (2:1-7, 14-17; 5:1-6)
- Hearing and doing (1:22-25; 2:14-26; 4:17)
- The danger of loose talk (1:19; 3:1-12)

AUTHORSHIP

According to the first verse, the author of the homily is James, a slave of God and of the Lord Jesus Christ. The New Testament mentions several different men by that name: James, the brother of Jesus (Mark 6:3); James, the son of Alphaeus, one of Jesus' disciples (Luke 6:15); James, the brother of John, one of the sons of Zebedee whom Jesus also called as a disciple (Mark 3:17); James, the father of Judas (not Judas Iscariot; Luke 6:16); James the younger, whose mother was with the women at the cross (Mark 15:40).

Traditionally, it was thought that the author of James was the brother of

Jesus. Although he was not a disciple during Jesus' lifetime (Mark 3:21, 31-35; John 7:3-5), he became a leading figure in Jerusalem after Jesus' resurrection. He probably became the head of the church after Peter left on his first missionary tour (Acts 12:17). Paul mentions him in Galatians 1:19 and 2:9 as one of the pillars of the church (see Acts 15) and one who may have opposed certain aspects of his ministry (Galatians 2:12).

Although it is easy to understand why Christians would want to read something written by the Lord's own brother, most scholars doubt that James was the true author of the letter of James. Jesus' name is only mentioned twice throughout the whole work (1:1; 2:1) and nothing is said about his relationship to the author. The homily is written in a highly polished Greek style, one that an uneducated worker like the brother of Jesus would not be likely to use. According to the Jewish historian Flavius Josephus, James died in 62 CE. But the homily clearly reflects the ideas and concerns of a much later period when Hebrews, Jude, and 1 and 2 Peter were also written. Some scholars think that James may have written parts of the original letter and that the final draft was composed by someone else who used his name to make sure that it would be widely read. It is impossible to be sure who the author was.

For reasons that are not completely clear, the letter of James was not fully accepted by the church until the fourth century. Questions about its authorship must have been raised from the start. Some Christians have been suspicious of its value, saying it has very little specifically Christian teaching in it. Some scholars have suggested, in fact, that it was originally written by Jews who lived outside of Palestine and was given a few Christian additions by Christian writers so it could be presented as the work of Jesus' brother. Indeed, during the Protestant Reformation, Martin Luther dismissed it as an "epistle of straw," one that was not of primary importance because it was not written by an apostle.

FAITH VERSUS WORKS

Despite suspicions concerning the value of James, the homily has been of great importance to Christians because it does take up important Christian themes. Scholars note that there are more than thirty-five indirect references to the teaching of Jesus in the epistle, twenty-five of which come from the Sermon on the Mount. The homily also takes up a number of ethical questions that are important in the rest of the New Testament and are significant for believers in any time.

Of particular importance, of course, is the discussion of faith and works that the author carefully develops. Although the apostle Paul argues in Romans 3–4 and Galatians 2–4 that people are put right with God only through their faith in Jesus Christ and that they cannot earn their salvation by works, the author of James lives in a time when people are content to mouth their beliefs without putting them into practice. It is not enough, he argues, to say that you believe in Jesus Christ, if you are not willing to follow him in the way you live. Christians may be saved by faith, but without the proof of actions and love expressed to one's neighbor in concrete deeds, faith is truly dead.

JAMES

Greeting

1 From James, a slave of God and of the Lord Jesus Christ.

To the twelve tribes who are scattered outside the land of Israel.

Greetings!

Stand firm

²My brothers and sisters, think of the various tests you encounter as occasions for joy. ³After all, you know that the testing of your faith produces endurance. ⁴Let this endurance complete its work so that you may be fully mature, complete, and lacking in nothing. ⁵But anyone who needs wisdom should ask God, whose very nature is to give to everyone without a second thought, without keeping score. Wisdom will certainly be given to those who ask. ⁶Whoever asks shouldn't hesitate. They should ask in faith, without doubting. Whoever doubts is like the surf of the sea, tossed and turned by the wind. ⁷People like that should never imagine that they will receive anything from the Lord. ⁸They are double-minded, unstable in all their ways.

⁹Brothers and sisters who are poor should find satisfaction in their high status. ¹⁰Those who are wealthy should find satisfaction in their low status, because they will die off like wildflowers. ¹¹The sun rises with its scorching heat and dries up the grass so that its flowers fall and its beauty is lost. Just like that, in the midst of their daily lives, the wealthy will waste away. ¹²Those who stand firm during testing are blessed. They are tried and true. They will receive the life God has promised to those who love him as their reward.

Our cravings versus God's gifts

¹³No one who is tested should say, "God is tempting me!" This is because God is not tempted by any form of evil, nor does he tempt anyone. ¹⁴Everyone is tempted by their own cravings; they are lured away and enticed by them. ¹⁵Once those cravings conceive, they give birth to sin; and when sin grows up, it gives birth to death.

¹⁶Don't be misled, my dear brothers and sisters. ¹⁷Every good gift, every perfect gift, comes from above. These gifts come down from the Father, the creator of the heavenly lights, in whose character there is no change at all. ¹⁸He chose to give us birth by his true word, and here is the result: we are like the first crop from the harvest of everything he created.

Welcoming and doing the word

¹⁹Know this, my dear brothers and sisters: everyone should be quick to listen, slow to speak, and slow to grow angry. ²⁰This is because an angry person doesn't produce God's righteousness. ²¹Therefore, with humility, set aside all moral filth and the growth of wickedness, and welcome the word planted deep inside you—the very word that is able to save you.

²²You must be doers of the word and not only hearers who mislead themselves. ²³Those who hear but don't do the word are like those who look at their faces in a mirror. ²⁴They look at themselves, walk away, and immediately forget what they were like. ²⁵But there are those who study the perfect law, the law of freedom, and continue to do it. They don't listen and then forget, but they put it into practice in their lives. They will be blessed in whatever they do.

²⁶If those who claim devotion to God don't control what they say, they mislead themselves. Their devotion is worthless. ²⁷True devotion, the kind that is pure and faultless before God the Father, is this: to care for orphans and widows in their difficulties and to keep the world from contaminating us.

Don't show favoritism

2 My brothers and sisters, when you show favoritism you deny the faithfulness of our Lord Jesus Christ, who has been resurrected in glory. ²Imagine two people coming into your meeting. One has a gold ring and fine clothes, while the other is poor, dressed in filthy rags. ³Then suppose that you were to take special notice of the one wearing fine clothes, saying, "Here's an excellent place. Sit here." But to the poor person you say, "Stand over there"; or, "Here, sit at my feet." ⁴Wouldn't you have shown favoritism among yourselves and become evil-minded judges?

⁵My dear brothers and sisters, listen! Hasn't God chosen those who are poor by worldly standards to be rich in terms of faith? Hasn't God chosen the poor as heirs of the kingdom he has promised to those who love him? ⁶But you have dishonored the poor. Don't the wealthy make life diffi-

JAMES

A name connected to the OT name Jacob.

1. James the son of Zebedee is referred to in church tradition as "James the Great/Major" (Matt 4:21; Mark 1:19; Luke 5:10). He is always among the first three in the four lists of the Twelve (Matt 10:2-4; Mark 3:16-19; Luke 6:14-16; Acts 1:13), indicating that he was remembered as important in the inner circles of Jesus' followers. His brother John was younger, to judge from the fact that James is always mentioned first. With their father, Zebedee, they were fishers on the Galilee Sea. Luke reports that they were partners with Peter and Andrew (Luke 5:10).

Jesus nicknamed both James and John "Boanerges, which means 'sons of Thunder'" (Mark 3:17), perhaps for their strong, brash personalities, as shown in their violence-prone anger toward a Samaritan village that refused Jesus entry (Luke 9:51-56) and in their request to Jesus for preeminence in God's kingdom (Mark 10:35-45; but Matt 20:20-28 puts this request in the mouth of their mother).

2. James the son of Alphaeus is called "James the Less/Minor" in tradition. "The son of Alphaeus" distinguishes him from the other, more prominent James the son of Zebedee. In the lists of the Twelve (Matt 10:2-4; Mark 3:16-19; Luke 6:14-16; Acts 1:13), he is named in the last third of the lists, showing his relative unimportance. He is not mentioned elsewhere in the NT.

3. James the son of Mary was not one of the Twelve. This James's mother was the Mary who, with the other women, was a witness of Jesus' crucifixion and the empty tomb (Matt 27:56; Mark 15:40; 16:1; Luke 24:10). He does not appear in the NT as a character, only in the phrase "Mary the mother of James" to distinguish her from Mary Magdalene, also at the crucifixion and the empty tomb.

4. James the father of a second Judas appearing in the Luke–Acts lists of the Twelve, but not in the lists in Matthew or Mark. This Judas is called "the son of James" to distinguish him from Judas Iscariot, who follows immediately in Luke's list.

5. James the brother of Jesus was not a follower of Jesus during his ministry, but he soon became the leader of the Jerusalem church, the traditional author of the canonical letter of James, and a Christian martyr. Also known as James the Just. See Acts 15; 1 Cor 15; Gal 1–2.

cult for you? Aren't they the ones who drag you into court? [7]Aren't they the ones who insult the good name spoken over you at your baptism?

[8]You do well when you really fulfill the royal law found in scripture, *Love your neighbor as yourself.*[a] [9]But when you show favoritism, you are committing a sin, and by that same law you are exposed as a lawbreaker. [10]Anyone who tries to keep all of the Law but fails at one point is guilty of failing to keep all of it. [11]The one who said, *Don't commit adultery,* also said, *Don't commit murder.*[b] So if you don't commit adultery but do commit murder, you are a lawbreaker. [12]In every way, then, speak and act as people who will be judged by the law of freedom. [13]There will be no mercy in judgment for anyone who hasn't shown mercy. Mercy overrules judgment.

Showing faith

[14]My brothers and sisters, what good is it if people say they have faith but do nothing to show it? Claiming to have faith can't save anyone, can it? [15]Imagine a brother or sister who is naked and never has enough food to eat. [16]What if one of you said, "Go in peace! Stay warm! Have a nice meal!"? What good is it if you don't actually give them what their body needs? [17]In the same way, faith is dead when it doesn't result in faithful activity.

[18]Someone might claim, "You have faith and I have action." But how can I see your faith apart from your actions? Instead, I'll show you my faith by putting it into practice in faithful action. [19]It's good that you believe that God is one. Ha! Even the demons believe this, and they tremble with fear. [20]Are you so slow? Do you need to be shown that faith without actions has no value at all? [21]What about Abraham, our father? Wasn't he shown to be righteous through his actions when he offered his son Isaac on the altar? [22]See, his faith was at work along with his actions. In fact, his faith was made complete by his faithful actions. [23]So the scripture was fulfilled that says, *Abraham believed God, and God regarded him as righteous.*[c] What is more, Abraham was called God's friend. [24]So you see that a person is shown to be righteous through faithful actions and not through faith alone. [25]In the same way, wasn't Rahab the prostitute shown to be righteous when she received the messengers as her guests and then sent them on by another road? [26]As the lifeless body is dead, so faith without actions is dead.

Taming the tongue

3 My brothers and sisters, not many of you should become teachers, because we know that we teachers will be judged more strictly. [2]We all make mistakes often, but those who don't make mistakes with their words have reached full maturity. Like a

[a]Lev 19:18 [b]Exod 20:13, 15 LXX (English: 20:13-14); Deut 5:17–18 [c]Gen 15:6

FAITH/FAITHFULNESS

The two words ("faith, faithfulness") provide the simplest rendering of the Greek *pistis* and the basic range of its meaning both in wider Greek usage and in the NT in particular. The basic range of the term in its actual usage, then, extends from confidence in someone/something else to the objective basis for such confidence: a believing on the basis that the one/object trusted is reliable—"trust, confidence, faith"; and that which evokes trust—"faithfulness, reliability, fidelity, commitment." This was the range of sense that use of the word *pistis* by Paul and other NT writers would have evoked among those who heard them.

bridled horse, they can control themselves entirely. [3]When we bridle horses and put bits in their mouths to lead them wherever we want, we can control their whole bodies.

[4]Consider ships: They are so large that strong winds are needed to drive them. But pilots direct their ships wherever they want with a little rudder. [5]In the same way, even though the tongue is a small part of the body, it boasts wildly.

Think about this: A small flame can set a whole forest on fire. [6]The tongue is a small flame of fire, a world of evil at work in us. It contaminates our entire lives. Because of it, the circle of life is set on fire. The tongue itself is set on fire by the flames of hell.

[7]People can tame and already have tamed every kind of animal, bird, reptile, and fish. [8]No one can tame the tongue, though. It is a restless evil, full of deadly poison. [9]With it we both bless the Lord and Father and curse human beings made in God's likeness. [10]Blessing and cursing come from the same mouth. My brothers and sisters, it just shouldn't be this way!

[11]Both fresh water and salt water don't come from the same spring, do they? [12]My brothers and sisters, can a fig tree produce olives? Can a grapevine produce figs? Of course not, and fresh water doesn't flow from a saltwater spring either.

Wisdom from above

[13]Are any of you wise and understanding? Show that your actions are good with a humble lifestyle that comes from wisdom. [14]However, if you have bitter jealousy and selfish ambition in your heart, then stop bragging and living in ways that deny the truth. [15]This is not the wisdom that comes down from above. Instead, it is from the earth, natural and demonic. [16]Wherever there is jealousy and selfish ambition, there is disorder and everything that is evil. [17]What of the wisdom from above? First, it is pure, and then peaceful, gentle, obedient, filled with mercy and good actions, fair, and genuine. [18]Those who make peace sow the seeds of justice by their peaceful acts.

Conflict with people and God

4 What is the source of conflict among you? What is the source of your disputes? Don't they come from your cravings that are at war in your own lives? [2]You long for something you don't have, so you commit murder. You are jealous for something you can't get, so you struggle and fight. You don't have because you don't ask. [3]You ask and don't have because you ask with evil intentions, to waste it on your own cravings.

[4]You unfaithful people! Don't you know that friendship with the world means hostility toward God? So whoever wants to be the world's friend becomes God's enemy. [5]Or do you suppose that scripture is meaningless? Doesn't God long for our faithfulness in[d] the life he has given to us?[e] [6]But he gives us more grace. This is why it says, *God stands against the proud, but favors the humble.*[f] [7]Therefore, submit to God. Resist the devil, and he will run away from you. [8]Come near to God, and he will come near to you. Wash your hands, you sinners. Purify your hearts, you double-minded. [9]Cry out in sorrow, mourn, and weep! Let your laughter become mourning and your joy become sadness. [10]Humble yourselves before the Lord, and he will lift you up.

[11]Brothers and sisters, don't say evil things about each other. Whoever insults or criticizes a brother or sister insults and criticizes the Law. If you find fault with the Law, you are not a doer of the Law but a judge over it. [12]There is only one lawgiver and judge, and he is able to save and to destroy. But you who judge your neighbor, who are you?

Warning the proud and wealthy

[13]Pay attention, you who say, "Today or tomorrow we will go to such-and-such a town. We will stay there a year, buying and selling, and making a profit." [14]You don't really know about tomorrow. What is your life? You are a mist that appears for only a short while before it vanishes. [15]Here's what you ought to say: "If the Lord wills, we

[d]Or *jealously longs for* [e]Or *Doesn't the spirit that God placed in us have jealous desires?* [f]Prov 3:34

will live and do this or that." [16]But now you boast and brag, and all such boasting is evil. [17]It is a sin when someone knows the right thing to do and doesn't do it.

5 Pay attention, you wealthy people! Weep and moan over the miseries coming upon you. [2]Your riches have rotted. Moths have destroyed your clothes. [3]Your gold and silver have rusted, and their rust will be evidence against you. It will eat your flesh like fire. Consider the treasure you have hoarded in the last days. [4]Listen! Hear the cries of the wages of your field hands. These are the wages you stole from those who harvested your fields. The cries of the harvesters have reached the ears of the Lord of heavenly forces. [5]You have lived a self-satisfying life on this earth, a life of luxury. You have stuffed your hearts in preparation for the day of slaughter. [6]You have condemned and murdered the righteous one, who doesn't oppose you.

Courageous patience

[7]Therefore, brothers and sisters, you must be patient as you wait for the coming of the Lord. Consider the farmer who waits patiently for the coming of rain in the fall and spring, looking forward to the precious fruit of the earth. [8]You also must wait patiently, strengthening your resolve, because the coming of the Lord is near. [9]Don't complain about each other, brothers and sisters, so that you won't be judged. Look! The judge is standing at the door!

[10]Brothers and sisters, take the prophets who spoke in the name of the Lord as an example of patient resolve and steadfastness. [11]Look at how we honor those who have practiced endurance. You have heard of the endurance of Job. And you have seen what the Lord has accomplished, for the Lord is full of compassion and mercy.

Final instructions

[12]Most important, my brothers and sisters, never make a solemn pledge—neither by heaven nor earth, nor by anything else. Instead, speak with a simple "Yes" or "No," or else you may fall under judgment.

[13]If any of you are suffering, they should pray. If any of you are happy, they should sing. [14]If any of you are sick, they should call for the elders of the church, and the elders should pray over them, anointing them with oil in the name of the Lord. [15]Prayer that comes from faith will heal the sick, for the Lord will restore them to health. And if they have sinned, they will be forgiven. [16]For this reason, confess your sins to each other and pray for each other so that you may be healed. The prayer of the righteous person is powerful in what it can achieve. [17]Elijah was a person just like us. When he earnestly prayed that it wouldn't rain, no rain fell for three and a half years. [18]He prayed again, God sent rain, and the earth produced its fruit.

[19]My brothers and sisters, if any of you wander from the truth and someone turns back the wanderer, [20]recognize that whoever brings a sinner back from the wrong path will save them from death and will bring about the forgiveness of many sins.

1 PETER

THEME

You are heirs of salvation through suffering.

TYPE AND STYLE OF WRITING

Until recently Bible commentators were convinced that 1 Peter, like James and 1 John, was not a genuine letter, but was a tract or a baptismal sermon written for new converts. Now, however, most scholars think that it really is a genuine letter written to real congregations in four different parts of Asia Minor (modern Turkey).

First Peter has the essential elements of a real letter: the naming of the author (1:1), comments to the recipients and wishes for their spiritual health (1:2), inclusion of the name of the church member who delivers it (Silvanus, 5:12), a farewell from the author and others who are with him (5:13), and a peace benediction (5:14).

First Peter differs from personal letters in one respect. It was not sent to just one person or family, but it is written for congregations in four different areas. For this reason it is called a "circular letter" and was meant to be read and passed on to other Christians who were meeting in neighboring homes, cities, or provinces.

The letter contains many different kinds of material. The author quotes or alludes to passages from the Old Testament in order to teach his readers about the Christian faith. The most obvious is 2:21-25, which is closely patterned after Isaiah 53:4-9. Numerous other passages are also quoted: Isaiah 40:6-9 in 1:24; Isaiah 28:16 in 2:6; Psalm 118:22 in 2:7; Isaiah 8:14 in 2:8; and Psalm 34:12-16 in 3:10-12, to mention just a few.

In addition to the use of scripture texts, the author of 1 Peter writes in a style that was popular in the first and second centuries called the "rhetorical style." It is highly polished, literate Greek, makes plays on words, has carefully constructed clauses, and uses compound negative words.

Other types of material are also used by the author. The letter is filled with advice given to servants and masters (2:18-20), husbands and wives (3:1-7), church leaders, called elders (5:1-4), and Christian believers in general (2:21-25; 3:8-12). First Peter also contains Christian hymns (1:20; 3:18-22), creeds, and prayers developed for new Christians.

MAJOR THEMES IN 1 PETER

First Peter has four major themes: (1) baptism and new birth, (2) encouragement in times of persecution, (3) the church as the true home of believers, and (4) advice for how to live successfully in a foreign culture.

AUTHORSHIP OF 1 PETER

Although the first verse is attributed to the apostle Peter and the conclusion of the letter mentions the names of those who were associated with him (see 5:12-13), it is generally agreed that 1 Peter was written by a follower or admirer of Peter who was probably a member of a school or circle that was committed to Peter's teachings. Peter was known in church tradition for his connection with Rome ("Babylon" in 5:13 is a code word for the capital of the Roman Empire; see Revelation 14:8). It was there that Peter died.

The highly literate Greek of 1 Peter is not the kind of language a fisherman from Galilee would have used, and some of the ideas in the letter come from periods that are relatively late in the development of the church. A number of passages show the influence of Paul's letter to the Romans, moreover, and indicate that 1 Peter was written at a time when its influence was well established, long after Peter and Paul had both died (about 64–65 CE).

RECIPIENTS OF THE LETTER

First Peter 1:1 indicates that the people who received the letter lived in five provinces of Asia Minor (what is now modern Turkey): Pontus, Galatia, Cappadocia, Asia, and Bithynia. The words "To God's chosen strangers in the world of the diaspora" do not necessarily mean that all of the readers were Jews. More likely, the phrase is used to describe all the Christians in the area, Jews and Gentiles, who felt like refugees in a region where they were persecuted because of their cultural upbringing and faith.

DATE

Because 1 Peter mentions persecution and suffering at the hands of government officials, it is often assumed that the letter was written during one of the periods when the Romans made life difficult for Christians: the reigns of the emperors Nero (54–68), Domitian (81–96), or Trajan (98–117). It is also possible that the persecution mentioned was not official in nature but was of the type that happened from time to time when refugees and unfamiliar religions were introduced into new areas.

Because references to 1 Peter appear in 2 Peter (3:1) and in the letter of Polycarp to the Philippians (both written during the second century), 1 Peter was probably sent to Asia Minor sometime at the end of the first century during Domitian's reign.

1 PETER

Greeting

1 Peter, an apostle of Jesus Christ,
To God's chosen strangers in the world of the diaspora, who live in Pontus, Galatia, Cappadocia, Asia, and Bithynia. ²God the Father chose you because of what he knew beforehand. He chose you through the Holy Spirit's work of making you holy and because of the faithful obedience and sacrifice of Jesus Christ.

May God's grace and peace be multiplied to you.

Thanksgiving

³May the God and Father of our Lord Jesus Christ be blessed! On account of his vast mercy, he has given us new birth. You have been born anew into a living hope through the resurrection of Jesus Christ from the dead. ⁴You have a pure and enduring inheritance that cannot perish—an inheritance that is presently kept safe in heaven for you. ⁵Through his faithfulness, you are guarded by God's power so that you can receive the salvation he is ready to reveal in the last time.

⁶You now rejoice in this hope, even if it's necessary for you to be distressed for a short time by various trials. ⁷This is necessary so that your faith may be found genuine. (Your faith is more valuable than gold, which will be destroyed even though it is itself tested by fire.) Your genuine faith will result in praise, glory, and honor for you when Jesus Christ is revealed. ⁸Although you've never seen him, you love him. Even though you don't see him now, you trust him and so rejoice with a glorious joy that is too much for words. ⁹You are receiving the goal of your faith: your salvation.

¹⁰The prophets, who long ago foretold the grace that you've received, searched and explored, inquiring carefully about this salvation. ¹¹They wondered what the Spirit of Christ within them was saying when he bore witness beforehand about the suffering that would happen to Christ and the glory that would follow. They wondered what sort of person or what sort of time they were speaking about. ¹²It was revealed to them that in their search they were not serving themselves but you. These things, which even angels long to examine, have now been proclaimed to you by those who brought you the good news. They did this in the power of the Holy Spirit, who was sent from heaven.

Response of obedience

¹³Therefore, once you have your minds ready for action and you are thinking clearly, place your hope completely on the grace that will be brought to you when Jesus Christ is revealed. ¹⁴Don't be conformed to your former desires, those that shaped you when you were ignorant. But, as obedient children, ¹⁵you must be holy in

BITHYNIA

A coastal province located in the northwest corner of Asia Minor, Bithynia was named for one of the Thracian tribes that settled there, subduing some of the native tribes, before the 8th century BCE. Paul planned to enter Bithynia, probably to reach Nicaea or Nicomedia in the western portion of the province, but he felt compelled to travel to Troas instead (Acts 16:7). Nonetheless, 1 Peter bears witness to a 1st-century Christian community there, since Bithynia is one of the five provinces to which the letter is addressed (1:1).

every aspect of your lives, just as the one who called you is holy. [16]It is written, *You will be holy, because I am holy.*[a] [17]Since you call upon a Father who judges all people according to their actions without favoritism, you should conduct yourselves with reverence during the time of your dwelling in a strange land. [18]Live in this way, knowing that you were not liberated by perishable things like silver or gold from the empty lifestyle you inherited from your ancestors. [19]Instead, you were liberated by the precious blood of Christ, like that of a flawless, spotless lamb. [20]Christ was chosen before the creation of the world, but was only revealed at the end of time. This was done for you, [21]who through Christ are faithful to the God who raised him from the dead and gave him glory. So now, your faith and hope should rest in God.

[22]As you set yourselves apart by your obedience to the truth so that you might have genuine affection for your fellow believers, love each other deeply and earnestly. [23]Do this because you have been given new birth—not from the type of seed that decays but from seed that doesn't. This seed is God's life-giving and enduring word. [24]Thus,

> All human life on the earth is like grass,
>   and all human glory
>   is like a flower in a field.
> The grass dries up and its flower falls off,
> [25] but the Lord's word endures forever.[b]

This is the word that was proclaimed to you as good news.

Your identity as believers

2 Therefore, get rid of all ill will and all deceit, pretense, envy, and slander. [2]Instead, like a newborn baby, desire the pure milk of the word. Nourished by it, you will grow into salvation, [3]since you have tasted that the Lord is good.

[4]Now you are coming to him as to a living stone. Even though this stone was rejected by humans, from God's perspective it is chosen, valuable. [5]You yourselves are being built like living stones into a spiri-

tual temple. You are being made into a holy priesthood to offer up spiritual sacrifices that are acceptable to God through Jesus Christ. [6]Thus it is written in scripture, *Look! I am laying a cornerstone in Zion, chosen, valuable. The person who believes in him will never be shamed.*[c] [7]So God honors you who believe. For those who refuse to believe, though, the stone the builders tossed aside has become the capstone. [8]This is a stone that makes people stumble and a rock that makes them fall. Because they refuse to believe in the word, they stumble. Indeed, this is the end to which they were appointed. [9]But you are a chosen race, a royal priesthood, a holy nation, a people who are God's own possession. You have become this people so that you may speak of the wonderful acts of the one who called you out of darkness into his amazing light. [10]Once you weren't a people, but now you are God's people. Once you hadn't received mercy, but now you have received mercy.

Life as strangers in the world

[11]Dear friends, since you are immigrants and strangers in the world, I urge that you avoid worldly desires that wage war against your lives. [12]Live honorably among the unbelievers. Today, they defame you, as if you were doing evil. But in the day when God visits to judge they will glorify him, because they have observed your honorable deeds.

[13]For the sake of the Lord submit to every human institution. Do this whether it means submitting to the emperor as supreme ruler, [14]or to governors as those sent by the emperor. They are sent to punish those doing evil and to praise those doing good. [15]Submit to them because it's God's will that by doing good you will silence the ignorant talk of foolish people. [16]Do this as God's slaves, and yet also as free people, not using your freedom as a cover-up for evil. [17]Honor everyone. Love the family of believers. Have respectful fear of God. Honor the emperor.

[18]Household slaves, submit by accepting the authority of your masters with all

---

[a]Lev 19:2 [b]Isa 40:6-8 [c]Isa 28:16

respect. Do this not only to good and kind masters but also to those who are harsh. [19]Now, it is commendable if, because of one's understanding of God, someone should endure pain through suffering unjustly. [20]But what praise comes from enduring patiently when you have sinned and are beaten for it? But if you endure steadfastly when you've done good and suffer for it, this is commendable before God.

[21]You were called to this kind of endurance, because Christ suffered on your behalf. He left you an example so that you might follow in his footsteps. [22]He committed no sin, nor did he ever speak in ways meant to deceive. [23]When he was insulted, he did not reply with insults. When he suffered, he did not threaten revenge. Instead, he entrusted himself to the one who judges justly. [24]He carried in his own body on the cross the sins we committed. He did this so that we might live in righteousness, having nothing to do with sin. By his wounds you were healed. [25]Though you were like straying sheep, you have now returned to the shepherd and guardian of your lives.

3 Wives, likewise, submit to your own husbands. Do this so that even if some of them refuse to believe the word, they may be won without a word by their wives' way of life. [2]After all, they will have observed the reverent and holy manner of your lives. [3]Don't try to make yourselves beautiful on the outside, with stylish hair or by wearing gold jewelry or fine clothes. [4]Instead, make yourselves beautiful on the inside, in your hearts, with the enduring quality of a gentle, peaceful spirit. This type of beauty is very precious in God's eyes. [5]For it was in this way that holy women who trusted in God used to make themselves beautiful, accepting the authority of their own husbands. [6]For example, Sarah accepted Abraham's authority when she called him *master*. You have become her children when you do good and don't respond to threats with fear.

[7]Husbands, likewise, submit by living with your wife in ways that honor her, knowing that she is the weaker partner. Honor her all the more, as she is also a co-heir of the gracious care of life. Do this so that your prayers won't be hindered.

[8]Finally, all of you be of one mind, sympathetic, lovers of your fellow believers, compassionate, and modest in your opinion of yourselves. [9]Don't pay back evil for evil or insult for insult. Instead, give blessing in return. You were called to do this so that you might inherit a blessing. [10]For

those who want to love life
and see good days
should keep their tongue from evil speaking
and their lips from speaking lies.
[11]They should shun evil and do good;
seek peace and chase after it.
[12]The Lord's eyes are on the righteous
and his ears are open to their prayers.
But the Lord cannot tolerate
those who do evil.[d]

[13]Who will harm you if you are zealous for good? [14]But happy are you, even if you suffer because of righteousness! Don't be terrified or upset by them. [15]Instead, regard Christ as holy in your hearts. Whenever anyone asks you to speak of your hope, be ready to defend it. [16]Yet do this with respectful humility, maintaining a good conscience. Act in this way so that those who malign your good lifestyle in Christ may be ashamed when they slander you. [17]It is better to suffer for doing good (if this could possibly be God's will) than for doing evil.

[18]Christ himself suffered on account of sins, once for all, the righteous one on behalf of the unrighteous. He did this in order to bring you into the presence of God. Christ was put to death as a human, but made alive by the Spirit. [19]And it was by the Spirit that he went to preach to the spirits in prison. [20]In the past, these spirits were disobedient—when God patiently waited during the time of Noah. Noah built an ark in which a few (that is, eight) lives were rescued through water. [21]Baptism is like that. It saves you now—not because it removes dirt from your body but because it is the mark of a good conscience toward

[d]Ps 34:12-16

God. Your salvation comes through the resurrection of Jesus Christ, [22]who is at God's right side. Now that he has gone into heaven, he rules over all angels, authorities, and powers.

4 Therefore, since Christ suffered as a human, you should also arm yourselves with his way of thinking. This is because whoever suffers is finished with sin. [2]As a result, they don't live the rest of their human lives in ways determined by human desires but in ways determined by God's will. [3]You have wasted enough time doing what unbelievers desire—living in their unrestrained immorality and lust, their drunkenness and excessive feasting and wild parties, and their forbidden worship of idols. [4]They think it's strange that you don't join in these activities with the same flood of unrestrained wickedness. So they slander you. [5]They will have to reckon with the one who is ready to judge the living and the dead. [6]Indeed, this is the reason the good news was also preached to the dead. This happened so that, although they were judged as humans according to human standards, they could live by the Spirit according to divine standards.

[7]The end of everything has come. Therefore, be self-controlled and clearheaded so you can pray. [8]Above all, show sincere love to each other, because love brings about the forgiveness of many sins. [9]Open your homes to each other without complaining. [10]And serve each other according to the gift each person has received, as good managers of God's diverse gifts. [11]Whoever speaks should do so as those who speak God's word. Whoever serves should do so from the strength that God furnishes. Do this so that in everything God may be honored through Jesus Christ. To him be honor and power forever and always. Amen.

Stand firm in the last times

[12]Dear friends, don't be surprised about the fiery trials that have come among you to test you. These are not strange happenings. [13]Instead, rejoice as you share Christ's suffering. You share his suffering now so that you may also have overwhelming joy when his glory is revealed. [14]If you are mocked because of Christ's name, you are blessed, for the Spirit of glory—indeed, the Spirit of God—rests on you.

[15]Now none of you should suffer as a murderer or thief or evildoer or rebel. [16]But don't be ashamed if you suffer as one who belongs to Christ. Rather, honor God as you bear Christ's name. Give honor to God, [17]because it's time for judgment to begin with God's own household. But if judgment starts with us, what will happen to those who refuse to believe God's good news? [18]If the righteous are barely rescued, what will happen to the godless and sinful? [19]So then, those who suffer because they follow God's will should commit their lives to a trustworthy creator by doing what is right.

5 Therefore, I have a request for the elders among you. (I ask this as a fellow elder and a witness of Christ's sufferings, and as one who shares in the glory that is about to be revealed.) I urge the elders: [2]Like shepherds, tend the flock of God among you. Watch over it. Don't shepherd because you must, but do it voluntarily for God. Don't shepherd greedily, but do it eagerly. [3]Don't shepherd by ruling over those entrusted to your care, but become examples to the flock. [4]And when the chief shepherd appears, you will receive an unfading crown of glory.

[5]In the same way, I urge you who are younger: accept the authority of the elders. And everyone, clothe yourselves with humility toward each other. God stands against the proud, but he gives favor to the humble.

[6]Therefore, humble yourselves under God's power so that he may raise you up in the last day. [7]Throw all your anxiety onto him, because he cares about you. [8]Be clearheaded. Keep alert. Your accuser, the devil, is on the prowl like a roaring lion, seeking someone to devour. [9]Resist him, standing firm in the faith. Do so in the knowledge that your fellow believers are enduring the same suffering throughout the world. [10]After you have suffered for a little while, the God of all grace, the one who called you into his eternal glory in Christ Jesus, will

himself restore, empower, strengthen, and establish you. ¹¹To him be power forever and always. Amen.

Final greeting

¹²I have written and sent these few lines to you by Silvanus. I consider him to be a faithful brother. In these lines I have urged and affirmed that this is the genuine grace of God. Stand firm in it. ¹³The fellow-elect church in Babylon greets you, and so does my son Mark. ¹⁴Greet each other with the kiss of love. Peace to you all who are in Christ.

ELDER (NT)

First Peter refers to only one form of leadership in addition to that of the apostles. This leadership is exercised by elders (5:1-5a) whose role is similar to that of Peter, the apostle (5:1a). The elder functions within the community in a role of oversight. This role, not yet an office, is like that of a shepherd, and it is not a paid position. If elders perform well, they will receive a reward from God in the future. In the meantime, they can expect that others in the community respect their authority.

A few other NT texts indicate that by the late 1st cent. "elder" was coming into general use as a title for those who exercised an authoritative leadership function. Thus, 2 and 3 John are written by "the elder" who provides directives for the church (2 John) and for the beloved Gaius (3 John). James 5:14 urges that when members of the community are ill, the elders of the assembly be summoned in order to pray over those who are sick and anoint them with oil. These elders appear to act collegially as did the council of elders who laid hands on Timothy (1 Tim 4:14).

The book of Revelation provides a vision of elders who function differently from the elders of the NT's Letters. These crowned elders take part in a heavenly liturgy. Twenty-four in number (Rev 4:4, 10; 5:8; 11:16; 19:4), they are seated on 24 thrones around a throne on which sits the one worthy of worship. These 24 elders are often portrayed alongside the four living creatures (Rev 4:9-10; 5:6, 8, 11, 14; 7:11; 14:3; 19:4). Twice, they are said to be surrounded by angels (Rev 5:11; 7:11).

2 PETER

THEME

The certainty of the second coming of Christ and the relation of that coming to Christian living

NATURE AND STYLE OF THE LETTER

Second Peter, although it claims to have been written by the apostle Peter (1:1, 13-19) shortly after the completion of 1 Peter (3:1), clearly comes from a very different environment from that which produced 1 Peter (or the Gospels and Acts, in which Peter played an important role). Along with Jude and Revelation, 2 Peter is one of the latest and most unusual writings of the early Christian church.

Second Peter is now an accepted part of the Bible, but in the early church many Christians doubted its scriptural value. The church leaders Eusebius (ca. 260–340 CE) and Jerome (ca. 345–420 CE) both reported doubt among many that it was Peter's work (and Eusebius himself rejected it), and it was not accepted as an inspired writing by the western church until the last part of the fourth century. In form and style 2 Peter has common features with later, non-biblical Christian writings often called "pseudepigrapha" (false writings).

Similarities can be found between 2 Peter and second-century Christian books that claimed to represent Peter's thoughts or give the history of his life (the Apocalypse of Peter, the Acts of Peter, the Preaching of Peter, and the Gospel of Peter).

Like James and 1 John, 2 Peter is not a real letter but is a sermon, a tract, or an encouraging homily. Its form is very similar to Jewish writings called "testimonials" or "valedictories." A testimonial was a farewell statement or "last will and testament" attributed to a famous person of faith that presented his final advice and predictions for the future (see 2 Peter 1:5-15; 3:3, 7, 10). Knowledgeable readers knew that the person represented in the testimonial had passed away long ago and that the author was really one of his disciples or someone who wanted to gain authority for his own teaching by using a well-known figure's name. Books written after the Old Testament was completed often used this style of writing. Good examples are found in The Assumption of Moses, The Testaments of the Twelve Patriarchs, The Testament of Job, and 1 Enoch.

Early Christians did not consider such a practice to be fraud but regarded it as merely a way to spread the master's teaching. For the first believers, attaching Peter's name to 2 Peter pointed to the wonderful tradition that stood behind this new "letter" being circulated in the church.

SOURCES

Second Peter is made up of a rich tapestry of different sources. It refers to the Old Testament (1:20-21; 2:5-10; 2:22; 3:8), but does not quote it directly. Extensive use is made of the New Testament letter of Jude, incorporating almost the whole book (most of verses 4-18) in 2:1-18 and 3:1-3. Clearly, the author of 2 Peter had Jude in front of him. As a comparison of the two writings shows, he adapts parts of Jude to address the unique circumstances of the church or churches to which he writes.

The author also draws on Jewish traditions outside the Old Testament (2:4, 11, 15) and his work has similarities to Christian letters and books written during the second century (such as 1 and 2 Clement and the Shepherd of Hermas).

Clear references are made to the Gospels (compare 1:14 to John 21:18; 1:16-18 to Mark 9:2-13 and its parallels; 2:20 to Matthew 12:45 and Luke 11:26; and 3:10 to Matthew 24:43 and Luke 12:39). In referring to the Gospels, the writer bolsters his connection to the apostle Peter.

Second Peter also makes an unusual statement about how difficult it is to understand Paul's writings (3:15-16), even though there is not much in the testimonial that resembles Paul's thought. Here Paul's letters have real authority, perhaps the authority of Scripture, and the author is worried about the way some Christians are misinterpreting them.

AUDIENCE

Because of the sources the author uses it is likely that he was writing to people who lived outside of Palestine and were influenced both by Jewish tradition and by pagan culture and religion. Verse 4 in chapter 1 indicates why he is writing the testimonial. He is worried that the Christian readers may lose their faith by being influenced by the corruption that is in the world. As 2:1-22 demonstrates, false teachers have come into the church, bringing destructive heresies and the denial of Jesus Christ as Lord (2:1, 20). They are also trying to get Christians to accept a system of conduct that is unchristian and unethical (1:5-8; 2:9-10, 18-22).

A second problem is that 2 Peter's readers are wondering whether Jesus will really come again as the prophets and apostles said he would (3:3-12). The testimonial is written to shore up their faith in and knowledge of Jesus Christ.

Although it is impossible to know for certain where the people who received 2 Peter lived, it is usually assumed that they were in Asia Minor (modern Turkey) or Egypt, places where Hellenistic culture and Judaism were both particularly strong. Because of the variety of temptations they faced (2:2-20), it is often suggested that they lived in a city, where any manner of evil could be found any time. Paul addresses similar concerns when he writes to the church in urban Corinth.

AUTHORSHIP

The author of 2 Peter is an unknown church leader who uses Peter's name to add authority to the advice he is sending to some churches. It is impossible to know who the author was or where the letter was written. Because 2 Peter has little in common with 1 Peter, there is little evidence to suggest that the author belonged to the same school or circle that influenced the writing of 1 Peter.

DATE

Because of 2 Peter's adaptation of Jude, itself one of the last New Testament books, its use of pagan religious terms, and its similarities to Christian writings that were produced in the second century, it must be assigned a relatively late date, somewhere between 100 and 135 CE. Commentators often suggest that 2 Peter was the last book in the New Testament to be written.

2 PETER

Greeting

1 From Simon Peter, a slave and apostle of Jesus Christ.

To those who received a faith equal to ours through the justice of our God and savior Jesus Christ.

²May you have more and more grace and peace through the knowledge of God and Jesus our Lord.

Christian life in outline

³By his divine power the Lord has given us everything we need for life and godliness through the knowledge of the one who called us by his own honor and glory. ⁴Through his honor and glory he has given us his precious and wonderful promises, that you may share the divine nature and escape from the world's immorality that sinful craving produces.

⁵This is why you must make every effort to add moral excellence to your faith; and to moral excellence, knowledge; ⁶and to knowledge, self-control; and to self-control, endurance; and to endurance, godliness; ⁷and to godliness, affection for others; and to affection for others, love. ⁸If all these are yours and they are growing in you, they'll keep you from becoming inactive and unfruitful in the knowledge of our Lord Jesus Christ. ⁹Whoever lacks these things is shortsighted and blind, forgetting that they were cleansed from their past sins.

¹⁰Therefore, brothers and sisters, be eager to confirm your call and election. Do this and you will never ever be lost. ¹¹In this way you will receive a rich welcome into the everlasting kingdom of our Lord and savior Jesus Christ.

Reminder of the Christian life

¹²So I'll keep reminding you about these things, although you already know them and stand secure in the truth you have. ¹³I think it's right that I keep stirring up your memory, as long as I'm alive. ¹⁴After all, our Lord Jesus Christ has shown me that I am about to depart from this life. ¹⁵I'm eager for you always to remember these things after my death.

Christ's return is true

¹⁶We didn't repeat crafty myths when we told you about the powerful coming of our Lord Jesus Christ. Quite the contrary, we witnessed his majesty with our own eyes. ¹⁷He received honor and glory from God the Father when a voice came to him from the magnificent glory, saying, "This is my dearly loved Son, with whom I am well-pleased." ¹⁸We ourselves heard this voice from heaven while we were with him on the holy mountain. ¹⁹In addition, we have a most reliable prophetic word, and you would do well to pay attention to it, just as you would to a lamp shining in a dark place, until the day dawns and the morning star rises in your hearts. ²⁰Most important, you must know that no prophecy of scripture represents the prophet's own understanding of things, ²¹because no prophecy ever came by human will. Instead, men and women led by the Holy Spirit spoke from God.

Appearance of false teachers

2 But false prophets also arose among the people. In the same way, false teachers will come among you. They will introduce destructive opinions and deny the master who bought them, bringing quick destruction on themselves. ²Many will follow them in their unrestrained immorality, and because of these false teachers the way of truth will be slandered. ³In their greed they will take advantage of you with lies. The judgment pronounced against them long ago hasn't fallen idle, nor is their destruction sleeping.

Active judgment of God

⁴God didn't spare the angels when they sinned but cast them into the lowest level of the underworld and committed them to chains of darkness, keeping them there until the judgment. ⁵And he didn't spare the ancient world when he brought a flood on the world of ungodly people, even though he protected Noah, a preacher of righteousness, along with seven others. ⁶God condemned the cities of Sodom and

Gomorrah to total destruction, reducing them to ashes as a warning to ungodly people. [7]And he rescued righteous Lot, who was made miserable by the unrestrained immorality of unruly people. ([8]While that righteous man lived among them he felt deep distress every day on account of the immoral actions he saw and heard.) [9]These things show that the Lord knows how to rescue the godly from their trials, and how to keep the unrighteous for punishment on the Judgment Day. [10]This is especially true for those who follow after the corrupt cravings of the sinful nature and defy the Lord's authority.

Evil character of the false teachers

These reckless, brash people aren't afraid to insult the glorious ones, [11]yet angels, who are stronger and more powerful, don't use insults when pronouncing the Lord's judgment on them. [12]These false teachers are like irrational animals, mere creatures of instinct, born to be captured and destroyed. They slander what they don't understand and, like animals, they will be destroyed. [13]In this way, they will receive payment for their wrongdoing.

They even enjoy unruly parties in broad daylight. They are blots and blemishes, taking delight in their seductive pleasures while feasting with you. [14]They are always looking for someone with whom to commit adultery. They are always on the lookout for opportunities to sin. They ensnare people whose faith is weak. They have hearts trained in greed. They are under God's curse. [15]Leaving the straight path, they have gone off course, following the way of Balaam son of Bosor, who loved the payment of doing wrong. [16]But Balaam was rebuked for his wrongdoing. A donkey, which has no voice, spoke with a human voice and put a stop to the prophet's madness.

[17]These false teachers are springs without water, mists driven by the wind. The underworld has been reserved for them. [18]With empty, self-important speech, they use sinful cravings and unrestrained immorality to ensnare people who have only just escaped life with those who have wandered from the truth. [19]These false teachers promise freedom, but they themselves are slaves of immorality; whatever overpowers you, enslaves you. [20]If people escape the moral filth of this world through the knowledge of our Lord and savior Jesus Christ, then get tangled up in it again and are overcome by it, they are worse off than they were before. [21]It would be better for them never to have known the way of righteousness than, having come to know it, to turn back from the holy commandment entrusted to them. [22]They demonstrate the truth of the proverb: "A dog returns to its own vomit, and a washed sow wallows in the mud."

Delay of Christ's coming in judgment

3 My dear friends, this is now my second letter to you. I have written both letters to stir up your sincere understanding with a reminder. [2]I want you to recall what the holy prophets foretold as well as what the Lord and savior commanded through your apostles. [3]Most important, know this: in the last days scoffers will come, jeering, living by their own cravings, [4]and saying, "Where is the promise of his coming? After

BALAAM

Balaam is a non-Israelite prophet or seer featured in Numbers 22–24 as the one who blessed Israel in defiance of King Balak of Moab, who had hired him to curse Israel. New Testament references to Balaam are uniformly negative, portraying him as a prototype of false prophets and teachers in the NT period (2 Pet 2:15; Jude 11; Rev 2:14).

all, nothing has changed—not since the beginning of creation, nor even since the ancestors died."

⁵But they fail to notice that, by God's word, heaven and earth were formed long ago out of water and by means of water. ⁶And it was through these that the world of that time was flooded and destroyed. ⁷But by the same word, heaven and earth are now held in reserve for fire, kept for the Judgment Day and destruction of ungodly people.

⁸Don't let it escape your notice, dear friends, that with the Lord a single day is like a thousand years and a thousand years are like a single day. ⁹The Lord isn't slow to keep his promise, as some think of slowness, but he is patient toward you, not wanting anyone to perish but all to change their hearts and lives. ¹⁰But the day of the Lord will come like a thief. On that day the heavens will pass away with a dreadful noise, the elements will be consumed by fire, and the earth and all the works done on it will be exposed.

¹¹Since everything will be destroyed in this way, what sort of people ought you to be? You must live holy and godly lives, ¹²waiting for and hastening the coming day of God. Because of that day, the heavens will be destroyed by fire and the elements will melt away in the flames. ¹³But according to his promise we are waiting for a new heaven and a new earth, where righteousness is at home.

Preparing for Christ's coming in judgment

¹⁴Therefore, dear friends, while you are waiting for these things to happen, make every effort to be found by him in peace— pure and faultless. ¹⁵Consider the patience of our Lord to be salvation, just as our dear friend and brother Paul wrote to you according to the wisdom given to him, ¹⁶speaking of these things in all his letters. Some of his remarks are hard to understand, and people who are ignorant and whose faith is weak twist them to their own destruction, just as they do the other scriptures.

Final instruction

¹⁷Therefore, dear friends, since you have been warned in advance, be on guard so that you aren't led off course into the error of sinful people, and lose your own safe position. ¹⁸Instead, grow in the grace and knowledge of our Lord and savior Jesus Christ. To him belongs glory now and forever. Amen.

1 JOHN

THEME

The message of the apostles is the standard of Christian truth and experience.

INTRODUCTION

First John is one of the most beautiful, elegant, and moving books in the New Testament. Through the use of simple and straightforward language (the whole book has a vocabulary of only 303 Greek words) the author introduces readers to the fundamentals of the Christian faith. Indeed, Martin Luther said he had never read a book with such simple, yet expressive, words.

First John is not really a letter but is more like a tract—a sermon or a guidebook for Christians. The author takes simple themes and shows them from two angles, from a positive and from a negative side, in order to make them easy to understand and give his readers an opportunity to choose between them. Throughout his tract he interweaves discussions about the beginning and the end of time (1:1; 2:17-18, 24; 3:8), life and death (1:1, 2; 2:25; 3:14-15; 5:11-12, 13), light and darkness (1:5-10; 2:8-11), truth and falsehood (1:6-10; 2:4-5, 21-24, 26-27; 3:7, 18-19; 4:1, 6; 5:20), and love and hatred (2:5, 9-11, 15; 3:11-18; 4:7-21; 5:1-5).

Although 1 John uses an uncomplicated style, it is not easy to determine the outline of its message. The argument does not move logically from one point to another but overlaps and interweaves the basic themes. It is not like a tightly argued law brief; it is more like a spiral of ideas twisted and turned around each other into a braided strand of pearls. However, 1 John 1:1-5 makes it clear that the basic objective is to bring a fundamental message about Jesus Christ so that readers might have fellowship with God and eternal life.

THE SITUATION OF 1 JOHN

Like many other books of the New Testament, 1 John was written because of problems created in the church by those who were opposed to the basic truth about Jesus Christ—rival preachers and teachers who tried to lead other believers astray. Scholars are not certain whether there was one group of opponents or more than one that troubled John and the Christians who were members of the church to which he wrote. John pits his own testimony against the message or messages they bring (1:2-3). In 2:18-19 he refers to them as "antichrists" who "went out from us" as if they were former members of his church who were trying to set up rival congregations. For this reason these opponents are often referred to as "secessionists," those who were dividing the Christian fellowship by trying to form new branches of it.

Although it is difficult to know what John's opponents taught, it is likely that they told people that Christians did not need to confess their sins to be forgiven (1:8-10; 2:1-2; 5:16-17) and that it was not necessary to accept Jesus as the Son of God to be close to God (2:22-25; 5:9-12). John's lengthy discussions of God's love and the necessity of extending that love to other people indicate that the opponents also failed to emphasize Christian forgiveness and reaching out to the needy, as God had forgiven and reached out to the church in love through Christ. John knew that his opponents' view of the nature of Jesus Christ was completely wrong. In his tract he is determined to correct that view and show his readers who Jesus really is, teach them what it means to live as Christians, keep them out of the darkness of sin, and lead them to the light of truth and eternal life.

AUTHORSHIP

The question of authorship in the three letters of John is extremely complicated, and Bible scholars disagree about the true identity of John. From a superficial point of view, it is clear that 1, 2, and 3 John are closely connected to the Gospel of John. For that reason scholars have traditionally held that the apostle John, the disciple of Jesus, wrote all four books.

Many of the themes are identical, and it is obvious that the purposes in 1 John 1:1-5; 5:11-15 and John 20:30-31 and 21:24-25 are very similar. Early church tradition also attributed Revelation to the same man (Revelation 1:1, 4, 9; 22:8), and it was believed that John wrote all his books from the city of Ephesus.

As early as the third century, however, Origen wrote that some church leaders doubted that all the books were by the apostle. Although Eusebius (fourth century) believed the Gospel and 1 John to be authentic, he referred in his writings to the "so-called" second and third letters of John, which, he said, might be the work of the evangelist or some other writer with the same name. Later, the man who translated the Bible into Latin, Jerome, said that the author of 1 John was not the same person who wrote 2 and 3 John.

Although some scholars still think that 1, 2, and 3 John, the Gospel of John, and the Revelation to John were all written by the apostle, most modern commentators are agreed that it is not that easy to determine who the authors of all of these books were. The most likely solution is that 1, 2, and 3 John were all written over a period of time by the same author, and that this John closely patterned his letters after the Gospel. Clearly the letters were written by someone who felt himself to be spiritually close to the author of the Gospel, and it is possible that he was even a student of his.

Most scholars recognize that the disciples who gathered around John the apostle at Ephesus formed a tightly-knit group that worked together to spread the truth about Jesus Christ by writing the last chapter of John's Gospel, the letters of John, and Revelation. It is possible that the letters of John were written because disagreement arose in the school about the proper interpretation of the Gospel and that the letters of John represent the "official" view of the majority of the members. The letters were thus written to refute the teaching of those who preached a different version and were trying to undermine the congregations established by the apostle and those who followed him.

PLACE AND DATE

Because of the problems of determining who wrote the three letters, it is also not possible to be certain where the epistles were written and who received them. They were probably composed in Ephesus, the home base of the Johannine "school," and were sent to churches in Asia Minor (modern Turkey) that the apostle and his disciples had founded. Since it is generally agreed that the Gospel of John could not have been written before 90–100 CE, the letters had to have been written sometime in the early part of the second century.

1 JOHN

Announcement about the word of life

1 We announce to you what existed from the beginning, what we have heard, what we have seen with our eyes, what we have seen and our hands handled, about the word of life. ²The life was revealed, and we have seen, and we testify and announce to you the eternal life that was with the Father and was revealed to us. ³What we have seen and heard, we also announce it to you so that you can have fellowship with us. Our fellowship is with the Father and with his Son, Jesus Christ. ⁴We are writing these things so that our joy can be complete.

The message: God is light

⁵This is the message that we have heard from him and announce to you: "God is light and there is no darkness in him at all." ⁶If we claim, "We have fellowship with him," and live in the darkness, we are lying and do not act truthfully. ⁷But if we live in the light in the same way as he is in the light, we have fellowship with each other, and the blood of Jesus, his Son, cleanses us from every sin. ⁸If we claim, "We don't have any sin," we deceive ourselves and the truth is not in us. ⁹But if we confess our sins, he is faithful and just to forgive us our sins and cleanse us from everything we've done wrong. ¹⁰If we claim, "We have never sinned," we make him a liar and his word is not in us.

Living in the light

2 My little children, I'm writing these things to you so that you don't sin. But if you do sin, we have an advocate with the Father, Jesus Christ the righteous one. ²He is God's way of dealing with our sins, not only ours but the sins of the whole world. ³This is how we know that we know him: if we keep his commandments. ⁴The one who claims, "I know him," while not keeping his commandments, is a liar, and the truth is not in this person. ⁵But the love of God is truly perfected in whoever keeps his word. This is how we know we are in him. ⁶The one who claims to remain in him ought to live in the same way as he lived.

⁷Dear friends, I'm not writing a new commandment to you, but an old commandment that you had from the beginning. The old commandment is the message you heard. ⁸On the other hand, I am writing a new commandment to you, which is true in him and in you, because the darkness is passing away and the true light already shines. ⁹The one who claims to be in the light while hating a brother or sister is in the darkness even now. ¹⁰The person loving a brother and sister stays in the light, and there is nothing in the light that causes a person to stumble. ¹¹But the person who hates a brother or sister is in the darkness and lives in the darkness, and doesn't know where to go because the darkness blinds the eyes.

Motivations for writing

¹²Little children, I'm writing to you because your sins have been forgiven through Jesus' name. ¹³Parents, I'm writing to you because you have known the one who has existed from the beginning. Young people, I'm writing to you because you have conquered the evil one. ¹⁴Little children, I write to you because you know the Father. Parents, I write to you because you have known the one who has existed from the beginning. Young people, I write to you because you are strong, the word of God remains in you, and you have conquered the evil one.

Warning about the world

¹⁵Don't love the world or the things in the world. If anyone loves the world, the love of the Father is not in them. ¹⁶Everything that is in the world—the craving for whatever the body feels, the craving for whatever the eyes see and the arrogant pride in one's possessions—is not of the Father but is of the world. ¹⁷And the world and its cravings are passing away, but the person who does the will of God remains forever.

Remaining in the truth

[18]Little children, it is the last hour. Just as you have heard that the antichrist is coming, so now many antichrists have appeared. This is how we know it is the last hour. [19]They went out from us, but they were not really part of us. If they had been part of us, they would have stayed with us. But by going out from us, they showed they all are not part of us. [20]But you have an anointing from the holy one, and all of you know the truth. [21]I don't write to you because you don't know the truth but because you know it. You know that no lie comes from the truth. [22]Who is the liar? Isn't it the person who denies that Jesus is the Christ? This person is the antichrist: the one who denies the Father and the Son. [23]Everyone who denies the Son does not have the Father, but the one who confesses the Son has the Father also.

[24]As for you, what you heard from the beginning must remain in you. If what you heard from the beginning remains in you, you will also remain in relationship to the Son and in the Father. [25]This is the promise that he himself gave us: eternal life. [26]I write these things to you about those who are attempting to deceive you. [27]As for you, the anointing that you received from him remains on you, and you don't need anyone to teach you the truth. But since his anointing teaches you about all things (it's true and not a lie), remain in relationship to him just as he taught you.

Remaining until Jesus appears

[28]And now, little children, remain in relationship to Jesus, so that when he appears we can have confidence and not be ashamed in front of him when he comes. [29]If you know that he is righteous, you also know that every person who practices righteousness is born from him.

3 See what kind of love the Father has given to us in that we should be called God's children, and that is what we are! Because the world didn't recognize him, it doesn't recognize us.

[2]Dear friends, now we are God's children, and it hasn't yet appeared what we will be. We know that when he appears we will be like him because we'll see him as he is. [3]And everyone who has this hope in him purifies himself even as he is pure. [4]Every person who practices sin commits an act of rebellion, and sin is rebellion. [5]You know that he appeared to take away sins, and there is no sin in him. [6]Every person who remains in relationship to him does not sin. Any person who sins has not seen him or known him.

Practicing sin or righteousness

[7]Little children, make sure no one deceives you. The person who practices righteousness is righteous, in the same way that Jesus is righteous. [8]The person who practices sin belongs to the devil, because the devil has been sinning since the beginning. God's Son appeared for this purpose:

JESUS CHRIST

"Jesus" was a name common among Jews before the rise of Christianity. The NT, including on occasion the Gospels, often adds "Christ" before or after the proper name. "Christ" is a transliteration of the Greek term *christos*, which means "anointed one." And this is a translation of the Hebrew term *mashiah* (which also means "anointed one"). Followers of Jesus originally used "Christ" to show Jesus' status as the king in the lineage of David who would fulfill Israel's royal expectations and liberate them from hardship. The strength of "Christ" as a title, however, soon faded, and "Jesus Christ" became a personal name, as it was already in Paul's letters.

to destroy the works of the devil. [9]Those born from God don't practice sin because God's DNA[a] remains in them. They can't sin because they are born from God. [10]This is how God's children and the devil's children are apparent: everyone who doesn't practice righteousness is not from God, including the person who doesn't love a brother or sister. [11]This is the message that you heard from the beginning: love each other. [12]Don't behave like Cain, who belonged to the evil one and murdered his brother. And why did he kill him? He killed him because his own works were evil, but the works of his brother were righteous.

Loving each other

[13]Don't be surprised, brothers and sisters, if the world hates you. [14]We know that we have transferred from death to life, because we love the brothers and sisters. The person who does not love remains in death. [15]Everyone who hates a brother or sister is a murderer, and you know that no murderer has eternal life residing in him. [16]This is how we know love: Jesus laid down his life for us, and we ought to lay down our lives for our brothers and sisters. [17]But if a person has material possessions and sees a brother or sister in need and that person doesn't care—how can the love of God remain in him?

[18]Little children, let's not love with words or speech but with action and truth. [19]This is how we will know that we belong to the truth and reassure our hearts in God's presence. [20]Even if our hearts condemn us, God is greater than our hearts and knows all things. [21]Dear friends, if our hearts don't condemn us, we have confidence in relationship to God. [22]We receive whatever we ask from him because we keep his commandments and do what pleases him. [23]This is his commandment, that we believe in the name of his Son, Jesus Christ, and love each other as he commanded us. [24]The person who keeps his commandments remains in God and God remains in him; and this is how we know that he remains in us,

because of the Spirit that he has given to us.

Testing the spirits

4 Dear friends, don't believe every spirit. Test the spirits to see if they are from God because many false prophets have gone into the world. [2]This is how you know if a spirit comes from God: every spirit that confesses that Jesus Christ has come as a human[b] is from God, [3]and every spirit that doesn't confess Jesus is not from God. This is the spirit of the antichrist, which you have heard is coming and is now already in the world. [4]You are from God, little children, and you have defeated these people because the one who is in you is greater than the one who is in the world. [5]They are from the world. So they speak from the world's point of view and the world listens to them. [6]We are from God. The person who knows God listens to us. Whoever is not from God doesn't listen to us. This is how we recognize the Spirit of truth and the spirit of error.

Love and God

[7]Dear friends, let's love each other, because love is from God, and everyone who loves is born from God and knows God. [8]The person who doesn't love does not know God, because God is love. [9]This is how the love of God is revealed to us: God has sent his only Son into the world so that we can live through him. [10]This is love: it is not that we loved God but that he loved us and sent his Son as the sacrifice that deals with our sins.

[11]Dear friends, if God loved us this way, we also ought to love each other. [12]No one has ever seen God. If we love each other, God remains in us and his love is made perfect in us. [13]This is how we know we remain in him and he remains in us, because he has given us a measure of his Spirit. [14]We have seen and testify that the Father has sent the Son to be the savior of the world. [15]If any of us confess that Jesus is God's Son, God remains in us and we remain in God.

[a]Or *genetic character* [b]Or *come in the flesh*

[16]We have known and have believed the love that God has for us.

God is love, and those who remain in love remain in God and God remains in them. [17]This is how love has been perfected in us, so that we can have confidence on the Judgment Day, because we are exactly the same as God is in this world. [18]There is no fear in love, but perfect love drives out fear, because fear expects punishment. The person who is afraid has not been made perfect in love. [19]We love because God first loved us. [20]If anyone says, I love God, and hates a brother or sister, he is a liar, because the person who doesn't love a brother or sister who can be seen can't love God, who can't be seen. [21]This commandment we have from him: Those who claim to love God ought to love their brother and sister also.

5 Everyone who believes that Jesus is the Christ has been born from God. Whoever loves someone who is a parent loves the child born to the parent. [2]This is how we know that we love the children of God: when we love God and keep God's commandments. [3]This is the love of God: we keep God's commandments. God's commandments are not difficult, [4]because everyone who is born from God defeats the world. And this is the victory that has defeated the world: our faith. [5]Who defeats the world? Isn't it the one who believes that Jesus is God's Son?

Testimony about Jesus

[6]This is the one who came by water and blood: Jesus Christ. Not by water only but by water and blood. And the Spirit is the one who testifies, because the Spirit is the truth. [7]The three are testifying—[8]the Spirit, the water, and the blood—and the three are united in agreement. [9]If we receive human testimony, God's testimony is greater, because this is what God testified: he has testified about his Son. [10]The one who believes in God's Son has the testimony within; the one who doesn't believe God has made God a liar, because that one has not believed the testimony that God gave about his Son. [11]And this is the testimony: God gave eternal life to us, and this life is in his Son. [12]The one who has the Son has life. The one who doesn't have God's Son does not have life.

Confidence in prayer

[13]I write these things to you who believe in the name of God's Son so that you can know that you have eternal life. [14]This is the confidence that we have in our relationship with God: If we ask for anything in agreement with his will, he listens to us. [15]If we know that he listens to whatever we ask, we know that we have received what we asked from him. [16]If anyone sees a brother or sister committing a sin that does not result in death, they should pray, and God will give life to them—that is, to those who commit sins that don't result in death. There is a sin that results in death—I'm not saying that you should pray about that. [17]Every unrighteous action is sin, but there is a sin that does not result in death.

Be on guard

[18]We know that everyone born from God does not sin, but the ones born from God

GOD'S SON

Biblical authors use "God's son" or its equivalents (e.g., "my son," "Son of the Most High") with reference to a variety of persons or groups. Most famously, "God's Son" appears in the NT as a title for Jesus and was taken up into the later development of Christian theology, from which it emerged as a primary component of creedal orthodoxy ("the only Son of God, eternally begotten of the Father, of one being with the Father").

guard themselves,[c] and the evil one cannot touch them. [19]We know we are from God, and the whole world lies in the power of the evil one. [20]We know that God's Son has come and has given us understanding to know the one who is true. We are in the one who is true by being in his Son, Jesus Christ. This is the true God and eternal life. [21]Little children, guard yourselves from idols!

---

[c]Or but the one who is born from God guards him from sin

2 JOHN

THEME

A warning against receiving and entertaining traveling false teachers

INTRODUCTION

Unlike 1 John, where the author does not identify himself, the writer of 2 John immediately says who he is in the very first verse, where he calls himself "the elder." For centuries Christians have debated the meaning of this ambiguous title and have tried to determine who the elder was. The task is complicated by the fact that the Greek term translated as elder can mean "old man," "respected person," or "a leader in the church" (see Acts 20:17; 1 Timothy 5:17; Titus 1:5; James 5:14; 1 Peter 5:1). Suggestions have been made that he was the apostle John in his old age; a man among a group of elders, who were each assigned different geographic areas in the church; a church leader named John who was not a disciple of Jesus and was not acquainted with the apostle John; or, as is most likely, a student of the apostle John who based his letters on the Gospel of John. In 2 and 3 John this John brings the apostle's message to the members of his church and refutes those who try to preach a different Christ. The title *elder* may indicate that the churches he is writing to are under his administrative oversight and that he functions somewhat as a bishop.

RECIPIENTS

Second John also differs from 1 John because it appears to be written to specific persons, the chosen gentlewoman and her children (verse 1), rather than to the church at large. Although most of the letters in the New Testament are written to congregations, a few, like 1 and 2 Timothy, Titus, and Philemon, purport to be written to individuals.

Unfortunately, the identity of the recipient of the letter is not clear, since the Greek words for "chosen gentlewoman" could have a number of different meanings. The word *chosen* can mean "called of God" or "noble," and was even used for a personal name in the ancient world. So suggestions have been made that "chosen gentlewoman" should be translated "the lady Electa," "the noble Kyria," or "Dear Lady." Such interpretations still do not explain who this woman is, why John refers to her children in verse 1, or why he ends the letter with "Your chosen sister's children greet you" (verse 13).

Realizing that the word *children* could refer to members of a congregation rather than the sons or daughters of a particular person, most scholars now think that "chosen gentlewoman" refers to a church rather than an individual. The word "chosen" refers, therefore, to the call of the church members to be Christians. Verse 13 indicates that the letter comes from another congregation that contains other children of God. Perhaps John uses symbolic language because he does not want his opponents to know where these churches are if his letter should fall into the wrong hands.

MAIN THEMES

Second John picks up several themes that are prominent in 1 John: truth (verse 2), love (verses 5-6), and the danger of deceivers and the Antichrist (verse 7). This letter appears to be a follow-up of 1 John and was written at a time when the situation described in the first letter had deteriorated. Although some of the children (members) are following the truth, others are still being deceived.

2 JOHN

Greeting

¹From the elder.

To the chosen gentlewoman and her children, whom I truly love (and I am not the only one, but also all who know the truth), ²because of the truth that remains with us and will be with us forever.

³Grace, mercy, and peace from God the Father and from Jesus Christ, the Son of the Father, will be ours who live in truth and love.

Love each other

⁴I was overjoyed to find some of your children living in the truth, just as we had been commanded by the Father. ⁵Now, dear friends, I am requesting that we love each other. It's not as though I'm writing a new command to you, but it's one we have had from the beginning. ⁶This is love: that we live according to his commands. This is the command that you heard from the beginning: live in love.

Reject false teachers

⁷Many deceivers have gone into the world who do not confess that Jesus Christ came as a human being. This kind of person is the deceiver and the antichrist. ⁸Watch yourselves so that you don't lose what we've worked for but instead receive a full reward. ⁹Anyone who goes too far and does not continue in the teaching about Christ does not have God. Whoever continues in this teaching has both the Father and the Son. ¹⁰Whoever comes to you who does not affirm this teaching should neither be received nor welcomed into your home, ¹¹because welcoming people like that is the same thing as sharing in their evil actions.

Plans to visit

¹²I have a lot to tell you. I don't want to use paper and ink, but I hope to visit you and talk with you face-to-face, so that our joy can be complete.

Final greeting

¹³Your chosen sister's children greet you.

ANTICHRIST

The antichrist is the adversary of God and Christ that comes in the end times. According to some sources he deceives many into false faith, and according to others he harasses the people of God. The term *antichrist* is not used in Revelation. It first appears in the Letters of John (1 John 2:18, 22; 2 John v. 7), and writers from the 2nd century onward refer to the antichrist as an agent of Satan, who combines traits of the man of lawlessness (2 Thess 2:1-3), the beast (Rev 13:1-10), and other enemies of God.

3 JOHN

THEME

Hospitality and financial assistance for traveling missionaries who teach true Christian doctrine

INTRODUCTION

Third John, unlike 1 and 2 John, seems to be a personal letter rather than a message or warning to a congregation. Although the author is likely the same as 2 John ("the elder," verse 1), the letter is addressed directly to Gaius.

This letter discusses some of the same subjects found in 1 and 2 John (truth, verses 3-4, 12; love, verse 6), but deals more specifically with three individuals. The letter brings encouragement to Gaius, chastises Diotrephes for failing to acknowledge the elder's authority, and praises Demetrius because true believers have testified to the truth of his life and ministry.

Third John is the shortest book in the New Testament, consisting of only 219 Greek words. Although it has some of the key vocabulary from 1 and 2 John (*truth, love, testifying*), 3 John is considerably different from its two predecessors. It is genuinely a letter since it is clearly written to an individual person rather than to a general audience or a congregation. Of all the so-called "letters" in the New Testament, moreover, 3 John has the closest resemblance to secular letters of the first and second centuries, even containing a wish for good health (verse 2).

The situation is also different from those presumed for 1 and 2 John. Two backgrounds are possible. Either 3 John is a totally independent writing that was sent to someone named Gaius to correct an isolated set of circumstances, or it continues to address the problems already discussed in the previous letters. Most commentators think the second possibility is the more likely. If so, deterioration of the situation described in 1 and 2 John must mean that more people are defecting to John's opponents and that he is getting more and more worried. The circumstances have become so critical that he has given up addressing his readers in general terms and is now being directly critical of one of the chief troublemakers, Diotrephes.

3 JOHN

Greeting

[1]From the elder.

To my dear friend Gaius, whom I truly love.

[2]Dear friend, I'm praying that all is well with you and that you enjoy good health in the same way that you prosper spiritually.

Encouragement for Gaius

[3]I was overjoyed when the brothers and sisters arrived and spoke highly of your faithfulness to the truth, shown by how you live according to the truth. [4]I have no greater joy than this: to hear that my children are living according to the truth. [5]Dear friend, you act faithfully in whatever you do for our brothers and sisters, even though they are strangers. [6]They spoke highly of your love in front of the church. You all would do well to provide for their journey in a way that honors God, [7]because they left on their journey for the sake of Jesus Christ without accepting any support from the Gentiles. [8]Therefore, we ought to help people like this so that we can be coworkers with the truth.

Criticism of Diotrephes

[9]I wrote something to the church, but Diotrephes, who likes to put himself first, doesn't welcome us. [10]Because of this, if I come, I will bring up what he has done—making unjustified and wicked accusations against us. And as if that were not enough, he not only refuses to welcome the brothers and sisters but stops those who want to do so and even throws them out of the church! [11]Dear friend, don't imitate what is bad but what is good. Whoever practices what is good belongs to God. Whoever practices what is bad has not seen God.

Approval of Demetrius

[12]Everyone speaks highly of Demetrius, even the truth itself. We also speak highly of him, and you know that what we say is true.

Final greeting

[13]I have a lot to say to you, but I don't want to use pen and ink. [14]I hope to see you soon, and we will speak face-to-face.

[15]Peace be with you. Your friends here greet you. Greet our friends there by name.

GAIUS

1. One of the first people baptized by Paul in Corinth (1 Cor 1:14). Probably of pagan origin, his wealth enabled him to host "the whole church" (Rom 16:23; cf. 1 Cor 14:23).

2. Gaius of Macedonia (Acts 19:29) was a traveling companion of Paul.

3. Gaius of Derbe (Acts 20:4) was also a traveling companion of Paul. Nothing else is known of them.

4. The apparent leader of a congregation to whom 3 John is addressed: "To my dear friend Gaius, whom I truly love" (v. 1).

THEME

God's judgment will fall on those in the church who undermine the faith and way of life once for all delivered to the saints.

NATURE AND STYLE

Jude, like 2 Peter, is sent to an unknown congregation or congregations and concerns the danger of false teachers. The author wants to keep his readers in the Christian fold, so he writes about the salvation we share and urges them to fight for the faith (verse 3). In verses 11-16 he gives several negative examples from Jewish tradition to show how bad the influence of his opponents is. What Christians are going through, he advises, is not surprising (verses 17-23). Those who understand the predictions of the apostles (verse 17) and are centered in the three-person God (verses 20-22) should expect such things. The letter ends with one of the most beautiful benedictions in the New Testament, in which believers are directed to the God and savior who will never let them fall (verses 24-25).

Jude has some similarities to other New Testament writings. Since it tries to preserve Jewish ethical values against pagan temptations, it is similar to James. Where it emphasizes the last days and the coming judgment of God, it is like 1 and 2 Peter and Revelation.

The style of the letter indicates that the author has been influenced by both Jewish and Greek thought. Many of his examples (Moses, Michael, Balaam) are from the Old Testament or later Jewish tradition. And his method of interpreting scripture is similar to that used in the Dead Sea Scrolls. The writer is also dependent on Jewish apocalyptic literature. Apocalyptic writings report mysterious revelations by God and his angels and portray the divine will for the last days. Mark 13 (and parallels in Matthew and Luke) and Revelation provide other New Testament examples. In Jude reference is made to 1 Enoch and The Assumption of Moses (verses 6, 9, 14-15).

The author is also very familiar with Hellenistic Greek ideas as his polished Greek style, his vocabulary, and his references to Greek religious and philosophical concepts clearly show. Jude must have been written to people in a culture that was strongly influenced by Jewish and Greek thought. The recipients probably lived either in Syria (where Jude may have been well-known), Asia Minor, or Egypt.

SITUATION

Although the whole letter is written to combat the godless persons mentioned in verse 4, it is never said who they really are. Scholars often argue that these persons might have been Gnostic heretics. These heretics thought they had special knowledge (*gnosis*) and liberty from God.

Since the writer of Jude never discusses the meaning of the word *knowledge*, however, as the author of 1 John repeatedly does, and since he is not concerned about elemental spirits or matters of the cosmos (key ideas in Gnostic philosophy) as Ephesians (1:20-21; 3:10, 18) is, it is more likely that Jude's opponents are not Gnostic heretics but church members. Jude indicates that they are involved in church life and regularly take communion (verse 12). Apparently the danger of their interpretation of the Christian faith is that they have misunderstood Jewish apocalyptic writings (verses 15-16) and are misleading the church about the nature of true Christian freedom. Perhaps they misunderstood Paul's teachings about Christian freedom and are urging members to become libertines (see verses 4, 10, 11, 15, 16 in comparison with Romans 1:18-32; 3:8; 6:1, 15; Galatians 5:1, 13). Whoever the opponents are, Jude has only the harshest words for them (verses 10-13, 16).

AUTHOR

The author calls himself "Jude, a slave of Jesus Christ and brother of James" (verse 1). The implication is that he is the brother of the writer of the book of James as well as the blood brother of Jesus (see Mark 6:3). This is unlikely, however, since the author of Jude does not identify himself with the apostles and sees them as respected men from the past (verse 17). Jude would have known the apostles well, his brother James being one of them (Acts 12:17; 15:13; 1 Corinthians 15:7; Galatians 1:19; 2:9, 12). It is also unusual that Jude refers to himself as Jesus' slave rather than his brother. Further, Jude, along with Jesus, was raised in a Jewish Aramaic-speaking environment in Galilee, and would not be familiar with the Hellenistic-Greek ideas that are found in this book.

Although it is often suggested that the author could be another Jude, the one mentioned in Acts 1:13 (the son of James) or the Judas Barsabbas of Acts 15:22-34, it is best to conclude that the writer of Jude, like James, borrows the name of one of Jesus' brothers in order to increase the value and authority of his own writing. Who he really was remains a mystery.

DATE

Because of the similarities of style and content, Jude was probably written around the same time as James, 1 Peter, and 1 John, at the end of the first century or the beginning of the second century.

JUDE

Greeting

¹Jude, a slave of Jesus Christ and brother of James.

To those who are called, loved by God the Father and kept safe by Jesus Christ.

²May you have more and more mercy, peace, and love.

Certain judgment of the false teachers

³Dear friends, I wanted very much to write to you concerning the salvation we share. Instead, I must write to urge you to fight for the faith delivered once and for all to God's holy people. ⁴Godless people have slipped in among you. They turn the grace of our God into unrestrained immorality and deny our only master and Lord, Jesus Christ. Judgment was passed against them a long time ago.

⁵I want to remind you of something you already know very well. The Lord, who once saved a people out of Egypt, later destroyed those who didn't maintain their faith. ⁶I remind you too of the angels who didn't keep their position of authority but deserted their own home. The Lord has kept them in eternal chains in the underworld until the judgment of the great day. ⁷In the same way, Sodom and Gomorrah and neighboring towns practiced immoral sexual relations and pursued other immoral sexual urges. By undergoing the punishment of eternal fire, they serve as a warning.

⁸Yet, even knowing this, these dreamers in the same way pollute themselves, reject authority, and slander the angels. ⁹The archangel Michael, when he argued with the devil about Moses' body, did not dare charge him with slander. Instead, he said, "The Lord rebuke you!" ¹⁰But these people slander whatever they don't understand. They are destroyed by what they know instinctively, as though they were irrational animals.

Prophecies about the false teachers

¹¹They are damned, for they follow in the footsteps of Cain. For profit they give themselves over to Balaam's error. They are destroyed in the uprising of Korah. ¹²These people are like jagged rocks just below the surface of the water waiting to snag you when they join your love feasts. They feast with you without reverence. They care only for themselves. They are waterless clouds carried along by the winds; fruitless autumn trees, twice dead, uprooted; ¹³wild waves of the sea foaming up their own shame; wandering stars for whom the darkness of the underworld is reserved forever.

¹⁴Enoch, who lived seven generations after Adam, prophesied about these people when he said, "See, the Lord comes with his countless holy ones, ¹⁵to execute judgment on everyone and to convict everyone about every ungodly deed they have committed in their ungodliness as well as all the harsh things that sinful ungodly people have said against him." ¹⁶These are faultfinding grumblers, living according to their own de-

---

ARCHANGEL

Meaning "chief angel" or "head angel," (1 Thess 4:16), *archangel* occurs only twice in the Bible (1 Thess 4:16; Jude v. 9), though the idea is more widespread, and the archangels Michael and Gabriel are named in both the OT and the NT. Christ's return will be accompanied by an unnamed archangel's victory shout (1 Thess 4:16), while Jude v. 9 calls Michael an archangel. One Second Temple tradition has four archangels, Michael, Gabriel, Raphael, and Sariel. Another has seven, adding the names Uriel, Raguel, and Remiel.

sires. They speak arrogant words and they show partiality to people when they want a favor in return.

[17] But you, dear friends, remember the words spoken beforehand by the apostles of our Lord Jesus Christ. [18] They said to you, "In the end time scoffers will come living according to their own ungodly desires." [19] These people create divisions. Since they don't have the Spirit, they are worldly.

A strategy for the faithful

[20] But you, dear friends: build each other up on the foundation of your most holy faith, pray in the Holy Spirit, [21] keep each other in the love of God, wait for the mercy of our Lord Jesus Christ, who will give you eternal life. [22] Have mercy on those who doubt. [23] Save some by snatching them from the fire. Fearing God, have mercy on some, hating even the clothing contaminated by their sinful urges.

Blessing

[24] To the one who is able
to protect you from falling,
and to present you blameless and
rejoicing before his glorious presence,
[25] to the only God our savior,
through Jesus Christ our Lord,
belong glory, majesty, power,
and authority,
before all time, now and forever.
Amen.

REVELATION

THEME

The triumph of Jesus Christ and his church

INTRODUCTION

Sometime between 81 and 91 CE, a Christian prophet named John was exiled on Patmos, an island in the Mediterranean about thirty miles off the coast of modern-day Turkey. While imprisoned on Patmos, John received the inspiration to write the book we know as Revelation.

WHO WAS JOHN?

The name John was common in Rome, and it was widely used in the church and in its stories: John the Baptist, John the son of Zebedee, John the author of the Gospel, John the writer of the letters, John the author of Revelation. Some traditions say that some of these were the same person; some say no. Of all of the writings we have by men named John, the Gospel and the first two letters seem most similar.

Revelation differs greatly from all of the others. It has a different style, different content, and different vocabulary. Most scholars think the writer of Revelation was not the same person who wrote the Gospel.

All we know about John is what we can learn from his book: He was a Christian prophet who used Old Testament images and symbols to describe God's glory, the evil of the times, and God's soon-to-occur intervention in history on behalf of the faithful. John spoke openly about Christ, even in times when Christians felt immense pressure to worship the emperor. He was faithful during times of persecution—so faithful that the authorities arrested him and exiled him on the island of Patmos—and he was convinced of God's plan to preserve the church to the end of time.

APOCALYPSE

John's book is sometimes called Revelation and sometimes The Apocalypse. Both words come down to the same thing. *Apocalypse* comes from two words in the Greek, one meaning "removing" and the other meaning "the cover." Something that reveals what has been concealed is apocalyptic. Therefore, the name that is given to Revelation and to many other books that promise to reveal God's hidden plan is *apocalypse*.

Revelation is the only apocalyptic book in the New Testament, though there are sections of other books that are like it, most notably Mark 13, Matthew 24, and Luke 21. Apocalyptic writing typically has most of these characteristics:

(1) The writings claim to have been written several years earlier by a well-known person, to have been hidden until "just the right time in history," and to have surfaced only recently. Apocalyptic books deal with the present events in a highly symbolic way, therefore, as though the long-dead author had foreseen them much earlier.

(2) It takes the form of a report of vivid and frightening visions.

(3) It uses symbols, especially combinations of numbers (for example, the number seven meant completeness or perfection to the Jews) or animals or strange creatures that have special meanings.

(4) It emphasizes a present crisis in history. History is portrayed as a struggle between good and evil that now rages toward its final battle. The end is near, and the reader must remain faithful even though the force of evil seems overwhelming. Properly read, the signs of the times show that God is in control.

(5) History has strayed beyond the limits of humans to redeem it, and has fallen entirely into the province of evil. Rescue comes only from beyond history, only from God.

(6) It makes many allusions to other books, usually those of prophets or other apocalyptic writers. It can do this because an apocalypse is, from the beginning, a written book—unlike those of Old Testament prophets or those about Jesus, which were first spoken and then later written down by disciples. The author of an apocalypse has had his vision, and he has his reference books to find the words and symbols he needs in order to describe and interpret that vision. That way he can write in a way that other readers of prophecies and apocalypses can well understand.

The book of Revelation has most of those characteristics. Although it does not claim that its author lived in the past or that it lay hidden long and only recently came to light, it does rely on striking visions. Combinations of numerical and animal symbols appear on every page. It describes a crisis of great magnitude occurring in history, spiraling to its end, and soon. It ascribes its authorship to a writer who bears a famous name in the church.

Further, through each vision the writer testifies to God's coming intervention and to God's presence in the here and now—the evil powers only think they are in control. Allusions to Isaiah, Exodus, Daniel, Ezekiel, Jeremiah, and Zechariah enliven and inform nearly every vision and parable. The book was certainly a written product from the onset; John is often told to write what he sees, and in 1:3 he promises a blessing to those who read the book aloud in church.

The book of Revelation, then, is an apocalypse. It is also a powerful Christian political tract for its time that radically rejected the way the Romans saw history. From John's point of view, the very things that supported Rome were the cause of crisis. Wealth and power combined to entice Christians who wanted somehow to have both the fruits of luxury and the benefits of discipleship. John could not allow secular wealth and power the sole right to interpret history. He wrote against the nation that surrounded him and against the influence it was having on the church.

HOW TO READ THE BOOK OF REVELATION

After reading any other book in the New Testament, Revelation comes as quite a surprise. Its images, bold pictures, and strident voice may make a reader feel uneasy. Its message is disturbing. The fact that it is unrelenting in its insistence that we pay attention only makes us more uneasy. Add to that its display of violence and carnage, and it is little wonder that Christians turn away from its pages.

But the book can be read with great profit. Through even its stormiest passages come rays of hope. John did not intend simply to frighten his readers. He wanted to strengthen them. The way he wrote would have been familiar to first-century Christians. But, because we do not know their tradition, we often fail to see what John was up to.

The following eight suggestions may help you bear with John's book until you become at ease with it. When you do, it will become easier to see the vision of the light that drove him to decry the world's darkness.

These eight suggestions are not "keys" to the book. They do not pretend that Revelation is a single large and secret code. They do offer you a way of identifying several of the things John does. When you begin to see how he works, and to recognize the patterns he uses, you may feel encouraged to venture interpretations of your own.

(1) Revelation, while it is unique in the New Testament, was not unusual in its time. There had been other books like it, some in the Old Testament, and some elsewhere.

(2) John did not write in a vacuum. He had a library, and Revelation was written by quoting sources from several other books in his library. Whatever John's visions were, he turned often to his favorite books to help him describe what he saw and to interpret it to his readers. Among his favorite books were these from the Old Testament: Genesis, Exodus, Psalms, Isaiah, Ezekiel, Jeremiah, and Daniel.

(3) Notice the patterns in Revelation. There are several sets of sevens—letters to seven churches, seven seals, seven bowls. The number seven is symbolic is this book. It refers to perfection or to completeness. Thus, the seven churches represent not only themselves, but all of the church. And look at the progression of the book. View it as a single extended sermon, making one point in several ways, each way more dramatic and powerful than the one before.

(4) Think of a stage and all of its apparatus. Imagine John as the playwright. On stage is the drama of the historical events challenging the first-century church. Backstage is God, who knows the true meaning of those events and who wants the players on stage to understand them as well.

The stage setting, seen by the Christians, is the Greek culture and the Roman government. Because of that, the players interpret the events as though they were all caused by and controlled by the Greeks and Romans.

John's book puts up new scenery. He decorates the stage with important symbols from the Old Testament, symbols that remind the players that God controls history. He puts up scenes of great natural devastation, far beyond what humans could do, to call attention to the God of the Creation. The real meaning of history, he wants them to see, comes not from Rome but from God.

As you read Revelation, remember that it was first read by people who saw only evidence of Roman power and success. They needed to see scenes that reminded them of God's essential role in history.

(5) Imagine yourself in a time of historical duress, in the presence of great temptation and evil. What assurances would you want? What signs would you look for? How would you console and encourage your fellow Christians or your children? Which images and stories from your religious tradition would you call on to remind them and yourself that history belongs to God and that it is important to keep the faith? In other words, imagine yourself in the position of John or his readers.

(6) Read the book through without worrying about the precise meaning of all of its signs and symbols. Keep track of its cumulative effect on yourself. Pay special attention to the effects of such passages as Revelation 21:3-4.

(7) Read this book as though it were a series of stories. Don't try to force connections. Let the stories stand on their own; think about them; see what connections emerge in your mind.

(8) Don't force premature conclusions about what the book means. Some think it is a detailed prediction of the course of human history. Others think it is a dramatic collection of stories and teachings meant to encourage Christians at all times to be faithful. Others think other things. Christians throughout history have produced a great variety of approaches to this book. So don't feel rushed to come up with the definitive interpretation.

REVELATION

Greetings

1 A revelation of Jesus Christ, which God gave him to show his servants what must soon take place. Christ made it known by sending it through his angel to his servant John, ²who bore witness to the word of God and to the witness of Jesus Christ, including all that John saw. ³Favored is the one who reads the words of this prophecy out loud, and favored are those who listen to it being read, and keep what is written in it, for the time is near.

⁴John, to the seven churches that are in Asia:

Grace and peace to you from the one who is and was and is coming, and from the seven spirits that are before God's throne, ⁵and from Jesus Christ—the faithful witness, the firstborn from among the dead, and the ruler of the kings of the earth.

To the one who loves us and freed us from our sins by his blood, ⁶who made us a kingdom, priests to his God and Father—to him be glory and power forever and always. Amen.

⁷Look, he is coming with the clouds! Every eye will see him, including those who pierced him, and all the tribes of the earth will mourn because of him. This is so. Amen. ⁸"I am the Alpha and the Omega," says the Lord God, "the one who is and was and is coming, the Almighty."

Christ appears to John

⁹I, John, your brother who shares with you in the hardship, kingdom, and endurance that we have in Jesus, was on the island called Patmos because of the word of God and my witness about Jesus. ¹⁰I was in a Spirit-inspired trance on the Lord's day, and I heard behind me a loud voice that sounded like a trumpet. ¹¹It said, "Write down on a scroll whatever you see, and send it to the seven churches: to Ephesus, Smyrna, Pergamum, Thyatira, Sardis, Philadelphia, and Laodicea."

¹²I turned to see who was speaking to me, and when I turned, I saw seven oil lamps burning on top of seven gold stands. ¹³In the middle of the lampstands I saw someone who looked like the Human One.[a] He wore a robe that stretched down to his feet, and he had a gold sash around his chest. ¹⁴His head and hair were white as white wool—like snow—and his eyes were like a fiery flame. ¹⁵His feet were like fine brass that has been purified in a furnace, and his voice sounded like rushing water. ¹⁶He held seven stars in his right hand, and from his mouth came a sharp, two-edged sword. His appearance was like the sun shining with all its power.

[a] Or *Son of Man*

ANGELS OF THE SEVEN CHURCHES

Mentioned only in Revelation 1:20 and addressed individually in letters to the churches (Rev 2:1, 8, 12, 18; 3:1, 7, 14), these angels have been identified as guardian angels of the churches and as heavenly personifications of the churches on earth. They have been seen as human leaders, such as bishops, or as messengers sent to John (Rev 1:4), and have been equated to stars (Rev 1:20).

[17]When I saw him, I fell at his feet like a dead man. But he put his right hand on me and said, "Don't be afraid. I'm the first and the last, [18]and the living one. I was dead, but look! Now I'm alive forever and always. I have the keys of Death and the Grave. [19]So write down what you have seen, both the scene now before you and the things that are about to unfold after this. [20]As for the mystery of the seven stars that you saw in my right hand and the seven gold lampstands, here is what they mean: the seven stars are the angels of the seven churches, and the seven lampstands are the seven churches.

Message to Ephesus

2 "Write this to the angel of the church in Ephesus:

These are the words of the one who holds the seven stars in his right hand and walks among the seven gold lampstands: [2]I know your works, your labor, and your endurance. I also know that you don't put up with those who are evil. You have tested those who say they are apostles but are not, and you have found them to be liars. [3]You have shown endurance and put up with a lot for my name's sake, and you haven't gotten tired. [4]But I have this against you: you have let go of the love you had at first. [5]So remember the high point from which you have fallen. Change your hearts and lives and do the things you did at first. If you don't, I'm coming to you. I will move your lampstand from its place if you don't change your hearts and lives. [6]But you have this in your favor: you hate what the Nico-laitans are doing, which I also hate. [7]If you can hear, listen to what the Spirit is saying to the churches. I will allow those who emerge victorious to eat from the tree of life, which is in God's paradise.

Message to Smyrna

[8]"Write this to the angel of the church in Smyrna:

These are the words of the one who is the first and the last, who died and came back to life: [9]I know your hardship and poverty (though you are actually rich). I also know the hurtful things that have been spoken about you by those who say they are Jews (though they are not, but are really Satan's synagogue). [10]Don't be afraid of what you are going to suffer. Look! The devil is going to throw some of you into prison in order to test you. You will suffer hardship for ten days. Be faithful even to the point of death, and I will give you the crown of life. [11]If you can hear, listen to what the Spirit is saying to the churches. Those who emerge victorious won't be hurt by the second death.

Message to Pergamum

[12]"Write this to the angel of the church in Pergamum:

These are the words of the one who has the sharp, two-edged sword: [13]I know that you are living right where Satan's throne is. You are holding on to my name, and you didn't break faith with me even at the time that Antipas, my faithful witness, was killed among you, where Satan lives. [14]But I have a few things against you, because you have some there who follow Balaam's teaching.

PATMOS

Patmos is the Aegean island where John received and wrote his vision (Rev 1:9). Patmos was probably not the backwater that is often assumed, with local cults to Apollo and Artemis. The text does not allow us to know whether John was on the island voluntarily. In later legend he was exiled there by the Roman emperor himself. John writes that he is on Patmos "because of the word of God." This may mean that John went to Patmos to hear the word preached.

Balaam had taught Balak to trip up the Israelites so that they would eat food sacrificed
to idols and commit sexual immorality. [15] In
the same way, you have some who follow
the Nicolaitans' teaching. [16] So change your
hearts and lives. If you don't, I am coming
to you soon, and I will make war on them
with the sword that comes from my mouth.
[17] If you can hear, listen to what the Spirit
is saying to the churches. I will give those
who emerge victorious some of the hidden manna to eat. I will also give to each of
them a white stone with a new name written on it, which no one knows except the
one who receives it.

Message to Thyatira

[18] "Write this to the angel of the church
in Thyatira:

These are the words of God's Son, whose
eyes are like a fiery flame, and whose feet
are like fine brass. [19] I know your works,
your love and faithfulness, your service and
endurance. I also know that the works you
have done most recently are even greater
than those you did at first. [20] But I have this
against you: you put up with that woman,
Jezebel, who calls herself a prophet. You
allow her to teach and to mislead my servants into committing sexual immorality and eating food sacrificed to idols. [21] I
gave her time to change her heart and life,
but she refuses to change her life of prostitution. [22] Look! I'm throwing her onto
a sickbed. I am casting those who have
committed adultery with her into terrible
hardship—if they don't change their hearts

from following her practices—[23] and I will
even put her children to death with disease.
Then all the churches will know that I'm the
one who examines minds and hearts, and
that I will give to each of you what your
actions deserve. [24] As for the rest of you in
Thyatira—those of you who don't follow
this teaching and haven't learned the so-
called "deep secrets" of Satan—I won't burden you with anything else. [25] Just hold on
to what you have until I come. [26] To those
who emerge victorious, keeping my practices until the end, I will give authority over
the nations—[27] to rule the nations with an
iron rod and smash them like pottery—
[28] just as I received authority from my
Father. I will also give them the morning
star. [29] If you can hear, listen to what the
Spirit is saying to the churches.

Message to Sardis

3 "Write this to the angel of the church in
Sardis:

These are the words of the one who holds
God's seven spirits and the seven stars: I
know your works. You have the reputation
of being alive, and you are in fact dead.
[2] Wake up and strengthen whatever you
have left, teetering on the brink of death,
for I've found that your works are far from
complete in the eyes of my God. [3] So remember what you received and heard. Hold
on to it and change your hearts and lives. If
you don't wake up, I will come like a thief,
and you won't know what time I will come
upon you. [4] But you do have a few people in
Sardis who haven't stained their clothing.

PERGAMUM

A city in western Asia Minor. The city's name refers to a citadel, since it
was built on top of an imposing hill that rose a thousand feet above the valley
below. Located about 15 mi. from the Aegean Sea, Pergamum was a major
political, cultural, and religious center. A Christian congregation was established at Pergamum by the last third of the 1st cent. CE. In Revelation 2:12-
17 this church is commended for its faith, which remained unwavering even
when a Christian named Antipas was killed in the city, either by the authorities or by mob action.

They will walk with me clothed in white because they are worthy. ⁵Those who emerge victorious will wear white clothing like this. I won't scratch out their names from the scroll of life, but will declare their names in the presence of my Father and his angels. ⁶If you can hear, listen to what the Spirit is saying to the churches.

Message to Philadelphia

⁷"Write this to the angel of the church in Philadelphia:

These are the words of the one who is holy and true, who has the key of David. Whatever he opens, no one will shut; and whatever he shuts, no one opens. ⁸I know your works. Look! I have set in front of you an open door that no one can shut. You have so little power, and yet you have kept my word and haven't denied my name. ⁹Because of this I will make the people from Satan's synagogue (who say they are Jews and really aren't, but are lying)—I will make them come and bow down at your feet and realize that I have loved you. ¹⁰Because you kept my command to endure, I will keep you safe through the time of testing that is about to come over the whole world, to test those who live on earth. ¹¹I'm coming soon. Hold on to what you have so that no one takes your crown. ¹²As for those who emerge victorious, I will make them pillars in the temple of my God, and they will never leave it. I will write on them the name of my God and the name of the city of my

God, the New Jerusalem that comes down out of heaven from my God. I will also write on them my own new name. ¹³If you can hear, listen to what the Spirit is saying to the churches.

Message to Laodicea

¹⁴"Write this to the angel of the church in Laodicea:

These are the words of the Amen, the faithful and true witness, the ruler^b of God's creation. ¹⁵I know your works. You are neither cold nor hot. I wish that you were either cold or hot. ¹⁶So because you are lukewarm, and neither hot nor cold, I'm about to spit you out of my mouth. ¹⁷After all, you say, 'I'm rich, and I've grown wealthy, and I don't need a thing.' You don't realize that you are miserable, pathetic, poor, blind, and naked. ¹⁸My advice is that you buy gold from me that has been purified by fire so that you may be rich, and white clothing to wear so that your nakedness won't be shamefully exposed, and ointment to put on your eyes so that you may see. ¹⁹I correct and discipline those whom I love. So be earnest and change your hearts and lives. ²⁰Look! I'm standing at the door and knocking. If any hear my voice and open the door, I will come in to be with them, and will have dinner with them, and they will have dinner with me. ²¹As for those who emerge victorious, I will allow them to sit with me on my throne, just as I emerged victorious and sat down with my Father on

^b Or *beginning*

SARDIS

Sardis, located in the Roman province of Asia (present-day Turkey), was about 50 mi. from Smyrna and Ephesus. It was the capital of the Lydian kingdom in the 7th and 6th centuries BCE and the home of the legendary King Croesus, who ruled from ca. 560 to ca. 547 BCE. Throughout ancient history, it remained an important city for succeeding empires, serving as a key city for the Persian, Seleucid, and Roman administrators. Revelation 1:11 and 3:1-6 mention the city, and Obadiah 20 refers to Sardis as "Sepharad."

his throne. ²²If you can hear, listen to what the Spirit is saying to the churches."

John sees God's heavenly throne

4 After this I looked and there was a door that had been opened in heaven. The first voice that I had heard, which sounded like a trumpet, said to me, "Come up here, and I will show you what must take place after this." ²At once I was in a Spirit-inspired trance and I saw a throne in heaven, and someone was seated on the throne. ³The one seated there looked like jasper and carnelian, and surrounding the throne was a rainbow that looked like an emerald. ⁴Twenty-four thrones, with twenty-four elders seated upon them, surrounded the throne. The elders were dressed in white clothing and had gold crowns on their heads. ⁵From the throne came lightning, voices, and thunder. In front of the throne were seven flaming torches, which are the seven spirits of God. ⁶Something like a glass sea, like crystal, was in front of the throne.

In the center, by the throne, were four living creatures encircling the throne. These creatures were covered with eyes on the front and on the back. ⁷The first living creature was like a lion. The second living creature was like an ox. The third living creature had a face like a human being. And the fourth living creature was like an eagle in flight. ⁸Each of the four living creatures had six wings, and each was covered all around and on the inside with eyes. They never rest day or night, but keep on saying,

"Holy, holy, holy is the Lord God Almighty,
who was and is and is coming."

⁹Whenever the living creatures give glory, honor, and thanks to the one seated on the throne, who lives forever and always, ¹⁰the twenty-four elders fall before the one seated on the throne. They worship the one who lives forever and always. They throw down their crowns before the throne and say,

¹¹"You are worthy, our Lord and God,
to receive glory and honor and power,
because you created all things.
It is by your will that they existed
and were created."

The Lamb takes the scroll

5 Then I saw a scroll in the right hand of the one seated on the throne. It had writing on the front and the back, and it was sealed with seven seals. ²I saw a powerful angel, who proclaimed in a loud voice, "Who is worthy to open the scroll and break its seals?" ³But no one in heaven or on earth or under the earth could open the scroll or look inside it. ⁴So I began to weep and weep, because no one was found worthy to open the scroll or to look inside it. ⁵Then one of the elders said to me, "Don't weep. Look! The Lion of the tribe of Judah, the Root of David, has emerged victorious so that he can open the scroll and its seven seals."

⁶Then, in between the throne and the four living creatures and among the elders, I saw a Lamb, standing as if it had been slain. It had seven horns and seven eyes, which are God's seven spirits, sent out into the whole earth. ⁷He came forward and took the scroll from the right hand of the one seated on the throne. ⁸When he took the scroll, the four living creatures and the twenty-four elders fell down before the Lamb. Each held a harp and gold bowls full of incense, which are the prayers of the saints. ⁹They took up a new song, saying,

"You are worthy to take the scroll
and open its seals,
because you were slain,
and by your blood
you purchased for God
persons from every tribe, language,
people, and nation.
¹⁰You made them a kingdom and priests
to our God,
and they will rule on earth."

¹¹Then I looked, and I heard the sound of many angels surrounding the throne, the living creatures, and the elders. They numbered in the millions—thousands upon thousands. ¹²They said in a loud voice,

"Worthy is the slaughtered Lamb
to receive power, wealth, wisdom,
and might,
and honor, glory, and blessing."

¹³And I heard every creature in heaven and on earth and under the earth and in the sea—I heard everything everywhere say,

"Blessing, honor, glory, and power belong
  to the one seated on the throne
    and to the Lamb
      forever and always."
[14]Then the four living creatures said,
"Amen," and the elders fell down and worshipped.

Opening the first six seals

6 Then I looked on as the Lamb opened
one of the seven seals. I heard one of
the four living creatures say in a voice like
thunder, "Come!" [2]So I looked, and there
was a white horse. Its rider held a bow and
was given a crown. And he went forth from
victory to victory.

[3]When the Lamb opened the second
seal, I heard the second living creature say,
"Come!" [4]Out came another horse, fiery red.
Its rider was allowed to take peace from the
earth so that people would kill each other.
He was given a large sword.

[5]When he opened the third seal, I heard
the third living creature say, "Come!" So I
looked, and there was a black horse. Its
rider held a balance for weighing in his
hand. [6]I heard what sounded like a voice
from among the four living creatures. It
said, "A quart of wheat for a denarion,[c] and
three quarts of barley for a denarion, but
don't damage the olive oil and the wine."

[7]When he opened the fourth seal, I heard
the voice of the fourth living creature say,
"Come!" [8]So I looked, and there was a pale
green horse. Its rider's name was Death,
and the Grave was following right behind.
They were given authority over a fourth of
the earth, to kill by sword, famine, disease,
and the wild animals of the earth.

[9]When he opened the fifth seal, I saw
under the altar those who had been slaughtered on account of the word of God and
the witness they had given. [10]They cried out
with a loud voice, "Holy and true Master,
how long will you wait before you pass judgment? How long before you require justice
for our blood, which was shed by those who
live on earth?" [11]Each of them was given
a white robe, and they were told to rest a
little longer, until their fellow servants and
brothers and sisters—who were about to be
killed as they were—were finished.

[12]I looked on as he opened the sixth seal,
and there was a great earthquake. The sun
became black as funeral clothing, and the
entire moon turned red as blood. [13]The
stars of the sky fell to the earth as a fig tree
drops its fruit when shaken by a strong
wind. [14]The sky disappeared like a scroll
being rolled up, and every mountain and
island was moved from its place. [15]Then the
kings of the earth, the officials and the generals, the rich and the powerful, and everyone, slave and free, hid themselves in caves
and in the rocks of the mountains. [16]They
called to the mountains and the rocks, "Fall
on us and hide us from the face of the one
seated on the throne and from the Lamb's
wrath! [17]The great day of their wrath has
come, and who is able to stand?"

One hundred forty-four thousand sealed

7 After this I saw four angels standing at
the four corners of the earth. They held
back the earth's four winds so that no wind
would blow against the earth, the sea, or
any tree. [2]I saw another angel coming up
from the east, holding the seal of the living
God. He cried out with a loud voice to the
four angels who had been given the power
to damage the earth and sea. [3]He said,
"Don't damage the earth, the sea, or the
trees until we have put a seal on the foreheads of those who serve our God."

[4]Then I heard the number of those
who were sealed: one hundred forty-four
thousand, sealed from every tribe of the
Israelites:

[5]From the tribe of Judah,
    twelve thousand were sealed;
  from the tribe of Reuben,
    twelve thousand;
  from the tribe of Gad,
    twelve thousand;
[6]from the tribe of Asher,
    twelve thousand;
  from the tribe of Naphtali,
    twelve thousand;

[c]A denarion was a day's pay for a laborer.

from the tribe of Manasseh,
 twelve thousand;
⁷from the tribe of Simeon,
 twelve thousand;
from the tribe of Levi,
 twelve thousand;
from the tribe of Issachar,
 twelve thousand;
⁸from the tribe of Zebulun,
 twelve thousand;
from the tribe of Joseph,
 twelve thousand;
from the tribe of Benjamin,
 twelve thousand were sealed.

The great crowd and seventh seal

⁹After this I looked, and there was a great crowd that no one could number. They were from every nation, tribe, people, and language. They were standing before the throne and before the Lamb. They wore white robes and held palm branches in their hands. ¹⁰They cried out with a loud voice:

"Victory belongs to our God
 who sits on the throne,
 and to the Lamb."

¹¹All the angels stood in a circle around the throne, and around the elders and the four living creatures. They fell facedown before the throne and worshipped God, ¹²saying,

"Amen! Blessing and glory
 and wisdom and thanksgiving
 and honor and power and might
 be to our God forever and always.
 Amen."

¹³Then one of the elders said to me, "Who are these people wearing white robes, and where did they come from?"

¹⁴I said to him, "Sir, you know."

Then he said to me, "These people have come out of great hardship. They have washed their robes and made them white in the Lamb's blood. ¹⁵This is the reason they are before God's throne. They worship him day and night in his temple, and the one seated on the throne will shelter them. ¹⁶They won't hunger or thirst anymore. No sun or scorching heat will beat down on them, ¹⁷because the Lamb who is in the midst of the throne will shepherd them. He will lead them to the springs of life-giving water,ᵈ and God will wipe away every tear from their eyes." ¹Then, when the Lamb opened the seventh seal, there was silence in heaven for about half an hour.

The first four trumpet plagues

²Then I saw the seven angels who stand before God, and seven trumpets were given to them. ³Another angel came and stood at the altar, and he held a gold bowl for burning incense. He was given a large amount of incense, in order to offer it on behalf of the prayers of all the saints on the gold altar in front of the throne. ⁴The smoke of the incense offered for the prayers of the saints rose up before God from the angel's hand. ⁵Then the angel took the incense container and filled it with fire from the altar. He threw it down to the earth, and there were thunder, voices, lightning, and an earthquake.

⁶Then the seven angels who held the seven trumpets got ready to blow them. ⁷The first angel blew his trumpet, and hail and fire mixed with blood appeared, and was thrown down to the earth. A third of the earth was burned up. A third of the trees were burned up. All the green grass was burned up. ⁸Then the second angel blew his trumpet, and something like a huge mountain burning with fire was thrown down into the sea. A third of the sea became blood, ⁹a third of the creatures living in the sea died, and a third of the ships were destroyed. ¹⁰Then the third angel blew his trumpet, and a great star, burning like a torch, fell from heaven. It fell on a third of the rivers and springs of water. ¹¹The star's name is Wormwood, and a third of the waters became wormwood, and many people died from the water, because it became so bitter. ¹²Then the fourth angel blew his trumpet, and a third of the sun was struck, and a third of the moon, and a third of the stars so that a third of them became dark. The day lost a third of its light, and the night lost a third of its light too.

ᵈOr the water of life

[13] Then I looked and I heard an eagle flying high overhead. It said with a loud voice, "Horror, horror, oh! The horror for those who live on earth because of the blasts of the remaining trumpets that the three angels are about to blow!"

The fifth and sixth trumpet plagues

9 Then the fifth angel blew his trumpet, and I saw a star that had fallen from heaven to earth, and he was given the key to the shaft of the abyss. [2] He opened the shaft of the abyss; and smoke rose up from the shaft, like smoke from a huge furnace. The sun and air were darkened by the smoke from the shaft. [3] Then locusts came forth from the smoke and onto the earth. They were given power like the power that scorpions have on the earth. [4] They were told not to hurt the grass of the earth or any green plant or any tree. They could only hurt the people who didn't have the seal of God on their foreheads. [5] The locusts weren't allowed to kill them, but only to make them suffer for five months—and the suffering they inflict is like that of a scorpion when it strikes a person. [6] In those days people will seek death, but they won't find it. They will want to die, but death will run away from them.

[7] The locusts looked like horses ready for battle. On their heads were what seemed to be gold crowns. Their faces were like human faces, [8] their hair was like women's hair, and their teeth were like lions' teeth. [9] In front they had what seemed to be iron armor upon their chests, and the sound of their wings was like the sound of many chariots and horses racing into battle.

[10] They also have tails with stingers, just like scorpions; and in their tails is their power to hurt people for five months. [11] Their king is an angel from the abyss, whose Hebrew name is Abaddon,[e] and whose Greek name is Apollyon.[f]

[12] The first horror has passed. Look! Two horrors are still coming after this.

[13] Then the sixth angel blew his trumpet, and I heard a voice from the four horns of the gold altar that is before God. [14] It said to the sixth angel, who had the trumpet, "Release the four angels who are bound at the great river Euphrates." [15] Then the four angels who had been made ready for that hour, day, month, and year were released to kill a third of humankind. [16] The number of cavalry troops was two hundred million. I heard their number. [17] And this is the way I saw the horses and their riders in the vision: they had breastplates that were fiery red, dark blue, and yellow as sulfur. The horses' heads were like lions' heads, and out of their mouths came fire, smoke, and sulfur. [18] By these three plagues a third of humankind was killed: by the fire, smoke, and sulfur coming out of their mouths. [19] The horses' power is in their mouths and their tails, for their tails are like snakes with heads that inflict injuries.

[20] The rest of humankind, who weren't killed by these plagues, didn't change their hearts and lives and turn from their handiwork. They didn't stop worshipping demons and idols made of gold, silver, bronze, stone, and wood—idols that can't see or hear or walk. [21] They didn't turn away from their murders, their spells and drugs, their sexual immorality, or their stealing.

[e] Destruction [f] Destroyer

APOLLYON

The name of the ruler of the abyss in Revelation 9:11 and a Greek translation of the Hebrew name Abaddon, which means, "destroyer." Ancient Jewish and Christian writers use many names for the leader of the demons, including Satan, Beelzebul, Mastema, and Semyaza.

John receives the open scroll

10 Then I saw another powerful angel coming down from heaven. He was robed with a cloud, with a rainbow over his head. His face was like the sun, and his feet were like fiery pillars. [2]He held an open scroll in his hand. He put his right foot on the sea and his left foot on the land. [3]He called out with a loud voice like a lion roaring, and when he called out, the seven thunders raised their voices. [4]When the seven thunders spoke, I was about to write, but I heard a voice from heaven say, "Seal up what the seven thunders have said, and don't write it down."

[5]Then the angel I saw standing on the sea and on the land raised his right hand to heaven. [6]He swore by the one who lives forever and always, who created heaven and what is in it, the earth and what is in it, and the sea and what is in it, and said, "The time is up. [7]In the days when the seventh angel blows his trumpet, God's mysterious purpose will be accomplished, fulfilling the good news he gave to his servants the prophets."

[8]Then the voice I heard from heaven spoke to me again and said, "Go, take the opened scroll from the hand of the angel who stands on the sea and on the land." [9]So I went to the angel and told him to give me the scroll. He said to me, "Take it and eat it. It will make you sick to your stomach, but sweet as honey in your mouth." [10]So I took the scroll from the angel's hand and ate it. And it was sweet as honey in my mouth, but when I swallowed it, it made my stomach churn. [11]I was told, "You must prophesy again about many peoples, nations, languages, and kings."

Two witnesses

11 Then I was given a measuring rod, which was like a pole. And I was told, "Get up and measure God's temple, the altar, and those who worship there. [2]But don't measure the court outside the temple. Leave that out, because it has been given to the nations, and they will trample the holy city underfoot for forty-two months. [3]And I will allow my two witnesses to prophesy for one thousand two hundred sixty days, wearing mourning clothes. [4]These are the two olive trees and the two lampstands that stand before the Lord of the earth. [5]If anyone wants to hurt them, fire comes out of their mouth and burns up their enemies. So if anyone wants to hurt them, they have to be killed in this way. [6]They have the power to close up the sky so that no rain will fall for as long as they prophesy. They also have power over the waters, to turn them into blood, and to strike the earth with any plague, as often as they wish.

[7]"When they have finished their witnessing, the beast that comes up from the abyss will make war on them, gain victory over them, and kill them. [8]Their dead bodies will lie on the street of the great city that is spiritually called Sodom and Egypt, where also their Lord was crucified. [9]And for three and a half days, members of the peoples, tribes, languages, and nations will look at their dead bodies, but they won't let their dead bodies be put in a tomb. [10]Those who live on earth will rejoice over them. They will celebrate and give each other gifts, because these two prophets had brought such pain to those who live on earth.

[11]"But after three and a half days, the breath of life from God entered them, and they stood on their feet. Great fear came over those who saw them. [12]Then they heard a loud voice from heaven say to them, 'Come up here.' And they went up to heaven in a cloud, while their enemies watched them. [13]At that hour there was a great earthquake, and a tenth of the city fell. Seven thousand people were killed by the earthquake, and the rest were afraid and gave glory to the God of heaven."

[14]The second horror is over. The third horror is coming soon.

Seventh trumpet

[15]Then the seventh angel blew his trumpet, and there were loud voices in heaven saying,

"The kingdom of the world has become
the kingdom of our Lord and his Christ,
and he will rule forever and always."

¹⁶ Then the twenty-four elders, who were seated on their thrones before God, fell on their faces and worshipped God. ¹⁷ They said,

"We give thanks to you,
Lord God Almighty,
who is and was,
    for you have taken your great power
        and enforced your rule.
¹⁸ The nations were enraged,
    but your wrath came.
The time came for the dead to be judged.
The time came to reward your servants,
    the prophets and saints,
    and those who fear your name,
        both small and great,
    and to destroy those
        who destroy the earth."

¹⁹ Then God's temple in heaven was opened, and the chest containing his covenant appeared in his temple. There were lightning, voices, thunder, an earthquake, and large hail.

A woman, her child, and the dragon

12 Then a great sign appeared in heaven: a woman clothed with the sun, with the moon under her feet and a crown of twelve stars on her head. ² She was pregnant, and she cried out because she was in labor, in pain from giving birth. ³ Then another sign appeared in heaven: it was a great fiery red dragon, with seven heads and ten horns, and seven royal crowns on his heads. ⁴ His tail swept down a third of

MICHAEL

1. An Asherite, the father of Sethur, who was one of the 12 spies sent to reconnoiter in Canaan (Num 13:13).

2. A Gadite who settled in Bashan in the days of Jotham and Jeroboam II (1 Chron 5:13).

3. A Gadite, the son of Jeshishai and father of Gilead (1 Chron 5:14).

4. A Levite singer, the great-grandfather of Asaph (1 Chron 6:40).

5. An Issacharite, son of Izrahiah, who served as a military leader in the time of David (1 Chron 7:3).

6. A Benjaminite, son of Beraiah, who resided in Jerusalem (1 Chron 8:16).

7. A military leader from the tribe of Manasseh who deserted Saul at Ziklag and was made a commander of David's forces (1 Chron 12:20).

8. An Issacharite, father of Omri, who oversaw Issachar during David's reign (1 Chron 27:18).

9. A son of King Jehoshaphat of Judah, who was assassinated when his older brother Jehoram assumed the throne (2 Chron 21:2-4).

10. The father of Zebadiah, who led 80 men back from Babylon with Ezra in the time of Artaxerxes (Ezra 8:8).

11. Archangel and heavenly prince. Michael and Gabriel are the only two angels mentioned by name in the Bible. In the OT Michael is identified only at Daniel 10:13, 21; 12:1, where he is described as "one of the highest leaders" or the "great leader" in charge of God's people.

In the NT, Michael is mentioned by name only twice, at Jude 9 and Revelation 12:7.

heaven's stars and threw them to the earth. The dragon stood in front of the woman who was about to give birth so that when she gave birth, he might devour her child. [5] She gave birth to a son, a male child who is to rule all the nations with an iron rod. Her child was snatched up to God and his throne. [6] Then the woman fled into the desert, where God has prepared a place for her. There she will be taken care of for one thousand two hundred sixty days.

Michael and the dragon

[7] Then there was war in heaven: Michael and his angels fought the dragon. The dragon and his angels fought back, [8] but they did not prevail, and there was no longer any place for them in heaven. [9] So the great dragon was thrown down. The old snake, who is called the devil and Satan, the deceiver of the whole world, was thrown down to the earth; and his angels were thrown down with him. [10] Then I heard a loud voice in heaven say,

"Now the salvation and power
   and kingdom of our God,
   and the authority of his Christ
      have come.
The accuser of our brothers and sisters,
   who accuses them day and night
      before our God,
   has been thrown down.
[11] They gained the victory over him
   on account of the blood of the Lamb
   and the word of their witness.
Love for their own lives
   didn't make them afraid to die.
[12] Therefore, rejoice, you heavens
   and you who dwell in them.
But oh! The horror for the earth and sea!
   The devil has come down to you
      with great rage,
   for he knows that he only has
      a short time."

The dragon pursues the woman

[13] When the dragon saw that he had been thrown down to the earth, he chased the woman who had given birth to the male child. [14] But the woman was given the two wings of the great eagle so that she could fly to her place in the desert. There she would be taken care of—out of the snake's reach—for a time and times and half a time. [15] Then from his mouth the snake poured a river of water after the woman so that the river would sweep her away. [16] But the earth helped the woman. The earth opened its mouth and swallowed the river that the dragon poured out of his mouth. [17] So the dragon was furious with the woman, and he went off to make war on the rest of her children, on those who keep God's commandments and hold firmly to the witness of Jesus.

The beast from the sea

[18] Then the dragon stood on the seashore, [1] and I saw a beast coming up out of the sea. It had ten horns and seven heads. Each of its horns was decorated with a royal crown, and on its heads were blasphemous names. [2] The beast I saw was like a leopard. Its feet were like a bear's, and its mouth was like a lion's mouth. The dragon gave it his power, throne, and great authority. [3] One of its heads appeared to have been slain and killed, but its deadly wound was healed. So the whole earth was amazed and followed the beast. [4] They worshipped the dragon because it had given the beast its authority. They worshipped the beast and said, "Who is like the beast, and who can fight against it?"

[5] The beast was given a mouth that spoke boastful and blasphemous things, and it was given authority to act for forty-two months. [6] It opened its mouth to speak blasphemies against God. It blasphemed God's name and his dwelling place (that is, those who dwell in heaven).

[7] It was also allowed to make war on the saints and to gain victory over them. It was given authority over every tribe, people, language, and nation. [8] All who live on earth worshipped it, all whose names hadn't been written—from the time the earth was made—in the scroll of life of the Lamb who was slain. [9] Whoever has ears must listen: [10] If any are to be taken captive, then into captivity they will go. If any are to be killed by the sword, then by the sword they will be

killed. This calls for endurance and faithfulness on the part of the saints.

The beast from the land

[11]Then I saw another beast coming up from the earth. It had two horns like a lamb, but it was speaking like a dragon. [12]It exercises all the authority of the first beast in its presence. It also makes the earth and those who live in it worship the first beast, whose fatal wound was healed. [13]It does great signs so that it even makes fire come down from heaven to earth in the presence of the people. [14]It deceives those who live on earth by the signs that it was allowed to do in the presence of the beast. It told those who live on earth to make an image for the beast who had been wounded by the sword and yet came to life again. [15]It was allowed to give breath to the beast's image so that the beast's image would even speak and cause anyone who didn't worship the beast's image to be put to death. [16]It forces everyone—the small and great, the rich and poor, the free and slaves—to have a mark put on their right hand or on their forehead. [17]It will not allow anyone to make a purchase or sell anything unless the person has the mark with the beast's name or the number of its name. [18]This calls for wisdom. Let the one who understands calculate the beast's number, for it's a human being's number. Its number is six hundred sixty-six.

The Lamb and the one hundred forty-four thousand

14 Then I looked, and there was the Lamb, standing on Mount Zion. With him were one hundred forty-four thousand who had his name and his Father's name written on their foreheads. [2]I heard a sound from heaven that was like the sound of rushing water and loud thunder. The sound I heard was like that of harpists playing their harps. [3]They sing a new song in front of the throne, the four living creatures, and the elders. And no one could learn the song except the one hundred forty-four thousand who had been purchased from the earth. [4]They weren't defiled with women, for these people who follow the Lamb wherever he goes are virgins. They were purchased from among humankind as early produce for God and the Lamb. [5]No lie came from their mouths; they are blameless.

Messages of three angels

[6]Then I saw another angel flying high overhead with eternal good news to proclaim to those who live on earth, and to every nation, tribe, language, and people. [7]He said in

BABYLON (NT)

The word *Babylon* occurs 12 times in the NT: four times in Matthew's genealogy of Jesus, once in Acts, once in 1 Peter, and six times in Revelation. In Matthew's genealogy the references to Babylon help organize the lineage of Jesus into three historical periods: Abraham to David, David to the Babylonian Exile, and the exile to Jesus the Christ (Matt 1:11, 12, 17). The Babylonian Exile began in the early 6th century BCE and marked the end of Israel's Davidic monarchy that ruled from Jerusalem. First Peter mentions Babylon once (5:13), but here the term is a political metaphor for Roman rule.

Half the NT references to Babylon come in the book of Revelation, where the term also serves as a metaphor for Rome. Revelation's attitude toward the Roman Empire is summarized in Revelation 14:8 when an angel proclaims, "Fallen, fallen is Babylon the great! She made all the nations drink the wine of her lustful passion."

a loud voice, "Fear God and give him glory, for the hour of his judgment has come. Worship the one who made heaven and earth, the sea and springs of water."

[8] Another angel, a second one, followed and said, "Fallen, fallen is Babylon the great! She made all the nations drink the wine of her lustful passion."

[9] Then another angel, a third one, followed them and said in a loud voice, "If any worship the beast and its image, and receive a mark on their foreheads or their hands, [10] they themselves will also drink the wine of God's passionate anger, poured full strength into the cup of his wrath. They will suffer the pain of fire and sulfur in the presence of the holy angels and the Lamb. [11] The smoke of their painful suffering goes up forever and always. There is no rest day or night for those who worship the beast and its image, and those who receive the mark of its name."

[12] This calls for the endurance of the saints, who keep God's commandments and keep faith with Jesus.

[13] And I heard a voice from heaven say, "Write this: Favored are the dead who die in the Lord from now on."

"Yes," says the Spirit, "so they can rest from their labors, because their deeds follow them."

Two harvests of the earth

[14] Then I looked, and there was a white cloud. On the cloud was seated someone who looked like the Human One.[g] He had a gold crown on his head and a sharp sickle in his hand. [15] Another angel came out of the temple, calling in a loud voice to the one seated on the cloud: "Use your sickle to reap the harvest, for the time to harvest has come, and the harvest of the earth is ripe." [16] So the one seated on the cloud swung his sickle over the earth, and the earth was harvested.

[17] Then another angel came out of the temple in heaven, and he also had a sharp sickle. [18] Still another angel, who has power over fire, came out from the altar. He said in a loud voice to the one who had the sharp

sickle, "Use your sharp sickle to cut the clusters in the vineyard of the earth, because its grapes are ripe." [19] So the angel swung his sickle into the earth, and cut the vineyard of the earth, and he put what he reaped into the great winepress of God's passionate anger. [20] Then the winepress was trampled outside the city, and the blood came out of the winepress as high as the horses' bridles for almost two hundred miles.[h]

Song of Moses and the Lamb

15 Then I saw another great and awe-inspiring sign in heaven. There were seven angels with seven plagues—and these are the last, for with them God's anger is brought to an end. [2] Then I saw what appeared to be a sea of glass mixed with fire. Those who gained victory over the beast, its image, and the number of its name were standing by the glass sea, holding harps from God. [3] They sing the song of Moses, God's servant, and the song of the Lamb, saying,

"Great and awe-inspiring
      are your works,
   Lord God Almighty.
   Just and true are your ways,
      king of the nations.
[4] Who won't fear you, Lord,
      and glorify your name?
      You alone are holy.
   All nations will come and fall down
      in worship before you,
         for your acts of justice
         have been revealed."

Seven bowl plagues

[5] After this I looked, and the temple in heaven—that is, the tent of witness—was opened. [6] The seven angels, who have the seven plagues, came out of the temple. They were clothed in pure bright linen and had gold sashes around their waists. [7] Then one of the four living creatures gave the seven angels seven gold bowls full of the anger of the God who lives forever and always. [8] The temple was filled with smoke from God's glory and power, and no one could go into

[g] Or Son of Man   [h] Or one thousand six hundred stades

the temple until the seven plagues of the seven last angels were brought to an end. **16** Then I heard a loud voice from the temple say to the seven angels, "Go and pour out the seven bowls of God's anger on the earth." [2]So the first angel poured his bowl on the earth, and a nasty and terrible sore appeared on the people who had the beast's mark and worshipped its image. [3]The second angel poured his bowl into the sea, and the sea turned into blood, like the blood of a corpse, and every living thing in the sea died. [4]The third angel poured his bowl into the rivers and springs of water, and they turned into blood. [5]Then I heard the angel of the waters say,

"You are just, holy one, who is and was,
    because you have given
        these judgments.
[6] They poured out the blood
    of saints and prophets,
        and you have given them blood
    to drink. They deserve it!"
[7] And I heard the altar say,
"Yes, Lord God Almighty,
    your judgments are true and just."

[8]The fourth angel poured his bowl on the sun, and it was allowed to burn people with fire. [9]The people were burned by intense heat, and they cursed the name of the God who had power over these plagues. But they didn't change their hearts and lives and give him glory. [10]The fifth angel poured his bowl over the beast's throne, and darkness covered its kingdom. People bit their tongues because of their pain, [11]and they

cursed the God of heaven because of their pains and sores; but they didn't turn away from what they had done.

[12]Then the sixth angel poured his bowl on the great river Euphrates. Its water was dried up so that the way was ready for the kings from the east. [13]Then I saw three unclean spirits, like frogs, come from the dragon's mouth, the beast's mouth, and the mouth of the false prophet. [14]These are demonic spirits that do signs. They go out to the kings of the whole world, to gather them for battle on the great day of God the Almighty. ([15]Look! I'm coming like a thief! Favored are those who stay awake and clothed so that they don't go around naked and exposed to shame.) [16]The spirits gathered them at the place that is called in Hebrew, Harmagedon.[i]

[17]Then the seventh angel poured his bowl into the air, and a loud voice came out from the temple, from the throne, saying, "It is done!" [18]There were lightning strikes, voices, and thunder, and a great earthquake occurred. The earthquake was greater than any that have occurred since there have been people on earth. [19]The great city split into three parts, and the cities of the nations fell. God remembered Babylon the great so that he gave her the wine cup of his furious anger. [20]Every island fled, and the mountains disappeared. [21]Huge hailstones weighing about one hundred pounds came down from heaven on the people. They cursed God for the plague of hail, because the plague was so terrible.

[i]Or Armageddon

HARMAGEDON/ARMAGEDDON

Occurs only in Revelation 16:16 as the site of an end-time battle that prepares the way for the millennium. The term *harmagedon* derives from the Hebrew for "mount of Megiddo." Several references to Megiddo occur in the OT. The ancient city of Megiddo (Josh 12:21; 17:11; Judg 1:27; 1 Kgs 4:12; 9:15; 2 Kgs 9:27; 1 Chron 7:29) sat on a mound in northwestern Palestine not far from Mount Carmel. Megiddo was next to two major trade routes, one of which carried traffic from Egypt to Syria.

Babylon and the beast

17 Then one of the seven angels who had the seven bowls spoke with me. "Come, he said, I will show you the judgment upon the great prostitute, who is seated on deep waters. ²The kings of the earth have committed sexual immorality with her, and those who live on earth have become drunk with the wine of her whoring."

³Then he brought me in a Spirit-inspired trance to a desert. There I saw a woman seated on a scarlet beast that was covered with blasphemous names. It had seven heads and ten horns. ⁴The woman wore purple and scarlet clothing, and she glittered with gold and jewels and pearls. In her hand she held a gold cup full of the vile and impure things that came from her activity as a prostitute. ⁵A name—a mystery—was written on her forehead: "Babylon the great, the mother of prostitutes and the vile things of the earth." ⁶I saw that the woman was drunk on the blood of the saints and the blood of Jesus' witnesses. I was completely stunned when I saw her.

⁷Then the angel said to me, "Why are you amazed? I will tell you the mystery of the woman and the seven-headed, ten-horned beast that carries her. ⁸The beast that you saw was and is not, and is about to come up out of the abyss and go to destruction. Those who live on earth, whose names haven't been written in the scroll of life from the time the earth was made, will be amazed when they see the beast, because it was and is not and will again be present. ⁹This calls for an understanding mind. The seven heads are seven mountains on which the woman is seated. They are also seven kings. ¹⁰Five kings have fallen, the one is, and the other hasn't yet come. When that king comes, he must remain for only a short time. ¹¹As for the beast that was and is not, it is itself an eighth king that belongs to the seven, and it is going to destruction. ¹²The ten horns that you saw are ten kings, who haven't yet received royal power. But they will receive royal authority for an hour, along with the beast. ¹³These kings will be of one mind, and they will give their power and authority to the beast. ¹⁴They will make war on the Lamb, but the Lamb will emerge victorious, for he is Lord of lords and King of kings. Those with him are called, chosen, and faithful."

¹⁵Then he said to me, "The waters that you saw, where the prostitute is seated, are peoples, crowds, nations, and languages. ¹⁶As for the ten horns that you saw, they and the beast will hate the prostitute. They will destroy her and strip her bare. They will devour her flesh and burn her with fire ¹⁷because God moved them to carry out his purposes. That is why they will be of one mind and give their royal power to the beast, until God's words have been accomplished. ¹⁸The woman whom you saw is the great city that rules over the kings of the earth."

Babylon's fall

18 After this I saw another angel coming down from heaven. He had great authority, and the earth was filled with light because of his glory. ²He called out with a loud voice, saying, "Fallen, fallen is Babylon the great! She has become a home for demons and a lair for every unclean spirit. She is a lair for every unclean bird, and a lair for every unclean and disgusting beast ³because all the nations have fallenʲ due to the wine of her lustful passion. The kings of the earth committed sexual immorality with her, and the merchants of the earth became rich from the power of her loose and extravagant ways."

⁴Then I heard another voice from heaven say, "Come out of her, my people, so that you don't take part in her sins and don't receive any of her plagues. ⁵Her sins have piled up as high as heaven, and God remembered her unjust acts. ⁶Give her what she has given to others. Give her back twice as much for what she has done. In the cup that she has poured, pour her twice as much. ⁷To the extent that she glorified herself and indulged her loose and extravagant ways, give her pain and grief. In her heart she says, 'I sit like a queen! I'm not a widow.

ʲCritical editions of the Gk New Testament read *have drunk.*

I'll never see grief.' [8]This is why her plagues will come in a single day—deadly disease, grief, and hunger. She will be consumed by fire because the Lord God who judges her is powerful.

[9]"The kings of the earth, who committed sexual immorality with her and shared her loose and extravagant ways, will weep and mourn over her when they see the smoke from her burning. [10]They will stand a long way off because they are afraid of the pain she suffers, and they will say, 'Oh, the horror! Babylon, you great city, you powerful city! In a single hour your judgment has come.'

[11]"The merchants of the earth will weep and mourn over her, for no one buys their cargoes anymore—[12]cargoes of gold, silver, jewels, and pearls; fine linen, purple, silk, and scarlet; all those things made of scented wood, ivory, fine wood, bronze, iron, and marble; [13]cinnamon, incense, fragrant ointment, and frankincense; wine, oil, fine flour, and wheat; cattle, sheep, horses, and carriages; and slaves, even human lives. [14]'The fruit your whole being craved has gone from you. All your glitter and glamour are lost to you, never ever to be found again.'

[15]"The merchants who sold these things, and got so rich by her, will stand a long way off because they fear the pain she suffers. They will weep and mourn, and say, [16]'Oh, the horror! The great city that wore fine linen, purple, and scarlet, who glittered with gold, jewels, and pearls—[17]in just one hour such great wealth was destroyed.'

"Every sea captain, every seafarer, sailors, and all who make their living on the sea stood a long way off. [18]They cried out as they saw the smoke from her burning and said, 'What city was ever like the great city?' [19]They threw dust on their heads, and they cried out, weeping and mourning. They said, 'Oh, the horror! The great city, where all who have ships at sea became so rich by her prosperity—in just one hour she was destroyed. [20]Rejoice over her, heaven—you saints, apostles, and prophets—because God has condemned her as she condemned you.'"

[21]Then a powerful angel picked up a stone that was like a huge millstone and threw it into the sea, saying, "With such violent force the great city of Babylon will be thrown down, and it won't be found anymore. [22]The sound of harpists and musicians, of pipers and trumpeters, will never be heard among you again. No craftsman of any kind will ever be found among you again. The sound of the hand mill will never be heard among you again. [23]The light of a lamp will never shine among you again. The sound of a bridegroom and bride will never be heard among you again because your merchants ran the world, because all the nations were deceived by the spell you cast, and because [24]the blood of prophets, of saints, and of all who have been slaughtered on the earth was found among you."[k]

Celebration in heaven

19 After this I heard what sounded like a huge crowd in heaven. They said,

"Hallelujah! The salvation and glory and
 power of our God!
[2] His judgments are true and just,
 because he judged the great prostitute,
  who ruined the earth by her whoring,
 and he exacted the penalty
  for the blood of his servants
  from her hand."
[3]Then they said a second time,
"Hallelujah! Smoke goes up from her
 forever and always."

[4]The twenty-four elders and the four living creatures fell down and worshipped God, who is seated on the throne, and they said, "Amen. Hallelujah!"

[5]Then a voice went out from the throne and said,

"Praise our God, all you his servants,
 and you who fear him,
  both small and great."

[6]And I heard something that sounded like a huge crowd, like rushing water and powerful thunder. They said,

"Hallelujah! The Lord our God,
 the Almighty,
  exercised his royal power!

[k]Or her

⁷ Let us rejoice and celebrate,
    and give him the glory,
    for the wedding day of the Lamb
        has come,
    and his bride has made herself ready.
⁸ She was given fine, pure white linen
        to wear,
    for the fine linen
        is the saints' acts of justice."

⁹ Then the angel said to me, "Write this: Favored are those who have been invited to the wedding banquet of the Lamb." He said to me, "These are the true words of God." ¹⁰ Then I fell at his feet to worship him. But he said, "Don't do that! I'm a servant just like you and your brothers and sisters who hold firmly to the witness of Jesus. Worship God! The witness of Jesus is the spirit of prophecy!"

Christ defeats the beast

¹¹ Then I saw heaven opened, and there was a white horse. Its rider was called Faithful and True, and he judges and makes war justly. ¹² His eyes were like a fiery flame, and on his head were many royal crowns. He has a name written on him that no one knows but he himself. ¹³ He wore a robe dyed[1] with blood, and his name was called the Word of God. ¹⁴ Heaven's armies, wearing fine linen that was white and pure, were following him on white horses. ¹⁵ From his mouth comes a sharp sword that he will use to strike down the nations. He is the one who will rule them with an iron rod. And he is the one who will trample the winepress of the Almighty God's passionate anger. ¹⁶ He has a name written on his robe and on his thigh: King of kings and Lord of lords.

¹⁷ Then I saw an angel standing in the sun, and he called out with a loud voice and said to all the birds flying high overhead, "Come and gather for God's great supper. ¹⁸ Come and eat the flesh of kings, the flesh of generals, the flesh of the powerful, and the flesh of horses and their riders. Come and eat the flesh of all, both free and slave, both small and great." ¹⁹ Then I saw that the beast and the kings of the earth and their armies had gathered to make war against the rider on the horse and his army. ²⁰ But the beast was seized, along with the false prophet who had done signs in the beast's presence. (He had used the signs to deceive people into receiving the beast's mark and into worshipping the beast's image.) The two of them were thrown alive into the fiery lake that burns with sulfur. ²¹ The rest were killed by the sword that comes from the mouth of the rider on the horse, and all the birds ate their fill of their flesh.

Satan confined

20 Then I saw an angel coming down from heaven, holding in his hand the key to the abyss and a huge chain. ² He

---

[1]Critical editions of the Gk New Testament read *dipped* or *covered with*.

MAGOG

Land from which Gog comes to make war on God's people (Ezek 38–39). Although it appears in the Table of Nations (Gen 10:2), in Ezekiel's use Magog is not an actual nation but symbolizes the archetypal northern enemy. Magog's armies come to make war on Israel and are defeated by God. Revelation draws on Ezekiel's imagery in portraying scenes of God's judgment. Gog and Magog appear metaphorically as opponents of God, the "nations that are at the four corners of the earth" (Rev 20:8). The narration of their destruction by fire echoes Ezekiel (see Ezek 38:22), as does the battle scene of Revelation 19:11-21 (esp. Rev 19:17-18, 21; cf. Ezek 39:4, 17-20). Magog also appears in end-time battle scenes in rabbinic writings.

seized the dragon, the old snake, who is the devil and Satan, and bound him for a thousand years. ³He threw him into the abyss, then locked and sealed it over him. This was to keep him from continuing to deceive the nations until the thousand years were over. After this he must be released for a little while.

The saints rule with Christ

⁴Then I saw thrones, and people took their seats on them, and judgment was given in their favor.ᵐ They were the ones who had been beheaded for their witness to Jesus and God's word, and those who hadn't worshipped the beast or its image, who hadn't received the mark on their forehead or hand. They came to life and ruled with Christ for one thousand years. ⁵The rest of the dead didn't come to life until the thousand years were over. This is the first resurrection. ⁶Favored and holy are those who have a share in the first resurrection. The second death has no power over them, but they will be priests of God and of Christ, and will rule with him for one thousand years.

Satan's defeat

⁷When the thousand years are over, Satan will be released from his prison. ⁸He will go out to deceive the nations that are at the four corners of the earth—Gog and Magog. He will gather them for battle. Their number is like the sand of the sea. ⁹They came up across the whole earth and surrounded the saints' camp, the city that God loves. But fire came down from heaven and consumed them. ¹⁰Then the devil, who had deceived them, was thrown into the lake of fire and sulfur, where the beast and the false prophet also were. There painful suffering will be inflicted upon them day and night, forever and always.

ᵐOr to them

SATAN (REVELATION)

In the beginning chapters of Revelation, "Satan" is used when John writes to the angels in the seven churches. Here the phrase "Satan's synagogue" is used twice (2:9 and 3:9) for those who are slandering the members of the churches and are falsely claiming to be Jews. These references appear to be associated with Satan (2:10) as one who is testing the people in the role of an adversary. "Satan's throne" and the place "where Satan lives" (2:13) apparently refer to the specific location of a particular individual who is testing the faith of the church members. The "deep secrets" of Satan (2:24) appear to be false teachings that test the faith.

Although the idea of Satan as an adversary who tests faith is possible, images in the book of Revelation also emphasize the struggle between the good God and Satan as the embodiment of evil. The devil who is also called Satan is identified with the dragon that was thrown down along with the angels (12:9). The dragon is an allusion to the monster that inhabited the chaotic waters when God created the world. In Psalm 74:13-14 the Lord is praised for having "shattered the heads of the sea monsters on the waters" and "crushed Leviathan's heads" (see also Ps 89:10).

At the end of Revelation the angel comes down to bind Satan (the devil, the dragon) and throw him into the abyss for a thousand years before he is released for a short time (20:1-3, 7).

Final judgment

[11]Then I saw a great white throne and the one who is seated on it. Before his face both earth and heaven fled away, and no place was found for them. [12]I saw the dead, the great and the small, standing before the throne, and scrolls were opened. Another scroll was opened too; this is the scroll of life. And the dead were judged on the basis of what was written in the scrolls about what they had done. [13]The sea gave up the dead that were in it, and Death and the Grave gave up the dead that were in them, and people were judged by what they had done. [14]Then Death and the Grave were thrown into the fiery lake. This, the fiery lake, is the second death. [15]Then anyone whose name wasn't found written in the scroll of life was thrown into the fiery lake.

New heaven and new earth

21 Then I saw a new heaven and a new earth, for the former heaven and the former earth had passed away, and the sea was no more. [2]I saw the holy city, New Jerusalem, coming down out of heaven from God, made ready as a bride beautifully dressed for her husband. [3]I heard a loud voice from the throne say, "Look! God's dwelling is here with humankind. He will dwell with them, and they will be his peoples. God himself will be with them as their God. [4]He will wipe away every tear from their eyes. Death will be no more. There will be no mourning, crying, or pain anymore, for the former things have passed away." [5]Then the one seated on the throne said, "Look! I'm making all things new." He also

said, "Write this down, for these words are trustworthy and true." [6]Then he said to me, "All is done. I am the Alpha and the Omega, the beginning and the end. To the thirsty I will freely give water from the life-giving spring. [7]Those who emerge victorious will inherit these things. I will be their God, and they will be my sons and daughters. [8]But for the cowardly, the faithless, the vile, the murderers, those who commit sexual immorality, those who use drugs and cast spells, the idolaters and all liars—their share will be in the lake that burns with fire and sulfur. This is the second death."

New Jerusalem

[9]Then one of the seven angels who had the seven bowls full of the seven last plagues spoke with me. "Come," he said, "I will show you the bride, the Lamb's wife." [10]He took me in a Spirit-inspired trance to a great, high mountain, and he showed me the holy city, Jerusalem, coming down out of heaven from God. [11]The city had God's glory. Its brilliance was like a priceless jewel, like jasper that was as clear as crystal. [12]It had a great high wall with twelve gates. By the gates were twelve angels, and on the gates were written the names of the twelve tribes of Israel's sons. [13]There were three gates on the east, three gates on the north, three gates on the south, and three gates on the west. [14]The city wall had twelve foundations, and on them were the twelve names of the Lamb's twelve apostles.

[15]The angel who spoke to me had a gold measuring rod with which to measure the city, its gates, and its wall. [16]Now the city

NEW HEAVEN/NEW EARTH

Revelation depicts John's vision of "a new heaven and a new earth" (21:1). The old heaven and earth have departed (cf. 20:11), along with the sea and its associations with chaos. The imagery is part of the cosmic upheaval associated with God's appearance at the end time (i.e., Rev 6:12-14). The destruction or transformation of creation is common in Jewish prophetic and apocalyptic traditions (e.g., Isa 65:17; 66:22) and the NT (Matt 5:18; Mark 13:30-31; Rom 8:21; 2 Pet 3:12-13).

was laid out as a square. Its length was the same as its width. He measured the city with the rod, and it was fifteen hundred miles.[n] Its length and width and height were equal. [17]He also measured the thickness of its wall. It was two hundred sixteen feet[o] thick, as a person—or rather, an angel—measures things. [18]The wall was built of jasper, and the city was pure gold, like pure glass. [19]The city wall's foundations were decorated with every kind of jewel. The first foundation was jasper, the second was sapphire, the third was chalcedony, and the fourth was emerald. [20]The fifth was sardonyx, the sixth was carnelian, the seventh was chrysolite, and the eighth was beryl. The ninth was topaz, the tenth was chrysoprase, the eleventh was jacinth, and the twelfth was amethyst. [21]The twelve gates were twelve pearls; each one of the gates was made from a single pearl. And the city's main street was pure gold, as transparent as glass.

[22]I didn't see a temple in the city, because its temple is the Lord God Almighty and the Lamb. [23]The city doesn't need the sun or the moon to shine on it, because God's glory is its light, and its lamp is the Lamb. [24]The nations will walk by its light, and the kings of the earth will bring their glory into it. [25]Its gates will never be shut by day, and there will be no night there. [26]They will bring the glory and honor of the nations into it. [27]Nothing unclean will ever enter it, nor anyone who does what is vile and deceitful, but only those who are registered in the Lamb's scroll of life.

22 Then the angel showed me the river of life-giving water,[p] shining like crystal, flowing from the throne of God and the Lamb [2]through the middle of the city's main street. On each side of the river is the tree of life, which produces twelve crops of fruit, bearing its fruit each month. The tree's leaves are for the healing of the nations. [3]There will no longer be any curse. The throne of God and the Lamb will be in it, and his servants will worship him. [4]They will see his face, and his name will be on their foreheads. [5]Night will be no more. They won't need the light of a lamp or the light of the sun, for the Lord God will shine on them, and they will rule forever and always.

Jesus is coming soon

[6]Then he said to me, "These words are trustworthy and true. The Lord, the God of the spirits of the prophets, sent his angel to show his servants what must soon take place.

[7]"Look! I'm coming soon. Favored is the one who keeps the words of the prophecy contained in this scroll."

[8]I, John, am the one who heard and saw these things. When I heard and saw them, I fell down to worship at the feet of the angel who had shown them to me. [9]But he said to me, "Don't do that! I'm a servant just like you and your brothers and sisters, the

---

[n]Or *twelve thousand stades*   [o]Or *one hundred forty-four pechon* (cubits)   [p]Or *the water of life*

NEW JERUSALEM

The culminating image of Revelation is John's vision of "the holy city, New Jerusalem" (Rev 21:2; cf. 21:10; 3:12), a vision of God's ultimate establishment of abundance and peace. The city metaphor has multiple, overlapping meanings. Many details of the city in Revelation 21:1–22:5 are familiar from the restoration of Jerusalem promised by the prophets (e.g., Isa 2:1-4; 49:18; 60–62; 65:17-25; Jer 31:38; Zech 14:6-11). The measuring of the city (Rev 21:15-21) alludes to Ezekiel's vision of the restored temple (Ezek 40–47), although in Revelation God dwells directly in the city. The city as bride evokes the notion of the marriage of the church to Christ (e.g., Eph 5:25-33).

prophets, and those who keep the words of this scroll. Worship God!" [10]Then he said to me, "Don't seal up the words of the prophecy contained in this scroll, because the time is near. [11]Let those who do wrong keep doing what is wrong. Let the filthy still be filthy. Let those who are righteous keep doing what is right. Let those who are holy still be holy.

[12]"Look! I'm coming soon. My reward is with me, to repay all people as their actions deserve. [13]I am the alpha and the omega, the first and the last, the beginning and the end. [14]Favored are those who wash their robes so that they may have the right of access to the tree of life and may enter the city by the gates. [15]Outside are the dogs, the drug users and spell-casters, those who commit sexual immorality, the murderers, the idolaters, and all who love and practice deception.

[16]"I, Jesus, have sent my angel to bear witness to all of you about these things for the churches. I'm the root and descendant of David, the bright morning star. [17]The Spirit and the bride say, 'Come!' Let the one who hears say, 'Come!' And let the one who is thirsty come! Let the one who wishes receive life-giving water[q] as a gift."

[18]Now I bear witness to everyone who hears the words of the prophecy contained in this scroll: If anyone adds to them, God will add to that person the plagues that are written in this scroll. [19]If anyone takes away from the words of this scroll of prophecy, God will take away that person's share in the tree of life and the holy city, which are described in this scroll.

[20]The one who bears witness to these things says, "Yes, I'm coming soon." Amen. Come, Lord Jesus!

[21]The grace of the Lord Jesus be with all.

[q]Or the water of life

INDEXES

INDEXES

ARTICLE INDEX

MAP INDEX

The first number for each code denotes the number of the map. The letter and the second number denote the square in which the item will be found.

— A —

'Araq el-Emir 10C4
Abdon 3B2, 9C3
Abel-beth-maacah 4C1, 5C1
Abel-meholah 3C3, 4C3, 5C3, 9C3
Abila 10C2, 13C2
Abilene 13D1 16C6
Accaron (Ekron) 13A4
Acco 1B2, 4B2, 6C2, 8B2
Achaia 12C3, 16B3
Achshaph 1B2, 3B2, 9C3
Achzib 1B2, 3B2, 7B2, 7B5, 9C3, 10B2
Adadah (Aroer) 1B6
Adasa 13B4
Adora 13B5
Adoraim 10B5
Adramyttium 16B4
Adullam 1B5, 3B5, 4B5, 5B5, 7B5, 10B5
Aduru 1C2
Aegyptus (Egypt) 12D4, 16D5
Aenon 13C3
Agrippias 13A5
Agrippina 13C3
Ai 1B4, 2D2, 3B4, 5B4
Aiath 7B4
Aijalon 1B4, 5B4
Akkad 6C5, 8B5
Akrabatta (Akrabattene) 10B4
Alema 10D2
Aleppo 6B2, 8A3
Alexandria 11A6, 12D4
Alexandrium 10C4, 13C4
Altar 14C3,
Alulos 13B5
Amalek 4A6
Amastris 12B4
Amathus 13C3
Amisus 12B5
Ammathus 13C2
Ammon 1D4, 2D2, 6D2, 7D4, 10C4
Ammonites 3D4, 4D4, 5D4, 9D4
Amorites 1C5
Amphipolis 16A3
Amu Darya 11C1, 11C3, 11C5
Anab 3B5, 9B5

Anaharath 1C3
Anat 6C4
Anathoth 4B4, 5B4, 7B4, 10B4, 13B4
Ancyra 12C4
Anthedon 10A5
Antioch 12C5, 16B6
Antioch in Pisdia 16B5
Antioch on the Chrysorhoas (Gerasa) 10C3
Antipatris (Pegai) 13B4 16C5
Antium 12B3
Antonia Fortress 15C3
Apamea 12C5
Aphairema 10B4
Aphek (Pegai) 1B4, 3B4, 5C2, 8C2, 9B4, 10B4
Apollonia 10A4, 12C4, 16A3
Apollonia Sozusa 13A4
Appian Way 16A2
Ar 1C5, 7C5
Arabah 4C4, 7C3
Arabia 6D3
Arabian Desert 8D3
Arabian Sea 11D2, 11D4, 11D6
Arachosia 11D4
Arad (city) 1B6, 3B6, 4B6, 8C2, 9B5
Arad (region) 1B5, 3B5, 9C5
Aram (Syria) 1D1
Ararat (Urartu) 8A4
Arbatta 10B3
Arbela 6B4, 10C2, 11B5, 13C2
Archelais 13C4, 16B5
Areopolis (Rabbathmoab) 13C5
Argob 1D2, 4D2
Aristobulias 13B5
Armenia 12B5
Arnon Gorge 4C5
Arnon R. 1C5, 2D3, 3C5, 4C5, 5C5, 7C5, 9C5, 13C5
Aroer 3C5, 4C5, 5C5, 7C5, 9C5
Arpad 6B2, 8A3
Arubboth 1B3
Arumah 3B4, 9C4
Aruna 1B3
Arus 13B4
Arvad 8B3

MAP 1

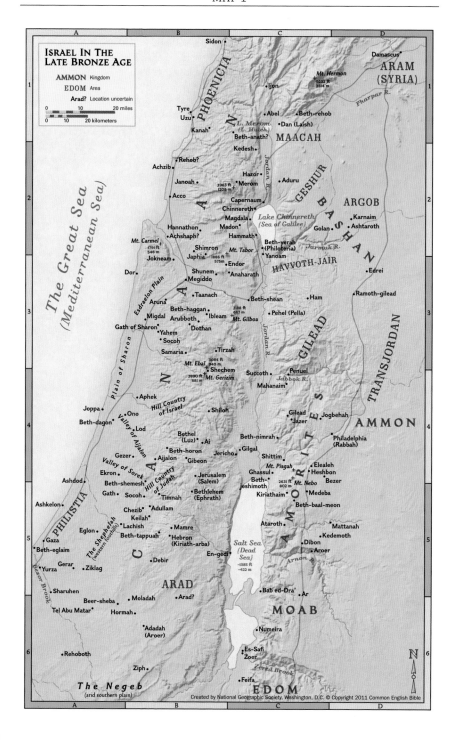

ISRAEL IN THE
LATE BRONZE AGE

AMMON Kingdom
EDOM Area
Arad? Location uncertain

0   10   20 miles
0   10   20 kilometers

The Great Sea
(Mediterranean Sea)

Sidon
Damascus
ARAM
(SYRIA)
Mt. Hermon
9232 ft
2814 m
Ijon
Abel
Beth-rehob
Tyre
Uzu
Kanah
L. Merom
(L. Huleh)
Dan (Laish)
PHOENICIA
MAACAH
Beth-anath?
Kedesh
Achzib
Rehob?
Janoah
Hazor
Aduru
Acco
Merom
3963 ft
1208 m
Capernaum
Chinnereth
GESHUR
BASHAN
ARGOB
Karnaim
Ashtaroth
Hannathon
Achshaph
Magdala
Madon
Hammath
Lake Chinnereth
(Sea of Galilee)
Golan
Mt. Carmel
1791 ft
546 m
Shimron
Jokneam
Mt. Tabor
1886 ft
575m
Beth-yerah
(Philoteria)
Yanoam
Jarmuk R.
Dor
Japhia
Endor
Anaharath
HAVVOTH-JAIR
Edrei
Shunem
Megiddo
Esdraelon Plain
Taanach
Beth-shean
Ham
Ramoth-gilead
Aruna
Beth-haggan
Arubboth
Ibleam
Migdal
Dothan
2188 ft
667 m
Mt. Gilboa
Pehel (Pella)
GILEAD
Gath of Sharon
Yahem
Socoh
Samaria
Tirzah
Jordan R.
Plain of Sharon
Mt. Ebal
3084 ft
940 m
Shechem
2890 ft
881 m
Mt. Gerizim
Succoth
Penuel
Mahanaim
Jabbok R.
TRANSJORDAN
Aphek
Ono
Joppa
Beth-dagon
Lod
Hill Country
of Israel
Shiloh
Gilead
Jazer
Jogbehah
AMMON
Valley of Aijalon
Bethel
(Luz)
Ai
Beth-horon
Jericho
Gilgal
Beth-nimrah
Philadelphia
(Rabbah)
Gezer
Aijalon
Gibeon
Shittim
Ghassul
Mt. Pisgah
Elealeh
Heshbon
Valley of Sorek
Ekron
Ashdod
Beth-shemesh
Gath
Socoh
Jerusalem
(Salem)
Beth-
jeshimoth
2631 ft
802 m
Mt. Nebo
Bezer
Timnah
Bethlehem
(Ephrath)
Kiriathaim
Medeba
Ashkelon
Chezib
Keilah
Adullam
Mamre
Hebron
(Kiriath-arba)
Beth-baal-meon
Eglon
Lachish
Beth-tappuah
Ataroth
Mattanah
Kedemoth
Gaza
Beth-eglaim
The Shephelah
(western foothills)
Salt Sea
(Dead
Sea)
-1385 ft
-422 m
Dibon
Aroer
Yurza
Gerar
Debir
Ziklag
En-gedi
Arnon R.
Sharuhen
ARAD
Bab ed-Dra'
Ar
Rehoboth
Beer-sheba
Moladah
Arad?
MOAB
Tel Abu Matar
Hormah
Numeira
Adadah
(Aroer)
Es-Safi
Zoer
Ziph
Feifa
EDOM
The Negeb
(arid southern plain)
Zered Brook

N

Created by National Geographic Society, Washington, D.C. © Copyright 2011 Common English Bible

Kishon Brook
Jordan R.
Pharpar R.
CANAAN
PHILISTIA
Hill Country
of Judah
AMORITES

MAP 2

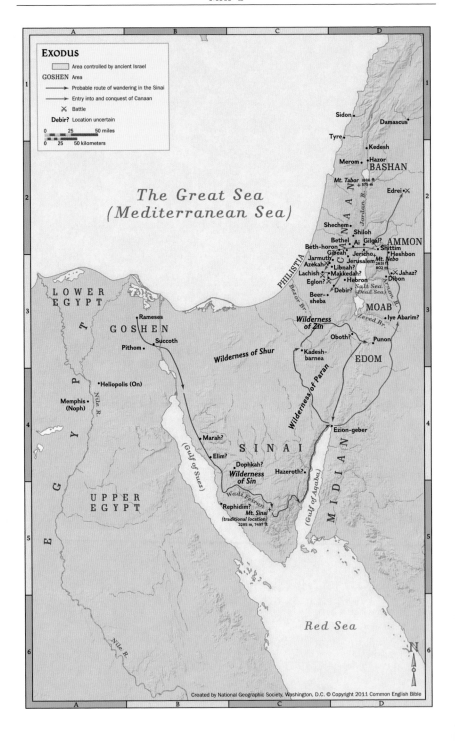

EXODUS

Area controlled by ancient Israel

GOSHEN Area

Probable route of wandering in the Sinai

Entry into and conquest of Canaan

✕ Battle

Debir? Location uncertain

0   25   50 miles

0   25   50 kilometers

*The Great Sea
(Mediterranean Sea)*

Sidon

Damascus

Tyre

Kedesh

Merom   Hazor

BASHAN

Mt. Tabor 1886 ft
+575 m

Edrei ✕

Shechem

Shiloh

Bethel   Gilgal?   **AMMON**

Ai

Beth-horon   Jericho   Shittim   Heshbon

Gibeah   Mt.   Nebo

Jarmuth ✕   Jerusalem   2631 ft
802 m

Azekah ✕   Libnah?

Lachish ✕   Makkedah? ✕   ✕ Jahaz?

Eglon? ✕   Hebron   Dibon

Debir? ✕   *Salt Sea
(Dead Sea)*

Beer-
sheba   **MOAB**

*Wilderness
of Zin*   Iye Abarim?

Oboth?

Kadesh-   Punon
barnea

Wilderness of Shur

Wilderness of Paran   **EDOM**

**L O W E R
E G Y P T**

Rameses

G O S H E N

Succoth

Pithom

Ezion-geber

Heliopolis (On)

Memphis
(Noph)

Marah?   **S I N A I**

Elim?

Dophkah?

*Wilderness
of Sin*   Hazeroth?

Wadi Feiran   **M I D I A N**

**U P P E R
E G Y P T**   Rephidim?

*Mt. Sinai
(traditional location)*
2285 m, 7497 ft

(Gulf of Suez)

(Gulf of Aqaba)

Nile R.

Red Sea

N

MAP 3

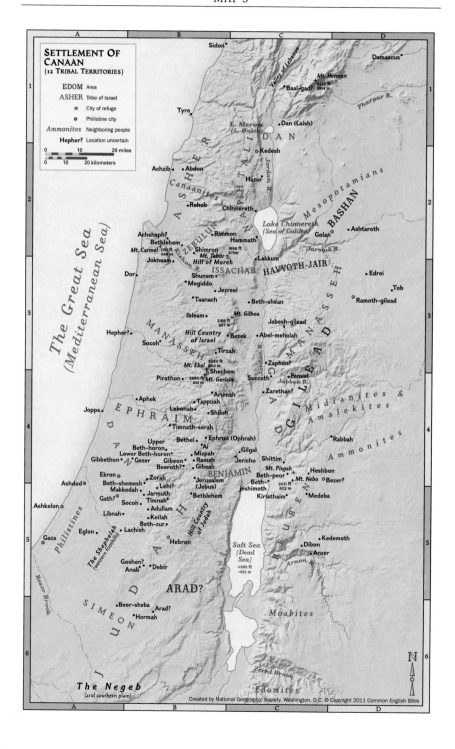

SETTLEMENT OF CANAAN
(12 TRIBAL TERRITORIES)

EDOM   Area
ASHER   Tribe of Israel
●   City of refuge
◉   Philistine city
Ammonites   Neighboring people
Hepher?   Location uncertain

0   10   20 miles
0   10   20 kilometers

Sidon

Damascus

Valley of Lebanon

Mt. Hermon
9232 ft
2814 m

Baal-gad?

Pharpar R.

Tyre

L. Merom
(L. Huleh)

Dan (Laish)

Kedesh

NAPHTALI

Jordan R.

Mesopotamians

BASHAN

Achzib   Abdon

Hazor

Ashtaroth

Rehob

Chinnereth

Lake Chinnereth
(Sea of Galilee)

Golan

Achshaph?
Bethlehem

ZEBULUN

Rimmon   Hammath

Jarmuk R.

Mt. Carmel 1791 ft
546 m

Shimron

1886 ft
575m

Jokneam

Hill of Moreh

Mt. Tabor

Lakkum

HAVVOTH-JAIR

Dor

ISSACHAR

Edrei

Shunem

Tob

Megiddo

Jezreel

Ramoth-gilead

Taanach

Beth-shean

Ibleam

Mt. Gilboa

Jabesh-gilead

2188 ft
667 m

Abel-meholah

Hepher?

MANASSEH

Hill Country
of Israel

Bezek

Socoh

Tirzah

MANASSEH

Zaphon?

3084 ft
940 m

Mt. Ebal

Shechem

GILEAD

Penuel

Pirathon

2890 ft
881 m

Mt. Gerizim

Succoth

Jabbok R.

Zarethan?

The Great Sea
(Mediterranean Sea)

Arumah

Aphek

Tappuah

Midianites &
Amalekites

Joppa

EPHRAIM

Lebonah

Shiloh

DAN

Timnath-serah

Upper
Beth-horon

Bethel

Ephron (Ophrah)

Gilgal

Rabbah

Lower Beth-horon

Ai

Mizpah

Ammonites

Gibbethon

Gezer

Gibeon

Ramah

Jericho

Shittim

Beeroth?

Gibeah

Ekron

BENJAMIN

Beth-peor

Heshbon

Ashdod

Beth-shemesh

Zorah

Jerusalem
(Jebus)

Beth-
jeshimoth

2631 ft
802 m

Mt. Nebo

Bezer?

Makkedah

Lehi?

Gath?

Jarmuth

Bethlehem

Kiriathaim

Medeba

Ashkelon

Socoh

Timnah

Adullam

JUDAH

Libnah

Keilah

Hill Country
of Judah

Beth-zur

Philistines

Eglon

Lachish

The Shephelah
(western foothills)

Hebron

Salt Sea
(Dead
Sea)
-1385 ft
-422 m

Kedemoth

Gaza

Dibon

Goshen?

Debir

Aroer

Anab

REUBEN

Arnon R.

SIMEON

ARAD?

Beer-sheba

Arad?

Hormah

Moabites

The Negeb
(arid southern plain)

Zered Brook

Besor Brook

Edomites

N

Created by National Geographic Society, Washington, D.C. © Copyright 2011 Common English Bible

MAP 4

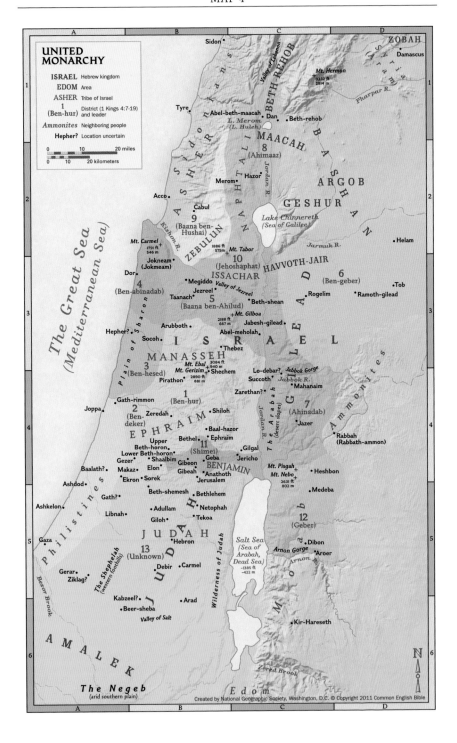

UNITED
MONARCHY

ISRAEL   Hebrew kingdom
EDOM   Area
ASHER   Tribe of Israel
1
(Ben-hur)   District (1 Kings 4:7-19)
and leader
Ammonites   Neighboring people
Hepher?   Location uncertain

0   10   20 miles
0   10   20 kilometers

ZOBAH
Damascus

Sidon

BETH-REHOB
Litani R.
Valley of Lebanon
Mt. Hermon
9232 ft
2814 m

Tyre
Abel-beth-maacah
Dan
Beth-rehob
L. Merom
(L. Huleh)

MAACAH
8
(Ahimaaz)

BASHAN
ARGOB

GESHUR

Merom
Hazor

Acco

Cabul
9
(Baana ben-
Hushai)

ZEBULUN

NAPHTALI

Jordan R.

Lake Chinnereth
(Sea of Galilee)

Helam

Mt. Carmel
1791 ft
546 m

Jokneam
(Jokmeam)

Dor

1886 ft
575m
Mt. Tabor

10
(Jehoshaphat)

ISSACHAR

Jarmuk R.

HAVVOTH-JAIR

6
(Ben-geber)

Tob

4
(Ben-abinadab)

Megiddo
Jezreel
Taanach

Valley of Jezreel

5
(Baana ben-Ahilud)

Beth-shean

2188 ft
667 m
Mt. Gilboa

Jabesh-gilead

Rogelim
Ramoth-gilead

The Great Sea
(Mediterranean Sea)

Kishon R.

Plain of Sharon

Hepher?

Socoh

Arubboth

Thebez

Abel-meholah

GILEAD

Lo-debar?
Succoth

Jabbok Gorge
Jabbok R.
Mahanaim

MANASSEH
3
(Ben-hesed)

Mt. Ebal
3084 ft
940 m
Mt. Gerizim
2890 ft
881 m
Pirathon

Shechem

Zarethan?

7
(Ahinadab)

Jazer

Ammonites

I S R A E L

Gath-rimmon

1
(Ben-hur)

2
(Ben-
deker)

Joppa

Zeredah
Shiloh

EPHRAIM

Baal-hazor
Ephraim

Upper
Beth-horon
Lower Beth-horon
Gezer
Makaz
Elon
Ekron   Sorek

Bethel

11
(Shimei)
Geba
Shaalbim   Gibeon   Jericho
Gibeah
Anathoth
Jerusalem

Gilgal

Jordan R.
The Arabah (desert slopes)

Mt. Pisgah
Mt. Nebo
2631 ft
802 m

Heshbon

Medeba

Baalath?

BENJAMIN

Ashdod

Gath?

Beth-shemesh
Bethlehem

Libnah

Adullam
Giloh

Netophah
Tekoa

12
(Geber)

Ashkelon

Gaza

JUDAH

Hebron

Salt Sea
(Sea of
Arabah,
Dead Sea)
-1385 ft
-422 m

Dibon
Arnon Gorge   Aroer

Philistines

The Shephelah
(western foothills)

13
(Unknown)

Debir   Carmel

Wilderness of Judah

Moab

Arnon R.

Gerar
Ziklag

Kabzeel?

Arad

Beer-sheba
Valley of Salt

Kir-Haresheth

Besor Brook

A M A L E K

The Negeb
(arid southern plain)

Zered Brook

E d o m

N

Created by National Geographic Society, Washington, D.C. © Copyright 2011 Common English Bible

MAP 5

MAP 6

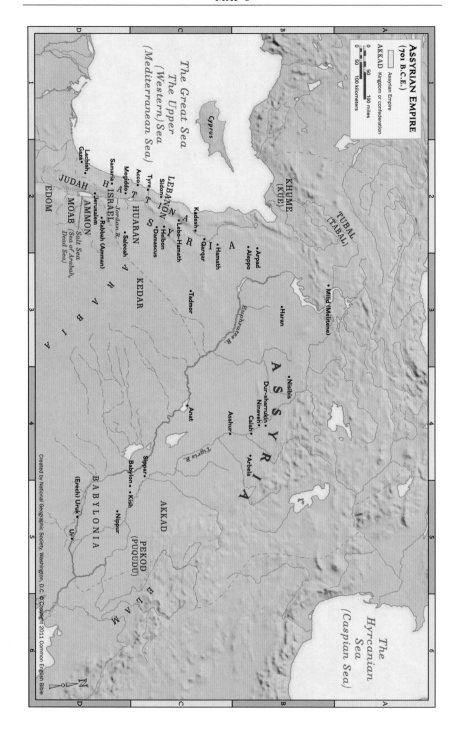

ASSYRIAN EMPIRE
(701 B.C.E.)

Assyrian Empire

AKKAD Kingdom or confederation

0   50   100 miles
0   50   100 kilometers

The Great Sea
The Upper
(Western) Sea
(Mediterranean Sea.)

Cyprus

KHUME
(KUE)

TUBAL
(TABAL)

Milid (Melitene)

Lachish•
Gaza•

JUDAH

EDOM

MOAB

AMMON

•Jerusalem

•Rabbah (Amman)

ISRAEL

Samaria•

Megiddo•

Acco•

Tyre•

Sidon•

LEBANON

Kadesh•

•Aleppo

•Arpad

•Hamath

•Qargar

•Helbon

•Damascus

•Lebo-Hamath

HUARAN

•Salecah

Jordan R.

Salt Sea
(Sea of Arabah,
Dead Sea)

KEDAR

•Tadmor

•Haran

Euphrates R.

ASSYRIA

Dur-sharrukin•
•Nineveh
Calah•

•Nisibis

Asshur•

•Arbela

•Anat

Tigris R.

Sippar•

Babylon• •Kish

BABYLONIA

(Erech) Uruk•

Ur•

•Nippur

AKKAD

PEKOD
(PUQUDU)

ELAM

The
Hyrcanian
Sea
(Caspian Sea.)

N

MAP 7

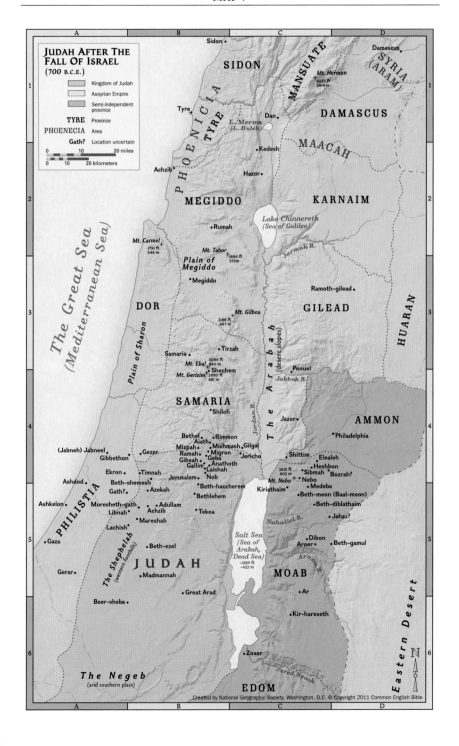

JUDAH AFTER THE FALL OF ISRAEL
(700 B.C.E.)

- Kingdom of Judah
- Assyrian Empire
- Semi-independent province

TYRE Province

PHOENECIA Area

Gath? Location uncertain

0   10   20 miles
0 10   20 kilometers

The Great Sea (Mediterranean Sea)

Sidon •

SIDON

Damascus •

SYRIA (ARAM)

MANSUATE

Mt. Hermon
9232 ft
3814 m

Tyre •

PHOENICIA
TYRE

Dan •

L. Merom
(L. Huleh)

DAMASCUS

Kedesh •

MAACAH

Achzib •

Hazor •

MEGIDDO

Lake Chinnereth
(Sea of Galilee)

KARNAIM

• Rumah

Mt. Carmel
1791 ft
546 m

Mt. Tabor
1886 ft
575m

Plain of Megiddo

Jarmuk R.

• Megiddo

Ramoth-gilead •

GILEAD

HUARAN

DOR

+ Mt. Gilboa
2188 ft
667 m

Plain of Sharon

Samaria •

• Tirzah

Mt. Ebal
3084 ft
940 m

Mt. Gerizim
2890 ft
881 m

Shechem

Penuel •

Jabbok R.

SAMARIA

• Shiloh

Jazer •

AMMON

Bethel •
Aiath •
• Rimmon

Mizpah •
Ramah •
Gibeah •
Gallim •

Michmash •
Migron •
Geba
Anathoth
Laishah

Gilgal •
Jericho •

Shittim •

Elealeh •
• Heshbon
Sibmah • Bozrah?

Philadelphia •

(Jabneh) Jabneel •
• Gezer

Ekron •
• Timnah

Beth-shemesh •

Jerusalem •
Nob •

Beth-haccherem •

2631 ft
802 m
Mt. Nebo +

• Nebo
Medeba •

Ashdod •

Gath? •
• Azekah

• Bethlehem

Kiriathaim •

• Beth-meon (Baal-meon)

Ashkelon •

Moresheth-gath •
Libnah •

Adullam •
Achzib •

• Tekoa

• Beth-diblathaim

Mareshah •

Nahaliel R.

• Jahaz?

Lachish •

PHILISTIA

The Shephelah
(western foothills)

• Beth-ezel

Dibon •

Aroer •
• Beth-gamul

• Gaza

JUDAH

Salt Sea
(Sea of
Arabah,
Dead Sea)
-1385 ft
-422 m

Arnon R.

MOAB

Gerar •

• Madmannah

• Great Arad

• Ar

Beer-sheba •

• Kir-hareseth

Eastern Desert

• Zoaer

*The Negeb
(arid southern plain)*

Zered Brook

EDOM

N

Created by National Geographic Society, Washington, D.C. © Copyright 2011 Common English Bible

MAP 8

BABYLONIA AND ISRAEL

EDOM Kingdom or confederation
Jewish exiles
From Canaan in Assyrian captivity
To Canaan in Assyrian captivity
From Babylonia in Assyrian captivity
Return under Sheshbazzar & Zerubbabel
Return under Ezra & Nehemiah

0   100   200 kilometers
0   100   200 miles

Created by National Geographic Society, Washington, D.C. © Copyright 2011 Common English Bible

MAP 9

EZEKIEL'S VISION OF 12 RESTORED TRIBES
(Ezek. 47:13-48:29)

ASHER — Tribe of Israel
••••••• — Tribal boundary (Envisioned by Ezekiel)
◎ — City of refuge
● — Philistine city
EDOM — Area
Ammonites — Neighboring people
Hepher? — Location uncertain

0   25   50 miles
0   25   50 kilometers

The Great Sea (Mediterranean Sea)

Haitela•
HAMATH
DAN
Byblos•   Labweh•   Zedad•   Qaryatein•   Zedad
ASHER
NAPHTALI
Sidon•   Damascus•
Valley of Lebanon
•Baal-gad?
Tyre•   •Dan (Laish)   MANASSEH
Kedesh•   *Jordan R.*
Achzib•   •Abdon   Hazor•
Canaanites   Mesopotamians
Rehob•   •Chinnereth   *Lake Chinnereth (Sea of Galilee)*   BASHAN   EPHRAIM
Achshaph•   •Rimmon   Golan•   Ashtaroth•
Bethlehem•   •Hammath   *Jarmuk R.*   Mt. Hauran +
Jokneam•   •Shimron   *Hill of Moreh*   HAVVOTH-JAIR   Edrei•
Dor•   Megiddo•   •Shunem   •Jezreel   *Jordan R.*   •Tob
Taanach•   •Ibleam   •Beth-shean   Ramoth-gilead•
Hepher?•   REUBEN   Bezek   •Jabesh-gilead
Socoh•   *Hill Country of Israel*   •Abel-meholah   GILEAD
Tirzah•   •Zaphon?
Pirathon•   ⊙Shechem   •Penuel
•Aphek   •Arumah   •Zarethan?   Jabbok R.   Midianites & Amalekites
Joppa•   Lebonah•   •Shiloh   •Tapphuah
JUDAH   •Timnath-serah   •Rabbah (Amman)
Bethel•   •Ephron (Ophrah)
Gibbethon•   Gezer•   Gibeon•   Mizpah•   •Gilgal   Shittim•   Ammonites
Ekron•   Beeroth?•   •Gibeah   •Jericho   Heshbon•
Ashdod•   Makkedah•   •Lehi?   ⊙Jerusalem (Jebus)   •Bezer
Ashkelon•   •Gath?   •Bethlehem   •Medeba
Libnah•   •Timnah   Kiriathaim•
Beth-zur•   •Keilah   *Hill Country of Judah*   •Kedemoth
Gaza•   Eglon•   •Hebron   BENJAMIN   Dibon•
The Shephelah (western foothills)   Goshen?•   •Anab   •Debir   *Salt Sea (Sea of Arabah, Dead Sea)*   •Aroer
SIMEON   ARAD?   Moabites   Arnon R.
Beer-sheba•   •Arad?   Hormah•
ISSACHAR
ZEBULUN   *Zered Br.*
The Negeb (arid southern plain)   Edomites
Wadi el-Arish   •Tamar
GAD
Kadesh-barnea•

N

MAP 10

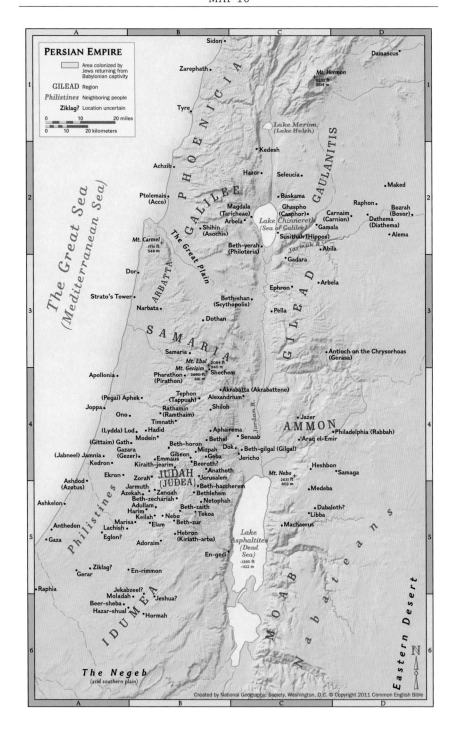

PERSIAN EMPIRE

Area colonized by
Jews returning from
Babylonian captivity

GILEAD Region

Philistines Neighboring people

Ziklag? Location uncertain

0   10   20 miles
0   10   20 kilometers

Sidon

Damascus

Zarephath

Mt. Hermon
9232 ft
2814 m

Tyre

Lake Merom
(Lake Huleh)

Kedesh

Achzib

Hazor

Seleucia

Maked

Ptolemais
(Acco)

Baskama

Raphon

Bozrah
(Bosor)

Magdala
(Taricheae)

Ghaspho
(Casphor)

Carnaim
(Carnion)

Dathema
(Diathema)

Shihin
(Asochis)

Arbela

Lake Chinnereth
(Sea of Galilee)

Gamala

Alema

Mt. Carmel
1791 ft
546 m

Susithah (Hippos)

Jarmuk R.

Beth-yerah
(Philoteria)

Abila

Dor

Gadara

Strato's Tower

Ephron

Arbela

Narbata

Beth-shan
(Scythopolis)

Pella

Dothan

Antioch on the Chrysorhoas
(Gerasa)

Samaria

Mt. Ebal
3084 m
940 m

Mt. Gerizim
2890 ft
881 m

Shechem

Apollonia

Pharathon
(Pirathon)

Akrabatta (Akrabattene)

Tephon
(Tappuah)

Alexandrium

(Pegai) Aphek

Rathamin
(Ramthaim)

Shiloh

Joppa

Ono

Timnath

Jazer

Philadelphia (Rabbah)

(Lydda) Lod

Hadid

Aphairema

Senaab

Araq el-Emir

(Gittaim) Gath

Modein

Bethel

Dok

Gazara
(Gezer)

Beth-horon

Mizpah

Geba

Beth-gilgal (Gilgal)

Heshbon

(Jabneel) Jamnia

Gibeon

Jericho

Kedron

Emmaus

Beeroth?

Samaga

Kiraith-jearim

Anathoth

Ekron

Zorah

Jerusalem

Mt. Nebo
2631 ft
802 m

Ashdod
(Azotus)

Jarmuth

Beth-haccherem

Azekah

Zanoah

Bethlehem

Medeba

Ashkelon

Beth-zechariah

Netophah

Adullam

Beth-zaith

Harim

Keilah

Nebo

Tekoa

Dabaloth?

Anthedon

Marisa

Elam

Beth-zur

Libba

Lachish

Machaerus

Gaza

Eglon?

Hebron
(Kiriath-arba)

Adoraim

Lake
Asphaltites
(Dead
Sea)
-1385 ft
-422 m

En-gedi

Ziklag?

En-rimmon

Gerar

Raphia

Jekabzeel?

Moladah

Jeshua?

Beer-sheba

Hazar-shual

Hormah

The Negeb
(arid southern plain)

SIDON

PHOENICIA

GALILEE

GAULANITIS

The Great Plain

The Great Sea
(Mediterranean Sea)

ARBATTA

GILEAD

SAMARIA

AMMON

JUDAH
(JUDEA)

Philistines

IDUMEA

MOAB

Nabateans

Eastern Desert

N

Created by National Geographic Society, Washington, D.C. © Copyright 2011 Common English Bible

MAP 11

HELLENISTIC KINGDOMS IN DANIEL

Babylonian Empire 626 – 539 B.C.E.
Median Empire 625 – 549 B.C.E.
MEDIA Region
Pteria? Location uncertain

0   400   800 miles
0   400   800 kilometers

Danube R.
Black Sea
PHRYGIA
Pteria?
CILICIA
CYPRUS
Mediterranean Sea
Sidon
Tyre
Jerusalem
Dead Sea
EGYPT
Nile R.
Red Sea
Euphrates R.
Tigris R.
Babylon
BABYLONIA
Caspian Sea
MEDIA
Persepolis
PERSIS
Persian Gulf
Amu Darya
Indus R.
Arabian Sea

Persian Empire 550 – 330 B.C.E.

Danube R.
Black Sea
PHRYGIA
CILICIA
CYPRUS
Mediterranean Sea
Damascus
Tyre
Jerusalem
Memphis
EGYPT
Nile R.
Red Sea
Euphrates R.
Tigris R.
Babylon
BABYLONIA
Caspian Sea
MEDIA
PARTHIA
Persepolis
PERSIS
Persian Gulf
Amu Darya
Maracanda
(Samarkand)
BACTRIA
ARACHOSIA
Indus R.
GEDROSIA
Arabian Sea

Macedonian Empire 334 – 323 B.C.E.
Extent of Roman Empire at 69 C.E. shown on Map 15

Danube R.
Pella
GREECE
Black Sea
PHRYGIA
CILICIA
CYPRUS
Mediterranean Sea
Damascus
Tyre
Alexandria
Gaza
Memphis
EGYPT
Nile R.
Red Sea
Euphrates R.
Tigris R.
Arbela
MEDIA
Babylon
BABYLONIA
Caspian Sea
Hectamopolis
Persepolis
PERSIS
Harmozia
Persian Gulf
Amu Darya
SOGDIANA
Maracanda
(Samarkand)
BACTRIA
DRANGIANA
PORUS
Multan
Indus R.
GEDROSIA
Arabian Sea
N

Created by National Geographic Society, Washington, D.C. © Copyright 2011 Common English Bible

MAP 12

MAP 13

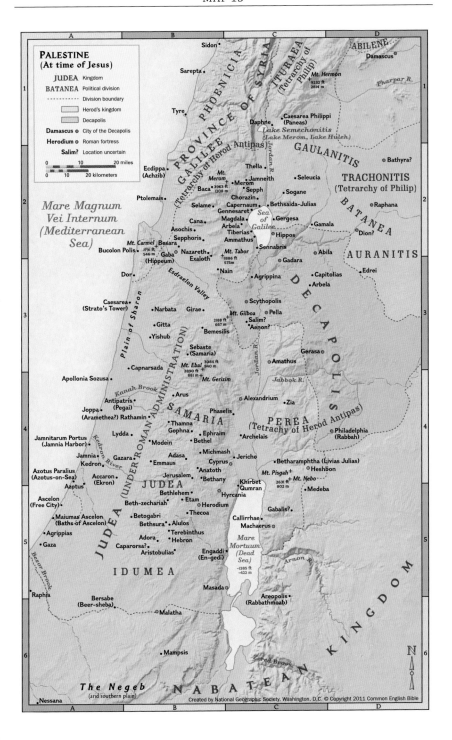

PALESTINE
(At time of Jesus)

JUDEA   Kingdom
BATANEA   Political division
- - - -   Division boundary
   Herod's kingdom
   Decapolis
Damascus ⊚   City of the Decapolis
Herodium ⊚   Roman fortress
Salim?   Location uncertain

0   10   20 miles
0   10   20 kilometers

Mare Magnum
Vei Internum
(Mediterranean
Sea)

ABILENE
Damascus ⊚
Pharpar R.

Sidon
Sarepta
Tyre
PHOENICIA
PROVINCE OF SYRIA
ITURAEA
(Tetrarchy of Philip)
Mt. Hermon
9232 ft
2814 m
Daphne
Caesarea Philippi
(Paneas)
Lake Semechonitis
(Lake Merom, Lake Huleh)
GALILEE
(Tetrarchy of Herod Antipas)
GAULANITIS
Bathyra?
TRACHONITIS
(Tetrarchy of Philip)
Thella
Jamneith
Mt. Merom
3963 ft
1208 m
Baca
Merom
Sepph
Chorazin
Seleucia
Sogane
BATANEA
Ptolemais
Selame
Capernaum
Bethsaida-Julias
Raphana
Gennesaret
Cana
Magdala
Sea of Galilee
Gergesa
AURANITIS
Asochis
Arbela
Hippos
Gamala
Dion?
Sepphoris
Tiberias
Ammathus
Sennabris
Abila
Besara
Nazareth
Mt. Tabor
1886 ft
575m
Gadara
Edrei
Bucolon Polis
Mt. Carmel
1791 ft
546 m
Gaba
(Hippeum)
Exaloth
Nain
Agrippina
Capitolias
Arbela
Dor
Esdraelon Valley
Scythopolis
Mt. Gilboa
2188 ft
667 m
Pella
DECAPOLIS
Caesarea
(Strato's Tower)
Narbata
Girae
Salim?
Aenon?
Gitta
Bemesilis
Yishub
Sebaste
(Samaria)
Gerasa
Capnarsada
Mt. Ebal
3084 ft
2890 ft
940 m
881 m
Mt. Gerizim
Amathus
Jabbok R.
Apollonia Sozusa
Arus
Alexandrium
Zia
Antipatris
(Pegai)
Phaselis
PEREA
(Tetrarchy of Herod Antipas)
Joppa
(Aramethea?) Rathamin
Thamna
Gophna
Ephraim
Archelais
Philadelphia
(Rabbah)
Lydda
Modein
Bethel
Jamnitarum Portus
(Jamnia Harbor)
Adasa
Michmash
Jamnia
Gazara
Emmaus
Cyprus
Jericho
Betharamphtha (Livias Julias)
Kedron
Accaron
(Ekron)
Anatoth
Jerusalem
Bethany
Heshbon
Azotus Paralius
(Azotus-on-Sea)
Mt. Pisgah
Mt. Nebo
2631 ft
802 m
Azotus
JUDEA
Bethlehem
Khirbet
Qumran
Medeba
Ascelon
(Free City)
Beth-zechariah
Etam
Hyrcania
Herodium
Thecoa
Gabalis?
Maiumas Ascelon
(Baths of Ascelon)
Betogabri
Callirrhae
Machaerus
Agrippias
Bethsura
Alulos
Gaza
Adora
Terebinthus
Hebron
Mare
Mortuum
(Dead
Sea)
Caparorsa?
Aristobulias
Engaddi
(En-gedi)
-1385 ft
-422 m
Arnon R.
IDUMEA
NABATEAN KINGDOM
Masada
Raphia
Bersabe
(Beer-sheba)
Areopolis
(Rabbathmoab)
Malatha
Mampsis
Zered Brook
The Negeb
(arid southern plain)
N
Nessana
Created by National Geographic Society, Washington, D.C. © Copyright 2011 Common English Bible

Jordan R.
Plain of Sharon
Kanah Brook
Kedron River
Beor Brook
JUDEA (UNDER ROMAN ADMINISTRATION)
SAMARIA

MAP 14

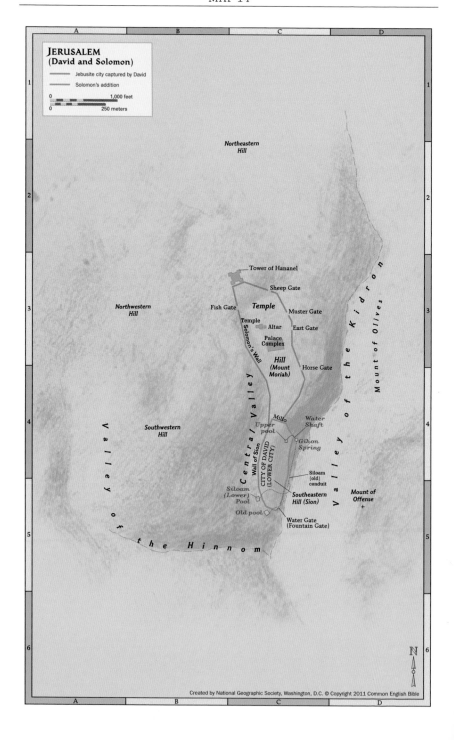

JERUSALEM
(David and Solomon)

Jebusite city captured by David
Solomon's addition

0   1,000 feet
0   250 meters

Northeastern
Hill

Tower of Hananel

Sheep Gate

Northwestern
Hill

Fish Gate   Temple   Muster Gate

Temple
Solomon's Wall   Altar   East Gate

Palace
Complex

Hill
(Mount
Moriah)   Horse Gate

Central Valley

Southwestern
Hill

Millo

Upper
pool   Water
Shaft

Wall of Sion

CITY OF DAVID
(LOWER CITY)   Gihon
Spring

Siloam
(old) conduit

Siloam
(Lower)
Pool   Southeastern
Hill (Sion)   Mount of
Offense
+

Old pool

Water Gate
(Fountain Gate)

Mount of Olives

Valley of the Kidron

Valley of the Hinnom

N

Created by National Geographic Society, Washington, D.C. © Copyright 2011 Common English Bible

MAP 15

MAP 16

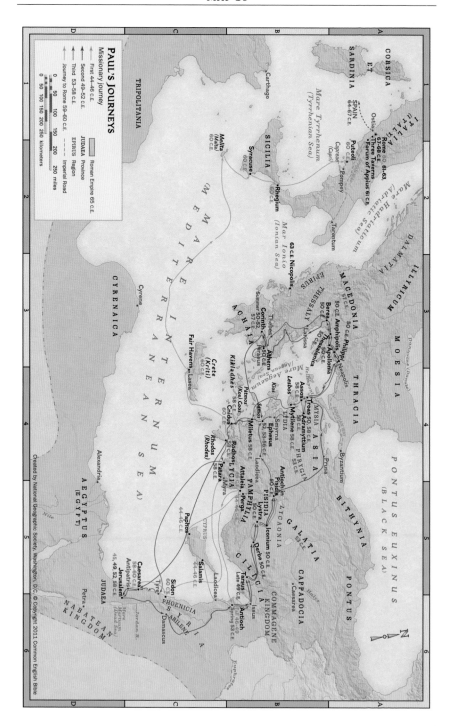

PAUL'S JOURNEYS
Missionary Journey

→ First 44–46 C.E.
→ Second 49–52 C.E.
→ Third 53–58 C.E.
→ Journey to Rome 59–60 C.E.

Roman Empire 65 C.E.
JUDAEA Province
EPIRUS Region
----- Imperial Road

0 50 100 150 200 250 kilometers
0 50 100 150 200 250 miles